English-Russian Dictionary-Phrasebook
of

Marina Frolova & Robert Powers

Rodnik Publishing Company
Seattle, Washington
2000

English-Russian Dictionary-Phrasebook of Love

Authors:	**Marina Frolova & Robert Powers**
Russian editor:	**Lidiya Zabokritskaya**
Technical editor:	**Isaak Zabokritskiy**

Published by:

Rodnik Publishing Company
P.O. Box 16727
Seattle, WA 98116-0727

Library of Congress Catalog Card Number: 00-191266
ISBN 1-929482-01-9

Printed in the United States of America

With infinite gratitude to
Lucy Schultz and Gary Cotkin
without whose faithful support
this work could not have been realized

Table of Contents

INTRODUCTION

Whoever becomes attracted to or falls in love with someone from another country soon finds out how difficult it can be to express their feelings to that person, gain the person's affections, and navigate the capricious waters of a relationship. As if it weren't enough of a challenge already, the language barrier confronts them at every turn.

Since Russian is not commonly studied in the West and not one of the easiest languages for English speakers to learn, the majority of those who look for love in Russia tend to rely on their Russian acquaintance's ability in English. More often than not, however, the knowledge of English claimed in an ad turns out to be rather gossamer. So, communication, especially of the romantic variety, is sometimes reduced to Tarzan basics. Or, inhibition of inhibitions, it goes through a translator.

To help those who go in pursuit of Russian romance rise above their language limitations, the authors have compiled here a collection of phrases and terms that hopefully will serve to connect the hearts and minds of both user and recipient in a beautiful and exciting way. Included are phrases that express love and affection, desire and passion, hopes and dreams, thoughts and feelings. Plus, there are many useful expressions for practical purposes. In short, we have given you here most of the language material needed to cultivate romance.

In using this dictionary-phrasebook, please be aware of the fact that in some cases the Russian phrases represent the best translation we could provide of the English phrases and, although they will be easily understood by a Russian, they are not necessarily what Russians themselves would think of to say for those particular ideas. This not withstanding, the chances are quite good that the person who receives such words will be thoroughly delighted to have them directed their way.

We wish you good success and ultimate happiness in your pursuit of love and romance, and we invite your comments – positive or negative – on the comment sheet on page 795.

How to Use the Dictionary

Main words

All phrases and terms in the dictionary are grouped under "**main words,**" which they contain. For example, the phrase "I never see beauty without thinking of you." is listed under the main word "beauty."

Some phrases appear in the dictionary more than once, because they contain more than one important main word. For example, the phrase "I find your charm and beauty hard to resist." is listed once under the main word "charm" and a second time under "beauty."

Sub-categories

When there are many terms and phrases under a main word, they are grouped under **sub-categories**. These sub-categories are prefaced by a label inside of a frame. The label first gives the main word and then a descriptor of the sub-category. For, example, the sub-category $\boxed{\textit{beloved: salutations in letters}}$ contains salutations containing the word "beloved." Similarly, $\boxed{\textit{conversation: verb terms}}$ is the category containing verb terms with the main word "conversation."

Parts of speech

Each listed main word is followed by its abbreviated part of speech, such as *n* for "noun," *vt* for "verb transitive," etc. (See "**Abbreviations Used in the Dictionary**" on page 10.)

Tilde substituting main word

For all terms, a **tilde** ~ substitutes for the main word of the term. For example, under the main word **cake**, "wedding cake" is listed as **wedding** ~. Similarly, "call back" under the main word "call" is given as ~ **back**.

Russian Verbs

Russian verbs are given with the **imperfective form** (in the infinitive) first, followed by a **slash**, and then the **perfective form** (in the infinitive). In some cases, only one form is given, because there is only one, or because one of the forms is not useful. To find out how a verb is conjugated, see **Appendix 3: Russian Verbs Conjugated** on page 689. To learn more about perfective and imperfective verbs, see the section **Verbs** in **Appendix 2: Russian Grammar** on page 686.

Following all transitive Russian verbs (those that take direct objects) and some intransitive verbs the grammatical case used with the verb is given in parentheses.

Slash = or

Throughout the dictionary a **slash** / is used to mean **"or,"** i.e., that you can choose one or the other. The choices are numbered, in parentheses, both on the English side and the Russian side. Hence, the term **beautifully** *(1,2)* **coiffured hair** прекра́сно *(1)* со́бранные / *(2)* уло́женные во́лосы can be said as either прекра́сно со́бранные во́лосы or прекра́сно уло́женные во́лосы. Sometimes the choices differ in meaning, sometimes they are the same.

The same is true of parts of phrases that are number and separated by a **slash** /. These will be preceded or followed -- or both -- by three dots. For example, in the phrase **Please call (me)** *(1)* **...anytime.** / *(2)* **...whenever you have time.** Пожа́луйста, звони́ (мне) *(1)* ...в любо́е вре́мя. / *(2)* ..., когда́ у тебя́ бу́дет вре́мя. you can choose to say **Please call (me) anytime.** Пожа́луйста, звони́ (мне) в любо́е вре́мя. or **Please call (me) whenever you have time.** Пожа́луйста, звони́ (мне), когда́ у тебя́ бу́дет вре́мя.

Parentheses = optional

Words or parts of phrases in **parentheses** are **optional**. In the example above, you could include or omit the word **(me)** in both English and Russian. In a very few cases, an English word in parentheses is optional in English, but has no counterpart in Russian: the sentence in Russian will be the same either way.

Women's speech

The Russian letter ж , followed by a colon : , in parentheses, indicates what a woman would say to a man. Otherwise, the phrase would be for a man talking to a woman. This difference is due to grammatical differences in speech for men and women. For more explanation of this, see **Appendix 2: Russian Grammar** on page 676.

Accents

Accents have been placed on all Russian words of two or more syllables to indicate which syllable is stressed when pronouncing the word. This feature is added for the convenience of learners; do not copy the accents when writing to a Russian.

Because of the size of capital letters, it was not possible to put accents on capitalized Russian vowels. Therefore, when you find a Russian word starting with a capitalized vowel, and there is no accent elsewhere, assume that the accent is on the capitalized vowel.

In Russian words that have ё, the ё has the stress of the word.

Alphabet pages

There are two **alphabet charts** in the book: one in **Appendix 1** on page 675, and the other in the form of a **tear-out page** on the last page of the book.

Russian Usage

In using this dictionary-phrasebook, please bear in mind that the Russian phrases in many cases represent the best translation we could provide of the English phrases and, although they will be easily understood by a Russian, they are not necessarily what Russians themselves would think of to say for those particular ideas.

Abbreviations Used in the Dictionary

English Abbreviations

abbrev	abbreviation
acc.	accusative (case)
adj	adjective
adv	adverb
coll.	collective
dat.	dative (case)
elec.	electrical
emot.	emotional
etc	etcetera
f	feminine
fam.	familiar
fig.	figurative
gen.	genitive (case)
instr.	instrumental (case)
LTR	long-term relation-ship
m	masculine
med.	medical
mil.	military
n	noun
neut	neuter
phys.	physical
pl	plural
pol.	polite
pp	past participle
pred	predicate
prep	preposition
prep.	prepositional (case)
reg.	registration
s.o.	someone
s.th.	something
univ.	university
veh.	vehicle
vi	verb intransitive
vt	verb transitive

Russian Abbreviations

ж	женщина (woman)
и т.д.	и так далее (etc)

A

abandon *vt* покида́ть / поки́нуть *(what, whom = acc.)*, оставля́ть / оста́вить *(what, whom = acc.)* ♦ ~ **oneself** всеце́ло отдава́ться / отда́ться *(to what = dat.)*.

> **abandon:** *desert*

I would never abandon you. Я никогда́ не поки́ну тебя́. ♦ **Don't abandon me.** Не покида́й меня́. ♦ **My husband abandoned me (and** *[1]* **my son /** *[2]* **my daughter /** *[3]* **my children).** Мой муж поки́нул меня́ (и *[1]* ...моего́ сы́на. / *[2]* ...мою́ дочь. / *[3]* ...мои́х дете́й.).

> **abandon:** *let oneself go*

I want to abandon myself to your lush beauty. Я хочу́ отда́ться твое́й роско́шной красоте́.

abandon *n* непринуждённость *f*, несде́ржанность *f* ♦ **I long to see you stretch out in languorous abandon as I place tiny kisses all over your beautiful body.** Я жа́жду уви́деть тебя́, раски́нувшуюся в то́мной непринуждённости, в то вре́мя, как я покрыва́ю кро́шечными поцелу́ями твоё прекра́сное те́ло. ♦ **When I look at your full, sensuous lips so promising of soft, sweet ecstasy, I am filled with an** *(1)* **enormous/** *(2)* **overpowering desire to kiss them with wild abandon to the very end of time.** Когда́ я смотрю́ на твои́ по́лные, чу́вственные гу́бы, обеща́ющие не́жный, сла́достный экста́з, меня́ наполня́ет *(1)* огро́мное / *(2)* невыноси́мое жела́ние целова́ть их бесконе́чно, соверше́нно забы́в обо всём.

abate *vt* ослабева́ть / ослабе́ть *(what = acc.)*, уменьша́ть / уме́ньшить *(what = acc.)*.

abdomen *n* живо́т.

abdominals *n, pl* мы́шцы живота́.

abide *vi (dwell)* жить, обита́ть ♦ **I cannot begin to express the love that abides in my heart for you.** Я не могу́ вы́разить ту любо́вь к тебе́, кото́рой полно́ моё се́рдце.

ability *n* спосо́бность *f*; уме́ние ♦ **I have no ability (whatsoever) to resist you.** Я (соверше́нно) не спосо́бен *(ж: спосо́бна)* сопротивля́ться тебе́.

abject *adj (wretched)* жа́лкий, -ая, -ое, -ие; *(extreme)* кра́йний, -яя, -ее, -ие ♦ **You don't know what abject loneliness I felt before I met you.** Ты не зна́ешь, како́е кра́йнее одино́чество я чу́вствовал *(ж: чу́вствовала)* до тех пор, пока́ не встре́тил *(ж:встре́тила)* тебя́. ♦ **Without you** *(1)* **here /** *(2)* **around I feel abject loneliness.** Без тебя́ *(1,2)*

Russian nouns are either masculine, feminine or neuter.
Adjectives with them will be the same.

ря́дом со мной я чу́вствую кра́йнее одино́чество.

ablaze *adv* в огне́, в пла́мени ♦ **Your beautiful** *(1)* **blue / (2) dark eyes have set my heart ablaze.** Твои́ прекра́сные *(1)* голубы́е / *(2)* тёмные глаза́ зажига́ют ого́нь в моём се́рдце.

able *vi:* ♦ **Are you able to come in May?** Ты смо́жешь прие́хать в ма́е? ♦ **I'm (not) able to come next month.** Я (не) смогу́ прие́хать в сле́дующем ме́сяце. ♦ **Were you able to get a visa?** Ты смогла́ *(ж: смог)* получи́ть ви́зу? ♦ **I was(n't) able to change the date.** Я (не) смог *(ж: смогла́)* измени́ть да́ту.

abominably *adv* отврати́тельно ♦ **I behaved abominably.** Я вёл *(ж: вела́)* себя́ отврати́тельно. ♦ **You behaved abominably.** Ты вела́ *(ж: вёл)* себя́ отврати́тельно.

abortion *n* або́рт ♦ **I think** *(1)* **I / (2) you should get an abortion.** Я ду́маю, *(1)* я /*(2)* ты должна́ сде́лать або́рт. ♦ **How about getting an abortion?** Что, е́сли сде́лать або́рт? ♦ **How much would it cost to get an abortion?** Ско́лько бу́дет сто́ить сде́лать або́рт? ♦ **Where could** *(1)* **I / (2) you get an abortion?** Где *(1)* ...я могу́... / *(2)* ...ты мо́жешь... сде́лать або́рт? ♦ *(1)* **You / (2) I could get an abortion at...** *(1)* Ты / *(2)* Я могла́ бы сде́лать або́рт в... ♦ **I (don't) want to get an abortion.** Я (не) хочу́ де́лать або́рт. ♦ **I don't believe in abortion.** Я про́тив або́рта. ♦ **I had an abortion.** Я сде́лала або́рт.

abound *vi* изоби́ловать, находи́ться / быть в большо́м коли́честве ♦ **I wish I could put into words the (tender) feelings that abound in my heart for you.** Я хоте́л бы вы́разить слова́ми (не́жные) чу́вства к тебе́, переполня́ющие моё се́рдце.

abounding *adj* оби́льный, -ая, -ое, -ые, изоби́льный, -ая, -ое, -ые ♦ **With abounding affection for you,** *(closing of a letter.)* С большо́й не́жностью к тебе́,

above-average *adj* вы́ше сре́днего ♦ **I'd say) I'm above-average in everything.** (Я бы сказа́л *[ж: сказа́ла]*,) я вы́ше сре́днего во всём.

abrasive *adj (rough)* ре́зкий, -ая, -ое, -ие; *(intolerable)* невыноси́мый, -ая, -ое, -ые, несно́сный, -ая, -ое, -ые; *(irritating)* раздражи́тельный, -ая, -ое, -ые ♦ **Frankly, your personality is a little too abrasive (for my liking).** Открове́нно, (на мой взгляд,) у тебя́ дово́льно ре́зкий хара́ктер.

abs *n, pl* мы́шцы живота́.

absence *n* отсу́тствие ♦ **Your absence makes a wasteland of my whole** *(1)* **day / (1) evening.** Твоё отсу́тствие де́лает пусты́м мой *(1)* день / *(2)* ве́чер.

absentminded *adj* рассе́янный, -ая, -ое, -ые.

absentmindedly *adv* рассе́янно.

absolute *adj* по́лный, -ая, -ое, -ые, соверше́нный, -ая, -ое, -ые, абсолю́тный, -ая, -ое, -ые.

absolutely *adv* соверше́нно, абсолю́тно.

abstemious *adj (in moderation)* уме́ренный, -ая, -ое, -ые, скро́мный, -ая, -ое, -ые.

abuse *vt* оскорбля́ть / оскорби́ть *(whom = acc.)* ♦ **You abuse me.** Ты оскорбля́ешь меня́. ♦ **He abused me** *(1)* **emotionally / (2) sexually.** Он оскорби́л меня́ *(1)* эмоциона́льно / *(2)* сексуа́льно. ♦ **He abused me (physically).** Он жесто́ко обраща́лся со мной.

abuse *n* 1. *(offense)* оскорбле́ние; 2. *(bad treatment)* жесто́кое обраще́ние; 3. *(misuse)* злоупотребле́ние ♦ **child** ~ жесто́кое обраще́ние с детьми́ ♦ **drug** ~ злоупотребле́ние нарко́тиками ♦ **emotional** ~ эмоциона́льное оскорбле́ние ♦ **physical** ~ жесто́кое физи́ческое обраще́ние ♦ **sexual** ~ 1. *(adult)* сексуа́льное оскорбле́ние, оскорби́тельные сексуа́льные притяза́ния; 2. *(child)* растле́ние (малоле́тного); совраще́ние (малоле́тного) ♦ **I'm tired of** *(1)* **your / (2) his abuse.** Я уста́ла от *(1)* твои́х / *(2)* его́ оскорбле́ний.

accent *n* акце́нт ♦ **I speak with a(n) (heavy) accent.** Я говорю́ с (си́льным) акце́нтом.

accentuate *vt* подчёркивать / подчеркну́ть *(what = acc.)* ♦ **Your dark hair accentuates**

Learn more about Russian customs in Appendix 15, page 782.

the soft loveliness of your face. Твои́ тёмные во́лосы подчёркивают мя́гкую красоту́ твоего́ лица́.

accept *vt* принима́ть / приня́ть *(what, whom = acc.)* ♦ **I want a woman who will accept me as I am.** Я хочу́ же́нщину, кото́рая при́мет меня́ таки́м, како́й я есть. ♦ **I want a man who will accept me as I am.** Я хочу́ мужчи́ну, кото́рый при́мет меня́ тако́й, кака́я я есть.

acceptance *n* приня́тие ♦ *(1,2)* **total** ~ *(1)* абсолю́тное / *(2)* по́лное приня́тие.

accessories *n, pl* аксессуа́ры, принадле́жности.

accompany *vt* сопровожда́ть *(whom = acc.)*, сопу́тствовать *(whom = dat.)* ♦ **May I accompany you?** Могу́ я сопровожда́ть тебя́?

accomplished *adj* 1. *(done)* зако́нченный, -ая, -ое, -ые, заверше́нный, -ая, -ое, -ые, вы́полненный, -ая, -ое, -ые; 2. *(proficient)* иску́сный, -ая, -ое, -ые, соверше́нный, -ая, -ое, -ые, состоя́вшийся, -аяся, -еєся, -иеся, наделённый (-ая, -ое, -ые) ма́ссой досто́инств ♦ **professionally ~** профессиона́льно состоя́вшийся ♦ **I didn't know you were an accomplished** *(1)* **painter** / *(2)* **artist.** Я не знал *(ж: знала)*, что ты состоя́вшийся *(1)* худо́жник / *(2)* арти́ст.

accord *n (harmony)* согла́сие, гармо́ния; *(volition)* жела́ние ♦ **I want you to do it of your own accord.** Я хочу́, чтобы ты де́лала *(ж: де́лал)* это по своему́ со́бственному жела́нию.

accusation *n* обвине́ние ♦ **Stop hurling accusations at me.** Прекрати́ осыпа́ть меня́ обвине́ниями. ♦ **You're constantly hurling (false) accusations at me.** Ты постоя́нно осыпа́ешь меня́ (ло́жными) обвине́ниями. ♦ **That accusation is (absolutely)** *(1)* **untrue** / *(2)* **false.** Это обвине́ние (абсолю́тно) *(1)* ло́жное / *(2)* оши́бочное.

accuse *vt* обвиня́ть / обвини́ть *(whom = acc., of what = в + prep.)* ♦ **You're accusing me of something I didn't do.** Ты обвиня́ешь меня́ в том, что я не де́лал *(ж: де́лала)*. ♦ **How could you accuse me of such a thing?** Как ты мо́жешь обвиня́ть меня́ в таки́х веща́х? ♦ **I'm not accusing you (of anything).** Я не обвиня́ю тебя́ (ни в чём).

ache *vi* 1. *(be in pain)* боле́ть; 2. *(yearn)* жа́ждать, (и́зо всех сил) стреми́ться ♦ **I ache with** *(1)* **longing** / *(2)* **love for you.** Я бо́лен *(ж: больна́)* от *(1)...* тоски́ по тебе́. / *(2) ...*любви́ к тебе́. ♦ **My heart aches with love for you.** Моё се́рдце боли́т от любви́ к тебе́. ♦ **I ache with desire for you.** Я до бо́ли жела́ю тебя́. ♦ **I ache (so much) for your touch.** Я (так) жа́жду твои́х прикоснове́ний. ♦ **I ache to** *(1) ...***be with you (again).** / *(2)...***see you (again).** Я жа́жду *(1) ...*быть с тобо́й (опя́ть). / *(2) ...*уви́деть тебя́ (опя́ть). ♦ **There are no words to describe how I hunger for you, how I ache for you, how I want you.** Нет слов, чтобы описа́ть, как я го́лоден по тебе́, как я страда́ю по тебе́ , как я хочу́ тебя́. ♦ **How I ache for the day when my mouth can at last claim yours.** Как я жа́жду того́ дня, когда́ мой рот смо́жет наконе́ц овладе́ть твои́м. ♦ **In the middle of the night I wake up, aching with desire for you.** Среди́ но́чи я просыпа́юсь, до бо́ли жела́я тебя́. ♦ **I've been aching to kiss you since the first** *(1)* **moment** / *(2)* **minute** / *(3)* **time I** *(4)* **met** / *(5)* **saw you.** Я горю́ жела́нием поцелова́ть тебя́ *(1) ...*с пе́рвого мгнове́ния,... / *(2) ...*с пе́рвой же мину́ты,... / *(3) ...*со вре́мени,... когда́ я *(4)* встре́тил *(ж: встре́тила)* / *(5)* уви́дел *(ж: уви́дела)* тебя́. ♦ **All day long after reading your ad in the personals (section) I've been aching to get home and write you this letter.** Весь день по́сле прочте́ния Ва́шего объявле́ния в отде́ле знако́мств я стреми́лся *(ж: стреми́лась)* прийти́ домо́й и написа́ть Вам это письмо́.

ache *n* боль *f* ♦ **~ of longing** боль тоски́, тоска́ ♦ **agonizing ~** мучи́тельная боль ♦ **constant ~** постоя́нная боль ♦ **overwhelming ~** непреодоли́мая боль ♦ **terrible ~** ужа́сная боль, ужа́сное страда́ние ♦ **tremendous ~** огро́мная боль ♦ **unbearable ~**

A slash always denotes "or."
You can choose the numbered words before or after the slash..

невыноси́мая боль ♦ **unrelenting** ~ жесто́кая боль.

| ache: phrases |

There is such an *(1)* **unbearable** / *(2)* **overwhelming** / *(3)* **tremendous ache in my heart for you.** В моём се́рдце и́з-за тебя така́я *(1)* невыноси́мая / *(2)* непреодоли́мая / *(3)* огро́мная боль. ♦ *(1)* **Since you left... /** *(2)* **Since we've been apart..., the ache in my heart never** *(3)* **...ceases.** / *(4)***...goes away.** *(1)* С тех пор, как ты ушла́ *(ж: ушёл)*... / *(2)* С тех пор, как мы расста́лись... боль в моём се́рдце никогда́ не *(3)* ...прекраща́ется. / *(4)* ...ухо́дит. ♦ **Only the sweet softness of your lips can quell the ache of longing that ravages my heart.** То́лько сла́дкая мя́гкость твои́х губ мо́жет подави́ть боль тоски́, разруша́ющей моё се́рдце. ♦ **Without you in my arms a perpetual ache of longing marauds my soul.** Постоя́нная тоска́ терза́ет мою́ ду́шу, когда́ тебя нет в мои́х объя́тиях. ♦ **I've never felt such a crazy ache of love in all my life.** Любо́вь никогда́ не причиня́ла мне тако́го ужа́сного страда́ния. ♦ **Every night brings me a throbbing ache of longing for your warm, beautiful softness.** Ка́ждая ночь прино́сит мне пульси́рующую боль жа́жды твое́й тёплой прекра́сной мя́гкости.

achiever *n* челове́к, достига́ющий це́ли *(1 term)* ♦ **high** ~ челове́к, всегда́ добива́ющийся своего́ *(1 term)*.

aching *adj* 1. боля́щий, -ая, -ее, -ие, но́ющий, -ая, -ее, -ие, больно́й, -а́я, -о́е, -ы́е; 2. *(heart)* тяжёлое, -ые.

aching *n* боль *f.*

achingly *adv* бо́льно.

acknowledge *vt* 1. *(admit)* признава́ть / призна́ть *(what = acc.)*; 2. *(confirm)* подтвержда́ть / подтверди́ть *(what = acc.)* ♦ **Please at least acknowledge that you have received this letter.** Пожа́луйста, по кра́йней ме́ре, подтверди *(polite: подтверди́те)* получе́ние э́того письма́.

acne *n* угри́, а́кне ♦ **I have an acne problem (on my face).** У меня угри́ (на лице́).

acquaintance *n* 1. *(act; state)* знако́мство; 2. *(person)* знако́мый *m*, знако́мая *f* ♦ **I don't believe I've made your acquaintance.** *(1,2)* **My name is...** Я не ду́маю, что знако́м *(ж: знако́ма)* с Ва́ми. *(1)* Моё и́мя... / *(2)* Меня зову́т... ♦ **It's a pleasure to make your acquaintance.** Это удово́льствие - познако́миться с Ва́ми. ♦ **I'm very happy to make your acquaintance.** Я о́чень рад *(ж: ра́да)* познако́миться с Ва́ми. ♦ **She's (just) an (old) acquaintance of mine.** Она́ то́лько моя ста́рая знако́мая. ♦ **He's (just) an (old) acquaintance of mine.** Он то́лько мой ста́рый знако́мый.

acquainted *adj* знако́м, -а, -о, -ы *(short forms)* ♦ **get better** ~ полу́чше познако́миться *(with whom = + с + instr.)* ♦ **I fervently** *(1)* **entreat** / *(2)* **implore you to** *(3)* **give** / *(4)* **grant me the opportunity to get better acquainted with you.** Я горячо́ *(1,2)* умоля́ю Вас *(3)* дать / *(4)* предоста́вить мне возмо́жность лу́чше узна́ть Вас. ♦ **I'd like to get better acquainted with you (first).** Я хоте́л *(ж: хоте́ла)* бы (снача́ла) полу́чше познако́миться с Ва́ми. ♦ **Let's get acquainted.** Дава́йте познако́мимся.

act *n* 1. де́йствие; 2. посту́пок ♦ ~ **of kindness** до́брый посту́пок ♦ ~ **of tenderness** не́жное де́йствие, не́жность *f* ♦ ~ **of gentleness** до́брый посту́пок ♦ **tactless** ~**(s)** *n* беста́ктность *f* ♦ **I caught her (him) in the act.** Я пойма́л её *(ж: пойма́ла его́)* на изме́не. ♦ **Your many acts of tenderness have enslaved my heart.** Не́жность, кото́рую ты так ще́дро дари́ла *(ж: дари́л)* мне, поработи́ла моё се́рдце. ♦ **You need to** *(1,2)* **get your act together.** Ты должна́ *(ж: до́лжен)* *(1)* собра́ться / *(2)* сконцентри́роваться.

active *adj* акти́вный, -ая, -ое, -ые, де́йствующий, -ая, -ее, -ие ♦ **I seek someone who is culturally active.** Я ищу́ того́, кто лю́бит культу́рное времяпрепровожде́ние. ♦ **I'm**

Common adult weights are given in Appendix 10, page 777.

a socially **active person.** Я люблю́ обще́ние.

activity *n* 1. *(action, pursuits) (often pl.)* де́ятельность *f*, де́йствия; 2. *(vigorous)* акти́вность *f* ♦ **erotic** ~**ies** эроти́ческие развлече́ния ♦ **extramarital** ~**s** свя́зи на стороне́, проведе́ние вре́мени на стороне́ ♦ **indoor** ~**ies** развлече́ния в помеще́нии ♦ **outdoor** ~**ies** акти́вный о́тдых на откры́том во́здухе ♦ **physical** ~**ies** физи́ческая де́ятельность ♦ **playful** ~**ies** и́гры, ша́лости ♦ **sexual** ~ сексуа́льная акти́вность ♦ **I enjoy activties that nurture mind, body and spirit.** Я люблю́ заня́тия, пита́ющие ум, те́ло и ду́шу. ♦ **I seek someone who enjoys outdoor activities.** Я ищу́ того́ кто лю́бит акти́вный о́тдых на откры́том во́здухе.

acute *adj* 1. о́стрый, -ая, -ое, -ые, проница́тельный, -ая, -ое, -ые; то́нкий, -ая, -ое, -ие ♦ ~ **jealousy** жгу́чая ре́вность ♦ ~ **pleasure** о́строе наслажде́ние.

acutely *adv* о́стро, проница́тельно.

ad *n* рекла́ма, объявле́ние ♦ **first-time** ~ пе́рвое объявле́ние ♦ **marriage** ~ бра́чное объявле́ние ♦ **my** ~ моё объявле́ние ♦ **personal** ~ ча́стное объявле́ние ♦ *(1,2)* **short** ~ *(1)* коро́ткое / *(2)* кра́ткое объявле́ние ♦ *(1,2)* **small** ~ *(1)* небольшо́е / *(2)* ма́ленькое объявле́ние ♦ **your** ~ *(familiar)* твоё объявле́ние; *(polite)* Ва́ше объявле́ние.

ad: verb terms

place a personal ~ **(in a newspaper)** помеща́ть / помести́ть ча́стное объявле́ние (в газе́ту) ♦ **print** *(1)* **my** / *(2)* **your** ~ **(in the newspaper)** напеча́тать *(1)* моё / *(2)* Ва́ше объявле́ние (в газе́те) ♦ **put a personal** ~ **in the newspaper** дава́ть / дать ча́стное объявле́ние в газе́ту.

ad: phrases

I read your ad in the personals. Я прочита́л *(ж: прочита́ла)* Ва́ше объявле́ние в отде́ле «ча́стных объявле́ний». ♦ **I saw your ad** *(1)* **...in the newspaper.** / *(2)* **...on the Internet.** Я уви́дел *(ж: уви́дела)* Ва́ше объявле́ние *(1)* ...в газе́те. / *(2)* ...на интерне́те. ♦ **I couldn't help but notice your ad. You're exceptionally** *(1)* **lovely** / *(2)* **handsome.** Я не мог *(ж: могла́)* не заме́тить Ва́шего объявле́ния. Ты исключи́тельно *(1)* краси́ва / *(2)* краси́в. ♦ **I was quite intrigued by your ad.** Я был *(ж: была́)* весьма́ заинтриго́ван *(ж: заинтриго́вана)* Ва́шим объявле́нием. ♦ **What a charming ad you had in the newspaper.** Како́е очарова́тельное объявле́ние Вы да́ли в газе́ту. ♦ **Your description in your ad** *(1,2)* **really sparked my interest.** То, как Вы описа́ли себя́ в объявле́нии, *(1)* ...разожгло́ мой интере́с. / *(2)* ...о́чень заинтересова́ло меня́. ♦ **All day long after reading your ad in the personals (section) I've been aching to get home and write you this letter.** Весь день по́сле прочте́ния Ва́шего объявле́ния в отде́ле зна-ко́мств я стреми́лся прийти́ домо́й и написа́ть Вам э́то письмо́. ♦ **The minute I read your ad, I knew I had to write to you.** В ту мину́ту, когда́ я чита́л *(ж: чита́ла)* Ва́ше объявле́ние, я по́нял *(ж: поняла́)*, что до́лжен *(ж: должна́)* написа́ть Вам. ♦ **When I saw your ad,** *(1)* **...I couldn't resist writing to you.** / *(2)* **...I immediately forgot about all the others.** Когда́ я уви́дел *(ж: уви́дела)* Ва́ше объявле́ние, *(1)* ...я не смог *(ж: смогла́)* удержа́ться, что́бы не написа́ть Вам. / *(2)* ...я то́тчас же забы́л *(ж: забы́ла)* обо всех остальны́х. ♦ **There were several other ads in the personals that were somewhat interesting, but yours struck an immediate chord in my heart and I knew with a certainty that there was no way I could not write to you.** В отде́ле знако́мств бы́ло не́сколько други́х интере́сных объявле́ний, но Ва́ше вы́звало неме́дленный о́тклик в моём се́рдце, и я твёрдо знал *(ж знала́)*, что не могу́ не написа́ть Вам. ♦ **The thought patterns that yielded your choice of words and sentences in your ad reveal the exact same raging hunger for love and affection that I harbor within me.** Мы́сли, вло́женные в слова́ и стиль Ва́шего объявле́ния, говоря́т о то́чно тако́й же неи́стовой жа́жде

An italicized ж: *in parentheses indicates a woman speaking*

любви́ и не́жности, кото́рая таи́тся во мне.

adamant *adj* непрекло́нный, -ая, -ое, -ые, твёрдый, -ая, -ое, -ые.

adamantly *adv* непрекло́нно, твёрдо ♦ **I'm adamantly opposed to that.** Я твёрдо э́тому сопротивля́юсь.

adapt *vi* приспоса́бливаться / приспосо́биться *(to what = + к + dat.)* ♦ **I'm willing to adapt to a new way of life.** Я гото́в *(ж: гото́ва)* приспосо́биться к но́вой жи́зни.

adaptable *adj* (легко́) приспоса́бливающийся, -аяся, -ееся, -иеся.

addict *n* 1. *(drugs)* наркома́н *m*, наркома́нка *f*; 2. *(other things)* фана́тик ♦ **drug** ~ наркома́н *m*, наркома́нка *f* ♦ **love** ~ фана́тик любви́ ♦ **sex** ~ фана́тик се́кса.

addicted *adj* пристрасти́вшийся, -аяся, -ееся, -иеся, пристра́стен, пристра́стна, -о, -ы *(short forms)*, во вла́сти *(to what = gen.)* ♦ **be** ~ пристрасти́ться *(to what = + к + dat.)*, предава́ться *(to what = dat.)*, быть во вла́сти *(to what = gen.)* ♦ **become** ~ пристрасти́ться *(to what = + к + dat.)*, оказа́ться во вла́сти *(to what = gen.)*.

| **addicted: phrases** |
I'm completely addicted to you. Я весь *(ж: вся)* в твое́й вла́сти. ♦ **I'm (1) absolutely / (2) completely / (3) totally addicted to (4) ...your beautiful body. / (5) ...your sweet / (6) heavenly / (7) wonderful kisses.** Я *(1-3)* по́лностью во вла́сти *(4)* ...твоего́ прекра́сного те́ла. / *(5)* ...твои́х сла́дких / *(6)* боже́ственных / *(7)* удиви́тельных поцелу́ев. ♦ **You've made me so addicted to love.** Ты сде́лала *(ж: сде́лал)* меня́ рабо́м любви́. ♦ **A person could easily become addicted to your lips.** Челове́к мо́жет легко́ оказа́ться во вла́сти твои́х губ.

addiction *n* пристра́стие ♦ **I know that I can never overcome my addiction to your (1) kisses / (2) love / (3) body.** Я зна́ю, что никогда́ не смогу́ освободи́ться от вла́сти *(1)* ...твои́х поцелу́ев. / *(2)* ...твое́й любви́. / *(3)* ...твоего́ те́ла.

addictive *adj* вызыва́ющий (-ая, -ее, -ие) привы́чку, легко́ пристрасти́ться ♦ **Your kisses are so addictive.** К твои́м поцелу́ям так легко́ пристрасти́ться.

address *n* а́дрес ♦ **brother's** ~ а́дрес бра́та ♦ **business** ~ *(company)* а́дрес фи́рмы; *(enterprise)* а́дрес предприя́тия ♦ **complete** ~ по́лный а́дрес ♦ **correct** ~ пра́вильный а́дрес ♦ **e-mail** ~ а́дрес электро́нной по́чты ♦ **father's** ~ а́дрес отца́ ♦ **forwarding** ~ а́дрес пересы́лки ♦ **friend's** ~ а́дрес дру́га ♦ **home** ~ дома́шний а́дрес ♦ **incomplete** ~ непо́лный а́дрес ♦ **incorrect** ~ непра́вильный а́дрес ♦ **Internet** ~ а́дрес в интерне́те ♦ **mailing** ~ почто́вый а́дрес ♦ **mother's** ~ а́дрес ма́тери ♦ **my** ~ мой а́дрес ♦ **new** ~ но́вый а́дрес ♦ **office** ~ а́дрес предприя́тия, служе́бный а́дрес ♦ **old** ~ ста́рый а́дрес ♦ **parents'** ~ а́дрес роди́телей ♦ **permanent** ~ постоя́нный а́дрес ♦ **previous** ~ пре́жний а́дрес ♦ **proper** ~ пра́вильный а́дрес ♦ **return** ~ обра́тный а́дрес ♦ **right** ~ пра́вильный а́дрес ♦ **sister's** ~ а́дрес сестры́ ♦ **temporary** ~ вре́менный а́дрес ♦ **work** ~ служе́бный а́дрес ♦ **wrong** ~ непра́вильный а́дрес ♦ **your** ~ *(familiar)* твой а́дрес; *(polite)* Ваш а́дрес ♦ **change** *(my / your)* ~ перее́хать ♦ **forget** *(1,2)* **your** ~ забы́ть *(1)* твой *(familiar)* / *(2)* Ваш *(polite)* а́дрес.

| **address: phrases** |
What's your address? Како́й у тебя́ а́дрес? ♦ **My (new) address is ___.** Мой (но́вый) а́дрес: ♦ **Please write (down) your address for me.** Напиши́, пожа́луйста, свой а́дрес. ♦ **Could you write down your address for me?** Не могла́ *(ж: мог)* бы ты написа́ть свой а́дрес для меня́? ♦ **I'll write down my address for you.** Я напишу́ для тебя́ свой а́дрес. ♦ **Let me write down (1) my / (2) your address.** Позво́ль мне написа́ть *(1)* свой / *(2)* твой а́дрес. ♦ **(1) This is... / (2) Here's... my (new) address.** *(1)* Это... / *(2)* Вот... мой (но́вый) а́дрес. ♦ **Write to me at this address...** Пиши́ мне по э́тому а́дресу... ♦ **I'm sorry I didn't write. I lost your address.** Прости́, что не писа́л *(ж: писа́ла)*. Я потеря́л *(ж:*

Procedures for getting married to a Russian
are outlined in Appendix 18, page 787.

потеряла) твой áдрес.

adjusted *adj* уравновéшенный, -ая, -ое, -ые ♦ **I'm seeking a single white female who is well-proportioned, educated and adjusted.** Я ищý одинóкую бéлую жéнщину, хорошó сложённую, образóванную и уравновéшенную.

admiration *n* восхищéние ♦ **boundless** ~ безграни́чное восхищéние ♦ **frank** ~ откровéнное восхищéние ♦ **great** ~ большóе восхищéние ♦ **infinite** ~ бесконéчное восхищéние ♦ **mutual** ~ взаи́мное восхищéние ♦ **my** ~ моё восхищéние ♦ **profound** ~ глубóкое восхищéние ♦ **reverent** ~ почти́тельное восхищéние ♦ **sincere** ~ и́скреннее восхищéние.

admiration: phrases

I'm full of admiration for you. Я пóлон *(ж: полнá)* восхищéния тобóй. ♦ *(1)* **I cannot begin to tell you...** / *(2)* **You don't know... how much admiration I have for you.** *(1)* Я не знáю, как сказáть тебé,... / *(2)* Ты не знáешь,... какóе огрóмное восхищéние ты вызывáешь во мне. ♦ **I am engulfed in** *(1)* **infinite** / *(2)* **boundless admiration of your** *(3)* **indescribable** / *(4)* **incomparable** / *(5)* **peerless** / *(6)* **exquisite** / *(7)* **beauty** / *(8)* **loveliness.** Я *(1)* бесконéчно / *(2)* безграни́чно восхищáюсь твоéй *(3)* неописýемой /*(4,5)* несравнéнной / *(6)* изы́сканной / *(7,8)* красотóй. ♦ **I gaze at your photo in reverent admiration.** Я вгля́дываюсь в твоё фóто в почти́тельном восхищéнии. ♦ **I've been filled with admiration for you since the first day we met.** Я пóлон *(ж: полнá)* восхищéния тобóй со дня нáшей пéрвой встрéчи.

admire *vt* любовáться / полюбовáться *(what, whom = + instr. or* на *+ acc.),* восхищáться / восхити́ться *(what, whom = instr.)* ♦ **secretly** ~ втáйне восхищáться *(what, whom = instr.)* ♦ **sincerely** ~ и́скренне восхищáться *(what, whom = instr.).*

admire: phrases

I admire so many things about you. Меня́ так мнóгое восхищáет в тебé. ♦ **I admire everything about you.** Я восхищáюсь всем в тебé. ♦ **I admire you (so much) (for your** *[1]* **courage** / *[2]* **gentleness** / *[3]* **honesty** / *[4]* **strength** / *[5]* **thoughtfulness** / *[6]* **wisdom.** / *[7]* **...kind heart.** / *[8]* **...compassion.)** Я (так си́льно) восхищáюсь тобóй (за *[1]* ...твою́ хрáбрость / *[2]* мя́гкость / *[3]* чéстность / *[4]* си́лу / *[5]* внимáтельность / *[6]* мýдрость. / *[7]* ...твоё дóброе сéрдце. / *[8]* ...твоё сострадáние.). ♦ **I admire you for your** *(1)* **...gentle** / *(2)* **thoughtful ways.** / *(3)* **...high principles.** Я восхищáюсь тобóй за *(1)* ...твою́ нéжность / *(2)* чýткость. / *(3)* ...твои́ высóкие при́нципы. ♦ **I admire you much more than I can say.** Я восхищáюсь тобóй бóльше, чем могý вы́сказать. ♦ **If you only knew how much I admired you.** Éсли бы ты тóлько знáла *(ж: знал)*, как си́льно я восхищён *(ж: восхищенá)* тобóй. ♦ **I've admired you** *(1)* **...since the first day we met.** / *(2)* **...for a long (, long) time.** Я восхищáюсь тобóй *(1)* ...со дня нáшей пéрвой встрéчи. / *(2)* ...ужé (давны́м) давнó. ♦ **You have many fine traits that I admire.** У тебя́ мнóго прекрáсных черт, котóрыми я любýюсь.

admirer *n* поклóнник *m*, поклóнница *f* ♦ **I imagine you have** *(1)* **...many...** / *(2)* **...quite a few... admirers.** Я представля́ю, что у Вас есть *(1)* ...мнóго... /*(2)* ...довóльно мнóго... поклóнников. ♦ **You can count me as one of your admirers.** Вы мóжете считáть меня́ одни́м из свои́х поклóнников. ♦ **This is your secret admirer writing this to you.** Ваш тáйный поклóнник пи́шет э́то Вам. ♦ **I've been an (ardent) admirer of yours ever since we first met.** Со дня нáшей пéрвой встрéчи я был Вáшим (пы́лким) поклóнником. ♦ **I've long been an admirer of yours.** Я ужé давнó Ваш поклóнник.

admit *vt* признавáть / признáть *(what = acc.)* ♦ **be afraid to** ~ боя́ться признáть *(what = acc.).*

admit *vi* признавáться / признáться ♦ **be afraid to** ~ боя́ться признáться.

A list of conjugated Russian verbs is given
in Appendix 3 on page 699

adolescent *adj* подростко́вый, -ая, -ое, -ые; ю́ношеский, -ая, -ое, -ие.

adolescent *n* подро́сток.

Adonis *n (exceptionally handsome young man)* Адо́нис, краса́вец.

adopt *vt (boy)* усыновля́ть / усынови́ть *(whom = acc.)*; *(girl)* удочеря́ть / удочери́ть *(whom = acc.)* ♦ **I** *(1,2)* **would be willing to adopt your** *(3)* **son** / *(4)* **daughter.** *(1)* Я гото́в... / *(2)* Я бы хоте́л... *(3)* ...усынови́ть твоего́ ма́льчика. / *(4)* ...удочери́ть твою́ де́вочку. ♦ **What do I have to do to adopt** *(1)* **him** / *(2)* **her?** Что я до́лжен сде́лать, что́бы *(1)* ...усынови́ть его́ ? / *(2)* ...удочери́ть её?

adoption *n (boy)* усыновле́ние; *(girl)* удочере́ние.

adorable *adj* восхити́тельный, -ая, -ое, -ые *(short forms:* восхити́телен, восхити́тельна, -о, -ы)*, преле́стный, -ая, -ое, -ые ♦ **You are so adorable.** Ты так восхити́тельна.

adoration *n* обожа́ние ♦ **boundless** ~ бесконе́чное обожа́ние ♦ **fervent** ~ пы́лкое обожа́ние ♦ **object of** ~ предме́т обожа́ния.

adoration: phrases

I promise you a lifetime of *(1)* **enduring** / *(2)* **unwavering** / *(3)* **unremitting** / *(4)* **steadfast love and adoration.** Я обеща́ю тебе́ на всю жизнь *(1)* бесконе́чную / *(2-4)* ве́рную любо́вь и обожа́ние. ♦ *(1)* **I intend...** / *(2)* **I'm going... to lavish love and tenderness and adoration upon you such as you have never dreamed of.** *(1)* Я подарю́ тебе́ таки́е любо́вь, не́жность и обожа́ние, о кото́рых ты никогда́ не могла́ и мечта́ть. ♦ **If by some miracle I am able someday to press my lips in fervent adoration to the exquisite loveliness of your sweet smile, I shall have nothing more to hope for or want.** Если бы каки́м-то чу́дом я смог в оди́н прекра́сный день с пы́лким обожа́нием прижа́ться губа́ми к изы́сканной пре́лести твое́й сла́дкой улы́бки, мне не́чего бы́ло бы бо́льше жела́ть. ♦ **You have a face that instantly inspires reverence and adoration.** У тебя́ лицо́, кото́рое мгнове́нно внуша́ет почте́ние и обожа́ние. ♦ **I gaze upon your divinely beautiful face in its silky frame of** *(1)* **golden** / *(2)* **auburn** / *(3)* **black hair and I am awash in fervent adoration.** Я вгля́дываюсь в твоё боже́ственно-прекра́сное лицо́ в шелкови́стом обрамле́нии *(1)* золоты́х / *(2)* золоти́сто-кашта́новых / *(3)* чёрных воло́с и я охва́чен пы́лким обожа́нием. ♦ **Every time I see you walk** *(1)* **...through the door...** / *(2)* **...down the hallway...** / *(3)* **...along the street...** / *(4)* **...past me...** / *(5)* **...into the room... my heart begins palpitating wildly and I am flooded with** *(6)* **exquisite** / *(7)* **overpowering** / *(8)* **dizzying sensations of adoration and desire for you.** Ка́ждый раз, когда́ я ви́жу, как ты *(1)* ...вхо́дишь в дверь... / *(2)* ...идёшь по коридо́ру... / *(3)* ...идёшь по у́лице... / *(4)* ...прохо́дишь ми́мо... / *(5)* ...вхо́дишь в ко́мнату... моё се́рдце начина́ет выска́кивать из груди́, и меня́ переполня́ют *(6)* о́стрые / *(7)* невыноси́мые / *(8)* головокружи́тельные чу́вства обожа́ния и жела́ния. ♦ **You make me want to innundate you with warm, tender affection, love, and adoration.** Ты вызыва́ешь во мне жела́ние затопи́ть тебя́ тёплой, не́жной любо́вью и обожа́нием.

adore *vt* обожа́ть *(what, whom = acc.)*, поклоня́ться *(what, whom = dat.)* ♦ **absolutely** ~ соверше́нно обожа́ть ♦ ~ **beyond measure** обожа́ть безме́рно ♦ ~ **madly** обожа́ть до безу́мия.

adore: I adore you

There is no way that you can comprehend the fervor with which I adore you. Нико́им о́бразом ты не мо́жешь поня́ть пыл, с кото́рым я обожа́ю тебя́. ♦ **I adore your eyes and sing to them.** Я обожа́ю твои́ глаза́ и воспева́ю их. ♦ **Oh, how I adore you!** О, как я обожа́ю тебя́! ♦ **Do you know what I adore most about you? The part that lies between the top of your head and the bottom of your feet.** Зна́ешь ли ты, что я обожа́ю бо́лее всего́ в тебе́? Я обожа́ю всё в тебе́ с головы́ до ко́нчиков ног. ♦ **You possess**

For Russian adjectives, the masculine form is spelled out,
followed by the feminine, neuter and plural endings

the kind of beauty that I could spend a lifetime adoring and never get enough of. Ты обладаешь такой красотой, которой я мог бы восхищаться всю жизнь, никогда не насыщаясь. ♦ **I adore** *(1)* **...you.** / *(2)* **...your face.** / *(3)* **...everything about you.** / *(4)* **...every part of you.** Я обожаю *(1)* ...тебя / *(2)* ...твоё лицо. / *(3)* ...всё в тебе . / *(4)* ...каждую частичку тебя. ♦ **I adore you with all my heart and soul.** Я обожаю тебя всем своим сердцем и душой. ♦ **I love you and adore you more than anything in this world.** Я люблю тебя и обожаю тебя больше всего в этом мире. ♦ **Can you possibly imagine how much I adore you?** Можешь ли ты представить себе, как сильно я обожаю тебя ? ♦ **I adore everything about you -- your beautiful eyes, your silky hair, your** *(1,2)* **sunny smile -- everything.** Я обожаю всё в тебе -- твои прекрасные глаза , твои шелковистые волосы, твою *(1)* солнечную / *(2)* ясную улыбку -- всё. ♦ **If you ever feel the generosity in your heart to bestow the ultimate joy in life to someone who adores you beyond measure, then put your sweet mouth against mine for one heavenly minute and you will have done it.** Если только в твоём сердце пробудится щедрость подарить величайшее наслаждение в жизни тому, кто обожает тебя безмерно, тогда на одну божественную минутку прижми свои сладкие губы к моим и ты это сделаешь. ♦ **Have I told you lately that I adore you?** Говорил *(ж: Говорила)* ли я тебе в последнее время, что я обожаю тебя? ♦ **Oh, how I'm going to adore you!** О, как я буду обожать тебя! ♦ **I'm thinking about you all the time and adoring you and wanting you.** Я всё время думаю о тебе, обожаю тебя и хочу тебя. ♦ **Now I will close my letter, but not before I tell you that I adore you and think about you every day and dream about you every night.** Теперь я закончу своё письмо, но не раньше, чем скажу тебе, что я обожаю тебя, думаю о тебе каждый день и мечтаю о тебе каждую ночь.

---
adore: *my lips will adore you*
---

(1) **I want to...** / *(2)* **I'm going to... adore every part of your** *(3)* **beautiful** / *(4)* **delectable** / *(5)* **luscious body with my lips.** *(1)* Я хочу... / *(2)* Я буду... нежить своими губами каждую частицу твоего *(3)* прекрасного / *(4)* восхитительного / *(5)* сочного тела. ♦ **How I long to hold you in my arms and adore the beauty of your face with soft, gentle, love-filled kisses.** Как жажду я держать тебя в объятиях и и покрывать твоёпрекрасное лицо мягкими, нежными, полными любви поцелуями. ♦ **Do you have any idea at all how many hours I could spend just adoring you with my lips?** Представляешь ли ты себе, сколько часов я смог бы провести только лаская тебя губами? ♦ **How fervently my lips could adore you.** Как пылко мои губы могли бы ласкать тебя. ♦ **My lips would reverently adore the graceful curve of your hips.** Мои губы будут почтительно обожать грациозные изгибы твоих бёдер. ♦ **And then my lips would adore the** *(1)* **creamy** / *(2)* **smooth column of your throat with soft, loving kisses.** А потом мои губы покроют твою *(1)* кремовую / *(2)* гладкую стройную шею мягкими, любящими поцелуями.

adoring *adj* обожающий, -ая, -ее, -ие ♦ **My adoring lips will uncover your most precious secret.** Мои обожающие губы раскроют твой самый заветный секрет.

adult *adj* взрослый, -ая, -ое, -ые.

adult *n* взрослый *m*, взрослая *f*, взрослые *pl* ♦ **consenting** ~ взрослый, согласный на отношения *m (1 term)*; взрослая, согласная на отношения *f (1 term)*.

adulterer *n* неверный муж.

adulteress *n* неверная жена.

adulterous *adj* внебрачный, -ая, -ое, -ые.

adultery *n* адюльтер ♦ **I don't want to commit adultery.** Я не хочу совершить адюльтер.

advances *n, pl* притязания ♦ **sexual** ~s сексуальные притязания.

See Appendix 18 for notes on sending mail to Russia and Ukraine.

advantage n 1. (superiority) преиму́щество; 2. (benefit) вы́года, по́льза ♦ **You took advantage of me.** Ты по́льзовалась (ж: по́льзовался) свои́м преиму́ществом на́до мно́й. ♦ **I would never (try to) take advantage of you.** Я никогда́ не бу́ду (пыта́ться) воспо́льзоваться свои́м преиму́ществом над тобо́й.

adventure n (serious) приключе́ние, авантю́ра; (fun) развлече́ния pl ♦ **~s in love and life** приключе́ния в любви́ и жи́зни ♦ **amorous** ~ аму́рное приключе́ние ♦ **clothing-free** ~ развлече́ния без оде́жды ♦ **enticing** ~ зама́нчивое приключе́ние ♦ **erotic** ~ эроти́ческое приключе́ние ♦ **innovative romantic ~s** но́вые романти́ческие приключе́ния ♦ **sexual** ~ сексуа́льное приключе́ние ♦ **steamy** ~ эроти́ческое приключе́ние ♦ **urban ~s** городски́е развлече́ния ♦ **weekend ~s** развлече́ния на выходны́х.

adventure: phrases

(1,2) **I have a lively sense of adventure.** (1) Я о́чень люблю́ приключе́ния. / (2) Я авантю́рный челове́к. ♦ **I seek someone with a sense of adventure.** Я ищу́ того́, кто лю́бит приключе́ния. ♦ **I'm into laughter, adventure, and having fun.** Я челове́к, лю́бящий смех, приключе́ния и развлече́ния.

adventure-loving adj лю́бящий (-ая, -ее, -ие) приключе́ния ♦ **be** ~ люби́ть приключе́ния ♦ **I'm an adventure-loving person.** Я люблю́ приключе́ния.

adventurer n иска́тель приключе́ний ♦ **spiritual** ~ челове́к, про́бующий разли́чные духо́вные иде́и (1 term).

adventuress n иска́тельница приключе́ний ♦ **spiritual** ~ же́нщина, про́бующая разли́чные духо́вные иде́и (1 term).

adventurous adj 1. (liking adventure) лю́бящий (-ая, -ее, -ие) приключе́ния; (courageous) сме́лый, -ая, -ое, -ые, отва́жный, -ая, -ое, -ые; 2. (enterprising) предприи́мчивый, -ая, -ое, -ые ♦ **be** ~ люби́ть приключе́ния.

adventurousness n скло́нность к приключе́ниям ♦ **sexual** ~ скло́нность к сексуа́льным приключе́ниям.

adversity n несча́стья pl, невзго́ды pl, превра́тности судьбы́ pl, напа́сти pl ♦ **Our love is going to prevail against this adversity, I promise you.** На́ша любо́вь оде́ржит верх над э́тими невзго́дами, я обеща́ю.

advice n сове́т (often pl: сове́ты) ♦ **bad** ~ плохо́й сове́т ♦ **excellent** ~ отли́чный сове́т ♦ **fatherly** ~ отцо́вский сове́т ♦ **friendly** ~ дру́жеский сове́т ♦ **good** ~ хоро́ший сове́т ♦ **motherly** ~ матери́нский сове́т ♦ **my** ~ мой сове́т ♦ **sensible** ~ разу́мный сове́т ♦ **smart** ~ у́мный сове́т ♦ **useful** ~ поле́зный сове́т ♦ **wonderful** ~ прекра́сный сове́т ♦ **your** ~ (familiar) тво́й сове́т; (polite) Ваш сове́т ♦ **follow** (1) **my** / (2) **your** ~ сле́довать / после́довать (1) моему́ / (2) твоему́ сове́ту.

advice: phrases

I will (1) **heed** / (2) **take your advice.** (1) Я обращу́ внима́ние на... / (2) Я приму́... тво́й сове́т. ♦ **I need your advice.** Мне ну́жен тво́й сове́т. ♦ **May I give you some advice?** Могу́ ли я дать тебе́ сове́т? ♦ **Let me give you some** ([1] **motherly** / [2] **fatherly** / [3] **good**) **advice.** Позво́ль мне дать тебе́ ([1] матери́нский / [2] отцо́вский / [3] хоро́ший) сове́т. ♦ **Thank you for your** ([1] **motherly** / [2] **fatherly** / [3] **good**) **advice.** Спаси́бо тебе́ за твой ([1] матери́нский / [2] отцо́вский / [3] хоро́ший) сове́т. ♦ **I appreciate your advice (very much).** Я (о́чень) ценю́ твой сове́т.

advise vt сове́товать / посове́товать (whom = dat.).

aerobics n аэро́бика ♦ **kiss ~s** аэро́бика поцелу́ев ♦ **sexual ~s** сексуа́льная аэро́бика ♦ **do** ~ занима́ться аэро́бикой ♦ **I want to introduce you to kiss aerobics.** Я хочу́ познако́мить тебя́ с аэро́бикой поцелу́ев.

aesthetic adj эстети́ческий, -ая, -ое, -ие.

When terms are listed after a main word, a tilde ~ is used to indicate the main word.

aesthetics *n* эсте́тика ♦ **I have a strong sense of aesthetics.** У меня́ хоро́ший эстети́ческий вкус.

affable *adj* приве́тливый, -ая, -ое, -ые.

affair *n* 1. *(matter)* де́ло; 2. *(love)* рома́н, связь *f*, любо́вная интри́га / исто́рия ♦ **adulterous** ~ внебра́чная связь, связь на стороне́ ♦ **brief (love)** ~ коро́ткая (любо́в-ная) связь ♦ **budding love** ~ расцвета́ющая любо́вная связь ♦ **business** ~s би́знес ♦ **casual** случа́йная связь ♦ **constant** ~s постоя́нные рома́ны ♦ **endless** ~s бесконе́чные рома́ны ♦ **extramarital** ~ внебра́чная связь, связь на стороне́ ♦ **fizzled** ~ неуда́вшаяся связь ♦ **full-blown love** ~ по́лностью разви́вшаяся любо́вная связь ♦ **grand love** ~ вели́кий рома́н ♦ **ill-starred love** ~ любо́вь, обречённая на неуда́чу *(1 term)* ♦ **illicit (love)** ~ та́йная (любо́вная) связь ♦ **love** ~ 1. рома́н, любо́вная интри́га; 2. любо́вная связь ♦ **personal** ~s ли́чные дела́ ♦ **private** ~s ли́чные дела́ ♦ **secret** ~ та́йный рома́н ♦ **sordid** ~ гну́сный рома́н ♦ **tawdry** ~ дешёвая связь ♦ **unhappy love** ~ неуда́чный рома́н ♦ **whirlwind** ~ урага́нная связь ♦ **wretched** ~ несча́стный рома́н, несча́стная связь ♦ **rush into an** ~ броса́ться / бро́ситься в любо́вную связь.

> **affair: phrases**

I'm (still) trying to get over an unhappy love affair. Я (до сих пор) пыта́юсь опра́виться от неуда́чного рома́на. ♦ **I can't handle a(n)** *(1)* **secret /** *(2)* **illicit (love) affair.** Я не могу́ вы́нести *(1,2)* та́йную (любо́вную) связь. ♦ **I don't want just an affair.** Я не хочу́ про́сто рома́на. ♦ **I'm not interested in just an affair.** Я не заинтересо́ван *(ж: заинтересо́вана)* про́сто в рома́не. ♦ **I had a(n) (brief) (love) affair with** *(1)* **him /** *(2)* **her.** У меня́ была́ (коро́ткая) (любо́вная) связь с *(1)* ней / *(2)* ним. ♦ **We had a(n) (brief) (love) affair.** У нас была́ (коро́ткая) (любо́вная) связь. ♦ **I don't have the stomach for an affair.** У меня́ не хвата́ет реши́тельности для рома́на. ♦ **I have some** *(1)* **business /** *(2)* **personal affairs to take care of.** У меня́ есть *(1)* ...би́знес, кото́рым... / *(2)* ...ли́чные дела́, кото́рыми... мне на́до занима́ться. ♦ **This is an affair of the heart.** Это де́ло се́рдца. ♦ **I** *(1)* **can't /** *(2)* **couldn't put up with her** *(his)* **endless affairs.** Я не *(1)* могу́ / *(2)* мог *(ж:могла́)* смири́ться с её *(ж: его́)* бесконе́чными рома́нами.

affectation *n* жема́нство.

affected *adj* жема́нный, -ая, -ое, -ые.

affection *n* не́жность *f*, любо́вь *f* ♦ **abounding** ~ больша́я не́жность ♦ **boundless** ~ безграни́чная не́жность ♦ **brotherly** ~ бра́тская любо́вь ♦ **great** ~ больша́я не́жность ♦ **obvious** ~ я́вный интере́с ♦ **sisterly** ~ се́стринская любо́вь ♦ **sweet** не́жная любо́вь ♦ **tender** ~ не́жная любо́вь ♦ **tremendous** ~ огро́мная любо́вь ♦ **warm** ~ тёплая любо́вь.

> **affection: verb & other terms**

be starved for ~ жа́ждать не́жности ♦ **crave** ~ жа́ждать не́жности ♦ **give** ~ дава́ть / дать не́жность *(to whom = dat.)*, дари́ть / подари́ть не́жность *(to whom = dat.)* ♦ **lack of** ~ отсу́тствие не́жности ♦ **lavish** ~ расточа́ть / расточи́ть не́жность *(on whom = dat.)*, ще́дро отдава́ть / отда́ть не́жность *(on whom = dat.)* ♦ **need** *(1,2)* ~ нужна́ *(1)* любо́вь / *(2)* не́жность *(person needing = dat.)* ♦ **(never) get enough of your** ~ (никогда́ не) насыща́ться / насы́титься твое́й любо́вью ♦ **show** ~ пока́зывать / показа́ть не́жность *(to whom = dat.)*, выража́ть / вы́разить любо́вь *(to whom = dat.)*, проявля́ть / прояви́ть не́жность *(to whom = dat.)* ♦ **win your** ~ завоева́ть твою́ привя́занность.

> **affection: I have affection to give**

I have so much affection to give (*[1]* **...to you. /** *[2]* **...to the right person).** Во мне так мно́го любви́ (и всю её я отда́м *[1]* ...тебе́. / *[2]* ...подходя́щему челове́ку.). ♦ **I have a great capacity for affection.** Во мне большо́й дар любви́.

A list of abbreviations used in the dictionary is given on page 10.

---

affection: *I love affection*

I love affection (*[1]* ... — in all its manifold forms. / *[2]* ...at all times.) Я люблю не́жность (*[1]* ... во всех её многообра́зных фо́рмах. / *[2]* ...во вся́кое вре́мя.) ♦ **I thrive on affection.** Я живу́ любо́вью. ♦ **I love to give affection and fill my partner with boundless pleasure and delight in an eager and selfless way.** Я люблю́ дари́ть своему́ партнёру не́жность, безграни́чное наслажде́ние и восхище́ние пы́лко и бескоры́стно.

affection: *I need affection*

(1) **I need / *(2)* crave affection -- and I have so much to give.** *(1)* Мне нужна́ не́жность... / *(2)* Я жа́жду не́жности... и я могу́ так мно́го дать. ♦ **I'm *(1)* so / *(2)* really / *(3)* totally starved for (love and) affection.** Я *(1)* так / *(2)* действи́тельно / *(3)* весь *(ж: вся)* жа́жду (любви́ и) не́жности. ♦ **I never get enough of your affection.** Я никогда́ не смогу́ насы́титься твое́й любо́вью. ♦ **The thought patterns that yielded your choice of words and sentences in your ad reveal the exact same raging hunger for love and affection that I harbor within me.** Мы́сли, вло́женные в слова́ и стиль Ва́шего объявле́ния, говоря́т о то́чно тако́й же неи́стовой жа́жде любви́ и не́жности, кото́рая таи́тся во мне. ♦ **Affection — oh, God, I am so starved for it!** Не́жность -- о, бо́же, я так жа́жду её! ♦ **I seek someone for mutual affection.** Я ищу́ челове́ка для взаи́мной любви́.

affection: *my affection for you*

(1) **I have... / *(2)* There is... (such) boundless affection in my heart for you.** *(1,2)* В моём се́рдце безграни́чная не́жность к тебе́. ♦ **This brief missive conveys only an iota of the affection that I nourish in my heart for you.** Это коро́ткое письмо́ несёт то́лько ма́лую то́лику той любви́ к тебе́, кото́рой полно́ моё се́рдце. ♦ **I have such a vast reservoir of tender affection to lavish upon you.** У меня́ для тебя́ тако́й огро́мный резервуа́р не́жной любви́. ♦ *(1)* **No doubt... / *(2)* I'm sure... you have noticed my obvious affection for you.** *(1)* Несомне́нно... / *(2)* Я уве́рен,... Вы заме́тили мой я́вный интере́с к Вам. ♦ **I guess my affection for you has been very obvious.** Я полага́ю, мой интере́с к Вам был соверше́нно очеви́ден. ♦ **You are the (one and only) object of (all) my affections.** Ты оди́н (еди́нственный) предме́т (всей) мое́й любви́. ♦ **It is much more than *(1)* sisterly / *(2)* brotherly affection that I *(3)* feel / *(4)* harbor for you.** То, что я *(3)* чу́вствую / *(4)* испы́тываю к тебе́, э́то мно́го бо́льше, чем *(1)* се́стринская / *(2)* бра́тская любо́вь.

affection: *I'll give you affection*

(1) **I want to... / *(2)* I'm going to... lavish love and affection on you beyond your wildest dreams.** *(1)* Я хочу́ ще́дро отда́ть... / *(2)* Я ще́дро отда́м... тебе́ свою́ любо́вь и не́жность сверх всех твои́х са́мых заве́тных жела́ний. ♦ **I want to spend all my days lavishing affection on you.** Я хочу́ провести́ все свои́ дни, расточа́я тебе́ не́жность. ♦ **I want to inundate you with love and affection.** Я хочу́ затопи́ть тебя́ любо́вью и не́жностью. ♦ **I want to fill your life with (constant) affection.** Я хочу́ напо́лнить твою́ жизнь (постоя́нной) не́жностью. ♦ **I will show you affection in every possible way (, every hour of every day of every year).** Все́ми возмо́жными спо́собами я бу́ду выража́ть тебе́ свою́ любо́вь (ка́ждый час ка́ждого дня ка́ждого го́да). ♦ **I want to express affection to you in all ways possible.** Я хочу́ вы́разить тебе́ свою́ любо́вь все́ми возмо́жными путя́ми. ♦ **I know that I would never get tired of *(1)* giving / *(2)* showing you affection.** Я зна́ю, что никогда́ не уста́ну *(1,2)* люби́ть тебя́. ♦ **I could just smother you with love and affection.** Я про́сто осы́плю тебя́ свое́й любо́вью и не́жностью. ♦ **You make me want to innundate you with warm, tender affection, love, and adoration.** Ты вызыва́ешь во мне жела́ние затопи́ть тебя́ тёплой, не́жной любо́вью и обожа́нием. ♦ **I wish I could spend all the hours of the day lavishing affection on you.**

The accents on Russian words are to show how to pronounce them..
You don't have to copy the accents when writing to someone.

Я жела́л бы проводи́ть все часы́, расточа́я тебе́ свою́ не́жность.

affection: *you give me affection*

I love the way you show me affection. Мне нра́вится то, как ты выража́ешь свою́ любо́вь. ♦ **You and your sweet affection are so precious to me.** Ты и твоя́ не́жная любо́вь - таки́е це́нности для меня́. ♦ **I pray that you can return my affection (in even a small measure).** Я молю́сь, что́бы ты смогла́ отве́тить на мою́ любо́вь (хотя́ бы немно́го). ♦ **If you can return even a tiny fraction of all the affection I give you, you will make me the happiest person alive.** Если ты смо́жешь верну́ть хотя́ бы кро́хотную части́чку всей той любви́, кото́рую я даю́ тебе́, ты сде́лаешь меня́ счастли́вейшим челове́ком среди́ живу́щих. ♦ **No one has ever shown me** *(1)* **...so much affection.** / *(2)* **...as much affection as you have.** Никто́ никогда́ не выража́л мне *(1)* ...так мно́го любви́. / *(2)* ...так мно́го любви́, как ты. ♦ **Your constant show of affection** *(1)* **...fills my heart with love for you.** / *(1)* **...makes me love you more and more.** Твоя́ постоя́нно выража́емая любо́вь *(1)* ...наполня́ет моё се́рдце любо́вью к тебе́. / *(2)* ...всё бо́льше и бо́льше уси́ливает мою́ любо́вь к тебе́. ♦ **I love (your) small signs of affection.** Я люблю́ (твои́) ма́ленькие зна́ки любви́. ♦ **Is it really only** *(1)* **sisterly /** *(2)* **brotherly affection that you** *(3)* **feel /** *(4)* **harbor for me?** Это пра́вда, что ты *(3)* чу́вствуешь / *(4)* испы́тываешь то́лько *(1)* сестри́нскую / *(2)* бра́тскую любо́вь ко мне?

affection: *your capacity for affection*

Your *(1)* **blue /** *(2)* **dark eyes and wide smile radiate affection.** Твои́ *(1)* голубы́е / *(2)* тёмные глаза́ и широ́кая улы́бка излуча́ют не́жность. ♦ **I perceive in you a reservoir of warmth and affection and tenderness that is very, very deep.** Я чу́вствую в тебе́ о́чень, о́чень глубо́кий резервуа́р серде́чности, любви́ и не́жности.

affection: *showing affection*

I think it's important to show affection. Я ду́маю, что э́то ва́жно пока́зывать свою́ не́жность. ♦ **Little signs of affection** *(1)* **...mean a lot to me. /** *(2)* **...are so important.** Ма́ленькие зна́ки любви́ *(1)* ...зна́чат мно́го для меня́. / *(2)* ...так ва́жны.

affection: *lack of affection*

I wish you would show me a little more affection. Я жела́л *(ж: жела́ла)* бы, что́бы ты была́ *(ж: был)* чуть нежне́е. ♦ **I feel so disillusioned by your lack of affection.** Я так разочаро́ван *(ж: разочаро́вана)* отсу́тствием у тебя́ не́жности. ♦ *(1)* **He /** *(2)* **She refuses to hug or kiss or show affection.** *(1)* Он / *(2)* Она́ отка́зывается обня́ть, поцелова́ть, прояви́ть не́жность.

affection: *trifling with affections*

You have trifled with my affections. Ты игра́ла *(ж: игра́л)* мое́й любо́вью. ♦ **Believe me, I would never trifle with your affections.** Пове́рь мне, я никогда́ не бу́ду игра́ть твое́й любо́вью.

affection: *closing of a letter*

With abounding affection for you, С большо́й не́жностью к тебе́, ♦ **In affection,** С любо́вью, ♦ **With** *(1,2)* **warm(est) affection,** С *(1)* большо́й / *(2)* огро́мной любо́вью.

affectionate *adj* не́жный, -ая, -ое, -ые *(short forms:* не́жен, не́жна, -о, -ы*),* лю́бящий, -ая, -ее, -ие ♦ **I need an affectionate, loving person with lots of hugs and kisses to give.** Мне ну́жен не́жный, лю́бящий челове́к, даря́щий мно́жество объя́тий и поцелу́ев. ♦ **Are you affectionate?** Ты не́жная? *(ж: Ты не́жный?).* ♦ **I'm (**[1] **very /** [2] **enormously /** [3] **tremendously /** [4] **unbelievably) affectionate (by nature).** Я (*[1]* о́чень / *[2,3]* чрезме́рно / *[4]* невероя́тно) не́жный *(ж не́жная)* (по нату́ре). ♦ **You won't believe how affectionate I am.** Ты не пове́ришь, как я не́жен *(ж: не́жна).* ♦ **You've never** *(1)* **met /** *(2)* **known anyone as affectionate as I am.** Ты никогда́ не *(1)* встреча́ла / *(2)*

If no accent is shown on a word with a capitalized vowel,
it means that the capitalized vowel is accented.

зна́ла никого́ тако́го не́жного, как я. ♦ **I've never** *(1)* **met** / *(2)* **known anyone as affectionate as you are.** Я никогда́ не *(1)* встреча́л *(ж: встреча́ла)* / *(2)* знал *(ж: зна́ла)* таку́ю не́жную *(ж: тако́го не́жного)*, как ты. ♦ *(1)* **You are so affectionate.** / *(2)* **You are such an affectionate person.** *(1,2)* Ты така́я не́жная. *(ж: Ты тако́й не́жный.)* ♦ **I love how affectionate you are.** Мне нра́вится, что ты така́я не́жная *(ж: тако́й не́жный)*.

affectionately *adv* не́жно, лю́бяще ♦ **Affectionately yours,** *(closing of a letter)* С любо́вью, *(оконча́ние письма́)*.

affinity *n* ро́дственность *f*, родство́, схо́дство; симпа́тия *(for whom = + к + dat.)* ♦ **From your very first letter I sensed an affinity between us.** С твоего́ са́мого пе́рвого письма́ я ощути́л *(ж: ощути́ла)* родство́ ме́жду на́ми.

affirmation *n* утвержде́ние ♦ **We will lose ourselves (every night) in the rapturous affirmation of our love.** Мы бу́дем растворя́ться (ка́ждую ночь) в восто́рженном утвержде́нии на́шей любви́. ♦ **That will be the ultimate affirmation of our love for each other.** Это бу́дет наивы́сшим подтвержде́нием на́шей любви́ друг к дру́гу.

affluent *adj (wealthy)* бога́тый, -ая, -ое, -ые; *(well-off)* состоя́тельный, -ая, -ое, -ые.

afire *adj* в огне́ ♦ **My desire for you sets me afire.** Страсть к тебе́ сжига́ет меня́. ♦ **I am afire with lust for you.** Я сгора́ю от вожделе́ния к тебе́. ♦ **The very thought of you sets my heart afire.** Сама́ мысль о тебе́ наполня́ет моё се́рдце огнём. ♦ **Your beautiful** *(1)* **blue** / *(2)* **dark eyes have set my heart afire.** Твои́ прекра́сные *(1)* голубы́е / *(2)* тёмные глаза́ поверга́ют в ого́нь моё се́рдце. ♦ **I want to kiss you and kiss you and kiss you until all your senses are afire with** *(1)* **need** / *(2)* **desire.** Я хочу́ целова́ть тебя́, целова́ть и целова́ть до тех пор, пока́ все твои́ чу́вства не погру́зятся в ого́нь *(1)* жела́ния / *(2)* стра́сти.

aflame *adj* в огне́ *(See phrases under* **afire***)*.

aflutter *adj* взволно́ванный, -ая, -ое, -ые, возбуждённый, -ая, -ое, -ые; трепе́щущий, -ая, -ее, -ие ♦ **My heart was all aflutter.** Моё се́рдце трепета́ло.

afraid *adj (Russian uses verb* боя́ться + *gen.)* ♦ **be** ~ боя́ться *(of what, whom =* gen.*)* ♦ **be ~ to admit** боя́ться призна́ться ♦ **I'm afraid of being hurt (again).** Я не хочу́ (опя́ть) страда́ть. ♦ **I** *(1)* **seek** / *(2)* **want someone who's not afraid to love.** Я *(1)* ищу́ / *(2)* хочу́ того́, кто не бои́тся люби́ть. ♦ **Don't be afraid.** Не бо́йся. ♦ **Are you afraid?** Ты бои́шься? ♦ **I'm (not) afraid** Я (не) бою́сь.

Afro *(hair style)* причёска в сти́ле «Афро».

after *prep* по́сле. *(+ gen.)*.

afterglow *n* о́тсвет ♦ **silken** ~ шелкови́стый о́тсвет, шелкови́стое свече́ние.

afternoon *n* (вре́мя) по́сле полу́дня ♦ **every** ~ ка́ждый день по́сле полу́дня ♦ **in the** ~ днём, по́сле полу́дня ♦ **Saturday** *(etc.)* ~ в суббо́ту по́сле полу́дня ♦ **this** ~ сего́дня днём, сего́дня по́сле полу́дня ♦ **tomorrow** ~ за́втра днём, за́втра по́сле полу́дня ♦ **yesterday** ~ вчера́ днём, вчера́ по́сле полу́дня.

aftershave (lotion) *n* лосьо́н по́сле бритья́.

age *vi* старе́ть / постаре́ть ♦ **To me, you will never fade nor age nor die.** Для меня́ ты никогда́ не увя́нешь, не соста́ришься, не умрёшь.

age *n* во́зраст ♦ ~ **open** *(personal ads)* во́зраст безразли́чен ♦ ~ **unimportant** во́зраст нева́жен ♦ **any** ~ любо́й во́зраст ♦ **approximate** ~ приблизи́тельный во́зраст ♦ **marriageable** ~ бра́чный во́зраст ♦ **mature** ~ зре́лый во́зраст ♦ **maximum** ~ преде́льный во́зраст ♦ **middle** ~ сре́дний во́зраст ♦ **my** ~ мо́й во́зраст ♦ **old** ~ ста́рческий во́зраст, ста́рость *f* ♦ **right** ~ подходя́щий во́зраст ♦ **same** ~ одного́ во́зраста ♦ **suitable** ~ подходя́щий во́зраст ♦ **twice** *(1)* **my** / *(2)* **your** ~ вдво́е ста́рше *(1)* меня́ / *(2)* тебя́ ♦ ~ **unimportant** во́зраст нева́жен ♦ **young** ~ молодо́й во́зраст ♦ **your** ~ *(familiar)*

Russian has 6 grammatical cases. For an explanation of them see the grammar appendix on page 686.

твой во́зраст; *(polite)* Ваш во́зраст ♦ ~ **difference** ра́зница в во́зрасте ♦ **girl of marriageable** ~ взро́слая де́вушка ♦ **tell-tale lines of** ~ преда́тельские морщи́ны, выдаю́щие во́зраст *(1 term)*.

> **age: phrases**

What's your age? Ско́лько Вам лет? ♦ **You look (much) younger than your age.** Вы вы́глядите (гора́здо) моло́же свои́х лет. ♦ *(1)* **Your age...** / *(2)* **Our age difference... doesn't matter to me.** *(1)* Твой во́зраст... / *(2)* На́ша ра́зница в во́зрасте... не име́ет значе́ния для меня́. ♦ **I don't care what age you are.** Меня́ не волну́ет твой во́зраст. ♦ **Our age difference is too** *(1)* **much** / *(2)* **great.** На́ша ра́зница в во́зрасте сли́шком *(1)* больша́я / *(2)* велика́. ♦ **I hope you won't mind the difference in our ages.** Я наде́юсь, ты не име́ешь ничего́ про́тив ра́зницы в на́шем во́зрасте. ♦ **I'm looking for someone around the same age.** Я ищу́ кого́-нибудь приблизи́тельно тако́го же во́зраста. ♦ **Do you know someone (around) my age?** Зна́ешь ли ты кого́-нибудь (приблизи́тельно) моего́ во́зраста? ♦ **You have a** *(1)* **beauty** / *(2)* **loveliness that age can never** *(3)* **dim** / *(4)* **diminish.** Ты так *(1,2)* краси́ва, что с года́ми твоя́ красота́ не мо́жет *(3)* потускне́ть / *(4)* уме́ньшиться. ♦ **I don't care what your age is, you** *(f)* **are still** *(1)* **exceptionally** / *(2)* **extraordinarily** / *(3)* **very** *(4)* **good-looking** / *(5)* **attractive** / *(6)* **beautiful.** Меня́ не волну́ет твой во́зраст, ты всё ещё *(1)* исключи́тельно / *(2)* чрезвыча́йно / *(3)* о́чень *(4)* интере́сная / *(5)* привлека́тельная / *(6)* краси́вая. ♦ **I don't care what your age is, you** *(m)* **are still** *(1)* **exceptionally** / *(2)* **extraordinarily** / *(3)* **very** *(4)* **good-looking** / *(5)* **attractive** / *(6)* **handsome.** Меня́ не волну́ет твой во́зраст, ты всё ещё *(1)* исключи́-тельно / *(2)* чрезвыча́йно / *(3)* о́чень *(4)* интере́сный / *(5)* привлека́тельный / *(1)* краси́вый.

ageless *adj* нестаре́ющий, -ая, -ее, -ие.

aggressive *adj* агресси́вный, -ая, -ое, -ые.

aggressively *adv* агресси́вно.

agile *adj* прово́рный, -ая, -ое, -ые *(short forms:* прово́рен, прово́рна, -о, -ы*)* ♦ **You're as agile as a cat.** Ты так прово́рна *(ж: прово́рен)*, как ко́шка *(ж: кот)*.

aging *adj* старе́ющий, -ая, -ее, -ие.

agitated *adj* взволно́ванный, -ая, -ое, -ые; возбуждённый, -ая, -ое, -ые ♦ *(1)* **be** / *(2)* **get** ~ *(1,2)* волнова́ться ♦ **There's no reason to** *(1)* **be** / *(2)* **get so (wildly) agitated.** Нет никако́й причи́ны так (ди́ко) *(1,2)* волнова́ться.

agitation *n* волне́ние; возбужде́ние.

aglow *pred adj* пыла́ющий, -ая, -ее, -ие, горя́щий, -ая, -ее, -ие ♦ **The things you** *(1)* **...say...** / *(2)* **...write in your letters... set my heart aglow.** То, что ты *(1)* ...говори́шь,... / *(2)* ...пи́шешь в свои́х пи́сьмах,... заставля́ет моё се́рдце пыла́ть. ♦ **A letter from you sets my heart aglow.** Письмо́ от тебя́ заставля́ет моё се́рдце пыла́ть. ♦ **Your** *(1)* **letter** / *(2)* **call set my heart aglow.** *(1)* Твоё письмо́ заста́вило... / *(2)* Твой звоно́к заста́вил... моё се́рдце пыла́ть.

agnostic *n* агно́стик.

agonize *vi* му́читься ♦ **I've been agonizing over** *(1)* **...this...** / *(2)* **...the decision** / *(3)* **question** / *(4)* **matter...** / *(5)* **...your proposal...** *(6)* **...all night long.** / *(7)* **...for the past two** / *(8)* **etc days.** / *(9)* **...for the past week** / *(10)* **month.** Меня́ му́чает *(1)* ...э́то... / *(2)* ...э́то реше́-ние... / *(3)* ...э́тот вопро́с... / *(4)* ...э́то де́ло... / *(5)* ...твоё предложе́ние... / *(6)* ...всю ночь напролёт. / *(7)* ...в после́дние два дня / *(8)* ит.д. дня. / *(9)* ...всю э́ту неде́лю. / *(10)* ...весь э́тот ме́сяц.

agony *n* му́ка, страда́ние, аго́ния; муче́ние, пы́тка ♦ **constant** ~ постоя́нная му́ка ♦ **sheer** ~ су́щая пы́тка ♦ *(1,2)* **sweet** ~ *(1)* сла́дкая / *(2)* сла́достная аго́ния ♦ **unbearable** ~

There are no articles ("a" or "the") in Russian.

невыноси́мая му́ка ♦ *(1)* **My love for you...** / *(2)* **My wanting you...** / *(3)* **My longing for you...** / *(4)* **My loneliness (without you)...** / *(5)* **The yearning in my heart for you...** **is an agony that I can** *(6)* **barely** / *(7)* **scarcely endure.** *(1)* Моя любо́вь к тебе́... / *(2)* Моё жела́ние тебя́... / *(3)* Моя́ тоска́ по тебе́... / *(4)* Моё одино́чество (без тебя́)... / *(5)* жа́жда тебя́ в моём се́рдце... - э́то му́ка, кото́рую я *(6,7)* едва́ могу́ вы́нести. ♦ **If you have any shred of compassion for me, you'll alleviate the agony of my yearning by sending me more photos of yourself.** Если у тебя́ есть хотя́ бы ма́лая то́лика состра-да́ния ко мне, ты облегчи́шь му́ку мое́й тоски́, посла́в мне ещё не́сколько свои́х фотогра́фий. ♦ **This being apart from you is sheer agony.** Быть в разлу́ке с тобо́й су́щая пы́тка. ♦ **Wanting you and not being able to have you is sheer agony.** Хоте́ть тебя́ и не име́ть возмо́жность быть с тобо́й су́щая пы́тка. ♦ **You can never know the sheer agony I go through** *(1)* **... being apart from you.** / *(2)* **... wanting you and not being able to have you.** Ты никогда́ не узна́ешь че́рез каку́ю пы́тку я прохожу́ *(1)* ...бу́дучи в разлу́ке с тобо́й. / *(2)* ...жела́я тебя́ и не име́я возмо́жность быть с тобо́й.

agree *vi* соглаша́ться / согласи́ться ♦ **Do you agree?** Ты согла́сна *(ж: согла́сен)*? ♦ **I (don't) agree.** Я (не) согла́сен *(ж: согла́сна)* ♦ **Do you think your** *(1)* **mother** / *(2)* **father will agree?** Ты ду́маешь, *(1)* ...твоя́ мать... / *(2)* ...тво́й оте́ц... согласи́тся? ♦ **I (don't) think** *(1)* **she** / *(2)* **he will agree.** Я (не) ду́маю, что *(1)* она́ / *(2)* он согласи́тся. ♦ **Do you think your parents will agree?** Ты ду́маешь, твои́ роди́тели соглася́тся? ♦ **I (don't) think they will agree.** Я (не) ду́маю, что они́ соглася́тся. ♦ **I can't help but agree.** Мне не остаётся ничего́ друго́го, как согласи́ться.

agreeable *adj* покла́дистый, -ая, -ое, -ые.

agreement *n* соглаше́ние ♦ **cohabitation** ~ нотариа́льно офо́рмленное соглаше́ние о совме́стной жи́зни ♦ **legal** ~ зако́нное соглаше́ние ♦ **separation** ~ соглаше́ние о разде́льной жи́зни ♦ **come to a mutual** ~ приходи́ть / прийти́ к взаи́мному согла-ше́нию ♦ **come to an** ~ приходи́ть / прийти́ к согла́сию.

aid *n*: ♦ **I wear a hearing aid.** Я ношу́ слухово́й аппара́т.

AIDS *acronym* СПИД.

air *n* 1. *(to breath)* во́здух; 2. *(aura)* атмосфе́ра; 3. *(attitude)* вид ♦ ~ **of importance** ва́жный вид ♦ ~ **of innocence** неви́нный вид ♦ ~ **of superiority** высокоме́рный вид ♦ **hot** ~ *(slang)* «бодя́га» ♦ **I'm so happy. I've been walking on air all** *(1)* **day** / *(2)* **week.** Я так сча́стлив *(ж: сча́стлива)*. Я лета́л *(ж: лета́ла)* как на кры́льях *(1)* ...весь день. / *(2)* ...всю неде́лю. ♦ **You have such an air of** *(1)* **confidence** / *(2)* **self-assurance about you.** Ты так *(1)* ...уве́ренна *(ж: уве́рен)* в себе́. / *(2)* ...самоуве́ренна *(ж: самоуве́рен)*.

air force *n* вое́нно-возду́шные си́лы (ВВС) ♦ **I'm in the Air Force.** Я в вое́нно-возду́ш-ных си́лах. ♦ **I'm a** *(1)* **Sergeant** / *(2)* **Lieutenant** / *(3)* *etc* **in the Air Force.** Я *(1)* сержа́нт / *(2)* лейтена́нт / *(3)* и т.д. вое́нно-возду́шных сил. ♦ **I served four years in the Air Force.** Я служи́л *(ж: служи́ла)* четы́ре го́да в вое́нно-возду́шных си́лах.

aisle *n* прохо́д *(ме́жду ряда́ми)* ♦ *(1)* **I want to...** / *(2)* **My most cherished dream is to...** *(3,4)* **walk down the aisle with you.** *(1)* Я хочу́... / *(2)* Моё са́мое заве́тное жела́ние... *(3)* пойти́ с тобо́й под вене́ц. / *(4)* ...жени́ться на тебе́. *(ж: Я хочу́ вы́йти за́муж за тебя́)*.

alabaster *adj* алеба́стровый, -ая, -ое, -ые.

Aladdin's lamp *n* ла́мпа Аладди́на ♦ **If I were to find Aladdin's lamp, I would just throw it away, because in you I have** *(1)* **...the fulfillment of all my wishes.** / *(2)* **...everything a person could wish for.** Если бы я нашёл *(ж: нашла́)* ла́мпу Аладди́на, то вы́бросил *(ж: вы́бросила)* бы её, потому́ что в тебе́ *(1)* ...исполне́ние всех мои́х жела́ний. / *(2)* ...всё, что челове́к мог бы пожела́ть.

alcohol *n* алкого́ль *m* ♦ **I don't drink alcohol.** Я не пью кре́пкие напи́тки.

This dictionary contains two Russian alphabet pages:
one in Appendix 1, page 685, and a tear-off page on page 799.

alcoholic *adj* алкого́льный, -ая, -ое, -ые.

alcoholic *n* алкого́лик *m*, алкоголи́чка *f*.

alcoholism *n* алкоголи́зм.

alienate *vt* отчужда́ть *(whom = acc.)*, отта́лкивать / оттолкну́ть *(whom = acc.)*.

alimony *n* алиме́нты *pl* ♦ **I (don't) have to pay her alimony.** Я (не) до́лжен плати́ть ей алиме́нты.

alive *adj* живо́й, -а́я, -о́е, -ы́е *(short forms:* жив, -а́, -о, -ы) ♦ **You make my body feel so tinglingly alive.** Благодаря́ тебе́ моё те́ло стано́вится таки́м тре́петно живы́м. ♦ **You make me feel vividly alive.** Благодаря́ тебе́, я чу́вствую, что живу́. ♦ **All my senses come alive when you touch me.** Все мои́ чу́вства ожива́ют, когда́ ты каса́ешься меня́

all *n* весь *m*, вся *f*, всё *neut*, все *pl* ♦ **All my love is yours.** Вся моя́ любо́вь -- тебе́. ♦ **You are my all and everything.** Ты для меня́ -- всё на све́те. ♦ **You are all that I ever want.** Ты всё, чего́ я то́лько хочу́. ♦ **You are all that I could ever hope for.** Ты всё, на что я то́лько наде́юсь. ♦ **Tell me all about it.** Расскажи́ мне всё об э́том.

all-consuming *adj* всеохва́тывающий, -ая, -ее, -ие, испепеля́ющий, -ая, -ее, -ие, всепоглоща́ющий, -ая, -ее, -ие ♦ **My entire being is** *(1)* **assailed /** *(2)* **tormented by the all-consuming need to take you in my arms and revel in the reservoir of your passion.** Я весь *(1)* охва́чен / *(2)* изму́чен всепоглоща́ющей жа́ждой заключи́ть тебя́ в объя́тия и упива́ться твое́й стра́стью.

all-encompassing *adj* всеохва́тывающий, -ая, -ее, -ие.

allergic *adj* аллерги́ческий, -ая, -ое, -ие ♦ **I'm allergic to** *(1)* **smoke /** *(2)* **cats /** *(3)* **dogs /** *(4)* **work.** У меня́ аллерги́я на *(1)* куре́ние / *(2)* ко́шек / *(3)* соба́к / *(4)* рабо́ту.

allergy *n* аллерги́я ♦ **I have an allergy (to** *[1]* **smoke /** *[2]* **cats /** *[3]* **dogs).** У меня́ аллерги́я (на *[1]* куре́ние / *[2]* ко́шек / *[3]* соба́к).

alleviate *vt* облегча́ть / облегчи́ть *(what = acc.)* ♦ **If you have any shred of compassion for me, you'll alleviate the agony of my yearning by sending me more photos of yourself.** Если у тебя́ есть хотя́ бы ма́лая то́лика сострада́ния ко мне, ты облегчи́шь му́ку мое́й тоски́, посла́в мне ещё не́сколько свои́х фотогра́фий.

all over 1. *(finished)* ко́нчен, -а, -о, -ы; 2. *(everywhere)* везде́ ♦ **It's all over between us.** Всё ко́нчено ме́жду на́ми.

all there: ♦ *(1)* **He's /** *(2)* **She's not all there.** *(1)* Он / *(2)* Она́ немно́го не в себе́.

allure *n (fascination, charm)* привлека́тельность *f*, обая́ние, шарм; *(enticement)* зама́нива-ние, привлече́ние, завлече́ние, прима́нка, собла́зн ♦ **I cannot escape the allure of your red, rose-petal lips.** Я не могу́ устоя́ть пе́ред собла́зном твои́х кра́сных, похо́жих на лепестки́ ро́зы губ. ♦ **You have such** *(1)* **overwhelming /** *(2)* **cogent /** *(3)* **tremendous physical allure.** Ты так *(1)* ошеломля́юще / *(2)* неоспори́мо / *(3)* протряса́юще (физи́-чески) привлека́тельна. ♦ **Your physical allure takes my breath completely away.** Твоя́ физи́ческая привлека́тельность оставля́ет меня́ бездыха́нным.

alluring *adj* соблазни́тельный, -ая, -ое, -ые, зама́нчивый, -ая, -ое, -ые, обольсти́тель-ный, -ая, -ое, -ые.

allusion *n* намёк ♦ **sexual ~s** сексуа́льные намёки.

alone 1. *(only one person)* оди́н *m*, одна́ *f*, одно́ *neut*; *(with no others)* одни́ *pl*; *(in private)* наедине́; 2. *(in peace)* в поко́е ♦ **for you ~** для тебя́ одно́й *(ж: одного́)* ♦ **leave ~** 1. *(go away from)* оставля́ть / оста́вить одну́ *(ж: одного́) (whom = acc.)*; 2. *(not bother)* оставля́ть / оста́вить в поко́е *(whom = acc.)*.

---

alone: phrases

I am *(1)* **terribly /** *(2)* **so alone.** Я *(1)* ужа́сно / *(2)* так одино́к *(ж: одино́ка).* ♦ **I'm tired of being alone.** Я уста́л *(ж: уста́ла)* от одино́чества. ♦ **Life is too short to spend it**

---

*Russian verbs conjugate for 6 persons:
I, familiar you, he-she-it, we, polite & plural you, and they.*

alone. Жизнь сли́шком коротка́ для того́, что́бы проводи́ть её в одино́честве. ♦ **I want to** *(1)* **...be alone with you.** / *(2)* **...see you alone.** Я хочу́ *(1)* ...побы́ть с тобо́й наедине́. / *(2)* ...уви́деться с тобо́й наедине́. ♦ **Is there someplace we can be alone?** Есть ли тако́е ме́сто, где мы могли́ бы побы́ть одни́? ♦ **We can be alone** *(1)* **...here.** / *(2)* **...there.** / *(3)* **...in this** / *(4)* **my room.** / *(5)* **...in my apartment** / *(6)* **house.** Мы смо́жем побы́ть одни́ *(1)* ...здесь. / *(2)* ...там. / *(3)* ...в э́той / *(4)* мое́й ко́мнате. / *(5)* ...в мое́й кварти́ре. / *(6)* ...в моём до́ме. ♦ **Leave me** *(1,2)* **alone.** Оста́вь меня́ *(1)* одного́ . / *(2)* ...в поко́е. ♦ **I need some time to be alone.** Мне тре́буется вре́мя, что́бы побы́ть наедине́ с собо́й.

aloof *adj* отчуждённый, -ая, -ое, -ые, отрешённый, -ая, -ое, -ые, сде́ржанный, -ая, -ое, -ые ♦ **~ manner** сде́ржанное поведе́ние ♦ **I wish you wouldn't hold yourself so aloof from me.** Я хоте́л *(ж: хоте́ла)* бы, что́бы ты не держа́ла *(держа́л)* себя́ так отчуждённо.

altar *n* алта́рь *m* ♦ **Your body** *(1)* **...is...** / *(2)* **...will be...** **my altar.** Твоё те́ло *(1)* ...-- мой алта́рь. / *(2)* ...бу́дет мои́м алтарём. ♦ **It's hard to believe that you've never made a trip to the altar with anyone.** Тру́дно пове́рить в то, что ты никогда́ ни с кем не соверша́ла путеше́ствия к алтарю́.

altruistic *adj* альтруисти́ческий, -ая, -ое, -ие, бескоры́стный, -ая, -ое, -ые.

always *adv* всегда́ ♦ **I feel as** *(1)* **though** / *(2)* **if I have always known you.** У меня́ тако́е чу́вство, *(1.2)* как бу́дто я всегда́ знал *(ж: зна́ла)* тебя́. ♦ **I love you always and forever.** Я люблю́ тебя́ наве́чно. ♦ **I will always be here for you (, you know that, don't you?).** Я всегда́ бу́ду здесь для тебя́ (, ты зна́ешь э́то, не так ли?). ♦ **You will always be (first) in my heart.** Ты всегда́ бу́дешь (пе́рвой *[ж: пе́рвым]*) в моём се́рдце. ♦ **No matter where I am or what I do, I always think of you.** Не ва́жно, где я и что де́лаю, я всегда́ ду́маю о тебе́. ♦ **I will always** *(1)* **cherish** / *(2)* **treasure** / *(3)* **revere the memories of the times we shared together.** Я всегда́ бу́ду *(1)* ...леле́ять / *(2)* храни́ть воспомина́ния... / *(3)* ...дорожи́ть воспомина́ниями... о вре́мени, проведённом вме́сте. ♦ **I remain yours always.** Я навсегда́ оста́нусь твои́м *(ж: твое́й)*.

amaranthine *adj (= never-fading)* неувяда́емый, -ая, -ое, -ые ♦ **Your beauty is amaranthine.** Твоя́ красота́ неувяда́ема. ♦ **Your amaranthine** *(1)* **beauty** / *(2)* **loveliness fills me with wonder.** Я изумлён твое́й неувяда́емой *(1,2)* красото́й.

amaze *vt* изумля́ть / изуми́ть *(whom = acc.)* ♦ **You constantly amaze me.** Ты постоя́нно изумля́ешь меня́.

amazed *adj* изумлён, изумлена́, -о́, -ы́ *(short forms)* ♦ **I am (totally) amazed at** *(1)* **...what your beauty does to me.** / *(2)* **...the profound** / *(3)* **overwhelming** / *(4)* **tremendous effect you have on my heart and mind.** Я (соверше́нно) изумлён *(1)* ...тем, что твоя́ красота́ де́лает со мно́й. / *(2)* ...глубо́ким / *(3)* ошеломля́ющим / *(4)* грома́дным эффе́ктом, кото́рый ты произво́дишь на моё се́рдце и ра́зум.

amazement *n* изумле́ние ♦ **ecstatic ~** восто́рженное изумле́ние ♦ **frank ~** открове́нное изумле́ние ♦ **rapturous ~** восто́рженное изумле́ние.

ambience *n* 1. *(surroundings)* окруже́ние; среда́; 2. *(atmosphere)* атмосфе́ра; *(spirit)* дух ♦ **Whenever you stand in front of something, it seems to take on your color, your light, and your ambience to create a beautiful picture.** Ты придаёшь всему́, что нахо́дится ря́дом с тобо́й, свой свет, цвет, и свою́ атмосфе́ру, создава́я прекра́сную карти́ну.

ambition *n* 1. *(desire to succeed)* честолю́бие; 2. *(aspiration)* стремле́ние; *(goal)* цель *f*; *(dream)* мечта́ ♦ **To gain a small measure of your precious love is my passionate ambition.** Получи́ть ка́плю твое́й драгоце́нной любви́ -- моё стра́стное стремле́ние ♦ **I'm completely devoid of any** *(1,2)* **ambition to do anything except hold you in my arms and**

There are two words for "you" in Russian:
familiar «ты» and polite / plural «вы» (See page 781)

make love to you. Я соверше́нно лишён каки́х-либо други́х *(1)* стремле́ний / *(2)* амби́-
ций, кро́ме того́, что́бы держа́ть тебя́ в объя́тиях и занима́ться любо́вью с тобо́й.

ambitious *adj* 1. *(full of ambition)* честолюби́вый, -ая, -ое, -ые; 2. *(industrious)* трудо-
люби́вый, -ая, -ое, -ые.

ambivalence *n* дво́йственность *f* ♦ *(1)* **I'm getting tired of...** / *(2)* **I'm really dismayed
at... your ambivalence (about our relationship).** *(1)* Мне надоеда́ет... / *(2)* Меня́
действи́тельно обескура́живает... твоя́ дво́йственность (в на́ших отноше́ниях).

ambivalent *adj* дво́йственный, -ая, -ое, -ые ♦ **You seem to be so ambivalent about** *(1)*
...our relationship / *(2)* **future. /** *(3)* **...marriage.** У тебя́, ка́жется, тако́е дво́йственое
отноше́ние к *(1)* ...на́шим отноше́ниям. / *(2)* ...на́шему бу́дущему. / *(3)* ...на́шему
заму́жеству.

ambrosia *n* амбро́зия ♦ **Your love and devotion are the nectar and ambrosia for my soul.**
Твоя́ любо́вь и пре́данность -- некта́р и амбро́зия для мое́й души́.

amenable *adj* покла́дистый, -ая, -ое, -ые.

amends *n, pl* компенса́ция, вознагражде́ние ♦ **make ~s** загла́живать / загла́дить вину́
(for what = + за + *acc., to whom* = + пе́ред + *instr.)* ♦ **I want to make amends (for** *[1]*
...what I've done. / *[2]* **...all that's happened in the past.).** Я хочу́ загла́дить вину́ (за *[1]*
...то, что я де́лал *[ж: де́лала]*. / *[2]* ...всё, что случи́лось в про́шлом.)

America *n* Аме́рика ♦ **from ~** из Аме́рики ♦ **in ~** в Аме́рике ♦ **to ~** в Аме́рику.

American *adj* америка́нский, -ая, -ое, -ие.

American *n* америка́нец *m*, америка́нка *f.*

amiability *n* благожела́тельность *f*, дружелю́бие; любе́зность *f* ♦ **social** *(1,2)* **~** *(1)* благо-
жела́тельность / *(2)* дружелю́бие к окружа́ющим.

amiable *adj* дружелю́бный, -ая, -ое, -ые, дру́жеский, -ая, -ое, -ие.

amiably *adv* дру́жески.

amore *n (Italian)* *(= love)* аму́р, любо́вь *f.*

amorous *adj* 1. влю́бчивый, -ая, -ое, -ые; 2. любо́вный, -ая, -ое, -ые; 3. влюблённый, -ая,
-ое, -ые ♦ **You write such (beautiful,) amorous letters.** Ты пи́шешь таки́е (прекра́сные,)
любо́вные пи́сьма. ♦ **I** *(1)* **like /** *(2)* **love your amorous letters.** *(1)* Мне нра́вятся... / *(2)*
Я люблю́... твои́ любо́вные пи́сьма. ♦ **Your letters are too amorous. We hardly know
each other.** Твои́ пи́сьма сли́шком любо́вные. Мы едва́ зна́ем друг дру́га. ♦ **You fill
me with such warm, amorous feelings.** Ты наполня́ешь меня́ таки́ми тёплыми, любо́в-
ными чу́вствами. ♦ **I've never** *(1)* **met /** *(2)* **known a person as amorous as you.** Я ни-
когда́ не *(1)* встреча́л *(ж: встреча́ла)* / *(2)* знал *(ж: зна́ла)* челове́ка, так лю́бящего,
как ты. ♦ **I love your amorous ways.** Мне нра́вится как ты выража́ешь свою́ влюблённость.

amorousness *n* влю́бчивость *f.*

amour *n* любо́вь *f* ♦ **You are my amour.** Ты моя́ любо́вь. ♦ **My sweet amour, I miss you
so much.** Моя́ не́жная любо́вь, я так си́льно по тебе́ скуча́ю.

amourette *n* любо́вная интри́жка.

amuse *vt* забавля́ть *(whom* = *acc.)*, развлека́ть *(whom* = *acc.)*.

amusement *n* развлече́ние, заба́ва; *(pleasure)* удово́льствие.

amusing *adj* заба́вный, -ая, -ое, -ые, смешно́й, -а́я, -о́е, -ы́е.

analytical *adj* аналити́ческий, -ая, -ое, -ие.

angel *n* а́нгел ♦ **beautiful ~** прекра́сный а́нгел ♦ **beloved ~** возлю́бленный а́нгел ♦
darling ~ дорого́й а́нгел ♦ **dear ~** дорого́й а́нгел ♦ **little ~** ангело́чек ♦ ♦ **love ~** а́нгел
любви́ ♦ **my ~** мой а́нгел ♦ **precious ~** драгоце́нный а́нгел ♦ **special ~** дорого́й а́нгел
♦ **sweet ~** дорого́й а́нгел.

Russian terms of endearment are given in Appendix 13, page 780

---

angel: *phrases*

My pure, beautiful Angel, I miss you more than words can say. Мой чи́стый, прекра́сный а́нгел, не могу́ вы́разить слова́ми, как я скуча́ю по тебе́. ♦ **You are God's loveliest angel.** Ты прекра́снейший а́нгел бо́жий. ♦ **You are my** *(1)* **special** / *(2)* **Botticelli angel.** Ты мой *(1)* дорого́й / *(2)* ботиче́ллиевский а́нгел. ♦ **You will always be my special angel.** Ты всегда́ бу́дешь мои́м дороги́м а́нгелом. ♦ **You have the face of an angel.** У тебя́ лицо́ а́нгела. ♦ **When I look at you, I see the face of an angel.** Смотря́ на тебя́, я ви́жу лицо́ а́нгела. ♦ **You have a face that was sculpted by angels.** У тебя́ лицо́, изва́янное а́нгелами. ♦ **I know that in a wedding dress you would look like an angel.** Я зна́ю, что в подвене́чном пла́тье ты бу́дешь похо́жа на а́нгела.

angelic *adj* а́нгелоподо́бный, -ая, -ое, -ые, а́нгельский, -ая, -ое, -ие.

angel-like *adj* а́нгелоподо́бный, -ая, -ое, -ые, а́нгельский, -ая, -ое, -ие ♦ ~ **face** а́нгелоподо́бное лицо́ ♦ ~ *(1,2)* **golden hair** а́нгельские *(1)* золоты́е / *(2)* золоти́стые во́лосы.

anger *vt* злить *(whom = acc.).*

anger *n* гнев ♦ **hot** ~ неи́стовый гнев ♦ *(1,2)* **pent-up** ~ *(1)* подавля́емый / *(2)* сде́ржанный гнев ♦ *(1,2)* **repressed** ~ *(1)* подавля́емый / *(2)* сде́ржанный гнев ♦ **unreasonable** ~ безрассу́дный гнев ♦ **fit of** ~ при́ступ гне́ва.

angrily *adv* серди́то.

angry *adj* серди́тый, -ая, -ое, -ые *(short forms:* серди́т, -а, -о, -ы*)* ♦ **be** ~ серди́ться ♦ **get** ~ серди́ться / рассерди́ться ♦ **It's impossible to stay angry with you.** На тебя́ невозмо́жно до́лго серди́ться. ♦ **I'm afraid to open my heart to you and tell you everything I feel, because I'm afraid you would be offended or shocked or angry and then stop writing to me.** Я бою́сь откры́ть тебе́ своё се́рдце и сказа́ть всё, что я чу́вствую, потому́ что страшу́сь того́, что ты оби́дишься, бу́дешь шоки́рована и́ли рассе́рдишься и переста́нешь писа́ть мне.

anguish *n* му́ка, муче́ние, боль *f* ♦ **My loneliness (without you) is an anguish that I can** *(1)* **barely** / *(2)* **scarcely endure.** Моё одино́чество (без тебя́) - э́то му́ка, кото́рую я *(1,2)* едва́ выношу́.

anguished *adj* мучи́тельный, -ая, -ое, -ые.

animal *n* живо́тное *(pl:* живо́тные*)* ♦ **party** ~ люби́тель вечери́нок ♦ **Don't act like an animal all the time.** Не поступа́й всё вре́мя как живо́тное.

animate *vt* оживля́ть / оживи́ть *(what = acc.)* ♦ **I know a lot of ways to animate a relationship.** Я зна́ю мно́го путе́й для оживле́ния отноше́ний.

animated *adj* оживлённый, -ая, -ое, -ые *(short forms:* оживлён, оживлена́, -о́, -ы́*)* ♦ **I love to see your face animated with joy.** Я люблю́ видеть твоё лицо́, оживлённое ра́достью.

ankle *n* лоды́жка ♦ **slim** ~s стро́йные лоды́жки ♦ **You have a (very)** *(1)* **delicate** / *(2)* **nice turn of ankle.** У тебя́ (о́чень) *(1)* ...изя́щные лоды́жки. / *(2)* ...прия́тной фо́рмы лоды́жки.

annoy *vt* досажда́ть / досади́ть *(whom = dat.),* надоеда́ть / надое́сть *(whom = dat.),* докуча́ть *(whom = dat.);* раздража́ть *(whom = acc.)*

annoyance *n* доса́да; раздраже́ние.

anonymous *adj* анони́мный, -ая, -ое, -ые.

anniversary *n* годовщи́на ♦ ~ **of our meeting** годовщи́на на́шей встре́чи ♦ **wedding** ~ годовщи́на сва́дьбы.

annul *vt* аннули́ровать *(what = acc.);* отменя́ть / отмени́ть *(what = acc.)* ♦ *(1)* **You should...** / *(2)* **I want to... annul the marriage.** *(1)* Ты должна́... / *(2)* Я хочу́... аннули́ровать брак.

> *Some of the Russian sentences are translations of things we say and are not what Russians themselves would normally say*

annulment *n* аннули́рование; отме́на ♦ *(1)* **You should... /** *(2)* **I want to...** *(3)* **get /** *(4)* **obtain an annulment (of the marriage).** *(1)* Ты должна́... / *(2)* Я хочу́... / *(3)* ...получи́ть аннули́рование... / *(4)* ...доби́ться аннули́рования... бра́ка.

anonymous *adj* анони́мный, -ая, -ое, -ые.

anonymously *adv* анони́мно.

answer *vi* отвеча́ть / отве́тить *(whom = dat., what = +* на *+ acc.)* ♦ **~ as soon as possible** отве́тить как мо́жно скоре́е ♦ **~ my** *(1)* **letter /** *(2)* **letters** отвеча́ть / отве́тить на *(1)* ...моё письмо́. / *(2)* ...мои́ пи́сьма ♦ **~ my** *(1)* **question /** *(2)* **questions** отвеча́ть / отве́тить на *(1)* ...мой вопро́с. / *(2)* ...мои́ вопро́сы ♦ **~** *(1,2)* **promptly** отвеча́ть / отве́тить *(1)* бы́стро / *(2)* неме́дленно ♦ **~** *(1,2)* **right away** отве́тить *(1)* сра́зу / *(2)* неме́дленно ♦ **~ sharply** ре́зко отве́тить ♦ **~ the phone** снима́ть / снять тру́бку ♦ **~ your** *(1)* **letter /** *(2)* **letters** отвеча́ть / отве́тить на *(1)* ...твоё *(polite: Ва́ше)* письмо́. / *(2)* ...твои́ *(polite: Ва́ши)* пи́сьма ♦ **~ your** *(1)* **question /** *(2)* **questions** отвеча́ть / отве́тить на *(1)* ...твой *(polite: Ваш)* вопро́с. / *(2)* ...твои́ *(polite: Ва́ши)* вопро́сы.

answer *n* отве́т ♦ **ambiguous ~** двусмы́сленный отве́т ♦ **evasive ~** укло́нчивый отве́т ♦ **her ~** её отве́т ♦ **his ~** его́ отве́т ♦ **my ~** мо́й отве́т ♦ **satisfactory ~** удовлетвори́тельный отве́т ♦ **saucy ~** 1. *(impudent)* де́рзкий отве́т; 2. *(brazenly flirtatious)* коке́тливий отве́т ♦ *(1,2)* **vague ~** *(1)* расплы́вчатый / *(2)* неопределённый отве́т ♦ **your ~ (to my letter)** *(familiar)* тво́й отве́т (на моё письмо́); *(polite)* Ваш отве́т (на моё письмо́).

anticipation *n* ожида́ние, предви́дение; предвкуше́ние ♦ **It sends a shiver of anticipation along my spine.** Это посыла́ет тре́пет предвкуше́ния по мое́й спине́. ♦ **My heart races (wildly) with anticipation at the prospect of seeing you.** Моё се́рдце (бе́шено) коло́тится в предвкуше́нии встре́чи с тобо́й. ♦ **Whenever I think about you, my body trembles in anticipation.** Когда́ бы я ни поду́мал *(ж: поду́мала)* о тебе́, моё те́ло трепе́щет в предвкуше́нии.

antiquing *n* собира́ние антиквариа́та ♦ **I enjoy antiquing.** Я получа́ю удово́льствие от собира́ния антиквариа́та.

anxiety *n* беспоко́йство ♦ **I'm filled with anxiety at the prospect.** Я охва́чен *(ж: охва́чена)* беспоко́йством за предстоя́щее.

any *adj* 1. *(questions* како́й-нибудь, -а́я-нибудь, -о́е-нибудь, -и́е-нибудь; 2. *(whichever, every)* любо́й, -а́я, -о́е, -ы́е, вся́кий, -ая, -ое, -ие.

anyone 1. *(questions and hypothetical sentences)* кто́-нибудь; 2. *(affirmative sentences)* любо́й; 3. *(negative sentences)* никого́ ♦ **Is there anyone else?** Существу́ет ли друго́й *(ж: друга́я)*? ♦ **There could never be anyone else for me.** Никто́ друго́й никогда́ не мог быть со мно́й.

anything *pron* 1. *(questions and hypothetical sentences)* что́-нибудь; 2. *(affirmative sentences)* вся́кое, всё; 3. *(negative sentences)* ничего́ ♦ **I love you more than anything (in this whole world).** Я люблю́ тебя́ бо́льше всего́ (на све́те). ♦ **I would do anything for you.** Я сде́лаю всё для тебя́. ♦ **You can do anything you want with me.** Ты мо́жешь де́лать со мной всё, что ты хо́чешь. ♦ **I will do anything** *(1)* **...you wish /** *(2)* **want. /** *(3)* **...to make you happy. /** *(4)* **...to prove that I love you.** Я сде́лаю всё, *(1)* ...что ты пожела́ешь / *(2)* захо́чешь. / *(3)* ...чтобы ты была́ сча́стлива *(ж: был сч́астлив).* / *(4)* ...что́бы доказа́ть, что я люблю́ тебя́.

anytime *adv* в любо́е вре́мя, всегда́.

anyway *adv* 1. *(nevertheless)* всё-таки; всё же; 2. *(in any case)* во вся́ком слу́чае.

anywhere *adv* 1. *(questions and hypothetical sentences)* *(location)* где́-нибудь; *(motion)* куда́-нибудь; 2. *(affirmative sentences)* *(location)* где уго́дно; *(motion)* куда́ уго́дно; 3. *(negative sentences)* *(location)* нигде́; *(motion)* никуда́.

Counting things in Russian is a bit involved.
See Appendix 4, Numbers, on page 756 .

apart *adv* 1. *(at a distance)* в отдале́нии; 2. *(separately)* разде́льно, по́рознь; врозь ♦ **be ~** быть врозь, быть далеко́ друг от дру́га ♦ **live ~** жить врозь.

apart: *phrases*

When we're apart, I go through the motions of living. Когда́ мы далеко́ друг от дру́га, я де́лаю вид, что живу́. ♦ **The thought of being apart from you** *(1)* **...pierces** / *(2)* **crushes my very soul.** / *(3)* **...makes me feel** *(4)* **physically** / *(5)* **genuinely ill.** Мысль о том, что́бы ты далеко́ от меня́ *(1)* ...пронза́ет / *(2)* разруша́ет мою́ ду́шу. / *(3)* ...де́лает меня́ *(4)* физи́чески / *(5)* по-настоя́щему больны́м *(ж: больно́й).* ♦ **Distance** *(1)* **holds** / *(2)* **keeps us apart, but our love binds us together.** Расстоя́ние *(1,2)* разделя́ет нас, но на́ша любо́вь соединя́ет нас. ♦ **Time and distance will never keep us apart.** Вре́мя и расстоя́ние никогда́ не разлуча́т нас. ♦ **Being apart from you, I suffer the** *(1)* **unspeakable** / *(2)* **unbearable.** Когда́ мы врозь, я страда́ю *(1)* несказа́нно / *(2)* невыноси́мо. ♦ **In all our lives I never want us to be apart another night.** Я не хочу́, что́бы в на́шей жи́зни была́ ещё одна́ ночь врозь. ♦ **Each** *(1)* **minute** / *(2)* **hour** / *(3)* **day that we are apart** *(4)* **...weighs on my heart...** / *(5)* **...seems like a(n) eternity** / *(6)* **(whole) lifetime.** *(1)* Ка́ждая мину́та... / *(2)* Ка́ждый час / *(3)* день... в разлу́ке *(4)* ...тяготи́т моё се́рдце. / *(5)* ...ка́жется ве́чностью / *(6)* (це́лой) жи́знью. ♦ **I simply cannot** *(1)* **bear** / *(2)* **endure being apart from you.** Я про́сто не могу́ *(1)* вы́нести / *(2)* вы́держать разлу́ку с тобо́й. ♦ **It is sheer agony to be apart from you.** Это су́щее муче́ние - быть с тобо́й врозь. ♦ **You're always with me, even when we're apart.** Ты всегда́ со мно́й, да́же когда́ мы далеко́ друг от дру́га.

apartment *n* кварти́ра ♦ **big** ~ больша́я кварти́ра ♦ *(1,2)* **comfortable** ~ *(1)* комфорта́бельная / *(2)* ую́тная кварти́ра ♦ **communal** ~ коммуна́льная кварти́ра, коммуна́лка ♦ **cooperative** ~ кооперати́вная кварти́ра ♦ **cozy** ~ ую́тная кварти́ра ♦ **cramped** ~ те́сная кварти́ра ♦ **four-room** ~ четырёхко́мнатная кварти́ра ♦ **furnished** ~ обста́вленная кварти́ра ♦ **large** ~ больша́я кварти́ра ♦ **my** ~ моя́ кварти́ра ♦ **new** ~ но́вая кварти́ра ♦ **nice** ~ хоро́шая кварти́ра ♦ **noisy** ~ шу́мная кварти́ра ♦ **old** ~ ста́рая кварти́ра ♦ **one-room** ~ однокомна́тная кварти́ра ♦ **our** ~ на́ша кварти́ра ♦ **poor** ~ плоха́я кварти́ра ♦ **quiet** ~ ти́хая кварти́ра ♦ **roomy** ~ просто́рная кварти́ра ♦ *(1,2)* **small** ~ *(1)* ма́ленькая / *(2)* небольша́я кварти́ра ♦ **spacious** ~ просто́рная кварти́ра ♦ **three-room** ~ трёхко́мнатная кварти́ра ♦ **two-room** ~ двухко́мнатная кварти́ра ♦ **unfurnished** ~ необста́вленная кварти́ра ♦ **your** ~ *(familiar)* твоя́ кварти́ра; *(polite)* Ва́ша кварти́ра.

apartment: *other terms*

~ rent пла́та за кварти́ру ♦ **find an** ~ найти́ кварти́ру ♦ **lease an** ~ брать / взять кварти́ру в аре́нду, арендова́ть кварти́ру ♦ **look for an** ~ иска́ть кварти́ру ♦ **move out of the** ~ выезжа́ть / вы́ехать из кварти́ры ♦ **move to a new** ~ переезжа́ть / перее́хать в но́вую кварти́ру ♦ **rent an** ~ снима́ть кварти́ру; арендова́ть кварти́ру.

ape *n*: ♦ **hairy** ~ *(slang)* «гиббо́н».

apologize *vi* извиня́ться / извини́ться *(to whom* = + перед + *instr., for what* = + за + *acc.)* ♦ **I apologize for all the hurtful things I said to you.** Я извиня́юсь за все оби́дные слова́, кото́рые сказа́л *(ж: сказа́ла)* тебе́.

apology *n* извине́ние ♦ **humble** ~ поко́рное извине́ние ♦ **sincere** ~ и́скреннее извине́ние ♦ **Please accept my (humble) apologies.** Пожа́луйста, прими́ мои́ (поко́рные) извине́ния. ♦ **I accept your apology.** Я принима́ю твоё извине́ние. ♦ **I guess an apology is in order.** Я полага́ю, что до́лжен *(ж: должна́)* извини́ться.

appeal *n* 1. *(attraction)* привлека́тельность *f,* притяга́тельность *f,* очарова́ние, обая́ние; 2. *(request)* про́сьба, мольба́ ♦ **delicate** ~ то́нкое очарова́ние ♦ **enormous** ~ огро́мная

---

*Russian has 2 different verbs for "go",
one for "on foot" and the other for "by vehicle"*

привлека́тельность ♦ **exotic** ~ экзоти́ческое очарова́ние ♦ **masculine** ~ мужска́я притяга́тельность ♦ **mysterious** ~ таи́нственное обая́ние ♦ **physical** ~ физи́ческая привлека́тельность ♦ **sex** ~ сексапи́льность *f*, сексуа́льная привлека́тельность ♦ **strong love** ~ си́льное любо́вное влече́ние ♦ **tremendous** ~ огро́мная привлека́тель-ность ♦ **your** ~ *(familiar)* твоя́ привлека́тельность, твоё обая́ние; *(polite)* Ва́ша при-влека́тельность, Ва́ше обая́ние ♦ **exert enormous** ~ облада́ть огро́мной привлека́-тельностью, быть чрезвыча́йно привлека́тельной *f* / привлека́тельным *m*.

> **appeal: phrases**

I cannot describe (and cannot resist) the appeal that you have for me. Я не могу́ описа́ть твою́ привлека́тельность (и не могу́ сопротивля́ться ей). ♦ **No one has ever had such an appeal for me.** Никто́ никогда́ не был так привлека́телен для меня́. ♦ **You have much more appeal for me than any other woman I've ever known.** Ты гора́здо привле-ка́тельнее, чем все други́е же́нщины, кото́рых я когда-ли́бо знал. ♦ **Such a magne-tic appeal you have for me!** Како́е магнети́ческое притяже́ние ты ока́зываешь на меня́! ♦ **The** *(1)* **strength** / *(2)* **force** / *(3)* **intensity** / *(4)* **magnitude of your appeal for me is beyond** *(5)* **description** / *(6)* **calculation** / *(7)* **definition.** *(1,2)* Си́лу / *(3)* Интенси́в-ность / *(4)* Магнети́зм твое́й привлека́тельности для меня́ невозмо́жно *(5)* описа́ть / *(6)* изме́рить / *(7)* определи́ть.

appeal *vi* привлека́ть / привле́чь *(to whom = acc.)*, интересова́ть *(to whom = acc.)*, нра́-виться / понра́виться *(to whom = dat.)* ♦ **You appeal to me (in so many ways).** Ты (так мно́гим) привлека́ешь меня́. ♦ **You appeal to me (much) more than I can tell you.** Ты привлека́ешь меня́ (гора́здо) бо́льше, чем я могу́ вы́разить слова́ми. ♦ **No** *(1)* **one** / *(2)* **person has ever appealed to me like you do.** *(1)* Никто́... / *(2)* Ни оди́н челове́к... никогда́ не привлека́л меня́ так, как ты. ♦ **Does the idea appeal to you?** Эта иде́я тебе́ нра́вится? ♦ **The idea appeals to me.** Иде́я нра́вится мне. ♦ **The idea doesn't appeal to me.** Иде́я не нра́вится мне. ♦ **She didn't** *(1,2)* **appeal to me.** Она́ не *(1)* интересова́ла / *(2)* тро́гала меня́. ♦ **He didn't** *(1,2)* **appeal to me.** Он не *(1)* интересова́л / *(2)* тро́гал меня́. ♦ *(1)* **She** / *(2)* **He doesn't** *(3,4)* **appeal to me.** *(1)* Она́ / *(2)* Он не *(3)* интересу́ет / *(4)* тро́гает меня́.

appealing *adj* привлека́тельный, -ая, -ое, -ые, *(short forms:* привлека́телен, привлека́-тельна, -о, -ы)* ♦ **To say that you are physically appealing is the understatement of the** *(1)* **year** / *(2)* **century.** Сказа́ть, что ты про́сто физи́чески привлека́тельна, -- э́то са́мое невероя́тное преуменьше́ние э́того *(1)* го́да / *(2)* ве́ка.

appearance *n* 1. *(looks)* вне́шний вид, о́блик, нару́жность *f*; 2. *(showing up)* появле́ние ♦ **pleasant** ~ прия́тная нару́жность ♦ **Appearances can be deceiving.** Нару́жность мо́-жет быть обма́нчива.

appease *vt* утоля́ть / утоли́ть *(whom = acc.)*.

appeasing *n* утоле́ние.

appetite *n* аппети́т ♦ ~ **for conversation** разгово́рчивость *f* ♦ ~ **for laughter** смешли́вость *f* ♦ ~ **for literature** любо́вь к литерату́ре ♦ ~ **for nature** любо́вь к приро́де ♦ ~ **for romance** страсть к рома́нам ♦ **enormous** ~ **for sex** огро́мный сексуа́льный аппети́т ♦ **healthy** ~ **for sex** норма́льный сексуа́льный аппети́т ♦ **insatiable** ~ неуёмный аппети́т ♦ **That fuels my appetite.** Это распаля́ет мой аппети́т.

appetizing *adj* аппети́тный, -ая, -ое, -ые ♦ **You're an appetizing little thing.** Ты аппети́т-ный кусо́чек.

apple *n* я́блоко ♦ *(1)* **You're...** / *(2)* **You've always been... the apple of my eye.** *(1)* Ты ... / *(2)* Ты всегда́... зени́ца моего́ о́ка.

application *n* за́явка, заявле́ние ♦ **fill out an** ~ заполня́ть / запо́лнить за́явку ♦ **make**

> *Dipthongs in Russian are made by adding* й
> *to the end of a vowel (*а, е, ё, о, у, э, ю, *and* я*)*

an ~ де́лать / сде́лать зая́вку *(for what* = + на + *acc.)*, подава́ть / пода́ть зая́вку *(for what* = + на + *acc.)* ♦ **submit an** ~ подава́ть / пода́ть зая́вку *(for what* = + на+ *acc.)*

apply *vi* подава́ть / пода́ть зая́вку *(for what* = + на + *acc.)* ♦ ~ **for a marriage license** подава́ть / пода́ть зая́вку на разреше́ние на (вступле́ние в) брак ♦ ~ **for a (***[1]* **fiancée** *f* / *[2]* **fiancé** *m*) **visa** подава́ть / пода́ть зая́вку на ви́зу (для *[1]* неве́сты / *[2]* жениха́)

appraisal *n* оце́нка. ♦ **studious** ~ чёткая оце́нка.

appreciate *vt* цени́ть *(what, whom* = *acc.)*; быть благода́рным *m* / благода́рной *f (what* = + за + *acc.)*, благодари́ть *(what* = + за + *acc.)* ♦ ~ **a good home** цени́ть хоро́ший дом*)* ♦ ~ **a good man** цени́ть хоро́шего мужчи́ну*)* ♦ ~ **a good woman** цени́ть хоро́шую же́нщину*)* ♦ ~ **love** цени́ть любо́вь*)* ♦ *(1,2)* **I appreciate everything you've done for me.** *(1)* Я ценю́... / *(2)* Я благодарю́ за ...всё, что ты сде́лала *(ж: сде́лал)* для меня́. ♦ **I appreciate your** *(1)* **kindness** / *(2)* **generosity** / *(3)* **help** / *(4)* **discretion** / *(5)* **thoughtfulness** / *(6)* **advice** / **(very much).** Я (о́чень) ценю́ *(1)* ...твою́ доброту́ / *(2)* ще́дрость / *(3)* по́мощь / *(4)* такти́чность. / *(5)* ...твоё внима́ние. / *(6)* ...тво́й сове́т. ♦ **I didn't appreciate** *(1)* ...**that remark.** / *(2)* ...**that.** / *(3)*...**what you did** / *(4)* **said.** Мне не понра́вилось *(1)* ...э́то замеча́ние. / *(2)* ...э́то. / *(3)* ...то, что ты сде́лала *(ж: сде́лал)* / *(4)* сказа́ла *(ж: сказа́л)*.

appreciated *adj* оценён, оценена́, -о́, -ы́ *(short forms)* ♦ **I want to always make you feel appreciated.** Я хочу́, чтобы ты всегда́ чу́вствовала *(ж: чу́вствовал)* , что я ценю́ тебя́.

appreciative *adj* высокоцен́ящий, -ая, -ее, -ие.

appreciation *n* призна́тельность *f*, благода́рность *f* ♦ **I want to show my appreciation.** Я хочу́ показа́ть свою́ благода́рность. ♦ **As a small token of my appreciation, I'd like to invite you to dinner.** Как ма́лый знак мое́й призна́тельности, я хоте́л бы пригласи́ть Вас на обе́д.

apprehensive *adj* опаса́ющийся, -аяся, -ееся, -иеся, жду́щий (-ая, -ее, -ие) со стра́хом.

approach *vt* 1. *(address tentatively)* обраща́ться / обрати́ться *(whom* = + с + *instr.)*; 2. *(come /go near)* приближа́ться / прибли́зиться *(what, whom* = + к + *dat.)*; *(come / go to on foot)* подходи́ть / подойти́ *(what, whom* = + к + *dat.)*; *(come / go to by veh.)* подъезжа́ть / подъе́хать *(what, whom* = + к + *dat.)* ♦ **I know it's not proper for me to approach you this way.** Я зна́ю, что мне не надлежи́т обраща́ться с тобо́й таки́м о́бразом.

approval *n* одобре́ние ♦ **I would move heaven and earth to earn your approval.** Я сдви́ну небеса́ и зе́млю, чтобы заслужи́ть твоё одобре́ние.

approve *vi* одобря́ть / одо́брить *(of what, whom* = *acc.)* ♦ **I hope your parents will approve of me.** Я наде́юсь, что твои́ роди́тели одо́брят меня́. ♦ **I hope your** *(1)* **mother** / *(2)* **father will approve of me.** Я наде́юсь, что *(1)* ...твоя́ мать... / *(2)* ...твой оте́ц... одо́брит меня́. ♦ **My** *(1)* **mother** / *(2)* **father doesn't approve...** / *(3)* **My parents don't approve...** *(4)* **of me staying out all night.** / *(5)* ...**of me marrying a foreigner.** / *(6)* ...**of me seeing you.** *(1)* Моя́ мать не одобря́ет... / *(2)* Мой оте́ц не одобря́ет... / *(3)* Мои́ роди́тели не одобря́ют... *(4)* ..., когда́ я нахожу́сь не до́ма всю ночь. / *(5)* ...брак с иностра́нцем. / *(6)* ...того́, что я встреча́юсь с тобо́й.

aquamarine *n* цвет морско́й волны́.

Aquarius *(Jan. 20 - Feb. 18)* Водоле́й *(20 января́ - 18 февраля́)*.

aquiver *adj* дрожа́, трепеща́ ♦ **The very thought of you sets my heart aquiver.** Сама́ мысль о тебе́ заставля́ет моё се́рдце трепета́ть. ♦ **This letter of yours was so unexpected. Your** *(1)* **sweet** / *(2)* **beautiful words of love have set my heart completely aquiver.** Это письмо́ от тебя́ бы́ло так неожи́данно. Твои́ *(1)* не́жные / *(2)* прекра́сные слова́ любви́ заставля́ют трепета́ть моё се́рдце.

Some phrases are listed under more than one main word.

arch *vt* изгибáть / изогнýть *(what = acc.)* ♦ ~ **your body upward** изгибáть / изогнýть (твою́) спи́ну ♦ ~ **your back** выгибáть / вы́гнуть (твою́) спи́ну.

arch *vi* изгибáться / изогнýться ♦ **I want to see your body arch in rampant desire.** Я хочý ви́деть твоё тéло изгибáющимся в безýдержной стрáсти.

arch *n (of the foot)* изги́б, свод ♦ **The delicate arches of your feet are so lovely.** Изя́щные изги́бы твои́х ступнéй так восхити́тельны.

ardent *adj* пы́лкий, -ая, -ое, -ие, стрáстный, -ая, -ое, -ые, горя́чий, -ая, -ее, -ие, задóрный, -ая, -ое, -ые.

ardor *n* пыл, страсть *f*, задóр ♦ **burning** ~ горя́чий пыл ♦ **fierce** ~ нéистовый пыл ♦ **ravenous** ~ ненасы́тный пыл ♦ **Nothing will ever** *(1)* **deflate /** *(2)* **diminish my ardor for you.** Ничтó никогдá не *(1,2)* умéньшит мою́ страсть к тебé. ♦ **Your ardor (for me) seems to have cooled (**[1] **considerably /** [2] **somewhat).** Твой пыл (ко мне), кáжется, (*[1]* весьмá / *[2]* немнóго) осты́л. ♦ **My ardor for you will never cool.** Мой пыл к тебé никогдá не осты́нет.

areola *n* околососкóвый кружóк.

argue *vi* ссóриться / поссóриться *(with whom = + с + instr.)* ♦ **always** ~ всегдá ссóриться ♦ **constantly** ~ постоя́нно ссóриться ♦ **often** ~ чáсто ссóриться ♦ ~ **incessantly** ~ вéчно ссóриться ♦ **seldom** ~ рéдко ссóриться ♦ **sometimes** ~ иногдá ссóриться ♦ **I don't want to argue (with you).** Я не хочý ссóриться (с тобóй). ♦ *(1,2)* **I don't like to argue.** *(1)* Мне не нрáвится... / *(2)* Я не люблю́.. ссóриться. ♦ **Let's not argue.** Давáй не ссóриться.

arguing *n* ссóры ♦ **constant** ~ постоя́нные ссóры ♦ **incessant** ~ вéчные ссóры.

argument *n* ссóра ♦ *(1,2)* **big** ~ *(1)* большáя / *(2)* крýпная ссóра ♦ **bitter** ~ жестóкая ссóра ♦ **childish** ~ дéтская ссóра ♦ **constant** ~s постоя́нные ссóры ♦ **dumb** ~ глýпая ссóра ♦ **incessant** ~s вéчные ссóры ♦ *(1,2)* **little** ~ *(1)* небольшáя / *(2)* мáленькая ссóра ♦ **loud** ~ шýмная ссóра ♦ **meaningless** ~ пустáя ссóра ♦ **minor** ~s мéлкие ссóры ♦ **noisy** ~ шýмная ссóра ♦ **senseless** ~ бессмы́сленная ссóра ♦ **serious** ~ серьёзная ссóра ♦ *(1,2)* **small** ~ *(1)* небольшáя / *(2)* мáленькая ссóра ♦ **ugly** ~ безобрáзная ссóра ♦ **avoid** ~ избегáть ссóры ♦ **cause an** ~ вызывáть / вы́звать ссóру ♦ **get into an** ~ ввязáться в ссóру *(with whom = + с + instr.)* ♦ **have a(n)** (*[1]* **big /** *[2]* **serious)** ~ (*[1]* крýпно / *[2]* серьёзно) ссóриться / поссóриться ♦ **start** *(1)* **an** ~ / *(2)* ~s начинáть / начáть *(1)* ссóру / *(2)* ссóры ♦ **I hate arguments.** Я ненави́жу ссóры.

argumentive *adj* вздóрный, -ая, -ое, -ые, сварли́вый, -ая, -ое, -ые.

Aries *(Mar. 21 - Apr. 19)* Овéн *(21 мáрта - 19 апрéля)*.

aristocrat *n* аристокрáт *m*, аристокрáтка *f*.

aristocratic *adj* аристократи́ческий, -ая, -ое, -ие.

arm *n* 1. рукá *(pl: рýки) (Note: Russian word includes the hand.)*; 2. *pl (embraces)* объя́тия ♦ **beautiful** ~s краси́вые рýки ♦ **big** ~s больши́е рýки ♦ **delicate** ~s хрýпкие рýки ♦ **hairy** ~s волосáтые рýки ♦ **long** ~s дли́нные рýки ♦ **long shapely** ~s дли́нные изя́щные рýки ♦ **muscular** ~s мускули́стые рýки ♦ **sinewy** ~s мускули́стые рýки ♦ **slender** ~s тóнкие рýки ♦ **small** ~s мáленькие рýки ♦ *(1,2)* **strong** ~s *(1)* крéпкие / *(2)* си́льные рýки ♦ **(sun)tanned** ~s загорéлые рýки ♦ **welcoming** ~s раскры́тые навстрéчу объя́тия ♦ **fall into** *(1)* **my /** *(2)* **your** ~s упáсть в *(1)* мои́ / *(2)* твои́ объя́тия ♦ **melt in** *(1)* **my /** *(2)* **your** ~s растáять в *(1)* мои́х / *(2)* твои́х объя́тиях ♦ **welcome with open** ~s принимáть / приня́ть с распростёртыми объя́тиями *(whom = acc.)*.

> **arm:** *I want to hold you in my arms*

I wish so much that I could hold you snugly in my arms and put soft, loving kisses all over your hair and face. Я так хотéл бы ую́тно устрóить тебя́ в свои́х объя́тиях и покры́ть мя́гкими, любя́щими поцелýями твои́ вóлосы и лицó. ♦ **The way you write to me**

The singular past tense of Russian verbs ends in -л (m) (usually), -ла (f) or -ло (n). the plural past tense ends in -li.

makes me want to take you in my arms and hug you and hug you and hug you and cover your sweet face with loving kisses. То, как ты пи́шешь мне, вызыва́ет во мне жела́ние заключи́ть тебя́ в объя́тия, обнима́ть, обнима́ть и обнима́ть тебя́ и покрыва́ть твоё не́жное лицо́ лю́бящими поцелу́ями. ♦ The overriding goal of my life is to eventually take you in my arms and make beautiful, beautiful, beautiful love with you. Гла́вная цель мое́й жи́зни - заключи́ть тебя́ в объя́тия и заня́ться бесконе́чно прекра́сной любо́вью с тобо́й. ♦ Everything I want, everything I dream of, everything I hope for is in your arms. Всё, чего́ я хочу́, всё, о чём мечта́ю, всё, на что наде́юсь, - всё в твои́х объя́тиях. ♦ I want to lose myself (to the world) in your arms. Я хочу́ скры́ться (от ми́ра) в твои́х объя́тиях. ♦ I want (so much) to (1) take / (2,3) hold you in my arms. Я (так) хочу́ (1) ...заключи́ть тебя́ в объя́тия / (2) ...обня́ть тебя́. / (3) ...держа́ть тебя́ в объя́тиях. ♦ I want (so much) to (1) put / (2) wrap my arms around you (3) ...and hold you tight. / (4) ...and cover you with kisses. / (5) ...and kiss you and kiss you and kiss you. Я (так) хочу́ (1,2) обви́ть тебя́ рука́ми (3) ...и держа́ть тебя́ кре́пко. / (4) ...и покрыва́ть тебя́ поцелу́ями. / (5) ...и целова́ть тебя́, целова́ть и целова́ть. ♦ I (1) long / (2) yearn for the (3) paradise / (4) heaven of your (5) precious / (6) dear / (7) wonderful arms. Я (1) тоску́ю / (2) томлю́сь по (3,4) ра́ю твои́х (5) драгоце́нных / (6) дороги́х / (7) удиви́тельных рук. ♦ I desire so ardently to hold you tenderly in my arms. Я так пы́лко жа́жду не́жно держа́ть тебя́ в объя́тиях. ♦ How I wish that I were holding you in my arms at this very minute, covering your beautiful face with adoring kisses. Как бы я жела́л держа́ть тебя́ в объя́тиях в э́ту са́мую мину́ту, покрыва́я твоё прекра́сное лицо́ обожа́ющими поцелу́ями. ♦ I want so desperately to be close to you, to hold you in my arms, to feel the warmth of you, to kiss you. Я отча́янно хочу́ быть ря́дом с тобо́й, держа́ть тебя́ в объя́тиях, чу́вствовать твоё тепло́, целова́ть тебя́. ♦ I want to hold you naked in my arms. Я хочу́ держа́ть тебя́ обнажённой в объя́тиях. ♦ I'm completely devoid of any (1,2) ambition to do anything except hold you in my arms and make love to you. Я соверше́нно лишён каки́х-ли́бо други́х (1) стремле́ний / (2) амби́ций, кро́ме того́, чтобы держа́ть тебя́ в объя́тиях и занима́ться любо́вью с тобо́й.

| arm: the urge to hold you in my arms |

The temptation to take you in my arms was almost more than I could bear. Искуше́ние заключи́ть тебя́ в объя́тия бы́ло почти́ невыноси́мо. ♦ I have such a(n) (powerful) urge to take you in my arms. У меня́ тако́е вла́стное побужде́ние заключи́ть тебя́ в объя́тия.

| arm: I dream of holding you in my arms |

To have you nestled snugly in my arms is my constant dream. Моя́ постоя́нная мечта́ - ты, ую́тно устро́ившаяся в мои́х объя́тиях. ♦ I dream of spending endless blissful hours holding you in my arms (and making tender love with you). Я мечта́ю проводи́ть бесконе́чные блаже́нные часы́, обнима́я тебя́ (и занима́ясь не́жной любо́вью с тобо́й).

| arm: I need your arms |

I need your arms around me. Мне нужны́ твои́ объя́тия. ♦ My arms are (so) lonely for your (1) ...softness. / (2) ...soft warm body. / (3) ...voluptuous charms. Мои́ ру́ки (так) одино́ки без (1) ...твое́й мя́гкости / (2) ...твоего́ мя́гкого тёплого те́ла. / (3) ...твои́х сладостра́стных пре́лестей. ♦ Only the sweet, soft magic of your beautiful body in my arms can assuage the desperate hunger that consumes me. То́лько не́жное, мя́гкое волшебство́ твоего́ прекра́сного те́ла в мои́х объя́тиях мо́жет утоли́ть отча́янный го́лод, кото́рый пожира́ет меня́. ♦ Without you in my arms a perpetual ache of longing marauds my soul. Постоя́нная боль тоски́ терза́ет мою́ ду́шу, когда́ тебя́ нет в мои́х объя́тиях.

| **arm**: *bliss in your arms* |

The happiness I've found in your arms is beyond *(1)* description / *(2)* words. Сча́стье, кото́рое я нашёл *(ж: нашла́)* в твои́х объя́тиях, невозмо́жно *(1)* ...описа́ть / *(2)* ...вы́разить слова́ми. ♦ It's such *([1]* tremendous / *[2]* infinite) bliss to *(3)* ...be in your arms. / *(4)* ...have you in my arms. Это тако́е *([1]* огро́мное / *[2]* безграни́чное) блаже́нство *(3)* ...быть в твои́х объя́тиях. / *(4)* ...обнима́ть тебя́. ♦ What *(1)* pure / *(2)* absolute bliss to *(3)* ...be in your arms. / *(4)* ...have you in my arms. Что за *(1)* и́стинное / *(2)* по́лное блаже́нство *(3)* ...быть в твои́х объя́тиях. / *(4)* ...обнима́ть тебя́. ♦ My heart breaks into rapture whenever I take you into my arms. Моё се́рдце наполня́ется восто́ргом всегда́, когда́ я держу́ тебя́ в объя́тиях. ♦ Your arms around me feel so *(1)* comforting / *(2)* wonderful. В твои́х рука́х, обвива́ющих меня́, так *(1)* ую́тно / *(2)* замеча́тельно. ♦ I find such comfort in your arms. Я нахожу́ тако́й ую́т в твои́х объя́тиях. ♦ One night in your arms is all I would ever ask to make my life complete. Одну́ ночь в твои́х объя́тиях - э́то всё, что я бы проси́л, что́бы моя́ жизнь ста́ла абсолю́тно счастли́вой.

| **arm**: *I'm going to take you in my arms* |

I'm going to sweep you into my arms (and cover you with kisses). Я схвачу́ тебя́ в объя́тия (и покро́ю поцелу́ями).

| **arm**: *journey to your arms* |

I am so eagerly awaiting this journey that I hope will lead to your heart and your arms. Я с таки́м нетерпе́нием жду э́той пое́здки, кото́рая, я наде́юсь, приведёт меня́ к твоему́ се́рдцу и к твои́м объя́тиям.

| **arm**: *the memory of you in my arms* |

At this moment *(1)* ...last week... / *(2)* ...last Sunday... / *(3)* ...last night... I was holding you in my arms. В то мгнове́ние *(1)* ...на про́шлой неде́ле... / *(2)* ...в про́шлое воскресе́нье... / *(3)* ...про́шлой но́чью... я держа́л тебя́ в свои́х объя́тиях.

| **arm**: *you in someone else's arms* |

I can't bear the thought of you in someone else's arms. Мысль о тебе́ в чьи́х-то объя́тиях невыноси́ма для меня́.

| **arm**: *lost my arm* |

I lost my *(1)* right / *(2)* left arm in *(3)* ...the (Vietnam) war. / *(4)* ...an accident. Я потеря́л *(ж: потеря́ла)* *(1)* пра́вую / *(2)* ле́вую ру́ку *(3)* ...на войне́ (во Вьетна́ме). / *(4)* ...в ава́рии.

Armenian *adj* армя́нский, -ая, -ое, -ие.

Armenian *n* 1. *(person)* армяни́н *m*, армя́нка *f* *(pl:* армя́не*)*; 2. *(language)* армя́нский язы́к ♦ speak ~ говори́ть по-армя́нски.

armful *n*: ♦ You're (really) a nice armful. Ты (действи́тельно) полна́ очарова́ния.

armor *n* броня́, кольчу́га ♦ You are my knight in shining armor. Ты мой ры́царь в сверка́ющей кольчу́ге. ♦ I wish I could break through the *([1]* heavy / *[2]* thick) armor that *(3)* encases / *(4)* envelopes your heart. Я хоте́л бы проби́ться сквозь *([1]* кре́пкую / *[2]* про́чную) броню́, кото́рая *(3)* обвола́кивает / *(4)* окружа́ет твоё се́рдце.

army *n* а́рмия ♦ I'm in the Army. Я в а́рмии. ♦ I'm a *(1)* Sergeant / *(2)* Lieutenant / *(3)* etc in the Army. Я *(1)* сержа́нт / *(2)* лейтена́нт / *(3)* и т.д. а́рмии. ♦ I served *(1)* two / *(3)* three years in the Army. Я служи́л *(ж: служи́ла)* *(1)* два / *(3)* три го́да в а́рмии.

aroma *n* арома́т ♦ delicate ~ то́нкий арома́т ♦ intoxicating ~ опьяня́ющий арома́т ♦ intoxicating ~ of innocence пьяня́щий арома́т неви́нности ♦ pleasant ~ прия́тный

Clock and calender time are discussed in Appendix 5, page 759.

аромáт ◆ **sweet** ~ слáдкий аромáт ◆ **wonderful** ~ чудéсный аромáт.

arousal *n* возбуждéние. ◆ **full** ~ пóлное возбуждéние.

arouse *vt* пробуждáть / пробудить *(what, whom = acc.)*, возбуждáть / возбудить *(what, whom = acc.)* ◆ ~ **desire** пробуждáть / пробудить страсть ◆ ~ **disgust** вызывáть / вызвать отвращéние ◆ ~ **emotions** пробуждáть / пробудить чýвства ◆ ~ **envy** вызывáть / вызвать зáвисть ◆ ~ **feelings** пробуждáть / пробудить чýвства ◆ ~ **passion** пробуждáть / пробудить страсть ◆ ~ **pity** пробуждáть / пробудить жáлость ◆ ~ **sympathy** пробуждáть / пробудить сочýвствие.

arouse: phrases

You don't know how you arouse me. Ты не знáешь, как ты возбуждáешь меня. ◆ **You arouse me more than any ten other** *(1)* **women** / *(2)* **men combined.** Ты возбуждáешь меня бóльше, чем дéсять других *(1)* жéнщин / *(2)* мужчин вмéсте. ◆ **You arouse a storm of** *(1)* **incredible** / *(2)* **fantastic sensations in me.** Ты возбуждáешь бýрю *(1)* невероятных / *(2)* фантастических чýвств во мне. ◆ **You** *(1-3)* **arouse such** *(4)* **...turbulent feelings...** / *(5)* **...beautiful emotions... in me.** Ты *(1)* пробуждáешь / *(2)* вызывáешь / *(3)* возбуждáешь такие *(4)* бýрные / *(5)* прекрáсные чýвства во мне. ◆ **You are truly a master at the art of arousing** *(1)* **me** / *(2)* **passion.** Ты, прáвда, мáстер в искýсстве возбуждáть *(1)* меня / *(2)* страсть. ◆ **When I have you in my arms, I'm going to arouse tides of sweet feeling in you that will sweep you into a storm of passion.** Когдá я заключý тебя в объятия, я разбужý потóк нéжных чýвств в тебé, котóрый брóсит тебя в бýрю стрáсти.

aroused *adj* возбуждённый, -ая, -ое, -ые *(short forms:* возбуждён, возбужденá, -ó, -ы́), пробуждённый, -ая, -ое, -ые *(short forms:* пробуждён, пробужденá, -ó, -ы́) ◆ **be** ~ быть возбуждённым *m* / возбуждённой *f (I'm aroused:* я возбуждён *[ж: возбужденá]. You're aroused:* ты возбужденá *[ж: возбуждён].)* ◆ **get** ~ возбуждáться / возбудиться, пробуждáться / пробудиться.

arousing *adj* возбуждáющий, -ая, -ее, -ие, пробуждáющий, -ая, -ее, -ие ◆ ~ **as hell** возбуждáющий (-ая, -ее, -ие) как чёрт.

arrangement *n* соглашéние. ◆ **discreet** ~ осмотрительное соглашéние.

array *n* мáсса, мнóжество ◆ **I'm going to treat you to an ever-changing array of pleasurable sensations.** Я бýду угощáть тебя мнóжеством всегдá-меняющихся доставляющих удовóльствие ощущéний.

arrest *vt* 1. *(apprehend)* арестóвывать / арестовáть *(whom = acc.)*; 2. *(stop)* прекращáть / прекратить *(what = acc.)* ◆ ~ **a relationship** прекращáть / прекратить отношéния.

arrive *vi (all modes)* прибывáть / прибыть; *(pedestrian, bus, train)* приходить / прийти; *(person by vehicle)* приезжáть / приéхать; *(flight)* прилетáть / прилетéть ◆ **What time will the** *(1)* **bus** / *(2)* **train** / *(3)* **flight arrive?** В какóе врéмя прибýдет *(1)* автóбус / *(2)* пóезд / *(3)* самолёт? ◆ **The** *(1)* **bus** / *(2)* **train** / *(3)* **flight will arrive at one (thirty).** *(See page 759 for other times.)* *(1)* Автóбус / *(2)* Пóезд / *(3)* Самолёт прибýдет в час (тридцать).

arrogance *n* надмéнность *f*, высокомéрие.

arrogant *adj* надмéнный, -ая, -ое, -ые, высокомéрный, -ая, -ое, -ые.

arrogantly *adv* надмéнно, высокомéрно.

arrow *n* стрелá ◆ **I've been struck all over by Cupid's arrows.** Я был пронзён *(ж: былá пронзенá)* стрéлами Купидóна.

art *n* искýсство ◆ ~ **of making love** искýсство любви ◆ ~ **of pleasure** искýсство наслаждéний ◆ ~ **of the kiss** искýсство поцелýя ◆ ~**s of love** любóвные наýки ◆ **martial** ~**s** боевы́е искýсства.

> *Reflexive verbs are those that end in* -ся *or* -сь.
> *The* -ся *or* -сь *also goes onto a past tense ending.*

art: phrases

I'm very interested in art. Я о́чень интересу́юсь иску́сством. ♦ **I have a passion for art and music.** У меня́ страсть к иску́сству и му́зыке. ♦ **What kind of art do you like?** Како́й вид иску́сства ты лю́бишь? ♦ **I want to give you endless, ecstasy-filled lessons in the art of making love.** Я хочу́ дава́ть тебе́ бесконе́чные, напо́лненные экста́зом уро́ки иску́сства любви́. ♦ **You are truly a (marvelous) master at the art of** *(1)* **...making love.** / *(2)* **...arousing me** / *(3)* **passion.** / *(4)* **...giving pleasure.** / *(5)* **...bewitching (me).** / *(6)* **...cheating** / *(7)* **deceiving (people).** Ты, пра́вда, (замеча́тельный) ма́стер в иску́сстве *(1)* ...любви́. / *(2)* ...возбужда́ть меня́ / *(3)* страсть. / *(4)* ...доставля́ть удово́льствия. / *(5)* ...очаро́вывать (меня́). / *(6,7)* ...обма́на (люде́й).

artful *adj* уме́лый, -ая, -ое, -ые, иску́сный, -ая, -ое, -ые ♦ *(1,2)* ~ **lover** *(1)* уме́лый / *(2)* иску́сный любо́вник.

articulate *vt* я́сно выража́ть.

articulate *adj* уме́ющий хорошо́ выража́ть свои́ мы́сли ♦ **be** ~ уме́ть хорошо́ выража́ть свои́ мы́сли ♦ **You're very articulate.** Ты о́чень хорошо́ уме́ешь выража́ть свои́ мы́сли.

artifice *n* иску́сная проде́лка, уло́вка.

artificial *adj* иску́сственный, -ая, -ое, -ые.

artist *n* 1. худо́жник; *(painter)* живопи́сец; 2. *(drama, music, etc)* арти́ст; 3. *(master)* арти́ст, ма́стер ♦ **con** ~ обма́нщик, жу́лик, моше́нник, «арти́ст» ♦ **make-out** ~ Дон-Жуа́н ♦ **serious** ~ серьёзный худо́жник.

artistic *adj* 1. *(of or about art)* худо́жественный, -ая, -ое, -ые; 2. *(having good taste or talent)* артисти́чный, -ая, -ое, -ые *(short forms:* артисти́чен, артисти́чна, -о, -ы*)*, артисти́ческий, -ая, -ое, -ие.

artsy *adj* претенду́ющий (-ая, -ее, -ие) на худо́жественность.

arty *adj (slang):* ♦ **be** ~ 1. *(involved in art)* занима́ться иску́сством; 2. *(interested in art)* интересова́ться иску́сством.

ashamed *pred adj* присты́женный, -ая, -ое, -ые ♦ **be** ~ стыди́ться *(of what = gen.)*, быть сты́дно *(person ashamed = dat., to do what = inf.)* ♦ **feel** ~ стыди́ться *(of what = gen.)*.

ashamed: phrases

Aren't you ashamed? Ра́зве тебе́ не сты́дно? ♦ **I'm (not)** *(1,2)* **ashamed (to tell you).** *(1)* Я (не) стыжу́сь, / *(2)* Мне (не) сты́дно (сказа́ть тебе́). ♦ **There's nothing to be ashamed of.** Нет ничего́, чего́ бы на́до бы́ло стыди́ться. ♦ **I wouldn't be ashamed to do anything for you.** Мне бы́ло бы не сты́дно сде́лать для тебя́ всё, что уго́дно. ♦ **I love you (with all my heart) and I'm not** *(1,2)* **ashamed to tell anyone.** Я люблю́ тебя́ (всем се́рдцем) и *(1)* ...я не стыжу́сь,,, / *(2)* ...мне не сты́дно... сказа́ть об э́том кому́ уго́дно.

ash-blond *adj* пе́пельный, -ая, -ое, -ые.

Asian *adj* азиа́тский, -ая, -ое, -ие.

Asian *n* азиа́т *m*, азиа́тка *f*.

ask *vt* спра́шивать / спроси́ть *(whom = acc., about what = + о + prep.)* ♦ ~ **a question** задава́ть / зада́ть вопро́с *(whom = dat.)* ♦ ~ **a lot of questions** задава́ть / зада́ть мно́го вопро́сов *(whom = dat.)* ♦ ~ **for** *vi* проси́ть / попроси́ть *(for what, whom = gen. or + о + prep.)* ♦ ~ **out** *vt* приглаша́ть / пригласи́ть пойти́ куда́-нибу́дь.

ask questions:

Feel free to ask me anything. Ты мо́жешь свобо́дно спра́шивать меня́ обо всём. ♦ **May I ask you a question?** Могу́ я зада́ть тебе́ вопро́с?

ask for:

I could never ask for more (in this *[1]* **life /** *[2]* **world) than** *(3)* **...you.** / *(4)* **...your love.** /

The time zones for many cities of the world
are given in Appendix 6, page 761.

(5) ...**to have you as my wife** / *(6)* **husband.** Никогда́ ни о чём бо́льшем (в э́той *[1,2]* жи́зни) не смог *(ж: смогла́)* бы проси́ть я кро́ме, как *(3)* ...о тебе́. / *(4)* ...о твое́й любви́. / *(5)* ...о том, чтобы ты ста́ла мое́й жено́й. / *(6)* ...о том, чтобы ты стал мои́м му́жем.

ask out:

I've been wanting to ask you out from the first moment I saw you. Я хоте́л пригласи́ть тебя́ пойти́ со мной куда́-нибу́дь с того́ моме́нта, как уви́дел тебя́.

aspiration *n* стремле́ние, жела́ние ♦ **My greatest aspiration in life is to** *(1)* ...**win your love** / *(2)* **heart.** / *(3)* ...**marry you.** / *(4)* ...**make you my bride.** / *(5)* ...**put my lips against yours.** / *(6)* ...**fill your body with indescribable** / *(7)* **infinite** *(8)* **pleasure** / *(9)* **ecstasy.** Са́мое си́льное стремле́ние мое́й жи́зни - *(1)* ...завоева́ть твою́ любо́вь. / *(2)* ...завоева́ть твоё се́рдце. / *(3)* ...жени́ться на тебе́. / *(4)* ...сде́лать тебя́ свое́й неве́стой. / *(5)* ...прижа́ться губа́ми к твои́м губа́м. / *(6)* ...напо́лнить твоё те́ло неопису́емым / *(7)* бесконе́чным *(8)* наслажде́нием / *(9)* экста́зом. ♦ **To gain a small measure of your precious love is my passionate aspiration.** Получи́ть ка́плю твое́й драгоце́нной любви́ - моё стра́стное жела́ние.

aspire *vi* стреми́ться ♦ **All I aspire to in this world is to** *(1)* **have** / *(2)* **win your love.** Всё, к чему́ я стремлю́сь в э́том ми́ре, - э́то *(1,2)* завоева́ть твою́ любо́вь. ♦ **To** *(1)* **have** / *(2)* **win your** *(3)* **precious** / *(4)* **wonderful love is the greatest** *(5)* **goal** / *(6)* **thing I can aspire to.** *(1,2)* Заслужи́ть твою́ *(3)* драгоце́нную / *(4)* удиви́тельную любо́вь -- велича́йшая *(5,6)* цель, к кото́рой я стремлю́сь.

ass *n (slang)* зад, по́па ♦ **little ~** по́пка.

assail *vt* охва́тывать / охвати́ть *(what, whom = acc.)*; *(sleep, thoughts)* наруша́ть / нару́шить *(what = acc.)* ♦ **My sleep, shallow and restless, was assailed by visions of your beautiful, voluptuous body.** Мой сон, неглубо́кий и беспоко́йный, был нару́шен виде́нием твоего́ прекра́сного, чу́вственного те́ла. ♦ **I'm constantly assailed by this primeval lusting for** *(1)* ...**you.** / *(2)* ...**your incredibly beautiful body.** Меня́ постоя́нно охва́тывает первобы́тное вожделе́ние к *(1)* ...тебе́. / *(2)* ...твоему́ невероя́тно прекра́сному те́лу. ♦ **The memories of those wonderful times (together) assail me night and day.** Воспомина́ния об э́том удиви́тельном вре́мени (, проведённом вме́сте) не оставля́ют меня́ но́чью и днём. ♦ **My entire being is assailed by the all-consuming need to take you in my arms and revel in the reservoir of your passion.** Я весь охва́чен всепоглоща́ющей жа́ждой заключи́ть тебя́ в объя́тия и упива́ться твое́й стра́стью.

assertive *adj* напо́ристый, -ая, -ое, -ые.

assuage *vt* 1. *(ease)* смягча́ть / смягчи́ть *(what = acc.)*; 2. *(appease)* утоля́ть / утоли́ть *(what = acc.)* ♦ **Only the sweet, soft magic of your beautiful body in my arms can assuage the desperate hunger that consumes me.** То́лько не́жное, мя́гкое волшебство́ твоего́ прекра́сного те́ла в мои́х объя́тиях мо́жет утоли́ть отча́янный го́лод, кото́рый пожира́ет меня́. ♦ **I fervently pray that in your heart you can somehow find the compassion to condescend to grant me just a few brief minutes to** *(1)* **meet** / *(2)* **talk with you and thereby assuage this unbearable longing that grips my soul.** Я горячо́ молю́сь, чтобы ты смогла́ найти́ сострада́ние в своём се́рдце и подари́ть мне то́лько не́сколько коро́тких мину́т *(1)* встре́чи / *(2)* разгово́ра с тобо́й, чтобы утоли́ть невыноси́мое жела́ние, охвати́вшее мою́ ду́шу.

assuaging *n* утоле́ние.

assure *vt* уверя́ть / уве́рить *(whom = acc.)*, гаранти́ровать *(whom = acc.)*.

astrology *n* астроло́гия ♦ **Do you believe in astrology?** Ты ве́ришь в астроло́гию? ♦ **I (don't) believe in astrology.** Я (не) ве́рю в астроло́гию.

Optional parts of sentences are preceded
or followed (or both) by three dots.

astute *adj* проница́тельный, -ая, -ое, -ые ♦ **emotionally** ~ душе́вно проница́тельный.

atheist *n* атеи́ст *m*, атеи́стка *f*.

atheistic *adj* атеисти́ческий, -ая, -ое, -ие.

athlete *n* спортсме́н *m*, спортсме́нка *f* ♦ **armchair** ~ люби́тель наблюда́ть спорт по телеви́зору.

athletic *adj* атлети́ческий, -ая, -ое, -ие ♦ **reasonably** ~ доста́точно спорти́вный, -ая, -ое, -ые.

athletic-minded *adj* лю́бящий (-ая, -ее, -ие) спорт ♦ **be** ~ люби́ть спорт.

athletics *n, pl* атле́тика, заня́тие спо́ртом.

atmosphere *n* атмосфе́ра ♦ **cozy** ~ ую́тная атмосфе́ра ♦ **friendly** ~ дру́жеская атмосфе́ра ♦ **homey** ~ дома́шняя атмосфе́ра ♦ **intimate** ~ инти́мная атмосфе́ра ♦ **pleasant** ~ прия́тная атмосфе́ра ♦ **quiet** ~ споко́йная атмосфе́ра ♦ **relaxed** ~ расслабля́ющая атмосфе́ра ♦ **romantic** ~ романти́ческая атмосфе́ра ♦ **tense** ~ напряжённая атмосфе́ра.

atrociously *adv* отврати́тельно, ужа́сно ♦ **I behaved atrociously.** Я вёл *(ж: вела́)* себя́ ужа́сно. ♦ **You behaved atrociously.** Ты вела́ *(ж: вёл)* себя́ ужа́сно.

attached *adj* привя́занный, -ая, -ое, -ые *(short forms:* привя́зан, -а, -ы); привя́занный, -ая, -ое, -ые ♦ **become** ~ привя́зываться / привяза́ться *(to whom* = + к + *dat.)* ♦ *(1)* **Can /** *(2)* **May I ask you a personal question? Are you attached?** *(1,2)* Могу́ я зада́ть тебе́ ли́чный вопро́с? У тебя́ кто́-то есть? ♦ **I normally wouldn't think of stealing someone else's** *(1)* **woman /** *(2)* **girl, but if you're attached, I'm afraid I'm going to have to make an exception.** Я обы́чно не поду́мал бы о кра́же чьей-ли́бо *(1)* же́нщины / *(2)* де́вушки, но е́сли ты свя́зана с ке́м-то, я бою́сь, что до́лжен сде́лать исключе́ние.

attachment *n* привя́занность *f* ♦ **emotional** ~ эмоциона́льная привя́занность ♦ **romantic** ~ романти́ческая привя́занность ♦ **strong** ~ си́льная привя́занность.

attempt *vi* пыта́ться / попыта́ться.

attempt *n* попы́тка ♦ **desperate** ~ отча́янная попы́тка ♦ **feeble** ~ сла́бая попы́тка ♦ **make an** ~ пыта́ться / попыта́ться ♦ **I made several attempts to call you.** Я не́сколько раз пыта́лся позвони́ть тебе́. ♦ **I made every attempt to** *(1)* **save /** *(2)* **salvage the marriage.** Я сде́лал *(ж: сде́лала)* всё, что возмо́жно для *(1,2)* спасе́ния бра́ка.

attention *n* внима́ние ♦ **all my** ~ всё моё внима́ние ♦ **a lot of** ~ большо́е внима́ние ♦ **constant** ~ постоя́нное внима́ние ♦ **devoted** ~ лю́бящее внима́ние ♦ *(1,2)* **main** ~ *(1)* гла́вное / *(2)* основно́е внима́ние ♦ **my** ~ моё внима́ние ♦ **loving** ~ лю́бящее внима́ние ♦ *(1,2)* **particular** ~ *(1)* осо́бое / *(2)* осо́бенное внима́ние ♦ **rapt** ~ восто́рженное внима́ние ♦ **requisite** ~ до́лжное внима́ние ♦ **serious** ~ серьёзное внима́ние ♦ *(1,2)* **special** ~ *(1)* осо́бое / *(2)* осо́бенное внима́ние ♦ **tremendous amount of** ~ огро́мное внима́ние ♦ **unremitting** ~ неосла́бное внима́ние ♦ **your** ~ *(familiar)* твоё внима́ние; *(polite)* Ва́ше внима́ние ♦ **center of** ~ центр внима́ния.

attention: verb terms

attract (my) ~ привлека́ть / привле́чь (моё) внима́ние ♦ **concentrate** ~ сосредото́чивать / сосредото́чить внима́ние *(on what, whom* = + на + *prep.)* ♦ **demand** ~ тре́бовать / потре́бовать внима́ния ♦ **focus** ~ сосредото́чивать / сосредото́чить внима́ние *(on what, whom* = + на + *prep.)* ♦ **occupy my** ~ занима́ть / заня́ть моё внима́ние ♦ **pay** ~ обраща́ть / обрати́ть внима́ние *(to what, whom* = + на + *acc.).*

attention: center of attention

You will always be the center of my attention. Ты всегда́ бу́дешь це́нтром моего́ внима́ния. ♦ **Your loveliness (undoubtedly) makes you the center of attention wherever you go.** Твоя́ красота́ (несомне́нно) де́лает тебя́ це́нтром внима́ния везде́, где

If you're not on familiar terms with a person,
the «ты» forms here will have to be changed to «Вы».

бы ты ни появи́лась.

attention: *caught my / your attention*

I'm so glad I caught your attention. Я так рад *(ж: ра́да)*, что я привлёк *(ж: привлекла́)* твоё внима́ние. ◆ **Your photo caught my attention** *(1)* ...**the instant I turned (the page) to it.** / *(2)* ...**instantly.** Твоя́ фотогра́фия привлекла́ к себе́ моё внима́ние *(1)* ...как то́лько я переверну́л *(ж: переверну́ла)* (страни́цу). / *(2)* ...мгнове́нно.

attention: *pay attention*

I promise that I will always pay attention to your *(1)* **happiness** / *(2)* **needs.** Я обеща́ю, что я всегда́ бу́ду уделя́ть внима́ние *(1)* ...твоему́ сча́стью. / *(2)* ...твои́м ну́ждам. ◆ **I will always give you my whole-hearted attention.** Я всегда́ бу́ду относи́ться к тебе́ с и́скренним внима́нием. ◆ **I wish you would pay a little more attention to me.** Я хоте́л *(ж: хоте́ла)* бы, что́бы ты обраща́ла *(ж: обраща́л)* немно́го бо́льше внима́ния на меня́. ◆ **I feel (**[*1*] **really /** [*2*] **very) bad about not paying more attention to you.** Я (*[1]* действи́тельно / *[2]* о́чень) сожале́ю, что не уделя́ю тебе́ доста́точного внима́ния.

attention: *your beauty demands attention*

Beauty such as yours demands attention. Така́я красота́, как твоя́, тре́бует внима́ния.

attention: *your photo*

How often my attention lingers on your photo. Как ча́сто моё внима́ние заде́рживается на твое́й фотогра́фии.

attention: *your attention does wonders*

All your attention does wonders for my *(1)* **morale** / *(2)* **self-esteem.** Твоё внима́ние - чудоде́йственное сре́дство для моего́ *(1)* ...душе́вного состоя́ния. / *(2)* ...самоува-же́ния.

attention: *lack of attention*

I feel so disillusioned by your lack of attention. Я так разочаро́ван *(ж: разочаро́вана)* отсу́тствием у тебя́ внима́ния.

attentive *adj* внима́тельный, -ая, -ое, -ые *(short forms:* внима́телен. внима́тельна, -о, -ы), предупреди́тельный, -ая, -ое, -ые ◆ **I would be so attentive, so focused on your needs and desires and likes and dislikes.** Я был бы так внима́телен, так сосредото́чен на твои́х ну́ждах и жела́ниях, на том, что ты лю́бишь и что не лю́бишь.

attire *n (outfit)* наря́д; *(clothes)* оде́жда ◆ **bridal** ~ сва́дебный наря́д ◆ **elegant** ~ элега́нтная оде́жда ◆ **formal** ~ форма́льная оде́жда.

attired *adj* наря́жен, -а, -о, -ы *(short forms)*; оде́т, -а, -о, -ы *(short forms)* ◆ **elegantly** ~ элега́нтно оде́т, -а, -ы ◆ **You look** *(1)* **beautiful /** *(2)* **gorgeous /** *(3)* **ravishing no matter what you're attired in.** Ты вы́глядишь *(1)* прекра́сно / *(2)* великоле́пно / *(3)* восхи-ти́тельно в любо́м наря́де.

attitude *n* отноше́ние ◆ **bad** ~ плохо́е отноше́ние ◆ **careless** ~ небре́жное отноше́ние ◆ **casual** ~ беспе́чное отноше́ние ◆ **caring** ~ бе́режное отноше́ние ◆ **cavalier** ~ высоко-ко́мерное отноше́ние ◆ **chauvinistic** ~ шовинисти́ческое отноше́ние ◆ **devil-may--care** ~ наплева́тельское отноше́ние ◆ **distrustful** ~ недове́рчивое отноше́ние ◆ **down--to-earth** ~ тре́звый взгляд ◆ **friendly** ~ дру́жеское отноше́ние ◆ **frivolous** ~ легко-мы́сленное отноше́ние ◆ **good** ~ хоро́шее отноше́ние ◆ **haughty** ~ высокоме́рное отноше́ние ◆ **healthy** ~ здоро́вое отноше́ние ◆ **humane** ~ гума́нное отноше́ние ◆ **incomprehensible** ~ непоня́тное отноше́ние ◆ **indifferent** ~ равноду́шное отноше́-ние ◆ **irresponsible** ~ безотве́тственное отноше́ние ◆ **laid-back** ~ споко́йное отноше́-ние ◆ **liberal** ~ либера́льное отноше́ние ◆ **lousy** ~ ужа́сное отноше́ние ◆ **mistrust-ful** ~ недове́рчивое отноше́ние ◆ **negative** ~ отрица́тельное отноше́ние ◆ **no-non-sense** ~ стро́гое отноше́ние ◆ **philosophical** ~ филосо́фское отноше́ние ◆ **poor** ~

A list of common places with their grammatical endings is given in Appendix 7, page 763.

плохо́е отноше́ние ♦ **positive (mental)** ~ позити́вное отноше́ние ♦ **proprietorial** ~ со́бственническое отноше́ние ♦ **puritanical** ~ пурита́нское отноше́ние ♦ **raptur ous** ~ восто́рженное отноше́ние ♦ **rice-pilaf** ~ наплева́тельское отноше́ние ♦ **serious** ~ серьёзное отноше́ние ♦ **strange** ~ стра́нное отноше́ние ♦ **sympathetic** сочу́вственное отноше́ние ♦ **terrible** ~ ужа́сное отноше́ние ♦ **upbeat** ~ *(optimistic)* оптимисти́чное отноше́ние; *(positive)* положи́тельное отноше́ние ♦ **your** ~ *(familiar)* твоё отноше́ние; *(polite)* Ва́ше отноше́ние.

attitude: phrases

I don't appreciate your proprietorial attitude toward me. Мне не нра́вится твоё со́бственническое отноше́ние ко мне. ♦ **I feel so disillusioned by your attitude (toward me).** Я так разочаро́ван *(ж: разочаро́вана)* твои́м отноше́нием (ко мне). ♦ **Your casual, laid-back attitude to life appeals to me.** Твоё беспе́чное, споко́йное отноше́ние к жи́зни нра́вится мне. ♦ **Your attitude toward me has been so icy lately.** После́днее вре́мя твоё отноше́ние ко мне бы́ло таки́м ледяны́м.

attorney *n* адвока́т ♦ *(1,2)* **adoption** ~ адвока́т по *(1)* усыновле́нию *(boy)* / *(2)* удочере́нию *(girl)* ♦ **defense** ~ защи́тник ♦ **divorce** ~ адвока́т по разво́ду ♦ **immigration** ~ адвока́т по иммиграцио́нным дела́м.

attract *vt* привлека́ть / привле́чь *(what, whom = acc.)*, увлека́ть / увле́чь *(what, whom = acc.)*; прельща́ть / прельсти́ть *(whom = acc.)* ♦ ~ **a mate** привлека́ть / привле́чь партнёра ♦ ~ **(my) attention** привлека́ть / привле́чь (моё) внима́ние ♦ **What first attracted me to you was your** *(1)* **...beautiful /** *(2)* **bewitching eyes. /** *(3)* **...dazzling /** *(4)* **cute /** *(5)* **lovely /** *(6)* **beautiful /** *(7)* **sweet /** *(8)* **bright smile.** Пе́рвое, что привлекло́ меня́ к тебе́ - *(1)* ...твои́ прекра́сные / *(2)* околдо́вывающие глаза́. / *(3)* ...твоя́ ослепи́тельная / *(4,5)* преле́стная / *(6)* прекра́сная / *(7)* ми́лая / *(8)* сия́ющая улы́бка.

attracted *adj* привлечён, привлечена́, -о́, -ы́ *(short forms)*, прельщён, прельщена́, -о́, -ы́ *(short forms)*; увлечён, увлечена́, -о́, -ы́ *(short forms)* ♦ **I'm** *(1)* **very /** *(2)* **tremendously /** *(3)* **overwhelmingly /** *(4)* **greatly /** *(5)* **so attracted to you.** Я *(1)* о́чень / *(2)* чрезвыча́йно / *(3)* безграни́чно / *(4)* си́льно / *(5)* так увлечён *(ж: увлечена́)* тобо́й. ♦ **I'm attracted to you far more than I've ever been attracted to anyone else.** Я увлечён *(ж: увлечена́)* тобо́й гора́здо бо́льше, чем когда́-либо был увлечён *(ж: была́ увлечена́)* кем-ли́бо ещё. ♦ **I was madly attracted to you from the very beginning.** Я был *(ж: была́)* безу́мно увлечён *(ж: увлечена́)* тобо́й с са́мого нача́ла. ♦ **What a wonderful act of Providence that we were attracted to one another.** Что за чу́до провиде́ния, что мы привлекли́ друг дру́га. ♦ **Do you know why I'm so attracted to you? It's your** *(1)* **...loving nature. /** *(2)* **...gentle /** *(3)* **loving ways. /** *(4)* **...sweet disposition. /** *(5)* **...wonderful personality.** Ты зна́ешь, почему́ я так увлечён *(ж: увлечена́)* тобо́й? За *(1)* ...твою́ лю́бящую нату́ру. / *(2)* ...твоё не́жное / *(3)* любо́вное обраще́ние. / *(4)* ...твой ми́лый нрав. / *(5)* ...твой удиви́тельный хара́ктер.

attraction *n* притяже́ние, тяготе́ние, влече́ние ♦ **ardent** ~ стра́стное влече́ние ♦ **elemental** ~ приро́дная привлека́тельность ♦ **inexplicable** ~ необъясни́мое влече́ние ♦ **magical** ~ волше́бное влече́ние ♦ **mere** ~ просто́е увлече́ние ♦ **mutual** ~ взаи́мное притяже́ние ♦ **physical** *(1,2)* ~ физи́ческое *(1)* влече́ние / *(2)* тяготе́ние ♦ **powerful** ~ мо́щное тяготе́ние ♦ **spiritual** ~ духо́вное влече́ние ♦ **strange** ~ стра́нное притяже́ние ♦ **strong love** ~ си́льное любо́вное влече́ние ♦ **strong physical** ~ си́льное физи́ческое тяготе́ние ♦ **tremendous (physical)** ~ грома́дное (физи́ческое) притяже́ние ♦ *(1,2)* **wild** ~ *(1)* ди́кое / *(2)* безу́мное притяже́ние ♦ **overwhelming power of** ~ сокруши́тельная си́ла притяже́ния.

Common adult heights are given in Appendix 9, page 776.

attraction: *phrases*

There is such a *(1,2)* **wild attraction between us.** Между на́ми тако́е *(1)* ди́кое / *(2)* безу́мное притяже́ние. ♦ **I've never felt such a(n) (powerful) attraction to anyone (as I feel toward you).** Я никогда́ ни к кому́ не чу́вствовал *(ж: чу́вствовала)* тако́го (мо́щного) тяготе́ния (, как к тебе́). ♦ **You can't deny it, there's a *(1)* powerful / *(2)* strong / *(3)* tremendous physical attraction between us.** Ты не мо́жешь отрица́ть существова́ния *(1)* мо́щного / *(2)* си́льного / *(3)* грома́дного физи́ческого притяже́ния ме́жду на́ми. ♦ **The physical attraction I feel toward you is overwhelming.** Физи́ческое тяготе́ние, кото́рое я чу́вствую к тебе́, ошеломля́ет. ♦ **There's no (true) love between us, it's a purely physical attraction.** Ме́жду на́ми нет (настоя́щей) любви́, э́то - исключи́тельно физи́ческое тяготе́ние.

attractive *adj* привлека́тельный, -ая, -ое, -ые *(short forms:* привлека́телен, привлека́тельна, -о, -ы*)*; симпати́чный, -ая, -ое, -ые; *(f only:)* хоро́шенькая, -ие, хороша́ собо́й ♦ **awfully** ~ чёрто́вски привлека́тельный *m*, -ая *f* ♦ **devastatingly** ~ сокруши́тельно привлека́тельный *m*, -ая *f* ♦ **exceptionally** ~ исключи́тельно привлека́тельный *m*, -ая *f* ♦ **extraordinarily** ~ чрезвыча́йно привлека́тельный *m*, -ая *f* ♦ **extremely** ~ исключи́тельно привлека́тельный *m*, -ая *f* ♦ **lethally** ~ ужа́сно привлека́тельный *m*, -ая *f* ♦ **mentally** ~ душе́вно привлека́тельный *m*, -ая *f* ♦ **overwhelmingly** ~ ошеломля́юще привлека́тельный *m*, -ая *f* ♦ **physically** ~ физи́чески привлека́тельный *m*, -ая *f* ♦ **terribly** ~ чёрто́вски привлека́тельный *m*, -ая *f* ♦ **unbelievably** ~ невероя́тно привлека́тельный *m*, -ая *f* ♦ **uncommonly** ~ необыкнове́нно привлека́тельный *m*, -ая *f* ♦ **unusually** ~ необыкнове́нно привлека́тельный *m*, -ая *f* ♦ **very** ~ о́чень привлека́тельный *m*, -ая *f*.

attractive: *phrases*

I don't care what your age is, you're still *(1)* **exceptionally** / *(2)* **extraordinarily** / *(3)* **very attractive.** Меня́ не волну́ет твой во́зраст, ты всё ещё *(1)* исключи́тельно / *(2)* чрезвыча́йно / *(3)* о́чень привлека́тельна *(ж: привлека́телен).* ♦ **You're far from being plain. You're *(1)* very / *(2)* extremely attractive.** Ты совсе́м не некраси́ва *(ж: некраси́в).* Ты *(1)* о́чень / *(2)* исключи́тельно привлека́тельна *(ж: привлека́телен).* ♦ **I find you *(1)* very / *(2)* exceptionally / *(3)* overwhelmingly attractive.** Я нахожу́, что ты *(1)* о́чень / *(2)* исключи́тельно / *(3)* ошеломля́юще привлека́тельна *(ж: привлека́телен).* ♦ **To say that you are attractive is the understatement of the *(1)* year / *(2)* century.** Сказа́ть, что ты про́сто привлека́тельна - э́то са́мое невероя́тное преуменьше́ние э́того *(1)* го́да / *(2)* ве́ка. ♦ **You make me feel attractive.** Ты заставля́ешь меня́ чу́вствовать себя́ привлека́тельной. ♦ **I consider myself attractive.** Я счита́ю себя́ привлека́тельным *(ж: привлека́тельной).*

attractiveness *n* привлека́тельность *f* ♦ **animal** ~ живо́тная привлека́тельность ♦ **virile** ~ му́жественная привлека́тельность.

attribute *n* ка́чество, (отличи́тельная) черта́, сво́йство ♦ **exceptional** ~s исключи́тельные ка́чества ♦ **feminine** ~s же́нские черты́ ♦ **marvelous** ~s замеча́тельные сво́йства ♦ **physical** ~s физи́ческие сво́йства ♦ **similar** ~s схо́дные ка́чества ♦ **womanly** ~s же́нские черты́ ♦ *(1,2)* **wonderful** ~s *(1)* удиви́тельные / *(2)* чуде́сные сво́йства.

attribute: *phrases*

You have so many attributes that I admire. У тебя́ так мно́го ка́честв, кото́рыми я восхища́юсь. ♦ **I've never *(1)* seen / *(2)* met anyone with so many extraordinary physical attributes (as you have).** Я никогда́ не *(1)* ви́дел *(ж: ви́дела)* / *(2)* встреча́л *(ж: встреча́ла)* никого́, тако́го физи́чески прекра́сного, как ты. ♦ **Your *(1)* beauty / *(2)* love-**

Words in parentheses are optional.

liness / *(3)* **charm is just one of your many exceptional attributes.** *(1,2)* Твоя́ красота́... / *(3)* Твоё обая́ние... - то́лько одно́ из мно́гих твои́х исключи́тельных ка́честв.

attuned *adj* настро́ен, -а, -о, -ы *(short forms)* ♦ **It's** *(1)* **marvelous** / *(2)* **wonderful how we're so attuned to each other.** Это *(1)* изуми́тельно / *(2)* удиви́тельно, как гармони́чно мы настро́ены друг на дру́га.

atypical *adj* нетипи́чный, -ая, -ое, -ые.

audacious *adj* 1. *(courageous)* сме́лый, -ая, -ое, -ые; 2. *(impudent)* на́глый, -ая, -ое, -ые; де́рзкий, -ая, -ое, -ие.

audacity *n* 1. *(courage)* сме́лость *f* ; 2. *(impudence)* на́глость *f* ; де́рзость *f.*

au naturel *Fr (naked)* голышо́м.

aunt *n* тётя.

aura *n* а́ура ♦ ~ **of temptation** а́ура собла́зна ♦ **powerful ~ of sexuality** мо́щная а́ура сексуа́льности ♦ **There is such an aura of calmness about you.** От тебя́ исхо́дит тако́е споко́йствие.

Australian *adj* австрали́йский, -ая, -ое, -ие.

Australian *n* австрали́ец *m*, австрали́йка *f.*

authoritarian *adj* авторита́рный, -ая, -ое, -ые.

authoritative *adj* авторите́тный, -ая, -ое, -ые.

autonomy *n* автоно́мия, незави́симость *f.*

autumn *n* о́сень *f* ♦ **in the ~** о́сенью ♦ **last ~** про́шлой о́сенью ♦ **next ~** сле́дующей о́сенью.

available *adj* 1. *(to be had)* име́ющиися, -аяся, -ееся, -иеся, досту́пный, -ая, -ое, -ые 2. *(not occupied)* свобо́дный, -ая, -ое, -ые *(short forms:* свобо́ден, свобо́дна, -о, -ы*)* ♦ **emotionally ~** свобо́дный (-ая, -ое, -ые) в свои́х чу́вствах, эмоциона́льно откры́тый, -ая, -ое, -ые ♦ **be ~** име́ться; быть в нали́чии ♦ **I won't be available tomorrow night.** Я не свобо́ден *(ж: свобо́дна)* за́втра ве́чером. ♦ **Is there a room available?** Есть свобо́дные ко́мнаты? ♦ *(1-3)* **Nothing is available.** *(1)* Всё за́нято. / *(2)* Свобо́дных мест / *(3)* ко́мнат нет.

average *adj* сре́дний, -яя, -ее, -ие.

average-looking *adj* обы́чный, -ая, -ое, -ые.

avert *vt* отвраща́ть / отврати́ть *(what = acc.)*, отводи́ть / отвести́ *(what = acc.)* ♦ **When my gaze fastened on your (beautiful) face, I couldn't avert it.** Когда́ мой взгляд устреми́лся на твоё (прекра́сное) лицо́, я не смог отвести́ от него́ глаз. ♦ **I couldn't avert my gaze (from** *[1]*...**you.** / *[2]* ...**your beautiful** / *[3]* **enchanting face.).** Я не смог *(ж: смогла́)* оторва́ть свой взгляд (от *[1]* ...тебя́. / *[2]* ...твоего́ прекра́сного / *[3]* очарова́тельного лица́.).

averted *adj (Russian uses verbs, such as* удержа́ться, отвести́, отврати́ть*)* ♦ **It was difficult to keep my eyes averted (from you).** Я не мог *(ж: могла́)* отвести́ глаз (от тебя́).

avid *adj* 1. *(ardent)* стра́стный, -ая, -ое, -ые, зая́длый, -ая, -ое, -ые; 2. *(greedy)* жа́дный, -ая, -ое, -ые ♦ **I'm an avid reader.** Я стра́стный чита́тель. ♦ **I promise you hours and hours of incredible ecstasy as my avid lips totally worship your loveliness.** Я обеща́ю тебе́ часы́ и часы́ невероя́тного экста́за в то вре́мя, как мои́ жа́дные гу́бы бу́дут поклоня́ться твое́й красоте́.

avidity *n* а́лчность *f*, жа́дность *f.*

avoid *vt* избега́ть / избежа́ть *(what, whom = acc.)*

avow *vt* признава́ть / призна́ть *(what = acc.)*, откры́то заявля́ть / заяви́ть *(what = acc.)*

awake *adj:* ♦ **I seek a person who is spiritually awake.** Я ищу́ челове́ка, кото́рого волну́ют вопро́сы ду́ха.

awaken *vt* пробужда́ть / пробуди́ть *(what, whom = acc.)*, буди́ть / разбуди́ть *(what,*

You can find common clothing sizes n Appendix 11 on page 778.

whom = acc.) ♦ ~ **feelings** пробужда́ть / пробуди́ть чу́вства.

awaken: phrases

Your love is the sun that awakens life within me. Твоя́ любо́вь - э́то со́лнце, пробужда́ющее жизнь во мне. ♦ **You awaken so much desire in me.** Ты пробужда́ешь так мно́го стра́сти во мне. ♦ **You have awoken such** *(1)* **wonderful /** *(2)* **incredible /** *(3)* **exquisite /** *(4)* **glorious /** *(5)* **heavenly feelings in me.** Ты пробуди́ла *(ж: пробуди́л)* во мне таки́е *(1)* удиви́тельные / *(2)* невероя́тные / *(3)* изы́сканные / *(4)* прекра́сные / *(5)* небе́сные чу́вства. ♦ **I'm going to awaken** *(1)* **...feelings in you that you didn't realize you had. /** *(2)* **...feelings of ecstasy in you such as you have never imagined possible.** Я разбужу́ в тебе́ *(1)* ...таки́е чу́вства, кото́рых ты в себе́ не подозрева́ешь. / *(2)* ...тако́й экста́з, како́й ты никогда́ не могла́ себе́ предста́вить. ♦ **If you were my woman, I would fill your life to overflowing with soft, gentle, eager, loving kisses that would awaken all sorts of warm, wonderful, exquisite feelings in you.** Е́сли бы ты была́ мое́й же́нщиной, я бы запо́лнил твою́ жизнь до краёв мя́гкими, не́жными, жа́ждущими, лю́бящими поцелу́ями, кото́рые пробуди́ли бы все са́мые тёплые, замеча́тельные, изы́сканные чу́вства в тебе́. ♦ **My warm breath will awaken all of your senses.** Моё тёплое дыха́ние пробу́дит все твои́ чу́вства.

awakening *n* пробужде́ние ♦ **blissful** ~ счастли́вое пробужде́ние ♦ **sexual** ~ сексуа́льное пробужде́ние.

aware *adj* 1. *(informed)* осведомлённый, -ая, -ое, -ые; *(knowing)* зна́ющий, -ая, -ее, -ие; 2. *(savvy)* разбира́ющийся -аяся, -ееся, -иеся, гра́мотный, -ая, -ое, -ые; 3. *(perceptive)* чу́ткий, -ая, -ое, -ие, понима́ющий, -ая, -ее, -ие ♦ **be artistically** ~ разбира́ться в иску́сстве ♦ **become** ~ узна́ть *(of what = + o + prep.)* ♦ **be completely** ~ быть по́лностью осведомлённым, -ой, -ым, -ыми ♦ **be instinctively** ~ инстинкти́вно знать ♦ **be mystically** ~ разбира́ться в ми́стике ♦ **be politically** ~ разбира́ться в поли́тике ♦ **be socially** ~ знать, как держа́ть себя́ в о́бществе *(1 term)* ♦ **be spiritually** ~ интересова́ться духо́вной жи́знью.

aware: phrases

When I *(1)* **became /** *(2)* **grew aware of your feelings for me, I was overcome with joy.** Когда́ я *(1,2)* узна́л *(ж: узна́ла)* о твои́х чу́вствах ко мне, я был охва́чен *(ж: была́ охва́чена)* ликова́нием. ♦ **I'm** *(1)* **acutely /** *(2)* **intensely aware of your situation.** Я *(1,2)* хорошо́ зна́ю твою́ ситуа́цию. ♦ **In case you're not aware, I'm trying to seduce you.** Ты ещё не догада́лась *(ж: догада́лся)*, что я пыта́юсь соблазни́ть тебя́.

awareness *n* осведомлённость; зна́ние ♦ **inner** ~ осозна́ние себя́.

awash *pred adj (Russian uses verb construction)* ♦ **My whole body is awash with fire, thinking about you.** Всё моё те́ло охва́тывает ого́нь при мы́сле о тебе́. ♦ **I gaze upon your divinely beautiful face in its silky frame of** *(1)* **golden /** *(2)* **auburn /** *(3)* **black hair and I am awash in fervent adoration.** Я вгля́дываюсь в твоё боже́ственно-прекра́сное лицо́ в шелкови́стом обрамле́нии *(1)* золоты́х / *(2)* золоти́сто-кашта́новых / *(3)* чёрных воло́с и я тону́ в пы́лком обожа́нии.

away *adj*: ♦ **Life is (so)** *(1)* **dismal /** *(2)* **dreary /** *(3)* **empty /** *(4)* **grey /** *(5)* **miserable when I'm away from you.** Жизнь (така́я) *(1)* мра́чная / *(2)* безотра́дная / *(3)* пуста́я / *(4)* се́рая / *(5)* печа́льная, когда́ я вдали́ от тебя́. ♦ **I simply cannot** *(1)* **bear /** *(2)* **endure being away from you.** Я про́сто не могу́ *(1)* вы́нести / *(2)* вы́держать разлу́ку с тобо́й. ♦ **It is sheer agony to be away from you.** Это су́щее муче́ние быть вдали́ от тебя́.

awe *n* благогове́ние ♦ **I am (***[1]* **always /** *[2]* **totally) in awe of** *(3)* **...you. /** *(4)* **...your (***[5]* **incredible /** *[6]* **shining /** *[7]* **incomparable /** *[8]* **peerless /** *[9]* **amaranthine /** *[10]* **exquisite) beauty.** Я (*[1]* всегда́) в (*[2]* по́лном) благогове́нии пе́ред *(3)* ...тобо́й. / *(4)* ...твое́й

For general rules of Russian grammar see Appendix 2 on page 686.

(*[5]* невероя́тной / *[6]* блиста́тельной / *[7,8]* несравне́нной / *[9]* неувяда́емой / *[10]* изы́сканной) красото́й.

awe-inspiring *adj* внуша́ющий (-ая, -ее, -ие) благогове́ние ♦ **be** ~ внуша́ть благогове́ние.

awesome *adj* 1. *(inspiring awe)* благогове́нный, -ая, -ое, -ые; 2. *(terrific)* фантасти́ческий, -ая, -ое, -ие, великоле́пный, -ая, -ое, -ые ♦ **totally** ~ *(fabulous)* соверше́нно потряса́ющий, -ая, -ее, -ие; *(incredible)* соверше́нно невероя́тный, -ая, -ое, -ые; *(wonderful)* соверше́нно замеча́тельный, -ая, -ое, -ые; *(delightful)* соверше́нно восхити́тельный, -ая, -ое, -ые.

awestruck *adj* охва́ченный (-ая, -ое, -ые) благогове́нием, прони́кнутый (-ая, -ое, -ые) благогове́нием, преиспо́лненный (-ая, -ое, -ые) благогове́ния ♦ **I was too awestruck to say anything.** Я засты́л *(ж: засты́ла)* в благогове́йном молча́нии. ♦ **When I** *(1)* **...looked at your photo,...** / *(2)* **...saw your face,... I was awestruck.** *(1)* Взгляну́в на твою́ фотогра́фию,... / *(2)* Уви́дев твоё лицо́,... я был охва́чен благогове́нием.

awful *adj* ужа́сный, -ая, -ое, -ые.

awfully *adv* 1. *(very)* о́чень, весьма́; 2. *(terribly)* ужа́сно.

awkward *adj* 1. неуклю́жий, -ая, -ее, -ие, нело́вкий, -ая, -ое, -ие; 2. неудо́бный, -ая, -ое, -ые, затрудни́тельный, -ая, -ое, -ые ♦ **I felt so awkward.** Я чу́вствовал *(ж: чу́вствовала)* себя́ так неудо́бно. ♦ **It** *(1)* **is** / *(2)* **was a(n)** (*[3]* **rather** / *[4]* **very**) **awkward situation.** *(1)* Это... / *(2)* Это была́... (*[3]* немно́го / *[4]* о́чень) неудо́бная ситуа́ция. ♦ **It would be a very awkward situation.** Это была́ бы о́чень неудо́бная ситуа́ция. ♦ **I feel** (*[1]* **rather** / *[2]* **very**) **awkward writing a letter to someone I don't know.** Я испы́тываю (*[1]* ...не́которое... / *[2]* ...си́льное...) неудо́бство писа́ть письмо́ челове́ку, кото́рого я не зна́ю.

awkwardness *n* 1. неуклю́жесть *f*, нело́вкость *f*; 2. *(discomfort)* неудо́бство ♦ **feeling of** ~ ощуще́ние нело́вкости.

Azerbaijanian *adj* азербайджа́нский, -ая, -ое, -ие.

Azerbaijanian *n* 1. *(person)* азербайджа́нец *m*, азербайджа́нка *f (pl:* азербайджа́нцы*)*; 2. *(language)* азербайджа́нский язы́к ♦ **speak** ~ говори́ть по-азербайджа́нски.

For transitive Russian verbs the cases that they take are shown
by means of an = sign and the Russian case. (abbreviated)

B

babe *n (slang) (woman)* же́нщина ♦ **beautiful** ~ краса́вица, красо́тка, краси́вая же́нщина ♦ **good-looking** ~ привлека́тельная же́нщина ♦ **gorgeous** ~ великоле́пная же́нщина.

baby *n* 1. *(infant)* ребёнок; 2. *(darling)* дорого́й *m*, дорога́я *f* ♦ **It would be so wonderful to have a baby with you.** Бы́ло бы так замеча́тельно име́ть ребёнка от тебя́. ♦ **Let's make a baby.** Дава́й сде́лаем ребёнка.

baby doll *n (slang)* 1. *(short negligee)* коро́ткий пеньюа́р; 2. *(sweetheart)* возлю́бленная.

baby-faced *adj* с ку́кольным лицо́м.

bachelor *n* холостя́к ♦ **confirmed** ~ убеждённый холостя́к ♦ **old** ~ ста́рый холостя́к.

bachelorette *n* неза́мужяя же́нщина.

bachelorhood *n* холостя́цкая жизнь ♦ **I'm totally ready and willing to give up my bachelorhood for you.** Для тебя́ я соверше́нно гото́в расста́ться со свое́й холостя́цкой жи́знью.

back *n* спина́ ♦ **little** ~ спи́нка ♦ **smooth** ~ гла́дкая спина́ ♦ **Let me rub your back.** Дай мне помасси́ровать твою́ спи́нку. ♦ *(1-3)* **Get off my back.** *(1)* Отвяжи́сь... / *(2)* Отцепи́сь... / *(3)* Отста́нь... от меня́.

backbone *n* си́льный хара́ктер ♦ **I like a man who has backbone.** Мне нра́вятся мужчи́ны с си́льным хара́ктером.

back down *vi* уступа́ть / уступи́ть.

background *n* 1. *(origin)* исто́ки, происхожде́ние; 2. *(biographical data)* биографи́ческие да́нные ♦ **educational** ~ образова́ние, подгото́вка ♦ **family** ~ происхожде́ние, семья́ ♦ **German** ~ неме́цкое происхожде́ние ♦ **social** ~ социа́льное происхожде́ние ♦ **I have a solid family background.** Я происхожу́ из кре́пкой семьи́.

back off *vi (slang)* отходи́ть / отойти́, отстава́ть / отста́ть, отва́ливать / отвали́ть ♦ *(1-3)* **Back off!** *(1)* Отойди́! / *(2)* Отста́нь! / *(3)* Отвали́!

back out *vi* уклоня́ться / уклони́ться, отка́зываться / отказа́ться, отступа́ть / отступи́ть ♦ ~ **gracefully** димпломати́чески отка́зываться / отказа́ться.

backrub *n* масса́ж спины́.

backstabber *n (slang)* челове́к, напада́ющий на друго́го челове́ка сза́ди *(explanation)*.

bad *adj* плохо́й, -а́я, -о́е, -и́е.

bad-looking *adj:* ♦ **not** ~ недурён собо́й *m*, недурна́ собо́й *f.*

badly *adv* пло́хо.

badminton *n* бадминто́н ♦ **I like to play badminton.** Я люблю́ игра́ть в бадминто́н.

Russian verbs have 2 forms: imperfective and perfective. They're given in that order

baffled *adj* озадáчен, -а, -о, -ы *(short forms)*, сбит (-а, -о, -ы) с тóлку *(short forms)*, постáвлен (-а, -о, -ы) в тупúк *(short forms)*, приведён (приведенá, -ó, -ы́) в замешáтельство *(short forms)*.

bag *n* 1. *(purse)* сýмка; 2. *(suitcase)* чемодáн; 3. *(sack)* мешóк ♦ **overnight** ~ дорóжная сýмка.

baggage *n* 1. *(suitcases)* багáж; 2. *(burdens; obligations)* груз; *(problems, inhibitions or undesired obligations)* проблéмы, брéмя, обýза ♦ **emotional** ~ эмоционáльное брéмя, эмоционáльные проблéмы ♦ **no** ~ не обременённый, -ая, -ое, -ые ♦ **I don't have any emotional baggage that's going to clutter up a relationship.** У меня нет никакúх эмоционáльных проблéм, котóрые бýдут мешáть отношéниям.

balanced *adj* уравновéшенный, -ая, -ое, -ые *(short forms:* уравновéшен, -а, -о, -ы*)* ♦ **emotionally** ~ эмоционáльно уравновéшен, -а, -о, -ы ♦ **spiritually** ~ духóвно уравновéшен, -а, -о, -ы.

bald *adj* лы́сый, -ые.

balding *adj* лысéющий, -ая, -ее, -ие.

ballad *n* баллáда ♦ **My heart sings ballads of love to you every minute of the day.** Кáждую минýту моё сéрдце поёт баллáды любвú к тебé.

balls *n (slang)* 1. *(testicles)* яúчки; 2. *(courage, audacity)* смéлость *f,* мýжество.

balm *n* бальзáм ♦ **edible** *(1,2)* **pleasure** ~ съедóбный бальзáм для *(1)* наслаждéния / *(2)* удовóльствия ♦ **lip** ~ бальзáм для губ.

banal *adj* банáльный, -ая, -ое, -ые.

banality *n* банáльность *f.*

band *n* 1. *(ribbon; tie)* лéнта, тесьмá; завя́зка; 2. *(ring)* кольцó; 3. *(orchestra)* оркéстр; 4. *(group)* отря́д ♦ **gold** ~ золотóе (обручáльное) кольцó ♦ **wedding** ~ обручáльное кольцó.

band together *vi (slang) (meet)* встречáться / встрéтиться; *(join together)* соединя́ться / соединúться ♦ **If you're a person with these qualities, let's band together.** Éсли ты человéк с э́тими кáчествами, давáй соединúмся.

bangs *n, pl (hair on forehead)* чёлочка ♦ **wear ~s** носúть чёлочку.

bankrupt *adj* несостоя́тельный, -ая, -ое, -ые ♦ **emotionally** ~ эмоционáльно несостоя́тельный, -ая, -ое, -ые.

banquet *n* банкéт ♦ **wedding** ~ свáдебный банкéт, брáчный пир.

bar *n* бар ♦ **singles'** ~ бар для одинóких ♦ **I don't like bars.** Я не люблю́ бáры ♦ **I stay out of bars.** Я не хожý в бáры.

barbarian *n* вáрвар ♦ **I'm sorry for the way I acted. I was a complete barbarian.** Извинú за мои постýпки. Я был (совершéнным) вáрваром. ♦ **You must think I'm a ([1] complete / [2] total) barbarian.** Ты должнá дýмать, что я ([1] закóнченный /[2] пóлный) вáрвар.

barbecue *n* барбекю́, приготовлéние жáренного мя́са на открытом вóздухе.

barbecue *vi & vt* жáрить / пожáрить мя́со на открытом вóздухе.

barbered *adj* аккурáтно подстрúженный, -ая, -ое, -ые.

bare-breasted *adj* с обнажённой грýдью.

bare-chested *adj* с обнажённой грýдью.

barefoot *adj* босóй, -áя, -óе, -ы́е.

barefoot *adv* босикóм ♦ **go around** ~ ходúть босикóм.

barfly *n (slang)* человéк, проводя́щий мнóго врéмени в бáрах *(explanation).*

barhop *vi* бéгать по бáрам, ходúть по бáрам.

barhopping *n* хождéние по бáрам.

---

*How to use the Cyrillic alphabet on the Internet
is the subject of Appendix 20 on page 789.*

barrier *n* барьер, препятствие, преграда ♦ **I can't** *(1)* **fathom** / *(2)* **understand** / *(3)* **surmount this polite barrier of coolness that you've erected.** Я не могу *(1,2)* понять / *(3)* преодолеть этот вежливый барьер холодности, который ты построила *(ж: построил).* ♦ **When we're together, I want you to let down all your (inner) barriers and just give yourself to me completely.** Когда мы вместе, я хочу, чтобы ты перешагнула через все свои внутренние барьеры и отдала мне себя полностью. ♦ **I promise I'm going to let down all my (inner) barriers and just give myself to you completely.** Я обещаю отбросить все свои (внутренние) барьеры и отдать тебе себя полностью.

base *n* 1. *(basis)* основа, базис, основание; 2. *(mil.)* база; 3. *(baseball)* база *(один из четырёх пунктов на углах бейсбольного поля)* ♦ **be off** ~ *(be mistaken)* ошибаться ♦ **I can't seem to get to first base with you.** Я, кажется, не могу добиться успеха с тобой. ♦ **You're way off base.** Ты совершенно ошибаешься. ♦ **I live on base.** *(mil.)* Я живу на базе. ♦ **I can't** *(1)* **...go off base.** / *(2)* **...leave base.** *(mil.)* Я не могу *(1)* ...выйти из базы. / *(2)* ...покинуть базу. ♦ **I have to go back to base.** *(mil.)* Я должен *(ж: должна)* вернуться на базу.

baseball *n* бейсбол ♦ **Do you know the American game of baseball?** Знаешь ли ты американскую игру бейсбол?

based: ♦ **be** ~ *(mil.)* базироваться ♦ **I'm based at** *(name of [1] base / [2] city)* . Я базируюсь *[1]* на ____ / *[2]* в ___.

bashful *adj* застенчивый, -ая, -ое, -ые; робкий, -ая, -ое, -ие ♦ ~**girl** застенчивая девушка ♦ **You don't have to be bashful with me.** Ты не должна *(ж: должен)* быть застенчивой *(ж: застенчивым)* со мной. ♦ **Don't be (so) bashful.** Не будь (так) застенчива *(ж: застенчив).*

bashfulness *n* застенчивость *f*; робость *f*.

basically *adv* в сущности; по существу; в основном.

bask *vi* 1. *(in the sun)* греться на солнце; 2. *(enjoy)* наслаждаться *(in what = instr.)*; *(luxuriate in the warmth of)* согреваться *(in what = instr.)* ♦ **I want to bask in the warmth of your sunshine.** Я хочу греться в твоих лучах. ♦ **I could bask forever in the warmth of your sunshine.** Я смог *(ж: смогла)* бы вечно греться в тепле твоих лучей.

basketball *n* баскетбол ♦ **I play basketball once in awhile.** Я играю изредка в баскетбол.

bastard *n (slang)* ублюдок.

bath *n* ванна ♦ **bubble** ~ пенистая ванна ♦ **Let's take a bath together.** Давай примем ванну вместе. ♦ **We'll take a bath together and I'll** *(1)* **put** / *(2)* **rub soap all over your body.** Мы примем ванну вместе и я *(1,2)* намылю всё твоё тело. ♦ **I dream of taking a bath with you by candlelight.** Я мечтаю принять с тобой ванну при свечах. ♦ **I want to take a long, leisurely bath together with you.** Мне хочется долго, неторопливо нежиться с тобой в ванне.

bathe *vt* купать *(what, whom = acc.)* ♦ **I love to bathe** *(1)* **...you.** / *(2)* **...your beautiful /** *(3)* **gorgeous body.** Я люблю купать *(1)* ...тебя. / *(2)* ...твоё прекрасное / *(3)* великолепное тело.

be *vi* быть *(I am:* я *[no translation of "am"]. You are:* ты *[no translation of "are"].).* ♦ **Be mine.** Будь моей *(ж: моим).* ♦ **I'm yours** *([1]* **always** / *[2]* **forever).** Я твой *(ж: твоя)* *([1,2]* навсегда). ♦ **I will always be yours.** Я всегда буду твоим *(ж: твоей).* ♦ **I want you (always) to be mine.** Я хочу, чтобы ты всегда была моей *(ж: был моим).* ♦ **I will always be** *(1)* **...yours.** /*(2)* **...faithful /** *(3)* **true to you.** Я всегда буду *(1)* ...твоим *(ж: твоей).* / *(2)* ...преданным *(ж: преданной)* / *(3)* верным *(ж: верной)* тебе. ♦ **Nothing matters except being with you.** Нет ничего важнее, чем быть с тобой. ♦ **We need to be together.** Нам надо быть вместе. ♦ **If only you could be with me now!**

Russian adjectives have long and short forms.
Where short forms are given, they are labeled as such.

Если бы ты то́лько могла́ *(ж: мог)* быть со мной сейча́с! ♦ **It has been set down by a divine will that I am yours and you are mine.** Э́то бы́ло во́лей провиде́ния, что ...я твой и ты моя́ *(ж: ...я твоя́ и ты мой).* ♦ **(1,2) What time will you be there?** *(1)* Когда́... / *(2)* В како́е вре́мя... ты бу́дешь там? ♦ **I'll be there at one (thirty).** *(See page 759 for other times.)* Я бу́ду там в час (три́дцать). ♦ **You haven't been yourself lately.** Ты не была́ са́мой *(ж: не был сами́м)* собо́й после́днее вре́мя.

beach *n* пляж ♦ **moonlit** ~ пляж, зали́тый лу́нным све́том *(1 term)* ♦ **nude** ~ нуди́стский пляж ♦ **topless** ~ пляж, где мо́жно находи́ться без бюстга́льтера *(1 term)* ♦ **I love to take long walks on the beach.** Я люблю́ соверша́ть до́лгие прогу́лки по пля́жу.

beads *n, pl* бу́сы.

beam *vi* сия́ть ♦ **You are beaming so happily in this photo.** Ты так сия́ешь сча́стьем на э́том фо́то. ♦ **I want to see your face beaming happily every morning.** Я хочу́ ка́ждое у́тро ви́деть твоё лицо́, сия́ющее сча́стем.

bear *vt* 1. *(hold, carry)* носи́ть *(what = acc.),* переноси́ть / перенести́ *(what = acc.);* 2. *(endure)* выде́рживать / вы́держать *(what, whom = acc.),* переноси́ть / перенести́ *(what, whom = acc.),* выноси́ть / вы́нести *(what, whom = acc.).*

┌─────────────────────┐
│ **bear: hold, carry** │
└─────────────────────┘

You can never know how much love I bear in my heart for you. Ты не представля́ешь, како́й огро́мной любо́вью к тебе́ полно́ моё се́рдце. ♦ **I bear no regrets.** Я ни о чём не жале́ю. ♦ **I bear no remorse.** У меня́ нет угрызне́ний со́вести. ♦ **I bear such (enormously) tender feelings for you.** Я по́лон таки́ми не́жными чу́вствами к тебе́.

┌─────────────────┐
│ **bear: endure** │
└─────────────────┘

I (simply) cannot *(1,2)* **bear** *(3)* **...being apart from you.** / *(4)* **...to be apart from you.** / *(5)* **...to think about it.** / *(6)* **...the thought of you in someone else's arms.** / *(7)* **...the thought of leaving you.** / *(8)* **...the thought of (ever) losing you.** Я не могу́ *(1)* вы́нести / *(2)* перенести́ *(3,4)* ...разлу́ку с тобо́й. / *(3,4)* ...быть вдалеке́ от тебя́. *(5)* ...мы́слей об э́том. / *(6)* ...мы́слей о тебе́ в чьи́х-то объя́тиях. / *(7)* ...мы́слей об отъе́зде. / *(8)* ...мы́слей о поте́ре тебя́. ♦ **The** *(1)* **longing** / *(2)* **yearning in my heart for you is** *(3)* **...more than I can bear.** / *(4)* **...an agony that I can hardly bear.** *(1)* Тоска́ по тебе́... / *(2)* Жа́жда тебя́... в моём се́рдце *(3)* ...вы́ше мои́х сил. / *(4)* ...- му́ка, кото́рую я едва́ могу́ вы́нести. ♦ **I want you so much I can't bear it.** Я так си́льно хочу́ тебя́, что не могу́ вы́держать. ♦ **The temptation to** *(1)* **...kiss you...** / *(2)* **...take you in my arms... was almost more than I could bear.** Искуше́ние *(1)* ...целова́ть тебя́... / *(2)* ...заключи́ть тебя́ в объя́тия... бы́ло почти́ невыноси́мо. ♦ **It was so intense (that) I could hardly bear it.** Э́то бы́ло так си́льно, что я едва́ мог *(ж: могла́)* вы́нести. ♦ **I can't bear it anymore.** Я э́того бо́льше не вы́несу.

bear *n* медве́дь *m* ♦ **teddy** ~ медвежо́нок ♦ **I want to be your teddy bear, so you can cuddle up with me all the time.** Я хочу́ быть твои́м медвежо́нком, что́бы ты могла́ всё вре́мя обнима́ться со мной.

beard *n* борода́ ♦ **black** ~ чёрная борода́ ♦ **bushy** ~ густа́я борода́ ♦ **cropped** ~ ко́ротко остри́женная борода́ ♦ **small** ~ боро́дка ♦ **tawny** ~ рыжева́то-кори́чневая борода́ ♦ **Your beard tickles.** Твоя́ борода́ щеко́чет. ♦ **I like the feel of your beard.** Мне нра́вится чу́вствовать твою́ бо́роду. ♦ **I think you'd look (much) better without a beard.** Я ду́маю, ты вы́глядишь гора́здо лу́чше без бороды́. ♦ **You look (very)** *(1)* **good** / *(2)* **distinguished** / *(3)* **handsome** / *(4)* **scholarly in / with a beard.** С бородо́й ты вы́глядишь (о́чень) *(1)* хорошо́ / *(2)* аристократи́чно / *(3)* краси́вым / *(4)* как учёный.

bearded *adj* борода́тый, -ые.

bearer *n* пода́тель, пода́ющий, предъяви́тель ♦ **ring** ~ *(at a wedding)* пода́ющий кольцо́

┌──┐
│ *Russian nouns are either masculine, feminine or neuter.* │
│ *Adjectives with them will be the same.* │
└──┘

(на свáдьбе).

bearing *n* осáнка ♦ **proud** ~ горделúвая осáнка. ♦ **regal** ~ цáрственная осáнка.

beat *adj (slang) (exhausted)* изнемогáл *m*, изнемогáла *f.*

beat *vt* бить / побúть *(what, whom= acc.)* ♦ **My** *(1,2)* **boyfriend** / *(3)* **husband** *(4)* **beats** / *(5)* **beat me (all the time).** Мой *(1)* сожúтель *(co-vivant)* / *(2)* любóвник *(lover)* / *(3)* муж (всё врéмя) *(4)* бьёт / *(5)* бил меня́. ♦ *(1,2,3)* **It beats me.** Я не имéю ни малéйшего *(1)* поня́тия / *(2)* представлéния. / *(3)* Я совсéм не зна́ю.

beat *n* 1. *(hitting)* удáр; 2. *(pulsation)* биéние; 3. *(rhythm)* ритм; такт ♦ **When our eyes** *(1)* **locked** / *(2)* **met, my heart skipped a beat.** Когдá нáши глазá *(1,2)* встрéтились, моё сéрдце зáмерло.

beau *n (boyfriend)* поклóнник.

beautiful *adj* прекрáсный, -ая, -ое, -ые, *(short forms:* прекрáсен, прекрáсна, -о, -ы)*, красúвый, -ая, -ое, -ые, *(short forms:* красúв, -а, -о, -ы)* ♦ **absolutely** ~ совершéнно прекрáсная ♦ **achingly** ~ исключúтельно красúвая ♦ **awesomely** ~ фантастúчески прекрáсная ♦ **awfully** ~ чертóвски красúвая ♦ ~ **beyond words** невероя́тно прекрáсная ♦ ~ **inside and out** прекрáсна внýтренне и внéшне ♦ ~ **to perfection** красúвая до совершéнства ♦ **bewitchingly** ~ обворожúтельно прекрáсная ♦ **dazzlingly** ~ ослепúтельно красúвая ♦ **devastatingly** ~ ошеломля́юще прекрáсная ♦ **dramatically** ~ драматúчески прекрáсная ♦ **enchantingly** ~ очаровáтельная и прекрáсная ♦ **exceptionally** ~ исключúтельно прекрáсная ♦ **exotically** ~ экзотúчески прекрáсная ♦ **exquisitely** ~ изы́сканно прекрáсная ♦ **extraordinarily** ~ чрезвычáйно прекрáсная ♦ **fantastically** ~ фантастúчески прекрáсная ♦ **incredibly** ~ невероя́тно прекрáсная ♦ **most** ~ сáмая прекрáсная ♦ **painfully** ~ исключúтельно красúвая ♦ **physically** ~ физúчески прекрáсная ♦ **quite** ~ весьмá красúвая ♦ **rhapsodically** ~ рапсодúчески прекрáсная ♦ **so** ~ так прекрáсна ♦ **startlingly** ~ исхóдно прекрáсная ♦ *(1,2)* **strikingly** ~ *(1)* потряса́юще / *(2)* поразúтельно прекрáсная ♦ **sublimely** ~ велúчественно прекрáсная ♦ **stunningly** ~ сногшибáтельно **sublimely** ~ велúчественно прекрáсная ♦ **terribly** ~ чертóвски красúвая ♦ **totally** ~ совершéнно прекрáсная ♦ **very** ~ óчень красúвая ♦ **be verging on** ~ быть почтú красúвой.

---
beautiful: *You're beautiful*

You are very beautiful. Ты óчень красúва. ♦ **You are (** *[1]* **so /** *[2]* **exceptionally /** *[3]* **absolutely /** *[4]* **totally /** *[5]* **incredibly /** *[5]* **fantastically) beautiful.** Ты *([1]* так / *[2]* исключúтельно / *[3]* совершéнно / *[4]* невероя́тно / *[5]* фантастúчески) прекрáсна. ♦ **You're the most beautiful** *(1)* **woman /** *(2)* **girl** *(3)* **...here. /** *(4)* **...in the room. /** *(5)* **...I know. /** *(6)* **...I've ever seen /** *(7)* **met (in all my life). /** *(8)* **...I've ever laid eyes on. /** *(9)* **...I could ever imagine. /** *(10)* **...anyone could ever desire. /** *(11)* **...on the face of this earth. /** *(12)* **...in this whole world.** Ты сáмая прекрáсная *(1)* жéнщина / *(2)* дéвушка *(3)* ...здесь. / *(4)* ...в э́той кóмнате. / *(5)* ..., котóрую я зна́ю. / *(6)* ...из всех, вúденных / *(7)* встрéченных мной (в жúзни). / *(8)* ...из всех, на котóрых я когдá-либо останáвливал взгляд. / *(9)* ...из всех, когдá-либо воображáемых мной. / *(10)* ..., котóрую желáет кáждый мужчúна. / *(11)* ...на землé. / *(12)* ...в цéлом мúре. ♦ **How beautiful you** *(1)* **are /** *(2)* **look!** Как *(1)* ...ты прекрáсна! / *(2)* ...прекрáсно ты вы́глядишь! ♦ **I've never** *(1)* **met /** *(2)* **seen anyone so beautiful (in all my life).** Я никогдá (в жúзни) не *(1)* встречáл / *(2)* вúдел такóй прекрáсной. ♦ **I am absolutely certain that I will never again meet anyone more enchantingly beautiful than you are.** Я совершéнно увéрен, что никогдá не встрéчу никогó очаровáтельнее и прекрáснее, чем ты. ♦ **You are so beautiful (that) you** *(1)* **hardly /** *(2)* **don't seem real.** Ты так прекрáсна, что *(1,2)* трýдно повéрить в твоё реáльное существовáние. ♦ **I don't think you (even)** *(1)* **...know... /** *(2)* **...realize...**

Learn more about Russian customs in Appendix 15, page 782.

/ (3) **...have any idea... how beautiful you are.** Я ду́маю, что ты (да́же) не *(1)* зна́ешь / *(2)* осознаёшь / *(3)* представля́ешь, как ты прекра́сна. ♦ **You have no idea how beautiful you are.** Ты да́же не представля́ешь, как ты прекра́сна. ♦ **You are (***[1]* **far /** *[2]* **much) more beautiful than I (ever) expected.** Ты (*[1]* намно́го / *[2]* ещё) краси́вее, чем я ожида́л. ♦ **Even in my most extravagant dreams I never conceived of anyone as beautiful as you.** Да́же в свои́х са́мых сумасбро́дных мечта́х я никогда́ не мог вообрази́ть таку́ю прекра́сную же́нщину, как ты. ♦ **I can't believe how** *(1,2)* **beautiful you are.** Я не могу́ пове́рить, что ты так *(1)* краси́ва / *(2)* прекра́сна. ♦ **To say that you are pretty would be vulgar. You are** *(1)* **exceptionally /** *(2)* **exquisitely /** *(3)* **strikingly beautiful.** Сказа́ть, что ты хоро́шенькая, бы́ло бы вульга́рно. Ты *(1)* исключи́тельно / *(2)* изы́сканно / *(3)* порази́тельно прекра́сна. ♦ **How is it possible for anyone to be so beautiful?** Как э́то возмо́жно быть столь прекра́сной? ♦ **You're beautiful inside and out.** Ты прекра́сна вну́тренне и вне́шне. ♦ **You're even more beautiful than my dreams.** Ты да́же краси́вее, чем мои́ мечты́. ♦ **Never in my wildest imagination did I ever think I could meet anyone as beautiful as you.** Никогда́, да́же в са́мых безу́мных мечта́х, я не ду́мал, что могу́ встре́тить кого́-ли́бо тако́го прекра́сного, как ты. ♦ **You seem to be getting more beautiful with every photo.** Ты, ка́жется, стано́вишься всё прекра́снее с ка́ждой фотогра́фией. ♦ **You're not ugly! You're beautiful!** Ты не уро́длива! Ты прекра́сна!

beautiful: words cannot describe

(1,2) **You are beautiful beyond words.** *(1)* Твоя́ красота́ вы́ше вся́ких слов. / *(2)* Ты невероя́тно краси́ва. ♦ **The word "beautiful"** *(1)* **...doesn't begin to describe you. /** *(2)* **...for you is far /** *(3)* **much too weak.** Сло́во «прекра́сная» *(1)* ...не спосо́бно описа́ть тебя́. / *(2,3)* ...сли́шком сла́бо. ♦ **Mere words are** *(1)* **...not enough... /** *(2)* **...inadequate... to describe how (awesomely)** *(3,4)* **beautiful you are.** Про́сто слов *(1,2)* не доста́точно, что́бы описа́ть, как (фантасти́чески) ты *(3)* краси́ва / *(4)* прекра́сна.

beautiful: an understatement

To say that you are beautiful is the understatement of the *(1)* **year /** *(2)* **century.** Сказа́ть, что ты про́сто краси́ва бы́ло бы преуменьше́нием *(1)* го́да / *(2)* ве́ка. ♦ **Beautiful is a much-abused word, but it's an understatement when applied to you.** Прекра́сная - сло́во, кото́рым ча́сто злоупотребля́ют, но э́то преуменьше́ние, когда́ оно́ обращено́ к тебе́.

beautiful: despite the years

The years have been *(1)* **very /** *(2)* **exceptionally kind to you. You're still** *(3)* **quite /** *(4)* **very beautiful.** Го́ды бы́ли *(1)* о́чень / *(2)* исключи́тельно благоскло́нны к тебе́. Ты всё ещё *(3)* весьма́ / *(4)* о́чень краси́ва. ♦ **I don't care what your age is, you're still** *(1)* **exceptionally /** *(2)* **extraordinarily /** *(3)* **very beautiful.** Меня́ не волну́ет твой во́зраст, ты всё ещё *(1)* исключи́тельно / *(2)* чрезвыча́йно / *(3)* о́чень краси́вая. ♦ **You get more and more beautiful as the time goes by.** Ты стано́вишься всё бо́лее и бо́лее прекра́сной.

beautiful: your features

You have such a beautiful *(1)* **figure /** *(2)* **smile /** *(3)* **neck /** *(4)* **derriere /** *(5)* **bottom /** *(6)* **face /** *(7)* **body /** *(8)* **mouth.** У тебя́ *(1)* ...така́я прекра́сная фигу́ра / *(2)* улы́бка / *(3)* ше́я / *(4,5)* по́па. / *(6)* ...тако́е прекра́сное лицо́ / *(7)* те́ло. / *(8)* ...тако́й прекра́сный рот. ♦ **You have such beautiful** *(1)* **eyes /** *(2)* **hair /** *(3)* **legs /** *(4)* **curves /** *(5)* **hips /** *(6)* **lips /** *(7)* **nipples /** *(8)* **buns /** *(9)* **breasts.** У тебя́ *(1)* ...таки́е прекра́сные глаза́ / *(2)* во́лосы / *(3)* но́ги / *(4)* фо́рмы / *(5)* бёдра / *(6)* гу́бы / *(7)* соски́. / *(8)* ...така́я прекра́сная по́па / *(9)* грудь. ♦ **What a beautiful** *(3)* **face /** *(2)* **body (you have)!** Что за прекра́сное *(1)* лицо́ / *(2)* те́ло (у тебя́)! ♦ **What a beautiful** *(1)* **hairdo /** *(2)* **smile /** *(3)* **figure /** *(4)* **shape /** *(5)*

A slash always denotes "or."
You can choose the numbered words before and after.

ass (you have)! Что за прекра́сная *(1)* причёска / *(2)* улы́бка / *(3)* фигу́ра / *(4)* фигу́ра / *(5)* по́пка (у тебя́)! ◆ **What beautiful** *(1)* **earrings** / *(2)* **fingernails** / *(3)* **legs** / *(4)* **hair (you have)!** Что за прекра́сные *(1)* се́рьги / *(2)* ...но́гти на рука́х... / *(3)* но́ги / *(4)* во́лосы (у тебя́)! ◆ **What beautiful** *(1)* **breasts** / *(2)* **buns (you have)!** Что за прекра́сная *(1)* грудь / *(2)* по́пка (у тебя́)! ◆ **Even in my dreams I've never seen such a beautiful body.** Да́же в мои́х снах я никогда́ не ви́дел тако́го прекра́сного те́ла. ◆ **The** *(1)* **memory** / *(2)* **thought of your beautiful body never leaves my mind.** *(1)* Воспомина́ние / *(2)* Мысль о твоём прекра́сном те́ле никогда́ не покида́ет меня́. ◆ **The image of your beautiful body never leaves my mind.** О́браз твоего́ прекра́сного те́ла никогда́ не покида́ет меня́.

> **beautiful:** *your clothes*

That's a (very) beautiful *(1)* **skirt** / *(2)* **blouse** / *(3)* **dress** / *(4)* **gown** / *(5)* **negligee** / *(6)* **outfit** / *(7)* **seater.** Это (о́чень) *(1)* ...краси́вая ю́бка / *(2)* блу́зка. / *(3,4)* ...краси́вое пла́тье / *(5)* неглиже́. / *(6)* ...краси́вый наря́д / *(7)* сви́тер. ◆ **What a beautiful** *(1)* **dress** / *(2)* **necklace (you have)!** Что за прекра́сное *(1)* пла́тье / *(2)* ожере́лье (у тебя́)! ◆ **What a beautiful outfit (you have)!** Что за прекра́сный наря́д (у тебя́)! ◆ **You look (**[1] **very** / [2] **absolutely** / [3] **positively) beautiful (in that).** (В э́том) ты вы́глядишь (*[1] (nothing)* / [2] соверше́нно / [3] про́сто) прекра́сно. ◆ **You look beautiful in any dress you wear, but I like you better unclothed.** Ты вы́глядишь прекра́сно в любо́м пла́тье, кото́рое ты но́сишь, но мне ты бо́льше нра́вишься без оде́жды.

> **beautiful:** *beautiful, but not married?*

How does it happen that someone so beautiful is not yet married? This is nothing short of a miracle. But I must say, I am extremely happy that the miracle exists. Как так случи́лось, что така́я прекра́сная ещё не за́мужем? Это про́сто чу́до. Но я до́лжен сказа́ть, что я чрезвыча́йно сча́стлив, что э́то чу́до существу́ет. ◆ **I'm astonished like I've never been astonished before that someone as beautiful as you** *(1)* **...is not married.** / *(2)* **...appears on the Internet.** Я изумлён так, как не́ был никогда́ пре́жде, что така́я прекра́сная, как Вы, *(1)* ...не за́мужем. / *(2)* ...появи́лась на Интерне́те.

> **beautiful:** *salutation*

My beautiful, beautiful, beautiful Veronica! Моя́ прекра́сная, прекра́сная, прекра́сная Верони́ка!

> **beautiful:** *everything beautiful in the world*

When I look at you, I see everything good and beautiful in the world. Когда́ я смотрю́ на тебя́, я ви́жу всё хоро́шее и прекра́сное в ми́ре.

beautifully *adv* прекра́сно, краси́во.

beauty *n* 1. *(quality)* красота́; 2. *(person)* краса́вица, красо́тка.

> **beauty:** *quality*

alluring ~ притяга́тельная красота́ ◆ **amaranthine** ~ неувяда́емая красота́ ◆ **bewitching** ~ обворожи́тельная красота́ ◆ **Botticelli-like** ~ ботиче́ллиевская красота́ ◆ **enchanting** ~ обворожи́тельная красота́ ◆ **ethereal** ~ эфеме́рная красота́ ◆ **everlasting** ~ бессме́ртная красота́ ◆ **exceptional** ~ исключи́тельная красота́ ◆ **exotic** ~ экзоти́ческая красота́ ◆ **extraordinary** ~ исключи́тельная красота́ ◆ *(1,2)* **exquisite** ~ *(1)* изы́сканная / *(2)* утончённая красота́ ◆ **flawless** ~ красота́ без изъя́на ◆ **inimitable** ~ неповтори́мая красота́ ◆ **inner** ~ вну́тренняя красота́ ◆ **masculine** ~ мужска́я красота́ ◆ *(1,2)* **natural** ~ *(1)* есте́ственная / *(2)* натура́льная красота́ ◆ **overpowering** ~ неотрази́мая красота́ ◆ **perfect** ~ соверше́нная красота́ ◆ **petal-fresh** ~ красота́ све́жая, как лепесто́к *(1 term)* ◆ **radiant** ~ сия́ющая красота́ ◆ **rare** ~ ре́дкая красота́ ◆ **regal** ~ ца́рственная красота́ ◆ **rubenesque** ~ ру́бенсовская красота́ ◆

Common adult weights are given in Appendix 10, page 777.

sensual ~ чу́вственная красота́ ♦ **serene** ~ споко́йная красота́ ♦ **Slavic** ~ славя́нская красота́ ♦ **spiritual** ~ духо́вная красота́ ♦ **sublime** ~ вели́чественная красота́ ♦ **unique** ~ неповтори́мая красота́ ♦ **unsurpassed** ~ непревзойдённая красота́ ♦ **wondrous** ~ ди́вная красота́.

beauty: person

athletic ~ атлети́ческая краса́вица ♦ **bathing** ~ красо́тка в купа́льном костю́ме ♦ **blonde** ~ белоку́рая краса́вица ♦ **blue-eyed** ~ голубогла́зая краса́вица ♦ **brown-eyed** ~ карегла́зая краса́вица ♦ **busty** ~ груда́стая краса́вица ♦ **curvaceous** ~ окру́глая краса́вица ♦ **fair-haired** ~ златовла́сая краса́вица ♦ *(1,2)* **fiery** *(3,4)* ~ *(1)* пы́лкая / *(2)* жгу́чая *(3)* краса́вица / *(4)* красо́тка ♦ **genuine** ~ настоя́щая краса́вица ♦ **passionate** ~ стра́стная краса́вица ♦ **petite** ~ ма́ленькая краса́вица ♦ **picture of** ~ пи́саная краса́вица ♦ **radiant** ~ сверка́ющая краса́вица ♦ **rare** ~ ре́дкая краса́вица ♦ **raving** ~ сногсшиба́тельная краса́вица ♦ **real** ~ настоя́щая краса́вица ♦ **Slavic** ~ славя́нская краса́вица ♦ **sleeping** ~ спя́щая краса́вица ♦ **statuesque** ~ ста́тная краса́вица ♦ **striking** ~ потряса́ющая краса́вица ♦ **stunning** ~ потряса́ющая краса́вица ♦ **succulent** ~ со́чная краса́вица ♦ **sultry** ~ зно́йная краса́вица ♦ **sun-kissed** ~ загоре́лая краса́вица ♦ **tall, blonde** ~ высо́кая, белоку́рая краса́вица ♦ **true** ~ настоя́щая краса́вица ♦ **voluptuous** ~ роско́шная краса́вица.

beauty: other terms

~ *(1,2)* **queen** *(1)* короле́ва / *(2)* боги́ня красоты́ ♦ **female with inner** ~ же́нщина с вну́тренней красото́й ♦ **person with inner** ~ челове́к с вну́тренней красото́й ♦ **woman with inner** ~ же́нщина с вну́тренней красото́й.

beauty: your beauty

You're in the flower of your beauty. Ты в расцве́те свое́й красоты́. ♦ **You radiate (**[1] **pure / **[2] **sheer / **[3] **perfect) beauty (and vitality).** Ты сия́ешь (*[1]* чи́стой / *[2]* абсолю́тной / *[3]* соверше́нной) красото́й (и жи́востью). ♦ **Your beauty is** *(1)* **indescribable** / *(2)* **incredible** / *(3)* **unforgettable** / *(4)* **incomparable** / *(5)* **perfect** / *(6)* **heavenly** / *(7)* **amaranthine** / *(8)* **dream-like** / *(9)* **breath-taking** / *(10)* **...very distracting.** / *(11)* **...just one of your many exceptional attributes.** Твоя́ красота́ *(1)* неопису́ема. / *(2)* невероя́тна. / *(3)* незабыва́ема. / *(4)* несравне́нна. / *(5)* соверше́нна. / *(6)* боже́ственна. / *(7)* неувяда́ема. / *(8)* ...похо́жа на мечту́. / *(9)* ...остана́вливает дыха́ние. / *(10)* ...приво́дит в си́льное смяте́ние. / *(11)* ... - то́лько одно́ из мно́гих твои́х исключи́тельных ка́честв. ♦ **Your beauty is like something** *(1)* **...straight out of paradise.** / *(2)* **...out of a dream** / *(3)* **fairytale.** Твоя́ красота́, как бу́дто, *(1)* ...пря́мо из ра́я. / *(2)* ...из мечты́ / *(3)* ска́зки. ♦ **You are** *(1,2)* **the essence** / *(3)* **the epitome** / *(4)* **a paragon of beauty.** Ты *(1)* су́щность / *(2)* квинтэссе́нция / *(3)* воплоще́ние / *(4)* образе́ц красоты́. ♦ **Mere words are** *(1)* **...not enough...** / *(2)* **...inadequate... to describe your (**[3] **ethereal /** [4] **incomparable) beauty.** Про́сто слов *(1,2)* недоста́точно, что́бы описа́ть твою́ (*[3]* небе́сную / *[4]* несравне́нную) красоту́. ♦ **You are a woman of striking beauty.** Ты же́нщина порази́тельной красоты́. ♦ **You are a vision of** *(1)* **breath-taking** / *(2)* **exquisite beauty.** Ты виде́ние *(1)* ...захва́тывающей дух... / *(2)* ...изы́сканной... красоты́. ♦ **You have classic beauty.** У тебя́ класси́ческая красота́. ♦ **You possess the kind of beauty that** *(1)* **...drives men to heroism.** / *(2)* **...wars have been fought over.** / *(3)* **...inspires masterpieces of art.** / *(4)* **...inspires great paintings.** / *(5)* **...makes all jewelry seem** *(6)* **needless /** *(7)* **trivial /** *(8)* **superfluous.** / *(9)* **...I would like to see reflected in the faces of all my children.** / *(10)* **...I could spend a lifetime adoring and never get enough of.** Ты облада́ешь тако́й красото́й, *(1)* ...кото́рая вдохновля́ет мужчи́н на герои́зм. / *(2)* ...и́з-за кото́рой возника́ли во́йны. / *(3)* ...кото́рая вдохновля́ет

An italicized ж in parentheses indicates a woman speaking.

шеде́вры иску́сства. / *(4)* ...кото́рая вдохновля́ет вели́ких худо́жников. / *(5)* ...кото́рая де́лает все драгоце́нности *(6)* нену́жными / *(7)* незначи́тельными / *(8)* изли́шними. / *(9)* ...кото́рую я бы хоте́л ви́деть отражённой в ли́цах всех свои́х дете́й. / *(10)* ...кото́рую я мог бы обожа́ть всю жизнь, никогда́ не насыща́ясь. ♦ **You are so innocently unaware of the haze of beauty that constantly envelopes you.** Ты так неви́нно не подозрева́ешь о ды́мке красоты́, постоя́нно обвола́кивающей тебя́. ♦ **What a shame to cover up the radiance of such beauty.** Как не сты́дно прикрыва́ть сия́ние тако́й красоты́.

| *beauty: the beauty of your face* |

Your face is a paragon of beauty. Твоё лицо́ образе́ц красоты́. ♦ **You have a face of infinite beauty (and sensitivity).** У тебя́ лицо́ безграни́чной красоты́ (и чу́вственности). ♦ **It is such a pleasure to** *(1)* **look /** *(2)* **gaze at the radiant beauty of your face in this photo.** Тако́е удово́льствие *(1)* ...смотре́ть на... / *(2)* ...вгля́дываться в... сия́ющую красоту́ твоего́ лица́ на э́той фотогра́фии. ♦ **I see in this photo a face of** *(1)* **exquisite /** *(2)* **unimaginable beauty crowned with an opulence of** *(3)* **golden /** *(4)* **chestnut /** *(5)* **raven hair.** Я ви́жу на э́той фотогра́фии лицо́ *(1)* изы́сканной / *(2)* невообрази́мой красоты́ в струя́щемся бога́тстве *(3)* золоты́х / *(4)* кашта́новых / *(5)* чёрных воло́с. ♦ **The unsurpassed beauty of your face reigns over all my thoughts.** Несравне́нная красота́ твоего́ лица́ вла́ствует над все́ми мои́ми по́мыслами.

| *beauty: no one can compare to you in beauty* |

No one (and nothing) (in this world) can hold a candle to your beauty. Никто́ (и ничто́) (в э́том ми́ре) не мо́жет сравни́ться красото́й с тобо́й. ♦ **You are the top of the mountain named Beauty and from where you stand there is only a downward view.** Ты верши́на горы́, называ́емой Красота́, и отту́да, где ты нахо́дишься, есть то́лько взгляд вниз. ♦ **No one in this whole world can ever surpass you in beauty.** Никто́ на всём све́те не смо́жет превзойти́ тебя́ в красоте́.

| *beauty: time can never diminish your beauty* |

You have a beauty that *(1)* **age /** *(2)* **time can never** *(3)* **dim /** *(4)* **diminish.** Ты так краси́ва, что с *(1,2)* года́ми твоя́ красота́ не мо́жет *(3)* потускне́ть / *(4)* уме́ньшиться.

| *beauty: I admire your beauty* |

I am engulfed in *(1)* **infinite /** *(2)* **boundless admiration of your** *(3)* **indescribable /** *(4)* **exquisite /** *(5)* **incomparable /** *(6)* **peerless beauty.** Я поглощён *(1)* бесконе́чным / *(2)* безграни́чным восхище́нием твое́й *(3)* неопису́емой / *(4)* изы́сканной / *(5,6)* несравне́нной красоты́. ♦ **I'm not impervious to your beauty.** Я не безразли́чен к твое́й красоте́. ♦ **I appreciate beauty. (And you certainly have a lot to appreciate.)** Я ценю́ красоту́. (И в тебе́, определённо, есть что цени́ть.)

| *beauty: I'm enchanted by your beauty* |

I am (*[1]* **completely /** *[2]* **totally /** *[3]* **entirely /** *[4]* **thoroughly /** *[5]* **utterly)** *(6)* **mesmerized /** *(7)* **bewitched /** *(8)* **enchanted /** *(9)* **entranced /** *(10)* **captivated /** *(11)* **dazzled by your (** *[12]* **incredible /** *[13]* **breath-taking /** *[14]* **shining /** *[15]* **heavenly /** *[16]* **radiant /** *[17]* **exquisite /** *[18]* **exotic) beauty.** Я (*[1,2]* по́лностью / *[1-5]* соверше́нно) *(6)* загипнотизи́рован / *(7)* околдо́ван / *(8,9)* очаро́ван / *(10)* пленён / *(11)* ослеплён твое́й (*[12]* невероя́тной / *[13]* ...остана́вливающей дыха́ние... / *[14]* сия́ющей / *[15]* небе́сной / *[16]* лучи́стой / *[17]* изы́сканной / *[18]* экзоти́ческой) красото́й. ♦ **My heart is** *(1)* **completely /** *(2)* **totally /** *(3)* **irredeemably /** *(4)* **hopelessly** *(5)* **enslaved /** *(6)* **captivated /** *(7)* **enraptured by your** *(8)* **shining /** *(9)* **radiant /** *(10)* **ethereal beauty.** Моё се́рдце *(1,2)* соверше́нно / *(3)* безвозвра́тно / *(4)* безнаде́жно *(5)* порабощено́ / *(6)* очаро́вано / *(7)* восхищён твое́й *(8)* сия́ющей / *(9)* лучи́стой / *(10)* неземно́й красото́й.

Procedures for getting married to a Russian are outlined in Appendix 18, page 787.

beauty: *I'm in awe of your beauty*

I am (totally) in awe of your (*[1]* **incredible** / *[2]* **shining** / *[3]* **incomparable** / *[4]* **peerless** / *[5]* **exquisite** / *[6]* **amaranthine** / *[7]* **sheer**) (physical) beauty. Я в (по́лном) благогове́нии пе́ред твое́й (*[1]* невероя́тной / *[2]* блиста́тельной / *[3,4]* несравне́нной / *[5]* изы́сканной / *[6]* неувяда́емой / *[7]* соверше́нной) (физи́ческой) красото́й.

beauty: *I've never seen such beauty*

(1) **In all my life...** / *(2)* **In all the places I've been in this world... I have never** *(3)* **beheld** / *(4)* **seen such** *(5)* **perfect** / *(6)* **heavenly** / *(7)* **dream-like** / *(8)* **incredible** / *(9)* **flawless** / *(10)* **exquisite beauty as yours.** *(1)* За всю жизнь... / *(2)* Ни в одно́м уголке́ ми́ра, где бы я ни побыва́л... я никогда́ не *(3)* созерца́л / *(4)* ви́дел тако́й *(5)* соверше́нной / *(6)* небе́сной / *(7)* ...похо́жей на мечту́... / *(8)* невероя́тной / *(9)* безупре́чной / *(10)* изы́сканной красоты́, как твоя́. ♦ **In your beauty their is a perfection such as I have never** *(1)* **beheld** / *(2)* **seen** / *(3)* **encountered.** В твое́й красоте́ тако́е соверше́нство, како́го я никогда́ не *(1,2)* ви́дел / *(3)* встреча́л.

beauty: *I never dreamed of such beauty*

I never *(1)* **knew** / *(2)* **imagined** / *(3)* **dreamt (that) such beauty** *(4)* **...was possible.** / *(5)* **... existed in this world.** *(1)* Я никогда́ не знал / *(2)* представля́л... / *(3)* Я никогда́ не мечта́л о том.... что така́я красота́ *(4)* ...возмо́жна. / *(5)* ...существу́ет в э́том ми́ре.

beauty: *I can't resist your beauty*

I find your charm and beauty very hard to resist. Я обнару́жил, что твоему́ обая́нию и красоте́ о́чень тру́дно сопротивля́ться. ♦ **I (simply) cannot resist your beauty.** Я (про́сто) не могу́ сопротивля́ться твое́й красоте́. ♦ **I have become a slave to your** *(1)* **incomparable** / *(2)* **shining beauty.** Я стал рабо́м твое́й *(1)* несравне́нной / *(2)* блиста́тельной красоты́. ♦ *(1,2)* **I am (completely) a slave to your beauty.** *(1)* Я (весь) во вла́сти твое́й красоты́. / *(2)* Я раб твое́й красоты́.

beauty: *all I can think of is your beauty*

Since the day we met I've been oblivious of all else except your *(1)* **breathtaking** / *(2)* **angelic beauty.** Со дня на́шей встре́чи я соверше́нно забы́л обо всём, кро́ме твое́й *(1)* ...захва́тывающей дух... / *(2)* ...а́нгельской... красоты́.

beauty: *I think of you when I see beauty*

I never see beauty without thinking of you. Когда́ я наслажда́юсь красото́й, я всегда́ ду́маю о тебе́.

beauty: *dreaming of your beauty*

How I dream of beholding your exquisite beauty sans clothes. Как я мечта́ю созерца́ть твою́ изы́сканную красоту́ без оде́жды.

beauty: *what your beauty does to me*

Your (*[1]* **exquisite** / *[2]* **exotic** / *[3]* **radiant** / *[4]* **exceptional** / *[5]* **ethereal** / *[6]* **amaranthine) beauty** *(7,8)* **...takes my breath away.** / *(9)* **...dazzles me.** / *(10)* **...thrills me through and through.** / *(11)* **...sets my head to whirling.** / *(12)* **...(constantly) sets my heart on fire.** / *(13)* **...fills me with wonder.** Твоя́ (*[1]* изы́сканная / *[2]* экзоти́ческая / *[3]* сия́ющая / *[4]* исключи́тельная / *[5]* небе́сная / *[6]* неувяда́емая) красота́ *(7)* ...захва́тывает дух. / *(8)* ...остана́вливает дыха́ние. / *(9)* ...ослепля́ет меня́. / *(10)* ...возбужда́ет всё во мне. / *(11)* ...вскружи́ла мою́ го́лову. / *(12)* ...(постоя́нно) воспламеня́ет моё се́рдце. / *(13)* ...изумля́ет меня́. ♦ **Your** *(1)* **incredible** / *(2)* **voluptuous beauty has me crazed with** *(3)* **lust** / *(4)* **desire.** Твоя́ *(1)* невероя́тная / *(2)* роско́шная красота́ сво́дит меня́ с ума́ от *(3)* вожделе́ния / *(4)* стра́сти. ♦ **Your beauty and sensuality overwhelm me.** Твоя́ красота́ и чу́вственность ошеломля́ют меня́. ♦ **Your breath-taking beauty haunts my** *(1)* **mind** / *(2)* **thoughts night and day.** Твоя́ захва́тывающая дух красота́ пресле́дует *(1)*

A list of conjugated Russian verbs is given
in Appendix 3 on page 699

...мою́ па́мять... / *(2)* ...мои́ мы́сли... но́чью и днём. ♦ **I am (totally) amazed at what your beauty does to me.** Я (соверше́нно) изумлён тем, что твоя́ красота́ де́лает со мной. ♦ **You** *(1)* **hypnotize** / *(2)* **overwhelm me with your (radiant) beauty.** Ты *(1)* гипнотизи́руешь / *(2)* ошеломля́ешь меня́ свое́й (сия́ющей) красото́й. ♦ **You have not the smallest idea how totally you have bewitched me and enthralled me with your incomparable, indescribable beauty.** Ты не име́ешь да́же мале́йшего представле́ния, как ты соверше́нно околдова́ла и увлекла́ меня́ свое́й несравне́нной, неопису́емой красото́й. ♦ **I have never met any woman in all my life whose beauty** *(1)* **enchanted /** *(2)* **enthralled me as yours has.** Я никогда́ в жи́зни не встреча́л же́нщины, красота́ кото́рой *(1)* очаро́вывала / *(2)* увлека́ла меня́, как твоя́. ♦ **The vision of your beauty in my mind overwhelms all other thoughts.** Твоя́ красота́ заполня́ет все мои́ мы́сли. ♦ **Your (incredible) beauty and (scintillating) charm have completely swept me away.** Твоя́ (невероя́тная) красота́ и (искря́щееся) обая́ние по́лностью покори́ли меня́. ♦ **You dazzle me with your charm and beauty and blithe spirit.** Ты пораж́аешь меня́ свои́м обая́нием, красото́й и весёлым хара́ктером. ♦ **Your incomparable** *(1)* **shining /** *(2)* **radiant beauty has cast an unbreakable spell over my heart.** Твоя́ несравне́нная *(1)* блестя́щая / *(2)* сия́ющая красота́ навсегда́ околдова́ла моё се́рдце. ♦ **Your beauty has a devastating effect on** *(1)* **...my will power. /** *(2)* **...my ability to concentrate. /** *(3)* **...my rational thinking.** Твоя́ красота́ разруша́юще де́йствует на *(1)* ...мою́ во́лю. / *(2)* ...мою́ спосо́бность концентри́роваться. / *(3)* ...моё рациона́льное мышле́ние. ♦ **The beauty of your smile captivates my heart.** Красота́ твое́й улы́бки пленя́ет моё се́рдце. ♦ **Your beauty and charm are an elixir to my soul.** Твоя́ красота́ и обая́ние - эликси́р мое́й души́. ♦ *(1)* **I burn... /** *(2)* **My whole body burns... with** *(3)* **longing /** *(4)* **hunger for** *(5)* **...you. /** *(6)* **...your soft, warm beauty.** *(1)* Я сгора́ю... / *(2)* Всё моё те́ло гори́т от *(3)* ...тоски́ по *(5 [+3])* ...тебе́. / *(6 [+3])* ...твое́й мя́гкой, тёплой красоте́. / *(4)* ...жа́жды *(5 [+4])* ...тебя́. / *(6 [+4])* ...твое́й мя́гкой, тёплой красоты́. ♦ **An extraordinary heat suffuses my whole body whenever I think about your voluptuous beauty.** Всегда́, когда́ бы я ни поду́мал о твое́й сла́достной красоте́, я весь охва́чен жа́ром. ♦ **Molten waves of desire sweep through** *(1)* **...my entire body... /** *(2)* **...every fiber and cell of my body... whenever I think of your exquisite, luscious beauty.** Бушу́ющие во́лны стра́сти проно́сятся че́рез *(1)* ...всё моё те́ло... / *(2)* ...все фи́бры и кле́тки моего́ те́ла,... когда́ бы я ни поду́мал о твое́й изы́сканной, со́чной красоте́. ♦ **Your beauty and sexiness just boggle my mind.** Твоя́ красота́ и сексуа́льность про́сто пораж́ают меня́.

| **beauty:** *what I want to do with your beauty* |

I want to celebrate your *(1)* **breath-taking /** *(2)* **fantastic /** *(3)* **incredible beauty with adoring kisses all over it.** Я хочу́ прославля́ть твою́ *(1)* ...перехва́тывающую дыха́ние... / *(2)* фантасти́ческую / *(3)* невероя́тную красоту́ обожа́ющими поцелу́ями. ♦ **My** *(1)* **hungry /** *(2)* **loving /** *(3)* **wandering /** *(4)* **roving lips will seek and find the hidden treasures of your** *(5)* **magnificent /** *(6)* **luscious beauty.** Мои́ *(1)* голо́дные / *(2)* любя́щие / *(3,4)* блужда́ющие гу́бы бу́дут иска́ть и находи́ть скры́тые сокро́вища твое́й *(5)* великоле́пной / *(6)* со́чной красоты́ ♦ **I want to abandon myself to your lush beauty.** Я хочу́ весь отда́ться твое́й роско́шной красоте́. ♦ **I want to behold all of your beauty sans clothes.** Я хочу́ созерца́ть всю твою́ красоту́ без оде́жды.

| **beauty:** *more than your beauty* |

There is *(1)* **something /** *(2)* **much more than your beauty that captivates** *(3)* **...me. /** *(4)* **...my heart.** Есть *(1)* не́что / *(2)* гора́здо бо́льшее, чем твоя́ красота́, что пленя́ет *(3)* ...меня́. / *(4)* ...моё се́рдце. ♦ **If you have a nature as generous as your beauty, you are**

For Russian adjectives, the masculine form is spelled out,
followed by the feminine, neuter and plural endings

truly heaven's special prize. Если твой харáктер такóй же замечáтельный, как твоя́ красотá, то ты и́стинный дар небéс.

    beauty: *don't turn your beauty on someone else*

I pray that you will never be so cruel as to try the power of your exceptional beauty *(1)* **...on someone else.** / *(2)* **...elsewhere.** Я молю́сь, чтóбы ты никогдá не былá так жестóка, чтóбы испы́тывать си́лу своéй исключи́тельной красоты́ *(1)* ...на ком-нибýдь ещё. / *(2)* ...где-нибýдь в другóм мéсте.

    beauty: *sayings*

Beauty is only skin deep. Красотá недолговéчна. ♦ **Beauty is in the eye(s) of the beholder.** Не по-хорошý мил, а по-ми́лу хорóш.

    beauty: *quotation*

"A thing of beauty is a joy forever." *(John Keats)* Красотá - вéчная рáдость. *Джон Китс*

beckon *vi* подзывáть / подозвáть кивкóм *(whom = acc.)*, мани́ть / помани́ть к себé *(whom = acc.)* ♦ ~ **seductively** подзывáть / подозвáть соблазни́тельно.

bed *n* кровáть *f*; постéль *f* ♦ **water** ~ рези́новый матрáс, напóлненный водóй *(1 term)* ♦ **fun in** ~ постéльные утéхи ♦ **get in** ~ ложи́ться / лечь в постéль ♦ **put to** ~ уклáдывать / уложи́ть в постéль *(whom = acc.)* ♦ **It would be so heavenly to crawl into bed with you.** Как божéственно бы́ло бы лечь с тобóй в постéль. ♦ **I'll come to your bed when everyone is asleep.** Я придý к тебé в постéль, когдá все уснýт. ♦ **Do you think I just hop from bed to bed?** Не дýмаешь ли ты, что я прóсто пры́гаю из однóй постéли в другýю? ♦ **I'm not the kind of** *(1)* **man /** *(2)* **person who hops from bed to bed.** Я не тот *(1)* мужчи́на / *(2)* человéк, котóрый пры́гает из однóй постéли в другýю. ♦ **I'm not the kind of woman who hops from bed to bed.** Я не та жéнщина, котóрая пры́гает из однóй постéли в другýю. ♦ **When we get to our room, I'm going to swing you into my arms and head straight for the bed.** Когдá мы придём в нáшу кóмнату, я возьмý тебя́ на рýки и отнесý пря́мо в постéль. ♦ **My** *(1)* **greatest /** *(2)* **most precious dream is to have you share my bed** *(3)* **...forever.** / *(4)* **...for the rest of my life.** Моя́ *(1)* величáйшая / *(2)* ...сáмая драгоцéнная... мечтá, чтóбы ты разделя́ла постéль со мной *(3)* ...навсегдá. / *(4)* ...до концá моéй жи́зни. ♦ **I (really) enjoy being in bed with you.** Я (действи́тельно) наслаждáюсь в постéли с тобóй. ♦ **Darling, if I ever get in the same bed with you, I'm going to make myself a slave to your desires and your pleasure and your satisfaction.** Дорогáя, éсли я окажýсь в однóй постéли с тобóй, я сдéлаю себя́ рабóм твои́х страстéй, твоегó наслаждéния и твоегó удовлетворéния. ♦ **We could spend the whole** *(1)* **day /** *(2)* **week rolling around in bed.** Мы могли́ бы провести́ *(1)* ...весь день... / *(2)* ...всю недéлю... в постéли. ♦ **We'll make a mess of the bed.** Мы устрóим беспоря́док в постéли. ♦ **I want to share my bed with you for the rest of my life.** Я хочý, чтóбы всю остáвшуюся жизнь мы спáли в однóй постéли.

bedevil *vt* 1. *(torment)* мýчить *(what, whom = acc.)*, терзáть *(what, whom = acc.)*; 2. *(confuse)* сбивáть с тóлку *(what, whom = acc.)* ♦ **The vision of your alluring, sexy loveliness bedevils my thoughts night and day.** Ви́дение твоéй замáнивающей, сексуáльной красоты́ мýчит мои́ мы́сли нóчью и днём.

beer *n* пи́во.

before *adv* рáньше; прéжде.

before *prep* до *(+ gen.)*, пéред *(+ instr.)*.

beg *vt* умоля́ть / умоли́ть *(whom = acc.)* ♦ **I beg you (with all my heart)** *(1)* **...to forgive me.** / *(2)* **...to give me one more chance.** / *(3)* **...not to leave me.** / *(4)* **...not to turn away from me.** / *(5)* **...to stay.** / *(6)* **...not to do it.** / *(7)* **...to meet with me just one time.** / *(8)* **...to let me**

See Appendix 19 for notes on sending mail to Russia and Ukraine.

see you (tonight). / *(9)* ...to grant me just a few minutes of your time to meet with you and talk with you (in person). Я умоля́ю тебя́ (от всего́ се́рдца) *(1)* ...прости́ть меня́. / *(2)* ...дать мне ещё оди́н шанс. / *(3)* ...не оставля́ть меня́. / *(4)* ...не отвора́чиваться от меня́. / *(5)* ...оста́ться. / *(6)* ...не де́лать э́того. / *(7)* ...встре́титься со мной то́лько оди́н раз. / *(8)* ...позво́лить мне уви́деть тебя́ (сего́дня ве́чером). / *(9)* ...удели́ть мне хотя́ бы не́сколько мину́т, чтобы я мог встре́титься с тобо́й и поговори́ть (ли́чно). ♦ **I'm going to swallow my pride and beg you (not to leave me).** Я поступлю́сь свое́й го́рдостью и бу́ду умоля́ть тебя́ (не оставля́ть меня́).

beguile *vt (entice)* соблазня́ть / соблазни́ть *(whom = acc., with what = instr.)*, зама́нивать / замани́ть *(whom = acc., with what = instr.)*; *(charm)* увлека́ть / увле́чь *(whom = acc.)* очаро́вывать / очарова́ть *(whom = acc.)* ♦ **You (really) beguile me with your wide-eyed innocence.** Ты (действи́тельно) очаро́вываешь меня́ свое́й наи́вной неви́нностью.

beguiling *adj* соблазни́тельный, -ая, -ое, -ые, зама́нчивый, -ая, -ое, -ые, околдо́вывающий, -ая, -ее, -ие ♦ **Such a beautiful, beguiling smile you have.** У тебя́ така́я прекра́сная, околдо́вывающая улы́бка. ♦ **I've never seen a more beguiling smile.** Я никогда́ не ви́дел бо́лее околдо́вывающей улы́бки.

behave *vi* 1. вести́ / повести́ себя́, поступа́ть / поступи́ть; 2. вести́ / повести́ себя́ хорошо́ / прили́чно ♦ **~ correctly** вести́ себя́ корре́ктно ♦ **I promise to behave like a gentleman.** Я обеща́ю вести́ себя́ как джентельме́н. ♦ **I'll behave like a saint, I promise.** Я бу́ду вести́ себя́ как свято́й, я обеща́ю. ♦ **I'm sorry for the way I behaved.** Я извиня́юсь за своё поведе́ние. ♦ **That was no way to behave.** Это бы́ло непра́вильное поведе́ние. ♦ **Behave yourself.** Веди́ себя́ прили́чно. ♦ **I behaved badly toward you (and I want to apologize).** Я пло́хо себя́ вёл *(ж: вела́)* по отноше́нию к тебе́ (, и я хочу́ извини́ться). ♦ **I behaved** *(1)* **abominably** / *(2)* **atrociously** / *(3)* **shamelessly.** Я вёл *(ж: вела́)* себя́ *(1)* отврати́тельно / *(2)* ужа́сно / *(3)* посты́дно. ♦ **You behaved** *(1)* **abominably** / *(2)* **atrociously** / *(3)* **shamelessly.** Ты вела́ *(ж: вёл)* себя́ *(1)* отврати́тельно / *(2)* ужа́сно / *(3)* посты́дно.

behavior *n* поведе́ние ♦ **correct ~** пра́вильное поведе́ние ♦ **disgraceful ~** позо́рное поведе́ние ♦ **gentlemanly ~** джентельме́нское поведе́ние ♦ **impeccable ~** безупре́чное поведе́ние ♦ **proper ~** надлежа́щее поведе́ние ♦ **puritanical ~** пурита́нское поведе́ние ♦ **rude ~** гру́бое поведе́ние ♦ **social ~** обще́ственное поведе́ние ♦ **unseemly ~** неподоба́ющее поведе́ние ♦ **I'm ashamed of my wanton behavior.** стыжу́сь своего́ непристо́йного поведе́ния. ♦ **I apologize for my wanton behavior.** Я извиня́юсь за своё непристо́йное поведе́ние.

behind *prep* за, позади́ ♦ **I'm behind you all the way.** Я окажу́ тебе́ по́лную подде́ржку.

behold *vt* созерца́ть *(what, whom = acc.)*, ви́деть *(what, whom = acc.)* ♦ *(1)* **In all my life...** / *(2)* **In all the places I've been in this world... I have never** *(3,4)* **beheld such** *(5)* **perfect** / *(6)* **heavenly** / *(7)* **dream-like** / *(8)* **incredible** / *(9)* **flawless** / *(10)* **exquisite beauty as yours.** *(1)* За всю жизнь... / *(2)* Ни в одно́м уголке́ ми́ра, где бы я ни побыва́л,... я никогда́ не *(3)* созерца́л / *(4)* ви́дел тако́й *(5)* соверше́нной / *(6)* небе́сной / *(7)* ...похо́жей на мечту́... / *(8)* невероя́тной / *(9)* безупре́чной / *(10)* изы́сканной красоты́, как твоя́. ♦ **The provocative curve of your breasts is such a pleasure to behold.** Тако́е удово́льствие созерца́ть соблазни́тельные изги́бы твое́й груди́. ♦ **I want to behold all of your beauty sans clothes.** Я хочу́ созерца́ть всю твою́ красоту́ без оде́жды.

being *n* 1. *(existence)* существова́ние, жизнь *f*; бытие́; 2. *(creature)* (живо́е) существо́, созда́ние; 3. *(essence)* существо́, суть *f* ♦ **fellow human ~** тако́й же челове́к (как я), *(pl:* все лю́ди, челове́чество) ♦ **human ~** челове́к *(pl:* лю́ди, челове́чество) ♦ **perfect**

When terms are listed after a main word, a tilde ~ is used to indicate the main word.

~ совершённое созда́ние ♦ **precious** ~ драгоце́нное существо́ ♦ **Our bodies will** *(1)* **fuse /** *(2)* **merge together into a single being.** На́ши тела́ *(1)* солью́тся / *(2)* соединя́тся в одно́ це́лое. ♦ **Visions of your voluptuous loveliness send fire licking through my arteries, igniting my entire being into an inferno of passionate desire.** Вид твое́й чу́вственной красоты́ вызыва́ет ого́нь, busсю́щий в мои́х арте́риях, посыла́ющий всё моё существо́ в ад стра́стного жела́ния. ♦ **I offer to you all my love, all my being, all my life.** Я предлага́ю тебе́ всю мою́ любо́вь, всё моё существо́, всю мою́ жизнь. ♦ **I love you to the very roots of my being.** Я люблю́ тебя́ до глубины́ души́. ♦ **Whenever I think of you, red-hot desire scorches my** *(1,2)* **innermost being.** Когда́ бы я не поду́мал о тебе́, обжига́ющая страсть опаля́ет всё *(1)* ...во мне. / *(1)* ...моё сокрове́нное. ♦ *(1)* **I want to... /** *(2)* **I'm going to... suffuse your entire being in the fiery rapture of climax.** *(1)* Я хочу́ зали́ть... / *(2)* Я залью́... всё твоё существо́ о́гненным восто́ргом орга́зма. ♦ **My** *(1)* **whole /** *(2)* **entire being cries out for you.** *(1,2)* Всё моё существо́ зовёт тебя́. ♦ **All the real pleasure I enjoy in this world is derived from being with you.** Ты исто́чник всех наслажде́ний, кото́рые я испы́тываю в э́том ми́ре. ♦ **I want you with every fiber of my being.** Я хочу́ тебя́ все́ми фи́брами мое́й души́. ♦ **My entire being is** *(1)* **assailed /** *(2)* **and tormented by the all-consuming need to take you in my arms and revel in the reservoir of your passion.** Я весь *(1)* охва́чен / *(2)* изму́чен всепоглоща́ющей жа́ждой заключи́ть тебя́ в объя́тия и упива́ться твое́й стра́стью.

Belarus *n* Белару́сь *f* ♦ **from** ~ из Белару́си ♦ **in** ~ в Белару́си ♦ **to** ~ в Белару́сь.

belie *vt* дава́ть неве́рное представле́ние *(what = + о + prep.)* ♦ **Your shyness and quiet nature belie the passion within you.** Твоя́ засте́нчивость и споко́йный хара́ктер даю́т неве́рное представле́ние о твое́й стра́стности.

belief *n* 1. *(faith, trust)* ве́ра, дове́рие; 2. *(opinion, conviction)* мне́ние, убежде́ние ♦ ~ **in God** ве́ра в Бо́га ♦ **deep** ~ глубо́кая ве́ра ♦ **erroneous** ~ оши́бочное мне́ние ♦ **firm** ~ твёрдая ве́ра; твёрдое убежде́ние ♦ **passionate** ~ горя́чая ве́ра ♦ **religious** ~s религио́зные ве́ры ♦ **sincere** ~ и́скренняя ве́ра.

believe *vt* ве́рить / пове́рить *(what, whom = + dat.)* ♦ **blindly** ~ сле́по ве́рить ♦ **deeply** ~ глубоко́ ве́рить ♦ **easily** ~ легко́ ве́рить ♦ **firmly** ~ твёрдо ве́рить ♦ **hard to** ~ тру́дно пове́рить ♦ **passionately** ~ горячо́ ве́рить ♦ **sincerely** ~ и́скренне ве́рить ♦ **willingly** ~ охо́тно ве́рить ♦ **make** *(1)* **you /** *(2)* **me believe** заставля́ть / заста́вить *(1)* тебя́ / *(2)* меня́ ве́рить ♦ **stop believing** переста́ть ве́рить ♦ **want to** ~ хоте́ть ве́рить ♦ **I find it (very)** *(1)* **hard /** *(2)* **difficult to believe that** *(3)* **...you're not married.** / *(4)* **...someone as beautiful as you is looking for someone in this world.** Мне (о́чень) *(1)* тяжело́ / *(2)* тру́дно пове́рить, что *(3)* ...ты не за́мужем. / *(4)* ...така́я прекра́сная, как ты, и́щет кого́-то в э́том ми́ре. ♦ **I can't believe how** *(1)* **beautiful /** *(2)* **lovely you are.** Я не могу́ пове́рить, что ты так *(1)* краси́ва / *(2)* прекра́сна. ♦ **Please believe me.** Пожа́луйста, пове́рь мне. ♦ **I (don't) believe you.** Я (не) ве́рю тебе́. ♦ **I'm trying to believe you.** Я пыта́юсь пове́рить тебе́.

believe *vi* ве́рить / пове́рить *(in what / whom = + в + acc.)* ♦ ~ **in God** ве́рить в Бо́га ♦ ~ **in life after death** ве́рить в загро́бную жизнь ♦ ~ **in miracles** ве́рить в чудеса́ ♦ **I believe in you, in myself, and in us.** Я ве́рю в тебя́, в себя́ и в нас. ♦ **Do you believe in love at first sight?** Ве́ришь ли ты в любо́вь с пе́рвого взгля́да?

believer *n* сторо́нник, ве́рующий, -ая, -ие ♦ **I used to be rather** *(1)* **cynical /** *(2)* **skeptical about love, but you've made me a believer in it.** Я был *(ж: была́)* до не́которой сте́пени *(1)* ци́ником / *(2)* ске́птиком относи́тельно любви́, но ты всели́ла *(ж: всели́л)* в меня́ ве́ру в неё.

belittle *vt* унижа́ть / унизи́ть *(whom = acc.).*

A list of abbreviations used in the dictionary is given on page 10.

bell *n* ко́локол, колоко́льчик ♦ **wedding ~s** сва́дебные колоко́льчики.

belle *n* краса́вица.

belly *n* 1. *(stomach)* живо́т; 2. *(paunch)* пу́зо ♦ **flat ~** пло́ский живо́т ♦ **pot ~** пу́зо (, как бо́чка) ♦ **young ~** молодо́й живо́т.

bellybutton *n (slang)* пуп ♦ **pierced ~** проко́лотый пуп ♦ **tattooed ~** татуиро́ванный пуп.

bellydancing *n* та́нец живота́.

belong *vi* принадлежа́ть *(to whom = dat.)* ♦ **We belong together.** Мы принадлежи́м друг дру́гу. ♦ **You belong to (only) me.** Ты принадлежи́шь (то́лько) мне. ♦ **I (don't) belong to (only) you.** Я (не) принадлежу́ (то́лько) тебе́.

Belorussian *adj* белору́сский, -ая, -ое, -ие.

Belorussian *n* 1. *(person)* белору́с *m*, белору́ска *f* 2. *(language)* белору́сский язы́к **speak ~** говори́ть по-белору́сски.

beloved *adj* возлю́бленный, -ая, -ое, -ые, люби́мый, -ая, -ое, -ые ♦ **~ face** люби́мое лицо́ ♦ **Oh, how I miss your beloved, beautiful face!** О, как я скуча́ю по твоему́ люби́мому, прекра́сному лицу́! ♦ **Whenever I look at your beloved face in this photo,** *(1)*...**my heart overflows with love for you.** / *(2)*...**I am filled with** *(3)* **enormous** / *(4)* **tremendous** / *(5)* **unbearable yearning to be with you (again).** Когда́ бы я ни взгляну́л на твоё люби́мое лицо́ на э́той фотогра́фии, *(1)* ...моё се́рдце переполня́ется любо́вью к тебе́. / *(2)* ...я перепо́лнен *(3)* огро́мной / *(4)* грома́дной / *(5)* невыноси́мой жа́ждой быть с тобо́й (опя́ть). ♦ **I just can't tell you enough how dear and precious and beloved you have become to me.** Я про́сто не могу́ доста́точно хорошо́ вы́разить тебе́, како́й дорого́й *(ж: каки́м дороги́м)*, драгоце́нной *(ж: драгоце́нным)* и люби́мой *(ж: люби́мым)* ты ста́ла *(ж: стал)* для меня́.

> **beloved:** *salutations in letters*

My *(1,2)* **beloved Angela,** Моя́ *(1)* возлю́бленная / *(2)* люби́мая Анже́ла, ♦ **Beloved of my heart, ...** Избра́нница *(ж: Избра́нник)* моего́ се́рдца,... ♦ **My** *(1,2)* **beloved darling...** Моя́ *(1)* возлю́бленная / *(2)* люби́мая... *(ж: Мой [1] возлю́бленный / [2] люби́мый...)* ♦ **My beloved sweetheart...** Моя́ возлю́бленная... *(ж: Мой возлю́бленный...)* ♦ **My beloved angel...** Мой люби́мый а́нгел...

belt *n* по́яс, ремень *m* ♦ **black garter ~** чёрная подвя́зка ♦ **chastity ~** по́яцелому́дрия ♦ **garter ~** по́яс с подвя́зками.

benefit *n* по́льза, вы́года ♦ **I'll give you the benefit of the doubt.** Я всё приму́ на ве́ру.

bent *n (tendency)* скло́нность *f* ♦ **athletic ~** скло́нность к атле́тике.

bereaved *adj* обездо́ленный, -ая, -ое, -ые.

beseech *vt* умоля́ть / умоли́ть *(whom = acc.)*, проси́ть / попроси́ть *(whom = acc.)* ♦ **I humbly beseech you.** Я смире́нно молю́ тебя́. ♦ **I beseech you (with all my heart)** *(1)* ...**to give me one more chance.** / *(2)* ...**not to turn away from** *me.* / *(3)* ...**to grant me just a few minutes of your time to meet with you and talk with you (in person).** / *(4)* ...**to meet with me** *(5)* **this** / *(6)* **tomorrow evening (***[7]***... at the Blue Moon Cafe...** / *[8]* ...**at the park entrance...** / *etc***) for just a half an hour.** Я умоля́ю тебя́ (от всего́ се́рдца) *(1)* ...дать мне ещё оди́н шанс. / *(2)* ...не отвора́чиваться от меня́. / *(3)* ...удели́ть мне хотя́ бы не́сколько мину́т, что́бы я мог встре́титься с тобо́й и поговори́ть (ли́чно). / *(4)* ...встре́титься со мной *(5)* сего́дня / *(6)* за́втра ве́чером (*[7]* ...в кафе́ «Голуба́я луна́»... / *[8]* ...у вхо́да в парк... / *и.т.д.*) хотя́ бы на по́лчаса́.

besotted *adj* опьянённый, -ая, -ое, -ые ♦ **I'm (totally) besotted with you.** Я (соверше́нно) опьянён *(ж: опьянена́)* тобо́й.

bespectacled *adj* очка́стый, -ая, -ое, -ые, в очка́х.

Please do us a favor:
Fill out and mail in the Feedback Sheet on page 795.

best *adj* (наи)лу́чший, -ая, -ее, -ие ♦ **I picked you (to write to), because I didn't want to settle for second best.** Я вы́брал тебя́ и написа́л тебе́, потому́ что не хочу́ ничего́ второсо́ртного. ♦ **I want to look my absolute best (for you).** Я хочу́ вы́глядеть наилу́чшим о́бразом (для тебя́).

bestow *vt* дава́ть / дать *(what = acc., to whom = dat.)*, дари́ть / подари́ть *(what = acc., to whom = dat.)*, одаря́ть / одари́ть *(what = instr., to whom = acc.)* ♦ **Oh, what consummate ecstasy I will bestow upon you when we swirl into the wild vortex of our passion.** О, како́й соверше́нный экста́з я подарю́ тебе́, когда́ мы закру́жимся в бе́шеном водоворо́те стра́сти. ♦ **If you ever feel the generosity in your heart to bestow the ultimate joy in life to someone who adores you beyond measure, then put your sweet mouth against mine for 60 heavenly seconds and you will have done it.** Если то́лько в твоём се́рдце пробу́дится ще́дрость подари́ть велича́йшее наслажде́ние в жи́зни тому́, кто обожа́ет тебя́ безме́рно, тогда́ прижми́ свои́ сла́дкие гу́бы к мои́м на шестьдеся́т *(= 60)* секу́нд, и ты э́то сде́лаешь. ♦ **I have a heart full of love to bestow upon you.** Я одарю́ тебя́ всей любо́вью, наполня́ющей моё се́рдце. ♦ **When at last my mouth claims yours, I will bestow more kisses upon it than it has ever known before.** Когда́ наконе́ц мой рот встре́тится с твои́м, я подарю́ ему́ бо́льше поцелу́ев, чем он когда́-либо пре́жде получа́л. ♦ **The one thing that would make all my dreams come true is for you to bestow upon me** *(1)* **exquisite /** *(2)* **supreme joys of your luscious all.** То́лько одно́ могло́ бы осуществи́ть все мои́ мечты́ -- э́то, что́бы ты подари́ла мне *(1)* изы́сканную / *(2)* исключи́тельную ра́дость всей твое́й роско́шной красоты́.

bet *vt:* ♦ **You bet!** Да, коне́чно!

betray *vt* 1. *(cheat)* предава́ть / преда́ть *(whom = acc.)*, изменя́ть / измени́ть *(whom = dat.)*; 2. *(give away)* выдава́ть / вы́дать *(what = acc.)* ♦ **I would never betray you.** Я никогда́ не изменю́ тебе́. ♦ **I guess I've betrayed my (true) feelings.** Я полага́ю, я вы́дал *(ж: вы́дала)* свои́ (и́стинные) чу́вства.

betrayal *n* преда́тельство, изме́на.

betrothal *n* обруче́ние, помо́лвка.

betrothed *adj* обручённый, -ая, -ое, -ые *(short forms:* обручён, обручена́, -о́, -ы́*)*.

better *adj* лу́чший, -ая, -ее, -ие.

better *adv* лу́чше ♦ **You're better off without** *(1)* **him /** *(2)* **her.** Тебе́ бу́дет лу́чше без *(1)* него́ / *(2)* неё.

bewilder *vt* озада́чивать / озада́чить *(whom = acc.)*; *(confuse)* сбива́ть / сбить с то́лку *(whom = acc.)* ♦ **You completely bewilder me (at times).** Ты (поро́й) соверше́нно озада́чиваешь меня́.

bewildered *adj* озада́чен, -а, -о, -ы *(short forms)* ♦ **I have to confess, I'm a little bewildered (by** *[1]* **...what you said. /** *[2]* **...your attitude /** *[3]* **behavior /** *[4]* **letter.).** Я до́лжен *(ж: должна́)* призна́ться, я немно́го озада́чен *(ж: озада́чена)* (тем, *[1]* ...что ты сказа́ла *[ж: сказа́л]*. / *[2]* ...твои́м отноше́нием / *[3]* поведе́нием / *[4]* письмо́м.)

bewildering *adj* озада́чивающий, -ая, -ее, -ие.

bewilderment *n* озада́ченность *f*, замеша́тельство.

bewitch *vt* околдо́вывать / околдова́ть *(whom = acc.)*, заколдо́вывать / заколдова́ть *(whom = acc.)*, завора́живать / заворожи́ть *(whom = acc.)*, обвора́живать / обворожи́ть *(whom = acc.)*; очаро́вывать / очарова́ть *(whom = acc.)* ♦ **You** *(1,2)* **bewitch me with your beautiful smile.** Ты *(1)* околдо́вываешь / *(2)* обвора́живаешь меня́ свое́й прекра́сной улы́бкой. ♦ **You have not the smallest idea how totally you have bewitched me and enthralled me with your incomparable, indescribable beauty.** Ты не име́ешь да́же мале́йшего представле́ния, как соверше́нно околдова́ла и

The accents on Russian words are to show how to pronounce them..
You don't have to copy the accents when writing to someone.

увлекла меня своей несравненной, невероятной красотой. ♦ **You are truly a master at the art of bewitching (me).** Ты, правда, мастер в искусстве очаровывать (меня).

bewitched *adj* околдован, -а, -о, -ы *(short forms)*, заколдован, -а, -о, -ы *(short forms)*, заворожён, заворожена, -о, -ы *(short forms)*, обворожён, обворожена, -о, -ы *(short forms)*; очарован, -а, -о, -ы *(short forms)* ♦ **I am** *(1)* **totally** / *(2)* **entirely** / *(3)* **completely bewitched by your** *(4)* **...([5] incredible** / *[6]* **breath-taking** / *[7]* **shining** / *[8]* **heavenly** / *[9]* **radiant** / *[10]* **exquisite) beauty.** / *(11)* **...delicious sensuality.** Я *(1-3)* совершенно околдован *(4)* ...твоей (*[5]* невероятной / *[6]* ...останавливающей дыхание... / *[7]* сияющей / *[8]* небесной / *[9]* лучистой / *[10]* изысканной) красотой. / *(11)* ...изысканной чувственностью. ♦ **You've got me bewitched, bothered and bewildered.** Ты меня околдовала, растревожила и озадачила. ♦ **No woman ever had me as bewitched, bothered and bewildered as you do.** Ни одна женщина никогда не околдовывала, не тревожила и не озадачивала меня так, как ты.

bewitching *adj* околдовывающий, -ая, -ее, -ие, заколдовывающий, -ая, -ее, -ие, завораживающий, -ая, -ее, -ие, обвораживающий, -ая, -ее, -ие; очаровывающий, -ая, -ее, -ие, обаятельный, -ая, -ое, -ые, обворожительный, -ая, -ое, -ые, чарующий, -ая, -ее, -ие ♦ **Your** *(1)* **smile** / *(2)* **innocence is so** *(3-5)* **bewitching.** Твоя *(1)* улыбка / *(2)* невинность такая *(3)* околдовывающая / *(4)* обвораживающая / *(5)* чарующая. ♦ **You are bewitching beyond my wildest** *(1)* **dreams** / *(2)* **fantasies.** Ты очаровательна сверх моих самых необузданных *(1)* мечтаний / *(2)* фантазий.

bi *n (slang) (bisexual)* бисексуал.

biceps *n, pl* бицепсы ♦ **You've got such** *(1)* **great** / *(2)* **incredible** / *(3)* **awesome** / *(4)* **big biceps.** У тебя такие *(1)* замечательные... / *(2)* невероятные... / *(3)* внушающие страх ... / *(4)* большие... бицепсы.

bi-curious *adj* интересующийся (-аяся, -ееся, -иеся) бисексуальными отношениями.

bicycle *vi* ездить на велосипеде.

bicycle *n* велосипед.

bicycling *n* езда на велосипеде ♦ **Would you like to go bicycling (with me)?** Не хотела *(ж: хотел)* бы ты поехать на велосипеде (со мной)? ♦ **Let's go bicycling (together).** Давай поедем на велосипедах (вместе).

bigamist *n* двоеженец *m.*

bigamy *n* двубрачие; двоеженство *m;* двоемужие *f.*

big-boned *adj* ширококостный, -ая, -ое, -ые.

big-bosomed *adj* грудастая, с большой грудью.

big-breasted *adj* грудастая, с большой грудью.

big-chested *adj* грудастая, с большой грудью.

big-hearted *adj* великодушный, -ая, -ое, -ые, благородный, -ая, -ое, -ые, большой души.

big-heartedness *n* великодушие, благородство.

big-mouth *n* болтун *m,* болтунья *f.*

bike *vi* кататься на велосипеде ♦ **I like to bike.** Я люблю кататься на велосипеде.

bike *n* велосипед.

biker *n* 1. *(bicycle)* велосипедист; 2. *(motorcycle)* мотоциклист ♦ **avid ~**1. *(bicycle)* азартный велосипедист; 2. *(motorcycle)* азартный мотоциклист.

biking *n* катание на велосипеде ♦ **mountain ~** катание на горном велосипеде ♦ **go (mountain) ~** кататься / покататься на (горном) велосипеде ♦ **It would be fun to go biking together.** Забавно было бы вместе покататься на велосипедах.

bikini *n* бикини *neut* ♦ **thong ~** крохотное бикини.

bilingual *adj* двуязычный, -ая, -ое, -ые, говорящий (-ая, -ее, -ие) на двух языках.

If no accent is shown on a word with a capitalized vowel,
it means that the capitalized vowel is accented.

billiards *n* билья́рд ♦ **I'll show you how to play billiards.** Я покажу́ тебе́, как игра́ть в билья́рд.

bimbo *n (slang)* сексапи́льная деви́ца без мозго́в.

bind *vt* 1. *(tie)* свя́зывать / связа́ть *(what, whom = acc.)*, соединя́ть / соедини́ть *(what, whom = acc.)*; 2. *(obligate)* обя́зывать / обяза́ть *(what, whom = acc.)* ♦ **Love and laughter bind us together.** Любо́вь и смех свя́зывают нас. ♦ **Distance** *(1)* **holds /** *(2)* **keeps us apart, but our love binds us together.** Расстоя́ние *(1,2)* разделя́ет нас, но на́ша любо́вь соединя́ет нас.

bionic *adj* биони́ческий, -ая, -ое, -ие.

bird *n* пти́ца ♦ **love** ~ любо́вник *m*, любо́вница *f*.

birding *n* наблюде́ние за пти́цами.

birdwatching *n* наблюде́ние за пти́цами ♦ **One of my favorite pastimes is birdwatching.** Одно́ из мои́х люби́мых заня́тий -- наблюде́ние за пти́цами.

birth *n* рожде́ние ♦ ~ **of a child** рожде́ние малыша́.

birthday *n* день рожде́ния.

birthmark *n* роди́мое пятно́; *(small)* ро́динка.

bisexual *adj* бисексуа́льный, -ая, -ое, -ые.

bisexual *n* бисексуа́л.

bit *n (piece)* кусо́к, кусо́чек ♦ **a little** ~ немно́го.

bitch *vi (vulgar slang) (complain)* жа́ловаться *(at whom = +* на *+ acc., about what = +* о *+ prep.)*, ворча́ть *(at whom = +* на *+ acc., about what = +* о *+ prep.)*, ныть *(about what = +* о *+ prep.)*.

bitch *n (slang)* 1. *(lewd / immoral woman)* су́ка, шлю́ха; *(prostitute)* проститу́тка; 2. *(malicious / spiteful woman)* зла́я / зло́бная же́нщина.

bite *vt* куса́ть / укуси́ть *(what, whom = acc.)* ♦ **Don't worry, I'm not going to bite you.** Не беспоко́йся, я тебя́ не съем. ♦ **I bit my tongue the whole time.** Я прику́сывал *(ж: прику́сывала)* язы́к всё вре́мя.

bitter *adj* го́рький, -ая, -ое, -ие, жесто́кий, -ая, -ое, -ие.

bitterness *n* го́речь *f*.

bittersweet *adj* сла́достно-го́рький, -ая, -ое, -ие ♦ ~ **memories** сла́достно-го́рькие воспомина́ния.

bizarre *adj* стра́нный, -ая, -ое, -ые, причу́дливый, -ая, -ое, -ые.

black *adj* чёрный, -ая, -ое, -ые.

black-haired *adj* чёрноволо́сый, -ая, -ое, -ые.

blacklist *n* чёрный спи́сок ♦ **I hope I'm not on your blacklist (for not calling you last night).** Я наде́юсь, что я не в твоём чёрном спи́ске (за то, что не звони́л *[ж: звони́ла]* тебе́ вчера́ ве́чером).

blackmail *vt* шантажи́ровать *(whom = acc.)*.

blackmail *n* шанта́ж.

blackness *n* чернота́ ♦ **I love the rich blackness of your hair.** Мне нра́вится роско́шная чернота́ твои́х воло́с.

blame *vt* обвиня́ть / обвини́ть *(whom = acc.)* ♦ **Don't blame me.** Не обвиня́й меня́. ♦ **I don't blame you.** Я не обвиня́ю тебя́. ♦ **I 'm not blaming you for anything.** Я ни в чём тебя́ не обвиня́ю.

blame *n* вина́ ♦ **The blame is all mine.** Вина́ вся моя́. ♦ **Why do you put the blame on me?** Почему́ ты обвиня́ешь меня́?

bland *adj* 1. *(weak)* сла́бый, -ая, -ое, -ые; 2. *(dull)* ску́чный, -ая, -ое, -ые, неинтере́сный, -ая, -ое, -ые; *(monotonous)* моното́нный, -ая, -ое, -ые ♦ **How pale and bland all other**

Russian has 6 grammatical cases. For an explanation of them see the grammar appendix on page 686.

women are before you. Как бледны́ и неинтере́сны все други́е же́нщины по сравне́нию с тобо́й.

blanket *n* одея́ло.

blatant *adj (obvious)* я́вный, -ая, -ое, -ые, очеви́дный, -ая, -ое, -ые ♦ ~ **lie** я́вная ложь.

blatantly *adv (obvious)* я́вно, очеви́дно.

blaze *vi* горе́ть, пыла́ть.

blaze *vt (a trail)* прокла́дывать / проложи́ть *(what = acc.)* ♦ **As my lips pay devoted homage to your nipples, my fingers will blaze a fiery trail over your skin.** В то вре́мя, как мои́ гу́бы ока́жут почти́тельное внима́ние твои́м соска́м, мои́ па́льцы бу́дут прокла́дывать о́гненный путь по твое́й ко́же.

bleak *adj* уны́лый, -ая, -ое, -ые, безра́достный, -ая, -ое, -ые, мра́чный, -ая, -ое, -ые ♦ **My life is bleak without you here.** Моя́ жизнь без тебя́ здесь безра́достна. ♦ **My days are bleak since you went away.** Дни мои́ безра́достны с тех пор, как ты уе́хала *(ж: уе́хал)*.

bleakness *n* безра́достность *f*, уны́ние, мра́чность *f* ♦ **With you gone, bleakness has** *(1)* **crept** / *(2)* **seeped into my soul.** С твои́м ухо́дом уны́ние *(1)* прокра́лось / *(2)* прони́кло в мою́ ду́шу.

blemish *n* пятно́.

blend *vi* соединя́ться / соедини́ться; подходи́ть друг дру́гу, сме́шиваться / смеша́ться, слива́ться / сли́ться ♦ **We blend so well together, don't you think?** Мы так хорошо́ подхо́дим друг дру́гу, не так ли? ♦ **Our bodies will blend (together) as one.** На́ши тела́ солью́тся (вме́сте) как одно́. ♦ **Darling, you and I are going to blend together** *(1,2)* **wonderfully.** Дорога́я, ты и я *(1)* великоле́пно / *(2)* превосхо́дно подойдём друг к дру́гу.

blend *n* смесь *f* ♦ **city-country** ~ смесь го́рода с дере́вней.

blending *n* смесь *f*, сочета́ние ♦ **You have a marvelous blending of spirit, charm and sensuality.** У тебя́ удиви́тельное сочета́ние души́, обая́ния и чу́вственности.

bless *vt* благословля́ть / благослови́ть *(whom = acc., with what = instr.)* ♦ **I thank God for blessing me with your (wonderful) love.** Я благодарю́ Бо́га за то, что он благослови́л меня́ твое́й (замеча́тельной) любо́вью. ♦ *(1)* **God** / *(2)* **Heaven has blessed me with** *(3)* **...you.** / *(4)* **...your** *(5)* **precious** / *(6)* **wonderful love.** *(1)* Бог благослови́л... / *(2)* Небеса́ благослови́ли... меня́ *(3)* ...тобо́й. / *(4)* ...твое́й *(5)* драгоце́нной / *(6)* замеча́тельной любо́вью. ♦ **God** *(1)* **definitely** / *(2)* **certainly blessed me when he made my path converge with yours.** Бог *(1,2)* несомне́нно благослови́л меня́, когда́ он соедини́л нас. ● **God could not have blessed me any more than when he brought you into my life.** Бог не мог бы бо́лее благослови́ть меня́, чем принести́ тебя́ в мою́ жизнь.

blessed *adj* благословлён, благословлена́, -о́, -ы́, осчастли́влен, -а, -о, -ы *(short forms)* ♦ **I am** *(1)* **so** / *(2)* **truly blessed to have your love.** Я *(1)* так / *(2)* действи́тельно благословлён *(ж: благословлена́)* твое́й любо́вью. ♦ **I believe that our love is blessed by God.** Я ве́рю, что на́ша любо́вь благословлена́ Бо́гом.

blessing *n* благослове́ние ♦ **What greater blessing could I (ever) ask for than your** *(1)* **wonderful** / *(2)* **beautiful** / *(3)* **precious love?** О како́м бо́льшем благослове́нии мог *(ж: могла́)* бы я проси́ть, чем о твое́й *(1)* замеча́тельной / *(2)* прекра́сной / *(3)* драгоце́нной любви́. ♦ **Your love is the** *(1)* **greatest** / *(2)* **most precious blessing in my life.** Твоя́ любо́вь -- *(1)* велича́йшее / *(2)* драгоце́ннейшее благослове́ние в мое́й жи́зни. ♦ **I could have no richer blessing than your love.** Я не мог *(ж: могла́)* бы име́ть бо́льшего блаже́нства, чем твое́й любви́. ♦ **I know my** *(1)* **mother** / *(2)* **father will give** *(3)* **her** / *(4)* **his blessing (to our marriage).** Я зна́ю, что *(1)* ...моя́ мать... / *(2)* ...мой оте́ц... даст *(3,4)* своё благослове́ние (на наш брак). ♦ **I know my parents will give their blessing**

There are no articles ("a" or "the") in Russian.

(to our marriage). Я зна́ю, что мои́ роди́тели даду́т своё благослове́ние (на наш брак). ♦ **It's a mixed blessing.** В э́том есть как положи́тельные, так и отрица́тельные сто́роны.

blind *adj* слепо́й, -а́я, -о́е, -ы́е *(short forms:* слеп, -а́, ы́*)* ♦ **partially ~** части́чно слепо́й, -а́я, -о́е, -ы́е ♦ **I'm not blind to** *(1)* **...what has been going on.** / *(2)* **...what you've been doing.** Я не слеп *(ж: слепа́)* к *(1)* ...происходя́щему. / *(2)* ...тому́, что ты де́лаешь. ♦ **You must think I'm blind.** Ты должно́ быть ду́маешь, что я слепо́й *(ж: слепа́я).* ♦ **They say love is blind.** Говоря́т, что любо́вь слепа́.

blinded *adj* ослеплённый, -ая, -ое, -ые *(short forms:* ослеплён, ослеплена́, -о́, -ы́*)* ♦ **I was blinded by the wild attraction between us.** Я был ослеплён *(ж: была́ ослеплена́)* безу́мным влече́нием к тебе́. ♦ **I was blinded by my love for you.** Я был ослеплён *(ж: была́ ослеплена́)* мое́й любо́вью к тебе́.

blinders *n, pl* шо́ры ♦ **You'll never have to put blinders on me — I have eyes only for you.** Тебе́ не на́до бу́дет надева́ть мне на глаза́ шо́ры -- я ви́жу то́лько тебя́.

blind-side *vt (slang) (take unawares, take by surprise)* огоро́шить *(whom = acc.),* си́льно удиви́ть *(whom = acc.).*

blind-sided *adj (slang) (taken unawares, taken by surprise)* огоро́шен, -а, -о, -ы *(short forms),* си́льно удивлён (удивлена́, -о́, -ы́) *(short forms),* сражён, сражена́, -о́, -ы́ *(short forms)* ♦ **I was completely blind-sided by her *(his)* decision to get divorced.** Я был *(ж: была́)* соверше́нно огоро́шен *(ж: огоро́шена)* её *(ж: его́)* реше́нием развести́сь.

blink *vt* мига́ть / мигну́ть, морга́ть / моргну́ть *(what = instr.)* ♦ **~** *(1)* **my /** *(2)* **your eyes** *(1,2)* морга́ть / моргну́ть.

bliss *n* блаже́нство ♦ **celestial ~** ра́йское блаже́нство ♦ **exquisite ~** упои́тельное блаже́нство ♦ **marital ~** супру́жеское блаже́нство ♦ *(1,2)* **perfect ~** *(1)* по́лное / *(2)* абсолю́тное блаже́нство ♦ **rapturous ~** упои́тельное блаже́нство ♦ **shared ~** пережи́тое (на́ми) блаже́нство ♦ **wedded ~** супру́жеское сча́стье ♦ **peaks of** *(1)* **celestial** / *(2)* **ethereal** / *(3)* **heavenly ~** верши́ны *(1-3)* неземно́го блаже́нства.

---
bliss: *phrases*

In your arms I have found such bliss as I've never known before. В твои́х объя́тиях я нашёл *(ж: нашла́)* тако́е блаже́нство, како́го я никогда́ не знал *(ж: зна́ла)* пре́жде. ♦ **I want to fill your life with never-ending bliss.** Я хочу́ напо́лнить твою́ жизнь бесконе́чным блаже́нством. ♦ *(1)* **What...** / *(2)* **It's such...** (*[3]* **tremendous /** *[4]* **infinite /** *[5]* **pure /** *[6]* **absolute) bliss to** *(7)* **...be in your arms.** / *(8)* **...have you in my arms.** *(1)* Что за... / *(2)* Это тако́е... (*[3]* огро́мное / *[4]* безграни́чное / *[5]* и́стинное / *[6]* по́лное) блаже́нство *(7)* ...быть в твои́х объя́тиях. / *(8)* ...обнима́ть тебя́. ♦ **I have never known such (*[1]* monumental /** *[2]* **total /** *[3]* **supreme /** *[4]* **absolute) bliss with anyone.** Я никогда́ не знал *(ж: зна́ла)* тако́го (*[1]* огро́много / *[2]* по́лного / *[3]* высоча́йшего / *[4]* абсолю́тного) блаже́нства с кем-ли́бо. ♦ **Oh, this is bliss!** О, э́то блаже́нство! ♦ **You transport me into bliss.** Ты перено́сишь меня́ в блаже́нство. ♦ **I will reveal the delightful secrets of love and bliss for you.** Я откро́ю тебе́ упои́тельные та́йны любви́ и блаже́нства. ♦ **I want to cause you nothing but bliss.** Я не хочу́ доста́вить тебе́ ничего́, кро́ме блаже́нства. ♦ **I want to** *(1)* **surround /** *(2)* **envelop you with (*[3]* endless /** *[4]* **infinite /** *[5]* **ever-lasting /** *[6]* **boundless) bliss.** Я хочу́ *(1)* окружи́ть / *(2)* оку́тать тебя́ (*[3,4]* бесконе́чным / *[5]* несконча́емым / *[6]* безграни́чным) блаже́нством.

blissful *adj* счастли́вый, -ая, -ое, -ые, блаже́нный, -ая, -ое, -ые ♦ **I dream of spending endless blissful hours holding you in my arms (and making tender love with you).** Я мечта́ю проводи́ть бесконе́чные блаже́нные часы́, обнима́я тебя́ (и занима́ясь

---

*This dictionary contains two Russian alphabet pages:
one in Appendix 1, page 685, and a tear-off page on page 799.*

нéжной любóвью с тобóй). ♦ **Always the sweet memories of those blissful** *(1)* **moments** / *(1)* **hours** / *(1)* **days come back to me.** Слáдкие воспоминáния о тех счастлúвых *(1)* момéнтах / *(1)* часáх / *(1)* днях всегдá возвращáются ко мне. ♦ **That was the most blissful** *(1)* **day** / *(2)* **evening that I've ever had.** Это был сáмый счастлúвый *(1)* день / *(2)* вéчер моéй жúзни. ♦ **That was the.most blissful night that I've ever had.** Это была сáмая счастлúвая ночь моéй жúзни. ♦ **That was the most blissful time that I've ever had.** Это бы́ло мойм самым счастлúвым врéмем. ♦ **That was the most blissful weekend that I've ever had.** Это бы́ли сáмые счастлúвые выходны́е (дни), котóрые у меня́ когдá-лúбо бы́ли. ♦ **Those moments (we shared together) were so blissful.** Те мгновéния (, котóрые мы провелú вмéсте) бы́ли такúми счастлúвыми. ♦ *(1)* **This...** / *(2)* **Being in your arms...** / *(3)* **Holding you in my arms... is so blissful.** *(1)* Это... / *(2)* Быть в твоúх объя́тиях... / *(3)* Держáть тебя́ в объя́тиях... такóе блажéнство.

blissfully *adv* счастлúво, блажéнно ♦ **smile** ~ рáдостно улыбáться ♦ **All this time you've been so blissfully unaware of my** *(1)* **feelings** / *(2)* **love for you.** Всё э́то врéмя ты так счáстливо не подозревáла *(ж: не подозревáл)* о *(1)* ...мойх чýвствах... / *(2)* ...моéй любвú... к тебé.

blithe *adj* 1. *(joyful)* весёлый, -ая, -ое, -ые, жизнерáдостный, -ая, -ое, -ые, счастлúвый, -ая, -ое, -ые; 2. *(casual)* беспéчный, -ая, -ое, -ые ♦ **You** *(1)* **are** / *(2)* **have such a blithe spirit.** *(1,2)* У тебя́ такóй весёлый харáктер. ♦ **You** *(1)* **enchant** / *(2)* **captivate me with your blithe spirit.** Ты *(1)* очарóвываешь / *(2)* пленя́ешь меня́ свойм весёлым харáктером. ♦ **Your (precious) blithe spirit** *(1)* **...pervades...** / *(2)* **...radiates through... (all) my thoughts wherever I go.** Мы́сли о тебé никогдá не покидáют меня́. Твоя́ жизнерáдостность и нéжность совершéнно покорúли меня́.

blithely *adv* вéсело, жизнерáдостно.

blitzkrieg *n* молниенóсная атáка ♦ **kissing** ~ молниенóсная атáка поцелýями ♦ **When we get together (again), I'm going to do a kissing blitzkrieg on you.** Когдá мы (опя́ть) бýдем вмéсте, я молниенóсно атакýю тебя́ поцелýями.

block *n* глы́ба ♦ **She's like a block of ice.** Онá как глы́ба льда.

blockhead *n* дубóвая головá, болвáн.

blonde *n* блондúнка ♦ **adventurous** ~ предприúмчивая блондúнка ♦ **alluring** ~ соблазнúтельная блондúнка ♦ **ash** ~ пéпельная блондúнка ♦ **beautiful** ~ прекрáсная блондúнка ♦ **bewitching** ~ очаровáтельная блондúнка ♦ **bleached** ~ обесцвéченная блондúнка ♦ **blue-eyed** ~ голубоглáзая блондúнка ♦ **bubbly** ~ искря́щаяся блондúнка ♦ **busty** ~ блондúнка с бю́стом, грудáстая блондúнка ♦ **captivating** ~ очаровáтельная блондúнка ♦ **classy** ~ клáссная блондúнка ♦ **curvy** ~ окрýглая блондúнка ♦ **cute** ~ хорóшенькая блондúнка ♦ **delicate** ~ изя́щная блондúнка ♦ **exotic** ~ экзотúческая блондúнка ♦ **faux** ~ *(dyed blonde)* крáшенная блондúнка ♦ **fiery** ~ пы́лкая блондúнка ♦ **golden-haired** ~ отливáющая зóлотом блондúнка ♦ *(1,2)* **good-looking** ~ *(1)* хорóшенкая / *(2)* симпатúчная блондúнка ♦ **gorgeous** ~ восхитúтельная блондúнка ♦ **green-eyed** ~ зеленоглáзая блондúнка ♦ **knockout** ~ сногсшибáтельная блондúнка ♦ **large pretty** ~ большáя привлекáтельная блондúнка ♦ **mercurial** ~ блондúнка с перемéнчивым харáктером ♦ **natural** ~ натурáльная блондúнка ♦ **platinum** ~ плáтиновая блондúнка ♦ **pretty** ~ хорóшенькая блондúнка ♦ **ravishing** ~ потрясáющая блондúнка ♦ **spunky** ~ пы́лкая блондúнка ♦ **statuesque** ~ стáтная блондúнка ♦ **strawberry** ~ рыжевáтая блондúнка ♦ **stunning** ~ сногсшибáтельная блондúнка ♦ **stylish** ~ мóдная блондúнка ♦ **succulent** ~ сóчная блондúнка ♦ **sultry** ~ знóйная блондúнка ♦ **Teutonic** ~ тевтóнская блондúнка ♦ **vibrant** ~ живáя блондúнка ♦ **They say that gentlemen prefer blondes.** Говоря́т,

---

Russian verbs conjugate for 6 persons:
I, familiar you, he-she-it, we, polite & plural you, and they.

что джентельме́ны предпочита́ют блонди́нок.

blonde *adj* светловоло́сый, -ая, -ое, -ые.

blond-haired *adj* светловоло́сый, -ая, -ое, -ые.

blood *n* кровь *f* ♦ **My blood becomes roaring fire whenever I even think about your soft, warm, beautiful body.** Моя́ кровь превраща́ется в бушу́ющий ого́нь вся́кий раз, когда́ я ду́маю о твоём мя́гком, тёплом, прекра́сном те́ле. ♦ **Just to look at your picture sends the blood rushing in my veins.** То́лько взгляд на твою́ фотогра́фию заставля́ет кровь быстре́е бежа́ть в мои́х ве́нах. ♦ **You can never** *(1)* **know** / *(2)* **imagine how you stoke the fires in my blood.** Ты не *(1)* ...зна́ешь,... / *(2)* ...мо́жешь вообрази́ть,... како́й ого́нь разжига́ешь в мое́й крови́. ♦ **I am** *(1)* **consumed** / *(2)* **engulfed by this fire that you have started racing through my blood.** Я *(1,2)* поглощён огнём, кото́рый ты разожгла́ в мое́й крови́.

blossom *vi* расцвета́ть / расцвести́ ♦ **So much love has blossomed in my heart for you.** В моём се́рдце расцвело́ больша́я любо́вь к тебе́. ♦ **This love that is blossoming in my heart for you is unlike anything I've ever known.** Эта любо́вь к тебе́, цвету́щая в моём се́рдце, непохо́жа ни на что друго́е, что бы́ло со мной.

blossom *n* цвет, цвете́ние.

blossoming *adj* цвету́щий, -ая, -ее, -ие.

blossoming *n* расцве́т ♦ ~ **of feeling** расцве́т чу́вства.

blouse *n* блу́зка ♦ **daring** ~ де́рзкая блу́зка ♦ **deep-cut** ~ глубоко́ вы́резанная блу́зка ♦ **sequined** ~ блестя́щая блу́зка ♦ **silk** ~ шёлковая блу́зка ♦ **That's a (very) beautiful blouse.** Это (о́чень) краси́вая блу́зка. ♦ **You make that** *(1,2)* **blouse very beautiful.** Ты де́лаешь э́ту *(1)* ко́фточку / *(2)* блу́зку соверше́нно прекра́сной.

blow *vt* раздува́ть / разду́ть *(what = acc.)* ♦ *(1)* **You're blowing...** / *(2)* **You've blown... this (all) out of proportion.** Ты *(1)* раздува́ешь / *(2)* раздува́ла *(ж: раздува́л)* э́то (совсе́м) несоразме́рно.

blow *n* уда́р ♦ **It is a staggering blow to me.** Это ошеломля́ющий уда́р для меня́. ♦ **It was a staggering blow to me.** Это бы́ло ошеломля́ющим уда́ром для меня́.

blown away: ♦ **I was just blown away** *([1]* ...**by your letter.** / *[2]* ...**when you kissed me.** / *[3]* ...**when you told me).** Я про́сто расцвёл *(ж: расцвела́)* *([1]* ...от твоего́ письма́. / *[2]* ..., когда́ ты поцелова́ла *[ж: поцелова́л]* меня́. / *[3]* ..., когда́ ты сказа́ла *[ж: сказа́л]* мне).

blowzy-looking *adj* неря́шливого ви́да.

blue *adj* 1. *(color)* си́ний, -яя, -ее, -ие; *(eyes)* голубо́й, -а́я, -о́е, -ы́е; 2. *(slang) (sad)* печа́льный, -ая, -ое, -ые ♦ **soft** ~ све́тло-си́ний, -яя, -ее, -ие ♦ **I feel so blue** *(1)* ...**without you here.** / *(2)* ...**since you left.** Я чу́вствую таку́ю печа́ль *(1)* ...без тебя́. / *(1)* ...с тех пор, как ты уе́хала *(ж: уе́хал)*. ♦ **I'm so blue** *(1)* ...**without you here.** / *(2)* ...**since you left.** Мне так печа́льно *(1)* ...без тебя́. / *(1)* ...с тех пор, как ты уе́хала *(ж: уе́хал)*. ♦ **I feel kind of blue today.** Мне ка́к-то печа́льно сего́дня.

blue *n* синь *f* ♦ **heavenly** ~ **of your eyes** небе́сная синь твои́х глаз.

blue-eyed *adj* голубогла́зый, -ая, -ое, -ые.

blue grass *(music)* (му́зыка) «блу́грасс».

bluenose *adj* пурита́нский, -ая, -ое, -ие.

blues 1. *(music)* блюз; 2. *(sadness)* хандра́ ♦ **have the** ~s хандри́ть.

blunder *vi* промахну́ться, сде́лать гру́бую оши́бку, гру́бо ошиби́ться.

blunder *n* прома́шка, гру́бая оши́бка ♦ **I've made a terrible blunder.** Я сде́лал *(ж:сде́-`лала)* ужа́сную оши́бку. ♦ **My marriage to** *(1)* **her** / *(2)* **him was a** *(3)* **real** / *(4)* **terrible blunder.** Мой брак с *(1)* ней / *(2)* ним был *(3)* действи́тельно / *(4)* ужа́сной

There are two words for "you" in Russian: familiar «ты» and polite / plural «вы» (See page 781).

ошибкой.

blunt *adj* резкий, -ая, -ое, -ие, прямой, -ая, -ое, -ые

bluntly *adv* прямо, резко, напрямик ♦ **put it** ~ сказать прямо.

blurt out *vt* сболтнуть *(what = acc.).*

blush *vi* краснеть / покраснеть, заливаться / залиться румянцем ♦ **I've made you blush.** Я заставил тебя покраснеть. ♦ **You make me blush.** Ты заставляешь меня краснеть. ♦ **You're blushing.** Ты краснеешь. ♦ **Why are you blushing?** Почему ты краснеешь?

blush *n (cosmetic)* румяна.

B.O. *abbrev* = **body odor** запах тела.

boa *n* боа.

board *n* доска ♦ **bulletin** ~ доска объявлений.

boast *vi* хвастаться ♦ **I don't mean to boast.** Я не хочу хвастаться. ♦ **I hope it doesn't sound like I'm boasting.** Я надеюсь, это не звучит так, как будто я хвастаюсь.

boastful *adj* хвастливый, -ая, -ое, -ые.

boat *n* лодка.

boater *n* катающийся (-аяся, -иеся) на лодке.

boating *n* катание на лодке ♦ **Would you like to go boating with me?** Не хотела *(ж: хотёл)* бы ты покататься на лодке со мной?

bod *n (slang) (body)* тело ♦ *(1,2)* **bare** ~ *(1)* голое / *(2)* обнажённое тело ♦ **beautiful** ~ прекрасное тело ♦ **great** ~ великолепное тело.

bodice *n (of a dress)* лиф *(плátья); (sleeveless waist, outer girdle)* корсаж ♦ **daring** ~ дерзкий лиф ♦ **lacy** ~ кружевной лиф.

body *n* тело *(pl: телá)* ♦ **athelete's** ~ тело спортсмена ♦ **athletic** ~ атлетическое тело ♦ **attractive** ~ привлекательное тело ♦ **beautiful** ~ прекрасное тело ♦ **beautifully contoured** ~ прекрасно очерченное тело ♦ **beloved** ~ любимое тело ♦ ~ **like music** тело как музыка ♦ **boyish** ~ юношеское тело ♦ **bronzed** ~ бронзовое тело ♦ **brown** ~ коричневое тело ♦ **burning** ~ разгорячённое тело ♦ **clean** ~ чистое тело ♦ **compliant** ~ послушное тело ♦ **coveted** ~ желанное тело ♦ **dark(-skinned)** ~ смуглое тело ♦ **delectable** ~ лакомое тело ♦ **delicate** ~ хрупкое тело ♦ **disturbingly exposed** ~ соблазнительно выставленное на показ тело ♦ **energetic** ~ энергетичное тело ♦ **entire** ~ всё тело ♦ **entwined** ~s сплетённые тела ♦ **expressive** ~ выразительное тело ♦ **fantastic** ~ великолепное тело ♦ *(1,2)* **fat** ~ *(1)* толстое / *(2)* полное тело ♦ **feminine** ~ женское тело ♦ **fit** ~ тренированное тело ♦ **flabby** ~ дряблое тело ♦ **flexible** ~ гибкое тело ♦ **fragile** ~ хрупкое тело ♦ **girlish** ~ девичье тело ♦ **girl's** ~ тело девушки ♦ **glistening** ~ сверкающее тело ♦ **glorious golden** ~ великолепное золотистое тело ♦ **good-looking** ~ привлекательное тело ♦ **gorgeous** ~ великолепное тело ♦ **graceful** ~ изящное тело ♦ **great** ~ великолепное тело ♦ **hairy** ~ волосатое тело ♦ **half-naked** ~ наполовину обнажённое тело ♦ **hard** ~ крепкое тело ♦ **healthy** ~ здоровое тело ♦ **heavenly** ~ божественное тело ♦ *(1,2)* **heavy** ~ *(1)* толстое / *(2)* полное тело ♦ **hot** ~ горячее тело ♦ **huge** ~ огромное тело ♦ **human** ~ человеческое тело ♦ **husky** ~ плотное тело ♦ **intertwined** ~ies переплетённые тела ♦ *(1,2)* **large** ~ *(1)* большое / *(2)* крупное тело ♦ *(1,2)* **lean** ~ *(1)* сухопарое / *(2)* худощавое тело ♦ **light** ~ лёгкое тело ♦ **lithe** ~ гибкое тело ♦ **little** ~ маленькое тело, тельце ♦ **long** ~ длинное тело ♦ **lovely** ~ прелестное тело ♦ **luscious** ~ сочное тело ♦ **magnificent** ~ великолепное тело ♦ **male** ~ мужское тело ♦ **marvelous** ~ восхитительное тело ♦ **masculine** ~ мужское тело ♦ **muscular** ~ мускулистое тело ♦ **my** ~ моё тело ♦ *(1,2)* **naked** ~ *(1)* обнажённое / *(2)* голое тело ♦ *(1,2)* **nice** ~ *(1)* привлекательное / *(2)* красивое тело ♦ *(1,2)* **nude** ~ *(1)* обнажённое / *(2)* голое тело ♦ **obedient** ~ послушное тело ♦ **old** ~ старое тело

Russian terms of endearment are given in Appendix 13, page 780.

♦ **perfect** ~ совершённое тéло ♦ **petite** ~ мáленькое тéло ♦ **pink** ~ рóзовое тéло ♦ **rubenesque** ~ рýбенсовское тéло ♦ **scrumptious** ~ аппетúтное тéло ♦ **sexy** ~ сексапúльное тéло ♦ **shapely** ~ пропорционáльное тéло ♦ **short** ~ корóткое тéло ♦ **skinny** ~ худóе тéло ♦ **sleep-warm** ~ тёплое óто сна тéло ♦ **small** ~ мáленькое тéло ♦ **smooth** ~ глáдкое тéло ♦ *(1,2)* **soft** ~ *(1)* нéжное / *(2)* мягкое тéло ♦ **solid(ly built)** ~ плóтное тéло ♦ **splendid** ~ великолéпное тéло ♦ **strong** ~ сúльное тéло ♦ **suntanned** ~ загорéлое тéло ♦ **superbly toned** ~ мускулúстое тéло ♦ **supple feminine** ~ подáтливое жéнское тéло ♦ **swaying** ~**ies** раскáчивающиеся телá ♦ **sweaty** ~ пóтное тéло ♦ **sweet** ~ слáдкое тéло ♦ **tanned** ~ загорéлое тéло ♦ **thin** ~ худóе тело ♦ **trim** ~ стрóйное тéло ♦ *(1,2)* **voluptuous** ~ *(1)* чýвственное / *(2)* роскóшное тéло ♦ **warm** ~ тёплое тéло ♦ **well conditioned** ~ тренирóванное тéло ♦ **wet** ~ мóкрое тéло ♦ **white** ~ бéлое тéло ♦ **whole** ~ всё тéло ♦ **wiry** ~ жúлистое тéло ♦ **young** ~ молодóе тéло ♦ **young girl's** ~ тéло молодóй дéвушки ♦ **your** ~ *(familiar)* твоё тéло; *(polite)* Вáше тéло ♦ **youthful** ~ молодóе тéло ♦ **from the very depths of the** ~ из сáмой глубины тéла ♦ **true closeness of mind, spirit and** ~ пóдлинная гармóния умá, дýха и тéла.

body: your body

You have such a (lithe, supple,) beautiful body. У тебя такóе (подáтливое, гúбкое,) прекрáсное тéло. ♦ **You have a** *([1]* **truly** */ [2]* **really)** *(3)* **great** */ (4)* **wonderful** */ (5)* **beautiful body.** У тебя *([1,2]* действúтельно) *(3)* великолéпное / *(4)* замечáтельное / *(5)* прекрáсное тéло. ♦ **What a(n)** *(1)* **beautiful** */ (2)* **gorgeous** */ (3)* **luscious** */ (4)* **fantastic** */ (5)* **terrific** */ (6)* **incredible body** */ (7)* **scrumptious (you have)!** Что за *(1)* прекрáсное / *(2)* великолéпное / *(3)* сóчное / *(4)* фантастúческое / *(5)* чудéсное / *(6)* невероятное / *(7)* аппетúтное тéло (у тебя)! ♦ **You have the** *(1)* **sexiest** */ (2)* **best** */ (3)* **most beautiful** */ (4)* **most luscious** */ (5)* **most gorgeous body I've ever seen in all my life.** У тебя *(1)* сáмое сексуáльное / *(2)* лýчшее / *(3)* прекрáснейшее / *(4)* сочнéйшее / *(5)* прекрáснейшее тéло, котóрое я когдá-либо в моéй жúзни вúдел. ♦ **You have a delightfully curvaceous body.** У тебя восхитúтельно окрýглое тéло. ♦ **You have the most** *(1)* **curvaceous** */ (2)* **tantalizing body I've ever** *(3)* **...seen.** */ (4)* **...laid eyes on.** Я никогдá не *(3,4)* вúдел такóго *(1)* ...окрýглого, красúвого... / *(2)* ...манящего... тéла. ♦ **Your body has such** *(1)* **lissome** */ (2)* **lithesome** */ (3)* **willowy grace.** В твоём тéле есть такáя *(1-3)* гúбкая грáция. ♦ **You have (such) a nice,** *(2)* **trim** */ (3)* **hard** */ (4)* **athletic body.** У тебя (такóе) красúвое, *(1)* стрóйное / *(2)* крéпкое / *(3)* атлетúческое тéло. ♦ **You have a** *(11* **well** */ (2)* **superbly** */ (3)* **nicely toned body.** У тебя *(1)* хорóшее / *(2)* мускулúстое / *(3)* ...хорошó тренирóванное... тéло. ♦ **Your body is perfect in its symmetry.** Твоё тéло так совершéнно в своéй симметрúи. ♦ **If you have a nature as generous as your body, you are truly heaven's special prize.** Éсли твой харáктер такóй же замечáтельный, как твоё тéло, то ты úстинный дар небéс. ♦ **That swimsuit was made for your beautifully contoured body.** Этот купáльник был сóздан для твоегó прекрáсного скульптýрного тéла. ♦ **Your body is so fragrant.** Твоё тéло такóе душúстое. ♦ **Your body exudes a sweetness like a meadow flower.** От твоегó тéла исхóдит слáдость, как от луговых цветóв. ♦ **Your body** *(1)* **...is...** */ (2)* **...will be... my altar.** Твоё тéло *(1)* ...-- мой алтáрь. / *(2)* ...бýдет мойм алтарём.

body: I love your body

Oh, (how) I love your (beautiful) body! О, (как) я люблю твоё (прекрáсное) тéло! ♦ **I** *(1)* **love** */ (2)* **adore your (rubenesque) body.** Я *(1)* люблю / *(2)* обожáю твоё (рýбенсовское) тéло. ♦ **I love the soft** *(1,2)* **contours of your body.** Я люблю мягкие *(1)* кóнтуры / *(2)* очертáния твоегó тéла. ♦ **I love the smell of your body.** Мне нрáвится

Some of the Russian sentences are translations of things we say and are not what Russians themselves would normally say.

за́пах твоего́ те́ла. ♦ **I love the way your body softens when I** *(1)* **touch /** *(2)* **caress you.** Мне нра́вится, как твоё те́ло расслабля́ется, когда́ я *(1)* каса́юсь / *(2)* ласка́ю тебя. ♦ **I love the way your body comes to life under my touch.** Мне нра́вится, как ожива́ет твоё те́ло под мои́ми прикоснове́ниями. ♦ **How I love to lie and gaze at the silken afterglow of your body.** Как я люблю́ лежа́ть и вгля́дываться в шелкови́стый о́тсвет твоего́ те́ла.

body: how wonderful it would be...

How absolutely wonderful it would be to climb between the sheets to nestle against your warm, soft, luscious body. Как соверше́нно замеча́тельно бы́ло бы зале́зть ме́жду простыня́ми и прильну́ть к твоему́ тёплому, мя́гкому, со́чному те́лу. ♦ **How heavenly it would be to relish the warm, wonderful softness of your body in the languor of half-sleep.** Как сла́достно бы́ло бы наслажда́ться тёплой, замеча́тельной мя́г-костью твоего́ те́ла в то́мном полусне́.

body: I dream of your body

How I dream of the day when I can peel away your silk underwear to reveal the full, *(1)* **glorious /** *(2)* **magnificent splendor of your beautiful, luscious body.** Как я мечта́ю о том дне, когда́ смогу́ сбро́сить с тебя́ шёлковое бельё, чтобы откры́ть напо́лненную до краёв, *(1)* великоле́пную / *(2)* замеча́тельную ро́скошь твоего́ прекра́сного, со́чного те́ла. ♦ **All of my daydreams and fantasies are filled with images of your exquisitely beautiful body.** Все мои́ мечты́ и фанта́зии запо́лнены о́бразом твоего́ изы́сканно прекра́сного те́ла. ♦ **My sleep, shallow and restless, was assailed by visions of your beautiful, voluptuous body.** Мой сон, неглубо́кий и беспоко́йный, был нару́шен ви́дением твоего́ прекра́сного, чу́вственного те́ла. ♦ **Even in my dreams I've never seen such a** *(1)* **beautiful /** *(2)* **luscious body.** Да́же в свои́х снах я никогда́ не ви́дел тако́го *(1)* прекра́сного / *(2)* со́чного те́ла. ♦ **I dream of filling your body with intense, exquisite pleasure day and night, night and day, for as long as God grants me the time.** Я мечта́ю наполня́ть твоё те́ло пы́лким, изы́сканным наслажде́нием день и ночь, ночь и день до конца́ даро́ванной мне Бо́гом жи́зни. ♦ **Do you have any idea how many times you have woken me up in the middle of the night with the power and magic of your beautiful, luscious, sexy body? I couldn't begin to tell you.** Зна́ешь ли ты, как ча́сто ты пробужда́ешь меня́ в середи́не но́чи си́лой и волшебство́м твоего́ пре-кра́сного, со́чного, сексуа́льного те́ла? Я про́сто не могу́ сказа́ть тебе́. ♦ **Many times at night I wake up with my body on fire from cavorting with you in one episode or another of the Kama Sutra.** Мно́го раз я просыпа́юсь но́чью с те́лом охва́ченным огнём от того́, что мы с тобо́й изуча́ем ту и́ли другу́ю главу́ Ка́ма Су́тры.

body: your body is in my thoughts

The *(1)* **memory /** *(2)* **thought of your** *(3)* **beautiful /** *(4)* **luscious /** *(5)* **wonderful body never leaves my mind.** *(1)* Воспомина́ние / *(2)* Мысль о твоём *(3)* прекра́сном / *(4)* со́чном / *(5)* замеча́тельном те́ле никогда́ не покида́ет меня́. ♦ **The vision of your lush, beautiful body fills my thoughts night and day.** Вид твоего́ роско́шного, прекра́сного те́ла заполня́ет мои́ мы́сли и днём и но́чью. ♦ **All I can think of, day and night, is your tantalizing body.** Всё, о чём я могу́ ду́мать день и ночь, э́то твоё маня́щее те́ло.

body: when I think about your body

My blood becomes roaring fire whenever I even think about your soft, warm, beautiful body. Моя́ кровь превраща́ется в бушу́ющий ого́нь вся́кий раз, когда́ я ду́маю о твоём мя́гком, тёплом, прекра́сном те́ле. ♦ **Whenever I think about you,** *(1)* **...my body trembles in anticipation. /** *(2)* **...physical desire flares up in me like a bright flame.** Когда́ бы я ни поду́мал *(ж: поду́мала)* о тебе́, *(1)* ...моё те́ло трепе́щет в предвку-

---

Counting things in Russian is a bit involved.
See Appendix 4, "Numbers," on page 756 .

шéнии. / *(2)* ...физи́ческая страсть вспы́хивает во мне, как я́ркое пла́мя. ♦ **Whenever I even think of your beautiful, *(1)* delectable / *(2)* luscious body, I am *(3)* filled / *(4)* seized with raging lust.** Когда́ бы я ни поду́мал о твоём прекра́сном, *(1)* преле́стном / *(2)* со́чном те́ле, меня́ *(3)* наполня́ет / *(4)* охва́тывает бе́шеная страсть.

> **body:** *I want your body*

My arms are (so) lonely for your soft warm body. Мои́ ру́ки (так) одино́ки без твоего́ мя́гкого тёплого те́ла. **I long for the day when I can *(1)* ...uncover all the secrets of your gorgeous body. / *(2)* ...luxuriate (again) in the warm, sweet splendor of your beautiful body.** Я тоску́ю по дню, когда́ смогу́ *(1)* ...пости́чь все та́йны твоего́ великоле́пного те́ла. / *(2)* ...наслажда́ться (опя́ть) тёплым, сла́достным великоле́пием твоего́ прекра́сного те́ла. ♦ **I spend these long, lonely nights yearning and burning for the warm, wonderful, heavenly magic of your beautiful body.** Я провожу́ э́ти до́лгие, одино́кие но́чи, сгора́я и тоску́я по тёплой, удиви́тельной, ра́йской ма́гии твоего́ прекра́сного те́ла. ♦ **It would be absolute heaven to lie next to you, hold you tenderly in my arms, look into your beautiful, dark eyes, kiss you ever so lovingly and adoringly, and feel the magic warmth of your body all through the night.** Бы́ло бы соверше́нно боже́ственно лежа́ть ря́дом с тобо́й, держа́ть тебя́ не́жно в свои́х рука́х, смотре́ть в твои́ прекра́сные тёмные глаза́, целова́ть тебя́ с любо́вью и обожа́нием и чу́вствовать волше́бное тепло́ твоего́ те́ла всю ночь. ♦ **I'm constantly assailed by this primeval lusting for your incredibly beautiful body.** Меня́ постоя́нно охва́тывает первобы́тное вожделе́ние к твоему́ невероя́тно прекра́сному те́лу.

> **body:** *my body aches for you*

My body aches to feel the fire that rages in the core of your womanhood. Моё тело жа́ждет почу́вствовать ого́нь, кото́рый бушу́ет в глубине́ твоей же́нственности. ♦ **There is no moment in the day when I don't long for your hands on my body.** В тече́ние дня нет и мину́ты, когда́ бы я не тоскова́л *(ж: тосковáла)* по твои́м рука́м, ласка́ющим меня́. ♦ **My whole body burns with longing for *(1)* ...you. / *(2)* ...your soft, warm beauty.** Всё моё те́ло гори́т от тоски́ по *(1)* ...тебе́. / *(2)* ...твое́й мя́гкой, тёплой красоте́. ♦ **My pulse just rockets when I look at your beautiful face and beautiful body.** Мой пульс то́тчас учаща́ется, как то́лько я взгля́ну на твоё прекра́сное лицо́ и те́ло. ♦ **Fire *(1)* licks / *(2)* sweeps / *(3)* pours / *(4)* rages through my veins whenever I think of your soft, warm, beautiful, luscious body and the oceans of ecstasy that it contains.** Ого́нь ...*(1)* ли́жет / *(2)* охва́тывает мои́ ве́ны... / ...*(3)* льётся / *(4)* бушу́ет в мои́х ве́нах... вся́кий раз, когда́ я ду́маю о твоём мя́гком, тёплом, прекра́сном, со́чном те́ле и океа́нах экста́за, кото́рые оно́ соде́ржит. ♦ **I want you with every fiber of my body.** Я хочу́ тебя́ все́ми фи́брами своего́ те́ла. ♦ **My body is clamoring for yours.** Моё те́ло взыва́ет твоё.

> **body:** *I need your body*

I need your beautiful body. Мне ну́жно твоё прекра́сное те́ло. ♦ **I'm *(1)* absolutely / *(2)* completely / *(3)* totally / *(4)* hopelessly addicted to your beautiful body.** Я *(1)* соверше́нно / *(2,3)* по́лностью / *(4)* безнаде́жно во вла́сти твоего́ прекра́сного те́ла. ♦ **I know that I can never overcome my addiction to your body.** Я зна́ю, что никогда́ не смогу́ освободи́ться от вла́сти твоего́ те́ла. ♦ **Only the sweet, soft magic of your beautiful body in my arms can assuage the desperate hunger that consumes me.** То́лько не́жное, мя́гкое волшебство́ твоего́ прекра́сного те́ла в мои́х объя́тиях мо́жет утоли́ть отча́янный го́лод, кото́рый пожира́ет меня́.

> **body:** *what I want to do with your body*

I want to revel in the sweetness of your *(1)* beautiful / *(2)* luscious body. Я хочу́ упи-

> *Russian has 2 different verbs for "go",*
> *one for "on foot" and the other for "by vehicle".*

ваться сладостью твоего *(1)* прекрасного / *(2)* сочного тела. ♦ *(1)* **I want to...** / *(2)* **I'm going to... adore every part of your** *(3)* **beautiful** / *(4)* **delectable** / *(5)* **luscious body with my lips.** *(1)* Я хочу... / *(2)* Я буду... обожать губами каждую частицу твоего *(3)* прекрасного / *(4)* лакомого / *(5)* сочного тела. ♦ *(1)* **I want to...** / *(2)* **I'm going to... pay homage to every inch of your beautiful body with my lips.** Своими губами я *(1)* ...хочу воздать... / *(2)* ...воздам... должное каждому дюйму твоего прекрасного тела.
♦ **My greatest aspiration in life is to fill your body with** *(1)* **indescribable** / *(2)* **infinite** *(3)* **pleasure** / *(4)* **ecstasy.** Стремление всей моей жизни -- наполнить твоё тело *(1)* неописуемым / *(2)* бесконечным *(3)* наслаждением / *(4)* экстазом. ♦ **My most cherised wish is to partake of the myriad** *(1,2)* **delights promised by that beautiful body of yours.** Моё самое заветное желание -- испытать мириады *(1)* восторгов / *(2)* наслаждений, обещаемых твоим прекрасным телом. ♦ **I want to feast my eyes on your beautiful nude body -- and then my lips.** Я хочу сначала пожирать твоё прекрасное обнажённое тело глазами, а потом губами. ♦ **I** *(1)* **yearn** / *(2)* **long so** *(3)* **mightily** / *(4)* **much to explore all the** *(5)* **luscious** / *(6)* **delicious secrets of your body.** Я так *(3,4)* сильно *(1)* жажду / *(2)* стремлюсь исследовать все *(5)* сочные / *(6)* восхитительные секреты твоего тела. ♦ **There is never a moment in the day when I don't long to caress your body with my hands (and lips).** В течение дня нет и минуты, когда бы мои руки (и губы) не жаждали ласкать твоё тело. ♦ **I want to** *(1,2)* **fill your body with** *(3)* **...indescribable pleasure.** / *(4)* **...so much pleasure that you will be** *(5)* **hurled** / *(6)* **flung** / *(7)* **rocketed into a cosmos of exploding ecstasy.** Я хочу *(1)* заполнить / *(2)* наполнить твоё тело *(3)* ...неописуемым наслаждением. / *(4)* ...таким огромным наслаждением, чтобы ты была *(5,6)* брошена / *(7)* запущена в космос взрывающегося экстаза. ♦ **I want to lose myself forever in the warmth of your body.** Я хочу навсегда погрузиться в теплоту твоего тела. ♦ **I want to give you a soft mini-nibble massage all over your body.** Я хочу массажировать всё твоё тело нежными крошечными поцелуями. ♦ **I want to tune your body with my mouth and hands until it sings.** Я хочу настраивать твоё тело ртом и руками до тех пор, пока оно не запоёт. ♦ **I want you to feel with your whole body how much I love you and in so doing make you love me with all your heart.** Я хочу, чтобы всем своим телом ты ощутила, как сильно я люблю тебя, и это принесёт тебе такую же любовь ко мне. ♦ **I want to become intimately familiar with the sensual topography of your (beautiful) body.** Я хочу близко познакомиться с чувственной топографией твоего (прекрасного) тела. ♦ **How I long to immerse myself in the soft, lingering fragrance of your body.** Как я жажду погрузиться в нежный аромат твоего тела. ♦ **I'd love to paint your body (with body paints). Will you let me?** Мне бы хотелось разрисовать твоё тело (красками для тела). Ты позволишь? ♦ **I want to see your body arch in rampant desire.** Я хочу видеть твоё тело, изгибающимся в безудержной страсти.

---

body: *what I'm going to do with your body*

First, I'll run my hands lightly over your body, and then my lips. Сначала мои руки мягко пробегут по твоему телу, а затем и губы. ♦ **I'll rub soap all over your body.** Я намылю всё твоё тело. ♦ **My (eager) lips will** *(1)* **...explore every** *(2)* **millimeter** / *(3)* **inch of your** *(4)* **beautiful** / *(5)* **delectable** / *(6)* **luscious body.** / *(7)* **...suffuse your body with exquisite pleasure.** / *(8)* **...make your body sing.** Мои нетерпеливые губы *(1)* ...исследуют каждый *(2)* миллиметр / *(3)* дюйм твоего *(4)* прекрасного / *(5)* лакомого / *(6)* сочного тела. / *(7)* ...затопят твоё тело изысканным наслаждением. / *(8)* ...заставят твоё тело петь. ♦ **I'm going to cover your beautiful body with (tender, loving) kisses.** Я покрою твоё прекрасное тело (нежными, любящими) поцелуями. ♦ **With my lips**

> *Dipthongs in Russian are made by adding* й
> *to the end of a vowel (*а, е, ё, о, у, э, ю, *and* я*)*

I'm going to make tingling sensations ripple all through your body. Мои́ гу́бы вы́зовут во́лны тре́пета, бегу́щие по всему́ твоему́ те́лу. ♦ **When my lips and tongue revel on your beautiful, luscious body, they will hear your** *(1)* **moans /** *(2)* **screams of** *(3)* **pleasure /** *(4)* **ecstasy in South Africa.** Когда́ мои́ гу́бы и язы́к бу́дут упива́ться твои́м прекра́сным, со́чным те́лом, твои́ *(1)* сто́ны / *(2)* кри́ки *(3)* наслажде́ния / *(4)* экста́за бу́дут слышны́ в Ю́жной Áфрике. ♦ **I'm going to make hot tingles run all through your body.** Я заста́влю горя́чую дрожь пробега́ть по всему́ твоему́ те́лу. ♦ **I'll make raging desire travel to every nerve ending of your body.** Я заста́влю бе́шеную страсть путеше́ствовать в ка́ждом не́рвном оконча́нии твоего́ те́ла. ♦ **I'm going to make waves of exquisite pleasure surge through your body.** Я вы́зову во́лны изы́сканного наслажде́ния, захлёстывающие твоё те́ло. ♦ **If I were there next to you, you'd have to use a crowbar to pry my lips off of your beautiful body.** Éсли бы я был там ря́дом с тобо́й, тебе́ пришло́сь бы испо́льзовать лом, что́бы оторва́ть мои́ гу́бы от своего́ прекра́сного те́ла. ♦ **I'm going to slowly kiss every inch of your body into paradise.** Я бу́ду ме́дленно целова́ть ка́ждый дюйм твоего́ те́ла до тех пор, пока́ ты не дости́гнешь вы́сшего блаже́нства. ♦ **My fingers and lips will spread warm** *(1)* **rings /** *(2)* **waves of joy throughout your beautiful, voluptuous body.** Мои́ па́льцы и гу́бы распространя́т тёплые *(1)* ко́льца / *(2)* во́лны наслажде́ния в твоём прекра́сном, роско́шном те́ле. ♦ **My fingers will stroll languidly, softly, adoringly along the svelte curve of your body.** Мои́ па́льцы ме́дленно, мя́гко, обожа́юще прогуля́ются по стро́йным окру́глостям твоего́ те́ла. ♦ **Your body is going to learn a new definition of the word** *(1)* **ecstasy /** *(2)* **love /** *(3)* **pleasure.** Твоё те́ло узна́ет но́вое определе́ние сло́ва *(1)* экста́з / *(2)* любо́вь / *(3)* наслажде́ние.

> **body:** *what you do to my body*

Such flames you kindle in my body! Како́е пла́мя ты зажига́ешь в моём те́ле! ♦ **You make my body come alive like** *(1)* **...never before. /** *(2)* **...no one has ever done.** С тобо́й моё те́ло ожива́ет так, как *(1)* ...никогда́ пре́жде. / *(2)* ...ни с кем пре́жде. ♦ **You send electric sensations shooting through** *(1)* **...my entire body. /** *(2)* **...every cell and fiber of my body.** Ты посыла́ешь электри́ческие заря́ды, простре́ливающие *(1)* ...всё моё те́ло. / *(2)* ...ка́ждую кле́тку и все фи́бры моего́ те́ла. ♦ **The sight of your beautiful face fills my whole body with warm excitement and floods my heart with feelings of love for you.** Взгляд на твоё прекра́сное лицо́ наполня́ет всё моё те́ло жа́рким возбужде́нием и затопля́ет се́рдце чу́вством любви́ к тебе́. ♦ **Molten waves of desire sweep through** *(1)* **...my entire body... /** *(2)* **...every fiber and cell of my body... whenever I think of your exquisite, luscious beauty.** Бушу́ющие во́лны стра́сти проно́сятся че́рез *(1)* ...всё моё те́ло... / *(2)* ...все фи́бры и кле́тки моего́ те́ла,... когда́ бы я ни поду́мал о твое́й изы́сканной, со́чной красоте́. ♦ **Liquid fire swirls through every fiber of my body.** Жи́дкий ого́нь проно́сится ви́хрем че́рез все фи́бры моего́ те́ла. ♦ **You own my mind, my heart, my body.** Ты владе́ешь мои́м умо́м, мои́м се́рдцем и мои́м те́лом.

> **body:** *what your body does to me*

Your beautiful, *(1)* **diminutive /** *(2)* **petite body really excites me.** Твоё прекра́сное, *(1)* ма́ленькое / *(2)* миниатю́рное те́ло так возбужда́ет меня́. ♦ **The soft, warm magic of your body transports me to a cosmic kaleidoscope of ecstasy.** Мя́гкая, тёплая ма́гия твоего́ те́ла перено́сит меня́ в косми́ческий калейдоско́п экста́за. ♦ **The magic of your beautiful, sensuous body has enslaved my soul.** Волшебство́ твоего́ прекра́сного, чу́вственного те́ла покори́ло мою́ ду́шу. ♦ **The silky sheen of your body invites my lips.** Шелкови́стый гля́нец твоего́ те́ла приглаша́ет мои́ гу́бы.

Some phrases are listed under more than one main word.

---

body: *our bodies together*

Our bodies will *(1)* **fuse /** *(2)* **merge together into a single being.** На́ши тела́ *(1)* солью́тся / *(2)* соединя́тся в одно́ це́лое. ♦ **Our bodies will fuse together in exquisite pleasure until we are** *(1)* **flung /** *(2)* **hurled into a wild sea of passion.** На́ши тела́ солью́тся в изы́сканном наслажде́нии до тех пор, пока́ мы не бу́дем *(1,2)* бро́шены в бе́шеное мо́ре стра́сти. ♦ **Our bodies are so** *(1)* **perfectly /** *(2)* **wonderfully orchestrated when we make love.** На́ши тела́ так *(1)* соверше́нно / *(2)* замеча́тельно настро́ены в унисо́н, когда́ мы занима́емся любо́вью. ♦ **Through the total orchestration of our bodies you and I together will produce the most beautiful symphony of love anyone has ever known.** Благодаря́ абсолю́тной сы́гранности на́ших тел, ты и я вме́сте создади́м таку́ю прекра́сную симфо́нию любви́, кото́рую никто́ никогда́ не знал.

body: *can't trust my own body*

When I'm around you, I can' t trust my own weak-willed body. Когда́ я ря́дом с тобо́й, я не могу́ доверя́ть своему́ со́бственному сла́бому те́лу.

bodyrub *n* масса́ж те́ла ♦ **sensual** ~ чу́вственный масса́ж те́ла.

bodysuit *n* обтя́гивающий комбинезо́н; *(aerobics)* спорти́вное трико́, костю́м для аэро́бики.

boggle *vt* поража́ть / порази́ть *(what = acc.)* ♦ **Your beauty and sexiness just boggle my mind.** Твоя́ красота́ и сексуа́льность про́сто поража́ют меня́.

Bohemian *adj* боге́мный, -ая, -ое, -ые ♦ **I don't care for a Bohemian lifestyle.** Мне не нра́вится боге́мный о́браз жи́зни.

bold *adj* 1. *(brave)* сме́лый, -ая, -ое, -ые, хра́брый, -ая, -ое, -ые; 2. *(audacious, brazen)* де́рзкий, -ая, -ое, -ие ♦ **Forgive me for being so bold.** Прости́ меня́ за то, что был таки́м де́рзким *(ж: была́ тако́й де́рзкой)*. ♦ **I hope I'm not being too bold.** Наде́юсь, я не́ был сли́шком де́рзким *(ж: не была́ сли́шком де́рзкой)*. ♦ **You're** *(1)* **quite /** *(2)* **very bold.** Ты *(1)* немно́го / *(2)* о́чень де́рзкая *(ж: де́рзкий)*.

boldly *adv* 1. *(bravely)* сме́ло, хра́бро; 2. *(audaciously, brazenly)* де́рзко.

bolt *vi (run off)* сбежа́ть, удра́ть.

bolt *n (lightning)* мо́лния, уда́р мо́лнии ♦ **The other** *(1)* **evening /** *(2)* **day /** *(3)* **night with you... /** *(4)* **Last night with you... /** *(5)* **Our time /** *(6)* **day /** *(7)* **evening /** *(8)* **night /** *(9)* **weekend together... was a lightning bolt of** *(10)* **happiness /** *(11)* **joy /** *(12)* **ecstasy.** *(1)* Тот ве́чер / *(2)* день с тобо́й был... / *(3)* Та / *(4)* Про́шлая ночь с тобо́й была́... / *(5)* На́ше вре́мя вме́сте бы́ло... / *(6)* Наш день / *(7)* ве́чер вме́сте был... / *(8)* На́ша ночь вме́сте была́... / *(9)* На́ши выходны́е вме́сте бы́ли... как мо́лния *(10)* сча́стья / *(11)* ра́дости / *(12)* экста́за.

bombshell *n (slang) (gorgeous woman)* сногшиба́тельная же́нщина ♦ **blonde** ~ сногшиба́тельная блонди́нка ♦ **Russian** ~ сногшиба́тельная ру́сская.

bond *vi* подходи́ть друг к дру́гу ♦ **We bond so well intellectually.** Мы интеллектуа́льно так хорошо́ подхо́дим друг к дру́гу.

bond *n* связь *f*; *pl* у́зы ♦ ~**s of friendship** у́зы дру́жбы ♦ ~**s of marriage** у́зы бра́ка ♦ ~**s of wedlock** у́зы бра́ка ♦ **emotional** ~ эмоциона́льная связь ♦ **inescapable** ~ неизбе́жная связь ♦ **love** ~**s** любо́вные у́зы ♦ **marital** ~**s** супру́жеские у́зы ♦ **spiritual** ~ духо́вная связь ♦ **This is a symbol of a bond between our souls.** Это си́мвол свя́зи на́ших душ. ♦ **Nothing will ever** *(1)* **break /** *(2)* **weaken this bond between us.** Ничто́ не *(1)* разорвёт / *(2)* осла́бит э́тих уз ме́жду на́ми.

bonding *n* у́зы, связь *f*.

bonehead *n* дубо́вая голова́, болва́н.

bon vivant *n* бонвива́н.

The singular past tense of Russian verbs ends in -л (m) (usually),
-ла (f) or -ло (n). the plural past tense ends in -li.

boobs *(also* **boobies)** *n, pl (slang) (breasts)* грудь *f.*

book *vt (reserve)* заказывать / заказа́ть *(what = acc.)*, брони́ровать / заброни́ровать *(what = acc.)* ♦ ~ **a room** зака́зывать / заказа́ть ко́мнату, брони́ровать / заброни́ровать ко́мнату ♦ ~ **a flight** брони́ровать / заброни́ровать биле́т на самолёт.

bookish *adj* кни́жный, -ая, -ое, -ые.

bookworm *n* книголю́б.

boost *vt* поднима́ть / подня́ть *(what = acc.)* ♦ **You've done so much to boost my self-esteem.** Ты так мно́го сде́лала *(ж: сде́лал)* для того́, что́бы подня́ть моё самоуваже́ние.

boost *n* подъём ♦ **emotional** ~ эмоциона́льный подъём.

boot *n* сапо́г; *(lady's)* бо́тик ♦ **high-heeled** ~**s** боти́нки на высо́ких каблука́х ♦ **pair of** ~**s** па́ра сапо́г; *(lady's)* па́ра бо́тиков.

bore *vt* надоеда́ть / надое́сть *(whom = dat.)*, наску́чить *pfv (whom = dat.)* ♦ **I don't want to bore you (with all the details).** Я не хочу́ надоеда́ть тебе́ (вся́кими подро́бностями). ♦ **I'm sorry, I must be boring you.** Прости́, я, должно́ быть, надоеда́ю тебе́. ♦ **I hope** *(1)* **...I'm not boring...** / *(2)* **...I don't bore...** / *(3)* **...I didn't bore... you.** Я наде́юсь, я не *(1,2)* надоеда́ю / *(3)* надое́л *(ж: надое́ла)* тебе́. ♦ **I hope my letter** *(1)* **...doesn't bore...** / *(2)* **...didn't bore... you.** Я наде́юсь, моё письмо́ не *(1)* ску́чное / *(2)* наску́чило тебе́. ♦ *(1,2)* **You never bore me.** *(1)* Ты никогда́ не надое́шь мне. / *(2)* Мне никогда́ не ску́чно с тобо́й.

bore *n* 1. *(boredom)* ску́ка; 2. *(boring person)* ску́чный челове́к, зану́да *both m & f* ♦ **It is such a (terrible) bore.** Это так (ужа́сно) ску́чно. ♦ *(1,2)* **She is such a (terrible) bore.** *(1)* Она́ так (ужа́сно) скучна́. / *(2)* Она́ така́я (ужа́сная) зану́да. ♦ *(1,2)* **He is such a (terrible) bore.** *(1)* Он так (ужа́сно) ску́чен. / *(2)* Он тако́й (ужа́сный) зану́да. ♦ **Forgive me for being such a bore.** Прости́ меня́ за то, что я был таки́м *(ж: была́ тако́й)* зану́дой. ♦ **I hope I'm not a bore.** Наде́юсь, ты не счита́ешь меня́ зану́дой.

bored *adj* ску́чен, скучна́, -ы́ *(short forms)*, ску́чно *(person bored = dat.)* ♦ be ~ скуча́ть, быть ску́чным *(person bored = dat.)* ♦ **Are you bored?** Тебе́ ску́чно? ♦ **I'm (not) bored.** Мне (не) ску́чно. ♦ **Are you bored (with this)?** Тебе́ наску́чило (э́то)? ♦ **I'm (really) bored with this.** Мне (действи́тельно) наску́чило э́то. ♦ **I'm (really) bored without you here.** Я (действи́тельно) скуча́л *(ж: скуча́ла)* без тебя́. ♦ **It's impossible to be bored around you.** Невозмо́жно скуча́ть ря́дом с тобо́й. ♦ **You look bored.** Ты вы́глядишь скуча́ющей *(ж: скуча́ющим)*. ♦ **I was so bored until** *(1)* **...I met you.** / *(2)* **...you came into my life.** Мне бы́ло так ску́чно, пока́ *(1)* ...я не встре́тил *(ж: встре́тила)* тебя́. / *(2)* ...ты не вошла́ *(ж: вошёл)* в мою́ жизнь. ♦ **I get (**[1] **so /** [2] **very /** [3] **really /** [4] **terribly /** [5] **dreadfully) bored when you're not here.** Я (*[1]* так / *[2]* о́чень / *[3]* пра́вда / *[4]* ужа́сно / *[5]* стра́шно) скуча́ю, когда́ тебя́ нет ря́дом.

boring *adj* ску́чный, -ая, -ое, -ые *(short forms:* ску́чен, скучна́, -ы́*)*, ску́чно ♦ *(1)* **This** / *(2)* **It is...** / *(3)* **That** / *(4)* **It was...** (*[5]* **kind of /** *[6]* **rather /** *[7]* **so /** *[8]* **very /** *[9]* **really /** *[10]* **terribly /** *[11]* **dreadfully) boring.** *(1,2)* Это... / *(3,4* Это бы́ло... (*[5]* немно́го / *[6]* доста́точно / *[7]* так / *[8]* о́чень / *[9]* пра́вда / *[10]* ужа́сно / *[11]* стра́шно) ску́чно. ♦ *(1)* **Everything** / *(2)* **Life is so boring without you (here).** *(1)* Всё так ску́чно,... / *(2)* Жизнь так скучна́,... е́сли тебя́ нет (ря́дом). ♦ *(1)* **Everything** / *(2)* **Life seemed so boring until I met you.** *(1)* Всё каза́лось таки́м ску́чным,... / *(2)* Жизнь каза́лась тако́й ску́чной,... пока́ я не встре́тил *(ж: встре́тила)* тебя́.

born *adj* роди́вшийся, -аяся, -еася, -иеся, рождён, рождена́, -о́, -ы́ *(short forms)* ♦ be ~ роди́ться ♦ **foreign** ~ роди́вшийся (-аяся, -иеся) за грани́цей; *(foreigner)* иностра́нец *m*, иностра́нка *f* ♦ **I wasn't born yesterday.** Я не вчера́ роди́лся *(ж: роди-*

Please do us a favor:
Fill out and mail in the Feedback Sheet on page 795.

лáсь). ♦ **I was born to be yours.** Я был рождён быть твои́м *(ж: Я была́ рождена́ быть твоéй).*

bosom *n* грудь *f* ♦ **beautiful** ~ прекра́сная грудь ♦ **big** ~ больша́я грудь ♦ **braless** ~ грудь без бюстга́льтера ♦ **creamy white** ~ крéмово-бéлая грудь ♦ **full** ~ пóлная грудь ♦ *(1,2)* **gorgeous** ~ *(1)* великолéпная / *(2)* пы́шная грудь ♦ **handsome** ~ краси́вая грудь ♦ **large** ~ больша́я грудь ♦ *(1,2)* **magnificent** ~ *(1)* великолéпная / *(2)* пы́шная грудь ♦ **snow-white** ~ белоснéжная грудь ♦ *(1,2)* **splendid** ~ *(1)* великолéпная / *(2)* пы́шная грудь ♦ **well-formed** ~ хорóшей фóрмы грудь.

bosomy *adj (1-3)* с *(1)* большóй / *(2)* пы́шной грýдью, *(3)* груда́стая ♦ **I (really) like** *(1,2)* **bosomy women.** Мне (действи́тельно) нра́вятся жéнщины с *(1)* большóй / *(2)* пы́шной грýдью. ♦ **I like it that you're bosomy.** Мне нра́вится, что у тебя́ больша́я грудь. ♦ **How wonderfully bosomy you are!** Кака́я у тебя́ замеча́тельно пы́шная грудь!

bossy *adj* распоряжа́ющийся (-яяся, -ееся, -иеся) всем, вла́стный, -ая, -ое, -ые ♦ **be** ~ люби́ть распоряжа́ться.

bother *vt* 1. *(disturb)* меша́ть / помеша́ть *(whom = dat.);* 2. *(worry)* беспокóить / обеспокóить *(whom = acc.)* ♦ **I don't want you to bother me (anymore).** Я не хочý, чтóбы ты когда́-либо опя́ть беспокóила *(ж: беспокóил)* меня́. ♦ **I don't want to bother you.** Я не хочý меша́ть тебé. ♦ **I hope I'm not bothering you.** Надéюсь, что я не меша́ю тебé. ♦ **You're bothering me.** Ты мне меша́ешь. ♦ **Please don't bother me (anymore).** Пожа́луйста, (бóльше никогда́) не беспокóй меня́. ♦ **It doesn't bother me (at all).** Это (совсéм) не меша́ет мне. ♦ **You don't bother me (at all).** Ты (совсéм) не меша́ешь мне. ♦ **Tell me what's bothering you.** Расскажи́ мне, что волнýет тебя́. ♦ **bottled up** сдéржанный, -ая, -ое, -ые, скры́тый, -ая, -ое, -ые, зажа́тый, -ая, -ое, -ые ♦ *(1)* **Don't keep... /** *(2)* **You always keep... /** *(3)* **You shouldn't keep... your feelings** *(4,5)* **bottled up inside you.** *(1)* Не держи́... / *(2)* Ты всегда́ дéржишь... / *(3)* Ты не должна́ *(ж: дóлжен)* держа́ть... свои́ чýвства, *(4)* зажа́тыми / *(5)* скры́тыми в себé.

bottom *n* 1. *(lowest point)* дно; 2. *(buttocks)* зад, пóпа, пóпка ♦ **full** ~ пóлная пóпа ♦ **gorgeous** ~ прекра́сный зад, прекра́сная пóпа ♦ **rounded** ~ окрýглый зад, окрýглая пóпа ♦ **shapely** ~ зад хорóшей фóрмы ♦ **You've got a really nice bottom.** У тебя́ действи́тельно краси́вая пóпка.

boudoir *n* будуа́р.

bounce around *idiom (slang) (go from place to place)* посеща́ть ра́зные места́ ♦ ~ **town** посеща́ть ра́зные места́ в гóроде.

bound: *(1)* **He /** *(2)* **She is bound to find out (sooner or later).** (Ра́ньше и́ли пóзже) *(1)* Он / *(2)* Она́ обяза́тельно узна́ет.

boundary *n* грани́ца ♦ **We've overstepped the boundary of no return.** Мы переступи́ли грани́цу невозврати́мо. ♦ **My love for you knows no boundaries.** Моя́ любóвь к тебé не зна́ет никаки́х грани́ц.

boundless *adj* безграни́чный, -ая, -ое, -ые, беспредéльный, -ая, -ое, -ые, безбрéжный, ая, -ое, -ые ♦ **Never have I felt such boundless passion for anyone.** Никогда́ я не чýвствовал *(ж: чýвствовала)* такóй беспредéльной стра́сти к комý-либо. ♦ *(1)* **I have... /** *(2)* **There is... such boundless affection in my heart for you.** *(1,2)* В моём сéрдце безграни́чная нéжность к тебé.

boundlessly *adv* безграни́чно, беспредéльно.

bounds *n, pl* грани́ца, предéлы ♦ **You've overstepped the bounds of propriety.** Ты переступи́ла *(ж: переступи́л)* грани́цу присто́йности.

bountiful *adj* щéдрый, -ая, -ое, -ые, оби́льный, -ая, -ое, -ые.

bouquet *n* букéт ♦ **bridal** ~ букéт для невéсты ♦ ~ **of roses** букéт роз.

Clock and calender time are discussed in Appendix 5, page 759.

bourgeois *adj* буржуа́зный, -ая, -ое, -ые.

bow *n (ribbon)* бант ♦ **small** ~ ба́нтик.

bow-legged *adj* кривоно́гий, -ая, -ое, -ие.

bowling *n* игра́ в ке́гли, игра́ в шары́ ♦ **Would you like to go bowling (with me)?** Не хоте́ла *(ж: хоте́л)* бы ты поигра́ть в ке́гли (со мной)? ♦ **Let's go bowling (together).** Дава́й (вме́сте) пойдём игра́ть в ке́гли.

boy *n* 1. *(child)* ма́льчик; 2. *(guy)* па́рень, молодо́й челове́к ♦ **country** ~ дереве́нский па́рень ♦ **indi(e)** ~ *(slang) (independent boy)* незави́симый молодо́й челове́к ♦ **transition** ~ *(boy between relationships)* молодо́й челове́к, то́лько что поко́нчивший с отноше́ниями *(explanation)* ♦ **ultimate** ~ превосхо́дный молодо́й челове́к.

boyfriend *n* друг, возлю́бленный, «па́рень» ♦ **ex-** ~ бы́вший возлю́бленный ♦ **former** ~ бы́вший возлю́бленный ♦ **last** ~ про́шлый возлю́бленный ♦ **no current** ~ нет постоя́нного дру́га, нет возлю́бленного ♦ **previous** ~ предыду́щий возлю́бленный ♦ **upscale** ~ друг вы́ше сре́днего у́ровня ♦ **Do you have a boyfriend?** У тебя́ есть возлю́бленный? ♦ **I don't have a boyfriend.** У меня́ нет возлю́бленного.

boyish *adj* мальчи́шеский, -ая, -ое, -ие; ю́ношеский, -ая, -ое, -ие.

boyishly *adv* мальчи́шески.

bra *n* бюстга́льтер, ли́фчик ♦ **edible** ~ съедо́бный бюстга́льтер ♦ **fishnet** ~ бюстга́льтер из се́тчатого материа́ла ♦ **flimsy (lace)** ~ лёгкий (кружево́й) бюстга́льтер ♦ **lacy** ~ кружево́й бюстга́льтер ♦ **leather** ~ ко́жаный бюстга́льтер ♦ **peek-a-boo** ~ бюстга́льтер с отве́рстиями (у соско́в) ♦ **push-up** ~ бюстга́льтер, поднима́ющий грудь *(1 term)* ♦ **shelf** ~ ни́зко вы́резанный бюстга́льтер ♦ **skimpy** ~ ма́ленький бюстга́льтер ♦ **closure of a** ~ застёжка бюстга́льтера ♦ **fastener of a** ~ застёжка бюстга́льтера ♦ **hook of a** ~ крючо́к бюстга́льтера ♦ **I** *(1)* **like /** *(2)* **love it when you don't wear a bra.** *(1)* Мне нра́вится, ... / *(2)* Я люблю́,... когда́ ты не но́сишь бюстга́льтер. ♦ **You look** *(1)* **fabulous /** *(2)* **fantastic without a bra.** Ты вы́глядишь *(1)* потряса́юще / *(2)* фантасти́чески без бюстга́льтера.

brag *vi* хва́статься ♦ **I don't mean to brag.** Я не хочу́ хва́статься. ♦ **I can't stand someone who brags all the time.** Я не терплю́ того́, кто всё вре́мя хва́стается.

braggart *n* хвасту́н.

braid *n* коса́ *(pl: ко́сы)* ♦ **hair in** ~s во́лосы, заплетённые в ко́сы *(1 term)* ♦ **long** ~s дли́нные ко́сы.

brain *n* 1. *(organ)* мозг; 2. *(mind, intellect)* рассу́док, ра́зум; ум, интелле́кт; *pl (slang) (intelligence)* мо́зги ♦ **keen** ~ о́стрый ум ♦ **sharp** ~ о́стрый ум ♦ **I like a** *(1)* **man /** *(2)* **woman with brains.** Мне нра́вится *(1)* мужчи́на / *(2)* же́нщина с мозга́ми.

brainwaves *n, pl* мозговы́е во́лны ♦ **I've been thinking about you a lot (lately). Have you received my brainwaves?** Я мно́го ду́маю о тебе́ (после́днее вре́мя). Получи́ла ли ты мои́ мозговы́е во́лны? ♦ **I've been sending you brainwaves all** *(1)* **day /** *(2)* **week long. Surely you've gotten some of them. And if you have, then you know how** *(3)* **tenderly /** *(4)* **warmly I've been thinking about you.** Я *(1)* ...весь день... / *(2)* ...всю неде́лю... посыла́ю тебе́ мозговы́е во́лны. Несомне́нно, ты получи́ла *(ж: получи́л)* не́которые из них. И е́сли ты получи́ла *(ж: получи́л)*, тогда́ ты зна́ешь, как *(3)* не́жно / *(4)* тепло́ я ду́маю о тебе́. ♦ **If you can unscramble my brainwaves, you'll know that I miss you (a lot).** Если ты смо́жешь расшифрова́ть мои́ мозговы́е во́лны, ты узна́ешь, что я (о́чень) скуча́ю по тебе́.

brainy *adj (slang)* у́мный, -ая, -ое, -ые, мозгови́тый, -ая, -ое, -ые.

brake *n* то́рмоз *(pl: тормоза́)* ♦ **I think its time to apply the brakes (to this relationship).** Я ду́маю, что сейча́с пора́ прекрати́ть (э́ти отноше́ния).

Reflexive verbs are those that end in -ся or -сь.
The -ся or -сь also goes onto a past tense ending.

brash *adj* 1. *(impetuous)* поры́вистый, -ая, -ое, -ые, стреми́тельный, -ая, -ое, -ые; 2. *(impudent)* наха́льный, -ая, -ое, -ые, де́рзкий, -ая, -ое, -ие.

brashness *n (impetuousness)* поры́вистость *f*, стреми́тельность *f.*

brassiere *n* бюстга́льтер *(See also entries under* **bra)** ♦ **I envy your brassiere. It gets to hold your beautiful breasts all day. I wish I could do the same.** Я зави́дую твоему́ бюстга́льтеру. Он подде́рживает твою́ прекра́сную грудь це́лый день. Я жела́л бы де́лать то же са́мое.

brat *n* отро́дье ♦ **You're a spoiled brat.** Ты изба́лованное отро́дье.

bravado *n* брава́да ♦ **false** ~ фальши́вая брава́да.

brawny *adj* мускули́стый, -ая, -ое, -ые.

brazen *adj* бессты́дный, -ая, -ое, -ые; на́глый, -ая, -ое, -ые.

break *vt* разрыва́ть / разорва́ть *(what = acc.)*; лома́ть / слома́ть *(what = acc.)* ♦ **~ off** *vt* порыва́ть / порва́ть *(what = acc.)*.

> **break:**

Nothing will ever break this bond between us. Ничто́ не разорвёт э́тих уз ме́жду на́ми. ♦ **I'm glad you broke the ice.** Я рад *(ж: ра́да)*, что ты слома́ла *(ж: слома́л)* лёд.

> **break off:**

Do you want to break off our *(1)* **engagement /** *(2)* **relationship?** Ты хо́чешь порва́ть *(1)* ...на́шу помо́лвку / *(2)* ...на́ши отноше́ния? ♦ **I (don't) want to break off our** *(1)* **engagement /** *(2)* **relationship.** Я (не) хочу́ порва́ть *(1)* ...на́шу помо́лвку / *(2)* ...на́ши отноше́ния.

break *vi* порва́ть ♦ **~ free** *vi* освобожда́ться / освободи́ться *(from what, whom = +* от *+ gen.)* ♦ **~ up** *vi* порва́ть.

> **break:**

I want to break with the past. Я хочу́ порва́ть с про́шлым.

> **break free:**

I want to break free from *(1)* **her /** *(2)* **him.** Я хочу́ освободи́ться от *(1)* неё / *(2)* него́. ♦ **I finally broke free from her.** Я наконе́ц освободи́лся от неё. ♦ **I finally broke free from him.** Я наконе́ц освободи́лась от него́.

[*break up:*]

Since we broke up, I've been feeling such abject despair. С тех пор, как мы порва́ли, я чу́вствую кра́йнее отча́яние.

breakup *n* прекраще́ние отноше́ний ♦ **I'm going through a breakup (with...).** Я сейча́с в проце́ссе прекраще́ния отноше́ний (с...).

breast *n* грудь *f (singular is mostly used)* ♦ *(1,2)* **lovely** ~s *(1)* прекра́сная / *(2)* краси́вая грудь ♦ **alabaster-like** ~s сло́вно алеба́стровая грудь ♦ *(1,2)* **ample** ~s *(1)* пы́шная / *(2)* больша́я грудь ♦ **bared** ~s обнажённая грудь ♦ *(1,2)* **beautiful** ~s *(1)* прекра́сная / *(2)* краси́вая грудь ♦ **best** ~s наилу́чшая грудь ♦ **big** ~s больша́я грудь ♦ **bountiful** ~s ще́драя грудь ♦ **creamy** ~s кре́мовая грудь ♦ **delectable** ~~s великоле́пная грудь ♦ **exciting** ~s возбужда́ющая грудь ♦ **exposed** ~s обнажённая грудь ♦ **fantastic** ~s фантасти́ческая грудь ♦ *(1,2)* **firm** ~s *(1)* твёрдая / *(2)* упру́гая грудь ♦ **flat** ~s пло́ская грудь ♦ *(1,2)* **full** ~s *(1)* пы́шная / *(2)* по́лная грудь ♦ **girlish** ~s де́вичья грудь ♦ **gorgeous** ~s великоле́пная грудь ♦ **high** ~s высо́кая грудь ♦ **huge** ~s огро́мная грудь ♦ **incredible** ~s невероя́тная грудь ♦ **jutting** ~s торча́щая грудь ♦ **little** ~s ма́ленькая грудь ♦ **magnificent** ~s великоле́пная грудь ♦ **milky white** ~s моло́чно-бе́лая грудь ♦ **pale** ~s бле́дная грудь ♦ **pear-shaped** ~s грушеви́дная грудь ♦ **pendulous** ~s вися́щая грудь ♦ **plump** ~s пы́шная грудь ♦ **sagging** ~s отви́слая грудь ♦ **sensitive** ~s чувстви́тельная грудь ♦ **sexy** ~s сексуа́льная грудь

The time zones for many cities of the world are given in Appendix 6, page 761.

♦ **shapely** ~s грудь хорошей формы ♦ **small** ~s маленькая грудь ♦ **swollen** ~s набухшая грудь ♦ **taut** ~s упругая грудь ♦ **thrusting** ~s торчащая грудь ♦ **well-rounded** ~s хорошо округлая грудь ♦ **yummy** ~s великолепная грудь.

breast: *verb terms*

bury my face into your ~s прятать / спрятать моё лицо в твоей груди ♦ **caress your ~(s)** ласкать твою грудь ♦ **feel your ~(s)** ощутать / ощутить твою грудь ♦ **hold your ~(s)** держать твою грудь ♦ **kiss your ~(s)** целовать твою грудь ♦ **nuzzle my face into your** ~s зарыться лицом в твоей груди ♦ **put my face in your** ~s класть / положить своё лицо на твою грудь ♦ **snuggle my face into your** ~s зарыться лицом в твоей груди, прильнуть моим лицом к твоей груди ♦ **squeeze your ~(s)** сжимать / сжать твою грудь ♦ **stroke your ~(s)** гладить твою грудь ♦ **suck (on) your ~(s)** сосать твою грудь ♦ **your ~s protrude** твоя грудь торчит.

breast: *other terms*

buds of the ~s бутоны сосков ♦ **coral tips of your** ~s коралловые кончики твоих грудей ♦ **creamy flesh of your** ~s кремовая плоть твоей груди ♦ **curve of your** ~s изгибы твоей груди ♦ **feel of your** ~s ощущение твоей груди ♦ **fullness of your** ~s полнота твоей груди ♦ **rich softness of your** ~s роскошная мягкость твоей груди ♦ **rounded globes of your** ~s округлые шары твоих грудей ♦ **soft mound of your ~** мягкий бугорок твоей груди ♦ **soft roundness of your** ~s мягкая округлость твоей груди ♦ **swell of your** ~s выпуклость твоих грудей.

breast: *your lovely breasts*

Such *(1)* lovely / *(2)* gorgeous / *(3)* beautiful / *(4)* big breasts you have. У тебя такая *(1)* красивая / *(2)* великолепная / *(3)* прекрасная / *(4)* большая грудь. ♦ **What *(1)* beautiful / *(2)* incredible / *(3)* fantastic / *(4)* sexy breasts (you have)!** Какая (у тебя) *(1)* прекрасная / *(2)* невероятная / *(3)* фантастическая / *(4)* сексуальная грудь! ♦ **You've got the *(1)* nicest / *(2)* firmest / *(3)* best / *(4)* biggest / *(5)* sexiest / *(6)* most beautiful breasts I've ever *(7)* seen / *(8)* known / *(9)* felt.** У тебя *(1)* ...изящнейшая... / *(2)* ...самая твёрдая... / *(3)* ...наилучшая... / *(4)* ...самая большая... / *(5)* ...сексуальнейшая... / *(6)* ...самая прекрасная... грудь, какую я когда-либо *(7)* видел / *(8)* знал / *(9)* чувствовал. ♦ **Your breasts are such a treat to the eye.** Твоя грудь так радует глаз. ♦ **The provocative curve of your breasts is such a pleasure to behold.** Такое удовольствие созерцать соблазнительные изгибы твоей груди.

breast: *I dream of your breasts*

I dream of *(1)* feeling / *(2)* caressing the soft roundness of your breasts. Я мечтаю *(1)* чувствовать / *(2)* ласкать мягкую округлость твоей груди. ♦ **I dream of lying beside you, my face snuggled into the rich softness of your breasts, lost in a deep cloud of your heavenly scent.** Я мечтаю о том, чтобы лежать рядом с тобой, зарывшись лицом в роскошную мягкость твоей груди, погрузившись в облако твоего божественного аромата.

breast: *I love your breasts*

Oh, (how) I love your (*[1]* beautiful / *[2]* sexy) breasts! О, (как) я люблю твою (*[1]* прекрасную / *[2]* сексуальную) грудь! ♦ **I love the way your breasts protrude (even when you wear a coat).** Мне нравится, как торчит твоя грудь (, даже когда ты одеваешь пальто). ♦ **How I love to feast my eyes on the creamy, full swell of your breasts.** Как я люблю пожирать глазами кремовую, полную выпуклость твоих грудей. ♦ **I love to watch your breasts heave when passion sweeps through you.** Я люблю видеть, как вздымается твоя грудь, когда страсть охватывает тебя. ♦ **I love the feel of your breasts.** Мне нравится ощущение твоей груди. ♦ **I (really) like big**

Optional parts of sentences are preceded
or followed (or both) by three dots.

breasts. Мне (действительно) нравится большая грудь.

breast: *what I love to do with your breasts*

I love to *(1)* **hold** / *(2)* **kiss** / *(3)* **squeeze the rounded globes of your breasts.** Я люблю *(1)* держать / *(2)* целовать / *(3)* сжимать округлые шары твоих грудей. ♦ **I love to put my face in your (warm, soft) breasts.** Я люблю класть моё лицо на твою (тёплую, мягкую) грудь. ♦ **I** *(1)* **love** / *(2)* **want to (gently) suck on your breast(s) (for hours and hours and hours).** Я *(1)* люблю / *(2)* хочу (нежно) сосать твою грудь (часами, часами и часами). ♦ **I** *(1)* **love** / *(2)* **want to gently caress your breasts, lingering on the** *(3)* **tips** / *(4)* **nipples.** Я *(1)* люблю / *(2)* хочу нежно ласкать твою грудь, задерживаясь на *(3)* кончиках / *(4)* сосках. ♦ *(1)* **What a magical feeling...** / *(2)* **I love the feeling... when my hand cups the fullness of your breast.** *(1)* Что за волшебство чувствовать... / *(2)* Я люблю ощущать... мою руку, наполненную полнотой твоей груди.

breast: *what I want to do with your breasts*

I want to stroke your breasts tenderly. Я хочу нежно гладить твою грудь. ♦ **I want to feel the fullness of your breasts** *(1)* **...with my mouth.** / *(2)* **...against my chest.** Я хочу ощутить полноту твоей груди *(1)* ...своими губами. / *(2)* ...прижавшись к тебе. ♦ *(1)* **I would love...** / *(2)* **I want...** *(3)* **bury** / *(4)* **snuggle** / *(5)* **nuzzle my face in your (warm, soft) breasts.** *(1)* Я бы хотел... / *(2)* Я хочу... *(3)* спрятать моё лицо в... / *(4)* ...прильнуть моим лицом к... / *(5)* ...зарыться лицом в... твоей (тёплой, мягкой) груди. ♦ *(1)* **I want to...** / *(2)* **I'm going to... brush my lips across the tips of your breasts, down your stomach and along your legs.** Я *(1)* хочу / *(2)* собираюсь коснуться губами твоих сосков, спуститься к твоему животу и пробежать вдоль твоих ног. ♦ **I envy your brassiere. It gets to hold your beautiful breasts all day. I wish I could do the same.** Я завидую твоему бюстгальтеру. Он поддерживает твою прекрасную грудь целый день. Я желал бы делать то же самое. ♦ **This is a locket with my photo in it. Wear it close to your breasts, because that's where I myself always want to be.** Это медальон с моей фотографией. Носи его на своей груди потому, что это то место, где я всегда хочу пребывать.

breast: *what I'm going to do with your breasts*

I'm going to make those rosy nubs on your breasts pulsate with pleasure. Я заставлю эти розовые шишечки твоих грудей пульсировать от наслаждения. ♦ **My mouth will trail along your neck to your shoulder and then down to your breast.** Мой рот будет путешествовать по твоей шее, к твоим плечам и затем вниз к твоей груди. ♦ *(1)* **I'm going to...** / *(2)* **I want to...** *(3)* **feast on...** / *(4)* **revel in... the firm, creamy flesh of your full breasts.** *(1)* Я буду... / *(2)* Я хочу... *(3)* ...пировать в упругой, крёмовой плоти... / *(4)* упиваться упругой, крёмовой плотью... твоей полной груди. ♦ **As my hand cups the fullness of your breast, my mouth will cover your beautiful face and smooth neck with adoring kisses.** В то время, как моя рука ощутит полноту твоей груди, мой рот покроет твоё прекрасное лицо и нежную шею обожающими поцелуями.

breath *n* дыхание ♦ **The first time I** *(1)* **...saw you...** / *(2)* **...looked at your beautiful face... it (nearly) took my breath away.** В первый раз, *(1)* ...увидав тебя... / *(2)* ...взглянув на твоё прекрасное лицо... я (почти) потерял дыхание. ♦ **Every time I think about you, it nearly takes my breath away.** Каждый раз, когда я думаю о тебе, я почти теряю дыхание. ♦ *(1)* **Your (exquisite) beauty...** / *(2)* **The copious splendor of your generous natural endowments...** *(3-5)* **takes my breath away.** *(1)* Твоя (совершенная) красота... / *(2)* Обильная роскошь того, что природа так щедро тебе дала,... *(3)* ...захватывает дух. / *(4)* ...останавливает дыхание. / *(5)* ...перехватывает моё дыхание. ♦ **My warm breath will awaken all of your senses.** Моё тёплое дыхание пробудит все твои чувства.

If you're not on familiar terms with a person, the «ты» forms will have to be changed to «Вы».

♦ **Your warm breath awakens all of my senses.** Твоё тёплое дыха́ние пробужда́ет все мои́ чу́вства. ♦ **You're like a breath of fresh air in my life.** Ты в мое́й жи́зни как глото́к све́жего во́здуха. ♦ *(1,2)* **You have bad breath.** У тебя́ *(1)* ...неприя́тное дыха́ние. / *(2)* ...за́пах и́зо рта.

breathe *vi* дыша́ть ♦ **I cannot even breathe without** *(1)* **...a thought...** / *(2)* **...thinking... of you.** Я не могу́ да́же дыша́ть *(1)* ...без мы́сли... / *(2)* ...не ду́мая... о тебе́.

breathing *n* дыха́ние ♦ **rapid and uneven** ~ бы́строе и неро́вное дыха́ние.

breath-taking *adj* поразѝтельный, -ая, -ое, -ые, захва́тывающий (-ая, -ее, -ие) дух ♦ **Your breath-taking beauty haunts my** *(1)* **mind** / *(2)* **thoughts night and day.** Твоя́ захва́тывающая дух красота́ пресле́дует *(1)* ...мою́ па́мять... / *(2)* ...мои́ мы́сли... но́чью и днём. ♦ **You are a vision of breath-taking** *(1)* **beauty** / *(2)* **loveliness.** Ты ви́дение (1,2) красоты́, захва́тывающей дух.

breathless *adj* 1. *(out of breath)* запыха́вшийся, -аясь, -еесь, -иесь; 2. *(very impressed)* бездыха́нный, -ая, -ое, -ые; 3. *(holding one's breath)* затаи́вший (-ая, -ее, -ие) дыха́ние ♦ **You leave me absolutely breathless.** Ты оставля́ешь меня́ соверше́нно бездыха́нным *(ж: бездыха́нной)*. ♦ **You gave me such an intense look that it left me breathless.** Ты одари́ла *(ж: одари́л)* меня́ таки́м пы́лким взгля́дом, что у меня́ перехвати́ло дыха́ние.

breed *n* поро́да ♦ **I guess you could say I'm a dying breed.** Я полага́ю, ты могла́ бы сказа́ть, что я из вымира́ющей поро́ды.

brew *n* *(slang) (beer)* пи́во ♦ **I like a brew now and then.** Поро́й я люблю́ пи́во.

bridal *adj* сва́дебный, -ая, -ое, -ые.

bride *n* неве́ста ♦ **beautiful** ~ прекра́сная неве́ста ♦ **beloved** ~ возлю́бленная неве́ста ♦ **blushing** ~ смущённая неве́ста ♦ **chaste** ~ непоро́чная неве́ста ♦ **virgin** ~ непоро́чная неве́ста ♦ **I'm waiting for the day when I can call you my bride.** Я жду того́ дня, когда́ назову́ тебя́ свое́й неве́стой. ♦ **Will you be my bride?** Ты бу́дешь мое́й неве́стой? ♦ **Oh, my beloved bride!** О, моя́ возлю́бленная неве́ста! ♦ **You'll be the most beautiful bride in the** *(1)* **...whole world.** / *(2)* **...history of Russia** / *(3)* **Ukraine.** Ты бу́дешь прекра́снейшей неве́стой в ...це́лом ми́ре. / *(2)* ...исто́рии Росси́и / *(3)* Украи́ны. ♦ **My greatest aspiration in life is to make you my bride.** Стремле́ние всей мое́й жи́зни -- сде́лать тебя́ свое́й неве́стой. ♦ **You are my soul's bride.** Ты неве́ста мое́й души́. ♦ **At the end of the ceremony, the groom kisses the bride.** В конце́ церемо́нии жени́х целу́ет неве́сту. ♦ **The bride's father is usually the one who gives her away at the wedding.** На сва́дьбе оте́ц неве́сты обы́чно тот, кто отдаёт её. ♦ **In America, the groom carries the bride over the threshold (of their home).** В Аме́рике жени́х перено́сит неве́сту че́рез поро́г (их до́ма).

bridegroom *n* жени́х.

bridesmaid *n* подру́га неве́сты.

bride-to-be *n* бу́дущая неве́ста.

bridge *n* мост ♦ **It's not a good idea to burn all your bridges behind you.** Это не лу́чшая иде́я сжечь за собо́й все мосты́. ♦ **I've burnt all my bridges behind me.** Я сжёг *(ж: сожгла́)* все мосты́ за собо́й.

briefs *n, pl* шо́рты, коро́ткие тру́сики ♦ **bikini** ~s тру́сики-бики́ни.

bright *adj* 1. *(luminous)* я́ркий, -ая, -ое, -ие; блестя́щий, -ая, -ее, -ие; 2. *(smart, clever)* смышлёный, -ая, -ое, -ые, сообрази́тельный, -ая, -ое, -ые, шу́стрый, -ая, -ое, -ые ♦ **brighter** я́рче ♦ *(1)* **Letters from you...** / *(2)* **Thoughts of you... make a bright day even brighter.** *(1)* Твои́ пи́сьма... / *(2)* Мы́сли о тебе́... де́лают я́ркий день ещё я́рче. ♦ **Your smile makes a bright day even brighter.** Твоя́ улы́бка де́лает я́ркий день ещё

A list of common places with their grammatical endings is given in Appendix 7, page 763.

я́рче. ♦ **My days are brighter because of you.** Благодаря́ тебе́ мои́ дни ста́ли я́рче.

brighten *vt* озаря́ть / озари́ть *(what = acc.)*, освеща́ть / освети́ть *(what = acc.)*, ра́довать / обра́довать *(what = acc.)*; оживля́ть / оживи́ть *(what = acc.)* ♦ *(1)* **You don't know...** / *(2)* **If you only knew... how (much) you** *(3,4)* **brighten** *(5)* **...my life** / *(6)* **...my days.** / *(7)* **...the hours of my life.** *(1)* Ты да́же не зна́ешь,... / *(2)* Е́сли бы ты то́лько зна́ла *(ж: знал)*,... как ты *(3)* озаря́ешь /*(4)* освеща́ешь *(5)* ...мою́ жизнь. / *(6)* ...мои́ дни. / *(7)* ...часы́ мое́й жи́зни. ♦ *(1)* **The (mere) thought...** / *(2)* **Thoughts... of you** *(3,4)* **brighten(s) up** *(5)* **...my day** / *(6)* **...everything in my world.** / *(7)* **...everything around me..** *(1,2)* (То́лько) мы́сли о тебе́ *(3)* озаря́ют / *(4)* освеща́ют *(5)* ...мой день / *(6)* ...всё в моём ми́ре. / *(7)* ...всё вокру́г меня́. ♦ **Your smile brightens (up) even a sunny day.** Твоя́ улы́бка освеща́ет да́же со́лнечный день. ♦ **You brighten my life with your** *(1)* **...sweet smile and loving ways.** / *(2)* **...effervescent** / *(3)* **sparkling personality.** Ты озаря́ешь мою́ жизнь свое́й *(1)* ...не́жной улы́бкой и любо́вью. / *(2)* ...кипу́чей / *(3)* искря́щейся нату́рой. ♦ **Your** *(1)* **effervescent** / *(2)* **sparkling personality brightens my life.** Твоя́ *(1)* кипу́чая / *(2)* искря́щаяся нату́ра озаря́ет мою́ жизнь. ♦ **Your letters lift my spirits and brighten my day more than I can describe to you.** Твои́ пи́сьма поднима́ют мой дух и освеща́ют мой день бо́лее, чем я могу́ описа́ть тебе́. ♦ **Your** *(1)* **call** / *(2)* **letter brightened my mood.** *(1)* Твой звоно́к по́днял... / *(2)* Твоё письмо́ по́дняло... моё настрое́ние. ♦ **No one brightens up my life like you do.** Никто́ не освеща́ет мою́ жизнь так, как ты. ♦ **Nothing brightens up my day like** *(1)* **...a letter from you.** / *(2)* **...thoughts of you.** Ничто́ так не освеща́ет мой день, как *(1)* ...письмо́ от тебя́. / *(2)* ...мы́сли о тебе́.

bright-eyed *adj* яркогла́зый, -ая, -ое, -ые.

brightness *n* я́ркость *f* ♦ **I never dreamed a smile could fill my life with so much warmth and brightness.** Я никогда́ не представля́л, что улы́бка смо́жет напо́лнить мою́ жизнь таки́м тепло́м и све́том.

brilliant *adj (very smart)* блестя́щий, -ая, -ее, -ие, о́чень у́мный, -ая, -ое, -ые.

brim *vi* наполня́ться / напо́лниться до краёв *(with what = instr.)* ♦ **I'm brimming over with happiness.** Я перепо́лнен *(ж: перепо́лнена)* сча́стьем. ♦ **I've never met a person who brimmed with (positive) energy the way you do.** Я никогда́ не встреча́л *(ж: встреча́ла)* челове́ка, кото́рый был бы так до краёв напо́лнен (положи́тельной) эне́ргией, как ты. ♦ **One thing I** *(1)* **admire** / *(2)* **like about you is that you're brimming with (positive) energy.** *(1)* Я любу́юсь тем... / *(2)* Мне нра́вится в тебе́ то,... что ты до краёв напо́лнена *(ж: напо́лнен)* (положи́тельной) эне́ргией. ♦ **I'm brimming with** *(1)* **eagerness** / *(2)* **impatience to** *(3)* **meet** / *(4)* **see you.** Я до краёв напо́лнен *(ж: напо́лнена) (1,2)* нетерпе́нием *(3)* встре́тить / *(4)* уви́деть тебя́. ♦ **My heart is brimming with love for you.** Моё се́рдце до краёв напо́лнено любо́вью к тебе́.

brisk *adj* живо́й, -а́я, -о́е, -ы́е, прово́рный, -ая, -ое, -ые

briskly *adv* жи́во, прово́рно.

broach *vt* направля́ть / напра́вить разгово́р, поднима́ть / подня́ть разгово́р, затра́гивать / затро́нуть вопро́с ♦ **I don't know how to broach the subject (with** *[1]* **him** / *[2]* **her** / *[3]* **them).** Я не зна́ю, как напра́вить разгово́р на э́ту те́му (с *[1]* ним / *[2]* ней / *[3]* ни́ми).

broad-minded *adj* широко́ мы́слящий, -ая, -ее, -ие, с широ́ким кругозо́ром.

broad-shouldered *adj* широкопле́чий, -ая, -ее, -ие.

broken *adj* сло́манный, -ая, -ое, -ые *(short forms:* сло́ман, -а, -о, -ы)́; разби́тый, -ая, -ое, -ые *(short forms:* разби́т, -а, -о, -ы*)* ♦ **emotionally** ~ эмоциона́льно сло́манный, -ая, -ое, -ые ♦ **My heart is (completely) broken.** Моё се́рдце (соверше́нно) разби́то.

Common adult heights are given in Appendix 9, page 776.

broken-hearted *adj* с разби́тым се́рдцем, неуте́шный, -ая, -ое, -ые.

broker *n* ♦ **marriage** ~ сват *m*, сва́ха *f.*

brooch *n* брошь *f*, бро́шка.

brood *vi* размышля́ть; заду́мываться.

brooding *n* размышле́ние.

brown *adj* кори́чневый, -ая, -ое, -ые; *(eyes)* ка́рий, -ая, -ое, -ые; *(hair)* кашта́новый, -ая, -ое, -ые.

brown-skinned *adj* с кори́чневой ко́жей.

bruise *n* синя́к.

brunette *n* брюне́т *m*, брюне́тка *f* ♦ **adventurous** ~ предприи́мчивая брюне́тка ♦ **alluring** ~ привлека́тельная брюне́тка ♦ **beautiful** ~ прекра́сная брюне́тка **bewitching** ~ очарова́тельная брюне́тка ♦ **busty** ~ груда́стая брюне́тка ♦ **classy** ~ кла́ссная брюне́тка ♦ **curvy** ~ окру́глая брюне́тка ♦ **exotic** ~ экзоти́ческая брюне́тка ♦ **fiery** ~ пы́лкая брюне́тка ♦ **gorgeous** ~ восхити́тельная брюне́тка ♦ **knockout** ~ сногшиба́тельная брюне́тка ♦ **large pretty** ~ больша́я привлека́тельная брюне́тка ♦ **long-haired** ~ длинноволо́сая брюне́тка ♦ **luscious** ~ со́чная брюне́тка ♦ **mercurial** ~ брюне́тка с переме́нчивым хара́ктером ♦ **petite** ~ миниатю́рная брюне́тка ♦ **statuesque** ~ ста́тная брюне́тка ♦ **stunning** ~ сногшиба́тельная брюне́тка ♦ **succulent** ~ со́чная брюне́тка ♦ **sultry** ~ зно́йная брюне́тка ♦ **vibrant** ~ жива́я брюне́тка.

brush *vt* 1. *(clean)* чи́стить / почи́стить *(what = acc.)*; 2. *(hair)* причёсывать / причеса́ть *(what = acc.)*; 3. *(with lips, fingers, hand)* (легко́) каса́ться / косну́ться *(what = gen., with what = instr.)* ♦ *(1)* **I want to...** / *(2)* **I'm going to... brush my lips across the tips of your breasts, down your stomach and along your legs.** Я *(1)* хочу́ / *(2)* собира́юсь косну́ться губа́ми твои́х соско́в, спусти́ться к твоему́ животу́ и пробежа́ть вдоль твои́х ног. ♦ **First, I want to brush my lips over your fingertips.** Снача́ла я хочу́ легко́ косну́ться губа́ми ко́нчиков твои́х па́льцев. ♦ **What pure heaven it would be to brush the top of your breasts with my lips.** Что за и́стинное блаже́нство бы́ло бы губа́ми легко́ косну́ться ко́нчиков твои́х груде́й. ♦ **When your hand brushed against my breast, warm shock waves went all through me.** Когда́ твоя́ рука́ легко́ косну́лась мое́й гру́ди, тёплые потряса́ющие во́лны прошли́ че́рез меня́.

brush-off *n (slang) (rejection)* отка́з, неприня́тие уха́живания ♦ **I hope you won't give me the brush-off.** Я наде́юсь, ты не отка́жешь мне. ♦ **Before you give me the brush-off, let me say just one thing.** Пре́жде, чем ты отка́жешь мне, позво́ль сказа́ть то́лько одну́ вещь.

brusque *adj* бесцеремо́нный, -ая, -ое, -ые; ре́зкий, -ое, -ие.

brutal *adj* жесто́кий, -ая, -ое, -ие.

brute *n* зверь *m*, живо́тное, скоти́на.

BS *abbrev* = **Bachelor of Science degree** сте́пень бакала́вра нау́к.

b.s. *(vulgar slang) (nonsense)* вздор, абсу́рд, глу́пости, ерунда́, дрянь *f* ♦ **That's a lot of b.s.** Это сплошно́й абсу́рд.

bubble over *vi* бить ключо́м.

bubbly *adj (slang) (lively, effervescent, loquacious)* искря́щийся, -аяся, -ееся, -иеся, пе́нящийся, -аяся, -ееся, -иеся.

buccaneerish *adj* похо́жий (-ая, -ее, -ие) на пира́та.

bud *vi* расцвета́ть / расцвести́.

bud *n (nipple of the breast)* буто́н ♦ ~**s of the breasts** буто́ны груде́й ♦ ~**s of passion** буто́ны стра́сти ♦ **coral** ~**s** кора́лловые буто́ны.

Buddhist *adj* будди́йский, -ая, -ое, -ие.

Words in parentheses are optional.

Buddhist *n* будди́ст *m*, будди́стка *f.*

budding *adj* расцвета́ющий, -ая, -ее, -ие.

buddy *n (slang)* прия́тель, друг ♦ **spiritual** ~ друг по ду́ху; задуше́вный друг.

buff *n (fan, enthusiast)* люби́тель, боле́льщик, энтузиа́ст ♦ **fitness** ~ энтузиа́ст здоро́вого о́браза жи́зни ♦ **movie** ~ люби́тель кино́ ♦ **sports** ~ спорти́вный боле́льщик ♦ **tennis** ~ те́ннисный боле́льщик ♦ **in the** ~ нагишо́м, голышо́м, в го́лом ви́де, обнажённый, -ая, -ое, -ые, го́лый, -ая, -ое, -ые.

bug *vt (slang) (annoy, irritate)* досажда́ть *(whom = acc.)*, раздража́ть *(whom = acc.)* ♦ **It (kind of) bugged me that you didn't even** *(1)* **call /** *(2)* **write.** То, что ты да́же не *(1)* позвони́ла *(ж: позвони́л)* / *(2)* написа́ла *(ж: написа́л)*, (немно́го) раздража́ло меня́.

bug *n* насеко́мое *(pl:* насеко́мые*)* ♦ **I've been bitten by the love bug.** Я в любо́вном помеша́тельстве.

build *n* (те́ло)сложе́ние ♦ **athletic** ~ атлети́ческое (те́ло)сложе́ние ♦ **husky** ~ кре́пкое (те́ло)сло́жение ♦ **medium** ~ сре́днее (те́ло)сложе́ние ♦ **muscular** ~ мускули́стое (те́ло)сложе́ние ♦ **powerful** ~ могу́чее (те́ло)сложе́ние ♦ **slim** ~ изя́щное (те́ло)-сложе́ние ♦ **stocky** ~ кре́пкое (те́ло)сложе́ние ♦ **I have a stocky build.** Я призе́мистый.

builder *n*: ♦ **body** ~ культури́ст.

building *n*: ♦ **body** ~ культури́зм.

build up *vt (raise)* поднима́ть / подня́ть *(what = acc.)* ♦ **You build me up and then you let me down.** Ты снача́ла поднима́ешь мой дух, а пото́м всё разруша́ешь.

build up *vi* нара́щивать, нака́пливаться ♦ **My feelings** *(1)* **...toward you... /** *(2)* **...about this... have been building up for** *(3)* **days /** *(4)* **weeks /** *(5)* **months now.** Мои́ чу́вства по отноше́нию к *(1)* тебе́ / *(2)* э́тому нака́пливаются уже́ *(3)* дня́ми / *(4)* неде́лями / *(5)* меся́цами. ♦ **My resentment has been building (up) for a long time.** Моё негодова́ние нака́пливается уже́ давно́. ♦ **These feelings have been building up in me for a long time.** Э́ти чу́вства нараста́ли во мне до́лгое вре́мя. ♦ **Sometimes I feel like I'm going to explode from the tremendous love-pressure that builds up inside of me for you.** Иногда́ я чу́вствую себя́ гото́вым взорва́ться от огро́много любо́вного напряже́ния, выраста́ющего во мне.

buildup *n* нара́щивание ♦ **gradual** ~ постепе́нное нара́щивание ♦ **slow** ~ ме́дленное нара́щивание.

built *adj* сложённый, -ая, -ое, -ые *(short forms:* сложён, сложена́, -о́, -ы́*)* ♦ **athletically** ~ атлети́чески сложён *m* / сложена́ *f* ♦ ~ **like a battleship** име́ющая прекра́сное те́ло ♦ **flawlessly** ~ безупре́чно сложена́ *f* ♦ **solidly** ~ кре́пко сложён *m* ♦ **You are very trimly built.** Ты о́чень пропорциона́льно сложена́ *(ж: сложён)*.

bull *n (slang)* 1. *(nonsense)* дрянь *f*, вздор, ерунда́, чепуха́, вра́ки; 2. *(lie)* ложь *f*, вра́ки.

bullshit *n (vulgar)* 1. *(nonsense)* дрянь *f*, вздор, ерунда́, вра́ки; 2. *(lie)* ложь *f*, вра́ки ; 3. *(unpleasantness)* неприя́тность *f* ; *(hassle)* тру́дность *f* ; *(red tape)* волоки́та; *(s.th. unnecessary)* ненужное; *(s.th. useless)* бесполе́зное.

bum *n (loafer, idler)* ло́дырь *m*, безде́льник; *(good-for-nothing)* никчёмный челове́к ♦ **beach** ~ безде́льник, проводя́щий всё вре́мя на пля́же *(explanation)* ♦ **outdoor sun** ~ безде́льник, проводя́щий всё вре́мя на со́лнце *(explanation)*.

bummer *n (slang) (unlucky / bad situation)* невезе́ние; *(blow)* уда́р; *(disappointment)* разочарова́ние; *(unpleasantness)* неприя́тность *f.*

bunny *n (slang)* крольчёнок ♦ **playful snuggle** ~ игри́вый крольчёнок.

buns *n, pl (slang) (buttocks)* за́дница, по́па, по́пка, ягоди́цы ♦ **beautiful** ~s прекра́сная по́п(к)а ♦ **bulbous** ~s больша́я, кру́глая по́па ♦ **fabulous** ~s потряса́ющая по́п(к)а

You can find common clothing sizes in Appendix 11 on page 778.

♦ **fantastic** ~s великоле́пная по́п(к)а ♦ **firm** ~s твёрдая по́п(к)а, твёрдые ягоди́цы ♦ **gorgeous** ~s прекра́сная по́п(к)а ♦ **nice** ~s прия́тная по́п(к)а ♦ **sexy** ~s сексуаль-ная по́п(к)а ♦ **tight** ~s пло́тные ягоди́цы ♦ **You have such beautiful buns.** У тебя́ така́я прекра́сная по́п(к)а. ♦ **What beautiful buns (you have)!** Что за прекра́сная по́п(к)а (у тебя́)! ♦ **Oh, (how) I love your (beautiful) buns!** О, (как) я люблю́ твою́ (прекра́сную) по́пку. ♦ **You've got the** *(1)* **nicest /** *(2)* **firmest /** *(3)* **best /** *(4)* **sexiest /** *(5)* **most beautiful buns I've ever** *(6)* **seen /** *(7)* **known /** *(8)* **felt.** У тебя́ *(1)* ...изя́щнейшая... / *(2)* ...са́мая твёрдая... / *(3)* ...наилу́чшая... / *(4)* ...са́мая сексуа́льная... / *(5)* ...са́мая прекра́сная... по́пка, кото́рую я когда́-ли́бо *(6)* ви́дел / *(7)* знал / *(8)* чу́вствовал.

buoy *vt (boost)* поднима́ть / подня́ть *(what = acc.); (encourage)* ободря́ть / ободри́ть *(whom = acc.)* ♦ **Your letters buoy my spirits.** Твои́ пи́сьма поднима́ют мой дух.

buoyed *adj (boosted)* по́днят, -а́, -о, -ы *(short forms); (encouraged)* ободрён, ободрена́, -о́, -ы́ *(short forms)* ♦ **I'm really buoyed up by the thought of seeing you (soon).** Я действи́тельно ободрён *(ж: ободрена́)* мы́слью, что ско́ро уви́жу тебя́.

bureau *n* конто́ра, бюро́; отде́л ♦ **marriage** ~ бра́чная конто́ра.

burden *vt* обременя́ть / обремени́ть *(what, whom = acc., with what = instr.)* ♦ **I don't want to burden you with all my problems.** Я не хочу́ обременя́ть тебя́ все́ми свои́ми пробле́мами. ♦ **I'm sorry to burden you with all my problems.** Прости́ за то, что я обременя́ю тебя́ все́ми свои́ми пробле́мами.

burden *n* но́ша, тя́жесть *f*, груз, бре́мя *neut* ♦ **share life's** ~ вме́сте нести́ бре́мя жи́зни ♦ **It's a great burden to carry.** Это тяжёлое бре́мя. ♦ **It's not a burden (at all) (for me).** Это (совсе́м) не бре́мя (для меня́).

burly *adj* дю́жий, -ая, -ее, -ие.

burn *vi* горе́ть *(with what = instr.)*, пыла́ть, сгора́ть *(with what = + от + gen.)*. ♦ ~ **with desire** сгора́ть от стра́сти ♦ ~ **with impatience** сгора́ть от нетерпе́ния ♦ *(1)* **I burn...** / *(2)* **My whole body burns... with hunger for** *(3)* **...you.** / *(4)* **...your soft, warm beauty.** *(1)* Я сгора́ю... / *(2)* Всё моё те́ло гори́т... от жа́жды *(3)* ...тебя́. / *(4)* ...твое́й мя́гкой, тёплой красоты́. ♦ *(1)* **I burn...** / *(2)* **My whole body burns... with longing for** *(3)* **...you.** / *(4)* **...your soft, warm beauty.** *(1)* Я сгора́ю... / *(2)* Всё моё те́ло гори́т... от тоски́ по *(3)* ...тебе́. / *(4)* ...твое́й мя́гкой, тёплой красоте́. ♦ **I burn with desire.** Я сгора́ю от стра́сти. ♦ **I'm burning inside.** Я внутри́ весь *(ж: вся)* горю́. ♦ **I'm going to cover you with a million kisses burning as though beneath the equator.** Я покро́ю тебя́ миллио́ном поцелу́ев, обжига́ющих, как со́лнце над эква́тором. ♦ **I spend these long, lonely nights yearning and burning for** *(1)* **...your soft, luscious warmth.** / *(2)* **...the warm, wonderful, heavenly magic of your beautiful body.** Я провожу́ э́ти до́лгие, одино́кие но́чи, сгора́я и тоску́я по *(1)* ...твоему́ мя́гкому ла́сковому теплу́. / *(2)* ...тёплой, удиви́тельной, боже́ственной ма́гии твоего́ прекра́сного те́ла. ♦ **I feel as if I burn at your every touch.** Я чу́вствую себя́ так, как бу́дто сгора́ю от ка́ждого твоего́ прикоснове́ния.

burning *adj* пыла́ющий, -ая, -ее, -ие, жгу́чий, -ая, -ее, -ие.

burrow *n* но́рка ♦ **soft** ~ мя́гкая но́рка.

burst *vi (heart)* разрыва́ться / разорва́ться ♦ ~ **out laughing** разрази́ться сме́хом, рас-хохота́ться ♦ **I love you so much I think my heart is going to burst.** Я люблю́ тебя́ так си́льно, что ка́жется моё се́рдце разорвётся. ♦ **Our kindled passion will burst into an uncontrollable, raging fire.** На́ша воспламени́вшаяся страсть разгори́тся некон-троли́руемым, бе́шеным огнём. ♦ **Promise you won't burst out laughing.** Обеща́й, что не разрази́шься сме́хом.

burst *n* взрыв ♦ ~ **of laughter** взрыв сме́ха.

For general rules of Russian grammar see Appendix 2 on page 686.

bury *vt* пря́тать / спря́тать *(what = acc.)* ♦ *(1)* **I would love to bury...** / *(2)* **I love to bury...** **my face in your (warm, soft) breasts.** *(1)* Я бы хоте́л спря́тать... / *(2)* Я люблю́ пря́тать... моё лицо́ в твои́ (тёплую, мя́гкую) грудь.

bus *n* авто́бус ♦ **What time will the bus** *(1,2)* **arrive** / *(3,4)* **depart?** В како́е вре́мя *(1)* прибу́дет / *(2)* придёт / *(3)* отпра́вится / *(4)* отойдёт авто́бус? ♦ **The bus will** *(1,2)* **arrive** / *(3,4)* **depart at one (thirty).** *(See page 759 for other times.)* Авто́бус *(1)* прибу́дет / *(2)* придёт / *(3)* отпра́вится / *(4)* отойдёт в час (три́дцать).

bushy-browed брова́стый, -ая, -ое, -ые.

business *n* 1. *(commercial)* де́ло, би́знес; 2. *(company, enterprise)* компа́ния, предприя́тие; 3. *(matters)* дела́ *pl* ♦ **urgent** ~ неотло́жные дела́ ♦ ~ **trip** командиро́вка, делова́я пое́здка ♦ **on** ~ по де́лу ♦ **establish a** ~ создава́ть / созда́ть де́ло ♦ **go into** *(1,2)* ~ заня́ться *(1)* де́лом / *(2)* би́знесом ♦ **manage a** ~ управля́ть предприя́тием ♦ **open a** ~ начина́ть / нача́ть де́ло ♦ **operate a** ~ управля́ть предприя́тием ♦ **run a** ~ управля́ть предприя́тием ♦ **start a** ~ начина́ть / нача́ть де́ло.

businessman *n* делово́й мужчи́на.

businesswoman *n* делова́я же́нщина.

busybody *n* навя́зчивый челове́к, су́ющий нос в чужи́е дела́ *(explanation)*.

bust *n* бюст ♦ **beautiful** ~ прекра́сный бюст ♦ **gorgeous** ~ великоле́пный бюст ♦ **voluptuous** ~ роско́шный бюст ♦ **What a gorgeous bust you have.** Что за великоле́пный бюст у тебя́.

bustier *n* бюстье́ ♦ **black lace** ~ *(of a bra)* чёрное шёлковое бюстье́ ♦ **open-bust** ~ бюстье́ с откры́той гру́дью.

bustline *n* бюст ♦ **sagging** ~ отви́сший бюст.

busty *adj* груда́стый, -ая, -ое, -ые, с бю́стом.

busy *adj* за́нятой, -а́я, -о́е, -ы́е *(short forms:* за́нят, -а, -о, -ы*)* ♦ **Are you busy** *(1)* **...tonight?** / *(2)* **...after work?** / *(3)* **...tomorrow (**[4] **morning** / [5] **afternoon** / [6] **evening)?** / *(7)* **...on Saturday?** *(See page 759 for other days.)* Ты (бу́дешь) за́нята *(ж:* за́нят*)* *(1)* ...сего́дня ве́чером? / *(2)* ...по́сле рабо́ты? / *(3)* ...за́втра (*[4]* у́тром / *[5]* в по́лдень / *[6]* ве́чером)? / *(7)* ...в суббо́ту? ♦ **I'm busy** *(1)* **...tonight.** / *(2)* **...tomorrow (**[3] **morning** / [4] **afternoon** / [5] **evening).** / *(6)* **...on Saturday.** *(See page 759 for other days.)* Я (бу́ду) за́нят *(ж:* за́нята*)* *(1)*...сего́дня ве́чером. / *(2)* ...за́втра (*[3]* у́тром / *[4]* в по́лдень / *[5]* ве́чером). / *(6)* ...в суббо́ту. ♦ **I'm not busy.** Я не за́нят *(ж:* за́нята*)*. ♦ **I won't be busy.** Я не бу́ду за́нят *(ж:* за́нята*)*.

butt *n* *(slang)* по́па, по́пка, за́дница ♦ **firm** ~ твёрдая за́дница ♦ **little** ~ по́пка.

butterfly *vi* ходи́ть по ба́бам ♦ **I don't butterfly with other women.** Я не хожу́ по ба́бам.

butterfly *n* ба́бочка, мотылёк ♦ **social** ~ легкомы́сленная, непостоя́нная же́нщина *(1 term)* ♦ **I'm not some kind of butterfly that flits from woman to woman.** Я не мотылёк, перелета́ющий от одно́й же́нщины к друго́й. ♦ **Whenever I think of** *(1)* **...it,...** / *(2)* **...meeting you for the first time,... I get butterflies in my stomach.** Когда́ бы я ни поду́мал *(1)* ...об э́том,... / *(2)* ...о пе́рвой встре́че с тобо́й,... я о́чень возбужда́юсь. ♦ **Butterflies took flight in my stomach.** Я о́чень волнова́лся *(ж:* волнова́лась*)*.

buttocks *n, pl* ягоди́цы, по́п(к)а ♦ *(1,2)* **firm** ~**s** *(1)* кре́пкие / *(2)* упру́гие ягоди́цы ♦ **shapely** ~**s** изя́щная по́п(к)а.

button *n* 1. *(clothing)* пу́говица; 2. *(control)* кно́пка ♦ **love** ~ *(slang) (clitoris)* кли́тор ♦ **You really know how to push all my sexual buttons.** Ты действи́тельно зна́ешь, как нажа́ть на все мои́ сексуа́льные кно́пки. ♦ **I want to find out how to push all your sexual buttons.** Я хочу́ узна́ть, как нажа́ть на все твои́ сексуа́льные кно́пки.

For transitive Russian verbs the cases that they take are shown by means of an = sign and the Russian case. (abbreviated)

buxom *adj* полногру́дная, -ые.

buxomness *n* по́лная грудь.

buy *vt* покупа́ть / купи́ть *(what = acc.)* ♦ **I want to buy** *(1)* **it** / *(2)* **them for you.** Я хочу́ купи́ть *(1)* э́то / *(2)* их для тебя́. ♦ **Let's buy** *(1)* **it** / *(2-4)* **one** / *(5)* **them.** Дава́й, ку́пим *(1)* э́то / *(2)* оди́н *m* / *(3)* одну́ *f* / *(4)* одно́ *neut* / *(5)* их. ♦ **I bought** *(1)* **this** / *(2)* **these for you.** Я купи́л *(ж: купи́ла)* *(1)* э́то / *(2)* их для тебя́. ♦ **I'll buy** *(1)* **it** / *(2-4)* **one** / *(5)* **them for you.** Я куплю́ *(1)* э́то / *(2)* оди́н *m* / *(3)* одну́ *f* / *(4)* одно́ *neut* / *(5)* их для тебя́.

buzz *n (slang) (call)* звоно́к ♦ **Give me a buzz.** Позвони́ мне.

bygones *n, pl* мину́вшее, про́шлое, пережи́тое; про́шлые оби́ды ♦ **Let's let bygones be bygones.** Пусть про́шлое бу́дет про́шлым. ♦ **Can we just let bygones be bygones (and start [1] over / [2] anew)?** Мо́жем мы про́сто позво́лить про́шлому быть про́шлым (и нача́ть *[1]* опя́ть / *[2]* снача́ла)?

Russian verbs have 2 forms: imperfective and perfective.
They're given in that order

C

cabaret *n* кабаре́ *neut.*

cabin *n* да́чный дом, небольшо́й за́городный дом, до́мик ♦ **romantic** ~ романти́ческий до́мик.

cad подле́ц.

caftan *n* кафта́н.

cage *n* кле́тка ♦ **rib** ~ грудна́я кле́тка ♦ **I feel like some bird in a cage.** Я ощуща́ю себя́ э́такой пти́чкой в кле́тке.

cake *n* торт; (сла́дкий) пиро́г; *(fancy cake)* пиро́жное; *(fruit cake)* кекс ♦ **birthday** ~ имени́нный пиро́г ♦ **wedding** ~ сва́дебный торт ♦ **You can't have your cake and eat it too.** Один пиро́г два ра́за не съешь.

calculating *adj (deliberate, purposeful)* расчётливый, -ая, -ое, -ые.

calculation *n* расчёт, измере́ние ♦ **The** *(1)* **strength /** *(2)* **force /** *(3)* **intensity /** *(4)* **magnitude of your appeal for me is beyond calculation** *(1,2)* Си́ла / *(3)* Интенси́вность / *(4)* Магнети́зм твое́й привлека́тельности для меня́ вы́ше вся́кой ме́ры.

calf *n* (calves *pl*) *(of the leg)* икра́ *(ноги́).*

calf-length *adj* длино́й до икры́.

call *vt* 1. *(out loud)* звать / позва́ть *(whom = acc.)*; 2. *(summon)* вызыва́ть / вы́звать *(what, whom = acc.)*; 3. *(by phone)* звони́ть / позвони́ть *(whom = dat., what = + в + acc.)*; созва́ниваться / созвони́ться *(whom = + с + instr.)* ♦ ~ **a taxi** вызыва́ть / вы́звать такси́, зака́зывать / заказа́ть такси́ ♦ ~ **back** *idiom* перезвони́ть *(whom = dat., what = + в + acc.)*, позвони́ть опя́ть *(whom = dat., what = + в + acc.)* ♦ ~ **each other** перезва́ниваться ♦ ~ **off** *vt* отменя́ть / отмени́ть *(what = acc.).*

---

call: *calling you on the phone*

I'll call you *(1)* **...tomorrow** *([2]* **morning /** *[3]* **afternoon /** *[4]* **evening)** */ (5)* **...at one (thirty).** *(See page 759 for other times.)* Я позвоню́ тебе́ *(1)* ...за́втра *([2]* у́тром / *[3]* днём / *[4]* ве́чером). / *(5)* ...в час (три́дцать). ♦ *(1)* **Can /** *(2)* **Could I call you?** *(1)* Могу́... / *(2)* Мог *(ж: могла́)* бы... я позвони́ть тебе́? ♦ **Would it be okay for me to call you?** Удо́бно ли бу́дет, е́сли я позвоню́ тебе́? ♦ *(1,2)* **What time shall I call?** *(1)* Когда́... / *(2)* В како́е вре́мя... до́лжен *(ж: должна́)* я позвони́ть? ♦ **I called you, but you weren't there.** Я звони́л *(ж: звони́ла)* тебе́, но тебя́ (там) не́ было. ♦ **I tried many times to call you.** Я мно́го раз пыта́лся *(ж: пыта́лась)* дозвони́ться тебе́. ♦ **I** *(1)* **didn't** */ (2)* **couldn't call you, because...** *(1)* Я не позвони́л *(ж: позвони́ла)*... / *(2)* Я не смог *(ж:*

Words in parentheses are optional.

смогла) позвони́ть... тебе́, потому́ что... ♦ **I'm sorry I didn't call. I lost your number.** Прости́, что я не позвони́л *(ж: позвони́ла).* Я потеря́л *(ж: потеря́ла)* твой но́мер. ♦ *(1)* **I intended... / (2) It was my intention... to call you.** *(1)* Я собира́лся *(ж: собира́лась)...* / *(2)* Мои́м наме́рением бы́ло... позвони́ть тебе́.

┌─────────────────────────────────┐
│ **call:** *calling me on the phone* │
└─────────────────────────────────┘

Would it be possible for you to call me? Смо́жешь ли ты позвони́ть мне? ♦ **Please call me** *(1)* **...tomorrow** *([2]* **morning** / *[3]* **afternoon** / *[4]* **evening)** / *(5)* **...at one (thirty).** *(See page 759 for other times.)* Пожа́луйста, позвони́ мне *(1)* ...за́втра *([2]* у́тром / *[3]* днём / *[4]* ве́чером). / *(5)* ...в час (три́дцать). ♦ **Please call (me)** *(1)* **...anytime.** / *(2)* **...whenever you have time.** Пожа́луйста, звони́ (мне) *(1)* ...в любо́е вре́мя. / *(2)* ..., когда́ у тебя́ бу́дет вре́мя. ♦ **Please (don't) call me at** *(1)* **...this number: 222-3344.** / *(2)* **...home.** / *(3)* **...my office.** / *(4)* **...work.** / *(5)* **...before 9:00 AM.** / *(6)* **...after 10 PM.** Пожа́луйста, (не) звони́ мне *(1)* ...по э́тому но́меру: 222-3344. / *(2)* ...домо́й. / *(3)* в мой о́фис. / *(4)* ...на рабо́ту. / *(5)* ...до девяти́ утра́. / *(6)* ...по́сле десяти́ ве́чера. ♦ *(1,2)* **What time will you call?** *(1)* Когда́... / *(2)* В како́е вре́мя... ты бу́дешь звони́ть? ♦ **If you call and I'm not there, please** *(1)* **...try again later.** / *(2)* **...leave a message.** Е́сли ты позвони́шь, а меня́ там не бу́дет, пожа́луйста, *(1)* ...попыта́йся ещё раз. / *(2)* ...оста́вь сообще́ние. ♦ **Did you call me?** Ты звони́ла *(ж: звони́л)* мне? ♦ **I waited for you to call me (but you didn't).** Я ждал *(ж: ждала́)* твоего́ звонка́ (, но ты не позвони́ла *[ж: позвони́л]*). ♦ **Why didn't you call me?** Почему́ ты не позвони́ла *(ж: позвони́л)* мне? ♦ **If** *(1)* **...someone else... / (2) ...a man... / (3) ...a woman... answers when you call, just hang up.** Е́сли *(1)* ...кто-нибудь друго́й... / *(2)* ...мужчи́на... / *(3)* ...же́нщина... отве́тит на твой звоно́к, про́сто положи́ тру́бку. ♦ **I don't want you to call me** *([1]* **anymore** / *[2]* **here** / *[3]* **there).** Я не хочу́, что́бы ты звони́ла *(ж: звони́л)* мне *([1]* бо́льше / *[2]* сюда́ / *[3]* туда́).

[**call:** *calling elsewhere on the phone*]

Where do you want to call to? Куда́ ты хо́чешь позвони́ть? ♦ **I want to call...** Я хочу́ позвони́ть...

[**call:** *by a name*]

People *(1,2)* **call me**   *(name)* . Все *(1)* зову́т / *(2)* называ́ют меня́ ____. ♦ **You can call me**   *(name)* . Ты мо́жешь называ́ть меня́ ____.

[**call:** *judge*]

I call it the way I see it. Я сужу́ о ситуа́ции по своему́.

[**call off:**]

I think we should call off the wedding. Я ду́маю, мы должны́ отмени́ть сва́дьбу. ♦ **I want to call off the wedding.** Я хочу́ отмени́ть сва́дьбу. ♦ **Why do you want to call off the wedding?** Почему́ ты хо́чешь отмени́ть сва́дьбу?

call *n* звоно́к ♦ **I'll give you a call** *(1)* **...tomorrow.** / *(2)* **...on Friday** / *(3)* **Saturday** / *(4)* **Sunday.** Я позвоню́ тебе́ *(1)* ... за́втра. / *(2)* ...в пя́тницу / *(3)* суббо́ту / *(4)* воскресе́нье. ♦ **Please give me a call** *([1]* **anytime** / *[2]* **sometime).** Пожа́луйста, звони́ мне *([1]* ...в любо́е вре́мя. / *[2]* ...как-нибудь). ♦ **I need to make a(n)** *(1)* **long-distance** / *(2)* **overseas call.** Мне ну́жно сде́лать *(1)* ...междугоро́дний звоно́к. / *(2)* ...звоно́к заграни́цу. ♦ **How do I make a(n)** *(1)* **long-distance** / *(2)* **overseas call?** Как мне позвони́ть *(1)* по междугоро́дке / *(2)* заграни́цу? ♦ *(1)* **Were there... / (2) Did I get... any calls?** *(1,2)* Кто-нибу́дь мне звони́л? ♦ **You had a call (...from...) (while you were out).** Тебе́ звони́ли (...из...) (пока́ тебя́ не бы́ло). ♦ **You didn't have any calls.** Тебе́ никто́ не звони́л. ♦ *(1)* **It really warmed my heart and lifted up my spirits... / (2) It was a tonic for my spirits... to get your call.** Твой звоно́к *(1)* ...действи́тельно согре́л моё се́рдце и по́дняло

┌───┐
│ *You can find common clothing sizes in Appendix 11 on page 778.* │
└───┘

настрое́ние. / (2) ...был элекси́ром для моего́ ду́ха. ♦ **Your call (really)** (1) ...**set my heart aglow.** / (2) ...**brightened my mood.** Твой звоно́к (действи́тельно) (1) ...заста́вил моё се́рдце пыла́ть. / (2) ...по́днял моё настрое́ние.

callipygian, callipygious *adj (having shapely buttocks)* с изя́щной по́пкой.

callous *adj* безжа́лостный, -ая, -ое, -ые.

callously *adv* безжа́лостно.

calm *adj* споко́йный, -ая, -ое, -ые ♦ **Just** (1) **remain** / (2) **stay** / (3) **keep calm.** То́лько (1-3) ...остава́йся споко́йной (*ж: споко́йным*). / (1-3) ...сохраня́й споко́йствие.

calm down *vi* успока́иваться / успоко́иться ♦ **Calm down, there's nothing to get upset about.** Успоко́йся, нет причи́ны для расстро́йства.

camaraderie *n* дух това́рищества.

camisole *n* (свобо́дная) ко́фта (*ночна́я или дома́шняя*) ♦ **lacy satin** ~ кружевна́я атла́сная ко́фта.

camp *vi* жить / пожи́ть в пала́тке.

campground *n* ке́мпинг.

camping *n (verb expression)* жить / пожи́ть в пала́тке ♦ **go** ~ жить / пожи́ть в пала́тке ♦ **Would you like to go camping (with me)?** Не хоте́ла (*ж: хоте́л*) бы ты пожи́ть в пала́тке со мной? ♦ **Let's go** (1,2) **camping (together).** Дава́й поживём в (1) пала́тке / (2) ке́мпинге (вме́сте).

can *vi* мочь / смочь *(infinitives are not used)* ♦ **Can you?** Не мо́жешь ли ты? ♦ **I can('t).** Я (не) могу́. ♦ **I could(n't).** Я (не) мог. *(ж: Я [не] могла́.)*

Canada *n* Кана́да ♦ **from** ~ из Кана́ды ♦ **in** ~ в Кана́де ♦ **to** ~ в Кана́ду.

Canadian *adj* кана́дский, -ая, -ое, -ие.

Canadian *n* кана́дец *m,* кана́дка *f.*

Cancer *(Jun. 21 - Jul. 22)* Рак *(21 ию́ня - 22 ию́ля)*

candle *n* свеча́ ♦ **You're trying to burn the candle at both ends. It won't work.** Ты пыта́ешься заже́чь свечу́ с двух концо́в. Не полу́чится.

candlelight *n* свет свечи́ ♦ **I dream of taking baths with you by candlelight.** Я мечта́ю приня́ть с тобо́й ва́нну при свеча́х. ♦ (1) **I want to have...** / (2) **I love... dinners by candlelight (with you).** (1) Я хочу́ обе́дать... / (2) Я люблю́ обе́ды... при свеча́х (с тобо́й).

candy *n* конфе́та *(usually pl:* конфе́ты*)* ♦ **bring** (1) **me** / (2) **you** ~ приноси́ть / принести́ (1) мне / (2) тебе́ конфе́ты.

cane *n* па́лка ♦ **I walk with a cane.** Я хожу́ с па́лкой.

canine-friendly *adj:* ♦ **be** ~ люби́ть соба́к.

canoe *vi* пла́вать на кано́э ♦ **I like to canoe.** Я люблю́ пла́вать на кано́э.

canoe *n* кано́э.

canoeing *n (Russian uses verb expression* пла́вать на кано́э*)* ♦ **Let's go canoeing!** Пошли́ пла́вать на кано́э!

cantankerous *adj* взло́рный, -ая, -ое, -ые, сварли́вый, -ая, -ое, -ые.

cap *n* ке́пка; *(fur)* ша́пка ♦ **fur** ~ ша́пка.

capacity *n* спосо́бность *f* ♦ **I have a great capacity** (1) ...**to love.** / (1) ...**for love** / (2) **affection. (I just need the right person.)** У меня́ огро́мная спосо́бность (1-3) люби́ть. (Мне то́лько ну́жен подходя́щий челове́к.)

cappuccino *n* капуччи́но *(кофе).*

caprice *n* капри́з ♦ **feminine** ~s же́нские причу́ды ♦ **sensual** ~ чу́вственный капри́з.

capricious *adj* капри́зный, -ая, -ое, -ые ♦ **be** ~ капри́зничать.

Capricorn *(Dec. 22 - Jan. 19)* Козеро́г *(22 декабря́ -19 января́).*

For general rules of Russian grammar see Appendix 2 on page 686.

captivate *vt* пленя́ть / плени́ть *(what, whom = acc.)*, очаро́вывать / очарова́ть *(what, whom = acc.)*, увлека́ть / увле́чь *(what, whom = acc.)* ♦ **You have** *(1,2)* **captivated my heart like no one else has ever done.** Ты *(1)* плени́ла *(ж: плени́л)* / *(2)* очарова́ла *(ж: очарова́л)* моё се́рдце, как никто́ и никогда́. ♦ **Your beautiful eyes have captivated me completely.** Твои́ прекра́сные глаза́ меня́ соверше́нно очарова́ли. ♦ **You (really) captivate me with your** *(1)* **...wide-eyed innocence.** / *(2)* **...blithe spirit.** Ты (действи́тельно) пленя́ешь меня́ *(1)* ...свое́й наи́вной неви́нностью. / *(2)* ...свои́м весёлым хара́ктером. ♦ **There is** *(1)* **something** / *(2)* **much more than your beauty that captivates** *(3)* **...me.** / *(4)* **...my heart.** Есть *(1)* не́что / *(2)* гора́здо бо́льшее, чем твоя́ красота́, что пленя́ет *(3)* ...меня́. / *(4)* ...моё се́рдце. ♦ **The sweet magic of your kisses captivates my soul.** Сла́дкое волшебство́ твои́х поцелу́ев пленя́ет мою́ ду́шу. ♦ **The** *(1)* **beauty** / *(2)* **radiance of your smile captivates my heart.** *(1)* Красота́ / *(2)* Сия́ние твое́й улы́бки пленя́ет моё се́рдце. ♦ **The copious splendor of your natural endowments captivates all my senses.** Великоле́пие твои́х приро́дных дарова́ний пленя́ет все мои́ чу́вства.

captivated *adj* пленён, пленена́, -о́, -ы́, очаро́ван, -а, -о, -ы *(short forms)* ♦ **I am** *(1)* **completely** / *(2)* **totally** / *(3)* **entirely** *(4)* **irredeemably** / *(5)* **hopelessly captivated by your** *([6]* **incredible** / *[7]* **breath-taking** / *[8]* **shining** / *[9]* **heavenly** / *[10]* **radiant** / *[11]* **ethereal** / *[12]* **exquisite) beauty.** Я *(1,2)* соверше́нно / *(3)* по́лностью / *(4)* безвозвра́тно / *(5)* безнадёжно пленён твое́й (*[6]* невероя́тной / *[7]* ...остана́вливающей дыха́ние... / *[8]* сия́ющей / *[9]* небе́сной / *[10]* лучи́стой / *[11]* неземно́й / *[12]* изы́сканной) красото́й. ♦ **I am** *(1)* **completely** / *(2)* **totally** *(3,4)* **captivated by your** *(5)* **...manifold charms.** / *(6)* **...vivacity and loveliness.** Я *(1)* по́лностью / *(2)* абсолю́тно *(3)* очаро́ван / *(4)* пленён *(5)* ...твои́ми многочи́сленными пре́лестями. / *(6)* ...твое́й жи́востью и красото́й.

captivating *adj* плени́тельный, -ая, -ое, -ые.

captive *n* пле́нник *m*, пле́нница *f*, пле́нный *m*, пле́нная *f* ♦ **The whole evening my** *(1)* **attention** / *(2)* **mind was captive to your intoxicating presence.** Весь ве́чер *(1)* ...моё внима́ние бы́ло... / *(2)* ...мой ум был... пле́нником твоего́ опьяня́ющего прису́тствия.

captivity *n* плен ♦ **emotional** ~ эмоциона́льный плен   **sensual** ~ чу́вственный плен.

capture *vt* пленя́ть / плени́ть *(whom = acc.)*, брать / взять в плен *(whom = acc.)* ♦ **You capture my heart every day.** Ты берёшь в плен моё се́рдце ка́ждый день.

car *n* 1. *(auto)* маши́на; 2. *(train)* ваго́н ♦ **drive a** ~ води́ть маши́ну ♦ **Do you have a car?** Есть у тебя́ маши́на? ♦ **I have a car.** У меня́ (есть) маши́на. ♦ **I don't have a car.** У меня́ нет маши́ны. ♦ **Can you drive a car?** Мо́жешь ты води́ть маши́ну? ♦ **I (can't) drive a car.** Я (не) могу́ води́ть маши́ну. ♦ **Does someone in your family have a car?** У кого́-либо в твое́й семье́ есть маши́на? ♦ **Do you know someone with a car?** Зна́ешь ли ты кого́-нибудь с маши́ной? ♦ **My** *(1)* **brother** / *(2)* **father** / *(3)* **uncle** / *(4)* **cousin** / *(5)* **friend** / *(6)* **co-worker has a car.** У моего́ *(1)* бра́та / *(2)* отца́ / *(3)* дя́ди / *(4)* ...двою́родного бра́та... / *(5)* дру́га / *(6)* сослужи́вца есть маши́на. ♦ **My** *(1)* **mother** / *(2)* **sister** / *(3)* **aunt** / *(4)* **cousin** / *(5)* **friend has a car.** У мое́й *(1)* ма́тери / *(2)* сестры́ / *(3)* тёти / *(4)* ...двою́родной сестры́... / *(5)* подру́ги есть маши́на.

carat *n* кара́т ♦ **It's a 2-carat diamond.** Это бриллиа́нт в два *(2)* кара́та.

card *n* 1. *(credit, business, etc)* ка́рточка; 2. *(playing)* ка́рта; 3. *(membership)* биле́т ♦ **ATM** ~ де́бетовая ка́рточка, ка́рточка для ба́нковского автома́та ♦ **business** ~ визи́тная ка́рточка, визи́тка ♦ **calling** ~ визи́тная ка́рточка, визи́тка ♦ **cash machine** ~ де́бетовая ка́рточка, ка́рточка для ба́нковского автома́та ♦ **credit** ~ креди́тная ка́рточка ♦ **Green Card** *(U.S. immigration document)* «грин кард» ♦ *(1)* **ID** / *(2)* **identification** ~ *(1,2)* удостовере́ние ли́чности, идентификацио́нная ка́рточка ♦ **play** ~s игра́ть в ка́рты.

For transitive Russian verbs the cases that they take are shown by means of an = sign and the Russian case (abbreviated).

care *vi* 1. *(have concern)* заботиться *(about what, whom* = + о + *prep.)*; 2. *(love)* любить *(about whom* = *acc.)* ♦ ~ **for** заботиться *(for whom* = + о + *prep.)*.

| *care: have concern* |

I care about your feelings. Я забочусь о твоих чувствах. ♦ **You don't seem to care about my feelings.** Ты, кажется, не заботишься о моих чувствах. ♦ **I don't care** (*[1]*...**who knows** / *[2]* **sees.** / *[3]* ...**what happens.** / *[4]* ...**where we go.** / *[5]* ...**how much it costs.** / *[6]* ...**how long I have to wait for you.**). Мне всё равно (*[1]*...кто знает / *[2]* видит. / *[3]* ...что происходит. / *[4]* ...куда мы идём. / *[5]* ...сколько это стоит. / *[6]* ...как долго мне придётся ждать тебя.). ♦ **I don't care what** *(1)* **he** / *(2)* **she thinks.** Мне всё равно, что *(1)* он / *(2)* она подумает. ♦ **I** *(1)* **could** / *(2)* **couldn't care less.** *(1,2)* Мне (совершенно) наплевать.

| *care: love* |

Do you care about me? Ты любишь меня? ♦ **I** (*[1]* **truly) care about you** (*[2]* **very much).** Я (*[1]* действительно / *[2]* очень) люблю тебя. ♦ **I care about you more than any other person** *(1)*...**on earth.** / *(2)* ...**in this world.** Я люблю тебя больше, чем кто-либо ещё *(1)* ...на земле. / *(2)* ...в этом мире. ♦ **You don't seem to care about me.** Ты, кажется, не любишь меня. ♦ **I can't escape the feeling that you don't care about me anymore.** Я не могу отделаться от чувства, что ты больше не любишь меня. ♦ **I need someone who cares.** Мне нужен кто-то, кто полюбит меня. ♦ **Happiness for me is knowing that you care about me.** Счастье для меня знать, что ты любишь меня.

| *care for:* |

I promise to love you and respect you and care for you all my life. Я обещаю любить тебя, уважать тебя и заботиться о тебе всю свою жизнь.

care *n* забота ♦ **loving ~** любящая забота ♦ **tender, loving ~** нежная, любящая забота ♦ **I** *(1)* **want** / *(2)* **plan to give you a lifetime of tender, loving care.** Я *(1)* хочу / *(2)* намерен *(ж: намерена)* окружить тебя нежностью и любовью на всю жизнь. ♦ **I'm going to give you more tender, loving care than you ever dreamed of.** Я дам тебе больше нежности и любви, чем ты когда-либо мечтала *(ж: мечтал)*. ♦ **I'll give you lots of tender, loving care.** Я подарю тебе много нежной, любящей заботы. ♦ **I take good care of myself.** Я слежу за собой.

careen *vi:* ♦ **Our relationship is careening off a cliff.** Наши (взаимо)отношения катятся со скалы.

career *n* карьера ♦ **put a ~ before one's** *(1)* **relationship** / *(2)* **marriage** поставить карьеру превыше *(1)* взаимоотношений / *(2)* брака ♦ **I personally believe it's misguided to put a career before one's relationship.** Лично я верю, что это неправильно поставить карьеру выше отношений.

career-driven *adj* занятый (-ая, -ые) своей карьерой.

career-minded *adj* занятый (-ая, -ые) своей карьерой.

carefree *adj* беззаботный, -ая, -ое, -ые.

careful *adj* осторожный, -ая, -ое, -ые (*short forms:* осторожен, осторожна, -о, -ы) ♦ **Please be careful.** Пожалуйста, будь осторожна *(ж: осторожен)*. ♦ **We have to be careful.** Мы должны быть осторожными. ♦ **I promise I'll be careful.** Я обещаю быть осторожным *(ж: осторожной)*.

careless *adj* неосторожный, -ая, -ое, -ые.

carelessly *adv* неосторожно.

caress *vt* ласкать *(whom, what* = *acc.)* ♦ **~ with the lips** ласкать губами *(what* = *acc.)* ♦ **~ with the tongue** ласкать языком *(what* = *acc.)* ♦ **gently ~** нежно ласкать ♦ **smoothly ~** нежно ласкать.

Russian verbs have 2 forms: imperfective and perfective.
They're given in that order

caress: *I love caressing*

I love to kiss, hug, caress, touch, hold hands, nibble, cuddle, rub against, stroke — you just name it. Я люблю́ целова́ть, обнима́ть, ласка́ть, каса́ться, держа́ться за́ руки, покусывать, сжима́ть в объя́тиях, тере́ться, гла́дить , ты то́лько назови́. ♦ **I love to be caressed.** Я люблю́, когда́ меня́ ласка́ют. ♦ **I love caressing** *(1)* **...your (***[2]* **soft /** *[3]* **smooth /** *[4]* **beautiful) buttocks /** *(5)* **breasts. /** *(6)* **...your (***[7]* **soft /** *[8]* **smooth /** *[9]* **beautiful) legs.** Я люблю́ ласка́ть *(1)* ...твою́ (*[2]* мя́гкую / *[3]* гла́дкую / *[4]* прекра́сную) по́пку / *(5)* грудь. / *(6)* ...твои́ (*[7]* мя́гкие / *[8]* гла́дкие / *[9]* прекра́сные) но́ги. ♦ **I love the way** *(1)* **...your body softens when I caress you. /** *(2)* **...you caress me.** Мне нра́вится, как *(1)* ...твоё те́ло расслабля́ется, когда́ я ласка́ю тебя́. / *(2)* ...ты ласка́ешь меня́.

caress: *I want to caress you*

I *(1)* **want /** *(2)* **love to gently caress** *(3)* **...you. /** *(4)* **...your beautiful body. /** *(5)* **...your heavenly soft loveliness. /** *(6)* **...your breasts, lingering on the** *(7)* **tips /** *(8)* **nipples. /** *(9)* **...your tongue with mine.** Я *(1)* хочу́ / *(2)* люблю́ не́жно ласка́ть *(3)* ...тебя́. / *(4)* ...твоё прекра́сное те́ло. / *(5)* ...твою́ боже́ственную, мя́гкую красоту́. / *(6)* ...твою́ грудь, заде́рживаясь на *(7)* ко́нчиках / *(8)* соска́х. / *(9)* ...твой язы́к мои́м. ♦ **I want to kiss you and caress you every night and every morning.** Я хочу́ целова́ть и ласка́ть тебя́ ка́ждую ночь и ка́ждое у́тро. ♦ **I have such a(n) (powerful) urge to caress you.** У меня́ тако́е вла́стное побужде́ние ласка́ть тебя́. ♦ **How I want to curl up with you, snuggle against your breast, feel the warmth of you, caress you, love you.** Как бы я хоте́л обня́ться с тобо́й, прижа́ться к твое́й гру́ди, чу́вствовать твоё тепло́, ласка́ть тебя́, люби́ть тебя́. ♦ **I could spend endless hours caressing you.** Я мог бы проводи́ть бесконе́чные часы́, ласка́я тебя́.

caress: *I'm going to caress you*

I'm going to caress every part of your body with my lips and my tongue. Я бу́ду ласка́ть ка́ждую части́цу твоего́ те́ла свои́ми губа́ми и языко́м. ♦ **I can't wait to hold you in my arms and kiss you and caress you and pleasure you all night long.** Я не могу́ дожда́ться мгнове́ния, когда́ я смогу́ обня́ть тебя́, целова́ть тебя́, ласка́ть тебя́ и доставля́ть наслажде́ние тебе́ всю ночь напролёт.

caress *n* ла́ска ♦ **ardent** ~**es** пы́лкие ла́ски ♦ **burning** ~**es** горя́чие ла́ски ♦ **delightful** ~**es** восхити́тельные ла́ски ♦ **feminine** ~**es** же́нские ла́ски ♦ **gentle** ~ не́жная ла́ска *(pl:* не́жные ла́ски*)* ♦ *(1,2)* **hungry** ~**es** *(1)* жа́дные / *(2)* голо́дные ла́ски ♦ **intimate** ~**es** инти́мные ла́ски ♦ **my** ~**es** мои́ ла́ски ♦ **rampant** ~**s** безуде́ржные ла́ски ♦ **rough** ~**es** гру́бые ла́ски ♦ **soft** ~**es** мя́гкие ла́ски ♦ **stimulating** ~**es** стимули́рующие ла́ски ♦ **the lightest of** ~**es** мягча́йшие ла́ски ♦ **warm** ~**es** тёплые ла́ски ♦ **your** ~**es** твои́ ла́ски.

caress: *phrases*

I *(1)* **love /** *(2)* **need your caresses.** *(1)* Я люблю́... / *(2)* Мне нужны́... твои́ ла́ски. ♦ **Your caresses are pure magic.** Твои́ ла́ски -- чисте́йшее волше́бство. ♦ **Whenever I think about your** *(1)* **gentle /** *(2)* **tender kisses and warm caresses, I realize why I can never get enough of you.** Когда́ я ду́маю о твои́х *(1,2)* не́жных поцелу́ях и тёплых ла́сках, я понима́ю, почему́ никогда́ не могу́ насы́титься тобо́й. ♦ **When we're together again, I'm going to cover you with kisses and caresses like you've never even dreamed of in your wildest dreams.** Когда́ мы бу́дем опя́ть вме́сте, я покро́ю тебя́ поцелу́ями и бу́ду ласка́ть так, как ты никогда́ да́же не мечта́ла в свои́х са́мых безу́мных мечта́х.

caressing *n* ла́ска ♦ **I like lots of touching and caressing and kissing.** Я люблю́ мно́го прикоснове́ний, ласк и поцелу́ев.

How to use the Cyrillic alphabet on the Internet is the subject of Appendix 20 on page 789.

caricature *n* карикату́ра.

caring *adj* забо́тливый, -ая, -ое, -ые ♦ **I'm a very caring person.** Я о́чень забо́тливый *(ж: забо́тливая)*. ♦ **You'e a very caring person.** Ты о́чень забо́тливая *(ж: забо́т-ливый)*. ♦ **I wish you could be more caring.** Я хоте́л бы, что́бы ты была́ бо́лее забо́тливой. *(ж: Я хоте́ла бы, что́бы ты был бо́лее забо́тливым.)* ♦ **You are so good and sweet and thoughtful and caring and loving.** Ты така́я хоро́шая *(ж: тако́й хоро́-ший)*, не́жная *(ж: не́жный)*, внима́тельная *(ж: внима́тельный)*, забо́тливая *(ж: забо́тливый)* и лю́бящая *ж:(лю́бящий)*.

caring *n* забо́та ♦ **mutual ~** взаи́мная забо́та ♦ **Your caring was just a facade.** Ты создава́ла *(ж: создава́л)* то́лько ви́димость забо́ты.

carnal *adj* пло́тский, -ая, -ое, -ие, чу́вственный, -ая, -ое, -ые ♦ **I try not to be so primitive and carnal in my thoughts about you, but I simply can't help it.** Я пыта́юсь не быть столь первобы́тным и чу́вственным, ду́мая о тебе́, но мне э́то про́сто не удаётся.

carnival *n* карнава́л ♦ **Let's** *(1,2)* **go to the carnival (together)!** Дава́й (вме́сте) *(1)* пойдём *(on foot)* / *(2)* пое́дем *(by veh.)* на карнава́л.

carriage *n (bearing; posture)* оса́нка ♦ **regal ~** ца́рственная оса́нка ♦ **Your carriage is (truly)** *(1)* **perfect /** *(2)* **marvelous.** Твоя́ оса́нка (действи́тельно) *(1)* соверше́нна / *(2)* восхити́тельна. ♦ **What** *(1)* **perfect /** *(2)* **marvelous carriage you have (when you walk).** Кака́я у тебя́ *(1)* великоле́пная / *(2)* изуми́тельная оса́нка (когда́ ты идёшь).

carrier *n (mail)* почтальо́н ♦ **mail ~** почтальо́н.

case *n* слу́чай ♦ **in ~** в том слу́чае, е́сли... *(1 term)* ♦ **just in ~** на вся́кий слу́чай.

casual *adj* небре́жный, -ая, -ое, -ые.

casually *adv* небре́жно.

catch *vt* лови́ть / пойма́ть *(what, whom = acc.)* ♦ **~ sight of** уви́деть *(what, whom = acc.)*, заме́тить *(what, whom = acc.)* ♦ **I caught her** *(him) (1).* **...in the act. /** *(2)* **...having sex with** *(person).* Я пойма́л *(ж: пойма́ла)* её *(ж: его́) (1)* ...на изме́не. / *(2)* ..., занима́ю-щейся *(ж: занима́ющимся)* се́ксом (с *(и́мя)*). ♦ **I'm so glad I caught your attention.** Я так рад *(ж: ра́да)*, что я привлёк *(ж: привлекла́)* твоё внима́ние. ♦ **Your photo caught my attention** *(1)* **...the instant I turned (the page) to it. /** *(2)* **...instantly.** Твоя́ фотогра́фия привлекла́ к себе́ моё внима́ние *(1)* ...как то́лько я переверну́л (стра-ни́цу). / *(2)* ...мгнове́нно.

catch *n* уло́в, уда́ча, добы́ча, пои́мка ♦ **As far as I'm concerned, you're the** *(1)* **...catch of the year. /** *(2)***...ultimate catch. /** *(3)* **...best catch of my life.** Что каса́ется меня́, ты *(1)* ...уда́ча го́да. / *(2)* ...наилу́чшая пои́мка. / *(3)* ...са́мый лу́чший уло́в мое́й жи́зни. ♦ **You may not know it, but you're a** *(1)* **good /** *(2)* **great catch.** Ты возмо́жно не зна́ешь того́, что ты *(1)* хоро́шая / *(2)* замеча́тельная добы́ча.

cathedral *n* собо́р.

Catholic *adj* католи́ческий, -ая, -ое, -ие.

Catholic *n* като́лик *m*, католи́чка *f.*

cat-loving *adj*: ♦ **be ~** люби́ть ко́шек.

catty *adj* язви́тельный, -ая, -ое, -ые; саркасти́ческий, -ая, -ое, -ие.

cause *vt* вызыва́ть / вы́звать *(what = acc.)*, причиня́ть / причини́ть *(what = acc.)* ♦ **You cause such turbulent feelings in** *(1)* **...me. /** *(2)* **...my heart.** Ты вызыва́ешь таки́е бу́рные чу́вства *(1)* ...во мне. / *(2)* ...в моём се́рдце.

caution *n* осторо́жность *f* ♦ **We have to use caution.** Мы должны́ быть осторо́жными. ♦ **Caution is necessary.** Осторо́жность необходи́ма.

cautious *adj* осторо́жный, -ая, -ое, -ые *(short forms:* осторо́жен, осторо́жна, -о, -ы).

cavalier *adj* 1. *(unconcerned, indifferent)* бесцеремо́нный, -ая, -ое, -ые; 2. *(high-handed,*

Russian adjectives have long and short forms.
Where short forms are given, they are labeled as such.

arrogant) надме́нный, -ая, -ое, -ые высокоме́рный, -ая, -ое, -ые ♦ **I treated you in a very cavalier manner.** Я обраща́лся *(ж: обраща́лась)* с тобо́й о́чень бесцеремо́нно. ♦ *(1)* **I'm sorry...** / *(2)* **I apologize... for treating you in such a cavalier manner.** *(1)* Я прошу́ проще́ния... / *(2)* Я извиня́юсь... за обраще́ние с тобо́й таки́м бесцеремо́нным о́бразом. ♦ **You treated me in a very cavalier manner.** Ты обраща́лась *(ж: обраща́лся)* со мно́й о́чень бесцеремо́нно.

caveman *n* пеще́рный челове́к ♦ **civilized** ~ цивилизо́ванный пеще́рный челове́к.

cavort *vi:* ♦ **Many times at night I wake up with my body on fire from cavorting with you in one episode or another of the Kama Sutra.** Мно́го раз я просыпа́юсь но́чью с те́лом, охва́ченным огнём от того́, что мы с тобо́й изуча́ем ту и́ли другу́ю главу́ Ка́ма Су́тры.

celebrate *vt* 1. *(commemorate)* пра́здновать / отпра́здновать *(what = acc.)*; 2. *(glorify)* прославля́ть / просла́вить *(what = acc.)* ♦ **Let's celebrate** *(1)* **...the day** / *(2)* **evening** / *(3)* **holiday(s)** / *(4)* **occasion.** / *(5)* **...being together.** Дава́й отпра́зднуем *(1)* ...день / *(2)* ве́чер / *(3)* пра́здник(и) / *(4)* слу́чай. / *(5)* ...возмо́жность быть вме́сте. ♦ **I want to celebrate** *(1)* **...my birthday...** / *(2)* **...New Year's...** / *(3)* **...the holiday... with you.** Я хочу́ отпра́здновать *(1)* ...свой день рожде́ния... / *(2)* ...Но́вый год... / *(3)* ...пра́здник... с тобо́й. ♦ **I want to celebrate your** *(1)* **breath-taking** / *(2)* **fantastic** / *(3)* **incredible beauty with adoring kisses all over it.** Я хочу́ прославля́ть твою́ *(1)* ...перехва́тывающую дыха́ние... / *(2)* фантасти́ческую / *(3)* невероя́тную красоту́ обожа́ющими поцелу́ями.

celebrate *vi* пра́здновать / отпра́здновать; *(make merry)* весели́ться ♦ **When** *(1)* **...you get here...** / *(2)* **...I get there..., we're going to (really) celebrate.** Когда́ *(1)* ...ты прие́дешь сюда́,... / *(2)* ...я прие́ду туда́,... у нас бу́дет (настоя́щий) пра́здник.

celebration *n* пра́здник ♦ **joyous** ~ ра́достный пра́здник ♦ **nuptial** ~ сва́дьба ♦ **simple, intimate** ~ проста́я, инти́мная сва́дьба ♦ **My heart ignites in celebration** *(1)* **...every time I get a letter from you.** / *(2)* **...every time I see your (*[3]* beautiful / *[4]* beloved) face.** / *(5)* **...at the mere thought of you.** Моё се́рдце загора́ется ра́достью *(1)* ...ка́ждый раз, когда́ я получа́ю письмо́ от тебя́. / *(2)* ...ка́ждый раз, когда́ я ви́жу твоё (*[3]* прекра́сное / *[4]* люби́мое) лицо́. / *(5)* ...от просто́й мы́сли о тебе́.

celestial *adj* небе́сный, -ая, -ое, -ые, неземно́й, -ая, -ое, -ые.

celibacy *n (no spouse)* безбра́чие; *(abstention)* воздержа́ние.

celibate *adj (not married)* не состоя́щий (-ая, -ие) в бра́ке; *(single, m)* холосто́й, -ы́е; *(single, f)* незаму́жняя, -ие; *(chaste)* целому́дренный, -ая, -ое, -ые ♦ **I've been celibate a long time.** Я до́лгое вре́мя не занима́лся *(ж: занима́лась)* любо́вью.

cell *n* кле́тка ♦ **You send electric sensations shooting through every cell and fiber of my body.** Ты посыла́ешь электри́ческие заря́ды, простре́ливающие ка́ждую кле́тку и все фи́бры моего́ те́ла. ♦ **Molten waves of desire sweep through every fiber and cell of my body whenever I think of your exquisite, luscious beauty.** Бушу́ющие во́лны стра́сти проно́сятся че́рез все фи́бры и кле́тки моего́ те́ла, когда́ бы я ни поду́мал о твое́й изы́сканной, со́чной красоте́.

cellphone *n* со́товый телефо́н.

center *vi* концентри́роваться, сосредото́чиваться / сосредото́читься ♦ **My thoughts center around you (night and day).** Все мои́ мы́сли сосредото́чены на тебе́ (но́чью и днём).

center *n* центр ♦ **fitness** ~ центр здоро́вья.

centerfold *n* центра́льная фотогра́фия *(в журна́ле для мужчи́н)* ♦ **You're every bit as beautiful as any centerfold girl (in a men's magazine).** Ты ка́ждой свое́й части́чкой

Russian nouns are either masculine, feminine or neuter.
Adjectives with them will be the same.

та́кже прекра́сна, как де́вушки с центра́льной фотогра́фии в журна́ле для мужчи́н.

cerebral *adj (slang)* интеллектуа́льный, -ая, -ое, -ые.

ceremony *n* церемо́ния ♦ **civil ~** *(wedding)* гражда́нская церемо́ния *(сва́дьба)* ♦ **double-ring ~** церемо́ния обме́на ко́льцами ♦ **graduation ~** выпускна́я церемо́ния ♦ **outdoor ~** сва́дебная церемо́ния на откры́том во́здухе ♦ **religious ~** *(wedding)* церко́вный обря́д *(венча́ния)*, религио́зная церемо́ния ♦ **wedding ~** сва́дебная церемо́ния ♦ **He will perform the (wedding) ceremony.** Он бу́дет вести́ (сва́дебную) церемо́нию.

certificate *n* свиде́тельство ♦ **birth ~** свиде́тельство о рожде́нии ♦ **marriage ~** свиде́тельство о бра́ке ♦ **You need to have your birth certificate translated.** Тебе́ ну́жно име́ть переведённое свиде́тельство о рожде́нии. ♦ **Do you have an English translation of your birth certificate?** У тебя́ есть англи́йский перево́д твоего́ свиде́тельства о рожде́нии?

cha-cha *n* ча-ча-ча.

chain *n* цепо́чка ♦ **gold ~** золота́я цепо́чка ♦ **silver ~** сере́бряная цепо́чка.

challenge *n* испыта́ние, про́ба (свои́х) сил; сло́жная зада́ча, пробле́ма ♦ *(1)* **Learning a new language...** / *(2)* **Getting used to a strange culture... will be a big challenge. But I will help you.** *(1)* Изуче́ние но́вого языка́... / *(2)* Привыка́ние к чужо́й культу́ре... бу́дет сло́жной зада́чей. Но я помогу́ тебе́.

champagne *n* шампа́нское *neut* ♦ **bottle of ~** буты́лка шампа́нского ♦ **~ and strawberries** шампа́нское и клубни́ка.

chance *n* шанс, возмо́жность *f* ♦ **another ~** друго́й шанс, ещё оди́н шанс ♦ **big ~** большо́й шанс ♦ **~ for** *(1,2)* **love** возмо́жность *(1)* люби́ть / *(2)* любви́ ♦ **good ~** хоро́шая возмо́жность ♦ **last ~** после́дняя возмо́жность ♦ **lucky ~** счастли́вый шанс ♦ **new ~** но́вый шанс, но́вая возмо́жность ♦ **only ~** еди́нственный шанс, еди́нственная возмо́жность ♦ **second ~** ещё оди́н шанс ♦ **willing to take a ~** гото́в *(ж: гото́ва)* рискну́ть.

chance: verb terms

get the ~ получи́ть возмо́жность ♦ **give** *(1)* **you** / *(2)* **me a** *(3,4)* **~** дать *(1)* тебе́ / *(2)* мне *(3)* возмо́жность / *(4)* шанс ♦ **miss the ~** упусти́ть возмо́жность ♦ **take a ~** рискова́ть / рискну́ть, идти́ на риск.

chance: phrases

I *(1)* **harbor** / *(2)* **entertain no illusions about my chances of winning your** *(3)* **heart** / *(4)* **love.** Я не *(1)* таю́ / *(2)* пита́ю никаки́х иллю́зий относи́тельно моего́ ша́нса *(3)* ...победи́ть твоё се́рдце. / *(4)* ...завоева́ть твою́ любо́вь. ♦ *(1)* **I beg** / *(2)* **beseech you (with all my heart) to...** / *(3* **I hope** / *(4)* **pray that you will... give me** *(5)* **...a second...** / *(6)* **...one more...** / *(7)* **...another... chance.** *(1,2)* Я умоля́ю тебя́ (от всего́ се́рдца) дать... / *(3)* Я наде́юсь / *(4)* молю́сь, что ты дашь мне *(5,6)* ...ещё оди́н... / *(7)* ...друго́й... шанс. ♦ **Please give me** *(1)* **...a second...** / *(2)* **...another... chance.** Пожа́луйста, дай мне *(1)* ...ещё оди́н... / *(2)* ...друго́й... шанс. ♦ **Will you give me another chance (to try and win your love)?** Дашь ли ты мне ещё оди́н шанс (попыта́ться заслужи́ть твою́ любо́вь)? ♦ **Is there any chance that** *(1)* **...I can see you (**[2]**...this weekend?** / [3] **...next month?** / [4] **...this [coming] summer?)?** / *(5)* **...you can take vacation?** / *(6)* **...you can come with me?** / *(7)* **...you can come here?** Есть ли како́й-то шанс, что *(1)* ...я смогу́ уви́деть тебя́ (**[2]** ...в э́ти выходны́е? / [3] ...в сле́дующем ме́сяце? / [4] ...э́тим ле́том?) / *(5)* ...ты смо́жешь взять о́тпуск? / *(6)* ...ты смо́жешь пое́хать со мной? / *(7)* ...ты смо́жешь прие́хать сюда́? ♦ **Thank you for giving me this chance for love.** Спаси́бо, что ты дала́ *(ж: дал)* мне э́ту возмо́жность люби́ть. ♦ **I thought I would never have a chance**

Learn more about Russian customs in Appendix 15, page 782.

for love (in my life). Я ду́мал *(ж: ду́мала)*, что никогда́ (в жи́зни) у меня́ не бу́дет возмо́жности любви́. ♦ **I never thought I would stand a chance with someone as beautiful as you.** Я никогда́ не ду́мал, что получу́ шанс с тако́й прекра́сной же́нщиной, как ты. ♦ **A chance like this comes only once in a lifetime.** Тако́й шанс, как э́тот, случа́ется раз в жи́зни.

change *vt* меня́ть / перемени́ть; изменя́ть / измени́ть ♦ ~ **clothes** переодева́ться / переоде́ться.

change *n* переме́на, измене́ние ♦ **The person I seek must not be afraid of change.** Челове́к, кото́рого я ищу́, не до́лжен боя́ться переме́н.

chapel *n* часо́вня ♦ **wedding** ~ сва́дебная часо́вня.

chaperon(e) *vt* сопровожда́ть *(whom = acc.).*

chaperon(e) *n* сопровожда́ющий *m*, сопровожда́ющая *f.*

chaperoned *adj* сопровождённый, -ая, -ое, -ые.

character *n* хара́ктер ♦ **easy-going**~ покла́дистый хара́ктер ♦ **fine**~ хоро́ший хара́ктер ♦ **good** ~ хоро́ший хара́ктер ♦ **impeccable moral** ~ безупре́чная нра́вственность ♦ **obsessive** ~ навя́зчивый хара́ктер ♦ **poor** ~ плохо́й хара́ктер ♦ **splendid** ~ великоле́пный хара́ктер ♦ **strong** ~ си́льный хара́ктер ♦ **vile** ~ гну́сный хара́ктер ♦ **volatile** ~ вспы́льчивый хара́ктер ♦ **strength of** ~ си́ла хара́ктера.

> *character: phrases*

What I value most is character. Что я ценю́ бо́лее всего́ -- э́то хара́ктер. ♦ **I can see that you have a very good character.** Я ви́жу, что у тебя́ о́чень хоро́ший хара́ктер. ♦ **I could immediately see that you're a person of** (*[1]* good / *[2]* splendid) **character.** Я мог *(ж: могла́)* сра́зу же определи́ть, что ты челове́к с (*[1]* хоро́шим / *[2]* великоле́пным) хара́ктером. ♦ **I know that you're a person of impeccable moral character.** Я зна́ю, что ты челове́к безупре́чной нра́вственности. ♦ **There is such genuine warmth in your character.** От тебя́ исхо́дит по́длинная вну́тренняя теплота́. ♦ **I'm (usually) a good judge of character.** Я (обы́чно) хорошо́ разбира́юсь в лю́дях. ♦ **Our characters were not compatible.** Мы не сошли́сь хара́ктерами.

characteristic *n* характери́стика, характе́рная осо́бенность ♦ **I'm seeking a person with similar** *(1,2)* **characteristics.** Я ищу́ челове́ка с похо́жими *(1)* осо́бенностями / *(2)* характери́стиками.

charade *n* шара́да, фарс ♦ **The whole thing was just a charade.** Всё э́то бы́ло всего́ лишь фа́рсом.

Chardonnay *n (wine)* Шардоне́.

charge *vt* заряжа́ть / заряди́ть *(what = acc.)* ♦ **You charge me with such (tremendous)** *(1)* **excitement /** *(2)* **passion.** Ты заряжа́ешь меня́ *(1)* ...таки́м (грома́дным) возбужде́нием. / *(2)* ...тако́й (грома́дной) стра́стью. ♦ **The very thought of you charges me with indescribable excitement.** Да́же мы́сли о тебе́ заряжа́ют меня́ невероя́тным возбужде́нием.

charge *n (leadership)* ли́дерство ♦ **I'm a take-charge kind of guy.** Я челове́к, беру́щий ли́дерство на себя́.

charisma *n* 1. *(attractive force)* хари́зма, притяга́тельная си́ла; 2. *(charm)* шарм, обая́ние ♦ **You have a lot of charisma.** В тебе́ мо́ре обая́ния. ♦ **I've never encountered such (powerful) charisma as you have.** Я никогда́ не ста́лкивалась с таки́м (могу́щественным) обая́нием, как у тебя́.

charismatic *adj* 1. *(exerting charisma)* харизмати́ческий, -ая, -ое, -ие; 2. *(charming)* обая́тельный, -ая, -ое, -ые.

charm *vt* очаро́вывать / очарова́ть *(whom = acc.).*

> *A slash always denotes "or."*
> *You can choose the numbered words before and after.*

charm *n* очарова́ние, обая́ние; пре́лесть; шарм; *pl:* пре́лести ♦ **bewitching ~s** кол-
довски́е ча́ры ♦ **boyish ~** ю́ношеское обая́ние ♦ **captivating feminine ~s** чару́ющие
же́нские пре́лести ♦ **exceptional ~** исключи́тельное обая́ние ♦ **extraordinary ~**
исключи́тельное обая́ние ♦ **feminine ~** же́нское обая́ние; *pl:* же́нские пре́лести ♦
girlish ~ деви́чье обая́ние ♦ **irresistible ~** неотрази́мый шарм ♦ **lucky ~** талисма́н
на сча́стье ♦ **lush feminine ~s** роско́шные же́нские пре́лести ♦ **magical ~s** вол-
ше́бные ча́ры ♦ **manifold ~s** многочи́сленные пре́лести ♦ **masculine ~** мужска́я
пре́лесть ♦ **persuasive ~** убеди́тельный шарм ♦ **physical ~s** физи́ческие пре́лести ♦
potent ~ могу́щественное обая́ние ♦ **prodigal ~** чрезме́рная пре́лесть ♦ **radiant
~** сия́ющее обая́ние ♦ **intillating ~** искря́щееся обая́ние ♦ **seductive ~** соблазни́-
тельный шарм ♦ **voluptuous ~s** сладостра́стные пре́лести ♦ **exude ~** излуча́ть
очарова́ние.

> *charm: Your charm*

Your charm is just one of your many exceptional attributes. Твоё обая́ние... -- то́лько
одно́ из мно́гих твои́х исключи́тельных ка́честв. ♦ **The magnetism of your charm
is (completely) irresistible.** Магнети́зм твоего́ обая́ния (соверше́нно) неотрази́м. ♦
You have such irresistible charm. В тебе́ тако́й неотрази́мый шарм. ♦ **Your** *(1,2)*
charm is very *(3)* **persuasive** / *(4)* **potent (, do you know that?).** Твоё *(1)* обая́ние / *(2)*
очарова́ние о́чень *(3)* убеди́тельно / *(4)* могу́щественно (, зна́ешь ли ты э́то?). ♦
Your charm is mesmerizing. Твоё очарова́ние гипнотизи́рует. ♦ **No man could resist
your charm.** Ни оди́н мужчи́на не смог бы устоя́ть пе́ред твои́м очарова́нием. ♦
You have a marvelous blending of spirit, charm and sensuality. У тебя́ удиви́тельное
сочета́ние души́, обая́ния и чу́вственности. ♦ **You exude charm.** Ты излуча́ешь
очарова́ние.

> *charm: How I regard your charm*

I'm not impervious to your charm. Я не безразли́чен к твоему́ обая́нию. ♦ **I (simply)
cannot resist your charms.** Я (про́сто) не могу́ сопротивля́ться твоему́ очарова́нию.
♦ **I find your charm and beauty very hard to resist.** Я обнару́жил, что твоему́ обая́нию
и красоте́ о́чень тру́дно сопротивля́ться. ♦ **I marvel at your physical charms.** Я вос-
хища́юсь твои́ми физи́ческими пре́лестями. ♦ **You dazzle me with your charm and
beauty and blithe spirit.** Ты поража́ешь меня́ свои́м обая́нием, красото́й и весёлым
хара́ктером. ♦ **Since the day we met I've been oblivious of** *(1)* **everything** / *(2)* **all else
except your radiant charm.** Со дня на́шей встре́чи я соверше́нно забы́л обо *(1,2)* всём
кро́ме твоего́ сия́ющего обая́ния.

> *charm: What your charm does to me*

You hypnotize me with your scintillating charm. Ты гипнотизи́руешь меня́ свои́м
искря́щимся обая́нием. ♦ **I am** *(1)* **completely** / *(2)* **totally** *(3)* **captivated** / *(4)* **enchanted**
/*(5)* **enthralled** / *(6)* **seduced** / *(7)* **mesmerized by your** *(8,9)* **...charm.** / *(10)* **...manifold
charms.** Я *(1)* по́лностью / *(2)* абсолю́тно *(3)* пленён /*(4)* околдо́ван / *(5)* очаро́ван /
(6) обольщён / *(7)* загипнотизи́рован *(8)* ...твои́м очарова́нием / *(9)* ша́рмом. / *(10)*
...твои́ми многочи́сленными пре́лестями. ♦ **My heart is (**[1] **completely** / [2] **totally)
enraptured by your charm and beauty.** Я (*[1,2]* соверше́нно) восхищён твои́м обая́-
нием и красото́й. ♦ **I cannot describe to you how deeply stirred I am by your manifold charms.** Я не могу́ описа́ть, как глубоко́ я взволно́ван твои́ми многочи́слен-
ными пре́лестями. ♦ **Your (incredible) beauty and (scintillating) charm** *(1)* **...have
completely swept me away.** / *(2)* **...are an elixir to my soul.** Твоя́ (невероя́тная) красота́
и (искря́щееся) обая́ние ...по́лностью покори́ли меня́. / ...-- эликси́р мое́й души́.

Common adult weights are given in Appendix 10, page 777.

| **charm:** *I'm lonely for your charms* |

My arms are (so) lonely for your voluptuous charms. Мои́ ру́ки (так) тоску́ют по твоему́ роско́шному те́лу.

| **charm:** *life's charms* |

You have made me rediscover life's charms. Ты помогла́ *(ж: помо́г)* мне опя́ть оцени́ть пре́лести жи́зни.

charmed *adj* очаро́ван, -а, -о, -ы *(short forms)* ♦ **I was so charmed at** *(1)* **seeing** / *(2)* **meeting you yesterday that I feel compelled to write this short note to you to tell you how (very) much it meant to me.** Я был так очаро́ван, *(1)* уви́дев / *(2)* встре́тив тебя́ вчера́ , что я чу́вствую непреодоли́мую потре́бность написа́ть э́ту коро́ткую запи́ску, что́бы сказа́ть тебе́ , как (о́чень) мно́го э́то зна́чит для меня́.

charmer *n* чароде́й *m*; чароде́йка, очарова́шка *f*, преле́стница, обая́тельный челове́к ♦ **You are** *(1)* **such** / *(2)* **really a charmer.** Ты *(1)* така́я / *(2)* про́сто очарова́шка.

charming *adj* очарова́тельный, -ая, -ое, -ые, обая́тельный, -ая, -ое, -ые, преле́стный, -ая, -ое, -ые, обворожи́тельный, -ая, -ое, -ые ♦ **utterly ~** соверше́нно очарова́тельный, -ая, -ое, -ые.

chase *vt* гоня́ться *(what = + за + instr.)* ♦ **~ away** прогоня́ть / прогна́ть прочь *(what, whom = acc.)* ♦ **~ rainbows** гоня́ться за недостижи́мым. ♦ *(1)* **Come** / *(2)* **Hurry back to me and chase away this terrible** *(3)* **pain** / *(4)* **scourge of loneliness (that grips my heart).** *(1)* Прийди́ / *(2)* Торопи́сь (обра́тно) ко мне и прогони́ прочь э́ту ужа́сную *(3)* боль / *(4)* ка́ру одино́чества (, кото́рая терза́ет моё се́рдце).

chaser *n* пресле́дователь ♦ **rainbow ~** тот, кто гоня́ется за недостижи́мым *(explanation)* ♦ **skirt ~** *(slang)* бе́гающий за все́ми ю́бками, ба́бник, волоки́та.

chasm *n* бе́здна ♦ **burning ~** горя́чая бе́здна ♦ **hot ~** горя́чая бе́здна.

chaste *adj* целому́дренный, -ая, -ое, -ые ♦ **remain ~** сохраня́ть / сохрани́ть целому́дрие.

chastise *vt* отчи́тывать / отчита́ть *(whom = dat.)* *(whom = acc.)*, устра́ивать / устро́ить разно́с.

chastity *n* целому́дрие ♦ **They say that chastity is curable if detected early.** Говоря́т, что целому́дрие ле́чится, е́сли обнару́жено во́время.

chat *vi* разгова́ривать *(with whom = + с + instr.)*, поболта́ть *(with whom = + с + instr.)*.

chat *n* разгово́р; *(Internet discussion)* диало́г ♦ **confidential ~** довери́тельный разгово́р ♦ *(1,2)* **long ~** *(1)* дли́нный / *(2)* до́лгий разгово́р ♦ **Let's go someplace and have a chat.** Дава́й пойдём куда́-нибудь и поговори́м. ♦ **I'd love to spend quiet evenings with you, having long fireside chats.** Я хоте́л *(ж: хоте́ла)* бы проводи́ть споко́йные вечера́ с тобо́й с до́лгими разгово́рами у ками́на.

chatterbox *n* *(slang)* болту́н *m*, болту́нья *f*.

chatty *adj* болтли́вый, -ая, -ое, -ые.

chauvinist *n* шовини́ст ♦ **male ~** мужчи́на-шовини́ст.

chauvinistic *adj* шовинисти́ческий, -ая, -ое, -ие.

cheapen oneself *vt* унижа́ть / уни́зить себя́ ♦ **I feel like I've cheapened myself.** Я чу́вствую, что уни́зил *(ж: уни́зила)* себя́.

cheat *vi* обма́нывать / обману́ть *(on whom = acc.)* ♦ **I have a** *(1)* **gut** / *(2)* **nagging feeling that you're cheating on me.** Я *(1)* ...инстинкти́вно... / *(2)* ...со щемя́щей бо́лью... чу́вствую, что ты обма́нываешь меня́. ♦ **I would never cheat on you.** Я никогда́ не бу́ду обма́нывать тебя́.

cheat(er) *n* обма́нщик *m*, обма́нщица *f* ♦ **be a ~** *(also:)* изменя́ть *(whom = dat.)*. ♦ **You're a cheat.** Ты обма́нщица *(ж: обма́нщик)*.

cheating *n* обма́н ♦ **You are truly a master at the art of cheating.** Ты, пра́вда, ма́стер в

An italicized ж in parentheses   indicates a woman speaking.

иску́сстве обма́на.

check *vt* проверя́ть / прове́рить *(what = acc.)* ♦ ~ **out** *vt (slang) (examine with great interest)* оки́дывать / оки́нуть оце́нивающим взгля́дом *(what, whom = acc.)* ♦ **I saw you checking** *(1)* **him** / *(2)* **her out.** Я ви́дел *(ж: ви́дела)*, что ты оки́нула *(1)* его́ *(ж: оки́нул [2] её)* оце́нивающим взгля́дом.

check *n* 1. *(control)* контро́ль; 2. *(examination)* прове́рка; 3. *(money)* чек ♦ **do a reality** ~ верну́ться к реа́льности ♦ **You really should try to keep your feelings in check.** Ты, действи́тельно, должна́ *(ж: до́лжен)* попыта́ться держа́ть под контро́лем свои́ чу́вства. ♦ **It's so hard for me to keep my feelings in check (when** *[1]* **...I'm around you.** / *[2]* **...I think about you.).** Мне так тру́дно уде́рживать под контро́лем свои́ чу́вства (, когда́ *[1]* ...я ря́дом с тобо́й. / *[2]* ...я ду́маю о тебе́.)

cheek *n* 1. *(on face)* щека́ *(pl:* щёки*)*; 2. *(buttocks)* окру́глость *f*; 3. *(impudence)* на́глость *f*; де́рзость *f* ♦ **crimson** ~**s** пунцо́вые щёки, тёмно-кра́сные щёки ♦ *(1,2)* **fat** ~**s** *(1)* по́лные / *(2)* то́лстые щёки ♦ **firm** ~**s of the buttocks** пло́тные окру́глости по́пки ♦ **little** ~**s** щёчки ♦ **rosy** ~**s** румя́ные щёки ♦ **smooth** ~**s** гла́дкие щёки ♦ *(1,2)* **soft** ~**s** *(1)* не́жные / *(2)* мя́гкие щёки ♦ *(familiar)* **your** ~**s** твои́ щёки; *(polite)*Ва́ши щёки ♦ **stroke your** ~ гла́дить / погла́дить тебя́ по щеке́.

---
cheek: phrases

I like dancing cheek to cheek with you. Мне нра́вится танцева́ть с тобо́й щека́ к щеке́. ♦ **You have such (rose-)petal-soft cheeks.** У тебя́ щёчки мя́гкие, как лепестки́ ро́зы. ♦ **I just want to kiss you on the cheek.** Я то́лько хочу́ поцелова́ть тебя́ в щёчку. ♦ **I'm going to make your cheeks get** *(1)* **flushed** / *(2)* **red all over.** Я заста́влю твои́ щёки *(1,2)* покры́ться румя́нцем. ♦ **How I'd love to rub my cheeks softly against the inside of your legs.** Как бы я хоте́л не́жно потере́ться щека́ми по вну́тренней стороне́ твои́х ног. ♦ **It's pure heaven just to fondle your cheek.** Э́то чисте́йшее наслажде́ние про́сто ласка́ть твою́ щеку́. ♦ **Your cheeks glow like a sunset promising a warm night.** Твои́ щёки пыла́ют как зака́т, обеща́ющий тёплую ночь. ♦ **You have a lot of cheek.** В тебе́ мно́го на́глости.

cheekbones *n, pl* ску́лы ♦ **high** ~**s** высо́кие ску́лы ♦ **high, delicate** ~**s** высо́кие, изя́щные ску́лы ♦ **prominent** ~**s** выступа́ющие ску́лы.

cheer *n* 1. *(gaiety)* весе́лье; 2. *(encouragement)* ободре́ние; 3. *(hurrah)* ура́.

cheer up *vt* подба́дривать / подбодри́ть *(whom = acc.).*

cheesecake *n (slang)* по́за, позволя́ющая же́нщине показа́ть но́ги, бёдра, те́ло *(1 explanation).*

chemise *n* соро́чка.

chemistry *n* 1. *(science)* хи́мия; 2. *(psychological)* (психологи́ческая) совмести́мость; 3. *(attraction)* тяготе́ние, притяже́ние, влече́ние ♦ **physical** ~ физи́ческое тяготе́ние ♦ **sexual** *(1,2)* ~ взаи́мное сексуа́льное *(1)* притяже́ние / *(2)* тяготе́ние ♦ **unique** ~ 1. *(attraction)* уника́льное влече́ние; 2. *(compatibility)* уника́льная совмести́мость ♦ **lots of** ~ си́льное взаи́мное тяготе́ние.

---
chemistry: phrases

We have such *(1)* **good** / *(2)* **great chemistry between us.** Мы так *(1)* хорошо́ / *(2)* превосхо́дно ла́дим друг с дру́гом. ♦ **I've never had such good chemistry with anyone (as I have with you).** Мне никогда́ не́ было ни с кем так хорошо́ (, как с тобо́й). ♦ **I'm looking for that special chemistry with a slender, attractive, good-natured single female.** Я ищу́ психологи́ческой совмести́мости со стро́йной, привлека́тельной, до́брой, одино́кой же́нщиной.

cherish *vt* дорожи́ть *(what, whom = instr.)*, леле́ять *(what, whom = acc.)*, бере́чь *(what, whom*

Procedures for getting married to a Russian
are outlined in Appendix 18, page 787.

= *acc.*), (бéрежно) храни́ть *(what, whom = acc.)*, нéжно люби́ть *(what, whom = acc.)*.

| **cherish:** *I cherish you / your love* |

I cherish *(1)* **...you (more than anything else in this world).** / *(2)* **...your love.** / *(3)* **...the closeness that we share.** / *(4)* **...everything about you.** / *(5)* **...our love above all else.** / / *(6)* **...the day that I met you.** Я дорожу́ *(1)* ...тобо́й (бо́льше, чем всем в э́том ми́ре). / *(2)* ...твоéй любо́вью. / *(3)* ...на́шей бли́зостью. / *(4)* ...всем о тебé. / *(5)* ...на́шей любо́вью превы́ше всего́. / *(6)* ...па́мятью о том дне, когда́ встрéтил *(ж: встрéтила)* тебя́. ◆ *(1)* **I will...** / *(2)* **I promise to... love you and cherish you** *(3)* **...forever.** / *(4)* **...till the end of time.** / *(5)* **...for (the rest of my) life.** / *(6)* **...until the day I die.** *(1)* Я бу́ду... / *(2)* Я обеща́ю... люби́ть тебя́ и леле́ять тебя́ *(3)* ...всегда́. / *(4)* ...вéчно. / *(5)* ...всю (оста́вшуюся) жизнь. / *(6)* ...до са́мой смéрти. ◆ **The more I know you, the more I love you and cherish you.** Чем бо́лее я узна́ю тебя́, тем бо́льше люблю́ и леле́ю.

| **cherish:** *I cherish the memories / times* |

I cherish *(1)* **...those memories.** / *(2)* **...the memories of the wonderful** *(3,4)* **moments** / *(5)* **hours** / *(6)* **times we spent together.** Я дорожу́ *(1)* ...э́тими воспомина́ниями. / *(2)* ...воспомина́ниями о прекра́сных *(3)* мину́тах / *(4)* мгновéниях / *(5)* часа́х / *(6)* времена́х, проведённых с тобо́й. ◆ **I will always cherish the memories of the** *(1)* **times** / *(2)* **moments we shared together.** Я всегда́ бу́ду леле́ять воспомина́ния о *(1)* времена́х / *(2)* мину́тах, кото́рые мы проводи́ли вдвоём. ◆ **Oh, my darling, how I cherish the moments that we** *(1)* **share** / *(2)* **spend together.** О, моя́ дорога́я, как я леле́ю в душé те мгновéния, кото́рые мы *(1)* разделя́ем / *(2)* прово́дим вмéсте. ◆ **I cherish every hour, every minute that I** *(1)* **share** / *(2)* **spend with you.** Я храню́ в сéрдце ка́ждый час, ка́ждую мину́ту, *(1)* разделённую / *(2)* проведённую с тобо́й. ◆ **How can I ever put into words how much I cherish our** *(1)* **life** / *(2)* **moments together?** Как описа́ть слова́ми, как бéрежно я храню́ воспомина́ния о *(1)* ...на́шей жи́зни... / *(2)* ...мгновéниях, проведённых вмéсте?

| **cherish:** *I cherish the hope* |

I cherish the (fervent) hope that *(1)* **...we can see each other soon.** / *(2)* **...you will accept my invitation.** / *(3)* **...you will want** / *(4)* **decide to correspond with me.** Я леле́ю (горя́чую) надéжду, что *(1)* ...мы ско́ро смо́жем уви́деть друг дру́га. / *(2)* ...ты при́мешь моё приглашéние. / *(3)* ...ты захо́чешь / *(4)* реши́шь перепи́сываться со мной.

| **cherish:** *I cherish your letters* |

I read your letters over and over again and I never cease to cherish them. Я чита́ю твои́ пи́сьма опя́ть и опя́ть и никогда́ не переста́ну дорожи́ть и́ми.

cherished *adj* леле́янный, -ая, -ое, -ые, взлеле́янный, -ая, -ое, -ые, дорого́й (-а́я, -о́е, -и́е) ◆ сéрдцу; незабвéнный, -ая, -ое, -ые, завéтный, -ая, -ое, -ые ◆ **My most cherished memories are of the times we** *(1)* **shared** / *(2)* **spent together.** Мои́ са́мые драгоцéнные воспомина́ния -- э́то воспомина́ния о врéмени, *(1,2)* проведённом вмéсте.

cherry *n (slang) (virginity)* дéвственность *f* ◆ **Listen, I'm not just trying to get your cherry. I truly love you.** Послу́шай, я не про́сто пыта́юсь лиши́ть тебя́ неви́нности. Я действи́тельно люблю́ тебя́. ◆ **I don't give a damn if someone broke your cherry already. It's totally unimportant.** Мне наплева́ть, éсли ты ужé не дéвушка. Это совершéнно не ва́жно.

chest *n* 1. *(breast, -s)* грудь *f*; 2. *(box, trunk)* я́щик, сунду́к; *(treasure)* сокро́вище ◆ **ample** ~ больша́я грудь ◆ *(1,2)* **bare** ~ *(1)* го́лая / *(2)* обнажённая грудь ◆ **big** ~ больша́я грудь ◆ *(1,2)* **broad** ~ *(1)* широ́кая / *(2)* си́льная грудь ◆ **flat** ~ пло́ская грудь ◆ **furry** ~ мехова́я грудь ◆ **hairless** ~ безволо́сая грудь ◆ **hairy** ~ волоса́тая грудь ◆ **massive** ~ масси́вная грудь ◆ **narrow** ~ у́зкая грудь ◆ *(1,2)* **powerful** ~ *(1)* мо́щная / *(2)* бога-

---

*A list of conjugated Russian verbs is given
in Appendix 3 on page 699*

ты́рская грудь ♦ *(1,2)* **strong ~** *(1)* кре́пкая / *(2)* си́льная грудь ♦ **tanned ~** загоре́лая грудь ♦ **treasure ~** сокро́вище.

chest: phrases

I *(1)* **love** / *(2)* **want to sleep with my head on your chest.** Я *(1)* люблю́ / *(2)* хочу́ спать голово́й на твое́й груди́. ♦ **You are a(n) (absolute) treasure chest of** *(1)* **sweetness** / *(2)* **delights** / *(3)* **love** / *(4)* **beauty** / *(5)* **goodness** / *(6)* **ecstasy** / *(7)* **pleasure.** Ты (абсолю́тное) сокро́вище *(1)* сла́дости / *(2)* восто́рга / *(3)* любви́ / *(4)* красоты́ / *(5)* доброты́ / *(6)* экста́за / *(7)* удово́льствия.

chested: ♦ **ample ~** с большо́й гру́дью ♦ **beautifully ~** с прекра́сной гру́дью ♦ **big ~** с большо́й гру́дью.

Chianti *n (Italian red wine)* Кья́нти.

chic *adj* элега́нтный, -ая, -ое, -ые, эффе́ктный, -ая, -ое, -ые, изы́сканный, -ая, -ое, -ые, шика́рный, -ая, -ое, -ые ♦ **My! How chic you look!** О, как шика́рно ты вы́глядишь! ♦ **You always dress so chic.** Ты всегда́ одева́ешься так шика́рно. ♦ **You look** *(1)* **quite** / *(2)* **very** *(3,4)* **chic in that** *(5)* **dress** / *(6)* **outfit.** Ты вы́глядишь *(1)* вполне́ / *(2)* о́чень *(3)* шика́рно / *(4)* элега́нтно в э́том *(5)* пла́тье / *(6)* наря́де. ♦ **That** *(1)* **dress** / *(2)* **outfit is very chic.** *(1)* Это пла́тье о́чень элега́нтно. / *(2)* Этот наря́д о́чень элега́нтен.

chick *n (slang) (girl, woman)* де́вушка; же́нщина ♦ **blonde ~** блонди́нка ♦ **cute ~** привлека́тельная де́вушка ♦ **sweet ~** не́жная де́вушка.

chicken *n (slang) (coward)* трус ♦ **no spring ~** не девчо́нка, не пе́рвой мо́лодости ♦ **be ~** тру́сить.

chide *vt* брани́ть / побрани́ть *(whom = acc.)*, упрека́ть / упрекну́ть *(whom = acc.)*; жури́ть / пожури́ть *(whom = acc.)*.

chiffon *adj* шифо́новый, -ая, -ое, -ые.

chiffon *n* шифо́н.

chignon *n (pony tail)* шиньо́н.

child *n* ребёнок, дитя́ *(pl* де́ти*)* ♦ **love ~** дитя́ любви́ ♦ **carry a ~** *(pregnant)* носи́ть ребёнка.

child: children OK

One child is okay. Оди́н ребёнок -- хорошо́. ♦ **I can accept a child** Я допуска́ю ребёнка.♦ **Children are okay with me.** Если у тебя́ де́ти, -- хорошо́. ♦ **I** *(1)* **like** / *(2)* **love children.** Я *(1,2)* люблю́ дете́й.

child: have children?

Do you have any children? У тебя́ есть де́ти? ♦ **I have** *(1)* **...one child.** / *(2)* **...two** / *(3)* **three children.** У меня́ есть *(1)* ...оди́н ребёнок. / *(2)*...два / *(3)* три ребёнка. ♦ **How old are your children?** Ско́лько лет твои́м де́тям? ♦ **I'm dedicated to my children.** Я пре́дан *(ж: пре́дана)* свои́м де́тям.

child: having children with you

I want so much to have a child that *(1)* **...looks** *(2)* **just** / *(3)* **exactly like you.** / *(4)* **...has your (beautiful) face and eyes.** Я о́чень хочу́ име́ть ребёнка *(1)* ...*(2)* по́лностью / *(3)* абсолю́тно похо́жего на тебя́. / *(4)* ...с твои́ми (прекра́сными) глаза́ми и лицо́м. ♦ **I've often dreamt of having children that look just like you.** Я часто́ мечта́ю име́ть дете́й, кото́рые вы́глядят то́чно, как ты. ♦ **I want you to be the** *(1)* **mother** / *(2)* **father of my children.** Я хочу́, чтобы ты *(1)* ...была́ ма́терью... / *(2)* ...был отцо́м... мои́х дете́й. ♦ **You're the only woman I've ever met with whom I'd like to have children.** Ты еди́нственная же́нщина, с кото́рой я хоте́л бы име́ть дете́й. ♦ **I'd like to have children (with you).** Я хоте́л бы име́ть дете́й (от тебя́) ♦ **I want all of my children to look just**

For Russian adjectives, the masculine form is spelled out,
followed by the feminine, neuter and plural endings

like you. Я хочу́, чтобы все мои́ де́ти вы́глядели то́чно, как ты. ◆ **You possess the kind of beauty that I would like to see reflected in the faces of all my children.** Ты облада́ешь тако́й красото́й, кото́рую я бы хоте́л ви́деть отражённой в ли́цах всех свои́х дете́й.

child-free *adj* безде́тный, -ая, -ое, -ые.

childish *adj* де́тский, -ая, -ое, -ие; ребя́ческий, -ая, -ое, -ие.

childishness *n* ребя́чество ◆ *(1)* **That's...** / *(2)* **This is... childishness.** *(1,2)* Это ребя́чество.

childless *adj* безде́тный, -ая, -ое, -ые.

child-like *adj* подо́бный (-ая, -ое, -ые) ребёнку.

chill *vi (slang) (relax, take it easy)* расслабля́ться / рассла́биться.

chilliness *n* холо́дность *f* ◆ **Why the chilliness all of a sudden?** Почему́ неожи́данная холо́дность?

chilling *n (slang) (relaxing, taking it easy)* расслабле́ние.

chilly *adj* холо́дный, -ая, -ое, -ые *(short forms:* хо́лоден, холодна́, хо́лодно, холодны́) ◆ **Why are so chilly toward me?** Почему́ ты так холодна́ *(ж: хо́лоден)* со мной? ◆ **You've been awfully chilly toward me lately.** Ты была́ ужа́сно холодна́ *(ж: хо́лоден)* со мной после́днее вре́мя. ◆ **I'm** *(1,2)* **sorry if I seemed chilly.** Я *(1)* извиня́юсь / *(2)* сожале́ю, е́сли я каза́лся холо́дным *(ж: каза́лась холо́дной).*

chin *n* подборо́док ◆ **cleft** ~ подборо́док с я́мочкой ◆ **double** ~ двойно́й подборо́док ◆ **I love the dimple on your chin.** Мне нра́вится я́мочка на твоём подборо́дке.

Chinese *adj* кита́йский, -ая, -ое, -ие.

Chinese *n* 1. *(person)* кита́ец *m*, китая́нка *f (pl:* кита́йцы); 2. *(language)* кита́йский язы́к ◆ **speak** ~ говори́ть по-кита́йски.

chips *n, pl* 1. *(potato)* чи́псы, 2. *(games)* фи́шки ◆ **When the chips are down, I'll be there to support you.** В реша́ющий моме́нт я бу́ду там, чтобы поддержа́ть тебя́.

chitchat *n* болтовня́; разгово́р, бесе́да *(о том о сём)* ◆ **pleasant** ~ прия́тный разгово́р.

chivalrous *adj* ры́царский, -ая, -ое, -ие ◆ **How chivalrous of you!** Как э́то по-ры́царски с твое́й стороны́! ◆ **How chivalrous you are!** Како́й ты ры́царь!

chivalry *n* ры́царство.

choice вы́бор ◆ **first** ~ пе́рвый вы́бор ◆ **second** ~ второ́й вы́бор ◆ **make a** ~ сде́лать вы́бор.

choker *n* коро́ткое ожере́лье.

chomp *vt:* ◆ *(1)* **She** / *(2)* **He is chomping at the bit to get married.** *(1)* Она́ жа́ждет вы́йти за́муж. / *(2)* Он жа́ждет жени́ться.

choose *vt* выбира́ть / вы́брать *(what, whom = acc.)* ◆ **I'm so glad I chose you.** Я так рад *(ж: ра́да),* что вы́брал *(ж: вы́брала)* тебя́. ◆ **There was no way I could choose anyone else.** Для меня́ бы́ло бы соверше́нно невозмо́жно вы́брать кого́-то друго́го.

choosy *adj* разбо́рчивый, -ая, -ое, -ые, привере́дливый, -ая, -ое, -ые.

chord *n* акко́рд, струна́ ◆ **There were several other ads in the personals that were somewhat interesting, but yours struck an immediate chord in my heart and I knew with a certainty that there was no way I could not write to you.** В отде́ле знако́мств бы́ло не́сколько други́х объявле́ний, чём-то интере́сных, но Ва́ше вы́звало неме́дленный о́тклик в моём се́рдце, и я твёрдо знал *(ж: зна́ла),* что не могу́ не написа́ть Вам. ◆ **I want to** *(1)* **hear** / *(2)* **make your vocal chords play all of Beethoven's symphonies in high C.** Я хочу́ *(1)* слы́шать / *(2)* заста́вить твои́ голосовы́е свя́зки игра́ть все симфо́нии Бетхо́вена на са́мой высо́кой но́те.

Christian *adj* христиа́нский, -ая, -ое, -ие.

Christian *n* христиа́нин *m*, христиа́нка *f* ◆ **born-again** ~ новообращённый христиа́нин *m*, новообращённая христиа́нка *f*.

See Appendix 19 for notes on sending mail to Russia and Ukraine.

chubby *adj* то́лстенький, -ая, -ое, -ие, пу́хленький, -ая, -ое, -ие, по́лненький, -ая, -ое, -ие, полнова́т, -а, -ы *(short forms)*; *(face)* круглоли́цый, -ая, -ое, -ые ♦ ~ **girl** пы́шка ♦ **I like it that you're a little chubby.** Мне нра́вится, что ты по́лненькая. ♦ **I like a chubby woman.** Мне нра́вятся по́лные же́нщины. ♦ **I hope you don't mind it that I'm a little chubby.** Я наде́юсь, ты не возвража́ешь, что я полнова́т *(ж: полнова́та)*.

chum *n (slang)* закады́чный друг.

chunky *n (slang) (overweight)* упи́танный, -ая, -ое, -ые

church *n* це́рковь *f* ♦ **Do you go to church (often)?** Ты (ча́сто) хо́дишь в це́рковь? ♦ **I (don't) go to church (*[1]* often / *[2]* regularly).** Я (не) хожу́ в це́рковь (*[1]* ча́сто / *[2]* регуля́рно). ♦ **I seek a person who is committed to church and family.** Я ищу́ челове́ка, кото́рому важна́ це́рковь и семья́.

churn *vi* крути́ться, верте́ться, кружи́ться ♦ **All my emotions were churning inside me.** Все чу́вства смеша́лись во мне.

chutzpah *n* 1. *(impudence)* на́глость *f*, наха́льство; 2. *(audacity)* де́рзость *f*, сме́лость *f*.

circa *prep* о́коло *(+ gen.)* ♦ *(age)* ~ **29-38** о́коло 29-38.

circle *n* круг ♦ ~ **of acquaintances** круг знако́мых ♦ ~ **of friends** круг друзе́й.

circulation *n* 1. *(use)* обраще́ние; 2. *(air)* циркуля́ция; 3. *(blood)* (крово)обраще́ние ♦ **I've been out of circulation for a long time.** Я не встреча́лся *(встреча́лась)* ни с кем до́лгое вре́мя.

circumstance *n* 1. *(occurrence)* обстоя́тельство, слу́чай; 2. *(condition) pl:* обстоя́тельства, усло́вия, положе́ние; 3. *(financial condition)* (материа́льное / фина́нсовое) положе́ние ♦ **compromising** ~s компромети́рующие обстоя́тельства ♦ **difficult** ~s тру́дные обстоя́тельства, тру́дное положе́ние ♦ *(1,2)* **financial** ~s *(1)* материа́льное / *(2)* фина́нсовое положе́ние.

citizen *n* граждани́н *m*, гражда́нка *f (pl:* гра́ждане*)* ♦ **American** ~ *n* америка́нский граждани́н *m*, америка́нская гражда́нка *f* ♦ **sexy senior** ~ сексуа́льный пенсионе́р ♦ **become a** ~ стать граждани́ном *m* / гражда́нкой *f*.

citizenship *n* гражда́нство ♦ **apply for** ~ запо́лнить и пода́ть докуме́нты на гражда́нство ♦ **get** ~ получи́ть гражда́нство.

civil *adj* 1. *(polite, mannerly)* ве́жливый, -ая, -ое, -ые; 2. *(citizen's)* гражда́нский, -ая, -ое, -ие.

civility *n* ве́жливость *f*, корре́ктность *f*.

clad *adj* оде́тый, -ая, -ое, -ые ♦ **scantily** ~ полуразде́тый, -ая, -ое, -ые, полуго́лый, -ая, -ое, -ые, полуоде́тый, -ая, -ое, -ые

claim *vt* 1. *(assert)* заявля́ть / заяви́ть *(what = acc.)*, утвержда́ть / утверди́ть *(what = acc.)*; 2. *(take)* овладе́ть *(what = instr.)* ♦ **How I ache for the day when my mouth can at last claim yours.** Как я страда́ю по тому́ дню, когда́ мой рот смо́жет наконе́ц овладе́ть твои́м. ♦ **When at last my mouth claims yours, I will** *(1)* **...deluge it with more kisses...** / *(2)* **...lavish /** *(3)* **bestow more kisses upon it... than it has ever known before.** Когда́ наконе́ц мой рот встре́тится с твои́м, я *(1)* ...затоплю́ его бо́льшим коли́чеством поцелу́ев,... / *(2,3)* ...подарю́ ему бо́льше поцелу́ев,... чем он когда́-либо пре́жде получа́л.

clamor *vi* крича́ть / кри́кнуть, шу́мно тре́бовать / потре́бовать, взыва́ть / воззва́ть ♦ **My body is clamoring for yours.** Моё те́ло взыва́ет к твому́. ♦ **My lips are clamoring for yours.** Мои́ гу́бы тре́буют твои́.

clamp down *vi* зажима́ть / зажа́ть *(on what = acc.)* ♦ **I have to clamp down on my feelings.** Я до́лжен *(ж: должна́)* зажа́ть свои́ чу́вства.

clandestine *adj* та́йный, -ая, -ое, -ые ♦ ~ **(love) affair** та́йная любо́вная связь ~ **meet-**

When terms are listed after a main word, a tilde ~
is used to indicate the main word.

ing тáйная встрéча.

clasp vt 1. *(hands)* сжимáть / сжать *(what = acc.);* 2. *(someone to oneself)* обнимáть / обня́ть *(whom = acc.)*, прижимáть / прижáть *(whom = acc.)* ♦ **We'll clasp hands (together) and walk along the beach.** Мы возьмёмся зá руки (вмéсте) и пойдём гуля́ть по пля́жу.

class n 1. *(school group)* класс; *(lesson)* урóк, заня́тие; 2. *(category)* класс; сорт, кáчество; 3. *(style)* класс, шик ♦ **man with ~** клáссный мужчи́на ♦ **woman with ~** клáссная жéнщина ♦ *(1)* **You have... /** *(2)* **You showed... a lot of class.** *(1)* У тебя́... / *(2)* Ты демонстри́ровала *(ж: демонстри́ровал)*... высóкий класс. ♦ **You exude class.** В Вас срáзу чýвствуется класс.

classic adj класси́ческий, -ая, -ое, -ие ♦ **You have classic beauty.** У тебя́ класси́ческая красотá. ♦ **You are indisputably unique and indisputably classic in the magnitude of your loveliness.** Ты бесспóрно уникáльна и бесспóрно класси́чна в своéй красотé.

classmate соучени́к *m*, соучени́ца *f*; *(univ.)* сокýрсник *m*, сокýрсница *f*.

classy adj клáссный, -ая, -ое, -ые ♦ **In my opinion, you're as classy as they come.** По моемý мнéнию, нет никогó, бóлее клáссного, чем ты.

claw n кóготь *m (pl:* кóгти*)* ♦ **One marriage was enough. I don't want anybody getting their claws into me again.** Однóй жени́тьбы бы́ло достáточно. Я не хочý, чтóбы ктó-нибудь опя́ть запусти́л в меня́ свои́ кóгти. ♦ **Draw in your claws.** Убери́ кóгти.

clean-cut adj подтя́нутый, -ая, -ое, -ые.

clear adj 1. *(easily visible)* отчётливый, -ая, -ое, -ые; 2. *(sound)* звóнкий, -ая, -ое, -ие, чи́стый, -ая, -ое, -ые; 3. *(understandable)* я́сный, -ая, -ое, -ые, поня́тный, -ая, -ое, -ые; 4. *(unimpeded)* свобóдный, -ая, -ое, -ые ♦ **You and I were meant to be together. That's crystal clear me.** Ты и я предназнáчены быть вмéсте. Это мне кристáльно я́сно.

clear-thinking adj я́сно дýмающий, -ая, -ее, -ие.

cleavage n щель *f*, расщéлина, «ручеёк».

clergy n духовéнство.

clergyman n свящéнник.

clever adj ýмный, -ая, -ое, -ые.

click vi 1. *(noise)* щёлкать / щёлкнуть; 2. *(slang: fit well together, get along well)* отли́чно лáдить (вмéсте) ♦ **You and I just seem to click (together).** Мы с тобóй, кáжется, отли́чно лáдим. ♦ **Something between us just clicked.** Мы прóсто почýвствовали взаи́мное притяжéние.

climax n оргáзм ♦ *(1)* **I want to... /** *(2)* **I'm going to suffuse your entire being in the fiery rapture of climax.** *(1)* Я хочý зали́ть... / *(2)* Я залью́... всё твоё существó óгненным востóргом оргáзма.

climax vi *(slang) (reach orgasm)* дости́чь оргáзма.

cling vi 1. *(hold onto)* цепля́ться *(to what, whom = +* за *+ acc.);* держáться *(to what, whom = +* за *+ acc.)*, удéрживать / удержáть *(to what = acc.);* 2. *(stick)* ли́пнуть *(to what = +* к *+ dat.),* прилипáть / прили́пнуть *(to what = +* к *+ dat.)* ♦ **~ seductively** соблазни́тельно облегáть ♦ **~ to a hope** цепля́ться за надéжду ♦ **~ to** *(1)* **me /** *(2)* **you /** *(3)* **him /** *(4)* **her** держáться за *(1)* меня́ / *(2)* тебя́ / *(3)* негó / *(4)* неё.

| cling: phrases |

I cling to the hope that *(1)* **...I can come over there before the end of the year. /** *(2)* **...my /** *(3)* **your visa will come through soon. /** *(4)* **...I can see you this month. /** *(5)* **...we can get married next spring.** Я цепля́юсь за надéжду, что *(1)* ...смогý приéхать тудá до концá гóда. / *(2)* ...моя́ / *(3)* твоя́ ви́за бýдет полýчена скóро. / *(4)* ...смогý уви́деть тебя́ в э́том мéсяце. / *(5)* ...мы мóжем пожени́ться слéдующей веснóй. ♦ **I will always cling to the memory of** *(1)* **...those days together. /** *(2)* **...those wonderful /** *(3)* **beautiful** *(4)* **hours**

A list of abbreviations used in the dictionary is given on page 10.

/ (5) **days we spent together.** / (6) **...our first kiss** / (7) **meeting.** Я бу́ду всегда́ вспомина́ть (1) ...об э́тих днях, проведённых вме́сте. / (2) ...об э́тих великоле́пных / (3) прекра́сных (4) часа́х / (5) днях, проведённых на́ми вме́сте. / (6) ...о на́шем пе́рвом поцелу́е. / (7) ...о на́шей пе́рвой встре́че. ♦ **Do I cling to you too much?** Не сли́шком ли си́льно я ли́пну к тебе́? ♦ **You cling to me too much.** Ты сли́шком ли́пнешь ко мне. ♦ **I love it when you cling to me (tightly).** Я люблю́, когда́ ты (кре́пко) прижима́ешься ко мне. ♦ **I want to cling to this small piece of heaven that we share.** Я хочу́ удержа́ть ма́ленький кусо́чек ра́я, кото́рый нас соединя́ет.

clinger *n* прилипа́ла.

clinginess *n* прили́пчивость *f.*

clinging *adj* 1. *(holding onto)* цепля́ющийся, -аяся, -ееся, -иеся; 2. *(sticking to)* прилипа́ющий, -ая, -ее, -ие.

clingy *adj* цепля́ющий, -ая, -ее, -ие; ли́пнущий, -ая, -ее, -ие.

clit *(slang)* = **clitoris** *n* кли́тор.

clitoris *n* кли́тор.

cloak *vt* скрыва́ть / скрыть *(what = acc.)* ♦ **You shouldn't cloak your emotions (so). You need to open up.** Ты не должна́ *(ж: до́лжен)* скрыва́ть свои́ эмо́ции (так). Ты должна́ *(ж: до́лжен)* раскры́ться.

clogs *n, pl (heavy wooden sandals)* тяжёлые деревя́нные санда́лии.

close *adj* бли́зкий, -ая, -ое, -ие ♦ ~ **resemblance** большо́е схо́дство.

close *adv* бли́зко ♦ **closer** бли́же ♦ **I like to have you close.** Мне нра́вится, когда́ ты во́зле меня́. ♦ **Whenever you get close to me, my knees begin to tremble.** Вся́кий раз, когда́ ты приближа́ешься ко мне, мои́ коле́ни начина́ют дрожа́ть. ♦ **Your letters always make me feel very close to you.** Твои́ пи́сьма всегда́ вызыва́ют во мне чу́вство большо́й бли́зости к тебе́. ♦ **Just being close to you sends the blood rushing in my veins.** Кровь начина́ет бе́шено струи́ться в мои́х ве́нах про́сто от того́, что ты ря́дом. ♦ **I want to** (1) **hold** / (2) **pull you close (to me) (and kiss you tenderly).** Я хочу́ (1) держа́ть / (2) притяну́ть тебя́ бли́зко (ко мне) (и целова́ть тебя́ не́жно). ♦ **I want so desperately to be close to you, to hold you in my arms, to feel the warmth of you, to kiss you.** Я отча́янно хочу́ быть ря́дом с тобо́й, держа́ть тебя́ в объя́тиях, чу́вствовать твоё тепло́, целова́ть тебя́.

close *vi* закрыва́ться / закры́ться ♦ (1,2) **What time does** (3-5) **it close?** (1) Когда́... / (2) В како́е вре́мя... (3) он *m* / (4) она́ *f* / (5) оно́ *neut* закрыва́ется? ♦ (1-3) **It closes at** (4) **one (thirty).** *(See page 759 for other times.)* (1) Он *m* / (2) Она́ *f* / (3) Оно́ *neut* закрыва́ется в (4) час (три́дцать).

closeness *n* 1. бли́зость *f*; о́бщность *f*, гармо́ния ♦ **constant** ~ постоя́нная бли́зость ♦ **emotional** ~ эмоциона́льная бли́зость ♦ **intimate** ~ инти́мная бли́зость ♦ **lifelong** ~ бли́зость на всю жизнь, бли́зость длино́ю в жизнь ♦ **spiritual** ~ духо́вная бли́зость ♦ **true** ~ **of mind, spirit and body** по́длинная гармо́ния ума́, ду́ха и те́ла ♦ **feel your** ~ чу́вствовать твою́ бли́зость ♦ **feelings of** ~ чу́вство бли́зости ♦ **Closeness to you means so much to me.** Быть ря́дом с тобо́й так мно́го зна́чит для меня́. ♦ **I love closeness** (1) **to** / (2) **with you.** Мне нра́вится быть (1,2) ря́дом с тобо́й. ♦ **I cherish the closeness that we share.** Я дорожу́ на́шей бли́зостью. ♦ **With you I have found warmth and compassion and closeness such as I've never known before.** В тебе́ я нашёл *(ж: нашла́)* таки́е теплоту́, сострада́ние и бли́зость, каки́х я никогда́ пре́жде не знал *(ж: зна́ла).*

closure *n* 1. *(conclusion)* заверше́ние; 2. *(fastener)* застёжка ♦ ~ **of a bra** застёжка бюстга́льтера.

The accents on Russian words are to show how to pronounce them..
You don't have to copy the accents when writing to someone.

clothed *adj* одétый, -ая, -ое, -ые *(short forms:* одéт, -а, -о, -ы*)*. ♦ **fully** ~ пóлностью одéт, -а, -ы ♦ **scantily** ~ недостáточно одéт, -а, -ы.

clothes *n, pl* одéжда ♦ **change** ~**s** переодевáться / переодéться ♦ **put** ~**s on** одевáться / одéться ♦ **take** ~**s off** 1. *vi (self)* раздевáться / раздéться 2. *vt (other)* раздевáть / раздéть *(whom = acc.)* ♦ **As far as I'm concerned, you don't need clothes.** Наскóлько я в éтом разбирáюсь, ты не нуждáешься в одéжде. ♦ **I want to behold all of your beauty sans clothes.** Я хочý созерцáть всю твою́ красотý без одéжды. ♦ **The first thing I want to do is divest you of all** *(1)* **those /***(2)* **your (useless) clothes.** Пéрвое, что я хочý сдéлать, éто снять с тебя́ все *(1)* éти / *(2)* твои́ (бесполéзные) одéжды.

clothing *n* одéжда.

clothing-free *adj* не одéтый, -ая, -ое, -ые, без одéжды.

cloud *n* óблако ♦ *(1)* **I've been on a cloud...** / *(2)* **My head's been in the clouds... ever since I** *(3)* **...met you.** / *(4)* **...talked with you.** / *(5)* **...read your letter.** / *(6)* **...all day /** *(7)* **week.** *(1)* Я был *(ж: былá)...* / *(2)* Моё сéрдце бы́ло... на облакáх, с тех пор, как я *(3)* ...встрéтил *(ж: встрéтила)* тебя́. / *(4)* ...говори́л *(ж: говори́ла)* с тобóй. / *(5)* ...прочёл *(ж: прочлá)* твоё письмó. / *(6)* ...весь день. / *(7)* ...всю недéлю. ♦ **I've been walking around on a cloud.** Я витáю в облакáх.

club *n* клуб ♦ **health** ~ клуб здорóвья ♦ **lonely hearts'** ~ клуб одинóких сердéц ♦ **pen-pal** ~ клуб друзéй по перепи́ске ♦ **singles'** ~ клуб одинóких.

clubbing *n*: ♦ **go** ~ ходи́ть по клýбам.

clue *n* ключ к разгáдке, ули́ка, информáция ♦ **I don't have a clue.** *(slang) (no idea)* Я поня́тия не имéю. ♦ *(1)* **He /** *(2)* **She (3,4) doesn't have a clue.** *(slang) (dense)* (1) Он / (2) Онá совершéнно *(3)* тупóй *m* / *(4)* тупáя *f*. ♦ **I have no clue what's going to happen.** Я не представля́ю, что случи́тся.

clueless *adj (slang)* тупóй, -ая, -ое, -ые, глýпый, -ая, -ое, -ые.

clutch *vt (grab)* схвáтывать / схвати́ть *(what, whom = acc.)*; *(squeeze)* сжимáть / сжать *(what, whom = acc.)*; *(press to oneself)* прижимáть / прижáть *(what, whom = acc.)* ♦ ~ **my arm** вцепи́ться в мою́ рýку ♦ ~ **tightly** *(hand, arm)* крéпко сжимáть; *(person to oneself)* крéпко прижимáть.

coat *n (overcoat)* пальтó; *(jacket)* кýртка; *(sport / suit coat)* пиджáк ♦ **beautiful** ~ прекрáсное пальтó ♦ **fur** ~ шýба; меховáя шýбка ♦ **lovely** ~ краси́вое пальтó ♦ **sport** ~ пиджáк ♦ *(1,2)* **stylish** ~ *(1)* мóдное / *(2)* элегáнтное пальтó ♦ **suit** ~ пиджáк ♦ **warm** ~ тёплое пальтó ♦ **winter** ~ зи́мнее пальтó ♦ **your** ~ *(familiar)* твоё пальтó; *(polite)* Вáше пальтó.

coax *vt* уговáривать / уговори́ть *(whom = acc.)*, задáбривать / задóбрить *(whom = acc.)*.

cock *n (slang) (penis)* пéнис, член.

cocktail *n* коктéйль *m*.

cocoon *n* кóкон ♦ **You're wrapped in a cocoon of self-pity.** Ты завёрнута в кóкон жáлости к себé.

coerce *vt* принуждáть / принуди́ть *(whom = acc.)*; заставля́ть / застáвить *(whom = acc.)* ♦ **I would never coerce** *(1)* **you /** *(2)* **anyone into a physical relationship.** Я *(1)* тебя́ / *(2)* никогó никогдá не бýду принуждáть к физи́ческим отношéниям.

coffee *n* кóфе *m*.

cognac *n* конья́к.

cohabitation *n* сожи́тельство.

cohort *n (slang)* 1. *(partner)* партнёр, спýтник *m*, спýтница *f*; 2. *(friend)* друг *m*, подрýга *f*.

coiffed *adj* причёсанный, -ая, -ое, -ые. *(See* **coiffured** *for other terms.)*

If no accent is shown on a word with a capitalized vowel, it means that the capitalized vowel is accented.

coiffure *n* причёска. ♦ **stylish** ~ мо́дная причёска.

coiffured *adj* причёсанный, -ая, -ое, -ые, уло́женный, -ая, -ое, -ые, со́бранный, -ая, -ое, -ые, у́бранный, -ая, -ое, -ые ♦ **beautifully** ~ с прекра́сной причёской ♦ **beautifully** *(1,2)* ~ **hair** прекра́сно *(1)* со́бранные / *(2)* уло́женные во́лосы ♦ **elegantly** ~ с элега́нтной причёской ♦ **elegantly** *(1,2)* ~ **hair** элега́нтно *(1)* со́бранные / *(2)* уло́женные волосы ♦ **splendidly** ~ с замеча́тельной причёской ♦ **splendidly** *(1,2)* ~ **hair** замеча́тельно *(1)* со́бранные / *(2)* уло́женные волосы ♦ **stylishly** ~ с мо́дной причёской ♦ **How** *(1)* **splendidly** / *(2)* **beautifully coiffured you are (in the photo).** Как *(1)* замеча́тельно / *(2)* прекра́сно ты причёсана (на фотогра́фии).

coitus *n* ко́итус, совокупле́ние.

cold *adj* холо́дный, -ая, -ое, -ые ♦ ~ **heart** холо́дное се́рдце ♦ ~ **look** холо́дный взгляд ♦ ~ **reception** холо́дный приём ♦ **get** ~ **feet** тру́сить / стру́сить.

cold-hearted *adj* бессерде́чный, -ая, -ое, -ые.

coldly *adv* хо́лодно.

coldness *n* холо́дность *f.*

collapse *vi* ру́шиться, разруша́ться / разру́шиться ♦ **I don't want our relationship to collapse.** Я не хочу́, чтобы на́ши отноше́ния ру́шились.

collar *n* воротни́к ♦ *(1,2)* **blue** ~ *(worker)* *(1)* голубой / *(2)* си́ний воротничо́к, рабо́чий *m*, рабо́чая *f* ♦ **white** ~ *(professional, office)* бе́лый воротничо́к, слу́жащий *m*, слу́жащая *f.*

college-educated *adj* с вы́сшим образова́нием.

colony *n* коло́ния ♦ **nudist** ~ нуди́стская коло́ния.

color *n* цвет *(pl:* цвета́*)* ♦ **man of** ~ цветно́й мужчи́на ♦ **woman of** ~ цветна́я же́нщина ♦ **What's your favorite color?** Како́й твой люби́мый цвет? ♦ **My favorite color is...** Мой люби́мый цвет...

color-blind *adj* гото́в (-а, -ы) обща́ться с челове́ком любо́й ра́сы ♦ **As concerns race, I'm color-blind.** Что каса́ется ра́сы, я соверше́нно безразли́чен *(ж: безразли́чна).*

colorless *adj* бесцве́тный, -ая, -ое, -ые.

column *n* *(newspaper)* коло́нка ♦ **penpal** ~ коло́нка с объявле́ниями друзе́й по перепи́ске ♦ **personal ad** ~ коло́нка с ча́стными объявле́ниями ♦ **And then my lips would adore the** *(1)* **creamy** / *(2)* **smooth column of your throat with soft, loving kisses.** А пото́м мои́ гу́бы покро́ют твою́ *(1)* кре́мовую / *(2)* гла́дкую стро́йную ше́ю мя́гкими, лю́бящими поцелу́ями.

combine *vi* соединя́ться / соедини́ться, сочета́ться ♦ **This is my main motivation: to come over there so that we can** *(1,2)* **combine together in heart and mind and body.** Моя́ гла́вная цель -- прие́хать к тебе́ для того́, чтобы мы смогли́ *(1)* соедини́ться / *(2)* сочета́ться се́рдцем, мы́слями и те́лом.

come *n* *(slang)* *(semen)* спе́рма, се́мя.

come *vi* 1. *(pedestrian, bus, train)* идти́ / пойти́, приходи́ть / прийти́ ; *(person by vehicle)* е́хать / пое́хать, приезжа́ть / прие́хать; 2. *(slang)* *(reach orgasm)* дости́чь орга́зма ♦ ~ **back** *vi* возвраща́ться / возврати́ться *or* верну́ться ♦ ~ **between** *vi* встава́ть / встать ме́жду *(what, whom = + instr.).* ♦ ~ **clean** *vi* *(slang)* *(confess)* признава́ться / призна́ться ♦ ~ **of** *vi* выходи́ть / вы́йти из, получа́ться / получи́ться из ♦ ~ **on** *vi* *(slang)* *(flirt with)* флиртова́ть *(to whom = + с + instr.).* ♦ ~ **over** *vi* приезжа́ть / прие́хать.

---

come: *come with me / you*

(1,2) **Come with me** (*[3]* **to my room** / *[4]* **apartment** / *[5]* **house).** *(1)* Пойдём *(on foot)* / *(2)* Пое́дем со мной *(by veh.)* (*[3]*...в мою ко́мнату / *[4]* кварти́ру. / *[5]* ...в мой дом.). ♦ **I'll** *(1,2)* **come with you.** Я *(1)* пойду́ *(on foot)* / *(2)* пое́ду *(by veh.)* с тобо́й.

Russian has 6 grammatical cases. For an explanation of them, see the grammar appendix on page 686.

come: *can / may come*

May I *(1,2)* **come with you?** Мо́жно я *(1)* пойду́ *(on foot)* / *(2)* пое́ду *(by veh.)* с тобо́й? ♦ **Yes, you may** *(1,2)* **come with me.** Да, ты мо́жешь *(1)* пойти́ *(on foot)* / *(2)* пое́хать *(by veh.)* со мной. ♦ **No, you can't** *(1,2)* **come with me.** Нет, ты не мо́жешь *(1)* пойти́ *(on foot)* / *(2)* пое́хать *(by veh.)* со мной. ♦ **Can you** *(1,2)* **come?** Ты мо́жешь *(1)* прийти́ *(on foot)* / *(2)* прие́хать *(by veh.)*? ♦ **I can('t)** *(1,2)* **come.** Я (не) могу́ *(1)* прийти́ *(on foot)* / *(2)* прие́хать *(by veh.)*. ♦ **Would it be possible for you to** *(1,2)* **come with me?** Смо́жешь ли ты *(1)* пойти́ *(on foot)* / *(2)* пое́хать *(by veh.)* со мной. ♦ **Would it be possible for you to** *(1,2)* **come** (*[3]* ...here... / *[4]* ...to my hotel...) **after work?** Смо́жешь ли ты *(1)* прийти́ *(on foot)* / *(2)* прие́хать *(by veh.)* (*[3]*...сюда́... / *[4]* ...в мою́ гости́ницу...) по́сле рабо́ты?

come: *when?*

(1,2) **What time ...will you** *(3,4)* **come?** *(1)* Когда́... / *(2)* В како́е вре́мя... *(3)* ... ты придёшь *(on foot)* / *(4)* прие́дешь *(by veh.)*? ♦ **I'll** *(1,2)* **come at one (thirty).** *(See page 759 for other times.)* Я *(1)* приду́ *(on foot)* / *(2)* прие́ду *(by veh.)* в час (три́дцать). ♦ *(1,2)* **What time** *(3)* **shall** / *(4)* **should I** *(5,6)* **come?** *(1)* Когда́... / *(2)* В како́е вре́мя... *(3,4)* до́лжен *(ж: должна́)* я *(5)* прийти́ *(on foot)* / *(6)* прие́хать *(by veh.)*? ♦ *(1,2)* **Come at one (thirty).** *(See page 759 for other times.)* *(1)* Приходи́ *(on foot)* / *(2)* Приезжа́й *(by veh.)* в час (три́дцать). ♦ **I intend to come there** *(1)* **...in the summer.** / *(2)* **...as soon as possible.** Я наме́рен *(ж: наме́рена)* прие́хать туда́ *(1)* ...ле́том. / *(2)* ...как мо́жно скоре́е.

come: *come to me*

Come to me. Подойди́ ко мне. ♦ **Come (a little) closer.** Подойди́ (немно́го) бли́же.

come: *happy you're coming*

When I found out you were coming, I felt shock waves of pure, unadulterated joy. Когда́ я узна́л *(ж: узна́ла)*, что ты прие́дешь, я ощути́л *(ж: ощути́ла)* во́лны и́стинного, настоя́щего ликова́ния.

come: *thankful you came into my life*

(1) **I thank God...** / *(2)* **I'm so happy** / *(3)* **grateful... that you came into my life.** *(1)* Я благодарю́ Бо́га,... / *(2)* Я так сча́стлив *(ж: сча́стлива)* / *(3)* благода́рен *(ж: благода́рна)*,... что ты вошла́ *(ж: вошёл)* в мою́ жизнь.

come between:

I don't want anything to ever come between us. Я не хочу́, чтобы что-нибудь когда́-либо вста́ло ме́жду на́ми. ♦ **Nothing (and nobody) will ever come between us.** Ничто́ (и никто́) никогда́ не вста́нет ме́жду на́ми.

come of:

Nothing will come of it. Ничего́ из э́того не вы́йдет. ♦ **I wonder if anything will come of our relationship.** Я хоте́л бы знать, полу́чится ли что́-либо из на́ших отноше́ний.

come on:

It seemed like you were coming on to *(1)* **me** / *(2)* **him.** Каза́лось, что ты флиртова́ла *(1)* со мной. / *(2)* с ним.

come over:

I cling to the hope that I can come over there before the end of the year. Я цепля́юсь за наде́жду, что смогу́ прие́хать туда́ до конца́ го́да.

comedian *n* ко́мик ♦ **freelance ~** шу́тник.

comedy *n* коме́дия.

comely *adj* милови́дный, -ая, -ое, -ые *(short forms:* милови́ден, милови́дна, -о, -ы*)* ♦ **It would be a definite understatement to say that you're quite comely.** Бы́ло бы опреде-

---

There are no articles ("a" or "the") in Russian.

лённым преуменьше́нием сказа́ть, что ты о́чень милови́дна.

comfort *n* 1. *(ease)* комфо́рт, ую́т; 2. *(solace)* утеше́ние ♦ **momentary** ~ момента́льное утеше́ние ♦ **You are my joy and comfort, my hope and my dreams — my everything.** Ты моя́ ра́дость и утеше́ние, моя́ наде́жда и моя́ мечта́ -- всё для меня́. ♦ **I find such comfort** *(1)* **...with you.** / *(2)* **...in your arms.** Я нахожу́ тако́й ую́т *(1)* ...с тобо́й. / *(2)* ...в твои́х объя́тиях.

comfortable *adj* удо́бный, -ая, -ое, -ые, ую́тный, -ая, -ое, -ые, комфорта́бельный, -ая, -ое, -ые ♦ **I don't feel comfortable with that.** Мне неудо́бно в тако́й ситуа́ции. ♦ **I feel (so) comfortable (spending time) with you.** Мне (так) прия́тно (проводи́ть вре́мя) с тобо́й. ♦ **I'm comfortable with who I am.** Я дово́лен *(ж: дово́льна)* собо́й. ♦ **I want a woman who is comfortable in jeans or a(n)** *(1)* **cocktail** / *(2)* **evening dress.** Я хочу́ же́нщину, кото́рой одина́ково удо́бно в джи́нсах и в *(1)* ...пла́тье для кокте́йля. / *(2)* ...вече́рном пла́тье. ♦ **I'm seeking a man who is comfortable in jeans or a tuxedo.** Я ищу́ мужчи́ну, кото́рому одина́ково удо́бно в джи́нсах и в смо́кинге.

comforting *adj* успокои́тельный, -ая, -ое, -ые, успока́ивающий, -ая, -ее, -ие ♦ **Your presence is so comforting.** Твоё прису́тствие так успока́ивает.

comingle *vt* сме́шивать / смеси́ть *(what = acc.)*, соединя́ть / соедини́ть *(what = acc.)* ♦ ~ **families** соединя́ть / соедини́ть се́мьи.

command *vt (control)* управля́ть *(what, whom = instr.)* ♦ **The fierce passion I feel for you commands all my thoughts and attention.** Си́льная страсть к тебе́ управля́ет все́ми мои́ми мы́слями и внима́нием.

command *n* прика́з ♦ **I am compelled to obey the silent command of your (**[1] **sensuous** / [2] **beautiful) lips.** Я вы́нужден повинова́ться безмо́лвным прика́зам твои́х (*[1]* чу́вственных / *[2]* прекра́сных) губ. ♦ **Your wish is my command.** Твоё жела́ние -- зако́н для меня́.

commend *vt* хвали́ть / похвали́ть *(what, whom = acc.)* ♦ **I must commend you (**[1]**...on your excellent taste in clothes** / [2] **music** / [3] **wine** / [4] **art.** / [5] **...on your thoughtfulness.** Я до́лжен *(ж: должна́)* похвали́ть тебя́ (за *[1]* ...твой превосхо́дный вкус в оде́жде / *[2]* му́зыке / *[3]* вине́ / *[4]* иску́сстве. / *[5]* ...твою́ внима́тельность.

comment *n* замеча́ние *(pl: замеча́ния)* ♦ **acerb** ~ язви́тельное замеча́ние ♦ **catty** ~ язви́тельное замеча́ние; сарка́сти́ческое замеча́ние ♦ **caustic** ~ е́дкое замеча́ние ♦ **cryptic** ~ зага́дочное замеча́ние ♦ **dumb** ~ глу́пое замеча́ние ♦ **funny** ~ *(humorous)* смешно́е замеча́ние ♦ **hilarious** ~ умори́тельное замеча́ние ♦ **indiscreet** ~ неосторо́жное замеча́ние ♦ **lewd** ~ непристо́йное замеча́ние ♦ **obscene** ~ непристо́йное замеча́ние ♦ **offhand** ~ бесцеремо́нное замеча́ние ♦ **outrageous** ~ дура́цкое замеча́ние ♦ **peculiar** ~ стра́нное замеча́ние ♦ **ridiculous** ~ не́лепое замеча́ние ♦ **rude** ~ гру́бое замеча́ние ♦ **sarcastic** ~ сарка́сти́ческое замеча́ние ♦ **saucy** ~ 1. *(impudent)* де́рзкое замеча́ние; 2. *(brazenly flirtatious)* коке́тливое замеча́ние ♦ **stupid** ~ глу́пое замеча́ние ♦ **sweet** ~ не́жное замеча́ние ♦ **thoughtless** ~ невнима́тельное замеча́ние ♦ **unkind** ~ недо́брое замеча́ние ♦ **witty** ~ остроу́мное замеча́ние ♦ **wry** ~ ирони́ческое замеча́ние ♦ **I didn't understand your (last) comment.** Я не по́нял *(ж: поняла́)* твоего́ (после́днего) замеча́ния.

commit *vi* принима́ть / приня́ть на себя́ обяза́тельства, свя́зывать / связа́ть себя́ (обяза́тельством), посвяща́ть / посвяти́ть себя́ ♦ **I seek someone who can commit to a long-term relationship.** Я ищу́ того́, кто мо́жет приня́ть на себя́ обяза́тельства до́лгих отноше́ний. ♦ **I'm ready to commit to the right person.** Я гото́в *(ж: гото́ва)* связа́ть себя́ с подходя́щим челове́ком.

commitment *n* обяза́тельство; обяза́тельность *f* ♦ **lasting** ~ постоя́нные обяза́тельства

This dictionary contains two Russian alphabet pages:
one in Appendix 1, page 685, and a tear-off page on page 799.

♦ **lifelong** ~ обяза́тельства на всю жизнь ♦ **long-term** ~ долгосро́чные обяза́тельства ♦ **verbal** ~ слове́сные обяза́тельства ♦ **act of** ~ де́йствие, налага́ющее обяза́тельства *(1 term)* ♦ **be on the cusp of** ~ быть на острие́ обяза́тельств ♦ **break** *(1)* **your** / *(2)* **my** ~ наруша́ть / нару́шить *(1)* твои́ / *(2)* мои́ обяза́тельства ♦ **lack of** ~ необяза́тельность *f* ♦ **level of** ~ сте́пень отноше́ний.

> **commitment:** *phrases*

I feel so disillusioned by your lack of commitment. Я так разочаро́ван твое́й необяза́тельностью. ♦ **Your commitment was just a facade.** Твоя́ пре́данность была́ то́лько показно́й. ♦ **I'm (not) afraid of making commitments.** Я (не) бою́сь дава́ть обяза́тельства. ♦ **I hope you're not one of those people who's afraid of making commitments.** Я наде́юсь, что ты не одна́ *(ж: один)* из тех, кото́рые боя́тся дава́ть обяза́тельства. ♦ **I take a commitment seriously.** Я отношу́сь серьёзно к обяза́тельствам. ♦ **I** *(1)* **seek** / *(2)* **want someone who** *(3)* **...will make a (long-term) commitment.** / *(4)* **...is ready for commitment.** / *(5)* **...is not afraid of commitment.** Я *(1)* ищу́ / *(2)* хочу́ того́, кто *(3)* ...даст (долгосро́чные) обяза́тельства. / *(4)* ...гото́в к обяза́тельствам. / *(5)* ...не бои́тся обяза́тельств. ♦ **What I** *(1)* **...want...** / *(2)* **...yearn for... most in a relationship is commitment.** Чего я *(1)* ...хочу́... / *(2)* ...жа́жду... бо́лее всего́ в отноше́ниях -- обяза́тельности. ♦ **Commitment is what really counts in a relationship.** Обяза́тельность -- вот, что действи́тельно ва́жно в отноше́ниях.

commitment-minded *adj* гото́вый (-ая, -ое, -ые) к серьёзным отноше́ниям.

committed *adj* пре́данный, -ая, -ое, -ые *(short forms:* пре́дан, -на, -но, -ны*)* ♦ **I seek a person who is committed to (church and) family.** Я ищу́ челове́ка, кото́рому важна́ (це́рковь и) семья́.

common *adj* о́бщий, -ая, -ее, -ие.

common *n*: ♦ **You and I** *([1]* **really)** *([2]* **seem to) have** *(3)* **...a lot...** / *(4)* **...many things... in common.** У тебя́ и у меня́ *([2]* , ка́жется,) *([1]* действи́тельно) есть *(3,4)* мно́го о́бщего. ♦ *(1)* **She** / *(2)* **He and I** *(3)* **have** / *(4)* **had nothing in common.** У *(1)* неё / *(2)* него́ и у меня́ *(3)* ...нет... / *(4)* ...не бы́ло... ничего́ о́бщего.

commonality *n* о́бщность *f* ♦ ~ **of interests** о́бщность интере́сов.

communicate *vt* 1. *(convey)* передава́ть / переда́ть *(what = acc., to whom = dat.)*; *(inform)* сообща́ть / сообщи́ть *(what = acc., to whom = dat.)*; *(express)* выража́ть / вы́разить *(what = acc., to whom = dat.)* ♦ **How I wish I could communicate all the** *([1]* **beautiful** / *[2]* **intense** / *[3]* **deep) feelings I have toward you.** Как бы я жела́л *(ж: жела́ла)*, что́бы я мог *(ж: могла́)* переда́ть все *([1]* прекра́сные / *[2]* пы́лкие / *[3]* глубо́кие) чу́вства, кото́рые я испы́тываю к тебе́. ♦ **Even in ordinary, everyday things I'm going to try to communicate to you how much I love you.** Да́же в обы́чных, повседне́вных дела́х я попыта́юсь вы́разить тебе́, как си́льно я люблю́ тебя́. ♦ **I will always try to communicate my love to you in all ways possible.** Я бу́ду всегда́ пыта́ться выража́ть мою́ любо́вь к тебе́ все́ми возмо́жными спо́собами. ♦ **I want you to communicate your thoughts and hopes and dreams and wishes to me.** Я хочу́, что́бы ты посвяти́ла *(ж: посвяти́л)* меня́ в свои́ мы́сли, наде́жды, мечты́ и жела́ния.

communicate *vi* объясня́ться, обща́ться ♦ **I hope that we can always communicate (well) together.** Я наде́юсь, что у нас всегда́ бу́дет (хоро́шее) взаимопонима́ние. ♦ **It's** *(1,2)* **hard to communicate with you.** С тобо́й *(1)* тру́дно / *(2)* тяжело́ обща́ться. ♦ **You and I communicate so well together.** Мы так хорошо́ понима́ем друг дру́га. ♦ **We don't seem to be communicating very well.** Мы, ка́жется, не о́чень хорошо́ понима́ем друг дру́га.

communicating *n* связь *f*, сообще́ние; коммуника́ция.

> *Russian verbs conjugate for 6 persons:*
> *I, familiar you, he-she-it, we, polite & plural you, and they.*

communication *n* 1. *(act or means)* связь *f*, сообще́ние; 2. *(mutual understanding)* взаимопонима́ние ♦ **good** ~ 1. хоро́шая связь; 2. хоро́шее взаимопонима́ние ♦ **committed to honest** ~ пре́данный (-ая, -ое, -ые) иде́е че́стного обще́ния.

***communication:** phrases*

Our commication system is *(1)* **...erratic.** / *(2)* **...not connected right.** / *(3)* **...missing something.** *(1-3)* Мы, ка́жется, не сли́шком хорошо́ понима́ем друг дру́га. ♦ **It's very important to me that we always have open communication (between us).** Для меня́ о́чень ва́жно, чтобы мы всегда́ бы́ли открове́нны друг с дру́гом. ♦ **I like good communication.** Мне нра́вится откры́тое обще́ние. ♦ **Let's always do our best to keep lines of communication open between us.** Дава́й де́лать всё возмо́жное для того́, что́бы мы всегда́ могли́ откры́то говори́ть друг с дру́гом. ♦ **You need never be fearful of communication with me. You can tell me anything.** Ты никогда́ не должна́ боя́ться обща́ться со мно́й. Ты мо́жешь расска́зывать мне всё.

communicative *n* общи́тельный, -ая, -ое, -ые, разгово́рчивый, -ая, -ое, -ые ♦ **openly** ~ открове́нный, -ая, -ое, -ые.

communicator *n*: ♦ **good** ~ откры́тый, открове́нный челове́к *(1 term)* ♦ **poor** ~ за́мкнутый челове́к ♦ **willing** ~ жела́ющий (-ая, -ее, -ие) обща́ться.

communion *n* обще́ние ♦ **intimate** ~ инти́мное обще́ние ♦ **spiritual** ~ духо́вное обще́ние ♦ **I want to totally abandon myself in the intimate communion of our bodies.** Я хочу́ по́лностью преда́ться инти́мному обще́нию на́ших тел.

compact *adj* компа́ктный, -ая, -ое, -ые; *(person)* ма́ленький, -ая, -ое, -ие ♦ **You're so nice and compact.** Ты така́я изя́щная и ма́ленькая.

companion *n* спу́тник *m*, спу́тница *f*, компаньо́н *m*, компаньо́нка *f*; друг *m*, подру́га *f* ♦ **athletic** ~ друг в заня́тиях спо́ртом ♦ **caring** ~ забо́тливый друг *m*, забо́тливая подру́га *f* ♦ **communicative** ~ коммуника́бельный друг ♦ **constant** ~ постоя́нный компаньо́н, постоя́нная компаньо́нка ♦ **dinner** ~ челове́к, с кото́рым вме́сте обе́дает *(explanation)* ♦ **fit** ~ спорти́вный друг ♦ **lifetime** ~ спу́тник *m* / спу́тница *f* жи́зни ♦ **running** ~ друг по бе́гу ♦ **smart** ~ у́мный друг *m*, у́мная подру́га *f* ♦ **travel** ~ компаньо́н *m* / компаньо́нка *f* в путеше́ствии.

***companion:** phrases*

You would be such a good companion for me. Ты была́ бы тако́й хоро́шей спу́тницей для меня́. *(ж: Ты был бы таки́м хоро́шим спу́тником для меня́.)* ♦ **I want to be your friend, your lover, your companion and your confidant.** Я хочу́ быть твои́м дру́гом *(ж: твое́й подру́гой)*, твои́м любо́вником *(ж: твое́й любо́вницей)*, твои́м спу́тником *(ж: твое́й спу́тницей)* и твои́м пове́ренным *(ж: твое́й пове́ренной)*. ♦ **You're the kind of loving companion I always dreamed of.** Ты та лю́бящая спу́тница, о кото́рой я всегда́ мечта́л. *(ж: Ты тот лю́бящий спу́тник, о кото́ром я всегда́ мечта́ла.)* ♦ **You're such a loving companion.** Ты така́я лю́бящая подру́га. *(ж: Ты тако́й лю́бящий друг.)*

companionship *n* дру́жеское обще́ние ♦ **constant** ~ постоя́нные дру́жеские отноше́ния ♦ **I need your companionship**. Мне нужна́ дру́жба с тобо́й. ♦ **I enjoy your companionship.** Я наслажда́юсь дру́жбой с тобо́й.

company *n* 1. *(companionship)* компа́ния, о́бщество; 2. *(firm)* фи́рма; 3. *(guest)* гость; *(guests)* го́сти ♦ **I love your company.** Мне нра́вится твоё о́бщество. ♦ **I (really) enjoy your company.** Я (действи́тельно) наслажда́юсь твои́м о́бществом. ♦ **When I'm in your company, I always feel so good.** В твоём о́бществе я всегда́ чу́вствую себя́ так хорошо́. ♦ **Two is company, three is a crowd.** Два челове́ка -- компа́ния, три -- толпа́.

There are two words for "you" in Russian:
familiar «ты» *and polite / plural* «вы» *(See page 781).*

comparison *n* сравнéние ♦ Any other woman pales in comparison with you. Любáя
другáя жéнщина мéркнет в сравнéнии с тобóй.

compassion *n* сострадáние, сочýвствие; жáлость*f* ♦ If you have any shred of compassion
for me, you'll alleviate the agony of my yearning by sending me more photos of yourself.
Éсли у тебя́ есть хотя́ бы мáлая тóлика сострадáния ко мне, ты облегчи́шь мýку
моéй тоски́, послáв мне ещё нéсколько свои́х фотогрáфий. ♦ With you I have found
warmth and compassion and closeness such as I've never known before. В тебé я нашёл
(ж: нашлá) таки́е теплотý, сострадáние и отзы́вчивость, каки́х я никогдá прéжде не
знал *(ж: знáла)*. ♦ I admire you for your compassion. Я восхищáюсь (тобóй) твои́м
сострадáнием. ♦ I fervently pray that in your heart you can somehow find the compassion to condescend to grant me just a few brief minutes to *(1)* meet / *(2)* talk with you
and thereby assuage this unbearable longing that grips my soul. Я горячó молю́сь, чтобы ты смоглá найти́ сострадáние в своём сéрдце и подари́ть мне тóлько нéсколько
корóтких минýт *(1)* встрéчи / *(2)* разговóра с тобóй, чтóбы утоли́ть невыноси́мую
тоскý, охвати́вшую мою́ дýшу.

compassionate *adj* сострадáтельный, -ая, -ое, -ые, сочýвствующий,-ая, -ее, -ие.
compassionately *adv* сострадáтельно.

compatibility *n* совмести́мость*f* ♦ sexual ~ сексуáльная совмести́мость ♦ Compatibility
in the bedroom isn't all that's important. Совмести́мость в спáльне -- э́то ещё не всё,
что вáжно. ♦ Compatibility is the key to a strong relationship. Совмести́мость --
ключ к прóчным отношéниям.

compatible *adj* совмести́мый, -ая, -ое, -ые, подходя́щий, -ая, -ее, -ие ♦ emotionally ~
эмоционáльно совмести́мый, -ая, -ое, -ые ♦ sexually ~ сексуáльно совмести́мый, -ая,
-ое, -ые. ♦ I'm looking for a compatible partner. Я ищý совмести́мого партнёра. ♦ I
feel sure in my heart that you and I will always be compatible. Моё сéрдце полнó увé-
ренностью, что мы всегдá бýдем совмести́мы друг с дрýгом. ♦ You and I are on such
a common wavelength that I really believe neither of us could ever find a more compatible partner. Мы с тобóй настóлько на однóй волнé, что я увéрен, ни оди́н из нас не
смóжет найти́ бóлее подходя́щего партнёра.

compel *vt* вынуждáть / вы́нудить *(what, whom = acc.)*, заставля́ть / застáвить *(what, whom*
= acc.), принуждáть / принуди́ть *(what, whom = acc.)*; побуждáть / побуди́ть *(what,*
whom = acc.) ♦ Your letter compels a response. Твоё письмó побуждáет к отвéту. ♦
My heart compels me to write this to you. Моё сéрдце побуждáет меня́ написáть тебé
э́то.

compelled *adj* вы́нужден, -а, -о, -ы *(short forms)* ♦ I am compelled to obey the silent
command of your *([1]* sensuous / *[2]* beautiful) lips. Я вы́нужден повиновáться без-
мóлвным прикáзам твои́х *([1]* чýвственных / *[2]* прекрáсных) губ.

compelling *adj* вынуждáющий, -ая, -ее, -ие ♦ hypnotically ~ вынуждáющий (-ая, -ее,
-ие) под гипнóзом.

competition *n* кóнкурс, конкурéнция, соревновáние ♦ You have no competition (with
me). У тебя́ нет конкурéнток *(ж: конкурéнтов)*. ♦ *(1)* There seems to be... / *(2)* I would
imagine there is... a lot of competition for your *(3)* attention / *(4)* friendship. *(1)* Кáжется... / *(2)* Я воображáю, что... мнóгие старáются заслужи́ть *(3)* ...твоё внимáние. / *(4)*
...твою́ дрýжбу. ♦ I don't worry about (a little) competition. (Мáленькое) соревновáние меня́ не волнýет.

complacency *n* самодовóльство.
complacent *adj* самодовóльный, -ая, -ое, -ые.
complement *n* дополнéние ♦ You're a perfect complement for me. Ты дополня́ешь меня́

Russian terms of endearment are given in Appendix 13, page 780.

превосхо́дно.

complete *adj* соверше́нный, -ая, -ое, -ые, по́лный, -ая, -ое, -ые ♦ **You make my life complete.** Ты наполня́ешь мою́ жизнь. ♦ **I have never felt as complete as I do with you.** Ни с кем моя́ жизнь не была́ тако́й напо́лненной, как с тобо́й. ♦ **You make me feel complete.** Ты заставля́ешь меня́ чу́вствовать полноту́ жи́зни.

complete *vt* заверша́ть / заверши́ть *(what, whom = acc.)*, доде́лать *(what, whom = acc.)*, дополня́ть / дополни́ть *(what, whom = acc.)* ♦ **You complete me.** Ты дополня́ешь меня́. ♦ **I'm searching for a good-hearted, affectionate, loving companion to complete my life.** Я ищу́ добросерде́чного, не́жного, лю́бящего челове́ка, кото́рый напо́лнит собо́й мою́ жизнь.

completely *adv* вполне́, по́лностью, соверше́нно.

complex *adj* сло́жный, -ая, -ое, -ые, тру́дный, -ая, -ое, -ые, запу́танный, -ая, -ое, -ые.

complex *n* ко́мплекс ♦ **inferiority** ~ ко́мплекс неполноце́нности ♦ **persecution** ~ ма́ния пресле́дования ♦ **full of ~s** весь в ко́мплексах ♦ **You seem to have a complex (about it).** У тебя́, ка́жется, ко́мплекс (по отноше́нию к э́тому).

complexion *n* 1. *(color)* цвет лица́, вид; 2. *(texture)* ко́жа ♦ **beautiful** ~ прекра́сный цвет лица́ ♦ **carmel** ~ светло-кори́чневое лицо́ ♦ **creamy** ~ не́жное лицо́ ♦ **fresh** ~ све́жий цвет лица́ ♦ **ivory** ~ ма́товая ко́жа ♦ **lovely** ~ прекра́сный цвет лица́ ♦ **marvelous** ~ изуми́тельный цвет лица́ ♦ **milky-white** ~ моло́чно-бе́лый цвет лица́ ♦ **olive** ~ оли́вковое лицо́ ♦ **ruddy** ~ румя́ное лицо́ ♦ **smooth** ~ гла́дкая ко́жа, гла́дкое лицо́ ♦ *(1,2)* **translucent** ~ *(1)* просве́чивающая / *(2)* прозра́чная ко́жа *(на лице́)* ♦ **You have such a (1) creamy / (2) smooth complexion.** У тебя́ тако́е *(1)* не́жное / *(2)* гла́дкое лицо́. ♦ **You have a (1) marvelous / (2) beautiful (3) lovely complexion.** У тебя́ *(1)* изуми́тельный / *(2,3)* прекра́сный цвет лица́.

compliant *adj* пода́тливый, -ая, -ое, -ые, усту́пчивый, -ая, -ое, -ые.

compliment *vt* хвали́ть / похвали́ть *(whom = acc.)*, де́лать / сде́лать комплиме́нт *(whom = dat.)*.

compliment *n* комплиме́нт ♦ **empty** ~ пусто́й комплиме́нт ♦ **idle** ~ пра́здный комплиме́нт ♦ **left-handed** ~ сомни́тельный комплиме́нт ♦ **nice** ~ прия́тный комплиме́нт ♦ **make a** ~ де́лать / сде́лать комплиме́нт *(to whom = dat.)*, говори́ть / сказа́ть комплиме́нт *(to whom = dat.)* ♦ **pay a** ~ де́лать / сде́лать комплиме́нт *(to whom = dat.)*, говори́ть / сказа́ть комплиме́нт *(to whom = dat.)*.

compliment: phrases

Thank you for the nice compliment. Благодарю́ за прия́тный комплиме́нт. ♦ **That's the nicest compliment anyone has ever made to me.** Это наилу́чший комплиме́нт из всех, когда́-либо сде́ланных мне. ♦ **It's not (just) a(n) (*[1]* empty / *[2]* idle) compliment — it's the truth.** Это не (про́сто) (*[1]* пусто́й / *[2]* пра́здный) комплиме́нт -- э́то пра́вда. ♦ **Stop fishing for compliments.** Переста́нь напра́шиваться на комплиме́нты.

comply *vi* исполня́ть / испо́лнить про́сьбу, подчиня́ться / подчини́ться *(with what = dat.)* ♦ **Your lips demand to be kissed, and my lips can only comply.** Твои́ гу́бы тре́буют поцелу́ев, и мои́ то́лько подчиня́ются.

compose *vt (write)* сочиня́ть / сочини́ть *(what = acc.)* ♦ ~ **oneself** успока́иваться / успоко́иться.

compose: write

I've never composed a letter like this before. Я никогда́ пре́жде не сочиня́л *(ж: сочиня́ла)* тако́го письма́, как э́то. ♦ **No one has ever composed such a (1) beautiful / (2) heart-warming / (3) sweet letter to me before.** Никто́ никогда́ пре́жде не сочиня́л тако́го *(1)* ...прекра́сного... / *(2)* ...согрева́ющего се́рдце... / *(3)* ...не́жного... письма́ ко

Some of the Russian sentences are translations of things we say and are not what Russians themselves would normally say.

мне. ♦ **You make me want to compose poetry for you.** Ты вызыва́ешь во мне жела́ние сочиня́ть стихи́ для тебя́.

> **compose:** *oneself*

Try to compose yourself. Постара́йся упоко́иться.

composed *adj* споко́йный, -ая, -ое, -ые, сде́ржанный, -ая, -ое, -ые; владе́ющий (-ая, -ее, -ие) собо́й ♦ **I'm amazed at how you always stay so composed.** Я изумлён *(ж: изумлена́)*, како́й споко́йной *(ж: каки́м споко́йным)* ты остаёшься.

composure *n* споко́йствие, хладнокро́вие, самооблада́ние ♦ **I'm sorry I lost my composure.** Прости́, я потеря́л *(ж: потеря́ла)* самооблада́ние. ♦ **I lost my composure when I saw the two of you together.** Я потеря́л *(ж: потеря́ла)* самооблада́ние, когда́ уви́дел *(ж: уви́дела)* вас вме́сте. ♦ **It was (very) hard for me to keep my composure.** Мне бы́ло (о́чень) тру́дно сохраня́ть самооблада́ние.

compromise *vi* пойти́ на компроми́сс *(on what= + o + prep.)*, пойти́ на соглаше́ние *(on what= + o + prep.)* ♦ **Let's compromise.** Дава́й пойдём на компроми́сс. ♦ **Can't we compromise (on this)?** Мо́жем мы пойти́ на компроми́сс (в э́том)? ♦ **I can't compromise on** *(1)* **...it.** / *(2)* **...my beliefs** / *(3)* **morals** / *(4)* **values.** Я не могу́ пойти́ на компроми́сс в вопро́се *(1)* ...об э́том. / *(2)* ...о мои́х убежде́ниях / *(3)* це́нностях. / *(4)* ...о мое́й мора́ли.

compromise *n* компроми́сс ♦ **make a ~** пойти́ на компроми́сс *(on what= + o + prep.)* ♦ **Suppose we make a compromise.** Предполо́жим, мы пойдём на компроми́сс. ♦ **How about a compromise?** Как о том, что́бы пойти́ на компроми́сс?

compromising *adj* компромети́рующий, -ая, -ее, -ие ♦ **I don't want to get caught in a compromising** *(1)* **position** / *(2)* **situation.** Я не хочу́ оказа́ться в компромети́рующем *(1,2)* положе́нии.

computer *n* компью́тер ♦ **personal ~ (PC)** персона́льный компью́тер.

con *vt (slang) (deceive)* обма́нывать / обману́ть *(whom = acc.)* ♦ **I would never con you (into doing anything).** Я никогда́ не бу́ду обма́нывать тебя́. ♦ **Believe me, I wouldn't con you — you're the most beautiful woman I've ever met.** Пове́рь мне, я не обма́нываю тебя́ -- ты са́мая прекра́сная же́нщина из всех, когда́-либо встре́ченных мно́ю. ♦ **I think you've been conning me (the whole time).** Я ду́маю, ты (всё вре́мя) обма́нывала *(ж: обма́нывал)* меня́. ♦ **You conned me (shamelessly).** Ты обма́нывала *(ж: обма́нывал)* меня́ (бессты́дно).

concede *vt (admit)* признава́ть / призна́ть *(what = acc.)* ♦ **I concede, no one has ever** *(1)* **...paid so much attention to me.** / *(2)* **...been so nice to me.** / *(3)* **...shown so much affection** / *(4)* **love for me.** Я признаю́, что никто́ никогда́ *(1)* не обраща́л тако́го внима́ния на меня́. / *(2)* ...не был так хоро́ш со мной. / *(3)* ...не выска́зывал так мно́го *(4)* не́жности / *(5)* любви́ ко мне. ♦ **Surely, in all honesty, you'll concede that no one has ever** *(1)* **...loved you as much as I do.** / *(2)* **...shown you as much love as I have.** Несомне́нно, е́сли по-че́стному, ты призна́ешься, что никто́ никогда́ *(1)* ...не люби́л тебя́ так си́льно, как я. / *(2)* ...не выка́зывал тебе́ так мно́го любви́, как я.

conceit *n* самомне́ние; тщесла́вие.

conceited *adj* с больши́м самомне́нием, тщесла́вный, -ая, -ое, -ые; высокоме́рный, -ая, -ое, -ые, чва́нный, -ая, -ое, -ые, чванли́вый, -ая, -ое, -ые.

conceive *vt* 1. *(give birth)* зача́ть *(ребёнка)*; 2. *(think up)* заду́мывать / заду́мать ♦ **I'm not able to conceive.** Я не спосо́бна зача́ть. ♦ **It doesn't matter to me that you're not able to conceive.** То, что ты не спосо́бна зача́ть, не име́ет значе́ния для меня́. ♦ **Even in my most extravagant dreams I never conceived of anyone as** *(1)* **beautiful** / *(2)* **lovely as you.** Да́же в свои́х са́мых сумасбро́дных мечта́х я никогда́ не мог вообрази́ть таку́ю

Counting things in Russian is a bit involved.
See Appendix 4, "Numbers," on page 756 .

(1,2) прекра́сную же́нщину, как ты.

concentrate *vi* сосредота́чиваться / сосредото́читься *(on what = + на + prep.)*, концентри́роваться *(on what = + на + prep.)* ♦ **With the vision of your beautiful face constantly in my thoughts, I am totally unable to concentrate on anything.** Твоё прекра́сное лицо́ постоя́нно в мои́х мы́слях, и я соверше́нно не в состоя́нии ни на чём сосредото́читься. ♦ **I can't concentrate on anything with this fever in my blood.** Этот жар в мое́й кро́ви не даёт мне сосредото́читься ни на чём.

concern *n* 1. *(care, solicitude)* забо́та, уча́стие; *(interest)* интере́с; 2. *(worry)* беспоко́йство; 3. *(regard)* отноше́ние; 4. *(matter)* де́ло ♦ **Your concern was just a facade.** Твоя́ забо́та была́ то́лько показно́й. ♦ **It made me feel good to hear your voice full of gentle concern.** Мне бы́ло о́чень прия́тно услы́шать твой го́лос, по́лный не́жной забо́ты.

concert *n* конце́рт ♦ *(1)* **I'd like to invite you...** / *(2)* **Would you like to go (with me)... to a concert** *(3)* **...tomorrow (evening).** / *(4)* **...this afternoon** / *(5)* **evening.** / *(6)* **...on Friday** / *(7)* **Saturday** / *(8)* **Sunday** *(9)* **afternoon** / *(10)* **evening.** / **?** *(1)* Я хоте́л *(ж: хоте́ла)* бы пригласи́ть тебя́... / *(2)* Не хоте́ла *(ж: хоте́л)* бы ты пойти́ (со мной)... на конце́рт *(3)* ...за́втра (ве́чером). / *(4)* ...сего́дня днём / *(5)* ве́чером. / *(6)* ...в пя́тницу / *(7)* суббо́ту / *(8)* воскресе́нье *(9)* днём / *(10)* ве́чером. / **?** ♦ **Let's go to a concert (together).** Дава́й пойдём на конце́рт (вме́сте).

conclusion *n* 1. *(end, close)* оконча́ние, заверше́ние; 2. *(final judgement)* (умо)заключе́ние, вы́вод ♦ **You're jumping to conclusions.** Ты де́лаешь поспе́шные вы́воды. ♦ **Don't jump to conclusions.** Не де́лай поспе́шных вы́водов.

concoction *n* смесь *f* ♦ **potent** ~ кре́пкая смесь.

concubine *n* нало́жница ♦ **I don't want to be your concubine.** Я не хочу́ быть твое́й нало́жницей.

concupiscence *n* 1. *(strong desire)* си́льное жела́ние; 2. *(lust)* похотли́вость *f*, вожделе́ние.

condemn *vt* осужда́ть / осуди́ть *(whom = acc.)* ♦ **Don't condemn me.** Не осужда́й меня́.

condescend *vi* снисходи́ть / снизойти́ ♦ **I fervently pray that in your heart you can somehow find the compassion to condescend to grant me just a few brief minutes to** *(1)* **meet** / *(2)* **talk with you and thereby assuage this fierce longing that grips my soul.** Я горячо́ молю́сь, что́бы ты смогла́ найти́ сострада́ние в своём се́рдце и подари́ть мне то́лько не́сколько коро́тких мину́т *(1)* встре́чи / *(2)* разгово́ра с тобо́й, что́бы утоли́ть невыноси́мое жела́ние, охвати́вшее мою́ ду́шу.

condescending *adj* снисходи́тельный, -ая, -ое, -ые.

condom *n* презервати́в ♦ **It's (**[1]** too /** [2]** so) dangerous without a condom.** (*[1]* Сли́шком / *[2]* Так) Опа́сно без презервати́ва.

condo(minium) *n* со́бственная кварти́ра.

conduct *n* поведе́ние ♦ **personal** ~ ли́чное поведе́ние.

confession *n* призна́ние ♦ ~ **of love** призна́ние в любви́ ♦ **I have a (small) confession to make. (I've wanted to go out with you ever since I met you.)** Я до́лжен *(ж: должна́)* сде́лать (ма́ленькое) призна́ние. (Я хоте́л *[ж: хоте́ла]* пойти́ вме́сте с тобо́й куда́-нибудь, как то́лько я встре́тил *[ж: встре́тила]* тебя́.)

confidant *n (man)* дове́ренное лицо́, пове́ренный *m*, напе́рсник ♦ **I want to be your friend, your lover, your companion and your confidant.** Я хочу́ быть твои́м дру́гом, твои́м любо́вником, твои́м спу́тником и твои́м пове́ренным.

confidante *n (woman)* дове́ренное лицо́, пове́ренная *f*, напе́рсница ♦ **I want to be your friend, your lover, your companion and your confidant.** Я хочу́ быть твои́м дру́гом, твое́й любо́вницей, твое́й спу́тницей и твое́й пове́ренной.

confide *vt* доверя́ть / дове́рить *(what = acc., to whom = dat.)* ♦ **You can confide your**

Russian has 2 different verbs for "go",
one for "on foot" and the other for "by vehicle".

problem to me. I promise I won't tell anyone. Ты мо́жешь дове́рить свою́ пробле́му мне. Я обеща́ю, что не расскажу́ никому́.

confide *vi* доверя́ться / дове́риться *(in whom = dat.)* ♦ **You can always confide in me.** Ты мо́жешь всегда́ дове́риться мне. ♦ **I know I can confide in you.** Я зна́ю, что могу́ дове́риться тебе́. ♦ **Can I confide in you?** Могу́ ли я дове́риться тебе́ ?

confidence *n* уве́ренность *f* ♦ **You seem to have a lack of confidence.** Ка́жется, у тебя́ не хвата́ет уве́ренности. ♦ **Your manner instills confidence.** Твои́ мане́ры внуша́ют уве́ренность. ♦ **You exude confidence.** Ты излуча́ешь уве́ренность. ♦ **You have such an air of confidence about you.** Ты так уве́ренна *(ж: уве́рен)* в себе́.

confident *adj* уве́ренный (-ая, -ое, -ые) в себе́, самоуве́ренный, -ая, -ое, -ые ♦ **sexually** ~ сексуа́льно уве́ренный, -ая, -ое, -ые.

conflict *n* конфли́кт.

conflict-free *adj* бесконфли́ктный, -ая, -ое, -ые.

conflicting *adj* противоречи́вые *(pl)* ♦ **I have conflicting emotions about *(1)* ...you. / *(2)* ...it. / *(3)* ...that. / *(4)* ...your proposal. / *(5)* ...the idea. / *(6)* ...marriage.** У меня́ противоре́чи́вые чу́вства по отноше́нию к *(1)* ...тебе́. / *(2,3)* ...э́тому. / *(4)* ...твоему́ предложе́нию. / *(5)* ...иде́е. / *(6)* ...жени́тьбе.

confront *vt* смотре́ть / посмотре́ть в лицо́ *(what, whom = dat.)*; стоя́ть лицо́м к лицу́ *(what, whom = + c + instr.)* ♦ **You're afraid to confront the truth. (You *[1]* love / *[2]* want me.)** Ты бои́шься посмотре́ть в лицо́ пра́вде. (Ты *[1]* лю́бишь / *[2]* хо́чешь меня́.)

confrontation *n* конфронта́ция ♦ **I don't want a confrontation (with *[1]* her / *[2]* him).** Я не хочу́ конфронта́ции (с *[1]* ней / *[2]* ним).

confuse *vt* 1. *(embarrass)* смуща́ть / смути́ть; 2. *(mix up)* пу́тать / спу́тать ♦ **Don't ~ love with desire.** Не пу́тай любо́вь с жела́нием.

confused *adj* смущённый, -ая, -ое, -ые, недоуме́нный, -ая, -ое, -ые ♦ **become (completely) ~** прийти́ в (по́лное) смяте́ние, сби́ться с то́лку.

confusing *adj* сби́вчивый, -ая, -ое, -ые, сбива́ющий (--ая, -ее, -ие) с то́лку; пу́таный, -ая, -ое, -ые.

congratulate *vt* поздравля́ть / поздра́вить *(whom = acc., on what = + c + instr.)* ♦ **I congratulate you (on your promotion, *etc*).** Я поздравля́ю тебя́ (с повыше́нием / *и т.д.*).

congratulation *n* поздравле́ние ♦ **Congratulations!** Поздравля́ю!

conjure up *vt* заду́мывать / заду́мать *(what = acc.)*; выду́мывать / вы́думать *(what = acc.)*, приду́мывать / приду́мать *(what = acc.)* ♦ **I'll try to conjure up some way to *(1)* ...meet you. / *(2,3)* ...come there. / *(4,5)* ...make it. / *(6)* ...do it.** Я попыта́юсь найти́ возмо́жность *(1)* ...встре́титься с тобо́й. / *(2,4)* ...прийти́ *(on foot)* / *(3,5)* прие́хать *(by veh.)* туда́. / *(6)* ...сде́лать э́то. ♦ **You conjure up more excuses than anyone I've ever met.** Ты приду́мываешь бо́льше отгово́рок, чем кто́-либо ещё.

connect *vi* 1. *(join, make a connection)* соединя́ться / соедини́ться, свя́зываться / свя́за́ться; 2. *(get along)* сочета́ться, подходи́ть *(with whom = dat.)* ♦ *(1)* **I'm looking for...** / *(2)* **I want... someone who can connect with me on every level.** *(1)* Я ищу́... / *(2)* Я хочу́... того́, кто бу́дет подходи́ть мне во всём. ♦ **You and I really connect together.** Ты и я действи́тельно подхо́дим друг к дру́гу. ♦ **It's fantastic how you and I connect so *(1)* perfectly / *(2)* well together.** Это фанта́стика, как ты и я так *(1)* превосхо́дно / *(2)* хорошо́ подхо́дим друг дру́гу. ♦ **You and I could share so many things, make so much wonderful love together, talk about so many things together, connect in heart, mind, and spirit so perfectly.** Ты и я смогли́ бы раздели́ть мно́гое, так мно́го занима́ться прекра́сной любо́вью, говори́ть о мно́гом друг с дру́гом, так соверше́нно соединя́ться се́рдцем, умо́м и ду́хом. ♦ **When our eyes connected, *(1)* ...I knew right away**

Dipthongs in Russian are made by adding й
*to the end of a vowel (*а, е, ё, о, у, э, ю, *and* я*).*

that you were the one. / *(2)* ...I knew I had to meet you. Когда́ на́ши глаза́ встре́тились, *(1)* ...я то́тчас знал *(ж: зна́ла)*, что ты та са́мая *(ж: тот са́мый). / (2)* ...я знал *(ж: зна́ла)*, что я до́лжен *(ж: должна́)* познако́миться с тобо́й.

connection *n* связь *f* ◆ **deep soul** ~ глубо́кая духо́вная связь ◆ **I'm seeking a heart-to-heart connection.** Я ищу́ ту, с кото́рой *(ж: того́, с кем)* смогу́ соедини́ться сердца́ми. ◆ **I have deep connections to the natural world.** У меня́ глубо́кая связь с приро́дой.

connotation *n* побо́чный отте́нок *(значе́ния)*, дополни́тельное значе́ние, подоплёка ◆ **romantic** ~ романти́ческий отте́нок ◆ **sexual** ~ сексуа́льная подоплёка ◆ **have a** ~ подразумева́ть *(of what = acc.)* ◆ **Everything I write to you has a special connotation — that I love you.** Всё то, что я пишу́ тебе́, име́ет осо́бый подте́кст , что я люблю́ тебя́.

connote *vt* означа́ть *(what = acc.).*

connubial *adj* бра́чный, -ая, -ое, -ые, супру́жеский, -ая, -ое, -ие.

conquest *n* завоева́ние, побе́да, покоре́ние ◆ **I hope I'm not just another conquest.** Я наде́юсь, что я не про́сто очередно́е завоева́ние. ◆ **Believe me, I'm not someone who's just trying to make a conquest.** Пове́рь мне, я не из тех, кто про́сто пыта́ется покоря́ть. ◆ **Am I just another conquest for you?** Я то́лько очередна́я побе́да для тебя́? ◆ **If you think you're just a conquest for me, you're wrong — I love you (with all my heart.)** Е́сли ты ду́маешь, что ты то́лько очередна́я побе́да для меня́, ты ошиба́ешься -- я люблю́ тебя́ (всем се́рдцем). ◆ **I'm not looking for an easy conquest — I want a *(1)* lasting / *(2)* permanent / *(3)* true relationship.** Я не ищу́ лёгкой побе́ды -- я хочу́ *(1)* дли́тельных / *(2)* постоя́нных / *(3)* ве́рных отноше́ний.

conscience *n* со́весть *f*, созна́ние ◆ **bad** ~ нечи́стая со́весть ◆ **clear** ~ чи́стая со́весть ◆ **guilty** ~ нечи́стая со́весть ◆ **quiet** ~ споко́йная со́весть ◆ **social** ~ социа́льная со́весть ◆ *(1,2)* **pangs of** ~ *(1)* угрызе́ния / *(2)* му́ки со́вести ◆ **My conscience is clear.** Моя́ со́весть чиста́. ◆ **My conscience *(1)* ...is bothering me. / *(2)* ...has been bothering me. / *(3)* ...bothered me.** Моя́ со́весть *(1,2)* ...беспоко́ит меня́ . / *(3)* ...беспоко́ила меня́. ◆ **Have you no conscience?** Ты не име́ешь со́вести? ◆ **You're a *(1)* man / *(2)* woman / *(3)* person without conscience (or morals).** Ты *(1)* мужчи́на / *(2)* же́нщина / *(3)* челове́к без со́вести (и́ли мора́ли). ◆ **My conscience wouldn't let me do that.** Моя́ со́весть не позво́лит мне де́лать э́то.

conscious *adj (aware)* сознаю́щий, -ая, -ее, -ие; созна́тельный, -ая, -ое, -ые ◆ **be** ~ осознава́ть / осозна́ть *(of what = acc.)*; обраща́ть / обрати́ть внима́ние *(of what = + на + acc.).* ◆ **I'm acutely conscious of your situation.** Я превосхо́дно осознаю́ твою́ ситуа́цию. ◆ **I'm very health conscious.** Я обраща́ю большо́е внима́ние на своё здоро́вье. ◆ **I'm glad that you're a *(1,2)* fitness conscious person.** Я рад *(ж: ра́да)*, что ты обраща́ешь внима́ние на *(1)* трениро́вки *(exercise). / (2)* здоро́вье *(health).*

consecrated *adj* свяще́нный, -ая, -ое, -ые ◆ **Any ground you stand on becomes for me a consecrated place.** Люба́я то́чка, на кото́рую ты ступи́ла, стано́вится свяще́нным ме́стом для меня́.

consensual *adj* по соглаше́нию.

consent *vi* соглаша́ться / согласи́ться *(to what = + на + acc.).* ◆ **Will *(1)* she / *(2)* he consent to a divorce?** Согласи́тся ли *(1)* она́ / *(2)* он на разво́д? ◆ *(1)* **She / *(2)* He will (not) consent to a divorce.** *(1)* Она́ / *(2)* Он (не) согласи́тся на разво́д. ◆ **Do you think your *(1)* parents / *(2)* mother / *(3)* father will consent to your getting married?** Ты ду́маешь, что *(1)* ...твои́ роди́тели соглася́тся... / *(2)* ...твоя́ мать согласи́тся... / *(3)* твой оте́ц согласи́тся... вы́дать тебя́ за́муж? ◆ *(1)* **I'm sure... / *(2)* I don't think... *(3)* they / *(4)* she / *(5)* he will consent (to my getting married).** *(1)* Я уве́рен *(ж: уве́рена),... / (2)* Я не

Some phrases are listed under more than one main word.

ду́маю,... что *(3)* ...они́ соглася́тся... / *(4)* ...она́ / *(5)* он согласи́тся... (на на́шу жени́тьбу).

consent *n* согла́сие ♦ **legal** ~ зако́нное согла́сие ♦ **mutual** ~ взаи́мное согла́сие ♦ **parental** ~ роди́тельское согла́сие ♦ **written** ~ пи́сьменное согла́сие ♦ **give** ~ дава́ть / дать согла́сие *(to whom = dat., for what = + на + acc.)* ♦ **We need to get your** *(1)* **parents'** / *(1)* **mother's** / *(1)* **father's consent to get married.** На́м на́до получи́ть согла́сие *(1)* ...твои́х роди́телей... / *(2)* ...твое́й ма́тери... / *(3)* ...твоего́ отца́... на жени́тьбу. ♦ **I (don't) need my** *(1)* **mother's** / *(2)* **father's** / *(3)* **parents' consent (to get married).** Мне (не) ну́жно согла́сие *(1)* ...мое́й ма́тери... / *(2)* ...моего́ отца́... / *(3)* ...мои́х роди́телей... (на брак.) ♦ **We need** *(1)* **her** / *(2)* **his** / *(3)* **their written consent (**[4]**...for you to get married.** / [5]**...to adopt the child.)** На́м ну́жно *(1)* её / *(2)* его́ / *(3)* их пи́сьменное согла́сие ([4] ...для тебя́ на брак. / [5] ...на усыновле́ние *[boy]* / [6] удочере́ние *[girl]* ребёнка). ♦ **Do you think your** *(1)* **parents** / *(2)* **mother** / *(3)* **father will give** *(4)* **their** / *(5)* **her** / *(6)* **his consent to get married?** Ты ду́маешь, *(1)* ...твои́ роди́тели даду́т... / *(2)* ...твоя́ мать даст... / *(3)* ...твой оте́ц даст... *(4-6)* согла́сие на на́шу жени́тьбу? ♦ *(1)* **I'm sure...** / *(2)* **I don't think...** *(3)* **they** / *(4)* **she** / *(5)* **he will give** *(6)* **their** / *(7)* **her** / *(8)* **his consent (to my getting married).** *(1)* Я уве́рен *(ж: уве́рена)*,... / *(2)* Я не ду́маю,... что *(3)* ...они́ даду́т... / *(4)* ...она́ / *(5)* он даст... *(6-8)* согла́сие (на на́шу жени́тьбу).

consider *vt* 1. *(regard)* счита́ть *(what, whom = acc., as what / whom = instr.)*; 2. *(think over)* обду́мывать / обду́мать *(what = acc.)* ♦ **~ a proposal** обду́мывать / обду́мать предложе́ние ♦ **I consider myself** *(1)* **good-looking** / *(2)* **attractive** / *(3)* **handsome** / *(4)* **outgoing** / *(5)* **sensitive** / *(6)* **easy-going.** Я счита́ю себя́ *(1,2)* привлека́тельным *(ж: привлека́тельной)* / *(3)* краси́вым / *(4)* общи́тельным *(ж: общи́тельной)* / *(5)* чу́тким *(ж: чу́ткой)* / *(6)* споко́йным *(ж: споко́йной)*.

considerate *adj* внима́тельный, -ая, -ое, -ые *(short forms:* внима́телен, внима́тельна, -о, -ы*)*, предупреди́тельный, -ая, -ое, -ые ♦ **You're very considerate.** Ты о́чень внима́тельна *(ж: внима́телен)*. ♦ **That** *(1)* **is** / *(2)* **was very considerate of you.** Э́то *(1)* - / *(2)* бы́ло о́чень внима́тельно с твое́й стороны́.

considerateness *n* внима́тельность *f*.

consideration *n* 1. *(factor, something to think about)* соображе́ние; 2. *(review, thinking about)* рассмотре́ние, обсужде́ние; 3. *(respect, thoughtfulness, attention)* уваже́ние, предупреди́тельность *f*, внима́ние ♦ **There are a** *(1)* **host** / *(2)* **lot** / *(3)* **number of (**[4] **critical** / [5] **important) considerations in this.** В э́том есть *(1)* мно́жество / *(2)* мно́го / *(3)* ряд ([4] крити́ческих / [5] ва́жных) соображе́ний. ♦ **Please try to have consideration for my** *(1)* **position** / *(2)* **situation.** Пожа́луйста, попыта́йся отнести́сь с уваже́нием к *(1)* ...моему́ положе́нию. / *(2)* ...мое́й ситуа́ции. ♦ **Please try to show a little consideration.** Пожа́луйста, попыта́йся вы́казать хотя́ бы како́е-то внима́ние. ♦ **You have no consideration for my** *(1)* **feelings** / *(2)* **position** / *(3)* **situation.** У тебя́ нет никако́го уваже́ния к *(1)* ...мои́м чу́вствам. / *(2)* ...моему́ положе́нию. / *(3)* ...мое́й ситуа́ции.

consolation *n* утеше́ние ♦ **That's a small consolation.** Э́то сла́бое утеше́ние. ♦ **If it's any consolation to you, I've told her** *(him)* **I don't want to see her** *(him)* **anymore.** Е́сли э́то како́е-нибудь утеше́ние для тебя́, я сказа́л *(ж: сказа́ла)* ей *(ж: ему́)*, что я бо́льше не хочу́ встреча́ться с ней *(ж: ним)*. ♦ **This gift is a small consolation for standing you up (**[1] **...the other day.** / [2] **...on Friday /** *etc.*) Э́тот пода́рок -- ма́ленькое утеше́ние за то, что я не пришёл на свида́ние ([1]...на днях. / [2]...в пя́тницу. / *и т.д.*).

console *vt* утеша́ть / уте́шить *(whom = acc.)* ♦ **I wish I could console you.** Я хоте́л *(ж: хоте́ла)* бы, что́бы я мог *(ж: могла́)* уте́шить тебя́.

consort *n* супру́г *m*, супру́га *f*.

The singular past tense of Russian verbs ends in -л (m) (usually), -ла (f) or -ло (n). the plural past tense ends in -li.

conspicuous *adj* заме́тный, -ая, -ое, -ые, броса́ющийся (-аяся, -ееся, -иеся) в глаза́ ♦ **You'd be conspicuous in a sack.** Ты была́ бы заме́тна да́же, е́сли бы наде́ла мешо́к.

constancy *n* постоя́нство ♦ **What I** *(1)* **...want...** */ (2)* **...yearn for... most in a relationship is constancy.** То, чего́ я *(1)* ...хочу́... */ (2)* ...жа́жду... бо́лее всего́ в отноше́ниях - постоя́нства.

constant *adj* постоя́нный, -ая, -ое, -ые, непреры́вный, -ая, -ое, -ые.

constantly *adv* постоя́нно, непреры́вно.

consultant *n* консульта́нт ♦ **bridal** ~ сва́дебный консульта́нт.

consume *vt* пожира́ть / пожра́ть *(what, whom = acc.)*, поглоща́ть / поглоти́ть *(what, whom = acc.)* ♦ ~ **the body** распаля́ть те́ло ♦ **Desire** *(1,2)* **consumes** *(3)* **...me...** */ (4)* **...my body... (every time I think of you).** Страсть *(1)* распаля́ет / *(2)* пожира́ет *(3)* ...меня́... */ (4)* ...моё те́ло... (всё вре́мя, когда́ я ду́маю о тебе́). ♦ **I've been consumed with love for you from the very first moment I laid eyes on you.** Я воспыла́л *(ж:воспыла́ла)* любо́вью к тебе́ с того́ са́мого моме́нта, как то́лько мои́ глаза́ уви́дели тебя́. ♦ **Only the sweet, soft magic of your beautiful body in my arms can assuage the desperate hunger that consumes me.** То́лько не́жное, мя́гкое волшебство́ твоего́ прекра́сного те́ла в мои́х объя́тиях мо́жет утоли́ть отча́янный го́лод, кото́рый пожира́ет меня́. ♦ **The yearning in my heart for you is an inferno that is consuming me.** Тоска́ по тебе́ в моём се́рдце - э́то ад, поглоща́ющий меня́. ♦ **The fierce** *(1)* **passion** */ (2)* **desire I feel for you is utterly consuming me.** *(1)* Неи́стовая страсть к тебе́... */ (2)* Неи́стовое жела́ние тебя́... по́лностью поглоща́ет меня́. ♦ **Misery consumes me.** Страда́ние изнуря́ет меня́.

consumed *adj* охва́чен, -а, -о, -ы *(short forms) (with what = instr., for whom = + к + dat.)*, поглощён, поглощена́ , -о́ , -ы́ *(short forms) (with what = instr., for whom = + к + dat.)*, пожира́ем, -а, -о, -ы *(short forms) (with what = instr., for whom = + к + dat.)*, съеда́ем, -а, -о, -ы *(short forms) (with what = instr., for whom = + к + dat.)* ♦ **I am (totally) consumed** *(1)* **by** */ (2)* **with desire for you.** Я (соверше́нно) поглощён *(1,2)* стра́стью к тебе́. ♦ **I am consumed by this fire that you have started racing through my blood.** Я поглощён огнём, кото́рый ты разожгла́ в мое́й крови́. ♦ **I lie in bed at night, consumed with desire,** *(1)* **fantasizing** */ (2)* **thinking about you.** Я лежу́ в посте́ли но́чью, пожира́емый стра́стью, *(1)* фантази́руя / *(2)* ду́мая о тебе́.

consummate *adj* соверше́нный, -ая, -ое, -ые, зако́нченный, -ая, -ое, -ые ♦ **Oh, what consummate ecstasy I will bestow upon you when we swirl into the wild vortex of our passion.** О, како́й соверше́нный экста́з я подарю́ тебе́, когда́ мы закру́жимся в бе́шеном водоворо́те стра́сти.

consummate *vt (marriage)* осуществля́ть / осуществи́ть *(what = acc.)* ♦ ~ **a marriage** осуществля́ть / осуществи́ть бра́чные отноше́ния, консуми́ровать брак.

contact *vt* свя́зываться / связа́ться *(whom = + с + instr.)* ♦ **Is there some way I can contact you?** Каки́м о́бразом я могу́ связа́ться с тобо́й?

contact *n* 1. *(touching)* соприкоснове́ние, конта́кт; 2. *(communication)* связь, конта́кт; 3. *pl (social)* знако́мства, свя́зи; 4. *pl (lenses)* конта́ктные ли́нзы ♦ **casual** ~ случа́йный конта́кт ♦ **eye** ~ (взаи́мный) конта́кт глаза́ми ♦ **genuine human** ~ и́скренний челове́ческий конта́кт ♦ **human** ~ челове́ческий конта́кт ♦ **initial** ~ нача́льный конта́кт ♦ **lots of eye** ~ ча́стая встре́ча глаза́ми ♦ **physical** ~ прикоснове́ние ♦ **social** *(1,2)* ~**s** *(1)* знако́мства / *(2)* свя́зи в о́бществе.

contact: *touching*

When my hand came in contact with yours, I *(1)* **... wanted to grab you (right there) and kiss you.** */ (2)* **...felt electricity** */ (3)* **fire** */ (4)* **thrills in every part of my body.** */ (5)* **...almost**

Please do us a favor:
Fill out and mail in the Feedback Sheet on page 795.

fainted / *(6)* **melted (on the spot).** Когда́ моя́ рука́ соприкаса́лась с твое́й, я *(1)* ...хоте́л *(ж: хоте́ла)* схвати́ть тебя́ (пря́мо здесь) и целова́ть. / *(2)* ...чу́вствовал *(ж: чу́вствовала)* электри́чество / *(3)* ого́нь / *(4)* тре́пет во всём те́ле. / *(5)* ...почти́ теря́л *(ж: теря́ла)* созна́ние... / *(6)* ...почти́ та́ял *(ж: та́яла)...* (на ме́сте).

contact: communication

How can I get in contact with you? Как я смогу́ контакти́ровать с тобо́й? ♦ **You can get in contact with me** *(1)* **...at this number.** / *(2)* **...at my home** / *(3)* **hotel** / *(4)* **office.** Ты смо́жешь контакти́ровать со мной *(1)* ...по э́тому но́меру. / *(2)* ...в моём до́ме. / *(3)* ...в гости́нице. / *(4)* ...в о́фисе. ♦ **I'll get in contact with you (**[1]**...as soon as I can /** [2] **arrive /** [3] **return. /** [4] **...tonight. /** [5] **...tomorrow [**(6) **morning /** (7) **afternoon /** (8) **evening]. /** [9] **...on Monday /** *etc.* **/** [10] **...next week.)** Я бу́ду контакти́ровать с тобо́й (*[1]* ...сра́зу же как смогу́. / *[2]* ...когда́ приду́ / *[3]* верну́сь. / *[4]* ...сего́дня ве́чером. / *[5]* ...за́втра у́тром. / *[6]* ...за́втра в по́лдень. / *[7]* ...за́втра ве́чером. / *[8]* ...в поне-де́льник. / *и т.д.* / *[9]* ...на сле́дующей неде́ле.)

contain *vt* 1. *(hold)* содержа́ть *(what = acc.)* 2. *(suppress)* сде́рживать / сдержа́ть *(what = acc.)* ♦ **When I** *(1)* **...felt your hand in mine...** / *(2)* **...read your letter..., I could hardly contain myself.** Когда́ я *(1)* ...чу́вствовал *(ж: чу́вствовала)* твою́ ру́ку в мое́й,... / *(2)* ...чита́л *(ж: чита́ла)* твоё письмо́,... я едва́ мог *(ж: могла́)* сдержа́ть себя́. ♦ **When you** *(1)* **...put your hand in mine...** / *(2)* **...said that you loved me, I could hardly contain myself.** Когда́ ты *(1)* ...вложи́ла *(ж: вложи́л)* свою́ ру́ку в мою́,... / *(2)* ...сказа́ла *(ж: сказа́л)*, что ты лю́бишь меня́,... я едва́ мог *(ж: могла́)* сде́рживать себя́. ♦ **Forgive me for writing such a steamy letter, but my thoughts of you mixed together with my feelings for you arouse passions in me that are difficult to contain.** Прости́ меня́ за тако́е чу́вственное письмо́, но мои́ мы́сли о тебе́, вме́сте с чу́вствами к тебе́, пробужда́ют во мне страсть, кото́рую тру́дно сдержа́ть. ♦ **I cannot contain the** *(1)* **fierce /** *(2)* **passionate longing in my heart to hold you in my arms (again).** Я не могу́ сдержа́ть *(1)* неи́стовую / *(2)* стра́стную жа́жду се́рдца (опя́ть) сжать тебя́ в объя́тиях.

contemplate *vt* 1. *(gaze at)* созерца́ть *(what, whom = acc.)*; 2. *(ponder)* размышля́ть *(what, whom = + о + prep.)*, разду́мывать *(what, whom = + о + prep.)*, обду́мывать *(what, whom = + о + prep.)*.

contemplation *n* 1. *(gazing at)* созерца́ние; 2. *(pondering)* размышле́ние, разду́мье ♦ **lustful ~** вожделе́нное созерца́ние.

contemplative *adj* созерца́тельный, -ая, -ое, -ые, заду́мчивый, -ая, -ое, -ые.

contemporary *adj* совреме́нный, -ая, -ое, -ые.

contempt *n* презре́ние ♦ **You're beneath contempt.** Ты да́же не заслу́живаешь пре-зре́ния. ♦ **I feel nothing but contempt for you.** Я не чу́вствую ничего́, кро́ме презре́ния к тебе́.

contemptible *adj* презре́нный, -ая, -ое, -ые.

contemptuous *adj* презри́тельный, -ая, -ое, -ые.

content *n (satisfaction)* удовлетворе́ние ♦ **to one's heart's ~** всласть, вдо́воль, ско́лько душе́ уго́дно. ♦ **We'll be all by ourselves and we can make love to our heart's content.** Мы бу́дем одни́ и смо́жем занима́ться любо́вью всла́сть.

contented *adj* дово́льный, -ая, -ое, -ые; удовлетворённый, -ая, -ое, -ые ♦ **I feel deeply contented (with...** [1] **you.** / [2] **...our relationship.** / [3] **...things the way they are.** / [4] **...having you in my life.).** Я чу́вствую себя́ глубоко́ удовлетворённым *(ж: удовлет-ворённой)* (с [1] ...тобо́й. / [2] ...на́шими отноше́ниями. / [3] ...дела́ми так, как они́ есть. / [4] ...тем, что ты есть в мое́й жи́зни.)

contentious *adj* вздо́рный, -ая, -ое, -ые, сварли́вый, -ая, -ое, -ые.

Clock and calender time are discussed in Appendix 5, page 759.

contentment *n* удовлетворённость *f* ♦ **moment of** ~ миг нéги ♦ **My little love-kitten, I want to make you always purr in contentment.** Мой мáленький люби́мый котёнок, я хочý, что́бы ты всегдá удовлетворённо мурлы́кала. ♦ **I've never known such contentment (with anyone).** Я никогдá (ни с кем) не знал *(ж: знáла)* такóй удовлетворённости. ♦ **I feel such blissful contentment (with you).** Я чýвствую такýю счастли́вую удовлетворённость (с тобóй).

continue *vt* продолжáть / продóлжить *(what = acc.)*.

continue *vi* продолжáться.

continuous *adj* непреры́вный, -ая, -ое, -ые.

continuously *adv* непреры́вно.

contour *n* кóнтур, очертáние; изги́б ♦ **beautiful** *(1,2)* ~s прекрáсные *(1)* очертáния / *(2)* контýры ♦ **delicate** *(1,2)* ~s нéжные *(1)* очертáния / *(2)* контýры ♦ **every** ~ **(of your body)** кáждый изги́б (твоегó тéла) ♦ **smooth** *(1,2)* ~s глáдкие *(1)* очертáния / *(2)* контýры ♦ **soft** *(1,2)* ~s мя́гкие *(1)* очертáния / *(2)* контýры ♦ **voluptuous** ~s роскóшные фóрмы.

contour: phrases

I love the ([1] **smooth /** [2] **delicate /** [3] **soft /** [4] **beautiful) (5,6) contours of your (7) face / (8) body.** Я люблю́ (*[1]* глáдкие / *[2]* нéжные / *[3]* мя́гкие / *[4]* прекрáсные) *(5)* очертáния / *(6)* контýры твоегó *(7)* лицá / *(8)* тéла. ♦ **I've never (1) known / (2) seen a woman with such voluptuous contours as you have.** Я никогдá не *(1)* знал / *(2)* ви́дел жéнщины с таки́ми роскóшными фóрмами, как у тебя́. ♦ **Endless hours of (1) delightful / (2) heavenly kissing are promised in the delicate contour of your lips.** Бесконéчные часы́ *(1)* восхити́тельных / *(2)* божéственных поцелýев обéщаны в изя́щном кóнтуре твои́х губ. ♦ **I like the way that dress emphasizes every contour of your body.** Мне нрáвится, как э́то плáтье подчёркивает кáждый изги́б твоегó тéла.

contoured очéрченный, -ая, -ое, -ые ♦ **beautifully** ~ **body** прекрáсно очéрченное тéло ♦ **That swimsuit was made for your beautifully contoured body.** Этот купáльник был сóздан для твоегó прекрáсного скульптýрного тéла.

contraception *n* контрацéпция.

contraceptive *n* контрацепти́в, противозачáточное срéдство.

contradiction *n* противорéчие ♦ **You're full of contradictions.** Ты полнá *(ж: пóлон)* противорéчий.

contrite *adj* кáющийся, -аяся, -ееся, -иеся ♦ ~ **letter** покая́нное письмó.

contrive *vi (manage)* умудря́ться / умудри́ться, ухитря́ться / ухитри́ться ♦ **I'll contrive somehow to** *(1)* **...meet you. /** *(2)* **...come there. /** *(3)* **...make it. /** *(4)* **...do it.** Я как-нибýдь умудрю́сь *(1)* ...встрéтить тебя́. / *(2)* ...прийти́ *(on foot)* / *(3)* приéхать *(by veh.)* тудá. / *(4)* ......прийти́ *(on foot)* / *(5)* приéхать *(by veh.)*. / *(6)* ...сдéлать э́то.

control *vt* контроли́ровать *(what, whom = acc.)* ♦ **I have no desire to control a person.** У меня́ нет никакóго желáния контроли́ровать человéка. ♦ **I have to learn how to control my baser instincts around you.** Я дóлжен научи́ться контроли́ровать свои́ ни́зшие инсти́нкты ря́дом с тобóй.

control *n* контрóль *m* ♦ **My desire for you is going absolutely out of control. (I can't think of anything else, but you.)** Моя́ страсть к тебé не поддаётся никакóму контрóлю. (Я не могý дýмать ни о чём, крóме тебя́.) ♦ **My heart goes out of control every time I think about you.** Моё сéрдце выхóдит из под контрóля, когдá бы я ни подýмал *(ж: подýмала)* о тебé. ♦ **This whole thing is out of control.** Всё э́то дéло не поддаётся контрóлю. ♦ **Whenever I'm in your arms, I feel such a willingness to give up control.** Вся́кий раз, когдá ты обнимáешь меня́, я ощущáю такýю готóвность перестáть

Reflexive verbs are those that end in -ся *or* -сь.
The -ся *or* -сь *also goes onto a past tense ending.*

сде́рживаться. ♦ **Try to get yourself under control.** Пыта́йся держа́ть себя́ под контро́лем. ♦ **Don't lose control (of yourself).** Не теря́й контро́ль (над собо́й). ♦ **I'm sorry, I lost control.** Я извиня́юсь, я потеря́л *(ж: потеря́ла)* контро́ль.

controlling *adj* контроли́рующий, -ая, -ее, -ие ♦ **I'm not a controlling person.** Я не тот челове́к, кото́рый контроли́рует други́х.

conversant *adj* осведомлённый, -ая, -ое, -ые; знако́мый (-ая, -ое, -ые) с чем-то.

conversation *n* разгово́р, бесе́да ♦ **absorbing** ~ увлека́тельный разгово́р ♦ **animated** ~ оживлённый разгово́р ♦ **cheerful** ~ весёлый разгово́р ♦ **~s of head and heart** у́мные и задуше́вные разгово́ры ♦ **delightful** ~ восхити́тельная бесе́да ♦ **e-mail** ~ разгово́р по электро́нной по́чте ♦ **emotional** ~ эмоциона́льный разгово́р ♦ **enlightening** ~ просвеща́ющий разгово́р ♦ **fascinating** ~ захва́тывающая бесе́да, увлека́тельный разгово́р ♦ **frank** ~ открове́нный разгово́р ♦ **friendly** ~ дру́жеский разгово́р ♦ **heart-to-heart** ~ задуше́вная бесе́да, задуше́вный разгово́р ♦ **heated** ~ горя́чий разгово́р ♦ **important** ~ ва́жный разгово́р ♦ **in-depth** ~ глубо́кий разгово́р ♦ **interesting** ~ интере́сный разгово́р ♦ **intimate** ~ инти́мная бесе́да, инти́мный разгово́р ♦ **lively** ~ оживлённый разгово́р ♦ *(1,2)* **long** ~ *(1)* дли́нный / *(2)* до́лгий разгово́р ♦ **long, drawn-out** ~ затяну́вшийся разгово́р ♦ **nice** ~ прия́тный разгово́р ♦ **one-sided** ~ односторо́нний разгово́р ♦ **open** ~ открове́нный разгово́р ♦ **our** ~ наш разгово́р ♦ **phone** ~ телефо́нный разгово́р, разгово́р по телефо́ну ♦ **pleasant** ~ прия́тный разгово́р ♦ *(1,2)* **private** ~ *(1)* ли́чный / *(2)* ча́стный разгово́р ♦ **quiet** ~ споко́йная бесе́да, споко́йный разгово́р ♦ **serious** ~ серьёзный разгово́р ♦ **sexually explicit** ~ сексуа́льно откры́тый разгово́р ♦ **short** ~ коро́ткий разгово́р ♦ **spirited** ~ оживлённый разгово́р ♦ **stimulating** ~ возбужда́ющий разгово́р; разгово́р, стимули́рующий интере́с *(1 term)* ♦ **thrilling** ~ волну́ющий разгово́р ♦ **unpleasant** ~ неприя́тны разгово́р ♦ **warm** ~ тёплый разгово́р.

conversation: *verb terms*

carry on a ~ вести́ разгово́р ♦ **continue our** ~ продолжа́ть / продо́лжить наш разгово́р ♦ *(1,2)* **end the** ~ *(1)* ко́нчить / *(2)* прекрати́ть разгово́р ♦ **get into a** ~ вступа́ть / вступи́ть в разгово́р *(with whom = + с + instr.)* ♦ **interrupt the** ~ прерыва́ть / прерва́ть разгово́р ♦ **join in the** ~ вступа́ть / вступи́ть в разгово́р ♦ *(1-3)* **open the** ~ *(1)* откры́ть / *(2)* нача́ть / *(3)* завести́ разгово́р ♦ *(1-3)* **start the** ~ *(1)* откры́ть / *(2)* нача́ть / *(3)* завести́ разгово́р ♦ *(1,2)* **stop the** ~ *(1)* ко́нчить / *(2)* прекрати́ть разгово́р.

conversation: *phrases*

I can tell where this conversation is leading. Я могу́ сказа́ть, куда́ ведёт э́тот разгово́р. ♦ **We need to have a (*[1]* long / *[2]* heart-to-heart) conversation together.** Нам необхо́дим (*[1]* до́лгий / *[2]* задуше́вный) разгово́р друг с дру́гом. ♦ **I like to share conversation (with you).** Я люблю́ бесе́довать (с тобо́й). ♦ **Conversation flows so naturally with you.** Разгово́р с тобо́й течёт так есте́ственно.

conversationalist *n* собесе́дник *m*, собесе́дница *f* ♦ **excellent** ~ прекра́сный собесе́дник *m*, прекра́сная собесе́дница *f* ♦ **good** ~ хоро́ший собесе́дник *m*, хоро́шая собесе́дница *f*.

convey *vt* передава́ть / переда́ть *(what = acc., to whom = dat.)*, выража́ть / вы́разить *(what = acc., to whom = dat.)*, сообща́ть / сообщи́ть *(what = acc., to whom = dat.)*; нести́ / понести́ *(what = acc.)* ♦ ~ **feelings** выража́ть / вы́разить чу́вства ♦ ~ **love** передава́ть / переда́ть любо́вь.

convey: *phrases*

This brief missive conveys only an iota of the affection that I nourish in my heart for you. Это коро́ткое письмо́ несёт то́лько ма́лую то́лику той любви́ к тебе́, кото́рой полно́

Depending on the subject, the possessive pronoun **свой (своя́, своё, свой)** *can be translated* **my, your, his, her, its, our** *or* **their.**

моё се́рдце. ◆ **I wish I could convey my feelings as well as you** *(1)* **...do.** / *(2)* **...have done.** Я хоте́л *(ж: хоте́ла)* бы уме́ть та́кже хорошо́ выража́ть свои́ чу́вства, как ты э́то *(1)* ...де́лаешь. / *(2)* ...де́лала *(ж: де́лал).* ◆ **You conveyed the impression that you** *(1)* **...cared about me.** / *(2)* **...didn't care about me (anymore).** / *(3)* **...wanted to have a relationship.** / *(4)* **...wanted to get married.** / *(5)* **...wanted to break up.** Создава́лось впечатле́ние, что ты *(1)* ...интересова́лась *(ж: интересова́лся)* мной. / *(2)* ...(бо́льше) не интересова́лась *(ж: интересова́лся)* мной. / *(3)* ...хоте́ла *(ж: хоте́л)* серьёзных отноше́ний. / *(4)* ...хоте́ла *(ж: хоте́л)* вступи́ть в брак. / *(5)* ...хоте́ла *(ж: хоте́л)* порва́ть. ◆ **I'm sorry if I conveyed that impression.** Я извиня́юсь, что созда́л *(ж: создала́)* тако́е впечатле́ние. ◆ **I didn't mean to convey that impression.** Я не хоте́л *(ж:хоте́ла)* созда́ть тако́е впечатле́ние. ◆ **I hope this letter conveys my meaning as I intend it.** Я наде́юсь, что э́то письмо́ то́чно передаёт то, что я ду́маю.

convict *n (prisoner)* заключённый *m*, заключённая *f*.

convince *vt* убежда́ть / убеди́ть *(whom = acc.).*

convinced *adj* убеждён, убеждена́, -о́, -ы́ *(short forms)* ◆ **I'm convinced that you don't love me anymore.** Я убеждён *(ж: убеждена́)*, что ты бо́льше не лю́бишь меня́.

convincing *adj* убеди́тельный, -ая, -ое, -ые ◆ **That's not a very convincing reason.** Это не о́чень убеди́тельная причи́на.

convivial *adj (sociable)* компане́йский, -ая, -ое, -ие; *(friendly)* дру́жеский, -ая, -ое, -ие.

cook *vt* гото́вить / пригото́вить *(what = acc.)* ◆ ~ **dinner** гото́вить обе́д ◆ **not ~ (very) well** гото́вить нева́жно ◆ ~ *(1,2)* **well** гото́вить *(1)* хорошо́ / *(2)* вку́сно.

cook *n* 1. по́вар; 2. челове́к, гото́вящий еду́ *(1 term)* ◆ **gourmet** ~ челове́к, гото́вящий изы́сканную еду́ *(1 term).* ◆ **not be a (very) good** ~ гото́вить нева́жно.

cooking *n* приготовле́ние (пи́щи), гото́вка ◆ **gourmet** ~ приготовле́ние пи́щи для гурма́нов.

cool *adj* 1. *(in temperature)* прохла́дный, -ая, -ое, -ые, све́жий, -ая, -ее, -ие; 2. *(unfriendly, unresponsive)* холо́дный, -ая, -ое, -ые, сухо́й, , -а́я, -бе, -и́е, равноду́шный, -ая, -ое, -ые, нела́сковый, -ая, -ое, -ые; 3. *(slang) (okay)* хорошо́; *(nice)* хоро́ший, -ая, -ее, -ие ◆ **You look very cool and fresh (in that outfit).** Ты вы́глядишь о́чень прохла́дной и све́жей (в э́том наря́де). ◆ **Your manner was (decidedly) cool.** Ты относи́лась *(ж: относи́лся)* (весьма́) прохла́дно. ◆ **You seem so cool toward me lately.** Ты ка́жешься тако́й равноду́шной *(ж: таки́м равноду́шным)* ко мне (после́днее вре́мя). ◆ **Why are you so cool toward me (lately)?** Почему́ ты так равноду́шна *(ж: равноду́шен)* ко мне (после́днее вре́мя). ◆ **Everything is cool between us.** *(slang)* Всё хорошо́ ме́жду на́ми.

cool *vi* остыва́ть / осты́ть ◆ **Has your passion (for me) cooled?** Твоя́ страсть (ко мне) осты́ла? ◆ **Your** *(1)* **desire** / *(2)* **passion** / *(3)* **love (for me) seems to have cooled (considerably).** Твоя́ *(1,2)* страсть / *(3)* любо́вь (ко мне), ка́жется, (весьма́) осты́ла. ◆ **My** *(1)* **ardor** / *(2)* **desire** / *(3)* **passion** / *(4)* **love for you will never cool.** *(1)* Мой пыл... / *(2,3)* Моя́ страсть / *(4)* любо́вь... к тебе́ никогда́ не осты́нет.

coordinator *n* координа́тор ◆ **wedding** ~ сва́дебный координа́тор.

copious *adj* оби́льный, -ая, -ое, -ые ◆ **The copious splendor of your natural endowments** *(1)* **...takes my breath away.** / *(2)* **...captivates all my senses.** Великоле́пие твои́х приро́дных дарова́ний *(1)* ...перехва́тывает моё дыха́ние. / *(2)* ...пленя́ет все мои́ чу́вства.

copiously *adv* оби́льно.

copper-haired *adj* медноволо́сый, -ая, -ое, -ые.

copulate *vi* совокупля́ться.

Optional parts of sentences are preceded or followed (or both) by three dots.

coquettish *adj* коке́тливый, -ая, -ое, -ые.

coral *adj* кора́лловый, -ая, -ое, -ые.

cordial *adj* серде́чный, -ая, -ое, -ые, раду́шный, -ая, -ое, -ые.

cordially *adv* серде́чно, раду́шно ♦ **greet ~** раду́шно встреча́ть / встре́тить *(whom = acc.).*

core *n* 1. *(center)* сердцеви́на, ядро́; 2. *(essence)* суть *f,* су́щность *f* ♦ *(1)* **Talking to you...** / *(2)* **Hearing your voice...** / *(3)* **The sound of your voice... on the phone (just) warms** *(4,5)* **me to the very core.** *(1)* Разгово́р с тобо́й... / *(2,3)* Звук твоего́ го́лоса... по телефо́ну согрева́ет *(4)* ...мою́ ду́шу. / *(5)* ...меня́ всего́. ♦ **The words you wrote in your letter warmed me to the very core.** Слова́, кото́рые ты написа́ла *(ж: написа́л)* в письме́, согре́ли мне ду́шу. ♦ **My body aches to feel the fire that rages in the core of your womanhood.** Моё те́ло жа́ждет почу́вствовать ого́нь, кото́рый бушу́ет в глубине́ твое́й же́нственности.

cornucopia *n* рог изоби́лия ♦ **~ of delight** рог, по́лный наслажде́ния *(1 term)* ♦ **~ of love** рог, по́лный любви́ *(1 term)* ♦ **~ of possibilities** изоби́лие возмо́жностей ♦ **I have a cornucopia of love that I want to bring to your life.** Я хочу́ принести́ в твою́ жизнь рог, по́лный любви́. ♦ **Our marriage will be a cornucopia of love.** Наш брак бу́дет, как рог, напо́лненный любо́вью. ♦ **You're a cornucopia of delight.** Ты рог, по́лный наслажде́ния. ♦ **I'm going to give you a cornucopia of** *(1)* **pleasure** / *(2)* **ecstasy** / *(3)* **love.** Я дам тебе́ рог, по́лный *(1)* наслажде́ния / *(2)* экста́за / *(3)* любви́.

corny *adj* бана́льный, -ая, -ое, -ые ♦ **~ joke** бана́льная шу́тка ♦ **I hope this letter doesn't sound corny to you.** Я наде́юсь, что э́то письмо́ не пока́жется бана́льным тебе́.

corpulent *adj* ту́чный, -ая, -ое, -ые, гру́зный, -ая, -ое, -ые.

correspond *vi* перепи́сываться *(with whom = + c + instr.),* вести́ перепи́ску *(with whom = + c + instr.)* ♦ **continue ~ing** продолжа́ть перепи́ску ♦ **stop ~ing** прекрати́ть перепи́ску.

correspondence *n* перепи́ска ♦ **lengthy ~** продолжи́тельная перепи́ска ♦ **lively ~** оживлённая перепи́ска ♦ **romantic ~** романти́ческая перепи́ска ♦ **be in ~** быть в перепи́ске *(with whom = + c + instr.)* ♦ **break off the ~** оборва́ть перепи́ску ♦ **carry on a ~** вести́ перепи́ску *(with whom = + c + instr.)* ♦ **end the ~** ко́нчить перепи́ску ♦ *(1-3)* **start up a ~** *(1)* нача́ть / *(2)* завяза́ть перепи́ску *(with whom = + c + instr.),* *(3)* нача́ть перепи́сываться *(with whom = + c + instr.).*

cosmic *adj* косми́ческий, -ая, -ое, -ие ♦ **The soft, warm magic of your body transports me to a cosmic kaleidoscope of ecstasy.** Мя́гкая, тёплая ма́гия твоего́ те́ла перено́сит меня́ в косми́ческий калейдоско́п экста́за.

cosmopolitan *adj* космополити́ческий, -ая, -ое, -ие.

cosmos *n* ко́смос ♦ **I want to fill your body with so much pleasure that you will be** *(1)* **hurled** / *(2)* **flung** / *(3)* **rocketed into a cosmos of exploding ecstasy.** Я хочу́ запо́лнить твоё те́ло таки́м огро́мным наслажде́нием, чтобы ты была́ *(1,2)* бро́шена / *(3)* запу́щена в ко́смос взрыва́ющегося экста́за. ♦ *(1)* **I want to...** / *(2)* **I'm going to... teach you how to soar through the cosmos.** *(1)* Я хочу́ научи́ть... / *(2)* Я научу́... тебя́, как взлете́ть в ко́смос.

cost *vi* сто́ить ♦ **How much ...does** *(1)* **it** / *(2)* **this** / *(3)* **that cost?** / **...do** *(4)* **they** / *(5)* **these** / *(6)* **those cost?** Ско́лько *(1-3)* ...э́то сто́ит? / *(4)* ...они́ / *(5,6)* э́ти стоя́т? ♦ *(1)* **It** / *(2)* **This** / *(3)* **That costs** *(price)* . *(1-3)* Э́то сто́ит *(цена́)* . ♦ *(1)* **They** / *(2)* **These** / *(3)* **Those cost** *(price)* . *(1)* Они́ / *(2,3)* Э́ти стоя́т *(цена́)* . ♦ **How much did** *(1)* **it** / *(2)* **this** / *(3)* **that** / *(4)* **they** / *(5)* **these** / *(6)* **those cost?** Ско́лько *(1-3)* ...э́то сто́ило? / *(4-6)* ...они́ сто́или? ♦ *(1)* **It** / *(2)* **This** / *(3)* **That** / *(4)* **They** / *(5)* **These** / *(6)* **Those cost** *(price)* .

If you're not on familiar terms with a person,
the «ты» forms will have to be changed to «Вы».

(1-3) Это сто́ило... / *(4-6)* Они́ сто́или... (цена́) .

cottage *n* котте́дж ♦ **cozy** ~ ую́тный котте́дж ♦ **romantic** ~ романти́ческий котте́дж.

couch *n* дива́н.

counseling *n* консульта́ция ♦ **marriage** ~ бра́чная консульта́ция ♦ **relationship** ~ консульта́ция, помога́ющая сохране́нию, нала́живанию отноше́ний *(explanation)* ♦ *(1)* **He** / *(2)* **She thinks we should undergo (marriage) counseling.** *(1)* Он / *(2)* Она́ счита́ет, что мы должны́ посети́ть (бра́чную) консульта́цию.

count *vt* счита́ть / сосчита́ть *(what = acc.)* ♦ **I (eagerly) count the days (and hours and minutes) until we can (at last) be together (again).** Я (нетерпели́во) счита́ю дни (, часы́ и мину́ты) до тех пор, пока́ мы (наконе́ц) (опя́ть) смо́жем быть вме́сте.

count *vi (be important)* име́ть значе́ние, быть ва́жным, быть са́мым гла́вным ♦ *(1)* **Commitment** / *(2)* **Loyalty** / *(3)* **Honesty is what really counts in a relationship.** *(1)* Обяза́тельность / *(2)* Ве́рность / *(3)* Че́стность -- вот, что действи́тельно ва́жно в отноше́ниях. ♦ **What really counts is whether you love me or not.** Са́мое гла́вное -- лю́бишь ты меня́ и́ли нет.

countenance *n (face)* лицо́, выраже́ние лица́ ♦ **It really lifts my spirits to see your lovely, smiling countenance (everyday).** Что действи́тельно поднима́ет моё настрое́ние -- э́то ви́деть твоё очарова́тельное, улыба́ющееся лицо́ (ка́ждый день).

counterpart *n* двойни́к *(Russian mostly uses short adjective* похо́ж, -а, -о, -ы *[= similar] or long adjective* подходя́щий, -ая, -ее, -ие *[= suitable] for this meaning)* ♦ **female** ~ подходя́щая же́нщина ♦ **male** ~ подходя́щий мужчи́на ♦ **shapely** ~ подходя́щая же́нщина с хоро́шей фигу́рой.

couple *vi (make love)* занима́ться любо́вью.

couple *n* па́ра ♦ *(1,2)* **beautiful** ~ *(1)* краси́вая / *(2)* прекра́сная па́ра ♦ *(1,2)* ~ **in love** влюблённая *(1)* па́ра / *(2)* па́рочка ♦ **elderly** ~ пожила́я па́ра ♦ **happy** ~ счастли́вая па́ра ♦ **inseparable** ~ неразлу́чная па́ра ♦ **lovely** ~ краси́вая па́ра ♦ **loving** ~ любя́щая па́ра ♦ **married** ~ супру́жеская па́ра ♦ **marvelous** ~ превосхо́дная па́ра ♦ **model** ~ приме́рная па́ра ♦ **newly engaged** ~ то́лько что обручи́вшаяся па́ра ♦ **nice** ~ *(good)* хоро́шая па́ра; *(pleasant)* прия́тная па́ра; *(sweet)* ми́лая па́ра ♦ **perfect** ~ превосхо́дная па́ра ♦ **splendid** ~ превосхо́дная па́ра ♦ **sweet** ~ ми́лая па́ра ♦ *(1-3)* **wonderful** ~ *(1)* замеча́тельная / *(2)* удиви́тельная / *(3)* чуде́сная па́ра ♦ *(1,2)* **young** ~ *(1)* ю́ная / *(2)* молода́я па́ра ♦ **a** ~ **(of) days** па́ра дней ♦ **a** ~ **(of) hours** па́ра часо́в ♦ **a** ~ **(of) months** па́ра ме́сяцев ♦ **a** ~ **(of) years** па́ра лет ♦ **No couple in this world has as many** *(1)* **attributes** / *(2)* **prospects** / *(3)* **possibilities for happiness as you and I.** Ни одна́ па́ра в э́том ми́ре не име́ет сто́лько *(1)* причи́н / *(2)* предпосы́лок / *(3)* возмо́жностей для сча́стья, как ты и я. ♦ **You and I make a perfect couple together.** Ты и я вме́сте -- превосхо́дная па́ра.

coupling *n (making love)* заня́тие любо́вью.

courage *n* хра́брость *f*, сме́лость *f*, бо́дрость *f* ду́ха ♦ **get up the** ~ набира́ться / набра́ться сме́лости ♦ **I admire you for your courage.** Я восхища́юсь (тобо́й) твое́й хра́бростью.

course *vi* течь, струи́ться, нести́сь ♦ **The sensual message in your eyes sends fire coursing through my veins.** Чу́вственный призы́в в твои́х глаза́х порожда́ет ого́нь, теку́щий в мои́х ве́нах. ♦ **Fire courses through my veins.** Ого́нь стру́ится сквозь мои́ ве́ны.

court *vt* уха́живать *(whom = + за + instr.)*.

courteous *adj* обходи́тельный, -ая, -ое, -ые.

courter *n* уха́живающий *(pl:* уха́живающие*)*.

courtesy *n* учти́вость *f*, ве́жливость *f* ♦ **I'm grateful for all the courtesy you have extended me.** Я благода́рен *(ж: благода́рна)* за всю ту учти́вость, кото́рую ты оказа́ла *(ж:*

A list of common places with their grammatical
endings is given in Appendix 7, page 763.

оказа́л) мне.

courting *n* уха́живание.

courtly *adj* ве́жливый, -ая, -ое, -ые, учти́вый, -ая, -ое, -ые.

courtship *n* уха́живание ♦ **This has been a whirlwind courtship, I admit.** Это уха́живание бы́ло как урага́н, я призна́юсь.

cousin *n* двою́родный брат *m*; двою́родная сестра́ *f.*

cover *vt* покрыва́ть / покры́ть *(what, whom = acc., with what = instr.)* ♦ **~ up** *(hide)* скрыва́ть / скрыть *(what = acc.)* ♦ **(1) I want to... / (2) I'm going to... (absolutely) cover you with (tender, [3] adoring / [4] loving) kisses.** Я (про́сто) (1) ...хочу́ покры́ть... / (2) ...покро́ю... тебя́ (не́жными, [3] обожа́ющими / [4] лю́бящими) поцелу́ями. ♦ **I'm going to cover you with a million kisses burning as though beneath the equator.** Я покро́ю тебя́ миллио́ном поцелу́ев, обжига́ющих, как со́лнце над эква́тором. ♦ **When we're together again, I'm going to cover you with kisses and caresses like you've never even dreamed of in your wildest dreams.** Когда́ мы бу́дем опя́ть вме́сте, я покро́ю тебя́ поцелу́ями и бу́ду ласка́ть так, как ты никогда́ да́же не мечта́ла в свои́х са́мых безу́мных мечта́х. ♦ **How I wish that I were holding you in my arms at this very minute, covering your beautiful face with adoring kisses.** Как бы я жела́л держа́ть тебя́ в объя́тиях в э́ту са́мую мину́ту, покрыва́я твоё прекра́сное лицо́ обожа́ющими поцелу́ями. ♦ **I'm going to cover your beautiful (1) face / (2) body with (tender, loving) kisses.** Я покро́ю твоё прекра́сное (1) лицо́ / (2) те́ло (не́жными, лю́бящими) поцелу́ями. ♦ **As my hand cups the fullness of your breast, my mouth will cover your beautiful face and smooth neck with adoring kisses.** В то вре́мя, как моя́ рука́ ощути́т полноту́ твое́й груди́, мой рот покро́ет твоё прекра́сное лицо́ и не́жную ше́ю обожа́ющими поцелу́ями. ♦ **I want to (1) put / (2) wrap my arms around you and cover you with kisses.** Я хочу́ (1,2) обви́ть тебя́ рука́ми и покры́ть поцелу́ями. ♦ **The way you write to me makes me want to take you in my arms and hug you and hug you and hug you and cover your sweet face with loving kisses.** То, как ты пи́шешь мне, вызыва́ет во мне жела́ние взять тебя́ на ру́ки, обнима́ть, обнима́ть и обнима́ть тебя́ и покрыва́ть твоё не́жное лицо́ лю́бящими поцелу́ями.

covert *adj* скры́тый, -ая, -ое, -ые.

covertly *adv* скры́тно.

covet *vt* жа́ждать *(what, whom = gen.)*; жела́ть / пожела́ть *(what = gen., whom = acc.)* ♦ **I shall never covet another (1) woman / (2) man.** Я никогда́ не пожела́ю (1) ...другу́ю же́нщину / (2) ...друго́го мужчи́ну. ♦ **I covet no one else except you.** Я не жела́ю никого́, кро́ме тебя́.

coveted *adj* вожделе́нный, -ая, -ое, -ые.

co-vivant *n (person that one lives with)* сожи́тель *m*, сожи́тельница *f.*

coward *n* трус.

cowardice *n* тру́сость *f.*

cowardly *adj* трусли́вый, -ая, -ое, -ые.

cowboy *n* ковбо́й.

cowgirl *n* де́вушка-ковбо́й.

coy *adj* 1. *(shy)* засте́нчивый, -ая, -ое, -ые, скро́мный, -ая, -ое, -ые; 2. *(feigning shyness)* жема́нный, -ая, -ое, -ые.

coyness *n* засте́нчивость *f*, скро́мность *f.*

coziness *n* ую́т.

cozy *adj* ую́тный, -ая, -ое, -ые.

cozy up (to) *vi (snuggle up)* обнима́ться / обня́ться *(to whom = + с + instr.)*, прижима́ться

Common adult heights are given in Appendix 9, page 776.

/ прижа́ться *(to whom = + к + dat.).*

crabbing *n (catching crabs)* ло́вля кра́бов ♦ **I want to take you crabbing sometime.** Я хочу́ когда́-нибудь позва́ть тебя́ лови́ть кра́бов. ♦ **We'll go crabbing together.** Мы пойдём лови́ть кра́бов вме́сте.

crabs *n, pl (slang) (pubic lice)* «пошляки́».

crass *adj* тупо́й, -а́я, -о́е, -ы́е, глу́пый, -ая, -ое, -ые.

craddle-robber *n (man who flirts with a much younger girl)* флирту́ющий с де́вушкой значи́тельно моло́же себя́; *(woman who flirts with a much younger guy)* флирту́ющая с мужчи́ной значи́тельно моло́же себя́; *(old lover of a young woman)* ста́рый любо́вник молодо́й же́нщины; *(old lover of a young man)* ста́рая любо́вница молодо́го челове́ка; *(old wife of a young man)* ста́рая жена́ молодо́го челове́ка.

crave *vt* жа́ждать *(what = gen., whom = acc.)* ♦ **I crave affection -- and I have so much to give.** Я жа́жду не́жности и могу́ так мно́го дать. ♦ **Only you can provide the fulfillment that I crave.** То́лько ты мо́жешь дать мне то удовлетворе́ние, кото́рого я жа́жду.

crawl *vi* 1. *(one time, one direction)* ползти́ / поползти́; *(often, always, 2 or more times)* по́лзать; 2. *(servilely)* пресмыка́ться ♦ **Don't expect me to come crawling to you.** Не ожида́й, что я бу́ду пресмыка́ться пе́ред тобо́й.

crazed *adj* поме́шанный, -ая, -ое, -ые, соше́дший (-ая, -ее, -ие) с ума́ ♦ **Your** *(1)* **incredible /** *(2)* **voluptuous beauty has me crazed with** *(3)* **lust /** *(4)* **desire.** Твоя́ *(1)* невероя́тная / *(2)* роско́шная красота́ сво́дит меня́ с ума́ от *(3)* вожделе́ния / *(4)* стра́сти.

crazily *adv* безу́мно ♦ **I'm crazily in love with you.** Я безу́мно люблю́ тебя́

crazy *adj* сумасше́дший, -ая, -ее, -ие, поме́шанный, -ая, -ые, безу́мный, -ая, -ое, -ые ♦ **be ~ about** бре́дить *(about whom = instr.)* ♦ **I'm crazy about you.** Я схожу́ с ума́ по тебе́. ♦ **(I promise you,) I'm going to** *(1)* **...make you go... /** *(2)* **...drive you... (absolutely) crazy (with** *[3]* **ecstasy /** *[4]* **pleasure).** (Я обеща́ю, что) я *(1)* ...(соверше́нно) сведу́ тебя́ с ума́... / *(2)* ...сде́лаю тебя́ (абсолю́тно) безу́мной... (от *[3]* экста́за / *[4]* наслажде́ния). ♦ **You drive me (absolutely) crazy.** Ты (соверше́нно) сво́дишь меня́ с ума́. ♦ **I don't want us to spend just one crazy night together — I want us to spend a lifetime of crazy nights together.** Я не хочу́, чтобы мы провели́ вме́сте одну́ безу́мную ночь -- я хочу́, чтобы мы провели́ вме́сте це́лую жизнь, по́лную безу́мных ноче́й.

cream *n* крем ♦ **edible massage ~** съедо́бный масса́жный крем ♦ **~ of the crop** наилу́чший, -ая, -ее, -ие.

creamy *adj* сли́вочный, -ая, -ое, -ые, кре́мовый, -ая, -ое, -ые ♦ **And then my lips would adore the** *(1)* **creamy /** *(2)* **smooth column of your throat with soft, loving kisses.** А пото́м мои́ гу́бы покро́ют твою́ *(1)* кре́мовую / *(2)* гла́дкую стро́йную ше́ю мя́гкими, лю́бящими поцелу́ями.

creamy-smooth *adj* сли́вочно-ма́товый, -ая, -ое, -ые.

create *vt* создава́ть / созда́ть *(what = acc.)* ♦ **I am** *(1)* **completely /** *(2)* **totally** *(3)* **...overcome by... /** *(4)* **...swept away by... /** *(5)* **...engulfed in... the rapture that you create with your** *(6)* **...skillful hands. /** *(7)* **...ardent kisses. /** *(8)* **...roving lips.** Я *(1)* по́лностью / *(2)* весь *(ж: вся)* *(3,4)* ...охва́чен *(ж: охва́чена)*... / *(5)* ...поглощён *(ж: поглощена́)*... упое́нием, кото́рое ты создаёшь свои́ми *(6)* ...уме́лыми рука́ми. / *(7)* ...пы́лкими поцелу́ями. / *(8)* ...блужда́ющими губа́ми. ♦ **I'm going to create a million little delicious pleasures all over your body that are going to course into one tremendous explosion of ecstasy.** Я созда́м миллио́н ма́леньких восхити́тельных наслажде́ний в твоём те́ле, кото́рые солью́тся в оди́н огро́мный взрыв экста́за. ♦ **I want to create a family (with you).** Я хочу́ созда́ть семью́ (с тобо́й). ♦ **My mission in life is going to be to create over-**

Words in parentheses are optional.

whelming sensations all through your body, night and day. Цель моéй жи́зни бу́дет ночь и день создава́ть ошеломля́ющие ощуще́ния во всём твоём те́ле.

creative *adj* тво́рческий, -ая, -ое, -ие, созида́тельный, -ая, -ое, -ые ♦ **I have a creative spirit.** Во мне дух созида́ния.

creature *n* созда́ние, тварь *f*, существо́ ♦ **beautiful** ~ прекра́сное созда́ние ♦ **beloved** ~ люби́мое существо́ ♦ **darling** ~ ми́лое существо́ ♦ **dear** ~ дорого́е существо́ ♦ **delightful** *(1,2)* ~ восхити́тельное *(1)* существо́ / *(2)* созда́ние ♦ **good-hearted** ~ добросерде́чное созда́ние ♦ **gorgeous** ~ великоле́пное созда́ние ♦ **innocent** ~ неви́нное созда́ние ♦ **lovable** ~ ми́лое созда́ние ♦ **lovely** ~ прекра́сное созда́ние ♦ **luscious** ~ со́чное созда́ние ♦ **perfect** ~ соверше́нное созда́ние ♦ **wild** ~ ди́кое созда́ние ♦ **wonderful** ~ удиви́тельное созда́ние.

creature: *phrases*

You are truly a creature of divine fascination. Ты и́стинно боже́ственно-преле́стное созда́ние. ♦ **You are (/[1] absolutely / [2] unquestionably) the (3) most beautiful / (4) loveliest / (5) fairest / (6) most gorgeous / (7) most luscious creature I have ever (8) ...met. / (9) ...laid eyes on. / (10) ...known (in all my life).** Ты *([1]* абсолю́тно / *[2]* безогово́рочно) *(3-5)* ...са́мое прекра́сное... / *(6)* ...са́мое великоле́пное... / *(7)* ...сочне́йшее... созда́ние из всех, *(8)* ...встре́ченных / *(9)* уви́денных мной. / *(10)* ...кото́рых я когда́-либо знал (в свое́й жи́зни). ♦ **You're the (1) most beautiful creature in all the world.** Ты прекрасне́йшее созда́ние в ми́ре. ♦ **You are such a (1) good-hearted / (2) lovable / (3) delightful / (4) wonderful creature.** Ты тако́е *(1)* добросерде́чное / *(2)* ми́лое / *(3)* восхити́тельное / *(4)* удиви́тельное созда́ние. ♦ **You're a wild creature.** Ты ди́кое созда́ние.

credentials *n, pl* 1. вери́тельные гра́моты; 2. *(diploma)* дипло́м.

creep *n (slang)* га́дина, подо́нок.

cretin *n* крети́н.

crevice *n* щель, расще́лина ♦ **That's such a(n) (1) fascinating / (2) interesting crevice.** Это така́я *(1)* плени́тельная / *(2)* интере́сная расще́лина.

crimson *adj* тёмно-кра́сный, -ая, -ое, -ые, мали́новый,-ая, -ое, -ые; багро́вый, -ая, -ое, -ые, пунцо́вый, -ая, -ое, -ые ♦ **~ cheeks** тёмно-кра́сные щёки ♦ **turn ~** красне́ть / покрасне́ть.

cringe *vi* страши́ться *(at what = gen.)* ♦ **How can I (1) get / (2) live through another (3) day / (4) month / (5) week without you by my side. I cringe at the prospect.** Как могу́ я *(1,2)* дожи́ть до *(3)* ...сле́дующего дня / *(4)* ме́сяца... / *(5)* ...сле́дующей неде́ли... без тебя́ ря́дом со мной. Я страшу́сь тако́й перспекти́вы.

crippled *adj* искале́ченный, -ая, -ое, -ые.

crisp *adj (invigorating)* све́жий, бодря́щий.

crisply *adv (invigoratingly)* све́же, бодря́ще.

critical *adj (criticizing)* критику́ющий, -ая, -ее, -ие, осужда́ющий, -ая, -ее, -ие.

criticism *n* кри́тика.

criticize *vt* критикова́ть *(whom = acc.)*.

croon *vt* напева́ть / напе́ть *(what = acc.)* ♦ **You make me want to croon love songs to you all night long.** Ты вызыва́ешь во мне жела́ние напева́ть тебе́ любо́вные пе́сни всю ночь напролёт.

cross *vi* пересека́ться / пересе́чься ♦ **I'm so happy that our paths crossed (in this [1] life / [2] world).** Я так сча́стлив *(ж: сча́стлива)*, что на́ши пути́ пересекли́сь *([1]* ...в э́той жи́зни. / *[2]* ...в э́том ми́ре.)

cross-eyed *adj* косогла́зый, -ая, -ые ♦ **I'm slightly cross-eyed.** У меня́ лёгкое косогла́зие.

You can find common clothing sizes in Appendix 11 on page 778.

cross-pollinate *vt* (перекрёстно) опыля́ть / опыли́ть *(what = acc.).*

crotch *n* пах.

crown *n* коро́на ♦ **~ of the head** маку́шка.

crowned (with) *adj* уве́нченный, -ая, -ое, -ые ♦ **I see in this photo a face of** *(1)* **exquisite / (2) unimaginable beauty crowned with an opulence of** *(3)* **golden / (4) chestnut / (5) raven hair.** Я ви́жу на э́той фотогра́фии лицо́ *(1)* изы́сканной / *(2)* невообрази́мой красоты́ в струя́щемся бога́тстве *(3)* золоты́х / *(4)* кашта́новых / *(5)* чёрных воло́с.

crude *adj* гру́бый, -ая, -ое, -ые ♦ **That was a crude remark.** Это бы́ло гру́бое замеча́ние.

crudely *adv* гру́бо.

cruel *adj* жесто́кий, -ая, -ое, -ие, бессерде́чный, -ая, -ое, -ые ♦ **You're so cruel (to me).** Ты так жесто́ка *(ж: жесто́к)* (со мной). ♦ **Don't be so cruel to me.** Не будь тако́й жесто́кой *(ж: таки́м жесто́ким)* со мной. ♦ **That was about the cruelest thing you could (ever) have done.** Это бы́ло почти́ са́мой жесто́кой ве́щью, кото́рую ты могла́ *(ж: мог)* когда́-либо сде́лать. ♦ **I'm sorry I've been so cruel to you.** Мне жаль, что я был так жесто́к с тобо́й. ♦ **It was really cruel of me. Please forgive me.** Это бы́ло действи́тельно жесто́ко с мое́й стороны́. Пожа́луйста, прости́ меня́. ♦ **How could you be so cruel and heartless?** Как могла́ ты быть тако́й жесто́кой и бессерде́чной? *(ж: Как мог ты быть таки́м жесто́ким и бессерде́чным?)* ♦ **You are so cruel the way you** *(1)* **hold / (2) keep your love from me.** Так жесто́ко то, что ты *(1,2)* сде́рживаешь свою́ любо́вь ко мне.

crumble *vi* ру́шиться ♦ **Our marriage is crumbling.** Наш брак ру́шится.

crush *vt* 1. *(by pressure)* дави́ть / раздави́ть *(what, whom = acc.);* 2. *(extinguish, stifle)* подавля́ть / подави́ть *(what, whom = acc.)* ♦ **The thought of** *(1)* **...losing you... / (2) ...being without you... / (3) ...being apart from you... crushes my very soul.** Мысль о том, чтобы *(1)* ...потеря́ть тебя́... / *(2)* ...быть без тебя́... / *(3)* ...быть вдали́ от тебя́... подавля́ет мою́ ду́шу.

crush *n (slang) (infatuation)* слепо́е увлече́ние ♦ **have a ~** потеря́ть го́лову *(on whom = + из-за + gen.)* ♦ **I feel just like I have a schoolgirl crush (on you).** Я чу́вствую себя́ шко́льницей, потеря́вшей го́лову (из-за тебя́).

crutches *n, pl* костыли́ ♦ **I walk on crutches.** Я хожу́ на костыля́х.

cry *vi* 1. *(call out)* вскри́кивать / вскри́кнуть; 2. *(weep)* пла́кать / запла́кать ♦ **~ out** 1. выкри́кивать; 2. звать / позва́ть *(for what, whom = acc.);* о́стро нужда́ться *(for what, whom = + в + prep.).*

cry: weep

Cry if you need to. (It's okay.) Let it all out. Попла́чь, е́сли тебе́ э́то ну́жно. (Всё норма́льно.) Изба́вься от э́того. ♦ **I don't want to make you cry.** Я не хочу́ (де́лать так), чтобы ты пла́кала. ♦ *(1,2)* **Why are you crying?** *(1)* Почему́ / *(2)* Отчего́ ты пла́чешь? ♦ **Please don't cry.** Пожа́луйста, не плачь. ♦ **I** *(1)* **want / (2) wanted to cry.** Мне *(1)* хо́чется / *(2)* хоте́лось пла́кать.

cry out:

I love the way you cry out. Мне о́чень нра́вится, как ты вскри́киваешь. ♦ **My** *(1)* **whole / (2) entire being cries out for you.** *(1,2)* Всё моё существо́ зовёт тебя́.

cry *n* крик ♦ **~ of pleasure** крик наслажде́ния ♦ **guttural ~** горта́нный крик ♦ **Every night I want you to serenade me with your moans and cries of pleasure.** Я хочу́, чтобы ка́ждую ночь ты исполня́ла для меня́ серена́ду сто́нов и кри́ков наслажде́ния.

cuckold *vt* наставля́ть / наста́вить рога́ *(whom = dat.),* изменя́ть / измени́ть *(whom = dat.)* ♦ **I don't want to be cuckolded (by anyone).** Я не хочу́, чтобы кто́-нибудь наста́вил мне рога́.

Depending on the subject, the possessive pronoun **свой (своя́, своё, свой)** *can be translated* **my, your, his, her, its, our** *or* **their***.*

cuckold *n* рогоносец, обманутый муж.

cuddle (up) *vi* прижиматься / прижаться *(with whom = + к + dat.)*, обниматься / обняться *(with whom = + с + instr.)*, сжимать в объятиях *(with whom = acc.)*, нежить.

> **cuddle:** *love to cuddle*

Do you like to cuddle? Тебе нравится обниматься? ♦ **I love to kiss, hug, caress, touch, hold hands, nibble, cuddle, rub against, stroke — you just name it.** Я люблю целовать, обнимать, ласкать, касаться, держаться за руки, покусывать, сжимать в объятиях, тереться, гладить -- ты только назови. ♦ **I love (1) ...to cuddle... / (2) ...cuddling up... (with you).** Я люблю *(1,2)* обниматься (с тобой).

> **cuddle:** *I want to cuddle with you*

I want to cuddle up with you. Я хочу ласкаться и обниматься с тобой. ♦ **I want to take you in my arms and caress you and kiss you and cuddle (up) with you.** Я хочу держать тебя в своих объятиях, ласкать, целовать и обнимать тебя. ♦ **How wonderful it would be to (1,2) cuddle up with you in bed every night.** Как замечательно было бы *(1)* ...обниматься с тобой... / *(2)* ...прижиматься друг к другу... в постели каждую ночь. ♦ **It would be wonderful to cuddle up with you on the couch and watch a video — until we thought of something else more enjoyable to do.** Было бы так замечательно прижаться друг к другу на диване и смотреть фильм до тех пор, пока мы не подумаем о том, чтобы заняться чём-то ещё более приятным.

> **cuddle:** *we can cuddle together*

Let's cuddle together. Давай прижмёмся друг к другу. ♦ **(I'll make a fire in the fireplace and) we can cuddle by the fire(light).** (Я зажгу огонь в камине и) мы сможем прижаться друг к другу у огня. ♦ **We can lie down on my couch (by the fireplace) and cuddle together.** Мы можем лежать на моём диване (около камина) и ласкать друг друга.

cuddle-bug *n (slang)* любимая *(любимый)*, которую *(которого)* очень приятно обнимать *(explanation)*.

cuddler *n* человек, который любит обнимать *(1 term)*.

cuddlesome *adj (no adjective in Russian, the term* приятно обниматься *is used)* ♦ **You're so cuddlesome.** С тобой так приятно обниматься.

cuddling *n* объятия *pl. (Russian mostly uses verbs. See* **cuddle** *above.)* ♦ **nocturnal ~** объятия ночью, *(verb term:)* обниматься ночью ♦ **Cuddling with you is (absolutely) heaven!** Обниматься с тобой -- (абсолютное) блаженство. ♦ **I never knew that cuddling with someone could be so heavenly.** Я никогда не знал, что обниматься с кем-либо может быть так божественно. ♦ **I (really) enjoy cuddling.** Я (действительно) наслаждаюсь объятиями.

cuddly *adj (no adjective in Russian, the term* приятно обниматься *is used)* ♦ **You are so (warm and) cuddly.** (Ты такая тёплая и) с тобой так приятно обниматься. ♦ **You look so cuddly and kissable in these photos I can hardly stand it!** На этих фотографиях ты выглядишь такой зовущей к объятиям и к поцелуям, что я едва могу вынести.

cue *n* намёк ♦ **nonverbal ~** намёк без слов ♦ **verbal ~** словесный намёк.

cuisine *n* кухня ♦ **exotic ~** экзотическая кухня ♦ **haute ~** изысканная кухня.

culminate *vi* достигать / достичь кульминации *(in what = + в + prep.)* ♦ **~ in orgasm** достигать / достичь кульминации в оргазме.

cultivated *adj* культурный, -ая, -ое, -ые, развитой, -ая, -ое, -ые.

culture *n* культура ♦ **singles' ~** культура одиноких ♦ **I relate to diverse cultures.** У меня есть интерес к разным культурам. ♦ **Getting used to a strange culture will be a big challenge. But I will help you.** Привыкание к чужой культуре будет сложной

For general rules of Russian grammar see Appendix 2 on page 686.

зада́чей. Но я помогу́ тебе́.

cultured *adj* культу́рный, -ая, -ое, -ые.

cum *n (slang) (semen)* спе́рма, се́мя.

cunnilingus *n* кунили́нгус *(ора́льное возбужде́ние же́нских половы́х о́рганов)*.

cunning *adj* хи́трый, -ая, -ое, -ые, кова́рный, -ая, -ое, -ые.

cup *vt* обхва́тывать / обхвати́ть *(what = acc.)* ♦ **As my hand cups the fullness of your breast, my mouth will cover your beautiful face and smooth neck with adoring kisses.** В то вре́мя, как моя́ рука́ ощути́т полноту́ твое́й груди́, мой рот покро́ет твоё прекра́сное лицо́ и не́жную ше́ю обожа́ющими поцелу́ями.

Cupid *n* Купидо́н ♦ **(I feel like) Cupid has shot an arrow right through my heart.** (Я чу́вствую, как) Купидо́н посла́л стрелу́ пря́мо в моё се́рдце. ♦ **The first moment I laid eyes on you, Cupid unloaded all his arrows into my heart.** В пе́рвый моме́нт, как то́лько я уви́дел тебя́, Купидо́н посла́л все свои́ стре́лы пря́мо в моё се́рдце. ♦ **If it seems to you that I'm staggering, it's because I've got Cupid's arrows sticking all over me.** Если тебе́ ка́жется, что я шата́юсь, так э́то потому́, что все стре́лы Купидо́на попа́ли пря́мо в меня́. ♦ **Your smile and Cupid's arrow came to me at the same time.** Твоя́ улы́бка и стре́лы Купидо́на дости́гли меня́ одновреме́нно.

curb *vt* обу́здывать *(what = acc.)* ♦ **It is impossible for me to curb my** *(1)* **desire** / *(2)* **passion when I'm** *(3)* **with** / *(4)* **around you.** Невозмо́жно для меня́ обу́здывать *(1)* ...моё жела́ние,... / *(2)* ...мою́ страсть,... когда́ я *(3)* ...с тобо́й. / *(4)* ...вблизи́ тебя́.

curiosity *n* любопы́тство ♦ **intense** ~ си́льное любопы́тство.

curious *adj* любопы́тный, -ая, -ое, -ые ♦ **intellectually** ~ любозна́тельный, -ая, -ое, -ые ♦ **I'm curious. Where did you study English?** Мне любопы́тно. Где ты изуча́ла *(ж: изуча́л)* англи́йский?

curl *vt (slang)*: ♦ **I'll curl your toes!** *(slang)* Я доста́влю тебе́ мо́ре наслажде́ния.

curl *n* ло́кон, завито́к; *pl* ку́дри, ло́коны, завитки́ ♦ **beautiful** ~s краси́вые ку́дри ♦ **black** ~s чёрные ку́дри ♦ **dark** ~ s тёмные ку́дри ♦ **golden** *(1,2)* ~s золоти́стые *(1)* завитки́ / *(2)* ку́дри ♦ **lavish** ~s густы́е ло́коны ♦ **magnificent golden** *(1,2)* ~s великоле́пные золоти́стые *(1)* завитки́ / *(2)* ку́дри ♦ **tiny** ~s ме́лкие кудря́шки ♦ **windblown** ~s развева́емые ве́тром ло́коны.

curl up *vi* сверну́ться в клубо́к *(with whom =* + с + *instr.)*, прильну́ть *(with whom =* + к + *dat.)*, прижима́ться / прижа́ться *(with whom =* + к + *dat.)* ♦ **I want to curl up with you** (*[1]*...**in bed.** / *[2]* ...**on the couch** / *[3]* **sofa.** / *[4]* ...**in front of the fireplace.**). Я хочу́ прильну́ть к тебе́ (*[1]*...в крова́ти. / *[2]* ...на дива́не / *[3]* софе́. / *[4]* ...пе́ред ками́ном.). ♦ **I dream of curling up with you all night long.** Я мечта́ю о том, что́бы прильну́ть к тебе́ на всю ночь. ♦ **Let's climb under the covers and curl up together.** Дава́й заберёмся под одея́ло и прижмёмся друг к дру́гу. ♦ **I love curling up with you.** Мне так нра́вится сверну́ться с тобо́й в клубо́к. ♦ **How I want to curl up with you, snuggle against your breast, feel the warmth of you, caress you, love you.** Как бы я хоте́л обня́ться с тобо́й, прижа́ться к твое́й груди́, чу́вствовать твоё тепло́, ласка́ть тебя́, люби́ть тебя́.

curly *adj* кудря́вый, -ая, -ое, -ые, курча́вый, -ая, -ое, -ые.

curly-haired / **-headed** *adj* кудря́вый, -ая, -ое, -ые.

current *n* 1. *(water)* пото́к, тече́ние; 2. *(emot.)* струя́; 3. *(elec.)* ток ♦ **like an electric** ~ как электри́ческий ток ♦ **I sense in you an underlying current of** *(1)* **disdain** / *(2)* **doubt** / *(3)* **indifference** / *(4)* **mistrust** / *(5)* **reluctance.** Я ощуща́ю в тебе́ скры́тое *(1)* пренебреже́ние / *(2)* сомне́ние / *(3)* равноду́шие / *(4)* недове́рие / *(5)* нежела́ние.

curvaceous *adj* окру́глый, -ая, -ое, -ые; соблазни́тельный, -ая, -ое, -ые, пы́шный, -ая, -ое,

---

For transitive Russian verbs the cases that they take are shown by means of an = sign and the Russian case (abbreviated).

-ые, с хоро́шей / изя́щной фигу́рой ♦ **You have the most curvaceous body I've ever seen.** Я никогда́ не ви́дел тако́го окру́глого, краси́вого те́ла.

curve *n (line)* крива́я; *(road, etc)* изги́б, изви́лина; *(body) (pl:)* изги́бы, фо́рмы, фигу́ра; окру́глости ♦ **alluring** ~s привлека́тельные изги́бы ♦ **beautiful** ~s прекра́сные фо́рмы, прекра́сная фигу́ра ♦ **delicate** ~s не́жные изги́бы ♦ **enticing** ~s соблазни́тельные изги́бы ♦ *(1-3)* **graceful** ~s *(1)* изя́щные ли́нии те́ла, *(2)* изя́щные / *(3)* грацио́зные изги́бы ♦ **exquisite** ~s соверше́нные ли́нии ♦ **luscious** ~s роско́шные фо́рмы ♦ **lush** ~s роско́шные фо́рмы ♦ **nicely proportioned** ~s о́чень пропорциона́льныое те́ло ♦ **perfect** ~s **of your breasts** соверше́нные ли́нии твое́й груди́ ♦**provocative** соблазни́тельные изги́бы ♦ **sensuous** ~s чу́вственные изги́бы ♦ **slender** ~s стро́йные изги́бы ♦ **soft feminine** ~s мя́гкие же́нственные фо́рмы ♦ **supple** ~s ги́бкие фо́рмы ♦ **svelte** *(1-3)* ~s стро́йные *(1)* изги́бы / *(2)* фо́рмы / *(3)* окру́глости, *(4)* стро́йная фигу́ра ♦ **tantalizing** ~s дразня́щая фигу́ра ♦ **youthful** ~s молоды́е изги́бы.

> **curve: phrases**

The provocative curve of your breasts is such a pleasure to behold. Тако́е удово́льствие созерца́ть соблазни́тельные изги́бы твое́й груди́. ♦ **You look so incredibly lovely with your** *([1]* **luscious** / *[2]* **svelte** / *[3]* **supple**) **curves** *(4,5)* **swathed in** *(6)* **silk** / *(7)* **chiffon.** Ты вы́глядишь тако́й невероя́тно краси́вой в *(6)* шёлке / *(7)* шифо́не, *(4)* оку́тывающем / *(5)* покрыва́ющем твои́ (*[1]* роско́шные / *[2]* стро́йные / *[3]* ги́бкие) фо́рмы. ♦ **My fingers will stroll languidly, softly, adoringly along the svelte curve of your body.** Мои́ па́льцы ме́дленно, мя́гко, обожа́юще прогуля́ются по стро́йным окру́глостям твоего́ те́ла. ♦ **You have such** *(1)* **tantalizing** / *(2)* **svelte** / *(3)* **beautiful curves.** У тебя́ така́я *(1)* дразня́щая / *(2)* стро́йная / *(3)* прекра́сная фигу́ра. ♦ **The delicate curves of your legs are so** *(1)* **alluring** / *(2)* **beautiful** /*(3)* **enticing.** Не́жные изги́бы твои́х ног так *(1)* привлека́тельны / *(2)* прекра́сны / *(3)* соблазни́тельны. ♦ **My lips would reverently adore the graceful curve of your hips.** Мои́ гу́бы бу́дут почти́тельно обожа́ть грацио́зные изги́бы твои́х бёдер.

curvy *adj* окру́глый, -ая, -ое, -ые ♦ **What a lovely, curvy figure you have!** Кака́я у тебя́ краси́вая, окру́глая фигу́ра!

custom *n* обы́чай; привы́чка ♦ **Russian** ~ ру́сский обы́чай ♦ **Ukrainian** ~ украи́нский обы́чай ♦ **I want to know more about your customs.** Я хочу́ бо́льше узна́ть об обы́чаях твое́й страны́. ♦ **Is that a custom in your country?** Это обы́чай твое́й страны́? ♦ **It's (not) a custom in** *(1)* **my** / *(2)* **our country.** Это (не) обы́чай *(1)*мое́й / *(2)* на́шей страны́. ♦ **That's against our customs.** У нас э́то не при́нято.

cut *vt:* ♦ ~ **in** *vi (on s.o. dancing)* отнима́ть / отня́ть партнёршу (на та́нцах) ♦ ~ **out** *vt (slang) (stop)* прекраща́ть / прекрати́ть *(what = acc.)* ♦ ~ **to the quick** *vt* оскорбля́ть / оскорби́ть до глубины́ души́ *(whom = acc.)*, задева́ть за живо́е *(whom = acc.)*.

> **cut in:**

May I cut in? Могу́ я разби́ть Вас?

> **cut out:**

Cut it out! Прекрати́!

> **cut to the quick:**

(1) **Your remark...** / *(2)* **What you said... really cut me to the quick.** *(1)* Твоё замеча́ние..., / *(2)* То, что ты сказа́ла *(ж: сказа́л)*..., действи́тельно, до глубины́ души́ оскорби́ло меня́.

cute *adj (f only)* хоро́шенькая, -ие, ми́ленькая, -ие, смазли́вая, -ые, преми́ленькая, -ие; *(m & f)* привлека́тельный, -ая, -ое, -ые, ми́лый, -ая, -ое, -ые; преле́стный, -ая, -ое, -ые ♦ **deliciously** *(1,2)* ~ восхити́тельно *(1)* ми́лая / *(2)* привлека́тельная ♦ **kinda** *(1,2)*

Russian verbs have 2 forms: imperfective and perfective.
They're given in that order.

~ дово́льно *(1)* ми́ленькая / *(2)* привлека́тельная.

cute: phrases

You're cute as a button. Ты така́я хоро́шенькая. ♦ **What a(n adorably) cute face you have.** Како́е преле́стное лицо́ у тебя́. ♦ **What a(n adorably) cute** *(1)* **mouth** / *(2)* **nose you have.** Како́й преле́стный *(1)* рот / *(2)* нос у тебя́. ♦ **You're just as cute as can be.** Ты са́мая хоро́шенькая на све́те.

cutie *n (slang)* хоро́шенькая де́вушка, красо́тка.

CW = country & western (music) (му́зыка) ка́нтри-энд-ве́стерн.

cyberlover *n* на́йденный на интерне́те возлю́бленный *m*, на́йденная на интерне́те возлю́бленная *f*.

cyberspace *n* киберпростра́нство, электро́нный эфир.

cycle *n (menstrual)* цикл ♦ **monthly** ~ ме́сячный цикл ♦ **your** ~ твой цикл.

cycling *n* езда́ на велосипе́де.

cynic *n* ци́ник.

cynical *adj* цини́чный, -ая, -ое, -ые ♦ **You shouldn't be (so) cynical about love.** Тебе́ не сле́довало бы быть (тако́й *[ж: таки́м]*) цини́чной *(ж: цини́чным)* в отноше́нии к любви́.

cynosure *n* путево́дная звезда́ ♦ **You are the cynosure of all my** *(1)* **thoughts** / *(2)* **dreams** / *(3)* **hopes** / *(4)* **desires.** / *(5)* **love** / *(6)* **life.** Ты путево́дная звезда́ *(1)* ...всех мои́х мы́слей / *(2)* мечта́ний / *(3)* наде́жд / *(4)* жела́ний. / *(5)* ...всей мое́й любви́ / *(6)* жи́зни.

---

*How to use the Cyrillic alphabet on the Internet
is the subject of Appendix 20 on page 789.*

D

dad *n (slang)* па́па ♦ **part-time ~** разведённый оте́ц, ребёнок кото́рого иногда́ живёт с ним *(explanation)* ♦ **single ~** одино́кий па́па.

daddy *n (slang)* па́па ♦ **sugar ~** бога́тый покло́нник.

dainty *adj* изя́щный, -ая, -ое, -ые; изы́сканный, -ая, -ое, -ые ♦ **~ hand** изя́щная рука́.

daisy *n* маргари́тка ♦ **sunny ~** со́лнечная маргари́тка.

dalliance *n* заи́грывание, флирт.

damnably *adv* ужа́сно, о́чень, чрезвыча́йно; а́дски, черто́вски.

damsel *n* деви́ца ♦ **~ in (1,2) distress** деви́ца в *(1)* го́ре / *(2)* беде́.

dance *vi* танцева́ть ♦ **~ close** танцева́ть прижа́вшись ♦ **~ in the moonlight** танцева́ть в лу́нном све́те ♦ **~ in the rain** танцева́ть под дождём ♦ **I'd like to dance around the world with you.** Я хоте́л *(ж: хоте́ла)* бы протанцева́ть по всему́ ми́ру с тобо́й. ♦ **We'll dance 'til dawn.** Мы бу́дем танцева́ть до рассве́та.

dance *n* 1. та́нец; 2. *(event)* та́нцы *pl* ♦ **fast ~** бы́стрый та́нец ♦ **folk ~** наро́дный та́нец ♦ **modern ~** совреме́нный та́нец ♦ **slow ~** ме́дленный та́нец ♦ *(1)* **I'd like to invite you...** / *(2)* **Would you like to go (with me)... to a dance** *(3)* **...tomorrow (evening).** / *(4)* **...this afternoon** / *(5)* **evening.** / *(6)* **...on Friday** / *(7)* **Saturday** / *(8)* **Sunday** *(9)* **afternoon** / *(10)* **evening.** / ? *(1)* Я хоте́л бы пригласи́ть тебя́... / *(2)* Не хо́чешь ли ты пойти́ (со мной)... на та́нцы *(3)* ...за́втра (ве́чером). / *(4)* ...сего́дня днём / *(5)* ве́чером. / *(6)* ...в пя́тницу / *(7)* суббо́ту / *(8)* воскресе́нье *(9)* днём / *(10)* ве́чером. / ?

dancer *n* танцо́р *m*, танцовщи́ца *f* ♦ **go-go ~** танцовщи́ца в дискоте́ке ♦ **smooth ~** грацио́зный иску́сный танцо́р ♦ *(1,2)* **I'm a good dancer.** *(1)* Я хоро́ший танцо́р. / *(2)* Я хорошо́ танцу́ю. ♦ **I'm not a good dancer.** Я пло́хо танцу́ю. ♦ **You're a (very) good dancer.** Ты (о́чень) хорошо́ танцу́ешь. ♦ **I'm not a very good dancer, but I like holding you.** Я не о́чень хоро́ший танцо́р, но мне нра́вится держа́ть тебя́ в та́нце.

dancing *n* та́нцы ♦ **ballroom ~** ба́льные та́нцы ♦ **disco ~** ди́ско ♦ **fast ~** бы́стрые та́нцы ♦ **Latin ~** лати́но-америка́нские та́нцы ♦ **slow ~** ме́дленные та́нцы ♦ **salsa ~** *(Latino style of dancing)* лати́но-америка́нский та́нец «са́лса» ♦ **techno ~** *(dancing to music with lots of synthesizing and a minimum of vocal)* та́нцы под синтези́рованную му́зыку ♦ **Would you like to go dancing (with me)?** Не пойдёшь ли ты танцева́ть (со мной)? ♦ **Let's go dancing (together).** Пойдём на та́нцы (вме́сте).

Dane *n* датча́нин *m*, датча́нка *f* *(pl:* датча́не).

Russian adjectives have long and short forms.
Where short forms are given, they are labeled as such.

danger *n* опа́сность *f.*

dangerous *adj* опа́сный, -ая, -ое, -ые *(short forms:* опа́сен, опа́сна, -о, -ы) ♦ **It's dangerous to be so close to you.** Быть так бли́зко к тебе́ опа́сно. ♦ **It's (***[1]* **too /** *[2]* **so) dangerous without (***3)* **...some kind of protection. /** *(4)* **...a condom.** (*[1]* Сли́шком / *[2]* Так) Опа́сно без *(3)* ...како́го-ли́бо предохране́ния. / *(4)* ...презервати́ва.

Danish *adj* да́тский, -ая, -ое, -ие.

Danish *n (language)* да́тский язы́к ♦ **speak** ~ говори́ть по-да́тски.

dapper *adj* щегольско́й, -а́я, -о́е, -и́е, наря́дный, -ая, -ое, -ые.

dare *vi* сметь / посме́ть; осме́ливаться / осме́литься ♦ **How dare you (***[1]***...say such a thing! /** *[2]* **...do such a thing! /** *[3]* **...come in here! /** *[4]* **...touch me like that!)!** Как ты посме́ла *(ж: посме́л)* (*[1]*...сказа́ть тако́е! / *[2]* ...сде́лать тако́е! / *[3]* ...прийти́ сюда́! / *[4]* ...косну́ться меня́ таки́м о́бразом!)!

daredevil *n* смельча́к, безрассу́дно сме́лый челове́к.

daring *adj* сме́лый, -ая, -ое, -ые, отва́жный, -ая, -ое, -ые.

daringly *adv* сме́ло ♦ **I write this to you daringly, I know, but I hope that it will reach your heart.** Я зна́ю, что пишу́ тебе́ сме́ло, но наде́юсь, что э́то дойдёт до твоего́ се́рдца.

dark *adj* 1. *(light, color)* тёмный, -ая, -ое, -ые; 2. *(complexion)* сму́глый, -ая, -ое, -ые ♦ **tall, ~ and handsome** высо́кий, сму́глый и краси́вый.

dark *n* темнота́ ♦ **This is a shot in the dark, but I decided to try anyway.** Это вы́стрел в темноту́, но я реши́л всё-таки попро́бовать. ♦ **I'm (completely) in the dark about it.** Я (соверше́нно) ничего́ об э́том не зна́ю. ♦ **Please don't keep me in the dark.** Пожа́луйста, не держи́ меня́ в неве́дении. ♦ **In the dark, just you and I together.** В темноте́, то́лько ты и я вме́сте.

dark-brown *adj* тёмно-кашта́новый, -ая, -ое, -ые, тёмно-ру́сый, -ая, -ое, -ые.

dark-complected *adj* сму́глый, -ая, -ое, -ые.

dark-eyed *adj* тёмноглазый, -ая, -ое, -ые.

dark-haired *adj* темноволо́сый, -ая, -ое, -ые.

darkness *n* темнота́.

dark-skinned *adj* темноко́жий, -ая, -ее, -ие.

darling *n* ми́лый, дорого́й *m;* ми́лая, дорога́я *f* ♦ **little** ~ голу́бка, ко́шечка, ду́шечка, ла́почка, дорогу́ша ♦ **precious** ~ драгоце́нный *m;* драгоце́нная *f* ♦ **Good morning, my dearly beloved little (***1,2)* **darling!** До́брое у́тро, моя́ не́жно люби́мая ма́ленькая *(1)* голу́бка / *(2)* ко́шечка! ♦ **You are my darling.** Ты моя́ дорога́я *(ж: мой дорого́й).* ♦ **My precious darling, I love you so very much.** Моя́ драгоце́нная *(ж: Мой драгоце́нный),* я так си́льно люблю́ тебя́. ♦ **Darling, would you like to have dinner out tonight?** Дорога́я *(ж: Дорого́й),* ты бы не хоте́ла *(ж: хоте́л)* пойти́ куда́-нибу́дь пообе́дать сего́дня ве́чером? ♦ **My darling, you mean everything to me.** Моя́ дорога́я *(ж: Мой дорого́й),* ты для меня́ всё.

dart *n* стрела́ ♦ **Cupid's ~s** стре́лы Купидо́на ♦ **love ~s** стре́лы любви́.

dashing *adj* лихо́й, -а́я, -о́е, -и́е, щегольско́й, -а́я, -о́е, -и́е, молодцева́тый, -ая, -ое, -ые.

date *vt (go out with someone, usually romantically) (single occasion)* идти́ / пойти́ на свида́ние *(whom =* + с + *instr.); (regularly)* встреча́ться *(whom =* + с + *instr.)* ♦ **Are you dating anyone?** Ты встреча́ешься с кем-нибу́дь? ♦ **I'm not dating anyone.** Я ни с кем не встреча́юсь. ♦ **I just date (***1)* **casually /** *(2)* **occasionally.** Я встреча́юсь *(1)* несерьёзно / *(2)* иногда́.

date *n* 1. *(calendar)* да́та; 2. *(appointment to meet)* свида́ние; 3. *(person met)* челове́к, с кото́рым встреча́ешься *(1 term)* ♦ **arranged** ~ свида́ние, кото́рое бы́ло организо́вано ке́м-то *(explanation)* ♦ **blind** ~ свида́ние с тем, с кем никогда́ ра́ньше не встреча́лся

Russian nouns are either masculine, feminine or neuter.
Adjectives with them will be the same.

(explanation) ♦ **disaster** ~ ужа́сное свида́ние ♦ **double** ~ *(No special term in Russian for this concept)* свида́ние двух молоды́х люде́й с двумя́ де́вушками *(explanation)* ♦ **first** ~ пе́рвое свида́ние ♦ **forthcoming** ~ предстоя́щее свида́ние ♦ **Friday's** ~ свида́ние в пя́тницу ♦ **last** ~ после́днее свида́ние ♦ **next** ~ сле́дующее свида́ние ♦ **upcoming** ~ предстоя́щее свида́ние ♦ **wedding** ~ да́та сва́дьбы ♦ **ask out on a** ~ приглаша́ть / пригласи́ть на свида́ние *(whom = acc.)* ♦ **We can go on a double date with them.** Мы мо́жем пойти́ куда́-нибу́дь вме́сте с ни́ми. ♦ **I have a dinner date this evening.** Я обе́даю сего́дня ве́чером с ке́м-то.

dateline *n* телефо́н, по кото́рому мо́жно звони́ть и инти́мно разгова́ривать с де́вушками и́ли мужчи́нами *(explanation)*.

dating *n* хожде́ние на свида́ния *(Russian prefers verb expression* ходи́ть на свида́ния*)* ♦ **I do a little (casual) dating.** Я хожу́ иногда́ на (несерьёзные) свида́ния. ♦ **I seek an attractive, educated, fun-loving woman for dating.** Я ищу́ привлека́тельную, лю́бящую развлече́ния же́нщину для встреч.

daughter *n* дочь ♦ **adopted** ~ удочерённая дочь ♦ **foster** ~ приёмная дочь ♦ **older** ~ ста́ршая дочь ♦ **oldest** ~ са́мая ста́ршая дочь ♦ **middle** ~ сре́дняя дочь ♦ **younger** ~ мла́дшая дочь ♦ **youngest** ~ са́мая мла́дшая дочь ♦ **I *(1,2)* would be willing to adopt your daughter.** *(1)* Я гото́в *(ж: гото́ва)*... / *(2)* Я бы хоте́л *(ж: хоте́ла)*... удочери́ть твою́ дочь.

daughter-in-law *n* неве́стка.

dawn *n* заря́.

day *n* день *m (pl:* дни*)* ♦ **all** ~ весь день ♦ **beautiful** ~ прекра́сный день ♦ **each** ~ ка́ждый день ♦ **every** ~ ка́ждый день ♦ **long awaited** ~ долгожда́нный день ♦ **red-letter** ~ па́мятный, ра́достный день *(1 term)* ♦ **the same** ~ в оди́н день ♦ **the whole** ~ весь день ♦ **Valentine's Day** День Свято́го Валенти́на *(праздник возлюбленных, 14-ое февраля́)* ♦ **wedding** ~ день сва́дьбы ♦ **wonderful** ~ замеча́тельный день.

day: other terms

~ **after** ~ день за днём ♦ **during the** ~ днём ♦ **for a** ~ 1. *(planned)* на день; 2. *(spent)* день ♦ **for one** ~ 1. *(planned)* на оди́н день; 2. *(spent)* оди́н день ♦ **for** *(1)* **two** / *(2)* **three** / *(3)* **four days** 1. *(planned)* на *(1)* два / *(2)* три / *(3)* четы́ре дня; 2. *(spent)* *(1)* два / *(2)* три / *(3)* четы́ре дня ♦ **in** *(1)* **a** / *(2)* **one** ~ *(in the space of)* в *(1,2)* оди́н день, за *(1,2)* оди́н день ♦ **in a** ~ *(after)* че́рез день ♦ **in** *(1)* **two** / *(3)* **three** ~**s** *(after)* че́рез *(1)* два / *(2)* три дня ♦ **on any day** в любо́й день ♦ **once a** ~ раз в день ♦ **(On) What day?** В како́й день?

day: phrases

(1) **That (*[2]* beautiful** / *[3]* **wonderful) day...** / *(4)* **Those (*[5]* beautiful** / *[6]* **wonderful) days... will** *(7)* **stay** / *(8)* **remain indelibly etched in my** *(9)* **mind** / *(10)* **memory** *(11)* **...forever.** / *(12)* **...for as long as I live.** *(1)* Э́тот *([2]* прекра́сный / *[3]* замеча́тельный*)* день оста́нется... / *(4)* Э́ти *([5]* прекра́сные / *[6]* замеча́тельные*)* дни *(7,8)* оста́нутся... в мое́й *(9,10)* па́мяти *(11)* ...навсегда́. / *(12)* ...до тех пор, пока́ я жив *(ж:жива́)*. ♦ **You made my day.** Ты сде́лала *(ж: сде́лал)* день хоро́шим для меня́. ♦ **Your** *(1)* **call** / *(2)* **letter made my day.** *(1)* Твой звоно́к сде́лал... / *(2)* Твоё письмо́ сде́лало... день хоро́шим для меня́. ♦ **I will always cling to the memory of those** *(1)* **wonderful** / *(2)* **beautiful days we spent together.** Я бу́ду всегда́ вспомина́ть об э́тих *(1)* великоле́пных / *(2)* прекра́сных днях, проведённых на́ми вме́сте.

daydream *vi* гре́зить наяву́ *(about what, whom = + о + prep.)*, мечта́ть *(about what, whom = + о + prep.)*, фантази́ровать *(about what, whom = + о + prep.)* ♦ **I daydream about you constantly.** Я постоя́нно мечта́ю о тебе́. ♦ **I spend private moments thinking about you, wondering about you, daydreaming about you.** Я провожу́ свои́ свобо́дные

Learn more about Russian customs in Appendix 15, page 782.

мину́ты, ду́мая о тебе́, представля́я себе́, чем ты сейча́с занима́ешься, мечта́я о тебе́. ♦ **Sometimes I daydream that we are all alone in a cabin at the seashore.** Иногда́ я мечта́ю, что мы совсе́м одни́ в до́мике на морско́м берегу́. ♦ **I'll be thinking and daydreaming about you as I wait for your** *(1)* **letter** / *(2)* **call.** Я бу́ду ду́мать и мечта́ть о тебе́ в то вре́мя, как я жду твоего́ *(1)* письма́ / *(2)* звонка́. ♦ **I hope I'm not just daydreaming.** Я наде́юсь, я не то́лько мечта́ю.

daydream *n* грёза, мечта́ ♦ **beautiful** ~ прекра́сная мечта́ ♦ **loving** ~ мечта́, по́лная любви́ *(1 term)* ♦ *(1,2)* **marvelous** ~ *(1)* замеча́тельная / *(2)* чуде́сная мечта́ ♦ **tender** ~ не́жная мечта́ ♦ *(1,2)* **wonderful** ~ *(1)* замеча́тельная / *(2)* чуде́сная мечта́.

---
daydream: phrases

My head is (constantly) filled with the most tender, loving daydreams about you. Моя́ голова́ (постоя́нно) запо́лнена нежне́йшими, по́лными любви́ мечта́ми о тебе́. ♦ **Love with you is like a** *(1)* **wonderful** / *(2)* **marvelous** / *(3)* **beautiful daydream.** Любо́вь с тобо́й похо́жа на *(1)* замеча́тельную / *(2)* чуде́сную / *(3)* прекра́сную мечту́. ♦ **All of my daydreams and fantasies are filled with images of your exquisitely beautiful** *(1)* **face** / *(2)* **body.** Все мои́ мечты́ и фанта́зии запо́лнены о́бразом твоего́ изы́сканно прекра́сного *(1)* лица́ / *(2)* те́ла. ♦ **You're my favorite daydream subject.** Ты гла́вный предме́т мои́х мечта́ний. ♦ **I will be back with you in my pre-falling-asleep daydreams — where you've been a permanent resident for a long time already.** Пе́ред тем, как забы́ться сном, я верну́сь к тебе́ в свои́х мечта́х, где ты и так была́ постоя́нным жи́телем давны́м давно́.

daylight *n* дневно́й свет ♦ **in broad** ~ при дневно́м све́те, публи́чно.

daytrip *n* однодне́вное путеше́ствие.

daze *n* ошеломле́ние, изумле́ние ♦ **That kiss really** *(1)* **...inflicted a daze on me.** / *(2)* **...put me in a daze.** Этот поцелу́й действи́тельно ошеломи́л меня́. ♦ **I'm still in a daze (from** *[1]* **...your letter.** / *[2]* **...that kiss.** / *[3]* **...what you told me.)** Я всё ещё в ошеломле́нии (от *[1]* ...твоего́ письма́. / *[2]* ...э́того поцелу́я. / *[3]* ...того́, что ты сказа́ла *[ж: сказа́л]* мне.).

dazzle *vt* ослепля́ть / ослепи́ть *(what, whom = acc.)*, поража́ть / порази́ть *(what, whom = acc.)* ♦ **Your** *(1)* **beauty** / *(2)* **loveliness** *(3,4)* **dazzles me.** Твоя́ *(1,2)* красота́ *(3)* ослепля́ет / *(4)* поража́ет меня́. ♦ **You dazzle me with your charm and beauty and blithe spirit.** Ты поража́ешь меня́ свои́м обая́нием, красото́й и весёлым хара́ктером.

dazzled *adj* ослеплён, ослеплена́, -о́, -ы́ *(short forms)* ♦ **I am (** *[1]* **completely** / *[2]* **totally) dazzled by** *(3)* **...you.** / *(4)* **...your beauty.** Я (*[1,2]* соверше́нно / *[1,2]* по́лностью) ослеплён *(3)* ...тобо́й. / *(4)* ...твое́й красото́й.

dazzling *adj* ослепи́тельный, -ая, -ое, -ые ♦ ~ **smile** ослепи́тельная улы́бка.

dead *adj (literally, not figuratively)* мёртвый, -ая, -ое, -ые ♦ **I** *(1)* **feel** / *(2)* **felt dead inside.** Я *(1)* чу́вствую / *(2)* почу́вствовал *(ж: почу́вствовала)*, как что́-то внутри́ оборва-ло́сь. ♦ **My love for** *(1)* **you** / *(2)* **her** / *(3)* **him is (** *[4]* **completely** / *[5]* **totally)** *(6,7)* **dead.** Моя́ любо́вь к *(1)* тебе́ / *(2)* ней / *(3)* нему́ (*[4]* по́лностью / *[5]* абсолю́тно) *(6)* прошла́ / *(7)* умерла́. ♦ **My feelings for** *(1)* **you** / *(2)* **her** / *(3)* **him are (** *[4]* **completely** / *[5]* **totally)** *(6,7)* **dead.** Мои́ чу́вства к *(1)* тебе́ / *(2)* ней / *(3)* нему́ (*[4]* по́лностью / *[5]* соверше́нно) *(6)* уга́сли / *(7)* у́мерли.

deadhead *n (slang)* ску́чный челове́к, зану́да.

deadpan *adj* невырази́тельный, -ая, -ое, -ые, ка́менный, -ая, -ое, -ые ♦ ~ **face** ка́менное лицо́.

deaf *adj* глухо́й, -а́я, -о́е, -и́е.

deal *n* де́ло ♦ **a great** ~ мно́го ♦ **(not) a big** ~ (не) ва́жно ♦ **It would mean a great deal to**

A slash always denotes "or."
You can choose the numbered words before and after.

me if you would go with me. Если ты пойдёшь со мной, э́то бу́дет о́чень мно́го зна́чить для меня́.

dear *adj* дорого́й, -а́я, -о́е, -и́е ♦ **~ to the heart** ми́лый (-ая, -ое, -ые) се́рдцу ♦ **You are so dear to me.** Ты так дорога́ *(ж: до́рог)* мне. ♦ **I just can't tell you enough how dear and precious and beloved you have become to me.** Я про́сто не могу́ доста́точно хорошо́ рассказа́ть тебе́, како́й дорого́й *(ж: каки́м дороги́м)*, драгоце́нной *(ж: драгоце́нным)* и люби́мой *(ж: люби́мым)* ты ста́ла *(ж: стал)* для меня́. ♦ **Nothing in the world is more dear to me than you.** Нет ничего́ в ми́ре, что бы́ло бы доро́же для меня́, чем ты.

debonair *adj* 1. *(carefree)* беззабо́тный, -ая, -ое, -ые, беспе́чный, -ая, -ое, -ые; *(light-hearted)* жизнера́достный, -ая, -ое, -ые, весёлый, -ая, -ое, -ые; 2. *(urbane)* изы́сканный, -ая, -ое, -ые, утончённый, -ая, -ое, -ые, изя́щный, -ая, -ое, -ые.

deceit *n* обма́н.

deceive *vt* обма́нывать / обману́ть *(whom = acc.)* ♦ **I would never deceive you.** Я никогда́ не обману́ тебя́. ♦ **You deceived me.** Ты обма́нывала *(ж: обма́нывал)* меня́. ♦ **You've been deceiving me (all along).** Ты обма́нывала *(ж: обма́нывал)* меня́ (всё э́то вре́мя). ♦ **How could you deceive me like this?** Как могла́ *(ж: мог)* ты так обма́нывать меня́? ♦ **You are truly a master at the art of deceiving people.** Ты, пра́вда, ма́стер в иску́сстве обма́на люде́й.

> **deceive:** *quotation*

"The tangled webs we weave when we practice to deceive." *(Anon.)* «Мы се́ти для себя́ плетём, когда́ друг дру́гу лжём.» *(Анон.)*

deceived *adj* обма́нутый, -ая, -ое, -ые *(short forms:* обма́нут, -а, -о, -ы).

deceiving *n* обма́н.

decency *n* 1. *(decorum)* прили́чие, благопристо́йность *f* ; *(modesty)* скро́мность *f*; 2. *(propriety)* поря́дочность *f* ; *(politeness)* ве́жливость *f* ♦ **You have no decency.** В тебе́ нет скро́мности. ♦ **You could have had the decency (at least) to** *(1)* **...let me know.** / *(2)***... write and tell me.** / *(3)* **...call me.** В тебе́ могла́ бы быть поря́дочность (по ме́ньшей ме́ре) *(1)* ...дать мне знать. / *(2)* ...написа́ть мне. / *(3)* ...позвони́ть мне.

decent *adj* 1. *(decorous, proper)* прили́чный, -ая, -ое, -ые, благопристо́йный, -ая, -ое, -ые; *(upstanding, honest)* поря́дочный, -ая, -ое, -ые; 2. *(good, kind)* до́брый, -ая, -ое, -ые; 3. *(good)* хоро́ший, -ая, -ее, -ие; *(not bad)* неплохо́й, -а́я, -о́е, -и́е.

decide *vt & vi* реша́ть / реши́ть *(what = acc.)* ♦ **~ quickly** бы́стро реши́ть ♦ **~ right away** сра́зу реши́ть ♦ **just (now)** ~ то́лько что реши́ть ♦ **suddenly** ~ вдруг реши́ть.

decision *n* реше́ние ♦ **correct** ~ пра́вильное реше́ние ♦ **final** ~ оконча́тельное реше́ние ♦ **hasty** ~ поспе́шное реше́ние ♦ **my** ~ моё реше́ние ♦ **quick** ~ бы́строе реше́ние ♦ **right** ~ пра́вильное реше́ние ♦ **smart** ~ у́мное реше́ние ♦ **stupid** ~ глу́пое реше́ние ♦ *(1,2)* **sudden** ~ *(1)* неожи́данное / *(2)* внеза́пное реше́ние ♦ **wise** ~ му́дрое реше́ние ♦ **your** ~ *(familiar)* твоё реше́ние; *(polite)* Ва́ше реше́ние ♦ **come to a** ~ прийти́ к реше́нию ♦ **make a** ~ принима́ть / приня́ть реше́ние.

> **decision:** *phrases*

I've come to a decision. Я пришёл *(ж: пришла́)* к реше́нию. ♦ **What is your decision?** Что ты реши́ла *(ж: реши́л)*? ♦ **Let me know what your decision is.** Сообщи́ мне о своём реше́нии.

decked out (in) *(slang) (dressed)* оде́т, -а, -ы *(short forms) (in what = + в + prep.)*.

declare *vt (love)* признава́ться / призна́ться ♦ **~ love** признава́ться / призна́ться в любви́.

decollete *adj* декольти́рованный, -ая, -ое, -ые.

decorous *adj* прили́чный, -ая, -ое, -ые, присто́йный, -ая, -ое, -ые.

Common adult weights are given in Appendix 10, page 777.

decorum *n* прили́чие, благопристо́йность *f* ♦ **The burning adoration of my lips will melt the pillars of your sophisticated decorum into rivers of molten lava.** Мои́ пла́менные, обожа́ющие гу́бы превратя́т твердыíню твое́й благопристо́йности в ре́ки распла́вленной ла́вы.

decree *n* реше́ние ♦ **divorce ~** реше́ние о разво́де, реше́ние суда́ о разво́де ♦ **I'm (still) waiting for my final (divorce) decree.** Я (всё ещё) жду моего́ оконча́тельного реше́ния о разво́де. ♦ **When will your (divorce) decree be final?** Когда́ ты полу́чишь реше́ние о разво́де? ♦ **My (divorce) decree should be final** *(1)* **...next month. /** *(2)* **...in a couple months.** Реше́ние о разво́де должно́ быть вы́дано *(1)* ...в сле́дующем ме́сяце. / *(2)* ...че́рез па́ру ме́сяцев.

dedicated *adj* пре́данный, -ая, -ое, -ые ♦ **spiritually ~** религио́зный, -ая, -ое, -ые.

deep *adj* глубо́кий, -ая, -ое, -ие ♦ **You seem to be a person who is very deep and reflective.** Ты ка́жешься глубо́ким и ду́мающим челове́ком.

deepen *vt* 1. углубля́ть / углуби́ть *(what = acc.)*; 2. *(strengthen, increase)* уси́ливать / уси́лить *(what = acc.)*, увели́чивать / увели́чить *(what = acc.)* ♦ **In the** *(1)* **days /** *(2)* **months /** *(3)* **years ahead I hope we can deepen our** *(4)* **love /** *(5)* **relationship.** В *(1-3)* бу́дущем я наде́юсь, мы смо́жем углуби́ть *(4)* ...на́шу любо́вь. / *(5)* ...на́ши отноше́ния.

deepen *vi* 1. углубля́ться / углуби́ться; 2. *(strengthen, increase)* уси́ливаться / уси́литься, увели́чиваться / увели́читься ♦ **I know that our love will deepen as** *(1,2)* **time goes by.** Я зна́ю, что на́ша любо́вь бу́дет уси́ливаться *(1)* ...с года́ми / *(2)* ...со вре́менем.

deeper глу́бже.

deeply *adv* глубоко́ ♦ **I love you deeply.** Я глубоко́ люблю́ тебя́. ♦ **I never knew I could love someone as deeply as you.** Я никогда́ не знал *(ж: зна́ла)*, что смогу́ полюби́ть кого́-то так глубоко́, как тебя́.

defect *n* недоста́ток, дефе́кт; поро́к.

defense *n* защи́та ♦ **You have broken down (all) my defenses.** Ты разру́шила *(ж: разру́шил)* (всю) мою́ защи́ту.

definition *n* определе́ние ♦ **The** *(1)* **strength /** *(2)* **force /** *(3)* **intensity /** *(4)* **magnitude of your appeal for me is beyond definition.** *(1,2)* Си́ла / *(3)* Интенси́вность / *(4)* Магнети́зм твое́й привлека́тельности для меня́ вы́ше вся́кого определе́ния. ♦ **I'm going to teach you a new definition of** *(1)* **kissing /** *(2)* **pleasure /** *(3)* **ecstasy /** *(4)* **passion.** Я научу́ тебя́ но́вому определе́нию *(1)* поцелу́я / *(2)* наслажде́ния / *(3)* экста́за / *(4)* стра́сти.

deflower *vt* лиша́ть де́вственности *(whom = acc.)*.

deflowering *n* дефлора́ция.

degenerate *adj* распу́щенный, -ая, -ое, -ые ♦ **morally ~** мора́льно распу́щенный.

degrading *adj* унизи́тельный, -ая, -ое, -ые ♦ **~ experience** унизи́тельный слу́чай.

degree *n* сте́пень ♦ **bachelor's ~** сте́пень бакала́вра ♦ **BA ~** сте́пень бакала́вра гуманита́рных нау́к ♦ **Bachelor of Arts ~** сте́пень бакала́вра гуманита́рных нау́к ♦ **BS ~** сте́пень бакала́вра (есте́ственных / то́чных) нау́к ♦ **Bachelor of Science ~** сте́пень бакала́вра (есте́ственных / то́чных) нау́к ♦ **doctor's ~** сте́пень до́ктора ♦ **graduate ~** учёная сте́пень ♦ **master's ~** сте́пень маги́стра ♦ **MA ~** сте́пень маги́стра гуманита́рных нау́к ♦ **Master of Arts ~** сте́пень маги́стра гуманита́рных нау́к ♦ **MS ~** сте́пень маги́стра (есте́ственных / то́чных) нау́к ♦ **MBA ~** сте́пень маги́стра би́знеса ♦ **Master of Business Administration ~** сте́пень маги́стра би́знеса ♦ **post-grad(uate) ~** учёная сте́пень.

degreed *adj* с вы́сшим образова́нием, око́нчивший (-ая, -ие) университе́т.

deja-vu *n* чу́вство узнава́ния ♦ **This whole situation is giving me a sense of deja-vu.** Я, ка́жется, был *(ж: была́)* уже́ в э́той ситуа́ции пре́жде. ♦ **This feels like deja-vu.** Я

An italicized ж in parentheses indicates a woman speaking.

чу́вствую, как бу́дто э́то уже́ бы́ло.

dejected *adj* уны́лый, -ая, -ое, -ые, удручённый, -ая, -ое, -ые, как в во́ду опу́щенный, -ая, -ое, -ые ◆ **Why are you so dejected?** Почему́ ты так удручена́ *(ж: удручён)?* ◆ **You look so dejected.** Ты вы́глядишь тако́й удручённой *(ж: таки́м удручённым)*.

delay *vt* заде́рживать / задержа́ть *(what, whom = acc.)* ◆ **be delayed** заде́рживаться / задержа́ться.

delay *n* заде́ржка; промедле́ние.

delectable *adj* ла́комый, -ая, -ое, -ые, восхити́тельный, -ая, -ое, -ые, преле́стный, -ая, -ое, -ые ◆ **~ thing** ла́комый кусо́чек ◆ **Whenever I even think of your beautiful, delectable body, I am (1) filled / (2) seized with raging lust.** Когда́ бы я ни поду́мал о твоём прекра́сном, со́чном те́ле, меня́ *(1)* наполня́ет / *(2)* охва́тывает бе́шеная страсть. ◆ **You are (1) absolutely / (2) so delectable.** Ты *(1)* соверше́нно / *(2)* так восхити́тельна. ◆ **I wish that I could kiss both your eyes very softly many, many, many times before moving on to other delectable parts.** Я хоте́л бы, чтобы я мог о́чень мя́гко целова́ть о́ба твои́х гла́за мно́го, мно́го, мно́го раз пре́жде, чем передви́нуться к други́м восхити́тельным частя́м.

deliberate *adj* наро́читый, -ая, -ое, -ые; наме́ренный, -ая, -ое, -ые; умы́шленный, -ая, -ое, -ые.

deliberately *adv* наро́чно; наме́ренно.

delicacy *n* 1. *(fineness)* то́нкость *f*, не́жность *f*; 2. *(tact)* делика́тность *f*, такт.

delicious *adj* 1. *(food)* (о́чень) вку́сный, -ая, -ое, -ые; 2. *(fig.)* восхити́тельный, -ая, -ое, -ые, преле́стный, -ая, -ое, -ые ◆ **You have such delicious power over my senses.** У тебя́ така́я сла́дкая власть над мои́ми чу́вствами. ◆ **I (1) yearn / (2) long so (3) mightily / (4) much to explore all the delicious secrets of your body.** Я так *(3,4)* си́льно *(1)* жа́жду / *(2)* стремлю́сь иссле́довать все восхити́тельные секре́ты твоего́ те́ла. ◆ **I am completely (1) ...under the spell of... / (2) ...bewitched / (3) entranced by... your delicious sensuality.** Я по́лностью *(1)* ...под ча́рами твое́й восхити́тельной чу́вственности. / *(2)* ...околдо́ван / *(3)* очаро́ван твое́й восхити́тельной чу́вственностью.

deliciously *adv* 1. *(very tastily)* о́чень вку́сно; 2. *(delightfully, enchantingly)* восхити́тельно, очарова́тельно, преле́стно ◆ **My loving kisses will lead you deliciously along the paths of heavenly pleasure until you reach cosmic ecstasy.** Мои́ лю́бящие поцелу́и поведу́т тебя́ по восхити́тельной тропе́ ра́йского наслажде́ния до косми́ческого экста́за.

delight *n* восто́рг, восхище́ние; наслажде́ние, удово́льствие ◆ **boundless** ~ безграни́чное восхище́ние ◆ **childish** ~ де́тский восто́рг ◆ **~s of love** восто́рги любви́ ◆ **great** ~ большо́й восто́рг ◆ **indescribable** ~ неопису́емый восто́рг ◆ **mutual ~s** взаи́мное удово́льствие ◆ **oral ~s** ора́льные наслажде́ния ◆ **physical ~s** 1. *(charms)* физи́ческие пре́лести 2. *(pleasures)* физи́ческие наслажде́ния ◆ **quivering** ~ тре́петный восто́рг ◆ **rapturous** ~ восто́рженное восхище́ние ◆ **sincere** ~ и́скренний восто́рг ◆ **total** ~ соверше́нный восто́рг ◆ **unparalleled** ~ небыва́лый восто́рг ◆ **utter** ~ соверше́нный восто́рг ◆ **(1-3) wild** ~ *(1)* ди́кий / *(2)* безу́мный / *(3)* бу́рный восто́рг.

> **delight:** *verb terms*

cause you ~ вы́звать у тебя́ восто́рг ◆ **experience** ~ испы́тывать / испыта́ть восто́рг ◆ **fill you with** ~ дари́ть / подари́ть тебе́ восто́рг, приводи́ть / привести́ тебя́ в восто́рг ◆ **ignite in** ~ загора́ться восто́ргом ◆ **shine with** ~ сия́ть от удово́льствия ◆ **tremble with** ~ трепета́ть от восто́рга.

> **delight:** *other terms*

cornucopia of ~ рог, по́лный наслажде́ния *(1 term)* ◆ **expression of** ~ выраже́ние восто́рга ◆ **feeling of** ~ чу́вство восто́рга ◆ **moans of** *(1,2)* ~ сто́ны *(1)* удово́льствия

---

*Procedures for getting married to a Russian
are outlined in Appendix 18, page 787.*

/ *(2)* наслаждéния ◆ **pinnacle of** ~ вершúна блажéнства.

delight: *I feel / felt delight*]

I was speechless with delight. От восхищéния я потеря́л *(ж: потеря́ла)* дар рéчи. ◆ **When I** *(1)* **...found your letter in my box...** / *(2)* **...saw your photo(s)...** / *(3)* **...read that you were coming... it was the pinnacle of delight for me.** Когда́ я *(1)* ...нашёл *(ж: нашла́)* твоё письмó в почтóвом я́щике,... / *(2)* ...увúдел *(ж: увúдела)* твою́ фотогра́фию,... / *(3)* ...прочита́л *(ж: прочита́ла)*, что ты прилета́ешь,... я был *(ж: была́)* на вершúне блажéнства. ◆ **This letter of yours was so unexpected. Your** *(1)* **sweet /** *(2)* **beautiful words of love have sent my heart into utter delight.** Это письмó от тебя́ бы́ло так неожи́данно. Твои́ *(1)* нéжные / *(2)* прекра́сные слова́ любви́ вызыва́ют в моём сéрдце пóлный востóрг. ◆ **My heart ignites in delight** *(1)* **...every time I get a letter from you.** / *(2)* **...every time I see your (**[3]**) beautiful /** [4]**) beloved) face.** / *(5)* **...at the mere thought of you.** Моё сéрдце загора́ется востóргом *(1)* ...ка́ждый раз, когда́ я получа́ю письмó от тебя́. / *(2)* ...ка́ждый раз, когда́ я ви́жу твоё (*[3]* прекра́сное / *[4]* люби́мое) лицó. / *(5)* ...от простóй мы́сли о тебé.

delight: *causing you delight*

I love to give affection and fill my partner with boundless pleasure and delight in a totally eager and selfless way. Я люблю́ дари́ть своему́ партнёру нéжность, безграни́чное наслаждéние и восхищéние пы́лко и бескоры́стно. ◆ **I'm going to initiate you into physical delights unlike any you've ever experienced.** Я познакóмлю тебя́ с физи́ческими наслаждéниями, не похóжими на те, что ты испы́тывала прéжде. ◆ **Every morning when you wake up, I want your face to be shining with delight.** Ка́ждое у́тро, когда́ ты просыпа́ешься, я хочу́, чтóбы твоё лицó сия́ло от удовóльствия. ◆ **Hopefully the neighbors will get used to hearing your moans of rapturous delight.** Надéюсь, сосéди привы́кнут к твои́м стóнам востóрженного удовóльствия. ◆ **The night air will be filled with your moans of rapturous delight.** Ночнóй вóздух напóлнится твои́ми стóнами востóрженного удовóльствия. ◆ **How I love to hear your moans of rapturous delight fill the (night) air.** Как я люблю́ слу́шать стóны твоегó востóрженного наслаждéния, заполня́ющие (ночнóй) вóздух.

delight: *the delights of your body*

My most cherished wish is to partake of the myriad delights promised by that beautiful body of yours. Моё са́мое завéтное жела́ние -- испыта́ть мириа́д востóргов, котóрые сули́т твоё прекра́сное тéло.

delight: *you're a delight*

You're a cornucopia of delight. Ты рог, пóлный наслаждéния.

delight: *mutual delights*

We'll spend the whole weekend partaking of mutual delights. Мы проведём весь уик-э́нд во взаи́мном удовóльствии.

delighted *adj* восхищён, восхищена́, -ó, -ы́ *(short forms)* ◆ **I was so delighted at** *(1)* **seeing /** *(2)* **meeting you yesterday that I feel compelled to write this short note to you to tell you how (very) much it meant to me.** Я был так восхищён *(ж: была́ так восхищена́) (1)* уви́дев / *(2)* встрéтив тебя́ вчера́, что я чу́вствую непреодоли́мую потрéбность написа́ть э́ту корóткую запи́ску, чтóбы сказа́ть тебé, как (óчень) мнóго э́то зна́чит для меня́.

delightful *adj* упои́тельный, -ая, -ое, -ые.

delirium *n* бред, исступлéние ◆ **joyful** ~ ра́достное исступлéние ◆ **Your letter has** *(1,2)* **plunged me into a joyful delirium.** Твоё письмó *(1)* погрузи́ло / *(2)* вве́ргло меня́ в ра́достное исступлéние.

A list of conjugated Russian verbs is given in Appendix 3 on page 699.

deluge *vt* затопля́ть / затопи́ть *(what = acc., with what = instr.)*, наводня́ть / наводни́ть *(what = acc., with what = instr.)* ♦ **When at last my mouth claims yours, I will deluge it with more kisses than it has ever known before.** Когда́ наконе́ц мой рот встре́тится с твои́м, я затоплю́ его́ бо́льшим коли́чеством поцелу́ев, чем он когда́-ли́бо пре́жде получа́л.

demand *vt* тре́бовать / потре́бовать *(what = gen. [abstract] or acc. [tangible] or* + чтобы... *[that...])* ♦ **Your lips demand to be kissed, and my lips can only comply.** Твои́ гу́бы тре́буют поцелу́ев, и мои́ то́лько подчиня́ются.

demand *n* тре́бование ♦ **excessive** ~s чрезме́рные тре́бования ♦ **persistent** ~s насто́йчивые тре́бования ♦ **unnatural** ~s ненорма́льные тре́бования.

demanding *adj* тре́бовательный, -ая, -ое, -ые ♦ **I wish you'd stop being so demanding.** Я хочу́, чтобы ты переста́ла быть тако́й тре́бовательной *(ж: ...переста́л быть таки́м тре́бовательным).* ♦ **I shouldn't be so demanding of you. I'm sorry.** Я не до́лжен быть таки́м тре́бовательным *(ж: Я не должна́ быть тако́й тре́бовательной)* к тебе́. Я извиня́юсь.

demeanor *n* поведе́ние, мане́ра держа́ться ♦ **elegant** ~ элега́нтная мане́ра поведе́ния ♦ **harsh** ~ гру́бое поведе́ние ♦ **pleasant** ~ ве́жливое поведе́ние ♦ **suave** ~ обходи́тельная мане́ра ♦ **When I first saw you, you seemed to have such a suave demeanor.** *(ж:)* Когда́ я впервы́е уви́дела тебя́, мне показа́лось, что у тебя́ така́я обходи́тельная мане́ра держа́ться.

demi-smile *n* полуулы́бка.

demon *n* де́мон, искуси́тель *m*, дья́вол ♦ **You're a regular demon.** Ты настоя́щий дья́вол. ♦ **I don't know what demons have gotten into you.** Я не зна́ю, каки́е де́моны прони́кли в тебя́.

demoralized *adj* деморализо́ванный, -ая, -ое, -ые *(short forms:* деморализо́ван, -а, -о, -ы.*)* ♦ **I feel (**[1] **completely /** [2] **so /** [3] **utterly /** [4] **very) demoralized.** Я чу́вствую себя́ *(*[1] по́лностью / [2] так / [3] кра́йне / [4] о́чень*)* деморализо́ванным *(ж: деморализо́ванной).*

demur *vi* возража́ть / возрази́ть.

demure *adj (shy)* засте́нчивый, -ая, -ое, -ые; *(modest)* скро́мный, -ая, -ое, -ые; *(restrained)* сде́ржанный, -ая, -ое, -ые.

denial *n* 1. *(rejection of truth)* отрица́ние; 2. *(refusal)* отка́з ♦ **be in** ~ не смотре́ть в лицо́ пра́вде *(about what* = + о + *prep.)*, отка́зываться смотре́ть в лицо́ пра́вде *(about what* = + о + *prep.)* ♦ **For a long time I've** (1,2) **been in denial about** (3) **...you. /** (4) **...our relationship.** До́лгое вре́мя я (1) ...не смотре́л *(ж: смотре́ла)*... / (2) ...отка́зывался *(ж: отка́зывалась)* смотре́ть... в лицо́ пра́вде (3) ...о тебе́. / (4) ...о на́ших отноше́ниях.

denim *n* 1. *(material)* гру́бая хлопчатобума́жная ткань *(для джи́нсов и т.д.)*; 2. *(jeans)* джи́нсы ♦ **You look** (1) **nice /** (2) **sexy in denim.** Ты вы́глядишь (1) ми́ло / (2) сексуа́льно в джи́нсах.

denizen *n* обита́тель ♦ **club** ~ обита́тель клу́бов.

deny *vt* отка́зывать / отказа́ть *(what = dat.)*, отрица́ть *(what = acc.)* ♦ **You're denying your own** (1) **body /** (2) **desires.** Ты отка́зываешь (1) ...своему́ со́бственному те́лу. / (2) ...свои́м со́бственным страстя́м.

depart *vi (all modes)* отправля́ться / отпра́виться; *(on foot)* уходи́ть / уйти́; *(bus, train)* отходи́ть / отойти́; *(flight)* вылета́ть / вы́лететь ♦ **What time will the** (1) **bus /** (2) **train /** (3) **flight depart?** В како́е вре́мя отпра́вится (1) авто́бус / (2) по́езд / (3) самолёт? ♦ **The** (1) **bus /** (2) **train /** (3) **flight will depart at one (thirty).** *(See page 759 for other times.)*

---

*For Russian adjectives, the masculine form is spelled out,
followed by the feminine, neuter and plural endings.*

(1) Автобус / *(2)* Поезд / *(3)* Самолёт отправится в час (тридцать).

depend (on) *vi* 1. *(rely on)* полагаться / положиться *(on what / whom* = + на + *acc.)*; 2. *(hinge on)* зависеть *(on what / whom* = + от + *gen.)* ♦ **Can I depend on you?** Могу я положиться на тебя? ♦ **You can (always) depend on me.** Ты (всегда) можешь положиться на меня. ♦ **I want you always to know that you can depend on me** *(1)* **...without reservation.** / *(2)* **...utterly.** Я хочу, чтобы ты всегда знала *(ж: знал)*, что ты можешь положиться на меня *(1)* ...без сомнений. / *(2)* ...полностью. ♦ **It depends on** *(1)* **...you.** / *(2)* **...my work schedule.** Это зависит от *(1)* ...тебя. / *(2)* ...моего рабочего графика.

dependable *adj* надёжный, -ая, -ое, -ые.

dependence *n* зависимость *f* ♦ **financial ~** материальная зависимость ♦ **It's nice to be able to have mutual dependence with someone.** Это хорошо, когда можно полагаться друг на друга. ♦ **Too much dependence is not a good thing.** Слишком большая зависимость -- это не хорошо.

dependency *n* зависимость *f.*

dependent *n* иждивенец *m*, иждивенка *f* ♦ **I have no dependents.** У меня нет иждивенцев.

depress *vt* удручать / удручить *(whom* = *acc.)*, подавлять / подавить *(whom* = *acc.)*, угнетать *(whom* = *acc.)*.

depressed *adj* подавлен, -а, -о, -ы, угнетён, угнетена, -о, -ы *(short forms)*, удручён, удручена, -о, -ы *(short forms)* ♦ **be ~** хандрить, быть подавленным *m* / подавленной *f* *(I'm depressed:* я подавлен *[ж: подавлена].* You're depressed: ты подавлена *[ж: подавлен].)*. ♦ *(1)* **become** / *(2)* **get ~** *(1,2)* приуныть *(past tense only)*.

┌──────────────────────┐
│ *depressed: phrases* │
└──────────────────────┘

I'm starting to *(1)* **get** / *(2)* **grow depressed about our relationship.** *(1,2)* Наши отношения начинают угнетать меня. ♦ **I'm (***[1]*** really /** *[2]* **very) depressed (about** *[3]* **...it.** / *[4]* **...our relationship.** / *[5]* **...the way things are going between us.).** Я (*[1]* действительно / *[2]* очень) подавлен *(ж: подавлена)* (*[3]* ...из-за этого. / *[4]* ...из-за наших отношений. /*[5]* ...тем, как всё складывается между нами.).

depression *n* депрессия, угнетённое / подавленное настроение.

deprived *adj* лишён, лишена, -о, -ы *(short forms).* ♦ **I've been deprived of love for** *(1)* **...so long.** / *(2)* **...so many years.** Я был лишён *(ж: была лишена)* любви *(1)* ...так долго. / *(2)* ...так много лет.

depth *n* глубина, глубь *f*; богатство чувств ♦ **burning ~s** горячие глубины ♦ **~ of character** глубина характера ♦ **~ of mind** глубина ума ♦ **~ of my feelings** глубина моих чувств ♦ **~ of my love** глубина моей любви ♦ **~ of soul** глубина души ♦ **~ of understanding** глубина понимания ♦ **emotional ~** эмоциональная глубина ♦ **liquid dark ~s of your eyes** мерцающая тёмная глубина твоих глаз ♦ **moist ~s** влажные глубины ♦ **secret ~s** таинственная глубина ♦ **spiritual ~** духовная глубина ♦ **velvet(y) ~s** бархатистая глубина ♦ **warm ~s** тёплая глубина.

┌──────────────────────┐
│ *depth: other terms* │
└──────────────────────┘

comprehend the ~ понимать / понять глубину, постигать / постигнуть глубину ♦ **fathom the ~** измерять / измерить глубину, постигать / постигнуть глубину ♦ **from the very ~s of the body** из самой глубины тела ♦ **know the ~** знать глубину ♦ *(1)* **man** / *(2)* **woman** / *(3)* **person of depth** глубокий *(1-3)* человек.

┌──────────────────────┐
│ *depth: of my feelings* │
└──────────────────────┘

The depth of my feelings for you is unlike anything I've known before. Глубина моих чувств к тебе непохожа на что-либо, что я знал *(ж: знала)* прежде. ♦ **If you could only know the depth of my feelings for you.** Если бы ты только могла *(ж: мог)* знать глубину моих чувств к тебе. ♦ **There are no words to describe the depth of the love that**

See Appendix 19 for notes on sending mail to Russia and Ukraine.

I bear in my heart for you. Нет слов, чтобы описáть глубину́ моéй любви́, котóрую я ношу́ в своём сéрдце для тебя́. ♦ **You've helped me to find a new depth to my feelings.** Ты помогáла *(ж: помогáл)* мне находи́ть нóвую глубину́ в мои́х чу́вствах. ♦ *(1,2)* **You can never know... /** *(3)* **You cannot begin to fathom... the depth of my love for you.** Ты никогдá не смóжешь *(1)* узнáть / *(2)* поня́ть / *(3)* измéрить ...глубину́ моéй любви́ к тебé.

depth: *spiritual depth*

I'm looking for someone who has emotional and spiritual depth. Я ищу́ человéка, обладáющего эмоционáльной и духóвной глубинóй. ♦ **To me, depth of soul is far more important than material well-being.** По мне, глубинá души́ горáздо важнéе, чем материáльное благополу́чие.

depth: *out of my depth*

I feel out of my depth with you. Я чу́вствую, что ты сли́шком хорошá *(ж: хорóш)* для меня́.

derisive *adj* насмéшливый, -ая, -ое, -ые.

derisively *adv* насмéшливо.

derriere *n (buttocks)* пóпа, пóпка ♦ **You have such a beautiful derriere.** У тебя́ такáя прекрáсная пóпа. ♦ **Such an exquisitely curved derriere you have.** Какáя у тебя́ изы́сканная кру́глая пóпка. ♦ **I love brushing my lips on your smooth, sculptured derriere.** Мне нрáвится касáться губáми твоéй глáдкой, скульпту́рной пóпки.

describe *vt* опи́сывать / описáть *(what, whom = acc.),* изображáть / изобрази́ть *(what, whom = acc.)* ♦ **I cannot describe the appeal that you have for me.** Я не могу́ описáть, как привлекáтельна ты для меня́. ♦ **The desire that I harbor in my heart for you goes beyond my power of words to describe.** Страсть к тебé, скрывáемая в моём сéрдце, превы́ше всех описáний. ♦ **It is beyond my power to describe to you the tremendous effect that your dear, sweet, loving letter has had upon me.** Я не в состоя́нии описáть тебé то огрóмное впечатлéние, котóрое твоé дорогóе, нéжное, лю́бящее письмó произвелó на меня́. ♦ **No language can describe my feelings (for you).** Никакóй язы́к не спосóбен описáть мои́ чу́вства (к тебé).

description *n* описáние ♦ **The happiness I've found in your** *(1)* **love /** *(2)* **arms is beyond description.** Счáстье, котóрое я нашёл *(ж: нашлá)* в *(1)* ...твоéй любви́,... / *(2)* ...твои́х объя́тиях,... невозмóжно описáть. ♦ **The** *(1)* **strength /** *(2)* **force /** *(3)* **intensity /** *(4)* **magnitude of your appeal for me is beyond description.** *(1,2)* Си́ла / *(3)* Интенси́вность / *(4)* Магнети́зм твоéй привлекáтельности для меня́ вы́ше вся́кого описáния.

desert *vt* покидáть / поки́нуть *(what, whom = acc.),* оставля́ть / остáвить *(what, whom = acc.)* ♦ **My husband deserted me (and my** *[1]* **son /** *[2]* **daughter /** *[3]* **children).** Мой муж поки́нул меня́ (и *[1]* ...моегó сы́на. / *[2]* ...мою́ дочь. / *[3]* ...мои́х детéй.). ♦ **I would never, never desert you.** Я никогдá, никогдá не остáвлю тебя́. ♦ **All of my reason has deserted me. I can think of nothing and no one except you.** Весь мой рассу́док остáвил меня́. Я не могу́ ду́мать ни о чём и ни о ком, крóме тебя́.

design *n* 1. *(pattern)* узóр; 2. *pl (devious plans)* у́мыслы ♦ **beautiful** ~ прекрáсный узóр ♦ *(1,2)* **fancy** ~ *(1)* затéйливый / *(2)* причу́дливый узóр ♦ **If you think I have designs on you, you're very wrong.** Если ты ду́маешь, что у меня́ есть какúе-то у́мыслы по отношéнию к тебé, ты óчень ошибáешься.

designed *adj* предназнáчен, -а, -о, -ы *(short forms)* ♦ ~ **for** *(1)* **loving /** *(2)* **kissing** предназнáчен (-а, -о, -ы) для *(1)* любви́ / *(2)* поцелу́ев.

desirability *n* желáтельность *f.*

desirable *adj* 1. *(preferred, advantageous)* желáтельный, -ая, -ое, -ые; 2. *(arousing erotic*

When terms are listed after a main word, a tilde ~ is used to indicate the main word.

longing) соблазни́тельный, -ая, -ое, -ые, жела́нный, -ая, -ое, -ые ♦ **You are *(1)* extremely / *(2)* so / *(3)* very desirable.** Ты *(1)* чрезвыча́йно / *(2)* так / *(3)* о́чень соблазни́тельна. ♦ **You are the most incredibly desirable woman I've ever *(1)* seen / *(2)* met / *(3)* known.** Ты са́мая соблазни́тельная же́нщина, кото́рую я когда́-ли́бо *(1)* ви́дел / *(2)* встре́тил / *(3)* знал. ♦ **I've never in my life met (or seen) anyone as (sexy and) desirable as you.** Я никогда́ в свое́й жи́зни не встреча́л (и не ви́дел) друго́й тако́й же (сексуа́льной и) соблазни́тельной, как ты.

desire *vi (feel desire for)* жела́ть / пожела́ть *(what, whom = gen.)*; жа́ждать *(what, whom = gen.)*; *(want)* хоте́ть *(what, whom = acc.)* ♦ ~ **ardently** жа́ждать пы́лко ♦ ~ **fervently** вожделе́нно хоте́ть ♦ ~ *(1,2)* **greatly** жела́ть *(1)* си́льно / *(2)* стра́стно ♦ ~ **intensely** жела́ть пы́лко ♦ ~ **passionately** жела́ть стра́стно ♦ ~ **tremendously** жа́ждать стра́стно ♦ ~ *(1,2)* **unbearably** жела́ть *(1)* нестерпи́мо / *(2)* невыноси́мо.

desire: *phrases*

I desire only you. Я жела́ю то́лько тебя́. ♦ **I desire so ardently to *(1)* ...take your hand in mine. / *(2)* ...hold you tenderly in my arms. / *(3)* ...feel you close to me (again).** Я так пы́лко жа́жду *(1)* ...взять тебя́ за́ руку. / *(2)* ...не́жно держа́ть тебя́ в объя́тиях. / *(3)* ...чу́вствовать тебя́ ря́дом (опя́ть). ♦ **Just to look at you is to desire you *(1)* greatly / *(2)* intensely / *(3)* unbearably.** То́лько смотре́ть на тебя́ -- зна́чит *(1)* си́льно / *(2)* пы́лко / *(3)* невыноси́мо жела́ть тебя́. ♦ **Not a minute passes that I don't desire you.** Не прохо́дит и мину́ты, что́бы я не жела́л *(ж: жела́ла)* тебя́. ♦ **I want to tell you plainly and openly: I desire you tremendously.** Я хочу́ сказа́ть тебе́ откры́то и открове́нно: я стра́стно жа́жду тебя́.

desire *n* жела́ние, страсть *f*; вожделе́ние; предме́т вожделе́ния ♦ **acute** ~ о́строе жела́ние ♦ **all-consuming** ~ всепоглоща́ющее жела́ние ♦ **ardent** ~ пы́лкая страсть ♦ **base** ~s ни́зменные жела́ния ♦ **burning** ~ горя́чее жела́ние ♦ ~ **never before experienced** неизве́данное жела́ние ♦ ~ **to please each other** жела́ние ра́довать друг дру́га ♦ **erotic** ~ эроти́ческое вожделе́ние ♦ **feminine** ~s же́нские жела́ния ♦ **fervent** ~ пы́лкая страсть ♦ **fierce** ~ неи́стовое жела́ние ♦ **fondest** ~ са́мое заве́тное жела́ние ♦ **frustrated** ~ тще́тное жела́ние ♦ *(1,2)* **great** ~ *(1)* большо́е / *(2)* си́льное жела́ние ♦ **insatiable** ~ ненасы́тная страсть ♦ **intense** ~ пы́лкое жела́ние ♦ **keen** ~ о́строе жела́ние ♦ **lascivious** ~ похотли́вое вожделе́ние ♦ **my** ~ моё жела́ние ♦ **natural** ~ есте́ственное жела́ние ♦ **no** ~ (нет) ни мале́йшего жела́ния ♦ **not the slightest** ~ (нет) ни мале́йшего жела́ния ♦ *(1-5)* **overwhelming** ~ *(1)* нестерпи́мое / *(2)* сокруши́тельное / *(3)* оглуши́тельное / *(4)* неодоли́мое / *(5)* ошеломля́ющее жела́ние ♦ **passionate** ~ стра́стное жела́ние ♦ **persistent** ~ насто́йчивое жела́ние ♦ **physical** ~ физи́ческая страсть ♦ **powerful** ~ могу́чее жела́ние ♦ **primeval** ~ первобы́тная страсть ♦ **primitive** ~ примити́вная страсть ♦ **pure** ~ настоя́щая страсть ♦ **raging** ~ бе́шеное жела́ние; бе́шеная страсть ♦ **rampant** ~ безу́держная страсть ♦ **red-hot** ~ обжига́ющая страсть ♦ **repressed** ~ сде́рживаемое жела́ние ♦ *(1,2)* **secret** ~ *(1)* сокрове́нное / *(2)* заве́тное жела́ние ♦ **seething** ~ горя́чее жела́ние ♦ **smoldering** ~ тле́ющая страсть ♦ **sultry** ~ зно́йная страсть ♦ *(1,2)* **tremendous** ~ *(1)* могу́чее / *(2)* огро́мное жела́ние ♦ **unadulterated** ~ и́стинная страсть ♦ **unbearable** ~ невыноси́мое жела́ние ♦ **uncontrollable** ~ неудержи́мое жела́ние ♦ **unflagging** ~ неослабева́ющая страсть ♦ **unquenchable** ~ неутоли́мое жела́ние ♦ **unquenched** ~ неутолённое жела́ние ♦ **urgent** ~ насто́йчивое жела́ние ♦ **your** ~ *(familiar)* твоё жела́ние; *(polite)* Ва́ше жела́ние.

desire: *verb terms*

ache with ~ до бо́ли жела́ть *(for what = gen, for whom = acc.)*. ♦ **arouse** ~ пробужда́ть / пробуди́ть страсть, вызыва́ть / вы́звать жела́ние ♦ **awaken** ~ пробужда́ть / пробу-

A list of abbreviations used in the dictionary is given on page 10.

дить страсть, вызывать / вызвать желание ♦ **burn with** *(1,2)* ~ гореть *(1)* желанием / *(2)* страстью, сгорать от страсти ♦ **enflame** ~ распалять желание ♦ **feel** ~ чувствовать желание ♦ **fight your own** ~ бороться со своей страстью ♦ **ignite the flame(s) of** ~ зажигать / зажечь пламя желания ♦ **restrain** *(1)* **my** / *(2)* **your** ~ сдерживать *(1,2)* своё желание ♦ **rouse** ~ пробуждать / пробудить страсть, вызывать / вызвать желание ♦ **satisfy** *(1)* **my** / *(2)* **your** ~s удовлетворять / удовлетворить *(1)* мои / *(2)* твои желания ♦ **suppress** *(1)* **my** / *(2)* **your** ~ подавлять / подавить *(1,2)* своё желание ♦ **surrender to** *(1)* **my** / *(2)* **your** ~ уступить *(1,2)* своему желанию.

desire: *other terms*

consumed by ~ пожираем *m* / пожираема *f* страстью *(for what, whom* = + к + *dat.),* охвачен *m* / охвачена *f* страстью *(for what, whom* = + к + *dat.).* ♦ **cynosure of my** ~s путеводная звезда моих желаний ♦ **feelings of** ~ страсть ♦ **fire(s) of** ~ огонь желания ♦ **flames of** ~ пламя желания ♦ **inferno of passionate** ~ ад страстного желания ♦ **intensity of physical** ~ накал физической страсти ♦ **my heart's** ~ желание моего сердца ♦ **overcome by** ~ охвачен *m* / охвачена *f* страстью *(for what, whom* = + к + *dat.).* ♦ **overwhelmed by** ~ охвачен *m* / охвачена *f* страстью *(for what, whom* = + к + *dat.).* ♦ **spark of** ~ искра желания ♦ **swept away by** ~ охвачен *m* / охвачена *f* страстью *(for what, whom* = + к + *dat.).* ♦ **tremendous surge of** ~ огромная волна желания ♦ **web of** ~ паутина желания.

desire: *you - my heart's desire*

You are my heart's desire. Ты желание моего сердца. ♦ **You are the cynosure of all my desires.** Ты путеводная звезда всех моих желаний.

desire: *I burn with desire*

I burn with desire. Я сгораю от страсти. ♦ **My desire for you sets me afire.** Страсть к тебе сжигает меня. ♦ **A flare of desire bursts inside of me any time I even think of you.** Огонь желания вспыхивает во мне, как только я подумаю о тебе. ♦ **Whenever I think of you, red-hot desire scorches my** *(1,2)* **innermost being.** Когда бы я не подумал о тебе, обжигающая страсть опаляет всё *(1)* ...во мне. / *(2)* ...моё сокровенное. ♦ *(1)* **Touching your hand...** / *(2)* **Hearing your voice...** / *(3)* **Smelling your perfume...** / *(4)* **Seeing your beautiful face...** / *(5)* **Seeing your beautiful figure... just adds fuel to the fire of my desire for you.** Когда я *(1)* ...касаюсь твоей руки, ... / *(2)* ...слышу твой голос,... / *(3)* ...вдыхаю твои духи,... / *(4)* ...вижу твоё прекрасное лицо,... / *(5)* ...вижу твою прекрасную фигуру,... огонь моей страсти к тебе разжигается ещё сильнее. ♦ **Visions of your voluptuous loveliness send fire licking through my arteries, igniting my entire being into an inferno of passionate desire.** Вид твоей чувственной красоты вызывает огонь, бушующий в моих артериях, посылающий всё моё существо в ад страстного желания. ♦ **Desire flames through me everytime** I *(1)* **...think about you.** / *(2)* **...look at you.** Страсть вспыхивает во мне каждый раз, когда я *(1)* ...думаю о тебе. / *(2)* ...смотрю на тебя. ♦ **Molten waves of desire surge through** *(1)* **...my entire body...** / *(2)* **...every fiber and cell of my body... whenever I think of your exquisite, luscious beauty.** Бушующие волны страсти проносятся через *(1)* ...всё моё тело... / *(2)* ...все фибры и клетки моего тела,... когда бы я ни подумал о твоей изысканной, сочной красоте.

desire: *I ache*

(1,2) **I ache with desire for you.** *(1)* Я болен от страсти к тебе. / *(2)* Я до боли желаю тебя. ♦ **In the middle of the night I wake up, aching with desire for you.** Среди ночи я просыпаюсь, до боли желая тебя.

> *The accents on Russian words are to show how to pronounce them. You don't have to copy the accents when writing to someone.*

desire: *I'm consumed*

I am (totally) *(1,2)* **consumed** *(3)* **by / *(4)* with desire for you.** Я (совершённо) *(1)* поглощён / *(2)* охва́чен *(3,4)* стра́стью к тебе́. ♦ **Desire consumes me (everytime I think of you).** Страсть охва́тывает меня́ (ка́ждый раз, когда́ я ду́маю о тебе́). ♦ **I lie in bed at night, consumed with desire,** *(1)* **fantasizing / *(2)* thinking about you.** Я лежу́ в посте́ли но́чью, охва́ченный стра́стью, *(1)* фантази́руя / *(2)* ду́мая о тебе́. ♦ **The fierce desire I feel for you** *(1)* **...is something I have never experienced before. / *(2)* ...is utterly consuming me. / *(3)* ...dominates all my thoughts and attention. / *(4)* ... overwhelms me.** Неи́стовое жела́ние тебя́ *(1)* ...э́то не́что тако́е, чего́ я никогда́ пре́жде не испы́тывал / *(2)* ...по́лностью поглоща́ет меня́. / *(3)* ...госпо́дствует над все́ми мои́ми мы́слями и внима́нием. / *(4)* ...переполня́ет меня́.

desire: *I'm flooded*

Every time I see you walk *(1)* **...through the door... / *(2)* ...down the hallway... / *(3)* ...along the street... / *(4)* ...past me... / *(5)* ...into the room... my heart begins palpitating wildly and I am flooded with** *(6)* **exquisite / *(7)* overpowering / *(8)* dizzying sensations of adoration and desire for you..** Ка́ждый раз, когда́ я ви́жу, как ты *(1)* ...вхо́дишь в дверь... / *(2)* ...идёшь по коридо́ру... / *(3)* ...идёшь по у́лице... / *(4)* ...прохо́дишь ми́мо... / *(5)* ...вхо́дишь в ко́мнату... моё се́рдце начина́ет выска́кивать из груди́, и меня́ переполня́ют *(6)* о́стрые / *(7)* невыноси́мые / *(8)* головокружи́тельные чу́вства обожа́ния и жела́ния.

desire: *I'm filled*

Whenever I look at you, I'm filled with pure, unadulterated desire. Вся́кий раз, когда́ бы я ни взгляну́л на тебя́, меня́ наполня́ет настоя́щая, и́стинная страсть. ♦ **When I look at your full, sensuous lips so promising of soft, sweet ecstasy, I am filled with an** *(1)* **enormous / *(2)* overpowering desire to kiss them with wild abandon to the very end of time.** Когда́ я смотрю́ на твои́ по́лные чу́вственные гу́бы, обеща́ющие не́жный, сла́достный экста́з, меня́ наполня́ет *(1)* огро́мное / *(2)* невыноси́мое жела́ние цело-ва́ть их бесконе́чно, соверше́нно забы́в обо всём. ♦ **Desire travels to every sensitive nerve ending in my body.** Страсть путеше́ствует в ка́ждом не́рве моего́ те́ла.

desire: *I'm overcome / overwhelmed*

I am *(1)* **overcome / *(2)* overwhelmed by desire for you.** Страсть к тебе́ *(1,2)* овладе́ла мной. ♦ **If I touch even your hand, I am** *(1)* **overcome / *(2)* overwhelmed by desire for you.** Е́сли я про́сто каса́юсь твое́й руки́, меня́ *(1,2)* охва́тывает жела́ние. ♦ **Whenever I'm near you, feelings of desire overcome me.** Всегда́, когда́ я ря́дом с тобо́й, страсть охва́тывает меня́. ♦ **I must tell you that I feel an overwhelming desire to kiss you. It possesses me night and day. I cannot shake it off.** Я до́лжен сказа́ть тебе́, что я ощуща́ю ошеломля́ющее жела́ние поцелова́ть тебя́. Оно́ владе́ет мной ночь и день. Я не могу́ ...стряхну́ть его́. / ...отде́латься от него́.

desire: *I'm swept away*

I am *(1)* **completely / *(2)* utterly / *(3)* totally swept away by my desire for you.** Я *(1,2)* по́лностью / *(3)* соверше́нно охва́чен *(ж: охва́чена)* стра́стью к тебе́.

desire: *out of control*

My desire for you is going absolutely out of control. (I can't think of anything else, but you.) Моя́ страсть к тебе́ не поддаётся никако́му контро́лю. (Я не могу́ ду́мать ни о чём, кро́ме тебя́.)

desire: *you awaken*

You awaken so much desire in me. Ты пробужда́ешь таку́ю стра́сть во мне. ♦ **Only you know how to ignite the flame of passionate desire in my heart.** То́лько ты зна́ешь,

---

If no accent is shown on a word with a capitalized vowel,
it means that the capitalized vowel is accented.

как зажéчь плáмя стрáстного желáния в моём сéрдце. ♦ **Your** *(1)* **incredible /** *(2)* **voluptuous beauty has me crazed with desire.** Твоя́ *(1)* невероя́тная / *(2)* роскóшная красотá свóдит меня́ с умá от стрáсти. ♦ **When we lie side by side and our legs entwine, it never fails to rouse desire in me.** Когдá мы лежи́м ря́дом и нáши нóги сплетены́, э́то всегдá пробуждáет страсть во мне. ♦ **Just the thought of your name turns on desire in my body like a light switch.** Прóсто мысль о твоём и́мени включáет страсть в моём тéле, как выключáтель свéт. ♦ **Everytime I think about you I feel such a *(* tremendous /** *(2)* **powerful surge of desire.** Всегдá, когдá я дýмаю о тебé, я чýвствую такýю *(1)* огрóмную / *(2)* мóщную волнý желáния.

desire: *torrid dream*

Every night my dreams roil in the most torrid scenes of *(1)* **passionate /** *(2)* **erotic desire for your sweet, warm, wonderful womanness.** Кáждую ночь в мои́х снах роя́тся сáмые знóйные сцéны *(1)*... стрáсти... / *(2)* ...эроти́ческого вожделéния... к твоéй слáдкой, тёплой, великолéпной жéнственности.

desire: *growing and growing*

The desire in my heart to see you grows ever more inflamed. Желáние уви́деть тебя́ всё бóлее воспламеня́ет моё сéрдце. ♦ **My desire for you grows stronger and stronger with each passing day.** Моя́ страсть к тебé станóвится сильнéе и сильнéе с кáждым проходя́щим днём. ♦ **Whenever** *(1)* **...I look at you,... /** *(2)* **...I think about you,... /** *(3)* **...you look at me,... my desire (for you) heightens (unbearably).** Когдá *(1)* ...бы я ни взгляну́л на тебя́,... / *(2)* ...я дýмаю о тебé... / *(3)* ...бы ты ни взгляну́ла на меня́,... моя́ жáжда (тебя́) возрастáет (невыноси́мо).

desire: *indescribable*

The desire that I harbor in my heart for you goes beyond my power of words to describe. Страсть к тебé, скрывáемая в моём сéрдце, превы́ше всех описáний.

desire: *never diminishing*

My desire for you *(1)* **...never wanes. /** *(2)* **...is unflagging.** Моя́ страсть к тебé *(1)* ...никогдá не умéньшится. / *(2)* ...неослабевáющая. ♦ **My desire for you is insatiable.** Моя́ страсть к тебé ненасы́тна. ♦ **It is impossible for me to curb my desire when I'm** *(1)* **with /** *(2)* **around you.** Невозмóжно для меня́ обýздывать моё желáние, когдá я *(1)* ...с тобóй. / *(2)* ...вблизи́ тебя́. ♦ **I'm wrapped in a cloak of desire for you twenty-four hours a day.** Я закýтан в плащ стрáсти к тебé двáдцать четы́ре часá в сýтки. ♦ **Nothing can dispel the seething desire in my heart to see you.** Ничтó не мóжет охлади́ть горя́чее желáние моегó сéрдца уви́деть тебя́.

desire: *I surrender*

My heart offers me no alternative but to surrender to my (raging) desire for you. Моё сéрдце не предлагáет мне другóй альтернати́вы, крóме как уступи́ть (бéшеной) стрáсти к тебé.

desire: *don't fight it*

Just let yourself go and surrender to your *(1,2)* **desire.** Прóсто позвóль себé быть самóй собóй и уступи́ *(1)* ...своéй стрáсти. / *(2)* ...своемý желáнию. ♦ **You're fighting your own desire. Why don't you just surrender to it (for once)?** Ты бóрешься со своéй стрáстью. Почемý бы тебé прóсто не уступи́ть ей (однáжды)? ♦ **You're denying your own desires.** Ты откáзываешь свои́м сóбственным стрáстям.

desire: *I'll arouse*

My lips will rouse flames of desire to leap from your soul and surge through your veins. Мои́ гýбы пробýдят плáмя желáния, котóрое бýдет бушевáть в тебé и струи́ться в вéнах. ♦ **I'll make raging desire travel to every nerve ending of your body.** Я застáвлю

Russian has 6 grammatical cases. For an explanation of them,
see the grammar appendix on page 686.

бе́шеную страсть путеше́ствовать в ка́ждом не́рвном оконча́нии твоего́ те́ла. ◆ **I want to kiss you and kiss you and kiss you until all your senses are aflame with desire.** Я хочу́ целова́ть тебя́, целова́ть и целова́ть до тех пор, пока́ все твои́ чу́вства не погру́зятся в ого́нь стра́сти. ◆ **I want to see your body arch in rampant desire.** Я хочу́ ви́деть твоё те́ло изгиба́ющимся в безу́держной стра́сти.

desire: *I'll fulfill your desires*

  Darling, if I ever get in the same bed with you, I'm going to make myself a slave to your desires and your pleasure and your satisfaction. Дорога́я, е́сли я окажу́сь в одно́й посте́ли с тобо́й, я сде́лаю себя́ рабо́м твои́х страсте́й, твоего́ наслажде́ния и твоего́ удовлетворе́ния. ◆ **I want to do everything I (possibly) can to fulfill your needs and desires.** Я хочу́ де́лать всё, что в мои́х си́лах для исполне́ния твои́х нужд и жела́ний. ◆ **Your needs and desires** *(1)* **...are...** / *(2)* **...will always be... my** *(3)* **central** / *(4)* **main priority.** Твои́ ну́жды и жела́ния *(1)* ...- мои́ *(3,4)* гла́вные приорите́ты. / *(2)* ...всегда́ бу́дут мои́ми *(3,4)* гла́вными приорите́тами. ◆ *(1)* **I'll be...** / *(2)* **I pledge myself to be... a slave to all your needs and desires.** *(1)* Я бу́ду... / *(2)* Я обязу́юсь быть... рабо́м всех твои́х нужд и жела́ний. ◆ **I would be so attentive, so focused on your needs and desires and likes and dislikes.** Я был бы так внима́телен, так сосредото́чен на твои́х ну́ждах и жела́ниях, и на том, что ты лю́бишь и что не лю́бишь.

desire: *dampened*

The thought of such a thing *(1)* **blankets** / *(2)* **smothers the fires of my desire.** Мысль об э́том *(1)* га́сит / *(2)* подавля́ет ого́нь моего́ жела́ния. ◆ **My desire ebbed out of me.** Моя́ страсть ослабе́ла во мне.

desire: *mutual*

  It's wonderful that we both have the desire to please each other. Замеча́тельно, что у нас обо́их есть жела́ние ра́довать друг дру́га. ◆ **We can indulge our desires.** Мы мо́жем преда́ться на́шим стра́стям.

desire: *keep the fires burning*

(1) **I know...** / *(2)* **You really know... how to keep the fires of desire burning.** *(1)* Я зна́ю,... / *(2)* Ты действи́тельно зна́ешь,... как подде́рживать ого́нь жела́ния.

desire: *don't confuse*

You must not confuse love with desire. Нельзя́ пу́тать любо́вь с жела́нием.

desired *adj* жела́нный, -ая, -ое, -ые ◆ **ardently** ~ вожделе́нный, -ая, -ое, -ые.

desire-swollen *adj* набу́хший (-ая, -ее, -ие) от жела́ния.

desolate *adj* поки́нутый, -ая, -ое, -ые, одино́кий, -ая, -ое, -ие; несча́стный, -ая, -ое, -ые ◆ **I've never felt so desolate.** Я никогда́ не чу́вствовал *(ж: чу́вствовала)* себя́ таки́м несча́стным *(ж: тако́й несча́стной).* ◆ **I feel so desolate** *(1)* **...since we parted.** / *(2)* **...since you left.** / *(3)* **...when I'm not with you.** Я чу́вствую себя́ таки́м несча́стным *(ж: тако́й несча́стной)* *(1)* ...с тех пор, как мы разошли́сь. / *(2)* ...с тех пор, как ты ушла́ *(ж: ушёл).* / *(3)* ..., когда́ я не с тобо́й.

despair *n* отча́яние ◆ *(1,2)* **complete** ~ *(1)* соверше́нное / *(2)* по́лное отча́яние ◆ **deep** ~ глубо́кое отча́яние ◆ **ineffible** ~ невырази́мое отча́яние ◆ **infinite** ~ бесконе́чное отча́яние ◆ **real** ~ настоя́щее отча́яние ◆ *(1,2)* **terrible** ~ *(1)* стра́шное / *(2)* ужа́сное отча́яние ◆ *(1,2)* **utter** ~ *(1)* соверше́нное / *(2)* по́лное отча́яние ◆ **drive me to** ~ доводи́ть / довести́ меня́ до отча́яния ◆ **fall into** ~ впасть в отча́яние ◆ **feeling of** ~ чу́вство отча́яния ◆ **I'm full of despair.** Я по́лон *(ж: полна́)* отча́яния. ◆ **I can't shake off this feeling of despair.** Я не могу́ стряхну́ть э́то чу́вство отча́яния. ◆ **I feel such terrible despair (since you left).** Я чу́вствую тако́е ужа́сное отча́яние (с тех пор, как ты ушла́ *[ж: ушёл]*). ◆ **Since we broke up, I've been feeling such abject despair.** С тех

There are no articles ("a" or "the") in Russian.

пор, как мы порва́ли, я чу́вствую кра́йнее отча́яние.

desperate *adj* отча́янный, -ая, -ое, -ые, безрассу́дный, -ая, -ое, -ые; безнадёжный, -ая, -ое, -ые, безвы́ходный, -ая, -ое, -ые ♦ **I'm desperate to** *(1)* **...see you.** / *(2)* **...hold you in my arms.** / *(3)* **...be with you.** Я отча́янно хочу́ *(1)* ...ви́деть тебя́. / *(2)* ...обня́ть тебя́. / *(3)* ...быть с тобо́й. ♦ **I need love -- physical and emotional -- and I feel almost desparate for both, almost like I'm suffocating for lack of air.** Мне нужна́ любо́вь физи́ческая и душе́вная, и я до отча́яния жа́жду их. Это почти́ похо́же на то, как бу́дто я задыха́юсь от недоста́тка во́здуха.

desperately *adv* отча́янно ♦ **I** *(1)* **long** / *(2)* **hunger (so) desperately for you.** Я (так) отча́янно *(1,2)* жа́жду тебя́.

desperation *n* отча́яние, безрассу́дство, безу́мие; кра́йность *f.*

despicable *adj* презре́нный, -ая, -ое, -ые, досто́ин *m* / досто́йна *f* презре́ния ♦ **You are utterly despicable.** Ты досто́йна *(ж: досто́ин)* по́лного презре́ния. ♦ **That was a despicable thing to** *(1)* **say** / *(2)* **do.** То, что ты сказа́ла *(ж сказа́л)* / сде́лала *(ж сде́лал)*, досто́йно презре́ния.

despise *vt* презира́ть *(what, whom = acc.)* ♦ **I despise** *(1)* **him** / *(2)* **her** / *(3)* **you.** Я презира́ю *(1)* его́ / *(2)* её / *(3)* тебя́.

destination *n* назначе́ние, цель *f*, ме́сто ♦ **romantic** ~ романти́ческое ме́сто.

destined *adj* назна́чен, -а, -о, -ы *(short forms)*, предназна́чен, -а, -о, -ы *(short forms)*, определён, определена́, -о́, -ы́ *(short forms)* ♦ **The union of our two spirits was destined to be.** Сою́з двух на́ших душ был предопределён.

destiny *n* судьба́ ♦ **It was Destiny that** *(1)* **...brought us together.** / *(2)* **...we should meet (like this).** Это была́ судьба́, *(1)* ...кото́рая свела́ нас вме́сте. / *(2)* ...что мы должны́ бы́ли встре́титься. ♦ **I can only believe that it was our destiny to meet.** Я могу́ то́лько ве́рить, что э́то была́ на́ша судьба́ встре́титься. ♦ **We are each other's destiny.** На́ша судьба́ -- быть друг с дру́гом. ♦ **Destiny hangs on small details.** Судьба́ ча́сто зави́сит от мелоче́й.

destroy *vt* 1. уничтожа́ть / уничто́жить *(what = acc.)*, разруша́ть / разру́шить *(what = acc.)*; 2. лома́ть / слома́ть *(what = acc.)* ♦ **You have completely destroyed all my will (to resist).** Ты по́лностью слома́ла *(ж: слома́л)* всю мою́ во́лю (сопротивля́ться). ♦ **You have destroyed my love for you.** Ты уби́ла *(ж: убил)* мою́ любо́вь к тебе́.

detail *n* подро́бность *f*, дета́ль *f* ♦ **Leave the details to me.** Оста́вь подро́бности для меня́.

detained *adj* заде́ржан, -а, -о, -ы *(short forms)* ♦ **I was unexpectedly detained.** Я был *(ж: была́)* неожи́данно заде́ржан *(ж: заде́ржана)*.

deter *vt* 1. *(hold back)* уде́рживать / удержа́ть *(what = acc.)*; 2. *(talk out of)* отгова́ривать / отговори́ть *(whom = acc.)*.

deterred *adj* 1. *(held back)* уде́ржан, -а, -о, -ы *(short forms)*; 2. *(talked out of)* отговорён, отговорена́, -о́, -ы́ *(short forms)* ♦ *(1,2)* **I will not be deterred.** Меня́ бу́дет не отговори́ть.

detestable *adj* отврати́тельный, -ая, -ое, -ые.

devastated *adj* потрясён, потрясена́, -о́, -ы́ *(short forms)* ♦ **I** *(1)* **am** / *(2)* **was (**[3] **totally** / [4] **utterly) devastated.** *(1)* Я... / *(2)* Я был *(ж: была́)* (**[3]** по́лностью / **[4]** соверше́нно) потрясён *(ж: потрясена́)*.

devastating *adj* опустоши́тельный, -ая, -ое, -ые, разруши́тельный, -ая, -ое, -ые, сокруши́тельный, -ая, -ое, -ые ♦ *(1)* **This being...** / *(2)* **My loneliness... without you is (totally) devastating.** *(1)* Это существова́ние... / *(2)* Моё одино́чество... без тебя́ (абсолю́тно) опустоша́ет.

deviant *n* челове́к с отклоне́ниями от норм поведе́ния ♦ **social** ~ челове́к с откло-

---

This dictionary contains two Russian alphabet pages:
one in Appendix 1, page 685, and a tear-off page on page 799.

нениями от норм обще́ственного поведе́ния.

devil *n* дья́вол, чёрт, бес ♦ **handsome** ~ краси́вый дья́вол ♦ **silver-tongued** ~ сладко-речи́вый дья́вол ♦ **You little devil!** Ты ма́ленький дья́вол! ♦ **What a devil you are!** Что за дья́вол ты!

devilish *adj* дья́вольский, -ая, -ое, -ие, чертовский, -ая, -ое, -ие.

devilishly *adv* чертовски, ужа́сно, стра́шно.

devil-may-care *adj* беззабо́тный, -ая, -ое, -ые, беспе́чный, -ая, -ое, -ые; наплева́тельский, -ая, -ое, -ие ♦ ~ **attitude** наплева́тельское отноше́ние.

devious *adj* 1. *(roundabout)* непрямо́й, -а́я, -о́е, -ы́е, око́льный, -ая, -ое, -ые; 2. *(sneaky)* хи́трый, -ая, -ое, -ые, неи́скренний, -яя, -ее, -ие.

devoid *adj* лишённый, -ая, -ое, -ые *(short forms:* лишён, лишена́, -о́, -ы́*) (of what = gen.)* ♦ **My life is so devoid of love.** Моя́ жизнь так лишена́ любви́. ♦ **I'm completely devoid of any (1,2) ambition to do anything except hold you in my arms and make love to you.** Я соверше́нно лишён каки́х-ли́бо други́х *(1)* стремле́ний / *(2)* амби́ций, кро́ме того́, чтобы держа́ть тебя́ в объя́тиях и занима́ться любо́вью с тобо́й.

devote *vt* посвяща́ть / посвяти́ть *(what = acc., to what = dat.)*; отдава́ть / отда́ть *(what = acc., to what = dat.)*; уделя́ть / удели́ть *(what = acc., to what = dat.)* ♦ ~ **all my energies** отдава́ть все свои́ си́лы ♦ ~ **my life** посвяща́ть / посвяти́ть свою́ жизнь ♦ **(1,2)** ~ **my time** *(1)* посвяща́ть / *(2)* уделя́ть своё вре́мя ♦ ~ **oneself** предава́ться / преда́ться *(to what = dat.)*.

devoted *adj* пре́данный, -ая, -ое, -ые *(short forms:* пре́дан, -а, -о, -ы*)* ♦ **I'm devoted to you.** Я пре́дан *(ж: пре́дана)* тебе́.

devotion *n* пре́данность *f*, си́льная привя́занность ♦ **constant** ~ постоя́нная пре́данность ♦ **dog-like** ~ соба́чья пре́данность ♦ **eternal** ~ ве́чная пре́данность ♦ **my** ~ моя́ пре́данность *(to what, whom = dat.)* ♦ **passionate** ~ стра́стная привя́занность ♦ **selfless** ~ беззаве́тная пре́данность ♦ **undying** ~ неумира́ющая пре́данность ♦ **unflagging** ~ неослабева́ющая пре́данность ♦ **your** ~ твоя́ пре́данность *(to what, whom = dat.)*.

devotion: phrases

Your devotion was just a facade. Твоя́ пре́данность была́ лишь ви́димостью. ♦ **On the altar of God I will make a lifetime (1,2) pledge of love and devotion to you.** Пе́ред Бо́жьим алтарём я дам тебе́ *(1)* обе́т / *(2)* обеща́ние любви́ и пре́данности на всю жизнь. ♦ **I will prove my devotion to you.** Я докажу́ мою́ пре́данность тебе́. ♦ **Always in your letters there is present the feeling of love and devotion.** В твои́х пи́сьмах всегда́ прису́тствуют чу́вства любви́ и пре́данности. ♦ **Your love and devotion are the nectar and ambrosia for my soul.** Твои́ любо́вь и пре́данность -- некта́р и амбро́зия для мое́й души́. ♦ **My devotion for you is unflagging.** Моя́ пре́данность тебе́ не ослабева́ет.

devour *vt* 1. *(consume)* пожира́ть / пожра́ть *(what = acc.)*, есть / съесть жа́дно *(what = acc.)*; 2. *(absorb avidly)* поглоща́ть / поглоти́ть *(what = acc.)* ♦ **I'm going to devour your face (1)** ...**with kisses.** / **(2)** ...**with my lips.** Я покро́ю твоё лицо́ *(1,2)* поцелу́ями. ♦ **I'm going to absolutely devour you.** Я по́лностью поглощу́ тебя́. ♦ **I want to devour your sweet (1) mouth / (2) lips.** Я хочу́ съесть *(1)* ...твой сла́дкий рот. / *(2)* ...твои́ сла́дкие гу́бы. ♦ **My mouth is going to devour yours.** Мой рот поглоти́т твой.

dewy-eyed *(1,2)* *adj* с *(1)* вла́жными / *(2)* увлажнёнными глаза́ми.

diabolical *adj* дья́вольский, -ая, -ое, -ие.

dialog *n* диало́г ♦ **romantic** ~ романти́ческий диало́г.

diamond *n* алма́з, бриллиа́нт ♦ **I guess I'm what you'd call a diamond in the rough.** Полага́ю, я то, что ты могла́ бы назва́ть необрабо́танным бриллиа́нтом.

diaphanous *adj* прозра́чный, -ая, -ое, -ые.

Depending on the subject, the possessive pronoun **свой** *(***своя́, своё, свои́***) can be translated* **my, your, his, her, its, our** *or* **their**.

die *vi* 1. *(humans)* умира́ть / умере́ть; 2. *(plants)* ги́бнуть / поги́бнуть, засыха́ть / засо́х-нуть, вя́нуть / увя́нуть; 3. *(slang) (want s.th. very much)* умира́ть от жела́ния ♦ **I've been dying to meet you for a long time.** Я до́лгое вре́мя умира́л *(ж: умира́ла)* от жела́ния встре́титься с Ва́ми. ♦ **I'm dying to (1,2) go there with you.** Я умира́ю от жела́ния *(1)* пойти́ *(on foot)* / *(2)* пое́хать *(by veh.)* туда́ с тобо́й. ♦ **To me, you will never fade nor age nor die.** Для меня́ ты никогда́ не увя́нешь, не соста́ришься, не умрёшь. ♦ **You are the (1) rose / (2) flower that never dies.** Ты *(1)* ...ро́за, кото́рая... / *(2)* ...цвето́к, кото́-рый... никогда́ не умрёт.

die down *vi (feelings)* умира́ть / умере́ть *(о чу́вствах)* ♦ **My feelings for (1) her / (2) him have (completely) died down.** Мои́ чу́вства к *(1)* ней / *(2)* нему́ (по́лностью) у́мерли.

die for *vi*: ♦ **He's to die for!** *(Slang)* Он фантасти́чески краси́в!

difference *n* 1. ра́зница; разли́чие; 2. *(argument)* разногла́сие ♦ **age** ~ ра́зница в во́зрасте, ра́зница во́зрастов ♦ **big** ~ больша́я ра́зница ♦ **~ in character** ра́зница хара́ктеров ♦ **~ in tastes** ра́зница во вку́сах, ра́зница вку́сов ♦ **~ of opinion** ра́зница взгля́дов, ра́зница во взгля́дах ♦ **insignificant** ~ незначи́тельная ра́зница ♦ **main** ~ основна́я ра́зница ♦ **only** ~ еди́нственная ра́зница ♦ **our age** ~ ра́зница на́ших лет ♦ **significant** ~ значи́тельная ра́зница ♦ **small** ~ небольша́я ра́зница ♦ **time** ~ ра́зница во вре́мени ♦ **tremendous** ~ огро́мная ра́зница ♦ **resolve** ~s устрани́ть разногла́сия.

---
difference: phrases

I hope our age difference won't (1) ...bother you. / (2) ...scare you off. / (3) ...discourage you. Я наде́юсь, ра́зница на́ших лет не *(1)* ...бу́дет волнова́ть тебя́. / *(2)* ... испуга́ет тебя́. / *(3)* ... обескура́жит тебя́. ♦ **Let's always try to discuss our differences openly.** Дава́й всегда́ обсужда́ть на́ши разногла́сия откры́то.

different *adj* 1. *(not the same)* разли́чный, -ая, -ое, -ые, ра́зный, -ая, -ое, -ые; 2. *(other)* друго́й, -а́я, -о́е, -и́е, ино́й, -а́я, -о́е, -ы́е; 3. *(various)* ра́зный, -ая, -ое, -ые ♦ **Things will be different, I promise.** Всё изме́нится, я обеща́ю.

differently *adv* по-друго́му.

diffident *adj* неуве́ренный (-ая, -ое, -ые) в себе́, ро́бкий, -ая, -ое, -ие, засте́нчивый, -ая, -ое, -ые.

dig *vt (slang) (like)* люби́ть *(what, whom = acc.)*, нра́виться *(thing or person liked is subject, person who likes = dat.)* ♦ **I dig traveling, the sun, laughter.** Я люблю́ путеше́ствия, со́лнце, смех.

dilemma *n* диле́мма ♦ **moral** ~ мора́льная диле́мма ♦ **solve a** ~ реши́ть диле́мму.

dim *vt* затемня́ть / затемни́ть *(what = acc.)* ♦ **You have a (1) beauty / (2) loveliness that (3) age / (4) time can never dim.** Ты так *(1,2)* краси́ва, что с *(3,4)* года́ми твоя́ красота́ не мо́жет потускне́ть.

dim *vi* тускне́ть / потускне́ть ♦ **You are the light that never dims.** Ты свет, кото́рый никогда́ не потускне́ет.

dimension *n* разме́р ♦ **I never realized that you had this profound spiritual dimension.** Я никогда́ не осознава́л *(ж: осознава́ла)*, что ты так духо́вно бога́та *(ж: бога́т)*.

diminish *vt* уменьша́ть / уме́ньшить *(what = acc.)*, ослабля́ть / осла́бить *(what = acc.)* ♦ **You have a (1) beauty / (2) loveliness that (3) age / (4) time can never diminish.** Ты так *(1,2)* краси́ва, что с *(3,4)* года́ми твоя́ красота́ не мо́жет уме́ньшиться.

diminutive *adj* ма́ленький, -ая, -ое, -ие ♦ **Your beautiful, diminutive (1) form / (2) body really excites me.** *(1)* Твоя́ прекра́сная, ма́ленькая фигу́ра... / *(2)* Твоё прекра́сное, ма́ленькое те́ло... так возбужда́ет меня́.

dimple *n* я́мочка *(на лице́)* ♦ **attractive** ~ симпати́чная я́м(оч)ка ♦ **charming** ~ очарова́тельная я́м(оч)ка ♦ **cute** ~ очарова́тельная я́м(оч)ка ♦ **enticing** ~ соблаз-

---

There are two words for "you" in Russian:
familiar «ты» and polite / plural «вы» (See page 781).

ни́тельная я́мочка ♦ **lovely ~** преле́стная я́м(оч)ка ♦ **You have a cute dimple on your chin.** У тебя́ преми́ленькая я́мочка на подборо́дке. ♦ **You have the cutest dimples (when you smile).** У тебя́ привлека́тельнейшая я́мочка (, когда́ ты улыба́ешься). ♦ **I love the dimple on your chin.** Я люблю́ я́мочку на твоём подборо́дке.

dine *vi* обе́дать / пообе́дать ♦ **I like to dine out.** Я люблю́ обе́дать в рестора́не. ♦ *(1,2)* **Shall we dine out tonight?** *(1)* Бу́дем ли мы... / *(2)* Пойдём ли... обе́дать в рестора́н сего́дня ве́чером?

dine *vt* угоща́ть / угости́ть обе́дом, корми́ть / накорми́ть ♦ **I'm going to wine and dine you to your heart's content.** Я напою́ тебя́ вино́м и угощу́ обе́дом до отва́ла.

dining *n* обе́д ♦ **fine ~** прекра́сный обе́д ♦ *(1,2)* **I enjoy dining out.** *(1)* Я наслажда́юсь обе́дом... / *(2)* Я люблю́ обе́дать... в рестора́не.

dinner *n* обе́д; у́жин ♦ **candlelight ~** у́жин при свеча́х ♦ **~ by candlelight** у́жин при све́те свече́й ♦ *(1)* **I'd like to invite you to...** / *(2)* **Would you like to go (with me) to...** / *(3)* **Let's have...** / *(4)* **Let's go to... dinner (together)** *(5)* **...tomorrow (evening).** / *(6)* **...this afternoon** / *(7)* **evening.** / *(8)* **...on Friday** / *(9)* **Saturday** / *(10)* **Sunday** *(11)* **afternoon** / *(12)* **evening.** / **?** *(1)* Я хоте́л бы пригласи́ть тебя́ на обе́д... / *(2)* Не хо́чешь ли ты пойти́ (со мной) на обе́д... / *(3,4)* Дава́й, пообе́даем (вме́сте)... *(5)* ...за́втра (ве́чером). / *(6)* ...сего́дня днём / *(7)* ве́чером. / *(8)* ...в пя́тницу / *(9)* суббо́ту / *(10)* воскресе́нье *(11)* днём / *(12)* ве́чером. / **?** ♦ **I enjoy candlelight dinners.** Я наслажда́юсь у́жинами при свеча́х.

diplomatic *adj* дипломати́ческий, -ая, -ое, -ие.

direct *adj* прямо́й, -а́я, -о́е, -ы́е.

directionless *adj* бесце́льный, -ая, -ое, -ые.

directly *adj* пря́мо.

directness *n* прямота́, открове́нность *f* ♦ **I was taken aback by the directness of your question.** Я был поражён *(ж: была́ поражена́)* прямото́й твоего́ вопро́са.

dirty *adj* 1. *(unclean)* гря́зный, -ая, -ое, -ые; 2. *(foul, obscene)* скве́рный, -ая, -ое, -ые, гря́зный, -ая, -ое, -ые, непристо́йный, -ая, -ое, -ые; 3. *(low, mean)* по́длый, -ая, -ое, -ые ♦ **~ language** скве́рный язы́к ♦ **~ mind** извращённый ум ♦ **~ mouth** гря́зный рот ♦ **~ story** са́льность *f*, непристо́йность *f* ♦ **~ words** непристо́йные слова́ ♦ **That was a (pretty) dirty thing to do.** Бы́ло (весьма́) по́дло сде́лать э́то.

dirty *adv (obscenely)* скве́рно, непристо́йно ♦ **talk ~** говори́ть непристо́йно.

dis *vt (slang) (belittle)* унижа́ть / унизи́ть *(whom = acc.)*; *(insult)* оскорбля́ть / оскорби́ть *(whom = acc.)*; *(criticize)* критикова́ть.

disability *n* инвали́дность *f*, нетрудоспосо́бность *f*.

disabled *adj (crippled)* искале́ченный, -ая, -ое, -ые; *(incapacitated)* нетрудоспосо́бный, -ая, -ое, -ые ♦ **~ person** инвали́д ♦ **partially ~** части́чно нетрудоспосо́бный.

disagree *vi* не соглаша́ться *(with whom = + с + instr.)* ♦ **I disagree (with you).** Я (с тобо́й) не согла́сен *(ж: согла́сна).*

disagreement *n* разногла́сие.

disappoint *vt* разочаро́вывать / разочарова́ть *(whom = acc.)* ♦ *(1)* **You don't know...** / *(2)* **You can't imagine... how much you have disappointed me.** *(1)* Ты не зна́ешь... / *(2)* Ты не мо́жешь предста́вить себе́..., как си́льно ты разочарова́ла *(ж: разочарова́л)* меня́. ♦ **God forbid that I should ever disappoint you.** Бо́же, не дай мне никогда́ разоча-ро́вывать тебя́. ♦ **I** *(1)* **realize** / *(2)* **know that I have disappointed you (and I beg you to forgive me).** Я *(1)* осознаю́ / *(2)* зна́ю, что я разочарова́л *(ж: разочарова́ла)* тебя́ (и я умоля́ю тебя́ прости́ть меня́). ♦ **Can you ever forgive me for disappointing you the way I have?** Мо́жешь ли ты когда́-нибудь прости́ть меня́ за то, что я так разоча-рова́л *(ж: разочарова́ла)* тебя́ ? ♦ **I never want to disappoint you (in any way).** Я не

Russian terms of endearment are given in Appendix 13, page 780.

хочу́ никогда́ разочарова́ть тебя́ (ни ко́им о́бразом). ♦ **I hope that I never do (or say) anything that will disappoint you.** Я наде́юсь, что я никогда́ не сде́лаю (и не скажу́) ничего́ тако́го, что разочару́ет тебя́. ♦ **You disappoint(ed) me** *(1)* **terribly /** *(2)* **enormously.** Ты разочарова́ла *(ж: разочарова́л)* меня́ *(1)* ужа́сно / *(2)* чрезвыча́йно. ♦ **How could you disappoint me like this?** Как могла́ *(ж: мог)* ты разочарова́ть меня́ так? ♦ **I feel like a swine for disappointing you the way I have.** Я чу́вствую себя́ свинье́й, что я так тебя́ разочарова́л.

disappointed *adj* разочаро́ванный, -ая, -ое, -ые *(short forms:* разочаро́ван, -а, -о, -ы*).*

> **disappointed:** *I am*

I'm (*[1]* **terribly /** *[2]* **really /** *[3]* **very) disappointed (in you).** Я (*[1]* ужа́сно / *[2]* действи́тельно / *[3]* о́чень) разочаро́ван *(ж: разочаро́вана)* в тебе́. ♦ **I can't (begin to) tell you how disappointed I am.** Я не могу́ приступи́ть к разгово́ру о том, как я разочаро́ван *(ж: разочаро́вана).*

> **disappointed:** *I was*

I was (*[1]* **massively /** *[2]* **enormously /** *[3]* **terribly /** *[4]* **really /** *[5]* **very) disappointed** *(6)* **... when you didn't show up. /** *(7)* **...when you didn't come. /** *(8)* **...when you didn't call me (as you** *[9]* **promised /** *[10]* **said you would). /** *(11)* **...when you told me that. /** *(12)* **...when I didn't find any mail from you (in my box). /** *(13)* **...that we couldn't (go somewhere and) make love. /** *(14)* **...that we couldn't be together alone. /** *(15)* **...by the way you treated me.** *(16)* **...when I found out (that you were** *[17]* **...married. /** *[18]* **...engaged /** *[19]* **...attached to someone else.).** Я был *(ж: была́)* (*[1,2]* си́льно / *[3]* ужа́сно / *[4]* действи́тельно / *[5]* о́чень) разочаро́ван *(ж разочаро́вана), (6)* ...когда́ ты не появи́лась *(ж: появи́лся).* / *(7)* ...когда́ ты не пришла́ *(ж: пришёл).* / *(8)* ...когда́ ты не позвони́ла *(ж: позвони́л)* мне (, как ты *[9,10]* обеща́ла *[ж: обеща́л]).* / *(11)* ...когда́ ты сказа́ла *(ж: сказа́л)* мне э́то. / *(12)* ...когда́ я не нашёл *(ж: нашла́)* ни одного́ письма́ от тебя́ (в моём почто́вом я́щике). / *(13)* ...что мы не могли́ (пойти́ куда́-нибудь и) заня́ться любо́вью. / *(14)* ...что мы не могли́ оста́ться одни́. / *(15)* ...тем, как ты обраща́лась *(ж: обраща́лся)* со мной. / *(16)* ...когда́ я узна́л *(ж: узна́ла)* (, что ты *[17]* ...за́мужем *[ж: жена́т.].* / *[18]* ...помо́лвлена *[ж: помо́лвлен.].* / *[19]* ...привя́зана к друго́му *[ж: привя́зан к друго́й].).* ♦ **I've never been so disappointed in my life.** Я никогда́ в жи́зни не́ был *(ж: не была́)* так разочаро́ван *(ж: разочаро́вана).* ♦ **I was always so disappointed in love (before I met you).** Я был так разочаро́ван *(ж: была́ так разочаро́вана)* в любви́ (до тех пор, пока́ я ни встре́тил *[ж: встре́тила]* тебя́).

> **disappointed:** *I would / will be*

I would be enormously disappointed if I didn't *(1)* **...meet you. /** *(2)* **...hear from you.** Я бу́ду стра́шно разочаро́ван *(ж: разочаро́вана),* е́сли я не *(1)* ...встре́чу тебя́. / *(2)* ...услы́шу ничего́ от тебя́. ♦ **I'll be (very) disappointed.** Я бу́ду (о́чень) разочаро́ван *(ж: разочаро́вана).*

> **disappointed:** *don't be*

I don't want you ever to be disappointed in me. Я не хочу́, что́бы ты когда́ -ли́бо разочарова́лась *(ж: разочарова́лся)* во мне. ♦ **I hope you won't be disappointed (** *[1]* **...when you see /** *[2]* **meet me in person. /** *[3]* **...with my looks /** *[4]* **appearance.).** Я наде́юсь, ты не бу́дешь разочаро́вана *(ж: разочаро́ван)* (*[1]* ...когда́ ты уви́дишь / *[2]* встре́тишь меня́ ли́чно. / *[3]* ...тем, как я вы́гляжу. / *[4]* ...мои́м вне́шним ви́дом.).

disappointing *adj* разочаро́вывающий, -ая, -ее, -ие.

disappointment *n* разочарова́ние ♦ *(1,2)* **big** ~ *(1)* большо́е / *(2)* жесто́кое разочарова́ние ♦ **biggest** ~ наибо́льшее разочарова́ние ♦ **bitter** ~ го́рькое разочарова́ние ♦ **crushing** ~ сокруши́тельное разочарова́ние ♦ ~ **in love** разочарова́ние в любви́ ♦ *(1,2)* **great** ~

Some of the Russian sentences are translations of things we say and are not what Russians themselves would normally say.

(1) большо́е / *(2)* жесто́кое разочарова́ние ♦ **huge** ~ огро́мное разочарова́ние ♦ **terrible** ~ ужа́сное разочарова́ние ♦ **tremendous** ~ грома́дное разочарова́ние.

disappointment: *it is*

It's a *(1)* **big** / *(2)* **huge** / *(3)* **tremendous disappointment (for me)** *(4)* **...not to be able to see you.** / *(5)* **...that you can't** *(6,7)* **...come.** / *(8)* **...be there.** / *(9,10)* **...not to be able to come** / *(11,12)* **go.** Это *(1)* большо́е / *(2)* огро́мное / *(3)* грома́дное разочарова́ние (для меня́) *(4)* ...не име́ть возмо́жности ви́деть тебя́. / *(5)* ...что ты не мо́жешь *(6)* ...прийти́ *(on foot).* / *(7)* прие́хать *(by veh.).* / *(8)* ...быть там. / *(9)* ...не име́ть возмо́жности прийти́ *(on foot)* / *(10)* прие́хать *(by veh.).* / *(11)* пойти́ *(on foot)* / *(12)* пое́хать *(by veh.).* ♦ **This is the biggest disappointment I've ever had in my life.** Это наибо́льшее разочарова́ние, бы́вшее когда́-либо в мое́й жи́зни.

disappointment: *it was*

It was a *(1)* **big** / *(2)* **huge** / *(3)* **tremendous disappointment (for me)** *(4)* **...not to be able to see you.** / *(5)* **...that you couldn't** *(6,7)* **...come.** / *(8)* **...be there.** / *(9)* **...to see you (there) with someone else.** / *(10,11)* **...not to be able to come** / *(12,13)* **go.** / *(14)* **...when you didn't call** / *(15)* **write.** Это бы́ло *(1)* больши́м / *(2)* огро́мным / *(3)* грома́дным разочарова́нием (для меня́) *(4)* ...не име́ть возмо́жности ви́деть тебя́. / *(5)* ...что ты не смогла́ *(ж: смог)* *(6)* ...прийти́ *(on foot).* / *(7)* прие́хать *(by veh.).* / *(8)* ...быть там. / *(9)* ...уви́деть тебя́ (там) с други́м *(ж: друго́й).* / *(10)* ...не име́ть возмо́жности прийти́ *(on foot)* / *(11)* прие́хать *(by veh.).* / *(12)* пойти́ *(on foot)* / *(13)* пое́хать *(by veh.).* / *(14)* ...когда́ ты не позвони́ла *(ж: позвони́л)* / *(15)* написа́ла *(ж: написа́л).*

disappointment: *of the year*

My heartfelt thanks to you for awarding me the Disappointment of the Year. Моё и́скреннее спаси́бо тебе́ за награжде́ние меня́ разочарова́нием го́да.

disappointment: *our relationship*

Our relationship together has been one disappointment after another. На́ши отноше́ния бы́ли одни́м разочарова́нием за други́м.

disapprove *vi* не одобря́ть / не одо́брить *(of what = acc.)* ♦ **My** *(1)* **mother** / *(2)* **father disapproves...** / *(3)* **My parents disapprove...** **of** *(4)* **...us being together.** / *(5)* **...me seeing you.** *(1)* Моя́ мать не одобря́ет... / *(2)* Мой оте́ц не одобря́ет... / *(3)* Мои́ роди́тели не одобря́ют... *(4)* на́ши взаимоотноше́ния. / *(5)* ..., что мы с тобо́й встреча́емся.

disarm *vt* обезору́живать *(whom = acc.)* ♦ **You (really) disarm me with your wide-eyed innocence.** Ты (действи́тельно) обезору́живаешь меня́ свое́й наи́вной неви́нностью.

disaster *n* бе́дствие, несча́стье, катастро́фа ♦ **The** *(1)* **relationship** / *(2)* **marriage was a disaster (from the start).** *(1)* Отноше́ния бы́ли... / *(2)* Брак был... катастро́фой (с са́мого нача́ла).

disarming *adj* обезору́живающий, -ая, -ее, -ие ♦ ~ **smile** обезору́живающая улы́бка.

disbelief *n* неве́рие; недове́рие ♦ **stare in** ~ смотре́ть в недоуме́нии.

disco(theque) *n* дискоте́ка.

discomfiture *n* замеша́тельство, расте́рянность *f.*

disconcerting *adj* смуща́ющий, -ая, -ее, -ие.

discord *n* разла́д.

discourage *vt* обескура́живать / обескура́жить *(whom = acc.).*

discouraged *adj* обескура́женный, -ая, -ое, -ые *(short forms:* обескура́жен, -а, -о, -ы*).*

discover *vt* открыва́ть / откры́ть *(what, whom = acc.)* ♦ **We can discover each other all over again.** Мы мо́жем откры́ть друг дру́га опя́ть. ♦ **We can spend many blissful hours discovering each other.** Мы мо́жем провести́ мно́го счастли́вых часо́в, открыва́я друг дру́га.

Counting things in Russian is a bit involved.
See Appendix 4, Numbers, on page 756 .

discreet *adj* осторо́жный, -ая -ое, -ые *(short forms:* осторо́жен, осторо́жна, -о, -ы*)*, осмотри́тельный, -ая -ое, -ые ♦ **Please be (as) discreet (as possible).** Пожа́луйста, будь (как мо́жно бо́лее) осторо́жна *(ж: осторо́жен).* ♦ **(I promise you) I'll be (very) discreet.** (Я обеща́ю,) я бу́ду (о́чень) осторо́жен *(ж: осторо́жна).* ♦ **You can count on me to be discreet.** Ты мо́жешь положи́ться на меня́, я бу́ду осторо́жен *(ж: осторо́жна).* ♦ **We have to be discreet (at all times).** Мы должны́ быть осторо́жны (всё вре́мя). ♦ **You have to be a little more discreet.** Ты должна́ *(ж: до́лжен)* быть немно́го бо́льше осторо́жной *(ж: осторо́жным).*

discretion *n* осмотри́тельность *f,* осторо́жность *f,* такти́чность *f* ♦ **I need your total discretion (in this).** Мне нужна́ твоя́ по́лная осмотри́тельность (в э́том). ♦ **Discretion assured.** *(personals ad)* Осторо́жность гаранти́руется. ♦ **Discretion (1) necessary / (2) essential.** *(personals ad)* Осторо́жность *(1,2)* необходи́ма. ♦ **I appreciate your discretion (very much).** Я (о́чень) ценю́ твою́ такти́чность.

discuss *vt* обсужда́ть / обсуди́ть *(what = acc.),* дискути́ровать *(what = acc.)* ♦ **There's something I want to discuss with you.** Есть не́что, что я хочу́ обсуди́ть с тобо́й. ♦ **Let's always try to discuss our (1) differences / (2) problems openly.** Дава́й всегда́ обсужда́ть на́ши *(1)* разногла́сия / *(2)* пробле́мы откры́то. ♦ **(1) Can / (2) Could we discuss it in private?** *(1)* Мо́жем... / *(2)* Не могли́ бы... мы обсуди́ть э́то наедине́? ♦ **I'd like to discuss (1) it / (2) something with you in private.** Я хоте́л *(ж: хоте́ла)* бы обсуди́ть *(1)* э́то / *(2)* что́-то с тобо́й наедине́.

discussion *n* обсужде́ние, дискуссия ♦ **frank** ~ открове́нное обсужде́ние ♦ **heart-to-heart** ~ дискуссия от се́рдца к се́рдцу ♦ **honest** ~ че́стное обсужде́ние ♦ **intimate** ~ инти́мное обсужде́ние ♦ **stimulating** ~ стимули́рующее обсужде́ние.

disdain *n* презре́ние; пренебреже́ние ♦ **aloof** ~ кра́йняя надме́нность ♦ **I sense in you an underlying current of disdain.** Я ощуща́ю в тебе́ скры́тое пренебреже́ние.

disdainful *adj* презри́тельный, -ая, -ое, -ые; пренебрежи́тельный, -ая, -ое, -ые.

disdainfully *adv* презри́тельно, пренебрежи́тельно.

disenchanted *adj* разочаро́ванный, -ая, -ое, -ые.

disenchantment *n* разочарова́ние.

disengage (oneself) *vi* освобожда́ться / освободи́ться *(from what, whom = + от + gen.)* ♦ *(1)* **I want to ... / (2) I'm trying to... disengage myself from (3) her / (4) him.** *(1)* Я хочу́... / *(2)* Я пыта́юсь... освободи́ться от *(3)* неё / *(4)* него́.

disgrace *vt* позо́рить / опозо́рить *(whom = acc.)*

disgrace *n* позо́р; бесче́стье ♦ **It will be... a (**[1]** big / **[2]** terrible) disgrace (for my family).** Это бу́дет... (**[1]** больши́м / **[2]** ужа́сным) позо́ром (для мое́й семьи́). ♦ **I don't want to put (1) ...you... / (2) ...your family... in disgrace.** Я не хочу́ опозо́рить *(1)* ...тебя́. / *(2)* ...твою́ семью́.

disgraced *n* опозо́рен, -а, -о, -ы ♦ **I'll be disgraced in the eyes of ...my (1) parents / (2) friends. / (3) ...people.** Я бу́ду опозо́рен *(ж: опозо́рена)* в глаза́х *(1)* ...мои́х роди́телей / *(2)* друзе́й. / *(3)* ...люде́й.

disgraceful *adj* позо́рный, -ая, -ое, -ые ♦ **I said some disgraceful things. I'm sorry.** Я сказа́л *(ж: сказа́ла)* не́что оби́дное. Я сожале́ю об э́том. ♦ **That was (utterly) disgraceful.** Это бы́ло (так) позо́рно.

disgruntled *adj* недово́льный, -ая, -ое, -ые, раздражённый, -ая, -ое, -ые.

disgruntlement *n* недово́льство, раздраже́ние.

disguise *vt* 1. *(change appearance)* маскирова́ть / замаскирова́ть *(what, whom = acc.);* 2. *(hide)* скрыва́ть / скрыть *(what = acc.)* ♦ ~ *(1)* **your / (2) my feelings** скрыва́ть / скрыть *(1,2)* свои́ чу́вства.

Russian has 2 different verbs for "go",
one for "on foot" and the other for "by vehicle".

disguise *n* маскиро́вка.

disguised *adj* 1. *(changed appearance)* замаскиро́ванный, -ая, -ое, -ые; 2. *(hidden)* скры́тый, -ая, -ое, -ые.

disgust *n* отвраще́ние ♦ **arouse** ~ пробужда́ть / пробуди́ть отвраще́ние.

disgusted *adj* чу́вствующий (-ая, -ее, -ие) отвраще́ние ♦ **I'm disgusted with the way you (1) ...act / (2) behave. / (3) ...treat me.** Я чу́вствую отвраще́ние к тому́, как ты *(1)* ...де́йствуешь / *(2)* поступа́ешь. / *(3)* ...обраща́ешься со мной.

disgusting *adj* отврати́тельный, -ая, -ое, -ые *(short forms:* отврати́телен, отврати́тельна, -о, -ы*)*, проти́вный, -ая, -ое, -ые ♦ **You're (absolutely) disgusting.** Ты (абсолю́тно) отврати́тельна *(ж: отврати́телен)*. ♦ **That's disgusting!** Это отврати́тельно!

dish *n* 1. *(cooked food)* блю́до; 2. *(slang) (attractive woman)* (краси́вая) же́нщина ♦ **luscious** ~ *(slang)* сексапи́льная же́нщина ♦ **What's your favorite dish?** Како́е твоё люби́мое блю́до? ♦ **My favorite dish is .....** Моё люби́мое блю́до....

disharmony *n* дисгармо́ния.

disheartened *adj* обескура́женный, -ая, -ое, -ые ♦ **be** ~ опуска́ть ру́ки.

dishonor *n* бесче́стие.

dishonorable *adj* бесче́стный, -ая, -ое, -ые; посты́дный, -ая, -ое, -ые.

disillusion *vt* разочаро́вывать / разочарова́ть *(whom = acc.)* ♦ **You don't know how you've disillusioned me.** Ты не зна́ешь, как ты разочарова́ла *(ж: разочарова́л)* меня́.

disillusioned *adj* разочаро́ван, -а, -о, -ы) *(short forms)* ♦ *(1)* **I feel...** / *(2)* **I'm...** *(3)* **so** / *(4)* **very disillusioned** (*[5]* **...by the way you treat me.** / *[6]* **...by your attitude.** / *[7]* **...by your lack of commitment** / *[8]* **sensitivity** / *[9]* **affection** / *[10]* **attention).** *(1)* Я чу́вствую себя́... / *(2)* Я... *(3)* так / *(4)* о́чень разочаро́ван *(ж: разочаро́вана)* (*[5]* ...тем, как ты обраща́ешься со мной. / *[6]* ...твои́м отноше́нием. / *[7]* ...твое́й необяза́тельностью. / *[8]* ...отсу́тствием у тебя́ понима́ния мои́х чувств. / *[9]* ...отсу́тствием у тебя́ не́жности / *[10]* внима́ния.

disillusionment *n* разочаро́ванность *f,* круше́ние иллю́зий.

disintegrate *vi* распада́ться / распа́сться ♦ **Our relationship disintegrated.** На́ши отноше́ния распа́лись. ♦ **Our marriage disintegrated.** Наш брак распа́лся.

dislike *vt* не люби́ть *(what, whom = acc.)*, не нра́виться *(person disliking = dat., thing / person disliked = subject).*

dislikes *n, pl* неприя́знь, антипа́тии; то, что не лю́бишь *(1 term)*; предубежде́ния ♦ **likes and** ~**s** пристра́стия и предубежде́ния; симпа́тии и антипа́тии ♦ **I would be so attentive, so focused on your needs and desires and likes and dislikes.** Я был бы так внима́телен, так сосредото́чен на твои́х ну́ждах и жела́ниях, и на том, что ты лю́бишь и что не лю́бишь. ♦ **I have a few dislikes.** У меня́ есть ко́е-каки́е антипа́тии.

dismal *adj (gloomy)* мра́чный, -ая, -ое, -ые; *(sad, depressed)* печа́льный, -ая, -ое, -ые; уны́лый, -ая, -ое, -ые, пода́вленный, -ая, -ое, -ые.

dismay *n* 1. *(disenchantment)* разочарова́ние; 2. *(consternation)* смяте́ние, замеша́тельство, трево́га.

disoriented *adj* сби́тый (-ая, -ое, -ые) с то́лку ♦ **I feel (a little) disoriented.** Я чу́вствую себя́ (немно́го) сби́тым *(ж: сби́той)* с то́лку.

disparity *n* нера́венство, несоотве́тствие ♦ **I hope you don't mind the (slight) disparity in our ages.** Я наде́юсь, что тебе́ не ва́жно (незначи́тельное) несоотве́тствие в на́шем во́зрасте. ♦ **The disparity in our ages doesn't bother me.** Несоотве́тствие в на́шем во́зрасте не волну́ет меня́.

dispassion *n* бесстра́стие.

dispel *vt* разгоня́ть / разогна́ть *(what = acc.)*, рассе́ивать / рассе́ять *(what = acc.);*

Dipthongs in Russian are made by adding й
*to the end of a vowel (*а, е, ё, о, у, э, ю, *and* я*).*

раста́пливать / растопи́ть *(what = acc.)* ♦ **~ fear and mistrust** раста́пливать / растопи́ть страх и недове́рие ♦ **Nothing can dispel the seething desire in my heart to see you.** Ничто́ не мо́жет охлади́ть горя́чее жела́ние моего́ се́рдца уви́деть тебя́. ♦ **You've dispelled all my loneliness.** Ты рассе́яла *(ж: рассе́ял)* всё моё одино́чество. ♦ **I'm going to dispel your loneliness once and for all.** Я рассе́ю твоё одино́чество раз и навсегда́.

display *vt* пока́зывать / показа́ть *(what = acc.)*, проявля́ть / прояви́ть *(what = acc.)* ♦ **~ love** пока́зывать / показа́ть любо́вь.

display *n* 1. *(show)* пока́з, демонстра́ция; 2. *(showing)* проявле́ние, демонстра́ция; 3. *(exhibit)* вы́ставка ♦ **~ of feeling** проявле́ние чувств ♦ **I go away from any encounter with you with my heart spinning wildly and my mind erupting in a fireworks display of love thoughts about you.** По́сле ка́ждой встре́чи с тобо́й я ухожу́ с бе́шено стуча́щим се́рдцем и с це́лым фейерве́рком любо́вных мы́слей о тебе́.

displease *vt* не нра́виться *(person displeased = dat., thing displeasing = subject)* ♦ **be displeased** не нра́виться, быть недово́льным *(short forms:* недово́лен, недово́льна, -о, -ы) *(I'm displeased:* я не дово́лен *[ж: дово́льна]. You're displeased:* ты не дово́льна *[ж: дово́лен].) (with what = instr.)* ♦ **I'm displeased with you.** Я недово́лен *(ж: недово́льна)* тобо́й. ♦ **If it displeases you, please tell me.** Е́сли э́то не нра́вится тебе́, скажи́ мне, пожа́луйста. ♦ **It displeased me very much.** Э́то мне о́чень не понра́вилось.

displeasure *n* неудово́льствие; недово́льство.

disposition *n* 1. *(temperament)* нрав; *(character)* хара́ктер; 2. *(mood)* настрое́ние ♦ **amiable** ~ общи́тельный хара́ктер ♦ **cheerful** ~ весёлый нрав ♦ **fickle** ~ непостоя́нный хара́ктер ♦ **friendly** ~ дружелю́бный хара́ктер ♦ **happy-go-lucky** ~ беспе́чный нрав, весёлость *f* ♦ **nasty** *(1,2)* ~ дурно́й *(1)* нрав / *(2)* хара́ктер ♦ **nice** ~ хоро́ший хара́ктер ♦ **obstinate** ~ стропти́вый нрав ♦ **pleasant** ~ прия́тный хара́ктер ♦ **sociable** ~ общи́тельный хара́ктер ♦ **sweet** ~ ми́лый нрав.

disposition: phrases

I hope this will *(1,2)* **soothe your disposition.** Я наде́юсь, что э́то *(1)* ...улу́чшит твоё настрое́ние. / *(2)* ...уте́шит тебя́. ♦ **I (really) admire your happy-go-lucky disposition.** Я (про́сто) восхища́юсь твои́м беспе́чным нра́вом. ♦ **Your happy-go-lucky disposition is like a refreshing breeze.** Твоя́ весёлость, как освежа́ющий бриз. ♦ **Do you know why I'm so attracted to you? It's your sweet disposition.** Ты зна́ешь, почему́ я так увлечён *(ж: увлечена́)* тобо́й? За твой ми́лый нрав.

disquieting *adj* беспоко́ящий, -ая, -ее, -ие, трево́жный, -ая, -ое, -ые.

disrobe *vi* раздева́ться / разде́ться.

disrupt *vt* разруша́ть / разру́шить *(what = acc.)*, разрыва́ть / разорва́ть *(what = acc.)* ♦ **It has completely disrupted my plans.** Э́то по́лностью разру́шило мои́ пла́ны. ♦ **I hope nothing disrupts our plans.** Я наде́юсь, ничто́ не разру́шит на́ши пла́ны.

dissatisfaction *n* неудовлетворённость *f.*

dissension *n* разла́д.

dissipate *vi* рассе́иваться / рассе́яться ♦ **It seems like the love we once had together has dissipated.** Ка́жется, что любо́вь, кото́рая у нас была́, рассе́ялась. ♦ **Our love has dissipated.** На́ша любо́вь рассе́ялась. ♦ **Our happiness has dissipated.** На́ше сча́стье рассе́ялось. ♦ **All my hopes have dissipated.** Все мои́ наде́жды рассе́ялись.

dissolve *vi* исчеза́ть / исче́знуть; та́ять / раста́ять; распада́ться / распа́сться ♦ **I completely dissolve whenever I think of** *(1)* ...**being with you.** / *(2)* ...**holding you in my arms.** / *(3)* ...**making love with you.** Я про́сто та́ю при мы́сли о том, что *(1)* ...ты ря́дом со мной. / *(2)* ...я держу́ тебя́ в объя́тиях. / *(3)* ...я занима́юсь любо́вью с тобо́й. ♦ **The**

Some phrases are listed under more than one main word.

moment I heard your voice, all my anger dissolved. В тот момéнт, когдá я услы́шал *(ж: услы́шала)* твой гóлос, весь мой гнев исчéз.

distance *vt* держáть на расстоя́нии *(oneself = not translated, from whom = acc.)* ♦ You've distanced yourself from me lately. Ты дéржишь меня́ на расстоя́нии послéднее врéмя.

distance *n* дистáнция, расстоя́ние ♦ safe ~ безопáсное расстоя́ние ♦ I promise to keep my distance. Обещáю держáть дистáнцию. ♦ I want to put as much distance as possible between *(1)* her / *(2)* him and me. Я хочу́ держáть *(1)* её / *(2)* егó на как мóжно бóльшем расстоя́нии. ♦ Distance *(1)* holds / *(2)* keeps us apart, but our love binds us together. Расстоя́ние *(1,2)* разделя́ет нас, но нáша любóвь соединя́ет нас. ♦ Time and distance will never keep us apart. Врéмя и расстоя́ние никогдá не разлучáт нас.

distant *adj* 1. *(far)* отдалённый, -ая, -ое, -ые, дáльний, -яя, -ее, -ие; 2. *(reserved)* сдéр-жанный, -ая, -ое, -ые ♦ You seem to have grown so distant (from me) lately. Ты, кáжется, так отдали́лась *(ж: отдали́лся)* (от меня́) за послéднее врéмя. ♦ You seem so distant. Ты кáжешься такóй отдали́вшейся *(ж: таки́м отдали́вшимся)*. ♦ I don't understand why you've become / grown so distant (from me). Я не понимáю, почему́ ты так отдали́лась *(ж: отдали́лся)* (от меня́). ♦ He is a distant relative. Он дáльний рóдственник. ♦ She is a distant relative. Онá дáльняя рóдственница.

distaste *n* неприя́знь *f*, отвращéние.

distasteful *adj (unpleasant)* неприя́тный, -ая, -ое, -ые; *(repugnant)* проти́вный, -ая, -ое, -ые ♦ I find it very distasteful. Я ду́маю, э́то óчень неприя́тно. ♦ Such an *(1)* idea / *(2)* prospect is very distasteful to me. Такáя *(1)* идéя / *(2)* перспекти́ва óчень неприя́тна для меня́. ♦ Such an *(1)* suggestion / *(2)* proposal is very distasteful to me. Такóе *(1,2)* предложéние óчень неприя́тно для меня́.

distinguished *adj* аристократи́чный, -ая, -ое, -ые, аристократи́ческий, -ая, -ое, -ие; импозáнтный, -ая, -ое, -ые ♦ You look (very) distinguished in / with a beard. С бородóй ты вы́глядишь (óчень) аристократи́чно.

distinguished-looking *adj* аристократи́чески вы́глядящий, -ая, -ее, -ие.

distract *vt* отвлекáть / отвлéчь *(what, whom = acc.)* ♦ The thought of your beautiful *(1)* face / *(2)* body continually distracts me. Мысль о твоём прекрáсном *(1)* лицé / *(2)* тéле постоя́нно отвлекáет меня́.

distracting *adj* приводя́щий (-ая, -ее, -ие) в смятéние; отвлекáющий, -ая, -ее, -ие ♦ be ~ приводи́ть в смятéние ♦ Your beauty is very distracting. Твоя́ красотá приводит в си́льное смятéние.

distress *n* 1. *(grief, suffering)* гóре, бедá; 2. *(need)* нуждá; *(danger)* бéдствие.

disturb *vt* мешáть / помешáть *(whom = dat.)* ♦ I don't want to disturb you. Я не хочу́ мешáть тебé.

ditto тóже.

ditty *n* пéсенка.

dive *vi* 1.*(into water)* ныря́ть / нырну́ть; 2. *(immerse oneself)* погружáться / погрузи́ться.

dive *n (slang) (club)* клуб ♦ funky ~ необы́чный клуб.

diverse *adj* разносторóнний, -яя, -ее, -ие ♦ I'm diverse. Я разносторóнний человéк.

diversion *n* 1. *(distraction)* отвлечéние; 2. *(amusement)* развлечéние ♦ romantic ~ ромáнти́ческое развлечéние ♦ Am I just a passing diversion for you? Я тóлько проходя́щее увлечéние для тебя́?

divine *adj* божéственный, -ая, -ое, -ые ♦ To love you is divine. Люби́ть тебя́ -- блажéн-ство.

divinity *n* божествó ♦ You are my divinity. Ты моё божествó.

divorce *n* развóд ♦ agreed-upon ~ развóд по взаи́мному соглашéнию ♦ bitter ~ гóрький

The singular past tense of Russian verbs ends in -л (m) (usually), -ла (f) or -ло (n). the plural past tense ends in -li.

развóд ♦ **uncontested** ~ развóд по взаи́мному соглашéнию ♦ **ask** *(1)* **her** / *(2)* **him for a** ~ проси́ть / попроси́ть *(1)* её / *(2)* егó о развóде ♦ ~ **decree** решéние о развóде, судéбное решéние о развóде ♦ **file for a** ~ подавáть / подáть (заявлéние) на развóд ♦ **get a** ~ получи́ть развóд, разводи́ться / развести́сь *(whom = + c + instr.)* ♦ **go through a** ~ проходи́ть / пройти́ чéрез развóд ♦ **go through with the** ~ разводи́ться / развести́сь ♦ **motive for a** ~ моти́в развóда ♦ **reason for a** ~ моти́в развóда ♦ **start** ~ **proceedings** начинáть / начáть дéло о развóде ♦ **sue for** ~ трéбовать / потрéбовать развóда (в судéбном поря́дке).

divorce: going to get one

(1) **I plan...** / *(2)* **I intend...** / *(3)* **I'm going... to get a divorce (from** *[4]* **her** / *[5]* **him).** *(1)* Я плани́рую... / *(2)* Я намéрен *(ж: намéрена)...* / *(3)* Я собирáюсь... получи́ть развóд (с *[4]* ней / *[5]* ним). ♦ **I'm going to file for a divorce.** Я бýду подавáть на развóд. ♦ **I'm going to ask** *(1)* **her** / *(2)* **him for a divorce.** Я бýду проси́ть *(1)* её / *(2)* егó о развóде.

divorce: I asked / filed for one

I asked *(1)* **her** / *(2)* **him for a divorce.** Я проси́л *(ж: проси́ла) (1)* её / *(2)* егó о развóде. ♦ *(1)* **She** / *(2)* **He won't give me a divorce.** *(1)* Онá / *(2)* Он не даст мне развóд. ♦ **Have you filed for divorce yet?** Ты ужé подалá *(ж: пóдал)* на развóд? ♦ **I've already filed for divorce.** Я ужé пóдал *(ж: подалá)* на развод. ♦ **I filed for divorce in March** / *etc.* Я пóдал *(ж: подалá)* на развóд в мáрте / *и т.п.*

divorce: how long?

There's a required waiting period after the divorce. Пóсле развóда существýет трéбуемый перио́д ожидáния. ♦ **How long will the divorce take?** Скóлько врéмени займёт развóд? ♦ **The divorce will (probably) take** *(1)* **...3 months.** / *(2)* **...about 3 months.** Развóд (вероя́тно) займёт *(1)* ...три мéсяца. / *(2)* ...óколо трёх мéсяцев. ♦ **When will the divorce be** *(1,2)* **final?** Когдá *(1)* закóнчится / *(2)* заверши́тся развóд? ♦ **The divorce will be** *(1,2)* **final next month.** Развóд *(1)* закóнчится / *(2)* заверши́тся в слéдующем мéсяце.

divorce: maybe not

I don't know if I can go through a divorce. Не знáю, могý ли я пройти́ чéрез развóд. ♦ **I just** *(1)* **can't** / *(2)* **couldn't stomach a divorce.** Я прóсто *(1)* ...не смогý... / *(2)* ...не смог *(ж: смоглá)* бы... вы́нести развóда. ♦ **A divorce would be so hard on my** *(1)* **children** / *(2)* **daughter** / *(3)* **son.** Развóд мог бы так тяжелó отрази́ться на *(1)* ...мои́х дéтях. / *(2)* ...моéй дóчери. / *(3)* ...моём сы́не. ♦ **If I got a divorce, I would lose** *(1)* **...my children.** / *(2)* **...my daughter.** / *(3)* **...my son.** / *(4)* **...everything.** Éсли бы я получи́л *(ж: получи́ла)* развóд, я бы потеря́л *(ж: потеря́ла) (1)* ...мои́х детéй. / *(2)* ...мою́ дочь. / *(3)* ...моегó сы́на. / *(4)* ...всё.

divorcé *n* разведённый муж.

divorced *adj* разведён, разведенá, -ó, -ы́ *(short forms)* ♦ **Are you divorced?** Ты разведенá *(ж: разведён)*? ♦ **I'm divorced.** Я разведён *(ж: разведенá)*. ♦ **How long have you been divorced?** Скóлько врéмени ты разведенá *(ж: разведён)*? ♦ **I've been divorced for two years.** Я разведён *(ж: разведенá)* ужé два гóда. ♦ **Why did you get divorced?** Почемý ты развелáсь *(ж: развёлся)*? ♦ **I got divorced because my** *(1)* **ex-wife** / *(2)* **ex-husband** *(3)* **...and I were not compatible.** / *(4)* **...was unfaithful (to me).** / *(5)* **...was cheating on me.** / *(6)* **...was running around all the time.** / *(7)* **...drank too much.** / *(8)* **...had a(n) (serious) alcohol problem.** / *(9)* **...was a drug addict.** / *(10)* **...was using drugs (all the time).** / *(11)* **...physically abused me.** / *(12)* **...lied to me all the time.** Я развёлся *(ж: развелáсь)*, потомý что *(1)* ...моя́ бы́вшая женá / *(2)* ...мой бы́вший муж *(3)* ...и я бы́ли несовмести́мы. / *(4)* ...былá невернá *(ж: был невéрен)* мне. / *(5)* ...обмáнывала *(ж: обмáны-*

Please do us a favor:
Fill out and mail in the Feedback Sheet on page 795.

вал) меня. / *(6)* ...всё вре́мя обма́нывала *(ж: обма́нывал)* меня. / *(7)* ...сли́шком мно́го пила́ *(ж: пил)*. / *(8)* ...име́ла *(ж: име́л)* серьёзную пробле́му с алкого́лем. / *(9)* ...была́ наркома́нкой *(ж: был наркома́ном)*. / *(10)* ...(всё вре́мя) употребля́ла *(ж: употребля́л)* нарко́тики. / *(11)* ...жесто́ко обраща́лась *(ж: обраща́лся)* со мной. / *(12)* ...лгала́ *(ж: лгал)* мне всё вре́мя. ♦ **I was completely blind-sided by her *(his)* decision to get divorced.** Я был *(ж: была́)* соверше́нно огоро́шен *(ж: огоро́шена)* её *(ж: его́)* реше́нием развести́сь.

divorcée *n* разведённая жена́.

dizzy *adj (dizzying)* головокружи́тельный, -ая, -ое, -ые ♦ **I *(1)* am / *(2)* feel dizzy.** У меня́ *(1,2)* кру́жится голова́. ♦ **The scent of your hair makes me feel (downright) dizzy with *(1)* love / *(2)* desire for you.** За́пах твои́х воло́с наполня́ет меня́ (соверше́нно) головокружи́тельным чу́вством *(1)* любви́ / *(2)* стра́сти к тебе́.

dizzying *adj* головокружи́тельный, -ая, -ое, -ые.

do *vt* 1. де́лать / сде́лать *(what = acc.)*; занима́ться *(what = instr.)*; 2. *vi (work)* рабо́тать, занима́ться ♦ **~ it lying (down)** занима́ться любо́вью лёжа ♦ **~ it sitting** занима́ться любо́вью си́дя ♦ **~ it standing (up)** занима́ться любо́вью сто́я.

do: will do

Will you do it? Бу́дешь ты де́лать это? ♦ **I will (not) do it.** Я (не) бу́ду де́лать э́то. ♦ **What are you going to do?** Что ты бу́дешь де́лать?

do: did

Did you do it? Ты сде́лала *(ж: сде́лал)* э́то? ♦ **I did it.** Я сде́лал *(ж: сде́лала)* э́то. ♦ **I didn't do it.** Я не сде́лал *(ж: сде́лала)* э́то. ♦ **What did you do?** Что ты де́лала *(ж: де́лал)*? ♦ **Why did you do that?** Почему́ ты сде́лала *(ж: сде́лал)* это? ♦ **You shouldn't have done that.** Ты не должна́ была́ *(ж: до́лжен был)* э́того де́лать.

do: for you

Everything I do, I do for you. Всё, что я де́лаю, я де́лаю для тебя́. ♦ **Everything I do is done with you in mind.** Что бы я ни де́лал *(ж: де́лала)*, я де́лаю с мы́слью о тебе́. ♦ **I would do anything for you.** Я сде́лаю всё для тебя́.

do: in your free time

What are you doing *(1)* ...tonight? / *(2)* ...after work? / *(3)* ...tomorrow (*[4]* morning / *[5]* afternoon / *[6]* evening)? / *(7)* ...on Friday? *(See page 759 for other days.)* Что ты де́лаешь *(1)* ...сего́дня ве́чером? / *(2)* ...по́сле рабо́ты? / *(3)* ...за́втра (*[4]* у́тром / *[5]* в по́лдень / *[6]* ве́чером)? / *(7)* ...в пя́тницу? ♦ **I'm not doing anything.** Я ничего́ не де́лаю.

do: don't want

I don't want to do it. Я не хочу́ э́того де́лать. ♦ **Don't!** Не на́до!

do: what to do

Tell me what to do. Скажи́ мне, что де́лать.

do: make love

I love to do it (with you). Я люблю́ занима́ться любо́вью (с тобо́й). ♦ **You can do anything you want with me.** Ты мо́жешь де́лать со мной всё, что ты хо́чешь.

do: what's your job?

(1,2) What do you do (for a living)? *(1)* Чем Вы занима́етесь? / *(2)* Кем Вы рабо́таете?

do: what I like to do

I like to do versus watch. Я люблю́ де́лать, а не смотре́ть. ♦ **I enjoy doing almost everything (in life).** Я наслажда́юсь почти́ всем (в жи́зни).

do: without you

I don't know what I would do without you. Я не зна́ю, что бы я де́лал *(ж: де́лала)* без тебя́.

Clock and calender time are discussed in Appendix 5, page 759.

---

do: what you do to me

You don't know what you do to me. Зна́ешь ли ты, что ты де́лаешь со мной?

do: we can do it

Deep down in my heart I know that we can do it. В глубине́ своего́ се́рдца я зна́ю, что мы мо́жем сде́лать э́то.

do: we need to

(1-3) **We need to do something about this.** *(1)* Мы должны́ что́-то с э́тим сде́лать. / *(2)* Мы должны́ ка́к-то реши́ть э́ту пробле́му. / *(3)* Мы должны́ что́-то предприня́ть.

do: quotation

"I want to do with you what spring does with the cherry trees." *Pablo Neruda* «Я хочу́ сде́лать с тобо́й то же, что весна́ де́лает с вишнёвыми дере́вьями.» *Пабло Неруда*

doctorate *n* до́кторская сте́пень.

document *n* докуме́нт ♦ **marriage ~s** бра́чные докуме́нты ♦ *(1,2)* **necessary ~s** *(1)* необ-ходи́мые / *(2)* ну́жные докуме́нты.

dog *n* соба́ка ♦ **cheating ~** неве́рная соба́ка ♦ *(1)* **I'm** / *(2)* **You're** / *(3)* **He's a lucky dog.** *(1)* Мне / *(2)* тебе́ / *(3)* ему́ везёт.

dog-loving *adj*: ♦ **be ~** люби́ть соба́к.

doll *n* ку́кла, ку́колка ♦ **You are an absolute doll.** Ты про́сто ку́колка.

dominance *n* госпо́дство ♦ **erotic ~** эроти́ческое госпо́дство.

dominant *adj* госпо́дствующий, -ая, -ее, -ие, вла́стный, -ая, -ое, -ые.

dominate *vt* госпо́дствовать *(what, whom =* + над + *instr., or* + в + *prep.)*, преоблада́ть *(what, whom =* + над + *instr.)* ♦ **You are the kind of woman that dominates a man's fantasies.** Ты тип же́нщины, кото́рый госпо́дствует в мужски́х фанта́зиях. ♦ **The fierce** *(1)* **passion** / *(2)* **desire I feel for you dominates all my thoughts and attention.** *(1)* Неи́стовая страсть к тебе́... / *(2)* Неи́стовое жела́ние тебя́... госпо́дствует над все́ми мои́ми мы́слями и внима́нием.

dominating *adj* госпо́дствующий, -ая, -ее, -ие, вла́ствующий, -ая, -ее, -ие ♦ **ruthlessly ~** беспоща́дно вла́ствующий.

domineering *adj* госпо́дствующий, -ая, -ее, -ие, вла́стный, -ая, -ое, -ые ♦ **~ character** вла́стный хара́ктер ♦ **~ personality** вла́стный хара́ктер ♦ **You're too domineering.** Ты сли́шком вла́стная *(ж: вла́стный)*. ♦ **I don't like a** *(1)* **woman** / *(2)* **man** / *(3)* **person who is domineering.** Я не люблю́ вла́стных *(1)* же́нщин *pl* / *(2)* мужчи́н *pl* / *(3)* люде́й *pl*.

doo-doo *n (slang) (trouble)* неприя́тности *pl* ♦ *(1)* **I'm...** / *(2)* **You're...** / *(3)* **We're... in deep doo-doo.** *(1)* У меня́... / *(2)* У тебя́... / *(3)* У нас... мно́го неприя́тностей.

doomed *adj* обречён, обречена́, -о́, -ы́ *(short forms)* ♦ **Our relationship is doomed.** На́ша привя́занность обречена́.

doormat *n* полови́к, ко́врик для вытира́ния ног ♦ **You've made me your doormat.** Ты сде́лала *(ж: сде́лал)* меня́ свои́м ко́вриком для вытира́ния ног. ♦ **I'm just your doormat, aren't I?** Я то́лько твой ко́врик для вытира́ния ног, не так ли?

doppelganger *n* второ́е «я».

dork *n (slang) (someone who acts weird or stupid)* чуда́к, приду́рок, челове́к со стра́н-ностями ♦ **real** *(1,2)* **~** настоя́щий *(1)* чуда́к / *(2)* приду́рок.

dorkiness *n (slang) (goofiness, craziness: trait)* чудакова́тость, ду́рость *f*; *(act)* чуда́чество, ду́рость *f* ♦ **boundless ~** беспреде́льная ду́рость.

dorky *adj (slang) (weird)* чудакова́тый, -ая, -ое, -ые, стра́нный, -ая, -ое, -ые; *(stupid)* глу́пый, -ая, -ое, -ые.

dote *vi (adore)* обожа́ть *(on / over whom = acc.)*; *(be crazy about)* сходи́ть с ума́ *(on / over whom =* + по + *dat.)*.

Reflexive verbs are those that end in -ся *or* -сь. *The* -ся *or* -сь *also goes onto a past tense ending.*

doting *adj (adoring)* обожа́ющий, -ая, -ее, -ие; *(crazy about)* безу́мно лю́бящий, -ая, -ее, -ие, сходя́щий (-ая, -ее, -ие) с ума́ (по + *dat.*).

double-date *vi (No special word in Russian for this concept.)* идти́ куда́-то вме́сте с друго́й па́рой.

doubt *vt* сомнева́ться *(what = + в + prep.)* ♦ **~ very much** о́чень сомнева́ться ♦ **strongly ~** си́льно сомнева́ться ♦ **begin to ~** начина́ть / нача́ть сомнева́ться ♦ **stop doubting** *(1)* **me** / *(2)* **you** переста́ть сомнева́ться *(1)* во мне / *(2)* в тебе́. ♦ **I doubt** *(1)* **... it.** / *(2)* **...that I can come this year.** Я сомнева́юсь *(1)* ...в э́том. / *(2)* ..., что могу́ прие́хать в э́том году́.

doubt *n* сомне́ние ♦ **great ~** большо́е сомне́ние ♦ **no ~** нет сомне́ния ♦ **serious ~s** серьёзные опасе́ния ♦ **slightest ~** мале́йшее сомне́ние ♦ **some ~** како́е-то сомне́ние ♦ **be in ~** сомнева́ться *(about what = + в + prep.)* ♦ **beyond any ~** вне вся́кого сомне́ния ♦ **dispel (all)** *(1)* **my** / *(2)* **your ~s** разве́ять (все) *(1)* мои́ / *(2)* твои́ сомне́ния ♦ **have ~s** име́ть сомне́ния ♦ **without any ~** без вся́кого сомне́ния.

doubt: phrases

I'll give you the benefit of the doubt. Я всё приму́ на ве́ру. ♦ **If you were to have even the slightest doubt about my love for you, it would cut into my heart like a knife.** Е́сли бы у тебя́ появи́лось хоть мале́йшее сомне́ние в мое́й любви́, э́то бы́ло бы для меня́ ножо́м в се́рдце. ♦ **I sense in you an underlying current of doubt.** Я ощуща́ю в тебе́ скры́тое сомне́ние. ♦ **Once and for all I want to silence your doubts (about** *[1]* **...me.** / *[2]* **...my love for you.).** Раз и навсегда́ я хочу́, что́бы замолча́ли твои́ сомне́ния (*[1]*...во мне. / *[2]* ...в мое́й любви́ к тебе́.)

dove *n* го́лубь *m* ♦ **May this letter come to you as a white dove heralding its love on a bright, spring day.** Пусть моё письмо́ прилети́т к тебе́, как бе́лый го́лубь, воспева́ющий свою́ любо́вь в я́ркий, весе́нний день.

dowdy *adj (lacking good taste)* безвку́сный, -ая, -ое, -ые; *(unstylish)* немо́дный, -ая, -ое, -ые; *(slovenly)* неря́шливый, -ая, -ое, -ые.

down *adj (sad, depressed)* упа́вший (-ая, -ее, -ие) ду́хом ♦ **be ~ (in the dumps)** пове́сить нос, приуны́ть, упа́сть ду́хом, впасть в уны́ние *(all used in past tense)* ♦ **be (kind of) ~** (немно́го) приуны́ть *(used in past tense)* ♦ **feel ~** пове́сить нос, приуны́ть, упа́сть ду́хом, впасть в уны́ние *(all used in past tense)* ♦ **feel kind of ~** немно́го приуны́ть *(used in past tense)* ♦ **I** *(1)* **am** / *(2)* **feel kind of down.** *(1,2)* Я немно́го приуны́л *(ж: приуны́ла).* ♦ *(1,2)* **Why are you so down (in the dumps)?** Почему́ ты *(1)* ...впа́ла *(ж: впал)* в уны́ние? / *(2)* ...упа́ла *(ж: упал)* ду́хом?

downer *n (slang)* что́-то *(1)* подавля́ющее / *(2)* угнета́ющее.

down-to-earth *adj (practical)* практи́чный, -ая, -ое, -ые; *(simple)* просто́й, -а́я, -о́е, -ы́е; *(sober)* тре́звый, -ая, -ое, -ые ♦ **~ attitude** тре́звый взгляд.

downy *adj* пуши́стый, -ая, -ое, -ые, мя́гкий (-ая, -ое, -ие) как пух.

dowry *n* прида́ное ♦ **traditional ~** традицио́нное прида́ное.

drain *vt* осуша́ть / осуши́ть *(what = acc.)*; *(drink to the bottom)* пить / вы́пить до дна *(what = acc.)*.

drain *vi (go away)* уходи́ть / уйти́; *(disappear)* исчеза́ть / изче́знуть; *(desert)* покида́ть / поки́нуть *(out of what, whom = acc.)* ♦ **If my lips ever come in contact with yours, all that (** *[1]* **cold /** *[2]* **sham)** *(3)* **haughtiness /** *(4)* **resistance is going to drain right out of you.** Е́сли мои́ гу́бы когда́-нибу́дь косну́тся твои́х губ, всё твоё (*[1]* холо́дное / *[2]* притво́рное) *(3)* высокоме́рие / *(4)* сопротивле́ние изче́знет. ♦ **When you** *(1)* **kiss /** *(2)* **touch me, all my resistance drains out of me.** Когда́ *(1)* ты целу́ешь / *(2)* каса́ешься меня́, всё сопротивле́ние покида́ет меня́.

---

*The time zones for many cities of the world
are given in Appendix 6, page 761.*

drama *n* драма.

dramatize *vt* драматизи́ровать *(what = acc.)*.

drawl *n* протя́жное произноше́ние, растя́гивание слов ♦ **I talk with a drawl.** Я говорю́, растя́гивая слова́.

drawn *adj* привлечён, привлечена́, -о́ , -ы́ *(short forms)* ♦ **be ~** испы́тывать тя́гу *(to whom = + к + dat.)* ♦ **feel ~** чу́вствовать притяже́ние *(to whom = + к + dat.)* ♦ **I have never been so (irresistibly) drawn to anyone in my life as I am to you.** Меня́ никогда́ в жи́зни так (неодоли́мо) не влекло́ к кому́-ли́бо, как к тебе́.

drawn-out *adj* затяжно́й, -а́я, -о́е, -ы́е, растя́нутый, -ая, -ое, -ые ♦ **I don't want a long drawn-out court battle.** Я не хочу́ затяжны́х суде́бных бата́лий.

dread *vt* страши́ться *(what = gen.)*, боя́ться *(what = gen.)* ♦ **I dread** *(1)* **...leaving you.** / *(2)* **...saying goodbye.** *(3)* **...telling him** / *(4)* **her.** Я бою́сь *(1)* ...оста́вить тебя́. / *(2)* ...сказа́ть до свида́ния. / *(3)* ...рассказа́ть ему́ / *(4)* ей.

dread *n* страх ♦ **My heart filled with dread.** Моё се́рдце напо́лнилось стра́хом.

dreadful *adj* ужа́сный, -ая, -ое, -ые, стра́шный, -ая, -ое, -ые.

dreadfully *adv* ужа́сно, стра́шно.

dream *vi* 1. *(in sleep)* ви́деть сон, сни́ться / присни́ться *(dreamer = dat., person / thing dreamed of = subject)* 2. *(consciously)* мечта́ть, гре́зить; *(fantasize)* фантази́ровать.

> **dream: I dream of you**

I dream of you (all the time). Ты сни́шься мне (всё вре́мя). ♦ **I dream of** *(1)* **...holding you (tenderly) in my arms.** / *(2)* **...kissing you all over.** / *(3)* **...making love with you.** / *(4)* **...having you as my wife** / *(5)* **husband.** Я мечта́ю о том, что́бы *(1)* ...(не́жно) обня́ть тебя́. / *(2)* ...целова́ть тебя́ всю. / *(3)* ...заня́ться любо́вью с тобо́й. / *(4)* ...ты была́ мое́й жено́й. / *(5)* ...ты был мои́м му́жем. ♦ **Now I will close my letter, but not before I tell you that I adore you and think about you every day and dream about you every night.** Тепе́рь я зако́нчу своё письмо́, но не ра́ньше, чем скажу́ тебе́, что я обожа́ю тебя́, ду́маю о тебе́ ка́ждый день и мечта́ю о тебе́ ка́ждую ночь. ♦ **Is it any wonder that I dream and fantasize about you in the most shamelessly erotic way day and night?** Не удиви́тельно ли, что я мечта́ю и фантази́рую о тебе́ са́мым бессты́дным эроти́ческим о́бразом день и ночь? ♦ **How I dream of beholding your exquisite beauty sans clothes.** Как я мечта́ю созерца́ть твою́ изы́сканную красоту́ без оде́жды. ♦ **You are the kind of woman that every man dreams about. And, lately, I find myself dreaming about you often.** Ты така́я же́нщина, о кото́рой мечта́ет ка́ждый мужчи́на. В после́днее вре́мя я ловлю́ себя́ на том, что ча́сто мечта́ю о тебе́.

> **dream: I dreamt of you**

I('ve) dreamt about you (so often). Ты (так ча́сто) сни́лась *(ж: сни́лся)* мне. ♦ **You are the woman that I've been dreaming of all my life.** Ты же́нщина, о кото́рой я мечта́л всю свою́ жизнь. ♦ **You are the man that I've been dreaming of all my life.** Ты мужчи́на, о кото́ром я мечта́ла всю свою́ жизнь. ♦ **You are the person that I've been dreaming of all my life.** Ты челове́к, о кото́ром я мечта́л *(ж: мечта́ла)* всю свою́ жизнь. ♦ **I guess I've only dreamt of meeting you.** Я ду́маю, мне то́лько сни́лась встре́ча с тобо́й. ♦ **I've always dreamt of meeting someone like you.** Я всегда́ мечта́л *(ж: мечта́ла)* о встре́че с ке́м-то, похо́жим на тебя́. ♦ **I've often dreamt of having children that look just like you.** Я ча́сто мечта́ю име́ть дете́й, кото́рые вы́глядят то́чно, как ты.

> **dream: I'll be dreaming of you**

In the meantime, you can be sure that I'll be dreaming about that beautiful, radiant smile of yours and how wonderful it would be to cover it with adoring kisses. Ме́жду тем, ты мо́жешь быть уве́рена, что я бу́ду мечта́ть об э́той сия́ющей твое́й улы́бке и как

---

*Optional parts of sentences are preceded
or followed (or both) by three dots.*

замеча́тельно бы́ло бы покры́ть её обожа́ющими поцелу́ями.

dream: *things you've never dreamt*

When we're together again, I'm going to cover you with kisses and caresses like you've never even dreamed of in your wildest dreams. Когда́ мы бу́дем опя́ть вме́сте, я покро́ю тебя́ поцелу́ями и бу́ду ласка́ть так, как ты никогда́ да́же не мечта́ла в са́мых безу́мных мечта́х. ♦ **I want to give you pleasure such as you have never known or dreamed of before.** Я хочу́ дать тебе́ тако́е наслажде́ние, кото́рого ты никогда́ не зна́ла и о кото́ром никогда́ пре́жде не мечта́ла.

dream: *various*

Surely I must be dreaming. Мне, должно́ быть, сни́тся. ♦ **I've dreamed of this moment.** Я так мечта́л *(ж: мечта́ла)* об э́той мину́те. ♦ **If you think so, you're dreaming.** Е́сли ты так ду́маешь, то ты мечта́тель. ♦ **Come dream with me.** Дава́й помечта́ем вме́сте.

dream *n* 1. *(in sleep)* сон; 2. *(conscious)* мечта́ ♦ *(1,2)* **beautiful** ~ *(1)* краси́вая / *(2)* прекра́сная мечта́ ♦ *(1,2)* **bad** ~ *(1)* плохо́й / *(2)* дурно́й сон ♦ **bright** ~s све́тлые мечты́ ♦ **cherished** ~ заве́тная мечта́ ♦ **cozy** ~ прия́тная мечта́ ♦ ~ **of happiness** мечта́ о сча́стье ♦ **ecstasy-filled** ~ сон, напо́лненный экста́зом *(1 term)* ♦ **empty** ~s пусты́е мечты́ ♦ **extravagant** ~ сумасбро́дная мечта́ ♦ **fondest** ~ заве́тная мечта́ ♦ **girlish** ~s де́вичьи мечты́ ♦ **good** ~ хоро́ший сон ♦ **happy** ~ ра́достный сон ♦ *(1,2)* **heavenly** ~ *(1)* ра́йская / *(2)* боже́ственная мечта́ ♦ **idyllic** ~ идилли́ческая мечта́ ♦ **magical** ~s **of love** волше́бные грёзы любви́ ♦ **most cherished** ~ са́мая заве́тная мечта́ ♦ **my** ~ *(1,2)* **come true** моя́ *(1)* сбы́вшаяся / *(2)* ожи́вшая мечта́ ♦ **nice** ~ хоро́ший сон ♦ **paradisiacal** ~ ра́йская мечта́ ♦ **pipe** ~ несбы́точная мечта́ ♦ **pleasant** ~ прия́тная мечта́ ♦ *(1,2)* **secret** ~ *(1)* заве́тная / *(2)* сокрове́нная мечта́ ♦ **strange** ~ стра́нный сон ♦ **terrible** ~ стра́шный сон ♦ **torrid** ~ жа́ркий сон ♦ **wet** ~ эроти́ческий сон, вызыва́ющий поллюцию *(1 term)* ♦ *(1,2)* **wonderful** ~ *(1)* замеча́тельный / *(2)* удиви́тельный сон.

dream: *verb terms*

be a ~ быть мечто́й ♦ **cherish the** ~ леле́ять мечту́ ♦ **live in a** ~ жить в ми́ре грёз ♦ **realize my** ~ осуществля́ть / осуществи́ть свою́ мечту́ ♦ **seem like a** ~ каза́ться мечто́й ♦ **share** ~s разделя́ть мечты́ ♦ **shatter my** ~s разби́ть мои́ мечты́ ♦ **walk around in a** ~ предава́ться мечта́м.

dream: *seen you in my dreams*

I've seen you so many times in my dreams. Я тебя́ так мно́го раз ви́дел *(ж: ви́дела)* во сне. ♦ **I know where I met you — in (all of) my dreams.** Я зна́ю, где я встре́тил тебя́, -- в(о) (всех) мои́х снах. ♦ **I'd know your face anywhere — I see it in all my dreams.** Я узна́л бы твоё лицо́ где уго́дно -- я ви́жу его́ во всех свои́х снах.

dream: *you - my dream come true*

(1,2) **You are my dream come true.** Ты *(1)* ...моя́ ожи́вшая мечта́. / *(2)* ...мой сон наяву́. ♦ **You are my every dream come true.** Ты де́лаешь ка́ждую мою́ мечту́ пра́вдой. ♦ **You fulfill all my hopes and dreams.** Ты испо́лнила *(ж: испо́лнил)* все мои́ наде́жды и мечты́. ♦ **You are the fulfillment of my dreams.** Ты исполне́ние мои́х снов. ♦ **You are my hopes and dreams, my strength and purpose, my joy and happiness. You are my life.** Ты мои́ наде́жды и мечты́, моя́ си́ла и цель, моя́ ра́дость и сча́стье. Ты моя́ жизнь. ♦ **You are my joy and comfort, my hope and my dreams — my everything.** Ты моя́ ра́дость и утеше́ние, моя́ наде́жда и моя́ мечта́ -- всё для меня́. ♦ **All my dreams belong to you.** Все мои́ мечты́ в тебе́. ♦ **You are the master of all my dreams.** Ты хозя́йка *(ж: хозя́ин)* всех мои́х мечта́ний. ♦ *(1)* **Being with you (like this)...** / *(2)* **Having your love... is a dream come true.** *(1)* Быть с тобо́й (как сейча́с) -- ... / *(2)* Чу́вствовать

If you're not on familiar terms with a person, the «ты» forms will have to be changed to «Вы».

твою любовь --... это просто сон наяву. ♦ **When I met you, all my dreams came true.** Когда́ я встре́тил *(ж: встре́тила)* тебя́, все мои́ мечты́ сбыли́сь.

dream: *the person of my dreams*

You are the *(1)* **man** / *(2)* **woman** / *(3)* **girl** / *(4)* **person of my dreams.** Ты *(1)* мужчи́на / *(2)* же́нщина / *(3)* де́вушка / *(4)* челове́к мое́й мечты́. ♦ *(1)* **I want to find...** / *(2)* **In you I've found...** the girl of my dreams.** *(1)* Я хочу́ найти́... / *(2)* В тебе́ я нашёл... де́вушку свое́й мечты́.

dream: *you - center of my dreams*

You are the cynosure of all my (hopes and) dreams. Ты путево́дная звезда́ всех мои́х (наде́жд и) мечта́ний. ♦ **All my future plans and dreams of happiness are centered around you.** Все мои́ пла́ны на бу́дущее, все мечты́ о сча́стье свя́заны с тобо́й.

dream: *making dreams come true*

You have made all my dreams come true. Благодаря́ тебе́ сбыли́сь все мои́ мечты́. ♦ **I want to make all your dreams come true.** Я хочу́ испо́лнить все твои́ мечты́. ♦ **The one thing that would make all my dreams come true is for you to bestow upon me the** *(1)* **exquisite** / *(2)* **supreme joys of your luscious all.** То́лько одно́ могло́ бы осуществи́ть все мои́ мечты́ -- это, что́бы ты подари́ла мне *(1)* изы́сканную / *(2)* исключи́тельную ра́дость всей твое́й роско́шной красоты́.

dream: *beyond my / your wildest dreams*

When I kissed you the first time, it was beyond my wildest dreams. Когда́ я впервы́е поцелова́л (ж: поцелова́ла) тебя́, это бы́ло превы́ше мои́х са́мых (стра́стных) мечта́ний. ♦ **You're even more beautiful than my dreams.** Ты да́же краси́вее, чем мои́ мечты́. ♦ **You are bewitching beyond my wildest dreams.** Ты очарова́тельна сверх мои́х са́мых необу́зданных мечта́ний. ♦ **Even in my dreams I've never seen such a** *(1)* **beautiful** / *(2)* **luscious body.** Да́же в свои́х снах я никогда́ не ви́дел тако́го *(1)* прекра́сного / *(2)* со́чного те́ла. ♦ **Even in my most extravagant dreams I never conceived of anyone as** *(1)* **beautiful** / *(2)* **lovely as you.** Да́же в свои́х са́мых сумасбро́дных мечта́х я никогда́ не мог вообрази́ть таку́ю *(1,2)* прекра́сную же́нщину, как ты. ♦ **When we're together again, I'm going to cover you with kisses and caresses like you've never even dreamed of in your wildest dreams.** Когда́ мы бу́дем опя́ть вме́сте, я покро́ю тебя́ поцелу́ями и бу́ду ласка́ть так, как ты никогда́ да́же не мечта́ла в свои́х са́мых безу́мных мечта́х.

dream: *torrid dreams of you*

Last night I had a *(1)* **wonderful** / *(2)* **torrid** / *(3)* **ecstasy-filled dream about you.** Про́шлой но́чью мне сни́лся *(1)* замеча́тельный / *(2)* жа́ркий / *(3)* ...напо́лненный экста́зом... сон о тебе́. ♦ **Every night my dreams roil in the most torrid scenes of** *(1)* **passionate** / *(2)* **erotic desire for your sweet, warm, wonderful womanness.** Ка́ждую ночь в мои́х снах роя́тся са́мые зно́йные сце́ны стра́сти / эроти́ческого вожделе́ния к твое́й сла́дкой, тёплой, великоле́пной же́нственности.

dream: *my cherished dream*

My most cherished dream is to kiss your beautiful face 25,000,000 times — in the first year. And then gradually increase the number of kisses. Моя́ са́мая заве́тная мечта́ - - целова́ть твоё прекра́сное лицо́ 25000000 *(два́дцать пять миллио́нов)* раз в наш пе́рвый год. И зате́м постепе́нно увели́чивать число́ поцелу́ев. ♦ **This cozy, idyllic, heavenly dream of having you as my loving wife is wonderful beyond any words that I can muster.** Эта прия́тная, идилли́ческая, боже́ственная мечта́ о том, что́бы ты была́ мое́й люби́мой жено́й, превы́ше любы́х слов, кото́рые я могу́ сказа́ть.

A list of common places with their grammatical endings is given in Appendix 7, page 763.

dream: *wonderful dreams*

That's just a paradisiacal dream! Это про́сто ра́йская мечта́! ♦ *(1)* **Our love...** / *(2)* **Love with you... is a beautiful dream.** *(1,2)* На́ша любо́вь -- прекра́сная мечта́.

dream: *your letters bring dreams*

I need your letters and the dreams they bring to sustain me through the long, empty nights. Мне нужны́ твои́ пи́сьма и мечты́, кото́рые они́ прино́сят, что́бы подде́рживать меня́ дли́нными, одино́кими нача́ми.

dream: *you in my dreams*

You are my favorite dream. Ты моя́ люби́мая мечта́. ♦ I know for sure that your beautiful eyes and face will monopolize my thoughts and dreams in the days ahead. Я соверше́нно уве́рен, что твои́ прекра́сные глаза́ и лицо́ запо́лнят все мои́ мы́сли и мечты́ на все бу́дущие дни. ♦ I think it would be such a nice feeling to sit close to you and talk with you in an intimate way for hours on end. This is going to be my new dream in the days ahead. Я ду́маю, как бы э́то бы́ло прекра́сно сиде́ть ря́дом с тобо́й и говори́ть о сокрове́нном бесконе́чные часы́. Э́то тепе́рь бу́дет мое́й но́вой мечто́й. ♦ My last waking thoughts and all of my dreams are of you. Мои́ после́дние мы́сли пе́ред сном и все мои́ мечты́ о тебе́. ♦ In the meantime, you can be sure that I'll be dreaming about that beautiful, radiant smile of yours and how wonderful it would be to cover it with adoring kisses. Ме́жду тем, ты мо́жешь быть уве́рена, что я бу́ду мечта́ть об э́той сия́ющей твое́й улы́бке и как замеча́тельно бы́ло бы покры́ть её обожа́ющими поцелу́ями.

dream: *kissing you in my dreams*

In the unbounded vistas of my dreams and fantasies I taste the exquisite sweetness of your lips a thousand, ten thousand, a million times, and each time am only impelled by the sheer ecstasy of the kiss to taste them once again. В безграни́чной верени́це мои́х снов и фанта́зий я вкуша́ю исключи́тельную сла́дость твои́х губ ты́сячу, де́сять ты́сяч, миллио́н раз и ка́ждый раз побужде́н и́стинным восто́ргом поцелу́я упива́ться им опя́ть. ♦ Kiss me in your dreams and my heart will feel it. Целу́й меня́ в свои́х снах, и моё се́рдце почу́вствует э́то.

dream: *bad dreams*

This is like a bad dream. Э́то похо́же на плохо́й сон. ♦ **My marriage** *(1)* **is** / *(2)* **was like a bad dream.** Мой брак *(1)* ...похо́ж... / *(2)* ...был похо́ж... на стра́шный сон.

dream: *various*

I hope this isn't (just) a dream. Я наде́юсь, э́то не (то́лько) сон. ♦ I've been walking around in a dream. Я предаю́сь мечта́м. ♦ Such dreams really help to spur me on. Таки́е мечты́ действи́тельно вдохновля́ют меня́. ♦ Thank you for this dream. Благодарю́ тебя́ за э́ту мечту́. ♦ I'm looking for a loving person to fill my dream. Я ищу́ лю́бящего челове́ка, воплоща́ющего мою́ мечту́. ♦ You have shattered all my dreams. Ты разби́ла *(ж: разби́л)* все мои́ мечты́.

dreamboat *n* 1. *(beautiful / handsome person)* краса́вица *f*, краса́вчик *m*; 2. *(subject of longing)* голуба́я мечта́.

dreamer *n* мечта́тель *m*, мечта́тельница *f* ♦ **beautiful** ~ прекра́сная мечта́тельница ♦ **hopeless** ~ безнадёжный мечта́тель ♦ My beautiful dreamer, how I adore you. Моя́ прекра́сная мечта́тельница, как я обожа́ю тебя́. ♦ My beautiful dreamer... Моя́ прекра́сная мечта́тельница... ♦ I know I'm a hopeless dreamer, but I can never stop wishing that someday you'll open your heart to me. Я зна́ю, что я безнадёжный мечта́тель, но не перестаю́ наде́яться, что одна́жды ты откро́ешь мне своё се́рдце.

dreaminess *n* мечта́тельность *f*.

Common adult heights are given in Appendix 9, page 776.

dreaming *n* мечтáние ♦ **You set me to dreaming.** Ты дéлаешь меня́ мечтáтелем.

dream-like *adj* скáзочный, -ая, -ое, -ые, похóжий (-ая, -ее, -ие) на мечту́ / сон, фантасти́ческий, -ая, -ое, -ие.

dreamy *adj* мечтáтельный, -ая, -ое, -ые ♦ **I** *(1)* **love /** *(2)* **adore your dreamy face.** Я *(1)* люблю́ / *(2)* обожáю твоё мечтáтельное лицó.

dreary *adj* тоскли́вый, -ая, -ое, -ые.

drench *vt* утопля́ть / утопи́ть *(what = acc.).* ♦ **I'm going to drench you in ecstasy.** Я утоплю́ тебя́ в экстáзе.

dress *vi* одевáться / одéться ♦ **You dress very** *(1)* **well /** *(2)* **nicely.** Ты óчень *(1,2)* хорошó одевáешься.

dress *n* плáтье ♦ **ankle-length** ~ плáтье длинóй до лоды́жек ♦ **backless** ~ плáтье с откры́той спинóй ♦ **beautiful** ~ прекрáсное плáтье ♦ **boldly revealing** ~ дéрзкое откры́тое плáтье ♦ **chiffon** ~ шифóновое плáтье ♦ **clingy** ~ облегáющее плáтье ♦ **cocktail** ~ плáтье для коктéйля ♦ **cut-out** ~ плáтье с вы́резами ♦ **daring** ~ смéлое плáтье ♦ **dark(-colored)** тёмное плáтье ♦ **different** ~ другóе плáтье ♦ **elegant** ~ элегáнтное плáтье ♦ **evening** ~ вечéрнее плáтье ♦ **everyday** ~ бу́дничное плáтье ♦ **expensive** ~ дорогóе плáтье ♦ **fancy** ~ наря́дное платье ♦ **figure-molding** ~ облегáющее платье ♦ **flimsy** ~ лёгкое плáтье ♦ **flowery** ~ цветáстое плáтье ♦ **house** ~ домáшнее плáтье ♦ *(1,2)* **knit(ted)** ~ *(1)* трикотáжное / *(2)* вя́заное плáтье ♦ **light** ~ лёгкое плáтье ♦ **light-colored** ~ свéтлое плáтье ♦ **long** ~ дли́нное плáтье ♦ **lovely** ~ прекрáсное плáтье ♦ **mini** ~ ми́ни-плáтье ♦ **modest** ~ скрóмное плáтье ♦ **my** ~ моё плáтье ♦ **new** ~ нóвое плáтье ♦ **nice** ~ хорóшее плáтье ♦ **nice-looking** ~ симпати́чное плáтье ♦ **old** ~ стáрое плáтье ♦ *(1-3)* **party** ~ *(1)* наря́дное / *(2)* прáздничное плáтье, *(3)* прáздничный наря́д ♦ **provocative** ~ вызывáющее плáтье ♦ **satin** ~ сати́новое плáтье ♦ **sexy** ~ соблазни́тельное плáтье ♦ **short** ~ корóткое плáтье ♦ **silk** ~ шёлковое плáтье ♦ **simple** ~ простóе плáтье ♦ **skimpy** ~ óчень откры́тое плáтье ♦ **sleeve** ~ обтя́гивающее плáтье ♦ **sleeveless** ~ плáтье без рукавóв ♦ **slinky** ~ плáтье в обтя́жку ♦ **smart-looking** ~ наря́дное плáтье ♦ **strapless** ~ плáтье без бретéлек ♦ **stretch** ~ обтя́гивающее плáтье ♦ *(1,2)* **stylish** ~ *(1)* мóдное / *(2)* шикáрное плáтье ♦ **summer** ~ лéтнее плáтье ♦ **tight(ly) (fitting)** ~ облегáющее платье ♦ **velvet** ~ бáрхатное плáтье ♦ *(1,2)* **wedding** ~ *(1)* свáдебное / *(2)* подвенéчное плáтье ♦ **wool** ~ шерстянóе плáтье ♦ **your** ~ *(familiar)* твоё плáтье; *(polite)* Вáше плáтье ♦ **disassemble your** ~ расстёгивать / расстегну́ть твоё плáтье ♦ **unbutton your** ~ расстёгивать / расстегну́ть твоё плáтье.

dress: phrases

What a *(1)* **beautiful /** *(2)* **lovely dress (you have on)!** Что за *(1,2)* прекрáсное плáтье (у тебя́)! ♦ **That's a (very) beautiful dress.** Это (óчень) краси́вое плáтье. ♦ **I like the way that dress emphasizes every contour of your body.** Мне нрáвится, как плáтье подчёркивает кáждый изги́б твоегó тéла. ♦ **The dress clings to you like a second skin.** Плáтье облегáет тебя́ как вторáя кóжа. ♦ **That dress doesn't leave much to the imagination.** Это плáтье не мнóго оставля́ет для воображéния. ♦ **You look beautiful in any dress you wear, but I like you better unclothed.** Ты вы́глядишь прекрáсно в любóм плáтье, котóрое ты нóсишь, но мне ты бóльше нрáвишься без одéжды. ♦ **I want a woman who is comfortable in jeans or a(n)** *(1)* **cocktail /** *(2)* **evening dress.** Я хочу́ жéнщину, котóрой одинáково удóбно в джи́нсах и в *(1)* ...плáтье для коктéйля. / *(2)* ...вечéрном плáтье.

dress: quotation

"A dress has no meaning unless it makes a man want to take it off." *Francoise Sagan, The Observer, 1969.* «Плáтье не имéет никакóго другóго значéния, как застáвить мужчи́ну захотéть снять егó.» *Франсуáза Сагáн, «Наблюдáтель», 1969.*

Words in parentheses are optional.

dressed *adj* одéт, -а, -о, -ы *(short forms).* ♦ **beautifully** ~ прекрáсно одéт *m* / одéта *f* ♦ **elegantly** ~ элегáнтно одéт *m* / одéта *f* ♦ **modestly** ~ скрóмно одéт *m* / одéта *f* ♦ **primly** ~ стрóго одéта *f* ♦ **quietly** ~ скрóмно одéт *m* / одéта *f* ♦ **simply** ~ прóсто одéт *m* / одéта *f* ♦ **stunningly** ~ потрясáюще одéта *f* ♦ **stylishly** ~ шикáрно одéта *f* ♦ **superbly** ~ великолéпно одéт *m* / одéта *f* ♦ *(1,2)* **soberly** ~ *(1)* спокóйно / *(2)* неярко одéт *m* / одéта *f* ♦ **get** ~ одевáться / одéться.

dresser *n* человéк, одевáющийся определённым óбразом *(1 term)* ♦ *(1,2)* **neat** ~ *(1)* аккурáтно / *(2)* изящно одéтый *m* / одéтая *f* ♦ **sharp** ~ прекрáсно одевáющийся человéк.

drift *vi* 1. *(float)* течь, плыть; 2. *(apart)* расходúться / разойтúсь, отдаляться / отдалúться ♦ ~ **apart** расходúться / разойтúсь друг от дрýга, удаляться / удалúться друг от дрýга ♦ ~ **away** *vi* уходúть / уйтú, удаляться / удалúться.

┌─────────────────┐
│ *drift: phrases* │
└─────────────────┘

You're *(1,2)* **drifting away from me.** Ты *(1)* ухóдишь / *(2)* удаляешься от меня. ♦ *(1)* **We...** / *(2)* **He** / *(3)* **She and I ...have drifted so far apart.** *(1)* Мы... / *(2)* Он / *(3)* Онá и я... так далекó удалúлись друг от дрýга. ♦ **I feel like you and I are drifting** *(1)* **...apart.** / *(2)* **...away from each other.** Я чýвствую, что ты и я *(1)* ...расхóдимся. / *(2)* ...отдаляемся друг от дрýга. ♦ **You've drifted away from me (in the last few** *[1]* **weeks /** *[2]* **months).** Ты отдалúлась *(ж: отдалúлся)* от меня (в послéдние нéсколько *[1]* недéль / *[2]* мéсяцев.). ♦ **My thoughts are constantly** *(1,2)* **drifting over to you.** Моú мýсли постоянно *(1)* обращáются / *(2)* текýт к тебé. ♦ **The love we had has drifted away.** Любóвь, котóрая былá у нас, ушлá.

drifter *n* бродяга.

drink *n* напúток ♦ **soft** ~ безалкогóльный напúток ♦ **strong** ~ спиртнóй напúток ♦ **Would you like to have a drink (with me)?** Не хотéла бы ты выпить (со мной)? ♦ **Could I** *(1)* **buy /** *(2)* **offer you a drink?** Могý я *(1)* купúть / *(2)* предложúть тебé выпить? ♦ **Let me** *(1)* **get** *(= buy)* **/** *(2)* **buy you a drink.** Позвóль мне *(1,2)* купúть тебé что-нибýдь выпить. ♦ *(1)* **I'll fix... /** *(2)* **Let me fix... you a drink.** *(1)* Я приготóвлю... / *(2)* Позвóль мне приготóвить... тебé выпить. ♦ **Let's have a drink (together).** Давáй выпьем (вдвоём).

drink *vt* пить / выпить *(what = acc.)* ♦ **Do you drink?** Ты пьёшь алкогóльные напúтки? ♦ **I don't drink (alcohol).** Я не пью (совсéм). ♦ **I drink** *(1)* **...a little. /** *(2)* **...very little. /** *(3)* **...very seldom. /** *(4)* **...occasionally. /** *(5)* **...sometimes. /** *(6)* **...socially.** Я пью *(1)* ...немнóго. / *(2)* ...совсéм немнóго. / *(3)* ...óчень рéдко. / *(4,5)* ...иногдá. / *(6)* ...в компáниях. ♦ **I drink a beer** *(1)* **...occasionally. /** *(2)* **...every now and then. /** *(3)* **...once in a great while.** Я пью пúво *(1,2)* ...иногдá. / *(3)* ...довóльно рéдко. ♦ **I** *(1)* **quit /** *(2)* **stopped drinking (a long time ago).** Я (давнó) *(1)* прекратúл *(ж: прекратúла)* / *(2)* перестáл *(ж: перестáла)* пить.

drinker *n* пьющий *m*, пьющая *f*; *(drunkard)* пьяница *m&f* ♦ **coffee** ~ кóфе пьющий *m* / пьющая *f* ♦ **heavy** ~ гóрький пьяница *m*, гóрькая пьяница *f* ♦ **light** ~ слегкá пьющий *m* / пьющая *f* ♦ **moderate** ~ в мéру пьющий *m* / пьющая *f* ♦ **non-drinker** непьющий *m*, непьющая *f* ♦ **tea** ~ чай пьющий *m* / пьющая *f*.

drinking *n* 1. питьё; 2. *(drunkenness)* пьянство ♦ **I can't handle** *(1)* **your /** *(2)* **his /** *(3)* **her drinking.** Я не могý вынести *(1)* твоё / *(2)* егó / *(3)* её пьянство.

drive *vt* доводúть / довестú *(what, whom = + acc.);* сводúть / сместú *(what, whom = acc.)* ♦ **I'm going to drive you crazy with ecstasy.** Я доведý тебя до безýмного экстáза. ♦ **You drive me (absolutely)** *(1)* **crazy /** *(2)* **wild.** Ты (совершéнно) свóдишь меня *(1,2)* с умá. ♦ **I promise you, I'm going to drive you (absolutely)** *(1)* **crazy /** *(2)* **wild.** Я обещáю, что я (совершéнно) сведý тебя *(1,2)* с умá. ♦ **I know so many wonderful ways to drive you**

You can find common clothing sizes in Appendix 11 on page 778.

(1) **crazy** / *(2)* **wild.** Мне изве́стно так мно́го замеча́тельных спо́собов довести́ тебя́ до *(1)* безу́мия / *(2)* исступле́ния. ♦ **I'm going to do things with you that will drive you (absolutely)** *(1)* **...crazy.** / *(2)* **...out of your mind.** / *(3)* **...wild.** Я сде́лаю с тобо́й тако́е, что доведёт тебя́ до (по́лного) *(1,2)* безу́мия. / *(3)* исступле́ния.

drive *n:* ♦ **We can go on** *(1)* **mountain** / *(2)* **scenic** / *(3)* **country drives together.** Мы (вме́сте) мо́жем пое́хать *(1)* ...в го́ры. / *(2)* ...в живопи́сные места́. / *(3)* ...по се́льской доро́ге.

droll *adj* заба́вный, -ая, -ое, -ые.

drool *vi* распуска́ть / распусти́ть слю́ни ♦ **I don't like it when someone drools all over me.** Я не люблю́, когда́ кто́-нибудь распуска́ет слю́ни на меня́.

drop *vt* роня́ть / урони́ть *(what = acc.)* ♦ ~ *(1)* **you** / *(2)* **me a** *(3)* **note** / *(4)* **line** написа́ть *(1)* тебе́ / *(2)* мне *(3)* запи́ску / *(4)* письмо́.

drown *vi* тону́ть / потону́ть, топи́ться / утопи́ться ♦ **I want us to drown in each other.** Я хочу́, чтобы мы утону́ли друг в дру́ге.

drug-free *adj:* ♦ **be ~** не употребля́ть нарко́тики.

drugs *n* 1. *(narcotics)* нарко́тики; 2. *(medicines)* медикаме́нты ♦ **I don't** *(1)* **do** / *(2)* **use drugs.** Я не *(1,2)* употребля́ю нарко́тики. ♦ **I don't want someone who uses drugs.** Мне не ну́жен челове́к, употребля́ющий нарко́тики.

drunk *adj* пья́ный, -ая, -ое, -ые ♦ **get ~** напива́ться / напи́ться ♦ **I think I'll go out and get** *(1-3)* **royally drunk.** Я ду́маю пойти́ куда́-нибудь и напи́ться *(1)* ...по-короле́вски. / *(2)* ...как сле́дует. / *(3)* ...до чёртиков.

dubious *adj* сомни́тельный, -ая, -ое, -ые.

dubiously *adv* сомни́тельно.

duckling *n:* ♦ **ugly ~** га́дкий утёнок.

dude *n (slang) (guy)* па́рень *m* ♦ **great-looking ~** краси́вый па́рень.

dulcet *adj* сла́дкий, -ая, -ое, -ие.

dull *adj (boring)* ску́чный, -ая, -ое, -ые.

dullsville *n (slang)* скучи́ща.

dumb *adj* глу́пый, -ая, -ое, -ые.

dumbfounded *adj* огоро́шен, -а, -о, -ы *(short forms)*, ошеломлён, ошеломлена́, -о́, -ы́ *(short forms)* ♦ **I was dumbfounded when I** *(1)* **heard** / *(2)* **read it.** Я был огоро́шен *(ж: была́ огоро́шена)*, *(1)* услы́шав / *(2)* прочита́в э́то.

dummy *n (bantering, affectionate)* глупы́ш *m*, глупы́шка *f.*

dump *vt* броса́ть / бро́сить *(what, whom = acc.)* ♦ *(1)* **She dumped...** / *(2)* **He dumped... me for someone else.** *(1)* Она́ бро́сила меня́ для друго́го. / *(2)* Он бро́сил меня́ для друго́й. ♦ **I'm afraid you'll get tired of me and dump me.** Я бою́сь, что ты уста́нешь от меня́ и бро́сишь меня́.

dupe *vt* дура́чить *or* одура́чивать / одура́чить *(whom = acc.)*, надува́ть / наду́ть *(whom = acc.)* ♦ **All this time** *(1)* **she** / *(2)* **he has been duping me.** Всё э́то вре́мя *(1)* ...она́ дура́чила... / *(2)* ...он дура́чил... меня́.

duped *adj* одура́чен, -а, -о, -ы *(short forms)* ♦ **I was completely duped by** *(1)* **her** / *(2)* **you.** Я был соверше́нно одура́чен *(1)* е́ю / *(2)* тобо́й. ♦ **I was completely duped by** *(1)* **him** / *(2)* **you.** Я была́ соверше́нно одура́чена *(1)* им / *(2)* тобо́й.

duplicity *n* двули́чность *f* ♦ **I'm sick (and tired) of your duplicity.** Мне осточерте́ла твоя́ двули́чность.

dust *n:* ♦ **edible honey ~** съедо́бная пчели́ная пыльца́.

Dutch *adj* голла́ндский, -ая, -ое, -ие.

Dutch *n* 1. *(people)* голла́ндцы; 2. *(language)* нидерла́ндский язы́к ♦ **speak ~** говори́ть по-нидерла́ндски.

For general rules of Russian grammar see Appendix 2 on page 686.

Dutchman n *(person)* голла́ндец m.

Dutchwoman n голла́ндка f.

dwell vi жить, пребыва́ть ♦ **If you could but know how much love dwells in my heart for you.** Е́сли бы ты могла́ *(ж: мог)* то́лько знать, кака́я больша́я любо́вь к тебе́ живёт в моём се́рдце.

dweller n жи́тель m, обита́тель m ♦ **city** ~ городско́й жи́тель.

---

*For transitive Russian verbs the cases that they take are shown
by means of an = sign and the Russian case (abbreviated).*

E

eager *adj* 1. *(impatient)* нетерпели́вый, -ая, -ое, -ые; 2. *(lips, mouth)* жа́дный, -ая, -ое, -ые
♦ **You can't imagine how eager I am for June to get here.** Ты не мо́жешь предста́вить, с каки́м нетерпе́нием я жду ию́ня. ♦ **I'm very eager to meet you in person.** Я с больши́м нетерпе́нием жду ли́чной встре́чи с тобо́й. ♦ **I love to give affection and fill my partner with boundless pleasure and delight in a totally eager and selfless way.** Я люблю́ дари́ть своему́ партнёру не́жность, безграни́чное наслажде́ние и восхище́ние пы́лко и бескоры́стно.

eagerly *adv* нетерпели́во, с нетерпе́нием ♦ **I look forward** *(1,2)* **eagerly to** *(3)* **...getting your next letter.** / *(4)* **...hearing from you.** Я *(1)* ...нетерпели́во / *(2)* ...с нетерпе́нием... жду *(3)* ...твоего́ сле́дующего письма́. / *(4)* ...услы́шать чтó-ли́бо от тебя́. ♦ **How eagerly I look forward to June.** С каки́м нетерпе́нием я жду ию́ня.

eagerness *n* пыл, рве́ние, нетерпе́ние ♦ **You have no idea with what joy and eagerness I wait for every letter from you.** Ты не представля́ешь, с како́й ра́достью и нетерпе́нием я жду ка́ждого твоего́ письма́. ♦ **I'm brimming with eagerness to** *(1)* **meet** / *(2)* **see you.** Я до краёв напо́лнен *(ж: напо́лнена)* нетерпе́нием *(1)* встре́тить / *(2)* уви́деть тебя́.

ear *n* у́хо *(pl:* у́ши*)* ♦ **big ~s** больши́е у́ши ♦ **both ~s** о́ба у́ха ♦ *(1,2)* **cute (little) ~s** *(1)* хоро́шенькие / *(2)* преле́стные у́шки ♦ **left ~** ле́вое у́хо ♦ **little ~** у́шко ♦ **lovely ~s** краси́вые у́ши ♦ **lovely (little) ~** преле́стное у́шко ♦ **pierced ~s** проко́лотые у́ши ♦ **right ~** пра́вое у́хо ♦ **shell-like ~s** ма́ленькие изя́щные у́ши ♦ *(1,2)* **small ~s** *(1)* небольши́е / *(2)* ма́ленькие у́ши ♦ **play it by ~** принима́ть / приня́ть реше́ние по хо́ду де́ла.

ear: phrases

I want to talk privately with your ear for a moment. Я хочу́ мину́тку пошепта́ться с твои́м ушко́м наедине́. ♦ **Oh, (you have) such a cute (little) ear!** О, у тебя́ тако́е хоро́шенькое *(ма́ленькое)* у́шко! ♦ **Your (cute little) ears are just pleading to be nibbled.** Твои́ *(изя́щные ма́ленькие)* у́шки про́сто взыва́ют к поцелу́ям. ♦ **I'm not some kid, wet behind the ears.** Я не ребёнок, мо́крый по са́мые у́ши. ♦ **I have a bad** *(1)* **right** / *(2)* **left ear.** Я пло́хо слы́шу *(1)* пра́вым / *(2)* ле́вым у́хом.

earlobe *n* ушна́я мо́чка ♦ *(1)* **I'd like...** / *(2)* **I love... to nibble on your earlobes.** *(1)* Я хоте́л бы... / *(2)* Я люблю́... поку́сывать мо́чки твои́х уше́й.

early *adv* ра́но ♦ **earlier** ра́ньше.

earnest *adj (serious)* серьёзный, -ая, -ое, -ые; *(sincere)* и́скренний, -яя, -ее, -ие.

Russian verbs have 2 forms: imperfective and perfective.
They're given in that order.

earnest *n* серьёзность *f* ◆ **What I say to you, I say in earnest.** То, что я говорю тебе, я говорю серьёзно. ◆ **I say this to you in all earnest.** Я говорю это тебе со всей серьёзностью.

earnestly *adv (seriously)* серьёзно; *(sincerely)* искренне.

earrings *n, pl* серьги ◆ **What** *(1)* **beautiful /** *(2)* **lovely earrings (you have)!** Что за *(1,2)* прекрасные серьги (у тебя)!

earth *n* земля ◆ **salt of the ~** соль земли ◆ **You are the most beautiful woman on the face of this earth.** Ты самая прекрасная женщина на земле.

earthy *adj* простецкий, -ая, -ое, -ие, грубоватый, -ая, -ое, -ые.

ease *vt* 1. *(make easier)* облегчать / облегчить *(what = acc.)*; 2. *(calm)* успокаивать / успокоить *(what = acc.)*; 3. *(free)* освобождать / освободить *(what = acc.)* ◆ **It (really)** *(1)* **eases /** *(2)* **eased my mind.** Это (действительно) *(1)* даёт / *(2)* дало мне душевный покой.

ease *n* 1. *(easiness)* лёгкость *f*; 2. *(freedom)* свобода, непринуждённость *f*; 3. *(rest)* покой ◆ **I feel so at ease with you.** Я чувствую себя так свободно с тобой. ◆ **You make me feel so at ease.** Ты даёшь мне чувство такой свободы. ◆ **I** *(1)* **feel /** *(2)* **felt (very) ill at ease.** Я *(1)* чувствую / *(2)* чувствовал *(чувствовала)* себя (очень) неловко. ◆ **Thank you for putting my mind at ease.** Спасибо тебе за то, что ты дала *(ж: дал)* мне душевный покой.

easy *adj* лёгкий, -ая, -ое, -ие ◆ **~ to get along with** уживчивый, -ая, -ое, -ые ◆ **You are so easy on the eyes.** Ты так радуешь глаз! ◆ **I've never met anyone as easy on the eyes as you are.** Я никогда не встречал никого, кто бы так радовал глаз, как ты. ◆ **You're easy to be with.** С тобой легко. ◆ **I think you'll find that I'm easy to be with.** Я думаю, ты узнаешь, что со мной легко. ◆ **It's so easy to talk with you.** Так легко говорить с тобой. ◆ **Nice and easy does it every time.** Медленно и спокойно - каждый раз успешно. ◆ **Take it easy.** 1. *(Be calm.)* Относись спокойно (к этому). 2. *(Don't worry.)* Не беспокойся. 3. *(Don't overdo it.)* Не усердствуй. 4. *(Don't rush.)* Не торопись.

easy-going *adj* добродушно-весёлый, -ая, -ое, -ые, покладистый, -ая, -ое, -ые, с лёгким характером, уживчивый, -ая, -ое, -ые ◆ **I'm an easygoing person.** Я человек с лёгким характером. ◆ **I have an easy-going nature.** У меня лёгкий характер. ◆ **I consider myself easy-going.** Я считаю себя человеком добродушным.

eat *vt* есть ◆ **~ breakfast** завтракать / позавтракать ◆ **~ dinner** обедать / пообедать ◆ **~ lunch** *(eat breakfast in the middle of the day)* завтракать / позавтракать (в середине дня); *(eat dinner in the middle of the day)* обедать / пообедать (в середине дня) ◆ **~ supper** ужинать / поужинать.

eavesdrop *vi* подслушивать / подслушать *(on whom = acc.)*.

ebony *adj* чёрный, -ая, -ое, -ые.

ebullience *n* кипение; *(радостное)* возбуждение; энтузиазм ◆ **Your ebullience is so refreshing.** Твоя кипучая натура необыкновенно приятна мне. ◆ **Your ebullience really** *(1)* **intrigues /** *(2)* **charms me.** Твоя жизненная энергия *(1,2)* очаровывает меня.

ebullient *adj* кипучий, -ая, -ее, -ие, полный (-ая, -ое, -ые) энтузиазма ◆ **You have such an ebullient nature.** У тебя такая кипучая натура.

eccentric *adj* эксцентричный, -ая, -ое, -ые, взбалмошный, -ая, -ое, -ые ◆ **~ person** взбалмошный человек.

echo *vi* отзываться / отозваться эхом.

echo *vt* отражать / отразить эхом ◆ **In my heart there is a love song that echoes your name.** В моём сердце звучит любовная песня, отражающая эхом твоё имя.

eclectic *adj* эклектический, -ая, -ое, -ие ◆ **~ tastes** эклектические вкусы.

eclipse *vt* затемнять / затемнить *(what, whom = + acc.)*, затмевать / затмить *(what, whom*

---

*How to use the Cyrillic alphabet on the Internet
is the subject of Appendix 20 on page 789.*

= + *acc.)* ♦ **My love for you is so deep and tender that it eclipses the range of human imagination.** Невозмо́жно предста́вить себе́ как глубока́ и нежна́ моя́ любо́вь к тебе́. ♦ **You have a** *(1)* **beauty /** *(2)* **loveliness that** *(3)* **age /** *(4)* **time can never** *(5,6)* **eclipse.** Ты так краси́ва, что с *(3,4)* года́ми твоя́ *(1,2)* красота́ не мо́жет *(5)* потускне́ть / *(6)* уме́ньшиться.

eco-minded *adj (concerned about ecology)* интересу́ющийся (-аяся, -ееся, -иеся) эколо́-гией.

ecstasy *n* экста́з, восто́рг ♦ **all-consuming** ~ всепоглоща́ющий восто́рг ♦ **cosmic** ~ косми́-ческий экста́з ♦ **genuine** ~ и́стинный восто́рг ♦ **heretofore unknown** *(1,2)* ~ неиз-ве́данный дото́ле *(1)* экста́з / *(2)* восто́рг ♦ **incredible** ~ невероя́тный экста́з ♦ **intoxi-cating** ~ упои́тельный экста́з, пьяня́щий восто́рг ♦ **mindless** ~ безу́мный экста́з ♦ **new-found** ~ но́вый экста́з ♦ **orgiastic** ~ разну́зданный экста́з ♦ **rapturous** ~ упои́-тельный экста́з ♦ **shuddering** ~ содрога́ющийся экста́з, дрожа́щий (-ая, -ее, -ие) в экста́зе ♦ **swirling** ~ вихрь экста́за ♦ **total** ~ по́лный экста́з ♦ **true** ~ и́стинный восто́рг ♦ **boundless waves of** ~ безбре́жные во́лны экста́за ♦ **experience** ~ испы́тывать / испы-та́ть экста́з ♦ **feasts of** ~ пиры́ экста́за ♦ **fiery plumes of** ~ о́гненные стру́и экста́за ♦ **moans of** ~ сто́ны экста́за ♦ **shiver of** ~ тре́пет экста́за ♦ **waves of** ~ во́лны экста́за ♦ **wings of** ~ кры́лья экста́за.

---

ecstasy: I'll give you ecstasy

I'm going to create a million little delicious pleasures all over your body that are going to course into one tremendous explosion of ecstasy. Я созда́м миллио́н ма́леньких восхити́тельных наслажде́ний по всему́ твоему́ те́лу, кото́рые солью́тся в оди́н огро́мный взрыв экста́за. ♦ **I want to cause you nothing but ecstasy.** Я не хочу́ доста́-вить тебе́ ничего́ кро́ме экста́за. ♦ **I'm going to drench you in ecstasy.** Я собира́юсь утопи́ть тебя́ в экста́зе. ♦ **I'm going to drive you crazy with ecstasy.** Я доведу́ тебя́ до безу́много экста́за. ♦ **I'm going to give you a cornucopia of ecstasy.** Я дам тебе́ рог, по́лный экста́за. ♦ **You're going to swirl in a kaleidoscope of ecstasy.** Ты закру́жишься в калейдоско́пе экста́за. ♦ **I'm going to awaken feelings of ecstasy in you such as you have never imagined possible.** Я разбужу́ в тебе́ тако́й экста́з, како́й ты никогда́ не могла́ себе́ предста́вить. ♦ **I want to fill your body with so much pleasure that you will be** *(1)* **hurled /** *(2)* **flung /** *(3)* **rocketed into a cosmos of exploding ecstasy.** Я хочу́ запо́л-нить твоё те́ло таки́м огро́мным наслажде́нием, чтобы ты была́ *(1,2)* бро́шена / *(3)* запу́щена в ко́смос взрыва́ющегося экста́за. ♦ **I want to fill your life with endless ecstasy.** Я хочу́ напо́лнить твою́ жизнь бесконе́чным экста́зом. ♦ **I want to give you more ecstasy than you've ever** *(1)* **... dreamed of. /** *(2)* **... imagined possible.** Я хочу́ дать тебе́ бо́льше экста́за, чем ты когда́-ли́бо *(1)* ... мечта́ла. / *(2)* ...представля́ла возмо́ж-ным. ♦ **Upward and upward and upward I want** *(1)* **...to propel /** *(2)* **send you into ecstasy. /** *(3)* **...you to soar into ecstasy.** Я хочу́ *(1,2)* ...посла́ть тебя́ всё вы́ше, вы́ше и вы́ше к верши́нам экста́за. / *(3)* ..., чтобы ты всё вы́ше, вы́ше и вы́ше пари́ла в экста́зе. ♦ **When my lips and tongue revel on your beautiful, luscious body, they will hear your** *(1)* **moans /** *(2)* **screams of ecstasy in South Africa.** Когда́ мои́ гу́бы и язы́к бу́дут упива́ться твои́м прекра́сным, со́чным те́лом, твои́ *(1)* сто́ны / *(2)* кри́ки экста́за бу́дут слышны́ в Ю́жной А́фрике. ♦ **My greatest aspiration in life is to fill your body with** *(1)* **indescribable /** *(2)* **infinite ecstasy.** Стремле́ние всей мое́й жи́зни -- напо́лнить твоё те́ло *(1)* неопису́емым / *(2)* бесконе́чным экста́зом. ♦ **I'm going to teach you a new definition of ecstasy.** Я научу́ тебя́ но́вому определе́нию экста́за. ♦ **Your body is going to learn a new definition of the word ecstasy.** Твоё те́ло узна́ет но́вое определе́ние сло́ва экста́з. ♦ **Oh, what consummate ecstasy I will bestow upon you**

Depending on the subject, the possessive pronoun **свой (своя́, своё, свой)** *can be translated* **my, your, his, her, its, our** *or* **their**.

when we swirl into the wild vortex of our passion. О, како́й соверше́нный экста́з я подарю́ тебе́, когда́ мы закру́жимся в бе́шеном водоворо́те стра́сти. ♦ **I promise you hours and hours of incredible ecstasy as my avid lips totally worship your loveliness.** Я обеща́ю тебе́ часы́ и часы́ невероя́тного экста́за в то вре́мя, как мои́ жа́дные гу́бы бу́дут поклоня́ться твое́й красоте́. ♦ **My loving kisses will lead you deliciously along the paths of heavenly pleasure until you reach cosmic ecstasy.** Мои́ лю́бящие поцелу́и поведу́т тебя́ по восхити́тельной тропе́ ра́йского наслажде́ния до косми́ческого экста́за. ♦ **I want to fill the night air with your moans of ecstasy.** Я хочу́ напо́лнить ночно́й во́здух твои́ми сто́нами экста́за. ♦ **I know so many delicious secrets about love — secrets that would make you just dizzy with ecstasy — and they're just going to waste right now.** Я зна́ю так мно́го восхити́тельных секре́тов любви́, секре́тов, кото́рые заста́вят тебя́ испыта́ть головокружи́тельный экста́з, и они́ про́сто ника́к не испо́льзуются сейча́с. ♦ **I'm going to fill you with as much ecstasy as your heart desires and your body can endure.** Я дам тебе́ сто́лько экста́за, ско́лько жа́ждет твоё се́рдце и смо́жет вы́нести твоё те́ло. ♦ **I love to give pleasure and ecstasy.** Я люблю́ дари́ть наслажде́ние и экста́з.

---

ecstasy: *you give me ecstasy*

You transport me into ecstasy. Ты дово́дишь меня́ до экста́за. ♦ **Fire** *(1)* **licks /** *(2)* **sweeps /** *(2)* **pours /** *(2)* **rages through my veins whenever I think of your soft, warm, beautiful, luscious body and the oceans of ecstasy that it contains.** Ого́нь ...*(1)* ли́жет / *(2)* охва́тывает мои́ ве́ны... / ...*(3)* льётся / *(4)* бушу́ет в мои́х ве́нах... вся́кий раз, когда́ я ду́маю о твоём мя́гком, тёплом, прекра́сном, со́чном те́ле и океа́нах экста́за, кото́рые оно́ соде́ржит. ♦ **You fill my life with ecstasy.** Ты наполня́ешь мою́ жизнь экста́зом. ♦ **Holding you in my arms would be** *(1)* **sheer /** *(2)* **pure /** *(3)* **absolute ecstasy.** Держа́ть тебя́ в объя́тиях бы́ло бы *(1)* полне́йшим / *(2)* и́стинным / *(3)* соверше́нным экста́зом. ♦ **The sheer ecstasy I get from being with you is something I can't describe.** Полне́йший экста́з, кото́рый я получа́ю, бу́дучи с тобо́й, невозмо́жно описа́ть. ♦ **I almost went out of my mind with ecstasy.** Я чуть не обезу́мел *(ж: обезу́мела)* от экста́за. ♦ **I almost collapsed from ecstasy.** Я почти́ изнемога́л *(ж: изнемога́ла)* от экста́за. ♦ **The soft, warm magic of your body transports me to a cosmic kaleidoscope of ecstasy.** Мя́гкая, тёплая ма́гия твоего́ те́ла перено́сит меня́ в косми́ческий калейдоско́п экста́за. ♦ **My heart ignites in ecstasy** *(1)* **...every time I get a letter from you. /** *(2)* **...every time I see your (**[3] **beautiful /** [4] **beloved) face. /** *(5)* **...at the mere thought of you.** Моё се́рдце вспы́хивает в экста́зе *(1)* ...ка́ждый раз, когда́ я получа́ю письмо́ от тебя́. / *(2)* ...ка́ждый раз, когда́ я ви́жу твоё (*[3]* прекра́сное / *[4]* люби́мое) лицо́. / *(5)* ...от просто́й мы́сли о тебе́.

---

ecstasy: *your lips, your kisses*

What an ecstasy to kiss you! Что за восто́рг целова́ть тебя́ ! ♦ **When our lips touch even for a brief moment, I am** *(1)* **thrown /** *(2)* **hurled into a vortex of (ineffable) ecstasy.** Когда́ на́ши гу́бы соприкаса́ются да́же на коро́ткое мгнове́ние, я *(1,2)* бро́шен *(ж: бро́шена)* в вихрь (невырази́мого) экста́за. ♦ **When our lips met the first time, I almost** *(1)* **fainted /** *(2)* **swooned from ecstasy.** Когда́ на́ши гу́бы встре́тились впервы́е, я почти́ *(1)* ...потеря́л *(ж: потеря́ла)* созна́ние... / *(2)* ...упа́л *(ж: упа́ла)* в о́бморок... от экста́за. ♦ **The sweet magic of your kisses sends me into endless ecstasy.** Сла́дкая ма́гия твои́х поцелу́ев приво́дит меня́ в несконча́емый восто́рг. ♦ **Kissing you is** *(1)* **sheer / (2) pure / (3) absolute ecstasy.** Целова́ть тебя́- *(1)* ...полне́йший / *(2)* и́стинный / *(3)* соверше́нный экста́з. ♦ **When I think of putting my lips against your lips I almost faint with ecstasy.** Мысль о том, что́бы прижа́ться мои́ми губа́ми к твои́м, приво́дит меня́

Russian adjectives have long and short forms.
Where short forms are given, they are labeled as such.

в состоя́ние полне́йшего экста́за. ♦ **When I look at your full, sensuous lips so promising of soft, sweet ecstasy, I am filled with an** *(1)* **enormous /** *(2)* **overpowering desire to kiss them with wild abandon to the very end of time.** Когда́ я смотрю́ на твои́ по́лные, чу́вственные гу́бы, обеща́ющие не́жный, сла́достный экста́з, меня́ наполня́ет *(1)* огро́мное / *(2)* невыноси́мое жела́ние целова́ть их бесконе́чно, соверше́нно забы́в обо всём. ♦ **The thought of kissing your sweet, beautiful lips makes me dizzy with ecstasy.** Мысль о поцелу́ях твои́х сла́дких, прекра́сных губ приво́дит меня́ в состоя́ние головокружи́тельного экста́за. ♦ **What a divine ecstasy to savor the sweetness of your lips.** Како́й боже́ственный восто́рг вкуша́ть сла́дость твои́х губ. ♦ **When our lips met the first time, I** *(1)* **...almost fainted /** *(2)* **swooned from ecstasy. /** *(3)* **...was overcome by ecstasy.** Когда́ на́ши гу́бы встре́тились впервы́е, я *(1,2)* ...чуть не лиши́лся *(ж: лиши́лась)* чувств от восто́рга. / *(3)* ...был охва́чен *(ж: была́ охва́чена)* экста́зом. ♦ **In the unbounded vistas of my dreams and fantasies I taste the exquisite sweetness of your lips a thousand, ten thousand, a million times, and each time am only impelled by the sheer ecstasy of the kiss to taste them once again.** В безграни́чной верени́це мои́х снов и фанта́зий я вкуша́ю исключи́тельную сла́дость твои́х губ ты́сячу, де́сять ты́сяч, миллио́н раз и ка́ждый раз побуждён и́стинным восто́ргом поцелу́я упива́ться им опя́ть.

---
ecstasy: *it was a lightning bolt of ecstasy*
---

(1) **The other night ... /** *(2)* **Last night... with you was a lightning bolt of ecstasy.** *(1)* Та ночь... / *(2)* Про́шлая ночь... с тобо́й была́ как мо́лния экста́за. ♦ **Our** *(1)* **time /** *(2)* **day / *(3)* evening / *(4)* night / *(5)* weekend together was a lightning bolt of ecstasy.** *(1)* Вре́мя, проведённое с тобо́й, бы́ло... / *(2)* Наш день / *(3)* ве́чер с тобо́й был... / *(4)* На́ша ночь была́... / *(5)* На́ши выходны́е бы́ли... как мо́лния экста́за.

---
ecstasy: *I've never known such*

I've never *(1)* **felt /** *(2)* **experienced /** *(3)* **known such (** *[4]* **...a kaleidoscope of... /** *[5]* **...tremendous...) ecstasy (with anyone).** Я никогда́ (ни с кем) не *(1)* чу́вствовал *(ж: чу́вствовала)* / *(2)* испы́тывал *(ж: испы́тывала)* / *(3)* знал *(ж: зна́ла)* тако́го *([4]* калейдоско́па / *[5]* потряса́ющего) экста́за. ♦ **I can never get over the wonder and ecstasy of your love.** Я никогда́ не переста́ну удивля́ться чу́ду и экста́зу твое́й любви́.

---
ecstasy: *it's you*

You are a(n absolute) treasure chest of ecstasy. Ты драгоце́нный исто́чник экста́за. ♦ **Loving you is one ecstasy after another.** Люби́ть тебя́ -- оди́н взрыв экста́за за други́м. ♦ **I look at you (in this photo) and I can imagine what pure ecstasy it would be to** *(1)* **... kiss you. /** *(2)* **...hold you in my arms. /** *(3)* **...make love with you.** Я смотрю́ на тебя́ (на э́той фотогра́фии) и представля́ю, каки́м и́стинным восто́ргом бы́ло бы *(1)* ...целова́ть тебя́. / *(2)* ...держа́ть тебя́ в объя́тиях. / *(3)* ...занима́ться любо́вью с тобо́й.

---
ecstasy: *together*

Together you and I are going to have feasts of ecstasy. У нас с тобо́й бу́дут пиры́ экста́за. ♦ **Together you and I can experience the ecstasy of unbridled passion.** Вме́сте ты и я смо́жем испыта́ть экста́з необу́зданной стра́сти. ♦ **As our bodies move in unison, we will climb the heavenly sweet path to ecstasy.** В то вре́мя, как на́ши тела́ бу́дут дви́гаться в унисо́н, мы бу́дем взбира́ться по блаже́нно-сла́дкой тропе́ к экста́зу. ♦ **I want (so much) to lose myself in the ecstasy of your embraces.** Я (так) хочу́ потеря́ть себя́ в экста́зе твои́х объя́тий.

---
ecstasy: *the feeling*

It's a feeling that blends ecstasy and *(1)* **wonder /** *(2)* **longing /** *(3)* **torment.** Э́то чу́вство -- смесь экста́за и *(1)* удивле́ния / *(2)* жа́жды / *(3)* му́ки.

> *Russian nouns are either masculine, feminine or neuter.*
> *Adjectives with them will be the same.*

ecstatic *adj* восто́рженный, -ая, -ое, -ые ♦ **I was ecstatic to find your letter in my box.** Я был *(ж: была́)* в восто́рге, когда́ нашёл *(ж: нашла́)* в почто́вом я́щике твоё письмо́.

edifice *n* зда́ние; сооруже́ние ♦ **~ of** *(1)* **my** / *(2)* **your happiness** зда́ние *(1)* моего́ / *(2)* твоего́ сча́стья.

educated *adj* образо́ванный, -ая, -ое, -ые *(short forms:* образо́ван, -а, -о, -ы) ♦ **well ~** хорошо́ образо́ван(ный) ♦ **college ~** получи́вший образова́ние в ко́лледже / университе́те, с вы́сшим образова́нием.

education *n* образова́ние ♦ *(1-3)* **college ~** образова́ние в *(1)* ко́лледже / *(2)* университе́те, *(3)* вы́сшее образова́ние ♦ **higher ~** вы́сшее образова́ние ♦ **high school ~** сре́днее образова́ние ♦ **musical ~** музыка́льное образова́ние ♦ *(1,2)* **university ~** образова́ние в *(1)* университе́те, *(2)* вы́сшее образова́ние ♦ **vocational ~** профессиона́льно-техни́ческое образова́ние ♦ **get** *(1)* **my** / *(2)* **your ~** получи́ть *(1,2)* своё образова́ние ♦ **have an ~** име́ть образова́ние.

effect *n* эффе́кт; влия́ние; де́йствие; возде́йствие ♦ *(1,2)* **devastating ~** *(1)* разруша́ющее / *(2)* губи́тельное де́йствие ♦ *(1,2)* **disastrous ~** *(1)* разруша́ющее / *(2)* губи́тельное де́йствие ♦ **good ~** хоро́шее влия́ние ♦ **great ~** большо́е влия́ние ♦ **instantaneous ~** мгнове́нное де́йствие ♦ **intense ~** интенси́вное де́йствие ♦ **magical ~** маги́ческое де́йствие ♦ **masterful ~** вла́стное влия́ние ♦ **negative ~** отрица́тельное влия́ние ♦ **nice ~** хоро́шее влия́ние ♦ **overwhelming ~** ошеломля́ющий эффе́кт ♦ **positive ~** положи́тельное влия́ние ♦ *(1,2)* **powerful** *(3,4)* **~** *(1)* сильное / *(2)* могу́щественное *(3)* возде́йствие / *(3,4)* влия́ние ♦ **profound ~** глубо́кий эффе́кт ♦ **reverse ~** обра́тное де́йствие ♦ *(1,2)* **ruinous ~** *(1)* разруша́ющее / *(2)* губи́тельное де́йствие ♦ *(1,2)* **tremendous ~** *(1)* огро́мный / *(2)* грома́дный эффе́кт ♦ **create an ~** создава́ть / созда́ть эффе́кт ♦ **have an ~** ока́зывать / оказа́ть де́йствие.

| *effect: phrases* |

You have a very unsettling effect on me. Ты выбива́ешь меня́ из колеи́. ♦ **You have an effect on my heart, mind and psyche that no amount of words, English or Russian, can ever suffice to describe.** У меня́ не хвата́ет слов, англи́йских и ру́сских, что́бы описа́ть возде́йствие, кото́рое ты ока́зываешь на моё се́рдце, мы́сли и ду́шу. ♦ **It is beyond my power to describe to you the tremendous effect that your dear, sweet, loving letter has had upon me.** Я не в состоя́нии описа́ть тебе́ то огро́мное впечатле́ние, кото́рое твоё дорого́е, не́жное, лю́бящее письмо́ произвело́ на меня́. ♦ **I am (totally) amazed at the** *(1)* **profound /** *(2)* **overwhelming /** *(3)* **tremendous effect you have on my heart and mind.** Я (соверше́нно) изумлён *(1)* глубо́ким / *(2)* ошеломля́ющим / *(3)* грома́дным эффе́ктом, кото́рый ты произво́дишь на моё се́рдце и ра́зум. ♦ **Your beauty has a devastating effect on** *(1)* **...my will power. /** *(2)* **...my ability to concentrate.** / *(3)* **...my rational thinking.** Твоя́ красота́ разруша́юще де́йствует на *(1)* ...мою́ во́лю. / *(2)* ...мою́ спосо́бность концентри́роваться. / *(3)* ...моё рациона́льное мышле́ние. ♦ **Your every glance has such a powerful effect on my senses.** Ка́ждый твой взгляд облада́ет таки́м могу́щественным возде́йствием на мои́ чу́вства.

effervescent *adj* кипу́чий, -ая, -ее, -ие, энерги́чный, -ая, -ое, -ые ♦ **You brighten my life with your effervescent personality.** Ты озаря́ешь мою́ жизнь свое́й кипу́чей нату́рой.

effort *n* 1. *(exertion)* уси́лие; 2. *(attempt)* попы́тка ♦ **desperate ~** отча́янное уси́лие ♦ **~ of will** уси́лие во́ли ♦ **emotional ~** душе́вное уси́лие ♦ *(1,2)* **futile ~** *(1)* тще́тное / *(2)* напра́сное уси́лие ♦ **great ~** большо́е уси́лие ♦ **last-ditch ~** после́дняя реши́тельная попы́тка ♦ **special ~** осо́бое уси́лие ♦ **tremendous ~** огро́мное уси́лие ♦ *(1,2)* **vain ~** *(1)* тще́тное / *(2)* напра́сное уси́лие ♦ **be worth the ~** сто́ить уси́лий ♦ **make every ~** приложи́ть все уси́лия ♦ **I'm going to make every (possible) effort to** *(1)* **...be a good**

Russian nouns are either masculine, feminine or neuter.
Adjectives with them will be the same.

husband / *(2)* **wife to you.** / *(3)* **...bring you happiness.** / *(4)* **...prove my love for you.** Я приложу́ все (возмо́жные) уси́лия, что́бы *(1)* ...быть хоро́шим му́жем. / *(2)* ...быть хоро́шей жено́й. / *(3)* ...принести́ тебе́ сча́стье. / *(4)* ...доказа́ть свою́ любо́вь к тебе́.

effusive *adj* экспанси́вный, -ая, -ое, -ые.

effusively *adv* экспанси́вно.

egalitarian *n* уравни́тельный, -ая, -ое, -ые, эгалита́рный, - ая, -ое, -ые.

egg *n*: ♦ **all-around good** ~ о́чень сла́вный па́рень.

egg on *vt* подстрека́ть / подстрекну́ть *(whom = acc.)*.

eggshells *n, pl* яи́чная скорлупа́ ♦ **With you, I always have the feeling that I'm walking on eggshells.** С тобо́й я всегда́ чу́вствую себя́ так, как бу́дто иду́ по то́нкому льду.

ego *n* 1. *(self)* э́го, я (сам), ли́чность *f*; 2. *(self-esteem)* самолю́бие; 3. *(conceit)* самомне́ние ♦ **big** ~ большо́е самомне́ние ♦ **her** ~ её «я» ♦ **his** ~ его́ «я» ♦ **inflated** ~ разду́тое самомне́ние ♦ **male** ~ мужско́е самолю́бие ♦ **my** ~ моё «я» ♦ **secure** ~ уве́ренное э́го ♦ **your** ~ твоё «я». ♦ **You just need** *(1)* **someone** / *(2)* **me to** *(3)* **...give your ego a boost.** / *(4)* **...pump up** / *(5)* **boost your ego.** *(1)* Тебе́ про́сто ну́жен челове́к... / *(2)* Я тебе́ про́сто ну́жен *(ж: нужна́)...* что́бы *(3)* ...поддержа́ть своё «я». / *(4)* ...нака́чивать / *(5)* подня́ть своё «я». ♦ **You really have a big ego.** Ты действи́тельно о́чень эгоисти́чна *(ж: эгоисти́чен).* ♦ **All I've ever been to you is just** *(1)* **...an ego trip.** / *(2)* **...a boost to your ego.** Я всегда́ был ну́жен *(ж: была́ нужна́)* тебе́ то́лько для *(1)* ...утвержде́ния своего́ «я». / *(2)* ...как подде́ржка твоего́ «я».

egotistical *adj* самовлюблённый, -ая, -ое, -ые, эгоисти́ческий, -ая, -ое, -ие.

elated *adj* в восто́рге, лику́ющий, -ая, -ее, -ие.

elation *n* восто́рг, бу́рная ра́дость; ликова́ние. ♦ **Knowing that you love me as much as I love you fills my heart with indescribable elation.** Уве́ренность, что ты лю́бишь меня́ так же си́льно, как я люблю́ тебя́, наполня́ет моё се́рдце невероя́тным ликова́нием.

elbow *n* ло́коть *m (pl:* ло́кти*)* ♦ **little** ~ локото́к.

electric *adj* электри́ческий, -ая, -ое, -ие; *(fig.)* удиви́тельный, -ая, -ое, -ые, волну́ющий, -ая, -ее, -ие ♦ **I crave the electric magic of your** *(1)* **touch** / *(2)* **tongue** / *(3)* **lips** / *(4)* **kisses.** Я жа́жду удиви́тельного волшебства́ *(1)* ...твоего́ прикоснове́ния. / *(2)* языка́ / *(3)* ...твои́х губ. / *(4)* поцелу́ев. ♦ **Your** *(1)* **...touch is...** / *(2)* **...kisses are... absolutely electric.** Твои́ *(1)* прикоснове́ния / *(2)* поцелу́и как разря́д электри́чества. ♦ **You have the most electric** *(1)* **touch** / *(2)* **kisses** / *(3)* **tongue I've ever felt** / **experienced.** Твои́ *(1)* прикос-нове́ния / *(2)* поцелу́и,.. / *(3)* Твой язы́к,.. -- сильне́йший электри́ческий заря́д. ♦ **Your fingers on mine were like an electric shock.** Твои́ па́льцы на мои́х бы́ли как электри́ческий шок.

electricity *n* электри́чество; *(fig.)* си́ла, эне́ргия ♦ **Your kisses have such** *(1)* **exquisite** / *(2)* **heavenly** / *(3)* **wonderful electricity in them.** В твои́х поцелу́ях така́я *(1)* исключи́тель-ная / *(2)* боже́ственная / *(3)* удиви́тельная си́ла. ♦ **I long for the magic electricity of your** *(1)* **lips** / *(2)* **kisses** / *(3)* **touch.** Я жа́жду маги́ческой си́лы *(1)* ...твои́х губ / *(2)* поцелу́ев. / *(3)* ...твоего́ прикоснове́ния. ♦ **There is such electricity in your** *(1)* **kisses** / *(2)* **lips** / *(3)* **touch.** *(1)* В тво́их поцелу́ях / *(2)* губа́х... / *(3)* В твоём прикоснове́нии... така́я си́ла. ♦ **There's so much electricity between us (everytime we're together).** (Ка́ждый раз, когда́ мы вме́сте,) ме́жду на́ми тако́е огро́мное притяже́ние. ♦ **I felt electricity jump between us (when** *[1]* **...we kissed** / *[2]* **...you looked at me).** Я чу́вствовал *(ж: чу́вствовала),* как электри́ческий разря́д проска́кивал ме́жду на́ми (, когда́ *[1]* ...мы целова́лись. / *[2]* ...ты смотре́ла *(ж: смотре́л)* на меня́).

electrify *vt (excite)* возбужда́ть / возбуди́ть *(what, whom = acc.)*, электризова́ть *(what = acc.)* ♦ **You** *(1,2)* **electrify my senses (whenever you** *[3]* **...touch me.** / *[4]* **...look at me.)**

Learn more about Russian customs in Appendix 15, page 782.

Ты *(1)* возбужда́ешь / *(2)* электризу́ешь мои́ чу́вства (, когда́ бы ни *[3]* ...коснýлась *(ж: коснýлся)* меня́. / *[4]* ...взгляну́ла *(ж: взгляну́л)* на меня́.).

elegance *n* элега́нтность *f* ♦ **enchanting** ~ очарова́тельная элега́нтность. ♦ **I stand in awe of your sartorial elegance.** Я испы́тываю благогове́ние пе́ред твои́м уме́нием одева́ться. ♦ **Such sartorial elegance!** Кака́я элега́нтность! ♦ **You have such elegance of movement.** В твои́х движе́ниях така́я элега́нтность.

elegant *adj* элега́нтный, -ая, -ое, -ые ♦ **You look absolutely elegant in that** *(1)* **dress** / *(2)* **outfit.** Ты вы́глядишь о́чень элега́нтной в э́том *(1)* пла́тье / *(2)* костю́ме. ♦ **You move (around) in such an elegant way.** Твои́ движе́ния так элега́нтны. ♦ **How elegant you look!** Как элега́нтно ты вы́глядишь!

elegantly *adv* элега́нтно ♦ **You move around so elegantly.** Ты дви́гаешься так элега́нтно.

elemental *adj* приро́дный, -ая, -ое, -ые.

elixir *n* эликси́р ♦ ~ **of life** эликси́р жи́зни ♦ **Your beauty and charm are an elixir to my soul.** Твоя́ красота́ и обая́ние -- эликси́р мое́й души́. ♦ **I want to spend a lifetime quaffing the elixir of your love.** Я хочу́ провести́ жизнь, упива́ясь эликси́ром твое́й любви́. ♦ **Reading one of your letters is like quaffing a magic elixir — it just makes me feel totally good through and through.** Чте́ние ка́ждого из твои́х пи́сем, как большо́й глото́к маги́ческого эликси́ра, -- оно́ наполня́ет меня́ замеча́тельным чу́вством.

elope *vi* та́йно сбежа́ть (с возлю́бленной *f* / возлю́бленным *m*) *(с це́лью жени́тьбы)* ♦ **Let's elope.** Дава́й сбежи́м.

elopement *n* побе́г (с возлю́бленной *f* / возлю́бленным *m*) *(с це́лью жени́тьбы)*.

else *adj*: ♦ **I think you have someone else.** Я ду́маю, у тебя́ есть кто́-то ещё. ♦ **Is there someone else?** Есть ли у тебя́ кто́-то ещё? ♦ **There's no one else (, I swear).** Нет никого́ друго́го (, я кляну́сь). ♦ **What else?** Что ещё? ♦ **Who else will be there?** Кто ещё бу́дет там?

elude *vt* избега́ть / избежа́ть *(what, whom = acc.)*, уклоня́ться / уклони́ться *(what, whom = + от + gen.)*; ускольза́ть / ускользну́ть *(what, whom = + от + gen.)* ♦ *(1)* **You're eluding...** / *(2)* **Don't try to elude...** *(3)* **...the question.** / *(4)* **...your responsibility.** / *(5)* **...reality.** *(1)* Ты ускольза́ешь... / *(2)* Не пыта́йся ускользну́ть... *(3)* ...от отве́та. / *(4)* ...от свое́й отве́тственности. / *(5)* ...от реа́льности.

e-mail *vt* посыла́ть / посла́ть электро́нное письмо́ *(whom = dat.)* ♦ **You can e-mail me at this address....** Ты мо́жешь посла́ть мне электро́нное письмо́ по э́тому а́дресу...

e-mail *n (system)* электро́нная по́чта; *(multiple messages)* электро́нные пи́сьма; *(one message)* электро́нное письмо́ ♦ **Your e-mail is so** *(1,2)* **uplifting for me.** Твои́ электро́нные пи́сьма так поднима́ют *(1)* ...мой дух. / *(2)* ...моё настрое́ние. ♦ **There are so many things I want to say to you that I feel too inhibited to say to you in e-mail.** Существу́ет так мно́го слов, кото́рые я хочу́ сказа́ть тебе́, но сли́шком стесня́юсь написа́ть в электро́нном письме́.

emanate *vi* исходи́ть *(from what = + из + gen.)*.

embarrass *vt* смуща́ть / смути́ть *(whom = acc.)*, приводи́ть / привести́ в замеша́тельство *(whom = acc.)*.

embarrassed *adj* смущён, смущена́, -о́, -ы́ *(short forms)* ♦ *(1,3)* **be** / *(2,4)* **get** ~ *(1,2)* смуща́ться / смути́ться, *(3,4)* стесня́ться / постесня́ться ♦ **I'm** (*[1]* **really** / *[2]* **so** / *[3]* **very** / *[4]* **terribly) embarrassed.** Я (*[1]* действи́тельно / *[2]* так / *[3]* о́чень / *[4]* ужа́сно) смущён *(ж: смущена́)*. ♦ **I was** (*[1]* **really** / *[2]* **so** / *[3]* **very** / *[4]* **terribly) embarrassed.** Я был *(ж: была́)* (*[1]* действи́тельно / *[2]* так / *[3]* о́чень / *[4]* ужа́сно) смущён *(ж: смущена́)*. ♦ **There's nothing to be embarrassed about.** Нет причи́ны для смуще́ния. ♦ **What's there to be embarrassed about?** Что в э́том тако́го, чего́ на́до стесня́ться?

A slash always denotes "or."
You can choose the numbered words before and after.

embarrassing *adj* смуща́ющий, -ая, -ее, -ие, стесни́тельный, -ая, -ое, -ые; затрудни́тель-ный, -ая, -ое, -ые, нело́вкий, -ая, -ое, -ие ♦ *(1,2)* ~ **situation** *(1)* затрудни́тельное / *(2)* нело́вкое положе́ние.

emboldened *adj* осмеле́вший, -ая, -ее, -ие.

embrace *vt* обнима́ть / обня́ть *(whom= acc.)* ♦ **I believe in embracing life.** Я хочу́ испыта́ть в жи́зни мно́гое. ♦ **It is perhaps pure folly to embrace such hopes, but my heart will not allow me to do otherwise.** Это, возмо́жно, чисте́йшее безрассу́дство леле́ять таки́е наде́жды, но моё се́рдце не позволя́ет мне ина́че.

embrace *n* объя́тие ♦ **dizzying** ~ умопомрачи́тельное объя́тие ♦ **enthusiastic** ~ восто́р-женное объя́тие ♦ **heated** ~ жа́ркое объя́тие ♦ **intoxicating** ~ умопомрачи́тельное объя́тие ♦ **passionate** ~ стра́стное объя́тие ♦ **possessive** ~ со́бственническое объя́тие ♦ **soft** ~ не́жное объя́тие ♦ **sweet** ~ сла́дкое объя́тие ♦ **tender** ~ не́жное объя́тие ♦ **tight** ~ кре́пкое объя́тие ♦ **warm** ~ тёплое объя́тие.

embrace: phrases

I love the way you reciprocate my embraces. Мне нра́вится то, как ты отвеча́ешь на мои́ объя́тия. ♦ **I want (so much) to lose myself in** *(1)* **...your embraces.** / *(2)* **...the ecstasy of your embraces.** Я (так) хочу́ потеря́ть себя́ в *(1)* ...твои́х объя́тиях. / *(2)* ...экста́зе твои́х объя́тий. ♦ **My heart yearns to show you my love in an endless stream of warm embraces and soft,** *(1)* **adoring /** *(2)* **loving kisses.** Моё се́рдце жа́ждет показа́ть тебе́ любо́вь в бесконе́чном пото́ке тёплых объя́тий и мя́гких, *(1)* обожа́ющих / *(2)* лю́бящих поцелу́ев.

embroiled *adj* запу́танный, -ая, -ое, -ые *(short forms:* запу́тан, -а, -о, -ы), впу́танный, -ая, -ое, -ые *(short forms:* впу́тан, -а, -о, -ы) ♦ **become** ~ связа́ться *(with whom = +* с *+ instr.)*, спу́таться *(with whom = +* с *+ instr.)* ♦ **I became** *(1,2)* **embroiled with** *(3)* **...the wrong person. /** *(4)* **...someone I didn't really care for.** Я *(1)* связа́лся *(ж: связа́лась)* / *(2)* спу́тался *(ж: спу́талась)* *(3)* ...не с тем челове́ком. / *(4)* ...с той *(ж: тем)*, кто мне реа́льно не был ну́жен.

emerald *adj* изумру́дный, -ая, -ое, -ые.

emerald *n* изумру́д.

emit *vt* испуска́ть / испусти́ть *(what = acc.)*; издава́ть / изда́ть *(what = acc.)* ♦ ~ **a sigh** испуска́ть / испусти́ть вздох.

emotion *n* эмо́ция, чу́вство ♦ **amorous** ~s чу́вства любви́ ♦ **beautiful** ~s прекра́сные чу́вства ♦ **conflicting** *(1,2)* ~s противоречи́вые *(1)* чу́вства / *(2)* эмо́ции ♦ **deep** ~ глубо́кие чу́вства ♦ **mixed** *(1,2)* ~s сме́шанные *(1)* чу́вства / *(2)* эмо́ции ♦ **positive** ~ положи́тельные эмо́ции ♦ **spontaneous** ~s стихи́йные эмо́ции ♦ **strange** *(1,2)* ~s стра́нные *(1)* чу́вства / *(2)* эмо́ции ♦ **sweet** ~s не́жные эмо́ции ♦ **tempestuous** *(1,2)* ~s бу́рные *(1)* чу́вства / *(2)* эмо́ции.

emotion: verb terms

arouse *(1,2)* ~s пробужда́ть / пробуди́ть *(1)* чу́вства / *(2)* эмо́ции ♦ **express** *(1,2)* ~s выража́ть / вы́разить *(1)* чу́вства / *(2)* эмо́ции ♦ **fill with deep** ~ наполня́ть / напо́лнить глубо́кими чу́вствами *(whom = acc.)* ♦ **hide** *(1)* **my /** *(2)* **your** ~s пря́тать *(1)* мои́ / *(2)* твои́ эмо́ции ♦ **take hold of one's** *(1,2)* ~s сде́рживать / сдержа́ть *(свои́)* *(1)* чу́вства / *(2)* эмо́ции.

emotion: other terms

eyes full of ~ глаза́, по́лные чувств *(1 term)* ♦ **floodgate of** ~s шлюз эмо́ций ♦ **gamut of** ~s га́мма эмо́ций ♦ **tremor of** ~ эмоциона́льная дрожь, эмоциона́льное потрясе́ние. ♦ **whirlpool of** ~ водоворо́т стра́сти.

Common adult weights are given in Appendix 10, page 777.

emotion: *expressing them*

I'm not very good at hiding my emotions. Я не сли́шком хорошо́ уме́ю скрыва́ть свои́ эмо́ции. ♦ **It's hard for me to express my emotions.** Мне тру́дно вы́разить свои́ чу́вства. ♦ **You shouldn't cloak your emotions (so). You need to open up.** Ты не должна́ *(ж: до́лжен)* (так) скрыва́ть свои́ эмо́ции. Ты должна́ *(ж: до́лжен)* раскры́ться.

emotion: *experiencing them*

I am tossed about in a sea of tempestuous emotions. Я бро́шен *(ж: бро́шена)* в мо́ре бу́рных эмо́ций. ♦ **My heart overflows with *(1,2)* emotion.** Моё се́рдце перепо́лнено *(1)* эмо́циями / *(2)* чу́вствами. ♦ **You arouse such beautiful emotions in me.** Ты пробужда́ешь таки́е прекра́сные чу́вства во мне. ♦ **All my emotions were churning inside me.** Все эмо́ции смеша́лись во мне. ♦ **I have conflicting emotions about *(1)* ...you. / *(2)* ...it. / *(3)* ...that. / *(4)* ...your proposal. / *(5)* ...the idea. / *(6)* ...marriage.** У меня́ противоречи́вые чу́вства по отноше́нию к *(1)* ...тебе́. / *(2,3)* ...э́тому. / *(4)* ...твоему́ предложе́нию. / *(5)* ...иде́е. / *(6)* ...жени́тьбе. ♦ **My emotions *(1)* overwhelmed / *(2)* swamped me so completely that *(3)* ...I was at a loss for words. / *(4)* ...I couldn't say anything. / *(5)* ...I was (utterly) tongue-tied.** Мои́ эмо́ции *(1)* ошеломи́ли / *(2)* затопи́ли меня́ всеце́ло так, что *(3)* ...я потеря́л *(ж: потеря́ла)* дар ре́чи. / *(4)* ...я ничего́ не мог *(ж: могла́)* сказа́ть. / *(5)* ...я был *(ж: была́)* (соверше́нно) безъязы́чным *(ж: безъязы́чной)*. ♦ **I was thrown into a violent whirlpool of emotion.** Я был бро́шен *(ж: была́ бро́шена)* в жу́ткий водоворо́т стра́сти. ♦ **It filled me with deep emotion.** Это напо́лнило меня́ глубо́кими чу́вствами. ♦ **It opened a floodgate of emotions for me.** Это откры́ло шлюз эмо́ций во мне.

emotion: *various aspects*

You play with my emotions. Ты игра́ешь мои́ми чу́вствами. ♦ **My emotions are out of whack.** Мои́ чу́вства не в поря́дке.

emotional *adj* эмоциона́льный, -ая, -ое, -ые ♦ *(1)* **I've been through... / *(2)* There is... / *(3)* There was... so much emotional turmoil.** *(1)* Я прошёл *(ж: прошла́)* че́рез... / *(2)* Есть... / *(3)* Бы́ло... тако́е си́льное эмоциона́льное смяте́ние.

emotionally *adv* эмоциона́льно.

empathic *adj* сочу́вствующий, -ая, -ее, -ие.

empathy *n* сочу́вствие ♦ **loving ~** не́жное сочу́вствие.

employed *adj*: ♦ **I'm happily employed.** У меня́ хоро́шая рабо́та.

emptiness *n* пустота́ ♦ **Until I met you I knew only loneliness and emptiness.** До тех пор, пока́ я не встре́тил *(ж: встре́тила)* тебя́, я знал *(ж: зна́ла)* то́лько одино́чество и пустоту́.

empty *adj* пусто́й, -а́я, -о́е, -ы́е ♦ *(1)* **Since you left... / *(2)* Without you here... I feel so empty inside.** *(1)* С тех пор, как ты ушла́ *(ж: ушёл)*... / *(2)* Без тебя́ здесь... я чу́вствую в душе́ таку́ю пустоту́. ♦ **My life would be (*[1]* absolutely / *[2]* terribly) empty without you (in it).** Моя́ жизнь была́ бы (*[1]* абсолю́тно / *[2]* ужа́сно) пусто́й без тебя́.

encase *vt* обвола́кивать *(what, whom = acc., with what = instr.)*, окружа́ть *(what, whom = acc., with what = instr.)*, оку́тывать *(what, whom = acc., with what = instr.)* ♦ **I wish I could break through the (*[1]* heavy / *[2]* thick) armor that *(3,4)* encases your heart.** Я хоте́л бы проби́ться сквозь (*[1]* кре́пкую / *[2]* про́чную) броню́, кото́рая *(3)* обвола́кивает / *(4)* окружа́ет твоё се́рдце.

encased *adj* упако́ванный, -ая, -ое, -ые *(short forms:* упако́ван, -а, -о, -ы*)* ♦ **You look so *(1)* gorgeous / *(2)* voluptuous / *(3)* svelte encased in *(4)* satin / *(5)* silk.** Ты вы́глядишь так *(1)* ...так великоле́пно / *(2)* роско́шно... / *(3)* ...тако́й стро́йной... упако́ванной в *(4)* а́тлас / *(5)* шёлк.

An italicized ж *in parentheses indicates a woman speaking.*

enchant *vt* очаро́вывать / очарова́ть *(whom = acc.)* ♦ **You (really) enchant me with your wide-eyed innocence.** Ты (действи́тельно) чару́ешь меня́ свое́й наи́вной неви́нностью. ♦ **You enchant me with your** *(1)* **...beautiful smile** / *(2)* **eyes.** / *(3)* **...blithe spirit.** Ты очаро́вываешь меня́ *(1)* ...свое́й прекра́сной улы́бкой. / *(2)* ...свои́ми прекра́сными глаза́ми. / *(3)* ...свои́м весёлым хара́ктером. ♦ **Your beautiful** *(1)* **smile** / *(2)* **eyes enchant(s) me (more than I can tell you).** *(1)* Твоя́ прекра́сная улы́бка очаро́вывает... / *(2)* Твои́ прекра́сные глаза́ очаро́вывают... меня́ (бо́льше, чем я могу́ вы́сказать). ♦ **I have never met any woman in all my life whose beauty enchanted me as yours has.** Я никогда́ в жи́зни не встреча́л же́нщины, красота́ кото́рой очаро́вывала бы меня́ так, как твоя́.

enchanted *adj* очаро́ван, -а, -о, -ы *(short forms)*, зачаро́ван, -а, -о, -ы *(short forms)*, околдо́ван, -а, -о, -ы *(short forms)* ♦ **I am** *(1,4)* **completely** / *(2,5)* **totally** / *(3,6)* **entirely** *(7-9)* **enchanted by your** *(10)* **...([11] incredible** / *[12]* **breath-taking** / *[13]* **shining** / *[14]* **heavenly** / *[15]* **radiant** / *[16]* **exquisite) beauty.** / *(17)* **...manifold charms.** Я *(1-3)* по́лностью / *(4-6)* соверше́нно *(7)* очаро́ван / *(8)* околдо́ван / *(9)* зачаро́ван *(10)* ...твое́й (*[11]* невероя́тной / *[12]* ...остана́вливающей дыха́ние... / *[13]* сия́ющей / *[14]* небе́сной / *[15]* лучи́стой / *[16]* изы́сканной) красото́й. / *(17)* ...твои́ми многочи́сленными пре́лестями.

enchanting *adj* очарова́тельный, -ая, -ое, -ые, обворожи́тельный, -ая, -ое, -ые, упои́тельный, -ая, -ое, -ые. ♦ **You have the most enchanting** *(1)* **eyes** / *(2)* **face** / *(3)* **smile that I've ever seen (in all my life).** У тебя́ *(1)* ...са́мые очарова́тельные глаза́, кото́рые... / *(2)* ...са́мое очарова́тельное лицо́, кото́рое... / *(3)* ...са́мая очарова́тельная улы́бка, кото́рую... я когда́-либо (в жи́зни) ви́дел. ♦ **Dear Maria with the enchanting eyes,** *(beginning of a letter)* Дорога́я Мари́я с плени́тельными глаза́ми, *(нача́ло письма́).* ♦ **You look (*[1]*absolutely** / *[2]* **positively) enchanting.** Ты вы́глядишь (*[1,2]* соверше́нно) очарова́тельно. ♦ **Your enchanting smile never leaves my thoughts.** Твоя́ очарова́тельная улы́бка никогда́ не покида́ет мои́ мы́сли. ♦ **Your smile is so enchanting.** Твоя́ улы́бка так очарова́тельна. ♦ **Your eyes are so enchanting.** Твои́ глаза́ так очарова́тельны.

enchantment *n* очарова́ние ♦ **I want to** *(1)* **loll** / *(2)* **lounge (forever) in the heavenly enchantment of your person.** Я хочу́ *(1)* не́житься / *(2)* не́житься (ве́чно) в твоём боже́ственном очарова́нии. ♦ **I want to** *(1)* **luxuriate** / *(2)* **revel (forever) in the heavenly enchantment of your person.** Я хочу́ *(1)* наслажда́ться / *(2)* упива́ться (ве́чно) твои́м боже́ственным очарова́нием.

enchantress *n* очарова́тельница, чаровни́ца.

encircle *vt* окружа́ть / окружи́ть *(what = acc., with what = instr.)*; охва́тывать / охвати́ть *(what = acc., with what = instr.)*; *(embrace)* обнима́ть / обня́ть *(what = + за + acc., whose = acc.)* ♦ **~ your waist** обнима́ть / обня́ть тебя́ за та́лию.

enclose *vt* *(insert)* вкла́дывать / вложи́ть *(what = acc., in what = + в + acc.)*; *(attach)* прилага́ть / приложи́ть *(what = acc., with / to what = + к + dat.)* ♦ **Oh, what feelings swept over me when your hand enclosed mine.** О, каки́е чу́вства охва́тывали меня́, когда́ моя́ рука́ была́ в твое́й. ♦ **I'm enclosing a** *(1)* **photo** / *(2)* **postcard.** Я вкла́дываю *(1)* фо́то / *(2)* откры́тку.

encompass *vt* охва́тывать / охвати́ть *(what, whom = acc.)*; заключа́ть / заключи́ть *(what, whom = acc.)*; окружа́ть / окружи́ть *(what, whom = acc.)* ♦ **I want to encompass you in my arms.** Я хочу́ заключи́ть тебя́ в объя́тиях.

encounter *n* встре́ча ♦ **amorous** ~s любо́вные встре́чи ♦ **casual** ~ случа́йная встре́ча ♦ **chance** ~ случа́йная встре́ча ♦ **erotic** ~ эроти́ческая встре́ча ♦ **first** ~ пе́рвая встре́ча

Procedures for getting married to a Russian are outlined in Appendix 18, page 787.

♦ **fleeting** ~ мимолётная встре́ча ♦ **intimate** ~ инти́мное свида́ние ♦ **passionate** ~ стра́стная встре́ча ♦ **romantic** ~ романти́ческая встре́ча ♦ **I go away from any encounter with you with my heart spinning wildly and my mind erupting in a fireworks display of love thoughts about you.** По́сле ка́ждой встре́чи с тобо́й я ухожу́ с бе́шено стуча́щим се́рдцем и с це́лым фейерве́рком любо́вных мы́слей о тебе́. ♦ **Believe me, I don't (just) want a casual sexual encounter (with you).** Пове́рь мне, я не хочу́ (про́сто) случа́йной сексуа́льной встре́чи (с тобо́й). ♦ **I don't believe in casual sexual encounters.** Я про́тив случа́йных сексуа́льных встреч.

encourage *vt* поощря́ть *(what, whom = acc.)* ♦ ~ **love** поощря́ть любо́вь.

end *vt* заверша́ть / заверши́ть, прекраща́ть / прекрати́ть, положи́ть коне́ц ♦ **I think we should** *(1,2)* **end our relationship.** Я ду́маю, мы должны́ *(1)* ...прекрати́ть на́ши отноше́ния. / *(2)* ...положи́ть коне́ц на́шим отноше́ниям. ♦ **Do you think we should** *(1,2)* **end our relationship.** Ты ду́маешь, нам сле́дует *(1)* ...прекрати́ть на́ши отношения? / *(2)* ...положи́ть коне́ц на́шим отноше́ниям? ♦ **Do you want to** *(1,2)* **end our relationship?** Ты хо́чешь *(1)* ...прекрати́ть на́ши отноше́ния? / *(2)* ...положи́ть коне́ц на́шим отноше́ниям?

end *vi* зака́нчиваться / зако́нчиться, прекраща́ться / прекрати́ться, конча́ться / ко́нчиться ♦ **Our love will never end.** На́ша любо́вь никогда́ не зако́нчится. ♦ **I don't want these (wonderful) moments (with you) to ever end.** Я не хочу́, что́бы э́ти (замеча́тельные) мину́ты (с тобо́й) когда́-нибудь прекрати́лись.

end *n* коне́ц, оконча́ние, заверше́ние ♦ **emotional dead** ~ эмоциона́льный тупи́к. ♦ **psychological dead** ~ психологи́ческий тупи́к. ♦ **rear** ~ *(slang) (buttocks)* за́дница, по́п(к)а. ♦ **This is leading to a dead end.** Это ведёт в тупи́к. ♦ **I will love you (and cherish you) till the end of time.** Я бу́ду люби́ть тебя́ и леле́ять до конца́ дней.

endear *vt (instill love)* внуши́ть любо́вь *(oneself* = + к себе́, *to whom = dat.);* *(cause to love)* заста́вить полюби́ть *(oneself* = + себя́, *to whom = acc.); (win over)* расположи́ть к себе́ *(to whom = acc.)* ♦ **You have endeared yourself to me** *(1)* **...so much.** / *(2)* **...more than I can ever tell you.** Ты внуши́ла *(ж: внуши́л)* мне *(1)* ...таку́ю большу́ю любо́вь к тебе́. / *(2)* ...любо́вь к тебе́ бо́льшую, чем я смогу́ вы́разить слова́ми.

endearing *adj (inspiring love)* внуша́ющий (-ая, -ее, -ие) любо́вь; *(captivating)* подкупа́ющий, -ая, -ее, -ие.

endearment *n* ла́ска, выраже́ние не́жности ♦ **casual** ~ небре́жное ла́сковое обраще́ние. ♦ *(1-3)* **term of** ~ ла́сковое *(1)* и́мя / *(2)* про́звище / *(3)* обраще́ние.

ending *n* оконча́ние ♦ **nerve** ~ не́рвное оконча́ние.

endless *adj* бесконе́чный, -ая, -ое, -ые.

endlessly *adv* бесконе́чно ♦ **Those beautiful** *(1)* **dark** / *(2)* **green eyes of yours intrigue me endlessly.** Эти твои́ прекра́сные *(1)* тёмные / *(2)* зелёные глаза́ интригу́ют меня́ бесконе́чно. ♦ **I want so much to hold you in my arms and kiss you endlessly.** Я так жа́жду обня́ть тебя́ и целова́ть бесконе́чно.

endowed *adj (given by nature)* наделённый, -ая, -ое, -ые, одарённый, ая, -ое, -ые; *(provided with)* обеспе́ченный, -ая, -ое, -ые ♦ **admirably** ~ превосхо́дно одарённый,-ая, -ые ♦ **anatomically well** ~ анатоми́чески хорошо́ одарённый ♦ **artistically** ~ артисти́чески одарённый, -ая, -ое, -ые ♦ **gluteally** ~ *(having big buttocks)* наделённый (-ая, -ые) большо́й по́пой ♦ **magnificently** ~ великоле́пно одарённый, -ые ♦ **superbly** ~ великоле́пно одарённый, -ые ♦ **well** ~ хорошо́ одарённый, -ые.

endowment *n* дарова́ние ♦ **The copious splendor of your natural endowments** *(1)* **...takes my breath away.** / *(2)* **...captivates all my senses.** Великоле́пие твои́х приро́дных дарова́ний *(1)* ...перехва́тывает моё дыха́ние. / *(2)* ...пленя́ет все мои́ чу́вства.

A list of conjugated Russian verbs is given
in Appendix 3 on page 699.

endurance *n* выно́сливость *f* ♦ **physical** ~ физи́ческая выно́сливость.

endure *vt* выде́рживать / вы́держать *(what, whom = acc.),* терпе́ть / потерпе́ть *(what, whom = acc.),* выноси́ть / вы́нести *(what, whom = acc.)* ♦ **My longing for you is an agony that I can scarcely endure.** Моя́ тоска́ по тебе́ -- э́то му́ка, кото́рую я едва́ выде́рживаю. ♦ **I want you so badly I can hardly endure it.** Я так си́льно хочу́ тебя́, что едва́ могу́ э́то вы́держать. ♦ **My loneliness (without you) is a(n)** *(1)* **agony /** *(2)* **torment /** *(3)* **anguish /** *(4)* **torture that I can** *(5)* **barely /** *(6)* **scarcely endure.** Моё одино́чество (без тебя́) -- э́то *(1,2)* ...муче́ние, кото́рое... / *(3)* ...му́ка / *(4)* пы́тка, кото́рую... я *(5,6)* едва́ выношу́. ♦ **I simply cannot endure being** *(1)* **apart /** *(2)* **away from you.** Я про́сто не могу́ вы́держать *(1,2)* разлу́ки с тобо́й. ♦ **I'm going to fill you with as much ecstasy as your heart desires and your body can endure.** Я дам тебе́ сто́лько экста́за, ско́лько жа́ждет твоё се́рдце и смо́жет вы́нести твоё те́ло.

enduring *adj* про́чный, -ая, -ое, -ые.

energetic *adj* энерги́чный, -ая, -ое, -ые.

energy *n* эне́ргия, си́ла ♦ **high** ~ высо́кая эне́ргия ♦ **positive** ~ положи́тельная эне́ргия ♦ **sexual** ~ сексуа́льная эне́ргия ♦ **One thing I** *(1)* **admire /** *(2)* **like about you is that you're brimming with (positive) energy.** *(1)* Я любу́юсь тем... / *(2)* Мне нра́вится в тебе́ то,... что ты до краёв напо́лнена (положи́тельной) эне́ргией. ♦ **I'm a high energy person.** Я о́чень энерги́чен *(ж: энерги́чна).*

enervate *vt* обесси́ливать / обесси́лить *(what = acc.),* расслабля́ть / рассла́бить *(what = acc.)* ♦ **Not having you** *(1)* **around /** *(2)* **here enervates my spirit terribly.** То, что тебя́ нет *(1)* ря́дом / *(2)* здесь ужа́сно ослабля́ет мой дух.

enervating *adj* обесси́ливающий, -ая, -ее, -ие, расслабля́ющий, -ая, -ее, -ие.

engaged *adj* обручённый, -ая, -ое, -ые *(short forms:* обручён, обручена́, -ы́), помо́лвленный, -ая, -ые ♦ ~ **to be married** быть обручён, обручена́, -ы́ *(short forms)* ♦ **newly** ~ неда́вно обручённый, -ая, -ые ♦ **get** ~ **(to be married)** обруча́ться / обручи́ться *(to whom = + с + instr.).*

engagement *n* обруче́ние, помо́лвка ♦ **When shall we announce our engagement?** Когда́ мы объя́вим о на́шей помо́лвке? ♦ **Let's announce our engagement next Saturday.** Дава́й объя́вим о на́шей помо́лвке в сле́дующую суббо́ту. ♦ *(1)* **What do you want to do,... /** *(2)* **Do you want to...** *(3,4)* **break (off) our engagement?** *(1)* Что ты хо́чешь сде́лать,... / *(2)* Ты хо́чешь... *(3)* порва́ть / *(4)* разорва́ть на́шу помо́лвку? ♦ **I (don't) want to** *(1,2)* **break (off) our engagement.** Я (не) хочу́ *(1)* порва́ть / *(2)* разорва́ть на́шу помо́лвку.

engaging *adj* привлека́тельный, -ая, -ое, -ые, обая́тельный, -ая, -ое, -ые ♦ **You have a very engaging** *(1)* **manner /** *(2)* **personality /** *(3)* **smile.** У тебя́ о́чень *(1)* ...обая́тельные мане́ры. / *(1)* ...обая́тельный хара́ктер. / *(1)* ...обая́тельная улы́бка.

England *n* А́нглия ♦ **from** ~ из А́нглии ♦ **in** ~ в А́нглии ♦ **to** ~ в А́нглию.

English *adj* англи́йский, -ая, -ое, -ие.

English *n (language)* англи́йский язы́к ♦ **speak** ~ говори́ть по-англи́йски ♦ **Do you speak English?** Вы говори́те по-англи́йски? ♦ **I speak only English, but I smile in any language.** Я говорю́ то́лько по-англи́йски, но улыба́юсь на всех языка́х.

Englishman *n* англича́нин *(pl:* англича́не).

Englishwoman *n* англича́нка.

engulf *vt* поглоща́ть / поглоти́ть *(what, whom = acc.)* ♦ ~ **the body** распаля́ть те́ло ♦ **Desire engulfs my body.** Страсть распаля́ет моё те́ло.

engulfed *adj* поглощён, поглощена́, -о́, -ы́ *(short forms)* ♦ **I am engulfed by** *(1)* **...a desperate yearning to** *(2)* **see /** *(3)* **be with /** *(4)* **hold you in my arms. /** *(5)* **...this fire that you**

For Russian adjectives, the masculine form is spelled out, followed by the feminine, neuter and plural endings.

have started racing through my blood. Я поглощён *(1)* ...отчаянным желанием *(2)* ...увидеть тебя. / *(3)* ...быть с тобой. / *(4)* ...обнять тебя. / *(5)* ...огнём, который ты разожгла в моей крови. ♦ **I am** *(1)* **completely /** *(2)* **totally engulfed in the rapture that you create with your** *(3)* **...skillful hands. /** *(4)* **...ardent kisses. /** *(5)* **...roving lips.** Я *(1)* полностью / *(2)* весь *(ж: вся)* поглощён *(ж: поглощена)* упоением, которое ты создаёшь своими *(3)* ...умелыми руками. / *(4)* ...пылкими поцелуями. / *(5)* ...блуждающими губами. ♦ **When I look into the deep blue depths of your eyes, I am engulfed by feelings of love.** Когда я смотрю в тёмно-синюю глубину твоих глаз, я (совершенно) поглощён любовью к тебе. ♦ **I am engulfed in** *(1)* **infinite /** *(2)* **boundless admiration of your** *(3)* **indescribable /** *(4)* **incomparable /** *(5)* **exquisite /** *(6)* **peerless** *(7)* **beauty /** *(8)* **loveliness.** Я поглощён *(1)* бесконечным / *(2)* безграничным восхищением твоей *(3)* неописуемой / *(4)* несравненной / *(5)* изысканной / *(6)* несравненной *(7,8)* красоты.

enhance *vt* улучшать / улучшить *(what = acc.)* ♦ **The dress enhances your natural loveliness.** Платье подчёркивает твою естественную прелесть. ♦ **You enhance my life in every way.** Ты делаешь мою жизнь лучше с каждым днём. ♦ **I'm looking for a partner to enhance my life.** Я ищу спутницу *(ж: спутника)*, с которой *(ж: с которым)* смогу улучшить свою жизнь.

enhancer *n* увеличение ♦ **(silicon-gel) breast ~s** (силиконовое) увеличение грудей.

enigma *n* загадка.

enigmatic *adj* загадочный, -ая, -ое, -ые.

enjoy *vt* наслаждаться *(what = instr.)* ♦ *(1)* **I want to... /** *(2)* **I'm going to... teach you how to enjoy (love).** *(1)* Я хочу научить... / *(2)* Я научу... тебя, как наслаждаться (любовью). ♦ **I (really) enjoy being (together) with you.** Для меня (действительно) наслаждение быть (вместе) с тобой. ♦ **I want someone who knows how to enjoy life.** Я хочу ту *(ж: того)*, кто знает, как наслаждаться жизнью. ♦ **I (really) enjoy cuddling.** Я (действительно) наслаждаюсь объятиями.

enjoyable *adj* приятный, -ая, -ое, -ые, *(Russians also use verb expression* доставлять удовольствие *= afford enjoyment)* ♦ **It would be wonderful to cuddle up with you on the couch and watch a video — until we thought of something else more enjoyable to do.** Было бы так замечательно прижаться друг к другу на диване и смотреть фильм до тех пор, пока мы не подумаем о том, чтобы заняться чём-то ещё более приятным.

enjoyment *n* удовольствие ♦ **You'll be surprised at how many ways I know to prolong your enjoyment.** Ты будешь удивлена тем, как много способов я знаю для продления твоего удовольствия.

enlighten *vt* просвещать / просветить *(what, whom = acc.)*.

enliven *vi* оживлять / оживить *(what = acc.)*.

ennui *n* скука; тоска.

enormous *adj* огромный, -ая, -ое, -ые, громадный, -ая, -ое, -ые.

enormously *adv* чрезвычайно, очень (и очень), крайне.

enough *adj & adv* достаточно *(+ gen.)* ♦ **~ love** достаточно любви ♦ **~ money** достаточно денег ♦ **not ~** недостаточно ♦ **My sloe-eyed siren, I can never get enough of you.** Моя тёмноглазая сирена, я никогда не смогу (вдоволь) тобой насытиться. ♦ **I never get enough of you.** Мне всегда тебя не хватает. ♦ **You're more than enough for me.** Ты более, чем достаточна *(ж: достаточен)* для меня. ♦ **That's enough.** Этого достаточно.

enrapture *vt* восхищать / восхитить *(what, whom = acc.)*, приводить / привести в восторг *(whom = acc.)* ♦ **You have totally enraptured my heart.** Ты совершенно восхитила *(ж:*

See Appendix 19 for notes on sending mail to Russia and Ukraine.

восхити́л) моё се́рдце. ♦ **Your blithe spirit and shining personality enrapture me completely.** Твой весёлый дух и сия́ющая индивидуа́льность невероя́тно восхища́ют меня́. ♦ **Your smile enraptures my soul.** Твоя́ улы́бка восхища́ет меня́.

enraptured *adj* восхищён, восхищена́, -о́, -ы́ *(short forms)* ♦ **My heart is** (*[1]* **completely** / *[2]* **totally) enraptured by your charm and beauty.** Я (*[1,2]* соверше́нно) восхищён твои́м обая́нием и красото́й.

enrich *vt* обогаща́ть *(what = acc.)* ♦ **You enrich my life more and more every day.** Ты всё бо́льше с ка́ждым днём обогаща́ешь мою́ жизнь.

enslave *vt* порабоща́ть / поработи́ть *(what, whom = acc.)*, покоря́ть / покори́ть *(what, whom = acc.)* ♦ **Your many acts of tenderness have enslaved my heart.** Не́жность, кото́рую ты так ще́дро дари́ла *(ж: дари́л)* мне, поработи́ла моё се́рдце. ♦ **My heart is** *(1)* **completely** / *(2)* **irredeemably** / *(3)* **hopelessly enslaved by your** *(4)* **shining** / *(5)* **radiant** / *(6)* **ethereal beauty.** Моё се́рдце *(1)* соверше́нно / *(2)* безвозвра́тно / *(3)* безнадёжно порабощено́ твое́й *(6)* сия́ющей / *(7)* лучи́стой / *(8)* неземно́й красото́й.
♦ **The magic of your beautiful, sensuous body has enslaved my soul.** Волшебство́ твоего́ прекра́сного, чу́вственного те́ла покори́ло мою́ ду́шу.

entangled *adj* запу́тан, -а, -о, -ы *(short forms)* ♦ **get** ~ спу́тываться / спу́таться *(with whom = + c + instr.)* ♦ **It was a mistake to get entangled with** *(1)* **you** / *(2)* **her** / *(3)* **him.** Это бы́ло оши́бкой связа́ться с *(1)* тобо́й / *(2)* ней / *(3)* ним.

entanglement *n* 1. *(involvment)* вовлече́ние; вовлечённость *f*; 2. *(complication)* затрудне́ние ♦ **I've always avoided emotional entanglements.** Я всегда́ избега́л эмоциона́льной вовлечённости.

enter *vt* 1. *(go in)* входи́ть / войти́ *(what = + в + acc.)*; 2. *(penetrate)* вонза́ться / вонзи́ться *(what = + в + acc.)*.

enterprising *adj* предприи́мчивый, -ая, -ое, -ые.

entertain *vt* 1. *(foster)* пита́ть *(what = acc.)*, леле́ять *(what = acc.)*; 2. *(amuse)* развлека́ть *(whom = acc.)*, забавля́ть *(whom = acc.)* ♦ **I entertain no illusions about** *(1)* **...your love** / *(2)* **feelings for me.** / *(3)* **...my chances of winning your heart** / *(4)* **love.** Я не пита́ю никаки́х иллю́зий относи́тельно *(1)* ...твое́й любви́ ко мне. / *(2)* ...твои́х чувств ко мне. / *(3)* ...моего́ ша́нса победи́ть твоё се́рдце. / *(4)* ...моего́ ша́нса завоева́ть твою́ любо́вь.

enthrall *vt* увлека́ть / увле́чь *(whom = acc.)*, очаро́вывать / очарова́ть *(whom = acc.)* ♦ **The sweet magic of your kisses enthralls me.** Сла́дкая ма́гия твои́х поцелу́ев очаро́вывает меня́. ♦ **You have not the smallest idea how totally you have bewitched me and enthralled me with your incomparable, indescribable beauty.** Ты не име́ешь да́же мале́йшего представле́ния, как ты соверше́нно околдова́ла меня́ и увлекла́ меня́ свое́й несравне́нной, невероя́тной красото́й. ♦ **I have never met any woman in all my life whose beauty enthralled me as yours has.** Я никогда́ в мое́й жи́зни не встреча́л же́нщины, красота́ кото́рой увлека́ла бы меня́, как твоя́.

enthralled *adj* очаро́ван, -а, -о, -ы, увлечён, увлечена́, -о́, -ы́, порабощён, порабощена́, -о́, -ы́ *(short forms)* ♦ **I am** (*[1]* **completely** / *[2]* **totally) enthralled by** *(3)* **...your manifold charms.** / *(4)* **...the sensual richness in your lips.** Я (*[1]* по́лностью / *[2]* соверше́нно) очаро́ван *(3)* ...твои́ми многочи́сленными пре́лестями. /*(4)* ...чу́вственностью твои́х губ. ♦ **I was so enthralled at** *(1)* **seeing** / *(2)* **meeting you yesterday that I feel compelled to write this short note to you to tell you how (very) much it meant to me.** Я был так очаро́ван, *(1)* уви́дев / *(2)* встре́тив тебя́ вчера́, что я чу́вствую непреодоли́мую потре́бность написа́ть э́ту коро́ткую запи́ску, что́бы сказа́ть тебе́, как (о́чень) мно́го э́то зна́чит для меня́. ♦ **When I first saw your** *(1,2)* **piquant smile, I was utterly**

When terms are listed after a main word, a tilde ~
is used to indicate the main word.

enthralled. Когда́ я впервы́е уви́дел твою́ *(1)* игри́вую / *(2)* соблазни́тельную улы́бку, я был соверше́нно очаро́ван.

enthralling *adj* увлека́тельный, -ая, -ое, -ые.

enthusiasm *n* энтузиа́зм; восто́рг ♦ **boundless** ~ безграни́чный энтузиа́зм ♦ **boyish** ~ мальчи́шеский энтузиа́зм ♦ **girlish** ~ де́вичий энтузиа́зм ♦ **great** ~ большо́й энтузиа́зм ♦ **show** ~ проявля́ть / прояви́ть энтузиа́зм ♦ **Nothing fires my enthusiasm as much as the** *(1)* **prospect /** *(2)* **thought of** *(3)* **...being with you. /** *(4)* **...seeing /** *(5)* **meeting you.** Ничто́ не зажига́ет мой энтузиа́зм так си́льно, как *(1)* перспекти́ва / *(2)* мысль *(3)* ...быть с тобо́й. / *(4)* ...уви́деть / *(5)* встре́тить тебя́.

enthusiastic *adj* восто́рженный, -ая, -ое, -ые; по́лный (-ая, -ое, -ые) энтузиа́зма ♦ ~ **for life** по́лный (-ая, -ое, -ые) жи́зненного энтузиа́зма.

enthusiastically *adv* восто́рженно, с восто́ргом; с энтузиа́змом.

entice *vt* перема́нивать / перемани́ть *(whom = acc.)*, зама́нивать / замани́ть *(whom = acc.)*, соблазня́ть / соблазни́ть *(whom = acc.)* ♦ **Could I possibly entice you to** *(1)* **...go on vacation to Hawaii with me? /** *(2)* **...go there with me? /** *(3)* **...spend a couple of weeks here with me? /** *(4)* **...go to dinner with me?** Могу́ ли я соблазни́ть тебя́ *(1)* ...пое́хать на о́тдых на Гава́йи со мной? / *(2)* ...пойти́ туда́ со мной? / *(3)* ...провести́ па́ру неде́ль здесь со мной? / *(4)* ...пойти́ на обе́д со мной? ♦ **Oh, how I wish I could entice you to** *(1)* **...come over here and live with me. /** *(2)* **...go on vacation with me.** О, как бы я жела́л соблазни́ть тебя́ *(1)* ...прие́хать сюда́ и жить со мной. / *(2)* ...пое́хать в о́тпуск со мной.

enticement *n* зама́нивание ♦ **That's an enticement I can't refuse.** Тако́му собла́зну я не могу́ сопротивля́ться.

enticing *adj* зама́нчивый, -ая, -ое, -ые, соблазни́тельный, -ая, -ое, -ые.

enticingly *adv* соблазни́тельно ♦ **I watch your mouth forming sounds, moving and undulating so supplely, so softly, so enticingly and I am seized with a raging impulse to fuse my own mouth together with it and once and for all revel in its sweet softness.** Я слежу́, как твой рот создаёт зву́ки, дви́гаясь и изгиба́ясь так ги́бко, так мя́гко, так соблазни́тельно, и я захва́чен бе́шеным и́мпульсом соедини́ть мой рот с твои́м, что́бы раз и навсегда́ пирова́ть в его́ сла́дкой не́жности.

entirety *n* полнота́, це́льность *f.*

entrance *n* вход ♦ **secret** ~ запре́тный вход ♦ **I'll wait for you by the entrance.** Я бу́ду ждать тебя́ у вхо́да.

entranced *adj* очаро́ван, -а, -о, -ы, заворожён, -а́, -о́, -ы́ *(short forms)* ♦ **I am** *(1)* **completely /** *(2)* **thoroughly** *(3,4)* **entranced by your** *(5)* **...(dark exotic) beauty /** *(6)* **loveliness. /** *(7)* **...delicious sensuality.** Я *(1, 2)* соверше́нно *(3)* заворожён / *(4)* очаро́ван твое́й *(5,6)* ...(сму́глой, экзоти́ческой) красото́й. / *(7)* ...восхити́тельной чу́вственностью. ♦ **When I first saw your** *(1, 2)* **piquant smile, I was utterly entranced.** Когда́ я впервы́е уви́дел твою́ *(1)* игри́вую / *(2)* соблазни́тельную улы́бку, я был соверше́нно очаро́ван.

entrancing *adj* очарова́тельный, -ая, -ое, -ые.

entreat *vt* умоля́ть *(whom = acc.)* ♦ **I fervently entreat you to** *(1)* **give /** *(2)* **grant me the opportunity to** *(3)* **...know you better. /** *(4)* **...get better acquainted with you. /** *(5)* **...speak with you. /** *(6)* **...see your beautiful face once again. /** *(7)* **...meet with you.** Я горячо́ умоля́ю Вас *(1)* дать / *(2)* предоста́вить мне возмо́жность *(3)* ...лу́чше узна́ть Вас. / *(4)* ...бли́же познако́миться с Ва́ми. / *(5)* ...поговори́ть с Ва́ми. / *(6)* ...уви́деть Ва́ше прекра́сное лицо́ ещё раз. / *(7)* ...встре́титься с Ва́ми.

entrepreneur *n* антрепренёр.

A list of abbreviations used in the dictionary is given on page 10.

entwine *vi* обвиваться / обвиться, вплетаться / вплестись, сплетаться / сплестись ♦ **Our hearts have entwined never(more) to part.** Наши сердца сплелись, чтобы никогда (более) не разделиться. ♦ **When we lie side by side and our legs entwine, it never fails to rouse desire in me.** Когда мы лежим рядом и наши ноги сплетены, это всегда пробуждает страсть во мне.

entwined *adj* сплетённый, -ая, -ое, -ые *(short forms:* сплетён, сплетена, -о, -ы*)* ♦ **We'll lie under some big, shady tree, fingers entwined, legs entwined, lips entwined, savoring each other's soul.** Мы будем лежать под большим тенистым деревом, пальцы сплетены, ноги сплетены, губы сплетены, вкушая души друг друга.

envelop *vt* окутывать / окутать *(what, whom = acc., with what = instr.)*, обволакивать *(what, whom = acc., with what = instr.)*, охватывать / охватить *(what, whom = acc., with what = instr.)*, окружать / окружить *(what, whom = acc., with what = instr.)* ♦ **You are so innocently unaware of the haze of beauty that constantly envelops you.** Ты так невинно не подозреваешь о дымке красоты, постоянно обволакивающей тебя. ♦ **The wildest thrill enveloped me (when [1] ...I kissed you. / [2] ...you kissed / [3] touched me.)** Самое дикое возбуждение охватило меня (, когда *[1]* ...я целовал *[ж: целовала]* тебя. / *[2]* ...ты целовала *[ж: целовал]* меня. / *[3]* ...ты касалась *[ж: касался]* меня. ♦ **I want to envelop you with (*[1]* endless / *[2]* infinite / *[3]* ever-lasting / *[4]* boundless) (5) bliss / (6) happiness.** Я хочу окутать тебя (*[1,2]* бесконечным / *[3]* нескончаемым / *[4]* безграничным) *(5)* блаженством / *(6)* счастьем. ♦ **I wish I could break through the (*[1]* heavy / *[2]* thick) armor that (3,4) envelops your heart.** Я хотел *(ж: хотела)* бы пробиться сквозь (*[1]* крепкую / *[2]* прочную) броню, которая *(3)* обволакивает / *(4)* окружает твоё сердце.

enviable *adj* завидный, -ая, -ое, -ые.

envious *adj* завистливый, -ая, -ое, -ые.

enviro *abbrev* = **environmental** относящийся (-аяся, -ееся, -иеся) к окружающей среде.

envision *vt* 1. *(imagine)* воображать / вообразить, представлять / представить; 2. *(foresee)* предвидеть, предусматривать / предусмотреть.

envy *vt* завидовать / позавидовать *(what, whom = dat.)* ♦ **I envy your brassiere. It gets to hold your beautiful breasts all day. I wish I could do the same.** Я завидую твоему бюстгальтеру. Он поддерживает твою прекрасную грудь целый день. Я желал бы делать то же самое. ♦ **I envy your stockings. They're wrapped around your legs all day. How I wish I could do the same.** Я завидую твоим чулкам. Они обёртывают твои ноги весь день. Как бы я желал делать то же самое.

envy *n* зависть *f* ♦ **arouse** ~ пробуждать / пробудить зависть.

epicenter *n* эпицентр.

epistle *n (letter)* письмо.

epistolary *adj (in or by letters)* письменный, -ая, -ое, -ые.

epitome *n* воплощение ♦ **You are the epitome of *(1)* beauty / *(2)* loveliness.** Ты воплощение *(1,2)* красоты.

epitomize *vt (embody)* воплощать / воплотить *(what = acc.)*, олицетворять / олицетворить *(what = acc.)*; *(represent)* представлять / представить *(what = acc.)*.

equality *n* равенство.

erect *adj (penis)* отвердевший, -ая, -ее, -ие ♦ **become / get** ~ отвердевать / отвердеть.

erotic *adj* эротический, -ая, -ое, -ие ♦ **I hope you won't be mad at me when I tell you that I no longer have any thoughts about you that are not erotic.** Я надеюсь, что ты не рассердишься на меня, когда я скажу, что у меня не осталось никаких других мыслей о тебе, кроме эротических.

The accents on Russian words are to show how to pronounce them. You don't have to copy the accents when writing to someone.

erotica *n* эро́тика ♦ **I'm hoping you have a penchant for erotica, the same as I.** Я наде́юсь, что у тебя́, так же как и у меня́, есть скло́нность к эро́тике.

erratic *adj* взба́лмошный, -ая, -ое, -ые ♦ ~ **person** взба́лмошный челове́к.

erroneous *adj* оши́бочный, -ая, -ое, -ые.

erudite *adj* эруди́рованный, -ая, -ое, -ые; *(learned)* учёный, -ая, -ое, -ые.

erupt *vi* изверга́ться ♦ **I go away from any encounter with you with my heart spinning wildly and my mind erupting in a fireworks display of love thoughts about you.** По́сле ка́ждой встре́чи с тобо́й я ухожу́ с бе́шено стуча́щим се́рдцем и с це́лым фейер-ве́рком любо́вных мы́слей о тебе́.

eruption *n* изверже́ние ♦ **I'm like a volcano on the verge of a full-scale eruption.** Я как вулка́н на гра́ни полномасшта́бного изверже́ния.

escape *vi* убега́ть / убежа́ть ♦ **Can't we escape for** *(1)* **...a while? /** *(2)* **...a few hours /** *(3)* **days? /** *(4)* **...a weekend?** Не могли́ ли бы мы убежа́ть на *(1)* ...не́которое вре́мя? / *(2)* ...не́сколько часо́в / *(3)* дней? / *(4)* ...выходны́е дни? ♦ **Darling, let's escape together for** *(1)* **...a weekend... /** *(2)* **...a week... /** *(3)* **...a few days...to some** *(4)* **far-off /** *(5)* **secluded /** *(6)* **quiet place.** Дорога́я *(ж: Дорого́й)*, дава́й убежи́м вме́сте на *(1)* ...выходны́е дни... / *(2)* ...неде́лю... / *(3)* ...не́сколько дней... куда́-нибудь в *(4)* далёкое / *(5)* уединённое / *(6)* споко́йное ме́сто.

escape *vt* 1. *(flee)* убега́ть / убежа́ть *(from what, whom = + от + gen.)*; 2. *(avoid)* избега́ть / избежа́ть *(what, whom = acc.)*; *(withstand)* устоя́ть *(what, whom = + перед + instr.)* ♦ **I cannot escape the allure of your red rose-petal lips.** Я не могу́ устоя́ть пе́ред собла́зном твои́х кра́сных, похо́жих на лепестки́ ро́зы губ.

escape *n* 1. *(running away)* побе́г; 2. *(secluded place)* уединённое ме́сто ♦ **romantic** ~ уединённое ме́сто для любо́вников.

escort *n* 1. *(guard)* эско́рт, охра́на; 2. *(partner)* партнёр, кавале́р ♦ **frequent** ~ ча́стый партнёр.

ESP *abbrev* = **extrasensory perception** внечу́вственное восприя́тие, экстрасе́нсорные спосо́бности, телепа́тия ♦ **You must have ESP. I was just thinking** *(1)* **...about you. /** *(2)* **...about calling you.** У тебя́, должно́ быть, экстрасе́нсорные спосо́бности. Я то́лько что ду́мал *(ж:ду́мала)* *(1)* ...о тебе́. / *(2)* ...о том, что́бы позвони́ть тебе́.

espresso *n* ко́фе экспре́ссо.

essence *n* су́щность *f* ♦ **My lips will draw the very essence from you.** Мои́ гу́бы вы́пьют са́мую су́щность твою́. ♦ **You are the** *(1,2)* **essence of** *(3)* **loveliness /** *(4)* **beauty.** Ты *(1)* су́щность / *(2)* квинтэссе́нция *(3,4)* красоты́.

essential *adj* необходи́мый, -ая, -ое, -ые, обяза́тельный, -ая, -ое, -ые, непреме́нный, -ая, -ое, -ые.

esteem *n* уваже́ние, почте́ние ♦ **great** ~ большо́е уваже́ние ♦ **high** ~ большо́е уваже́ние ♦ **This gift is a tiny token of my love and esteem for you.** Этот пода́рок -- ма́ленький си́мвол мое́й любви́ и уваже́ния к тебе́. ♦ **You know (that) I hold you in very high esteem.** Ты зна́ешь, (что) я отношу́сь к тебе́ с о́чень больши́м уваже́нием. ♦ **My esteem for you is absolutely the highest.** Моё уваже́ние к тебе́ безусло́вно высоча́йшее.

Estonian *adj* эсто́нский, -ая, -ое, -ие.

Estonian *n* 1. *(person)* эсто́нец *m*, эсто́нка *f (pl:* эсто́нцы*)*; 2. *(language)* эсто́нский язы́к ♦ **speak** ~ говори́ть по-эсто́нски.

estranged *(1,2) adj* живу́щий (-ая, -ее, -ие) *(1)* разде́льно / *(2)* отде́льно ♦ **My** *(1)* **wife /** *(2)* **husband and I are estranged.** Мы с *(1)* жено́й / *(2)* му́жем живём разде́льно.

etceteras *n, pl (other things)* други́е ве́щи.

etched *adj* вы́гравированный, -ая, -ое, -ые ♦ **That (**[*1*] **beautiful /** [*2*] **wonderful)** *(3)*

If no accent is shown on a word with a capitalized vowel, it means that the capitalized vowel is accented.

moment / *(4)* **day will** *(5)* **stay** / *(6)* **remain indelibly etched in my** *(7)* **mind** / *(8)* **memory** *(9)* **...forever.** / *(10)* **...for as long as I live.** Этот (*[1]* прекра́сный / *[2]* замеча́тельный) *(3)* моме́нт / *(4)* день *(5,6)* оста́нется вы́гравиро́ванным несмыва́емо в мое́й *(7,8)* па́мяти *(9)* ...навсегда́. / *(10)* ...пока́ я жив *(ж: жива́)*. ♦ **Those** (*[1]* **beautiful** / *[2]* **wonderful**) *(3)* **hours** / *(4)* **days will** *(5)* **stay** / *(6)* **remain indelibly etched in my** *(7)* **mind** / *(8)* **memory** *(9)* **...forever.** / *(10)* **...for as long as I live.** Эти (*[1]* прекра́сные / *[2]* замеча́тельные) *(3)* часы́ / *(4)* дни *(5,6)* оста́нутся вы́гравированными несмыва́емо в мое́й *(7,8)* па́мяти *(9)* ...навсегда́. / *(10)* ...пока́ я жив *(ж: жива́)*.

eternal *adj* ве́чный, -ая, -ое, -ые ♦ **I want you to be my eternal** *(1)* **mate** / *(2)* **partner.** Я хочу́, чтобы ты была́ мои́м ве́чным *(1)* ...спу́тником жи́зни. / *(2)* ...партнёром. ♦ **Our souls will join together in eternal love.** На́ши ду́ши солью́тся вме́сте в ве́чной любви́.

eternally *adv* ве́чно, наве́чно, наве́ки ♦ **I want to be together with you eternally.** Я хочу́ ве́чно быть вме́сте с тобо́й. ♦ **I love you eternally.** Я люблю́ тебя́ наве́ки. ♦ **I am eternally yours.** Я наве́чно твой *(ж: твоя́)*.

eternity *n* ве́чность *f* ♦ **Each** *(1)* **minute** / *(2)* **hour** / *(3)* **day that we are apart seems like an eternity.** *(1)* Ка́ждая мину́та... / *(2)* Ка́ждый час / *(3)* день... в разлу́ке ка́жется ве́чностью. ♦ **The days will seem like an eternity to me.** Дни пока́жутся мне це́лой ве́чностью.

ethereal *adj* эфи́рный, -ая, -ое, -ые, неземно́й, -а́я, -о́е, -ы́е ♦ **My heart is** *(1)* **completely** / *(2)* **irredeemably** / *(3)* **hopelessly** *(4)* **enslaved** / *(5)* **captivated by your ethereal beauty.** Моё се́рдце *(1)* соверше́нно / *(2)* безвозвра́тно / *(3)* безнадёжно *(4)* порабощено́ / *(5)* очаро́вано твое́й неземно́й красото́й.

etherealness *n* эфи́рность *f*, возду́шность *f*, лёгкость *f*.

ethical *adj* эти́ческий, -ая, -ое, -ие, эти́чный, -ая, -ое, -ие, мора́льный, -ая, -ое, -ые.

ethics *n, pl* э́тика, мора́ль *f*, нра́вственность *f* ♦ **high** ~s высо́кая мора́ль ♦ **social** ~s э́тика обще́ния.

etiquette *n* этике́т ♦ **rules of** ~ пра́вила этике́та.

euphoria *n* эйфори́я ♦ **Your kisses induce such sensual euphoria.** Твои́ поцелу́и вызыва́ют таку́ю чу́вственную эйфори́ю. ♦ **I've been in a state of euphoria** *(1)* **...all day.** / *(2)* **...all week.** / *(3)* **...since you called.** / *(4)* **...since I read your letter.** Я был *(ж: была́)* в состоя́нии эйфори́и *(1)* ...весь день. / *(2)* ...всю неде́лю. / *(3)* ...с тех пор, как ты позвони́ла *(ж: позвони́л)*. / *(4)* ...с тех пор, как я прочита́л *(ж: прочита́ла)* твоё письмо́.

euphoric *adj* эйфори́ческий, -ая, -ое, -ие.

Europe *n* Евро́па ♦ **from** ~ из Евро́пы ♦ **in** ~ в Евро́пе ♦ **to** ~ в Евро́пу.

European *adj* европе́йский, -ая, -ое, -ие.

evade *vt* уклоня́ться / уклони́ться *(what, whom* = + от + *gen.)*, увёртываться / увернуться *(what, whom* = + от + *gen.)*; избега́ть / избежа́ть *(what, whom* = *acc.)*.

evaporate *vi (vanish)* улету́читься ♦ **The feelings that I felt for you in the beginning have evaporated forever.** Чу́вства, кото́рые я испы́тывал *(ж: испы́тывала)* к тебе́ в нача́ле, безвозвра́тно улету́чились.

evasive *adj* укло́нчивый, -ая, -ое, -ые ♦ ~ **answer** укло́нчивый отве́т.

evasiveness *n* укло́нчивость *f*.

even-featured *adj (face)* плоսколи́цый, -ая, -ое, -ые.

evening *n* ве́чер ♦ **beautiful** ~ прекра́сный ве́чер ♦ **every** ~ ка́ждый ве́чер ♦ **fantastic** ~ фантасти́ческий ве́чер ♦ **in the** ~ ве́чером ♦ **long-awaited** ~ долгожда́нный ве́чер ♦ **memorable** ~ па́мятный ве́чер ♦ **nice** ~ хоро́ший ве́чер ♦ **pleasant** ~ прия́тный ве́чер ♦ *(1,2)* **quiet** ~ *(1)* споко́йный / *(2)* ти́хий ве́чер ♦ **Saturday** *(etc.)* ~ в суббо́ту ве́чером

Russian has 6 grammatical cases. For an explanation of them,
see the grammar appendix on page 686.

♦ **summer** ~ ле́тний ве́чер ♦ **the whole** ~ весь ве́чер ♦ **this** ~ сего́дня ве́чером ♦ **tomorrow** ~ за́втра ве́чером ♦ **unforgettable** ~ незабыва́емый ве́чер ♦ **warm** ~ тёплый ве́чер ♦ *(1,2)* **wonderful** ~ *(1)* чуде́сный / *(2)* чу́дный ве́чер ♦ **yesterday** ~ вчера́ ве́чером ♦ **We could spend quiet evenings at home.** Мы смо́жем проводи́ть споко́йные вечера́ до́ма. ♦ **It was an unforgettable evening.** Это был незабыва́емый ве́чер. ♦ **Those were unforgettable evenings.** Это бы́ли незабыва́емые вечера́. ♦ *(1)* **Yesterday** / *(2)* **That evening (with you) was** *(3)* **fantastic** / *(4)* **heavenly** / *(5)* **wonderful.** *(1)* Вчера́шний / *(2)* Этот ве́чер (с тобо́й) был *(3)* фантасти́ческим / *(4)* боже́ственным / *(5)* чуде́сным.

even-minded *adj* уравнове́шенный, -ая, -ое, -ые, споко́йный, -ая, -ое, -ые.

event *n* собы́тие ♦ **cultural** ~s культу́рные собы́тия ♦ **exciting** ~ волну́ющее собы́тие ♦ **happy** ~ ра́достное собы́тие ♦ **joyful** ~ ра́достное собы́тие ♦ **sporting** ~s спорти́вные собы́тия.

even-tempered *adj* уравнове́шенный, -ая, -ое, -ые, невозмути́мый, -ая, -ое, -ые.

eventual *adj* коне́чный, -ая, -ое, -ые, оконча́тельный, -ая, -ое, -ые.

eventually *adv* в конце́ концо́в.

ever *adv* когда́-либо; когда́-нибудь.

everlasting *adj* несконча́емый, -ая, -ое, -ые, ве́чный, -ая, -ое, -ые, бесконе́чный, -ая, -ое, -ые, постоя́нный, -ая, -ое, -ые ♦ **I want our lives to be an everlasting symphony of love.** Я хочу́, что́бы на́ша жизнь была́ бесконе́чной симфо́нией любви́. ♦ **Our souls will join together in everlasting love.** На́ши ду́ши соединя́тся вме́сте в ве́чной любви́.

every *adj* 1. *(each)* ка́ждый, -ая, -ое; 2. *(all)* все.

everybody *pron* все.

everyone *pron* все.

everything *pron* всё ♦ **I will do everything to prove that I love you.** Я бу́ду де́лать всё, что́бы доказа́ть, что я люблю́ тебя́. ♦ **You are my all and everything.** Ты для меня́ - - всё на све́те. ♦ **You are (my) everything.** Ты всё для меня́. ♦ **You mean everything to me.** Ты означа́ешь для меня́ всё. ♦ **Everything I want, everything I dream of, everything I hope for is in your arms.** Всё, чего́ я хочу́, всё, о чём мечта́ю, всё, на что наде́юсь, всё в твои́х рука́х. ♦ **I would give everything** (*[1]* **...in this world...** / *[2]* **...that I have...**) *(3)* **...to have your love.** / *(4)* **...to have you as my wife.** Я отда́л бы всё (*[1]*...на све́те... / *[2]* ...что, у меня́ есть...), *(3)* ...что́бы получи́ть твою́ любо́вь. / *(4)* ...что́бы ты ста́ла мое́й жено́й. ♦ **You are my joy and comfort, my hope and my dreams — my everything.** Ты моя́ ра́дость и утеше́ние, моя́ наде́жда и моя́ мечта́ -- всё для меня́. ♦ **You are everything that matters to me in this world.** Ты всё, что име́ет значе́ние для меня́ в э́том ми́ре. ♦ **Tell me everything (about it).** Расскажи́ мне всё (об э́том).

everywhere *adv* везде́, всю́ду.

evolve *vi* развива́ться / разви́ться *(into what = + в + acc.)*.

evolved *adj* ра́звитый, -ая, -ое, -ые ♦ **I seek a single woman who's educated, evolved and happy.** Я ищу́ одино́кую же́нщину, образо́ванную, ра́звитую и счастли́вую.

ex *n (former wife)* бы́вшая жена́; *(former husband)* бы́вший муж; *(former girlfriend)* бы́вшая возлю́бленная; *(former boyfriend)* бы́вший возлю́бленный.

exacerbate *vt (intensify)* уси́ливать / уси́лить *(what = acc.)*; *(aggravate)* обостря́ть / обостри́ть *(what = acc.)*.

exasperate *vt* выводи́ть / вы́вести из себя́ *(whom = acc)*, раздража́ть / раздражи́ть *(whom = acc)*.

exasperated *adj* вы́веден (-а, -о, -ы) из себя́ *(short forms)*, раздражён, раздражена́, -о́, -ы́ *(short forms)*.

There are no articles ("a" or "the") in Russian.

exasperating *adj* раздража́ющий, -ая, -ее, -ие.

exasperation *n* раздраже́ние; доса́да.

ex-boyfriend бы́вший возлю́бленный.

excellent *adj* превосхо́дный, -ая, -ое, -ые, отли́чный, -ая, -ое, -ые ♦ ~ **with kids** превосхо́дно с детьми́.

exceptional *adj* исключи́тельный, -ая, -ое, -ые, необы́чный, -ая, -ое, -ые ♦ **You're exceptional.** Ты исключи́тельна. *(ж: Ты исключи́телен.).*

exceptionally *adv* исключи́тельно, необы́чно.

excite *vt* возбужда́ть / возбуди́ть *(what, whom = acc.)*, будора́жить / взбудора́жить *(what = acc.)* ♦ **You excite me (**[1] **enormously /** [2] **tremendously).** Ты возбужда́ешь меня́ (*[1]* безме́рно / *[2]* бесконе́чно). ♦ **The clean, masculine smell of you excites me.** Твой чи́стый мужско́й за́пах возбужда́ет меня́. ♦ **You excite** *(1)* **...me...** / *(2)* **...my senses... more than you can imagine.** Ты возбужда́ешь *(1)* ...меня́... / *(2)* ...мои́ чу́вства... бо́лее, чем мо́жешь предста́вить себе́.

excited *adj* возбуждённый, -ая, -ое, -ые *(short forms:* возбуждён, возбуждена́, -о́, -ы́*)*, взволно́ванный, -ая, -ое, -ые *(short forms:* взволно́ван, -а, -о, -ы*)* ♦ **get** *(1)* **me /** *(2)* **you (so)** ~ приводи́ть / привести́ *(1)* меня́ / *(2)* тебя́ в (тако́е) волне́ние ♦ **You make me feel strangely excited.** Ты вызыва́ешь во мне стра́нное возбужде́ние. ♦ **Don't get excited.** Не волну́йся. ♦ **I'm (so) excited.** Я (так) взволно́ван *(ж: взволно́вана).*

excitement *n* возбужде́ние, волне́ние ♦ **blissful** ~ блаже́нное возбужде́ние ♦ **deep** ~ глубо́кое волне́ние ♦ **dizzying** ~ головокружи́тельное возбужде́ние ♦ **inner** *(1,2)* ~ вну́треннее *(1)* возбужде́ние / *(2)* волне́ние ♦ **overwhelming** ~ ошеломля́ющее возбужде́ние ♦ **sweet** *(1,2)* ~ сла́дкое *(1)* возбужде́ние / *(2)* волне́ние ♦ **tremendous** *(1,2)* ~ огро́мное *(1)* возбужде́ние / *(2)* волне́ние ♦ *(1,2)* **wild** ~ *(1)* бу́рное / *(2)* ди́кое возбужде́ние ♦ *(1,2)* **pitch of** ~ *(1)* у́ровень / *(2)* си́ла возбужде́ния ♦ **tremble with** ~ дрожа́ть от возбужде́ния.

excitement: phrases

I love to feel the excitement grow in you. Я люблю́ чу́вствовать в тебе́ всё возраста́ющее возбужде́ние. ♦ **Excitement just tingled through me when I** *(1)* **saw /** *(2)* **met** / *(3)* **kissed you.** Я про́сто трепета́л *(ж: трепета́ла)* от волне́ния, когда́ *(1)* уви́дел *(ж: уви́дела)* / *(2)* встре́тил *(ж: встре́тила)* / *(3)* поцелова́л *(ж: поцелова́ла)* тебя́. ♦ **I've never known such excitement with anyone (as I know with you).** Я никогда́ ни с кем не знал *(ж: зна́ла)* тако́го возбужде́ния (, как с тобо́й). ♦ **I felt such (**[1] **dizzying /** [2] **wild /** [3] **overwhelming) excitement when I first** *(4)* **saw /** *(5)* **met /** *(6)* **kissed you.** Я чу́вствовал *(ж: чу́вствовала)* тако́е (*[1]* головокружи́тельное / *[2]* бу́рное / *[3]* ошеломля́ющее) возбужде́ние, когда́ я впервы́е *(4)* уви́дел *(ж: уви́дела)* / *(5)* встре́тил *(ж: встре́тила)* / *(6)* поцелова́л *(ж: поцелова́ла)* тебя́. ♦ **Oh, if you only knew the intensity of my** *(1,2)* **excitement whenever** *(3)* **...I'm near you.** / *(4)* **...I think about you.** О, е́сли бы ты то́лько зна́ла *(ж: знал)* си́лу моего́ *(1)* возбужде́ния / *(2)* волне́ния вся́кий раз, когда́ я *(3)* ...ря́дом с тобо́й. / *(4)* ...ду́маю о тебе́. ♦ **I feel such a (tremendous) rush of excitement every time I think of you.** Меня́ охва́тывает тако́е (огро́мное) возбужде́ние вся́кий раз, когда́ я ду́маю о тебе́. ♦ **The pitch of excitement I feel when I** *(1)* **... see /** *(2)* **hold you...** / *(3)* **...think about you... is** *(4)* **unbearable /** *(5)* **indescribable.** Си́ла возбужде́ния, кото́рое я ощуща́ю, когда́ *(1)* ...ви́жу / *(2)* обнима́ю тебя́,... / *(3)* ...ду́маю о тебе́,... *(4)* невыноси́ма / *(5)* неопису́ема. ♦ **The sight of your beautiful face fills my whole body with warm excitement and floods my heart with feelings of love for you.** Взгляд на твоё прекра́сное лицо́ наполня́ет всё моё те́ло жа́рким возбужде́нием и затопля́ет се́рдце чу́вством любви́ к тебе́.

---

*This dictionary contains two Russian alphabet pages:
one in Appendix 1, page 685, and a tear-off page on page 799.*

exciting *adj* возбужда́ющий, -ая, -ее, -ие, волну́ющий, -ая, -ее, -ие ♦ **sexually** ~ сексуа́льно возбужда́ющий, -ая, -ее, -ие ♦ ~ **in bed** возбужда́ющий (-ая, -ее, -ие) в посте́ли ♦ **You're the most exciting thing that ever happened to me.** Никто́ никогда́ не возбужда́л меня́ так, как возбужда́ешь ты.

excruciating *adj* мучи́тельный, -ая, -ое, -ые, невыноси́мый, -ая, -ое, -ые ♦ **The** *(1)* **pleasure** / *(2)* **sensation** *(3)* **...bordered on being...** / *(4)* **...was almost... excruciating.** *(1)* Наслажде́ние / *(2)* Чу́вство *(3)* ...бы́ло на гра́ни невыноси́мого. / *(4)* ...бы́ло почти́ невыноси́мым. ♦ **This loneliness (without you) is excruciating.** Одино́чество (без тебя́) мучи́тельно.

excursion *n (organized)* экску́рсия; *(trip)* пое́здка; *(walk)* прогу́лка.

excuse *n* 1. *(apology)* извине́ние; 2. *(justification)* оправда́ние; *(alibi)* отгово́рка, предло́г ♦ **flimsy** ~ неубеди́тельная отгово́рка ♦ **lame** ~ неубеди́тельная отгово́рка ♦ **poor** ~ плоха́я отгово́рка ♦ **I have an excuse.** У меня́ есть оправда́ние. ♦ **I have no excuse.** У меня́ нет оправда́ния. ♦ **I'm tired of your excuses.** Я уста́л *(ж: уста́ла)* от твои́х отгово́рок. ♦ **I don't want to hear your excuses.** Я не хочу́ слы́шать твои́ оправда́ния. ♦ **You** *(1)* **conjure** / *(2)* **think up more excuses than anyone I've ever met.** Ты *(1,2)* приду́мываешь бо́льше отгово́рок, чем кто́-либо ещё.

exec *abbrev* = **executive** руководя́щий рабо́тник, администра́тор.

exercise *vi* упражня́ться, тренирова́ться ♦ **I** *(1,2)* **exercise regularly.** Я *(1)* трениру́юсь / *(2)* упражня́юсь регуля́рно.

exercise *n (also pl)* заря́дка ♦ **do e~s** де́лать заря́дку.

exercise-oriented *adj* трениру́ющийся, -аясь, -иесь.

exert *vt* ока́зывать / оказа́ть *(what = acc.).*

ex-girlfriend бы́вшая возлю́бленная.

exhausted *adj* изнурённый, -ая, -ое, -ые, утомлённый, -ая, -ое, -ые.

exhibit *n* вы́ставка ♦ **art** ~ вы́ставка карти́н.

exhibitionist *n* эксгибициони́ст.

exhilarate *vt (cheer, gladden)* весели́ть / развесели́ть *(whom = acc.); (enliven)* оживля́ть / оживи́ть *(whom = acc.).*

exhilerating *adj* волну́ющий, -ая, -ее, -ие, возбужда́ющий, -ая, -ее, -ие, опьяня́ющий, -ая, -ее, -ие ♦ **Being with you is exhilerating.** Так волну́юще быть с тобо́й. ♦ **Your kisses are exhilerating.** Твои́ поцелу́и так опьяня́ют.

exhilaration *n (pleasant excitement)* прия́тное возбужде́ние; *(joyful mood)* ра́достное настрое́ние; *(cheer)* весёлость ♦ **I feel such exhilaration (being with you).** Я ощуща́ю тако́е прия́тное возбужде́ние (, когда́ я с тобо́й).

ex-husband *n* бы́вший муж.

existence *n (life)* жизнь *f* ♦ **solitary** ~ одино́кая жизнь.

existentialist *n* экзистенциали́ст.

exit *n* вы́ход ♦ **I'll wait for you by the exit.** Я бу́ду ждать тебя́ у вы́хода.

ex-love *n* бы́вшая любо́вь.

ex-lover *n* бы́вший любо́вник *m*, бы́вшая любо́вница *f*.

ex-military *adj* бы́вший (-ая, -ее, -ие) вое́нный, -ая, -ое, -ые.

exotic *adj* экзоти́ческий, -ая, -ое, -ие; -**ally** *adv* экзоти́чески.

expect *vi* ожида́ть *(what, whom = gen.)* ♦ **You are (** *[1]* **far /** *[2]* **much) more beautiful than I (ever) expected.** Ты (*[1]* намно́го / *[2]* ещё) краси́вее, чем я ожида́л.

expectation *n* 1. *(awaiting)* ожида́ние; 2. *(hope)* наде́жда ♦ *(1)* **She /** *(2)* **He had... /** *(3)* **You have... unrealistically high expectations of me.** *(1)* Она́ возлага́ла... / *(2)* Он возлага́л... / *(3)* Ты возлага́ешь... нереа́льно больши́е наде́жды на меня́. ♦ **The expectation to see**

Depending on the subject, the possessive pronoun **свой (своя́, своё, свои́)** *can be translated* **my, your, his, her, its, our** *or* **their**.

your beloved face again makes me feel hot and feverish. Ожида́ние опя́ть уви́деть твоё
люби́мое лицо́ вызыва́ет во мне жар и лихора́дочное возбужде́ние. ♦ **Your expectations of me are unrealistic.** То, чего́ ты ожида́ешь от меня́, нереа́льно. ♦ **You have
such inflated expectations (of me).** Ты ждёшь (от меня́) сли́шком мно́гого.

expensive *adj* дорого́й, -а́я, -о́е, -и́е ♦ *(1)* **It's** / *(2)* **That's** (*[3]* **rather** / *[4]* **too** / *[5]* **very** / *[6]*
terribly) expensive. *(1,2)* Это (*[3]* доста́точно / *[4]* сли́шком / *[5]* о́чень / *[6]* ужа́сно)
дорого́е. ♦ *(1)* **It's** / *(2)* **That's not** (*[3]* **so** / *[4]* **too** / *[5]* **very) expensive.** *(1,2)* Это не (*[3]*
так / *[4]* сли́шком / *[5]* о́чень) дорого́е.

experience *vt* испы́тывать / испыта́ть *(what = acc.)* ♦ **~ pleasure** испы́тывать / испыта́ть
наслажде́ние ♦ **Together you and I can experience the ecstasy of unbridled passion.**
Вме́сте ты и я смо́жем испыта́ть экста́з необу́зданной стра́сти.

experience *n* 1. *(accumulated knowledge / practice)* о́пыт; 2. *(occurrence)* слу́чай, о́пыт,
происше́ствие ♦ **bizarre ~** стра́нный слу́чай ♦ **cosmic ~** фантасти́ческий слу́чай ♦
degrading ~ унизи́тельный слу́чай ♦ **ecstatic ~** экста́з ♦ **embarrassing ~** *(See sentence
under "phrases")* ♦ *(1,2)* **funny ~** 1. *(amusing)* смешно́й слу́чай; 2. *(strange)* стра́нный
слу́чай ♦ **great ~** 1. *(accumulated knowledge / practice)* большо́й о́пыт; 2. *(occurrence)*
замеча́тельный о́пыт ♦ **interesting ~** интере́сный слу́чай ♦ **life ~** жи́зненный о́пыт ♦
love ~ любо́вное пережива́ние ♦ **my ~** мой о́пыт ♦ **once-in-a-lifetime ~** происше́ствие,
случи́вшееся одна́жды в жи́зни *(1 term)* ♦ *(1,2)* **personal ~** *(1)* со́бственный / *(2)*
ли́чный о́пыт ♦ **romantic ~** романти́ческий о́пыт ♦ **sexual ~** сексуа́льный о́пыт ♦ *(1,2)*
similar ~ *(1)* подо́бный / *(2)* похо́жий слу́чай ♦ **strange ~** стра́нный слу́чай ♦ *(1,2)*
unusual ~ *(1)* необы́чный / *(2)* необыкнове́нный слу́чай ♦ *(1,2)* **vast ~** *(1)* огро́мный
/ *(2)* бога́тый о́пыт ♦ **wonderful ~** замеча́тельный о́пыт ♦ **your ~** *(familiar)* твой о́пыт;
(polite) Ваш о́пыт ♦ **share ~s** разделя́ть пережива́ния.

---
experience: *phrases*

    It was a very embarrassing experience. Я был *(ж: была́)* ужа́сно смущён *(ж: сму-
щена́).* **Our relationship was a sweet and sour experience.** В на́ших отноше́ниях бы́ло
и сла́дкое и го́рькое. ♦ **I'm open to new experiences.** Я откры́т *(ж: откры́та)* всему́
но́вому.

experienced *adj* о́пытный, -ая, -ое, -ые *(short forms:* о́пытен, о́пытна, -о, -ы*)* ♦ **You seem
to be (very) experienced.** Ты ка́жешься о́чень о́пытной *(ж: о́пытным).* ♦ **I'm not very
experienced.** Я не о́чень о́пытен *(ж: о́пытна).* ♦ **I'm glad you're experienced.** Я рад
(ж: ра́да), что ты о́пытна *(ж: о́пытен).*

experiment *vi* эксперименти́ровать ♦ **We can experiment together in the ways of love.** Мы
мо́жем вме́сте эксперименти́ровать на поля́х любви́.

expertise *n* эксперти́за ♦ **erotic ~** эроти́ческая эксперти́за.

explain *vt* объясня́ть / объясни́ть *(what = acc., to whom = dat.)* ♦ **Please let me explain.**
Пожа́луйста, позво́ль мне объясни́ть. ♦ **I can explain (everything).** Я могу́ объясни́ть
(всё). ♦ **No language can explain my feelings (for you).** Никако́й язы́к не спосо́бен
объясни́ть мои́ чу́вства (к тебе́).

explanation *n* объясне́ние ♦ **I owe you an explanation.** Я до́лжен *(ж: должна́)*
объясни́ться с тобо́й.

explode *vi* взорва́ться ♦ **Sometimes I feel like I'm going to explode from the tremendous
love-pressure that builds up inside of me for you.** Иногда́ я чу́вствую себя́ гото́вым
взорва́ться от огро́много любо́вного напряже́ния, нараста́ющего во мне.

exploit *n* по́двиг ♦ **I don't** *(1)* **care** / *(2)* **want to hear about your sexual exploits.** Я не *(1,2)*
хочу́ слы́шать о твои́х сексуа́льных по́двигах.

exploration *n* иссле́дование ♦ **We can engage in culinary explorations together.** Мы

---

*There are two words for "you" in Russian:
familiar* «ты» *and polite / plural* «вы» *(See page 781).*

мóжем занимáться кулинáрными исслéдованиями вмéсте.

explore *vt* исслéдовать *(what = acc.)*, изучáть *(what = acc.)* ♦ ~ **possibilities** исслéдовать возмóжности ♦ **I want to explore the universe with you.** Я хочý исслéдовать Вселéнную вмéсте с тобóй. ♦ **I find myself eager to have you explore me.** *(ж:)* Я горю́ нетерпéнием быть исслéдованной тобóй. ♦ **I** *(1)* **yearn /** *(2)* **long so** *(3)* **mightily /** *(4)* **much to explore all the** *(5)* **luscious /** *(6)* **delicious secrets of your body.** Я так *(3,4)* си́льно *(1)* жáжду / *(2)* стремлю́сь исслéдовать все *(5)* сóчные / *(6)* восхити́тельные секрéты твоегó тéла. ♦ **My eager lips will explore every** *(1)* **millimeter /** *(2)* **inch of your** *(3)* **beautiful /** *(4)* **delectable /** *(5)* **luscious body.** Мои́ нетерпели́вые гýбы исслéдуют кáждый *(1)* миллимéтр / *(2)* дюйм твоегó *(3)* прекрáсного / *(4)* лáкомого / *(5)* сóчного тéла. ♦ **We can explore areas of mutual interest.** Мы мóжем занимáться тем, что интерéсно нам обóим. ♦ **We can go on weekend** *(1)* **jaunts /** *(2)* **trips to explore new places.** В выходны́е дни мы мóжем отпрáвиться в *(1,2)* поéздку исслéдовать нóвые местá. ♦ **I enjoy exploring** *(1)* **...(art) galleries. /** *(2)* **...new places.** Я наслаждáюсь посещéнием *(1)* ...(худóжественных) галерéй. / *(2)* ...нóвых мест.

exploring *n* исслéдование ♦ **We can indulge in some passionate exploring of each other.** Мы мóжем предáться стрáстному исслéдованию друг дрýга.

explosion *n* взрыв ♦ **dazzling** ~ искромётный взрыв ♦ **I'm going to create a million little delicious pleasures all over your body that are going to course into one tremendous explosion of ecstasy.** Я создáм миллиóн мáленьких восхити́тельных наслаждéний по всемý твоемý тéлу, котóрые солью́тся в оди́н огрóмный взрыв экстáза.

exposed *adj* 1. *(revealed)* вы́ставленный, -ая, -ое, -ые на покáз; *(bare, open)* обнажённый, -ая, -ое, -ые, откры́тый, -ая, -ое, -ые; 2. *(film)* экспони́рованный, -ая, -ое, -ые ♦ **disturbingly** ~ **body** соблазни́тельно вы́ставленное на покáз тéло ♦ *(1,2)* ~ **breast** *(1)* обнажённая / *(2)* откры́тая грудь ♦ ~ **film** экспони́рованная плёнка.

express *vt* выражáть / вы́разить *(what = acc.)* ♦ ~ *(1)* **my /** *(2)* **your feelings** выражáть / вы́разить *(1,2)* свои́ чýвства ♦ ~ **love** выражáть / вы́разить любóвь.

express: phrases

There is no way that I can express in words how (very much) I love you (and *[1]* need / *[2]* want you). Я не могý вы́разить словáми, как (óчень си́льно) я люблю́ тебя́ (и *[1]* ...нуждáюсь в тебé. / *[2]* ...хочý тебя́). ♦ **Words alone cannot express the love that I feel for you in my heart.** Одни́ми словáми невозмóжно вы́разить ту любóвь к тебé, котóрой напóлнено моё сéрдце. ♦ **I wish I could express my feelings as well as you** *(1)* **...do. /** *(2)* **...have done.** Я хотéл бы умéть так же хорошó выражáть свои́ чувствá, как ты э́то *(1)* ...дéлаешь. / *(2)* ...дéлала *(ж: дéлал).* ♦ **No language can express my feelings (for you)** Никакóй язы́к не спосóбен вы́разить мои́ чýвства (к тебé). ♦ **How can I express all the love I feel in my heart for you?** Как мне вы́разить всю ту любóвь к тебé, котóрую я чýвствую в своём сéрдце? ♦ **It's hard for me to express my emotions.** Мне трýдно вы́разить свои́ чýвства. ♦ **I've never seen a mouth that expresses sensuality the way yours does.** Я никогдá не ви́дел рот, котóрый выражáет такýю чýвственность, как твой.

expression *n* выражéние ♦ *(1,2)* **arrogant** ~ *(1)* высокомéрное / *(2)* надмéнное выражéние ♦ **blank** ~ ничегó не выражáющее лицó ♦ **calm** ~ спокóйное выражéние ♦ **cheerful** ~ весёлое выражéние ♦ **cold** ~ холóдное лицó ♦ **determined** ~ реши́тельное выражéние ♦ **disappointed** ~ разочарóванное выражéние ♦ **dreamy** ~ мечтáтельное выражéние ♦ **dumb** ~ глýпое выражéние ♦ **embarrassed** ~ смущённое выражéние ♦ ~ **of delight** востóрженное выражéние ♦ ~ **of disappointment** выражéние разочарóвания ♦ ~ **of happiness** выражéние счáстья ♦ ~ **of joy** выражéние рáдости ♦ ~ **of**

Russian terms of endearment are given in Appendix 13, page 780.

sadness выраже́ние печа́ли ♦ ~ **of surprise** выраже́ние удивле́ния ♦ ~ **of worry** выраже́ние беспоко́йства ♦ *(1,2)* **friendly** ~ *(1)* приве́тливое / *(2)* дру́жеское выраже́ние ♦ **frightened** ~ испу́ганное выраже́ние ♦ **funny** ~ 1. *(humorous)* смешно́е выраже́ние; 2. *(strange)* стра́нное выраже́ние ♦ **genuine** ~ и́скреннее выраже́ние ♦ **gentle** ~ кро́ткое выраже́ние ♦ *(1,2)* **gloomy** ~ *(1)* мра́чное / *(2)* угрю́мое выраже́ние ♦ **good-natured** ~ добро́ду́шное выраже́ние ♦ **happy** ~ счастли́вое выраже́ние ♦ *(1,2)* **haughty** ~ *(1)* высокоме́рное / *(2)* надме́нное выраже́ние ♦ **hauntingly lovely** ~ запомина́ющееся краси́вое лицо́ ♦ **hurt** ~ оби́женное выраже́ние ♦ **impassive** ~ бесстра́стное выраже́ние ♦ **indifferent** ~ равноду́шное выраже́ние ♦ **intelligent** ~ у́мное выраже́ние ♦ **joyful** ~ ра́достное выраже́ние ♦ **naive** ~ наи́вное выраже́ние ♦ **odd** ~ стра́нное выраже́ние ♦ **pained** ~ страда́льческое выраже́ние ♦ **peaceful** ~ споко́йное выраже́ние ♦ **petulant** ~ раздражи́тельное выраже́ние ♦ *(1,2)* **puzzled** ~ *(1)* озада́ченное / *(2)* неодоумева́ющее выраже́ние ♦ *(1,2)* **quizzical** ~ *(1)* вопроша́ющее / *(2)* недоуме́нное выраже́ние ♦ **sad** ~ печа́льное выраже́ние ♦ **satisfied** ~ дово́льное выраже́ние ♦ *(1,2)* **serene** ~ *(1)* споко́йное / *(2)* безмяте́жное выраже́ние ♦ **serious** ~ серьёзное выраже́ние ♦ **smug** ~ самодово́льное выраже́ние ♦ **somber** ~ мра́чное выраже́ние ♦ **sorrowful** ~ гру́стное выраже́ние ♦ **sour** ~ ки́слое выраже́ние ♦ **stern** ~ суро́вое выраже́ние ♦ **strange** ~ стра́нное выраже́ние ♦ **stupid** ~ глу́пое выраже́ние ♦ **sulky** ~ оби́женное выраже́ние ♦ **sullen** ~ угрю́мое выраже́ние ♦ **surprised** ~ удивлённое выраже́ние ♦ **sympathetic** ~ сочу́вственное выраже́ние ♦ **tired** ~ уста́лое выраже́ние ♦ **ultimate** ~ максима́льное выраже́ние ♦ **unhappy** ~ несча́стное выраже́ние ♦ **worried** ~ озабо́ченное выраже́ние ♦ **devoid of** ~ лишённый (-ая, -ое, -ые) выраже́ния.

| **expression:** *phrases* |

I love the dreamy expression on your face. Я люблю́ мечта́тельное выраже́ние на твоём лице́. ♦ *(1)* **This is...** / *(2)* **That** / *(3)* **It will be ... the ultimate expression of our love for each other.** *(1,2)* Это максима́льное выраже́ние... / *(3)* Это бу́дет максима́льным выраже́нием... на́шей любви́ друг к дру́гу. ♦ **I hope that what I've written to you here doesn't sound mushy. Everything that I've said is a genuine expression of how I feel about you.** Наде́юсь, то, что я написа́л, не звучи́т сли́шком сентимента́льно. Всё, о чём я написа́л - и́скреннее выраже́ние мои́х чувств к тебе́. ♦ *(1)* **This...** / *(2)* **This gift... is just a small expression of my unending love for you.** *(1)* Это... / *(2)* Этот пода́рок... - то́лько ма́ленький си́мвол мое́й несконча́емой любви́ к тебе́.

expressive *adj* вырази́тельный, -ая, -ое, -ые ♦ **emotionally** ~ эмоциона́льный, -ая, -ое, -ые.

exquisite *adj* изы́сканный, -ая, -ое, -ые, преле́стный, -ая, -ое, -ые, соверше́нный, -ая, -ое, -ые ♦ **You are a vision of exquisite** *(1)* **beauty** / *(2)* **loveliness.** Ты виде́ние изы́сканной *(1,2)* красоты́.

ex-spouse n бы́вший супру́г *m*, бы́вшая супру́га *f*.

extend *vt* 1. *(reach out)* вытя́гивать / вы́тянуть *(what = acc., to whom = dat.)*; 2. *(show)* ока́зывать / оказа́ть *(what = acc., to whom = dat.)* ♦ ~ *(1)* **my** / *(2)* **your hand** вы́тянуть *([1,2]* свою́) ру́ку *(to whom = dat.)* ♦ **I'm (very) grateful for all the** *(1)* **courtesy** / *(2)* **hospitality you have extended me.** Я о́чень благода́рен *(ж: благода́рна)* за *(1)* ...всю учти́вость, ока́занную мне. / *(2)* ...всё гостеприи́мство, ока́занное мне.

extramarital *adj* внебра́чный, -ая, -ое, -ые, на стороне́ ♦ ~ **affair** связь на стороне́ ♦ ~ **activities** свя́зи на стороне́, проведе́ние вре́мени на стороне́.

extraordinarily *adv* чрезвыча́йно, исключи́тельно, необыча́йно.

extraordinary *adj* чрезвыча́йный, -ая, -ое, -ые, исключи́тельный, -ая, -ое, -ые, необы-

---

> *Some of the Russian sentences are translations of things we say and are not what Russians themselves would normally say.*

чáйный, -ая, -ое, -ые.

extreme *adj* крáйний, -яя, -ее, -ие, чрезвычáйный, -ая, -ое, -ые.

extremely *adv* крáйне, чрезвычáйно.

exuberance *n* богáтство, изобѝлие, избѝток ♦ ~ **of heart** богáтство сéрдца, обѝлие сердéчности ♦ **Your letters** *(1)* **manifest /** *(2)* **display such an exuberance of heart.** Твоѝ пѝсьма *(1)* обнарýживают / *(2)* покáзывают такóе обѝлие сердéчности.

extroverted *adj* с открѝтой натýрой.

exuberant *adj* бьѝющий (-ая, -ее, -ие) ключóм.

exude *vt* выделя́ть / вы́делить *(what = acc.)*; излучáть / излучѝть *(what = acc.)* ♦ ~ **happiness** излучáть рáдость ♦ ~ **heat** лучѝться теплóм ♦ **You exude** *(1)* **charm /** *(2)* **con fidence.** Ты излучáешь *(1)* очаровáние / *(2)* увéренность. ♦ **You exude class.** В Вас срáзу чýвствуется класс. ♦ **Your body exudes a sweetness like a meadow flower.** От твоегó тéла исхóдит слáдость, как от луговы́х цветóв. ♦ **You exude a genuine joy for living.** Ты излучáешь пóдлинную рáдость жѝзни.

ex-wife *n* бы́вшая женá.

eye *vt* смотрéть / посмотрéть *(what, whom = + на + acc.)* ♦ ~ *(someone)* **thoughtfully** смотрéть / посмотрéть задýмчиво *(what, whom = + на + acc.)* ♦ ~ *(someone)* **suspiciously** смотрéть / посмотрéть подозрѝтельно *(what, whom = + на + acc.)* ♦ ~ *(someone)* **up and down** смотрéть / посмотрéть вверх и вниз *(what, whom = + на + acc.)*.

eye *n* глаз *(pl: глазá)* ♦ **absorbing** ~**s** привлекáтельные глазá ♦ **almond(-shaped)** ~**s** миндалевѝдные глазá ♦ **amber** ~**s** янтáрные глазá ♦ **awesome** ~**s** замечáтельные глазá ♦ **beautiful** ~**s** прекрáсные глазá ♦ **bedroom** ~**s** сексуáльные глазá ♦ **beloved** ~**s** любѝмые глазá ♦ *(1,2)* **bewitching blue** ~**s** *(1)* чарýющие / *(2)* обворожѝтельные голубы́е глазá ♦ **big** *(1)* **blue /** *(2)* **brown** ~**s** большѝе *(1)* голубы́е / *(2)* кáрие глазá ♦ **black** ~ синя́к ♦ **blazing blue** ~**s** сия́ющие голубы́е глазá ♦ **bloodshot** ~**s** крáсные глазá ♦ *(1,2)* **blue** ~**s** *(1)* голубы́е / *(2)* сѝние глазá ♦ **blue-grey** ~**s** сéро-голубы́е глазá ♦ **blue laughing** ~**s** голубы́е смею́щиеся глазá ♦ **both** ~**s** óба глáза ♦ **bottomless (dark)** ~**s** бездóнные (тёмные) глазá ♦ *(1,2)* **bright** ~**s** *(1)* свéтлые / *(2)* живы́е глазá ♦ **brilliant dark** ~**s** тёмные, блестя́щие глазá ♦ **brown** ~**s** кáрие глазá ♦ **chestnut-brown** ~**s** кáрие глазá ♦ **closed** ~**s** закры́тые глазá ♦ **cold** ~**s** холóдные глазá ♦ *(1,2)* **come-on** ~**s** *(1)* зовýщие / *(2)* маня́щие глазá ♦ **compelling** ~**s** подчиня́ющие себé глазá ♦ **cornflower-blue** ~**s** василькóво-голубы́е глазá ♦ **dancing** ~**s** танцýющие глазá ♦ **dark** ~**s** тёмные глазá ♦ *(1)* **dark /** *(2)* **blue** ~**s filled with vivid intelligence** *(1)* тёмные / *(2)* голубы́е глазá, пóлные живóго умá *(1 term)* ♦ **dark, piercing** ~**s** тёмные пронѝзывающие глазá ♦ **deep dark** ~**s** глубóкие тёмные глазá ♦ **deep-set** ~**s** глубокó посáженные глазá ♦ *(1,2)* **dreamer's** ~**s** глазá *(1)* мечтáтеля *m* / *(2)* мечтáтельницы *f* ♦ **emerald green** ~**s** изумрýдно-зелёные глазá ♦ **enchanting** ~**s** пленѝтельные глазá ♦ **enormous** ~**s** огрóмные глазá ♦ **envious** ~**s** завѝстливые глазá ♦ **exotic** ~**s** экзотѝческие глазá ♦ **expressive** ~**s** вырази́тельные глазá ♦ **extraordinary** ~**s** удивѝтельные глазá ♦ ~**s as blue as bluebells** глазá голубы́е, как колокóльчик *(1 term)* ♦ ~**s of the clearest** *(1)* **green /** *(2)* **blue** глазá я́рко *(1)* зелёные / *(2)* голубы́е. ♦ ~**s full of emotion** глазá, пóлные чувств *(1 term)* ♦ **fathomless** ~**s** бездóнные глазá ♦ **feline** ~**s** кошáчьи глазá ♦ *(1,2)* **flashing** ~**s** *(1)* сверкáющие / *(2)* горя́щие глазá ♦ **fluorescent blue** ~**s** светя́щиеся голубы́е глазá ♦ **friendly** ~**s** привéтливые глазá ♦ *(1,2)* **gentle** ~**s** *(1)* нéжные / *(2)* крóткие глазá ♦ **green** ~**s** зелёные глазá ♦ **gunsmoke grey** ~**s** ды́мчато-сéрые глазá ♦ **hazel-blue** ~**s** карé-голубы́е глазá ♦ **hazel** ~**s** светло-кáрие глазá ♦ **ice-blue** ~**s** глазá ледянóй голубизны́ ♦ **indigo** ~**s** глазá цвéта индѝго ♦ *(1,2)* **innocent(-looking)** ~**s** *(1)* невѝнные / *(2)* чѝстые глазá ♦ **innocent-seeming** ~**s** кáжущиеся невѝнными глазá ♦ **intelligent** ~**s** ýмные

Counting things in Russian is a bit involved.
See Appendix 4, "Numbers," on page 756 .

глаза́ ♦ **intense brown** ~s пы́лкие ка́рие глаза́ ♦ **intriguing** ~s интригу́ющие глаза́ ♦ **iridescent** ~s ра́дужные глаза́ ♦ **jade green** ~s глаза́ цве́та нефри́та ♦ **jet-dark** ~s чёрные глаза́ ♦ **kind(ly)** ~s до́брые глаза́ ♦ **large, luminous** ~s огро́мные, блестя́щие глаза́. ♦ **laughing** ~s смею́щиеся глаза́ ♦ **left** ~ ле́вый глаз ♦ **light brown** ~s светло-ка́рие глаза́ ♦ **light-colored** ~s све́тлые глаза́ ♦ **liquid brown** ~s вла́жные ка́рие глаза́ ♦ **liquid** ~s я́сные глаза́ ♦ **lively** ~s живы́е глаза́ ♦ **love-filled** ~s влюблённые глаза́ ♦ **lovely** ~s прекра́сные глаза́ ♦ **lovesick** ~s снеда́емые любо́вью глаза́ ♦ **love-struck** ~s влюблённые глаза́ ♦ *(1,2)* **luminous (green)** ~s *(1)* сия́ющие / *(2)* светя́щиеся (зелёные) глаза́ ♦ **made-up** ~s подкра́шенные глаза́ ♦ **mellifluous brown** ~s медоточи́вые ка́рие глаза́ ♦ **mesmerizing (brown)** ~s гипнотизи́рующие (ка́рие) глаза́ ♦ **misty-green** ~s ды́мчато-зелёные глаза́ ♦ **my** ~s мои́ глаза́ ♦ **mysterious** ~s таи́нственные глаза́ ♦ **nutmeg** ~s глаза́ цве́та муска́тного оре́ха ♦ **oloroso-colored** ~s золоти́сто-ка́рие глаза́ ♦ **onyx** ~s чёрные глаза́ ♦ **open** ~s откры́тые глаза́ ♦ **over-large** ~s огро́мные глаза ♦ **pale-blue** ~s бле́дно-голубы́е глаза́ ♦ **pansy** ~s фиоле́товые глаза́ **penetrating (hazel)** ~s проница́тельные (све́тло-ка́рие) глаза́ ♦ **perfectly made-up** ~s великоле́пно подкра́шенные глаза́ ♦ **pleasant** ~s до́брые глаза́ ♦ **puppy(-dog / -like)** ~s щеня́чьи глаза́ ♦ **rapture-filled** ~s восто́рженные глаза́ ♦ **red** ~s кра́сные глаза́ ♦ **right** ~ пра́вый глаз ♦ *(1,2)* **sad** ~s *(1)* печа́льные / *(2)* гру́стные глаза́ ♦ **sapphire blue** ~s сапфи́рно-голубы́е глаза́ ♦ **sexy** ~s сексуа́льные глаза́ ♦ **sharp** ~s зо́ркие глаза́ ♦ **silvery** ~s серебри́стые глаза́ ♦ **silvery grey** ~s серебри́сто-се́рые глаза́ ♦ *(1,2)* **slanted** ~s *(1)* у́зкие / *(2)* раско́сые глаза́; *(almond-shaped)* миндалеви́дные глаза́ ♦ *(1,2)* **slanting** ~s *(1)* у́зкие / *(2)* раско́сые глаза; *(almond-shaped)* миндалеви́дные глаза́ ♦ **sleepy** ~s со́нные глаза́ ♦ **smiling (blue)** ~s смею́щиеся (голубы́е) глаза́ ♦ **smokey-blue** ~s ды́мчато-голубы́е глаза́ ♦ **solemn (brown)** ~s серьёзные (ка́рие) глаза́ ♦ *(1-3)* **sparkling** ~s *(1)* искря́щиеся / *(2)* сия́ющие / *(3)* сверка́ющие глаза́ ♦ **sparkly** ~s сверка́ющие глаза́ ♦ **starry** ~s лучи́стые глаза́, сия́ющие как звёзды глаза́ ♦ **steel grey** ~s пронзи́тельно-се́рые глаза́ ♦ **striking blue** ~s порази́тельные голубы́е глаза́ ♦ **sympathetic** ~s сочу́вствующие глаза́ ♦ **tear-filled** ~s запла́канные глаза́ ♦ **tearful** ~s запла́канные глаза́ ♦ **tired** ~s уста́лые глаза́ ♦ **troubled** ~s беспоко́йные глаза́ ♦ **twinkling** ~s сверка́ющие глаза́ ♦ **unbelievable blue** ~s невероя́тные голубы́е глаза́ ♦ **unreadable** ~s зага́дочные глаза́ ♦ **violet** ~s василько́вые глаза́ ♦ **violet blue** ~s василько́во-си́ние глаза́ ♦ **vivid blue** ~s я́рко-голубы́е глаза́ ♦ **vivid** ~s живы́е глаза́ ♦ **watery** ~s вла́жные глаза́ ♦ **wide open** ~s широко́ распа́хнутые глаза́ ♦ **your** ~s *(informal)* твои́ глаза́; *(polite)* Ва́ши глаза́.

---

eye: *verb terms*

avert *(1)* **my** / *(2)* **your** ~s отводи́ть / отвести́ *(1,2)* глаза́ (в сто́рону) ♦ **blink** *(1)* **my** / *(2)* **your** ~s *(1,2)* морга́ть / моргну́ть ♦ **close** *(1)* **my** / *(2)* **your** ~s закрыва́ть / закры́ть *(1,2)* глаза́ ♦ **open** *(1)* **my** / *(2)* **your** ~s открыва́ть / откры́ть *(1,2)* глаза́ ♦ **have an ~ for fashion** име́ть вкус к оде́жде ♦ **look in** *(1)* **my** / *(2)* **your** ~s смотре́ть в *(1)* мои́ / *(2)* твои́ глаза́ ♦ **look** *(1)* **me** / *(2)* **you in the ~** посмотре́ть *(1)* мне / *(2)* тебе́ в глаза́ ♦ **make a pass at** *(1)* **him** / *(2)* **her with your** ~s флиртова́ть с *(1)* ним / *(2)* ней глаза́ми ♦ **turn** *(1)* **my** / *(2)* **your** ~s **away** отводи́ть / отвести́ *([1,2]* свои́) глаза́ (в сто́рону).

---

eye: *other terms*

(1,2) **dark shadows under** *(3)* **my** / *(4)* **your** ~s *(1)* тёмные / *(2)* чёрные кру́ги под *(3)* мои́ми / *(4)* твои́ми глаза́ми ♦ *(1)* **easy** / *(2)* **EZ on the** ~s *(1,2)* привлека́тельная ♦ **heavenly blue of your** ~s небе́сная синь твои́х глаз ♦ **liquid dark depths of your** ~s мерца́ющая тёмная глубина́ твои́х глаз ♦ **tears in your** ~s слёзы на твои́х глаза́х ♦ **with bags under the** ~s с мешка́ми под глаза́ми.

Russian has 2 different verbs for "go",
one for "on foot" and the other for "by vehicle".

eye: *your beautiful eyes*

You have such beautiful eyes. У тебя такие прекрасные глаза. ♦ **Your eyes and your hair are absolutely gorgeous. They stay in my memory constantly.** Твои глаза и волосы совершенно великолепны. Они постоянно в моей памяти. ♦ **What first attracted me to you was your *(1)* beautiful / *(2)* bewitching eyes.** Первое, что привлекло меня к тебе, - твои *(1)* прекрасные / *(2)* околдовывающие глаза. ♦ **The image of your sweet smile and beautiful eyes was in my mind all the time.** Твоя нежная улыбка и прекрасные глаза были всегда в моих мыслях. ♦ **It is such a pleasure to look at your big, beautiful *(1)* dark / *(2)* blue eyes and the radiant loveliness of your face in your photos.** Такое наслаждение видеть твои большие, прекрасные *(1)* тёмные / *(2)* голубые глаза и сияющую красоту твоего лица на фотографиях. ♦ **Here's to your (incredibly) beautiful (*[1]* blue / *[2]* dark) eyes.** *(toast)* За твои (невероятно) прекрасные (*[1]* голубые / *[2]* тёмные) глаза. ♦ **Many, many times during the day, no matter where I am, I see your beautiful, *(1)* dark / *(2)* blue eyes and your long, shiny, *(3)* black / *(4)* blonde / *(5)* brown hair in my mind's eye.** Много, много раз в течение дня, где бы я ни был, в воображении вижу твои прекрасные, *(1)* тёмные / *(2)* голубые глаза и твои длинные, блестящие *(3)* чёрные / *(4)* светлые / *(5)* каштановые волосы. ♦ **Dear Maria with the enchanting eyes,** *(beginning of a letter)* Дорогая Мария с пленительными глазами,*(начало письма)*. ♦ **Every time I talk with you and look into your beautiful face, all I can see in front of my eyes for hours and hours afterwards are your enchanting, sparkling eyes, your smooth white skin, your *(1)* enticing / *(2)* kissable red lips, and your angel-like golden hair.** Каждый раз после того, как я говорю с тобой и смотрю на твоё прекрасное лицо, всё, что потом часами встаёт перед моими глазами, - твои очаровывающие, сверкающие глаза, твоя мягкая, белая кожа, твои *(1)* ...манящие... / *(2)* ...зовущие к поцелуям... красные губы и твои ангельские золотые волосы.

eye: *various qualities of your eyes*

Your eyes sparkle with mirth. Твои глаза искрятся весельем. ♦ **Do you know that you have stars in yours eyes?** Знаешь ли ты, что в твоих глазах звёзды? ♦ **When I look into your eyes, I see the stars.** Когда я смотрю в твои глаза, я вижу звёзды. ♦ **You have eyes that are bright with intelligence.** В твоих глазах светится ум. ♦ **Your eyes flash with such vitality.** Твои глаза так полны жизни. ♦ **I love the way your luminous eyes flash.** Мне нравится, как сверкают твои светящиеся глаза. ♦ **Your *(1)* blue / *(2)* dark / *(3)* green eyes are so captivating.** Твои *(1)* голубые / *(2)* тёмные / *(3)* зелёные глаза так очаровывают. ♦ **No wonder the sky is grey today. All the blue is in your eyes.** Не удивительно, что небо сегодня серое. Вся его голубизна в твоих глазах. ♦ **Your eyes sparkle like burnished turquoise.** Твои глаза искрятся, как полированная бирюза. ♦ **Your eyes are like limpid pools.** Твои глаза как прозрачные озёра. ♦ **Your *(1)* blue / *(2)* dark eyes and wide smile radiate *(3)* warmth / *(4)* affection.** Твои *(1)* голубые / *(2)* тёмные глаза и широкая улыбка излучают *(3)* теплоту / *(4)* нежность. ♦ **You have the most enchanting eyes that I've ever seen (in all my life).** У тебя самые очаровательные глаза, которые я когда-либо видел (во всей своей жизни). ♦ **Even in the dark(ness) your face seemed illumined by your eyes.** Даже в темноте твоё лицо кажется освещённым твоими глазами. ♦ **I can't forget your eyes.** Я не могу забыть твоих глаз. ♦ **The best artist in the world could not do justice to your eyes.** Лучший художник мира не способен оценить по достоинству твои глаза.

eye: *what your eyes do to me*

Your beautiful eyes melt my heart. Твои прекрасные глаза растопили моё сердце. ♦ **Each time I gaze into your eyes, I am inundated with the most intense feelings of love and**

Dipthongs in Russian are made by adding й
*to the end of a vowel (*а, е, ё, о, у, э, ю, *and* я).

adoration that I've ever experienced. Всякий раз, когда я вглядываюсь в твои глаза, я затоплен такими пылкими чувствами любви и обожания, каких никогда не испытывал. ♦ **I know for sure that your beautiful eyes and face will monopolize my thoughts and dreams in the days ahead.** Я совершенно уверен, что твои прекрасные глаза и лицо заполнят все мои мысли и мечты на все будущие дни. ♦ **I look at your dark, exotic, sensual eyes and I am thrilled to the very center of my heart.** Я смотрю в твои тёмные экзотические, чувственные глаза и моё сердце трепещет от волнения. ♦ **When I look into the dark irises of your eyes, I am (1) drawn / (2) sucked into a wild vortex of passion.** Когда я вглядываюсь в тёмную радужную оболочку твоих глаз, вихрь бешеной страсти засасывает меня. ♦ **When I look into the deep blue depths of your eyes, I am (completely) (1) transfixed. / (2) engulfed / (3) overcome by feelings of love.** Когда я смотрю в тёмно-синюю глубину твоих глаз, я (совершенно) (1) пронзён *(ж: пронзена)* / (2) поглощён *(поглощена)* / (3) охвачен *(ж: охвачена)* любовью к тебе. ♦ **Your beautiful blue eyes subjugate me utterly.** Твои прекрасные голубые глаза совершенно покорили меня. ♦ **Those beautiful (1) dark / (2) green eyes of yours intrigue me endlessly.** Эти твои прекрасные (1) тёмные / (2) зелёные глаза интригуют меня бесконечно. ♦ **The dark lambent flame in your eyes thrills me to the core of my being.** Меня всего охватывает тёмное сверкающее пламя твоих глаз. ♦ **Your beautiful eyes enchant me ([1] ...more than I can tell you. / [2] ...no end.).** Твои прекрасные глаза очаровывают меня ([1] ...больше, чем я могу высказать. / [2] ...без конца). ♦ **The sensual message in your eyes sends fire coursing through my veins.** Чувственный призыв в твоих глазах порождает огонь, текущий в моих венах. ♦ **You hypnotize me with your (1) beautiful / (2) exotic / (3) dark eyes.** Ты гипнотизируешь меня своими (1) прекрасными / (2) экзотическими / (3) тёмными глазами.

   | *eye: what your eyes did to me* |

You seduced me with your eyes. Ты глазами соблазняла *(ж: соблазнял)* меня. ♦ **The way your eyes roved so unashamedly over me just made me burn.** То, как бесстыдно твои глаза блуждали по мне, обжигало меня. ♦ **Your beautiful (1) blue / (2) dark eyes have set my heart (3) ablaze / (4) afire.** Твои прекрасные (1) голубые / (2) тёмные глаза повергают (3,4) в огонь моё сердце. ♦ **Your magical green eyes flecked with gold have subjugated all my thoughts.** Твои волшебные зелёные глаза с золотистыми крапинками взяли в плен все мои мысли.

   | *eye: love your eyes* |

Your eyes and your lips — oh! I could write a whole book of love poems dedicated to them. Твои глаза и губы -- О! Я мог бы написать целую книгу любовной лирики, посвящённой им. ♦ **I adore your eyes and sing to them.** Я обожаю твои глаза и воспеваю их. ♦ **I love to look ([1] directly / [2] deep) into your eyes when I (3) ...kiss you. / (4) ...make love with you.** Я люблю смотреть ([1] прямо / [2] глубоко) в твои глаза, когда (3) ...целую тебя. / (4) ...занимаюсь любовью с тобой.

   | *eye: kiss your eyes* |

I wish that I could kiss both your eyes very softly many, many, many times — before moving on to other delectable parts. Я хотел бы, чтобы я мог очень мягко целовать оба твоих глаза много, много, много раз прежде, чем передвинуться к другим восхитительным частям.

   | *eye: looking into your eyes* |

It's such a thrill to gaze into the dark irises of your eyes. Такое возбуждение - смотреть в тёмные зрачки твоих глаз. ♦ **It would be absolute heaven to lie next to you, hold you tenderly in my arms, look into your beautiful, dark eyes, kiss you ever so lovingly and**

> *Some phrases are listed under more than one main word.*

adoringly, and feel the magic warmth of your body all through the night.** Бы́ло бы так замеча́тельно лежа́ть ря́дом с тобо́й, держа́ть тебя́ не́жно в объя́тиях, смотре́ть в твои́ прекра́сные тёмные глаза́, целова́ть тебя́ с любо́вью и обожа́нием, чу́вствовать волше́бное тепло́ твоего́ те́ла всю ночь. ♦ **Do you know what I see when I look into your eyes? All the wonders and delights of paradise.** Ты зна́ешь, что я ви́жу, когда́ смотрю́ в твои́ глаза́? Все чудеса́ и восто́рги ра́я.

> **eye:** *when our eyes met*

When our eyes *(1)* **locked /** *(2)* **met /** *(3)* **connected,** *(4)* **...I knew right away that you were the one for me. /** *(5)* **...I knew I had to meet you. /** *(6)* **...I knew I had to have you. /** *(7)* **... I almost fainted with desire. /** *(8,9)* **...my heart skipped a beat. /** *(10)* **...I felt such a feeling as I've never felt before.** Когда́ на́ши глаза́ *(1-3)* встре́тились, *(4)* ...я то́тчас знал *(ж: зна́ла)*, что ты бу́дешь мое́й еди́нственной *(ж: мои́м еди́нственным)..* / *(5)* ...я знал *(ж: зна́ла)*, что я до́лжен *(ж: должна́)* познако́миться с тобо́й. / *(6)* ...я знал *(ж: зна́ла)*, что до́лжен *(ж: должна́)* быть с тобо́й / *(7)* ...я почти́ теря́л *(ж: теря́ла)* созна́ние от стра́сти. / *(8)* ...моё се́рдце заколоти́лось / *(9)* за́мерло. / *(10)* ...я ощуща́л *(ж: ощуща́ла)* тако́е чу́вство, как никогда́ пре́жде.

> **eye:** *had my eye on you*

I had my eye on you *(1)* **...for a long time. /** *(2)* **...since the day I first** *(3)* **saw /** *(4)* **met you.** Я положи́л взгляд на тебя́ *(1)* ...давно́. /*(2)* ...с того́ дня, когда́ я впервы́е *(3)* уви́дел / *(4)* встре́тил тебя́.

> **eye:** *eyes only for you*

I only have eyes for you. Я ви́жу то́лько тебя́.

> **eyes:** *can't take my eyes off you*

It's impossible for me to take my eyes off of you. Мне невозмо́жно отвести́ глаз от тебя́. ♦ **My eyes never left you for a second.** Мои́ глаза́ не оставля́ли тебя́ ни на секу́нду. ♦ **I cannot fill my eyes enough with the sight of your** *(1)* **beloved /** *(2)* **angelic /** *(3)* **beautiful face.** Я не могу́ нагляде́ться на твоё *(1)* люби́мое / *(2)* а́нгельское / *(3)* прекра́сное лицо́. ♦ **I could not** *(1)* **draw /** *(2)* **take my eyes away from** *(3)* **you /** *(4)* **yours.** Я не мог *(1,2)* отвести́ глаза́ от *(3)* тебя́ / *(4)* твои́х.

> **eye:** *easy on the eyes*

You're definitely not hard on the eyes. Ты определённо привлека́тельна. ♦ **You are so easy on the eyes.** Ты так ра́дуешь глаз! ♦ **I've never met anyone as easy on the eyes as you are.** Я никогда́ не встреча́л никого́, кто бы так ра́довал глаз, как ты.

> **eye:** *happiness and love in your eyes*

I want to always see *(1)* **love /** *(2)* **happiness** *(3,5)* **shining /** *(4,6)* **reflected in your eyes.** Я хочу́ всегда́ ви́деть *(1)* ...любо́вь, *(3)* сия́ющую / *(4)* отража́ющуюся... / *(2)* ...сча́стье, *(5)* сия́ющее / *6)* отража́ющееся... в твои́х глаза́х. ♦ **I hope that your beautiful** *(1)* **dark / ** *(2)* **blue eyes are shining with happiness to receive my letter.** Я наде́юсь, что твои́ прекра́сные *(1)* тёмные / *(2)* голубы́е глаза́ засия́ют сча́стьем, когда́ ты полу́чишь моё письмо́.

> **eye:** *feast my eyes*

I want to feast my eyes on your beautiful nude body-- and then my lips. Я хочу́ снача́ла пожира́ть твоё прекра́сное обнажённое те́ло глаза́ми, а пото́м губа́ми.

> **eye:** *catching my / your eye*

Your smile caught my eye. Твоя́ улы́бка бро́силась мне в глаза́. ♦ **I'm glad I caught your eye.** Я рад *(ж: ра́да)*, что пойма́л *(ж: пойма́ла)* твой взгляд.

> **eye:** *windows of the soul*

Eyes are the windows of the soul. Глаза́ -- зе́ркало души́.

> *The singular past tense of Russian verbs ends in -л (m) (usually), -ла (f) or -ло (n). the plural past tense ends in -li.*

eye: *attracting ladies' eyes*

I'm sure you draw all the ladies' eyes. Я увéрена, ты привлекáешь все жéнские взгля́ды.

eye: *sight for sore eyes*

You're a sight for sore eyes. Как я рад вас ви́деть.

eye: *see eye to eye*

We don't see eye to eye. Мы разошли́сь во взгля́дах. ♦ **We never see eye to eye (on anything).** Мы никогдá (ни на что) не смóтрим одинáковыми глазáми. ♦ **You and I see eye to eye on so many things.** Ты и я смóтрим одинáковыми глазáми на такóе мнóжество вещéй.

eye: *unfaithful eyes*

You have roving eyes. Твои́ глазá не пропускáют ни одногó мужчи́ну *(ж: одну́ жéн-щину).* ♦ **You were making cow's eyes at him *(her)* all night long.** Ты весь вéчер стро́и-ла емý *(ж: стро́ил ей)* глáзки. ♦ **I saw you making eyes at each other.** Я ви́дел *(ж: ви́дела),* вы стро́или глáзки друг дру́гу. ♦ **You made a pass at *(1)* him / *(2)* her with your eyes.** Ты постре́ливала *(ж: постре́ливал)* в *(1)* негó / *(2)* неё глазáми.

eye: *keep an eye on you*

It looks like I have to keep an eye on you (all the time). Выхóдит, что я всё врéмя дóлжен *(ж: должнá)* не спускáть с тебя́ глаз.

[**eye: *pulling the wool over mine***]

Don't think you can pull the wool over my eyes. Не ду́май, что ты мóжешь обману́ть меня́.

eye: *look me in the eye*

Can you look me in the eye and tell me that? Мóжешь ты посмотрéть мне в глазá и рассказáть мне э́то?

eye: *lost an eye*

I lost my *(1)* right / *(2)* left eye in *(3)* ...the (Vietnam) war. / *(4)* ...an accident. Я потеря́л *(ж: потеря́ла) (1)* прáвый / *(2)* лéвый глаз *(3)* ...на войнé (во Вьетнáме). / *(4)* ...в авáрии.

eyebrow *n* бровь *f (pl:* брóви*)* ♦ **beautiful** ~s краси́вые брóви ♦ **black** ~s чёрные брóви ♦ **blond** ~s свéтлые брóви ♦ *(1,2)* **bushy** ~s *(1)* густы́е / *(2)* кусти́стые брóви ♦ **plucked** ~s вы́щипанные брóви ♦ **thick** ~s **brows** тóлстые брóви ♦ **shaggy** ~s мохнáтые брóви ♦ **thin** ~s тóнкие брóви ♦ **tinted** ~s крáшеные брóви ♦ **That's going to raise a lot of eyebrows.** Мнóгие поднимут брóви. ♦ **I don't want to raise eyebrows.** Я не хочý поднимáть брóви.

eye-catching *adj* привлекáтельный, -ая, -ое, -ые.

eye-eat *vt* поедáть глазáми ♦ **You were eye-eating him *(her)* all evening.** Ты поедáла егó *(ж: поедáл её)* глазáми весь вéчер.

eyeful *n* 1. *(pleasing sight)* восхити́тельное зрéлище; 2. *(attractive woman)* прелéстная жéнщина ♦ **You're quite an eyeful.** Ты совершéнно прелéстная жéнщина.

eyeglasses *n, pl* очки́.

eyelash *n* ресни́ца ♦ **beautiful** ~es краси́вые ресни́цы ♦ **black** ~es чёрные ресни́цы ♦ **blonde** ~es свéтлые ресни́цы ♦ **curled** ~es зáгнутые (квéрху) ресни́цы ♦ **dark** ~es тёмные ресни́цы ♦ *(1-3)* **false** ~es *(1)* накладны́е / *(2)* наклéенные / *(3)* иску́сственные ресни́цы ♦ **fluffy** ~es пуши́стые ресни́цы ♦ **fluttering** ~es трепéщущие ресни́цы ♦ **heavy** ~es тяжёлые ресни́цы ♦ **long (black)** ~es дли́нные (чёрные) ресни́цы ♦ **painted** ~es накрáшенные ресни́цы ♦ **red** ~es ры́жие ресни́цы ♦ **short** ~es корóткие ресни́цы ♦ **thick** ~es густы́е ресни́цы ♦ **your** ~es *(familiar)* твои́ ресни́цы; *(polite)* Вáши ресни́цы

Please do us a favor:
Fill out and mail in the Feedback Sheet on page 795.

  ♦ **flutter ~es** взма́хивать / взмахну́ть ресни́цами.

eyelid *n* ве́ко ((*pl:* ве́ки).

eyeliner *n* каранда́ш для глаз.

eye-power *n* си́ла взгля́да.

eye shadow *n* те́ни для век.

eyesight *n* зре́ние ♦ **good** ~ хоро́шее зре́ние ♦ **perfect** ~ отли́чное зре́ние ♦ **poor** ~ плохо́е зре́ние ♦ **weak** ~ сла́бое зре́ние.

EZ *abbrev* = **easy** лёгкий, -ая, -ое, -ие.

Clock and calender time are discussed in Appendix 5, page 759.

F

fab *adj (slang)* = **fabulous** невероя́тный, -ая, -ое, -ые, потряса́ющий, -ая, -ее, -ие.

fabric *n* ткань *f* ♦ **thin** ~ то́нкая ткань.

fabulous *adj* невероя́тный, -ая, -ое, -ые, потряса́ющий, -ая, -ее, -ие ♦ **You are an absolutely fabulous lover.** Ты соверше́нно потряса́ющая любо́вница *(ж: потрясáющий любóвник).* ♦ **You look (**[1]** absolutely /** [2]** positively) fabulous.** Ты вы́глядишь *(*[1,2]* про́сто)* потряса́юще.

facade *n* ви́димость *f* ♦ **Your** *(1)* **caring /** *(2)* **concern /** *(3)* **commitment /** *(4)* **devotion /** *(5)* **love /** *(6)* **sincerity was just a** *(7,8)* **facade.** Твоя́ *(1,2)* забо́та / *(3,4)* пре́данность / *(5)* любо́вь / *(6)* и́скренность была́ то́лько *(7)* показно́й / *(8)* ви́димостью.

face *vt* справля́ться / спра́виться *(what = + с + acc.),* смотре́ть / посмотре́ть в лицо́ *(whom = dat.),* встреча́ть / встре́тить лицо́м *(what, whom = acc.)* ♦   **Side by side I know we can face whatever life brings.** Вме́сте, я зна́ю, мы мо́жем сме́ло встре́тить всё, что преподнесёт нам жизнь.

face *n* лицо́ ♦ **angelic** ~ а́нгельское лицо́ ♦ **attractive** ~ симпати́чное лицо́ ♦ **austere** ~ стро́гое лицо́ ♦ **baby** ~ 1. *(face)* ку́кольное лицо́, ли́чико; 2. *(person)* ку́колка, краcо́тка ♦ **bearded** ~ борода́тое лицо́ ♦ *(1,2)* **beautiful** ~ *(1)* краси́вое / *(2)* прекра́сное лицо́ ♦ **broad** ~ широ́кое лицо́ ♦ **cheerful** ~ весёлое лицо́ ♦ **child's** ~ де́тское лицо́ ♦ **classically beautiful** ~ класси́чески краси́вое лицо́ ♦ **clean** ~ чи́стое лицо́ ♦ **clean shaven** ~ чи́сто вы́бритое лицо́ ♦ **common** ~ просто́е лицо́ ♦ **cute** ~ хоро́шенькое ли́чико ♦ **dark** ~ смýглое лицо́ ♦ **darkly handsome** ~ смýглое краси́вое лицо́ ♦ **deadpan** ~ ка́менное лицо́ ♦ **dear** ~ дорого́е лицо́ ♦ **dirty** ~ гря́зное лицо́ ♦ **expressive** ~ вырази́тельное лицо́ ♦ ~ **quick to smile** улы́бчивое лицо́ ♦ ~ **that smiles easily** улы́бчивое лицо́ ♦ **amiliar** ~ знако́мое лицо́ ♦ **freckled** ~ весну́шчатое лицо́ ♦ **fresh** ~ све́жее лицо́ ♦ **friendly** ~ приве́тливое лицо́ ♦ **gentle** ~ не́жное лицо́ ♦ **girlish** ~ де́вичье лицо́ ♦ **gloomy** ~ угрю́мое лицо́ ♦ *(1,2)* **good-looking** ~ *(1)* симпати́чное / *(2)* интере́сное лицо́ ♦ **happy** ~ ра́достное лицо́ ♦ **haughty** ~ надме́нное лицо́ ♦ **heart-shaped** ~ ова́льное ли́чико с о́стрым подбородко́м ♦ **innocent** ~ неви́нное лицо́ ♦ *(1,2)* **intelligent** ~ *(1)* интеллиге́нтное / *(2)* у́мное лицо́ ♦ **kind(ly)** ~ до́брое лицо́ ♦ **kissie** ~ лицо́, со́зданное для поцелу́ев *(1 term)* ♦ **large** ~ крýпное лицо́ ♦ **laughing** ~ смею́щееся лицо́ ♦ **lively** ~ живо́е лицо́ ♦ *(1-7)* **long** ~ *(sad, gloomy)* *(1)* грýстное лицо́, *(2)* печа́льный / *(3)* ки́слый / *(4)* уны́лый / *(5)* мра́чный вид; *(6) (distressed)* огорчённый вид; *(7) (disappointed)* разочаро́ванный вид ♦ **love-soft**

Reflexive verbs are those that end in -ся *or* -сь.
The -ся *or* -сь *also goes onto a past tense ending.*

ened ~ смягчённое любо́вью лицо́ ♦ **lovely** ~ прекра́сное лицо́ ♦ **madonna-like** ~ лицо́ мадо́нны ♦ **magnetic** ~ притя́гивающее лицо́ ♦ **mean** ~ злбе лицо́ ♦ **mobile** ~ по-дви́жное лицо́ ♦ **narrow** ~ у́зкое лицо́ ♦ **nice** ~ *(attractive)* симпати́чное лицо́; *(pleasant)* прия́тное лицо́ ♦ **noble** ~ благоро́дное лицо́ ♦ **ordinary** ~ просто́е лицо́ ♦ **pale** ~ бле́дное лицо́ ♦ **petulant** ~ раздражённое лицо́ ♦ **placid** ~ споко́йное лицо́ ♦ **plain** ~ *(ordinary)* просто́е лицо́; *(unattractive)* некраси́вое лицо́ ♦ *(1,2)* **pleasant** ~ *(1)* прия́тное / *(2)* откры́тое лицо́ ♦ **pock-marked** ~ рябо́е лицо́ ♦ **poker** ~ ка́менное лицо́ ♦ *(1-3)* **pretty** ~ *(1)* милови́дное / *(2)* смазли́вое / *(3)* ми́лое лицо́ ♦ **puffed-up** ~ одут-лова́тое лицо́ ♦ **puffy** ~ одутлова́тое лицо́ ♦ **red** ~ кра́сное лицо́ ♦ **round(ed)** ~ кру́глое лицо́ ♦ **round pudgy** ~ кру́глое по́лное лицо́ ♦ **ruddy** ~ румя́ное лицо́ ♦ *(1,2)* **sad** ~ *(1)* печа́льное / *(2)* гру́стное лицо́ ♦ **serene** ~ споко́йное лицо́ ♦ **serenely beautiful** ~ споко́йное прекра́сное лицо́ ♦ *(1,2)* **sleepy** ~ *(1)* со́нное / *(2)* за́спанное лицо́ ♦ **small** ~ небольшо́е лицо́ ♦ **smiling** ~ улыба́ющееся лицо́ ♦ **smooth** ~ не́жное лицо́ ♦ **stern** ~ стро́гое лицо́ ♦ **strange** ~ *(unfamiliar)* незнако́мое лицо́ ♦ **striking** ~ порази́тельное лицо́ ♦ **strong, masculine** ~ реши́тельное, мужско́е лицо́ ♦ **stuckup** ~ надме́нное лицо́ ♦ **sullen** ~ угрю́мое лицо́ ♦ **(sun)tanned** ~ загоре́лое лицо́ ♦ **tear-stained** ~ запла́канное лицо́ ♦ **tear-streaked** ~ лицо́ с по́лосами слёз ♦ **tired** ~ уста́лое лицо́ ♦ **ugly** ~ некра-си́вое лицо́ ♦ **unfamiliar** ~ незнако́мое лицо́ ♦ **unshaven** ~ небри́тое лицо́ ♦ **weather-beaten** ~ обве́тренное лицо́ ♦ **weathered** ~ обве́тренное лицо́ ♦ **weather-tanned** ~ лицо́, покры́тое зага́ром *(1 term)* ♦ **wholesome freckled** ~ пы́шущее здоро́вьем вес-ну́шчатое лицо́ ♦ **wise** ~ му́дрое лицо́ ♦ **worried** ~ озабо́ченное лицо́ ♦ **wrinkled** ~ морщи́нистое лицо́ ♦ **~ to** ~ лицо́м к лицу́ ♦ **stroke your** ~ гла́дить твоё лицо́ ♦ **wear a long** ~ *(sad, gloomy)* име́ть гру́стное лицо́, име́ть печа́льный / ки́слый / уны́лый / мра́чный вид; *(distressed)* име́ть огорчённый вид; *(disappointed)* име́ть разочаро́-ванный вид.

---

face: *your beautiful face*

What a *(1)* **cute** / *(2)* **beautiful** / *(3)* **lovely face (you have)!** Что за *(1)* ми́лое / *(2,3)* пре-кра́сное лицо́ (у тебя́)! ♦ *(1)* **You've got...** / *(2)* **You have... the** ...*(3)* **cutest** / *(4)* **loveliest** / *(5)* **most beautiful** / *(6)* **most angelic** / *(7)* **most enchanting** / *(8)* **most adorable** / *(9)* **most heavenly... face I've ever seen (in all my life).** *(1,2)* У тебя́ са́мое *(3)* ...ми́ленькое / *(4,5)* прекра́сное / *(6)* а́нгельское / *(7)* очарова́тельное / *(8)* восхити́тельное / *(9)* боже́ст-венное... лицо́ из всех, ви́денных мной (в жи́зни). ♦ **Your face is a paragon of** *(1)* **beauty** / *(2)* **loveliness.** Твоё лицо́ - образе́ц *(1,2)* красоты́. ♦ **You have a face of infinite beauty (and sensuality).** У тебя́ лицо́ безграни́чной красоты́ (и чу́вственности). ♦ **If the rest of you is (half) as beautiful as your face, then heaven holds no greater promises for me.** Если и всё остально́е в тебе́ (хотя́ бы наполови́ну) так же прекра́сно, как твоё лицо́, тогда́ мне не о чем бо́льше проси́ть небеса́. ♦ **Your face is exquisite.** Твоё лицо́ преле́стно. ♦ **Even in the dark(ness) your face seemed illumined by your eyes.** Да́же в темноте́ твоё лицо́ ка́жется освещённым твои́ми глаза́ми. ♦ **Your dark hair accen-tuates the soft loveliness of your face.** Твои́ тёмные во́лосы подчёркивают мя́гкую красоту́ твоего́ лица́. ♦ **I wish I were an artist so that I could capture the exquisite beauty of your face in a painting.** Я хоте́л бы быть худо́жником для того́, чтобы в карти́не запечатле́ть изы́сканную красоту́ твоего́ лица́. ♦ **Your face is so incredibly beautiful, like nothing else I've ever seen.** Твоё лицо́ так невероя́тно прекра́сно, как ни одно́ друго́е, кото́рое я пре́жде ви́дел. ♦ **You have the face of an angel.** У тебя́ лицо́ а́нгела. ♦ **You have a face that was sculpted by angels.** У тебя́ лицо́, изва́янное а́нге-лами. ♦ **You have** *(1)* **...such a...** / *(2)* **...an exceptionally... beautiful face.** У тебя́ *(1)* тако́е / *(2)* исключи́тельно прекра́сное лицо́. ♦ **You have a face that is (absolutely)**

The time zones for many cities of the world are given in Appendix 6, page 761.

enchanting in its loveliness. У тебя́ лицо́, красота́ кото́рого (соверше́нно) очаро́-вывает. ♦ **Your face is so full of sensuality.** Твоё лицо́ так по́лно чу́вственности.

> *face: the effect of your beautiful face*

You have a face that instantly inspires reverence and adoration. У тебя́ лицо́, кото́рое мгнове́нно внуша́ет благогове́ние и обожа́ние. ♦ **Your face makes all other faces drab and plain by comparison.** Все други́е ли́ца вы́глядят ту́склыми и неинтере́сными по сравне́нию с твои́м.

> *face: your face in my thoughts and dreams*

The unsurpassed beauty of your face reigns over all my thoughts. Непревзойдённая красота́ твоего́ лица́ вла́ствует над все́ми мои́ми по́мыслами. ♦ **After seeing your (beautiful) face, I haven't been able to think of anything else.** Уви́дев Ва́ше (прекра́сное) лицо́, я не могу́ ду́мать ни о чём друго́м. ♦ **Everywhere I go, everything I do, the radiant beauty of your face fills my thoughts.** Везде́, куда́ бы я ни пошёл, во всём, что бы я ни де́лал, сия́ющая красота́ твоего́ лица́ заполня́ет мои́ мы́сли. ♦ **I know for sure that your beautiful eyes and face will monopolize my thoughts and dreams in the days ahead.** Я соверше́нно уве́рен, что твои́ прекра́сные глаза́ и лицо́ запо́лнят все мои́ мы́сли и мечты́ на все бу́дущие дни. ♦ **In all my dreams I see your beautiful face (framed by the splendor of your golden hair).** Во всех свои́х снах я ви́жу твоё прекра́сное лицо́ (в опра́ве из роско́шных золоты́х воло́с). ♦ **With the vision of your beautiful face constantly in my thoughts, I am totally unable to concentrate on anything.** Твоё прекра́сное лицо́ постоя́нно в мои́х мы́слях, и я соверше́нно не в состоя́нии ни на чём сосредото́читься. ♦ **The thought of your beautiful face continually distracts me.** Мысль о твоём прекра́сном лице́ постоя́нно отвлека́ет меня́. ♦ **Your face has been on my mind ever since.** Твоё лицо́ с тех пор постоя́нно бы́ло пе́редо мной. ♦ **All of my daydreams and fantasies are filled with images of your exquisitely beautiful face.** Твоё изы́сканно прекра́сное лицо́ заполня́ет все мои́ мечты́ и фанта́зии. ♦ **I'd know your face anywhere -- I see it in all my dreams.** Я узна́л бы твоё лицо́ где уго́дно -- я ви́жу его́ во всех свои́х снах.

> *face: your beauty in the faces of my children*

You possess the kind of beauty that I would like to see reflected in the faces of all my children. Ты облада́ешь тако́й красото́й, кото́рую я бы хоте́л ви́деть отражённой в ли́цах всех свои́х дете́й.

> *face: when I saw your face*

When I saw your face I *(1)* **...felt a thunderbolt of love go straight to my heart.** / *(2)* **...was awestruck.** Когда́ я уви́дел твоё лицо́, *(1)* ...мо́лния любви́ попа́ла пря́мо в моё се́рдце. / *(2)* ...я был охва́чен *(ж: была́ охва́чена)* благогове́нием. ♦ **The minute I saw your face,** *(1)* **...I knew I had to write to you.** / *(2)* **...my heart demanded that I write to you.** / *(3)* **...I forgot everyone else I had seen before.** / *(4)* **...my heart was in your captivity.** / *(5)* **...I realized how unlucky my life had been up till then.** / *(6)* **...I knew you were the (one and only) person I wanted to meet** С той мину́ты, как я уви́дел Ва́ше лицо́, *(1)* ...я знал, что до́лжен написа́ть Вам. / *(2)* ...моё се́рдце тре́бовало, чтобы я написа́л Вам. / *(3)* ...я забы́л всех, кого́ я ви́дел ра́ньше. / *(4)* ...моё се́рдце бы́ло покорено́. / *(5)* ...я по́нял, как неуда́чна моя́ жизнь была́ до сих пор. / *(6)* ...я знал, что Вы тот (еди́нственный) челове́к, кото́рого я хоте́л встре́тить. ♦ **I was really astonished to see such a(n) (incredibly) beautiful face looking at me from the Internet.** Я был действи́тельно изумлён, уви́дев тако́е (невероя́тно) прекра́сное лицо́, смотре́вшее на меня́ с Интерне́та.

> *face: seeing your face*

I cannot fill my eyes enough with the sight of your *(1)* **beloved** / *(2)* **angelic** / *(3)* **beautiful**

> *Optional parts of sentences are preceded*
> *or followed (or both) by three dots.*

face. Я не могу́ нагляде́ться на твоё *(1)* люби́мое / *(2)* а́нгельское / *(3)* прекра́сное лицо́. ♦ **It is such a pleasure to** *(1)* **look /** *(2)* **gaze at** *(3,4)* **your big, beautiful** *(5)* **dark /** *(6)* **blue eyes and the radiant** *(7)* **beauty /** *(8)* **loveliness of** *(9,10)* **your face in this photo.** Тако́е удово́льствие *(1)* ...смотре́ть на... / *(2)* ...вгля́дываться в... *(3)* твои́ *(familiar)* / *(4)* Ва́ши *(polite)* больши́е, прекра́сные *(5)* тёмные / *(6)* голубы́е глаза́ и сия́ющую *(7,8)* красоту́ *(9)* твоего́ *(familiar)* / *(10)* Ва́шего *(polite)* лица́ на э́той фотогра́фии. ♦ **I want to wake up and see your beautiful face every morning.** Ка́ждое у́тро я хочу́ просыпа́ться и ви́деть твоё прекра́сное лицо́. ♦ **When I look at you, I see the face of an angel.** Смотря́ на тебя́, я ви́жу лицо́ а́нгела. ♦ **I see in this photo a face of** *(1)* **exquisite /** *(2)* **unimaginable beauty crowned with an opulence of** *(3)* **golden /** *(4)* **chestnut /** *(5)* **raven hair.** Я ви́жу на э́той фотогра́фии лицо́ *(1)* изы́сканной / *(2)* невообрази́мой красоты́ в стру́ящемся бога́тстве *(3)* золоти́стых / *(4)* кашта́новых / *(5)* чёрных воло́с. ♦ **I forgot where I was after seeing your face.** Я забы́л обо всём, уви́дев Ва́ше *(polite)* лицо́. ♦ **I couldn't avert my gaze from your** *(1)* **beautiful /** *(2)* **enchanting face.** Я не мог отвести́ свой взгляд от твоего́ *(1)* прекра́сного / *(2)* очарова́тельного лица́. ♦ **Every time my eyes are open, I want to look at your beautiful, lovable, angelic face.** Всегда́, когда́ мои́ глаза́ откры́ты, я хочу́ ви́деть твоё прекра́сное, люби́мое, а́нгельское лицо́.

> **face:** *what I feel when I see your face*

Whenever I look at your beloved face in this photo, *(1)***...my heart overflows with love for you. /** *(2)* **...I am filled with enormous /** *(3)* **tremendous /** *(4)* **unbearable yearning to be with you (again).** Когда́ бы я ни взгляну́л *(ж: взгляну́ла)* на твоё люби́мое лицо́ на э́той фотогра́фии, *(1)* ...моё се́рдце переполня́ется любо́вью к тебе́. / *(2)* ...я перепо́лнен огро́мной / *(3)* грома́дной / *(4)* невыноси́мой жа́ждой быть с тобо́й (опя́ть). ♦ **Every time I talk with you and look into your beautiful face, all I can see in front of my eyes for hours and hours afterwards are your enchanting, sparkling eyes, your smooth white skin, your** *(1)* **enticing /** *(2)* **kissable red lips, and your angel-like golden hair.** Ка́ждый раз по́сле того́, как я говорю́ с тобо́й и смотрю́ на твоё прекра́сное лицо́, всё, что пото́м часа́ми встаёт пе́ред мои́ми глаза́ми - твои́ очаро́вывающие, сверка́ющие глаза́, твоя́ мя́гкая, бе́лая ко́жа, твои́ *(1)* ...маня́щие... / *(2)* ...зову́щие к поцелу́ям... кра́сные гу́бы и твои́ а́нгельские золоти́стые во́лосы. ♦ **My pulse just rockets when I look at your beautiful face (and beautiful body).** Мой пульс то́тчас учаща́ется, как то́лько я взгляну́ на твоё прекра́сное лицо́ (и те́ло). ♦ **My heart ignites in** *(1)* **celebration /** *(2)* **delight /** *(3)* **ecstasy /** *(4)* **jubilation every time I see your (**[5]* **beautiful /** *[6]* **beloved) face.** Моё се́рдце *(1)* ...загора́ется ра́достью / *(2)* восто́ргом... / *(3)* ...вспы́хивает в экста́зе... / *(4)* ...лику́ет... ка́ждый раз, когда́ я ви́жу твоё (*[5]* прекра́сное / *[6]* люби́мое) лицо́. ♦ **The sight of your beautiful face** *(1)* **...fills my whole body with warm excitement and floods my heart with feelings of love for you. /** *(2)* **...makes me dream of all the pleasures in paradise.** Взгляд на твоё прекра́сное лицо́ *(1)* ...наполня́ет всё моё те́ло жа́рким возбужде́нием и затопля́ет се́рдце чу́вством любви́ к тебе́. / *(2)* ...заставля́ет мечта́ть о всех наслажде́ниях ра́я. ♦ **To pull out your photos and look at the face and form of the person who is writing all these nice things to me almost makes me swoon into a faint.** Вы́нуть твои́ фотогра́фии и ви́деть лицо́ и фигу́ру челове́ка, пи́шущего мне все э́ти прия́тные слова́, -- э́то дово́дит меня́ почти́ до о́бморока. ♦ **Seeing your beautiful face just adds fuel to the fire of my desire for you.** Когда́ я ви́жу твоё прекра́сное лицо́, ого́нь мое́й стра́сти к тебе́ разжига́ется ещё сильне́е. ♦ **The expectation to see your beloved face again makes me feel hot and feverish.** Ожида́ние опя́ть уви́деть твоё люби́мое лицо́ вызыва́ет во мне жар и

> *If you're not on familiar terms with a person,*
> *the «ты» forms will have to be changed to «Вы».*

лихора́дочное возбужде́ние.

---
face: *the image of your face*

The image of your beautiful face is forever alive in my heart. Твоё прекра́сное лицо́ всегда́ живёт в моём се́рдце.

---
face: *I like / love your face*

(Oh, how) I *(1)* love / *(2)* (absolutely) adore your (*[3]* dreamy / *[4]* beautiful / *[5]* angelic) face. (О, как) я *(1)* люблю́ / *(2)* (про́сто) обожа́ю твоё (*[3]* мечта́тельное / *[4]* прекра́сное / *[5]* а́нгельское) лицо́. ♦ **I gaze upon your divinely beautiful face in its silky frame of *(1)* golden / *(2)* auburn / *(3)* black hair and I am awash in fervent adoration.** Я вгля́дываюсь в твоё боже́ственно-прекра́сное лицо́ в шелкови́стом обрамле́нии *(1)* золоти́стых / *(2)* золоти́сто-кашта́новых / *(3)* чёрных воло́с и тону́ в пы́лком обожа́нии. ♦ **What rapture it is to gaze at your love-softened face.** Что за восто́рг -- вгля́дываться в твоё смягчённое любо́вью лицо́. ♦ **To see your face is to adore it.** Ви́деть твоё лицо́ -- зна́чит обожа́ть его́. ♦ **There are faces in this world that immediately captivate the heart. Yours is one of those. And certainly it is the most captivating that I personally have ever seen.** Есть ли́ца в э́том ми́ре, кото́рые неме́дленно пленя́ют сердца́. Твоё одно́ из них. И несомне́нно, твоё лицо́ -- са́мое плени́тельное из всех, ви́денных мной. ♦ **I really like your (beautiful) face. It is one of the most beautiful faces I have ever seen.** Мне действи́тельно нра́вится твоё (прекра́сное) лицо́. Это одно́ из прекра́снейших лиц, ви́денных мной.

---
face: *I want to kiss your face*

I've never seen a face that I wanted to kiss more than I want to kiss yours. Я никогда́ не ви́дел лица́, кото́рое я хоте́л бы целова́ть бо́льше, чем хочу́ целова́ть твоё. ♦ **How heavenly it would be to take your beautiful face softly in my hands and kiss it lovingly all over, many, many, many times.** Как боже́ственно бы́ло бы не́жно взять в ру́ки твоё прекра́сное лицо́ и любо́вно покры́ть его́ поцелу́ями мно́го, мно́го, мно́го раз. ♦ **I'm going to *(1)* cover / *(2)* shower your beautiful face with (tender, loving) kisses.** Я *(1)* покро́ю / *(2)* затоплю́ твоё прекра́сное лицо́ (не́жными, лю́бящими) поцелу́ями. ♦ **My favorite pleasure in life is kissing your beautiful face.** Са́мое большо́е наслажде́ние в мое́й жи́зни -- целова́ть твоё прекра́сное лицо́. ♦ **You have the kind of face that I could kiss (on) for hours and hours.** У Вас тако́е лицо́, кото́рое я мог бы целова́ть часа́ми. ♦ **I could spend endless hours kissing your beautiful face.** Я мог бы провести́ бесконе́чные часы́, целу́я твоё прекра́сное лицо́. ♦ **How I wish that I were holding you in my arms at this very minute, covering your beautiful face with (adoring) kisses.** Как бы я жела́л держа́ть тебя́ в объя́тиях в э́ту са́мую мину́ту, покрыва́я твоё прекра́сное лицо́ (обожа́ющими) поцелу́ями. ♦ **As my hand cups the fullness of your breast, my mouth will cover your beautiful face and smooth neck with (adoring) kisses.** В то вре́мя, как моя́ рука́ ощути́т полноту́ твое́й груди́, мой рот покро́ет твоё прекра́сное лицо́ и не́жную ше́ю (обожа́ющими) поцелу́ями. ♦ **The way you write to me makes me want to take you in my arms and hug you and hug you and hug you and cover your sweet face with loving kisses.** То, как ты пи́шешь мне, вызыва́ет во мне жела́ние взять тебя́ на ру́ки, обнима́ть, обнима́ть и обнима́ть тебя́ и покрыва́ть твоё не́жное лицо́ лю́бящими поцелу́ями. ♦ **I wish so much that I could hold you snugly in my arms and put soft, loving kisses all over your hair and face.** Я так хоте́л бы ую́тно устро́ить тебя́ в свои́х объя́тиях и покры́ть мя́гкими, лю́бящими поцелу́ями твои́ во́лосы и лицо́. ♦ **I want to kiss your dear, beloved face.** Я хочу́ целова́ть твоё дорого́е, люби́мое лицо́.

A list of common places with their grammatical endings is given in Appendix 7, page 763.

face: *I miss your face*
I miss your beloved, beautiful face. Я скуча́ю по твоему́ люби́мому, прекра́сному лицу́.

face: *sucker for a pretty face*
I guess I'm a sucker for a pretty face. Пожа́луй, меня́ сли́шком привлека́ют краси́вые ли́ца.

face: *look me in the face*
Look me in the face and say that. Взгляни́ в моё лицо́ и скажи́ э́то.

fact *n* факт ♦ **actual** ~ действи́тельный факт ♦ **indisputable** ~ неоспори́мый факт ♦ **plain** ~ просто́й факт ♦ **simple** ~ просто́й факт ♦ **surprising** ~ удиви́тельный факт.

fade *vi* вя́нуть / увя́нуть, увяда́ть / увя́нуть; угаса́ть / уга́снуть ♦ **You are the** *(1)* **rose /** *(2)* **flower that never fades.** Ты *(1)* ...ро́за, кото́рая... / *(2)* ...цвето́к, кото́рый... никогда́ не увя́нет. ♦ **To me, you will never fade nor age nor die.** Для меня́ ты никогда́ не увя́нешь, не соста́ришься, не умрёшь.

fail *vi* оказа́ться не в состоя́нии, прова́ливаться / провали́ться, ослабе́ть, потерпе́ть неуда́чу ♦ ~ **in love** потерпе́ть неуда́чу в любви́, не име́ть успе́ха в любви́, оказа́ться несостоя́тельным в любви́ ♦ **If all else fails, I'll call you from the airport.** В любо́м слу́чае я позвоню́ тебе́ из аэропо́рта. ♦ **Up to now, I seem always to have failed in love.** Ка́жется, до сих пор у меня́ никогда́ не́ было успе́ха в любви́.

failure *n* неуспе́х, неуда́ча, прова́л ♦ ~ **to understand each other** взаи́мное недопонима́ние.

faint *vi* лиши́ться чувств, упа́сть в о́бморок ♦ **When our lips met the first time, I almost fainted from ecstasy.** Когда́ на́ши гу́бы встре́тились впервы́е, я чуть не лиши́лся *(ж: лиши́лась)* чувств от восто́рга.

fair *adj* 1. *(honest; evenhanded)* справедли́вый, -ая, -ое, -ые; 2. *(fair-haired)* белоку́рый, -ая, -ое, -ые; *(hair)* све́тлый, -ая, -ое, -ые; *(skin)* бе́лый, -ая, -ое, -ые; 3. *(beautiful)* краси́вый, -ая, -ое, -ые ♦ ~ **hair** све́тлые во́лосы ♦ ~ **lady** краси́вая да́ма ♦ ~ **person** 1. *(evenhanded)* справедли́вый челове́к; 2. *(fair-haired)* белоку́рый челове́к, блонди́н *m*, блонди́нка *f* ♦ ~ **skin** бе́лая ко́жа.

fair *n* я́рмарка ♦ **book** ~ кни́жная я́рмарка ♦ **international** ~ междунаро́дная я́рмарка ♦ **spring** ~ весе́нняя я́рмарка ♦ **trade** ~ торго́вая я́рмарка ♦ **Would you like to** *(1,2)* **go to the fair (with me)?** Не хоте́ла *(ж: хоте́л)* бы ты *(1)* пойти́ *(on foot)* / *(2)* пое́хать *(by veh.)* на я́рмарку (со мной)?

fair-haired *adj* светловоло́сый, -ая, -ое, -ые, белоку́рый, -ая, -ое, -ые, златовла́сый, -ая, -ое, -ые.

fair-minded *adj* справедли́вый, -ая, -ое, -ые.

fairness *n* справедли́вость *f* ♦ **In all fairness** *(1)* ...**I must tell you.** / *(2)* ...**you should have told me.** Справедли́вости ра́ди *(1)* ...я до́лжен *(ж: должна́)* рассказа́ть тебе́. / *(2)* ...ты должна́ была́ *(ж: до́лжен был)* рассказа́ть мне.

fairytale *n* ска́зка.

faith *n* 1. *(belief)* ве́ра; *(trust)* дове́рие; 2. *(religious)* ве́ра, рели́гия ♦ **act of** ~ акт дове́рия ♦ **Have faith in me.** Пове́рь в меня́. ♦ **I have (a lot of) faith in you.** Я (так си́льно) ве́рю в тебя́.

faithful *adj* ве́рный, -ая, -ое, -ые *(short forms:* ве́рен, верна́, -о, -ы́*)* ♦ **It is my solemn vow to you that I will always** *(1)* **be /** *(2)* **remain faithful to you.** Даю́ тебе́ торже́ственную кля́тву, что я всегда́ *(1)* ...бу́ду... / *(2)* ...бу́ду остава́ться... ве́рным *(ж: ве́рной)* тебе́. ♦ **I will always be faithful to you.** Я всегда́ бу́ду ве́рен *(ж: верна́)* тебе́. ♦ **I'm always faithful to you.** Я всегда́ ве́рен *(ж: верна́)* тебе́. ♦ **I have always been faithful to you**

Common adult heights are given in Appendix 9, page 776.

(both in thought and in deed). Я всегда́ был ве́рен *(ж: была́ верна́)* тебе́ (как в мы́слях, так и в посту́пках). ♦ **Your faithful** (name) *(closing of a letter)* Твой пре́-данный *(ж: Твоя́ пре́данная)* (имя). ♦ **Let us promise always to be faithful to** *(1)* **...each other.** / *(2)* **...one another.** Дава́й пообеща́ем всегда́ быть ве́рными *(1,2)* друг дру́гу.

fake *adj* фальши́вый, -ая, -ое, -ые, подде́льный, -ая, -ое, -ые.

fake *vt* подде́лывать / подде́лать *(what = acc.)*, фальсифици́ровать *(what = acc.)* ♦ ~ **it** де́лать / сде́лать вид ♦ **With him I used to just fake an orgasm.** С ним я привы́кла то́лько подде́лывать / фальсифици́ровать орга́зм.

fall *vi* 1. па́дать / упа́сть; 2. *(in love)* влюби́ться *(with whom = + в + acc.)* ♦ ~ **apart** *vi* разва́ливаться / развали́ться ♦ ~ **in love** влюби́ться *(with whom = + в + acc.)*.

> **fall apart:**

My *(1)* **life** / *(2)* **marriage is falling apart.** *(1)* Моя́ жизнь... / *(2)* Мой брак... разва́ли-вается. ♦ **Our relationship is falling apart.** На́ши отноше́ния разва́ливаются.

> **fall for:** *be taken in*

I was really a fool to fall for that story. Я был *(ж: была́)* действи́тельно дурако́м *(ж: ду́рой)*, что попа́л *(ж: попа́ла)* в э́ту исто́рию. ♦ **I fell for it hook, line and sinker.** Я попа́лся *(ж: попа́лась)* на крючо́к.

> **fall in love:**

(I have to confess:) I've fallen head over heels in love with you. (Я до́лжен *[ж: должна́]* призна́ться,) я потеря́л *(ж: потеря́ла)* го́лову от любви́ к тебе́. ♦ **I'm falling** *(1)* **...in love with...** / *(2)* **...for... you.** *(past tense in Russian:)* *(1,2)* Я влюби́лся *(ж: влюби́лась)* в тебя́. ♦ *(1)* **The first time I met you,...** / *(2)* **The moment I** *(3)* **saw** / *(4)* **met you,...** **I fell** *(5,6)* **head over heels in love with you.** *(1)* С пе́рвой на́шей встре́чи... / *(2)* В тот моме́нт, когда́ я *(3)* уви́дел *(ж: уви́дела)* / *(4)* встре́тил *(ж: встре́тила)* тебя́,... я влюби́лся *(ж: влюби́лась)* в тебя́ *(5)* ...без па́мяти. / *(6)* ...безу́мно. ♦ **I don't know why I fell for** *(1)* **her** / *(2)* **him.** Я не зна́ю, почему́ я влюби́лся *(ж: влюби́лась)* в *(1)* неё / *(2)* него́. ♦ **I fell for you the first time I saw you.** Я влюби́лся *(ж:влюби́лась)* в тебя́ с пе́рвого взгля́да. ♦ **I really fell (hard) for you.** Я действи́тельно (си́льно) влюби́лся *(ж:влю-би́лась)* в тебя́. ♦ **I've never fallen for anyone like I have for you.** Я никогда́ ни в кого́ не влюбля́лся *(ж: влюбля́лась)* так, как в тебя́. ♦ **Don't think I just fell for your pretty face. There are many things I like about you.** Не ду́май, что я влюби́лся в тебя́ то́лько за твоё преле́стное лицо́. Существу́ет мно́го друго́го, что я люблю́ в тебе́.

fall *n (autumn)* о́сень *f* ♦ **in the** ~ о́сенью ♦ **last** ~ про́шлой о́сенью ♦ **next** ~ сле́дующей о́сенью.

falling out *n* несогла́сие, размо́лвка ♦ **I'm sorry about the falling out that we had.** Я извиня́юсь за размо́лвку, кото́рая была́ у нас.

falsies *n, pl (slang) (false breasts, breast padding)* *(1)* фальши́вая / *(2)* подде́льная грудь.

falter *vi* 1. *(stammer)* запина́ться / запну́ться; 2. *(waver)* колеба́ться / поколеба́ться; *(weaken)* слабе́ть / осла́бнуть ♦ **My love for you will never falter.** Моя́ любо́вь к тебе́ никогда́ не осла́бнет.

familiar *adj* 1. *(known, acquainted)* знако́мый, -ая, -ое, -ые *(short forms:* знако́м, -а, -о, -ы)*; 2. *(overly free, presumptuous)* фамилиа́рный, -ая, -ое, -ые ♦ **You look so familiar. I'm sure I've** *(1)* **seen** / *(2)* **met you before.** Вы вы́глядите тако́й знако́мой *(ж: таки́м знако́мым)*. Я уве́рен *(ж: уве́рена)*, что я *(1)* ви́дел *(ж: ви́дела)* / *(2)* встреча́л *(ж: встреча́ла)* Вас пре́жде.

familiarity *n* 1. *(close acquaintance with a person)* бли́зкое знако́мство, бли́зкие отноше́-ния, бли́зость *f* ; *(knowledge of a subject / thing)* (хоро́шее) знако́мство; 2. *(overly informal behavior, presumptuousness)* фамилиа́рность *f*.

Words in parentheses are optional.

family *n* семья ♦ **big** ~ больша́я семья ♦ *(1,2)* **broken** ~ *(1)* непо́лная / *(2)* разби́тая семья́ ♦ **close-knit** ~ спа́янная семья́ ♦ **good** ~ хоро́шая семья́ ♦ **happy** ~ счастли́вая семья́ ♦ **model** ~ образцо́вая семья́ ♦ **my** ~ моя́ семья́ ♦ **no** ~ нет семьи́ ♦ **our** ~ на́ша семья́ ♦ **patriarchal** ~ патриарха́льная семья́ ♦ **poor** ~ бе́дная семья́ ♦ *(1,2)* **small** ~ *(1)* ма́ленькая / *(2)* небольша́я семья́ ♦ **wealthy** ~ бога́тая семья́ ♦ **well-to-do** ~ обеспе́-ченная семья́ ♦ **working** ~ рабо́чая семья́ ♦ **your** ~ *(familiar)* твоя́ семья́; *(polite)* Ва́ша семья́.

family: verb terms:

build a ~ созда́ть семью́ ♦ **destroy the** ~ разруша́ть / разру́шить семью́ ♦ **feed the** ~ корми́ть семью́ ♦ **make a** ~ созда́ть семью́ ♦ **start a** ~ созда́ть семью́ ♦ **support a** ~ содержа́ть семью́.

family: other terms:

leader of the ~ ли́дер семьи́ ♦ **leadership in a** ~ главе́нство в семье́ ~ ♦ **life** жизнь в семье́ ♦ ~ **member** член семьи́ ♦ **head of the** ~ глава́ семьи́ ♦ **in a** ~ **way** бере́менная, в интере́сном положе́нии.

family: phrases:

I want to create a family (with you). Я хочу́ созда́ть семью́ (с тобо́й). ♦ **I'm a person who loves life and family.** Я челове́к, кото́рый лю́бит жизнь и семью́. ♦ **I want to start a family.** Я хочу́ созда́ть семью́. ♦ **I seek a person who is committed to church and family.** Я ищу́ челове́ка, кото́рому важна́ це́рковь и семья́. ♦ *(1)* **I dream of building...** / *(2)* **I want to build... a family (together) with you.** *(1)* Я мечта́ю... / *(2)* Я хочу́... созда́ть (с тобо́й) семью́. ♦ **(Having a) family is my number one** *(1,2)* **priority.** Семья́ - моя́ первоочередна́я *(1)* цель / *(2)* зада́ча.

family-minded *adj* скло́нный (-ая, -ое, -ые) к семе́йной жи́зни, заинтересо́ванный (-ая, -ое, -ые) в созда́нии семьи́.

family-oriented *adj* скло́нный (-ая, -ое, -ые) к семе́йной жи́зни, заинтересо́ванный (-ая, -ые) в созда́нии семьи́.

fancy *adj* 1. *(high-class)* изы́сканный, -ая, -ое, -ые, вы́сшего ка́чества; *(stylish)* мо́дный, -ая, -ое, -ые, наря́дный, -ая, -ое, -ые; 2. *(elaborate)* зате́йливый, -ая, -ое, -ые; *(intricate)* замыслова́тый, -ая, -ое, -ые; *(whimsical)* причу́дливый, -ая, -ое, -ые ♦ *(1,2)* ~ **design** *(1)* зате́йливый / *(2)* причу́дливый узо́р ♦ ~ **dress** наря́дное пла́тье ♦ ~ **hairdo** зате́йливая причёска.

fancy *vt* нра́виться *(what, whom = subject; the person who fancies = dat.)*, люби́ть *(what, whom = acc.)* ♦ *(1)* **He** / *(2)* **She fancies you.** Ты *(1)* ему́ / *(2)* ей нра́вишься.

fancy *n* 1. *(liking)* увлече́ние, скло́нность *f*, пристра́стие; 2. *(imagination)* воображе́ние, фанта́зия; 3. *(whim)* при́хоть *f*, капри́з ♦ **We can do whatever strikes our fancy.** Мы мо́жем де́лать всё, что нам нра́вится.

fanny *n (slang) (buttocks)* по́па.

fantasize *vi* фантази́ровать *(about what = + о + prep.)* ♦ **Is it any wonder that I dream and fantasize about you in the most shamelessly erotic way day and night?** Не удиви́тельно ли, что я мечта́ю и фантази́рую о тебе́ бессты́дным эроти́ческим о́бразом день и ночь?

fantastic *adj* фантасти́чный, -ая, -ое, -ые, замеча́тельный, -ая, -ое, -ые ♦ **That was (absolutely) fantastic.** Это бы́ло (соверше́нно) фантасти́чно. ♦ **You are (absolutely) fantastic.** Ты (соверше́нно) фантасти́чна *(ж: фантасти́чен).* ♦ **No-one is as fantastic in bed as you are.** Никто́ не мо́жет быть так фантасти́чен в посте́ли, как ты. ♦ **I can imagine that you'd be (absolutely) fantastic in bed.** Я представля́ю, что ты (соверше́нно) фантасти́чна *(ж: фантасти́чен)* в посте́ли.

You can find common clothing sizes in Appendix 11 on page 778.

fantastically *adv* фантастически ♦ **It is so fantastically wonderful to make love with you.** Это так фантастически прекрасно заниматься любовью с тобой.

fantasy *n* фантазия ♦ **bridal** ~ свадебные фантазии ♦ **favorite** ~ любимая фантазия ♦ **lustful** ~ похотливая фантазия ♦ **sensual** ~ чувственная фантазия ♦ **wild** ~ необузданная фантазия ♦ **act out (our) sexual ~ies** воплотить (наши) сексуальные фантазии.

---
fantasy: phrases

In the unbounded vistas of my dreams and fantasies I taste the exquisite sweetness of your lips a thousand, ten thousand, a million times, and each time am only impelled by the sheer ecstasy of the kiss to taste them once again. В безграничной веренице моих снов и фантазий я вкушаю исключительную сладость твоих губ тысячу, десять тысяч, миллион раз, и каждый раз я побуждён упиваться опять истинным восторгом поцелуя. ♦ **You are the kind of woman that dominates a man's fantasies.** Ты тип женщины, которая господствует в мужских фантазиях. ♦ **All of my daydreams and fantasies are filled with images of your exquisitely beautiful** *(1)* **face /** *(2)* **body.** Все мои мечты и фантазии заполнены твоим изысканно прекрасным *(1)* лицом / *(2)* телом. ♦ **You are bewitching beyond my wildest fantasies.** Ты очаровательна сверх моих самых необузданных фантазий. ♦ **You're even better than my fantasies.** Ты даже лучше, чем в моих фантазиях. ♦ **My favorite activity these days is to lie in bed at night and** *(1)* **...indulge my fantasies... /** *(2)* **...lose myself in fantasies... about you.** Моё любимое занятие в эти дни лежать на кровати ночью и *(1)* ...предаваться моим фантазиям... / *(2)* ...забыться в фантазиях... о тебе. ♦ **You fulfill all my fantasies.** Ты исполняешь все мои фантазии. ♦ **You are every** *(1)* **man's /** *(2)* **woman's fantasy.** Ты мечта *(1)* ...каждого мужчины. / *(2)* ...каждой женщины. ♦ **You're a fantasy come true.** Ты сбывшаяся фантазия. ♦ **You are all my fantasies come true.** Ты все мои сбывшиеся фантазии. ♦ **In your letter you made a suggestion that has been fueling my fantasies ever since.** В своём письме ты сделала *(ж: сделал)* предложение, которое с тех пор воспламеняет мои фантазии. ♦ **The two of us can act out our sexual fantasies together.** Вместе мы можем воплотить (наши) сексуальные фантазии.

far *adj* далёк, далека, -о, -и *(short forms)* ♦ **How far do you live from here?** Как далеко отсюда ты живёшь? ♦ **I live (not) far from here.** Я живу (не) далеко отсюда. ♦ **How far is it?** Как далеко это? ♦ **It's (**[1]** not /** [2] **rather) far.** Это (**[1]** не / **[2]** достаточно) далеко. ♦ **I don't want to go too far.** Я не хочу идти слишком далеко. ♦ **This has gone too far.** Это зашло слишком далеко.

farewell *n* прощание ♦ **tearful** ~ прощание, полное слёз *(1 term)* ♦ **bid** *(1)* **you /** *(2)* **him /** *(3)* **her** ~ прощаться / попрощаться с *(1)* тобой / *(2)* ним / *(3)* ней ♦ **Farewell!** Прощай!

farsighted *adj* дальнозоркий, -ая, -ое, -ие.

fascinate *vt* очаровывать / очаровать *(whom = acc.)* ♦ **You fascinate me (no end).** Ты очаровываешь меня (бесконечно).

fascinated *adj* очарован, -а, -о, -ы *(short forms)* ♦ **When I first saw your (**[1]** bright /** [2] **piquant) smile, I was utterly fascinated.** Когда я впервые увидел твою (**[1]** сияющая / [2] пикантную) улыбку, я был совершенно очарован.

fascinating *adj* очаровательный, -ая, -ое, -ые ♦ **utterly** ~ совершенно очаровательный, -ая, -ое, -ые.

fascination *n* 1. *(charm, enchantment)* обаяние, очарование, прелесть *f*; 2. *(intense absorption)* восхищение ♦ **all-consuming** ~ всепоглощающее восхищение ♦ **You are truly a creature of divine fascination.** Ты истинно божественно-прелестное создание.

fashion *n* стиль *m*, мода ♦ **latest** ~ последняя мода ♦ **new** ~ новый стиль, новая мода ♦ **old** ~ старый стиль, старая мода ♦ **You really have a flair for fashion.** У тебя

For general rules of Russian grammar see Appendix 2 on page 686.

действи́тельно есть чу́вство сти́ля.

fashionable *adj* мо́дный, -ая, -ое, -ые, фешене́бельный, -ая, -ое, -ые.

fasten *vi (eyes)* устремля́ться / устреми́ться *(on what = + на + acc.)* ♦ **When my gaze fastened on your (beautiful) face, I couldn't avert it.** Когда́ мой взгляд устреми́лся на твоё (прекра́сное) лицо́, я не смог отвести́ от него́ глаз.

fastidious *adj* 1. *(discriminating)* привере́дливый, -ая, -ое, -ые, разбо́рчивый, -ая, -ое, -ые; 2. *(refined)* утончённый, -ая, -ое, -ые.

fat *adj* то́лстый, -ая, -ое, -ые, по́лный, -ая, -ое, -ые, ту́чный, -ая, -ое, -ые.

fate *n* судьба́, рок ♦ **blind ~** слепа́я судьба́ ♦ **cruel ~** жесто́кая судьба́ ♦ **happy ~** счаст-ли́вая судьба́ ♦ **gift of ~** пода́рок судьбы́ ♦ **tempt ~** искуша́ть судьбу́ ♦ **(I** *[1]* **feel /** *[2]* **believe that)** *(3,4)* **...Fate (has)...** / *(5,6)* **...it was Fate that... brought us together.** (Я *[1]* чу́вствую / *[1]* ве́рю, что) *(3,5)* ...Рок свёл... / *(4,6)* ...Судьба́ свела́... нас вме́сте. ♦ **It was Fate that we met.** То, что мы встре́тились, была́ судьба́. ♦ **Fate** *(1)* **brought /** *(2)* **put us together** *(3)* **...that day /** *(4)* **evening /** *(5)* **morning /** *(6)* **night.** Судьба́ *(1)* свела́ / *(2)* соедини́ла нас *(3)* ...в тот день / *(4)* ве́чер. / *(5)* ...в то у́тро. / *(6)* ...в ту ночь. ♦ **Fate guided me to you.** Сама́ судьба́ привела́ меня́ к тебе́. ♦ **Fate guided us to each other (and I am so grateful).** Судьба́ свела́ нас вме́сте (и я я так ей благода́рен *[ж: благода́рна]*).

father *n* оте́ц ♦ **bad ~** плохо́й оте́ц ♦ **foster ~** приёмный оте́ц ♦ **good ~** хоро́ший оте́ц ♦ **my ~** мой оте́ц ♦ **my** *(1)* **own /** *(2)* **real ~** мой *(1,2)* родно́й оте́ц ♦ **wonderful ~** пре-кра́сный оте́ц ♦ **your ~** *(familiar)* твой оте́ц; *(polite)* Ваш оте́ц ♦ **I want you to be the father of my children.** Я хочу́, чтобы ты был отцо́м мои́х дете́й.

fatherhood *n* отцо́вство.

father-in-law *n (wife's father)* тесть *m; (husband's father)* свёкор.

fathom *vt* 1. *(measure depth)* измеря́ть / изме́рить глубину́; 2. *(comprehend)* понима́ть / поня́ть, постига́ть / пости́гнуть ♦ **You cannot (possibly) fathom the depths of the love that fills my heart for you.** Ты не мо́жешь пости́гнуть всю глубину́ той любви́ к тебе́, кото́рой запо́лнено моё се́рдце.

fathomless *adj* неизмери́мый, -ая, -ое, -ые *(short forms:* неизмери́м, -а, -о, -ы), бездо́н-ный, -ая, -ое, -ые, непостижи́мый, -ая, -ое, -ые ♦ **My love for you is fathomless.** Моя́ любо́вь к тебе́ неизмери́ма.

fault *n* 1. *(blame)* вина́; 2. *(defect)* недоста́ток ♦ **It's (not)** *(1)* **my /** *(2)* **your fault.** Это (не) *(1)* моя́ / *(2)* твоя́ вина́. ♦ **It was (not)** *(1)* **my /** *(2)* **your fault.** Это была́ (не) *(1)* моя́ /*(2)* твоя́ вина́. ♦ **You're always looking for faults.** Ты всегда́ и́щешь винова́тых. ♦ **I'm not the sort of person who goes around finding faults in people all the time.** Я не из тех люде́й, кото́рые всегда́ и́щут недоста́тки в лю́дях. ♦ **I know I have a lot of faults, but** *(1)* **...I hope you can overlook them. /** *(2)* **...I'll try hard to improve.** Я зна́ю, что у меня́ мно́го недоста́тков, но *(1)* ...я наде́юсь, что ты мо́жешь проигнори́ровать их. / *(2)* ...я бу́ду о́чень стара́ться испра́вить их.

faultfinding *n* приди́рчивость *f*, приди́рки *pl.*

faux *adj* 1. *(artificial)* иску́сственный, -ая, -ое, -ые; 2. *(hair: dyed)* кра́шенные.

faux pas *n* ло́жный шаг, беста́ктность *f* ; оши́бка ♦ **social ~** оши́бка в поведе́нии в о́бществе.

favor *n* одолже́ние ♦ **I plead of you to grant me this one small favor.** Я умоля́ю тебя́ сде́лать мне одно́ ма́ленькое одолже́ние. ♦ **Could you (please) do me a (**[1]** small /** [2] **big) favor?** (Пожа́луйста) Не смогла́ *(ж: смог)* бы ты сде́лать для меня́ (*[1]* ма́лень-кое / *[2]* большо́е) одолже́ние? ♦ **I have a (**[1]** small /** [2] **big) favor to ask of you.** Я хочу́ попроси́ть тебя́ о(б) (*[1]* ма́леньком / *[2]* большо́м) одолже́нии. ♦ **Thanks for the favor.** Спаси́бо за одолже́ние.

For transitive Russian verbs the cases that they take are shown by means of an = sign and the Russian case (abbreviated).

fawn-eyed *adj* оленеглазый, -ая, -ое, -ые.

fawn over *vi* 1. *(make a play for)* заигрывать *(over whom = + с + instr.)*; 2. *(curry favor)* вилять хвостом *(over whom = + перед + instr.)*, заискивать *(over whom = + перед + instr.)*, подлизываться *(over whom = + к + dat.)* ♦ **You were fawning (all) over** *(1)* **him** / *(2)* **her.** *(1)* Ты слишком заигрывала с ним. / *(2)* Ты слишком заигрывал с ней.

fear *vt* бояться *(what, whom = gen.)*.

fear *n* 1.*(fright)* боязнь *f*, страх; 2. *(concern)* опасение ♦ **desperate** ~ отчаянный страх ♦ ~ **of being alone** боязнь одиночества ♦ ~ **of being hurt** боязнь быть обиженной ♦ ~ **of loss** страх потери ♦ **real** ~ настоящий страх ♦ **unreasonable** ~ неразумный страх ♦ **dispel** ~ растапливать / растопить страх ♦ **I have such a fear of losing your love.** Во мне такой страх потери твоей любви.

fearful *adj*: ♦ **be** ~ бояться *(of what = gen.)* ♦ **You need never be fearful of communication with me. You can tell me anything.** Ты никогда не должна бояться общаться со мной. Ты можешь рассказывать мне всё.

feast *vi* лакомиться / полакомиться *(on what = instr.)*, пировать *(on what = + на + prep.)*, упиваться *(on what = instr.)*; *vt* пожирать / пожрать *(what = instr., on what = acc.)* ♦ **I want to feast my eyes on your beautiful nude body -- and then my lips.** Я хочу сначала пожирать твоё прекрасное обнажённое тело глазами, а потом губами. ♦ **I want to feast (**[1]** endlessly /** [2] **night and day) on your lips.** Я хочу упиваться (*[1]* бесконечно / *[2]* ночь и день) твоими губами. ♦ **Every night our mouths will feast on each other's.** Каждую ночь наши рты будут пировать друг в друге. ♦ *(1)* **I'm going to...** / *(2)* **I want to... feast on the firm, creamy flesh of your full breasts.** *(1)* Я буду... / *(2)* Я хочу... пировать в упругой, кремовой плоти твоей полной груди. ♦ **How I love to feast my eyes on the creamy, full swell of your breasts.** Как я люблю пожирать глазами кремовую, полную выпуклость твоих грудей.

feast *n* 1. *(banquet)* пир; 2. *(pleasure)* наслаждение ♦ **sweet** ~ **of satisfying sex** нежное наслаждение удовлетворяющим сексом ♦ **Together you and I are going to have feasts of ecstasy.** У нас с тобой будут пиры экстаза.

feature *n* черта, особенность *f* ♦ **attractive** ~s привлекательные черты (лица) ♦ *(1,2)* **beautiful** ~s *(1)* прекрасные / *(2)* красивые черты (лица) ♦ **beloved** ~s любимые черты (лица) ♦ **captivating** ~s пленительные особенности ♦ **dark** ~s смуглое лицо ♦ **delicate** *(1,2)* ~s *(of the face)* тонкие *(1)* черты / *(2)* особенности (лица) ♦ **exquisite tiny** ~s изысканное маленькое лицо ♦ **facial** *(1,2)* ~s *(1)* черты / *(2)* особенности лица ♦ **fine** *(1,2)* ~s *(of the face)* тонкие *(1)* черты / *(2)* особенности (лица) ♦ **hard chiseled** ~s грубо вылепленное лицо ♦ *(1,2)* **lovely** ~s *(1)* прекрасные / *(2)* красивые черты (лица) ♦ **oriental** ~s восточный тип лица ♦ **rough(-hewn)** ~s суровые очертания лица, грубые черты ♦ **sharp** ~s острые черты лица ♦ **soft** ~s мягкие черты (лица) ♦ **striking** ~s поразительные черты (лица) ♦ **unique** ~s неповторимые черты.

fed up *adj (slang)* сытый (-ая, -ое, -ые) по горло ♦ **be** ~ быть сытым по горло *(with what = instr.)*.

feed *vt* кормить *(whom = acc.)* ♦ ~ **a line** льстить *(to whom = dat.)* ♦ **You're feeding me a line.** Ты льстишь мне. ♦ **Don't think I'm just feeding you a line.** Не думай, что я просто льщу тебе.

feel *vt* чувствовать / почувствовать *(what, whom = acc.)*, ощущать / ощутить *(what, whom = acc.)* ♦ **I desire so ardently to feel you close to me (again).** Я так пылко жажду почувствовать тебя рядом (опять). ♦ **I want so much to feel you.** Я так хочу почувствовать тебя. ♦ **Beside what I feel for you, everything else is** *(1)* **insignificant** / *(2)* **trivial.** По сравнению с тем, что я чувствую к тебе, всё остальное так *(1)* незначительно /

(2) тривиа́льно. ♦ **When I feel you respond, my heart overflows with love for you.** Когда́ я чу́вствую, что ты отвеча́ешь мне, моё се́рдце переполня́ется любо́вью к тебе́. ♦ **I love to feel the excitement grow in you.** Я люблю́ чу́вствовать, как возбужде́ние нараста́ет в тебе́. ♦ **I love to feel you inside of me.** Я люблю́ чу́вствовать тебя́ во мне. ♦ **I feel so much love for you.** Я чу́вствую огро́мную любо́вь к тебе́. ♦ **I've never felt so much love for anyone (in my whole life) (as I feel for you).** Я никогда́ (в жи́зни) не чу́вствовал *(ж: чу́вствовала)* тако́й огро́мной любви́ к кому́-либо (, как я чу́вствую к тебе́).

feel *vi* 1. чу́вствовать / почу́вствовать (себя́); 2. *(regard)* относи́ться / отнести́сь *(toward whom = + к + dat.)* ♦ ~ **subconsciously** подсозна́тельно чу́вствовать ♦ ~ **the same** чу́вствовать то же са́мое ♦ ~ **unappreciated** чу́вствовать себя́ неоценённым *m* / неоценённой *f.*

> **feel:** *how I feel about you*

You know how I feel about you. Ты зна́ешь, как я отношу́сь к тебе́. ♦ *(1)* **You can't begin to know /** *(2)* **imagine... /** *(3)* **No words can express... what I feel for you in my heart.** *(1)* Ты не зна́ешь / *(2)* представля́ешь... / *(3)* Никаки́ми слова́ми невозмо́жно переда́ть..., те чу́вства к тебе́, кото́рыми полно́ моё се́рдце. ♦ **I've never** *(1,2)* **felt this way about anyone (before).** Я никогда́ (пре́жде) и ни к кому́ не *(1)* ...относи́лся *(ж: относи́лась)* так. / *(2)* ...испы́тывал *(ж: испы́тывала)* таки́х чувств. ♦ **I've never felt so much in love with anyone (in my whole life) (as I feel with you).** Я никогда́ (в жи́зни) не был *(ж: была́)* так влюблён *(ж: влюблена́)* в кого́-либо (, как я влюблён *[ж:влюблена́]* в тебя́). ♦ **It's not easy for me to say how I feel, but I hope you know how much I love you.** Мне нелегко́ сказа́ть, что я чу́вствую, но я наде́юсь, ты зна́ешь, как си́льно я тебя́ люблю́. ♦ **I hope that what I've written to you here doesn't sound mushy. Everything that I've said is a genuine expression of how I feel about you.** Наде́юсь, то, что я написа́л, не звучи́т сли́шком сентимента́льно. Всё, о чём я написа́л, и́скреннее выраже́ние мои́х чувств к тебе́. ♦ **I feel like I've known you all my life.** Я чу́вствую, что я зна́ю тебя́ всю свою́ жизнь. ♦ **I've never felt so drawn to anyone as I feel toward you.** Я никогда́ ни к кому́ не чу́вствовал *(ж: чу́вствовала)* тако́го притяже́ния, како́е я чу́вствую к тебе́.

> **feel:** *how you make me feel*

You make me feel complete. Ты заставля́ешь меня́ чу́вствовать полноту́ жи́зни. ♦ **You make me feel so** *(1)* **wonderful /** *(2)* **heavenly /** *(3)* **good.** Ты вызыва́ешь во мне таки́е *(1)* великоле́пные / *(2)* боже́ственные / *(3)* хоро́шие чу́вства. ♦ **You make me feel so good and so warm with all the nice things you say to me in your letters.** Мне так хорошо́ и тепло́ от всех прия́тных слов, обращённых ко мне в твои́х пи́сьмах. ♦ **I love the way you make me feel.** Мне нра́вятся чу́вства, кото́рые ты вызыва́ешь во мне. ♦ **I love the way I feel when I'm with you.** Мне нра́вятся мои́ ощуще́ния, когда́ я ря́дом с тобо́й. ♦ **You don't know** *(1)* **...how (wonderful) you make me feel. /** *(2)* **...how wonderful I feel in your arms.** Ты да́же не зна́ешь, *(1)* ...каки́е (удиви́тельные) ощуще́ния ты вызыва́ешь во мне. / *(2)* ...как замеча́тельно я чу́вствую себя́ в твои́х объя́тиях. ♦ **There are no words to tell you how you make me feel.** Нет слов, что́бы рассказа́ть тебе́, каки́е ты вызыва́ешь во мне чу́вства.

> **feel:** *I feel good*

I haven't felt so *(1)* **good /** *(2)* **happy in years.** Я мно́го лет не чу́вствовал *(ж: чу́вствовала)* *(1)* ...себя́ так хорошо́. / *(2)* ...тако́го сча́стья.

> **feel:** *how it feels*

How *(1)* **does /** *(2)* **did it feel (for you)?** Что ты *(1)* чу́вствуешь / *(2)* чу́вствовала *(ж:*

How to use the Cyrillic alphabet on the Internet is the subject of Appendix 20 on page 789.

чу́вствовал)? ◆ **It** *(1)* **feels** / *(2)* **felt** *(3)* **okay** / *(4)* **good** / *(5)* **nice** / *(6)* **beautiful** / *(7)* **wonderful** / *(8)* **marvelous** / *(9)* **fantastic** / *(10)* **incredible** / *(11)* **heavenly** / *(12)* **divine** / *(13)* **great** / *(14)* **terrific** / *(15)* **out of this world.** *(1)* Это... / *(2)* Это бы́ло... *(3,4)* хорошо́ / *(5)* прия́тно / *(6)* прекра́сно / *(7)* чуде́сно / *(8)* замеча́тельно / *(9)* фантасти́чно / *(10)* невероя́тно / *(11,12)* боже́ственно / *(13-15)* великоле́пно.

---
feel: *how I'll make you feel*
---

(1) **I want you to know...** / *(2)* **I'm going to teach you... what it feels like to be a woman.** *(1)* Я хочу́, чтобы ты узна́ла,... / *(2)* Я научу́ тебя́,... что э́то зна́чит чу́вствовать себя́ же́нщиной. ◆ **Wait till you see how good it makes you feel.** Уви́дишь, как хорошо́ ты почу́вствуешь себя́ от э́того. ◆ **I want to always make you feel appreciated.** Я хочу́, чтобы ты всегда́ чу́вствовала *(ж: чу́вствовал)*, что я ценю́ тебя́. ◆ **I want you always to let me know how you feel.** Я хочу́, чтобы ты всегда́ дава́ла *(ж: дава́л)* мне возмо́жность знать, что ты чу́вствуешь. ◆ **I don't want to make you feel bad.** Я не хочу́ оби́деть тебя́.

---
feel: *I feel bad*

I feel terrible about the way I've *(1)* **neglected** / *(2)* **treated you.** Я о́чень сожале́ю, что я так *(1)* ...пренебрега́л *(ж: пренебрега́ла)* тобо́й. / *(2)* ...обраща́лся *(ж: обраща́лась)* с тобо́й. ◆ **I've never felt** *(1)* **...so bad** / *(2)* **terrible** / *(3)* **bleak** / *(4)* **rotten.** / *(5)* **...so miserable** / *(6)* **desolate** / *(7)* **shattered.** Я никогда́ пре́жде не чу́вствовал себя́ *(1)* ...так пло́хо / *(2)* ужа́сно / *(3)* уны́ло / *(4)* отврати́тельно. / *(5)* ...таки́м несча́стным / *(6)* опустошённым / *(7)* потрясённым.

---
feel: *feel at home*

I want you to feel at home (here). Я хочу́, чтобы ты чу́вствовала *(ж: чу́вствовал)* себя́ (здесь) как до́ма. ◆ **I really feel at home (***[1]* **...here.** / *[2]* **...with you.***).** Я действи́тельно чу́вствую себя́ *([1]* ...здесь. / *[2]* ...с тобо́й) как до́ма.

feel *n* ощуще́ние ◆ **The feel of your fingers on my** *(1)* **neck** / *(2)* **hand** / *(3)* **leg is so sensuous.** Ощуще́ние твои́х па́льцев на мое́й *(1)* ше́е / *(2)* руке́ / *(3)* ноге́ так чу́вственно. ◆ **I love the feel of** *(1)* **...it.** / *(2)* **...your mouth** / *(3)* **tongue (there).** / *(4)* **...your hands** / *(5)* **lips (there)** / *(6)* **breasts.** Мне нра́вится ощуще́ние *(1)* ...э́того. / *(2)* ...твоего́ рта / *(3)* языка́ (там). / *(4)* ...твои́х рук / *(5)* губ (там). / *(6)* ...твое́й груди́.

feeling *n* чу́вство, ощуще́ние ◆ **all-encompassing** ~ всёпоглоща́ющее чу́вство ◆ **ambivalent** ~s дво́йственные чу́вства ◆ **amorous** ~s любо́вные чу́вства ◆ **aroused** ~s взбудора́женные чу́вства ◆ **awkward** ~ нело́вкое чу́вство ◆ **beautiful** ~s прекра́сные чу́вства ◆ **crazy** ~ безу́мное чу́вство ◆ **deep** ~s глубо́кие чу́вства ◆ **enduring** ~s про́чные чу́вства ◆ **enormous** ~ огро́мное чу́вство ◆ **exquisite** ~s изы́сканные чу́вства ◆ ~ **of awkwardness** ощуще́ние нело́вкости ◆ ~ **of bitterness** чу́вство го́речи ◆ ~ **of boredom** чу́вство ску́ки ◆ ~ **of depression** чу́вство уны́ния ◆ ~s **of ecstasy** экста́з ◆ ~ **of elation** чу́вство припо́днятости ◆ ~ **of excitement** чу́вство возбужде́ния ◆ ~ **of guilt** чу́вство вины́ ◆ ~ **of jealousy** чу́вство ре́вности ◆ ~ **of joy** чу́вство ра́дости ◆ ~ **of loneliness** чу́вство одино́чества ◆ ~ **of love** чу́вство любви́ ◆ ~ **of melancholy** чу́вство тоски́ ◆ ~ **of peace** чу́вство поко́я ◆ ~ **of pity** чу́вство жа́лости ◆ ~ **of regret** чу́вство сожале́ния ◆ ~ **of relief** чу́вство облегче́ния ◆ ~ **of sadness** чу́вство печа́ли ◆ ~ **of satisfaction** чу́вство удовлетворе́ния ◆ ~ **of security** чу́вство безопа́сности ◆ ~ **of self-worth** самооце́нка ◆ **fuzzy** ~s прия́тные чу́вства ◆ **glorious** ~s прекра́сные чу́вства ◆ **happy** ~ ра́достное чу́вство ◆ **heavenly** ~s небе́сные чу́вства ◆ **incredible** ~s невероя́тные чу́вства ◆ **intense** ~s пы́лкие чу́вства ◆ **inner** ~s вну́тренние чу́вства ◆ **intoxicating flow of** ~s пьяня́щий пото́к ощуще́ний ◆ **joyous** ~ ра́достное чу́вство ◆ **lasting** ~s про́чные чу́вства ◆ **loving** ~s лю́бящие чу́вства ◆ **my** ~s мои́ чу́вства ◆

Russian adjectives have long and short forms.
Where short forms are given, they are labeled as such.

nagging ~ щемя́щее чу́вство ✦ **new** ~ но́вое чу́вство ✦ **nice** ~ прия́тное чу́вство ✦ **odd** ~ стра́нное чу́вство ✦ **overwhelming** ~s ошеломля́ющие чу́вства ✦ **passionate** ~ стра́стное чу́вство ✦ **pleasant** ~s прия́тные чу́вства ✦ **powerful** ~s могу́щественные чу́вства ✦ **primeval** ~s первобы́тные чу́вства ✦ **pure** ~ чи́стое чу́вство ✦ **rapturous** ~ упои́тельное чу́вство ✦ **reciprocated** ~ отве́тное чу́вство ✦ **returned** ~ отве́тное чу́вство ✦ **sensual** ~s сладостра́стные ощуще́ния ✦ **strange** ~ стра́нное чу́вство ✦ **strong** ~ си́льное чу́вство ✦ **strong f**~s про́чные чу́вства ✦ **such a** ~ тако́е чу́вство ✦ **such** ~s таки́е чу́вства ✦ **sweet** ~s не́жные чу́вства ✦ *(1,2)* **tender** ~s *(1)* серде́чные / *(2)* не́жные чу́вства ✦ **tremendous** ~s грома́дные чу́вства ✦ **troubled** ~ беспоко́йное чу́вство ✦ **true** ~s и́стинные чу́вства ✦ **turbulent** ~s бу́рные чу́вства ✦ **unchanged** ~ неизме́нное чу́вство ✦ **unfamiliar** ~ незнако́мое чу́вство ✦ **warm** ~ тёплое чу́вство ✦ *(1,2)* **wonderful** ~ *(1)* удиви́тельные / *(2)* замеча́тельные чу́вства ✦ **worried** ~ беспоко́йное чу́вство ✦ **your** ~s *(familiar)* твои́ чу́вства; *(polite)* Ва́ши чу́вства.

feeling: *verb terms*

arouse ~s задева́ть / заде́ть чу́вства, пробужда́ть / пробуди́ть чу́вства ✦ **capture** ~s захва́тывать / захвати́ть в плен чу́вства ✦ **describe** *(1)* **my** / *(2)* **your** ~s опи́сывать / описа́ть *(1,2)* свои́ чу́вства ✦ **display** ~s проявля́ть чу́вства ✦ **experience** ~s испы́тывать чу́вства ✦ **explain** *(1)* **my** / *(2)* **your** ~s объясня́ть / объясни́ть *(1,2)* свои́ чу́вства ✦ **express** *(1)* **my** / *(2)* **your** ~s выража́ть / вы́разить *(1,2)* свои́ чу́вства ✦ **harbor strong** ~s пита́ть си́льные чу́вства *(for whom = + к + dat.)* ✦ **hide** *(1)* **my** / *(2)* **your** ~s пря́тать *(1,2)* свои́ чу́вства ✦ **hurt** *(1)* **my** / *(2)* **your** ~s ра́нить *(1)* мои́ / *(2)* твои́ чу́вства ✦ **intensify** ~s уси́ливать / уси́лить чу́вства ✦ **keep** *(1)* **my** / *(2)* **your** ~s **locked up** держа́ть *(1,2)* свои́ чу́вства за́пертыми ✦ **kill** ~s убива́ть / уби́ть чу́вства ✦ **pretend** ~s притворя́ться в чу́вствах ✦ **reveal** *(1)* **my** / *(2)* **your** ~s выка́зывать / вы́казать *(1,2)* свои́ чу́вства ✦ **share** *(1)* **my** / *(2)* **your** ~s дели́ться *(1,2)* свои́ми чу́вствами ✦ **sort out one's** ~s разбира́ться / разобра́ться в свои́х чу́вствах ✦ **take** ~s **seriously** воспринима́ть / восприня́ть чу́вства всерьёз.

feeling: *other terms*

blossoming of ~ расцве́т чу́вства ✦ **depth of my** ~s глубина́ мои́х чувств ✦ **display of** ~ проявле́ние чувств ✦ **flood of** ~s пото́к чувств ✦ **gamut of** ~s га́мма чувств ✦ **intensity of my** ~s интенси́вность мои́х чувств ✦ **nature of my** ~s хара́ктер мои́х чувств ✦ **range of** ~s диапазо́н чувств ✦ **regard for** *(1)* **my** / *(2)* **your** ~s уваже́ние к *(1,2)* свои́м чу́вствам ✦ **spectrum of** ~s диапазо́н чувств ✦ **storm of** ~s бу́ря чувств ✦ **surge of** ~ прили́в чувств ✦ **stream of** ~s пото́к ощуще́ний ✦ **tides of sweet** ~ пото́к не́жных чувств ✦ **torrent of** ~s водопа́д чувств ✦ **vortex of** ~s вихрь чувств.

feeling: *can't hold back my feelings*

I can't hold back my feelings any longer. Я не могу́ бо́льше сде́рживать свои́ чу́вства. ✦ **It's really hard for me to keep my feelings (for you) in check.** Действи́тельно тру́дно для меня́ держа́ть чу́вства (к тебе́) под контро́лем. ✦ **I've tried and tried to fight my feelings for you (but it's no use).** Я пыта́лся и пыта́лся *(ж: пыта́лась и пыта́лась)* боро́ться с чу́вствами к тебе́ (но безуспе́шно). ✦ **Forgive me for writing such a steamy letter, but my thoughts of you mixed together with my feelings for you arouse passions in me that are difficult to contain.** Прости́ меня́ за тако́е чу́вственное письмо́, но мои́ мы́сли о тебе́ вме́сте с чу́вствами к тебе́, пробужда́ют во мне страсть, кото́рую тру́дно сдержа́ть. ✦ **I have to clamp down on my feelings.** Я до́лжен *(ж: должна́)* зажа́ть свои́ чу́вства.

feeling: *my feelings for you*

If you only knew what tender, loving feelings I harbor for you. Если бы ты то́лько зна́ла

Russian nouns are either masculine, feminine or neuter.
Adjectives with them will be the same.

(ж: знал), какое нежное чувство любви к тебе я таю. ♦ **I** *(1)* **bear** / *(2)* **have** / *(3)* **harbor such tender feelings for you.** *(1)* Я ношу... / *(2)* У меня есть... / *(3)* Я скрываю... такие сердечные чувства к тебе. ♦ **No language can** *(1)* **explain** / *(2)* **describe** / *(3)* **express my feelings (for you).** Никакой язык не способен *(1)* объяснить / *(2)* описать / *(3)* выразить мои чувства (к тебе). ♦ **My feelings** *(1)* **...toward you...** / *(2)* **...about this... have been building up for** *(3)* **days** / *(4)* **weeks** / *(5)* **months now.** Мои чувства по отношению к *(1)* тебе / *(2)* этому накапливаютсяуже *(3)* днями / *(4)* неделями / *(5)* месяцами. ♦ **The depth of my feelings for you is unlike anything I've known before.** Глубина моих чувств к тебе непохожа на что-либо, что я знал *(ж: знала)* прежде. ♦ **If you could only know the depth of my feelings for you.** Если бы ты только могла *(ж: мог)* знать глубину моих чувств к тебе. ♦ **I am** *(1)* **completely** / *(2)* **utterly** / *(3)* **totally swept away by my feelings for you.** Я *(1,2)* полностью / *(3)* весь во власти своих чувств к тебе. ♦ **Each time I think of you, it sends a sweet arrow of feeling straight into my heart.** Мысли о тебе всегда посылают нежные стрелы чувств в моё сердце. ♦ **If the feeling that's raging through my heart for you isn't love, then I guess I'm really out of touch with what love is.** Если чувство к тебе, бушующее в моём сердце, не любовь, тогда я просто не понимаю, что такое любовь. ♦ **What enormous, exquisite, intense feeling grips my heart for you right now!** Какое огромное, изысканное, пылкое чувство к тебе охватывает моё сердце сейчас! ♦ **I've been masking my (true) feelings for you for a long time.** Я долгое время скрывал *(ж: скрывала)* мои (истинные) чувства к тебе. ♦ **My feelings for you will never waver.** Мои чувства к тебе никогда не поколеблются.

feeling: *the feelings your letters stir in me*

Your letters always give me such a warm feeling. Твои письма всегда вызывают во мне такие тёплые чувства. ♦ **Your letters release a flood of warm,** *(1)* **tender** / *(2)* **loving feelings for you in my heart.** Твои письма высвобождают в моём сердце поток тёплых, *(1)* нежных / *(2)* любящих чувств к тебе. ♦ **Your letters, the things you say in them, stir up such huge waves of tender, warm feelings in me toward you.** Твои письма, то, что ты говоришь в них, возбуждают во мне такие огромные волны нежных, тёплых чувств к тебе. ♦ **The very fact that you write to me at all gives me warm feelings, and then the things you say in your letters intensify those feelings a thousand-fold.** Просто факт, что ты пишешь мне, вызывает во мне тёплые чувства, и затем то, что ты говоришь в своих письмах, усиливает эти чувства в тысячу раз.

feeling: *it would be a nice feeling*

I think it would be such a nice feeling to sit close to you and talk with you in an intimate way for hours on end. This is going to be my new dream in the days ahead. Я думаю, как прекрасно было бы сидеть рядом с тобой и говорить о сокровенном бесконечные часы. Это теперь будет моей новой мечтой.

feeling: *the feelings you give me*

You have awoken such *(1)* **wonderful** / *(2)* **incredible** / *(3)* **exquisite** / *(4)* **glorious** / *(5)* **heavenly feelings in me.** Ты пробудила *(ж: пробудил)* во мне такие *(1)* удивительные / *(2)* невероятные / *(3)* изысканные / *(4)* прекрасные / *(5)* небесные чувства. ♦ **You fill me with such warm, amorous feelings.** Ты наполняешь меня такими тёплыми, любовными чувствами. ♦ **You give me such** *(1)* **...sensual...** / *(2)* **...sensuous...** / *(3)* **...warm, fuzzy... feelings.** Ты вызываешь во мне *(1)* ...такую чувственность. / *(2)* ...такие сладострастные чувства. / *(3)* ...такие тёплые, приятные чувства. ♦ **Oh, what feelings swept over me when** *(1)* **...my hand enclosed yours.** / *(2)* **...your hand enclosed mine.** О, какие чувства охватывали меня, когда *(1)* ...твоя рука была в моей. / *(2)* ...моя рука была в твоей. ♦ **When you do that, it sends sweet arrows of feeling along my**

Learn more about Russian customs in Appendix 15, page 782.

spine. Когда́ ты де́лаешь так, э́то посыла́ет стре́лы не́жных чувств вдоль всего́ моего́ позвоно́чника. ♦ **You** *(1)* **arouse** / *(2)* **cause** / *(3)* **stir up such turbulent feelings in** *(4)* **...me.** / *(5)* **...my heart.** Ты *(1)* пробужда́ешь / *(2)* вызыва́ешь / *(3)* возбужда́ешь таки́е бу́рные чу́вства *(4)* ...во мне. / *(5)* ...в моём се́рдце. ♦ **I've never known anyone in my life that could penetrate to the very core of my soul and stir up all my feelings the way you can.** Я никогда́ в свое́й жи́зни не знал *(ж: зна́ла)* кого́-либо ещё, кто мог бы проника́ть в са́мую глубину́ мое́й души́ и возбужда́ть мои́ чу́вства так, как ты. ♦ **The thought of your beautiful, luscious body arouses such primeval feelings in me.** Мы́сли о твоём прекра́сном, со́чном те́ле пробужда́ют таки́е первобы́тные чу́вства во мне. ♦ **I get a fluttery feeling in my stomach whenever I** *(1)* **...think about you.** / *(2)* **...see you.** Моё се́рдце трепе́щет вся́кий раз, когда́ бы я ни *(1)* ...поду́мал *(ж: поду́мала)* о тебе́. / *(2)* ...уви́дел *(ж: уви́дела)* тебя́. ♦ **Never have I had such feelings as I** *(1)* **have** / *(2)* **experience** / *(3)* **had** / *(4)* **experienced with you.** Никогда́ я не испы́тывал *(ж: испы́тывала)* таки́х чувств, каки́е я *(1,2)* испы́тываю / *(3,4)* испы́тывал *(ж: испы́тывала)* с тобо́й. ♦ **My feelings** *(1)* **overwhelmed** / *(2)* **swamped me so completely that** *(3)* **...I was at a loss for words.** / *(4)* **...I couldn't say anything.** / *(5)* **...I was (utterly) tongue-tied.** Мои́ чу́вства *(1)* ошеломи́ли / *(2)* затопи́ли меня́ всеце́ло так, что *(3)* ...я потеря́л *(ж: потеря́ла)* дар ре́чи. / *(4)* ...я ничего́ не мог *(ж: могла́)* сказа́ть. / *(5)* ...я был *(ж: была́)* (соверше́нно) безъязы́чным *(ж: безъязы́чной).* ♦ **You give me (such) a (wonderful) feeling of security.** Ты даёшь мне (тако́е) (замеча́тельное) чу́вство безопа́сности. ♦ **You've helped me to find a new depth to my feelings.** Ты помога́ла *(ж: помога́л)* мне находи́ть но́вую глубину́ в мои́х чу́вствах.

feeling: *these terrific feelings*

(1) **This is...** / *(2)* **That was... the most** *(3)* **beautiful** / *(4)* **heavenly** / *(5)* **wonderful feeling I have ever experienced.** *(1)* Э́то... / *(2)* Э́то бы́ло... са́мое *(3)* прекра́сное / *(4)* небе́сное / *(5)* удиви́тельное чу́вство, кото́рое я когда́-либо испы́тывал *(ж: испы́тывала).* ♦ **I wish this feeling** *(1)* **could** / *(2)* **would go on forever.** Я хоте́л *(ж: хоте́ла)* бы, *(1,2)* что́бы э́то чу́вство никогда́ не уга́сло. ♦ **It's a feeling that blends ecstasy and** *(1)* **wonder** / *(2)* **longing** / *(3)* **torment.** Э́то чу́вство -- смесь экста́за и *(1)* удивле́ния / *(2)* жа́жды / *(3)* му́ки. ♦ **This is such an all-encompassing feeling.** Э́то тако́е всёпоглоща́ющее чу́вство. ♦ **I don't want to lose this feeling.** Я не хочу́ потеря́ть э́то чу́вство. ♦ **These feelings have been building up in me for a long time.** Э́ти чу́вства нараста́ли во мне до́лгое вре́мя. ♦ **I hadn't realized that such** *(1)* **powerful** / *(2)* **tremendous** / *(3)* **overwhelming feelings could exist between a man and a woman.** Я не понима́л, что таки́е *(1)* могу́чие / *(2)* грома́дные / *(3)* ошеломля́ющие чу́вства мо́гут существова́ть ме́жду мужчи́ной и же́нщиной.

feeling: *give in to your feelings*

Just give in to your feelings. Про́сто отда́йся свои́м чу́вствам. ♦ **Why do you clamp down on your feelings? You need to open up and let yourself go.** Почему́ ты сде́рживаешь свои́ чу́вства? Тебе́ на́до раскры́ться и позво́лить твои́м чу́вствам вы́йти нару́жу. ♦ *(1)* **Don't keep...** / *(2)* **You always keep... your feelings (**[3] **locked** / [4] **bottled up) inside you.** *(1)* Не держи́... / *(2)* Ты всегда́ де́ржишь... свои́ чу́вства (*[3,4]* зажа́тыми) в себе́. ♦ **You keep your feelings locked behind a mask of indifference.** Ты де́ржишь свои́ чу́вства за́пертыми под ма́ской равноду́шия. ♦ **You shouldn't keep your feelings bottled up inside you.** Ты не должна́ *(ж: до́лжен)* держа́ть свои́ чу́вства скры́тыми внутри́ себя́.

feeling: *the feelings I'll give you*

I'm going to awaken feelings in you *(1)* **...such as you have never imagined possible.** / *(2)* **...that you didn't realize you had.** Я разбужу́ в тебе́ таки́е чу́вства, кото́рых ты *(1)* ...никогда́ не могла́ себе́ предста́вить. / *(2)* ...в себе́ не подозрева́ешь. ♦ **When I have you**

A slash always denotes "or."
You can choose the numbered words before and after.

in my arms, I'm going to arouse tides of sweet feeling in you that will sweep you into a storm of passion. Когда́ я заключу́ тебя́ в объя́тия, я разбужу́ пото́к не́жных чувств в тебе́, кото́рый бро́сит тебя́ в бу́рю стра́сти. ♦ **The feelings are going to move like warm honey through your loins.** Чу́вства разолью́тся по твои́м бёдрам сла́дкой исто́мой. ♦ **If you were my woman, I would fill your life to overflowing with soft, gentle, eager, loving kisses that would awaken all sorts of warm, wonderful, exquisite feelings in you.** Е́сли бы ты была́ мое́й же́нщиной, я бы запо́лнил твою́ жизнь до краёв мя́гкими, не́жными, жа́ждущими, лю́бящими поцелу́ями, кото́рые пробуди́ли бы все са́мые тёплые, замеча́тельные, изы́сканные чу́вства в тебе́. ♦ **We would have so much fun together and I would fill you with such beautiful feelings that you would never let go of me.** У нас бы́ло бы сто́лько весе́лья, и я бы напо́лнил тебя́ таки́ми прекра́сными чу́вствами, что ты никогда́ бы не захоте́ла поки́нуть меня́.

---
feeling: *your feelings for me*

When I *(1)* **became /** *(2)* **grew aware of your feelings for me, I was overcome with joy.** Когда́ я узна́л *(ж: узна́ла)* о твои́х чу́вствах ко мне, я был охва́чен *(ж: была́ охва́чена)* ликова́нием. ♦ **I** *(1)* **harbor /** *(2)* **entertain no illusions about your feelings for me.** Я не *(1)* таю́ / *(2)* пита́ю никаки́х иллю́зий относи́тельно твои́х чувств ко мне. ♦ **You're mistaken in your feeling for me.** Ты ошиба́ешься в свои́х чу́вствах ко мне.

---
feeling: *expressing feelings*

I wish I could *(1)* **...convey /** *(2)* **express my feelings as well as you** *(3)* **...do. /** *(4)* **...have done. /** *(5)* **...put into words the (tender) feelings that abound in my heart for you.** Я хоте́л *(ж: хоте́ла)* бы уме́ть ...та́кже хорошо́ *(1,2)* выража́ть свои́ чу́вства, как ты э́то *(3)* де́лаешь. / *(4)* де́лала *(ж: де́лал)*. / *(5)* ...вы́разить слова́ми (не́жные) чу́вства к тебе́, переполня́ющие моё се́рдце. ♦ **How I wish I could communicate all the (**[1] **beautiful /** [2] **intense /** [3] **deep) feelings I have toward you.** Как бы я жела́л, что́бы я мог переда́ть все (*[1]* прекра́сные / *[2]* пы́лкие / *[3]* глубо́кие) чу́вства, кото́рые я испы́тываю к тебе́.

---
feeling: *mutual feelings*

Your feelings (for me) are (very much) reciprocated. Твои́ чу́вства (ко мне) (абсолю́тно) взаи́мны. ♦ **I want you to know that the feelings you expressed to me are reciprocated 100%. I feel exactly the same about you.** Я хочу́, что́бы ты зна́ла *(ж: знал)*, что чу́вства, кото́рые ты вы́сказала *(ж: вы́сказал)* ко мне, на сто проце́нтов взаи́мны. Я чу́вствую абсолю́тно то же по отноше́нию к тебе́. ♦ **The feeling is mutual.** Чу́вство взаи́мно. ♦ **You and I are incredibly alike in the nature and intensity of our feelings.** Мы с тобо́ей невероя́тно похо́жи хара́ктером и интенси́вностью чувств.

---
feeling: *sharing feelings*

I want you to share your feelings with me. Я хочу́, что́бы ты дели́лась *(ж: дели́лся)* свои́ми чу́вствами со мной. ♦ **I want someone that I can share my feelings with.** Я хочу́ кого́-то, с кем я смог *(ж: смогла́)* бы дели́ться свои́ми чу́вствами. ♦ **Dear, you can always reveal your feelings to me.** Дорога́я, ты мо́жешь всегда́ выка́зывать мне свои́ чу́вства.

---
feeling: *regard for feelings*

It would be nice if you would show a little more sensitivity to my feelings. Бы́ло бы так хорошо́, е́сли бы ты вы́казала *(ж: вы́казал)* немно́го бо́льше понима́ния мои́х чувств. **You seem to have no regard (at all) for my feelings.** Ты ка́жется не пита́ешь (никако́го) уваже́ния к мои́м чу́вствам. ♦ **I care about your feelings.** Я забо́чусь о твои́х чу́вствах. **You don't seem to care about my feelings.** Ты, ка́жется, не забо́тишься о мои́х чу́вствах.

---
feeling: *hurt feelings*

I don't want to hurt your feelings. Я не хочу́ ра́нить твои́ чу́вства. ♦ **I (**[1] **honestly /** [2]

Common adult weights are given in Appendix 10, page 777.

truly) didn't mean to hurt your feelings. Я (*[1]* ...действительно... / *[2]* ...на самом деле...) не хотел (*ж: хотела*) ранить твои чувства. ♦ *(1)* **I'm** (*[2]* **very** / *[3]* **terribly) sorry...** / *(4)* **Please forgive me...** *(5)* **that** / *(6)* **if I hurt your feelings.** *(1)* Я (*[2]* очень / *[3]* ужасно) сожалею... / *(4)* Прости, пожалуйста,... *(5)* что / *(6)* , если я ранил (*ж: ранила*) твои чувства. ♦ **You hurt my feelings** (*[1]* ...**a lot.** / *[2]* ...**more than you'll ever know.** / *[3]* ...**more than I can tell you.**). Ты ранила (*ж: ранил*) мои чувства (*[1]* ...очень. / *[2]* ...даже больше, чем ты думаешь. / *[3]* ...более, чем я могу сказать тебе.)

---

feeling: *pretended feelings*

I think you're just pretending to *(1,2)* **have feelings for me.** Я думаю, ты только притворяешься, что *(1)* испытываешь / *(2)* имеешь какие-то чувства ко мне. ♦ **I wonder if you're not just pretending your feelings for me.** Я хотел (*ж: хотела*) бы знать, не притворяешься ли ты, что испытываешь какие-то чувства ко мне. ♦ **I can't pretend feelings (that I don't have).** Я не могу притворяться в чувствах (, которые я не испытываю).

---

feeling: *confused feelings*

I can't sort out my feelings. Я не могу разобраться в своих чувствах. ♦ **My feelings are in turmoil.** Мои чувства в смятении.

---

feeling: *controlling feelings*

You really should try to keep your feelings in check. Ты действительно должна (*ж: должен*) попытаться держать под контролем свои чувства. ♦ **It's so hard for me to keep my feelings in check (when** *[1]* ...**I'm around you.** / *[2]* ...**I think about you.**). Мне так трудно удерживать под контролем свои чувства (когда *[1]* ...я рядом с тобой. / *[2]* ...я думаю о тебе.)

---

feeling: *dead feelings*

My feelings for *(1)* **you** / *(2)* **her** / *(3)* **him are** (*[4]* **completely** / *[5]* **totally)** *(6,7)* **dead.** Мои чувства к *(1)* тебе / *(2)* ней / *(3)* нему (*[4]* полностью / *[5]* совершенно) *(6)* угасли / *(7)* умерли. ♦ **The feelings that I felt for you in the beginning are irretrievably gone.** Чувства, которые я испытывал (*ж: испытывала*) к тебе в начале, безвозвратно улетучились.

---

feeling: *other kinds of feelings*

Sometimes *(1)* ...**I get...** / *(2)* ...**you give me... such a smothered feeling.** *(1,2)* Иногда из-за тебя у меня такое ощущение, что что-то душит меня. ♦ **My feelings of self-worth have** *(1)* ...**gone steadily down.** / *(2)* ...**really been battered** / *(3)* **hammered.** Моя самооценка *(1)* ...шла постоянно вниз. / *(2)* ...действительно была разрушена / *(3)* разбита. ♦ **My feelings** *(1)* **are** / *(2)* **were vulnerable.** Мои чувства *(1)* ...ранимы. / ...были ранимыми. ♦ **I can't escape the feeling that** *(1)* ...**you don't care about me anymore.** / *(2)* ...**I don't mean anything to you anymore.** Я не могу отделаться от чувства, что *(1)* ...ты больше не любишь меня. / *(2)* ...я больше ничего не значу для тебя. ♦ **With you, I always have the feeling that I'm walking on eggshells.** С тобой, я всегда чувствую себя, сидящим на пороховой бочке. ♦ **I have a cold, hollow feeling in my stomach.** Во мне холод и пустота. ♦ **I have a** *(1)* **gut** / *(2)* **nagging feeling that you're** *(3)* ...**seeing someone else.** / *(4)* ... **cheating on me.** Я *(1)* ...инстинктивно... / *(2)* ...со щемящей болью... чувствую, что ты *(3)* ...встречаешься с кем-то ещё. / *(4)* ... обманываешь меня.

---

feeling: *person of feeling*

I'm a person of feeling. Я человек чувства.

feign *vt* притворяться *(what = instr.)* ♦ ~ *(1,2)* **sleep** притворяться *(1)* спящим *m* / *(2)* спящей *f*.

feisty *adj* 1. *(quarrelsome, cantakerous)* сварливый, -ая, -ое, -ые, вздорный, -ая, -ое, -ые;

(troublesome) скло́чный, -ая, -ое, -ые; *(persistent)* упо́рный, -ая, -ое, -ые; *(straight-forward)* прямолине́йный, -ая, -ое, -ые; 2. *(brave)* сме́лый, -ая, -ое, -ые, отва́жный, -ая, -ое, -ые.

feline *adj* коша́чий, -ая, -ее, -ие.

feline-friendly *adj*: ♦ **be ~** люби́ть ко́шек.

fella' *n (slang) (fellow)* па́рень *m* ♦ **my ~** *(my boyfriend)* мой па́рень.

female *adj* же́нский, -ая, -ое, -ие.

female *n* же́нщина *(people only, not animals) (See also* **gal**, **girl**, **lady** *and* **woman)** ♦ **caring** ~ забо́тливая же́нщина ♦ **chatty** ~ разгово́рчивая же́нщина ♦ **Christian** ~ же́нщина-христиа́нка ♦ **classy** ~ кла́ссная же́нщина ♦ **compassionate** ~ сострада́тельная же́нщина ♦ **ebony** ~ же́нщина чёрная как смоль, чёрная же́нщина ♦ **energetic** ~ энерги́чная же́нщина ♦ **eye-catching** ~ привлека́тельная же́нщина ♦ **fascinating** ~ очарова́тельная же́нщина ♦ **~ of bright interior** вну́тренне я́ркая же́нщина ♦ **~ with inner beauty** же́нщина с вну́тренней красото́й ♦ **fit** ~ спорти́вная же́нщина ♦ **full-figured** ~ по́лная же́нщина ♦ **fun** ~ же́нщина, с кото́рой ве́село *(1 term)* ♦ **fun-loving** ~ же́нщина, лю́бящая развлече́ния *(1 term)* ♦ **highly sexed** ~ о́чень сексуа́льная же́нщина ♦ **insightful** ~ проница́тельная же́нщина ♦ **ivory** ~ же́нщина цве́та слоно́вой ко́сти, бе́лая же́нщина ♦ **loving** ~ лю́бящая же́нщина ♦ **outgoing** ~ же́нщина-экстраве́рт ♦ **pierced** ~ же́нщина с ко́льцами на те́ле ♦ **professional** ~ высококвалифици́рованная же́нщина ♦ **romantic** ~ романти́ческая же́нщина ♦ **sexually confident** ~ сексуа́льно уве́ренная же́нщина ♦ **shapely** ~ стро́йная же́нщина, же́нщина с хоро́шей фигу́рой ♦ **similar** ~ же́нщина с подо́бными ка́чествами ♦ **spiritual** ~ же́нщина с духо́вной жи́знью ♦ **stylish** ~ шика́рная же́нщина ♦ **submissive** ~ поко́рная же́нщина ♦ **thin** ~ то́нкая же́нщина ♦ **uninhibited** ~ же́нщина без ко́мплексов ♦ **unique** ~ уника́льная же́нщина ♦ **vivacious** ~ жива́я же́нщина ♦ **well-proportioned** ~ хорошо́ сложённая же́нщина.

feminine *adj* 1. *(female)* же́нский, -ая, -ое, -ие; 2. *(womanly)* же́нственный, -ая, -ое, -ые.

feminism *n* фемини́зм.

feminist *n* фемини́стка.

femme fatale *n (French)* роkова́я же́нщина.

fervent *adj* пы́лкий, -ая, -ое, -ие ♦ **You have no idea with what fervent yearning I wait for each letter from you.** Ты не представля́ешь, с каки́м стра́стным жела́нием я жду ка́ждого твоего́ письма́.

fervently *adv* пы́лко, горячо́.

fervor *n* горя́чность *f*, пыл ♦ **respond with equal** ~ отвеча́ть / отве́тить с таки́м же пы́лом ♦ **There is no way that you can comprehend the fervor with which I adore you.** Ты не мо́жешь пости́гнуть пыл, с кото́рым я обожа́ю тебя́.

fest *n* пра́здник; пир ♦ **love ~** пра́здник любви́, пир любви́ ♦ **I want to have a love fest with you every night.** Я хочу́, чтобы пра́здник любви́ был с тобо́й ка́ждую ночь.

festival *n* фестива́ль *m* ♦ **autumn ~** осе́нний фестива́ль ♦ **Christmas ~** рожде́ственский фестива́ль ♦ **wine ~** ви́нный фестива́ль ♦ **How would you like to** *(1,2)* **go to the festival with me on Saturday?** Не хоте́ла *(ж: хоте́л)* бы ты *(1)* пойти́ *(on foot)* / *(2)* пое́хать *(by veh.)* на фестива́ль со мной в суббо́ту? ♦ **You make my** *(1)* **life /** *(2)* **world a daily festival of love.** Ты превраща́ешь *(1)* ...мою́ жизнь... / *(2)* ...мой мир... в ежедне́вный пра́здник любви́.

fetish *n* фе́тиш, и́дол, куми́р.

feud *vi (quarrel)* ссо́риться / поссо́риться *(with whom =* + с + *instr.).*

feud *n (quarrel)* ссо́ра.

---

*Procedures for getting married to a Russian
are outlined in Appendix 18, page 787.*

fever *n* жар ♦ **I can't concentrate on anything with this fever in my blood.** Этот жар в моёй крóви не даёт мне сосредотóчиться ни на чём.

feverish *adj* возбуждённый, -ая, -ое, -ые ♦ **The expectation to see your beloved face again makes me feel hot and feverish.** Ожидáние увúдеть твоё любúмое лицó опя́ть вызывáет во мне жар и лихорáдочное возбуждéние.

few *n* нéсколько ♦ **a ~ days** нéсколько дней ♦ **a ~ hours** нéсколько часóв ♦ **a ~ months** нéсколько мéсяцев ♦ **a ~ years** нéсколько лет.

fiancé *n* женúх.

fiancée *n* невéста.

fiber *n* фúбра ♦ **Liquid fire swirls through every fiber of my body.** Жúдкий огóнь пронóсится вúхрем чéрез все фúбры моегó тéла. ♦ **You send electric sensations shooting through every cell and fiber of my body.** Ты посылáешь электрúческие заря́ды, прострéливающие кáждую клéтку и все фúбры моегó тéла. ♦ **I want you with every fiber of my** *(1)* **being /** *(2)* **body.** Я хочý тебя́ всéми фúбрами *(1)* ...своéй душú. / *(2)* ...своегó тéла. ♦ **Molten waves of desire surge through every fiber and cell of my body whenever I think of your exquisite, luscious beauty.** Бушýющие вóлны стрáсти пронóсятся чéрез все фúбры и клéтки моегó тéла, когдá бы я ни подýмал о твоéй изы́сканной, сóчной красотé.

fickle *adj* непостоя́нный, -ая, -ое, -ые, перемéнный, -ая, -ое, -ые, неустóйчивый, -ая, -ое, -ые.

fidelity *n* вéрность *f* ♦ **vow ~** кля́сться / покля́сться в вéрности ♦ **What I** *(1)* **...want... /** *(2)* **...yearn for... most in a relationship is fidelity** Чегó я *(1)* ...хочý... / *(2)* ...жáжду... бóлее всегó в отношéниях - вéрности. ♦ **"Your idea of fidelity is not having more than one man in bed at the same time." "***Darling***"** *(movie)* «Твоё поня́тие вéрности - э́то имéть в постéли одновремéнно не бóлее, чем одногó мужчúну.» «*Дорогáя*» *(фильм)*

fidget *vi* вертéться, ёрзать.

field *n* 1. *(land)* пóле; 2. *(sports)* площáдка; 3. *(of endeavor)* óбласть *f* ; *(specialty)* специáльность *f* ♦ **~ of love** любóвное пóприще ♦ **I'm not a guy who plays the field.** Я не тот мужчúна, котóрый волочúтся за всéми жéнщинами.

fiend *n* 1. *(demon)* дья́вол; злодéй; 2. *(maniac)* манья́к ♦ **sex ~** сексуáльный манья́к.

fierce *adj* неúстовый, -ая, -ое, -ые ♦ **The fierce** *(1)* **passion /** *(2)* **desire I feel for you** *(3)* **...is something I have never experienced before. /** *(4)* **...is utterly consuming me. /** *(5)* **...dominates all my thoughts and attention. /** *(6)* **... overwhelms me.** *(1)* Неúстовая страсть к тебé... / *(2)* Неúстовое желáние тебя́... *(3)* ...э́то нéчто такóе, чегó я никогдá прéжде не испы́тывал / *(4)* ...пóлностью поглощáет меня́. / *(5)* ...госпóдствует над всéми моúми мы́слями и внимáнием. / *(6)* ...переполня́ет меня́.

fiercely *adv* неúстово, горячó, сúльно.

fierceness *n* неúстовство ♦ **~ of a kiss** неúстовство поцелýя.

fiery *adj* óгненный, -ая, -ое, -ые, жгýчий, -ая, -ее, -ие ♦ *(1)* **I want to... /** *(2)* **I'm going to suffuse your entire being in the fiery rapture of climax.** *(1)* Я хочý залúть... / *(2)* Я залью́... всё твоё существó óгненным востóргом оргáзма.

fight *vt* борóться *(what, whom* = + с + *instr.)* ♦ **You're fighting your own desire. Why don't you just surrender to it (for once)?** Ты бóрешься со своéй стрáстью. Почемý бы тебé прóсто не уступúть ей (однáжды)?

figure *n* фигýра ♦ *(1,2)* **athletic ~** *(1)* атлетúческая / *(2)* спортúвная фигýра ♦ *(1,2)* **beautiful ~** *(1)* прекрáсная / *(2)* красúвая фигýра ♦ **bewitching ~** обворожúтельная фигýр(к)а ♦ **breath-taking ~** умопомрачúтельная фигýра ♦ **classical ~** классúческая фигýра ♦ **curvaceous ~** стрóйная фигýра ♦ **curved ~** стрóйная фигýра ♦ **decent ~**

A list of conjugated Russian verbs is given in Appendix 3 on page 699.

неплохáя фигýра ♦ *(1-3)* **delicate** ~ *(1)* стрóйная / *(2)* точёная / *(3)* хрýпкая фигýра ♦ **fabulous** ~ потрясáющая фигýра ♦ *(1-3)* **fantastic** ~ *(1)* великолéпная / *(2)* замечáтельная / *(3)* фантастúческая фигýра ♦ **feminine** ~ жéнственная фигýра ♦ **fine** ~ красúвая фигýра ♦ *(1,2)* **full** ~ *(1)* пóлная / *(2)* дорóдная фигýра ♦ **girlish** ~ дéвичья фигýра ♦ **good** ~ хорóшая фигýра ♦ *(1,2)* **gorgeous** ~ *(1)* великолéпная / *(2)* замечáтельная фигýра ♦ **graceful** ~ грациóзная фигýра ♦ *(1,2)* **great** ~ *(1)* великолéпная / *(2)* превосхóдная фигýра ♦ **hourglass** ~ точёная фигýра, осúная тáлия, тóнкая фигýра, фигýра как песóчные часы́ ♦ *(1,2)* **incredible** ~ *(1)* изумúтельная / *(2)* невероя́тная фигýра ♦ **junoesque** ~ фигýра как у Юнóны ♦ **lanky** ~ долговя́зая фигýра ♦ **lithesome girlish** ~ гúбкий девúчий стан ♦ *(1,2)* **lovely** ~ *(1)* прекрáсная / *(2)* красúвая фигýра ♦ **luscious** ~ сóчная фигýра ♦ **lush** ~ роскóшная фигýра ♦ **magnetic** ~ привлекáтельная фигýра ♦ **marvelous** ~ удивúтельная фигýра ♦ **mouth-watering** ~ соблазнúтельная фигýра ♦ **my** ~ моя́ фигýра ♦ **nice** ~ хорóшая фигýра ♦ **pretty good** ~ неплохáя фигýра ♦ **provocative** ~ соблазнúтельная фигýра ♦ **rubenesque** ~ рýбенсовская фигýра ♦ **shapely** ~ стрóйная фигýра ♦ **skinny** ~ худáя фигýра ♦ *(1,2)* **slender** ~ *(1)* тóнкая / *(2)* стрóйная фигýра ♦ *(1,2)* **slim** ~ *(1)* тóнкая / *(2)* стрóйная фигýра ♦ **stately** ~ стáтная фигýра ♦ **striking** ~ поразúтельная фигýра ♦ **stunning** ~ потрясáющая фигýра ♦ **such a** ~ такáя фигýра ♦ **terrific** ~ великолéпная фигýра ♦ *(1,2)* **voluptuous** ~ *(1)* чýвственная / *(2)* роскóшная фигýра ♦ *(1,2)* **well-built** ~ *(1)* лáдная / *(2)* склáдная фигýра ♦ *(1,2)* **well-proportioned** ~ *(1)* лáдная / *(2)* склáдная фигýра ♦ *(1,2)* **well-rounded** ~ *(1)* лáдная / *(2)* склáдная фигýра ♦ *(1,2)* **willowy** ~ *(1)* стрóйная / *(2)* гúбкая фигýра ♦ **wonderful** ~ замечáтельная фигýра ♦ **your** ~ *(familiar)* твоя́ фигýра; *(polite)* Вáша фигýра.

---
figure: phrases

Seeing your beautiful figure just adds fuel to the fire of my desire for you. Когдá я вúжу твою́ прекрáсную фигýру, огóнь моéй стрáсти к тебé разжигáется ещё сильнéе. ♦ **You have a(n)** *(1)* **incredible** / *(2)* **marvelous** / *(3)* **beautiful** / *(4)* **gorgeous figure.** У тебя́ *(1)* невероя́тная / *(2)* удивúтельная / *(3)* прекрáсная / *(4)* великолéпная фигýра. ♦ **You (still) have a girlish figure.** У тебя́ (до сих пор) дéвичья фигýра. ♦ **What a(n)** *(1)* **beautiful** / *(2)* **gorgeous** / *(3)* **fantastic** / *(4)* **terrific** / *(5)* **incredible** / *(6,7)* **willowy figure (you have)!** Что за *(1)* красúвая / *(2)* прекрáсная / *(3)* фантастúческая / *(4)* великолéпная / *(5)* невероя́тная / *(6)* стрóйная / *(7)* гúбкая фигýра (у тебя́)! ♦ **Why you would want to cover up a figure like that, I can't imagine.** Почемý ты хóчешь скрыть такýю фигýру, я не понимáю. ♦ **It's a (n absolute)** *(1)* **crime** / *(2)* **sin** / *(3)* **blasphemy to cover up a figure like yours.** Это (прóсто) *(1)* преступлéние / *(2)* грех / *(3)* богохýльство скрывáть такýю фигýру, как твоя́. ♦ **You have such a beautiful figure.** У тебя́ такáя прекрáсная фигýра. ♦ **I really love a rubenesque figure.** Мне óчень нрáвится рýбенсовская фигýра. ♦ **I** *(1)* **love** / *(2)* **adore your rubenesque figure.** Я *(1)* люблю́ / *(2)* обожáю твою́ рýбенсовскую фигýру.

figure-molding *adj* плóтно-облегáющий, -ая, -ее, -ие.

file *vi* подавáть / подáть *(for what = + на + acc.)* ♦ **I'm going to file for a divorce.** Я собирáюсь подáть на развóд.

fill *vt* заполня́ть / заполнить *(what = + acc., with what = + instr.)*, наполня́ть / наполнить *(what = + acc., with what = + instr.)* ♦ **You fill my life with love.** Ты наполня́ешь мою́ жизнь любóвью. ♦ **I want to fill your body with so much pleasure that you will be** *(1)* **hurled** / *(2)* **flung** / *(3)* **rocketed into a cosmos of exploding ecstasy.** Я хочý заполнить твоё тéло такúм огрóмным наслаждéнием, чтóбы ты былá *(1,2)* брóшена / *(3)* запýщена в кóсмос взрывáющегося экстáза. ♦ **I dream of filling your body with intense,**

> *For Russian adjectives, the masculine form is spelled out,*
> *followed by the feminine, neuter and plural endings.*

exquisite pleasure day and night, night and day, for as long as God grants me the time. Я мечта́ю наполня́ть твоё те́ло пы́лким, изы́сканным наслажде́нием день и ночь, ночь и день до конца́ даро́ванной мне бо́гом жи́зни. ♦ The *(1,2)* magic of the spring fills my heart with longing to be with you. *(1)* Волшебство́ / *(2)* Ма́гия весны́ наполня́ет моё се́рдце жа́ждой быть с тобо́й. ♦ If you were my woman, I would fill your life to overflowing with soft, gentle, eager, loving kisses that would awaken all sorts of warm, wonderful, exquisite feelings in you. Если бы ты была́ мое́й же́нщиной, я бы запо́лнил твою́ жизнь до краёв мя́гкими, не́жными, жа́ждущими, лю́бящими поцелу́ями, кото́рые пробуди́ли бы все са́мые тёплые, замеча́тельные, изы́сканные чу́вства в тебе́.

fill *n* по́лное насыще́ние ♦ **get one's fill** получи́ть по́лное насыще́ние.

film *n* 1. *(for cameras)* плёнка; 2. *(movie)* фильм ♦ **indi(e) ~s** *(films by independent producers)* фи́льмы, сде́ланные незави́симыми продю́серами *(1 term)*.

finally *adv* в конце́ концо́в, наконе́ц.

find *vt* находи́ть / найти́ *(whom, what = + acc.)* ♦ **~ complete harmony** обрести́ по́лную гармо́нию ♦ **~ happiness** найти́ сча́стье ♦ **I am so** *(1)* **happy** / *(2)* **grateful that I found you (in this world).** Я так *(1)* сча́стлив *(ж: счастли́ва)* / *(2)* благода́рен *(ж: благо-да́рна)*, что я нашёл *(ж: нашла́)* тебя́ (в э́том ми́ре). ♦ **I am so lucky that I found you (in this world).** Мне так повезло́, что я нашёл *(ж: нашла́)* тебя́ (в э́том ми́ре). ♦ **My** *(1)* **hungry** / *(2)* **loving** / *(3)* **wandering** / *(4)* **roving lips will seek and find the hidden treasures of your** *(5)* **magnificent** / *(6)* **luscious beauty.** Мои́ *(1)* голо́дные / *(2)* лю́бящие / *(3,4)* блужда́ющие гу́бы бу́дут иска́ть и находи́ть скры́тые сокро́вища твое́й *(5)* великоле́пной / *(6)* со́чной красоты́.

find *n* нахо́дка ♦ **Someone like you is a rare find.** Тако́й челове́к, как ты, -- ре́дкая нахо́дка.

finesse *n* иску́сность *f*, мастерство́ ♦ **You won't believe what** *(1)* **marvelous** / *(2)* **satisfying finesse I have at giving a massage.** Ты не смо́жешь пове́рить, каки́м *(1)* изуми́тельным / *(2)* удовлетворя́ющим иску́сством масса́жа я владе́ю.

finger *n* па́лец *(pl:* па́льцы) ♦ **aristocratic ~s** аристократи́ческие па́льцы ♦ **beautiful ~s** краси́вые па́льцы ♦ **dainty ~s** изя́щные па́льцы ♦ **~s of the gods** волше́бные па́льцы ♦ **4th ~ of the left hand** *(counting the thumb) (the finger that the marriage ring is worn on in the U.S.)* четвёртый па́лец ле́вой руки́, безымя́нный па́лец ♦ **gentle ~s** не́жные па́льцы ♦ **hot ~s** горя́чие па́льцы ♦ **index ~** указа́тельный па́лец ♦ **little ~** *(smallest on the hand)* мизи́нец ♦ **little ~s** па́льчики ♦ **long ~s** дли́нные па́льцы ♦ **lovely ~s** краси́вые па́льцы ♦ **middle ~** сре́дний па́лец ♦ **mischievous ~s** шаловли́вые па́льцы ♦ **nimble ~s** ло́вкие па́льцы ♦ **ring ~** *(on the left hand in America, on the right in Russia)* па́лец с обруча́льным кольцо́м *(в Аме́рике - па́лец на ле́вой руке́, в Росси́и - на пра́вой)*, безымя́нный па́лец *(4th finger of each hand, ring or no ring)* ♦ **sensitive ~s** чу́ткие па́льцы ♦ **slender ~s** то́нкие па́льцы ♦ **warm ~s** тёплые па́льцы.

finger: phrases

The touch of your fingers is fire. Прикоснове́ние твои́х па́льцев -- э́то пла́мя. ♦ Your fingers on mine were like an electric shock. Твои́ па́льцы на мои́х бы́ли как электри́ческий шок. ♦ *(1)* He / *(2)* She (obviously) has you *(3,4)* wrapped around *(5)* his / *(6)* her finger. *(1)* Он / *(2)* Она́ (очеви́дно) *(3)* обвёл *m* / *(4)* обвела́ *f* тебя́ вокру́г *(5,6)* па́льца. ♦ My fingers and lips will spread warm *(1)* rings / *(2)* waves of joy throughout your beautiful, voluptuous body. Мои́ па́льцы и гу́бы распространя́т тёплые *(1)* ко́льца / *(2)* во́лны наслажде́ния в твоём прекра́сном, роско́шном те́ле. ♦ My fingers will stroll languidly, softly, adoringly along the svelte curve of your body. Мои́ па́льцы

See Appendix 19 for notes on sending mail to Russia and Ukraine.

ме́дленно, мя́гко, обожа́юще прогуля́ются по стро́йным окру́глостям твоего́ те́ла.

fingernails *n, pl* но́гти па́льца (руки́) ♦ **beautiful** ~s краси́вые но́гти (на па́льцах) ♦ **little** ~s ноготки́ (на па́льцах) ♦ **long** ~s дли́нные но́гти (на па́льцах) ♦ **lovely** ~s краси́вые но́гти (на па́льцах) ♦ **What** *(1)* **beautiful /** *(2)* **lovely fingernails (you have)!** Каки́е *(1,2)* краси́вые но́гти (у тебя́) на рука́х!

fingertip *n* ко́нчик па́льца ♦ **My fingertips will glide over your body, scattering delicious pleasure in their path.** Ко́нчики мои́х па́льцев бу́дут скользи́ть по твоему́ те́лу, рассе́ивая восхити́тельное наслажде́ние на своём пути́.

Finn *n* финн *m*, фи́нка *f*.

Finnish *adj* фи́нский, -ая, -ое, -ие.

Finnish *n* фи́нский язы́к ♦ **speak** ~ говори́ть по-фи́нски.

fire *n* 1. ого́нь *m*, пла́мя *neut*; 2. *(ardor)* пыл ♦ **bright** ~ я́ркий ого́нь ♦ **flowing** ~ теку́щий ого́нь ♦ **great** ~ большо́й ого́нь ♦ **liquid** ~ жи́дкий ого́нь ♦ *(1-3)* **raging** ~ *(1)* бушу́ющий / *(2)* бе́шеный ого́нь, *(3)* бушу́ющее пла́мя ♦ *(1-3)* **roaring** ~ *(1)* бушу́ющий / *(2)* бе́шеный ого́нь, *(3)* бушу́ющее пла́мя ♦ **sensuous** ~ чу́вственный ого́нь ♦ **uncontrollable** ~ неконтроли́руемый ого́нь ♦ **add fuel to the** ~ добавля́ть / доба́вить жа́ру в ого́нь ♦ **fan the** ~ раздува́ть / разду́ть ого́нь ♦ **light my** ~ зажига́ть ого́нь во мне ♦ **play with** ~ игра́ть с огнём ♦ **put out the** ~ гаси́ть / погаси́ть ого́нь ♦ **start a** ~ разжига́ть / разже́чь ого́нь ♦ **turn to** ~ превраща́ться / преврати́ться в ого́нь ♦ **light my** ~ зажига́ть / заже́чь ого́нь во мне ♦ **put out the** ~ унима́ть / уня́ть пожа́р. ♦ **turn to** ~ преврати́ться в ого́нь.

fire: *when I think of you*

Fire *(1)* **licks /** *(2)* **sweeps /** *(3)* **pours /** *(4)* **rages /** *(5)* **courses through my veins whenever I think of your soft, warm, beautiful, luscious body and the oceans of ecstasy that it contains.** Ого́нь ...*(1)* ли́жет / *(2)* охва́тывает мои́ ве́ны... / ...*(3)* льётся / *(4)* бушу́ет в мои́х ве́нах... / ...струи́тся сквозь мои́ ве́ны... вся́кий раз, когда́ я ду́маю о твоём мя́гком, тёплом, прекра́сном, со́чном те́ле и океа́нах экста́за, кото́рые оно́ содер́жит. ♦ **My blood becomes roaring fire whenever I even think about your soft, warm, beautiful body.** Моя́ кровь превраща́ется в бушу́ющий ого́нь вся́кий раз, когда́ я ду́маю о твоём мя́гком, тёплом, прекра́сном те́ле. ♦ **Visions of your voluptuous loveliness send fire licking through my arteries, igniting my entire being into an inferno of passionate desire.** Вид твое́й чу́вственной красоты́ вызыва́ет ого́нь, бушу́ющий в мои́х арте́риях, посыла́ющий всё моё существо́ в ад стра́стного жела́ния. ♦ **My whole body is awash with fire, thinking about you.** Всё моё те́ло охва́тывает ого́нь при мы́сле о тебе́.

fire: *you set me on fire*

Your beauty (constantly) sets my heart on fire. Твоя́ красота́ (постоя́нно) воспламеня́ет моё се́рдце. ♦ *(1)* **Touching your hand... /** *(2)* **Hearing your voice... /** *(3)* **Smelling your perfume... /** *(4)* **Seeing your beautiful face... /** *(5)* **Seeing your beautiful figure... just adds fuel to the fire of my desire for you.** Когда́ я *(1)* ...каса́юсь твое́й руки́, ... / *(2)* ...слы́шу твой го́лос,... / *(3)* ...вдыха́ю твои́ духи́,... / *(4)* ...ви́жу твоё прекра́сное лицо́,... / *(5)* ...ви́жу твою́ прекра́сную фигу́ру,... ого́нь мое́й стра́сти к тебе́ разжига́ется ещё сильне́е. ♦ **You can never** *(1)* **know /** *(2)* **imagine how you stoke the fires in my** *(3)* **heart /** *(4)* **blood.** Ты не *(1)* ...зна́ешь,... / *(2)* ...мо́жешь вообрази́ть,... како́й ого́нь разжига́ешь в *(3)* ...моём се́рдце. / *(4)* ...мое́й крови́. ♦ **I am** *(1)* **consumed /** *(2)* **engulfed by this fire that you have started racing through my blood.** Я *(1,2)* поглощён огнём, кото́рый ты разожгла́ в мое́й крови́. ♦ **You really light my fire.** Ты действи́тельно зажига́ешь ого́нь во мне. ♦ **No one lights my fire like you do.** Никто́ не зажи-

The time zones for many cities of the world are given in Appendix 6, page 761.

гáет такóго огня́ во мне, как ты. ♦ **You have a** *(1)* **kiss /** *(2)* **touch of fire.** *(1)* Твой поцелу́й... / *(2)* Твоё прикосновéние... -- э́то огóнь. ♦ **Your touch is like fire.** Твоё прикосновéние, как огóнь. ♦ **Your kisses are like fire.** Твои́ поцелу́и, как огóнь. ♦ **The sensual message in your eyes sends fire coursing through my veins.** Чу́вственный призы́в в твои́х глазáх возбуждáет огóнь, теку́щий в мои́х вéнах.

fire: *fire is upon me*

The sensation spreads through my loins like liquid fire. Чу́вство разливáется по мои́м бёдрам, как жи́дкий огóнь. ♦ **Liquid fire swirls through** *(1)* **...me. /** *(2)* **...every fiber of my body.** Жи́дкий огóнь проно́сится ви́хрем чéрез *(1)* ...меня́. / *(2)* ...все фи́бры моегó тéла. ♦ **Many times at night I wake up with my body on fire from cavorting with you in one episode or another of the Kama Sutra.** Мнóго раз я просыпáюсь нóчью с тéлом, охвáченным огнём от тогó, что мы с тобóй изучáем ту и́ли другу́ю главу́ Кáма Су́тры. ♦ **Nothing can quench the fire that rages inside me except your love.** Ничтó, крóме твоéй любви́, не мóжет утоли́ть огóнь, бушу́ющий во мне. ♦ **My body aches to feel the fire that rages in the core of your womanhood.** Моё тéло жáждет почу́вствовать огóнь, котóрый бушу́ет в глубинé твоéй жéнственности.

fire: *set your soul on fire*

One of these days I'm going to break through that protective bubble of reserve that you live in and set your soul on fire. Однáжды я прорву́сь чéрез защи́тную оболóчку сдéржанности, в котóрой ты живёшь, и зажгу́ огóнь в твоéй душé.

fire: *our passion*

Our kindled passion will burst into an uncontrollable, raging fire. Нáша воспламени́вшаяся страсть разгори́тся неконтроли́руемым, бéшеным огнём.

fire: *quotation*

"Purify me with a great fire of divine love." *Liane de Pougy* «Очи́сти меня́ вели́ким огнём небéсной любви́.» *Ля́ян де Пуш*

fire: *beach fire*

We can build a beach fire. Мы мóжем зажéчь костёр на пля́же.

fireball *n* «огóнь» *m*.

firelight *n* óгненный свет ♦ **I would love to cuddle with you by firelight.** Я бы хотéл *(ж: хотéла)* обня́ться с тобóй у огня́.

firestorm *n* óгненный шторм ♦ *(1)* **I want to... /** *(2)* **I'm going to... ignite a firestorm of passion in you.** *(1)* Я хочу́ зажéчь... / *(2)* Я зажгу́... óгненный шторм стрáсти в тебе.

fireworks *n, pl* фéйервéрк ♦ **I go away from any encounter with you with my heart spinning wildly and my mind erupting in a fireworks display of love thoughts about you.** Пóсле кáждой встрéчи с тобóй я ухожу́ с бéшено стучáщим сéрдцем и с цéлым фейер-вéрком любóвных мы́слей о тебé.

fish *vi* уди́ть ры́бу, лови́ть ры́бу.

fishing *n* ры́бная лóвля.

fishy *adj (slang) (suspicious)* подозри́тельный, -ая, -ое, -ые ♦ **It seems a bit fishy.** Вы́глядит нéсколько подозри́тельно.

fit *adj (healthy)* здорóвый, -ая, -ое, -ые; *(in good shape)* в хорóшем состоя́нии ♦ **emotionally** ~ эмоционáльно здорóвый ♦ **physically** ~ физи́чески здорóвый ♦ **reasonably** ~ достáточно здорóвый ♦ **I try to** *(1,3)* **keep /** *(2,4)* **stay fit.** Я пытáюсь *(1,2)* ...поддéрживать фóрму. / *(3,4)* ...оставáться в фóрме.

fit *vt* подходи́ть / подойти́ *(whom = dat.)* ♦ ~ **snugly** ую́тно устрáиваться / устрóиться ♦ **How does** *(1)* **it /** *(2)* **that fit?** Как тебé подхóдит *(1,2)* э́то? ♦ **How do** *(1)* **they /** *(2)* **those fit?** Как *(1,2)* они́ тебé подхóдят? ♦ *(1-3)* **It /** *(4)* **This /** *(5)* **That fits you** *(6)* **...perfectly.**

When terms are listed after a main word, a tilde ~
is used to indicate the main word.

/ *(7)* ...(very) well. / *(8)* ...beautifully. *(1)* Он *m* / *(2)* Она́ *f* / *(3)* Оно́ *neut* / *(4,5)* Это тебе́ *(6)* замеча́тельно / *(7)* (о́чень) хорошо́ / *(8)* прекра́сно подхо́дит. ◆ *(1)* **They** / *(2)* **These** / *(3)* **Those fit you** *(4)* **...perfectly.** / *(5)* **...(very) well.** / *(6)* **...beautifully.** *(1)* Они́ / *(2,3)* Эти тебе́ *(4)* замеча́тельно / *(5)* (о́чень) хорошо́ / *(6)* прекра́сно подхо́дят.

fit *n (Russian uses verb* подходи́ть *for meaning of "match")* ◆ **You and I are a perfect fit.** Ты и я превосхо́дно подхо́дим друг к дру́гу.

fitness *n* здоро́вье. ◆ **physical** ~ физи́ческое здоро́вье.

fitness-oriented *adj* трениру́ющийся, -аяся, -ееся, -иеся ◆ **I seek someone who is fitness-oriented.** Я ищу́ того́, кто трениру́ется.

fixated *adj* зафикси́рован, -а, -о, -ы *(short forms)*; заци́клен, -а, -о, -ы *(short forms)* ◆ **I'm not a person who is fixated on making money.** Я не тот челове́к, кото́рый заци́клен то́лько на добыва́нии де́нег.

flabbergasted *adj* изумлённый, -ая, -ое, -ые, поражённый, -ая, -ое, -ые ◆ **I'm flabbergasted by your** *(1)* **accusation** / *(2)* **comment** / *(3)* **remark.** Я поражён *(ж: поражена́)* твои́м *(1)* извине́нием / *(2,3)* замеча́нием.

flair *n* спосо́бности, скло́нность *f*, вкус ◆ **You really have a flair for fashion.** У тебя́ действи́тельно есть чу́вство сти́ля.

flake *n (slang) (worthless person)* никче́мный челове́к.

flamboyant *adj (ostentatious)* показно́й, -а́я, -о́е, -ы́е, броса́ющийся (-аяся, -ееся, -иеся) в глаза́; *(fancy)* вы́чурный, -ая, -ое, -ые; *(flowery)* цвети́стый, -ая, -ое, -ые; *(gaudy)* пы́шный, -ая, -ое, -ые.

flame *vi* вспы́хивать / вспы́хнуть, пыла́ть ◆ **Desire flames through me everytime I** *(1)* **...think about you.** / *(2)* **...look at you.** Страсть вспы́хивает во мне ка́ждый раз, когда́ я *(1)* ...ду́маю о тебе́. / *(2)* ...смотрю́ на тебя́.

flame *n* пла́мя *neut* ◆ **bright** ~ я́ркое пла́мя ◆ **burning** ~ горя́чее пла́мя ◆ **~ of desire** пла́мя жела́ния ◆ **hot** ~ горя́чее пла́мя ◆ **intense** ~ интенси́вное пла́мя ◆ **lambent** ~ сверка́ющее пла́мя ◆ **searing** ~ **of passion** жгу́чее пла́мя стра́сти ◆ **sensual** ~ чу́вственное пла́мя ◆ **burst into** ~ вспы́хивать / вспы́хнуть пла́менем ◆ **enveloped in ~s** объя́т (-а, -о, -ы) пла́менем ◆ *(1)* **ignite** / *(2)* **kindle a flame** ~ *(1,2)* заже́чь пла́мя.

flame: phrases

I know that the flame that you have kindled in my heart will never go out. Я зна́ю, что пла́мя, кото́рое ты зажгла́ *(ж: зажёг)* в моём се́рдце, никогда́ не пога́снет. ◆ **If you only knew what (wild) flames you have kindled inside me.** Е́сли бы ты то́лько зна́ла *(ж: знал)*, како́е (ди́кое) пла́мя ты зажгла́ *(ж: зажёг)* во мне. ◆ **Such flames you kindle in my body!** Како́е пла́мя ты зажига́ешь в моём те́ле! ◆ **The dark lambent flame in your eyes thrills me to the core of my being.** Меня́ всего́ охва́тывает тёмное сверка́ющее пла́мя твои́х глаз. ◆ **Whenever I think about you, physical desire flares up in me like a bright flame.** Когда́ бы я не поду́мал о тебе́, физи́ческая страсть вспы́хивает во мне, как я́ркое пла́мя. ◆ **When you touch me, I burst into flames.** Когда́ ты каса́ешься меня́, я вспы́хиваю пла́менем. ◆ **My lips will rouse flames of** *(1)* **desire** / *(2)* **passion to leap from your soul and surge through your veins.** Мои́ гу́бы пробу́дят пла́мя *(1)* жела́ния / *(2)* стра́сти, кото́рое бу́дет бушева́ть в тебе́ и струи́ться в ве́нах. ◆ **Only you know how to ignite the flame of passionate desire in my heart.** То́лько ты зна́ешь, как заже́чь пла́мя стра́стного жела́ния в моём се́рдце.

flame-red *adj* о́гненно-кра́сный, -ая, -ое, -ые.

flaming *adj* пыла́ющий, -ая, -ее, -ие.

flare *n* вспы́шка ◆ **A flare of desire bursts inside of me any time I even think of you.** Ого́нь жела́ния вспы́хивает во мне, как то́лько я поду́маю о тебе́.

A list of abbreviations used in the dictionary is given on page 10.

flare up *vi* вспы́хивать / вспы́хнуть ♦ **Whenever I think about you, physical desire flares up in me like a bright flame.** Когда́ бы я ни поду́мал о тебе́, физи́ческая страсть вспы́хивает во мне, как я́ркое пла́мя.

flash *vt* вспы́хивать / вспы́хнуть *(what = instr.)*, сверка́ть / сверкну́ть *(what = instr.)* ♦ **When you flashed your** *(1)* **beautiful** / *(2)* **gorgeous** / *(3)* **dazzling smile at me, my heart went into a lunar orbit.** Когда́ ты сверкну́ла *(1)* прекра́сной / *(2)* великоле́пной / *(3)* ослепи́тельной улы́бкой, моё се́рдце взлете́ло на лу́нную орби́ту.

flash *n* блеск ♦ **fiery ~ of your dark eyes** горя́чий блеск твои́х тёмных глаз.

flat-chested *adj* плоскогру́дый, -ая, -ое, -ые.

flatter *vt* льстить / польсти́ть *(whom = dat.)*.

flattened *adj*: ♦ **feel ~** соверше́нно разочарова́ться.

flattered *adj* польщён, польщена́, -о́, -ы́ *(short forms)*.

flattering *adj* 1. *(meant to flatter)* льсти́вый, -ая, -ое, -ые 2. *(complimentary)* ле́стный, -ая, -ое, -ые.

flattery *n* лесть *f* ♦ **That's not (just) flattery. It's** *(1)* **...a fact.** / *(2)* **...the truth.** Это не (про́сто) лесть. Это *(1)* факт / *(2)* пра́вда. ♦ **Flattery will get you** *(1)* **nowhere** / *(2)* **everywhere.** С ле́стью ты *(1)* ...никогда́ не... / *(2)* ...всегда́... дости́гнешь успе́ха.

flaw *n* недоста́ток, изъя́н, дефе́кт ♦ **No matter what your flaws and shortcomings are, I love you (with all my heart).** Не име́ет значе́ния, каки́е у тебя́ недоста́тки и несовер-ше́нства, я люблю́ тебя́ (всем се́рдцем).

flawless *adj* безупре́чный, -ая, -ое, -ые, без изъя́на ♦ **~ beauty** красота́ без изъя́на ♦ **~ English** безупре́чный англи́йский.

flawlessly *adv* безупре́чно.

fleeting *adj* мимолётный, -ая, -ое, -ые.

flesh *n* плоть *f* ♦ **burning ~** разгорячённая плоть ♦ **creamy ~** кре́мовая плоть ♦ **firm ~** упру́гая плоть ♦ **hard ~** твёрдая плоть ♦ **hardened male ~** затверде́вшая мужска́я плоть ♦ **hot ~** горя́чая плоть ♦ **male ~** мужска́я плоть ♦ **moist ~** вла́жная плоть ♦ **pulsing ~** пульси́рующая плоть ♦ **soft, pale ~** мя́гкая, бле́дная плоть ♦ **virile ~** му́жественная плоть ♦ **pleasures of the ~** наслажде́ния пло́ти ♦ **We can spend** *(1)* **a week** / *(2)* **two weeks** / *(3)* **the weekend enjoying the pleasures of the flesh.** Мы мо́жем провести́ *(1)* ...неде́лю... / *(2)* ...две неде́ли... / *(3)* ...выходны́е дни,... наслажда́ясь удово́льствиями пло́ти. ♦ *(1)* **I'm going to...** / *(2)* **I want to...** *(3)* **feast on...** / *(4)* **revel in... the firm, creamy flesh of your full breasts.** *(1)* Я бу́ду... / *(2)* Я хочу́... *(3)* ...пирова́ть в упру́гой, кре́мовой пло́ти... / *(4)* упива́ться упру́гой, кре́мовой пло́тью... твое́й по́лной груди́. ♦ **I'm flesh and blood.** Я кровь и плоть.

flexible *adj* 1. *(bendable)* ги́бкий, -ая, -ое, -ие; 2. *(schedules, etc)* свобо́дный, -ая, -ое, -ые.

flick *n (slang) (movie)* фильм.

flicker *n* мерца́ние, про́блеск ♦ **Is there any flicker of hope that we can see each other** *(1)* **...next week** / *(2)* **month?** / *(3)* **...soon?** Есть ли како́й-ли́бо про́блеск наде́жды, что мы смо́жем уви́деть друг дру́га *(1)* ...на сле́дующей неде́ле? / *(2)* ...в сле́дующем ме́сяце? / *(3)* ...ско́ро?

flight *n* самолёт; полёт ♦ **What time will the flight** *(1,2)* **arrive** / *(3,4)* **depart?** В како́е вре́мя *(1)* прибу́дет / *(2)* прилети́т / *(3)* отпра́вится / *(4)* вы́летит самолёт? ♦ **The flight will** *(1,2)* **arrive** / *(3,4)* **depart at** *(5)* **one (thirty).** *(See page 759 for other times.)* Самолёт *(1)* прибу́дет / *(2)* прилети́т / *(3)* отпра́вится / *(4)* вы́летит в *(5)* час (три́дцать).

flighty *adj* легкомы́сленный, -ая, -ое, -ые, ве́треный, -ая, -ое, -ые, капри́зный, -ая, -ое, -ые, взбалмо́шный, -ая, -ое, -ые.

flimsy *adj* 1. *(frail)* хру́пкий, -ая, -ое, -ие, непро́чный, -ая, -ое, -ые; 2. *(skimpy)* лёгкий,

---

The accents on Russian words are to show how to pronounce them. You don't have to copy the accents when writing to someone.

-ая, -ое, -ие, недоста́точный, -ая, -ое, -ые ♦ ~ **blouse** лёгкая блу́зка ♦ ~ **dress** лёгкое пла́тье.

fling *vt* броса́ть / бро́сить *(what, whom = acc.)*, швыря́ть / швырну́ть *(what, whom = acc.)* ♦ ~ *(1)* **myself** / *(2)* **yourself** *(1,2)* броса́ться / бро́ситься ♦ **I shouldn't have flung myself at you the way I have.** Я не до́лжен был *(ж: должна́ была́)* броса́ться к тебе́ так безу́держно. ♦ **What a fool I've been to fling myself at you (**[1] **so wantonly** / [2] **shamelessly).** *(ж:)* Како́й ду́рой я была́, бро́сившись к тебе́ так (*[1]* безу́держно / *[2]* бессты́дно).

fling *n (brief affair)* коро́ткая связь ♦ **brief** ~ кра́ткая связь ♦ **casual** ~ несерьёзная связь; случа́йная связь ♦ **meaningless** ~ бессмы́сленная связь ♦ **Is this just going to be a brief fling?** Это бу́дет то́лько коро́ткой свя́зью? ♦ **Do you just want to have a (brief) fling (with me)?** Ты хо́чешь то́лько (коро́ткую) связь (со мной)? ♦ **I'm not interested in just having a fling (with you).** Я не заинтересо́ван *(ж: заинтересо́вана)* (то́лько) в коро́ткой свя́зи (с тобо́й).

flip *adj (slang) (flippant)* де́рзкий, -ая, -ое, -ие, непочти́тельный, -ая, -ое, -ые ♦ ~ **answer** де́рзкий отве́т.

flip (out) *vi (slang) (get angry)* серди́ться / рассерди́ться; *(go into a rage)* прийти́ в я́рость.

flip-flop *vi* колеба́ться / поколеба́ться.

flip-flops *n, pl:* ♦ **do** ~ колоти́ться / заколоти́ться ♦ **You make my heart do flip-flops.** Ты заставля́ешь моё се́рдце колоти́ться. ♦ **The first** *(1)* **time** / *(2)* **moment I saw you, my heart did flip-flops.** В пе́рвый *(1)* раз / *(2)* моме́нт, когда́ я уви́дел *(ж: уви́дела)* тебя́, моё се́рдце заколоти́лось.

flippant *adj* де́рзкий, -ая, -ое, -ие, непочти́тельный, -ая, -ое, -ые.

flirt *vi* флиртова́ть, коке́тничать, заи́грывать ♦ **I really liked the way you flirted with me.** Мне действи́тельно понра́вилось, как ты флиртова́ла *(ж: флиртова́л)* со мной.

flirt *n (woman)* коке́тка; *(man)* люби́тель пофлиртова́ть ♦ **big-time** ~ нейстовая коке́тка ♦ **outrageous** ~ бессты́дная коке́тка.

flirtation *n* флирт, коке́тничание, коке́тство, заи́грывание.

flirtatious *adj* коке́тливый, -ая, -ое, -ые, лю́бящий (-ая, -ие) флиртова́ть ♦ **You're the most flirtatious girl I ever met.** Я никогда́ не встреча́л де́вушку, кото́рая бы так люби́ла флиртова́ть, как ты. ♦ **You're the most flirtatious** *(1)* **person** / *(2)* **guy I ever met.** Я никогда́ не встреча́ла *(1)* челове́ка / *(2)* па́рня, кото́рый бы так люби́л флиртова́ть, как ты.

flirtatiously *adv* коке́тливо.

flirting *n* флирт, коке́тничание, коке́тство, заи́грывание ♦ **extracurricular** ~ флирт на стороне́ ♦ **little bit of** ~ лёгкий флирт.

flirty *adj* коке́тливый, -ая, -ое, -ые.

flock *vi* толпи́ться ♦ **I imagine** *(1)* **men** / *(2)* **women flock around you.** Я вообража́ю, что *(1)* мужчи́ны / *(2)* же́нщины толпя́тся вокру́г тебя́.

flood *vt* наводня́ть / наводни́ть *(what = acc., with what = instr.)*, затопля́ть / затопи́ть *(what = acc., with what = instr.)*; *(light)* залива́ть / зали́ть *(what = acc., with what = instr.)*, освеща́ть / освети́ть *(what = acc., with what = instr.)* ♦ ~ **the (whole) body** разлива́ться / разли́ться по всему́ те́лу ♦ **The sight of your beautiful face fills my whole body with warm excitement and floods my heart with feelings of love for you.** Взгляд на твоё прекра́сное лицо́ наполня́ет всё моё те́ло жа́рким возбужде́нием и затопля́ет се́рдце чу́вством любви́ к тебе́. ♦ **Each time I look at your photo, the (**[1] **beautiful** / [2] **sweet** / [3] **wonderful) memories come flooding back into my mind.** Ка́ждый раз, когда́ я смотрю́ на твою́ фотогра́фию, (*[1]* прекра́сные / *[2]* сла́дкие / *[3]* замеча́тельные)

If no accent is shown on a word with a capitalized vowel,
it means that the capitalized vowel is accented.

воспоминáния опя́ть затопля́ют меня́. ♦ **Your letters flood my life with** *(1)* **sunbeams** / *(2)* **sunshine.** Твои́ пи́сьма освеща́ют мою́ жизнь *(1)* ...со́лнечными луча́ми. / *(2)* ...со́лнечным све́том. ♦ **All these sunbeams that flood the day — it is your smile shining down on me.** Все э́ти со́лнечные лучи́, кото́рые залива́ют день -- э́то твоя́ улы́бка, сия́ющая на меня́. ♦ **Every time you smile at me, you flood my world with love.** Вся́кий раз, когда́ ты улыба́ешься мне, ты затопля́ешь мой мир любо́вью.

flood *n (fig.)* пото́к ♦ **Your letters release a flood of warm,** *(1)* **tender** / *(2)* **loving feelings for you in my heart.** Твои́ пи́сьма высвобожда́ют в моём се́рдце пото́к тёплых, *(1)* не́жных / *(2)* лю́бящих чувств к тебе́.

flooded *adj* зато́плен, -а, -о, -ы, перепо́лнен, -а, -о, -ы ♦ **Every time I see you walk** *(1)* **...through the door...** / *(2)* **...down the hallway...** / *(3)* **...along the street...** / *(4)* **...past me...** / *(5)* **...into the room... my heart begins palpitating wildly and I am flooded with** *(6)* **exquisite** / *(7)* **overpowering** / *(8)* **dizzying sensations of adoration and desire for you.** Ка́ждый раз, когда́ я ви́жу, как ты *(1)* ...вхо́дишь в дверь... / *(2)* ...идёшь по коридо́ру... / *(3)* ...идёшь по у́лице... / *(4)* ...прохо́дишь ми́мо... / *(5)* ...вхо́дишь в ко́мнату... моё се́рдце начина́ет выска́кивать из груди́, и меня́ переполня́ют *(6)* о́стрые / *(7)* невыноси́мые / *(8)* головокружи́тельные чу́вства обожа́ния и жела́ния.

floodgates *n, pl* шлю́зы ♦ **You have opened the floodgates of my womanhood.** Ты откры́л шлю́зы мое́й же́нственности. ♦ **It opened a floodgate of emotions for me.** Это откры́ло шлюз эмо́ций во мне.

floozy *n* распу́тная же́нщина, шлю́ха.

florid *adj (face)* кра́сный, -ая, -ое, -ые.

flounder *vi* бара́хтаться ♦ **I'm floundering in a morass of** *(1)* **misery** / *(2)* **loneliness without you.** Без тебя́ я бара́хтаюсь в боло́те *(1)* страда́ния / *(2)* одино́чества.

flourish *vi* цвести́, процвета́ть ♦ **From our two hearts we will create a love that will flourish to the end of our lives.** Двумя́ на́шими сердца́ми мы создади́м любо́вь, кото́рая бу́дет цвести́ до конца́ на́ших жи́зней. ♦ **I know that our romance will flourish till the end of our days.** Я зна́ю, что наш рома́н бу́дет цвести́ до конца́ на́ших дней.

flow *vi* течь, ли́ться.

flow *n* пото́к ♦ **intoxicating ~ of** *(1)* **feelings** / *(2)* **sensations** пьяня́щий пото́к *(1,2)* ощуще́ний.

flower *n* цвето́к *(pl:* цветы*)* ♦ **beautiful ~** прекра́сный цвето́к ♦ **bright ~** я́ркий цвето́к **favorite ~** люби́мый цвето́к ♦ **fragrant ~** души́стый цвето́к ♦ **glorious ~ of love** великоле́пный цвето́к любви́ ♦ **magnificent ~ of love** великоле́пный цвето́к любви́ ♦ **passion ~** цвето́к стра́сти ♦ **pretty ~** краси́вый цвето́к ♦ **succulent ~** со́чный цвето́к ♦ **wilted ~** увя́дший цвето́к ♦ **bring ~s** приноси́ть / принести́ цветы́ *(to whom = dat.).* ♦ **give ~s** дари́ть / подари́ть цветы́ *(to whom = dat.)* ♦ **send ~s** посыла́ть / посла́ть цветы́ *(to whom = dat.).*

---
flower: phrases

You are a perfect flower. Ты соверше́нный цвето́к. ♦ **You're the most beautiful flower there is.** Ты са́мый прекра́сный из существу́ющих цвето́в. ♦ **You are the flower that never** *(1)* **dies** / *(2)* **fades.** Ты цвето́к, кото́рый никогда́ не *(1)* умрёт / *(2)* увя́нет. ♦ **Your body exudes a sweetness like a meadow flower.** От твоего́ те́ла исхо́дит сла́дость, как от лугов́ы́х цвето́в. ♦ **Imagine that you're a flower filled with nectar and I'm the world's thirstiest hummingbird.** Предста́вь, что ты цвето́к, по́лный некта́ра, и я истомлённейший жа́ждой коли́бри. ♦ **I long to see you stretch out in languorous abandon as I place tiny kisses about your bosom and down your stomach.** Я жа́жду уви́деть тебя́, раски́нувшуюся в то́мной непринуждённости, в то вре́мя, как я

Russian has 6 grammatical cases. For an explanation of them, see the grammar appendix on page 686.

размещаю крошечные поцелуи вокруг твоей груди и вниз по твоему животу.

flowerlike *adj* похожий (-ая, -ее, -ие) на цветок, подобный (-ая, -ое, -ые) цветку ♦ **You are so delicate and** *(1,2)* **flowerlike.** Ты такая хрупкая и *(1)* ...похожая на цветок. / *(2)* ...подобна цветку. ♦ **I've never met a** *(1)* **woman /** *(2)* **girl as delicate and flowerlike as you.** Я никогда не встречал *(1)* женщины / *(2)* девушки, такой хрупкой и так подобной цветку, как ты.

flowery *adj* 1. *(having flowers)* цветочный, -ая, -ое, -ые; 2. *(fancy)* цветистый, -ая, -ое, -ые ♦ ~ **words** цветистые слова.

fluid *adj* 1. *(liquid)* жидкий, -ая, -ое, -ие; 2. *(smooth)* плавный, -ая, -ое, -ые, гладкий, -ая, -ое, -ие.

fluidly *adv* плавно, гладко.

flung *adj* брошен, -а, -о, -ы *(short forms)* ♦ **I want to fill your body with so much pleasure that you will be flung into a cosmos of exploding ecstasy.** Я хочу заполнить твоё тело таким огромным наслаждением, чтобы ты была брошена в космос взрывающегося экстаза. ♦ **Our bodies will fuse together in exquisite pleasure until we are flung into a wild sea of passion.** Наши тела сольются в изысканном наслаждении до тех пор, пока мы не будем брошены в бешеное море страсти.

flush *vi* краснеть / покраснеть, вспыхивать / вспыхнуть ♦ ~ **hotly** жарко покраснеть.

flushed *adj* покрасневший, -ая, -ее, -ие, вспыхнувший, -ая, -ее, -ие ♦ **What a divine treat to see your face beautifully flushed and well-kissed after we make love.** Что за божественное наслаждение видеть твоё лицо, прекрасно раскрасневшееся и зацелованное после нашей близости.

fluster *vt* волновать / взволновать *(whom = acc.)*, возбуждать / возбудить *(whom = acc.)*.

flustered *adj* взволнован, -а, -о, -ы, возбуждён, возбуждена, -о, -ы *(short forms)*.

flutter *vi* 1. *(hands)* порхать / порхнуть; 2. *(eyelashes)* взмахивать / взмахнуть *(ресницами)* ♦ **I like the way your hands flutter over me.** Мне нравится, как твои руки порхают по моему телу.

fluttery *adj* дрожащий, -ая, -ее, -ие, трепещущий, -ая, -ее, -ие ♦ **I get a fluttery feeling in my stomach whenever I** *(1)* ...**think about you. /** *(2)* ...**see you.** Моё сердце трепещет всякий раз, когда бы я ни *(1)* ...подумал *(ж: подумала)* о тебе. / *(2)* ...увидел *(ж: увидела)* тебя.

flux *n*: ♦ **Our relationship is in a state of flux.** Наши отношения в состоянии постоянного изменения.

focused *adj* сосредоточен, -а, -о, -ы *(short forms)* ♦ **I would be so attentive, so focused on your needs and desires and likes and dislikes.** Я был бы так внимателен, так сосредоточен на твоих нуждах и желаниях, и на том, что ты любишь и что не любишь.

follow *vt* идти / пойти *(whom = +* за *+ instr.),* следовать / последовать *(whom = +* за *+ instr.)* ♦ *(1)* **I'd /** *(2)* **I'll follow you to the ends of the earth.** *(1)* Я пошёл *(ж: пошла)* бы... / *(2)* Я пойду... за тобой на край света.

folly *n* безрассудство, глупость ♦ **It is perhaps pure folly to embrace such hopes, but my heart will not allow me to do otherwise.** Это, возможно, чистейшее безрассудство лелеять такие надежды, но моё сердце не позволяет мне иначе.

fond of *(like strongly, love)* любить *(what, whom = acc.); (like)* нравиться *(of what, whom = subject of the verb, person who is fond = dat.); (regard fondly)* хорошо относиться *(of whom = +* к *+ dat.)* ♦ **I'm genuinely fond of you.** Я искренне люблю тебя. ♦ **I'm fond of you, but I don't love you.** Я очень хорошо к тебе отношусь, но я не люблю тебя.

fondle *vt* ласкать *(what = acc.),* нежно поглаживать *(what = acc.)* ♦ **I love to fondle your (beautiful) breasts.** Я люблю ласкать твою (прекрасную) грудь. ♦ **I love it when you**

There are no articles ("a" or "the") in Russian.

fondle my breasts. Мне нра́вится, когда́ ты ласка́ешь мою́ грудь.

fondness *n* симпа́тия *(for whom = + к + dat.)* ♦ **develop a ~ for each other** проника́ть / прони́кнуть друг к дру́гу симпа́тией.

food *n* 1. пи́ща; пита́ние; еда́ 2. *(mental, etc)* пи́ща; 3. *(groceries)* проду́кты ♦ **ethnic ~** этни́ческая пи́ща.

fool *vt* обма́нывать / обману́ть; дура́чить / одура́чить; проводи́ть / провести́ ♦ **You (really) fooled me.** Ты (действи́тельно) провела́ *(ж: провёл)* меня́.

fool *n* дура́к *m*, ду́ра *f*. ♦ **big ~** большо́й дура́к *m*, больша́я ду́ра *f* ♦ **clumsy ~** неуклю́жий дура́к *m*, неуклю́жая ду́ра *f* ♦ **complete ~** соверше́нный дура́к *m*, соверше́нная ду́ра *f* ♦ **little ~** дурачо́к *m*, ду́рочка *f* ♦ **naive ~** наи́вный дура́к *m*, наи́вная ду́рочка *f* ♦ **sentimental ~** сентимента́льный дура́к *m*, сентимента́льная ду́ра *f* ♦ **sweet ~** дурачо́к *m*, ду́рочка *f* ♦ **terrible ~** ужа́сный дура́к *m*, ужа́сная ду́ра *f*

fool: phrases

I'm such a clumsy fool. Я тако́й неуклю́жий дура́к. *(ж: Я така́я неуклю́жая ду́ра.)* ♦ **You must think I'm a (***[1]* **big /** *[2]* **terrible /** *[3]* **complete) fool.** Ты должна́ ду́мать, что я (*[1]* большо́й / *[2]* ужа́сный / *[3]* соверше́нный) дура́к. *(ж: Ты до́лжен ду́мать, что я больша́я / ужа́сная / соверше́нная ду́ра.)* ♦ **What a fool I've been to fling myself at you (***[1]* **so wantonly /** *[2]* **shamelessly).** *(ж:)* Како́й ду́рой я была́, бро́сившись к тебе́ так (*[1]* безу́держно / *[2]* бессты́дно). ♦ **Do you take me for a fool?** Ты меня́ принима́ешь за дурака́ *(ж ду́ру)*? ♦ **I'm not a fool.** Я не дура́к *(ж: ду́ра)*. ♦ **What a fool I** *(1)* **...am. /** *(2)* **...have been. /** *(3)* **...was.** Что за дура́к *(ж: ду́ра)* *(1)* ...я. / *(2,3)* ...я был *(ж: была́)*. ♦ **Oh, you sweet fool, how could you think that I didn't love you?** О, ду́рочка *(ж: дурачо́к)*, как ты могла́ *(ж:мог)* поду́мать, что я не люблю́ тебя́?

fool around *vi* 1. *(play)* игра́ть, развлека́ться; *(kid around)* шути́ть; *(act foolish)* дура́читься, валя́ть дурака́; 2. *(chase women)* волочи́ться; *(philander)* изменя́ть / измени́ть; 3. *(engage in petting)* занима́ться пе́ттингом, игра́ть, ласка́ть ♦ **I'm not the kind of person who fools around.** Я не тот челове́к, кото́рый изме́нит. ♦ **I don't want someone who fools around.** Я не хочу́ челове́ка, кото́рый мо́жет измени́ть. ♦ **I think you've been fooling around (on me).** Я ду́маю, что ты изменя́ла *(ж: изменя́л)* мне.

foolish *adj* 1. *(dumb)* глу́пый, -ая, -ое, -ые *(short forms:* глуп, -а́, -о, -ы́)*; 2. *(idiotic, ridiculous)* дура́цкий, -ая, -ое, -ие, неле́пый, -ая, -ое, -ые ♦ **I** *(1)* **feel /** *(2)* **felt (***[3]* **really /** *[4]* **so /** *[5]* **very) foolish.** Я *(1)* чу́вствую / *(2)* чу́вствовал *(ж: чу́вствовала)* себя́ (*[3]* действи́тельно / *[4]* так / *[5]* о́чень) глу́пым *(ж: глу́пой)*. ♦ **It would be foolish for us to** *(1)* **...get married (now). /** *(2)* **...have a baby now.** Бы́ло бы глу́по для нас *(1)* ...жени́ться (сейча́с). / *(2)* ...име́ть ребёнка сейча́с. ♦ **It was foolish of me (to** *[1]* **say /** *[2]* **write that to you).** С мое́й стороны́ бы́ло глу́по (*[1]* сказа́ть / *[2]* написа́ть э́то тебе́). ♦ **Forgive me for being so foolish.** Прости́ меня́ за то, что я был *(ж: была́)* так глуп *(ж: глупа́)*. ♦ **I hope you don't think I'm being foolish.** Я наде́юсь, ты не ду́маешь, что я глуп *(ж: глупа́)*.

foot *n* нога́ *(includes the leg)*; ступня́ *(specifically the foot, but less commonly used)* ♦ **bare feet** босы́е но́ги ♦ **dainty feet** изя́щные сту́пни ♦ **left ~** ле́вая ступня́ ♦ **pretty feet** преле́стные сту́пни ♦ **right ~** пра́вая ступня́ ♦ **get cold feet** тру́сить / стру́сить ♦ **You're so cute in your bare feet.** Ты така́я симпати́чная босико́м. ♦ **I want to get off on the right foot with you.** Я хочу́ стартова́ть с пра́вой ноги́ с тобо́й. ♦ **I'm afraid we got off on the wrong foot.** Я бою́сь, что мы на́чали с ле́вой ноги́. ♦ **I lost my** *(1)* **right /** *(2)* **left foot in** *(3)* **...the (Vietnam) war. /** *(4)* **...an accident.** Я потеря́л *(ж: потеря́ла)* *(1)* пра́вую / *(2)* ле́вую ступню́ *(3)* ...на войне́ (во Вьетна́ме). / *(4)* ...в ава́рии.

This dictionary contains two Russian alphabet pages: one in Appendix 1, page 685, and a tear-off page on page 799.

football *n (American)* (америка́нский) футбо́л.

footsie *n (slang)* каса́ние ного́й чьей-то ноги́ *(explanation)* ♦ **play ~ with** *(1)* **me** / *(2)* **you** каса́ться ного́й *(1)* мое́й / *(2)* твое́й ноги́ ♦ **I saw you playing footsie with** *(1)* **her** / *(2)* **him (under the table).** Я ви́дел *(ж: ви́дела)*, как ты каса́лась его́ *(ж: каса́лся её)* ноги́ свое́й ного́й (под столо́м). ♦ **You really made me hot when you started playing footsie with me.** Ты действи́тельно разожгла́ *(ж: разжёг)* меня́, когда́ ты ста́ла *(ж: стал)* каса́ться меня́ ного́й.

forbid *vt* запреща́ть / запрети́ть *(what = acc., whom = dat.)* ♦ *(1)* **My mother** / *(2)* **father forbids...** / *(3)* **My parents forbid...** **me to** *(4)* **...see you.** / *(5,6)* **...go (there) (with you).** / *(7)* **...go out with anyone (alone).** *(1)* Моя́ мать запреща́ет... / *(2)* Мой оте́ц запреща́ет... / *(3)* Мои́ роди́тели запреща́ют... мне *(4)* ...встреча́ться с тобо́й. / *(5)* ...е́хать *(by veh.)* / *(6)* идти́ *(on foot)* (с тобо́й) (туда́). / *(7)* ...ходи́ть куда́-либо с ке́м-то (одно́й).

forbidden *adj (modify nouns)* запре́тный, -ая, -ое, -ые; *(predicate use)* запрещён, запрещена́, -о́, -ы́ *(short forms)* ♦ **It's forbidden** *(1)* **...to smoke (here).** / *(2)* **...to take pictures** (*[3]* **here** / *[4]* **there).** Воспреща́ется *(1)* ...кури́ть (здесь). / *(2)* ...фотографи́ровать (*[3]* здесь / *[4]* там).

force *vt* заставля́ть / заста́вить *(whom = acc.)*, вынужда́ть / вы́нудить *(whom = acc.)*, принужда́ть / принуди́ть *(whom = acc.)* ♦ **I don't want to force you to do something you don't want to do.** Я не хочу́ заставля́ть тебя́ де́лать то, что ты не хо́чешь де́лать. ♦ **Please don't try to force me.** Пожа́луйста, не пыта́йся принужда́ть меня́.

force *n* си́ла ♦ **enormous ~** грома́дная си́ла ♦ **~ of attraction** притяга́тельная си́ла ♦ **great ~** больша́я си́ла ♦ **hurricane ~** урага́нная си́ла ♦ **magical ~** волше́бная си́ла ♦ **magnetic ~** притяга́тельная си́ла ♦ **powerful ~** могу́чая си́ла ♦ **such ~** така́я си́ла ♦ **tremendous ~** огро́мная си́ла ♦ **wild primitive ~** ди́кая примити́вная си́ла ♦ **The force of your appeal for me is beyond** *(1)* **description** / *(2)* **definition** / *(3)* **calculation.** Си́ла твое́й привлека́тельности для меня́ вы́ше *(1)* ...вся́кого описа́ния / *(2)* определе́ния. / *(3)* ...вся́кой ме́ры. ♦ **I am completely swept away by the force of your magnetism.** Я по́лностью сметён *(ж: сметена́)* с ног си́лой твоего́ магнети́зма.

forced *adj* заста́влен, -а, -о, -ы *(short forms)*, вы́нужден, -а, -о, -ы *(short forms)*, принуждён, принуждена́, -о́, -ы́ *(short forms)* ♦ **I was forced into marrying her.** Я был вы́нужден жени́ться на ней. ♦ **I was forced into marrying him.** Я была́ вы́нуждена вы́йти за него́ за́муж.

foreboding *n* дурно́е предчу́ствие ♦ **sense of ~** предчу́вствие дурно́го.

forefinger *n* указа́тельный па́лец.

forehead *n* лоб ♦ *(1,2)* **broad ~** *(1)* широ́кий / *(2)* высо́кий лоб ♦ **high ~** высо́кий лоб.

foreplay *n* любо́вная игра́, предвари́тельные игры, увертю́ра, эроти́ческое стимули́рование, ла́ски до полово́го а́кта ♦ **I like lots and lots of foreplay.** Я люблю́ до́лгие, до́лгие предвари́тельные и́гры.

forever *adv* навсегда́, наве́чно ♦ **Forever thine,** *(closing of a letter)* Навсегда́ твой *(ж: твоя́).* ♦ **I love you always and forever.** Я люблю́ тебя́ всегда́ и наве́чно. ♦ **You have changed my life forever.** Ты навсегда́ измени́ла *(ж: измени́л)* мою́ жизнь. ♦ *(1,2)* **My forever Lisa,...** *(salutation of a letter)* *(1)* Ве́чно моя́... / *(2)* Моя́ навсегда́... Ли́за, *(приве́тствие в письме́).*

forget *vt* забыва́ть / забы́ть *(what, whom = acc., about what, whom = + о + prep.)* ♦ **You make me forget everything else** *(1)* **...around me.** / *(2)* **...in the world.** Ты заставля́ешь меня́ забы́ть обо всём *(1)* ...окружа́ющем. / *(2)* ...на све́те. ♦ **You make me forget**

Depending on the subject, the possessive pronoun **свой (своя́, своё, свой)** *can be translated* **my, your, his, her, its, our** *or* **their**.

all about *(1)* **...my work.** / *(2)* **...other women.** / *(3)* **...my worries** / *(4)* **problems.** / *(5)* **...her** / *(6)* **him.** Ты заставляешь меня совсем забыть *(1)* ...о моей работе. / *(2)* ...других женщин / *(3)* мужчин. / *(4)* ...мои заботы / *(5)* проблемы. / *(6)* ...её / *(7)* его. ♦ *(1)* **I want to...** / *(2)* **I'm going to... make you (completely) forget** *(3)* **...all other men** / *(4)* **women.** / *(5)* **...those terrible years.** / *(6)* **...your loneliness of the past.** / *(7)* **...the past.** *(1)* Я хочу заставить... / *(2)* Я заставлю... тебя (полностью) забыть *(3)* ...всех остальных мужчин / *(4)* женщин. / *(5)* ...эти ужасные годы. / *(6)* ...твоё одиночество в прошлом. / *(7)* ...прошлое. ♦ **I don't want you to forget me.** Я не хочу, чтобы ты забыла *(ж: забыл)* меня. ♦ **Don't forget (me).** Не забудь (меня).

forgetful *adj* забывчивый, -ая, -ое, -ые.

forgive *vt* прощать / простить *(what, whom = acc.)* ♦ **Do you forgive me?** Ты прощаешь меня? ♦ **I forgive you.** Я прощаю тебя. ♦ **Please forgive me (for** *[1]* **...what I've done.** / *[2]* **...what I said.** / *[3]* **...for hurting** / *[4]* **offending you.)** Прости меня, пожалуйста, (за *[1]* ...то, что я сделал *[ж: сделала]* . / *[2]* ...то, что я сказал *[ж: сказала]* . / *[3]* ...обиду / *[4]* оскорбление.)

forgiveness *n* прощение ♦ **I humbly beg your forgiveness.** Я смиренно умоляю тебя о прощении.

forgiving *adj* прощающий, -ая, -ее, -ие; великодушный, -ая, -ое, -ые.

forgotten *adj* забытый, -ая, -ое, -ые ♦ **long ~** давно забытый, -ая, -ое, -ые.

forlorn *adj (forsaken)* заброшенный, -ая, -ое, -ые, покинутый, -ая, -ое, -ые; *(lonely)* одинокий, -ая, -ое, -ие.

form *n* фигура ♦ **Your beautiful,** *(1)* **diminutive** / *(2)* **petite form really excites me.** Твоя прекрасная, *(1)* маленькая / *(2)* миниатюрная фигура так возбуждает меня. ♦ **I dream of the day when my eyes can savor the delights of your unclad form.** Я мечтаю о том дне, когда мои глаза смогут восхищённо смаковать твоё обнажённое тело.

formed *adj* сложённый, -ая, -ое, -ые *(short forms:* сложён, сложена, -ó, -ы*)* ♦ **beautifully ~** прекрасно сложён, сложена, -ó, -ы *(short forms)*.

former *adj* бывший, -ая, -ее, -ие, прежний, -яя, -ее, -ие.

formerly *adv* прежде, раньше.

forsake *vt* оставлять / оставить *(what, whom = acc.)*, покидать / покинуть *(what, whom = acc.)*, отказываться / отказаться *(what, whom = + от +acc.)* ♦ **I promise you that I will forsake all others.** Я обещаю тебе, что я покину всех других. ♦ **Please do not forsake me.** Пожалуйста, не покидай меня. ♦ **You have (completely) forsaken me.** Ты (окончательно) покинула *(ж: покинул)* меня. ♦ **What have I done that has made you forsake me (this way)?** Что же я сделал *(ж: сделала)* такого, что заставило тебя покинуть меня (таким образом)? ♦ **I will never forsake you.** Я никогда не покину тебя.

forthcoming *adj* предстоящий, -ая, -ее, -ие.

forthright *adj* откровенный, -ая, -ое, -ые, прямодушный, -ая, -ое, -ые, прямолинейный, -ая, -ое, -ые.

fortify *vt* укреплять / укрепить *(what, whom = acc.)*, придавать / придать силы *(what, whom = dat.)* ♦ **I know that we will be together** *(1)* **soon** / *(2)* **again** / *(3)* **someday, and this** *(4)* **knowledge** / *(5)* **realization fortifies my** *(6)* **soul** / *(7)* **spirit.** Я знаю, что мы *(1)* скоро / *(2)* опять / *(3)* однажды будем вместе, и *(4,5)* знание это укрепляет *(6)* ...мою душу. / *(7)* ...мой дух.

forty-ish *adj* около сорока лет.

forty-something *adj* за сорок.

forward *adj (overly familiar)* развязный, -ая, -ое, -ые, фамильярный, -ая, -ое, -ые ♦ **I hope you won't think it forward of me.** Я надеюсь, ты не подумаешь, что это слишком

There are two words for "you" in Russian:
familiar «ты» and polite / plural «вы» (See page 781).

фамилья́рно с мое́й стороны́.

forward-looking *adj* дальнови́дный, -ая, -ое, -ые, предусмотри́тельный, -ая, -ое, -ые.

foster *adj* приёмный, -ая, -ое, -ые ♦ ~ **father** приёмный оте́ц ♦ ~ **mother** приёмная мать ♦ ~ **parents** приёмные роди́тели.

foster *vt* 1. *(nurture)* леле́ять *(what = acc.)*, пита́ть *(what = acc.)*, взра́щивать / взрасти́ть *(what = acc.)*; 2. *(promote)* благоприя́тствовать *(what = dat.)*, спосо́бствовать *(what = dat.)* ♦ **I want to foster a love in your heart that will grow ever stronger as the years go by.** Я хочу́ взрасти́ть таку́ю любо́вь в твоём се́рдце, кото́рая бу́дет станови́ться то́лько сильне́е с года́ми.

foundation *n* 1. *(basis)* основа́ние; осно́ва, ба́зис, ба́за; 2. *(of a building)* фунда́мент ♦ **Love and respect form the foundation of a strong and lasting marriage.** Любо́вь и уваже́ние создаю́т фунда́мент кре́пкого и продолжи́тельного бра́ка.

fox *n (woman)* (сексуа́льно привлека́тельная) красо́тка; *(man)* (сексуа́льно привлека́тельный) краса́вец ♦ **attractive Belorussian** ~ привлека́тельная белору́сская красо́тка ♦ **silver** ~ *(middle-aged man)* «сере́бряный лис», мужчи́на сре́дних лет.

fragile *adj* хру́пкий, -ая, -ое, -ие, сла́бый, -ая, -ое, -ые ♦ ~ **beauty** хру́пкая красота́.

fragrance *n* 1. *(aroma)* арома́т, благоуха́ние; 2. *(perfume)* духи́ *pl.* ♦ **delicate** ~ не́жное благоуха́ние ♦ ~ **of your body** арома́т твоего́ те́ла ♦ ~ **of your hair** арома́т твои́х воло́с ♦ **haunting** ~ пресле́дующее (меня́) благоуха́ние ♦ **heady** ~ хмельно́й арома́т ♦ **intoxicating** ~ пьяня́щий арома́т ♦ **lingering** ~ не́жный арома́т ♦ **soft** ~ то́нкий арома́т ♦ **sweet, intoxicating** ~ сла́дкий пьяня́щий арома́т ♦ **your** ~ твой арома́т.

fragrance: phrases

The delicate fragrance that you wear intoxicates me. Не́жное благоуха́ние твои́х духо́в опьяня́ет. ♦ **The fragrance of you is like the breath of roses.** Твой арома́т как дыха́ние роз. ♦ **I love the delicate, haunting fragrance** *(1)* **...of your hair.** / *(2)* **...that you wear.** Я люблю́ не́жное, пресле́дующее меня́ благоуха́ние *(1)* ...твои́х воло́с. / *(2)* ...твои́х духо́в. ♦ **The fragrance of roses emanates from your soul.** Твоя́ душа́ благоуха́ет ро́зами. ♦ **How I long to immerse myself in the soft, lingering fragrance of your** *(1)* **hair** / *(2)* **body** / *(3)* **person.** Как я жа́жду погрузи́ться в не́жный арома́т *(1)* ...твои́х воло́с. / *(2,3)* ...твоего́ те́ла. ♦ **The fragrance of your perfume will haunt me for the rest of my life.** Арома́т твои́х духо́в оста́нется со мной на всю жизнь.

fragrant *adj* души́стый, -ая, -ое, -ые, арома́тный, -ая, -ое, -ые ♦ **Your body is so fragrant.** Твоё те́ло тако́е души́стое. ♦ **Your hair is so fragrant.** Твои́ во́лосы таки́е души́стые.

frailty *n* сла́бость *f* ♦ **human** ~**ies** челове́ческие сла́бости.

frame *n* 1. *(picture)* ра́ма, ра́мка; 2. *(phys. build)* (те́ло)сложе́ние ♦ **fine-honed** ~ прекра́сно вы́точенное те́ло ♦ ~ **of mind** настрое́ние ♦ **large** ~ кру́пное те́ло ♦ **small** ~ ма́ленькое те́ло.

framed *adj* обрамлённый, -ая, -ое, -ые, в опра́ве ♦ **In all my dreams I see your beautiful face framed by the splendor of your golden hair.** Во всех свои́х снах я ви́жу твоё прекра́сное лицо́ в опра́ве из роско́шных золоти́стых воло́с.

frank *adj* открове́нный, -ая, -ое, -ые, и́скренний, -яя, -ее, -ие, откры́тый, -ая, -ое, -ые ♦ **I'll be frank with you — I want to make love with you.** Бу́ду открове́нен *(ж: открове́нна)* с тобо́й -- я хочу́ заня́ться с тобо́й любо́вью.

frankly *adv* открове́нно, и́скренне, откры́то ♦ **Frankly, my Dear, I don't give a damn.** Открове́нно говоря́, дорога́я, мне наплева́ть.

frankness *n* открове́нность *f*, и́скренность *f*, прямота́ ♦ **I admire (your) frankness.** Я восхища́юсь (твое́й) и́скренностью.

frantic *adj* 1. *(frenzied)* неи́стовый, -ая, -ое, -ые, безу́мный, -ая, -ое, -ые, бе́шеный, -ая,

Russian terms of endearment are given in Appendix 13, page 780.

-ое, -ые; 2. *(desparate)* отча́янный, -ая, -ое, -ые.

frantically *adv* 1. *(frenziedly)* нейстово, безу́мно, бе́шено, до бе́шенства; 2. *(desparately)* отча́янно.

fraternity *n* студе́нческое бра́тство.

freak (out) *vi (slang) (get real nervous)* о́чень волнова́ться; *(get scared)* испуга́ться; *(lose self-control)* теря́ть / потеря́ть самооблада́ние, расстра́иваться / расстро́иться.

free *adj* 1. *(at liberty, available)* свобо́дный, -ая, -ое, -ые; 2. *(no cost)* беспла́тный, -ая, -ое, -ые. ♦ **set** ~ опуска́ть / опусти́ть на во́лю *(whom = acc.)* ♦ **Are you free** *(1)* **...tonight?** */ (2)* **...after work?** */ (3)* **...tomorrow (** *[4]* **morning** / *[5]* **afternoon** / *[6]* **evening)?** */ (7)* **...on Sunday?** *(See page 759 for other days.)* Вы свобо́дны *(1)* ...сего́дня ве́чером? */ (1)* ...по́сле рабо́ты? */ (1)* ...за́втра *([4]* у́тром / *[5]* в по́лдень / *[6]* ве́чером)? */ (1)* ...в воскресе́нье? ♦ **I'm free** *(1)* **...tonight.** */ (2)* **...after work.** */ (3)* **...tomorrow (** *[4]* **morning** / *[5]* **afternoon** / *[6]* **evening).** */ (7)* **...on Sunday.** *(See page 759 for other days.)* */ (10)* **...after six** / *(11)* **twelve o'clock.** Я свобо́ден *(ж: свобо́дна) (1)* ...сего́дня ве́чером. */ (2)* ...по́сле рабо́ты. */ (3)* ...за́втра (*[4]* у́тром / *[5]* в по́лдень / *[6]* ве́чером). */ (7)* ...в воскресе́нье. */ (10)* ...по́сле шести́ / *(11)* двена́дцати. ♦ **Feel free to ask me anything.** Ты мо́жешь свобо́дно спра́шивать меня́ обо всём.

freedom *n* свобо́да ♦ **individual** ~ ли́чная свобо́да ♦ **I love my freedom.** Я люблю́ свою́ свобо́ду.

freeload *vi* угоща́ться на дармовщи́ну, жить за чужо́й счёт.

freeloader *n* нахле́бник, прижива́льщик *m*, прижива́лка *f.*

freeloading *adj* лю́бящий (-ая, -ее, -ие) жить за чужо́й счёт.

freespirited *adj* свобо́дный (-ая, -ое, -ые) ду́хом.

free-thinking *adj* вольноду́мный, -ая, -ое, -ые.

freeze *vi (cold)* мёрзнуть / замёрзнуть, замерза́ть / замёрзнуть; *(fear, etc)* цепене́ть / оцепене́ть, ледене́ть / оледене́ть, замира́ть / замере́ть.

French *adj* францу́зский, -ая, -ое, -ие.

French *n* францу́зский язы́к ♦ **speak** ~ говори́ть по-францу́зски.

Frenchman *n* францу́з.

Frenchwoman *n* францу́женка.

frenzied *adj* нейстовый, -ая, -ое, -ые, взбе́шеный, -ая, -ое, -ые, безу́мный, -ая, -ое, -ые, бе́шеный, -ая, -ое, -ые, исступлённый, -ая, -ое, -ые.

frenziedly *adv* нейстово, безу́мно, бе́шено, до бе́шенства.

frenzy *n* бе́шенство, я́рость *f* ; нейстовство; иступле́ние ♦ **feeding** ~ бе́шеный аппети́т ♦ **I'm going to go into a frenzy of kissing you.** Я бу́ду нейстово целова́ть тебя́.

frequent *adj* ча́стый, -ая, -ое, -ые.

frequently *adv* ча́сто.

fresh *adj* 1. све́жий, -ая, -ее, -ие; 2. *(slang) (forward)* де́рзкий, -ая, -ое, -ие ♦ **get** ~ *(slang)* пристава́ть / приста́ть *(with whom* = + к + *dat.)* ♦ **You look very cool and fresh (in that outfit).** Ты вы́глядишь о́чень прохла́дной и све́жей (в э́том наря́де).

freshness *n* све́жесть *f.*

fret *vi* беспоко́иться ♦ **There's no need to fret (about it).** Не на́до (об э́том) беспоко́иться.

Friday *n* пя́тница ♦ **by** ~ к пя́тнице ♦ **last** ~ в про́шлую пя́тницу ♦ **next** ~ в сле́дующую пя́тницу ♦ **on** ~ в пя́тницу.

friend *n* друг *m (pl:* друзья), подру́га *f* ♦ **best** ~ лу́чший друг *m*, лу́чшая подру́га *f* ♦ **bosom** ~ закады́чный друг *m*, закады́чная подру́га *f* ♦ **casual** ~ знако́мый *m*, знако́мая *f (pl:* знако́мые)* ♦ **childhood** ~ друг де́тства *m*, подру́га де́тства *f* ♦ **close** ~ бли́зкий друг *m*, бли́зкая подру́га *f* ♦ **devoted** ~преданный друг *m*, пре́данная подру́га *f* ♦ **faithful**

~ ве́рный друг *m*, ве́рная подру́га *f* ♦ ~ **of the** *(1,2)* **family** друг *(1)* до́ма / *(2)* семьи́ ♦ **good** ~ хоро́ший друг *m*, хоро́шая подру́га *f* ♦ **inseparable** ~**s** неразлу́чные друзья́ ♦ **mutual** ~ о́бщий друг *m*, о́бщая подру́га *f* ♦ **my** ~ мой друг *m (pl:* мои́ друзья́), моя́ подру́га *f* ♦ **new** ~ но́вый друг *m*, но́вая подру́га *f* ♦ *(1,2)* **old** ~ *(1)* ста́рый / *(2)* да́вний друг *m*, *(1)* ста́рая / *(2)* да́вняя подру́га *f* ♦ **online** ~ друг на интерне́те ♦ **only** ~ еди́нственный друг *m*, еди́нственная подру́га *f* ♦ **pillow** ~**s** друзья́ по поду́шке ♦ **real** ~ настоя́щий друг *m*, настоя́щая подру́га *f* ♦ **school** ~ шко́льный друг *m*, шко́льная подру́га *f* ♦ **staunch** ~ пре́данный друг *m*, пре́данная подру́га *f* ♦ **true** ~ настоя́щий друг *m*, настоя́щая подру́га *f* ♦ **your** ~ твой друг *m (pl:* твои́ друзья́), твоя́ подру́га *f*; *(polite)* Ваш друг *m (pl:* Ва́ши друзья́), Ва́ша подру́га *f (familiar)*.

friend: *other terms*

be ~**s** дружи́ть *(with whom = +* с *+ instr.)*, быть друзья́ми ♦ **become** ~**s** подружи́ться ♦ **circle of** ~**s** круг друзе́й ♦ **know how to be a good** ~ уме́ть быть хоро́шим дру́гом ♦ **make** ~**s** подружи́ться *(with whom = +* с *+ instr.)* ♦ *(1)* **remain** / *(2)* **stay** ~**s** *(1,2)* остава́ться / оста́ться друзья́ми.

friend: *phrases*

I hope we can stay friends. Я наде́юсь, мы смо́жем оста́ться друзья́ми. ♦ **First, let's just be friends.** Снача́ла дава́йте про́сто бу́дем друзья́ми. ♦ **I'd like to just be friends first.** Я хоте́л *(ж: хоте́ла)* бы снача́ла быть про́сто друзья́ми. ♦ **Can we just be friends?** Мо́жем мы быть то́лько друзья́ми? ♦ **I can't just be friends with you. I love you too much.** Я не могу́ то́лько дружи́ть с тобо́й. Я сли́шком тебя́ люблю́. ♦ **I hope we can always be both friends and lovers.** Я наде́юсь, мы смо́жем всегда́ быть и друзья́ми и любо́вниками. ♦ **I like socializing with friends.** Мне нра́вится обще́ние с друзья́ми. ♦ **I enjoy socializing with friends.** Я наслажда́юсь обще́нием с друзья́ми. ♦ **I want you to be my wife, my friend, my lover.** Я хочу́, что́бы ты была́ мое́й жено́й, мои́м дру́гом, мое́й любо́вницей. ♦ **I feel like the luckiest person in this part of the universe to have you as my dear, close, and beloved friend.** Я чу́вствую себя́ счастли́вейшим челове́ком в э́той ча́сти вселе́нной, потому́ что ты мой дорого́й, бли́зкий и люби́мый друг.

friendliness *n* дружелю́бие ♦ **There is a tempest in my heart** *(1,2)* **caused by your sweet, innocent friendliness.** Твоё ми́лое, неви́нное дружелю́бие *(1)* сотвори́ло / *(2)* вы́звало бу́рю в моём се́рдце.

friendly *adj* дру́жеский, -ая, -ое, -ие ♦ **cat** ~ люби́тель ко́шек ♦ **distantly** ~ сде́ржанно-дру́жеский ♦ **dog** ~ люби́тель соба́к ♦ **herb** ~ лю́бящий (-ая, -ее, -ие) марихуа́ну ♦ **pet** ~ люби́тель (дома́шних) живо́тных.

friendship *n* дру́жба ♦ **blossoming** ~ расцвета́ющая дру́жба ♦ **casual** ~ знако́мство ♦ *(1,2)* **close** ~ *(1)* бли́зкая / *(2)* те́сная дру́жба ♦ *(1,2)* ~ **of many years** *(1)* долголе́тняя / *(2)* многоле́тняя дру́жба ♦ **great** ~ больша́я дру́жба ♦ **long** ~ до́лгая дру́жба ♦ *(1,2)* **old** ~ *(1)* ста́рая / *(2)* да́вняя дру́жба ♦ **our** ~ на́ша дру́жба ♦ *(1,2)* **real** ~ *(1)* настоя́щая / *(2)* и́стинная дру́жба ♦ *(1,2)* **strong** ~ *(1)* про́чная / *(2)* кре́пкая дру́жба ♦ *(1,2)* **true** ~ *(1)* настоя́щая / *(2)* и́стинная дру́жба ♦ **warm** ~ те́сная дру́жба ♦ **bonds of** ~ у́зы дру́жбы ♦ **nature of our** ~ хара́ктер на́шей дру́жбы ♦ **share** ~ разделя́ть дру́жбу ♦ **stamp of** ~ печа́ть дру́жбы ♦ **I desire friendship leading to a long-term relationship.** Я хочу́ дру́жбу, кото́рая приведёт к дли́тельным отноше́ниям. ♦ **I don't want our friendship to dissolve.** Я не хочу́, что́бы на́ша дру́жба разру́шилась.

friend-ville *n (slang) (a relationship that is purely friendly, not romantic)* про́сто дру́жеские отноше́ния ♦ **I want to leave friend-ville behind.** Я хочу́ бо́льше, чем про́сто дру́жбы.

frigid *adj* сексуа́льно холо́дный, -ая, -ое, -ые, фриги́дный, -ая, -ое, -ые.

Counting things in Russian is a bit involved.
See Appendix 4, Numbers, on page 756 .

frill *n* обо́рка, рюш.

frilly *adj* отде́ланный (-ая, -ое, -ые) обо́рками.

frisbee *n* лета́ющая таре́лка *(для игры)* ♦ **throw a** ~ броса́ть / бро́сить лета́ющую таре́лку.

frisky *adj* ре́звый, -ая, -ое, -ые; игри́вый, -ая, -ое, -ые ♦ **You're a frisky one, aren't you.** Ты игри́вая *(ж: игри́вый)*, не так ли? ♦ **I'm quite frisky by nature.** Я дово́льно игри́вый *(ж: игри́вая)* по нату́ре.

frivolity *n* легкомы́слие.

frivolous *adj* легкомы́сленный, -ая, -ое, -ые.

frog *n (slang) (undesirable suitor)* неподходя́щий кавале́р.

frolic *n* ша́лость *f* ♦ **I have a penchant for fun and frolic.** У меня́ накло́нность / скло́нность к весе́лью и ша́лости. ♦ **We can spend** *(1)* **long /** *(2)* **blissful hours in pleasureful frolic.** Мы мо́жем проводи́ть *(1)* до́лгие / *(2)* счастли́вые часы́ в ша́лостях, по́лных наслажде́ния.

frolicking *adj* веселя́щийся, -аяся, -ееся, иеся, развлека́ющийся, -аяся, -ееся, иеся ♦ **I wish to meet a good-looking, adventurous single female for funky frolicking fun.** Я хочу́ встре́тить хорошо́ вы́глядящую же́нщину, со скло́нностью к приключе́ниям для весёлых, шаловли́вых развлече́ний.

frolicsome *adj* шаловли́вый, -ая, -ое, -ые.

frown *vi* хму́риться / нахму́риться.

frown *n* хму́рый взгляд.

frugal *adj* бережли́вый, -ая, -ое, -ые, эконо́мный, -ая, -ое, -ые ♦ *(1,2)* **creatively** ~ *(1)* тво́рчески / *(2)* разу́мно эконо́мный, -ая, -ое, -ые.

fruit *n* фрукт, плод ♦ **forbidden** ~ **(of pleasure)** запре́тный плод (наслажде́ния).

frump *n* старомо́дно и пло́хо оде́тая же́нщина.

frumpy *adj (old-fashioned)* старомо́дный, -ая, -ое, -ые; *(poorly dressed)* безвку́сно / пло́хо оде́тый, -ая, -ое, -ые; *(unattractive)* непривлека́тельный, -ая, -ое, -ые.

frustrate *vt* 1. *(upset, disrupt)* расстра́ивать / расстро́ить *(what = acc.)*; 2. *(defeat expectation)* разочаро́вывать / разочарова́ть *(what = acc.)*.

frustrated *adj* разочаро́ванный, -ая, -ое, -ые.

frustrating *adj* разочаро́вывающий, -ая, -ее, -ие.

frustration *n* разочарова́ние.

fuel *vt* распаля́ть / распали́ть *(what = acc.)* ♦ **That fuels my appetite.** Это распаля́ет мой аппети́т.

fulfill *vt* выполня́ть / вы́полнить *(what = acc.)*, исполня́ть / испо́лнить *(what = acc.)*; осуществля́ть / осуществи́ть *(what = acc.)* ♦ **You and I will get married and fulfill our purpose (in life).** Ты и я поже́нимся и дости́гнем на́шей це́ли (в жи́зни). ♦ **I want to do everything I (possibly) can to fulfill your needs and desires.** Я хочу́ де́лать всё, что в мои́х си́лах для исполне́ния твои́х нужд и жела́ний.

fulfilling *adj* удовлетворя́ющий, -ая, -ее, -ие ♦ **mutually** ~ взаи́мно удовлетворя́ющий.

fulfillment *n* 1. *(satisfaction)* удовлетворе́ние; 2. *(accomplishment)* выполне́ние, исполне́ние; осуществле́ние ♦ **complete** ~ по́лное удовлетворе́ние ♦ **mutual** ~ взаи́мное удовлетворе́ние ♦ **Only you can provide the fulfillment that I crave.** То́лько ты мо́жешь дать то удовлетворе́ние, кото́рого я жа́жду. ♦ **I seek a playmate for mutual fulfillment.** Я ищу́ партнёра для взаи́много удовлетворе́ния.

full *adj* по́лный, -ая, -ое, -ые *(short forms:* по́лон, полна́, -о́, -ы́*)*; запо́лненный, -ая, -ое, -ые *(short forms:* запо́лнен, -а, -о, -ы*)* ♦ **You are so full of yourself.** Ты так запо́лнен сам собо́й. ♦ **My heart is full of love for you.** Моё се́рдце полно́ любо́вью к тебе́.

full-bodied *adj (heavy, overweight)* полноте́лый, -ая, -ое, -ые.

Russian has 2 different verbs for "go",
one for "on foot" and the other for "by vehicle".

full-figured *adj* по́лный, -ая, -ое, -ые.

fullness *n* полнота́ ♦ ~ **of pleasure** полнота́ наслажде́ния ♦ **I want to feel the fullness of your breasts** *(1)* **...with my mouth.** / *(2)* **...against my chest.** Я хочу́ ощути́ть полноту́ твое́й гру́ди *(1)* ...губа́ми. / *(2)*, ...прижа́вшись к тебе́. ♦ **As my hand cups the fullness of your breast, my mouth will cover your beautiful face and smooth neck with adoring kisses.** В то вре́мя, как моя́ рука́ ощути́т полноту́ твое́й гру́ди, мой рот покро́ет твоё прекра́сное лицо́ и не́жную ше́ю обожа́ющими поцелу́ями.

fun *n* заба́ва, поте́ха, весе́лье, удово́льствие; развлече́ние ♦ **flirtatious** ~ весёлый флирт ♦ **lusty** ~ чу́вственное развлече́ние ♦ **naughty** ~ неприли́чное развлече́ние ♦ **romantic** ~ романти́ческое удово́льствие ♦ **sensual** ~ чу́вственное наслажде́ние ♦ **uninhibited** ~ несде́рживаемое удово́льствие ♦ **wild** ~ ди́кое весе́лье ♦ **full of** ~ по́лный (-ая, -ое, -ые) задо́ра ♦ **have** ~ весели́ться.

fun: in general

(1) **I'm** / *(2)* **You're** *(3)* **...(a lot of) fun (to be around).** / *(4)* **...more fun than a barrel of monkeys.** *(1)* Со мной... / *(2)* С тобо́й *(3)* ...(о́чень) ве́село. / *(2)* ...веселе́е, чем с бо́чкой обезья́н. ♦ **I'll do anything for fun.** Я де́лаю всё для весе́лья. ♦ **It's so much fun being with you.** Тако́е удово́льствие быть с тобо́й. ♦ **It's always fun being with you.** Это всегда́ удово́льствие быть с тобо́й. ♦ **It will be (a lot of) fun.** Это бу́дет (о́чень) ве́село. ♦ **It's no fun (here) without you.** Без тебя́ (здесь) совсе́м не ве́село. ♦ **You seem like (a lot of) fun.** Ка́жется, что с тобо́й (о́чень) ве́село. ♦ **I want someone with a sense of fun.** Я хочу́ челове́ка, лю́бящего развлече́ния ♦ **I wish to meet a good-looking, adventurous single female for funky frolicking fun.** Я хочу́ встре́тить хорошо́ вы́глядящую же́нщину, со скло́нностью к приключе́ниям для весёлых, шаловли́вых развлече́ний..

fun: have fun

I have a *(1,2)* **penchant for fun and frolic.** У меня́ *(1)* накло́нность / *(2)* скло́нность к весе́лью и ша́лости. ♦ **We always have so much fun together.** Мы всегда́ вме́сте так ве́село прово́дим вре́мя. ♦ **We had so much fun together (that time).** Мы так ве́село провели́ время вме́сте (в э́тот раз). ♦ **I had a lot of fun.** Мне бы́ло о́чень ве́село. ♦ **We'll have a lot of fun together.** Вме́сте мы о́чень ве́село проведём вре́мя. ♦ **I've never had so much fun (with anyone).** Мне никогда́ не бы́ло так ве́село (с кем-либо). ♦ **Let's have fun together.** Дава́й весели́ться вме́сте. ♦ *(1,2)* **We can have (a lot of) fun together.** *(1)* Мы мо́жем (о́чень) весели́ться вме́сте. / *(2)* Нам мо́жет быть (о́чень) ве́село вдвоём. ♦ **I'm into laughter, adventure, and having fun.** Я челове́к, лю́бящий смех, приключе́ния и развлече́ния. ♦ **We would have so much fun together and I would fill you with such beautiful feelings that you would never let go of my arm.** У нас бы́ло бы сто́лько весе́лья, и я бы напо́лнил тебя́ таки́ми прекрасными чу́вствами, что ты никогда́ бы не захоте́ла поки́нуть меня́. ♦ **We can have some clothing-free fun together.** Мы мо́жем развлека́ться без оде́жды.

fun: make fun of

I would never make fun of you. Я никогда́ не бу́ду насмеха́ться над тобо́й.

funky *adj (slang)* 1. *(out of the ordinary)* необы́чный, -ая, -ое, -ые, из ря́да вон выходя́щий, -ая, -ее, -ие; *(kind of wild)* дикова́тый, -ая, -ое, -ые; *(fun)* весёлый, -ая, -ое, -ые; 2. *(earthy, raw)* просте́цкий, -ая, -ое, -ие, грубова́тый, -ая, -ое, -ые; 3. *(music)* в сти́ле «фанк» ♦ **I wish to meet a good-looking, adventurous single female for funky frolicking fun.** Я хочу́ встре́тить хорошо́ вы́глядящую же́нщину, со скло́нностью к приключе́ниям для весёлых, шаловли́вых развлече́ний.

fun-loving *(1,2,3) adj* лю́бящий (-ая, -ее, -ие) *(1)* весе́лье / *(2)* заба́вы / *(3)* развлече́ния.

Dipthongs in Russian are made by adding й
*to the end of a vowel (*а, е, ё, о, у, э, ю, *and* я*).*

funny *adj* 1. *(amusing)* смешно́й, -а́я, -о́е, -ы́е, заба́вный, -ая, -ое, -ые; 2. *(strange)* стра́н-ный,-ая, -ое, -ые; 3. *(improper)* неприли́чный, -ая, -ое, -ие, нескро́мный, -ая, -ое, -ые ♦ ~ **as hell** заба́вный (-ая, -ое, -ые) как чёрт ♦ **That's (not) funny.** Это (не) смешно́ ♦ **Don't try anything funny.** Не пыта́йся сде́лать ничего́ неприли́чного.

fun-spirited *adj* с весёлой нату́рой.

fur *n* мех.

fur *adj* мехово́й, -а́я, -о́е, -ы́е.

furious *adj (intense, violent)* я́ростный, -ая, -ое, -ые, неи́стовый, -ая, -ое, -ые, бе́шеный, -ая, -ое, -ые ♦ **be** ~ быть в я́рости ♦ *(1)* **He** / *(2)* **She was furious.** *(1)* Он был... / *(2)* Она́ была́... в я́рости.

furtive *adj* та́йный, -ая, -ое, -ые, сде́ланный (-ая, -ое, -ые) укра́дкой.

furtively *adv* та́йно, укра́дкой.

fury *n* я́рость *f*, бе́шенство ♦ **"Heaven has no Rage like Love to Hatred turn'd, Nor Hell a Fury, like a Woman scorned."** *William Congreve, "The Mourning Bride" (1697)* «На небеса́х нет тако́й я́рости, как любо́вь, обращённая в не́нависть, в аду́ нет тако́го бе́шенства, как же́нщина отве́ргнутая.» *Ви́льям Ко́нгрив, «Скорбя́щая неве́ста».*

fuse *vt (mouths, bodies)* соединя́ть / соедини́ть *(what = acc., to what = + с + instr.)* ♦ **I watch your mouth forming sounds, moving and undulating so supplely, so softly, so enticingly and I am seized with a raging impulse to fuse my own mouth together with it and once and for all revel in its sweet softness.** Я слежу́, как твой рот создаёт зву́ки, дви́гаясь и изгиба́ясь так ги́бко, так мя́гко, так соблазни́тельно, и я охва́чен бе́шеным и́мпульсом соедини́ть мой рот с твои́м, что́бы раз и навсегда́ пирова́ть в его́ сла́дкой не́жности.

fuse *vi* слива́ться / сли́ться ♦ **Our bodies will fuse together into a single being.** На́ши тела́ солью́тся в одно́ це́лое.

fusion *n* соедине́ние, слия́ние ♦ ~ **of mind and body** душе́вное и теле́сное слия́ние.

fuss *n* шум ♦ *(1)* **cause** / *(2)* **make** / *(3)* **raise a** ~ *(1-3)* поднима́ть / подня́ть шум.

fussy *adj (finicky)* привере́дливый, -ая, -ое, -ые, разбо́рчивый, -ая, -ое, -ые ♦ **I'm (not too) fussy about such things.** Я (не сли́шком) привере́длив в таки́х веща́х.

futile *adj* тще́тный, -ая, -ое, -ые, напра́сный,-ая, -ое, -ые, бесполе́зный, -ая, -ое, -ые ♦ **It all seems so futile.** Это всё ка́жется таки́м тще́тным. ♦ *(1)* **This** / *(2)* **It is futile.** *(1,2)* Это тще́тно.

futilely *adv* тще́тно, бесполе́зно, напра́сно.

futility тще́тность *f*, пустота́, бесполе́зность *f* ♦ *(1)* **Our relationship** / *(2)* **marriage...** / *(3)* **This** / *(4)* **It... is an exercise in futility.** *(1)* На́ши отноше́ния... / *(2)* Наш брак... / *(3,4)* Это... упражне́ния в пустоте́.

future *adj* бу́дущий, -ая, -ее, -ие.

future *n* бу́дущее *(adjectival noun)* ♦ **beautiful** ~ прекра́сное бу́дущее ♦ *(1,2)* **bright** ~ *(1)* све́тлое / *(2)* блестя́щее бу́дущее ♦ **gloomy** ~ мра́чное бу́дущее ♦ **great** ~ большо́е бу́дущее ♦ **happy** ~ счастли́вое бу́дущее ♦ **our** ~ на́ше бу́дущее ♦ *(1,2)* **wonderful** ~ *(1)* прекра́сное / *(2)* удиви́тельное бу́дущее ♦ **dream of the** ~ мечта́ть о бу́дущем ♦ **foresee a** ~ предви́деть бу́дущее ♦ **hope for the** ~ *vi* наде́яться на бу́дущее ♦ **hope for the** ~ *n* наде́жда на бу́дущее ♦ **in the** ~ в бу́дущем ♦ **in the near** ~ в ближа́йшее вре́мя, в ближа́йшем бу́дущем ♦ **plan for the** ~ плани́ровать на бу́дущее *(what = acc.).* ♦ **plans for the** ~ пла́ны на бу́дущее ♦ **I pray that our future together will be bright and beautiful.** Я молю́сь, что́бы на́ше бу́дущее вме́сте бы́ло я́рким и прекра́сным. ♦ **I pray that you and I will have a wonderful (, happy) future together.** Я молю́сь о том, что́бы у нас с тобо́й бы́ло удиви́тельное (, счастли́вое) бу́дущее вме́сте.

Some phrases are listed under more than one main word.

G

gaiety *n* весе́лье; весёлость *f* ♦ **full of ~** по́лный (-ая, -ые) весе́лья.

gain *vt* 1. *(get, obtain)* получа́ть / получи́ть *(what = acc.)*, приобрета́ть / приобрести́ *(what = acc.)*; *(earn)* зараба́тывать / зарабо́тать *(what = acc.)*; 2. *(achieve)* достига́ть / дости́гнуть *(what = gen.)*, добива́ться / доби́ться *(what = gen.)*; *(win)* завоёвывать / завоева́ть *(what = acc.)*; 3. *(derive benefit)* извлека́ть / извле́чь по́льзу / вы́году.

> **gain: phrases**

What do you hope to gain? Что ты наде́ешься получи́ть? ♦ **I have everything to gain and nothing to lose.** У меня́ ничего́ нет и мне не́чего теря́ть. ♦ **To gain a small measure of your precious love is my passionate *(1)* ambition / *(2)* aspiration.** Получи́ть ка́плю твое́й драгоце́нной любви́ - моё стра́стное *(1)* стремле́ние / *(2)* жела́ние.

gait *n* похо́дка.

gal *n (slang)* девчо́нка, де́вушка *(See also* **girl, female** *and* **woman)** ♦ **atypical ~** необы́чная де́вушка ♦ **country ~** дереве́нская де́вушка ♦ **(1,2) cute little ~** *(1)* ми́лая / *(2)* симпати́чная ма́ленькая де́вушка ♦ **full-figured ~** по́лная де́вушка ♦ **(1,2) good-looking ~** *(1)* привлека́тельная / *(2)* симпати́чная де́вушка ♦ **nice ~** 1. *(pleasant)* прия́тная де́вушка; 2. *(upstanding)* поря́дочная де́вушка ♦ **old-fashioned ~** де́вушка, приде́рживающаяся ста́рых идеа́лов *(1 term)*.

gal-pal *n (slang)* подру́жка.

gall *n* на́глость *f* ♦ **You have the gall to *(1)* ...say that. / *(2)* ...come here.** У тебя́ хвата́ет на́глости *(1)* ...говори́ть э́то. / *(2)* ...прийти́ сюда́.

gallant *n (chivalrous)* гала́нтный, -ая, -ое, -ые.

gallantly *adv* гала́нтно.

gamble *vi* 1. *(bet)* игра́ть в аза́ртные и́гры, игра́ть на де́ньги; 2. *(risk)* рискова́ть.

gambling *n* аза́ртные и́гры, и́гры на де́ньги.

gambol *vi* резви́ться.

game *n* 1. *(play)* игра́; 2. *(prey)* дичь ♦ **fair ~** дичь, на кото́рую разрешено́ охо́титься *(1 term)*. ♦ **head ~s** хи́трые и́гры ♦ **mating ~** па́рная игра́ ♦ **play a ~ of cat and mouse** хитри́ть.

> **game: phrases**

(1,2) **No games.** *(1)* Не на́до игр. / *(2)* Нет вре́мени развлека́ться. ♦ **No head games.** Не на́до (хи́трых) игр. ♦ **I don't believe in playing games (with people).** Я не скло́нен *(ж: скло́нна)* игра́ть (с людьми́). ♦ **Stop playing games.** Переста́нь игра́ть. ♦ **Please don't**

> *The singular past tense of Russian verbs ends in -л (m) (usually), -ла (f) or -ло (n). the plural past tense ends in -li.*

play games with me. Пожа́луйста, со мной не на́до игр. ◆ **Life is too short for games.** Жизнь сли́шком коротка́ для игр. ◆ **I have no time for games.** У меня́ нет вре́мени для игр. ◆ **I hate head games.** Я ненави́жу хи́трые и́гры. ◆ **Would you like to go to a** *(1)* **soccer /** *(2)* **basketball /** *(3)* **baseball game?** Не хоте́ла *(ж: хоте́л)* бы ты пойти́ на *(1)* футбо́л / *(2)* баскетбо́л / *(3)* бейсбо́л? ◆ **Let's go to a** *(1)* **soccer /** *(2)* **basketball /** *(3)* **baseball game (together).** Дава́й пойдём на *(1)* футбо́л / *(2)* баскетбо́л / *(3)* бейсбо́л.

game-playing *n* и́гры ◆ **I'm past the game-playing stage.** Я прошёл ста́дию игры́.

gaming *n* и́гры *(на компью́тере)* ◆ **PC** ~ и́гры на (персона́льном) компью́тере.

gams *n, pl (slang)* но́ги.

gamut *n* га́мма ◆ ~ **of emotions** га́мма эмо́ций ◆ ~ **of feelings** га́мма чувств ◆ ~ **of moods** га́мма настрое́ний.

gangliness *n* углова́тость *f* ◆ **youthful** ~ ю́ношеская углова́тость.

gangly *adj* долговя́зый, -ая, -ое, -ые, нескла́дный, -ая, -ое, -ые.

gap *n (disparity)* про́пасть, разры́в ◆ **age** ~ про́пасть в года́х.

garden *n* сад ◆ **I want to spend endless hours planting delicious fruits of pleasure in the secret garden of your body.** Я хочу́ провести́ бесконе́чные часы́, сажа́я восхити́тельные фру́кты наслажде́ния в секре́тном саду́ твоего́ те́ла. ◆ **You make my** *(1)* **life /** *(2)* **world a Garden of Eden.** Ты превраща́ешь *(1)* ...мою́ жизнь... / *(2)* ...мой мир... в ра́йский сад.

gardening *n* садово́дство ◆ **flower** ~ цвето́чное садово́дство.

garish *adj* 1. *(flashy)* сли́шком я́ркий, -ая, -ое, -ие, крича́щий, -ая, -ее, -ие, бро́ский, -ая, -ое, -ие; 2. *(flamboyant)* я́ркий, -ая, -ое, -ие, броса́ющийся (-аяся, -еєся, -иеся) в глаза́; цвети́стый, -ая, -ое, -ые; показно́й, -а́я, -о́е, -ы́е.

garter *n* подвя́зка ◆ **bridal** ~ сва́дебная подвя́зка.

gasp *vi* задыха́ться / задохну́ться ◆ ~ **deeply** глубоко́ задыха́ться / задохну́ться.

gathering *n* собра́ние; встре́ча ◆ **intimate** ~ инти́мное собра́ние ◆ **social** ~ встре́ча друзе́й.

gauche *adj* неуклю́жий, -ая, -ее, -ие, нело́вкий, -ая, -ое, -ие, неповоро́тливый, -ая, -ое, -ые ◆ **feel** *(1,2)* ~ чу́вствовать себя́ неуклю́жим *m* / неуклю́жей *f.*

gawk *vi* тара́щить глаза́ *(at what, whom = + на + acc.).*

gay *adj* гомосексуа́льный, -ая, -ое, -ые.

gay *n* гомосексуали́ст.

gaze *vi* (приста́льно) смотре́ть *(at what, whom = + на + acc.),* гляде́ть *(at what, whom = + на + acc.),* вгля́дываться *(at what, whom = + в + acc.)* ◆ ~ **lovingly** смотре́ть с любо́вью ◆ ~ **tenderly** смотре́ть не́жно ◆ ~ **wistfully** смотре́ть заду́мчиво.

gaze: *phrases*

I gaze upon your divinely beautiful face in its silky frame of *(1)* **golden /** *(2)* **auburn /** *(3)* **black hair and I am awash in fervent adoration.** Я вгля́дываюсь в твоё боже́ственно прекра́сное лицо́ в шелкови́стом обрамле́нии *(1)* золоти́стых / *(2)* золоти́сто-кашта́новых / *(3)* чёрных воло́с и я тону́ в пы́лком обожа́нии. ◆ **What rapture it is to gaze at your love-softened face.** Что за восто́рг вгля́дываться в твоё смягчённое любо́вью лицо́. ◆ **It's such a thrill to gaze into the dark irises of your eyes.** Тако́е наслажде́ние смотре́ть в тёмные зрачки́ твои́х глаз. ◆ **Each time I gaze into your eyes, I am inundated with the most intense feelings of love and adoration that I've ever experienced.** Вся́кий раз, когда́ я вгля́дываюсь в твои́ глаза́, меня́ затопля́ют таки́е пы́лкие чу́вства любви́ и обожа́ния, каки́х я никогда́ не испы́тывал.

gaze *n* (приста́льный) взгляд ◆ **admiring** ~ любу́ющийся взгляд ◆ **ardent** ~ стра́стный взгляд ◆ **dark** ~ мра́чный взгляд ◆ **distant** ~ отрешённый взгляд ◆ **gentle** ~ не́жный

Please do us a favor:
Fill out and mail in the Feedback Sheet on page 795.

взгляд ♦ **intent** ~ внима́тельный взгляд ♦ **intimate** ~ инти́мный взгляд ♦ **lustful** ~ похотли́вый взгляд ♦ **open** ~ откры́тый взгляд ♦ **smoldering** ~ призы́вный взгляд ♦ **tender** ~ не́жный взгляд ♦ **virile** ~ мужско́й взгляд ♦ **warm** ~ тёплый взгляд.

gaze: phrases

I was so thrilled when I noticed I had fallen into your gaze. Я был *(ж: была́)* так си́льно взволно́ван *(ж: взволно́вана)*, когда́ я заме́тил *(ж: заме́тила)*, что ты смо́тришь на меня́. ♦ **I couldn't avert my gaze (from** *[1]* **...you. /** *[2]* **...your** *[3]* **beautiful /** *[4]* **enchanting face.).** Я не смог *(ж: смогла́)* отвести́ свой взгляд *(от [1] ...тебя́. / [2] ...твоего́ [3] прекра́сного / [4] очарова́тельного лица́.).*

geek *n (slang)* чуда́к.

gem *n* драгоце́нный ка́мень, драгоце́нность *f* ♦ **To me, you are the rarest of gems.** Для меня́ ты редча́йшая драгоце́нность.

Gemini *(May 21 - Jun. 21)* Близнецы́ *(21 ма́я - 21 ию́ня).*

gene *n* ген ♦ **rogue** ~ анома́льный ген ♦ **All of your genes are in perfect orchestration.** Все твои́ ге́ны соверше́нно оркерстри́рованы.

general *n:* ♦ **in** ~ вообще́.

generally *adv* 1. *(usually)* обы́чно, как пра́вило; 2. *(in general)* вообще́.

generosity *n* ще́дрость *f*, великоду́шие ♦ **I'm very generous of self.** Я о́чень ще́дрый. ♦ **I appreciate your generosity (very much).** Я (о́чень) ценю́ твою́ ще́дрость. ♦ **I'm (very) grateful for all the generosity you have shown me.** Я (о́чень) благода́рен *(ж: благода́рна)* за всю ту ще́дрость, кото́рую ты проявля́ла *(ж: проявля́л)* ко мне.

generous *adj* ще́дрый, -ая, -ое, -ые, великоду́шный, -ая, -ое, -ые ♦ **emotionally** ~ эмоциона́льно ще́дрый, -ая, -ое, -ые ♦ ~ **to a fault** чрезме́рно ще́дрый.

generously *adv* ще́дро.

genial *adj* гениа́льный, -ая, -ое, -ые.

gent *n* джентльме́н.

gentle *adj (soft, kind)* мя́гкий, -ая, -ое, -ие, до́брый, -ая, -ое, -ые; *(tender)* не́жный, -ая, -ое, -ые, ла́сковый, -ая, -ое, -ые; *(meek)* кро́ткий, -ая, -ое, -ие ♦ **You'll find me sinfully gentle.** Ты найдёшь меня́ гре́шно не́жным. ♦ *(1)* **I'll be... /** *(2)* **I'm... as gentle as a lamb.** *(1)* Я бу́ду... / *(2)* Я ... не́жен, как ягнёнок. ♦ **You are so gentle.** Ты так нежна́ *(ж: не́жен).* ♦ **You are such a gentle lover.** Ты така́я не́жная любо́вница. *(ж: Ты тако́й не́жный любо́вник.)* ♦ **I love your gentle touch.** Я люблю́ твои́ не́жные прикоснове́ния. ♦ **I love how gentle you are to me.** *(ж:)* Мне нра́вится, что ты не́жен со мной. ♦ **Please be gentle.** *(ж:)* Пожа́луйста, будь не́жным.

gentle-hearted *adj* добросерде́чный, -ая, -ое, -ые, мя́гкий, -ая, -ое, -ие.

gentleman *n* джентльме́н ♦ **active** ~ энерги́чный джентльме́н ♦ **compassionate** ~ сострада́тельный джентльме́н ♦ **cultured** ~ культу́рный джентльме́н ♦ **established** ~ 1. устро́енный джентльме́н; 2. джентльме́н, про́чно стоя́щий на нога́х *(1 term)* ♦ ~ **of integrity** че́стный джентльме́н ♦ ~ **of means** джентльме́н со сре́дствами ♦ ~ **of the old school** джентльме́н ста́рой шко́лы ♦ **Latino** ~ латино-америка́нский джентльме́н ♦ **loving** ~ лю́бящий джентльме́н ♦ **nice** ~ прия́тный джентльме́н ♦ **old-fashioned** ~ джентльме́н ста́рой зака́лки ♦ **optimistic** ~ оптими́ст ♦ **perfect** ~ превосхо́дный джентльме́н ♦ **real** ~ настоя́щий джентльме́н ♦ *(1,2)* **refined** ~ *(1)* изы́сканный / *(2)* утончённый джентльме́н ♦ **romantic** ~ романти́ческий джентльме́н, рома́нтик ♦ **\$ecure** ~ фина́нсово обеспе́ченный джентльме́н ♦ **traveled** ~ мно́го путеше́ствовавший джентльме́н ♦ **understanding** ~ понима́ющий джентльме́н ♦ **unique** ~ уника́льный джентльме́н ♦ **well-groomed** ~ хорошо́ вы́глядящий джентльме́н ♦ **well-mannered** ~ джентльме́н с хоро́шими мане́рами ♦ **worldly** ~ умудрённый

Clock and calender time are discussed in Appendix 5, page 759.

джентельме́н ♦ **I promise to behave like a gentleman.** Я обеща́ю вести́ себя́ как джентльме́н.

gentleness *n* мя́гкость *f*, доброта́, не́жность *f* ♦ **act of** ~ акт доброты́, мя́гкое де́йствие ♦ **person of** ~ до́брый челове́к ♦ **I admire you for your gentleness.** Я восхища́юсь- твое́й мя́гкостью. ♦ **There is a gentleness** *(1)* **in** */ (2)* **about you that I would never have thought possible.** *(1,2)* В тебе́ така́я не́жность, каку́ю я никогда́ не мог *(ж: могла́)* бы да́же предста́вить. ♦ **When I initiate your body into _intimacy_, it will be with infinite love and consummate gentleness.** Когда́ я познако́млю твоё те́ло с инти́мной бли́зостью, я сде́лаю э́то с бесконе́чной любо́вью и и́стинной не́жностью.

gently *adv (softly)* мя́гко, не́жно; *(carefully)* осторо́жно.

genuine *adj* настоя́щий, -ая, -ее, -ие.

Georgian *adj* грузи́нский, -ая, -ое, -ие.

Georgian *n* 1. *(person)* грузи́н *m*, грузи́нка *f (pl:* грузи́ны*)*; 2. *(language)* грузи́нский язы́к ♦ **speak** ~ говори́ть по-грузи́нски.

German *adj* неме́цкий, -ая, -ое, -ие.

German *n* 1. *(person)* не́мец *m*, не́мка *f (pl:* не́мцы*)*; 2. *(language)* неме́цкий язы́к ♦ **speak** ~ говори́ть по-неме́цки.

gesticulate *vi* жестикули́ровать.

gesture *n* жест ♦ **beautiful** ~ прекра́сный жест ♦ **childlike** ~ де́тский жест ♦ **courting** ~ уха́живающий жест ♦ **courtly** ~ жест ве́жливости ♦ **elegant** ~ изя́щный жест ♦ **eloquent** ~ красноречи́вый жест ♦ **face-saving** ~ жест, сохраня́ющий лицо́ *(1 term)*. ♦ **flirtatious** ~ коке́тливый жест ♦ **friendly** ~ дру́жеский жест ♦ **graceful** ~ грацио́зный жест ♦ **impatient** ~ нетерпели́вый жест ♦ **noble** ~ благоро́дный жест ♦ **rude** ~ гру́бый жест ♦ **small** ~s ма́ленькие же́сты ♦ **strange** ~ стра́нный жест ♦ **sweet** ~ не́жный жест ♦ **theatrical** ~ театра́льный жест ♦ **thoughtful** ~ внима́тельный жест ♦ **make a** ~ де́лать / сде́лать жест ♦ **That was a very thoughtful gesture.** Это был о́чень внима́тельный жест.

get *vt* 1. *(receive)* получа́ть / получи́ть *(what = acc.)*; 2. *(fetch)* брать / взять *(what = acc.)*; *(bring)* приноси́ть / принести́ *(what = acc.)*; 3. *(obtain)* достава́ть / доста́ть *(what = acc.)*; *(buy)* покупа́ть / купи́ть *(what = acc.)*; 4. *(achieve)* достига́ть / дости́гнуть *(what = gen.)*.

get: idioms

~ **along** ла́дить *(with whom = + с + instr.)* ♦ ~ **anywhere** достига́ть / дости́гнуть успе́ха, достига́ть / дости́гнуть свое́й це́ли, добива́ться / доби́ться успе́ха ♦ ~ **back** *vi* 1. *(return)* возвраща́ться / верну́ться; 2. *(slang) (contact later, call again)* позвони́ть поздне́е *(to whom = dat.)* ♦ ~ **back together** воссоединя́ться / воссоедини́ться ♦ **easy to** ~ **along with** ужи́вчивый, -ая, -ое, -ые ♦ ~ **enough of** насыща́ться / насы́титься *(of what / whom = instr.)* ♦ ~ **fresh** вести́ себя́ развя́зно *(with whom = + с + instr.)* ♦ ~ **(a)hold of yourself** контроли́ровать себя́, держа́ть себя́ в рука́х ♦ ~ **you in bed** *(slang)* «тащи́ть тебя́ в посте́ль» ♦ ~ *(1)* **my** */ (2)* **your own way** идти́ *(1,2)* свои́м со́бственным путём ♦ ~ **nowhere** ничего́ не дости́гнуть ♦ ~ **off** *vi* 1. *(exit)* слеза́ть / слезть, вылеза́ть / вы́лезти; выходи́ть / вы́йти; 2. *(of work)* освобожда́ться / освободи́ться ♦ ~ **off by ourselves** *(find seclusion)* уединя́ться / уедини́ться ♦ ~ **out** *vi (leave)* убира́ться / убра́ться ♦ ~ **over** 1. *(feelings, loss)* поборо́ть *(what = acc.)*; *(obstacles, problems)* преодолева́ть / преодоле́ть *(what = acc.)*; 2. *(believe it's true)* нади ви́ться *(what = dat.)* ♦ ~ **over with** *(finish)* зако́нчить *(what = acc.)*, поко́нчить *(what = acc.)*, заверши́ть *(what = acc.)* ♦ ~ **somewhere** достига́ть / дости́гнуть успе́ха, доби́ться успе́ха, достига́ть / дости́гнуть свое́й це́ли, добива́ться / доби́ться успе́ха ♦ ~ **together** *vi (meet)* встреча́ться / встре́титься.

Reflexive verbs are those that end in -ся or -сь.
The -ся or -сь also goes onto a past tense ending.

get along:

I want somebody I can talk to and get along with in my old age. Я хочу́ того́, с кем смогу́ говори́ть и ла́дить в ста́рости. ♦ **You and I don't seem to get along very well anymore.** Ты и я, похо́же, не о́чень хорошо́ ла́дим друг с дру́гом после́днее вре́мя.

get anywhere:

I just can't (seem to) get anywhere with you. Я так и не могу́ (, ка́жется,) доби́ться у тебя́ успе́ха.

get back: *contact later*

I'll get back to you *(1)* **...later.** / *(2)* **...tomorrow.** / *(3)* **...as soon as I can.** Я позвоню́ тебе́ опя́ть *(1)* ...поздне́е. / *(2)* ...за́втра. / *(3)* ...сра́зу же как то́лько смогу́. ♦ *(1)* **When...** / *(2)* **How soon... can you get back to me?** *(1,2)* Когда́ ты смо́жешь позвони́ть мне опя́ть?

get back: *return*

When I get back, I'll call you. Когда́ верну́сь, я позвоню́ тебе́.

get enough of:

I can never get enough of you. Я никогда́ не смогу́ насы́титься тобо́й. ♦ **Whenever I think about your** *(1)* **gentle** / *(2)* **tender kisses and warm caresses, I realize why I can never get enough of you.** Когда́ я ду́маю о твои́х *(1,2)* не́жных поцелу́ях и тёплых ла́сках, я понима́ю почему́ никогда́ не могу́ насы́титься тобо́й.

get hold:

(1,2) **Get hold of yourself.** *(1)* Контроли́руй себя́. / *(2)* Держи́ себя́ в рука́х.

get into:

What has gotten into you? Что случи́лось с тобо́й? ♦ **I don't know what's gotten into me.** Я не зна́ю, что случи́лось со мной. ♦ **I don't let myself get into anybody very** *(1,2)* **heavily.** Я не позволя́ю себе́ быть втя́нутым *(ж: втя́нутой)* в о́чень *(1)* глубо́кие / *(2)* бли́зкие отноше́ния с кем-нибу́дь.

get my / your own way:

I'm used to getting my (own) way. Я привы́к *(ж: привы́кла)* идти́ мои́м со́бственным путём. ♦ **Do you think you can always get your own way?** Ты ду́маешь, что ты всегда́ смо́жешь идти́ свои́м со́бственным путём? ♦ **You seem to be one of these people that think they can always get their own way.** Ты, ка́жется, одна́ *(ж: один)* из тех люде́й, кото́рые ду́мают, что они́ мо́гут всегда́ идти́ свои́м со́бственным путём.

get off: *free oneself*

Would it be possible to meet you after you get off work? Мо́жно ли бу́дет встре́тить тебя́ по́сле рабо́ты? ♦ **I'll meet you after I get off work.** Я встре́чу тебя́ по́сле рабо́ты. ♦ **Would it be possible for you to get** *(1)* **...today** / *(2)* **tomorrow** *(3,4)* **off?** Смо́жешь ли ты получи́ть *(3)*...свобо́дный день... / *(4)* ...выходно́й... *(1)* сего́дня / *(2)* за́втра? ♦ **Would it be possible for you to get** *(1)* **two** / *(2)* **three days off?** Смо́жешь ли ты получи́ть *(1)* два / *(2)* три дня свобо́дные? ♦ **Would it be possible for you to get** *(1)* **...a week off?** / **...**(2) **two** / *(3)* **three weeks off?** Бу́дет ли возмо́жно для тебя́ получи́ть *(1)* ...свобо́дную неде́лю? / ...(2) две / *(3)* три неде́ли свобо́дные? ♦ **I can('t) get off** *(1)***..this** / *(2)* **tomorrow** *(3)* **afternoon** / *(4)* **evening.** Я (не) могу́ освободи́ться *(1+3)* ...сего́дня в по́лдень. / *(1+4)* ...сего́дня ве́чером. / *(2+3)* за́втра в по́лдень. / *(2+4)* ...за́втра ве́чером.

get off: *remove yourself*

(1-3) **Get off my back.** *(1)* Отвяжи́сь... / *(2)* Отцепи́сь... / *(3)* Отста́нь... от меня́.

[get out:]

Get out of here! Убира́йся отсю́да!

Depending on the subject, the possessive pronoun **свой** (**своя́, своё, свои́**) *can be translated* **my, your, his, her, its, our** *or* **their**.

get over:

I can't get over *(1)* **...how you've treated me.** / *(2)* **...our breakup.** / *(3)* **...what you said.** / *(4)* **...your leaving.** / *(5)* **...what has happened (between us).** Я не могу́ вы́нести *(1)* ...того́, как ты обраща́лась *(ж: обраща́лся)* со мной. / *(2)* ...на́шего разры́ва. / *(3)* ...того́, что ты сказа́ла *(ж: сказа́л).* / *(4)* ...твоего́ ухо́да. / *(5)* ...того́, что произошло́ (ме́жду на́ми). ♦ **I can never get over the wonder and ecstasy of your love.** Я никогда́ не смогу́ надиви́ться чу́ду и экста́зу твое́й любви́. ♦ **I'm (still) trying to get over an unhappy love affair.** Я (до сих пор) пыта́юсь опра́виться от неуда́чного рома́на. ♦ **You'll soon get over your shyness.** Ты ско́ро преодоле́ешь свою́ стесни́тельность.

[*get over with: finish*]

I want to get *(1)* **...it...** / *(2)* **...the divorce... over with.** Я хочу́ поко́нчить с *(1)* э́тим / *(2)* разво́дом.

get through:

How can I get through another *(1)* **day** / *(2)* **month** / *(3)* **week without you by my side. I cringe at the prospect.** Как могу́ я дожи́ть до *(1)* ...сле́дующего дня / *(2)* ме́сяца... / *(3)* ...сле́дующей неде́ли... без тебя́ ря́дом со мной. Я страшу́сь тако́й перспекти́вы.

get together:

Let's get together tomorrow for *(1)* **coffee** / *(2)* **lunch** / *(3)* **dinner.** Дава́й встре́тимся за́втра и вме́сте *(1)* ...вы́пьем ко́фе. / *(2)* ...пообе́даем. / *(3)* ...поу́жинаем. ♦ **The sooner we get together, the sooner we can realize our love and be happy.** Чем ра́ньше мы ока́жемся вме́сте, тем скоре́е мы смо́жем воплоти́ть на́шу любо́вь и быть сча́стливы.

getaway *n* 1. *(secluded place)* уединённое ме́сто; 2. *(trip)* пое́здка ♦ **adult** ~ уединённое ме́сто для взро́слых ♦ **lovers'** ~ уединённое ме́сто для любо́вников ♦ **weekend** ~ пое́здка на выходны́е (дни).

get-together *n* встре́ча ♦ **social** ~ встре́ча друзе́й.

GIB *abbrev* = **great in bed** о́чень хоро́ш *m* / хороша́ *f* в посте́ли.

giddiness *n* 1. *(dizziness)* головокруже́ние; 2. *(frivolity)* легкомы́слие, ве́треность *f.*

giddy *adj* 1. *(dizzy)* чу́вствующий (-ая, -ее, -ие) головокруже́ние; 2. *(frivolous)* легко-мы́сленный, -ая, -ое, -ые, ве́треный, -ая, -ое, -ые; 3. *(emotionally dizzy)* опьянённый, -ая, -ое, -ые ♦ **make** ~ опьяня́ть / опьяни́ть до головокруже́ния *(whom = acc.).*

gift *n* пода́рок *(pl:* пода́рки) ♦ **beautiful** ~ прекра́сный пода́рок ♦ **birthday** ~ пода́рок на день рожде́ния ♦ **Christmas** ~ рожде́ственский пода́рок ♦ **expensive** ~ дорого́й пода́рок ♦ **~ of fate** пода́рок судьбы́ ♦ **humble** ~ скро́мный пода́рок ♦ **love** ~ пода́рок в знак любви́ ♦ **lovely** ~ краси́вый пода́рок ♦ **New Year's** ~ нового́дний пода́рок ♦ **nice** ~ хоро́ший пода́рок ♦ **precious** ~ драгоце́нный пода́рок ♦ **small** ~ ма́ленький пода́рок ♦ **wedding** ~ сва́дебный пода́рок ♦ *(1,2)* **wonderful** ~ *(1)* замеча́тельный / *(2)* удиви́тельный пода́рок.

gift: verb terms

bring you a ~ приноси́ть / принести́ тебе́ пода́рок ♦ **buy you a** ~ покупа́ть / купи́ть тебе́ пода́рок ♦ **give you a** ~ де́лать / сде́лать тебе́ пода́рок ♦ **send you a** ~ посыла́ть / посла́ть тебе́ пода́рок.

gift: phrases

You are the biggest (, most precious) gift in my life. Ты са́мый большо́й (, са́мый драго-це́нный) пода́рок в мое́й жи́зни. ♦ **Having** *(1)* **...you in my life...** / *(2)* **...your love... is the greatest, most wonderful gift that God could give me.** *(1)* Ты... / *(2)* Твоя́ любо́вь... -- э́то са́мый лу́чший, са́мый удиви́тельный пода́рок, кото́рый я получи́л *(ж: получи́ла)* от Бо́га. ♦ **Please accept this** *(1)* **small** / *(2)* **humble gift.** Пожа́луйста, прими́ э́тот *(1)* ма́ленький / *(2)* скро́мный пода́рок. ♦ **I want to give you a small gift.** Я хочу́

The time zones for many cities of the world are given in Appendix 6, page 761.

(1) ма́ленький / *(2)* скро́мный пода́рок. ♦ **I want to give you a small gift.** Я хочу́ вручи́ть тебе́ ма́ленький пода́рок. ♦ **Thank you for the** *([1]* **beautiful** / *[2]* **lovely** / *[3]* **wonderful** / *[4]* **nice) gift.** Спаси́бо за *([1]* прекра́сный / *[2]* краси́вый / *[3]* замеча́тельный / *[4]* хоро́ший) пода́рок. ♦ **I'm sorry, I can't accept the gift.** Извини́те, я не могу́ приня́ть э́тот пода́рок. ♦ **You are the most precious gift any man could ever have.** Ты са́мый драгоце́нный пода́рок для любо́го мужчи́ны. ♦ **Here's a small gift for my special lady.** Это ма́ленький пода́рок для дорого́й мне же́нщины. ♦ **I'm not God's gift to women (by any means).** Я (нико́им о́бразом) не Бо́жий дар для же́нщин.

gifted *adj* одарённый, -ая, -ое, -ые ♦ **intellectually** ~ интеллектуа́льно одарённый, -ая, -ое, -ые.

giggle *vi* хихи́кать.

gigolo *n* альфо́нс.

gin *n* джин.

girl *n* 1. де́вушка; *(child)* де́вочка; 2. *(girlfriend)* подру́га, возлю́бленная ♦ **adult** ~ взро́слая де́вушка ♦ *(1-3)* **attractive** ~ *(1)* симпати́чная / *(2)* привлека́тельная / *(3)* интере́сная де́вушка ♦ **bashful** ~ засте́нчивая де́вушка ♦ **beautiful** ~ краси́вая де́вушка ♦ **black-haired** ~ де́вушка с чёрными волоса́ми ♦ **blond** ~ белоку́рая де́вушка, блонди́нка ♦ **blossoming** ~ цвету́щая де́вушка ♦ **blue-eyed** ~ голубогла́зая де́вушка, де́вушка с голубы́ми глаза́ми ♦ **capable** ~ спосо́бная де́вушка ♦ **caring** ~ забо́тливая де́вушка ♦ *(1-3)* **charming** ~ *(1)* обая́тельная / *(2)* очарова́тельная / *(3)* преле́стная де́вушка ♦ **cheerful** ~ весёлая де́вушка ♦ **cherry** ~ *(slang) (virgin)* де́вственница ♦ **chubby** ~ пы́шка ♦ **compassionate** ~ чу́ткая де́вушка ♦ **considerate** ~ внима́тельная де́вушка ♦ **country** ~ дереве́нская де́вушка ♦ **down-to-earth** ~ проста́я де́вушка ♦ **fair-haired** ~ белоку́рая де́вушка ♦ **fashion-conscious** ~ мо́дная де́вушка ♦ **fawn-eyed** ~ оленегла́зая де́вушка ♦ **flighty** ~ легкомы́сленная де́вушка ♦ **flirtatious** ~ коке́тливая де́вушка ♦ **flirty** ~ коке́тливая де́вушка ♦ **flower** ~ *(at a wedding)* цвето́чница, де́вочка с цвета́ми *(на сва́дьбе)* ♦ ~ **of medium height** де́вушка сре́днего ро́ста ♦ ~ **of my dreams** де́вушка мое́й мечты́ ♦ ~ **with light brown hair** ру́сая де́вушка ♦ **good** ~ хоро́шая де́вушка ♦ *(1-3)* **good-looking** ~ *(1)* симпати́чная / *(2)* привлека́тельная / *(3)* интере́сная де́вушка ♦ **graceful** ~ грацио́зная де́вушка ♦ **gregarious** ~ общи́тельная де́вушка ♦ **grey-eyed** ~ серогла́зая де́вушка ♦ **grownup** ~ взро́слая де́вушка ♦ **hardworking** ~ трудолюби́вая де́вушка ♦ **heavy(set)** ~ по́лная де́вушка ♦ *(1,2)* **hip** ~ *(1)* осведомлённая / *(2)* зна́ющая девушка ♦ **impressionable** ~ впечатли́вая де́вушка ♦ **indi(e)** ~ *(independent girl)* незави́симая де́вушка ♦ **industrious** ~ трудолюби́вая де́вушка ♦ **innocent** ~ неви́нная де́вушка ♦ **intelligent** ~ у́мная де́вушка ♦ **kind-hearted** ~ отзы́вчивая де́вушка ♦ **lovely** ~ краси́вая де́вушка ♦ **modern** ~ совреме́нная де́вушка ♦ **modest** ~ скро́мница, скро́мная де́вушка ♦ **my** ~ *(girlfriend)* моя́ подру́га, моя́ возлю́бленная ♦ **naive** ~ наи́вная де́вушка ♦ **naughty** ~ испо́рченная де́вушка; неприли́чная де́вушка ♦ **nice** ~ 1. *(pleasant)* прия́тная де́вушка; 2. *(up standing)* поря́дочная де́вушка ♦ **nice, refined** ~ ми́лая, воспи́танная де́вушка ♦ **ordinary** ~ обыкнове́нная де́вушка ♦ **pinup** ~ краси́вая де́вушка, «карти́нка» ♦ **plump** ~ пы́шка, по́лная де́вушка ♦ **poor** ~ бе́дная де́вушка ♦ *(1,2)* **pretty** ~ *(1)* хоро́шенькая / *(2)* милови́дная де́вушка ♦ **proud** ~ 1. го́рдая де́вушка; 2. *(vain)* самолюби́вая де́вушка ♦ **quiet** ~ ти́хая де́вушка ♦ **red-haired** ~ де́вушка с ры́жими волоса́ми ♦ **refined** ~ культу́рная де́вушка ♦ **regular** ~ обы́чная де́вушка ♦ **right** ~ подходя́щая де́вушка ♦ **rosy-cheeked** ~ краснощёкая де́вушка ♦ **serious** ~ серьёзная де́вушка ♦ **shapely** ~ ста́тная де́вушка ♦ **short** ~ невысо́кая де́вушка ♦ **shy** ~ засте́нчивая де́вушка ♦ **skinny** ~ ху́денькая де́вушка ♦ **slender** ~ стро́йная де́вушка ♦ **slim**

Optional parts of sentences are preceded
or followed (or both) by three dots.

~ то́ненькая де́вушка ♦ **smart** ~ у́мная де́вушка ♦ **strapping** ~ ро́слая де́вушка ♦ **stylish** ~ мо́дная де́вушка ♦ **suntanned** ~ загоре́лая де́вушка ♦ **sweet** ~ ми́лая де́вушка ♦ **tall** ~ высо́кая де́вушка ♦ *(1,2)* **thin** ~ *(1)* худа́я / *(2)* то́ненькая де́вушка ♦ **thoughtful** ~ внима́тельная де́вушка ♦ **timid** ~ ро́бкая де́вушка ♦ **transition** ~ *(girl between relationships)* де́вушка, то́лько что поко́нчившая с отноше́ниями *(explanation)* ♦ **trusting** ~ дове́рчивая де́вушка ♦ **ultimate** ~ превосхо́дная де́вушка ♦ **unattractive** ~ некраси́вая де́вушка ♦ **uninhibited** ~ де́вушка без ко́мплексов ♦ **village** ~ дереве́нская де́вушка ♦ *(1,2)* **vivacious** ~ *(1)* жива́я / *(2)* жизнера́достная де́вушка ♦ **wholesome** ~ 1. *(good character)* здравомы́слящая де́вушка; 2. *(robust)* цвету́щая де́вушка ♦ **young** ~ ю́ная де́вушка; *(early teens)* моло́денькая де́вушка ♦ **zaftig** ~ *(luscious girl)* со́чная де́вушка.

girl: phrases

I'm looking for the girl next door. Я ищу́ здравомы́слящую де́вушку. ♦ **They say that girls are made of sugar and spice and everything nice. Is that true of you?** Говоря́т, что де́вушки сде́ланы из са́хара и пря́ностей и из всего́ прекра́сного. Подхо́дит ли э́то к тебе́?

girlfriend *n* подру́га, возлю́бленная, «де́вушка» ♦ **ex-girlfriend** бы́вшая возлю́бленная ♦ **former** ~ бы́вшая возлю́бленная ♦ **last** ~ после́дняя возлю́бленная ♦ **no current** *(1,2)* ~ *(personal ads)* нет *(1)* подру́ги / *(2)* возлю́бленной сейча́с ♦ **previous** ~ предыду́щая возлю́бленная **Do you have a girlfriend?** У тебя́ есть возлю́бленная? ♦ **I don't have any girlfriend.** У меня́ нет возлю́бленной.

girlish *adj* деви́чий, деви́чья, -е, -и ♦ **You (still) have a girlish figure.** У тебя́ (до сих пор) деви́чья фигу́ра.

girth *n (circumference)* обхва́т.

give *vt* дава́ть / дать *(what = acc., to whom = dat.)*; отдава́ть / отда́ть *(what = acc., to whom = dat.)* ♦ ~ **in** *vi* отдава́ться / отда́ться *(to what, whom = dat.)* ♦ ~ **up** *vt (relinquish)* отка́зываться / отказа́ться *(what, whom = + от + gen.)*. ♦ ~ **way** уступа́ть / уступи́ть ме́сто *(to what, whom = dat.)*.

give: phrases

Thank you for everything you give me. Спаси́бо тебе́ за всё, что ты даёшь мне. ♦ **I have so much to give (to the right** *[1]* **man /** *[2]* **woman /** *[3]* **person).** Я так мно́го мог *(ж: могла́)* бы дать (*[1]* ...подходя́щей же́нщине. / *[2]* подходя́щему мужчи́не / *[3]* челове́ку.). ♦ **I can hardly wait to look at you gloriously naked, ready to give yourself to me.** Я не могу́ дожда́ться того́ мгнове́ния, когда́ уви́жу твоё прекра́сное те́ло обнажённым, гото́вым отда́ть себя́ мне. ♦ **When you give yourself to me, you're going to be rewarded with more pleasure than you ever dreamed of.** Когда́ ты отда́шься мне, ты бу́дешь вознаграждена́ таки́м наслажде́нием, о кото́ром не могла́ да́же мечта́ть. ♦ **In a relationship you have to give something of yourself.** Во взаимоотноше́ниях ты до́лжен отдава́ть части́цу себя́.

give in:

Just give in to your feelings. Про́сто отда́йся свои́м чу́вствам.

give up:

I don't want to give you up. Я не могу́ отказа́ться от тебя́.

giver *n* даю́щий *m*, даю́щая *f* ♦ **I'm a giver, not a taker.** Я даю́щий *(ж: даю́щая)*, а не беру́щий *(ж: беру́щая)*.

giving *adj* ще́дрый, -ая, -ое, -ые ♦ **You are a very giving person.** Ты о́чень ще́дрый челове́к.

glamo(u)r *n* очарова́ние, волшебство́; шик ♦ **I've never** *(1)* **seen /** *(2)* **encountered such**

If you're not on familiar terms with a person,
the «ты» forms will have to be changed to «Вы».

intense glamour as you *(3)* **have** / *(4)* **project.** Я никогда́ не *(1)* ви́дел / *(2)* встреча́л тако́го очарова́ния, кото́рое *(3)* ...есть в тебе́. / *(4)* ...ты излуча́ешь.

glamo(u)rous *adj* очарова́тельный, -ая, -ое, -ые; обольсти́тельный, -ая, -ое, -ые; шика́р-ный, -ая, -ое, -ые.

glance *n* взгляд ♦ **admiring** ~ любу́ющийся взгляд ♦ **bashful** ~ засте́нчивый взгляд ♦ **quick** ~ бы́стрый взгляд ♦ **sexy** ~ сексуа́льный взгляд ♦ **sidelong** ~ косо́й взгляд ♦ **wistful** ~ мечта́тельный взгляд ♦ **catch** *(1)* **your** / *(2)* **my** ~ пойма́ть *(1)* твой / *(2)* мой взгляд ♦ **Your every glance has such a powerful effect on my senses.** Ка́ждый твой взгляд так си́льно возде́йствует на мои́ чу́вства.

glass *n* стака́н ♦ **liquor** ~ рю́мка ♦ **shot** ~ рю́м(оч)ка ♦ **wine** ~ бока́л.

glasses *n, pl* очки́ ♦ **tinted** ~s цветны́е очки́ ♦ **I wear glasses.** Я ношу́ очки́.

glide *vi* скользи́ть ♦ **My fingertips will glide over your body, scattering delicious pleasure in their path.** Ко́нчики мои́х па́льцев бу́дут скользи́ть по твоему́ те́лу, рассе́ивая восхити́тельное наслажде́ние на своём пути́. ♦ **I like the way you glide so softly across a room.** Мне нра́вится, как мя́гко ты скользи́шь по ко́мнате.

glimpse *n (fleeting impression)* мимолётное впечатле́ние; *(quick look)* бы́стрый взгляд ♦ **fleeting** ~ мимолётный взгляд ♦ **catch a** ~ взгляну́ть одни́м глазко́м, уви́деть мелько́м.

glisten *vi* блесте́ть, сверка́ть.

glistening *adj* блестя́щий, -ая, -ее, -ие, сверка́ющий, -ая, -ее, -ие.

glitter *vi* блесте́ть ♦ **I want your eyes always to glitter with joy.** Я хочу́, что́бы твои́ глаза́ всегда́ блесте́ли от ра́дости.

glitter *n* блеск.

globe *n* гло́бус; шар ♦ **silky** ~s шелкови́стые окру́глости ♦ **soft** ~s мя́гкие окру́глости ♦ **I love to** *(1)* **hold** / *(2)* **kiss** / *(3)* **squeeze the rounded globes of your breasts.** Я люблю́ *(1)* держа́ть / *(2)* целова́ть / *(3)* сжима́ть окру́глые шары́ твои́х груде́й.

glorious *adj* великоле́пный, -ая, -ое, -ые, чуде́сный, -ая, -ое, -ые, прекра́сный, -ая, -ое, -ые, восхити́тельный, -ая, -ое, -ые.

gloss *n* 1. блеск; 2. блеск для губ ♦ **coral lip** ~ кора́лловый блеск для губ ♦ **lip** ~ блеск для губ.

glossy *adj (hair)* блестящие *pl.*

glove *n* перча́тка ♦ **pair of** ~s па́ра перча́ток.

glow *vi* свети́ться; сверка́ть ♦ ~ **with happiness** сверка́ть ра́достью.

glow *n* 1. о́тблеск, за́рево; 2. румя́нец ♦ **Your skin has such a natural glow.** На твое́й ко́же тако́й натура́льный румя́нец.

glower *vi* серди́то смотре́ть / посмотре́ть.

glowing *adj (radiant)* сия́ющий, -ая, -ее, -ие..

glow-in-the-dark *adj* светя́щийся (-аяся, -ееся, -иеся) в темноте́.

glue *n* клей ♦ **I'm going to stick to you like glue.** Я собира́юсь прили́пнуть к тебе́, как клей.

glum *adj* мра́чный, -ая, -ое, -ые.

glumness *n* мра́чность *f.*

gnaw *vi* 1. *(chew on)* грызть *(what = acc.)*; 2. *(torment)* му́чить *(what = acc.)* ♦ **I've had a lot of doubt gnawing at my mind.** У меня́ бы́ло мно́жество сомне́ний, му́чающих меня́. ♦ **The suspicion has been gnawing at my mind for some time now that you've got someone else.** Подозре́ние, что у тебя́ есть кто́-то ещё, му́чает меня́ уже́ дово́льно давно́.

go *vi* ходи́ть *(on foot - repeated)*, идти́ / пойти́ *(on foot - one direction)*; е́здить *(by veh. -*

A list of common places with their grammatical endings is given in Appendix 7, page 763.

repeated) , éхать / поéхать *(by veh. - one direction)*; *(head)* отправля́ться / отпра́виться.

| go: idioms |

~ all the way занима́ться / заня́ться сéксом ♦ **~ down** *vi (slang) (have oral sex)* занима́ться / заня́ться ора́льным сéксом *(on whom = + с + instr.)* ♦ **~ in for** *(s.th.)* *vi* занима́ться *(for what = instr.)* ♦ **~ on** 1. *(continue)* продолжа́ть / продо́лжить, 2. *(happen)* происходи́ть / произойти́, случа́ться / случи́ться ♦ **~ out** *vi (on a date)* пойти́ куда́-нибудь.

| go: can / can't go |

Can you *(1,2)* **go (with me)?** Мо́жешь ты *(1)* пойти́ *(on foot)* / *(2)* поéхать *(by veh.)* (со мной)? ♦ **I can('t)** *(1,2)* **go (with you).** Я (не) могу́ *(1)* пойти́ *(on foot)* / *(2)* поéхать *(by veh.)* (с тобо́й). ♦ **May I** *(1,2)* **go with you?** Мо́жно я пойду́ / поéду с тобо́й? ♦ **Yes, you may** *(1,2)* **go with me.** Да, ты мо́жешь *(1)* пойти́ *(on foot)* / *(2)* поéхать *(by veh.)* со мной. ♦ **No, you can't** *(1,2)* **go with me.** Нет, ты не мо́жешь *(1)* пойти́ *(on foot)* / *(2)* поéхать *(by veh.)* со мной. ♦ **(Please)** *(1,2)* **go with me.** (Пожа́луйста), *(1)* пойдём *(on foot)* / *(2)* поéдем *(by veh.)* со мной.

| go: where? |

Where are you *(1,2)* **going?** Куда́ ты *(1)* идёшь *(on foot)* / *(2)* éдешь *(by veh.)*? ♦ **I'm** *(1,2)* **going** *(3)* **...to the market** / *(4)* **beach** / *(5)* **store** / *(6)* **university** / *(7)* **park.** / *(8)* **...to work** / *(9)* **school.** / *(10)* **...to a friend's house.** /*(11)* **...to a movie** / *(12)* **play** / *(13)* **concert** / *(14)* **party.** / *(15)* **...home.** Я *(1)* *(on foot:)* иду́ / *(2)* *(by veh.:)* éду *(3)* ...на ры́нок / *(4)* пляж. / *(5)* ...в магази́н / *(6)* университéт / *(7)* парк. / *(8)* ...на рабо́ту. / *(9)* ...в шко́лу. / *(10)* ...в дом моего́ дру́га. / *(11)* ...в кино́ / *(12)* теа́тр. / *(13)* ...на концéрт / *(14)* вечери́нку. / *(15)* ...домо́й.

| go: will / will not |

I will (not) *(1,2)* **go (there).** Я (не) *(1)* пойду́ *(on foot)* / *(2)* поéду *(by veh.)* (туда́). ♦ **I'm (not)** *(1,2)* **going to go (there).** Я (не) *(1)* пойду́ *(on foot)* / *(2)* поéду *(by veh.)* (туда́). ♦ **Whither thou goest I will go.** Куда́ бы ты ни пошла́ *(ж: пошёл)*, я пойду́ за тобо́й.

| go: have to / don't have to |

I (don't) have to *(1,2)* **go (** *[3]* **...home.** / *[4]* **...to work** / *[5]* **school).** Мне (не) на́до *(1)* пойти́ *(on foot)* / *(2)* поéхать *(by veh.)* (*[3]* ...домо́й. / *[4]* ...на рабо́ту. / *[5]* ...в шко́лу). ♦ **I must go.** *(1)* Я до́лжен *(ж: должна́)* пойти́ *(on foot)* / *(2)* поéхать *(by veh.)*.

| go: go too far |

This has gone too far. Это зашло́ сли́шком далеко́. ♦ *(love:)* **I don't want to go too far.** Я не хочу́ заходи́ть сли́шком далеко́. *(в отношéниях)*

| go: let go |

Don't be so inhibited. Let yourself go. Не будь тако́й сдéржанной *(ж: таки́м сдéр-жанным)*. Дай себé во́лю. ♦ **Let me go.** Отпусти́ меня́. ♦ **Let go of** *(1)* **...me!** / *(2)* **...of my arm!** Отпусти́ *(1)* ...меня́! / *(2)* ...мою́ ру́ку!

| go all the way: |

I don't want to go all the way with you. At least, not yet. Я не хочу́ занима́ться сéксом с тобо́й. По кра́йней мéре, не сейча́с. ♦ **I really want to go all the way with you.** Я действи́тельно хочу́ занима́ться сéксом с тобо́й. ♦ **I don't think it's a good idea to go all the way with someone before marriage.** Я не ду́маю, что э́то хоро́шая идéя занима́ться сéксом с кéм-либо до бра́ка. ♦ **Please don't try to push me into going all the way with you.** Пожа́луйста, не пыта́йся наста́ивать на том, что́бы я занима́лась с тобо́й любо́вью.

| go in for: |

I don't go in for such things. Я не занима́юсь таки́ми дела́ми.

Common adult heights are given in Appendix 9, page 776.

go on:

There's a party going on at *(1)* our / *(2)* their / *(3)* his / *(4)* her place. У *(1)* нас / *(2)* них / *(3)* него / *(4)* неё вечеринка. ♦ I think something is going on between you two. Я думаю, что-то происходит между вами двумя. ♦ I swear, nothing is going on between us. Я клянусь, ничего не происходит между нами.

go out:

I'd like (very much) to go out with you sometime. How about *(1)* ...this evening? / *(2)* ...tomorrow (evening)? / *(3)* ... next Saturday? / *(4)* ...in five minutes? Я (очень) хотел бы однажды пойти куда-нибудь с тобой. Может быть, *(1)* ...этим вечером? / *(2)* ...завтра (вечером)? / *(3)* ...в следующую субботу? / *(4)* ...через пять минут? ♦ I have a small confession to make: I've wanted to go out with you ever since I met you. Я должен *(ж:должна)* сделать маленькое признание: Я хотел *(ж: хотела)* пойти вместе с тобой куда-нибудь, как только я встретил *(ж: встретила)* тебя. ♦ (How) would you like to go out to dinner with me *(1)* ...this evening? / *(2)* ...tomorrow (evening)? / *(3)* ... next Saturday? Не хотела бы ты пообедать со мной *(1)* ...сегодня вечером? / *(2)* ...завтра (вечером)? / *(3)* ...в следующую субботу? ♦ Let's (you and I) go out to dinner *(1)* ...this evening. / *(2)* ...tomorrow (evening). / *(3)* ...next Saturday. Давай (ты и я) поужинаем *(1)* ...сегодня вечером. / *(2)* ...завтра (вечером). / *(3)* ...в следующую субботу. ♦ Let's not go out tonight. Let's just stay here and *(1)* ...cuddle up together. / *(2)* ...make love. Давай никуда не пойдём сегодня вечером. Давай просто останемся здесь и *(1)* ...прижмёмся друг к другу. / *(2)* ...займёмся любовью.

go through with:

Do you want to go through with the wedding? Ты хочешь замуж *(ж: жениться)*? ♦ I (don't) want to go through with the wedding. Я (не) хочу жениться *(ж: замуж)*.

go *n (try)* попытка ♦ **give it a ~** попытаться ♦ **give it another ~** попытаться ещё раз.

goal *n* цель *f* ♦ To *(1)* have / *(2)* win your *(3)* precious / *(4)* wonderful love is the greatest goal I can aspire to. *(1,2)* Заслужить твою *(3)* драгоценную / *(4)* удивительную любовь - величайшая цель, к которой я стремлюсь.

goal-oriented *adj* целеустремлённый, -ая, -ое, -ые.

goatee *n* козлиная бородка ♦ **red ~** рыжая козлиная бородка.

God; god *n* 1. *(God)* Бог; 2. *(other)* бог ♦ **nectar of the ~s** божественный нектар ♦ I am so grateful to God for bringing us together. Я так благодарен Богу за то, что он соединил нас вместе. ♦ I thank God for *(1)* ...bringing you into my life. / *(2)* ...blessing me with your love. Я благодарю Бога за то, что он *(1)* ...послал тебя в мою жизнь. / *(2)* ...благословил меня твоей любовью. ♦ You are the most wonderful person that God could ever have brought into my life. Ты самый замечательный человек, которого Бог мог бы когда-либо послать в мою жизнь.

goddess *n* богиня ♦ **beautiful ~** прекрасная богиня ♦ **blonde ~** светловолосая богиня ♦ **love ~** богиня любви ♦ You are my goddess of love. Ты моя богиня любви. ♦ My beautiful, blond-haired goddess. Моя прекрасная, светловолосая богиня.

goer: ♦ **film ~** любитель ходить в кино.

go-getter *n* энергичный, предприимчивый человек *(1 term)*.

gold *adj* золотой, -ая, -ое, -ые.

gold *n* золото ♦ **thick silken ~** *(hair)* густое шелковистое золото *(волос)*.

golden *adj* золотой, -ая, -ое, -ые; *(incl. hair)* золотистый, -ая, -ое, -ые, отливающий (-ая, -ее, -ие) золотом.

gold-digger *n (slang) (No equivalent word in Russian. Explanation:)* человек, вытягивающий деньги у *(1)* любовника *m* / *(2)* любовницы *f*.

Words in parentheses are optional.

golden-haired *adj* златовла́сый, -ая, -ое, -ые, златоку́дрый, -ая, -ое, -ые.

golden-skinned *adj* золотистоко́жий, -ая, -ее, -ие, с золоти́стой ко́жей.

golf *vi* игра́ть в гольф ♦ **I like to golf occasionally.** Мне нра́вится, и́зредка игра́ть в гольф.

golf *n* гольф ♦ **Would you like to play golf (with me)?** Не хоте́ла *(ж: хоте́л)* бы ты сыгра́ть в гольф (со мной)? ♦ **Come on, I'll teach you how to play golf.** Дава́й, я бу́ду учи́ть тебя́ игра́ть в гольф.

golfer *n* игро́к в гольф ♦ **avid** ~ стра́стный игро́к в гольф.

golfing *n* игра́ в гольф.

gone: ♦ **I feel such a terrible hollowness with you gone.** Я чу́вствую таку́ю ужа́сную пустоту́ по́сле твоего́ отъе́зда.

good *adj* 1. *(general)* хоро́ший, -ая, -ее, -ие; 2. *(kind, nice)* до́брый, -ая, -ое, -ые; 3. *(good at) (with* к + *dat.)* спосо́бен, спосо́бна, -ы *(short forms)* ♦ **pretty** ~ неплохо́й, -а́я, -о́е, -и́е ♦ **That was so good!** Это бы́ло так хорошо́! ♦ **You are so good.** Ты така́я хоро́шая. *(ж: Ты тако́й хоро́ший.).* ♦ **No one is as good as you are.** Ты лу́чше всех. ♦ **You're a good** *(1)* **man** / *(2)* **person.** Ты хоро́ший *(1)* мужчи́на / *(2)* челове́к. ♦ **You're a good woman.** Ты хоро́шая же́нщина. ♦ *(1)* **It's...** / *(2)* **It was... so good** *(3)* **...to see you (again).** / *(4)* **...to hear from you (again).** *(1)* Так хорошо́... / *(2)* Бы́ло так хорошо́... *(3)* ...уви́деть тебя́ (опя́ть). / *(4)* ...услы́шать тебя́ (опя́ть). ♦ **You are so good and sweet and thoughtful and caring and loving.** Ты така́я хоро́шая *(ж: тако́й хоро́ший)*, не́жная *(ж: не́жный)*, внима́тельная *(ж: внима́тельный)*, забо́тливая *(ж: забо́тливый)* и любя́щая *(ж: любя́щий)*. ♦ **You're the best.** Ты лу́чше всех. ♦ **When I look at you, I see everything good and beautiful in the world.** Когда́ я смотрю́ на тебя́, я ви́жу всё хоро́шее и прекра́сное в ми́ре. ♦ **I (don't) feel good about myself.** Я (не) дово́лен *(ж: дово́льна)* собо́й. ♦ **It's important to feel good about yourself.** Ва́жно быть дово́льным собо́й.

goodbye *n* проща́ние ♦ **We said our goodbyes.** Мы сказа́ли на́ше «проща́й». ♦ **I think it's time we said our goodbyes.** Я ду́маю, вре́мя для нас сказа́ть «проща́й».

Goodbye! *int (1,2:)* *(1)* До свида́ния! / *(2)* Проща́й!

good-hearted *adj* добросерде́чный, -ая, -ое, -ые.

good-heartedness *n* добросерде́чность *f* ♦ **No one in this whole world can ever surpass you in good-heartedness.** Никто́ на всём све́те не смо́жет превзойти́ тебя́ в добросерде́чности. ♦ **You nourish my soul with your good-heartedness.** Ты пита́ешь мою́ ду́шу свое́й добросерде́чностью. ♦ **My heart yearns so fiercely to have a partner like you in life, one who combines a gentle spirit with sexuality, good-heartedness, intelligence, and a loving nature.** Моё се́рдце так неи́стово жа́ждет тако́го спу́тника жи́зни, как ты, тако́го, кто соединя́ет мя́гкий хара́ктер с сексуа́льностью, добросерде́чием, интеллиге́нтностью и любя́щей нату́рой.

good-looking *adj (male or female)* краси́вый, -ая, -ое, -ые, интере́сный, -ая, -ое, -ые, привлека́тельный -ая, -ое, -ые; *(female only)* хоро́шенькая, -ие, симпати́чная, -ые, миловидная, -ые, смазли́вая, -ые *f*, хороша́ собо́й ♦ **awfully** ~ черто́вски привлека́тельный *m*, -ая *f* ♦ **exceptionally** ~ исключи́тельно привлека́тельный *m*, -ая *f* ♦ **extraordinarily** ~ чрезвыча́йно привлека́тельный *m*, -ая *f* ♦ **terribly** ~ черто́вски привлека́тельный *m*, -ая *f* ♦ **uncommonly** ~ необыкнове́нно привлека́тельный *m*, -ая *f* ♦ **unusually** ~ необыкнове́нно привлека́тельный *m*, -ая *f* ♦ **very** ~ о́чень привлека́тельный *m*, -ая *f*.

---
good-looking: phrases

You're a very *(1-3)* **good-looking** *(4)* **woman** / *(5)* **girl.** Ты о́чень *(1)* краси́вая / *(2)* привлека́тельная / *(3)* интере́сная *(4)* же́нщина / *(5)* де́вушка. ♦ **You're the** *(1-3)* **best-**

You can find common clothing sizes in Appendix 11 on page 778.

looking *(4)* **woman** / *(5)* **girl** *(6)* **...here.** / *(7)* **...in this whole place.** / *(8)* **...in the room.** / *(9)* **...I know.** / *(10)* **...I've ever met.** Ты са́мая *(1)* краси́вая / *(2)* привлека́тельная / *(3)* интере́сная *(4)* же́нщина / *(5)* де́вушка *(6,7)* ...здесь. / *(8)* ...в э́той ко́мнате. / *(9)* ..., кото́рую я зна́ю. / *(10)* ...из всех, встре́ченных мной. ♦ **You're a very** *(1-3)* **good-looking** *(4)* **guy** / *(5)* **man.** Ты о́чень *(1)* краси́вый / *(2)* привлека́тельный / *(3)* интере́с-ный *(4)* па́рень / *(5)* мужчи́на. ♦ **You're the** *(1,2)* **best-looking** *(3)* **guy** / *(4)* **man** *(5)* **...here.** / *(6)* **...in this whole place.** / *(7)* **...in the room.** / *(8)* **...I know.** / *(9)* **...I've ever met.** Ты са́мый *(1)* краси́вый / *(2)* привлека́тельный *(3)* па́рень / *(4)* мужчи́на *(5,6)* ...здесь. / *(7)* ...в э́той ко́мнате. / *(8)* ..., кото́рого я зна́ю. / *(9)* ...из всех, встре́ченных мной. ♦ **To say that you're (exceptionally)** *(1,2)* **good-looking is a** *(3)* **gross** / *(4)* **huge under-statement.** Сказа́ть, что ты (исключи́тельно) *(1)* краси́ва *(ж: краси́в)* / *(2)* привлека́-тельна *(ж: привлека́телен)* - э́то *(3)* большо́е / *(4)* огро́мное преуменьше́ние. ♦ **I don't care what your age is, you are still** *(1)* **exceptionally** / *(2)* **extraordinarily** / *(3)* **very** *(4-6)* **good-looking.** Меня́ не волну́ет твой во́зраст, ты всё ещё *(1)* исключи́тельно / *(2)* чрезвыча́йно / *(3)* о́чень *(4)* интере́сна *(ж: интере́сен)* / *(5)* привлека́тельна *(ж: привлека́телен)* / *(6)* краси́ва *(ж: краси́в)*. ♦ **You're far from being plain. You're** *(1)* **very** / *(2)* **extremely** *(3,4)* **good-looking.** Ты совсе́м не некраси́ва *(ж: некраси́в)*. Ты *(1)* о́чень / *(2)* исключи́тельно *(3)* привлека́тельна *(ж: привлека́телен)* / *(4)* краси́ва *(ж: краси́в)*. ♦ **I've been told that I'm good-looking.** Мне говоря́т, что я привлека́телен *(ж: привлека́тельна)*. ♦ **I consider myself good-looking.** Я счита́ю себя́ привлека́-тельным *(ж: привлека́тельной)*.

good-natured *adj* доброду́шный, -ая, -ое, -ые ♦ **indolently** ~ лени́во доброду́шный.

goodness *n* доброта́, любе́зность *f*, великоду́шие ♦ **You have so much goodness in you.** В тебе́ так мно́го доброты́. ♦ **I've never met a person with as much goodness in their heart as you have.** Я никогда́ не встреча́л *(ж: встреча́ла)* челове́ка с тако́й доброто́й в се́рдце, как у тебя́. ♦ **When I read your letters, I feel with my heart how much goodness and sweetness and love there is in you.** Когда́ я чита́ю твои́ пи́сьма, всем се́рдцем чу́вствую, как мно́го в тебе́ доброты́, не́жности и любви́. ♦ **Your sweet, pure goodness pulls me irresistibly to you.** Твоя́ не́жная, чи́стая доброта́ притя́гивает меня́ к тебе́ непреодоли́мо.

goofy *adj (slang)* глу́пый, -ая, -ое, -ые, бестолко́вый, -ая, -ое, -ые.

gorgeous *adj (magnificent)* великоле́пный, -ая, -ое, -ые, превосхо́дный, -ая, -ое, -ые; *(beautiful)* прекра́сный, -ая, -ое, -ые ♦ **drop-dead** ~ сногсшиба́тельная ♦ **exotically** ~ экзоти́чески краси́вая, -ые ♦ **You are** *(1)* **absolutely** / *(2)* **positively gorgeous.** Ты *(1)* абсолю́тно / *(2)* про́сто прекра́сна.

gorgeously *adv (magnificently)* великоле́пно, превосхо́дно; *(beautifully)* прекра́сно.

gossip *vi* спле́тничать.

gossip *n* слух, спле́тня *(often pl: спле́тни)* ♦ **cruel** ~ жесто́кая спле́тня ♦ *(1,2)* **malicious** ~ *(1)* зло́бная / *(2)* злонаме́ренная спле́тня ♦ *(1,2)* **mindless** ~ *(1)* глу́пая / *(2)* бес-смы́сленная спле́тня ♦ **ridiculous** ~ неле́пая спле́тня ♦ **vicious** ~ зло́стная спле́тня ♦ **That's malicious gossip.** Это злонаме́ренная спле́тня.

gothboy *n (slang) (boy caught up in gothic culture)* па́рень, кото́рый увлека́ется го́тской культу́рой *(explanation)*.

Gothic, gothic *adj* го́тский, -ая, -ое, -ие.

gourmand *n* гурма́н.

gown *n* (вече́рнее) пла́тье ♦ **beautiful** ~ краси́вое пла́тье ♦ **backless** ~ вече́рнее пла́тье с откры́той спино́й ♦ **boldly revealing** ~ де́рзко откры́тое пла́тье ♦ **bridal** ~ сва́дебное пла́тье ♦ **chiffon** ~ шифо́новое пла́тье ♦ **clinging black** ~ облега́ющее чёрное пла́тье

For general rules of Russian grammar see Appendix 2 on page 686.

♦ **cocktail** ~ пла́тье для кокте́йлей, вече́рнее пла́тье ♦ **daring** ~ сме́лое пла́тье ♦ **dressing** ~ хала́т, пеньюа́р ♦ **evening** ~ вече́рнее пла́тье ♦ **lace** ~ кружевно́е пла́тье ♦ **lovely** ~ краси́вое пла́тье ♦ **sleeveless** ~ пла́тье без рукаво́в ♦ *(1,2)* **wedding** ~ *(1)* подвене́чное / *(2)* сва́дебное пла́тье ♦ **That's a (very) beautiful gown.** Это (о́чень) краси́вое пла́тье.

grab *vt* схвати́ть *(what, whom = acc.)*; *(in one's arms)* схвати́ть в объя́тия *(what, whom = acc.)*. ♦ **I'd like to grab you and kiss you right now.** Я хоте́л бы пря́мо сейча́с схвати́ть тебя́ в объя́тия и целова́ть и целова́ть.

grace *n* гра́ция, грацио́зность *f* ♦ **bewitching** ~ обворожи́тельная гра́ция ♦ **casual** ~ небре́жная гра́ция ♦ **easy** ~ лёгкая гра́ция ♦ **feline** ~ коша́чья гра́ция ♦ **flawless** ~ безупре́чная гра́ция ♦ ~ **of movement** гра́ция движе́ний ♦ **lissome** ~ ги́бкая гра́ция ♦ **lithesome** ~ ги́бкая гра́ция ♦ **natural** ~ есте́ственная гра́ция ♦ **proud** ~ го́рдая гра́ция ♦ **seductive** ~ соблазни́тельная гра́ция ♦ **willowy** ~ ги́бкая гра́ция ♦ **full of** ~ по́лный (-ая, -ое, -ые) гра́ции, грацио́зный, -ая, -ое, -ые, изя́щный, -ая, -ое, -ые ♦ **poetry and** ~ поэ́зия и гра́ция.

| *grace: phrases* |

You have the grace of a trained dancer. У тебя́ гра́ция трениро́ванной танцо́вщицы. ♦ **Your body has such** *(1)* **lissome /** *(2)* **lithesome /** *(3)* **willowy grace.** В твоём те́ле есть така́я *(1-3)* ги́бкая гра́ция. ♦ **You move with such lithesome grace.** Ты дви́гаешься с тако́й ги́бкой гра́цией. ♦ **I long to adore the tender grace of your** *(1)* **neck /** *(2)* **throat with my lips.** Я стра́стно жела́ю губа́ми ощути́ть не́жную грацио́зность *(1)* ...твое́й ше́и. / *(2)* ...твоего́ го́рла.

graceful *adj* грацио́зный, -ая, -ое, -ые, изя́щный, -ая, -ое, -ые ♦ **socially** ~ прия́тный (-ая, -ое, -ые) в обще́нии.

gracefully *adv* грацио́зно, изя́щно.

grade *n* 1. *(quality)* ка́чество, сорт; *(qualifying level)* высота́; 2. *(rank)* ранг; 3. *(in school)* класс ♦ **make the** ~ быть на до́лжной высоте́.

gradual *adj* постепе́нный, -ая, -ое, -ые.

gradually *adv* постепе́нно.

graduate *n* око́нчивший (-ая, -ие) уче́бное заведе́ние; выпускни́к *m*, выпускни́ца *f* ♦ **I'm a** *(1)* **college /** *(2)* **university graduate.** Я око́нчил *(ж: око́нчила)* *(1,2)* университе́т.

grandchild *n* внук *m;* вну́чка *f.*

grandchildren *n, pl* вну́ки *m or both;* вну́чки *f.*

granddaughter *n* вну́чка.

grandeur *n* великоле́пие ♦ ~ **of your feminine beauty** великоле́пие твое́й же́нской красоты́.

grandfather *n* де́душка.

grandmother *n* ба́бушка.

grandson *n* внук.

granite-jawed *adj* с грани́тным подборо́дком.

grant *vt*, предоставля́ть / предоста́вить*(what = acc., to whom = dat.)*, дава́ть / дать *(what = acc., to whom = dat.)*; уделя́ть / удели́ть *(what = acc., to whom = dat.)* ♦ **I** *(1)* **beg /** *(2)* **beseech you (with all my heart) to grant me just a few minutes of your time to meet with you and talk with you (in person).** Я *(1,2)* умоля́ю тебя́ (от всего́ се́рдца) удели́ть мне хотя́ бы не́сколько мину́т, что́бы я мог встре́титься с тобо́й и поговори́ть (ли́чно). ♦ **I fervently pray that in your heart you can somehow find the compassion to condescend to grant me just a few brief minutes to** *(1)* **meet /** *(2)* **talk with you and thereby assuage this unbearable longing that grips my soul.** Я горячо́ молю́сь, что́бы ты смогла́ найти́

For transitive Russian verbs the cases that they take are shown by means of an = sign and the Russian case (abbreviated).

сострада́ние в своём се́рдце и подари́ть мне то́лько не́сколько коро́тких мину́т *(1)* встре́чи / *(2)* разгово́ра с тобо́й, что́бы утоли́ть невыноси́мое жела́ние, охвати́вшее мою́ ду́шу.

granted *adj*: ♦ **take for ~** принима́ть / приня́ть как до́лжное *(what, whom = acc.)*, счита́ть само́ собо́й разуме́ющимся ♦ **You seem to just take me for granted.** Ты, ка́жется, счита́ешь себя́ в пра́ве де́лать всё, что тебе́ хо́чется, не счита́ясь с мои́ми жела́ниями. ♦ **Do you think you can take me for granted all the time?** Ду́маешь, ты всегда́ в пра́ве де́лать всё, что тебе́ хо́чется, не счита́ясь с мои́ми жела́ниями? ♦ **Darling, I would never take you for granted.** Дорога́я, я всегда́ бу́ду счита́ться с твои́ми жела́ниями. ♦ **I would never take you for granted.** Я никогда́ не при́нял *(ж: приняла́)* бы тебя́ как до́лжное. ♦ **I'm not the kind who takes** *(1)* **women /** *(2)* **men /** *(3)* **people for granted.** Я не из тех, кто принима́ет *(1)* же́нщин / *(2)* мужчи́н / *(3)* люде́й как до́лжное.

grape(s) *n* виногра́д *sing. & pl* ♦ **sour ~s** зе́лен виногра́д.

grapevine *n* слу́хи *pl* ♦ **I heard (it) on the grapevine that...** Бы́ли слу́хи, что...

grasp *vt* 1. *(grab hold)* схва́тывать / схвати́ть *(what = acc.)*; 2. *(squeeze)* сжима́ть / сжать *(what = acc.)*; 3. *(understand, catch)* понима́ть / поня́ть *(what = acc.)*, постига́ть / пости́чь *(what = acc.)*, ула́вливать / улови́ть *(what = acc.)* ♦ **I liked the way you grasped my hand.** Мне нра́вилось, как ты сжима́ла *(ж: сжима́л)* мою́ ру́ку. ♦ **I can't grasp** *(1)* **...what you're saying. /** *(2,3)* **...your point. /** *(4)* **...the meaning.** Я не могу́ улови́ть *(1)* ...о чём ты говори́шь. / *(2)* ...смысл / *(3)* соль. / *(4)* ...значе́ние.

grateful *adj* благода́рен, благода́рна, -о, -ы *(short forms) (for =* за + *acc.)* ♦ **I am so grateful that I found you (in this world).** Я так благода́рен *(ж: благода́рна)*, что я нашёл *(ж: нашла́)* тебя́ (в э́том ми́ре). ♦ **I am so grateful to God for bringing us together.** Я так благода́рен *(ж: благода́рна)* Бо́гу за то, что он соедини́л нас вме́сте.

gratification *n* удовлетворе́ние ♦ **love ~** любо́вное удовлетворе́ние ♦ **I'm not just interested in my own gratification.** Я заинтересо́ван не то́лько в своём со́бственном удовлетворе́нии.

great *adj* 1. *(large)* большо́й, -а́я, -ое, -и́е; 2. *(marvelous, wonderful)* великоле́пный, -ая, -ое, -ые, чуде́сный, -ая, -ое, -ые, замеча́тельный, -ая, -ое, -ые ♦ **That was (absolutely) great.** Э́то бы́ло (соверше́нно) великоле́пно. ♦ **You are (absolutely) great.** Ты (соверше́нно) великоле́пна *(ж: великоле́пен)*.

great *adv* прекра́сно, великоле́пно.

greedily *adv* жа́дно.

greedy *adj* жа́дный, -ая, -ое, -ые ♦ **insatiably ~** ненасы́тно жа́дный, -ая, -ое, -ые ♦ **You'd better** *(1,2)* **save up all your** *(3)* **sweetness /** *(4)* **honey, because I'm going to be unbelievably greedy with you.** Ты лу́чше *(1)* сохраня́й / *(2)* копи́ *(3)* ...всю свою́ сла́дость,... / *(4)* ...весь свой мёд,... потому́ что я бу́ду невероя́тно жа́ден.

green *adj* зелёный, -ая, -ое, -ые.

Green Card *n (U.S. immigration document)* «грин кард».

green-eyed *adj* зеленогла́зый, -ая, -ое, -ые.

greet *vt* приве́тствовать *(what, whom = acc.)* ♦ **~ cordially** ра́душно встреча́ть / встре́тить ♦ **~ warmly** тепло́ приве́тствовать.

greeting *n* приве́тствие; ~s *pl* приве́т ♦ **cheerful ~** бо́дрое приве́тствие ♦ **cool ~** прохла́дное приве́тствие ♦ **cordial ~** серде́чное приве́тствие ♦ **friendly ~** дру́жеское приве́тствие; ~s *pl* дру́жеский приве́т ♦ **frosty ~** ледяно́е приве́тствие ♦ **hearty ~s** серде́чный приве́т ♦ **tender ~** не́жное приве́тствие ♦ **warm ~** тёплое приве́тствие; ~s *pl* большо́й приве́т ♦ *(1,2)* **warmest ~s** *(1)* горя́чий / *(2)* серде́чный приве́т ♦ **convey**

Russian verbs have 2 forms: imperfective and perfective.
They're given in that order.

my ~s передáть мой привéт *(to whom = dat.)* ♦ **send (my) ~s** посылáть / послáть привéт *(to whom = dat.)* ♦ **Greetings from Chicago!** Привéт из Чикáго! ♦ **The warm greeting that you gave me has stayed in my mind ever since.** Твоё тёплое привéтствие до сих пор в моéй пáмяти.

gregarious *adj* общи́тельный, -ая, -ое, -ые.

grey *adj* сéрый, -ая, -ое, -ые ♦ **My world is dark grey. There was no mail from you today.** Мой ми́р тёмносéрый. Не бы́ло пи́сем от тебя́ сегóдня.

grief *n* гóре ♦ **I'm sorry for** *(1)* **...causing you so much grief.** / *(2)* **...(all) the grief that I've caused you.** Прости́ *(1)* ..., что я причини́л *(ж: причини́ла)* тебé так мнóго гóря. / *(2)* ...за всё то гóре, котóрое я причини́л *(ж: причини́ла)* тебé.

grin *vi* ухмыля́ться / ухмылну́ться.

grin *n* ухмы́лка ♦ **big ~** широ́кая ухмы́лка ♦ **ridiculous ~** нелéпая ухмы́лка ♦ **sexy ~** сексуáльная ухмы́лка ♦ **silly ~** глу́пая ухмы́лка.

grip *vt* 1. *(grasp)* хватáть / схвати́ть *(what = acc.)*, сжимáть / сжать *(what = acc.)*; 2. *(envelop)* охвáтывать / охвати́ть *(what = acc.)* ♦ **I love it when you grip my hand firmly as we walk along the street.** Я люблю́, когдá ты, гуля́я со мной по у́лице, крéпко сжимáешь мою́ ру́ку. ♦ **I fervently pray that in your heart you can somehow find the compassion to condescend to grant me just a few brief minutes to** *(1)* **meet** / *(2)* **talk with you and thereby assuage this unbearable longing that grips my soul.** Я горячó молю́сь, чтóбы ты смоглá найти́ сострадáние в своём сéрдце и подари́ть мне тóлько нéсколько корóтких мину́т *(1)* встрéчи / *(2)* разговóра с тобóй, чтóбы утоли́ть невыноси́мое желáние, охвати́вшее мою́ ду́шу.

gripped *adj* охвáчен, -а, -о, -ы *(short forms)* ♦ **Whenever I think of you, I am gripped by an intensely sweet agony.** Вся́кий раз, когдá бы я ни подýмал о тебé, пы́лкое, слáдостное страдáние охвáтывает меня́.

groggy *adj* не по себé, не в своéй тарéлке ♦ *(1,2)* **I was groggy with sleep.** Я не мог *(ж: моглá)* *(1)* ...очу́хаться... / *(2)* ...прийти́ в себя́... ото сна.

groin *n* пах.

groom *n* жени́х ♦ **handsome ~** краси́вый жени́х ♦ **You are my soul's groom.** Ты жени́х моéй души́.

grooming *n* ухóд за собóй ♦ **careful ~** тщáтельный ухóд за собóй ♦ **good ~** хорóший ухóд за собóй ♦ **poor ~** плохóй ухóд за собóй ♦ **sloppy ~** небрéжный ухóд за собóй.

groove *vi* *(slang)* *(enjoy)* наслаждáться *(on what = instr.)*; *(like)* нрáвиться *(person liking = dat., thing liked = subject of verb)* ♦ **I groove on Italian food.** Мне нрáвится итальянская пи́ща.

grope *vi* нащу́пывать; ощу́пывать.

grotto *n* грóтик ♦ **~ of pleasure** грóтик наслаждéний ♦ **hot ~** горя́чий грóтик ♦ **moist ~** влáжный грóтик ♦ **soft ~** мя́гкий грóтик.

grouch *n* злю́ка, злю́чка.

ground *n* 1. *(soil)* пóчва, земля́; 2. *(basis, reason)* основáние, причи́на ♦ **You have to stand your ground.** Ты должнá *(ж: дóлжен)* стоя́ть на своём. ♦ **I want a person who has their feet on the ground.** Я хочу́ человéка, стоя́щего обéими ногáми на землé. ♦ **Any ground you stand on becomes for me a consecrated place.** Любáя тóчка, на котóрую ты ступи́ла, станóвится свящéнным мéстом для меня́.

grounded *adj* 1. *(stable)* стаби́льный, -ая, -ое, -ые; *(reliable)* соли́дный, -ая, -ое, -ые; 2. *(pragmatic)* практи́чный, -ая, -ое, -ые; 3. *(deprived of driving rights)* лишённый (-ая, -ое, -ые) води́тельских прав.

group *n* гру́ппа ♦ **chat ~** *(Internet)* диалóговая гру́ппа ♦ **singles ~** гру́ппа холостякóв.

How to use the Cyrillic alphabet on the Internet
is the subject of Appendix 20 on page 789.

grouse *vi* ворча́ть.

grow *vi* 1. расти́ / вы́расти; 2. *(increase)* возраста́ть / возрасти́, увели́чиваться / увели́читься; 3. *(become)* станови́ться / стать ♦ ~ **apart** *vi* отдаля́ться / отдали́ться друг от дру́га ♦ **My love for you grows more and more every day.** Моя́ любо́вь к тебе́ стано́вится бо́льше и бо́льше с ка́ждым днём. ♦ **Over these past** *(1)* **weeks** / *(2)* **months I have really grown to love you.** В тече́ние э́тих проше́дших *(1)* неде́ль / *(2)* ме́сяцев я действи́тельно полюби́л *(ж: полюби́ла)* тебя́. ♦ **I pray that in the** *(1)* **days** / *(2)* **years ahead you can grow to love me even half as much as I love you.** Я молю́сь о том, что́бы с *(1)* дня́ми / *(2)* года́ми ты полюби́ла *(ж: полюби́л)* меня́ хотя́ бы на полови́ну так си́льно, как я люблю́ тебя́. ♦ **I want someone to grow with.** Я хочу́ ту *(ж: того́),* с кем бы мог *(ж: могла́)* расти́.

> **grow apart:**

We've grown apart, you and I. Мы отдали́лись друг от дру́га, ты и я. ♦ **My** *(1)* **husband** / *(2)* **wife and I have grown apart.** *(1)* Мой муж... / *(2)* Моя́ жена́... и я отдали́лись друг от дру́га.

growth *n* рост ♦ **emotional** ~ эмоциона́льный рост ♦ **personal** ~ рост ли́чности, персона́льный рост ♦ **spiritual** ~ духо́вный рост.

growth-oriented *adj* расту́щий, -ая, -ее, -ие, продолжа́ющий (-ая, -ее, -ие) расти́ ♦ **I seek a growth-oriented person.** Я ищу́ челове́ка, продолжа́ющего расти́.

gruff *adj (rough)* грубова́тый, -ая, -ое, -ые; *(brusque)* ре́зкий, -ая, -ое, -ие; *(ungracious)* неприве́тливый, -ая, -ое, -ые.

grumpy *adj* сварли́вый, -ая, -ое, -ые, раздражи́тельный, -ая, -ое, -ые.

G-string *n* кро́хотные тру́сики.

guard *n* 1. *(defense)* охра́на; стра́жа; 2. *(person)* сто́рож ♦ **catch** *(1)* **me** / *(2)* **you off** ~ заста́ть *(1)* меня́ / *(2)* тебя́ враспло́х ♦ **let down one's** ~ осла́бить охра́ну ♦ **I can't let down my guard** *(1)* **with** / *(2)* **around you for a minute.** Я не могу́ ни на мину́ту осла́бить охра́ну *(1,2)* вокру́г тебя́. ♦ **It was a mistake for me to let down my guard** *(1)* **with** / *(2)* **around you.** Мое́й оши́бкой бы́ло осла́бить охра́ну *(1,2)* вокру́г тебя́. ♦ **You caught me off guard.** Ты заста́ла *(ж: заста́л)* меня́ враспло́х. ♦ **Your proposal caught me off guard.** Твоё предложе́ние заста́ло меня́ враспло́х.

guest *n* гость *m*, го́стья *f (pl:* го́сти) ♦ **wedding** ~ гость, приглашённый на сва́дьбу *(1 term).*

guileless *adj* простоду́шный, -ая, -ое, -ые.

guilt *n* вина́ ♦ **I've carried my share of guilt.** Я нёс *(ж: несла́)* свою́ до́лю вины́. ♦ **I feel a surge of guilt every time I think of** *(1)* **it** / *(2)* **her** / *(3)* **him** / *(4)* **them.** Меня́ охва́тывает о́строе чу́вство вины́ вся́кий раз, когда́ я ду́маю *(1)* ...об э́том. / *(2)* ...о ней / *(3)* нём / *(4)* них. ♦ **You don't know how much guilt I feel.** Ты не зна́ешь, как си́льно я чу́вствую свою́ вину́. ♦ **You don't need to feel any guilt.** Ты не должна́ *(ж: до́лжен)* чу́вствовать никако́й вины́.

guilty *adj* винова́тый, -ая, -ое, -ые *(short forms:* винова́т, -а, -о, -ы) ♦ **I feel (** *[1]* **so** / *[2]* **very) guilty (about** *[3]* **...it.** / *[4]* **...what I've done.** / *[5]* **...not telling you.)** Я чу́вствую себя́ (*[1]* таки́м *[ж: тако́й]* / *[2]* о́чень) винова́тым *(ж: винова́той)* (за *[3]* ...э́то. / *[4]* ...то, что сде́лал *[ж: сде́лала]* / *[5]* ...то, что не сказа́л *[ж: сказа́ла]* тебе́.) ♦ **You make me feel (** *[1]* **so** / *[2]* **very) guilty.** Ты заставля́ешь меня́ чу́вствовать (*[1]* таку́ю / *[2]* большу́ю) вину́.

gumption *n* сме́лость *f.*

gush *vi (make an unrestrained display of affection, etc)* излива́ть *(чу́вства)* ♦ ~ **effusively** экспанси́вно излива́ть чу́вства.

Russian adjectives have long and short forms.
Where short forms are given, they are labeled as such.

gusto *n* смак.

guts *n, pl (slang)* му́жество; дух ♦ **You have a lot of guts.** У тебя́ большо́е му́жество.

gutter *n* сто́чная кана́ва ♦ **have your mind in the** ~ быть непристо́йным.

guttural *adj* горта́нный, -ая, -ое, -ые

guy *n (slang)* па́рень *m*, молодо́й челове́к *(See also* **boy**, **male** *and* **man)** ♦ **above-average** ~ незауря́дный молодо́й челове́к ♦ **atypical** ~ необы́чный молодо́й челове́к ♦ **burly** ~ ро́слый па́рень ♦ **clean-cut** ~ подтя́нутый молодо́й челове́к ♦ **compassionate** ~ сострада́тельный молодо́й челове́к ♦ **decent** ~ хоро́ший па́рень ♦ **exceptional** ~ незауря́дный па́рень ♦ **fit** ~ спорти́вный па́рень ♦ **friendly** ~ дружелю́бный па́рень ♦ **fun** ~ весёлый па́рень ♦ **good** ~ хоро́ший па́рень ♦ ~ **of my dreams** мужчи́на мое́й мечты́ ♦ **handsome** ~ краса́вчик ♦ *(1,2)* **hip** ~ *(1)* осведомлённый / *(2)* зна́ющий па́рень ♦ **husky** ~ дю́жий па́рень ♦ **kind-hearted** ~ добросерде́чный молодо́й челове́к ♦ **lethally handsome** ~ роково́й краса́вец ♦ **lucky** ~ *(see phrases below)* ♦ **modest** ~ скро́мник ♦ **naughty** ~ неприли́чный ма́лый ♦ **nice** ~ хоро́ший па́рень ♦ **old-fashioned** ~ молодо́й челове́к, приде́рживающийся ста́рых идеа́лов *(1 term)* ♦ **ready-for-relationship** ~ молодо́й челове́к, гото́вый вступи́ть в отноше́ния *(1 term)* ♦ **regular** ~ обы́чный па́рень ♦ **right** ~ подходя́щий па́рень ♦ **single** ~ холостя́к ♦ **striking** ~ потряса́ющий па́рень ♦ **swell** ~ замеча́тельный па́рень ♦ **trusting** ~ дове́рчивый па́рень ♦ **well-rounded** ~ всесторо́нне разви́тый па́рень.

guy: phrases

(1) **I'm** / *(2)* **You're** / *(3)* **He's a lucky guy.** *(1)* Мне / *(2)* тебе́ / *(3)* ему́ везёт. ♦ **I'm just a regular guy.** Я про́сто обы́чный па́рень.

gym(nasium) *n* спорти́вный зал.

gym-toned *adj* спорти́вный, -ая, -ое, -ые; нака́ченный, -ая, -ое, -ые ♦ **You have quite a gym-toned physique.** У тебя́ весьма́ нака́ченные му́скулы.

gypsy *adj* цыга́нский, -ая, -ое, -ие ♦ **I have a gypsy heart. I love to travel and enjoy life.** У меня́ цыга́нское се́рдце. Я люблю́ путеше́ствовать и наслажда́ться жи́знью.

gypsy *n* цыга́н *m*, цыга́нка *f* ♦ **I guess there's a little bit of gypsy in my** *(1)* **soul** / *(2)* **heart.** Я предполага́ю, что в *(1)* ...мое́й душе́... / *(2)* ...моём се́рдце... есть не́что цыга́нское.

gyrate *vi* враща́ться (по кру́гу); изгиба́ться.

gyration *n* враще́ние.

Russian nouns are either masculine, feminine or neuter.
Adjectives with them will be the same.

H

habit *n* привы́чка, характе́рная черта́ ♦ **Bohemian** ~s боге́мские привы́чки ♦ *(1,2)* **bad** ~ *(1)* плоха́я / *(2)* дурна́я привы́чка ♦ **drinking** ~ вы́пивка, привы́чка пить, привы́чка к вы́пивке ♦ **drug** ~ наркома́ния ♦ **good** ~s хоро́шие привы́чки ♦ **similar** ~s похо́жие привы́чки ♦ **acquire the** ~ приобрета́ть / приобрести́ привы́чку ♦ **be in the** ~ име́ть привы́чку ♦ **get into the** ~ входи́ть / войти́ в привы́чку, приобрета́ть / приобрести́ привы́чку ♦ **make a** ~ **(of)** име́ть привы́чку ♦ *(1,2)* **I have clean, tidy habits.** *(1)* Я аккура́тный и опря́тный *(ж: Я аккура́тная и опря́тная).* / *(2)* Я люблю́ чистоту́ и опря́тность. ♦ **I have no** *(1,2)* **bad habits.** У меня́ нет *(1)* плохи́х / *(2)* дурны́х привы́чек. ♦ **I'm looking for someone with similar habits.** Я ищу́ челове́ка с похо́жими привы́чками.

hair *n* во́лосы *pl* ♦ **abundant raven** ~ густы́е во́лосы цве́та вороно́го крыла́ ♦ **angel-like golden** ~ а́нгельские золоты́е во́лосы ♦ **ash-colored** ~ пе́пельные во́лосы ♦ **ash grey** ~ пе́пельные во́лосы ♦ **ash blonde** ~ све́тло-пе́пельные во́лосы ♦ *(1,2)* **auburn** ~ *(1)* рыжева́тые / *(2)* золоти́сто-кашта́новые во́лосы ♦ **beautiful** ~ прекра́сные во́лосы ♦ **beautifully** *(1,2)* **coiffured** ~ прекра́сно *(1)* со́бранные / *(2)* уло́женные во́лосы ♦ **black** ~ чёрные во́лосы ♦ *(1,2)* **blonde** ~ *(1)* све́тлые / *(2)* белоку́рые во́лосы ♦ **blonde** ~ **in a ponytail** белоку́рые во́лосы, причёсанные в ко́нский хвост *(1 term)* ♦ **bouncy** ~ упру́гие во́лосы ♦ **braided** ~ заплетённые во́лосы ♦ **bright red** ~ я́рко ры́жие во́лосы ♦ **brilliant red** ~ блестя́щие ры́жие во́лосы ♦ **brown** ~ кашта́новые во́лосы ♦ **brown** ~ **in a ponytail** кашта́новые во́лосы, причёсанные в ко́нский хвост *(1 term)* ♦ **brunette** ~ тёмно-кашта́новые во́лосы ♦ **burnished auburn** ~ блестя́щие золоти́сто-кашта́новые во́лосы ♦ **cinnamon** ~ све́тло-кашта́новые во́лосы ♦ **clean** ~ чи́стые во́лосы ♦ **coarse** ~ жёсткие во́лосы ♦ **combed** ~ причёсанные во́лосы ♦ **copper** ~ во́лосы цве́та ме́ди ♦ *(1-3)* **curly** ~ *(1)* вью́щиеся / *(2)* кудря́вые / *(3)* курча́вые во́лосы ♦ **dark** ~ тёмные во́лосы ♦ **dark copper** ~ во́лосы цве́та тёмной ме́ди ♦ *(1,2)* **dark brown** ~ *(1)* тёмно-ру́сые / *(2)* тёмно-кашта́новые во́лосы ♦ **dark-red** ~ тёмно-ры́жие во́лосы ♦ **dirty** ~ гря́зные во́лосы ♦ **dishevelled** ~ растрёпанные во́лосы ♦ **dishwater blonde** ~ светло-ру́сые во́лосы ♦ **dyed** ~ кра́шеные во́лосы ♦ **elegantly** *(1,2)* **coiffured** ~ элега́нтно *(1)* со́бранные / *(2)* уло́женные во́лосы ♦ *(1,2)* **fair** ~ *(1)* све́тлые / *(2)* белоку́рые во́лосы ♦ **fiery** ~ о́гненные во́лосы ♦ **fiery red** ~ о́гненно-ры́жие во́лосы ♦ **fine, clean, shining** ~ прекра́сные, чи́стые, блестя́щие во́лосы ♦ **fine-spun golden** ~ то́нкие золоти́стые во́лосы ♦ **flowing** ~ распу́щенные во́лосы ♦ **fluffy** ~ пуши́стые

Learn more about Russian customs in Appendix 15, page 782.

во́лосы ♦ **fragrant** ~ души́стые во́лосы ♦ **frizzy** ~ вью́щиеся во́лосы ♦ **glossy** ~ блестя́щие во́лосы ♦ **golden** ~ золоти́стые во́лосы, отлива́ющие зо́лотом во́лосы ♦ **good** ~ хоро́шие во́лосы ♦ **gorgeous** ~ прекра́сные во́лосы ♦ **greasy** ~ жи́рные во́лосы ♦ **grey** ~ седы́е во́лосы ♦ **greying** ~ седе́ющие во́лосы ♦ **~ in a bun** во́лосы, причёсанные в у́зел *(1 term)* ♦ **~ in a ponytail** во́лосы, причёсанные в ко́нский хвост *(1 term)* ♦ **~ in braids** во́лосы, заплетённые в ко́сы *(1 term)* ♦ **~ like burnished gold** во́лосы, похо́жие на полиро́ванное зо́лото *(1 term)* ♦ **~ plaited with ribbons** ко́сы, заплетённые ле́нтами *(1 term)* ♦ **~ pulled back severely** во́лосы, стро́го затя́нутые наза́д *(1 term)* ♦ **~ tied back** во́лосы, затя́нутые наза́д *(1 term)* ♦ **honey-colored / -gold** ~ медо́во-золоти́стые во́лосы ♦ **inky black** ~ во́лосы чёрные, как смоль *(1 term)* ♦ **iron-grey** ~ седы́е во́лосы ♦ **light brown** ~ све́тло-кашта́новые во́лосы, ру́сые во́лосы ♦ **light-colored** ~ све́тлые во́лосы ♦ **long** ~ дли́нные во́лосы ♦ **loose** ~ распу́щенные во́лосы ♦ **lovely** ~ прекра́сные во́лосы ♦ **lustrous (blonde)** ~ блестя́щие (све́тлые) во́лосы ♦ **luxuriant** ~ пы́шные во́лосы ♦ **luxurious** ~ роско́шные во́лосы ♦ **my** ~ мои́ во́лосы ♦ **natural curly** ~ приро́дно вью́щиеся во́лосы ♦ **nice facial** ~ *(mustache)* краси́вые усы́; *(beard)* краси́вая борода́; *(both)* краси́вые усы́ и борода́ ♦ **nice** ~ хоро́шие во́лосы ♦ **night black** ~ во́лосы цве́та но́чи ♦ **pale** ~ блёклые во́лосы ♦ **pale-blond** ~ све́тлые во́лосы ♦ **pubic** ~ лобко́вые во́лосы ♦ **raven** ~ во́лосы цве́та вороно́го крыла́ ♦ **receding** ~ залы́сины *pl*, реде́ющие во́лосы ♦ **red** ~ ры́жие во́лосы ♦ *(1,2)* **reddish-blond** ~ *(1)* рыжева́тые / *(2)* све́тло-ры́жие во́лосы ♦ **red-gold** ~ золоти́сто-ры́жие во́лосы ♦ **rich brown** ~ роско́шные кашта́новые во́лосы ♦ *(1,2)* **ruffled** ~ *(1)* взъеро́шенные / *(2)* взлохма́ченные во́лосы ♦ *(1,2)* **rumpled** ~ *(1)* взъеро́шенные / *(2)* взлохма́ченные во́лосы ♦ **russet-brown** ~ кашта́новые во́лосы ♦ **salt-and-pepper** ~ во́лосы с про́седью ♦ **sandy blonde** ~ во́лосы цве́та све́тлого песка́ ♦ **scented** ~ арома́тные во́лосы ♦ **shining** ~ блестя́щие во́лосы ♦ *(1,2)* **short** ~ *(1)* коро́ткие / *(2)* стри́женые во́лосы ♦ **short-cropped** ~ ко́ротко стри́женые во́лосы ♦ **shoulder-length** ~ во́лосы длино́й до плеч ♦ **silky (**[1] **blonde /** [2] **dark)** ~ шёлковистые ([1] све́тлые / [2] тёмные) во́лосы ♦ **silver** ~ золоты́е во́лосы ♦ **sleek brown** ~ гла́дкие кашта́новые во́лосы ♦ **smooth** ~ гла́дкие во́лосы ♦ **soft** ~ мя́гкие во́лосы ♦ *(1,2)* **sparse** ~ *(1)* ре́дкие / *(2)* жи́дкие во́лосы ♦ **straight** ~ прямы́е во́лосы ♦ **sun-bleached** ~ во́лосы, посветле́вшие от со́лнца *(1 term)* ♦ **tangled** ~ спу́танные во́лосы ♦ **tawny** ~ рыжева́то-кашта́новые во́лосы ♦ **thick** ~ густы́е во́лосы ♦ *(1,2)* **thin** ~ *(1)* ре́дкие / *(2)* жи́дкие во́лосы ♦ **thinning** ~ реде́ющие во́лосы ♦ **tinted** ~ кра́шеные во́лосы ♦ *(1,2)* **tousled** ~ *(1)* взъеро́шенные / *(2)* взлохма́ченные во́лосы ♦ **uncombed** ~ непричёсанные во́лосы ♦ **untidy** ~ растрёпанные во́лосы ♦ **wavy** ~ волни́стые во́лосы ♦ **wet** ~ мо́крые во́лосы ♦ **white** ~ бе́лые во́лосы ♦ **wiry** ~ жёсткие во́лосы ♦ **wiry chest** ~ жёсткие во́лосы на груди́ ♦ **wonderful** ~ чуде́сные во́лосы ♦ **your** ~ *(familiar)* твои́ во́лосы; *(polite)* Ва́ши во́лосы.

___
hair: *verb terms*
___

brush *(1)* **your /** *(2)* **my** ~ *(1,2)* причёсываться / причеса́ться щёткой ♦ **comb** *(1)* **your /** *(2)* **my** ~ *(1,2)* причёсываться / причеса́ться ♦ **cut** *(1)* **your /** *(2)* **my** ~ *(1,2)* стри́чься / остри́чься ♦ **dye** *(1)* **your /** *(2)* **my** ~ *(1,2)* покра́сить во́лосы ♦ *(1)* **fling /** *(2)* **toss your** ~ *(1,2)* отбра́сывать / отбро́сить (свои́) во́лосы ♦ **let your** ~ **out** отпуска́ть / отпусти́ть во́лосы ♦ **preen one's** ~ прихора́шиваться ♦ **rumple** *(1)* **your /** *(2)* **my** ~ еро́шить / взъеро́шить *(1)* тебе́ / *(2)* мне во́лосы ♦ **wash** *(1)* **your /** *(2)* **my** ~ *(1,2)* мыть / вы́мыть во́лосы ♦ **wear** *(1)* **your /** *(2)* **my** ~ *(3)* **long /** *(4)* **short** носи́ть *(3)* дли́нные / *(4)* коро́ткие *(1,2)* во́лосы.

___
hair: *other terms*
___

flowing ripples of your ~ струя́щаяся волни́стость твои́х воло́с ♦ **fragrance of your** ~

___
A slash always denotes "or."
You can choose the numbered words before and after.
___

арома́т твои́х воло́с ♦ **halo of** *(1)* **golden** / *(2)* **black** ~ орео́л *(1)* золоти́стых / *(2)* чёрных воло́с ♦ **highlights in your** ~ отблестки све́та в твои́х волоса́х ♦ **lock of your** ~ ло́кон твои́х воло́с ♦ **luster of your** ~ блеск твои́х воло́с ♦ **pitchblack mane of** ~ смоляна́я гри́ва воло́с ♦ **ringlet of your** ~ прядь твои́х воло́с ♦ **sheen of your** ~ сия́ние твои́х воло́с ♦ **silky strands of** ~ шёлковистые пря́ди воло́с ♦ **silky wave of** ~ шелкови́стая волна́ воло́с ♦ **smell of your** ~ за́пах твои́х воло́с ♦ **soft waves of** ~ мя́гкие во́лны воло́с ♦ **tangle of shining** ~ сия́ющие спу́танные во́лосы ♦ **wild mane of golden** ~ ди́кая гри́ва золоти́стых воло́с.

hair: *how you wear your hair*

I like the way you wear your hair. Мне нра́вится, как ты причёсываешь во́лосы. ♦ **It's so beautiful the way your hair cascades around your shoulders.** Как прекра́сно твои́ во́лосы стру́ятся вокру́г твои́х плеч. ♦ **I like your hair loose.** Я люблю́ твои́ распу́щенные во́лосы.

♦ **Your hair looks** *(1)* **nice** / *(2)* **pretty** / *(3)* **beautiful** *(4)* **...that way.** / *(5)* **...long** / *(6)* **short.** / *(7)* **...shoulder length.** / *(8)* **...in braids.** / *(9)* **...in a pony tail.** / *(10)* **...tied back.** Твои́ во́лосы вы́глядят *(1)* хорошо́ / *(2)* преле́стно / *(3)* прекра́сно *(4)* ...причёсанными так. / *(5)* ...дли́нными / *(6)* коро́ткими. / *(7)* ...длино́й до плеч. / *(8)* ...заплетёнными в ко́сы. / *(9)* ...когда́ ты де́лаешь хвост. / *(10)* ...затя́нутыми наза́д. ♦ **I (really) like your hair** *(1)* **...that way.** / *(2)* **...long** / *(3)* **short.** / *(4)* **...shoulder length.** / *(5)* **...in braids.** / *(6)* **...in a pony tail.** / *(7)* **...tied back.** Мне (о́чень) нра́вятся твои́ во́лосы *(1)* ...причёсанными так. / *(2)* ...дли́нными / *(3)* коро́ткими. / *(4)* ...длино́й до плеч. / *(5)* ...заплетёнными в ко́сы. / *(6)* ...когда́ ты де́лаешь хвост. / *(7)* ...затя́нутыми наза́д. ♦ **Please don't (ever) cut your hair.** Пожа́луйста, (никогда́) не обреза́й свои́х воло́с.

hair: *about my hair*

I wear my hair *(1,2)* **in a bun.** Я ношу́ во́лосы *(1)* ...узло́м. / *(2)* ..., со́бранные в у́зел. **My hair falls to my waist.** Мои́ во́лосы спада́ют до та́лии. ♦ **I have all my hair.** Я сохрани́л все свои́ во́лосы.

hair: *your beautiful hair*

You have such beautiful hair. У тебя́ таки́е прекра́сные во́лосы. ♦ **What** *(1)* **beautiful /** *(2)* **lovely /** *(3)* **gorgeous hair (you have)!** Что за *(1-3)* прекра́сные во́лосы (у тебя́)! ♦ **Your hair is really beautiful when it's all let out (like this).** Твои́ во́лосы действи́тельно прекра́сны, когда́ они́ распу́щены (, как сейча́с). ♦ **Your hair looks beautiful (***[1]***...that way. /** *[2]* **...with the flower in it.)** Твои́ во́лосы вы́глядят прекра́сно (*[1]*...так. / *[2]* ...с цветко́м в них.) ♦ **Your eyes and your hair are absolutely gorgeous. They stay in my memory constantly.** Твои́ глаза́ и во́лосы соверше́нно великоле́пны. Они́ постоя́нно в мое́й па́мяти. ♦ **I gaze upon your divinely beautiful face in its silky frame of** *(1)* **golden /** *(2)* **auburn /** *(3)* **black hair and I am awash in fervent adoration.** Я вгля́дываюсь в твоё боже́ственно-прекра́сное лицо́ в шелкови́стом обрамле́нии *(1)* золоти́стых / *(2)* золоти́сто-кашта́новых / *(3)* чёрных воло́с, и я тону́ в пы́лком обожа́нии. ♦ **In all my dreams I see your beautiful face framed by the splendor of your golden hair.** Во всех свои́х снах я ви́жу твоё прекра́сное лицо́ в опра́ве из роско́шных золоти́стых воло́с. ♦ **I see in this photo a face of** *(1)* **exquisite /** *(2)* **unimaginable beauty crowned with an opulence of** *(3)* **golden /** *(4)* **chestnut /** *(5)* **raven hair.** Я ви́жу на э́той фотогра́фии лицо́ *(1)* изы́сканной / *(2)* невообрази́мой красоты́ в стру́ящемся бога́тстве *(3)* золоты́х / *(4)* кашта́новых / *(5)* чёрных воло́с. ♦ **With your** *(1)* **blonde /** *(2)* **black /** *(3)* **red hair and** *(4)* **creamy /** *(5)* **pale /** *(6)* **bronze /** *(7)* **golden skin you are the most striking woman I have ever** *(8)* **seen /** *(9)* **met.** Со свои́ми *(1)* све́тлыми / *(2)* чёрными / *(3)* ры́жими волоса́ми и *(4)* не́жной / *(5)* бле́дной / *(6)* бро́нзовой / *(7)* золоти́стой ко́жей ты са́мая потряса́ющая

Common adult weights are given in Appendix 10, page 777.

же́нщина, кото́рую я когда́-ли́бо *(8)* ви́дел / *(9)* встреча́л. ♦ **Many, many times during the day, no matter where I am, I see your beautiful, *(1)* dark / *(2)* blue eyes and your long, shiny, *(3)* black / *(4)* blonde / *(5)* brown hair in my mind's eye.** Мно́го, мно́го раз в тече́ние дня, незави́симо от того́, где я, в своём воображе́нии ви́жу твои́ прекра́сные, *(1)* тёмные / *(2)* голубы́е глаза́ и твои́ дли́нные, блестя́щие *(3)* чёрные / *(4)* све́тлые / *(5)* кашта́новые во́лосы. ♦ **Every time I talk with you and look into your beautiful face, all I can see in front of my eyes for hours and hours afterwards are your enchanting, sparkling eyes, your smooth white skin, your *(1)* enticing / *(2)* kissable red lips, and your angel-like golden hair.** Ка́ждый раз по́сле того́, как я говорю́ с тобо́й и смотрю́ на твоё прекра́сное лицо́, всё что пото́м часа́ми встаёт пе́ред мои́ми глаза́ми - твои́ очаро́вывающие, сверка́ющие глаза́, твоя́ мя́гкая, бе́лая ко́жа, твои́ *(1)* ...маня́щие... / *(2)* ...зову́щие к поцелу́ям... кра́сные гу́бы и твои́ а́нгельские золоти́стые во́лосы. ♦ **Your milky white skin and shining blonde hair sing siren-like sonnets to me.** Твоя́ молочнобе́лая ко́жа и блестя́щие све́тлые во́лосы, подо́бно сире́нам, пою́т мне соне́ты.

hair: *various qualities of your hair*

The luster of your hair is so *(1)* gorgeous / *(2)* magnificent. Блеск твои́х воло́с так *(1)* изуми́телен / *(2)* великоле́пен. ♦ **Your hair has such a *(1)* coppery / *(2)* golden / *(3)* toffee-rich / *(4)* velvety / *(5)* rich sheen.** У твои́х воло́с тако́й *(1)* ме́дный / *(2)* золото́й / *(3)* ири́совый / *(4)* ба́рхатный / *(5)* роско́шный блеск. ♦ **Your hair is the color of white gold.** Твои́ во́лосы цве́та бе́лого зо́лота. ♦ **Your blond hair seems to be full of sunlight.** Твои́ све́тлые во́лосы ка́жутся напо́лненными со́лнечным све́том. ♦ **Your hair is so fragrant.** Твои́ во́лосы таки́е души́стые. ♦ **Your hair has a reddish cast.** Твои́ во́лосы отлива́ют краснова́тым отте́нком. ♦ **Your dark hair accentuates the soft loveliness of your face.** Твои́ тёмные во́лосы подчёркивают мя́гкую красоту́ твоего́ лица́. ♦ **Your hair looks lustrous.** У тебя́ блестя́щие во́лосы. ♦ **The bright highlights in your hair are like a starry summer night.** Я́ркие блёстки в твои́х волоса́х как звёздная ле́тняя ночь.

hair: *what I love about your hair*

I love the smell of your hair. Я люблю́ за́пах твои́х воло́с. ♦ **I love the way your (rich brown) hair *(1)* ...flows around your face. / *(2)* ...cascades around your shoulders.** Мне нра́вится, как твои́ (роско́шные кашта́новые) во́лосы *(1)* ...струя́тся вокру́г твоего́ лица́. / *(2)* ...каска́дом струя́тся по твои́м плеча́м. ♦ **I love the rich blackness of your hair.** Мне нра́вится роско́шная чернота́ твои́х воло́с.

hair: *what I love / would love to do with your hair*

I love to run my *(1)* hand / *(2)* fingers through the abundant flowing ripples of your hair. Я люблю́ погружа́ть *(1)* ру́ки / *(2)* па́льцы в оби́льную струя́щуюся волни́стость твои́х воло́с. ♦ **How I long to immerse myself in the soft, lingering fragrance of your hair.** Как я жа́жду погрузи́ться в не́жный арома́т твои́х воло́с. ♦ **My fingers just revel in the thickness of your dark hair.** Мои́ па́льцы про́сто наслажда́ются в густоте́ твои́х тёмных воло́с. ♦ ***(1)* I love watching... / *(2)* I'd love to watch... you brush your hair.** *(1)* Я люблю́... / *(2)* Я хоте́л бы... наблюда́ть, как ты расчёсываешь во́лосы. ♦ **What pure pleasure it would be to run my hands through the abundant flowing ripples of your hair.** Каки́м и́стинным наслажде́нием бы́ло бы пробежа́ть рука́ми че́рез оби́льную струя́щуюся волни́стость твои́х воло́с. ♦ **I wish so much that I could hold you snugly in my arms and put soft, loving kisses all over your hair and face.** Я так хоте́л бы ую́тно устро́ить тебя́ в свои́х объя́тиях и покры́ть мя́гкими, лю́бящими поцелу́ями твои́ во́лосы и лицо́.

hair: *let it out*

Loosen your hair. Распусти́ свои́ во́лосы. ♦ **Unpin your hair.** Расколи́ свои́ во́лосы. ♦ **Take the *(1)* pins / *(2)* combs / *(3)* clips out of your hair and let it out.** Убери́ *(1)* зако́лки

An italicized ж *in parentheses indicates a woman speaking.*

/ *(2)* гре́бни / *(3)* шпи́льки из воло́с и позво́ль им рассы́паться.

hair: *a lock of your hair*

(1) **Send me...** / *(2)* **I'd love to have... a lock of your hair (to carry around with me).** *(1)* Пошли́ мне... / *(2)* Я бы хоте́л име́ть... ло́кон твои́х воло́с (, чтобы носи́ть с собо́й). ♦ **Could you please send me a ringlet of your hair?** Пожа́луйста, не могла́ бы ты посла́ть мне прядь свои́х воло́с?

haircut *n* стри́жка ♦ **brush** ~ стри́жка ёжиком ♦ **GI** ~ вое́нная стри́жка.

hairdo *n* причёска ♦ **beautiful** ~ прекра́сная причёска ♦ **fancy** ~ зате́йливая причёска ♦ **gorgeous** ~ прекра́сная причёска ♦ **lovely** ~ прекра́сная причёска ♦ **What a** *(1)* **beautiful** / *(2)* **lovely** / *(3)* **gorgeous hairdo (you have)!** Что за *(1-3)* прекра́сная причёска (у тебя́)!

hairline *n* ли́ния воло́с *(на голове́)* ♦ **receding** ~ залы́сины *pl* ♦ **hairspray** *n* лак для воло́с.

hairpiece *n* паричо́к, накла́дка (из иску́сственных воло́с).

hairstyle *n* причёска ♦ **no-nonsense** ~ стро́гая причёска.

halcyon *adj* безмяте́жный, -ая, -ое, -ые, споко́йный, -ая, -ое, -ые ♦ **I constantly rerun the memories of those halcyon days.** Я постоя́нно возвраща́юсь к воспомина́ниям об э́тих безмяте́жных днях.

half *n* полови́на ♦ *(Ad:)* **Affectionate homebody seeks other half.** Лю́бящий домосе́д и́щет свою́ полови́ну.

half-slip *n* ни́жняя ю́бка.

halo *n* орео́л ♦ ~ **of** *(1)* **golden** / *(2)* **black hair** орео́л *(1)* золоти́стых / *(2)* чёрных воло́с.

hand *n* рука́ ♦ **beautiful** ~s краси́вые ру́ки ♦ **both** ~s о́бе руки́ ♦ *(1,2,)* **dainty** ~ *(1)* изя́щная / *(2)* то́нкая рука́ ♦ **burning** *(1,2)* ~s горя́чие *(1)* ладо́ни / *(2)* ру́ки ♦ **gentle** ~s ла́сковые ру́ки ♦ ~ **in** ~ рука́ об руку ♦ **hot** *(1,2)* ~s горя́чие *(1)* ладо́ни / *(2)* ру́ки ♦ **left** ~ ле́вая рука́ ♦ **little** ~ ру́чка ♦ **lovely** ~s краси́вые ру́ки ♦ *(1,2)* **masterful** ~ *(1)* иску́сные / *(2)* уме́лые ру́ки ♦ **my** ~s мои́ ру́ки ♦ **nimble** ~s ло́вкие ру́ки ♦ **right** ~ пра́вая рука́ ♦ *(1,2)* **skillful** ~ *(1)* иску́сные / *(2)* уме́лые ру́ки ♦ **slender** ~s то́нкие ру́ки ♦ **small** ~s ма́ленькие ру́ки ♦ **soft** ~s мя́гкие ру́ки ♦ *(1,2)* **strong** ~s *(1)* си́льные / *(2)* кре́пкие ру́ки ♦ **warm** *(1,2)* ~s тёплые *(1)* ладо́ни / *(2)* ру́ки ♦ **white** ~s бе́лые ру́ки ♦ **your** ~s *(familiar)* твои́ ру́ки; *(polite)* Ва́ши ру́ки.

hand: *other terms*

get the upper ~ брать / взять верх, оде́рживать / одержа́ть верх ♦ **hold** ~s держа́ться за́ руки ♦ **hold your** ~ (in mine) держа́ть твою́ ру́ку (в свое́й) ♦ **in your** ~s в твои́х рука́х ♦ **pressure of your** ~ давле́ние твое́й руки́. ♦ **take you by the** ~ взять тебя́ за́ руку. ♦ **take your** ~ (in mine) взять тебя́ за́ руку ♦ **walk** ~ **in** ~ идти́ рука́ об руку.

hand: *holding your hand*

How nice it would be to take your hand in mine and stroll through the park. Как бы́ло бы прия́тно взять тебя́ за́ руку и броди́ть по па́рку. ♦ **I love the feel of your hand in mine.** Я люблю́ чу́вствовать твою́ ру́ку в свое́й. ♦ **I desire so ardently to take your hand in mine.** Я так пы́лко жа́жду взять тебя́ за́ руку. ♦ **I love to hold your hand in mine (when we walk together).** Я люблю́ держа́ть твою́ ру́ку в свое́й (, когда́ мы гуля́ем вме́сте). ♦ **How my heart yearns to feel the soft pressure of your hand in mine (again).** Как жа́ждет моё се́рдце (опя́ть) почу́вствовать не́жное давле́ние твое́й руки́ в мое́й. ♦ **I remember how we walked along the** *(1)* **beach** / *(2)* **street, holding hands together.** Я по́мню, как мы гуля́ли по *(1)* пля́жу / *(2)* у́лице, держа́сь за́ руки. ♦ **I want to take a long walk along the beach, holding your hand in mine.** Я хочу́ до́лго гуля́ть по пля́жу, держа́ твою́ ру́ку в свое́й. ♦ **Touching your hand just adds fuel to the fire of my desire for you.** Когда́ я каса́юсь твое́й руки́, ого́нь мое́й стра́сти к тебе́ разжига-

Procedures for getting married to a Russian are outlined in Appendix 18, page 787.

ется ещё сильнée.

| **hand:** *holding hands* |

I love to kiss, hug, caress, touch, hold hands, nibble, cuddle, rub against, stroke — you just name it. Я люблю́ целова́ть, обнима́ть, ласка́ть, каса́ться, держа́ться за ру́ки, покусывать, сжима́ть в объя́тиях, тере́ться, гла́дить -- ты то́лько назови́.

| **hand:** *my hands on you* |

There is never a moment in the day when I don't long to caress your body with my hands (and lips). В тече́ние дня нет и мину́ты, когда́ бы мои́ ру́ки (и гу́бы) не жа́ждали ласка́ть твоё те́ло. ♦ **First, I'll run my hands lightly over your body, and then my lips.** Снача́ла мои́ ру́ки мя́гко пробегу́т по твоему́ те́лу, а зате́м и гу́бы. ♦ **I want to tune your body with my mouth and hands until it sings.** Я хочу́ настра́ивать твоё те́ло свои́м ртом и рука́ми до тех пор, пока́ оно́ не запоёт.

| **hand:** *your hands on me* |

I love it when your hands wander over my body. Я люблю́, когда́ твои́ ру́ки блужда́ют по моему́ те́лу. ♦ **You have such masterful hands.** У тебя́ таки́е иску́сные ру́ки. ♦ **The touch of your masterful hands melts my bones.** Прикоснове́ние твои́х иску́сных рук пла́вит мои́ ко́сти. ♦ **I'm putty in your hands.** Я гли́на в твои́х рука́х. ♦ **There is no moment in the day when I don't long for your hands on my body.** В тече́ние дня нет и мину́ты, когда́ бы я не тоскова́л *(ж: тоскова́ла)* по твои́м рука́м, ласка́ющим меня́. ♦ **I am** *(1)* **completely /** *(2)* **totally** *(3)* **...overcome by... /** *(4)* **...swept away by... /** *(5)* **...engulfed in... the rapture that you create with your skillful hands.** Я *(1)* по́лностью / *(2)* весь *(ж: вся) (3,4)* ...охва́чен *(ж: охва́чена)... /* *(5)* ...поглощён *(ж: поглощена́)...* упое́нием, кото́рое ты создаёшь свои́ми уме́лыми рука́ми. ♦ **I love the feel of your hands.** Мне нра́вится ощуще́ние твои́х рук. ♦ **I like the way your hands flutter over me.** Мне нра́вится, как твои́ ру́ки порха́ют по моему́ те́лу.

| **hand:** *various phrases* |

I wash my hands of this whole *(1)* **affair /** *(2)* **relationship.** В э́тих *(1)* дела́х / *(2)* отноше́ниях я умыва́ю ру́ки. ♦ **This whole thing is getting out of hand.** Всё идёт бесконтро́льно. ♦ **I lost my** *(1)* **right /** *(2)* **left hand in** *(3)* **...the (Vietnam) war. /** *(4)* **...an accident.** Я потеря́л *(ж: потеря́ла) (1)* пра́вую / *(2)* ле́вую ру́ку *(3)* ...на войне́ (во Вьетна́ме). / *(4)* ...в ава́рии.

hand-holding *n (Russians use verb expression* держа́ться за́ руки.*)*

handicapped *adj* неполноце́нный, -ая, -ое, -ые, ограни́ченный, -ая, -ое, -ые.

hand-in-hand *adv* рука́ в руке́.

handkerchief *n* носово́й плато́к ♦ **scented** ~ наду́шенный носово́й плато́к ♦ **silk** ~ шёлковый носово́й плато́к.

handle *vt* 1. *(deal / cope with)* име́ть де́ло *(what, whom = + c + instr.)*, справля́ться / спра́виться *(what, whom = + c + instr.)*; 2. *(tolerate, endure)* терпе́ть / потерпе́ть *(what = acc.)*, выде́рживать / вы́держать *(what = acc.)*, выноси́ть / вы́нести *(what = acc.)* ♦ **I can't handle** *(1)* **...a(n) secret /** *(2)* **illicit (love) affair. /** *(3)* **...your /** *(4)* **his /** *(5)* **her (constant) jealousy. /** *(6)* **...your /** *(7)* **his /** *(8)* **her drinking.** Я не могу́ вы́нести *(1,2)* ...та́йную (любо́вную) связь. / *(3)* ...твою́ / *(4)* его́ / *(5)* её (постоя́нную) ре́вность. / *(6)* ...твоё / *(7)* его́ / *(8)* её пья́нство. ♦ **I can't handle the situation.** Я не могу́ спра́виться с ситуа́цией.

handle *n:* ♦ **love** ~s *(slang)* отложе́ние жи́ра на бока́х.

handsome *adj* краси́вый, *(pl:)* -ые *(short forms:* краси́в, -ы) ♦ **boyishly** ~ мальчи́шески краси́в ♦ *(1-3)* **devastatingly** ~ *(1)* сокруши́тельно / *(2)* ослепи́тельно / *(3)* ги́бельно краси́вый ♦ **devilishly** ~ чертóвски краси́вый ♦ **exceptionally** ~ исключи́тельно

A list of conjugated Russian verbs is given in Appendix 3 on page 699.

краси́вый ♦ **extraordinarily** ~ чрезвыча́йно краси́вый ♦ **tall, dark and** ~ высо́кий, сму́глый и краси́вый ♦ **tall, white and** ~ высо́кий, бе́лый и краси́вый ♦ **very** ~ о́чень краси́вый.

---
handsome: phrases

I consider myself handsome. Я счита́ю себя́ краси́вым. ♦ **You are exceptionally handsome.** Ты потряса́юще краси́в. ♦ **I don't care what your age is, you're still** *(1)* **exceptionally** / *(2)* **extraordinarily** / *(3)* **very handsome.** Меня́ не волну́ет твой во́зраст, ты всё ещё *(1)* исключи́тельно / *(2)* чрезвыча́йно / *(3)* о́чень краси́вый. ♦ **The years have been** *(1)* **very** / *(2)* **exceptionally kind to you. You're still** *(3)* **quite** / *(4)* **very handsome.** Го́ды бы́ли *(1)* о́чень / *(2)* исключи́тельно благоскло́нны к тебе́. Ты всё ещё *(3,4)* о́чень краси́в. ♦ **You're the most handsome man** *(1)* **...here.** / *(2)* **...in the room.** / *(3)* **...I know.** / *(4)* **...I've ever met.** Ты са́мый краси́вый мужчи́на ...здесь. / ...в э́той ко́мнате. / ..., кото́рого я зна́ю. / ...из всех, встре́ченных мной.

handy *adj* иску́сный, -ая, -ое, -ые, с рука́ми ♦ **I'm handy around the house.** Для до́ма я челове́к с рука́ми.

handyman *n* ма́стер на все ру́ки.

hang *vi* ве́шаться *(on whom* = + на + *prep.)* ♦ ~ **around** *idiom* слоня́ться ♦ ~ **out** *vi (slang)* 1. *(lounge around in malls, coffee shops, etc)* слоня́ться (без де́ла); 2. *(spend time with)* проводи́ть вре́мя *(with whom* = + с + *instr.)*.

hanging out *n (slang)* 1. *(lounging around in malls, coffee shops, etc)* безде́льничание, хожде́ние без де́ла; 2. *(spending time with)* проведе́ние вре́мени *(with whom* = + с + *instr.)*.

hangover *n* похме́лье ♦ **nurse a** ~ пыта́ться изба́виться от похме́лья.

hang up *vt (tel.)* ве́шать / пове́сить тру́бку.

hangup *n (slang)* 1. *(inhibition)* ско́ванность *f*, ко́мплекс; 2. *(prejudice)* предрассу́док ♦ **I have no hangups (whatsoever).** Во мне нет (никаки́х) ко́мплексов. ♦ **I hope you don't have any hangups about sex.** Наде́юсь, у тебя́ нет никаки́х ко́мплексов в отноше́нии се́кса.

hanker for *vi (slang)* жела́ть *(what, whom* = *acc.)*, хоте́ть *(what, whom* = *acc.)*, хоте́ться *(person hankering* = *dat., thing hankered for* = *gen.)* ♦ **I hanker for some tender, loving care.** Мне хо́чется не́жной, лю́бящей забо́ты.

hanky-panky *n (slang)* 1. *(deception)* обма́н; *(infidelity)* изме́на; 2. *(petting)* стра́стные ла́ски; 3. *(making love)* заня́тие любо́вью.

happen *vi* случа́ться / случи́ться, происходи́ть / произойти́ ♦ **What (has) happened?** Что случи́лось? ♦ *(1,2)* **Tell me what happened.** *(1)* Расскажи́ / *(2)* Скажи́ мне, что случи́лось. ♦ **We can meet each other in person and see what happens from there.** Мы мо́жем встре́титься и посмотре́ть, что из э́того вы́йдет. ♦ **What's happened to us?** Что же случи́лось с на́ми.

happiness *n* сча́стье; ра́дость *f* ♦ **a little** ~ немно́го сча́стья ♦ **a lot of** ~ мно́го сча́стья ♦ **boundless** ~ безграни́чное сча́стье ♦ **brief** ~ кратковре́менное сча́стье ♦ **celestial** ~ неземно́е сча́стье ♦ **complete** ~ по́лное сча́стье ♦ **creative** ~ созида́тельное сча́стье ♦ **earthly** ~ земно́е сча́стье ♦ **endless** ~ бесконе́чное сча́стье ♦ **enormous** ~ огро́мное сча́стье ♦ **ephemeral** ~ мимолётное сча́стье ♦ **eternal** ~ ве́чное сча́стье ♦ *(1,2)* **everlasting** ~ *(1)* несконча́емое / *(2)* ве́чное сча́стье ♦ **everyday** ~ каждодне́вные ра́дости ♦ **fleeting** ~ кратковре́менное сча́стье ♦ *(1,2)* **genuine** ~ *(1)* настоя́щее / *(2)* и́стинное сча́стье ♦ **great** ~ вели́кая ра́дость, большо́е сча́стье, вели́кое сча́стье ♦ **greatest** ~ са́мое большо́е сча́стье ♦ **illusory** ~ иллюзо́рное сча́стье ♦ ~ **in** *(1)* **my** / *(2)* **your heart** сча́стье в *(1)* моём / *(2)* твоём се́рдце ♦ **infinite** ~ бесконе́чное сча́стье ♦ **lasting** ~ продолжи́тельное сча́стье ♦ **long-awaited** ~ долгожда́нное сча́стье ♦ **much** ~ мно́го

For Russian adjectives, the masculine form is spelled out,
followed by the feminine, neuter and plural endings.

сча́стья ♦ **my** ~ моё сча́стье ♦ **ordinary** ~ обы́чная ра́дость ♦ **our** ~ на́ше сча́стье ♦ **personal** ~ ли́чное сча́стье ♦ *(1,2)* **real** ~ *(1)* настоя́щее / *(2)* и́стинное сча́стье ♦ **simple** ~ просто́е сча́стье ♦ **such** ~ тако́е сча́стье ♦ **tremendous** ~ огро́мное сча́стье ♦ *(1,2)* **true** ~ *(1)* настоя́щее / *(2)* и́стинное сча́стье ♦ **unexpected** ~ неожи́данное сча́стье ♦ **what** ~ како́е сча́стье ♦ **your** ~ *(familiar)* твоё сча́стье; *(polite)* Ва́ше сча́стье.

happiness: *verb terms*

beam with ~ сия́ть сча́стьем ♦ **bring** *(1)* **you** / *(2)* **me** ~ приноси́ть / принести́ *(1)* тебе́ / *(2)* мне сча́стье ♦ *(1,2)* **experience** ~ *(1)* испы́тывать / *(2)* пережива́ть счастье ♦ **exude** ~ излуча́ть ра́дость ♦ **feel** ~ чу́вствовать сча́стье ♦ **find** ~ найти́ сча́стье ♦ *(1,2)* **glow with** ~ *(1)* сия́ть / *(2)* свети́ться сча́стьем ♦ **look for** ~ иска́ть сча́стье ♦ **radiate** ~ излуча́ть ра́дость ♦ **revel in** ~ пирова́ть в сча́стье ♦ **search for** ~ иска́ть сча́стье ♦ *(1,2)* **shine with** ~ *(1)* сия́ть / *(2)* свети́ться сча́стьем ♦ **thirst for** ~ жа́ждать сча́стья.

happiness: *other terms*

dream of ~ *n* мечта́ о сча́стье ♦ **edifice of** *(1)* **my** / *(2)* **your** ~ зда́ние *(1)* моего́ / *(2)* твоего́ сча́стья ♦ **feeling of** ~ чу́вство сча́стья ♦ **harmony of love and** ~ гармо́ния любви́ и сча́стья ♦ **lightning bolt of** ~ мо́лния сча́стья ♦ *(1,2)* **modicum of** ~ *(1)* глото́к / *(2)* крупи́ца сча́стья ♦ **moment of** ~ моме́нт сча́стья ♦ **surge of** ~ волна́ сча́стья ♦ **tears of** ~ слёзы сча́стья.

happiness: *with you*

I revel in the happiness I have found with you. Я пиру́ю в сча́стье, кото́рое нашёл *(ж: нашла́)* с тобо́й. ♦ **What moments of complete happiness I have** *(1)* **known** / *(2)* **experienced with you.** Каки́е моме́нты по́лного сча́стья я *(1)* знал *(ж: зна́ла)* / *(2)* пережива́л *(ж: пережива́ла)* с тобо́й. ♦ **The happiness I've found in your** *(1)* **love** / *(2)* **arms is beyond** *(3)* **description** / *(4)* **words.** Сча́стье, кото́рое я нашёл *(ж: нашла́)* в *(1)* ...твое́й любви́,... / *(2)* ...твои́х объя́тиях,... невозмо́жно *(3)* ...описа́ть. / *(4)* ...вы́разить слова́ми. ♦ **The greatest happiness I can imagine is to spend my life with you, sharing love and all joys and tribulations.** Са́мое большо́е сча́стье, кото́рое я могу́ себе́ предста́вить, э́то прожи́ть всю жизнь с тобо́й, деля́ любо́вь, ра́дость и невзго́ды.

happiness: *I feel happiness*

I'm brimming over with happiness. Я перепо́лнен *(ж: перепо́лнена)* сча́стьем. ♦ *(1,2)* **My heart overflows with happiness.** *(1)* Моё се́рдце перепо́лнено сча́стьем. / *(2)* Сча́стье переполня́ет моё се́рдце. ♦ **Every time I think of you, I** *(1)* **feel** / *(2)* **experience such a surge of happiness.** Ка́ждый раз, когда́ я ду́маю о тебе́, я *(1)* чу́вствую / *(2)* пережива́ю таку́ю огро́мную волну́ сча́стья. ♦ **I've never experienced such happiness (in all my life).** Я никогда́ не испы́тывал *(ж: испы́тывала)* тако́го сча́стья (в мое́й жи́зни).

happiness: *you are my happiness*

You are my love, my life, my happiness. Ты моя́ любо́вь, моя́ жизнь, моё сча́стье. ♦ **You are my hope and dreams, my strength and purpose, my joy and happiness. You are my life.** Ты мои́ наде́жды и мечты́, моя́ си́ла и цель, моя́ ра́дость и сча́стье. Ты моя́ жизнь. ♦ **All my future plans and dreams of happiness are centered around you.** Все мои́ пла́ны на бу́дущее, все мечты́ о сча́стье свя́заны с тобо́й. ♦ **Thank you for bringing so much love and joy and happiness into my life.** Спаси́бо тебе́, что принесла́ *(ж: принёс)* так мно́го любви́, ра́дости и сча́стья в мою́ жизнь. ♦ **My greatest happiness would be to have you as my wife.** Как бесконе́чно я был бы сча́стлив, е́сли бы ты ста́ла мое́й жено́й. ♦ **My greatest happiness would be to have you as my husband.** Как бесконе́чно я была́ бы сча́стлива, е́сли бы ты стал мои́м му́жем. ♦ **My greatest happiness is loving you.** Моё са́мое большо́е сча́стье - люби́ть тебя́. ♦ **Happiness for me is** *(1)* **...sharing my life with you.** / *(2)* **...getting letters from you.** / *(3)* **...knowing that you care about me.** Сча́стье для

See Appendix 19 for notes on sending mail to Russia and Ukraine.

меня -- это *(1)* ...разделять с тобой жизнь. / *(2)* ...получать твои письма. / *(3)* ...знать, что ты любишь меня.

happiness: *your happiness*

I promise that I will always pay attention to your happiness. Я обещаю, что всегда буду уделять внимание твоему счастью. ♦ **I never want to see anything but pleasure in your eyes, love on your lips, and happiness in your heart.** Я всегда хочу видеть только наслаждение в твоих глазах, любовь на твоих губах и счастье в твоём сердце. ♦ **I want to envelop you with (*[1]* endless / *[2]* infinite / *[3]* ever-lasting / *[4]* boundless) happiness.** Я хочу окутать тебя (*[1,2]* бесконечным / *[3]* нескончаемым / *[4]* безграничным) счастьем. ♦ **I hope that your beautiful *(1)* dark / *(2)* blue eyes are shining with happiness to receive my letter.** Я надеюсь, что твои прекрасные *(1)* тёмные / *(2)* голубые глаза засияют счастьем, когда ты получишь моё письмо. ♦ **I want to always see happiness shining in your eyes.** Я хочу всегда видеть счастье, сияющее в твоих глазах. ♦ **I will do everything I possibly can to bring you (everlasting) happiness.** Я буду делать всё возможное для твоего (вечного) счастья. ♦ **I'm going to make every (possible) effort to bring you happiness.** Я приложу все (возможные) усилия, чтобы принести тебе счастье.

happiness: *our happiness*

Our happiness has dissipated. Наше счастье рассеялось. ♦ **No couple in this world has as many *(1)* attributes / *(2)* prospects / *(3)* possibilities for happiness as you and I.** Ни одна пара в этом мире не имеет столько *(1)* причин / *(2)* предпосылок / *(3)* возможностей для счастья, как ты и я.

happiness: *unexpected happiness*

I never thought that a random meeting with a stranger would bring such boundless happiness into my life. Я никогда не думал *(ж: думала)*, что случайная встреча с иностранкой *(ж: иностранцем)* принесёт такое безграничное счастье в мою жизнь. ♦ **Our *(1)* time / *(2)* day / *(3)* evening / *(4)* night / *(5)* weekend together was a lightning bolt of happiness.** *(1)* Наше время вместе было... / *(2)* Наш день / *(3)* вечер вместе был... / *(4)* Наша ночь вместе была... / *(5)* Наши выходные вместе были... как молния счастья.

happiness: *in general*

I just want a modicum of happiness in life. Я только хочу крупицу счастья в жизни. ♦ **I don't want happiness at such a price.** Я не хочу счастья за такую цену.

happiness: *sayings*

Money can't buy happiness. За деньги нельзя купить счастье. ♦ **Happiness comes from within.** Счастье приходит изнутри.

happy *adj* счастливый, -ая, -ое, -ые *(short forms:* счастлив, -а, -о, -ы) ♦ **deeply** ~ глубоко счастливый, -ая, -ое, -ые ♦ **(1,2) enormously** ~ *(1)* невероятно / *(2)* неимоверно счастливый, -ая, -ое, -ые ♦ **gloriously** ~ невообразимо счастливый, -ая, -ое, -ые ♦ **happiest** счастливейший, ая, ее, ие ♦ **immeasurably** ~ неизмеримо счастливый, -ая, -ое, -ые ♦ **(1,2) infinitely** ~ *(1)* безгранично / *(2)* бесконечно счастливый, -ая, -ое, -ые ♦ **marvelously** ~ удивительно счастливый, -ая, -ое, -ые ♦ **perpetually** ~ счастливый (-ая, -ое, -ые) навсегда ♦ **really** ~ по-настоящему счастливый, -ая, -ое, -ые ♦ **so** ~ так счастлив, -а, -о, -ы *(short forms)* ♦ **supremely** ~ бесконечно счастливый, -ая, -ое, -ые, в высшей степени счастливый, -ая, -ое, -ые ♦ **(1,2) tremendously** ~ *(1)* невероятно / *(2)* неимоверно счастливый, -ая, -ое, -ые ♦ **truly** ~ по-настоящему счастливый, -ая, -ое, -ые ♦ **very** ~ очень счастливый, -ая, -ое, -ые ♦ **be** ~ радоваться / обрадоваться *(about what = instr.)*; быть счастливым *m* / счастливой *f* ♦ **feel** ~ чувствовать себя

When terms are listed after a main word, a tilde ~
is used to indicate the main word.

счастли́вым *m* / счастли́вой *f* ♦ **make ~** ра́довать / пора́довать *(whom = acc.)* ♦ **seem ~** каза́ться счастли́вым *m* / счастли́вой *f.*

happy: *you make me happy*

Do you know how happy *(1)* **...you make me?** / *(2)* **...you have made me?** Ты зна́ешь, каки́м счастли́вым *(ж: какой счастли́вой)* *(1)* ...ты де́лаешь меня́? / *(2)* ...ты сде́лала *(ж: сде́лал)* меня́? ♦ **You make me ...***(1)* **so** / *(2)* **very happy.** / *(3)* **...happier than I can possibly describe to you.** Ты де́лаешь меня́ *(1)* ...таки́м *(ж: такой)* / *(2)* о́чень счастли́вым *(ж: счастли́вой).* / *(3)* ...счастли́вее, чем я (наве́рно) могу́ описа́ть тебе́. ♦ **You make me happy beyond** *(1)* **description** / *(2)* **words.** Сча́стье, кото́рое ты даёшь мне, невозмо́жно *(1)* ...описа́ть. / *(2)* ...вы́разить слова́ми. ♦ **No one has ever made me as happy as you do.** Никто́ никогда́ не приноси́л мне сто́лько сча́стья, как ты. ♦ **You make my life (so very) happy.** Ты де́лаешь мою́ жизнь тако́й счастли́вой. ♦ **You've made me the happiest** *(1)* **person** / *(2)* **guy** / *(3)* **man alive.** Ты сде́лала меня́ са́мым счастли́вым *(1)* челове́ком / *(2)* па́рнем / *(3)* мужчи́ной на све́те. ♦ **You've made me the happiest** *(1)* **girl** / *(2)* **woman** / *(3)* **person alive.** Ты сде́лал меня́ ...са́мой счастли́вой *(1)* де́вушкой / *(2)* же́нщиной... / *(3)* ...са́мым счастли́вым челове́ком... на све́те. ♦ **You (***[1]* **really /** *[2]* **simply /** *[3]* **just) can't imagine how happy** *(4)* **it /** *(5)* **that makes me.** Ты *([1]* действи́тельно / *[2]* про́сто / *[3]* ника́к) не мо́жешь вообрази́ть, каки́м счастли́вым *(4,5)* ты де́лаешь меня́.

happy: *I'm happy because of you*

I'm (*[1]* **so /** *[2]* **enormously /** *[3]* **gloriously /** *[4]* **infinitely /** *[5]* **tremendously /** *[6]* **supremely) happy (knowing) that** *(7)* **...are mine.** / *(8)* **...you love me.** / *(9)* **...belong to me.** / *(10)* **...I have your love in this world.** / *(11)* **...your heart belongs to me.** / *(12)* **...I found you (in this world).** / *(13)* **...you are in my life.** Я *([1]* так / *[2]* неимове́рно / *[3]* невообрази́мо / *[4]* бесконе́чно / *[5]* безграни́чно / *[6]* в вы́сшей сте́пени) сча́стлив *(ж: сча́стлива)* (знать), что *(7)* ...ты моя́ *(ж: мой).* / *(8)* ...ты лю́бишь меня́. / *(9)* ...ты принадлежи́шь мне. *(10)* ...в э́том ми́ре у меня́ есть твоя́ любо́вь. / *(11)* ...твоё се́рдце принадлежи́т мне. / *(12)* ...я нашёл *(ж: нашла́)* тебя́ (в э́том ми́ре). / *(13)* ...ты есть в мое́й жи́зни. ♦ **I have never been so happy with anyone.** Я никогда́ не́ был *(ж: не была́)* так сча́стлив *(ж: сча́стлива)* ни с кем. ♦ **With your love I am the happiest** *(1)* **man** / *(2)* **woman in the world.** С твое́й любо́вью я *(1)* ...счастли́вейший мужчи́на... / *(2)* ...счастли́вейшая же́нщина... в ми́ре. ♦ **I never** *(1)* **knew** / *(2)* **dreamed** / *(3)* **imagined I could be so happy with anyone.** Я никогда́ не *(1)* ...знал *(ж: зна́ла)...,* / *(2)* ...мечта́л *(ж: мечта́ла)...,* / *(3)* ...представля́л себе́ *(ж: представля́ла себе́)...,* что я мог *(ж: могла́)* бы быть таки́м счастли́вым *(ж: тако́й счастли́вой)* с кем-нибу́дь. ♦ **How happy I am to have** *(1)* **...you in my life.** / *(2)* **...your love.** Как я сча́стлив *(ж: сча́стлива),* что *(1)* ...ты есть в мое́й жи́зни. / *(2)* ...у меня́ есть твоя́ любо́вь. ♦ **I am happier with you than I ever** *(1)* **thought** / *(2)* **imagined** / *(3)* **dreamed I could be.** С тобо́й я счастли́вее, чем когда́-либо *(1)* ...ду́мал *(ж: ду́мала).* / *(2)* ...представля́л себе́ *(ж: представля́ла себе́).* / *(3)* ...мечта́л *(ж: мечта́ла).* ♦ **My life has never been happier since I met you.** Моя́ жизнь ста́ла мно́го счастли́вее с тех пор, как я встре́тил *(ж: встре́тила)* тебя́. ♦ **With you by my side I would feel so uplifted and inspired and happy.** С тобо́й я бы чу́вствовал *(ж: чу́вствовала)* тако́й подъём, вдохнове́ние и сча́стье.

happy: *make you happy*

I will do anything to make you happy. Я сде́лаю всё, что́бы ты была́ сча́стлива *(ж: был сча́стлив).* ♦ **Teach me how to make you happy.** Научи́ меня́, как сде́лать тебя́ счастли́вой *(ж: счастли́вым).* ♦ **My greatest desire (in life) is to make you perpetually happy.** Моё наибо́льшее жела́ние (в жи́зни) - сде́лать тебя́ счастли́вой *(ж: быть счастли́вым)* навсегда́. ♦ **I want to always make you happy.** Я хочу́ всегда́ дава́ть тебе́

A list of abbreviations used in the dictionary is given on page 10.

счáстье.

happy: I'd be happy

Nothing would make me happier than *(1)* **...to meet you in person.** / *(2)* **...to correspond with you.** Ничтó не смоглó бы сдéлать меня счастлúвее, чем *(1)* ...лúчная встрéча с Вáми. / *(2)* ...перепúска с Вáми.

happy-go-lucky *adj* беззабóтный, -ая, -ое, -ые, беспéчный, -ая, -ое, -ые, весёлый, -ая, -ое, -ые ♦ **I (really) admire your happy-go-lucky disposition.** Я (действúтельно) восхищáюсь твоúм беспéчным харáктером. ♦ **Your happy-go-lucky** *(1)* **disposition** / *(2)* **manner is like a refreshing breeze.** *(1)* Твоя́ весёлость,... / *(2)* Твой беспéчный харáктер,... как освежáющий бриз.

happy-spirited *adj* жизнерáдостный, -ая, -ое, -ые

harass *vt* 1. беспокóить *(whom = acc.)*, тревóжить *(whom = acc.)*; 2. приставáть *(whom = + к + dat.)* ♦ **sexually** ~ сексуáльно приставáть.

harassment *n* причинéние беспокóйства; преслéдование, издевáтельство ♦ **sexual** ~ сексуáльное домогáтельство.

harbor *vt* укрывáть / укры́ть *(what = acc.)*, скрывáть / скрыть *(what = acc.)*, затáивать / затаúть *(what = acc.)*, таúть *(what = acc.)*, пря́тать ♦ **If you only knew what tender, loving feelings I harbor for you.** Éсли бы ты тóлько знáла *(ж: знал)*, какúе нéжные чýвства любвú к тебé я таю́. ♦ **How can I describe to you all the love that I harbor for you in my heart?** Как мне описáть тебé всю любóвь, котóрая таúтся в моём сéрдце? ♦ **The desire that I** *(1,2)* **harbor in my heart for you goes beyond my power of words to describe.** Страсть к тебé, *(1)* скрывáемую / *(2)* спря́танную в моём сéрдце, невозмóжно описáть словáми. ♦ **I harbor no illusions about** *(1)* **...your love** / *(2)* **feelings for me.** / *(3)* **...my chances of winning your heart** / *(4)* **love.** Я не таю́ никакúх иллю́зий относúтельно *(1)* ...твоéй любвú ко мне. / *(2)* ...твоúх чувств ко мне. / *(3)* ...моегó шáнса победúть твоё сéрдце. / *(4)* ...моегó шáнса завоевáть твою́ любóвь. ♦ **I harbor such tender feelings for you.** Я таю́ такúе нéжные чýвства к тебé. ♦ **The thought patterns that yielded your choice of words and sentences in your ad reveal the exact same raging hunger for love and affection that I harbor within me.** Мы́сли, родúвшие вы́бор слов и предложéний в Вáшем объявлéнии, говоря́т о тóчно такóй же неúстовой жáжде любвú и нéжности, котóрая таúтся во мне. ♦ **Is it really only** *(1)* **sisterly** / *(2)* **brotherly affection that you harbor for me?** Это прáвда, что ты испы́тываешь тóлько *(1)* сéстринскую / *(2)* брáтскую любóвь ко мне? ♦ **It is much more than** *(1)* **sisterly** / *(2)* **brotherly affection that I harbor for you.** То, что я испы́тываю к тебé, э́то мнóго бóльше, чем *(1)* сéстринская / *(2)* брáтская любóвь.

hard *adj* 1. *(difficult)* трýдный, -ая, -ое, -ые; 2. *(firm)* твёрдый, -ая, -ое, -ые; *(penis)* твёрдый, -ая, -ое, -ые, отвердéвший, -ая, -ее, -ие ♦ **become** / **get** ~ *(penis)* отвердевáть / отвердéть. ♦ ~ **to get** трýдно завоевáть, быть недостýпной *(with whom = + с + instr.)* ♦ **Why do you always play hard to get (with me)?** Почемý ты всегдá так недостýпна со мной? ♦ **Playing hard to get, eh?** Игрáешь в недостýпность, а?

hard-body *adj* с *(1)* сúльным / *(2)* крéпким тéлом.

hardbody *n (slang)* мужчúна с *(1)* сúльным / *(2)* крéпким тéлом.

hardened *adj* закалённый, -ая, -ое, -ые.

hard-headed *adj (stubborn)* упря́мый, -ая, -ое, -ые.

hard-hearted *adj* жестокосердéчный, -ая, -ое, -ые, бесчýвственный, -ая, -ое, -ые, бессердéчный, -ая, -ое, -ые ♦ **You are so hard-hearted (to me).** Ты так бессердéчна *(ж: бессердéчен)* (со мной). ♦ **Why are you so hard-hearted (to me)?** Почемý ты так бессердéчна *(ж: бессердéчен)* (со мной)?

---

*The accents on Russian words are to show how to pronounce them.
You don't have to copy the accents when writing to someone.*

hard-heartedness *n* жестокосе́рдие, бесчу́вствие.

hardness *n* твёрдость *f,* про́чность *f* ♦ **You have such an athletic hardness to your body.** У тебя́ тако́е кре́пкое атлети́ческое те́ло. ♦ **I admire your athletic hardness.** Меня́ восхища́ет твоё кре́пкое атлети́ческое те́ло. ♦ **I need your hardness.** Мне нужна́ твоя́ твёрдость.

hardship *n* лише́ния *pl* ♦ **I've had more than my fair share of hardship.** На мою́ до́лю вы́пало лише́ний бо́лее чем доста́точно.

hardworking *adj* усе́рдный, -ая, -ое, -ые, мно́го рабо́тающий, -ая, -ее, -ие, трудолюби́-вый, -ая, -ое, -ые.

harelip *n* «за́ячья губа́», расще́лина (ве́рхней) губы́, незараще́ние (ве́рхней) губы́.

harmless *adj* безвре́дный, -ая, -ое, -ые.

harmonious *adj* гармони́чный, -ая, -ое, -ые, гармони́ческий, -ая, -ое, -ие.

harmony *n* гармо́ния ♦ **complete** ~ по́лная гармо́ния ♦ ~ **of love and happiness** гармо́ния любви́ и сча́стья ♦ **perfect** ~ соверше́нная гармо́ния ♦ **sexual** ~ сексуа́льная гармо́ния ♦ **such** ~ така́я гармо́ния ♦ **tenuous** ~ ша́ткая гармо́ния ♦ **total** ~ по́лная гармо́ния ♦ **wonderful** ~ удиви́тельная гармо́ния ♦ **feel** ~ чу́вствовать гармо́нию ♦ **find complete** ~ обрести́ по́лную гармо́нию.

> **harmony: phrases**

I feel such *(1)* **wonderful** / *(2)* **perfect** / *(3)* **total harmony in** *(4)* **...all areas of our relationship.** / *(5)* **...everything we do together.** Я чу́вствую таку́ю *(1)* удиви́тельную / *(2)* соверше́нную / *(3)* по́лную гармо́нию *(4)* ...во всех аспе́ктах на́ших отноше́ний. / *(5)* ...во всём, что мы де́лаем вме́сте. ♦ **I've never felt such harmony with another person (as I feel with you).** Тако́й гармо́нии (, каку́ю я чу́вствую с тобо́й,) я никогда́ не чу́вствовал *(ж: чу́вствовала)* ни с кем други́м.

harrowing *adj (agonizing)* мучи́тельный, -ая, -ое, -ые.

hasty *adj* поспе́шный, -ая, -ое, -ые.

hat *n* шля́па ♦ **beautiful** ~ прекра́сная шля́па ♦ **wonderful** ~ восхити́тельная шля́па.

hate *vt* ненави́деть *(what, whom = acc.)* ♦ **How I hate to stop talking to you.** Я хочу́, что́бы наш разгово́р никогда́ не прерыва́лся. ♦ **I hate** *(1)* **you** / *(2)* **him** / *(3)* **her** / *(4)* **it** / *(5)* **them.** Я ненави́жу *(1)* тебя́ / *(2)* его́ / *(3)* её / *(4)* э́то / *(5)* их. ♦ **Please don't hate me.** Пожа́-луйста, не на́до ненави́деть меня́. ♦ **Do you hate me (so much)?** Ты ненави́дишь меня́ (так си́льно)? ♦ **I (don't) hate you.** Я тебя́ (не) ненави́жу. ♦ **You act like you hate me.** Ты де́йствуешь так, как бу́дто ты ненави́дишь меня́.

hate, hatred *n* не́нависть *f.*

haughtiness *n* надме́нность *f,* высокоме́рие ♦ **If my lips ever come in contact with yours, all that (**[1]** cold /** [2]** sham) haughtiness is going to drain right out of you.** Е́сли мои́ гу́бы когда́-нибудь косну́тся твои́х губ, всё твоё (**[1]** холо́дное /** [2]** притво́рное) высоко-ме́рие изче́знет.

haughty *adj* надме́нный, -ая, -ое, -ые, высокоме́рный, -ая, -ое, -ые.

haunt *vt* ча́сто посеща́ть *(whom, what = acc.),* пресле́довать *(whom, what = acc.),* остава́ться / оста́ться *(whom = + с + instr.)* ♦ **Your (breath-taking) beauty haunts my** *(1)* **mind /** *(2)* **thoughts night and day.** Твоя́ (захва́тывающая дух) красота́ пресле́дует *(1)* ...мою́ па́мять... / *(2)* ...мои́ мы́сли... но́чью и днём. ♦ **You haunt me.** Твой о́браз пресле́дует меня́. ♦ **The fragrance of your perfume will haunt me for the rest of my life.** Арома́т твои́х духо́в оста́нется со мной на всю жизнь.

haute couture *n* дорога́я мо́дная оде́жда.

hauteur *n* надме́нность *f,* высокоме́рие.

have *vt (tangible things: the person who has = + у + gen. + есть*; the thing had = no change);*

> *If no accent is shown on a word with a capitalized vowel,*
> *it means that the capitalized vowel is accented.*

(intangible) иметь *(what = acc.).* *(* есть is included if possession or existence is the question, otherwise it is omitted. See following 2 examples.)* ♦ **I have a car.** У меня есть машина. ♦ **I have a blue car.** У меня синяя машина. ♦ **I've had enough.** *(idiom)* Меня достало.

have to *(must)* надо *(person that has to = dat.),* нужно *(person that has to = dat.);* должен, должна, -но, -ны ♦ **I have to (1,2) go.** Мне надо *(1)* пойти *(on foot)* / *(2)* поехать *(by veh.).* ♦ **I don't have to (1,2) go.** Я не *(1)* пойду *(on foot)* / *(2)* поеду *(by veh.).*

haven *n* приют ♦ ~ **for love** приют любви.

havoc *n* хаос, опустошение, разорение ♦ **You've really (1) played / (2) wreaked havoc with (3) ...my emotions / (4) feelings. / (5) ... my normal / (6) quiet everyday life.** Ты действительно *(1,2)* внесла *(ж: внёс)* хаос в *(3,4)* ...мои чувства. / *(5)* ...мою нормальную / *(6)* спокойную ежедневную жизнь.

haze *n* дымка, марево ♦ **You are so innocently unaware of the haze of beauty that constantly envelops you.** Ты так невинно не подозреваешь о дымке красоты, постоянно обволакивающей тебя.

head *n* голова ♦ **bald** ~ лысая голова ♦ **beautiful** ~ красивая голова ♦ **beautifully shaped** ~ прекрасная форма головы ♦ **clear** ~ ясная голова ♦ **empty** ~ пустая голова ♦ *(1,2)* **good** ~ *(1)* умная / *(2)* светлая голова ♦ **hard** ~ упрямая натура ♦ ~ **over heels** по уши, без памяти ♦ **little** ~ головка, головушка ♦ **shaved** ~ бритая голова.

head: *other terms*

fall ~ **over heels in love with you** потерять голову от любви к тебе, влюбиться в тебя по уши ♦ **set my** ~ **to whirling** вскружить мою голову ♦ **lose (1) my / (2) your** ~... терять / потерять *(1,2)* голову ♦ **press (1) your / (1) my** ~ **to (1) my / (1) your chest** прижиматься / прижаться *(1,2)* головой к *(3)* моей / *(4)* твоей груди.

head: *head over heels*

(1) **The first time I met you,... / (2) The moment I (3) saw / (4) met you,... I (5,6) fell head over heels in love with you.** *(1)* С первой нашей встречи... / *(2)* В тот момент, когда я *(3)* увидел *(ж: увидела)/ (4)* встретил *(ж: встретила)* тебя,... я *(5)* ...потерял *(ж: потеряла)* голову от любви к тебе. / *(6)* ...влюбился *(ж: влюбилась)* в тебя по уши. ♦ *(1,2)* **I'm head over heels in love with you.** *(1)* Я потерял *(ж: потеряла)* голову от любви к тебе. / *(2)* Я влюблён *(ж: влюблена)* в тебя по уши. ♦ **(I have to confess:) I've fallen head over heels in love with you.** (Я должен *[ж: должна]* признаться,) я потерял *(ж: потеряла)* голову от любви к тебе.

head: *set my head to whirling*

You set my head to whirling. Ты вскружила *(ж: вскружил)* мне голову. ♦ **Your (1) radiant / (2) exceptional / (3) ethereal beauty sets my head to whirling.** Твоя *(1)* сияющая / *(2)* исключительная / *(3)* небесная красота вскружила мою голову.

head: *you turn heads*

You turn everybody's head when you walk into a room. Ты привлекаешь к себе все взгляды, когда входишь в комнату. ♦ **You're the kind of (1) woman / (2) girl who turns heads wherever you go.** Ты из тех *(1)* женщин / *(2)* девушек, к которым поворачиваются головы везде, где бы они не были.

head: *various phrases*

(1) **I want to... / (2) I'm going to... cover you with ([3] adoring / [4] loving) kisses from head to toe.** *(1)* Я хочу покрыть... / *(2)* Я покрою... тебя *([3]* обожающими / *[4]* любящими) поцелуями с головы до пальчиков ног. ♦ *(1)* **You have... / (2) He / (3) She has... a good head on (4) your / (5) his / (6) her shoulders.** У *(1)* тебя / *(2)* него / *(3)* неё хорошая голова на *(4-6)* плечах. ♦ **I want a person who has their head together.** Я ищу человека с головой. ♦ **You're going to give me a swelled head.** Ты поднимаешь моё самомне-

---

Russian has 6 grammatical cases. For an explanation of them, see the grammar appendix on page 686.

ние. ♦ **I felt like I was going out of my head.** Я чу́вствовал *(ж: чу́вствовала)*, что схожу́ с ума́. ♦ **I lost my head.** Я потеря́л *(ж: потеря́ла)* го́лову. ♦ **You go to my head like wine.** Ты кру́жишь мне го́лову, как вино́. ♦ **Wine always goes to my head.** Вино́ всегда́ ударя́ет мне в го́лову.

headache *n* головна́я боль ♦ **I don't want to become a headache to you.** Я не хочу́ стать твое́й головно́й бо́лью. ♦ **What a headache this is!** Это действи́тельно головна́я боль!

headcase *n* у́мственно ненорма́льный челове́к.

headstrong *adj* своенра́вный, -ая, -ое, -ые.

head-turner *n* привлека́ющая к себе́ взгля́ды.

head-turning *adj* привлека́ющая взгля́ды к себе́.

heady *adj* опьяня́ющий, -ая, -ее, -ие, пьяня́щий, -ая, -ее, -ие.

heal *vt* зале́чивать / залечи́ть *(what = acc.)*, изле́чивать / излечи́ть *(what = acc.)* ♦ **Time heals all wounds.** Вре́мя зале́чивает все ра́ны.

health *n* здоро́вье ♦ *(1,2)* **excellent ~** *(1)* прекра́сное / *(2)* отме́нное здоро́вье ♦ **I'm in** *(1)* **excellent /** *(2)* **good /** *(3)* **perfect health.** У меня́ *(1)* прекра́сное / *(2)* хоро́шее / *(3)* превосхо́дное здоро́вье.

health-conscious *adj* беспоко́ющийся (-аяся, -еся, -иеся) о здоро́вье.

healthy *adj* здоро́вый, -ая, -ое, -ые ♦ **emotionally ~** эмоциона́льно здоро́вый, -ая, -ое, -ые ♦ **physically ~** физи́чески здоро́вый, -ая, -ое, -ые ♦ **My goal is to be healthy, wealthy and wise.** Моя́ цель - быть здоро́вым, бога́тым и му́дрым *(ж: здоро́вой, бога́той и му́дрой)*. ♦ **I want a person who is emotionally healthy.** Я хочу́ встре́тить эмоциона́льно здоро́вого челове́ка.

hear *vt* слы́шать / услы́шать *(what, whom = acc.)* ♦ **I look forward eagerly to hearing from you.** Я с нетерпе́нием жду услы́шать что́-либо от тебя́. ♦ **It's been so long since I heard from you.** Прошло́ так мно́го вре́мени с тех пор, как я слы́шал *(ж: слы́шала)* что́-либо о тебе́. ♦ **Can you hear me?** Ты меня́ слы́шишь? ♦ **I can('t) hear you.** Я (не) слы́шу тебя́. ♦ **I don't want to hear** *(1)* **it /** *(2)* **this.** Я не хочу́ *(1,2)* э́то слы́шать. ♦ **I hear what you're saying.** Я слы́шал *(ж: слы́шала)*, что ты сказа́ла *(ж: сказа́л)*. ♦ **I've heard it all before.** Я всё э́то уже́ слы́шал *(ж: слы́шала)*. ♦ **Hearing your voice just adds fuel to the fire of my desire for you.** Когда́ я слы́шу твой го́лос, ого́нь мое́й стра́сти к тебе́ разжига́ется ещё сильне́е.

hearing *n* слух ♦ **hard of ~** тугоу́хий, -ая, -ие, туго́й (-а́я, -и́е) на у́хо ♦ **I'm hard of hearing.** Я тугоу́хий *(ж: тугоу́хая)*. ♦ **I have bad hearing.** У меня́ плохо́й слух.

heart *n* се́рдце ♦ **accessible ~** се́рдце свобо́дно ♦ **big ~** большо́е се́рдце ♦ **broken ~** разби́тое се́рдце ♦ **clamoring ~** взыва́ющее се́рдце ♦ **cold ~** холо́дное се́рдце ♦ **country ~** челове́к, лю́бящий се́льскую жизнь *(explanation)* ♦ **cruel ~** жесто́кое се́рдце ♦ **devoted ~** пре́данное се́рдце ♦ **faithful ~** ве́рное се́рдце ♦ *(1,2)* **gentle ~** *(1)* до́брое / *(2)* не́жное се́рдце ♦ **good ~** до́брое се́рдце ♦ **~ of gold** золото́е се́рдце ♦ **~ of stone** ка́менное се́рдце ♦ **honest ~** че́стное се́рдце ♦ **huge ~** грома́дное се́рдце ♦ **inexperienced ~** нео́пытное се́рдце ♦ *(1,2)* **kind ~** *(1)* до́брое / *(2)* отзы́вчивое се́рдце ♦ **loving ~** лю́бящее се́рдце ♦ **open ~** откры́тое се́рдце ♦ **pounding ~** колотя́щееся се́рдце ♦ **pure ~** чи́стое се́рдце ♦ **simple ~** просто́е се́рдце ♦ **sinking ~** замира́ющее се́рдце ♦ *(1,2)* **soft ~** *(1)* до́брое / *(2)* мя́гкое се́рдце ♦ **true ~** ве́рное се́рдце ♦ *(1,2)* **warm ~** *(1)* до́брое / *(2)* отзы́вчивое се́рдце ♦ **wildly** *(1,3)* **beating /** *(2,4)* **pounding ~** бе́шенно *(1,2)* бью́щееся / *(3,4)* колоти́вшееся се́рдце.

heart: *verb terms*

break *(1)* **my /** *(2)* **your ~** разби́ть *(1)* моё / *(2)* твоё сердце ♦ **cry** *(1)* **my /** *(2)* **your ~ out** *(1,2:)* го́рько рыда́ть, выпла́кивать все глаза́, вы́плакаться ♦ **eat** *(1)* **my /** *(2)* **your ~ out**

There are no articles ("a" or "the") in Russian.

(1,2:) изводи́ться, страда́ть мо́лча, исстрада́ться ♦ **give** *(1)* **my** / *(2)* **your** ~ **to** *(3)* **you** / *(4)* **me** отдава́ть / отда́ть *(1)* моё / *(2)* твоё се́рдце *(3)* тебе́ / *(4)* мне ♦ **lose** ~ опуска́ть ру́ки ♦ **lose my ~ to you** отда́ть моё се́рдце тебе́ ♦ **open** *(1)* **my** / *(2)* **your** ~ открыва́ть / откры́ть *(1,2)* свою́ ду́шу *(to whom = dat.)* ♦ **pour out** *(1)* **my** / *(2)* **your** ~ излива́ть / изли́ть свои́ чу́вства *(to whom = dat.)* ♦ **put all my ~ in(to)** вложи́ть всё моё се́рдце в *(what = acc.)* ♦ **speak to the** ~ доходи́ть / дойти́ до се́рдца ♦ **steal** *(1)* **my** / *(2)* **your** ~ похити́ть *(1)* моё / *(2)* твоё се́рдце ♦ *(1,2)* **touch** *(3)* **my** / *(4)* **your** ~ *(1)* тро́гать / тро́нуть / *(2)* затра́гивать / затро́нуть *(3)* моё / *(4)* твоё се́рдце ♦ **wear my ~ on my sleeve** не (уме́ть) скрыва́ть свои́х чувств, выставля́ть напока́з свои́ чу́вства, душа́ нараспа́шку *(I wear...* у меня́ душа́ нараспа́шку.*)* ♦ *(1-3)* **win** *(4)* **my** / *(5)* **your** ~ *(1)* завоева́ть / *(2)* покори́ть / *(3)* победи́ть *(4)* моё / *(5)* твоё се́рдце.

heart: *other terms*

dear to the ~ ми́лый (-ая, -ое, -ые) се́рдцу ♦ **deep in my** ~ в глубине́ (мое́й) души́ ♦ **exuberance of** ~ бога́тство се́рдца ♦ **from the bottom of my** ~ от всей души́, от всего́ се́рдца, всей душо́й, всем се́рдцем ♦ **in the** *(1)* **innermost** / *(2)* **secret recesses of the** ~ в *(1,2)* тайника́х души́ ♦ **key to** *(1)* **my** / *(2)* **your** ~ ключ к *(1)* моему́ / *(2)* твоему́ се́рдцу ♦ **king of my** ~ коро́ль моего́ се́рдца ♦ **matters of the** ~ серде́чные дела́ ♦ **pain in the** ~ серде́чная боль ♦ **prince of my** ~ принц моего́ се́рдца ♦ **princess of my** ~ принце́сса моего́ се́рдца ♦ **queen of my** ~ короле́ва моего́ се́рдца ♦ **winner of ladies'** ~s завоева́тель да́мских серде́ц ♦ **with a heavy** ~ с тяжёлым се́рдцем ♦ **with all my** ~ от всей души́, от всего́ се́рдца, всей душо́й, всем се́рдцем ♦ **with my whole** ~ от всей души́, от всего́ се́рдца, всей душо́й, всем се́рдцем.

heart: *what you do to my heart*

There is a tempest in my heart *(1,2)* **caused by your sweet, innocent friendliness.** Твоё ми́лое, неви́нное дружелю́бие *(1)* сотвори́ло / *(2)* вы́звало бу́рю в моём се́рдце. ♦ **I am (totally) amazed at the** *(1)* **profound** / *(2)* **overwhelming** / *(3)* **tremendous effect you have on my heart and mind.** Я (соверше́нно) изумлён *(ж: изумлена́)* *(1)* глубо́ким / *(2)* ошеломля́ющим / *(3)* грома́дным эффе́ктом, кото́рый ты произво́дишь на моё се́рдце и ра́зум. ♦ **You make my heart** *(1)* **...do flip-flops.** / *(2)* **...sing (with joy).** Ты заставля́ешь моё се́рдце *(1)* ...колоти́ться. / *(2)* ...петь (от ра́дости). ♦ **You capture my heart every day.** Ты пленя́ешь моё се́рдце ка́ждый день. ♦ **Because of you there's a song in my heart.** Благодаря́ тебе́ пе́сня в моём се́рдце. ♦ **There is springtime in my heart because of you.** Из-за тебя́ в моём се́рдце весна́. ♦ **Every time I see you walk** *(1)* **...through the door...** / *(2)* **...down the hallway...** / *(3)* **...along the street...** / *(4)* **...past me...** / *(5)* **...into the room... my heart begins palpitating wildly and I am flooded with** *(6)* **exquisite** / *(7)* **overpowering** / *(8)* **dizzying sensations of adoration and desire for you.** Ка́ждый раз, когда́ я ви́жу, как ты *(1)* ...вхо́дишь в дверь... / *(2)* ...идёшь по коридо́ру... / *(3)* ...идёшь по у́лице... / *(4)* ...прохо́дишь ми́мо... / *(5)* ...вхо́дишь в ко́мнату... моё се́рдце начина́ет выска́кивать из груди́, и меня́ переполня́ют *(6)* о́стрые / *(7)* невыноси́мые / *(8)* головокружи́тельные чу́вства обожа́ния и жела́ния. ♦ **I go away from any encounter with you with my heart spinning wildly and my mind erupting in a fireworks display of love thoughts about you.** По́сле ка́ждой встре́чи с тобо́й я ухожу́ с бе́шено стуча́щим се́рдцем и с це́лым фейерве́рком любо́вных мы́слей о тебе́. ♦ **You have an effect on my heart, mind and psyche that no amount of words, English or Russian, can ever suffice to describe.** У меня́ не хвата́ет слов, англи́йских и ру́сских, что́бы описа́ть возде́йствие, кото́рое ты ока́зываешь на моё се́рдце, мы́сли и ду́шу. ♦ **Your constant show of affection fills my heart with love for you.** Твоя́ постоя́нно выража́емая любо́вь наполня́ет моё се́рдце любо́вью к тебе́. ♦ **You can never** *(1)* **know** / *(2)* **imagine how you stoke the fires in my**

This dictionary contains two Russian alphabet pages:
one in Appendix 1, page 685, and a tear-off page on page 799.

heart. Ты не *(1)* ...зна́ешь,... / *(2)* ...мо́жешь вообрази́ть,... како́й ого́нь разжига́ешь в моём се́рдце. ♦ **Kiss me in your dreams and my heart will feel it.** Целу́й меня́ в свои́х снах, и моё се́рдце почу́вствует э́то. ♦ **You own my mind, my heart, my body.** Ты владе́ешь мои́м умо́м, мои́м се́рдцем и мои́м те́лом.

> ***heart:*** *what you did to my heart*

You have touched my heart in a way no one else ever has. Ты затро́нула *(ж: затро́нул)* моё се́рдце так, как никто́ никогда́ ещё э́того не де́лал. ♦ **You have found the key to my heart.** Ты нашла́ *(ж: нашёл)* ключ к моему́ се́рдцу. ♦ **You have *(1)* created / *(2)* caused a tempest in my heart.** Ты *(1)* сотвори́ла / *(2)* вы́звала бу́рю в моём се́рдце. ♦ **You have totally enraptured my heart.** Ты соверше́нно покори́ла *(ж: покори́л)* моё се́рдце. ♦ **You have hooked my heart (and I never want to get off the hook).** Ты пойма́ла *(ж: пойма́л)* моё се́рдце на крючо́к (, и я никогда́ не хоте́л *[ж: хоте́ла]* бы сорва́ться с него́). ♦ **You put a song in my heart.** Ты напо́лнила *(ж: напо́лнил)* пе́сней моё се́рдце. ♦ **I was sure you would hear the (*[1]* rapid / *[2]* wild) thudding of my heart (when *[3]* ...we met / *[4]* danced. / *[5]* ...I stood next to you.).** Я был уве́рен *(ж: была́ уве́рена)*, что ты слы́шала *(ж: слы́шал)* (*[1]* бы́строе / *[2]* ди́кое) бие́ние моего́ се́рдца (, когда́ *[3]* ...мы встре́тились / *[4]* танцева́ли. / *[5]* ...я стоя́л *[ж: стоя́ла]* ря́дом с тобо́й.) ♦ **Your many acts of tenderness have enslaved my heart.** Не́жность, кото́рую ты так ще́дро дари́ла *(ж:дари́л)* мне, порабо́тила моё се́рдце. ♦ **I know that the flame that you have kindled in my heart will never go out.** Я зна́ю, что пла́мя, кото́рое ты зажгла́ *(ж: зажёг)* в моём се́рдце, никогда́ не пога́снет. ♦ **Your sweet nature has impinted itself on my heart.** Твоя́ све́тлая ли́чность запа́ла в мою́ ду́шу. ♦ **You made my heart lurch.** *(ж:)* Ты пове́рг моё се́рдце в смяте́ние. **It warmed my heart through and through.** Это так согре́ло моё се́рдце.

> ***heart:*** *when I saw you*

The first *(1)* time / *(2)* moment I saw you, my heart did flip-flops. В пе́рвый *(1)* раз / *(2)* моме́нт, когда́ я уви́дел *(ж: уви́дела)* тебя́, моё се́рдце заколоти́лось. ♦ **When I looked at *(1)* ...you... / *(2)* ...your picture... the first time, my heart said, "This is the one you've been waiting for."** Когда́ я пе́рвый раз уви́дел *(ж: уви́дела)* *(1)* ...тебя́,... / *(2)* ...твою́ фотогра́фию,... моё се́рдце сказа́ло: «Это та еди́нственная, кото́рую ты ждал *(ж: тот еди́нственный, кото́рого ты ждала́)*.» ♦ **My heart lightened at the sight of you.** У меня́ светле́ло на се́рдце, когда́ я ви́дел *(ж: ви́дела)* тебя́.

> ***heart:*** *how my heart feels*

My heart feels like a wilderness that has turned green at the first touch of spring. Моё се́рдце, как пусты́ня, нача́вшая зелене́ть от пе́рвого прикоснове́ния весны́. ♦ **What enormous, exquisite, intense feeling grips my heart for you right now!** Како́е огро́мное, изы́сканное, пы́лкое чу́вство к тебе́ охва́тывает моё се́рдце сейча́с! ♦ **Every time the phone has rung, my heart has palpitated.** Как то́лько зазвони́т телефо́н, у меня́ выска́кивает се́рдце. ♦ **My heart has awoken for the first time.** Моё се́рдце впервы́е просну́лось.

> ***heart:*** *how my heart felt*

(When our eyes *[1]* locked / *[2]* met,) my heart *(3)* missed / *(4)* skipped a beat. (Когда́ на́ши глаза́ *[1,2]* встре́тились,) моё се́рдце *(3,4)* за́мерло. ♦ **My heart *(1)* ...was all aflutter. / *(2,3)* ...was racing. / *(4)* ...soared up into the sky.** Моё се́рдце *(1)* ...трепета́ло. / *(2)* ...си́льно / *(3)* ча́сто заби́лось. / *(4)* ...взлете́ло в небеса́. ♦ **I could feel my heart pounding.** Я чу́вствовал *(ж: чу́вствовала)*, как колоти́лось моё се́рдце. ♦ **I found my heart racing.** Я почу́вствовал *(ж: почу́вствовала)*, что моё се́рдце застуча́ло.

> ***heart:*** *what your beauty does to my heart*

Your beauty constantly sets my heart on fire. Твоя́ красота́ постоя́нно воспламеня́ет моё

> *Russian verbs conjugate for 6 persons:*
> *I, familiar you, he-she-it, we, polite&plural you, and they.*

сéрдце. ♦ **My heart is** *(1)* **completely** / *(2)* **irredeemably** / *(3)* **hopelessly** *(4)* **enslaved** / *(5)* **captivated by your** *(6)* **shining** / *(7)* **radiant** / *(8)* **ethereal beauty.** Моё сéрдце *(1)* совершéнно / *(2)* безвозврáтно / *(3)* безнадёжно *(4)* порабощенó / *(5)* очарóвано твоéй *(6)* сияющей / *(7)* лучúстой / *(8)* неземнóй красотóй. ♦ **I look at your dark, exotic, sensual eyes and I am thrilled to the very center of my heart.** Я смотрю в твоú тёмные экзотúческие, чýвственные глазá и ощущáю сúльное волнéние в своём сéрдце. ♦ **The image of your beautiful face is forever alive in my heart.** Твоё прекрáсное лицó всегдá живёт в моём сéрдце. ♦ **My heart ignites in** *(1)* **celebration** / *(2)* **delight** / *(3)* **ecstasy** / *(4)* **jubilation** *(5)* **...every time I see your** *([6]* **beautiful** / *[7]* **beloved) face.** Моё сéрдце *(1)* ...загорáется рáдостью / *(2)* востóргом... / *(3)* ...вспыхивает в экстáзе... / *(4)* ...ликýет... *(5)* ...кáждый раз, когдá я вúжу твоё *([6]* прекрáсное / *[7]* любúмое) лицó. ♦ **Whenever I look at your beloved face in this photo, my heart overflows with love for you.** Когдá бы я ни взглянýл *(ж: взглянýла)* на твоё любúмое лицó на éтой фотогрáфии, моё сéрдце переполняется любóвью к тебé. ♦ **My heart is** *([1]* **completely** / *[2]* **totally) enraptured by your charm and beauty.** Я *([1,2]* совершéнно) восхищён твоúм обаянием и красотóй. ♦ **The sight of your beautiful face fills my whole body with warm excitement and floods my heart with feelings of love for you.** Взгляд на твоё прекрáсное лицó наполняет всё моё тéло жáрким возбуждéнием и затопляет сéрдце чýвством любвú к тебé.

heart: *what your beauty has done to my heart*

Your beautiful *([1]* **blue** / *[2]* **dark) eyes** *(3)* **...have set my heart** *(4)* **ablaze** / *(5)* **afire.** / *(6)* **...melt my heart.** Твоú прекрáсные *([1]* голубыe / *[2]* тёмные) глазá *(3)* ...повéргли *(4,5)* в огóнь моё сéрдце. / *(6)* ...растопúли моё сéрдце. ♦ **Your incomparable** *(1)* **shining** / *(2)* **radiant beauty has cast an unbreakable spell over my heart.** Твоя несравнéнная *(1)* блестящая / *(2)* сияющая красотá навсегдá околдовáла моё сéрдце.

heart: *what your smile does to my heart*

Your *([1]* **warm** / *[2]* **gentle** / *[3]* **radiant** / *[4]* **beautiful) smile reached deep inside me and touched my heart.** Твоя *([1]* тёплая / *[2]* нéжная / *[3]* сияющая / *[4]* прекрáсная) улыбка пронúкла глубокó в меня и коснýлась моегó сéрдца. ♦ **The** *(1)* **beauty** / *(2)* **radiance of your smile captivates my heart.** *(1)* Красотá / *(2)* сияние твоéй улыбки пленяет моё сéрдце. ♦ **Your smile fills the empty places of my heart.** Твоя улыбка заполняет пустотý в моём сéрдце.

heart: *your place in my heart*

You will always be *(1)* **...(first) in...** / *(2)* **...close to... my heart.** Ты всегдá бýдешь *(1)* ...(пéрвой *[ж: пéрвым]*) в моём сéрдце. / *(2)* ...близкá *(ж: блúзок)* моемý сéрдцу. ♦ **Your place in my heart will never change.** Твоё мéсто в моём сéрдце вéчно. ♦ **No one will ever take your place in my heart.** Никтó никогдá не займёт твоегó мéста в моём сéрдце. ♦ **You are the** *(1)* **princess** / *(2)* **prince** / *(3)* **treasure** / *(4)* **...constant beat... of my heart.** Ты *(1)* принцéсса / *(2)* принц / *(3)* сокрóвище / *(4)* ...постоянное биéние... моегó сéрдца. ♦ **You are my** *(1)* **...heart.** / *(2)* **...heart's desire.** / *(3)* **...heart and soul.** Ты *(1)* ...моё сéрдце. / *(2)* ...страсть моегó сéрдца. / *(3)* ...душá и сéрдце. ♦ **No matter where you are, you're always in my heart.** Не имéет значéния, где ты - ты всегдá в моём сéрдце. ♦ **I'll always have a tender spot for you in my heart.** В моём сéрдце всегдá найдётся нéжноемéсто для тебя. ♦ **You are the one who** *(1)* **...holds my heart completely.** / *(2)* **...will hold my heart forever.** Ты едúнственная *(ж: едúнственный)*, кто *(1)* ...пóлностью покорúла *(ж: покорúл)* моё сéрдце. / *(2)* ...завладéла *(ж: завладéл)* моúм сéрдцем навсегдá. ♦ **You are** *(1)* **always** / *(2)* **ever in my heart.** Ты *(1,2)* всегдá в моём сéрдце. ♦ **You are firmly** *(1,4)* **implanted** / *(2,5)* **embedded** / *(3,6)* **cemented in my heart, my mind, and my soul.** Ты нáкрепко *(1-3)* вошлá / *(4-6)* врослá в моё сéрдце, ум и дýшу. ♦ **I have you locked in my heart (forever).** Я

There are two words for "you" in Russian: familiar «ты» and polite / plural «вы» (See page 781).

(навсегда́) заключи́л *(ж: заключи́ла)* тебя́ в своём се́рдце. ♦ **You have my heart now and always.** Моё се́рдце принадлежи́т тебе́ сейча́с и навсегда́. ♦ **My heart is (so) full of you.** Моё се́рдце полно́ тобо́й.

---

heart: *my heart toward you*

My heart is always with you. Моё се́рдце всегда́ с тобо́й. ♦ **My heart is yours forever and beyond.** Моё се́рдце -- твоё наве́чно и ещё да́льше. ♦ **My heart belongs to you.** Моё се́рдце принадлежи́т тебе́. ♦ **You are the only one my heart is beating for.** Ты еди́нственная *(ж: еди́нственный)*, для кого́ бьётся моё се́рдце. ♦ **I sense with absolute sureness that you are the person in this world that my heart has been yearning to find during these many years.** Я абсолю́тно уве́рен *(ж: уве́рена)*, что ты тот челове́к в э́том ми́ре, кото́рого моё се́рдце жа́ждало найти́ в тече́ние мно́гих лет. ♦ **This is an affair of the heart.** Это де́ло се́рдца. ♦ **Not a minute passes that my heart doesn't call out your name in** *(1)* **desperate** / *(2)* **tortured longing.** Не прохо́дит и мину́ты, чтобы моё се́рдце не называ́ло твоё и́мя в *(1)* отча́янной / *(2)* мучи́тельной жа́жде. ♦ **I can never shut you out of my heart.** Ты всегда́ бу́дешь в моём се́рдце. ♦ **My heart offers me no alternative but to surrender to my (raging) desire for you.** Моё се́рдце не предлага́ет мне друго́й альтернати́вы, кро́ме как уступи́ть (бе́шеной) стра́сти к тебе́. ♦ **My heart was made for you.** Моё се́рдце бы́ло со́здано для тебя́. ♦ **My heart yearns for you terribly.** Моё се́рдце отча́янно жа́ждет тебя́. ♦ **My heart knows it's you for me (— forever).** Моё се́рдце зна́ет -- ты для меня́ (навсегда́). ♦ **My heart sings ballads of love to you every minute of the day.** Ка́ждую мину́ту моё се́рдце поёт балла́ды любви́ к тебе́. ♦ **I hope you will make this springtime stay in my heart** *(1)* **always** / *(2)* **forever.** Я наде́юсь, что ты помо́жешь э́той весне́ оста́ться в моём се́рдце *(1)* навсегда́ / *(2)* наве́чно. ♦ **Deep down in my heart I know that** *(1)* **...I can never love anyone but you.** / *(2)* **...you are the person for me.** / *(3)* **...we can do it.** / *(4)* **...we were meant for each other.** / *(5)* **...our relationship will endure.** / *(6)* **...you're the one I want to marry.** / *(7)* **...this will (not) work.** / *(8)* **...this is (not) right.** В глубине́ се́рдца я зна́ю, что *(1)* ...никогда́ не смогу́ полюби́ть никого́, кро́ме тебя́. / *(2)* ...ты челове́к для меня́. / *(3)* ...мы мо́жем сде́лать э́то. / *(4)* ...мы предназна́чены друг для дру́га. / *(5)* ...на́ши отноше́ния бу́дут продолжа́ться. / *(6)* ...ты та, на ком я хочу́ жени́ться *(ж: ...ты тот, за кого́ я хочу́ вы́йти за́муж)*. / *(7)* ...э́то (не) полу́чится. / *(8)* ...э́то (не) пра́вильно. ♦ **The garden of my heart can only bloom when you're with me.** Сад в моём се́рдце мо́жет цвести́ то́лько, когда́ ты со мной. ♦ **My heart will never change for any reason.** Ни по каки́м причи́нам никогда́ не изме́нится моё се́рдце. ♦ **I promise to always listen (to you) with my heart.** Я обеща́ю всегда́ слы́шать (тебя́) се́рдцем.

---

heart: *the love in my heart for you*

My heart *(1)* **... is (so) full of love...** / *(2-4)* **...overflows** / *(5)* **is brimming** / *(6)* **aches with love... (for you).** Моё се́рдце *(1)* ...полно́ / *(2)* перепо́лнено / *(3)* истека́ет / *(4)* переполня́ется / *(5)* ...до краёв напо́лнено... любо́вью... / *(6)* ...боли́т от любви́... (к тебе́). ♦ **How can I describe to you all the love that I harbor for you in my heart?** Как мне описа́ть тебе́ всю ту любо́вь, кото́рая таи́тся в моём се́рдце? ♦ **There are no words to describe how much love my heart holds for you.** Нет слов, чтобы описа́ть, како́й любо́вью к тебе́ полно́ моё се́рдце. ♦ **There is no way to measure how much love my heart holds for you.** Невозмо́жно изме́рить, како́й любо́вью к тебе́ напо́лнено моё се́рдце. ♦ **If you could but know how much love dwells in my heart for you.** Если бы ты то́лько могла́ *(ж: мог)* знать, како́й огро́мной любо́вью к тебе́ полно́ моё се́рдце. ♦ **I have a heart full of love to bestow upon you.** Я одарю́ тебя́ всей любо́вью, наполня́ющей моё се́рдце. ♦ *(1)* **You can't begin to know** / *(2)* **imagine...** / *(3)* **No words can express... what I feel for you in my heart.** *(1)* Ты не зна́ешь / *(2)* представля́ешь... / *(3)* Никаки́ми слова́ми невозмо́жно переда́ть... чу́вства

Russian terms of endearment are given in Appendix 13, page 780.

к тебе, наполня́ющие моё се́рдце. ♦ **You cannot possibly fathom the depths of the love that fills my heart for you.** Ты, вероя́тно, не мо́жешь пости́гнуть всю глубину́ любви́ к тебе́, наполня́ющую моё се́рдце. ♦ **I love you so much I think my heart is going to burst.** Я люблю́ тебя́ так си́льно, что ка́жется моё се́рдце разорвётся.

---
heart: *I give / gave my heart to you*

I gave my heart to you as soon as I saw you. Я отда́л *(ж: отдала́)* тебе́ своё се́рдце сра́зу же, как я уви́дел *(ж: уви́дела)* тебя́. ♦ **In case you haven't noticed, I stand before you with heart in hand.** В том слу́чае, е́сли ты не заме́тила, я стою́ пе́ред тобо́й с мои́м се́рдцем на ладо́нях.

---
heart: *what happens to my heart when I think of you*

My heart *(1)* **...sings...** / *(2)* **...fills with love and joy... whenever I think of you.** Моё се́рдце *(1)* **...поёт...** / *(2)* **...наполня́ется любо́вью и ра́достью... вся́кий раз, когда́ я ду́маю о тебе́. ♦ **Each time I think of you my heart smiles.** Ка́ждый раз, когда́ я ду́маю о тебе́, моё се́рдце улыба́ется. ♦ **My heart ignites in** *(1)* **celebration** / *(2)* **delight** / *(3)* **ecstasy** / *(4)* **jubilation** *(5)* **...at the mere thought of you.** Моё се́рдце *(1)* **...загора́ется ра́достью** / *(2)* восто́ргом... / *(3)* ...вспы́хивает в экста́зе... / *(4)* ...лику́ет... *(5)* ...от просто́й мы́сли о тебе́. ♦ **My heart beats so fast (whenever I** *[1]***...think about you.** / *[2]***...hear your voice.** / *[3]***...am near you).** Моё се́рдце так бе́шенно бьётся (всегда́, когда́ бы я ни *[1]* ...поду́мал *[ж: поду́мала]* о тебе́. / *[2]* ...услы́шал *[ж: услы́шала]* твой го́лос. / *[3]* ...был *[ж: была́]* ря́дом с тобо́й. ♦ **My heart races (wildly)** *(1)* **...with anticipation at the prospect of seeing you.** / *(2)* **......at the thought of seeing you.** Моё се́рдце (бе́шено) коло́тится *(1)* ...в предвкуше́нии встре́чи с тобо́й. / *(2)* ...от мы́сли о встре́че с тобо́й. ♦ **My heart goes out of control every time I think about you.** Моё се́рдце выхо́дит из под контро́ля, когда́ бы я ни поду́мал *(ж: поду́мала)* о тебе́. ♦ **It brings a thrill to my heart whenever the** *(1)* **thought** / *(2)* **vision of you creeps into my mind for even a second.** Моё се́рдце трепе́щет вся́кий раз, когда́ *(1)* ...мысль о тебе́... / *(2)* ...твой о́браз... возника́ет пе́редо мно́ю хотя́ бы на мгнове́ние. ♦ **The (very) thought of** *(1)* **...you...** / *(2)* **...meeting you...** / *(3)* **...seeing you...** / *(4)* **...holding you in my arms...** / *(5)* **...kissing your beautiful mouth...** *(6)* **...sets my heart aquiver** / *(7)* **aflame.** / *(8)* **...causes my heart to thunder.** (Сама́) мысль *(1)* ...о тебе́... *(2,3)* ...о встре́че с тобо́й... / *(4)* ...о том, чтобы держа́ть тебя́ в объя́тиях... / *(5)* ...о том, чтобы целова́ть твой прекра́сный рот... *(6)* ...заставля́ет моё се́рдце трепета́ть. / *(7)* ...наполня́ет моё се́рдце огнём. / *(8)* ...заставля́ет моё се́рдце греме́ть. ♦ **If you hear something that sounds like faraway drums, it's just the rapid beat of my heart as I think about you.** Если ты услы́шишь не́что, звуча́щее как отдалённый бараба́н, э́то то́лько учащённые бие́ния моего́ се́рдца, когда́ я ду́маю о тебе́.

---
heart: *the effect on my heart of your letters / calls*

It really warmed my heart and lifted up my spirits to *(1)* **...get your call** / *(2)* **letter.** / *(3)* **...hear your (beloved) voice on the phone.** / *(4)* **...see you again.** Что действи́тельно согре́ло моё се́рдце и по́дняло настрое́ние, так э́то *(1)* ...твой звоно́к./ *(2)* ...твоё письмо́. / *(3)* ...твой люби́мый го́лос по телефо́ну. / *(4)* ...на́ша после́дняя встре́ча. ♦ **Your letters warm my heart more than you can ever know.** Твои́ пи́сьма согрева́ют моё се́рдце бо́лее, чем ты да́же мо́жешь предста́вить. ♦ **My heart ignites in** *(1)* **celebration** / *(2)* **delight** / *(3)* **ecstasy** / *(4)* **jubilation** *(5)* **...every time I get a letter from you.** Моё се́рдце *(1)* ...загора́ется ра́достью / *(2)* восто́ргом... / *(3)* ...вспы́хивает в экста́зе... / *(4)* ...лику́ет... *(5)* ...ка́ждый раз, когда́ я получа́ю письмо́ от тебя́. ♦ **The things you** *(1)* **...say...** / *(2)* **...write in your letters... set my heart aglow.** То, что ты *(1)* ...говори́шь,... / *(2)* ...пи́шешь в свои́х пи́сьмах,... заставля́ет моё се́рдце пыла́ть. ♦ **A letter from you sets my heart aglow.** Письмо́ от тебя́ заставля́ет моё се́рдце пыла́ть. ♦ **Your** *(1)* **letter** / *(2)* **call set my heart**

Some the of Russian sentences are translations of things we say and are not what Russians themselves would normally say.

aglow. *(1)* Твоё письмо́ заста́вило... / *(2)* Твой звоно́к заста́вил... моё се́рдце пыла́ть. ♦ **Your letters** *(1)* **manifest** / *(2)* **display such an exuberance of heart.** Твои́ пи́сьма *(1)* обнару́живают / *(2)* пока́зывают тако́е оби́лие серде́чности. ♦ **This letter of yours was so unexpected. Your** *(1)* **sweet** / *(2)* **beautiful words of love have** *(3)* **...set my heart completely aquiver.** / *(4)* **...sent my heart into utter delight.** Это письмо́ от тебя́ бы́ло так неожи́данно. Твои́ *(1)* не́жные / *(2)* прекра́сные слова́ любви́ *(3)* ...заставля́ют моё се́рдце трепета́ть. / *(4)* ...вызыва́ют в моём се́рдце по́лный восто́рг. ♦ **Your words really** *(1)* **stirred** / *(2)* **touched my heart.** Твои́ слова́ действи́тельно *(1)* ...растро́гали меня́. / *(2)* ...тро́нули моё се́рдце. ♦ **Remember to smile for me in your photos. I want to see the same kind of sunshine on your face that your letters bring to my heart.** Не забу́дь улыба́ться на свои́х фо́то. Я хочу́ ви́деть тако́й же со́лнечный свет на твоём лице́, како́й твои́ пи́сьма прино́сят в моё се́рдце.

> **heart:** *your name and my heart*

My heart rejoices at the sound of your name. Моё се́рдце лику́ет от зву́ка твоего́ и́мени. ♦ **In my heart there is a love song that echoes your name.** В моём се́рдце звучи́т любо́вная пе́сня, э́хом отража́ющая твоё и́мя.

> **heart:** *your ad's effect on my heart*

There were several other ads in the personals that were somewhat interesting, but yours struck an immediate chord in my heart and I knew with a certainty that there was no way I could not write to you. В отде́ле знако́мств бы́ло не́сколько други́х объявле́ний, чём-то интере́сных, но Ва́ше вы́звало неме́дленный о́тклик в моём се́рдце, и я твёрдо знал *(ж: зна́ла)*, что не могу́ не написа́ть Вам.

> **heart:** *your kind of heart*

You are the sweetest of all hearts. Ты са́мая дорога́я на све́те. ♦ **I admire you for your kind heart.** Я восхища́юсь твои́м до́брым се́рдцем. ♦ **You have such a good, loving heart.** У тебя́ тако́е до́брое, лю́бящее се́рдце. ♦ **The sunshine of your heart has melted away all of my loneliness.** Со́лнечный свет твоего́ се́рдца растопи́л всё моё одино́чество. ♦ **You have a heart (made) of** *(1)* **ice** / *(2)* **snow.** Твоё се́рдце (сде́лано) и́зо *(1,2)* льда.

> **heart:** *your heart toward me*

If you have any tender spot for me in your heart, you'll let me *(1)* **see** / *(2)* **meet you (again).** Если в твоём се́рдце есть хотя́ бы каки́е-то до́брые чу́вства ко мне, ты позво́лишь мне *(1)* уви́деться / *(2)* встре́титься с тобо́й (опя́ть). ♦ **Try to listen with your heart (to the things I tell you here).** Постара́йся услы́шать се́рдцем (то, что я говорю́ тебе́ здесь).

> **heart:** *winning your heart*

I write this to you daringly, I know, but I hope that it will reach your heart. Я зна́ю, что пишу́ тебе́ сме́ло, но наде́юсь, что э́то дойдёт до твоего́ се́рдца. ♦ **My greatest aspiration in life is to win your heart.** Стремле́ние всей мое́й жи́зни -- завоева́ть твоё се́рдце. ♦ **I will do everything (I possibly can) to win your heart.** Я сде́лаю всё (возмо́жное), что́бы завоева́ть твоё се́рдце. ♦ **I** *(1)* **harbor** / *(2)* **entertain no illusions about my chances of winning your heart.** Я не *(1)* таю́ / *(2)* пита́ю никаки́х иллю́зий относи́тельно моего́ ша́нса победи́ть твоё се́рдце. ♦ **I wish I could break through the (*[1]* heavy / *[2]* thick) armor that** *(3)* **encases** / *(4)* **envelops your heart.** Я хоте́л бы проби́ться сквозь (*[1]* кре́пкую / *[2]* про́чную) броню́, кото́рая *(3)* обвола́кивает / *(4)* окружа́ет твоё се́рдце.

> **heart:** *your heart belongs to me*

i'm so (*[1]* enormously / *[2]* gloriously / *[3]* infinitely / *[4]* tremendously) happy knowing that your heart belongs to me. Я так (*[1]* неимове́рно / *[2]* бесконе́чно / *[3]* невообрази́мо / *[4]* безграни́чно) сча́стлив *(ж: сча́стлива)* знать, что твоё се́рдце принадлежи́т мне.

Counting things in Russian is a bit involved.
See Appendix 4, "Numbers," on page 756 .

heart: *journey to your heart*

I am so eagerly awaiting this journey that I hope will lead to your heart and your arms. Я с таки́м нетерпе́нием жду э́той пое́здки, кото́рая, я наде́юсь, приведёт меня́ к твоему́ се́рдцу и к твои́м объя́тиям.

heart: *I want to fill your heart with love*

I want to foster a love in your heart that will grow ever stronger as the years go by. Я хочу́ взрасти́ть любо́вь в твоём се́рдце, кото́рая бу́дет станови́ться то́лько сильне́е с года́ми.
♦ **I want to fill your heart with** *(1)* **...boundless /** *(2)* **undying love. /** *(3)* **...an ocean of love.** Я хочу́ напо́лнить твоё се́рдце *(1)* ...безграни́чной / *(2)* неумира́ющей любо́вью. / *(3)* ...океа́ном любви́.

heart: *your love's effect on my heart*

Knowing that you love me as much as I love you fills my heart with indescribable *(1)* **joy /** *(2)* **elation /** *(3)* **rapture.** Зна́ние, что ты лю́бишь меня́ так же си́льно, как я люблю́ тебя́, наполня́ет моё се́рдце *(1)* ...невероя́тной ра́достью. / *(2)* ...невероя́тным ликова́нием / *(3)* восто́ргом. ♦ **If you win my heart, you win the world.** Е́сли ты победи́шь моё се́рдце, ты победи́шь мир.

heart: *open your heart*

I know I'm a hopeless dreamer, but I can never stop wishing that someday you'll open your heart to me. Я зна́ю, что я безнадёжный мечта́тель, но не перестаю́ наде́яться, что одна́жды ты откро́ешь мне своё се́рдце. ♦ *(1)* **I want you to... /** *(2)* **I pray that you'll... open your heart to me.** *(1)* Я хочу́,... / *(2)* Я молю́сь,... чтобы ты откры́ла мне своё се́рдце. ♦ **I beseech you to open your heart to me.** Я молю́ тебя́ откры́ть мне своё се́рдце. ♦ **Open your heart to me and you will find that mine is open even more to you.** Откро́й своё се́рдце мне и ты узна́ешь, что моё откры́то для тебя́ да́же бо́лее. ♦ **Please don't lock me out of your heart.** Пожа́луйста, не прогоня́й меня́ из своего́ се́рдца. ♦ **Why have you locked me out of your heart?** Почему́ ты прогна́ла меня́ из своего́ се́рдца? ♦ **Tell me what's in your heart.** Расскажи́ мне, что у тебя́ на се́рдце. ♦ **Look in your heart and answer.** Взгляни́ в своё се́рдце и отве́ть. ♦ **Listen to your heart.** Слу́шай своё се́рдце.

heart: *opening my heart to you*

You're the first person I've really opened (up) my heart to. Ты пе́рвый челове́к, кото́рому я действи́тельно откры́л *(ж: откры́ла)* своё се́рдце. ♦ **I'm afraid to open my heart to you and tell you everything I feel, because I'm afraid you would be offended or shocked or angry and then stop writing to me.** Я бою́сь откры́ть тебе́ своё се́рдце и сказа́ть всё, что я чу́вствую, потому́ что страшу́сь того́, что ты оби́дишься, бу́дешь шоки́рована или рассе́рдишься и переста́нешь писа́ть мне. ♦ **How I wish you could understand everything that's in my heart.** Как бы я хоте́л *(ж: хоте́ла)*, чтобы ты смогла́ *(ж: смог)* поня́ть всё, что у меня́ на се́рдце. ♦ **I wish I could tell you everything that's in my heart.** Я хоте́л *(ж: хоте́ла)* бы рассказа́ть тебе́ всё, что у меня́ на се́рдце.

heart: *our two hearts*

Our two hearts beat as one. На́ши два се́рдца бью́тся, как одно́. ♦ **From our two hearts we will create a love that will** *(1)* **...flourish to the end of our lives. /** *(2)* **...last till the end of time. /** *(3)* **...grow ever stronger, ever more beautiful.** На́ши два се́рдца создаду́т любо́вь, кото́рая *(1)* ...бу́дет цвести́ до конца́ на́ших жи́зней. / *(2)* ...бу́дет продолжа́ться пока́ существу́ет мир. / *(3)* ...вы́растет ещё сильне́е, ещё бо́лее прекра́сной. ♦ **Our hearts have entwined never(more) to part.** На́ши сердца́ сплели́сь, чтобы никогда́ (бо́лее) не раздели́ться. ♦ **When I** *(1)* **...talk with you... /** *(2)* **...read your letters... I feel that our two hearts caress. Do you feel the same?** Когда́ я *(1)* ...говорю́ с тобо́й,... / *(2)* ...чита́ю твои́ пи́сьма,... я чу́вствую, что на́ши два се́рдца ласка́ют друг дру́га. Чу́вствуешь ли ты

Russian has 2 different verbs for "go",
one for "on foot" and the other for "by vehicle".

э́то? ♦ **We'll lie in each other's arms and our hearts will speak together.** Мы бу́дем лежа́ть в объя́тиях друг дру́га, и на́ши сердца́ бу́дут говори́ть друг с дру́гом. ♦ **I pray that our two hearts will always speak together.** Я молю́сь о том, что́бы на́ши два се́рдца всегда́ говори́ли друг с дру́гом. ♦ **You and I — two hearts, one love.** Ты и я два се́рдца, одна́ любо́вь. ♦ **You and I could share so many things, make so much wonderful love together, talk about so many things together, connect in heart, mind, and spirit so perfectly.** Ты и я смогли́ бы раздели́ть мно́гое: так мно́го занима́ться прекра́сной любо́вью, говори́ть о мно́гом друг с дру́гом, так соверше́нно соединя́ться се́рдцем, умо́м и ду́хом.

heart: *what my heart seeks*

My heart is searching for *(1)* **...the right person in life.** / *(2)* **...its mate.** / *(3)* **...([4] true** / *[5]* **genuine) love.** Моё се́рдце и́щет *(1)* ...пра́вильного спу́тника жи́зни. / *(1)* ...себе́ па́ру. / *(1)* ...([4] по́длинную / [5] и́скреннюю) любо́вь. ♦ **I have my heart set on seeing you next week.** Моё се́рдце настро́ено на встре́чу с тобо́й на сле́дующей неде́ле. ♦ **I can only follow the dictates of my heart.** Я могу́ сле́довать то́лько веле́ниям своего́ се́рдца. ♦ **A good heart means more (to me) than good looks.** До́брое се́рдце зна́чит бо́льше (для меня́), чем вне́шняя красота́.

heart: *my heart's yearning*

I feel impelled by the acute longing in my heart to write you this letter. Стра́стное стремле́ние се́рдца заставля́ет меня́ написа́ть Вам э́то письмо́. ♦ **My heart is thirsty for your kisses.** Моё се́рдце жа́ждет твои́х поцелу́ев. ♦ **My heart yearns to be with you (there) right now.** Моё се́рдце жа́ждет быть с тобо́й (там) пря́мо сейча́с. ♦ **How my heart yearns to feel the soft pressure of your hand in mine (again).** Как жа́ждет моё се́рдце (опя́ть) почу́вствовать не́жное давле́ние твое́й руки́. ♦ **My heart yearns to show you my love in an endless stream of warm embraces and soft,** *(1)* **adoring** / *(2)* **loving kisses.** Моё се́рдце жа́ждет показа́ть тебе́ свою́ любо́вь в бесконе́чном пото́ке тёплых объя́тий и мя́гких, *(1)* обожа́ющих / *(2)* лю́бящих поцелу́ев. ♦ **My heart yearns so fiercely to have a partner like you in life, one who combines a gentle spirit with sexuality, good-heartedness, intelligence, and a loving nature.** Моё се́рдце так нейстово жа́ждет тако́го спу́тника жи́зни, как ты, тако́го, кто соединя́ет мя́гкий хара́ктер с сексуа́льностью, добросерде́чием, интеллиге́нтностью и лю́бящей нату́рой. ♦ **There is such a(n)** *(1)* **unbearable** / *(2)* **overwhelming** / *(3)* **tremendous** / *(4)* **unrelenting** / *(5)* **agonizing ache in my heart for you.** В моём се́рдце и́з-за тебя́ така́я *(1)* невыноси́мая / *(2)* неопреодоли́мая / *(3)* огро́мная / *(4)* жесто́кая / *(5)* мучи́тельная боль. ♦ **Since** *(1)* **...you left...** / *(2)* **...we've been apart...** **, the ache in my heart never** *(3)* **...ceases.** / *(4)* **...goes away.** С тех пор, как *(1)* ...ты ушла́... / *(2)* ...мы разлучи́лись... боль в моём се́рдце никогда́ не *(3)* ...прекраща́ется. / *(4)* ...ухо́дит. ♦ **Only the sweet softness of your lips can quell the ache of longing that ravages my heart.** То́лько сла́дкая мя́гкость твои́х губ мо́жет подави́ть боль тоски́, разруша́ющей моё се́рдце. ♦ **With you gone, I feel such a pain in my heart.** Когда́ ты не со мной, я чу́вствую таку́ю серде́чную боль.

heart: *my heart*

I have a very *(1)* **loving** / *(2)* **compassionate heart.** У меня́ о́чень *(1)* лю́бящее / *(2)* сострада́тельное се́рдце. ♦ **My heart is** *(1)* **accessible** / *(2)* **available.** Моё се́рдце *(1,2)* свобо́дно. ♦ **I have a large void in my heart which perhaps you can fill.** В моём се́рдце огро́мная пустота́, кото́рую ты, возмо́жно, смо́жешь запо́лнить. ♦ **I have a gypsy heart. I love to travel and enjoy life.** У меня́ цыга́нское се́рдце. Я люблю́ путеше́ствовать и наслажда́ться жи́знью. ♦ **I guess there's a little bit of gypsy in my heart.** Я предполага́ю, что в моём се́рдце есть не́что цыга́нское. ♦ **I'm just a kid at heart.** Я се́рдцем про́сто дитя́. ♦ **I'm still (very) young at heart.** Я всё ещё (о́чень) мо́лод *(ж: молода́)* се́рдцем.

Dipthongs in Russian are made by adding й
*to the end of a vowel (*а, е, ё, о, у, э, ю, *and* я*).*

♦ **I'm a romantic at heart.** Я в своём се́рдце рома́нтик. ♦ **I live from the heart.** Я живу́ се́рдцем.

| **heart:** *my heart on my sleeve* |

I guess I wear my heart on my sleeve. Я полага́ю, что у меня́ душа́ нараспа́шку.

| **heart:** *heart to heart* |

I want to sit and talk with you heart to heart. Я хочу́ посиде́ть и поговори́ть с тобо́й от се́рдца к се́рдцу. ♦ **I would like very much to have a real heart-to-heart** *(1)* **talk /** *(2)* **discussion with you.** Я о́чень хоте́л бы по-настоя́щему *(1,2)* поговори́ть с тобо́й от се́рдца к се́рдцу. ♦ **My heart** *(1)* **wants /** *(2)* **yearns to speak to your heart.** Моё се́рдце *(1)* хо́чет / *(2)* жа́ждет говори́ть с твои́м се́рдцем. ♦ *(1)* **These flowers are... /** *(2)* **This gift is... from my heart to your heart.** *(1)* Э́ти цветы́... / *(2)* Э́тот пода́рок... от всего́ се́рдца. ♦ **This comes from my heart to yours.** Э́то идёт из моего́ се́рдца к твоему́.

| **heart:** *a good handle on your heart* |

I want a *(1)* **woman /** *(2)* **man who has a good handle on** *(3)* **her /** *(4)* **his heart and mind.** Я хочу́ *(1)* ...таку́ю же́нщину, кото́рая... / *(2)* ...тако́го мужчи́ну, кото́рый... хорошо́ владе́ет *(3,4)* свои́м се́рдцем и умо́м.

| **heart:** *change of heart* |

I hope you haven't *(1,2)* **had a change of heart.** Я наде́юсь, что *(1) (feelings)* ...твои́ чу́вства не измени́лись. / *(2) (mind)* ...ты не переду́мала *(ж: переду́мал).* ♦ **If you have a change of heart, be honest with me and tell me so.** Е́сли *(1) (feelings)* ...твои́ чу́вства изме́нятся,... / *(2) (mind)* ...ты переду́маешь,... будь честна́ *(ж: че́стен)* со мной и скажи́ э́то.

| **heart:** *broken heart(s)* |

Please don't break my heart. Пожа́луйста, не разбива́йте моё се́рдце. ♦ **You broke my heart.** Ты разби́ла *(ж: разби́л)* моё се́рдце. ♦ **My heart is (completely) broken.** Моё се́рдце (соверше́нно) разби́то. ♦ **My heart is breaking.** Моё се́рдце разбива́ется. ♦ **I('ve) had my heart broken (***[1]* **...a few times. /** *[2]* **...more than once. /** *[3]* **...too many times.).** Моё се́рдце бы́ло разби́то (*[1]* ...не́сколько раз. / *[2]* ...не раз. / *[3]* ...сли́шком мно́го раз.) ♦ **It really cut me to the heart.** Э́то (действи́тельно) рани́ло меня́ в са́мое се́рдце. ♦ **If you don't want me to suffer from a broken heart, you'll write to me at least once a week.** Е́сли ты не хо́чешь, что́бы я страда́л *(ж: страда́ла)* от разби́того се́рдца, ты бу́дешь писа́ть мне по ме́ньшей ме́ре раз в неде́лю. ♦ **I've been suffering from a broken heart (because you haven't written to me lately).** Я страда́ю от разби́того се́рдца (, потому́ что ты не писа́ла *[ж: писа́л]* мне после́днее вре́мя). ♦ **I don't want you to suffer from a broken heart.** Я не хочу́, что́бы ты страда́ла *(ж: страда́л)* от разби́того се́рдца. ♦ **I wonder how many hearts you've broken (and never even realized it).** Я хоте́л бы знать, ско́лько серде́ц ты разби́ла *(ж: разби́л)* (и никогда́ да́же э́того не зна́ла *[ж: знал]*). ♦ **You must have a trail of broken hearts** *(1)* **...behind you. /** *(2)* **...leading from your door.** У тебя́ должна́ быть тропа́, у́стланная разби́тыми сердца́ми *(1)* ...позади́. / *(2)* ...веду́щая от твое́й две́ри. ♦ **The fact that you're not married can only mean that you've left behind a trail of broken hearts.** Тот факт, что ты до сих пор не за́мужем *(ж: жена́т),* мо́жет означа́ть то́лько, что ты оста́вила *(ж: оста́вил)* позади́ тропу́, у́стланную разби́тыми сердца́ми.

| **heart:** *heavy heart* |

There is such heaviness in my heart (since you left). У меня́ на се́рдце така́я тя́жесть по́сле твоего́ ухо́да).

| **heart:** *cross my heart* |

I cross my heart. Я кляну́сь.

Some phrases are listed under more than one main word.

heart: *carve a heart*

I'll carve a heart with our initials on a tree. Я вы́режу се́рдце с на́шими инициа́лами на де́реве.

heart: *salutations in letters*

(1,2) **Dear heart,** *(1)* Се́рдце моё, / *(2)* Душа́ моя́, ♦ *(1,2)* **My (own) dear heart,** *(1)* Се́рдце / *(2)* Серде́чко моё! ♦ **Beloved of my heart,** Избра́нница *(ж: Избра́нник)* моего́ се́рдца,...

heart: *sayings*

What the heart thinks, the tongue speaks. Что на уме́, то и на языке́. ♦ **Faint heart never won fair lady.** Ро́бкое се́рдце никогда́ не покори́ло краси́вую же́нщину. ♦ **It's the heart that counts.** Са́мое ва́жное -- э́то то, что чу́вствует се́рдце.

heartache *n* душе́вная боль, душе́вные му́ки; страда́ние ♦ **agonizing** ~ мучи́тельная душе́вная боль ♦ **constant** ~ постоя́нная душе́вная боль ♦ **intense** ~ си́льная душе́вная боль ♦ **tremendous** ~ ужа́сная душе́вная боль ♦ **unbearable** ~ непереноси́мая душе́вная боль ♦ **You've caused me so much heartache.** Ты причини́ла *(ж: причини́л)* мне тако́е страда́ние. ♦ **You've caused me more heartache than you can imagine.** Ты принесла́ *(ж: принёс)* мне бо́льше срада́ний, чем мо́жешь себе́ предста́вить. ♦ **I never want to cause you any heartache.** Я не хочу́ никогда́ быть причи́ной твои́х страда́ний. ♦ **I've suffered so much heartache (** *[1]* **...in the past.** / *[2]* **...in my life.** / *[3]* **...because of you.)** Я страда́л *(ж: страда́ла)* так мно́го (*[1]*...в про́шлом. / *[2]* ...в свое́й жи́зни. / *[3]* ...из-за тебя́.). ♦ **I've had more than my fair share of heartache.** На мою́ до́лю вы́пало бо́лее, чем доста́точно страда́ний.

heartbeat *n* бие́ние се́рдца, пульса́ция се́рдца ♦ **My heartbeat escalates every time** *(1)* **...I think about you.** / *(2)* **...I look at your photo.** / *(3)* **...I see you.** / *(4)* **...I hear your voice.** / *(5)* **...you touch me.** Бие́ние моего́ се́рдца учаща́ется ка́ждый раз, когда́ *(1)* ...я ду́маю о тебе́. / *(2)* ... я смотрю́ на твою́ фотогра́фию. / *(3)* ...я ви́жу тебя́. / *(4)* ...я слы́шу твой го́лос. / *(5)* ...ты каса́ешься меня́.

heartbreak *n* большо́е го́ре; жесто́кое разочарова́ние.

heartbreaker *n* 1. *(person who breaks hearts)* челове́к, разбива́ющий сердца́ *(1 term)*; 2. *(big disappointment)* большо́е разочарова́ние ♦ **It was a real heartbreaker for me not to be able to come over there this summer.** То, что я не смог *(ж: смогла́)* прие́хать туда́ э́тим ле́том, бы́ло действи́тельно больши́м разочарова́нием для меня́.

hearten *vt* ободря́ть / ободри́ть *(whom = acc.)*; воодушевля́ть / воодушеви́ть *(whom = acc.)*.

heartening *adj* обнадёживающий, -ая, -ее, -ие, ободря́ющий, -ая, -ее, -ие.

heartfelt *adj* и́скренний, -яя, -ее, -ие, серде́чный, -ая, -ое, -ые.

heartless *adj* бессерде́чный, -ая, -ое, -ые, безжа́лостный, -ая, -ое, -ые ♦ **How** *(1)* **can** / *(2)* **could you be so (cruel and) heartless?** Как *(1)* мо́жешь / *(2)* могла́ *(ж: мог)* ты быть тако́й (жесто́кой и) бессерде́чной *(ж: таки́м [жесто́ким и] бессерде́чным?)*? ♦ **What a heartless swine you are.** Кака́я ты бессерде́чная свинья́. ♦ **That was about the most heartless thing you could (ever) have done.** Это была́ са́мая бессерде́чная вещь, кото́рую ты (когда́-либо) могла́ *(ж: мог)* бы сде́лать. ♦ **You are** *(1)* **really** / *(2)* **truly heartless (, do you know that?).** Ты *(1)* действи́тельно / *(2)* по-настоя́щему бессерде́чная *(ж: бессерде́чный)* (, ты зна́ешь?). ♦ **How could I have been so heartless to you?** Как мог *(ж: могла́)* я быть таки́м бессерде́чным *(ж: такой бессерде́чной)* с тобо́й? ♦ **The way you** *(1)* **keep** / *(2)* **hold your love from me is totally heartless.** То, как ты *(1,2)* отка́зываешь мне в любви́, соверше́нно бессерде́чно. ♦ **The most heartless thing you could ever do to me is to say that a thousand kisses are enough for one night.** Са́мое

The singular past tense of Russian verbs ends in -л (m) (usually), -ла (f) or -ло (n). the plural past tense ends in -li.

бессерде́чное, что ты могла́ бы когда́-нибудь сде́лать, э́то сказа́ть мне, что ты́сячи поцелу́ев доста́точно для одно́й но́чи.

heart-rending *adj* душераздира́ющий, -ая, -ее, -ие.

heartsick *adj* удручён, удручена́, -о́, -ы́, пода́влен, -а, -о, -ы *(short forms).*

heartstrings *n, pl (responsive feelings)* серде́чные стру́ны; *(deepest feelings)* глубоча́йшие чу́вства ♦ **pull my ~s** взволнова́ть меня́ до глубины́ души́ ♦ **That really tugs at my heartstrings.** Это действи́тельно задева́ет все мои́ серде́чные стру́ны.

heartthrob *n* возлю́бленный *m*, возлю́бленная *f.*

heart-to-heart *adj* задуше́вный, -ая, -ое, -ые, инти́мный, -ая, -ое, -ые, серде́чный, -ая, -ое, -ые, по ду́шам ♦ **I'm seeking a heart-to-heart connection.** Я ищу́ ту, с кото́рой *(ж: того́, с кем)* смогу́ соедини́ться сердца́ми.

heartwarming *adj* ра́достный, -ая, -ое, -ые.

heart-winning *adj* побежда́ющий (-ая, -ее, -ие) сердца́, завоёвывающий (-ая, -ее, -ие) сердца́.

heart-wrenching *adj* разрыва́ющий (-ая, -ее, -ие) се́рдце.

heat *n* теплота́, тепло́; жар ♦ **moist ~** вла́жная теплота́ ♦ **searing ~** обжига́ющий жар ♦ **feel the ~ of your body** ощуща́ть / ощути́ть тепло́ твоего́ те́ла ♦ **I want to feel all the heat centered in the core of your womanhood.** Я хочу́ ощути́ть всё тепло́, спря́танное в глубине́ твое́й же́нственности. ♦ **An extraordinary heat suffuses my whole body whenever** *(1)* **...the vision of your perfect loveliness comes into my mind.** / *(2)* **...I think about your voluptuous beauty.** / *(3)* **...I look at your photo.** Всегда́, когда́ бы *(1)* ...твоя́ превосхо́дная красота́ ни вста́ла в мое́й па́мяти,... / *(2)* ...я ни поду́мал о твоём прекра́сном сла́достном те́ле,... / *(3)* ...я ни смотре́л на твою́ фотогра́фию,... я весь охва́чен жа́ром.

heave *vi* вздыма́ться ♦ **I love to watch your breasts heave when passion sweeps through you.** Я люблю́ ви́деть, как вздыма́ется твоя́ грудь, когда́ страсть охва́тывает тебя́.

heaven *n* 1. *(sky)* не́бо, небеса́ *pl*; 2. *(paradise)* небеса́ *pl*, рай; 3. *(God)* Небеса́ ♦ **absolute ~** соверше́нно боже́ственно ♦ **~ on earth** рай на земле́ ♦ **for ~'s sake** ра́ди Бо́га ♦ **have ~ to share** име́ть рай, для того́, чтобы подели́ться *(with whom = + с + instr.)* *(1 term)* ♦ **in ~** в раю́ ♦ **in (the) seventh ~** на седьмо́м не́бе.

> **heaven:** *I'm in heaven*

I think I'm in heaven. Мне ка́жется, что я в раю́. ♦ **I feel like I'm in heaven.** Я чу́вствую себя́, как в раю́. ♦ **This must be what heaven is like.** Должно́ быть на э́то похо́ж рай. ♦ **Now I know the true meaning of heaven.** Тепе́рь я зна́ю, что тако́е рай.

> **heaven:** *you are heaven*

You are my heaven on earth. Ты мой рай на земле́. ♦ **If you have a nature as generous as your** *(1)* **beauty** / *(2)* **body, you are truly heaven's special prize.** Если Ваш хара́ктер тако́й же замеча́тельный, как *(1)* ...Ва́ша красота́... / *(2)* ...Ва́ше те́ло..., то Вы и́стинный дар небе́с. ♦ **If the rest of you is (half) as beautiful as your face, then heaven holds no greater promises for me.** Если и всё остально́е в Вас (хотя́ бы наполови́ну) так же прекра́сно, как Ва́ше лицо́, тогда́ мне не о чём бо́льше проси́ть небеса́.

> **heaven:** *heaven with you*

Cuddling with you is (absolutely) heaven! Обнима́ться с тобо́й (про́сто) рай. ♦ **I** *(1)* **long** / *(2)* **yearn for the heaven of your** *(3)* **precious** / *(4)* **dear** / *(5)* **wonderful arms.** Я *(1,2)* тоску́ю по ра́ю твои́х *(3)* драгоце́нных / *(4)* дороги́х / *(5)* замеча́тельных рук. ♦ **It would be absolute heaven to lie next to you, hold you tenderly in my arms, look into your beautiful, dark eyes, kiss you ever so lovingly and adoringly, and feel the magic warmth of your body all through the night.** Бы́ло бы так замеча́тельно лежа́ть ря́дом с тобо́й,

---

держа́ть тебя́ не́жно в объя́тиях, смотре́ть в твои́ прекра́сные тёмные глаза́, целова́ть тебя́ с любо́вью и обожа́нием и чу́вствовать волше́бное тепло́ твоего́ те́ла всю ночь. ♦ **Heaven holds no sweeter treat than the taste of your beautiful lips.** У небе́с нет бо́лее сла́дкого угоще́ния, чем вкус твои́х прекра́сных губ.

heaven: *Heaven made us for each other*

I am convinced that Heaven made us for each other. Я убеждён *(ж: убеждена́)*, что небеса́ со́здали нас друг для дру́га.

heaven: *that we share*

I want to cling to this small piece of heaven that we share. Я хочу́ удержа́ть ма́ленький ку́сочек ра́я, кото́рый нас соединя́ет.

heaven: *expressions*

Good heavens! Бо́же мой! ♦ **Thank heavens!** Сла́ва Бо́гу!

heavenly *adj* боже́ственный, -ая, -ое, -ые, небе́сный, -ая, -ое, -ые, неземно́й, -а́я, -о́е, -ы́е; *(fig.)* замеча́тельный, -ая, -ое, -ые, великоле́пный, -ая, -ое, -ые, прекра́сный, -ая, -ое, -ые ♦ **That** *(1)* **is** / *(2)* **was (absolutely) heavenly.** *(1)* Это... *(2)* Это бы́ло... (абсолю́тно) боже́ственно. ♦ **It would be so heavenly to crawl into bed with you.** Бы́ло бы так прекра́сно лечь с тобо́й в посте́ль. ♦ **How heavenly it would be to take your beautiful face softly in my hands and kiss it lovingly all over, many, many, many times.** Как боже́ственно бы́ло бы не́жно взять в ру́ки твоё прекра́сное лицо́ и любо́вно покры́ть его́ поцелу́ями мно́го, мно́го, мно́го раз. ♦ **There is nothing as heavenly as** *(1)* **... holding you in my arms.** / *(2)* **... kissing your beautiful mouth.** / *(3)* **... making love with you.** / *(4)* **... looking in your beautiful eyes.** / *(5)* **... cuddling with you.** / *(6)* **... feeling your touch on my body.** / *(7)* **... feeling your lips against mine.** Нет ничего́ боже́ственней, чем *(1)* ...держа́ть тебя́ в объя́тиях. / *(2)* ...целова́ть твой прекра́сный рот. / *(3)* ...занима́ться любо́вью с тобо́й. / *(4)* ...смотре́ть в твои́ прекра́сные глаза́. / *(5)* ...обнима́ться с тобо́й. / *(6)* ...чу́вствовать твоё прикоснове́ние на моём те́ле. / *(7)* ...чу́вствовать твои́ гу́бы на свои́х. ♦ **I look at your beautiful face in this photo and I can imagine how heavenly it would be to** *(1)* **...hold you in my arms.** / *(2)* **... kiss your sweet little mouth.** / *(3)* **... make love with you.** / *(4)* **... cuddle up with you.** / *(5)* **... feel your lips against mine.** / *(6)* **... feel the warmth of you.** Я смотрю́ на твоё прекра́сное лицо́ на э́той фотогра́фии, и я могу́ предста́вить себе́ как боже́ственно бы́ло бы *(1)* ...держа́ть тебя́ в объя́тиях. / *(2)* ...целова́ть твой сла́дкий ма́ленький рот. / *(3)* ...занима́ться любо́вью с тобо́й. / *(4)* ...обнима́ться с тобо́й. / *(5)* ...чу́вствовать твои́ гу́бы на свои́х. / *(6)* ...чу́вствовать твоё тепло́. ♦ **You have the most heavenly face I have ever seen.** У тебя́ са́мое изуми́тельное лицо́ из всех, когда́-либо ви́денных мной. ♦ **I yearn for the heavenly lushness of your beautiful body.** Я тоску́ю по боже́ственной ро́скоши твоего́ прекра́сного те́ла.

heavens *n, pl* поднебе́сье.

heaviness *n* тя́жесть *f* ♦ **There is such heaviness in my heart (since you left).** У меня́ на се́рдце така́я тя́жесть (по́сле твоего́ ухо́да).

heaving *adj* вздыма́ющийся, -аяся, -еяся, -иеся ♦ ~ **breasts** вздыма́ющаяся грудь.

heavy *adj* 1. *(heavy in weight)* тяжёлый, -ая, -ое, -ые; 2. *(fat)* то́лстый, -ая, -ое, -ые.

heavy-hearted *adj* с тяжёлым се́рдцем.

heavyset *adj* то́лстый, -ая, -ое, -ые.

hedonist *n* гедони́ст.

hedonistic *adj* гедонисти́ческий, -ая, -ое, -ие.

heel *n* 1. пя́тка 2. *(pl) (high-heeled shoes)* ту́фли на высо́ких каблука́х, каблуки́; 3. *(contemptible person)* подле́ц, негодя́й ♦ **little** ~ пя́точка ♦ **spike** ~**s** то́нкие и высо́кие

Clock and calender time are discussed in Appendix 5, page 759.

каблуки́, ту́фли на шпи́льках ♦ **You look gorgeous in high heels.** Ты вы́глядишь великоле́пно на высо́ких каблука́х.

height *n* 1. *(person)* рост 2. *(thing)* высота́; *pl* верши́ны, высо́ты ♦ **above average ~** вы́ше сре́днего ро́ста ♦ **dizzying ~s of passion** головокружи́тельные верши́ны стра́сти ♦ **heavenly ~s** заобла́чная высота́ ♦ **medium ~** сре́дний рост ♦ **It was the heights for me.** Это бы́ло верши́ной для меня́. ♦ **I'm going to take you to new heights of dizzying passion.** Я подниму́ тебя́ к но́вым верши́нам головокружи́тельной стра́сти. ♦ **I want to take you on a daily (1) ...excursion to... / (2) ...tour of... the heights of pleasure.** Я хочу́ повести́ тебя́ на *(1)* ...ежедне́вную экску́рсию... / *(2)* ...ежедне́вный тур... к верши́нам наслажде́ния.

heighten *vt (increase)* повыша́ть / повы́сить *(what = acc.)*; *(strengthen)* уси́ливать / уси́лить *(what = acc.)* ♦ **My desire (for you) heightens whenever (1) ...I think about you. / (2) ...you look at me.** Моя́ жа́жда (тебя́) возраста́ет вся́кий раз, когда́ *(1)* ...я ду́маю о тебе́. / *(2)* ...бы ты ни взгляну́ла *(ж: взгляну́л)* на меня́.

heighten *vi* увели́чиваться / увели́читься ♦ **Whenever I look at you, my desire heightens (unbearably).** Когда́ бы я ни взгляну́л *(ж: взгляну́ла)* на тебя́, моё жела́ние увели́чивается (невыноси́мо).

heir *n* насле́дник.

heiress *n* насле́дница.

hell *n* ад, преиспо́дняя ♦ **This being apart from you is sheer hell.** Быть без тебя́ - су́щий ад. ♦ **Wanting you and not being able to have you is sheer hell.** Хоте́ть тебя́ и не име́ть возмо́жности быть с тобо́й -- су́щая пы́тка. ♦ **You can never know the sheer hell I go through (1) ... being apart from you. / (2) ... wanting you and not being able to have you.** Ты никогда́ не узна́ешь че́рез каку́ю пы́тку я прохожу́, *(1)* ... бу́дучи в разлу́ке с тобо́й. / *(2)* ...жела́я тебя́ и не име́я возмо́жности быть с тобо́й. ♦ **(1) He / (2) She has made my life (a) hell.** *(1)* Он преврати́л... / *(2)* Она́ преврати́ла... мою́ жизнь в ад. ♦ **(1) He / (2) She is... / (3) You're... hell to live with.** Жить с *(1)* ним / *(2)* ней / *(3)* тобо́й -- э́то су́щий ад. ♦ **The last few (1) days / (2) weeks / (3) months without you have been hell.** После́дние *(1)* дни / *(2)* неде́ли / *(3)* ме́сяцы без тебя́ бы́ли а́дом. ♦ *(1,2)* **Go to hell!** *(1)* Пошла́ *(ж: Пошёл)* к чёрту! / *(2)* Иди́ к чёрту! ♦ **What the hell (1) ...does that mean? / (2) ...are you doing? / (3) ...is going on? / (4) ...can / (5) should I do?** Что э́то, чёрт возьми́, *(1)* ...зна́чит? / *(2)* ...ты де́лаешь? / *(3)* ...происхо́дит? / *(4)* ...я могу́ / *(5)* до́лжен *(ж: должна́)* де́лать? ♦ **What the hell are you talking about?** О чём, чёрт возьми́, ты говори́шь? ♦ **How the hell (1) ...do I know? / (2) ...should I know? / (3) ...would I know?** Отку́да, чёрт возьми́, я *(1)* ...зна́ю? / *(2)* ...до́лжен *(ж: должна́)* знать? / *(3)* ...мог *(ж: могла́)* бы знать? ♦ **That's a hell of a (1) ...thing to do / (2) say. / (3) ...way to show your love.** Черто́вски пло́хо *(1)* ...де́лать / *(2)* говори́ть так. / *(3)* ...выка́зывать свою́ любо́вь таки́м о́бразом.

---

hell: quotation

"Heaven has no Rage like Love to Hatred turn'd, Nor Hell a Fury, like a Woman scorned." *William Congreve, "The Mourning Bride" (1697)* «На небеса́х нет тако́й я́рости, как любо́вь, обращённая в не́нависть, в аду́ нет тако́го бе́шенства, как же́нщина отве́ргнутая.» *Ви́льям Ко́нгрив, «Скорбя́щая неве́ста», (1697).*

help *vt* помога́ть / помо́чь *(whom = dat.)* ♦ **(1) I want... / (2) I'd like... to help you.** *(1)* Я хочу́... / *(2)* Я хоте́л *(ж: хоте́ла)* бы... помо́чь тебе́. ♦ **Tell me how I can help (you).** Скажи́ мне, как я могу́ помо́чь тебе́. ♦ **I (1) can / (2) will help you.** *(1)* Я могу́ помо́чь... / *(2)* Я помогу́... тебе́. ♦ **I can't help you.** Я не могу́ помо́чь тебе́. ♦ **I can't help myself.** Я не могу́ с собо́й спра́виться. ♦ **Are you mad at me for loving you? I know I shouldn't,**

Reflexive verbs are those that end in -ся or -сь.
The -ся or -сь also goes onto a past tense ending.

but I can't help it. It just happens all by itself. Ты óчень сéрдишься на меня за любóвь к тебé? Я знáю, что не дóлжен *(ж: должнá)*, но я не могý ничегó с э́тим подéлать, так случи́лось самó по себé.

help *n* пóмощь *f* ♦ **I appreciate your help (very much).** Я (óчень) ценю́ твою́ пóмощь. ♦ **I need your help.** Мне нужнá твоя́ пóмощь.

helpful *adj* готóвый (-ая, -ое, -ые) помóчь, услýжливый, -ая, -ое, -ые.

helpfulness *n* готóвность *f* помóчь *(1 term).*

helpless *adj* беспóмощный, -ая, -ое, -ые.

helplessness *n* беспóмощность *f.*

helpmate *n* помóщник *m*, помóщница *f* ♦ **I want to take care of you and be your helpmate in every way.** Я хочý забóтиться о тебé и во всём тебé помогáть.

herbage *n (slang) (marijuana)* марихуáна.

herb-intolerant *adj (stated in a personal ad)* Курящих марихуáну прошý не беспокóить.

herbivore *n (slang) (user of marijuana)* куря́щий (-ая, -ие) марихуáну.

herbly *adj (slang) (using marijuana)* куря́щий (-ая, -ие) марихуáну.

hermit *n* отшéльник.

hero *n* герóй ♦ **You are my hero.** Ты мой герóй. ♦ **You will always be my hero.** Ты всегдá бýдешь мои́м герóем.

heroism *n* герои́зм ♦ **You have the kind of beauty that drives men to heroism.** У тебя́ такáя красотá, котóрая вдохновля́ет мужчи́н на герои́зм.

herpes *n* герпéс ♦ **dormant** ~ латéнтный герпéс ♦ **infrequent** ~ нечáстый герпéс.

hesitate *vi* колебáться / поколебáться, сомневáться ♦ *(1,2)* **He who hesitates is lost.** *(1)* Теря́ет тот, кто колéблется. / *(2)* Промедлéние смéрти подóбно.

hesitation *n* колебáние ♦ **without** ~ без колебáний.

heterosexual *adj* гетеросексуáльный, -ая, -ое, -ые.

hickey *n* засóс, синя́к, краснотá, кровоподтёк *(на шéе пóсле дóлгого поцелýя).*

hide *vt* пря́тать / спря́тать *(what = acc.),* скрывáть / скрыть *(what = acc.)* ♦ **I'm not very good at hiding my emotions.** Я не óчень умéю пря́тать свои́ эмóции. ♦ **You're hiding something from me.** Ты скрывáешь чтó-то от меня́. ♦ **I'm not hiding anything from you.** Я не скрывáю ничегó от тебя́. ♦ **I would never hide anything from you.** Я не бýду никогдá ничегó от тебя́ скрывáть.

hide *vi* пря́таться / спря́таться, скрывáться / скры́ться, таи́ться.

hideaway *n* убéжище; гнёздышко ♦ **honeymoon** ~ гнёздышко для медóвого мéсяца.

high *adj* высóкий, -ая, -ое, -ие *(short forms:* высóк, -á, -о, -и́) ♦ **highest** наивы́сший, -ая, -ее, -ие ♦ **You are my highest and most precious.** Ты моя́ наивы́сшая и наибóльшая драгоцéнность.

high-achieving *adj* успéшный, -ая, -ое, -ые, дости́гший (-ая, -ее, -ие) успéха.

high-caliber *adj* высóкого кали́бра.

high-handed *adj* влáстный, -ая, -ое, -ые, своевóльный, -ая, -ое, -ые.

high-handedness *adj* влáстность *f*, своевóлие.

high-power *adj* óчень энерги́чный, -ая, -ое, -ые.

hike *vi* ходи́ть пешкóм (в лесý *[woods]),* броди́ть по лéсу *(woods).*

hiker *n* люби́тель ходи́ть пешкóм, ходóк ♦ **avid** ~ азáртный ходóк, стрáстный люби́тель похóдов.

hiking *n* похóд ♦ **Would you like to go hiking (with me)?** Не хотéла *(ж: хотéл)* бы ты пойти́ в похóд (со мнóй)? ♦ **Let's go hiking (together).** Давáй пойдём в похóд (вмéсте).

hinder *vt* мешáть / помешáть *(what, whom = dat.),* препя́тствовать / воспрепя́тствовать

---

*The time zones for many cities of the world
are given in Appendix 6, page 761.*

(what, whom = dat.).

hindrance *n* помéха, препя́тствие ♦ **A child is no hindrance.** Ребёнок - не помéха.

hint *vi* намека́ть / намекну́ть.

hint *n* намёк ♦ **gentle** ~ то́нкий намёк ♦ **subtle** ~ то́нкий намёк ♦ **drop a** ~ оброни́ть намёк, намекну́ть ♦ **take a** ~ понима́ть / поня́ть намёк.

hip *adj (slang)* зна́ющий (-ая, -ее, -ие) (что к чему́), (хорошо́) разбира́ющийся, -аяся, -ееся, -иеся, осведомлённый, -ая, -ое, -ые ♦ **be** ~ знать что к чему́, хорошо́ разби-ра́ться, быть не про́мах.

hip *n* бедро́ *(pl: бёдра)* ♦ **alluring** ~s соблазни́тельные бёдра ♦ **beautiful** ~s прекра́сные бёдра ♦ **(1,2) firm** ~s *(1)* упру́гие / *(2)* пло́тные бёдра ♦ **gorgeous** ~s великоле́пные бёдра ♦ **lovely** ~s прекра́сные бёдра ♦ **narrow** ~s у́зкие бёдра ♦ **slender** ~s стро́йные бёдра ♦ **swing your** ~s верте́ть бёдрами ♦ **You have such beautiful hips.** У тебя́ таки́е прекра́сные бёдра. ♦ **My lips would reverently adore the graceful curve of your hips.** Мои́ гу́бы бу́дут почти́тельно обожа́ть грацио́зные изги́бы твои́х бёдер.

hippie *n* хи́ппи.

hipster *n (slang)* знато́к культу́ры ♦ **handsome** ~ краси́вый знато́к культу́ры.

hit *vt* ударя́ть / уда́рить *(whom = acc.)* ♦ ~ **back** *(slang) (call back)* верну́ть звоно́к *(whom = dat.)*; перезвони́ть *(whom = dat.)* ♦ ~ **it off** *(slang)* ла́дить / пола́дить *(with whom = + с + instr.)* ♦ ~ **on** *(slang) (flirt)* флиртова́ть *(whom = + с + instr.)* ♦ ~ **up** *vt (slang) (call)* звони́ть / позвони́ть *(whom = dat.)*; *(send a message)* посыла́ть / посла́ть сообще́ние *(whom = dat.)*.

hit back:

Hit me back. *(call back)* Перезвони́ мне.

hit it off:

You and I just seemed to hit it off together from the very start. Ты и я, каза́лось, хорошо́ ла́дили с са́мого нача́ла. ♦ **I'm glad we hit it off so well with each other.** Я рад *(ж: ра́да)*, что мы так хорошо́ ла́дим друг с дру́гом. ♦ **It's wonderful the way we hit it off together.** Прекра́сно, что мы так хорошо́ ла́дим друг с дру́гом. ♦ **We just didn't seem to hit it off together.** Похо́же, что мы про́сто не подходи́ли друг дру́гу. ♦ **Before we talk about a long-term relationship, we have to see how we hit it off together (in person).** Пре́жде, чем говори́ть о дли́тельных отноше́ниях, мы должны́ поня́ть, подходим ли мы друг дру́гу.

hit on:

I can imagine a lot of guys are hitting on you. *(flirting)* Я представля́ю, что мно́гие мужчи́ны флирту́ют с тобо́й.

hit up:

Hit me up. *(call)* Позвони́ (мне). ; *(send a message)* Пошли́ (мне) сообще́ние.

hitch *n (problem, difficulty)* зами́нка, помéха; *(delay* заде́ржка*)* ♦ **There's a (small) hitch.** Существу́ет (небольша́я) помéха.

hitched *adj (slang) (married)* жена́т *m*, за́мужем *f* ♦ **get** ~ жени́ться *m*, вы́йти за́муж *f*.

hobby *n* хо́бби *neut., indecl. (pl:* хо́бби*)* ♦ **What are your hobbies and interests?** Каки́е у Вас хо́бби и интере́сы? ♦ **Some of my hobbies and interests are...** Не́которые из мои́х хо́бби и интере́сов: ... ♦ **As for hobbies and interests, I like to...** Насчёт хо́бби и интере́сов, мне нра́вится...

hockey *n* хокке́й ♦ **field** ~ хокке́й на траве́ ♦ **ice** ~ хокке́й на льду ♦ **tonsil** ~ *(slang)* францу́зский поцелу́й.

hold *vt* 1. держа́ть *(what, whom = acc.)*; 2. *(embrace)* обнима́ть / обня́ть *(whom = acc.)* ♦ ~ **back** *vt* сде́рживать / сдержа́ть, уде́рживать / удержа́ть *(what, whom = acc.)*.

---

*Optional parts of sentences are preceded
or followed (or both) by three dots.*

hold: *I want to hold you*

I want to *(1)* **put /** *(2)* **wrap my arms around you and hold you tight.** *(1,2)* Я хочу́ обви́ть тебя́ рука́ми и держа́ть тебя́ кре́пко. ♦ **I want to hold you** *(1)* **...in my arms. /** *(2)* **...tenderly. /** *(3)* **...close (to me) (and kiss you tenderly).** Я хочу́ держа́ть тебя́ *(1)* ...в объя́тиях. / *(2)* ...не́жно. / *(3)* ...бли́зко (ко мне) (и целова́ть тебя́ не́жно). ♦ **I** *(1,2)* **want so much to hold you** *(3)* **...tightly against me. /** *(4)* **...in my arms and kiss you endlessly.** Я так *(1)* ...жа́жду... / *(2)* ...си́льно хочу́... *(3)* ...прижа́ть тебя́ кре́пко к себе́. / *(4)* ...обня́ть тебя́ и целова́ть бесконе́чно. ♦ **I desire so ardently to hold you tenderly in my arms.** Я так жа́жду не́жно держа́ть тебя́ в объя́тиях. ♦ **I ache so terribly to hold you in my arms (again).** Я так отча́янно жа́жду (опя́ть) заключи́ть тебя́ в объя́тия. ♦ **It would be absolute heaven to lie next to you, hold you tenderly in my arms, look into your beautiful, dark eyes, kiss you ever so lovingly and adoringly, and feel the magic warmth of your body all through the night.** Это бы́ло бы так прекра́сно лежа́ть ря́дом с тобо́й, держа́ть тебя́ не́жно в объя́тиях, смотре́ть в твои́ прекра́сные тёмные глаза́, целова́ть тебя́ с любо́вью и обожа́нием и чу́вствовать волше́бное тепло́ твоего́ те́ла всю ночь. ♦ **I dream of holding you (tenderly) in my arms.** Я мечта́ю о том, что́бы (не́жно) обня́ть тебя́. ♦ **If only I could hold you** *(1)* **...close to me,... /** *(2)* **...in my arms,...(for a little while,) it would be so wonderful.** Е́сли бы то́лько я смог *(1)* ...прижа́ть тебя́ ко мне... / *(2)* ...обня́ть тебя́... (на мгнове́ние), э́то бы́ло бы так замеча́тельно. ♦ **How I wish that I were holding you in my arms at this very minute, covering your beautiful face with adoring kisses.** Как бы я жела́л держа́ть тебя́ в объя́тиях в э́ту са́мую мину́ту, покрыва́я твоё прекра́сное лицо́ обожа́ющими поцелу́ями. ♦ **I'm completely devoid of any** *(1,2)* **ambition to do anything except hold you in my arms and make love to you.** Я соверше́нно лишён каки́х-либо други́х *(1)* стремле́ний / *(2)* амби́ций, кро́ме жела́ния держа́ть тебя́ в свои́х объя́тиях и занима́ться любовью с тобо́й. ♦ **I wish so much that I could hold you snugly in my arms and put soft, loving kisses all over your hair and face.** Я так хоте́л бы ую́тно устро́ить тебя́ в объя́тиях и покры́ть мя́кими, лю́бящими поцелу́ями твои́ во́лосы и лицо́. ♦ **The thought of holding you in my arms causes my heart to thunder.** Да́же мысль о том, что́бы обня́ть тебя́, заставля́ет моё се́рдце греме́ть. ♦ **It's been so long since I held you in my arms.** Прошло́ так мно́го вре́мени с тех пор, как я держа́л *(ж: держа́ла)* тебя́ в объя́тиях.

hold: *I can't wait to hold you*

I can't wait to hold you again. Я не могу́ дожда́ться того́ мгнове́ния, когда́ я сно́ва обниму́ тебя́. ♦ **I can't wait to hold you in my arms and kiss you and caress you and pleasure you all night long.** Я не могу́ дожда́ться мгнове́ния, когда́ я смогу́ обня́ть тебя́, и целова́ть тебя́ и ласка́ть тебя́, и доставля́ть наслажде́ние тебе́ всю ночь напролёт.

hold: *I love holding you*

I love holding *(1)* **...you in my arms. /** *(2)* **...hands with you.** Мне нра́вится *(1)* ...обнима́ть тебя́. / *(2)* ...держа́ться за руки с тобо́й.

hold: *you hold me*

I love the way you hold me. Мне о́чень нра́вится, как ты обнима́ешь меня́. ♦ **I need you to hold me.** Мне ну́жно, что́бы ты обняла́ *(ж: о́бнял)* меня́.

hold: *hold hands*

I would love to hold hands with you and walk along the beach. Мне хоте́лось бы взя́ться за́ руки с тобо́й и гуля́ть по пля́жу.

hold: *hold your breasts*

I love to hold the rounded globes of your breasts. Я люблю́ держа́ть окру́глые шары́ твои́х груде́й.

If you're not on familiar terms with a person,
the «ты» forms will have to be changed to «Вы».

---

hold: *past holding*

At this moment *(1)* **...last week...** / *(2)* **...last Sunday...** / *(3)* **...last night... I was holding you in my arms.** В то мгновéние *(1)* ...на прóшлой недéле... / *(2)* ...в прóшлое воскресéнье... / *(3)* ...прóшлой нóчью... я держáл тебя́ в своих объя́тиях.

hold: *all I have to hold*

You're the only thing I have to hold onto (in life). Ты еди́нственное, за что я держýсь (в жи́зни).

hold: *get hold*

Get hold of yourself. Держи́ себя́ в рукáх.

hold back:

It was hard to hold back my tears. Мне бы́ло трýдно сдержáть слёзы. ♦ **I can't hold back my feelings any longer.** Я не могý бóльше сдéрживать свои́ чýвства.

hold *vi* держáться ♦ **~ back** *vi* сдéрживаться / сдержáться ♦ **~ off** задéрживаться / задержáться ♦ **Hold still (a minute).** Не дви́гайся (минýточку). ♦ **I think we should hold off on getting married until next** *(1)* **month** / *(2)* **year.** Я дýмаю, что мы должны́ подождáть с брáком до слéдующего *(1)* мéсяца / *(2)* гóда.

holding *n* *(Russian uses verb)* держáть ♦ **My favorite pleasure in life is** *(1)* **...holding you tight.** / *(2)* **...holding you in my arms.** Сáмое большóе наслаждéние в моéй жи́зни -- *(1)* ...прижáть тебя́ крéпко. / *(2)* ...держáть тебя́ в объя́тиях.

holistic *adj* цéлостный, -ая, -ое, -ые.

hollowness *n* пустотá ♦ **I feel such a terrible hollowness with you gone.** Я чýвствую такýю ужáсную пустотý пóсле твоегó отъéзда.

homage *n* почтéние, уважéние, пóчесть *f* ♦ **This is my homage to you.** Это знак моегó уважéния к тебé. ♦ *(1)* **I want to...** / *(2)* **I'm going to... pay homage to every inch of your beautiful** *(3)* **body** / *(4)* **self with my lips.** Свои́ми губáми я *(1)* ...хочý воздáть... / *(2)* ...воздáм... пóчесть кáждому дю́йму твоегó прекрáсного *(3,4)* тéла. ♦ **As my lips pay devoted homage to your nipples, my fingers will blaze a trail over your burning skin.** В то врéмя, как мои́ гýбы окáжут почти́тельное внимáние твои́м соскáм, мои́ пáльцы бýдут проклáдывать óгненный путь по твоéй кóже.

home *n* 1. *(house)* дом; 2. *(homeward)* домóй; 3. *(at home)* дóма ♦ **cozy ~** ую́тный дом ♦ **mobile ~** дом на колёсах ♦ **trailer ~** дом на колёсах ♦ **at ~** дóма ♦ **I have found my true home in you.** Я нашёл в тебé моё и́стинное пристáнище. ♦ *(1)* **I dream of building...** / *(2)* **I want to build... a home (together) with you.** Я *(1)* мечтáю / *(2)* хочý создáть дом (вмéсте) с тобóй. ♦ **We could spend quiet** *(1)* **evenings** / *(2)* **nights at home.** Мы смóжем проводи́ть спокóйные *(1,2)* вечерá дóма. ♦ **I dream of a cozy home with you.** Я мечтáю об ую́тном дóме с тобóй. ♦ **I'm** *(1,2)* **going home.** Я *(1)* идý *(on foot)* / *(2)* éду *(by veh.)* домóй. ♦ **I have to** *(1,2)* **go home.** Я дóлжен *(ж: должнá) (1)* идти́ *(on foot)* / *(2)* éхать *(by veh.)* домóй.

homebody *n* домосéд *m*, домосéдка *f*.

homegrown *adj* *(slang)* *(from the local area)* мéстный, -ая, -ое, -ые.

homelife *n* домáшняя жизнь.

homely *adj* некраси́вый, -ая, -ое, -ые, невзрáчный, -ая, -ое, -ые.

homemaker *n* хозя́йка дóма; мать семéйства.

homeowner *n* владéлец дóма *m*; владéлица дóма *f*.

homewrecker *n* человéк, разрушáющий чужýю семью́ *(1 term)*.

homey *adj* домáшний, -яя, -ее, -ие.

honest *adj* чéстный, -ая, -ое, -ые ♦ **brutally ~** жестóко правди́вый, -ая, -ое, -ые ♦ **completely ~** абсолю́тно чéстный, -ая, -ое, -ые ♦ **emotionally ~** эмоционáльно чéст-

---

A list of common places with their grammatical endings is given in Appendix 7, page 763.

ный, -ая, -ое, -ые ♦ **painfully** ~ совершéнно чéстный, -ая, -ое, -ые ♦ **refreshingly** ~ необыкновéнно чéстный, -ая, -ое, -ые ♦ **totally** ~ абсолю́тно чéстный, -ая, -ое, -ые ♦ **Please be honest with me.** Пожáлуйста, будь чéстной *(ж: чéстным)* со мной. ♦ *(1)* **I'm going to...** / *(2)* **I'll...** / *(3)* **I want to... be (completely) honest with you.** *(1,2)* Я бýду... / *(3)* Я хочý быть... (совершéнно) чéстным *(ж: чéстной)* с тобóй. ♦ **If you (really) value our relationship, you'll be completely honest with me.** Éсли ты (действительно) цéнишь нáши отношéния, ты бýдешь совершéнно чéстной *(ж: чéстным)* со мной.

honestly *adv* чéстно ♦ **speak** ~ говорить прáвду ♦ **Tell me honestly.** Скажи мне чéстно.

honesty *n* чéстность *f* ♦ **relationship based on** ~ отношéние оснóвано на чéстности ♦ **I appreciate honesty.** Я ценю́ чéстность. ♦ **I give total honesty and I expect total honesty.** Я до концá чéстен и ожидáю пóлной чéстности. ♦ **I admire you for your honesty.** Я восхищáюсь (тобóй) твоéй чéстностью. ♦ **Honesty is what really counts in a relationship.** Чéстность - вот, что действительно вáжно в отношéниях. ♦ **What I** *(1)* **...want...** / *(2)* **...yearn for... most in a relationship is honesty.** Чегó я *(1)* ...хочý... / *(2)* ...жáжду... бóлее всегó в отношéниях - чéстности.

honey *n* 1. мёд; 2. *(term of endearment)* дорогáя *f*, дорогóй *m* ♦ **rivers of (molten)** ~ рéки / потóки (расплáвленного) мёда ♦ **The sweet honey of your lips is just** *(1)* **heavenly** / *(2)* **wonderful** / *(3)* **paradise.** Слáдкий мёд твоих губ -- прóсто *(1)* божéственный / *(2)* прекрáсный / *(3)* рай. ♦ **You'd better save up all your honey, because I'm going to be unbelievably greedy with you.** Ты лýчше *(1)* сохраняй / *(2)* копи весь свой мёд, потомý что я бýду невероя́тно жáден. ♦ **Your lips taste like honey.** У твоих губ вкус мёда. ♦ **The feelings are going to move like warm honey through your loins.** Чýвства разолью́тся по твоим бёдрам слáдкой истóмой. ♦ **When you do that, I feel like my bones have turned to honey and are slowly melting away.** Когдá ты так дéлаешь, я чýвствую, что мои кóсти размягчáются и мéдленно тáют. ♦ **Oh, Honey, I love you!** О, дорогáя *(ж: дорогóй)*, я люблю́ тебя !

Honeybun *(term of endearment)* дорогáя *f*, дорогóй *m*.

honeybunch *(term of endearment)* милый *m*, милая *f*, миленькая, дýшечка, лáпушка ♦ **Honey bunch, you mean everything to me.** Милая *(ж: Милый)*, ты значишь всё для меня́.

honey bunny *(term of endearment)* зáйчик ♦ **My little honey bunny, I can hardly wait to have you in my arms again.** Мой дорогóй, мáленький зáйчик, я с трудóм могý дождáться мгновéния, когдá я опя́ть обнимý тебя́.

honeycake *n (term of endearment)* милая ♦ **I miss you, my little honeycake.** Я скучáю по тебé, моя́ милая.

honeyed *adj* льстивый, -ая, -ое, -ые ♦ ~ **words** льстивые словá.

honeymoon *n* медóвый мéсяц ♦ **be on a** ~ проводить медóвый мéсяц ♦ **go on a** ~ поéхать в свáдебное путешéствие, провести медóвый мéсяц ♦ **I want to take you on a lifelong honeymoon.** Я хочý предложить тебé медóвый мéсяц длинóй в жизнь. ♦ **For a honeymoon I want to take you** *(1,2)* **to** *(name of place).* Я хочý провести с тобóй медóвый мéсяц *(1)* на / *(2)* в *(назвáние мéста).* ♦ **Where would you like to go for / on a honeymoon?** Где бы ты хотéла *(ж: хотéл)* провести медóвый мéсяц? ♦ **Let's go to Bermuda for / on our honeymoon.** Давáй, проведём медóвый мéсяц на Бермýдах.

honor *n* честь *f* ♦ **high** ~ высóкая честь ♦ **I give you my word of honor.** Я даю́ тебé моё чéстное слóво.

honorable *adj* чéстный, -ая, -ое, -ые ♦ **I thought you were honorable.** Я дýмал *(ж: дýмала),* что ты чéстная *(ж: чéстный).*

hook *vt* подцепить на крючóк *(what, whom = acc.).*

Common adult heights are given in Appendix 9, page 776.

hook *n* крючо́к ♦ ~ **of a bra** крючо́к бюстга́льтера ♦ **You've got me on your hook.** Ты подцепи́ла *(ж: подцепи́л)* меня́ на крючо́к..

hook, line and sinker *(idiom)* по́лностью, целико́м, без оста́тка, сра́зу и безоговоро́чно ♦ **I fell for the story hook, line and sinker.** Я сра́зу и безоговоро́чно пове́рил *(ж: пове́рила)* в э́ту исто́рию. ♦ **I fell for it hook, line and sinker.** Я попа́лся *(ж: попа́лась)* на крючо́к.

hook up *vi (slang) (get together, meet)* встреча́ться / встре́титься *(with whom = + с + instr.)*.

hope *vi* наде́яться ♦ **You are all that I could ever hope for.** Ты всё, на что я то́лько наде́юсь. ♦ **I fervently hope that** *(1)* **...you'll give me the chance to meet you in person.** / *(2)* **...I can see you** *([3]* **again** / *[4]* **tonight** / *[5]* **tomorrow).** / *(6)* **...we can see each other** *(7)* **...soon.** / *(8)* **...in the summer.** / *(9)* **...next week** / *(10)* **month** / *(11)* **year.** Я горячо́ наде́юсь, что *(1)* ...ты дашь мне шанс встре́титься с тобо́й наедине́. / *(2)* ...я смогу́ уви́деть тебя́ (*[3]* опя́ть / *[4]* сего́дня ве́чером / *[5]* за́втра). / *(6)* ...мы смо́жем уви́деться друг с дру́гом *(7)* ...ско́ро. / *(8)* ...ле́том. / *(9)* ...на сле́дующей неде́ле. / *(10)* ...в сле́дующем ме́сяце / *(11)* году́.

hope *n* наде́жда ♦ **abiding** ~ постоя́нная наде́жда ♦ **all my** ~**s** все мои́ наде́жды ♦ **bright** ~ све́тлая наде́жда ♦ **constant** ~ постоя́нная наде́жда ♦ **faint** ~ сла́бая наде́жда ♦ **fervent** ~ пы́лкая наде́жда ♦ **great** ~ больша́я наде́жда ♦ **joyful** ~ ра́достная наде́жда ♦ **last** ~ после́дняя наде́жда ♦ **my** ~ моя́ наде́жда ♦ **no** ~ **(at all)** нет (никако́й) наде́жды ♦ **only** ~ еди́нственная наде́жда ♦ **renewed** ~ воскре́сшая наде́жда ♦ **slightest** ~ мале́йшая наде́жда ♦ *(1,2)* **strong** ~ *(1)* си́льная / *(2)* твёрдая наде́жда ♦ **such** ~**s** таки́е наде́жды ♦ **timid** ~ ро́бкая наде́жда ♦ **tiniest** ~ са́мая кро́хотная наде́жда ♦ **tiny** ~ кро́хотная наде́жда ♦ **undying** ~ неумира́ющая наде́жда ♦ **vain** ~ напра́сная наде́жда ♦ **vague** ~ сму́тная наде́жда ♦ **weak** ~ сла́бая наде́жда ♦ **flicker of** ~ про́блеск наде́жды.

hope: verb terms

arouse the ~ пробужда́ть / пробуди́ть наде́жду ♦ **betray** *(1)* **my** / *(2)* **your** ~**s** обману́ть *(1)* мои́ / *(2)* твои́ наде́жды ♦ **cherish the** ~ леле́ять наде́жду ♦ **cling to the** ~ цепля́ться / уцепи́ться за наде́жду ♦ **embrace the** ~ леле́ять наде́жду ♦ **fill me with** ~ наполня́ть / напо́лнить меня́ наде́ждой ♦ **give (me)** ~ подава́ть / пода́ть (мне) наде́жду ♦ **live in the** ~ **(that...)** жить наде́ждой (, что...) ♦ **(not) lose** ~ (не) теря́ть / потеря́ть наде́жду ♦ **nourish the** ~ пита́ть наде́жду.

hope: you are my hope

You are my hope (and inspiration). Ты моя́ наде́жда (и вдохнове́ние). ♦ **You are my hope and dreams, my strength and purpose, my joy and happiness. You are my life.** Ты мои́ наде́жды и мечты́, моя́ си́ла и цель, моя́ ра́дость и сча́стье. Ты моя́ жизнь. ♦ **You are my joy and comfort, my hope and my dreams — my everything.** Ты моя́ ра́дость и утеше́ние, моя́ наде́жда и моя́ мечта́ -- всё для меня́. ♦ **You are the cynosure of all my hopes (and dreams).** Ты путево́дная звезда́ всех мои́х наде́жд (и мечта́ний). ♦ **You fulfill all my hopes and dreams.** Ты испо́лнила *(ж: испо́лнил)* все мои́ наде́жды и мечты́.

hope: I have hope

I cling to the hope that *(1)* **...I can come over there before the end of the year.** / *(2)* **...my** / *(3)* **your visa will come through soon.** / *(4)* **...I can see you this month.** / *(5)* **...we can get married next spring.** Я цепля́юсь за наде́жду, что *(1)* ...смогу́ прие́хать туда́ до конца́ го́да. / *(2)* ...моя́ / *(3)* твоя́ ви́за бу́дет полу́чена ско́ро. / *(4)* ...смогу́ уви́деть тебя́ в э́том ме́сяце. / *(5)* ...мы мо́жем пожени́ться сле́дующей весно́й. ♦ **Hope has ignited in my heart.** Наде́жда зажгла́сь в моём се́рдце. ♦ **It is perhaps pure folly to embrace**

Words in parentheses are optional.

such hopes, but my heart will not allow me to do otherwise. Это, возмо́жно, чисте́йшее безрассу́дство леле́ять таки́е наде́жды, но моё се́рдце не позволя́ет мне ина́че. ◆ **You fill me with hope.** Ты наполня́ешь меня́ наде́ждой. ◆ **In my heart there lives the hope that the day will come when...** В душе́ мое́й живёт наде́жда, что наста́нет день, когда́...

┌─────────────────┐
│ *hope: any hope?* │
└─────────────────┘
Is there any flicker of hope that we can see each other *(1)* **...next week /** *(2)* **month? /** *(3)* **...soon?** Есть ли како́й-ли́бо про́блеск наде́жды, что мы смо́жем уви́деть друг дру́га *(1)* ...на сле́дующей неде́ле? / *(2)* ...в сле́дующем ме́сяце? / *(3)* ...ско́ро?

┌─────────────┐
│ *hope: gone* │
└─────────────┘
All my hopes have dissipated. Все мои́ наде́жды рассе́ялись.

hopeless *adj* безнадёжный, -ая, -ое, -ые ◆ **It's (completely) hopeless (between us).** На́ши отноше́ния (абсолю́тно) безнадёжны. ◆ **I know it's (completely) hopeless, but I love you (with all my heart).** Я зна́ю, что э́то (соверше́нно) безнадёжно, но я (всем се́рдцем) люблю́ тебя́.

hopelessly *adv* безнадёжно ◆ **I'm hopelessly in love with you.** Я безнадёжно влюблён *(ж: влюблена́)* в тебя́.

horizon *n* горизо́нт ◆ **I want someone to explore new horizons with.** Я хочу́ того́, с кем смогу́ открыва́ть но́вые горизо́нты.

hormone *n* гормо́н ◆ **All of your hormones are in perfect orchestration.** Все твои́ гормо́ны в соверше́нной гармо́нии.

horoscope *n* гороско́п ◆ **Do you believe in horoscopes?** Ты ве́ришь в гороско́п? ◆ **I (don't) believe in horoscopes.** Я (не) ве́рю в гороско́п.

horrible *adj* ужа́сный, -ая, -ое, -ые, стра́шный, -ая, -ое, -ые.

horribly *adv* ужа́сно, стра́шно.

horrified *adj* 1. *(frightened)* напу́ган, -а, -о, -ы *(short forms)*; 2. *(shocked)* шоки́рован, -а, -о, -ы *(short forms).*

horse *n* ло́шадь *f*, конь *m.*

horseplay *n* баловство́, озорство́ ◆ **wild ~** разну́зданное весе́лье.

hose *vt (slang) (spoil, ruin)* по́ртить / испо́ртить *(what = acc.)* ◆ **It hosed my entire day.** Это испо́ртило весь мой день.

hospitable *adj* гостеприи́мный, -ая, -ое, -ые.

hospitality *n* гостеприи́мство ◆ **friendly ~** дру́жеское гостеприи́мство ◆ **gracious ~** ми́лое гостеприи́мство ◆ *(1)* **extend /** *(2)* **show ~** *(1,2)* ока́зывать / оказа́ть гостеприи́мство *(to whom = dat.)* ◆ **I'm very grateful for all the hospitality you extended to me.** Я о́чень благода́рен *(ж: благода́рна)* за гостеприи́мство, кото́рое ты оказа́ла *(ж: оказа́л)* мне.

host *n* хозя́ин ◆ **good ~** гостеприи́мный хозя́ин.

hostess *n* хозя́йка ◆ **charming ~** очарова́тельная хозя́йка ◆ **good ~** гостеприи́мная хозя́йка.

hostile *adj* вражде́бный, -ая, -ое, -ые ◆ **You seemed so hostile to me. Why?** Ты каза́лась тако́й вражде́бной *(ж: каза́лся таки́м вражде́бным)* ко мне. Почему́? ◆ **I'm really sorry if I seemed hostile to you.** Мне о́чень жаль, е́сли я каза́лся вражде́бным *(ж: каза́лась вражде́бной)* к тебе́. ◆ **I didn't mean to** *(1)* **sound /** *(2)* **seem so hostile.** Я не хоте́л *(ж: хоте́ла)* *(1,2)* каза́ться таки́м вражде́бным *(ж: вражде́бной).* ◆ **Why are you so hostile toward me lately?** Почему́ ты така́я вражде́бная *(ж: тако́й вражде́б-ный)* (по отноше́нию) ко мне в после́днее вре́мя?

hostility *n* вражде́бность *f*; вражде́бное отноше́ние; вражда́ ◆ **masked ~** замаскиро́-

┌──┐
│ *You can find common clothing sizes in Appendix 11 on page 778.*   │
└──┘

ванная враждёбность ♦ **open** ~ откры́тая враждёбность ♦ **feelings of** ~ враждёбность, враждёбные чу́вства ♦ **I don't think it's any** *(1)* **reason** / *(2)* **cause for hostility.** Я не ду́маю, что есть *(1)* ...кака́я-либо причи́на... / *(2)* ...како́й-либо по́вод... для враждёбности.

hot *adj* горя́чий, -ая, -ее, -ие; пы́лкий, -ая, -ое, -ие, стра́стный, -ая, -ое, -ые, возбуждённый, -ая, -ое, -ые ♦ **become burning** ~ распаля́ться / распали́ться ♦ **get** ~ станови́ться / стать горя́чим *(ж: горя́чей)*, пыла́ть, горе́ть ♦ **make you** ~ зажига́ть / заже́чь тебя́ ♦ **You (always)** *(1)* **get** / *(2)* **make me so** *(3-6)* **hot.** *(1,2)* С тобо́й я (всегда́) *(3)* ...так стра́стен *(ж: стра́стна)* / *(4)* пы́лок *(ж: пылка́)* / *(5)* возбуждён *(ж: возбуждена́)* / *(6)* ...стано́влюсь таки́м горя́чим *(ж: тако́й горя́чей)*. ♦ **Everytime I think about** *(1)* **...you** / *(2)* **...your beautiful body, I get so (terribly)** *(3,4)* **hot.** Ка́ждый раз, ду́мая о *(1)* ...тебе́, / *(2)* ...твоём прекра́сном те́ле, я весь *(ж: вся)* *(3)* горю́ / *(4)* пыла́ю. ♦ **You don't know how hot I get thinking about you.** Ты не представля́ешь, каки́м горя́чим я становлю́сь, ду́мая о тебе́. ♦ **I want to make you so hot that you'll never let me go.** Я хочу́ заже́чь тебя́ так, что́бы ты никогда́ не дала́ мне уйти́. ♦ **I'm hot on the dance floor.** Я прекра́сный танцо́р.

hotel *n* оте́ль *m*, гости́ница ♦ **big** ~ больша́я гости́ница ♦ **cheap** ~ дешёвая гости́ница ♦ **clean** ~ чи́стая гости́ница ♦ **expensive** ~ дорога́я гости́ница ♦ **fancy** ~ *(expensive)* дорого́й оте́ль; *(high-class)* оте́ль вы́сшего кла́сса ♦ **good** ~ хоро́шая гости́ница ♦ **nice** ~ хоро́шая гости́ница ♦ **quiet** ~ ти́хая гости́ница ♦ *(1,2)* **small** ~ *(1)* ма́ленькая / *(2)* небольша́я гости́ница.

hotel: *verb terms*

book a room at a ~ заказа́ть но́мер в гости́нице ♦ **find a** ~ найти́ гости́ницу ♦ **get a room at a** ~ снять но́мер в гости́нице ♦ **look for a** ~ иска́ть гости́ницу ♦ *(1,2)* **stay at a** ~ *(1)* останови́ться / *(2)* жить в гости́нице.

hotlips *n,pl* горя́чие гу́бы.

hot-tempered *adj* вспы́льчивый, -ая, -ое, -ые.

hotty *n (slang) (passionate woman)* стра́стная же́нщина.

hour *n* час *(pl: часы́)* ♦ **a couple (of)** ~s па́ра часо́в ♦ **a few** ~s не́сколько часо́в ♦ **for an** ~ 1. *(in the future)* на час; 2. *(in the past)* час ♦ **for** *(1)* **two** / *(3)* **three** ~s 1. *(planned)* на *(1)* два / *(2)* три часа́; 2. *(planned)* *(1)* два / *(2)* три часа́ ♦ **half an** ~ полчаса́ ♦ **an** ~ **and a half** полтора́ часа́ ♦ **in an** ~ 1. *(after)* че́рез час; 2. *(in the space of)* за оди́н час ♦ **in** *(1)* **two** / *(2)* **three** ~s 1. *(after)* че́рез *(1)* два / *(2)* три часа́; 2. *(in the space of)* за *(1)* два / *(2)* три часа́ ♦ **a many** ~s мно́го часо́в ♦ **several** ~s не́сколько часо́в.

hour: *phrases*

We can spend *(1)* **long** / *(2)* **blissful hours in pleasureful frolic.** Мы мо́жем проводи́ть *(1)* до́лгие / *(2)* счастли́вые часы́ в ша́лостях, по́лных наслажде́ния. ♦ **Those (**[1] **beautiful** / [2] **wonderful) hours will** *(3)* **stay** / *(4)* **remain indelibly etched in my** *(5)* **mind** / *(6)* **memory** *(7)* **...forever.** / *(8)* **...for as long as I live.** Эти (*[1]* прекра́сные / *[2]* замеча́тельные) часы́ *(3,4)* оста́нутся вы́гравированными несмыва́емо в мое́й *(5,6)* па́мяти *(7)* ...навсегда́. / *(8)* ...пока́ я жив *(ж: жива́)*.

hour-gasm *n (hour-long orgasm)* часово́й орга́зм.

house *n* дом ♦ **big** ~ большо́й дом ♦ **new** ~ но́вый дом ♦ **old** ~ ста́рый дом ♦ **single-family** ~ дом длдя одно́й семьй ♦ *(1,2)* **small** ~ *(1)* небольшо́й / *(2)* ма́ленький дом ♦ **two-story** ~ двухэта́жный дом.

housebroken *adj (slang) (used to living in a relationship, easy to live with)* приу́ченный, -ая, -ое, -ые; *(proper, behaved)* благопристо́йный, -ая, -ое, -ые, сми́рный, -ая, -ое, -ые.

household *adj* 1. *(family)* семе́йный, -ая, -ое, -ые; 2. *(care of the house)* хозя́йственный,

---

For general rules of Russian grammar see Appendix 2 on page 686.

-ая, -ое, -ые.

household *n* 1. *(family)* семья; 2. *(care of the house)* хозяйство.

housekeeping *n*: ♦ *(1)* **flare** / *(2)* **talent for** ~ *(1,2)* хозяйственность *f* ♦ **efficiency at** ~ хозяйственность *f.*

housewife *n* домохозяйка.

housework *n* домашняя работа.

how *adv* как ♦ ~ **about** как насчёт *(+ gen.)* ♦ ~ **come** почему (же) ♦ ~ **many** сколько ♦ ~ **much** сколько.

hubby *(slang) (husband)* муженёк.

hue *n (shade)* оттенок; *(color)* цвет ♦ **delicate in** ~ нежный оттенок.

huff and puff *vi* тяжело дышать.

hug *vt* обнимать / обнять ♦ ~ **fiercely** неистово обнимать / обнять ♦ ~ **tenderly** нежно обнимать / обнять ♦ ~ **tightly** крепко обнимать / обнять ♦ ~ **warmly** горячо обнимать / обнять ♦ **I love to kiss, hug, caress, touch, hold hands, nibble, nuzzle, cuddle, rub against, stroke — you just name it.** Я люблю целовать, обнимать, ласкать, касаться, держаться за руки, покусывать, прижаться, сжимать в объятиях, тереться, гладить - ты только назови. ♦ **The way you write to me makes me want to take you in my arms and hug you and hug you and hug you and cover your sweet face with loving kisses.** То, как ты пишешь мне, вызывает во мне желание взять тебя на руки, обнимать, обнимать и обнимать тебя и покрывать твоё нежное лицо любящими поцелуями.

hug *n* объятие ♦ **bear** ~ медвежье объятие ♦ **spontaneous** ~ спонтанное объятие ♦ **warm** ~ тёплое объятие ♦ **give a hug** обнимать / обнять *(to whom = acc.)* ♦ **I hug you.** Я обнимаю тебя. ♦ **Give me a hug.** Обними меня. ♦ **I need an affectionate, loving person with lots of hugs and kisses to give.** Мне нужен нежный, любящий человек, дарящий множество объятий и поцелуев. ♦ **I send you many hugs and kisses, each one filled with much love.** Я посылаю тебе объятия и поцелуи, каждый из которых полон любви. ♦ **I miss your hugs and kisses (more than I can tell you).** Я скучаю по твоим объятиям и поцелуям (больше, чем могу высказать).

hug-a-bear *n (term of endearment for a man)* милый медвежонок.

huggable *adj (Russians use verb expressions: 1-3)* *(1)* великолепно / *(2)* замечательно / *(3)* приятно обнимать *(who is = acc.)* ♦ **Mmmm! You are so huggable!** О! Тебя так приятно обнимать! ♦ **You're the most huggable little** *(1)* **thing** / *(2)* **person I've ever met.** Лучше всех в мире обнимать тебя. ♦ **What a huggable delight you are!** Как восхитительно обнимать тебя!

human *adj* человеческий, -ая, -ое, -ие.

human *n* человек ♦ ~ **being** человек.

humane *adj* человеческий, -ая, -ое, -ие ♦ **in a** ~ **way** по-человечески.

humble *adj* смиренный, -ая, -ое, -ые, скромный, -ая, -ое, -ые, покорный, -ая, -ое, -ые ♦ **Please accept my humble apologies.** Прими, пожалуйста, мои покорные извинения.

humbly *adv* смиренно, скромно, покорно ♦ **I humbly beg your forgiveness.** Я смиренно умоляю тебя о прощении. ♦ **I humbly beseech you.** Я смиренно молю тебя.

humdrum *adj* однообразный, -ая, -ое, -ые, неинтересный, -ая, -ое, -ые ♦ **It all seemed so exciting at first, but lately it's gotten** *(1)* **rather** / *(2)* **awfully humdrum.** Это всё казалось таким волнующим сначала, но в последнее время это стало *(1)* достаточно / *(2)* ужасно однообразным. ♦ **It was a humdrum relationship.** Это были неинтересные отношения. ♦ **It was a humdrum marriage.** Это было неинтересное замужество. ♦ **I'm saddled with an empty, humdrum marriage.** Я обременён *(ж: обременена)*

For transitive Russian verbs the cases that they take are shown by means of an = sign and the Russian case (abbreviated).

пусты́м, неинтере́сным бра́ком. ♦ **It's a (rather) humdrum job.** Это (дово́льно) одно-
обра́зная рабо́та. ♦ **I lead a (rather) humdrum life.** Я веду́ (дово́льно) однообра́зную
жизнь. ♦ **No one can accuse you of being humdrum.** Никто́ не мо́жет обвини́ть тебя́
в однообра́зии.

humiliate *vt* унижа́ть / уни́зить *(whom = acc.)* ♦ **Why must you always humiliate me (***[1,2]***
in front of other people)?** Почему́ ты должна́ *(ж: до́лжен)* всегда́ уни́зить меня́ (*[1]*
...в прису́тствии други́х люде́й? / *[2]* ...пе́ред людьми́?)? ♦ **You humiliated me.** Ты
уни́зила *(ж: уни́зил)* меня́.

humiliated *adj* уни́женный, -ая, -ое, -ые, *(short forms:* уни́жен, -а, -о, -ы) ♦ **I** *(1)* **feel / (2)**
felt so humiliated. Я *(1)* чу́вствую / *(2)* чу́вствовал *(ж: чу́вствовала)* себя́ таки́м
уни́женным *(ж: тако́й уни́женной).* ♦ **I was never so humiliated in all my life.** Я
никогда́ в жи́зни не был так уни́жен *(ж: не была́ так уни́жена).*

humiliating *adj* унизи́тельный, -ая, -ое, -ые ♦ **That was the most humiliating thing that**
ever happened to me. Это бы́ло са́мое унизи́тельное из всего́, что когда́-либо слу-
ча́лось со мной. ♦ **It's (absolutely) humiliating.** Это (соверше́нно) унизи́тельно.

humiliation *n* униже́ние.

humility *n* смире́ние, скро́мность; поко́рность ♦ **with great ~** с больши́м смире́нием.

hummingbird *n* коли́бри ♦ **Imagine that you're a flower filled with nectar and I'm the**
world's thirstiest hummingbird. Предста́вь, что ты цвето́к, по́лный некта́ра, и я
истомлённейший жа́ждой коли́бри.

humor *n* ю́мор ♦ **creative ~** созида́тельный ю́мор ♦ **deadpan ~** ю́мор под простачка́ ♦
dry ~ сде́ржанный ю́мор ♦ **engaging ~** подкупа́ющий ю́мор ♦ **offbeat ~** оригина́льный
ю́мор ♦ **sarcastic ~** саркасти́чный ю́мор.

humor: *other terms*

caustic sense of ~ ко́лкое чу́вство ю́мора ♦ **good sense of ~** хоро́шее чу́вство ю́мора
♦ **great sense of ~** замеча́тельное чу́вство ю́мора ♦ **impish sense of ~** шаловли́вое
чу́вство ю́мора ♦ **irreverent sense of ~** ничего́ не щадя́щее чу́вство ю́мора ♦ **keen**
sense of ~ о́строе чу́вство ю́мора ♦ **lively sense of ~** живо́е чу́вство ю́мора ♦ **marvelous**
sense of ~ замеча́тельное чу́вство ю́мора ♦ **quirky sense of ~** необы́чное чу́вство
ю́мора ♦ **sense of ~** чу́вство ю́мора ♦ **shocking sense of ~** шоки́рующее чу́вство ю́мора
♦ **spicy sense of ~** о́строе чу́вство ю́мора ♦ **tremendous sense of ~** огро́мное чу́вство
ю́мора ♦ **wicked sense of ~** озорно́й ю́мор ♦ **witty sense of ~** о́строе чу́вство ю́мора
♦ **wry sense of ~** то́нкий ю́мор.

humor: *phrases*

Sometimes I have a rather caustic sense of humor. Иногда́ мой ю́мор быва́ет ко́лким.
♦ **I have a good sense of humor.** У меня́ хоро́шее чу́вство ю́мора. ♦ **I love your sense**
of humor. Мне нра́вится твоё чу́вство ю́мора. ♦ **I'm filled to the brim with humor.** Я
до краёв по́лон *(ж: полна́)* ю́мором. ♦ **I want a relationship touched with humor.** Я
хочу́ отноше́ний, прони́кнутых ю́мором. ♦ **I value wisdom, kindness and humor.** Я
ценю́ му́дрость, доброту́ и ю́мор.

humorless *adj* лишённый (-ая, -ое, -ые) чу́вства ю́мора.

humorous *adj* смешно́й, -а́я, -о́е, -ы́е, заба́вный, -ая, -ое, -ые.

hunger *vi* жа́ждать *(for what = gen., for whom = acc.),* быть голо́дным (-ой, -ым, -ыми) *(I*
hunger: я го́лоден *[ж: голодна́]. You hunger:* ты голодна́ *[ж: го́лоден].) (for what, whom*
= + по + dat.) ♦ **I hunger (so much) for your love.** Я (так) жа́жду твое́й любви́. ♦ **I**
hunger for the wonderful warmth and softness of your body. Я го́лоден по удиви́тель-
ному теплу́ и мя́гкости твоего́ те́ла. ♦ **I hunger (so desparately) for you.** Я так
отча́янно жа́жду тебя́. ♦ **There are no words to describe how I hunger for you, how I**

Russian verbs have 2 forms: imperfective and perfective.
They're given in that order.

ache for you, how I want you. Нет слов, чтобы описа́ть, как я го́лоден *(ж: голодна́)* по тебе́, как я страда́ю по тебе́, как я хочу́ тебя́.

hunger *n* 1. *(physical)* го́лод; 2. *(emotional)* жа́жда *(for what, whom = gen.)* ◆ **The thought patterns that yielded your choice of words and sentences in your ad reveal the exact same raging hunger for love and affection that I harbor within me.** Мы́сли, роди́вшие вы́бор слов и предложе́ний в Ва́шем объявле́нии, говоря́т о то́чно тако́й же неи́стовой жа́жде любви́ и не́жности, кото́рая таи́тся во мне. ◆ **Only the sweet, soft magic of your beautiful body in my arms can assuage the desperate hunger that consumes me.** То́лько не́жное, мя́гкое волшебство́ твоего́ прекра́сного те́ла в мои́х объя́тиях мо́жет утоли́ть отча́янный го́лод, кото́рый пожира́ет меня́. ◆ *(1)* **I burn...**/ *(2)* **My whole body burns... with hunger for** *(3)* **...you.** / *(4)* **...your soft, warm beauty.** *(1)* Я сгора́ю... / *(2)* Всё моё те́ло гори́т... от жа́жды *(3)* ...тебя́. / *(4)* ...твое́й мя́гкой, тёплой красоты́.

hunk *n (slang) (very handsome guy)* краса́вец ◆ **intelligent** ~ у́мный краса́вец ◆ **He's such a hunk.** Он тако́й краса́вец.

hunky *adj (slang) (handsome)* краси́вый, -ые.

hunting *n* охо́та ◆ **husband** ~ охо́та за му́жем ◆ **wife** ~ охо́та за жено́й.

hurled *adj* бро́шен, -а, -о, -ы, забро́шен, -а, -о, -ы *(short forms)* ◆ **I want to fill your body with so much pleasure that you will be hurled into a cosmos of exploding ecstasy.** Я хочу́ запо́лнить твоё те́ло таки́м огро́мным наслажде́нием, что ты бу́дешь бро́шена в ко́смос взрыва́ющегося экста́за. ◆ **Our bodies will fuse together in exquisite pleasure until we are hurled into a wild sea of passion.** На́ши тела́ солью́тся в изы́сканном наслажде́нии до тех пор, пока́ мы не бу́дем бро́шены в бе́шеное мо́ре стра́сти.

hurried *adj* спе́шный, -ая, -ое, -ые, торопли́вый, -ая, -ое, -ые ◆ *(1,2)* **I don't like to feel hurried.** Мне не нра́вится, когда́ *(1) (someone:)* кто́-то / *(2) (something:)* что́-то подгоня́ет меня́. ◆ **I** *(1)* **feel** / *(2)* **felt so hurried.** Я *(1)* чу́вствую / *(2)* чу́вствовал *(ж: чу́вствовала)* таку́ю спе́шку.

hurry *n* спе́шка ◆ **Why are you in such an all-fired hurry?** Почему́ ты спеши́шь, как на пожа́р?

hurt *vt* 1. *(offend)* обижа́ть / оби́деть *(whom = acc.); (emotionally)* ра́нить *(whom = acc.)*; 2. *(physically)* де́лать / сде́лать бо́льно *(whom = dat.)*, причиня́ть / причини́ть боль *(whom = dat.)* ◆ **I don't want to hurt** *(1)* **...you.** / *(2)* **...your feelings.** Я не хочу́ *(1)* ...оби́деть тебя́. / *(2)* ...ра́нить твои́ чу́вства. ◆ **You hurt my feelings (**[1] **...a lot.** / [2] **...more than you'll ever know.** / [3] **...more than I can tell you.).** Ты ра́нила *(ж: ра́нил)* мои́ чу́вства (*[1]* ...о́чень. / *[2]* ...да́же бо́льше, чем ты ду́маешь. / *[3]* ...бо́лее, чем я могу́ сказа́ть тебе́.). ◆ **I didn't mean to hurt** *(1)* **...you.** / *(2)* **...your feelings.** Я не хоте́л *(ж: хоте́ла)* ра́нить *(1)* ...тебя́. / *(2)* ...твои́ чу́вства. ◆ **I'm sorry I hurt** *(1)* **...you.** / *(2)* **...your feelings.** Прости́, я ра́нил *(ж: ра́нила)* *(1)* ...тебя́. / *(2)* ...твои́ чу́вства. ◆ **Please forgive me if I hurt** *(1)* **...you.** / *(2)* **...your feelings.** Прости́, пожа́луйста, е́сли я *(1)* ...оби́дел *(ж: оби́дела)* тебя́. / *(2)* ...ра́нил *(ж: ра́нила)* твои́ чу́вства. ◆ **I'm afraid of being hurt (again).** Я не хочу́ (опя́ть) страда́ть.

hurt *vi* боле́ть; быть больны́м, -о́й,-ы́м,-ы́ми ◆ **I want so badly to fall in love that it hurts.** Я си́льно до бо́ли хочу́ влюби́ться. ◆ **I'm afraid of being hurt (again).** Я не хочу́ (опя́ть) страда́ть.

hurt *n* боль *f* ◆ **I'm sorry for the hurt I've caused you.** Я извиня́юсь за боль, причинённую тебе́ мной. ◆ **I still haven't gotten over the hurt.** Я всё ещё не преодоле́л *(ж: преодоле́ла)* боль.

hurtful *adj (causing hurt)* ра́нящий, -ая, -ее, -ие; *(insulting)* оскорби́тельный, -ая, -ое, -ые;

How to use the Cyrillic alphabet on the Internet
is the subject of Appendix 20 on page 789.

(offensive) обидный, -ая, -ое, -ые ♦ **I said some very hurtful things and I'm sorry.** Я сказал *(ж: сказала)* некие очень ранящие слова, и я извиняюсь. ♦ **I apologize for all the hurtful things I said to you.** Я извиняюсь за все обидные слова, которые я сказал *(ж: сказала)* тебе.

husband *n* муж ♦ **attentive** ~ внимательный муж ♦ **bad** ~ плохой муж ♦ **beloved** ~ любимый муж ♦ **caring** ~ заботливый муж ♦ *(1,2)* **deceased** ~ *(1)* умерший / *(2)* покойный муж ♦ **ex-husband** бывший муж ♦ **fine** ~ хороший муж ♦ **first** ~ первый муж ♦ **former** ~ бывший муж ♦ **good** ~ хороший муж ♦ **jealous** ~ ревнивый муж ♦ **kind** ~ добрый муж ♦ *(1,2)* **late** ~ *(1)* умерший / *(2)* покойный муж ♦ **loving** ~ любящий муж ♦ **model** ~ образцовый муж ♦ **my** ~ мой муж ♦ **no** ~ нет мужа ♦ **perfect** ~ отличный муж ♦ **poor** ~ плохой муж ♦ **second** ~ второй муж ♦ **thoughtful** ~ внимательный муж ♦ **wonderful** ~ удивительный муж ♦ **your** ~ *(familiar)* твой муж; *(polite)* Ваш муж.

husband: verb terms

become your ~ стать твоим мужем ♦ **divorce** *(1)* my / *(2)* **your** ~ развестись с *(1,2)* мужем ♦ **find a** ~ найти (себе) мужа ♦ *(1,2)* **leave** *(3)* my / *(4)* **your** ~ *(1)* оставить / *(2)* бросить *(3,4)* мужа ♦ **separate from** *(1)* my / *(2)* **your** ~ расстаться с *(1,2)* мужем ♦ **stop loving my** ~ разлюбить мужа.

husband: phrases

I dream of having you as my husband. Я мечтаю о том, чтобы ты был моим мужем. ♦ **My greatest happiness would be to have you as my husband.** Как бесконечно я была бы счастлива, если бы ты стал моим мужем. ♦ **I could never ask for more (in this [1] life / [2] world) than to have you as my husband.** Я никогда не смогла бы просить ни о чём большем (в этой *[1,2]* жизни), чем о том, чтобы ты стал моим мужем. ♦ **My husband deserted me (and my [1] son / [2] daughter / [3] children).** Мой муж покинул меня (и *[1]* ...моего сына. / *[2]* ...мою дочь. / *[3]* ...моих детей.) ♦ **I'm going to make every (possible) effort to be a good husband to you.** Я приложу все (возможные) усилия, чтобы быть хорошим мужем.

husband-to-be *n* будущий муж.

husk *n* шелуха ♦ **I'm a dry husk without you.** Я сухая шелуха без тебя.

huskily *adv* 1. *(body)* сильно, крепко; 2. *(voice)* хрипло, сипло.

husky *adj* 1. *(body)* сильный, -ая, -ое, -ые, крепкий, -ая, -ое, -ие, рослый, -ая, -ое, -ые, здоровённый, -ая, -ое, -ые; 2. *(voice)* хриплый, -ая, -ое, -ые, сиплый, -ая, -ое, -ые ♦ **I have a (rather) husky build.** Я (достаточно) крепко скроен. ♦ **Your husky voice is quite sexy.** Твой хриплый голос очень сексуален.

hussy *n* нахальная девка ♦ **I didn't know I was getting mixed up with a brazen hussy.** *(joking)* Я не знал, что я спутался с нахальной девкой. *(шутка)*

hygiene *n:* ♦ **good (personal)** ~ чистоплотность *f*, опрятность *f*, аккуратность *f*.

hyper-intelligent *adj* высоко-интеллигентный, -ая, -ое, -ые.

hypersexed *adj* гиперсексуальный, -ая, -ое, -ые.

hypnotic *adj* гипнотический, -ая, -ое, -ие ♦ **There's something (very) hypnotic about you.** Есть что-то (очень) гипнотическое вокруг тебя.

hypnotize *vt* гипнотизировать / загипнотизировать *(whom = acc.)* ♦ **You hypnotize me with your** *(1)* **...scintillating charm.** / *(2)* **...dazzling smile.** / *(3)* **...radiant beauty.** / *(4)* **...beautiful** / *(5)* **exotic** / *(6)* **dark eyes.** Ты гипнотизируешь меня *(1)* ...своим искрящимся обаянием. / *(2)* ...своей ослепительной улыбкой. *(3)* ...своей сияющей красотой. / *(4)* ...своими прекрасными / *(5)* экзотическими / *(6)* тёмными глазами.

hypnotized *adj* загипнотизирован, -а, -о, -ы *(short forms)*.

Russian adjectives have long and short forms.
Where short forms are given, they are labeled as such.

hypocrisy *n* лицеме́рие.

hypocrite *n* лицеме́р *m*, лицеме́рка *f*.

hypocritical *adj* лицеме́рный, -ая, -ое, -ые ♦ **be ~** лицеме́рить.

hysteria *n* исте́рика.

hysterical *adj* истери́ческий, -ая, -ое, -ие, истери́чный, -ая, -ое, -ые ♦ **Don't get hysterical.** Не устра́ивай исте́рику.

hysterics *n, pl* исте́рика; *(fit)* припа́док истери́и ♦ **You don't have to go into hysterics (all the time).** Ты не должна́ *(ж: до́лжен)* впада́ть в исте́рику (всё вре́мя). ♦ **Don't go into hysterics.** Не впада́й в исте́рику. ♦ **You went into hysterics (and wouldn't listen to anything I said).** Ты устро́ила *(ж: устро́ил)* исте́рику (и не слы́шала *[ж: слы́шал]* ничего́ того́, что я сказа́л *[ж:сказа́ла]*).

Russian nouns are either masculine, feminine or neuter.
Adjectives with them will be the same.

I

ice *n* лёд ♦ **I'm glad you broke the ice.** Я рад, что ты слома́ла *(ж: слома́л)* лёд.

ice-breaker *n* слова́, явля́ющиеся по́водом для нача́ла разгово́ра *(explanation)*.

ice-skate *vi* ката́ться на конька́х ♦ **Do you know how to ice-skate?** Ты уме́ешь ката́ться на конька́х?

ice-skating *n* ката́ние на конька́х.

iconoclastic *adj* напра́вленный (-ая, -ое, -ые) про́тив предрассу́дков.

icy *adj* ледяно́й, -а́я, -о́е, -ы́е ♦ **Your attitude toward me has been so icy lately.** После́днее вре́мя твоё отноше́ние ко мне бы́ло таки́м ледяны́м.

ID *abbrev* = **identification** *n* удостовере́ние ли́чности.

idea *n* 1. *(original thought)* иде́я, мысль *f*; 2. *(notion, concept)* представле́ние, поня́тие; 3. *(opinion)* мне́ние ♦ **approximate** ~ приме́рное представле́ние ♦ **bad** ~ плоха́я иде́я ♦ **brilliant** ~ блестя́щая иде́я ♦ **clever** ~ у́мная иде́я ♦ **crazy** ~ сумасше́дшая иде́я ♦ **different** ~ друга́я иде́я ♦ **dumb** ~ глу́пая иде́я ♦ **excellent** ~ превосхо́дная иде́я ♦ **fantastic** ~ фантасти́ческая иде́я ♦ **funny** ~ 1. *(strange)* стра́нная иде́я; 2. *(amusing)* смешна́я иде́я ♦ **general** ~ о́бщее представле́ние ♦ **glorious** ~ выдаю́щаяся иде́я ♦ **good** ~ хоро́шая иде́я ♦ *(1,2)* **goofy** ~ *(1)* глу́пая / *(2)* неле́пая иде́я ♦ *(1,2)* **great** ~ *(1)* превосхо́дная / *(2)* вели коле́пная иде́я ♦ **loony** ~ сумасше́дшая иде́я ♦ *(1,2)* **marvel-ous** ~ *(1)* чуде́сная / *(2)* удиви́тельная иде́я ♦ *(1,2)* **neat** ~ *(1)* отли́чная / *(2)* замеча́тель-ная иде́я ♦ **no** ~ никако́го представле́ния ♦ **not the foggiest** *(1,2)* ~ ни мале́йшего *(1)* поня́тия / *(2)* представле́ния ♦ **original** *(1,2)* ~ оригина́льная *(1)* иде́я / *(2)* мысль ♦ **ridiculous** ~ неле́пая иде́я ♦ **rough** ~ приме́рное представле́ние ♦ **smart** ~ у́мная иде́я ♦ *(1,2)* **splendid** ~ *(1)* превосхо́дная / *(2)* великоле́пная иде́я ♦ **strange** ~ стра́нная иде́я ♦ **stupid** ~ глу́пая иде́я ♦ *(1,2)* **super** ~ *(1)* превосхо́дная / *(2)* великоле́пная иде́я ♦ *(1,2)* **terrific** ~ *(1)* превосхо́дная / *(2)* великоле́пная иде́я ♦ *(1,2)* **weird** *(3,4)* ~ *(1)* стра́нная / *(2)* неле́пая *(3)* иде́я / *(4)* мысль ♦ *(1,2)* **wonderful** ~ *(1)* чуде́сная / *(2)* удиви́тельная иде́я.

idea: *phrases*

I haven't the *(1)* **foggiest** / *(2)* **slightest** *(3,4)* **idea.** Я не име́ю ни *(1,2)* мале́йшего *(3)* поня́тия / *(4)* представле́ния. ♦ **Please don't get the wrong idea (about me).** Не получи́ ло́жного представле́ния (обо мне). ♦ **Somebody may get the wrong idea.** Кто́-то мо́жет получи́ть ло́жное представле́ние. ♦ **I hope** *(1)* **you** / *(2)* **they don't get the wrong**

Learn more about Russian customs in Appendix 15, page 782.

idea. Я наде́юсь, что *(1)* ...ты не полу́чишь... / *(2)* ...они не полу́чат... ло́жного представле́ния. ♦ **What a glorious idea that is!** Что за выдаю́щаяся иде́я! ♦ **I have an idea.** У меня́ есть иде́я. ♦ **I'm always open to new ideas.** Я всегда́ откры́т *(ж: откры́та)* но́вым иде́ям.

ideal *adj* идеа́льный, -ая, -ое, -ые ♦ **I think you're an ideal partner.** Я ду́маю, ты идеа́льный партнёр. ♦ **You are ideal for me.** Ты идеа́льна *(ж: идеа́лен)* для меня́. ♦ **You are my ideal** *(1)* **woman** / *(2)* **man.** Ты мой идеа́л *(1)* же́нщины / *(2)* мужчи́ны. ♦ **I've never met anyone as ideal for me as you are.** Тако́й идеа́льной *(ж: Тако́го идеа́льного)* для меня́, как ты, я никогда́ не встреча́л *(ж: встреча́ла).* ♦ **You have an (absolutely) ideal** *(1)* **figure** / *(2)* **body.** У тебя́ (абсолю́тно) *(1)* ...идеа́льная фигу́ра. / *(2)* ...идеа́льное те́ло. ♦ **As a lover you are ideal.** Как любо́вница *(ж: любо́вник)* ты идеа́л. ♦ **What an ideal lover you are!** Что за идеа́льная *(ж: идеа́льный)* ты любо́вница *(ж: любо́вник)*! ♦ **Everything (with you) was (just) ideal.** Всё (с тобо́й) бы́ло (про́сто) идеа́льным. ♦ **We had an ideal time together.** Мы провели́ идеа́льное вре́мя друг с дру́гом. ♦ **It was such an ideal evening together.** Ве́чер, проведённый вме́сте, был идеа́лен. ♦ **It was such an ideal time together.** Вре́мя, проведённое вме́сте, бы́ло идеа́льно. ♦ **In you I have found my ideal** *(1)* **man** / *(2)* **woman** / *(3)* **lover.** В тебе́ я нашёл *(ж: нашла́)* мой идеа́л *(1)* мужчи́ны / *(2)* же́нщины / *(3)* любо́вницы *(ж: любо́вника).*

ideal *n* идеа́л ♦ **You are my ideal** *([1]* **as a lover** / *[2]* **for a partner** / *[3]* **for a husband** / *[4]* **for a wife).** Ты мой идеа́л *([1]* как любо́вница *[ж: любо́вник]* / *[2]* партнёр / *[3]* муж / *[4]*жена́). ♦ **You are my ideal in every respect.** Ты мой идеа́л в любо́м отноше́нии.

idealist *n* идеали́ст ♦ **optimistic ~** оптимисти́ческий идеали́ст.

idealistic *adj* идеалисти́ческий, -ая, -ое, -ие.

idealize *vt* идеализи́ровать *(what, whom = acc.)* ♦ **You don't know to what extent I idealize you.** Ты не зна́ешь, в како́й ме́ре я идеализи́рую тебя́. ♦ **You idealize me too much.** Ты сли́шком си́льно идеализи́руешь меня́. ♦ **Please don't idealize me.** Пожа́луйста, не идеализи́руй меня́.

identification *n* удостовере́ние ли́чности.

identify (with) *vi* отождествля́ть себя́ *(with what, whom = + с + instr.)* ♦ **I can identify with your** *(1)* **experience** / *(2)* **feelings** / *(3)* **situation.** У меня́ *(1)* ...(был) тожде́ственный о́пыт. / *(2)* ...(бы́ли) тожде́ственные чу́вства. / *(3)* ...(была́) тожде́ственная ситуа́ция.

identity *n* ли́чность *f.*

idiosyncracy *n* своеобра́зие, стра́нная привы́чка, стра́нность *f* ♦ **It's one of my idiosyncracies (that I** *[1]* **...like to walk in the rain.** / *[2]* **...etc.).** Это одна́ из мои́х стра́нных привы́чек (что я *[1]* ...люблю́ гуля́ть под дождём. / *[2]* ...и т.д.).

idiot *n* идио́т *m*, идио́тка *f* ♦ **absolute ~** абсолю́тный идио́т *m*, абсолю́тная идио́тка *f* ♦ **complete ~** кру́глый идио́т *m*, кру́глая идио́тка *f* ♦ **I would be an absolute idiot ever to let you go.** Я был *(ж: была́)* бы абсолю́тным идио́том *(ж: абсолю́тной идио́ткой)*, е́сли бы то́лько позво́лил *(ж: позво́лила)* тебе́ уйти́.

idiotic *adj* идио́тский, -ая, -ое, -ие.

idolize *vt* поклоня́ться *(whom = dat.)*, обожа́ть *(whom = acc.)* ♦ **I idolize you** *(1)* **...beyond words.** / *(2)* **..more than you'll ever know.** Я обожа́ю тебя́ *(1)* ...невырази́мо. / *(2)* ...бо́лее, чем ты да́же зна́ешь.

idolizing *n* обожа́ние, преклоне́ние.

idyllic *adj* идилли́ческий, -ая, -ое, -ие ♦ **It was such an idyllic time with you.** Вре́мя, проведённое с тобо́й, бы́ло иди́ллией. ♦ **It was such an idyllic vacation with you.** Наш о́тпуск был иди́ллией. ♦ **It was such an idyllic weekend with you.** Выходны́е, проведённые вме́сте, бы́ли иди́ллией.

A slash always denotes "or."
You can choose the numbered words before and after.

ignite *vt* зажига́ть / заже́чь *(what = acc.)* ♦ **Visions of your voluptuous loveliness send fire licking through my arteries, igniting my entire being into an inferno of passionate desire.** Вид твое́й чу́вственной красоты́ вызыва́ет ого́нь, бушу́ющий в мои́х арте́риях, посыла́ющий всё моё существо́ в ад стра́стного жела́ния. ♦ **You ignite so much passion in me.** Ты зажига́ешь огро́мную страсть во мне. ♦ **(1) I want to... / (2) I'm going to... ignite a firestorm of passion in you.** *(1)* Я хочу́ заже́чь... / *(2)* Я зажгу́... о́гненный шторм стра́сти в тебе́. ♦ **Only you know how to ignite the flame of passionate desire in my heart.** То́лько ты зна́ешь, как заже́чь пла́мя стра́стного жела́ния в моём се́рдце. ♦ **You ignite passion in me so easily.** Ты так легко́ разжига́ешь страсть во мне. ♦ **I'm going to ignite fires of passion in you that will rage for a lifetime.** Я разожгу́ тако́й ого́нь стра́сти в тебе, кото́рый бу́дет бушева́ть всю жизнь.

ignite *vi (feelings)* зажига́ться / заже́чься, вспы́хивать / вспы́хнуть ♦ **My heart ignites in (1) celebration / (2) delight / (3) ecstasy / (4) jubilation (5) ...every time I get a letter from you. / (6) ...every time I see your ([7] beautiful / [8] beloved) face. / (9) ...at the mere thought of you.** Моё се́рдце *(1)* ...загора́ется ра́достью / *(2)* восто́ргом... / *(3)* ...вспы́хивает в экста́зе... / *(4)* ...лику́ет... *(5)* ...ка́ждый раз, когда́ я получа́ю письмо́ от тебя́. / *(6)* ...ка́ждый раз, когда́ я ви́жу твоё (*[7]* прекра́сное / *[8]* люби́мое) лицо́. / *(9)* ...от просто́й мы́сли о тебе́. ♦ **Hope has ignited in my heart.** Наде́жда зажгла́сь в моём се́рдце.

ignore *vt* игнори́ровать *(what, whom = acc.)* ♦ **I'm going to ignore all your protests.** Я бу́ду игнори́ровать все твои́ проте́сты. ♦ **You've been ignoring me lately.** Ты игнори́руешь меня́ после́днее вре́мя. ♦ **I'm not ignoring you.** Я не игнори́рую тебя́.

ill *adj* бо́лен, больна́, больны́ *(short forms)* ♦ **be** ~ боле́ть, быть больны́м *m* / больно́й *f (I'm ill:* я бо́лен *[ж: больна́]. You're ill:* ты больна́ *[ж: бо́лен].)*

ill at ease *adj phrase:* ♦ **be** ~ конфу́зиться, смуща́ться ♦ **feel** ~ смуща́ться, чу́вствовать смуще́ние.

ill-concealed *adj* пло́хо скры́тый, -ая, -ое, -ые.

illicit *adj* незако́нный, -ая, -ое, -ые, запрещённый, -ая, -ое, -ые.

illicitness *n* незако́нность *f*, запре́т.

ill-starred *adj* несчастли́вый, -ая, -ое, -ые.

illusion *n* иллю́зия, мира́ж, при́зрак ♦ **girlish** ~s де́вичьи иллю́зии ♦ **(1,2) entertain** ~s *(1)* таи́ть / *(2)* пита́ть иллю́зии ♦ **(1,2) harbor** ~s *(1)* таи́ть / *(2)* пита́ть иллю́зии ♦ **I (1) entertain / (2) harbor no illusions about (3) ...you. / (4) ...your love / (5) feelings for me. / (6) ...marriage. / (7) ...men. / (8) ...women. / (9) ...my chances with you. / (10) ...my chances of winning your heart / (11) love.** Я не *(1)* таю́ / *(2)* пита́ю никаки́х иллю́зий о *(3)* ...тебе́. / *(4)* ...твое́й любви́ ко мне. / *(5)* ...твои́х чу́вствах ко мне. / *(6)* ...бра́ке. / *(7)* ...мужчи́нах. / *(8)* ...же́нщинах. / *(9)* ...мои́х возмо́жностях с тобо́й. / *(10)* ...моём ша́нсе победи́ть твоё се́рдце. / *(11)* ...моём ша́нсе завоева́ть твою́ любо́вь.

illusory *adj* при́зрачный, -ая, -ое, -ые.

ILY *abbrev* = **I love you.** Я люблю́ тебя́.

image *n* 1. *(picture)* изображе́ние; 2. *(vision)* о́браз, о́блик; виде́ние ♦ **The image of your beautiful face is forever alive in my heart.** Твоё прекра́сное лицо́ ве́чно живёт в моём се́рдце. ♦ **The image of your (1) beautiful / (2) luscious / (3) wonderful body never leaves my mind.** Виде́ние твоего́ *(1)* прекра́сного / *(2)* со́чного / *(3)* великоле́пного те́ла никогда́ не покида́ет меня́. ♦ **The image of your sweet smile and beautiful eyes was in my mind all the time.** Твоя́ не́жная улы́бка и прекра́сные глаза́ бы́ли всегда́ в мои́х мы́слях.

imagination *n* воображе́ние ♦ **active** ~ живо́е воображе́ние ♦ **artistic** ~ худо́жественное

Common adult weights are given in Appendix 10, page 777.

воображе́ние ♦ **creative** ~ тво́рческое воображе́ние ♦ **fertile** ~ бога́тое воображе́ние ♦ **fervent** ~ пы́лкое воображе́ние ♦ **great** ~ большо́е воображе́ние ♦ **human** ~ челове́ческое воображе́ние ♦ **inexhaustible** ~ неиссяка́емое воображе́ние ♦ **lively** ~ живо́е воображение ♦ **my** ~ моё воображе́ние ♦ **poetic** ~ поэти́ческое воображе́ние ♦ **rich** ~ бога́тое воображе́ние ♦ **wild** ~ ди́кое воображе́ние ♦ **your** ~ *(familiar)* твоё воображе́ние; *(polite)* Ва́ше воображе́ние.

imagination: *verb terms*

arouse my ~ пробужда́ть / пробуди́ть моё воображе́ние ♦ **capture my** ~ захвати́ть моё воображе́ние ♦ **excite my** ~ волнова́ть моё воображе́ние ♦ **give play to my** ~ дава́ть / дать во́лю своему́ воображе́нию ♦ **have an** ~ име́ть воображе́ние ♦ **nourish my** ~ пита́ть моё воображе́ние ♦ **possess an** ~ облада́ть воображе́нием.

imagination: *other terms*

food for the ~ пи́ща для воображе́ния ♦ **richness of** ~ бога́тство воображе́ния.

imagination: *phrases*

Never in my wildest imagination did I ever think I could meet anyone as *(1)* beautiful / *(2)* wonderful as you. Никогда́, да́же в са́мых ди́ких безу́мных мечта́х, я не ду́мал, что могу́ встре́тить кого́-либо тако́го *(1)* прекра́сного / *(2)* замеча́тельного, как ты. ♦ **My love for you is so deep and tender that it eclipses the range of human imagination.** Моя́ любо́вь к тебе́ так глубока́ и нежна́, что э́то вы́ше челове́ческого воображе́ния. ♦ **My imagination constantly carries me to you.** Моё воображе́ние постоя́нно перено́сит меня́ к тебе́.

imagine *vt* вообража́ть / вообрази́ть, представля́ть / предста́вить себе́ *(what = acc.)* ♦ **Love with you is more beautiful than I ever imagined.** Любо́вь с тобо́й намно́го прекра́снее, чем я представля́л *(ж: представля́ла)* себе́. ♦ **I can't imagine *(1)* ...life without you. / *(2)* ...being with anyone else (but you).** Я не могу́ предста́вить себе́ жизнь *(1)* ...без тебя́. / *(2)* ...с ке́м-либо ещё *(кро́ме тебя́)*. ♦ **Can you (possibly) imagine how much I love you?** Мо́жешь ли ты предста́вить себе́, как си́льно я люблю́ тебя́ ? ♦ **You cannot imagine how much I love you.** Ты не мо́жешь предста́вить себе́, как си́льно я люблю́ тебя́. ♦ **You are the most beautiful woman I could ever imagine.** Ты са́мая прекра́сная же́нщина из всех когда́-либо вообража́емых мной.

imbibe *vt (drink)* пить.

imbued (with) *adj* вдохновлён, вдохновлена́, -о́, -ы́ *(short forms)*.

imitate *vt* подража́ть *(what, whom = dat.)* ♦ *(1)* **I want to... / *(2)* I'm going to... teach you how to imitate a volcano.** *(1)* Я хочу́ научи́ть... / *(2)* Я научу́... тебя́, как подража́ть вулка́ну.

immaculate *adj* 1. *(pure)* чи́стый, -ая, -ое, -ые; 2. *(irreproachable)* безупре́чный, -ая, -ое, -ые, безукори́зненный, -ая, -ое, -ые.

immature *adj* незре́лый, -ая, -ое, -ые.

immaturity *n* незре́лость *f.*

immediate *adj* неме́дленный, -ая, -ое, -ые.

immediately *adv* неме́дленно.

immensity *n* безме́рность *f,* беспреде́льность *f,* безграни́чность *f* ♦ **There are no words to describe the immensity of the love that I bear in my heart for you.** Нет слов, что́бы описа́ть безме́рность той любви́ к тебе́, кото́рой полно́ моё се́рдце.

immerse *vt* погружа́ть / прогрузи́ть *(what, whom = acc.)* ♦ **How I long to immerse myself in the soft, lingering fragrance of your *(1)* hair / *(2)* body / *(3)* person.** Как я жа́жду погрузи́ться в не́жный арома́т *(1)* ...твои́х воло́с. / *(2,3)* ...твоего́ те́ла.

immigrant *n* иммигра́нт *m,* иммигра́нтка *f.*

An italicized ж in parentheses indicates a woman speaking.

immoral *adj* безнра́вственный, -ая, -ое, -ые.

imp *n* шалу́н, чертёнок, бесёнок ♦ **You're a mischievous little imp!** Ты непослу́шный ма́ленький чертёнок!

imparidise *vt* переноси́ть / перенести́ в рай *(whom = acc.)*, доводи́ть / довести́ до бла-же́нства *(whom = acc.)* ♦ **The sweetness of your lips imparidises me.** Сла́дость твои́х губ перено́сит меня́ в рай. ♦ **You have no idea at all how you have imparidised me with your tender, loving ways.** Ты про́сто не представля́ешь, как твоя́ не́жность, любо́вное отноше́ние перено́сит меня́ в рай. ♦ **You simply imparidise me -- like no one has ever done.** Ты так дово́дишь меня́ до блаже́нства, как никто́ и никогда́ пре́жде.

imparidised *adj* перенесён (перенесена́, -о́, -ы́) в рай *(short forms)* ♦ **I want to spend long, languorous hours imparadised in your** *(1)* **arms /** *(2)* **embraces.** Я хочу́ проводи́ть до́лгие, то́мные часы́ в раю́ твои́х *(1)* рук / *(2)* объя́тий. ♦ **Oh, how I** *(1)* **yearn /** *(2)* **long to be imparadised...in your** *(3)* **arms /** *(4)* **embraces. /** *(5)* **...in the warm, beautiful softness of you.** О, как я *(1,2)* жа́жду ра́я ...твои́х *(3)* рук / *(4)* объя́тий. / *(5)* ...твое́й тёплой, прекра́сной мя́гкости.

impart *vt* 1. *(endow)* придава́ть / прида́ть *(what = acc., to what, whom = dat.)*, наделя́ть / надели́ть *(what = acc., to what, whom = dat.)*; 2. *(pass along)* передава́ть / переда́ть *(what = acc., to what, whom = dat.)*, сообща́ть / сообщи́ть *(what = acc., to what, whom = dat.)*; дели́ться / подели́ться *(мы́слями, чу́вствами)* ♦ **You impart sweetness to** *(1)* **...every-thing around you. /** *(2)* **...all my hopes and dreams.** Ты придаёшь не́жность *(1)* ...всему́, окружа́ющему тебя́. / *(1)* ...всем мои́м наде́ждам и мечта́м.

impassioned *adj* стра́стный, -ая, -ое, -ые *(short forms:* стра́стен, страстна́, -о, -ы*)* ♦ **I hope you're a person who is as impassioned with life as I am.** Я наде́юсь, что ты челове́к с тако́й же стра́стью к жи́зни, как я.

impassive *adj (devoid of passion / emotion)* бесстра́стный, -ая, -ое, -ые; *(devoid of interest)* безразли́чный -ая, -ое, -ые.

impatience *n* нетерпе́ние ♦ **burn with ~** сгора́ть от нетерпе́ния ♦ **I'm brimming with impatience to** *(1)* **meet /** *(2)* **see you.** Я до краёв напо́лнен нетерпе́нием *(1)* встре́тить / *(2)* уви́деть тебя́.

impatient *adj* нетерпели́вый, -ая, -ое, -ые.

impatiently *adv* нетерпели́во.

impeccable *adj* безупре́чный, -ая, -ое, -ые, безукори́зненный, -ая, -ое, -ые ♦ **I know that you're a person of impeccable moral character.** Я зна́ю, что ты челове́к безупре́чной нра́вственности. ♦ **You look impeccable.** Ты вы́глядишь безупре́чно.

impel *vt* побужда́ть / побуди́ть *(what, whom = acc.)*; принужда́ть / принуди́ть *(what, whom = acc.)*, заставля́ть / заста́вить *(what, whom = acc.)*.

impelled *adj* побуждён, побуждена́, -о́, -ы́ *(short forms)*; принуждён, принуждена́, -о́, -ы́ *(short forms)* ♦ **I feel impelled by the acute longing in my heart to write you this letter.** Стра́стное стремле́ние моего́ се́рдца заставля́ет меня́ написа́ть Вам э́то письмо́. ♦ **In the unbounded vistas of my dreams and fantasies I taste the exquisite sweetness of your lips a thousand, ten thousand, a million times, and each time am only impelled by the sheer ecstasy of the kiss to taste them once again.** В безграни́чной верени́це мои́х снов и фанта́зий я вкуша́ю исключи́тельную сла́дость твои́х губ ты́сячу, де́сять ты́сяч, миллио́н раз и ка́ждый раз побуждён и́стинным восто́ргом поцелу́я упива́ться им опя́ть.

impertinent *adj* де́рзкий, -ая, -ое, -ие

impervious *adj* 1. *(impenetrable)* непроница́емый, -ая, -ое, -ые; 2. *(oblivious)* глухо́й, -а́я, -о́е, -и́е *(short forms:* глух, -а́, -о, -и*)*; *(blind)* слепо́й, -а́я, -о́е, -ы́е *(short forms:* слеп,

---

Procedures for getting married to a Russian
are outlined in Appendix 18, page 787.

-á, -о, -ы) ♦ **I'm not impervious to your** *(1)* **beauty** / *(2)* **loveliness** / *(3)* **charm.** Я не безразли́чен *(1,2)* ...к твое́й красоте́. / *(3)* ...к твоему́ обая́нию.

impetuous *adj* опроме́тчивый, -ая, -ое, -ые, стреми́тельный, -ая, -ое, -ые, поры́вистый, -ая, -ое, -ые.

impetuously *adv* опроме́тчиво.

implore *vt* умоля́ть / умоли́ть *(whom = acc.)*, взмоли́ться ♦ **fervently** ~ горячо́ умоля́ть ♦ **I implore you.** Я умоля́ю тебя́. ♦ **I fervently implore you to** *(1)* **give** / *(2)* **grant me the opportunity to** *(3)* **...know you better.** / *(4)* **...get better acquainted with you.** / *(5)* **...speak with you.** / *(6)* **...see your beautiful face once again.** / *(7)* **...meet with you.** Я горячо́ умоля́ю Вас *(1)* дать / *(2)* предоста́вить мне возмо́жность *(3)* ...лу́чше узна́ть Вас. / *(4)* ...бли́же познако́миться с Ва́ми. / *(5)* ...поговори́ть с Ва́ми. / *(6)* ...уви́деть Ва́ше прекра́сное лицо́ ещё раз. / *(7)* ...встре́титься с Ва́ми.

imploring *adj* умоля́ющий, -ая, -ее, -ие.

importance *n* ва́жность *f*, значе́ние, значи́тельность *f*, зна́чимость *f* ♦ **air of** ~ ва́жный вид ♦ **You are of infinite worth and importance** *(1)* **...in my life** / *(2)* **...to me.** Ты бесконе́чная це́нность и ва́жность *(1)* ...мое́й жи́зни. / *(2)* ...для меня́.

important *adj* ва́жный, -ая, -ое, -ые ♦ **It's (not) (very) important.** Это (не) (о́чень) ва́жно.

imposing *adj* импоза́нтный, -ая, -ое, -ые.

impotence *n* импоте́нция ♦ **He suffers from impotence.** Он страда́ет от импоте́нции. ♦ **Viagra is a good remedy for impotence.** Ви́агра - хоро́шее сре́дство от импоте́нции.

impotent *adj* 1. *(powerless)* бесси́льный, -ая, -ое, -ые 2. *(sexually)* импоте́нтный, -ая, -ое, -ые.

impress *vt* производи́ть / произвести́ впечатле́ние *(whom = + на + acc.)*, поража́ть / порази́ть *(whom = acc.)* ♦ **I won't try to impress you. (I'll just be me.)** Я не бу́ду пыта́ться порази́ть Вас. (Я про́сто бу́ду са́мим *[ж: са́мой]* собо́й.)

impression *n* впечатле́ние ♦ **bad** ~ плохо́е впечатле́ние ♦ **big** ~ большо́е впечатле́ние ♦ **deceptive** ~ обма́нчивое впечатле́ние ♦ **deep** ~ глубо́кое впечатле́ние ♦ **definite** ~ определённое впечатле́ние ♦ **different** ~ друго́е впечатле́ние ♦ **exceptional** ~ исключи́тельное впечатле́ние ♦ *(1,2)* **false** ~ *(1)* неве́рное / *(2)* ло́жное впечатле́ние ♦ **favorable** ~ благоприя́тное впечатле́ние ♦ **first** ~ пе́рвое впечатле́ние ♦ **good** ~ хоро́шее впечатле́ние ♦ **indelible** ~ неизглади́мое впечатле́ние ♦ **lasting** ~ усто́йчивое впечатле́ние ♦ **marvelous** ~ великоле́пное впечатле́ние ♦ **my** ~ моё впечатле́ние ♦ **negative** ~ отрица́тельное впечатле́ние ♦ **nice** ~ прия́тное впечатле́ние ♦ **overall** ~ о́бщее впечатле́ние ♦ **positive** ~ положи́тельное впечатле́ние ♦ **previous** ~ пре́жнее впечатле́ние ♦ **strange** ~ стра́нное впечатле́ние ♦ **striking** ~ потряса́ющее впечатле́ние ♦ **strong** ~ си́льное впечатле́ние ♦ **tremendous** ~ огро́мное впечатле́ние ♦ **unforgettable** ~ незабыва́емое впечатле́ние ♦ **vague** ~ сму́тное впечатле́ние ♦ **vivid** ~ я́ркое впечатле́ние ♦ **wonderful** ~ замеча́тельное впечатле́ние ♦ *(1,2)* **wrong** ~ *(1)* неве́рное / *(2)* ло́жное впечатле́ние ♦ **your** ~ *(familiar)* твоё впечатле́ние; *(polite)* Ва́ше впечатле́ние.

impression: *verb terms*

create the ~ созда́ть впечатле́ние ♦ **leave the** ~ оста́вить впечатле́ние ♦ **make an** ~ производи́ть / произвести́ впечатле́ние *(on whom = + на + acc.)* ♦ **ruin** *(1)* **my** / *(2)* **your** ~ по́ртить / испо́ртить *(1)* моё / *(1)* твоё впечатле́ние ♦ **spoil** *(1)* **my** / *(2)* **your** ~ по́ртить / испо́ртить *(1)* моё / *(1)* твоё впечатле́ние ♦ **strengthen my** ~ уси́лить моё впечатле́ние.

impression: *phrases*

I hope you *(1)* **don't** / *(2)* **won't get the wrong impression (about me).** Я наде́юсь, ты *(1,2)*

A list of conjugated Russian verbs is given in Appendix 3 on page 699.

не полу́чишь неве́рное впечатле́ние (обо мне). ♦ **I'm sorry if I gave you the wrong impression.** Я сожале́ю, е́сли произвёл *(ж: произвела́)* на тебя́ неве́рное впечатле́ние. ♦ **You conveyed the impression that you** *(1)* **...cared about me.** / *(2)* **...didn't care about me (anymore).** / *(3)* **...wanted to have a relationship.** / *(4)* **...wanted to get married.** / *(5)* **...wanted to break up.** Создава́лось впечатле́ние, что ты *(1)* ...интересова́лась *(ж: интересова́лся)* мной. / *(2)* ...(бо́льше) не интересова́лась *(ж: интересова́лся)* мной. / *(3)* ...хоте́ла *(ж: хоте́л)* серьёзных отноше́ний. / *(4)* ...хоте́ла *(ж: хоте́л)* вступи́ть в брак. / *(5)* ...хоте́ла *(ж: хоте́л)* порва́ть. ♦ **I'm sorry if I conveyed that impression.** Я извиня́юсь, что со́здал *(ж: создала́)* тако́е впечатле́ние. ♦ **I didn't mean to convey that impression.** Я не хоте́л *(ж: хоте́ла)* созда́ть тако́е впечатле́ние.

impressionability *n* впечатли́тельность *f.*

impressionable *adj* впечатли́тельвый, -ая, -ое, -ые.

imprint *n* отпеча́ток, печа́ть *f*, след ♦ **Your loving nature has left an imprint on my soul that will never go away.** Ты оста́вила *(ж: оста́вил)* отпеча́ток в мое́й душе́, кото́рый никогда́ не исче́знет.

impromptu *adj (improvised)* импровизи́рованный, -ая, -ое, -ые; *(unexpected)* неожи́данный, -ая, -ое, -ые; *(chance)* случа́йный, -ая, -ое, -ые ♦ *(1,2)* ~ **visit** *(1)* неожи́данный / *(2)* случа́йный визи́т.

improper *adj* 1. *(unsuitable)* неподходя́щий, -ая, -ое, -ые; 2. *(indecent)* неприли́чный, -ая, -ое, -ые; 3. *(incorrect)* непра́вильный, -ая, -ое, -ые.

impudent *adj* де́рзкий, -ая, -ое, -ие, на́глый, -ая, -ое, -ые.

impulse *n* и́мпульс, поры́в; жела́ние ♦ **burning** ~ жгу́чий и́мпульс, горя́чее побужде́ние ♦ **inner** ~ вну́тренний и́мпульс ♦ **irresistible** ~ непреодоли́мый и́мпульс, неопреодоли́мое жела́ние ♦ **lascivious** ~ похотли́вый и́мпульс ♦ **overpowering** ~ неудержи́мое жела́ние ♦ **raging** ~ бе́шеный и́мпульс ♦ *(1,2)* **sudden** ~ внеза́пный *(1)* и́мпульс / *(2)* поры́в ♦ **uncontrollable** ~ неконтроли́руемый и́мпульс ♦ **wild** ~ безу́мный и́мпульс ♦ **on** ~ непроизво́льно, подда́вшись поры́ву.

impulse: phrases

I watch your mouth forming sounds, moving and undulating so supplely, so softly, so enticingly and I am seized with a raging impulse to fuse my own mouth together with it and once and for all revel in its sweet softness. Я слежу́, как твой рот создаёт зву́ки, дви́гаясь и изгиба́ясь так ги́бко, так мя́гко, так соблазни́тельно, и я захва́чен бе́шеным и́мпульсом соедини́ть мой рот с твои́м, что́бы раз и навсегда́ пирова́ть в его́ сла́дкой не́жности. ♦ **Just on impulse I decided to write to you.** Я реши́л *(ж: реши́ла)* написа́ть тебе́, про́сто подда́вшись поры́ву. ♦ **I bought it for you on impulse.** Я купи́л *(ж: купи́ла)* э́то для тебя́, подда́вшись поры́ву. ♦ **I have an overpowering impulse to kiss you.** У меня́ неудержи́мое жела́ние поцелова́ть тебя́. ♦ **I'm not ashamed of my impulses.** Я не стыжу́сь свои́х и́мпульсов.

impulsive *adj* импульси́вный, -ая, -ое, -ые ♦ **You're** *(1)* **too** / *(2)* **very impulsive.** Ты *(1)* сли́шком / *(2)* о́чень импульси́вная *(ж: импульси́вный).* ♦ **You shouldn't be so impulsive.** Ты не должна́ *(ж: до́лжен)* быть тако́й импульси́вной *(ж: таки́м импульси́вным).* ♦ **It was an impulsive thing to do.** Э́то бы́ло сде́лано импульси́вно.

impulsively *adv* импульси́вно.

inadequacy *n* недоста́точность *f* ; неадеква́тность *f.*

inadequate *adj* недоста́точный, -ая, -ое, -ые; неадеква́тный, -ая, -ое, -ые.

inamorata *n (female lover)* возлю́бленная, любо́вница.

inamorato *n (male lover)* возлю́бленный, любо́вник.

inattentive *adj* невнима́тельный, -ая, -ое, -ые *(short forms:* невнима́телен,

---

For Russian adjectives, the masculine form is spelled out, followed by the feminine, neuter and plural endings.

невнима́тельна, -о, -ы) ♦ *(1)* **He** / *(2)* **She is very inattentive to my needs.** *(1)* Он о́чень невнима́телен... / *(2)* Она́ о́чень невнима́тельна... ко мне.

inattentiveness *n* невнима́тельность *f*.

incense *n* ла́дан, фимиа́м.

incensed *adj* разгне́ванный, -ая, -ое, -ые.

incessant *adj* беспреста́нный, -ая, -ое, -ые, непреры́вный, -ая, -ое, -ые, бесконе́чный, -ая, -ое, -ые.

incessantly *adv* беспреста́нно, непреры́вно, бесконе́чно.

inclined *adj* скло́нный, -ая, -ое, -ые *(short forms:* скло́нен, скло́нна, -о, -ы), предрас-поло́женный, -ая, -ое, -ые ♦ **musically** ~ музыка́льный, -ая, -ое, -ые ♦ **be** ~ проявля́ть скло́нность, быть скло́нным *m* / скло́нной *f* *(I'm inclined:* я скло́нен *[ж: скло́нна]*. *You're inclined:* ты скло́нна *[ж: скло́нен]*) ♦ **be humorously** ~ люби́ть ю́мор.

income *n* дохо́д ♦ **above-average** ~ дохо́д вы́ше сре́днего ♦ **good** ~ хоро́ший дохо́д ♦ **great** ~ великоле́пный дохо́д ♦ **high** ~ высо́кий дохо́д ♦ **personal** ~ ли́чный дохо́д ♦ **steady** ~ усто́йчивый дохо́д.

incomparable *adj* несравне́нный, -ая, -ое, -ые, несравни́мый, -ая, -ое, -ые.

incomparably *adv* несравне́нно, несравни́мо.

incongruous *adj* несообра́зный, -ая, -ое, -ые, несоотве́тствующий, -ая, -ее, -ие.

inconsolable безуте́шный, -ая, -ое, -ые, неуте́шный, -ая, -ое, -ые.

inconvenience *vt* затрудня́ть / затрудни́ть *(whom = acc.)*, утружда́ть *(whom = acc.)*, причиня́ть / причини́ть неудо́бство *(whom = dat.)* ♦ **I don't want to inconvenience you.** Я не хочу́ утружда́ть тебя́.

inconvenient *adj* неудо́бный, -ая, -ое, -ые.

incredible *adj* невероя́тный, -ая, -ое, -ые ♦ **You look incredible!** Ты вы́глядишь великоле́пно! ♦ **That was (absolutely) incredible.** Э́то бы́ло (соверше́нно) невероя́тно. ♦ **You are (absolutely) incredible.** Ты (соверше́нно) невероя́тна *(ж: невероя́тен)*.

incredibly *adv* невероя́тно.

incredulity *n* недове́рие.

incredulous *adj* недове́рчивый, -ая, -ое, -ые, скепти́ческий, -ая, -ое, -ие.

indecent *adj* неприли́чный, -ая, -ое, -ые, непристо́йный, -ая, -ое, -ые, нескро́мный, -ая, -ое, -ые.

indecision *n* нереши́тельность *f*, неуве́ренность *f* ♦ **Your indecision is rendering you helpless.** Твоя́ нереши́тельность де́лает тебя́ беспо́мощной *(ж: беспо́мощным)*.

indecisive *adj* нереши́тельный, -ая, -ое, -ые.

independence *n* незави́симость *f*.

independent *adj* незави́симый, -ая, -ое, -ые.

indescribable *adj* неопису́емый, -ая, -ое, -ые, несказа́нный, -ая, -ое, -ые ♦ **What my lips are going to do to your beautiful body is indescribable.** То, что мои́ гу́бы сде́лают с твои́м прекра́сным те́лом, неопису́емо.

indescribably *adv* неопису́емо.

Indian *n* 1. *(India)* инди́ец *m*, индиа́нка *f*; 2. *(America)* инде́ец *m*, индиа́нка *f*.

indi(e) *abbrev (slang)* = **independent** незави́симый, -ая, -ое, -ые.

indifference *n* равноду́шие, безразли́чие ♦ **callous** ~ безду́шное безразли́чие ♦ **mask of** ~ ма́ска равноду́шия ♦ **I sense in you an underlying current of indifference.** Я ощуща́ю в тебе́ скры́тое равноду́шие. ♦ **You keep your feelings locked behind a mask of indifference.** Ты де́ржишь свои́ чу́вства за́пертыми под ма́ской равноду́шия.

indifferent *adj* безразли́чный, -ая, -ое, -ые, равноду́шный, -ая, -ое, -ые.

indiscrete *adj* неосторо́жный, -ая, -ое, -ые, неблагоразу́мный, -ая, -ое, -ые, опроме́т-

See Appendix 19 for notes on sending mail to Russia and Ukraine.

чивый, -ая, -ое, -ые ♦ **That was** *(1)* **very /** *(2)* **rather indiscrete.** Это бы́ло *(1)* о́чень / *(2)* доста́точно неосторо́жно. ♦ **That was a very indiscrete thing to do.** Бы́ло о́чень неосторо́жно сде́лать э́то. ♦ **If you do something indiscrete,** *(1)* **he /** *(2)* **she will find out and there will be trouble.** Если ты сде́лаешь что́-то неосторо́жно, *(1)* он / *(2)* она́ узна́ет, и бу́дут пробле́мы.

indiscretion *n* неосмотри́тельность *f* ♦ **commit an** ~ соверши́ть неосмотри́тельность.

indispensable *adj* необходи́мый, -ая, -ое, -ые.

individual *n* челове́к *(See also terms under* **person**)*.* ♦ **compassionate** ~ сострада́тельный челове́к ♦ **uninhibited** ~ челове́к без ко́мплексов.

individualist *n* индивидуали́ст ♦ **eclectic** ~ эклекти́ческий индивидуали́ст.

individualistic *adj* индивидуалисти́ческий, -ая, -ое, -ие.

induce *vt* вызыва́ть / вы́звать *(what = acc.)*, побужда́ть / побуди́ть *(what = acc.)* ♦ **Your kisses induce such sensual euphoria.** Твои́ поцелу́и вызыва́ют таку́ю чу́вственную эйфори́ю.

indulgent *adj* снисходи́тельный, -ая, -ое, -ые.

ineffable *adj* невырази́мый, -ая, -ое, -ые, несказа́нный, -ая, -ое, -ые ♦ **When our lips touch even for a brief moment, I am** *(1)* **thrown /** *(2)* **hurled into a vortex of ineffable ecstasy.** Когда́ на́ши гу́бы соприкаса́ются да́же на коро́ткое мгнове́ние, я *(1,2)* бро́шен *(ж: бро́шена)* в вихрь невырази́мого экста́за.

inept *adj* неспосо́бный, -ая, -ое, -ые.

inescapable *adj* неизбе́жный, -ая, -ое, -ые.

inescapably *adj* неизбе́жно.

inevitable *adj* неизбе́жный, -ая, -ое, -ые ♦ **escape the** ~ противостоя́ть неизбе́жному.

inevitably *adv* неизбе́жно.

inexperience *n* неискушённость *f.*

inexperienced *adj* нео́пытный, -ая, -ое, -ые, *(short forms:* нео́пытен, нео́пытна, -о, -ы) ♦ **I'm (**[1] **very /** [2] **completely) inexperienced at love.** Я *(*[1]*)* о́чень / *[2]* соверше́нно) нео́пытен *(ж: нео́пытна)* в любви́.

inexplicable *adj* необъясни́мый, -ая, -ое, -ые.

inexplicably *adv* необъясни́мо.

infatuated *adj* увлечён, -увлечена́, -о́, -ы́ *(short forms)* ♦ **become** ~ стра́стно увле́чься *(with whom = instr.)* ♦ **Do you think I'm just infatuated with you? Well, you're very, very wrong -- I love you.** Ты ду́маешь, я то́лько увлечён *(ж: увлечена́)* тобо́й? Ты о́чень, о́чень неправа́ *(ж: непра́в)* -- я тебя́ люблю́. ♦ **I guess I was infatuated with you.** Я полага́ю, я был увлечён *(ж: была́ увлечена́)* тобо́й.

infatuation *n* (слепо́е) увлече́ние ♦ **mad** ~ безрассу́дное увлече́ние ♦ **It's not love, it's just infatuation.** Это не любо́вь, э́то то́лько слепо́е увлече́ние. ♦ **It's not infatuation, it's (genuine) love.** Это не увлече́ние, э́то (настоя́щая) любо́вь. ♦ **I don't care to be the object of your infatuation.** Меня́ не устра́ивает быть объе́ктом твоего́ слепо́го увле-че́ния. ♦ **You don't really love me. It's just infatuation.** Ты на са́мом де́ле не лю́бишь меня́. Это то́лько увлече́ние. ♦ **I know for an absolute certainty that what I feel for you is no mere infatuation. It's love if there ever was love.** Я абсолю́тно то́чно зна́ю, что моё чу́вство к тебе́ не про́сто увлече́ние. Это любо́вь, е́сли когда́-нибудь существова́ла любо́вь. ♦ **I thought at first it was love, but I guess it was just infatuation.** Снача́ла я ду́мал *(ж: ду́мала)*, что э́то была́ любо́вь, но я полага́ю, э́то бы́ло то́лько увлече́ние.

inferno *n* ад ♦ **Visions of your voluptuous loveliness send fire licking through my arteries, igniting my entire being into an inferno of passionate desire.** Вид твое́й чу́вственной красоты́ вызыва́ет ого́нь, бушу́ющий в мои́х арте́риях, посыла́ющий всё моё

When terms are listed after a main word, a tilde ~
is used to indicate the main word.

существо́ в ад стра́стного жела́ния. ♦ **The yearning in my heart for you is an inferno that is consuming me.** Тоска́ по тебе́ в моём се́рдце -- э́то ад, поглоща́ющий меня́.

infidelity *n* изме́на, неве́рность *f* ♦ **marital** ~ супру́жеская неве́рность.

infinite *adj* бесконе́чный, -ая, -ое, -ые *(short forms:* бесконе́чен, бесконе́чна, -о, -ы*)* ♦ **My love for you is infinite.** Моя́ любо́вь к тебе́ бесконе́чна.

infinitely *adv* бесконе́чно.

infinity *n* бесконе́чность *f* ♦ **for all** ~ наве́чно ♦ **I pledge my heart and soul to you for all infinity.** Я обеща́ю своё се́рдце и ду́шу тебе́ наве́чно.

inflame *vt* разжига́ть / разже́чь *(what = acc.)*; воспламеня́ть / воспламени́ть *(what = acc.)*.

inflamed *adj (set afire)* воспламенённый, -ая, -ое, -ые; *(aroused)* возбуждённый, -ая, -ое, -ые ♦ **The desire in my heart to see you grows ever more inflamed.** Жела́ние уви́деть тебя́ всё бо́лее воспламеня́ет моё се́рдце.

influence *n* влия́ние ♦ **You have a tremendous influence over** *(1)* **...all my thoughts and actions.** / *(2)* **...everything I do.** Ты ока́зываешь огро́мное влия́ние на *(1)* ...все мои́ мы́сли и посту́пки. / *(2)* ...на всё, что я де́лаю.

influential *adj* влия́тельный, -ая, -ое, -ые.

inform *vt* сообща́ть / сообщи́ть *(whom = dat., of what = acc.)*; извеща́ть / извести́ть *(whom = acc., of what = + о + prep.)*.

information *n* информа́ция, спра́вки ♦ **Could you get the information for me?** Мо́жешь ты получи́ть информа́цию для меня́? ♦ **I'll get the information for you.** Я получу́ информа́цию для тебя́. ♦ **I couldn't get the information.** Я не мог *(ж: могла́)* получи́ть информа́цию.

informed *adj* зна́ющий, -ая, -ее, -ие, осведомлённый, -ая, -ое, -ые *(short forms:* осве-домлён, осведомлена́, -о́, -ы́*)*. ♦ **be** ~ знать *(about what = + о + prep.)*, быть осведом-лённым *m* / осведомлённой *f (I'm informed:* я осведомлён *[ж: осведомлена́]. You're informed:* ты осведомлена́ *[ж: осведомлён].) (about what = + о + prep.)*.

infuriate *vt* выводи́ть / вы́вести из себя́ *(whom = acc.)*, разъяря́ть / разъяри́ть *(whom = acc.)*, беси́ть / взбеси́ть *(whom = acc.)*.

infuriated *adj* разъярённый, -ая, -ое, -ые, разгне́ванный, -ая, -ое, -ые.

infuriating *adj* разъяря́ющий, -ая, -ее, -ие, приводя́щий (-ая, -ее, -ие) в я́рость.

infusive *adj* вдохновля́ющий, -ая, -ее, -ие, воодушевля́ющий, -ая, -ее, -ие.

ingenue *n* молода́я неви́нная де́вушка ♦ **dewy-eyed** ~ молода́я неви́нная наи́вная де́вушка.

ingratitude *n* неблагода́рность *f.*

inhibit *vt* 1. *(restrain)* сде́рживать *(what, whom = acc.)*; 2. *(hinder)* препя́тствовать *(what, whom = dat.)*, меша́ть *(what, whom = dat.)*. ♦ **Your maidenly sense of propriety is inhib-iting you (way) too much.** Твоё де́вичье чу́вство благопристо́йности сли́шком си́льно сде́рживает тебя́.

inhibited *adj* сде́ржанный, -ая, -ое, -ые, ско́ванный, -ая, -ое, -ые, стеснённый, -ая, -ое, -ые ♦ **You've got to stop being so inhibited.** Ты должна́ переста́ть быть тако́й сде́р-жанной. ♦ **You don't need to be inhibited with me.** Тебе́ не ну́жно быть сде́ржанной со мной. ♦ **Don't be so inhibited. Let yourself go.** Не будь тако́й сде́ржанной *(ж: сде́ржанным)*. Дай себе́ во́лю. ♦ **You should try to be less inhibited.** Тебе́ на́до пы-та́ться быть ме́нее ско́ванной *(ж: ско́ванным)*.

inhibition *n* сде́ржанность *f*, ско́ванность *f*, стесни́тельность *f*, стесне́ние, сде́рживание (чувств), подавле́ние (чувств); ко́мплекс, ограниче́ния *pl* ♦ **I'm going to help you** *(1)* **...get rid of all your inhibitions.** / *(2)* **...overcome your inhibitions and learn the true meaning of** *(3)* **joy** / *(4)* **pleasure** / *(5)* **love** / *(6)* **passion.** Я помогу́ тебе́ *(1)* ...изба́виться

A list of abbreviations used in the dictionary is given on page 10.

от всей твоéй сдéржанности. / *(2)* ...преодолéть твою́ сдéржанность и поня́ть и́стинное значéние *(3)* рáдости / *(4)* наслаждéния / *(5)* любви́ / *(6)* стрáсти. ♦ **You've got to learn how to overcome your inhibitions.** Тебé нáдо научи́ться преодолевáть свою́ сдéржанность. ♦ **You need to throw off your inhibitions and let yourself go.** Тебé ну́жно отбрóсить твою́ сдéржанность и раскрепости́ться. ♦ **When we're together you can** *(1)* **discard** /*(2)* **shed** / *(3)* **jettison** / *(4)* **lose all your** *(5,6)* **inhibitions.** Когдá мы вмéсте, ты мóжешь *(1,2)* отбрóсить / *(3)* ...вы́бросить за борт... / *(4)* забы́ть всю свою́ *(5)* стесни́тельность / *(6)* сдéржанность. ♦ **Just let (all) your inhibitions go.** Отбрóсь (всю) свою́ сдéржанность. ♦ **It's perfectly okay to let your inhibitions go.** Не бу́дет ничегó плохóго, éсли ты отбрóсишь свою́ сдéржанность. ♦ **I'm looking for a** *(1)* **woman** / *(2)* **partner** / *(3)* **mate without inhibitions.** Я ищу́ жéнщину / партнёршу / супру́гу без кóмплексов. ♦ **I have no inhibitions (at all).** У меня́ (совсéм) нет кóмплексов.

inimitable *adj* неповтори́мый, -ая, -ое, -ые ♦ ~ **beauty** *adj* неповтори́мая красотá.

initials *n, pl* инициáлы.

initiate *vt* знакóмить / познакóмить *(whom = acc.)* ♦ **I am so grateful to you for initiating me into this sweet, intoxicating ritual of love.** Я так благодáрен *(ж: благодáрна)* тебé за то, что ты познакóмила *(ж: познакóмил)* меня́ со слáдким, опьяня́ющим ритуáлом любви́. ♦ **I'm going to initiate you into physical delights unlike any you've ever experienced.** Я познакомлю тебя́ с физи́ческими наслаждéниями, не похóжими на те, что ты испы́тывала прéжде.

initiative *n* инициати́ва ♦ **take the** ~ взять инициати́ву на себя́.

innate *adj* врождённый, -ая, -ое, -ые, прирóдный, -ая, -ое, -ые.

innermost *adj* глубочáйший, -ая, -ее, -ие, сокровéнный, -ая, -ое, -ые ♦ **Whenever I think of you, red-hot desire scorches my innermost being.** Когдá бы я ни подýмал о тебé, обжигáющая страсть опаля́ет всё во мне.

innocence *n* неви́нность *f,* непорóчность *f* ♦ **bewitching** ~ чарýющая неви́нность ♦ **captivating** ~ плени́тельная неви́нность ♦ **gentle** ~ нéжная неви́нность ♦ **precious** ~ драгоцéнная неви́нность ♦ **refreshing** ~ ми́лая наи́вность, очаровáтельная неви́нность ♦ **wide-eyed** ~ наи́вная неви́нность ♦ **Your (gentle) innocence is so** *(1)*   **cap tivating** / *(2)***endearing** / *(3)* **precious** / *(4)* **refreshing** / *(5)* **bewitching.** Твоя́ (нéжная) неви́нность так *(1)* плени́тельна / *(2)* покоря́юща / *(3)* драгоцéнна / *(4)* освежáюща / *(5)* чарýюща. ♦ **You (really)** *(1)* **...throw me off balance...** / *(2)* **...beguile** / *(3)* **captivate** / *(4)* **disarm** / *(5)* **enchant me... with your wide-eyed innocence.** Ты (действи́тельно) *(1)* ...вывóдишь меня́ из равновéсия... / *(2)* ...очарóвываешь / *(3)* пленя́ешь / *(4)* обезорýживаешь / *(5)* чарýешь меня́... своéй наи́вной неви́нностью.

innocent *adj* неви́нный, -ая, -ое, -ые ♦ **You** *(1)* **look** / *(2)* **seem as innocent as a lamb.** Ты *(1)* вы́глядишь / *(2)* кáжешься неви́нной, как овéчка.

innocent *n* неви́нный *m*, неви́нная *f* ♦ **Don't play the injured innocent with me.** Не игрáй со мной в оби́женную неви́нность.

innovative *adj* созидáтельный, -ая, -ое, -ые.

innuendo *n* (кóсвенный) намёк, инсинуáция ♦ **malicious** ~**s** злóбные намёки ♦ **sly** ~**s** хи́трые намёки.

inquisitive *adj* любознáтельный, -ая, -ое, -ые.

insane *adj* безу́мный, -ая, -ое, -ые, сумасшéдший, -ая, -ее, -ие.

insanely *adv* безу́мно ♦ **My** *(1)* **(ex-)boyfriend** / *(2)* **(ex-)husband** / *(3)* **(ex-)girlfriend** / *(4)* **(ex-)wife is insanely jealous (of me).** *(1)* Мой (бы́вший) друг / *(2)* муж... / *(3)* Моя́ (бы́вшая) дéвушка / *(4)* женá... безу́мно ревну́ет (меня́).

insatiable *adj* ненасы́тный, -ая, -ое, -ые, жáдный, -ая, -ое, -ые ♦ **My** *(1)* **passion** / *(2)* **desire**

The accents on Russian words are to show how to pronounce them.
You don't have to copy the accents when writing to someone.

/ *(3)* **love for you is insatiable.** Моя *(1,2)* страсть / *(3)* любо́вь к тебе́ ненасы́тна. ♦ **If I seem insatiable (when we make love), it's your fault.** Если я кажу́сь тебе́ ненасы́тным *(ж: ненасы́тной)*, (когда́ мы занима́емся любо́вью,) э́то твоя́ вина́.

insatiably *adv* ненасы́тно; жа́дно ♦ ~ **responsive** ненасы́тный, -ая, -ое, -ые.

inscription *n (on a ring)* на́дпись *f* ♦ ~ **on a ring** на́дпись на кольце́.

insecure *adj* неуве́ренный, -ая, -ое, -ые.

insecurity *n* неуве́ренность (в са́мом себе́).

insensitive *adj* нечувстви́тельный, -ая, -ое, -ые, невоспри́имчивый, -ая, -ое, -ые.

inseparable *adj* нераздели́мый, -ая, -ое, -ые *(short forms:* нераздели́м, -а, -о, -ы*)*, неразлу́чный, -ая, -ое, -ые ♦ **We are inseparable.** Мы неразделимы.

in-shape *adj* в хоро́шей фо́рме.

inside *prep* внутри́ ♦ **It's who you are inside that counts.** Ва́жно кто ты внутри́.

inside out: ♦ **It turns me inside out to think of you with another** *(1)* **man /** *(2)* **woman.** Мысль о том, что ты *(1)* ...с други́м мужчи́ной... / *(2)* ...с друго́й же́нщиной... выво́дит меня́ из себя́. ♦ **I know** *(1)* **you /** *(2)* **him /** *(3)* **her /** *(4)* **them inside out.** Я всё зна́ю о *(1)* тебе́ / *(2)* нём / *(3)* ней / *(4)* них.

insidious *adj* кова́рный, -ая, -ое, -ые.

insight *n* понима́ние ♦ **give an** ~ дать поня́ть *(whom = dat.)* ♦ **Your letter gave me an insight into your situation.** Твоё письмо́ да́ло мне возмо́жность поня́ть твою́ ситуа́цию.

insignificant *adj* незначи́тельный, -ая, -ое, -ые.

insincere *adj* неи́скренний, -яя, -ее, -ие.

insincerity *n* неи́скренность *f* ♦ *(1)* **I hate... /** *(2)* **I can't stand... insincerity.** *(1)* Я ненави́жу... / *(2)* Я не могу́ терпе́ть... неи́скренность.

insinuate *vt* намека́ть / намекну́ть *(what = acc.)* ♦ **What are you insinuating?** На что ты намека́ешь? ♦ **Are you insinuating that I'm unfaithful?** Ты намека́ешь, что я не ве́рен *(ж: верна́)* тебе́? ♦ **I'm not insinuating anything (of the sort).** Я ни на что (тако́е) не намека́ю.

insinuation *n* намёк, инсинуа́ция ♦ **lewd** ~ непристо́йный намёк.

insist *vi* наста́ивать / настоя́ть *(on what = + на + prep.)*.

insistent *adj* насто́йчивый, -ая, -ое, -ые, настоя́тельный, -ая, -ое, -ые.

insistently *adv* насто́йчиво.

insolence *n* на́глость *f*, наха́льство, де́рзость *f*.

insolent *adj* на́глый, -ая, -ое, -ые, наха́льный, -ая, -ое, -ые, де́рзкий, -ая, -ое, -ие.

insolently *adv* на́гло, наха́льно, де́рзко.

inspiration *n* вдохнове́ние ♦ **You are my inspiration (and hope).** Ты моё вдохнове́ние (и наде́жда). ♦ **You give me the inspiration** *(1)* **...to carry on. /** *(2)* **...to keep going. /** *(3)* **...achieve my goals.** Ты вдохновля́ешь меня́ *(1,2)* ...продолжа́ть. / *(3)* ...в достиже́нии мои́х це́лей.

inspire *vi* 1. *(motivate, stir)* вдохновля́ть / вдохнови́ть *(what, whom = acc.)*; 2. *(evoke)* внуша́ть / внуши́ть *(what = acc.)* ♦ **You inspire love.** Ты внуша́ешь любо́вь. ♦ **I can't tell you how much you inspire me (**[1] **in ...my work. /** [2] **...everything I do.).** Невозмо́жно вы́разить, как ты вдохновля́ешь меня́ (**[**1**]**...в рабо́те. / **[**2**]** ...во всём, что я де́лаю.) ♦ **You possess the kind of beauty that inspires** *(1)* **...masterpieces of art. /** *(2)* **...great paintings.** Ты облада́ешь тако́й красото́й, кото́рая вдохновля́ет *(1)* ...шеде́вры иску́сства. / *(2)* ...вели́ких худо́жников.

inspired *adj* вдохновлённый, -ая, -ое, -ые *(short forms:* вдохновлён, вдохновлена́, -о́, -ы́*)* ♦ **With you by my side I would feel so uplifted and inspired and happy.** С тобо́й я бы чу́вствовал *(ж: чу́вствовала)* тако́й подъём, вдохнове́ние и сча́стье.

If no accent is shown on a word with a capitalized vowel,
it means that the capitalized vowel is accented.

inspiring *adj* вдохновля́ющий, -ая, -ее, -ие ♦ **sensually ~** чу́вственно вдохновля́ющий, -ая, -ее, -ие.

instill *vt* внуша́ть / внуши́ть *(what = acc.)* ♦ **Your manner instills confidence.** Твои́ мане́ры внуша́ют уве́ренность.

instinct *n* инсти́нкт ♦ **animal ~** звери́ный инсти́нкт ♦ **base ~s** ни́зменные инсти́нкты ♦ **baser ~s** ни́зшие инсти́нкты ♦ **basest ~s** са́мые ни́зменные инсти́нкты ♦ **blind ~** слепо́й инсти́нкт ♦ **first ~** пе́рвое побужде́ние ♦ **maternal ~s** матери́нские инсти́нкты ♦ **my ~s** мои́ инсти́нкты ♦ **prudish ~s** стыдли́вые инсти́нкты ♦ **by ~** инстинкти́вно ♦ **I'm going to trust my instincts (about you).** Я дове́рю свое́й интуи́ции (о тебе́). ♦ **I have to learn how to control my baser instincts around you.** Я до́лжен научи́ться контроли́ровать свои́ ни́зшие инсти́нкты ря́дом с тобо́й. ♦ **You (really) need to overcome your prudish instincts.** Ты (действи́тельно) должна́ преодоле́ть свои́ стыдли́вые инсти́нкты. ♦ **My instincts prompt me to** *(1)* **...just leave you. /** *(2)* **...forget about you. /** *(3,4)* **...go home. /** *(5)* **...run off with you (and** *[6,7]* **get married).** Мой инсти́нкт подска́зывает мне *(1)* ...про́сто оста́вить тебя́. / *(2)* ...забы́ть о тебе́. / *(3)* ...уе́хать *(by veh.)* / *(4)* уйти́ *(on foot)* домо́й. / *(5)* ...убежа́ть с тобо́й (и *[6]* ...жени́ться *m.* / *[7]* ...вы́йти за́муж *f.*).

instinctive *adj* инстинкти́вный, -ая, -ое, -ые.

instinctively *adv* инстинкти́вно ♦ **know ~** знать инстинкти́вно.

insufferable *adj* невыноси́мый, -ая, -ое, -ые, нестерпи́мый, -ая, -ое, -ые.

insult *vt* оскорбля́ть / оскорби́ть *(what, whom = acc.)* ♦ **You have insulted me.** Ты оскорби́ла *(ж: оскорби́л)* меня́. ♦ **I didn't mean to insult you.** Я не хоте́л *(ж: хоте́ла)* оскорби́ть тебя́. ♦ **I'm sorry** *(1)* **that /** *(2)* **if I insulted you.** Прости́ *(1)* ...за то, что... / *(2)* ...е́сли... оскорби́л *(ж оскорби́ла)* тебя́.

insult *n* оскорбле́ние, оби́да ♦ **That's an insult.** Это оскорбле́ние. ♦ **That was an insult.** Это бы́ло оскорбле́нием. ♦ **That's an insult to my intelligence.** Ты ду́маешь, что я глуп *(ж: глупа́).*

intangible *adj* неосяза́емый, -ая, -ое, -ые, неулови́мый, -ая, -ое, -ые, непостижи́мый, -ая, -ое, -ые.

integrity *n* че́стность *f*, прямота́, поря́дочность *f* ♦ **personal ~** ли́чная че́стность ♦ **person of high ~** о́чень че́стный челове́к ♦ **I'm a person of integrity.** Я че́стный челове́к. ♦ **You can be sure that I'm a person of (high) integrity.** Ты мо́жешь быть уве́рена *(ж: уве́рен),* что я (высоко́) поря́дочный челове́к. ♦ **Integrity means everything to me.** Че́стность гла́вное для меня́.

intellect *n* интелле́кт, ум ♦ *(1-3)* **keen ~** *(1)* о́стрый / *(2)* проница́тельный / *(3)* то́нкий ум ♦ *(1,2)* **powerful ~** *(1)* могу́чий / *(2)* си́льный интелле́кт ♦ *(1,2)* **robust ~** *(1)* здра́вый / *(2)* я́сный ум ♦ **scintillating** *(1,2)* **~** искря́щийся *(1)* интелле́кт / *(2)* ум ♦ **vibrant** *(1,2)* **~** живо́й *(1)* интелле́кт / *(2)* ум ♦ **vigorous** *(1,2)* **~** живо́й *(1)* интелле́кт / *(2)* ум.

intellectual *adj* интеллектуа́льный, -ая, -ое, -ые ♦ **You have quite an intellectual (turn of) mind.** У тебя́ весьма́ интеллектуа́льный склад ума́.

intellectual *n* интеллектуа́л.

intellectually *adv* интеллектуа́льно ♦ **We bond so well intellectually.** Мы интеллектуа́льно так хорошо́ подхо́дим друг к дру́гу.

intelligence *n* ум, рассу́док, интелле́кт ♦ **You're a woman of (high) intelligence.** Ты (о́чень) у́мная (же́нщина). ♦ **You're a man of (high) intelligence.** Ты (о́чень) у́мный (мужчи́на). ♦ **That's an insult to my intelligence.** Ты ду́маешь, что я глуп *(ж глупа́).* ♦ **My heart yearns so fiercely to have a partner like you in life, one who combines a gentle spirit with sexuality, good-heartedness, intelligence, and a loving nature.** Моё се́рдце

Russian has 6 grammatical cases. For an explanation of them, see the grammar appendix on page 686.

так неи́стово жа́ждет тако́го спу́тника жи́зни, как ты, тако́го, кто соединя́ет мя́гкий хара́ктер с сексуа́льностью, добросерде́чием, интеллиге́нтностью и любя́щей нату́рой.

intelligent *adj* разу́мный, -ая, -ое, -ые, у́мный, -ая, -ое, -ые ♦ **exceptionally** ~ исключи́тельно у́мный, -ая, -ое, -ые ♦ **liberally** ~ либера́льно интеллиге́нтный, -ая, -ое, -ые ♦ **remarkably** ~ необыкнове́нно у́мный, -ая, -ое, -ые ♦ **very** ~ о́чень у́мный, -ая, -ое, -ые ♦ **You are a remarkably intelligent person.** Ты необыкнове́нно у́мный челове́к.

intend *vi* намерева́ться; собира́ться ♦ **My parents want to know if you intend to marry me.** *(ж:)* Мои́ роди́тели хотя́т знать, наме́рен ли ты жени́ться на мне. ♦ **I'm going to tell my parents I intend to marry you.** Я скажу́ свои́м роди́телям, что наме́рен жени́ться на тебе́ *(ж: наме́рена вы́йти за́муж за тебя́.).* ♦ **I intend to** *(1)* **...come there in the summer.** / *(2)* **...marry you (as soon as possible).** / *(3)* **...get a divorce.** Я наме́рен *(ж: наме́рена) (1)* ...прие́хать туда́ ле́том. / *(2)* ...жени́ться на тебе́ *(ж: вы́йти за́муж за тебя́)* (как мо́жно скоре́е). / *(3)* ...получи́ть разво́д. ♦ **I intended to** *(1)* **call** / *(2)* **write** / *(3)* **tell you.** Я собира́лся *(ж: собира́лась) (1)* позвони́ть / *(2)* написа́ть / *(3)* сказа́ть тебе́.

intense *adj* интенси́вный, -ая, -ое, -ые, си́льный, -ая, -ое, -ые ♦ **It was so intense (that) I could hardly bear it.** Это бы́ло так си́льно, что я едва́ мог *(ж: могла́)* вы́нести.

intensely *adv* интенси́вно, си́льно.

intensify *vt* уси́ливать / уси́лить *(what = acc.)* ♦ **The very fact that you write to me at all gives me warm feelings, and then the things you say in your letter intensify those feelings a thousand-fold.** Про́сто факт, что ты пи́шешь мне, вызыва́ет во мне тёплые чу́вства, и зате́м то, что ты говори́шь в свои́х пи́сьмах, уси́ливает э́ти чу́вства в ты́сячу раз.

intensity *n* интенси́вность *f*, си́ла ♦ **sheer** ~ и́стинная си́ла ♦ **wild** ~ ди́кая си́ла ♦ ~ **of feeling** нака́л чу́вства ♦ ~ **of love** си́ла любви́ ♦ ~ **of physical desire** нака́л физи́ческой стра́сти ♦ ~ **of your passion** си́ла твое́й стра́сти ♦ **The sheer intensity of your passion was** *(1)* **fantastic** / *(2)* **incredible** / *(3)* **unbelievable.** Интенси́вность твое́й стра́сти была́ про́сто *(1)* фантасти́ческой / *(2,3)* невероя́тной. ♦ **I was surprised at the sheer intensity of your passion.** Я был про́сто поражён *(ж: поражена́)* и́стинной си́лой твое́й стра́сти. ♦ **The** *(1,2)* **intensity of your appeal for me is beyond** *(3)* **description** / *(4)* **definition** / *(5)* **calculation.** *(1)* Интенси́вность / *(2)* Си́ла твое́й привлека́тельности для меня́ вы́ше *(3)* ...вся́кого описа́ния / *(4)* определе́ния. / *(5)* ...вся́кой ме́ры. ♦ **There are no words to describe the intensity of the love that I bear in my heart for you.** Нет слов, что́бы описа́ть си́лу той любви́ к тебе́, кото́рой полно́ моё се́рдце. ♦ **You and I are incredibly alike in the nature and intensity of our feelings.** Мы с тобо́й невероя́тно похо́жи хара́ктером и интенси́вностью на́ших чувств.

intention *n* наме́рение ♦ **good** ~s хоро́шие наме́рения ♦ **honorable** ~s че́стные наме́рения ♦ **lofty** ~s высо́кие наме́рения ♦ **noble** ~s благоро́дные наме́рения ♦ **serious** ~s серьёзные наме́рения ♦ **slightest** ~ мале́йшее наме́рение.

| **intention:** *phrases* |

I have no intention of losing you. У меня́ нет наме́рения потеря́ть тебя́. ♦ **It's my intention to** *(1)* **...marry you.** / *(2)* **...tell him** / *(3)* **her** / *(4)* **them.** / *(5)* **...come there next spring.** Моё наме́рение - *(1)* ...жени́ться на тебе́ *(ж: вы́йти за тебя́ за́муж).* / *(2)* ...сказа́ть ему́ / *(3)* ей / *(4)* им. / *(5)* ...прие́хать туда́ сле́дующей весно́й. ♦ **It was my intention to** *(1)* **call** / *(2)* **write** / *(3)* **tell you.** Моё наме́рение бы́ло *(1)* позвони́ть / *(2)* написа́ть / *(3)* сказа́ть тебе́. ♦ **The road to hell is paved with good intentions.** Хоро́шими наме́рениями вы́мощена доро́га в ад. ♦ **I'll change my mind and forget my honorable intentions.** Я переду́маю и забу́ду свои́ че́стные наме́рения. ♦ **I don't think you have**

There are no articles ("a" or "the") in Russian.

even the slightest intention of marrying me. Я не ду́маю, что у тебя́ есть хотя́ бы мале́йшее наме́рение вы́йти за меня́ за́муж *(ж: жени́ться на мне).*

intentional *adj* наме́ренный, -ая, -ое, -ые, умы́шленный, -ая, -ое, -ые.

intentionally *adv* наме́ренно, умы́шленно.

interchange *n* обме́н ♦ **I hope there will always be a constant interchange of love between us.** Я наде́юсь, что ме́жду на́ми всегда́ бу́дет постоя́нный обме́н любо́вью.

intercourse *n (sexual)* половы́е сноше́ния *pl,* половы́е отноше́ния *pl* ♦ **passionate ~** стра́стное заня́тие любо́вью ♦ **wild ~** необу́зданное заня́тие любо́вью ♦ **I don't want to have intercourse (with you).** Я не хочу́ име́ть половы́х отноше́ний (с тобо́й). ♦ **I've never had intercourse with anyone.** Я никогда́ ни с кем не име́л *(ж: име́ла)* сексуа́льных отноше́ний.

interdependence *n* взаимозави́симость *f* ♦ **There's always interdependence in a good relationship.** Всегда́ есть взаимозави́симость в хоро́ших отноше́ниях.

interdependent *adj* взаимозави́симый, -ая, -ое, -ые ♦ **I want us to always be interdependent (and to share all things).** Я хочу́, что́бы мы всегда́ зави́сели друг от дру́га (и дели́ли всё в жи́зни).

interest *vt* интересова́ть / заинтересова́ть *(whom = acc.)* ♦ **You interest me (very much).** Вы меня́ (о́чень) заинтересова́ли.

interest *n* интере́с ♦ **artistic ~s** худо́жественные интере́сы ♦ **broad ~s** широ́кие интере́сы ♦ **burning ~** горя́чий интере́с ♦ **common ~s** о́бщие интере́сы ♦ **considerable ~** значи́тельный интере́с ♦ **cultural ~s** культу́рные интере́сы ♦ **deep ~** глубо́кий интере́с ♦ **diverse ~s** ра́зные интере́сы ♦ **eclectic ~s** эклекти́ческие интере́сы ♦ **enormous ~** огро́мный интере́с ♦ **genuine ~** и́скренний интере́с ♦ **great ~** большо́й интере́с ♦ **healthy ~ in the opposite sex** здоро́вый интере́с к противополо́жному по́лу ♦ **intense ~** напряжённый интере́с ♦ **keen ~** живо́й интере́с ♦ **literary ~s** литерату́рные интере́сы ♦ **lively ~** живо́й интере́с ♦ **my ~s** мои́ интере́сы ♦ **particular ~** осо́бый интере́с ♦ **personal ~s** ли́чные интере́сы ♦ **romantic ~** романти́ческий интере́с ♦ *(1,2)* **similar ~s** *(1)* о́бщие / *(2)* похо́жие интере́сы ♦ **sincere ~** и́скренний интере́с ♦ **spiritual ~s** духо́вные интере́сы ♦ **tremendous ~** огро́мный интере́с ♦ **unique ~s** уника́льные интере́сы ♦ **usual ~s** обы́чные интере́сы ♦ **varied ~s** разнообра́зные интере́сы ♦ **what ~s** каки́е интере́сы ♦ **your ~s** *(familiar)* твои́ интере́сы; *(polite)* Ва́ши интере́сы.

interest: other terms

arouse my ~ пробужда́ть / пробуди́ть мой интере́с ♦ **commonality of ~s** о́бщность интере́сов ♦ **have ~** име́ть интере́с *(in what = + к + dat.)* ♦ **lack of ~** отсу́тствие интере́са ♦ **small spark of ~** ма́ленькая и́скорка интере́са.

interest: phrases

Tell me about your interests. *(polite)* Расскажи́те мне о свои́х интере́сах. ♦ **We have many similar interests.** У нас мно́го о́бщих интере́сов. ♦ **I'm** *(1)* **glad /** *(2)* **pleased that we have so many interests in common.** Я рад *(ж: ра́да),* что у нас так мно́го о́бщих интере́сов. ♦ **We can explore areas of mutual interest.** Мы мо́жем занима́ться тем, что интере́сно нам обо́им. ♦ **What are your hobbies and interests?** Каки́е у Вас люби́мые заня́тия и интере́сы? ♦ **I have varied interests.** У меня́ разнообра́зные интере́сы. ♦ **My interests are varied.** Мои́ интере́сы разнообра́зны. ♦ **I seek a** *(1)* **lady /** *(2)* **woman /** *(3)* **gentleman /** *(4)* **man /** *(5)* **person with similar interests.** Я ищу́ *(1,2)* же́нщину / *(3)* джентельме́на / *(4)* мужчи́ну / *(5)* челове́ка с похо́жими интере́сами. ♦ **Your description in your ad** *(1,2)* **really sparked my interest.** То, как ты описа́ла *(ж: описа́л)* себя́ в объявле́нии, *(1)* ...разожгло́ мой интере́с. / *(2)* ...о́чень заинтересова́ло меня́.

interested *adj* заинтересо́ван, -а, -о, -ы *(short forms).* ♦ **be ~** интересова́ться *(in what =*

This dictionary contains two Russian alphabet pages: one in Appendix 1, page 685, and a tear-off page on page 799.

instr.) ♦ **What are you interested in?** Что Вас интересу́ет? ♦ **What (kind of) things are you interested in?** Каки́е у Вас интере́сы? ♦ **Are you interested in** *(1)* **art** / *(2)* **music** / *(3)* **literature** / *(4)* **sports** / *(5)* **etc** *(in what = instr.).***?** Вы интересу́етесь *(1)* иску́сством / *(2)* му́зыкой / *(3)* литерату́рой / *(4)* спо́ртом / *(5)* *и т. д.*? ♦ **I'm (not) interested in** *(1)* **art** / *(2)* **etc** *(in what = instr.)*. Я (не) интересу́юсь *(1)* иску́сством / *(2)* *и т. д.*

interface *vi* свя́зываться / связа́ться *(with whom = + с + instr.)* ♦ **~ over e-mail** свя́зываться / связа́ться по электро́нной по́чте *(with whom = + с + instr.).*

interfere *vi* меша́ть / помеша́ть, вме́шиваться / вмеша́ться *(in what = + в + acc.)* ♦ **I didn't mean to** *(1,2)* **interfere.** Я не хоте́л *(ж: хоте́ла)* *(1)* помеша́ть / *(2)* вмеша́ться. ♦ **I'm sorry if I interfered.** Прости́, е́сли (я) помеша́л *(ж: помеша́ла)*. ♦ *(1)* **He** / *(2)* **She has...** / *(3)* **You have... no right to interfere in** *(4,7)* **your** / *(5,8)* **my** *(6)* **life** / *(9)* **affairs.** *(1)* Он / *(2)* Она́ не име́ет... / *(3)* Ты не име́ешь... пра́ва вме́шиваться в ...*(4)* твою́ / *(5)* мою́ *(6)* жизнь. / ... *(7)* твои́ / *(8)* мои́ *(9)* дела́. ♦ **Please don't interfere.** Пожа́луйста, не вме́шивайся. ♦ **I don't want you to interfere in my life.** Я не хочу́, чтобы ты вме́шивалась *(ж: вме́шивался)* в мою́ жизнь. ♦ **Forgive me for interfering (in your personal affairs).** Прости́ меня́ за вмеша́тельство (в твои́ ли́чные дела́).

interference *n* вмеша́тельство.

interlude *n* 1. *(interval)* промежу́ток, интерва́л; 2. *(theater)* антра́кт; 3. *(romantic)* связь ♦ **intimate ~** инти́мная связь ♦ **romantic ~** романти́ческая связь.

internalize *vt* усва́ивать / усво́ить *(what = acc.).*

interpret *vt* 1. *(explain, make sense of)* толкова́ть *(what = acc.)*; истолко́вывать / истолкова́ть *(what = acc.)*, объясня́ть / объясни́ть *(what = acc.)*, расце́нивать / расцени́ть *(what = acc.)*; 2. *(translate orally)* переводи́ть / перевести́ (у́стно) *(what = acc.)* ♦ **How should I interpret** *(1)* **...your letter?** / *(2)* **...what you said?** / *(3)* **...all this?** Как я до́лжен *(ж: должна́)* расце́нивать *(1)* ...твоё письмо́? / *(2)* ...то, что ты сказа́ла *(ж: сказа́л)*? / *(3)* ...всё э́то? ♦ **Is there somebody (here) who could interpret (for** *[1]* **me** / *[2]* **us)?** Есть ли (здесь) кто́-нибудь, кто смог бы перевести́ (для *[1]* меня́ / *[2]* нас)? ♦ *(1)* **He** / *(2)* **She can interpret for** *(3)* **you** / *(4)* **us.** *(1)* Он / *(2)* Она́ мо́жет перевести́ для *(3)* тебя́ / *(4)* нас.

interrupt *vt* перебива́ть / переби́ть *(what, whom = acc.)*, прерыва́ть / прерва́ть *(what, whom = acc.)* ♦ **I'm sorry to** *(1,2)* **interrupt you.** Извини́ за то, что *(1)* переби́л / *(2)* прерва́л *(ж: [1] переби́ла / [2] прерва́ла)* тебя́.

interruption *n* 1. *(interrupting)* прерыва́ние; 2. *(disturbance)* поме́ха; *(intrusion)* вмеша́тельство, вторже́ние; 3. *(break)* переры́в.

intertwine *vi* сплета́ться / сплести́сь.

intimacy *n* бли́зость *f*, инти́мность *f*; бли́зкие отноше́ния ♦ **blissful ~** счастли́вая инти́мность ♦ **caring ~** лю́бящая бли́зость ♦ **delightful ~** восхити́тельная инти́мность ♦ **emotional ~** эмоциона́льная бли́зость ♦ **exciting ~** возбужда́ющая инти́мность ♦ **false ~** неи́скренняя бли́зость ♦ **lifelong ~** бли́зость длино́ю в жизнь ♦ **mutual ~** взаи́мная бли́зость ♦ **online ~** бли́зкие отноше́ния по интерне́ту ♦ **sensuous ~** чу́вственная инти́мность ♦ **true ~** настоя́щая инти́мность ♦ **warm ~** тёплая бли́зость ♦ **wonderful ~** замеча́тельная инти́мность.

intimacy: other terms

be afraid of ~ боя́ться бли́зости ♦ **enjoy ~** наслажда́ться бли́зостью ♦ **fear of ~** страх пе́ред бли́зостью ♦ **magic of ~** ма́гия инти́мности ♦ **share ~** разделя́ть бли́зость *(with whom = + с + instr.).*

intimacy: phases

It's so wonderful to share intimacy with you. Так замеча́тельно разделя́ть бли́зость с тобо́й. ♦ **I've never known such** *(1)* **blissful** / *(2)* **wonderful intimacy with anyone.** Я

Russian verbs conjugate for 6 persons:
I, familiar you, he-she-it, we, polite&plural you, and they.

никогда ни с кем не знал *(знала)* такой *(1)* счастливой / *(2)* замечательной близости. ♦ **You need to shed your fear of intimacy.** Ты должна *(ж: должен)* отбросить свой страх перед близостью. ♦ **I think you're afraid of intimacy.** Я думаю, ты боишься близости. ♦ *(1)* **Don't be... /** *(2)* **You must not be... afraid of intimacy.** *(1)* Не бойся... / *(2)* Ты не должна *(ж: должен)* бояться... близости. ♦ **I want to give you a world of warm, caring intimacy.** Я хочу дать тебе мир тёплой, любящей близости. ♦ **When I initiate your body into intimacy, it will be with infinite love and consummate gentleness.** Когда я познакомлю твоё тело с интимной близостью, я сделаю это с бесконечной любовью и истинной нежностью. ♦ **What heaven it would be to have some lazy, languorous, uninterrupted time to share love and intimacy with you.** Как замечательно было бы провести с тобой ленивое, томное, непрерываемое время, наполненное любовью и близостью.

intimate *adj* интимный, -ая, -ое, -ые, близкий, -ая, -ое, -ие, сокровенный, -ая, -ое, -ые ♦ **I think it would be such a nice feeling to sit close to you and talk with you in an intimate way for hours on end. This is going to be my new dream in the days ahead.** Я думаю, как бы это было прекрасно сидеть рядом с тобой и говорить о сокровенном бесконечные часы. Это теперь будет моей новой мечтой. ♦ **I want to totally abandon myself in the intimate communion of our bodies.** Я хочу полностью предаться интимному общению наших тел. ♦ **I have never been intimate with anyone.** Я никогда ни с кем не был близок *(ж: не была близка)*.

intimately *adv* интимно, близко ♦ **I've never known a man intimately.** Я никогда не знала мужчину интимно. ♦ **I want us to know each other intimately.** Я хочу, чтобы мы близко узнали друг друга. ♦ **It's wonderful that we know each other so intimately.** Это прекрасно, что мы так близко знаем друг друга.

into *prep*: ♦ **be ~** *(prep) (slang) (be very interested in, be actively involved in)* очень интересоваться *(what = instr.)*, любить *(what = acc.)*, активно участвовать *(what = + в + prep.)* ♦ **I'm into** *(1)* **movies /** *(2)* **sports /** *(3)* **biking /** *(4)* **skiing /** *(5)* **laughing.** Я люблю *(1)* кино / *(2)* спорт / *(3)* велосипед / *(4)* лыжи / *(5)* смех. ♦ **I'm into** *(1)* **biking /** *(2)* **skiing.** Я заядлый *(1)* велосипедист / *(2)* лыжник. ♦ **I'm not into watching TV.** Я не интересуюсь телевизором.

intolerable *adj* невыносимый, -ая, -ое, -ые, нестерпимый, -ая, -ое, -ые.

intoxicate *vt* опьянять / опьянить *(what = acc.)* ♦ **You intoxicate me with passion.** Ты опьяняешь меня страстью. ♦ **You really know how to intoxicate (a person).** Ты действительно знаешь, как опьянить (человека).

intoxicating *adj* опьяняющий, -ая, -ее, -ие, пьянящий, -ая, -ее, -ие, упоительный, -ая, -ое, -ые ♦ **The whole evening my** *(1)* **attention /** *(2)* **mind was captive to your intoxicating presence.** Весь вечер *(1)* ...моё внимание было... / *(2)* ...мой ум был... пленником твоего опьяняющего присутствия.

intrigue *vt* интриговать *(whom = + acc.)* ♦ **You (really) intrigue me.** Ты (действительно) интригуешь меня. ♦ **Those beautiful** *(1)* **dark /** *(2)* **green eyes of yours intrigue me endlessly.** Эти твои прекрасные *(1)* тёмные / *(2)* зелёные глаза интригуют меня бесконечно.

intrigued *adj* заинтригован, -а, -о, -ы *(short forms)*, заинтересован, -а, -о, -ы *(short forms)* ♦ **I was quite intrigued by your ad.** Я был *(ж: была)* весьма заинтригован *(ж: заинтригована)* твоим объявлением.

intriguing *adj* интригующий, -ая, -ее, -ие ♦ **You have such intriguing eyes.** У тебя такие интригующие глаза.

introspective *adj* интроспективный, -ая, -ое, -ые, занимающийся (-аяся, -еся, -иеся)

There are two words for "you" in Russian:
familiar «ты» and polite / plural «вы» (See page 781).

самоана́лизом.

introvert *n* интрове́рт ♦ **gregarious** ~ общи́тельный интрове́рт.

introverted *adj* сосредото́чен (-а, -о, -ы) на са́мом себе *(short forms)*, интрове́ртный, -ая, -ое, -ые.

intrude *vi* вторга́ться / вто́ргнуться *(on what = + в + acc.)*; *(abuse)* злоупотребля́ть / злоупотреби́ть *(on what = instr.)* ♦ **I don't want to intrude on your** *(1)* **...hospitality.** / *(2)* **...private life.** Я не хочу́ *(1)* ...злоупотребля́ть твои́м гостеприи́мством. / *(2)* ...вторга́ться в твою́ ли́чную жизнь.

intruder *n* навя́зчивый челове́к ♦ **unwanted** ~ нежела́тельный челове́к.

intrusion *n* вторже́ние.

intuition *n* интуи́ция ♦ **feminine** ~ же́нская интуи́ция ♦ **keen** ~ о́страя интуи́ция ♦ **woman's** ~ же́нская интуи́ция ♦ **My woman's intuition tells me that something** *(1)* **...isn't right.** / *(2)* **...is going on.** Моя́ же́нская интуи́ция подска́зывает мне, что что́-то *(1)* ...не так. / *(2)* ...происхо́дит. ♦ **It's my woman's intuition.** Это моя́ же́нская интуи́ция.

intuitive *adj* интуити́вный, -ая, -ое, -ые.

intuitively *adv* интуити́вно ♦ **I knew intuitively that you were the one for me.** Я интуити́вно знал *(ж: зна́ла)*, что ты моя́ еди́нственная *(ж: мой еди́нственный)*.

inundate *vt* 1. *(water)* наводня́ть / наводни́ть *(what = acc.)*; 2. *(affection, love)* затопля́ть / затопи́ть *(what, whom = acc., with what = instr.)* ♦ **Each time I gaze into your eyes, I am inundated with the most intense feelings of love and adoration that I've ever experienced.** Вся́кий раз, когда́ я вгля́дываюсь в твои́ глаза́, я зато́плен таки́ми пы́лкими чу́вствами любви́ и обожа́ния, каки́х я никогда́ не испы́тывал. ♦ *(1)* **You make me want...** / *(2)* **I want... to inundate you with warm, tender love and affection.** *(1)* Ты вызыва́ешь во мне жела́ние... / *(2)* Я хочу́... затопи́ть тебя́ тёплой, не́жной любо́вью..

invade *vt* 1. вторга́ться / вто́ргнуться; 2. *(emotion)* наводня́ть / наводни́ть *(what = acc.)* ♦ **My mouth is going to do its fervent work on you until the need to surrender invades your whole body.** Мой рот бу́дет де́лать свою́ пы́лкую рабо́ту до тех пор, пока́ потре́бность капитули́ровать не наводни́т всё твоё те́ло.

invigorating *adj* бодря́щий, -ая, -ее, -ие, стимули́рующий, -ая, -ее, -ие.

invitation *n* приглаше́ние ♦ **birthday (party)** ~ приглаше́ние на день рожде́ния ♦ **brazen** ~ бессты́дное приглаше́ние ♦ ~ **to a concert** приглаше́ние на конце́рт ♦ ~ **to dinner** приглаше́ние на обе́д ♦ ~ **to the theater** приглаше́ние в теа́тр ♦ ~ **to visit** приглаше́ние в го́сти ♦ **my** ~ моё приглаше́ние ♦ **official** ~ официа́льное приглаше́ние ♦ **personal** ~ ли́чное приглаше́ние ♦ **special** ~ осо́бое приглаше́ние ♦ **wedding** ~ приглаше́ние на сва́дьбу ♦ **written** ~ пи́сьменное приглаше́ние ♦ **your** ~ *(familiar)* твоё приглаше́ние; *(polite)* Ва́ше приглаше́ние.

invitation: *other terms*

accept *(1)* **my** / *(2)* **your** ~ приня́ть *(1)* моё / *(2)* твоё приглаше́ние ♦ **decline** *(1)* **my** / *(2)* **your** ~ отклони́ть *(1)* моё / *(2)* твоё приглаше́ние ♦ *(1)* **give** / *(2)* **offer** / *(3)* **extend an** ~ *(1-3)* приглаша́ть / пригласи́ть *(whom = acc.)* ♦ **letter of** ~ письмо́ с приглаше́нием ♦ **receive** *(1)* **my** / *(2)* **your** ~ получи́ть *(1)* моё / *(2)* твоё приглаше́ние ♦ **refuse** *(1)* **my** / *(2)* **your** ~ отклони́ть *(1)* моё / *(2)* твоё приглаше́ние ♦ **send** *(1)* **me** / *(2)* **you an** ~ посла́ть *(1)* мне / *(2)* тебе́ приглаше́ние. ♦ **send out** ~**s** рассыла́ть / разосла́ть приглаше́ния *(to whom = dat.)*.

invitation: *phrases*

Thank you for your invitation (to dinner). Спаси́бо за *(твоё)* приглаше́ние *(на обе́д)*. ♦ *(1-3)* **I'm sorry, I can't accept your invitation.** *(1)* О́чень жаль, но... / *(2)* Извини́, но...

Russian terms of endearment are given in Appendix 13, page 780.

/ *(3)* К сожале́нию... я не могу́ приня́ть твоё приглаше́ние.

invite *vt* приглаша́ть / пригласи́ть *(whom = acc., to what = + на or в + acc.)* ♦ **I'd like to invite you to** *(1)* **...dinner...** / *(2)* **...a birthday party...** / *(3)* **...a party** / *(4)* **concert** / *(5)* **ballet** / *(6)* **dance** / *(7)* **play** / *(8)* **movie...** / *(9)* **...my home...** / *(10)* **...meet my parents...** *(11)* **...tomorrow (evening).** / *(12)* **...this afternoon** / *(13)* **evening.** / *(14)* **...on Friday** / *(15)* **Saturday** / *(16)* **Sunday** *(17)* **afternoon** / *(18)* **evening.** *(1)* Я хоте́л *(ж: хоте́ла)* бы пригласи́ть тебя́ *(1)* ...на обе́д... / *(2)* ...на день рожде́ния... / *(3)* ...на вечери́нку / *(4)* конце́рт / *(5)* бале́т / *(6)* та́нцы... / *(7)* ...в теа́тр / *(8)* кино́... / *(9)* ...ко мне домо́й... / *(10)* ...на встре́чу с мои́ми роди́телями... *(11)* ...за́втра (ве́чером). / *(12)* ...сего́дня днём / *(13)* ве́чером. / *(14)* ...в пя́тницу / *(15)* суббо́ту / *(16)* воскресе́нье *(17)* днём / *(18)* ве́чером. ♦ **As a small token of my appreciation, I'd like to invite you to dinner.** Как ма́лый знак мое́й призна́тельности, я хоте́л бы пригласи́ть Вас на обе́д. ♦ **Thank you for inviting me.** Спаси́бо за приглаше́ние. ♦ **The silky sheen of your body invites my lips.** Шелкови́стый гля́нец твоего́ те́ла приглаша́ет мои́ гу́бы.

inviting *adj* соблазни́тельный, -ая, -ое, -ые, зама́нчивый, -ая, -ое, -ые, маня́щий, -ая, -ее, -ие, зову́щий, -ая, -ее, -ие, привлека́тельный, -ая, -ое, -ые ♦ **The soft curves of your lips are so inviting.** Мя́гкие изги́бы твои́х губ так привлека́тельны.

invitingly *adv* приглаша́юще ♦ **~ kissable** приглаша́ющий (-ая, -ее, -ие) к поцелу́ям.

involved *adj*, 1. *(romantically)* свя́зан, -а, -о, -ы *(short forms)*, в связи́, вовлечён, вовлечена́, -о́, -ы́ *(short forms)*; 2. *(activities) (verb is used:)* уча́ствовать ♦ **culturally ~** 1. *(interested)* интересу́ющийся (-аяся, -ееся, -иеся) иску́сством; 2. *(active in)* занима́ющийся (-аяся, -ееся, -иеся) иску́сством ♦ **get ~ with a married man** связа́ться с жена́тым челове́ком, вступи́ть в бли́зкие отноше́ния с жена́тым челове́ком ♦ **get ~ with a married woman** связа́ться с за́мужней же́нщиной, вступи́ть в бли́зкие отноше́ния с за́мужней же́нщиной ♦ **~ with another man** свя́зана с други́м мужчи́ной ♦ **~ with another woman** свя́зан с друго́й же́нщиной ♦ **romantically ~** любо́вно свя́зан, -а, -ы *(short forms)*.

involved: phrases

Are you romantically involved with anyone? У тебя́ есть возлю́бленный *(ж: возлю́бленная)*? ♦ **I'm not romantically involved with anyone.** У меня́ нет возлю́бленной *(ж: возлю́бленного)*. ♦ **I was involved with someone (at the time).** Я был *(ж: была́)* в связи́ с ке́м-то (в то вре́мя). ♦ **I'm not involved with anyone (***[1]***...at the present time. /** *[2]* **...right now.)** Я не свя́зан *(ж: свя́зана)* ни с кем (*[1]* ...в настоя́щее вре́мя. / *[2]* ...сейча́с.).

involvement *n* 1. *(participation)* уча́стие, вовлечённость *f*; 2. *(romantic)* отноше́ния ♦ **romantic ~** романти́ческие отноше́ния, романти́ческая связь ♦ **~ with another** *(1)* **man** / *(2)* **woman** связь с *(1)* ...други́м мужчи́ной / *(2)* ...друго́й же́нщиной.

IQ *abbrev* = **intelligence quotient** показа́тель у́мственных спосо́бностей ♦ **high ~** высо́кий показа́тель у́мственных спосо́бностей ♦ **low ~** ни́зкий показа́тель у́мственных спосо́бностей ♦ **normal ~** норма́льный показа́тель у́мственных спосо́бностей.

iris *n (eye)* ра́дужная оболо́чка *(гла́за)* ♦ **When I look into the dark irises of your eyes, I am** *(1)* **drawn** / *(2)* **sucked into a wild vortex of passion.** Когда́ я вгля́дываюсь в тёмную ра́дужную оболо́чку твои́х глаз, меня́ *(1)* втя́гивает / *(2)* заса́сывает в ди́кий вихрь стра́сти. ♦ **It's such a thrill to gaze into the dark irises of your eyes.** Тако́е возбужде́ние смотре́ть в тёмные зрачки́ твои́х глаз.

Irishman *n* ирла́ндец.

Irishwoman *n* ирла́ндка.

iron *n* желе́зо ♦ **red-hot branding ~** раскалённое клеймо́.

Some of the Russian sentences are translations of things we say and are not what Russians themselves would normally say.

ironic *adj* ирони́ческий, -ая, -ое, -ие.

ironically *adv* ирони́чески.

irony *n* иро́ния.

irrational *adj* неразу́мный, -ая, -ое, -ые, нерациона́льный, -ая, -ое, -ые ♦ **You're** *(1,2)* **being irrational.** Ты *(1)* ...ведёшь себя́... / *(2)* ...поступа́ешь... неразу́мно.

irrationality *n* неразу́мность *f*, нелоги́чность *f*; безрассу́дность *f*.

irrelevant *adj* неуме́стный, -ая, -ое, -ые.

irrepressible *adj* неуёмный, -ая, -ое, -ые.

irresistible *adj* непреодоли́мый, -ая, -ое, -ые, неотрази́мый, -ая, -ое, -ые ♦ **You have a (personal) magnetism that** *(1)* **...is...** / *(2)* **...I find... irresistible.** У тебя́ тако́й магнети́зм, кото́рому *(1,2)* невозмо́жно сопротивля́ться. ♦ **The magnetism of your** *(1)* **charm** / *(2)* **personality is (completely) irresistible.** Магнети́зм *(1)* ...твоего́ обая́ния... / *(2)* ...твое́й индивидуа́льности... (соверше́нно) неотрази́м. ♦ **You are** *(1)* **utterly** / *(2)* **absolutely irresistible.** Ты *(1)* соверше́нно / *(2)* абсолю́тно неотрази́ма *(ж: неотрази́м).* ♦ **I find you** *(1)* **totally** / *(2)* **utterly irresistible.** Я нахожу́ тебя́ *(1,2)* соверше́нно неотрази́мой *(ж: неотрази́мым).* ♦ **You have such irresistible charm.** В тебе́ тако́й неотрази́мый шарм.

irresistibly *adj* непреодоли́мо, неотрази́мо.

irresponsible *adj* безотве́тственный, -ая, -ое, -ые.

irreverence *n* непочти́тельность *f*, неуваже́ние.

irreverent *adj* непочти́тельный, -ая, -ое, -ые, неуважи́тельный, -ая, -ое, -ые.

irritability *n* раздражи́тельность *f*.

irritable *adj* раздражи́тельный, -ая, -ое, -ые.

irritate *vt* раздража́ть *(whom = acc.).*

irritated *adj* раздражён, раздражена́, -о, -ы *(short forms).* ♦ **be ~** быть раздражённым *m* / раздражённой *f (I'm irritated:* я раздражён *[ж: раздражена́]. You're irritated:* ты раздражена́ *[ж: раздражён].)* ♦ **get ~** раздража́ться ♦ **I hope you're not irritated with me.** Наде́юсь, я не раздража́ю тебя́.

irritating *adj* раздражи́тельный, -ая, -ое, -ые.

irritation *n* раздраже́ние.

Islamic *adj* мусульма́нский, -ая, -ое, -ие.

isolated *adj* изоли́рованный, -ая, -ое, -ые, обосо́бленный, -ая, -ое, -ые.

isolation *n* изоля́ция.

it *pron* 1. *(personal)* он *m*, она́ *f*, оно́ *neut*; 2. *(indefinite)* э́то; 3. *(impersonal) Not translated (See examples)* ♦ **It's nice to be with you.** Хорошо́ быть с тобо́й. ♦ **It's hot.** Жа́рко.

Counting things in Russian is a bit involved.
See Appendix 4, Numbers, on page 756 .

J

jacket *n* ку́ртка; *(women's)* жаке́т, ко́фта; *(sport coat)* пиджа́к ♦ **sport(s)** ~ пиджа́к.

Jacuzzi *n* джаку́зи.

jade *adj* сде́ланный (-ая, -ое, -ые) из нефри́та.

jade *n* нефри́т.

jaded *adj* пресы́щенный, -ая, -ое, -ые.

jailbait *n (slang)* де́вушка-подро́сток (связь с кото́рой запреща́ется зако́ном), несовершенноле́тняя де́вушка.

Japanese *adj* япо́нский, -ая, -ое, -ие.

Japanese *n* 1. *(person)* япо́нец *m*, япо́нка *f (pl:* япо́нцы*)*; 2. *(language)* япо́нский язы́к ♦ **speak** ~ говори́ть по-япо́нски.

jasmine *n* жасми́н ♦ **I love the scent of jasmine** *(1)* **...in your hair.** / *(2)* **...on you.** Я люблю́ за́пах жасми́на *(1)* ...в твои́х волоса́х. / *(2)* ...от тебя́.

jaunt *n (slang) (trip)* пое́здка ♦ **We can go on weekend jaunts to explore new places.** В выходны́е дни мы мо́жем отпра́виться в пое́здку иссле́довать но́вые места́.

jaunty *adj* бо́йкий, -ая, -ое, -ие, живо́й, -а́я, -о́е, -ы́е, задо́рный, -ая, -ое, -ые.

jawline *n* ли́ния подборо́дка.

jazz *n* джаз.

jealous *adj* ревни́вый, -ая, -ое, -ые *(short forms:* ревни́в, ревни́ва, ревни́вы*)* ♦ **insanely** ~ безу́мно ревни́в *m* / ревни́ва *f* ♦ **madly** ~ безу́мно ревни́в *m* / ревни́ва *f* ♦ **unreasonably** ~ беспричи́нно ревни́в *m* / ревни́ва *f* ♦ **wildly** ~ ди́ко ревни́в *m* / ревни́ва *f* ♦ **be** ~ ревнова́ть *(of whom* = + к + *dat.)* ♦ **get** ~ приревнова́ть.

jealous: phrases

Are you jealous (of *[1]* **him** / *[2]* **her)?** Ты ревну́ешь (*[1]* его́ / *[2]* её)? ♦ **I'm (not) jealous.** Я (не) ревну́ю. ♦ **Are you a jealous person?** Ты ревни́ва *(ж: ревни́в)*? ♦ **I'm a jealous person.** Я ревни́в *(ж: ревни́ва)*. ♦ **You make me jealous.** Ты заставля́ешь меня́ ревнова́ть. ♦ **I feel (***[1]* **so** / *[2]* **very) jealous (when you** *[3]* **...talk** / *[4]* **dance with other** *[5]* **guys** / *[6]* **men** / *[7]* **girls** / *[8]* **women.** / *[9]* **...look at other guys** / *[10]* **men** / *[11]* **girls** / *[12]* **women.)** Я (*[1]* так / *[2]* ужа́сно) ревну́ю (, когда́ ты *[3]* ...разгова́риваешь / *[4]* танцу́ешь с други́ми *[5]* парня́ми / *[6]* мужчи́нами / *[7]* де́вушками / *[8]*же́нщинами. / *[9]* ...смо́тришь на други́х парне́й / *[10]* мужчи́н / *[11]* де́вушек / *[12]* же́нщин.). ♦ **You never have to be jealous about me.** Ты никогда́ не должна́ *(ж: не до́лжен)* ревнова́ть меня́. ♦ **Don't be jealous of** *(1)* **him** / *(2)* **her.** Не ревну́й *(1)* его́ / *(2)* её. ♦ **My** *(1)*

Russian has 2 different verbs for "go",
one for "on foot" and the other for "by vehicle".

(ex-)boyfriend / *(2)* (ex-)husband / *(3)* (ex-)girlfriend / *(4)* (ex-)wife is insanely jealous (of me). *(1)* Мой (бывший) друг / *(2)* муж... / *(3)* Моя (бывшая) девушка / *(4)* жена... безумно ревнует (меня).

jealousy *n* ревность *f* ♦ acute ~ жгучая ревность ♦ blind ~ ослеплённая ревность ♦ constant ~ постоянная ревность ♦ fierce ~ яростная ревность ♦ rampant ~ яростная ревность ♦ almost die of ~ чуть не умереть от ревности ♦ pangs of ~ муки ревности.

| jealousy: *jealousy in me* |

I feel such (*[1]* rampant / *[2]* fierce) jealousy anytime you look at *(1)* ...someone else. / *(2)* ...another man / *(3)* woman. Я испытываю такую (*[1,2]* яростную) ревность всегда, когда ты смотришь на *(1)* ...другого *(ж: другую)*. / *(2)* ...другого мужчину. / *(3)* ...другую женщину. ♦ I was blinded by jealousy. Я был ослеплён *(ж: была ослеплена)* ревностью. ♦ Jealousy winged through me. Ревность пронизывала меня. ♦ I *(1)* feel / *(2)* felt like I could explode with jealousy. Я чувствую / чувствовал *(ж: чувствовала)*, что я могу / мог *(ж: могла)* бы взорваться от ревности. ♦ I'm green with jealousy. Я ужасно ревную.

| jealousy: *jealousy in you and others* |

I can't handle *(1)* your / *(2)* his / *(3)* her (constant) jealousy. Я не могу вынести *(1)* твою / *(2)* его / *(3)* её (постоянную) ревность. ♦ You're blinded by jealousy. Ты ослеплена *(ж: ослеплён)* ревностью. ♦ There is no *(1)* reason / *(2)* cause for such jealousy. Нет *(1)* причины / *(2)* повода для такой ревности.

| jealousy: *quotations* |

"In jealousy there is more self-love than love." *(La Rochefoucauld)* «В ревности больше себялюбия, чем любви.» *(Ла Рашфуко)*. ♦ "He who loves without jealousy does not truly love." *The Zohar* «Тот, кто любит без ревности, не любит по-настоящему.» *Зохар.*

jeans *n, pl* джинсы ♦ *(1,2)* blue j~s *(1)* синие / *(2)* голубые джинсы ♦ *(1)* hip- / *(2)* thigh-hugging ~s обтягивающие *(1,2)* бёдра джинсы ♦ oversized ~s очень большие джинсы ♦ I want a woman who is comfortable in jeans or a(n) *(1)* cocktail / *(2)* evening dress. Я хочу женщину, которой одинаково удобно в джинсах и в *(1)* ...платье для коктейля. / *(2)* ...вечернем платье. ♦ I'm seeking a man who is comfortable in jeans or a tuxedo. Я ищу мужчину, которому одинаково удобно в джинсах и в смокинге.

Jehovah's Witness *n* свидетель Иеговы.

jelly *n* желе ♦ K-Y ~ *(lubricating jelly for sex)* желе К-У *(смазывающее желе для сёкса)*.

jeopardize *vt* подвергать / подвергнуть опасности *(what, whom = acc.)*, ставить / поставить под угрозу *(what, whom = acc.)*.

jeopardy *n* опасность *f.*

jerk *n* дрянь *f*; идиот ♦ big-time ~ большая дрянь, подонок ♦ immature ~ незрелый идиот.

jest *vi* шутить / пошутить ♦ I was (just) jesting. Я (просто) шутил *(ж: шутила)*.

jet lag *n* усталость от перелёта через несколько часовых поясов ♦ *(1)* I have... / *(2)* I'm suffering from... jet lag. *(1)* Я устал *(ж: устала)*,... / *(2)* Я мучаюсь,... потому что перелетел *(ж: перелетела)* через несколько часовых поясов.

Jew *n* еврей.

jewelry *n* драгоценности, ювелирные украшения ♦ You possess the kind of beauty that makes all jewelry seem *(1)* needless / *(2)* trivial / *(3)* superfluous. Ты обладаешь такой красотой, которая делает все драгоценности *(1)* ненужными / *(2)* незначительными / *(3)* излишними.

Jewess *n* еврейка.

Dipthongs in Russian are made by adding й
*to the end of a vowel (*а, е, ё, о, у, э, ю, *and* я*).*

Jewish *adj* еврейский, -ая, -ое, -ие.

Jezebel *n* распутная женщина.

jilt *vt* бросать / бросить ради другого *(whom = acc.).*

jilted *adj (for another man:)* брошенный ради другого; *(for another woman:)* брошенная ради другой.

jingle *n (slang) (telephone call)* (телефонный) звонок ♦ *(1,2)* **Give me a jingle.** *(1)* Позвони / *(2)* Звякни мне.

jitters *n, pl (nervousness)* нервность *f*, нервное волнение, нервное состояние ♦ **bridal ~s** нервное состояние перед свадьбой ♦ **wedding ~s** нервное состояние перед свадьбой ♦ **get / have the ~s** нервничать ♦ **have wedding ~s** нервничать перед свадьбой ♦ **You've got a case of bridal jitters. You'll be okay.** Ты нервничаешь перед свадьбой. Всё будет хорошо.

jittery *adj* нервный, -ая, -ое, -ые.

jive *vt (slang)* 1. *(talk nonsense)* болтать чепуху *(whom = dat.);* 2. *(deceive)* обманывать / обмануть *(whom = acc.),* разыгрывать / разыграть *(whom = acc.).*

jive *n (slang)* 1. *(empty talk)* пустая болтовня; 2. *(deceit)* обман, разыгрывание.

job *n* работа ♦ **dead-end ~** бесперспективная работа ♦ **full-time ~** работа с полной занятостью ♦ **part-time ~** работа с неполной занятостью ♦ **stable ~** стабильная работа ♦ **steady ~** постоянная работа ♦ **I have a good job.** У меня хорошая работа. ♦ **I have a** *(1)* **fulltime /** *(2)* **part-time job.** Я работаю *(1)* полную / *(2)* неполную рабочую неделю.

jock *n (slang) (athlete)* спортсмен.

jog *vi* бежать трусцой.

jogger *n* бегун трусцой ♦ **avid ~** азартный бегун трусцой.

jogging *n* бег трусцой.

join *vt (a person, group, etc)* присоединяться / присоединиться *(whom = + к + dat.)* ♦ **~together** *vi* сливаться / слиться ♦ *(1)* **May /** *(2)* **Could I join you?** *(1)* Могу ли... / *(2)* Не могу ли... я присоединиться к Вам? ♦ **Come join me.** Присоединяйся ко мне. ♦ **Please join** *(1)* **me /** *(2)* **us.** Пожалуйста, присоединяйтесь *(1)* ...ко мне. / *(2)* ...к нам. ♦ **Won't you** *(1,2)* **join me (for** *[3]* **...dinner? /** *[4]* **...lunch? /** *[5]* **...a drink /** *[6]* **cocktail?)?** Не *(1)* ...составишь ли ты мне компанию... / *(2)* ...присоединишься ли ты ко мне...(*[3]* ...поужинать? / *[4]* ...пообедать? / *[5]* ...выпить? / *[6]* ...на коктейль?)? ♦ **Thank you, I'd love to join you.** Спасибо, я согласна ...присоединиться к тебе. / ...составить тебе компанию. ♦ **I'll join you later.** Я присоединюсь к тебе позднее. ♦ **Our souls will join together in** *(1)* **eternal /** *(2)* **everlasting love.** Наши души сольются вместе в *(1,2)* вечной любви.

joining *n* слияние ♦ **ultimate sexual ~** максимальное сексуальное слияние.

joke *vi* шутить / пошутить *(about what, whom = + о + prep.)* ♦ **Are you joking?** Ты шутишь? ♦ **Surely you're joking?** Конечно, ты шутишь? ♦ *(1)* **I'm... /** *(2)* **I was... (just) joking.** Я (просто) *(1)* шучу / *(2)* шутил *(ж: шутила).* ♦ **Stop joking.** Перестань шутить.

joke *n* шутка ♦ **It's a joke.** Это шутка. ♦ **I was just making a joke.** Я просто пошутил *(ж: пошутила).* ♦ **I'll tell you a joke.** Я расскажу тебе шутку.

jolly *adj* весёлый, -ая, -ое, -ые.

jolt *n* толчок ♦ **It gave me a bitter jolt.** Это было ужасным ударом для меня.

journey *n* поездка; путешествие *(See also entries under* **trip***.).* ♦ **life's ~** путешествие по жизни ♦ **I am so eagerly awaiting this journey that I hope will lead to your heart and your arms.** Я с таким нетерпением жду этой поездки, которая, я надеюсь, приведёт

Some phrases are listed under more than one main word.

меня́ к твоему́ се́рдцу и к твои́м объя́тиям.

jovial *adj* весёлый, -ая, -ое, -ые.

joy *n* ра́дость *f*; ликова́ние ♦ **brief** ~ коро́ткая ра́дость ♦ **constant** ~ постоя́нная ра́дость ♦ **cosmic** ~ косми́ческое ликова́ние ♦ **divine** ~ ди́вная ра́дость ♦ **fleeting** ~ мимолёт-ная ра́дость ♦ *(1-3)* **genuine** ~ *(1)* неподде́льная / *(2)* по́длинная / *(3)* и́стинная ра́дость ♦ **great** ~ больша́я ра́дость ♦ **greatest** ~ велича́йшая ра́дость ♦ **immeasurable** ~ неиз-мери́мая ра́дость ♦ **immense** ~ огро́мная ра́дость ♦ **indescribable** ~ невероя́тная ра́дость ♦ **nfinite** ~ бесконе́чная ра́дость ♦ **inner** ~ вну́треннее удово́льствие ♦ **irrepressible** ~ безу́держная ра́дость ♦ **~ of intimate closeness** ра́дость инти́мной бли́зости ♦ **~ of love** ра́дость любви́ ♦ **my** ~ моя́ ра́дость ♦ **only** ~ еди́нственная ра́дость ♦ **pure** ~ и́стинная ра́дость ♦ **quiet** ~ ти́хая ра́дость ♦ **rampant** ~ неи́стовое ликова́ние ♦ **shared** ~ разделённая ра́дость ♦ **sincere** ~ и́скренняя ра́дость ♦ **small** ~ ма́ленькая ра́дость ♦ **such** ~ така́я ра́дость ♦ **tremendous** ~ огро́мная ра́дость ♦ *(1,2)* **unadulterated** ~ *(1)* настоя́щая / *(2)* неподде́льная ра́дость ♦ **unbounded** ~ безгра-ни́чная ра́дость ♦ **what** ~ кака́я ра́дость ♦ **wild** ~ бу́рная ра́дость.

---
joy: verb terms
---

beam with ~ сия́ть от ра́дости, сия́ть ра́достью ♦ **be** *(1)* **crazy** / *(2)* **wild with** ~ *(1,2)* шале́ть / ошале́ть от ра́дости ♦ **be speechless with** ~ потеря́ть дар ре́чи от ра́дости ♦ **bring** ~ приноси́ть / принести́ ра́дость *(to whom = dat.)* ♦ **burst with** ~ разрыва́ться / разорва́ться от ра́дости ♦ **dance with** ~ пляса́ть от ра́дости ♦ **experience** ~ испы́тывать / испыта́ть ра́дость ♦ **exude** ~ излуча́ть ра́дость ♦ **feel** ~ чу́вствовать / почу́вствовать ра́дость ♦ **fill with** ~ *vt* наполня́ть / напо́лнить ра́достью *(what, whom = acc.)* ♦ **fill with** ~ *vi* наполня́ться / напо́лниться ра́достью ♦ **find** ~ находи́ть / найти́ ра́дость ♦ **give** ~ дава́ть / дать ра́дость *(to whom = dat.)* ♦ **glitter with** ~ блесте́ть от ра́дости ♦ **go** *(1)* **crazy** / *(2)* **wild with** ~ *(1,2)* шале́ть / ошале́ть от ра́дости ♦ **jump with** ~ пры́гать / пры́гнуть от ра́дости ♦ **radiate** ~ свети́ться ра́достью ♦ **share** ~ дели́ть ра́дость ♦ **shine with** ~ свети́ться от ра́дости, свети́ться ра́достью.

---
joy: other terms
---

bundle of ~ *(baby)* ребёнок, младе́нец ♦ **feeling of** ~ чу́вство ра́дости ♦ **full of** ~ напо́лненный (-ая, -ое, -ые) ра́достью ♦ **kaleidoscope of** ~ калейдоско́п ра́дости ♦ **lightning bolt of** ~ мо́лния ра́дости ♦ **paean of** ~ побе́дная пе́сня ра́дости ♦ **shriek of** ~ вопль удово́льствия ♦ **source of** ~ исто́чник ра́дости ♦ **tears of** ~ слёзы ра́дости ♦ **wave of** ~ волна́ ра́дости.

---
joy: joy and my heart

(1,2) **My heart overflows with joy.** *(1)* Моё се́рдце перепо́лнено ра́достью. / *(2)* Ра́дость переполня́ет моё се́рдце. ♦ **My heart fills with love and joy whenever I think of you.** Моё се́рдце наполня́ется любо́вью и ра́достью вся́кий раз, когда́ я ду́маю о тебе́. ♦ **My heart is full of joy.** Моё се́рдце полно́ ра́дости. ♦ **Knowing that you love me as much as I love you fills my heart with indescribable joy.** Созна́ние того́, что ты лю́бишь меня́ так же си́льно, как я люблю́ тебя́, наполня́ет моё се́рдце невероя́тной ра́достью.

---
joy: the joy I feel / felt

When I *(1)* **read** / *(2)* **hear your words of love, I feel** *(3)* **cosmic** / *(4)* **rampant joy in the deepest part of my soul.** Когда́ я *(1)* чита́ю / *(2)* слы́шу твои́ слова́ любви́, я чу́вствую *(3)* косми́ческое / *(4)* неи́стовое ликова́ние в мое́й душе́. ♦ **I've never** *(1)* **felt** / *(2)* **experienced** / *(3)* **known such a kaleidoscope of joy.** Я никогда́ не *(1)* чу́вствовал *(ж: чу́вствовала)* / *(2)* испы́тывал *(ж: испы́тывала)* / *(3)* знал *(ж: зна́ла)* тако́го калейдо-ско́па ра́дости. ♦ **When I** *(1)* **became** / *(2)* **grew aware of your feelings for me, I was overcome with joy.** Когда́ я узна́л *(ж: узна́ла)* о твои́х чу́вствах ко мне, я был

The singular past tense of Russian verbs ends in -л (m) (usually),
-ла (f) or -ло (n). the plural past tense ends in -li.

охва́чен *(ж: была́ охва́чена)* ликова́нием. ♦ **When** *(1)* ... **I saw you,...** */ (2)* ...**I heard your voice,...** */ (3)* ...**I found** */ (4)* **read your letter,...** */ (5)* ...**I found out you were coming,...** */ (6)* ...**you said you loved me,...** **I felt shock waves of pure, unadulterated joy.** Когда́ *(1)* ...я ви́дел *(ж: ви́дела)* тебя́,... */ (2)* ...я слы́шал *(ж: слы́шала)* твой го́лос,... */ (3)* ...я нашёл *(ж: нашла́)* */ (4)* чита́л *(ж: чита́ла)* твоё письмо́,... */ (5)* ...я узна́л *(ж: узна́ла)*, что ты прие́дешь,... */ (6)* ,,,ты сказа́ла *(ж: сказа́л)*, что лю́бишь меня́,... я ощути́л *(ж: ощути́ла)* во́лны и́стинного, настоя́щего ликова́ния. ♦ **I was** *(1)* ...**speechless...** */ (2)* ...**beside myself... with joy.** Я *(1)* ...потеря́л *(ж: потеря́ла)* дар ре́чи... */ (2)* ...был *(ж: была́)* вне себя́... от ра́дости. ♦ **I am full to bursting with the joy of being near you.** Я про́сто разрыва́юсь от ра́дости, когда́ ты ря́дом. ♦ **I could not contain my joy.** Я не мог *(ж: могла́)* сдержа́ть свое́й ра́дости. ♦ **My heart thrilled with joy.** Моё се́рдце трепета́ло от ра́дости.

joy: *the joy of your letters*

Your letters are a source of *(1)* **constant /** *(2)* **immeasurable /** *(3)* **infinite joy to me.** Твои́ пи́сьма -- э́то исто́чник *(1)* постоя́нной */ (2)* неизмери́мой */ (3)* бесконе́чной ра́дости для меня́. ♦ **You have no idea with what joy and eagerness I wait for every letter from you.** Ты не представля́ешь, с како́й ра́достью и нетерпе́нием я жду ка́ждого твоего́ письма́. ♦ **Your letter brought me more joy than anything else in the world could do, except you in person.** Твоё письмо́ принесло́ мне бо́льше ра́дости, чем что́-либо ещё в ми́ре, кро́ме тебя́ ли́чно.

joy: *a lightning bolt of joy*

Our *(1)* **time /** *(2)* **day /** *(3)* **evening /** *(4)* **night /** *(5)* **weekend together was a lightning bolt of joy.** *(1)* На́ше вре́мя вме́сте бы́ло... */ (2)* Наш день */ (3)* ве́чер вме́сте был... */ (4)* На́ша ночь вме́сте была́... */ (5)* На́ши выходны́е вме́сте бы́ли... как мо́лния ра́дости.

joy: *you are my joy*

You are my joy and comfort, my hope and my dreams — my everything. Ты моя́ ра́дость и утеше́ние, моя́ наде́жда и моя́ мечта́ -- всё для меня́. ♦ **You are my hope and dreams, my strength and purpose, my joy and happiness. You are my life.** Ты мои́ наде́жды и мечты́, моя́ си́ла и цель, моя́ ра́дость и сча́стье. Ты моя́ жизнь. ♦ **You are the (greatest) joy of my life.** Ты (са́мая больша́я) ра́дость мое́й жи́зни. ♦ **You are a constant joy to me.** Ты моя́ постоя́нная ра́дость. ♦ **You're a joy to be around.** Ра́дость быть с тобо́й. ♦ **My greatest joy is having you for / as my** *(1)* **love /** *(2)* **wife /** *(3)* **sweetheart /** *(4)* **own.** Моя́ велича́йшая ра́дость, что ты моя́ *(1)* любо́вь */ (2)* жена́ */ (3)* возлю́бленная *(ж: мой возлю́бленный)* */ (4)* моя́ *(ж: мой)*.

joy: *you give me joy*

You fill my heart with so much joy. Ты наполня́ешь моё се́рдце тако́й огро́мной ра́достью. ♦ **Oh, the joy that you give me!** О, каку́ю ра́дость ты даёшь мне! ♦ **Thank you for bringing so much love and joy and happiness into my life.** Спаси́бо тебе́, что принесла́ *(ж: принёс)* так мно́го любви́, ра́дости и сча́стья в мою́ жизнь. ♦ **You've brought so much joy into my life.** Ты принесла́ *(ж: принёс)* так мно́го ра́дости в мою́ жизнь.

joy: *sharing joy with you*

You are the person with whom I want to (always) share life's joys and sorrows. Ты тот челове́к, с кото́рым я хочу́ (всегда́) дели́ть все мои́ ра́дости и печа́ли. ♦ **The greatest happiness I can imagine is to spend my life with you, sharing love and all joys and tribulations**. Са́мое большо́е сча́стье, кото́рое я могу́ себе́ предста́вить -- э́то прожи́ть всю жизнь с тобо́й, деля́ любо́вь, ра́дость и невзго́ды.

Please do us a favor:
Fill out and mail in the Feedback Sheet on page 795.

joy: bestow joy on me

If you ever feel the generosity in your heart to bestow the ultimate joy in life to someone who adores you beyond measure, then put your sweet mouth against mine for 60 heavenly seconds and you will have done it. Если то́лько в твоём се́рдце пробу́дится ще́дрость подари́ть велича́йшее наслажде́ние в жи́зни тому́, кто обожа́ет тебя́ безме́рно, тогда́ прижми́ свои́ сла́дкие гу́бы к мои́м на шестдеся́т (= 60) секу́нд и ты э́то сде́лаешь. ◆ The one thing that would make all my dreams come true is for you to bestow upon me the *(1)* exquisite / *(2)* supreme joys of your luscious all. То́лько одно́ могло́ бы осуществи́ть все мои́ мечты́ -- э́то, чтобы ты подари́ла мне *(1)* изы́сканную / *(2)* исключи́тельную ра́дость всей твое́й роско́шной красоты́.

joy: causing you joy

I want to cause you nothing but joy. Я не хочу́ доста́вить тебе́ ничего́, кро́ме ра́дости. ◆ My fingers and lips will spread warm *(1)* rings / *(2)* waves of joy throughout your beautiful, voluptuous body. Мои́ па́льцы и гу́бы распространя́т тёплые *(1)* ко́льца / *(2)* во́лны наслажде́ния в твоём прекра́сном, роско́шном те́ле. ◆ If there's one gift in the world I'd like to give you, it's the joy that you give me every day. Если существу́ет одна́ вещь в ми́ре, кото́рую я хоте́л *(ж: хоте́ла)* бы подари́ть тебе́, то э́то та ра́дость, кото́рую ты да́ришь мне ка́ждый день.

joy: joy in you

You exude a genuine joy for living. Ты излуча́ешь по́длинную ра́дость жи́зни. ◆ I want your eyes always to glitter with joy. Я хочу́, чтобы твои́ глаза́ всегда́ блесте́ли от ра́дости. ◆ I love to see your face animated with joy. Я люблю́ ви́деть твоё лицо́, оживлённое ра́достью.

joy: quotations

"A thing of beauty is a joy forever." *John Keats.* Красота́ -- ве́чная ра́дость. *Джон Китс.*

joyless *adj* безра́достный, -ая, -ое, -ые.

jubilation *n* ликова́ние ◆ My heart ignites in jubilation *(1)* ...every time I get a letter from you. / *(2)* ...every time I see your (*[3]* beautiful / *[4]* beloved) face. / *(5)* ...at the mere thought of you. Моё се́рдце лику́ет *(1)* ...ка́ждый раз, когда́ я получа́ю письмо́ от тебя́. / *(2)* ...ка́ждый раз, когда́ я ви́жу твоё (*[3]* прекра́сное / *[4]* люби́мое) лицо́. / *(5)* ...от просто́й мы́сли о тебе́.

jubilee *n* юбиле́й.

judgement *n* 1. *(capacity to judge)* рассуди́тельность *f*; *(good sense)* здра́вый смысл, благоразу́мие; 2. *(opinion)* мне́ние, взгляд, сужде́ние; 3. *(criticism, condemnation)* кри́тика, осужде́ние ◆ **cast** ~ суди́ть *(on whom = acc.)*, критикова́ть *(on whom = acc.)* ◆ **pass** ~ суди́ть *(on whom = acc.)*, критикова́ть *(on whom = acc.)* ◆ **person of good** ~ здравомы́слящий челове́к ◆ **trust** *(1)* **my** / *(2)* **your** ~ доверя́ть *(1)* моему́ / *(2)* твоему́ мне́нию.

juice *n* сок.

juicinesse *n* со́чность *f*.

juicy *adj* со́чный, -ая, -ое, -ые ◆ You're so hot and juicy. Ты така́я горя́чая и со́чная.

jump *vi* пры́гать / пры́гнуть ◆ ~ **with joy** пры́гать / пры́гнуть от ра́дости.

jump *vt:* ◆ ~ **ship** *(slang)* разорва́ть отноше́ния, уйти́, поко́нчить *(with whom = + с + instr.)*, оста́вить *(whom = acc.)*.

justice of the peace *n* мирово́й судья́.

Clock and calender time are discussed in Appendix 5, page 759.

K

kaleidoscope *n* калейдоско́п ♦ ~ **of ecstasy** калейдоско́п экста́за ♦ ~ **of joy** калейдоско́п ра́дости ♦ ~ **of passion** калейдоско́п стра́сти ♦ **The soft, warm magic of your body transports me to a cosmic kaleidoscope of ecstasy.** Мя́гкая, тёплая ма́гия твоего́ те́ла перено́сит меня́ в косми́ческий калейдоско́п экста́за. ♦ **I've never** *(1)* **felt /** *(2)* **experienced /** *(3)* **known such a kaleidoscope of** *(4)* **passion /** *(5)* **ecstasy /** *(6)* **joy.** Я никогда́ не *(1)* чу́вствовал *(ж: чу́вствовала) /* *(2)* испы́тывал *(ж: испы́тывала) /* *(3)* знал *(ж: зна́ла)* тако́го калейдоско́па *(4)* стра́сти / *(5)* экста́за / *(6)* ра́дости. ♦ **You're going to swirl in a kaleidoscope of** *(1)* **passion /** *(2)* **ecstasy.** Ты закру́жишься в калейдоско́пе *(1)* стра́сти / *(2)* экста́за.

Kama Sutra *n* Ка́ма-Су́тра ♦ **Many times at night I wake up with my body on fire from cavorting with you in one episode or another of the Kama Sutra.** Мно́го раз я просыпа́юсь но́чью с те́лом, охва́ченным огнём, от того́, что мы с тобо́й изуча́ем ту и́ли другу́ю главу́ Ка́ма-Су́тры.

karaoke *n* карао́ке.

karma *n* ка́рма.

kayak *n* кая́к.

kayak *vi* пла́вать на кая́ке ♦ **I enjoy kayaking** Я наслажда́юсь пла́ваньем на кая́ке.

kayaking *n* пла́ванье на кая́ке ♦ **Have you ever gone kayaking?** Ты когда-нибудь пла́вала *(ж: пла́вал)* на кая́ке?

Kazakh *adj* каза́хский, -ая, -ое, -ие.

Kazakh *n* 1. *(person)* каза́х *m,* каза́шка *f (pl:* каза́хи*)*; 2. *(language)* каза́хский язы́к ♦ **speak** ~ говори́ть по-каза́хски.

keep *vt* 1. *(hold)* держа́ть *(what, whom = acc.)*; 2. *(maintain)* содержа́ть *(what, whom = acc.)*; 3. *(hide)* скрыва́ть / скрыть *(what = acc.)* ♦ ~ **a woman** содержа́ть же́нщину ♦ **I would never keep anything from you.** Я никогда́ и ничего́ не бу́ду скрыва́ть от тебя́. ♦ **I think you're keeping something from me.** Я ду́маю, ты скрыва́ешь что́-то от меня́.

keepsake *n* па́мятный пода́рок ♦ *(1)* **This /** *(2)* **Here is a small keepsake of our trip for you.** *(1)* Это / *(2)* Вот ма́ленький пода́рок для тебя́ в па́мять о на́шей пое́здке.

key *n* ключ ♦ **apartment** ~ ключ от кварти́ры ♦ **house** ~ ключ от до́ма ♦ ~ **to happiness** ключ сча́стья ♦ ~ **to your heart** ключ к твоему́ се́рдцу ♦ **room** ~ ключ от ко́мнаты ♦ **You have found the key to my heart.** Ты нашла́ *(ж: нашёл)* ключ к моему́ се́рдцу.

Reflexive verbs are those that end in -ся or -сь.
The -ся or -сь also goes onto a past tense ending.

khakis *n, pl* хáки *neut., nondeclin.*

kick *vt* ударя́ть / уда́рить ного́й *(what, whom = acc.)* ♦ ~ **it** *(slang)* *(have a good time)* хорошо́ проводи́ть / провести́ вре́мя ♦ ~ **myself** грызть себя́, руга́ть себя́; *(stronger)* уби́ть себя́ ♦ ~ **off** *vt* сбра́сывать / сбро́сить *(what = acc.)* ♦ ~ **out** *vt* выгоня́ть / вы́гнать *(whom = acc.)*.

>> **kick it:**

We can go and **kick it.** *(slang)* Мы мо́жем пойти́ и хорошо́ провести́ вре́мя.

>> **kick myself:**

I **kick myself for** *(1)* ...**not calling** / *(2)* **telling you (sooner).** / *(3)* ...**not remembering.** Я руга́ю себя́ за то, что *(1)* ...не позвони́л *(ж: позвони́ла)*. / *(2)* ...не сказа́л *(ж: сказа́ла)* тебе́ (ра́ньше). / *(3)* ...не по́мнил *(ж: по́мнила)*.

>> **kick off:**

Kick off your shoes and relax. Сбрось свои́ ту́фли и рассла́бься.

>> **kick out:**

Please don't kick me out. Пожа́луйста, не выгоня́й меня́. ♦ **I ought to kick you out.** Я до́лжен *(ж: должна́)* вы́гнать тебя́. ♦ **I kicked her out.** Я вы́гнал её. ♦ **I kicked him out.** Я вы́гнала его́. ♦ **She kicked me out.** Она́ вы́гнала меня́. ♦ **He kicked me out.** Он вы́гнал меня́.

kick *n (enjoyment)* удово́льствие; *pl (slang) (fun)* удово́льствие; *(excitement)* волне́ние ♦ **I get a kick out of watching you do aerobics.** Я получа́ю удово́льствие, наблюда́я, как ты занима́ешься аэро́бикой. ♦ **I get my kicks from water skiing.** Я получа́ю удово́льствие от ката́ния на во́дных лы́жах.

kid *vt (joke)* шути́ть / пошути́ть, разы́грывать / разыгра́ть *(whom = acc.)* ♦ **Are you kidding (me)?** Ты ...шу́тишь? / ...разы́грываешь меня́? ♦ *(1)* **I'm...** / *(2)* **I was...** (*[3]* **just** / *[4]* **not) kidding (you).** Я (*[3]* то́лько / *[4]* не) *(1)* шучу́ / *(2)* шути́л *(ж: шути́ла)*.

kid *n (child)* ребёнок *(pl:* де́ти*)* ♦ **I love kids.** Я люблю́ дете́й. ♦ *(1,2)* **Kids ok.** *(1)* Де́ти -- не поме́ха. / *(2)* Мо́жно с детьми́. ♦ **Kids don't matter.** Де́ти -- не поме́ха. ♦ **No kids.** Без дете́й. ♦ **I'm just a kid at heart.** Я се́рдцем про́сто дитя́.

kid-free *adj* безде́тный, -ая, -ое, -ые.

kid-friendly *adj:* ♦ **be** ~ *(like)* люби́ть дете́й; *(get along well)* хорошо́ ла́дить с детьми́.

kid-loving *adj* лю́бящий (-ая, -ее, -ие) дете́й.

kill *vt* уби́ть *(what, whom = acc.)* ♦ **You have killed my love for you.** Ты уби́ла *(ж: уби́л)* мою́ любо́вь к тебе́.

kind *adj* до́брый, -ая, -ое, -ые *(short forms:* добр, -а́, -ы́*)* ♦ **The years have been** *(1)* **very /** *(2)* **exceptionally kind to you. You're still** *(3)* **quite /** *(4)* **very handsome.** Го́ды бы́ли *(1)* о́чень / *(2)* исключи́тельно благоскло́нны к тебе́. Ты всё ещё *(3,4)* о́чень краси́в. ♦ **You're a kind** *(1)* **man /** *(2)* **person.** Ты до́брый *(1)* мужчи́на / *(2)* челове́к. ♦ **You're a kind woman.** Ты до́брая же́нщина. ♦ **That** *(1)* **is /** *(2)* **was very kind of you.** *(1)* Это... / *(2)* Это бы́ло... о́чень любе́зно с твое́й стороны́. ♦ **You are (so) kind (to me).** Ты (так) добра́ *(ж: добр)* (ко мне). ♦ **You were (so) kind (to me).** Ты была́ *(ж: был)* (так) добра́ *(ж: добр)* (ко мне). ♦ **Please be kind enough to return my photo if you don't wish to correspond.** Пожа́луйста, бу́дьте добры́ верну́ть моё фо́то, е́сли Вы не хоти́те перепи́сываться.

kind *n* сорт, вид, тип; род ♦ **any** ~ **of** како́й-нибудь, -а́я-нибудь, -о́е-нибудь, -и́е-нибудь ♦ **different** ~**s (of things)** разли́чные (ве́щи) ♦ **other** ~**s (of things)** други́е (ве́щи) ♦ **some** ~ **of** како́й-то, -а́я-то, -о́е-то, -и́е-то ♦ **that** ~ тако́й, -а́я, -о́е, -и́е ♦ **this** ~ тако́й, -а́я, -о́е, -и́е ♦ **what kind of** како́й, -а́я, -о́е, -и́е ♦ **I'm not that kind of** *(1)* **woman /** *(2)* **girl /** *(3)* **man /** *(4)* **person.** Я не того́ ти́па *(1)* же́нщина / *(2)* де́вушка / *(3)* мужчи́на /

The time zones for many cities of the world are given in Appendix 6, page 761.

(4) человéк. ♦ **What kind of** *(1)* **woman** / *(2)* **girl** / *(3)* **man** / *(4)* **person do you think I am?**
К какóму тѝпу *(1)* жéнщин / *(2)* дéвушек / *(3)* мужчѝн / *(4)* людéй ты меня́ отнóсишь?
♦ **I like** *(1)* **this** / *(2)* **that kind of** *(3)* **bread** / *(4)* **music** / *(5)* **beer.** *(1,2)* Мне нрáвится *(3)*
...э́тот хлеб. / *(4)* ...э́та му́зыка. / *(5)* ...э́то пѝво. ♦ **What kind?** Какóй (-áя, -óе, -ѝе)?
♦ **What kind of camera do you have?** Какóй у тебя́ фотоаппарáт? ♦ **What kind of dog
do you have?** Какáя у тебя́ собáка? ♦ **What kind of wine is that?** Какóе э́то винó?
What kind of music tapes do you have? Какѝе музыкáльные кассéты у тебя́ есть? ♦
You're *(1,2)* **one of a kind.** Ты *(1)* ...уникáльный человéк. / *(2)* ...уникáльная лѝчность.
kind-hearted *adj* добросердéчный, -ая, -ое, -ые, отзы́вчивый, -ая, -ое, -ые, дóбрый, -ая,
-ое, -ые, с дóбрым сéрдцем ♦ **You are such a kind-hearted person.** Ты такóй добросердéчный человéк. ♦ **I've never met anyone as kind-hearted as you.** Я никогдá не
встречáл *(ж: встречáла)* человéка столь добросердéчного, как ты. ♦ **You are so
kind-hearted (to me).** Ты так добрá *(ж: добр)* (ко мне).
kind-heartedness *n* добросердéчие, отзы́вчивость *f*.
kindle *vt* зажигáть / зажéчь *(what = acc.)*, воспламеня́ть / воспламенѝть *(what = acc.)* ♦
I know that the flame that you have kindled in my heart will never go out. Я знáю, что
плáмя, котóрое ты зажглá *(ж: зажёг)* в моём сéрдце, никогдá не погáснет. ♦ **If you
only knew what (wild) flames you have kindled inside me.** Если бы ты тóлько знáла *(ж:
знал)*, какóе (нейстовое) плáмя ты зажглá *(ж: зажёг)* во мне. ♦ **Such flames you
kindle in my body!** Какóе плáмя ты зажигáешь в моём тéле! ♦ **Your touch kindles fire
in me.** Твоё прикосновéние разжигáет во мне огóнь.
kindled *adj* зажжённый, -ая, -ое, -ые, воспламенѝвшийся, -аяся, -ееся, -иеся ♦ **Our
kindled passion will burst into an uncontrollable, raging fire.** Нáша воспламенѝвшаяся
страсть разгорѝтся неконтролѝруемым, бéшеным огнём.
kindness *n* добротá, любéзность *f*, внимáние ♦ **act of** ~ дóбрый посту́пок ♦ ~ **of heart**
душéвная добротá ♦ **milk of human** ~ мягкосердéчие, добротá ♦ **Thank you for your
kindness.** Спасѝбо за твою́ добротý. ♦ **You've shown me so much kindness.** Ты проя-
вѝла *(ж: проявѝл)* так мнóго доброты́ ко мне. ♦ **I appreciate your kindness (very
much).** Я (óчень) ценю́ твою́ добротý. ♦ **From kindness comes love.** Из доброты́
прихóдит любóвь. ♦ **There's no** *(1,2)* **...milk of human kindness... in** *(3)* **you** / *(4)* **him**
/ *(5)* **her.** В *(3)* тебé / *(4)* нём / *(5)* ней нет *(1)* доброты́ / *(2)* мягкосердéчия. ♦ **I value
wisdom, kindness and humor.** Я ценю́ му́дрость, добротý и ю́мор.
kindred *adj* рóдственный, -ая, -ое, -ые.
king-size *adj* óчень большóй, -áя, -óе, -ѝе, огрóмный, -ая, -ое, -ие; *(beds)* óчень широ́кий,
-ая, -ое, -ие ♦ ~ **bed** óчень широ́кая кровáть.
kinky *adj* 1. *(perverted)* извращённый, -ая, -ое, -ые; 2. *(quirky, eccentric)* со стрáнностями,
с вы́вертами.
Kirghiz *adj* кирги́зский, -ая, -ое, -ие.
Kirghiz *n* 1. *(person)* кирги́з *m*, кирги́зка *f (pl:* кирги́зы*)*; 2. *(language)* кирги́зский язы́к
♦ **speak** ~ говорѝть по-кирги́зски.
kiss *vt* целовáть / поцеловáть *(what, whom = acc.)* ♦ ~ **adoringly** целовáть / поцеловáть
обожáюще, целовáть / поцеловáть с обожáнием ♦ ~ **again** целовáть / поцеловáть
опя́ть ♦ ~ **all over** целовáть вездé ♦ ~ **ardently** целовáть / поцеловáть пы́лко ♦ ~ **a
thousand times** целовáть ты́сячу раз ♦ ~ **deeply** целовáть / поцеловáть крéпко ♦ ~
endlessly целовáть бесконéчно ♦ ~ **everything** целовáть / поцеловáть всё ♦ ~ **everywhere** целовáть / поцеловáть вездé, покрывáть / покры́ть поцелу́ями ♦ ~ **fiercely**
целовáть / поцеловáть нейстово ♦ ~ **firmly** крéпко целовáть / поцеловáть *(on what =
+ в + acc., whom = acc.)* ♦ ~ **forcefully** целовáть / поцеловáть насѝльно ♦ ~ **frequently**

---

*Optional parts of sentences are preceded
or followed (or both) by three dots.*

целова́ть ча́сто ♦ **~ full(y) on the mouth** целова́ть / поцелова́ть пря́мо в гу́бы ♦ **~ gently** целова́ть / поцелова́ть мя́гко ♦ **~ goodnight** 1. *(bedtime)* целова́ть / поцелова́ть пе́ред сном; 2. *(parting)* целова́ть / поцелова́ть, расстава́ясь ве́чером ♦ **~ here** целова́ть / поцелова́ть сюда́ ♦ **~ in** *(1,2)* **public** целова́ть на *(1)* лю́дях / *(2)* пу́блике ♦ **~ (1-3) it** целова́ть / поцелова́ть *(1,2)* его́ *m & neut* / *(3)* её *f* ♦ **~ lightly** целова́ть не́жно, слегка́ каса́ясь губа́ми *(1 term)* ♦ **~ long** целова́ть до́лго ♦ **~ *(1,2)* lovingly** целова́ть / поцелова́ть *(1)* лю́бяще / *(2)* любо́вно, целова́ть / поцелова́ть с любо́вью ♦ **~ me** целова́ть / поцелова́ть меня́ ♦ **~ on the breast** целова́ть / поцелова́ть в грудь *(whom = acc.)* ♦ **~ on the cheek** целова́ть / поцелова́ть в щёку *(whom = acc.)* ♦ **~ on the lips** целова́ть / поцелова́ть в гу́бы *(whom = acc.)* ♦ **~ on the mouth** целова́ть / поцелова́ть в гу́бы *(whom = acc.)* ♦ **~ on the neck** целова́ть / поцелова́ть в ше́ю *(whom = acc.)* ♦ **~ over and over** целова́ть сно́ва и сно́ва ♦ **~ passionately** целова́ть / поцелова́ть стра́стно ♦ **~ reverently** целова́ть / поцелова́ть почти́тельно ♦ **~ roughly** целова́ть / поцелова́ть гру́бо ♦ **~ softly** целова́ть / поцелова́ть мя́гко ♦ **~ tenderly** целова́ть / поцелова́ть не́жно ♦ **~ them** целова́ть / поцелова́ть их ♦ **~ there** целова́ть / поцелова́ть туда́ ♦ **~ wetly** целова́ть / поцелова́ть вла́жно ♦ **~ with a slow, tender passion** целова́ть с ме́дленной, не́жной стра́стью ♦ **~ with feeling** целова́ть / поцелова́ть с чу́вством ♦ **~ you** *(familiar)* целова́ть / поцелова́ть тебя́; *(polite)* целова́ть / поцелова́ть Вас.

kiss: other terms

desire to ~ жела́ние целова́ть / поцелова́ть ♦ **stop kissing** переста́ть целова́ть *(whom = acc.)* ♦ **temptation to ~ you** искуше́ние поцелова́ть тебя́ ♦ **urge to ~ you** побужде́ние поцелова́ть тебя́.

kiss: I want to kiss you

(1) **I want to...** / *(2)* **I'm going to... kiss you** (*[3]* **...again and again.** / *[4]* **...all over.** / *[5]* **...endlessly.** / *[6]* **...long and slow.** / *[7]* **...like you've never been kissed before in all your life.** / *[8]* **...and kiss you and kiss you.**). *(1)* Я хочу́... / *(2)* Я бу́ду... целова́ть (*[8]* , целова́ть и целова́ть) тебя́ (*[3]*...сно́ва и сно́ва. / *[4]* ...всю. / *[5]* ...бесконе́чно. / *[6]* ...до́лго и ме́дленно. / *[7]* ...как никто́ никогда́ в твое́й жи́зни не целова́л тебя́.). ♦ **I want to** *(1)* **put** / *(2)* **wrap my arms around you and kiss you and kiss you and kiss you.** Я хочу́ *(1,2)* обви́ть тебя́ рука́ми и целова́ть, целова́ть и целова́ть тебя́. ♦ **I want to kiss you and kiss you and kiss you until all your senses are aflame with** *(1)* **need** / *(2)* **desire.** Я хочу́ целова́ть тебя́ и целова́ть, и целова́ть до тех пор, пока́ все твои́ чу́вства не погру́зятся в ого́нь *(1)* жела́ния / *(2)* стра́сти. ♦ **I've been aching to kiss you since the first** *(1)* **moment** / *(2)* **minute** / *(3)* **time I** *(4)* **met** / *(5)* **saw you.** Я горю́ жела́нием целова́ть тебя́ *(1)* ...с пе́рвого мгнове́ния,... / *(2)* ...с пе́рвой же мину́ты,... / *(3)* ...со вре́мени,... когда́ я *(4)* встре́тил / *(5)* уви́дел тебя́. ♦ **I must tell you that I feel an overwhelming desire to kiss you. It possesses me night and day. I cannot** *(1,2)* **shake it off.** Я до́лжен сказа́ть тебе́, что я ощуща́ю ошеломля́ющее жела́ние поцелова́ть тебя́. Оно́ владе́ет мной ночь и день. Я не могу́ *(1)* ...стряхну́ть его́. / *(2)* ...отде́латься от него́. ♦ **Sometimes I feel as though I will absolutely burst if I cannot kiss you.** Иногда́ я чу́вствую себя́ так, как бу́дто я взорву́сь, е́сли не смогу́ поцелова́ть тебя́. ♦ **Those beautiful, perfectly formed, alluring lips of yours just call to me to kiss them — and, oh, I want to spend many, many, many hours answering that call with my own lips.** Твои́ прекра́сные, соверше́нной фо́рмы, зама́нивающие гу́бы про́сто взыва́ют ко мне о поцелу́ях, и, о, я хочу́ проводи́ть мно́гие, мно́гие, мно́гие часы́, отвеча́я на э́тот призы́в свои́ми губа́ми. ♦ **It's hard for me to think of you without wanting to hold you tenderly in my arms and kiss you and kiss you and kiss you — ever so lovingly and ever so adoringly.** Мне тру́дно ду́мать о тебе́ без жела́ния держа́ть тебя́ не́жно в объя́тиях и целова́ть, целова́ть, и целова́ть о́чень лю́бяще и о́чень обожа́юще.

> *If you're not on familiar terms with a person,*
> *the «ты» forms will have to be changed to «Вы».*

♦ **It would not be possible to kiss you as much as I want to kiss you.** Бы́ло бы невозмо́жно целова́ть тебя́ сто́лько, ско́лько я хочу́. ♦ **I want so much to hold you in my arms and kiss you endlessly.** Я так жа́жду обня́ть тебя́ и целова́ть бесконе́чно. ♦ **I want so desperately to be close to you, to hold you in my arms, to feel the warmth of you, to kiss you.** Я отча́янно хочу́ быть ря́дом с тобо́й, держа́ть тебя́ в объя́тиях, чу́вствовать твоё тепло́, целова́ть тебя́. ♦ **I have such a(n)** *(1)* ...**(powerful) urge...** */ (2)* ...**overpowering impulse... to kiss you.** У меня́ тако́е *(1)* ...(вла́стное) побужде́ние... */ (2)* ...неудержи́мое жела́ние... поцелова́ть тебя́.

> **kiss:** *my dream is to kiss you*

What pure heaven it would be to kiss you lightly on the lips. Каки́м и́стинным наслажде́нием бы́ло бы легко́ целова́ть тебя́ в гу́бы. ♦ **My most cherished dream is to kiss your beautiful face 25,000,000 times — in the first year. And then gradually increase the number of kisses.** Моя́ са́мая заве́тная мечта́ -- целова́ть твоё прекра́сное лицо́ 25 000 000 *(два́дцать пять миллио́нов)* раз в наш пе́рвый год. И затем постепе́нно увели́чивать число́ поцелу́ев. ♦ **How heavenly it would be to take your beautiful face softly in my hands and kiss it lovingly all over, many, many, many times.** Как бы́ло бы замеча́тельно не́жно взять в ру́ки твоё прекра́сное лицо́ и любо́вно покры́ть его́ поцелу́ями мно́го, мно́го, мно́го раз. ♦ **It would be absolute heaven to lie next to you, hold you tenderly in my arms, look into your beautiful, dark eyes, kiss you ever so lovingly and adoringly, and feel the magic warmth of your body all through the night.** Бы́ло бы соверше́нно чуде́сно лежа́ть ря́дом с тобо́й, держа́ть тебя́ не́жно в объя́тиях, смотре́ть в твои́ прекра́сные тёмные глаза́, целова́ть тебя́ с любо́вью и обожа́нием и чу́вствовать волше́бное тепло́ твоего́ те́ла всю ночь.

> **kiss:** *I want to kiss your face*

I've never seen a face that I wanted to kiss more than I want to kiss yours. Я никогда́ не ви́дел лица́, кото́рое я хоте́л бы целова́ть бо́льше, чем хочу́ целова́ть твоё. ♦ **I just want to kiss you on the cheek.** Я хочу́ то́лько поцелова́ть тебя́ в щёчку. ♦ **I wish that I could kiss both your eyes very softly many, many, many times — before moving on to other delectable parts.** Я хоте́л бы, что́бы я мог о́чень мя́гко целова́ть о́ба твои́х гла́за мно́го, мно́го, мно́го раз пре́жде, чем передви́нуться к други́м восхити́тельным частя́м.

> **kiss:** *I want to kiss your body*

I dream of kissing you all over. Я мечта́ю о том, что́бы целова́ть тебя́ всю. ♦ *(1)* **I want to...** */ (2)* **I'm going to... kiss your** *(3)* ...**face** */ (4)* **mouth** */ (5)* **stomach** */ (6)* **waist** */ (7)* **head** */ (8)* **neck** */ (9)* **breasts** */ (10)* **chest** */ (11)* **back** */ (12)* **hair** */ (13)* **shoulders** */ (14)* **arms** */ (15)* **hands** */ (16)* **fingers** */ (17)* **nipples** */ (18)* **hips** */ (19)* **thighs** */ (20)* **legs** */ (21)* **feet** */ (22)* **toes** *([23]*...**adoringly.** */ [24]* ...**tenderly.** */ [25]* ...**gently.** */ [26]* ...**slowly and lovingly.** */ [27]*...**over and over.** */ [28]*...**a thousand times.** */ [29]* ...**all** */ [30]* **every day and** *[31]* **all** */ [32] ***every night.** */ [33]* ...**like no one has ever kissed it** */ [34]* **them before.** */ [35]* ...**until you beg me to stop.** */ [36]* ...**until you explode with ecstasy.)** *(1)* Я хочу́... */ (2)* Я бу́ду... целова́ть *(3)* ...твоё лицо́ */ (4)* ...твой рот */ (5)* живо́т */ (6)* ...твою́ та́лию */ (7)* го́лову */ (8)* ше́ю */ (9,10)* грудь */ (11)* спи́ну */ (12)* ...твои́ во́лосы */ (13)* пле́чи */ (14,15)* ру́ки */ (16)* па́льцы */ (17)* соски́ */ (18,19)* бёдра */ (20)* но́ги */ (21)* сту́пни */ (22)* ...твои́ па́льцы на нога́х *([23]*...с обожа́нием. */ [24,25]* ...не́жно. */ [26]* ...ме́дленно, с любо́вью. */ [27]* ...сно́ва и сно́ва. */ [28]* ...ты́сячу раз. */ [29]* ...весь */ [30]* ка́ждый день и *[31]* всю */ [32]* ка́ждую ночь. */ [33,34]*...как никто́ никогда́ не целова́л. */ [35]* ...пока́ ты не бу́дешь умоля́ть меня́ прекрати́ть. */ [36]* ...пока́ ты не взорвёшься в экста́зе.). ♦ *(1)* **I want to...** */ (2)* **I'm going to... kiss every square millimeter of your beautiful, luscious body.** *(1)* Я хочу́... */ (2)* Я бу́ду... целова́ть ка́ждый квадра́тный миллиме́тр твоего́ прекра́сного, со́чного те́ла.

Common adult heights are given in Appendix 9, page 776.

kiss: *I kiss you*

I kiss you (*[1]* tenderly / *[2]* lovingly / *[3]* softly / *[4]* adoringly) (*[5]*...in all my dreams. / *[6]* ...a thousand times.). Я целу́ю тебя́ (*[1]* не́жно / *[2]* любо́вно / *[3]* мя́гко / *[4]* обожа́юще) (*[5]*...во всех мои́х мечта́х. / *[6]* ...ты́сячу раз.). ♦ **I kiss you a thousand times for the *(1)* sweet / *(2)* wonderful / *(3)* love-filled / *(4)* precious letter that you *(5)* sent / *(6)* wrote to me.** Я целу́ю тебя́ ты́сячу раз за *(1)* ми́лое / *(2)* удиви́тельное / *(3)* ...по́лное любви́... / *(4)* драгоце́нное письмо́, кото́рое ты *(5)* посла́ла / *(6)* написа́ла мне. ♦ **Every time I kiss you, I'm telling you straight from my heart that I love you.** Ка́ждый раз, когда́ я целу́ю тебя́, я говорю́ тебе́ пря́мо от се́рдца к се́рдцу, что я люблю́ тебя́. ♦ **I don't want to stop kissing you.** Я не хочу́ переста́ть целова́ть тебя́. ♦ **I can never resist the *(1,2)* temptation of kissing you.** Я никогда́ не могу́ устоя́ть пе́ред *(1)* собла́зном / *(2)* искуше́нием поцелова́ть тебя́. ♦ **It's been so long since I kissed you.** Прошло́ так мно́го вре́мени с тех пор, как я целова́л *(ж: целова́ла)* тебя́. ♦ *(1)* **Show** / *(2)* **Tell me where to kiss you.** *(1)* Покажи́ / *(2)* Скажи́ мне, куда́ поцелова́ть тебя́.

kiss: *I love to kiss*

I love to kiss, hug, caress, touch, hold hands, nibble, cuddle, rub against, stroke — you just name it. Я люблю́ целова́ть, обнима́ть, ласка́ть, каса́ться, держа́ться за ру́ки, поку́сывать, сжима́ть в объя́тиях, тере́ться, гла́дить -- ты то́лько назови́.

kiss: *I love to kiss you*

I love to kiss the rounded globes of your breasts. Я люблю́ целова́ть окру́глые шары́ твои́х груде́й.

kiss: *the thought of kissing you*

The thought of kissing your beautiful mouth causes my heart to thunder. Мысль о том, чтобы целова́ть твой прекра́сный рот заставля́ет моё се́рдце учащённо би́ться.

kiss: *the temptation to kiss you*

The temptation to kiss you was almost more than I could bear. Искуше́ние целова́ть тебя́ бы́ло почти́ невыноси́мо.

kiss: *the first time I kissed you*

The first time I kissed you, it was like being *(1)* hit / *(2)* touched by lightning. В пе́рвый раз, когда́ я поцелова́л *(ж: поцелова́ла)* тебя́, э́то бы́ло как *(1)* уда́р / *(2)* прикоснове́ние мо́лнии. ♦ **I will always treasure the memory of the first time I kissed you.** Я бу́ду всегда́ храни́ть па́мять о вре́мени, когда́ впервы́е поцелова́л *(ж: поцелова́ла)* тебя́. ♦ **I cannot describe the passion that seized my soul when I first kissed you.** Не могу́ описа́ть страсть, охвати́вшую мою́ ду́шу, когда́ я впервы́е поцелова́л тебя́.

kiss: *you kiss me*

I love the way you kiss (me). Мне о́чень нра́вится, как ты (меня́) целу́ешь. ♦ **Kiss me (*[1]*...again. / *[2]* ...like that again. / *[3]* ...long. / *[4]* ...softly. / *[5]* ...tenderly. / *[6]* ...here. / *[7]* ...all over. / *[8]* ...with feeling. / *[9]* ...on the lips.).** Поцелу́й меня́ (*[1]*...сно́ва. / *[2]* ...вот так сно́ва. / *[3]* ...до́лго. / *[4]* ...мя́гко. / *[5]* ...не́жно. / *[6]* ...вот сюда́. / *[7]* ...везде́. / *[8]* ...с чу́вством. / *[9]* ...в гу́бы.) ♦ **Kiss me in your dreams and my heart will feel it.** Целу́й меня́ в свои́х снах, и моё се́рдце почу́вствует э́то. ♦ **When you kiss me, all my resistance drains out of me.** Когда́ ты целу́ешь меня́, всё сопротивле́ние покида́ет меня́.

kiss: *can't stop kissing you*

I'm so afraid that when I see you (again), I will not be able to stop kissing you. Я так бою́сь, что когда́ я встре́чу тебя́ (опя́ть), не смогу́ переста́ть целова́ть тебя́.

kiss: *kiss and tell*

I'm not the kind to kiss and tell. Я не тот тип, кото́рый снача́ла целу́ет, а пото́м всем расска́зывает об э́том.

Words in parentheses are optional.

kiss: closing of a letter

I kiss you and hug you (many times). Целу́ю и обнима́ю тебя́ (мно́го раз).

kiss *n* поцелу́й *m (pl:* поцелу́и) ♦ **adoring** ~ обожа́ющий поцелу́й *(pl:* обожа́ющие поцелу́и) ♦ *(1,2)* **ardent** ~ *(1)* пы́лкий / *(2)* стра́стный поцелу́й *(pl: [1]* пы́лкие / *[2]* стра́стные поцелу́и) ♦ **blown** ~ возду́шный поцелу́й ♦ **brotherly** ~ бра́тский поцелу́й ♦ *(1,2)* **burning** ~ *(1)* обжига́ющий / *(2)* жгу́чий поцелу́й *(pl: [1]* обжига́ющие / *[2]* жгу́чие поцелу́и) ♦ **chaste** ~ целому́дренный поцелу́й ♦ **clinging** ~ уде́рживающий поцелу́й ♦ **cold** ~ холо́дный поцелу́й ♦ **demanding** ~ тре́бовательный поцелу́й ♦ **eager** ~**es** жа́ждущие поцелу́и ♦ **farewell** ~ проща́льный поцелу́й ♦ **fatherly** ~ отцо́вский поцелу́й ♦ **first** ~ пе́рвый поцелу́й ♦ **formal** ~ форма́льный поцелу́й ♦ **French** ~ францу́зский поцелу́й ♦ **frenzied** ~ исступлённый поцелу́й *(pl:* исступлённые поцелу́и) ♦ **friendly** ~ дру́жеский поцелу́й ♦ **gentle** ~ не́жный поцелу́й *(pl:* не́жные поцелу́и) ♦ **goodbye** ~ проща́льный поцелу́й ♦ **goodnight** ~ поцелу́й на ночь ♦ **heady** ~**es** опьяня́ющие поцелу́и ♦ **heavenly** ~ боже́ственный поцелу́й *(pl:* боже́ственные поцелу́и) ♦ **hesitant** ~ неуве́ренный поцелу́й ♦ **innocent** ~ неви́нный поцелу́й ♦ **insistent** ~ насто́йчивый поцелу́й ♦ **intoxicating** ~ пьяня́щий поцелу́й ♦ **lazy** ~ лени́вый поцелу́й ♦ *(1,2)* **lingering** ~ *(1)* продолжи́тельный / *(2)* ме́дленный поцелу́й ♦ **lips-only** ~ поцелу́й то́лько губа́ми ♦ **listless** ~ вя́лый поцелу́й ♦ **long** ~ до́лгий поцелу́й ♦ **long, wet** ~**es** до́лгие, вла́жные поцелу́и ♦ **love-filled** ~ поцелу́й по́лный любви́ *(pl:* поцелу́и по́лные любви́) ♦ *(1,2)* **loving** ~ *(1)* любо́вный / *(2)* лю́бящий поцелу́й *(pl:* лю́бящие поцелу́и) ♦ **motherly** ~ матери́нский поцелу́й ♦ **my** ~ мой поцелу́й *(pl:* мои́ поцелу́и) ♦ **nervous** ~ не́рвный поцелу́й ♦ **parting** ~ проща́льный поцелу́й ♦ **passionate** ~ стра́стный поцелу́й *(pl:* стра́стные поцелу́и) ♦ *(1,2)* **perfect** ~ *(1)* превосхо́дный / *(2)* соверше́нный поцелу́й ♦ **perfunctory** ~ бе́глый поцелу́й ♦ **pleasurable** ~**es** доставля́ющие удово́льствие поцелу́и ♦ **romantic** ~ романти́ческий поцелу́й ♦ **rough** ~ гру́бый поцелу́й ♦ **searching, hungry** ~ и́щущий, голо́дный поцелу́й ♦ **sensual** ~ сладостра́стный поцелу́й ♦ **sensuous** ~ сладостра́стный поцелу́й ♦ **sisterly** ~ се́стринский поцелу́й ♦ **slow** ~ ме́дленный поцелу́й *(pl:* ме́дленные поцелу́и) ♦ **small** ~**es** ме́лкие поцелу́и ♦ **soft** ~ мя́гкий поцелу́й *(pl:* мя́гкие поцелу́и) ♦ **soul** ~ поцелу́й от души́ ♦ **soul-searing** ~ обжига́ющий ду́шу поцелу́й ♦ **sweet** ~ сла́дкий поцелу́й *(pl:* сла́дкие поцелу́и) ♦ **sweetest** ~ са́мый сла́дкий поцелу́й ♦ **tantalizing** ~ дразня́щий поцелу́й ♦ **tender** ~ не́жный поцелу́й *(pl:* не́жные поцелу́и) ♦ **tentative** ~ про́бный поцелу́й ♦ **tiny** ~**es** кро́шечные поцелу́и ♦ **tongue** ~ поцелу́й языко́м ♦ **wet** ~ вла́жный поцелу́й ♦ **wonderful** ~ удиви́тельный поцелу́й *(pl:* удиви́тельные поцелу́и) ♦ **your** ~ твой поцелу́й *(pl:* твои́ поцелу́и).

kiss: verb terms

be addicted to your ~**es** быть во вла́сти твои́х поцелу́ев ♦ **bestow** ~**es** дари́ть / подари́ть поцелу́и *(on what, whom = dat.)* ♦ **blow you a** ~ посыла́ть / посла́ть тебе́ возду́шный поцелу́й ♦ **cover you with** ~**es** покрыва́ть / покры́ть тебя́ поцелу́ями ♦ **crave your** ~**es** жа́ждать твои́х поцелу́ев ♦ **deluge with** ~**es** затопи́ть поцелу́ями *(whom = acc.)* ♦ **lavish** ~**es** дари́ть / подари́ть поцелу́и *(on what, whom = dat.)* ♦ **miss your** ~**es** скуча́ть по твои́м поцелу́ям ♦ **need your** ~**es** нужны́ твои́ поцелу́и *(person needing = dat. [I = мне])* ♦ **place** ~**es** размеща́ть поцелу́и ♦ **place** ~**es all over** покры́ть поцелу́ями *(what, whom = acc.)* ♦ **receive** ~**es** получа́ть / получи́ть поцелу́и ♦ **seal a letter with a** ~ запеча́тать письмо́ поцелу́ем ♦ **send you** *(1)* **a** ~ / *(2)* ~**es** посыла́ть / посла́ть тебе́ *(1)* поцелу́й / *(2)* поцелу́и ♦ **share a romantic** ~ обме́ниваться / обменя́ться лю́бящим поцелу́ем ♦ **shower you with** ~**es** покрыва́ть / покры́ть тебя́ поцелу́ями, затопля́ть / затопи́ть тебя́ поцелу́ями ♦ **steal a** ~ сорва́ть поцелу́й.

You can find common clothing sizes in Appendix 11 on page 778.

kiss: *other terms*

(1,2) **a lot of** ~es *(1)* мно́го / *(2)* мно́жество поцелу́ев ♦ **ecstasy of your** ~es восто́рг твои́х поцелу́ев ♦ **endless stream of** ~es бесконе́чный пото́к поцелу́ев ♦ **fierceness of a** ~ неи́стовство поцелу́я ♦ **honey sweetness of your** ~ медо́вая сла́дость твоего́ поцелу́я ♦ **magic of your** ~es волшебство́ твои́х поцелу́ев ♦ *(1,2)* **many** ~es *(1)* мно́го / *(2)* мно́жество поцелу́ев ♦ **rain of** ~es град поцелу́ев ♦ *(1,2)* **searing** *(3,4)* **trail of** ~es *(1)* пото́к / *(2)* след *(3)* жгу́чих / *(4)* обжига́ющих поцелу́ев ♦ **sweetness of your** ~es сла́дость твои́х поцелу́ев. ♦ **taste of your** ~es вкус твои́х поцелу́ев

kiss: *who's got kisses?*

I need an affectionate, loving person with lots of hugs and kisses to give. Мне ну́жен не́жный, лю́бящий челове́к, даря́щий мно́жество объя́тий и поцелу́ев.

kiss: *how your kisses are*

You have a kiss of fire. Твой поцелу́й -- э́то ого́нь. ♦ **Your kisses are like fire.** Твои́ поцелу́и, как ого́нь. ♦ **Your kisses are so addictive.** К твои́м поцелу́ям так легко́ пристрасти́ться.

kiss: *your sweet kiss(es)*

In the unbounded vistas of my dreams and fantasies I taste the exquisite sweetness of your lips a thousand, ten thousand, a million times, and each time am only impelled by the sheer ecstasy of the kiss to taste them once again. В безграни́чной верени́це мои́х снов и фанта́зий я вкуша́ю исключи́тельную сла́дость твои́х губ ты́сячу, де́сять ты́сяч, миллио́н раз и ка́ждый раз побуждён и́стинным восто́ргом поцелу́я упива́ться им опя́ть. ♦ **That was the softest, sweetest kiss I've ever known.** Это был са́мый не́жный, са́мый сла́дкий поцелу́й в мое́й жи́зни. ♦ **The taste of your kisses is still on my lips.** Вкус твои́х поцелу́ев всё ещё на мои́х губа́х.

kiss: *I need your kisses*

I need (your) kisses. Мне нужны́ (твои́) поцелу́и. ♦ **My heart is thirsty for your kisses.** Моё се́рдце жа́ждет твои́х поцелу́ев. ♦ **I know that I can never overcome my addiction to your kisses.** Я зна́ю, что никогда́ не смогу́ освободи́ться от вла́сти твои́х поцелу́ев. ♦ **I'm** *(1)* **absolutely** / *(2)* **completely** / *(3)* **totally** / *(4)* **hopelessly addicted to your** *(5)* **sweet** / *(6)* **heavenly** / *(7)* **wonderful kisses.** Я *(1)* соверше́нно / *(2,3)* по́лностью / *(4)* безнадёжно во вла́сти твои́х *(5)* сла́дких / *(6)* боже́ственных / *(7)* удиви́тельных поцелу́ев.

kiss: *I miss your kisses*

I miss your hugs and kisses (more than I can tell you). Я скуча́ю по твои́м объя́тиям и поцелу́ям (бо́льше, чем могу́ вы́сказать).

kiss: *can't get enough*

Whenever I think about your *(1)* **gentle** / *(2)* **tender kisses and warm caresses, I realize why I can never get enough of you.** Когда́ я ду́маю о твои́х *(1,2)* не́жных поцелу́ях и тёплых ла́сках, я понима́ю почему́ никогда́ не могу́ насы́титься тобо́й. ♦ **The most heartless thing you could ever do to me is to say that a thousand kisses are enough for one night.** Са́мое бессерде́чное, что ты могла́ бы когда́-нибудь сде́лать, э́то сказа́ть мне, что ты́сячи поцелу́ев доста́точно для одно́й но́чи.

kiss: *don't be stingy with them*

Don't be stingy with your kisses. Не будь скупа́ *(ж: скуп)* в поцелу́ях.

kiss: *what your kisses do / did to me*

I am *(1)* **completely** / *(2)* **totally** *(3)* **...overcome by...** / *(4)* **...swept away by...** / *(5)* **...engulfed in... the rapture that you create with your ardent kisses.** Я *(1)* по́лностью / *(2)* весь *(ж: вся)* *(3,4)* ...охва́чен *(ж: охва́чена)...* / *(5)* ...поглощён *(ж: поглощена́)...* упое́нием, кото́рое ты создаёшь свои́ми пы́лкими поцелу́ями. ♦ **The sweet magic of your kisses** *(1)*

For general rules of Russian grammar see Appendix 2 on page 686.

...enthralls me. / *(2)* ...captivates my soul. / *(3)* ...sends me into endless ecstasy. Сла́дкое волшебство́ твои́х поцелу́ев *(1)* ...очаро́вывает меня́. / *(2)* ...пленя́ет мою́ ду́шу. / *(3)* ...приво́дит меня́ в несконча́емый восто́рг. ♦ **Your** *(1)* **kiss** / *(2)* **kisses (just)** *(3,4)* **wiped my mind blank.** *(1)* Твой поцелу́й... / *(2)* Твои́ поцелу́и... (про́сто) *(3+1)* опустоши́л / *(4+2)* опустоши́ли меня́. ♦ **Your kisses** *(1)* ...set me on fire. / *(2)* ...induce such sensual euphoria. Твои́ поцелу́и *(1)* ...воспламеня́ют меня́. / *(2)* ...вызыва́ют таку́ю чу́вственную эйфори́ю. ♦ **Your kiss shook me like I've never been shaken before.** Потрясе́ние от твоего́ поцелу́я бы́ло сильне́йшим в мое́й жи́зни. ♦ **That kiss really** *(1)* **...inflicted a daze on me.** / *(2)* **...put me in a daze.** Э́тот поцелу́й действи́тельно ошеломи́л меня́. ♦ **I'm still in a daze from that kiss.** Я всё ещё ошеломлён (*ж: ошеломлена́*) э́тим поцелу́ем.

---
kiss: *kissing you*

I would like to be the lucky person in this world who teaches you what kind of magic a kiss can hold. Я хоте́л бы быть тем счастли́вым челове́ком в э́том ми́ре, кото́рый у́чит тебя́ тому́, како́е волшебство́ мо́жет быть в поцелу́ях. ♦ **I long to see you stretch out in languorous abandon as I place tiny kisses about your bosom and down your stomach.** Я жа́жду уви́деть тебя́, раски́нувшуюся в то́мной непринуждённости, в то вре́мя, как я размеща́ю кро́шечные поцелу́и вокру́г твое́й груди́ и вниз по твоему́ животу́. ♦ **My loving kisses will lead you deliciously along the paths of heavenly pleasure until you reach cosmic ecstasy.** Мои́ лю́бящие поцелу́и поведу́т тебя́ по восхити́тельной тропе́ ра́йского наслажде́ния до косми́ческого экста́за. ♦ **If you were my woman, I would fill your life to overflowing with soft, gentle, eager, loving kisses that would awaken all sorts of warm, wonderful, exquisite feelings in you.** Е́сли бы ты была́ мое́й же́нщиной, я бы запо́лнил твою́ жизнь до краёв мя́гкими, не́жными, жа́ждущими, лю́бящими поцелу́ями, кото́рые пробуди́ли бы все са́мые тёплые, замеча́тельные, изы́сканные чу́вства в тебе́.

---
kiss: *shower / cover you with kisses*
---

(1) **I want to...** / *(2)* **I'm going to...** / *([3]* **...sweep you into my arms and...** / *[4]* **...put** / *[5]* **wrap my arms around you and...)** *(6)* **cover** / *(7)* **shower** *(8)* **...you...** / *(9)* **...your beautiful** *(10)* **face** / *(11)* **body...** **with (tender,** *[12]* **adoring** / *[13]* **loving) kisses.** *(1)* Я хочу́ (*[3+1]* схвати́ть тебя́ в свои́ объя́тия и... / *[4+1, 5+1]* обви́ть тебя́ рука́ми и...) *(6+1,7+1)* покры́ть... / *(2)* Я (*[3+2]*...схвачу́ / *[4+2, 5+2]* обовью́... тебя́ и) *(6+2,7+2)* покро́ю... *(8)* ...тебя́... / *(9)* ...твоё прекра́сное *(10)* лицо́ / *(11)* те́ло... (не́жными, *[12]* обожа́ющими / *[13]* лю́бящими) поцелу́ями. ♦ **I'm going to shower your lips and face and neck with small kisses.** Я покро́ю твои́ гу́бы, лицо́, ше́ю каска́дом ме́лких поцелу́ев. ♦ **I'm going to cover you with a million kisses burning as though beneath the equator.** Я покро́ю тебя́ миллио́ном поцелу́ев, обжига́ющих, как со́лнце над эква́тором. ♦ **When we're together (again), I'm going to cover you with kisses and caresses like you've never even dreamed of in your wildest dreams.** Когда́ мы (опя́ть) бу́дем вме́сте, я покро́ю тебя́ поцелу́ями и бу́ду ласка́ть так, как ты никогда́ не мечта́ла в свои́х са́мых необу́зданных мечта́х. ♦ **When at last my mouth claims yours, I will** *(1)* **...deluge it with more kisses...** / *(2)* **...lavish** / *(3)* **bestow more kisses upon it... than it has ever known before.** Когда́ наконе́ц мой рот встре́тится с твои́м, я *(1)* ...затоплю́ его́ бо́льшим коли́чеством поцелу́ев,... / *(2,3)* ...подарю́ ему́ бо́льше поцелу́ев,... чем он когда́-либо пре́жде получа́л. ♦ **I'm going to place kisses lovingly all over your body.** Я покро́ю всё твоё те́ло лю́бящими поцелу́ями. ♦ **As my hand cups the fullness of your breast, my mouth will cover your beautiful face and smooth neck with adoring kisses.** В то вре́мя, как моя́ рука́ ощути́т полноту́ твое́й груди́, мой рот покро́ет твоё прекра́сное лицо́ и не́жную ше́ю обожа́ющими поцелу́ями. ♦

For transitive Russian verbs the cases that they take are shown by means of an = sign and the Russian case (abbreviated).

When we meet in the airport, I'm going to swing you around (and around) and shower you with kisses. Когда́ мы встре́тимся в аэропорту́, я закружу́ тебя́ на рука́х и затоплю́ поцелу́ями. ♦ How I wish that I were holding you in my arms at this very minute, covering your beautiful face with adoring kisses. Как бы я жела́л держа́ть тебя́ в объя́тиях в э́ту са́мую мину́ту, покрыва́я твоё прекра́сное лицо́ обожа́ющими поцелу́ями. ♦ I want to celebrate your (1) breath-taking / (2) fantastic / (3) incredible beauty with adoring kisses all over it. Я хочу́ прославля́ть твою́ (1) ...перехва́тывающую дыха́ние... / (2) фанта́сти́ческую / (3) невероя́тную красоту́ обожа́ющими поцелу́ями. ♦ (1) I want to... / (2) I'm going to... rain (tantalizing) kisses (3) ...on your sweet, beloved face. / (4) ...across the back of your neck. (1) Я хочу́ затопи́ть... / (2) Я затоплю́... (дразня́щими) поцелу́ями (3) ...твоё не́жное, люби́мое лицо́. / (4) ...твою́ ше́йку сза́ди. ♦ My heart yearns to show you my love in an endless stream of warm embraces and soft, (1) adoring / (2) loving kisses. Моё се́рдце жа́ждет показа́ть тебе́ свою́ любо́вь в бесконе́чном пото́ке тёплых объя́тий и мя́гких, (1) обожа́ющих / (2) любя́щих поцелу́ев. ♦ In the meantime, you can be sure that I'll be dreaming about that beautiful, radiant smile of yours and how wonderful it would be to cover it with adoring kisses. Ме́жду тем, ты мо́жешь быть уве́рена, что я бу́ду мечта́ть об э́той сия́ющей твое́й улы́бке и как замеча́тельно бы́ло бы покры́ть её обожа́ющими поцелу́ями. ♦ They say the human body has 20 million pores*. I want to put a kiss of love on each one of yours (every day). Говоря́т, что в челове́ческом те́ле 20 (два́дцать) милио́нов пор. Я хочу́ (ка́ждый день) дари́ть поцелу́й любви́ ка́ждой из твои́х. (* wild guess) ♦ The way you write to me makes me want to take you in my arms and hug you and hug you and hug you and cover your sweet face with loving kisses. То, как ты пи́шешь мне, вызыва́ет во мне жела́ние заключи́ть тебя́ в объя́тия, обнима́ть, обнима́ть и обнима́ть тебя́ и покрыва́ть твоё не́жное лицо́ любя́щими поцелу́ями. ♦ I wish so much that I could hold you snugly in my arms and put soft, loving kisses all over your hair and face. Мне бы так хоте́лось ую́тно устро́ить тебя́ в свои́х объя́тиях и покры́вать мя́гкими, любя́щими поцелу́ями твои́ во́лосы и лицо́.

kiss: I send you kisses

I send you many hugs and kisses, each one filled with much love. Я посыла́ю тебе́ объя́тия и поцелу́и, ка́ждый из кото́рых по́лон любви́. ♦ I want to send you another kiss before I go to sleep, to tell you that I love you. Я хочу́ посла́ть тебе́ ещё оди́н поцелу́й пе́ред тем, как пойти́ спать, что́бы сказа́ть: «Я люблю́ тебя́.» ♦ Across the (1) ...many miles (that separate us)... / (2) ...vast ocean... I blow you a soft, tender kiss. (Did you catch it?) Че́рез (1) ...мно́гие ми́ли (, разделя́ющие нас,)... / (2) ...необъя́тный океа́н... я посыла́ю тебе́ мя́гкий, не́жный поцелу́й. (Ты пойма́ла его́?) ♦ (1) I'm blowing... / (2) I blow... you a kiss. Did you catch it? How was it? Я (1) посыла́ю / (2) шлю тебе́ возду́шный поцелу́й. Ты пойма́ла (ж: пойма́л) его́? Как э́то бы́ло? ♦ I blow you a kiss — aimed right at your (beautiful) smile. Я посыла́ю тебе́ поцелу́й, наце́ленный пря́мо в твою́ (прекра́сную) улы́бку. ♦ I loved your "Sweet kisses" and with this letter I send you two for every one that you sent me. Мне о́чень понра́вились твои́ «Сла́дкие поцелу́и», и с э́тим письмо́м я посыла́ю тебе́ по два на ка́ждый, кото́рый ты посла́ла (ж: посла́л) мне.

kiss: your reward -- kisses

Your reward will be a (tender) kiss. Твое́й награ́дой бу́дет (не́жный) поцелу́й. ♦ As a small reward, I'm going to give you five million kisses. Как ма́ленькую награ́ду я подарю́ тебе́ пять миллио́нов поцелу́ев.

kiss: sealed with a kiss

This letter is sealed with a kiss. Это письмо́ запеча́тано поцелу́ем.

> *Russian verbs have 2 forms: imperfective and perfective.*
> *They're given in that order.*

kiss: first kiss

I will always cling to the memory of our first kiss. Я бу́ду всегда́ вспомина́ть о на́шем пе́рвом поцелу́е. ♦ **Your sweet kiss is proof we are meant to be together.** Твой сла́дкий поцелу́й -- доказа́тельство того́, что мы предназна́чены быть вме́сте. ♦ **The kiss lasted only an instant, but the memory of it** *(1)* **...shines forever bright in my mind.** / *(2)* **...has lingered warmly in my mind ever since.** Поцелу́й продолжа́лся то́лько мгнове́ние, но па́мять о нём *(1)* ...я́рко и навсегда́ запечатле́лась во мне. / *(2)* ...с тех пор остаётся во мне.

kiss: quotation

"A kiss on your heart, and then one a little lower down, much lower down." *Napoleon Bonaparte to Josephine* «Поцелу́й на се́рдце, и зате́м оди́н пони́же, мно́го ни́же.» *Наполео́н Бонапа́рт к Жозефи́не.*

kissable *adj* сла́дкий (-ая, -ое, -ие) для поцелу́ев, зову́щий (-ая, -ее, -ие) к поцелу́ям, со́зданный (-ая, -ое, -ые) для поцелу́ев ♦ **invitingly** ~ приглаша́ющий (-ая, -ее, -ие) к поцелу́ям ♦ **You look so cuddly and kissable in these photos I can hardly stand it!** Ты вы́глядишь тако́й зову́щей к объя́тиям и к поцелу́ям, что я едва́ могу́ вы́нести э́то. ♦ **You've got the most kissable mouth in the world.** Твой рот са́мый сла́дкий на све́те. ♦ **Your mouth looks so kissable.** Твой рот так и про́сит поцелу́ев. ♦ **What a kissable mouth! I just can't stop kissing it!** Что за сла́дкий рот! Я про́сто не могу́ переста́ть целова́ть его́! ♦ **You are kissable all over.** Ты вся со́здана для поцелу́ев. ♦ **There is no part of you that isn't kissable.** Ка́ждую части́чку тебя́ хо́чется поцелова́ть.

kisser *n* 1. *(one who kisses)* целу́ющий *m*, целу́ющая *f*; 2. *(slang: mouth)* рот ♦ **great** ~ замеча́тельно целу́ющийся *m* / целу́ющаяся *f* ♦ **You're a** *(1)* **fantastic** / *(2)* **great** / *(3)* **terrific kisser.** Ты целу́ешь *(1)* фантасти́чески / *(2)* великоле́пно / *(3)* изуми́тельно.

kissing *n* *(act)* *(Russian mostly uses verb* целова́ть*)*; *(kiss)* поцелу́й; *(kisses)* поцелу́и ♦ **delightful** ~ восхити́тельные поцелу́и ♦ **heavenly** ~ боже́ственные поцелу́и ♦ *(1-3)* ~ **in public** поцелу́и *(1)* ...в о́бществе / *(2)* ...на лю́дях / *(3)* ...на пу́блике ♦ **soul** ~ (до́лгий) францу́зский поцелу́й ♦ **art of** ~ иску́сство поцелу́ев ♦ *(1)* **designed** / *(2)* **made for** ~ *(1)* предназна́чен (-а, -о, -ы) / *(2)* со́здан (-а, -о, -ы) для поцелу́ев ♦ **I'm going to teach you a new definition of kissing.** Я научу́ тебя́ но́вому определе́нию *(1)* поцелу́я. ♦ **I like lots of touching and caressing and kissing.** Я люблю́ мно́го прикоснове́ний, ласк и поцелу́ев. ♦ **My favorite pleasure in life is kissing your beautiful** *(1)* **mouth** / *(2)* **face.** Са́мое большо́е наслажде́ние в мое́й жи́зни целова́ть *(1)* ...твой прекра́сный рот. / *(2)* ...твоё прекра́сное лицо́. ♦ **You have really mastered the art of kissing.** Ты действи́тельно ма́стер в иску́сстве поцелу́ев. ♦ **You have lips that were made for kissing.** У тебя́ гу́бы, кото́рые бы́ли со́зданы для поцелу́ев. ♦ **When we get together (again), I'm going to do a kissing blitzkrieg on you.** Когда́ мы (опя́ть) бу́дем вме́сте, я молниено́сно атаку́ю тебя́ поцелу́ями. ♦ **Endless hours of** *(1)* **delightful** / *(2)* **heavenly kissing are promised in the delicate contour of your lips.** Бесконе́чные часы́ *(1)* восхити́тельных / *(2)* боже́ственных поцелу́ев обе́щаны в изя́щном ко́нтуре твои́х губ.

kiss-off *n* *(slang)* «отста́вка» ♦ **give** *(someone)* **the** ~ дать отста́вку *(to whom = dat.)* ♦ **It looks like you're giving me the kiss-off.** Э́то вы́глядит так, как бу́дто ты дала́ мне отста́вку.

kissy *adj* со́зданный (-ая, -ое, -ые) для поцелу́ев ♦ **I love your kissy face.** Я люблю́ твоё лицо́, со́зданное для поцелу́ев.

kitten *n* котёнок ♦ **You're my sweet little sex kitten.** Ты мой сла́дкий, ма́ленький, сексуа́льный котёнок. ♦ **You're my soft, warm, cuddly kitten.** Ты мой мя́гкий, тёплый, не́жный котёнок. ♦ **It's a real turn-on to watch you stretch like a kitten.**

How to use the Cyrillic alphabet on the Internet is the subject of Appendix 20 on page 789.

know

Действи́тельно возбужда́ет смотре́ть, как ты потя́гиваешься, сло́вно котёнок.

knee *n* коле́но *(pl:* коле́ни) ♦ **bad** ~ больно́е коле́но ♦ **left** ~ ле́вое коле́но ♦ **little** ~ коле́нка ♦ **right** ~ пра́вое коле́но ♦ **round** ~s кру́глые коле́ни ♦ **skinny** ~s худы́е коле́ни ♦ **smooth** ~s гла́дкие коле́ни ♦ **on bent** ~ сто́я на (одно́м) коле́не ♦ **I'm going to propose to you on bent knee.** Я, преклони́в коле́но, бу́ду проси́ть твое́й руки́.

knight *n* ры́царь *m* ♦ **You are my knight in shining armor.** Ты мой ры́царь в сия́ющей кольчу́ге.

knockers *n, pl (slang)* грудь.

knock off *vt* 1. *(slang)* сноси́ть / снести́ *(what, whom = acc.)*, сбива́ть / сбить *(what, whom = acc.)*, сража́ть / срази́ть *(what, whom = acc.)*; 2. *(slang) (stop, quit)* прекраща́ть / прекрати́ть *(what = acc.)* ♦ **I'll knock your socks off!** Я сражу́ тебя́! ♦ **Knock it off!** Прекрати́!

knockout *n (slang) (very beautiful woman)* прекра́сная же́нщина.

knock up *vt (slang) (make pregnant)* сде́лать ребёнка *(whom = dat.)*.

knot *vi* сжима́ться ♦ **I feel my stomach knot whenever I think of you with** *(1)* **him /** *(2)* **her.** Я чу́вствую, как сжима́ется моё се́рдце, когда́ бы ни поду́мал *(ж: поду́мала)* о тебе́ с *(1)* ним / *(2)* ней.

knot *n* у́зел ♦ **love** ~ любо́вный у́зел ♦ **tie the** ~ *(get married) (man)* жени́ться; *(woman)* вы́йти за́муж; *(both)* связа́ть у́зами бра́ка, пожени́ться.

know *vt (have knowledge)* знать *(what, whom = acc.)*; *(get to know)* узна́ть *(what, whom = acc.)* ♦ **(get to)** ~ **each other better** получше познако́миться, лу́чше узна́ть друг дру́га ♦ ~ **better** лу́чше знать ♦ ~ **for sure** знать наверняка́ ♦ ~ **how** *(to do s.th.)* уме́ть ♦ ~ **myself** знать себя́ ♦ ~ **well** хорошо́ знать ♦ ~ **yourself** знать себя́ ♦ **process of get ting to** ~ **each other** проце́сс узнава́ния.

> **know:** *knowing you*

(1) **I feel as though /** *(2)* **if... /** *(3)* **I feel like... /** *(4)* **It seems to me (somehow) that... I've known you** *(5)* **...always. /** *(6)* **...for a long (long) time. /** *(7)* **...all my life.** *(1.2)* У меня́ тако́е чу́вство, как бу́дто... / *(3)* Я чу́вствую так, как бу́дто... / *(4)* Мне ка́жется, что... я знал *(ж: зна́ла)* тебя́ *(5)* ...всегда́. / *(6)* ...давны́м давно́. / *(7)* ...всю жизнь. ♦ **You're** *(1)* **so /** *(2)* **very /** *(3)* **infinitely /** *(4)* **excitingly different from anyone I've ever known before.** Ты *(1)* так / *(2)* о́чень / *(3)* бесконе́чно / *(4)* возбужда́юще отлича́ешься от всех, кого́ я когда́-либо знал *(ж зна́ла)* ра́ньше. ♦ **The more I know you, the more I love you and cherish you.** Чем бо́лее я узнаю́ тебя́, тем бо́льше люблю́ и леле́ю. ♦ **I know** *(1)* **you /** *(2)* **him /** *(3)* **her /** *(4)* **them inside out.** Я всё зна́ю о *(1)* тебе́ / *(2)* нём / *(3)* ней / *(4)* них.

> **know:** *know you better*

(1) **I'd like (very much)... /** *(2)* **I long... (3,4) ...(to get) to know you better. /** *(5)* **...to know more about you.** *(1)* Я (о́чень) хоте́л *(ж: хоте́ла)* бы... / *(2)* Я жа́жду... *(3)* ...узна́ть Вас лу́чше. / *(4)* ...познако́миться с тобо́й лу́чше. / *(5)* ...узна́ть бо́льше о Вас. ♦ **I think it would be so nice to know you.** Бы́ло бы так хорошо́ познако́миться с Ва́ми. ♦ **I'll tell you more about it when we get to know one another (better).** Я расскажу́ Вам бо́льше об э́том, когда́ мы (лу́чше) узна́ем друг дру́га. ♦ **I want to take it slow and get to know you (better).** Я хочу́ не спеши́ть и лу́чше узна́ть Вас. ♦ **I fervently** *(1)* **entreat /** *(2)* **implore you to (3) give /** *(4)* **grant me the opportunity to know you better.** Я горячо́ *(1,2)* умоля́ю Вас *(3)* дать / *(4)* предоста́вить мне возмо́жность лу́чше узна́ть Вас.

> **know:** *know someone intimately*

I've never known a man intimately. Я никогда́ не зна́ла мужчи́ну инти́мно.

> *Russian adjectives have long and short forms.*
> *Where short forms are given, they are labeled as such.*

| *know: you don't know* |

You don't know what you do to me. Зна́ешь ли ты, что ты де́лаешь со мной?

[*know: who will know?*]

Nobody will know. Никто́ не бу́дет знать.

| *know: I should know* |

I should *(1)* **...know...** / *(2)* **...have known... better (than to** *[3]* **...listen to you.** / *[4]* **...believe you.** / *[5]* **...get mixed up with you.)** Я *(1,2)* до́лжен был *(ж: должна́ была́)* бы знать лу́чше (пре́жде чем, *[3]* ...слу́шать тебя́. / *[4]* ...ве́рить тебе́. / *[5]* ...связа́ться с тобо́й.)

knowledge *n* зна́ние ♦ **I marvel at the extent of your knowledge.** Я восхища́юсь обши́рностью твои́х зна́ний.

Korean *adj* коре́йский, -ая, -ое, -ие.

Korean *n* 1. *(person)* коре́ец *m*, коре́янка *f (pl:* коре́йцы*)*; 2. *(language)* коре́йский язы́к ♦ **speak** ~ говори́ть по-коре́йски.

L

labyrinth *n* лабири́нт ♦ **I am lost in love's labyrinth.** Я потеря́лся в любо́вном лабири́нте.

lack *vt* 1. *(not have)* нужда́ться *(what = + в + prep.)*, не име́ть *(what = gen.)*; 2. *(not have enough of)* не хвата́ть *(person lacking = dat., thing lacked = gen.)*, недостава́ть *(person lacking = dat., thing lacked = gen.)*.

lack *n* недоста́ток, отсу́тствие ♦ **~ of love** недоста́ток любви́ ♦ **I feel so disillusioned by your lack of** *(1)* **commitment /** *(2)* **sensitivity /** *(3)* **affection /** *(4)* **attention.** Я так разочаро́ван *(ж: разочаро́вана)* *(1)* ...твое́й необяза́тельностью. / *(2)* ...отсу́тствием у тебя́ понима́ния мои́х чувств. / *(3)* ...отсу́тствием у тебя́ не́жности / *(4)* внима́ния.

lad *n (boy)* ма́льчик; *(young man)* молодо́й челове́к.

lady *n* же́нщина, ле́ди, да́ма *(See also* **woman, female** *and* **girl**) ♦ **above-average ~** незауря́дная же́нщина ♦ **city-country ~** же́нщина, лю́бящая как городску́ю, так и дереве́нскую жизнь *(explanation)* ♦ **classy ~** кла́ссная же́нщина ♦ **compassionate ~** сострада́тельная же́нщина ♦ **country ~** дереве́нская же́нщина ♦ **energetic ~** энерги́чная же́нщина ♦ **dragon ~** же́нщина-драко́н ♦ **full-figured ~** по́лная же́нщина ♦ **fun ~** весёлая же́нщина ♦ **homegrown ~** ме́стная же́нщина ♦ **~ of high energy** о́чень энерги́чная же́нщина ♦ **~ with a special spark** же́нщина с осо́бенной и́скоркой ♦ **nice ~** прия́тная же́нщина ♦ **old-fashioned ~** же́нщина ста́рой зака́лки ♦ **optimistic ~** оптимисти́чная же́нщина ♦ **outgoing ~** же́нщина-экстрове́рт ♦ **romantic ~** романти́ческая же́нщина ♦ **social ~** же́нщина, лю́бящая встреча́ться с друзья́ми *(1 term)* ♦ *(1,2)* **stylish ~** *(1)* мо́дная / *(2)* шика́рная же́нщина ♦ **submissive ~** поко́рная же́нщина ♦ **true ~** настоя́щая да́ма ♦ **uninhibited ~** же́нщина без ко́мплексов ♦ **unique ~** уника́льная же́нщина ♦ **vivacious ~** жива́я же́нщина ♦ **well-groomed ~** хорошо́ выгля́дящая же́нщина.

> ### lady: phrases

Here's a small gift for my special lady. Э́то ма́ленький пода́рок для дорого́й мне же́нщины. ♦ **I'm lucky to have found a lady with so much inner beauty.** Я сча́стлив, найдя́ же́нщину с тако́й вну́тренней красото́й. ♦ **I'm looking for a lady with a special spark.** Я ищу́ же́нщину с осо́бенной и́скоркой.

lady-killer *n (slang)* Дон Жуа́н, покори́тель же́нских серде́ц.

ladylove *n* зазно́ба.

Learn more about Russian customs in Appendix 15, page 782.

laid *pp*: ♦ **get ~** *(slang)* занима́ться любо́вью ♦ **I'm not interested in just getting laid.** Я не заинтересо́ван *(ж: заинтересо́вана)* то́лько в заня́тии любо́вью.

laid back *adj (slang) (easy-going)* споко́йный, -ая, -ое, -ые.

lambent *adj* сверка́ющий, -ая, -ее, -ие, лучи́стый, -ая, -ое, -ые ♦ **The dark lambent flame in your eyes thrills me to the core of my being.** Тёмное сверка́ющее пла́мя твои́х глаз возбужда́ет всё моё естество́.

lambikin *n (term of endearment)* не́жное обраще́ние к же́нщине *(explanation). (See Terms of Endearment on page 780.)*

lane *n* доро́жка; тропи́нка ♦ **lovers' ~** уединённая доро́га, тропа́ или тропи́нка, где любо́вники мо́гут занима́ться любо́вью *(explanation)* ♦ **To (1,2) go there again was a (3) journey / (4) trip down memory lane.** *(1)* Пойти́ *(on foot)* / *(2)* Пое́хать *(by veh.)* туда́ опя́ть бы́ло как *(3,4)* путеше́ствие в про́шлое.

language *n* язы́к ♦ **body ~** язы́к те́ла ♦ **foreign ~** иностра́нный язы́к ♦ *(1,2)* **nasty ~** *(1)* гря́зный / *(2)* непристо́йный язы́к ♦ **obscene ~** непристо́йный язы́к ♦ **~ of love** язы́к любви́ ♦ **find a common ~** находи́ть / найти́ о́бщий язы́к.

---
language: phrases

What (other) languages do you speak? На каки́х (ещё) языка́х Вы говори́те? ♦ **What languages do you know?** Каки́е языки́ Вы зна́ете? ♦ **I speak** *(1)* **two** / *(2)* **three** / *(3)* **four** / *(4)* **five languages.** Я говорю́ на *(1)* двух / *(2)* трёх / *(3)* четырёх / *(4)* пяти́ языка́х. ♦ **The languages I speak are Russian, Ukrainian, English, and French.** Языки́, на кото́рых я говорю́ : ру́сский, украи́нский, англи́йский и францу́зский. ♦ **I don't speak any (*[1]* foreign / *[2]* other) languages.** Я не говорю́ ни на каки́х (*[1]* иностра́нных / *[2]* други́х) языка́х. ♦ **Learning a new language will be a big challenge. But I will help you.** Изуче́ние но́вого языка́ бу́дет сло́жной зада́чей. Но я помогу́ тебе́. ♦ **The language of love is universal.** Язы́к любви́ универса́лен. ♦ **No language can** *(1)* **explain** / *(2)* **describe** / *(3)* **express my feelings (for you).** Никако́й язы́к не спосо́бен *(1)* объясни́ть / *(2)* описа́ть / *(3)* вы́разить мои́ чу́вства (к тебе́). ♦ **I'm going to fill you with so much passion that you'll be saying things in languages that don't exist in this world.** Я напо́лню тебя́ тако́й стра́стью, что ты заговори́шь на языка́х, кото́рые не существу́ют в э́том ми́ре.

languid *adj* то́мный, -ая, -ое, -ые.

languidly *adv* то́мно.

languor *n* 1. *(dreaminess)* мечта́тельное состоя́ние; то́мность *f*; 2. *(lassitude)* исто́ма ♦ **blissful ~** блаже́нная исто́ма ♦ **pleasant ~** прия́тная исто́ма ♦ **How heavenly it would be to relish the warm, wonderful softness of your body in the languor of half-sleep.** Как сла́достно бы́ло бы наслажда́ться тёплой, замеча́тельной мя́гкостью твоего́ те́ла в то́мном полусне́.

languorous *adj* то́мный, -ая, -ое, -ые ♦ **We can spend languorous hours in each other's arms.** Мы мо́жем проводи́ть то́мные часы́ в объя́тиях друг дру́га.

lanky *adj* долговя́зый, -ая, -ое, -ие.

lap *n* 1. *(knees in sitting position)* коле́ни *pl*; 2. *(skirt)* подо́л *(ю́бки)* ♦ **sit on** *(1)* **my** / *(2)* **your ~** сиде́ть у *(1)* меня́ / *(2)* тебя́ на коле́нах.

large *adj* большо́й, -а́я, -о́е, -и́е.

large-breasted *adj* груда́стая, с большо́й гру́дью.

lashes *n, pl* ресни́цы *(See also* **eyelash**) ♦ *(1-3)* **false ~s** *(1)* накладны́е / *(2)* накле́енные / *(3)* иску́сственные ресни́цы ♦ **heavy ~s** тяжёлые ресни́цы ♦ **long ~s** дли́нные ресни́цы ♦ **thick ~s** густы́е ресни́цы.

lass *n* де́вушка.

A slash always denotes "or."
You can choose the numbered words before and after.

last *adj* 1. *(final)* после́дний, -яя, -ее, -ие; 2. *(previous in time)* про́шлый, -ая, -ое, -ые.

last *vi* 1. *(continue)* дли́ться; продолжа́ться; 2. *(endure)* продолжа́ть выде́рживать, вы́держать ♦ **I** *(1)* **hope /** *(2)* **pray that our love will last forever.** Я *(1)* наде́юсь / *(2)* молю́сь, чтобы наша́ любо́вь продолжа́лась ве́чно. ♦ **I want our love to last** *(1)* **...forever. /** *(2)* **...until the end of time.** Я хочу́, что́бы наша́ любо́вь дли́лась *(1)* ...ве́чно. / *(2)* ...до конца́ на́шей жи́зни. ♦ **Our marriage lasted only 3 years.** Наш брак дли́лся то́лько три го́да. ♦ **I don't know how I'm going to last another** *(1)* **day /** *(2)* **month /** *(3)* **week without you (here) (by my side).** Я не зна́ю, как я вы́держу ещё *(1)* ...оди́н день / *(2* ме́сяц... / *(3)* ...одну́ неде́лю... без тебя́ (здесь) (со мной).

last *n:* ♦ **at ~** наконе́ц ♦ **at long ~** в конце́ концо́в.

latch onto соедини́ться *(whom = + с + instr.)*, подцепля́ть / подцепи́ть *(onto what, whom = acc.)* ♦ **I'm so glad I latched onto you.** Я так рад *(ж: ра́да)*, что соедини́лся *(ж: соедини́лась)* с тобо́й.

late *adj* 1. *(not on time)* опозда́вший, -ая, -ее, -ие; 2. *(occuring late)* по́здний, -яя, -ее, -ие; 3. *(deceased)* поко́йный, -ая, -ое, -ые ♦ **be ~** опа́здывать / опозда́ть *(for what = +* на *+ acc.).*

late *adv* по́здно.

lately *adv* (в) после́днее вре́мя.

later по́зже.

latte *n* ко́фе-ла́тте.

Latvian *adj* латви́йский, -ая, -ое, -ие.

Latvian *n* 1. *(person)* латы́ш *m*, латы́шка *f (pl:* латыши́); 2. *(language)* латы́шский язы́к ♦ **speak ~** говори́ть по-латы́шски.

laugh *vi* смея́ться *(at what, whom = +* над *+ instr.)* ♦ **~ melodiously** мелоди́чно смея́ться ♦ **I laugh easily.** Я легко́ смею́сь. ♦ **I like a person who can laugh easily.** Мне нра́вятся лю́ди, кото́рые легко́ смею́тся. ♦ **I like a person with a ready laugh.** Мне нра́вится челове́к, всегда́ гото́вый смея́ться. ♦ **I like to laugh.** Я люблю́ смея́ться. ♦ **I'm able to laugh at myself.** Я спосо́бен *(ж: спосо́бна)* смея́ться над сами́м *(ж: само́й)* собо́й. ♦ **If you're looking for someone who likes to laugh and have a good time, then write to me.** Если Вы и́щете того́, кто лю́бит смех и хоро́шее времяпрепровожде́ние, тогда́ напиши́те мне. ♦ **Promise you won't burst out laughing.** Обеща́й, что не разрази́шься сме́хом.

laugh *n* смех ♦ **belly ~** смех до ко́лик в животе́ ♦ **melodic ~** мелоди́чный смех ♦ **sexy ~** сексуа́льный смех.

laughter *n* смех ♦ **contagious ~** зарази́тельный смех ♦ **continual ~** непреры́вный смех ♦ *(1,2)* **happy ~** *(1)* ра́достный / *(2)* счастли́вый смех ♦ **merry ~** весёлый смех ♦ **tender ~** не́жный смех ♦ **unbridled ~** необу́зданный смех ♦ **vivacious ~** живо́й смех ♦ **burst of ~** взрыв сме́ха ♦ **share ~** дели́ть / раздели́ть смех ♦ **I'm into laughter, adventure, and having fun.** Я челове́к, лю́бящий смех, приключе́ния и развлече́ния.

lava *n* ла́ва ♦ *(1,2)* **molten ~** *(1)* раскалённая / *(2)* распла́вленная ла́ва ♦ **rivers of ~** ре́ки ла́вы ♦ **The burning adoration of my lips will melt the pillars of your sophisticated charm into rivers of molten lava.** Мои́ пла́менные, обожа́ющие гу́бы превратя́т тверды́ню твое́й благопристо́йности в ре́ки распла́вленной ла́вы.

lavender *n* лава́нда.

lavish *adj* ще́дрый, -ая, -ое, -ые.

lavish *vt* осыпа́ть / осы́пать *(what = instr., on whom = acc.)*, расточа́ть / расточи́ть *(what = acc., on whom = dat.)*; излива́ть / изли́ть *(what = acc., on whom = +* на *+ acc.)* ♦ **You lavish me with praise. I don't deserve it.** Ты расточа́ешь мне похвалы́. Я не заслу́жи-

Common adult weights are given in Appendix 10, page 777.

ваю их. ♦ **No one has ever lavished so much praise on me.** Никто́ никогда́ не расточа́л мне так мно́го похва́л. ♦ **I'm going to lavish love and affection on you** *(3)* **...beyond your wildest dreams.** / *(4)* **...such as you have never imagined.** Я затоплю́ тебя́ свое́йлюбо́вью и не́жностью *(3)* ...сверх всех твои́х са́мых заве́тных жела́ний. / *(4)* ...так, как ты никогда́ не вообража́ла. ♦ **I want to spend all my days lavishing affection on you.** Я хочу́ провести́ все свои́ дни, расточа́я тебе́ не́жность. ♦ **I have such a vast reservoir of tender affection to lavish upon you.** У меня́ грома́дный запа́с любви́ и не́жности, и весь его́ я хочу́ изли́ть на тебя́. ♦ **When at last my mouth claims yours, I will lavish more kisses upon it than it has ever known before.** Когда́ наконе́ц мой рот встре́тится с твои́м, я подарю́ ему́ бо́льше поцелу́ев, чем он когда́-либо пре́жде получа́л.

lavishly *adv* ще́дро.

law *n* зако́н ♦ **immigration** ~ зако́н об иммигра́ции ♦ **Russian** ~ зако́н Росси́и ♦ **state** ~ зако́н шта́та ♦ **Ukrainian** ~ зако́н Украи́ны.

lawyer *n* адвока́т ♦ **divorce** ~ адвока́т по дела́м о разво́дах.

lay *vt* класть / положи́ть *(what = acc.)* ♦ **I lay all my love and all my life at your feet.** Я кладу́ всю мою́ любо́вь и всю мою́ жизнь к твои́м нога́м.

lazily *adv* лени́во.

laziness *n* лень *f.*

lazy *adj* лени́вый, -ая, -ое, -ые.

lead *n* ли́дерство ♦ **I'm the kind of person who likes to take the lead.** Я челове́к, лю́бящий брать ли́дерство. ♦ **I'm going to let you take the lead.** Я позво́лю тебе́ взять ли́дерство.

leader *n* ли́дер ♦ ~ **of the family** ли́дер семьи́

lean *adj (thin)* то́щий, -ая, -ее, -ие, худо́й, -а́я, -о́е, -ы́е, сухопа́рый, -ая, -ое, -ые.

lean *vi* прислоня́ться / прислони́ться, отки́дываться / отки́нуться, отклоня́ться / отклони́ться; наклоня́ться / наклони́ться.

leap *vi:* ♦ **I leaped into the marriage too quickly.** Я жени́лся *(ж: вы́скочила за́муж)* сли́шком бы́стро. ♦ **I leaped into the relationship too quickly.** Я вступи́л *(ж: вступи́ла)* в бли́зкие отноше́ния сли́шком бы́стро.

learn *vt* 1. *(gain knowledge, learn how)* вы́учить *(what = acc.)*; научи́ться *(what = dat.)*; 2. *(find out)* узнава́ть / узна́ть *(what = acc.)*.

learn *vi* учи́ться ♦ ~ **about** узнава́ть / узна́ть *(about what* = + о + *prep.)* ♦ **be willing to** ~ хоте́ть учи́ться.

least *adj* наиме́ньший, -ая, -ее, -ие, мале́йший, -ая, -ее, -ие.

least *adv (with adjectives)* наиме́нее; *(with verbs)* ме́ньше всего́ ♦ ~ **of all** ме́ньше всего́.

least *n* са́мое ме́ньшее, минима́льное коли́чество ♦ **at** ~ по кра́йней ме́ре; по ме́ньшей ме́ре; хотя́ бы ♦ **The least you could do is** *(1)* **...call** / *(2)* **tell me.** / *(3)* **...let me know.** По ме́ньшей ме́ре ты мо́жешь *(1)* ...позвони́ть / *(2)* сказа́ть мне. / *(3)* ...дать мне знать. ♦ **The least you could have done was** *(1)* **...call** / *(2)* **tell me.** / *(3)* **...let me know.** По ме́ньшей ме́ре, то, что ты могла́ *(ж: мог)* бы сде́лать - э́то *(1)* ...позвони́ть / *(2)* сказа́ть мне. / *(3)* ...дать мне знать.

leave *vt* 1. *(on foot)* уходи́ть / уйти́ *(what* = + из + *gen., whom* = + от+ *gen.)*; *(by vehicle)* уезжа́ть / уе́хать *(what* = + из + *gen., whom* = + от + *gen.)*; 2. *(not take)* оставля́ть / оста́вить *(what, whom = acc.)*; *(abandon)* покида́ть / поки́нуть *(what, whom = acc.)* ♦ ~ **alone** 1. *(leave unaccompanied)* оставля́ть / оста́вить одного́ *m* / одну́ *f (whom = acc.)*; 2. *(leave in peace)* оставля́ть / оста́вить *(whom = acc.)*.

---
leave: depart

Please (don't) leave. Пожа́луйста, (не) уходи́. ♦ **I don't want to leave.** Я не хочу́ уходи́ть. ♦ **I don't want you to leave.** Я не хочу́, что́бы ты уходи́ла *(ж: уходи́л)*. ♦

An italicized ж *in parentheses indicates a woman speaking.*

Why are you leaving? Почему́ ты ухо́дишь? ♦ **I'm leaving (because...).** Я ухожу́ (, потому́ что....).

| **leave:** *not take; abandon* |

I never want to leave *(1)* **...you.** */ (2)* **...your side.** Я не хочу́ никогда́ покида́ть *(1,2)* тебя́. ♦ **I will never leave** *(1)* **...you.** */ (2)* **...your side.** Я никогда́ не оста́влю *(1,2)* тебя́. ♦ **Please (don't) leave me.** Пожа́луйста, (не) оста́вь меня́. ♦ **I don't want you ever to leave me.** Я не хочу́, чтобы ты когда́-нибудь поки́нула *(ж: покѝнул)* меня́. ♦ **Whenever I leave you, it's like leaving my heart in tiny pieces.** Вся́кий раз, когда́ я оставля́ю тебя́, э́то разбива́ет моё се́рдце. ♦ **She left me for another** *(1)* **guy** */ (2)* **man.** Она́ оста́вила меня́ ра́ди *(1,2)* друго́го. ♦ **He left me for another woman.** Он оста́вил меня́ ра́ди друго́й же́нщины. ♦ **I** *(1)* **can't** */ (2)* **couldn't stand to leave you.** *(1)* Я не могу́... */ (2)* Я не смог *(ж: смогла́)* бы... вы́нести разлу́ку с тобо́й. ♦ **I give you my word, I'll never, ever, ever leave you again.** Я даю́ тебе́ сло́во, что я никогда́, никогда́ не оста́влю тебя́ опя́ть.

| **leave alone:** *unaccompanied* |

I'll never leave you alone. Я никогда́ не оста́влю тебя́ одну́. ♦ **Please don't leave me alone.** Пожа́луйста, не оставля́й меня́ одного́ *(ж: одну́)*. ♦ **I don't want to leave you alone.** Я не хочу́ оставля́ть тебя́ одну́ *(ж: одного́)*. ♦ **I'm afraid of what will happen if I leave you alone.** Я бою́сь того́, что случи́тся, е́сли я оста́влю тебя́ одну́ *(ж: одного́)*.

| **leave alone:** *in peace* |

I want to be left alone. 1. *(in solitude)* Я хочу́ оста́ться оди́н *(ж: одна́)*. 2. *(not be bothered)* Не меша́й мне. ♦ **Leave me alone.** Оста́вь меня́ в поко́е.

lech *n (slang) (lecher)* развра́тник.

lecher *n* развра́тник.

lecherous *adj* развра́тный, -ая, -ое, -ые, распу́тный, -ая, -ое, -ые.

lechery *n* развра́т, распу́тство.

leer *vi* смотре́ть / посмотре́ть с вожделе́нием *(at whom = +* на *+ acc.)*, броса́ть / бро́сить плотоя́дные взо́ры *(at whom = +* на *+ acc.)*.

leering *n (see Russian verb expressions under* **leer***)*.

left-leaning *adj* ле́вых полити́ческих взгля́дов.

left out: ♦ **I** *(1)* **feel** */ (2)* **felt (kind of) left out.** Я *(1)* чу́вствую / *(2)* чу́вствовал *(ж: чу́вствовала)* себя́ (немно́го) ли́шним *(ж: ли́шней)*.

left-handed: ♦ **~ person** левша́ ♦ **I'm left-handed.** Я левша́.

leg *n* нога́ ♦ **bare ~s** го́лые но́ги ♦ **beautiful ~s** краси́вые но́ги ♦ **bow ~s** кривы́е но́ги ♦ **cute little ~s** но́женьки ♦ *(1,2)* **fat ~s** *(1)* по́лные / *(2)* то́лстые но́ги ♦ **gorgeous ~s** прекра́сные но́ги ♦ *(1,2)* **heavy ~s** *(1)* по́лные / *(2)* то́лстые но́ги ♦ **left ~** ле́вая нога́ ♦ **great ~s** великоле́пные но́ги ♦ **little ~s** но́жки ♦ **long ~s** дли́нные но́ги ♦ **lovely ~s** краси́вые но́ги ♦ **marvelously shaped ~s** но́ги ди́вной фо́рмы ♦ **muscular ~s** мускули́стые но́ги ♦ **my ~s** мои́ но́ги ♦ **pretty ~s** очарова́тельные но́ги ♦ **right ~** пра́вая нога́ ♦ **shapely ~s** изя́щные но́ги ♦ **short ~s** коро́ткие но́ги ♦ **skinny ~s** худы́е но́ги ♦ *(1,2)* **slender ~s** *(1)* стро́йные / *(2)* то́нкие но́ги ♦ *(1,2)* **slim ~s** *(1)* стро́йные / *(2)* то́нкие но́ги ♦ **smooth ~s** гла́дкие но́ги ♦ **straight ~s** прямы́е но́ги ♦ **such beautiful ~s** таки́е краси́вые но́ги ♦ **sun-browned ~s** загоре́лые но́ги ♦ **(sun)tanned ~s** загоре́лые но́ги ♦ **thin ~s** худы́е но́ги ♦ **your ~s** *(familiar)* твои́ ноги́; *(polite)* Ва́ши но́ги ♦ **graceful curve of your ~s** изя́щная ли́ния твои́х ног ♦ **slenderness of your ~s** стро́йность твои́х ног.

| **leg:** *your beautiful legs* |

What *(1)* **beautiful** */ (2)* **gorgeous** */ (3)* **sexy** */ (4)* **fantastic legs (you have)!** Что за *(1)*

---

*Procedures for getting married to a Russian
are outlined in Appendix 18, page 787.*

прекра́сные / *(2)* великоле́пные / *(3)* сексуа́льные / *(4)* фантасти́ческие но́ги (у тебя́)!
♦ **You've got the** *(1)* **...best...** / *(2)* **...nicest** / *(3)* **sexiest** / *(4)* **most beautiful** / *(5)* **most gorgeous... legs I've ever seen.** У тебя́ *(1)* ...наилу́чшие... ...са́мые *(2)* изя́щные / *(3)* сексуа́льные / *(4)* прекра́сные / *(5)* великоле́пные... но́ги, кото́рые я когда́-либо ви́дел. ♦ **You have such beautiful legs.** У тебя́ таки́е прекра́сные но́ги. ♦ **How** *(1)* **beautiful** / *(2)* **sexy your legs are, sheathed in sheer, black stockings.** Как *(1)* прекра́сны / *(2)* сексуа́льны твои́ но́ги, обтя́нутые прозра́чными чёрными чулка́ми. ♦ **You look so sexy when you cross your legs**. Ты вы́глядишь так сексуа́льно, когда́ кладёшь но́гу на́ ногу.

leg: *what I want to do with your legs*
I want to nuzzle my face in your legs. Я хочу́ зары́ть лицо́ в твои́х нога́х. ♦ **How I'd love to rub my cheeks softly against the inside of your legs.** Как бы я хоте́л не́жно поте́ре́ться щека́ми по вну́тренней стороне́ твои́х ног. ♦ **I want to brush my lips across the tips of your breasts, down your stomach and along your legs.** Я хочу́ косну́ться губа́ми твои́х соско́в, спусти́ться к твоему́ животу́ и пробежа́ть вдоль твои́х ног. ♦ **I envy your stockings. They're wrapped around your legs all day. How I wish I could do the same.** Я зави́дую твои́м чулка́м. Они́ обёртывают твои́ но́ги весь день. Как бы я жела́л де́лать то́ же са́мое. ♦ **Your legs are going to be tap-dancing in the air.** Твои́ но́ги бу́дут танцева́ть чечётку в во́здухе. ♦ **When we lie side by side and our legs entwine, it never fails to rouse desire in me.** Когда́ мы лежи́м ря́дом и на́ши но́ги сплетены́, это всегда́ пробужда́ет страсть во мне.

leg: *my legs*
My legs went limp at the knees. Я почу́вствовал сла́бость в коле́нях. ♦ **I lost my** *(1)* **right** / *(2)* **left leg in** *(3)* **...the (Vietnam) war.** / *(4)* **...an accident.** Я потеря́л *(ж: потеря́ла)* *(1)* пра́вую / *(2)* ле́вую но́гу *(3)* ...на войне́ (во Вьетна́ме). / *(4)* ...в ава́рии.
leggy *adj* со стро́йными но́жками.
leisurely *adj* неторопли́вый, -ая, -ое, -ые, ме́дленный, -ая, -ое, -ые.
lens *n* ли́нза ♦ **contact ~es** конта́ктные ли́нзы.
Leo *(Jul. 23 - Aug. 22)* Лев *(23 ию́ля - 22 а́вгуста)*.
less *adj* ме́ньше ♦ **~ than 60 kg** < 60 кг, ме́ньше шести́десяти *(60)* килогра́ммов *(кг)*.
less *adv (with adjectives)* ме́нее; *(with verbs)* ме́ньше ♦ **love ~** люби́ть ме́ньше *(whom = acc.)*.
lesson *n* уро́к ♦ **bitter ~** жесто́кий уро́к.
let *vt* дава́ть / дать *(whom = dat.)*, позволя́ть / позво́лить *(whom = dat.)* ♦ **~ down** *vt* разоча́ро́вывать / разочарова́ть *(whom = acc.)*; подводи́ть / подвести́ *(whom = acc.)* ♦ **~ go** *vt* 1. *(thoughts)* выки́дывать / вы́кинуть *(из головы́)* *(what = acc.)*; 2. *(release)* выпуска́ть / вы́пустить *(what, whom = acc.)*, отпуска́ть / отпусти́ть *(what, whom = acc.)*; 3. *(allow to go)* позволя́ть / позво́лить идти́ *(whom = dat.)*, дава́ть / дать уйти́ *(whom = dat.)* ♦ **~ go** *vi* дава́ть / дать себе́ во́лю; дава́ть / дать во́лю свои́м чу́вствам ♦ **~** *(1)* **me** / *(2)* **you know** дава́ть / дать *(1)* мне / *(2)* тебе́ знать ♦ **~ oneself in for** вля́паться *(for what = + в + acc.)* ♦ **~ out** *vt* отпуска́ть / отпусти́ть *(what, whom = acc.)*.

let down:
I'll never let you down (again). Я никогда́ не разочару́ю тебя́ (опя́ть). ♦ **You (really) let me down.** Ты (действи́тельно) меня́ разочарова́ла *(ж: разочарова́л)*. ♦ **You build me up and then you let me down.** Ты снача́ла поднима́ешь мой дух, а пото́м всё разруша́ешь.

let go *[vt]:*
I never want to let you go. Я не хочу́ когда́-либо позво́лить тебе́ уйти́. ♦ **Don't ever let me go.** Не отпуска́й меня́ никогда́. ♦ **I'll never let you go.** Я никогда́ не позво́лю

*A list of conjugated Russian verbs is given
in Appendix 3 on page 699.*

тебе́ уйти́. ♦ **Why do you clamp down on your feelings? You need to open up and let yourself go.** Почему́ ты сде́рживаешь свои́ чу́вства? Тебе́ на́до раскры́ться и позво́-лить свои́м чу́вствам вы́йти нару́жу.

let go [vi]:

I have a hard time letting go. Мне тру́дно дать во́лю свои́м чу́вствам. ♦ **I can let go.** Я могу́ дать себе́ во́лю. ♦ **You have to learn to let yourself go. And I'm going to help you.** Ты должна́ научи́ться дава́ть себе́ во́лю. И я помогу́ тебе́. ♦ *(1)* **I want to...** / *(2)* **I'm going to...** **teach you how to let yourself go.** *(1)* Я хочу́ научи́ть... / *(2)* Я научу́... тебя́, как дать себе́ во́лю. ♦ **Just let yourself go and surrender to your *(1,2)* desire.** Про́сто позво́ль себе́ быть само́й собо́й и уступи́ *(1)* ...свое́й стра́сти. / *(2)* ...своему́ жела́нию.

let oneself in for:

I didn't realize what I was letting myself in for. Я не по́нял *(ж: поняла́),* во что вля́пался *(вля́палась).*

let out:

Cry if you need to. (It's okay.) Let it all out. Попла́чь, е́сли тебе́ э́то ну́жно. (Всё норма́льно.) Изба́вься от э́того.

let-down *n* разочарова́ние ♦ **big** ~ большо́е разочарова́ние.

lethargic *adj* вя́лый, -ая, -ое, -ые, со́нный, -ая, -ое, -ые.

lethargy *n* вя́лость *f.*

letter *n* письмо́ (*pl:* пи́сьма) ♦ **affectionate** ~ не́жное письмо́ ♦ **airmail** ~ письмо́ авиа-по́чтой ♦ **anonymous** ~ анони́мное письмо́ ♦ **brief** ~ коро́ткое письмо́ ♦ **contrite** ~ пока́янное письмо́ ♦ **desultory love** ~ несвя́зное любо́вное письмо́ ♦ **detailed** ~ подро́бное письмо́ ♦ **erotic** ~ эроти́ческое письмо́ ♦ **express** ~ сро́чное письмо́ ♦ **follow-up** ~ повто́рное письмо́ ♦ **funny** ~ 1. *(humorous)* смешно́е письмо́; 2. *(strange)* стра́нное письмо́ ♦ **important** ~ ва́жное письмо́ ♦ **interesting** ~ интере́сное письмо́ ♦ **last** ~ предыду́щее письмо́ ♦ ~ **by express mail** сро́чное письмо́ ♦ **long** ~ дли́нное письмо́ ♦ **love** ~ любо́вное письмо́ ♦ **my** ~ моё письмо́ ♦ **next** ~ сле́дующее письмо́ ♦ **official** ~ официа́льное письмо́ ♦ **obscene** ~ неприли́чное письмо́ ♦ **previous** ~ предыду́щее письмо́ ♦ **registered** ~ заказно́е письмо́ ♦ **sensuous** ~ чу́вственное письмо́ ♦ **sexy** ~ сексуа́льное письмо́ ♦ **short** ~ коро́ткое письмо́ ♦ **special delivery** ~ сро́чное письмо́ ♦ **steamy** ~ пла́менное письмо́ ♦ **sweet** ~ ми́лое письмо́ ♦ **tear-stained** ~ письмо́ с ка́плями слёз ♦ **terse** ~ кра́ткое письмо́ ♦ **this** ~ э́то письмо́ ♦ **undated** ~ недати́рованное письмо́ ♦ **your** ~ *(familiar)* твоё письмо́; *(polite)* Ва́ше письмо́.

letter: verb terms

answer *(1)* **my** / *(2)* **your** ~ отвеча́ть / отве́тить на *(1)* моё / *(2)* твоё письмо́ ♦ **compose a** ~ составля́ть / соста́вить письмо́ ♦ **deliver a** ~ доставля́ть / доста́вить письмо́ ♦ **drop the** ~ **in the mailbox** броса́ть / бро́сить письмо́ в я́щик, опуска́ть / опусти́ть письмо́ в я́щик ♦ **enclose in the** ~ вкла́дывать / вложи́ть в письмо́ *(what = acc.)* ♦ **exchange** ~**s** обме́ниваться пи́сьмами *(with whom = + с + instr.)* ♦ **forward the** ~ пересыла́ть / пересла́ть письмо́ *(to whom = dat.)* ♦ **get** *(1)* **my** / *(2)* **your** ~ получа́ть / получи́ть *(1)* моё / *(2)* твоё письмо́ ♦ **give a** ~ *(from someone)* передава́ть / переда́ть письмо́ *(to whom = dat.)* ♦ **mail the** ~ броса́ть / бро́сить письмо́ в я́щик, опуска́ть / опусти́ть письмо́ в я́щик ♦ **print out the** ~ *(computer)* распеча́тывать / распеча́тать письмо́ ♦ **put the** ~ **in the mail** *(drop in the box)* броса́ть / бро́сить письмо́ в я́щик, опуска́ть / опусти́ть письмо́ в я́щик; *(send)* посыла́ть / посла́ть письмо́, отправля́ть / отпра́вить письмо́ ♦ **read** *(1)* **my** / *(2)* **your** ~ чита́ть / прочита́ть *(1)* моё / *(2)* твоё письмо́ ♦ **receive** *(1)* **my**

For Russian adjectives, the masculine form is spelled out,
followed by the feminine, neuter and plural endings.

/ *(2)* **your** ~ получа́ть / получи́ть *(1)* моё / *(2)* твоё письмо́ ♦ **rewrite a** ~ перепи́сывать / переписа́ть письмо́ ♦ **send a** ~ посыла́ть / посла́ть письмо́ *(to whom = dat.)*, отправля́ть / отпра́вить письмо́ *(to whom = dat.)* ♦ **take the** ~ **to the post office** относи́ть / отнести́ письмо́ на по́чту ♦ **tear up the** ~ разорва́ть письмо́ ♦ **translate** *(1)* **my** / *(2)* **your** ~ переводи́ть / перевести́ *(1)* моё / *(2)* твоё письмо́ ♦ **wait for your** ~ ждать твоего́ письма́ ♦ **write a** ~ писа́ть / написа́ть письмо́ *(to whom = dat.)*.

letter: other terms

at the *(1)* **beginning** / *(2)* **end of your** ~ в *(1)* нача́ле / *(2)* конце́ твоего́ письма́ ♦ **beginning of the** ~ нача́ло письма́ ♦ **contents of the** ~ содержа́ние письма́ ♦ **copy of** *(1)* **my** / *(2)* **your** ~ ко́пия *(1)* моего́ / *(2)* твоего́ письма́ ♦ **date of** *(1)* **my** / *(2)* **your** ~ да́та *(1)* моего́ / *(2)* твоего́ письма́ ♦ **end of the** ~ коне́ц письма́ ♦ **ending of the** ~ оконча́ние письма́ ♦ **in** *(1)* **my** / *(2)* **your** ~ в *(1)* моём / *(2)* твоём письме́ ♦ **packet of** ~**s** па́чка пи́сем.

letter: receiving letters

Did you *(1)* **get** / *(2)* **receive my letter?** Ты получи́ла *(ж: получи́л)* моё письмо́? ♦ **I wrote you a letter. Did you** *(1)* **get** / *(2)* **receive it?** Я написа́л *(ж: написа́ла)* тебе́ письмо́. Ты *(1,2)* получи́ла *(ж: получи́л)* его́? ♦ **I** *(1)* **got** / *(2)* **received your letter.** Я *(1,2)* получи́л *(ж: получи́ла)* твоё письмо́. ♦ **I didn't** *(1)* **get** / *(2)* **receive your letter (yet).** Я (ещё) не *(1,2)* получи́л *(ж: получи́ла)* твоё письмо́. ♦ **Another of your uplifting letters arrived today.** Ещё одно́ твоё поднима́ющее дух письмо́ пришло́ сего́дня. ♦ **Now I have another one of your letters, filled with your sweet, gentle, loving, caring spirit.** Тепе́рь у меня́ есть ещё одно́ твоё письмо́, напо́лненное твое́й не́жной, мя́гкой любя́щей, забо́тливой душо́й. ♦ **I hope that your beautiful** *(1)* **dark** / *(2)* **blue eyes are shining with happiness to receive my letter.** Я наде́юсь, что твои́ прекра́сные *(1)* тёмные / *(2)* голубы́е глаза́ заси́яют сча́стьем, когда́ ты полу́чишь моё письмо́. ♦ **Your (**[1]** sweet** / **[2]** loving** / **[3]** love-filled** / **[4]** wonderful** / **[5]** heart-warming) letter** *(6)* **came** / *(7)* **arrived** *(8)* **yesterday** / *(9)* **this** *(10)* **morning** / *(11)* **afternoon** / *(12)* **evening.** Твоё (**[1]** ми́лое / **[2]** любя́щее / **[3]** ...по́лное любви́... / **[4]** замеча́тельное / **[5]** ...согрева́ющее се́рдце...) письмо́ *(6)* пришло́ / *(7)* при́было *(8)* вчера́ / *(9)* сего́дня *(10)* у́тром / *(11)* днём / *(12)* ве́чером.

letter: so happy to hear from you

(1) **I was (so) happy** / *(2)* **overjoyed...** / *(3)* **I was (so) delighted** / *(4)* **elated ... to find your letter in my box (**[5]** this** / **[6]** yesterday** [7] **morning** / [8] **afternoon** / [9] **evening).** *(1)* Я был *(ж: была́)* (так) ...сча́стлив *(ж: сча́стлива)*,... / *(2)* ...перепо́лнен *(ж: перепо́лнена)* ра́достью,... / *(3)* Я был *(ж: была́)* в (тако́м) восто́рге,... / *(4)* Я так обра́довался *(ж: обра́довалась)*,... когда́ нашёл *(ж: нашла́)* в почто́вом я́щике твоё письмо́ (**[5]** сего́дня / **[6]** вчера́ [7] у́тром / [8] днём / [9] ве́чером). ♦ **You can't imagine how happy I was to get your letter (and your photo). My heart is still rejoicing.** Ты не мо́жешь вообрази́ть, как сча́стлив я был *(ж: как сча́стлива я была́)*, получи́в твоё письмо́ (и твою́ фотогра́фию). Моё се́рдце до сих пор ра́дуется. ♦ *(1)* **I've been on a cloud...** / *(2)* **My head's been in the clouds... ever since I read your letter.** *(1)* Я был *(ж: была́)*... / *(2)* Моё се́рдце бы́ло... на облака́х, с тех пор, как я прочёл *(ж: прочла́)* твоё письмо́. ♦ **I love** *(1)* **...your letters.** / *(2)* **...to get letters from you.** Я люблю́ *(1)* ...твои́ пи́сьма. / *(2)* ...получа́ть твои́ пи́сьма. ♦ **I kiss you a thousand times for the** *(1)* **sweet** / *(2)* **wonderful** / *(3)* **love-filled** / *(4)* **precious letter that you** *(5)* **sent** / *(6)* **wrote to me.** Я целу́ю тебя́ ты́сячу раз за *(1)* ми́лое / *(2)* удиви́тельное / *(3)* по́лное любви́ / *(4)* драгоце́нное письмо́, кото́рое ты *(5)* посла́ла / *(6)* написа́ла мне. ♦ **My heart breaks into rapture whenever I find a letter from you in my box.** Моё се́рдце наполня́ется восто́ргом всегда́, когда́ я нахожу́ письмо́ от тебя́ в почто́вом я́щике. ♦ **My heart ignites in** *(1)* **celebration** / *(2)* **delight** / *(3)* **ecstasy** / *(4)* **jubilation every time I get a letter from you.** Моё се́рдце *(1)* ...загора́ется ра́достью / *(2)* восто́ргом... / *(3)*

See Appendix 19 for notes on sending mail to Russia and Ukraine.

...вспы́хивает в экста́зе... / *(4)* ...лику́ет... ка́ждый раз, когда́ я получа́ю письмо́ от тебя́.
♦ **Happiness for me is getting letters from you.** Сча́стье для меня́ получа́ть твои́ пи́сьма.

---
letter: *the effect your letter had on me*

Your letter *(1)* **...warmed my heart more than I can tell you.** / *(2)* **...really brightened my mood.** / *(3)* **...made a bright spring day even brighter and more beautiful for me.** / *(4)* **...set my heart aglow.** / *(5,6)* **...has plunged me into a joyful delirium.** / *(7)* **...really shook me.** Твоё письмо́ *(1)* ...согре́ло моё се́рдце бо́лее, чем я могу́ вы́разить. / *(2)* ...действи́тельно подня́ло моё настрое́ние. / *(3)* ...сде́лало да́же я́ркий весе́нний день ещё я́рче и прекра́снее. / *(4)* ...заста́вило моё се́рдце пыла́ть. / *(5)* ...погрузи́ло / *(6)* вве́ргло меня́ в ра́достное исступле́ние. / *(7)* ...про́сто потрясло́ меня́. ♦ **It is beyond my power to describe to you the tremendous effect that your dear, sweet, loving letter has had upon me.** Я не в состоя́нии описа́ть тебе́ то огро́мное впечатле́ние, кото́рое твоё дорого́е, не́жное, лю́бящее письмо́ произвело́ на меня́. ♦ **This letter of yours was so unexpected. Your** *(1)* **sweet /** *(2)* **beautiful words of love have** *(3)* **...set my heart completely aquiver. /** *(4)* **...sent my heart into utter delight.** Это письмо́ от тебя́ бы́ло так неожи́данно. Твои́ *(1)* не́жные / *(2)* прекра́сные слова́ любви́ *(3)* ...заставля́ют моё се́рдце трепета́ть. / *(4)* ...вызыва́ют в моём се́рдце по́лный восто́рг. ♦ **Your letter** *(1)* **...brought me more joy...** / *(2)* **...gave me more delight... than anything else in the world could do, except you in person.** Твоё письмо́ *(1)* ...принесло́ мне бо́льше ра́дости,... / *(2)* ...доста́вило мне бо́льше удово́льствия,... чем что́-либо ещё в ми́ре могло́ бы, кро́ме тебя́ само́й *(ж: самого́)*. ♦ **When I** *(1)* **found /** *(2)* **read your letter, I felt shock waves of pure, unadulterated joy.** Когда́ я *(1)* нашёл *(ж: нашла́)* / *(2)* чита́л *(ж: чита́ла)* твоё письмо́, то ощути́л *(ж: ощути́ла)* во́лны и́стинного, настоя́щего ликова́ния. ♦ **It really warmed my heart and lifted up my spirits to get your letter.** Что действи́тельно согре́ло моё се́рдце и по́дняло настрое́ние, так э́то -- твоё письмо́. ♦ **How your letter has** *(1)* **raised /** *(2)* **uplifted my spirits.** Как твоё письмо́ *(1,2)* подня́ло мой дух. ♦ **It was a tonic for my spirits to get your letter.** Твоё письмо́ бы́ло эликси́ром для моего́ ду́ха. ♦ **I'm still in a daze from your letter.** Я всё ещё в ошеломле́нии от твоего́ письма́.

---
letter: *the effect your letters have on me in general*

Your letters *(1)* **...warm my heart more than you can ever know. /** *(2)* **...flood my life with** *(3)* **sunbeams /** *(4)* **sunshine. /** *(5)* **...(really) keep me going. /** *(6)* **...sustain me through my loneliness. /** *(7)* **...lift my spirits and brighten my day (more than I can describe to you). /** *(8)* **...release a flood of warm,** *(9)* **tender /** *(10)* **loving feelings for you in my heart. /** *(11)* **...always give me such a warm feeling. /** *(12)* **...always fill my heart with love for you. /** *(13)* **...make me feel very close to you.** Твои́ пи́сьма *(1)* ...согрева́ют моё се́рдце бо́льше, чем ты да́же мо́жешь предста́вить. / *(2)* ...освеща́ют мою́ жизнь *(3)* ...со́лнечными луча́ми. / *(4)* ...со́лнечным све́том. / *(5)* ...(действи́тельно) подде́рживают моё существова́ние. / *(6)* ...подде́рживают меня́ в моём одино́честве. / *(7)* ...поднима́ют мой дух и освеща́ют мой день (бо́лее, чем я могу́ описа́ть тебе́). / *(8)* ...высвобожда́ют в моём се́рдце пото́к тёплых, *(9)* не́жных / *(10)* лю́бящих чувств к тебе́. / *(11)* ...всегда́ вызыва́ют во мне таки́е тёплые чу́вства. / *(12)* ...всегда́ наполня́ют моё се́рдце любо́вью к тебе́. / *(13)* ...вызыва́ют во мне чу́вство большо́й бли́зости к тебе́. ♦ **Your letters are** *(1)* **...a source of** *(2)* **constant /** *(3)* **immeasurable /** *(4)* **infinite joy to me. /** *(5,6)* **...so uplifting for me.** Твои́ пи́сьма *(1)* ...-- э́то исто́чник *(2)* постоя́нной / *(3)* неизмери́мой / *(4)* бесконе́чной ра́дости для меня́. / *(5)* ...так поднима́ют мой дух. / *(6)* ...так поднима́ют моё настрое́ние. ♦ **Your letters, the things you say in them, stir up such huge waves of tender, warm feelings in me toward you.** Твои́ пи́сьма, то, что ты говори́шь в них, возбужда́ют во мне таки́е огро́мные во́лны не́жных, тёплых чувств к тебе́. ♦ **Letters from you make**

> *When terms are listed after a main word, a tilde ~*
> *is used to indicate the main word.*

a **bright day even brighter.** Твои пи́сьма де́лают я́ркий день ещё я́рче. ♦ **A letter from you** *(1)* **...turns the most dismal day into sunshine.** / *(2)* **...sets my heart aglow.** Письмо́ от тебя́ *(1)* ...превраща́ет са́мый мра́чный день в день, напо́лненный со́лнечным све́том. / *(2)* ...заставля́ет моё се́рдце пыла́ть. ♦ **Nothing** *(1)* **brightens** / *(2)* **sparkles up my day like a letter from you.** Ничто́ так не *(1)* освеща́ет / *(2)* озаря́ет мой день, как письмо́ от тебя́. ♦ *(1)* **If you only knew...** / *(2)* **I can't tell you... how much your letters** *(3)* **(up)lift** / *(4)* **raise my spirits.** *(1)* Е́сли бы то́лько зна́ла,... / *(2)* Я да́же не могу́ описа́ть тебе́,... как си́льно твои́ пи́сьма *(3,4)* поднима́ют мой дух. ♦ **My spirits are so uplifted by your letters.** Твои́ пи́сьма так поднима́ют мой дух. ♦ **Reading one of your letters is like** *(1)* **...quaffing a magic elixir — it just makes me feel totally good through and through.** / *(2)* **...climbing into a nice, warm bath and just sitting and luxuriating in it.** Чте́ние ка́ждого из твои́х пи́сем -- э́то как *(1)* ...большо́й глото́к маги́ческого эликси́ра, оно́ наполня́ет меня́ замеча́тельным чу́вством. / *(2)* ...погрузи́ться в прия́тную, тёплую ва́нну и про́сто сиде́ть и наслажда́ться. ♦ **Remember to smile for me in your photos. I want to see the same kind of sunshine on your face that your letters bring to my heart.** Не забу́дь улыба́ться на свои́х фо́то. Я хочу́ ви́деть тако́й же со́лнечный свет на твоём лице́, како́й твои́ пи́сьма прино́сят в моё се́рдце. ♦ **You make me feel so good and so warm with all the nice things you say to me in your letters.** Мне так хорошо́ и тепло́ от всех прия́тных слов, обращённых ко мне в твои́х пи́сьмах. ♦ **When I read your letters, I feel with my heart how much goodness and sweetness and love there is in you.** Когда́ чита́ю твои́ пи́сьма, я всем се́рцем чу́вствую, как мно́го в тебе́ доброты́, не́жности и любви́. ♦ **I read your letter and then went to bed and it was just like you were there in bed next to me.** Я прочита́л *(ж: прочита́ла)* твоё письмо́ и пошёл *(ж: пошла́)* спать и каза́лось, как бу́дто ты здесь в посте́ли ря́дом со мной.

letter: *how many times have I read your letter?*

I (have) read your letter *(1)* **...over and over.** / *(2)* **...many times(, I can't even remember how many times).** / *(3)* **...8 times from beginning to end.** Я перечи́тывал *(ж: перечи́тывала)* твоё письмо́ *(1)* ...сно́ва и сно́ва. / *(2)* ...мно́го раз(, не могу́ да́же вспо́мнить ско́лько). / *(3)* ...во́семь раз от нача́ла до конца́. ♦ **I read your letters over and over again and I never cease to** *(1)* **cherish** / *(2)* **treasure them.** Я перечи́тываю твои́ пи́сьма сно́ва и сно́ва и всегда́ бу́ду *(1,2)* дорожи́ть и́ми. ♦ **I'm reading all your letters over and over as I wait for the next one.** Я перечи́тываю все твои́ пи́сьма опя́ть и опя́ть в то вре́мя, как я ожида́ю сле́дующего. ♦ **I read each one of your letters over and over again.** Я перечи́тываю ка́ждое твоё письмо́ опя́ть и опя́ть.

letter: *your letter(s)*

That was a *(1)* **wonderful** / *(2)* **sweet** / *(3)* **heart-warming letter that you wrote to me.** Письмо́, кото́рое ты написа́ла *(ж: написа́л)* мне, *(1)* ...замеча́тельное. / *(2)* ...ми́лое. / *(3)* ...согрева́ет се́рдце. ♦ **That was the** *(1)* **nicest** / *(2)* **sweetest** / *(3)* **most wonderful** / *(4)* **most heart-warming** / *(5)* **most loving letter anyone has ever written to me.** Э́то бы́ло са́мое *(1)* ми́лое / *(2)* сла́дкое / *(3)* замеча́тельное / *(4)* ...согрева́ющее се́рдце... / *(5)* лю́бящее письмо́, кото́рое я когда́-либо получа́л *(ж: получа́ла)*. ♦ **No one has ever composed such a** *(1)* **beautiful** / *(2)* **heart-warming** / *(3)* **sweet letter to me before.** Никто́ никогда́ пре́жде не сочиня́л тако́го *(1)* ...прекра́сного... / *(2)* ...согрева́ющего се́рдце... / *(3)* ...не́жного... письма́ ко мне. ♦ **Always in your letters there is present the feeling of love and devotion.** В твои́х пи́сьмах всегда́ прису́тствуют чу́вства любви́ и пре́данности. ♦ **Please never give a thought to how you write to me in English. You write wonderful letters.** Пожа́луйста, никогда́ не ду́май о том, как ты пи́шешь мне на англи́йском. Ты пи́шешь великоле́пные пи́сьма. ♦ **How should I interpret your letter?** Как я до́лжен *(ж: должна́)*

A list of common places with their grammatical endings is given in Appendix 7, page 763.

расце́нивать твоё письмо́? ♦ **In your letter you said...** В своём письме́ ты сказа́ла *(ж: сказа́л)...*

---
letter: *I need your letters*

I need your letters (and the dreams they bring to sustain me through the long, empty nights). Мне нужны́ твои́ пи́сьма (и мечты́, кото́рые они́ прино́сят, что́бы подде́рживать меня́ дли́нными, одино́кими ноча́ми). ♦ **Your letters mean a lot to me.** Твои́ пи́сьма зна́чат мно́го для меня́.

---
letter: *waiting for your letters*

I look forward *(1,2)* eagerly to getting your next letter. Я *(1)* ...нетерпели́во / *(2)* ...с нетерпе́нием... жду твоего́ сле́дующего письма́. ♦ **You have no idea with what *(1)* ...joy and eagerness... / *(2)* ...fervent yearning... I wait for every letter from you.** Ты не представля́ешь, с *(1)* ...како́й ра́достью и нетерпе́нием... / *(2)* ...каки́м стра́стным жела́нием... я жду ка́ждого твоего́ письма́. ♦ **It seemed like years since I had gotten your last letter.** Каза́лось, прошли́ го́ды с тех пор, как я получи́л *(ж: получи́ла)* твоё после́днее письмо́. ♦ **Two weeks without a letter from you are in reality a long, slow torture.** Две неде́ли без письма́ от тебя́ действи́тельно дли́тельная, ме́дленная му́ка. ♦ **The days between your letters go by so slowly and so emptily.** Дни ме́жду твои́ми пи́сьмами прохо́дят так ме́дленно и так пу́сто.

---
letter: *no letter - I'm sad*

My world is grey. I feel so *(1)* dismal / *(2)* sad / *(3)* downhearted / *(4)* miserable. There was no letter from you (again) today. Мой мир сер. Я так *(1)* угнетён *(ж: угнетена́)* / *(2)* печа́лен *(ж: печа́льна)* / *(3)* уны́л *(ж: уны́ла)* / *(4)* несча́стен *(ж: несча́стна)*. Сего́дня от тебя́ (опя́ть) нет письма́. ♦ **It's been so long since I had a letter from you.** Так мно́го вре́мени прошло́ с тех пор, как я получи́л *(ж: получи́ла)* твоё письмо́. ♦ **When I go to my mailbox and find no letter from you inside, my whole day seems *(1)* dreary / *(2)* empty.** Когда́ я иду́ к моему́ почто́вому я́щику и не нахожу́ в нём письма́ от тебя́, це́лый день ка́жется *(1)* мра́чным / *(2)* пусты́м.

---
letter: *this letter to you*

All day long after reading your ad in the personals (section) I've been aching to get home and write you this letter. Весь день по́сле прочте́ния Ва́шего объявле́ния в отде́ле знако́мств я стреми́лся прийти́ домо́й и написа́ть Вам э́то письмо́. ♦ **I feel impelled by the acute longing in my heart to write you this letter.** Стра́стное стремле́ние моего́ се́рдца заставля́ет меня́ написа́ть Вам э́то письмо́. ♦ **I feel (*[1]* rather / *[2]* very) awkward writing a letter to someone I don't know.** Я испы́тываю (*[1]* ...до не́которой сте́пени... / *[2]* ...си́льное...) неудо́бство писа́ть письмо́ челове́ку, кото́рого я не зна́ю. ♦ **I've never composed a letter like this before.** Я никогда́ пре́жде не сочиня́л *(ж: сочиня́ла)* тако́го письма́, как э́то. ♦ **I hope this letter *(1)* ...conveys my meaning as I intend it. / *(2)* ...doesn't sound corny to you.** Я наде́юсь, что э́то письмо́ *(1)* ...то́чно передаёт то, что я ду́маю. / *(2)* ...не пока́жется бана́льным тебе́. ♦ **This is just a short letter to reach across the miles and touch you.** Это то́лько коро́ткое письмо́, кото́рое пройдёт ми́ли и коснётся тебя́. ♦ **May this letter come to you as a white dove heralding its love on a bright, spring day.** Пусть моё письмо́ прилети́т к тебе́, как бе́лый го́лубь, воспева́ющий свою́ любо́вь в я́ркий, весе́нний день. ♦ **Forgive me for writing such a steamy letter, but my thoughts of you mixed together with my feelings for you arouse passions in me that are difficult to contain.** Прости́ меня́ за тако́е чу́вственное письмо́, но мои́ мы́сли о тебе́, вме́сте с чу́вствами к тебе́, пробужда́ют во мне страсть, кото́рую тру́дно сдержа́ть. ♦ **I was thinking about you so much that I had to stop my work and write this letter to you.** Я так мно́го ду́мал *(ж: ду́мала)* о тебе́, что был вы́нужден *(ж: была́ вы́нуждена)* прекра-

---

A list of abbreviations used in the dictionary is given on page 10.

ти́ть рабо́тать и написа́ть тебе́ э́то письмо́. ♦ **If you don't answer my letter, you're going to miss out on meeting someone with a very warm, loving heart and affectionate nature.** Если Вы не отве́тите на моё письмо́, то упу́стите возмо́жность встре́чи с челове́ком с о́чень тёплым, лю́бящим се́рдцем и не́жной душо́й. ♦ **Now I will close my letter, but not before I tell you that I adore you and think about you every day and dream about you every night.** Тепе́рь я зако́нчу своё письмо́, но не ра́ньше, чем скажу́ тебе́, что я обожа́ю тебя́, ду́маю о тебе́ ка́ждый день и мечта́ю о тебе́ ка́ждую ночь. ♦ **I loved your "Sweet kisses" and with this letter I send you two for every one that you sent me.** Мне о́чень понра́вились твои́ «Сла́дкие поцелу́и» и с э́тим письмо́м я посыла́ю тебе́ по два на ка́ждый, кото́рый ты посла́ла *(ж: посла́л)* мне. ♦ **This letter is sealed with a kiss.** Это письмо́ запеча́тано поцелу́ем. ♦ **I'm sealing this letter with a kiss.** Я запеча́тываю э́то письмо́ поцелу́ем.

> **letter:** *writing to you*

I hope my letters don't bore you. Наде́юсь, мои́ пи́сьма не наску́чили тебе́. ♦ **I feel** *(1,2)* **restricted when I write to you, because I'm afraid** *(3)* **...someone... / (4)... your mother... / (5) ...your father... will read my letters.** Я чу́вствую *(1)* сде́ржанность / *(2)* стеснён- ность, когда́ пишу́ тебе́, потому́ что бою́сь, что *(3)* ...кто́-то... / *(4)* ...твоя́ ма́ма... / *(5)* ...твой па́па... прочита́ет мои́ пи́сьма.

level-headed *adj* разу́мный, -ая, -ое, -ые, осмы́сленный, -ая, -ое, -ые.

levity *n* легкомы́слие, неуме́стная весёлость ♦ **I'm prone to frequent levity.** Я скло́нен *(ж: скло́нна)* к ча́стому легкомы́слию.

lewd *adj* похотли́вый, -ая, -ое, -ые, развра́тный, -ая, -ое, -ые, распу́тный, -ая, -ое, -ые.

liaison *n* связь *f* ♦ **amorous** ~ любо́вная связь ♦ **electronic** ~ связь по интерне́ту ♦ **romantic** ~ романти́ческая связь.

liberal *adj* либера́льный, -ая, -ое, -ые ♦ **politically** ~ полити́чески либера́льный, -ая, -ое, -ые, с либера́льными полити́ческими взгля́дами ♦ **religiously** ~ либера́льный (-ая, -ое, -ые) к рели́гиям.

liberty *n* 1. *(freedom)* свобо́да; 2. *(excessive familiarity)* во́льность *f* ♦ **take ~s** позволя́ть / позво́лить себе́ во́льности *(with whom = + с + instr.)* ♦ **take the ~** брать / взять на себя́ сме́лость, осме́ливаться / осме́литься ♦ **I hope you won't mind my taking the liberty of writing to you in this way.** Я наде́юсь, Вы не бу́дете возража́ть, что я взял на себя́ сме́лость писа́ть Вам в э́том ду́хе. ♦ **You had no right to take liberties (with me).** У тебя́ нет никаки́х прав позволя́ть себе́ во́льности (со мной).

libido *n* либи́до ♦ **great** ~ великоле́пное либи́до ♦ **healthy** ~ здоро́вое либи́до ♦ **high** ~ си́льное либи́до ♦ **strong** ~ си́льное либи́до.

Libra *(Sep. 23 - Oct. 22)* Весы́ *(23 сентября́ - 22 октября́).*

license *n* разреше́ние, лице́нзия ♦ **driver's** ~ води́тельские права́ ♦ **marriage** ~ разреше́- ние на брак ♦ **Where do we** *(1)* **apply / (2) file for a marriage license?** Куда́ мы обрати́мся за разреше́нием на брак? ♦ **Here in my state we will have to get a marriage license.** Здесь в моём шта́те нам необходи́мо бу́дет получи́ть разреше́ние на брак.

lick *vt* лиза́ть *(what = acc.)* ♦ **Fire licks through my veins whenever I think of your soft, warm, beautiful, luscious body and the oceans of ecstasy that it contains.** Ого́нь ли́жет мои́ ве́ны вся́кий раз, когда́ я ду́маю о твоём мя́гком, тёплом, прекра́сном, со́чном те́ле и океа́нах экста́за, кото́рые оно́ соде́ржит. ♦ **I'd love to lick you softly all over.** Я хоте́л бы лиза́ть тебя́ не́жно всю.

licking *n* лиза́ние.

lie *vi* 1. *(recline)* лежа́ть; 2. *(speak untruthfully)* лгать / солга́ть *(about what = + о + prep., to whom = dat.)* ♦ ~ **back** отки́нуться ♦ ~ **down** ложи́ться / лечь.

> *The accents on Russian words are to show how to pronounce them.*
> *You don't have to copy the accents when writing to someone.*

lie: recline

I want to lie with you in my arms. Я хочу́ лежа́ть с тобо́й в мои́х объя́тиях. ♦ **How heavenly it is when you lie snugly in my arms afterward, fragrant with love, drifting into sleep.** Како́е э́то блаже́нство, когда́ пото́м ты лежи́шь, ую́тно устро́ившись в мои́х объя́тиях, па́хнущая любо́вью, погружа́ющаяся в сон.

lie: speak untruthfully

(1,2) **You're lying (to me).** *(1)* Ты говори́шь (мне) непра́вду. / *(2)* Ты лжёшь (мне). ♦ *(1,2)* **I'm not lying (to you).** *(1)* Я не говорю́ (тебе́) непра́вду. / *(2)* Я не лгу (тебе́). ♦ **I would never** *(1,2)* **lie to you.** Я никогда́ не бу́ду *(1)* ...говори́ть тебе́ непра́вду. / *(2)* ...лгать тебе́. ♦ **Please don't** *(1,2)* **lie to me.** Пожа́луйста, не *(1)* ...говори́ мне непра́вду. / *(2)* ...лги мне.

lie *n* ложь *f*, непра́вда ♦ **absolute** ~ соверше́нная ложь ♦ **big** ~ больша́я ложь ♦ **blatant** ~ я́вная ложь ♦ **brazen** ~ на́глая ложь ♦ **complete** ~ соверше́нная ложь ♦ **(god)damn** ~ прокля́тая ложь ♦ **heinous** ~ отврати́тельная ложь ♦ **malicious** ~ зло́бная ложь **outrageous** ~ возмути́тельная ложь ♦ **rotten** ~ безнра́вственная ложь ♦ **shameful** ~ постыдная ложь ♦ **such a** ~ така́я ложь ♦ **tell a** *(1,2)* ~ говори́ть / сказа́ть непра́вду, лгать / солга́ть *(about what =* + o + *prep., to whom = dat.)* ♦ **That's a** *([1]* **complete** /*[2]* **malicious** / *[3]* **rotten** / *[4]* **goddamn** / *[5]* **heinous) lie.** Это *([1]* соверше́нная / *[2]* зло́бная / *[3]* безнра́вственная / *[4]* прокля́тая / *[5]* отврати́тельная) ложь. ♦ **You told me a lie.** Ты сказа́ла *(ж: сказа́л)* мне непра́вду. ♦ **I** *(1)* ...**hate**... / *(2)* ...**can't stand**... **lies.** Я *(1)* ...ненави́жу... / *(2)* ...терпе́ть не могу́... лжи.

life *n* жизнь *f* ♦ **active** ~ акти́вная жизнь ♦ **all** *(1)* **my** / *(2)* **your life** всю *(1)* мою́ / *(2)* твою́ жизнь ♦ **bachelor** ~ холостя́цкая жизнь ♦ **barren** ~ беспло́дная жизнь ♦ **bleak** ~ уны́лая жизнь ♦ **boring** ~ ску́чная жизнь ♦ *(1,2)* **busy** ~ *(1)* акти́вная / *(2)* занята́я жизнь ♦ *(1-3)* **carefree** ~ *(1)* беспе́чная / *(2)* беззабо́тная / *(3)* раздо́льная жизнь ♦ **child-free** ~ жизнь без дете́й ♦ **city** ~ городска́я жизнь ♦ **comfortable** ~ комфорта́бельная жизнь ♦ **country** ~ дереве́нская жизнь ♦ **cozy** ~ ую́тная жизнь ♦ **cultural** ~ культу́рная жизнь ♦ **difficult** ~ тру́дная жизнь ♦ **dismal** ~ мра́чная жизнь ♦ **diverse** ~ разносторо́нняя жизнь ♦ **double** ~ двойна́я жизнь ♦ **drab** ~ ску́чная жизнь ♦ **dreary** ~ безотра́дная жизнь ♦ **dull** ~ ску́чная жизнь ♦ **easy** ~ лёгкая жизнь ♦ **empty** ~ пуста́я жизнь ♦ **eventful** ~ жизнь, по́лная собы́тий *(1 term)*; полнокро́вная жизнь ♦ **everyday** ~ повседне́вная жизнь ♦ *(1,2)* **exciting** ~ *(1)* захва́тывающая / *(2)* волну́ющая жизнь ♦ **family** ~ семе́йная жизнь ♦ **fantasy** ~ жизнь, по́лная фанта́зий *(1 term)* ♦ *(1,2)* **free** ~ *(1)* свобо́дная / *(2)* раздо́льная жизнь ♦ **grey** ~ се́рая жизнь ♦ **gypsy** ~ бродя́чая жизнь ♦ **happy** ~ счастли́вая жизнь ♦ **hard** ~ тяжёлая жизнь ♦ *(1,2)* **hectic** ~ *(1)* лихора́дочная / *(2)* кипу́чая жизнь ♦ **idle** ~ пра́здная жизнь ♦ **interesting** ~ интере́сная жизнь ♦ **intimate** ~ инти́мная жизнь ♦ *(1)* **joyful** / *(2)* **joyous** ~ *(1,2)* ра́достная жизнь ♦ ~ **nowadays** ны́нешняя жизнь ♦ ~ **of the party** душа́ компа́нии ♦ ~ **together** совме́стная жизнь ♦ **lonely** ~ одино́кая жизнь ♦ **long** ~ до́лгая жизнь ♦ **love** ~ любо́вная жизнь ♦ **married** ~ супру́жество, супру́жеская жизнь ♦ **meaningless** ~ бессмы́сленная жизнь ♦ **merciless** ~ безжа́лостная жизнь ♦ **military** ~ вое́нная жизнь ♦ *(1,2)* **miserable** ~ *(1)* печа́льная / *(2)* несча́стная жизнь ♦ *(1,2)* **monotonous** ~ *(1)* однообра́зная / *(2)* ску́чная жизнь ♦ **my** ~ моя́ жизнь ♦ **new** ~ но́вая жизнь ♦ **nomadic** ~ бродя́чая жизнь ♦ *(1,2)* **ordinary** ~ *(1)* обы́чная / *(2)* обыкнове́нная жизнь ♦ **peaceful** ~ ми́рная жизнь ♦ **personal** ~ ли́чная жизнь ♦ **present(-day)** ~ ны́нешняя жизнь ♦ **quiet** ~ споко́йная жизнь ♦ **real** ~ реа́льная жизнь ♦ **rural** ~ се́льская жизнь ♦ **sad** ~ печа́льная жизнь ♦ *(1,2)* **sex** ~ *(1)* полова́я / *(2)* сексуа́льная жизнь ♦ **single** ~ холоста́я жизнь ♦ **social** ~ вре́мя, проведённое с друзья́ми и знако́мыми

If no accent is shown on a word with a capitalized vowel,
it means that the capitalized vowel is accented.

(explanation), обще́ние с друзья́ми ♦ **solitary** ~ одино́кая жизнь ♦ **spiritual** ~ духо́вная жизнь ♦ **stressful** ~ напряжённая жизнь ♦ **tranquil** ~ безмяте́жная жизнь ♦ **turbulent** ~ бу́рная жизнь ♦ **unpretentious** ~ скро́мная жизнь ♦ **unsettled** ~ неустро́енная жизнь ♦ *(1,2)* **well-ordered** ~*(1)* упоря́доченная / *(2)* нала́женная жизнь ♦ *(1,2)* **wonderful** ~*(1)* замеча́тельная / *(2)* удиви́тельная жизнь ♦ **your** ~ *(familiar)* твоя́ жизнь; *(polite)* Ва́ша жизнь.

life: *verb terms*

awaken ~ **in me** пробужда́ть / пробуди́ть жизнь во мне ♦ **brighten my** ~ озаря́ть / озари́ть мою́ жизнь ♦ **build a** ~ стро́ить жизнь ♦ **change** *(1)* **my** / *(2)* **your** ~ изменя́ть / измени́ть *(1)* мою́ / *(2)* твою́ жизнь ♦ **come into** *(1)* **my** / *(2)* **your** ~ войти́ в *(1)* мою́ / *(2)* твою́ жизнь ♦ **come to** ~ *(awaken)* ожива́ть ♦ **embrace** ~ испыта́ть в жи́зни мно́гое ♦ **enhance my** ~ де́лать мою́ жизнь лу́чше ♦ **enjoy** ~ **(to the fullest)** (максима́льно) наслажда́ться жи́знью ♦ **join my** ~ **to yours** соедини́ть мою́ жизнь с твое́й ♦ **lead a (normal)** ~ вести́ (норма́льную) жизнь ♦ **live a comfortable** ~ комфорта́бельно жить ♦ **make a** ~ создава́ть / созда́ть жизнь ♦ **make my** ~ **complete** наполня́ть / напо́лнить мою́ жизнь ♦ **put my** ~ **in order** устра́ивать / устро́ить свою́ жизнь ♦ **rebuild my** ~ перестра́ивать / перестро́ить свою́ жизнь ♦ **ruin** *(1)* **my** / *(2)* **your** ~ по́ртить / испо́ртить *(1)* мне / *(2)* тебе́ жизнь ♦ **share (all) my** ~ **with you** разделя́ть / раздели́ть (всю) мою́ жизнь с тобо́й ♦ **share our lives together** вме́сте прожи́ть на́шу жизнь, соедини́ть на́ши жи́зни ♦ *(1,2)* **spend (all)** *(3)* **my** / *(4)* **your** ~ *(1)* провести́ / *(2)* прожи́ть (всю) *(3,4)* свою́ жизнь ♦ **start a new** ~ начина́ть / нача́ть но́вую жизнь.

life: *other terms*

cynosure of my ~ путево́дная звезда́ мое́й жи́зни ♦ **for** ~ на всю жизнь ♦ **full of** ~ по́лный (-ая, -ые) жи́зни ♦ **high point of my** ~ верши́на мое́й жи́зни ♦ **in** *(1)* **my** / *(2)* **your** ~ в *(1)* мое́й / *(2)* твое́й жи́зни ♦ ~ *(1,2)* **partner** *(1)* спу́тник / *(2)* спу́тница жи́зни ♦ **light of my** ~ свет мое́й жи́зни ♦ **love of my** ~ любо́вь мое́й жи́зни ♦ **lover of** ~ лю́бящий *m* / лю́бящая *f* жизнь ♦ **outlook on** ~ мировоззре́ние ♦ **part of my** ~ часть мое́й жи́зни ♦ **passion for** ~ страсть к жи́зни ♦ **satisfied with** ~ дово́льный (-ая, -ое, -ые) жи́знью *(short forms:* дово́лен, дово́льна, -о, -ы жи́знью*)* ♦ **star of my** ~ звезда́ мое́й жи́зни ♦ **thirst for** ~ жа́жда жи́зни ♦ **void in my** ~ пустота́ в мое́й жи́зни ♦ **web of** ~ паути́на жи́зни.

life: *I'm happy you're in my life*

I am so happy that you are in my life. Я так сча́стлив *(ж: сча́стлива)*, что ты есть в мое́й жи́зни. ♦ **I'm so glad (that) you're part of my life.** Я так рад *(ж: ра́да)*, (что) ты часть мое́й жи́зни. ♦ **My life has never been happier since I met you.** Моя́ жизнь ста́ла мно́го счастли́вее с тех пор, как я встре́тил тебя́. ♦ **With you, I live the life I once only dreamed.** С тобо́й я живу́ жи́знью, о кото́рой я пре́жде то́лько мечта́л *(ж: мечта́ла)*. ♦ **Thank you with all my heart and soul for coming into my life.** Всем свои́м се́рдцем и душо́й благодарю́ тебя́ за прихо́д в мою́ жизнь. ♦ **Thank you for being part of my life — the most important part.** Благодарю́ тебя́ за то, что ты са́мая лу́чшая часть мое́й жи́зни.

life: *you've changed my life*

You have changed my life (forever). Ты (навсегда́) измени́ла *(ж: измени́л)* мою́ жизнь. ♦ **Since I met you, my whole life has changed.** С тех пор, как я встре́тил *(ж: встре́тила)* тебя́, вся моя́ жизнь измени́лась.

life: *where have you been all my life?*

Where *(1,2)* **have you been all my life?** Где ты *(1)* была́ *(ж: был)* / *(2)* пропада́ла *(ж: пропада́л)* всю мою́ жизнь?

life: *you fill my life with love*

You fill my life with love. Ты наполня́ешь мою́ жизнь любо́вью. ♦ **Your love is the sun**

Russian has 6 grammatical cases. For an explanation of them,
see the grammar appendix on page 686.

that awakens life within me. Твоя любовь -- это солнце, пробуждающее жизнь во мне.

> **life:** *you are my love in life*

What more could I ask for than you as my love in life? О чём ещё я мог *(ж: могла)* бы просить, кроме того, чтобы ты была *(ж: был)* моей любовью на всю жизнь. ♦ **You are the love and light of my life.** Ты любовь и свет моей жизни. ♦ **You are and always will be the love of my life.** Ты любовь моей жизни сейчас и будешь ею всегда. ♦ **I could never ask for more in this life than your love.** Твоя любовь -- это единственное, о чём бы я мог *(ж: могла)* просить небеса.

> **life:** *you are the best in my life*

You are the best thing in my life. Ты лучшее, что есть у меня в жизни. ♦ **You are the most wonderful person that God could ever have brought into my life.** Ты самый замечательный человек, которого Бог мог бы когда-либо послать в мою жизнь. ♦ **Having you in my life is the greatest, most wonderful gift that God could give me.** Ты это самый лучший, самый удивительный подарок, который я получил *(ж: получила)* от Бога. ♦ **It's truly wonderful to have you in my life.** То, что ты есть в моей жизни, действительно замечательно.

> **life:** *you are my life*

You are my hope and dreams, my strength and purpose, my joy and happiness. You are my life. Ты мои надежды и мечты, моя сила и цель, моя радость и счастье. Ты моя жизнь. ♦ **You are my love, my life, my happiness.** Ты моя любовь, моя жизнь, моё счастье. ♦ **You are my love and my life - always.** Ты моя любовь и моя жизнь навсегда. ♦ **My life and soul!** *(heading of a letter)* Моя жизнь и душа! ♦ **You are the life of my life (and the soul of my soul).** Ты жизнь моей жизни (и душа моей души). ♦ **My entire life is in you.** Вся моя жизнь в тебе. ♦ **You are the** *(1)* **cynosure /** *(2)* **star /** *(3)* **music of my life.** Ты *(1)* ...путеводная звезда... / *(2)* ...звезда... / *(3)* ...музыка... моей жизни. ♦ **You are my life made whole.** С тобой моя жизнь стала полной.

> **life:** *you enhance my life*

You brighten my life with your sweet smile and loving ways. Ты озаряешь мою жизнь своей нежной улыбкой и любовью. ♦ **You enhance my life in every way.** Ты делаешь мою жизнь лучше с каждым днём. ♦ **You enrich my life more and more every day.** Ты всё больше с каждым днём обогащаешь мою жизнь. ♦ **You give my life a whole new meaning.** Ты придаёшь моей жизни совершенно новый смысл. ♦ *(1)* **Meeting you...** / *(2)* **This... is the high point of my life.** *(1)* Встреча с тобой... / *(2)* Это... вершина моей жизни. ♦ **You light up my life.** Ты освещаешь мою жизнь.

> **life:** *you make my life...*

You make my life complete. Ты наполняешь мою жизнь. ♦ **With you my life lacks nothing.** С тобой моя жизнь совершенно полна. ♦ **You make my life a** *(1)* **...Garden of Eden. /** *(2)* **...paradise. /** *(3)* **...daily festival of love.** Ты превращаешь мою жизнь *(1)* ...в райский сад. / *(2)* ...в рай. / *(3)* ...в ежедневный праздник любви. ♦ **You fill my life with music.** Ты наполняешь мою жизнь музыкой. ♦ **You fill a (huge) void in my life.** Ты заполняешь (огромную) пустоту в моей жизни. ♦ **One night in your arms is all I would ever ask to make my life complete.** Одну ночь с тобой -- это всё, что я бы просил, чтобы моя жизнь стала абсолютно счастливой.

> **life:** *you and I sharing life*

I want to join my life to yours. Я хочу соединить мою жизнь с твоей. ♦ **I pray that our lives will always be joined (in love).** Я молюсь, чтобы наши жизни были всегда соединены (в любви). ♦ **I am so happy that we have joined lives.** Я так счастлив *(ж: счастлива)*, что мы соединили жизни. ♦ **You are the person with whom I want to**

There are no articles ("a" or "the") in Russian.

(always) share life's joys and sorrows. Ты тот человек, с которым я хочу (всегда) делить все мои радости и печали. ♦ **I'd like to spend the rest of my life with you.** Я хотел *(ж: хотела)* бы провести остаток жизни с тобой. ♦ **There is no one else I would rather spend my life with.** Нет больше никого на свете, с кем бы я предпочёл *(ж: предпочла)* прожить свою жизнь. ♦ **The greatest happiness I can imagine is to spend my life with you, sharing love and all joys and tribulations.** Самое большое счастье, которое я могу себе представить -- это прожить всю жизнь с тобой, деля любовь, радость и невзгоды. ♦ **You and I will live a long, happy life together.** Ты и я (вместе) проживём долгую, счастливую жизнь. ♦ **Let's share our lives together.** Давай вместе проживём нашу жизнь. ♦ **I want to *(1)* share / *(2)* spend (all) my life with you.** Я хочу *(1)* разделить / *(2)* провести (всю) свою жизнь с тобой. ♦ **Side by side I know we can *(1)* face / *(2)* surmount whatever life brings.** Вместе, я знаю, мы можем *(1)* ...смело встретить... / *(2)* ...преодолеть... всё, что преподнесёт нам жизнь. ♦ **Life is best when shared (with someone you love).** Жизнь наиболее прекрасна, когда разделена (с тем, кого ты любишь). ♦ **You are the person with whom I want to (always) share life's joys and sorrows.** Ты тот человек, с которым я хочу (всегда) делить все мои радости и печали. ♦ **The two of us will share a(n) *(1)* cozy / *(2)* exciting / *(3)* joyful life together.** Мы будем вести *(1)* уютную / *(2)* волнующую / *(3)* радостную жизнь вместе. ♦ **Happiness for me is sharing my life with you.** Счастье для меня -- это разделять с тобой жизнь. ♦ **We can live a comfortable life together.** Мы можем комфортабельно жить вместе.

life: you and I - partners for life

I want you to be my partner for life. Я хочу, чтобы ты была моей спутницей *(ж: был моим спутником)* жизни. ♦ **I want to go through life (together) with you (as my *[1]* mate / *[2]* partner).** Я хочу пройти по жизни (вместе) с тобой (как *[1]* супруг *[ж: супруга]* / *[2]* спутник *[ж: спутница]*). ♦ **I love you and I cannot think of another woman *(man)* on this planet who I would prefer to spend my life with more than you.** Я люблю тебя и не могу подумать о другой женщине *(ж: другом мужчине)* на этой планете, с которой *(ж: которым)* я предпочёл *(ж: препочла)* бы более, чем с тобой, провести жизнь. ♦ **I'm looking for a partner to enhance my life.** Я ищу партнёра, с которым смогу улучшить свою жизнь. ♦ **Let's be Valentines for life.** Давай будем возлюбленными на всю жизнь.

life: without you life = 0

Without you my life would be *(1)* so / *(2)* totally / *(3)* completely meaningless. Без тебя моя жизнь была бы *(1)* так / *(2)* совершенно / *(3)* полностью бессмысленна. ♦ **Life is (so) *(1)* dismal / *(2)* dreary / *(3)* empty / *(4)* grey / *(5)* miserable when I'm *(6)* away / *(7)* separated from you.** Жизнь (такая) *(1)* мрачная / *(2)* безотрадная / *(3)* пустая / *(4)* серая / *(5)* печальная, когда я *(6)* ...вдали от тебя. / *(7)* ...разделён *(ж: разделена)* с тобой. ♦ **I can't imagine *(1)* ...life... / *(2)* ...what my life would be like... without you.** Я не могу представить *(1)* ...жизнь... / *(2)* ..., какой была бы моя жизнь... без тебя. ♦ **How *(1)* empty / *(2)* bleak / *(3)* barren / *(4)* drab / *(5)* grey / *(6)* dull my life would be if I had never met you.** Как *(1)* пуста / *(2)* уныла / *(3)* бесплодна / *(4)* скучна / *(5)* сера / *(6)* тускла моя жизнь была бы, если бы я никогда не встретил *(ж: встретила)* тебя. ♦ **Life would be so empty without you.** Жизнь была бы так пуста без тебя.

life: love life

You've enhanced my love life *(1)* enormously / *(2)* immeasurably. Ты *(1)* ...очень сильно... / *(2)* ...неизмеримо... улучшила *(ж: улучшил)* мою любовную жизнь. ♦ **I'm definitely going to enhance your love life.** Я обязательно улучшу твою любовную жизнь.

life: social life

My social life is (not) very active. Я (не) очень часто встречаюсь с друзьями. ♦ **My**

---

*This dictionary contains two Russian alphabet pages:
one in Appendix 1, page 685, and a tear-off page on page 799.*

social life has declined. Я стал *(ж: ста́ла)* ре́же встреча́ться с друзья́ми.

> *life: family life*

I love life and family. Я люблю́ жизнь и семью́.

> *life: my life*

I have a busy life. Я о́чень за́нят *(ж: за́нята).* ♦ **I lead** *(1)* **...a rather quiet...** / *(2)* **...an ordinary... life.** Я веду́ *(1)* ...дово́льно споко́йную... / *(2)* ...обыкнове́нную... жизнь. ♦ **I have my life in order.** Моя́ жизнь организо́вана. ♦ **My life is so devoid of love.** Моя́ жизнь так лишена́ любви́. ♦ **My life was very boring and empty until I met you.** Моя́ жизнь была́ о́чень ску́чной и пусто́й до тех пор, пока́ я не встре́тил *(ж: встре́тила)* тебя́. ♦ **That's the story of my life.** *(ironic)* Э́то исто́рия мое́й жи́зни *(ирони́чески).*

> *life: zest for life*

I have a passion for life. У меня́ есть страсть к жи́зни. ♦ **I want someone who has a passion for life (like me).** Я хочу́ ту *(ж: того́),* у кого́ така́я же страсть к жи́зни (, как у меня́). ♦ **I want someone who knows how to enjoy life.** Я хочу́ ту *(ж: того́),* кто зна́ет, как наслажда́ться жи́знью. ♦ **I'm looking for someone who is as fascinated with life as I am.** Я ищу́ того́, кто так же очаро́ван жи́знью, как я. ♦ **I believe in embracing life.** Я хочу́ испыта́ть в жи́зни мно́гое.

> *life: respect for all life*

I place importance on respect for all life. Я счита́ю ва́жным уважа́ть всё живо́е.

> *life: I offer you my life*

I offer to you all my love, all my being, all my life. Я предлага́ю тебе́ всю мою́ любо́вь, всё моё существо́, всю мою́ жизнь.

> *life: you body comes to life*

I love the way your body comes to life under my touch. Мне нра́вится, как твоё те́ло ожива́ет под мои́ми рука́ми.

> *life: someone in your / my life*

Do you have someone (else) in your life? Есть ли кто́-нибудь (ещё) в твое́й жи́зни? ♦ **I don't have anyone (else) in my life.** В мое́й жи́зни нет друго́й *(ж: друго́го).*

> *life: story of your life*

(1) **I want to hear...** / *(2)* **Tell me... the story of your life.** *(1)* Я хочу́ слы́шать... / *(2)* Расскажи́ мне... исто́рию твое́й жи́зни.

> *life: beautiful - and short*

Life is *(1)* **beautiful** / *(2)* **short.** Жизнь *(1)* прекра́сна / *(2)* коротка́.

> *life: too short*

Life is too short *(1)* **...to spend it alone.** / *(2)* **...for games.** Жизнь сли́шком коротка́ для *(1)* ...того́, что́бы проводи́ть её в одино́честве. / *(2)* ...игр.

> *life: double life*

I don't *(1)* **like** / *(2)* **want to lead a double life.** Я не *(1)* люблю́ / *(2)* хочу́ вести́ двойну́ю жизнь.

> *life: one day at a time*

I believe in taking life one day at a time. Я ду́маю, что жить ну́жно сего́дняшним днём.

lifelong *adj* пожи́зненный, -ая, -ое, -ые, длино́й в жизнь, на всю жизнь ♦ **I want you to be my lifelong** *(1)* **mate** / *(2)* **partner.** Я хочу́, что́бы ты *(1)* ...была́ мое́й супру́гой *(ж: был мои́м супру́гом)...* / *(2)* ...была́ *(ж: был)* мои́м спу́тником... на всю жизнь.

lifestyle *n* о́браз жи́зни, стиль жи́зни ♦ **active** ~ акти́вный о́браз жи́зни ♦ **balanced** ~ разме́ренный о́браз жи́зни ♦ **casual** ~ неорганизо́ванный, легкомы́сленный о́браз жи́зни *(1 term)* ♦ **clean** ~ чи́стый о́браз жи́зни ♦ **disciplined** ~ дисциплини́рованный о́браз жи́зни ♦ **flexible** ~ ги́бкий стиль жи́зни ♦ **fun** ~ весёлый жи́зненный стиль ♦

Russian verbs conjugate for 6 persons:
I, familiar you, he-she-it, we, polite&plural you, and they.

healthy ~ здоро́вый о́браз жи́зни ♦ **holistic health** ~ о́браз жи́зни, в кото́ром ва́жен це́лостный подхо́д к здоро́вью *(explanation)* ♦ **laid-back** ~ рассла́бленный стиль жи́зни.

lifetime *n* (це́лая) жизнь, продолжи́тельность жи́зни ♦ *(1,2)* **enchanting** ~ *(1)* восхити́-тельная / *(2)* волше́бная жизнь ♦ ~ **of love** це́лая жизнь в любви́ ♦ **whole** ~ це́лая жизнь ♦ **wonderful** ~ прекра́сная жизнь ♦ **love of a** ~ любо́вь всей жи́зни ♦ **once in a** ~ раз в жи́зни.

lifetime: *phrases*

(1,2) **We'll spend an enchanting lifetime together.** *(1)* Вме́сте мы проведём волше́бную жизнь. / *(2)* У нас бу́дет восхити́тельная жизнь. ♦ **You possess the kind of beauty that I could spend a lifetime adoring and never get enough of.** Ты облада́ешь тако́й красо-то́й, кото́рую я мог бы обожа́ть всю жизнь, никогда́ не насыща́ясь. ♦ **Each** *(1)* **minute** / *(2)* **hour** / *(3)* **day that we are apart seems like a (whole) lifetime.** *(1)* Ка́ждая мину́та... / *(2)* Ка́ждый час / *(3)* день... в разлу́ке ка́жется (це́лой) жи́знью. ♦ **You are the love of a lifetime. None could ever be greater or more beautiful.** Ты любо́вь всей жи́зни. Никака́я друга́я никогда́ не смо́жет быть лу́чше и́ли прекра́снее. ♦ **We have a lifetime of love ahead of us.** У нас впереди́ це́лая жизнь в любви́.

light *adj* 1. *(not dark)* све́тлый, -ая, -ое, -ые; 2. *(not heavy)* лёгкий, -ая, -ое, -ие.

light *vt (ignite)* зажига́ть / заже́чь *(what = acc.)* ♦ ~ **my fire** зажига́ть / заже́чь ого́нь во мне ♦ ~ **up** *vt* освеща́ть / освети́ть *(what = acc.)*.

light: *ignite*

You really light my fire. Ты действи́тельно зажига́ешь ого́нь во мне. ♦ **No one lights my fire like you do.** Никто́ не зажига́ет тако́го огня́ во мне, как ты.

light up:

You light up my (whole) life. Ты освеща́ешь (всю) мою́ жизнь. ♦ **Your love lights up my whole life.** Твоя́ любо́вь освеща́ет всю мою́ жизнь. ♦ **I want to light up your life.** Я хочу́ освети́ть твою́ жизнь. ♦ **You have a smile that would light up a city.** У тебя́ улы́бка, кото́рая спосо́бна освети́ть го́род.

light *n* свет ♦ **dim** ~**s** ту́склые огни́ ♦ **inner** ~ вну́тренний свет ♦ ~ **of love** свет любви́ ♦ ~ **of my life** свет мое́й жи́зни ♦ **urban** ~**s** городски́е огни́ ♦ **You are the light that never** *(1)* **...dims.** / *(2)* **...goes out.** Ты свет, кото́рый никогда́ не ...поме́ркнет / ...пога́с-нет. ♦ **You are my (brightly shining) light of love.** Ты мой (я́рко горя́щий) свет любви́. ♦ **You are the (love and) light of my life.** Ты (любо́вь и) свет мое́й жи́зни. ♦ **I'm be-ginning to see the light.** Для меня́ всё начина́ет проясня́ться.

lighten *vi* светле́ть ♦ ~ **up** *vi (slang)* веселе́ть / повеселе́ть ♦ **My heart lightened at the sight of you.** У меня́ светле́ло на се́рдце, когда́ я ви́дел тебя́. ♦ **Lighten up. Stop complaining all the time.** Повеселе́й. Переста́нь жа́ловаться всё вре́мя.

light-eyed *adj* светлогла́зый, -ая, -ое, -ые.

light-haired *adj* светловоло́сый, -ая, -ое, -ые.

light-headed *adj* (*Russian uses verb expression* чу́вствовать головокруже́ние) ♦ **I feel light-headed.** Я чу́вствую головокруже́ние.

lighthearted *adj (carefree)* беспе́чный, -ая, -ое, -ые, беззабо́тный, -ая, -ое, -ые; *(merry)* весёлый, -ая, -ое, -ые.

lighting *n* освеще́ние; свет ♦ **dim** ~ ту́склый свет ♦ **subdued** ~ смягчённый свет.

lightning *n* мо́лния ♦ **When your lips first met mine, it was like being touched by lightning.** Когда́ твои́ гу́бы впервы́е встре́тились с мои́ми, э́то бы́ло как уда́р мо́лнии. ♦ **The first time I** *(1)* **saw** / *(2)* **kissed you, it was like being** *(3)* **hit** / *(4)* **touched by lightning.** В пе́рвый раз, когда́ я *(1)* уви́дел *(ж: уви́дела)* / *(2)* поцелова́л *(ж: поцелова́ла)* тебя́,

---

There are two words for "you" in Russian:
familiar «ты» and polite / plural «вы» (See page 781).

э́то бы́ло как *(3)* уда́р / *(4)* прикоснове́ние мо́лнии. ♦ **Our** *(1)* **time** / *(2)* **day** / *(3)* **evening** / *(4)* **night** / *(5)* **weekend together was a lightning bolt of** *(6)* **happiness** / *(7)* **joy** / *(8)* **ecstasy.** *(1)* На́ше вре́мя вме́сте бы́ло... / *(2)* Наш день / *(3)* ве́чер вме́сте был... / *(4)* На́ша ночь вме́сте была́... / *(5)* На́ши выходны́е вме́сте бы́ли... как мо́лния *(6)* сча́стья / *(7)* ра́дости / *(8)* экста́за.

likable *adj* прия́тный, -ая, -ое, -ые, ми́лый, -ая, -ое, -ые, симпати́чный, -ая, -ое, -ые.

like *vt* нра́виться / понра́виться *(what, whom = subject; person who likes = dat.)*, люби́ть *(what = acc.)* ♦ **Would you like to** *(1)* **...go to dinner...** / *(2)* **...go to a concert** / *(3)* **party** / *(4)* **movie...** / *(5)* **...go bicycling** / *(6)* **bowling** / *(7)* **camping** / *(8)* **dancing** / *(9)* **hiking** / *(10)* **rollerblading** / *(11)* **shopping** / *(12)* **swimming** / *(13)* **sailing** / *(14)* **sightseeing** / *(15)* **skiing...** / *(16)* **...go for a walk** / *(17)* **ride...** / *(18)* **...go on a trip...** / *(19)* **...play tennis** / *(20)* **golf...** / *(21)* **...have a drink...** / *(22)* **...have lunch... (with me)?** Не хоте́ла *(ж: хоте́л)* бы ты *(1)* ...пойти́ на обе́д... / *(2)* ...пойти́ на конце́рт / *(3)* вечери́нку... / *(4)* ...пойти́ в кино́... / *(5)* ...поката́ться на велосипе́де... / *(6)* ...поигра́ть в ке́гли... / *(7)* ...пожи́ть в пала́тке... / *(8)* ...пойти́ на та́нцы... / *(9)* ...пойти́ в похо́д... / *(10)* ...поката́ться на ро́ликах... / *(11)* ...пойти́ за поку́пками... / *(12)* ...попла́вать... / *(13)* ...попла́вать на я́хте... / *(14)* ...осмотре́ть достопримеча́тельности... / *(15)* ...поката́ться на лы́жах... / *(16)* ...пойти́ на прогу́лку... / *(17)* ...поката́ться на маши́не... / *(18)* ...попутеше́ствовать... / *(19)* ...поигра́ть в те́ннис / *(20)* гольф... / *(21)* ...вы́пить... / *(22)* ...пообе́дать... (со мной)? ♦ **Yes, I'd like that.** Да, я бы хоте́л *ж: хоте́ла)*. ♦ **I like you.** *(familiar:)* Ты мне нра́вишься. / *(polite:)* Вы мне нра́витесь. ♦ *(1)* **Tell** / *(2)* **Teach me what you like (best).** *(1)* Скажи́ мне,... / *(2)* Научи́ меня́,... что тебе́ нра́вится (бо́льше всего́).

like-minded *adj* ду́мающий (-ая, -ие) одина́ково, лю́бящий (-ая, -ие) одина́ковые ве́щи.

likes *n, pl* пристра́стия; симпа́тии ♦ **~s and dislikes** пристра́стия и предубежде́ния; симпа́тии и антипа́тии ♦ **I would be so attentive, so focused on your needs and desires and likes and dislikes.** Я был бы так внима́телен, так сосредото́чен на твои́х ну́ждах и жела́ниях, и на том, что ты лю́бишь и что не лю́бишь.

liking *n* симпа́тия *(for whom = + к + dat.)*; расположе́ние ♦ **take a ~ to each other** проника́ться / прони́кнуться друг к дру́гу симпа́тией.

lily-of-the-valley *n* ла́ндыш.

limbo *n* неопределённость *f*, неопределённое / подве́шенное состоя́ние, неизве́стность *f* ♦ **You left me in limbo.** Ты оста́вила *(ж: оста́вил)* меня́ в неопределённом состоя́нии. ♦ **The whole** *(1)* **thing** / *(2)* **matter is in limbo.** *(1,2)* Всё пови́сло в во́здухе.

limbs *n, pl* коне́чности ♦ **slender ~s** стро́йные коне́чности.

limit *n* преде́л ♦ **There is no limit to my love for you.** Мое́й любви́ к тебе́ нет преде́ла.

limitless *adj* беспреде́льный, -ая, -ое, -ые ♦ **My love for you is limitless.** Моя́ любо́вь к тебе́ беспреде́льна.

   limp *adj* сла́бый, -ая, -ое, -ые, вя́лый, -ая, -ое, -ые ♦ **go ~** размя́кнуть; станов
и́ться / стать сла́бым (-ой, -ым, -ыми) ♦ *(1,2)* **My legs went limp at the knees.** *(1)* Мои́ но́ги осла́бли в коле́нях. / *(2)* Я почу́вствовал *(ж: почу́вствовала)* сла́бость в коле́нях.

limp *vi* хрома́ть.

limp *n* хромота́ ♦ **walk with a ~** хрома́ть.

limpid *adj* прозра́чный, -ая, -ое, -ые ♦ **Your eyes are like limpid pools.** Твои́ глаза́ как прозра́чные озёра.

line *n* 1. *(slang) (something a man says to attract a woman)* привлече́ние внима́ния; та́ктика; 2. *(written)* строка́ ♦ **great ~** замеча́тельная та́ктика *(для привлече́ния же́нщин)* ♦ **pickup ~** та́ктика для привлече́ния же́нщин ♦ **tell-tale ~s of age** преда́тельские морщи́ны, выдаю́щие во́зраст *(1 term)* ♦ **be out of ~** отклони́ться от ку́рса.

Russian terms of endearment are given in Appendix 13, page 780.

| *line: tactic* |

I really mean it. This is not just some kind of a line that I'm giving you. Я действительно считаю так. Это не просто способ привлечь твоё внимание. ♦ **You probably give the same line to every girl you meet.** Вы, вероятно, так же завлекаете каждую девушку, с которой встречаетесь. ♦ **That's a** *(1)* **nice /** *(2)* **great line...but I don't believe it.** Это *(1)* хорошая / *(2)* замечательная тактика, но я не верю Вам. ♦ **You're feeding me a line.** Вы льстите мне. ♦ **Don't think I'm just feeding you a line.** Не думайте, что я просто льщу Вам.

| *line: written* |

Drop me a line (*[1]* **...sometime. /** *[2]* **...when you have time /** *[3]* **a chance.)** Напиши мне (*[1]* ...когда-нибудь. / *[2]* ...когда у тебя будет время. / *[3]* ...по возможности.) ♦ **I'll drop you a line.** Я напишу тебе.

| *line: out of line* |

I think you're a little bit out of line. Я думаю, ты слегка отклонилась *(ж: отклонился)* от курса.

liner *n (eyes, lips)* карандаш ♦ **eye** ~ карандаш для (подведения) глаз ♦ **lip** ~ карандаш для губ.

linger *vi* медлить, задерживаться ♦ **How often my attention lingers on your photo.** Как часто моё внимание задерживается на твоей фотографии. ♦ **I want** *(1)* **my /** *(2)* **your lips to linger for hours on** *(3)* **yours /** *(4)* **mine.** Я хочу, чтобы *(1)* мои / *(2)* твои губы задерживались часами на *(3)* твоих / *(4)* моих.

lingerie *n* дамское бельё ♦ **intimate** ~ соблазнительное дамское бельё ♦ **lacy** ~ кружевное дамское бельё ♦ **sexy** ~ сексуальное дамское бельё.

lingering *adj* долгий, -ая, -ое, -ие, затянувшийся, -аяся, -ееся, -иеся, длительный, -ая, -ое, -ые ♦ ~ **glance** долгий взгляд ♦ **How I long to immerse myself in the soft, lingering fragrance of your** *(1)* **hair /** *(2)* **body /** *(3)* **person.** Как я жажду погрузиться в нежный аромат *(1)* ...твоих волос. / *(2,3)* ...твоего тела.

link *vt* соединять / соединить *(whom, what = acc.)*

lion-hearted *adj* храбрый, -ая, -ое, -ые, неустрашимый, -ая, -ое, -ые.

lip *n* губа *(pl:* губы) ♦ **adoring** ~s обожающие губы ♦ *(1,2)* **alluring** ~s *(1)* соблазнительные / *(2)* заманивающие губы ♦ **attractively full** ~s привлекательно-полные губы ♦ **avid** ~s жадные губы ♦ *(1,2)* **beautiful** ~s *(1)* прекрасные / *(2)* красивые губы ♦ **blood-red** ~s кроваво-красные губы ♦ **burning** ~s пламенные губы ♦ **capricious** ~s капризные губы ♦ **chapped** ~s потрескавшиеся губы ♦ **cherry** ~s вишнёвые губы ♦ **cold** ~s холодные губы ♦ **colorless** ~s бесцветные губы ♦ **crimson** ~s алые губы ♦ *(1,2)* **dry** ~s *(1)* сухие / *(2)* пересохшие губы ♦ **eager** ~s нетерпеливые губы ♦ **enticing** ~s заманчивые губы ♦ **fantastic** ~s фантастические губы ♦ *(1,2)* **full** ~s *(1)* полные / *(2)* пухлые губы ♦ **full, voluptuous lower** ~ полная, сладострастная нижняя губа ♦ **full, sensual** ~s полные, чувственные губы ♦ **hare** ~ «заячья губа», расщелина (верхней) губы, незаращение (верхней) губы ♦ **heavenly** ~s божественные губы ♦ **honeyed** ~s медовые губы ♦ **honey-sweet** ~s губы, сладкие как мёд *(1 term)* ♦ *(1,2)* **hot** ~s *(1)* жаркие / *(2)* горячие губы ♦ **hungry** ~s голодные губы ♦ **incredible** ~s невероятные губы ♦ *(1,2)* **inviting** ~s *(1)* зовущие / *(2)* привлекательные губы ♦ **kissable** ~s созданные для поцелуев губы, зовущие к поцелуям губы ♦ **kiss-swollen** ~s распухшие от поцелуев губы ♦ **little** ~ губка ♦ **lower** ~ нижняя губа ♦ **luscious** ~s сочные губы ♦ **lushly sensuous** ~s полные, чувственные губы ♦ **magic** ~s волшебные губы ♦ **moist** ~s влажные губы ♦ **painted** ~s крашеные губы ♦ **pale** ~s бледные губы ♦ **parched** ~s запёкшиеся губы ♦ **parted** ~s раскрытые губы ♦ **perfect** ~s совершённые

Some of the Russian sentences are translations of things we say and are not what Russians themselves would normally say.

губы ◆ **perfectly formed** ~s губы совершённой фóрмы ◆ **pierced** ~ прокóлотая губá ◆ **puckered** ~s поджáтые гýбы ◆ **ravenous** ~s изголодáвщиеся гýбы ◆ *(1-3)* **red** ~s *(1)* áлые / *(2)* крáсные / *(3)* вишнёвые гýбы ◆ **ripe** ~s гýбы (крáсные), как вúшни *(1 term)* ◆ **rose petal** ~s похóжие на лепесткú рóзы гýбы ◆ **rough** ~s шершáвые гýбы ◆ *(1,2)* **roving** ~s *(1)* блуждáющие / *(2)* капрúзные гýбы ◆ **scarlet** ~s áлые гýбы ◆ **skillful** ~s искýсные гýбы ◆ *(1,2)* **soft** ~s *(1)* нéжные / *(2)* мя́гкие гýбы ◆ **split** ~ рассечённая губá ◆ **sulky** ~s надýтые гýбы ◆ **sweet** ~s слáдкие гýбы ◆ **swollen** ~s припýхшие гýбы ◆ *(1,2)* **tantalizing** ~s *(1)* дразня́щие / *(2)* соблазнúтельные гýбы ◆ **tempting** ~s соблазнúтельные гýбы ◆ **tender** ~s нéжные гýбы ◆ **tensed** ~s напряжённые гýбы ◆ **thick** ~s тóлстые гýбы ◆ **thin** ~s тóнкие гýбы ◆ **trembling** ~s дрожáщие гýбы ◆ **upper** ~ вéрхняя губá ◆ **velvety red** ~s бáрхатные вишнёвые гýбы ◆ *(1,2)* **wandering** ~s *(1)* блуждáющие / *(2)* капрúзные гýбы ◆ **warm** ~s тёплые гýбы ◆ **wonderful** ~s замечáтельные гýбы ◆ **wondrous** ~s чудéсные гýбы ◆ **yearning** ~s жáждущие гýбы.

lips: verb terms

feel *(1)* my / *(2)* your ~s чýвствовать / почýвствовать *(1)* мой / *(2)* твой гýбы, ощущáть / ощутúть *(1)* мой / *(2)* твой гýбы ◆ **lick** *(1)* my / *(2)* your ~s облúзывать / облизáть *(1,2)* гýбы ◆ **move** *(1)* my / *(2)* your ~s двúгать / двúнуть *(1,2)* губáми ◆ **press** *(1)* my / *(2)* your ~s прижимáться / прижáться (*[1,2]* своúми) губáми *(to what = + к + dat.)* ◆ **pucker** *(1)* my / *(2)* your ~s вы́тянуть *(1,2)* гýбы ◆ **purse** *(1)* my / *(2)* your ~s мóрщить / смóрщить *(1,2)* гýбы ◆ **touch with** *(1)* my / *(2)* your ~s касáться (*[1,2]* своúми) губáми *(what = gen.).*

lips: other terms

contour of your ~s очертáния твоúх губ ◆ **corners of your** ~s уголкú твоúх губ ◆ **feel of** *(1)* my / *(2)* your ~s ощущéние *(1)* моúх / *(2)* твоúх губ ◆ **movement of your** ~s движéние твоúх губ ◆ **petals of the** ~s лепесткú губ ◆ **shape of your** ~s фóрма твоúх губ ◆ **soft redness of your** ~s áлая мя́гкость твоúх губ ◆ **taste of your** ~s вкус твоúх губ.

lips: your wonderful lips

Your lips are absolutely *(1)* **incredible** / *(2)* **fantastic** / *(3)* **wonderful** / *(4)* **heavenly.** Твой гýбы совершéнно *(1)* невероя́тные / *(2)* фантастúческие / *(3)* замечáтельные / *(4)* потрясáющие. ◆ **You have such (soft,) beautiful (, kissable) lips.** У тебя́ такúе (мя́гкие,) прекрáсные (, сóзданные для поцелýев,) гýбы. ◆ **You have perfect lips.** У тебя́ совершéнные гýбы. ◆ **You have lips that were made for kissing.** У тебя́ гýбы, котóрые бы́ли сóзданы для поцелýев. ◆ **Your lips look so** *(1)* **soft** / *(2)* **inviting** / *(3)* **enticing** / *(4)* **tempting** / *(5)* **sweet.** Твой гýбы вы́глядят такúми *(1)* мя́гкими / *(2)* зовýщими / *(3)* замáнчивыми / *(4)* соблазнúтельными / *(5)* слáдкими. ◆ **How soft and inviting your lips look.** Какúми мя́гкими и приглашáющими вы́глядят твой гýбы. ◆ **You have such a sensual richness in your lips.** В твоúх губáх такáя чýвственность. ◆ **The soft curves of your lips are so** *(1)* **tantalizing** / *(2)* **inviting.** Мя́гкие изгúбы твоúх губ так *(1)* маня́щи / *(2)* привлекáтельны. ◆ **Your lips are fuller and softer than any I've ever (1) known / (2) kissed / (3) seen.** Твой гýбы полнée и мя́гче всех тех, котóрые я когдá-либо *(1)* знал / *(2)* целовáл / *(3)* вúдел. ◆ **You have the most** *(1)* **wonderful** / *(2)* **heavenly lips in this world.** У тебя́ сáмые *(1)* замечáтельные / *(2)* божéственные гýбы в э́том мúре. ◆ **No one in this whole world has lips more wonderful than yours.** Ни у когó во всём э́том мúре нет губ бóлее замечáтельных, чем у тебя́. ◆ **Your eyes and your lips — oh! I could write a whole book of love poems dedicated to them.** Твой глазá и гýбы -- О! Я мог бы написáть цéлую кнúгу любóвной лúрики, посвящённой им. ◆ **Endless hours of** *(1)* **delightful** / *(2)* **heavenly kissing are promised in the delicate contour of your lips.** Бесконéчные часы́ *(1)* восхитúтельных / *(2)* божéственных поцелýев обéщаны в изя́щном кóнтуре твоúх губ. ◆ **Your lips shame the red, red rose.** Крáсные, крáсные рóзы стесня́ются твоúх губ. ◆

Counting things in Russian is a bit involved.
See Appendix 4, Numbers, on page 756 .

Your lips are like wine, and tonight I want to get drunk. Твои гу́бы, как вино́, и сего́дня ве́чером я хочу́ напи́ться.

---
lips: *the allure of your lips*

I am (completely) *(1)* mesmerized / *(2)* enthralled by the *(3)* ...sensual richness in... / *(4)* ...shiny sensuality of... your lips. Я (соверше́нно) *(1)* загипнотизи́рован / *(2)* очаро́ван (*[4]* я́ркой) *(3,4)* чу́вственностью твои́х губ. ♦ **I cannot escape the allure of your red rose-petal lips.** Я не могу́ устоя́ть пе́ред собла́зном твои́х кра́сных, похо́жих на лепестки́ ро́зы губ. ♦ **Those beautiful, perfectly formed, alluring lips of yours just call to me to kiss them — and, oh, I want to spend many, many, many hours answering that call with my own lips.** Твои́ прекра́сные, соверше́нной фо́рмы, зама́нивающие гу́бы про́сто взыва́ют ко мне о поцелу́ях и, о, я хочу́ проводи́ть до́лгие, до́лгие часы́, отвеча́я на э́тот призы́в свои́ми губа́ми. ♦ **I am compelled to obey the silent command of your (*[1]* sensuous / *[2]* beautiful) lips.** Я вы́нужден повинова́ться безмо́лвным прика́зам твои́х (*[1]* чу́вственных / *[2]* прекра́сных) губ. ♦ **Your lips demand to be kissed, and my lips can only comply.** Твои́ гу́бы тре́буют поцелу́ев, и мои́ то́лько подчиня́ются. ♦ **A man could easily become addicted to your lips.** Мужчи́на мо́жет легко́ пристрасти́ться к твои́м губа́м.

---
lips: *thoughts of your lips*

The thought of kissing your sweet, beautiful lips makes me dizzy with ecstasy. Мысль о поцелу́ях твои́х сла́дких, прекра́сных губ, приво́дит меня́ в состоя́ние головокру́жи́тельного экста́за. ♦ **All I can think about is the *(1)* exquisite / *(2)* heavenly *(3)* softness / *(4)* beauty / *(5)* magic of your lips.** Всё, о чём я могу́ ду́мать, э́то о(б) *(1)* ...изы́сканной / *(2)* боже́ственной *(3)* мя́гкости / *(4)* красоте́ ... / *(1)* ...изы́сканном / *(2)* боже́ственном *(5)* волшебстве́... твои́х губ. ♦ **When I think of putting my lips against your lips I almost faint with ecstasy.** Мысль о том, что́бы прижа́ться губа́ми к твои́м, приво́дит меня́ в состоя́ние полне́йшего экста́за. ♦ **I must confess, I am totally obsessed with thoughts of your beautiful dark eyes and full, *(1)* tantalizing / *(2)* alluring lips.** Я до́лжен призна́ться, что абсолю́тно одержи́м мы́слями о твои́х прекра́сных тёмных глаза́х и по́лных, *(1)* дразня́щих / *(2)* соблазни́тельных губа́х. ♦ **Every time I talk with you and look into your beautiful face, all I can see in front of my eyes for hours and hours afterwards are your enchanting, sparkling eyes, your smooth white skin, your *(1)* enticing / *(2)* kissable red lips, and your angel-like golden hair.** Ка́ждый раз по́сле того́, как я говорю́ с тобо́й и смотрю́ на твоё прекра́сное лицо́, всё, что пото́м часа́ми встаёт пе́ред мои́ми глаза́ми -- твои́ очаро́вывающие, сверка́ющие глаза́, твоя́ мя́гкая, бе́лая ко́жа, твои́ *(1)* ...маня́щие... / *(2)* ...зову́щие к поцелу́ям... кра́сные гу́бы и твои́ а́нгельские золоти́стые во́лосы.

---
lips: *I dream of your lips*

I dream of the heavenly moment when my lips take possession of your mouth. Я мечта́ю о ра́йском мгнове́нии, когда́ мои́ гу́бы овладе́ют твои́м ртом.

---
lips: *give me an hour with those lips*

God, please *(1)* give / *(2)* grant me just one *(3)* precious / *(4)* divine hour with those *(5)* heavenly / *(6)* beautiful lips. Бог, пожа́луйста, *(1)* дай / *(2)* подари́ мне то́лько оди́н *(3)* драгоце́нный / *(4)* бесце́нный час с э́тими *(5)* боже́ственными / *(6)* прекра́сными губа́ми.

---
lips: *I love your lips*

How I love your velvety red lips. Как я люблю́ твои́ ба́рхатные вишнёвые гу́бы. ♦ **I love the beautiful red curve of your lips.** Я люблю́ краси́вый изги́б твои́х кра́сных губ. ♦ **I love the sweet taste of your lips.** Я люблю́ сла́дкий вкус твои́х губ. ♦ **When you press your beautiful lips to mine, *(1)* ...all the rest of the world disappears. / *(2)* ...nothing else matters. / *(3)* ...I'm on top of the clouds. / *(4)* ...I feel all the bliss of heaven.** Когда́ твои́ прекра́сные

---

*Russian has 2 different vrbs for "go",
one for "on foot" and the other for "by vehicle".*

гу́бы прижима́ются к мои́м, *(1)* ...весь остально́й мир исчеза́ет. / *(2)* ...ничего́ бо́льше не име́ет значе́ния. / *(3)* ...я на верши́не облако́в. / *(4)* ...я чу́вствую всё блаже́нство ра́я. ♦ **Oh, the ecstasy of your lips!** О, экста́з твои́х губ! ♦ **I love it when you part your lips and let my tongue go into your mouth.** Я люблю́, когда́ ты приоткрыва́ешь гу́бы и позволя́ешь моему́ языку́ войти́ в твой рот.

lips: *the sweetness of your lips*

There is more sweetness in your lips than in all the beehives of the world. В твои́х губа́х бо́льше сла́дости, чем во всех у́льях ми́ра. ♦ **The sweetness of your lips imparidises me.** Сла́дость твои́х губ перено́сит меня́ в рай. ♦ **To savor the sweetness of your lips is so** *(1)* **divine** / *(2)* **wonderful** / *(3)* **heavenly.** Вкуша́ть сла́дость твои́х губ -- э́то так *(1)* боже́ственно / *(2)* удиви́тельно / *(3)* замеча́тельно. ♦ **What a divine ecstasy to savor the sweetness of your lips.** Что за боже́ственный экста́з -- вкуша́ть сла́дость твои́х губ. ♦ **Only the sweet softness of your lips can quell the ache of longing that ravages my heart.** То́лько сла́дкая мя́гкость твои́х губ мо́жет подави́ть боль тоски́, разруша́ющей моё се́рдце. ♦ **Heaven holds no sweeter treat than the taste of your beautiful lips.** У небе́с нет бо́лее сла́дкого угоще́ния, чем вкус твои́х прекра́сных губ. ♦ **The taste of your kisses is still on my lips.** Вкус твои́х поцелу́ев всё ещё на мои́х губа́х. ♦ **Your lips taste like honey.** У твои́х губ вкус мёда. ♦ **I've never (in my life) tasted such wonderful lips.** Я никогда́ (в жи́зни) не целова́л *(ж: целова́ла)* таки́х замеча́тельных губ.

lips: *I long for your lips*

My heart aches with longing to press my lips to yours. Я горю́ жела́нием прижа́ться губа́ми к твои́м губа́м. ♦ **How tremendously I** *(1)* **long** / *(2)* **yearn for the** *(3)* **feel** / *(4)* **taste** / *(5)* **softness** / *(6)* **sweetness of your (***[7]* **beautiful** / *[8]* **heavenly) lips.** Как сильна́ моя́ *(1,2)* тоска́ по *(3)* ощуще́нию / *(4)* вку́су / *(5)* мя́гкости / *(6)* сла́дости твои́х (*[7]* прекра́сных / *[8]* боже́ственных) губ. ♦ **I want to press my lips against yours and never take them away.** Я хочу́ прижа́ть свои́ гу́бы к твои́м навсегда́. ♦ **My greatest aspiration in life is to put my lips against yours.** Са́мое си́льное стремле́ние мое́й жи́зни -- прижа́ться губа́ми к твои́м губа́м. ♦ **When I look at your full, sensuous lips so promising of soft, sweet ecstasy, I am filled with an** *(1)* **enormous** / *(2)* **overpowering desire to kiss them with wild abandon to the very end of time.** Когда́ я смотрю́ на твои́ по́лные чу́вственные гу́бы, обеща́ющие не́жный, сла́достный экста́з, меня́ наполня́ет *(1)* огро́мное / *(2)* невыноси́мое жела́ние целова́ть их бесконе́чно, соверше́нно забы́в обо всём. ♦ **I want** *(1)* **my** / *(2)* **your lips to linger for hours on** *(3)* **yours** / *(4)* **mine.** Я хочу́, чтобы *(1)* мои́ / *(2)* твои́ гу́бы заде́рживались часа́ми на *(3)* твои́х / *(4)* мои́х. ♦ **I want to feast (***[1]* **endlessly** / *[2]* **night and day) on your lips.** Я хочу́ упива́ться (*[1]* бесконе́чно / *[2]* ночь и день) твои́ми губа́ми. ♦ **I want to put my lips against your lips and hold them there forever.** Я хочу́ соедини́ть свои́ гу́бы с твои́ми и оста́вить их там навсегда́. ♦ **I want to savor your lips night and day (for the rest of my life).** Я хочу́ смакова́ть вкус твои́х губ но́чью и днём (всю оста́вшуюся жизнь). ♦ **I want to devour your sweet lips.** Я хочу́ съесть твои́ сла́дкие гу́бы. ♦ **My lips are clamoring for yours.** Мои́ гу́бы тре́буют тебя́.

lips: *when our lips meet / met*

When our lips met the first time, *(1)* **...I almost fainted** / *(2)* **swooned from ecstasy.** / *(3)* **...I was overcome by ecstasy.** / *(4)* **...it was like being touched by lightning.** Когда́ на́ши гу́бы встре́тились впервы́е, *(1)* ...я чуть не лиши́лся *(ж: лиши́лась)* чувств от восто́рга. / *(2)* ...я за́мер *(ж: замерла́)* от восто́рга. / *(3)* ...я был охва́чен *(ж: была́ охва́чена)* экста́зом. / *(4)* ...э́то бы́ло как уда́р мо́лнии. ♦ **Your lips seared mine.** Твои́ гу́бы обжига́ли мои́. ♦ **When our lips touch even for a brief moment, I am** *(1)* **thrown** / *(2)* **hurled into a vortex of (ineffable) ecstasy.** Когда́ на́ши гу́бы соприкаса́ются да́же на коро́ткое мгнове́ние, я

Dipthongs in Russian are made by adding й
*to the end of a vowel (*а, е, ё, о, у, э, ю, *and* я*).*

(1,2) брóшен *(ж: брóшена)* в вихрь (невырази́мого) экстáза. ♦ **If my lips ever come in contact with yours, all that (*[1]* cold / *[2]* sham) *(3)* haughtiness / *(4)* resistance is going to drain right out of you.** Если мои́ гýбы когдá-нибудь коснýтся Вáших губ, всё Вáше *([1]* холóдное / *[2]* притвóрное) *(3)* высокомéрие / *(4)* сопротивлéние изчéзнет.

lips: *what I want to do to you with my lips*

I want to put my lips all over you. Я хочý тебя́ покры́ть поцелýями. ♦ **(1) I want to... / (2) I'm going to... adore (3) ...your body... / (4) ...every part of your (5) beautiful / (6) delectable / (7) luscious body... with my lips.** *(1)* Я хочý... / *(2)* Я бýду... обожáть губáми *(3)* ...твоё тéло. / *(4)* ...кáждую части́цу твоегó *(5)* прекрáсного / *(6)* лáкомого / *(7)* сóчного тéла. ♦ **(1) I want to... / (2) I'm going to... pay homage to every inch of your beautiful (3) body / (4) self with my lips.** *(1)* Я хочý губáми воздáть... / *(2)* Я губáми воздáм... пóчесть кáждому дю́йму твоегó прекрáсного *(3,4)* тéла. ♦ **I want to feast my eyes on your beautiful nude body — and then my lips.** Я хочý сначáла пожирáть твоё прекрáсное обнажённое тéло глазáми, а потóм губáми. ♦ **I long to adore the tender grace of your (1) neck / (2 throat with my lips.** Я стрáстно желáю ощути́ть нéжную грациóзность *(1)*...твоéй шéи... / *(2)* ...твоегó гóрла... губáми. ♦ **I want to put my lips on every (1) ...square millimeter... / (2) ...atom... of your beautiful body.** Я хочý коснýться губáми кáждого *(1)* ...квадрáтного миллимéтра... / *(2)* ...áтома... твоегó прекрáсного тéла. ♦ **I want to brush my lips across the tips of your breasts, down your stomach and along your legs.** Я хочý коснýться губáми твои́х соскóв, спусти́ться к твоемý животý и пробежáть вдоль твои́х ног. ♦ **My lips would reverently adore the graceful curve of your hips.** Мои́ гýбы бýдут почти́тельно обожáть грациóзные изги́бы твои́х бёдер. ♦ **Believe me, my little Darling, if my wish ever comes true to (1) get / (2) put my lips on you, you're going to need a crowbar to pry me loose.** Повéрь мне, моя́ мáленькая прéлесть, éсли мои́ мечты́ коснýться тебя́ губáми когдá-нибудь сбýдутся, тебé потрéбуется лом, чтóбы оторвáть меня́. ♦ **How nice it would be to bury my face in your neck and let my lips run wild.** Как прия́тно бы́ло бы зары́ться лицóм в твоéй шéе и дать вóлю губáм.

lips: *your body invites my lips*

The silky sheen of your body invites my lips. Шелкови́стый гля́нец твоегó тéла приглашáет мои́ гýбы.

lips: *I love putting my lips on your body*

I love brushing my lips on your smooth sculptured derriere. Я люблю́ касáться губáми твоéй глáдкой краси́вой пóпки.

lips: *what I'll do to you with my lips*

What my lips are going to do to your beautiful body is indescribable. То, что мои́ гýбы сдéлают с твои́м прекрáсным тéлом, неописýемо. ♦ **My (1) yearning / (2) adoring / (3) eager / (4) hungry / (5) ravenous / (6) loving / (7) wandering / (8) roving lips will (9) ...seek and find the hidden treasures of your (10) magnificent / (11) luscious beauty. / (12) ...explore every (13) millimeter / (14) inch of your (15) beautiful / (16) delectable / (17) luscious body. / (18) ...uncover your most precious secret. / (19) ...draw the very essence from you. / (20) ...suffuse your body with exquisite pleasure.** Мои́ *(1)* жáждущие / *(2)* обожáющие / *(3)* нетерпели́вые / *(4)* голóдные / *(5)* изголодáвшиеся / *(6)* лю́бящие / *(7,8)* блуждáющие гýбы *(9)* ...бýдут искáть и находи́ть скры́тые сокрóвища твоéй *(10)* великолéпной / *(11)* сóчной красоты́. / *(12)* ...исслéдуют кáждый *(13)* миллимéтр / *(14)* дюйм твоегó *(15)* прекрáсного / *(16)* лáкомого / *(17)* сóчного тéла. / *(18)* ...раскрóют твой сáмый завéтный секрéт. / *(19)* ...вы́пьют сáмую сýщность твою́. / *(20)* ...затóпят твоё тéло изы́сканным наслаждéнием. ♦ **My lips will (1) ...make your body sing. / (2) ...send sweet thrills racing through your body. / (3) ...spoil you such as you never dreamed of in your whole life. / (4)**

Some phrases are listed under more than one main word.

...rouse flames of *(5)* **desire /** *(6)* **passion to leap from your soul and surge through your veins.** Мои губы *(1)* ...заставят твоё тело петь. / *(2)* ...пошлют сладкий трепет по всему твоему телу. / *(3)* ...будут баловать тебя так, как ты никогда даже не мечтала. / *(4)* ...пробудят пламя *(5)* желания / *(6)* страсти, которое будет бушевать в тебе и струиться в венах. ♦ **My lips will roam hungrily across your cheek, your neck, your shoulders...** Мои голодные губы будут путешествовать по твоим щекам, шее, плечам... ♦ **I'm going to caress every part of your body with my lips and my tongue.** Я буду ласкать каждую частичку твоего тела губами и языком. ♦ **I'm going to devour your face with my lips.** Я покрою твоё лицо поцелуями. ♦ **First, I'll run my hands lightly over your body, and then my lips.** Сначала мои руки мягко пробегут по твоему телу, а затем губы. ♦ **With my lips I'm going to make tingling sensations ripple all through your body.** Мои губы вызовут волны трепета, бегущие по всему твоему телу. ♦ **When my lips and tongue revel on your beautiful, luscious body, they will hear your** *(1)* **moans /** *(2)* **screams of** *(3)* **pleasure /** *(4)* **ecstasy in South Africa.** Когда мои губы и язык будут упиваться твоим прекрасным, сочным телом, твои *(1)* стоны / *(2)* крики *(3)* наслаждения / *(4)* экстаза будут слышны в Южной Африке. ♦ **My lips and tongue will give you no** *(1)* **peace /** *(2)* **rest.** Мои губы и язык не дадут тебе *(1)* покоя / *(2)* отдыха. ♦ **My fingers and lips will spread warm waves of joy throughout your beautiful, voluptuous body.** Мои пальцы и губы распространят тёплые волны наслаждения в твоём прекрасном, роскошном теле. ♦ **My lips are going to softly trace the outline of your** *(1)* **mouth /** *(2)* **body /** *(3)* **breasts.** Мои губы мягко очертят контур *(1)* ...твоего рта / *(2)* тела. / *(3)* ...твоей груди. ♦ **I promise you hours and hours of incredible ecstasy as my avid lips totally worship your loveliness.** Я обещаю тебе часы и часы невероятного экстаза в то время, как мои жадные губы будут поклоняться твоей красоте. ♦ **As my lips pay devoted homage to your nipples, my fingers will blaze a trail over your burning skin.** В то время, как мои губы окажут почтительное внимание твоим соскам, мои пальцы будут прокладывать огненный путь по твоей коже. ♦ **The burning adoration of my lips will melt the pillars of your sophisticated decorum into rivers of molten lava.** Мои пламенные, обожающие губы превратят твердыню твоей благопристойности в реки расплавленной лавы.

lips: *adoring you with my lips*

Do you have any idea at all how many hours I could spend just adoring you with my lips? Представляешь ли ты себе, сколько часов я смог бы провести, только обожая тебя губами? ♦ **How fervently my lips could adore you.** Как пылко мои губы могли бы обожать тебя. ♦ **You can just lie there and let me adore your whole body with my lips.** Ты можешь просто лежать и позволь мне обожать твоё тело губами. ♦ **If by some divine miracle I am able someday to press my lips in fervent adoration to the exquisite loveliness of your sweet smile, I shall have nothing more to hope for or want.** Если бы каким-то божественным чудом я смог в один прекрасный день с пылким обожанием прижаться губами к изысканной прелести твоей сладкой улыбки, мне нечего было бы больше желать.

lips: *I love to feel your lips*

I love to feel your (hot, moist) lips *(1)* **...on me /** *(2)* **...there. /** *(3)* **...moving softly over my body.** Я люблю чувствовать твои (жаркие, влажные) губы *(1)* ...на мне / *(2)* ...там. / *(3)* ..., мягко движущиеся по моему телу. ♦ **I am** *(1)* **completely /** *(2)* **totally** *(3)* **...overcome by... /** *(4)* **...swept away by... /** *(5)* **...engulfed in... the rapture that you create with your roving lips.** Я *(1)* полностью / *(2)* весь *(ж: вся)* *(3,4)* ...охвачен *(ж: охвачена)*... / *(5)* ...поглощён *(ж: поглощена)*... упоением, которое ты создаёшь своими блуждающими губами.

The singular past tense of Russian verbs ends in -л (m) (usually),
-ла (f) or -ло (n). the plural past tense ends in -li.

| lips: tell me where to put my lips |

Tell me where you want me to put my lips -- that's where I'll put them. Скажи́ мне, где ты хо́чешь, что́бы я каса́лся губа́ми, там я и прикосну́сь. ♦ **Where would you like my lips?** Где бы ты хоте́ла *(ж: хоте́л)* мои́ гу́бы? ♦ **Show me where to put my lips.** Покажи́ мне, где бы ты хоте́ла *(ж: хоте́л)* мои́ гу́бы. ♦ **Put your lips *(1)* here / *(2)* there.** Прикосни́сь твои́ми губа́ми *(1)* здесь / *(2)* там.

| lips: quotation |

Her lips are lilies, flowing with liquid myrrh. *(Song of Songs)* Её гу́бы -- ли́лии, истека́ющие жи́дкой ми́ррой. ♦ **Your lips suck forth my soul.** *(A paraphrase of Christopher Marlowe)* Твои́ поцелу́и покоря́ют мою́ ду́шу.

lipstick *n* (губна́я) пома́да ♦ **beautiful** ~ краси́вая пома́да ♦ **bright** ~ я́ркая пома́да ♦ **glossy** ~ блестя́щая пома́да ♦ **pink** ~ ро́зовая пома́да ♦ **red** ~ кра́сная пома́да ♦ **color of** ~ цвет (губно́й) пома́ды ♦ **soft shade of** ~ мя́гкий отте́нок (губно́й) пома́ды ♦ **I want to feast on your lipstick** Я хочу́ пирова́ть на твое́й пома́де.

lissome *adj* ги́бкий, -ая, -ое, -ие *(See phrases under* **lithesome***)*.

listen *vi* слу́шать *(to whom = acc.)* ♦ ~ **attentively** слу́шать внима́тельно ♦ ~ **carefully** слу́шать внима́тельно ♦ ~ **intently** слу́шать сосредото́ченно ♦ ~ **to me** слу́шать меня́ ♦ ~ **to music** слу́шать му́зыку ♦ ~ **to you** слу́шать тебя́ ♦ ~ **with interest** слу́шать с интере́сом ♦ ~ **with pleasure** слу́шать с удово́льствием ♦ ~ **with the heart** слы́шать се́рдцем ♦ **be able to** ~ уме́ть слу́шать ♦ **know how to** ~ уме́ть слу́шать ♦ **Try to listen with your heart (to the things I tell you here).** Постара́йся услы́шать се́рдцем (то, что я говорю́ тебе́ здесь). ♦ **I promise to always listen (to you) with my heart.** Я обеща́ю всегда́ слы́шать (тебя́) се́рдцем. ♦ **I love listening to your stories.** Мне нра́вится слу́шать твои́ исто́рии.

listener *n* слу́шатель *m.,* слу́шательница *f* ♦ **gentle** ~ понима́ющий слу́шатель *m*, понима́ющая слу́шательница *f* ♦ **good** ~ хоро́ший слу́шатель *m*, хоро́шая слу́шательница *f* ♦ **receptive** ~ воспри́имчивый слу́шатель *m*, воспри́имчивая слу́шательница *f*.

listless *adj* вя́лый, -ая, -ое, -ые.

literate *adj* гра́мотный, -ая, -ое, -ые.

literature *n* литерату́ра.

lithe *adj* ги́бкий, -ая, -ое, -ие ♦ **You are so lithe and supple (*[1]*...in the way you move. / *[2]* ...in your movements).** Ты така́я ги́бкая и пласти́чная (*[1]* ..., когда́ дви́гаешься. / *[2]* ...в движе́нии.). ♦ **You have such a lithe, supple, beautiful body.** У тебя́ тако́е податливое, ги́бкое, краси́вое те́ло.

litheness *n* ги́бкость *f* ♦ **I marvel at your litheness.** Я восхища́юсь твое́й ги́бкостью.

lithesome *adj* ги́бкий, -ая, -ое, -ие ♦ **Your body has such lithesome grace.** В твоём те́ле есть така́я ги́бкая гра́ция. ♦ **You move with such lithesome grace.** Ты дви́гаешься с тако́й ги́бкой гра́цией.

Lithuanian *adj* лито́вский, -ая, -ое, -ие.

Lithuanian *n* 1. *(person)* лито́вец *m*, лито́вка *f* *(pl:* лито́вцы*)*; 2. *(language)* лито́вский язы́к ♦ **speak** ~ говори́ть по-лито́вски.

little *adj* ма́ленький, -ая, -ое, -ие; 2. *(small amount)* ма́ло ♦ ~ **chance** ма́ло ша́нсов ♦ ~ **hope** ма́ло наде́жды ♦ ~ **time** ма́ло вре́мени.

little *adv* ма́ло.

little *n* ма́ло ♦ **a** ~ немно́го *(+ gen.)* ♦ ~ **by** ~ ма́ло-пома́лу.

live *vi* жить ♦ ~ **a boring life** жить ску́чно ♦ ~ **a carefree life** жить беззабо́тно ♦ ~ **alone** жить одному́ *m* / одно́й *f*, жить в одино́честве ♦ ~ **a lonely life** жить одино́ко ♦ ~ **a long time** до́лго жить ♦ ~ **and let** ~ живи́ и дай жить други́м ♦ ~ **an interesting life** жить

Please do us a favor:
Fill out and mail in the Feedback Sheet on page 795.

интере́сно ♦ **~ as a bachelor** жить холостяко́м ♦ **~ a** *(1)* **secluded** / *(2)* **solitary life** жить *(1,2)* уединённо ♦ **~ a wonderful life** жить прекра́сно ♦ **~ comfortably** жить безбе́дно ♦ **~ for my** *(1)* **children** / *(2)* **son** / *(3)* **daughter** / *(4)* **family** жить для *(1)* дете́й / *(2)* сы́на / *(3)* до́чери / *(4)* семьи́ ♦ **~ happily ever after** жить сча́стливо всю жизнь ♦ **~ in harmony** жить в гармо́нии ♦ **~ in the hope** жить наде́ждой ♦ **~ like a monk** жить как мона́х ♦ **~ on a pension** жить на пе́нсию ♦ **~ on my salary** жить на (свою) зарпла́ту ♦ **~ quietly** жить споко́йно ♦ **~ simply** жить про́сто ♦ **~ together (with** *[1]* **me** / *[2]* **you)** жить вме́сте (*[1]* со мной / *[2]* с тобо́й) ♦ **~ well** жить хорошо́ ♦ **~ with my** *(1)* **mom** / *(2)* **mother** / *(3)* **dad** / *(4)* **father** / *(5)* **parents** / *(6)* **children** / *(7)* **son** / *(8)* **daughter** жить с *(1)* ма́мой / *(2)* ма́терью / *(3)* па́пой / *(4)* отцо́м / *(5)* роди́телями / *(6)* детьми́ / *(7)* сы́ном / *(8)* до́черью.

---
live: *live life*

I want to marry you and live happily ever after. Я хочу́ жени́ться на тебе́ *(ж: Я хочу́ вы́йти за́муж за тебя́)* и жить сча́стливо всю жизнь. ♦ **How can I live through another** *(1)* **day** / *(2)* **month** / *(3)* **week without you by my side. I cringe at the prospect.** Как могу́ я дожи́ть до *(1)* ...сле́дующего дня / *(2)* ме́сяца... / *(3)* ...сле́дующей неде́ли... без тебя́ ря́дом со мной. Я страшу́сь тако́й перспекти́вы. ♦ **I'm the kind of person who lives simply.** Я челове́к, кото́рый живёт про́сто. ♦ **I believe two people should try to live in balance.** Я ве́рю: два челове́ка должны́ пыта́ться жить в гармо́нии. ♦ **You only live once.** Ты живёшь то́лько раз. ♦ **You've given me something to live for.** Ты дала́ *(ж: дал)* мне то, ра́ди чего́ сто́ит жить. ♦ **I felt like I had nothing to live for until I met you.** Я чу́вствовал *(ж: чу́вствовала)* себя́ так, как бу́дто у меня́ не́ было ничего́, ра́ди чего́ сто́ит жить, до тех пор, пока́ не встре́тил *(ж: встре́тила)* тебя́.

---
live: *reside*

Where do you live? Где Вы живёте? ♦ **I live at** __(address)__ . Я живу́ __(а́дрес)__ . ♦ **Do you live alone?** Вы живёте одна́ *(ж: один)*? ♦ **I (don't) live alone.** Я (не) живу́ оди́н *(ж: одна́)*? ♦ **Would you be willing to live together with me (without being married)?** Жела́ешь ли ты жить вме́сте со мной (без бра́ка)? ♦ **We could live together (in** *[1]* **my** / *[2]* **your apartment).** Мы могли́ бы жить вме́сте (в мое́й / твое́й кварти́ре). ♦ **I want to live together with you.** Я хочу́ жить вме́сте с тобо́й.

---
live: *live and let live*
---

(1) **My philosophy is,...** / *(2)* **I believe in...** / *(3)* **I always say,... live and let live.** *(1)* Моя́ филосо́фия,... / *(2)* Я ве́рю,... / *(3)* Я всегда́ говорю́,... живи́ и дай жить други́м.

lively *adj* 1. *(active, full of life)* живо́й, -а́я, -о́е, -ы́е, по́лный (-ая, -ое, -ые) жи́зни; 2. *(animated)* оживлённый, -ая, -ое, -ые; 3. *(brisk)* задо́рный, -ая, -ое, -ые; *(spirited, merry)* весёлый, -ая, -ое, -ые.

living *n* 1. *(life)* жизнь *f*; 2. *(lifestyle)* о́браз жи́зни ♦ **organic ~** органи́ческий о́браз жи́зни ♦ **~ together** сожи́тие ♦ **You have now become the whole point of my living.** Ты ста́ла *(ж: стал)* для меня́ тепе́рь всем смы́слом жи́зни. ♦ **You exude a genuine joy for living.** Ты излуча́ешь по́длинную ра́дость жи́зни.

loads *n, pl* у́йма ♦ **We have loads of time.** У нас у́йма вре́мени.

lobes *n, pl* мо́чки ♦ **ear ~s** мо́чки у́ха.

lock *vt* запира́ть / запере́ть *(what, whom = acc.)* ♦ **~ up** *vt* запира́ть / запере́ть *(what, whom = acc.)* ♦ **I'd lock you up if you were mine.** Я бы за́пер тебя́, е́сли бы ты была́ моя́. ♦ **Make sure you lock the door.** Убеди́сь, что дверь закры́та. ♦ **Don't lock the door.** Не запира́й дверь. ♦ **Can you lock out all the memories that we've shared?** Мо́жешь ли ты вы́бросить из па́мяти всё, что бы́ло у нас?

lock *vi* 1. запира́ться / запере́ться; 2. *(eyes)* встреча́ться / встре́титься ♦ **The moment our**

Clock and calender time are discussed in Appendix 5, page 759.

eyes locked, I knew *(1)* **...you were the one for me.** / *(2)* **...I had to have you.** В тот момéнт, когдá нáши глазá встрéтились, я знал *(ж: знáла)*, что *(1)* ...ты бýдешь моéй едúнственной *(ж: мойм едúнственным)*. / *(2)* ...я дóлжен *(ж: должнá)* быть с тобóй.

lock *n* 1. *(doors, etc)* замóк; 2. *(hair)* лóкон ♦ ~ **of hair** лóкон ♦ *(1)* **Send me...** / *(2)* **I'd love to have... a lock of your hair (to carry around with me).** *(1)* Пошлú мне... / *(2)* Я бы хотéл *(ж: хотéла)* имéть ... лóкон твойх волóс (носúть с собóй).

locked up: ♦ **be ~ in oneself** замыкáться в своём чýвстве.

locket *n* медальóн ♦ **This is a locket with my photo in it. Wear it close to your breasts, because that's where I myself always want to be.** Это медальóн с моéй фотогрáфией. Носú егó на своéй грудú потомý, что э́то то мéсто, где я всегдá хочý пребывáть.

loins *n, pl* бёдра ♦ **My loins throb (unmercifully) for you night and day.** Моё естествó трепéщет (нещáдно) по тебé ночь и день. ♦ **I lie in the dark, thinking about you, and my loins throb unmercifully.** Я лежý в темнотé, дýмая о тебé, и моё естествó трепéщет нещáдно. ♦ **The sensation spreads through my loins like liquid fire.** Чýвство разливáется по бёдрам, как жúдкий огóнь. ♦ **The feelings are going to move like warm honey through your loins.** Чýвства разолью́тся по твойм бёдрам слáдкой истóмой.

loll *vi* нéжиться, валя́ться, лентя́йничать, бездéльничать ♦ **I want to loll forever in the heavenly enchantment of your person.** Я хочý вéчно нéжиться в твоём божéственном очаровáнии.

loneliness *n* одинóчество ♦ **abject** ~ крáйнее одинóчество ♦ **agonizing** ~ мучúтельное одинóчество ♦ **awful** ~ ужáсное одинóчество ♦ **dreadful** ~ стрáшное одинóчество ♦ **excruciating** ~ мучúтельное одинóчество ♦ **monastic** ~ монастырское одинóчество ♦ **oppressive** ~ гнетýщее одинóчество ♦ **terrible** ~ ужáсное одинóчество ♦ **unbearable** ~ невыносúмое одинóчество ♦ **utter** ~ совершéнное одинóчество.

loneliness: *I suffer(ed) loneliness*

I've had so much loneliness in my life. В жúзни я был *(ж: былá)* так чáсто одинóк *(ж: одинóка)*. ♦ **Until I met you I knew only loneliness and emptiness.** До тех пор, покá я не встрéтил *(ж: встрéтила)* тебя́, я знал *(ж: знáла)* тóлько одинóчество и пустотý. ♦ **You can't imagine the loneliness I** *(1)* **...have suffered.** / *(2)* **...have lived through.** / *(3)* **...live with (day in and day out).** Ты не мóжешь вообразúть одинóчество *(1)* ...от котóрого я страдáл *(ж: страдáла)*. / *(2)* ...чéрез котóрое я прошёл *(ж: прошлá)*. / *(3)* ...с котóрым я живý (день за днём). ♦ **I've had more than my fair share of loneliness.** На мою́ дóлю вы́пало одинóчества бóлее чем достáточно. ♦ **You don't know what** *(1)* **abject** / *(2)* **terrible loneliness I felt before I met you.** Ты не знáешь, какóе *(1)* крáйнее / *(2)* ужáсное одинóчество я чýвствовал *(ж: чýвствовала)* до тех пор, покá не встрéтил *(ж: встрéтила)* тебя́.

loneliness: *loneliness without you*

This loneliness (without you) is *(1)* **unbearable** / *(2)* **excruciating.** Это одинóчество (без тебя́) *(1)* невыносúмо / *(2)* мучúтельно. ♦ **My loneliness (without you) is a(n)** *(1)* **agony** / *(2)* **torment** / *(3)* **anguish** / *(4)* **torture that I can** *(5)* **barely** / *(6)* **scarcely endure.** Моё одинóчество (без тебя́) -- э́то *(1,2)* ...мучéние, котóрое... / *(3)* ...мýка / *(4)* пы́тка, котóрую... я *(5,6)* едвá выношý. ♦ **My loneliness without you** *(1)* **...is (totally) devastating.** / *(2)* **...is utterly oppressive.** / *(3)* **...crushes** / *(4)* **ravages my** *(5)* **soul** / *(6)* **spirit.** Моё одинóчество без тебя́ *(1)* ...(абсолю́тно) опустошáет. / *(2)* ...чрезвычáйно гнетýщее. / *(3)* ...подавля́ет / *(4)* опустошáет *(5)* ...мою́ дýшу. / *(6)* ...мой дух. ♦ **Without you** *(1)* **here** / *(2)* **around I feel such** *(3)* **abject** / *(4)* **terrible loneliness.** Без тебя́ *(1)* здесь / *(2)* вблизú я чýвствую такóе *(3)* крáйнее / *(4)* ужáсное одинóчество. ♦ **I'm floundering in a morass of loneliness without you.** Без тебя́ я барáхтаюсь в болóте одинóчества.

Reflexive verbs are those that end in -ся or -сь.
The -ся or -сь also goes onto a past tense ending.

| loneliness: *banishing loneliness* |

You've *(1)* **banished** / *(2)* **dispelled all my loneliness.** Ты *(1,2)* рассéяла *(ж: рассéял)* моё одинóчество. ♦ **The sunshine of your** *(1)* **heart** / *(2)* **love has melted away all of my loneliness.** Сóлнечный свет *(1)* ...твоегó сéрдца... / *(2)* ...твоéй любви́... растопи́л всё моё одинóчество. ♦ **I'm going to** *(1)* **banish** / *(2)* **dispel your loneliness once and for all.** Я *(1,2)* рассéю твоё одинóчество раз и навсегдá. ♦ *(1)* **I want to...** / *(2)* **I'm going to... make you (completely) forget your loneliness of the past.** Я хочý застáвить... / *(2)* Я застáвлю... тебя́ (пóлностью) забы́ть твоё одинóчество в прóшлом. ♦ *(1)* **Come** / *(2)* **Hurry back to me and chase away this terrible** *(3)* **pain** / *(4)* **scourge of loneliness (that grips my heart).** *(1)* Прийди́ / *(2)* Торопи́сь (обрáтно) ко мне и прогони́ прочь э́ту ужáсную *(3)* боль / *(4)* кáру одинóчества (, котóрая терзáет моё сéрдце). ♦ **Your letters (really) sustain me through my loneliness.** Твои́ пи́сьма (действи́тельно) поддéрживают меня́ в моём одинóчестве.

lonely *adj* одинóкий, -ая, -ое, -ие *(short forms:* одинóк, -а, -о, -и*)* ♦ **feel ~** чýвствовать себя́ одинóким *m* / одинóкой *f,* испы́тывать одинóчество ♦ **lead a ~ life** вести́ одинóкий óбраз жи́зни.

| lonely: *I'm lonely* |

I'm (*[1]* **so** / *[2]* **very** / *[3]* **terribly) lonely (without you).** Я (*[1]* так / *[2]* óчень / *[3]* ужáсно) одинóк *(ж: одинóка)* (без тебя́). ♦ **I've never felt so lonely.** Я никогдá не чýвствовал *(ж: чýвствовала)* такóго одинóчества. ♦ **I'm a very lonely person.** Я óчень одинóкий человéк. ♦ **In my heart I feel so lonely.** В моём сéрдце такóе одинóчество. ♦ **I get (a little) lonely sometimes.** Временáми я чýвствую (нéкое) одинóчество. ♦ **How lonely it is (here).** Как одинóко (здесь). ♦ **How lonely I am (here).** Как я (здесь) одинóк *(ж: одинóка).* ♦ **Are you as lonely as I am?** Ты так же одинóка *(ж: одинóк),* как я?

| lonely: *lonely without you* |

I get so (terribly) lonely (*[1]* **...without you here.** / *[2]* **...in the evenings.** / *[3]* **...that I can hardly stand it.**) / *[4]* **...that I could scream.).** Я так (ужáсно) одинóк *(ж: одинóка)* (*[1]* ...здесь без тебя́. / *[2]* ...вечерáми. / *[3]* ..., что с трудóм выдéрживаю э́то. / *[4]* ..., что хóчется кричáть.) ♦ **The nights are so (***[1]* **agonizingly** / *[2]* **torturously** / *[3]* **dreadfully** / *[4]* **terribly) lonely without you.** Нóчи так (*[1,2]* мучи́тельно / *[3]* ужáсно / *[4]* стрáшно) одинóки без тебя́. ♦ **I'll be (***[1]* **very** / *[2]* **terribly) lonely** *(3)* **...without you.** / *(4)* **...while you're away.** Я бýду (*[1]* óчень / *[2]* ужáсно) одинóк *(ж: одинóка)* *(3)* ...без тебя́. / *(4)* ...когдá ты не со мной. ♦ **Before I met you, I was always (***[1]* **so** / *[2]* **terribly) lonely.** До тогó, как я встрéтил *(ж: встрéтила)* тебя́, я всегдá был *(ж: былá)* (*[1]* так / *[2]* ужáсно) одинóк *(ж: одинóка).* ♦ **I spend these long, lonely nights yearning and burning for** *(1)* **...your soft, luscious warmth.** / *(2)* **...the warm, wonderful, heavenly magic of your beautiful body.** Я провожý э́ти дóлгие, одинóкие нóчи, сгорáя и тоскýя по *(1)* ...твоемý мя́гкому лáсковому теплý. / *(2)* ...тёплой, удиви́тельной, рáйской мáгии твоегó прекрáсного тéла.

| lonely: *you'll never be lonely again* |

I'm going to be with you all the time and you'll never be lonely again. Я бýду ря́дом с тобóй всё врéмя, и ты никогдá бóльше не бýдешь одинóка *(ж: одинóк).*

loner *n* человéк, лю́бящий дéйствовать в одинóчку *(1 term);* нелюди́м, дикáрь *m,* дикáрка *f* ♦ **I've been a loner by choice.** Я был одинóк *(ж: былá одинóка)* по сóбственному вы́бору.

lone-wolf *n* бирю́к.

long *adj* 1. *(length, distance)* дли́нный, -ая, -ое, -ые; 2. *(time)* дóлгий, -ая, -ое, -ие ♦ **It's been**

---

*The time zones for many cities of the world
are given in Appendix 6, page 761.*

so long since I *(1)* **...heard from you.** / *(2)* **...had a letter from you.** / *(3)* **...held you in my arms.** / *(4)* **...kissed you.** Прошло́ так мно́го вре́мени с тех пор, как я *(1)* ...слы́шал *(ж: слы́шала)* что́-либо о тебе́. / *(2)* ...получи́л *(ж: получи́ла)* твоё письмо́. / *(3)* ...держа́л *(ж: держа́ла)* тебя́ в объя́тиях. / ...целова́л *(ж: целова́ла)* тебя́. ♦ **So long!** Пока́!

long *vi* жа́ждать *(for what, whom = gen.)*, стра́стно жела́ть *(for what, whom = gen.)*; тоскова́ть *(for what, whom = + по + dat.)*, скуча́ть *(for what, whom = + по + dat.)* ♦ **You don't know how I long to be loved (by someone like you).** Ты не зна́ешь, как я тоску́ю о том, что́бы быть люби́мым *(ж: люби́мой)* (ке́м-нибудь таки́м, как ты). ♦ **I long desperately for you.** Я отча́янно жа́жду тебя́. ♦ **I long (so mightily) for** *(1)* **...your (sweet) kisses.** / *(2)* **...the paradise** / *(3)* **heaven of your** *(4)* **precious** / *(5)* **dear** / *(6)* **wonderful arms.** / *(7)* **...the day when I can luxuriate (again) in the warm, sweet splendor of your beautiful body.** Я тоску́ю по *(1)* ...твои́м (сла́дким) поцелу́ям. / *(2)* ...ра́ю / *(3)* небеса́м твои́х *(4)* драгоце́нных / *(5)* дороги́х / *(6)* удиви́тельных рук. / *(7)* ...дню, когда́ я (опя́ть) смогу́ наслажда́ться тёплым, сла́достным великоле́пием твоего́ прекра́сного те́ла. ♦ **I long so** *(1)* **mightily** / *(2)* **much to explore all the** *(3)* **luscious** / *(4)* **delicious secrets of your body.** Я так *(1,2)* стремлю́сь иссле́довать все *(3)* со́чные / *(4)* восхити́тельные секре́ты твоего́ те́ла. ♦ **There is no moment in the day when I don't long for your hands on my body.** В тече́ние дня нет и мину́ты, когда́ бы я не тоскова́л *(ж: тоскова́ла)* по твои́м рука́м, ласка́ющим меня́. ♦ **There is never a moment in the day when I don't long to caress your body with my hands (and lips).** В тече́ние дня нет и мину́ты, когда́ бы мои́ ру́ки (и гу́бы) не жа́ждали ласка́ть твоё те́ло.

long-awaited *adj* долгожда́нный, -ая, -ое, -ые.

longed for *adj* вожделе́нный, -ая, -ое, -ые.

long-haired *adj* длинноволо́сый, -ая, -ое, -ые.

longing *n* жа́жда, си́льное жела́ние, тоска́ ♦ **acute** ~ стра́стное стремле́ние ♦ **desperate** ~ отча́янная жа́жда ♦ **fierce** ~ **(to be touched)** неи́стовая жа́жда (прикоснове́ния) ♦ **~ (for you) in my heart** тоска́ (по тебе́) в моём се́рдце ♦ **intense** ~ си́льная жа́жда ♦ **my** ~ **(for you)** моя́ жа́жда (тебя́), моя́ тоска́ по тебе́ ♦ **obsessive** ~ навя́зчивая жа́жда ♦ **passionate** ~ страстна́я жа́жда ♦ **primitive** ~**s** примити́вные жела́ния ♦ **~ for you** жа́жда тебя́ ♦ **sweet** ~ сла́дкое жела́ние ♦ **tortured** ~ мучи́тельная жа́жда ♦ **unbearable** ~ невыноси́мая тоска́ ♦ **untamed** ~ неукроти́мая тоска́ ♦ **urgent** ~**s** настоя́тельные жела́ния.

longing: *other terms*

ache of ~ боль тоски́, боль жа́жды ♦ **ache with** ~ горе́ть жела́нием ♦ **burn with** ~ сгора́ть от тоски́ ♦ **waves of** ~ во́лны жела́ния.

longing: *for you*

My longing for you is *(1)* **downright** / *(2)* **absolutely painful.** Моя́ жа́жда тебя́ *(1)* соверше́нно / *(2)* абсолю́тно мучи́тельна. ♦ **I feel such a desperate longing for you.** Я так отча́янно жа́жду тебя́. ♦ **The longing in my heart for you is** *(1)* **...more than I can bear.** / *(2)* **...an agony that I can hardly bear.** / *(3)* **...unbearable.** Тоска́ по тебе́ в моём се́рдце *(1)* ...вы́ше мои́х сил. / *(2)* ...-- му́ка, кото́рую я едва́ могу́ вы́нести. / *(3)* ...невыноси́ма. ♦ **I have such an** *(1)* **intense** / *(1)* **obsessive longing for you.** У меня́ така́я *(1)* си́льная / *(2)* навя́зчивая жа́жда тебя́. ♦ **I ache with longing for you.** Я бо́лен *(ж: больна́)* от тоски́ по тебе́. ♦ *(1)* **I burn...** / *(2)* **My whole body burns... with longing for** *(3)* **...you.** / *(4)* **...your soft, warm beauty.** *(1)* Я сгора́ю... / *(2)* Всё моё те́ло гори́т... от тоски́ по *(3)* ...тебе́. / *(4)* ...твое́й мя́гкой, тёплой красоте́. ♦ **Not a minute passes that my heart doesn't call out your name in** *(1)* **desperate** / *(2)* **tortured longing.** Не прохо́дит и мину́ты, что́бы моё се́рдце не называ́ло твоё и́мя в *(1)* отча́янной / *(2)* мучи́тельной

---

*Optional parts of sentences are preceded
or followed (or both) by three dots.*

жа́жде. ♦ **Every night brings me a throbbing ache of longing for your warm, beautiful softness.** Ка́ждая ночь прино́сит мне пульси́рующую боль жа́жды твое́й тёплой прекра́сной мя́гкости.

longing: *for your lips*

My heart aches with longing to press my lips to yours. Я горю́ жела́нием прижа́ться губа́ми к твои́м губа́м. ♦ **Only the sweet softness of your lips can quell the ache of longing that ravages my heart.** То́лько сла́дкая мя́гкость твои́х губ мо́жет подави́ть боль тоски́, разруша́ющей моё се́рдце. **The** *(1,2)* **magic of the spring fills my heart with longing to be with you.** *(1)* Волшебство́ / *(2)* Ма́гия весны́ наполня́ет моё се́рдце жа́ждой быть с тобо́й.

longing: *to hold you in my arms*

I cannot *(1)* **overcome** / *(2)* **surmount** / *(3)* **abate** / *(4)* **contain the** *(5)* **fierce** / *(6)* **passionate longing in my heart to hold you in my arms (again).** Я не могу́ *(1)* преодоле́ть / *(2)* побоpо́ть / *(3)* уме́ньшить / *(4)* сдержа́ть *(5)* неи́стовую / *(6)* стра́стную жа́жду се́рдца (опя́ть) держа́ть тебя́ в объя́тиях.

longing: *to see you*

I fervently pray that in your heart you can somehow find the compassion to condescend to grant me just a few brief minutes to *(1)* **meet** / *(2)* **talk with you and thereby assuage this unbearable longing that grips my soul.** Я горячо́ молю́сь, что́бы ты смогла́ найти́ сострада́ние в своём се́рдце и подари́ть мне то́лько не́сколько коро́тких мину́т *(1)* встре́чи / *(2)* разгово́ра с тобо́й, что́бы утоли́ть невыноси́мое жела́ние, охвати́вшее мою́ ду́шу.

longing: *compels me to write you*

I feel impelled by the acute longing in my heart to write you this letter. Стра́стное стремле́ние моего́ се́рдца заставля́ет меня́ написа́ть Вам э́то письмо́.

longing: *conveying my longing*

When I talk with you on the phone, it seems as though I'm never able to convey the love and longing that I feel in my heart for you. Когда́ я говорю́ с тобо́й по телефо́ну, ка́жется, что я никогда́ не смогу́ переда́ть ту любо́вь к тебе́ и тоску́ по тебе́, кото́рыми полно́ моё се́рдце.

longing: *envelop(ed) me*

Waves of longing *(1)* **envelop** / *(2)* **enveloped me.** Во́лны жела́ния *(1)* охва́тывают / *(2)* охва́тывали меня́.

longing: *blended with ecstasy*

It's a feeling that blends ecstasy and longing. Э́то чу́вство -- смесь экста́за и жа́жды.

look *vi* 1. *(see)* смотре́ть / посмотре́ть *(at what, whom = + на + acc.)* 2. *(have an appearance)* вы́глядеть ♦ **~ around (for)** огля́дываться / огляде́ться (в по́иске) *(whom = gen.)* ♦ **~ for** иска́ть *(what, whom = acc.)* ♦ **~ forward** ждать с нетерпе́нием *(to what = gen.)*, предвкуша́ть ♦ **~ over from head to toe** огля́дывать / огляде́ть с ног до головы́ *(whom = acc.)* ♦ **~ radiant** блестя́ще вы́глядеть ♦ **~ the other way** не замеча́ть, не обраща́ть внима́ния.

look: *see*

I only have to look at you to want you. Мне сто́ит то́лько взгляну́ть на тебя́, и мной овладева́ет жела́ние. ♦ **Just to** *(1,2)* **look at you is to desire you** *(3,4)* **greatly** / *(5)* **intensely** / *(6)* **unbearably.** То́лько *(1)* смотре́ть / *(2)* взгляну́ть на тебя́ зна́чит жела́ть тебя́ *(3)* си́льно / *(4)* стра́стно / *(5)* пы́лко / *(6)* невыноси́мо. ♦ **I love looking at you.** Я люблю́ смотре́ть на тебя́. ♦ **The way you look at me turns my legs to jelly.** То, как ты смо́тришь на меня́, де́лает мои́ но́ги ва́тными. ♦ **When you look at me, I forget**

If you're not on familiar terms with a person,
the «ты» forms will have to be changed to «Вы».

everything else in the world. Когда́ ты смо́тришь на меня́, я забыва́ю о́бо всём на све́те. ♦ **Every time you look at me, I melt.** Ка́ждый раз, когда́ ты смо́тришь на меня́, я та́ю. ♦ **I like the way you look at me.** Мне нра́вится, как ты смо́тришь на меня́. ♦ **When I looked at** *(1)* **...you...** / *(2)* **...your picture... the first time, my heart said, "This is the one you've been waiting for."** Когда́ я пе́рвый раз уви́дел *(ж: уви́дела)* *(1)* ...тебя́,... / *(2)* ...твою́ фотогра́фию,... моё се́рдце сказа́ло: «Это та еди́нственная, кото́рую ты ждал *(ж: тот еди́нственный, кото́рого ты ждала́).*»

look: appear

(1) **That sweater *(It)*...** / *(2)* **That blouse *(It)*...** / *(3)* **That dress *(It)*... looks** *(4)* **great** / *(5)* **terrific** / *(6)* **beautiful on you.** *(1)* Этот сви́тер *(m It = Он)*... / *(2)* Эта блу́зка *(f It = Она́)*... / *(3)* Это пла́тье *(neut It = Оно́)*... *(4)* великоле́пно / *(5)* потряса́юще / *(6)* прекра́сно вы́глядит на тебе́. ♦ **Those pants *(They)* look** *(1)* **great** / *(2)* **terrific** / *(3)* **beautiful on you.** Эти брю́ки *(They = Они́)* вы́глядят *(1)* замеча́тельно / *(2)* потряса́юще / *(3)* прекра́сно на тебе́. ♦ **You look** *(1)* **beautiful** / *(2)* **fantastic** / *(3)* **gorgeous** / *(4)* **great** / *(5)* **terrific in** *(6)* **...that sweater *(it)*.** / *(7)* **...that blouse *(it)*.** / *(8)* **...that dress *(it)*.** / *(9)* **...those pants *(them)*.** Ты вы́глядишь *(1)* прекра́сно / *(2)* фантасти́чески / *(3,4)* великоле́пно / *(5)* потряса́юще в *(6)* ...э́том сви́тере *(m it = нём)*. / *(7)* ...в э́той блу́зке *(f it = ней)*. / *(8)* ...в э́том пла́тье *(neut it = нём)*. / *(9)* ... в э́тих брю́ках *(them = них)*. ♦ **You would look** *(1)* **beautiful** / *(2)* **great in** *(3)* **...any-thing.** / *(4)* **...a potato sack.** Ты вы́глядела бы *(1)* прекра́сно / *(2)* здо́рово *(3)* ...в чём уго́дно. / *(4)* ...да́же в мешке́. ♦ **You look (*[1]* absolutely** / *[2]* **positively) ravishing.** Ты вы́глядишь *([1]* абсолю́тно / *[2]* соверше́нно) восхити́тельно. ♦ **You look impeccable.** Ты вы́глядишь безупре́чно. **You look very cool and fresh (in that outfit).** ♦ (В э́том наря́де) ты вы́глядишь тако́й прохла́дной и све́жей.

look for:

I'm looking for someone like *(1)* **me** / *(2)* **myself.** Я ищу́ челове́ка, ...похо́жего на меня́. / ...тако́го же, как я сам *(ж: сама́).* ♦ **I'm still looking.** Я всё ещё ищу́.

look forward:

I look forward *(1,2)* **eagerly to** *(3)* **...getting your next letter.** / *(4)* **...hearing from you.** Я *(1)* ...нетерпели́во / *(2)* ...с нетерпе́нием... жду *(3)* ...твоего́ сле́дующего письма́. / *(4)* ...услы́шать что́-либо от тебя́. ♦ **How eagerly I look forward to June.** С каки́м нетерпе́нием я жду ию́ня. ♦ **I look forward (*[1]* so** / *[2]* **very much) to** *(3)* **...hearing from you.** / *(4)* **...seeing you (again).** / *(5)* **...meeting you in person.** / *(6)* **...being with you (again).** / *(7)* **...holding you in my arms (again) (and kissing you).** / *(8)* **...spending the rest of my life with you.** / *(9)* **...your letter** / *(10)* **call** / *(11)* **coming.** / *(12)* **...my vacation (there).** / *(13)* **...our vacation together.** Я с (*[1]* таки́м / *[2]* больши́м) нетерпе́нием жду *(3)* ...твоего́ звонка́. / *(4)* ...встре́чи с тобо́й (опя́ть). / *(5)* ...ли́чной встре́чи с тобо́й. / *(6)* ...вре́мени, когда́ мы (опя́ть) бу́дем вме́сте. / *(7)* ...той мину́ты, когда́ я смогу́ (опя́ть) обня́ть (и поцелова́ть) тебя́. / *(8)* ...той мину́ты, когда́ ты войдёшь в мою́ жизнь навсегда́. / *(9)* ...твоего́ письма́ / *(10)* звонка́ / *(11)* прихо́да. / *(12)* ...моего́ о́тпуска (с тобо́й). / *(13)* ...на́шего о́тпуска вме́сте. **I look forward very much to spending time with you.** Я не могу́ дожда́ться того́ вре́мени, кото́рое мы проведём вме́сте.

look *n* **1.** *(the way one looks at someone; glance)* взгляд; **2.** *(appearance)* вид, о́блик; **3.** *(expression)* выраже́ние ♦ **come-hither** ~ подзыва́ющий взгляд ♦ **coy** ~ засте́нчивый взгляд ♦ **deadpan** ~ ничего́ не выража́ющий взгляд ♦ **frigid** ~ холо́дный взгляд ♦ **happy** ~ *(expression)* ра́достное выраже́ние ♦ **idolizing** ~ обожа́ющий взгляд ♦ **intense** ~ пы́лкий взгляд ♦ **lingering** ~ до́лгий взгляд ♦ ~ **of indignation** возмущённый взгляд ♦ **lustful** ~ похотли́вый взгляд ♦ **meaningful** ~ многозначи́тельный взгляд ♦ **penetrating** ~ проница́тельный взгляд ♦ **probing** ~ и́щущий взгляд ♦ **provocative** ~ при-

A list of common places with their grammatical endings is given in Appendix 7, page 763.

зы́вный взгляд ♦ **puzzled** ~ недоумева́ющий взгляд ♦ **reproachful** ~ укори́зненный
взгляд ♦ *(1)* **sad** ~ *(expression)* (1) печа́льное / (2) гру́стное выраже́ние ♦ **searching** ~
и́щущий взгляд ♦ **shocked** ~ шоки́рованное выраже́ние ♦ **strange** ~ 1. *(glance)* стра́н-
ный взгляд; 2. *(expression)* стра́нное выраже́ние ♦ **tender** ~ не́жный взгляд ♦ **to exchange a (long)** ~ обменя́ться (до́лгим) взгля́дом *(with whom = + с + instr.)* ♦ **give a**
~ взгляну́ть *(whom = + на + acc.)*.

look: phrases

You gave me such a frigid look! Ты взгляну́ла *(ж: взгляну́л)* на меня́ так хо́лодно. ♦
You gave me such an intense look that it left me breathless. Ты одари́ла *(ж: одари́л)*
меня́ таки́м пы́лким взгля́дом, что у меня́ перехвати́ло дыха́ние. ♦ **You gave me such
meaningful looks, it just made me melt inside.** Ты дари́ла *(ж: дари́л)* мне таки́е много-
значи́тельные взгля́ды, что я про́сто весь пла́вился *(ж: вся пла́вилась)*. ♦ **I'd like to
get a closer look (at you).** Я хоте́л бы взгляну́ть (на тебя́) побли́же.

look-alike *n* похо́жий *m*, похо́жая *f* ♦ **I'm a Madonna look-alike.** Я похо́жа на Мадо́нну.
looker *n*: ♦ **not a bad** ~ не дурну́шка.
looks *n, pl* (вне́шний) вид, вне́шность *f*, нару́жность *f* ♦ **boyish good** ~s мальчи́шески
хоро́ший вид ♦ **charming** ~s очарова́тельная вне́шность ♦ **dark good** ~s сму́глая
красота́ ♦ **decent** ~s прили́чный вид ♦ **devastating (good)** ~s сокруши́тельная привле-
ка́тельность ♦ **fabulous** *(1,2)* ~s потряса́ющая *(1)* привлека́тельность / *(2)* красота́
♦ **good** ~s хоро́ший вне́шний вид, привлека́тельность, красота́ ♦ **irresistible good** ~s
неотрази́мая привлека́тельность ♦ **nice** ~s прия́тная вне́шность ♦ **passable** ~s удовле-
твори́тельный вид ♦ **pleasant** ~s прия́тная нару́жность ♦ **It was your dark good looks
that attracted me to you.** Это твоя́ сму́глая красота́ привлекла́ меня́ к тебе́. ♦ **A good
heart means more (to me) than good looks.** До́брое се́рдце зна́чит бо́льше (для меня́),
чем вне́шняя красота́.

loony *adj (slang)* полоу́мный, -ая, -ое, -ые, сумасбро́дный, -ая, -ое, -ые, рехну́вшийся,
-аяся, -ееся, -иеся.
loop *n*: ♦ **I've been out of the loop for quite some time.** Я дово́льно до́лго ни с кем не
встреча́лся *(ж: встреча́лась)*.
loopy *adj (slang) (goofy, kind of crazy)* глу́пый, -ая, -ое, -ые; бестолко́вый, -ая, -ое, -ые.
loose *adj* распу́щенный, -ая, -ое, -ые, безнра́вственный, -ая, -ое, -ые ♦ ~ **morals** мора́ль-
ная распу́щенность ♦ ~ **woman** безнра́вственная же́нщина.
loosen up *vi (slang) (relax)* расслабля́ться / рассла́биться.
loquacious *adj* болтли́вый, -ая, -ое, -ые.
lose *vt* теря́ть / потеря́ть *(what, whom = acc.)* ♦ ~ **oneself** теря́ть / потеря́ть себя́ *(in what,
whom = + в + prep.)*; пря́таться / спря́таться *(in what, whom = + в + prep.)*, скрыва́ться
/ скры́ться *(in what, whom = + в + prep.)*; погружа́ться / погрузи́ться *(in what, whom =
+ в + acc.)*; растворя́ться / раствори́ться *(in what, whom = + в + acc.)* ♦ ~ **one's mind**
теря́ть / потеря́ть рассу́док ♦ ~ **out** *vi (slang)* не име́ть успе́ха.

lose: phrases

I don't want to risk losing you. Я не хочу́ рискова́ть потеря́ть тебя́. ♦ **I don't know
what I would do if I ever lost you.** Я не зна́ю, что стал *(ж: ста́ла)* бы я де́лать, е́сли бы
потеря́л *(ж: потеря́ла)* тебя́. ♦ **God forbid that I should ever lose you.** Не дай Бог мне
когда́-нибудь тебя́ потеря́ть. ♦ **I pray that I will never lose you.** Я молю́сь о том, что́бы
никогда́ не потеря́ть тебя́. ♦ **My world would be totally** *(1)* **empty** / *(2)* **black if I were
ever to lose you.** Мой мир ста́нет совсе́м *(1)* пусты́м / *(2)* чёрным, е́сли я когда́-нибудь
потеря́ю тебя́. ♦ **The thought of losing you** *(1)* **pierces** / *(2)* **crushes my very soul.** Мысль
о поте́ре тебя́ *(1)* пронза́ет / *(2)* подавля́ет мою́ ду́шу. ♦ *(1)* **I never...** / *(2)* **I don't ever...**

Common adult heights are given in Appendix 9, page 776.

want to lose you. *(1,2)* Я всегда хочу быть с тобой. ♦ **I have no intention of losing you.** У меня нет намерения потерять тебя. ♦ **I can't bear the thought of (ever) losing you.** Для меня невыносима мысль о том, что я когда-либо потеряю тебя.

lose oneself:

I want (so much) to *(1,2)* **lose myself (to the world) in your** *(3)* **arms /** *(4)* **embraces.** Я (так) хочу *(1)* ...потерять себя... / *(2)* ...скрыться... (от мира) в твоих *(3,4)* объятиях. ♦ **I want to lose myself completely in your soft, warm, luscious body.** Я хочу весь погрузиться в твоё мягкое, тёплое, сочное тело. ♦ **I want to lose myself in your lush beauty.** Я хочу потеряться в твоей роскошной красоте. ♦ **We will lose ourselves (every night) in the rapturous affirmation of our love.** Мы будем растворяться (каждую ночь) в восторженном утверждении нашей любви. ♦ **We will lose ourselves (***[1]*** blissfully /** ***[2]*** **ravenously) in each other.** Мы (*[1]* счастливо / *[2]* жадно) растворимся друг в друге.

loser *n (slang)* никчёмный человек.

losing *n* проигрыш, потеря.

loss *n* потеря, лишение ♦ **feeling of** ~ чувство потери ♦ **I'm at a loss for words.** Я просто не нахожу слов.

lost *pp*: ♦ **I'd be lost without you.** Мне было бы плохо без тебя.

lot *n*: ♦ **a** ~ **(of)** много *(of what = gen.)*, многое *(no of)* ♦ **lots (of)** много *(of what = gen.)* ♦ **I have a lot to offer the right** *(1)* **woman /** *(2)* **man.** Многое я могу предложить *(1)* ...подходящей женщине. / *(2)* ...подходящему мужчине.

Lothario *n* волокита, Дон Жуан ♦ **true** ~ настоящий волокита.

lotion *n* лосьон ♦ **spread on suntan** ~ мазать / намазать лосьон для загара.

lottery *n* лотерея ♦ **I feel like someone who has just won the New York State Lottery.** Я чувствую себя, как будто я только что выиграл в Нью-Йоркской лотерее.

lounge *vi* нежиться, валяться, лентяйничать, бездельничать ♦ **I want to lounge forever in the heavenly enchantment of your person.** Я хочу вечно нежиться в твоём божественном очаровании.

louse *n (slang)* паршивый человек, гнида.

lovability *n* привлекательность *f*.

lovable *adj* милый, -ая, -ое, -ые, привлекательный, -ая, -ое, -ые ♦ **How lovable you are.** Как ты привлекательна. ♦ **You have such a lovable smile.** У тебя такая милая улыбка. ♦ **My lovely, lovable Love, Natasha...** *(heading of a letter.)* Моя красавица, милая любовь, Наташа... *(начало письма).* ♦ **How absolutely lovely — and lovable — you look in your photos!** Как совершенно прекрасно и очаровательно ты выглядишь на фотографиях.

love *vt* любить / полюбить *(what, whom = acc.)* ♦ ~ **ardently** любить пылко ♦ ~ **blindly** любить слепо ♦ ~ **boundlessly** любить безгранично ♦ ~ **deeply** любить глубоко ♦ ~ **desparately** любить отчаянно ♦ ~ **devotedly** любить преданно ♦ ~ **endlessly** любить бесконечно ♦ ~ **eternally** любить вечно ♦ ~ **fervently** любить пылко ♦ ~ **fiercely** любить до неистовства, любить горячо ♦ ~ **intensely** любить горячо ♦ ~ **joyfully** радостно любить ♦ ~ **like crazy** любить безумно ♦ ~ **madly** любить безумно ♦ ~ **more than anything in the world** любить больше всего на свете ♦ ~ **passionately** любить страстно ♦ ~ **romantically** любить романтически ♦ ~ **secretly** любить тайно ♦ ~ **selflessly** любить беззаветно ♦ ~ **tenderly** любить нежно ♦ ~ **truly** любить по-настоящему ♦ ~ *(1,2)* **very much** любить *(1)* очень / *(2)* сильно ♦ ~ **with all my heart** любить всем сердцем ♦ ~ **without drama** любить без драматических эффектов.

love: I love you...

I love you. Я люблю тебя. ♦ **I love you** *(1)* **very (very, very) /** *(2)* **so much.** Я люблю тебя

Words in parentheses are optional.

(1) о́чень (о́чень, о́чень) / *(2)* так си́льно. ♦ **I love you** *(1)* **boundlessly** / *(2)* **deeply** / *(3)* **desparately** / *(4)* **endlessly** / *(5)* **eternally** / *(6,7)* **fervently** / *(8)* **(always and) forever** / *(9)* **madly** / *(10,11)* **passionately** / *(12)* **totally** / *(13)* **wildly** Я люблю́ тебя́ *(1)* безграни́чно / *(2)* глубоко́ / *(3)* отча́янно / *(4)* бесконе́чно / *(5)* наве́ки / *(6)* горячо́ / *(7)* пы́лко / *(8)* (всегда́ и) наве́чно / *(9)* безу́мно / *(10)* ...стра́стно / *(11)* пы́лко / *(12)* ...всем се́рдцем. / *(13)* ди́ко. ♦ **I love you** *(1)* **...with all my heart (and soul).** / *(2)* **...with all my being.** / *(3)* **...with all the power of my soul.** / *(4)* **...with every fiber in my body and with all the energy of my soul.** / *(5)* **...to the bottom-most depths of my heart.** / *(6)* **...to the very roots of my being.** Я люблю́ тебя́ *(1)* ...всем се́рдцем (и всей душо́й). / *(2)* ...всем свои́м существо́м. / *(3)* ...всей си́лой свое́й души́. / *(4)* ...все́ми фи́брами своего́ те́ла и всей си́лой свое́й души́. / *(5)* ...всем се́рдцем. / *(6)* ...до глубины́ души́. ♦ **I love you** *(1)* **...as I have never loved anyone before.** / *(2)* **...as no man has ever loved a woman.** / *(3)* **...more than (any) words can ever express.** / *(4)* **...(much) more than you will ever know.** / *(5)* **...more than anything (in this whole world).** / *(6)* **...more than (my own) life.** / *(7)* **...more than any other woman in my whole life.** Я люблю́ тебя́ *(1)* ..., как никого́ и никогда́ пре́жде. / *(2)* ..., как ни оди́н мужчи́на никогда́ не люби́л же́нщину. / *(3)* ...бо́льше, чем э́то мо́жно вы́разить слова́ми. / *(4)* ...(намно́го) бо́льше, чем ты предполага́ешь. / *(5)* ...бо́льше всего́ (на све́те). / *(6)* ...бо́льше (свое́й) жи́зни. / *(7)* ...сильне́е, чем каку́ю-либо другу́ю же́нщину в свое́й жи́зни. ♦ **I love you now more than ever.** Сейча́с я люблю́ тебя́ бо́льше, чем когда́-либо. ♦ **I love you more and more (with each passing day).** Я люблю́ тебя́ бо́льше и бо́льше (с ка́ждым днём). ♦ **I love you so much I think my heart is going to burst.** Я люблю́ тебя́ так си́льно, что, ка́жется, моё се́рдце собира́ется разорва́ться. ♦ **I love you** *(1)* **...in every sort of way.** / *(2)* **...rain or shine.** / *(3)* **...to the highest degree you can imagine.** Я люблю́ тебя́ *(1)* ...вся́чески. / *(2)* ..., когда́ пло́хо и когда́ хорошо́. / *(3)* ...так си́льно, как ты не мо́жешь да́же вообрази́ть. ♦ **I love you** *(1)* **...all the way up to the sky.** / *(2)* **...beyond any human capacity to define or measure.** Моя́ любо́вь к тебе́ *(1)* ...необъя́тна, как не́бо. / *(2)* ...вы́ше челове́ческой возмо́жности определи́ть и́ли изме́рить. ♦ **I love you enough to want your happiness.** Я люблю́ тебя́ доста́точно, что́бы хоте́ть твоего́ сча́стья.

| *love: I've grown to love you* |

I've grown to love you so much (in such a short time). Моя́ любо́вь к тебе́ вы́росла так си́льно (за тако́е коро́ткое вре́мя). ♦ **Over these past** *(1)* **weeks** / *(2)* **months I have really grown to love you.** В тече́ние э́тих проше́дших *(1)* неде́ль / *(2)* ме́сяцев я действи́тельно полюби́л *(ж: полюби́ла)* тебя́.

| *love: the more I know you...* |

The more I'm around you, the more I love you. Чем бо́льше я ря́дом с тобо́й, тем сильне́е я люблю́ тебя́. ♦ **The more I know you, the more I love you and cherish you.** Чем бо́лее я узнаю́ тебя́, тем бо́льше люблю́ и леле́ю.

| *love: I love everything about you* |

I love *(1)* **...everything about you.** / *(2)* **...every part of you.** Я люблю́ *(1)* ...всё в тебе́. / *(2)* ...ка́ждую части́чку тебя́.

| *love: to know you is to love you* |

To know you is to love you. Знать тебя́ -- зна́чит люби́ть тебя́. ♦ **How would it be possible not to love you.** Невозмо́жно не люби́ть тебя́.

| *love: I'll tell the world* |

I want to tell the whole world that I love you. Я хочу́ рассказа́ть всему́ ми́ру, что я люблю́ тебя́. ♦ **I love you (with all my heart) and I'm not ashamed to tell anyone.** Я люблю́ тебя́ (всем се́рдцем) и не стыжу́сь сказа́ть об э́том кому́ уго́дно.

You can find common clothing sizes in Appendix 11 on page 778.

___love: *loving you*___

To love you is divine. Любить тебя -- божéственно. ♦ **Nothing matters but loving you.** Всё остальнóе, по сравнéнию с любóвью к тебé, не знáчит ничегó.

___love: *hopeless, but I love you*___

I know it's (completely) hopeless, but I love you (with all my heart). Я знáю, что э́то (совершéнно) безнадёжно, но я (всем сéрдцем) люблю́ тебя́.

___I ove: *I know I shouldn't love you*___

Are you mad at me for loving you? I know I shouldn't, but I can't help it. It just happens all by itself. Ты óчень сéрдишься на меня́ за любóвь к тебé? Я знáю, что не дóлжен *(ж: должнá)*, но я не могý ничегó с э́тим подéлать, так случи́лось самó по себé.

___love: *if you hear a rumor that I love you*___

If you hear a rumor that I love you, it's true. Éсли до тебя́ дошёл слух, что я люблю́ тебя́, так э́то прáвда.

___love: *I've loved you since...*___

I have loved you ever since I first *(1)* saw / *(2)* met you. Я полюби́л *(ж: полюби́ла)* тебя́ с тогó пéрвого рáза, как *(1)* уви́дел *(ж: уви́дела)* / *(2)* встрéтил *(ж: встрéтила)* тебя́. ♦ **Sometimes I think I've loved you *(1)* ...forever. / *(2)* ...all my life.** Иногдá я дýмаю, что я люби́л *(ж: люби́ла)* тебя́ *(1)* ...всегдá. / *(2)* ...всю мою́ жизнь.

___love: *to say I love you is not enough*___

To say "I love you" *(1)* ... just doesn't seem enough. / *(2)* ...seems like such an understatement. / *(3)* ...is the understatement of the year / *(4)* century. Прóсто сказáть «Я люблю́ тебя́» *(1)* ...кáжется не достáточно. / *(2)* ...звучи́т, как преуменьшéние. / *(3)* ... -- сáмое большóе преуменьшéние гóда / *(4)* вéка.

___love: *it's so easy to love you*___

It's so easy to love you. Так легкó люби́ть тебя́.

[*love: have I told you lately that I love you?*]

Have I told you lately that I love you? Говори́л *(ж: Говори́ла)* ли я тебé в послéднее врéмя, что люблю́ тебя́?

___love: *every time I kiss you*___

Every time I kiss you, I'm telling you straight from my heart that I love you. Кáждый раз, когдá целýю тебя́, я говорю́ тебé пря́мо от сéрдца к сéрдцу, что люблю́ тебя́.

___love: *I will always love you*___

I will always love you. Я бýду люби́ть тебя́ всегдá. ♦ **I will love you (and *[1,2]* cherish you) *(3)* ...until the day I die. / *(4)* ...until the end of time. / *(5,6)* ...forever.** Я бýду люби́ть (и *[1]* берéчь / *[2]* лелéять) тебя́ *(3)* ...до сáмой смéрти. / *(4)* ...до концá врéмени. / *(5)* ...вéчно / *(6)* ...всегдá.

___love: *I will never stop loving you*___

I will never stop loving you. Я никогдá не перестáну люби́ть тебя́. ♦ **It's not likely that I will ever stop loving you.** Э́то прóсто невероя́тно, что я когдá-нибудь тебя́ разлюблю́. ♦ **I can't stop loving you.** Я не могý перестáть люби́ть тебя́.

___love: *I promise to love you*___

I promise to love you and *(1)* ...respect you and care for you all my life. / *(2)* ...cherish you for the rest of our lives. Я обещáю люби́ть тебя́ *(1)* ..., уважáть тебя́ и забóтиться о тебé всю свою́ жизнь. / *(2)* ...и лелéять тебя́ всю остáвшуюся жизнь. ♦ **I *(1)* pledge / *(2)* promise that I will do everything (I possibly can) to prove that I love you.** Я *(1,2)* обещáю сдéлать всё, (что смогý,) чтóбы доказáть тебé свою́ любóвь.

___love: *I'll do everything to prove I love you*___

I will do everything to prove that I love you. Я бýду дéлать всё, чтóбы доказáть, что

For general rules of Russian grammar see Appendix 2 on page 686.

люблю тебя. ♦ **I love you and** *(1)* **...I want to... /** *(2)* **...I'm going to... spend the rest of my life proving it to you.** Я люблю тебя и *(1)* ...хочу провести ... / *(2)* ...проведу... всю оставшуюся жизнь, доказывая это тебе. ♦ **Even in ordinary, everyday things I'm going to try to communicate to you how much I love you.** Даже в обычных, повседневных делах я попытаюсь выразить тебе, как сильно я люблю тебя.

love: you're the only one I could love

You are the only person I could ever love. Ты единственная, которую я мог бы полюбить. *(ж: Ты единственный, которого я могла бы полюбить.)* ♦ **I love you and I cannot think of another woman** *(man)* **on this planet who I would prefer to spend my life with more than you.** Я люблю тебя и не могу подумать о другой женщине *(ж: другом мужчине)* на этой планете, с которой *(ж: которым)* предпочёл *(ж: препочла)* бы более, чем с тобой, провести жизнь. ♦ **Deep down in my heart I know that I can never love anyone but you.** В глубине своего сердца я знаю, что никогда не смогу полюбить никого, кроме тебя.

love: you're the only one I've ever loved

You are the only one I have ever loved. Ты единственная, которую я любил и люблю. *(ж: Ты единственный, которого я любила и люблю.)* ♦ **You are the only** *(1)* **woman /** *(2)* **man I have ever truly loved.** Ты *(1)* ...единственная женщина, которую... / *(2)* ...единственный мужчина, которого... я когда-либо по-настоящему любил *(ж: любила).*

love: there are no words to tell you

(1) **There are no words to tell you... /** *(2)* **I search in vain for the right words to tell you... /** *(3)* **There is no way that I can express in words... how much I love you (and** *[4]* **need /** *[5]* **want you).** *(1)* Нет слов, чтобы сказать,... / *(2)* Я ищу напрасно такие слова, которые рассказали бы тебе,... / *(3)* Я не могу выразить словами,... как сильно я люблю тебя (и *[4]* ...нуждаюсь в тебе. / *[5]* ...хочу тебя).

love: you can't imagine how much I love you

Can you (possibly) imagine how much I love you? Можешь ли ты себе представить, как сильно я люблю тебя? ♦ **You cannot imagine how much I love you.** Ты не можешь себе представить, как сильно я люблю тебя.

love: it's not easy for me to say

It's not easy for me to say how I feel, but I hope you know how much I love you. Мне нелегко сказать, что я чувствую, но я надеюсь, ты знаешь, как сильно я тебя люблю.

love: I never knew...

I never knew I could love someone as deeply as you. Я никогда не знал *(ж: знала),* что смогу полюбить кого-то так глубоко, как тебя.

love: why I love you

I love you for so many reasons (, but most of all I love you 'cause you're you). Я люблю тебя по многим причинам (, но больше всего за то, что ты есть ты). ♦ **For everything you are, for everything you do, I love you with all my heart.** За всё, что есть ты, за всё, что ты делаешь, я люблю тебя всем своим сердцем. ♦ **I love you for yourself alone.** Я люблю тебя за то, что ты есть ты. ♦ **I love you even more because I believe you like me for my own sake and nothing else.** Я люблю тебя ещё больше, потому что верю, ты любишь меня за меня самого *(ж: саму)* и ни за что больше. ♦ **It's all the little things that make me love you so much.** Я так сильно люблю тебя за все эти маленькие знаки внимания. ♦ **I love you because you have a way of bringing out the very best in me.** Я люблю тебя, потому что ты пробуждаешь самое лучшее во мне.

love: because I love you

Because I love you, I want to walk hand in hand with you across the years. Я хочу пройти

For transitive Russian verbs the cases that they take are shown by means of an = sign and the Russian case (abbreviated).

с тобо́й рука́ о́б руку по жи́зни, потому́ что я люблю́ тебя́.

love: *I love you no matter what*

No matter what your flaws and shortcomings are, I love you (with all my heart). Не име́ет значе́ния, каки́е у тебя́ недоста́тки и несоверше́нства, я люблю́ тебя́ (всем се́рдцем).

love: *I thought I'd never love again*

I thought I would never love again (until I met you). Я ду́мал *(ж: ду́мала)*, что никогда́ уже́ опя́ть не полюблю́ (, пока́ не встре́тил *[ж: встре́тила]* тебя́).

love: *I hope you can love me half as much*

I pray that in the (1) days / (2) years ahead you can grow to love me even half as much as I love you. Я молю́сь о том, что́бы с *(1)* дня́ми / *(2)* года́ми ты полюби́ла *(ж: полюби́л)* меня́ хотя́ бы наполови́ну так си́льно, как я люблю́ тебя́.

love: *I'm so happy you love me*

I'm so ([1] enormously / [2] gloriously / [3] infinitely / [4] tremendously) happy knowing that you love me. Я так *([1]* неимове́рно / *[2]* бесконе́чно / *[3]* невообрази́мо / *[4]* безме́рно) сча́стлив *(ж: сча́стлива)* знать, что ты лю́бишь меня́. ♦ **When you said you loved me, I felt shock waves of pure, unadulterated joy.** Когда́ ты сказа́ла *(ж: сказа́л)*, что лю́бишь меня́, я ощути́л *(ж: ощути́ла)* во́лны и́стинного, настоя́щего ликова́ния.

love: *love me*

Love me! Люби́ меня́!

love: *still?*

Do you still love me? Ты всё ещё лю́бишь меня́? ♦ **Tell me you (still) love me.** Скажи́ мне, что (всё ещё) лю́бишь меня́.

love: *I love your...*

Oh, (how) I love (1) ...your (beautiful) body / (2) face! / (3) ...your (beautiful) breasts / (4) ass / (5) buns! О, (как) я люблю́ *(1)* ...твоё (прекра́сное) те́ло / *(2)* лицо́! / *(3)* ...твою́ (прекра́сную) грудь / *(4,5)* по́пку! ♦ **I love your gentle touch and the warmth I feel at your side.** Мне нра́вится твоё не́жное прикоснове́ние и тепло́, исходя́щее от тебя́.

love: *what I love doing with you*

I love (1) ...holding hands with you. / (2) ...holding you in my arms. / (3) ...cuddling up with you. / (4) ...listening to your stories. Мне нра́вится *(1)* ...держа́ться за́ руки с тобо́й. / *(2)* ...обнима́ть тебя́. / *(3)* ...обнима́ться с тобо́й. / *(4)* ...слу́шать твои́ исто́рии. ♦ **I love looking at you.** Я люблю́ смотре́ть на тебя́.

love: *I love what you do*

I love the things you do to me. Мне нра́вится то, что ты де́лаешь со мной. ♦ **I love the way you make me feel.** Мне нра́вятся те чу́вства, кото́рые ты вызыва́ешь во мне. ♦ **I love the way I feel when I'm with you.** Мне нра́вятся мои́ ощуще́ния, когда́ я ря́дом с тобо́й. ♦ **I love the way you (1) ...touch me. / (2) ...kiss me. / (3) ...do that. / (4) ...hold me. / (5) ...squeeze. / (6) ...cry out. / (7) ...caress me.** Мне о́чень нра́вится, как ты *(1)* ...каса́ешься меня́. / *(2)* ...целу́ешь меня́. / *(3)* ...де́лаешь э́то. / *(4)* ...обнима́ешь меня́. / *(5)* ...сжима́ешь. / *(6)* ...вскри́киваешь. / *(7)* ...ласка́ешь меня́. ♦ **I love that!** Я люблю́ э́то! ♦ **Your constant show of affection makes me love you more and more.** Твоя́ постоя́нно выража́емая любо́вь всё бо́льше и бо́льше уси́ливает мою́ любо́вь к тебе́.

love: *I love to make love with you*

I love to make love (with you). Я люблю́ занима́ться любо́вью (с тобо́й).

love: *I want you to feel how much I love you*

I want you to feel with your whole body how much I love you and in so doing make you love me with all your heart. Я хочу́, что́бы всем свои́м те́лом ты ощути́ла, как си́льно я люблю́ тебя́, и э́то принесёт тебе́ таку́ю же любо́вь ко мне. ♦ **I still love you (as**

Russian verbs have 2 forms: imperfective and perfective.
They're given in that order.

much as ever). Я всё ещё люблю́ тебя́ (так же си́льно, как всегда́).

| *love: you'll love it* |

You're going to love it. Ты полю́бишь э́то.

| *love: if one truly loves a woman* |

Personally, I've always been infused with the conviction that if you truly love a woman and care for her, you do everything you possibly can to fill her with pleasure and suffuse her with love. Ли́чно я всегда́ был наделён убежде́нием, что е́сли действи́тельно лю́бишь же́нщину и забо́тишься о ней, то де́лаешь всё возмо́жное, что́бы напо́лнить её наслажде́нием и затопи́ть любо́вью.

| *love: loving each other* |

We love each other. Мы лю́бим друг дру́га. ♦ **If we truly love one another, we can do it.** Если мы действи́тельно лю́бим друг дру́га, мы мо́жем сде́лать э́то.

| *love: seeking someone not afraid to love* |

I *(1)* seek / *(2)* want someone who's not afraid to love. Я *(1)* ищу́ / *(2)* хочу́ того́, кто не бои́тся люби́ть.

| *love: I have a great capacity* |

I have a great capacity to love. I just need the right person. У меня́ огро́мная спосо́бность люби́ть. Мне то́лько ну́жен подходя́щий челове́к.

| *love: it's never too late* |

It's never too late to love. Никогда́ не по́здно люби́ть.

| *love: I don't love you* |

I don't love you (anymore). Я (бо́льше) не люблю́ тебя́.

| *love: quotations* |

"You can give without loving, but you cannot love without giving." *Ami Carmichael.* «Возмо́жно отдава́ть без любви́, но невозмо́жно люби́ть, не отдава́я.» *Ами Ка́рмайкл.* ♦ **"He who loves without jealousy does not truly love."** *The Zohar* «Тот, кто лю́бит без ре́вности, не лю́бит по-настоя́щему.» *Зоха́р.*

love *n* любо́вь *f* ♦ **all** *(1)* **my** / *(2)* **your** ~ вся *(1)* моя́ / *(2)* твоя́ любо́вь ♦ **ardent** ~ пы́лкая любо́вь ♦ **beautiful** ~ прекра́сная любо́вь ♦ **blind** ~ слепа́я любо́вь ♦ **blissful** ~ счастли́вая любо́вь ♦ **boundless** ~ безграни́чная любо́вь ♦ **budding** ~ расцвета́ющая любо́вь ♦ **burning** ~ горя́чая любо́вь ♦ **casual** ~ несерьёзная любо́вь ♦ **crazy** ~ безу́мная любо́вь ♦ **deep** ~ глубо́кая любо́вь ♦ **devoted** ~ пре́данная любо́вь ♦ **earnest** ~ и́скренняя любо́вь ♦ **enduring** ~ продолжа́ющаяся любо́вь ♦ *(1,2)* **eternal** ~ *(1)* бесконе́чная / *(2)* ве́чная любо́вь ♦ **everlasting** ~ бесконе́чная любо́вь ♦ **fervent** ~ пы́лкая любо́вь ♦ **fierce** ~ неи́стовая любо́вь ♦ **first** ~ пе́рвая любо́вь ♦ **great** ~ больша́я любо́вь ♦ **greatest** ~ велича́йшая любо́вь ♦ **inspired** ~ вдохнове́нная любо́вь ♦ **lasting** ~ про́чная любо́вь ♦ ~ **online** любо́вь по интерне́ту ♦ ~ **without clouds** безо́блачная любо́вь ♦ **marital** ~ супру́жеская любо́вь ♦ **mature** ~ зре́лая любо́вь ♦ **mutual** ~ взаи́мная любо́вь ♦ **my** ~ **(for you)** моя́ любо́вь (к *[familiar]* тебе́ / *[polite]* Вам) ♦ **no other** ~ никака́я друга́я любо́вь ♦ **one-sided** ~ односторо́нняя любо́вь ♦ **only** ~ еди́нственная любо́вь ♦ **our** ~ на́ша любо́вь ♦ **overpowering** ~ сокруша́ющая любо́вь ♦ **passionate** ~ стра́стная любо́вь ♦ **platonic** ~ платони́ческая любо́вь ♦ *(1-3)* **puppy** ~ *(1)* ребя́ческая / *(2)* де́тская любо́вь, *(3)* ю́ношеское увлече́ние ♦ **pure** ~ чи́стая любо́вь ♦ **real** ~ настоя́щая любо́вь ♦ **selfish** ~ эгоисти́чная любо́вь ♦ **sensual** ~ чу́вственная любо́вь ♦ **slow, passionate** ~ ме́дленная, стра́стная любо́вь ♦ **spiritual** ~ духо́вная любо́вь ♦ **sublime** ~ возвы́шенная любо́вь ♦ **such (a)** ~ така́я любо́вь ♦ **tender** ~ не́жная любо́вь ♦ **timid** ~ ро́бкая любо́вь ♦ **transient** ~ мимолётная любо́вь ♦ **true** ~ настоя́щая любо́вь ♦ **ultimate** ~ велича́йшая любо́вь ♦ **unconditional** ~

How to use the Cyrillic alphabet on the Internet is the subject of Appendix 20 on page 789.

безусло́вная любо́вь ♦ *(1,2)* **unending** ~ *(1)* бесконе́чная / *(2)* несконча́емая любо́вь ♦ **universal** ~ вселе́нская любо́вь ♦ *(1,2)* **unrequited** ~ *(1)* неразделённая / *(2)* безотве́тная любо́вь, любо́вь без взаи́мности ♦ **unselfish** ~ бескоры́стная любо́вь ♦ **well-balanced** ~ гармони́чная любо́вь ♦ **wonderful** ~ замеча́тельная любо́вь ♦ **young** ~ ю́ношеская любо́вь ♦ **your** ~ **(for me)** *(informal)* твоя́ любо́вь (ко мне); *(polite)* Ва́ша любо́вь (ко мне).

love: verb terms

be (crazy) in ~ (безу́мно) влюби́ться *(with whom = + в + prep.)* *(used in past tense)* ♦ **believe in** ~ ве́рить в любо́вь ♦ **be worthy of your** ~ заслу́живать / заслужи́ть твою́ любо́вь ♦ **burn with** ~ сгора́ть от любви́ ♦ **carry** ~ нести́ любо́вь ♦ **cherish your** ~ дорожи́ть твое́й любо́вью ♦ **conceal** *(1)* **my** / *(2)* **your** ~ скрыва́ть / скрыть *(1,2)* свою́ любо́вь, таи́ть *(1,2)* свою́ любо́вь ♦ **convey** ~ передава́ть / переда́ть любо́вь ♦ **declare** *(1)* **my** / *(1)* **your** ~ признава́ться / призна́ться в любви́ *(to whom = dat.)*, объясня́ться / объясни́ться в любви́ *(to whom = dat.)* ♦ **deserve your** ~ заслу́живать / заслужи́ть твою́ любо́вь ♦ **display** ~ пока́зывать / показа́ть любо́вь ♦ **encourage** ~ поощря́ть любо́вь ♦ **enjoy** ~ наслажда́ться любо́вью ♦ **express** *(1)* **my** / *(2)* **your** ~ выража́ть / вы́разить *(1,2)* свою́ любо́вь ♦ **fail in** ~ не име́ть успе́ха в любви́ ♦ **fall in** ~ влюби́ться *(with whom = + в + acc.)* ♦ **fall in** ~ *(1)* **impetuously** / *(2)* **impulsively** влюби́ться *(1,2)* опроме́тчиво *(with whom = + в + acc.)* ♦ **fall out of** ~ разлюби́ть *(with whom = acc.)* ♦ **feel** ~ чу́вствовать / почу́вствовать любо́вь ♦ **hide** *(1)* **my** / *(2)* **your** ~ скрыва́ть / скрыть *(1,2)* свою́ любо́вь, таи́ть *(1,2)* свою́ любо́вь ♦ **keep your** ~ бере́чь твою́ любо́вь ♦ **kill** *(1)* **my** / *(2)* **your** ~ убива́ть / уби́ть *(1)* мою́ / *(2)* твою́ любо́вь ♦ **live without** ~ жить без любви́ ♦ **lose your** ~ теря́ть / потеря́ть твою́ любо́вь ♦ **make** ~ занима́ться любо́вью *(to / with whom = + с + instr.)*, предава́ться любо́вным уте́хам *(to / with whom = + с + instr.)* ♦ **make** ~ **from the** *(1)* **back** / *(2)* **rear** занима́ться любо́вью *(1,2)* сза́ди ♦ **make** ~ **lying down** занима́ться любо́вью лёжа ♦ **make** ~ **sideways** занима́ться любо́вью на боку́ ♦ **make** ~ **sitting down** занима́ться любо́вью си́дя ♦ **make** ~ **standing up** занима́ться любо́вью сто́я ♦ **marry for** ~ *(man)* жени́ться по любви́; *(woman)* вы́йти за́муж по любви́ ♦ **proclaim** ~ признава́ться / призна́ться в любви́, объясня́ться / объясни́ться в любви́ ♦ **speak of** ~ говори́ть о любви́ ♦ **treasure your** ~ дорожи́ть твое́й любо́вью ♦ **win your** ~ завоёвывать / завоева́ть твою́ любо́вь.

love: other terms

being in ~ влюблённость*f* ♦ **confession of** ~ призна́ние в любви́ ♦ **couple in** ~ влюблённая па́р(очк)а ♦ **delights of** ~ восто́рги любви́ ♦ **expression of** ~ выраже́ние любви́ ♦ **feeling of** ~ чу́вство любви́ ♦ **fervent melody of** ~ стра́стная мело́дия любви́ ♦ **field of** ~ любо́вное по́прище ♦ **full of** ~ любвеоби́льный, -ая, -ое, -ые ♦ **glorious flower of** ~ великоле́пный цвето́к любви́ ♦ **harmony of** ~ **and happiness** гармо́ния любви́ и сча́стья ♦ **intensity of my** ~ си́ла мое́й любви́ ♦ **invincible magic of** ~ всепобежда́ющая ма́гия любви́ ♦ **joy of** ~ ра́дость любви́ ♦ **magical dreams of** ~ волше́бные грёзы любви́ ♦ **ocean(s) of** ~ океа́н(ы) любви́ ♦ **palace of** ~ дворе́ц любви́ ♦ **power of** ~ си́ла любви́ ♦ **prolonged feeling of** ~ дли́тельное чу́вство любви́ ♦ **queen of** ~ боги́ня любви́ ♦ **secure feeling of** ~ усто́йчивое чу́вство любви́ ♦ **strength of** *(1)* **my** / *(2)* **our** ~ си́ла *(1)* мое́й / *(2)* на́шей любви́.

love: I'm in love with you

I'm afraid I'm falling in love with you. Бою́сь, что я влюбля́юсь в тебя́. ♦ **The fact of the matter is, ...I'm in love with you. / ...I've fallen in love with you.** Де́ло в том, что ...я люблю́ тебя́. / ...я влюблён *(ж: влюблена́)* в тебя́. ♦ **(I have to confess,)** *(1)* **I've fallen... /** *(2)* **I'm... head over heels in love with you.** (Я до́лжен *[ж: должна́]* призна́ться,) *(1,2)* Я потеря́л *(ж: потеря́ла)* го́лову от любви́ к тебе́. ♦ **I'm (**[1]** madly /** [2]** crazily /** [3]** rapturously / [4]** wildly /** [5]** totally /** [6]** hopelessly) in love with you.** Я (*[1,2]* безу́мно / *[3]*

Russian adjectives have long and short forms.
Where short forms are given, they are labeled as such.

восто́рженно / *[4]* ди́ко / *[5]* безграни́чно / *[6]* безнадёжно) влюблён *(ж: влюблена́)* в тебя́. ♦ **I can no longer mask the fact that I'm in love with you.** Я не могу́ до́льше скрыва́ть тот факт, что я люблю́ тебя́. ♦ **I go away from any encounter with you with my heart spinning wildly and my mind erupting in a fireworks display of love thoughts about you.** По́сле ка́ждой встре́чи с тобо́й я ухожу́ с бе́шено стуча́щим се́рдцем и с це́лым фейерве́рком любо́вных мы́слей о тебе́.

> *love: proclaiming my love*

You may think it impossible that someone could proclaim love for you after knowing you such a short time, but what you have done to my heart gives it no other choice than to make this proclamation. Ты веро́ятно ду́маешь, что невозмо́жно объясня́ться в любви́ по́сле тако́го коро́ткого вре́мени знако́мства, но то, что ты де́лаешь с мои́м се́рдцем, не оставля́ет ему́ никако́го друго́го вы́бора, кро́ме как объясни́ться. ♦ **I suppose it's too early to speak of love, but I must tell you, I have very strong, tender feelings for you.** Я допуска́ю, что ещё сли́шком ра́но говори́ть о любви́, но я до́лжен *(ж: должна́)* сказа́ть, что у меня́ о́чень си́льные, не́жные чу́вства к тебе́.

> *love: hunger for love*

The thought patterns that yielded your choice of words and sentences in your ad reveal the exact same raging hunger for love and affection that I harbor within me. Мы́сли, роди́вшие вы́бор слов и предложе́ний в Ва́шем объявле́нии, говоря́т о то́чно тако́й же неи́стовой жа́жде любви́ и не́жности, кото́рая таи́тся во мне.

> *love: your letters bring love*

Your letters always fill my heart with love for you. Твои́ пи́сьма всегда́ наполня́ют моё се́рдце любо́вью к тебе́. ♦ **Always in your letters there is present the feeling of love and devotion.** В твои́х пи́сьмах всегда́ прису́тствуют чу́вства любви́ и пре́данности. ♦ **When I read your letters, I feel with my heart how much goodness and sweetness and love there is in you.** Чита́я твои́ пи́сьма, я всем се́рдцем чу́вствую, как мно́го в тебе́ доброты́, не́жности и любви́.

> *love: your words of love bring happiness*

When I *(1)* read / *(2)* hear your words of love, I feel *(3)* cosmic / *(4)* rampant joy in the deepest part of my soul. Когда́ я *(1)* чита́ю / *(2)* слы́шу твои́ слова́ любви́, я чу́вствую *(3)* косми́ческое / *(4)* неи́стовое ликова́ние в мое́й душе́. ♦ **This letter of yours was so unexpected. Your *(1)* sweet / *(2)* beautiful words of love have *(3)* ...set my heart completely aquiver. / *(4)* ...sent my heart into utter delight.** Это письмо́ от тебя́ бы́ло так неожи́данно. Твои́ *(1)* не́жные / *(2)* прекра́сные слова́ любви́ *(3)* ...заставля́ют моё се́рдце трепета́ть. / *(4)* ...вызыва́ют в моём се́рдце по́лный восто́рг.

> *love: you were made for love*

You were made for love. Ты была́ со́здана *(ж: был со́здан)* для любви́.

> *love: love pictures of you*

I paint love pictures to you in all my thoughts. В своём воображе́нии я рису́ю карти́ны любви́ с тобо́й. ♦ **All my thoughts are filled with love pictures of you.** Все мои́ мы́сли полны́ любо́вными карти́нами о тебе́.

> *love: thoughts of love*

I'll be thinking of you — warm, tender, affectionate thoughts, full of love. Мои́ мы́сли о тебе́ бу́дут тёплыми, не́жными и напо́лненными любо́вью.

> *love: my heart sings love songs to you*

My heart sings ballads of love to you every minute of the day. Ка́ждую мину́ту моё се́рдце поёт балла́ды любви́ к тебе́.

> *love: I send you love*

Russian nouns are either masculine, feminine or neuter.
Adjectives with them will be the same.

I send you many hugs and kisses, each one filled with much love. Я посыла́ю тебе́ мно́го объя́тий и поцелу́ев, ка́ждый из кото́рых по́лон любви́.

___love: *I want / need your love*___

I need your love. Мне нужна́ твоя́ любо́вь. ◆ **My greatest aspiration in life is to win your love.** Са́мое си́льное стремле́ние мое́й жи́зни -- завоева́ть твою́ любо́вь. ◆ **All I aspire to in this world is to *(1)* have / *(2)* win your love.** Всё, к чему́ я стремлю́сь в э́том ми́ре, -- *(1,2)* завоева́ть твою́ любо́вь. ◆ **To *(1)* have / *(2)* win your *(3)* precious / *(4)* wonderful love is the greatest *(5)* goal / *(6)* thing I can aspire to.** *(1,2)* Заслужи́ть твою́ *(3)* драгоце́нную / *(4)* удиви́тельную любо́вь -- велича́йшая *(5,6)* цель, к кото́рой я стремлю́сь. ◆ **I'm pleading for your love.** Я молю́ о твое́й любви́. ◆ **I will do everything (I possibly can) to win your love.** Я сде́лаю всё, (что смогу́,) что́бы завоева́ть твою́ любо́вь.

___love: *give me your love*___

Give me your love — all of it. Подари́ мне всю свою́ любо́вь. ◆ **Shower me with your love.** Изле́й на меня́ свою́ любо́вь.

___love: *only your love can quench the fires*___

Nothing can quench the fire that rages inside me except your love. Ничто́, кро́ме твое́й любви́, не мо́жет утоли́ть ого́нь, бушу́ющий во мне.

___love: *never felt so much love*___

I've never felt so much love for anyone (in my whole life) (as I feel for you). Никогда́ в жи́зни я не чу́вствовал *(ж: чу́вствовала)* тако́й огро́мной любви́ (, как я чу́вствую к тебе́). ◆ **I've never felt so much in love with anyone (in my whole life) (as I feel with you).** Я никогда́ (в жи́зни) не был *(ж: была́)* так влюблён *(ж: влюблена́)* в кого́-то (, как я влюблён *[ж: влюблена́]* в тебя́). ◆ **I've never been so deeply in love with anyone.** Я никого́ никогда́ так глубоко́ не люби́л *(ж: люби́ла)*. ◆ **I've never felt such a crazy ache of love in all my life.** Никогда́ в жи́зни я так си́льно не срада́л *(страда́ла)* от любви́. ◆ **I am lost in love's labyrinth.** Я потеря́лся *(ж: потеря́лась)* в любо́вном лабири́нте. ◆ **This love that is blossoming in my heart for you is unlike anything I've ever known.** Эта любо́вь к тебе́, цвету́щая в моём се́рдце, непохо́жа ни на что друго́е, что бы́ло со мной.

___love: *I have so much love for you*___

I feel so much love for you. Я чу́вствую огро́мную любо́вь к тебе́. ◆ **My heart *(1-3)* ...overflows... / *(4-6)* ...is overflowing / *(7)* brimming... with love (for you).** Моё се́рдце *(1,4)* ...перепо́лнено / *(2,5)* переполня́ется... / *(3,6)* истека́ет / *(7)* ...до краёв напо́лнено... любо́вью (к тебе́). ◆ **My heart is (so) full of love for you.** Моё се́рдце полно́ любо́вью к тебе́. ◆ **I ache with love for you.** Я бо́лен *(ж: больна́)* от любви́ к тебе́. ◆ **I feel all kinds of love for you at one time.** Я ощуща́ю все ви́ды любви́ к тебе́ в одно́ и то же вре́мя. ◆ **If you could but know how much love dwells in my heart for you.** Если бы ты то́лько могла́ *(ж: мог)* знать, како́й огро́мной любо́вью к тебе́ полно́ моё се́рдце. ◆ **I have a heart full of love to bestow upon you.** Я одарю́ тебя́ всей любо́вью, наполня́ющей моё се́рдце. ◆ **So much love has blossomed in my heart for you.** В моём се́рдце расцвела́ огро́мная любо́вь к тебе́. ◆ **I am *(1)* completely / *(2)* utterly / *(3)* totally swept away by my love for you.** Я *(1-3)* весь охва́чен *(ж: вся охва́чена)* любо́вью к тебе́. ◆ **I have a cornucopia of love that I want to bring to your life.** Я хочу́ принести́ в твою́ жизнь рог, по́лный любви́. ◆ **I'm going to give you a cornucopia of love.** Я дам тебе́ рог, по́лный любви́. ◆ **All that my soul yearns to express at this moment is embodied in one word -- love.** Всё, что моя́ душа́ жа́ждет вы́разить в э́тот миг, воплоща́ется в одно́м сло́ве -- любо́вь. ◆ **My love for you is insatiable.** Моя́ любо́вь к тебе́ ненасы́тна. ◆ **I must confess, I am sick with love for you.** Я до́лжен *(ж: должна́)* призна́ться, я бо́лен *(ж: больна́)* от любви́ к тебе́.

Learn more about Russian customs in Appendix 15, page 782.

love: if this isn't love, what is?

If the feeling that's raging through my heart for you isn't love, then I guess I'm really out of touch with what love is. Если чу́вство к тебе́, бушу́ющее в моём се́рдце не любо́вь, тогда́ я про́сто не понима́ю, что тако́е любо́вь. ♦ **This is love.** Вот э́то и есть любо́вь.

love: I fall in love with you again each day

Each time a new day dawns, I fall in love with you all over again. Ка́ждое у́тро, на рассве́те я влюбля́юсь в тебя́ опя́ть.

love: love at first sight

It was love at first sight. Это была́ любо́вь с пе́рвого взгля́да. ♦ **Do you believe in love at first sight?** Ве́ришь ли ты в любо́вь с пе́рвого взгля́да? ♦ **The moment I** *(1)* **saw / (2) met you, I fell head over heels in love with you.** В тот моме́нт, когда́ я *(1)* уви́дел *(ж: уви́дела)/* *(2)* встре́тил *(ж: встре́тила)* тебя́, я влюби́лся *(ж: влюби́лась)* в тебя́ без па́мяти. ♦ **I've been consumed with love for you from the very first moment I laid eyes on you.** Я воспыла́л любо́вью к тебе́ с того́ са́мого моме́нта, как мой взгляд останови́лся на тебе́.

love: love from the very beginning

I've been in love with you since the first day I *(1)* **met / (2) saw you.** Я полюби́л тебя́ с пе́рвого дня, *(1)* встре́тив / *(2)* уви́дев тебя́. ♦ **I've been (hopelessly) in love with you since the first time I met you.** С пе́рвой на́шей встре́чи я (безнадёжно) влюблён *(ж: влюблена́)* в тебя́.

The first time I met you, I fell head over heels in love with you. С пе́рвой на́шей встре́чи я по́ уши влюби́лся *(ж: влюби́лась)* в тебя́.

love: when I think of you my heart fills with love

My heart fills with love and joy whenever I think of you. Моё се́рдце наполня́ется любо́вью и ра́достью вся́кий раз, когда́ я ду́маю о тебе́. ♦ **I can't think about you without instantly feeling love for you.** Сто́ит то́лько поду́мать о тебе́, как то́тчас чу́вство любви́ возника́ет во мне. ♦ **Every time I think of you, a warm wave of love washes through me.** Вся́кий раз, когда́ бы я ни поду́мал о тебе́, тёплые во́лны любви́ залива́ют меня́.

love: the sight of you fills me with love

The sight of your beautiful face fills my whole body with warm excitement and floods my heart with feelings of love for you. Взгляд на твоё прекра́сное лицо́ наполня́ет всё моё те́ло жа́рким возбужде́нием и затопля́ет се́рдце чу́вством любви́ к тебе́.

love: I can't express / describe my love

I cannot begin to express the love that abides in my heart for you. В моём се́рдце така́я любо́вь, кото́рую невозмо́жно вы́разить. ♦ **There are no words to** *(1)* **...tell you... / (2) ...describe... how much love (3) ...there is in my heart for you. / (4) ...my heart holds for you.** Нет слов, что́бы *(1+3)* ...рассказа́ть, како́й огро́мной любо́вью к тебе́ полно́ моё се́рдце. / *(2+4)* ...описа́ть, любо́вь к тебе́, наполня́ющую моё се́рдце. ♦ **How can I describe to you all the love that I harbor for you in my heart?** Как мне описа́ть тебе́ всю ту любо́вь, кото́рая таи́тся в моём се́рдце? ♦ **There are no words to describe the** *(1)* **depth / (2) immensity / (3) vastness / (4) intensity of the love that I bear in my heart for you.** Нет слов, что́бы описа́ть *(1)* глубину́ / *(2,3)* безме́рность / *(4)* си́лу той любви́ к тебе́, кото́рой полно́ моё се́рдце. ♦ **Words alone cannot express the love that I feel for you in my heart.** Невозмо́жно вы́разить слова́ми всю ту любо́вь к тебе́, кото́рой полно́ моё се́рдце. ♦ **How can I express all the love I feel in my heart for you?** Как мне вы́разить тебе́ всю ту любо́вь, кото́рой полно́ моё се́рдце? ♦ **When I talk with you on the phone, it seems as though I'm never able to convey the love and longing that I feel in my heart for you.** Когда́ я говорю́ с тобо́й по телефо́ну, ка́жется, что никогда́ не смогу́ переда́ть ту любо́вь к тебе́ и тоску́ по тебе́, кото́рыми полно́ моё се́рдце.

A slash always denotes "or."
You can choose the numbered words before and after.

---

love: *you can never know the depth of my love*

You can never fully know the *(1)* **depth** / *(2)* **extent** / *(3)* **vastness of my love.** Ты никогда́ не смо́жешь по́лностью узна́ть *(1)* глубину́ / *(2)* си́лу / *(3)* необъя́тность мое́й любви́. ♦ **My love for you is so deep and tender that it eclipses the range of human imagination.** Моя́ любо́вь к тебе́ так глубока́ и нежна́, что э́то за преде́лами челове́ческого воображе́ния. ♦ **You can never know how much love I bear in my heart for you.** Ты не представля́ешь, каку́ю огро́мную любо́вь к тебе́ я ношу́ в своём се́рдце. ♦ **You can't begin to fathom the depths of the love that fills my heart for you.** Ты не мо́жешь пости́гнуть всю глубину́ той любви́ к тебе́, кото́рой полно́ моё се́рдце.

---

love: *all my love is yours*

All my love is *(1)* **...yours.** / *(2)* **...for you alone.** Вся моя́ любо́вь *(1)* ...-- э́то ты. / *(2)* ...то́лько для тебя́ одно́й *(ж: одного́)*. ♦ **I offer to you all my love, all my being, all my life.** Я предлага́ю тебе́ всю мою́ любо́вь, всё моё существо́, всю мою́ жизнь. ♦ **I give you my unconditional love.** Я безогово́рочно отдаю́ тебе́ мою́ любо́вь. ♦ **I offer you love -- boundless and wonderful and true.** Я предлага́ю тебе́ любо́вь безграни́чную, замеча́тельную и ве́рную.

---

love: *love without strings*

My love for you is without (any) strings. Моя́ любо́вь не ста́вит тебе́ (никаки́х) усло́вий.

---

love: *I'll prove my love to you*

I'm going to make every (possible) effort to prove my love for you. Я приложу́ все (возмо́жные) уси́лия, что́бы доказа́ть тебе́ свою́ любо́вь.

---

love: *I want to show you love*

I want to show you my love in every possible way. Я хочу́ вы́разить тебе́ свою́ любо́вь все́ми возмо́жными сре́дствами. ♦ **I want to spend all my time showing you love.** Я хочу́ всё вре́мя выка́зывать тебе́ свою́ любо́вь. ♦ **I want to show you what true love is all about.** Я хочу́ показа́ть тебе́, что тако́е и́стинная любо́вь. ♦ **Darling, I want so very much to (see you and talk with you and) show you love in all the ways that it's possible to show love.** Дорога́я *(ж: Дорого́й)*, я так хочу́ (уви́деть тебя́, говори́ть с тобо́й и) демонстри́ровать тебе́ свою́ любо́вь все́ми возмо́жными сре́дствами. ♦ **My heart yearns to show you my love in an endless stream of warm embraces and soft,** *(1)* **adoring** / *(2)* **loving kisses.** Моё се́рдце жа́ждет показа́ть тебе́ любо́вь в бесконе́чном пото́ке тёплых объя́тий и мя́гких, *(1)* обожа́ющих / *(2)* лю́бящих поцелу́ев.

---

love: *I want you always to feel love*

I never want to see anything but pleasure in your eyes, love on your lips, and happiness in your heart. Я всегда́ хочу́ ви́деть то́лько наслажде́ние в твои́х глаза́х, любо́вь на твои́х губа́х и сча́стье в твоём се́рдце. ♦ **I want to always see love reflected in your eyes.** Я всегда́ хочу́ ви́деть любо́вь, отража́ющуюся в твои́х глаза́х. ♦ **I want to foster a love in your heart that will grow ever stronger as the years go by.** Я хочу́ взрасти́ть любо́вь в твоём се́рдце, кото́рая бу́дет станови́ться то́лько сильне́е с года́ми. ♦ **Personally, I've always been infused with the conviction that if you truly love a woman and care for her, you do everything you possibly can to fill her with pleasure and suffuse her with love.** Ли́чно я всегда́ был наделён убежде́нием, что е́сли действи́тельно лю́бишь же́нщину и забо́тишься о ней, то де́лаешь всё возмо́жное, что́бы напо́лнить её наслажде́нием и затопи́ть любо́вью. ♦ **I want to feel love spring from your heart.** Я хочу́ чу́вствовать любо́вь, струя́щуюся из твоего́ се́рдца.

---

love: *I want to inundate you with love*

I want to inundate you with love and affection. Я хочу́ затопи́ть тебя́ любо́вью и не́жностью. ♦ **You make me want to innundate you with warm, tender affection, love, and**

Common adult weights are given in Appendix 10, page 777.

adoration.Ты вызыва́ешь во мне жела́ние затопи́ть тебя́ тёплой, не́жной любо́вью и обожа́нием. ♦ **I could just smother you with love and affection.** Я про́сто осы́плю тебя́ свое́й любо́вью и не́жностью. ♦ **I want to envelop you with (***[1]* **endless /** *[2]* **infinite /** *[3]* **ever-lasting /** *[4]* **boundless) love.** Я хочу́ оку́тать тебя́ (*[1,2]* бесконе́чной / *[3]* несконча́емой / *[4]* безграни́чной) любо́вью. ♦ *(1)* **I want to... /** *(2)* **I'm going to... lavish love and affection on you beyond your wildest dreams.** *(1)* Я хочу́ изли́ть... / *(2)* Я бу́ду излива́ть... на тебя́ свою́ любо́вь и не́жность сверх всех твои́х са́мых заве́тных жела́ний.

---
love: *my love for you grows*
---

(1) **The love we share... /** *(2)* **My love for you...** *(3)* **...grows stronger (, brighter and deeper)...** */ (4)* **...grows more and more... /** *(5)* **...soars higher and higher...** *(6)* **...with every passing day.** */ (7)* **...every day.** *(1)* Любо́вь, кото́рую мы разделя́ем,... / *(2)* Моя́ любо́вь к тебе́... *(3)* ...стано́вится всё сильне́е (, светле́е и глу́бже)... / *(4)* ...стано́вится бо́льше и бо́льше... */ (5)* ...взлета́ет всё вы́ше и вы́ше... *(6,7)* с ка́ждым (*[6]* проходя́щим) днём. ♦ **The love for you in my heart has grown and strengthened.** Любо́вь к тебе́ в моём се́рдце вы́росла и укрепи́лась. ♦ **The love that I carry for you in my heart flourishes and deepens ever more with each passing day.** Любо́вь к тебе́, кото́рой напо́лнено моё се́рдце, расцвета́ет всё сильне́е и стано́вится всё глу́бже с ка́ждым проходя́щим днём.

---
love: *my love for you has no limit*

My love for you is *(1)* **...fathomless. /** *(2)* **unmeasurable. /** *(3)* **infinite. /** *(4)* **limitless. /** *(5)* **...beyond measure.** Моя́ любо́вь к тебе́ *(1,2)* ...неизмери́ма. / *(3)* бесконе́чна. / *(4)* беспреде́льна. / *(5)* ...вы́ше всех измере́ний. ♦ **My love for you** *(1)* **...is as boundless as the ocean. /** *(2)* **...is as timeless as eternity. /** *(3)* **...is as endless as the stars. /** *(4)* **...goes beyond the stars. /** *(5)* **...transcends everything else (in this world). /** *(6)* **...transcends all** *(7,8)* **bounds.** */ (9)* **...knows no boundaries.** Моя́ любо́вь к тебе́ *(1)* ...бездо́нна, как океа́н. / *(2)* ...безвре́менна, как ве́чность. / *(3)* ...бесконе́чна, как звёзды. / *(4)* ...-- вы́ше звёзд. / *(5)* ...превосхо́дит всё друго́е (в э́том ми́ре). / *(6)* ... превосхо́дит все *(7)* преде́лы / *(8)* грани́цы. / *(9)* ...не зна́ет никаки́х грани́ц. ♦ **There is no limit to my love for you.** Мое́й любви́ к тебе́ нет преде́ла. ♦ **There is no way to measure how much love my heart holds for you.** Невозмо́жно изме́рить глубину́ той любви́ к тебе́, кото́рой напо́лнено моё се́рдце.

---
love: *my love for you is above all else*

Next to my love for you, all else is *(1)* **immaterial /** *(2)* **insignificant /** *(3)* **trivial.** Ря́дом с мое́й любо́вью к тебе́ всё остально́е *(1)* несуще́ственно / *(2)* незначи́тельно / *(3)* тривиа́льно.

---
love: *never doubt my love*

If you were to have even the slightest doubt about my love for you, it would cut into my heart like a knife. Е́сли бы у тебя́ появи́лось хоть мале́йшее сомне́ние в мое́й любви́, э́то бы́ло бы для меня́ ножо́м в се́рдце.

---
love: *my love for you will never change*

My love for you will never *(1)* **waver /** *(2)* **falter.** Моя́ любо́вь к тебе́ не *(1)* разве́ется / *(2)* осла́бнет никогда́. ♦ **My love for you has never wavered since the day I met you.** С того́ дня, когда́ я встре́тил *(ж: встре́тила)* тебя́, моя́ любо́вь к тебе́ никогда́ не ослабева́ла. ♦ **My love for you is unflagging.** Моя́ любо́вь к тебе́ неосла́бна. ♦ **Nothing** *(1)* **will /** *(2)* **could ever change my love for you.** Ничто́ никогда́ не *(1)* ...изме́нит... / *(2)* ...смогло́ бы измени́ть... мою́ любо́вь к тебе́. ♦ **These vows of love that I make to you now will endure for as long as my time on this earth.** Э́ти обе́ты любви́, кото́рые я даю́ тебе́ сейча́с, бу́дут дли́ться сто́лько, ско́лько моя́ жизнь на э́той земле́.

An italicized ж *in parentheses indicates a woman speaking.*

love: *I pledge my life to our love*

I promise to devote my life to our love. Я обеща́ю посвяти́ть свою́ жизнь на́шей любви́. ♦ **I promise *(1-3)* to live in your love for all the days of my life.** Я обеща́ю *(1)* храни́ть / *(2)* леле́ять / *(3)* бере́чь твою́ любо́вь до конца́ мои́х дней. ♦ **I *(1)* pledge / *(2)* promise that I will do everything (I possibly can) to make our love grow ever stronger, ever deeper, ever more beautiful.** Я *(1,2)* обеща́ю сде́лать всё, (что смогу́,) что́бы сде́лать на́шу любо́вь ещё сильне́е, ещё глу́бже, ещё прекра́снее. ♦ **I promise you a lifetime of *(1)* unwavering / *(2)* enduring / *(3)* unremitting / *(4)* steadfast love and adoration.** Я обеща́ю тебе́ на всю жизнь *(1)* непоколеби́мую / *(2)* кре́пкую / *(3)* неослабева́ющую / *(4)* сто́йкую любо́вь и обожа́ние. ♦ **On the altar of God I will make a lifetime *(1,2)* pledge of love and devotion to you.** Пе́ред Бо́жьим алтарём я дам тебе́ *(1)* обе́т / *(2)* обеща́ние любви́ и пре́данности на всю жизнь. ♦ **I will do everything I possibly can to make our love flourish and deepen.** Я бу́ду де́лать всё, что смогу́, что́бы на́ша любо́вь расцвета́ла и углубля́лась.

love: *you are my love*

You are my love, my life, my happiness (-- always). Ты моя́ любо́вь, моя́ жизнь, моё сча́стье (навсегда́). ♦ **You are my first and only love.** Ты моя́ пе́рвая и еди́нственная любо́вь. ♦ **You are (and always will be) the love of my life.** Ты любо́вь мое́й жи́зни (и бу́дешь е́ю всегда́). ♦ **You are my one and only love.** Ты моя́ одна́ еди́нственная любо́вь. ♦ **You are the love of my life.** Ты любо́вь мое́й жи́зни. ♦ **You will always be the love of my life.** Ты всегда́ бу́дешь еди́нственной любо́вью мое́й жи́зни. ♦ **You are my goddess of love.** Ты моя́ боги́ня любви́. ♦ **You are (forever) my one true love.** Ты (навсегда́) моя́ еди́нственная настоя́щая любо́вь. ♦ **You are the cynosure of all my love.** Ты путево́дная звезда́ мое́й любви́. ♦ **You are my (brightly shining) light of love.** Ты мой (я́рко горя́щий) свет любви́. ♦ **You are the love of a lifetime. None could ever be greater or more beautiful.** Ты любо́вь всей жи́зни. Никто́ никогда́ не смо́жет быть лу́чше или прекра́снее. ♦ **What more could I ask for than you as my love in life.** Чего́ ещё я мог *(ж: могла́)* бы жела́ть кро́ме того́, что́бы ты была́ *(ж: был)* мое́й любо́вью на всю жизнь.

love: *sharing love with you*

I want to spend endless hours sharing love and tenderness with you. Я хочу́ проводи́ть бесконе́чные часы́, наслажда́ясь любо́вью и не́жностью с тобо́й. ♦ **The greatest happiness I can imagine is to spend my life with you, sharing love and all joys and tribulations.** Са́мое большо́е сча́стье, кото́рое я могу́ себе́ предста́вить, -- э́то прожи́ть всю жизнь с тобо́й, деля́ любо́вь, ра́дости и невзго́ды.

love: *what your love is to me*

Having your love is a dream come true. Твоя́ любо́вь -- э́то сон, ста́вший я́вью ♦ **Your love and devotion are the nectar and ambrosia for my soul.** Твои́ любо́вь и пре́данность -- некта́р и амбро́зия для мое́й души́. ♦ **I'm the luckiest guy in the world to have your love.** Я счастли́вейший мужчи́на на све́те потому́, что у меня́ есть твоя́ любо́вь. ♦ **I can't describe how much it means to me to have your love.** Я не в си́лах описа́ть, как мно́го зна́чит для меня́ твоя́ любо́вь. ♦ **All things around me are sweetened by the magic of your love.** Все ве́щи вокру́г меня́ освещены́ волшебство́м твое́й любви́.

love: *your love = happiness*

I'm so happy to have your love. Я так сча́стлив *(ж: сча́стлива)* твое́й любо́вью. ♦ **I'm so (*[1]* enormously / *[2]* tremendously / *[3]* gloriously / *[4]* infinitely) happy knowing that I have your love in this world.** Я так (*[1,2]* неимове́рно / *[3]* бесконе́чно / *[4]* невообрази́мо) сча́стлив *(ж: сча́стлива)* знать, что в э́том ми́ре у меня́ есть твоя́ любо́вь. ♦ **I revel in the boundless luxury of your love.** Я пиру́ю в беспреде́льной ро́скоши твое́й любви́. ♦ **My greatest joy is having you for / as my love.** Моя́ велича́йшая ра́дость, что

Procedures for getting married to a Russian are outlined in Appendix 18, page 787.

ты моя любовь. ♦ **Knowing that you love me as much as I love you fills my heart with indescribable** *(1)* **joy /** *(2)* **elation /** *(3)* **rapture.** Сознание, что ты любишь меня так же сильно, как я люблю тебя, наполняет моё сердце *(1)* ...невероятной радостью. / *(2)* ...невероятным ликованием / *(3)* восторгом. ♦ **The happiness I've found in your love is beyond** *(1)* **description /** *(2)* **words.** Счастье, которое я нашёл *(ж: нашла)* в твоей любви, невозможно *(1)* ...описать / *(2)* ...выразить словами.

---
love: what your love does to me

The sunshine of your love has melted away all of my loneliness. Солнечный свет твоей любви растопил всё моё одиночество. ♦ **Your constant show of affection fills my heart with love for you.** Твоя постоянно выражаемая любовь наполняет моё сердце любовью к тебе. ♦ **Your love is the sun that awakens life within me.** Твоя любовь -- это солнце, пробуждающее жизнь во мне. ♦ **Your love makes me starry-eyed.** Твоя любовь делает меня мечтателем.

---
love: your love is wonderful

Your love is all that is good and wonderful and precious in this world. Твоя любовь -- это всё, что есть хорошего, удивительного и драгоценного в этом мире. ♦ **Love with you is more beautiful than I ever imagined.** Любовь с тобой намного прекраснее, чем я представлял *(ж: представляла)* себе. ♦ **Your love is the** *(1)* **greatest /** *(2)* **most wonderful / *(3)* most beautiful I've ever known.** Твоя любовь -- *(1)* ...величайшее,... / *(2)* ...самое замечательное,... / *(3)* ...самое прекрасное,... что я когда-либо знал *(ж: знала)*. ♦ **You're the most wonderful love a person could ever have.** Любовь к тебе -- самое замечательное, что может быть дано человеку. ♦ **Love with you is a beautiful dream.** Любовь с тобой -- прекрасная мечта. ♦ **What paradise it is to bask in the wonderful warmth of your love.** Какое райское наслаждение -- чудесное тепло твоей любви. ♦ **I can never get over the wonder and ecstasy of your love.** Я никогда не смогу надивиться чуду и экстазу твоей любви. ♦ **I never thought that love could be this** *(1)* **beautiful /** *(2)* **deep /** *(3)* **wonderful.** Я никогда не думал *(ж: думала)*, что любовь может быть такой *(1)* прекрасной / *(2)* глубокой / *(3)* замечательной.

---
love: you make my life a festival of love

You make my *(1)* **life /** *(2)* **world a daily festival of love.** Ты превращаешь *(1)* ...мою жизнь... / *(2)* ...мой мир... в ежедневный праздник любви.

---
love: once in a lifetime

A love like this comes only once in a lifetime. Такая любовь, как эта, бывает только раз в жизни.

---
love: I could never ask for more than your love

I could never ask for more (in this *[1]* **life /** *[2]* **world) than your love.** Я никогда не мог *(ж: могла)* бы желать ничего большего (в *[1]* ...этой жизни... / *[2]* ...этом мире...), чем твоей любви. ♦ **Nothing Nothing in this world is more important to me than your love.** Ничто в этом мире не важно для меня так, как твоя любовь. ♦ **Nothing means as much to me as your love.** Ничто не значит для меня так много, как твоя любовь. ♦ **What more could I ask for than your love.** Чего более могу я просить, чем твоей любви. ♦ **Your love is the only reward I ever want.** Твоя любовь -- единственная награда, которую я хочу.

---
love: the blessing of your love
---

(1) **God /** *(2)* **Heaven has blessed me with your** *(3)* **precious /** *(4)* **wonderful love.** *(1)* Бог благословил... / *(2)* Небеса благословили... меня твоей *(3)* драгоценной / *(4)* замечательной любовью. ♦ **I thank God for blessing me with your wonderful love.** Я благодарю Бога за то, что он благословил меня твоей замечательной любовью. ♦

A list of conjugated Russian verbs is given in Appendix 3 on page 699.

What greater blessing could I (ever) ask for than your *(1)* wonderful / *(2)* beautiful / *(3)* precious love? О како́м бо́льшем благослове́нии мог *(ж: могла́)* бы я проси́ть, чем о твое́й *(1)* замеча́тельной / *(2)* прекра́сной / *(3)* драгоце́нной любви́. ♦ **Your love is the *(1)* greatest / *(2)* most precious blessing in my life.** Твоя́ любо́вь -- *(1)* велича́йшее / *(2)* драгоце́ннейшее благослове́ние в мое́й жи́зни. ♦ **There is no greater blessing for me than your love.** Для меня́ нет бо́льшего благослове́ния, чем твоя́ любо́вь. ♦ **I am truly blessed to have your love.** Я действи́тельно благословлён *(ж: благословлена́)* твое́й любо́вью. ♦ **Having your love is the greatest, most wonderful gift that God could give me.** Твоя́ любо́вь -- э́то са́мый лу́чший, са́мый удиви́тельный пода́рок, кото́рый я получи́л *(ж: получи́ла)* от Бо́га. ♦ **I could have no richer blessing than your love.** Я не мог *(ж: могла́)* бы име́ть бо́льшего блаже́нства, чем твоя́ любо́вь. ♦ **I believe that our love is blessed by God.** Я ве́рю, что на́ша любо́вь благословлена́ Бо́гом.

> *love: you've shown me so much love*

You have shown me *(1)* ...so much love. / *(2)* ...more love than I have ever known. Ты дава́ла *(ж: дава́л)* мне *(1)* ...так мно́го любви́. / *(2)* ...бо́льше любви́, чем я когда́-либо знал *(ж: зна́ла)*.

> *love: I've learned love from you*

They say love is a learned phenomenon and I believe it, because I learned it from you. Говоря́т, что любо́вь -- изу́ченное явле́ние, и я верю́ в э́то, потому́ что изучи́л *(ж: изучи́ла)* её благодаря́ тебе́. ♦ **From being with you, I have learned *(1)* ...what love really is. / *(2)* ...the true meaning of love.** Находя́сь ря́дом с тобо́й, я по́нял *(ж: поняла́)*, *(1)* ...что тако́е настоя́щая любо́вь. / *(2)* ...и́стинное значе́ние любви́. ♦ **You have taught me the true meaning of love.** Ты откры́ла *(ж: откры́л)* мне и́стинное значе́ние любви́. ♦ **You have shown me what true love is all about.** Ты показа́ла *(ж: показа́л)* мне, что тако́е и́стинная любо́вь.

> *love: I used to be skeptical about love*

I used to be rather *(1)* cynical / *(2)* skeptical about love, but you've made me a believer in it. Я был *(ж: была́)* до не́которой сте́пени *(1)* ци́ником / *(2)* ске́птиком относи́тельно любви́, но ты заста́вила *(ж: заста́вил)* меня́ пове́рить в неё.

> *love: I want your love forever*

I want to spend a lifetime quaffing the elixir of your love. Я хочу́ провести́ жизнь, упива́ясь эликси́ром твое́й любви́. ♦ **I want to grow old together with you, my Love.** Я хочу́ соста́риться вме́сте с тобо́й, моя́ любо́вь. ♦ **I want to travel love's highway together with you (for the rest of my life).** Я хочу́ путеше́ствовать доро́гой любви́ вме́сте с тобо́й (всю оста́вшуюся жизнь). ♦ **I want our lives to be an everlasting symphony of love.** Я хочу́, что́бы на́ша жизнь была́ бесконе́чной симфо́нией любви́. ♦ **Forever isn't long enough to be in love with you.** Ве́чность сли́шком коротка́ для на́шей любви́.

> *love: you fill my life with love*

You fill my life with love. Ты наполня́ешь мою́ жизнь любо́вью. ♦ **You make me feel such love as I have never known in all my life.** Ты заставля́ешь меня́ чу́вствовать таку́ю любо́вь, кото́рой я никогда́ в жи́зни не знал *(ж: зна́ла)*. ♦ **Every time you smile at me, you flood my world with love.** Вся́кий раз, когда́ ты улыба́ешься мне, ты затопля́ешь мой мир любо́вью.

> *love: thank you for bringing me love*

Thank you for bringing so much love and joy and happiness into my life. Спаси́бо тебе́, что принесла́ *(ж: принёс)* так мно́го любви́, ра́дости и сча́стья в мою́ жизнь. ♦ **Thank you for giving me this chance for love.** Спаси́бо, что дала́ *(ж: дал)* мне э́ту возмо́жность люби́ть. ♦ **I am so thankful for your love.** Я так благода́рен *(ж: благода́рна)* за твою́

> *For Russian adjectives, the masculine form is spelled out,*
> *followed by the feminine, neuter and plural endings.*

любо́вь. ♦ **I am so grateful to you for initiating me into this sweet, intoxicating ritual of love.** Я так благода́рен *(ж: благода́рна)* тебе́ за то, что посвяти́ла *(ж: посвяти́л)* меня́ в сла́дкий, опьяня́ющий ритуа́л любви́.

love: *I'm addicted to your love*

You've made me so addicted to love. Ты сде́лала *(ж: сде́лал)* меня́ рабо́м любви́. ♦ **I know that I can never overcome my addiction to your love.** Я зна́ю, что никогда́ не смогу́ освободи́ться от вла́сти твое́й любви́. ♦ **You have made me a slave of love.** Ты сде́лала *(ж: сде́лал)* меня́ рабо́м *(ж: рабо́й)* любви́.

love: *our love*

Our love is special and sacred. На́ша любо́вь -- осо́бая и свяще́нная. ♦ **Our love is like the sky — big and beautiful and forever.** На́ша любо́вь, как не́бо, -- больша́я, прекра́сная и ве́чная. ♦ **Let's make our love last forever.** Пусть на́ша любо́вь продолжа́ется ве́чно. ♦ **Our love is going to prevail against this adversity, I promise you.** На́ша любо́вь оде́ржит верх над э́тими невзго́дами, я обеща́ю. ♦ **You and I — two hearts, one love.** Мы два се́рдца, одна́ любо́вь. ♦ **I hope there will always be a constant interchange of love between us.** Я наде́юсь, что ме́жду на́ми всегда́ бу́дет постоя́нный обме́н любо́вью. ♦ **Our love remains** *(1)* **...strong.** / *(2)* **...as strong as ever.** На́ша любо́вь остаётся *(1)* ...си́льной. / *(2)* ...тако́й же си́льной, как всегда́. ♦ **Our love is a beautiful dream.** На́ша любо́вь -- прекра́сная мечта́. ♦ **In the** *(1)* **days** / *(2)* **months** / *(3)* **years ahead I hope we can deepen our love.** В *(1-3)* бу́дущем, я наде́юсь, мы смо́жем углуби́ть на́шу любо́вь. ♦ **I know that our love will deepen as** *(1,2)* **time goes by.** Я зна́ю, что на́ша любо́вь бу́дет уси́ливаться *(1)* ...с года́ми / *(2)* ...со вре́менем. ♦ **The sooner we get together, the sooner we can realize our love and be happy.** Чем ра́ньше мы ока́жемся вме́сте, тем скоре́е мы смо́жем воплоти́ть на́шу любо́вь и быть сча́стливы. ♦ **Our love is the real thing.** У нас настоя́щая любо́вь.

love: *love binds us together*

Distance *(1)* **holds** / *(2)* **keeps us apart, but our love binds us together.** Расстоя́ние *(1,2)* разделя́ет нас, но на́ша любо́вь соединя́ет нас. ♦ *(1,2)* **We have love as our guide.** *(1)* Любо́вь -- наш гид. / *(2)* Любо́вь ведёт нас.

love: *our love is forever*

Our love *(1)* **...is forever.** / *(2)* **...is here to stay.** / *(3)* **...shall be endless.** На́ша любо́вь *(1)* ...навсегда́. / *(2)* ...оста́нется. / *(3)* ...бу́дет бесконе́чна. ♦ **From our two hearts we will create a love that** *(1)* **...will flourish to the end of our lives.** / *(2)* **...will last till the end of time.** / *(3)* **...will grow ever stronger, ever more beautiful.** Ме́жду двумя́ на́шими сердца́ми мы создади́м любо́вь, кото́рая *(1)* ...бу́дет цвести́ до конца́ на́ших дней. / *(2)* ...бу́дет продолжа́ться пока́ существу́ет мир. / *(3)* ...вы́растет ещё сильне́е, ещё бо́лее прекра́сной. ♦ **Our souls will join together in** *(1)* **eternal** / *(2)* **everlasting love.** На́ши ду́ши солью́тся вме́сте в *(1,2)* ве́чной любви́. ♦ **I** *(1)* **...hope** / *(2)* **pray that our love will...** / *(3)* **...want our love to...** *(4,5)* **last** *(6)* **...forever.** / *(7)* **...until the end of time.** Я *(1)* наде́юсь / *(2)* молю́сь / *(3)* хочу́, что́бы на́ша любо́вь *(4)* продолжа́лась / *(5)* дли́лась *(6)* ...ве́чно. / *(7)* ...до конца́ на́шей жи́зни. ♦ **We have** *(1,2)* **a lifetime of love ahead of us.** У нас впереди́ *(1)* ...любо́вь длино́й в жизнь. / *(2)* ...це́лая жизнь в любви́.

love: *the ultimate expression of our love*

(1) **This is...** / *(2)* **That** / *(3)* **It will be ... the ultimate expression of our love for each other.** *(1)* Это максима́льное выраже́ние... / *(2,3)* Это бу́дет максима́льным выраже́нием... на́шей любви́ друг к дру́гу. ♦ **That will be the ultimate affirmation of our love for each other.** Это бу́дет наивы́сшим подтвержде́нием на́шей любви́ друг к дру́гу.

See Appendix 19 for notes on sending mail to Russia and Ukraine.

love: *our marriage will be filled with love*

Our marriage will be a cornucopia of love. Наш брак бу́дет, как рог, напо́лненный любо́вью.

love: *I'll teach you to enjoy love*

(1) **I want to...** / *(2)* **I'm going to... teach you how to enjoy love.** *(1)* Я хочу́ научи́ть... / *(2)* Я научу́... тебя́, как наслажда́ться любо́вью. ♦ **Your body is going to learn a new definition of the word love.** Твоё те́ло узна́ет но́вое определе́ние сло́ва любо́вь.

love: *secrets of love*

I will reveal to you the delightful secrets of love and bliss. Я откро́ю тебе́ упои́тельные та́йны любви́ и блаже́нства. ♦ **I know so many delicious secrets about love — secrets that would make you just dizzy with ecstasy — and they're just going to waste right now.** Я зна́ю так мно́го восхити́тельных секре́тов любви́ -- секре́ты, кото́рые заста́вят тебя́ испыта́ть головокружи́тельный экста́з, и они́ про́сто ника́к ни испо́льзуются сейча́с.

love: *I want to make love with you*

I want to make love with you (*[1]* **...all night long.** / *[2]* **...again).** Я хочу́ (*[1]* ...всю ночь напролёт... / *[2]* ...опя́ть...) занима́ться любо́вью с тобо́й. ♦ **I dream of making love with you.** Я мечта́ю о том, что́бы заня́ться любо́вью с тобо́й. ♦ **I want so much to make love with you.** Я так жа́жду занима́ться любо́вью с тобо́й. ♦ **I want to make love with you** *(1)* **...by moonlight.** / *(2)* **...under the moon and stars.** Я хочу́ занима́ться любо́вью с тобо́й *(1)* ...при лу́нном све́те. / *(2)* ...под луно́й и звёздами. ♦ **Darling, I must tell you that I'm really starved to make love with you.** Дорога́я, я до́лжен сказа́ть тебе́, что я действи́тельно жа́жду заня́ться любо́вью с тобо́й. ♦ **I have such a(n) (powerful) urge to make love with you.** У меня́ тако́е вла́стное побужде́ние заня́ться любо́вью с тобо́й. ♦ **I'm completely devoid of any** *(1,2)* **ambition to do anything except hold you in my arms and make love to you.** Я соверше́нно лишён каки́х-либо други́х *(1)* стремле́ний / *(2)* амби́ций, кро́ме того́, что́бы держа́ть тебя́ в объя́тиях и занима́ться любо́вью с тобо́й. ♦ **The overriding goal of my life is to eventually take you in my arms and make beautiful, beautiful, beautiful love with you.** Гла́вная цель мое́й жи́зни -- заключи́ть тебя́ в объя́тия и заня́ться бесконе́чно прекра́сной любо́вью с тобо́й. ♦ **I dream of spending endless blissful hours holding you in my arms and making tender love with you.** Я мечта́ю проводи́ть бесконе́чные блаже́нные часы́, держа́ тебя́ в объя́тиях и занима́ясь не́жной любо́вью с тобо́й. ♦ **How wonderful** / *(2)* **heavenly it** *(3)* **...is...** / *(4)* **...would be... to hold you in my arms and revel in the timeless expression of (human) love.** Как *(1)* чуде́сно / *(2)* замеча́тельно *(3)* - / *(4)* ...бы́ло бы... держа́ть тебя́ в объя́тиях и упива́ться бесконе́чным выраже́нием (челове́ческой) любви́. ♦ **What heaven it would be to have some lazy, languorous, uninterrupted time to share love and intimacy with you.** Как замеча́тельно бы́ло бы провести́ с тобо́й лени́вое, то́мное, непрерыва́емое вре́мя, напо́лненное любо́вью и бли́зостью. ♦ **I want to give you endless, ecstasy-filled lessons in the art of making love.** Я хочу́ дава́ть тебе́ бесконе́чные, напо́лненные экста́зом уро́ки иску́сства любви́.

love: *making love with you*

Let's not go out tonight. Let's just stay here and make love. Дава́й никуда́ не пойдём сего́дня ве́чером, про́сто оста́немся здесь и займёмся любо́вью. ♦ **I love to make love (with you).** Я люблю́ занима́ться любо́вью (с тобо́й). ♦ **It is so (fantastically) wonderful to make love with you.** Так (фантасти́чески) прекра́сно занима́ться любо́вью с тобо́й. ♦ **Making love with you is so** *(1)* **wonderful** / *(2)* **heavenly.** Занима́ться любо́вью с тобо́й так *(1)* замеча́тельно / *(2)* изуми́тельно. ♦ **How heavenly it is when you lie snugly in my arms afterward, fragrant with love, drifting into sleep.** Како́е э́то блаже́нство, когда́ пото́м ты

When terms are listed after a main word, a tilde ~
is used to indicate the main word.

лежи́шь, ую́тно устро́ившись в мои́х объя́тиях, па́хнущая любо́вью, погружа́ющаяся в сон. ♦ **When I initiate your body into intimacy, it will be with infinite love and consummate gentleness.** Когда́ я познако́млю твоё те́ло с инти́мной бли́зостью, то сде́лаю э́то с бесконе́чной любо́вью и и́стинной не́жностью. ♦ **I can never resist the** *(1,2)* **temptation of making love with you.** Я никогда́ не могу́ устоя́ть пе́ред *(1)* собла́зном / *(2)* искуше́нием заня́ться с тобо́й любо́вью. ♦ **If I seem insatiable (when we make love), it's your fault.** Если я кажу́сь тебе́ ненасы́тным, (когда́ мы занима́емся любо́вью,) э́то твоя́ вина́. ♦ **You are such a (***[1]*** wonderful /** *[2]* **marvelous) master of the art of making love.** Ты тако́й (*[1,2]* замеча́тельный) ма́стер в иску́сстве любви́. ♦ **I may be past my prime, but I still love to make love.** Я, мо́жет быть, уже́ минова́л свой расцве́т, но всё ещё люблю́ занима́ться любо́вью. ♦ **Our bodies are so** *(1)* **perfectly /** *(2)* **wonderfully orchestrated when we make love.** На́ши тела́ так *(1)* соверше́нно / *(2)* замеча́тельно настро́ены в унисо́н, когда́ мы занима́емся любо́вью. ♦ **Through the total orchestration of our bodies you and I together will produce the most beautiful symphony of love anyone has ever known.** Благодаря́ абсолю́тной сы́гранности на́ших тел, мы вме́сте создади́м таку́ю прекра́сную симфо́нию любви́, како́й никто́ никогда́ не знал. ♦ **I'd love it if you would let me see you when we make love.** Мне бы понра́вилось, е́сли бы ты позво́лила мне ви́деть тебя́, когда́ мы занима́емся любо́вью. ♦ **We can experiment together in the ways of love.** Мы мо́жем вме́сте эксперименти́ровать на поля́х любви́. ♦ **What a divine treat to see your face beautifully flushed and well-kissed after we make love.** Что за боже́ственное наслажде́ние ви́деть твоё лицо́, прекра́сно раскрасне́вшееся и зацело́ванное по́сле на́шей бли́зости. ♦ **You and I could share so many things, make so much wonderful love together, talk about so many things together, connect in heart, mind, and spirit so perfectly.** Мы вме́сте смогли́ бы наслажда́ться мно́гим, так мно́го занима́ться прекра́сной любо́вью, говори́ть о мно́гом друг с дру́гом, так соверше́нно соединя́ться се́рдцем, умо́м и ду́хом.

| *love: we'll lose ourselves in love* |

We will lose ourselves (every night) in the rapturous acclamation of our love. Мы бу́дем растворя́ться (ка́ждую ночь) в восто́рженном утвержде́нии на́шей любви́. ♦ **And every night we will reignite our passion and revel in our boundless, undiminishable love.** И ка́ждую ночь мы бу́дем опя́ть зажига́ть на́шу страсть и пирова́ть в на́шей безграни́чной, неугаси́мой любви́. ♦ **We can spend two weeks together there and just lose ourselves in love.** Мы мо́жем провести́ две неде́ли там вме́сте и про́сто погрузи́ться в любо́вь.

| *love: I don't want to make love with you* |

I don't want to make love (with you). Я не хочу́ занима́ться любо́вью (с тобо́й).

| *love: a token of my love* |

(1) **This... /** *(2)* **This gift... is just a small** *(3)* **expression /** *(4)* **token of my unending love for you.** *(1)* Это... / *(2)* Этот пода́рок... -- то́лько ма́ленький *(3)* си́мвол / *(4)* знак мое́й несконча́емой любви́ к тебе́. ♦ **This gift is a tiny token of my love (and esteem) for you.** Этот пода́рок -- ма́ленький си́мвол мое́й любви́ (и уваже́ния) к тебе́. ♦ **This ring is a promise of my (***[1]*** enduring /** *[2]* **eternal /** *[3]* **unending) love for you.** Это кольцо́ -- зало́г мое́й (*[1]* про́чной / *[2]* ве́чной / *[3]* несконча́емой) любви́ к тебе́. ♦ **This ring is a symbol of our** *(1)* **enduring /** *(2)* **everlasting love.** Это кольцо́ -- си́мвол на́шей *(1)* дли́тельной / *(2)* ве́чной любви́.

| *love: your voice - a serenade of love* |

Your voice in my ear is like a serenade of love. Твой го́лос в мои́х уша́х как серена́да любви́.

A list of abbreviations used in the dictionary is given on page 10.

love: *I'm searching for love*

(1) **My heart is...** / *(2)* **I'm...** *(3)* **looking** / *(4)* **searching for** (*[5,6]* **true** / *[7]* **genuine** / *[8]* **real**) **love.** *(1)* Моё се́рдце *(3,4)* и́щет... / *(2)* Я *(3,4)* ищу́... (*[5]* по́длинную / *[6]* и́стинную / *[7,8]* настоя́щую) любо́вь. ♦ **I want so badly to fall in love that it hurts.** Я до бо́ли хочу́ влю-би́ться. ♦ **I'm so starved for love and I think you are too.** Я так жа́жду любви́ и, ду́маю, ты то́же. ♦ **I want to share love and fun with a special** *(1)* **woman** / *(2)* **man** / *(3)* **person.** Я хочу́ наслажда́ться любо́вью и весе́льем с *(1)* ...подходя́щей же́нщиной. / *(2)* ...под-ходя́щим мужчи́ной / *(3)* челове́ком. ♦ **I need love -- physical and emotional -- and I feel almost desparate for both, almost like I'm suffocating for lack of air.** Мне нужна́ любо́вь физи́ческая и душе́вная, и я до отча́яния жа́жду их. Это почти́ похо́же на то, как бу́дто я задыха́юсь от недоста́тка во́здуха.

love: *my capacity for love*

I have a great capacity for love. Я ощуща́ю в себе́ большу́ю спосо́бность люби́ть. ♦ **I can give and receive love.** Я могу́ дава́ть и получа́ть любо́вь. ♦ **I have so much love in my heart to give to the right person. And I really have the feeling that this right person is you.** В моём се́рдце так мно́го любви́, кото́рую я хочу́ подари́ть заслу́живающему её челове́ку. И я определённо чу́вствую, что э́тот челове́к ты. ♦ **To someone who gives me all their love without reservation, I** *(1)* **could** / *(2)* **would pour out twice as much love and affection in return.** На ту *(ж: того́)*, кто отда́ст мне всю свою́ любо́вь безоговоро́чно, я в отве́т *(1)* ...мог *(ж: могла́)* бы изли́ть... / *(2)* ...изли́л *(ж: излила́)* бы... вдво́е бо́льше любви́ и не́жности.

love: *no love in my life*

I've been deprived of love for *(1)* **...so long.** / *(2)* **...so many years.** Я был лишён *(ж: была́ лишена́)* любви́ *(1)* ...так до́лго. / *(2)* ...так мно́го лет. ♦ **My life is so devoid of love.** Моя́ жизнь так лишена́ любви́. ♦ **I thought I would never have a chance for love (in my life).** Я ду́мал *(ж: ду́мала)*, что никогда́ (в жи́зни) у меня́ не бу́дет возмо́жности люби́ть.

love: *failed / unlucky in love*

I never thought I could be lucky in love — until I met you. Я никогда́ не ду́мал *(ж: ду́мала)*, что мне могло́ бы повезти́ в любви́, пока́ не встре́тил *(ж: встре́тила)* тебя́. ♦ **Up to now, I seem always to have failed in love.** Ка́жется, до сих пор у меня́ никогда́ не бы́ло успе́ха в любви́. ♦ **I was always so disappointed in love (before I met you).** Я был всегда́ так разочаро́ван *(ж: была́ так разочаро́вана)* в любви́ (до тех пор, пока́ не встре́тил [*ж: встре́тила*] тебя́). ♦ **I always seemed to look for love in the wrong places.** Каза́лось, что я всегда́ иска́л *(ж: иска́ла)* любо́вь не там, где на́до.

love: *life without love*

Life without love is like a tree without blossom or fruit. Жизнь без любви́ подо́бна нецвету́щему и неплодонося́щему де́реву.

love: *love based on trust / respect / understanding*

Our love is based on trust and respect and understanding. На́ша любо́вь осно́вана на дове́рии, уваже́нии и взаимопонима́нии. ♦ **I want a love based on trust and respect and understanding.** Я хочу́, что́бы в осно́ве любви́ бы́ли дове́рие, уваже́ние и взаимопо-нима́ние. ♦ **Love and respect form the foundation of a strong and lasting marriage.** Любо́вь и уваже́ние создаю́т фунда́мент кре́пкого и продолжи́тельного бра́ка.

love: *marry only for love*

I believe a person should marry only for love. Я ду́маю, что челове́к до́лжен жени́ться то́лько по любви́.

love: *poetry from love*

I want poetry from love. Я хочу́ поэ́зии в любви́.

> *The accents on Russian words are to show how to pronounce them.*
> *You don't have to copy the accents when writing to someone.*

love: *past love*
(1) **He** / *(2)* **She** *(3,4)* **was a long-ago love.** *(1)* Он / *(2)* Она́ когда́-то давно́ *(3)* был *m* / *(4)* была́ *f* мое́й любо́вью. ♦ **It's from a long-ago love.** Это из пре́жней любви́.

love: *love does strange things*
Love does strange things to people. Любо́вь де́лает стра́нные ве́щи с людьми́.

love: *not one-sided*
Love should not be all on one side. Любо́вь должна́ быть взаи́мной.

love: *don't confuse love with desire*
You must not *(1,2)* **confuse love with desire.** Нельзя́ пу́тать любо́вь с жела́нием.

love: *love versus infatuation*
I know for an absolute certainty that what I feel for you is no mere infatuation. It's love if there ever was love. Я абсолю́тно то́чно зна́ю, что моё чу́вство к тебе́ не про́сто увлече́ние. Это любо́вь, е́сли когда́ -нибудь существова́ла любо́вь. ♦ **I thought at first it was love, but I guess it was just infatuation.** Снача́ла я ду́мал *(ж: ду́мала)*, что э́то была́ любо́вь, но я полага́ю, э́то бы́ло то́лько увлече́ние.

love: *platonic love*
Our love is (purely) platonic. На́ша любо́вь (соверше́нно) платони́ческая. ♦ **I don't want just platonic love.** Я не хочу́ то́лько платони́ческой любви́. ♦ **I want you to understand that my love for you is purely platonic.** Я хочу́, что́бы ты поняла́ *(ж: по́нял)*, что моя́ любо́вь к тебе́ соверше́нно платони́ческая.

love: *love gone*
Have you fallen out of love with me? Ты меня́ разлюби́ла *(ж: разлюби́л)*? ♦ **It seems like the love we once had together has dissipated.** Ка́жется, что любо́вь, кото́рая у нас была́, рассе́ялась. ♦ **Our love has dissipated.** На́ша любо́вь рассе́ялась. ♦ **The love we had has drifted away.** Любо́вь, кото́рая была́ у нас, ушла́. ♦ **You have** *(1)* **destroyed** / *(2)* **killed my love for you.** Ты *(1,2)* уби́ла *(ж: уби́л)* мою́ любо́вь к тебе́.

love: *is your love true?*
You profess your love for me, but *(1)* **...is it true** / *(2)* **real** / *(3)* **genuine?** / *(4)* **...how deep** / *(5)* **strong is it?** Ты признаёшься мне в любви́, но *(1)* ...пра́вда ли э́то? / *(2,3)* ...настоя́щая ли она́? / *(4)* ...как глубока́ / *(5)* сильна́ ли она́?

love: *your love - not true*
Your love was just a facade. Твоя́ любо́вь была́ то́лько ви́димостью.

love: *give me another chance*
Will you give me another chance to try and win your love? Дашь ли ты мне ещё оди́н шанс попыта́ться заслужи́ть твою́ любо́вь?

love: *I want to rekindle your love*
I want to rekindle the flames of love in your heart. Я хочу́ вновь воспламени́ть пла́мя любви́ в твоём се́рдце.

love: *I'm still in love with you*
I'm still in love with you. Я всё ещё люблю́ тебя́.

love: *in love with love / marriage*
I think you're just in love with love. Я ду́маю, что ты про́сто лю́бишь любо́вь. ♦ **You seem to be in love with the idea of marriage. (I'm not.)** Тебе́, похо́же, нра́вится иде́я о бра́ке. (Мне нет.)

love: *no illusions*
I *(1)* **harbor** / *(2)* **entertain no illusions about** *(3)* **...your love for me.** / *(4)* **...my chances of winning your love.** Я не *(1)* таю́ / *(2)* пита́ю никаки́х иллю́зий относи́тельно *(3)* ...твое́й любви́ ко мне. / *(4)* ...моего́ ша́нса завоева́ть твою́ любо́вь. ♦ **I've given up**

If no accent is shown on a word with a capitalized vowel,
it means that the capitalized vowel is accented.

my (girlish) illusions about love. Я отказа́лась от мои́х (деви́чьих) иллю́зий о любви́.

| *love: don't be cynical about love* |

You shouldn't be (so) cynical about love. Тебе́ не сле́довало бы быть (тако́й цини́чной *[ж: таки́м цини́чным]*) в отноше́нии к любви́.

| *love: possessive love* |

Your love is *(1)* **too /** *(2)* **so possessive.** Твоя́ любо́вь *(1)* сли́шком / *(2)* така́я со́бственническая.

| *love: afraid of losing your love* |

I have such a fear of losing your love. Во мне тако́й страх поте́ри твое́й любви́.

| *love: closing of a letter* |

All my love, С (огро́мной) любо́вью, ♦ **Love always,** Люблю́ навсегда́, ♦ **Yours, with** *(1)* **undying /** *(2)* **unremitting love...** Твой, с *(1)* неумира́ющей / *(2)* неослабева́ющей любо́вью... .

| *love: sayings* |

Love makes the world go round. Любо́вь дви́жет ми́ром. ♦ **Love is the reward of love.** Отве́тная любо́вь -- лу́чшая награ́да. ♦ **Love** *(1)* **begets /** *(2)* **breeds love.** Любо́вь *(1,2)* порожда́ет (отве́тную) любо́вь. ♦ **No herb will cure love.** Боле́знь любви́ неизлечи́ма. ♦ *(1,2)* **Love knows no barriers.** *(1)* Для любви́ нет прегра́д. / *(2)* Любо́вь побежда́ет всё. ♦ *(1)* **Anything goes... /** *(2,3)* **All's fair... in love and war.** В любви́ и на войне́ *(1)* ...всё годи́тся. / *(2)* ...всё че́стно. / *(3)* ...все сре́дства хороши́. ♦ **Love is like the coming of a fiery angel.** Любо́вь -- как прихо́д о́гненного а́нгела. ♦ **The language of love is universal.** Язы́к любви́ универса́лен. ♦ **Love offers no apology.** Не извиня́йтесь за любо́вь. ♦ **Love is the wind that** *(1,2)* **lifts our wings.** Любо́вь -- э́то ве́тер, кото́рый *(1)* ...расправля́ет на́ши кры́лья. / *(2)* ...несёт нас на свои́х кры́льях. ♦ **If you have to keep love in a cage, it was not yours to begin with.** Е́сли ты должна́ *(ж: до́лжен)* держа́ть любо́вь в кле́тке, зна́чит она́ была́ не твоя́ с са́мого нача́ла. ♦ **Love is all there is.** Любо́вь -- э́то всё. ♦ **(They say) love is blind.** (Говоря́т, что) любо́вь слепа́. ♦ **Never underestimate the power of love.** Никогда́ не преуменьша́й си́лу любви́. ♦ **Money can't buy love.** За де́ньги нельзя́ купи́ть любо́вь. ♦ **Love cannot be forced.** Наси́льно мил не бу́дешь. ♦ **The strongest motivator in the world is love.** Любо́вь дви́жет ми́ром. ♦ **From kindness comes love.** Из доброты́ прихо́дит любо́вь. ♦ **Love has its ups and downs.** У любви́ есть свои́ подъёмы и спу́ски. ♦ **They say that love is a many-splendored thing.** Говоря́т, что любо́вь великоле́пна во мно́гих отноше́ниях.

| *love: quotations* |

"Heaven has no Rage like Love to Hatred turn'd, Nor Hell a Fury, like a Woman scorned." *William Congreve, "The Mourning Bride" (1697)* «На небеса́х нет тако́й я́рости, как любо́вь, обращённая в не́нависть, в аду́ нет тако́го бе́шенства, как же́нщина отве́ргнутая.» *Ви́льям Ко́нгрив, «Скорбя́щая неве́ста», 1697.* ♦ **"Purify me with a great fire of divine love."** *Liane de Pougy* «Очи́сти меня́ вели́ким огнём небе́сной любви́.» *Ля́ян де Пуж.* ♦ **"There are as many kinds of love in the world as there are hearts."** *L.N. Tolstoy* «Ско́лько на све́те серде́ц, сто́лько родо́в любви́.» *Л.Н. Толсто́й.* ♦ **"Our hours in love have wings; in absence, crutches."** *Colley Cibber, "Xerxes"* «У на́ших часо́в любви́ есть кры́лья; у часо́в разлу́ки -- костыли́.» *Ка́ли Си́бер «Ксеркс».*

lovebirds *n, pl* влюблённые.

lovebite *n* засо́с, синя́к, краснота́, кровоподтёк *(на ше́е по́сле до́лгого поцелу́я).*

love-bug *n* любо́вь, стре́лы любви́, стре́лы Купидо́на ♦ **I've been bitten all over by the love-bug.** Любо́вь насти́гла меня́.

loved *adj* люби́мый, -ая, -ое, -ые ♦ **You make me feel loved.** С тобо́й я чу́вствую себя́

Russian has 6 grammatical cases. For an explanation of them,
see the grammar appendix on page 686.

люби́мым *(ж: люби́мой)*. ♦ **No one has ever made me feel loved like you do.** Никто́ никогда́ не дал мне почу́вствовать себя́ люби́мым *(ж: люби́мой)* так, как э́то сде́лала *(ж: сде́лал)* ты. ♦ **You don't know how I long to be loved (by someone like you).** Ты не зна́ешь, как я тоску́ю о том, чтобы быть люби́мым *(ж: люби́мой)* (ке́м-нибудь таки́м, как ты).

lovefest *n* до́лгие часы́ любо́вных ласк, пир любви́.

love-kitten *n* люби́мый котёнок ♦ **My little love-kitten, I want to make you always purr in contentment.** Мой ма́ленький люби́мый котёнок, я хочу́, чтобы ты всегда́ удовлетворённо мурлы́кала.

loveliness *n* красота́; пре́лесть *f (See also* **beauty**) ♦ **alluring** ~ зама́нивающая красота́ ♦ **amaranthine** ~ неувяда́емая красота́ ♦ **breathtaking** ~ захва́тывающая дух красота́ ♦ **ethereal** ~ небе́сная красота́ ♦ **exceptional** ~ исключи́тельная красота́ ♦ **exquisite** ~ изы́сканная красота́, изы́сканная пре́лесть ♦ **incomparable** ~ несравне́нная красота́ ♦ **indescribable** ~ неописуемая красота́ ♦ **natural** ~ есте́ственная пре́лесть ♦ **peerless** ~ несравне́нная красота́ ♦ **radiant** ~ сия́ющая красота́ ♦ **sexy** ~ сексуа́льная красота́ ♦ **soft** ~ мя́гкая красота́ ♦ **voluptuous** ~ чу́вственная красота́ ♦ **epitome of** ~ воплоще́ние красоты́ ♦ *(1,2)* **essence of** ~ *(1)* су́щность / *(2)* квинтэссе́нция красоты́ ♦ *(1,2)* **paragon of** ~ *(1)* этало́н / *(2)* образе́ц красоты́.

---
loveliness: *your loveliness*

You have a loveliness that *(1)* **age** / *(2)* **time can never** *(3)* **dim** / *(4)* **diminish.** Ты так краси́ва, что с *(1,2)* года́ми твоя́ красота́ не мо́жет *(3)* потускне́ть / *(4)* уме́ньшиться. ♦ **You are the epitome of loveliness.** Ты воплоще́ние красоты́. ♦ **You are indisputably unique and indisputably classic in the magnitude of your loveliness.** Ты бесспо́рно уника́льна и бесспо́рно класси́чна в свое́й красоте́. ♦ **You are a vision of** *(1)* **breathtaking** / *(2)* **exquisite loveliness.** Ты виде́ние *(1)* ...захва́тывающей дух... / *(2)* ...изы́сканной... красоты́. ♦ **Your dark hair accentuates the soft loveliness of your face.** Твои́ тёмные во́лосы подчёркивают мя́гкую красоту́ твоего́ лица́. ♦ **Mere words are** *(1)* **...not enough...** / *(2)* **...inadequate... to describe your (**[3] **ethereal** / [4] **incomparable) loveliness.** Про́сто слов *(1,2)* не доста́точно, чтобы описа́ть твою́ ([3] небе́сную / [4] несравне́нную) красоту́. ♦ **Your loveliness is** *(1,2)* **sans pareil.** Твоя́ красота́ *(1)* несравне́нна / *(2)* бесподо́бна. ♦ **No one in this whole world can ever surpass you in loveliness.** Никто́ на всём све́те не смо́жет превзойти́ тебя́ в красоте́. ♦ **The dress enhances your natural loveliness.** Пла́тье подчёркивает твою́ есте́ственную пре́лесть. ♦ **You are the** *(1,2)* **essence of loveliness.** Ты *(1)* су́щность / *(2)* квинтэссе́нция красоты́. ♦ *(1)* **Your face is...** / *(2)* **You are... a paragon of loveliness.** *(1)* Твоё лицо́... / *(2)* Ты... образе́ц красоты́. ♦ **You have a face that is (absolutely) enchanting in its loveliness.** У тебя́ лицо́, красота́ кото́рого (соверше́нно) очаро́вывает. ♦ **Your loveliness is just one of your many exceptional attributes.** Твоя́ красота́ -- то́лько одно́ из мно́гих твои́х исключи́тельных ка́честв.

---
loveliness: *how I regard your loveliness*

It is such a *(1,2)* **pleasure to** *(3)* **look** / *(4)* **gaze at your big, beautiful** *(5)* **dark** / *(6)* **blue eyes and the radiant loveliness of your face in** *(7)* **...this photo.** / *(8)* **...your photos.** Тако́е *(1)* удово́льствие / *(2)* наслажде́ние *(3)* ...смотре́ть на... / *(4)* ...вгля́дываться в... твои́ больши́е, прекра́сные *(5)* тёмные / *(6)* голубы́е глаза́ и сия́ющую красоту́ твоего́ лица́ на *(7)* ...э́той фотогра́фии. / *(8)* ...твои́х фотогра́фиях. ♦ **I marvel at your exceptional loveliness.** Я восхища́юсь твое́й исключи́тельной красото́й. ♦ **I had heard a lot about you, but nothing prepared me for your loveliness.** Я слы́шал мно́го о тебе́, но не был подгото́влен к твое́й красоте́. ♦ **The wording of your ad didn't prepare me**

There are no articles ("a" or "the") in Russian.

at all for your (exceptional) loveliness. Формулирóвка в Вáшем объявлéнии совсéм не подготóвила меня к Вáшей (исключúтельной) красотé. ♦ **I'm not impervious to your loveliness.** Я не безразлúчен к твоéй красотé.

loveliness: *how your loveliness affects me*

I am ([1] completely / [2] totally / [3] utterly) *(4,5)* **entranced /** *(6)* **captivated /** *(7)* **mes merized by your (vivacity and) loveliness.** Я ([1] пóлностью / [2,3] совершéнно) (4) восхищáюсь / (5,6) очарóван / (7) загипнотизúрован твоéй (жúвостью и) красотóй. ♦ **I am engulfed in** *(1)* **infinite /** *(2)* **boundless admiration of your** *(3)* **indescribable /** *(4)* **incomparable /** *(5)* **peerless /** *(6)* **exquisite loveliness.** Я поглощён (1) бесконéчным / (2) безгранúчным восхищéнием твоéй (3) неописýемой / (4,5) несравнéнной / (6) изыс- канной красотóй. ♦ **An extraordinary heat suffuses my whole body whenever the vision of your perfect loveliness comes into my mind.** Всегдá, когдá бы я ни подýмал о твоём прекрáсном слáдостном тéле, я весь охвáчен жáром. ♦ **Your loveliness** *(1,2)* **dazzles me.** Твоя красотá (1) ослепляет / (2) поражáет меня. ♦ **I (simply) cannot resist your loveliness.** Я (прóсто) не могý сопротивляться твоéй красотé. ♦ **Your amaranthine loveliness fills me with wonder.** Я изумлён твоéй неувядáемой красотóй. ♦ **The vision of your (alluring, sexy) loveliness** *(1)* **...bedevils my thoughts night and day. /** *(2)* **...over- whelms all other thoughts in my mind.** Твоя (замáнивающая, сексуáльная) красотá *(1)* ...мýчает меня нóчью и днём. / *(2)* ...подавляет все другúе мысли. ♦ **Visions of your voluptuous loveliness send fire licking through my arteries, igniting my entire being into an inferno of passionate desire.** Твоя чýвственная красотá вызывáет огóнь, бушýю- щий в моúх артéриях, посылáющий всё моё существó в ад стрáстного желáния.

loveliness: *I worship your loveliness*

I promise you hours and hours of incredible ecstasy as my avid lips totally worship your loveliness. Я обещáю тебé часы и часы невероятного экстáза в то врéмя, как моú жáдные гýбы бýдут поклоняться твоéй красотé. ♦ **If by some divine miracle I am able someday to press my lips in fervent adoration to the exquisite loveliness of your sweet smile, I shall have nothing more to hope for or want.** Éсли бы какúм-то божéственным чýдом я смог в одúн прекрáсный день с пылким обожáнием прижáться губáми к изысканной прéлести твоéй слáдкой улыбки, мне нéчего было бы бóльше желáть.

lovelorn *adj* страдáющий (-ая, -ее, -ие) от безнадёжной любвú.

lovely *adj* красúвый, -ая, -ое, -ые, прекрáсный, -ая, -ое, -ые; прелéстный, -ая, -ое, -ые *(See also* **beautiful** *)* ♦ **absolutely** ~ совершéнно прекрáсная ♦ **fantastically** ~ фан- тастúчески прекрáсная ♦ **incredibly** ~ невероятно прекрáсная ♦ **physically** ~ физú- чески прекрáсная ♦ **rhapsodically** ~ вызывáющая востóрг своéй красотóй ♦ **very** ~ óчень красúвая.

lovely: *phrases*

You are *(1)* **incredibly /** *(2)* **fantastically lovely.** Ты (1) невероятно / (2) фантастúчески прекрáсна. ♦ **I can't believe how lovely you are.** Я не могý повéрить, что ты так прекрáсна. ♦ **I don't think you** *(1)* **know /** *(2)* **realize how lovely you are.** Я дýмаю, что ты не (1) знáешь / (2) осознаёшь, как ты прекрáсна. ♦ **You have no idea how lovely your are.** Ты дáже не представляешь, как ты прекрáсна. ♦ **How absolutely lovely — and lovable — you look in your photos!** Как совершéнно прекрáсно и очаровáтельно ты выглядишь на фотогрáфиях! ♦ **Even in my most extravagant dreams I never con- ceived of anyone as lovely as you.** Дáже в своúх сáмых сумасбрóдных мечтáх я ни- когдá не мог вообразúть такýю (1,2) прекрáсную жéнщину, как ты. ♦ **You are so lovely physically, and when this is superimposed upon your sweet, warm, caring, loving nature, it has an extremely powerful effect on me — like the world's biggest laser firing**

This dictionary contains two Russian alphabet pages:
one in Appendix 1, page 685, and a tear-off page on page 799.

straight into my eyes. Ты так прекра́сна физи́чески, что когда́ э́то накла́дывается на твою́ не́жную, тёплую, забо́тливую, лю́бящую нату́ру, э́то ока́зывает осо́бо могу́щественное де́йствие на меня́, как бу́дто наибо́льший в ми́ре ла́зер све́тит пря́мо в мои́ глаза́.

lovemaking *n* заня́тие любо́вью, (любо́вная) бли́зость, любо́вные ла́ски / уте́хи ◆ **early morning** ~ занима́ться любо́вью ра́но у́тром *(verb expression)* ◆ **furious** ~ *(verb expression)* неи́стово занима́ться любо́вью ◆ **gourmet** ~ великоле́пный секс ◆ **marathon** ~ непреры́вное заня́тие любо́вью ◆ **slow, tantalizing** ~ ме́дленно, дразня́ще занима́ться любо́вью *(verb expression)* ◆ **tempestuous** ~ бу́рный секс.

| *lovemaking: phrases* |

You're quite *(1)* **adept** / *(2)* **well-versed in (the art of) lovemaking.** Ты о́чень *(1,2)* искушена́ *(ж: искушён)* в иску́сстве любви́. ◆ **Our lovemaking sessions are so wonderful.** Вре́мя, когда́ мы занима́емся любо́вью, замеча́тельно. ◆ **My thoughts go back again and again to our wonderful lovemaking sessions.** Мои́ мы́сли опя́ть и опя́ть возвраща́ются к замеча́тельному вре́мени на́шей бли́зости. ◆ **The (**[1] **sweet /** [2] **warm /** [3] **precious) memories of our wonderful lovemaking sessions go through my mind** *(4)* **constantly /** *(5)* **unceasingly /** *(6)* **night and day.** (*[1]* Сла́достные / *[2]* тёплые / *[3]* драгоце́нные) воспомина́ния о замеча́тельном вре́мени на́шей бли́зости *(4)* постоя́нно / *(5)* непреры́вно / *(6)* ...но́чью и днём... вспы́хивают в мое́й па́мяти. *[1]*

lovemate *n* влюблённый *m*, влюблённая *f*, любо́вник *m*, любо́вница *f*.

love-pressure *n* любо́вное напряже́ние ◆ **Sometimes I feel like I'm going to explode from the tremendous love-pressure that builds up inside of me for you.** Иногда́ я чу́вствую себя́ гото́вым взорва́ться от огро́много любо́вного напряже́ния, нараста́ющего во мне.

lover *n* 1. *(partner in love)* любо́вник *m*; любо́вница *f*; возлю́бленный *m*, возлю́бленная *f*; 2. *(enthusiast)* люби́тель *m* / люби́тельница *f* ◆ **abandoned** ~ поки́нутый любо́вник *m*, поки́нутая любо́вница *f* ◆ **artful** ~ уме́лый любо́вник *m*, уме́лая любо́вница *f* ◆ **beach** ~ люби́тель *m* / люби́тельница *f* пля́жей ◆ **best** ~ са́мый лу́чший любо́вник *m*, са́мая лу́чшая любо́вница *f* ◆ **book** ~ книголю́б ◆ **cat** ~ люби́тель *m* / люби́тельница *f* ко́шек ◆ **classical music** ~ люби́тель *m* / люби́тельница *f* класси́ческой му́зыки ◆ **culture-crossed** ~s любо́вники с ра́зными культу́рами ◆ **dog** ~ люби́тель *m* / люби́тельница *f* соба́к ◆ **dream** ~ удиви́тельный любо́вник *m*, удиви́тельная любо́вница *f* ◆ **enthusiastic** ~ восто́рженный любо́вник *m*, восто́рженная любо́вница *f* ◆ **equal opportunity** ~ челове́к, не забо́тящийся о ра́се его́ любо́вника и́ли любо́вницы *(explanation)* ◆ **excellent** ~ отме́нный любо́вник *m*, отме́нная любо́вница *f* ◆ **exquisite** ~ утончённый любо́вник *m*, утончённая любо́вница *f* ◆ **fabulous** ~ потряса́ющий любо́вник *m*, потряса́ющая любо́вница *f* ◆ **fantastic** ~ фантасти́ческий любо́вник *m*, фантасти́ческая любо́вница *f* ◆ **fearful** ~ трусли́вый любо́вник *m*, трусли́вая любо́вница *f* ◆ **former** ~ пре́жний любо́вник *m*, пре́жняя любо́вница *f* ◆ **horse** ~ люби́тель *m* / люби́тельница *f* лошаде́й ◆ **hungry** ~ голо́дный любо́вник *m*, голо́дная любо́вница *f* ◆ **ideal** ~ идеа́льный любо́вник *m*, идеа́льная любо́вница *f* ◆ **imaginative** ~ изобрета́тельный любо́вник *m*, изобрета́тельная любо́вница *f* ◆ **incredible** ~ невероя́тный любо́вник *m*, невероя́тная любо́вница *f* ◆ **innovative** ~ созида́тельный любо́вник *m*, созида́тельная любо́вница *f* ◆ **insatiable** ~ ненасы́тный любо́вник *m*, ненасы́тная любо́вница *f* ◆ **jazz** ~ люби́тель *m* / люби́тельница *f* джа́за ◆ ~ **for long term** любо́вник *m* / любо́вница *f* на до́лгое вре́мя ◆ ~ **of life** лю́бящий (-ая, -ие) жизнь ◆ **magnificent** ~ изуми́тельный любо́вник *m*, изуми́тельная любо́вница *f* ◆ **music** ~ люби́тель *m* / люби́тельница *f* му́зыки ◆ **nature** ~ люби́тель *m* / люби́тельница *f* приро́ды ◆ **out-**

door(s) ~ люби́тель приро́ды ♦ **phenomenal** ~ феномена́льный любо́вник *m*, феноме-на́льная любо́вница *f* ♦ **scorned** ~ отве́ргнутый любо́вник *m*, отве́ргнутая любо́вница *f* ♦ **sensitive** ~ чувстви́тельный любо́вник *m*, чувстви́тельная любо́вница *f* ♦ **sun** ~ люби́тель *m* / люби́тельница *f* со́лнца ♦ *(1,2)* **superb** ~ *(1)* великоле́пный / *(2)* отме́н-ный любо́вник *m;* *(1)* великоле́пная / *(2)* отме́нная любо́вница *f* ♦ **terrific** ~ потряса́-ющий любо́вник *m*, потряса́ющая любо́вница *f* ♦ **tireless** ~ неутоми́мый любо́вник *m*, неутоми́мая любо́вница *f* ♦ **travel** ~ люби́тель *m* / люби́тельница *f* путеше́ствий ♦ *(1,2)* **wonderful** ~ *(1)* замеча́тельный / *(2)* удиви́тельный любо́вник *m*, *(1)* замеча́тель-ная / *(2)* удиви́тельная любо́вница *f* ♦ **become** ~s стать любо́вниками.

| **lover:** *you're a great lover* |

You are the most *(1)* **wonderful** / *(2)* **fantastic lover anyone ever had.** Ни у кого́ никогда́ не бы́ло тако́й *(1)* удиви́тельной / *(2)* фантасти́ческой любо́вницы *(ж: тако́го (1) удиви́тельного / (2) фантасти́ческого любо́вника)*, как ты. ♦ **What a** *(1)* **wonderful** / *(2)* **fantastic lover you are.** Кака́я ты *(1)* замеча́тельная / *(2)* фантасти́ческая любо́в-ница. *(ж: Како́й ты [1] замеча́тельный / [2] фантасти́ческий любо́вник.)* ♦ **You are (really) a(n)** *(1)* **terrific** / *(2)* **fabulous** / *(3)* **incredible** / *(4)* **wonderful** / *(5)* **dream** / *(6)* **mar-velous** / *(7)* **fantastic** *(female)* **lover.** Ты (действи́тельно) *(1,2)* потряса́ющая / *(3)* неверо́ятная / *(4)* замеча́тельная / *(5)* удиви́тельная / *(6)* изуми́тельная / *(7)* фантасти́-ческая любо́вница *f*. ♦ **You are (really) a(n)** *(1)* **terrific** / *(2)* **fabulous** / *(3)* **incredible** / *(4)* **wonderful** / *(5)* **dream** / *(6)* **marvelous** / *(7)* **fantastic** *(male)* **lover.** Ты (действи́тельно) *(1,2)* потряса́ющий / *(3)* неверо́ятный / *(4)* замеча́тельный / *(5)* удиви́тельный / *(6)* изуми́тельный / *(7)* фантасти́ческий любо́вник *m*. ♦ **You're the lover of my dreams.** Ты любо́вница *(ж: любо́вник)* мои́х мечта́ний. ♦ **Your prowess as a lover is without** *(1)* **equal** / *(2)* **compare.** Твоё досто́инство как любо́вника *(1)* ...не име́ет себе́ ра́вных. / *(2)* ...вне сравне́ния. ♦ **You're the best lover I've ever had — by far.** Из всех любо́вниц *(ж: любо́вников)*, кото́рые бы́ли у меня́, ты са́мая лу́чшая *(ж: са́мый лу́чший)*.

| **lover:** *I want you as my lover* |

I want you to be my wife, my friend, my lover. Я хочу́, что́бы ты была́ мое́й жено́й, мои́м дру́гом, мое́й любо́вницей. ♦ **I want to be your friend, your lover, your com-panion and your confidant.** Я хочу́ быть твои́м дру́гом, твои́м любо́вником, твои́м спу́тником и твои́м пове́ренным *(ж: твое́й подру́гой, твое́й любо́вницей, твое́й спу́тницей и твое́й пове́ренной)*.

loverlike *adj* как любо́вник *m* / любо́вница *f.*

love-sick *adj* томя́щийся (-аяся, -ееся, -иеся) от любви́, снеда́емый (-ая, -ое, -ые) любо́вью.

love-softened *adj* смягчённый (-ая, -ое, -ые) любо́вью.

love-struck *adj* безу́мно влюблённый, -ая, -ое, -ые.

lovestyle *n* о́браз любви́, стиль любви́ ♦ **You have a very passionate lovestyle.** Ты о́чень стра́стная любо́вница *(ж: стра́стный любо́вник)*.

lovey-dovey *adj* томя́щийся (-аяся, -ееся, иеся) от любви́.

loving *adj* лю́бящий, -ая, -ее, -ие, не́жный, -ая, -ое, -ые, любвеоби́льный, -ая, -ое, -ые ♦ **deeply** ~ глубоко́ лю́бящий, -ая, -ее, -ие ♦ **very** ~ о́чень не́жный, -ая, -ое, -ые.

| **loving:** *you're very loving* |

You are so good and sweet and thoughtful and caring and loving. Ты така́я хоро́шая *(ж: тако́й хоро́ший)*, не́жная *(ж: не́жный)*, внима́тельная *(ж: внима́тельный)*, забо́т-ливая *(ж: забо́тливый)* и лю́бящая *(ж: лю́бящий)*. ♦ **You are the most loving woman** *(1)* **...I've ever met.** / *(2)* **...there has ever been.** Ты са́мая лю́бящая же́нщина *(1)* ...из всех. / *(2)* ..., кото́рая когда́-либо существова́ла. ♦ **You are the most loving man** *(1)*

There are two words for "you" in Russian:
familiar «ты» and polite / plural «вы» (See page 771).

...I've ever met. / *(2)* **...there has ever been.** Ты са́мый лю́бящий мужчи́на *(1)* ...из всех. / *(2)* ..., кото́рый когда́-либо существова́л. ♦ **You are the most loving person** *(1)* **...I've ever met.** / *(2)* **...there has ever been.** Ты са́мая не́жная *(ж: са́мый не́жный) (1)* ...из всех. / *(2)* ..., кото́рая *(ж: кото́рый)* когда́-либо существова́ла *(ж: существова́л)*. ♦ **You're a very loving person.** Ты о́чень не́жная *(ж: не́жный)*. ♦ **No one is more loving and tender than you are.** Нет никого́ бо́лее лю́бящего и не́жного, чем ты.

> **loving:** *I'm very loving*

I'm a very loving person. Я о́чень не́жный *(ж: не́жная)*. ♦ **I am the most loving, affectionate, tender male you are ever likely to hear about, much less meet in this world.** Я наибо́лее лю́бящий, не́жный, ла́сковый мужчи́на из всех, о кото́рых ты слы́шала, а тем бо́лее встреча́ла в э́том ми́ре. ♦ **I am the most loving, affectionate, tender female you are ever likely to hear about, much less meet in this world.** Я наибо́лее лю́бящая, не́жная, ла́сковая же́нщина из всех, о кото́рых ты слы́шал, а тем бо́лее встреча́л в э́том ми́ре.

> **loving:** *loving toward you*

I could be so loving to you. You have no idea at all. Я мог *(ж: могла́)* бы быть таки́м лю́бящим *(ж: тако́й лю́бящей)* с тобо́й. Ты да́же не представля́ешь. ♦ **From the very first day, I've felt so loving toward you.** С са́мого пе́рвого дня я почу́вствовал *(ж: почу́вствовала)* таку́ю любо́вь к тебе́. ♦ **In all my life I have never thought or imagined or said to myself so many sweet, tender, adoring, devoted, admiring, idolizing, loving words about any person on the face of this earth as I do when I** *(1)* **...finish talking to you in person.** / *(2)* **...look at your photo.** Во всей свое́й жи́зни я никогда́ не ду́мал, вообража́л или говори́л так мно́го не́жных, обожа́ющих, посвящённых, восхищённых, идеализи́рующих, любо́вных слов кому́-либо на э́той земле́, как я де́лаю *(1)* ...по́сле разгово́ра с тобо́й. / *(2)* ...когда́ смотрю́ на твоё фо́то. ♦ *(1)* **I want to...** / *(2)* **I'm going to... do all kinds of loving, pleasure-giving things with you.** *(1)* Я хочу́ дать... / *(2)* Я дам... тебе́ все ви́ды любви́ и наслажде́ния.

> **loving:** *need a loving person*

I'm looking for a loving person to fill my dream. Я ищу́ лю́бящего челове́ка, воплоща́ющего мою́ мечту́. ♦ **I need an affectionate, loving person with lots of hugs and kisses to give.** Мне ну́жен не́жный, лю́бящий челове́к, да́рящий мно́жество объя́тий и поцелу́ев.

> **loving:** *try to be more loving*

If you (really) value our relationship, try to be more loving. Если ты (действи́тельно) це́нишь на́ши отноше́ния, попыта́йся быть бо́лее лю́бящей *(ж: лю́бящим)*.

> **loving:** *closing of a letter*

Your loving   *(name)*   Лю́бящий *(ж: лю́бящая)* тебя́   *(и́мя)* .

loving *n* любо́вь *(Russian more commonly uses verb* люби́ть*)* ♦ **marathon** ~ непреры́вное заня́тие любо́вью ♦ **designed for** ~ со́здан (-а, -о, -ы) для любви́ *(short forms)* ♦ **made for** ~ со́здан (-а, -о, -ы) для любви́ *(short forms)* ♦ **My greatest happiness is loving you.** Моё са́мое большо́е сча́стье -- люби́ть тебя́.

lovingly *adv* лю́бяще, с любо́вью, не́жно ♦ **Lovingly,** *(closing of a letter)* С любо́вью, *(оконча́ние письма́)*.

loyal *adj* ве́рный, -ая, -ое, -ые *(short forms:* ве́рен, верна́, -о, -ы́), пре́данный, -ая, -ое, -ые *(short forms:* пре́дан, -а, -о, -ы*)* ♦ **fiercely** ~ чрезвыча́йно ве́рный, -ая, -ое, -ые ♦ **I'm the kind of person who is fiercely loyal.** Я из тех, кто чрезвыча́йно ве́рен.

loyalty *n* ве́рность *f* ♦ **Loyalty is what really counts in a relationship.** Ве́рность -- вот, что действи́тельно ва́жно в отноше́ниях. ♦ **What I** *(1)* **...want...** / *(2)* **...yearn for... most in**

> *Russian terms of endearment are given in Appendix 13, page 780.*

a relationship is loyalty. Чего я *(1)* ...хочу... / *(2)* ...жажду... более всего в отношениях -- верности.

LTR *abbrev = (1,2)* **long term relationship** *(1)* долгие / *(2)* длительные отношения ♦ **I seek someone who can commit to a LTR.** Я ищу кого-нибудь, кто может принять на себя обязательства долгих отношений.

luck *n* 1. удача, счастье; везение; *(success)* успех; 2. *(fate)* судьба ♦ **bad** ~ несчастье, невезение ♦ **fantastic** ~ фантастическая удача, фантастическое счастье; фантастический успех ♦ **good** ~ удача, счастье; успех ♦ **rotten** ~ несчастье, невезение.

luck: phrases

(1,2) **Good luck!** *(1)* Счастливо! / *(2)* Желаю успеха! ♦ **With any luck at all we can meet on Friday.** При некоторой удаче мы можем встретиться в пятницу. ♦ **Don't push your luck.** Не искушай судьбу. ♦ **I wish you** *(1)* ...(lots of) **luck.** / *(2)* ...**all the luck in the world.** Я желаю тебе *(1)* ...(много) удачи. / *(2)* ...всё счастье мира. ♦ **What enormous good luck it was to find someone like you in this vast, crazy world.** Что за великая удача найти такую *(ж: такого),* как ты, в этом громадном, сумасшедшем мире.

luckily *adv* к счастью.

lucky *adj* удачливый, -ая, -ое, -ые, счастливый, -ая, -ое, -ые **be** ~ *(See phrases below).*

lucky: phrases

I am so lucky to have *(1)* ...**you as my own.** / *(2)* ...**your love.** / *(3)* ...**someone as wonderful as you.** Мне так повезло, что *(1)* ...ты моя *(ж: мой).* / *(2)* ...у меня есть твоя любовь. / *(3)* ...у меня есть такая замечательная *(ж:такой замечательный),* как ты. ♦ **How lucky I am to have met you (in this vast, unkind world).** Как мне повезло, что я встретил *(ж: встретила)* тебя (в этом огромном, недобром мире). ♦ **I am so lucky that I found you (in this world).** Мне так повезло, что я нашёл *(ж: нашла)* тебя (в этом мире). ♦ **I was (really) lucky.** Мне (действительно) повезло. ♦ **I'm the luckiest** *(1)* **guy** / *(2)* **man** / *(3)* **person** / *(4)* **girl** / *(5)* **woman in the world to have your love.** Я *(1,2)* ...счастливейший мужчина / *(3)* человек... / *(4)* ...счастливейшая девушка / *(5)* женщина... на свете потому, что у меня есть твоя любовь. ♦ **I feel like the luckiest person in this part of the universe to have you as my dear, close, and beloved friend.** Я чувствую себя счастливейшим человеком в этой части вселенной, потому что ты мой дорогой, близкий и любимый друг. ♦ **I am really lucky to have found someone as good and loving and devoted as you in this big, muddled world.** Я действительно везучий *(ж: везучая),* так как нашёл *(ж: нашла)* такого хорошего, любящего и преданного человека, как ты, в этом большом, беспорядочном мире.

luminous *adj* сияющий, -ая, -ее, -ие.

lunch *n* ленч, второй завтрак ♦ **romantic** ~ романтический ленч ♦ **Would you like to have lunch (with me)?** Хочешь ты пойти на ленч (со мной)? ♦ **How would you like to have lunch? I know a good place.** Не хотели ли бы Вы пойти на ленч? Я знаю хорошее место. ♦ **Let's go have lunch (together).** Давай пойдём на ленч (вместе). ♦ **Would you like to have lunch?** Пойдёте ли Вы на ленч? ♦ **Let's go to lunch (together).** Давай пойдём на ленч (вместе).

lurch *vi:* ♦ **You made my heart lurch.** Ты повергла *(ж: поверг)* моё сердце в смятение.

lure *vt* привлекать / привлечь *(whom = acc.);* соблазнять / соблазнить *(whom = acc.),* завлекать / завлечь *(whom = acc.),* вовлекать / вовлечь *(whom = acc.),* заманивать / заманить *(whom = acc.)* ♦ **You** *(1,2)* **lured me into this (relationship).** Ты *(1)* вовлекла *(ж: вовлёк)* / *(2)* заманила *(ж: заманил)* меня в эти отношения. ♦ **You have my permission to lure me anywhere.** У тебя есть моё разрешение завлекать меня куда угодно.

Russian terms of endearment are given in Appendix 13, page 780.

luscious *adj* со́чный, -ая, -ое, -ые ♦ **What a (beautiful,) luscious body you have.** Что за (прекра́сное,) со́чное у тебя́ те́ло. ♦ **You have the most luscious body I've ever seen (in all my life).** У тебя́ сочне́йшее те́ло, кото́рое я когда́-либо (в жи́зни) ви́дел. ♦ **Even in my dreams I've never seen such a luscious body.** Да́же в свои́х снах я никогда́ не ви́дел тако́го со́чного те́ла. ♦ **You are the most luscious creature I've ever known (in all my life).** Ты сочне́йшее созда́ние, кото́рое я когда́-либо знал (в жи́зни). ♦ **The (1) memory / (2) thought / (3) image of your luscious body never leaves my mind.** *(1)* Воспомина́ние / *(2,3)* Мысль о твоём со́чном те́ле... никогда́ не покида́ет меня́. ♦ **Whenever I even think of your beautiful, luscious body, I am (1) filled / (2) seized with raging lust.** Когда́ бы я ни поду́мал о твоём прекра́сном, со́чном те́ле, меня́ *(1)* наполня́ет / *(2)* охва́тывает бе́шеная страсть. ♦ **I (1) yearn / (2) long so (3) mightily / (4) much to explore all the luscious secrets of your body.** Я так *(3,4)* си́льно *(1)* жа́жду / *(2)* стремлю́сь иссле́довать все со́чные секре́ты твоего́ те́ла.

lush *adj* 1. *(luxuriant)* роско́шный, -ая, -ое, -ые, пы́шный, -ая, -ое, -ые; бу́йный, -ая, -ое, -ые;*(voluptuous)* роско́шный, -ая, -ое, -ые; 2. *(succulent)* со́чный, -ая, -ое, -ые. ♦ **I want to (1) abandon / (2) lose myself in your lush beauty.** Я хочу́ *(1)* ...весь отда́ться твое́й роско́шной красоте́. / *(2)* ...потеря́ть себя́ в твое́й роско́шной красоте́. ♦ **The vision of your lush, beautiful body fills my thoughts night and day.** Я постоя́нно днём и но́чью ви́жу пе́ред собо́й твой роско́шное, прекра́сное те́ло.

lush *n (slang)* пья́ница.

lushness *n* ро́скошь *f* ♦ **I yearn for the heavenly lushness of your beautiful body.** Я жа́жду изуми́тельной ро́скоши твоего́ прекра́сного те́ла.

lust *vi* вожделе́ть, испы́тывать / испыта́ть вожделе́ние ♦ **I've lusted after you for months.** Я испы́тываю вожделе́ние к тебе́ в тече́ние ме́сяцев. ♦ **I've never lusted after anyone like I lust after you.** Я испы́тываю к тебе́ тако́е вожделе́ние, како́го никогда́ ни к кому́ не испы́тывал.

lust *n* вожделе́ние, по́хоть *f* ♦ **burning** ~ сжига́ющее вожделе́ние ♦ **raging** ~ я́ростное вожделе́ние, бе́шеная страсть ♦ **volcanic** ~ вулани́ческое вожделе́ние ♦ **be afire with** ~ сгора́ть от вожделе́ния ♦ **be crazy with** ~ обезу́меть от вожделе́ния ♦ **fill me with** ~ наполня́ть / напо́лнить меня́ вожделе́нием.

lust: phrases

I am afire with lust for you. Я сгора́ю от вожделе́ния к тебе́. ♦ **Whenever I even think of your beautiful, (1) delectable / (2) luscious body, I am (3) filled / (4) seized with raging lust.** Когда́ бы я ни поду́мал о твоём прекра́сном, *(1)* преле́стном / *(2)* со́чном те́ле, меня́ *(3)* наполня́ет / *(4)* охва́тывает бе́шеная страсть. ♦ **You fill me with (raging) lust.** Ты наполня́ешь меня́ (я́ростным) вожделе́нием. ♦ **I'm (1) absolutely / (2) totally crazed with lust for you.** Я *(1)* абсолю́тно / *(2)* соверше́нно обезу́мел от вожделе́ния к тебе́. ♦ **(1) The very sight of you... / (2) Just looking at your picture... fills me with lust.** То́лько взгляд *(1)* ...на тебя́... / *(2)* ...на твою́ фотогра́фию... наполня́ет меня́ вожделе́нием. ♦ **Your (1) incredible / (2) voluptuous beauty has me crazed with lust.** Твоя́ *(1)* невероя́тная / *(2)* роско́шная красота́ сво́дит меня́ с ума́ от вожделе́ния.

luster *n* блеск ♦ **The luster of your hair is so (1) gorgeous / (2) magnificent.** Блеск твои́х воло́с так *(1)* изуми́телен / *(2)* великоле́пен.

lustful *adj* похотли́вый, -ая, -ое, -ые.

lusting *n* по́хоть *f*, вожделе́ние ♦ **I'm constantly assailed by this primeval lusting for (1) ...you. / (2) ...your incredibly beautiful body.** Меня́ постоя́нно охва́тывает первобы́тное вожделе́ние к *(1)* ...тебе́. / *(2)* ...твоему́ невероя́тно прекра́сному те́лу.

lustrous *adj* блестя́щий, -ая, -ее, -ие, глянцеви́тый, -ая, -ое, -ые ♦ **Your hair looks**

Some of the Russian sentences are translations of things we say and are not what Russians themselves would normally say.

lustrous. У тебя блестящие волосы.

Lutheran *adj* лютеранский, -ая, -ое, -ие.

luxuriant *adj* роскошный, -ая, -ое, -ые.

luxuriate *vi* наслаждаться, упиваться ♦ **I want to** *(1,2)* **luxuriate forever in the heavenly enchantment of your person.** Я хочу *(1)* наслаждаться / *(2)* упиваться вечно твоим божественным очарованием. ♦ **I long for the day when I can luxuriate (again) in the warm, sweet splendor of your beautiful body.** Я тоскую по дню, когда смогу (опять) наслаждаться тёплым, сладостным великолепием твоего прекрасного тела.

luxurious *adj* роскошный, -ая, -ое, -ые ♦ **You have such luxurious power over my senses.** У тебя такая удивительная власть над моими чувствами.

luxury *n* роскошь *f* ♦ **I revel in the boundless luxury of your love.** Я пирую в беспредельной роскоши твоей любви.

lycra *n (material)* лайкра *(вид материала).*

lyrical *adj* лирический, -ая, -ое, -ие.

lyrics *n, pl (of a song)* слова (песни), текст (песни).

Counting things in Russian is a bit involved.
See Appendix 4, Numbers, on page 756 .

M

MA *abbrev* = **Master of Arts degree** сте́пень маги́стра гуманита́рных нау́к.

macho *adj* му́жественный, -ая, -ое, -ые; кре́пкий, -ая, -ое, -ие; энерги́чный, -ая, -ое, -ые.

mad *adj* 1. *(crazy)* сумасше́дший, -ая, -ее, -ие, безу́мный, -ая, -ое, -ые, полоу́мный, -ая, -ое, -ые; 2. *(wild, violent)* бе́шеный, -ая, -ое, -ые, неи́стовый, -ая, -ое, -ые ♦ **be ~** *(angry)* серди́ться ♦ **be ~ about** *(infatuated)* бре́дить *(whom = instr.)* ♦ **get ~** *(angry)* серди́ться / рассерди́ться ♦ **I'm going to make you go (absolutely) mad with pleasure.** Ты испы́тываешь (соверше́нно) безу́мное наслажде́ние. ♦ **Are you mad at me for loving you?** Ты се́рдишься на меня́ за то, что я люблю́ тебя́?

made *adj* сде́лан, -а, -о, -ы, со́здан, -а, -о, -ы *(short forms)* ♦ **You and I were made for** *(1)* **...one another.** / *(2)* **...each other.** Ты и я бы́ли со́зданы *(1,2)* друг для дру́га.

madly *adv* безу́мно, до безу́мия ♦ **I'm madly in love with you.** Я безу́мно люблю́ тебя́.

madness *n* сумаше́ствие, безу́мие, бе́шенство; безрассу́дство ♦ **absolute ~** абсолю́тное безрассу́дство ♦ **~ of passion** безу́мие стра́сти ♦ **sheer ~** абсолю́тное безрассу́дство ♦ **Some kind of madness came over me.** Не́кий вид безу́мия нашёл на меня́.

magic *n* ма́гия, волшебство́ ♦ **heavenly ~** ра́йская ма́гия ♦ **invincible ~ of love** всепобежда́ющая ма́гия любви́ ♦ **~ of intimacy** ма́гия инти́мности ♦ **~ of your body** волшебство́ твоего́ те́ла ♦ **~ of your kisses** волшебство́ твои́х поцелу́ев ♦ **~ of your love** волшебство́ твое́й любви́ ♦ **natural ~** есте́ственная ма́гия ♦ **soft ~** мя́гкая ма́гия ♦ **sweet ~** не́жное волшебство́; сла́дкое волшебство́ ♦ **warm ~** тёплая ма́гия ♦ **wonderful ~** удиви́тельная ма́гия ♦ **your ~** твоя́ ма́гия.

magic: of your smile

There's such magic in your smile. В твое́й улы́бке тако́е волшебство́.

magic: of your kisses

The sweet magic of your kisses *(1)* **...enthralls me.** / *(2)* **...captivates my soul.** / *(3)* **...sends me into endless ecstasy.** Сла́дкое волшебство́ твои́х поцелу́ев *(1)* ...очаро́вывает меня́. / *(2)* ...пленя́ет мою́ ду́шу. / *(3)* ...приво́дит меня́ в несконча́емый восто́рг.

magic: of your love

All things around me are sweetened by the magic of your love. Все ве́щи вокру́г меня́ освещены́ волшебство́м твое́й любви́.

magic: of your body

The soft, warm magic of your body transports me to a cosmic kaleidoscope of ecstasy. Мя́гкая, тёплая ма́гия твоего́ те́ла перено́сит меня́ в косми́ческий калейдоско́п

Russian has 2 different verbs for "go", one for "on foot" and the other for "by vehicle".

экста́за. ♦ **Only the sweet, soft magic of your beautiful body in my arms can assuage the desperate hunger that consumes me.** То́лько не́жное, мя́гкое волшебство́ твоего́ прекра́сного те́ла в мои́х объя́тиях мо́жет утоли́ть отча́янный го́лод, пожира́ющий меня́. ♦ **I'm starved for the warm magic of** *(1)* **...you.** / *(2)* **...your beautiful body.** Я жа́жду тёплой ма́гии *(1)* ...твое́й. / *(2)* ...твоего́ прекра́сного те́ла. ♦ **I spend these long, lonely nights yearning and burning for the warm, wonderful, heavenly magic of your beautiful body** Я провожу́ э́ти до́лгие, одино́кие но́чи, сгора́я и тоску́я по тёплой, удиви́тельной, ра́йской ма́гии твоего́ прекра́сного те́ла. ♦ **The magic of your beautiful, sensuous body has enslaved my soul.** Волшебство́ твоего́ прекра́сного, чу́вственного те́ла покори́ло мою́ ду́шу.

magic: of you

You have a natural magic that is impossible to resist. Ты облада́ешь есте́ственной ма́гией, кото́рой невозмо́жно сопротивля́ться.

magic: magic of spring

The *(1,2)* **magic of the spring fills my heart with longing to be with you.** *(1)* Волшебство́ / *(2)* Ма́гия весны́ наполня́ет моё се́рдце стремле́нием быть с тобо́й. ♦ **I want to share the magic of the spring with you.** Я хочу́ раздели́ть волшебство́ весны́ с тобо́й.

magic: of a kiss

I would like to be the lucky person in this world who teaches you what kind of magic a kiss can hold. Я хоте́л бы быть тем счастли́вым челове́ком в э́том ми́ре, кото́рый у́чит тебя́ волшебству́ поцелу́ев.

magic: it happens

Sometimes magic happens. Иногда́ волше́бное случа́ется.

magical *adj* волше́бный, -ая, -ое, -ые, маги́ческий, -ая, -ое, -ие ♦ **I'll never forget those wonderful, magical moments with you.** Я никогда́ не забу́ду э́тих удиви́тельных, волше́бных мину́т, проведённых с тобо́й. ♦ **What a magical night that was (together).** Како́й волше́бной была́ э́та ночь (, проведённая вме́сте). ♦ **You have a magical touch.** Твои́ прикоснове́ния волше́бны.

magnanimity *n* великоду́шие.

magnanimous *adj* великоду́шный, -ая, -ое, -ые.

magnet *n* магни́т.

magnetic *adj* магнети́ческий, -ая, -ое, -ие ♦ **Such a magnetic appeal you have for me!** Како́е магнети́ческое притяже́ние ты ока́зываешь на меня́!

magnetism *n* магнети́зм ♦ **animal ~** живо́тный магнети́зм ♦ **hypnotic ~** гипноти́ческий магнети́зм ♦ **inner ~** вну́тренний магнети́зм ♦ *(1,2)* **irresistible ~** *(1)* непреодоли́мый / *(2)* неотрази́мый магнети́зм ♦ **You have a (personal) magnetism that** *(1)* **...is...** / *(2)* **...I find... irresistible.** У тебя́ тако́й магнети́зм, кото́рому *(1,2)* невозмо́жно сопроти́вля́ться. ♦ **The magnetism of your** *(1)* **charm** / *(2)* **personality is (completely) irresistible.** Магнети́зм *(1)* ...твоего́ обая́ния... / *(2)* ...твое́й индивидуа́льности... (соверше́нно) неотрази́м. ♦ **I am completely swept up away the force of your magnetism.** Я соверше́нно смете́н *(ж: сметена́)* с ног си́лой твоего́ магнети́зма. ♦ **You have a magnetism that sweeps me away.** У тебя́ тако́й магнети́зм, кото́рый смета́ет меня́ с ног.

magnificence *n* великоле́пие ♦ **~ of your feminine beauty** великоле́пие твое́й же́нской красоты́.

magnificent *adj* великоле́пный, -ая, -ое, -ые, изуми́тельный, -ая, -ое, -ые ♦ **totally ~** абсолю́тно изуми́тельный, -ая, -ое, -ые ♦ **You are magnificent.** Ты изуми́тельна *(ж: изуми́телен).* ♦ **You are a magnificent lover.** Ты изуми́тельная любо́вница *(ж: изуми́тельный любо́вник).*

Dipthongs in Russian are made by adding й
*to the end of a vowel (*а, е, ё, о, у, э, ю, *and* я).

magnificently *adv* великоле́пно.

magnitude *n* величина́; си́ла ♦ **The magnitude of your appeal for me is beyond** *(1)* **description** / *(2)* **definition** / *(3)* **calculation.** Си́ла твое́й привлека́тельности для меня́ вы́ше *(1)* ...вся́кого описа́ния / *(2)* определе́ния. / *(3)* ...вся́кой ме́ры.

maid *n* 1. *(young woman)* де́ва; деви́ца; де́вушка; 2. *(worker)* го́рничная, служа́нка ♦ **old** ~ ста́рая де́ва ♦ **~ of honor** подру́жка неве́сты ♦ **remain an old ~** оста́ться в ста́рых де́вах.

maiden *n* де́ва, деви́ца, де́вушка ♦ **This, my fair maiden, is for you.** Это, моя́ прекра́сная, для тебя́. ♦ **Never was there a maiden more fair (than you).** Никогда́ не́ было де́вушки бо́лее прекра́сной (, чем ты).

maidenhead *n* де́вственность *f*, непоро́чность *f*.

maidenhood *n* деви́чество.

maidenly *adj* деви́чий, -ья, -ье, -ьи ♦ **Your maidenly sense of propriety is inhibiting you (way) too much.** Твоё деви́чье чу́вство благопристо́йности сли́шком си́льно сде́рживает тебя́. ♦ **Your maidenly sense of propriety is preventing us from sharing wonderful moments together.** Если бы не твоё деви́чье чу́вство благопристо́йности, у нас могли́ бы быть великоле́пные моме́нты.

mail *vt* отправля́ть / отпра́вить *(what = acc., to whom = dat.)* ♦ **~ a letter (to you)** отпра́вить (тебе́) письмо́ ♦ **~ a package (to you)** отпра́вить (тебе́) посы́лку.

mail *n* по́чта ♦ **voice ~** автоотве́тчик ♦ **~ carrier** почтальо́н ♦ **I'll send it to you by** *(1)* **...airmail.** / *(2)* **...express mail.** / *(3)* **...registered mail.** / *(4,5)* **...surface mail.** Я пошлю́ э́то тебе́ *(1)* ...авиапо́чтой. / *(2)* ...экспре́сс-по́чтой. / *(3)* ...заказны́м. / *(4)* ...обы́чной / *(5)* просто́й по́чтой. ♦ **I got your e-mail.** Я получи́л твоё электро́нное письмо́. ♦ **I'll let you know by e-mail.** Я сообщу́ тебе́ электро́нной по́чтой. ♦ **You can leave a message on my voice mail.** Ты мо́жешь оста́вить сообще́ние на моём автоотве́тчике. ♦ **My world is dark grey. There was no mail from you today.** Мой мир -- тёмносерый. Не́ было пи́сем от тебя́ сего́дня.

mailman *n* почтальо́н.

make *vt* 1. *(produce, fabricate, accomplish, cause to do or become)* де́лать / сде́лать *(what, whom = acc.)*; 2. *(compel; cause to)* заставля́ть / заста́вить *(what, whom = acc.)*; 3. *(arrive in time)* успева́ть / успе́ть *(for what = + к + dat. or + на + acc.)*; 4. *(love)* занима́ться / заня́ться *(what = + instr., with whom = с + instr.)* ♦ **~ up** *vt* 1. *(compose)* составля́ть / соста́вить *(what = acc.)*; 2. *(think up)* выду́мывать / вы́думать *(what = acc.)*; 3. *(compensate)* возмеща́ть / возмести́ть *(what = acc., to whom = dat.)*.

> **make:** *make happy*

You make me *(1)* **so** / *(2)* **very happy.** Ты де́лаешь меня́ *(1)* таки́м *(ж: тако́й)* / *(2)* о́чень счастли́вым *(ж: счастли́вой).* ♦ **You've made me the happiest** *(1)* **person** / *(2)* **guy** / *(3)* **man alive.** Ты сде́лала меня́ са́мым счастли́вым *(1)* челове́ком / *(2)* па́рнем / *(3)* мужчи́ной на све́те. ♦ **You've made me the happiest** *(1)* **girl** / *(2)* **woman** / *(3)* **person alive.** Ты сде́лал меня́ ...са́мой счастли́вой *(1)* де́вушкой / *(2)* же́нщиной... / *(3)* ...са́мым счастли́вым челове́ком... на све́те.

> **make:** *make me love you*

It's all the little things that make me love you so much. Я так си́льно люблю́ тебя́ за все́ э́ти ма́ленькие зна́ки внима́ния.

> **make:** *make love*

I want so much to make love with you. Я так жа́жду занима́ться любо́вью с тобо́й. ♦ **I love to make love with you.** Я люблю́ занима́ться любо́вью с тобо́й. ♦ **It is so (fantastically) wonderful to make love with you.** Так (фантасти́чески) прекра́сно зани-

---

Some phrases are listed under more than one main word.

ма́ться любо́вью с тобо́й. ♦ **I want to make you melt in my arms.** Я хочу́, что́бы ты та́яла в мои́х рука́х.

make: make me feel

I love the way you make me feel. Мне нра́вятся те чу́вства, кото́рые ты вызыва́ешь во мне.

make: exaggerate

You're making too much of it. Ты раздува́ешь э́то сли́шком. ♦ **You're making mountains out of molehills.** Ты де́лаешь из му́хи слона́.

make up: compensate

I promise I'll make it up to you (later). Я обеща́ю, что возмещу́ тебе́ э́то (поздне́е).

make up: think up

You made up the whole story (, didn't you?). Ты вы́думала *(ж: вы́думал)* це́лую исто́рию (, не так ли?).

make *n (slang) (seduction)*: ♦ **He's just trying to put the make on you.** Он про́сто пыта́ется затащи́ть тебя́ в посте́ль. ♦ **Don't think I'm just trying to put the make on you. I would never do that.** Не ду́май, что я про́сто пыта́юсь затащи́ть тебя́ в посте́ль. Я никогда́ не бу́ду де́лать э́то.

maker *n*: ♦ **memory** ~ челове́к, оставля́ющий прекра́сные воспомина́ния *(explanation)* ♦ **music** ~ музыка́нт.

make up *vi (become reconciled)* мири́ться / помири́ться.

makeup *n* макия́ж, косме́тика, грим ♦ **heavy** ~ оби́льная косме́тика ♦ **minimal** ~ ми́нимум косме́тики ♦   **freshen** *(1,2)* **my** ~ освежи́ть *(1)* ...мой макия́ж. / *(2)* ...мою́ косме́тику.

male *adj* мужско́й, -а́я, -о́е, -и́е ♦ **primitively** ~ примити́вно-мужско́й ♦ **ruggedly** ~ гру́бо мужско́й ♦ **totally** ~ по́лностью мужско́й.

male *n* мужчи́на *(See also* **boy, guy** *and* **man)** ♦ **caring** ~ забо́тливый мужчи́на ♦ **compassionate** ~ сострада́тельный мужчи́на ♦ **energetic** ~ энерги́чный мужчи́на ♦ **fit** ~ спорти́вный мужчи́на ♦ **fun-loving** ~ лю́бящий развлече́ния мужчи́на ♦ **insightful** ~ проница́тельный мужчи́на ♦ **loving** ~ лю́бящий мужчи́на ♦ **pierced** ~ мужчи́на с ко́льцами на те́ле ♦ **professional** ~ высококвалифици́рованный мужчи́на ♦ **red-blooded** ~ норма́льный мужчи́на ♦ **romantic** ~ романти́ческий мужчи́на ♦ **similar** ~ похо́жий мужчи́на ♦ **spiritual** ~ духо́вный мужчи́на ♦ **uninhibited** ~ мужчи́на без ко́мплексов.

maleness *n* му́жественность *f* ♦ **virile** ~ зре́лая му́жественность.

malice *n* зло́ба ♦ **I bear you no malice.** Я не пита́ю зло́бы к тебе́.

malicious *adj* зло́бный, -ая, -ое, -ые, злой, -а́я, -о́е, -ы́е, злонаме́ренный, -ая, -ое, -ые ♦ **That's malicious gossip.** Это злонаме́ренная спле́тня. ♦ **That was a malicious thing to say.** Бы́ло зло с твое́й стороны́ сказа́ть э́то.

mama *n* ма́ма ♦ **hot** ~ горя́чая же́нщина.

man *n* мужчи́на ♦ **American** ~ америка́нец ♦ **amiable** ~ приве́тливый мужчи́на ♦ **another** ~ друго́й мужчи́на ♦ **appreciative** ~ высоко́ це́нящий мужчи́на ♦ **Armenian** ~ армя́нин ♦ **Asian** ~ азиа́т ♦ **attractive** ~ привлека́тельный мужчи́на ♦ **Australian** ~ австра́лиец ♦ **Azerbaijanian** ~ азербайджа́нец ♦ **bad** ~ плохо́й мужчи́на ♦ **bald** ~ лы́сый мужчи́на ♦ **Belorussian** ~ белору́с ♦ **best** ~ *(at a wedding)* дру́жка ♦ **big** ~ кру́пный мужчи́на ♦ **big-hearted** ~ ще́дрый мужчи́на, мужчи́на с больши́м се́рдцем ♦ **black** ~ чёрный мужчи́на ♦ **blue-eyed** ~ синегла́зый мужчи́на ♦ **broad-shouldered** ~ широкопле́чий мужчи́на ♦ **caring** ~ забо́тливый мужчи́на ♦ **Canadian** ~ кана́дец ♦ **Carribean** ~ мужчи́на с Кари́бских острово́в ♦ **charming** ~ обая́тельный мужчи́на

The singular past tense of Russian verbs ends in -л (m) (usually),
-ла (f) or -ло (n). the plural past tense ends in -li.

♦ **cheerful** ~ весёлый мужчи́на ♦ **Chinese** ~ кита́ец ♦ **Christian** ~ христиа́нин ♦ **clean-cut young** ~ подтя́нутый молодо́й челове́к ♦ **college-educated** ~ мужчи́на с вы́сшим образова́нием ♦ **compassionate** ~ сострада́тельный мужчи́на ♦ **considerate** ~ внима́тельный мужчи́на ♦ **cultured** ~ культу́рный мужчи́на ♦ **dark(-complected)** ~ сму́глый мужчи́на ♦ **dark-eyed** ~ черногла́зый мужчи́на ♦ **dependable** ~ надёжный мужчи́на ♦ **devoted** ~ пре́данный мужчи́на ♦ **dirty old** ~ ста́рый козёл, гря́зный старика́шка ♦ **divorced** ~ разведённый мужчи́на ♦ **domineering** ~ вла́стный мужчи́на ♦ **dumb** ~ глу́пый мужчи́на ♦ *(1,2)* **educated** ~ *(1)* образо́ванный / *(2)* интеллиге́нтный мужчи́на ♦ *(1,2)* **elderly** ~ *(1)* немолодо́й / *(2)* пожило́й мужчи́на ♦ **emotionally generous** ~ эмоциона́льно ще́дрый мужчи́на ♦ **energetic** ~ энерги́чный мужчи́на ♦ **enlisted** ~ **(EM)** солда́т ♦ **Estonian** ~ эсто́нец ♦ **family** ~ семе́йный мужчи́на ♦ *(1,2)* **fat** ~ *(1)* по́лный / *(2)* то́лстый мужчи́на ♦ **fine quality** ~ мужчи́на прекра́сных ка́честв ♦ **Finnish** ~ финн ♦ **fit** ~ спорти́вный мужчи́на ♦ **friendly** ~ дружелю́бный мужчи́на ♦ **generous** ~ ще́дрый мужчи́на ♦ **Georgian** ~ грузи́н ♦ **good** ~ хоро́ший мужчи́на ♦ *(1-3)* **good-hearted** ~ *(1)* до́брый / *(2)* добросерде́чный мужчи́на, *(3)* мужчи́на с до́брым се́рдцем ♦ *(1-3)* **good-looking** ~ *(1)* привлека́тельный / *(2)* симпати́чный / *(3)* интере́сный мужчи́на ♦ **good-looking young** ~ привлека́тельный молодо́й челове́к ♦ **good--natured** ~ доброду́шный мужчи́на ♦ **grey-haired** ~ седо́й мужчи́на ♦ **handsome** ~ краси́вый мужчи́на ♦ **hard-working** ~ трудолюби́вый мужчи́на ♦ **Hawaiian** ~ мужчи́на с Гава́йев ♦ *(1,2)* **heavy(-set)** ~ *(1)* по́лный / *(2)* то́лстый мужчи́на ♦ **Hispanic** ~ лати́но-америка́нский мужчи́на ♦ **honest** ~ че́стный мужчи́на ♦ **husky** ~ си́льный мужчи́на ♦ **impressive** ~ представи́тельный мужчи́на ♦ **Indian** ~ 1. *(India)* инди́ец 2. *(America)* инде́ец ♦ **industrious** ~ трудолюби́вый мужчи́на ♦ **intelligent** ~ у́мный мужчи́на ♦ **interesting** ~ интере́сный челове́к ♦ **Japanese** ~ япо́нец ♦ **jealous** ~ ревни́вый мужчи́на ♦ **Jewish** ~ евре́й ♦ **Kazakh** ~ каза́х ♦ **kind** ~ до́брый мужчи́на ♦ **kindhearted** ~ отзы́вчивый мужчи́на ♦ **Kirghiz** ~ кирги́з ♦ **Korean** ~ коре́ец ♦ **ladies'** ~ да́мский уго́дник, ба́бник ♦ **Latvian** ~ латы́ш ♦ **lazy** ~ лени́вый мужчи́на ♦ *(1,2)* **lean** ~ *(1)* сухопа́рый / *(2)* сухоща́вый мужчи́на ♦ **Lithuanian** ~ лито́вец ♦ **lonely** ~ одино́кий мужчи́на ♦ **loving** ~ лю́бящий мужчи́на ♦ ~ **of depth** глубо́кий мужчи́на ♦ ~ **of experience** о́пытный мужчи́на ♦ ~ **of high energy** о́чень энерги́чный мужчи́на ♦ ~ **of my dreams** мужчи́на мое́й мечты́ ♦ ~ **of passion** стра́стный мужчи́на ♦ ~ **with emotional substance** эмоциона́льный мужчи́на ♦ **married** ~ жена́тый мужчи́на ♦ **mean** ~ злой мужчи́на ♦ **modest** ~ скро́мный мужчи́на ♦ **Moldovan** ~ молдава́нин ♦ **Mongolian** ~ монго́л ♦ **motorcycle** ~ мотоцикли́ст ♦ **multi-dimensional** ~ многосторо́нний мужчи́на ♦ **neat** ~ аккура́тный мужчи́на ♦ **nervous** ~ не́рвный мужчи́на ♦ *(1,2)* **nice** ~ *(1)* прия́тный / *(2)* симпати́чный мужчи́на ♦ **old** ~ ста́рый мужчи́на, стари́к ♦ **older** ~ мужчи́на ста́рше *(than whom = gen.)* ♦ **one-woman** ~ однолю́б ♦ **open-hearted** ~ великоду́шный мужчи́на ♦ **outgoing** ~ мужчи́на-экстраве́рт ♦ **passionate** ~ стра́стный мужчи́на ♦ **polite** ~ ве́жливый мужчи́на ♦ *(1,2)* **quiet** ~ *(1)* споко́йный / *(2)* ти́хий мужчи́на ♦ **real** ~ настоя́щий мужчи́на ♦ **red-blooded** ~ норма́льный мужчи́на ♦ **refined** ~ культу́рный мужчи́на ♦ **reliable** ~ надёжный мужчи́на ♦ **remarkable** ~ замеча́тельный мужчи́на ♦ **robust** ~ цвету́щий мужчи́на ♦ **romantic** ~ романти́ческий мужчи́на ♦ **Russian** ~ ру́сский ♦ **self-assured** ~ самоуве́ренный мужчи́на ♦ **self-confident** ~ самоуве́ренный мужчи́на ♦ **sensible** ~ здравомы́слящий мужчи́на ♦ **sensitive** ~ чувстви́тельный мужчи́на ♦ **serious** ~ серьёзный мужчи́на ♦ **sharp-minded** ~ остроу́мный мужчи́на ♦ **sharp-witted** ~ остроу́мный мужчи́на ♦ **short** ~ невысо́кий мужчи́на ♦ **simple** ~ просто́й мужчи́на ♦ *(1-4)* **single** ~ *(1)* одино́кий / *(2)* нежена́тый / *(3)* холосто́й мужчи́на, *(4)* холостя́к ♦ **skinny** ~ худо́й мужчи́на ♦ **slender** ~ стро́йный мужчи́на ♦ **slim** ~ стро́йный мужчи́на

Please do us a favor:
Fill out and mail in the Feedback Sheet on page 795.

♦ **smart** ~ у́мный мужчи́на ♦ **smartly dressed** ~ подтя́нутый мужчи́на ♦ **sophisticated** ~ о́пытный мужчи́на ♦ **spiritual** ~ духо́вный мужчи́на ♦ **statuesque** ~ ста́тный мужчи́на ♦ **stout** ~ соли́дный мужчи́на ♦ **strange** ~ 1. *(odd)* стра́нный мужчи́на; 2. *(unknown)* незнако́мый мужчи́на ♦ **strong** ~ си́льный мужчи́на ♦ **stubborn** ~ упря́мый мужчи́на ♦ **stupid** ~ глу́пый мужчи́на ♦ **successful** ~ мужчи́на, доби́вшийся успе́ха *(1 term)* ♦ **suntanned** ~ загоре́лый мужчи́на ♦ **Tadzhik** ~ таджи́к ♦ **tall** ~ высо́кий мужчи́на ♦ **thin** ~ худо́й мужчи́на ♦ **thoughtful** ~ внима́тельный мужчи́на ♦ **trim** ~ подтя́нутый мужчи́на ♦ **Turkmen** ~ туркме́н ♦ **Ukrainian** ~ украи́нец ♦ **ultimate** ~ превосхо́дный мужчи́на ♦ **uninhibited** ~ мужчи́на без ко́мплексов ♦ **unique** ~ уника́льный мужчи́на ♦ **university-educated** ~ мужчи́на с вы́сшим образова́нием ♦ **unmarried** ~ нежена́тый мужчи́на ♦ **Uzbek** ~ узбе́к ♦ *(1,2)* **warm-hearted** ~ *(1)* серде́чный / *(2)* отзы́вчивый мужчи́на; до́брый мужчи́на ♦ **warm, loving** ~ тёплый, лю́бящий мужчи́на ♦ **weak** ~ сла́бый мужчи́на ♦ **well-educated** ~ интелли́гентный мужчи́на ♦ **well-established** ~ соли́дный мужчи́на ♦ **well-groomed** ~ подтя́нутый мужчи́на ♦ **white** ~ бе́лый мужчи́на ♦ **wholesome family** ~ здравомы́слящий семе́йный мужчи́на ♦ *(1,2)* **wonderful** ~ *(1)* замеча́тельный / *(2)* удиви́тельный мужчи́на ♦ **worldly** ~ умудрённый мужчи́на ♦ **young** *(1,2)* ~ молодо́й *(1)* челове́к / *(2)* мужчи́на.

man: phrases

You are the man *(1)* ...of my dreams. / *(2)* ...that I've been waiting for all my life. / *(3)* ...that I've been dreaming of all my life. Ты мужчи́на *(1)* ...мое́й мечты́. / *(2)* ...кото́рого я ждала́ всю жизнь. / *(3)* ..., о кото́ром я мечта́ла всю свою́ жизнь. ♦ **You are the only man** *(1)* ...for me. / *(2)* ...in my life. / *(3)* ...I have ever truly loved. Ты еди́нственный мужчи́на *(1)* ...для меня́. / *(2)* ...в мое́й жи́зни. / *(3)* ..., кото́рого я когда-либо по-настоя́щему люби́ла. ♦ *(1)* **I want...** / *(2)* **I'm looking for... an older man.** Я *(1,2)* ищу́ мужчи́ну ста́рше себя́. ♦ **I've given up my girlish illusions about men.** Я отказа́лась от мои́х деви́чьих иллю́зий о мужчи́нах. ♦ **I'm a one-woman man.** Я однолю́б. ♦ **I don't need another man.** Друго́го мужчи́ны мне не ну́жно.

manage *vi* умудри́ться.

mane *n* гри́ва ♦ **pitchblack** ~ **of hair** смоляна́я гри́ва воло́с ♦ **thick grey** ~ густа́я седа́я гри́ва ♦ **wild** ~ **of golden hair** ди́кая гри́ва золоти́стых воло́с.

maneuver *n* манёвр ♦ **clever** ~ у́мный манёвр ♦ **deft** ~ ло́вкий манёвр ♦ **sleazy** ~ по́длый манёвр ♦ **slick** ~ хи́трый манёвр ♦ **underhanded** ~ закули́сный манёвр.

manhood *n* 1. *(male maturity)* возмужа́лость *f*; 2. *(masculinity)* му́жественность *f* ♦ **You're a prime specimen of manhood.** Ты эта́лон му́жественности.

maniac *n* манья́к ♦ **sex** ~ сексуа́льный манья́к.

manic *adj* маниака́льный, -ая, -ое, -ые.

manipulate *vt* манипули́ровать *(what, whom = instr.)* ♦ **I think you've been manipulating me.** Я ду́маю, что ты манипули́руешь мной. ♦ **I'm not the kind of person to manipulate someone.** Я не тот челове́к, кото́рый манипули́рует ке́м-либо. ♦ **I feel like I've been manipulated (by you).** Я чу́вствую, что ты манипули́ровала *(ж: манипули́ровал)* мной.

manipulative *adj* манипули́рующий, -ая, -ее, -ие ♦ **He** *(1)* **is** / *(2)* **was (so) manipulative.** Он (всегда́) *(1)* кру́тит / *(2)* крути́л други́ми. ♦ **She** *(1)* **is** / *(2)* **was (so) manipulative.** Она́ (всегда́) *(1)* кру́тит / *(2)* крути́ла други́ми. ♦ **You are (so) manipulative.** Ты челове́к, (всегда́) манипули́рующий други́ми.

manipulator *n* челове́к, манипули́рующий други́ми *(1 term)*.

manliness *n* му́жественность *f*.

Clock and calender time are discussed in Appendix 5, page 759.

manly *adj* мужественный, -ая, -ое, -ые.

manner *n* 1. *(behavior)* манера; поведение; 2. *pl: (etiquette)* манеры; 3. *(way)* образ ♦ **affectionate** ~ ласковое обращение ♦ **aloof** ~ сдержанное поведение ♦ **cavalier** ~ бесцеремонные манеры; бесцеремонный образ ♦ **cold** ~ холодные манеры ♦ **condescending** ~ снисходительные манеры ♦ **cultured** ~s культурные манеры ♦ **daring** ~ смелая манера ♦ **engaging** ~ обаятельные манеры ♦ **gentle** ~ мягкая манера ♦ **happy-go-lucky** ~ беспечный характер ♦ **icy** ~ ледяная манера, ледяное поведение ♦ **insolent** ~ наглова́тые манеры ♦ **polished** ~s изысканные манеры ♦ **reassuring** ~ убеждающая манера ♦ **refined** ~s изысканные манеры ♦ **sensuous** ~ чувственность *f* ♦ **teasing** ~ дразнящие манеры.

| **manner: phrases** |

(1,2) **Your happy-go-lucky manner is like a refreshing breeze.** *(1)* Твоя весёлость,... / *(2)* Твой беспечный характер,... как освежающий бриз. ♦ **You have very** *(1)* **cultured /** *(2)* **refined /** *(3)* **polished ,manners.** У тебя очень *(1)* культурные / *(2,3)* изысканные манеры. ♦ **I thought it would be bad manners (for me to do that).** Я думал *(ж: думала)*, было бы некрасиво (, если бы я сделал *[ж: сделала]* это). ♦ **You have a very engaging manner.** У тебя очень обаятельные манеры. ♦ *(1)* **I treated you...** / *(2)* **You treated me... in a very cavalier manner.** *(1)* Я обращался *(ж: обращалась)* с тобой... / *(2)* Ты обращалась *(ж: обращался)* со мной... очень бесцеремонно. ♦ *(1)* **I'm sorry...** / *(2)* **I apologize... for treating you in such a cavalier manner.** *(1)* Я прошу прощения... / *(2)* Я извиняюсь... за обращение с тобой таким бесцеремонным образом. ♦ **Your manner toward me has been so icy lately.** В последнее время твоё поведение со мной такое ледяное.

mannerism 1. манеры *pl*, особенность *f*; 2. манерность *f* ♦ **nervous** ~ нервные манеры ♦ **elegant** ~ элегантные манеры.

many *adj* много *(+ gen.)* ♦ **not** ~ не много ♦ **too** ~ слишком много ♦ **very** ~ очень много.

many-splendored *adj* великолепный (-ая, -ое, -ые) в многих отношениях ♦ **They say that love is a many-splendored thing.** Говорят, что любовь великолепна во многих отношениях.

maraud *vt* разорять / разорить *(what = acc.)*; терзать *(what = acc.)* ♦ **Without you in my arms a perpetual ache of longing marauds my soul.** Когда тебя нет в моих объятиях, постоянная боль тоски терзает мою душу.

march *n* марш ♦ **wedding** ~ свадебный марш.

Marine Corps *n* морская пехота ♦ **I'm in the Marine Corps.** Я в морской пехоте. ♦ **I'm a** *(1)* **Sergeant /** *(2)* **Lieutenant /** *(3)* *etc* **in the Marine Corps.** Я *(1)* сержант / *(2)* лейтенант / *(3)* и т.д. морской пехоты. ♦ **I served three years in the Marine Corps.** Я служил три года в морской пехоте.

mark *n:* ♦ **black-and-blue** ~ синяк ♦ **kiss** ~ засос, синяк, краснота, кровоподтёк *(на коже после долгого поцелуя)*.

marriage *n* брак, супружество; женитьба; *(f:)* замужество; *(process)* бракосочетание ♦ **arranged** ~ устроенный брак ♦ **civil** ~ гражданский брак ♦ **common-law** ~ незарегистрированный брак *(после 7 лет совместной жизни)*, гражданский брак ♦ **critically wounded** ~ брак с большими проблемами ♦ **forced** ~ бракосочетание по физическому принуждению ♦ **foreign** ~ брак, заключённый за границей *(1 term)* ♦ **former** ~ прежний брак ♦ **future** ~ будущий брак ♦ **happy** ~ счастливый брак ♦ **harmonious** ~ гармоничный брак ♦ **ideal** ~ идеальный брак ♦ **ill-conceived** ~ необдуманный брак ♦ **invalid** ~ недействительный брак ♦ **legal** ~ законный брак ♦ **long** ~ долгий брак ♦ **loveless** ~ брак без любви ♦ **loving** ~ семейная жизнь, полная любви *(1 term)* ♦ ~ **by**

Reflexive verbs are those that end in -ся *or* -сь.
The -ся *or* -сь *also goes onto a past tense ending.*
---

proxy брак по дове́ренности ♦ **~ for love** брак по любви́ ♦ **~ of convenience** брак по расчёту ♦ **mixed ~** сме́шанный брак ♦ **Palace of ~** Дворе́ц бракосочета́ния ♦ **phony ~** фикти́вный брак ♦ **previous ~** пре́жний брак ♦ **sham ~** фикти́вный брак ♦ **short ~** коро́ткий брак ♦ **surrogate ~** фикти́вный брак ♦ **unhappy ~** несчастли́вый брак ♦ **valid ~** действи́тельный брак.

marriage: *verb terms*

be joined in ~ сочета́ться бра́ком ♦ **consummate a ~** осуществля́ть / осуществи́ть бра́чные отноше́ния ♦ **enter (into) a ~** вступа́ть / вступи́ть в брак ♦ **give in ~** отдава́ть / отда́ть за́муж *(whom = acc.)* ♦ **go into a ~** вступа́ть / вступи́ть в брак ♦ **neglect a ~** пренебрега́ть бра́ком ♦ **put a career before one's marriage** поста́вить карье́ру превы́ше бра́ка.

marriage: *other terms*

annulment of a ~ расторже́ние бра́ка ♦ **bonds of ~** у́зы бра́ка ♦ **preparing for ~** подгото́вка к бра́ку ♦ **problems of ~** пробле́мы бра́ка.

marriage: *what makes a good one*

Love and respect form the foundation of a strong and lasting marriage. Любо́вь и уваже́ние создаю́т фунда́мент кре́пкого и продолжи́тельного бра́ка.

marriage: *ours will be great*

You and I will have a *(1)* **beautiful /** *(2)* **wonderful marriage (, I'm sure of it).** У нас бу́дет *(1)* прекра́сный / *(2)* замеча́тельный брак (, я в э́том уве́рен *[ж: уве́рена]*). ♦ **Our marriage will be** *(1)* **...beautiful /** *(2)* **great /** *(3)* **wonderful. /** *(4)* **...a cornucopia of love.** Наш брак бу́дет *(1)* ...прекра́сным / *(2,3)* замеча́тельным. / *(4)* ..., как рог, напо́лненный любо́вью.

marriage: *and career*

(1,2) **I would never put a career before my marriage.** *(1)* Я никогда́ не поста́влю карье́ру вы́ше, чем се́мью. / *(2)* Я никогда́ не предпочту́ карье́ру семье́.

marriage: *not yet*

You seem to be in love with the idea of marriage. (I'm not.) Тебе́, похо́же, о́чень нра́вится иде́я о бра́ке. (Мне нет.) ♦ **I never mentioned marriage.** Я никогда́ не упомина́л *(ж: упомина́ла)* о жени́тьбе. ♦ **I know you have marriage on your mind, but I'm not ready for it yet.** Я зна́ю, что ты ду́маешь о бра́ке, но я ещё не гото́в *(ж: гото́ва)* к нему́.

marriage: *bad ones*

The marriage was a disaster (from the start). Брак был катастро́фой с са́мого нача́ла. ♦ **Our marriage** *(1)* **...is in shambles. /** *(2)* **...is down the tube. /** *(3)* **...is on the rocks. /** *(4)* **...is crumbling. /** *(5)* **...is /** *(6)* **was a sham.** *(7)* **...is an exercise in futility. /** *(8)* **...has become a stale routine.** Наш брак *(1,2)* ...разру́шился. / *(3,4)* ...разва́ливается. / *(3,4)* ...ру́шится. / *(3,4)* ...на мели́. / *(5)* ... фикти́вный. / *(6)* ...был фикти́вным. *(7)* ...- упражне́ния в пустоте́. / *(8)* ...стал однообра́зной рути́ной. ♦ **Our marriage has been on-again, off-again.** Наш брак прерыва́лся и начина́лся опя́ть. ♦ **Our marriage lasted only 5 years.** Наш брак дли́лся то́лько пять лет. ♦ **My marriage (to** *[1]* **her /** *[2]* **him) ...was a** *(3)* **real /** *(4)* **terrible blunder. / ...**(5)* **is /** *(6)* **was like a bad dream.** Мой брак (с *[1]* ней / *[2]* ним) ...был *(3)* действи́тельно / *(4)* ужа́сной оши́бкой. / *(5)* ...(*[6]* был) похо́ж на стра́шный сон. ♦ **I leaped into the marriage too quickly.** Я жени́лся сли́шком бы́стро *(ж: Я вы́скочила за́муж).* ♦ **I've given up my illusions about marriage.** Я отказа́лся *(ж: отказа́лась)* от мои́х иллю́зий о бра́ке.

marriage: *getting out*

Why don't you *(1)* **get /** *(2)* **pull out of the** *(3,4)* **marriage?** Почему́ бы тебе́ не *(1,2)*

---

*The time zones for many cities of the world
are given in Appendix 6, page 761.*

поко́нчить со *(3)* ...свое́й семе́йной жи́знью? / *(4)* ...свои́м бра́ком. ♦ **I want (to** *[1]* **get** / *[2]* **pull) out of the marriage.** Я хочу́ *(1,2)* поко́нчить *(3)* ...со свое́й семе́йной жи́знью. / *(4)* ...с(о свои́м) бра́ком.

marriage: *arrangement*

My parents want to arrange my marriage. Мои́ роди́тели хотя́т устро́ить мой брак.

marriageable *adj* взро́слый, -ая, -ое, -ые, дости́гший (-ая, -ее, -ие) бра́чного во́зраста. ♦ ~ **age** бра́чный во́зраст.

marriage-mad *adj* чрезме́рно жа́ждущий жени́ться *m*, чрезме́рно жа́ждущая вы́йти за́муж *f.*

marriage-minded *adj* заинтересо́ванный (-ая, -ое, -ые) в бра́ке, ду́мающий (-ая, -ее, -ие) о бра́ке, настро́енный (-ая, -ое, -ые) на брак.

married *adj (man)* жена́тый *(short forms:* жена́т, -ы); *(woman)* заму́жняя *(short form:* за́мужем) ♦ **legally** ~ официа́льно в бра́ке ♦ **officially** ~ официа́льно в бра́ке.

married: *verb terms*

agree to get ~ *(woman)* согласи́ться вы́йти за́муж ♦ **be** ~ *(man)* жени́ться / жени́ться *(to whom* = + на + *prep.)*; *(woman)* выходи́ть / вы́йти за́муж *(to whom* = + за + *acc.)*; обвенча́ться ♦ **be** ~ **under common law** стать жена́тыми по́сле семи́ лет совме́стного прожива́ния ♦ **decide not to get** ~ *(man)* реши́ть не жени́ться; *(woman)* реши́ть не выходи́ть за́муж ♦ **decide to get** ~ *(man)* реши́ть жени́ться; *(woman)* реши́ть вы́йти за́муж ♦ *(1,2)* **force** *(3)* **me** / *(4)* **you to get** ~ *(1)* заста́вить / *(2)* принуди́ть *(3)* меня́ / *(4)* тебя́ жени́ться *m*; *(woman) (1)* заста́вить / *(2)* принуди́ть *(3)* меня́ / *(4)* тебя́ вы́йти за́муж ♦ **get** ~ *(man)* жени́ться / жени́ться *(to whom* = + на + *prep.)*; *(woman)* выходи́ть / вы́йти за́муж *(to whom* = + за + *acc.)*; *(both)* пожени́ться, обвенча́ться ♦ **get** ~ **early** *(man)* жени́ться ра́но; *(woman)* вы́йти за́муж ра́но ♦ **get** ~ **late** *(man)* жени́ться по́здно; *(woman)* вы́йти за́муж по́здно ♦ **get** ~ **old** *(man)* жени́ться пожилы́м; *(woman)* вы́йти за́муж пожило́й ♦ **get** ~ **young** *(man)* жени́ться молоды́м; *(woman:)* вы́йти за́муж молодо́й. ♦ **intend to get** ~ *(man:)* собира́ться жени́ться; *(woman:)* собира́ться вы́йти за́муж ♦ **plan to get** ~ *(man:)* собира́ться жени́ться; *(woman:)* собира́ться вы́йти за́муж ♦ **want to get** ~ *(man:)* хоте́ть жени́ться; *(woman:)* хоте́ть вы́йти за́муж.

married: *getting married to you*

I dream of *(1)* **being** / *(2)* **getting married to you.** Я мечта́ю *(1,2)* жени́ться на тебе́ *(ж:* [1,2] *вы́йти за́муж за тебя́.).* ♦ **I can think of nothing more wonderful than to be married to you.** Я не могу́ предста́вить ничего́ бо́лее замеча́тельного, чем брак с тобо́й. ♦ **I can't wait until we're** *(1,2)* **married.** Я не могу́ дожда́ться, когда́ мы *(1)* ...всту́пим в брак. / *(2)* ...поже́нимся. ♦ **I cling to the hope that we can get married next spring.** Я цепля́юсь за наде́жду, что мы мо́жем пожени́ться сле́дующей весно́й. ♦ **Let's get married outdoors.** Дава́й устро́им сва́дьбу на откры́том во́здухе. ♦ **We could get married outdoors.** У нас мо́жет быть сва́дьба на откры́том во́здухе.

married: *my / your status*

(1) **Can** / *(2)* **May I ask you a personal question? Are you married?** *(1,2)* Могу́ я зада́ть Вам ли́чный вопро́с? Вы за́мужем? *(ж: Вы жена́ты?)* ♦ **I'm still legally married.** Я до сих пор официа́льно в бра́ке. ♦ **How does it happen that someone so beautiful is not yet married? This is nothing short of a miracle. But I must say, I am extremely happy that the miracle exists.** Как так случи́лось, что така́я прекра́сная ещё не за́мужем? Это про́сто чу́до. Но я до́лжен сказа́ть, что я чрезвыча́йно сча́стлив, что э́то чу́до существу́ет. ♦ **I didn't know I was getting mixed up with a married woman.** Я не знал, что связа́лся с заму́жней же́нщиной. ♦ **I didn't know I was getting mixed up with a married man.** Я не зна́ла, что связа́лась с жена́тым мужчи́ной.

---

*Optional parts of sentences are preceded
or followed (or both) by three dots.*

married: *gotta think about it*

I have a lot to think about before getting married (again). Пре́жде, чем (опя́ть) жени́ться *(ж: вы́йти за́муж)*, я до́лжен *(ж: должна́)* о мно́гом поду́мать.

married: *too soon*

I wound up married before I knew anything about life. Я оказа́лся *(ж: оказа́лась)* в бра́ке пре́жде, чем узна́л *(ж: узна́ла)* что́-либо о жи́зни.

marry *vt (man)* 1. жени́ться / жени́ться *(whom = + на + prep.)*; *(woman)* выходи́ть / вы́йти за́муж *(whom = + за + acc.)*; *(both)* обвенча́ться *(whom = + с + instr.)*; 2. *(unite 2 people)* венча́ть / обвенча́ть *(whom = acc.)*.

marry: *verb terms*

agree to ~ *([1]* **you** / *[2]* **me)** *(woman)* согласи́ться вы́йти за́муж (за *[1]* тебя́ / *[2]* меня́) ♦ **decide not to ~** *([1]* **you** / *[2]* **me)** *(man)* реши́ть не жени́ться (на *[1]* тебе́ / *[2]* мне); *(woman)* реши́ть не выходи́ть за́муж (за *[1]* тебя́ / *[2]* меня́) ♦ **decide to ~** *([1]* **you** / *[2]* **me)** *(man)* реши́ть жени́ться (на *[1]* тебе́ / *[2]* мне); *(woman)* реши́ть вы́йти за́муж (за *[1]* тебя́ / *[2]* меня́) ♦ **(1,2) force (3) me** / **(4) you to ~** *(man)* *(1)* заста́вить / *(2)* прину́дить *(3)* меня́ / *(4)* тебя́ жени́ться; *(woman)* *(1)* заста́вить / *(2)* принуди́ть *(3)* меня́ / *(4)* тебя́ вы́йти за́муж ♦ **intend to ~** *([1]* **you** / *[2]* **me)** *(man)* собира́ться жени́ться (на *[1]* тебе́ / *[2]* мне); *(woman)* собира́ться вы́йти за́муж (за *[1]* тебя́ / *[2]* меня́) ♦ **persuade you to ~ me** *(m to f:)* уговори́ть тебя́ вы́йти за́муж за меня́ ♦ **plan to ~** *([1]* **you** / *[2]* **me)** *(man)* собира́ться жени́ться (на *[1]* тебе́ / *[2]* мне); *(woman)* собира́ться вы́йти за́муж (за *[1]* тебя́ / *[2]* меня́) ♦ **want to ~** *([1]* **you** / *[2]* **me)** *(man)* хоте́ть жени́ться (на *[1]* тебе́ / *[2]* мне); *(woman)* хоте́ть вы́йти за́муж (за *[1]* тебя́ / *[2]* меня́).

marry: *I want to marry you*

(1) Say... / (2) Tell me... you'll (3,4) marry me. *(1,2)* Скажи́ что *(3)* *(m to f:)* ...вы́йдешь за меня́ (за́муж). / *(4)* *(f to m:)* ...же́нишься на мне. ♦ **Will you marry me?** Ты вы́йдешь за́муж за меня́ *(ж: же́нишься на мне)*? ♦ **I want (more than anything) to marry you.** (Бо́льше всего́) я хочу́ жени́ться на тебе́. *(ж: я хочу́ вы́йти за́муж за тебя́).* ♦ **Please marry me.** Пожа́луйста, вы́йди за́муж за меня́. ♦ **Deep down in my heart I know that you're the one I want to marry.** В глубине́ своего́ се́рдца я зна́ю, что ты та, на ком я хочу́ жени́ться *(ж: ...ты тот, за кого́ я хочу́ вы́йти за́муж).* ♦ **If you would like to make me the happiest person in the world, marry me.** Е́сли ты хо́чешь сде́лать меня́ счастли́вейшим челове́ком в ми́ре, вы́йди за меня́ за́муж. ♦ **I want to marry you and live happily ever after.** Я хочу́ жени́ться на тебе́ *(ж: вы́йти за́муж за тебя́)* и жить сча́стливо всю жизнь. ♦ **My greatest aspiration in life is to marry you.** Са́мое си́льное стремле́ние мое́й жи́зни -- жени́ться на тебе́. ♦ **I can't wait to marry you.** Я не могу́ дожда́ться на́шей жени́тьбы.

marry: *I can't / don't want to*

I don't want to marry you. Я не хочу́ жени́ться на тебе́. *(ж: Я не хочу́ выходи́ть за́муж за тебя́.)* ♦ **I'm sorry, I can't marry you.** Я сожале́ю, я не могу́ ...жени́ться на тебе́ *(ж: ...вы́йти за́муж за тебя́).*

marry: *intentions*

My parents want to know if you intend to marry me. *(ж:)* Мои́ роди́тели хотя́т знать, наме́рен ли ты жени́ться на мне. ♦ **I'm going to tell my parents I intend to marry you.** Я скажу́ свои́м роди́телям, что наме́рен жени́ться на тебе́ *(ж: наме́рена вы́йти за́муж за тебя́.).* ♦ **I intend to marry you (as soon as possible).** Я наме́рен *(ж: наме́рена)* жени́ться на тебе́ *(ж: вы́йти за́муж за тебя́)* (как мо́жно скоре́е). ♦ **I have no intention of marrying you.** У меня́ нет наме́рения ...жени́ться на тебе́ *(ж: ...вы́йти за тебя́ за́муж).* ♦ **I don't think you have the slightest intention of marrying me.** Я не

If you're not on familiar terms with a person,
the «ты» forms will have to be changed to «Вы».

ду́маю, что у тебя́ есть хотя́ бы мале́йшее наме́рение вы́йти за меня́ за́муж *(ж: жени́ться на мне)*.

marry: *Welsh saying*

There's an old Welsh saying that if you put a sprig of mistletoe under your pillow, you'll dream of the man that will marry you. В Уэ́лсе существу́ет ста́рое предсказа́ние о том, что, е́сли положи́ть ве́точку оме́лы под поду́шку, то уви́дишь во сне мужчи́ну, кото́рый же́нится на тебе́.

marry *vi (man or couple)* жени́ться; *(woman)* выходи́ть / вы́йти за́муж; *(either or both)* обвенча́ться, вступи́ть в брак ♦ ~ **early** *(man)* жени́ться ра́но; *(woman)* вы́йти за́муж ра́но; *(either or both)* вступи́ть в брак ра́но ♦ ~ **for love** *(man)* жени́ться по любви́; *(woman)* вы́йти за́муж по любви́ ♦ ~ **for money** *(man)* жени́ться по расчёту; *(woman)* вы́йти за́муж по расчёту ♦ ~ **into money** *(man)* жени́ться на деньга́х; *(woman)* вы́йти за́муж за де́ньги ♦ ~ **late** *(man)* жени́ться по́здно; *(woman)* вы́йти за́муж по́здно; *(either or both)* вступи́ть в брак по́здно ♦ ~ **old** *(man)* жени́ться пожилы́м; *(woman)* вы́йти за́муж пожило́й; *(either or both)* вступи́ть в брак пожилы́м *m* / пожило́й *f* / пожилы́ми *pl* ♦ ~ **young** *(man)* жени́ться молоды́м; *(woman)* вы́йти за́муж молодо́й; *(either or both)* вступи́ть в брак молоды́м *m* / молодо́й *f* / молоды́ми *pl* ♦ **I believe a person should marry only for love.** Я ду́маю, что челове́к до́лжен жени́ться то́лько по любви́.

martial arts *n, pl* иску́сства бо́я.

martini *n* марти́ни *neut.*

marvel *vi* восхища́ться *(at what = instr.)* ♦ **I marvel at** *(1)* ...**your litheness.** / *(2)* ...**the extent of your knowledge.** / *(3)* ...**your exceptional loveliness.** / *(4)* ...**your physical charms.** / *(5)* ...**your ability to speak** / *(6)* **write** *(7)* **English** / *(8)* **Russian.** Я восхища́юсь *(1)* ...твое́й ги́бкостью. / *(2)* ...обши́рностью твои́х зна́ний. / *(3)* ...твое́й исключи́тельной красото́й. / *(4)* ...твои́ми физи́ческими преле́стями. / *(5)* ...твое́й спосо́бностью говори́ть / *(6)* писа́ть *(7)* по-англи́йски / *(8)* по-ру́сски.

marvel *n* чу́до.

marvelous *adj* удиви́тельный, -ая, -ое, -ые, чуде́сный, -ая, -ое, -ые, изуми́тельный, -ая, -ое, -ые.

marvelously *adv* удиви́тельно, чуде́сно, изуми́тельно.

mascara *n* тушь для ресни́ц ♦ **a touch of** ~ немно́го ту́ши (на ресни́цах).

masculine *adj* му́жественный, -ая, -ое, -ые ♦ **overwhelmingly** ~ потряса́юще му́жественный.

masculinity *n* му́жественность *f* ♦ **appealing** ~ вызыва́ющая му́жественность ♦ **magnificent** ~ великоле́пная му́жественность ♦ **marvelous** ~ великоле́пная му́жественность ♦ **splendid** ~ великоле́пная му́жественность ♦ **virile** ~ зре́лая му́жественность.

mask *vt* пря́тать / спря́тать *(what = acc.)*, скрыва́ть / скрыть *(what = acc.)* ♦ **I've been masking my (true) feelings for you for a long time.** Я до́лгое вре́мя скрыва́л *(ж: скрыва́ла)* мои́ (и́стинные) чу́вства к тебе́. ♦ **I can no longer mask the fact that I'm in love with you.** Я не могу́ до́льше скрыва́ть тот факт, что я люблю́ тебя́.

mask *n* ма́ска ♦ ~ **of indifference** ма́ска равноду́шия.

massage *vt* массажи́ровать / помассажи́ровать *(what, whom = acc.)* ♦ **Let me gently massage your** *(1)* **neck** / *(2)* **back** / *(3)* **shoulders** / *(4)* **legs** / *(5)* **arms.** Позво́ль мне не́жно помассажи́ровать *(1)* ...твою́ ше́ю / *(2)* спи́ну. / *(3)* ...твои́ пле́чи / *(4)* но́ги / *(5)* ру́ки.

massage *n* масса́ж ♦ **awesome** ~ великоле́пный масса́ж ♦ **erotic** ~ эроти́ческий масса́ж ♦ **foot** ~ масса́ж ступне́й ♦ **full body** ~ масса́ж всего́ те́ла ♦ **gentle** ~ не́жный масса́ж ♦ **sensual** ~ чу́вственный масса́ж ♦ **thorough** ~ о́бщий масса́ж ♦ **I want to give you**

A list of common places with their grammatical endings is given in Appendix 7, page 763.

a soft mini-nibble massage all over your body. Я хочу́ массажи́ровать всё твоё те́ло не́жными кро́шечными поцелу́ями. ♦ **You won't believe what** *(1)* **marvelous** / *(2)* **satisfying finesse I have at giving a massage.** Ты не смо́жешь пове́рить, каки́м *(1)* изуми́тельным / *(2)* удовлетворя́ющим иску́сством масса́жа я владе́ю.

master *n* ма́стер ♦ **You are truly a master at the art of** *(1)* **...making love.** / *(2)* **...arousing me** / *(3)* **passion.** / *(4)* **...giving pleasure.** / *(5)* **...bewitching (me).** / *(6)* **...cheating** / *(7)* **deceiving (people).** Ты, пра́вда, ма́стер в иску́сстве *(1)* ...любви́. / *(2)* ...возбужда́ть меня́ / *(3)* страсть. / *(4)* ...доставля́ть удово́льствия. / *(5)* ...очаро́вывать (меня́). / *(6,7)* ...обма́на (люде́й).

masterful *adj (expert)* ма́стерский, -ая, -ое, -ие.

masterfully *adv (expertly)* ма́стерски.

masterpiece *n* шеде́вр ♦ **You possess the kind of beauty that inspires masterpieces of art.** Ты облада́ешь тако́й красото́й, кото́рая вдохновля́ет на шеде́вры иску́сства.

mastery *n* мастерство́ ♦ **erotic** ~ эроти́ческое госпо́дство ♦ **exquisite** ~ утончённое мастерство́ ♦ **seductive** ~ мастерство́ обольще́ния.

masturbate *vi* мастурби́ровать.

masturbation *n* мастурба́ция.

match *vt* 1. *(compare with, equal)* сравни́ться *(what, whom* = + c + *instr., in what* = + в + *prep.)*; 2. *(go with)* подходи́ть *(what* = + к + *dat.)*; гармони́ровать *(what* = + c + *instr.)*; 3. *(correspond to)* соотве́тствовать *(what* = *dat.)* ♦ **No one can match** *(1)* **...you in any way.** / *(2)* **...your (exquisite) beauty.** / *(3)* **...your sweet nature.** Никто́ не мо́жет сравни́ться с тобо́й *(1)* ...ни в чём. / *(2)* ...в (соверше́нной) красоте́. / *(3)* ...в доброте́ хара́ктера. ♦ **I'll try to match** *(1)* **her** / *(2)* **him up with someone.** Я попыта́юсь *(1)* её / *(2)* его́ с ке́м-то познако́мить.

match *n* 1. *(mate)* па́ра; 2. *(to light fire)* спи́чка ♦ **ideal** ~ идеа́льная па́ра ♦ **You're an ideal match for me.** Ты идеа́льная па́ра для меня́.

matching *adj* подходя́щий, -ая, -ее, -ие ♦ ~ **jacket** подходя́щий жаке́т ♦ ~ **robe** подходя́щий хала́т ♦ ~ **shoes** подходя́щие ту́фли.

matchless *adj* несравне́нный, -ая, -ое, -ые.

matchmaker *n* сват *m*, сва́ха *f* ♦ **would-be** ~ начина́ющий сват *m*, начина́ющая сва́ха *f*.

matchmaking *n* сватовство́.

mate *n* 1. *(partner)* партнёр; спу́тник *m* / спу́тница *f* жи́зни; 2. *(spouse)* супру́г *m*, супру́га *f*; 3. *(friend)* прия́тель *m*, друг ♦ **classmate** соучени́к *m*, соучени́ца *f* ♦ **eternal** ~ ве́чный спу́тник жи́зни ♦ **lifelong** ~ супру́г *m* / супру́га *f* на всю жизнь ♦ **pillow** ~ 1. *(husband)* муж; *(wife)* жена́; 2. *(lover)* любо́вник *m*, любо́вница *f* ♦ **roommate** живу́щий *m* / живу́щая *f* в одно́й кварти́ре ♦ **soul** ~ задуше́вный друг ♦ **I want to walk by your side forever as your soul mate.** Я хочу́ прошага́ть с тобо́й жизнь, как твой задуше́вный друг. ♦ **I want you to be my** *(1)* **lifelong** / *(2)* **eternal mate.** Я хочу́, что́бы ты была́ *(ж: был)* *(1)* ...мое́й супру́гой *(ж: мои́м супру́гом)* на всю жизнь. / *(2)* ...мое́й ве́чной спу́тницей *(ж: мои́м ве́чным спу́тником)* жи́зни.

mateless *adj* 1. *(no spouse)* не име́ющий супру́ги *m*, не име́ющая супру́га *f*; 2. *(no permanent partner)* не име́ющий (-ая, -ие) постоя́нного партнёра ♦ **I'm mateless.** 1. *(no spouse)* У меня́ нет супру́ги *(ж: супру́га)*; 2. *(no permanent partner)* У меня́ нет постоя́нного партнёра.

material *n* материа́л ♦ **filmy** ~ **of a dress** о́чень то́нкий материа́л пла́тья.

materialist *n* материали́ст ♦ **superficial** ~ пове́рхностный материали́ст.

materialistic *adj* материалисти́ческий, -ая, -ое, -ие.

mate-seeker *n* и́щущий супру́гу *m*, и́щущая супру́га *f*.

Common adult heights are given in Appendix 9, page 776.

matrimony *n* супру́жество.

matron *n* матро́на; мать семе́йства ♦ ~ **of honor** заму́жняя подру́га неве́сты *(на сва́дьбе).*

matter *vi* име́ть значе́ние ♦ **Nothing matters except being with you.** Нет ничего́ важне́е, чем быть с тобо́й.

matter *n (question, subject)* вопро́с, предме́т обсужде́ния; *(affair)* де́ло ♦ **another** ~ друго́е де́ло ♦ **business** ~s дела́ *pl,* деловы́е вопро́сы ♦ **complicated** ~ сло́жное де́ло ♦ **confidential** ~ не подлежа́щее разглаше́нию де́ло ♦ **delicate** ~ делика́тное де́ло ♦ **different** ~ друго́е де́ло ♦ **difficult** ~ тру́дное де́ло ♦ *(1,2)* **easy** ~ *(1)* лёгкое / *(2)* просто́е де́ло ♦ **financial** ~s фина́нсовые дела́ ♦ **important** ~ ва́жное де́ло; ва́жный вопро́с ♦ **involved** ~ сло́жное де́ло ♦ ~**s of the heart** серде́чные дела́ ♦ **no joking** ~ не шу́точное де́ло ♦ **no laughing** ~ не шу́точное де́ло ♦ **personal** ~ ли́чное де́ло; ли́чный вопро́с ♦ **private** ~ ли́чное де́ло; ли́чный вопро́с ♦ **serious** ~ серьёзное де́ло ♦ **simple** ~ просто́е де́ло ♦ **small** ~ небольшо́е де́ло ♦ **trivial** ~ пустя́к ♦ *(1,2)* **urgent** ~ *(1)* сро́чное / *(2)* неотло́жное де́ло.

> ### matter: phrases

What's the matter? В чём де́ло? ♦ **Tell me what the matter is.** Расскажи́ мне, в чём де́ло. ♦ **No matter where I am or what I do, I always think of you.** Не ва́жно, где я и что де́лаю, я всегда́ ду́маю о тебе́.

mature *adj* 1. *(developed, reached maturity)* зре́лый, -ая, -ое, -ые; 2. *(middle-aged)* сре́днего во́зраста, в сре́дних года́х; *(older)* престаре́лый, -ая, -ое, -ые ♦ **emotionally** ~ эмоциона́льно зре́лый, -ая, -ое, -ые.

MBA *abbrev* = **Master of Business Administration** ~ сте́пень маги́стра би́знеса.

mean *adj* злой, -а́я, -о́е, -ы́е ♦ **be** *(1,2)* ~ **to** *(3)* **me** / *(4)* **you** *(1)* пло́хо / *(2)* гру́бо обраща́ться / обрати́ться *(3)* со мной / *(4)* с тобо́й.

mean *vt* 1. *(have meaning)* зна́чить *(what = acc.),* означа́ть *(what = acc.);* 2. *(intend)* предназнача́ть *(what = acc., for whom = + для + gen.);* 3. *(have in mind)* подразумева́ть *(what, whom = acc.),* име́ть в виду́ *(what, whom = acc.); vi* 4. *(tell the truth)* говори́ть / сказа́ть пра́вду; 5. *(intend, plan)* намерева́ться ♦ **not** ~ **much** не мно́го зна́чить.

> ### mean: say truly / seriously

Do you mean it? Ты говори́шь пра́вду? ♦ **I (really) mean it.** Я (действи́тельно) говорю́ пра́вду. ♦ *(1,2)* **I don't (really) mean it.** *(1)* Это непра́вда. / *(2)* Это несерьёзно. ♦ **I meant it.** Я говори́л *(ж: говори́ла)* пра́вду. ♦ *(1,2)* **I didn't mean it.** *(1)* Это была́ непра́вда. / *(2)* Это бы́ло не серьёзно.

> ### mean: have in mind

(1,2) **What do you mean?** *(1)* Что ты име́ешь в виду́? / *(2)* Что э́то означа́ет? ♦ *(1)* **What I mean is...** / *(2)* **I mean (that)...** *(1,2)* Я име́ю в виду́, что... ♦ **Do you** *(1)* **know** / *(2)* **understand what I mean?** Тепе́рь ты *(1)* зна́ешь / *(2)* понима́ешь, что я име́ю в виду́? ♦ **I (don't)** *(1)* **know** / *(2)* **understand what you mean.** Я не *(1)* зна́ю / *(2)* по́нял *(ж: поняла́),* что ты име́ешь в виду́.

> ### mean: what I mean to you

Do I mean anything (at all) to you? Я зна́чу для тебя́ хоть что́-нибудь? ♦ **I don't mean a thing to you.** Я не зна́чу ничего́ для тебя́.

> ### mean: what you mean to me

You mean *(1)* **...a lot...** / *(2)* **...everything...** / *(3)* **...so much... to me.** Ты зна́чишь *(1)* ...мно́го... / *(2)* ...всё... / *(3)* ...так мно́го... для меня́. ♦ **You mean more and more to me with each passing day.** Ты зна́чишь всё бо́льше и бо́льше для меня́ с ка́ждым проходя́щим днём. ♦ **You mean the world to me.** Ты для меня́ -- весь мир. ♦ *(1)* **You don't**

Words in parentheses are optional.

know... / (2) **You'll never know...** / (3) **You can't guess** / (4) **imagine...** / (5) **If you only knew...** / (6) **I can't describe...** (7) **...how much you mean to me.** / (8) **...how much it means to me to have your love.** *(1)* Ты не зна́ешь,... / *(2)* Ты никогда́ не узна́ешь,... / *(3)* Ты не мо́жешь предположи́ть / *(4)* вообрази́ть,... / *(5)* Е́сли бы ты то́лько зна́ла *(ж: знал)*,... / *(6)* Я не в си́лах описа́ть,... *(7)* ...как мно́го ты зна́чишь для меня́. / *(8)* ...как мно́го зна́чит для меня́ твоя́ любо́вь. ◆ **I search in vain for the right words to tell you how much you mean to me.** Я ищу́ напра́сно таки́е слова́, кото́рые рассказа́ли бы тебе́, как мно́го ты зна́чишь для меня́. ◆ **You mean more to me than anything in the whole wide world.** Ты зна́чишь для меня́ бо́льше, чем всё друго́е в це́лом огро́мном ми́ре.

mean: *what your love means to me*

Nothing means as much to me as your love. Ничто́ не зна́чит для меня́ так мно́го, как твоя́ любо́вь.

mean: *what I mean to you*

I can't escape the feeling that I don't mean anything to you anymore. Я не могу́ отде́латься от чу́вства, что я бо́льше ничего́ не зна́чу для тебя́.

mean: *meant for each other*

Deep down in my heart I know that we were meant for each other. В глубине́ своего́ се́рдца я зна́ю, что мы предназна́чены друг для дру́га.

meaning *n* значе́ние; смысл ◆ **double** ~ двойно́й смысл ◆ **great** ~ большо́е значе́ние ◆ *(1,2)* **hidden** ~ *(1)* спря́танный / *(2)* та́йный смысл ◆ **important** ~ ва́жное значе́ние ◆ **new** ~ но́вое значе́ние ◆ **real** ~ настоя́щее значе́ние ◆ **true** ~ и́стинное значе́ние ◆ **vague** ~ *(uncertain)* неопределённый смысл; *(elusive)* неулови́мый смысл ◆ **full of** ~ по́лный (-ая, -ое, -ые) смы́сла; многозначи́тельный, -ая, -ое, -ые ◆ **give** ~ придава́ть / прида́ть смысл ◆ **have** ~ име́ть значе́ние ◆ **You have taught me the true meaning of love.** Ты откры́ла *(ж: откры́л)* мне и́стинное значе́ние любви́. ◆ **You give my life a whole new meaning.** Ты придаёшь мое́й жи́зни соверше́нно но́вый смысл. ◆ **I hope this letter conveys my meaning as I intend it.** Я наде́юсь, что э́то письмо́ то́чно передаёт то, что я ду́маю.

meaningful *adj* 1. *(having meaning)* зна́чащий, -ая, -ее, -ие; 2. *(significant)* многозначи́тельный, -ая, -ое, -ые ◆ **glance** многозначи́тельный взгляд ◆ ~ **look** многозначи́тельный взгляд ◆ ~ **smile** многозначи́тельная улы́бка.

meaningless *adj* бессмы́сленный, -ая, -ое, -ые ◆ **Without you my life would be** *(1)* **so** / *(2)* **totally** / *(3)* **completely meaningless.** Без тебя́ моя́ жизнь была́ бы *(1)* так / *(2)* соверше́нно / *(3)* по́лностью бессмы́сленна.

mean-spirited *adj* по́длый, -ая, -ое, -ые, ни́зкий, -ая, -ое, -ие.

measure *n* 1. измере́ние, ме́ра; 2. *(step)* ме́ра ◆ **precautionary** ~s ме́ры предосторо́жности ◆ **beyond** ~ вы́ше вся́кой ме́ры, беспреде́лен, беспреде́льна, -о, -ы *(adj, short forms)* ◆ **My love for you is beyond measure.** Моя́ любо́вь к тебе́ вы́ше вся́кой ме́ры.

mediocre *adj* посре́дственный, -ая, -ое, -ые.

meditate *vi* 1. *(dwell in thought)* размышля́ть; 2. *(contemplate spiritually)* медити́ровать.

meditation *n* 1. *(deep thought)* размышле́ние; 2. *(spiritual contemplation)* медита́ция.

meet *vt* встреча́ть / встре́тить *(what, whom = acc.)*.

meet: *first meeting*

I don't believe I've met you. *(1,2)* **My name is...** Я не ду́маю, что знако́м *(ж: знако́ма)* с Ва́ми. *(1)* Моё и́мя... / *(2)* Меня́ зову́т... ◆ **It's a pleasure to meet you.** Удово́льствие познако́миться с Ва́ми. ◆ **It's a real pleasure to meet you.** Э́то замеча́тельно позна-ко́миться с Ва́ми. ◆ **I'm (very)** *(1)* **happy** / *(2)* **pleased** / *(3)* **glad to meet you.** Я (о́чень) *(1-3)* рад *(ж: ра́да)* познако́миться с Ва́ми.

You can find common clothing sizes in Appendix 11 on page 778.

meet: *how I feel about meeting you*

I've never met anyone like you before. Я никогда́ пре́жде не встреча́л *(ж: встреча́ла)* никого́ тако́го, как ты. ♦ **I was so** *(1)* **charmed** / *(2)* **delighted** / *(3)* **enthralled at meeting you yesterday that I feel compelled to write this short note to you to tell you how (very) much it meant to me.** Я был так *(1)* очаро́ван / *(2)* восхищён / *(3)* увлечён, встре́тив Вас вчера́, что чу́вствую непреодоли́мую потре́бность написа́ть э́ту коро́ткую запи́ску, что́бы сказа́ть Вам, как (о́чень) мно́го э́то зна́чит для меня́. ♦ **I am absolutely certain that I will never again meet anyone more enchantingly beautiful than you are.** Я соверше́нно уве́рен, что никогда́ опя́ть не встре́чу никого́ очарова́тельнее и прекра́снее, чем ты. ♦ **I've never met anyone (in all my life) as wonderful as you.** Я никогда́ (в жи́зни) не встреча́л *(ж: встреча́ла)* никого́ тако́го замеча́тельного, как ты. ♦ **How** *(1)* **empty** / *(2)* **bleak** / *(3)* **barren** / *(4)* **drab** / *(5)* **grey** / *(6)* **dull my life would be if I had never met you.** Как *(1)* пуста́ / *(2)* уны́ла / *(3)* беспло́дна / *(4)* ску́чна / *(5)* се́ра / *(6)* ту́скла моя́ жизнь была́ бы, е́сли бы я никогда́ не встре́тил *(ж: встре́тила)* тебя́. ♦ **From the first moment I** *(1)* **noticed** / *(2)* **saw you, I wanted to meet you.** С пе́рвой мину́ты, когда́ я *(1)* заме́тил *(ж: заме́тила)* / *(2)* уви́дел *(ж: уви́дела)* тебя́, я хоте́л *(ж: хоте́ла)* познако́миться с тобо́й. ♦ *(1)* **I've been on a cloud...** / *(2)* **My head's been in the clouds... ever since I met you** *(1)* Я был *(ж: была́)...* / *(2)* Моё се́рдце бы́ло... на облака́х, с тех пор, как я встре́тил *(ж: встре́тила)* тебя́.

meet: *I've wanted to meet you*

I wish I could have met you many years ago. Я хоте́л *(ж: хоте́ла)* бы встре́тить тебя́ мно́го лет наза́д. ♦ **I've wanted so much to meet you** Я так си́льно хоте́л *(ж: хоте́ла)* встре́тить Вас. ♦ **I've been** *(1)* **wanting** / *(2)* **waiting to meet you** *(3)* **...for a long (, long) time.** / *(4)* **...all my life.** Я *(1)* хоте́л *(ж: хоте́ла)* / *(2)* ждал *(ж: ждала́)* встре́чи с Ва́ми *(3)* ...до́лгое (, до́лгое) вре́мя. / *(4)* ...всю жизнь.

meet: *met you before?*

Where have I met you before? Где я встреча́л *(ж: встреча́ла)* Вас ра́ньше? ♦ **It seems to me I've met you before.** Мне ка́жется, что я встреча́л *(ж: встреча́ла)* Вас ра́ньше. ♦ **You look so familiar. I'm sure I've** *(1)* **seen** / *(2)* **met you before.** Вы вы́глядите тако́й знако́мой *(ж: таки́м знако́мым).* Я уве́рен *(ж: уве́рена),* что *(1)* ви́дел *(ж: уви́дела)* / *(2)* встреча́л *(ж: встреча́ла)* Вас пре́жде. ♦ **I know where I met you — in (all of) my dreams.** Я зна́ю, где встреча́л Вас, -- в(о) (всех) мои́х снах.

meet: *where to meet*

Where shall I meet you? Где я тебя́ встре́чу? ♦ *(1)* **I'll meet you...** / *(2)* **Meet me...** *(3)* **...at / on the corner of Sadovaya and Pushkin streets.** / *(4)* **...in front of the Main Library.** / *(5)* **...by the entrance to the Opera House.** / *(6)* **...at the airport** / *(7)* **train station** / *(8)* **bus station.** / *(9)* **...right here.** / *(10)* **...right over there.** *(1)* Я встре́чу тебя́... / *(2)* Встре́ть меня́... *(3)* ...на углу́ Садо́вой и Пу́шкинской. / *(4)* ...у Центра́льной библиоте́ки. / *(5)* ...у вхо́да в Оперный теа́тр. / *(6)* ...в аэропорту́. / *(7)* ...на вокза́ле. / *(8)* ...на автобусной ста́нции. / *(9)* ...пря́мо здесь. / *(10)* ...пря́мо там.

meet: *when to meet*

(1,2) **What time shall I meet you?** *(1)* В кото́ром часу́ мы уви́димся? / *(2)* В како́е вре́мя мы встре́тимся? ♦ *(1)* **I'll meet you...** / *(2)* **Meet me... at one (thirty).** *(See page 759 for other times.)* *(1)* Я встре́чу тебя́... / *(2)* Встре́ть меня́... в час (три́дцать). ♦ **Would it be possible to meet you** *(1)* **...this afternoon** / *(2)* **evening?** / *(3)* **...tonight?** / *(4)* **...tomorrow (**[5]** morning** / [6] **afternoon** / [7] **evening)?** / *(8)* **...after work?** / *(9)* **...after you get off work?** Возмо́жно ли встре́титься с тобо́й *(1)* ...(сего́дня) в по́лдень? / *(2)* ...(сего́дня) ве́чером? / *(3)* ...сего́дня но́чью? / *(4)* ...за́втра ([5] у́тром / [6] в по́лдень / [7] ве́чером)? / *(8,9)*

For general rules of Russian grammar see Appendix 2 on page 686.

...после рабо́ты?

meet: *love to meet you*

I would love to meet you (in person). Я хоте́л *(ж: хоте́ла)* бы встре́титься с Ва́ми (ли́чно). ♦ **If you have any tender spot for me in your heart, you'll let me meet you (again).** Если в Ва́шем се́рдце есть хотя́ бы каки́е-то до́брые чу́вства ко мне, Вы позво́лите мне встре́титься с Ва́ми (опя́ть).

meet: *the thought of meeting you*

The thought of meeting you causes my heart to thunder. Мысль о встре́че с тобо́й заставля́ет моё се́рдце греме́ть.

meet *vi* 1. *(come together)* встреча́ться / встре́титься *(with whom = + с + instr.)*; 2. *(get acquainted)* знако́миться / познако́миться *(with whom = + с + instr.)* ♦ ~ **online** встреча́ться / встре́титься на интерне́те.

meet: *I'm glad we met*

I'm so *(1)* **glad /** *(2)* **happy that we've finally met.** Я так *(1)* рад *(ж: ра́да)* / *(2)* сча́стлив *(ж: сча́стлива)*, что мы в конце́ концо́в встре́тились. ♦ **Since I met you, my whole life has changed.** С тех пор, как я встре́тил *(ж: встре́тила)* тебя́, вся моя́ жизнь измени́лась. ♦ **I will always treasure the memory of the day we met.** Я бу́ду всегда́ дорожи́ть па́мятью о дне на́шей встре́чи.

meet: *when our eyes met*

When our eyes met, I knew I had to meet you. Когда́ на́ши глаза́ встре́тились, я знал *(ж: зна́ла)*, что я до́лжен *(ж: должна́)* познако́миться с тобо́й.

meet: *met before?*

Haven't we met before? Встреча́лись ли мы ра́ньше? ♦ **Didn't we meet at _____?** Не встреча́лись ли мы у ___? ♦ **We met at _____ .** Мы встреча́лись у ___.

meet: *where to meet*

Where shall we meet? Где мы встре́тимся? ♦ **Let's meet** *(1)* **...at / on the corner of Sadovaya and Pushkin streets. /** *(2)* **...in front of the Main Library. /** *(3)* **...by the entrance to the Opera House. /** *(4)* **...at the airport /** *(5)* **train station /** *(6)* **bus station. /** *(7)* **...right here. /** *(8)* **...right over there.** Дава́й встре́тимся *(1* ...на углу́ Садо́вой и Пу́шкинской. / *(2)* ...у Центра́льной библиоте́ки. / *(3)* ...у вхо́да в Оперный теа́тр. / *(4)* ...в аэропорту́. / *(5)* ...на вокза́ле. / *(6)* ...на авто́бусной ста́нции. / *(7)* ...пря́мо здесь. / *(8)* ...пря́мо там.

meet: *when to meet*

When can we meet? Когда́ мы мо́жем встре́титься? ♦ *(1)* **We can meet next... /** *(2)* **Let's try to meet...** *(3)* **summer /** *(4)* **fall /** *(5)* **winter /** *(6)* **spring.** *(1)* Мы мо́жем встре́титься... / *(2)* Дава́й попыта́емся встре́титься... *(3)* ...сле́дующим ле́том. / *(4)* ...сле́дующей о́сенью / *(5)* зимо́й / *(6)* весно́й. ♦ *(1,2)* **What time shall we meet?** *(1)* В кото́ром часу́... / *(2)* В како́е вре́мя... мы встре́тимся? ♦ *(1)* **Let's meet... /** *(2)* **We'll meet... at one (thirty).** *(See page 759 for other times.)* *(1)* Дава́й встре́тимся... / *(2)* Мы встре́тимся... в час (три́дцать).

meet: *please, let's meet*

We need to meet and talk together. Нам на́до встре́титься и поговори́ть. ♦ **We must meet! We absolutely must!** Мы должны́ встре́титься! Обяза́тельно должны́! ♦ **I fervently** *(1)* **entreat /** *(2)* **implore you to** *(3)* **give /** *(4)* **grant me the opportunity to meet with you.** Я горячо́ *(1,2)* умоля́ю Вас *(3)* дать / *(4)* предоста́вить мне возмо́жность встре́титься с Ва́ми. ♦ **I** *(1)* **beg /** *(2)* **beseech you (with all my heart) to grant me just a few minutes of your time to meet with you and talk with you (in person).** Я *(1,2)* умоля́ю Вас (от всего́ се́рдца) удели́ть мне хотя́ бы не́сколько мину́т, что́бы я мог встре́титься с Ва́ми и поговори́ть (ли́чно). ♦ **I beseech you (with all my heart) to meet with me** *(1)*

For transitive Russian verbs the cases that they take are shown by means of an = sign and the Russian case (abbreviated).

this / (2) **tomorrow evening** (*[3]* ... **at the Blue Moon Cafe...** / *[4]* ...**at the park entrance...** / etc) **for just a half an hour.** Я умоля́ю Вас (от всего́ се́рдца) встре́титься со мной *(1)* сего́дня / (2) за́втра ве́чером (*[3]* ...в кафе́ «Голуба́я луна́»... / *[4]* ...у вхо́да в парк... / *и.т.д.*) хотя́ бы на полчаса́.

meet: *meet in person*
We can meet each other in person and see what happens from there. Мы мо́жем встре́-титься и посмотре́ть, что из э́того вы́йдет.

meeting *n* встре́ча; свида́ние ♦ **brief** ~ коро́ткая встре́ча ♦ **chance** ~ случа́йное свида́ние, случа́йная встре́ча ♦ **exciting** ~ волну́ющая встре́ча ♦ **first (fateful)** ~ пе́рвая (роко-ва́я) встре́ча ♦ **forthcoming** ~ предстоя́щая встре́ча ♦ **frequent** ~s ча́стые встре́чи ♦ **happy** ~ счастли́вая встре́ча ♦ **joyous** ~ ра́достная встре́ча ♦ **last** ~ после́дняя встре́ча ♦ **long-awaited** ~ долгожда́нная встре́ча ♦ **memorable** ~ па́мятная встре́ча ♦ **next** ~ сле́дующая встре́ча ♦ **pleasant** ~ прия́тная встре́ча ♦ **previous** ~ предыду́щая встре́ча ♦ **short** ~ коро́ткая встре́ча ♦ **unexpected** ~ неожи́данная встре́ча ♦ **unforgettable** ~ незабыва́емая встре́ча.

meeting: *verb terms*
arrange a ~ устро́ить встре́чу ♦ **avoid** ~ избега́ть встре́чи ♦ **cancel our** ~ отмени́ть на́шу встре́чу ♦ **look forward to our** ~ ждать на́шей встре́чи ♦ **postpone our** ~ отло-жи́ть на́шу встре́чу.

meeting: *phrases*
I never thought that a random meeting with a stranger would bring such boundless happiness into my life. Я никогда́ не ду́мал *(ж: ду́мала)*, что случа́йная встре́ча с иностра́нкой *(ж: иностра́нцем)* принесёт тако́е безграни́чное сча́стье в мою́ жизнь. ♦ **Meeting you is the best thing that ever happened to me.** Встре́ча с тобо́й -- са́мое лу́чшее, что когда́-нибудь случа́лось со мной. ♦ **I guess I've only dreamt of meeting you.** Я ду́маю, мне то́лько сни́лась встре́ча с Ва́ми. ♦ **I've always dreamt of meeting someone like you.** Я всегда́ мечта́л о встре́че с ке́м-то, похо́жим на тебя́. ♦ **I will always cling to the memory of our first meeting.** Я бу́ду всегда́ вспомина́ть о на́шей пе́рвой встре́че.

melancholic *adj* меланхоли́чный, -ая, -ое, -ые.

melancholy *adj* меланхоли́чный, -ая, -ое, -ые ♦ **Your letter seemed so melancholy.** Твоё письмо́ показа́лось таки́м меланхоли́чным. ♦ **I feel (***[1]*** rather /** *[2]* **a bit) melancholy.** Я ощуща́ю (*[1]* не́кую / *[2]* лёгкую) меланхо́лию.

melancholy *n* меланхо́лия. ♦ **I can't seem to shake this melancholy that has taken hold of me.** Я, ка́жется, не могу́ стряхну́ть меланхо́лию, охвати́вшую меня́. ♦ **Since you went away, my days are filled with melancholy.** С тех пор, как ты ушла́ *(ж: ушёл)*, мои́ дни напо́лнены меланхо́лией.

mellow *adj* смягчи́вшийся, -аяся, -ееся, -иеся, подобре́вший, -ая, -ее, -ие, добро́ду́шный, -ая, -ое, -ые ♦ **You seem like a mellow sort of person.** Вы, ка́жется, доброду́шный челове́к.

mellow *vi* станови́ться / стать мя́гче, смягча́ться / смягчи́ться ♦ **I've mellowed with age.** С года́ми я стал *(ж: ста́ла)* мя́гче. ♦ **I've mellowed a lot since then.** Я стал *(ж: ста́ла)* намно́го мя́гче с тех пор.

melodic *adj* мелоди́чный, -ая, -ое, -ые ♦ **Your name sounds melodic to me.** Твоё и́мя звучи́т мелоди́чно для меня́. ♦ **Your name has a melodic quality to it.** В твоём и́мени звучи́т мело́дия.

melodiousness *n* мелоди́чность ♦ ~ **of your voice** мелоди́чность твоего́ го́лоса.

melody *n* мело́дия ♦ **fervent** ~ **of love** стра́стная мело́дия любви́.

Russian verbs have 2 forms: imperfective and perfective.
They're given in that order.

melons *n, pl (slang) (big breasts)* большáя грудь.

melt *vt* растопля́ть / растопи́ть *(what = acc.)* ◆ **The sunshine of your** *(1)* **heart /** *(2)* **love has melted away all of my loneliness.** Со́лнечный свет *(1)* ...твоего́ се́рдца... / *(2)* ...твое́й любви́... растопи́л всё моё одино́чество. ◆ **Your beautiful eyes melt my heart.** Твои́ прекра́сные глаза́ растопи́ли моё се́рдце. ◆ **The burning adoration of my lips will melt the pillars of your sophisticated decorum into rivers of molten lava.** Мои́ пла́менные, обожа́ющие гу́бы превратя́т тверды́ню твое́й благопристо́йности в ре́ки распла́вленной ла́вы.

melt *vi* 1. *(become liquid)* та́ять / раста́ять; пла́виться, расплавля́ться / распла́виться; 2. *(dissolve)* растворя́ться / раствори́ться ◆ **~ in my arms** раста́ять в мои́х объя́тиях ◆ *(1)* **When you touch me, ... /** *(1)* **Every time you look at me,... I (just) melt.** *(1)* Когда́ ты каса́ешься меня́,... / *(2)* Ка́ждый раз, когда́ ты смо́тришь на меня́,... я (про́сто) та́ю. ◆ **I want to make you melt in my arms.** Я хочу́, что́бы ты та́яла в мои́х объя́тиях. ◆ **I want to feel you melt again and again.** Я хочу́ чу́вствовать, как ты та́ешь опя́ть и опя́ть. ◆ **I want to melt into you (and become part of you).** Я хочу́ раствори́ться в тебе́ (и стать ча́стью тебя́). ◆ **You gave me such meaningful looks, it just made me melt inside.** Ты дари́ла *(ж: дари́л)* мне таки́е многозначи́тельные взгля́ды, что я про́сто весь пла́вился *(ж: вся пла́вилась)*. ◆ **When you do that, I feel like my bones have turned to honey and are slowly melting away.** Когда́ ты так де́лаешь, я чу́вствую, что мои́ ко́сти размягча́ются и ме́дленно та́ют.

meltdown *n* расплавле́ние ◆ **When I get you in my arms, you're going to experience a sensual meltdown.** Когда́ я заключу́ тебя́ в объя́тия, ты вся раста́ешь.

member *n* член ◆ **family ~** член семьи́ ◆ **male ~** *(penis)* мужско́е естество́.

memento *n* сувени́р, напомина́ние ◆ *(1)* **This /** *(2)* **Here is a little memento that I want you to** *(3)* **have /** *(4)* **keep.** *(1)* Это / *(2)* Вот ма́ленький сувени́р, кото́рый я хочу́, что́бы *(3)* ...был у тебя́. / *(4)* ...ты храни́ла *(ж: храни́л)*. ◆ **I will always treasure this memento of the (**[1] **wonderful /** [2] **happy) time we spent together.** Мне всегда́ бу́дет до́рого э́то напомина́ние о (**[1]** замеча́тельном/ **[2]** счастли́вом вре́мени, проведённом на́ми вме́сте.

memorable *adj* незабыва́емый, -ая, -ое, -ые.

memory *n* 1. *(ability)* па́мять *f*; 2. *(recollection)* воспомина́ние ◆ **bad ~ies** плохи́е воспомина́ния ◆ **beautiful ~ies** прекра́сные воспомина́ния ◆ **bitter ~ies** го́рькие воспомина́ния ◆ **bittersweet ~ies** го́рько-сла́дкие воспомина́ния ◆ *(1,2)* **bright ~ies** *(1)* я́ркие / *(2)* све́тлые воспомина́ния ◆ **childhood ~ies** де́тские воспомина́ния ◆ *(1,2)* **distant ~ies** *(1)* далёкие / *(2)* отдалённые воспомина́ния ◆ **erotic ~ies** эроти́ческие воспомина́ния ◆ **exciting ~ies** волну́ющие воспомина́ния ◆ **exquisite ~** изы́сканное воспомина́ние ◆ **fond ~** дорого́е воспомина́ние ◆ **good ~ies** хоро́шие воспомина́ния ◆ **good ~** *(ability to remember)* хоро́шая па́мять ◆ **happy ~ies** ра́достные воспомина́ния ◆ **~ies of my youth** воспомина́ния о мое́й мо́лодости ◆ *(1,2)* **nice ~ies** *(1)* хоро́шие / *(2)* прия́тные воспомина́ния ◆ *(1,2)* **painful ~ies** *(1)* тяжёлые / *(2)* боле́зненные воспомина́ния ◆ **pleasant ~ies** прия́тные воспомина́ния ◆ **precious ~ies** драгоце́нные воспомина́ния ◆ **rapturous ~ies** восто́рженные воспомина́ния ◆ **sad ~ies** гру́стные воспомина́ния ◆ **such ~ies** таки́е воспомина́ния ◆ **sweet ~** сла́дкое воспомина́ние ◆ **terrible ~ies** стра́шные воспомина́ния ◆ **unpleasant ~ies** неприя́тные воспомина́ния ◆ *(1)* **these /** *(2)* **those ~ies** *(1,2)* э́ти воспомина́ния ◆ **vague ~** сму́тное воспомина́ние ◆ **warm ~ies** тёплые воспомина́ния ◆ *(1-3)* **wonderful ~ies** *(1)* замеча́тельные / *(2)* прекра́сные / *(3)* чуде́сные воспомина́ния.

How to use the Cyrillic alphabet on the Internet is the subject of Appendix 20 on page 789.

memory: *verb terms*

awaken ~s будить / пробудить воспоминания, вызывать / вызвать воспоминания ♦ **bring back ~s** оживлять / оживить воспоминания ♦ **bring forth ~s** вызывать / вызвать воспоминания ♦ **cherish the ~s** дорожить воспоминаниями ♦ **keep the ~s** хранить воспоминания ♦ **recapture a ~** восстанавливать / восстановить в памяти ♦ **share ~s** делиться воспоминаниями ♦ **treasure the ~s** дорожить воспоминаниями.

memory: *memories of you*

I treasure the sweet potpourri of memories that you have given me. Я дорожу сладкими воспоминаниями о тебе. ♦ **The** *(1)* **memory of your** *(2)* **beautiful /** *(3)* **luscious /** *(4)* **wonderful body never leaves my mind.** *(1)* Воспоминание о твоём *(2)* прекрасном / *(3)* сочном / *(4)* замечательном теле никогда не покидает меня. ♦ **Each time I look at your photo, the (***[1]* **beautiful /** *[2]* **sweet /** *[3]* **wonderful) memories come flooding back into my mind.** Каждый раз, когда я смотрю на твою фотографию, (*[1]* прекрасные / *[2]* сладкие / *[3]* замечательные) воспоминания опять затопляют меня. ♦ **Your eyes and your hair are absolutely gorgeous. They stay in my memory constantly.** Твои глаза и волосы совершенно великолепны. Они постоянно в моей памяти.

memory: *times spent together*

That vacation is such a sweet potpourri of memories for me. Этот отпуск такой сладкий букет воспоминаний для меня. ♦ **Always the sweet memories of those blissful** *(1)* **moments /** *(2)* **hours /** *(3)* **days come back to me.** Сладкие воспоминания о тех счастливых *(1)* моментах / *(2)* часах / *(3)* днях всегда возвращаются ко мне.

memory: *I cherish the memories*

(1) **I cherish /** *(2)* **treasure... /** *(3)* **I will always cherish /** *(4)* **treasure... the memories (of the** *[wonderful]* *[5]* **times /** *[6]* **moments /** *[7]* **hours we** *[8]* **shared /** *[9]* **spent together).** *(1)* Я дорожу воспоминаниями... / *(2)* Я храню воспоминания... / *(3)* Я всегда буду дорожить воспоминаниями... / *(4)* Я всегда буду хранить воспоминания... (о *[прекрасных]* *[5]* ...времени, которое... / *[6]* ...минутах / *[7]* часах, которые... мы *[8,9]* провели вдвоём). ♦ *(1)* **I cherish... /** *(2)* **I will always treasure... the memory of** *(3)* **...the wonderful time we spent together. /** *(4)* **...the first time I kissed you. /** *(5)* **...the day we met. /** *(6)* **...that day (that we spent together).** *(1)* Я дорожу... / *(2)* Я буду всегда дорожить... памятью *(3)* ...о замечательном времени, проведённом вместе. / *(4)* ...о времени, когда я впервые поцеловал тебя. / *(5)* ...о дне нашей встречи. / *(6)* ...о том дне (который мы провели вместе).

memory: *the memories of those times...*

The sweet potpourri of memories from those days we spent together suffuses my thoughts night and day. Букет сладких воспоминаний о днях, проведённых вместе, заполняет мои мысли ночью и днём. ♦ **I constantly rerun the memories of** *(1)* **...that time. /** *(2)* **...those (halcyon) days. /** *(1)* **...our trip /** *(4)* **vacation.** Я постоянно возвращаюсь к воспоминаниям *(1)* ...об этом времени. / *(2)* ...об этих безмятежных днях. / *(3)* ...о нашем путешествии / *(4)* отпуске. ♦ **The** *(1)* **memory /** *(2)* **memories of the (wonderful) times (***[we spent]* **together)** *(3)* **...assails /** *(4)* **assail me night and day. /** *(5,6)* **...will last forever.** *(1)* Память о... / *(2)* Воспоминания об... (удивительном) времени (, проведённом вместе) *(3)* ...не оставляет / *(4)* оставляют меня ночью и днём. / *(5)* ...будет *sing.* / *(6)* будут *pl* жить всегда. ♦ **That (***[1]* **beautiful /** *[2]* **wonderful)** *(3)* **moment /** *(4)* **day... will** *(5)* **stay /** *(6)* **remain indelibly etched in my memory** *(7)* **...forever. /** *(8)* **...for as long as I live.** Этот (*[1]* прекрасный / *[2]* замечательный) *(3)* момент / *(4)* день *(5,6)* останется выгравированным несмываемо в моей памяти *(7)* ...навсегда. / *(8)* ...пока я жив *(ж: жива).* ♦ **Those (***[1]* **beautiful /** *[2]* **wonderful)** *(3)* **hours /** *(4)* **days... will** *(5)* **stay /** *(6)* **remain indelibly etched in my memory** *(7)* **...forever. /** *(8)* **...for as long as I live.** Эти (*[1]*

Russian adjectives have long and short forms.
Where short forms are given, they are labeled as such.

прекра́сные / *[2]* замеча́тельные) *(3)* часы́ / *(4)* дни *(5,6)* оста́нутся вы́гравирован-
ными несмыва́емо в мое́й па́мяти *(7)* ...навсегда́. / *(8)* ...пока́ я жив *(ж: жива́)*. ♦ **All
I do is relive old memories (of our times together).** Всё, что я де́лаю, -- пережива́ю
вновь ста́рые воспомина́ния (о вре́мени, проведённом вме́сте). ♦ **It filled me with so
many memories.** Это заполня́ло меня́ таки́м мно́жеством воспомина́ний.

memory: our lovemaking

The (*[1]* **sweet** / *[2]* **warm** / *[3]* **precious) memories of our wonderful love-making go
through my mind** *(4)* **constantly** / *(5)* **unceasingly** / *(6)* **night and day.** (*[1]* Сла́достные /
[2] тёплые / *[3]* драгоце́нные) воспомина́ния о замеча́тельном вре́мени на́шей
бли́зости *(4)* постоя́нно / *(5)* непреры́вно / *(6)* ...но́чью и днём... вспы́хивают в мое́й
па́мяти.

ménage à trois *n Fr (3 people together in a love affair)* инти́мность втроём.

mend *vt* 1. *(general repair)* чини́ть / почини́ть *(what = acc.)*, ремонти́ровать / отремон-
ти́ровать *(what = acc.)*, исправля́ть / испра́вить *(what = acc.)*; 2. *(relationship)* нала́-
живать / нала́дить *(what = acc.)* ♦ **Do you think we can mend our relationship?** Ты
ду́маешь, мы мо́жем нала́дить на́ши отноше́ния? ♦ **Dear, we can mend our relationship, I know we can.** Дорога́я, мы мо́жем нала́дить на́ши отноше́ния, я зна́ю, мы
мо́жем.

menstruate *vi* менструи́ровать.

mention *vt* упомина́ть / упомяну́ть *(what, whom = + о + prep.)*, ссыла́ться / сосла́ться
(what, whom = + на + acc.) ♦ **I never mentioned marriage.** Я никогда́ не упомина́л *(ж:
упомина́ла)* о жени́тьбе.

meow *n* мя́у ♦ **You're really the cat's meow.** Ты действи́тельно са́мая замеча́тельная *(ж:
са́мый замеча́тельный)*.

mercenary *adj* коры́стный, -ая, -ое, -ые, наёмный, -ая, -ое, -ые.

mercurial *adj* переме́нчивый, -ая, -ое, -ые, с переме́нчивым хара́ктером, непостоя́н-
ный, -ая, -ое, -ые.

merge *vi* соединя́ться / соедини́ться, слива́ться / сли́ться ♦ ~ **into one** слива́ться / сли́ться
воеди́но ♦ **Our bodies will merge together into a single being.** На́ши тела́ соединя́тся
в одно́ це́лое.

mermaid *n* руса́лка.

mesh *vi* подходи́ть друг дру́гу, ла́дить ♦ **We seem to mesh together so** *(1)* **well** / *(2)* **perfectly.** Мы, ка́жется, подхо́дим друг дру́гу *(1)* ...так хорошо́. / *(2)* ...отли́чно. ♦ **We
just seemed to mesh right from the beginning.** Мы, ка́жется, подходи́ли друг дру́гу с
са́мого нача́ла. ♦ **I've never meshed with anyone as well as I do with you.** Никто́ друго́й
никогда́ не подходи́л мне так хорошо́, как ты.

mesmerize *vt* гипнотизи́ровать / загипнотизи́ровать *(whom = acc.)* ♦ **I am mesmerized by
your** *(1)* **charm** / *(2)* **beauty** / *(3)* **loveliness.** Я загипнотизи́рован *(1)* ...твои́м очаро-
ва́нием. / *(2,3)* ...твое́й красото́й.

mesmerized *adj* загипнотизи́рован, -а, -о, -ы *(short forms)* ♦ **I am (*[1]* completely** / *[2]*
totally / *[3]* **entirely** / *[4]* **utterly) mesmerized by** *(5)* **...your (*[6]* incredible** / *[7]* **breath-
taking** / *[8]* **shining** / *[9]* **heavenly** / *[10]* **radiant** / *[11]* **exquisite) beauty** / *(12)* **loveliness.**
/ *(13)* **...the (shiny) sensuality of your lips.** Я (*[1]* по́лностью / *[2]* абсолю́тно / *[3,4]*
соверше́нно) загипнотизи́рован *(5,12)* ...твое́й (*[6]* невероя́тной / *[7]* ...оста́навлива-
ющей дыха́ние... / *[8]* сия́ющей / *[9]* небе́сной / *[10]* лучи́стой / *[11]* изы́сканной)
красото́й. / *(13)* ...(я́ркой) чу́вственностью твои́х губ. ♦ **You have me mesmerized by
your charisma.** Ты гипнотизи́руешь меня́ свои́м обая́нием.

mesmerizing *adj* гипнотизи́рующий, -ая, -ее, -ие, гипноти́ческий, -ая, -ое, -ие ♦ **Your**

---

*Russian nouns are either masculine, feminine or neuter.
Adjectives with them will be the same.*

charm is mesmerizing. Твоё очарова́ние гипнотизи́рует.

mess *n* 1. *(disorder)* беспоря́док, «барда́к»; 2. *(difficulty)* неприя́тность ♦ **I've** *(1,2)* **made a (terrible) mess of things.** Я *(1)* загуби́л *(ж: загуби́ла)* / *(2)* провали́л *(ж: провали́ла)* (ужа́сно) всё де́ло. ♦ **What a mess!** 1. *(disorder)* Како́й беспоря́док!; 2. *(difficulty)* Кака́я неприя́тность! ♦ **Everything is a mess.** Всё перепу́талось.

mess around *vi* 1. *(play)* игра́ть, развлека́ться; *(kid around)* шути́ть; *(act foolish)* дура́читься; 2. *(pet)* игра́ть, ласка́ть; 3. *(philander)* изменя́ть.

message *vt (send a message)* посыла́ть / посла́ть сообще́ние *(whom = dat.)*; *(leave a message)* оставля́ть / оста́вить сообще́ние *(whom = dat.)* ♦ **Message me.** *(send)* Пошли́ мне сообще́ние. ; *(leave)* Оста́вь мне сообще́ние.

message *n* сообще́ние; письмо́; посла́ние ♦ **e-mail** ~ е-мейл ♦ **important** ~ ва́жное сообще́ние ♦ **last** ~ после́днее сообще́ние ♦ **my** ~ моё сообще́ние ♦ **obscene** ~ неприли́чное сообще́ние; *(letter)* неприли́чное письмо́; *(note)* неприли́чная запи́ска ♦ **previous** ~ предыду́щее сообще́ние ♦ **sensual** ~ *(eyes)* чу́вственный призы́в ♦ *(1,2)* **short** ~ *(1)* коро́ткое / *(2)* кра́ткое сообще́ние ♦ **urgent** ~ сро́чное сообще́ние ♦ **your** ~ *(familiar)* твоё сообще́ние; *(polite)* Ва́ше сообще́ние.

message: verb terms

hear *(1)* **your** / *(2)* **my** ~ слыша́ть *(1)* твоё / *(2)* моё сообще́ние ♦ **leave** (*[1]* **you** / *[2]* **me**) **a** ~ оставля́ть / оста́вить (*[1]* тебе́ / *[2]* мне) сообще́ние ♦ **listen to** *(1)* **your** / *(2)* **my** ~ слу́шать *(1)* твоё / *(2)* моё сообще́ние ♦ **read** *(1)* **your** / *(2)* **my** ~ чита́ть / прочита́ть *(1)* твоё / *(2)* моё сообще́ние ♦ **receive** *(1)* **your** / *(2)* **my** ~ получа́ть / получи́ть *(1)* твоё / *(2)* моё сообще́ние ♦ **send** *(1)* **you** / *(2)* **me a** ~ посыла́ть / посла́ть *(1)* тебе́ / *(2)* мне сообще́ние ♦ **wait for a** ~ ждать сообще́ния.

message: phrases

That was an enticing message that you sent me. Ты присла́ла *(ж: присла́л)* мне соблазни́тельное посла́ние. ♦ **Your endearing messages mean so much to me.** Твои́ ла́сковые пи́сьма зна́чат так мно́го для меня́. ♦ **If I'm not** *(1)* **home** / *(2)* **there, please leave a message.** Если я не *(1)* до́ма / *(2)* там, пожа́луйста, оста́вь мне сообще́ние. ♦ **I left (you) a message (on your answering machine).** Я оста́вил *(ж: оста́вила)* (тебе́) сообще́ние (на твоём автоотве́тчике). ♦ **The sensual message in your eyes sends fire coursing through my veins.** Чу́вственный призы́в в твои́х глаза́х порожда́ет ого́нь, теку́щий в мои́х ве́нах. ♦ **Your e-mail messages are so** *(1,2)* **uplifting for me.** Твои́ электро́нные пи́сьма так поднима́ют *(1)* ...мой дух. / *(2)* ...моё настрое́ние.

messaging *n (Internet)* обме́н сообще́ниями ♦ **instant** ~ **(IM)** мгнове́нный обме́н сообще́ниями.

metalhead *n (slang) (fan of heavy metal rock music)* фана́т тяжёлого ро́ка.

metaphysical *adj* метафизи́ческий, -ая, -ое, -ие.

mid 30's (40's, 50's, etc) за три́дцать *(30)* (со́рок *[40]*, пятьдеся́т *[50]*, и т.д.) ♦ **I'm in my mid 30's (40's, 50's, etc).** Мне за три́дцать *(30)* (со́рок *[40]*, пятьдеся́т *[50]*, и т.д.).

middle-age(d) *adj* сре́дних лет.

mid-life *n* середи́на жи́зни.

midriff *n* (коро́ткая) ко́фточка с откры́той та́лией ♦ **You look** *(1)* **great** / *(2)* **nice in a bare midriff.** Ты вы́глядишь *(1)* великоле́пно / *(2)* ми́ло в коро́ткой ко́фточке с откры́той та́лией.

mild-mannered *adj* с мя́гкими мане́рами.

military *adj* вое́нный, -ая, -ое, -ые.

mind *vi* возража́ть, име́ть *(что́-либо)* про́тив ♦ **Would you mind(, if...)?** Ты не бу́дешь возража́ть(, е́сли...)? ♦ **If you don't mind...** Если ты не про́тив... ♦ *(1,2)* **I don't mind.**

Learn more about Russian customs in Appendix 15, page 782.

(1) Я не возража́ю. / *(2)* Я ничего́ не име́ю про́тив.

mind *n* 1. *(mental capacity, reason)* ум, ра́зум ; интелле́кт; 2. *(memory)* па́мять; 3. *(mood)* настрое́ние; 4. *(opinion)* мне́ние ♦ **analytical** ~ аналити́ческий ум ♦ **brilliant** ~ блестя́щий ум ♦ **decisive** ~ конкре́тный ум ♦ **developed** ~ ра́звитая пси́хика ♦ *(1,2)* **dirty** ~ *(1)* извращённый / *(2)* гря́зный ум *(not used jokingly)* ♦ **distinct** ~ я́сный ум ♦ **exceptional** ~ недю́жинный ум ♦ **great** ~ большо́й ум ♦ **inquisitive** ~ пытли́вый разум ♦ **keen** ~ о́стрый ум ♦ **observing** ~ наблюда́тельный ум ♦ **open** ~ откры́тый ум ♦ **practical** ~ практи́ческий ум ♦ *(1,2)* **quick** ~ *(1)* живо́й / *(2)* сметли́вый ум ♦ **remarkable** ~ недю́жинный ум ♦ **strong** ~ си́льный ум ♦ **talented** ~ тала́нтливый ум ♦ **weak** ~ сла́бый ум ♦ **wonderful** ~ удиви́тельный ум.

---
mind: *other terms*
---

blow my ~ потряса́ть меня́ ♦ **enrich the** ~ обогаща́ть ум ♦ **go out of** *(1,3)* my / *(2,4)* your ~ *(1,2)* сходи́ть / сойти́ с ума́, *(3,4)* обезу́меть ♦ **lose one's** ~ теря́ть / потеря́ть рассу́док ♦ **on my** ~ в мои́х мы́слях ♦ **state of** ~ состоя́ние рассу́дка ♦ **with an open** ~ без предубежде́ний, откры́то.

---
mind: *you're on my mind*

You were on my mind all day. Ты была́ *(ж: был)* в мои́х мы́слях весь день. ♦ **You're on my mind every minute (and every hour) of** *(1)* **the** / *(2)* **every day.** Ты в мои́х мы́слях ка́ждую мину́ту (и ка́ждый час) *(1,2)* ка́ждого дня. ♦ **You fill my mind every moment of the day (and night).** Ты заполня́ешь мои мы́сли ка́ждое мгнове́ние дня (и но́чи). ♦ **My mind is filled with thoughts of you every moment from the time I wake up.** С са́мого моего́ пробужде́ния ка́ждое мгнове́ние все мои мы́сли запо́лнены тобо́й. ♦ **I (just) can't** *(1)* **get** / *(2)* **put you out of my mind.** Я (про́сто) не могу́ *(1)* ...изба́виться от воспомина́ний о тебе́. / *(2)* ...вы́бросить тебя́ из свое́й головы́. ♦ **You are firmly** *(1)* **implanted** / *(2)* **embedded** / *(3)* **cemented in my heart, my mind, and my soul.** Ты на́крепко *(1-3)* вошла́ / *(1-3)* вросла́ в моё се́рдце, ум и ду́шу. ♦ **You own my mind, my heart, my body.** Ты владе́ешь мои́м умо́м, мои́м се́рдцем и мои́м те́лом.

---
mind: *what you do to my mind*

I go away from any encounter with you with my heart spinning wildly and my mind erupting in a fireworks display of love thoughts about you. По́сле ка́ждой встре́чи с тобо́й я ухожу́ с бе́шено стуча́щим се́рдцем и с це́лым фейерве́рком любо́вных мы́слей о тебе́. ♦ **You have an effect on my heart, mind and psyche that no amount of words, English or Russian, can ever suffice to describe.** У меня́ не хвата́ет слов, англи́йских и ру́сских, что́бы описа́ть возде́йствие, кото́рое ты ока́зываешь на моё се́рдце, мы́сли и ду́шу. ♦ **Your (incredible) beauty** *(1)* **sets** / *(2)* **sends my mind (to) spinning.** Твоя́ (невероя́тная) красота́ *(1,2)* вызыва́ет у меня́ головокруже́ние. ♦ **You** *(1)* **set** / *(2)* **send my mind (to) spinning.** Ты *(1,2)* вызыва́ешь у меня́ головокруже́ние. ♦ **When you take off your clothes, it (just) blows my mind.** Когда́ ты снима́ешь оде́жду, э́то (про́сто) потряса́ет меня́. ♦ **When you said "I love you," it really blew my mind.** Когда́ ты сказа́ла *(ж: сказа́л)*: «Я люблю́ тебя́», э́то действи́тельно потрясло́ меня́. ♦ **Your kisses (just) wiped my mind blank.** Твои́ поцелу́и (про́сто) опустоши́ли меня́. ♦ **I am (totally) amazed at the** *(1)* **profound** / *(2)* **overwhelming** / *(3)* **tremendous effect you have on my heart and mind.** Я (соверше́нно) изумлён *(1)* глубо́ким / *(2)* ошеломля́ющим / *(3)* грома́дным эффе́ктом, кото́рый ты произво́дишь на моё се́рдце и ра́зум. ♦ **The words you write sparkle in my mind like sunbeams.** Слова́, кото́рые ты пи́шешь, сверка́ют в мое́й па́мяти как со́лнечные лучи́.

---
mind: *memories etched in my mind*

That (*[1]*** beautiful / ***[2]*** wonderful)** *(3)* **moment** / *(4)* **day... will** *(5)* **stay** / *(6)* **remain in-**

A slash always denotes "or."
You can choose the numbered words before and after.

delibly etched in my mind *(7)* ...**forever.** / *(8)* ...**for as long as I live.** Этот *([1]* прекра́сный / *[2]* замеча́тельный) *(3)* моме́нт / *(4)* день *(5,6)* оста́нется вы́гравированным несмыва́емо в мое́й па́мяти *(7)* ...навсегда́. / *(8)* ...пока́ я жив *(ж: жива́).* ◆ **Those** *([1]* **beautiful** / *[2]* **wonderful)** *(3)* **hours** / *(4)* **days... will** *(5)* **stay** / *(6)* **remain indelibly etched in my mind** *(7)* ...**forever.** / *(8)* ...**for as long as I live.** Эти *([1]* прекра́сные / *[2]* замеча́тельные) *(3)* часы́ / *(4)* дни *(5,6)* оста́нутся вы́гравированными несмыва́емо в мое́й па́мяти *(7)* ...навсегда́. / *(8)* ...пока́ я жив *(ж: жива́).* ◆ **The memory is etched in my mind.** Это воспомина́ние вы́гравированно в мое́й па́мяти.

> *mind: connecting together in mind*

You and I could share so many things, make so much wonderful love together, talk about so many things together, connect in heart, mind, and spirit so perfectly. Ты и я смогли́ бы раздели́ть мно́гое, так мно́го занима́ться прекра́сной любо́вью, говори́ть о мно́гом друг с дру́гом, так соверше́нно соединя́ться се́рдцем, умо́м и ду́хом.

> *mind: your intellectual mind*

You have (quite) an intellectual (turn of) mind. У тебя́ интеллектуа́льный склад ума́.

> *mind: have a good handle on your mind*

I want a *(1)* **woman** / *(2)* **man who has a good handle on** *(3)* **her** / *(4)* **his heart and mind.** Я хочу́ *(1)* ...таку́ю же́нщину, кото́рая... / *(2)* ...тако́го мужчи́ну, кото́рый... хорошо́ владе́ет *(3,4)* свои́м се́рдцем и умо́м.

> *mind: what's on your mind?*

Is there something on your mind? Ты о чём-то заду́малась *(ж: заду́мался)*? ◆ **What's on your mind?** Что у тебя́ на уме́ ?

> *mind: with you in mind*

Everything I do is done with you in mind. Что бы я ни де́лал *(ж: де́лала)*, я де́лаю с мы́слью о тебе́.

> *mind: drive you out of your mind*

I'm going to do things with you that will drive you (absolutely) out of your mind. Я сде́лаю с тобо́й тако́е, что доведёт тебя́ до (по́лного) безу́мия.

> *mind: almost out of my mind*

I almost went out of my mind when you left me. Я чуть не потеря́л *(ж: потеря́ла)* рассу́док, когда́ ты поки́нула *(ж: поки́нул)* меня́.

> *mind: never change my mind*

Nothing will make me change my mind. Ничто́ не заста́вит меня́ измени́ть своё реше́ние.

> *mind: read your mind*

(1) **I can't...** / *(2)* **I wish I could... read your mind.** *(1)* Я не могу́... / *(2)* Я бы жела́л *(ж: жела́ла)*, что́бы я мог *(ж: могла́)*... чита́ть твои́ мы́сли.

> *mind: know your own mind*

I don't think you know your own mind. Я не ду́маю, что ты зна́ешь, чего́ ты хо́чешь.

> *mind: speak my mind*

I'm not afraid to speak my mind. Я не бою́сь выска́зывать своё мне́ние.

> *mind: saying*

Out of sight, out of mind. С глаз доло́й, из се́рдца вон.

mind-boggling *adj* си́льно-поража́ющий, соверше́нно невероя́тный.

mind-set психоло́гия.

mine *pron* мой, моя́, моё, мои́ ◆ **You are mine and mine alone.** Ты моя́ и то́лько моя́. *(ж: Ты мой и то́лько мой.)* ◆ **I know that if I don't ask you to be mine, I'm going to regret it for the rest of my life.** Я зна́ю, что е́сли я не попрошу́ тебя́ быть мое́й, то бу́ду

Common adult weights are given in Appendix 10, page 777.

сожалеть об этом до конца своей жизни.

mingle *vt* смешивать / смешать *(what = acc.)* ♦ **I'd love to mingle souls with you.** Я хотел *(ж: хотела)* бы слиться душой с тобой.

mini *n (miniskirt)* мини, минию́бка.

mini-nibble *adj* массажировать крошечными поцелуями ♦ **I want to give you a soft mininibble massage all over your body.** Я хочу массажировать всё твоё тело нежными крошечными поцелуями.

miniskirt *n* минию́бка.

minister *n* пастор ♦ **nondenominational** ~ священник, объединяющий все религии *(1 term)*.

mink *n* норка.

minx *n (slang) (hussy)* дерзкая девчонка.

miracle *n* чудо *(pl:* чудеса*)* ♦ **How does it happen that someone so beautiful is not yet married? This is nothing short of a miracle. But I must say, I am extremely happy that the miracle exists.** Как так случилось, что такая прекрасная ещё не замужем? Это просто чудо. Но я должен сказать, что я чрезвычайно счастлив, что это чудо существует. ♦ **If by some divine miracle I am able someday to press my lips in fervent adoration to the exquisite loveliness of your sweet smile, I shall have nothing more to hope for or want.** Если бы каким-то божественным чудом я смог в один прекрасный день с пылким обожанием прижаться губами к изысканной прелести твоей сладкой улыбки, мне нечего было бы больше желать.

mirth *n* веселье ♦ **Your eyes sparkle with mirth.** Твои глаза искрятся весельем.

miscarriage *n* выкидыш ♦ *(1,2)* **I had a miscarriage.** *(1)* У меня был выкидыш. / *(2)* Я потеряла ребёнка.

miscarry *vi* потерять ребёнка ♦ **I miscarried.** Я потеряла ребёнка.

mischief *n* озорство, проказы, шалости ♦ **You're full of mischief.** Ты полон проказ.

mischievous *adj* озорной, -ая, -ое, -ые, шаловливый, -ая, -ое, -ые ♦ **You're a mischievous little imp!** Ты непослушный маленький чертёнок!

misconstrue *vt* неправильно истолковывать / истолковать *(what = acc.)*.

miserable *adj* несчастный, -ая, -ое, -ые *(short forms:* несчастен, несчастна, -о, -ы*)*, жалкий, -ая, -ое, -ие ♦ **I am (**[1]** totally / **[2]** thoroughly / **[3]** absolutely / **[4]** completely) miserable without you.** Я (*[1,2]* совершенно / *[3]* абсолютно / *[4]* совсем) несчастен *(ж: несчастна)* без тебя. ♦ **You'll leave me and I'll wind up miserable.** Ты уедешь, и я буду несчастен *(ж: несчастна)*. ♦ **I'd be miserable without you.** Без тебя я был *(ж: была)* бы так несчастен *(ж: несчастна)*.

misery *n* страдание ♦ **abject** ~ жалкое страдание ♦ **acute** ~ острое страдание ♦ *(1,2)* **sheer** ~ *(1)* сущее / *(2)* абсолютное страдание ♦ **total** ~ полное страдание ♦ **utter** ~ полно страдание ♦ **morass of** ~ болото страдания.

misery: phrases

This being apart from you is sheer misery. Быть без тебя - сущее страдание. ♦ **Wanting you and not being able to have you is sheer misery.** Хотеть тебя и не иметь возможности быть с тобой - сущее страдание. ♦ **You can never know the sheer misery I go through** *(1)* **... being apart from you.** / *(2)* **... wanting you and not being able to have you.** Ты никогда не узнаешь, через какую пытку я прохожу *(1)* ...будучи в разлуке с тобой. / *(2)*, ...желая тебя и не имея возможности быть с тобой. ♦ **Misery consumes me.** Страдание пожирает меня. ♦ **I'm floundering in a morass of misery without you.** Без тебя я барахтаюсь в болоте страдания.

misgiving *n* 1. *(apprehension)* опасение *(foreboding)* предчувствие дурного; 2. *(doubt)*

An italicized ж in parentheses indicates a woman speaking.

сомне́ние ♦ **experience ~s** испы́тывать опасе́ние ♦ **have ~s** 1. *(foreboding)* предчу́вст-вовать дурно́е; 2. *(doubt)* сомнева́ться, (у *[I]* меня́ / *[you]* тебя́) есть сомне́ния ♦ **I have misgivings (about this).** У меня́ есть сомне́ния (насчёт э́того). ♦ **I don't want you to have any misgivings (about this).** Я не хочу́, что́бы у тебя́ бы́ли каки́е-либо сом-не́ния (насчёт э́того).

misjudge *vt (judge incorrectly)* непра́вильно оце́нивать / оцени́ть *(what, whom = acc.)*; *(underestimate)* недооце́нивать / недооцени́ть *(what, whom = acc.)*.

misread *vt* 1. *(read incorrectly)* непра́вильно чита́ть / прочита́ть *(what = acc.)*; 2. *(mis-understand)* непра́вильно истолко́вывать / истолкова́ть *(what = acc.)* ♦ **You misread** *(1)* **...my meaning.** / *(2)* **...my intentions** / *(3)* **feelings.** *(past tense)* Ты непра́вильно истол-кова́ла *(ж: истолкова́л)* *(1)* ...то, что я сказа́л *(ж: сказа́ла)*. / *(2)* ...мои́ наме́рения / *(3)* чу́вства. ♦ **I'll try to say this very clearly, because I don't want my feelings to be misread.** Я попыта́юсь вы́разить э́то о́чень я́сно, потому́ что не хочу́, что́бы мои́ чу́вства бы́ли непра́вильно истолко́ваны.

miss *vt* 1. *(long for)* скуча́ть / соску́читься *(what, whom = + по + dat.)*; 2. *(fail to meet)* не заста́ть *(whom = acc.)*; 3. *(be late for)* опа́здывать / опозда́ть *(what = + на + acc.)*; 4. *(let slip by)* упуска́ть / упусти́ть *(what = acc.)* ♦ **~ a train** опозда́ть на по́езд ♦ **~ a flight** опозда́ть на самолёт ♦ **~ an opportunity** упусти́ть возмо́жность ♦ **~ out** *vi* упуска́ть / упусти́ть возмо́жность.

miss: phrases

I miss you (*[1]*** desparately** / **[2,3] terribly** / **[4] unbearably** / **[5] very much).** Я (*[1]* от-ча́янно / *[2]* ужа́сно / *[3]* стра́шно / *[4]* невыноси́мо / *[5]* о́чень си́льно) скуча́ю по тебе́. ♦ **I miss you more than I can (ever) tell you.** Нет слов, что́бы вы́разить, как я скуча́ю по тебе́. ♦ **I miss you (much) more than you'll ever know.** Я скуча́ю по тебе́ (намно́го) бо́льше, чем ты ду́маешь. ♦ **My pure beautiful Angel, I miss you so more than words can say.** Мой чи́стый, прекра́сный а́нгел, не могу́ вы́разить слова́ми, как я скуча́ю по тебе́. ♦ **I miss you even more than I could have believed.** Я скуча́ю по тебе́ да́же бо́льше, чем мог *(ж: могла́)* бы предста́вить. ♦ **I miss your hugs and kisses (more than I can tell you).** Я скуча́ю по твои́м объя́тиям и поцелу́ям (бо́льше, чем могу́ вы́сказать). ♦ **Did you miss** *(1,2)* **me?** Ты скуча́ла *(ж: скуча́л)* *(1)* ...по мне? / *(2)* ...без меня́? ♦ **I missed you a lot.** Я о́чень по тебе́ соску́чился *(ж: соску́чилась)*. ♦ **How I miss you.** Как я по тебе́ соску́чился. ♦ **You'll never know how much I missed you.** Ты и предста́вить себе́ не мо́жешь, как я скуча́л *(ж: скуча́ла)* по тебе́. ♦ **If you can unscramble my brainwaves, you'll know that I miss you (a lot).** Е́сли ты смо́жешь рас-шифрова́ть мои́ мозговы́е во́лны, ты узна́ешь, что я (о́чень) скуча́ю по тебе́.

miss out:

If you don't answer my letter, you're going to miss out on meeting someone with a very warm, loving heart and affectionate nature. Е́сли Вы не отве́тите на моё письмо́, то упу́стите возмо́жость встре́чи с челове́ком с о́чень тёплым, лю́бящим се́рдцем и не́жной душо́й.

miss *n (unmarried woman)* мисс, де́вушка, незаму́жняя же́нщина ♦ **You seemed like such a prim and proper miss.** Ты каза́лась тако́й чо́порной.

missing *adj* отсу́тствующий, -ая, -ее, -ие, недостаю́щий, -ая, -ее, -ие ♦ **With you not here, it** *(1)* **feels** / *(2)* **is like part of me is missing.** Без тебя́ здесь, *(1)* ...ка́жется... / *(2)* ...как бу́дто... ча́сти меня́ недостаёт.

missive *n* письмо́ ♦ **This brief missive conveys only an iota of the affection that I nourish in my heart for you.** Э́то коро́ткое письмо́ несёт то́лько ма́лую то́лику той любви́, кото́рой полно́ моё се́рдце.

Procedures for getting married to a Russian are outlined in Appendix 18, page 787.

mistletoe *n* омёла ♦ **If you stand under mistletoe, it means I can kiss you.** Если ты стоишь под омёлой, это значит, я могу целовать тебя. ♦ **I** *(1)* **swear** / *(2)* **promise I'm going to** *(3,4)* **catch you under the mistletoe.** Я *(1)* клянусь / *(2)* обещаю, что *(3)* застигну / *(4)* поймаю тебя под омёлой (, чтобы поцеловать). ♦ **There's an old Welsh saying that if you put a sprig of mistletoe under your pillow, you'll dream of the man that will marry you.** В Уэлсе существует старое предсказание о том, что, если положишь веточку омёлы под подушку, то увидишь во сне мужчину, который женится на тебе.

mistreat *vt* плохо обращаться *(whom* = + с + *instr.)*; жестоко обращаться *(whom* = + с + *instr.)* ♦ **I would never mistreat you.** Я никогда не буду плохо обращаться с тобой. ♦ *(1)* **Does** / *(2)* **Did he mistreat you?** Он плохо *(1)* обращается / *(2)* обращался с тобой?

mistress *n (lover)* любовница; *(kept lover)* содержанка.

mistrust *n* недоверие ♦ **dispel** ~ растапливать / растопить недоверие. ♦ **I sense in you an underlying current of mistrust.** Я ощущаю в тебе скрытое недоверие.

mixed up *adj*: ♦ **be** ~ путаться / спутаться, связываться / связаться ♦ **get** ~ путаться / спутаться, связываться / связаться ♦ **I didn't know I was getting mixed up with** *(1)* **...a married woman.** / *(2)* **...a brazen hussy.** Я не знал, что я связался с *(1)* ...замужней женщиной. / *(2)* ...нахальной девкой. ♦ **I didn't know I was getting mixed up with a married man.** Я не знала, что я связалась с женатым мужчиной.

mix-up *n* путаница ♦ **There was a mix-up (in the schedule).** Была путаница (в расписании). ♦ **I'm sorry about the mix-up.** Я извиняюсь за путаницу.

moan *n* стон ♦ **blissful** ~ радостный стон ♦ ~**s of ecstasy** стоны экстаза ♦ ~**s of** *(1,2)* **pleasure** стоны *(1)* удовольствия / *(2)* наслаждения ♦ ~**s of rapturous** *(1,2)* **delight** стоны восторженного *(1)* удовольствия / *(2)* наслаждения ♦ **sensual** ~ сладострастный стон.

---
moan: *phrases*

I want to fill the night air with your moans of ecstasy. Я хочу наполнить ночной воздух твоими стонами экстаза. ♦ **I want to spend the whole night listening to your moans of pleasure.** Я хочу провести всю ночь, слушая твои стоны наслаждения. ♦ **When my lips and tongue revel on your beautiful, luscious body, they will hear your moans of** *(1)* **pleasure** / *(2)* **ecstasy in South Africa.** Когда мои губы и язык будут упиваться твоим прекрасным, сочным телом, твои стоны *(1)* наслаждения / *(2)* экстаза будут слышны в Южной Африке. ♦ **Every night I want you to serenade me with your moans and cries of pleasure.** Каждую ночь я хочу слышать серенаду из твоих стонов и криков наслаждения. ♦ **Those moans that escaped your lips told me more than a million words.** Эти стоны, которые слетали с твоих губ, говорили мне больше, чем миллион слов. ♦ **How I love to hear your moans of rapturous delight fill the (night) air.** Как я люблю слушать стоны твоего восторженного наслаждения, заполняющие (ночной) воздух. ♦ **Hopefully the neighbors will get used to hearing your moans of rapturous delight.** Надеюсь, соседи привыкнут к твоим стонам восторженного удовольствия. ♦ **The night air will be filled with your moans of rapturous delight.** Ночной воздух наполнится твоими стонами восторженного удовольствия.

moan *vi* стонать ♦ ~ **blissfully** радостно стонать ♦ ~ **with pleasure** стонать от наслаждения ♦ **The sweetest music to my ears is to hear you moan with pleasure.** Сладчайшая музыка для моего слуха -- твои стоны наслаждения.

mobile *adj* мобильный, -ая, -ое, -ые, подвижный, -ая, -ое, -ые ♦ ~ **home** мобильный дом, дом на колёсах ♦ **upwardly** ~ с хорошими профессиональными возможностями.

mocha *n* мокко.

mock *vt* насмехаться *(what, whom* = + над + *instr.)*, высмеивать / высмеять *(what, whom*

A list of conjugated Russian verbs is given
in Appendix 3 on page 699.

= *acc.)* ♦ **Are you mocking me?** Ты насмеха́ешься на́до мной? ♦ **I'm not mocking you. Don't think so.** Я не насмеха́юсь над тобо́й. Не ду́май так.

mockery *n* насме́шка.

model *vi (pose)* пози́ровать / попози́ровать ♦ **I'd like to have you model (**[1]** in the nude / [2] in a negligee) for me.** Я хоте́л бы, что́бы ты пози́ровала мне (*[1]* обнажённой / *[2]* в неглиже́). ♦ **Would you model (**[1]** in the nude / [2] in a negligee) for me?** Не попози́руешь ли ты мне (*[1]* обнажённой / *[2]* в неглиже́)?

model *n* образе́ц ♦ **~ of patience** образе́ц терпе́ния.

moderation *n* уме́ренность *f.*

modest *adj* скро́мный, -ая, -ое, -ые ♦ **~ guy** скро́мник ♦ **~ girl** скро́мница ♦ **~ person** скро́мник. ♦ **You're too modest.** Ты сли́шком скро́мная *(ж: скро́мный).*

modesty *n* скро́мность *f* ♦ **fake ~** ло́жная скро́мность.

modicum *n* крупи́ца, чу́точка, минима́льное коли́чество, о́чень ма́лое коли́чество ♦ **I just want a modicum of happiness in life.** Я то́лько хочу́ крупи́цу сча́стья в жи́зни.

moist *adj* вла́жный, -ая, -ое, -ые.

Moldavian *n* молда́вский язы́к ♦ **speak ~** говори́ть по-молда́вски.

Moldovan *adj* молда́вский, -ая, -ое, -ие.

Moldovan *n* молдова́нин *m*, молдова́нка *f.*

mole *n* ро́динка.

molten *adj* раскалённый, -ая, -ое, -ые ♦ **Molten waves of desire sweep through *(1)* ...my entire body... / *(2)* ...every fiber and cell of my body... whenever I think of your exquisite, luscious beauty.** Бушу́ющие во́лны стра́сти проно́сятся че́рез *(1)* ...всё моё те́ло... / *(2)* ...все фи́бры и кле́тки моего́ те́ла,... когда́ бы я ни поду́мал о твое́й изы́сканной, со́чной красоте́.

mom *n (slang)* ма́ма ♦ **single ~** ма́ма-одино́чка.

moment *n* моме́нт, миг, мгнове́ние ♦ **agonizing ~s** мучи́тельные моме́нты ♦ **any ~** любо́й моме́нт ♦ **beautiful ~** прекра́сный моме́нт ♦ **blissful** *(1,2)* **~s** счастли́вые *(1)* мгнове́ния / *(2)* моме́нты ♦ **electric ~** электризу́ющий моме́нт ♦ **favorable ~** благоприя́тный моме́нт ♦ **happy ~s** счастли́вые мгнове́ния ♦ **illusory ~** иллюзо́рный моме́нт ♦ **intimate ~s** инти́мные моме́нты ♦ **joyous ~** ра́достное мгнове́ние ♦ **long, intense ~** дли́тельный, напряжённый моме́нт ♦ **long awaited ~** долгожда́нный моме́нт ♦ **~ of bliss** миг блаже́нства ♦ **~ of contentment** миг не́ги ♦ **~ of supreme pleasure** миг наивы́сшего наслажде́ния ♦ **~s of passion** моме́нты стра́сти ♦ **magic(al) ~** волше́бный моме́нт ♦ **nervous ~** не́рвный моме́нт ♦ **precious ~** драгоце́нный миг ♦ **present ~** настоя́щий моме́нт ♦ **private ~s** 1. *(intimate)* инти́мные моме́нты; 2. *(personal, free)* ли́чное вре́мя, свобо́дные моме́нты ♦ **propitious ~** благоприя́тный моме́нт ♦ **rapturous ~** упои́тельный моме́нт ♦ **right ~** подходя́щий моме́нт ♦ *(1,2)* **sacred ~s** *(1)* драгоце́нные / *(2)* святы́е моме́нты ♦ **sensual ~** чу́вственный моме́нт ♦ **sensuous ~s** чу́вственные моме́нты ♦ **special ~s** осо́бые моме́нты ♦ **tense ~** напряжённый моме́нт ♦ *(1,2)* **this ~** *(1)* э́тот / *(2)* да́нный моме́нт ♦ *(1-3)* **wonderful ~** *(1)* удиви́тельный / *(2)* замеча́тельный моме́нт, *(3)* чуде́сный миг ♦ **at this ~** в э́тот моме́нт ♦ **(up) to** *(1)* **this / *(2)* that ~** (вплоть) до *(1,2)* э́того моме́нта.

> **moment: great moments with you**

Always the sweet memories of those blissful moments come back to me. Сла́дкие воспомина́ния о тех счастли́вых моме́нтах всегда́ возвраща́ются ко мне. ♦ **I'll never forget those wonderful, magical moments with you.** Я никогда́ не забу́ду э́тих удиви́тельных, волше́бных мину́т, проведённых с тобо́й. ♦ **That (**[1]** beautiful / [2] wonderful) moment. will *(3)* stay / *(4)* remain indelibly etched in my *(5)* mind / *(6)* mem-**

For Russian adjectives, the masculine form is spelled out,
followed by the feminine, neuter and plural endings.

ory *(7)* ...**forever.** / *(8)* ...**for as long as I live**. Этот (*[1]* прекра́сный / *[2]* замеча́тельный) моме́нт *(3,4)* оста́нется вы́гравированным несмыва́емо в мое́й *(5,6)* па́мяти *(7)* ...навсегда́. / *(8)* ...пока́ я жив *(ж: жива́)*. ♦ **The moments I spend with you are the most precious of my life**. Мину́ты, проведённые с тобо́й, -- са́мые драгоце́нные в мое́й жи́зни. ♦ **At this moment** *(1)* ...**last week...** / *(2)* ...**last Sunday...** / *(3)* ...**last night... I was holding you in my arms**. В то мгнове́ние *(1)* ...на про́шлой неде́ле... / *(2)* ...в про́шлое воскресе́нье... / *(3)* ...про́шлой но́чью... я держа́л тебя́ в объя́тиях.

┌─────────────────────────────────────┐
│ ***moment: hoped-for moments*** │
└─────────────────────────────────────┘
I hope we can steal a few private moments together. Я наде́юсь, мы смо́жем похи́тить не́сколько мгнове́ний, что́бы побы́ть то́лько вдвоём. ♦ **I want (so much) to** *(1)* ...**enjoy tender moments...** / *(2)* ...**share sensual moments... with you.** Я (так) хочу́ *(1)* ...наслажда́ться не́жными мину́тами... / *(2)* ...разделя́ть чу́вственные моме́нты... с тобо́й.

┌─────────────────────────────────────┐
│ ***moment: never a dull one*** │
└─────────────────────────────────────┘
There's never a dull moment (with *[1]* **me** / *[2]* **you).** Никогда́ не быва́ет ску́чно (*[1]* со мной / *[2]* с тобо́й). ♦ **I haven't known a dull moment since I met you.** Я никогда́ не скуча́л *(ж: скуча́ла)* с моме́нта на́шей встре́чи.

mommy *n* ма́ма.

Monday *n* понеде́льник ♦ **by ~** к понеде́льнику ♦ **last ~** в про́шлый понеде́льник ♦ **next ~** в сле́дующий понеде́льник ♦ **on ~** в понеде́льник.

money *n* де́ньги ♦ *(1)* **dig** / *(2)* **scrape up the ~** *(1,2)* выкра́ивать / вы́кроить де́ньги ♦ **I'll send you some money (** *[1]*...**to buy it.** / *[2]* ...**to pay for it.** / *[3]* ...**for the ticket** / *[4]* **trip** / *[5]* **cost** / *[6]* **postage.).** Я пошлю́ тебе́ не́которую су́мму де́нег (*[1]*...купи́ть э́то. / *[2]* ...заплати́ть за э́то. / *[3]* ...на биле́т / *[4]* путеше́ствие / *[5]* изде́ржки. / *[6]* ...почто́вые расхо́ды.) ♦ **I'll send you some money every month.** Я бу́ду посыла́ть тебе́ не́которую су́мму де́нег ка́ждый ме́сяц. ♦ **I'll** *(1)* **transfer** / *(2)* **wire the money to your bank account.** Я *(1)* переведу́ / *(2)* телеграфи́рую де́ньги на твой счёт в ба́нке. ♦ **I'll send you the money via Western Union.** Я пошлю́ тебе́ де́ньги че́рез «Ве́стерн Ю́нион». ♦ **I'll send you the rest of the money later.** Я пошлю́ тебе́ остальны́е де́ньги поздне́е. ♦ **How much money do you need?** Ско́лько тебе́ на́до де́нег? ♦ **I don't have enough money (at the present time).** У меня́ (сейча́с) не доста́точно де́нег. ♦ **Did you receive the money that I sent to you (on** *[date]* **)?** Получи́ла *(ж: Получи́л)* ли ты де́ньги, кото́рые я посла́л *(ж: посла́ла)* тебе́ *(да́та)*? ♦ **Money can't buy** *(1)* **happiness** / *(2)* **love.** За де́ньги нельзя́ купи́ть *(1)* сча́стье / *(2)* любо́вь. ♦ **I don't care about money.** Де́ньги не волну́ют меня́.

Mongolian *adj* монго́льский, -ая, -ое, -ие.

Mongolian *n* 1. *(person)* монго́л *m*, монго́лка *f*; 2. *(language)* монго́льский язы́к ♦ **speak ~** говори́ть по-монго́льски.

monogamous *adj* монога́мный, -ая, -ое, -ые ♦ **I'm looking for a monogamous relationship.** Я ищу́ монога́мных отноше́ний.

monogamy *n* монога́мия ♦ **I want monogamy.** Я хочу́ монога́мии.

monotonous *adj (boring)* однообра́зный, -ая, -ое, -ые, ску́чный, -ая, -ое, -ые

monotony *n* однообра́зие ♦ **break the ~** наруша́ть / нару́шить однообра́зие .

monster *n* чудо́вище, монстр ♦ **green-eyed ~** *(jealousy)* ре́вность *f*.

month *n* ме́сяц ♦ **all ~** весь ме́сяц ♦ **every ~** ка́ждый ме́сяц ♦ **for a (whole) ~** *(planned)* на (це́лый) ме́сяц **for one ~** *(planned)* на оди́н ме́сяц ♦ **for** *(1)* **two** / *(2)* **three** / *(3)* **four ~s** *(planned)* на *(1)* два / *(2)* три / *(3)* четы́ре ме́сяца. ♦ **for five ~s** *(planned)* на пять ме́сяцев ♦ **in a ~** 1. *(after)* че́рез ме́сяц; 2. *(in the space of)* за оди́н ме́сяц ♦ **in** *(1)* **two** / *(2)* **three** / *(3)* **four ~s** 1. *(after)* че́рез *(1)* два / *(2)* три / *(3)* четы́ре ме́сяца; 2. *(in the space*

┌──┐
│ *See Appendix 19 for notes on sending mail to Russia and Ukraine.* │
└──┘

of) за *(1)* два / *(2)* три / *(3)* четы́ре ме́сяца ♦ **last** ~ в про́шлом ме́сяце ♦ **long** ~s до́лгие ме́сяцы ♦ *(1,2)* **next** ~ в *(1)* сле́дующем / *(2)* бу́дущем ме́сяце ♦ **once a** ~ раз в ме́сяц ♦ **this** ~ в э́том ме́сяце ♦ **a whole** ~ це́лый ме́сяц ♦ **the whole** ~ весь ме́сяц.

mooch *vt* выпра́шивать / вы́просить *(what = acc., from whom = + у + gen.)*, попроша́йничать *(what = acc., from whom = + у + gen.)*.

moocher *n* попроша́йка.

mood *n* настрое́ние ♦ **angry** ~ серди́тое настрое́ние ♦ *(1-3)* **bad** ~ *(1)* плохо́е / *(2)* дурно́е / *(3)* скве́рное настрое́ние ♦ **bright** ~ све́тлое настрое́ние ♦ *(1,2)* **cheerful** ~ *(1)* бо́дрое / *(2)* весёлое настрое́ние ♦ *(1,2)* **cheery** ~ *(1)* бо́дрое / *(2)* весёлое настрое́ние ♦ **depressed** ~ пода́вленное настрое́ние ♦ **dismal** ~ пода́вленное настрое́ние ♦ **downcast** ~ уны́лое настрое́ние ♦ **elated** ~ припо́днятое настрое́ние ♦ **excellent** ~ отли́чное настрое́ние ♦ **feisty** ~ сварли́вое настрое́ние ♦ *(1,2)* **foul** ~ *(1)* отврати́тельное / *(2)* мёрзкое настрое́ние ♦ **good** ~ хоро́шее настрое́ние ♦ **grey** ~ мра́чное настрое́ние ♦ **grouchy** ~ ворчли́вое настрое́ние ♦ **happy** ~ счастли́вое настрое́ние ♦ **joyful** ~ ра́достное настрое́ние ♦ *(1,2)* **lousy** ~ *(1)* ужа́сное / *(2)* жу́ткое настрое́ние ♦ **marvelous** ~ превосхо́дное настрое́ние ♦ **melancholy** ~ уны́лое настрое́ние ♦ *(1-3)* **nasty** ~ *(1)* дурно́е / *(2)* раздражи́тельное / *(3)* скве́рное настрое́ние ♦ **playful** ~ игри́вое настрое́ние ♦ *(1,2)* **rotten** ~ *(1)* отврати́тельное / *(2)* мёрзкое настрое́ние ♦ **sad** ~ уны́лое настрое́ние ♦ **somber** ~ угрю́мое настрое́ние ♦ **sour** ~ ки́слое настрое́ние ♦ **sullen** ~ мра́чное настрое́ние ♦ **sunny** ~ со́лнечное настрое́ние ♦ *(1,2)* **terrible** ~ *(1)* ужа́сное / *(2)* жу́ткое настрое́ние ♦ **wonderful** ~ прекра́сное настрое́ние ♦ **brighten** *(1)* **my** / *(2)* **your mood** поднима́ть / подня́ть *(1)* моё / *(2)* твоё настрое́ние ♦ **gamut of** ~s га́мма настрое́ний.

┌─────────────────────┐
│ **mood:** *your mood* │
└─────────────────────┘

You're in a *(1)* **bright** / *(2)* **good** / *(3)* **happy** / *(4)* **sunny** / *(5)* **bad** / *(6)* **grouchy** / *(7)* **lousy** / *(8)* **somber** / *(9)* **sour mood today.** Ты в *(1)* све́тлом / *(2)* хоро́шем / *(3)* счастли́вом / *(4)* со́лнечном / *(5)* плохо́м / *(6)* ворчли́вом / *(7)* ужа́сном / *(8)* угрю́мом / *(9)* ки́слом настрое́нии сего́дня. ♦ **Your** *(1)* **cheery** / *(2)* **happy** / *(3)* **sunny mood is very infectious.** Твоё *(1)* бо́дрое / *(2)* счастли́вое / *(3)* со́лнечное настрое́ние о́чень зарази́тельно. ♦ **Why are you in such a** *(1)* **sour** / *(2)* **bad** / *(3)* **grey** / *(4)* **sullen mood?** Отчего́ ты в тако́м *(1)* ки́слом / *(2)* плохо́м / *(3,4)* мра́чном настрое́нии? ♦ **I want you always to be in a** *(1)* **happy** / *(2)* **joyful mood.** Я хочу́, что́бы ты всегда́ была́ *(ж: был)* в *(1)* счастли́вом / *(2)* ра́достном настрое́нии. ♦ **I know some very nice ways to** *(1)* **put** / *(2)* **get you in the mood.** Мне изве́стно не́сколько прекра́сных спо́собов *(1,2)* привести́ тебя́ в настрое́ние занима́ться любо́вью.

┌─────────────────────┐
│ **mood:** *my mood* │
└─────────────────────┘

I'm sorry I was in such a *(1)* **sour** / *(2)* **bad** / *(3)* **grey mood.** Извиня́юсь, что я был *(ж: была́)* в тако́м *(1)* ки́слом / *(2)* плохо́м / *(3)* мра́чном настрое́нии. ♦ **My mood always improves when I have you around.** У меня́ всегда́ поднима́ется настрое́ние, когда́ ты ря́дом. ♦ **Your** *(1)* **call** / *(2)* **letter brightened my mood.** *(1)* Твой звоно́к по́днял... / *(2)* Твоё письмо́ по́дняло... моё настрое́ние. ♦ **I'm (really) not in the mood (** *[1]*...**for that** / *[2]* **games** / *[3]* **jokes.** / *[4]* ...**for making love.** / *[5]* ...**to do that.** / *[6,7]* ...**to go.** / *[8]* ...**to discuss it.)** Я (действи́тельно) не в настрое́нии (*[1]* ...для э́того / *[2]* игр / *[3]* шу́ток. / *[4]* ...занима́ться любо́вью. / *[5]* ...де́лать э́то. / *[6]* ...идти́ *[on foot]* / *[7]* е́хать *[by veh.]*. / *[8]* ...обсужда́ть э́то.)

moodiness *n* угрю́мость *f.*

moody *adj (morose)* угрю́мый, -ая, -ое, -ые, уны́лый, -ая, -ое, -ые.

moon *n* луна́ ♦ **full** ~ по́лная луна́ ♦ **honey-colored** ~ медо́вого цве́та луна́ ♦ **silvery**

summer ~ серебри́стая ле́тняя луна́ ◆ **"I'll be looking at the moon, but I'll be seeing you."** *(Words of a song)* «Я бу́ду смотре́ть на луну́, но ви́деть тебя́.» *(Слова́ из пе́сни)*

moonbeam *n* луч лу́нного све́та.

moonlight *n* лу́нный свет ◆ **dance in the** ~ танцева́ть в лу́нном све́те ◆ **I want to make love with you by moonlight.** Я хочу́ занима́ться любо́вью с тобо́й при лу́нном све́те. ◆ **I want to dance with you in the moonlight.** Я хочу́ танцева́ть с тобо́й в лу́нном све́те. ◆ **You** *(1)* **look** / *(2)* **looked so beautiful in the moonlight.** Ты *(1)* вы́глядишь / *(2)* вы́гля- дела тако́й прекра́сной в лу́нном све́те.

moonlit *adj* освещённый (-ая, -ое, -ые) луно́й.

moon-struck *adj* 1. *(romantically sentimental)* вздыха́ющий (-ая, -ее, -ие) под луно́й; 2. *(mad)* поме́шанный, -ая, -ое, -ые.

moral *adj* нра́вственный, -ая, -ое, -ые, мора́льный, -ая, -ое, -ые ◆ **I know that you're a person of impeccable moral character.** Я зна́ю, что ты челове́к безупре́чной нра́вст- венности.

morale *n* душе́вное состоя́ние, мора́льный дух ◆ **All your attention does wonders for my morale.** Твоё внима́ние - чудоде́йственное сре́дство для моего́ душе́вного состоя́ния.

moralist *n* морали́ст.

moralistic *adj* поуча́ющий, -ая, -ее, -ие, нравоучи́тельный, -ая, -ее, -ие ◆ **I hope I don't sound too moralistic.** Наде́юсь, я не кажу́сь сли́шком поуча́ющим *(ж: поуча́ющей)*.

moralize *vi* морализова́ть; поуча́ть.

morals *n, pl* мора́ль *f*, но́рмы поведе́ния, нра́вы; нра́вственность *f* ◆ **high** ~s высо́кая мора́ль ◆ **old-fashioned** ~s ста́рые но́рмы поведе́ния ◆ **strong** ~s высо́кая мора́ль ◆ *(1,2)* **man of good** ~s *(1)* высоконра́вственный / *(2)* поря́дочный мужчи́на ◆ *(1,2)* **person of good** ~s *(1)* высоконра́вственный / *(2)* поря́дочный челове́к ◆ *(1,2)* **woman of good** ~s *(1)* высоконра́вственная / *(2)* поря́дочная же́нщина ◆ **man of loose** ~s распу́- щенный мужчи́на ◆ *(1,2)* **person of loose** ~s *(1)* распу́щенный / *(2)* безнра́вственный челове́к ◆ **woman of loose** ~s распу́щенная же́нщина ◆ **man without** ~s безнра́вст- венный мужчи́на ◆ **person without** ~s безнра́вственный челове́к ◆ **woman without** ~s безнра́вственная же́нщина.

---
morals: *phrases*

Have you no morals (at all)? У Вас (совсе́м) нет мора́ли? ◆ **You're a** *(1)* **man** / *(2)* **wo- man** / *(3)* **person without (conscience or) morals.** Ты *(1)* мужчи́на / *(2)* же́нщина / *(3)* челове́к без (со́вести и) мора́ли.

more *adj* 1. *(greater quantity)* бо́льше *(+ gen.)*; 2. *(additional)* ещё бо́лее; бо́льше ◆ ~ **love** бо́льше любви́ ◆ ~ **than 35 years old** > 35 лет, бо́льше тридцати́ пяти́ (35) лет ◆ ~ **time** бо́льше вре́мени.

more *adv* 1. *(greater extent)* бо́льше *(+ gen.)*; 2. *(used with adj & adv for comparative)* бо́лее ◆ **I love you more than you love me.** Я люблю́ тебя́ бо́льше, чем ты лю́бишь меня́. ◆ **You're more beautiful than your friend.** Ты бо́лее краси́вая, чем твоя́ подру́га.

mores *n, pl* нра́вы ◆ **sexual** ~s сексуа́льные нра́вы.

morning *n* у́тро ◆ **every** ~ ка́ждое у́тро ◆ **in the** ~ у́тром ◆ **Monday** *(etc)* ~ в понеде́льник у́тром ◆ **this** ~ сего́дня у́тром ◆ **tomorrow** ~ за́втра у́тром ◆ **yesterday** ~ вчера́ у́тром.

moron *n* слабоу́мный *m*, слабоу́мная *f*, идио́т *m*, идио́тка *f*.

morose *adj* мра́чный, -ая, -ое, -ые, угрю́мый, -ая, -ое, -ые.

morosely *adv* мра́чно, угрю́мо.

Moslem *adj* мусульма́нский, -ая, -ое, -ие.

Moslem *n* мусульма́нин *m*, мусульма́нка *f*.

A list of abbreviations used in the dictionary is given on page 10.

mosque *n* мечéть *f* .

motel *n* мотéль *m*.

mother *n* мать *f* ♦ **foster ~** приёмная мать ♦ **I want you to be the mother of my children.** Я хочý, чтóбы ты былá мáтерью моúх детéй.

motherhood *n* материнство.

mother-in-law *n* *(husband's mom)* свекрóвь *f* ; *(wife's mom)* тёща.

motion *n* движéние ♦ **When we're apart, I go through the motions of living.** Когдá мы далекó друг от дрýга, я дéлаю вид, что живý.

motivate *vt* побуждáть / побудúть *(whom = acc.)* ♦ **I need someone like you to motivate me.** Чтóбы побуждáть меня, мне нýжен такóй человéк, как ты. ♦ **You really motivate me** (*[1]* **...to achieve my goals.** / *[2]* **...to improve myself.**) Ты действúтельно побуждáешь меня (*[1]*...к достижéнию моúх цéлей. / *[2]* ...к самосовершéнству.)

motivation *n* мотивáция, вдохновéние ♦ **You are my motivation.** Ты моё вдохновéние. ♦ **You give me the motivation** *(1)* **...to carry on.** / *(2)* **...to keep going.** Ты побуждáешь меня *(1,2)* продолжáть. ♦ **This is my main motivation: to come over there so that we can** *(1,2)* **combine together in heart and mind and body.** Моя глáвная цель -- приéхать к тебé для тогó, чтóбы мы смоглú *(1)* соединúться / *(2)* сочетáться сéрдцем, мýслями и тéлом.

motive *n* мотúв ♦ **ulterior ~** скрýтый мотúв ♦ **questionable ~s** сомнúтельные мотúвы.

motorcycle *n* мотоцúкл.

motorhome *n* дáча на колёсах.

motor scooter *n* мотóрный скýтер.

mound *n* *(breasts)* хóлмик, бугорóк, гóрка *(грудú)* ♦ **delightful ~s** восхитúтельные бугоркú ♦ **perfect ~s** совершéнные хóлмики ♦ **pliant ~s** подáтливые бугоркú ♦ *(1,2)* **soft *(3,4)* ~s** *(1)* мягкие / *(2)* нéжные *(3)* бугоркú / *(4)* хóлмики *(грудú)*.

mouth *n* рот ♦ **beautiful ~** прекрáсный рот ♦ **big ~** большóй рот ♦ **charming ~** очаровáтельный рóт(ик) ♦ **cute ~** привлекáтельный рóт(ик) ♦ **dirty ~** грязный рот ♦ **eager ~** нетерпелúвый рот ♦ **enchanting ~** очаровáтельный рóт(ик) ♦ **firm ~** твёрдый рот ♦ *(1,2)* **full ~** *(1)* пóлный / *(2)* пýхлый рот ♦ **generous ~** пóлный рот ♦ **glossy ~** глянцевый рот ♦ **greedy ~** жáдный рот ♦ **hot ~** горячий рот ♦ **insistent ~** рот, стремящийся к поцелýям *(1 term)* ♦ **inviting ~** манящий рот ♦ **liquid ~** влáжный рот ♦ **little ~** рóтик, мáленький рот ♦ **lovely ~** прекрáсный рот ♦ **moist ~** влáжный рот ♦ **noble ~** благорóдный рот ♦ **open ~** открýтый рот ♦ **petite ~** мáленький рот ♦ **pouty ~** надýтые гýбы ♦ **pretty ~** красúвый рот ♦ **rosebud ~** рот как рóзовый бутóн ♦ **sensual ~** чýвственный рот ♦ **sensuous ~** чувствúтельный рот ♦ **sexy ~** сексуáльный рот ♦ **small ~** мáленький рот ♦ **soft ~** мягкий рот ♦ **sweet ~** слáдкий рот ♦ **tantalizing ~** манящий рот ♦ **tempting ~** соблазнúтельный рот ♦ **wicked ~** грéшный рот ♦ **wide ~** большóй рот ♦ **wonderful (little) ~** чудéсный рóт(ик).

mouth: *other terms*

close your ~ закрывáть / закрýть рот ♦ **contour of your ~** очертáние твоегó рта ♦ **moist recesses of the ~** влáжные ложбúнки рта ♦ **open your ~** открывáть / открýть рот.

mouth: *your beautiful mouth*

You have such a beautiful mouth. У тебя такóй прекрáсный рот. ♦ **Yours is a mouth that I can only think of as beautiful.** Едúнственное, что я могý дýмать о твоём рте, - - он прекрáсен. ♦ **I've never seen a mouth that expresses sensuality the way yours does.** Я никогдá не вúдел рта, котóрый выражáет такýю чýвственность, как твой. ♦ **That mouth of yours... It's so cute! So sweet-looking! So tempting!** Твой рот... Он так привлекáтелен! Такóй слáдкий! Такóй соблазнúтельный! ♦ **Such an inviting mouth you**

The accents on Russian words are to show how to pronounce them. You don't have to copy the accents when writing to someone.

have. Такóй манящий рот у тебя. ♦ **You have the most tantalizing mouth I've ever laid eyes on.** У тебя такóй манящий рот, какóго я ещё никогдá не вúдел. ♦ **I love the smell of your mouth.** Мне нрáвится арóмат твоегó дыхáния.

> **mouth:** *I want to kiss your mouth*

I watch your mouth forming sounds, moving and undulating so supplely, so softly, so enticingly and I am seized with a raging impulse to fuse my own mouth together with it and once and for all revel in its sweet softness. Я слежý, как твой рот создаёт звýки, двúгаясь и изгибáясь так гúбко, так мягко, так соблазнúтельно, и я охвáчен бéшеным úмпульсом соединúть мой рот с твоúм, чтóбы раз и навсегдá пировáть в егó слáдкой нéжности. ♦ **Never in all my life have I wanted to kiss someone's mouth as much as I want to kiss yours.** Никогдá ничéй рот так сúльно не хотéл целовáть я, как твой. ♦ **I want to devour your sweet mouth.** Я хочý съесть твой слáдкий рот. ♦ **How I ache for the day when my mouth can at last claim yours.** Как жáжду я тогó дня, когдá мой рот смóжет наконéц овладéть твоúм. ♦ **How I long to taste the warm recesses of your mouth (again).** Как жáжду я (опять) вкушáть тёплые глубúны твоегó рта.

> **mouth:** *I dream of kissing your mouth*

I dream of the heavenly moment when my lips take possession of your mouth. Я мечтáю о рáйском мгновéнии, когдá моú гýбы овладéют твоúм ртом. ♦ **If you ever feel the generosity in your heart to bestow the ultimate joy in life to someone who adores you beyond measure, then put your sweet mouth against mine for 60 heavenly seconds and you will have done it.** Если тóлько в твоём сéрдце пробýдится щéдрость подарúть величáйшее наслаждéние в жúзни томý, кто обожáет тебя безмéрно, тогдá прижмú свои слáдкие гýбы к моúм на шестдесят *(= 60)* секýнд, и ты это сдéлаешь. ♦ **All I can think of, day and night, is your tantalizing mouth.** Всё, о чём я могý дýмать день и ночь, -- твой манящий рот. ♦ **The thought of kissing your beautiful mouth causes my heart to thunder.** Мысль о том, чтóбы целовáть твой прекрáсный рот заставляет моё сéрдце гремéть.

> **mouth:** *I love to kiss your mouth*

My favorite pleasure in life is kissing your beautiful mouth. Сáмое большóе наслаждéние моéй жúзни -- целовáть твой прекрáсный рот. ♦ **I love to put my tongue in your mouth.** Мне нрáвится класть язык в твой рот. ♦ **I love to feel your tongue in my mouth.** Мне нрáвится чýвствовать во рту твой язык.

> **mouth:** *how your mouth feels*

Your mouth feels so *(1)* wonderful / *(2)* fantastic / *(3)* incredible! Ощущéние твоегó рта так *(1)* замечáтельно / *(2)* фантастúчно / *(3)* невероятно! ♦ **What a wonderful liquid mouth you have!** Что за прекрáсный влáжный рот у тебя! ♦ **I love the feel of your mouth (there).** Мне нрáвится ощущéние твоегó рта (там).

> **mouth:** *what my mouth will do to you*

My mouth will trail along your neck to your shoulder and then down to your breast. Моú гýбы бýдут путешéствовать вдоль твоéй шéи, к твоúм плечáм и затéм вниз к твоéй грудú. ♦ **As my hand cups the fullness of your breast, my mouth will cover your beautiful face and smooth neck with adoring kisses.** В то врéмя, как моя рукá ощутúт полнотý твоéй грудú, мой рот покрóет твоё прекрáсное лицó и нéжную шéю обожáющими поцелýями. ♦ **My mouth is going to do its fervent work on you until the need to surrender invades your whole body.** Мой рот бýдет дéлать свою пылкую рабóту до тех пор, покá потрéбность капитулúровать ни наводнúт всё твоё тéло. ♦ **I want to tune your body with my mouth and hands until it sings.** Я хочý настрáивать твоё тéло своúм ртом и рукáми до тех пор, покá онó не запоёт. ♦ **I'll show you the most talented, eager mouth you have**

> *If no accent is shown on a word with a capitalized vowel,*
> *it means that the capitalized vowel is accented.*

ever heard or dreamed of. Я продемонстри́рую тебе́ са́мый уме́лый, пы́лкий рот, о кото́ром ты то́лько могла́ мечта́ть. ♦ **When at last my mouth claims yours, I will** *(1)* **...deluge it with more kisses...** / *(2)* **...lavish** / *(3)* **bestow more kisses upon it... than it has ever known before.** Когда́ наконе́ц мой рот встре́тится с твои́м, я *(1)* ...затоплю́ его́ больши́м коли́чеством поцелу́ев,... / *(2,3)* ...подарю́ ему́ бо́льше поцелу́ев,... чем он когда́-либо пре́жде получа́л.

> **mouth:** *what our mouths will do*

Every night our mouths will feast on each other's. Ка́ждую ночь на́ши рты бу́дут пирова́ть друг в дру́ге.

move *vi* 1. *(perform motion)* дви́гаться / дви́нуться; 2. *(change residences)* переезжа́ть / перее́хать ♦ **~ fast** бы́стро дви́гаться ♦ **~ in** посели́ться *(with whom = + c + instr.)* ♦ **~ in unison** дви́гаться в унисо́н ♦ **~ out** *vi (leave)* уезжа́ть / уе́хать; *(move)* переезжа́ть / перее́хать ♦ **~ slowly** ме́дленно дви́гаться.

> **move:** *the way you move*

You are so lithe and supple in the way you move. Ты така́я ги́бкая и пласти́чная, когда́ дви́гаешься. ♦ **You move with such lithesome grace.** Ты дви́гаешься с тако́й ги́бкой гра́цией. ♦ **When you move like that, it just drives me out of my mind.** Когда́ ты де́лаешь таки́е движе́ния, ты сво́дишь меня́ с ума́. ♦ **I like the way you move.** Мне нра́вится, как ты дви́жешься.

> **move out:**

I can't live with *(1)* **her** / *(2)* **him** / *(3)* **them anymore. I'm going to move out.** Я бо́льше не могу́ жить с *(1)* ней / *(2)* ним / *(3)* ни́ми. Я уе́ду. ♦ **Why don't you move out?** Почему́ ты не перее́дешь?

movement *n* движе́ние *(pl: движе́ния)* ♦ **beautiful ~s** краси́вые движе́ния ♦ **expressive** ~s вырази́тельные движе́ния ♦ **fluid ~s** пла́вные движе́ния ♦ **frenzied ~s** исступлён-ные движе́ния ♦ **furious ~s** я́ростные движе́ния ♦ **graceful ~** движе́ние, по́лное гра́ции *(1 term)* ♦ **graceful ~s** грацио́зные движе́ния ♦ **lovely ~s** краси́вые движе́ния ♦ **rhythmic ~s** ритми́чные движе́ния ♦ **slow ~** ме́дленное движе́ние ♦ **smooth ~s** пла́вные движе́ния ♦ **undulating ~** волнообра́зное движе́ние ♦ **control ~s** управля́ть движе́ниями ♦ **You are so lithe and supple in your movements.** Ты така́я ги́бкая и пласти́чная в движе́нии.

movie *n* 1. *(film)* фильм; 2. *(theater)* кино́(теа́тр) ♦ **adult ~** фильм для взро́слых ♦ **erotic ~** эроти́ческий фильм ♦ **indi(e) ~s** *(movies made by independent producers)* фи́льмы, сде́ланные незави́симыми продю́серами *(1 term)* ♦ **watch** *(1)* **a ~** / *(2)* **~s** смотре́ть / посмотре́ть *(1)* фильм / *(2)* фи́льмы.

> **movie:** *phrases*

(1) **I'd like to invite you...** / *(2)* **Would you like to go (with me)... to a movie** *(3)* **...tomorrow (evening).** / *(4)* **...this afternoon** / *(5)* **evening.** / *(6)* **...on Friday** / *(7)* **Saturday** / *(8)* **Sunday** *(9)* **afternoon** / *(10)* **evening.** / **?** *(1)* Я хоте́л бы пригласи́ть тебя́... / *(2)* Не хо́чешь ли ты пойти́ (со мной)... в кино́ *(3)* ...за́втра (ве́чером). / *(4)* ...сего́дня днём / *(5)* ве́чером. / *(6)* ...в пя́тницу / *(7)* суббо́ту / *(8)* воскресе́нье *(9)* днём / *(10)* ве́чером. / **?** ♦ **Would you like to go to a movie (with me)?** Не хоте́ла *(ж: хоте́л)* бы ты пойти́ в кино́ (со мной)? ♦ **Let's go to a movie (together).** Дава́й пойдём в кино́ (вме́сте).

moving *adj* тро́гательный, -ая, -ое, -ые, волну́ющий, -ая, -ее, -ие ♦ **Your story is deeply moving.** Твоя́ исто́рия глубоко́ волну́ет.

moxie *n* 1. *(pluck; audacity)* сме́лость *f*, де́рзость *f*; 2. *(ingenuity)* ло́вкость *f*, уме́ние.

MS *abbrev* = **Master of Science degree** сте́пень маги́стра (есте́ственных / то́чных) нау́к.

much *adj, adv* мно́го ♦ **not ~** немно́го ♦ **too ~** сли́шком мно́го ♦ **very ~** о́чень мно́го.

Russian has 6 grammatical cases. For an explanation of them,
see the grammar appendix on page 686.

muffler *n* кашне́, шарф.

mule-headed *adj (slang) (stubborn)* упря́мый, -ая, -ое, -ые, тупоголо́вый, -ая, -ое, -ые.

multi-cultured *adj* широко́ культу́рный, -ая, -ое, -ые.

multi-faceted *adj* многогра́нный, -ая, -ое, -ые.

multi-talented *adj* име́ющий (-ая, -ее, -ие) мно́го тала́нтов.

mundane *adj* земно́й, -а́я, -о́е, -ы́е ♦ **share the** ~ разделя́ть обы́чную земну́ю жизнь.

murmur *vt* бормота́ть; шепта́ть.

murmur *n* 1. *(whisper)* шёпот; *(mumble)* бормота́ние; 2. *(grumble)* ро́пот ♦ **throaty** ~ хри́плый шёпот.

muscle *n* мы́шца; му́скул ♦ **hard-corded** *(1,2)* ~**s** кре́пкие *(1)* мы́шцы / *(2)* му́скулы ♦ **stomach** ~**s** мы́шцы живота́.

muscular *adj* мускули́стый, -ая, -ое, -ые.

musculature *n* мускулату́ра.

muse *n* му́за ♦ *(1)* **I want to... /** *(2)* **I hope I can... be your muse.** *(1)* Я хочу́ быть... / *(2)* Я наде́юсь, что смогу́ стать ... твое́й му́зой. ♦ **I need you to be my muse.** Я нужда́юсь в тебе́, как в свое́й му́зе.

mushy *adj* слаща́вый, -ая, -ое, -ые, сли́шком сентимента́льный, -ая, -ое, -ые ♦ **I hope that what I've written to you here doesn't sound mushy. Everything that I've said is a genuine expression of how I feel about you.** Наде́юсь, то, что я написа́л, не звучи́т сли́шком сентимента́льно. Всё, о чём я написа́л, -- и́скреннее выраже́ние мои́х чувств к тебе́.

music *n* му́зыка ♦ **alternative** ~ альтернати́вная му́зыка ♦ **blue grass** ~ му́зыка «блу́-грасс» ♦ **classical** ~ класси́ческая му́зыка ♦ **country-western (CW)** ~ ковбо́йская му́зыка, му́зыка «ка́нтри» ♦ **folk** ~ наро́дная му́зыка ♦ **good** ~ хоро́шая му́зыка ♦ **gothic** ~ му́зыка го́ттов ♦ **hardcore** ~ металли́ческий рок ♦ **industrial** ~ ди́кая, неконтроли́руемая му́зыка *(1 term)* ♦ **instrumental** ~ инструмента́льная му́зыка ♦ **loud** ~ гро́мкая му́зыка ♦ **New Age** ~ совреме́нная му́зыка "New Age" ♦ **organ** ~ орга́нная му́зыка ♦ **popular** ~ популя́рная му́зыка ♦ **raucous** ~ о́чень гро́мкая, пронзи́тельная му́зыка ♦ **rock** ~ рок-му́зыка ♦ **romantic** ~ романти́ческая му́зыка ♦ **sensual** ~ чу́вственная му́зыка ♦ **sentimental** ~ сентимента́льная му́зыка ♦ **soft** ~ ти́хая му́зыка, мя́гкая прия́тная му́зыка ♦ **spiritual** ~ религио́зная му́зыка ♦ **sweetest** ~ сладча́йшая му́зыка ♦ **what kind of** ~ кака́я му́зыка ♦ **wonderful** ~ чуде́сная му́зыка.

music: other terms

all kinds of ~ все ви́ды му́зыки ♦ **beat of the** ~ ритм му́зыки; такт му́зыки. ♦ **body like** ~ те́ло как му́зыка ♦ **enjoy** ~ наслажда́ться му́зыкой ♦ **listen to** ~ слу́шать му́зыку ♦ ~ **maker** музыка́нт ♦ **study** ~ учи́ться му́зыке.

music: phrases

You fill my life with music. Ты наполня́ешь мою́ жизнь му́зыкой. ♦ **You are the music of my life.** Ты му́зыка мое́й жи́зни. ♦ **The sweetest music to my ears is to hear you moan with pleasure.** Сладча́йшая му́зыка для моего́ слу́ха -- твои́ сто́ны наслажде́ния. ♦ **I have a passion for arts and music.** У меня́ страсть к иску́сству и му́зыке. ♦ **Music stokes me.** Му́зыка возбужда́ет меня́.

musical *adj* музыка́льный, -ая, -ое, -ые ♦ **Your voice is as musical as Apollo's lute.** Твой го́лос та́кже музыка́лен, как лю́тня Аполло́на.

musicality *n* музыка́льность *f.*

musician *n* музыка́нт *m,* музыка́нтка *f.*

must *v aux* 1. *(necessity)* до́лжен, должна́, -но́, -ны́; на́до; 2. *(strong probability)* должно́ быть ♦ ~ **not** нельзя́; не на́до; не до́лжен, не должна́, -но́, -ны́ ♦ **I must** *(1,2)* **go.** Я до́лжен *(ж: должна́)* *(1)* пойти́ *(on foot)* / *(2)* пое́хать *(by veh.).*

There are no articles ("a" or "the") in Russian.

mustache *n* усы́ ◆ **bushy** ~ густы́е усы́ ◆ **dashing** ~ лихи́е усы́ ◆ **handsome** ~ краси́вые усы́ ◆ **sensible** ~ небольши́е, аккура́тные усы́ *(1 term)* ◆ **thin** ~ то́нкие усы́.

mustang *n* муста́нг.

mutuality *n* взаи́мность *f.*

mysterious *adj* таи́нственный, -ая, -ое, -ые, зага́дочный, -ая, -ое, -ые.

mysteriously *adv* таи́нственно, зага́дочно.

mystery *n* та́йна ◆ **You have a hint of mystery about you.** В тебе́ есть что́-то зага́дочное.

mystical *adj* мисти́ческий, -ая, -ое, -ие.

mystically *adv* мисти́чно.

mystified *adj* озада́чен, -а, -о, -ы *(short forms)* ◆ **I'm completely mystified.** Я соверше́нно озада́чен *(ж: озада́чена).*

mystify *vt* озада́чивать / озада́чить *(whom = acc.)* ◆ **You (**[1] **really) mystify me (**[2] **at times).** (*[2]* Времена́ми) ты (*[1]* действи́тельно) озада́чиваешь меня́.

mystifying *adj* зага́дочный, -ая, -ое, -ые.

mystique *n* таи́нственность *f,* зага́дочность *f* ◆ **feminine** ~ же́нская зага́дочность.

---

*This dictionary contains two Russian alphabet pages:
one in Appendix 1, page 685, and a tear-off page on page 799.*

N

nag *vt* му́чить *(what = acc.)*, изводи́ть *(what = acc.)* ◆ **This has been nagging my conscience (for** *[1]* **...weeks.** / *[2]* **...a long time.)** Это му́чает мою́ со́весть (уже́ *[1]* ...неде́лями. / *[2]* ...до́лгое вре́мя.).

nag *vi* пили́ть, придира́ться *(at whom = + к + dat.),* ворча́ть ◆ **Please don't nag at me.** Пожа́луйста, не придира́йся ко мне. ◆ *(1)* **She** / *(2)* **He nags (at me)** *(3)* **...terribly.** / *(4)* **...all the time.** *(1)* Она́ / *(2)* Он *(3)* ...ужа́сно... / *(4)* ...всё вре́мя... придира́ется (ко мне). ◆ **I can't stand to have someone nagging at me.** Я терпе́ть не могу́, когда́ кто́-то придира́ется ко мне.

nagging *adj* ворчли́вый, -ая, -ое, -ые; сварли́вый, -ая, -ое, -ые.

nagging *n* приди́рки, ворча́нье ◆ **Her constant nagging killed my love for her.** Её постоя́нные приди́рки уби́ли мою́ любо́вь к ней. ◆ **I can't stand nagging.** Я терпе́ть не могу́ приди́рки.

nails *n, pl (fingernails)* но́гти ◆ **manicured ~s** наманикю́ренные но́гти.

naive *adj* наи́вный, -ая, -ое, -ые.

naivete *n* наи́вность *f* ◆ **youthful ~** ю́ная наи́вность.

naivety *n* наи́вность *f.*

naked *adj* го́лый, -ая, -ое, -ые, обнажённый, -ая, -ое, -ые ◆ **absolutely** *(1,2)* ~ абсолю́тно *(1)* го́лый / *(2)* обнажённый ◆ **buck** *(1,2)* ~ соверше́нно *(1)* го́лый / *(2)* обнажённый ◆ *(1,2)* **completely** *(3,4)* ~ *(1)* соверше́нно / *(2)* по́лностью *(3)* го́лый / *(4)* обнажённый ◆ **stark** *(1,2)* ~ соверше́нно *(1)* го́лый / *(2)* обнажённый ◆ **totally** *(1,2)* ~ по́лностью *(1)* го́лый / *(2)* обнажённый.

naked: phrases

I want to hold you naked in my arms. Я хочу́ держа́ть тебя́ в объя́тиях обнажённой. ◆ **Sometimes I feel naked when you look at me.** Иногда́ я чу́вствую себя́ го́лой, когда́ ты смо́тришь на меня́. ◆ **I can hardly wait to look at you gloriously naked, ready to give yourself to me.** Я не могу́ дожда́ться того́ мгнове́ния, когда́ уви́жу твоё прекра́сное те́ло обнажённым, гото́вым отда́ть себя́ мне. ◆ **I want to** *(1)* **...take a photo...** / *(1)* **...paint a picture... of you lying naked (on a** *[1]* **couch** / *[2]* **bed).** Я хочу́ *(1)* ...сфотографи́ровать тебя́... / *(2)* ...нарисова́ть тебя́... лежа́щей обнажённой (на *[1]* дива́не / *[2]* посте́ли).

nakedness *n* нагота́ ◆ **complete ~** соверше́нная нагота́.

name *n (first)* и́мя *neut.; (last)* фами́лия; *(pets)* кли́чка; *(things)* назва́ние ◆ **family ~**

Russian verbs conjugate for 6 persons:
I, familiar you, he-she-it, we, polite&plural you, and they.

фами́лия♦ ♦ **first** ~ и́мя *neut* ♦ **given** ~ и́мя *neut* ♦ **last** ~ фами́лия ♦ **maiden** ~ де́вичья
фами́лия ♦ **middle** ~ 1. *(Western:)* второ́е и́мя; 2. *(Russian:)* о́тчество *(based on father's
first name)* ♦ *(1,2)* **pet** ~ *(1)* уменьши́тельное / *(2)* ласка́тельное и́мя.

---

name: *what's your name?*

What's your name? Как Вас зову́т? ♦ **My name is** __. Меня́ зову́т ___. ♦ **What's your**
(1) **first** / *(2)* **given name?** Как Ва́ше *(1,2)* и́мя? ♦ **My** *(1)* **first** / *(2)* **given name is** __. Моё
(1,2) и́мя ___. ♦ **What's your** *(1)* **last** / *(2)* **family name?** Как Ва́ша *(1,2)* фами́лия? ♦
My *(1)* **last** / *(2)* **family name is** __. Моя́ *(1,2)* фами́лия ___. ♦ **What's your middle name**
(= patronymic)? Как Ва́ше о́тчество? ♦ **My middle name** *(= patronymic)* **is** __. Моё
о́тчество ___. ♦ **What's your middle name** *(western)?* Как Ва́ше второ́е и́мя? ♦ **My**
middle name *(western)* **is** __. Моё второе имя ___.

---

name: *your name is special to me*

You don't know how I love to hear the sound of my name coming from your lips. Ты не
зна́ешь, как мне нра́вится звуча́ние моего́ и́мени, слета́ющего с твои́х губ. ♦ **Not a**
minute passes that my heart doesn't call out your name (in *[1]* **desperate /** *[2]* **tortured**
longing). Не прохо́дит и мину́ты, чтобы моё се́рдце не называ́ло твоё и́мя (в *[1]* от-
ча́янной / *[2]* мучи́тельной жа́жде). ♦ **Your name is like music in my ears. I say it aloud**
to myself time and time again. Твоё и́мя звучи́т как му́зыка в мои́х уша́х. Я повторя́ю
его́ себе́ опя́ть и опя́ть. ♦ **Your (precious) name reverberates** *(1)* **through /** *(2)* **in my**
thoughts like a sacred chant intoned in awed reverence. Твоё (драгоце́нное) и́мя э́хом
отзыва́ется *(1,2)* в мои́х мы́слях, как свяще́нная песнь, интони́рованная с благо-
гове́йным почте́нием. ♦ **I say your name (to myself) over and over and over again.** Я
повторя́ю (себе́) твоё и́мя опя́ть и опя́ть. ♦ **I like saying your name.** Мне нра́вится
произноси́ть твоё и́мя. ♦ **I savor the sound of your name on my lips.** Мои́ гу́бы
смаку́ют звук твоего́ и́мени.

nape *n* заты́лок ♦ ~ **of the neck** заты́лок.

narcissistic *adj* самовлюблённый, -ая, -ое, -ые.

narrow-minded *adj* ограни́ченно-мы́слящий, -ая, -ее, -ие, узкомы́слящий, -ая, -ее, -ие.

nasty *adj* 1. *(disgusting, vile)* ме́рзкий, -ая, -ое, -ые, проти́вный, -ая, -ое, -ые, отврати́-
тельный, -ая, -ое, -ые; 2. *(obscene)* гря́зный, -ая, -ое, -ые, непристо́йный, -ая, -ое, -ые;
3. *(mean, ill-tempered)* зло́бный, -ая, -ое, -ые, раздражи́тельный, -ая, -ое, -ые, дурно́й,
-а́я, -бе, -ы́е ♦ ~ *(1,2)* **disposition** дурно́й *(1)* нрав / *(2)* хара́ктер ♦ *(1,2)* ~ **language** *(1)*
гря́зный / *(2)* непристо́йный язы́к ♦ *(1,2)* ~ **mood** *(1)* дурно́е / *(2)* раздражи́тельное
настрое́ние ♦ ~ **remark** 1. *(indecent)* непристо́йное замеча́ние; 2. *(venomous)* ядови́тое
замеча́ние ♦ ~ *(1,2)* **temper** дурно́й *(1)* нрав / *(2)* хара́ктер ♦ *(1,2)* ~ **words** *(1)* гря́зные
/ *(2)* непристо́йные слова́.

natty *adj* наря́дный, -ая, -ое, -ые.

natural *adj* 1. *(from nature)* есте́ственный, -ая, -ое, -ые; 2. *(normal)* норма́льный, -ая, -ое,
-ые, обы́чный, -ая, -ое, -ые ♦ **I admire you for being so natural and unaffected.** Я
восхища́юсь твое́й есте́ственностью и и́скренностью. ♦ **It feels so natural talking to**
you. Я чу́вствую себя́ так есте́ственно, говоря́ с тобо́й. ♦ **I have deep connections to**
the natural world. У меня́ глубо́кая связь с приро́дой.

naturalness *n* есте́ственность *f.*

nature *n* 1. *(character)* хара́ктер, нату́ра; 2. *(outdoors)* приро́да ♦ **artistic** ~ артисти́ческая
нату́ра ♦ **caring** ~ забо́тливая нату́ра ♦ **cheerful, loving** ~ весёлая, лю́бящая нату́ра
♦ **friendly** ~ дру́жеская нату́ра ♦ **gallant** ~ гала́нтная нату́ра ♦ *(1-3)* **gentle** ~ *(1)*
кро́ткий / *(2)* мя́гкий хара́ктер, *(3)* не́жная нату́ра ♦ **hedonistic** ~ гедонисти́ческая
нату́ра ♦ **hot-tempered** ~ вспы́льчивый хара́ктер ♦ **impulsive** ~ импульси́вный

There are two words for "you" in Russian:
familiar «ты» *and polite / plural* «вы» *(See page 771).*

хара́ктер ♦ **obstinate** ~ стропти́вый нрав ♦ **passionate** ~ стра́стная нату́ра ♦ **quiet** ~ споко́йная нату́ра ♦ **uninhibited** ~ несде́ржанный хара́ктер ♦ **volatile** ~ вспы́льчивый хара́ктер ♦ **warm, merry** ~ тёплый, весёлый хара́ктер.

nature: *your nature*

There is such genuine warmth in your nature. В твоём хара́ктере така́я и́скренняя теплота́. ♦ **If you have a nature as generous as your** *(1)* **beauty /** *(2)* **body, you are truly heaven's special prize.** Если твой хара́ктер тако́й же замеча́тельный, как *(1)* ...твоя́ красота́... / *(2)* ...твоё те́ло..., то ты и́стинный дар небе́с. ♦ **Your loving nature has left an imprint on my soul that will never go away.** Ты оста́вила тако́й отпеча́ток в мое́й душе́, кото́рый никогда́ не исче́знет. ♦ **You are so lovely physically, and when this is superimposed upon your sweet, warm, caring, loving nature, it has an extremely power-ful effect on me — like the world's biggest laser firing straight into my eyes.** Ты так прекра́сна физи́чески, и когда́ э́то накла́дывается на твою́ не́жную, тёплую, забо́т-ливую, лю́бящую нату́ру, э́то ока́зывает осо́бо могу́щественное де́йствие на меня́, как бу́дто наибо́льший в ми́ре ла́зер све́тит пря́мо в мои́ глаза́. ♦ **You have a very passionate nature.** У тебя́ о́чень стра́стная нату́ра.

nature: *the kind of nature I seek*

My heart yearns so fiercely to have a partner like you in life, one who combines a gentle spirit with sexuality, good-heartedness, intelligence, and a loving nature. Моё се́рдце так нени́стово жа́ждет тако́го спу́тника жи́зни, как ты, тако́го, кто соединя́ет мя́г-кий хара́ктер с сексуа́льностью, добросерде́чием, интеллиге́нтностью и лю́бящей нату́рой.

nature: *we're alike in nature*

You and I are incredibly alike in the nature and intensity of our feelings. Мы с тобо́й невероя́тно похо́жи хара́ктером и интенси́вностью на́ших чувств.

nature: *my nature*

I have a very passionate nature. У меня́ о́чень стра́стная нату́ра.

nature: *the nature of people and relationships*

That's the nature of *(1)* **men /** *(2)* **women.** Такова́ су́щность *(1)* мужчи́н / *(2)* же́нщин. ♦ **I believe in the reciprocal nature of a relationship.** Я ве́рю во взаи́мность в отноше́-ниях. ♦ **You can't overlook the reciprocal nature of a relationship.** В отноше́ниях нельзя́ пренебрега́ть взаи́мностью.

nature: *Mother Nature*

You have a whole lot of nature going for you. Тебе́ о́чень мно́го дано́ от приро́ды. ♦ *(1)* **Let's let... /** *(2)* **We'll just let... nature take its course.** *(1)* Дава́й позво́лим... / *(2)* Мы то́лько позво́лим... приро́де идти́ свои́м есте́ственным путём.

nature-oriented *adj*: ♦ **be** ~ интересова́ться приро́дой.

naturist *n* нуди́ст.

naughty *adj* 1. *(mischievous)* шаловли́вый, -ая, -ое, -ые, озорно́й, -а́я, -о́е, -ы́е, непослу́ш-ный, -ая, -ое, -ые; 2. *(risque)* риско́ванный, -ая, -ое, -ые, пика́нтный, -ая, -ое, -ые.

navel *n* пупо́к, пуп.

navy *n* вое́нно-морско́й флот ♦ **I'm in the Navy.** Я в вое́нно-морско́м фло́те. ♦ **I'm** *(1)* **a Petty Officer /** *(2)* **an Ensign /** *(3) etc* **in the Navy.** Я *(1)* у́нтер-офице́р / *(2)* лейтена́нт / *(3) и т.д.)* вое́нно-морско́го фло́та. ♦ **I served four years in the Navy.** Я служи́л четы́ре го́да в вое́нно-морско́м фло́те.

near *adv* бли́зко, ря́дом, вблизи́ ♦ **I am full to bursting with the joy of being near you.** Я про́сто взрыва́юсь от ра́дости, когда́ ты ря́дом.

near-naked *adj* полуобнажённый, -ая, -ое, -ые.

Russian terms of endearment are given in Appendix 13, page 780.

nearsighted *adj* близору́кий, -ая, -ое, -ие.

neat *adj* аккура́тный, -ая, -ое, -ые ♦ ~ **and tidy** аккура́тный, -ая, -ое, -ые.

necessary *adj* необходи́мый, -ая, -ое, -ые; ну́жный, -ая, -ое, -ые *(short forms:* ну́жен, нужна́, ну́жно, нужны́*)* ♦ **It's (not) necessary.** Это (не) ну́жно.

neck *vi (slang)* целова́ться.

neck *n* ше́я ♦ **beautiful** ~ краси́вая ше́я ♦ **delicate** ~ хру́пкая ше́я ♦ **finely shaped** ~ точёная ше́я ♦ **graceful** ~ точёная ше́я ♦ **little** ~ ше́йка ♦ **long** ~ дли́нная ше́я ♦ **lovely** ~ преле́стная ше́йка ♦ **scoop** ~ *(of a dress)* дово́льно ни́зкий, кру́глый вы́рез (спе́реди) *(пла́тья)* ♦ **short** ~ коро́ткая ше́я ♦ **slender** ~ то́нкая ше́я ♦ **soft white** ~ мя́гкая бе́лая ше́я ♦ **thin** ~ худа́я ше́я ♦ **white** ~ белосне́жная ше́йка ♦ **your** ~ *(familiar)* твоя́ ше́я; *(polite)* Ва́ша ше́я.

> ### *neck: phrases*

I long to adore the tender grace of your neck with my lips. Я стра́стно хочу́ ощути́ть не́жную грацио́зность твое́й ше́и свои́ми губа́ми. ♦ **As my hand cups the fullness of your breast, my mouth will cover your beautiful face and smooth neck with adoring kisses.** В то вре́мя, как моя́ рука́ ощути́т полноту́ твое́й груди́, мой рот покро́ет твоё прекра́сное лицо́ и не́жную ше́ю обожа́ющими поцелу́ями. ♦ **I want to nuzzle my face against your neck.** Я хочу́ прижа́ться лицо́м к твое́й ше́е. ♦ **How nice it would be to bury my face in your neck and let my lips run wild.** Как прия́тно бы́ло бы зары́ться лицо́м в твое́й ше́е и дать во́лю губа́м.

necklace *n* ожере́лье; *(beads)* бу́сы *pl* ♦ **What a** *(1)* **beautiful** / *(2)* **lovely necklace (you have)!** Что за *(1,2)* прекра́сное ожере́лье (у тебя́)!

neckline *n* вы́рез *(пла́тья)* ♦ **alluring** ~ *(of a dress)* соблазни́тельный вы́рез (пла́тья) ♦ *(1,2)* **low-cut** ~ *(1)* глубо́кий / *(2)* ни́зкий вы́рез ♦ **plunging** ~ глубо́кий вы́рез ♦ **I loved the plunging neckline of the gown you wore that night.** Мне нра́вился глубо́кий вы́рез пла́тья, в кото́ром ты была́ в тот ве́чер. ♦ **No one looks as** *(1)* **voluptuous** / *(2)* **beautiful** / *(3)* **awesome with a plunging neckline as you do.** Никто́ не вы́глядит так *(1)* роско́шно / *(2)* прекра́сно / *(3)* потряса́юще в пла́тье с глубо́ким вы́резом, как ты.

nectar *n* 1. некта́р; 2. цвето́чный сок, медо́к ♦ ~ **of the gods** боже́ственный некта́р ♦ **sweet** ~ сла́дкий некта́р ♦ **Your love and devotion are the nectar and ambrosia for my soul.** Твои́ любо́вь и пре́данность -- некта́р и амбро́зия для мое́й души́. ♦ **Imagine that you're a flower filled with nectar and I'm the world's thirstiest hummingbird.** Предста́вь, что ты цвето́к, по́лный некта́ра, и я истомлённейший жа́ждой ко́либри. ♦ **I long for the sweet nectar of your kisses.** Я тоску́ю по сла́дкому некта́ру твои́х поцелу́ев.

need *vt* нужда́ться *(what* = + в + *prep.),* ну́жен, нужна́, -о, -ы *(I need:* мне ну́жен, нужна́, -о, -ы. *You need:* тебе́ ну́жен, нужна́, -о, -ы) *(the thing needed is the subject, the one who needs is in the dative case).*

> ### *need: phrases*

I need you *(Lit.: You are needed to me.)* (*[1]*...**desperately.** / *[2]* ...**very much.** / *[3]* ...**more than anything.** / *[4]* ...**as never before.** / *[5]* ...**every day and in every way.** / *[6]* ... **like I need air to live.**) Ты нужна́ *(ж: ну́жен)* мне (*[1]*...до отча́яния. / *[2]* ...о́чень-о́чень. / *[3]* ...бо́льше всего́ на све́те. / *[4]* ..., как никогда́ пре́жде. / *[5]* ...всегда́ и везде́. / *[6]* ..., как во́здух.) ♦ **All I need to make me happy is you.** Всё, что мне ну́жно для сча́стья, э́то ты. ♦ **If you only knew how much I need you (and want you).** Е́сли б ты то́лько зна́ла *(ж: знал),* как ты нужна́ *(ж: ну́жен)* мне (и как я хочу́ тебя́). ♦ **I need an affectionate, loving person with lots of hugs and kisses to give.** Мне ну́жен не́жный, лю́бящий челове́к, даря́щий мно́жество объя́тий и поцелу́ев. ♦ **I will always be here**

> *Some of the Russian sentences are translations of things we say and are not what Russians themselves would normally say.*

when(ever) you need me. Когда́ бы я ни был ну́жен *(ж: была́ нужна́)* тебе́, я всегда́ бу́ду ря́дом. ♦ **I need your** *(1)* **...warmth (and softness).** / *(2)* **...tenderness.** / *(3)* **...hardness.** / *(4)* **...love.** Мне нужна́ твоя́ *(1)* теплота́ (и мя́кость). / *(2)* не́жность. / *(3)* твёрдость. / *(4)* любо́вь. ♦ **I need your beautiful body.** Мне ну́жно твоё прекра́сное те́ло. ♦ **I need your** *(1)* **...kisses (like I need air to breathe).** / *(2)* **...caresses.** / *(3)* **...arms around me.** Мне нужны́ твои́ *(1)* поцелу́и (, как во́здух). / *(2)* ла́ски. / *(3)* объя́тия. ♦ **I don't need anything from you.** Мне ничего́ от тебя́ не на́до.

need *n* нужда́, потре́бность *f* ♦ **burning** ~ горя́чее жела́ние ♦ **~s and desires** ну́жды и жела́ния ♦ **primitive aching** ~ инстинкти́вное боле́зненное жела́ние ♦ **primitive** ~ примити́вное жела́ние ♦ **unfulfilled sexual ~s** неосуществлённые сексуа́льные жела́ния ♦ **urgent** ~ безотлага́тельное жела́ние.

---
need: desire

My entire being is *(1)* **assailed** / *(2)* **tormented by the all-consuming need to take you in my arms and revel in the reservoir of your passion.** Я весь *(1)* охва́чен / *(2)* изму́чен всепоглоща́ющей жа́ждой заключи́ть тебя́ в объя́тия и упива́ться твое́й стра́стью. ♦ **My mouth is going to do its fervent work on you until the need to surrender invades your whole body.** Мой рот бу́дет де́лать свою́ пы́лкую рабо́ту до тех пор, пока́ потре́бность капитули́ровать ни наводни́т всё твоё те́ло. ♦ **I want to kiss you and kiss you and kiss you until all your senses are aflame with need.** Я хочу́ целова́ть тебя́, целова́ть и целова́ть до тех пор, пока́ все твои́ чу́вства не погру́зятся в ого́нь жела́ния.

---
need: your / my needs

Your needs and desires *(1)* **...are...** / *(2)* **...will always be... my** *(3)* **central** / *(4)* **main priority.** Твои́ ну́жды и жела́ния *(1)* -- мои́ *(3,4)* гла́вные приорите́ты. / *(2)* ...всегда́ бу́дут мои́ми *(3,4)* гла́вными приорите́тами. ♦ *(1)* **I'll be...** / *(2)* **I pledge myself to be... a slave to all your needs and desires.** *(1)* Я бу́ду... / *(2)* Я обязу́юсь быть... рабо́м всех твои́х нужд и жела́ний. ♦ **I want to do everything I (possibly) can to fulfill your needs and desires.** Я хочу́ де́лать всё, что в мои́х си́лах для исполне́ния твои́х нужд и жела́ний. ♦ **It would be nice if you would show a little more sensitivity to my needs.** Бы́ло бы так хорошо́, е́сли бы ты вы́казала *(ж: вы́казал)* немно́го бо́льше понима́ния мои́х потре́бностей. ♦ **I would be so attentive, so focused on your needs and desires and likes and dislikes.** Я был бы так внима́телен, так сосредото́чен на твои́х ну́ждах и жела́ниях, и на том, что ты лю́бишь и что не лю́бишь. ♦ *(1)* **He** / *(2)* **She is very inattentive to my needs.** *(1)* Он о́чень невнима́телен... / *(2)* Она́ о́чень невнима́тельна... к мои́м жела́ниям. ♦ **I'm a man who is sensitive to a woman's needs.** Я мужчи́на, кото́рый обраща́ет внима́ние на же́нские потре́бности.

needie *n, pl (slang) (person in need)* нужда́ющийся, -аяся, -иеся.

needle *vt (taunt, tease)* язви́ть, дразни́ть *(whom = acc.)* ♦ **I'm sorry, I don't mean to needle you (about that).** Прости́, я не ду́мал *(ж: ду́мала)* насмеха́ться над тобо́й (за э́то).

neglect *vt* 1. *(not pay proper attention to)* пренебрега́ть *(what, whom = instr.)*; не забо́титься *(what, whom = + о + prep.)*; 2. *(forget, fail to)* забыва́ть / забы́ть *(what, whom = acc.)*, упуска́ть / упусти́ть и́з виду *(what, whom = acc.)* ♦ **I feel terrible about the way I've neglected you.** Я о́чень сожале́ю, что я так пренебрега́л *(ж: пренебрега́ла)* тобо́й.

neglected *adj* забы́тый, -ая, -ое, -ые.

negligee *n* неглиже́ *neut* ♦ **black** ~ чёрное неглиже́ ♦ **lace** ~ кружевно́й пеньюа́р ♦ **red** ~ кра́сное неглиже́ ♦ **see-through** ~ прозра́чное неглиже́ ♦ **semi-transparent** ~ полупрозра́чный пеньюа́р ♦ **I love to watch you walk around in your (see-through) negligee.** Я люблю́ наблюда́ть, как ты хо́дишь в своём (прозра́чном) неглиже́. ♦ **I love it when**

Counting things in Russian is a bit involved.
See Appendix 4, Numbers, on page 756 .

you wear a (see-through) **negligee.** Я люблю́, когда́ ты надева́ешь (прозра́чное) неглиже́.

neo-animist *adj* нео-аними́ст.

nephew *n* племя́нник.

nerd *n (slang)* 1. *(dim-wit)* тупи́ца, болва́н; 2. *(too scholarly)* челове́к, сли́шком лю́бящий нау́ку *(1 term).*

nerve *n* 1. *(anatomy)* нерв; 2. *(courage)* прису́тствие ду́ха, му́жество; 3. *(impudence)* на́-глость.

> **nerve: nervous system**

I'm a bundle of nerves. Я-- клубо́к не́рвов.

> **nerve: courage**

I finally found the nerve (to *[1]* call / *[2]* write you). В конце́ концо́в я набра́лся ду́ха *([1]* позвони́ть / *[2]* написа́ть тебе́). ♦ **I didn't have the nerve (to *[1]* call / *[2]* tell you).** Я не набра́лся ду́ха *([1]* позвони́ть / *[2]* сказа́ть тебе́).

> **nerve: impudence**

You (really) have a lot of nerve (*[1]* ...to tell me that. / *[2]* ...to say that. / *[3]* ...to come here. / *[4]* ...to do that.) У тебя́ (действи́тельно) мно́го на́глости *([1]* ...рассказа́ть мне э́то. / *[2]* ...сказа́ть э́то. / *[3]* ...прийти́ сюда́. / *[4]* ...сде́лать э́то.).

> **nerve: sensitive spot**

What you *(1)* said / *(2)* wrote really *(3,4)* touched a nerve. То, что ты *(1)* сказа́ла *(ж: сказа́л)* / *(2)* написа́ла *(ж: написа́л)*, действи́тельно *(3)* расстра́ивает / *(4)* волну́ет.

nervous *adj* не́рвный, -ая, -ое, -ые, нерво́зный, -ая, -ое, -ые ♦ **be** ~ не́рвничать; беспоко́иться, волнова́ться ♦ **feel** ~ не́рвничать; беспоко́иться, волнова́ться ♦ **make** *(1)* **me** / *(2)* **you** ~ раздража́ть *(1)* меня́ / *(2)* тебя́, нерви́ровать *(1)* меня́ / *(2)* тебя́.

> **nervous: phrases**

Why are you so *(1,2)* nervous? Почему́ ты так *(1)* не́рвничаешь / *(2)* беспоко́ишься? ♦ **Don't be *(1,2)* nervous.** Не *(1)* не́рвничай / *(2)* беспоко́йся. ♦ **You don't have to be *(1,2)* nervous.** Не на́до *(1)* не́рвничать / *(2)* беспоко́иться. ♦ **There's nothing to be nervous about.** Не о чём беспоко́иться. ♦ **I'm (not) nervous (about it.** Я (не) беспоко́юсь (об э́том).

nervously *adv* не́рвно.

nervousness *n* 1. *(anxiety, timidity)* боязли́вость *f*, ро́бость *f*; 2. *(physical)* не́рвность *f*.

nest *n* гнездо́, гнёздышко ♦ **cozy** ~ ую́тное гнёздышко ♦ **curly** ~ **of hair** кудря́вое гнёздышко волос ♦ **golden** ~ золото́е гнёздышко ♦ **secret** ~ заве́тное гнёздышко ♦ **That's going to be our love nest for the next 4 weeks.** Это бу́дет на́шим любо́вным гнёздыш-ком на ближа́йшие четы́ре неде́ли. ♦ **We're going to make that (place) our love nest.** Мы сде́лаем э́то (ме́сто) на́шим любо́вным гнёздышком. ♦ **I want to go to some secluded place and make a love nest together with you.** Я хочу́ отпра́виться в не́кое уединённое ме́сто и постро́ить любо́вное гнёздышко с тобо́й.

nester *n (slang) (someone who likes homelife)* домосе́д ♦ **empty** ~ *(parent whose children have grown up and left home)* роди́тель, у кото́рого де́ти вы́росли и оста́вили дом *(explanation).*

nestle *vi* льнуть / прильну́ть *(to or against whom = + к + dat.)*, прижима́ться / прижа́ться *(to or against whom = + к + dat.)* ♦ **How absolutely wonderful it would be to climb between the sheets to nestle against your warm, soft, luscious body.** Как замеча́тельно бы́ло бы зале́зть ме́жду простыня́ми и прильну́ть к твоему́ тёплому, мя́гкому, со́чному те́лу. ♦ **To have you nestled snugly in my arms is my constant dream.** Моя́ постоя́нная мечта́ -- ты, ую́тно устро́ившаяся в мои́х объя́тиях.

> *Russian has 2 different vrbs for "go",*
> *one for "on foot" and the other for "by vehicle".*

net *n* сеть *f* ♦ **seductive** ~ обольстительная сеть.

neurosis *n* невроз.

neurotic *adj* невротический, -ая, -ое, ие, нервный, -ая, -ое, -ые ♦ **slightly** ~ слегка нервный.

never *adv* никогда.

never-ending *adj* никогда не кончающийся, -аяся, -еся, -иеся, бесконечный, -ая, -ое, -ые ♦ **I want fill your life with never-ending bliss.** Я хочу наполнить твою жизнь бесконечным блаженством.

new *adj* новый, -ая, -ое, -ые.

newfound *adj* вновь обретённый, -ая, -ое, -ые.

newlywed *adj* новобрачный, -ая, -ое, -ые.

newlyweds *n, pl* новобрачные, молодожёны.

newness *n* новизна.

next *adj* 1. *(next after preceding)* следующий, -ая, -ее, -ие; 2. *(next in time)* следующий, -ая, -ее, -ие, будущий, -ая, -ее, -ие.

nibble *vt* покусывать *(what = acc.)* ♦ ~ **eagerly** исступлённо покусывать ♦ **I love to kiss, hug, caress, touch, hold hands, nibble, cuddle, rub against, stroke — you just name it.** Я люблю целовать, обнимать, ласкать, касаться, держаться за руки, покусывать, сжимать в объятиях, тереться, гладить, ты только назови. ♦ **I want to nibble on your** *(1)* **breast** / *(2)* **neck** / *(3)* **ear.** Я хочу покусывать губами *(1)* ...твою грудь / *(2)* шею / *(3)* ...твоё ухо. ♦ **Your (cute little) ears are just pleading to be nibbled.** Твои (изящные маленькие) ушки прямо взывают к покусыванию.

nibbling *n (with the lips)* покусывание (губами) *(Note: better to use verb* покусывать) ♦ **I like nibbling on your** *(1)* **breast** / *(2)* **neck** / *(3)* **ear.** Мне нравится покусывать губами *(1)* ...твою грудь / *(2)* шею / *(3)* ...твоё ухо.

nice *adj* 1. *(good, pleasant)* хороший, -ая, -ее, -ие приятный, -ая, -ое, -ые милый, -ая, -ое, -ые, симпатичный, -ая, -ое, -ые; 2. *(polite)* любезный, -ая, -ое, -ые ♦ **How nice.** Как приятно. ♦ **You're a very easy** *(1)* **woman** / *(2)* **girl to be nice to.** Ты *(1)* женщина / *(2)* девушка, с которой легко быть милым. ♦ **You're a very easy** *(1)* **man** / *(2)* **guy to be nice to.** Ты *(1)* мужчина / *(2)* парень, с которым легко быть милой. ♦ **You're a very easy person to be nice to.** Ты человек, с которым легко быть милым *(ж: милой)*. ♦ **Nice and easy does it every time.** Медленно и спокойно -- каждый раз успешно.

nice-looking *adj* симпатичный, -ая, -ое, -ые, миловидный, -ая, -ое, -ые, привлекательный, -ая, -ое, -ые; *(f:)* славненькая.

niche *n* 1. *(recess)* ниша 2. *(haven)* приют; *(secluded place)* укромное место ♦ *(1,2)* **secluded** ~ *(1)* укромное / *(2)* уединённое место.

nickname *n* прозвище, уменьшительное имя.

niece *n* племянница.

night *n* ночь *f*; *(evening)* вечер ♦ **entire** ~ целая ночь ♦ **every** ~ каждую ночь ♦ *(1,2)* **exciting** ~**s** *(1)* великолепные / *(2)* прекрасные ночи ♦ **Friday (etc.)** ~ *(night)* в пятницу ночью; *(evening)* в пятницу вечером ♦ **lonely** ~**s** одинокие ночи ♦ **long** ~**s** долгие ночи ♦ **love-filled** ~**s** ночи, наполненные любовью *(1 term)* ♦ **mad** ~**s** безумные ночи ♦ **idyllic** ~**s** идиллические ночи ♦ **last** ~ *(night)* прошлой ночью; *(evening)* вчера вечером ♦ **memorable** ~ памятная ночь ♦ **moonless** ~ безлунная ночь ♦ **moonlit** ~ лунная ночь ♦ ~ **after** ~ ночь за ночью ♦ **passion-filled** ~**s** ночи, наполненные страстью *(1 term)* ♦ **quiet** ~ тихая ночь ♦ **quiet** ~**s** *(evenings)* спокойные вечера ♦ **sleepless** ~**s** бессонные ночи ♦ **starry** ~ звёздная ночь ♦ **summer** ~ летняя ночь ♦ **tomorrow** ~ *(night)* завтра ночью; *(evening)* завтра вечером ♦ **warm** ~**s** тёплые ночи ♦ **winter** ~**s**

Dipthongs in Russian are made by adding й
*to the end of a vowel (*а, е, ё, о, у, э, ю, *and* я*).*

зимние но́чи ♦ **whole ~** це́лая ночь ♦ **at ~** но́чью ♦ **during the ~** но́чью ♦ **in the ~** но́чью ♦ **spend the ~** проводи́ть / провести́ ночь.

night: *lonely nights*

I spend these long, lonely nights yearning and burning for *(1)* **...your soft, luscious warmth.** / *(2)* **...the warm, wonderful, heavenly magic of your beautiful body.** Я провожу́ э́ти до́лгие, одино́кие но́чи, сгора́я и тоску́я по *(1)* ...твоему́ мя́гкому, ла́сковому теплу́. / *(2)* ...тёплой, удиви́тельной, ра́йской ма́гии твоего́ прекра́сного те́ла. ♦ **The nights are so (***[1]* **agonizingly /** *[2]* **torturously /** *[3]* **dreadfully /** *[4]* **terribly) lonely without you.** Но́чи так (*[1,2]* мучи́тельно / *[3]* ужа́сно / *[4]* стра́шно) одино́ки без тебя́. ♦ **I've spent so many lonely nights.** Я провёл *(ж: провела́)* так мно́го одино́ких ноче́й.

night: *nights together*

We could have such idyllic days and nights together. У нас могло́ бы быть мно́го идилли́ческих ноче́й. ♦ **One night together with you is** *(1)* **...all I could ask from God /** *(2)* **Heaven.** / *(3)* **...the pinnacle /** *(4)* **apex of my** *(5)* **dreams /** *(6)* **desires.** Одна́ ночь вме́сте с тобо́й *(1)* ...всё, что я могу́ проси́ть у Бо́га / *(2)* небе́с. / *(3,4)* ...верши́на мои́х *(5)* мечта́ний / *(6)* жела́ний. ♦ **One night together with you, and there is nothing** *(1)* **else /** *(2)* **more I could** *(3)* **...want. /** *(4)* **...ask for.** Одна́ ночь с тобо́й, и не́чего *(1)* ещё / *(2)* бо́льше *(3)* жела́ть / *(4)* проси́ть. ♦ **I like late nights on the town.** Мне нра́вятся по́здние но́чи в го́роде. ♦ *(1)* **Last /** *(2)* **That night (with you) was** *(3)* **fantastic /** *(4)* **heavenly /** *(5)* **wonderful**. *(1)* Про́шлая / *(2)* Эта ночь (с тобо́й) была́ *(3)* фантасти́ческой / *(4)* боже́ственной / *(5)* великоле́пной. ♦ **We could spend quiet nights at home.** Мы смо́жем проводи́ть споко́йные вечера́ до́ма.

night: *sleepless nights*

You've caused me so many sleepless nights. Из-за тебя́ я провёл *(ж: провела́)* так мно́го бессо́нных ноче́й. ♦ **I've spent (so) many sleepless nights** *(1)* **...thinking about you.** / *(2)* **...asking myself why you broke up with me.** / *(3)* **...wondering why you went away.** Я провёл *(ж: провела́)* (так) мно́го бессо́нных ноче́й *(1)* ...ду́мая о тебе́. / *(2)* ...спра́шивая себя́, почему́ ты порва́ла *(ж: порва́л)* со мной. / *(3)* ...пыта́ясь поня́ть, почему́ ты ушла́ *(ж: ушёл)*.

night: *the night is young*

The night is young (and you're so beautiful). Ночь то́лько начала́сь (и ты так прекра́сна).

nightgown *n* ночна́я руба́шка ♦ **satin ~** атла́сная ночна́я руба́шка.

nightie *n* (коро́ткая) ночна́я руба́шка ♦ **flannel ~** флане́левая ночна́я руба́шка ♦ **peekaboo ~** прозра́чная ночна́я руба́шка ♦ **silk ~** шёлковая ночна́я руба́шка.

nightlife *n* ночна́я жизнь.

nightmare *n* кошма́р.

nightmarish *adj* кошма́рный, -ая, -ое, -ые.

night owl *n* полуно́чник.

nighttime *n* ночно́е вре́мя.

nimble *adj* ло́вкий, -ая, -ое, -ие.

nipple *n* сосо́к, сосо́чек, буто́н ♦ **beautiful ~s** краси́вые сосо́чки ♦ **big ~s** больши́е сосо́чки ♦ **nice ~s** краси́вые сосо́чки ♦ **rosy ~s** ро́зовые сосо́чки ♦ **sweet ~s** сла́дкие сосо́чки ♦ **rim around the ~** *(areola)* околососко́вый кружо́к.

nipple: *phrases*

I *(1)* **love /** *(2)* **want to gently caress your breasts, lingering on the nipples.** Я *(1)* люблю́ / *(2)* хочу́ не́жно ласка́ть твою́ грудь, заде́рживаясь на соска́х. ♦ **I** *(1)* **love /** *(2)* **want to gently suck on your nipples.** Я *(1)* люблю́ / *(2)* хочу́ не́жно соса́ть твои́ соски́. ♦ **As**

Some phrases are listed under more than one main word.

my lips pay devoted homage to your nipples, my fingers will blaze a trail over your burning skin. В то вре́мя, как мои́ гу́бы ока́жут почти́тельное внима́ние твои́м соска́м, мои́ па́льцы бу́дут прокла́дывать о́гненный путь по твое́й ко́же. ♦ **...as I lovingly massage your breast and tug at your nipples with my lips.** ...в то вре́мя, как я любо́вно масси́рую твою́ грудь и потя́гиваю со́ски губа́ми.

noble *adj* благоро́дный, -ая, -ое, -ые.

noble-minded *adj* благоро́дный, -ая, -ое, -ые, великоду́шный, -ая, -ое, -ые.

nobody *pron* никто́ ♦ **There is nobody (else) (in my life) except you.** (В мое́й жи́зни) Нет никого́ кро́ме тебя́.

nocturnal *adj* ночно́й, -а́я, -о́е, -ы́е.

nomadic *adj* кочево́й, -а́я, -о́е, -ы́е.

non-career-minded *adj* не интересу́ющийся (-аяся, -ееся, -иеся) карье́рой **I'm looking for a woman who is non-career-minded.** Я ищу́ же́нщину, не интересу́ющуюся карье́рой.

nonchalance *n* беспе́чность *f*, беззабо́тность *f*.

nonchalant *adj* беспе́чный, -ая, -ое, -ые, беззабо́тный, -ая, -ое, -ые.

nonchalantly *adv* беспе́чно, беззабо́тно.

noncommital *adj* укло́нчивый, -ая, -ое, -ые.

nonconforming *adj* инакомы́слящий, -ая, -ее, -ие.

nonconformist *n* инакомы́слящий, -ая, -ие, инакове́рующий, -ая, -ие.

non-conservative *adj* либера́льный, -ая, -ое, -ые.

nondate *n* неромантти́ческая встре́ча.

nondrinker *n* непью́щий *m*, -ая *f*, -ие *pl* .

non-flaky *adj* 1. *(good character)* с хоро́шим хара́ктером; 2. *(mentally stable, normal)* норма́льный, -ая, -ое, -ые; 3. *(reliable)* надёжный, -ая, -ое, -ые.

nonjudgmental *adj* неосужда́ющий, -ая, -ее, -ие, не скло́нный (-ая, -ое, -ые) суди́ть други́х ♦ **I'm a non-judgmental person.** Я не скло́нен *(ж: скло́нна)* суди́ть други́х.

nonmaterialistic *adj* нематериалисти́ческий, -ая, -ое, -ие

no-nonsense *adj* стро́гий, -ая, -ое, -ие, тре́бовательный, -ая, -ое, -ые ♦ ~ **attitude** стро́гое отноше́ние.

nonpromiscuous *adj* не развра́тный, -ая, -ое, -ые, нераспу́щенный, -ая, -ое, -ые.

non-repulsive *adj* неомерзи́тельный, -ая, -ое, -ые, небезобра́зный, -ая, -ое, -ые.

nonsense *n* чепуха́ ♦ **utter** ~ соверше́нная чепуха́.

nonsmoker *n* некуря́щий *m*, -ая *f*, -ие *pl*.

non-vegetarian *n* не вегетариа́нец *m*, не вегетариа́нка *f*.

no one *pron* никто́ ♦ **There is no one (else) (in my life) except you.** (В мое́й жи́зни) нет никого́ кро́ме тебя́.

Nordic *adj* норди́ческий, -ая, -ое, -ие.

normal *adj* норма́льный, -ая, -ое, -ые ♦ **reasonably** ~ доста́точно норма́льный, -ая, -ое, -ые.

Norwegian *adj* норве́жский, -ая, -ое, -ие.

Norwegian *n* 1. *(person)* норве́жец *m*, норве́жка *f (pl:* норве́жцы*)*; 2. *(language)* норве́жский язы́к ♦ **speak** ~ говори́ть по-норве́жски.

nose *n* нос ♦ **aquiline** ~ орли́ный нос ♦ **arched** ~ горба́тый нос, нос с горби́нкой ♦ **Asian** ~ восто́чный нос ♦ **beautiful** ~ краси́вый нос ♦ **big** ~ большо́й нос ♦ **broad** ~ широ́кий нос ♦ **broken** ~ разби́тый нос ♦ **button** ~ нос-пу́говка ♦ **delicate** ~ то́нкий нос ♦ **elegant** ~ изя́щный но́сик ♦ **flat** ~ пло́ский нос ♦ **little** ~ ма́ленький нос, но́сик ♦ **long** ~ дли́нный нос ♦ **oriental** ~ восто́чный нос ♦ **pert** ~ де́рзкий нос ♦ **petite** ~ ма́ленький

The singular past tense of Russian verbs ends in -л (m) (usually), -ла (f) or -ло (n). the plural past tense ends in -li.

нос ♦ **pointed** ~ о́стрый нос ♦ **Roman** ~ ри́мский нос ♦ **short** ~ коро́ткий нос ♦ **slender** ~ то́нкий нос ♦ **slim patrician** ~ небольшо́й аристократи́ческий нос ♦ **small** ~ ма́ленький нос ♦ **snub** ~ вздёрнутый нос ♦ **straight** ~ прямо́й нос ♦ **turned-up** ~ курно́сый нос, слегка́ приподня́тый нос ♦ **upturned** ~ курно́сый нос, слегка́ приподня́тый нос ♦ **tip of your** ~ ко́нчик твоего́ но́са.

nose: phrases

I don't mean to poke my nose into your (personal) business. Я не хочу́ сова́ть свой нос в твои́ (ли́чные) дела́. ♦ **Forgive me for poking my nose into your (personal) business.** Прости́ меня́ за то, что сова́л *(ж: сова́ла)* свой нос в твои́ (ли́чные) дела́.

nostril *n* ноздря́.

note *n* запи́ска ♦ **brief** ~ кра́ткая запи́ска ♦ **important** ~ ва́жная запи́ска ♦ **little** ~ ма́ленькая запи́ска ♦ **love** ~ любо́вная запи́ска ♦ **precious** ~ драгоце́нная запи́ска ♦ **short** ~ кра́ткая запи́ска ♦ **leave a** ~ оставля́ть / оста́вить запи́ску ♦ **write** *(1)* me / *(2)* you a ~ писа́ть / написа́ть *(1)* мне / *(2)* тебе́ запи́ску. ♦ **I** *(1)* **got** / *(2)* **found** / *(3)* **read your (precious) note.** Я получи́л *(ж: получи́ла)* / нашёл *(ж: нашла́)* / прочита́л *(ж: прочита́ла)* твою́ (драгоце́нную) запи́ску.

nothing ничего́ ♦ *(1-3)* **sweet ~s** *(1)* не́жности, *(2)* не́жные / *(3)* сла́дкие слова́ ♦ **I want to lie next to you and whisper sweet nothings in your ear.** Я хочу́ лежа́ть ря́дом с тобо́й и шепта́ть не́жные слова́ в твоё у́хо. ♦ **Nothing ventured, nothing gained.** Волко́в боя́ться -- в лес не ходи́ть.

notice *vt* замеча́ть / заме́тить *(what, whom = acc.)* ♦ **From the first moment I noticed you, I wanted to meet you.** С пе́рвой мину́ты, когда́ я заме́тил *(ж: заме́тила)* тебя́, я хоте́л *(ж: хоте́ла)* познако́миться с тобо́й. ♦ **How could I not notice you? You're so beautiful.** Как я мог тебя́ не заме́тить? Ты так прекра́сна. ♦ **I noticed you on the subway** *(metro). (See page 763 for other places.)* Я заме́тил *(ж: заме́тила)* тебя́ в метро́. ♦ **I couldn't help but notice your ad. You're exceptionally lovely.** Я не мог не заме́тить твоего́ объявле́ния. Ты исключи́тельно краси́ва.

notion *n* поня́тие, представле́ние ♦ **You have the wrong notion about me.** У тебя́ ло́жное представле́ние обо мне. ♦ **What gave you that notion?** Отку́да у тебя́ тако́е мне́ние?

nourish *vt* пита́ть *(what, whom = acc., with what = instr, for whom = + к + dat..)*, леле́ять *(what = acc., for whom = + к + dat.)*.

nourish: phrases

You nourish my soul with your *(1)* **...thoughtfulness** / *(2)* **sweetness** / *(3)* **good-heartedness.** / *(4)* **...loving ways.** Ты пита́ешь мою́ ду́шу *(1)* ...свои́м внима́нием. / *(2)* ...свое́й не́жностью. / *(3)* добросерде́чностью. / *(4)* любо́вью. ♦ **This brief missive conveys only an iota of the affection that I nourish in my heart for you.** Это коро́ткое письмо́ несёт то́лько ма́лую то́лику той любви́ к тебе́, кото́рой полно́ моё се́рдце. ♦ **I want a relationship that will nourish my soul.** Я хочу́ отноше́ний, кото́рые бу́дут пита́ть мою́ ду́шу. ♦ **Your** *(1)* **sweet** / *(2)* **wonderful love nourishes my soul.** Твоя́ *(1)* не́жная / *(2)* замеча́тельная любо́вь пита́ет мою́ ду́шу.

nourishment *n* пита́ние, пи́ща ♦ *(1)* **You are...** / *(2)* **Your love is... the nourishment of my soul.** *(1)* Ты... / *(2)* Твоя́ любо́вь... -- пи́ща для мое́й души́.

novelty *n* новизна́.

now *adv* сейча́с, тепе́рь ♦ **~ and then** времена́ми, вре́мя от вре́мени, иногда́ ♦ **right** ~ сейча́с.

nub *n* ши́шечка, утолще́ние, буто́н ♦ **crimson** ~ пунцо́вый буто́н ♦ **soft** ~ не́жный буто́н ♦ **I'm going to make those rosy nubs on your breasts pulsate with pleasure.** Я заста́влю э́ти ро́зовые ши́шечки твои́х груде́й пульси́ровать от наслажде́ния.

Please do us a favor:
Fill out and mail in the Feedback Sheet on page 795.

Nubian *n* нуби́ец *m*, нуби́йка *f.*

nubile *adj (girl)* дости́гшая бра́чного во́зраста, созре́вшая.

nude *adj* го́лый, -ая, -ое, -ые, наго́й, -а́я, -о́е, -и́е, обнажённый, -ая, -ое, -ые ◆ **I love it when you're completely nude.** Я люблю́, когда́ ты абсолю́тно нага́я / го́лая. ◆ **I want to** *(1)* **...take a photo...** */ (1)* **...paint a picture... of you lying nude (on a** *[1]* **couch** */ [2]* **bed).** Я хочу́ *(1)* ...сфотографи́ровать тебя́... */ (2)* ...нарисова́ть тебя́... лежа́щей обнажённой (на *[1]* дива́не / *[2]* посте́ли).

nude *n* нагота́ ◆ **in the** ~ нагишо́м ◆ **Would you pose in the** *(1,2)* **nude for me (sometime)?** Не попози́руешь ли ты мне *(1)* обнажённой / *(2)* наго́й (когда́ -нибу́дь)?

nudism *n* нуди́зм.

nudist *n* нуди́ст *m*, нуди́стка *f.*

numb *adj* 1. 1. *(emotionally)* оцепене́лый, -ая, -ое, -ые; ошеломлённый, -ая, -ое, -ые; 2. *(from cold)* окочене́лый, -ая, -ое, -ые ◆ **be(come)** ~ 1. *(emotionally)* оцепене́ть; 2. *(from cold)* окочене́ть ◆ **I'm too numb to talk (about it).** Я сли́шком ошеломлён *(ж: ошеломлена́)*, что́бы говори́ть (об э́том).

number *n* 1. *(tel., apt., etc)* но́мер; 2. *(numeral)* число́ ◆ **apartment** ~ но́мер кварти́ры ◆ **bus** ~ но́мер авто́буса ◆ **fax** ~ но́мер фа́кса ◆ *(1,2)* **flight** ~ но́мер *(1)* ре́йса / *(2)* полёта ◆ **house** ~ но́мер до́ма ◆ **lucky** ~ счастли́вый но́мер ◆ **passport** ~ но́мер па́спорта ◆ **room** ~ но́мер ко́мнаты ◆ **route** ~ но́мер маршру́та ◆ **(tele)phone** ~ но́мер телефо́на, телефо́н ◆ **train** ~ но́мер по́езда.

> **number:** *verb terms*

find the ~ найти́ но́мер ◆ **forget the** ~ забыва́ть / забы́ть но́мер ◆ **know the** ~ знать но́мер ◆ **look up the** ~ иска́ть но́мер ◆ **not know the** ~ не знать но́мер ◆ **remember the** ~ 1. *(memorize)* запомина́ть / запо́мнить но́мер; 2. *(recall)* вспомина́ть / вспо́мнить но́мер ◆ **write down the** ~ запи́сывать / записа́ть но́мер.

> **number:** *phrases*

What's your *(1,2)* **(phone) number?** Како́й у Вас *(1)* ...но́мер телефо́на? */ (2)* ...телефо́н? ◆ **Could you give me your phone number?** Не могли́ бы Вы дать мне свой но́мер телефо́на? ◆ **My (new)** *(1,2)* **(phone) number is __.** Мой (но́вый) *(1)* ...но́мер телефо́на . */ (2)* ...телефо́н. ___ ◆ **Here's my (new) (phone) number.** Это мой (но́вый) но́мер телефо́на. ◆ **Could you write down your phone number for me?** Вы не могли́ бы записа́ть свой но́мер телефо́на для меня́? ◆ **Write down the number.** Запиши́ но́мер. ◆ **I'll write down my phone number for you.** Я запишу́ Вам свой но́мер телефо́на. ◆ **I (don't) know the number.** Я (не) зна́ю но́мер. ◆ **Don't forget the number.** Не забу́дь но́мер. ◆ **I forgot the number.** Я забы́л *(ж: забы́ла)* но́мер. ◆ **I'm sorry I didn't call. I lost your number.** Прости́, что я не позвони́л *(ж: позвони́ла)*. Я потеря́л *(ж: потеряла)* твой но́мер.

numbing *adj* оцепеня́ющий, -ая, -ее, -ие, ошеломля́ющий, -ая, -ее, -ие.

nuptial *adj* бра́чный, -ая, -ое, -ые, сва́дебный, -ая, -ое, -ые.

nuptials *n, pl* сва́дьба ◆ **impending** ~s предстоя́щая сва́дьба.

nurture *vt* 1. *(raise, cultivate)* воспи́тывать / воспита́ть *(whom = acc.)*, обуча́ть / обучи́ть *(whom = acc.)*; 2. *(foster)* леле́ять *(what = acc.)*, пита́ть *(what = acc.)* ◆ **I enjoy activities that nurture mind, body and spirit.** Я люблю́ заня́тия, пита́ющие ум, те́ло и ду́шу.

nurturing *adj* 1. *(cultivating)* воспи́тывающий, -ая, -ее, -ие; 2. *(fostering)* пита́ющий, -ая, -ее, -ие.

nut *n (slang) (enthusiast)* поме́шанный *m*, поме́шанная *f* ◆ **golf** ~ поме́шанный *m* / поме́шанная *f* на го́льфе ◆ **sports** ~ поме́шанный *m* / поме́шанная *f* на спо́рте ◆ **tennis** ~ поме́шанный *m* / поме́шанная *f* на те́ннисе.

Clock and calender time are discussed in Appendix 5, page 759.

nuts *pred adj (slang) (crazy)* сумасше́дший, -ая, -ее, -ие, безу́мный, -ая, -ое, -ые ♦ **drive ~s** своди́ть / свести́ с ума́ *(whom = acc.)* ♦ *(1,2)* **You gotta be nuts!** *(1)* Ты, должно́ быть, сумасше́дшая *(ж: сумасше́дший)*! / *(2)* Ты сошла́ *(ж: сошёл)* с ума́!

nutty *adj (slang) (= crazy)* поме́шанный, -ая, -ое, -ые *(short forms:* поме́шан, -а, -о, -ы*)* ♦ **little ~** слегка́ поме́шанный, -ая, -ое, -ые.

nuzzle *vt* зары́ться *(what = acc., in what = + в + prep.),* ты́каться *(what = acc., in what = + в + acc.)*; прижима́ться / прижа́ться *(what = instr., against / into what = + к + dat.)* ♦ **I want to nuzzle my face** *(1)* **...against your neck.** / *(2)* **...in your breasts** / *(3)* **legs.** Я хочу́ *(1)* ...прижа́ться лицо́м к твое́й ше́е. / *(2)* ...зары́ться лицо́м в ...твое́й груди́. / *(3)* ...твои́х нога́х.

nymph *n* ни́мфа ♦ **You're the most thrilling little nymph I've ever run into.** Ты са́мая возбужда́ющая ма́ленькая ни́мфа из когда́-либо встре́ченных мной.

nymphet *n* нимфе́тка.

nymphomaniac *n* нимфома́нка.

Reflexive verbs are those that end in -ся or -сь.
The -ся or -сь also goes onto a past tense ending.

O

oafish *adj* глу́пый, -ая, -ое, -ые; несклáдный, -ая, -ое, -ые.

oats *n, pl*: ♦ **I've sown all my wild oats (long ago).** Я уже перебеси́лся (давны́м давно́).

obese *adj* ту́чный, -ая, -ое, -ые, жи́рный, -ая, -ое, -ые.

obey *vt* повиновáться *(what, whom = dat.)*, слу́шаться *(what, whom = dat.)*, подчиня́ться *(what, whom = dat.)* ♦ **I am compelled to obey the silent command of your ([1] sensuous / [2] beautiful) lips.** Я вы́нужден повиновáться безмо́лвным прикáзам твои́х *([1]* чу́вственных */ [2]* прекрáсных) губ.

obligation *n* обязáтельство, обя́занность *f* ♦ **I don't want to get sucked into a web of obligations.** Я не хочу́ быть запу́танным в паути́не обязáтельств.

oblivion *n* забвéние ♦ **sensual ~** чу́вственное забвéние.

oblivious *adj* не замечáющий, -ая, -ее, -ие, не обращáющий (-ая, -ее, -ие) внимáния ♦ **Since the day we met I've (1,2) been oblivious of (3) everything / (4) all else except (5) ...you. / (6) ...your radiant charm. / (7) ....your sunny / (8) vivacious personality. / (9) ...your breathtaking / (10) angelic beauty.** С того́ дня, когдá мы встрéтились, я *(1)* не замечáл */ (2)* ви́дел *(3,4)* ничего́, кро́ме *(5)* ...тебя́. */ (6)* ...твоего́ сия́ющего очаровáния. */ (7)* ...твоéй со́лнечной */ (8)* живо́й индивидуáльности. */ (9)* ...твоéй перехвáтывающей дыхáние красоты́. */ (10)* ...твоéй áнгельской красоты́.

obnoxious *n* проти́вный, -ая, -ое, -ые, несно́сный, -ая, -ое, -ые.

obscene *adj* непристо́йный, -ая, -ое, -ые, неприли́чный, -ая, -ое, -ые.

obsess *vt* преслéдовать, овладевáть ♦ **The vision of your (1,2) gentle loveliness obsesses my thoughts.** Твоя́ *(1)* мя́гкая */ (2)* нéжная красотá владéет мои́ми мы́слями. ♦ **The exquisite memories of the beautiful moments we shared together obsess my mind night and day.** Изы́сканные воспоминáния прекрáсных мину́т, проведённых вмéсте, преслéдуют меня́ но́чью и днём.

obsessed *pp* одержи́м, -а, -ы *(short forms)* ♦ **~ with sex** одержи́мый (-ая, -ые) сéксом ♦ **I must confess, I am totally obsessed with thoughts of (1) ...you. / (2) ...your wonderful feminine charms. / (3) ...your enchanting beauty. / (4) ...your beautiful dark eyes and full, tantalizing lips.** Я до́лжен признáться, что абсолю́тно одержи́м мы́слями о *(1)* ...тебé. */ (2)* ...твоéй очаровáтельной красотé. */ (3)* ...твои́х замечáтельных жéнских прéлестях. */ (4)* ...твои́х прекрáсных тёмных глазáх и по́лных, дразня́щихся губáх.

obsession *n* одержи́мость *f.*

obsessive *adj* навя́зчивый, -ая, -ое, -ые *(short forms:* навя́зчив, -а, -о, -ы) ♦ **~ character**

The time zones for many cities of the world
are given in Appendix 6, page 761.

навязчивый характер ♦ **Your love is** *(1)* **too** / *(2)* **so obsessive.** Твоя любовь *(1)* слишком / *(2)* так навязчива.

obstinate *adj* строптивый, -ая, -ое, -ые.

obvious *adj* 1. *(readily perceived by senses)* очевидный, -ая, -ое, -ые, явный, -ая, -ое, -ые; 2. *(readily perceived by mind)* ясный, -ая, -ое, -ые, понятный, -ая, -ое, -ые.

obviously *adv* очевидно, явно; *(clearly)* ясно; *(certainly)* конечно; *(unquestionably)* безусловно.

occasion *n* 1. *(event)* событие; случай; 2. *(time)* раз; 3. *(opportunity)* возможность, случай ♦ **special** ~ особенный случай.

occasional *adj (Note: Russians use verb with words* «время от времени» *[from time to time] or* «иногда» *[sometimes].)*

occasionally *adv* временами, время от времени, иногда.

ocean *n* океан.

oddball *n (slang)* чудак.

odor *n* запах ♦ **delicate** ~ тонкий запах.

off *prep*: ♦ ~ **and on** время от времени

---
off: phrases

Would it be possible for you to get *(1)*...**today** / *(2)* **tomorrow** *(3,4)* **off?** Сможешь ли ты получить *(3)*...свободный день... / *(4)* ...выходной... *(1)* сегодня / *(2)* завтра? ♦ **Would it be possible for you to get** *(1)* **two** / *(2)* **three days off?** Сможешь ли ты получить *(1)* два / *(2)* три свободных дня? ♦ **Would it be possible for you to get** *(1)* ...**a week off?** / ...*(2)* **two** / *(3)* **three weeks off?** Сможешь ли ты получить *(1)* ...свободную неделю? / ...*(2)* две / *(3)* три свободных недели? ♦ **I can('t) get off** *(1)*..**this** / *(2)* **tomorrow** *(3)* **afternoon** / *(4)* **evening.** Я (не) могу освободить *(3)* полдень / *(4)* вечер *(1)* сегодня / *(2)* завтра.

offbeat *adj* нетрадиционный, -ая, -ое, -ые, необычный, -ая, -ое, -ые, оригинальный, -ая, -ое, -ые.

offend *vt* обижать / обидеть *(whom = acc.)*, оскорблять / оскорбить *(whom = acc.)* ♦ **I hope that my romantic overtures have not offended you, but I could not restrain myself from making them.** Надеюсь, что моя романтическая увертюра не оскорбила тебя, я не смог сдержаться. ♦ **I don't want to** *(1,2)* **offend you.** Я не хочу *(1)* оскорбить / *(2)* обидеть тебя. ♦ **I didn't mean to offend you.** Я не хотел *(ж: хотела)* обидеть тебя. ♦ **I hope I didn't offend you.** Надеюсь, я не обидел *(ж: обидела)* тебя. ♦ **I hope that what I say here (in my letter) doesn't offend you.** Надеюсь, то, что я сказал *(ж: сказала)* здесь (в письме), не обидет тебя. ♦ **I'm sorry** *(1)* **that** / *(2)* **if I offended you.** Мне очень жаль, *(1)* что / *(2)* если я обидел *(ж: обидела)* тебя.

offended *adj* обижен, -а, -о, -ы *(short forms)*, оскорблён, оскорблена, -о, -ы *(short forms)* ♦ **be** ~ обижаться / обидеться, оскорбляться / оскорбиться ♦ **I'm afraid to open my heart to you and tell you everything I feel, because I'm afraid you would be offended or shocked or angry and then stop writing to me.** Я боюсь открыть тебе своё сердце и сказать всё, что я чувствую, потому что страшусь того, что ты обидишься, будешь шокирована или рассердишься и перестанешь писать мне.

offensive *adj* обидный, -ая, -ое, -ые; *(insulting)* оскорбительный, -ая, -ое, -ые.

offer *vt* предлагать / предложить *(what = acc., to whom = dat.)* ♦ **I offer to you all my love, all my being, all my life.** Я предлагаю тебе всю мою любовь, всё моё существо, всю мою жизнь. ♦ **I'm ready to offer more than a hundred percent of myself.** Я готов *(ж: готова)* предложить себя более, чем на сто процентов. ♦ **I have a lot to offer the right** *(1)* **woman** / *(2)* **man** / *(3)* **person.** У меня есть много, что предложить *(1)* ...подходящей женщине. / *(2)* ...подходящему мужчине / *(3)* человеку.

---

*Optional parts of sentences are preceded
or followed (or both) by three dots.*

office *n* бюро́, о́фис, конто́ра, канцеля́рия; *(small)* кабине́т ◆ **home** ~ дома́шний о́фис ◆ **private** ~ ли́чный кабине́т ◆ **registry** ~ бюро́ за́писей а́ктов гражда́нского состоя́ния (ЗАГС).

off-kilter *adj (slang) (unusual, goofy)* стра́нный, -ая, -ое, -ые, с причу́дами.

off-the-wall *adj (slang) (odd)* стра́нный, -ая, -ое, -ые.

often *adv* ча́сто.

oil *n* ма́сло ◆ **creamy** ~ густо́е (космети́ческое) ма́сло ◆ **massage** ~ ма́сло для масса́жа ◆ **scented** ~ арома́тное ма́сло.

okay *pred adj* хорошо́, в поря́дке ◆ **Everything** *(1)* ...is... / *(2)* ...will be... *(3,4)* **okay.** *(1)* Всё... / *(2)* Всё бу́дет... *(3)* ...хорошо́. / *(4)* ...в поря́дке.

okay *adv (well)* хорошо́; *(not bad)* непло́хо.

old *adj* ста́рый, -ая, -ое, -ые ◆ **I want to grow old together with you, my Love.** Я хочу́ соста́риться вме́сте с тобо́й, моя́ любо́вь.

old-fashioned *adj* старомо́дный, -ая, -ое, -ые.

olympics *n, pl* олимпиа́да ◆ **pleasure** ~**s** олимпиа́да наслажде́ния ◆ **I want you to participate with me in the pleasure olympics. (Let the games begin.)** Я хочу́, чтобы ты уча́ствовала вме́сте со мной в олимпиа́де наслажде́ния. (Дава́й начнём и́гры.)

on-again, off-again коле́блющийся, -аяся, -ееся, -иеся ◆ **be** ~ прерыва́ться и начина́ться опя́ть ◆ **Our marriage has been on-again, off-again.** Мно́го раз наш брак прерыва́лся и начина́лся опя́ть. ◆ **Our relationship has been on-again, off-again.** На́ши отноше́ния прерыва́лись и начина́лись опя́ть.

one *n* 1. оди́н *m*, одна́ *f*, одно́ *neut*; 2. *(person)* челове́к ◆ **dear** ~ дорого́й *m*, дорога́я *f* ◆ **loved** ~ люби́мый *m*, люби́мая *f*.

one: you are the one

You are my one and only. Ты моя́ одна́ еди́нственная. *(ж: Ты мой оди́н еди́нственный.)* ◆ **You are my one and only love.** Ты моя́ одна́ еди́нственная любо́вь. ◆ **You are the only one my heart is beating for.** Ты еди́нственная *(ж: еди́нственный)*, для кого́ бьётся моё се́рдце. ◆ **You are the only one I have ever loved.** Ты еди́нственная, кото́рую я люби́л и люблю́. *(ж: Ты еди́нственный, кото́рого я люби́ла и люблю́.)* ◆ **I swore (that) if I ever met the right one, that would be it. And you're the one.** Я кля́лся *(ж: кляла́сь)*, что, е́сли когда́-либо встре́чу подходя́щего для себя́ челове́ка, э́то бу́дет всё. И ты э́тот челове́к.

one: we will be one

You and I will be as one. Ты и я бу́дем как одно́ це́лое. ◆ **I feel that we have become one with each other.** Я чу́вствую, что мы ста́ли одни́м це́лым. ◆ **I can't wait until we are one.** Я не могу́ дожда́ться вре́мени, когда́ мы ста́нем одни́м це́лым.

one-sided *adj* односторо́нний, -яя, -ее, -ие.

online на интерне́те ◆ **love** ~ любо́вь на интерне́те ◆ **meet** ~ встреча́ться / встре́титься на Интерне́те.

only *adj* еди́нственный, -ая, -ое, -ые ◆ **You are my one and only.** Ты моя́ одна́ еди́нст-венная. *(ж: Ты мой оди́н еди́нственный.)* ◆ **You are my one and only love.** Ты моя́ одна́ еди́нственная любо́вь. ◆ **You are the only person I** *(1)* ...**could ever love.** / *(2)* ...**want in this whole world.** Ты еди́нственный челове́к, *(1)* ...кото́рого я то́лько мог *(ж: могла́)* полюби́ть. / *(2)* ...кото́рый ну́жен мне в э́том ми́ре. ◆ **You are the only one I have ever loved.** Ты еди́нственная, кото́рую я люби́л и люблю́. *(ж: Ты еди́нственный, кого́ я люби́ла и люблю́.)* ◆ **You're the only** *(1)* **woman** / *(2)* **girl for me.** Ты еди́нственная *(1)* же́нщина / *(2)* де́вушка для меня́. ◆ **You're the only** *(1)* **man** / *(2)* **guy for me.** Ты еди́нственный *(1)* мужчи́на / *(2)* па́рень для меня́. ◆ **It's only you that I want.** Ты

If you're not on familiar terms with a person,
the «ты» forms will have to be changed to «Вы».

единственная, которую я хочу. *(ж: Ты единственный, которого я хочу.)* ♦ **You are the only one my heart is beating for.** Ты единственная *(ж: единственный)*, для кого бьётся моё сердце.

ooze *vt* сочиться *(what = instr.).*

opal *adj* опаловый, -ая, -ое, -ые.

opal *n* опал.

open *adj* открытый, -ая, -ое, -ые *(short forms:* открыт, -а, -о, -ы*)* ♦ **be ~ (to)** быть открытым *m* / открытой *f (to what =* + к + *dat.)* ♦ **I want someone who is emotionally open.** Я хочу кого-нибудь, кто эмоционально открыт. ♦ **It's best to have everything in the open.** Лучше всего, чтобы всё было открыто.

open *vi* открываться / открыться ♦ **~ up** *vi (emotionally)* раскрываться / раскрыться, открываться / открыться.

open: phrases

(1,2) **What time does** *(3-5)* **it open?** *(1)* Когда... / *(2)* В какое время... *(3)* он *m* / *(4)* она *f* / *(5)* оно *neut* открывается? ♦ *(1-3)* **It opens at** *(4)* **one (thirty).** *(See page 759 for other times.)* *(1)* Он *m* / *(2)* Она *f* / *(3)* Оно *neut* открывается в *(4)* час (тридцать).

open: open up

I want somebody I can open up to. Я хочу того, с кем я смогу быть открытым *(ж: открытой).* ♦ **Why do you clamp down on your feelings? You need to open up and let yourself go.** Почему ты сдерживаешь свои чувства? Тебе надо раскрыться и позволить твоим чувствам выйти наружу. ♦ **You need to open up more.** Тебе нужно быть более открытой *(ж: открытым).* ♦ **I wish you would open up more.** Я хочу, чтобы ты была более открытой *(ж: был более открытым).* ♦ **You shouldn't cloak your emotions (so). You need to open up.** Ты не должна *(ж: должен)* скрывать свои эмоции (так). Ты должна *(ж должен)* раскрыться.

open-hearted *adj* 1. *(straightforward* чистосердечный, -ая, -ое, -ые; 2. *(big-hearted, kind)* великодушный, -ая, -ое, -ые, добрый, -ая, -ое, -ые*).*

open-minded *adj* 1. *(unprejudiced)* непредубеждённый, -ая, -ое, -ые, непредвзятый, -ая, -ое, -ые; 2. *(receptive)* восприимчивый, -ая, -ое, -ые; *(broadminded)* с широким кругозором.

openness *n* открытость *f* ♦ **emotional ~** эмоциональная открытость ♦ **What I** *(1)* **...want...** / *(2)* **...yearn for... most in a relationship is openness.** Чего я *(1)* ...хочу... / *(2)* ...жажду... более всего в отношениях -- открытости.

opera *n* опера.

operator *n (tel.)* телефонистка ♦ **smooth ~** *(slang)* 1. *(smooth-tongued)* сладкоречивый мужчина; *(lady-killer)* сердцеед; *(irresistible)* неотразимый мужчина; 2. *(skilled in sex)* мужчина, искушённый в сексе *(1 term).*

opinionated *adj* самоуверенный, -ая, -ое, -ые, своевольный, -ая, -ое, -ые, упрямый, -ая, -ое, -ые, упорствующий (-ая) в своих мнениях.

opportunity *n* возможность *f*, шанс ♦ **nice ~** первая возможность ♦ **good ~** хорошая возможность ♦ **last ~** последняя возможность ♦ **missed ~** упущенная возможность ♦ **nice ~** хорошая возможность ♦ **only ~** единственная возможность ♦ **wonderful ~** прекрасная возможность.

opportunity: verb terms

afford me the ~ давать / дать мне возможность ♦ **get the ~** получить возможность ♦ **give me the ~** давать / дать мне возможность ♦ **grant me the ~** предоставить мне возможность ♦ **have the ~** иметь возможность ♦ **miss the ~** упустить возможность ♦ **pass up the ~** упустить возможность ♦ **present (me) the ~** предоставить (мне) воз-

A list of common places with their grammatical endings is given in Appendix 7, page 763.

мо́жность ♦ **take advantage of the** ~ воспо́льзоваться возмо́жностью ♦ **take the** ~ испо́льзовать возмо́жность.

---
opportunity: *phrases*

I hope you'll *(1)* **afford /** *(2)* **give me the opportunity to** *(3)* **...see you again. /** *(4)* **...get to know you better.** Я наде́юсь, что ты *(1,2)* дашь мне возмо́жность *(3)* ...уви́деть тебя́ опя́ть. / *(4)* ...узна́ть тебя́ лу́чше. ♦ **I wouldn't miss the opportunity for anything.** Я бы ни за что не упусти́л *(ж: упусти́ла)* э́ту возмо́жность. ♦ **I can't pass up the opportunity.** Я не могу́ упусти́ть возмо́жности. ♦ *(1)* **Now /** *(2)* **That is our best opportunity.** *(1)* Тепе́рь / *(2)* Это наш лу́чший шанс. ♦ **I fervently** *(1)* **entreat /** *(2)* **implore you to** *(3)* **give /** *(4)* **grant me the opportunity to** *(4)* **...know you better. /** *(5)* **...get better acquainted with you. /** *(6)* **...speak with you. /** *(7)* **...see your beautiful face once again. /** *(8)* **...meet with you.** Я горячо́ умоля́ю Вас *(1)* дать / *(2)* предоста́вить мне возмо́жность *(3)* ...лу́чше узна́ть Вас. / *(4)* ...бли́же познако́миться с Ва́ми. / *(5)* ...поговори́ть с Ва́ми. / *(6)* ...уви́деть Ва́ше прекра́сное лицо́ ещё раз. / *(7)* ...встре́титься с Ва́ми.

oppressive *adj* гнету́щий, -ая, -ее, -ие, угнета́ющий, -ая, -ее, -ие ♦ **My loneliness without you is utterly oppressive.** Без тебя́ меня́ так гнетёт одино́чество.

opulence *n (plenty, profusion)* бога́тство, изоби́лие ♦ **I see in this photo a face of** *(1)* **exquisite /** *(2)* **unimaginable beauty crowned with an opulence of** *(3)* **golden /** *(4)* **chestnut /** *(5)* **raven hair.** Я ви́жу на э́той фотогра́фии лицо́ *(1)* изы́сканной / *(2)* невообрази́мой красоты́ в струя́щемся бога́тстве *(3)* золоты́х / *(4)* кашта́новых / *(5)* чёрных воло́с.

oral *adj* ора́льный, -ая, -ое, -ые, ротово́й, -а́я, -о́е, -ы́е.

orally *adv* ора́льно, в рот.

orange *adj* ора́нжевый, -ая, -ое, -ые.

orbit *n* орби́та ♦ **When you flashed your** *(1)* **beautiful /** *(2)* **gorgeous /** *(3)* **dazzling smile at me, my heart went into a lunar orbit.** Когда́ ты сверкну́ла *(1)* прекра́сной / *(2)* великоле́пной / *(3)* ослепи́тельной улы́бкой, моё се́рдце взлете́ло на лу́нную орби́ту.

orchestrated *adj* оркестро́ван, -а, -о, -ы *(short forms)* ♦ **Our bodies are so** *(1)* **perfectly /** *(2)* **wonderfully orchestrated when we make love.** На́ши тела́ так *(1)* соверше́нно / *(2)* замеча́тельно настро́ены в унисо́н, когда́ мы занима́емся любо́вью.

orchestration *n* оркестро́вка ♦ **All of your** *(1)* **hormones /** *(2)* **genes are in perfect orchestration.** Все твои́ *(1)* гормо́ны / *(2)* ге́ны в соверше́нной гармо́нии. ♦ **Through the total orchestration of our bodies you and I together will produce the most beautiful symphony of love anyone has ever known.** Благодаря́ абсолю́тной сы́гранности на́ших тел, ты и я вме́сте создади́м таку́ю прекра́сную симфо́нию любви́, кото́рой никто́ никогда́ не знал.

orchid *n* орхиде́я.

ordeal *n* тяжёлое испыта́ние, суд бо́жий.

order *vt* зака́зывать / заказа́ть *(what = acc.)* ♦ **~around** распоряжа́ться *(whom= instr..)* ♦ **~ by mail** зака́зывать / заказа́ть по по́чте ♦ **~ on the Internet** зака́зывать / заказа́ть по интерне́ту ♦ **in ~ to** для того́, чтобы *(1 term)* ♦ **out of ~** не в поря́дке, не рабо́тает.

ordinarily *adv* обы́чно, обыкнове́нно.

ordinary *adj* обы́чный, -ая, -ое, -ые, обыкнове́нный, -ая, -ое, -ые.

organ *n* о́рган ♦ **sex(ual)** ~ полово́й о́рган.

organize *vt* организова́ть *(what = acc.)*.

organized *adj* организо́ванный, -ая, -ое, -ые.

orgasm *n* орга́зм ♦ **cosmic** ~ косми́ческий орга́зм ♦ **earth-shattering** ~ зе́млю-разбива́ющий орга́зм ♦ **earth-splitting** ~ зе́млю-расщепля́ющий орга́зм ♦ **explosive** ~

Common adult heights are given in Appendix 9, page 776.

взрывно́й орга́зм ♦ **frequent** ~s ча́стые орга́змы ♦ **mind-blowing** ~ ошеломля́ющий орга́зм ♦ **multiple** ~s многокра́тные орга́змы ♦ **over-the-top** ~ си́льный оргазм ♦ **powerful** ~ си́льный орга́зм ♦ **prolonged** ~ продлённый орга́зм ♦ **simultaneous** ~ одновреме́нный орга́зм ♦ **tremendous** ~ грандио́зный орга́зм ♦ **volcanic** ~ вулкани́ческий орга́зм.

orgasm: *verb terms*

achieve ~ достига́ть / дости́гнуть орга́зма ♦ **experience an** ~ испы́тывать / испыта́ть орга́зм ♦ *(1,2)* **fake an** ~ *(1)* подде́лывать / подде́лать / *(2)* фальсифици́ровать орга́зм ♦ **feel an** ~ чу́вствовать / почу́вствовать орга́зм ♦ **give you an** ~ дать тебе́ орга́зм ♦ **give you** ~s дава́ть тебе́ орга́змы ♦ **have an** ~ испы́тывать / испыта́ть орга́зм, достига́ть / дости́гнуть орга́зма, (**I had an** ~ у меня́ был орга́зм) ♦ **reach** ~ достига́ть / дости́гнуть орга́зма.

orgasm: *phrases*

(1) **I want to make you feel...** / *(2)* **I felt...** *(3)* **...a tidal wave...** / *(4)* **...a tremendous ripple... of orgasm.** *(1)* Я хочу́ заста́вить тебя́ почу́вствовать... / *(2)* Я чу́вствовала... *(3)* ...приливну́ю волну́... / *(4)* ...грома́дный пото́к... орга́зма. ♦ **I've never experienced an orgasm** (*[1]*...**like that.** / *[2]*...**in my whole life**). Я никогда́ не испы́тывала орга́зма (*[1]* ...как э́тот. / *[2]* ...во всей жи́зни.) ♦ **Did you have an orgasm?** У тебя́ был орга́зм? ♦ **That was such a(n)** (*[1]* **fantastic** / *[2]* **incredible** / *[3]* **tremendous**) **orgasm!** Это был тако́й (*[1]* фантасти́ческий / *[2]* невероя́тный / *[3]* грома́дный) орга́зм. ♦ **I'm going to give you the biggest, most beautiful orgasm you ever dreamed of.** Я дам тебе́ тако́й си́льный, прекра́сный орга́зм, о кото́ром ты про́сто не мечта́ла. ♦ **I'm going to teach you how to have multiple orgasms.** Я научу́ тебя́, как получи́ть многокра́тные орга́змы. ♦ **With him I used to just** *(1,2)* **fake an orgasm.** С ним я привы́кла то́лько *(1)* подде́лывать / *(2)* фальсифици́ровать орга́зм. ♦ **I love the way you quake just before you have an orgasm.** Мне нра́вится, как ты трепе́щешь пе́ред орга́змом.

orgasmic *adj* 1. *(of or about orgasm)* орга́зма; *(by orgasm)* орга́змом; 2. *(easily experiencing orgasm)* легко́ получа́ющая *(f)* орга́зм *(Russian mostly uses the following verb expression)* ♦ **be** ~ легко́ испы́тывать орга́зм ♦ **highly** ~ о́чень легко́ испы́тывающая орга́зм ♦ **I never guessed you were so orgasmic.** Я никогда́ не предполага́л, что ты бу́дешь так легко́ испы́тывать орга́зм. ♦ **You're going to be so orgasmic you won't believe it.** Ты бу́дешь так легко́ испы́тывать орга́зм, как ты не смогла́ бы да́же вообрази́ть. ♦ **I want to give you orgasmic pleasure such as you have never known or dreamed of before.** Я хочу́ дать тебе́ тако́е наслажде́ние орга́змом, кото́рого ты никогда́ не зна́ла и о кото́ром никогда́ пре́жде не мечта́ла.

orgiastic *adj* разну́зданный, -ая, -ое, -ые.

orgy *n* о́ргия ♦ **You and I are going to have our own private orgy.** У тебя́ и у меня́ бу́дет на́ша со́бственная о́ргия.

Oriental *adj* восто́чный, -ая, -ое, -ые.

orientation *n* ориента́ция ♦ ~ **in space and time** ориента́ция в простра́нстве и вре́мени.

oriented *adj* ориенти́рованный, -ая, -ое, -ые ♦ **growth** ~ с гото́вностью развива́ться.

original *adj* оригина́льный, -ая, -ое, -ые.

originality *n* оригина́льность *f.*

orphan *n* сирота́ ♦ **love** ~ *(male)* тот, кого́ никогда́ не люби́ли *(1 term)*; *(female)* та, кото́рую никогда́ не люби́ли *(1 term)*.

ostensibly *adv* по-ви́димому, я́кобы.

ostentatious *adj* показно́й, -а́я, -о́е, -ы́е; мишу́рный, -ая, -ое, -ые; хвастли́вый, -ая, -ое, -ые.

Words in parentheses are optional.

other *adj* другóй, -áя, -óе, -и́е ♦ **There is no other** *(1)* **woman** / *(2)* **man in my life.** В моéй жи́зни нет *(1)* ...другóй жéнщины. / *(2)* ...другóго мужчи́ны.

otherwise *adv* ина́че.

outburst *n* взрыв, вспы́шка ♦ **emotional** ~ эмоциона́льный взрыв ♦ **hysterical** ~ истери́ческий взрыв ♦ ~ **of anger** взрыв гнéва ♦ ~ **of tears** взрыв слёз.

outdoors *n* вне дóма, на открытом вóздухе ♦ **I like to explore the outdoors.** Мне нра́вится иссле́довать нóвые места́. ♦ **Let's get married outdoors.** Дава́й устрóим сва́дьбу на открытом вóздухе. ♦ **We could get married outdoors.** У нас мóжет быть сва́дьба на открытом вóздухе.

outdoorsman *n* *(hunter)* охóтник; *(fisherman)* рыболóв; люби́тель развлечéний на открытом вóздухе.

outdoorswoman *n* жéнщина, лю́бящая быть на открытом вóздухе *(1 term)*.

outdoorsy *adj* лю́бящий *(ж: лю́бящая)* быть на открытом вóздухе, лю́бящий *(ж: лю́бящая)* прирóду ♦ **I'm somewhat outdoorsy. I like to go camping and hiking.** Я (до нéкоторой стéпени) люблю́ проводи́ть врéмя на открытом вóздухе. Я люблю́ отдыха́ть с пала́ткой и ходи́ть в похóды.

outfit *n* *(clothes)* наря́д, костю́м, анса́мбль *m* ♦ *(1,2)* **beautiful** ~ *(1)* краси́вый / *(2)* прекра́сный наря́д ♦ **cool** ~ *(slang)* *(nice-looking)* шика́рный наря́д ♦ **elegant** ~ изя́щный наря́д ♦ **French maid** ~ наря́д францу́зской гóрничной ♦ **genie** ~ наря́д джи́н(н)а, наря́д жéнщины востóка ♦ **harem** ~ гарéмный наря́д ♦ **new** ~ обнóвка, нóвый комплéкт одéжды ♦ **wedding** ~ сва́дебный наря́д ♦ **What a** *(1)* **beautiful** / *(2)* **lovely outfit (you have)!** Что за *(1,2)* прекра́сный наря́д (у тебя́)! ♦ **That's a (very) beautiful outfit.** Это (óчень) краси́вый наря́д.

outgoing *adj* общи́тельный, -ая, -ое, -ые.

outing *n* времяпровождéние вне дóма; экску́рсия ♦ **country** *(1,2)* ~**s** за́городная *(1)* экску́рсия / *(2)* поéздка ♦ **We could go for outings on the weekends.** Мы мóжем уéхать куда́-нибудь на выходны́е. ♦ **I like casual outings.** Я люблю́ развлечéния вне дóма.

outlandish *adj* дикóвинный, -ая, -ое, -ые.

outlook *n* взгляд, тóчка зрéния, мировоззрéние ♦ **healthy** ~ норма́льная тóчка зрéния ♦ ~ **on life** мировоззрéние ♦ **positive** ~ положи́тельный взгляд ♦ **similar** ~ одина́ковый взгляд ♦ **You and I have a similar outlook on life.** У нас одина́ковый взгляд на жизнь.

outpouring *n* излия́ние ♦ ~**s of the soul** душéвные излия́ния.

outraged *adj* *(offended)* оскорблён, -оскорблена́, -ó, -ы́ *(short forms)*; *(indignant)* возмущён, -возмущена́, -ó, -ы́ *(short forms)*.

outrageous *adj* *(offensive)* оскорби́тельный, -ая, -ое, -ые; *(revolting)* возмути́тельный, -ая, -ое, -ые; 2. *(excessive)* чрезмéрный, -ая, -ое, -ые, непомéрный, -ая, -ое, -ые.

outrageously *adv* 1. *(offensively)* оскорби́тельно; *(revoltingly)* возмути́тельно; 2. *(terribly)* ужа́сно.

outset *n* нача́ло ♦ **from the (very)** ~ с са́мого нача́ла.

outspoken *adj* прямóй, -а́я, -óе, -ы́е, откровéнный, -ая, -ое, -ые.

outstanding *adj* 1. *(foremost)* выдаю́щийся, -аяся, -ееся, -иеся; 2. *(exceptional)* исключи́тельный, -ая, -ое, -ые; *(great)* великолéпный, -ая, -ое, -ые.

over *adj* *(finished)* (за)кóнчен, -а, -о, -ы *(short forms)* ♦ **It's (all) over (between** *(1)* **...us.** / *(2)* **...her** / *(3)* **him and me.).** Мéжду *(1)* ...на́ми... / *(2)* ...ней / *(3)* ним и мной... всё кóнчено.

overanxious *adj* чрезмéрно озабóченный, -ая, -ое, -ые.

overbearing *adj* вла́стный, -ая, -ое, -ые.

overboard *adv*: **go** ~ *(overdo)* заходи́ть / зайти́ сли́шком далекó; *(try too hard)* пере-

---

You can find common clothing sizes in Appendix 11 on page 778.

стара́ться; *(go to great lengths)* лезть из ко́жи вон.

overcoat *n* пальто́.

overcome *adj* охва́чен, -а, -о, -ы *(short forms)*, *(verbs frequently used:)* охва́тывать / охва-ти́ть *(thing overcome by = subject; who or what is overcome = acc.)*, овладе́ть *(thing overcome by = subject; who or what is overcome = acc.)*.

| overcome: phrases |

I am overcome by desire for you. Страсть к тебе́ овладе́ла мной. ♦ **If I touch even your hand, I am overcome by desire for you.** Сто́ит мне косну́ться твое́й руки́, как меня́ охва́тывает жела́ние. ♦ **I am** *(1)* **completely** / *(2)* **totally overcome by the rapture that you create with your** *(3)* **...skillful hands.** / *(4)* **...ardent kisses.** / *(5)* **...roving lips.** Я *(1)* по́лностью / *(2)* весь охва́чен *(ж: вся охва́чена)* упое́нием, кото́рое ты создаёшь свои́ми *(3)* ...уме́лыми рука́ми. / *(4)* ...пы́лкими поцелу́ями. / *(5)* ...блужда́ющими губа́ми. ♦ **When I look into the deep blue depths of your eyes, I am overcome by feelings of love.** Когда́ я смотрю́ в тёмно-си́нюю глубину́ твои́х глаз, я (весь) охва́чен *(ж: [вся] охва́чена)* любо́вью к тебе́. ♦ **When our lips met the first time, I was overcome by ecstasy.** Когда́ на́ши гу́бы встре́тились впервы́е, я был охва́чен *(ж: была́ охва́чена)* экста́зом. ♦ **When I** *(1)* **became** / *(2)* **grew aware of your feelings for me, I was overcome with joy.** Когда́ я *(1,2)* узна́л *(ж: узна́ла)* о твои́х чу́вствах ко мне, я был охва́чен *(ж: была́ охва́чена)* ликова́нием.

overcome *vt* 1. *(surmount)* преодолева́ть / преодоле́ть *(what = acc.)*; 2. *(grip, overwhelm)* охва́тывать / охвати́ть *(what, whom = acc.)*.

| overcome: surmount |

You (really) need to overcome your prudish instincts. Ты (действи́тельно) должна́ преодоле́ть свои́ стыдли́вые инсти́нкты. ♦ **I'll help you overcome your shyness.** Я помогу́ тебе́ преодоле́ть засте́нчивость. ♦ **I cannot overcome the** *(1)* **fierce** / *(2)* **passionate longing in my heart to hold you in my arms (again).** Я не могу́ преодоле́ть *(1)* неи́стовую / *(2)* стра́стную жа́жду се́рдца (опя́ть) держа́ть тебя́ в объя́тиях.

| overcome: overwhelm |

Whenever I'm near you, feelings of desire overcome me. Всегда́, когда́ я ря́дом с тобо́й, страсть охва́тывает меня́.

overconfidence *n* чрезме́рная уве́ренность.

overconfident *adj* сли́шком уве́ренный, -ая, -ое, -ые.

overdress *vi* одева́ться / оде́ться сли́шком наря́дно.

overdrink *vi* сли́шком мно́го пить.

overexert *vt:* ♦ ~ *(1)* **myself** / *(2)* **yourself** *(1,2)* перенапряга́ться / перенапря́чься

overflow *vi* перелива́ться / перели́ться *(with what = instr.)*, переполня́ться / перепо́лниться *(with what = instr.)* ♦ **Whenever I look at your beloved face in this photo, my heart overflows with love for you.** Когда́ бы я ни взгляну́л *(ж: взгляну́ла)* на твоё люби́мое лицо́ на э́той фотогра́фии, моё се́рдце переполня́ется любо́вью к тебе́. ♦ **My heart overflows with** *(1)* **love** / *(2)* **emotion** / *(3)* **joy** / *(4)* **happiness.** Моё се́рдце перепо́лнено *(1)* любо́вью / *(2)* эмо́циями / *(3)* ра́достью / *(4)* сча́стьем. ♦ **My heart overflows with love for you.** Моё се́рдце переполня́ется любо́вью к тебе́.

overflowing *n (Russian uses verbs. See overflow.)* ♦ **If you were my woman, I would fill your life to overflowing with soft, gentle, eager, loving kisses that would awaken all sorts of warm, wonderful, exquisite feelings in you.** Е́сли бы ты была́ мое́й же́нщиной, я бы запо́лнил твою́ жизнь до краёв мя́гкими, не́жными, жа́ждущими, лю́бящими поцелу́ями, кото́рые пробуди́ли бы все са́мые тёплые, замеча́тельные, изы́сканные чу́вства в тебе́.

For general rules of Russian grammar see Appendix 2 on page 686.

overhear *vt* подслу́шивать / подслу́шать *(what = acc.)* ♦ **I overheard your conversation.** Я подслу́шал *(ж: подслу́шала)* твой разгово́р.

overindulge *vi (drink too much)* сли́шком мно́го пить / вы́пить.

overjoyed *adj* о́чень счастли́вый, -ая, -ое, -ые, вне себя́ от ра́дости.

overlook *vt (not notice)* не замеча́ть / не заме́тить *(what = gen.)*, пропуска́ть / пропусти́ть *(what = acc.)*.

overnight *adj* 1. *(for a night)* на ночь; 2. *(the whole night)* всю ночь ♦ ~ **stay** ночле́г ♦ ~ **stop** остано́вка на ночь.

overnight *adv* 1. *(for a night)* на ночь; 2. *(the whole night)* всю ночь ♦ **stay** ~ ночева́ть.

overpowering *adj* неотрази́мый, -ая, -ое, -ые ♦ ~ **beauty** неотрази́мая красота́.

overreact *vi* сли́шком си́льно реаги́ровать *(to what = +* на + *acc.)*.

overtime *adv* сверхуро́чно ♦ **work** ~ рабо́тать сверхуро́чно.

overtired *adj:* ♦ **be** ~ переутоми́ться.

overture *n* увертю́ра ♦ **romantic** ~ романти́ческая увертю́ра ♦ **sexual** ~ сексуа́льная увертю́ра ♦ **I hope that my romantic overtures have not offended you, but I could not restrain myself from making them.** Наде́юсь, что моя́ романти́ческая увертю́ра не оскорби́ла тебя́, я не смог сдержа́ться.

overweight *adj (a little)* упи́танный, -ая, -ое, -ые, толстова́т, -а, -о, -ы *(short forms)*, тяжелова́т, -а, -о, -ы *(short forms)*, в те́ле; *(a lot)* то́лстый, -ая, -ое, -ые, гру́зный, -ая, -ое, -ые ♦ **a (little) bit** ~ немно́го полнова́т, -а, -о, -ы ♦ **considerably** ~ име́ть значи́тельный изли́шний вес *(verb expression)* ♦ **slightly** ~ немно́го полнова́т, -а, -о, -ы ♦ **somewhat** ~ немно́го полнова́т, -а, -о, -ы ♦ **I'm a (little) bit overweight(, but I'm going to take it off).** Я немно́го тяжелова́т *(ж: тяжелова́та)* (, но я собира́юсь сбро́сить вес).

overwhelm *vt* ошеломля́ть / ошеломи́ть *(what, whom = acc.)*; охва́тывать / охвати́ть *(what, whom = acc.)*, овладева́ть / овладе́ть *(what, whom = instr.)*; сокруша́ть / сокруши́ть *(what, whom = acc.)*.

overwhelm: phrases

Your beauty and sensuality overwhelm me. Твоя́ красота́ и чу́вственность ошеломля́ют меня́. ♦ **You overwhelm me with your** *(1)* **beauty** / *(1)* **sweetness.** Ты ошеломля́ешь меня́ свое́й *(1)* красото́й / *(1)* добро́той. ♦ **The vision of your** *(1)* **beauty** / *(2)* **loveliness in my mind overwhelms all other thoughts.** Твоя́ *(1,2)* красота́ подавля́ет все други́е мы́сли. ♦ **The fierce** *(1)* **passion** / *(2)* **desire I feel for you overwhelms me.** *(1)* Неи́стовая страсть к тебе́... / *(2)* Неи́стовое жела́ние тебя́... переполня́ет меня́. ♦ **My** *(1)* **emotions** / *(2)* **feelings overwhelmed me so completely that** *(3)* **...I was at a loss for words.** / *(4)* **...I couldn't say anything.** / *(5)* **...I was utterly tongue-tied.** Мои́ *(1)* эмо́ции *(2)* чу́вства ошеломи́ли меня́ всеце́ло так, что *(3)* ...я потеря́л *(ж: потеря́ла)* дар ре́чи. / *(4)* ...я ничего́ не мог *(ж: могла́)* сказа́ть. / *(5)* ...я был *(ж: была́)* (соверше́нно) безъязы́чным *(ж: безъязы́чной)*.

overwhelmed *adj* охва́чен, -а, -о, -ы *(short forms)*, ошеломлён, ошеломлена́, -о́, -ы́ *(short forms)*, поражён, поражена́, -о́, -ы́ *(short forms)*, потрясён, потрясена́, -о́, -ы́ *(short forms) (verbs frequently used:)* охва́тывать / охвати́ть *(thing overwhelmed by = subject; who or what is overwhelmed = acc.)*, овладе́ть *(thing overwhelmed by = subject; who or what is overwhelmed = acc.)*.

overwhelmed: phrases

I'm (really) overwhelmed by *(1)* **...you.** / *(2)* **...your affections for me.** / *(3)* **...all of your attention.** / *(4)* **...your invitation** / *(5)* **proposal.** Я (действи́тельно) потрясён *(ж: потрясена́)* *(1)* ...тобо́й. / *(2)* ...твои́ми не́жными чу́вствами ко мне. / *(3)* ...твои́м возде́йствием на меня́. / *(4)* ...твои́м приглаше́нием / *(5)* предложе́нием. ♦ **I feel overwhelmed**

For transitive Russian verbs the cases that they take are shown by means of an = sign and the Russian case (abbreviated).

(by it all). Я чу́вствую себя́ потрясённым *(ж: потрясённой)* (всем э́тим). ♦ **I am overwhelmed by desire for you.** Страсть к тебе́ овладе́ла мно́ю. ♦ **If I touch even your hand, I am overwhelmed by / with desire for you.** Сто́ит мне косну́ться твое́й руки́, как меня́ охва́тывает жела́ние. ♦ **I'm overwhelmed with hurt.** Моё се́рдце перепо́лнилось бо́лью.

overwhelming *adj* неодоли́мый, -ая, -ое, -ые.

owl *n* сова́ ♦ **night ~** *(slang)* ночна́я сова́.

own *adj* со́бственный, -ая, -ое, -ые ♦ *(1,2)* **Your own** *(+ name) (closing of a letter)* *(1)* Всегда́ твой *(ж: твоя́) (+ и́мя)* / *(2)* Твой *(ж: Твоя́)* всегда́ *(+ и́мя)* .

owner *n* владе́лец ♦ *(1,2)* **business ~** владе́лец *(1)* предприя́тия / *(2)* фи́рмы ♦ **home ~** владе́лец до́ма ♦ **pet ~** владе́лец живо́тного.

ox *n* вол, бык.

Depending on the subject, the possessive pronoun **свой** (**своя́, своё, свой**) *can be translated* **my, your, his, her, its, our** *or* **their**.

P

pace *n* 1. *(step)* шаг; 2. *(walking speed)* шаг, скóрость *f;* 3. *(tempo)* темп, скóрость ♦ **set the** ~ задавáть / задáть темп ♦ **I like a slow, leisurely pace (in life).** Я люблю́ мéдленный, нетороплúвый стиль жúзни.

package *n* посы́лка ♦ *(1)* **get** / *(2)* **receive a** ~ *(1,2)* получáть / получúть посы́лку *(from whom* = + от + *gen.)* ♦ **send** *(1)* **you** / *(2)* **me a** ~ отправля́ть / отпрáвить *(1)* тебé / *(2)* мне посы́лку.

paean *n* пеан, ликýющая песнь, побéдная пéсня ♦ ~ **of joy** побéдная пéсня рáдости.

page *n* странúца ♦ **first** ~ пéрвая странúца ♦ **last** ~ послéдняя странúца ♦ **second** ~ вторáя странúца ♦ **web** ~ веб-странúца.

pain *n* боль *f* ♦ **agonizing** ~ мучúтельная боль ♦ **awful** ~ ужáсная боль ♦ **incessant** ~ нестихáющая боль ♦ ~ **in the heart** сердéчная боль ♦ ~ **in the** *(1)* **neck** *(slang)* / *(2)* **ass** *(vulg.)* / *(3)* **butt** *(vulg.)* / *(4)* **rear** *(slang) (1-4)* головнáя боль ♦ ~ **of loneliness** боль одинóчества ♦ ~ **of loss** боль утрáты ♦ ~ **of parting** боль расставáния ♦ **such** ~ такáя боль ♦ **terrible** ~ ужáсная боль ♦ **unbearable** ~ невыносúмая боль ♦ **unrelenting** ~ нестихáющая боль ♦ **cause** *(1)* **you** / *(2)* **me** ~ вызывáть / вы́звать у *(1)* тебя́ / *(2)* меня́ боль, причиня́ть / причинúть *(1)* тебé / *(2)* мне боль ♦ **ease** ~ смягчáть / смягчúть боль ♦ *(1)* **Come** / *(2)* **Hurry back to me and chase away this terrible pain of loneliness (that grips my heart).** *(1)* Прийдú / *(2)* Торопúсь (обрáтно) ко мне и прогонú прочь э́ту ужáсную боль одинóчества (, котóрая тéрзает моё сéрдце). ♦ **With you gone, I feel such a pain in my heart.** Когдá ты не со мной, я чýвствую такýю сердéчную боль.

painful *adj* 1. *(physical)* болéзненный, -ая, -ое, -ые; 2. *(mental)* мучúтельный, -ая, -ое, -ые, тя́гостный, -ая, -ое, -ые.

painfully *adv* 1. *(physical)* болéзненно; 2. *(mental)* мучúтельно, тя́гостно.

paint *vt* 1. *(create paintings)* писáть / написáть *(what, whom* = *acc.)*; 2. *(depict, portray)* рисовáть / нарисовáть *(what, whom* = *acc.)*; 3. *(apply paint)* расскрáшивать / раскрáсить *(what, whom* = *acc.)* ♦ **I paint love pictures to you in all my thoughts.** Все моú мы́сли полны́ картúнами любвú с тобóй. ♦ **I'd love to paint your body with body paints. Will you let me?** Мне бы хотéлось раскрáсить твоё тéло крáсками для тéла. Ты позвóлишь?

paint *n* крáска ♦ **edible body** ~ съедóбная крáска для тéла ♦ **I'd love to paint your beautiful body with body paints.** Я хотéл бы раскрáсить твоё прекрáсное тéло крáсками для тéла.

painter *n (artistic)* худóжник, живопúсец ♦ **portrait** ~ портретúст.

---

*Russian verbs have 2 forms: imperfective and perfective.
They're given in that order.*

painting *n* 1. *(activity)* раскра́шивание; 2. *(the art)* жи́вопись *f*; 3. *(work of art)* карти́на; ро́спись *f* ♦ **body** ~ раскра́шивание те́ла ♦ **You possess the kind of beauty that inspires great paintings.** Ты облада́ешь тако́й красото́й, кото́рая вдохновля́ет вели́киххудо́жников.

pal *n* това́рищ, прия́тель, друг ♦ **hangout** ~ друг, с кото́рым слоня́ешься вме́сте *(explanation)* ♦ **true** ~ настоя́щий това́рищ.

palace *n* дворе́ц ♦ ~ **of love** дворе́ц любви́ ♦ ~ **of Marriage** *(Russian office for civil marriages)* Дворе́ц бракосочета́ния.

pal around *vi* развлека́ться с *(прия́телем)* ♦ **I want someone to pal around with.** Я ищу́ того́, с кем смогу́ развле́каться.

pale *adj* бле́дный, -ая, -ое, -ые *(short forms:* бле́ден, бледна́, -о, -ы*)* ♦ **How pale and bland all other woman are before you.** Как бле́дны и неинтере́сны все други́е же́нщины по сравне́нию с тобо́й.

pale *vi* ме́ркнуть / поме́ркнуть ♦ **Any other woman pales in comparison with you.** Люба́я друга́я же́нщина ме́ркнет в сравне́нии с тобо́й.

palimony *n* алиме́нты, кото́рые пла́тятся челове́ку, с кото́рым сожи́тельствовал *(explanation).*

pallor *n* бле́дность *f.*

palm *n (of the hand)* ладо́нь *f* ♦ **I'll read your palm.** Я прочита́ю по твое́й ладо́ни.

palpitate *vi* уча́щённо би́ться ♦ **Every time the phone has rung, my heart has palpitated.** Как то́лько зазвони́т телефо́н, у меня́ выска́кивает се́рдце. ♦ **Every time I see you walk** *(1)* **...through the door.** / *(2)* **...down the hallway...** / *(3)* **...along the street...** / *(4)* **...past me...** / *(5)* **...into the room... my heart begins palpitating wildly and I am flooded with** *(6)* **exquisite** / *(7)* **overpowering** / *(8)* **dizzying sensations of adoration and desire for you.** Ка́ждый раз, когда́ я ви́жу, как ты *(1)* ...вхо́дишь в дверь... / *(2)* ...идёшь по коридо́ру... / *(3)* ...идёшь по у́лице... / *(4)* ...прохо́дишь ми́мо... / *(5)* ...вхо́дишь в ко́мнату... моё се́рдце начина́ет выска́кивать из груди́, и меня́ переполня́ют *(6)* о́стрые / *(7)* невыноси́мые / *(8)* головокружи́тельные чу́вства обожа́ния и жела́ния.

pamper *vt* ба́ловать / изба́ловать *(whom = acc.)*, не́жить *(whom = acc.)*, изне́живать / изне́жить *(whom = acc.)* ♦ **I** *(1)* **intend** / *(2)* **want to pamper you like you've never** *(1)* **...imagined possible.** / *(2)* **...been pampered before in your whole life.** Я собира́юсь / *(2)* хочу́ ба́ловать тебя́ так, *(1)* ...как ты никогда́ и вообрази́ть не могла́. / *(2)* ...как никто́ никогда́ в жи́зни не ба́ловал тебя́. ♦ **Every day I'm going to look for new ways to pamper you.** Ка́ждый день я бу́ду стреми́ться по-но́вому ба́ловать тебя́. ♦ **Let's have a contest to see who can pamper who the most. But I'm sure I'll win.** Дава́й, устро́им соревнова́ние: кто мо́жет лу́чше ба́ловать друго́го. Но я уве́рен *(ж: уве́рена)*, что вы́играю. ♦ **I want to spend the rest of my life pampering you.** Я хочу́ провести́ оста́ток свое́й жи́зни, балу́я тебя́.

pampered *adj* избало́ванный, -ая, -ое, -ые, изне́женный, -ая, -ое, -ые ♦ **You're going to be the most pampered woman in the whole country.** Ты бу́дешь са́мой избало́ванной же́нщиной в стране́. ♦ **Do you like to be pampered? You're going to be -- a lot!** Ты лю́бишь, что́бы тебя́ ба́ловали? Я бу́ду тебя́ о́чень ба́ловать!

pampering *n* баловство́ ♦ **mutual** ~ взаи́мное баловство́.

panache *n* цвети́стость *f*, я́ркость *f.*

pang *n* уко́л; *pl* му́ки, муче́ния ♦ ~ **of conscience** уко́л со́вести ♦ ~**s of jealousy** му́ки ре́вности.

panic *n* па́ника ♦ **Panic gripped me.** Па́ника охвати́ла меня́.

panties *n, pl* тру́сики ♦ **black** ~**s** чёрные тру́сики ♦ **crotchless** ~**s** тру́сики с откры́той

How to use the Cyrillic alphabet on the Internet
is the subject of Appendix 20 on page 789.

промéжностью ♦ **edible** ~s съедóбные трýсики ♦ **open-crotch** ~s трýсики с откры́той промéжностью ♦ **pretty** ~ прелéстные трýсики ♦ **red** ~s крáсные трýсики ♦ **sheer** ~s прозрáчные трýсики ♦ **silk** ~s шёлковые трýсики ♦ **I want to take off your panties** *(1)* **...and kiss you all over.** / *(2)* **...and kiss everything they're hiding.** / *(3)* **...with my tongue** / *(4)* **lips.** Я хочý снять с тебя́ трýсики *(1)* ...и целовáть тебя́ всю. / *(2)* ...и целовáть всё то, что они́ пря́чут. / *(3)* ...свои́м языкóм. / *(4)* ...свои́ми губáми.

panti-girdle *n* трýсики с резúнками.

pants *n, pl (long)* брю́ки; штаны́; *(short)* шóрты ♦ **capri** ~s брю́ки «кáпри» ♦ **flare-legged** ~s расклёшенные брю́ки ♦ **form-fitting** ~s подчёркивающие фóрмы брю́ки ♦ **hot** ~s корóткие обтя́гивающие шóрты ♦ **low-slung** ~s брю́ки, котóрые нóсятся нúже тáлии *(explanation)* ♦ **suit** ~s костю́мные брю́ки, брю́ки костю́ма ♦ **pair of** ~s брю́ки; штаны́ ♦ **I want to watch you take off your pants.** Я хочý смотрéть, как ты снимáешь брю́ки.

pantyhose *n* колгóтки *pl* ♦ **crotchless** ~ колгóтки с откры́той промéжностью ♦ **sheer** ~ прозрáчные колгóтки ♦ **I love taking off your pantyhose.** Я люблю́ снимáть твои́ колгóтки.

pantywaist *n* нéженка.

paper *n* 1. бумáга; 2. *(pl) (documents)* докумéнты ♦ **marriage** ~s брáчные бумáги.

paradise *n (heaven)* рай; *(bliss)* блажéнство ♦ **absolute** ~ абсолю́тный рай ♦ **beautiful** ~ прекрáсный рай ♦ **endless** ~ бесконéчный рай ♦ **genuine** ~ настоя́щий рай ♦ **real** ~ настоя́щий рай ♦ **sheer** ~ и́стинный рай ♦ **wonderful** ~ чудéсный рай.

paradise: phrases

You transport me into paradise. Ты перенóсишь меня́ в рай. ♦ **For me, to think of spending time with you in the same house is like imagining what paradise would be like.** Для меня́ дýмать о том, чтóбы провести́ врéмя с тобóй в однóм дóме -- э́то воображáть, как бýдто я в раю́. ♦ **To me, you are the gate of paradise.** Для меня́ ты вратá в рай. ♦ **I** *(1)* **long** / *(2)* **yearn for the paradise of your** *(3)* **precious** / *(4)* **dear** / *(5)* **wonderful arms.** Я *(1)* тоскýю / *(2)* томлю́сь по рáю твои́х *(3)* драгоцéнных / *(4)* дороги́х / *(5)* удиви́тельных рук. ♦ **You make my** *(1)* **life** / *(2)* **world a paradise.** Ты превращáешь *(1)* ...мою́ жизнь... / *(2)* ...мой мир... в рай. ♦ **I want to take up permanent residence in the paradise of making love with you.** Я хочý заня́ть постоя́нную резидéнцию в раю́ блúзости с тобóй. ♦ **Making love with you is** *(1)* **sheer** /*(2)* **absolute paradise.** Занимáться любóвью с тобóй -- *(1)* и́стинный / *(2)* абсолю́тный рай. ♦ **With your** *(1)* **sweet** / *(2)* **tender** / *(3)* **gentle love you have** *(4,5)* **transformed my life into a paradise.** Своéй *(1)* слáдкой / *(2)* нéжной / *(3)* мя́гкой любóвью ты *(4)* преврати́ла / *(5)* преобрази́ла мою́ жизнь в рай. ♦ **Oh, Darling, I'm in paradise!** О, дорогáя, я в раю́! ♦ **What an absolute paradise!** Что за абсолю́тный рай! ♦ **This is paradise!** Это рай! ♦ **Your kisses send me to paradise.** Твои́ поцелýи перенóсят меня́ в рай. ♦ **I want to make your life a(n)** *([1]* **endless** / *[2]* **beautiful) paradise of love.** Я хочý сдéлать твою́ жизнь *([1]* бесконéчным / *[2]* прекрáсным) рáем любви́. ♦ **I feel like a stranger in paradise.** Я чýвствую себя́ как чужестрáнец в раю́. ♦ **The sight of your beautiful face makes me dream of all the pleasures in paradise.** Твоё прекрáсное лицó заставля́ет мечтáть о всех наслаждéниях рáя.

paradisiacal *adj* рáйский, -ая, -ое, -ие ♦ ~ **relationship** рáйские отношéния ♦ **That's just a paradisiacal dream!** Это прóсто рáйская мечтá!

paragon *n* эталóн, образéц ♦ **You are a paragon of** *(1)* **loveliness** / *(2)* **beauty** / *(3)* **seductiveness** / *(4)* **voluptuousness** / *(5)* **sexiness** / *(6)* **vivacity.** Ты эталóн *(1,2)* красоты́ / *(3)* соблазни́тельности / *(4)* чýвственности / *(5)* сексуáльности / *(6)* жи́вости. ♦ **Your**

Russian adjectives have long and short forms.
Where short forms are given, they are labeled as such.

face is a paragon of *(1)* **beauty** / *(2)* **loveliness.** Твоё лицо -- образе́ц *(1,2)* красоты́. ◆
I'm no paragon of virtue, but I have my principles. Я не образе́ц доброде́тели, но у
меня́ есть свои́ при́нципы.

parcel *n* посы́лка *(See phrases under* **package***).*

parents *n, pl* роди́тели ◆ **both** ~s о́ба роди́теля ◆ **foster** ~s приёмные роди́тели ◆ **my** ~s
мои́ роди́тели ◆ **your** ~s *(familiar)* твои́ роди́тели; *(polite)* Ва́ши роди́тели.

park *n* парк ◆ **amusement** ~ парк с развлече́ниями ◆ **entertainment** ~ парк с развле-
че́ниями.

parka *n* па́рка.

part *vi* расстава́ться / расста́ться, расходи́ться / разойти́сь, разлуча́ться / разлучи́ться
◆ ~ **(as) friends** расстава́ться / расста́ться друзья́ми ◆ ~ **for good** расста́ться навсегда́
◆ ~ **out** расста́ться навсегда́.

part *n* 1. часть *f*, части́ца; 2. *(role)* роль *f* ◆ **best** ~ лу́чшая часть ◆ **big** ~ больша́я часть
◆ **easy** ~ лёгкая часть, са́мое лёгкое ◆ **every** ~ **of** *(1)* **my** / *(2)* **your body** ка́ждая части́ца
(1) моего́ / *(2)* твоего́ те́ла ◆ **first** ~ пе́рвая часть ◆ **hard** ~ тру́дная часть, са́мое тру́д-
ное ◆ **important** ~ ва́жная часть ◆ **last** ~ после́дняя часть ◆ **main** ~ основна́я часть
◆ **my** ~ 1. моя́ часть; 2. *(role)* моя́ роль ◆ **other** ~ друга́я часть ◆ **small** ~ небольша́я
часть ◆ **special** ~ осо́бая части́ца ◆ **worst** ~ ху́дшая часть ◆ **your** ~ 1. твоя́ часть;
2. *(role)* твоя́ роль ◆ **do** *(1)* **my** / *(2)* **your** ~ де́лать / сде́лать *(1,2)* свою́ часть ◆ **for my**
~ с мое́й стороны́ ◆ **take** ~ принима́ть / приня́ть уча́стие *(in what = +* в *+ prep.).*

> **part: phrases**

You are a special part of my life. Ты осо́бая части́ца мое́й жи́зни. ◆ **Thank you for
being part of my life.** Спаси́бо тебе́ за то, что ты ста́ла *(ж: стал)* части́цей мое́й
жи́зни. ◆ **You will always be a part of me.** Ты всегда́ бу́дешь ча́стью меня́. ◆ **I wish
that I could kiss both your eyes very softly many, many, many times — before moving on
to other delectable parts.** Я хоте́л бы о́чень мя́гко целова́ть о́ба твои́х гла́за мно́го,
мно́го, мно́го раз пре́жде, чем передви́нуться к други́м восхити́тельным места́м.

participate *vi* уча́ствовать *(in what = +* в *+ prep.).*

participation *n* уча́стие.

participatory *adj* уча́ствующий, -ая, -ее, -ие.

parting *n* 1. *(separation)* расстава́ние, разлу́ка; 2. *(leave-taking)* проща́ние ◆ **pain of** ~ боль
расстава́ния ◆ **I can't stand the thought of parting from you.** Я не могу́ переста́ть
ду́мать о проща́нии с тобо́й. ◆ **Parting is such sweet sorrow.** Сладка́ го́речь расста-
ва́ния.

partner *n* партнёр, спу́тник *m*, спу́тница *f* ◆ **athletic** ~ партнёр по спо́рту ◆ **awesome
female** ~ потряса́ющая же́нщина ◆ **awesome male** ~ потряса́ющий мужчи́на ◆ *(1,2)*
compatible ~ *(1)* подходя́щий / *(2)* совмести́мый партнёр ◆ **cuddling** ~ партнёр, кото́-
рого прия́тно обнима́ть *(1 term)* ◆ **dancing** ~ партнёр по та́нцам ◆ **energetic** ~ энер-
ги́чный партнёр ◆ **eternal** ~ ве́чный партнёр ◆ **former** ~ бы́вший партнёр ◆ **hiking**
~ друг по похо́дам ◆ **life** ~ спу́тник *m* / спу́тница *f* жи́зни ◆ **lifelong** ~ спу́тник *m* /
спу́тница *f* на всю жи́знь ◆ **magnificent** ~ замеча́тельный партнёр ◆ ~s **in the game
of life** партнёры в жи́зненной игре́ ◆ **passionate** ~ стра́стный друг ◆ **peer** ~ ра́вный
партнёр ◆ **previous** ~ предыду́щий партнёр ◆ **snuggle** ~ партнёр, кото́рого прия́тно
обнима́ть *(1 term)* ◆ **suitable** ~ подходя́щий партнёр ◆ **swing** ~ партнёр по сви́нгу
◆ **tennis** ~ те́ннисный партнёр ◆ **workout** ~ партнёр по трениро́вкам.

> **partner: verb terms**

change ~s меня́ть / перемени́ть партнёров ◆ **find a** ~ найти́ партнёра ◆ *(1)* **look** / *(2)*
search for a ~ *(1,2)* иска́ть партнёра ◆ **want a** ~ хоте́ть партнёра ◆ **yearn for a** ~

> *Russian nouns are either masculine, feminine or neuter.
> Adjectives with them will be the same.*

жа́ждать партнёра.

partner: phrases

I'm *(1)* **looking** / *(2)* **searching for a** *(3)* **compatible** / *(4)* **life partner.** Я *(1,2)* ищу́ *(3)* ...совмести́мого партнёра. / *(4)* ...спу́тницу *(ж: спу́тника)* жи́зни. ♦ **I don't ever want to change partners again.** Я не хочу́ опя́ть меня́ть партнёров. ♦ **You and I are on such a common wavelength that I really believe neither of us could ever find a more** *(1)* **suitable** / *(2)* **compatible partner.** Мы с тобо́й насто́лько на одно́й волне́, что я уве́рен *(ж: уве́рена)*, ни оди́н из нас не смо́жет найти́ бо́лее *(1,2)* подходя́щего партнёра. ♦ **I give myself to you as your partner.** Я отдаю́ себя́ тебе́. ♦ **I want you to be my** *(1)* **...eternal partner.** / *(2)* **...partner for life.** Я хочу́, что́бы ты была́ *(ж: был)* мои́м *(1)* ...ве́чным партнёром. / *(2)* ...спу́тником жи́зни. ♦ **What more could I ask for than you as my lifelong partner.** О чём бо́льшем мог *(ж: могла́)* бы я проси́ть, чем о тебе́, как моём спу́тнике на всю жизнь. ♦ **I'm looking for a partner to enhance my life.** Я ищу́ партнёра, с кото́рым смогу́ улу́чшить свою́ жизнь. ♦ **My heart yearns so fiercely to have a partner like you in life, one who combines a gentle spirit with sexuality, good-heartedness, intelligence, and a loving nature.** Моё се́рдце так нейстово жа́ждет тако́го спу́тника жи́зни, как ты, тако́го, кто́ соединя́ет мя́гкий хара́ктер с сексуа́льностью, добросерде́чием, интеллиге́нтностью и лю́бящей нату́рой. ♦ **I want you for my snuggle partner.** Ты челове́к, к кото́рому я хочу́ прильну́ть. ♦ **You're the best snuggle partner a person could have.** Ты наилу́чший на све́те партнёр для объя́тий.

partnership *n (relationship)* взаимоотноше́ния *pl* ♦ **loving** ~ любо́вныевзаимоотноше́ния.

party *vi* быть на вечери́нке, быть в компа́нии; ходи́ть на вечери́нки ♦ **I like to party sometimes.** Мне иногда́ нра́вится быть в компа́нии.

party *n* ве́чер, вечери́нка, компа́ния ♦ **anniversary** ~ ежего́дная вечери́нка ♦ **bachelor** ~ холостя́цкая пиру́шка *(пе́ред сва́дьбой)* ♦ **birthday** ~ день рожде́ния ♦ **costume** ~ костюми́рованная вечери́нка ♦ **crazy** ~ безу́мная вечери́нка ♦ **dinner** ~ обе́д **engagement** ~ вечери́нка по по́воду помо́лвки ♦ **farewell** ~ проща́льный ве́чер, проща́льная вечери́нка ♦ **get-acquainted** ~ вечери́нка с це́лью знако́мства с но́выми людьми́ ♦ **goodbye** ~ проща́льный ве́чер, проща́льная вечери́нка ♦ **graduation** ~ выпускна́я вечери́нка, вечери́нка по слу́чаю оконча́ния *(1) (school)* шко́лы / *(2) (university)* университе́та / *(3) (college)* ко́лледжа ♦ **impromptu** ~ вечери́нка экспро́мтом ♦ **keg** ~ вечери́нка с бочо́нком пи́ва ♦ **promotion** ~ вечери́нка по слу́чаю повыше́ния по слу́жбе ♦ **wedding** ~ сва́дьба ♦ **welcome** ~ приве́тственная вечери́нка ♦ **wild** ~ ди́кая вечери́нка.

party: other terms

give a ~ устра́ивать / устро́ить ве́чер(и́нку) ♦ **go to a** ~ идти́ / пойти́ на ве́чер(и́нку) ♦ **have a** ~ устра́ивать / устро́ить ве́чер(и́нку) ♦ **host a** ~ устра́ивать / устро́ить ве́чер(и́нку) ♦ **life of the** ~ душа́ компа́нии ♦ ~ **pooper** некомпане́йский челове́к ♦ **throw a** ~ устра́ивать / устро́ить вечер(и́нку).

party: sentences

(1) **I'd like to invite you...** / *(2)* **Would you like to go (with me)... to a party** *(3)* **...tomorrow (evening).** / **?** / *(4)* **...this afternoon** / *(5)* **evening.** / **?** / *(6)* **...on Friday** / *(7)* **Saturday** / *(8)* **Sunday** *(9)* **afternoon** / *(10)* **evening.** / **?** *(1)* Я хоте́л *(ж: хоте́ла)* бы пригласи́ть тебя́... / *(2)* Не хоте́ла *(ж: хоте́л)* бы ты пойти́ (со мной)... на вечери́нку *(3)* ...за́втра (ве́чером). / **?** / *(4)* ...сего́дня днём / *(5)* ве́чером. / **?** / *(6)* ...в пя́тницу / *(7)* суббо́ту / *(8)* воскресе́нье *(9)* днём / *(10)* ве́чером. / **?**

party-goer *n* ходя́щий (-ая, -ые) на вечери́нки.

partying *n*: ♦ **I've given up partying.** Я поко́нчил *(ж: поко́нчила)* с вечери́нками.

Learn more about Russian customs in Appendix 15, page 782.

party pooper *n (slang)* некомпанейский человек.

pass *vi* проходить / пройти *(past = + ми́мо + gen.)*, дви́гаться / дви́нуться *(past = + ми́мо + gen.)* ♦ **Don't pass me by.** Не пройди́ ми́мо меня́. ♦ **You could easily pass for twenty / thirty.** Ты мо́жешь легко́ сойти́ за двадцатиле́тнюю *(ж: двадцатиле́тнего)* / тридцатиле́тнюю *(ж: тридцатиле́тнего)*.

pass *n:* ♦ **make a ~** пыта́ться уха́живать *(at whom = + за + instr.)* ♦ **make a ~ (at someone) with one's eyes** флиртова́ть глаза́ми *(at whom = + с + instr.)*, постре́ливать *(at whom = + с + instr.)* ♦ **You made a pass at** *(1)* **him /** *(2)* **her with your eyes.** Ты постре́ливала *(ж: постре́ливал)* в *(1)* него́ / *(2)* неё гла́зками. ♦ **I imagine a lot of guys must make passes at you.** Я представля́ю, что вероя́тно мно́жество мужчи́н флирту́ют с тобо́й. ♦ **A lot of guys make passes at me, but I don't pay any attention.** Мно́жество мужчи́н флирту́ют со мной, но я не обраща́ю внима́ния.

passion *n* 1. страсть *f*; 2. стра́стность *f* ♦ *(1,2)* **raging ~** *(1)* бу́рная / *(2)* исступлённая страсть ♦ **abiding ~** неистреби́мая страсть ♦ *(1,2)* **all-consuming ~** *(1)* испепеля́ющая / *(2)* всепоглоща́ющая страсть ♦ **animal ~** живо́тная страсть ♦ **blazing ~** опаля́ющая страсть ♦ **boundless ~** беспреде́льная страсть ♦ **burning ~** горя́чий пыл, сжига́ющая страсть ♦ **consuming ~** всепоглоща́ющая страсть ♦ **creative ~** созида́тельная страсть ♦ **desperate ~** отча́янная страсть ♦ **dizzying ~** головокружи́тельная страсть ♦ **earth-shaking ~** землесотряса́ющая страсть ♦ **exploding ~** взрыва́ющаяся страсть ♦ *(1,2)* **fierce ~** *(1)* неи́стовая / *(2)* я́ростная страсть ♦ **fiery ~** о́гненная страсть ♦ **frenzied ~** исступлённая стра́сть ♦ **great ~** больша́я страсть ♦ **hoarded ~** нако́пленная страсть ♦ **incredible ~** невероя́тная страсть ♦ **insatiable ~** ненасы́тная страсть ♦ **intense ~** интенси́вная страсть ♦ **never-ending ~** бесконе́чная страсть ♦ **possessive ~** со́бственническая страсть ♦ **quivering ~** тре́петная стра́стность ♦ **raging ~** бе́шеная страсть ♦ *(1,2)* **red-hot ~** *(1)* обжига́ющая / *(2)* жа́ркая страсть ♦ **savage ~** ди́кая страсть ♦ **searing ~** опаля́ющая страсть ♦ **selfless ~** беззаве́тная стра́сть ♦ **slow, tender ~** ме́дленная, не́жная страсть ♦ **smouldering ~** затаённая страсть ♦ **stormy ~** бу́рная страсть ♦ **swirling ~** бурля́щая страсть ♦ **tender ~** не́жная страсть ♦ *(1,2)* **unbridled ~** *(1)* разну́зданная / *(2)* необу́зданная страсть ♦ **unfulfilled ~** неосуществлённая страсть ♦ *(1-3)* **unrestrained ~** *(1)* несде́ржанная / *(2)* безу́держная / *(3)* необу́зданная страсть ♦ **vast ~** огро́мная страсть ♦ **whirlwind ~** взвихрённая страсть ♦ *(1,2)* **white-hot ~** *(1)* бе́шеная / *(2)* раскалённая страсть ♦ **wild ~** ди́кая страсть.

passion: verb terms

abandon oneself to ~ предава́ться / преда́ться стра́сти ♦ **arouse ~** пробужда́ть /пробуди́ть страсть, возбужда́ть / возбуди́ть страсть ♦ **awaken ~** пробужда́ть / пробуди́ть страсть, возбужда́ть / возбуди́ть страсть ♦ **experience ~** испы́тывать / испыта́ть страсть ♦ **feel ~** чу́вствовать / почу́вствовать страсть ♦ **fill** *(1)* **me /** *(2)* **you with ~** наполня́ть / напо́лнить *(1)* меня́ / *(2)* тебя́ стра́стью ♦ **ignite ~** разжига́ть / разже́чь страсть ♦ **intoxicate me with ~** опьяня́ть меня́ стра́стью ♦ **kindle ~** воспламеня́ть / воспламени́ть страсть ♦ **know ~** знать / позна́ть страсть ♦ **share ~** разделя́ть страсть *(with whom = + с + instr.)* ♦ **soar into ~** пари́ть в стра́сти ♦ **stir ~s** пробужда́ть / пробуди́ть стра́сти *(in whom = + в + prep.)*, всколыхну́ть стра́сти *(in whom = + в + prep.)*.

passion: other terms

art of arousing ~ иску́сство возбужда́ть страсть ♦ **burning flame of ~** жгу́чее пла́мя стра́сти ♦ **dizzying heights of ~** головокружи́тельные верши́ны стра́сти ♦ **firestorm of ~** о́гненный шторм стра́сти ♦ **fit of ~** поры́в стра́сти ♦ **flame(s) of** *(1,2)* **~** пла́мя *(1)* жела́ния / *(2)* стра́сти ♦ *(1,2)* **intensity of your ~** *(1)* интенси́вность / *(2)* си́ла твое́й стра́сти ♦ **kaleidoscope of ~** калейдоско́п стра́сти ♦ **moments of ~** моме́нты стра́сти

A slash always denotes "or."
You can choose the numbered words before and after.

♦ ~ **for art** страсть к иску́сству ♦ ~ **for life** страсть к жи́зни ♦ ~ **for music** страсть к му́зыке ♦ **sea of** ~ мо́ре стра́сти ♦ **source of** ~ исто́чник стра́сти ♦ **storm of** ~ шторм стра́сти ♦ **surge of** ~ прили́в стра́сти ♦ **tide of** ~ прили́в стра́сти ♦ **tremor of** ~ дрожь стра́сти ♦ *(1,2)* **vortex of** ~ *(1)* вихрь / *(2)* водоворо́т стра́сти ♦ **wild sea of** ~ бе́шеное мо́ре стра́сти.

---
passion: *my passion for you*

Never have I felt such boundless passion for anyone. Никогда́ я не чу́вствовал *(ж: чу́вствовала)* тако́й беспреде́льной стра́сти к кому́-либо. ♦ **My passion for you is insatiable.** Моя́ страсть к тебе́ ненасы́тна. ♦ **I've never** *(1)* **felt** / *(2)* **experienced** / *(3)* **known such** *(4)* **...passion...** / *(5)* **...a kaleidoscope of passion... with anyone (in my whole life).** Я никогда́ ни с кем (в жи́зни) не *(1)* чу́вствовал *(ж: чу́вствовала)* / *(2)* испы́тывал *(ж: испы́тывала)* / *(3)* знал *(ж: зна́ла)* *(4)* ...тако́й стра́сти. / *(5)* ...тако́го калейдоско́па стра́сти. ♦ **I didn't realize I was capable of such** *(1)* **intense** / *(2)* **wild** / *(3)* **unrestrained passion.** Я не осознава́л *(ж: осознава́ла)*, что был спосо́бен *(ж: была́ спосо́бна)* на таку́ю *(1)* си́льную / *(2)* ди́кую / *(3)* необу́зданную страсть. ♦ **My passion for you will never cool.** Моя́ страсть к тебе́ никогда́ не осты́нет. ♦ **I love you with a passion that is more than fierce.** Я люблю́ тебя́ со стра́стью, кото́рая бо́лее, чем неи́стовая. ♦ **My entire being is** *(1)* **assailed** / *(2)* **tormented by the all-consuming need to take you in my arms and revel in the reservoir of your passion.** Я весь *(1)* охва́чен / *(2)* изму́чен всепоглоща́ющей жа́ждой заключи́ть тебя́ в объя́тия и упива́ться твое́й стра́стью. ♦ **The fierce passion I feel for you** *(1)* **...is something I have never experienced before.** / *(2)* **...is utterly consuming me.** / *(3)* **...dominates all my thoughts and attention.** / *(4)* **... overwhelms me.** Неи́стовая страсть к тебе́ *(1)* ...э́то не́что тако́е, чего́ я никогда́ пре́жде не испы́тывал *(ж: испы́тывала)* / *(2)* ...по́лностью поглоща́ет меня́. / *(3)* ...госпо́дствует над все́ми мои́ми мы́слями и внима́нием. / *(4)* ...переполня́ет меня́. ♦ **I cannot describe the passion that seized my soul when I first** *(1)* **saw** / *(2)* **kissed you.** Не могу́ описа́ть страсть, охвати́вшую мою́ ду́шу, когда́ я впервы́е *(1)* уви́дел *(ж: уви́дела)* / *(2)* поцелова́л *(ж: поцелова́ла)* тебя́. ♦ **It is impossible for me to curb my passion when I'm** *(1)* **with** / *(2)* **around you.** Невозмо́жно для меня́ обу́здывать мою́ страсть, когда́ я *(1)* ...с тобо́й. / *(2)* ...вблизи́ тебя́.

---
passion: *you arouse my passion*

You *(1,4)* **arouse** / *(2,5)* **stir** / *(3,6)* **awake such passion in me.** *(1-3)* Ты возбужда́ешь / *(4-6)* пробужда́ешь таку́ю страсть во мне. ♦ **You intoxicate me with passion.** Ты опьяня́ешь меня́ стра́стью. ♦ **You ignite passion in me so easily.** Ты так легко́ разжига́ешь страсть во мне. ♦ **You stir passions in me** *(1)* **...that no one else would ever be able to do.** / *(2)* **...such as I've never** *(3)* **known** / *(4)* **experienced in all my life.** Ты всколыхну́ла *(ж: всколыхну́л)* стра́сти во мне *(1)* ...каки́е никто́ ещё не смог всколыхну́ть. / *(2)* ...каки́е я никогда́ в жи́зни не *(3)* знал *(ж: зна́ла)* / *(4)* испы́тывал *(ж: испы́тывала)*. ♦ **When I look into the dark irises of your eyes, I am** *(1)* **drawn** / *(2)* **sucked into a wild vortex of passion.** Когда́ я вгля́дываюсь в тёмную ра́дужную оболо́чку твои́х глаз, я *(1)* втя́гиваюсь / *(2)* заса́сываюсь в ди́кий вихрь стра́сти. ♦ **Forgive me for writing such a steamy letter, but my thoughts of you mixed together with my feelings for you arouse passions in me that are difficult to contain.** Прости́те меня́ за тако́е чу́вственное письмо́, но мои́ мы́сли о Вас, вме́сте с чу́вствами к Вам, пробужда́ют во мне страсть, кото́рую тру́дно сдержа́ть. ♦ **You are truly a master at the art of arousing passion.** Ты, пра́вда, ма́стер в иску́сстве возбужда́ть страсть.

---
passion: *I'll arouse your passion*

You're going to swirl in a kaleidoscope of passion. Ты закру́жишься в калейдоско́пе

Common adult weights are given in Appendix 10, page 777.

стра́сти. ♦ **I want to see passion dance in your eyes.** Я хочу́ ви́деть та́нец стра́сти в твои́х глаза́х. ♦ **I want to make all the passion in you leap into a wild storm.** Я хочу́, чтобы вся твоя́ стра́стность переросла́ в бе́шеный шторм. ♦ *(1)* **I want to...** / *(2)* **I'm going to...** *(3)* **...ignite a firestorm of passion in you.** / *(4)* **...teach you a new definition of passion.** / *(5)* **...fill you with so much passion that you'll be saying things in languages that don't exist in this world.** / *(6)* **...take you to new heights of dizzying passion.** / *(7)* **...ignite fires of passion in you that will rage for a lifetime.** *(1+3)* Я хочу́ заже́чь... / *(2+3)* Я зажгу́... о́гненный шторм стра́сти в тебе́. / *(1+4)* Я хочу́ научи́ть... / *(2+4)* Я научу́... тебя́ но́вому определе́нию стра́сти. / *(1+5)* Я хочу́ напо́лнить... / *(2+5)* Я напо́лню... тебя́ тако́й стра́стью, что ты заговори́шь на языка́х, кото́рые не существу́ют в э́том ми́ре. / *(1+6)* Я хочу́ подня́ть... / *(2+6)* Я подниму́... тебя́ к но́вым верши́нам головокружи́тельной стра́сти. / *(1+7)* Я хочу́ разже́чь... / *(2+7)* Я разожгу́... тако́й ого́нь стра́сти в тебе́, кото́рый бу́дет бушева́ть всю жизнь. ♦ **I love to watch your breasts heave when passion sweeps through you.** Я люблю́ ви́деть, как вздыма́ется твоя́ грудь, когда́ страсть охва́тывает тебя́. ♦ **One of these days I'm going to teach you the true meaning of passion.** В оди́н из э́тих дней я обучу́ тебя́ и́стинному понима́нию стра́сти. ♦ **Upward and upward and upward I want** *(1)* **...to propel** / *(2)* **send you into passion.** / *(3)* **...you to soar into passion.** Я хочу́ *(1,2)* ...подня́ть тебя́ всё вы́ше, вы́ше и вы́ше к верши́нам стра́сти. / *(3)* ..., чтобы ты всё вы́ше, вы́ше и вы́ше пари́ла в стра́сти. ♦ **When I** *(1)* **have** / *(2)* **get you in my arms (again),** **I'm going to** *(3)* **...love you with** *(4)* **fierce** / *(5)* **savage passion.** / *(6)* **...arouse tides of sweet feeling in you that will sweep you into a storm of passion.** Когда́ я (опя́ть) *(1,2)* заключу́ тебя́ в объя́тия, то *(3)* ...бу́ду люби́ть тебя́ с *(4)* я́ростной / *(5)* ди́кой стра́стью. / *(6)* ...разбужу́ пото́к не́жных чувств в тебе́, кото́рый бро́сит тебя́ в бу́рю стра́сти. ♦ **My lips will rouse flames of** *(1,2)* **passion to leap from your soul and surge through your veins.** Мои́ гу́бы пробу́дят пла́мя *(1)* жела́ния / *(2)* стра́сти, кото́рое бу́дет бушева́ть в тебе́ и струи́ться в ве́нах. ♦ **Oh, how I'm going to stir your passions!** О, как я разбужу́ твою́ страсть. ♦ **I will always be your faithful navigator in the Sea of Passion.** Я всегда́ бу́ду твои́м ве́рным шту́рманом в мо́ре стра́сти. ♦ **That's just a small promise of the passion to come.** Это то́лько ма́ленькое обеща́ние приходя́щей стра́сти.

---
passion: *the passion in you*

Your shyness and quiet nature belie the passion within you. Твоя́ засте́нчивость и споко́йный хара́ктер даю́т неве́рное представле́ние о твое́й стра́стности. ♦ **I was surprised at the sheer intensity of your passion.** Я был поражён *(ж: была́ поражена́)* и́стинной си́лой твое́й стра́сти. ♦ **I love the way you respond with so much passion.** Мне нра́вится, что ты отвеча́ешь мне с тако́й большо́й стра́стью. ♦ **The sheer intensity of your passion was** *(1)* **fantastic** / *(2)* **incredible** / *(3)* **unbelievable.** Интенси́вность твое́й стра́сти была́ про́сто *(1)* фантасти́ческой / *(2,3)* невероя́тной. ♦ **Has your passion (for me) cooled?** Твоя́ страсть (ко мне) осты́ла? ♦ **Your passion (for me) seems to have cooled.** Твоя́ страсть (ко мне), ка́жется, осты́ла.

---
passion: *our passion together*

I love to share passion with you. Мне нра́вится разделя́ть страсть с тобо́й. ♦ **It's so wonderful to share passion with you.** Так замеча́тельно разделя́ть страсть с тобо́й. ♦ **I want to spend the rest of my life sharing passion with you.** Я хочу́ провести́ оста́ток жи́зни, разделя́я страсть с тобо́й. ♦ **Our kindled passion will burst into an uncontrollable, raging fire.** На́ша воспламени́вшаяся страсть разгори́тся неконтроли́руемым, бе́шенным огнём. ♦ **And every night we will reignite our passion and revel in our boundless, undiminishable love.** И ка́ждую ночь мы бу́дем опя́ть зажига́ть на́шу страсть и пирова́ть в на́шей безграни́чной, неугаси́мой любви́. ♦ **Oh, what consummate ecs-**

An italicized ж in parentheses indicates a woman speaking.

tasy I will bestow upon you when we swirl into the wild vortex of our passion. О, какой совершенный экстаз я подарю тебе, когда мы закружимся в бешеном водовороте страсти. ♦ **Together you and I can experience the ecstasy of unbridled passion.** Вместе ты и я сможем испытать экстаз необузданной страсти. ♦ **Our bodies will fuse together in exquisite pleasure until we are** *(1)* **flung /** *(2)* **hurled into a wild sea of passion.** Наши тела сольются в изысканном наслаждении до тех пор, пока мы не будем *(1,2)* брошены в бешеное море страсти.

passion: *for life, etc*

I have a passion for life. У меня есть страсть к жизни. ♦ **I have a(n)** *(1)* **abiding /** *(2)* **great /** *(3)* **vast passion for** *(4)* **life /** *(5)* **living.** У меня *(1)* неистребимая / *(2)* большая / *(3)* огромная страсть к *(4,5)* жизни. ♦ **I have a passion for arts and music.** У меня страсть к искусству и музыке.

passion: *quotation*

"**Passion cannot be beautiful without excess; one either loves too much or not enough.**" — *Pascal,* Pensées «Страсть не может быть прекрасной без избытка; человек либо любит слишком сильно, либо недостаточно.» *Паскаль.*

passionate *adj* страстный, -ая, -ое, -ые, пылкий, -ая, -ое, -ие; задорный, -ая, -ое, -ые ♦ **extremely** ~ чрезвычайно страстный, -ая, -ое, -ые ♦ **fiercely** ~ неистово страстный ♦ **frantically** ~ неистово страстный ♦ **incredibly** ~ невероятно страстный ♦ **insatiably** ~ ненасытно страстный. ♦ **savagely** ~ дико страстный ♦ **wildly** ~ дико страстный.

passionate: *phrases*

That was the most passionate kiss anyone has ever give me. Это был самый страстный поцелуй, который когда-либо кто-то дарил мне. ♦ **I never** *(1)* **guessed /** *(1)* **imagined that you were so passionate.** Я никогда не *(1)* предполагал *(ж: предполагала)* / *(2)* воображал *(ж: воображала)*, что ты такая страстная *(ж: такой страстный)*. ♦ **You are** *(1)* **so /** *(2)* **very** *(3,4)* **passionate.** Ты *(1)* очень / *(2)* такая *(3)* страстная / *(4)* пылкая. *(ж: Ты [1] очень / [2] такой [3] страстный / [4] пылкий.)* ♦ **You were so passionate (in my arms).** Ты была такой страстной (в моих объятиях). ♦ **I'm usually very placid and quiet, but you make me so passionate.** Я обычно очень спокойный *(ж: спокойная)*, но ты делаешь меня таким страстным *(ж: такой страстной)*. ♦ **You are the most passionate lover I have ever known.** Ты самая страстная любовница из всех, бывших у меня, *(ж: Ты самый страстный любовник из всех, бывших у меня.)* ♦ *(1)* **You /** *(2)* **I have a very passionate nature.** У *(1)* тебя / *(2)* меня очень страстная натура. ♦ **I'm passionate about painting.** Я страстный художник.

passionately *adv* страстно, пылко ♦ **I want to kiss you passionately (**[1]**...all over. /** [2]**...on every part of your body.).** Я хочу целовать тебя страстно *(*[1]*...всю. /* [2] *...каждую частицу твоего тела.).* ♦ **You responded so** *(1,2)* **passionately.** Ты отвечала так *(1)* страстно / *(2)* пылко. ♦ **I was astonished at how passionately you responded.** Я был удивлён, как страстно ты отвечала. ♦ **I love you** *(1,2)* **passionately.** Я люблю тебя *(1)* страстно / *(2)* пылко.

passion-filled *adj* наполненный (-ая, -ое, -ые) страстью.

past *adj* прошлый, -ая, -ое, -ые.

past *n* прошлое *(adjectival noun)* ♦ **in the** ~ в прошлом ♦ **I don't care about the past.** Меня не интересует твоё прошлое. ♦ **Everybody has a past.** У каждого есть прошлое. ♦ **Julia is in the past.** Юлия -- в прошлом. ♦ **I'd prefer not to talk about my (lurid) past.** Я предпочту не говорить о своём (страшном) прошлом. ♦ **I want to break with the past.** Я хочу порвать с прошлым. ♦ *(1)* **I want to... /** *(2)* **I'm going to... make you (completely) forget** *(3)* **...your loneliness of the past. /** *(4)* **...the past.** *(1)* Я хочу заставить... /

Procedures for getting married to a Russian are outlined in Appendix 18, page 787.

(2) Я заста́влю... тебя́ (по́лностью) забы́ть *(3)* ...твоё одино́чество в про́шлом. / *(4)* ...про́шлое.

pastor *n* па́стор.

pat *vt* погла́живать *(whom = acc., on what = +* по *+ dat.)* ♦ **~ on the back** погла́живать по спине́.

patch up *vt (relations)* ула́живать / ула́дить *(what = acc.),* нала́живать / нала́дить *(what = acc.)* ♦ **~ things up** ула́живать / ула́дить дела́, нала́живать / нала́дить отноше́ния ♦ **I hope we can patch things up (between us).** Наде́юсь, что мы смо́жем нала́дить (на́ши) отноше́ния.

paternal *adj* отцо́вский, -ая, -ое, -ие.

paternity *n* отцо́вство.

path *n* путь *m,* тропа́ ♦ **Cupid's ~** тропа́ Купидо́на ♦ **~ of least resistance** путь наиме́ньшего сопротивле́ния ♦ *(1)* **It's amazing...** / *(2)* **I'm so** *(3)* **glad** / *(4)* **happy... that our paths crossed (in this** *[5]* **...life.** / *[6]* **[...big, crowded.]** **world).** *(1)* Это удиви́тельно,... / *(2)* Я так *(3)* рад *(ж: ра́да)* / *(4)* сча́стлив *(ж: сча́стлива),...* что на́ши пути́ пересекли́сь *([5]* ...в э́той жи́зни. / *[6]* ...в э́том *[*большо́м, многолю́дном*]* ми́ре.).

pathetic *adj* жа́лкий, -ая, -ое, -ие.

patience *n* терпе́ние ♦ **admirable ~** похва́льное терпе́ние ♦ **great ~** большо́е терпе́ние ♦ **tremendous ~** огро́мное терпе́ние ♦ **wonderful ~** удиви́тельное терпе́ние.

patience: other terms

a lot of ~ большо́е терпе́ние, мно́го терпе́ния ♦ **display ~** проявля́ть / прояви́ть терпе́ние ♦ **exhibit ~** проявля́ть / прояви́ть терпе́ние ♦ **have ~** име́ть терпе́ние ♦ **lose ~** теря́ть / потеря́ть терпе́ние ♦ **model of ~** образе́ц терпе́ния ♦ **show ~** проявля́ть / прояви́ть терпе́ние.

patience: phrases

You have a lot of patience. У тебя́ мно́го терпе́ния. ♦ **Please have patience with me.** Пожа́луйста, будь терпели́ва *(ж: терпели́в)* со мной. ♦ **You'll find that I have a lot of patience.** Ты узна́ешь, что у меня́ большо́е терпе́ние.

patient *adj* терпели́вый, -ая, -ое, -ые *(short forms:* терпели́в, -а , -о, -ы*)* ♦ **Please be patient with me.** Пожа́луйста, будь терпели́ва *(ж: терпели́в)* со мной. ♦ **I'm very patient.** Я о́чень терпели́в *(ж: терпели́ва).* ♦ **If you (really) value our relationship, try to be more patient.** Если ты (действи́тельно) це́нишь на́ши отноше́ния, попыта́йся быть бо́лее терпели́вой *(ж: терпели́вым).*

pattern *n* 1. *(model; type)* образе́ц; 2. *(design)* рису́нок, узо́р ♦ **flower(y) ~** цвето́чный узо́р ♦ **pretty ~** краси́вый узо́р ♦ **I like the pattern of your dress.** Мне нра́вится узо́р твоего́ пла́тья. ♦ **The thought patterns that yielded your choice of words and sentences in your ad reveal the exact same raging hunger for love and affection that I harbor within me.** Мы́сли, роди́вшие вы́бор слов и предложе́ний в Ва́шем объявле́нии, говоря́т о то́чно тако́й же неи́стовой жа́жде любви́ и не́жности, кото́рая таи́тся во мне.

paw *vt* ла́пать *(what, whom = acc.).*

pay *vi* плати́ть / заплати́ть *(for what = +* за *+ acc.)* ♦ **Let me pay for it.** Позво́ль мне заплати́ть за э́то. ♦ **I'll pay for it.** Я заплачу́ за э́то. ♦ **Did you pay (for it) (already)?** Ты заплати́ла *(ж: заплати́л)* (за э́то) (уже́)? ♦ **I paid (for it) (already)** Я заплати́л *(ж: заплати́ла)* (за э́то) (уже́). ♦ **I didn't pay (for it) (yet).** Я (ещё) не заплати́л *(ж: заплати́ла)* (за э́то).

peace *n* 1. *(no war)* мир; 2. *(tranquility)* споко́йствие, поко́й ♦ **~ and quiet** мир и тишина́ ♦ **wonderful ~** удиви́тельное споко́йствие.

peaceful *adj (tranquil)* споко́йный, -ая, -ое, -ые, ти́хий, -ая, -ое, -ие.

---

*A list of conjugated Russian verbs is given
in Appendix 3 on page 699.*

peacefulness *n* споко́йствие ♦ **happy and radiant** ~ счастли́вое и сия́ющее споко́йствие.

peach *n* пе́рсик ♦ **ripe** ~ созре́вший пе́рсик ♦ **You're as luscious as a ripe peach.** Ты со́чная, как созре́вший пе́рсик.

peak *n* верши́на ♦ **~ of pleasure** верши́на наслажде́ния ♦ **~s of** *(1)* **celestial** / *(2)* **ethereal** / *(3)* **heavenly bliss** верши́ны *(1-3)* неземно́го блаже́нства ♦ **soar to the ~ of pleasure** взлете́ть на верши́ну наслажде́ния ♦ **My lips will travel first to one sensitive peak, then to the other.** Мои́ гу́бы бу́дут путеше́ствовать снача́ла к одно́й чувстви́тельной верши́нке, зате́м к друго́й.

pearl *n* же́мчуг *(pl:* жемчуга́*)* ♦ **rope of ~s** ни́тка же́мчуга ♦ **seed ~s** жемчу́жины ♦ **string of ~s** ни́тка же́мчуга.

pecs, pectorals *n, pl (pectorals)* грудны́е мы́шцы.

peculiar *adj (strange)* стра́нный, -ая, -ое, -ые.

peculiarity *n* осо́бенность *f*, характе́рная черта́.

peek *vi* загля́дывать / загляну́ть, подгля́дывать ♦ **Don't peek!** Не подгля́дывай! ♦ **I promise I won't peek.** Обеща́ю, я не бу́ду подгля́дывать.

peel *vt (clothes)* сбра́сывать / сбро́сить *(what = acc.)* ♦ **How I dream of the day when I can peel away your silk underwear to reveal the full,** *(1)* **glorious** / *(2)* **magnificent splendor of your of your beautiful, luscious body.** Как я мечта́ю о том дне, когда́ смогу́ сбро́сить с тебя́ шёлковое бельё, что́бы откры́ть напо́лненную до краёв, *(1)* великоле́пную / *(2)* замеча́тельную ро́скошь твоего́ прекра́сного, со́чного те́ла.

peepers *n, pl (slang) (eyes)* глаза́.

peerless *adj* несравне́нный, -ая, -ое, -ые ♦ **I am totally in awe of your peerless physical beauty.** Я в по́лном благогове́нии пе́ред твое́й несравне́нной физи́ческой красото́й. ♦ **You are peerless among women.** Среди́ же́нщин ты несравне́нна.

peignoir *n (woman's loose negligee or dressing gown)* пенью́ар.

pelvis *n* таз.

pen *vt (write)* писа́ть / написа́ть ♦ **I'll try to pen you another letter soon.** Я попыта́юсь вско́ре написа́ть тебе́ ещё одно́ письмо́.

pen *n* ру́чка.

penchant *n* накло́нность *f*, скло́нность *f* ♦ **I have a penchant for fun and frolic.** У меня́ скло́нность к весе́лью и ша́лости. ♦ **I'm hoping you have a penchant for erotica, the same as I.** Я наде́юсь, что у тебя́, так же как и у меня́, есть скло́нность к эро́тике.

pendant *n* куло́н, подве́ска.

penetrate *vt* проника́ть / прони́кнуть *(what = acc.)* ♦ **~ deeply** проника́ть / прони́кнуть глубоко́ ♦ **~ inside** проника́ть / прони́кнуть внутрь.

penetration *n* проникнове́ние ♦ **deep ~** глубо́кое проникнове́ние.

penis *n* пе́нис.

penpal *n* друг по перепи́ске *(pl:* друзья́ по перепи́ске*)*.

pension *n* пе́нсия ♦ **government** ~ госуда́рственная пе́нсия ♦ **military** ~ вое́нная пе́нсия ♦ **I** *(1)* **get** / *(2)* **receive a (monthly) pension.** Я (ежеме́сячно) *(1,2)* получа́ю пе́нсию.

pensioner *n* пенсионе́р *m*, пенсионе́рка *f*.

people *n, pl* лю́ди.

perceptible *adj* улови́мый, -ая, -ое, -ые ♦ **barely** ~ едва́ улови́мый, -ая, -ое, -ые

perceptive *adj* воспринима́ющий, -ая, -ее, -ие, восприи́мчивый, -ая, -ое, -ые, прони- ца́тельный, -ая, -ое, -ые ♦ **You're very perceptive.** Ты о́чень проница́тельная *(ж: про- ница́тельный)*.

perfect *adj* превосхо́дный, -ая, -ое, -ые, соверше́нный, -ая, -ое, -ые ♦ **Mr. Perfect** совер- ше́нство, соверше́нный челове́к ♦ **picture** ~ соверше́нный (-ая, -ое, -ые), как карти́на

For Russian adjectives, the masculine form is spelled out, followed by the feminine, neuter and plural endings.

(1 term) ♦ **Don't expect that I'm Mr. Perfect.** Не ожида́й, что я соверше́нство. ♦ **Everything about you is perfect.** Всё в тебе́ соверше́нно. ♦ **I'm not perfect. (Who is?)** Я не соверше́нство. (Да и кто соверше́нство?) ♦ **I don't expect you to be perfect.** Я не жду от тебя́ соверше́нства. ♦ **You look picture perfect in that dress.** В э́том пла́тье ты вы́глядишь соверше́нной карти́ной.

perfectly *adv* прекра́сно, превосхо́дно, соверше́нно.

perfection *n* соверше́нство ♦ **heavenly** ~ боже́ственное соверше́нство ♦ **In your beauty their is a perfection such as I have never** *(1)* **beheld** / *(2)* **seen** / *(3)* **encountered.** В твое́й красоте́ тако́е соверше́нство, како́го я никогда́ не *(1)* замеча́л / *(2)* ви́дел / *(3)* встреча́л. ♦ **You are as close to perfection as a rose.** Ты так же близка́ к соверше́нству, как ро́за. ♦ **You are perfection itself.** Ты само́ соверше́нство.

perfidious *adj* преда́тельский, -ая, -ое, -ие, веролóмный, -ая, -ое, -ые, кова́рный, -ая, -ое, -ые.

perfume *n* духи́ *pl* ♦ **cheap** ~ дешёвые духи́ ♦ **delicate** ~ не́жные духи́ ♦ **favorite** ~ люби́мые духи́ ♦ **intoxicating** ~ опьяня́ющие духи́ ♦ **seductive** ~ соблазни́тельные духи́ ♦ **scent of** ~ арома́т духо́в ♦ **Smelling your perfume just adds fuel to the fire of my desire for you.** Когда́ я вдыха́ю твои́ духи́, ого́нь мое́й стра́сти к тебе́ разжига́ется ещё сильне́е. ♦ **Just smelling your perfume sends the blood rushing in my veins.** Кровь начина́ет бе́шено струи́ться в мои́х ве́нах про́сто от арома́та твои́х духо́в. ♦ **The fragrance of your perfume will haunt me for the rest of my life.** Арома́т твои́х духо́в оста́нется со мной на всю жизнь.

perfumed *adj* наду́шенный, -ая, -ое, -ые.

perfunctory *adj (cursory)* пове́рхностный, -ая, -ое, -ые, бе́глый, -ая, -ое, -ые; *(careless)* небре́жный, -ая, -ое, -ые.

period *n* 1. пери́од; 2. *(menstrual period)* (менструа́льный) пери́од ♦ **There's a required waiting period after the divorce.** По́сле разво́да существу́ет тре́буемый пери́од ожида́ния. ♦ **I'm overdue with my period.** Мой пери́од запа́здывает. ♦ **My period is late.** Мой пери́од по́здно. ♦ **Are you having your period?** У тебя́ сейча́с пери́од? ♦ **I have my period.** У меня́ сейча́с пери́од. ♦ **My period (just) started.** Мой пери́од (то́лько) начался́. ♦ **When will your period be finished?** Когда́ твой пери́од зако́нчится? ♦ **My period will be finished in two days.** Мой пери́од зако́нчится че́рез два дня.

permanence *n* постоя́нство, неизме́нность *f* ♦ ~ **of marriage** постоя́нство бра́ка.

permeate *vt* пропи́тывать / пропита́ть *(what = acc.)*; прони́зывать *(what = acc.)*.

perpetual *adj* ве́чный, -ая, -ое, -ые, бесконе́чный, -ая, -ое, -ые; постоя́нный, -ая, -ое, -ые; пожи́зненный, -ая, -ое, -ые.

perpetually *adv* ве́чно; постоя́нно; пожи́зненно ♦ **You seem to be perpetually unhappy.** Ты всегда́ вы́глядишь несча́стной *(ж: несча́стным)*. ♦ **My greatest desire (in life) is to make you perpetually happy.** Моё наибо́льшое жела́ние (в жи́зни) -- сде́лать тебя́ счастли́вой *(ж: был счастли́вым)* навсегда́.

perplexed *adj* озада́ченный, -ая, -ое, -ые, сби́тый (-ая, -ое, -ые) с то́лку, ошеломлённый, -ая, -ое, -ые, недоуме́нный, -ая, -ое, -ые, недоумева́ющий, -ая, -ее, -ие ♦ **I'm afraid I'm a bit perplexed (about it all).** Я бою́сь, я немно́го озада́чен *(ж: озада́чена)* / ошеломлён *(ж: ошеломлена́)* (всем э́тим).

perplexing *adj* озада́чивающий, -ая, -ее, -ие, ошеломля́ющий, -ая, -ее, -ие.

persnickety *adj (slang)* разбо́рчивый, -ая, -ое, -ые, привере́дливый, -ая, -ое, -ые.

person *n* 1. *(individual)* челове́к *(pl:* лю́ди), ли́чность *f*; 2. *(body)* те́ло ♦ **absent-minded** ~ рассе́янный челове́к ♦ **active** ~ акти́вный челове́к ♦ **adventurous** ~ лю́бящий приключе́ния челове́к ♦ **aggressive** ~ напо́ристый челове́к ♦ **all-around** ~ всесторо́нний

See Appendix 19 for notes on sending mail to Russia and Ukraine.

человéк ♦ **ambitious** ~ честолюби́вый человéк ♦ **another** ~ другóй человéк ♦ **arrogant** ~ высокомéрный человéк ♦ **assertive** ~ напóристый человéк ♦ **awful** ~ ужа́сный человéк ♦ **bad** ~ плохóй человéк ♦ **boring** ~ ску́чный человéк ♦ **brave** ~ хра́брый человéк ♦ **candid** ~ откровéнный человéк ♦ **can-do** ~ 1. *(capable)* умéлый человéк; 2. *(decisive)* реши́тельный человéк ♦ **capable** ~ спосóбный человéк ♦ **capricious** ~ капри́зный человéк ♦ **carefree** ~ беззабóтный человéк ♦ **caring** ~ забóтливый человéк ♦ **cautious** ~ осторóжный человéк ♦ **charming** ~ обая́тельный человéк ♦ *(1,2)* **cheerful** ~ *(1)* бóдрый / *(2)* весёлый человéк ♦ **clever** ~ умный человéк; сообрази́тельный человéк ♦ **communicative** ~ общи́тельный человéк ♦ **compassionate** ~ сострада́тельный человéк ♦ **complex** ~ слóжный человéк ♦ **conceited** ~ тщесла́вный человéк ♦ **conscientious** ~ добросóвестный человéк ♦ **confident** ~ увéренный (в себé) человéк ♦ **considerate** ~ внима́тельный человéк ♦ **controlling** ~ человéк, стремя́щийся всегда́ быть хозя́ином положéния *(explanation)*. ♦ *(1,2)* **courteous** ~ *(1)* вéжливый / *(2)* любéзный человéк ♦ **cowardly** ~ трусли́вый человéк ♦ **crude** ~ гру́бый человéк ♦ **cruel** ~ жестóкий человéк ♦ **cultivated** ~ культу́рный человéк ♦ **cynical** ~ цини́чный человéк ♦ **decent** ~ поря́дочный человéк ♦ **different** ~ другóй человéк ♦ **difficult** ~ тру́дный человéк ♦ **diligent** ~ стара́тельный человéк ♦ **disgusting** ~ отврати́тельный человéк ♦ **easy-going** ~ лёгкий человéк ♦ **eccentric** ~ взбалмóшный человéк ♦ **eclectic** ~ человéк с тóнким вку́сом ♦ **educated** ~ образóванный человéк ♦ **emotional** ~ эмоциона́льный человéк ♦ **energetic** ~ энерги́чный человéк ♦ **erratic** ~ взбалмóшный человéк ♦ **exceptional** ~ исключи́тельный человéк ♦ **fair** ~ справедли́вый человéк ♦ **forgetful** ~ забы́вчивый человéк ♦ **frank** ~ откровéнный человéк ♦ *(1,2)* **friendly** ~ *(1)* привéтливый / *(2)* дружелю́бный человéк ♦ **frivolous** ~ легкомы́сленный человéк ♦ **fun** ~ весёлый человéк ♦ **funny** ~ 1. *(humorous)* смешнóй человéк; 2. *(strange)* стра́нный человéк ♦ **fussy** ~ суетли́вый человéк ♦ **generic** ~ обы́чный человéк ♦ **generous** ~ щéдрый человéк ♦ **genial** ~ гениа́льный человéк ♦ **gentle** ~ мя́гкий человéк ♦ *(1,2)* **gifted** ~ *(1)* дарови́тый / *(2)* одарённый человéк ♦ *(1,2)* **gloomy** ~ *(1)* мра́чный / *(2)* хму́рый человéк ♦ **good** ~ хорóший человéк ♦ **good-for-nothing** ~ никуды́шный человéк ♦ **good-natured** ~ доброду́шный человéк ♦ **greedy** ~ жа́дный человéк ♦ **happy-go-lucky** ~ беспéчный человéк ♦ **happy** ~ счастли́вый человéк ♦ **hardworking** ~ усéрдный человéк ♦ **heartless** ~ бессердéчный человéк ♦ **honest** ~ чéстный человéк ♦ **humane** ~ гума́нный человéк ♦ **immoral** ~ безнра́вственный человéк ♦ **impressionable** ~ впечатли́тельный человéк ♦ **inner** ~ душа́ ♦ **independent** ~ самостоя́тельный человéк ♦ **industrious** ~ трудолюби́вый человéк ♦ **insensitive** ~ бесчу́вственный человéк ♦ **intelligent** ~ у́мный человéк ♦ **interesting** ~ интерéсный человéк ♦ **irritable** ~ раздражи́тельный человéк ♦ **jealous** ~ ревни́вый человéк ♦ **kind** ~ дóбрый человéк ♦ **kind-hearted** ~ отзы́вчивый человéк ♦ **lazy** ~ лени́вый человéк ♦ **lively** ~ подви́жный человéк ♦ **lonely** ~ одинóкий человéк ♦ **lucky** ~ счастли́вый человéк, счастли́вец ♦ **married** ~ жена́тый человéк ♦ **marvelous** ~ превосхóдный человéк ♦ **mean** ~ злой человéк ♦ **modest** ~ скрóмник, скрóмный человéк. ♦ **mysterious** ~ таи́нственный человéк ♦ **naive** ~ наи́вный человéк ♦ **narrow(-minded)** ~ ограни́ченный человéк ♦ **neat** ~ аккура́тный человéк ♦ **nervous** ~ беспокóйный человéк ♦ **nice** ~ прия́тный человéк ♦ **night** ~ полунóчник ♦ **objective** ~ объекти́вный человéк ♦ **observant** ~ наблюда́тельный человéк ♦ **optimistic** ~ оптими́ст ♦ *(1,2)* **ordinary** ~ *(1)* обыкновéнный / *(2)* обы́чный человéк ♦ **organized** ~ организóванный человéк ♦ **patient** ~ терпели́вый человéк ♦ ~ **in love** влюблённый человéк ♦ ~ **of high energy** чрезвыча́йно энерги́чный человéк ♦ ~ **of (high) integrity** (óчень) чéстный человéк ♦ ~ **of (high) principle(s)** принципиа́льный человéк ♦ ~ **of my dreams** человéк моéй мечты́ ♦ ~ **with inner beauty** человéк с вну́тренней красотóй ♦ ~ **without morals**

When terms are listed after a main word, a tilde ~
is used to indicate the main word.

безнра́вственный челове́к ♦ ~ **without principles** беспринци́пный челове́к ♦ **plastic** ~ бесчу́вственный челове́к ♦ *(1,2)* **polite** ~ *(1)* ве́жливый / *(2)* любе́зный челове́к ♦ **positive** ~ положи́тельный челове́к ♦ **practical** ~ практи́чный челове́к ♦ **promiscuous** ~ распу́щенный челове́к ♦ *(1,2)* **pushy** ~ *(1)* вла́стный / *(2)* напо́ристый челове́к ♦ **quality** ~ челове́к с высо́кими ка́чествами ♦ **quiet** ~ споко́йный челове́к ♦ **real** ~ реа́льный челове́к ♦ **reasonable** ~ разу́мный челове́к ♦ **reliable** ~ надёжный челове́к ♦ **remarkable** ~ замеча́тельный челове́к ♦ *(1,2)* **reserved** ~ *(1)* сде́ржанный / *(2)* за́мкнутый челове́к ♦ **resourceful** ~ нахо́дчивый челове́к ♦ **responsible** ~ отве́тственный челове́к ♦ **reticent** ~ скры́тный челове́к ♦ **romantic** ~ романти́чный челове́к ♦ **savvy** ~ зна́ющий челове́к ♦ **secretive** ~ скры́тный челове́к ♦ **self-confident** ~ самоуве́ренный челове́к ♦ **self-controlled** ~ вы́держанный челове́к ♦ **self-reliant** ~ самостоя́тельный челове́к ♦ **self-restrained** ~ вы́держанный челове́к ♦ **sensible** ~ здравомы́слящий челове́к ♦ **sensitive** ~ чувстви́тельный челове́к ♦ **sentimental** ~ сентимента́льный челове́к ♦ **serious** ~ серьёзный челове́к ♦ **shallow** ~ пове́рхностный челове́к ♦ **shrewd** ~ проница́тельный челове́к ♦ **shy** ~ засте́нчивый челове́к ♦ *(1,2)* **silent** ~ *(1)* неразгово́рчивый / *(2)* молчали́вый челове́к ♦ **simple** ~ просто́й челове́к ♦ **sincere** ~ и́скренний челове́к ♦ **single** ~ холосто́й челове́к ♦ **sociable** ~ общи́тельный челове́к ♦ **sophisticated** ~ утончённый челове́к ♦ **spiritual** ~ духо́вный челове́к ♦ **splendid** ~ отли́чный челове́к ♦ **spoiled** ~ избало́ванный челове́к ♦ **spontaneous** ~ спонта́нный челове́к ♦ *(1,2)* **stiff** ~ *(1)* напряжённый / *(2)* холо́дный челове́к ♦ **stingy** ~ скупо́й челове́к ♦ **straightforward** ~ прямо́й челове́к ♦ **strange** ~ стра́нный челове́к ♦ **strict** ~ стро́гий челове́к ♦ **strong** ~ си́льный челове́к ♦ **stubborn** ~ упря́мый челове́к ♦ **stupid** ~ глу́пый челове́к ♦ **superficial** ~ пове́рхностный челове́к ♦ *(1,2)* **sympathetic** ~ *(1)* отзы́вчивый / *(2)* чу́ткий челове́к ♦ *(1,2)* **taciturn** ~ *(1)* неразгово́рчивый / *(2)* молчали́вый челове́к ♦ **tactful** ~ такти́чный челове́к ♦ **take-charge** ~ лиди́рующий челове́к ♦ **talkative** ~ разгово́рчивый челове́к ♦ **talented** ~ тала́нтливый челове́к ♦ **terrible** ~ ужа́сный челове́к ♦ **thinking** ~ мы́слящий челове́к ♦ **thoughtful** ~ внима́тельный челове́к ♦ **timid** ~ ро́бкий челове́к ♦ **trusting** ~ дове́рчивый челове́к ♦ **truthful** ~ правди́вый челове́к ♦ **unbearable** ~ невыноси́мый челове́к ♦ **uninhibited** ~ челове́к без ко́мплексов ♦ **unpredictable** ~ непредсказу́емый челове́к ♦ **unselfish** ~ бескоры́стный челове́к ♦ **unusual** ~ необыкнове́нный челове́к ♦ **vain** ~ тщесла́вный челове́к ♦ **warm(-hearted)** ~ серде́чный челове́к ♦ **weak** ~ сла́бый челове́к ♦ **well-balanced** ~ хорошо́ уравнове́шенный челове́к ♦ **well-bred** ~ воспи́танный челове́к ♦ **well-mannered** ~ воспи́танный челове́к ♦ **well-organized** ~ организо́ванный челове́к ♦ **well-read** ~ начи́танный челове́к ♦ **well-rounded** ~ всесторо́нне разви́тый челове́к, всесторо́нний челове́к ♦ **whimsical** ~ капри́зный челове́к ♦ **wise** ~ му́дрый челове́к ♦ **witty** ~ остроу́мный челове́к ♦ *(1-3)* **wonderful** ~ *(1)* замеча́тельный / *(2)* прекра́сный / *(3)* удиви́тельный челове́к.

person: sentences

I want to *(1)* **loll** / *(2)* **lounge** / *(3)* **luxuriate** / *(4)* **revel forever in the heavenly enchantment of your person.** Я хочу́ ве́чно *(1,2)* ...не́житься в твоём боже́ственном очарова́нии. / *(3)* ...наслажда́ться / *(4)* упива́ться твои́м боже́ственным очарова́нием. ♦ **How I long to immerse myself in the soft, lingering fragrance of your person.** Как я жа́жду погрузи́ться в не́жный арома́т твоего́ те́ла. ♦ **Deep down in my heart I know that you are the person for me.** В глубине́ се́рдца я зна́ю, что ты челове́к для меня́. ♦ **I need you to make me a better person than I am.** Мне нужна́ *(ж: ну́жен)* ты для того́, что́бы стать лу́чше, чем я есть. ♦ **It's the inner person that counts.** Душа́ -- вот, что гла́вное. ♦ *(1)* **You're...** / *(2)* **I'm... that kind of person.** *(1)* Ты / *(2)* Я тако́й челове́к. ♦ **I have so much love in my heart to give to the right person. And I really have the feeling that this right person is you.**

A list of abbreviations used in the dictionary is given on page 10.

В моём се́рдце так мно́го любви́, кото́рую я хочу́ подари́ть заслу́живающему её челове́ку. И я определённо чу́вствую, что э́тот челове́к ты. ♦ **You are the person** *(1)* **...of my dreams.** / *(2)* **...that I've been waiting for all my life.** / *(3)* **...that I've been dreaming of all my life.** Ты челове́к *(1)* ...мое́й мечты́. / *(2)* ...кото́рого я ждал *(ж: ждала́)* всю жизнь. / *(3)* ..., о кото́ром я мечта́л *(ж: мечта́ла)* всю свою́ жизнь.

persona *n (social front)* «ма́ска», показна́я сторона́ ли́чности; *(image)* «и́мидж» ♦ **strong** ~ си́льный «и́мидж».

personable *adj* представи́тельный, -ая, -ое, -ые.

personal *adj* ли́чный, -ая, -ое, -ые ♦ *(1)* **Can** / *(2)* **May I ask you a personal question? Are you** *(3)* **attached** / *(4)* **married?** *(1,2)* Могу́ я зада́ть Вам ли́чный вопро́с? *(3)* ...У Вас кто́-то есть? / *(4)* ...Вы за́мужем? *(ж: Вы жена́ты?)* ♦ **Am I being too personal?** Я был сли́шком беста́ктным? *(ж: Я была́ сли́шком беста́ктной?)* ♦ **That's (a little too) personal.** Это (немно́го) беста́ктно.

personality *n* хара́ктер; нату́ра, ли́чность *f*, индивидуа́льность *f* ♦ **abrasive** ~ ре́зкий хара́ктер ♦ **beautiful** ~ прекра́сные осо́бенности хара́ктера ♦ **charming** *(1-3)* ~ обая́тельная *(1)* индивидуа́льность / *(2)* ли́чность, *(3)* обая́тельный хара́ктер ♦ **cheerful** ~ весёлый хара́ктер ♦ **complex** ~ сло́жный хара́ктер ♦ **dynamic** ~ динами́чный хара́ктер ♦ **ebullient** ~ кипу́чая ли́чность ♦ *(1,2)* **effervescent** ~ кипу́чая *(1)* нату́ра / *(2)* ли́чность ♦ **engaging** ~ привлека́тельная ли́чность, обая́тельный хара́ктер ♦ **genial** ~ гениа́льная ли́чность ♦ **gentle** ~ мя́гкий хара́ктер ♦ **great** ~ замеча́тельная ли́чность ♦ **kaleidoscope** ~ (постоя́нно) меня́ющаяся ли́чность ♦ *(1,2)* **nice** ~ *(1)* прия́тный / *(2)* хоро́ший хара́ктер ♦ **outgoing** ~ общи́тельный хара́ктер ♦ **polished** ~ отто́ченная ли́чность ♦ **quiet** ~ споко́йный хара́ктер ♦ **radiant** ~ лучеза́рная ли́чность, лучи́стая индивидуа́льность ♦ **scintillating** ~ искря́щаяся индивидуа́льность, искря́щийся хара́ктер ♦ **shining** ~ сия́ющая ли́чность ♦ **sparkling** ~ сверка́ющая индивидуа́льность, искря́щаяся нату́ра ♦ **spontaneous** ~ спонта́нная ли́чность ♦ **sprightly** ~ весёлый хара́ктер ♦ **strong** ~ си́льный хара́ктер ♦ **sunny** ~ со́лнечная ли́чность ♦ **terrific** ~ великоле́пная ли́чность ♦ **type A** ~ хара́ктер ти́па A ♦ **type B** ~ хара́ктер ти́па Б ♦ **vivacious** ~ жизнера́достная ли́чность ♦ **warm** ~ тёплый хара́ктер ♦ **well-rounded** ~ це́льность нату́ры ♦ **winning** ~ побежда́ющая ли́чность, победи́тельный хара́ктер ♦ **wonderful** ~ замеча́тельная ли́чность, удиви́тельный хара́ктер ♦ **your** ~ *(familiar)* твоя́ нату́ра; *(polite)* Ва́ша нату́ра.

---

personality: phrases

You brighten my life with your *(1)* **effervescent** / *(2)* **sparkling personality.** Твоя́ *(1)* кипу́чая / *(2)* искря́щаяся нату́ра озаря́ет мою́ жизнь. ♦ **There is such genuine warmth in your personality.** В твое́й индивидуа́льности тако́е и́скреннее тепло́. ♦ **The magnetism of your personality is (completely) irresistible.** Магнети́зм твое́й индивидуа́льности (соверше́нно) неотрази́м. ♦ **You have such a warm, outgoing personality.** У тебя́ тако́й тёплый, общи́тельный хара́ктер. ♦ **You have such a** *(1)* **sparkling** / *(2)* **scintillating** / *(3)* **charming** / *(4)* **radiant personality.** У тебя́ така́я *(1)* сверка́ющая / *(2)* искря́щаяся / *(3)* обая́тельная / *(4)* лучи́стая индивидуа́льность. ♦ **Your** *(1)* **charming** / *(2)* **warm** / *(3)* **gentle** / *(4)* **scintillating personality has me completely under its spell.** Твой *(1)* обая́тельный / *(2)* тёплый / *(3)* мя́гкий / *(4)* искря́щийся хара́ктер по́лностью меня́ очарова́л. ♦ **Do you know why I'm so attracted to you? It's your wonderful personality.** Ты зна́ешь, почему́ я так увлечён *(ж: увлечена́)* тобо́й? За твой удиви́тельный хара́ктер. ♦ **You have a very** *(1)* **engaging** / *(2)* **vivacious personality.** У тебя́ о́чень *(1)* обая́тельный / *(2)* живо́й хара́ктер. ♦ **Your blithe spirit and shining personality enrapture me completely.** Твой весёлый дух и сия́ющая индивидуа́льность совер-

---

The accents on Russian words are to show how to pronounce them. You don't have to copy the accents when writing to someone.

ше́нно восхища́ют меня́. ♦ **Since the day we met I've been oblivious of** *(1)* **everything / (2) all else except your (3) sunny / (4) vivacious personality.** Со дня на́шей встре́чи я могу́ ду́мать *(1,2)* то́лько о тебе́, о твое́й *(3)* со́лнечной / *(4)* живо́й индивидуа́льности. ♦ **Frankly, your personality is a little too abrasive (for my liking).** Открове́нно, на мой взгляд, у тебя́ дово́льно ре́зкий хара́ктер.

personals *n, pl (personal ads)* объявле́ния «ты и я», ча́стные / ли́чные / бра́чные объявле́ния; *(section)* отде́л знако́мств. ♦ **online ~s** ли́чные объявле́ния на интерне́те. ♦ **All day long after reading your ad in the personals (section) I've been aching to get home and write you this letter.** Весь день по́сле прочте́ния Ва́шего объявле́ния в отде́ле знако́мств я стреми́лся прийти́ домо́й и написа́ть Вам э́то письмо́. ♦ **There were several other ads in the personals that were somewhat interesting, but yours struck an immediate chord in my heart and I knew with a certainty that there was no way I could not write to you.** В отде́ле знако́мств бы́ло не́сколько други́х объявле́ний, чём-то интере́сных, но Ва́ше вы́звало неме́дленный о́тклик в моём се́рдце, и я твёрдо знал *(ж: зна́ла),* что не могу́ не написа́ть Вам. ♦ **I read your ad in the personals.** Я прочита́л *(ж: прочита́ла)* Ва́ше объявле́ние в отде́ле «ча́стных объявле́ний». ♦ **I never** *(1)* **dreamed / (2) thought I could meet someone so nice (and [3] beautiful / [4] handsome) through the personals.** Я никогда́ не *(1)* мечта́л *(ж: мечта́ла)* / *(2)* ду́мал *(ж: ду́мала),* что смогу́ встре́тить кого́-либо тако́го ми́лого (и *[3]* прекра́сного / *[4]* краси́вого) по объявле́нию.

perspective *n* аспе́кт, то́чка зре́ния ♦ **different ~** друга́я то́чка зре́ния.

perspiration *n* пот.

perspire *vi* поте́ть.

persuade *vt* 1. *(induce)* угова́ривать / уговори́ть *(whom = acc.);* 2. *(convince)* убежда́ть / убеди́ть *(whom = acc.)* ♦ **I hope I can persuade you to** *(1)* **...come with me. / (2) ...meet me. / (3) ...let me see you.** Я наде́юсь, что смогу́ убеди́ть Вас *(1)* ...пойти́ *(on foot)* / пое́хать *(by veh.)* со мной. / *(2)* ...встре́титься со мной. / *(3)* ...позво́лить мне уви́деться с Ва́ми.

persuasion *n* 1. *(persuading)* убежде́ние; 2. *(conviction, opinion)* убежде́ние, мне́ние; 3. *(religious belief)* вероиспове́дание ♦ **I'm of the same persuasion.** У меня́ таки́е же убежде́ния.

persuasive *adj* убеди́тельный, -ая, -ое, -ые ♦ **Your charm is very persuasive.** Твоё обая́ние о́чень убеди́тельно.

persuasively *adv* убеди́тельно.

pert *adj* 1. *(lively, spirited)* бо́йкий, -ая, -ое, -ие, задо́рный, -ая, -ое, -ые; 2. *(chic)* шика́рный, -ая, -ое, -ые, элега́нтный, -ая, -ое, -ые.

pertness *n* бо́йкость *f.*

pervade *vt* наполня́ть *(what, whom = acc.);* насыща́ть *(what, whom = acc.);* прони́зывать *(what, whom = acc.);* пропи́тывать *(what, whom = acc.);* распространя́ться *(what, whom = + по + dat.)* ♦ **Your blithe spirit pervades my thoughts wherever I go.** Я постоя́нно ду́маю о твое́й сия́ющей жизнера́достности.

perverse *adj* превра́тный, -ая, -ое, -ые, поро́чный, -ая, -ое, -ые, извращённый, -ая, -ое, -ые.

perversion *n* совраще́ние, извраще́ние.

pervert *n* извраще́нец.

perverted *adj* извращённый, -ая, -ое, -ые, поро́чный, -ая, -ое, -ые.

pessimism *n* пессими́зм.

pessimist *n* пессими́ст.

> *If no accent is shown on a word with a capitalized vowel,*
> *it means that the capitalized vowel is accented.*

pessimistic *adj* пессимисти́ческий, -ая, -ое, -ие.

pester *vt* надоеда́ть *(whom = dat.)*, докуча́ть *(whom = dat.)* ♦ **I don't mean to pester you.** Я не хоте́л *(ж: хоте́ла)* надоеда́ть тебе́.

pet *vi* целова́ть и ласка́ть.

pet *n* дома́шнее живо́тное; *(pl:)* дома́шние живо́тные.

petal *n* лепесто́к ♦ **delicate ~s** не́жные лепестки́ ♦ **~s of the lips** лепестки́ губ.

petal-fresh *adj* све́жий (-ая, -ее, -ие), как лепесто́к.

petal-soft *adj* мя́гкий, (-ая, -ое, -ие) как лепесто́к *(1 term)* ♦ **You have such (rose-)petal-soft *(1)* cheeks / *(2)* skin.** У тебя́ *(1)* ...таки́е мя́гкие, как лепестки́ (ро́зы), щёчки. / *(2)* ...така́я мя́гкая, как лепесто́к (ро́зы), ко́жа.

petite *adj* миниатю́рный, -ая, -ое, -ые, ма́ленький, -ая, -ое, -ие ♦ **Your beautiful, petite *(1)* form / *(2)* body really excites me.** *(1)* Твоя́ прекра́сная, миниатю́рная фигу́ра... / *(2)* Твоё прекра́сное, миниатю́рное те́ло... так возбужда́ет меня́.

petrified *adj* окамене́лый, -ая, -ое, -ые, оцепене́вший, -ая, -ее, -ие.

petticoat *n* ни́жняя ю́бка.

pettiness *n* ме́лочность *f* ♦ **I can't stand pettiness.** Я не выношу́ ме́лочности.

petting *n* поцелу́и и ла́ски, пе́ттинг ♦ **heavy ~** горя́чие поцелу́и и ла́ски.

petty *adj* ме́лкий, -ая, -ое, -ие, незначи́тельный, -ая, -ое, -ые.

petulance *n* 1. раздражи́тельность *f*; 2. раздраже́ние, дурно́е настрое́ние.

petulant *adj* раздражи́тельный, -ая, -ое, -ые.

petulantly *adv* раздражи́тельно.

Ph.D. *abbrev* = **Philosophy Doctor (degree)** до́ктор филосо́фии.

philander *vi* 1. *(flirt)* флиртова́ть, заи́грывать; 2. *(two-time)* развра́тничать, ходи́ть по ба́бам; изменя́ть / измени́ть *(whom = acc.)* ♦ **I'm not the kind who philanders.** Я не тот, кто развра́тничает. ♦ **I hope you never philander.** Я наде́юсь, ты никогда́ не развра́тничаешь. ♦ **If you would ever philander on me, that would be the end (of our relationship).** Е́сли бы ты когда́-нибудь измени́ла *(ж: измени́л)* мне, э́то был бы коне́ц (на́ших отноше́ний).

philanderer *n* 1. Дон Жуа́н; 2. развра́тник, ба́бник ♦ **You're just a rotten, no-good philanderer.** Ты то́лько отврати́тельный ба́бник.

philandering *n* 1. *(flirting)* флирт, заи́грывание; 2. *(two-timing)* развра́тничание, развра́т, распу́тничество ♦ **I don't believe in philandering.** Я не люблю́ развра́тничать. ♦ **I despise philandering.** Я презира́ю развра́т. ♦ **Don't accuse me of philandering.** Не обвиня́й меня́ в распу́тничестве.

phone *n* телефо́н ♦ **cellular ~** со́товый телефо́н ♦ **Every time the phone has rung, my heart has palpitated.** Как то́лько зазвони́т телефо́н, у меня́ выска́кивает се́рдце.

phony *adj* фальши́вый, -ая, -ое, -ые, подде́льный, -ая, -ое, -ые, ло́жный, -ая, -ое, -ые.

phony *n* 1. *(person) (deceiver)* обма́нщик; *(pretender)* притво́рщик; 2. *(thing)* подде́лка, фальши́вка, «ли́па».

photo *n* фотогра́фия *(pl:* фотогра́фии*)* ♦ **bad ~** плоха́я фотогра́фия ♦ **black-and-white ~** чёрно-бе́лая фотогра́фия ♦ **color ~** цветна́я фотогра́фия ♦ **current ~** неда́вняя фотогра́фия ♦ **enlarged ~** увели́ченная фотогра́фия ♦ **excellent ~** отли́чная фотогра́фия ♦ **faded ~** потускне́вшая фотогра́фия ♦ **family ~** семе́йная фотогра́фия ♦ **flattering ~** льстя́щая фотогра́фия ♦ **good ~** хоро́шая фотогра́фия ♦ **great ~** великоле́пная фотогра́фия ♦ **group ~** группова́я фотогра́фия ♦ **large ~** больша́я фотогра́фия ♦ **my ~** моя́ фотогра́фия ♦ **new ~** но́вая фотогра́фия ♦ **old ~** ста́рая фотогра́фия ♦ **only ~** еди́нственная фотогра́фия ♦ **passport ~** па́спортная фотогра́фия ♦ **perfect ~** отли́чная фотогра́фия ♦ **poor ~** плоха́я фотогра́фия ♦ **precious ~** дорога́я

Russian has 6 grammatical cases. For an explanation of them, see the grammar appendix on page 686.

фотогра́фия ♦ **recent** ~ неда́вняя фотогра́фия ♦ **sexually explicit** ~ открове́нно сексуа́льная фотогра́фия ♦ *(1,2)* **small** ~ *(1)* небольша́я / *(2)* ма́ленькая фотогра́фия ♦ **souvenir** ~ па́мятная фотогра́фия ♦ **splendid** ~ великоле́пная фотогра́фия ♦ **terrific** ~ великоле́пная фотогра́фия ♦ **wedding** ~ сва́дебная фотогра́фия ♦ **your** ~ *(informal)* твоя́ фотогра́фия; *(polite)* Ва́ша фотогра́фия.

photo: verb terms

cherish your ~ дорожи́ть твое́й фотогра́фией ♦ **enlarge the** ~ увели́чивать / увели́чить фотогра́фию. ♦ **get** *(1)* **my** / *(2)* **your** ~ *(receive)* получа́ть / получи́ть *(1)* мою́ / *(2)* твою́ фотогра́фию. ♦ **give this** ~ дава́ть / дать э́ту фотогра́фию *(to whom = dat.)*; *(as a gift)* дари́ть / подари́ть э́ту фотогра́фию *(to whom = dat.)* ♦ **hang the** ~ **(on the wall)** пове́сить фотогра́фию (на сте́ну) ♦ **keep** *(1)* **my** / *(2)* **your** ~ храни́ть *(1)* мою́ / *(2)* твою́ фото-гра́фию ♦ **look at your** ~ смотре́ть / посмотре́ть на твою́ фотогра́фию ♦ **put your** ~ **in my wallet** класть / положи́ть твою́ фотогра́фию в (свой) бума́жник ♦ **put your** ~ **on my night table** ста́вить / поста́вить твою́ фотогра́фию на свою́ ту́мбочку ♦ **receive** *(1)* **my** / *(2)* **your** ~ получа́ть / получи́ть *(1)* мою́ / *(2)* твою́ фотогра́фию ♦ **see your** ~ ви́деть / уви́деть твою́ фотогра́фию ♦ **send a** ~ посыла́ть / посла́ть фотогра́фию *(to whom = dat.)* ♦ **show the** ~ пока́зывать / показа́ть фотогра́фию *(to whom = dat.)* ♦ **tear up** *(1)* **my** / *(2)* **your** / *(3)* **his** / *(4)* **her** ~ разорва́ть *(1)* мою́ / *(2)* твою́ / *(3)* его́ / *(4)* её фотогра́фию ♦ **throw away** *(1)* **my** / *(2)* **your** ~ выбра́сывать / вы́бросить *(1)* мою́ / *(2)* твою́ фотогра́фию ♦ **treasure your** ~ дорожи́ть твое́й фотогра́фией.

photo: other terms

quality of the ~ ка́чество фотогра́фии ♦ **size of the** ~ разме́р фотогра́фии.

photo: beautiful you

Your photos are beautiful — but they don't even do you justice. Твои́ фотогра́фии прекра́сные, но да́же они́ не оце́нивают тебя́ до́лжным о́бразом. ♦ **How absolutely lovely — and lovable — you look in your photos!** Как соверше́нно прекра́сно и очарова́тельно ты вы́глядишь на фотогра́фиях. ♦ **You look so cuddly and kissable in these photos I can hardly stand it!** Ты вы́глядишь тако́й зову́щей к объя́тиям и к поцелу́ям, что я едва́ могу́ вы́нести э́то. ♦ **You seem to be getting more beautiful with every photo.** Ты, ка́жется, стано́вишься всё прекра́снее с ка́ждой фотогра́фией. ♦ **I see in this photo a face of** *(1)* **exquisite** / *(2)* **unimaginable beauty crowned with an opulence of** *(3)* **golden** / *(4)* **chestnut** / *(5)* **raven hair.** Я ви́жу на э́той фотогра́фии лицо́ *(1)* изы́сканной / *(2)* невообрази́мой красоты́ в струя́щемся бога́тстве *(3)* золоти́стых / *(4)* кашта́новых / *(5)* чёрных воло́с.

photo: I look at yours again and again

I can't stop looking at your *(1)* **photo** / *(2)* **photos.** Я не могу́ переста́ть смотре́ть на *(1)* ...твою́ фотогра́фию / *(2)* ...твои́ фотогра́фии. ♦ **How can I stop thinking about you when I can't stop looking at your photo?** Как могу́ я переста́ть ду́мать о тебе́, е́сли не могу́ переста́ть смотре́ть на твою́ фотогра́фию? ♦ **How often my attention lingers on your photo.** Как ча́сто моё внима́ние заде́рживается на твое́й фотогра́фии. ♦ **I look at your** *([1]* **beautiful** / *[2]* **lovely) photo over and over (again).** Я смотрю́ на твою́ *([1,2]* прекра́сную) фотогра́фию опя́ть и опя́ть. ♦ **I take your photos with me wherever I go and I look at them again and again and again.** Куда́ бы я ни пошёл, твои́ фо́то со мной, и я смотрю́ на них сно́ва и сно́ва. ♦ **No matter how often I look at your photo, the moment I put it away I want to take it back out and look at it again.** Не име́ет значе́ния, как ча́сто я смотрю́ на твоё фо́то, в тот моме́нт, когда́ я убира́ю его́, я хочу́ вы́нуть и смотре́ть на него́ опя́ть.

There are no articles ("a" or "the") in Russian.

photo: *pleasure looking at you*

It really is an enormous pleasure for me to look at your photos, Sweetheart. Про́сто огро́мное наслажде́ние для меня́ смотре́ть на твои́ фо́то, дорога́я. ♦ **To pull out your photos and look at the face and form of the person who is writing all these nice things to me almost makes me swoon into a faint.** Вы́нуть твои́ фотогра́фии и ви́деть лицо́ и фигу́ру челове́ка, пи́шущего мне все э́ти прия́тные слова́, э́то почти́ дово́дит меня́ до о́бморока. ♦ **An extraordinary heat suffuses my whole body whenever I look at your photo.** Всегда́, когда́ бы я ни смотре́л *(ж: смотре́ла)* на твою́ фотогра́фию, я весь охва́чен *(ж: вся охва́чена)* жа́ром. ♦ **When I looked at your photo, I was awestruck.** Взгляну́в на твою́ фотогра́фию, я был охва́чен благогове́нием. ♦ **It is such a pleasure to look at your big, beautiful *(1)* dark / *(2)* blue eyes and the radiant loveliness of your face in your photos.** Тако́е наслажде́ние ви́деть твои́ больши́е, прекра́сные *(1)* тёмные / *(2)* голубы́е глаза́ и сия́ющую красоту́ твоего́ лица́ на фотогра́фиях. ♦ **Just looking at your photo sends the blood rushing in my veins.** Кровь начина́ет бе́шено струи́ться в мои́х ве́нах про́сто от взгля́да на твоё фо́то.

photo: *send more photos*

Would it be possible for you to send me more photos (of yourself)? Не могли́ бы Вы присла́ть мне ещё фотогра́фий (свои́х)? ♦ **I want you to go to a photography studio and have some photos taken.** Я хочу́, что́бы ты пошла́ *(ж: пошёл)* в фо́тоателье́ и сфотографи́ровалась *(ж: сфотографи́ровался).* ♦ **Remember to smile for me in your photos. I want to see the same kind of sunshine on your face that your letters bring to my heart.** Не забу́дь улыба́ться на свои́х фо́то. Я хочу́ ви́деть тако́й же со́лнечный свет на твоём лице́, како́й твои́ пи́сьма прино́сят в моё се́рдце. ♦ **If you have any shred of compassion for me, you'll alleviate the agony of my yearning by sending me more photos of yourself.** Е́сли у тебя́ есть хотя́ бы ма́лая то́лика сострада́ния ко мне, ты облегчи́шь му́ку мое́й тоски́, посла́в мне ещё не́сколько свои́х фотогра́фий. ♦ **My new hobby is going to be collecting photos of you.** Мои́м но́вым увлече́нием бу́дет коллекциони́рование твои́х фо́то. ♦ **I'm going to have big enlargements made of your photo and put them all over my *(1)* apartment / *(2)* house.** Я увели́чу твою́ фотогра́фию и разве́шу ко́пии по *(1)* ...всей свое́й кварти́ре. / *(2)* ...всему́ своему́ до́му. ♦ **I want to fill my *(1)* apartment / *(2)* room / *(3)* house with photos of you.** Я хочу́ напо́лнить *(1)*...мою́ кварти́ру / *(2)* ко́мнату... / *(3)* ...мой дом... твои́ми фотогра́фиями.

photo: *about your photo*

I put your photo in my wallet. Я положи́л *(ж: положи́ла)* твою́ фотогра́фию в (свой) бума́жник. ♦ **I put your photo on my night table.** Я поста́вил *(ж: поста́вила)* твою́ фотогра́фию на свою́ ту́мбочку. ♦ **Your photo caught my attention *(1)* ...the instant I turned (the page) to it. / *(2)* ...instantly.** Твоя́ фотогра́фия привлекла́ к себе́ моё внима́ние *(1)* ...как то́лько я переверну́л (страни́цу). / *(2)* ...мгнове́нно.

photo: *my photo(s)*

I'll send you *(1)* ...a photo... / *(2)* ...some (more) photos... *(3)* ...in my next letter. / *(4)* ...next time. Я пошлю́ тебе́ *(1)* ...фотогра́фию... / *(2)* ...(ещё) не́сколько фотогра́фий... *(3)* ...в моём сле́дующем письме́. / *(4)* ...в сле́дующий раз. ♦ **I'm sending you *(1)* ...a photo... / *(2)* ...a couple photos... / *(3)* ...some photos... (of myself) with this letter.** Я посыла́ю тебе́ *(1)* ...(мою́) фотогра́фию... / *(2)* ...па́ру / *(3)* не́сколько (мои́х) фотогра́фий... в э́том письме́. ♦ **I'm enclosing a photo (of myself).** Я вкла́дываю (моё) фо́то.

photo: *personal ads*

Must include current photo for a *(1)* reply / *(2)* response. В отве́тном письме́ должно́ быть фо́то. ♦ ***(1,2)* Photo appreciated.** *(1)* Хорошо́ с фотогра́фией. / *(2)* Жела́тельно фо́то.

This dictionary contains two Russian alphabet pages: one in Appendix 1, page 685, and a tear-off page on page 799.

photograph *n* фотогра́фия *(See* **photo***).*

photographer *n* фото́граф ♦ **Please go to a professional photographer and have some photos** *(1)* **made /** *(2)* **taken.** Пожа́луйста, пойди́ к профессиона́льному фото́графу и *(1,2)* сде́лай не́сколько фотогра́фий.

photography *n* фотогра́фия.

physical *adj* физи́ческий, -ая, -ое, -ие.

physicality *n (physical appearance)* вне́шность *f.*

physically *adv* физи́чески.

physique *n* те́ло, (те́ло)сложе́ние *(See also* **body***)* ♦ **athletic** ~ атлети́ческое (те́ло)сложе́ние ♦ **bodybuilder's** ~ телосложе́ние культури́ста ♦ **great** ~ замеча́тельное те́ло ♦ **lean hard** ~ кре́пкое (те́ло)сложе́ние ♦ **marvelous** ~ чуде́сное те́ло ♦ **muscular** ~ мускули́стое те́ло ♦ **perfect** ~ соверше́нное те́ло ♦ **youthful** ~ молодо́е те́ло ♦ **You have a** *(1)* **marvelous /** *(2)* **great /** *(3)* **muscular physique.** У тебя́ *(1)* чуде́сное / *(2)* замеча́тельное / *(3)* мускули́стое те́ло. ♦ **An athlete would envy your physique.** Любо́й атле́т мог бы позави́довать твои́м физи́ческим да́нным.

pick *vt* выбира́ть / вы́брать *(what, whom = acc.)* ♦ ~ **up** *vt (slang)* «снима́ть / снять» *(whom = acc.)* ♦ **I picked you (to write to), because I didn't want to settle for second best.** Я вы́брал тебя́ и написа́л тебе́, потому́ что я не хочу́ ничего́ второсо́ртного.

pickup *n (slang)* 1. *(woman for a brief sexual affair)* случа́йная знако́мая для се́кса; *(prostitue)* проститу́тка; 2. *(truck)* пика́п.

picky *adj* разбо́рчивый, -ая, -ое, -ые, привере́дливый, -ая, -ое, -ые.

picnic *vi* устра́ивать / устро́ить пикни́к ♦ **We can picnic on the beach.** Мы мо́жем устро́ить пикни́к на пля́же.

picnic *n* пикни́к ♦ **I like to go on picnics.** Я люблю́ пикни́ки. ♦ **We could make a picnic in the park.** Мы могли́ бы устро́ить пикни́к в па́рке.

picture *n* 1. карти́на; 2. *(photo)* фотогра́фия ♦ ~ **of beauty** пи́саная краса́вица ♦ **recent** ~ неда́вняя фотогра́фия ♦ **Whenever you stand in front of something, it seems to take on your color, your light and your ambience to create a beautiful picture.** Ты придаёшь всему́, что нахо́дится ря́дом с тобо́й, свой свет, цвет, и свою́ атмосфе́ру, создава́я прекра́сную карти́ну. ♦ **You and I are like pieces of a puzzle that, when fitted together, form a beautiful picture.** Ты и я как кусо́чки головоло́мки, кото́рые, бу́дучи подо́гнаны друг к дру́гу, создаю́т прекра́сную карти́ну.

picture-perfect *adj* как на карти́не.

pie: ♦ **cutie** ~ *term of endearment* пы́шечка, ми́лочка, дорогу́ша.

piece *n* кусо́к ♦ **Don't go to pieces.** Не впада́й в исте́рику.

pierce *vt* пронза́ть / пронзи́ть *(what = acc.)*; прока́лывать / проколо́ть *(what = acc.)* ♦ ~ **ears** прока́лывать / проколо́ть у́ши ♦ **The thought of** *(1)* **...losing you... /** *(2)* **...being without you... /** *(3)* **...being apart from you... pierces my very soul.** Мысль о том, что́бы *(1)* ...потеря́ть тебя́... / *(2)* ...быть без тебя́... / *(3)* ...быть вдали́ от тебя́... пронза́ет мою́ ду́шу.

pierced *adj* проко́лотый, -ая, -ое, -ые ♦ ~ **ears** проко́лотые у́ши ♦ ~ **tongue** проко́лотый язы́к ♦ ~ **lip** проко́лотая губа́.

piercing *n:* ♦ **body** ~ проко́лы ра́зных часте́й те́ла *(с це́лью вста́вить ко́льца).*

pig *n* свинья́.

pigeon-toed *adj* косола́пый, -ая, -ое, -ые.

pigtail *n* коси́чка ♦ **short** ~**s** коро́тенькие коси́чки.

pillar *n* столб ♦ **The burning adoration of my lips will melt the pillars of your sophisticated decorum into rivers of molten lava.** Мои́ пла́менные, обожа́ющие гу́бы превратя́т

Russian verbs conjugate for 6 persons:
I, familiar you, he-she-it, we, polite&plural you, and they.

твердьíню твоéй благопристóйности в рéки расплáвленной лáвы.

pimple *n* пупьíрышек; прьíщик.

pinch *vt* ущипнýть *(what, whom = acc.).*

pinch *n* щипóк ♦ **give a ~** ущипнýть *(whom = acc.).*

pine *vi* 1. *(languish)* чáхнуть; 2. *(yearn)* жáждать *(for what = gen., for whom = acc.),* тосковáть *(for what, whom = + по + dat.)* ♦ **I pine for you day and night.** Я тоскýю по тебé день и ночь.

ping-pong *n* пинг-пóнг.

pink *adj* рóзовый, -ая, -ое, -ые ♦ **~ as an apple blossom** рóзовый (-ая, -ое, -ые) как яблочный цвет ♦ **You look fantastic in those hot-pink shorts.** Ты вьíглядишь фантастúчески в этих ярко рóзовых шóртах.

pinnacle *n* вершúна, кульминациóнный пункт, кульминáция ♦ **~ of delight** кульминáция восхищéния ♦ **~ of pleasure** кульминáция наслаждéния ♦ **When I** *(1)* **...found your letter in my box...** / *(2)* **...saw your photo...** / *(3)* **...read that you were coming... it was the pinnacle of delight for me.** Когдá я *(1)* ...нашёл *(ж: нашлá)* твоё письмó в почтóвом ящике,... / *(2)* ...увúдел *(ж: увúдела)* твою фотогрáфию,... / *(3)* ...прочитáл *(ж: прочитáла),* что ты прилетáешь,... я был *(ж: былá)* на вершúне блажéнства.

pinup *n (slang)* красúвая дéвушка, «картúнка».

piper *n* дýдочник, флейтúст ♦ **One of these days you'll have to pay the piper.** В одúн из этих дней ты должнá *(ж: дóлжен)* бýдешь платúть по счетáм.

piquant *adj* пикáнтный, -ая, -ое, -ые, игрúвый, -ая, -ое, -ые, соблазнúтельный, -ая, -ое, -ые ♦ **When I first saw your** *(1,2)* **piquant smile, I was utterly** *(3)* **fascinated /** *(4)* **enthralled /** *(5)* **entranced.** Впервьíе увúдев твою *(1)* игрúвую / *(2)* соблазнúтельную улыбку, я был совершéнно *(3)* очарóван / *(4)* порабощён / *(5)* очарóван.

pique *vt* возбуждáть / возбудúть *(what = acc.)* ♦ **You have (really) piqued my interest.** Ты (действúтельно) возбудúла *(ж: возбудúл)* мой интерéс.

pirouette *vi* дéлать / сдéлать пируэт.

Pisces *(Feb. 19 - Mar. 20)* Рыба *(19 февраля - 20 мáрта).*

pit *n:* ♦ **I had the feeling in the pit of my stomach that you were going to leave me.** У меня сосýщее чýвство под лóжечкой, что ты собирáешься остáвить меня.

pitch *n* ýровень *m;* стéпень *f;* сúла; интенсúвность *f* ♦ **~ of excitement** ýровень возбуждéния ♦ **The pitch of excitement I feel when I** *(1)* **... see /** *(2)* **hold you... /** *(3)* **...think about you... is** *(4)* **unbearable /** *(5)* **indescribable.** Сúла возбуждéния, котóрое я ощущáю, когдá *(1)* ...вúжу / *(2)* обнимáю тебя,... / *(3)* ...дýмаю о тебé,... *(4)* невыносúма / *(5)* неописýема.

pity *vt* жалéть *(whom = acc.)* ♦ **I pity you.** Я жалéю тебя.

pity *n* жáлость *f* ♦ **arouse ~** пробуждáть / пробудúть жáлость ♦ **I don't** *(1)* **want /** *(2)* **need your pity.** Я не *(1)* ...хочý... / *(2)* ...нуждáюсь в... твоéй жáлости. ♦ **It's a pity that** *(1)* **...we're so far apart. /** *(2,3)* **...you can't come /** *(4)* **stay. /** *(5,6)* **...I can't come /** *(7)* **stay.** Жаль, что *(1)* ...мы так далекó друг от дрýга. / *(2)* ...ты не мóжешь прийтú *(on foot)* / *(3)* приéхать *(by veh.)* / *(4)* остáться. / *(5)* ...я не могý прийтú *(on foot)* / *(6)* приéхать *(by veh.)* / *(7)* остáться.

pixie *n* эльф; фéя.

pizzaz *n* 1. *(style)* стиль *m,* класс, шик; 2. *(cheerfulness)* бóдрость *f,* весёлость *f;* 3. *(fire, ardor)* огонёк, азáрт ♦ **You really have a lot of pizzaz.** В тебé действúтельно есть огонёк. ♦ **You will find that I have a lot of pizzaz.** Ты узнáешь, что во мне есть огонёк.

placate *vt* успокáивать / успокóить *(whom = acc.),* утихомúривать / утихомúрить *(whom = acc.).*

There are two words for "you" in Russian:
familiar «ты» *and polite / plural* «вы» *(See page 771).*

place *vt* ста́вить / поста́вить *(what = acc., where = + в or* на *+ acc.)*, помеща́ть / помести́ть *(what = acc., where = + в or* на *+ acc.)* ♦ **~ an ad in a newspaper** помести́ть объявле́ние в газе́ту. ♦ **I'm going to place kisses lovingly all over your body.** Я покро́ю всё твоё те́ло лю́бящими поцелу́ями.

place *n* ме́сто ♦ **bad** ~ плохо́е ме́сто ♦ **beautiful** ~ прекра́сное ме́сто ♦ **consecrated** ~ свяще́нное ме́сто ♦ **cozy** ~ ую́тное ме́сто ♦ **delightful** ~ восхити́тельное ме́сто ♦ **empty** ~ пусто́е ме́сто ♦ **favorite** ~ люби́мое ме́сто ♦ **good** ~ хоро́шее ме́сто ♦ **heavenly** ~ боже́ственное ме́сто ♦ **hot** ~ горя́чее ме́сто ♦ **juicy** ~ со́чное ме́сто ♦ **little** ~ ма́ленькое ме́сто, месте́чко ♦ **moist** ~ вла́жное ме́сто ♦ **most forbidden** ~ са́мое запре́тное месте́чко ♦ **my** ~ *(house)* мой дом; *(apartment)* моя́ кварти́ра; *(at my place)* у меня́; *(to my place)* ко мне ♦ **sacred** ~ свяще́нное ме́сто ♦ *(1,2)* **secluded** ~ *(1)* уедине́нное / *(2)* укро́мное ме́сто ♦ **secret** ~ тайни́к, та́йное ме́сто ♦ **sensitive** ~ чувстви́тельное ме́сто ♦ **soft** ~ мя́гкое ме́сто ♦ **sweet** ~ сла́дкое ме́сто ♦ **warm** ~ тёплое ме́сто ♦ **wet** ~ мо́крое ме́сто ♦ *(1,2)* **wonderful** ~ *(1)* удиви́тельное / *(2)* чуде́сное ме́сто ♦ **your** ~ *(house) (familiar)* твой дом; *(polite)* Ваш дом; *(apartment) (familiar)* твоя́ кварти́ра; *(polite)* Ва́ша кварти́ра; *(at your place) (familiar)* у тебя́; *(polite)* у Вас; *(to your place) (familiar)* к тебе́; *(polite)* к Вам.

> **place: phrases**

Any ground you stand on becomes for me a consecrated place. Люба́я то́чка, на кото́рую ты ступи́ла, стано́вится свяще́нным ме́стом для меня́. ♦ **Then I'm going to proceed from your face down to my other favorite places.** Пото́м я отпра́влюсь от твоего́ лица́ вниз к други́м мои́м люби́мым места́м.

plain *adj* 1. *(simple)* просто́й -а́я, -о́е, -ы́е; 2. *(clear)* я́сный, -ая, -ое, -ые; 3. *(unattractive)* некраси́вый, -ая, -ое, -ые ♦ **You're far from being plain. You're** *(1)* **very** / *(2)* **extremely** *(3)* **attractive** / *(4)* **good-looking.** Ты совсе́м не некраси́ва *(ж: некраси́в)*. Ты *(1)* о́чень / *(2)* исключи́тельно *(3,4)* привлека́тельна *(ж: привлека́телен)*.

plain-looking *adj (ordinary)* обы́чно-вы́глядящий, -ая, -ее, -ие; *(unattractive)* некраси́вый, -ая, -ое, -ые, невзра́чный, -ая, -ое, -ые.

plan *n* план ♦ *(1,2)* **detailed** ~ *(1)* подро́бный / *(2)* дета́льный план ♦ **good** ~ хоро́ший план ♦ **great** ~ великоле́пный план ♦ **~s for the future** пла́ны на бу́дущее ♦ **travel** ~s пла́ны путеше́ствия ♦ **vacation** ~s отпускны́е пла́ны ♦ **wedding** ~s сва́дебные пла́ны ♦ **change** ~s измени́ть пла́ны ♦ **make** ~s де́лать / сде́лать пла́ны ♦ *(1)* **I have to...** / *(2)* **You have to...** / *(3)* **We have to... make plans.** *(1)* Я до́лжен *(ж: должна́)*... / *(2)* Ты должна́ *(ж: до́лжен)*... / *(3)* Мы должны́... сде́лать пла́ны. ♦ **I have a plan.** У меня́ есть план. ♦ **What are your plans?** Каки́е у тебя́ пла́ны? ♦ **All my future plans and dreams of happiness are centered around you.** Все мои́ пла́ны на бу́дущее, все мечты́ о сча́стье свя́заны с тобо́й. ♦ **It has completely disrupted my plans.** Это по́лностью разру́шило мои́ пла́ны. ♦ **I hope nothing disrupts our plans.** Я наде́юсь, ничто́ не разру́шит на́ши пла́ны.

plane *n* 1. *(level)* план; 2. *(airplane)* самолёт ♦ **on a physical** ~ в физи́ческом пла́не ♦ **on a psychological** ~ в психологи́ческом пла́не.

platitude *n* бана́льность *f.*

platonic *adj* платони́ческий, -ая, -ое, -ие ♦ **Our love is (purely) platonic.** На́ша любо́вь *(соверше́нно)* платони́ческая. ♦ **Our relationship is (purely) platonic.** На́ши отноше́ния *(соверше́нно)* платони́ческие. ♦ **I don't want just** *(1)* **...platonic love.** / *(2)* **...a platonic relationship.** Я не хочу́ то́лько *(1)* ...платони́ческой любви́. / *(2)* ...платони́ческих отноше́ний. ♦ **I want to keep our relationship platonic.** Я хочу́ сохрани́ть на́ши отноше́ния платони́ческими. ♦ **I want you to understand that my love for you**

Russian terms of endearment are given in Appendix 13, page 780.

is purely platonic. Я хочу́, что́бы ты поняла́ *(ж: по́нял)*, что моя́ любо́вь к тебе́ соверше́нно платони́ческая.

plausible *adj* правдоподо́бный, -ая, -ое, -ые.

play *vt* игра́ть *(game = + в + acc.; mus. instr. = + на + prep.)* ♦ **~ around** 1. *(play)* игра́ть, развлека́ться; *(kid around)* шути́ть; *(act foolish)* дура́читься; 2. *(philander)* име́ть внебра́чные половы́е свя́зи; 3. *(chase after women)* волочи́ться за же́нщинами; 3. *(engage in petting)* занима́ться пе́ттингом, ласка́ть, игра́ть ♦ **~ hard to get** *(slang)* притворя́ться недотро́гой ♦ **~ music** занима́ться му́зыкой, исполня́ть му́зыку, музици́ровать ♦ **~ *(1)* outdoors / *(2)* outside** игра́ть *(1,2)* на све́жем во́здухе ♦ **~ the field** *(slang)* волочи́ться за же́нщинами ♦ **I think you just play the wolf all the time.** Я ду́маю, ты всё вре́мя то́лько изобража́ешь из себя́ ба́бника. ♦ **It's time to start playing more and working less.** Сейча́с вре́мя для того́, что́бы нача́ть бо́льше развлека́ться и ме́ньше рабо́тать.

play *n* 1. *(recreation)* игра́; *(fun)* заба́ва; 2. *(flirt)* заи́грывание; 3. *(drama)* пье́са, представле́ние ♦ **discreet ~** та́йный секс ♦ **fair ~** че́стная игра́, игра́ по пра́вилам ♦ **I'm not making a play for anyone.** Я не заи́грываю ни с кем. ♦ **You were making a play for him** *(her)*. Ты заи́грывала с ним *(ж: заи́грывал с ней)*.

playact *vi* притворя́ться, изобража́ть ♦ **Do you think I'm just playacting? You're crazy.** Ты ду́маешь, что я то́лько притворя́юсь? Ты сумасше́дшая *(ж: сумасше́дший)*. ♦ **You were just playacting the whole time.** Ты всё вре́мя то́лько притворя́лась *(ж: притворя́лся)*.

playboy *n* волоки́та, «плейбо́й», пове́са.

player *n* игро́к ♦ **game ~** 1. *(cooperates with others)* челове́к, ла́дящий с други́ми людьми́ *(1 term)*; 2. *([1] insincere, [2] not serious, [3] deceptive)* *(1)* неи́скренний / *(2)* несерьёзный / *(3)* обма́нывающий челове́к.

playful *adj* игри́вый, -ая, -ое, -ые; шаловли́вый, -ая, -ое, -ые. ♦ **eternally ~** неизме́нно игри́вый, -ая, -ое, -ые.

playfulness *n* игри́вость *f* ; шаловли́вость *f*.

playgirl *n* распу́тная молода́я же́нщина.

playing *n* игра́, и́гры *pl* ; *(music)* исполне́ние ♦ **~ music** исполне́ние му́зыки ♦ **~ *(1)* outdoors / *(2)* outside** и́гры *(1,2)* на све́жем во́здухе ♦ **I'm past the game playing stage.** Я прошёл *(ж: прошла́)* ста́дию игры́.

playmate *n* партнёр *(в игре)* ♦ **sexual ~** сексуа́льный партнёр ♦ ***(1,2)* sexy ~** *(1)* сексуа́льно привлека́тельный / *(2)* сексапи́льный партнёр ♦ **I seek a playmate for mutual fulfillment.** Я ищу́ партнёра для взаи́много удовлетворе́ния.

plaything *n* игру́шка ♦ **Am I just your (occasional) plaything?** Я то́лько (случа́йная) игру́шка для тебя́? ♦ **I'm not looking for a plaything, I want a lasting relationship.** Я не ищу́ игру́шку, я хочу́ дли́тельных отноше́ний.

plead *vi* 1. *(beseech)* умоля́ть *(of whom = acc.)*; 2. *(appeal)* взыва́ть ♦ **I plead of you to grant me this one small favor.** Я умоля́ю тебя́ сде́лать мне одно́ ма́ленькое одолже́ние. ♦ **I'm pleading for your love.** Я молю́ о твое́й любви́. ♦ **Your (cute little) ears are just pleading to be nibbled.** Твои́ (изя́щные ма́ленькие) у́шки пря́мо взы́вают к поку́сыванию.

please *adv* пожа́луйста.

please *vt* угожда́ть / угоди́ть *(whom = dat.)*; доставля́ть / доста́вить удово́льствие *(whom = dat.)* ♦ **I'm not hard to please.** Мне не тру́дно угоди́ть. ♦ **I'm (very) easy to please.** Мне (о́чень) легко́ угоди́ть. ♦ **You're hard to please.** Тебе́ тру́дно угоди́ть. ♦ **Does it please you?** Э́то тебе́ нра́вится? ♦ **It *(1)* pleases / *(2)* pleased me (very much) (that you**

Some of the Russian sentences are translations of things we say and are not what Russians themselves would normally say.

[3,4] ...came. / *[5]* ...called me. / *[6]* ...wrote to me. / ...*[7]* thought about me.). Мне *(1)* доставля́ет / *(2)* доста́вило (огро́мное) удово́льствие (то, что ты *[3]* ...пришла́ *[ж: пришёл] [on foot]* / *[4]* прие́хала *[ж: прие́хал] [by veh.].* / *[5]* ...звони́ла *[ж: звони́л].* / *[6]* ...писа́ла *[ж: писа́л].* / *[7]* ...ду́мала *[ж: ду́мал]* бо́бо мне.) ♦ **Nothing would please me more.** Ничего́ не могло́ бы доста́вить мне бо́льшего удово́льствия. ♦ **It would please me no end.** Это доста́вило бы мне бесконе́чное удово́льствие. ♦ **You can't please everyone.** Всем не угоди́шь.

pleasurability *n* возмо́жность получи́ть удово́льствие.

pleasurable *adj* доставля́ющий (-ая, -ее, -ие) удово́льствие, прия́тный, -ая, -ое, -ые.

pleasure *vt* дава́ть / дать наслажде́ние *(whom = dat.)*, дари́ть / подари́ть наслажде́ние *(whom = dat.)*, доставля́ть / доста́вить удово́льствие *(whom = dat.)* ♦ **We can pleasure each other for hours on end.** Мы мо́жем дари́ть наслажде́ние друг дру́гу бесконе́чными часа́ми. ♦ **I want to pleasure you for hours on end.** Я хочу́ дари́ть тебе́ наслажде́ние бесконе́чными часа́ми. ♦ **It's so much fun to pleasure you.** Так прия́тно дари́ть тебе́ наслажде́ние.

pleasure *n* наслажде́ние, удово́льствие ♦ **acute** ~ о́строе наслажде́ние ♦ *(1,2)* **boundless** ~ *(1)* безме́рное / *(2)* безграни́чное наслажде́ние ♦ *(1,2)* **carnal** ~s *(1)* чу́вственные / *(2)* пло́тские наслажде́ния ♦ **cosmic** ~ косми́ческое наслажде́ние. ♦ **delicious** ~ восхити́тельное наслажде́ние ♦ **distinct** ~ своеобра́зное удово́льствие ♦ **endless** ~ несконча́емое наслажде́ние ♦ **enormous** ~ огро́мное наслажде́ние ♦ **erotic** ~эроти́ческое наслажде́ние ♦ **exquisite** ~ изы́сканное наслажде́ние ♦ **fierce** ~ ди́кое удово́льствие ♦ **genuine** *(1,2)* ~ и́стинное *(1)* наслажде́ние / *(2)* удово́льствие ♦ **great** ~ большо́е удово́льствие ♦ **guilty** ~ наслажде́ние с чу́вством вины́ ♦ **heavenly** ~ ра́йское наслажде́ние ♦ **incomparable** *(1,2)* ~ несравне́нное *(1)* удово́льствие / *(2)* наслажде́ние ♦ **indescribable** ~ неопису́емое наслажде́ние ♦ *(1,2)* **infinite** ~ *(1)* бесконе́чное / *(2)* безме́рное наслажде́ние ♦ **intense** ~ пы́лкое наслажде́ние ♦ **love's** ~s любо́вные наслажде́ния ♦ **matchless** *(1,2)* ~ несравне́нное *(1)* удово́льствие / *(2)* наслажде́ние ♦ *(1,2)* **particular** ~ *(1)* осо́бенное / *(2)* осо́бое удово́льствие ♦ *(1-3)* ~s **of the flesh** *(1)* удово́льствия / *(2)* наслажде́ние пло́ти, *(3)* пло́тские наслажде́ния ♦ **mindless** ~ безу́мное наслажде́ние ♦ **orgasmic** ~ наслажде́ние орга́змом ♦ **outdoor** ~s развлече́ния на откры́том во́здухе ♦ **pure** ~ настоя́щее наслажде́ние ♦ **rapturous** ~ упои́тельное наслажде́ние ♦ **real** ~ и́стинное удово́льствие ♦ **sexual** ~ сексуа́льное наслажде́ние ♦ **sheer** ~ полне́йшее наслажде́ние ♦ **simple** ~s (**of life**) просто́е наслажде́ние (жи́знью) ♦ *(1,2)* **special** ~ *(1)* осо́бенное / *(2)* осо́бое удово́льствие ♦ **such** *(1,2)* ~ тако́е *(1)* удово́льствие / *(2)* наслажде́ние ♦ **timeless** ~ бесконе́чное наслажде́ние ♦ **tremendous** *(1,2)* ~ огро́мное *(1)* удово́льствие / *(2)* наслажде́ние ♦ **true** ~ и́стинное наслажде́ние ♦ **unadulterated** ~ настоя́щее удово́льствие ♦ **unbelievable** ~ невероя́тное наслажде́ние ♦ **unfathomable** ~ необъя́тное наслажде́ние ♦ **unmatched** *(1,2)* ~ несравне́нное *(1)* удово́льствие / *(2)* наслажде́ние ♦ **unrivaled** *(1,2)* ~ несравне́нное *(1)* удово́льствие / *(2)* наслажде́ние ♦ **vicarious** ~ чужо́е удово́льствие.

pleasure: verb terms

derive ~ получа́ть / получи́ть удово́льствие ♦ **experience** *(1,2)* ~ испы́тывать / испыта́ть *(1)* удово́льствие / *(2)* наслажде́ние ♦ **feel** ~ ощуща́ть / ощути́ть удово́льствие ♦ **find** ~ находи́ть / найти́ удово́льствие ♦ **get** ~ получа́ть / получи́ть удово́льствие ♦ **give** ~ доставля́ть / доста́вить удово́льствие *(to whom = dat.)* ♦ **moan with** ~ стона́ть от наслажде́ния ♦ **prolong the** ~ продлева́ть / продли́ть удово́льствие ♦ **shiver with** ~ дрожа́ть от наслажде́ния ♦ **soar to the peak of** ~ взлете́ть на верши́ну наслажде́ния ♦ **squirm with** ~ извива́ться от наслажде́ния ♦ **tremble with** ~ дрожа́ть от наслаж-

Counting things in Russian is a bit involved.
See Appendix 4, "Numbers," on page 756 .

дения. ♦ **wiggle with** ~ извива́ться от наслажде́ния.

pleasure: *other terms*

all kinds of ~ вся́кие удово́льствия ♦ **art of** ~ иску́сство наслажде́ний ♦ **cornucopia of** ~ рог, по́лный наслажде́ния *(1 term)* ♦ **cries of** ~ кри́ки наслажде́ния ♦ **feeling of** ~ чу́вство удово́льствия ♦ **fruits of** ~ фру́кты наслажде́ния ♦ **fullness of** ~ полнота́ наслажде́ния ♦ **heights of** ~ верши́ны наслажде́ния ♦ **moans of** ~ сто́ны наслажде́ния ♦ **moment of supreme** ~ миг наивы́сшего наслажде́ния ♦ **pinnacle of** ~ кульмина́ция наслажде́ния ♦ **symphony of** ~ симфо́ния наслажде́ния.

pleasure: *I want to give you pleasure*

I want to take you on a daily *(1)* **...excursion to... /** *(2)* **...tour of... the heights of pleasure.** Я хочу́ повести́ тебя́ на *(1)* ...ежедне́вную экску́рсию... / *(2)* ...ежедне́вный тур... к верши́нам наслажде́ния. ♦ **I never want to see anything but pleasure in your eyes, love on your lips, and happiness in your heart.** Я всегда́ хочу́ ви́деть то́лько наслажде́ние в твои́х глаза́х, любо́вь на твои́х губа́х и сча́стье в твоём се́рдце. ♦ **I want to see you glow with pleasure.** Я хочу́ ви́деть тебя́ пыла́ющую от наслажде́ния. ♦ **I want to cause you nothing but pleasure.** Я не хочу́ доста́вить тебе́ ничего́, кро́ме наслажде́ния. ♦ **I want to fill your body with so much pleasure that you will be** *(1)* **hurled /** *(2)* **flung /** *(3)* **rocketed into a cosmos of exploding ecstasy.** Я хочу́ запо́лнить твоё те́ло таки́м огро́мным наслажде́нием, что́бы ты была́ *(1,2)* бро́шена / *(3)* запу́щена в ко́смос взрыва́ющегося экста́за. ♦ **I want to spend endless hours planting delicious fruits of pleasure in the secret garden of your body.** Я хочу́ провести́ бесконе́чные часы́, сажа́я восхити́тельные фру́кты наслажде́ния в секре́тном саду́ твоего́ те́ла. ♦ **I want to spend the whole night listening to your moans of pleasure.** Я хочу́ провести́ всю ночь, слу́шая твои́ сто́ны наслажде́ния. ♦ **I want to** *(1)* **...flood your senses... /** *(2)* **...fill your body... with indescribable pleasure.** Я хочу́ *(1)* ...затопи́ть твои́ чу́вства... / *(2)* ...напо́лнить твоё те́ло... неопису́емым наслажде́нием. ♦ **I want to give you orgasmic pleasure such as you have never known or dreamed of before.** Я хочу́ дать тебе́ тако́е наслажде́ние орга́змом, кото́рого ты никогда́ не зна́ла и о кото́ром никогда́ пре́жде не мечта́ла. ♦ **My greatest aspiration in life is to fill your body with** *(1)* **indescribable /** *(2)* **infinite pleasure.** Стремле́ние всей мое́й жи́зни - напо́лнить твоё те́ло *(1)* неопису́емым / *(2)* бесконе́чным наслажде́нием. ♦ **I dream of filling your body with intense, exquisite pleasure day and night, night and day, for as long as God grants me the time.** Я мечта́ю наполня́ть твоё те́ло пы́лким, изы́сканным наслажде́нием день и ночь, ночь и день до конца́ даро́ванной мне Бо́гом жи́зни. ♦ **Every night I want you to serenade me with your moans and cries of pleasure.** Ка́ждую ночь я хочу́ слы́шать серена́ду из твои́х сто́нов и кри́ков наслажде́ния. ♦ **How many ways could I give you pleasure? I want to** *(1)* **find /** *(2)* **learn them all.** Сколько́ми ра́зными путя́ми я мог бы доста́вить тебе́ наслажде́ние? Я хочу́ *(1)* найти́ / *(2)* изучи́ть их все. ♦ **Teach me** *(1)* **...what gives you pleasure. /** *(2)* **...how I can give you the most pleasure.** Научи́ меня́, *(1)* ...что доставля́ет тебе́ наслажде́ние. / *(1)* ...как я смогу́ доста́вить тебе́ наибо́льшее наслажде́ние.

pleasure: *I'll give you pleasure*

I'm going to give you a cornucopia of pleasure. Я дам тебе́ рог, по́лный наслажде́ния. ♦ **I'm going to make waves of exquisite pleasure surge through your body.** Я вы́зову во́лны изы́сканного наслажде́ния, захлёстывающие твоё те́ло. ♦ **I'm going to make you go (absolutely)** *(1)* **crazy /** *(2)* **mad with pleasure.** Я сде́лаю тебя́ (абсолю́тно) *(1,2)* безу́мной от наслажде́ния. ♦ **I'm going to make those rosy nubs on your breasts pulsate with pleasure.** Я заста́влю э́ти ро́зовые ши́шечки твои́х груде́й пульси́ровать от наслаж-де́ния. ♦ **Darling, if I ever get in the same bed with you, I'm going to make myself a slave**

Russian has 2 different vrbs for "go",
one for "on foot" and the other for "by vehicle".

to your desires and your pleasure and your satisfaction. Дорога́я, е́сли я окажу́сь в одно́й посте́ли с тобо́й, я сде́лаю себя́ рабо́м твои́х страсте́й, твоего́ наслажде́ния и твоего́ удовлетворе́ния. ♦ **My fingertips will glide over your body, scattering delicious pleasure in their path.** Ко́нчики мои́х па́льцев бу́дут скользи́ть по твоему́ те́лу, рассе́ивая восхити́тельное наслажде́ние на своём пути́. ♦ **Exquisite pleasure will shoot through every *(1)* cell / *(2)* molecule / *(3)* fiber of your body.** Изы́сканное наслажде́ние бу́дет струи́ться че́рез ...ка́ждую *(1)* кле́тку / *(2)* моле́кулу... / *(3)* ...все фи́бры...твоего́ те́ла. ♦ **You're going to experience pleasure on a scope and scale you never dreamed of.** Ты испыта́ешь наслажде́ние в таки́х сфе́рах и масшта́бах, о каки́х ты никогда́ не мечта́ла. ♦ **I'm going to create a million little delicious pleasures all over your body that are going to course into one tremendous explosion of ecstasy.** Я созда́м миллио́н ма́леньких восхити́тельных наслажде́ний по всему́ твоему́ те́лу, кото́рые солью́тся в оди́н огро́мный взрыв экста́за. ♦ **My loving kisses will lead you deliciously along the paths of heavenly pleasure until you reach cosmic ecstasy.** Мои́ лю́бящие поцелу́и поведу́т тебя́ по восхити́тельной тропе́ ра́йского наслажде́ния до косми́ческого экста́за. ♦ **Your silky skin will breath pleasure as I caress it lovingly with my lips.** Твоя́ шёлковая ко́жа бу́дет дыша́ть удово́льствием, когда́ я бу́ду любо́вно ласка́ть её губа́ми. ♦ ***(1)* Your body is going to learn... / *(2)* I'm going to teach you... a new definition of the word pleasure.** *(1)* Твоё те́ло узна́ет но́вое определе́ние... / *(2)* Я научу́ тебя́ но́вому определе́нию... сло́ва наслажде́ние. ♦ **When my lips and tongue ravish your beautiful, luscious body, they will hear your *(1)* moans / *(2)* screams of pleasure in South Africa.** Когда́ мои́ гу́бы и язы́к бу́дут упива́ться твои́м прекра́сным, со́чным те́лом, твои́ *(1)* сто́ны / *(2)* кри́ки наслажде́ния бу́дут слышны́ в Ю́жной Африке. ♦ **My eager lips will suffuse your body with exquisite pleasure.** Мои́ нетерпели́вые гу́бы зато́пят твоё те́ло изы́сканным наслажде́нием. ♦ **When you give yourself to me, you're going to be rewarded with more pleasure than you ever dreamed of.** Когда́ ты отда́шься мне, ты бу́дешь вознаграждена́ таки́м наслажде́нием, о кото́ром не могла́ да́же мечта́ть. ♦ **I promise you, when I get you in my arms, I'm going to give you such enormous pleasure as you've never had nor ever even dreamed of before.** Я обеща́ю тебе́, что, когда́ обниму́ тебя́, я дам тебе́ тако́е огро́мное наслажде́ние, како́го у тебя́ никогда́ не бы́ло и о кото́ром ты да́же никогда́ пре́жде не мечта́ла. ♦ **You have never met or heard of anyone in your life who would be as zealous and whole-hearted at giving you pleasure as I would.** Ты никогда́ в жи́зни не встреча́ла никого́ и не слы́шала ни о ком, кто бы так беззаве́тно жа́ждал дава́ть тебе́ наслажде́ние, как я.

pleasure: *I love to give pleasure*

I love to give (you) pleasure (and ecstasy). Мне нра́вится дари́ть (тебе́) наслажде́ния (и экста́з). ♦ **I love to give affection and fill my partner with boundless pleasure and delight in a totally eager and selfless way.** Я люблю́ дари́ть своему́ партнёру не́жность, безграни́чное наслажде́ние и восхище́ние пы́лко и бескоры́стно. ♦ **Personally, I've always been infused with the conviction that if you truly love a woman and care for her, you do everything you possibly can to fill her with pleasure and suffuse her with love.** Ли́чно я всегда́ был наделён убежде́нием, что е́сли ты действи́тельно лю́бишь же́нщину и забо́тишься о ней, то ты де́лаешь всё возмо́жное, что́бы напо́лнить её наслажде́нием и затопи́ть любо́вью.

pleasure: *my favorite pleasure*

My favorite pleasure in life is *(1)* ...holding you tight. / *(2)* ...holding you in my arms. / *(3)* ...kissing your beautiful mouth / *(4)* face. Са́мое большо́е наслажде́ние в мое́й жи́зни -- *(1)* ...прижа́ть тебя́ кре́пко. / *(2)* ...держа́ть тебя́ в объя́тиях. / *(3)* ...целова́ть твой

Dipthongs in Russian are made by adding й
*to the end of a vowel (*а, е, ё, о, у, э, ю, *and* я*).*

прекра́сный рот. / *(4)* ...целова́ть твоё прекра́сное лицо́. ♦ **The sweetest music to my ears is to hear you moan with pleasure.** Сладча́йшая му́зыка для моего́ слу́ха -- твои́ сто́ны наслажде́ния. ♦ **All the real pleasure I enjoy in this world is derived from being with you.** Ты исто́чник всех наслажде́ний, кото́рые я испы́тываю в э́том ми́ре.

pleasure: *enjoying pleasure together*

We can spend *(1)* **a week** / *(2)* **two weeks** / *(3)* **the weekend enjoying the pleasures of the flesh.** Мы мо́жем провести́ *(1)* ...неде́лю... / *(2)* ...две неде́ли... / *(3)* ...выходны́е дни,... наслажда́ясь удово́льствиями пло́ти. ♦ **With you it would be so easy to set the world record for giving someone pleasure.** С тобо́й бы́ло бы так легко́ установи́ть мирово́й реко́рд наслажде́ний. ♦ **We can steal a little pleasure for ourselves.** Мы мо́жем укра́сть для себя́ немно́го наслажде́ния. ♦ **Our bodies will fuse together in exquisite pleasure until we are** *(1)* **flung** / *(2)* **hurled into a wild sea of passion.** На́ши тела́ солью́тся в изы́сканном наслажде́нии до тех пор, пока́ мы не бу́дем *(1,2)* бро́шены в бе́шеное мо́ре стра́сти. ♦ **I want you to participate with me in the pleasure olympics. (Let the games begin.)** Я хочу́, что́бы ты уча́ствовала со мной вме́сте в олимпиа́де наслажде́ния. (Дава́й начнём и́гры.)

pleasure: *I get pleasure*

I've never experienced such pleasure with anyone. Я никогда́ ни с кем не испы́тывал *(ж: испы́тывала)* тако́го наслажде́ния. ♦ **The pleasure** *(1)* **...bordered on being...** / *(2)* **...was almost... excruciating.** Чу́вство *(1)* ...бы́ло на грани́це невыноси́мого. / *(2)* ...бы́ло почти́ невыноси́мым. ♦ **I have never felt such** *(1)* **huge** / *(2)* **tremendous** / *(3)* **enormous waves of pleasure.** Я никогда́ не чу́вствовал *(ж: чу́вствовала)* таки́х *(1)* огро́мных / *(2,3)* грома́дных волн наслажде́ния. ♦ **You fill me with such** *(1)* **huge** / *(2)* **tremendous** / *(3)* **enormous waves of pleasure.** Ты наполня́ешь меня́ таки́ми *(1)* огро́мными / *(2,3)* грома́дными во́лнами наслажде́ния. ♦ **It is such a pleasure to** *(1)* **look** / *(2)* **gaze at the radiant** *(3)* **loveliness** / *(4)* **beauty of your face in this photo.** Тако́е удово́льствие *(1)* ...смотре́ть на... / *(2)* ...вгля́дываться в... сия́ющую *(3,4)* красоту́ твоего́ лица́ на э́той фотогра́фии. ♦ **The provocative curve of your breasts is such a pleasure to behold.** Тако́е удово́льствие созерца́ть соблазни́тельные изги́бы твое́й груди́. ♦ **You are truly a master at the art of giving pleasure.** Ты, пра́вда, ма́стер в иску́сстве доставля́ть удово́льствия.

pleasure: *secrets of pleasure*

You'll be surprised at how many ways I know to prolong your pleasure. Ты бу́дешь удивлена́, ско́лько я зна́ю спо́собов для продле́ния твоего́ наслажде́ния. ♦ **You can't even imagine what secrets I know for giving you pleasure on a cosmic level.** Ты да́же не мо́жешь предста́вить себе́, каки́е секре́ты я зна́ю для того́, что́бы доста́вить тебе́ косми́ческое наслажде́ние.

pleasure: *life's simple pleasures*

I search for someone with whom to enjoy life's simple pleasures. Я ищу́ того́, с кем смогу́ наслажда́ться просты́ми удово́льствиями жи́зни.

pleasure: *pleasures of paradise*

The sight of your beautiful face makes me dream of all the pleasures in paradise. Твоё прекра́сное лицо́ заставля́ет мечта́ть о всех наслажде́ниях ра́я.

pleasure: *never too old*

One is never too old to delight in carnal pleasures. Никто́ никогда́ не быва́ет сли́шком стар для того́, что́бы находи́ть удово́льствия в чу́вственных наслажде́ниях.

pleasure-filled *adj* напо́лненный (-ая, -ое, -ые) наслажде́нием / удово́льствием ♦ **The two of us** *(1)* **will** / *(2)* **can share pleasure-filled** *(3)* **hours** / *(4)* **days together.** Мы вдвоём *(1)*

---

*Dipthongs in Russian are made by adding й
to the end of a vowel (а, е, ё, о, у, э, ю, and я).*

бу́дем / (2) смо́жем разделя́ть напо́лненные наслажде́нием (3) часы́ / (4) дни.

pleasureful adj (full of pleasure) по́лный (-ая, -ое, -ые) наслажде́ния / удово́льствия, доставля́ющий (-ая, -ее, -ие) наслажде́ние / удово́льствие; (pleasant) прия́тный, -ая, -ое, -ые ♦ **We can spend** (1) **long** / (2) **blissful hours in pleasureful frolic.** Мы мо́жем проводи́ть (1) до́лгие / (2) счастли́вые часы́ в ша́лостях, по́лных наслажде́ния.

pleasure-giver n даю́щий m / даю́щая f наслажде́ние.

pleasure-giving adj: ♦ (1) **I want to...** / (2) **I'm going to... do all kinds of loving, pleasure-giving things with you.** (1) Я хочу́ испыта́ть... / (2) Я испыта́ю... все ви́ды любви́ и наслажде́ния с тобо́й.

pleasure-taker n принима́ющий m / принима́ющая f наслажде́ние.

pleasuring n: (Russian uses verbs. See **pleasure** vt) ♦ **mutual** ~ (verb expression:) дари́ть взаи́мное наслажде́ние ♦ **I love** (1,2) **pleasuring you.** Я люблю́ (1) дава́ть / (2) дари́ть тебе́ удово́льствие. ♦ **I want to devote my life to pleasuring you.** Я хочу́ посвяти́ть свою́ жизнь тому́, что́бы дари́ть тебе́ наслажде́ние. ♦ **I never tire of pleasuring you.** Мне никогда́ не надоеда́ет дари́ть тебе́ наслажде́ние.

pledge vi обеща́ть / пообеща́ть (whom = dat.) ♦ **I pledge my** (1) **life** / (2) **love to you.** Я обеща́ю свою́ (1) жизнь / (2) любо́вь тебе́. ♦ **I pledge** (1-3) **to live in your love for all the days of my life.** Я обеща́ю (1) храни́ть / (2) леле́ять / (3) бере́чь твою́ любо́вь до конца́ мои́х дней. ♦ **I pledge that I will do everything (I possibly can)** (1) **...to prove that I love you.** / (2) **...to make our love grow ever stronger, ever deeper, ever more beautiful.** Я обеща́ю сде́лать всё, (что смогу́,) (1) ...что́бы доказа́ть тебе́ свою́ любо́вь./ (2) ...что́бы сде́лать на́шу любо́вь ещё сильне́е, ещё глу́бже, ещё прекра́снее.

pledge n обе́т, обеща́ние ♦ **On the altar of God I will make a lifetime** (1,2) **pledge of love and devotion to you.** Пе́ред Бо́жьим алтарём я дам тебе́ (1) обе́т / (2) обеща́ние любви́ и пре́данности на всю жизнь.

pliant adj (flexible) ги́бкий, -ая, -ое, -ие; (malleable) мя́гкий, -ая, -ое, -ие, пласти́чный, -ая, -ое, -ые.

plight n (1) плохо́е / (2) тру́дное положе́ние.

ploy n хи́трость f, приём ♦ **artful** ~s иску́сные уло́вки ♦ **cheap** ~ дешёвый приём ♦ **deliberate** ~ обду́манный приём.

plump adj по́лный, -ая, -ое, -ые, пу́хлый, -ая, -ое, -ые, окру́глый, -ая, -ое, -ые; (woman) пы́шный, -ая, -ое, -ые ♦ **delightfully** ~ восхити́тельно по́лный ♦ **pleasingly** ~ прия́тно по́лный ♦ **pleasantly** ~ прия́тно по́лный ♦ ~ **girl** пы́шка.

plunge n (decisive step) реши́тельный шаг ♦ **take the** ~ 1. (take a decisive step) реши́ться, сде́лать реши́тельный шаг; 2. (get married) пожени́ться.

plus n плюс ♦ **Skier a plus.** (personal ads) Лы́жник плюс.

poem n стихотворе́ние; поэ́ма. ♦ **Your eyes and your lips — oh! I could write a whole book of love poems dedicated to them**. Твои́ глаза́ и гу́бы -- О! Я мог бы написа́ть це́лую кни́гу любо́вной ли́рики, посвящённой им.

poetic adj поэти́ческий, -ая, -ое, -ие.

poetry n поэ́зия ♦ ~ **and grace** поэ́зия и гра́ция ♦ **You bring out the poetry in my soul.** Ты пробужда́ешь поэ́зию в мое́й душе́. ♦ **Everyday I write poetry to you in my heart.** Ка́ждый день в моём се́рдце я сочиня́ю тебе́ стихи́. ♦ **You make me want to compose poetry for you.** Ты вызыва́ешь во мне жела́ние сочиня́ть стихи́ для тебя́.

point n 1. (dot / spot in space; stage) то́чка; пункт; 2. (gist) суть; 3. (place) ме́сто, пункт; 4. (moment) моме́нт; 5. (purpose, sense) смысл; 6. (characteristic) сторона́, (отличи́тельная) черта́; 7. (good impression, approval) хоро́шее впечатле́ние, одобре́ние; 8. (scoring) очко́ ♦ **good** ~s хоро́шие сто́роны ♦ **good and bad** ~s (character) положи-

---

Some phrases are listed under more than one main word.

тельные и отрица́тельные черты́ *(хара́ктера)* ♦ **pulse** ~ пульси́рующая то́чка ♦ **strong** ~ си́льная сторона́, си́льное ме́сто ♦ **weak** ~ сла́бая сторона́, сла́бое ме́сто ♦ **get the** *(1,2)* ~ поня́ть *(1)* смысл / *(2)* соль ♦ **make** ~s производи́ть / произвести́ хоро́шее впечатле́ние *(with whom* = + у + *gen.),* получа́ть / получи́ть *([1]* твоё / *[2]* моё) одобре́ние *([1] with you* = твоё , *[2] with me* = моё*)* ♦ **not get the** *(1,2)* ~ не поня́ть *(1)* смы́сла / *(2)* со́ли ♦ **score major** ~s производи́ть / произвести́ огро́мное впечатле́ние *(with whom* = + у + *gen.),* заслу́живать / заслужи́ть *([1]* твоё / *[2]* моё) одобре́ние *([1] with you* = твоё , *[2] with me* = моё *).*

> **point: phrases**

There's no point in arguing. Нет смы́сла в спо́ре. ♦ **What's the point (of it)?** Како́й смысл (в э́том)? ♦ **You have now become the whole point of my living.** Ты ста́ла *(ж: стал)* для меня́ тепе́рь всем смы́слом жи́зни. ♦ **I want you to know, you made a lot of points with me with the letter you wrote.** Я хочу́, чтобы ты зна́ла *(ж: знал),* что произвела́ *(ж: произвёл)* огро́мное впечатле́ние на меня́ свои́м письмо́м.

poise *n* самооблада́ние, вы́держка, уравнове́шенность *f* ♦ **You have a lot of poise.** Ты хорошо́ уме́ешь владе́ть собо́й.

polished *adj (elegant, refined)* изы́сканный, -ая, -ое, -ые, элега́нтный, -ая, -ое, -ые ♦ **You have very polished manners.** У тебя́ о́чень изы́сканные мане́ры.

polite *adj* ве́жливый, -ая, -ое, -ые, обходи́тельный, -ая, -ое, -ые.

politeness *n* ве́жливость *f.*

politics *n* поли́тика ♦ **progressive** ~ прогресси́вная поли́тика.

polygamy *n* многобра́чие, полига́мия; многожёнство.

pompous *adj* напы́шенный, -ая, -ое, -ые, по́лный (-ая, -ое, -ые) ва́жности.

pool *n* 1. пруд; озерцо́; 2. *(swimming)* бассе́йн ♦ **swimming** ~ бассе́йн для пла́вания ♦ **Your eyes are like limpid pools.** Твои́ глаза́ как прозра́чные озёра.

poor *adj* 1. *(lacking material well-being)* бе́дный, -ая, -ое, -ые; 2. *(unfortunate)* бе́дный, -ая, -ое, -ые, несча́стный, -ая, -ое, -ые ♦ ~ **(little) thing** бедня́жка *f.*

pore *n* по́ра ♦ **They say the human body has 20 million* pores. I want to put a kiss of love on each one of yours (every day).** Говоря́т, что в челове́ческом те́ле 20 (два́дцать) милио́нов пор. Я хочу́ (ка́ждый день) дари́ть поцелу́й любви́ ка́ждой из них. *(* wild guess)*

port *n* порт ♦ **I seek a home port.** *(personal ads)* Я ищу́ прича́л.

portly *adj* по́лный, -ая, -ое, -ые, доро́дный, -ая, -ое, -ые.

portrait *n* портре́т ♦ **I want you to go to a photography studio and have a portrait made.** Я хочу́, чтобы ты пошла́ *(ж: пошёл)* в фотосту́дию и заказа́ла *(ж: заказа́л)* свой потре́т.

pose *vi* пози́ровать / попози́ровать ♦ **Would you pose in the nude for me (sometime)?** Не попози́руешь ли ты мне обнажённой / наго́й (когда́ -нибудь)? ♦ **Would you pose for me?** Бу́дешь ли ты пози́ровать для меня́? ♦ **I'd love to have you pose in the nude.** Мне хоте́лось бы, чтобы ты пози́ровала обнажённой *(ж: пози́ровал обнажённым).*

pose *n* по́за ♦ *(1,2)* **provocative** ~ *(1)* соблазни́тельная / *(2)* маня́щая по́за ♦ **sexy** ~ секса-пи́льная по́за.

poser *n (slang) (pretender, phony person)* позёр.

position *n* пози́ция; по́за ♦ **missionary** ~ пози́ция с мужчи́ной све́рху ♦ **uncomfortable** ~ неудо́бная пози́ция ♦ **vulnerable** ~ уязви́мое положе́ние ♦ **switch** ~s изменя́ть / измени́ть пози́ции ♦ **I want to try every position** *([1]* ...imaginable... / *[2]* ...in the Kama Sutra...) **with you.** Я хочу́ испро́бовать с тобо́й ка́ждую из всех поз *([1]* ...кото́рые мо́жно себе́ предста́вить. / *[2]* ... из Ка́ма-Су́тры.).

> *The singular past tense of Russian verbs ends in -л (m) (usually),*
> *-ла (f) or -ло (n). the plural past tense ends in -li.*

possess *vt* обладáть *(what, whom = instr.)*, владéть *(what, whom = instr.)* ♦ ~ **a woman** обладáть жéнщиной ♦ **I must tell you that I feel an overwhelming desire to kiss you. It possesses me night and day. I cannot** *(1,2)* **shake it off.** Я дóлжен сказáть тебé, что ощущáю ошеломля́ющее желáние поцеловáть тебя́. Онó владéет мной ночь и день. Я не могý *(1)* ...стряхнýть егó. / *(2)* ...отдéлаться от негó.

possession *n* владéние, обладáние ♦ **I dream of the heavenly moment when my lips take possession of your mouth.** Я мечтáю о рáйском мгновéнии, когдá мои́ гýбы овладéют твои́м ртом.

possessive *adj* сóбственнический, -ая, -ое, -ие ♦ **I wish you wouldn't be so possessive.** Мне хотéлось бы, чтоб ты не была́ такóй сóбственницей *(ж: был таки́м сóбственником).* ♦ **You're too possessive.** Ты сли́шком большáя сóбственница *(ж: большóй сóбственник).*

possessiveness *n* сóбственничество, чýвство сóбственности.

possible *adj* возмóжный, -ая, -ое, -ые *(short forms:* возмóжен, возмóжна, -о, -ы), вероя́тный, -ая, -ое, -ые *(short forms:* вероя́тен, вероя́тна, -о, -ы) ♦ **Would it be possible to** *(1)* **see** / *(2)* **meet you** *(3)* **...this afternoon** / *(4)* **evening?** / *(5)* **...tonight?** / *(6)* **...tomorrow** (*[7]* **morning** / *[8]* **afternoon** / *[9]* **evening)?** / *(10)* **...after work?** / *(11)* **...after you get off work?** Мóжно ли *(1,2)* встрéтиться с тобóй *(3)* ...(сегóдня) в пóлдень? / *(4)* ...(сегóдня) вéчером? / *(5)* ...сегóдня нóчью? / *(6)* ...зáвтра (*[7]* ýтром / *[8]* в пóлдень / *[9]* вéчером)? / *(10,11)* ...пóсле рабóты? ♦ **Would it be possible for you ...to** *(1,2)* **go** / *(3,4)* **come with me?** / *(5,6)* **...to come** (*[7]* **here)** / (*[8]* **to my hotel) after work?** / *(9)* **...to call me?** / *(10)* **...to stay (with me) overnight?** / *(11)* **...to stay (with me) all night?** / *(12)* **...to send me more photos (of yourself)?** / *(13)* Смóжешь ли ты *(1,3)* ...пойти́ *(on foot)* / *(2,4)* поéхать *(by veh.)* со мной. / *(5)* ...прийти́ *(on foot)* / *(6)* приéхать *(by veh.)* (*[7]* ...сюдá... / *[8]* ...в мою́ гости́ницу...) пóсле рабóты? / *(9)* ...позвони́ть мне? / *(10)* ...остáться (со мной) на ночь? / *(11)* ...остáться (со мной) на всю ночь? / *(12)* ...послáть мне ещё нéсколько фотогрáфий (свои́х)? ♦ **Would it be possible for you to** *(1)* **get** / *(1)* **take** *(3)* **...today** / *(4)* **tomorrow off?** / *(5)* **...a week off?** / *(6)* **... two** / *(7)* **three days off?** / *(8)* **...two** / *(9)* **three weeks off?** / *(10)* **....a vacation** (*[11]* **while I'm here** / *[12]* **there)?** Смóжешь ли ты *(1)* ...получи́ть / *(2)* взять *(3)* ...свобóдный день сегóдня / *(4)* зáвтра? / *(5)* ...свобóдную недéлю? / *(6)* ...два / *(7)* три свобóдных дня? / *(8)* ...две / *(9)* три свобóдных недéли? / *(10)* ...óтпуск (*[11]* покá я здесь / *[12]* там)? ♦ **Would it be possible** *(1)* **...to stay at your house** / *(2)* **apartment?** / *(3)* **...to visit you?** / *(4)* **...to get my visa extended?** / *(5)* **...to stay for another day** / *(6)* **week?** / *(7)* **...to fix it** (*[8]* **today** / *[9]* **soon** / *[10]* **by tomorrow)?** Бýдет ли возмóжно *(1)* ...останови́ться в твоём дóме? / *(2)* ...останови́ться в твоéй кварти́ре? / *(3)* ...посети́ть тебя́? / *(4)* ...продли́ть мою́ ви́зу? / *(5)* ...остáться ещё на оди́н день? / *(6)* ...остáться ещё на однý недéлю? / *(7)* ...привести́ в поря́док э́то (*[8]* сегóдня? / *[9]* скóро? / *[10]* ...к зáвтрашнему дню?)?

possibility *n* возмóжность *f* ♦ **endless ~ies** бесконéчные возмóжности ♦ **cornucopia of ~ies** изоби́лие возмóжностей ♦ **explore ~ies** исслéдовать возмóжности.

posterior *n (buttocks)* зáдница, пóпа ♦ **shapely ~** окрýглая пóпа.

postcard *n* откры́тка ♦ **I wrote you a postcard. Did you** *(1)* **get** / *(2)* **receive it?** Я написáл *(ж: написáла)* тебé откры́тку. Ты её *(1,2)* получи́ла *(ж: получи́л)?* ♦ **I** *(1)* **got** / *(2)* **received your postcard.** Я *(1,2)* получи́л *(ж: получи́ла)* твою́ откры́тку.

postman *n* почтальóн.

postmark *n* почтóвый штéмпель.

postmarked *adj* проштампóванный, -ая, -ое, -ые *(short forms:* проштампóван, -а, -о, -ы) ♦ **The letter was postmarked August 14th.** Письмó бы́ло проштампóвано 14-ым (= че-

---

Please do us a favor:
Fill out and mail in the Feedback Sheet on page 795.

ты́рнадцатым) а́вгуста.

postpone *vt* откла́дывать / отложи́ть *(what = acc.)* ♦ **Why postpone the inevitable?** Заче́м откла́дывать неизбе́жное? ♦ **Do you want to postpone the wedding?** Ты хо́чешь отложи́ть сва́дьбу? ♦ **I (don't) want to postpone the wedding.** Я (не) хочу́ откла́дывать сва́дьбу. ♦ **We (don't) have to postpone the wedding.** Мы (не) должны́ откла́дывать сва́дьбу.

postponement *n* отсро́чка ♦ ~ **of the wedding** отсро́чка сва́дьбы.

posture *n* оса́нка ♦ **bad** ~ плоха́я оса́нка ♦ **good** ~ хоро́шая оса́нка.

post-wedding *adj* послесва́дебный, -ая, -ое, -ые.

posy *n* буке́т цвето́в.

pot *n (slang) (marijuana)* марихуа́на ♦ **sex** ~ *(slang)* сексапи́льная же́нщина.

potato *n* карто́шка ♦ **couch** ~ лежебо́ка.

potent *adj* 1. могу́щественный, -ая, -ое, -ые, сильноде́йствующий, -ая, -ее, -ие; 2. спосо́бный (-ая, -ое, -ые) к полово́му а́кту ♦ **You have such potent charm.** Ты облада́ешь таки́м могу́щественным обая́нием. ♦ **Your charm is** *(1)* **very /** *(2)* **exceedingly potent, do you know that?** Твоё очарова́ние *(1)* о́чень / *(2)* чрезвыча́йно могу́щественно, зна́ешь ли ты э́то?

potential *n* потенциа́л ♦ **romance** ~ рома́н возмо́жен.

potion *n* зе́лье ♦ **love** ~ любо́вное зе́лье.

potpourri *n* поппури́; *(fig.)* буке́т ♦ **I treasure the sweet potpourri of memories that you have given me.** Я дорожу́ сла́дкими воспомина́ниями о тебе́. ♦ **That vacation is such a sweet potpourri of memories for me.** Этот о́тпуск тако́й сла́дкий буке́т воспомина́ний для меня́. ♦ **The sweet potpourri of memories from those days we spent together suffuses my thoughts night and day.** Буке́т сла́дких воспомина́ний о днях, прове-дённых вме́сте, заполня́ет мои́ мы́сли но́чью и днём.

pound *vi (heart)* колоти́ться ♦ **begin to** ~ заколоти́ться ♦ **My heart began to pound.** Моё се́рдце заколоти́лось. ♦ **Whenever I** *(1)* **...see you... /** *(2)* **...think about you... /** *(3)* **...am near you..., it makes my heart begin to pound.** Когда́ бы я ни *(1)* ...уви́дел *(ж: уви́дела)* тебя́,... / *(2)* ...поду́мал *(ж: поду́мала)* о тебе́,... / *(3)* ...был *(ж: была́)* ря́дом с тобо́й,... моё се́рдце начина́ет колоти́ться. ♦ **I could feel my heart pounding.** Я почу́вствовал *(ж: почу́вствовала)*, как заколоти́лось моё се́рдце.

pounding *adj* колотя́щийся, -аяся, -ееся, -иеся ♦ ~ **heart** колотя́щееся се́рдце.

pour out *vt* излива́ть / изли́ть *(what = acc.)* ♦ **To someone who gives me all their love without reservation, I** *(1)* **could /** *(2)* **would pour out twice as much love and affection, or more, in return.** На ту *(ж: того́)*, кто отда́ст мне всю свою́ любо́вь безогово́рочно, я в отве́т *(1)* ...мог *(ж: могла́)* бы изли́ть... / *(2)* ...изли́л *(ж: излила́)* бы... вдво́е бо́льше любви́ и не́жности.

pout *vi* ду́ться, надува́ть / наду́ть гу́бы ♦ ~ **seductively** соблазни́тельно надува́ть / наду́ть гу́бы.

pout *n* 1. наду́тые гу́бы; 2. *(slang) (mouth)* рот.

poverty *n* бе́дность *f*, нищета́ ♦ **spiritual** ~ духо́вное убо́жество ♦ **Poverty doesn't frighten me.** Бе́дность не пуга́ет меня́.

powder *n* пу́дра ♦ **body** ~ пу́дра для те́ла.

power *n* 1. *(force, strength)* си́ла, эне́ргия, мощь; 2. *(control)* власть *f* ♦ **delicious** ~ сла́дкая власть ♦ **elemental** ~ приро́дная си́ла ♦ **enchanting** ~ чару́ющая власть ♦ **exquisite** ~ сла́дкая власть ♦ **great** ~ больша́я си́ла ♦ **intellectual** ~ интеллектуа́льная си́ла, си́ла ума́ ♦ **intoxicating** ~ маги́ческая власть ♦ **irresistible** ~ непреодоли́мая си́ла ♦ **latent** *(1,2* ~ скры́тая *(1)* си́ла / *(2)* власть ♦ **luxurious** ~ удиви́тельная власть ♦ **masculine**

Clock and calender time are discussed in Appendix 5, page 759.

~ мужска́я си́ла ♦ ~ **of your beauty** си́ла твое́й красоты́ ♦ **psychic** ~ духо́вая си́ла ♦ **raw masculine** ~ гру́бая мужска́я си́ла ♦ **seductive** ~ си́ла обольще́ния ♦ **staying** ~ спосо́бность до́лго занима́ться любо́вью ♦ **tremendous** ~ огро́мная си́ла ♦ **seek** ~ пыта́ться дости́чь власть.

---
power: *phrases*

You have such *(1)* luxurious / *(2)* **total** / *(3)* **delicious** / *(4)* **exquisite power over my senses.** У тебя́ така́я *(1,2)* удиви́тельная / *(3,4)* сла́дкая власть над мои́ми чу́вствами. ♦ **The desire that I** *(1,2)* **harbor in my heart for you goes beyond my power of words to describe.** Страсть к тебе́, кото́рую я *(1)* таю́ / *(2)* пита́ю в своём се́рдце, невозмо́жно описа́ть слова́ми. ♦ **There is about you an aura of raw, masculine power.** От тебя́ исхо́дит гру́бая мужска́я си́ла. ♦ **You have an intoxicating power over me.** У тебя́ маги́ческая власть на́до мной.

practical *adj* практи́ческий, -ая, -ое, -ие; практи́чный, -ая, -ое, -ые ♦ ~ **advice** практи́ческий сове́т ♦ ~ **idea** практи́ческая иде́я ♦ ~ **mind** практи́ческий ум ♦ ~ **person** практи́чный челове́к.

practice *vt*: ♦ **You should practice what you preach.** Дела́ должны́ соотве́тствовать слова́м.

praise *n* похвалы́ *pl* ♦ **You lavish me with praise. I don't deserve it.** Ты расточа́ешь мне похвалы́. Я не заслу́живаю их. ♦ **No one has ever lavished so much praise on me.** Никто́ никогда́ не расточа́л так мно́го похва́л мне.

prank *n* вы́ходка.

pray *vi* моли́ться *(to whom = dat., for what = + о + prep.)* ♦ **fervently** ~ горячо́ моли́ться ♦ **secretly** ~ та́йно моли́ться ♦ **I just pray to the heavens above that no one has already snatched you up.** Я то́лько молю́ небеса́, что́бы Вы не́ были подхва́чены ке́м-то други́м. ♦ **I fervently pray that in your heart you can somehow find the compassion to condescend to grant me just a few brief minutes to** *(1)* **meet** / *(2)* **talk with you and thereby assuage this unbearable longing that grips my soul.** Я горячо́ молю́сь, что́бы Вы смогли́ найти́ сострада́ние в своём се́рдце и подари́ть мне то́лько не́сколько коро́тких мину́т *(1)* встре́чи / *(2)* разгово́ра с Ва́ми, что́бы утоли́ть невыноси́мую тоску́, охвати́вшую мою́ ду́шу.

prayer моли́тва ♦ **say a** ~ чита́ть / проче́сть моли́тву ♦ **You're the answer to my** *(1)* **prayer** / *(2)* **prayers.** Ты отве́т на *(1)* ...мою́ моли́тву. / *(2)* ...мои́ моли́твы.

precious *adj* драгоце́нный, -ая, -ое, -ые, це́нный, -ая, -ое, -ые ♦ **It is** *(1)* **unbelievable** / *(2)* **incredible how precious you have become to me.** Это *(1,2)* невероя́тно, како́й драгоце́нной ты ста́ла *(ж: стал)* для меня́. ♦ **You are my highest and most precious.** Ты моя́ наивы́сшая драгоце́нность. ♦ **How precious you are to me.** Как драгоце́нна *(ж: драгоце́ннен)* ты для меня́. ♦ **You are the most precious thing in the world to me.** Ты для меня́ са́мое дорого́е сокро́вище на све́те. ♦ **My precious darling.** Моя́ драгоце́нная *(ж: Мой драгоце́нный)*. ♦ **You are so precious to me.** Ты так драгоце́нна *(ж: драгоце́ннен)* для меня́. ♦ **You are precious beyond words.** Ты огро́мная це́нность для меня́ ♦ **You are the most precious thing in my life.** Ты са́мое драгоце́нное, что есть у меня́ в жи́зни. ♦ **You are more precious (to me) than** *(1)* **...all the gold and diamonds in the world.** / *(2)* **...anything else in the world.** / *(3)* **...I can ever tell you.** / *(4)* **...I can ever describe to you.** / *(5)* **...life itself.** Ты драгоце́ннее *(для меня́)*, чем *(1)* ...всё зо́лото ми́ра. / *(2)* ...всё остально́е в ми́ре. / *(3)* ...я могу́ вы́сказать. / *(4)* ...я смогу́ когда́-либо описа́ть тебе́. / *(5)* ...сама́ жизнь. ♦ **I just can't tell you enough how dear and precious and beloved you have become to me.** Я про́сто не могу́ вы́разить тебе́, како́й дорого́й *(ж: каки́м дороги́м)*, драгоце́нной *(ж: драгоце́нным)* и люби́мой *(ж: люби́мым)* ты ста́ла *(ж:*

Reflexive verbs are those that end in -ся *or* -сь.
The -ся *or* -сь *also goes onto a past tense ending.*

стал) для меня. ♦ **The moments I spend with you are the most precious of my life.** Минуты, проведённые с тобой, -- самые драгоценные в моей жизни.

predilection *n* пристрастие ♦ **sexual** ~**s** сексуальные пристрастия.

predestination *n* предопределение.

predestined *adj* предопределён, предопределена, -о, -ы *(short forms)* ♦ **I believe we were predestined to meet.** Я верю, что наша встреча была предопределена.

predicament *n (difficult)* затруднительное / неприятное положение; *(awkward)* неловкое положение.

preen *vt* прихорашиваться ♦ ~ **one's hair** прихорашиваться.

prefer *vt* предпочитать *(what, whom = acc.).*

preferable *adj* предпочтительный, -ая, -ое, -ые.

preferably *adj* предпочтительно.

preferred *pp (Russian uses adverb* предпочтительно.*)* ♦ **Dancer preferred.** *(personal ad)* Предпочтительно: умеющая *(ж: умеющий)* танцевать.

preference *n* предпочтение; преимущество ♦ **sexual** ~ сексуальное предпочтение; *pl:* сексуальные пристрастия ♦ *(1)* **He** / *(2)* **She has a preference for other** *(3)* **men** / *(4)* **women.** У *(1)* него / *(2)* неё есть преимущество перед другими *(3)* мужчинами / *(4)* женщинами.

pregnancy *n* беременность *f* ♦ **false** ~ ложная беременность ♦ **unwanted** ~ нежелательная беременность.

pregnant *adj* беременная, -ые *(short forms:* беременна, -ы*)* ♦ **get** ~ забеременеть ♦ **I'm (not) pregnant.** Я (не) беременна. ♦ **Are you sure you're pregnant?** Ты уверена, что ты беременна? ♦ **I'm (not) sure that I'm pregnant.** Я (не) уверена, что беременна. ♦ **How many months pregnant are you?** Сколько у тебя месяцев беременности? ♦ **I'm** *(1)* **two** / *(2)* **three** / *(3)* **etc months pregnant.** У меня двух- / трёх- / *и т.д.* месячная беременность. ♦ **I (don't) want to make you pregnant.** Я (не) хочу, чтобы ты забеременела. ♦ **I (don't) want to get pregnant.** Я (не) хочу забеременеть.

prejudice *n* предрассудок *(often pl:* предрассудки*)*; предубеждение ♦ **racial** ~ расовые предрассудки.

prejudiced *adj* предубеждённый, -ая, -ое, -ые *(short forms:* предубеждён, предубеждена, -о, -ы*)*.

prelude *n* прелюдия ♦ **magical** ~ волшебная прелюдия.

premarital *adj* предсвадебный, -ая, -ое, -ые.

pre-nuptial *adj* предсвадебный, -ая, -ое, -ые.

preparation *n* приготовление, подготовка ♦ ~**s for the wedding** приготовления к свадьбе.

prepare *vt* готовить / приготовить *(what = acc.).*

prepared *adj* приготовлен, -а, -о, -ы *(short forms)*, подготовлен, -а, -о, -ы *(short forms)* ♦ **emotionally** ~ эмоционально подготовлен ♦ **mentally** ~ интеллектуально подготовлен.

presence *n* присутствие ♦ **close** ~ близкое присутствие ♦ **intoxicating** ~ опьяняющее присутствие ♦ **magnetic** ~ магнетическое присутствие ♦ **my** ~ моё присутствие ♦ **your** ~ *(familiar)* твоё присутствие; *(polite)* Ваше присутствие ♦ **Your presence is so comforting.** Твоё присутствие так успокаивает. ♦ **The whole evening my** *(1)* **attention** / *(2)* **mind was captive to your intoxicating presence.** Весь вечер *(1)* ...моё внимание было... / *(2)* ...мой ум был... пленником твоего опьяняющего присутствия. ♦ **Who could be unaware of your magnetic presence?** Кто мог бы не заметить твоего магнетического присутствия? ♦ **I** *(1)* **feel** / *(2)* **felt your presence so strongly.** Я так сильно

The time zones for many cities of the world are given in Appendix 6, page 761.

(1) ощуща́ю / *(2)* ощуща́л *(ж: ощуща́ла)* твоё прису́тствие.

present *adj* 1. *(on hand)* прису́тствующий, -ая, -ее, -ие; 2. *(current)* ны́нешний, -яя, -ее, -ие, тепе́решний, -яя, -ее, -ие, настоя́щий, -ая, -ее, -ие ♦ **be** ~ прису́тствовать.

press *vt* прижима́ть / прижа́ть *(what, whom = acc., to what, whom = + к + dat.)* ♦ ~ *(1)* **your** / *(1)* **my head to** *(1)* **my** / *(1)* **your chest** прижима́ться / прижа́ться *(1,2)* голово́й к *(3)* мое́й / *(4)* твое́й груди́. ♦ **I want to press you tightly against me.** Я хочу́ кре́пко прижа́ть тебя́ к себе́.

pressed *adj* сжат, -а, -о, -ы *(short forms)* ♦ **I was hard pressed to keep from crying.** Мне сто́ило больши́х уси́лий удержа́ться от слёз.

pressure *vt* дави́ть *(whom = + на + acc.)*, вынужда́ть / вы́нудить *(whom = acc.)* ♦ ~ *(someone)* **into (having) sex** принужда́ть / принуди́ть к се́ксу *(whom = acc.)* ♦ **I'm not going to pressure you.** Я не собира́юсь дави́ть на тебя́. ♦ **Please don't pressure me (to have sex).** Пожа́луйста, не принужда́й меня́ (занима́ться любо́вью).

pressure *n* давле́ние ♦ **a lot of** ~ большо́е давле́ние ♦ **great** ~ большо́е давле́ние ♦ **high blood** ~ гипертони́я, высо́кое давле́ние кро́ви ♦ **psychological** ~ психологи́ческое давле́ние ♦ **under** ~ под давле́нием ♦ **There's no pressure.** 1. *(not urgent)* Не сро́чно. / 2. *(not mandatory)* Не обяза́тельно ♦ **I don't want to put (any) pressure on you.** Я не хочу́ дави́ть на тебя́. ♦ **I've been under a lot of pressure lately.** Я был *(ж: была́)* под больши́м давле́нием после́днее вре́мя.

pressured *adj* принуждён, принуждена́, -о, -ы *(short forms)* ♦ **I don't want to feel pressured to have sex.** Я не хочу́ чу́вствовать никако́го принужде́ния к се́ксу.

prestige *n* прести́ж.

presumptuous *adj* сли́шком самоуве́ренный, -ая, -ое, -ые, самонаде́янный, -ая, -ое, -ые; высокоме́рный, -ая, -ое, -ые.

pretend *vt* притворя́ться / притвори́ться *(what = + в + prep.)* ♦ ~ **to be** *(1-4)* **unattached** притворя́ться *(1)* нежена́тым *(unmarried, m)* / *(2)* незаму́жней *(unmarried, f)* / *(3)* свобо́дным *(free, m)* / *(4)* свобо́дной *(free, f)* ♦ **I think you're just pretending your feelings for me.** Я ду́маю, ты то́лько притворя́ешься, что испы́тываешь каки́е-то чу́вства ко мне. ♦ **I wonder if you're not just pretending your feelings for me.** Я хоте́л *(ж: хоте́ла)* бы знать, не притворя́ешься ли ты, что испы́тываешь каки́е-то чу́вства ко мне. ♦ **I can't pretend feelings (that I don't have).** Я не могу́ притворя́ться в чу́вствах (, кото́рые я не испы́тываю). ♦ **You just pretend to have feelings for me.** Ты то́лько притворя́ешься, что име́ешь чу́вства ко мне. ♦ **You (just) pretend to love me (, but you don't).** Ты (то́лько) притворя́ешься, что лю́бишь меня́ (, но ты не лю́бишь).

pretense *n* притво́рство ♦ **It was all a pretense, wasn't it?** Это всё бы́ло притво́рством, не так ли?

pretty *adj* смазли́вый, -ая, -ое, -ые, милови́дный, -ая, -ое, -ые, привлека́тельный, -ая, -ое, -ые, преле́стный, -ая, -ое, -ые, краси́вый, -ая, -ое, -ые, хоро́шенькая, -ие, хороша́ собо́й ♦ **outstandingly** ~ неправдоподо́бно краси́вая ♦ ~ **as a picture** хоро́шенькая, как карти́нка *(1 term)* ♦ **To say that you are pretty would be vulgar. You are** *(1)* **exceptionally** / *(2)* **exquisitely** / *(3)* **strikingly beautiful.** Сказа́ть, что ты хоро́шенькая, бы́ло бы вульга́рно. Ты *(1)* исключи́тельно / *(2)* изы́сканно / *(3)* порази́тельно краси́ва. ♦ **You are absolutely the prettiest** *(1)* **woman** / *(2)* **girl I've ever** *(3)* **seen** / *(4)* **met.** Ты са́мая хоро́шенькая из всех *(1)* же́нщин / *(2)* де́вушек, *(3)* ви́денных / *(4)* встре́ченных мной. ♦ **You have a very pretty smile.** У тебя́ о́чень краси́вая улы́бка. ♦ **You don't know how pretty you are.** Ты не зна́ешь, как ты хороша́. ♦ **What a pretty dress!** Како́е краси́вое пла́тье! ♦ **What a pretty blouse!** Кака́я краси́вая блу́зка! ♦ **What a pretty outfit!** Како́й краси́вый наря́д! ♦ **How pretty your are!** Как ты хороша́! ♦ **I've seen**

Optional parts of sentences are preceded
or followed (or both) by three dots.

pretty women in my time, but none as pretty as you. Я видáл красúвых жéнщин в своéй жúзни, но ни однá не былá так хорошá, как ты. ♦ **You are exotically pretty.** Ты экзотúчески прелéстна.

pretty *adv (rather)* довóльно, достáточно.

prevail *vi* торжествовáть / восторжествовáть *(against what = + над + instr.)*, брать / взять верх *(against what = + над + instr.)*, одéрживать / одержáть верх *(against what = + над + instr.)* ♦ **Our love is going to prevail against this adversity, I promise you.** Нáша любóвь одéржит верх над э́тими невзгóдами, я обещáю.

prevent *vt* предотвращáть / предотвратúть *(what = acc.)*, мешáть / помешáть *(what, whom = dat.)* ♦ **Your maidenly sense of propriety is preventing us from sharing wonderful moments together.** Éсли бы не твоё дéвичье чýвство благопристóйности, у нас моглú бы быть великолéпные момéнты.

previous *adj* предыдýщий, -ая, -ее, -ие.

previously *adv* рáньше; рáнее; прéжде.

price *n* ценá ♦ **ticket** ~ ценá на билéт.

priceless *adj* бесцéнный, -ая, -ое, -ые ♦ **You're priceless.** Ты бесцéнна *(ж: бесцéнен)*.

prickly *adj* колю́чий, -ая, -ее, -ие.

pride *n* 1. *(satisfaction, sense of delight)* гóрдость *f*; 2. *(self-esteem)* самолю́бие ♦ **false** ~ чвáнство ♦ **great** ~ большáя гóрдость ♦ **tremendous** ~ огрóмная гóрдость ♦ **feel** ~ чýвствовать гóрдость ♦ **fill me with** ~ напóлнить меня́ гóрдостью ♦ **hurt** *(1)* **my** / *(2)* **your** ~ задéть *(1)* моё / *(2)* твоё самолю́бие ♦ **take** ~ гордúться *(in what = instr.)* ♦ **with** ~ с гóрдостью.

---
pride: phrases

Whenever I go someplace with you, I feel such tremendous pride. Когдá я идý с тобóй кудá-нибудь, я чýвствую такýю огрóмную гóрдость. ♦ **Having you as my** *(1)* **woman** / *(2)* **man fills me with (tremendous) pride.** То, что ты *(1)* ...моя́ жéнщина... / *(2)* ...мой мужчúна... наполня́ет меня́ (огрóмной) гóрдостью. ♦ **I'm going to swallow my pride and beg you not to** *(1)* ...**leave.** / *(2)* ...**leave me.** Я поступлю́сь своéй гóрдостью и бýду умоля́ть тебя́ не *(1)* ...уходúть. / *(2)* ...оставля́ть меня́. ♦ **I just swallow my pride.** Я прóсто поступáюсь своéй гóрдостью. ♦ **Transcend your pride.** Переступú свою́ гóрдость. ♦ **Is this your pride speaking?** Э́то твоя́ гóрдость говорúт? ♦ **It was a blow to my pride.** Э́то неслó мне удáр моемý самолю́бию. ♦ **You've stripped me of all my pride.** Из-за тебя́ я потеря́л *(ж: потеря́ла)* всю мою́ гóрдость. ♦ **My pride is (badly) hurt.** Моё самолю́бие (жестóко) рáнено.

priest *n* свящéнник.

prig *n* педáнт, формалúст, ханжá.

prim *adj* чóпорный, -ая, -ое, -ые ♦ **The first time I saw you, you looked so prim.** Когдá я пéрвый раз встрéтил тебя́, ты вы́глядела такóй чóпорной. ♦ **You** *(1)* **look** / *(2)* **looked so prim in that** *(3)* **dress** / *(4)* **outfit.** Ты *(1)* вы́глядишь / *(2)* вы́глядела так чóпорно в э́том *(3)* плáтье / *(4)* наря́де.

prime *n* расцвéт, начáло ♦ **You're really in your prime.** Ты действúтельно в сáмом расцвéте. ♦ **I may be past my prime, but I still love to make love.** Я, мóжет быть, ужé миновáл мой расцвéт, но я всё ещё люблю́ занимáться любóвью.

primeval *adj* первобы́тный, -ая, -ое, -ые ♦ **I'm constantly assailed by this primeval lusting for** *(1)* ...**you.** / *(2)* ...**your incredibly beautiful body.** Меня́ постоя́нно охвáтывает первобы́тное вожделéние к *(1)* ...тебé. / *(2)* ...твоемý невероя́тно прекрáсному тéлу.

primitive *adj* примитúвный, -ая, -ое, -ые, первобы́тный, -ая, -ое, -ые ♦ **I try not to be so primitive and carnal in my thoughts about you, but I simply can't help it.** Я пытáюсь не

If you're not on familiar terms with a person, the «ты» forms will have to be changed to «Вы».

быть столь первобы́тным и чу́вственным, ду́мая о тебе́, но мне э́то про́сто не удаётся.

primitiveness *n* примити́вность *f.*

primly *adv* чо́порно ♦ **You were so primly dressed.** Ты была́ так чо́порно оде́та. ♦ **You dress so primly (at times).** Твоя́ оде́жда (иногда́) так чо́порна.

prince *n* принц ♦ **dashing** ~ удало́й принц ♦ ~ **charming** ска́зочный принц ♦ **You are my prince charming.** Ты мой ска́зочный принц. ♦ **I seek someone who can be my spiritual prince charming.** *(ж:)* Я ищу́ того́, кто бу́дет мои́м ска́зочным при́нцем ду́ха.

princess *n* принце́сса ♦ **Asian** ~ азиа́тская принце́сса ♦ **blonde** ~ белоку́рая принце́сса ♦ **my little** ~ моя́ ма́ленькая принце́сса ♦ **Nubian** ~ нуби́йская принце́сса ♦ **Russian** ~ ру́сская принце́сса ♦ **spicy** ~ пика́нтная принце́сса.

principle *n* при́нцип ♦ **high** ~s высо́кие при́нципы ♦ **moral** ~s мора́льные усто́и ♦ **strong** ~s твёрдые при́нципы ♦ **I admire you for your high principles.** Я восхища́юсь тобо́й за твои́ высо́кие при́нципы. ♦ **I'm a** *(1)* **man** / *(2)* **woman** / *(3)* **person of principle.** Я *(1)* мужчи́на / *(2)* же́нщина / *(3)* челове́к с при́нципами. ♦ **I'm a person with (high) principles.** Я челове́к высо́ких при́нципов. ♦ **Have you no principles (at all)?** Вы не име́ете при́нципов? ♦ **I have strong principles.** У меня́ твёрдые при́нципы. ♦ **That's against my principles.** Это про́тив мои́х при́нципов. ♦ **Sex before marriage is against my principles.** Секс до жени́тьбы -- э́то про́тив мои́х при́нципов. ♦ **I'm no paragon of virtue, but I have my principles.** Я не образе́ц доброде́тели, но у меня́ есть свои́ при́нципы.

principled *adj* принципиа́льный, -ая, -ое, -ые, с твёрдыми при́нципами.

prioritize *vt* устана́вливать / установи́ть приорите́ты.

priority *n* поря́док очерёдности, очерёдность *f,* сро́чность *f,* приорите́т ♦ **first** *(1,2)* ~ первоочередна́я *(1)* цель / *(2)* зада́ча, первоочерёдность *f* ♦ **number one** *(1,2)* ~ первоочередна́я *(1)* цель / *(2)* зада́ча, первоочерёдность *f* ♦ **top** *(1,2)* ~ первоочередна́я *(1)* цель / *(2)* зада́ча, первоочерёдность *f* ♦ **(Having a) family is my number one** *(1,2)* **priority.** Семья́ - моя́ первоочередна́я *(1)* цель / *(2)* зада́ча. ♦ **Your needs and desires are my** *(1)* **central** / *(2)* **main priority.** Твои́ ну́жды и жела́ния -- мои́ *(1,2)* гла́вные приорите́ты. ♦ **Your needs and desires will always be my** *(1)* **central** / *(2)* **main priority.** Твои́ ну́жды и жела́ния всегда́ бу́дут мои́ми гла́вными приорите́тами.

privacy *n* уедине́ние ♦ *(1)* **find** / *(2)* **have** ~ *(1,2)* уединя́ться / уедини́ться ♦ **Sometimes I like privacy.** Иногда́ я люблю́ уедине́ние.

private *adj* 1. *(personal)* ча́стный, -ая, -ое, -ые; ли́чный, -ая, -ое, -ые; 2. *(confidential)* конфиденциа́льный, -ая, -ое, -ые, секре́тный, -ая, -ое, -ые, та́йный, -ая, -ое, -ые ♦ **in** ~ наедине́, конфиденциа́льно, секре́тно, с гла́зу на глаз ♦ *(1)* **Can** / *(2)* **Could we discuss it in private?** *(1)* Мо́жем... / *(2)* Не могли́ бы... мы обсуди́ть э́то наедине́? ♦ **I'd like to discuss** *(1)* **it** / *(2)* **something with you in private.** Я хоте́л *(ж: хоте́ла)* бы обсуди́ть *(1)* э́то / *(2)* что́-то с тобо́й наедине́. ♦ **I want to talk with you (about it) in private.** Я хочу́ поговори́ть с тобо́й (об э́том) наедине́. ♦ **Is there someplace we can talk in private?** Есть здесь ме́сто, где мы мо́жем поговори́ть наедине́?

prize *n* приз, пре́мия, награ́да ♦ **If you have a nature as generous as your** *(1)* **beauty** / *(2)* **body, you are truly heaven's special prize.** Если Ваш хара́ктер тако́й же замеча́тельный, как *(1)* ...Ва́ша красота́... / *(2)* ...Ва́ше те́ло..., то Вы и́стинный дар небе́с.

probe *vt* прощу́пывать / прощу́пать *(what = acc.).*

probing *n* прощу́пывание.

problem *n* пробле́ма, зада́ча ♦ **big** ~ больша́я пробле́ма ♦ **complicated** ~ сло́жная проблéма ♦ *(1,2)* **difficult** ~ *(1)* слóжная / *(2)* трýдная проблéма ♦ *(1,2)* **main** ~ *(1)* основнáя / *(2)* глáвная проблéма ♦ **serious** ~ серьёзная проблéма ♦ **small** ~ мáленькая проблéма ♦ **run into a** ~ столкнýться с проблéмой ♦ **solve the** ~ реши́ть проблéму ♦ **work out the** ~ реши́ть проблéму.

  | **problem: *phrases*** |

Is there a problem (about this)? В э́том проблéма? ♦ **There's a (***[1]*** small /** ***[2]*** **big) problem.** Существýет (*[1]* мáленькая / *[2]* большáя) проблéма. ♦ **There's no problem.** Нет проблéм. ♦ **It poses a problem.** Это -- проблéма. ♦ **What's the problem?** В чём проблéма? ♦ **The problem is that...** Проблéма в том, что... ♦ **Please tell me what the problem is.** Пожáлуйста, скажи́ мне, в чём проблéма. ♦ **You can confide your problem in me. I promise I won't tell anyone.** Ты мóжешь довéрить свою́ проблéму мне. Я обещáю, что не расскажý никомý. ♦ **Let's always try to discuss our problems openly.** Давáй всегдá обсуждáть нáши проблéмы откры́то. ♦ **Let's always try to work out our problems together.** Давáй всегдá решáть нáши проблéмы вмéсте. ♦ **I know we can work out our problems if we try.** Я знáю, мы мóжем реши́ть нáши проблéмы, éсли мы попытáемся. ♦ **We'll solve this problem somehow.** Эту проблéму мы кáк-нибудь реши́м.

proceed *vi* 1. *(continue, go on)* продолжáть, идти́ дáлее; 2. *(go, head)* идти́ / пойти́, отправля́ться / отпрáвиться ♦ **Then I'm going to proceed from your face down to my other favorite places.** Потóм я отпрáвлюсь от твоегó лицá вниз к други́м мои́м люби́мым местáм.

proclaim *vt:* ♦ ~ **love** признавáться / признáться в любви́, объясня́ться / объясни́ться в любви́ ♦ **You may think it impossible that someone could proclaim love for you after knowing you such a short time, but what you have done to my heart gives it no other choice than to make this proclamation.** Ты, вероя́тно, дýмаешь, что невозмóжно объясня́ться в любви́ пóсле такóго корóткого врéмени знакóмства, но то, что ты дéлаешь с мои́м сéрдцем, не оставля́ет ему никакóго другóго вы́бора, крóме как объясни́ться.

prodigal *adj* чрезмéрный, -ая, -ое, -ые, расточи́тельный, -ая, -ое, -ые ♦ ~ **charm** чрезмéрная прéлесть.

profess *vt* заявля́ть / заяви́ть, откры́то признавáть / признáть *(what = acc.)* ♦ ~ **love** признавáться / признáться в любви́ ♦ **You profess your love for me, but *(1)* ...is it true /** ***(2)*** **real /** ***(3)*** **genuine? /** ***(4)*** **...how deep /** ***(5)*** **strong is it?** Ты признаёшься мне в любви́, но *(1)* ...прáвда ли э́то? / *(2,3)* ...настоя́щая ли онá? / *(4)* ...как глубокá / *(5)* сильнá онá?

professional *n* профессионáл ♦ **high-tech** ~ профессионáл высóкой технолóгии.

profile *n* прóфиль *m*.

progressive *adj* прогресси́вный, -ая, -ое, -ые ♦ **politically** ~ с прогресси́вными полити́ческими взгля́дами.

project *n* проéкт ♦ **I like to work on home projects.** Я люблю́ дéлать всё в дóме свои́ми рукáми.

prolong *vt* продли́ть *(what = acc.)* ♦ **You'll be surprised at how many ways I know to prolong your *(1)* enjoyment /** ***(2)*** **pleasure.** Ты бýдешь удивленá тем, как мнóго спóсобов я знáю для продлéния твоегó *(1)* удовóльствия / *(2)* наслаждéния.

prolonging *n* продлéние.

promiscuity *n* (половáя) распýщенность *f*, (половóе) распýтство ♦ *(1)* **I cannot... /** ***(2)*** **I will not... tolerate promiscuity.** *(1)* Я не могý... / *(2)* Я не бýду... терпéть (половóй) распýщенности.

promiscuous *adj* распýщенный, -ая, -ое, -ые *(short forms:* распýщен, -а, -о, -ы*)*, беспоря-

Common adult heights are given in Appendix 9, page 776.

дочный, -ая, -ое, -ы ♦ **I don't believe in being promiscuous.** Я про́тив (полово́й) распу́щенности. ♦ **I'm not a promiscuous person.** Я не распу́щенный челове́к. ♦ **If I ever find out that you're promiscuous, that's the end (of it).** Если я когда́-нибудь узна́ю, что ты изменя́ешь, тогда́ э́то коне́ц. ♦ **If there's anything I can't stand, it's promiscuous behavior.** Если я чего́-то не терплю́, так э́то распу́тства.

promise *vi* обеща́ть / пообеща́ть *(what = acc., to whom = dat.)* ♦ **~ to love, honor and obey** обеща́ть люби́ть, уважа́ть и слу́шаться ♦ **I promise that I will always pay attention to your** *(1)* **happiness /** *(2)* **needs.** Я обеща́ю, что всегда́ бу́ду уделя́ть внима́ние *(1)* ...твоему́ сча́стью. / *(2)* ...твои́м ну́ждам. ♦ **I promise** *(1-3)* **to live in your love for all the days of my life.** Я обеща́ю *(1)* храни́ть / *(2)* леле́ять / *(3)* бере́чь твою́ любо́вь до конца́ мои́х дней. ♦ **I promise that I will do everything (I possibly can)** *(1)* **...to prove that I love you. /** *(2)* **...to make our love grow ever stronger, ever deeper, ever more beautiful.** Я обеща́ю сде́лать всё, (что смогу́,) *(1)* ...чтобы доказа́ть тебе́ свою́ любо́вь./ *(2)* ...чтобы сде́лать на́шу любо́вь ещё сильне́е, ещё глу́бже, ещё прекра́снее. ♦ **I promise to love you and** *(1)* **...respect you and care for you... /** *(2)* **...cherish you...** *(3)* **...all my life. /** *(4)* **...for the rest of our lives.** Я обеща́ю люби́ть тебя́ *(1)* ..., уважа́ть тебя́ и забо́титься о тебе́... / *(2)* ...и леле́ять тебя́... *(3)* ...всю свою́ жизнь. / *(4)* ...всю оста́в-шуюся жизнь.
♦ **I can't promise anything.** Я ничего́ не могу́ обеща́ть.

promise *n* обеща́ние ♦ **empty ~s** пусты́е обеща́ния ♦ **firm ~** твёрдое обеща́ние ♦ **hollow ~s** пусты́е обеща́ния ♦ **my ~** моё обеща́ние ♦ **solemn ~** торже́ственное обеща́ние ♦ **usual ~s** очередны́е обеща́ния ♦ **vague ~** сму́тное обеща́ние ♦ **your ~** *(familiar)* твоё обеща́ние; *(polite)* Ва́ше обеща́ние ♦ **break** *(1)* **my /** *(2)* **your ~** нару́шить *(1,2)* своё обеща́ние ♦ **forget** *(1)* **my /** *(2)* **your ~** забы́ть *(1,2)* своё обеща́ние ♦ **fulfill** *(1)* **my /** *(2)* **your ~** вы́полнить *(1,2)* своё обеща́ние ♦ **give** *(1)* **me /** *(2)* **you** *(3)* **your /** *(4)* **my ~** дава́ть / дать *(1)* мне / *(2)* тебе́ *(3,4)* своё обеща́ние ♦ **keep** *(1)* **my /** *(2)* **your ~** сдержа́ть *(1,2)* своё обеща́ние ♦ **make good on** *(1)* **my /** *(2)* **your ~** испо́лнить *(1,2)* своё обеща́ние ♦ **This ring is a promise of my (**[1] **enduring /** [2] **eternal /** [3] **unending) love for you.** Это кольцо́ -- зало́г мое́й (*[1]* про́чной / *[2]* ве́чной / *[3]* несконча́емой) любви́ к тебе́ ♦ **That's a promise.** Обеща́ю.

prompt *vt* 1. *(impel)* побужда́ть / побуди́ть *(what, whom = acc.)*; толка́ть / толкну́ть *(what, whom = acc.)*; 2. *(cue)* подска́зывать / подсказа́ть *(whom = dat.)* ♦ **My instincts prompt me to** *(1)* **...just leave you. /** *(2)* **...forget about you. /** *(3,4)* **...go home. /** *(5)* **...run off with you (and** *[6,7]* **get married).** Мои́ инсти́нкты подска́зывают мне *(1)* ...про́сто оста́вить тебя́. / *(2)* ...забы́ть о тебе́. / *(3)* ...уе́хать *(by veh.)* / *(4)* уйти́ *(on foot)* домо́й. / *(5)* ...убежа́ть с тобо́й (и *[6]* ...жени́ться. / *[7]* ...вы́йти за́муж.).

prone *adj* скло́нный, -ая, -ое, -ые *(short forms:* скло́нен, скло́нна, -о, -ы*)* ♦ **I'm prone to frequent levity.** Я скло́нен *(ж: скло́нна)* к ча́стому легкомы́слию. ♦ **You shouldn't be so prone to suspicion.** Ты не должна́ *(ж: до́лжен)* быть так скло́нна *(ж: скло́нен)* к подозри́тельности.

pronounce *vt* 1. *(words)* произноси́ть / произнести́ *(what = acc.)*; 2. *(declare)* объявля́ть / объяви́ть *(what = acc.)*, заявля́ть / заяви́ть *(what = acc.)*; *(marriage)* называ́ть / назва́ть *(whom = acc., as what = instr.)* ♦ **I dream of the day when they pronounce us man and wife.** Я мечта́ю о дне, когда́ нас назову́т му́жем и жено́й.

pronto *adv (slang) (quick)* бы́стро, жи́во.

proof *n* доказа́тельство ♦ **Your sweet kiss is proof we are meant to be together.** Твой сла́дкий поцелу́й - доказа́тельство того́, что нам предназна́чено быть вме́сте.

propel *vt* стимули́ровать *(what, whom = acc.)*, дви́гать / дви́нуть вперёд *(what, whom = acc.)* ♦ **Upward and upward and upward I want to propel you into** *(1)* **ecstasy /** *(2)*

Words in parentheses are optional.

passion. Я хочу́ поднима́ть тебя́ всё вы́ше, вы́ше и вы́ше к верши́нам *(1)* экста́за / *(2)* стра́сти.

property *n (characteristic)* 1. осо́бенность *f*, черта́; ка́чество; 2. *(belonging)* со́бственность *f*, иму́щество ♦ **I've never met anyone with as many desirable properties as you have.** Я никогда́ ещё не встреча́л *(ж: встреча́ла)* нико́го с таки́м мно́жеством прия́тных мне ка́честв, как у тебя́.

prophetic *adj* проро́ческий, -ая, -ое, -ие ♦ **Our very first meeting was prophetic.** На́ша са́мая пе́рвая встре́ча была́ проро́ческой.

propinquity *n* схо́дство.

proportion *n* пропо́рция, разме́ры, соотноше́ние ♦ **Junoesque ~s** пропо́рции Юно́ны ♦ **You** *(1)* **...are blowing...** / *(2)* **have blown... this (**[*1*] **all /** [*2*] **completely) out of proportion.** Ты *(1)* раздува́ешь / *(2)* раздува́ла *(ж: раздува́л)* э́то (*[1]* совсе́м / *[2]* соверше́нно) несоизмери́мо.

proportional *adj* пропорциона́льный, -ая, -ое, -ые.

proportioned *adj* пропорциона́лен, пропорциона́льна, -о, -ы *(short forms)*, сложён, сложена́, -о́, -ы́ *(short forms)* ♦ **You're extremely** *(1,2)* **well proportioned.** Ты чрезвыча́йно *(1)* ...хорошо́ сложена́. / *(1)* ...пропорциона́льна. ♦ **I would say that I'm (fairly) well proportioned.** Я хоте́л *(ж: хоте́ла)* бы сказа́ть, что я (доста́точно) хорошо́ сложён *(ж: сложена́).*

proposal *n* предложе́ние ♦ **marriage ~** предложе́ние (вы́йти за́муж) ♦ **tempting ~** зама́нчивое предложе́ние ♦ **accept** *(1)* **my /** *(2)* **your ~** приня́ть *(1)* моё / *(2)* твоё предложе́ние ♦ **consider** *(1)* **my /** *(2)* **your ~** обду́мывать / обду́мать *(1)* моё / *(2)* твоё предложе́ние ♦ **make a ~** де́лать / сде́лать предложе́ние *(to whom = dat.).*

propose *vt* 1. *(suggest)* предлага́ть / предложи́ть *(what = acc., to whom = dat.)*; 2. *(marriage)* де́лать / сде́лать предложе́ние *(to whom = dat.)* ♦ **I'm proposing to you. Will you marry me?** Я де́лаю тебе́ предложе́ние. Вы́йдешь ли ты за меня́ за́муж? ♦ **Are you proposing (marriage) to me?** Ты де́лаешь мне предложе́ние? ♦ **Please understand, I'm not proposing marriage.** Пожа́луйста, пойми́, я не предлага́ю брак. ♦ **What would your parents say if I proposed marriage to you?** Что сказа́ли бы твои́ роди́тели, е́сли бы я сде́лал тебе́ предложе́ние?

proprietorial *adj* со́бственнический, -ая, -ое, -ие ♦ **I don't appreciate your proprietorial attitude toward me.** Мне не нра́вится твоё со́бственническое отноше́ние ко мне.

propriety *n* присто́йность *f* ♦ **Your maidenly sense of propriety is inhibiting you (way) too much.** Твоё де́вичье чу́вство благопристо́йности сли́шком си́льно сде́рживает тебя́. ♦ **Your maidenly sense of propriety is preventing us from sharing wonderful moments together.** Е́сли бы не твоё де́вичье чу́вство благопристо́йности, у нас могли́ бы быть великоле́пные моме́нты. ♦ **You've overstepped the bounds of propriety.** Ты переступи́ла *(ж: переступи́л)* грани́цу присто́йности.

prospect *n* перспекти́ва ♦ **bright ~s** ра́дужные перспекти́вы ♦ **My heart races (wildly) with anticipation at the prospect of seeing you.** Моё се́рдце (бе́шено) коло́тится в предвкуше́нии встре́чи с тобо́й. ♦ **How can I** *(1)* **get /** *(2)* **live through another** *(3)* **day** / *(4)* **month /** *(5)* **week without you by my side. I cringe at the prospect.** Как могу́ я *(1,2)* дожи́ть до *(3)* ...сле́дующего дня / *(4)* ме́сяца... / *(5)* ...сле́дующей неде́ли... без тебя́ ря́дом со мной. Я страшу́сь тако́й перспекти́вы.

protect *vt* защища́ть / защити́ть *(what, whom = acc.).*

protection *n* защи́та, предохране́ние ♦ **It's (**[*1*] **too /** [*2*] **so) dangerous without some kind of protection.** (*[1]* Сли́шком / *[2]* Так) опа́сно без како́го-либо предохране́ния.

protest *n* проте́ст ♦ **I'm going to ignore all your protests.** Я бу́ду игнори́ровать все твои́

You can find common clothing sizes in Appendix 11 on page 778.

протéсты.

Protestant *adj* протестáнтский, -ая, -ое, -ие.

Protestant *n* протестáнт *m*, протестáнтка *f.*

protrude *vi* торчáть, выдавáться нарýжу ♦ **I love the way your breasts protrude (even when you wear a coat).** Мне нрáвится, как торчи́т твоя́ грудь (, дáже когдá ты одевáешь пальтó).

proud *adj* гóрдый, -ая, -ое, -ые *(short forms:* горд, -á, -о, -ы́) ♦ **I'm proud to** *(1)* ...**have you by my side.** / *(2)* ...**have you with me.** / *(3)* ...**go places with you.** / *(4)* ...**have a girlfriend** / *(5)* **wife as beautiful as you.** / *(6)* ...**have a boyfriend** / *(7)* **husband as handsome as you.** Я горд *(ж: гордá)* *(1)* ...тем, что ты ря́дом со мной. / *(2)* ...тем, что ты со мной. / *(3)* ...посещáть рáзные местá с тобóй. / *(4)* ...имéть дéвушку / *(5)* женý такýю прекрáсную, как ты. / *(6)* ...имéть дрýга / *(7)* мýжа такóго краси́вого, как ты. ♦ **I would be proud to** *(1)* ...**have you by my side.** / *(2)* ...**have you with me.** / *(3)* ...**go places with you.** / *(4)* ...**have a girlfriend** / *(5)* **wife as beautiful as you.** / *(6)* ...**have a boyfriend** / *(7)* **husband as handsome as you.** Я был бы горд *(ж: былá бы гордá)* *(1)* ...éсли бы ты былá *(ж: был)* ря́дом со мной. / *(2)* ...éсли бы ты былá *(ж: был)* со мной. / *(3)* ...посещáть рáзные местá с тобóй. / *(4)* ...имéть дéвушку / *(5)* женý такýю прекрáсную, как ты. / *(6)* ...имéть дрýга / *(7)* мýжа такóго краси́вого, как ты.

prove *vt* докáзывать / доказáть *(what = acc., to whom = dat.)* ♦ **I love you and** *(1)* ...**I want to...** / *(2)* ...**I'm going to... spend the rest of my life proving it to you.** Я люблю́ тебя́ и *(1)* ...я хочý провести́... / *(2)* ...я проведý... остáток моéй жи́зни, докáзывая э́то тебé. ♦ **I will do everything to prove that I love you.** Я сдéлаю всё, чтóбы доказáть, что я люблю́ тебя́.

provider *n* корми́лец *(семьи́)* ♦ **be a good ~** хорошó обеспéчивать семью́.

provocative *adj (alluring)* соблазни́тельный, -ая, -ое, -ые, пикáнтный, -ая, -ое, -ые, маня́щий, -ая, -ее, -ие; вызывáющий, -ая, -ее, -ие, призы́вный, -ая, -ое, -ые ♦ **The provocative curve of your breasts is such a pleasure to behold.** Такóе удовóльствие созерцáть соблазни́тельные изги́бы твоéй груди́.

prowess *n* мастерствó, совершéнство, умéние; си́ла ♦ **I'm really impressed by your physical prowess.** Я действи́тельно пораженá твоéй физи́ческой си́лой. ♦ **Your prowess as a lover is** *(1,2)* **without equal.** Твоё достóинство как любóвника *(1)* ...не имéет себé рáвных. / *(2)* ...вне сравнéния.

prude *n* 1. *(puts on modest / proper airs)* ханжá, блюсти́тель нрáвов; 2. *(extremely modest / proper)* скрóмница, недотрóга ♦ **You're such a prude!** 1. Какáя ты ханжá! 2. Какáя ты скрóмница! ♦ **Don't be such a prude.** 1. Не будь такóй ханжóй. 2. Не будь такóй скрóмницей.

prudent *adj* благоразýмный, -ая, -ое, -ые, рассуди́тельный, -ая, -ое, -ые.

prudish *adj* 1. *(putting on modest / proper airs)* хáнжеский, -ая, -ое, -ие; 2. *(extremely modest / proper)* изли́шне скрóмный, -ая, -ое, -ые, стыдли́вый, -ая, -ое, -ые ♦ **You're being prudish.** Ты ведёшь себя́ по-хáнжески. ♦ **Don't be so prudish.** Не веди́ себя́ по-хáнжески. ♦ **That's a** *([1,2]* **rather) prudish attitude.** Это *([1]* довóльно / *[2]* скорéе) хáнжеское отношéние. ♦ **You (really) need to overcome your prudish instincts.** Ты(действи́тельно) должнá преодолéть свои́ стыдли́вые инсти́нкты.

psyche *n* пси́хика, душá, дух ♦ **complex ~** слóжная пси́хика ♦ **complicated ~** слóжная пси́хика ♦ **female ~** жéнская пси́хика ♦ **male~** мужскáя пси́хика ♦ **You have subjugated the innermost part of my psyche.** Ты покори́ла мою́ дýшу. ♦ **You have an effect on my heart, mind and psyche that no amount of words, English or Russian, can ever suffice to describe.** У меня́ не хватáет слов, англи́йских и рýсских, чтóбы описáть

For general rules of Russian grammar see Appendix 2 on page 686.

воздействие, которое ты оказываешь на моё сердце, мысли и душу. ✦ **You have really invaded my psyche, do you know that?** Ты действительно вторглась *(ж: вторгся)* в мою душу, знаешь ли ты это?

psyched (up) *adj (slang) (excited)* возбуждён, возбуждена, -о, -ы *(short forms)*, взволнован, -на, -о, -ы *(short forms)* ✦ **be ~** *(slang) (be excited)* быть взволнованным *m* / взволнованной *f*. ✦ **I'm really psyched up about** *(1)* **...meeting** / *(2)* **seeing you.** / *(3)* **...coming over there.** Я действительно очень возбуждён *(ж: возбуждена)* *(1,2)* ...предстоящей встречей с тобой. / *(3)* ...предстоящим приездом туда.

psycho *n (slang)* псих.

public *n* народ, публика ✦ **in ~** публично.

pucker (up) *vi* морщить / наморщить.

pudgy *adj (slang)* толстый, -ая, -ое, -ые, пухлый, -ая, -ое, -ые.

pull *vt* тянуть / потянуть *(what, whom = acc.)*; *(to oneself)* притягивать / притянуть *(what, whom = acc.)* ✦ **~ away** *vi* отталкиваться / оттолкнуться *(from whom = + от + gen.)* ✦ **~ out** *vi (of a relationship)* покончить *(of what = + с + instr.)* ✦ **I want to pull you close (to me) (and kiss you tenderly).** Я хочу притянуть тебя близко (ко мне) (и целовать тебя нежно).

> **pull away:**

Why do you pull away from me? Почему ты отталкиваешь меня?

> **pull out:**

Why don't you pull out of the marriage? Почему бы тебе не покончить со своей семейной жизнью? ✦ **I want to pull out of the marriage.** Я хочу покончить со своей семейной жизнью.

pulsate *vi* пульсировать ✦ **I'm going to make those rosy nubs on your breasts pulsate with pleasure.** Я заставлю эти розовые шишечки твоих грудей пульсировать от наслаждения.

pulse *n* 1. *(heart's)* пульс; 2. *(slang) (interest, liking)* интерес, любовь ✦ **My pulse just** *(1,2)* **rockets when** *(3)* **...I get close to you.** / *(4)* **...you do that (to me).** / *(5)* **...I look at your beautiful face (and beautiful body).** / *(6)* **...I even think about you.** Мой пульс *(1)* скачет / *(2)* учащается, как только *(3)* ...я оказываюсь рядом с тобой. / *(5)* ...ты делаешь это (со мной). / *(5)* ...я взгляну на твоё прекрасное лицо (и тело). *(6)* ...я просто думаю о тебе. ✦ **Hopefully, you're someone with a pulse for urban adventures and outdoor pleasures.** Надеюсь, что Вам нравятся развлечения и в городе и на природе.

pulsing *adj* пульсирующий, -ая, -ее, -ие.

pump *vt:* ✦ **~ iron** *(slang) (lift weights)* поднимать / поднять вес.

pumps *n, pl (women's shoes)* (женские) туфли на каблуках ✦ **low-heeled ~s** (женские) туфли на низких каблуках.

pure *adj* чистый, -ая, -ое, -ые ✦ **~ and perfect** чистый (-ая, -ое, -ые) и совершенный (-ая, -ое, -ые).

purify *vt* очищать / очистить *(what, whom = acc.)* ✦ **"Purify me with a great fire of divine love."** *Liane de Pougy* «Очисти меня великим огнём небесной любви.» *Лаян де Пуж*

puritanical *adj* пуританский, -ая, -ое, -ие, строгий, -ая, -ое, -ие ✦ **~ attitude** пуританское отношение ✦ **~ behavior** пуританское поведение ✦ **~ ways** пуританские манеры.

purity *n* чистота ✦ **symbol of ~** символ чистоты.

purple *adj* лиловый, -ая, -ое, -ые.

purpose *n* цель *f*, стремление, намерение; назначение; предназначение ✦ **immoral ~s** аморальные цели ✦ **selfish ~s** эгоистические цели ✦ **vile ~s** низкие намерения ✦ **on ~** нарочно ✦ **to no ~** напрасно ✦ **It has no purpose.** Это бесцельно. ✦ **What's the**

For transitive Russian verbs the cases that they take are shown by means of an = sign and the Russian case (abbreviated).

purpose (of going on like this)? Какóй смысл (продолжáть так, как сейчáс)? ♦ **You and I together will fulfill our purpose (in life).** Вмéсте мы осуществи́м нáше предназначéние (в жи́зни). ♦ **You are my hopes and dreams, my strength and purpose, my joy and happiness. You are my life.** Ты мои́ надéжды и мечты́, моя́ си́ла и цель, моя́ рáдость и счáстье. Ты моя́ жизнь.

purr *vi* мурлы́кать ♦ **My little love-kitten, I want to make you always purr in contentment.** Мой мáленький люби́мый котёнок, я хочу́, чтóбы ты всегдá удовлетворённо мурлы́кала.

pursue *vt (a woman)* ухáживать *(whom = + за + instr.)* ♦ **~ romance** искáть ромáнтику ♦ **I've never pursued a woman before.** Я никогдá прéжде не ухáживал за жéнщиной. ♦ **I don't normally pursue women (, but with you I can't help myself).** Я обы́чно не ухáживаю за жéнщинами (, но ря́дом с тобóй не могу́ с собóй спрáвиться).

pursuit *n* 1. *(chasing)* преслéдование, погóня; 2. *(activity)* заня́тие, времяпрепровождéние ♦ **cultural ~s** культу́рное времяпрепровождéние ♦ **leisure ~s** заня́тия в свобóдное врéмя ♦ **~ of happiness** погóня за счáстьем ♦ **I enjoy cultural pursuits.** Я наслаждáюсь культу́рным времяпрепровождéнием.

push *vt*: ♦ **I'm pushing 50.** Мне под пятьдеся́т.

pushover *n* жéнщина лёгкого поведéния ♦ **What do you think I am — some kind of pushover?** Ты ду́маешь, что я жéнщина лёгкого поведéния? ♦ **I am not just a pushover.** Я не жéнщина лёгкого поведéния. ♦ **You must think I'm a pushover.** Ты вероя́тно ду́маешь, что я жéнщина лёгкого поведéния. ♦ **You treat me like I was some kind of pushover.** Ты обращáешься со мной, как бу́дто я жéнщина лёгкого поведéния. ♦ **I am not just a pushover.** Я не жéнщина лёгкого поведéния.

pushy *adj (slang)* влáстный, -ая, -ое, -ые, напóристый, -ая, -ое, -ые, пробивнóй, -áя, -óе, -ы́е ♦ **Sometimes you're a little too pushy.** Иногдá ты сли́шком напóристая *(ж: напóристый)*. ♦ **I don't like pushy *(1)* women / *(2)* men / *(3)* people.** Я не люблю́ напóристых *(1)* жéнщин / *(2)* мужчи́н / *(3)* людéй. ♦ **Don't be so pushy (with me).** Не будь такóй напóристой *(ж: таки́м напóристым)* (со мной). ♦ **I'm not (at all) pushy.** Я (совсéм) не напóристый *(ж: напóристая)*. ♦ **I'm not a pushy person.** Я не напóристый человéк.

pussy *n (slang) (vagina)* влагáлище, вáгина.

pussycat *n (slang) (little darling [female])* ки́ска *(нéжное обращéние)*.

put *vt* класть / положи́ть *(what = acc, where = + в or на + acc.)*. ♦ **~ down** *(belittle)* унижáть / унизи́ть *(whom = acc.)*; *(insult)* оскорбля́ть / оскорби́ть *(whom = acc.)*; *(criticize)* критиковáть. ♦ **~ off** *vt* 1. *(postpone)* отклáдывать / отложи́ть *(what = acc.)*, отсрóчивать / отсрóчить *(what = acc.)*; 2. *(get rid of, shake off)* отдéлываться / отдéлаться *(whom = + от + gen.)* ♦ **~ on** *vt* 1. *(clothing)* надевáть / надéть *(what = acc.)*; 2. *(slang) (deceive, lie)* обмáнывать / обману́ть *(whom = acc.)*, лгать / солгáть *(whom = dat.)*; 3. *(slang) (joke)* шути́ть / пошути́ть *(whom = + с + instr.)* ♦ **~ out** *vt* выбрáсывать / выбросить *(what = acc.)* ♦ **~ over** *vt (deceive)* обмáнывать / обману́ть *(whom = acc.)* ♦ **~ up with** смиря́ться / смири́ться *(with what = + с + instr.)*.

| **put:** |

I want you to put your *(1)* **...head on my shoulders.** / *(2)* **...hand in mine.** Я хочу́, чтóбы ты *(1)* ...положи́ла гóлову мне на плечó. / *(2)* ...далá мне ру́ку.

| **put off:** |

Please don't get the idea that I'm trying to put you off. Пожáлуйста, не ду́май, что я пытáюсь отдéлаться от тебя́. ♦ **Why have you been putting me off?** Почему́ ты пытáлась *(ж: пытáлся)* отдéлаться от меня́? ♦ **I'm sorry I've put off writing to you for**

Russian verbs have 2 forms: imperfective and perfective.
They're given in that order.

so long. Извини́, что я так до́лго не писа́л *(ж: писа́ла)* тебе́. ♦ **Please don't put it off.** Пожа́луйста, не откла́дывай э́то.

put on:

You're putting me on. 1. *(lying)* Ты лжёшь мне. 2. *(joking)* Ты шу́тишь.

put out:

You can just put marriage out of your head. Вы́брось из головы́ мы́сли о бра́ке. ♦ **I can't put you out of my mind.** Я не могу́ вы́бросить тебя́ из головы́.

put over:

Are you trying to put something over on me? Ты пыта́ешься обману́ть меня́?

put up with:

I *(1)* **can't** / *(2)* **couldn't put up with her** *(his)* **endless affairs.** Я не *(1)* могу́ / *(2)* мог *(ж: могла́)* смири́ться с её *(ж: его́)* бесконе́чными рома́нами.

putter *vi* де́лать ме́лкие рабо́ты.

puttering *n (Russians use verb expression* де́лать ме́лкие рабо́ты*).*

put together *(slang)* сложена́ ♦ **well ~** хорошо́ сложена́.

putty *n* зама́зка ♦ **I'm putty in your hands.** Я-- гли́на в твои́х рука́х.

puzzle *vt* озада́чивать / озада́чить *(whom = acc.)* ♦ **You (really) puzzle me (at times).** Ты (действи́тельно) (иногда́) озада́чиваешь меня́. ♦ **Your** *(1)* **attitude** / *(2)* **behavior puzzles me (a great deal).** Твоё *(1)* отноше́ние / *(2)* поведе́ние (о́чень) озада́чивает меня́.

puzzle *n* 1. *(mystery)* зага́дка; 2. *(toy)* головоло́мка; *(jigsaw)* составна́я карти́нка ♦ **You and I are like pieces of a puzzle that, when fitted together, form a beautiful picture.** Ты и я как кусо́чки головоло́мки, кото́рые, бу́дучи подо́гнаны друг к дру́гу, создаю́т прекра́сную карти́ну.

puzzled *adj* озада́ченный, -ая, -ое, -ые *(short forms:* озада́чен, -а, -о, -ы*)* ♦ **I'm (really) puzzled** *(1)* **...by the way you act.** / *(2)* **...by the things you say.** / *(3)* **...as to how you feel about me.** / *(4)* **...as to what you want.** Я (в са́мом де́ле) озада́чен *(ж: озада́чена) (1)* ...твои́м поведе́нием. / *(2)* ...тем, что ты говори́шь. / *(3)* ...тем, что ты чу́вствуешь по отноше́нию ко мне. / *(4)* ...тем, что ты хо́чешь.

Pygmalionism *n (falling in love with statues)* пигмалиони́зм *(= влюбля́ться в ста́туи).*

How to use the Cyrillic alphabet on the Internet is the subject of Appendix 20 on page 789.

Q

quadriceps *n, pl* четырёхглавая мы́шца.

quaff *vt* пить больши́ми глотка́ми ♦ **Reading one of your letters is like quaffing a magic elixir — it just makes me feel totally good through and through.** Чте́ние ка́ждого из твои́х пи́сем как большо́й глото́к маги́ческого эликси́ра -- оно́ наполня́ет меня́ замеча́тельным чу́вством.

quaint *adj* необы́чный, -ая, -ое, -ые, причу́дливый, -ая, -ое, -ые.

quake *vi* трепета́ть.

quality *adj (high quality)* высо́кого ка́чества, высокока́чественный, -ая, -ое, -ые.

quality *n (characteristic)* ка́чество, сво́йство; *(feature)* осо́бенность *f* ♦ **endearing** ~**ies** располага́ющие ка́чества; привлека́ющие ка́чества ♦ **exceptional** ~**ies** исключи́тельные ка́чества ♦ **fine** ~**ies** хоро́шие ка́чества ♦ **good** ~**ies** хоро́шие ка́чества ♦ **great** ~**ies** замеча́тельные ка́чества ♦ **marvelous** ~**ies** замеча́тельные ка́чества ♦ **moral** ~**ies** нра́вственные досто́инства ♦ **nice** ~**ies** хоро́шие ка́чества ♦ **physical** ~**ies** физи́ческие досто́инства ♦ **seductive** ~ *(voice)* обольсти́тельное звуча́ние ♦ *(1,2)* **similar** ~**ies** *(1)* схо́дные / *(2)* похо́жие ка́чества.

---
quality: *phrases*

You have a *(1)* **breathless** / *(2)* **seductive** / *(3)* **suggestive quality to your voice that really turns me on.** В твоём го́лосе есть *(1)* захва́тывающее / *(2)* обольсти́тельное / *(3)* соблазни́тельное звуча́ние, кото́рое действи́тельно заво́дит меня́. ♦ **You have so many** *(1)* **exceptional** / *(2)* **fine** / *(3)* **nice** / *(4)* **good** / *(5)* **marvelous qualities.** У тебя́ так мно́го *(1)* исключи́тельных / *(2-4)* хоро́ших / *(5)* замеча́тельных ка́честв. ♦ **I seek a** *(1)* **lady** / *(2)* **gentleman with similar qualities.** Я ищу́ *(1)* же́нщину / *(2)* мужчи́ну с таки́ми же ка́чествами.

quarrel *vi* ссо́риться / поссо́риться *(with whom =* + с + *instr.)* ♦ **always** ~ всегда́ ссо́риться **constantly** ~ постоя́нно ссо́риться ♦ **often** ~ ча́сто ссо́риться ♦ ~ **incessantly** ~ ве́чно ссо́риться ♦ **seldom** ~ ре́дко ссо́риться ♦ **sometimes** ~ иногда́ ссо́риться ♦ **I don't want to quarrel (with you).** Я не хочу́ ссо́риться (с тобо́й).

quarrel *n* ссо́ра ♦ *(1,2)* **big** ~ *(1)* больша́я / *(2)* кру́пная ссо́ра ♦ **childish** ~ де́тская ссо́ра *(1,2)* **little** ~ *(1)* небольша́я / *(2)* ма́ленькая ссо́ра ♦ **loud** ~ шу́мная ссо́ра ♦ **lover's** ~ ссо́ра любо́вников ♦ **senseless** ~ пуста́я ссо́ра ♦ **serious** ~ серьёзная ссо́ра ♦ *(1,2)* **small** ~ *(1)* ма́ленькая / *(2)* небольша́я ссо́ра ♦ **ugly** ~ безобра́зная ссо́ра ♦ **avoid** ~ избега́ть ссо́ры ♦ **have a** *([1]* **big** / *[2]* **serious)** ~ *([1]* кру́пно / *[2]* серьёзно) ссо́риться /

Counting things in Russian is a bit involved.
See Appendix 4, Numbers, on page 756 .

поссо́риться ◆ **start** *(1)* **a ~** / *(2)* **~s** начина́ть / нача́ть *(1)* ссо́ру / *(2)* ссо́ры ◆ **I hate quarrels.** Я ненави́жу ссо́ры.

quarreling *n* ссо́ры ◆ **constant ~** постоя́нные ссо́ры ◆ **incessant ~** ве́чные ссо́ры.

quarrelsome *adj* вздо́рный, -ая, -ое, -ые, сварли́вый, -ая, -ое, -ые.

quarters: ◆ **I can't wait to** *(1)* **be** / *(2)* **get in close quarters with you.** Я не могу́ дожда́ться того́ моме́нта, когда́ мы *(1)* бу́дем / *(2)* ста́нем близки́.

queen *n* 1. *(royalty)* короле́ва; 2. *(fig.)* боги́ня, цари́ца ◆ **beauty** *(1,2)* **~** *(1)* короле́ва / *(2)* боги́ня красоты́ ◆ **~ of love** боги́ня любви́.

queen-size *adj* большо́й, -а́я, -о́е, -и́е, кру́пный, -ая, -ое, -ые ◆ **I** *(1)* **like** / *(2)* **prefer a queen-size woman.** Я *(1)* люблю́ / *(2)* предпочита́ю кру́пных же́нщин. ◆ **~ bed** широ́кая двухспа́льная крова́ть.

quell *vt* подавля́ть / подави́ть *(what = acc.)*, успока́ивать / успоко́ить *(what = acc.)* ◆ **Only the sweet softness of your lips can quell the ache of longing that ravages my heart.** То́лько сла́дкая мя́гкость твои́х губ мо́жет подави́ть боль тоски́, разруша́ющей моё се́рдце.

quench *vt* утоля́ть / утоли́ть *(what = acc.)* ◆ **Nothing can quench the fire that rages inside me except your love.** Ничто́, кро́ме твое́й любви́, не мо́жет утоли́ть ого́нь, бушу́ющий во мне.

querulous *adj (habitually complaining)* ве́чно жа́лующийся, -аяся, -ееся, -иеся; *(whining)* но́ющий, -ая, -ее, -ие; *(grouchy)* ворчли́вый, -ая, -ое, -ые, брюзгли́вый, -ая, -ое, -ые.

question *n* вопро́с ◆ **a few ~s** не́сколько вопро́сов ◆ **awkward ~** щекотли́вый вопро́с ◆ **different ~** друго́й вопро́с ◆ **difficult ~** тру́дный вопро́с ◆ **direct ~** прямо́й вопро́с ◆ **foolish ~** глу́пый вопро́с ◆ **important ~** ва́жный вопро́с ◆ **leading ~** наводя́щий вопро́с ◆ **logical ~** поня́тный вопро́с ◆ **main ~** гла́вный вопро́с ◆ **many ~s** мно́го вопро́сов ◆ **my ~** мой вопро́с ◆ **next ~** сле́дующий вопро́с ◆ **only ~** еди́нственный вопро́с ◆ **personal ~** ли́чный вопро́с ◆ **philosophical ~** филосо́фский вопро́с ◆ **ridiculous ~** неле́пый вопро́с ◆ **serious ~** серьёзный вопро́с ◆ **several ~s** не́сколько вопро́сов ◆ **simple ~** просто́й вопро́с ◆ **strange ~** стра́нный вопро́с ◆ **stupid ~** глу́пый вопро́с ◆ **ticklish ~** щекотли́вый вопро́с ◆ **your ~** *(familiar)* твой вопро́с; *(polite)* Ваш вопро́с.

question: verb terms

answer *(1)* **my** / *(2)* **your ~** отвеча́ть / отве́тить на *(1)* мой / *(2)* твой вопро́с ◆ **ask** (*[1]* **you** / *[2]* **me**) **a ~** задава́ть / зада́ть (*[1]* тебе́ / *[2]* мне) вопро́с ◆ **ignore** *(1)* **my** / *(2)* **your ~** пренебрега́ть / пренебре́чь *(1)* мои́м / *(2)* твои́м вопро́сом ◆ **repeat your ~** повторя́ть / повтори́ть (свой) вопро́с ◆ **understand** *(1)* **my** / *(2)* **your ~** понима́ть / поня́ть *(1)* мой / *(2)* твой вопро́с.

question: phrases

Can I ask you a (personal) question? Могу́ я зада́ть тебе́ (ли́чный) вопро́с? ◆ **Would you mind if I asked you a (personal) question?** Не возража́ете ли Вы, е́сли я зада́м Вам (ли́чный) вопро́с?

questionable *adj* сомни́тельный, -ая, -ое, -ые.

questionnaire *n* анке́та ◆ **fill out a ~** заполня́ть / запо́лнить анке́ту ◆ **I filled out a questionnaire.** Я запо́лнил *(ж:запо́лнила)* анке́ту.

quick-tempered *adj* вспы́льчивый, -ая, -ое, -ые.

quick-witted *adj* 1. *(witty)* остроу́мный, -ая, -ое, -ые; 2. *(sharp-minded)* нахо́дчивый, -ая, -ое, -ые.

quiet *adj* ти́хий, -ая, -ое, -ие; споко́йный, -ая, -ое, -ые.

quiet *n* тишина́ ◆ **peace and ~** мир и тишина́.

quietly *adv* ти́хо.

> *Russian has 2 different vrbs for "go",*
> *one for "on foot" and the other for "by vehicle".*

quirk *n* причу́да, вы́верт, стра́нность *f* ♦ **I'm not without a few quirks, I suppose.** Полага́ю, что я не без не́которых причу́д. ♦ **I've got a quirk or two, I suppose.** Полага́ю, что éсть у меня́ одна́-две причу́ды. ♦ **I hope you can overlook my quirks.** Я наде́юсь, ты смо́жешь прости́ть мои причу́ды.

quirky *adj (peculiar)* стра́нный, -ая, -ое, -ые, необы́чный, -ая, -ое, -ые, причу́дливый, -ая, -ое, -ые, с причу́дами.

quite *adv* 1. *(somewhat)* дово́льно; 2. *(entirely)* совсе́м, вполне́.

quiver *vi* дрожа́ть, трепета́ть ♦ **You make me quiver all over.** Ты заставля́ешь меня́ всего́ *(ж: всю)* трепета́ть. ♦ **I love the way you quiver (when I do that to you).** Мне нра́вится, как ты трепе́щешь (, когда́ я де́лаю э́то).

Dipthongs in Russian are made by adding й
*to the end of a vowel (*а, е, ё, о, у, э, ю, *and* я).

R

R&B *abbrev* = **rhythm and blues** (му́зыка) «ритм и блюз».

rabbi *n* равви́н.

race *vi (run, stream)* пробега́ть / пробежа́ть ♦ ~ **through your whole body** пробежа́ть по всему́ твоему́ те́лу ♦ **Many thoughts raced through my mind.** Мно́го мы́слей пробега́ло в мое́й голове́. ♦ **My lips will send sweet thrills racing through your body.** Мои́ гу́бы пошлю́т сла́дкий тре́пет по всему́ твоему́ те́лу.

race *n* 1. *(human type)* ра́са; 2. *(contest)* го́нки; бег ♦ **any** ~ любо́й ра́сы ♦ **human** ~ челове́ческий род, род людско́й ♦ ~ **open** *(personal ad)* ра́са безразли́чна ♦ ~ **unimportant** ра́са не важна́. ♦ **Race open.** *(personal ad)* Ра́са не име́ет значе́ния. ♦ **Race doesn't matter.** Ра́са не име́ет значе́ния. ♦ **As concerns race, I'm color-blind.** Что каса́ется ра́сы, я соверше́нно безразли́чен *(ж: безразли́чна).*

racist *adj* раси́стский, -ая, -ое, -ие.

racist *n* раси́ст.

radiance *n* сия́ние, блеск ♦ **The radiance of your smile** *(1)* **...captivates...** / *(2)* **...has captivated... my heart.** Сия́ние твое́й улы́бки *(1)* пленя́ет / *(2)* плени́ло моё се́рдце. ♦ **And there you stood in all your radiance.** И там ты стоя́ла во всём своём бле́ске. ♦ **What a shame to cover up the radiance of such beauty.** Как не сты́дно прикрыва́ть сия́ние тако́й красоты́.

radiant *adj* сия́ющий, -ая, -ее, -ие, светя́щийся, -аяся, -еёся, -иеся, блестя́щий, -ая, -ее, -ие ♦ **exquisitely** ~ изы́сканно сия́ющий, -ая, -ее, -ие ♦ ~ **beauty** сия́ющая красота́ ♦ **look** ~ блестя́ще вы́глядеть. ♦ **You look nothing short of radiant.** Ты вы́глядишь про́сто блестя́ще.

radiate *vt* 1. *(emit)* излуча́ть / излучи́ть *(what = acc.),* исходи́ть *(what = subject, source of radiating = + от + gen.);* 2. *(manifest glowingly)* сия́ть *(what = instr.),* лучи́ться *(what = instr.); (suffuse)* прони́зывать ♦ ~ **affection** излуча́ть не́жность ♦ ~ **happiness** излуча́ть ра́дость ♦ **Your precious blithe spirit radiates through all my thoughts.** Ты с твое́й драгоце́нной жизнера́достностью прони́зываешь все мои́ мы́сли. ♦ **Sunshine radiates from you.** Со́лнечное сия́ние исхо́дит от тебя́. ♦ **Your** *(1)* **blue** / *(2)* **dark eyes and wide smile radiate** *(3)* **warmth** / *(4)* **affection.** Твои́ *(1)* голубы́е / *(2)* тёмные глаза́ и широ́кая улы́бка излуча́ют *(3)* теплоту́ / *(4)* не́жность. ♦ **You radiate (**[1] **pure** / [2] **sheer** / [3] **perfect) beauty (and vitality).** Ты сия́ешь (*[1]* чи́стой / *[2]* абсолю́тной / *[3]* соверше́нной) красото́й (и жи́востью).

Russian nouns are either masculine, feminine or neuter.
Adjectives with them will be the same.

rage *vi* бушева́ть   ♦ **Nothing can quench the fire that rages inside me except your love.** Ничто́, кро́ме твое́й любви́, не мо́жет утоли́ть ого́нь, бушу́ющий во мне. ♦ **My body aches to feel the fire that rages in the core of your womanhood.** Моё те́ло жа́ждет почу́вствовать ого́нь, кото́рый бушу́ет в глубине́ твое́й же́нственности. ♦ **Fire rages through my veins whenever I think of your soft, warm, beautiful, luscious body and the oceans of ecstasy that it contains.** Ого́нь бушу́ет в мои́х ве́нах вся́кий раз, когда́ я ду́маю о твоём мя́гком, тёплом, прекра́сном, со́чном те́ле и океа́нах экста́за, кото́рые оно́ соде́ржит. ♦ **If the feeling that's raging through my heart for you isn't love, then I guess I'm really out of touch with what love is.** Если чу́вство к тебе́, бушу́ющее в моём се́рдце, не любо́вь, тогда́ я про́сто не понима́ю, что тако́е любо́вь.

rage *n* я́рость *f*, раж, гнев, бе́шенство   ♦ **helpless** ~ бесси́льный гнев.

---
rage: phrases

(1,2) **He flew into a rage.** *(1)* Он впал в раж. / *(2)* Он пришёл в я́рость. ♦ *(1,2)* **She flew into a rage.** *(1)* Она́ впа́ла в раж. / *(2)* Она́ пришла́ в я́рость. ♦ *(1)* **He** / *(2)* **She will fly into a rage if** *(3)* **he** / *(4)* **she finds out.** *(1)* Он / *(2)* Она́ придёт в я́рость, е́сли *(3)* он / *(4)* она́ узна́ет.

raging *adj* неи́стовый, -ая, -ое, -ые, бе́шеный, -ая, -ое, -ые, исступлённый, -ая, -ое, -ые ♦ **The thought patterns that yielded your choice of words and sentences in your ad reveal the exact same raging hunger for love and affection that I harbor within me.** Мы́сли, роди́вшие вы́бор слов и предложе́ний в Ва́шем объявле́нии, говоря́т о то́чно тако́й же неи́стовой жа́жде любви́ и не́жности, кото́рая таи́тся во мне. ♦ **Whenever I even think of your beautiful,** *(1)* **delectable** / *(2)* **luscious body, I am** *(3)* **filled** / *(4)* **seized with raging lust.** Когда́ бы я ни поду́мал о твоём прекра́сном, *(1)* преле́стном / *(2)* со́чном те́ле, меня́ *(3)* наполня́ет / *(4)* охва́тывает бе́шеная страсть.

rain *n* дождь *m* ♦ **dance in the** ~ танцева́ть под дождём ♦ **We'll dance in the rain together.** Мы бу́дем вме́сте танцева́ть под дождём.

rainbow *n* ра́дуга ♦ *(1,2)* **It seems like I'm always chasing rainbows.** *(1)* Похо́же, я всегда́ гоня́юсь за ра́дугой. / *(2)* Ка́жется, я всегда́ пыта́юсь дости́чь недостижи́мого. ♦ *(1)* **I want to...** / *(2)* **I'm going to... teach you how to ride rainbows.** *(1)* Я хочу́ научи́ть... / *(2)* Я научу́... тебя́, как скака́ть на ра́дуге.

raincoat *n* дождеви́к, плащ.

raise *vt (children)* поднима́ть / подня́ть *(whom = acc.)*, расти́ть / вы́растить *(whom = acc.)*, воспи́тывать / воспита́ть *(whom = acc.)* ♦ **I don't want to raise any more kids.** Я бо́льше не хочу́ расти́ть дете́й. ♦ **I raised two** *(1)* **children** / *(2)* **kids.** Я вы́растил *(ж: вы́растила)* двои́х *(1,2)* дете́й.

rambunctious *adj* бу́йный, -ая, -ое, -ые; неугомо́нный, -ая, -ое, -ые, непоко́рный, -ая, -ое, -ые.

rampant *adj (raging)* неи́стовый, -ая, -ое, -ые; *(furious)* я́рый, -ая, -ое, -ые; *(unrestrained)* безу́держный, -ая, -ое, -ые ♦ **I want to see your body arch in rampant desire.** Я хочу́ ви́деть твоё те́ло, изгиба́ющимся в безу́держной стра́сти.

randiness *n* по́хоть *f.*

randy *adj* сексуа́льно возбуждённый, -ая, -ое, -ые; похотли́вый, -ая, -ое, -ые.

range *n* диапазо́н ♦ ~ **of feelings** диапазо́н чувств.

rape *vt* наси́ловать / изнаси́ловать *(whom = acc.)* ♦ *(1,2)* **I was raped.** *(1)* Меня́ изнаси́ловали. / *(2)* Я была́ изнаси́лована.

rape *n* изнаси́лование ♦ **statutory** ~ изнаси́лование несовершенноле́тней.

rapport *n* взаимопонима́ние ♦ **strong** ~ по́лная гармо́ния ♦ **develop a** ~ развива́ть / разви́ть взаимопонима́ние ♦ **establish a** ~ устана́вливать / установи́ть

Learn more about Russian customs in Appendix 15, page 782.

взаимопонима́ние ♦ **You and I have such good rapport.** Мы с тобо́й отли́чно ла́дим.

rapture *n* восто́рг, восхище́ние, упое́ние ♦ **all-consuming ~** всепоглоща́ющий восто́рг ♦ **fiery ~** о́гненный восто́рг ♦ **open ~** я́вный восто́рг.

rapture: *phrases*

What rapture it is to gaze at your love-softened face. Что за восто́рг -- вгля́дываться в твоё смягчённое любо́вью лицо́. ♦ *(1)* **I want to...** / *(2)* **I'm going to... suffuse your entire being in the fiery rapture of climax.** *(1)* Я хочу́ запо́лнить... / *(2)* Я запо́лню... всё твоё существо́ о́гненным восто́ргом орга́зма. ♦ **Knowing that you love me as much as I love you fills my heart with indescribable rapture.** Зна́ние, что ты лю́бишь меня́ так же си́льно, как я люблю́ тебя́, наполня́ет моё се́рдце невероя́тным восто́ргом. ♦ **I am** *(1)* **completely** / *(2)* **totally** *(3)* **...overcome by...** / *(4)* **...swept away by...** / *(5)* **...engulfed in... the rapture that you create with your** *(6)* **...skillful hands.** / *(7)* **...ardent kisses.** / *(8)* **...roving lips.** Я *(1)* по́лностью / *(2)* весь *(ж: вся)* *(3,4)* ...охва́чен *(ж: охва́чена)...* / *(5)* ...поглощён *(ж: поглощена́)...* упое́нием, кото́рое ты создаёшь свои́ми *(6)* ...уме́лыми рука́ми. / *(7)* ...пы́лкими поцелу́ями. / *(8)* ...блужда́ющими губа́ми. ♦ **My heart breaks into rapture whenever I** *(1)* **...see you.** / *(2)* **...hear your voice on the phone.** / *(3)* **...find a letter from you in my box.** / *(4)* **...take you into my arms.** Моё се́рдце наполня́ется восто́ргом всегда́, когда́ я *(1)* ...ви́жу тебя́. / *(2)* ...слы́шу твой го́лос по телефо́ну. / *(3)* ...нахожу́ письмо́ от тебя́ в почто́вом я́щике. / *(4)* ...держу́ тебя́ в объя́тиях.

rapturous *adj* восто́рженный, -ая, -ое, -ые, упои́тельный, -ая, -ое, -ые ♦ **We will lose ourselves (every night) in the rapturous affirmation of our love.** (Ка́ждую ночь) Мы бу́дем отдава́ть себя́ восто́рженному утвержде́нию на́шей любви́.

rapturously *adv* восто́рженно ♦ **I'm rapturously in love with you.** Я восто́рженно люблю́ тебя́.

rare *adj* ре́дкий, -ая, -ое, -ие.

rarely *adj* ре́дко.

rash *adj (hasty)* поспе́шный, -ая, -ое, -ые; *(impetuous)* опроме́тчивый, -ая, -ое, -ые; *(not thought out)* необду́манный, -ая, -ое, -ые; *(reckless)* безрассу́дный, -ая, -ое, -ые.

rashly *adv* поспе́шно; опроме́тчиво; необду́манно; безрассу́дно.

rather *adv* 1. *(somewhat)* дово́льно, до не́которой сте́пени; 2. *(sooner, preferably)* лу́чше, скоре́е, предпочти́тельнее ♦ **What would you rather do?** Чем бы ты предпочла́ *(ж: предпочёл)* заня́ться? ♦ **I'd rather spend time with you (than do anything else).** Я (всему́) предпочёл *(ж: предпочла́)* бы провести́ вре́мя с тобо́й. ♦ **I'd rather not talk about it?** Я предпочёл *(ж: предпочла́)* бы не говори́ть об э́том.

rational *adj* 1. *(reasonable)* благоразу́мный, -ая, -ое, -ые; рассуди́тельный, -ая, -ое, -ые; рациона́льный, -ая, -ое, -ые; 2. *(reasoning)* разу́мный, -ая, -ое, -ые, мы́слящий, -ая, -ее, -ие.

rationality *n* рациона́льность *f*, разу́мность *f*.

rationalization *n* рационализа́ция ♦ **All of the rationalizations that I can conjure up cannot keep me from wanting you night and day (with all my heart).** Весь мой рационали́зм не мо́жет удержа́ть меня́ от того́, чтобы (всем се́рдцем) не жела́ть тебя́ день и ночь.

rationalize *vt, vi (justify)* опра́вдывать / оправда́ть *(what = acc.)*; *(explain logically)* логи́чески обосно́вывать *(what = acc.)*, дава́ть разу́мное объясне́ние *(what = + o + prep.)*.

raunchy *adj* гря́зный, -ая, -ое, -ые, поха́бный, -ая, -ое, -ые.

ravage *vt* разруша́ть / разру́шить *(what = acc.)* ♦ **~ the soul** опустоша́ть / опустоши́ть ду́шу ♦ **Desire ravages my body.** Страсть распаля́ет моё те́ло. ♦ **Only the sweet softness of your lips can quell the ache of longing that ravages my heart.** То́лько сла́дкая мя́гкость твои́х губ мо́жет подави́ть боль тоски́, разруша́ющей моё се́рдце.

raven *adj* чёрный (-ая, -ое, -ые), как во́роново крыло́ *(1 term)*.

raven-haired *adj* с волоса́ми цве́та во́ронова крыла́.

ravenous *adj* жа́дный, -ая, -ое, -ые, изголода́вшийся, -аяся, -ееся, -иеся ♦ **My ravenous lips will uncover your most precious secret.** Мои́ изголода́вшиеся гу́бы раскро́ют твой са́мый заве́тный секре́т.

ravenously *adv* жа́дно.

ravishing *adj* восхити́тельный, -ая, -ое, -ые ♦ **You look (***[1]* **absolutely /** *[2]* **positively) ravishing (in that** *[3]* **dress /** *[4]* **outfit).** Ты вы́глядишь (*[1]* абсолю́тно / *[2]* совершённо) восхити́тельной (в э́том *[3]* пла́тье / *[4]* костю́ме). ♦ **How ravishing you look.** Как восхити́тельно ты вы́глядишь.

rawk *n (slang) (rock music)* рок(-му́зыка).

re-energize *vt* возбужда́ть опя́ть *(what, whom = acc.)*, пробужда́ть опя́ть *(what, whom = acc.)*.

reach *vt* 1. *(go / come to)* достига́ть / дости́гнуть *(what, whom = gen.)*, добира́ться / добра́ться *(what, whom = + до + gen.)*, доходи́ть / дойти́ *(what, whom = + до + gen.)*; 2. *(contact)* связа́ться *(whom = + с + instr.)* ♦ **I write this to you daringly, I know, but I hope that it will reach your heart.** Я зна́ю, что пишу́ тебе́ сме́ло, но наде́юсь, что э́то дойдёт до твоего́ се́рдца. ♦ **This is just a short letter to reach across the miles and touch you.** Это то́лько коро́ткое письмо́, кото́рое пройдёт ми́ли и коснётся тебя́. ♦ **Is there some away I can reach you?** Каки́м о́бразом я могу́ связа́ться с тобо́й?

reach out *vi (appeal)* апелли́ровать *(to whom = + к + dat.)*.

react *vi* реаги́ровать / отреаги́ровать; отзыва́ться / отозва́ться ♦ **I enjoy making you react** *(1)* **...like that. /** *(2)* **...that way.** Я наслажда́юсь, заставля́я тебя́ реаги́ровать *(1)* ...так. / *(2)* ...таки́м о́бразом. ♦ **I love it when you react** *(1)* **...like that. /** *(2)* **...that way.** Я люблю́, когда́ ты реаги́руешь *(1)* ...так. / *(2)* ...таки́м о́бразом.

reaction *n* реа́кция.

read *vt* чита́ть / прочита́ть *(what = acc.)*; *(reread)* перечи́тывать / перечита́ть *(what = acc.)* ♦ **I read your letter over and over (again).** *(past)* Я перечи́тывал *(ж: перечи́тывала)* твоё письмо́ сно́ва и сно́ва. ♦ **I read your letters over and over (again).** *(present)* Я чита́ю твои́ пи́сьма сно́ва и сно́ва. ♦ **We could read to each other in the evenings.** Мы мо́жем чита́ть друг дру́гу вечера́ми.

reader *n* чита́тель ♦ **avid** ~ стра́стный чита́тель ♦ **voracious** ~ ненасы́тный чита́тель ♦ **I'm an avid reader.** Я стра́стный чита́тель.

readiness *n* подготовлённость *f* ♦ **mental** ~ психологи́ческая подготовлённость ♦ **psychological** ~ психологи́ческая подготовлённость.

reading *n* чте́ние.

ready *adj* гото́вый, -ая, -ое, -ые *(short forms:* гото́в, -а, -о, -ы*)* ♦ **mentally** ~ психологи́чески гото́в, -а, -ы ♦ **psychologically** ~ психологи́чески гото́в, -а , -ы ♦ ~ **to play** гото́в *m* / гото́ва *f* игра́ть ♦ **If you're a person who's ready for** *(1,2)* **excitement, then we should meet.** Если Вы челове́к, гото́вый к *(1)* волну́ющей / *(2)* возбужда́ющей жи́зни, тогда́ мы должны́ встре́титься.

real *adj* 1. *(actual)* реа́льный, -ая, -ое, -ые, действи́тельный, -ая, -ое, -ые 2. *(genuine)* настоя́щий, -ая, -ее, -ие ♦ **Let's be real.** Бу́дем реали́стами. ♦ **This is the real thing.** Это настоя́щее. ♦ **Our love is the real thing.** На́ша любо́вь настоя́щая. ♦ **I want someone who is real.** Я хочу́ реа́льного челове́ка.

realist *n* реали́ст ♦ **I'm a romantic realist.** Я романти́ческий реали́ст.

reality *n* реа́льность *f*, действи́тельность *f* ♦ **cold** ~ холо́дная реа́льность ♦ **tangible** ~

Common adult weights are given in Appendix 10, page 777.

осяза́емая реа́льность ◆ **sense of** ~ ощуще́ние реа́льности ◆ **do a** ~ **check** верну́ться к реа́льности.

realize *vt* 1. *(become aware)* осознава́ть / осозна́ть *(what = acc.),* (я́сно) понима́ть / поня́ть *(what = acc.);* 2. *(fulfill, bring to life)* выполня́ть / вы́полнить *(what = acc.),* осуществля́ть / осуществи́ть *(what = acc.),* реализова́ть *(what = acc.);* претворя́ть / претвори́ть в жизнь *(what = acc.).*

realized: ◆ **be** ~ преврати́ться в реа́льность.

really *adv (truly)* действи́тельно; *(very, extremely)* о́чень, кра́йне.

rear *n (slang) (buttocks)* за́дница, по́па; *(little)* по́пка.

reason *n* 1. *(cause, basis)* причи́на, основа́ние; 2. *(motive, grounds)* моти́в, основа́ние; *(consideration)* соображе́ние; 3. *(intellect)* ра́зум; *(common sense; sanity)* (здра́вый) рассу́док ◆ **another** ~ друга́я причи́на ◆ *(1,2)* **any** ~ *(1)* вся́кая / *(2)* люба́я причи́на ◆ **convincing** ~ убеди́тельная причи́на ◆ **different** ~ друга́я причи́на ◆ **different** ~**s** ра́зные причи́ны ◆ **important** ~ ва́жная причи́на ◆ **main** ~ гла́вная причи́на ◆ **only** ~ еди́нственная причи́на ◆ **personal** ~**s** ли́чные причи́ны ◆ **real** ~ настоя́щая причи́на ◆ **secret** ~ скры́тая причи́на ◆ **simple** ~ проста́я причи́на ◆ **special** ~ осо́бая причи́на ◆ **strong** ~**s** про́чные причи́ны ◆ **true** ~ и́стинная причи́на ◆ *(1,2)* **unknown** ~ *(1)* неизве́стная / *(2)* непоня́тная причи́на ◆ **valid** ~ уважи́тельная причи́на ◆ **various** ~**s** ра́зные причи́ны.

reason: *other terms*

(1,2) **be the** ~ *(1)* быть / *(2)* явля́ться причи́ной ◆ **come up with a good** ~ приду́мывать / приду́мать хоро́ший предло́г ◆ **explain the** ~ объясня́ть / объясни́ть причи́ну ◆ **find out the** ~ узна́ть причи́ну ◆ **for** *(1)* **this** / *(2)* **that** ~ по *(1,2)* э́той причи́не ◆ **know the** ~ знать причи́ну ◆ **lose** ~ теря́ть / потеря́ть рассу́док ◆ **see the** ~ ви́деть причи́ну ◆ **think up a good** ~ приду́мывать / приду́мать хоро́ший предло́г.

reason: *phrase*

All of my reason has deserted me. I can think of nothing and no one except you. Весь мой рассу́док оста́вил меня́. Я не могу́ ду́мать ни о чём и ни о ком, кро́ме тебя́.

reasonable *adj* разу́мный, -ая, -ое, -ые ◆ *(1)* **It's** / *(2)* **That's** (*[3]* **quite** / *[4]* **very**) **reasonable.** *(1,2)* Это (*[3]* вполне́ / *[4]* о́чень) разу́мно.

reassurance *n* 1. *(comfort, solace)* утеше́ние; 2. *(calming)* успока́ивание; *(encouragement)* ободре́ние; *(cheering up)* подба́дривание ◆ **whisper words of** ~ 1. *(comfort, solace)* шепта́ть / прошепта́ть слова́ утеше́ния *(to whom = dat.);* 2. *(encouragement)* шепта́ть / прошепта́ть слова́ одобре́ния *(to whom = dat.).*

rebound *n* отско́к, рикоше́т, отда́ча ◆ **romance on the** ~ рома́н-рикоше́том, но́вый рома́н сра́зу же по́сле оконча́ния предыду́щего.

rebuff *vt* (ре́зко) отка́зывать / отказа́ть *(whom = dat.),* дава́ть / дать отпо́р *(whom = dat.)* ◆ **Even though you rebuffed me before, I want to ask you again.** Да́же, хотя́ ты ре́зко отказа́ла мне ра́ньше, я хочу́ проси́ть тебя́ опя́ть. ◆ **I** *(1)* **hope** / *(2)* **pray (with all my heart) that you will not rebuff me.** Я *(1)* наде́юсь / *(2)* молю́сь (всем се́рдцем), что ты не отка́жешь мне. ◆ **Even if you rebuff me, my feelings for you will remain unchanged.** Да́же, е́сли ты отка́жешь мне, мои́ чу́вства к тебе́ оста́нутся неизме́нными.

recall *vt* вспомина́ть / вспо́мнить *(what, whom = acc.),* припомина́ть / припо́мнить *(what, whom = acc.)* ◆ **clearly** ~ я́сно вспомина́ть / вспо́мнить ◆ **often** ~ ча́сто вспомина́ть ◆ *(1,2)* **suddenly** ~ *(1)* неожи́данно / *(2)* вдруг вспо́мнить ◆ **vaguely** ~ припомина́ть / припо́мнить; неопределённо вспомина́ть / вспо́мнить.

receive *vt* получа́ть / получи́ть *(what = acc.).*

recent *adj* после́дний, -яя, -ее, -ие ◆ **in** ~ *(1)* **days** / *(2)* **weeks** / *(3)* **months** / *(4)* **years** в

An italicized ж in parentheses indicates a woman speaking.

после́дние *(1)* дни / *(2)* неде́ли / *(3)* ме́сяцы / *(4)* го́ды.

recently *adv* (в) после́днее вре́мя.

reception *n* приём ◆ **cold** ~ холо́дный приём ◆ **friendly** ~ дру́жеский приём ◆ **icy** ~ ледяно́й приём ◆ **nice** ~ хоро́ший приём ◆ **warm** ~ тёплый приём ◆ **wedding** ~ сва́дебный приём.

recess *n* тайни́к, укро́мное месте́чко, ложби́нка, укро́мная пеще́рка ◆ **moist** ~**s of the mouth** вла́жные ложби́нки рта ◆ **secret** ~ укро́мная пеще́рка ◆ **And I will** *(1,2)* **fill the secret recesses of your body with fiery plumes of ecstasy.** И я *(1)* напо́лню / *(2)* запо́лню тайники́ твоего́ те́ла о́гненными стру́ями экста́за. ◆ **How I long to taste the warm recesses of your mouth (again).** Как жа́жду я (опя́ть) вкуша́ть тёплые глуби́ны твоего́ рта.

recipe *n* 1. *(cooking)* реце́пт; 2.*(plot)* сюже́т ◆ **A week together in Hawaii! That sounds like a marvelous recipe for romance.** Неде́ля вме́сте на Гава́йях! Это звучи́т, как изуми́тельный сюже́т для рома́на.

recipient *n* получа́тель *m*.

reciprocal *adj* взаи́мный, -ая, -ое, -ые, обою́дный, -ая, -ое, -ые.

reciprocate *vt* отвеча́ть (взаи́мностью) *(what = + на + acc.)* ◆ **Your feelings (for me) are (very much) reciprocated.** Твои́ чу́вства (ко мне) (абсолю́тно) взаи́мны. ◆ **I love the way you reciprocate my embraces.** Мне нра́вится то, как ты отвеча́ешь на мои́ объя́тия.

reciprocation *n* отве́тное де́йствие.

recluse *n* затво́рник *m*, затво́рница *f*, отше́льник *m*, отше́льница *f*.

reclusive *adj* затво́рнический, -ая, -ое, -ие, отше́льнический, -ая, -ое, -ие.

recognition 1. *(knowing)* узнава́ние; 2. *(admission)* призна́ние ◆ **flash of** ~ вспы́шка узнава́ния.

recognize *vt* 1. *(know)* узнава́ть / узна́ть *(what, whom = acc.)*; 2. *(admit)* признава́ть / призна́ть *(what = acc.)*.

reconcile *vt* примиря́ть / примири́ть *(what = acc.)* ◆ ~ **oneself** смиря́ться / смири́ться *(to what = + с + instr.)*, примиря́ться / примири́ться *(to what = + с + instr.)* ◆ **I've reconciled myself to** *(1)* **...it.** / *(2)* **...the situation.** Я смири́лся *(ж: смири́лась)* с *(1)* э́тим / *(2)* ситуа́цией. ◆ **I can't reconcile myself to** *(1)* **...it.** / *(2)* **...being apart from you.** Я не могу́ смири́ться с *(1)* э́тим. / *(2)* ...тем, что мы врозь.

reconciled *adj* примирён, примирена́, -о́, -ы́ *(short forms)* ◆ **be** ~ мири́ться / помири́ться *(with whom = + с + instr.)* ◆ **I don't think it's possible to be reconciled with** *(1)* **him** / *(2)* **her.** Я не ду́маю, что с *(1)* ним / *(2)* ней возмо́жно помири́ться.

reconciliation *n* примире́ние ◆ *(1)* **He** / *(2)* **She wants a reconciliation.** *(1)* Он / *(2)* Она́ хо́чет примире́ния.

record *n* 1. *(written)* за́пись; исто́рия; учёт; документа́ция; 2. *(sports)* реко́рд; 3. *(phonograph)* грампласти́нка ◆ *(1,2)* **adoption** ~**s** за́писи об *(1)* удочере́нии *(daughter)* / *(2)* усыновле́нии *(son)* ◆ **birth** ~ за́пись о рожде́нии ◆ **court** ~**s** протоко́лы суде́бного заседа́ния ◆ **death** ~ за́пись о сме́рти ◆ **divorce** ~**s** за́писи о разво́де ◆ **educational** ~**s** вы́писка из дипло́ма; *(Russian)* вы́писка из зачётной кни́жки ◆ **employment** ~**s** за́писи о рабо́те; *(Russian)* за́писи в трудово́й кни́жке ◆ **marriage** ~ за́пись о регистра́ции бра́ка ◆ **medical** ~**s** медици́нская документа́ция; медици́нская ка́рт(очк)а ◆ **police** ~ полице́йское досье́ ◆ **school** ~**s** шко́льный та́бель; аттеста́т ◆ *(1,2)* **obtain** ~**s** *(1)* приобрести́ / *(2)* получи́ть за́писи ◆ **request** ~**s** попроси́ть за́писи ◆ **I want to set the record straight.** Я хочу́ внести́ я́сность.

recreation *n* развлече́ние.

Procedures for getting married to a Russian are outlined in Appendix 18, page 787.

recreational *adj* для развлече́ния ♦ **I enjoy the usual recreational stuff.** Я наслажда́юсь обы́чными развлече́ниями.

recriminations *n, pl* взаи́мные обвине́ния ♦ **engage in ~s** броса́ть / бро́сить обвине́ния друг дру́гу.

rectitude *n* 1. *(correctness)* пра́вильность *f*; 2. *(honesty)* че́стность *f*; 3. *(morality)* нра́вственность *f* ♦ **moral ~** незы́блемые мора́льные усто́и.

red *adj* кра́сный, -ая, -ое, -ые ♦ **You** *(1)* **look** / *(2)* **looked** *(3)* **stunning** / *(4)* **gorgeous** / *(5)* **fantastic in that (fiery) red blouse.** Ты *(1)* вы́глядишь / *(2)* вы́глядела *(3)* сногсшиба́тельно / *(4)* великоле́пно / *(5)* фантасти́чески в э́той (о́гненно-)кра́сной блу́зке.

redden *vi* красне́ть / покрасне́ть.

redhead *n* ры́жий *m*, ры́жая *f*, рыжеволо́сый *m*, рыжеволо́сая *f* ♦ *(1,2)* **adventurous ~** *(1)* сме́лая / *(2)* предприи́мчивая рыжеволо́сая ♦ **alluring ~** соблазни́тельная рыжеволо́сая ♦ **beautiful ~** прекра́сная рыжеволо́сая ♦ **bewitching ~** очарова́тельная рыжеволо́сая ♦ **bubbly ~** искря́щаяся рыжеволо́сая ♦ **busty ~** рыжеволо́сая с бю́стом, груда́стая рыжеволо́сая ♦ **captivating ~** очарова́тельная рыжеволо́сая ♦ **classy ~** кла́ссная рыжеволо́сая ♦ **curvy ~** окру́глая рыжеволо́сая ♦ **exotic ~** экзоти́ческая рыжеволо́сая ♦ **faux ~** кра́шенная рыжеволо́сая ♦ **fiery ~** пы́лкая рыжеволо́сая ♦ **full-bodied ~** по́лная рыжеволо́сая ♦ **gorgeous ~** восхити́тельная рыжеволо́сая ♦ **green-eyed ~** зеленогла́зая рыжеволо́сая ♦ **knockout ~** сногшиба́тельная рыжеволо́сая ♦ **mercurial ~** рыжеволо́сая с переме́нчивым хара́ктером ♦ **natural ~** с натура́льными ры́жими волоса́ми ♦ **ravishing ~** потряса́ющая рыжеволо́сая ♦ **spicy ~** пика́нтная рыжеволо́сая ♦ **spunky ~** пы́лкая рыжеволо́сая ♦ **statuesque ~** ста́тная рыжеволо́сая ♦ **stunning ~** сногшиба́тельная рыжеволо́сая ♦ **succulent ~** со́чная рыжеволо́сая ♦ **sultry ~** сногшиба́тельная рыжеволо́сая ♦ **tasty ~** зно́йная рыжеволо́сая ♦ **vibrant ~** жива́я рыжеволо́сая ♦ **zesty ~** пика́нтная рыжеволо́сая ♦ **If you're looking for a redhead with style, I'm your person.** *(ж:)* Если ты и́щешь рыжеволо́сую со сти́лем, я та, кого́ ты и́щешь.

red-hot *adj* пы́лкий, -ая, -ое, -ие, пыла́ющий, -ая, -ее, -ие, горя́чий, -ая, -ее, -ие, обжига́ющий, -ая, -ее, -ие, раскалённый, -ая, -ое, -ые ♦ **Whenever I think of you, red-hot desire scorches my** *(1,2)* **innermost being.** Когда́ бы я не поду́мал о тебе́, обжига́ющая страсть опаля́ет всё *(1)* ...во мне. / *(2)* ...моё сокрове́нное.

redness *n* краснота́ ♦ **soft ~ of your lips** а́лая мя́гкость твои́х губ.

reel *vi* кружи́ться, верте́ться ♦ **My head is still reeling from** *(1)* **...the surprise** / *(2)* **shock.** / *(3)* **...what you wrote in your letter.** Моя́ голова́ всё ещё кру́жится от *(1)* ...удивле́ния / *(2)* шо́ка. / *(3)* ...того́, что ты написа́ла *(ж: написа́л)* в письме́.

refined *adj* утончённый, -ая, -ое, -ые, изы́сканный, -ая, -ое, -ые, изя́щный, -ая, -ое, -ые.

refinement *n* утончённость *f*, изы́сканность *f*; изя́щество; то́нкость *f* ♦ *(1-3)* **You have such an air of refinement.** *(1) (m to f:)* Ты так изя́щна. *(2)* Ты так изы́сканна. / *(3) (f to m:)* У тебя́ таки́е утончённые мане́ры.

reflective *adj* заду́мчивый, -ая, -ое, -ые, мы́слящий, -ая, -ее, -ие, размышля́ющий, -ая, -ее, -ие, ду́мающий, -ая, -ее, -ие ♦ **You seem to be a person who is very deep and reflective.** Ты ка́жешься глубо́ким и ду́мающим челове́ком.

reflex *n* рефле́кс.

refrain *vi* возде́рживаться / воздержа́ться *(from what = + от + gen.)*.

refresh *vt* освежа́ть / освежи́ть *(what = acc.)* ♦ **Refresh my** *(1)* **memory** / *(2)* **mind.** *(1,2)* Напо́мни мне. ♦ **Your** *(1)* **sparkling** / *(2)* **vivacious** / *(3)* **cheerful personality refreshes my spirit.** Твоя́ *(1)* искря́щаяся / *(2)* жизнера́достная / *(3)* бо́драя нату́ра освежа́ет мой дух.

A list of conjugated Russian verbs is given
in Appendix 3 on page 699.

refreshing *adj* освежа́ющий, -ая, -ее, -ие, необыкнове́нно прия́тный, -ая, -ое, -ые ♦ ~ **innocence** очарова́тельная неви́нность.

refreshingly *adv* освежа́юще.

refusal *n* отка́з ♦ **I will accept no refusal.** Я не приму́ отка́за.

refuse *vi* отка́зываться / отказа́ться ♦ *(1)* **He /** *(2)* **She refuses to hug or kiss or show affection.** *(1)* Он / *(2)* Она́ отка́зывается обня́ть, поцелова́ть, показа́ть не́жность.

regain *vt (get back)* получа́ть / получи́ть обра́тно *(what = acc.)*; *(restore)* восстана́вливать / восстанови́ть *(what = acc.)* ♦ ~ **one's composure** обрета́ть / обрести́ самооблада́ние ♦ ~ **one's voice** сно́ва обрета́ть / обрести́ го́лос.

regal *adj* короле́вский, -ая, -ое, -ие, ца́рский, -ая, -ое, -ие ♦ **You look truly regal.** Ты вы́глядишь и́стинной короле́вой.

regard *vt (consider)* счита́ть *(what, whom = acc., as what = instr.)*.

regard *n* 1. внима́ние; 2. уваже́ние; оце́нка ♦ **show** ~ ока́зывать / оказа́ть внима́ние *(for whom = dat.)* ♦ **I have a lot of regard for you.** Я испы́тываю большо́е уваже́ние к тебе́. ♦ **You just do what you want to do without any regard for** *(1)* **...me. /** *(2)* **...my feelings. /** *(3)* **...what I want.** Ты про́сто де́лаешь то, что хо́чешь де́лать, без вся́кого внима́ния *(1)* ...ко мне. / *(2)* ...к мои́м чу́вствам. / *(3)* ...к тому́, что я хочу́. ♦ **You seem to have no regard (at all) for my feelings.** Ты ка́жется не пита́ешь (никако́го) уваже́ния к мои́м чу́вствам. ♦ **You have no regard for my** *(1)* **feelings /** *(2)* **situation.** Ты не оце́ниваешь *(1)* мои́ чу́вства / *(2)* мою́ ситуа́цию. ♦ **You know that I hold you in the highest regard.** Ты зна́ешь, что я с огро́мным уваже́нием отношу́сь к тебе́. ♦ **Warmest regards,** *(closing of a letter)* Са́мые тёплые приве́ты, *(оконча́ние письма́).*

reggae *n* му́зыка «ре́гги».

registry *n* 1. *(place of reg.)* регистрату́ра; *(vital statistics)* отде́л за́писей а́ктов гражда́нского состоя́ния; 2. *(register, log)* журна́л за́писей; рее́стр; реги́стр ♦ ~ **office** *(Russia)* отде́л за́писей а́ктов гражда́нского состоя́ния (ЗАГС).

regret *n* сожале́ть *(what = + о + prep.)* ♦ **I know that if I don't ask you to be mine, I'm going to regret it for the rest of my life.** Я зна́ю, что е́сли я не попрошу́ тебя́ быть мое́й, то бу́ду сожале́ть об э́том до конца́ свое́й жи́зни.

regret *n* сожале́ние ♦ **I bear no regrets.** Я ни о чём не жале́ю.

reign *vi* госпо́дствовать *(over what = + над + instr.)*, вла́ствовать *(over what = + над + instr.)* ♦ **The unsurpassed beauty of your face reigns over all my thoughts.** Непревзойдённая красота́ твоего́ лица́ вла́ствует над все́ми мои́ми по́мыслами.

reignite *vt* зажига́ть / заже́чь опя́ть *(what = acc.)*, разжига́ть / разже́чь опя́ть *(what = acc.)* ♦ **And every night we will reignite our passion and revel in our boundless, undiminishable love.** И ка́ждую ночь мы бу́дем опя́ть зажига́ть на́шу страсть и пирова́ть в на́шей безграни́чной, неугаси́мой любви́.

reincarnation *n* перевоплоще́ние.

reject *vt* отверга́ть / отве́ргнуть *(whom = dat.)*; отклоня́ть / отклони́ть *(what = acc.)* ♦ **callously** ~ безжа́лостно отверга́ть / отве́ргнуть.

rejected *adj* отве́ргнутый, -ая, -ые; отклонённый, -ая, -ое, -ые ♦ **feel** ~ чу́вствовать себя́ отве́ргнутым *(ж: отве́ргнутой).*

rejection *n* отка́з; отклоне́ние ♦ **fear of** ~ страх отка́за ♦ **I've always been (a little bit) afraid of rejection.** Я всегда́ (немно́го) боя́лся *(ж: боя́лась)* отка́за.

rejoice *vi* ра́доваться / обра́доваться *(in what = instr.)*; весели́ться; ликова́ть ♦ ~ **in this night** ра́доваться / обра́доваться э́той но́чью ♦ **You can't imagine how happy I was to get your letter (and your photo). My heart is still rejoicing.** Ты не мо́жешь вообрази́ть, как сча́стлив я был, получи́в твоё письмо́ (и твою́ фотогра́фию). Моё се́рдце до сих

For Russian adjectives, the masculine form is spelled out, followed by the feminine, neuter and plural endings.

пор ра́дуется. ♦ **My heart rejoices at the sound of your name.** Моё се́рдце весели́тся от зву́ков твоего́ и́мени.

relate *vi* относи́ться *(to what, whom* = + к + *dat.)*, име́ть отноше́ние *((to what, whom* = + к + *dat.)* ♦ **I can't relate sexually to** *(1)* **her** / *(2)* **him.** *(1)* Он / *(2)* Она́ меня́ сексуа́льно не интересу́ет.

relating *n* отноше́ние.

relation *n* отноше́ние ♦ **intimate ~s** инти́мные отноше́ния ♦ **sexual ~s** сексуялмные отноше́ния.

relationship *n* отноше́ние *(usually pl:* отноше́ния*)*, связь *f* ♦ **adulterous ~** внебра́чная связь ♦ **awful ~** ужа́сные отноше́ния ♦ **bad ~** плохи́е отноше́ния ♦ **beautiful ~** прекра́сные отноше́ния ♦ **budding ~** расцвета́ющие отноше́ния ♦ **business ~** делов́ые отноше́ния ♦ **casual long-term ~** дли́тельные отноше́ния без наме́рения жени́ться ♦ **close ~** бли́зкие отноше́ния ♦ **committed ~** пре́данные отноше́ния ♦ **complementary ~** взаимодополня́ющие отноше́ния ♦ **critically wounded ~** отноше́ния с больши́ми пробле́мами ♦ **crummy ~** отврати́тельные отноше́ния ♦ **decent ~** неплохи́е отноше́ния ♦ **devoted (long-term) ~** пре́данные (дли́тельные) отноше́ния ♦ **disappointing ~** разочаро́вывающие отноше́ния ♦ **empty ~** пусты́е отноше́ния ♦ **eventual long-term ~** в бу́дущем дли́тельные отноше́ния ♦ **exciting ~** возбужда́ющие отноше́ния ♦ **exclusive ~** исключи́тельные отноше́ния ♦ **friendly ~** дру́жеские отноше́ния ♦ **fulfilling ~** удовлетворя́ющие отноше́ния ♦ **give-and-take ~** даю́щие и беру́щие отноше́ния ♦ **harmonious ~** гармони́чные отноше́ния ♦ **ill-conceived ~** необду́манные отноше́ния ♦ **interpersonal ~** межли́чностные отноше́ния ♦ **intimate ~** инти́мные отноше́ния ♦ **laid-back ~** лёгкие, прия́тные отноше́ния *(1 term)* ♦ **life-long ~** отноше́ния длино́ю в жизнь ♦ **long-term ~** дли́тельные отноше́ния ♦ **lopsided ~** неравноме́рные отноше́ния ♦ **lousy ~** ме́рзкие отноше́ния ♦ **mature ~** зре́лые отноше́ния ♦ *(1,2)* **meaningful ~** *(1)* и́стинные / *(2)* серьёзные отноше́ния ♦ **monogamous long-term ~** монога́мные дли́тельные отноше́ния ♦ **monogamous ~** монога́мные отноше́ния ♦ **nightmarish ~** кошма́рные отноше́ния ♦ **normal ~** норма́льные отноше́ния ♦ **one-sided ~** односторо́нние отноше́ния ♦ **ongoing meaningful ~** продолжа́ющиеся серьёзные отноше́ния ♦ **our ~** на́ши отноше́ния ♦ **paradisiacal ~** ра́йские отноше́ния ♦ **personal ~** ли́чные отноше́ния ♦ **physical ~** физи́ческие отноше́ния ♦ **platonic ~** платони́ческие отноше́ния ♦ **possible long-term ~** возмо́жные дли́тельные отноше́ния ♦ **powerful ~** великоле́пные отноше́ния ♦ **previous ~** пре́жние отноше́ния ♦ **quality ~** ка́чественные отноше́ния ♦ **~ based on** *(1)* **honesty** / *(2)* **respect** / *(3)* **trust** отноше́ние осно́вано на *(1)* че́стности / *(2)* уваже́нии / *(3)* дове́рии ♦ **~ of equals** ра́вные отноше́ния ♦ **~ touched with humor** отноше́ния, прони́кнутые ю́мором *(1 term)* ♦ **rock-solid ~** о́чень про́чные отноше́ния ♦ **sensual long-term ~** чу́вственные дли́тельные отноше́ния ♦ **sexual ~** сексуа́льные отноше́ния ♦ **short ~** коро́ткие отноше́ния ♦ **short-term ~** кратковре́менные отноше́ния ♦ **sincere ~** и́скренние отноше́ния ♦ *(1,2)* **solid ~** *(1)* кре́пкие / *(2)* про́чные отноше́ния ♦ **sordid ~** коры́стные отноше́ния ♦ **stable ~** стаби́льные отноше́ния ♦ **strained ~** натя́нутые отноше́ния ♦ **terrible ~** ужа́сные отноше́ния ♦ **this ~** э́ти отноше́ния ♦ **what kind of ~** каки́е отноше́ния ♦ **wonderful ~** замеча́тельные отноше́ния.

---
relationship: *verb terms*
---

arrest our ~ прекрати́ть на́ши отноше́ния ♦ **bail out of a ~** прекрати́ть отноше́ния ♦ *(1,2)* **break (off) a ~** *(1)* порва́ть / *(2)* разорва́ть отноше́ния ♦ **clarify our ~** вы́яснить на́ши отноше́ния ♦ **coerce** *(1)* **me** / *(2)* **you into a physical ~** принужда́ть / принуди́ть *(1)* меня́ / *(2)* тебя́ к физи́ческим отноше́ниям ♦ **commit to a long-term ~** приня́ть на

See Appendix 19 for notes on sending mail to Russia and Ukraine.

себя́ обяза́тельства до́лгих отноше́ний ♦ **continue our** ~ продолжа́ть на́ши отно-ше́ния ♦ **deepen our** ~ углуби́ть на́ши отноше́ния ♦ **develop a** ~ развива́ть / разви́ть отноше́ния ♦ **end our** ~ прекрати́ть на́ши отноше́ния, положи́ть коне́ц на́шим отноше́ниям ♦ **enliven** ~ оживля́ть / оживи́ть отноше́ния ♦ **enter a** ~ вступа́ть / вступи́ть в отноше́ния *(with whom* = + с + *instr.)* ♦ **establish a harmonious** ~ нала́дить гармони́чные отноше́ния ♦ **force** *(1)* **me** / *(2)* **you into a physical** ~ принужда́ть / принуди́ть *(1)* меня́ / *(2)* тебя́ к физи́ческим отноше́ниям ♦ **form a personal** ~ **online** *(on the Internet)* созда́ть ли́чные отноше́ния че́рез интерне́т ♦ **get our** ~ **back on track** нала́дить на́ши отноше́ния ♦ **get our** ~ **out of the ditch** нала́дить на́ши отноше́ния ♦ **jump into a** ~ вступи́ть в отноше́ния сли́шком бы́стро ♦ **keep our** ~ **secret** держа́ть на́ши отноше́ния в секре́те ♦ **maintain our** ~ подде́рживать на́ши отноше́ния ♦ **make our** ~ **work** подде́рживать на́ши отноше́ния ♦ **mend our** ~ нала́дить на́ши отноше́ния ♦ **neglect the** ~ пренебрега́ть отноше́ниями ♦ **put a career before one's** ~ поста́вить карье́ру превы́ше взаимоотноше́ний ♦ **put our** ~ **in the ditch** испо́ртить на́ши отноше́ния ♦ **resurrect our** ~ восстанови́ть на́ши отноше́ния ♦ **revive our** ~ восстанови́ть на́ши отноше́ния ♦ **(be) ripe for a** ~ созре́ть для отноше́ний ♦ **ruin a** ~ по́ртить / испо́ртить отноше́ния ♦ **sabotage a** ~ расша́тывать / расшата́ть отноше́ния ♦ **screw up a** ~ по́ртить / испо́ртить отноше́ния ♦ **sever a** ~ разорва́ть отноше́ния ♦ **solidify our** ~ укрепля́ть / укрепи́ть на́ши отноше́ния ♦ **start a** ~ начина́ть / нача́ть отноше́ния ♦ **sustain a long-term (intimate)** ~ подде́рживать дли́тельные (инти́мные) отноше́ния ♦ **terminate our** ~ прекрати́ть на́ши отноше́ния ♦ **unclutter a** ~ упоря́дочить отноше́ния ♦ **value a** ~ цени́ть отноше́ния.

---

relationship: *other terms*

core of the ~ суть отноше́ний ♦ **nature of our** ~ хара́ктер на́ших отноше́ний ♦ **reciprocal nature of a** ~ взаи́мность в отноше́ниях ♦ **stability of a** ~ стаби́льность отноше́ний ♦ **tension in a** ~ напряжённость в отноше́ниях.

---

relationship: *what I seek in a relationship*

(1) **I'm looking for...** / *(2)* **I'm seeking...** / *(3)* **I hope to find... a** *(4)* **long-term** / *(5)* **solid relationship (with someone).** *(1,2)* Я ищу́... / *(3)* Я наде́юсь найти́... челове́ка для *(4)* дли́тельных / *(5)* про́чных отноше́ний. ♦ **I'm interested in a serious long-term relationship.** Я заинтересо́ван *(ж: заинтересо́вана)* в дли́тельных серьёзных отноше́ниях. ♦ **I want a relationship** *(1)* **...that will nourish my soul.** / *(2)* **...touched with humor.** Я хочу́ отноше́ний, *(1)* ...кото́рые бу́дут пита́ть мою́ ду́шу. / *(2)* ...прони́кнутых ю́мором. ♦ **I'm not looking for an easy conquest — I want a** *(1)* **lasting** / *(2)* **permanent** / *(3)* **true relationship.** Я не ищу́ лёгкой побе́ды -- я хочу́ *(1)* дли́тельных / *(2)* постоя́нных / *(3)* ве́рных отноше́ний. ♦ **I seek someone who can commit to a long-term relationship.** Я ищу́ кого́-нибудь, кто мо́жет приня́ть на себя́ обяза́тельства до́лгих отноше́ний. ♦ **What I** *(1)* **...want...** / *(2)* **...yearn for... most in a relationship is** *(3)* **commitment** / *(4)* **constancy** / *(5)* **fidelity** / *(6)* **loyalty** / *(7)* **honesty** / *(8)* **openness** / *(9)* **togetherness.** Чего я *(1)* ...хочу́... / *(2)* ...жа́жду... бо́лее всего́ в отноше́ниях - *(3)* обяза́тельности / *(4)* постоя́нства / *(5,6)* ве́рности / *(7)* че́стности / *(8)* откры́тости / *(9)* совме́стности. ♦ **I desire friendship leading to a long-term relationship.** Я хочу́ дру́жбу, кото́рая приведёт к дли́тельным отноше́ниям.

---

relationship: *what's needed in a relationship*

It takes two to make a relationship work. Ну́жен обою́дный труд, что́бы подде́рживать отноше́ния. ♦ **A relationship can't survive on just the love of one person.** Отноше́ния не мо́гут вы́жить то́лько на любви́ одного́. ♦ **I believe in the reciprocal nature of a relationship.** Я ве́рю во взаи́мность в отноше́ниях. ♦ **Compatibility is the key to a strong**

When terms are listed after a main word, a tilde ~
is used to indicate the main word.

relationship. Совмести́мость -- ключ к про́чным отноше́ниям.

| relationship: *we'll have a great relationship* |

We're going to have a *(1)* **beautiful /** *(2)* **wonderful relationship together.** У нас бу́дут *(1)* прекра́сные / *(2)* замеча́тельные отноше́ния. ♦ **Together I know we can create a powerful relationship.** У нас мо́гут быть великоле́пные взаимоотноше́ния. ♦ **Deep down in my heart I know that our relationship will endure.** В глубине́ своего́ се́рдца я зна́ю, что на́ши отноше́ния бу́дут продолжа́ться.

| relationship: *maybe a long-term relationship* |

Perhaps this can blossom into a long-term relationship. Возмо́жно, что э́то преврати́тся в дли́тельные отноше́ния. ♦ **In this way (perhaps) we can sow the seeds of a meaningful relationship.** Таки́м о́бразом (возмо́жно) мы смо́жем посе́ять семена́ и́стинных отноше́ний.

| relationship: *harmony in our relationship* |

I feel such *(1)* **wonderful /** *(2)* **perfect /** *(3)* **total harmony in all areas of our relationship.** Я чу́вствую таку́ю *(1)* удиви́тельную / *(2)* соверше́нную / *(3)* по́лную гармо́нию во всех аспе́ктах на́ших отноше́ний.

| relationship: *I can liven a relationship* |

I know a lot of ways to *(1)* **animate /** *(2)* **enliven a relationship.** Я зна́ю мно́го путе́й для *(1,2)* оживле́ния отноше́ний.

| relationship: *get our relationship on solid ground* |

First we need to get our relationship on solid ground. Пре́жде всего́ мы должны́ дать на́шим отноше́ниям твёрдую осно́ву.

| relationship: *no putting career before relationship* |

I personally believe it's misguided to put a career before one's relationship. Я ли́чно ве́рю, что э́то непра́вильно поста́вить карье́ру вы́ше отноше́ний.

| relationship: *platonic relationships* |

I don't want (just) a platonic relationship. Я не хочу́ (то́лько) платони́ческих отноше́ний. ♦ **I want to keep our relationship platonic.** Я хочу́ сохрани́ть на́ши отноше́ния платони́ческими. ♦ **Our relationship is (purely) platonic.** На́ши отноше́ния (соверше́нно) платони́ческие.

| relationship: *I would never coerce you* |

I would never (try to) coerce *(1)* **you /** *(2)* **anyone into a physical relationship.** Я *(1)* тебя́ / *(2)* никого́ никогда́ не бу́ду принужда́ть к физи́ческим отноше́ниям.

| relationship: *improving our relationship* |

(In the *[1]* **days /** *[2]* **months /** *[3]* **years ahead) I hope we can deepen our relationship.** (В *[1-3]* бу́дущем) я наде́юсь, мы смо́жем углуби́ть на́ши отноше́ния. ♦ **I'll do everything I can to solidify our relationship.** Я бу́ду де́лать всё, что я смогу́ для укрепле́ния на́ших отноше́ний.

| relationship: *reviving our relationship* |

I want so much to revive our relationship. Я так стра́стно хочу́ восстанови́ть на́ши отноше́ния.

| relationship: *I don't want ours to go bad* |

I never want for our relationship to become a stale routine. Я не хочу́, что́бы на́ши отноше́ния ста́ли бу́дничной рути́ной. ♦ **I don't want our relationship to collapse.** Я не хочу́, что́бы на́ши отноше́ния разру́шились. ♦ **I don't want to** *(1)* **screw up /** *(2)* **ruin our relationship.** Я не хочу́ *(1,2)* испо́ртить на́ши отноше́ния.

| relationship: *if you really care about our relationship* |

If you (really) value our relationship, *(1)* **...you'll be completely honest with me. /** *(2)* **...you**

A list of abbreviations used in the dictionary is given on page 10.

won't hide things from me. / *(3)* **...you won't do things like that.** / *(4)* **...try to be more loving** / *(5)* **understanding** / *(6)* **sharing** / *(7)* **patient.** Если ты (действи́тельно) це́нишь на́ши отноше́ния, *(1)* ...ты бу́дешь соверше́нно че́стной *(ж: че́стным)* со мной. / *(2)* ...ты не бу́дешь ничего́ от меня́ скрыва́ть. / *(3)* ...ты не бу́дешь де́лать тако́го. *(4)* ...попыта́йся быть бо́лее лю́бящей *(ж: лю́бящим)* / *(5)* понима́ющей *(ж: понима́ющим)* / *(6)* уча́стливой *(ж: уча́стливым)* / *(7)* терпели́вой *(ж: терпели́вым).*

---
relationship: *mending our relationship*

Do you think we can *(1)* **patch up** / *(2)* **mend our relationship?** Ты ду́маешь, мы мо́жем *(1,2)* нала́дить на́ши отноше́ния? ♦ **Dear, we can** *(1)* **patch up** / *(2)* **mend our relationship, I know we can.** Дорога́я, мы мо́жем *(1,2)* нала́дить на́ши отноше́ния, я зна́ю, мы мо́жем.

---
relationship: *no illusions about them*

I've given up my illusions about relationships. Я отказа́лась от мои́х иллю́зий об отноше́ниях.

---
relationship: *someone trying to sabotage ours*
---

(1) **He** / *(2)* **She is trying to sabotage our relationship.** *(1)* Он / *(2)* Она́ пыта́ется расшата́ть на́ши отноше́ния.

---
relationship: *skeptical / depressed about ours*

For a long time I've *(1,2)* **been in denial about our relationship.** До́лгое вре́мя я *(1)* ...не смотре́л *(ж: смотре́ла)*... / *(2)* ...отка́зывался *(ж: отка́зывалась)* смотре́ть... в лицо́ пра́вде о на́ших отноше́ниях. ♦ **I'm** *([1]* **really** / *[2]* **very) depressed about our relationship.** Я *([1]* действи́тельно / *[2]* о́чень) пода́влен *(ж: пода́влена)* и́з-за на́ших отноше́ний.

---
relationship: *on-off, love-hate, sweet-sour, up-down*

Our relationship has been on-again, off-again. Мно́го раз на́ши отноше́ния прерыва́лись и начина́лись опя́ть. ♦ **We seem to have a love-hate relationship.** Ка́жется, на́ши отноше́ния коле́блются ме́жду любо́вью и не́навистью. ♦ **Our relationship was a sweet and sour experience.** В на́ших отноше́ниях бы́ло и сла́дкое и го́рькое. ♦ **Any relationship has its ups and downs.** В любы́х взаимоотноше́ниях есть свои́ подъёмы и спу́ски.

---
relationship: *ours is in trouble*

Our relationship *(1)* **...is...** / *(2)* **...has gotten** / *(3)* **become...** *(4)* **very** / *(5)* **rather** *(6,7)* **lopsided.** На́ши отноше́ния *(1)* получи́лись / *(2,3)* ста́ли *(4)* о́чень / *(5)* доста́точно *(6)* неравноме́рными / *(7)* односторо́нними. ♦ **Our relationship** *(1)* **...seems...** / *(2)* **...has become... so empty.** На́ша связь *(1)* ка́жется / *(2)* ста́ла тако́й пусто́й. ♦ **Our relationship is ...in shambles.** / **...on the rocks.** / **...careening off a cliff.** / **...an exercise in futilty.** На́ши (взаимо)отноше́ния ...разру́шились. / ...разва́ливаются. / ...ка́тятся со скалы́. / ...-- упражне́ния в пустоте́. ♦ **I feel like our relationship is beginning to unravel.** Я чу́вствую, как на́ши отноше́ния начина́ют разва́ливаться. ♦ **It seems like our relationship has gone awry.** Ка́жется, что на́ши отноше́ния зашли́ в тупи́к. ♦ **The relationship was a disaster (from the start).** Отноше́ния бы́ли катастро́фой с са́мого нача́ла. ♦ **Our relationship is doomed.** На́ша привя́занность обречена́. ♦ **You've (completely)** *(1)* **screwed up** / *(2)* **ruined our relationship.** Ты (по́лностью) *(1,2)* испо́ртила *(ж: испо́ртил)* на́ши отноше́ния. ♦ **Your behavior has** *(1)* **sabotaged** / *(2)* **undermined our relationship.** Твоё поведе́ние *(1,2)* расшата́ло на́ши отноше́ния.

---
relationship: *my relationship with her / him*

My relationship with *(1)* **him** / *(2)* **her is so empty.** Моя́ связь с *(1)* ним / *(2)* ней так пуста́.

---
relationship: *past relationships*

I just got out of a bad relationship. Я то́лько что ко́нчил *(ж: ко́нчила)* отноше́ния. ♦ **It was a(n)** *([1]* **totally** / *[2]* **completely) empty relationship.** Э́то была́ *([1]* абсолю́тно / *[2]*

The accents on Russian words are to show how to pronounce them.
You don't have to copy the accents when writing to someone.

совершéнно) пустáя связь. ♦ **I leaped into the relationship too quickly.** Я вступи́л *(ж: вступи́ла)* в бли́зкие отношéния сли́шком бы́стро.

| *relationship: end the relationship* |

Do you *(1)* **...think we should...** / *(2)* **...want to...** *(3)* **break off** / *(4,6)* **end** / *(5,6)* **terminate our relationship?** Ты *(1)* ...дýмаешь, нам слéдует... / *(2)* ...хóчешь... *(3)* ...порвáть / *(4,5)* прекрати́ть нáши отношéния? / *(6)* ...положи́ть конéц нáшим отношéниям? ♦ **I (don't) want to** *(1)* **break off** / *(2)* **end** / *(3)* **terminate our relationship.** Я (не) хочý *(1)* порвáть / *(2,3)* прекрати́ть нáши отношéния. ♦ **I think we should** *(1)* **end** / *(2)* **terminate our relationship.** Я дýмаю, мы должны́ *(1)* ...прекрати́ть нáши отношéния. / *(2)* ...положи́ть конéц нáшим отношéниям.

relationship-oriented *adj*: ♦ **I'm relationship-oriented.** Я хочý стаби́льных отношéний.
relative *adj* относи́тельный, -ая, -ое, -ые.
relative *n* рóдственник *m*, рóдственница *f* ♦ **close** ~ бли́зкий рóдственник *m*, бли́зкая рóдственница *f* ♦ **distant** ~ далёкий рóдственник *m*, далёкая рóдственница *f*.
relatively *adv* относи́тельно, довóльно, сравни́тельно.
relax *vi* 1. *(release tension)* расслабля́ться / рассла́биться; 2. *(rest)* отдыха́ть ♦ **Sometimes I like to just relax at home.** Иногдá мне нрáвится прóсто отдыхáть дóма.
relaxed *adj (free and easy, unconstrained)* непринуждённый, -ая, -ое, -ые, раскóванный, -ая, -ое, -ые.
relaxing *adj* расслабля́ющий, -ая, -ее, -ие.
release *vt* освобождáть / освободи́ть *(what, whom = acc.)*; отпускáть / отпусти́ть *(what, whom = acc.)*.
relent *vi* смягчáться / смягчи́ться, сми́лостивиться, уступáть / уступи́ть.
reliable *adj* надёжный, -ая, -ое, -ые.
relief *n* облегчéние.
relieved *adj* облегчённый, -ая, -ое, -ые ♦ **feel** ~ чýвствовать облегчéние.

| *relieved: phrases* |

I felt so relieved *(1)* **...to get your letter.** / *(2)* **...to get your call.** Я почýвствовал *(ж: почýвствовала)* такóе облегчéние *(1)* ..., получи́в твоё письмó. / *(2)* ...пóсле твоегó звонкá. ♦ **I feel so relieved** *(1)* **...that you understand.** / *(2)* **...that you're okay.** / *(3)* **...that you haven't changed your mind.** / *(4)* **...to hear that you still love me.** Я чýвствую такóе облегчéние от тогó, что *(1)* ...ты понялá *(ж: пóнял)*. / *(2)* ...всё хорошó с тобóй. / *(3)* ...ты не передýмала *(ж: передýмал)*. / *(4)* ...ты всё ещё лю́бишь меня́.
religious *adj* религиóзный, -ая, -ое, -ые.
relinquish *vt* бросáть / брóсить *(what = acc.)*, оставля́ть / остáвить *(what = acc.)* ♦ ~ **hope** оставля́ть / остáвить надéжду.
relish *vt (enjoy)* наслаждáться *(what = instr.)*, получáть удовóльствие / наслаждéние *(what = + от + gen.)*; *(savor)* смаковáть *(what = acc.)* ♦ **How heavenly it would be to relish the warm, wonderful softness of your body in the languor of half-sleep.** Как слáдостно бы́ло бы наслаждáться тёплой, замечáтельной мя́гкостью твоегó тéла в тóмном полуснé.
reluctance *n* нежелáние, неохóта, нерасположéние ♦ **I sense in you an underlying current of reluctance.** Я ощущáю в тебé скры́тое нежелáние.
reluctant *adj* неохóтный, -ая, -ое, -ые ♦ **be** ~ дéлать с неохóтой.
reluctantly *adv* неохóтно.
remark *n* замечáние ♦ **bitter** ~ гóрькое замечáние ♦ **careless** ~ небрéжное замечáние ♦ **catty** ~ язви́тельное замечáние; саркасти́ческое замечáние ♦ *(1,2)* **caustic** ~ *(1)* кóлкое / *(2)* éдкое замечáние ♦ **disparaging** ~ пренебрежи́тельное замечáние ♦ **dumb**

---

*If no accent is shown on a word with a capitalized vowel,
it means that the capitalized vowel is accented.*

~ дура́цкое замеча́ние ♦ **insulting** ~ оби́дное замеча́ние ♦ **mean** ~ зло́е замеча́ние ♦ **nasty** ~ 1. *(indecent)* непристо́йное замеча́ние; 2. *(venomous)* ядови́тое замеча́ние ♦ **obscene** ~ неприли́чное замеча́ние ♦ **offhanded** ~ бесцеремо́нное замеча́ние ♦ **sarcastic** ~ саркасти́ческое замеча́ние ♦ **saucy** ~ 1. *(impudent)* де́рзкое замеча́ние ; 2. *(brazenly flirtatious)* коке́тливое замеча́ние ♦ **sly** ~ хи́трое замеча́ние ♦ **stinging** ~ язви́тельное замеча́ние ♦ **stupid** ~ глу́пое замеча́ние ♦ **teasing** ~ дразня́щее замеча́ние ♦ **thoughtless** ~ необду́манное замеча́ние ♦ **unflattering** ~ нелёстное замеча́ние ♦ **ungracious** ~ неве́жливое замеча́ние ♦ **witty** ~ остроу́мное замеча́ние ♦ **make a** ~ сде́лать замеча́ние ♦ **That was a** *(1)* **dumb** / *(2)* **stupid** / *(3)* **thoughtless remark that I made.** С мое́й стороны́ э́то бы́ло *(1)* дура́цким / *(2)* глу́пым / *(3)* необду́манным замеча́нием .

remarried *adj (man)* опя́ть жена́т, -ы *(short forms); (woman)* опя́ть за́мужем *(short form).*

remarry *vi (man or couple)* опя́ть жени́ться *(whom = + на + prep.); (woman)* опя́ть выходи́ть / вы́йти за́муж *(whom = + за + acc.).*

remember *vt* по́мнить / вспо́мнить *(what, whom = acc.)* ♦ **Do you remember?** По́мнишь ли ты? ♦ **Oh, how I remember.** О, как я по́мню. ♦ **I will always remember** *(1)* **...the moments** / *(2)* **days** / *(3)* **hours that we spent together.** / *(4)* **...the time that we spent together.** Я всегда́ бу́ду по́мнить *(1)* ...мину́ты / *(2)* дни / *(3)* часы́, проведённые на́ми вме́сте. / *(4)* ...вре́мя, проведённое на́ми вме́сте.

remembrance *n* па́мять, воспомина́ние; *(reminder)* напомина́ние ♦ **I will (always) keep this as a** *(1,2)* **remembrance (of our** *[3]* **time** / *[4]* **evening** / *[5]* **weekend together).** Я (всегда́) бу́ду храни́ть э́то как *(1)* па́мять / *(2)* воспомина́ние (*[3]* о вре́мени... / *[4]* о ве́чере... / *[5]* о выходны́х днях... вме́сте). ♦ **Please keep this as a small remembrance (of our time together).** Пожа́луйста, сохрани́ э́то как ма́ленькое напомина́ние (о вре́мени, проведённом на́ми вме́сте).

reminder *n* напомина́ние ♦ **gentle** ~ намёк ♦ **painful** ~ боле́зненное воспомина́ние.

remorse *n* угрызе́ние со́вести; раска́яние ♦ **I feel (**[1]** great** / **[2]** **such) remorse for what I've done (to** *[3]* **you** / *[4]* **her** / *[5]* **him** / *[6]* **them).** Я испы́тываю (**[1]** си́льное / **[2]** тако́е) угрызе́ние со́вести за то, что я сде́лал *(ж: сде́лала)* (по отноше́нию к *[3]* тебе́ / *[4]* ней / *[5]* нему́ / *[6]* ним). ♦ **I feel no remorse (at all).** Я не испы́тываю (никаки́х) угрызе́ний со́вести. ♦ **I bear no remorse.** У меня́ нет угрызе́ний со́вести.

remorseful *adj* по́лный (-ая, -ое, -ые) раска́яния.

remote *adj* 1. *(distant)* отдалённый, -ая, -ое, -ые, да́льний, -яя, -ее, -ие; *(secluded)* уединённый, -ая, -ое, -ые, глухо́й,-а́я, -о́е, -и́е; 2. *(estranged)* отчуждённый, -ая, -ое, -ые ♦ ~ **place** уединённое ме́сто.

remoteness *n* 1. *(distance)* отдалённость *f*; 2. *(estrangement)* отчуждённость *f*.

remove *vt* 1. *(take away)* убира́ть / убра́ть *(what = acc.);* 2. *(take off)* снима́ть / снять *(what = acc.)* ♦ **Please remove your** *(1)* **hand** /*(2)* **arm.** Убери́, пожа́луйста, свою́ *(1,2)* ру́ку. ♦ **Let me remove that (for you).** *(garment)* Позво́ль мне снять э́то (для тебя́).

rendezvous *n* свида́ние, ме́сто встре́чи ♦ **fun-filled** ~ свида́ние, запо́лненное развлече́ниями *(1 term)* ♦ **joyful** ~ ра́достное свида́ние ♦ **love(r's)** ~ любо́вное свида́ние ♦ **secret** ~ та́йное свида́ние ♦ **set a** ~ назна́чить свида́ние ♦ *(1,2)* **Suppose we set a rendezvous for Saturday?** *(1)* Что ты ду́маешь о том, что́бы нам встре́титься в суббо́ту? / *(2)* Мо́жет быть мы встре́тимся в суббо́ту?

repartee *n* 1. *(quick, witty reply)* остроу́мный отве́т; 2. *(adroitness & cleverness in reply)* остроу́мие, нахо́дчивость *f*.

reply *n* отве́т ♦ **fast** ~ бы́стрый отве́т ♦ **immediate** ~ неме́дленный отве́т ♦ **laconic** ~ лакони́чный отве́т ♦ **long** ~ дли́нный отве́т ♦ **quick** ~ бы́стрый отве́т ♦ **saucy** ~ 1. *(impu-*

Russian has 6 grammatical cases. For an explanation of them,
see the grammar appendix on page 686.

dent) дéрзкий отвéт ; 2. *(brazenly flirtatious)* кокéтливый отвéт ♦ **serious** ~ серьёзный отвéт ♦ *(1,2)* **short** ~ *(1)* корóткий / *(2)* крáткий отвéт ♦ **terse** ~ лакони́чный отвéт ♦ **your** ~ *(familiar)* твой отвéт; *(polite)* Ваш отвéт.

reply: *verb terms*

compose a ~ писáть / написáть отвéт ♦ **receive** *(1)* **my** / *(2)* **your** ~ получи́ть *(1)* мой / *(2)* твой отвéт ♦ **send a** ~ посылáть / послáть отвéт ♦ **wait for your** ~ ждать твоегó отвéта ♦ **write a** ~ писáть / написáть отвéт.

reply: *phrases*

I sent you a reply a week ago. Я послáл *(ж: послáла)* тебé отвéт недéлю назáд. ♦ **Please send me a reply as soon as possible.** Пожáлуйста, пошли́ мне отвéт как мóжно скорéй. ♦ **Please send me a reply by** *(1)* **...e-mail.** / *(2)* **...fax.** / *(3)* **...express mail.** Пожáлуйста, пошли́ мне отвéт *(1)* ...электрóнной пóчтой. / *(2)* ...фáксом. / *(3)* ...срóчной пóчтой. ♦ **I want serious replies (only).** Я хочý серьёзных отвéтов (тóлько). *(на объявлéние)*

reprehensible *adj* предосуди́тельный, -ая, -ое, -ые.

represent *vt* представля́ть / предстáвить *(what = acc.)*, изображáть / изобрази́ть ♦ **You represent all of my (most cherished) hopes and dreams.** Ты воплощáешь все мои́ (сáмые сокровéнные) надéжды и мечты́.

reproach *vt* упрекáть / упрекнýть *(whom = acc., for what = + за + acc.)* ♦ **Can you reproach me (for** *[1]* **...my feelings?** / *[2]* **...loving you?)?** Мóжешь ты упрекнýть меня́ (за *[1]* ...мои́ чýвства? / *[2]* ...любóвь к тебé?)?

reproach *n* упрёк ♦ **silent** ~ молчали́вый упрёк ♦ **stinging** ~ язви́тельный упрёк ♦ **undeserved** ~ незаслýженный упрёк ♦ **unfair** ~ несправедли́вый упрёк.

reptilian *n (slang) (obnoxious person)* гад, проти́вный человéк.

repudiate *vt* отрекáться / отрéчься *(whom = + от + gen.)* ♦ **Why are you repudiating me?** Почемý ты отрекáешься от меня́?

repulse *vt (push away / back)* оттáлкивать / оттолкнýть *(whom = acc.)*; *(rebuff)* давáть / дать отпóр *(whom = dat.)*.

repulsive *adj* оттáлкивающий, -ая, -ее, -ие, омерзи́тельный, -ая, -ое, -ые.

reputation *n* репутáция ♦ **bad** ~ плохáя репутáция ♦ **good** ~ хорóшая репутáция.

reputation: *verb terms*

blemish *(1)* **my** / *(2)* **your** ~ запятнáть *(1)* мою́ / *(2)* твою́ репутáцию ♦ **damage** *(1)* **my** / *(2)* **your** ~ пóртить / испóртить *(1)* мою́ / *(2)* твою́ репутáцию ♦ **harm** *(1)* **my** / *(2)* **your** ~ поврeждáть / повреди́ть *(1)* мою́ / *(2)* твою́ репутáцию ♦ **risk** *(1)* **my** / *(2)* **your** ~ рисковáть *(1,2)* своéй репутáцией ♦ **spoil** *(1)* **my** / *(2)* **your** ~ пóртить / испóртить *(1)* мою́ / *(2)* твою́ репутáцию ♦ **uphold** *(1)* **my** / *(2)* **your** ~ поддéрживать *(1,2)* свою́ репутáцию.

reputation: *phrases*

I'm putting my reputation on the line. Я рискýю своéй репутáцией. ♦ **I have a good reputation. I don't want to** *(1)* **risk** / *(2)* **spoil it.** У меня́ хорóшая репутáция. Я не хочý *(1)* ...рисковáть ей. / *(2)* ...испóртить её. ♦ **I won't do anything to** *(1)* **harm** / *(2)* **blemish your reputation.** Я не сдéлаю ничегó, что мóжет *(1)* ...повреди́ть твоéй репутáции. / *(2)* ...запятнáть твою́ репутáцию. ♦ **I wouldn't think of harming your reputation.** Я ни за что не хотéл *(ж:хотéла)* бы повреди́ть твоéй репутáции.

require *vt* трéбовать / потрéбовать *(what = gen.)*.

required *adj* трéбуемый, -ая, -ое, -ые; необходи́мый, -ая, -ое, -ые.

requirement *n* трéбование.

resent *vt* негодовáть *(what = + на + acc.)*, обижáться *(what = + на + acc.)* ♦ **I resent** *(1)* **...what you said.** / *(2)* **...that remark** / *(3)* **comment** / *(4)* **accusation** / *(5)* **insinuation.** / *(6)*

There are no articles ("a" or "the") in Russian.

...being treated like *(7)* **this** / *(8)* **that.** Я обижа́юсь *(1)* ...на то, что ты сказа́ла *(ж: сказа́л).* / *(2,3)* ...на э́то замеча́ние. / *(4)* ...на э́то обвине́ние. / *(5)* ...на э́тот намёк. / *(6)* ...е́сли со мной обраща́ются *(7,8)* так.

resentful *adj* оби́женный, -ая, -ое, -ые.

resentment *n* негодова́ние, оби́да, возмуще́ние ♦ **My resentment has been building (up) for a long time.** Моё негодова́ние нака́пливается уже́ давно́.

reservation *n* 1. *(booking, order)* предвари́тельный зака́з; *(booked seat)* заброни́рованное ме́сто 2. *(limitation)* огово́рка ♦ **make ~s** *(seats)* заброни́ровать места́; *(room)* заброни́ровать но́мер ♦ **without ~** безогово́рочно, без огово́рок ♦ **I have a reservation.** У меня́ есть бро́ня. ♦ **To someone who gives me all their love without reservation, I** *(1)* **could** / *(2)* **would pour out twice as much love and affection, or more, in return.** На ту *(ж: того́),* кто отда́ст мне всю свою́ любо́вь безогово́рочно, я в отве́т *(1)* ...мог *(ж: могла́)* бы изли́ть... / *(2)* ...изли́л *(ж: излила́)* бы... вдво́е бо́льше любви́ и не́жности.

reserve *vt (order ahead)* зака́зывать / заказа́ть зара́нее *(what = acc.)*; *(book)* брони́ровать / заброни́ровать *(what = acc.)* ♦ **~ a (hotel) room** заброни́ровать но́мер ♦ **~** *(1)* **a seat** / *(2)* **seats** заброни́ровать *(1)* ме́сто / *(2)* места́.

reserve *n* 1. *(supply)* запа́с, резе́рв; 2. *(restraint)* сде́ржанность *f* ♦ **One of these days I'm going to break through that protective bubble of reserve that you live in and set your soul on fire.** Одна́жды я прорву́сь че́рез защи́тную оболо́чку сде́ржанности, в кото́рой ты живёшь, и зажгу́ ого́нь в твое́й душе́.

reserved *adj* 1. *(reticent)* сде́ржанный, -ая, -ое, -ые *(short forms:* сде́ржан, -на, -но, -ны*),* за́мкнутый, -ая, -ое, -ые *(short forms:* за́мкнут, -а, -о, -ы*);* 2. *(ordered ahead)* зака́занный (-ая, -ое, -ые) зара́нее; *(booked)* заброни́рованный, -ая, -ое, -ые ♦ **politely ~** ве́жливо-сде́ржанный, -ая, -ое, -ые ♦ **~ seat** заброни́рованное ме́сто *(pl:* заброни́рованные места́*).*

reservoir *n* резервуа́р, запа́с ♦ **I perceive in you a reservoir of warmth and affection and tenderness that is very, very deep.** Я чу́вствую в тебе́ о́чень, о́чень глубо́кий запа́с серде́чности, любви́ и не́жности. ♦ **I have such a vast reservoir of tender affection to lavish upon you.** У меня́ тако́й грома́дный, запа́с любви́ и не́жности, кото́рый я хочу́ изли́ть на тебя́. ♦ **My entire being is** *(1)* **assailed** / *(2)* **tormented by the all-consuming need to take you in my arms and revel in the reservoir of your passion.** Я весь *(1)* охва́чен / *(2)* изму́чен всепоглоща́ющей жа́ждой заключи́ть тебя́ в объя́тия и упива́ться твое́й стра́стью.

resist *vt* сопротивля́ться *(what, whom = dat.)* ♦ **~ the temptation** сопротивля́ться искуше́нию, устоя́ть пе́ред собла́зном.

---
resist: phrases

I couldn't resist the temptation (of *[1]* **calling** / *[2]* **contacting** / *[3]* **seeing you [again]).** Я не мог *(ж: могла́)* сопротивля́ться искуше́нию (*[1]* ...позвони́ть Вам... / *[2]* ...обща́ться с Ва́ми... / *[3]* ...уви́деть Вас... [опя́ть]). ♦ **When we** *(1)* **sat** / *(2)* **stood together there, I could hardly resist the temptation to kiss you.** Когда́ мы *(1)* сиде́ли / *(2)* стоя́ли там вме́сте, я едва́ мог сопротивля́ться искуше́нию поцелова́ть тебя́. ♦ **The temptation to** *(1)* **...kiss you...** / *(2)* **...take you in my arms... was almost more than I could resist.** Искуше́нию *(1)* ...целова́ть тебя́... / *(2)* ...заключи́ть тебя́ в объя́тия... бы́ло почти́ невозмо́жно сопротивля́ться. ♦ **I have no ability (whatsoever) to resist you.** Я (соверше́нно) не спосо́бен *(ж: спосо́бна)* сопротивля́ться тебе́. ♦ *(1)* **Who...** / *(2)* **What man... can resist someone as beautiful as you?** *(1)* Кто... / *(2)* Како́й мужчи́на... мо́жет сопротивля́ться тако́й красоте́, как твоя́. ♦ **I (simply) cannot resist** *(1)* **...you.** / *(2)* **...your charms** / *(3)* **beauty** / *(4)* **loveliness.** Я (про́сто) не могу́ сопротивля́ться *(1)*

This dictionary contains two Russian alphabet pages:
one in Appendix 1, page 685, and a tear-off page on page 799.

...тебе́. / (2) ...твоему́ очарова́нию. / (3,4) ...твое́й красоте́. ♦ **It's (**[*1*] **too /** [*2*] **so) hard to resist you.** (*[1]* Сли́шком / *[2]* Так) тру́дно сопротивля́ться тебе́. ♦ **I find your charm and beauty very hard to resist.** Я обнару́жил, что твоему́ обая́нию и красоте́ о́чень тру́дно сопротивля́ться. ♦ **I cannot describe and cannot resist the appeal that you have for me.** Я не могу́ описа́ть твою́ привлека́тельность и не могу́ сопроти-вля́ться ей.

resistance *n* сопротивле́ние ♦ **cold** ~ холо́дное сопротивле́ние ♦ **sham** ~ притво́рное сопротивле́ние ♦ **stubborn** ~ упо́рное сопротивле́ние ♦ **offer** ~ ока́зывать / оказа́ть сопротивле́ние *(to what, whom = dat.)* ♦ **overcome** *(1)* **my /** *(2)* **your** ~ преодоле́ть *(1)* моё / *(2)* твоё сопротивле́ние ♦ **If my lips ever come in contact with yours, all that (**[*1*] **cold /** [*2*] **sham) resistance is going to drain right out of you.** Е́сли мои́ гу́бы когда́-нибудь косну́тся твои́х губ, всё твоё (*[1]* холо́дное / *[2]* притво́рное) сопротивле́ние изче́з-нет. ♦ **When you** *(1)* **kiss /** *(2)* **touch me, all my resistance drains out of me.** От твои́х *(1)* поцелу́ев / *(2)* прикоснове́ний всё сопротивле́ние покида́ет меня́.

resonant *adj* зву́чный, -ая, -ое, -ые, зво́нкий, -ая, -ое, -ие.

resonate *vi* резони́ровать.

respect *vt* уважа́ть *(what, whom = acc., for what = +* за *+ acc.)* ♦ ~ **a lot** о́чень уважа́ть ♦ ~ **highly** высоко́ уважа́ть ♦ ~ **sincerely** и́скренне уважа́ть ♦ ~ **very much** о́чень уважа́ть.

---
respect: *phrases*

I respect you *(1)* **...a lot. /** *(2)* **...very much.** Я *(1,2)* о́чень тебя́ уважа́ю. ♦ **I respect your ideals and ambitions and dreams.** Я уважа́ю твои́ идеа́лы, стремле́ния и мечты́. ♦ **I promise to love you and respect you and care for you all my life.** Я обеща́ю люби́ть тебя́, уважа́ть тебя́ и забо́титься о тебе́ всю свою́ жизнь. ♦ **I believe it's important to respect oneself.** Я счита́ю, что ва́жно уважа́ть себя́. ♦ **The way you act, I don't think you re-spect me.** Су́дя по твои́м де́йствиям, я ду́маю, что ты не уважа́ешь меня́. ♦ **I'm afraid you won't respect me (if I do that).** Бою́сь, что ты переста́нешь уважа́ть меня́ (, е́сли я сде́лаю э́то). ♦ **If you (truly) respect me, you won't do that.** Е́сли ты (действи́тельно) уважа́ешь меня́, ты э́того не сде́лаешь. ♦ **I need you to respect me.** Мне ну́жно, чтобы ты уважа́ла *(ж: уважа́л)* меня́. ♦ *(1)* **I think... /** *(2)* **You act as though... you don't respect me.** *(1)* Я ду́маю, что... / *(2)* Ты де́лаешь так, как бу́дто... ты не уважа́ешь меня́. ♦ **I want to respect myself in the morning.** Я хочу́ уважа́ть себя́ у́тром.

respect *n* уваже́ние ♦ **deep** ~ глубо́кое уваже́ние ♦ **deepest** ~ глубоча́йшее уваже́ние ♦ **great** ~ большо́е уваже́ние ♦ **greatest** ~ велича́йшее уваже́ние ♦ **infinite** ~ бесконе́ч-ное уваже́ние ♦ **mutual** ~ взаи́мное уваже́ние ♦ **profound** ~ глубоча́йшее уваже́ние ♦ **sincere** ~и́скреннее уваже́ние ♦ **tremendous** ~огро́мное уваже́ние.

---
respect: *other terms*
---

gain *(1)* **my /** *(2)* **your** ~ заслужи́ть *(1)* моё / *(2)* твоё уваже́ние ♦ **have** ~ испы́тывать уваже́ние *(for whom = +* к *+ dat.)* ♦ **lack of** ~ недоста́точное уваже́ние ♦ **lose** *(1)* **my /** *(2)* **your** ~ потеря́ть *(1)* моё / *(2)* твоё уваже́ние ♦ **relationship based on** ~ отноше́ние осно́вано на уваже́нии ♦ **show** *(1)* **me /** *(2)* **you** ~ ока́зывать / оказа́ть *(1)* мне / *(2)* тебе́ уваже́ние.

---
respect: *phrases*

I have nothing but respect for you. Я не испы́тываю к тебе́ ничего́, кро́ме уваже́ния. ♦ **I have** *(1)* **great /** *(2)* **the greatest respect for** *(3)* **you /** *(4)* **her /** *(5)* **him /** *(6)* **them.** Я испы́тываю к *(3)* тебе́ / *(4)* ней / *(5)* нему́ / *(6)* ним *(1)* большо́е / *(2)* велича́йшее уваже́ние. ♦ **I** *(1)* **need /** *(2)* **want your respect.** *(1)* Мне ну́жно,... / *(2)* Я хочу́,... чтобы ты меня́ уважа́ла *(ж: уважа́л).* ♦ **You never show me any respect.** Ты никогда́ не

Russian verbs conjugate for 6 persons:
I, familiar you, he-she-it, we, polite&plural you, and they.

проявля́ешь никако́го уваже́ния ко мне. ♦ **I wish you would show me more respect.** Мне хоте́лось бы, что́бы ты ока́зывала *(ж: ока́зывал)* мне бо́льше уваже́ния. ♦ **Mutual respect is very important in a relationship** Взаи́мное уваже́ние о́чень ва́жно в отноше́ниях. ♦ **Your lack of respect (for me)** *(1)* **hurts /** *(2)* **offends /** *(3)* **bothers me (very much).** Твоё недоста́точное уваже́ние (ко мне) о́чень *(1)* ра́нит / *(2)* оскорбля́ет / *(3)* беспоко́ит меня́. ♦ **Love and respect form the foundation of a strong and lasting marriage.** Любо́вь и уваже́ние создаю́т фунда́мент кре́пкого и продолжи́тельного бра́ка. ♦ **Our love is based on trust and respect and understanding.** На́ша любо́вь осно́вана на дове́рии, уваже́нии и взаимопонима́нии. ♦ **I want a love based on trust and respect and understanding.** Я хочу́, что́бы в осно́ве любви́ бы́ли дове́рие, уваже́ние и взаимопонима́ние.

respectability *n* респекта́бельность *f.*

respectable *adj* добропоря́дочный, -ая, -ое, -ые.

respectful *adj* почте́нный, -ая, -ое, -ые, респекта́бельный, -ая, -ое, -ые прили́чный, -ая, -ое, -ые.

resplendent *adj* блиста́тельный, -ая, -ое, -ые, великоле́пный, -ая, -ое, -ые; пы́шно оде́тый, -ая, -ое, -ые ♦ **You look resplendent in that** *(1)* **outfit /** *(2)* **suit /** *(3)* **dress.** Ты вы́глядишь великоле́пно в э́том *(1)* наря́де / *(2)* костю́ме / *(3)* пла́тье.

respond *vi* отвеча́ть / отве́тить *(to what = + на + acc., to whom = dat.),* отклика́ться / откли́кнуться *(to what = + на + acc.),* реаги́ровать / прореаги́ровать *(to what = + на + acc.)* ♦ **~ instinctively** реаги́ровать инстинкти́вно.

> **respond:** *how you respond*

I love the way you respond with so much passion. Мне нра́вится, что ты отвеча́ешь мне с тако́й большо́й стра́стью. ♦ **When I feel you respond, my heart overflows with love for you.** Когда́ я чу́вствую, что ты отвеча́ешь мне, моё се́рдце переполня́ется любо́вью к тебе́. ♦ **I'm going to make you respond with so much passion you won't believe it.** Ты не пове́ришь, с како́й стра́стью я заста́влю тебя́ отве́тить мне. ♦ **You responded so** *(1,2)* **passionately.** Ты отвеча́ла так *(1)* стра́стно / *(2)* пы́лко. ♦ **I was astonished at how passionately you responded.** Я был удивлён, как стра́стно ты отвеча́ла. ♦ **I** *(1)* **like /** *(2)* **love the way you respond.** *(1)* Мне нра́вится,... / *(2)* Я люблю́,... как ты отвеча́ешь. ♦ **Nobody responds the way you do.** Никто́ не отвеча́ет так, как ты. ♦ **I'm going to give you so much love that you won't have any choice but to respond in the same way.** Я дам тебе́ так мно́го любви́, что у тебя́ не бу́дет ино́го вы́бора, кро́ме как отве́тить мне тем же. ♦ **When I show you love and affection, you never seem to respond.** Когда́ я выка́зываю тебе́ любо́вь и не́жность, ка́жется что, ты никогда́ не реаги́руешь.

> **respond:** *how I respond*

I respond well to affection. Я хорошо́ реаги́рую на не́жность. ♦ **I'm sorry I'm so slow in responding (to your** *[1]* **letter /** *[2]* **call).** Извини́те, что я так не ско́ро отвеча́ю *([1]*...на ва́ше письмо́. / *[2]* ...на ваш звоно́к.).

response *n* 1. *(answer)* отве́т; 2. *(reaction)* о́тклик, реа́кция ♦ **emotional ~** эмоциона́льная реа́кция ♦ **instinctive ~** инстинкти́вная реа́кция ♦ **mad ~** безу́мный о́тклик ♦ *(1,2)* **passionate ~** *(1)* пы́лкий / *(2)* стра́стный отве́т ♦ **feel your ~** чу́вствовать / почу́вствовать твой о́тклик.

> **response:** *phrases*

I called your house, but there was no response. Я позвони́л *(ж: позвони́ла)* тебе́ домо́й, но отве́та не бы́ло. ♦ **What kind of a response is that?** Как ты отвеча́ешь? ♦ *(1,2)* **Why do you give me no response?** *(1)* Почему́ Вы не даёте... / *(2)* Почему́ ты не даёшь... мне

There are two words for "you" in Russian:
familiar «ты» *and polite / plural* «вы» *(See page 771).*

ответа? ♦ **Such a** *(1,2)* **passionate response!** Такой *(1)* пылкий / *(2)* страстный ответ!
♦ **Please try to give me a response as soon as you can.** Пожалуйста, постарайся дать мне
ответ как можно скорее.

responsibility *n* ответственность *f (for what, whom* = + за + *acc.)* ♦ **big** ~ большая ответственность ♦ **full** ~ полная ответственность ♦ **heavy** ~ тяжёлая ответственность ♦ **her**
~ её ответственность ♦ **his** ~ его ответственность ♦ **huge** ~ огромная ответственность ♦ **moral** ~ моральная ответственность ♦ **my** ~ моя ответственность ♦ **no** ~ (нет)
никакой ответственности *(for what, whom* = + за + *acc.)* ♦ **our** ~ наша ответственность
♦ **personal** ~ личная ответственность ♦ **terrible** ~ страшная ответственность ♦ **their**
~ их ответственность ♦ **tremendous** ~ огромная ответственность ♦ **whose** ~ чья
ответственность ♦ **your** ~ *(familiar)* твоя ответственность; *(polite)* Ваша ответственность.

responsibility: verb terms

accept ~ брать / взять на себя ответственность, принимать / принять на себя ответственность ♦ **assume** ~ брать / взять на себя ответственность, принимать / принять на
себя ответственность ♦ **avoid** ~ увиливать / увильнуть от ответственности ♦ **feel** ~
чувствовать / почувствовать ответственность ♦ **shirk** ~ увиливать / увильнуть от
ответственности ♦ **take (on)** ~ брать / взять на себя ответственность, принимать /
принять на себя ответственность.

responsibility: other terms

part of the ~ доля ответственности ♦ **sense of** ~ чувство ответственности.

responsible *adj* ответственный, -ая, -ое, -ые ♦ **financially** ~ финансово ответственный,
-ая, -ое, -ые ♦ **morally** ~ морально ответственный.

responsive *adj* отзывчивый, -ая, -ое, -ые ♦ **insatiably** ~ ненасытный, -ая, -ое, -ые.

responsiveness *n* отзывчивость *f.*

rest *vi* отдыхать / отдохнуть ♦ ~ **assured** быть спокоен *m* / спокойна *f* ♦ ~ **easy** *(not worry)*
не беспокоиться, не волноваться ♦ **You may rest assured that I will take care of it.** Ты
можешь быть спокойна *(ж: спокоен)*, что я позабочусь об этом. ♦ **Let's rest (a little).**
Давай (немного) отдохнём. ♦ **I won't rest until I get you over here.** Я не успокоюсь,
пока ты не будешь здесь.

rest *n* 1. *(resting)* отдых; 2. *(break)* передышка, перерыв, пауза; 3. *(remainder)* остаток,
остальное ♦ **spend the** ~ **of my days** проводить / провести остаток (моих) дней ♦ **take
a** ~ отдыхать / отдохнуть; сделать передышку.

rest: phrases

When I get there, you're not going to get much rest. Когда я приеду туда, у тебя не
будет передышки. ♦ **I need some rest. (I've been working too hard.)** Мне нужен отдых.
(Я слишком много работаю.). ♦ **What do you do the rest of the time?** Что ты делаешь
в остальное время? ♦ **'ll cherish the memory for the rest of my life.** Я буду лелеять
воспоминания об этом всю оставшуюся жизнь. ♦ **I'll send you the rest of the money
later.** Я пошлю тебе остальные деньги позднее.

restaurant *n* ресторан ♦ **fancy** ~ модный ресторан ♦ **good** ~ хороший ресторан.

restrain *vt* сдерживать / сдержать *(what, whom* = *acc.)*, удерживать / удержать *(what,
whom* = *acc.)* ♦ ~ **oneself** сдерживаться / сдержаться ♦ **It's difficult for me to restrain
my feelings whenever I** *(1)* **...think about you.** / *(2)* **...am around you.** Мне трудно сдерживать свои чувства, когда бы я ни *(1)* ...подумал о тебе. / *(2)* ...был рядом с тобой.
♦ **Please restrain yourself.** Пожалуйста, сдержись.

restrained *adj* сдержанный, -ая, -ое, -ые.

restraint *n* сдержанность *f*, замкнутость *f*, отчуждённость *f*, скованность *f* ♦ **lack of**

Russian terms of endearment are given in Appendix 13, page 780.

emotional ~ эмоциона́льная несде́ржанность ♦ **without** ~ свобо́дно, не стесня́ясь.

> **restraint:** *phrases*

I want there never to be any restraint between us. Я хочу́, что́бы ме́жду на́ми никогда́ не бы́ло никако́й отчуждённости. ♦ **Let's promise each other that we will never have any restraint between us.** Дава́й пообеща́ем друг дру́гу, что никогда́ не бу́дет никако́й отчуждённости ме́жду на́ми. ♦ **I never feel any restrain when I'm with you.** С тобо́й я никогда́ не чу́вствую никако́й ско́ванности. ♦ **I'll try to show a little more restraint.** Я попыта́юсь быть немно́го бо́лее сде́ржанным.

restricted *adj (limited)* ограни́ченный, -ая, -ое, -ые *(short forms:* ограни́чен, -а, -о, -ы) ♦ **I don't want you to feel restricted (when you write to me).** Я не хочу́, что́бы ты чу́вствовала *(ж: чу́вствовал)* ско́ванность (когда́ пи́шешь мне). ♦ **I feel** *(1,2)* **restricted when I write to you, because I'm afraid** *(3)* **...someone... /** *(4)***... your mother... /** *(5)* **...your father... will read my letters.** Я чу́вствую *(1)* сде́ржанность / *(2)* стеснённость, когда́ пишу́ тебе́ потому́, что бою́сь, что *(3)* ...кто́-то... / *(4)* ...твоя́ ма́ма... / *(5)* ...твой па́па... прочита́ет мои́ пи́сьма.

retire *vi* уходи́ть / уйти́ в отста́вку *(from what* = + из + *gen.),* уходи́ть / уйти́ на пе́нсию *(from what* = + из + *gen.)* ♦ **I retired from the** *(1)* **Army /** *(2)* **Air Force /** *(3)* **Navy /** *(4)* **Marine Corps.** Я ушёл *(ж: ушла́)* в отста́вку из *(1)* ...а́рмии. / *(2)* ...вое́нно-возду́шных сил. / *(3)* ...вое́нно-морско́го фло́та. / *(4)* ...морско́й пехо́ты. ♦ **I retired from the government.** Я ушёл *(ж: ушла́)* на пе́нсию с рабо́ты на госуда́рственной слу́жбе.

retired *adj* отставно́й, -а́я, -о́е, -ы́е, в отста́вке, на пе́нсии ♦ **recently** ~ неда́вно вы́шедший (-ая, -ие) на пе́нсию ♦ **I'm a retired Army** *(1)* **NCO /** *(2)* **officer.** Я арме́йский *(1)* сержа́нт / *(2)* офице́р в отста́вке.

retiree *n (civilian* пенсионе́р *m,* пенсионе́рка *f;* (*mil.*) отставни́к) ♦ **military** ~ отставни́к, вое́нный пенсионе́р *m,* вое́нная пенсионе́рка *f.*

retreat *n* 1. *(withdrawal)* отступле́ние, отхо́д; 2. *(secluded house)* уединённый дом; *(secluded lodge)* уединённое ме́сто ♦ **idyllic** ~ идилли́ческое уединённое ме́сто ♦ **romantic** ~ романти́ческое уединённое ме́сто.

retro *adj (slang) (from the past)* ре́тро.

return *vi (come / go back)* возвраща́ться / возврати́ться *or* верну́ться.

return *vt (give back)* возвраща́ть / возврати́ть *or* верну́ть *(what = acc., to whom = dat.).*

return *n* возвраще́ние ♦ **in** ~ в отве́т ♦ **To someone who gives me all their love without reservation, I** *(1)* **could /** *(2)* **would pour out twice as much love and affection, or more, in return.** На ту *(ж: того́),* кто отда́ст мне всю свою́ любо́вь безогово́рочно, я в отве́т *(1)* ...мог *(могла́)* бы изли́ть... / *(2)* ...изли́л *(ж: излила́)* бы... вдво́е бо́льше любви́ и не́жности.

reunion *n* воссоедине́ние.

reunite *vi* воссоединя́ться / воссоедини́ться.

reveal *vt* 1. *(show; uncover)* пока́зывать / показа́ть *(what = acc.),* обнару́живать / обнару́жить *(what = acc.);* 2. *(disclose)* открыва́ть / откры́ть *(what = acc.)* ♦ ~ **a secret** открыва́ть / откры́ть та́йну.

> **reveal:** *phrases*

The thought patterns that yielded your choice of words and sentences in your ad reveal the exact same raging hunger for love and affection that I harbor within me. Мы́сли, роди́вшие вы́бор слов и предложе́ний в Ва́шем объявле́нии, говоря́т о то́чно тако́й же неи́стовой жа́жде любви́ и не́жности, кото́рая таи́тся во мне. ♦ **How I dream of the day when I can peel away your silk underwear to reveal the full,** *(1)* **glorious /** *(2)* **magnificent splendor of your of your beautiful, luscious body.** Как я мечта́ю о том дне,

---

> *Some of the Russian sentences are translations of things we say and are not what Russians themselves would normally say.*

когда́ смогу́ сбро́сить с тебя́ шёлковое бельё, что́бы откры́ть напо́лненную до краёв, *(1)* великоле́пную / *(2)* замеча́тельную ро́скошь твоего́ прекра́сного, со́чного те́ла.
♦ **That** *(1)* **dress** / *(2)* **blouse** / *(3)* **nightgown reveals more than it conceals.** *(1)* Это пла́тье... / *(2)* Эта блу́зка... / *(3)* Эта ночна́я руба́шка... пока́зывает бо́льше, чем скрыва́ет.

revealing *adj (garments)* откры́тый, -ая, -ое, -ые ♦ **boldly ~ dress** де́рзкое откры́тое пла́тье ♦ **~ blouse** откры́тая блу́зка.

revel *vi* 1. *(enjoy, delight in)* наслажда́ться *(in what = instr.)*, упива́ться *(in what = instr.)*; весели́ться *(in what = + в + prep.)*; 2. *(feast, carouse)* пирова́ть *(in what = + в + prep.)*, кути́ть *(in what = + в + prep.)*.

> **revel:** *I revel in happiness*

I revel in the happiness I have found with you. Я пиру́ю в сча́стье, кото́рое нашёл *(ж: нашла́)* с тобо́й.

> **revel:** *I revel in your love*

I revel in the boundless luxury of your love. Я пиру́ю в беспреде́льной ро́скоши твое́й любви́.

> **revel:** *I want to revel in you*

I want to revel (forever) in the *(1)* **...sweetness of your** *(2)* **beautiful** / *(3)* **luscious body.** / *(4)* **...heavenly enchantment of your person.** Я хочу́ упива́ться (ве́чно) *(1)* ...сла́достью твоего́ *(2)* прекра́сного / *(3)* со́чного те́ла. / *(4)* ...небе́сным очарова́нием твое́й ли́чности. ♦ **How** *(1)* **wonderful** / *(2)* **heavenly it** *(3)* **...is...** / *(4)* **...would be.. to hold you in my arms and revel in the timeless expression of (human) love.** Как *(1)* удиви́тельно / *(2)* прекра́сно *(3)* *(nothing)* / *(4)* ...бы́ло бы... держа́ть тебя́ в объя́тиях и упива́ться бесконе́чным выраже́нием (челове́ческой) любви́. ♦ **I watch your mouth forming sounds, moving and undulating so supplely, so softly, so enticingly and I am seized with a raging impulse to fuse my own mouth together with it and once and for all revel in its sweet softness.** Я слежу́, как твой рот создаёт зву́ки, дви́гаясь и изгиба́ясь так ги́бко, так мя́гко, так соблазни́тельно, и я охва́чен бе́шеным и́мпульсом соедини́ть мой рот с твои́м, что́бы раз и навсегда́ пирова́ть в его́ сла́дкой не́жности. ♦ *(1)* **I want to...** / *(2)* **I'm going to... revel in the firm, creamy flesh of your full breasts.** *(1)* Я хочу́... / *(2)* Я бу́ду... упива́ться упру́гой, кре́мовой пло́тью твое́й по́лной груди́. ♦ **My entire being is** *(1)* **assailed** / *(2)* **tormented by the all-consuming need to take you in my arms and revel in the reservoir of your passion.** Я весь *(1)* охва́чен / *(2)* изму́чен всепоглоща́ющей жа́ждой заключи́ть тебя́ в объя́тия и упива́ться твое́й стра́стью.

> **revel:** *I will revel in you*

How my fingers will revel in the thickness of your dark hair. Как мои́ па́льцы бу́дут наслажда́ться в густоте́ твои́х тёмных воло́с. ♦ **When my lips and tongue revel on your beautiful, luscious body, they will hear your** *(1)* **moans** / *(2)* **screams of** *(3)* **pleasure** / *(4)* **ecstasy in South Africa.** Когда́ мои́ гу́бы и язы́к бу́дут упива́ться твои́м прекра́сным, со́чным те́лом, твои́ *(1)* сто́ны / *(2)* кри́ки *(3)* наслажде́ния / *(4)* экста́за бу́дут слышны́ в Ю́жной Африке.

> **revel:** *we'll revel in passion*

And every night we will reignite our passion and revel in our boundless, undiminishable love. И ка́ждую ночь мы бу́дем опя́ть зажига́ть на́шу страсть и пирова́ть в на́шей безграни́чной, неугаси́мой любви́.

revere *vt* 1. *(honor, respect)* почита́ть *(what, whom = acc.)*, чтить *(what, whom = acc.)*, уважа́ть *(what, whom = acc.)*; 2. *(hold dear)* дорожи́ть *(what, whom = instr.)* ♦ **I will always revere the memories of the** *(1)* **times** / *(2)* **moments we shared together.** Я всегда́

Counting things in Russian is a bit involved.
See Appendix 4, Numbers, on page 756 .

бу́ду дорожи́ть воспомина́ниями о *(1)* времена́х / *(2)* мину́тах, кото́рые мы проводи́ли вдвоём.

reverence *n* почте́ние; почти́тельность *f* ♦ **You have a face that instantly inspires reverence and adoration.** У тебя́ лицо́, кото́рое мгнове́нно внуша́ет уваже́ние и обожа́ние. ♦ **Your (precious) name reverberates** *(1)* **through /** *(2)* **in my thoughts like a sacred chant intoned in awed reverence.** Твоё (драгоце́нное) и́мя э́хом отзыва́ется *(1,2)* в мои́х мы́слях, как свяще́нная песнь, интони́рованная с благогове́йным почте́нием.

reverent *adj* почти́тельный, -ая, -ое, -ые ♦ **I gaze at your photo in reverent admiration.** Я вгля́дываюсь в твоё фо́то в почти́тельном восхище́нии.

reverently *adv* почти́тельно ♦ **I gaze reverently upon your angelic face (in your photo).** Я вгля́дываюсь почти́тельно в твоё а́нгельское лицо́ (на твое́й фотогра́фии). ♦ **My lips would reverently adore the graceful curve of your hips.** Мои́ гу́бы бу́дут почти́тельно обожа́ть грацио́зные изги́бы твои́х бёдер.

reverie *(or* **revery)** *n* 1. *(musing)* мечта́ние; мечта́тельность *f*; 2. *(dream)* мечта́, грёза; *(fantasy)* фанта́зия ♦ **pleasant** ~ прия́тная мечта́тельность ♦ **be lost in** *(1,2)* ~ погружа́ться / погрузи́ться в *(1)* мечты́ / *(2)* грёзы, мечта́ть.

revive *vt* восстана́вливать / восстанови́ть *(what = acc.)*; оживля́ть / оживи́ть *(what = acc.)* **I want so much to revive our relationship.** Я так стра́стно хочу́ восстанови́ть на́ши отноше́ния.

revolt *vt* вызыва́ть / вы́звать отвраще́ние *(whom = + у + gen.)* ♦ **I was revolted by what you** *(1)* **said /** *(2)* **suggested.** То, что ты *(1)* сказа́ла *(ж: сказа́л)* / *(2)* предложи́ла *(ж: предложи́л)*, вы́звало отвраще́ние во мне.

revolting *adj* отврати́тельный, -ая, -ое, -ые.

reward *vt* вознагражда́ть / вознагради́ть *(whom = acc., with what = instr.)* ♦ **What can I do to reward you?** Что я могу́ сде́лать, что́бы вознагради́ть тебя́? ♦ **When you give yourself to me, you're going to be rewarded with more pleasure than you ever dreamed of.** Когда́ ты отда́шься мне, ты бу́дешь вознаграждена́ таки́м наслажде́нием, о кото́ром не могла́ да́же мечта́ть.

reward *n* награ́да, вознагражде́ние ♦ **small** ~ ма́ленькая награ́д ♦ **give a** ~ вознагражда́ть / вознагради́ть *(to whom = acc.)*.

reward: *phrases*

I'm going to give you a nice reward for your sweet letter. Do you know what it is? Я хорошо́ вознагражу́ тебя́ за твоё не́жное письмо́. Ты зна́ешь как? ♦ **Your love is the only reward I ever want.** Твоя́ любо́вь - еди́нственная награ́да, кото́рую я хочу́. ♦ **Your reward will be a (tender) kiss.** Твое́й награ́дой бу́дет (не́жный) поцелу́й. ♦ **As a small reward, I'm going to give you five million kisses.** Как ма́ленькую награ́ду я подарю́ тебе́ пять миллио́нов поцелу́ев. ♦ **What would you like for a reward?** Что бы ты хоте́ла *(ж: хоте́л)* в награ́ду?

rhapsodical *adj* рапсоди́ческий, -ая, -ое, -ие.

rhapsodically *adv* рапсоди́чески.

rhapsody *n* рапсо́дия.

rhyme *n* ри́фма ♦ **no** ~ **or reason** нет никако́го смы́сла.

rhythm and blues *n* (му́зыка) «ритм и блюз».

rhythm *n* ритм.

ribbon *n* ле́нта ♦ **tie with a** ~ завяза́ть ле́нтой ♦ **with a** ~ **in your hair** с ле́нтой в волоса́х.

rice *n* рис ♦ **shower** ~ **on the bride and groom** *(after the wedding ceremony)* осыпа́ть / осы́пать жениха́ и неве́сту ри́сом *(по́сле бра́чной церемо́нии)* ♦ **throw** ~ **at the bride and groom** *(after the wedding ceremony)* осыпа́ть / осы́пать жениха́ и неве́сту ри́сом

Russian has 2 different vrbs for "go", one for "on foot" and the other for "by vehicle".

(по́сле бра́чной церемо́нии).

richness *n* 1. *(wealth)* бога́тство; 2. *(brightness)* я́ркость; 3. *(beauty)* красота́ ♦ **sensual ~** чу́вственность *f* ♦ **You add so much richness to my daily life.** Ты вно́сишь так мно́го красоты́ в мою́ повседне́вную жизнь. ♦ **You have such a sensual richness in your lips.** В твои́х губа́х така́я чу́вственность. ♦ **I am enthralled by the sensual richness in your lips.** Я очаро́ван чу́вственностью твои́х губ.

riddance *n*: ♦ **Good riddance!** Тем лу́чше!

ride *vi (often, round trips)* е́здить; *(one time & one direction)* е́хать / пое́хать ♦ **(Please) ride with me.** (Пожа́луйста,) Пое́дем со мной.

ride *n* прогу́лка; пое́здка ♦ **amusement park ~** аттракцио́н в (развлека́тельном) па́рке ♦ **boat ~** пое́здка на ло́дке ♦ **motorcycle ~s** пое́здки на мотоци́кле ♦ **give** *(1)* **me /** *(2)* **you a ~** подвезти́ *(1)* меня́ / *(2)* тебя́ ♦ **go for a ~** ката́ться / поката́ться.

ridiculous *adj* неле́пый, -ая-, ое, -ые, смехотво́рный, -ая-, ое, -ые ♦ **I** *(1)* **feel /** *(1)* **felt (**[3] **a little /** [4] **rather) ridiculous.** Я *(1)* чу́вствую / *(2)* чу́вствовал *(ж: чу́вствовала)* себя́ (*[3]* немно́го / *[4]* доста́точно) неле́по. ♦ **Don't be ridiculous!** Не глупи́! ♦ **That's** *(1-3)* **ridiculous.** Это *(1)* глу́по / *(2)* неле́по / *(3)* смешно́.

rift *n* раско́л, разры́в ♦ **What has caused this rift between us?** Что вы́звало э́тот разры́в ме́жду на́ми? ♦ **I feel that there's a rift between us (and I want with all my heart to close it).** Я чу́вствую э́ту про́пасть ме́жду на́ми (и хочу́ от всего́ се́рдца преодоле́ть ее). ♦ **There's a rift between us and we have to bridge it.** В на́ших отноше́ниях появи́лась тре́щина, и нам на́до заде́лать её.

right *adj* 1. *(correct)* пра́вильный, -ая, -ое, -ые; 2. *(suitable, fitting)* подходя́щий, -ая, -ее, -ие; *(deserving)* заслу́живающий, -ая, -ее, -ие; 3. *(opposite of left)* пра́вый, -ая, -ое, -ые.

right: *phrases*

I have so much love in my heart to give to the right person. And I really have the feeling that this right person is you. В моём се́рдце так мно́го любви́, кото́рую я хочу́ подари́ть заслу́живающему её челове́ку. И я определённо чу́вствую, что э́тот челове́к ты. ♦ **I'm looking for** *(1)* **Miss /** *(2)* **Mr. Right.** Я ищу́ *(1)* ...подходя́щую спу́тницу... / *(2)* ...подходя́щего спу́тника... жи́зни. ♦ **I'm looking for Ms. Right.** Я ищу́ подходя́щую для меня́ же́нщину. ♦ **Deep down in my heart I know that this is (not) right.** В глубине́ се́рдца я зна́ю, что э́то (не) пра́вильно. ♦ **I'm sorry to tell you this, but I just don't think you're the right person for me.** Извини́ за то, что скажу́ тебе́ э́то, но мне не ка́жется, что ты подходя́щий челове́к для меня́. ♦ **Are you all right?** Ты в поря́дке? ♦ **I'm all right.** Я в по́лном поря́дке.

right *n* пра́во ♦ **have the ~** име́ть пра́во ♦ **not have the ~** не име́ть пра́ва.

right-handed *adj* праворукий, -ая, -ое, -ие.

right winger *n* челове́к «пра́вых» взгля́дов.

rigid *adj* 1. *(hard, inflexible)* жёсткий, -ая, -ое, -ие, твёрдый, -ая, -ое, -ые; 2. *(strict)* стро́гий, -ая, -ое, -ие; 3. *(tense)* напряжён, напряжена́, -о́, -ы́ *(short forms)*.

ring *n* кольцо́ ♦ **beautiful ~** краси́вое кольцо́ ♦ **bellybutton ~** кольцо́ на пупке́ ♦ **betrothal ~** обруча́льное кольцо́ ♦ **cheap ~** дешёвое кольцо́ ♦ **diamond ~** *(1 diamond)* кольцо́ с бриллиа́нтом; *(more than 1)* кольцо́ с бриллиа́нтами ♦ **elegant ~** изя́щное кольцо́ ♦ **engagement ~** обруча́льное кольцо́ ♦ **expensive ~** дорого́е кольцо́ ♦ **gold ~** золото́е кольцо́ ♦ **hollow ~** ду́тое кольцо́ ♦ **lip ~** кольцо́ для губ ♦ **navel ~** кольцо́ на пупке́ ♦ **plain ~** просто́е кольцо́ ♦ **pledge ~** обруча́льное кольцо́ ♦ **silver ~** сере́бряное кольцо́ ♦ **simple ~** просто́е кольцо́ ♦ **thin ~** то́нкое кольцо́ ♦ **tongue ~** кольцо́ для языка́ ♦ **wedding ~** *(Russia, commonly)* обруча́льное кольцо́; *(America, with 2-ring set)* сва́дебное кольцо́ ♦ **wide ~** широ́кое кольцо́.

Dipthongs in Russian are made by adding й
*to the end of a vowel (*а, е, ё, о, у, э, ю, *and* я).

ring: *verb terms*

buy a ~ покупа́ть / купи́ть кольцо́ ♦ **exchange ~s** обме́ниваться / обменя́ться ко́льцами ♦ **give a** ~ дари́ть / подари́ть кольцо́ *(to whom = dat.)* ♦ **give back a** ~ верну́ть кольцо́ *(to whom = dat.)* ♦ **put the ~ on your finger** надева́ть / наде́ть кольцо́ на твой па́лец ♦ **take off a** ~ снима́ть / снять кольцо́ ♦ **wear a** ~ носи́ть кольцо́.

ring: *other terms*

inscription on a ~ на́дпись на кольце́ ♦ **~ size** разме́р кольца́.

ring: *phrases*

This ring is a symbol of our *(1)* **enduring** / *(2)* **everlasting love**. Это кольцо́ - си́мвол на́шей *(1)* дли́тельной / *(2)* ве́чной любви́. ♦ **This ring is a promise of my (**[1]**enduring** / **[2] eternal** / **[3] unending) love for you**. Это кольцо́ -- зало́г мое́й (*[1]* про́чной / *[2]* ве́чной / *[3]* несконча́емой) любви́ к тебе́. ♦ **We'll exchange rings**. Мы обменя́емся ко́льцами. ♦ **It will be the happiest day of my life when I** *(1)* **put** / *(2)* **slide a ring on your finger**. День, когда́ я *(1,2)* наде́ну тебе́ на па́лец кольцо́, бу́дет счастли́вейшим в мое́й жи́зни. ♦ **As soon as possible I** *(1)* **intend** / *(2)* **want to put a ring on your finger**. Как мо́жно скоре́е я *(1)* наме́рен / *(2)* хочу́ наде́ть кольцо́ на твой па́лец. ♦ **I hope the ring isn't too** *(1)* **small** / *(2)* **big for you**. Я наде́юсь, что кольцо́ не (сли́шком) *(1)* мало́ / *(2)* велико́ тебе́. ♦ **The ring is too** *(1)* **small** / *(2)* **big for me**. Кольцо́ (сли́шком) *(1)* мало́ / *(2)* велико́ мне.

ringlet (of hair) *n* завито́к (воло́с).

ripple *vi* журча́ть ♦ **With my lips I'm going to make tingling sensations ripple all through your body**. Мои́ гу́бы вы́зовут во́лны тре́пета, бегу́щие по всему́ твоему́ те́лу.

ripples *n, pl (hair)* волни́стость *f* ♦ **What pure pleasure it would be to run my hands through the abundant flowing ripples of your hair**. Каки́м и́стинным наслажде́нием бы́ло бы пробежа́ть рука́ми че́рез оби́льную струя́щуюся волни́стость твои́х воло́с. ♦ **I love to run my hand through the abundant flowing ripples of your hair**. Я люблю́ погружа́ть ру́ки в оби́льную струя́щуюся волни́стость твои́х воло́с.

riser *n:* ♦ **I'm an early riser**. Я встаю́ ра́но.

risk *vt* рискова́ть *(what = instr.)* ♦ **I don't want to risk losing you**. Я не хочу́ рискова́ть поте́рей тебя́.

risk *n* риск ♦ **Take a risk on me**. Рискни́ со мной. ♦ **It's a (big) risk**. Это (большо́й) риск. ♦ **It's too much of a risk**. Сли́шком мно́го ри́ска. ♦ *(1,2)* **I'm willing to take the risk**. *(1)* Я охо́тно рискну́. / *(2)* Я гото́в *(ж: гото́ва)* рискова́ть. ♦ **I don't want to take the risk**. Я не хочу́ рискова́ть. ♦ **Don't worry, there's no risk (involved)**. Не беспоко́йся, нет никако́го ри́ска. ♦ **There's too much of a risk without a condom**. Сли́шком риско́ванно без презервати́ва.

risky *adj* риско́ванный, -ая, -ое, -ые ♦ **It's too risky (without a condom)**. Сли́шком риско́ванно (без презервати́ва).

risque *adj* риско́ванный, -ая, -ое, -ые.

ritual *n* ритуа́л ♦ **boy-meets-girl ~** ритуа́л знако́мства ю́ноши и де́вушки ♦ **courting ~** ритуа́л уха́живания ♦ **I am so grateful to you for initiating me into this sweet, intoxicating ritual of love**. Я так благода́рен *(ж: благода́рна)* тебе́ за то, что ты познако́мила *(ж: познако́мил)* меня́ со сла́дким, опьяня́ющим ритуа́лом любви́.

rival *n* сопе́рник, сопе́рница ♦ **Believe me, you have no rival in my life**. Верь мне, что в мое́й жи́зни у тебя́ нет сопе́рницы *(ж: сопе́рника)*.

river *n* река́ ♦ *(1,2)* **~s of (molten) honey** *(1)* ре́ки / *(2)* пото́ки (распла́вленного) мёда.

roadtrip *n* путеше́ствие на маши́не.

roam *vi (wander)* броди́ть; *(travel)* путеше́ствовать ♦ **My lips will roam hungrily across**

Some phrases are listed under more than one main word.

your cheek, your neck, your shoulders... Мои голо́дные гу́бы бу́дут путеше́ствовать по твои́м щека́м, ше́е, плеча́м...

robbed *pp:* ♦ ~ **of strength** расслабленный, -ая, -ое, -ые.

robust *adj* кре́пкий, -ая, -ое, -ие, си́льный, -ая, -ое, -ые, дю́жий, -ая, -ее, -ие.

robustly *adv* кре́пко.

rock *vt* 1. *(shake up)* трясти́ / тряхну́ть *(what, whom = acc.),* потряса́ть / потрясти́ *(what, whom = acc.)*; 2. *(back and forth)* кача́ть / качну́ть *(what, whom = acc.)* ♦ **You rock my world.** Ты сотрясла́ *(ж: сотря́с)* мой мир.

rock *n* ка́мень *m* ♦ **You are my rock.** Ты моя́ опо́ра. ♦ **You are the rock in my life.** Ты опо́ра мое́й жи́зни. ♦ **Our marriage is on the rocks.** Наш брак разва́ливается. ♦ **Our relationship is on the rocks.** На́ши отноше́ния разва́ливаются. ·

rock climbing *n* скалола́зание.

rocket *vi* 1. *(rocket)* взлета́ть / взлете́ть; 2. *(pulse)* учаща́ться / участи́ться ♦ **My pulse just rockets when** *(1)* **...I get close to you.** / *(2)* **...you do that (to me).** / *(3)* **...I look at your beautiful face (and beautiful body).** Мой пульс то́тчас учаща́ется, как то́лько *(1)* ...я ока́зываюсь ря́дом с тобо́й. / *(2)* ...ты де́лаешь э́то (со мной). / *(3)* ...я взгляну́ на твоё прекра́сное лицо́ (и те́ло).

rocketed *adj* запу́щен, -а, -о, -ы *(short forms)* ♦ **I want to fill your body with so much pleasure that you will be rocketed into a cosmos of exploding ecstasy.** Я хочу́ запо́лнить твоё те́ло таки́м огро́мным наслажде́нием, что́бы ты была́ запу́щена в ко́смос взрыва́ющегося экста́за.

rock-n-roll *n* рок-н-ролл.

roil *vi* рои́ться ♦ **Every night my dreams roil in the most torrid scenes of passionate / erotic desire for your sweet, warm, wonderful womanness.** Ка́ждую ночь в мои́х снах ро́ятся са́мые зно́йные сце́ны стра́стного / эроти́ческого вожделе́ния к твое́й сла́дкой, тёплой, великоле́пной же́нственности.

role *n* роль *f* ♦ **big** ~ больша́я роль ♦ **central** ~ центра́льная роль ♦ **difficult** ~ тру́дная роль ♦ **leading** ~ гла́вная роль ♦ **main** ~ гла́вная роль ♦ **new** ~ но́вая роль ♦ **secondary** ~ второстепе́нная роль ♦ **unfamiliar** ~ незнако́мая роль ♦ **play a** ~ игра́ть роль ♦ **I don't want to play a secondary role (in your life).** Я не хочу́ игра́ть второстепе́нную роль (в твое́й жи́зни).

roll *vi* кати́ться ♦ ~ **in the hay** *(slang)* занима́ться любо́вью ♦ **I'd love to roll in the hay with you.** Я хоте́л бы заня́ться любо́вью с тобо́й. ♦ **We could spend the whole** *(1)* **day** / *(2)* **week rolling around in bed.** Мы могли́ бы провести́ *(1)* ...весь день... / *(2)* ...всю неде́лю... в посте́ли.

rollerblade *vi* ката́ться на ро́ликах (с одни́м по́лозом) ♦ **I'll teach you how to rollerblade.** Я научу́ тебя́, как ката́ться на однопо́лозных ро́ликах.

rollerblader *n:* ♦ **be a** ~ ката́ться на ро́ликах (на одно́м по́лозе). ♦ **I'm a rollerblader.** Я ката́юсь на ро́ликах (с одни́м по́лозом).

rollerblading *n* ката́ние на ро́ликах (с одни́м по́лозом) ♦ **I go rollerblading often.** Я ча́сто ката́юсь на однопо́лозных ро́ликах. ♦ **Would you like to go rollerblading (with me)?** Не хоте́ла *(ж: хоте́л)* бы ты поката́ться на ро́ликах (со мной)? ♦ **Let's go rollerblading (together).** Дава́й поката́емся на ро́ликах (вме́сте).

roller-skate *vi* ката́ться на ро́ликах ♦ **Do you know how to roller-skate?** Ты уме́ешь ката́ться на ро́ликах?

roller-skating *n* ката́ние на ро́ликах.

roly-poly *adj (slang)* по́лный, -ая, -ое, -ые.

romance *vt* уха́живать *(whom = + за + instr.),* волочи́ться *(whom = + за + instr.)* ♦ **No one**

The singular past tense of Russian verbs ends in -л (m) (usually), -ла (f) or -ло (n). the plural past tense ends in -li.

has ever romanced me the way you have. Никто́ ещё не уха́живал за мной так, как ты. ♦ **I think you're *(1,2)* romancing someone else.** Я ду́маю, что ты *(1)* уха́живаешь / *(2)* волочи́шься за ке́м-то ещё. ♦ **I want to be romanced.** Я хочу́ быть люби́мым *(ж: люби́мой)*.

romance *n* 1. *(affair)* рома́н; 2. *(story)* любо́вная исто́рия, рома́н; 3. *(romantic quality)* рома́нтика ♦ **e-mail** ~ рома́н по электро́нной по́чте ♦ **enduring** ~ бессме́ртный рома́н ♦ **extracurricular** ~ рома́н на стороне́ ♦ **old-fashioned** ~ старомо́дный рома́н ♦ **online** ~ рома́н на интерне́те ♦ **potential** ~ возмо́жный рома́н ♦ ~ **on the rebound** рома́н-рикоше́том, но́вый рома́н сра́зу же по́сле оконча́ния предыду́щего ♦ **tragic** ~ траги́ческий рома́н ♦ **year-round** ~ круглогоди́чный рома́н.

─────────────────
romance: *verb terms*
─────────────────
pursue ~ иска́ть рома́нтику ♦ **start a** ~ заводи́ть / завести́ рома́н, начина́ть / нача́ть рома́н.

─────────────────
romance: *phrases*
─────────────────
I know that our romance will flourish till the end of our days. Я зна́ю, что наш рома́н бу́дет цвести́ до конца́ на́ших дней. ♦ **The spirit of romance floats in the air.** Дух рома́нтики вита́ет в во́здухе. ♦ **A week together in Hawaii! That sounds like a marvelous recipe for romance.** Неде́ля вме́сте на Гава́йях! Это звучи́т, как изуми́тельный сюже́т для рома́на. ♦ **My idea of romance is...** Моё представле́ние о рома́нтике -- ... ♦ *(1)* **This** / *(2)* **That is not my idea of romance.** *(1,2)* Это не моё представле́ние о рома́нтике. ♦ *(1)* **I'm afraid...** / *(2)* **I think...** / *(3)* **It seems like... our romance has gone** *(4)* **awry** / *(5,6)* **sour.** *(1)* Я бою́сь,... / *(2)* Я ду́маю,... / *(3)* Ка́жется,... наш рома́н *(4)* ...зашёл в тупи́к. / *(5)* ...скис. / *(6)* ...не уда́лся. ♦ **The romance (in our** *[1]* **relationship** / *[2]* **marriage) is dead.** Нет бо́льше рома́нтики (*[1]*...в на́ших отноше́ниях. / *[2]* ...в на́шем бра́ке.).

romantic *adj* романти́ческий, -ая, -ое, -ие ♦ **highly** ~ чрезвыча́йно романти́ческий, -ая, -ое, -ие ♦ **hopelessly** ~ безнадёжно романти́ческий, -ая, -ое, -ие ♦ **I'm wildly romantic.** Я -- стра́стный рома́нтик ♦ **I'm (one of these people who is) hopelessly romantic.** Я-- (оди́н из тех, кто) безнадёжный рома́нтик. ♦ **I'm (very) romantic at heart.** Се́рдцем я --(большо́й) рома́нтик.

romantic *n* рома́нтик ♦ **I'm a hopeless romantic.** Я безнаде́жный рома́нтик. ♦ **I'm a romantic at heart.** Се́рдцем я рома́нтик.

romanticize *vt* романтизи́ровать *(what = acc.)*, представля́ть / предста́вить в идеализи́рованном ви́де *(what = acc.)*.

romp *vi* вози́ться / провози́ться ♦ **We can romp in the sack all weekend long.** Мы мо́жем провози́ться в посте́ли все выходны́е.

romp *n* возня́ ♦ **I don't just want a romp in the** *(1)* **hay** / *(2)* **sack (with you).** Я не хочу́ то́лько *(1,2)* посте́ли (с тобо́й).

room *n* 1. *(in a building)* ко́мната; 2. *(space)* ме́сто ♦ *(1)* **adjacent** / *(2)* **adjoining** ~s *(1,2)* сме́жные ко́мнаты ♦ **chat** ~ страни́ца на интерне́те, по кото́рой лю́ди мо́гут разгова́ривать друг с дру́гом, посыла́я электро́нные сообще́ния друг дру́гу *(explanation)* ♦ ~ **for one (person)** *(hotel)* но́мер на одного́ ♦ ~ **for two** *(hotel)* но́мер на двои́х ♦ **hotel** ~ но́мер ♦ **quiet** ~ *(hotel)* ти́хий но́мер ♦ ~ **with a** *(1)* **bathroom** / *(2)* **shower** *(hotel)* но́мер с *(1)* ва́нной / *(2)* ду́шем.

roomie *n (slang) (sharing an apartment)* сосе́д *m* / сосе́дка *f* по кварти́ре; *(sharing a room)* сосе́д *m* / сосе́дка *f* по ко́мнате.

roommate *n (apartment)* сосе́д *m* / сосе́дка *f* по кварти́ре; *(room)* сосе́д *m* / сосе́дка *f* по ко́мнате.

Please do us a favor:
Fill out and mail in the Feedback Sheet on page 795.

ropes: ♦ *(1)* **I can show you... /** *(2)* **You can show me... the ropes.** *(1)* Я могу́ ввести́ тебя́... / *(2)* Ты мо́жешь ввести́ меня́... (по́лностью) в курс де́ла.

rose *n* ро́за ♦ **beautiful** ~ прекра́сная ро́за ♦ **deep red** ~ тёмно-кра́сная ро́за ♦ **bouquet of** ~**s** буке́т роз ♦ **dozen** ~**s** дю́жина роз.

rose: phrases

The fragrance of you is like the breath of roses. Твой арома́т как дыха́ние роз. ♦ **If I had the money, I would send you a dozen red roses everyday.** Е́сли бы у меня́ бы́ли де́ньги, я бы посыла́л тебе́ дю́жину кра́сных роз ка́ждый день. ♦ **You are the rose that never** *(1)* **dies /** *(2)* **fades.** Ты ро́за, кото́рая никогда́ не *(1)* умрёт / *(2)* увя́нет. ♦ **The fragrance of roses eminates from your soul.** Твоя́ душа́ благоуха́ет ро́зами. ♦ **You are as close to perfection as a rose.** Ты так же близка́ к соверше́нству, как ро́за. ♦ **"One rose, one tender thought of you."** *Movie: "Darling Lily"* «Одна́ ро́за, одна́ не́жная мысль о тебе́.» *Фильм «Дорога́я Лили́».*

rosy-cheeked *adj* розовощёкий, -ая, -ое, -ие, румя́ный, -ая, -ое, -ые.

rotund *adj (plump)* пу́хлый, -ая, -ое, -ые.

rotundity *n* пу́хлость *f.*

roué распу́тник ♦ **old** ~ ста́рый распу́тник.

rouge *n* румя́на.

rough it *vi* жить без удо́бств, терпе́ть лише́ния ♦ **I love roughing it.** Мне нра́вится жить без удо́бств. ♦ **I'm not afraid to rough it.** Я не бою́сь жить без удо́бств. ♦ **We'll have to rough it** *(1)* **...in the beginning. /** *(2)* **...for a while.** Мы должны́ бу́дем жить без удо́бств *(1)* ...в нача́ле. / *(2)* ...не́которое вре́мя.

round *adj* окру́глый, -ая, -ое, -ые ♦ **You're soft and round in all the right places.** Ты мя́гкая и окру́глая во всех ну́жных места́х.

round *n (drinks)* круг, по кру́гу.

roundness *n* окру́глость *f* ♦ **exciting** ~ **of your hips** волну́ющая окру́глость твои́х бёдер ♦ **I dream of** *(1)* **feeling /** *(2)* **caressing the soft roundness of your breasts.** Я мечта́ю *(1)* чу́вствовать / *(2)* ласка́ть мя́гкую окру́глость твое́й груди́.

rouse *vt* буди́ть / пробуди́ть *(what, whom = acc.),* пробужда́ть / пробуди́ть *(what, whom = acc.),* будора́жить / взбудора́жить *(what = acc.)* ♦ **My lips will rouse flames of** *(1)* **desire /** *(2)* **passion to leap from your soul and surge through your veins.** Мои́ гу́бы пробу́дят пла́мя *(1)* жела́ния / *(2)* стра́сти, кото́рое бу́дет бушева́ть в тебе́ и струи́ться в ве́нах.

routine *n* рути́на ♦ **daily** ~ повседне́вные дела́ ♦ **stale** ~ однообра́зная рути́на ♦ **We've gotten locked into a stale routine.** Мы завя́зли в однообра́зной рути́не. ♦ **Our marriage has become a stale routine.** Наш брак стал однообра́зной рути́ной. ♦ **I never want for our relationship to become a stale routine.** Я не хочу́, что́бы на́ши отноше́ния ста́ли бу́дничной рути́ной.

roving *adj* блужда́ющий, -ая, -ее, -ие ♦ **My roving lips will uncover your most precious secret.** Мои́ блужда́ющие гу́бы раскро́ют твой са́мый заве́тный секре́т.

RSVP *abbrev* = **Repondez s'il vous plait.** *(French: Please reply.)* Про́сьба отве́тить.

rub *vt* тере́ть *(what = acc.);* потира́ть / потере́ть *(what = acc.);* растира́ть / растере́ть *(what = acc.)* ♦ ~ **the wrong way** гла́дить про́тив ше́рсти *(whom = acc.)* ♦ ~ **it in** растравля́ть / растрави́ть ра́ну ♦ **I'll rub your** *(1)* **back /** *(2)* **neck.** Я бу́ду растира́ть тебе́ *(1)* спи́ну / *(2)* ше́ю. ♦ **We can rub each other with soap.** Мы мо́жем намы́лить друг дру́га.

rub *vi* тере́ться / потере́ться *(against what, whom = + о + acc.)* ♦ **When you rub against me like that, it makes me hot all over.** Меня́ всего́ *(ж: всю)* броса́ет в жар, когда́ ты трёшься о меня́, как сейча́с. ♦ **I love to kiss, hug, caress, touch, hold hands, nibble, cuddle, rub against, stroke — you just name it.** Я люблю́ целова́ть, обнима́ть, ласка́ть,

---

Clock and calender time are discussed in Appendix 5, page 759.

касаться, держаться за́ руки, поку́сывать, сжима́ть в объя́тиях, тере́ться, гла́дить - - ты то́лько назови́.

rub *n* натира́ние, растира́ние; масса́ж, масси́рование ♦ **back** ~ масса́ж спины́ ♦ **candle-lit back** ~ масси́рование спины́ при свеча́х ♦ **sensual back** ~ чу́вственный масса́ж спины́.

rubber *n (slang)* презервати́в.

rubdown *n* масса́ж ♦ **sensual** ~ чу́вственный масса́ж.

rubenesque *adj* ру́бенсовский, -ая, -ое, -ие ♦ **I really love a rubenesque figure.** Мне о́чень нра́вится ру́бенсовская фигу́ра. ♦ **I** *(1)* **love /** *(2)* **adore your rubenesque** *(3)* **figure /** *(4)* **body.** Я *(1)* люблю́ / *(2)* обожа́ю *(3)* ...твою́ ру́бенсовскую фигу́ру. / *(4)* ...твоё ру́бенсовское те́ло.

ruin *vt* по́ртить / испо́ртить *(what = acc.)* ♦ **You've (completely) ruined our relationship.** Ты (по́лностью) испо́ртила *(ж: испо́ртил)* на́ши отноше́ния. ♦ **I don't want to ruin our relationship.** Я не хочу́ испо́ртить на́ши отноше́ния.

rule *n* пра́вило ♦ **as a** ~ как пра́вило ♦ **I'm the kind of person who believes in playing by the rules.** Я тот челове́к, кото́рый ве́рит в игру́ по пра́вилам.

rumba *vi* танцева́ть ру́мбу.

rumba *n* ру́мба.

rumor *n* слух, молва́ ♦ **If you hear a rumor that I love you, it's true.** Е́сли до тебя́ дошёл слух, что я люблю́ тебя́, так э́то пра́вда. ♦ **That's just a(n)** (*[1]* **empty /** *[2]* **stupid /** *[3]* **malicious) rumor.** Э́то про́сто (*[1]* пусто́й / *[2]* глу́пый / *[3]* зло́бный) слух. ♦ **Don't listen to** *(1,2)* **rumors.** Не слу́шай *(1)* слу́хов / *(2)* спле́тен. ♦ **Rumors have been** *(1)* **...circulating. /** *(2)* **...going around.** Слу́хи *(1)* распространя́лись / *(2)* ходи́ли.

rump *n (slang) (buttocks)* по́па; *(little)* по́пка.

rumple *vt* взъеро́шить *(what = acc.)* ♦ **I want to rumple your hair — in bed.** Я хочу́ взъеро́шить тебе́ во́лосы в посте́ли.

rumpled *adj* 1. *(hair)* взъеро́шенный, -ая, -ое, -ые; 2. *(clothes)* измя́тый, -ая, -ое, -ые, жёваный, -ая, -ое, -ые.

run *vt* пробега́ть / пробежа́ть *(what = instr., up / down what = + по + dat.)* ♦ **I love it when you run your hand up and down my spine.** Мне нра́вится, когда́ ты пробега́ешь руко́й вверх и вниз по моему́ позвоно́чнику. ♦ **I** *(1)* **love /** *(2)* **want to run my hand up and down your spine.** Я *(1)* люблю́ / *(2)* хочу́ пробега́ть руко́й вверх и вниз по твоему́ позвоно́чнику. ♦ **The way it is with you, you run hot one day and cold the next.** С тобо́й так, оди́н день ты горяча́ как пла́мень, друго́й - холодна́ как лёд.

run *vi (repeatedly, around)* бе́гать; *(one direction, one time)* бежа́ть / побежа́ть ♦ ~ **away** *vi* убега́ть / убежа́ть, оставля́ть / оста́вить *(from whom = acc.)*, покида́ть / покину́ть *(from whom = acc.)* ♦ **You're not going to** *(1,2)* **run away from me anymore.** Ты бо́льше не *(1)* оста́вишь / *(2)* поки́нешь меня́.

runner *n* бегу́н.

running *n* бе́ганье.

rush *vt* торопи́ть / поторопи́ть *(what, whom = acc.)* ♦ **I don't think we should rush things.** Я не ду́маю, что мы должны́ торопи́ть собы́тия. ♦ **Don't you think we're rushing this too much?** Не ду́маешь ли ты, что мы сли́шком э́то торо́пим? ♦ **Is there any way we can rush this?** Существу́ет ли путь уско́рить э́то?

rush *vi* 1. *(hurry)* спеши́ть, торопи́ться; 2. *(dash)* броса́ться / бро́ситься ♦ ~ **into your arms** броса́ться / бро́ситься тебе́ в объя́тия.

rush *n* 1. *(hurry)* спе́шка; 2. *(surge)* поры́в, бросо́к; прили́в ♦ **in a** ~ в спе́шке ♦ **What a rush it was!** Как э́то взволнова́ло! ♦ **I feel such a (tremendous) rush of excitement**

Reflexive verbs are those that end in -ся or -сь.
The -ся or -сь also goes onto a past tense ending.

every time I think of you. Меня́ охва́тывает тако́е (огро́мное) возбужде́ние вся́кий раз, когда́ я ду́маю о тебе́. ♦ **Whenever I even think of you, I get a warm, sensuous rush all through my body.** Вся́кий раз, когда́ я ду́маю о тебе́, я ощуща́ю тёплый, чу́вственный прили́в во всём те́ле.

rushed *adj (Russian uses verb* торопи́ть*)* ♦ **I don't want you to feel rushed.** Я не хочу́, чтобы ты чу́вствовала, что я тороплю́ тебя́. ♦ **I feel kind of rushed.** Я чу́вствую, что меня́ торо́пят.

Russia *n* Росси́я ♦ **from** ~ из Росси́и ♦ **in** ~ в Росси́и ♦ **to** ~ в Росси́ю.

Russian *adj* ру́сский, -ая, -ое, -ие.

Russian *n* 1. *(person)* ру́сский *m*, ру́сская *f (pl:* ру́сские*)*; 2. *(language)* ру́сский язы́к ♦ **know** ~ знать ру́сский язы́к ♦ **read** ~ чита́ть по-ру́сски ♦ **speak (a little bit of)** ~ говори́ть (немно́го) по-ру́сски ♦ **understand (a little bit of)** ~ понима́ть (немно́го) по-ру́сски ♦ **write** ~ писа́ть по-ру́сски.

ruthless *adj* безжа́лостный, -ая, -ое, -ые.

ruthlessness *n* безжа́лостность *f.*

RV *abbrev* = **recreational vehicle** жило́й автофурго́н (для о́тдыха), да́ча на колёсах ♦ **We can go for long trips together in my RV.** Мы смо́жем пое́хать в дли́тельные путеше́ствия в моём автофурго́не.

The time zones for many cities of the world are given in Appendix 6, page 761.

S

sabotage *vt* расша́тывать / расшата́ть *(what = acc.)*; разруша́ть / разру́шить *(what = acc.)*
  ♦ **Your behavior has sabotaged our relationship.** Твоё поведе́ние разру́шило на́ши отноше́ния. ♦ *(1)* **He /** *(2)* **She is trying to sabotage our relationship.** *(1)* Он / *(2)* Она́ пыта́ется разру́шить на́ши отноше́ния.

sachet *n* саше́, сухи́е духи́ ♦ **lavender** ~ лава́ндовое саше́.

sack *n (slang) (bed)* посте́ль *f* ♦ **I'd love to** *(1)* **hop /** *(2)* **jump in the sack with you.** Я бы хоте́л *(1,2)* пры́гнуть в посте́ль с тобо́й. ♦ **We can romp in the sack all weekend long.** Мы мо́жем провози́ться в посте́ли все выходны́е.

sacred *adj* свяще́нный, -ая, -ое, -ые ♦ **Our love is special and sacred.** На́ша любо́вь осо́бая и свяще́нная.

sacrifice *vt* же́ртвовать / поже́ртвовать *(what, whom = instr., for what, whom = + ра́ди + gen.)* ♦ ~ **everything** же́ртвовать / поже́ртвовать всем ♦ ~ **nothing** ниче́м не же́рт-вовать / поже́ртвовать.

sacrifice *n* же́ртва ♦ **any** ~ люба́я же́ртва ♦ **big** ~ больша́я же́ртва ♦ **great** ~ больша́я же́ртва ♦ **tremendous** ~ огро́мная же́ртва.

sad *adj* печа́льный, -ая, -ое, -ые, гру́стный, -ая, -ое, -ые ♦ **I'm sad to tell you this.** Мне тяжело́ сказа́ть тебе́ э́то. ♦ **I** *(1)* **feel /** *(2)* **felt so sad.** Я *(1)* чу́вствую / *(2)* чу́вствовал *(ж: чу́вствовала)* таку́ю печа́ль. ♦ **I'm sorry I've made you sad.** Извини́, что опеча́-лил *(ж: опеча́лила)* тебя́. ♦ *(1,2)* **I want nothing sad to pass from me to you.** Я не хочу́ *(1)* ...никаки́х печа́лей тебе́ принести́. / *(2)* ...ниче́м опеча́лить тебя́.

saddled *adj* осёдлан, -а, -о, -ы, обременён, обременена́, -о́, -ы́ *(short forms)* ♦ **I don't want to be saddled with** *(1)* **...a wife and kids. /** *(2)* **...a lot of responsibilities.** Я не хочу́ быть обременён *(1)* ...жено́й и детьми́. / *(2)* ...мно́жеством обя́занностей. ♦ **I'm saddled with an empty, humdrum marriage.** Я обременён *(ж: обременена́)* пусты́м, одно-обра́зным бра́ком.

sadly *adv* печа́льно, гру́стно; *(unfortunately)* к сожале́нию, к несча́стью.

sadness *n* печа́ль *f*, грусть *f*.

safe *adj* безопа́сный, -ая, -ое, -ые ♦ **Quit playing it safe!** Прекрати́ осторо́жную игру́!

safely *adv* безопа́сно.

sagacious *adj* проница́тельный, -ая, -ое, -ые; благоразу́мный, -ая, -ое, -ые, здравомы́с-лящий, -ая, -ее, -ие.

Sagittarius *(Nov. 22 - Dec. 21)* Стреле́ц *(22 ноября́ - 21 декабря́)*.

Common adult heights are given in Appendix 9, page 776.

sail *vi* ката́ться на *(1)* (па́русной) ло́дке / *(2)* я́хте.

sailboat *n* па́русная ло́дка, я́хта.

sailing *n* пла́вание под паруса́ми, ката́ние на (па́русной) ло́дке / я́хте ♦ **We can go sailing together.** Мы мо́жем вме́сте поката́ться на (па́русной) ло́дке. ♦ **Would you like to go sailing (with me)?** Не хоте́ла *(ж: хоте́л)* бы ты поплы́ть на я́хте (со мной)?

saint *n* свято́й ♦ **I'll behave like a saint, I promise.** Я бу́ду вести́ себя́ как свято́й, я обеща́ю.

Saint Valentine *n* свято́й Валенти́н.

Saint Valentine's Day *n* день свято́го Валенти́на *(14-ое февраля́, пра́здник влюблённых)*

sake *n (Japanese rice wine)* саке́, япо́нская ри́совая во́дка.

salacious *adj* 1. *(indecent, lewd, obscene)* непристо́йный, -ая, -ое, -ые, скабрёзный, -ая, -ое, -ые; 2. *(lecherous, lewd)* распу́тный, -ая, -ое, -ые, развра́тный, -ая, -ое, -ые; *(lustful)* похотли́вый, -ая, -ое, -ые.

salt of the earth *n* соль земли́ ♦ **You'll like my father. He's a salt-of-the-earth kind of guy.** Тебе́ понра́вится мой оте́ц. Он из тех, кото́рых называ́ют «соль земли́».

salubrious *adj (healthful)* здоро́вый, -ая, -ое, -ые; целе́бный, -ая, -ое, -ые.

same *adj* тот же (са́мый), та же (са́мая), то же (са́мое), те же (са́мые), одина́ковый, -ая, -ое, -ые.

same *n* то же са́мое ♦ **feel the ~** чу́вствовать то же са́мое.

sanctimonious *adj* ха́нжеский, -ая, -ое, -ие.

sand *n* песо́к ♦ **I'm a person who loves sun, surf and sand.** Я челове́к, лю́бящий со́лнце, прибо́й и песо́к.

sandals *n, pl* санда́лии, босоно́жки ♦ **high-heeled** *(1,2)* **~s** *(1)* санда́лии / *(2)* босоно́жки на высо́ких каблука́х ♦ **stiletto ~s** босоно́жки на то́нком каблуке́ ♦ **strappy ~s** босоно́жки с ремешка́ми.

sane *adj* норма́льный, -ая, -ые ♦ **questionably ~** сомни́тельно норма́льный, -ая, -ые.

sangfroid *n* самооблада́ние, хладнокро́вие.

sanguine *adj (optimistic)* оптимисти́чный, -ая, -ое, -ые.

sans *prep* без ♦ *(1)* **I want to behold...** / *(2)* **How I dream of beholding... all of your (exquisite) beauty sans clothes.** *(1)* Я хочу́... / *(2)* Как я мечта́ю... созерца́ть всю твою́ (изы́сканную) красоту́ без оде́жды.

sans pareil *(French: without parallel)* несравне́нен, несравне́нна, -о, -ы, беспдо́бен, беспдо́бна, -о, -ы *(short forms)* ♦ **Your loveliness is** *(1,2)* **sans pareil.** Твоя́ красота́ *(1)* несравне́нна / *(2)* беспдо́бна.

sarcasm *n* сарка́зм ♦ **You take refuge behind sarcasm.** Ты пря́чешься под сарка́змом.

sardonic *adj* сардони́ческий, -ая, -ое, -ие.

sassy *adj* 1. *(impudent)* де́рзкий, -ая, -ое, -ие; 2. *(sharp, clever)* бо́йкий, -ая, -ое, -ие.

satin *adj* атла́сный, -ая, -ое, -ые.

satin *n* атла́с ♦ **You look so** *(1)* **gorgeous** / *(2)* **voluptuous** / *(3)* **svelte encased in satin.** Ты вы́глядишь так *(1)* ...так великоле́пно / *(2)* роско́шно... / *(3)* ...тако́й стро́йной... упако́ванной в атла́с.

satisfaction *n* удовлетворе́ние ♦ **Darling, if I ever get in the same bed with you, I'm going to make myself a slave to your desires and your pleasure and your satisfaction.** Дорога́я, е́сли я окажу́сь в одно́й посте́ли с тобо́й, я сде́лаю себя́ рабо́м твои́х страсте́й, твоего́ наслажде́ния и твоего́ удовлетворе́ния.

satisfied *adj* удовлетворённый, -ая, -ое, -ые *(short forms:* удовлетворён, удовлетворена́, -о́, -ы́) ♦ **~ with life** дово́лен (дово́льна, -о, -ы) жи́знью *(short forms)*.

Words in parentheses are optional.

satisfied: *phrases*

I think it's important to be satisfied with oneself. Я ду́маю, что э́то ва́жно -- быть удо-влетворённым сами́м собо́й. ♦ **I'm (not) satisfied sexually (with** *[1]* **her /** *[2]* **you).** *(m:)* Я (не) удовлетворён сексуа́льно (с *[1]* ней / *[2]* тобо́й). ♦ **I'm (not) satisfied sexually (with** *[1]* **him /** *[2]* **you).** *(f:)* Я (не) удовлетворена́ сексуа́льно (с *[1]* ним / *[2]* тобо́й). ♦ **I'm going to keep you satisfied for the rest of your life.** Я бу́ду удовлетворя́ть тебя́ всю твою́ жизнь. ♦ **I know I'll always be satisfied with you.** Я зна́ю, что я всегда́ бу́ду удовлетворён *(ж: удовлетворена́)* с тобо́й.

satisfy *vt* удовлетворя́ть / удовлетвори́ть *(whom = acc.)* ♦ *(1)* **He /** *(2)* **She doesn't satisfy me sexually.** *(1)* Он / *(2)* Она́ не удовлетворя́ет меня́ сексуа́льно. ♦ **No one ever satisfied me (sexually) the way you do.** Никто́ никогда́ не удовлетворя́л меня́ (сексуа́льно) так, как ты. ♦ **You satisfy me completely.** Ты меня́ по́лностью удовлетворя́ешь. ♦ **I promise you I'm going to satisfy you every day for the rest of your life.** Я обеща́ю тебе́, что бу́ду удовлетворя́ть тебя́ ка́ждый день всю твою́ жизнь.

Saturday *n* суббо́та ♦ **by ~** к суббо́те ♦ **last ~** в про́шлую суббо́ту ♦ **next ~** в сле́дующую суббо́ту ♦ **on ~** в суббо́ту.

saucy *adj* 1. *(impudent)* де́рзкий, -ая, -ое, -ие; 2. *(brazenly flirtatious)* коке́тливый, -ая, -ое, -ые.

saucy-looking *adj* де́рзкого ви́да.

savage *adj* 1. *(uncivilized)* ди́кий, -ая, -ое, -ие, ва́рварский, -ая, -ое, -ие; 2. *(ferocious)* жесто́кий, -ая, -ое, -ие, свире́пый, -ая, -ое, -ые.

savagely *adv* 1. *(uncivilized)* ди́ко, ва́рварски; 2. *(ferociously)* жесто́ко, свире́по.

savagery *n* 1. *(uncivilized)* ди́кость *f*; 2. *(ferocity)* жесто́кость *f*, свире́пость *f*.

savor *vt* вкуша́ть / вкуси́ть *(what = acc.)*, смакова́ть *(what = acc.)*; наслажда́ться *(what = instr.)* ♦ **To savor the sweetness of your lips is so** *(1)* **divine /** *(2)* **heavenly /** *(3)* **wonderful.** Вкуша́ть сла́дость твои́х губ так *(1,2)* замеча́тельно / *(3)* удиви́тельно. ♦ **What a divine ecstasy to savor the sweetness of your lips.** Что за боже́ственный восто́рг -- вкуша́ть сла́дость твои́х губ. ♦ **How I long to savor the soft warmth of your body next to mine.** Как я жа́жду вкуша́ть мя́гкое тепло́ твоего́ те́ла ря́дом с мои́м. ♦ **I savor every** *(1)* **moment /** *(2)* **second that we spend together.** Я смаку́ю ка́ждое *(1,2)* мгнове́ние, проведённое вме́сте с тобо́й. ♦ **We'll lie under some big, shady tree, fingers entwined, legs entwined, lips entwined, savoring each other's soul.** Мы бу́дем лежа́ть под большим тени́стым де́ревом, па́льцы сплетены́, но́ги сплетены́, гу́бы сплетены́, вкуша́я ду́ши друг дру́га. ♦ **I savor the sound of your name on my lips.** Мои́ гу́бы смаку́ют звук твоего́ и́мени. ♦ **I dream of the day when my eyes can savor the delights of your unclad form.** Я мечта́ю о том дне, когда́ мои́ глаза́ смо́гут восхищённо смакова́ть твоё обнажённое те́ло.

savvy *adj (clever, quick-witted)* смека́листый, -ая, -ое, -ые, сметли́вый, -ая, -ое, -ые; *(able to figure out)* разбира́ющийся, -аяся, -ееся, -иеся; *(understanding)* понима́ющий, -ая, -ее, -ие.

savvy *n (know-how)* уме́ние; *(brains)* ра́зум, рассу́док; *(comprehension)* понима́ние; *(quick-wittedness, sharpness)* смётка ♦ **cultural ~** понима́ние культу́ры.

say *vt* говори́ть / сказа́ть *(what = acc., to whom = dat.)* ♦ **How can you say such a thing?** Как ты мо́жешь сказа́ть тако́е? ♦ **How should I interpret what you said?** Как я до́лжен *(ж: должна́)* расце́нивать то, что ты сказа́ла *(ж: сказа́л)*? ♦ *(1)* **There are so many things...** / *(2)* **There's so much... I want to say to you.** *(1,2)* Так мно́го я хочу́ сказа́ть тебе́. ♦ **No matter what I say to you, it never seems to be enough.** Что бы я ни сказа́л *(ж: сказа́ла)* тебе́, э́того никогда́ не бу́дет доста́точно.

You can find common clothing sizes in Appendix 11 on page 778.

scamper *vi* скака́ть, (бы́стро) бе́гать ♦ **I like to watch you scamper around the room with no clothes on.** Мне нра́вится смотре́ть, как ты бе́гаешь по ко́мнате обнажённой.

scar *n* рубе́ц, шрам ♦ **~ on the stomach** шрам на животе́.

scare *vt* пуга́ть / испуга́ть *(whom = acc.)*.

scared *adj* испу́ганный, -ая, -ое, -ые ♦ **be / get** ~ пуга́ться / испуга́ться.

scarf *n* шарф.

scarlet *adj* а́лый, -ая, -ое, -ые.

scarred *adj* 1. *(physical)* покры́т (-а, -о, -ы) рубца́ми / шра́мами *(short forms)*; обезобра́женный, -ая, -ое, -ые; 2. *(emotional)* ра́нен, -а, -о, -ы *(short forms)* ♦ **emotionally** ~ эмоциона́льно ра́нен, -а, -о, -ы *(short forms)*.

scary *adj* жу́ткий, -ая, -ое, -ие, ужа́сный, -ая, -ое, -ые.

scatter *vt (flowers)* разбра́сывать / разброса́ть *(what = acc.)*; *(pleasure, etc)* рассе́ивать / рассе́ять *(what = acc.)* ♦ **My fingertips will glide over your body, scattering delicious pleasure in their path.** Ко́нчики мои́х па́льцев бу́дут скользи́ть по твоему́ те́лу, рассе́ивая восхити́тельное наслажде́ние на своём пути́.

scene *n* 1. *(place of occurrence)* ме́сто *(де́йствия / собы́тия)*; 2. *(play, movie)* сце́на; 3. *(uproar)* сце́на, сканда́л; 4. *(picture)* карти́на ; 5. *(view)* вид; 6. *(mileu, culture)* мир ♦ **bar** ~ мир ба́ров, ба́ры, развлече́ния в ба́ре ♦ **gay** ~ мир гомосексуа́лов ♦ **intimate** ~ инти́мная сце́на ♦ **love** ~ любо́вная сце́на ♦ **personal-ad** ~ мир персона́льных объявле́ний ♦ **make a** ~ **in public** устра́ивать / устро́ить публи́чную сце́ну.

> **scene: phrases**

I don't care for the bar scene. Я не интересу́юсь ба́рами. ♦ **The bar scene is a waste of time.** Вре́мя в ба́ре -- вы́брошенное вре́мя. ♦ **I especially enjoy the music scene.** Я осо́бенно наслажда́юсь ми́ром му́зыки. ♦ **I've been away from the dating scene for quite a while.** Я обходи́лся без свида́ний дово́льно до́лго. ♦ **Please don't make a scene.** Пожа́луйста, не устра́ивай сце́ну.

scent *n* за́пах, арома́т ♦ *(1,2)* **alluring** ~ *(1)* маня́щий / *(2)* соблазни́тельный за́пах ♦ **aromatic** ~ арома́т, прия́тный за́пах ♦ *(1,2)* **bewitching** ~ *(1)* обворожи́тельный / *(2)* чару́ющий за́пах ♦ **exotic** ~ экзоти́ческий арома́т ♦ *(1,2)* **heady** ~ *(1)* хмельно́й / *(2)* головокружи́тельный за́пах ♦ **heavenly** ~ боже́ственный арома́т ♦ **intoxicating** ~ опьяня́ющий арома́т ♦ **masculine** ~ мужско́й за́пах ♦ **musky** ~ му́скусный арома́т ♦ **pungent** ~ си́льный арома́т ♦ ~ **of flowers** арома́т цвето́в ♦ **soft** ~ не́жный за́пах ♦ **sweet** ~ сла́дкий за́пах ♦ **wholesome** ~ прия́тный за́пах ♦ **wonderful** ~ чуде́сный за́пах.

> **scent: phrases**

I love the scent of jasmine *(1)* **...in your hair.** / *(2)* **...on you.** Я люблю́ за́пах жасми́на *(1)* ...в твои́х волоса́х. / *(2)* ...от тебя́. ♦ **The scent of your hair makes** *(1)* **...my heart /** *(2)* **pulse** *(3)* **race /** *(4)* **flutter. /** *(5)* **...my knees feel weak. /** *(6)* **...me feel (downright) dizzy with** *(7)* **love /** *(8)* **desire for you.** За́пах твои́х воло́с *(1)* ...заставля́ет моё се́рдце / *(2)* мой пульс *(3)* ускоря́ться / *(4)* трепета́ть. / *(5)* ...заставля́ет чу́вствовать сла́бость в коле́нях. / *(6)* ...наполня́ет меня́ (соверше́нно) головокружи́тельным чу́вством *(7)* любви́ / *(8)* стра́сти к тебе́. ♦ **I dream of lying beside you, my face snuggled into the rich softness of your breasts, lost in a deep cloud of your heavenly scent.** Я мечта́ю о том, что́бы лежа́ть ря́дом с тобо́й, зары́вшись лицо́м в роско́шную мя́гкость твое́й груди́, погрузи́вшись в о́блако твоего́ боже́ственного арома́та.

scented *adj* наду́шенный, -ая, -ое, -ые ♦ ~ **handkerchief** наду́шенный носово́й плато́к.

schmooze *vi (slang) (chatter)* болта́ть.

scholarly *adj* учёный, -ая, -ое, -ые ♦ **You look (very) scholarly** *(1)* **in /** *(2)* **with a beard.** *(1,2)*

For general rules of Russian grammar see Appendix 2 on page 686.

С бородо́й ты (о́чень) похо́ж на учёного.

school *n* шко́ла ♦ **I have to** *(1,2)* **go to school.** Я до́лжен *(ж: должна́)* *(1)* пойти́ *(on foot)* / *(2)* пое́хать *(by veh.)* в шко́лу.

schoolboy *n* шко́льник ♦ **(Sometimes) I feel like a schoolboy (around you).** (Иногда́) я чу́вствую себя́ шко́льником (ря́дом с тобо́й).

schoolgirl *n* шко́льница ♦ **(Sometimes) I feel like a schoolgirl (around you).** (Иногда́) я чу́вствую себя́ шко́льницей (ря́дом с тобо́й).

schoolgirlish *adj* веду́щая себя́ как шко́льница.

scintillating *adj* искри́стый, -ая, -ое, -ые, искря́щийся, -аяся, -ееся, -иеся, сверка́ющий, -ая, -ее, -ие ♦ **Your incredible beauty and scintillating charm have completely swept me away.** Твоя́ (невероя́тная) красота́ и искря́щееся обая́ние по́лностью покори́ли меня́.

scoff *vi* насмеха́ться *(at what, whom = + над + instr.)*, осме́ивать *(at what, whom = acc.)* ♦ **Don't scoff at me.** Не насмеха́йся на́до мной.

scorch *vt* пали́ть / опали́ть *(what = acc.)* ♦ **Whenever I think of you, red-hot desire scorches my innermost being.** Когда́ бы я не поду́мал о тебе́, обжига́ющая страсть опаля́ет всё во мне.

scorched *adj* опалённый, -ая, -ое, -ые.

scorn *vt (reject)* отверга́ть / отве́ргнуть *(what, whom = acc.)* ♦ **"Heaven has no Rage like Love to Hatred turn'd, Nor Hell a Fury, like a Woman scorned."** *William Congreve, "The Mourning Bride" (1697).* «На небеса́х нет тако́й я́рости, как любо́вь, обращённая в не́нависть, в аду́ нет тако́го бе́шенства, как же́нщина отве́ргнутая.» *Ви́льям Ко́нгрив, «Скорбя́щая неве́ста», (1697).*

scorn *n* презре́ние, пренебреже́ние ♦ **Why do you treat me with such scorn?** Почему́ ты обраща́ешься со мной так презри́тельно? ♦ **You heap so much scorn on me.** Ты выплё-скиваешь так мно́го презре́ния на меня́. ♦ **I have nothing but scorn for you.** У меня́ не оста́лось ничего́, кро́ме презре́ния к тебе́.

scorned *adj* отве́ргнутый, -ая, -ое, -ые.

scornful *adj* презри́тельный, -ая, -ое, -ые.

Scorpio *(Oct. 23 - Nov. 21)* Скорпио́н *(23 октября́ - 21 ноября́).*

scotch *n (whiskey)* скотч.

scoundrel *n* негодя́й, подле́ц.

scourge *n* ка́ра, бич ♦ *(1)* **Come /** *(2)* **Hurry back to me and chase away this terrible scourge of loneliness (that grips my heart).** *(1)* Прийди́ / *(2)* Торопи́сь (обра́тно) ко мне и про-гони́ прочь э́ту ужа́сную ка́ру одино́чества (, кото́рая терза́ет моё се́рдце).

scowl *n (1)* серди́тый / *(2)* злой взгляд ♦ **dark ~** гро́зный взгляд.

scream *vi* вскри́кивать / вскри́кнуть; вопи́ть; (пронзи́тельно) крича́ть ♦ **I want to make you scream with** *(1)* **pleasure /** *(2)* **delight /** *(3)* **ecstasy.** Я хочу́ заста́вить тебя́ крича́ть *(1)* ...от наслажде́ния / *(2)* восто́рга / *(3)* ...в экста́зе. ♦ **I get so (terribly) lonely that I could scream.** Я так (ужа́сно) одино́к *(ж: одино́ка)*, что хо́чется крича́ть. ♦ **When I get you in my arms I'm going to make you scream with** *(1)* **pleasure /** *(2)* **delight /** *(3)* **ecstasy.** В свои́х объя́тиях я заста́влю тебя́ крича́ть *(1)* ...от наслажде́ния / *(2)* восто́рга / *(3)* ...в экста́зе. ♦ **I love the way you scream out when we make love.** Я люблю́, как ты вскри́киваешь, когда́ мы занима́емся любо́вью.

scream *n* (пронзи́тельный) крик, вопль *m* ♦ **When my lips and tongue revel on your beautiful, luscious body, they will hear your screams of** *(1)* **pleasure /** *(2)* **ecstasy in South Africa.** Когда́ мои́ гу́бы и язы́к бу́дут упива́ться твои́м прекра́сным, со́чным те́лом, твои́ кри́ки *(1)* наслажде́ния / *(2)* экста́за бу́дут слышны́ в Ю́жной Африке. ♦ **When**

For transitive Russian verbs the cases that they take are shown by means of an = sign and the Russian case (abbreviated).

I *(1)* **get /** *(2)* **take you in my arms, they're going to hear your screams of** *(3)* **pleasure /** *(4)* **ecstasy /** *(5)* **delight in Argentina.** Когда́ я *(1,2)* заключу́ тебя́ в объя́тия, твои́ во́пли *(3)* наслажде́ния / *(4)* экста́за / *(5)* восто́рга услы́шат в Аргенти́не. ♦ **I want to fill the** *(1)* **night /** *(2)* **nights with your screams of** *(3)* **pleasure /** *(4)* **ecstasy /** *(5)* **delight.** Я хочу́ напо́лнить *(1)* ночь / *(2)* но́чи твои́ми кри́ками *(3)* наслажде́ния / *(4)* экста́за / *(5)* восто́рга.

screen *vt* отбира́ть / отобра́ть *(what, whom = acc.)* ♦ **~ out the weirdos** отсе́ивать люде́й со стра́нностями.

screening *n* отбо́р.

screw up *vt (slang)* изга́живать / изга́дить *(what = acc.)*, по́ртить / испо́ртить *(what = acc.)* ♦ **I've (really) screwed up everything. I'm sorry.** Я (действи́тельно) испо́ртил *(ж: испо́ртила)* всё. Мне жаль. ♦ **You've (completely) screwed up our relationship.** Ты (по́лностью) испо́ртила *(ж: испо́ртил)* на́ши отноше́ния. ♦ **I don't want to screw up things between us.** Я не хочу́ испо́ртить на́ши отноше́ния.

scrumptious *adj* сногсшиба́тельный, -ая, -ое, -ые, аппети́тный, -ая, -ое, -ые ♦ **What a** *(1,2)* **scrumptious body you have!** Что за *(1)* сногсшиба́тельное / *(2)* аппети́тное те́ло у тебя́! ♦ **You are absolutely scrumptious.** Ты соверше́нно сногсшиба́тельна.

scrupulous *adj* 1. *(honest)* че́стный, -ая, -ое, -ые, добросо́вестный, -ая, -ое, -ые; 2. *(meticulous)* безупре́чный, -ая, -ое, -ые; скрупулёзный, -ая, -ое, -ые, дото́шный, -ая, -ое, -ые.

scrupulously *adv* 1. *(honestly)* че́стно, добросо́вестно 2. *(meticulously)* безупре́чно; скрупулёзно, дото́шно.

scrutinize *vt* (приста́льно) рассма́тривать / рассмотре́ть *(what = acc.)* ♦ **I don't like to have someone scrutinize my every move.** Мне не нра́вится, когда́ кто́-то приста́льно контроли́рует ка́ждое моё движе́ние.

scuba *n* ску́ба, аквала́нг ♦ **I often go** *(1,2)* **scuba diving.** Я ча́сто ныря́ю с *(1)* аквала́нгом / *(2)* ску́бой.

sculpt *vt* вая́ть / извая́ть *(what = acc.)* ♦ **You have a face that was sculpted by angels.** У тебя́ лицо́, извая́нное а́нгелами.

sculpture *n* скульпту́ра ♦ **When I look at you, it reminds me of a Michelangelo sculpture.** Когда́ я смотрю́ на тебя́, то вспомина́ю скульпту́ру Микела́нджело.

sea *n* мо́ре ♦ **I will always be your faithful navigator in the Sea of Passion.** Я всегда́ бу́ду твои́м ве́рным шту́рманом в мо́ре стра́сти. ♦ **Our bodies will fuse together in exquisite pleasure until we are** *(1)* **flung /** *(2)* **hurled into a wild sea of passion.** На́ши тела́ солью́тся в изы́сканном наслажде́нии до тех пор, пока́ мы не бу́дем *(1,2)* бро́шены в бе́шеное мо́ре стра́сти.

seal *vt* запеча́тывать / запеча́тать *(what = acc., with what = instr.)* ♦ **I'm sealing this letter with a kiss.** Я запеча́тываю э́то письмо́ поцелу́ем.

sealed *adj* запеча́тан, -а, -о, -ы *(short forms)* ♦ **This letter is sealed with a kiss.** Это письмо́ запеча́тано поцелу́ем.

sear *vt* обжига́ть / обже́чь *(what, whom = acc.)* ♦ **Your lips seared mine.** Твои́ гу́бы обжига́ли мои́. ♦ **Desire sears my body.** Страсть распаля́ет моё те́ло.

search *vt* иска́ть *(for what, whom = acc.)* ♦ **I'm searching for someone like** *(1)* **me /** *(2)* **myself.** Я ищу́ челове́ка, ...похо́жего на себя́. / ...тако́го же, как я сам *(ж: сама́)*.

searching *n* по́иск ♦ **I need to do some soul searching (about this).** Мне на́до тща́тельно поду́мать об э́том. ♦ **I've done a lot of soul searching (about** *[1]* **it /** *[2]* **us) (and I've decided...).** Я до́лго размышля́л *(ж: размышля́ла)* (*[1]* об э́том / *[2]* о нас) (и я реши́л *[ж: реши́ла]*...).

seared *adj* опалённый, -ая, -ое, -ые.

> *Russian verbs have 2 forms: imperfective and perfective.*
> *They're given in that order.*

searing *adj* жгу́чий, -ая, -ее, -ие, обжига́ющий, -ая, -ее, -ие ♦ ~ **trail of kisses** жгу́чий след поцелу́ев.

seashore *n* морско́й бе́рег.

seasoned *adj (experienced)* о́пытный, -ая, -ое, -ые; *(hardened)* закалённый, -ая, -ое, -ые.

seat *n* 1. *(place to sit)* ме́сто; сиде́нье; 2. *(rear end)* зад ♦ **back ~ of a car** за́днее сиде́нье маши́ны ♦ **You can have my seat.** *(bus, metro or streetcar)* Вы мо́жете сесть на моё ме́сто. ♦ **Is this seat** *(1)* **vacant /** *(2)* **taken?** Это ме́сто *(1)* свобо́дно / *(2)* за́нято? ♦ **This seat is** *(1)* **occupied /** *(2)* **taken.** Это ме́сто *(1,2)* за́нято.

secluded *adj* уединённый, -ая, -ое, -ые.

seclusion *n* уедине́ние ♦ **find ~** уединя́ться / уедини́ться.

secrecy *n* таи́нственность.

secret *n* секре́т, та́йна ♦ **deep dark ~** полне́йшая та́йна ♦ *(1,2)* **deep ~** *(1)* глубо́кая / *(2)* сокрове́нная та́йна ♦ *(1,2)* **delicious ~s** *(1)* восхити́тельные / *(2)* упои́тельные секре́ты ♦ *(1,2)* **delightful ~s** *(1)* восхити́тельные / *(2)* упои́тельные секре́ты ♦ **heart's ~** серде́чная та́йна ♦ **innermost ~s** сокрове́нные секре́ты ♦ **luscious ~s** со́чные секре́ты ♦ **most precious ~** са́мый заве́тный секре́т ♦ **my ~** моя́ та́йна ♦ **~s of love** секре́ты любви́ ♦ **our ~** на́ша та́йна ♦ *(1,2)* **terrible ~** *(1)* стра́шная / *(2)* ужа́сная та́йна ♦ **your ~** *(familiar)* твоя́ та́йна; *(polite)* Ва́ша та́йна.

> #### secret: verb terms

keep a ~ храни́ть та́йну ♦ **keep ~** держа́ть в секре́те *(what = acc.)*, храни́ть в та́йне *(what = acc.)* ♦ **reveal a ~** *(uncover)* раскрыва́ть / раскры́ть та́йну; *(show)* открыва́ть / откры́ть та́йну.

> #### secret: your secrets

I *(1)* **yearn /** *(2)* **long so** *(3)* **mightily /** *(4)* **much to explore all the** *(5)* **luscious /** *(6)* **delicious secrets of your body.** Я так *(3,4)* си́льно *(1)* жа́жду / *(2)* стремлю́сь иссле́довать все *(5)* со́чные / *(6)* восхити́тельные секре́ты твоего́ те́ла. ♦ **My** *(1)* **yearning /** *(2)* **adoring /** *(3)* **roving /** *(4)* **ravenous lips will uncover your most precious secret.** Мои́ *(1)* жа́ждущие / *(2)* обожа́ющие / *(3)* блужда́ющие / *(4)* изголода́вшиеся гу́бы раскро́ют твой са́мый заве́тный секре́т. ♦ **I long for the day when I can uncover all the secrets of your gorgeous body.** Я тоску́ю по дню, когда́ я смогу́ пости́чь все та́йны твоего́ великоле́пного те́ла.

> #### secret: secrets of love and pleasure

I will reveal the delightful secrets of love and bliss for you. Я откро́ю тебе́ упои́тельные та́йны любви́ и блаже́нства. ♦ **You can't even imagine what secrets I know for giving you pleasure on a cosmic level.** Ты да́же не мо́жешь предста́вить себе́, каки́е секре́ты я зна́ю для того́, чтобы доста́вить тебе́ косми́ческое наслажде́ние. ♦ **I know so many delicious secrets about love — secrets that would make you just dizzy with ecstasy — and they're just going to waste right now.** Я зна́ю так мно́го восхити́тельных секре́тов любви́ -- секре́ты, кото́рые заста́вят тебя́ испыта́ть головокружи́тельный экста́з, и они́ про́сто ника́к ни испо́льзуются сейча́с.

secretive *adj* скры́тый, -ая, -ое, -ые, за́мкнутый, -ая, -ое, -ые ♦ **be ~** таи́ться.

section *n* 1. *(of a newspaper, store, agency, etc)* отде́л, се́кция; 2. *(part)* часть; 3. *(of a book)* разде́л ♦ **All day long after reading your ad in the personals section I've been aching to get home and write you this letter.** Весь день по́сле прочте́ния Ва́шего объявле́ния в отде́ле знако́мств я стреми́лся прийти́ домо́й и написа́ть Вам э́то письмо́.

secular *adj* све́тский, -ая, -ое, -ие, мирско́й, -а́я, -о́е, -и́е.

secure *adj* усто́йчивый, -ая, -ое, -ые *(short forms:* усто́йчив, -а, -о, -ы), стаби́льный, -ая, -ое, -ые, обеспе́ченный, -ая, -ое, -ые *(short forms:* обеспе́чен, -а, -о, -ы), безопа́сный,

---

How to use the Cyrillic alphabet on the Internet is the subject of Appendix 20 on page 789.

-ая, -ое, -ые ♦ **emotionally** ~ эмоциона́льно усто́йчив, -а, -о, -ы ♦ *(1,2)* **financially** ~ *(1)* материа́льно / *(2)* фина́нсово обеспе́чен, -а, -о, -ы ♦ ~ **with self** уве́ренный (-ая, -ые) в себе́ ♦ *(1,2)* **$ecure** *(financially secure)* *(1)* материа́льно / *(2)* фина́нсово обеспе́чен, -а, -о, -ы.

security *n* 1. *(safety)* безопа́сность *f*; 2. *(material well-being)* обеспе́чение ♦ **financial** ~ материа́льное обеспе́чение ♦ **$ecurity = financial security** фина́нсовое благополу́чие ♦ **sense of** ~ чу́вство безопа́сности

sedate *adj (quiet)* споко́йный, -ая, -ое, -ые; *(staid)* степе́нный, -ая, -ое, -ые.

seduce *vt* соблазня́ть / соблазни́ть *(whom = acc.)*; обольща́ть / обольсти́ть *(whom = acc.)* ♦ **In case you're not aware, I'm trying to seduce you.** Ты ещё не догада́лась *(ж: догада́лся)*, что я пыта́юсь соблазни́ть тебя́.

seduced *adj* обольщённый, -ая, -ое, -ые, соблазнённый, -ая, -ое, -ые ♦ **be** ~ **by your charm** быть обольщённым *(ж: обольщённой)* твои́м очарова́нием.

seducer *n* соблазни́тель *m*, соврати́тель *m*.

seduction *n* обольще́ние ♦ **experienced in** ~ о́пытный (-ая, -ые) в обольще́нии.

seductive *adj* соблазни́тельный, -ая, -ое, -ые, обольсти́тельный, -ая, -ое, -ые ♦ **You're enormously seductive, you know that?** Зна́ешь ли ты, как бесконе́чно ты обольсти́тельна? ♦ **Do you have any idea how seductive you are?** Зна́ешь ли ты, как ты обольсти́тельна?

seductively *adv* соблазни́тельно, обольсти́тельно.

seductiveness *n* соблазни́тельность *f* ♦ **You are a paragon of seductiveness.** Ты этало́н соблазни́тельности.

seductress *n* соблазни́тельница ♦ **You're my sultry seductress.** Ты моя́ зно́йная соблазни́тельница.

see *vt* 1. *(visually)* ви́деть / уви́деть *(what, whom = acc.)*; 2. *(romantically)* встреча́ться *(whom = + с + instr.)*; 3. *(consult)* сове́товаться / посове́товаться *(whom = + с + instr.)* ♦ ~ **each other** ви́деться, встреча́ться / встре́титься.

> **see: when can I see you?**

When can I see you (again)? Когда́ я уви́жу тебя́ (опя́ть)? ♦ **Would it be possible to see you** *(1)* ...**this afternoon** / *(2)* **evening?** / *(3)* ...**tonight?** / *(4)* ...**tomorrow (**[5] **morning** / [6] **afternoon** / [7] **evening)?** / *(8)* ...**after work?** / *(9)* ...**after you get off work?** Мо́жно ли встре́титься с тобо́й *(1)* ...(сего́дня) в по́лдень? / *(2)* ...(сего́дня) ве́чером? / *(3)* ...сего́дня но́чью? / *(4)* ...за́втра (*[5]* у́тром / *[6]* в по́лдень / *[7]* ве́чером)? / *(8,9)* ...по́сле рабо́ты?

> **see: I want to see you**

I want to see you ([1] **again** / [2] **tomorrow** / [3] **soon).** Я хочу́ уви́деть тебя́ (*[1]* опя́ть / *[2]* за́втра / *[3]* вско́ре). **I want to see you** *(1)* **often** / *(2)* **everyday.** Я хочу́ ви́деть тебя́ *(1)* ...ча́сто. / *(2)* ...ка́ждый день. ♦ **I can't wait to see you.** Мне не те́рпится уви́деть тебя́. ♦ **Darling, I want so very much to see you and (talk with you and) show you love in all the ways that it's possible to show love.** Дорога́я *(ж: Дорого́й)*, я так си́льно хочу́ уви́деть тебя́ и (говори́ть с тобо́й и) продемонстри́ровать тебе́ свою́ любо́вь все́ми возмо́жными спо́собами. ♦ **I really think about you a lot and wish with all my heart that I could see you.** Я, действи́тельно, мно́го ду́маю о тебе́ и всем се́рдцем жела́ю уви́деть тебя́.

> **see: I hope I can see you**

I fervently hope that *(1)* ...**you'll give me the chance to see you in person.** / *(2)* ...**I can see you (**[3] **again** / [4] **tonight** / [5] **tomorrow).** / *(6)* ...**we can see each other** *(7)* ...**soon.** / *(8)* ...**in the summer.** / *(9)* ...**next week** / *(10)* **month** / *(11)* **year.)** Я горячо́ наде́юсь, что *(1)*

Russian adjectives have long and short forms.
Where short forms are given, they are labeled as such.

...ты дашь мне возмо́жность уви́деться с тобо́й. / *(2)* ...смогу́ уви́деть тебя́ (*[3]* опя́ть / *[4]* сего́дня ве́чером / *[5]* за́втра). / *(6)* ...мы смо́жем уви́деться *(7)* ...вско́ре. / *(8)* ...ле́том. / *(9)* ...на сле́дующей неде́ле. / *(10)* ...в сле́дующем ме́сяце / *(11)* году́. ♦ **I cling to the hope that I can see you this month.** Я цепля́юсь за наде́жду, что смогу́ уви́деть тебя́ в э́том ме́сяце.

see: *please let me see you*

I fervently *(1)* **entreat** / *(2)* **implore you to** *(3)* **give** / *(4)* **grant me the opportunity to see your beautiful face once again.** Я горячо́ *(1,2)* умоля́ю Вас *(3)* дать / *(4)* предоста́вить мне возмо́жность уви́деть Ва́ше прекра́сное лицо́ ещё раз. ♦ **If you have any tender spot for me in your heart, you'll let me see you (again).** Е́сли в Ва́шем се́рдце есть хотя́ бы каки́е-то до́брые чу́вства ко мне, Вы позво́лите мне уви́деться с Ва́ми (опя́ть).

see: *the thought of seeing you*

The thought of seeing you causes my heart to thunder. Мысль о встре́че с тобо́й заставля́ет моё се́рдце учащённо би́ться.

see: *whenever I see you*

Every time I see you walk *(1)* **...through the door...** / *(2)* **...down the hallway...** / *(3)* **...along the street...** / *(4)* **...past me...** / *(5)* **...into the room... my heart begins palpitating wildly and I am flooded with** *(6)* **exquisite** / *(7)* **overpowering** / *(8)* **dizzying sensations of adoration and desire for you.** Ка́ждый раз, когда́ я ви́жу, как ты *(1)* ...вхо́дишь в дверь... / *(2)* ...идёшь по коридо́ру... / *(3)* ...идёшь по у́лице... / *(4)* ...прохо́дишь ми́мо... / *(5)* ...вхо́дишь в ко́мнату... моё се́рдце начина́ет выска́кивать из груди́, и меня́ переполня́ют *(6)* о́стрые / *(7)* невыноси́мые / *(8)* головокружи́тельные чу́вства обожа́ния и жела́ния. ♦ **My heart breaks into rapture whenever I see you.** Моё се́рдце наполня́ется восто́ргом всегда́, когда́ я ви́жу тебя́. ♦ **I get a fluttery feeling in my stomach whenever I see you.** Моё се́рдце трепе́щет вся́кий раз, когда́ бы я ни уви́дел *(ж: уви́дела)* тебя́.

see: *I see you everywhere*

I see you everywhere I go. Где бы я ни был *(ж: была́)*, ты постоя́нно со мной.

see: *when I saw you*

I was so *(1)* **charmed** / *(2)* **delighted** / *(3)* **enthralled at meeting you yesterday that I feel compelled to write this short note to you to tell you how (very) much it meant to me.** Я был *(ж: была́)* так *(1)* очаро́ван *(ж: очаро́вана)* / *(2)* восхищён *(ж: восхищена́)* / *(3)* увлечён *(ж: увлечена́)*, уви́дев Вас вчера́, что я чу́вствую непреодоли́мую потре́бность написа́ть э́ту коро́ткую запи́ску, что́бы сказа́ть Вам, как (о́чень) мно́го э́то зна́чит для меня́. ♦ **The first time I saw you, it was like being** *(1)* **hit** / *(2)* **touched by lightning.** В пе́рвый раз, когда́ я уви́дел *(ж: уви́дела)* тебя́, э́то бы́ло как *(1)* уда́р / *(2)* прикоснове́ние мо́лнии. ♦ **When I saw you, I felt shock waves of pure, unadulterated joy.** Когда́ я уви́дел *(ж: уви́дела)* тебя́, я ощути́л *(ж: ощути́ла)* во́лны и́стинного, настоя́щего ликова́ния. ♦ **I cannot describe the passion the seized my soul when I first saw you.** Не могу́ описа́ть страсть, охвати́вшую мою́ ду́шу, когда́ я впервы́е уви́дел *(ж: уви́дела)* тебя́.

see: *seeing someone*

Are you seeing anyone? Ты с ке́м-нибудь встреча́ешься? ♦ **I'm not seeing anyone.** Я ни с кем не встреча́юсь. ♦ **I felt in the pit of my stomach that you were seeing someone else.** Я чу́вствовал *(ж: чу́вствовала)* в глубине́ души́, что ты встреча́лась с други́м *(ж: встреча́лся с друго́й)*. ♦ **I have a** *(1)* **gut** / *(2)* **nagging feeling that you're seeing someone else.** Я *(1)* ...инстинкти́вно... / *(2)* ...со щемя́щей бо́лью... чу́вствую, что ты встреча́ешься с ке́м-то ещё.

see: *what do you see in him / her?*

What do you see in him? Что ты нашла́ в нём? ♦ **What do you see in her?** Что ты нашёл

Russian nouns are either masculine, feminine or neuter.
Adjectives with them will be the same.

в ней?

| **see:** *see you when we make love* |

I'd love it if you would let me see you when we make love. Мне бы понра́вилось, е́сли бы ты позво́лила мне ви́деть тебя́, когда́ мы занима́емся любо́вью.

| **see:** *I don't want to see you* |

I don't want to see you anymore. Я не хочу́ тебя́ бо́льше ви́деть.

| **see:** *parting expression* |

See you soon. До ско́рого свида́ния.

seeing *n* ви́дение ♦ **My heart races (wildly) at the** *(1)* **prospect** / *(2)* **thought of seeing you.** Моё се́рдце (бе́шено) коло́тится *(1)* ...в предвкуше́нии встре́чи... / *(2)* ......от мы́сли о встре́че... с тобо́й. ♦ **Seeing your beautiful** *(1)* **face** / *(2)* **figure just adds fuel to the fire of my desire for you.** Когда́ я ви́жу *(1)* ...твоё прекра́сное лицо́,... / *(2)* ...твою́ прекра́сную фигу́ру,... ого́нь мое́й стра́сти к тебе́ разжига́ется ещё сильне́е.

seek *vt* иска́ть *(what, whom = acc.)* ♦ **My** *(1)* **hungry** / *(2)* **loving** / *(3)* **wandering** / *(4)* **roving lips will seek and find the hidden treasures of your** *(5)* **magnificent** / *(6)* **luscious beauty.** Мои́ *(1)* голо́дные / *(2)* лю́бящие / *(3,4)* блужда́ющие гу́бы бу́дут иска́ть и находи́ть скры́тые сокро́вища твое́й *(5)* великоле́пной / *(6)* со́чной красоты́.

seeker *n* и́щущий *m,* и́щущая *f,* иска́тель *m,* иска́тельница *f* ♦ **adventure** ~ иска́тель *m* / иска́тельница *f* приключе́ний ♦ **challenge** ~ иска́тель *m* / иска́тельница *f* тру́дностей ♦ *(1,2)* **fun** ~ иска́тель *m* / иска́тельница *f (1)* удово́льствий / *(2)* развлече́ния ♦ **sun** ~ челове́к, лю́бящий со́лнце *(1 term).*

seemingly *adv* по-ви́димому, су́дя по ви́ду, каза́лось бы.

seep in *vi (be realized)* сообража́ть / сообрази́ть, доходи́ть / дойти́ ♦ **It finally seeped in that she** *(f: he) (1)* **...was seeing someone else.** / *(2)* **...didn't care about me.** До меня́ дошло́, наконе́ц, что *(1)* ...она́ встреча́лась *(ж: он встреча́лся)* с ке́м-то ещё. / *(2)* ...она́ не люби́ла *(ж: он не люби́л)* меня́.

seethe *vi* быть охва́ченным *m* / охва́ченной *f (with what = instr.)* ♦ ~ **in (one's) veins** клокота́ть в ве́нах.

seething *adj* бурля́щий, -ая, -ее, -ие ♦ **Nothing can dispel the seething desire in my heart to see you.** Ничто́ не мо́жет охлади́ть горя́чее жела́ние моего́ се́рдца уви́деть тебя́.

selective *adj* избира́тельный, -ая, -ое, -ые.

self *n* своё «я», со́бственное «я», со́бственная персо́на ♦ **share** *(1)* **my** / *(2)* **your inner** ~ подели́ться *(1,2)* свои́м вну́тренним ми́ром *(with whom = + c + instr.)* ♦ *(1)* **I want to...** / *(2)* **I'm going to... pay homage to every inch of your beautiful self with my lips.** *(1)* Я хочу́ возда́ть... / *(2)* Я возда́м... губа́ми по́честь ка́ждому дю́йму твоего́ прекра́сного те́ла.

self-absorbed *adj* поглощён (поглощена́, -о́, -ы́) сами́м собо́й *(short forms)*, эгоцентри́чный, -ая, -ое, -ые.

self-absorption *n* погруже́ние в себя́.

self-assurance *n* самоуве́ренность *f* ♦ **You have such an air of self-assurance about you.** Ты так самоуве́ренна *(ж: самоуве́рен).*

self-assured *adj* самоуве́ренный, -ая, -ое, -ые *(short forms:* самоуве́рен, -на, -но, -ны*).*

self-aware *adj* зна́ющий (-ая, -ее, -ие) себя́ ♦ **be** ~ знать себя́.

self-blame *n* самообвине́ние.

self-centered *adj* эгоисти́чный, -ая, -ое, -ые.

self-confidence *n* уве́ренность *f* в себе́ ♦ **sexual** ~ сексуа́льная состоя́тельность ♦ **gain** ~ приобрета́ть / приобрести́ уве́ренность в себе́ ♦ **lose** ~ теря́ть / потеря́ть уве́ренность в себе́.

Learn more about Russian customs in Appendix 15, page 782.

---

self-confidence: *phrases*

You need more self-confidence. Тебе ну́жно быть бо́лее уве́ренной *(ж: уве́ренным)* в себе́. ♦ **It (has) *(1)* eroded / *(2)* undermined my self-confidence.** Это *(1)* разру́шило / *(2)* подорва́ло мою́ уве́ренность в себе́. ♦ **You mustn't let it undermine your self-confidence.** Не позволя́й э́тому подорва́ть твою́ уве́ренность в себе́.

self-conscious *adj* засте́нчивый, -ая, -ое, -ые.

self-consciousness *n* засте́нчивость *f.*

self-critical *adj* самокрити́чный, -ая, -ое, -ые.

self-deceiving *adj* обма́нывающий (-ая, -ее, -ие) себя́.

self-deception *n* самообма́н.

self-denial *n* самоотрече́ние ♦ **engage in** ~ отка́зывать себе́.

self-destruction *n* самоуничтоже́ние, саморазруше́ние.

self-destructive *adj* самоуничтожа́ющий, -ая, -ее, -ие.

self-discipline *n* самодисципли́на, вну́тренняя дисципли́на.

self-discovery *n* откры́тие самого́ себя́.

self-employed *adj*: ♦ **be** ~ рабо́тать на себя́.

self-esteem *n* самоуваже́ние ♦ **low** ~ ни́зкое самоуваже́ние ♦ **gain** ~ приобрета́ть / приобрести́ чу́вство самоуваже́ния ♦ **lose** ~ теря́ть / потеря́ть чу́вство самоуваже́ния.

self-esteem: *phrases*

You've done so much to boost my self-esteem. Ты так мно́го сде́лала *(ж: сде́лал)* для того́, что́бы подня́ть моё самоуваже́ние. ♦ **My self-esteem has been (badly) eroded by the experience.** Испыта́ния (си́льно) подорва́ли моё самоуваже́ние. ♦ **All your attention does wonders for my self-esteem.** Твоё внима́ние -- чудоде́йственное сре́дство для моего́ самоуваже́ния.

self-honesty *n* че́стность с сами́м собо́й.

self-image *n* самооце́нка ♦ **negative** ~ отрица́тельная самооце́нка ♦ **positive** ~ положи́тельная самооце́нка.

self-indulgent *adj* потво́рствующий (-ая, -ее, -ие) свои́м жела́ниям.

selfish *adj* эгоисти́чный, -ая, -ое, -ые ♦ **I'm never selfish in love.** Я никогда́ не быва́ю эго́истом в любви́.

selfishly *adv* эгоисти́чно.

selfishness *n* эгои́зм, эгоисти́чность *f*

self-knowledge *n* самосозна́ние.

selfless *adj* самоотве́рженный, -ая, -ое, -ые, самозабве́нный, -ая, -ое, -ые, бескоры́стный, -ая, -ое, -ые ♦ **I love to give affection and fill my partner with boundless pleasure and delight in a totally eager and selfless way.** Я люблю́ дари́ть своему́ партнёру не́жность, безграни́чное наслажде́ние и восхище́ние пы́лко и бескоры́стно.

selflessly *adv* самозабве́нно.

selflessness *n* самозабве́ние.

self-love *n* себялю́бие.

self-pity *n* жа́лость *f* к (самому́) себе́ ♦ **tears of** ~ слёзы жа́лости к самому́ себе́ ♦ **wallow in** ~ бара́хтаться в жа́лости к самому́ себе́ ♦ *(1)* **You've got to stop...** / *(2)* **Stop... wallowing in self-pity.** *(1)* Ты должна́ *(ж: до́лжен)* переста́ть... / *(2)* Переста́нь... бара́хтаться в жа́лости к само́й *(ж: самому́)* себе́. ♦ **You're wrapped in a cocoon of self-pity.** Ты завёрнута в ко́кон жа́лости к себе́.

self-possessed *adj* хладнокро́вный, -ая, -ое, -ые, наделённый (-ая, -ое, -ые) самооблада́нием, невозмути́мый, -ая, -ое, -ые.

self-possession *n* самооблада́ние, вы́держка.

A slash always denotes "or."
You can choose the numbered words before and after.

self-reliance *n* увéренность *f* в себé.

self-reliant *adj* увéренный (-ая, -ое, -ые) в себé.

self-restraint *n* самооблада́ние, сде́ржанность *f.*

self-revelation *n* саморазоблачéние.

self-righteous *adj* увéренный (-ая, -ое, -ые) в своéй правотé, ха́нжеский, -ая, -ое, -ие.

self-righteously *adv* ха́нжески.

self-sacrifice *n* самопожéртвование.

self-satisfied *adj* самодовóльный, -ая, -ое, -ые.

self-seeking *adj* своекорьíстный, -ая, -ое, -ые.

self-sufficiency *n* самостоя́тельность *f*, независимость *f.*

self-sufficient *adj* самостоя́тельный, -ая, -ое, -ые, незави́симый, -ая, -ое, -ые.

self-taught *adj* -самоýчка ◆ ~ **cook** пóвар-самоýчка ◆ ~ **painter** худóжник-самоýчка.

self-torture *n* самоистяза́ние.

self-willed *adj* своевóльный, -ая, -ое, -ые.

self-worth *n* самоуважéние ◆ **feelings of** ~ чýвство самоуважéния ◆ **My feelings of self-worth have** *(1)* **...gone steadily down.** / *(2)* **...really been battered** / *(3)* **hammered.** Моё самоуважéние *(1)* ...шло постоя́нно вниз. / *(2)* ...действи́тельно былó разрýшено / *(3)* разби́то.

semi-athletic *adj*: ◆ **be** ~ немнóго занима́ться спóртом.

semi-traditional *adj* части́чно приде́рживающийся (-аяся, -ееся, -иеся) тради́ций ◆ **I'm semi-traditional.** Я части́чно приде́рживаюсь тради́ций.

semi-transparent *adj* полупрозра́чный, -ая, -ое, -ые

send *vt* посыла́ть / посла́ть *(what = acc., to whom = dat.),* отправля́ть / отпра́вить *(what = acc., to whom = dat.)*

send-off *n* прóводы *pl.*

senior *n* пенсионéр *m*, пенсионéрка *f* ◆ **sexy** ~ сексуа́льный пенсионéр *m*, сексуа́льная пенсионéрка *f.*

sensation *n* чýвство; ощущéние ◆ **beautiful** ~ прекра́сное ощущéние ◆ **cosmic** ~ косми́ческое ощущéние ◆ **dizzy(ing)** *(1,2)* ~ головокружи́тельное *(1)* чýвство / *(2)* ощущéние ◆ **electric** ~s электри́ческие заря́ды ◆ **erotic** ~ эроти́ческое ощущéние ◆ **excruciating** ~ невыноси́мое чýвство ◆ **exquisite** *(1,2)* ~s изьíсканные *(1)* чýвства / *(2)* ощущéния ◆ **fantastic** ~ фантасти́ческое чýвство ◆ **giddy** ~ головокружи́тельное ощущéние, головокружéние ◆ **heady** ~ опьяня́ющее ощущéние ◆ **incredible** ~ невероя́тное чýвство ◆ **overpowering** ~ невыноси́мое чýвство ◆ **overwhelming** ~ ошеломля́ющее ощущéние ◆ **pleasant** *(1,2)* ~ прия́тное *(1)* чýвство / *(2)* ощущéние ◆ **pleasurable** ~ ощущéние, доставля́ющее удовóльствие *(1 term)* ◆ **rapturous** ~s востóрженные ощущéния ◆ **tingling** ~ пока́лывающее ощущéние, дрожь *f* ◆ **voluptuous** ~ чýвственное ощущéние ◆ **wonderful** ~ замеча́тельное ощущéние ◆ **intoxicating flow of** ~s пьяня́щий потóк ощущéний ◆ **stream of** ~s потóк ощущéний ◆ **torrent of** ~s водопа́д ощущéний.

---

sensation: *I get sensations*

Every time I see you walk *(1)* **...through the door...** / *(2)* **...down the hallway...** / *(3)* **...along the street...** / *(4)* **...past me...** / *(5)* **...into the room... my heart begins palpitating wildly and I am flooded with** *(6)* **exquisite** / *(7)* **overpowering** / *(8)* **dizzying sensations of adoration and desire for you.** Ка́ждый раз, когда́ я ви́жу, как ты *(1)* ...вхóдишь в дверь... / *(2)* ...идёшь по коридóру... / *(3)* ...идёшь по ýлице... / *(4)* ...прохóдишь ми́мо... / *(5)* ...вхóдишь в кóмнату... моё сéрдце начина́ет выска́кивать из грудй, и меня́ переполня́ют *(6)* óстрые / *(7)* невыноси́мые / *(8)* головокружи́тельные чýвства обожа́ния и

Common adult weights are given in Appendix 10, page 777.

желáния. ♦ **You send electric sensations shooting through** *(1)* **...my entire body.** / *(2)* **...every cell and fiber of my body.** Ты посылáешь электрúческие заря́ды, простре́-ливающие *(1)* ...всё моё те́ло. / *(2)* ...кáждую кле́тку и все фúбры моего́ те́ла. ♦ **A hot tingling sensation goes all through my body whenever you look at me.** Жáркая дрожь пронúзывает всё моё те́ло вся́кий раз, когдá ты смóтришь на меня́. ♦ **I feel a hot tingling sensation whenever you** *(1)* **...come close to me.** / *(2)* **...look at me.** Я чýвствую жáркую дрожь вся́кий раз, когдá ты *(1)* ...приближáешься ко мне. / *(2)* ...смóтришь на меня́. ♦ **You arouse a storm of** *(1)* **incredible** / *(2)* **fantastic sensations in me.** Ты возбуждáешь бýрю *(1)* невероя́тных / *(2)* фантастúческих чувств во мне. ♦ **You arouse such** *(1)* **beautiful** / *(2)* **wonderful sensations in me.** Ты пробуждáешь такúе *(1)* прекрáсные / *(2)* замечáтельные ощуще́ния во мне. ♦ **I was drugged by the sensations that filled me.** Я был пьян *(ж: былá пьянá)* от чувств, запóлнивших меня́.

┌───┐
│ *sensation: I'll give you sensations* │
└───┘

With my lips I'm going to make tingling sensations ripple all through your body. Моú гýбы вы́зовут вóлны тре́пета, бегýщие по всемý твоемý те́лу. ♦ **My mission in life is going to be to create wonderful sensations all through your body, night and day.** Це́лью моéй жúзни бýдет день и ночь создавáть чуде́сные ощуще́ния во всём твоём те́ле. ♦ **I'm going to unleash in you a storm of the most** *(1)* **exquisite** / *(2)* **incredible** / *(3)* **fantastic sensations you've ever** *(4)* **experienced** / *(5)* **felt (in your whole life).** Я брóшу тебя́ в шторм бóлее *(1)* изы́сканных / *(2)* невероя́тных / *(3)* фантастúческих чувств, чем те, котóрые ты когдá-либо *(4)* испы́тывала / *(5)* чýвствовала (в своéй жúзни). ♦ **I'm going to treat you to an ever-changing array of pleasurable sensations.** Я бýду угощáть тебя́ мнóжеством всегдá меня́ющихся, доставля́ющих удовóльствие ощуще́ний.

sense *vt* чýвствовать / почýвствовать *(what = acc.)*; ощущáть / ощутúть *(what = acc.)*; чýять / почýять *(what = acc.)* ♦ **I sense a change in you.** Я чýвствую измене́ние в тебе́. ♦ **I sensed that you had feelings for me.** Я чýвствовал *(чýвствовала)*, что у тебя́ есть чýвства ко мне.

sense *n* чýвство ♦ **common** *(1,2)* ~ здрáвый *(1)* рассýдок / *(2)* смысл ♦ **great** ~ **of humor** замечáтельное чýвство ю́мора ♦ **impish** ~ **of humor** шаловлúвое чýвство ю́мора ♦ **keen** ~ **of humor** óстрое чýвство ю́мора ♦ **lively** ~ **of humor** живóе чýвство ю́мора ♦ **quirky sense of** ~ необы́чное чýвство ю́мора ♦ **shocking** ~ **of humor** шокúрующее чýвство ю́мора ♦ **spicy** ~ **of humor** óстрое чýвство ю́мора ♦ **come to** *(1)* **my** / *(2)* **your ~s** *(1,2)* приходúть / прийтú в себя́.

┌─────────────────────────┐
│ *sense: of humor* │
└─────────────────────────┘

I have a good sense of humor. У меня́ хорóшее чýвство ю́мора. ♦ **I love your sense of humor.** Мне нрáвится твоё чýвство ю́мора. ♦ **Sometimes I have a rather caustic sense of humor.** Иногдá у меня́ довóльно éдкое чýвство ю́мора.

┌──────────────────────────────┐
│ *sense: of adventure* │
└──────────────────────────────┘

(1,2) **I have a lively sense of adventure.** *(1)* Я óчень люблю́ приключе́ния. / *(2)* Я авантю́рный челове́к. ♦ **I seek someone with a sense of adventure.** Я ищý тогó, кто лю́бит приключе́ния.

┌──────────────────────────────────────┐
│ *sense: what you do to my senses* │
└──────────────────────────────────────┘

You have such *(1)* **luxurious** / *(2)* **total** / *(3)* **delicious** / *(4)* **exquisite power over my senses.** У тебя́ такáя *(1)* удивúтельная / *(2)* пóлная / *(3)* слáдкая / *(4)* потрясáющая власть над моúми чýвствами. ♦ **All my senses come alive when you touch me.** Все моú чýвства оживáют, когдá ты касáешься меня́. ♦ **Your warm breath awakens all of my senses.** Твоё тёплое дыхáние пробуждáет все моú чýвства. ♦ **You make my senses soar.** Ты заставля́ешь моú чýвства парúть. ♦ **You** *(1,2)* **electrify my senses (whenever you** *[3]*

┌───┐
│   *An italicized* ж *in parentheses   indicates a woman speaking.* │
└───┘

...touch me. / *[4]* **...look at me.**) Ты *(1)* возбужда́ешь / *(2)* электризу́ешь мои́ чу́вства (, когда́ бы ни *[3]* ...косну́лась *(ж: косну́лся)* меня́. / *[4]* ...взгляну́ла *(ж: взгляну́л)* на меня́.) ◆ **You have sent my senses reeling.** Из-за тебя́ все мои́ чу́вства пришли́ в смяте́ние. ◆ **Your every glance has such a powerful effect on my senses.** Ка́ждый твой взгляд так си́льно возде́йствует на мои́ чу́вства. ◆ **You excite my senses more than you can imagine.** Ты возбужда́ешь мои́ чу́вства бо́лее, чем ты мо́жешь предста́вить.

| *sense: what I want to do to your senses* |

I want to flood your senses with indescribable pleasure. Я хочу́ напо́лнить твои́ чу́вства неопису́емым наслажде́нием. ◆ **I want to kiss you and kiss you and kiss you until all your senses are aflame with** *(1)* **need** / *(2)* **desire.** Я хочу́ целова́ть тебя́, целова́ть и целова́ть до тех пор, пока́ всё в тебе́ не воспламени́тся *(1)* жела́нием / *(2)* стра́стью. ◆ **I'm going to give you such enjoyable sensations.** Я дам тебе́ тако́е наслажде́ние. ◆ **My warm breath will awaken all of your senses.** Моё тёплое дыха́ние пробу́дит все твои́ чу́вства.

| *sense: in every sense of the word* |

I'm yours in every sense of the word. Я твой *(ж: твоя́)* в по́лном смы́сле э́того сло́ва.

sensibility *n* восприи́мчивость *f* ◆ **artistic ~ies** восприи́мчивость к иску́сству.

sensible *adj* разу́мный, -ая, -ое, -ые, рассуди́тельный, -ая, -ое, -ые, здравомы́слящий, -ая, -ее, -ие ◆ **Let's be sensible (about this).** Дава́й взгля́нем разу́мно (на э́то).

sensitive *adj* 1. чувстви́тельный, -ая, -ое, -ые; 2. *(impressionable)* чу́ткий, -ая, -ое, -ие ◆ **unduly ~** сли́шком чувстви́тельный, -ая, -ое, -ые ◆ **I consider myself sensitive.** Я счита́ю себя́ чу́тким *(ж: чу́ткой)*.

sensitivity *n* 1. чувстви́тельность *f*; 2. *(understanding)* понима́ние ◆ **~ to touch** чувстви́тельность к прикоснове́нию ◆ **person of ~** чувстви́тельный челове́к.

| *sensitivity: phrases* |

I feel so disillusioned by your lack of sensitivity. Я так разочаро́ван *(ж: разочаро́вана)* отсу́тствием у тебя́ понима́ния мои́х чувств. ◆ **It would be nice if you would show a little more sensitivity (to my** *[1]* **feelings** / *[2]* **needs).** Бы́ло бы так хорошо́, е́сли бы ты вы́казала *(ж: вы́казал)* немно́го бо́льше понима́ния (мои́х *[1]* чувств / *[2]* потре́бностей). ◆ **You have a face of infinite beauty and sensitivity.** У тебя́ лицо́ безграни́чной красоты́ и чу́вственности.

sensual *adj* чу́вственный, -ая, -ое, -ые ◆ **deliciously ~** восхити́тельно чу́вственный ◆ **excitingly ~** возбужда́юще чу́вственный ◆ **exquisitely ~** изы́сканно чу́вственный ◆ **radiantly ~** излуча́юще чу́вственный ◆ **wickedly ~** гре́шно чу́вственный.

| *sensual: phrases* |

You make me feel (/*[1]* **so** / *[2]* **excitingly) sensual.** Ты вызыва́ешь во мне (*[1]* таку́ю / *[2]* возбужда́ющую) чу́вственность. ◆ **You are so deliciously sensual.** Ты восхити́тельно чу́вственна. ◆ **You look wickedly sensual.** Ты вы́глядишь грешно́ чу́вственной.

sensualist *n* чу́вственный челове́к.

sensuality *n* чу́вственность *f*, сладостра́стие ◆ **Your beauty and sensuality overwhelm me.** Твоя́ красота́ и чу́вственность покоря́ют меня́. ◆ **I'm completely mesmerized by the shiny sensuality of your lips.** Я соверше́нно загипнотизи́рован я́ркой чу́вственностью твои́х губ. ◆ **I've never seen a mouth that expresses sensuality the way yours does.** Я никогда́ не ви́дел рот, кото́рый выража́ет таку́ю чу́вственность, как твой. ◆ **I am completely** *(1)* **...under the spell of...** / *(2)* **...bewitched** / *(3)* **entranced by... your delicious sensuality.** Я по́лностью *(1)* ...под ча́рами твое́й восхити́тельной чу́вственности. / *(2)* ...околдо́ван / *(3)* очаро́ван твое́й восхити́тельной чу́вственностью. ◆

Procedures for getting married to a Russian
are outlined in Appendix 18, page 787.

Your face is so full of sensuality. Твоё лицо так полно чувственности. ♦ **You have a marvelous blending of spirit, charm and sensuality.** У тебя удивительное сочетание души, обаяния и чувственности.

sensuous *adj* чувственный, -ая, -ое, -ые ♦ **You are such a sensuous** *(1)* **person** / *(2)* **man** / *(3)* **lover.** Ты такой чувственный *(1)* человек *(m)* / *(2)* мужчина / *(3)* любовник. ♦ **You are such a sensuous** *(1)* **woman** / *(2)* **lover.** Ты такая чувственная *(1)* женщина / *(2)* любовница *(f)*.

sentence *n* 1. *(gram.)* предложение, фраза; 2. *(prison)* приговор.

sentiment *n* 1. *(feeling)* чувство; 2. *(sentimentality)* сентиментальность *f* ♦ **romantic ~s** романтические чувства ♦ **tender ~s** нежные чувства ♦ **You fill my soul with so many tender sentiments.** Ты наполняешь мою душу такими нежными чувствами.

sentimental *adj* сентиментальный, -ая, -ое, -ые.

sentimentality *n* сентиментальность *f*.

separate *vt* разлучать / разлучить *(whom = acc.)*.

separated *adj* 1. *(apart)* в разлуке, врозь; 2. *(split up)* отделён (отделена, -ы), врозь ♦ **Life is (so)** *(1)* **dismal** / *(2)* **dreary** / *(3)* **empty** / *(4)* **grey** / *(5)* **miserable when I'm separated from you.** Жизнь (такая) *(1)* мрачная / *(2)* безотрадная / *(3)* пустая / *(4)* серая / *(5)* печальная, когда я в разлуке с тобой. ♦ *(1)* **My wife...** / *(2)* **My husband... and I are separated.** *(1)* Моя жена... / *(2)* Мой муж... и я живём врозь.

separation *n* разлучение, разлука.

sequined *adj* расшитый (-ая, -ое, -ые) блёстками.

serenade *vt* петь серенаду ♦ **Every night I want you to serenade me with your moans and cries of pleasure.** Каждую ночь я хочу слушать серенаду из твоих стонов и криков наслаждения.

serenade *n* серенада ♦ **Your voice in my ear is like a serenade of love.** Твой голос в моих ушах как серенада любви.

serene *adj* безмятежный, -ая, -ое, -ые, спокойный, -ая, -ое, -ые.

serious *adj* серьёзный, -ая, -ое, -ые *(short forms:* серьёзен, серьёзна, -о, -ы*)* ♦ **I'm getting (very) serious about you.** Я (всё более) серьёзен *(ж: серьёзна)* по отношению к тебе. ♦ **I've never been this serious about anybody.** Я ни к кому никогда не относился *(ж: относилась)* так серьёзно. ♦ **You're getting too serious.** Ты становишься слишком серьёзной *(ж: серьёзным).* ♦ **Are you serious?** Ты серьёзно? ♦ **I'm (not) serious.** Я (не) серьёзно.

seriously *adv* серьёзно, всерьёз ♦ **I take** *(1)* **...you...** / *(2)* **...everything you say... seriously.** Я принимаю *(1)* ...тебя... / *(2)* ...всё, что ты говоришь,... серьёзно.

serious-minded *adj* серьёзный, -ая, -ое, -ые.

seriousness *n* серьёзность *f* ♦ **in all ~** со всей серьёзностью.

sermon *n* нравоучение.

service *n (1. ceremony; 2. military service)* 1. *(restaurants, hotels, etc)* обслуживание, сервис; 2. *(assistance)* услуга; 3. *(mil.)* (военная) служба; 4. *(relig.)* богослужение, служба ♦ **computer dating ~** служба знакомств через компьютер ♦ **dating ~** служба знакомств ♦ **introduction ~** служба знакомств ♦ **military ~** военная служба ♦ **religious ~** религиозная служба, богослужение ♦ **wedding ~** свадебный сервис ♦ **I've been in the (military) service for two years.** Я уже два года на (военной) службе.

servitude *n* рабство ♦ **I would like to spend** *(1)* **...the rest of my days...** / *(2)* **...all my hours... in attentive servitude to you.** Я хотел *(ж: хотела)* бы провести *(1)* ...остаток моих дней... / *(2)* ...все мои часы... твоим внимательным рабом *(ж: твоей внимательной рабой).*

A list of conjugated Russian verbs is given in Appendix 3 on page 699.

session *n* сéссия; врéмя ♦ **love-making** ~ врéмя заня́тия любо́вью ♦ **steamy make-out** ~ врéмя стра́стного заня́тия любо́вью ♦ **Our love-making sessions are so wonderful.** Врéмя, когда́ мы занима́емся любо́вью, замеча́тельно. ♦ **My thoughts go back again and again to our wonderful love-making sessions.** Мои́ мы́сли сно́ва и сно́ва возвраща́ются к замеча́тельному врéмени на́шей бли́зости. ♦ **The** *([1]* **sweet /** *[2]* **warm /** *[3]* **precious) memories of our wonderful love-making sessions go through my mind** *(4)* **constantly /** *(5)* **unceasingly /** *(6)* **night and day.** *([1]* Сла́достные / *[2]* Тёплые / *[3]* Драгоцéнные) воспомина́ния о замеча́тельном врéмени на́шей бли́зости *(4)* постоя́нно / *(5)* непреры́вно / *(6)* ...но́чью и днём... вспы́хивают в мое́й па́мяти.

set *vt (place, put)* ста́вить / поста́вить *(what = acc.)* ♦ ~ **a date** назнача́ть / назна́чить да́ту ♦ **I hope this will set your mind at ease.** Я надéюсь, что э́то принесёт тебé душéвный поко́й. ♦ **I'd like to set you straight about that.** Я хотéл *(ж: хотéла)* бы рассказа́ть тебé пра́вду об э́том. ♦ **Your kisses set me on fire.** Твои́ поцелу́и воспламеня́ют меня́.

set *n* гарниту́р, набо́р ♦ **peignoir** ~ пеньюа́р.

settle *vi* успока́иваться / успоко́иться *(for what = +* на *+ prep.)* ♦ ~ **down** *vi* остепени́ться.

settle down:

I'm (really) ready to settle down. Я (действи́тельно) гото́в остепени́ться. ♦ **I don't think I'm ready to settle down yet.** Не ду́маю, что я ужé гото́в остепени́ться.

settle for:

I wouldn't settle for less. Я не стал *(ж: ста́ла)* бы успока́иваться на мéньшем.

sever *vt* разрыва́ть / разорва́ть *(what = acc.)* ♦ ~ **a relationship** разрыва́ть / разорва́ть отноше́ния.

sex *n* секс ♦ **beautiful** ~ прекра́сный секс ♦ **casual** ~ случа́йный секс ♦ **cosmic** ~ косми́ческий секс ♦ **enjoyable** ~ секс, даю́щий наслажде́ние *(1 term)* ♦ **extramarital** ~ внебра́чный секс ♦ **fantastic** ~ фантасти́ческий секс ♦ **gentle** ~ 1. *(women)* прекра́сный пол; 2. *(love-making)* нéжный секс ♦ **gourmet** ~ изы́сканный секс ♦ **gymnastic** ~ гимнасти́ческий секс ♦ **hot** ~ горя́чий секс ♦ **incredible** ~ невероя́тный секс ♦ **marathon** ~ непреры́вный секс ♦ **opposite** ~ противополо́жный пол ♦ **oral** ~ ора́льный секс ♦ **passionate** ~ стра́стный секс ♦ **quiet** ~ споко́йный секс ♦ **satisfying** ~ удовлетворя́ющий секс ♦ **sensual** ~ чу́вственный секс ♦ **terrific** ~ чудéсный секс ♦ **wild** ~ необу́зданный секс ♦ **wonderful** ~ чудéсный секс.

sex: verb terms

have ~ занима́ться сéксом *(with whom = +* с *+ instr.)*, имéть секс *(with whom = +* с *+ instr.)*; *(make love)* занима́ться любо́вью *(with whom = +* с *+ instr.)* ♦ **initiate** ~ сдéлать почи́н к заня́тию сéксом ♦ **pressure** *(someone)* **into (having)** ~ принужда́ть / принуди́ть к сéксу *(whom = acc.)*.

sex: phrases

I want to have sex with you every night. Я хочу́ занима́ться любо́вью с тобо́й ка́ждую ночь. ♦ **I've never had sex with a** *(1)* **girl /** *(2)* **woman before.** Я никогда́ не был в сексуа́льных отноше́ниях с *(1)* дéвушкой / *(2)* жéнщиной ра́ньше. ♦ **I've never had sex with a** *(1)* **boy /** *(2)* **man before.** Я никогда́ не была́ в сексуа́льных отноше́ниях с *(1)* ю́ношей / *(2)* мужчи́ной ра́ньше. ♦ **I'm so ignorant about sex. You have to teach me.** Я так несвéдущ *(ж: несвéдуща)* в сéксе. Ты должна́ *(ж: до́лжен)* учи́ть меня́. ♦ **I don't want to have sex (with you).** Я не хочу́ занима́ться любо́вью (с тобо́й). ♦ **All you think about is sex.** Все твои́ мы́сли о сéксе. ♦ **I'm not just interested in sex.** Я заинтересо́ван *(ж: заинтересо́вана)* не то́лько в сéксе. ♦ **Sex is important, but it's not everything.** Секс о́чень ва́жен, но э́то не всё. ♦ **Sex isn't everything in life. But I have to say that for me it's very important.** Секс -- не всё в жи́зни. Но до́лжен *(ж: должна́)*

For Russian adjectives, the masculine form is spelled out,
followed by the feminine, neuter and plural endings.

сказа́ть, что для меня́ э́то о́чень ва́жно. ♦ **I caught her *(him)* having sex with** _(person)_. Я пойма́л *(ж: пойма́ла)* её *(ж: его́)*, занима́ющейся *(ж: занима́ющимся)* любо́вью (с _(и́мя))_.

sex-crazed *adj* сексуа́льно-поме́шанный, -ая, -ое, -ые.

sexiness *n* сексуа́льность *f*, сексапи́льность *f* ♦ **You are a paragon of sexiness.** Ты этало́н сексуа́льности. ♦ **Your beauty and sexiness just boggle my mind.** Твоя́ красота́ и сексуа́льность про́сто поража́ют меня́.

sex-starved *adj* сексуа́льно голо́дный, -ая, -ое, -ые.

sexual *adj* сексуа́льный, -ая, -ое, -ые ♦ **highly** ~ высоко́-сексуа́льный, -ая, -ое, -ые.

sexuality *n* сексуа́льность *f* ♦ **aggressive** ~ агресси́вная сексуа́льность ♦ **animal** ~ живо́т-ная сексуа́льность ♦ **powerful aura of** ~ мо́щная а́ура сексуа́льности ♦ **My heart yearns so fiercely to have a partner like you in life, one who combines a gentle spirit with sexuality, good-heartedness, intelligence, and a loving nature.** Моё се́рдце неи́стово жа́ждет тако́го спу́тника жи́зни, как ты, тако́го, кто соединя́ет мя́гкий хара́ктер с сексуа́льностью, добросерде́чием, интеллиге́нтностью и лю́бящей нату́рой.

sexy *adj* сексуа́льный, -ая, -ое, -ые, сексапи́льный, -ая, -ое, -ые ♦ **exquisitely** ~ изы́сканно сексуа́льный, -ая, -ое, -ые ♦ **I've never in my life ever met or seen anyone as sexy and desirable as you.** Я никогда́ в жи́зни не встреча́л и не ви́дел друго́й тако́й же сексуа́льной и соблазни́тельной, как ты. ♦ **You look so sexy when you cross your legs.** Ты вы́глядишь так сексуа́льно, когда́ кладёшь но́гу на но́гу. ♦ **I like it when you talk sexy.** Мне нра́вится, когда́ ты говори́шь сексуа́льно.

sexy-looking *adj* сексапи́льный, -ая, -ое, -ые.

shabbily *adv* некраси́во ♦ **I've treated you shabbily.** Я обраща́лся *(ж: обраща́лась)* с тобо́й некраси́во. ♦ **I apologize for treating you so shabbily.** Я извиня́юсь за тако́е некраси́вое обхожде́ние с тобо́й. ♦ **You really treated me shabbily.** Ты действи́тельно обходи́лась *(ж: обходи́лся)* со мной некраси́во.

shabby *adj* 1. *(mean)* по́длый, -ая, -ое, -ые; *(low)* ни́зкий, -ая, -ое, -ие; 2. *(undeserved, unfair)* недосто́йный, -ая, -ое, -ые, несправедли́вый, -ая, -ое, -ые ♦ **not** ~ неплохо́й, -а́я, -о́е, -и́е ♦ ~ **treatment** недосто́йное обраще́ние.

shack up *(slang)* жить (как любо́вники) *(with whom = + с + instr.)*.

shades *n, pl (slang) (sunglasses)* со́лнечные очки́.

shadow *n* тень *f* ♦ **eye** ~ те́ни для век.

shaggy *adj* мохна́тый, -ая, -ое, -ые.

shaggy-haired *adj* лохма́тый, -ая, -ое, -ые, вихра́стый, -ая, -ое, -ые.

shake *vt* 1. трясти́ / тряхну́ть *(what, whom = acc.)*; 2. *(stir feelings)* потряса́ть / потрясти́ *(what, whom = acc.)* ♦ ~ **off** *vt* стряхну́ть *(what = acc.)*, отде́латься *(what = + от + gen.)* ♦ ~ **up** *vt (stir feelings)* потряса́ть / потрясти́ *(what, whom = acc.)*. ♦ **Your letter really shook me.** Твоё письмо́ про́сто потрясло́ меня́. ♦ **Your kiss shook me like I've never been shaken before.** Потрясе́ние от твоего́ поцелу́я бы́ло сильне́йшим в мое́й жи́зни.

shake off:

I must tell you that I feel an overwhelming desire to kiss you. It possesses me night and day. I cannot *(1,2)* **shake it off.** Я до́лжен сказа́ть тебе́, что я ощуща́ю ошеломля́ющее жела́ние поцелова́ть тебя́. Оно́ владе́ет мной ночь и день. Я не могу́ *(1)* ...стряхну́ть его́. / *(2)* ...отде́латься от него́.

shallow *adj* 1. *(water)* ме́лкий, -ая, -ое, -ие; 2. *(superficial)* пове́рхностный, -ая, -ое, ые, неглубо́кий, -ая, -ое, -ие; *(limited)* ограни́ченный, -ая, -ое, ые; *(empty)* пусто́й, -а́я, -о́е, ы́е ♦ *(1,2)* ~ **intellect** *(1)* неглубо́кий / *(2)* пове́рхностный ум ♦ *(1,2)* ~ **mind** *(1)* неглубо́кий / *(2)* пове́рхностный ум ♦ ~ **person** ограни́ченный челове́к.

See Appendix 19 for notes on sending mail to Russia and Ukraine.

shambles *n, pl* руи́ны, разва́лины ◆ **Our relationship is in shambles.** На́ши (взаимо) отно-ше́ния разру́шились. ◆ **Our marriage is in shambles.** Наш брак разру́шился.

shame *n* стыд, позо́р ◆ *(1,2)* **Shame on you!** *(1)* Позо́р тебе́! / *(2)* Сты́дно!

shameful *adj* позо́рный, -ая, -ое, -ые, посты́дный, -ая, -ое, -ые.

shameless *adj* бессты́дный, -ая, -ое, -ые ◆ **It was shameless of me.** С мое́й стороны́ э́то бы́ло позо́рно. ◆ **What I did was really shameless.** То, что я сде́лал *(ж: сде́лала)*, бы́ло действи́тельно позо́рно. ◆ **You must think I'm** *(1)* **really /** *(2)* **completely /** *(3)* **utterly shameless.** Ты, должно́ быть, ду́маешь, что мне *(1)* действи́тельно / *(2,3)* соверше́нно незнако́мо чу́вство стыда́. ◆ **You are** *(1)* **really /** *(2)* **completely /** *(3)* **utterly shameless.** Тебе́ *(1)* действи́тельно / *(2,3)* соверше́нно незнако́мо чу́вство стыда́.

shamelessly *adv* бессты́дно ◆ **What a fool I've been to fling myself at you shamelessly.** *(ж:)* Како́й глу́пой я была́, бро́сившись к тебе́ так бессты́дно. ◆ **I behaved shamelessly.** Я вёл *(ж: вела́)* себя́ посты́дно. ◆ **You behaved shamelessly.** Ты вела́ *(ж: вёл)* себя́ посты́дно.

shamelessness *n* бессты́дство.

shape *n* фо́рма, фигу́ра ◆ **beautiful** ~ прекра́сная фигу́ра ◆ **excellent** ~ *(physical condition)* превосхо́дное физи́ческое состоя́ние, превосхо́дная физи́ческая фо́рма ◆ **fantastic** ~ *(figure)* фантасти́ческая фигу́ра ◆ **good** ~ 1. *(figure)* хоро́шая фигу́ра; 2. *(physical condition)* хоро́шее физи́ческое состоя́ние ◆ **great** ~ 1. *(figure)* замеча́тельная фигу́ра; 2. *(physical condition)* замеча́тельное физи́ческое состоя́ние, замеча́тельная физи́че-ская фо́рма ◆ **hourglass** ~ фигу́ра, как песо́чные часы́ *(1 term)*, оси́ная та́лия ◆ **lovely** ~ прекра́сная фигу́ра ◆ **slender** ~ стро́йная фигу́ра ◆ **wonderful** ~ замеча́тель-ная фигу́ра.

shape: phrases

What a *(1)* **fantastic /** *(2)* **beautiful shape (you have)!** Что за *(1)* фантасти́ческая / *(2)* прекра́сная фигу́ра (у тебя́)! ◆ **I keep myself in good shape.** Я держу́ себя́ в хоро́шей фо́рме. ◆ **I'm in (good) shape.** Я в (хоро́шей физи́ческой) фо́рме. ◆ **You look like you're in (**[1] **good /** [2] **excellent /** [3] **great) shape.** Ты вы́глядишь челове́ком в (*[1]* хоро́шей / *[2]* превосхо́дной / *[3]* замеча́тельной) физи́ческой фо́рме. ◆ **I try to** *(1)* **keep /** *(2)* **stay in shape.** Я пыта́юсь *(1)* ...держа́ть себя́... / *(2)* ...остава́ться... в фо́рме. ◆ **I'm a little bit out of shape.** Я немно́го не в фо́рме. ◆ **I'm trying to get in shape (again).** Я пыта́юсь (опя́ть) прийти́ в фо́рму.

share *vt* дели́ть *(what = acc., with whom =* + с + *instr.)*, разделя́ть / раздели́ть *(what = acc., with whom =* + с + *instr.)*, дели́ться *(what = instr., with whom =* + с + *instr.)*; *(enjoy to-gether)* наслажда́ться вме́сте *(what = instr.)* ◆ ~ **amore** разделя́ть любо́вь ◆ ~ **equally** дели́ть по́ровну ◆ ~ **love** разделя́ть любо́вь ◆ ~ **one's inner self** подели́ться свои́м вну́тренним ми́ром *(with whom =* + с + *instr.)* ◆ ~ **time** проводи́ть / провести́ вре́мя вме́сте.

share: time

The time we share together is so precious to me. Вре́мя, кото́рое мы прово́дим вме́сте, так до́рого для меня́. ◆ **I love the time we share together.** Мне нра́вится вре́мя, кото́-рое мы прово́дим вме́сте. ◆ **The time we share is always special.** Вре́мя, кото́рое мы прово́дим вме́сте, всегда́ осо́бенное. ◆ **Let's share these precious days.** Дава́й прове-дём вме́сте э́ти драгоце́нные дни. ◆ **The two of us** *(1)* **will /** *(2)* **can share pleasure-filled** *(3)* **hours /** *(4)* **days together.** Вме́сте мы *(1)* ...бу́дем проводи́ть... / *(2)* ...смо́жем провести́... напо́лненные наслажде́нием *(3)* часы́ / *(4)* дни.

share: life

The greatest happiness I can imagine is to spend my life with you, sharing love and all

---

When terms are listed after a main word, a tilde ~
is used to indicate the main word.

joys and tribulations. Са́мое большо́е сча́стье, кото́рое я могу́ себе́ предста́вить, -- э́то прожи́ть всю жизнь с тобо́й, деля́ любо́вь, все ра́дости и невзго́ды. ♦ **Let's share our lives together.** Дава́й вме́сте проживём на́шу жизнь. ♦ **I want to share all my life with you.** Я хочу́ прожи́ть всю свою́ жизнь с тобо́й. ♦ **The two of us will share a(n)** *(1)* **cozy** / *(2)* **exciting** / *(3)* **joyful life together.** Мы бу́дем вести́ *(1)* ую́тную / *(2)* волну́ю-щую / *(3)* ра́достную жизнь. ♦ **The two of us will share all of life's joys and sorrows.** Вдвоём мы бу́дем разделя́ть все ра́дости и печа́ли жи́зни.

share: *love and intimacy*

I love to share passion with you. Я наслажда́юсь бли́зостью с тобо́й. ♦ **It's so wonderful to share passion with you.** Бли́зость с тобо́й прекра́сна. ♦ **I want to spend the rest of my life sharing passion with you.** Я хочу́ провести́ оста́ток свое́й жи́зни, наслажда́ясь бли́зостью с тобо́й. ♦ **I want to spend endless hours sharing love and tenderness with you.** Я хочу́ проводи́ть бесконе́чные часы́, деля́ любо́вь и не́жность с тобо́й. ♦ **I cherish the closeness that we share.** Я дорожу́ на́шей бли́зостью.

share: *experiences*

I want a partner in life who has a willingness to share (everything). Я хочу́ найти́ спу́т-ницу *(ж: спу́тника)* жи́зни, кото́рая гото́ва *(ж: кото́рый гото́в)* разделя́ть всё со мной. ♦ **I want to share** *(1)* **...my hopes and dreams...** / *(2)* **...all things in life...** / *(3)* **...my vacation...** / *(4)* **...sunsets...** / *(5)* **...quiet evenings... with you.** Я хочу́ *(1)* ...подели́ться свои́ми наде́ждами и мечта́ми с тобо́й. / *(2)* ..., чтобы всё в жи́зни у нас бы́ло о́бщим. / *(3)* ...провести́ свой о́тпуск с тобо́й. / *(4)* ...любова́ться зака́тами с тобо́й. / *(5)* ...проводи́ть споко́йные вечера́ с тобо́й. ♦ **It would be so** *(1)* **nice** / *(2)* **wonderful to share** *(3)* **...(beautiful) sunsets...** / *(4)* **...(intimate) conversation...** / *(5)* **...(long) walks...** / *(6)* **...candlelight** / *(7)* **intimate dinners... with you.** Бы́ло бы так *(1)* хорошо́ / *(2)* замеча́-тельно наслажда́ться вме́сте *(3)* ...(прекра́сными) зака́тами... / *(4)* ...(инти́мными) разгово́рами... / *(5)* ...(дли́тельными) прогу́лками... / *(6)* ...у́жинами при свеча́х... / *(7)* ...инти́мными у́жинами... с тобо́й. ♦ **We can share** *(1)* **...new experiences...** / *(2)* **...life's finer things... together.** С тобо́й мы смо́жем вме́сте наслажда́ться *(1)* ...но́вым о́пы-том. / *(2)* ...всем прекра́сным в жи́зни. ♦ **I need someone to share the good and bad times.** Мне ну́жен кто́-то, кто бу́дет дели́ть со мной ра́дости и печа́ли. ♦ **I'm looking for someone to share fun times with.** Я ищу́ кого́-нибудь, чтобы вме́сте развлека́ться. ♦ **You and I could share so many things, make so much wonderful love together, talk about so many things together, connect in heart, mind, and spirit so perfectly.** Мы с тобо́й смогли́ бы наслажда́ться вме́сте мно́гим, так мно́го занима́ться любо́вью, говори́ть о мно́гом друг с дру́гом, так соверше́нно соединя́ться се́рдцем, умо́м и ду́хом. ♦ **I like to share conversation (with you).** Я люблю́ бесе́довать (с тобо́й).

share: *feelings*

Let's always share our feelings together. Дава́й всегда́ дели́ться на́шими чу́вствами. ♦ **I want you to share your feelings with me.** Я хочу́, чтобы ты дели́лась *(ж: дели́лся)* свои́ми чу́вствами со мной. ♦ **I want someone that I can share my feelings with.** Я хочу́ кого́-то, с кем я смог *(ж: смогла́)* бы дели́ться свои́ми чу́вствами. ♦ **I want to share in your hopes and dreams and anxieties.** Я хочу́ разделя́ть твои́ наде́жды, мечты́ и трево́ги.

share: *problems*

You can always share your problems with me. Ты всегда́ мо́жешь подели́ться свои́ми пробле́мами со мной.

share *n* до́ля, часть *f* ♦ **I've had more than my fair share of** *(1)* **heartache** / *(2)* **trouble** / *(3)* **unhappiness** / *(4)* **hardship** / *(5)* **loneliness.** На мою́ до́лю вы́пало бо́лее, чем доста́-

---

A list of abbreviations used in the dictionary is given on page 10.

точно *(1)* страданий / *(2)* неприятностей / *(3)* несчастий / *(4)* лишений / *(5)* одиночества.

shared *adj* разделённый, -ая, -ое, -ые ♦ **Life is best when shared (with someone you love).** Жизнь наиболее прекрасна, когда разделена (с тем, кого ты любишь).

sharing *adj (Russian uses verb* разделять*)* ♦ **I'm a sharing person.** Я человек, готовый разделять всё с любимой *(ж: любимым).* ♦ **If you (really) value our relationship, try to be more sharing.** Если ты (действительно) ценишь наши отношения, попытайся быть более участливой *(ж: участливым).*

sharing *n* деление ♦ **spiritual** ~ разделение духовных интересов.

sharp-eyed *adj* остроглазый, -ая, -ое, -ые.

sharp-tongued *adj* остроязычный, -ая, -ое, -ые.

shatter *vt* разбивать / разбить *(what = acc.)* ♦ **You have shattered all my dreams.** Ты разбила *(ж: разбил)* все мои мечты.

shave *vt* брить / побрить *(what, whom = acc.)* ♦ ~ **a beard** сбрить бороду.

shave *vi* бриться / побриться.

shaved *adj* бритый, -ая, -ое, -ые ♦ **partially** ~ частично бритый.

shaven *adj* выбритый, -ая, -ое, -ые ♦ **clean** ~ чисто выбритый ♦ **smooth** ~ гладковыбритый.

sheathed *adj* обтянутый, -ая, -ое, -ые, вложен, -а, -о, -ы *(short forms)* ♦ **You look so sexy with your legs sheathed in sheer, black stockings.** Ты выглядишь так сексуально с ногами, обтянутыми прозрачными чёрными чулками. ♦ **How** *(1)* **beautiful** / *(2)* **sexy your legs are, sheathed in sheer, black stockings.** Как *(1)* прекрасны / *(2)* сексуальны твои ноги в прозрачных, чёрных чулках.

she-devil *n* дьяволица.

sheen *n* блеск, сияние; глянец ♦ **Your hair has such a** *(1)* **beautiful** / *(2)* **rich sheen.** У твоих волос такое *(1)* прекрасное / *(2)* роскошное сияние. ♦ **The silky sheen of your body invites my lips.** Шелковистый глянец твоего тела приглашает мои губы.

sheepish *adj* 1. застенчивый, -ая, -ое, -ые, робкий, -ая, -ое, -ие, смущённый, -ая, -ое, -ые ♦ **I feel very sheepish after the way I acted (toward) you the other day.** Я чувствую сильное смущение от того, что так поступил *(ж: поступила)* (с тобой) на днях.

sheer *adj* 1. *(see-through)* прозрачный, -ая, -ое, -ые; 2. *(utter, absolute)* сущий, -ая, -ее, -ие, полнейший, -ая, -ее, -ие, абсолютный, -ая, -ое, -ые, совершенный, -ая, -ое, -ые, настоящий, -ая, -ее, -ие ♦ ~, **black stockings** прозрачные чёрные чулки ♦ ~ **gown** прозрачное платье.

| **sheer: see-through** |

I like it when you wear a sheer gown. Мне нравится, когда ты надеваешь прозрачное платье. ♦ **Wear a sheer gown for me.** Надень прозрачное платье для меня. ♦ **Do you have a sheer gown?** У тебя есть прозрачное платье?

| **sheer: utter** |

(1) **Holding you in my arms...** / *(2)* **Kissing you...** *(3)* **...was...** / *(4)* **...would be... sheer** *(5)* **ecstasy** / *(6)* **heaven.** *(1)* Держать тебя в объятиях... / *(2)* Целовать тебя... *(3)* ...было... / *(4)* ...было бы... истинным *(5)* экстазом. / *(6)* блаженством. ♦ *(1)* **Kissing you...** / *(2)* **Being (together) with you... is sheer** *(1)* **ecstasy** / *(2)* **heaven.** *(1)* Целовать тебя... / *(2)* Быть (вместе) с тобой... - *(1)* ...истинный экстаз / *(2)* ...истинное блаженство. ♦ **The sheer** *(1)* **pleasure** / *(2)* **ecstasy I get from being with you is something I can't describe.** *(1)* Истинное удовольствие, которое... / *(2)* Истинный экстаз, который... я получаю с тобой, невозможно описать. ♦ **I am totally in awe of your sheer physical beauty.** Я в полном благоговении перед твоей совершенной физической красотой. ♦ **I was**

The accents on Russian words are to show how to pronounce them.
You don't have to copy the accents when writing to someone.

surprised at the sheer intensity of your passion. Я был про́сто поражён и́стинной интенси́вностью твое́й стра́сти. ♦ *(1)* This being apart from you... / *(2)* Wanting you and not being able to have you... is sheer *(3)* hell / *(4)* torture / *(5)* agony / *(6)* misery. *(1)* Быть в разлу́ке с тобо́й... / *(2)* Жела́ть тебя́ и не име́ть возмо́жности быть с тобо́й... -- *(3)* ...су́щий ад. / *(4,5)* ...су́щая пы́тка. / *(6)* ...су́щее страда́ние.

sheet *n* 1. *(bed)* простыня́; 2. *(paper, metal)* лист ♦ How (absolutely) wonderful it would be to climb between the sheets to nestle against your warm, soft, luscious body. Как замеча́тельно бы́ло бы зале́зть ме́жду простыня́ми и прильну́ть к твоему́ тёплому, мя́гкому, со́чному те́лу. ♦ Oh, God, I want to get you between the sheets! О, Бо́же, как я хочу́ быть с тобо́й в посте́ли!

sherry *n* хе́рес.

shimmer *vi* мерца́ть ♦ I like the way your hair shimmers in the *(1)* light / *(2)* moonlight. Мне нра́вится, как мерца́ют твои́ во́лосы в *(1)* ...све́те. / *(2)* ...лу́нном све́те.

shimmering *adj* мерца́ющий, -ая, -ее, -ие, блестя́щий, -ая, -ее, -ие.

shine *vi* свети́ть, сия́ть ♦ Every morning when you wake up, I want your face to be shining with delight. Ка́ждое у́тро, когда́ ты просыпа́ешься, я хочу́, что́бы твоё лицо́ сия́ло от удово́льствия. ♦ I hope that your beautiful *(1)* dark / *(2)* blue eyes are shining with happiness to receive my letter. Я наде́юсь, что твои́ прекра́сные *(1)* тёмные / *(2)* голубы́е глаза́ засия́ют сча́стьем, когда́ ты полу́чишь моё письмо́.

shirt *n* руба́шка ♦ blouse ~ блу́за-руба́шка.

shirtless *adj* без руба́шки.

shiver *vi* дрожа́ть; трясти́сь; трепета́ть.

shiver *n* дрожь *f*, тре́пет, содрога́ние ♦ ~ of ecstasy тре́пет экста́за ♦ A shiver danced along my spine. Дрожь пробежа́ла по мое́й спине́. ♦ I'm going to send delicious shivers up and down your spine. Упои́тельный тре́пет, по́сланный мной, пробежи́т вверх и вниз по твое́й спине́. ♦ I'm going to make delicious shivers dance all over you. Я заста́влю всё твоё те́ло блаже́нно трепета́ть. ♦ My adoring mouth will send glorious shivers racing down your spine. Мой обожа́ющий рот пошлёт упои́тельный тре́пет по твое́й спине́.

shock *vt* возмуща́ть / возмути́ть *(whom = acc.)*, шоки́ровать *(whom = acc.)* ♦ Nothing shocks me. Ничего́ не смуща́ет меня́. ♦ Does that shock you? Это шоки́рует тебя́? ♦ That doesn't shock me. Это меня́ не шоки́рует. ♦ Did I shock you? Я шоки́ровал *(ж: шоки́ровала)* тебя́? ♦ You *(1)* ...didn't shock... / *(2)* ...shocked... me. Ты ...не шоки́ровала *(ж: не шоки́ровал)*... / ...шоки́ровала *(ж: шоки́ровал)*... меня́.

shock *n* уда́р, потрясе́ние; шок ♦ I've never suffered a shock like that before. Я никогда́ пре́жде не испы́тывал *(ж: испы́тывала)* тако́го потрясе́ния. ♦ It was really a shock. Это бы́ло настоя́щим шо́ком. ♦ What a shock! Како́й уда́р! ♦ I'm (still) in a state of shock. Я (до сих пор) в состоя́нии шо́ка. ♦ Your fingers on mine were like an electric shock. Твои́ па́льцы на мои́х бы́ли как электри́ческий шок.

shocked *adj* 1. *(startled; horrified)* потрясён, потрясена́, -о́, -ы́ *(short forms)*; 2. *(scandalized)* шоки́рован, -а, -о, -ы *(short forms)*, возмущён, возмущена́, -о́, -ы́ *(short forms)* ♦ Are you shocked? Ты шоки́рована *(ж: шоки́рован)*? ♦ I'm (not) shocked. Я (не) шоки́рован *(ж: шоки́рована)*. ♦ I'm not easily shocked. Меня́ не легко́ шоки́ровать. ♦ I'm afraid to open my heart to you and tell you everything I feel, because I'm afraid you would be offended or shocked or angry and then stop writing to me. Я бою́сь откры́ть тебе́ своё се́рдце и сказа́ть всё, что я чу́вствую, потому́ что страшу́сь того́, что ты оби́дишься, бу́дешь шоки́рована или рассе́рдишься и переста́нешь писа́ть мне.

shocking *adj* возмути́тельный, -ая, -ое, -ые, сканда́льный, -ая, -ое, -ые ♦ ~ experience

---

If no accent is shown on a word with a capitalized vowel,
it means that the capitalized vowel is accented.

возмути́тельный слу́чай. ♦ **Nothing is too shocking for me.** Ничто́ не шоки́рует меня́.
♦ **Is that shocking (for you)?** Это шоки́рует (тебя́)?

shoe *n* боти́нок, полуботи́нок; *(woman's)* ту́фля ♦ **high-heeled** ~s ту́фли на высо́ких каблука́х ♦ **low-heeled** ~s ту́фельки на ни́зких каблучка́х ♦ **old** ~s ста́рые ту́фли ♦ **spike** ~s же́нские ту́фли на высо́ких, то́нких каблука́х ♦ **pair of** ~s па́ра боти́нок; па́ра ту́фель.

shook up *adj (idiomatic for "shaken up")* возбуждён, возбуждена́, -о́, -ы́ *(short forms)* ♦ **You've got me all shook up.** Ты меня́ всего́ возбуди́ла *(ж: всю возбуди́л).* ♦ **Every time I look at you, I get all shook up.** Ка́ждый раз, когда́ я смотрю́ на тебя́, я весь *(ж: вся)* возбужда́юсь.

shoot *vt*: ♦ ~ **the breeze** болта́ть.

shoot *vi* проноси́ться / пронести́сь, мча́ться / промча́ться ♦ **You send electric sensations shooting through** *(1)* **...my entire body.** / *(2)* **...every cell and fiber of my body.** Ты посыла́ешь электри́ческие заря́ды, простре́ливающие *(1)* ...всё моё те́ло. / *(2)* ...ка́ждую кле́тку и все фи́бры моего́ те́ла.

shop around *vi* 1. присма́триваться к це́нам *(товаров) (for what = gen.)*; 2. подыски́вать / подыска́ть *(for what = acc.)*, иска́ть *(for what, whom = acc.)* ♦ **I'm shopping around for someone who's interested in a long-term relationship.** Я ищу́ того́, кто заинтересо́ван в дли́тельных отноше́ниях.

shopping *n*: ♦ **Would you like to go shopping (with me)?** Не хоте́ла *(ж: хоте́л)* бы ты пойти́ *(on foot)* / пое́хать *(by veh.)* за поку́пками (со мной)? ♦ **Let's** *(1,2)* **go shopping (together) (for** *[3]* **...some clothes for you.** / *[4]* **...something nice** / *[5]* **pretty for you.** / *[6]* **...a new dress** / *[7]* **coat for you.)** Дава́й *(1)* пойдём / *(2)* пое́дем за поку́пками (вме́сте) (за *[3]* ...оде́ждой для тебя́. / *[4]* ...че́м-нибудь прия́тным / *[5]* привлека́тельным для тебя́. / *[6]* ...но́вым пла́тьем / *[7]* пальто́ для тебя́.).

short *adj* 1. *(time or length)* коро́ткий, -ая, -ое, -ие; 2. *(height)* невысо́кий, -ая, -ое, -ие, ни́зкого ро́ста; *(low)* ни́зкий, -ая, -ое, -ие ♦ ~ **woman** невысо́кая же́нщина, же́нщина ни́зкого ро́ста ♦ **to make a long story** ~ коро́че говоря́.

shortcoming *n* недоста́ток, несоверше́нство ♦ **No matter what your flaws and shortcomings are, I love you (with all my heart).** Не име́ет значе́ния, каки́е у тебя́ недоста́тки и несоверше́нства, я люблю́ тебя́ (всем се́рдцем). ♦ **I hope you can block out my shortcomings.** Наде́юсь, ты смо́жешь не обраща́ть внима́ния на мои́ недоста́тки.

shorts *n, pl* трусы́ ♦ **boxer** ~s дли́нные трусы́.

short-waisted *adj* с коро́ткой та́лией.

shot *n*: ♦ **This is a shot in the dark, but I decided to try anyway.** Это вы́стрел в темноту́, но я реши́л *(ж: реши́ла)* всё-таки попро́бовать.

shoulder *n* плечо́ *(pl: пле́чи)*; *(little)* плечико ♦ **bare** ~s обнажённые пле́чи ♦ **beautiful** ~s краси́вые пле́чи ♦ **broad, powerful** ~s широ́кие, могу́чие пле́чи ♦ **creamy** ~s кре́мовые пле́чи ♦ **delicate** ~s хру́пкие пле́чики ♦ **little** ~s пле́чики ♦ **lovely** ~s краси́вые пле́чи ♦ **milky white** ~s моло́чно-бе́лые пле́чи ♦ **powerful** ~s могу́чие пле́чи ♦ **rounded** ~s окру́глые пле́чи ♦ **shapely** ~s пле́чи краси́вой фо́рмы ♦ **slender** ~s у́зкие пле́чи ♦ **smooth** ~s гла́дкие пле́чи ♦ **soft** ~s не́жные пле́чи ♦ **sore** ~ больно́е плечо́ ♦ **shrug** *(1)* **my** / *(2)* **your shoulders** жать / пожа́ть *(1,2)* плеча́ми.

> **shoulder: phrases**

You have such delicate shoulders. У тебя́ таки́е хру́пкие пле́чи. ♦ **I need your shoulder to lean on (in difficult times).** Мне ну́жно твоё плечо́, что́бы прислони́ться (в тру́дное вре́мя). ♦ **What do you have a chip on your shoulder about?** Почему́ ты и́щешь по́вод для ссо́ры? ♦ **You always seem to be carrying a chip on your shoulder.** Ты, ка́жется,

---

Russian has 6 grammatical cases. For an explanation of them,
see the grammar appendix on page 686.

всегда́ и́щешь по́вод для ссо́ры. ♦ **Now you give me the cold shoulder.** В после́днее вре́мя ты ока́зываешь мне холо́дный приём. ♦ **You sure gave me the cold shoulder.** Ты действи́тельно хо́лодно встре́тила *(ж: встре́тил)* меня́. ♦ **Why have you turned a cold shoulder to me?** Почему́ ты хо́лодно встреча́ешь меня́?

shove away *vt* отта́лкивать / оттолкну́ть *(what, whom = acc.).*

show *vt* 1. *(display)* пока́зывать / показа́ть *(what = acc., to whom = dat.);* 2. *(demonstrate, extend)* проявля́ть / прояви́ть *(what = acc., to whom = dat.),* выка́зывать / вы́казать *(what = acc., to whom = dat.);* *(give)* дава́ть / дать *(what = acc., to whom = dat.);* 3. *(express)* выража́ть / вы́разить *(what = acc., to whom = dat.).*

> **show: phrases**

I want to show you my love in every possible way. Я хочу́ вы́разить тебе́ свою́ любо́вь все́ми возмо́жными спо́собами. ♦ **I want to spend all my time showing you love.** Я хочу́, что́бы всё моё вре́мя бы́ло о́тдано мое́й любви́ к тебе́. ♦ **You have shown me** *(1)* **...so much love.** / *(2)* **...more love than I have ever known.** Ты дала́ *(ж: дал)* мне *(1)* ...так мно́го любви́. / *(2)* ...бо́льше любви́, чем я когда́-либо знал *(ж: зна́ла).* ♦ **Darling, I want so very much to (see you and talk with you and) show you love in all the ways that it's possible to show love.** Дорога́я *(ж: Дорого́й),* я так си́льно хочу́ (уви́деть тебя́ и говори́ть с тобо́й и) показа́ть тебе́ любо́вь все́ми возмо́жными спо́собами. ♦ **Show me where to** *(1)* **...kiss you.** / *(2)* **...put my lips.** Покажи́ мне, *(1)* ...куда́ поцелова́ть тебя́. / *(2)* ...где бы ты хоте́ла *(ж: хоте́л)* мои́ гу́бы.

show *n* 1. *(demonstration)* пока́з, демонстра́ция 2. *(performance)* спекта́кль, представле́ние, зре́лище, шо́у ♦ **Your constant show of affection** *(1)* **...fills my heart with love for you.** / *(1)* **...makes me love you more and more.** Твоя́ постоя́нно выража́емая любо́вь *(1)* ...наполня́ет моё се́рдце любо́вью к тебе́. / *(2)* ...всё бо́льше и бо́льше уси́ливает мою́ любо́вь к тебе́.

shower *vt (kisses)* затопля́ть / затопи́ть *(whom = acc., with what = instr.),* залива́ть / зали́ть *(whom = acc., with what = instr.);* *(gifts)* засыпа́ть / засы́пать *(whom = acc., with what = instr.)* ♦ **When we meet in the airport, I'm going to swing you around (and around) and shower you with kisses.** Когда́ мы встре́тимся в аэропорту́, я закружу́ тебя́ на рука́х и затоплю́ поцелу́ями. ♦ **I'm going to shower your face with (tender, loving) kisses.** Я затоплю́ твоё лицо́ (не́жными, лю́бящими) поцелу́ями. ♦ **Shower me with your love.** Излéй на меня́ свою́ любо́вь.

shower *n* душ ♦ **wedding** ~ приём госте́й в до́ме неве́сты с преподнесе́нием сва́дебных пода́рков ♦ **take a** ~ **(together)** принима́ть / приня́ть душ (вме́сте).

shrew *n* меге́ра, сварли́вая же́нщина.

shrewish *adj* сварли́вый, -ая, -ое, -ые, ворчли́вый, -ая, -ое, -ые.

shriek *n* визг, вопль *m* ♦ ~ **of joy** вопль удово́льствия.

shrug *vt* пожима́ть / пожа́ть *(what = instr.)* ♦ ~ **off** *vt* отма́хиваться / отмахну́ться *(what* = + от + *gen.),* отмета́ть / отмести́ *(what = acc.),* не реаги́ровать *(what* = + на + *acc.),* не обраща́ть / не обрати́ть внима́ния *(what* = + на + *acc.)* ♦ ~ **your shoulders** пожима́ть / пожа́ть плеча́ми ♦ **Why do you shrug your shoulders?** Почему́ ты пожима́ешь плеча́ми?

shudder *n* дрожь *f,* содрога́ние, тре́пет ♦ **ecstatic** ~ тре́пет экста́за.

shuddering *adj* дрожа́щий, -ая, -ее, -ее; вздра́гивающий, -ая, -ее, -ее ♦ ~ **ecstasy** дрожа́щий (-ая, -ее, -ие) в экста́зе.

shun *vt* избега́ть *(what, whom = acc.),* держа́ться в стороне́ *(what, whom* = + от + *gen.),* остерега́ться *(what, whom* = + от + *gen.).*

shut out *vt:* ♦ **I can never shut you out of my** *(1)* **heart** / *(2)* **thoughts.** Ты всегда́ бу́дешь в

> *There are no articles ("a" or "the") in Russian.*

(1) ...моём се́рдце. / *(2)* ...мои́х мы́слях.

shut up *vi (slang) (stop talking)* замолча́ть.

shy *adj* засте́нчивый, -ая, -ое, -ые ♦ **You don't have to be shy with me.** Ты не должна́ *(ж: до́лжен)* быть засте́нчивой *(ж: засте́нчивым)* со мной. ♦ *(1,2)* **Don't be (so) shy.** *(1)* Не будь (так) засте́нчива *(ж: засте́нчив).* / *(2)* Не (так) стесня́йся. ♦ **I'm basically a shy person.** Я в су́щности засте́нчивый челове́к.

shyness *n* засте́нчивость *f* ♦ **girlish ~** де́вичья засте́нчивость ♦ **Your shyness and quiet nature belie the passion within you.** Твоя́ засте́нчивость и споко́йный хара́ктер даю́т неве́рное представле́ние о твое́й стра́стности. ♦ **I'll help you overcome your shyness.** Я помогу́ тебе́ преодоле́ть засте́нчивость. ♦ **You'll soon get over your shyness.** Ты ско́ро преодоле́ешь свою́ стесни́тельность.

sibling *n* родно́й брат *m*, родна́я сестра́ *f.*

sick *adj* больно́й, -а́я, -о́е, -ы́е *(short forms:* бо́лен, больна́, -о, -ы́ *)* ♦ **be ~** быть больны́м *m* / больно́й *f (I'm sick:* я бо́лен *[ж: больна́]. You're sick:* ты больна́ *[ж: бо́лен].),* боле́ть ♦ **get ~** заболе́ть ♦ **I must confess, I am sick with love for you.** Я до́лжен *(ж: должна́)* призна́ться, я бо́лен *(ж: больна́)* от любви́ к тебе́. ♦ **You make me sick.** Меня́ тошни́т от тебя́. ♦ **I'm sick (and tired) of your duplicity.** Мне осточерте́ла твоя́ двули́чность.

side *n* сторона́ ♦ **~, by ~** бок о бок; ря́дом ♦ **on the flip ~** с друго́й стороны́ ♦ **Side by side I know we can** *(1)* **face** / *(2)* **surmount whatever life brings.** Вме́сте, я зна́ю, мы мо́жем *(1)* ...сме́ло встре́тить... / *(2)* ...преодоле́ть... всё, что преподнесёт нам жизнь. ♦ **I have a fun-loving side.** Я люблю́ развлече́ния. ♦ **I seek someone with a humorous side.** Я ищу́ челове́ка с ю́мором. ♦ **I seek someone with a** *(2)* **passionate** / *(3)* **romantic side.** Я ищу́ *(1)* стра́стного / *(2)* романти́чного челове́ка. ♦ **Tell me your side.** Расскажи́ мне твой вариа́нт.

sideburns *n, pl* бачки́.

sideways *adv* на боку́ ♦ **make love ~** занима́ться любо́вью на боку́.

sigh *vi* вздыха́ть / вздохну́ть ♦ **~ blissfully** вздыха́ть сча́стливо ♦ **~ contentedly** вздыха́ть удовлетворённо ♦ **~ heavily** вздыха́ть тяжело́.

sigh *n* вздох ♦ **blissful ~** счастли́вый вздох ♦ **contented ~** удовлетворённый вздох ♦ **gentle ~** мя́гкий вздох ♦ **~ of ecstasy** вздох экста́за ♦ **~ of pleasure** вздох наслажде́ния ♦ **~ of relief** вздох облегче́ния ♦ **weary ~** утомлённый вздох ♦ **emit a ~** испуска́ть / испусти́ть вздох ♦ **All night long I want to hear the music of your ecstasy-filled sighs.** Всю ночь я хочу́ слы́шать му́зыку твои́х вздо́хов, напо́лненных экста́зом.

sight *n* 1. *(vision)* зре́ние; 2. *(s.th. seen)* вид; *(spectacle)* зре́лище; *(scenic)* *(pl)* достопримеча́тельности; 3. *(look)* взгляд; 4. *(gun)* прице́л ♦ **catch ~ of** уви́деть *(what, whom = acc.),* заме́тить *(what, whom = acc.)* ♦ **magnificent ~** ди́вное зре́лище ♦ **marvelous ~** ди́вное зре́лище.

sight: phrases

Out of sight, out of mind. С глаз доло́й, из се́рдца вон. ♦ **My heart lightened at the sight of you.** У меня́ светле́ло на се́рдце, когда́ я ви́дел *(ж: ви́дела)* тебя́. ♦ **The sight of your beautiful face** *(1)* **...makes me dream of all the pleasures in paradise.** / *(2)* **...fills my whole body with warm excitement and floods my heart with feelings of love for you.** (Взгляд на) твоё прекра́сное лицо́ *(1)* ...заставля́ет мечта́ть о всех наслажде́ниях ра́я. / *(2)* ...напо́лняет всё моё те́ло жа́рким возбужде́нием и затопля́ет се́рдце чу́вством любви́ к тебе́.

sightseeing *n* осмо́тр достопримеча́тельностей ♦ **go ~** осма́тривать / осмотре́ть достопримеча́тельности ♦ **Would you like to go sightseeing (with me)?** Не хоте́ла *(ж: хоте́л)* бы ты осмотре́ть достопримеча́тельности (со мной)? ♦ **Let's go sightseeing**

This dictionary contains two Russian alphabet pages:
one in Appendix 1, page 685, and a tear-off page on page 799.

(together). Дава́й осмо́трим достопримеча́тельности (вме́сте). ♦ **We could do week-end sightseeing together.** Мы смогли́ бы в выходны́е дни осмотре́ть достопримеча́тельности вме́сте.

sign *n* знак ♦ **~s of affection** зна́ки любви́ ♦ **zodiac** ~ знак зодиа́ка *(See various zodiac signs under* **zodiac***)* ♦ **Little signs of affection mean a lot to me.** Ма́ленькие зна́ки любви́ зна́чат мно́го для меня́. ♦ **I love (your) small signs of affection.** Я люблю́ (твои́) ма́ленькие зна́ки любви́.

signal *n* сигна́л; знак ♦ **come-hither** ~ призыва́ющие сигна́лы ♦ **courtship** ~ знак уха́-живания ♦ **fiery** ~s о́гненные сигна́лы ♦ **gender** ~s зна́ки по́ла ♦ **love** ~s любо́вные зна́ки, знаки любви́ ♦ **sexual** ~s сексуа́льные зна́ки ♦ **give** ~s дава́ть / дать сигна́лы *(to whom = dat.)* ♦ **send love** ~s посыла́ть / посла́ть любо́вные сигна́лы *(to whom = dat.)* ♦ **My eyes were sending you love signals all evening. (Did you read them?)** Мои́ глаза́ посыла́ли тебе́ любо́вные сигна́лы весь ве́чер. (Ты прочла́ *[ж: прочёл]* их?)

silence *n* тишина́, молча́ние ♦ **awkward** ~ нело́вкое молча́ние ♦ **complete** ~ по́лное молча́ние ♦ **dead** ~ мёртвая тишина́ ♦ **gloomy** ~ угрю́мое молча́ние ♦ **long** ~ до́лгое молча́ние ♦ **my** ~ моё молча́ние ♦ **strained** ~ напряжённая тишина́ ♦ **total** ~ по́лное молча́ние ♦ **uncomfortable** ~ неудо́бное молча́ние ♦ **your** ~ *(familiar)* твоё мол-ча́ние; *(polite)* Ва́ше молча́ние ♦ **lapse into** ~ впасть в молча́ние.

silent *adj* молчали́вый, -ая, -ое, -ые ♦ **be** ~ молча́ть ♦ **keep** ~ храни́ть молча́ние.

silhouette *n* силуэ́т.

silhouetted *adj* вы́рисованный (-ая, -ое, -ые) на фо́не ♦ **be** ~ вырисо́вываться ♦ **You looked so** *(1)* **beautiful /** *(2)* **lovely silhouetted against the moonlit** *(3)* **sky /** *(4)* **window.** Ты так *(1)* прекра́сно / *(2)* преле́стно вырисо́вываешься на фо́не освещённого луно́й *(3)* не́ба / *(4)* окна́.

silk *n* шёлк ♦ **You look so** *(1)* **gorgeous /** *(2)* **voluptuous /** *(3)* **svelte encased in silk.** Ты вы́глядишь *(1)* ...так великоле́пно / *(2)* роско́шно... / *(3)* ...тако́й стро́йной... упако́-ванной в шёлк. ♦ **Your touch is raw silk.** Твоё прикоснове́ние -- про́сто шёлк. ♦ **Your skin is as smooth as silk.** Твоя́ ко́жа так же нежна́ как шёлк.

silky *adj* шелкови́стый, -ая, -ое, -ые.

silliness *n* глу́пость ♦ **inspired** ~ вдохнове́нная глу́пость.

silly *adj* глу́пый, -ая, -ое, -ые ♦ **act** ~ де́йствовать глу́по; поступа́ть / поступи́ть глу́по. ♦ **feel** ~ чу́вствовать себя́ глу́по ♦ **I** *(1)* **feel /** *(2)* **felt so silly.** Я *(1)* чу́вствую / *(2)* чу́вствовал себя́ *(ж: чу́вствовала)* так глу́по. ♦ **You probably think I'm acting silly.** Ты, вероя́тно, ду́маешь, что я поступа́ю глу́по. ♦ **I am silly with love for you.** Я глупе́ю от любви́ к тебе́.

silver-haired *adj* с посеребрёнными (седино́й) волоса́ми.

silver-maned *adj* с посеребрёнными (седино́й) волоса́ми.

silver-tongued *adj* сладкоречи́вый, -ая, -ое, -ые ♦ ~ **devil** сладкоречи́вый дья́вол.

similar *adj* схо́жий, -ая, -ее, -ие, подо́бный, -ая, -ое, -ые.

simple *adj* просто́й, -а́я, -о́е, -ы́е.

simplicity *n* простота́ ♦ **I cherish simplicity.** Я люблю́ простоту́.

sin *n* грех ♦ **It's not a sin to make love.** Это не грех занима́ться любо́вью. ♦ **We have committed no sin.** Мы не соверша́ли никако́го греха́.

sincere *adj* и́скренний, -яя, -ее, -ие *(short forms:* и́скренен, и́скренна, -о, -и*)* ♦ **I'm sincere in everything I say (to you).** Я и́скренен *(ж: и́скренна)* во всём, что я говорю́ (тебе́). ♦ **My feelings for you are** *(1)* **completely /** *(2)* **very sincere.** Мои́ чу́вства к тебе́ *(1)* со-верше́нно / *(2)* о́чень и́скренни.

sincerely *adv* и́скренне ♦ **I sincerely hope that** *(1)* **...you can get your visa soon. /** *(2)*

Russian verbs conjugate for 6 persons:
I, familiar you, he-she-it, we, polite&plural you, and they.

...**everything goes according to plan.** Я и́скренне наде́юсь, что *(1)* ...ты вско́ре получишь ви́зу. / *(2)* ...всё идёт согла́сно пла́ну.

sincerity и́скренность *f* ♦ **I want sincerity in a relationship.** Я хочу́ и́скренности в отно-
ше́ниях. ♦ **Your sincerity was just a facade.** Твоя́ и́скренность была́ то́лько ви́ди-
мостью.

sinewy *adj* мускули́стый, -ая, -ое, -ые, си́льный, -ая, -ое, -ые ♦ **~ arms** мускули́стые
ру́ки.

sinful *adj* гре́шный, -ая, -ое, -ые.

sing *vi* петь / спеть ♦ **My heart sings whenever I think of you.** Моё се́рдце поёт вся́кий
раз, когда́ я ду́маю о тебе́. ♦ **You make my heart sing (with joy).** Ты заставля́ешь моё
се́рдце петь (от ра́дости). ♦ **I want to tune your body with my mouth and hands until
it sings.** Я хочу́ настра́ивать твоё те́ло свои́м ртом и рука́ми до тех пор, пока́ оно́ не
запоёт. ♦ **My lips will make your body sing.** Мои́ гу́бы заста́вят твоё те́ло петь.

singing *n* пе́ние ♦ **A crazy, wild singing was in my ears.** Безу́мное, ди́кое пе́ние звуча́ло
в мои́х уша́х.

single *adj* холосто́й *m;* незаму́жняя *f* ♦ **remain / stay ~s** остава́ться холосты́м *(ж: неза-
му́жней)* ♦ **No wonder you're still single — you're constantly** *(1)* **busy /** *(2)* **working.** Не
удиви́тельно, что ты всё ещё одна́ *(ж: оди́н),* -- ты постоя́нно *(1)* занята́ *(ж: за́нят)*
/ *(2)* рабо́таешь. ♦ **I've been single too long.** Я был холосты́м *(ж: была́ незаму́жней)*
сли́шком до́лго. ♦ **I'm** *(1)* **sick /** *(2)* **tired of being single.** *(1)* Я бо́лен *(ж: больна́)* / уста́л
(ж: уста́ла) от одино́чества. / *(2)* Я уста́л *(ж: уста́ла)* быть одино́ким *(ж: одино́кой).*
♦ **I have a friend who is single. Can you introduce** *(1)* **him /** *(2)* **her to someone?** У меня́
есть друг *(ж: подру́га),* у кото́рого *(ж: у кото́рой)* никого́ нет. Мо́жешь ли ты *(1)* его́
/ *(2)* её с ке́м-нибудь познако́мить?

singleness *n* безбра́чие.

sink *vi (heart)* оборва́ться ♦ **~ in** *vi* дойти́; устоя́ться ♦ **My heart sank.** Моё се́рдце обо-
рва́лось. ♦ **Let's let it sink in and go from there.** Дава́й дади́м э́тому устоя́ться и
посмо́трим, что полу́чится.

sip *n* (ма́ленький) глото́к, небольшо́е коли́чество ♦ **take a ~** отпи́ть.

siren *n* сире́на ♦ **My sloe-eyed siren, I can never get enough of you.** Моя́ темногла́зая
сире́на, я никогда́ не смогу́ насы́титься тобо́й.

sit *vi (in position)* сиде́ть; *(down)* сади́ться / сесть ♦ **Is anyone sitting here?** Кто́-нибудь
сиди́т здесь? ♦ **Please sit down.** *(polite:)* Пожа́луйста, сади́тесь. ♦ **Do you mind if I sit**
(1) **...here? /** *(2)* **...with you?** *(polite:)* Вы не возража́ете, е́сли я ся́ду *(1)* ...сюда́? / *(2)* ...с
Ва́ми? ♦ **You can sit** *(1)* **...here. /** *(2)* **...next to me. /** *(3)* **...with me. /** *(4)* **...at my table.**
(polite:) Вы мо́жете сесть *(1)* ...сюда́. / *(2)* ...ря́дом со мной. / *(3)* ...со мной. / *(4)* ...за
мой стол. ♦ **Come sit** *(1)* **...with me. /** *(2)* **...at my table.** Приди́те и ся́дьте *(1)* ...со мной.
/ *(2)* ...за мой стол. ♦ **Let's sit** *(1)* **here /** *(2)* **(over) there.** Дава́й ся́дем *(1)* здесь / *(2)* (вон)
там.

site *n* 1. *(place)* ме́сто; 2. *(web)* сайт ♦ **web ~** веб-сайт.

situation *n* ситуа́ция, положе́ние, состоя́ние ♦ **awkward ~** нело́вкое положе́ние ♦ **complicated ~** сло́жное положе́ние ♦ **compromising ~** компроми́ссная ситуа́ция ♦ **critical
~** крити́ческое положе́ние ♦ **dating ~** свида́ние ♦ **desperate ~** отча́янное положе́ние
♦ *(1,2)* **difficult ~** *(1)* тру́дное / *(2)* тяжёлое положе́ние ♦ **embarrassing ~** смуща́ющая
ситуа́ция ♦ **family ~** семе́йная ситуа́ция ♦ **financial ~** фина́нсовая ситуа́ция ♦ **foolish
~** дура́цкое положе́ние ♦ **funny ~** *(humorous)* смешно́е положе́ние ♦ **hopeless ~** без-
вы́ходное положе́ние ♦ **marital ~** ситуа́ция в бра́ке ♦ **marriage ~** ситуа́ция в бра́ке
♦ **money ~** де́нежная ситуа́ция ♦ **my ~** моё положе́ние, моя́ ситуа́ция ♦ **nightmarish**

There are two words for "you" in Russian:
familiar «ты» and polite / plural «вы» (See page 771).

~ кошма́рная ситуа́ция ◆ **sticky** ~ *(difficult)* тру́дная ситуа́ция; *(unpleasant)* неприя́т-
ная ситуа́ция ◆ **terrible** ~ ужа́сное положе́ние ◆ **ticklish** ~ щекотли́вое положе́ние
◆ **unpleasant** ~ неприя́тное положе́ние, неприя́тная ситуа́ция ◆ **your** ~ *(familiar)* твоё
положе́ние, твоя́ ситуа́ция; *(polite)* Ва́ше положе́ние, Ва́ша ситуа́ция ◆ **I couldn't
stand the situation (any longer).** Я не мог *(ж: могла́)* (до́льше) терпе́ть э́ту ситуа́цию.
sixty-nine *(slang) (mutual oral sex)* взаи́мный ора́льный секс.
size *n* разме́р ◆ **dress** ~ разме́р пла́тья ◆ **ring** ~ разме́р кольца́ ◆ **shoe** ~ разме́р ту́фель
◆ **what** ~ како́й разме́р.
skate *vi* 1. *(iceskate)* ката́ться на конька́х; 2. *(roller-skate)* ката́ться на ро́ликах.
skating *n* 1. *(iceskating)* ката́ние на конька́х; 2. *(roller-skating)* ката́ние на ро́ликах ◆ **ice**
~ ката́ние на конька́х ◆ **inline** ~ *(rollerblading)* ката́ние на ро́ликах с одни́м по́лозом.
ski *vi* ката́ться на лы́жах.
skier *n* лы́жник *m*, лы́жница *f* ◆ *(1,2)* **avid** ~ *(1)* аза́ртный / *(2)* стра́стный лы́жник *m*, *(1)*
аза́ртная / *(2)* стра́стная лы́жница *f.*
skiing *n* ката́ние на лы́жах ◆ **water** ~ ката́ние на во́дных лы́жах ◆ **jet** ~ ката́ние на
во́дном ску́тере ◆ **Would you like to go skiing (with me)?** Не хоте́ла *(ж: хоте́л)* бы ты
пойти́ на лы́жах (со мной)? ◆ **Let's go skiing (together).** Дава́й пойдём на лы́жах
(вме́сте).
skill *n* мастерство́; уме́ние; иску́сство ◆ **good communication** ~s хоро́шая коммуни-
ка́бельность ◆ **impeccable social** ~s блестя́щие на́выки обще́ния ◆ **social** *(1,2)* ~s *(1)*
на́выки / *(2)* культу́ра обще́ния ◆ **possess social** ~s владе́ть культу́рой обще́ния.
skillful *adj* уме́лый, -ая, -ое, -ые.
skimpy *adj* ску́дный, -ая, -ое, -ые; лёгкий, -ая, -ое, -ие.
skin *n* ко́жа ◆ **baby soft** ~ ко́жа не́жная, как у ребёнка *(1 term)* ◆ **bronze** ~ бро́нзовая
ко́жа ◆ **bronzed** ~ загоре́лая ко́жа ◆ **clear** ~ чи́стая ко́жа ◆ **copper(-toned)** ~ ме́дная
ко́жа ◆ **creamy(-toned)** ~ кре́мовая ко́жа ◆ **creamy-smooth** ~ сли́вочно-ма́товая
ко́жа ◆ **dark** ~ тёмная ко́жа ◆ **delicate** ~ не́жная ко́жа ◆ **ebony** ~ чёрная ко́жа ◆ **exquisite** ~ изуми́тельная ко́жа ◆ *(1,2)* **fair** ~ *(1)* све́тлая / *(2)* бе́лая ко́жа ◆ **golden** ~
золоти́стая ко́жа ◆ *(1,2)* **heated** ~ *(1)* разогре́тая / *(2)* горя́чая ко́жа ◆ **ivory** ~ ко́жа
цве́та слоно́вой ко́сти ◆ **pale** ~ бле́дная ко́жа ◆ **pearly** ~ жемчу́жная ко́жа ◆ **satin**
~ атла́сная ко́жа ◆ **satin-smooth** ~ атла́сно-не́жная ко́жа ◆ **sensitive** ~ чувстви́тельная
ко́жа ◆ **sensually soft** ~ чу́вственно-не́жная ко́жа ◆ **silken** ~ шёлковая ко́жа ◆ **silky**
~ шелкови́стая ко́жа ◆ ~ **and bones** ко́жа да ко́сти ◆ ~ **like a(n)** *(1)* **peach** / *(2)* **apricot**
ко́жа как *(1)* пе́рсик / *(2)* абрико́с ◆ **snow-white** ~ белосне́жная ко́жа ◆ *(1,2)* **softly
tanned** ~ ко́жа с *(1)* лёгким / *(2)* мя́гким зага́ром ◆ **swarthy** ~ сму́глая ко́жа ◆ **tanned**
~ загоре́лая ко́жа ◆ **tender** ~ не́жная ко́жа ◆ *(1,2)* **velvet(y)** ~ *(1)* бархати́стая / *(2)*
ба́рхатная ко́жа ◆ **velvety soft** ~ бархати́сто-мя́гкая ко́жа ◆ **your** ~ *(familiar)* твоя́
ко́жа; *(polite)* Ва́ша ко́жа.

> **skin:** *your beautiful skin*

You have such (rose-)petal-soft skin. У тебя́ така́я мя́гкая, как (ро́зовый) лепесто́к,
ко́жа. ◆ **Your skin has such a natural glow.** На твое́й ко́же тако́й натура́льный ру-
мя́нец. ◆ **You have such perfect skin.** У тебя́ превосхо́дная ко́жа. ◆ **Your skin is** *(1)*
...soft as velvet / *(2)* **a baby /** *(3)* **a kitten.** Твоя́ ко́жа мя́гкая, как *(1)* ...ба́рхат. / *(2)*
...ко́жа ребёнка. / *(3)* ...у котёнка. ◆ **The rich smoothness of your skin is so** *(1)* **exciting**
/ *(2)* **wonderful to touch.** Изуми́тельная гла́дкость твое́й ко́жи *(1)* ...так возбужда́ет /
(3) ...удиви́тельна при прикоснове́нии. ◆ **With your** *(1)* **blonde /** *(2)* **black /** *(3)* **red hair**
and *(4)* **creamy /** *(5)* **pale /** *(6)* **bronze /** *(7)* **golden skin you are the most striking woman**
I have ever *(8)* **seen /** *(9)* **met.** Со свои́ми *(1)* све́тлыми / *(2)* чёрными / *(3)* ры́жими

Russian terms of endearment are given in Appendix 13, page 780.

волоса́ми и *(4)* не́жной / *(5)* бле́дной / *(6)* бро́нзовой / *(7)* золоти́стой ко́жей ты са́мая потряса́ющая же́нщина, кото́рую я когда́-либо *(8)* ви́дел / *(9)* встреча́л.

skin: *how your skin affects me*

The rich smoothness of your skin excites my touch unimaginably. Прикоснове́ние к твое́й изуми́тельно гла́дкой ко́же невероя́тно возбужда́ет меня́. ♦ **Your milky white skin and shining blonde hair sing siren-like sonnets to me.** Твоя́ молочнобе́лая ко́жа и блестя́щие све́тлые во́лосы, подо́бно сире́нам, пою́т мне соне́ты. ♦ **Every time I talk with you and look into your beautiful face, all I can see in front of my eyes for hours and hours afterwards are your enchanting, sparkling eyes, your smooth white skin, your *(1)* enticing / *(2)* kissable red lips, and your angel-like golden hair.** Ка́ждый раз по́сле того́, как я говорю́ с тобо́й и смотрю́ на твоё прекра́сное лицо́, всё, что пото́м часа́ми встаёт пе́ред мои́ми глаза́ми -- твои́ очаро́вывающие, сверка́ющие глаза́, твоя́ мя́г-кая, бе́лая ко́жа, твои́ *(1)* ...маня́щие... / *(2)* ...зову́щие к поцелу́ям... кра́сные гу́бы и твои́ а́нгельские золоты́е во́лосы.

skin: *my fingers on your skin*

As my lips pay devoted homage to your nipples, my fingers will blaze a trail over your burning skin. В то вре́мя, как мои́ гу́бы ока́жут почти́тельное внима́ние твои́м соска́м, мои́ па́льцы бу́дут прокла́дывать о́гненный путь по твое́й ко́же.

skinny *adj* то́щий, -ая, -ее, -ие, худо́й, -а́я, -о́е, -ы́е, худоща́вый, -ая, -ое, -ые.

skintight *adj* в обтя́жку, обтя́гивающий, -ая, -ее, -ие (, как перча́тка).

skirt *n* ю́бка ♦ **daring** ~ де́рзкая ю́бка ♦ **provocative** ~ вызыва́юще коро́ткая ю́бка ♦ **short** ~ коро́ткая ю́бка ♦ **That's a (very) beautiful skirt.** Это (о́чень) краси́вая ю́бка.

skirt-chaser *n (slang)* ба́бник, волоки́та.

skittish *adj* игри́вый, -ая, -ое, -ые.

skort *n (full skirt separated like shorts)* ю́бка-шо́рты.

sky *n* не́бо ♦ *(1,2)* **blue** ~ *(1)* си́нее / *(2)* голубо́е не́бо ♦ *(1,2)* **clear** ~ *(1)* чи́стое / *(2)* я́сное не́бо ♦ **endless** ~ бесконе́чное не́бо ♦ **starry night** ~ звёздное ночно́е не́бо ♦ **summer** ~ ле́тнее не́бо ♦ *(1,2)* **blue of the** ~ *(1)* синева́ / *(2)* голубизна́ не́ба.

sky: *phrases*

Whether our skies our clear or stormy, let us always fly together as one. И в чи́стом не́бе, и в штормово́м дава́й всегда́ лета́ть вме́сте. ♦ **I love you all the way up to the sky.** Моя́ любо́вь к тебе́ необъя́тна, как не́бо. ♦ **Our love is like the sky — big and beautiful and forever.** На́ша любо́вь, как небо́, -- больша́я, прекра́сная и ве́чная.

skydiving *n* затяжны́е прыжки́ с парашю́том.

slacker *n (slang)* безде́льник *m*, безде́льница *f*.

slacks *n, pl* сла́ксы, брю́ки ♦ **pair of** ~s брю́ки.

Slav *n* славяни́н *m*, славя́нка *f (pl:* славя́не*).*

slave *n* раб *m*, раба́ *f* ♦ **I have become a slave to your** *(1)* **incomparable /** *(2)* **shining beauty.** Я стал рабо́м твое́й *(1)* несравне́нной / *(2)* блиста́тельной красоты́. ♦ **I am (complete-ly)** *(1,2)* **...your slave. /** *(3,4)* **...a slave to your beauty.** Я (по́лностью) *(1)* ...в твое́й вла́сти. / *(2)* ...твой раб *(ж: твоя́ раба́).* / *(3)* ...во вла́сти твое́й красоты́. / *(4)* ...раб твое́й красоты́. ♦ **I want to be your slave.** Я хочу́ быть твои́м рабо́м *(ж: рабо́й).* ♦ **I have this overwhelming desire to be a slave to you.** У меня́ всепоглоща́ющее жела́ние быть твои́м рабо́м *(ж: твое́й рабо́й).* ♦ **You have made me a slave of love.** Ты сде́лала *(ж: сде́лал)* меня́ рабо́м *(ж: рабо́й)* любви́. ♦ *(1)* **I'll be... /** *(2)* **I pledge myself to be... a slave to all your needs and desires.** *(1)* Я бу́ду... / *(2)* Я обязу́юсь быть... рабо́м всех твои́х нужд и жела́ний. ♦ **Darling, if I ever get in the same bed with you, I'm going to make myself a slave to your desires and your pleasure and your satisfaction.** Дорога́я,

---

Some of the Russian sentences are translations of things we say and are not what Russians themselves would normally say.

éсли я окажу́сь в одно́й посте́ли с тобо́й, я сде́лаю себя́ рабо́м твои́х страсте́й, твоего́ наслажде́ния и твоего́ удовлетворе́ния.

Slavic *adj* славя́нский, -ая, -ое, -ие.

slavish *adj* ра́бский, -ая, -ое, -ие.

sleazy *adj* 1. *(ethically low)* по́длый, -ая, -ое, -ые, ни́зкий, -ая, -ое, -ие; 2. *(unsightly, sloppy)* неря́шливый, -ая, -ое, -ые; *(shabby)* жа́лкий, -ая, -ое, -ие, убо́гий, -ая, -ое, -ие.

sleep *vi* спать / поспа́ть ♦ **~ around** спать с кем попа́ло ♦ **~ in** проспа́ть до́льше обы́чного ♦ **~ like a log** спать мёртвым сном ♦ **~ soundly** кре́пко спать ♦ **~ together** спать вме́сте ♦ **~ with a** *(1)* **man** / *(2)* **woman** переспа́ть с *(1)* мужчи́ной / *(2)* же́нщиной.

> **sleep:** *I love to watch you sleep*

(1) **I love to...** / *(2)* **I want to...** *(3)* **look** / *(4)* **gaze at** *(5)* **...you...** / *(6)* **...your beautiful face... when you're sleeping.** *(1)* Мне нра́вится... / *(2)* Я хочу́... *(3,4)* смотре́ть на *(5)* ...тебя́,... / *(6)* ...твоё прекра́сное лицо́,... когда́ ты спишь. ♦ **You're so** *(1)* **pretty** / *(2)* **angelic** / *(3)* **beautiful** / *(4)* **lovely** *(5)* **adorable when you're sleeping**. Ты так *(1)* хороша́ / *(2)* ангелоподо́бна / *(3)* прекра́сна / *(4)* краси́ва / *(5)* восхити́тельна, когда́ спишь.

> **sleep:** *I can't sleep*

I can't sleep without you. Я не могу́ спать без тебя́. ♦ **I couldn't sleep, thinking about you.** Я не мог *(ж: могла́)* спать, ду́мая о тебе́. ♦ **I didn't sleep a wink.** Я не сомкну́л *(ж: сомкну́ла)* глаз.

> **sleep:** *sleep together*

I want so much to sleep with you. Я так хочу́ спать с тобо́й. ♦ **No one will know if we sleep together.** Никто́ не узна́ет, е́сли мы бу́дем спать вме́сте. ♦ **I can't sleep with you.** Я не могу́ спать с тобо́й. ♦ **We can't sleep together.** Мы не мо́жем спать вме́сте. ♦ **Sleep at my place tonight.** Спи у меня́ сего́дня. ♦ **We don't sleep in the same bed anymore.** Мы бо́льше не спим в одно́й посте́ли.

> **sleep:** *I don't sleep around*

I'm not the kind of person who sleeps around. Я не тот челове́к, кото́рый спит с кем попа́ло.

sleep *n* сон ♦ **deep ~** глубо́кий сон ♦ *(1,2)* **restless ~** *(1)* беспоко́йный / *(2)* трево́жный сон ♦ **sound ~** кре́пкий сон ♦ **troubled ~** трево́жный сон ♦ **My sleep, shallow and restless, was assailed by visions of your beautiful, voluptuous body.** Мой сон, неглубо́кий и беспоко́йный, был нару́шен виде́нием твоего́ пре́красного, чу́вственного те́ла.

sleepless *adj* бессо́нный, -ая, -ое, -ые ♦ **I've had so many sleepless nights because of you.** У меня́ бы́ло так мно́го бессо́нных ноче́й и́з-за тебя́.

sleepyhead *n* со́ня, со́нная тете́ря.

slender *adj* то́нкий, -ая, -ое, -ие, стро́йный, -ая, -ое, -ые.

slenderness *n* то́нкость *f*, стро́йность *f*.

slight *adj* 1. *(not great)* небольшо́й, -а́я, -о́е, -и́е; 2. *(slim)* худоща́вый, -ая, -ое, -ые, то́нкий, -ая, -ое, -ие, изя́щный, -ая, -ое, -ые ♦ **You're a slight thing.** Ты изя́щное созда́ние.

slight *n* пренебреже́ние, неуваже́ние.

slightly *adv* слегка́, едва́, немно́го.

slim *adj* то́нкий, -ая, -ое, -ие, стро́йный, -ая, -ое, -ые.

slinky *adj* облега́ющий, -ая, -ее, -ие, в обтя́жку ♦ **~dress** облега́ющее пла́тье ♦ **~evening gown** облега́ющий вече́рний туале́т.

slip *vi:* ♦ **~ away** *vi* уходи́ть / уйти́ незаме́тно ♦ **~ in** *vi* проска́льзывать / проскользну́ть *(into what* = + в + *acc.)*, прокра́дываться / прокра́сться *(into what* = + в + *acc.)* ♦ **~ out** *vi* выска́льзывать / вы́скользнуть *(out of what* = + из + *gen.)*.

Counting things in Russian is a bit involved.
See Appendix 4, Numbers, on page 756 .

slip:
I wish you could come slip between the sheets with me right now. Я хотéл *(ж: хотéла)* бы, чтóбы ты пришлá *(ж: пришёл)* ко мне в постéль пря́мо сейчáс.

slip in:
I'll slip into your *(1)* **bedroom /** *(2)* **room later.** Я проскользну́ в твою́ *(1)* спáльню / *(2)* кóмнату позднéе.

slip out:
I'll slip out in the morning. Я вы́скользну у́тром.

slip *n (woman's undergarment)* комбинáция, сорóчка ♦ **satin ~** атлáсная комбинáция ♦ **~ of the tongue** обмóлвка, оговóрка.

slip on *vt (put on)* накидывать / накинуть *(what = acc.)*, надевáть / надéть *(what = acc.)* ♦ **~ a blouse** надевáть / надéть блу́зку.

slippers *n, pl* домáшние ту́фли, тáпочки ♦ **Marabou ~s** пуши́стые тáпочки.

sloe-eyed *adj* темноглáзая *f* ♦ **My sloe-eyed siren, I can never get enough of you.** Моя́ темноглáзая сирéна, я никогдá не смогу́ насы́титься тобóй.

slothful *adj* неря́шливый, -ая, -ое, -ые, неопря́тный, -ая, -ое, -ые.

sloppiness *n* неря́шливость *f.*

sloppy *adj* неря́шливый, -ая, -ое, -ые.

slovenly *adj* 1. *(lazy)* лени́вый, -ая, -ое, -ые; 2. *(sloppy)* неря́шливый, -ая, -ое, -ые.

slow *adj* мéдленный, -ая, -ое, -ые ♦ **I want to take it slow and get to know you (better).** Я не хочу́ спеши́ть и хочу́ лу́чше узнáть Вас.

slow-dance *vi* мéдленно танцевáть.

slowly *adv* мéдленно.

slowness *n* медли́тельность *f* ♦ **deliberate ~** нарочи́тая медли́тельность ♦ **tantalizing ~** сладострáстная медли́тельность.

slut *n* потаску́ха.

sly *adj* хи́трый, -ая, -ое, -ые, лóвкий, -ая, -ое, -ие ♦ **~ fox** хитрéц ♦ **on the ~** тайкóм, потихóньку, укрáдкой, под сурди́нку ♦ **I think you're seeing someone else on the sly.** Я ду́маю, что ты встречáешься с кéм-то ещё укрáдкой. ♦ *(1)* **She /** *(2)* **He has been seeing someone else on the sly.** Онá / Он встречáется с кéм-то ещё укрáдкой.

smack *n (slang) (noisy kiss)* (звóнкий) поцелу́й ♦ **~ on the lips** звóнкий поцелу́й.

smacker *n (slang) (mouth)* рот.

small *adj* мáленький, -ая, -ое, -ие.

small *n:* ♦ **~ of your back** твоя́ поясни́ца.

small-boned *adj* узкокóстный, -ая, -ое, -ые.

smart *adj* 1. *(intelligent, clever)* у́мный, -ая, -ое, -ые, тóлковый, -ая, -ое, -ые; *(bright)* шу́стрый, -ая, -ое, -ые; 2. *(stylish)* шикáрный, -ая, -ое, -ые; *(elegant)* наря́дный, -ая, -ое, -ые, элегáнтный, -ая, -ое, -ые ♦ **~ as a whip** чрезвычáйно у́мный, -ая, -ое, -ые.

smell *n* 1. *(general)* зáпах; *(fragrance)* аромáт, благоухáние; 2. *(unpleasant)* дурнóй зáпах, вонь *f* ♦ **I love the smell of** *(1)* **...you. /** *(2)* **...your hair /** *(3)* **mouth /** *(4)* **body.** Мне нрáвится *(1)* ...твой зáпах. / *(2)* ...зáпах твои́х волóс. / *(3)* ...аромáт твоегó дыхáния. / *(4)* ...зáпах твоегó тéла. ♦ **The clean, masculine smell of you excites me.** Твой чи́стый мужскóй зáпах возбуждáет меня́.

smelling *n* вдыхáние ♦ **Smelling your perfume just adds fuel to the fire of my desire for you.** Когдá я вдыхáю твои́ духи́, огóнь моéй стрáсти к тебé разжигáется ещё сильнéе.

smile *vi* улыбáться / улыбну́ться ♦ **~ affectionately** лю́бяще улыбáться / улыбну́ться ♦ **~ back** улыбáться / улыбну́ться в отвéт ♦ **~ blissfully** рáдостно улыбáться / улыбну́ться ♦ **~ bravely** улыбáться / улыбну́ться хрáбро ♦ **~ from ear to ear** широкó

Russian has 2 different vrbs for "go",
one for "on foot" and the other for "by vehicle".

улыба́ться / улыбну́ться ✦ ~ **politely** ве́жливо улыба́ться / улыбну́ться ✦ ~ **radiantly** лучеза́рно улыба́ться / улыбну́ться ✦ ~ **sadly** гру́стно улыба́ться / улыбну́ться ✦ ~ **shyly** засте́нчиво улыба́ться / улыбну́ться ✦ ~ **tenderly** не́жно улыба́ться / улыбну́ться.

smile: *phrases*

I see you smile in all the sunbeams. Я ви́жу твою́ улы́бку в ка́ждом со́лнечном луче́. ✦ **I like the way you smile.** Мне нра́вится, как ты улыба́ешься. ✦ **Remember to smile for me in your photos. I want to see the same kind of sunshine on your face that your letters bring to my heart.** Не забу́дь улыба́ться на свои́х фо́то. Я хочу́ ви́деть тако́й же со́лнечный свет на твоём лице́, како́й твои́ пи́сьма прино́сят в моё се́рдце. ✦ **I smile a lot.** Я ча́сто улыба́юсь. ✦ **I smile to myself thinking of you.** Я улыба́юсь, ду́мая о тебе́.

smile *n* улы́бка ✦ *(1,2)* **affectionate** ~ *(1)* не́жная / *(2)* ла́сковая улы́бка ✦ *(1,2)* **alluring** ~ *(1)* завлека́ющая / *(2)* маня́щая улы́бка ✦ **artificial** ~ иску́сственная улы́бка ✦ **beautiful** ~ прекра́сная улы́бка ✦ **blissful** ~ блаже́нная улы́бка ✦ *(1,2)* **beguiling** ~ *(1)* соблазни́тельная / *(2)* завора́живающая улы́бка ✦ *(1-3)* **bewitching** ~ *(1)* обворожи́тельная / *(2)* очарова́тельная / *(3)* чару́ющая улы́бка ✦ **bright** ~ сия́ющая улы́бка ✦ *(1,2)* **captivating** ~ *(1)* плени́тельная / *(2)* очарова́тельная улы́бка ✦ *(1,2)* **charming** ~ *(1)* обая́тельная / *(2)* очарова́тельная улы́бка ✦ **cheerful** ~ весёлая улы́бка ✦ **cold** ~ холо́дная улы́бка ✦ **comely** ~ ми́лая улы́бка ✦ **contented** ~ дово́льная улы́бка ✦ **cute** ~ ми́лая улы́бка ✦ **dazzling** ~ ослепи́тельная улы́бка ✦ **disarming** ~ обезору́живающая улы́бка ✦ *(1-3)* **enchanting** ~ *(1)* обворожи́тельная / *(2)* очарова́тельная / *(3)* чару́ющая улы́бка ✦ **endearing** ~ подкупа́ющая улы́бка ✦ *(1,2)* **engaging** ~ *(1)* привлека́тельная / *(2)* обая́тельная улы́бка ✦ **enigmatic** ~ зага́дочная улы́бка ✦ *(1,2)* **forced** ~ *(1)* вы́нужденная / *(2)* натя́нутая улы́бка ✦ **frequent** ~ ча́стая улы́бка ✦ **friendly** ~ приве́тливая улы́бка ✦ **frost-white** ~ белозу́бая улы́бка ✦ *(1-3)* **gentle** ~ *(1)* мя́гкая / *(2)* ла́сковая / *(3)* кро́ткая улы́бка ✦ **gleaming** ~ сия́ющая улы́бка ✦ **glowing** ~ сия́ющая улы́бка ✦ **gorgeous** ~ великоле́пная улы́бка ✦ **gracious** ~ ми́лостивая улы́бка ✦ **great** ~ замеча́тельная улы́бка ✦ *(1,2)* **halfhearted** ~ *(1)* безразли́чная / *(2)* равноду́шная улы́бка ✦ *(1,2)* **happy** ~ *(1)* ра́достная / *(2)* счастли́вая улы́бка ✦ **heart-melting** ~ улы́бка, от кото́рой та́ет се́рдце ✦ **hesitant** ~ нереши́тельная улы́бка ✦ **icy** ~ ледяна́я улы́бка ✦ **impudent** ~ наха́льная улы́бка ✦ **indulgent** ~ снисходи́тельная улы́бка ✦ **inviting** ~ приглаша́ющая улы́бка ✦ **killer** ~ убива́ющая улы́бка ✦ *(1-3)* **lovely** ~ *(1)* прекра́сная / *(2)* краси́вая / *(3)* привлека́тельная улы́бка ✦ **loving** ~ влюблённая улы́бка ✦ **mocking** ~ насме́шливая улы́бка ✦ *(1,2)* **nice** ~ *(1)* прия́тная / *(2)* сла́вная улы́бка ✦ **plastic** ~ неи́скренняя улы́бка ✦ **pleasant** ~ прия́тная улы́бка ✦ **pretty** ~ привлека́тельная улы́бка ✦ *(1,2)* **provocative** ~ *(1)* соблазни́тельная / *(2)* маня́щая улы́бка ✦ *(1-3)* **radiant** ~ *(1)* лучи́стая / *(2)* сия́ющая / *(3)* лучеза́рная улы́бка ✦ **sad** ~ гру́стная улы́бка ✦ **sardonic** ~ сардони́ческая усме́шка ✦ **satisfied** ~ дово́льная улы́бка ✦ **saucy** ~ коке́тливая улы́бка ✦ **secretive** ~ скры́тая улы́бка ✦ **seductive** ~ обольща́ющая улы́бка ✦ **sensual** ~ чу́вственная улы́бка ✦ **serene** ~ беззабо́тная улы́бка ✦ **shy** ~ засте́нчивая улы́бка ✦ ~ **laden with charm** очаро́вывающая улы́бка ✦ ~ **of sweet intimacy** не́жная, инти́мная улы́бка ✦ **sly** ~ хи́трая улы́бка ✦ **soft sensuous** ~ мя́гкая чу́вственная улы́бка ✦ **stunning** ~ умопомрачи́тельная улы́бка ✦ **sunny** ~ со́лнечная улы́бка ✦ **sunshine** ~ со́лнечная улы́бка ✦ *(1,2)* **sweet** ~ *(1)* ми́лая / *(2)* ла́сковая улы́бка ✦ **teasing** ~ дразня́щая улы́бка ✦ *(1,2)* **tender** ~ *(1)* не́жная / *(2)* ла́сковая улы́бка ✦ **toothpaste** ~ белозу́бая улы́бка ✦ **vibrant** ~ оживлённая улы́бка ✦ **vivacious** ~ оживлённая улы́бка ✦ **warm** ~ тёплая улы́бка ✦ **white-toothed** ~ белозу́бая улы́бка ✦ **wicked** ~ гре́шная улы́бка ✦ **wide, charming** ~ широ́кая, обая́тельная улы́бка ✦ *(1,2)* **winning** ~ *(1)* под-

---

Dipthongs in Russian are made by adding й
*to the end of a vowel (*а, е, ё, о, у, э, ю, *and* я*).*

купа́ющая / *(2)* побежда́ющая улы́бка ♦ **crack a** ~ улыбну́ться ♦ **quick to** ~ улы́бчивый, -ая, -ое, -ые.

---

smile: *your smile and its qualities*

You have such a beautiful smile. У тебя́ така́я прекра́сная улы́бка. ♦ **What a beautiful smile (you have)!** Что за прекра́сная улы́бка (у тебя́)! ♦ **You have the most beautiful smile I've ever seen.** Твоя́ улы́бка -- са́мая прекра́сная из всех, ви́денных мной. ♦ **You have the loveliest of smiles.** Твоя́ улы́бка -- краси́вейшая из улы́бок. ♦ **Your** *(1)* **blue /** *(2)* **dark eyes and wide smile radiate** *(3)* **warmth /** *(4)* **affection.** Твои́ *(1)* голу́бые / *(2)* тёмные глаза́ и широ́кая улы́бка излуча́ют *(3)* теплоту́ / *(4)* не́жность. ♦ **You have the most enchanting smile that I've ever seen (in all my life).** (Во всей жи́зни) ни у кого́ я не ви́дел тако́й очарова́тельной улы́бки, как у тебя́. ♦ **Your smile makes a bright day even brighter.** Твоя́ улы́бка де́лает я́ркий день ещё я́рче. ♦ **I love the sunshine of your smile.** Я люблю́ со́лнечный свет твое́й улы́бки. ♦ **All these sunbeams that flood the day — it is your smile shining down on me.** Твоя́ сия́ющая улы́бка для меня́ -- э́то со́лнечные лучи́, прони́зывающие день. ♦ **Such a beautiful, beguiling smile you have.** У тебя́ така́я прекра́сная, околдо́вывающая улы́бка. ♦ **I've never seen a more beguiling smile.** Я никогда́ не ви́дел бо́лее околдо́вывающей улы́бки. ♦ **There's such magic in your smile.** В твое́й улы́бке тако́е волшебство́. ♦ **You have a very engaging smile.** У тебя́ о́чень обая́тельная улы́бка. ♦ **You have a smile** *(1)* **...like a lighthouse by the sea. /** *(2)* **...that would light up a city.** У тебя́ улы́бка *(1)* ...как мая́к на морско́м берегу́. / *(2)* ..., кото́рая спосо́бна освети́ть го́род. ♦ **Your smile is so** *(1,2)* **bewitching.** Твоя́ улы́бка така́я *(1)* околдо́вывающая / *(2)* обвора́живающая. ♦ **What first attracted me to you was your** *(1)* **dazzling /** *(2)* **cute /** *(3)* **lovely /** *(4)* **beautiful /** *(5)* **sweet /** *(6)* **bright smile.** Пе́рвое, что привлекло́ меня́ к тебе́ -- *(1)* ...твоя́ ослепи́тельная / *(2,3)* преле́стная / *(4)* прекра́сная / *(5)* ми́лая / *(6)* сия́ющая улы́бка. ♦ **Your loving smile is such a precious sight.** Тако́е сча́стье ви́деть твою́ лю́бящую улы́бку. ♦ **I want to spend the rest of my days basking in the sunshine of your smile.** Я хочу́ провести́ остальны́е дни, гре́ясь в со́лнечном све́те твое́й улы́бки.

---

smile: *your smile in my thoughts*

Your enchanting smile never leaves my thoughts. Твоя́ очарова́тельная улы́бка всегда́ со мной. ♦ **The image of your sweet smile and beautiful eyes was in my mind all the time.** Твоя́ не́жная улы́бка и прекра́сные глаза́ бы́ли всегда́ в мои́х мы́слях.

---

smile: *what your smile does / did to me*

Your (beautiful) smile *(1)* **...fills the empty places of my heart. /** *(2)* **...enraptures my soul. /** *(3)* **...enchants me (**[4] **...more than I can tell you. /** [5] **...no end.** Твоя́ (прекра́сная) улы́бка *(1)*...заполня́ет пустоту́ в моём се́рдце. / *(2)* ...восхища́ет мою́ ду́шу. / *(3)* ...очаро́вывает меня́ (*[4]*...бо́льше, чем я могу́ вы́сказать. / *[5]* ...без конца́. ♦ **You** *(1)* **enchant /** *(2)* **hypnotize /** *(3-5)* **bewitch me with your** *(6)* **beautiful /** *(7)* **dazzling smile.** Ты *(1)* очаро́вываешь / *(2)* гипнотизи́руешь / *(3)* околдо́вываешь / *(4)* заколдо́вываешь / *(5)* обвора́живаешь меня́ свое́й *(6)* прекра́сной / *(7)* ослепи́тельной улы́бкой. ♦ **The** *(1)* **beauty /** *(2)* **radiance of your smile captivates my heart.** *(1)* Красота́ / *(2)* сия́ние твое́й улы́бки пленя́ет моё се́рдце. ♦ **When you flashed your** *(1)* **beautiful /** *(2)* **gorgeous /** *(3)* **dazzling smile at me, my heart went into a lunar orbit.** Когда́ ты сверкну́ла *(1)* прекра́сной / *(2)* великоле́пной / *(3)* ослепи́тельной улы́бкой, моё се́рдце взлете́ло на лу́нную орби́ту. ♦ **Your (**[1] **warm /** [2] **gentle /** [3] **radiant /** [4] **beautiful) smile reached deep inside me and touched my heart.** Твоя́ (*[1]* тёплая / *[2]* не́жная / *[3]* сия́ющая / *[4]* прекра́сная) улы́бка прони́кла глубоко́ в меня́ и косну́лась моего́ се́рдца. ♦ **When I first saw your** *(1,2)* **piquant smile, I was utterly** *(3)* **fascinated /** *(4)* **enthralled /** *(5)* **entranced.** Когда́ я

Some phrases are listed under more than one main word.

впервы́е уви́дел твою́ *(1)* игри́вую / *(2)* соблазни́тельную улы́бку, я был соверше́нно *(3)* очаро́ван / *(4)* порабощён / *(5)* очаро́ван. ♦ **You brighten my life with your sweet smile and loving ways.** Ты озаря́ешь мою́ жизнь свое́й не́жной улы́бкой и любо́вью. ♦ **I never dreamed a smile could fill my life with so much warmth and brightness.** Я никогда́ не представля́л, что улы́бка смо́жет напо́лнить мою́ жизнь таки́м тепло́м и све́том. ♦ **Every time you smile at me, you flood my world with love.** Вся́кий раз, когда́ ты улыба́ешься мне, ты затопля́ешь мой мир любо́вью. ♦ **Your smile caught my eye.** Твоя́ улы́бка бро́силась мне в глаза́.

smile: kiss your smile

(1) **I kiss...** / *(2)* **I want to kiss... your beautiful smile — and everything connected to it.** *(1)* Я целу́ю... / *(2)* Я хочу́ целова́ть... твою́ прекра́сную улы́бку и всё, соединённое с ней. ♦ **Keep that beautiful smile turned on.** Сохраня́й э́ту прекра́сную улы́бку. ♦ **In the meantime, you can be sure that I'll be dreaming about that beautiful, radiant smile of yours and how wonderful it would be to cover it with adoring kisses.** Ме́жду тем, ты мо́жешь быть уве́рена, что я бу́ду мечта́ть об твое́й сия́ющей улы́бке, и о том, как замеча́тельно бы́ло бы покры́ть её обожа́ющими поцелу́ями. ♦ **If by some divine miracle I am able someday to press my lips in fervent adoration to the exquisite loveliness of your sweet smile, I shall have nothing more to hope for or want.** Е́сли бы каки́м-то боже́ственным чу́дом я смог в оди́н прекра́сный день с пы́лким обожа́нием при-жа́ться губа́ми к изы́сканной пре́лести твое́й сла́дкой улы́бки, мне не́чего бы́ло бы бо́льше жела́ть. ♦ **I'd like to taste your smile.** Я хоте́л бы попро́бовать твою́ улы́бку.

smirk *n* самодово́льная улы́бка.

smitten *pp*: ♦ *(1)* **I'm...** / *(2)* **I've become... (quite) smitten with you.** *(1,2)* Я (совсе́м) влю-би́лся *(ж: влюби́лась)* в тебя́.

smoker *n* куря́щий *m*, куря́щая *f (pl:* куря́щие*)* ♦ **ex-smoker** бы́вший куря́щий *m*, бы́в-шая куря́щая *f* ♦ **heavy** ~ мно́го куря́щий *m*, мно́го куря́щая *f* ♦ **light** ~ немно́го куря́щий *m*, немно́го куря́щая *f* ♦ **moderate** ~ уме́ренно куря́щий *m*, уме́ренно куря́-щая *f* ♦ **nonsmoker** не куря́щий *m*, не куря́щая *f* ♦ **reformed** ~ бы́вший куря́щий *m*, бы́вшая куря́щая *f*.

smolder *vi* тлеть.

smoldering *adj* тле́ющий, -ая, -ее, -ие.

smooch *vi (slang) (kiss)* целова́ть / поцелова́ть *(whom = acc.)*.

smooching *n (slang) (kissing)* поцелу́и.

smooth *adj* гла́дкий, -ая, -ое, -ие ♦ **Your body is so smooth.** У тебя́ тако́е гла́дкое те́ло. ♦ **Your** *(1)* **skin** / *(2)* **back** / *(3)* **neck** / *(4)* **hand** / *(5)* **arm is so smooth.** У тебя́ така́я гла́дкая *(1)* ко́жа / *(2)* спина́ / *(3)* ше́я / *(4,5)* рука́. ♦ **Your** *(1)* **legs** / *(2)* **cheeks** / *(3)* **breasts** / *(4)* **arms** / *(5)* **shoulders** / *(6)* **buttocks** / *(7)* **buns** / *(8)* **hips are so smooth.** У тебя́ таки́е гла́дкие *(1)* но́ги / *(2)* щёки / *(3)* гру́ди / *(4)* ру́ки / *(5)* пле́чи / *(6,7)* я́годицы / *(8)* бёдра.

smoothie, smoothy *n (slang) (smooth-tongued)* сладкоречи́вый мужчи́на; *(lady-killer)* сер-дцее́д; *(irresistible)* неотрази́мый мужчи́на.

smoothly *adv* гла́дко.

smoothness *n* гла́дкость *f* ♦ **rich** ~ изуми́тельная гла́дкость ♦ **The rich smoothness of your skin is so** *(1)* **exciting** / *(2)* **wonderful to touch.** Изуми́тельная гла́дкость твое́й ко́жи так *(1)* возбужда́ет / *(3)* удиви́тельна при прикоснове́нии. ♦ **The rich smoothness of your skin excites my touch unimaginably.** Прикоснове́ние к твое́й изуми́тельно гла́дкой ко́же невероя́тно возбужда́ет меня́.

smooth-tongued *adj* сладкоречи́вый, -ая, -ое, -ые.

The singular past tense of Russian verbs ends in -л (m) (usually),
-ла (f) or -ло (n). the plural past tense ends in -li.

smother *vt* 1. *(whom = acc.)* души́ть / задуши́ть; 2. *(cover)* гу́сто покрыва́ть / покры́ть *(what, whom = acc., with what = instr.)*, оку́тывать / оку́тать *(what, whom = acc., with what = instr.)*; *(deluge)* засыпа́ть / засы́пать *(what, whom = acc., with what = instr.)*, осыпа́ть / осы́пать *(what, whom = acc., with what = instr.)* ♦ **I could just smother you with love and affection.** Я могу́ про́сто оку́тать тебя́ любо́вью и не́жностью.

smug *adj* самодово́льный, -ая, -ое, -ые.

smugness *n* самодово́льство.

snag *n* зами́нка, загво́здка ♦ **There's a snag.** Есть загво́здка.

snap *vi (speak angrily)* набра́сываться / набро́ситься *(at whom = + на + acc.)*, огрыза́ться / огрызну́ться *(at whom = + на + acc.)*.

snappish *adj (nagging)* приди́рчивый, -ая, -ое, -ые; *(quarrelsome)* сварли́вый, -ая, -ое, -ые; *(irritable)* раздражи́тельный, -ая, -ое, -ые.

snatch *vt* хвата́ть / схвати́ть *(what, whom = acc.)*; подхва́тывать / подхвати́ть *(what, whom = acc.)* ♦ **I just pray to the heavens above that no one has already snatched you up.** Я то́лько молю́ небеса́, чтобы ты не была́ подхва́чена ке́м-то други́м.

sneak *vi*: ♦ **~ around** *vi (go out secretly with another [1]* **woman** / *[2]* **man)** встреча́ться тайко́м с *(1)* ...друго́й же́нщиной / *(2)* ...други́м мужчи́ной, тайко́м изменя́ть ♦ **~ in** *vi* проска́льзывать / проскользну́ть *(into what = + в + acc.)* ♦ **~ out** *vi* 1. *(slip out)* выска́льзывать / вы́скользнуть *(out of what = + из + gen.)*; 2. *(sneak around)* (тайко́м) изменя́ть.

> **sneak around:**

I think you've been sneaking around on me. Я ду́маю, что ты тайко́м изменя́ешь мне. ♦ **I'm tired of all your sneaking around.** Я уста́л от твои́х постоя́нных изме́н.

> **sneak in:**

I'll sneak into your room later. Я проскользну́ в твою́ ко́мнату поздне́е.

> **sneak out:**

I'll sneak out in the morning. Я вы́скользну у́тром. ♦ **I would never sneak out on you.** Я никогда́ не бу́ду изменя́ть тебе́.

sneakers *n, pl* те́ннисные ту́фли, ке́ды.

sneaky *adj* лука́вый, -ая, -ое, -ые.

snip *n* челове́чишка, пусто́е ме́сто ♦ **You little snip!** Ты пусто́е ме́сто!

snit *n (slang) (disagreeable person)* брюзга́ ♦ **humorless ~** брюзга́ с отсу́тствием ю́мора.

snob *n* сноб.

snooty *adj* спеси́вый, -ая, -ое, -ые, задира́ющий (-ая, -ее, -ие) нос, ва́жничающий, -ая, -ее, -ие.

snorkeling *n* подво́дное пла́вание с ма́ской и тру́бкой ♦ **Have you ever gone snorkeling?** Пла́вала *(ж: Пла́вал)* ли ты когда́-либо под водо́й с ма́ской и тру́бкой?

snow *vt* (хи́тро) обма́нывать / обману́ть *(whom = acc.)*.

snowbird *n (slang) (retired person)* пенсионе́р *m*, пенсионе́рка *f* ♦ **lady ~** *(retired lady)* пенсионе́рка.

snowboarding *n* ката́ние на сно́уборде, сно́убординг ♦ **go ~** ката́ться на сно́уборде.

snub *vt* пренебрега́ть / пренебре́чь *(whom = instr.)*, унижа́ть *(whom = acc.)* ♦ **It seemed like you were snubbing me.** Каза́лось, ты пренебрега́ла *(ж: пренебрега́л)* мной. ♦ **I wasn't snubbing you.** Я не пренебрега́л *(ж: пренебрега́ла)* тобо́й.

snub-nosed *adj* курно́сый, -ая, -ое, -ые.

snuggle (up) *vt* ую́тно устро́иться *(what = instr., in / against what, with whom = + к + dat.)*, прильну́ть *(what = instr., in / against what, with whom = + к + dat.)*, прижа́ться *(what = instr., in / against what, with whom = + к + dat.)*.

Please do us a favor:
Fill out and mail in the Feedback Sheet on page 795.

snuggle: *phrases*

I want to snuggle up with you. Я хочу́ прижа́ться к тебе́. ♦ *(1)* **I would love...** / *(2)* **I love... to snuggle my face in your (warm, soft) breasts.** *(1)* Я бы хоте́л... / *(2)* Я так люблю́... прильну́ть лицо́м к твое́й (тёплой, мя́гкой) груди́. ♦ **How I want to curl up with you, snuggle against your breast, feel the warmth of you, caress you, love you.** Как бы я хоте́л обня́ться с тобо́й, прижа́ться к твое́й груди́, чу́вствовать твоё тепло́, ласка́ть тебя́, люби́ть тебя́.

soar *vi* 1. пари́ть; 2. вспа́рхивать / вспорхну́ть; взлета́ть / взлете́ть, взмыва́ть / взмыть ♦ **~ to the peak of pleasure** взлете́ть на верши́ну наслажде́ния.

soar: *phrases*

My love for you soars higher and higher with each passing day. Моя́ любо́вь к тебе́ взлета́ет всё вы́ше и вы́ше с ка́ждым днём. ♦ **Upward and upward and upward I want you to soar into** *(1)* **ecstasy** / *(2)* **passion.** Я хочу́, чтобы ты всё вы́ше, вы́ше и вы́ше пари́ла в *(1)* экста́зе / *(2)* стра́сти. ♦ **My heart soared up into the sky.** Моё се́рдце взлете́ло в небеса́. ♦ *(1)* **I want to...** / *(2)* **I'm going to... teach you how to soar through the cosmos.** *(1)* Я хочу́ научи́ть... / *(2)* Я научу́... тебя́, как взлете́ть в ко́смос. ♦ **You make my senses soar.** Ты заставля́ешь мои́ чу́вства пари́ть. ♦ **When I gave your hand a squeeze and you squeezed back, my heart soared to the moon.** Когда́ я сжима́л *(ж: сжима́ла)* твою́ ру́ку, и ты в отве́т сжима́ла *(ж: сжима́л)* мою́, моё се́рдце воспаря́ло ввысь.

s.o.b. *abbrev (profane)* = **son of a bitch** су́кин сын.

sob *n* рыда́нье; всхли́пывание.

sob *vi* рыда́ть; всхли́пывать/ всхлипну́ть.

sober *adj* тре́звый, -ая, -ое, -ые ♦ **cold stone ~** соверше́нно тре́звый.

sociable *adj* общи́тельный, -ая, -ое, -ые.

social *adj* 1. *(about society)* обще́ственный, -ая, -ое, -ые, социа́льный, -ая, -ое, -ые; 2. *(friendly)* дру́жеский, -ая, -ое, -ие ♦ **~ behavior** обще́ственное поведе́ние ♦ **~ gathering** встре́ча друзе́й ♦ **~ get-together** встре́ча друзе́й ♦ **~ life** вре́мя, проведённое с друзья́ми и знако́мыми *(explanation)*, обще́ние с друзья́ми ♦ **~ visit** дру́жеский визит, посеще́ние друзе́й.

socialize *vi* обща́ться *(with whom = + с + instr.)*.

socializing *n* обще́ние ♦ **I like socializing with friends.** Мне нра́вится обща́ться с друзья́ми. ♦ **I enjoy socializing with friends.** Я наслажда́юсь обще́нием с друзья́ми.

sociopath *n* социопа́т.

sock *n* носо́к *(pl:* носки́*)* ♦ **pair of ~s** па́ра носко́в.

sofa *n* дива́н ♦ **~ spud** *(slang)* лежебо́ка.

so far *adv* пока́ что; пока́ ещё; до сих пор.

soft *adj* мя́гкий, -ая, -ое, -ие ♦ **~ as silk** мя́гкий (-ая, -ое, -ие), как шёлк *(1 term)* ♦ **velvety ~** бархати́сто-мя́гкий, -ая, -ое, -ые ♦ **Your skin is** *(1)* **...soft as velvet** / *(2)* **a baby** / *(3)* **a kitten.** Твоя́ ко́жа мя́гкая, как *(1)* ...ба́рхат. / *(2)* ...ко́жа ребёнка. / *(3)* ...у котёнка. ♦ **You're soft and round in all the right places.** Ты мя́гкая и окру́глая во всех ну́жных места́х.

soften *vi* расслабля́ться ♦ **I love the way your body softens when I** *(1)* **touch** / *(2)* **caress you.** Мне нра́вится, как твоё те́ло расслабля́ется, когда́ я *(1)* каса́юсь / *(2)* ласка́ю тебя́.

soft-hearted *adj* мягкосерде́чный, -ая, -ое, -ые, до́брый, -ая, -ое, -ые, отзы́вчивый, -ая, -ое, -ые.

softly *adv* мя́гко.

softness *n* мя́гкость *f* ♦ **curving ~** окру́глая мя́гкость ♦ **enchanting ~** упои́тельная мя́г-

---

Clock and calender time are discussed in Appendix 5, page 759.

кость ♦ **radiant** ~ светя́щаяся мя́гкость ♦ **rich** ~ роско́шная мя́гкость.

softness: phrases

Only the sweet softness of your lips can quell the ache of longing that ravages my heart. То́лько сла́дкая мя́гкость твои́х губ мо́жет подави́ть боль тоски́, разруша́ющей моё се́рдце. ♦ **My arms are (so) lonely for your softness.** Мои́ ру́ки (так) тоску́ют по твое́й мя́гкости. ♦ **I watch your mouth forming sounds, moving and undulating so supplely, so softly, so enticingly and I am seized with a raging impulse to fuse my own mouth together with it and once and for all revel in its sweet softness.** Я слежу́, как твой рот создаёт зву́ки, дви́гаясь и изгиба́ясь так ги́бко, так мя́гко, так соблазни́тельно, и я охва́чен бе́шеным и́мпульсом соедини́ть мой рот с твои́м, что́бы раз и навсегда́ пирова́ть в его́ сла́дкой не́жности. ♦ **I get a melting softness inside me whenever** *(1)* ...**I see /** *(2)* **touch you. /** *(3)* ...**I think about you. /** *(4)* ...**I hear your voice on the phone. /** *(5)* ...**you kiss /** *(6)* **touch me.** Всё во мне та́ет вся́кий раз, когда́ *(1)* ...я ви́жу / *(2)* каса́юсь тебя́. / *(3)* ...я ду́маю о тебе́ / *(4)* ...я слы́шу твой го́лос по телефо́ну. / *(5)* ...ты целу́ешь / *(6)* каса́ешься меня́. ♦ **Every night brings me a throbbing ache of longing for your warm, beautiful softness.** Ка́ждая ночь прино́сит мне невыноси́мую тоску́ по твоему́ тёплому прекра́сному не́жному те́лу. ♦ **How heavenly it would be to relish the warm, wonderful softness of your body in the languor of half-sleep.** Как сла́достно бы́ло бы наслажда́ться тёплой, замеча́тельной мя́гкостью твоего́ те́ла в то́мном полусне́.

soft-spoken *adj* ти́хий, -ая, -ое, -ие.

softy *n (slang)* тря́пка.

soiree *n (evening party)* вечери́нка.

solace *n* утеше́ние ♦ **find ~ (in the wilderness)** найти́ утеше́ние (в пусты́не).

solemn *adj* 1. *(serious)* серьёзный, -ая, -ое, -ые; 2. *(ceremonies, oaths)* торже́ственный, -ая, -ое, -ые.

solemnly *adv* 1. серьёзно; 2. торже́ственно.

solicitude *n* озабо́ченность *f*; забо́тливость *f.*

solid *adj* 1. *(strong, sturdy)* кре́пкий, -ая, -ое, -ие, си́льный, -ая, -ое, -ые; 2. *(upstanding)* соли́дный, -ая, -ое, -ые; *(reliable)* надёжный, -ая, -ое, -ые ♦ **~ relationship** кре́пкие отноше́ния.

solidify *vt* затвердева́ть / затверде́ть *(what = acc.)*, укрепля́ть / укрепи́ть *(what = acc.)* ♦ **I'll do everything I can to solidify our relationship.** Я бу́ду де́лать всё, что я смогу́ для укрепле́ния на́ших отноше́ний.

solitary *adj* одино́кий, -ая, -ое, -ие ♦ **~ existence** одино́кая жизнь ♦ **~ life** одино́кая жизнь.

solitude *n* одино́чество, уедине́ние ♦ **intimate ~** инти́мное уедине́ние ♦ **Help me break these chains of solitude.** Помоги́ мне сбро́сить око́вы одино́чества.

So long! Пока́!

solve *vt* реша́ть / реши́ть *(what = acc.)* ♦ **We'll solve this problem somehow.** Эту пробле́му мы ка́к-нибудь реши́м.

solvent *adj* платёжеспосо́бный, -ая, -ое, -ые.

somebody *pron (indefinite)* кто́-нибудь; *(definite)* кто́-то.

someday *adv (indefinite)* когда́-нибудь; ка́к-нибудь; *(definite)* когда́-то.

somehow *adv (indefinite)* ка́к-нибудь; *(definite)* ка́к-то ♦ **We'll solve this problem somehow.** Эту пробле́му мы ка́к-нибудь реши́м.

someone *pron (indefinite)* кто́-нибудь; *(definite)* кто́-то.

something *pron (indefinite)* что́-нибудь; *(definite)* что́-то ♦ **Something old, something new, something borrowed, something blue.** Что́-нибудь ста́рое, что́-нибудь но́вое, что́-

---

Reflexive verbs are those that end in -ся *or* -сь.
The -ся *or* -сь *also goes onto a past tense ending.*

нибудь заимствованное, что-нибудь голубое. ♦ **There's something about you.** Что́-то в тебе́ есть.

sometimes *adv* иногда́, времена́ми.

somewhat *adv* дово́льно, до не́которой сте́пени.

somewhere *adv (location: indefinite)* где́-нибудь; *(location: definite)* где́-то; *(direction: indefinite)* куда́-нибудь; *(direction: definite)* куда́-то.

son *n* сын *(pl:* сыновья́) ♦ older ~ ста́рший сын ♦ oldest ~ са́мый ста́рший сын ♦ middle ~ сре́дний сын ♦ younger ~ мла́дший сын ♦ youngest ~ са́мый мла́дший сын ♦ **I would be willing to adopt your son.** Я бы хоте́л *(ж: хоте́ла)* усынови́ть твоего́ ма́льчика.

song *n* пе́сня ♦ folk ~ наро́дная пе́сня ♦ love ~ любо́вная пе́сня ♦ my favorite ~ моя́ люби́мая пе́сня ♦ new ~ но́вая пе́сня ♦ old ~ ста́рая пе́сня ♦ our (favorite) ~ на́ша (люби́мая) пе́сня ♦ ~ of love пе́сня любви́ ♦ your favorite ~ *(familiar)* твоя́ люби́мая пе́сня; *(polite)* Ва́ша люби́мая пе́сня ♦ melody of a ~ мело́дия пе́сни ♦ sing a ~ петь / спеть пе́сню ♦ words of a ~ слова́ пе́сни.

song: *phrases*

You have filled my *(1)* **life /** *(2)* **heart with a song of love.** Ты напо́лнила *(ж: напо́лнил) (1)* ...мою́ жизнь... / *(2)* ...моё се́рдце... пе́сней любви́. ♦ **In my heart there is a love song that echoes your name.** В моём се́рдце звучи́т любо́вная пе́сня, э́хом отража́ющая твоё и́мя. ♦ **Since I met you, all I want to do is listen to love songs.** С тех пор, как я встре́тил *(ж: встре́тила)* тебя́, всё, чего́ я хочу́, э́то слу́шать пе́сни любви́. ♦ **You put a song in my heart.** Ты напо́лнила *(ж: напо́лнил)* пе́сней моё се́рдце. ♦ **Because of you there's a song in my heart.** Благодаря́ тебе́ в моём се́рдце пе́сня. ♦ **You make me want to croon love songs to you all night long.** Ты вызыва́ешь во мне жела́ние напева́ть тебе́ любо́вные пе́сни всю ночь напролёт.

son-in-law *n* зять *m*.

sonnet *n* соне́т ♦ spring ~ весе́нний соне́т ♦ **Your milky white skin and shining blonde hair sing siren-like sonnets to me.** Твоя́ молочнобе́лая ко́жа и блестя́щие све́тлые во́лосы, подо́бно сире́нам, пою́т мне соне́ты.

sonofabitch *n (profane)* су́кин сын.

soon *adv* ско́ро, вско́ре ♦ sooner скоре́е; ра́ньше.

sophist *n* фило́соф, мысли́тель *m*.

sophisticate *n* зна́ющий *m*, зна́ющая *f (pl:* зна́ющие) ♦ city ~ зна́ющий *m* го́род, зна́ющая *f* го́род.

sophisticated *adj* 1. *(experienced)* искушённый, -ая, -ое, -ые, о́пытный, -ая, -ое, -ые; 2.*(refined)* изощрённый, -ая, -ое, -ые, изы́сканный, -ая, -ое, -ые, утончённый, -ая, -ое, -ые.

sophistication *n* изощрённость *f*, изы́сканность *f*, утончённость *f* ♦ **Please forgive my lack of sophistication.** Пожа́луйста, прости́, что я недоста́точно изощрён *(ж: изощрена́)*.

sorcery *n* волшебство́, колдовство́ ♦ **I don't know what sorcery you've been practicing on me that makes me love you so much, but I don't want you to stop.** Я не зна́ю, каки́м волше́бным сре́дством ты де́лаешь мою́ любо́вь тако́й си́льной, но я хочу́, чтобы ты продолжа́ла в том же ду́хе.

sordid *adj (base, vile)* по́длый, -ая, -ое, -ые, ни́зкий, -ая, -ое, -ие; гну́сный, -ая, -ое, -ые.

sore *n* бодя́чка; я́зва ♦ *(1,2)* cold ~ *(on the lip)* *(1)* просту́да / *(2)* лихора́дка на губе́.

sorority *n* социа́льная организа́ция для де́вушек *(в университе́те)*, же́нская общи́на, же́нское земля́чество.

sorrow *n* печа́ль *f* ♦ **You are the person with whom I want to (always) share life's joys and sorrows.** Ты тот челове́к, с кото́рым я хочу́ (всегда́) дели́ть все мои́ ра́дости и печа́ли. ♦ **Since you went away my days are wrapped in sorrow.** С тех пор, как ты

The time zones for many cities of the world
are given in Appendix 6, page 761.

уéхала *(ж: уéхал)*, мои́ дни полны́ печа́лью.

sorry *adj* жаль ♦ **feel ~** *(regret)* сожалéть *(about what = + о + prep.)*; *(sympathize)* сочу́вст-
вовать *(for whom = dat.)*, жаль *(person sorry = dat., person for whom sorry = acc.)* ♦   *(1,2)*
I'm sorry. *(apology)* (1) Извини́ (*[polite:]* Извини́те). / *(2)* Прости́ (*[polite:]* Прости́те).
♦ **I'm sorry for you.** Мне тебя́ жаль. ♦ **I'm sorry for what I said.** Я сожалéю о том,
что я сказа́л *(ж: сказа́ла)*. ♦ **I'm sorry to say...** К сожалéнию...

sort *n* сорт, тип ♦ **I'm not that sort of** *(1)* **woman** / *(2)* **girl** / *(3)* **man** / *(4)* **person.** Я не того́
со́рта *(1)* жéнщина / *(2)* дéвушка / *(3)* мужчи́на / *(4)* человéк. ♦ **What sort of** *(1)* **woman**
/ *(2)* **girl** / *(3)* **man** / *(4)* **person do you think I am?** К какóму сóрту *(1)* жéнщин / *(2)*
дéвушек / *(3)* мужчи́н / *(4)* людéй ты меня́ отнóсишь? ♦ *(1)* **He** / *(2)* **She is not a bad
sort.** *(1)* Он / *(2)* Она́ человéк неплохóй. ♦ **You seem like a decent sort.** *(polite you)* Вы
ка́жетесь хорóшим человéком.

sorts *n, pl*: ♦ **I feel a little out of sorts.** Я чу́вствую себя́ невáжно.

soul *adj* задушéвный, -ая, -ое, -ые.

soul *n* душа́ ♦ *(1,2)* **adventurous ~** *(1)* отвáжный / *(2)* смéлый дух ♦ **artist's ~** душа́
худóжника ♦ **beautiful ~** прекрáсная душа́ ♦ **clear ~** я́сная душа́ ♦ **fiery ~** горя́чая
душа́ ♦ **good ~** дóбрая душа́ ♦ **happy ~** счастли́вая душа́ ♦ **honest ~** чéстная душа́ ♦
my ~ моя́ душа́ ♦ **noble ~** благорóдная душа́ ♦ **passionate ~** горя́чая душа́ ♦ **poet's
~** душа́ поэ́та ♦ **pure ~** чи́стая душа́ ♦ **restless ~** мяту́щаяся душа́ ♦ **Russian ~** ру́сская
душа́ ♦ **sensitive ~** чу́ткая душа́ ♦ **simple ~** простáя душа́ ♦ **timid ~** рóбкая душа́ ♦
tired ~ устáлая душа́ ♦ **tortured ~** страдáющая душа́ ♦ **unique ~** уникáльная душа́
♦ **wizard's ~** колдóвская душа́ ♦ **your ~** *(familiar)* твоя́ душа́; *(polite)* Ва́ша душа́.

    | *soul: other terms* |

beauty of your ~ красотá твоéй души́ ♦ **outpourings of the ~** ду́шевные излия́ния ♦ *(1)*
pureness / *(2)* **purity of your ~** *(1,2)* чистотá твоéй души́.

    | *soul: what you are to my soul* |

Your beauty and charm are an elixir to my soul. Твоя́ красотá и обая́ние - эликси́р
моéй души́. ♦ *(1)* **You are...** / *(2)* **Your love is... the nourishment of my soul.** *(1)* Ты... /
(2) Твоя́ любóвь... -- пи́ща для моéй души́. ♦ **You are the soul of my soul (and the life
of my life).** Ты душа́ моéй души́ (и жизнь моéй жи́зни). ♦ **You are the** *(1)* **wife** / *(2)*
husband of my soul. Ты *(1)* ...женá, котóрую... / *(2)* ...муж, котóрого... прóсит моя́
душа́. ♦ **You are my soul's** *(1)* **bride** / *(2)* **groom.** Ты *(1)* невéста / *(2)* жени́х моéй души́.
♦ **You are my heart and soul.** Ты моя́ душа́ и сéрдце. ♦ **You are firmly** *(1,4)* **implanted**
/ *(2,5)* **embedded** / *(3,6)* **cemented in my heart, my mind, and my soul.** Ты нáкрепко *(1-
3)* вошлá / *(4-6)* вросла́ в моё сéрдце, ум и ду́шу. ♦ **Your love and devotion are the
nectar and ambrosia for my soul.** Твои́ любóвь и прéданность -- нектáр и амбрози́я
для моéй души́. ♦ **My soul has never sung as it does for you.** Моя́ душа́ никогда́ не пéла
так, как она́ поёт для тебя́. ♦ **"All my soul follows you, love — encircles you — and I
live in being yours."** *Robert Browning.* «Вся моя́ душа́ тя́нется к тебé, любóвь окру-
жáет тебя́, и я живу́, принадлежá тебé.». *Рóберт Брáунинг.*

    | *soul: what you do to my soul* |

You nourish my soul with your *(1)* **...thoughtfulness** / *(2)* **sweetness** / *(3)* **goodhearted-
ness.** / *(4)* **...loving ways.** Ты питáешь мою́ ду́шу *(1)* ...свои́м внимáнием. / *(2)* ...своéй
нéжностью. / *(3)* добросердéчностью. / *(4)* любóвью. ♦ **You bring out the poetry in my
soul.** Ты пробуждáешь поэ́зию в моéй душé. ♦ **Your smile enraptures my soul.** Твоя́
улы́бка восхищáет мою́ ду́шу. ♦ **Your** *(1)* **sweet** / *(2)* **wonderful love nourishes my soul.**
Твоя́ *(1)* нéжная / *(2)* замечáтельная любóвь питáет мою́ ду́шу. ♦ **I know that we will
be together** *(1)* **soon** / *(2)* **again** / *(3)* **someday, and this** *(4)* **knowledge** / / *(5)* **realization**

---

*Optional parts of sentences are preceded
or followed (or both) by three dots.*

fortifies my soul. Я зна́ю, что мы *(1)* ско́ро / *(2)* опя́ть / *(3)* одна́жды бу́дем вме́сте, и *(4,5)* и э́та мысль укрепля́ет мой ду́х. ♦ **I've never known anyone in my life that could penetrate to the very core of my soul and stir up all my feelings the way you can.** Я никогда́ в жи́зни не знал *(ж: зна́ла)* кого́-либо ещё, кто мог бы проника́ть в са́мую глубину́ мое́й души́ и возбужда́ть мои́ чу́вства так, как ты. ♦ **The magic of your beautiful, sensuous body has enslaved my soul.** Волшебство́ твоего́ прекра́сного, чу́вственного те́ла покори́ло мою́ ду́шу. ♦ **You have captured my soul (entirely).** Ты захвати́ла *(ж: захвати́л)* (в плен) мою́ ду́шу (целико́м). ♦ **The sweet magic of your kisses captivates my soul.** Сла́дкое волшебство́ твои́х поцелу́ев пленя́ет мою́ ду́шу. ♦ **You fill my soul with so many tender sentiments.** Ты напо́лнил *(ж: напо́лнила)* мою́ ду́шу таки́ми не́жными чу́вствами. ♦ **I cannot describe the passion that seized my soul when I first** *(1)* **saw /** *(2)* **kissed you.** Не могу́ описа́ть страсть, охвати́вшую мою́ ду́шу, когда́ я впервы́е *(1)* уви́дел *(ж: уви́дела)* / *(2)* поцелова́л *(ж: поцелова́ла)* тебя́.

> **soul:** *your soul*

The fragrance of roses eminates from your soul. Твоя́ душа́ благоуха́ет ро́зами. ♦ **You are such a** *(1)* **gentle /** *(2)* **tender soul.** У тебя́ така́я *(1)* мя́гкая / *(2)* не́жная душа́. ♦ **You are the** *(1)* **gentlest /** *(2)* **most tender soul I have ever** *(3)* **known /** *(4)* **met.** Я никогда́ не *(3)* знал *(ж: зна́ла)* / *(4)* встреча́л *(ж: встреча́ла)* тако́й *(1)* мя́гкой / *(2)* не́жной души́, как твоя́. ♦ **I want you to open your soul to me.** Я хочу́, что́бы ты откры́ла мне свою́ ду́шу. ♦ **I want to feel touched by your soul.** Я хочу́ чу́вствовать прикоснове́ние твое́й души́.

> **soul:** *my soul is yours*

I gave my soul to you as soon as I saw you. Я отда́л *(ж: отдала́)* мою́ ду́шу тебе́ сра́зу же, как уви́дел *(ж: уви́дела)* тебя́. ♦ **My soul shall never be untrue to yours.** Моя́ душа́ никогда́ не изме́нит твое́й. ♦ **I want to open your soul to you.** Я хочу́ откры́ть тебе́ свою́ ду́шу.

> **soul:** *our souls together*

This is a symbol of a bond between our souls. Это си́мвол свя́зи на́ших душ. ♦ **I'd love to mingle souls with you.** Я хоте́л *(ж: хоте́ла)* бы сли́ться душо́й с тобо́й. ♦ **We'll lie under some big, shady tree, fingers entwined, legs entwined, mouths entwined, savoring each other's soul.** Мы бу́дем лежа́ть под больши́м тени́стым де́ревом, па́льцы сплетены́, но́ги сплетены́, гу́бы сплетены́, вкуша́я ду́ши друг дру́га.

> **soul:** *set your soul on fire*

One of these days I'm going to break through that protective bubble of reserve that you live in and set your soul on fire. Одна́жды я собира́юсь прорва́ться че́рез защи́тную оболо́чку сде́ржанности, в кото́рой ты живёшь, и заже́чь ого́нь в твое́й душе́.

> **soul:** *my soul*

My soul has *(1)* **...come alive. /** *(2)* **...awakened (for the first time).** Моя́ душа́ *(1)* ...ожила́. / *(2)* ...просну́лась (впервы́е). ♦ *(1)* **I want... /** *(2)* **I need to be able... to keep a portion of my soul to call my own.** *(1)* Я хочу́... / *(2)* Я до́лжен *(ж: должна́)* сохрани́ть часть свое́й души́ для себя́. ♦ **My soul was so** *(1)* **lonesome /** *(2)* **lonely before I met you.** Моя́ душа́ была́ так *(1,2)* одино́ка до того́, как я встре́тил *(ж: встре́тила)* тебя́. ♦ **My soul has always been so** *(1)* **lonesome /** *(2)* **lonely.** Моя́ душа́ всегда́ была́ так *(1,2)* одино́ка. ♦ **I want a relationship that will nourish my soul.** Я хочу́ отноше́ний, кото́рые бу́дут пита́ть мою́ ду́шу. ♦ **All that my soul yearns to express at this moment is** *(1)* **embodied /** *(2)* **enclosed in one word -- love.** Всё, что моя́ душа́ жа́ждет вы́разить в э́тот миг, *(1,2)* воплоща́ется в одно́м сло́ве -- любо́вь. ♦ **I guess there's a little bit of gypsy in my soul.** Я предполага́ю, что в мое́й душе́ есть не́что цыга́нское.

> *If you're not on familiar terms with a person,*
> *the «ты» forms will have to be changed to «Вы».*

soul: my soul aches

My loneliness without you *(1)* **crushes /** *(2)* **ravages my soul.** Моё одиночество без тебя *(1)* подавляет / *(2)* опустошает мою душу. ♦ **Without you in my arms a perpetual ache of longing marauds my soul.** Постоянная боль тоски терзает мою душу, когда тебя нет в моих объятиях. ♦ **With you gone, bleakness has** *(1)* **crept /** *(2)* **seeped into my soul.** С твоим уходом уныние *(1)* прокралось / *(2)* проникло в мою душу. ♦ **The thought of** *(1)* **...losing you... /** *(2)* **...being without you... /** *(3)* **...being apart from you... (4) pierces /** *(5)* **crushes my very soul.** Мысль о том, чтобы *(1)* ...потерять тебя... / *(2)* ...быть без тебя... / *(3)* ...быть вдали от тебя... *(4)* пронзает / *(5)* подавляет мою душу. ♦ **Something has died in my soul.** Что-то умерло в моей душе.

soul: the longing in my soul

I fervently pray that in your heart you can somehow find the compassion to condescend to grant me just a few brief minutes to *(1)* **meet /** *(2)* **talk with you and thereby assuage this unbearable longing that grips my soul.** Я горячо молюсь, чтобы ты смогла найти сострадание в своём сердце и подарить мне только несколько коротких минут *(1)* встречи / *(2)* разговора с тобой, чтобы утолить невыносимое желание, охватившее мою душу.

soul: searching my soul

I've been searching my soul (about *[1]* **...this. /** *[2]* **...the idea of marriage. /** *[3]* **...about our relationship.)** Я спрашиваю своё сердце (*[1]* ...об этом. / *[2]* ...об идее жениться. / *[3]* ...о наших отношениях.). ♦ **I need to search my soul (a little more) (about this).** (Об этом) я должен *(ж: должна)* (ещё) немного поговорить со своим сердцем.

soul: salutation of a letter

My life and soul! Моя жизнь и душа!

soul: saying

Eyes are the windows of the soul. Глаза - зеркало души.

soulful *adj* душевный, -ая, -ое, -ые, задушевный, -ая, -ое, -ые.

soulmate *n* задушевный друг *m & f*, задушевная подруга *f*, друг по духу ♦ **energetic ~** энергичный задушевный друг ♦ **gentle ~** нежный задушевный друг ♦ **happy ~** счастливый задушевный друг *m*, счастливая задушевная подруга *f* ♦ **I want to be your soul-mate for the rest of my life.** Я хочу быть твоим задушевным другом на всю оставшуюся жизнь. ♦ **You are my soulmate forever.** Ты мой задушевный друг навечно. ♦ **You are the perfect soul-mate for me.** Ты превосходный задушевный друг для меня. ♦ **My dear soulmate,** *(salutation of a letter)* Мой дорогой задушевный друг, *(начало письма).*

soul-rending *adj* разрывающий (-ая, -ее, -ие) душу.

soul-stirring *adj* волнующий (-ая, -ее, -ие) душу.

sound *adj* 1. *(healthy)* здоровый, -ая, -ое, -ые; 2. *(reliable)* надёжный, -ая, -ое, -ые; 3. *(sensible)* здравый, -ая, -ое, -ые, обоснованный, -ая, -ое, -ые; 4. *(solid)* прочный, -ая, -ое, -ые *(solid)* ♦ **spiritually ~** душевно здоровый.

sound *vi* звучать ♦ **You** *(1)* **sound /** *(2)* **sounded (** *[3]* **a little /** *[4]* **rather /** *[5]* **very) upset.** Твой голос *(1)* звучит / *(2)* звучал (*[3]* немного / *[4]* довольно / *[5]* очень) огорчённо.

sound *n* звук ♦ **beautiful ~** красивый звук ♦ **exciting ~** волнующий звук ♦ **melodic ~** мелодичный звук ♦ **nice ~** приятный звук ♦ **~ of your laughter** звук твоего смеха ♦ **~ of your name** звук твоего имени ♦ **~ of your pleasure** звук твоего наслаждения ♦ **~ of your sighs** звуки твоих вздохов ♦ **~ of your voice** звуки твоего голоса ♦ **sultry ~** чувственный звук ♦ **I savor the sound of your name on my lips.** Мои губы смакуют звук твоего имени.

A list of common places with their grammatical endings is given in Appendix 7, page 763.

sour *adj* ки́слый, -ая, -ое, -ые ♦ *(1)* **I'm afraid...** / *(2)* **I think... our romance has** *(3,4)* **gone sour.** *(1)* Я бою́сь,... / *(2)* Я ду́маю,... наш рома́н *(3)* ...скис. / *(4)* ...не уда́лся.

source *n* исто́чник ♦ ~ **of passion** исто́чник стра́сти.

sourpuss *n (slang)* ворчу́н, брюзга́.

spa *n* 1. куро́рт; 2. исто́чник ♦ **health** ~ куро́рт с минера́льными во́дами.

space *n* 1. *(room; place)* ме́сто; 2. *(slang) (freedom)* свобо́да; *(personal life)* ли́чная жизнь ♦ **I need breathing space.** Мне на́до немно́го свобо́ды. ♦ **I believe in giving a person their space.** Я ду́маю, что челове́ку на́до дава́ть возмо́жность име́ть свою́ ли́чную жизнь. ♦ **I feel like I have no space to breathe.** Я чу́вствую, что не могу́ свобо́дно дыша́ть. ♦ **I know you need your space. Everyone does.** Я зна́ю, что тебе́ нужна́ твоя́ ли́чная жизнь. Ка́ждому нужна́.

spacy *adj (slang) (scatter-brained, flighty)* легкомы́сленный, -ая, -ое, -ые, ве́треный, -ая, -ое, -ые.

spandex *n* спа́ндекс.

Spanish *adj* испа́нский, -ая, -ое, -ие.

Spanish *n (language)* испа́нский язы́к ♦ **speak** ~ говори́ть по-испа́нски.

spark *vt* зажига́ть / заже́чь *(what = acc.)*, разжига́ть / разже́чь *(what = acc.)* ♦ **Your description in your ad** *(1,2)* **really sparked my interest.** То, как ты описа́ла *(ж: описа́л)* себя́ в объявле́нии, *(1)* ...разожгло́ мой интере́с. / *(2)* ...о́чень заинтересова́ло меня́.

spark *n* 1. и́скра, и́скорка 2. *pl: (slang) (romantic excitement)* (романти́ческое) возбужде́ние, (романти́ческие) и́скры ♦ **I'm looking for a lady with a special spark.** Я ищу́ же́нщину с осо́бенной и́скоркой. ♦ **We can get together and see if there are any sparks.** Мы мо́жем встре́титься и посмотре́ть, вспы́хнут ли и́скры романти́ческого интере́са. ♦ **I could use a few sparks in my life right now.** Мое́й жи́зни сейча́с не помеша́ли бы не́сколько романти́ческих искр. ♦ **Your touch causes sparks.** Твоё прикоснове́ние вызыва́ет и́скры. ♦ **When our lips came together, the sparks flew.** Когда́ на́ши гу́бы встре́тились, посы́пались и́скры.

sparkle *vi* искри́ться, сверка́ть / сверкну́ть, сия́ть ♦ **Your eyes sparkle like burnished turquoise.** Твои́ глаза́ искря́тся, как полиро́ванная бирюза́. ♦ **I want to make you sparkle.** Я хочу́, что́бы ты сия́ла. ♦ **The words you write sparkle in my mind like sunbeams.** Слова́, кото́рые ты пи́шешь, сверка́ют в мое́й па́мяти как со́лнечные лучи́. ♦ **Your eyes sparkle with mirth.** Твои́ глаза́ искря́тся весе́льем.

sparkle up *vt (brighten)* озаря́ть / озари́ть; *(liven up)* оживля́ть / оживи́ть ♦ **Thoughts of you sparkle up my day.** Мы́сли о тебе́ озаря́ют мой день. ♦ **Nothing sparkles up my day like** *(1)* **...a letter from you.** / *(2)* **...thoughts of you.** Ничто́ так не озаря́ет мой день, как *(1)* ...письмо́ от тебя́. / *(2)* ...мы́сли о тебе́.

sparkling *adj* сверка́ющий, -ая, -ее, -ие, искря́щийся, -аяся, -ееся, - иеся ♦ **Your sparkling personality brightens my life.** Твоя́ искря́щаяся нату́ра озаря́ет мою́ жизнь. ♦ **You brighten my life with your sparkling personality.** Ты озаря́ешь мою́ жизнь свое́й искря́щейся нату́рой.

speak *vi* говори́ть / поговори́ть *(with whom* = + с + *instr.)* ♦ ~ **of love** говори́ть о любви́ ♦ **I marvel at your ability to speak** *(1)* **English** / *(2)* **Russian.** Я восхища́юсь твое́й спосо́бностью говори́ть *(1)* по-англи́йски / *(2)* по-ру́сски. ♦ **I fervently** *(1)* **entreat** / *(2)* **implore you to** *(3)* **give** / *(4)* **grant me the opportunity to speak with you.** Я горячо́ *(1,2)* умоля́ю Вас *(3)* дать / *(4)* предоста́вить мне возмо́жность поговори́ть с Ва́ми.

special *adj* осо́бенный, -ая, -ое, -ые, осо́бый, -ая, -ое, -ые ♦ **someone** ~ осо́бый челове́к ♦ **that** ~ **someone** э́тот осо́бый челове́к.

Common adult heights are given in Appendix 9, page 776.

| **special: phrases** |

You are (*[1]* **so** / *[2]* **very**) *(3,4)* **special to me.** Ты (*[1]* так / *[2]* óчень) *(3)* ...мнóго знáчишь... / *(4)* ...важнá *(ж: вáжен)*... для меня. ♦ **You and I are special together.** Нáши отношéния -- э́то нéчто осóбенное. ♦ **How special you are to me.** Как мнóго ты для меня знáчишь. ♦ **You have a special place in my heart.** Ты занимáешь осóбое мéсто в моём сéрдце. ♦ **Our love is special and sacred.** Нáша любóвь осóбая и свящéнная. ♦ **I'm looking for a special lady.** Я ищý осóбую жéнщину. ♦ **You are so unique and so special.** Ты так уникáльна *(ж: уникáлен)*. ♦ **You're my special** *(1)* **girl** / *(2)* **lady** / *(3)* **woman.** Ты моя́ люби́мая *(1)* дéвушка / *(2)* лéди / *(3)* жéнщина. ♦ **You're my special** *(1)* **guy** / *(2)* **man.** Ты мой люби́мый *(1)* пáрень / *(2)* мужчи́на.

specimen *n* образéц ♦ **You're a prime specimen of** *(1)* **manhood** / *(2)* **womanhood.** Ты эталóн *(1)* мýжественности / *(2)* жéнственности.

specs *n, pl (slang) (spectacles)* очки́.

spectacular *adj* эффéктный, -ая, -ое, -ые ♦ **You look spectacular.** Ты вы́глядишь эффéктно.

spectrum *n* диапазóн ♦ **~ of feelings** диапазóн чувств.

speech *n* речь *f* ♦ **flowery ~** цвети́стая речь.

speechless *adj* потеря́вший (-ая, -ее, -ие) дар рéчи *(Note: better to use verb* потеря́ть) ♦ **I was speechless with** *(1)* **delight** / *(2)* **joy** / *(3)* **surprise.** Я потеря́л *(ж: потеря́ла)* дар рéчи от *(1)* восхищéния / *(2)* рáдости / *(3)* удивлéния. ♦ **You left me speechless.** Из-за тебя́ я потеря́л *(ж: потеря́ла)* дар рéчи.

spell *n* заклинáние, чáры *pl.*, колдовствó ♦ **break the ~** рассéять чáры ♦ **I can't believe how easily I slipped under the spell of your charm.** Я не могý повéрить, как легкó я поддáлся очаровáнию твоéй прéлести. ♦ **You have cast a love spell over me.** Я околдóван твои́ми чáрами. ♦ **Your** *(1)* **charming** / *(2)* **warm** / *(3)* **gentle** / *(4)* **scintillating personality has me completely under its spell.** Твой *(1)* обая́тельный / *(2)* тёплый / *(3)* мя́гкий / *(4)* искря́щийся харáктер пóлностью меня́ очаровáл. ♦ **I am completely under the spell of your delicious sensuality.** Я пóлностью под чáрами твоéй восхити́тельной чýвственности. ♦ **I have fallen (completely) under your spell.** Я (пóлностью) покорён твои́ми чáрами. ♦ **Your incomparable** *(1)* **shining** / *(2)* **radiant beauty has cast an unbreakable spell over my heart.** Твоя́ несравнéнная *(1)* блестя́щая / *(2)* сия́ющая красотá навсегдá околдовáла моё сéрдце.

spellbound *adv* заворожённо ♦ **watch ~** смотрéть заворожённо.

spend *vt* 1. *(time)* проводи́ть / провести́; 2. *(money)* трáтить / истрáтить ♦ **~ the (whole) night** проводи́ть / провести́ (всю) ночь.

spent *adj* 1. *(exhausted)* изнурённый, -ая, -ое, -ые, устáлый, -ая, -ое, -ые; 2. *(used up)* истощённый, -ая, -ое, -ые; исчéрпанный, -ая, -ое, -ые ♦ **emotionally ~** эмоционáльно исчéрпанный, -ая, -ое, -ые ♦ **physically ~** физи́чески устáлый, -ая, -ое, -ые.

sperm *n* спéрма.

spice *n* пря́ность *f* ♦ **They say that girls are made of sugar and spice and everything nice. Is that true of you?** Говоря́т, что дéвушки сдéланы из сáхара и пря́ностей и из всегó прекрáсного. Подхóдит ли э́то к тебé?

spice up *vt (slang)* оживля́ть / оживи́ть *(what = acc.)*, добавля́ть / добáвить остроты́ *(what = + в + acc.)* ♦ **I'm looking for an affectionate, happy-spirited girl to spice up my life.** Я ищý любя́щую, жизнерáдостную дéвушку, чтóбы добáвить остроты́ в мою́ жизнь.

spiffy *adj* 1. *(smart, dapper, elegant)* наря́дный, -ая, -ое, -ые, щегольскóй, -áя, -óе, -и́е, элегáнтный, -ая, -ое, -ые; 2. *(stylish)* мóдный, -ая, -ое, -ые, сти́льный, -ая, -ое, -ые.

spin *vi* крути́ть, кружи́ться, вертéться ♦ **I go away from any encounter with you with my**

Words in parentheses are optional.

heart spinning wildly and my mind erupting in a fireworks display of love thoughts about you. После ка́ждой встре́чи с тобо́й я ухожу́ с бе́шено стуча́щим се́рдцем и с це́лым фейерве́рком любо́вных мы́слей о тебе́.

spine *n* позвоно́чник ♦ **I love it when you run your hand up and down my spine.** Мне нра́вится, когда́ ты пробега́ешь руко́й вверх и вниз по моему́ позвоно́чнику. ♦ **I** *(1)* **love / (2) want to run my hand up and down your spine.** *(1)* Мне нра́вится... / *(2)* Я хочу́... пробега́ть руко́й вверх и вниз по твоему́ позвоно́чнику. ♦ **I'm going to send delicious shivers up and down your spine.** Упои́тельный тре́пет, по́сланный мной, пробежи́т вверх и вниз по твое́й спине́.

spinster *n* ста́рая де́ва ♦ **One thing is definitely sure: you are never going to be a spinster.** Одно́ соверше́нно я́сно: ты никогда́ не бу́дешь ста́рой де́вой.

spinsterhood *n* стародеви́чество.

spirit *n* дух, душа́; *pl:* настрое́ние, дух ♦ **adventurous** ~ авантю́рный хара́ктер ♦ **blithe** ~ весёлый хара́ктер, весёлая нату́ра ♦ **caring** ~ забо́тливая нату́ра ♦ **Christmas** ~ рожде́ственское настрое́ние ♦ **creative** ~ созида́тельный дух ♦ **devil-may-care** ~ беспе́чность *f* ♦ **enthusiastic** ~ восто́рженная душа́, по́лная этузиа́зма душа́ ♦ **evil** ~ злой дух ♦ **(1,2) exuberant** ~ *(1)* жизнера́достный / *(2)* неудержи́мый хара́ктер ♦ **free** ~ свобо́дный дух ♦ **holiday** ~ пра́здничное настрое́ние ♦ **jubilant** ~s лику́ющий дух ♦ **proud** ~ го́рдая душа́ ♦ **sensual feminine** ~ чу́вственный же́нский хара́ктер ♦ **timid** ~ ро́бкая душа́ ♦ **kindred** ~ ро́дственный дух ♦ **New Age** ~ дух Но́вой э́ры ♦ **nomadic** ~ кочу́ющий дух ♦ **youthful** ~ молодо́й дух.

spirit: other terms

in good ~s в хоро́шем настрое́нии ♦ **in high** ~s в припо́днятом настрое́нии ♦ **in low** ~s в пода́вленном настрое́нии ♦ **true closeness of mind,** ~ **and body** по́длинная гармо́ния ума́, ду́ха и те́ла.

spirit: your spirit

You *(1)* **are / (2) have such a blithe spirit.** *(1,2)* У тебя́ тако́й весёлый хара́ктер. ♦ **You** *(1)* **enchant / (2) captivate me with your blithe spirit.** Ты *(1)* очаро́вываешь / *(2)* пленя́ешь меня́ свои́м весёлым хара́ктером. ♦ **Your precious blithe spirit radiates through all my thoughts.** Твоя́ драгоце́нная жизнера́достность прони́зывает все мои́ мы́сли. ♦ **Your blithe spirit pervades my thoughts wherever I go.** Где бы я ни был *(ж: была́)*, твоя́ жизнера́достность озаря́ет всю мою́ жизнь. ♦ **Your blithe spirit and shining personality enrapture me completely.** Твой весёлый дух и сия́ющая индивидуа́льность невероя́тно восхища́ют меня́. ♦ **You dazzle me with your charm and beauty and blithe spirit.** Ты поража́ешь меня́ свои́м обая́нием, красото́й и весёлым хара́ктером. ♦ **You have a marvelous blending of spirit, charm and sensuality.** У тебя́ удиви́тельное сочета́ние души́, обая́ния и чу́вственности. ♦ **Now I have another one of your letters, filled with your sweet, gentle, loving, caring spirit.** Тепе́рь у меня́ есть ещё одно́ твоё письмо́, напо́лненное твое́й не́жной, мя́гкой лю́бящей, забо́тливой душо́й. ♦ **My heart yearns so fiercely to have a partner like you in life, one who combines a gentle spirit with sexuality, good-heartedness, intelligence, and a loving nature.** Моё се́рдце так неи́стово жа́ждет тако́го спу́тника жи́зни, как ты, тако́го, кто соединя́ет мя́гкий хара́ктер с сексуа́льностью, добросерде́чием, интеллиге́нтностью и лю́бящей нату́рой.

spirit: what you do for my spirit

You are sunshine to my spirit. Ты со́лнечный свет мое́й души́. ♦ **You bring sunshine to my spirit.** Ты прино́сишь со́лнечный свет в мою́ ду́шу. ♦ **I know that we will be together** *(1)* **soon / (2) again / (3) someday, and this (4) knowledge / (5) realization fortifies my spirit.** Я зна́ю, что мы *(1)* ско́ро / *(2)* опя́ть / *(3)* одна́жды бу́дем вме́сте, и *(4,5)*

You can find common clothing sizes in Appendix 11 on page 778.

эта мысль укрепляет мой дух.

| spirit: *you uplift my spirits* |

If you only knew how much your letters *(1)* **lift** / *(2)* **raise my spirits.** Если бы только знала, как сильно твои письма *(1,2)* поднимают мой дух. ♦ **Your letters lift my spirits and brighten my day more than I can describe to you.** Твои письма поднимают мой дух и освещают мой день более, чем я могу описать тебе. ♦ **I can't tell you how much your letters uplift my spirits.** Я даже не могу описать тебе, как твои письма поднимают мой дух. ♦ **How your letter has uplifted my spirits.** Как твоё письмо подняло мой дух. ♦ **My spirits are so uplifted by your letters.** Твои письма так поднимают мой дух. ♦ **It really warmed my heart and lifted up my spirits to** *(1)* **...get your call** / *(2)* **letter.** / *(3)* **...hear your (beloved) voice on the phone.** / *(4)* **...see you again.** Что действительно согрело моё сердце и подняло настроение, так это *(1)* ...твой звонок./ *(2)* ...твоё письмо. / *(3)* ...твой любимый голос по телефону. / *(4)* ...наша последняя встреча. ♦ **It was a tonic for my spirits to get your** *(1)* **call** / *(2)* **letter.** *(1)* Твой звонок был... / *(2)* Твоё письмо было... эликсиром для моего духа.

| spirit: *our spirits* |

You and I are kindred spirits. Ты и я родственные души. ♦ **The union of our two spirits was destined to be.** Союз наших двух душ был предопределён. ♦ **You and I could share so many things, make so much wonderful love together, talk about so many things together, connect in heart, mind, and spirit so perfectly.** Мы с тобой смогли бы так многим наслаждаться вместе, так много заниматься прекрасной любовью, говорить о многом друг с другом, так совершенно соединяться сердцем, умом и духом.

| spirit: *creative spirit* |

I have a creative spirit. Во мне дух созидания.

| spirit: *someone who is rich in spirit* |

I seek a person who is rich in spirit. Я ищу человека, богатого духом.

| spirit: *my spirit suffers* |

My loneliness without you *(1)* **crushes** / *(2)* **ravages my spirit.** Моё одиночество без тебя *(1)* подавляет / *(2)* опустошает мой дух.

| spirit: *protection from evil spirits* |

They say it will protect you from evil spirits. Говорят, это защитит тебя от злого духа.

spirited *adj* жизнерадостный, -ая, -ое, -ые, живой, -ая, -ое, -ые, энергичный, -ая, -ое, -ые, оживлённый, -ая, -ое, -ые.

spiritual *adj* духовный, -ая, -ое, -ые ♦ **deeply ~** глубокодуховный, -ая, -ое, -ые ♦ **I want someone who will share spiritual experiences with me.** Я хочу того, кто разделит духовные поиски со мной.

spirituality *n* духовность *f*, одухотворённость *f*.

spitfire *n* злюка, злючка, «порох» ♦ **You can be a real spitfire at times.** Ты временами можешь быть действительно злой.

splendid *adj (great, fine, wonderful)* великолепный, -ая, -ое, -ые, чудный, -ая, -ое, -ые, прекраснейший, -ая, -ее, -ие, чудесный, -ая, -ое, -ые.

splendidly *adv* великолепно, чудно, прекрасно, чудесно.

splendor *n* великолепие, роскошь *f* ♦ **How I dream of the day when I can peel away your silk underwear to reveal the full,** *(1)* **glorious** / *(2)* **magnificent splendor of your beautiful, luscious body.** Как я мечтаю о том дне, когда смогу сбросить с тебя шёлковое бельё, чтобы открыть наполненную до краёв, *(1)* великолепную / *(2)* замечательную роскошь твоего прекрасного, сочного тела. ♦ **In all my dreams I see your beautiful face framed by the splendor of your golden hair.** Во всех своих снах я вижу твоё пре-

For general rules of Russian grammar see Appendix 2 on page 686.

кра́сное лицо́ в опра́ве из роско́шных золоты́х воло́с. ♦ **I long for the day when I can luxuriate (again) in the warm, sweet splendor of your beautiful body.** Я то́скую по дню, когда́ я смогу́ наслажда́ться (опя́ть) тёплым, сла́достным великоле́пием твоего́ прекра́сного те́ла. ♦ **The copious splendor of your natural endowments** *(1)* **...takes my breath away. /** *(2)* **...captivates all my senses.** Великоле́пие твои́х приро́дных дарова́ний *(1)* ...перехва́тывает моё дыха́ние. / *(2)* ...пленя́ет все мои́ чу́вства.

spoil *vt* 1. *(pamper)* балова́ть / избалова́ть *(whom = acc.)*; 2. *(damage)* по́ртить / испо́ртить *(what = acc.)* ♦ **Let me spoil you.** Позво́ль мне балова́ть тебя́. ♦ **I'm going to spoil you** *(1)* **...outrageously /** *(2)* **shamelessly. /** *(3)* **...beyond your wildest dreams.** Я избалу́ю тебя́ *(1,2)* ...чрезме́рно. / *(3)* ...свы́ше всех твои́х необу́зданных мечта́ний. ♦ **I'm going to spoil you rotten.** Я соверше́нно избалу́ю тебя́. ♦ **I want to spoil you like you've never** *(1)* **...imagined possible. /** *(2)* **...been spoiled before in all your life.** Я хочу́ балова́ть тебя́ так, *(1)* ...как ты никогда́ не могла́ вообрази́ть. / *(2)* ...как тебя́ никогда́ не балова́ли пре́жде. ♦ **I could just spoil you shamelessly in love.** Я мог *(ж: могла́)* бы про́сто бессо́вестно избалова́ть тебя́ в любви́. ♦ **My lips will spoil you such as you never dreamed of in your whole life.** Мои́ гу́бы избалу́ют тебя́ так, как ты никогда́ не могла́ мечта́ть. ♦ **What could be more fun than spoiling each other?** Что могло́ бы доста́вить бо́льше удово́льствия, чем балова́ть друг дру́га?

spoiled *adj* изне́женный, -ая, -ое, -ые, избало́ванный, -ая, -ое, -ые.

spoiling *n (Russians use verb* балова́ть*)* ♦ **mutual** ~ *(verb expression)* баловать друг дру́га.

spoilsport *n* тот, кто по́ртит удово́льствие други́м *(explanation)*.

spoken for свя́зан, -а, -о, -ы *(short forms)* ♦ **I sure hope you're not already spoken for.** Я о́чень наде́юсь, что ты ещё ни с кем не свя́зана *(ж: свя́зан)*.

spontaneity *n* спонта́нность *f*; стихи́йность *f* ♦ **I like spontaneity in a** *(1)* **person /** *(2)* **relationship.** Мне нра́вится спонта́нность в *(1)* челове́ке / *(2)* отноше́ниях.

spontaneous *adj* самопроизво́льный, -ая, -ое, -ые, спонта́нный, -ая, -ое, -ые.

spoon *vi (slang)* целова́ться и обнима́ться, занима́ться пе́ттингом.

spooning *n (slang)* пе́ттинг, поцелу́и и объя́тия *(Note: better to use verbs)*.

sports *n* спорт *(only singular in Russian)* ♦ **outdoor** ~ спорт на откры́том во́здухе ♦ **spectator** ~ зре́лищный спорт ♦ **light** ~ лёгкий спорт.

sports-minded *adj* лю́бящий (-ая, -ее, -ие) спорт.

spot *n* 1. *(place)* ме́сто; *(in the heart)* уголо́к; 2. *(restaurant)* рестора́н; *(club)* клуб; *(tavern)* каба́к; 3. *(situation)* положе́ние; 4. *(stain, soiled place)* пятно́ ♦ **bald** ~ лы́сина ♦ **cozy** ~ ую́тное ме́сто ♦ **difficult** ~ тру́дное положе́ние ♦ **G** ~ Г-зо́на, зо́на Гра́фенберга ♦ **Grafenberg** ~ зо́на Гра́фенберга, Г-зо́на ♦ **nice little** ~ хоро́ший рестора́н; хоро́ший клуб ♦ **soft** ~ *(in the heart)* не́жный уголо́к, не́жное ме́сто *(в се́рдце)* ♦ **tender** ~ *(in the heart)* не́жный уголо́к, не́жное ме́сто *(в се́рдце)* ♦ **tight** ~ тру́дное положе́ние ♦ **tough** ~ тру́дное положе́ние ♦ **have a soft** ~ пита́ть сла́бость *(for whom = + к + dat.)*.

---
spot: phrases

I will always have a tender spot for you in my heart. В своём се́рдце я навсегда́ сохраню́ не́жный уголо́к для тебя́. ♦ **If you have any tender spot for me in your heart, you'll let me** *(1)* **see /** *(2)* **meet you (again).** Если в твоём се́рдце сохрани́лся не́жный уголо́к для меня́, ты позво́лишь мне (опя́ть) *(1)* ...уви́деть тебя́. / *(2)* ...встре́титься с тобо́й.

spouse *n* супру́г *m*, супру́га *f* ♦ **former** ~ бы́вший супру́г *m*, бы́вшая супру́га *f*.

sprawl *vi* растя́гиваться / растяну́ться ♦ **We can sprawl together** *(1)* **...in bed. /** *(2)* **...in front of the fireplace. /** *(3)* **...on the couch /** *(4)* **floor /** *(5)* **grass.** Мы мо́жем растяну́ться вме́сте *(1)* ...в крова́ти. / *(2)* ...пе́ред ками́ном. / *(3)* ...на дива́не / *(4)* полу́ / *(5)* траве́.

spread *vi* распространя́ться / распространи́ться ♦ ~ **through the whole body** разлива́ться

For transitive Russian verbs the cases that they take are shown by means of an = sign and the Russian case. (abbreviated).

/ разли́ться по всему́ те́лу. ♦ **The sensation spreads through my loins like liquid fire.** Чу́вство разлива́ется по моему́ те́лу, как жи́дкий ого́нь.

spread *vt* наноси́ть / нанести́, нама́зывать / нама́зать ♦ ~ **on suntan lotion** ма́зать / нама́зать лосьо́н для зага́ра.

spring *n* весна́ ♦ **in the** ~ весно́й ♦ **last** ~ про́шлой весно́й ♦ **next** ~ сле́дующей весно́й.

spring: phrases

My heart feels like a wilderness that has turned green at the first touch of spring. Моё се́рдце, как пусты́ня, нача́вшая зелене́ть от пе́рвого прикоснове́ния весны́. ♦ **The *(1,2)* magic of the spring fills my heart with longing to be with you.** *(1)* Волшебство́ / *(2)* Ма́гия весны́ наполня́ет моё се́рдце жа́ждой быть с тобо́й. ♦ **I want to share the magic of the spring with you.** Я хочу́ раздели́ть волшебство́ весны́ с тобо́й. ♦ **"I want to do with you what spring does with the cherry trees."** *Pablo Neruda* «Я хочу́ сде́лать с тобо́й то же, что весна́ де́лает с вишнёвыми дере́вьями.» *Па́бло Неру́да.*

springtime *n* весна́ ♦ **There is springtime in my heart because of you.** Из-за тебя́ в моём се́рдце весна́. ♦ **I hope you will make this springtime stay in my heart *(1)* always / *(2)* forever.** Я наде́юсь, что ты помо́жешь э́той весне́ оста́ться в моём се́рдце *(1)* навсегда́ / *(2)* наве́чно.

spunk *n (ardor, spirit)* пыл, жар, жи́вость, пы́лкость *f* ♦ **You really *(1)* have / *(2)* show a lot of spunk.** *(1,2)* Ты действи́тельно полна́ жи́вости.

spunky *adj (spirited)* живо́й, -а́я, -о́е, -ы́е, энерги́чный, -ая, -ое, -ые; темпера́ментный, -ая, -ое, -ые.

spur on *vt* вдохновля́ть *(whom = acc.)* ♦ **Such dreams really help to spur me on.** Таки́е мечты́ действи́тельно вдохновля́ют меня́.

squeal *vi* визжа́ть / завизжа́ть.

squeal *n* визг ♦ **delightful** ~ восхищённый визг ♦ ~ **of delight** визг восто́рга.

squeeze *vt* сжима́ть / сжать *(what, whom = acc.)* ♦ **I love to squeeze the rounded globes of your breasts.** Я люблю́ сжима́ть окру́глые шары́ твои́х груде́й.

squeeze *n* 1. *(squeezing)* сжа́тие, сжима́ние; *(hand squeeze)* пожа́тие; *(embrace)* объя́тие; 2. *(slang) (girlfriend)* возвлю́бленная, люби́мая де́вушка, подру́га ♦ **friendly** ~ дру́жеское объя́тие ♦ **my old** ~ моя́ бы́вшая подру́га ♦ **When I gave your hand a squeeze and you squeezed back, my heart soared to the moon.** Когда́ я сжима́л *(ж: сжима́ла)* твою́ ру́ку, и ты в отве́т сжима́ла *(ж: сжима́л)* мою́, моё се́рдце воспаря́ло ввысь. ♦ *(1)* **I'm his...** / *(2)* **She's my... new *(3,4)* squeeze.** *(1)* Я его́... / *(2)* Она́ моя́... но́вая *(3)* подру́га / *(4)* возлю́бленная.

squire *n (lady's escort)* кавале́р.

squirm *vi* выгиба́ться / вы́гнуться, ко́рчиться / ско́рчиться, извива́ться ♦ ~ **with pleasure** извива́ться от наслажде́ния.

stab *vt* ра́нить кинжа́лом *(whom = acc.)* ♦ *(1)* **I don't want to...** / *(2)* **I can't... stab *(3)* her / *(4)* him in the back.** Я не *(1)* хочу́ / *(2)* могу́ де́йствовать за *(3)* её / *(4)* его́ спино́й.

stability *n* усто́йчивость *f*, стаби́льность *f* ♦ ~ **of a relationship** стаби́льность отноше́ний.

stable *adj* усто́йчивый, -ая, -ое, -ые *(short forms:* усто́йчив, -а, -о, -ы), стаби́льный, -ая, -ое, -ые ♦ **emotionally** ~ эмоциона́льно стаби́льный, -ая, -ое, -ые ♦ **financially** ~ материа́льно обеспе́чен, -а, -о, -ы, фина́нсово стаби́льный, -ая, -ое, -ые ♦ **mentally** ~ психи́чески стаби́льный, -ая, -ое, -ые.

stacked *adj (slang)* аппети́тная, с *(1)* пы́шной / *(2)* роско́шной фигу́рой ♦ **I've never seen a woman as stacked as you are.** Я никогда́ не встреча́л же́нщины с тако́й роско́шной фигу́рой, как твоя́.

stamina *n* выно́сливость *f* ♦ **You have a lot of *(1,2)* stamina!** Ско́лько у тебя́ *(1)* выно́с-

---

Russian verbs have 2 forms: imperfective and perfective.
They're given in that order.

ли́вости / *(2)* си́лы!

stamp *n* 1. *(imprint)* печа́ть *f*; 2. *(postage)* ма́рка ♦ ~ **of friendship** печа́ть дру́жбы.

stance *n* по́за, пози́ция.

stand *vt (endure)* выде́рживать / вы́держать *(what, whom = acc.)*, переноси́ть / перенести́ *(what, whom = acc.)*, выноси́ть / вы́нести *(what, whom = acc.) (See also expressions under* **bear)** ♦ **I want you so much I can't stand it.** Я так си́льно хочу́ тебя́, что не могу́ вы́держать. ♦ **I get so (terribly) lonely that I can hardly stand it.** Я так (ужа́сно) одино́к *(ж: одино́ка)*, что с трудо́м выде́рживаю э́то. ♦ **I** *(1)* **can't /** *(2)* **couldn't stand to leave you.** *(1)* Я не могу́... / *(2)* Я не смог *(ж: смогла́)* бы... вы́нести разлу́ки с тобо́й. ♦ **I can't stand the idea of being away from you.** Я не могу́ вы́нести мысль о том, что́бы быть без тебя́.

stand *vi* стоя́ть ♦ *(1)* **Nothing /** *(2)* **Nobody will stand in** *(3)* **...our way. /** *(4)* **...the way of our love.** *(1)* Ничто́ / *(2)* Никто́ не вста́нет *(3)* ...на на́шем пути́. / *(4)* ...на пути́ на́шей любви́.

stand *n (slang)* связь *f* ♦ **one-night** ~ связь на одну́ ночь ♦ **I don't like one-night stands.** Я не интересу́юсь свя́зями на одну́ ночь. ♦ **I don't want (this to be) a one-night stand.** Я не хочу́ свя́зи на одну́ ночь.

stand-offish *adj (unfriendly)* неприве́тливый, -ая, -ое, -ые; *(unsociable)* необщи́тельный, -ая, -ое, -ые; *(cold)* холо́дный, -ая, -ое, -ые; *(haughty)* высокоме́рный, -ая, -ое, -ые.

stand up *vt (make someone wait in vain)* заставля́ть / заста́вить ждать напра́сно *(whom = acc.)* ♦ **I'm sorry I stood you up.** Я извиня́юсь, я заста́вил *(ж: заста́вила)* тебя́ ждать напра́сно. ♦ **I didn't mean to stand you up.** Я не хоте́л *(ж: хоте́ла)* заста́вить тебя́ ждать напра́сно. ♦ **Promise you won't stand me up.** Обеща́й, ты не заста́вишь меня́ ждать напра́сно. ♦ **I won't stand you up, I promise.** Я не заста́влю тебя́ жда́ть напра́сно, обеща́ю.

star *n* звезда́ *(pl:* звёзды*)* ♦ **bright** ~ я́ркая звезда́ ♦ **falling** ~ па́дающая звезда́ ♦ **lucky** ~ счастли́вая звезда́ ♦ **shooting** ~ па́дающая звезда́ ♦ ~ **of my life** звезда́ мое́й жи́зни ♦ **unlucky** ~ несчастли́вая звезда́ ♦ **look at the** ~**s** смотре́ть на звёзды ♦ **reach the** ~**s** дости́чь звёзд ♦ **gaze at the** ~**s** смотре́ть на звёзды.

> ### star: phrases

Do you know that you have stars in yours eyes? Зна́ешь ли ты, что в твои́х глаза́х звёзды? ♦ **When I look into your eyes, I see the stars.** Когда́ я смотрю́ в твои́ глаза́, я ви́жу звёзды. ♦ **I thank my lucky stars that** *(1)* **...I met you (in this world). /** *(2)* **...our paths converged in life. /** *(3)* **...you came into my life. /** *(4)* **...I found you in this big, crazy world.** Я благодарю́ мою́ звезду́ уда́чи за то, что *(1)* ...я встре́тил *(ж: встре́тила)* тебя́ (в э́том ми́ре). / *(2)* ...на́ши жи́зненные тро́пы пересекли́сь. / *(3)* ...ты вошла́ *(ж: вошёл)* в мою́ жизнь. / *(4)* ...я нашёл *(ж: нашла́)* тебя́ в э́том большо́м, сумасше́дшем ми́ре. ♦ **I'll put stars in your eyes (on the first date).** Я зажгу́ звёзды в твои́х глаза́х (при пе́рвом же на́шем свида́нии). ♦ **I want to lie with you outside on a clear, summer night and gaze at the stars.** Я́сной ле́тней но́чью я хочу́ лежа́ть с тобо́й и смотре́ть на звёзды. ♦ **You are the star of my life.** Ты звезда́ мое́й жи́зни. ♦ **It's written in the stars that the two of us should be together.** Звёздами бы́ло предназна́чено нам быть вме́сте.

stare *vi* при́стально смотре́ть *(at whom, whom* = + на + *acc.)*, уста́виться *(at whom, whom* = + на + *acc.)* ♦ ~ **coldly** хо́лодно уста́виться.

stare *n* при́стальный взгляд ♦ **cold** ~ холо́дный при́стальный взгляд.

stargazing *n* созерца́ние звёзд.

starry *adj* звёздный, -ая, -ое, -ые ♦ ~ **night** звёздная ночь.

adj не от ми́ра сего́, мечта́тельный, -ая, -ое, -ые ♦ **Your love makes me starry-**

How to use the Cyrillic alphabet on the Internet
is the subject of Appendix 20 on page 789.

eyed. Твоя́ любо́вь де́лает меня́ мечта́телем.

starve *vi* жа́ждать *(for what = gen.)*; умира́ть от жела́ния ♦ **I'm starving for affection.** Я жа́жду любви́ и не́жности.

starved *adj (Russian generally uses the verb* жа́ждать *(+ gen.) for the meaning of "crave")* ♦ **be ~** жа́ждать *(for what, whom = gen.)* ♦ **I'm (**[1] **so / [2] really / [3] totally / [4] enormously / [5] terribly) starved for** (6) **...you. /** (7) **...love (and I think you are too). /** (8) **...affection. /** (9) **...intimacy. /** (10) **...sex.** (11) **...your (**[12] **burning / [13] sweet) kisses.** Я ([1] так / [2] действи́тельно / [3] весь *(ж: вся)* / [4] ужа́сно / [5] стра́шно жа́жду (6) ...тебя́. / (7) ...любви́ (и, ду́маю, ты то́же). / (8) ...не́жности. / (9) бли́зости / (10) се́кса / (11) ...твои́х ([12] горя́чих / [13] сла́дких) поцелу́ев. ♦ **Affection — Oh, my dear, I am so starved for it!** Не́жность -- о, моя́ дорога́я *(ж: мой дорого́й)*, я так жа́жду её! ♦ **Darling, I must tell you that I'm really starved to make love with you.** Дорога́я, я до́лжен сказа́ть тебе́, что я действи́тельно жа́жду заня́ться любо́вью с тобо́й. ♦ **Oh, Sweetheart, I'm so terribly starved for you.** О, дорога́я *(ж: дорого́й)*, я так си́льно жа́жду тебя́.

state *n* 1. *(condition)* состоя́ние; 2. *(U.S.)* штат ♦ **~ of bewilderment** замеша́тельство ♦ **~ of mind** состоя́ние рассу́дка ♦ **Our relationship is in a state of flux.** На́ши отноше́ния не устоя́лись. ♦ **You have me in a state right now where I don't know if I'm walking, spinning or floating.** Я сейча́с в тако́м состоя́нии, что не зна́ю хожу́ ли я, враща́юсь ли и́ли плыву́. ♦ **I live in the state of California.** Я живу́ в шта́те Калифо́рния. ♦ **I'm from the state of New York.** Я из шта́та Нью Йо́рк.

stationed *adj* размещён, размещена́, -о, -ы *(short forms)* ♦ **be ~** бази́роваться ♦ **I'm stationed at** _(name of [1] base / [2] city)_ . Я бази́руюсь [1] на ___ / [2] в ___ .

statistics *n* 1. стати́стика; 2. *(dimensions)* разме́ры ♦ **vital ~s** *(measurements around the bust, waist and hips)* разме́ры бю́ста, та́лии и бёдер ♦ **perfect ~s** превосхо́дные разме́ры бю́ста, та́лии и бёдер.

statue *n* статуя; статуэ́тка ♦ **carved ~** вы́сеченная стату́я ♦ **Standing there like that, you look like an exquisite alabaster statue.** Сто́я там так, ты похо́жа на изя́щную алеба́стровую статуэ́тку.

statuesque *adj* ста́тный, -ая, -ое, -ые, скульпту́рный, -ая, -ое, -ые ♦ **~ beauty** ста́тная краса́вица ♦ **~ blonde** ста́тная блонди́нка ♦ **~ brunette** ста́тная брюне́тка.

stature *n* рост ♦ **medium ~** сре́днего ро́ста ♦ **short ~** невысо́кого ро́ста.

status *n* ста́тус, положе́ние, состоя́ние ♦ **equal ~** ра́вный ста́тус ♦ **marital ~** семе́йное положе́ние.

stay *vi* 1. *(remain)* остава́ться / оста́ться; 2. *(live)* жить, остана́вливаться / останови́ться ♦ **Where are you staying?** Где ты останови́лась *(ж: останови́лся)*? ♦ **I'm staying at** _(name)_ . Я останови́лся *(ж: останови́лась)* в _(назва́ние)_ . ♦ **Would it be possible for you to stay (with me)** (1) **...overnight? /** (2) **...all night?** Смо́жешь ли ты оста́ться (со мной) (1) ... на ночь? / (2) ... на всю ночь? ♦ **I can('t) stay with you (** [5]**...tonight. / [2] ...all night. / [3] ...tomorrow.).** Я (не) могу́ оста́ться с тобо́й ([5]...сего́дня но́чью. / [2] ...на всю ночь. / [3] ...за́втра.). ♦ **Would it be possible** (1) **...to stay at your house /** (2) **apartment? /** (3)**...to stay for another day /** (4) **week?** Бу́дет ли возмо́жно (1) ...останови́ться в твоём до́ме? / (2) ...останови́ться в твое́й кварти́ре? / (3) ...оста́ться ещё на оди́н день? / (4) ...оста́ться ещё на одну́ неде́лю? ♦ **You can('t) stay** (1) **...at my house /** (2) **apartment. /** (3) **...for another day /** (4) **week.** Ты (не) мо́жешь (1) ...останови́ться в моём до́ме. / (2) ...останови́ться в мое́й кварти́ре. / (3) ...оста́ться ещё на оди́н день. / (4) ...оста́ться ещё на одну́ неде́лю. ♦ **I try to stay** (1) **...fit. /** (2) **...in shape.** Я пыта́юсь остава́ться (1,2) в фо́рме.

Russian adjectives have long and short forms.
Where short forms are given, they are labeled as such.

STD-free *adj (free of sexually transmitted diseases)* нет заболеваний, передающихся сексуальным путём *(1 term)*.

steadfast *adj* стойкий, -ая, -ое, -ие, непоколебимый, -ая, -ое, -ые.

steadfastly *adv* настойчиво.

steadfastness *n* стойкость *f*, непоколебимость *f*.

steal *vt* красть / украсть *(what = acc.)* ♦ **~ a kiss** сорвать поцелуй ♦ **You've stolen my heart (completely) away.** Ты похитила моё сердце. ♦ **I've never stolen anything in my life — except a kiss.** В своей жизни я никогда ничего не украл, кроме поцелуя. ♦ **I normally wouldn't think of stealing someone else's** *(1)* **woman** / *(2)* **girl, but if you're attached, I'm afraid I'm going to have to make an exception.** Я обычно не подумал бы о краже чьей-то *(1)* женщины / *(2)* девушки, но, если ты связана с кем-то, я боюсь, что должен сделать исключение.

steal in *vi* проскальзывать / проскользнуть *(into what = + в + acc.)*, прокрадываться / прокрасться *(into what = + в + acc.)* ♦ **I'll steal into your room later on (when they're asleep).** Я проскользну в твою комнату позднее (, когда они уснут).

steal out *vi* выскальзывать / выскользнуть *(out of what = + из + gen.)* ♦ **I'll steal out in the morning.** Я выскользну утром.

steamy *adj* 1. *(erotic)* эротический, -ая, -ое, -ие; 2. *(passionate)* страстный, -ая, -ое, -ые.

stepbrother *n* сводный брат.

stepdaughter *n* падчерица.

stepfather *n* отчим.

stepmother *n* мачеха.

step out *vi* встречаться / встретиться с другой *(ж: другим)*, ходить на сторону ♦ **I would never step out on you.** Я никогда не буду встречаться с кем-либо другим.

stepsister *n* сводная сестра.

stepson *n* пасынок.

sterile *adj (infertile)* бесплодный, -ая, -ое, -ые *(short forms:* бесплоден, бесплодна, -ы*)*; стерильный, -ая, -ое, -ые ♦ **I can't have children. I'm sterile.** Я не могу иметь детей. Я бесплоден.

stick *vi (adhere to)* прилипать / прилипнуть *(to what, whom = + к + dat.)*; приставать / пристать *(to what, whom = + к + dat.)*, привязываться / привязаться *(to what, whom = + к + dat.)* ♦ **I'm going to stick to you like glue.** Я собираюсь прилипнуть к тебе, как клей.

stick *n* палка ♦ **swizzle ~** соломинка.

stick-slender *adj* стройная как берёза.

sticky *adj* 1. *(adhesive)* липкий, -ая, -ое, -ие, клейкий -ая, -ое, -ие; 2. *(difficult)* трудный, -ая, -ое, -ые, сложный, -ая, -ое, -ые ♦ **The whole** *(1)* **situation** / *(2)* **affair** *(3)* **...has gotten...** / *(4)* **...is getting... too sticky.** Вся *(1)* ситуация / *(2)* связь *(3)* ...становилась... / *(4)* ...становится... слишком сложной.

stiff *adj* 1. *(rigid)* жёсткий, -ая, -ое, -ие; 2. *(tense)* одеревенелый, -ая, -ое, -ые, деревянный, -ая, -ое, -ые, напряжённый, -ая, -ое, -ые; 3. *(not cordial)* холодный, -ая, -ое, -ые, чопорный, -ая, -ое, -ые.

stiffen *vi* столбенеть / остолбенеть, цепенеть / оцепенеть; костенеть / окостенеть.

stigma *n* клеймо позора.

still *adj* тихий, -ая, -ое, -ие ♦ **Still waters** *(1)* **run** / *(2)* **flow deep.** *(1,2)* В тихом омуте черти водятся.

still *adv* ещё.

stimulate *vt* возбуждать *(what = acc.)*, стимулировать *(what = acc.)*.

stimulating *adj* возбуждающий, -ая, -ее, -ие, стимулирующий, -ая, -ее, -ие ♦ **mentally**

Russian nouns are either masculine, feminine or neuter.
Adjectives with them will be the same.

~ у́мственно возбужда́ющий, -ая, -ее, -ие ♦ **visually** ~ зри́тельно возбужда́ющий, -ая, -ее, -ие.

stinginess *n* ску́пость *f*, ска́редность *f*.

stingy *adj* скупо́й, -а́я, -о́е, -ы́е *(short forms:* скуп, -а́, -о, -ы*)*, ска́редный, -ая, -ое, -ые ♦ **When it comes to love, I'm not at all stingy.** Когда́ э́то каса́ется любви́, я совсе́м не скуп *(ж: скупа́)*. ♦ **Don't be stingy with your kisses.** Не будь скупа́ *(ж: скуп)* в поцелу́ях.

stir *vt* пробужда́ть / пробуди́ть *(what = acc.)*; возбужда́ть / возбуди́ть *(what = acc.)*, волнова́ть *(what, whom = acc.)* ♦ ~ **feelings** пробужда́ть / пробуди́ть чу́вства ♦ ~ **my heart** растро́гать меня́, тро́нуть моё се́рдце ♦ ~ **passion** пробужда́ть / пробуди́ть страсть ♦ ~ **up** возбужда́ть / возбуди́ть *(what = acc.)*, будора́жить / взбудора́жить *(what = acc.)*.

stir:

Your words really stirred my heart. Твои́ слова́ действи́тельно растро́гали меня́. ♦ **Oh, how I'm going to stir your passions!** О, как я разбужу́ твою́ страсть.

stir up:

You *(1-3)* **stir up such turbulent feelings in** *(4)* **...me.** / *(5)* **...my heart.** Ты *(1)* пробужда́ешь / *(2)* вызыва́ешь / *(3)* возбужда́ешь таки́е бу́рные чу́вства *(4)* ...во мне. / *(5)* ...в моём се́рдце. ♦ **I've never known anyone in my life that could penetrate to the very core of my soul and stir up all my feelings the way you can.** Я никогда́ в свое́й жи́зни не знал *(ж: зна́ла)* кого́-либо ещё, кто мог бы проника́ть в са́мую глубину́ мое́й души́ и возбужда́ть мои́ чу́вства так, как ты.

stirred *adj* взволно́ван, -а, -о, -ы *(short forms)* ♦ **I cannot describe to you how deeply stirred I am by your manifold charms.** Я не могу́ описа́ть, как глубоко́ я взволно́ван твои́ми многочи́сленными пре́лестями.

stirring *adj* волну́ющий, -ая, -ее, -ие.

stockings *n, pl* чулки́ ♦ **black** ~s чёрные чулки́ ♦ **dark** ~s тёмные чулки́ ♦ **fishnet** ~s чулки́ в се́точку ♦ **patterned** ~s чулки́ с узо́ром ♦ **sheer, black** ~s прозра́чные чёрные чулки́.

stockings: *phrases*

How *(1)* **beautiful** / *(2)* **sexy your legs are in sheer, black stockings.** Как *(1)* прекра́сны / *(2)* сексуа́льны твои́ но́ги в прозра́чных, чёрных чулка́х. ♦ **I envy your stockings. They're wrapped around your legs all day. How I wish I could do the same.** Я зави́дую твои́м чулка́м. Они́ обёртывают твои́ но́ги весь день. Как бы я жела́л де́лать то́же са́мое.

stocky *adj* корена́стый, -ая, -ое, -ые, призе́мистый, -ая, -ое, -ые, кре́пкий, -ая, -ое, -ие ♦ **My build is (rather) stocky.** Я (дово́льно) призе́мистый. ♦ **I have a** *(1,2)* **stocky build.** Я *(1)* корена́стый / *(2)* призе́мистый.

stoic *adj* стои́ческий, -ая, -ое, -ие.

stoically *adv* стои́чески.

stoke *vt* разжига́ть / разже́чь *(what = acc.)*; возбужда́ть *(what, whom = acc.)* ♦ **You can never** *(1)* **know** / *(2)* **imagine how you stoke the fires in my** *(3)* **heart** / *(4)* **blood.** Ты не *(1)* ...зна́ешь,... / *(2)* ...мо́жешь вообрази́ть,... како́й ого́нь разжига́ешь в *(3)* ...моём се́рдце. / *(4)* ...мое́й кро́ви. ♦ **Music stokes me.** Му́зыка возбужда́ет меня́.

stomach *vt* выноси́ть / вы́нести *(what, whom = acc.)*, терпе́ть / потерпе́ть *(what, whom = acc.)*, сноси́ть / снести́ *(what, whom = acc.)* ♦ **I just** *(1)* **can't** / *(2)* **couldn't stomach a divorce.** Я то́лько *(1)* ...не смогу́... / *(2)* ...не смог *(ж: смогла́)* бы... вы́нести разво́да.

stomach *n* живо́т; *(little)* живо́тик ♦ **bare** ~ го́лый живо́т ♦ **big** ~ большо́й живо́т ♦ **fat** ~ то́лстый живо́т ♦ **flat** ~ пло́ский живо́т ♦ **hard** ~ твёрдый живо́т ♦ **little** ~ живо́тик

Learn more about Russian customs in Appendix 15, page 782.

♦ **my** ~ мой живо́т ♦ *(1,2)* **small** ~ *(1)* небольшо́й / *(2)* ма́ленький живо́т ♦ **soft** ~ мя́г-кий живо́т ♦ **tanned** ~ загоре́лый живо́т ♦ **tight** ~ туго́й живо́т ♦ **your** ~ твой живо́т ♦ **scar on the** ~ шрам на животе́.

---
stomach: *phrases*

You have such a flat stomach. У тебя́ тако́й пло́ский живо́т. ♦ *(1)* **I want to...** / *(2)* **I'm going to... brush my lips across the tips of your breasts, down your stomach and along your legs.** Я *(1)* хочу́ / *(2)* собира́юсь косну́ться губа́ми твои́х соско́в, спусти́ться к твоему́ живо́ту и пробежа́ть вдоль твои́х ног. ♦ **Whenever I think of** *(1)* **...it,** / *(2)* **...meeting you for the first time, I get butterflies in my stomach.** Когда́ бы я ни поду́мал *(ж: поду́мала)* *(1)* ...об э́том,... / *(2)* ...о пе́рвой встре́че с тобо́й,... я о́чень возбужда́юсь. ♦ **I felt in the pit of my stomach that you were** *(1)* **...seeing someone else.** / *(2)* **...being untrue.** / *(3)* **...were going to leave me.** Я чу́вствовал *(ж: чу́вствовала)* в глубине́ души́, что ты *(1)* ...встреча́лась с други́м *(ж: встреча́лся с друго́й).* / *(2)* ...была́ неверна́ *(ж: был неве́рен).* / *(3)* ...собира́ешься оста́вить меня́. ♦ **I have a cold, hollow feeling in my stomach.** Во мне хо́лод и пустота́. ♦ **I don't have the stomach for an affair.** У меня́ не хвата́ет ду́ха для рома́на.

stone *n* ка́мень *m* ♦ **precious** ~ драгоце́нный ка́мень ♦ **I'm not made of stone.** Я не ка́мен-ный *(ж: ка́менная).*

stony *adj* ка́менный, -ая, -ое, -ые ♦ **You were so cold and stony to me.** Ты была́ холодна́, как лёд, со мной. ♦ **Why the** *(1,2)* **stony silence?** Почему́ тако́е *(1)* ледяно́е / *(2)* ка́менное молча́ние?

stop *vt* перестава́ть / переста́ть ♦ *(1-3)* **Stop it!** *(1)* Останови́сь! / *(2)* Переста́нь! / *(3)* Прекрати́! ♦ **Stop doing that!** Переста́нь так де́лать! ♦ **I don't want to stop kissing you.** Я не хочу́ переста́ть целова́ть тебя́. ♦ **I will never stop loving you.** Я никогда́ не переста́ну люби́ть тебя́.

stop *vi* остана́вливаться / останови́ться.

storm *n* бу́ря, урага́н, шторм ♦ **I want to make all the passion in you leap into a wild storm.** Я хочу́, что́бы вся твоя́ стра́стность переросла́ в бе́шеный шторм. ♦ **You arouse a storm of** *(1)* **incredible** / *(2)* **fantastic sensations in me.** Ты возбужда́ешь бу́рю *(1)* невероя́тных / *(2)* фантасти́ческих чувств во мне. ♦ **I'm going to unleash in you a storm of the most** *(1)* **exquisite** / *(2)* **incredible** / *(3)* **fantastic sensations you've ever** *(4)* **experienced** / *(5)* **felt (in your whole life).** Я бро́шу тебя́ в шторм бо́лее *(1)* изы́сканных / *(2)* невероя́тных / *(3)* фантасти́ческих чувств, чем те, кото́рые ты когда́-либо *(4)* испы́тывала / *(5)* чу́вствовала (в свое́й жи́зни). ♦ **When I have you in my arms, I'm going to arouse tides of sweet feeling in you that will sweep you into a storm of passion.** Когда́ я заключу́ тебя́ в объя́тия, я разбужу́ пото́к не́жных чувств в тебе́, кото́рый бро́сит тебя́ в бу́рю стра́сти.

story *n* расска́з, исто́рия ♦ **dirty** ~ са́льность *f*, непристо́йность *f* ♦ **love's old** ~ ста́рая исто́рия любви́ ♦ **love** ~ 1. *(fiction)* любо́вный рома́н, *(1)* расска́з / *(2)* по́весть / *(3)* рома́н о любви́; 2. *(account)* любо́вная исто́рия ♦ **That's the story of my life.** *(ironic)* Это исто́рия мое́й жи́зни. *(ирони́чески)* ♦ *(1)* **I want to hear...** / *(2)* **Tell me... the story of your life.** *(1)* Я хочу́ слы́шать... / *(2)* Расскажи́ мне... исто́рию твое́й жи́зни.

straight *adj* 1. *(not curved)* прямо́й, -а́я, -о́е, -ы́е; 2. *(slang) (not homosexual)* ♦ негомо-сексуа́льный, -ая, -ое, -ые.

straightforward *adj (frank)* открове́нный, -ая, -ое, -ые; *(honest)* че́стный, -ая, -ое, -ые.

straight-laced *adj* чо́порный, -ая, -ое, -ые, пурита́нский, -ая, -ое, -ие.

straight-shooter *n (1)* открове́нный / *(2)* че́стный челове́к.

straight-shooting *adj (frank)* открове́нный, -ая, -ое, -ые; *(honest)* че́стный, -ая, -ое, -ые.

A slash always denotes "or."
You can choose the numbered words before and after.

strain *n* напряже́ние ◆ **It's causing a strain in our relationship.** Это вызыва́ет напряже́ние в на́ших отноше́ниях.

strand *n* прядь *f* ◆ **golden ~ of hair** золота́я прядь воло́с ◆ **silky ~s of hair** шелкови́стые пря́ди воло́с.

strange *adj* 1. *(odd)* стра́нный, -ая, -ое, -ые; 2. *(unfamiliar)* незнако́мый, -ая, -ое, -ые.

strangely *adv* стра́нно.

stranger *n* 1. *(unknown person)* незнако́мец, незнако́мый челове́к; 2. *(poet.) (alien)* чужестра́нец ◆ **complete ~** соверше́нно незнако́мый челове́к ◆ **~s in the night** ночны́е незнако́мцы ◆ **perfect ~** соверше́нно незнако́мый челове́к ◆ **total ~** соверше́нно незнако́мый челове́к ◆ **virtual ~** факти́чески незнако́мый ◆ **You and I are like (total) strangers** *(1)* **anymore /** *(2)* **lately /** *(3)* **nowadays.** Ты и я как (соверше́нно) незнако́мые *(1-3)* после́днее вре́мя.

strap *n* 1. *(general)* реме́нь *m*; 2. *(shoulder strap)* ля́мка; 3. *(undergarments)* брете́лька.

strapless *adj* без брете́лек.

straw *n* соло́м(инк)а ◆ **I know I'm grasping at straws, but can't we just talk things over one more time?** Я зна́ю, что пыта́юсь ухвати́ться за соло́минку, но не могли́ бы мы про́сто обсуди́ть дела́ ещё оди́н раз?

stray *vi* отбива́ться / отби́ться ◆ **My** *(1)* **wife /** *(2)* **husband and I have strayed apart.** На́ши с *(1)* жено́й / *(2)* му́жем доро́ги разошли́сь.

streak *n* 1. *(characteristic)* жи́лка, черта́; 2. *(hair with color)* прядь *f* ◆ **blonde ~** белоку́рая прядь ◆ **grey ~** седа́я прядь ◆ **nervous ~** нерво́зность *f* ◆ **reddish ~** ры́жая прядь ◆ **romantic ~** романти́ческая жи́лка ◆ **wild ~** распу́щенность *f*, гру́бость *f*.

stream *n* 1. *(small river)* руче́й; 2. *(copious flow)* пото́к ◆ **~ of** *(1)* **feelings /** *(2)* **sensations** пото́к *(1,2)* ощуще́ний ◆ **From far away I send you an endless stream of loving thoughts.** Издалека́ я посыла́ю тебе́ бесконе́чный пото́к любо́вных мы́слей. ◆ **My heart yearns to show you my love in an endless stream of warm embraces and soft,** *(1)* **adoring /** *(2)* **loving kisses.** Моё се́рдце жа́ждет показа́ть тебе́ свою́ любо́вь в бесконе́чном пото́ке тёплых объя́тий и мя́гких, *(1)* обожа́ющих / *(2)* лю́бящих поцелу́ев.

strength *n* си́ла; про́чность *f* ◆ **ageless ~** нестаре́ющая си́ла ◆ **emotional ~** эмоциона́льная си́ла ◆ **great ~** больша́я си́ла ◆ **inner ~** вну́тренняя си́ла ◆ *(1-3)* **moral ~** *(1)* мора́льная / *(2)* нра́вственная / *(3)* душе́вная си́ла ◆ **physical ~** физи́ческая си́ла ◆ **primitive ~** примити́вная си́ла ◆ **spiritual ~** духо́вная си́ла ◆ **robbed of ~** рассла́бленный, -ая, -ое, -ые ◆ **overwhelming ~** вла́стная си́ла.

> **strength:** *phrases*

You are my hope and dreams, my strength and purpose, my joy and happiness. You are my life. Ты мои́ наде́жды и мечты́, моя́ си́ла и цель, моя́ ра́дость и сча́стье. Ты моя́ жизнь. ◆ **I admire you for your strength.** Я восхища́юсь тобо́й за твою́ си́лу. ◆ **You are (such) a tower of strength** *(1)* **...to me. /** *(2)* **...in my life.** *(1,2)* Я за тобо́й как за ка́менной стено́й. ◆ **You give me the strength** *(1)* **...to carry on. /** *(2)* **...to keep going.** Ты даёшь мне си́лы *(1,2)* продолжа́ть. ◆ **The strength of your appeal for me is beyond** *(1)* **description /** *(2)* **definition /** *(3)* **calculation.** Си́ла твое́й привлека́тельности для меня́ вы́ше *(1)* ...вся́кого описа́ния / *(2)* определе́ния. / *(3)* ...вся́кой ме́ры.

stretch *vt* натя́гивать / натяну́ть *(what = acc.)* ◆ **~ the truth** вытя́гивать / вы́тянуть пра́вду, преувели́чивать ◆ **Aren't you stretching the truth a little?** Ты немно́го преувели́чиваешь?

stretch *vi* потя́гиваться / потяну́ться ◆ **~ languidly** то́мно потя́гиваться ◆ **~ out** *vi* растя́гиваться / растяну́ться ◆ **I long to see you stretch out in languorous abandon as I place tiny kisses about your bosom and down your stomach.** Я жа́жду уви́деть тебя́,

---

Common adult weights are given in Appendix 10, page 777.

раскинувшуюся в томной непринуждённости, в то время, как я размещаю крошечные поцелуи вокруг твоей груди и вниз по твоему животу.

strict *adj* строгий, -ая, -ое, -ие.

striking *adj* поразительный, -ая, -ое, -ые, потрясающий, -ая, -ее, -ие ♦ **With your** *(1)* **blonde** / *(2)* **black** / *(3)* **red hair and** *(4)* **creamy** / *(5)* **pale** / *(6)* **bronze** / *(7)* **golden skin you are the most striking woman I have ever** *(8)* **seen** / *(9)* **met.** Со своими *(1)* светлыми / *(2)* чёрными / *(3)* рыжими волосами и *(4)* нежной / *(5)* бледной / *(6)* бронзовой / *(7)* золотистой кожей ты самая потрясающая женщина, которую я когда-либо *(8)* видел / *(9)* встречал. ♦ **You are a woman of striking beauty.** Ты женщина поразительной красоты. ♦ **That's a striking outfit that you're wearing.** Ты носишь поразительный наряд. ♦ **You certainly are striking (tonight).** Ты определённо поразительна (сегодня вечером). ♦ **You are the most striking woman I have ever** *(1)* **met** / *(2)* **seen.** Ты наиболее поразительная женщина, которую я когда-либо *(1)* встречал / *(2)* видел.

string *n* 1. верёвка, бечёвка; 2. *(thread)* нитка; 3. *(pl: conditions)* условия ♦ **heart ~s** с струны сердца ♦ **~ of beads** нитка бус ♦ **~ of pearls** нитка жемчуга ♦ **with no ~s attached** без каких-либо условий.

> **string: phrases**

I just want a *(1)* **simple** / *(2)* **casual relationship with no strings attached.** Я хочу только простых отношений без каких-либо условий. ♦ **I'd just like to go out with you occasionally. No strings attached.** Я просто хочу иногда встречаться с тобой. Без каких-либо условий. ♦ **My love for you is without (any) strings.** Моя любовь не ставит тебе (никаких) условий. ♦ **There are no strings attached.** Не ставится никаких условий. ♦ **The sweet letters you write pull at my heart strings more than I can tell you.** Нежные письма, написанные тобой, затрагивают струны моего сердца более, чем я могу выразить.

string along *vt (deceive)* водить за нос *(whom= acc.)*, обманывать / обмануть *(whom= acc.)* ♦ **All this time you've just been stringing me along.** Всё это время ты водила *(ж: водил)* меня за нос. ♦ **Don't think I'm just stringing you along. I really want to marry you.** Не думай, что я просто вожу тебя за нос. Я действительно хочу на тебе жениться *(ж: хочу выйти за тебя замуж)*.

strip *vi* раздеваться / раздеться.

striptease *n* стриптиз ♦ **Will you do a striptease for me?** Ты покажешь мне стриптиз? ♦ **I want you to do a slow, tantalizing striptease for.** Я хочу, чтобы ты показала мне медленный, дразнящий стриптиз. ♦ **If you want, I'll do a striptease for you.** Если хочешь, я покажу тебе стриптиз.

stroke *vt* гладить / погладить *(what, whom = acc.)* ♦ *(1,2)* **gently ~** *(1)* ласково / *(2)* нежно гладить ♦ **~ your cheek** гладить тебя по щеке ♦ **~ your face** гладить твоё лицо ♦ *(1,2)* **tenderly ~** *(1)* ласково / *(2)* нежно гладить.

> **stroke: phrases**

I love to kiss, hug, caress, touch, hold hands, nibble, cuddle, rub against, stroke — you just name it. Я люблю целовать, обнимать, ласкать, касаться, держаться за руки, покусывать, сжимать в объятиях, тереться, гладить -- ты только назови. ♦ **I like to have my body sensually stroked.** Мне нравится, когда чувственно ласкают моё тело. ♦ **I love the way you gently stroke my** *(1)* **legs** / *(2)* **back** / *(3)* **breast** / *(4)* **body.** Мне нравится, как ты нежно гладишь *(1)* ...мои ноги. / *(2)* ...мою спину / *(3)* грудь. / *(4)* ...моё тело. ♦ **I** *(1)* **want** / *(2)* **love to** *([3]* **gently** / *[4]* **tenderly) stroke your** *(5)* **legs** / *(6)* **back** / *(7)* **breasts.** Я *(1)* хочу / *(2)* люблю *([3,4]* нежно / *[3,4]* ласково) гладить *(5)* ...твои

An italicized ж *in parentheses indicates a woman speaking.*

но́ги. / *(6)* ...твою́ спи́ну / *(7)* грудь. ♦ **Oh, how I love to softly stroke your** *(1)* **face** / *(2)*
body / *(3)* **neck** / *(4)* **breasts** / *(5)* **legs** / *(6)* **thighs.** О, как я люблю́ не́жно погла́живать
(1) ...твоё лицо́ / *(2)* те́ло. / *(3)* ...твою́ ше́ю / *(4)* грудь. / *(5)* ...твои́ но́ги / *(6)* бёдра.
stroking *n* погла́живание.
stroll *vi* гуля́ть / погуля́ть ♦ **How I would love to stroll with you (hand in hand)** *(1)* **...along**
the beach. / *(2)* **...on a country road (in autumn)** / *(3)* **...in the park.** / *(4)* **...and look in the**
shop windows. Как бы я хоте́л *(ж: хоте́ла)* гуля́ть с тобо́й (рука́ в руке́) *(1)* ...по
пля́жу. / *(2)* ...по просёлочной доро́ге (о́сенью). / *(3)* ...в па́рке. / *(4)* ...и загля́дывать
в о́кна магази́нов. ♦ **I want to stroll side by side with you along a country lane when the**
leaves are falling from the trees. Я хочу́ прогу́ливаться бок о́ бок с тобо́й по просёлочной доро́ге, когда́ ли́стья опада́ют с дере́вьев. ♦ **My fingers will stroll languidly, softly,**
adoringly along the svelte curve of your body. Мои́ па́льцы ме́дленно, мя́гко, обожа́ю-
ще прогуля́ются по стро́йным окру́глостям твоего́ те́ла.
stroll *n* прогу́лка ♦ **go for a** ~ 1. *(one time)* пойти́ на прогу́лку, погуля́ть; 2. *(often)* гуля́ть,
соверша́ть прогу́лки, ходи́ть на прогу́лку ♦ **go for** ~s гуля́ть, соверша́ть прогу́лки,
ходи́ть на прогу́лку ♦ **take a** ~ 1. *(one time)* пойти́ на прогу́лку, погуля́ть; 2. *(often)*
гуля́ть, соверша́ть прогу́лки , ходи́ть на прогу́лку ♦ **take** ~s гуля́ть, соверша́ть
прогу́лки, ходи́ть на прогу́лку.

stroll: phrases

Would you like to go for a stroll? Не хоте́ла *(ж: хоте́л)* бы ты пойти́ на прогу́лку? ♦
Let's go for a stroll. Дава́й пойдём на прогу́лку. ♦ **I** *(1)* **like** / *(2)* **love to take (long) strolls**
(3) **...in the park.** / *(4)* **...in the evening.** / *(5)* **...along the beach.** Я *(1,2)* люблю́ (до́лго)
гуля́ть *(3)* ...в па́рке. / *(4)* ...ве́чером. / *(5)* ...по пля́жу. ♦ **How nice it would be to take**
a (long) stroll with you *(1)* **...along the beach.** / *(2)* **...on a country road (in autumn)** / *(3)*
...in some park. Как прия́тно бы́ло бы (до́лго) гуля́ть с тобо́й *(1)* ...по пля́жу. / *(2)*
...просёлочной доро́гой (о́сенью). / *(3)* ...в како́м-нибудь па́рке. ♦ **I want to take** *(1)*
midnight / *(2)* **moonlight** / *(3)* **moonlit strolls with you.** Я хочу́ соверша́ть прогу́лки с
тобо́й *(1)* ...в по́лночь. / *(2)* ...при лу́нном све́те. / *(3)* ...под луно́й. ♦ **I'd love to take**
(long) strolls with you *(1)* **...in the park.** / *(2)* **...on the beach.** / *(3)* **...around the city.** Я бы
хоте́л *(ж: хоте́ла)* соверша́ть (дли́тельные) прогу́лки с тобо́й *(1)* ...в па́рке. / *(2)* ...по
пля́жу. / *(3)* ...по го́роду.
strolling *n* прогу́лка.
strong *adj* си́льный, -ая, -ое, -ые ♦ **My love for you** *(1)* **grows** / *(2)* **gets stronger every day.**
Моя́ любо́вь к тебе́ *(1,2)* стано́вится сильне́е с ка́ждым днём. ♦ **I'm over 50, but still**
going strong. Мне бо́льше пяти́десяти *(50)*, но я ещё остаю́сь си́льным.
stronger сильне́е.
strong-minded *adj (independently thinking)* самостоя́тельно мы́слящий, -ая, -ее, -ие; *(deci-*
sive) реши́тельный, -ая, -ое, -ые.
strong-willed *adj* реши́тельный, -ая, -ое, -ые, волево́й, -а́я, -о́е, -ы́е, своенра́вный, -ая,
-ое, -ые.
struggle *vi* боро́ться *(against what, whom = + про́тив + gen.)*.
stubble *n (beard)* щети́на ♦ **two days of** ~ двухдне́вная щети́на.
stubborn *adj* упря́мый, -ая, -ое, -ые ♦ **Don't be so stubborn.** Не будь тако́й упря́мой *(ж:*
таки́м упря́мым). ♦ **You're** *(1)* **so** / *(2)* **awfully stubborn.** Ты *(1)* так / *(2)* ужа́сно упря́ма
(ж: упря́м). ♦ **What a stubborn person you are!** Что за упря́мый ты челове́к!
stubbornly *adv* упря́мо.
stubbornness *n* упря́мство.
stuck-up *adj* высокоме́рный, -ая, -ое, -ые, зано́счивый, -ая, -ое, -ые, чва́нный, -ая, -ое,

---

Procedures for getting married to a Russian
are outlined in Appendix 18, page 787.

-ые, чванли́вый, -ая, -ое, -ые.

stud *n (slang)* жеребе́ц.

studio *n* сту́дия; ателье́, мастерска́я ♦ **photography** ~ фотосту́дия, фотоателье́ ♦ **I want you to go to a photography studio and have** *(1)* **...a portrait made. /** *(2)* **...some photos taken.** Я хочу́, что́бы ты пошла́ *(ж: пошёл)* в фотосту́дию и *(1)* ...заказа́ла *(ж: заказа́л)* свой потре́т. / *(2)* ...сфотографи́ровалась *(ж: сфотографи́ровался)*.

studious *adj* стара́тельный, -ая, -ое, -ые.

studiously *adv* стара́тельно ♦ ~ **avoid** стара́тельно избега́ть *(whom, what = acc.)*.

study *vt* 1. *(a subject)* изуча́ть / изучи́ть *(what = acc.)*; 2. *(observe)* наблюда́ть *(what, whom = + за + instr.)* ♦ **What are you studying (at the university)?** Что ты изуча́ешь (в университе́те)? ♦ **I'm studying history /** *etc.* Я изуча́ю исто́рию / *и т.п.* ♦ **The only thing I've studied today has been your photograph.** Еди́нственное, что я изуча́л сего́дня, была́ твоя́ фотогра́фия. ♦ **What I would really like to study is you — in the nude.** Что бы я действи́тельно хоте́л изуча́ть -- э́то тебя́ обнажённую. ♦ **I was studying you (intently) from** *(1)* **...a distance. /** *(2)* **...across the room.** Я наблюда́л *(ж: наблюда́ла)* за тобо́й (при́стально) *(1)* ...издалека́. / *(2)* ...че́рез ко́мнату.

stuff *n (things)* ве́щи *pl*, иму́щество; *(merchandise)* това́ры ♦ **I enjoy the usual recreational stuff.** Я наслажда́юсь обы́чными развлече́ниями.

stunned *adj* потрясён, потрясена́, -о́, -ы́ *(short forms)*, ошеломлён, ошеломлена́, -о́, -ы́ *(short forms)* ♦ **I was stunned when I found out (you were married).** Я был потрясён *(ж: была́ потрясена́)*, когда́ узна́л *(ж: узна́ла)* (, что ты за́мужем *[ж: жена́т]*).

stunning *adj* сногсшиба́тельный, -ая, -ое, -ые, потряса́ющий, -ая, -ее, -ие ♦ **You look (***[1]* **absolutely /** *[2]* **positively) stunning (in that** *[3]* **dress /** *[4]* **outfit)!** Ты вы́глядишь (*[1]* абсолю́тно / *[2]* про́сто) потряса́юще (в э́том *[3]* пла́тье / *[4]* костю́ме). ♦ **You're the most stunning woman I've ever** *(1)* **seen /** *(2)* **known /** *(3)* **met in all my life.** Ты са́мая потряса́ющая же́нщина, кото́рую мне довело́сь *(1)* ви́деть / *(2)* знать / *(3)* встре́тить в мое́й жи́зни.

stunningly *adv* потряса́юще.

stupid *adj* глу́пый, -ая, -ое, -ые *(short forms:* глуп, -а́, -о, -ы*)*, тупо́й, -а́я, -о́е, -ы́е ♦ ~ **idea** глу́пая иде́я ♦ ~ **mistake** глу́пая оши́бка ♦ ~ **remark** глу́пое замеча́ние ♦ ~ **suggestion** глу́пое предложе́ние ♦ ~ **thing** глу́пость *f*.

stupid: phrases

That was a stupid thing I *(1)* **said /** *(2)* **did.** Я *(1)* сказа́л *(ж: сказа́ла)* / *(2)* сде́лал *(ж: сде́лала)* глу́пость. ♦ **That was a stupid thing you** *(1)* **said /** *(2)* **did.** Ты *(1)* сказа́ла *(ж: сказа́л)* / *(2)* сде́лала *(ж: сде́лал)* глу́пость. ♦ **I'm so stupid.** Я так глуп *(ж: глупа́)*. ♦ **I was so stupid.** Я был *(ж: была́)* так глуп *(ж: глупа́)*. ♦ **Don't do anything stupid.** Не де́лай глу́постей.

stupidity *n* глу́пость *f*.

stupidly *adv* глу́по.

stupor *n* оцепене́ние.

stutter *vi* заика́ться.

style *n* 1. *(way)* стиль *m*; *(manner)* мане́ра; 2. *(chic, class)* шик, блеск, ро́скошь *f* ; *(taste)* вкус; 3. *(fashion)* мо́да, фасо́н ♦ **country** ~ дереве́нский стиль ♦ **elegant** ~ изя́щный стиль ♦ **hair** ~ причёска ♦ **individual** ~ индивидуа́льный стиль ♦ **latest** ~ нове́йший фасо́н ♦ **modern** ~ совреме́нный стиль ♦ **new** ~ но́вый стиль ♦ **nice** ~ хоро́ший стиль ♦ **old** ~ ста́рый стиль ♦ **simple** ~ просто́й стиль ♦ **strange** ~ стра́нный стиль ♦ ~ **of living** о́браз жи́зни ♦ **I (really) like your style.** Мне (о́чень) нра́вится твой стиль. ♦ **If you're looking for a redhead with style, I'm your person** *(ж:)* Е́сли ты и́щешь рыже-

A list of conjugated Russian verbs is given in Appendix 3 on page 699.

волóсую со стúлем, я та, когó ты úщешь.

styled *n* стилизóванный, -ая, -ое, -ые.

stylish *adj* мóдный, -ая, -ое, -ые.

stylishly *adv* мóдно.

suave *adj* учтúвый, -ая, -ое, -ые ♦ **When I first saw you, you seemed** *(1)* **...so suave.** / *(2)* **...to have such a suave demeanor.** *(ж:)* Когдá я впервьíе увúдела тебя́, *(1)* ...ты казáлся такúм учтúвым. / *(2)* ...казáлось, что у тебя́ такúе вéжливые манéры.

subconscious *adj* подсознáтельный, -ая, -ое, -ые.

subconsciously *adv* подсознáтельно ♦ **feel ~** подсознáтельно чýвствовать.

subdue *vt* покоря́ть / покорúть *(what, whom = acc.)*, подчиня́ть / подчинúть *(what, whom = acc.)*.

subdued *adj* 1. *(restrained)* подáвленный, -ая, -ое, -ые; 2. *(softened)* смягчённый, -ая, -ое, -ые; *(muted)* приглушённый, -ая, -ое, -ые ♦ **~ mood** подáвленное настрóение ♦ **~ voice** приглушённый гóлос.

subject *n* предмéт, тéма ♦ **dangerous ~** опáсная тéма ♦ **deep ~** глубóкая тéма ♦ **delicate ~** деликáтная тéма ♦ **engrossing ~** захвáтывающая тéма ♦ **favorite ~** любúмая тéма ♦ **great ~** великолéпная тéма ♦ **interesting ~** интерéсная тéма ♦ *(1,2)* **main ~** *(1)* глáвная / *(2)* основнáя тéма ♦ **safe(r) ~** (бóлее) безопáсная тéма ♦ **taboo ~** запрéтная тéма ♦ **touchy ~** деликáтная тéма ♦ **unpleasant ~** неприя́тная тéма.

subjugate *vt* покоря́ть / покорúть *(what, whom = acc.)*, брать / взять в плен *(what, whom = acc.)* ♦ **Your magical green eyes flecked with gold have subjugated all my thoughts.** Твоú волшéбные зелёные глазá с золотьíми крáпинками взя́ли в плен все моú мьíсли.

sublimate *vt* возвышáть / возвьíсить *(what = acc.)*.

sublime *adj* возвьíшенный, -ая, -ое, -ые, велúчественный, -ая, -ое, -ые ♦ **~ love** возвьíшенная любóвь.

submission *n* покóрность *f* ♦ **instinct of ~** инстúнкт покóрности.

submissive *adj* покóрный, -ая, -ое, -ые, смирéнный, -ая, -ое, -ые.

submissiveness *n* покóрность *f*.

submit *vi* покоря́ться / покорúться *(to what, whom = dat.)*, подчиня́ться / подчинúться *(to what, whom = dat.)*.

subservient *adj* раболéпный, -ая, -ое, -ые.

substance *n* 1. *(matter)* веществó; 2. *(essence)* сýщность *f*, существó, суть ♦ **controlled ~** запрещённое веществó, наркóтик ♦ **man of ~** состоя́тельный человéк ♦ **man with emotional ~** эмоционáльный мужчúна ♦ **woman with emotional ~** эмоционáльная жéнщина.

substance-free *adj* не испóльзующий (-ая, -ее, -ие) наркóтики.

subtle *adj* тóнкий, -ая, -ое, -ие.

subtlety *n* тóнкость *f*.

subtly *adv* тóнко.

succeed *vi (in doing something)* удавáться / удáсться *(subject = dat., verb = 3rd person sing.)*, сумéть сдéлать ♦ **I hope I succeed in coming there this year.** Я надéюсь, мне удáстся приéхать тудá в э́том годý.

success *n* успéх ♦ **great ~** большóй успéх ♦ **achieve ~** достúгнуть успéха ♦ **have ~** имéть успéх.

successful *adj* успéшный, -ая, -ое, -ые.

succulent *adj* сóчный, -ая, -ое, -ые ♦ **~ flower** сóчный цветóк.

succumb *vi* поддавáться / поддáться, уступáть / уступúть ♦ **~ to a temptation** под-

---

For Russian adjectives, the masculine form is spelled out,
followed by the feminine, neuter and plural endings.

дава́ться / подда́ться собла́зну ♦ **I have completely succumbed to your beauty.** Я ника́к не мог устоя́ть пе́ред твое́й красото́й.

suck *vi* соса́ть *(what = acc.)* ♦ **I** *(1)* **love** / *(2)* **want to (gently) suck on your** *(3)* **breast(s)** / *(4)* **nipples.** Я *(1)* люблю́ / *(2)* хочу́ (не́жно) соса́ть *(3)* ...твою́ грудь. / *(4)* ...твои́ соски́.

sucker *n (dupe)* проста́к ♦ **I guess I'm a sucker for a pretty face.** Пожа́луй, меня́ сли́шком привлека́ют краси́вые ли́ца.

sudden *adj* неожи́данный, -ая, -ое, -ые, внеза́пный, -ая, -ое, -ые.

suddenly *adv* неожи́данно, вдруг, внеза́пно.

suffer *vt (experience)* испы́тывать / испыта́ть *(what = acc.)* ♦ **Being apart from you, I suffer the** *(1)* **unspeakable** / *(2)* **unbearable.** Когда́ мы врозь, я страда́ю *(1)* несказа́нно / *(2)* невыноси́мо.

suffer *vi* страда́ть / пострада́ть *(from what = + от + gen.)* ♦ **I've really suffered a lot because of you. You can't imagine.** Ты предста́вить не мо́жешь, как мно́го я страда́л *(ж: страда́ла)* из-за тебя́. ♦ **Can't you see that I'm suffering?** Ви́дишь ли ты, что я страда́ю? ♦ **If you don't want me to suffer from a broken heart, you'll write to me at least once a week.** Е́сли ты не хо́чешь, что́бы моё се́рдце бы́ло разби́то, ты бу́дешь писа́ть мне по ме́ньшей ме́ре раз в неде́лю. ♦ **I've been suffering from a broken heart (because you haven't written to me lately).** Я страда́ю и моё се́рдце разби́то (, потому́ что ты не писа́ла *[ж: писа́л]* мне после́днее вре́мя). ♦ **I don't want you to suffer from a broken heart.** Я не хочу́, что́бы твоё се́рдце бы́ло разби́то и ты страда́ла *(ж: страда́л)*.

sufficient *adj* доста́точно *(+ gen.)* ♦ **~ money** доста́точно де́нег.

suffocate *vt* души́ть / задуши́ть *(what, whom = acc.)* ♦ **After you** *(1)* **...went away...** / *(2)* **...left... , this** *(3)* **house** / *(4)* **apartment suffocates me.** По́сле того́, как ты *(1,2)* уе́хала *(ж: уе́хал) (by veh.)* / *(1,2)* ушла́ *(ж: ушёл) (on foot)*, *(3)* ...э́тот дом... / *(4)* ...э́та кварти́ра... ду́шит меня́.

suffuse *vt* залива́ть / зали́ть *(what, whom = acc., with what = instr.)*; покрыва́ть / покры́ть *(what, whom = acc., with what = instr.)*; заполня́ть / запо́лнить *(what, whom = acc., with what = instr.)*, наполня́ть / напо́лнить *(what, whom = acc., with what = instr.)*, затопля́ть / затопи́ть *(what, whom = acc., with what = instr.)*.

suffuse: phrases

(1) **I want to...** / *(2)* **I'm going to suffuse your entire being in the fiery rapture of climax.** *(1)* Я хочу́ напо́лнить... / *(2)* Я напо́лню... всё твоё существо́ о́гненным восто́ргом орга́зма. ♦ **Personally, I've always been infused with the conviction that if you truly love a woman and care for her, you do everything you possibly can to fill her with pleasure and suffuse her with love.** Ли́чно я всегда́ был наделён убежде́нием, что, е́сли действи́тельно лю́бишь же́нщину и забо́тишься о ней, то де́лаешь всё возмо́жное, что́бы напо́лнить её наслажде́нием и затопи́ть любо́вью. ♦ **An extraordinary heat suffuses my whole body whenever** *(1)* **...the vision of your perfect loveliness comes into my mind.** / *(2)* **...I think about your voluptuous beauty.** / *(3)* **...I look at your photo.** Всегда́, когда́ бы *(1)* ...твоя́ превосхо́дная красота́ ни вста́ла в мое́й па́мяти,... / *(2)* ...ни поду́мал о твоём прекра́сном сла́достном те́ле,... / *(3)* ...ни смотре́л на твою́ фотогра́фию,... я весь охва́чен жа́ром. ♦ **The sweet potpourri of memories from those days we spent together suffuses my thoughts night and day.** Буке́т сла́дких воспомина́ний о днях, проведённых вме́сте, заполня́ет мои́ мы́сли но́чью и днём. ♦ **My eager lips will suffuse your body with exquisite pleasure.** Мои́ нетерпели́вые гу́бы затопя́т твоё те́ло изы́сканным наслажде́нием.

sugar *n* 1. са́хар; 2. *(slang) (kisses)* поцелу́и ♦ **Do you want some sugar?** Ты хо́чешь поцелу́ев? ♦ **Give me some sugar.** Поцелу́й меня́. ♦ **I could spend the whole day giving you**

See Appendix 19 for notes on sending mail to Russia and Ukraine.

sugar. Я могу́ провести́ це́лый день, целу́я тебя́. ♦ **I'd like to spin some sugar with you.** Я хоте́л *(ж: хоте́ла)* бы целова́ться с тобо́й. ♦ **They say that girls are made of sugar and spice and everything nice. Is that true of you?** Говоря́т, что де́вушки сде́ланы из са́хара и пря́ностей и из всего́ прекра́сного. Подхо́дит ли э́то к тебе́?

sugar daddy *n (slang)* пожило́й бога́тый мужчи́на.

Sugarlips *n name of endearment* «Са́харные гу́бы».

Sugar Pie *name of endearment* Сла́дкая ♦ **I can never love anyone as much as you, Sugar Pie.** Я не смогу́ никогда́ никого́ так си́льно люби́ть, как тебя́, моя́ сла́дкая.

suggest *vt* предлага́ть / предложи́ть *(what = acc., to whom = dat.)*

suggestion *n* предложе́ние *(See also* **proposal***)* ♦ **saucy** ~ коке́тливое предложе́ние ♦ **In your letter you made a suggestion that has been fueling my fantasies ever since.** В своём письме́ ты сде́лала *(ж: сде́лал)* предложе́ние, кото́рое с тех пор воспламеня́ет мои́ фанта́зии.

suggestive *adj (seductive)* соблазни́тельный, -ая, -ое, -ые.

suit *vt* подходи́ть *(whom = dat.)*.

suit *n* 1. *(clothing)* костю́м; 2. *(lawsuit)* суде́бный проце́сс, иск ♦ **bathing** ~ купа́льник, купа́льный костю́м ♦ **beautiful** ~ краси́вый костю́мтвое́йтвое́й ♦ **black** ~ чёрный костю́м ♦ **dark** ~ тёмный костю́м ♦ **dark blue** ~ тёмно-си́ний костю́м ♦ **dress** ~ наря́дный костю́м ♦ **paternity** ~ суде́бный проце́сс по установле́нию отцо́вства ♦ **swim(ming)** ~ купа́льник, купа́льный костю́м ♦ **three-piece (business)** ~ костю́м-тро́йка ♦ **What a sexy** *(1)* **bathing /** *(2)* **swim(ming) suit!** Како́й сексуа́льный *(1,2)* купа́льник!

suitable *adj* подходя́щий, -ая, -ее, -ие ♦ **You and I are on such a common wavelength that I really believe neither of us could ever find a more suitable partner.** Мы с тобо́й так настро́ены на одну́ волну́, что я уве́рен *(ж: уве́рена)*, ни оди́н из нас не смо́жет найти́ бо́лее подходя́щего партнёра.

suite *n (hotel)* но́мер-люкс ♦ **honeymoon** ~ но́мер-люкс, в кото́ром прово́дят медо́вый ме́сяц *(explanation)*.

suited *adj (Russians use verb* подходи́ть*)* ♦ **I think you and I are perfectly suited to each other.** Ду́маю, мы отли́чно подхо́дим друг к дру́гу. ♦ *(1)* **She /** *(2)* **He and I are just not suited to each other.** Мы с *(1)* ней / *(2)* ним про́сто не подхо́дим друг к дру́гу.

suitor *n* покло́нник ♦ **ardent** ~ стра́стный покло́нник ♦ **persistent** ~ упо́рный покло́нник.

sulk *vi* ду́ться *(about what =* + о + *prep.)*.

sullen *adj* угрю́мый, -ая, -ое, -ые, серди́тый, -ая, -ое, -ые.

sultry *adj* 1. *(torrid)* зно́йный, -ая, -ое, -ые, пы́лкий, -ая, -ое, -ие; *(passionate)* стра́стный, -ая, -ое, -ые; 2. *(voluptuous)* сладостра́стный, -ая, -ое, -ые; *(sensual)* чу́вственный, -ая, -ое, -ые.

summer *n* ле́то ♦ **in the** ~ ле́том ♦ **last** ~ про́шлым ле́том ♦ **next** ~ сле́дующим ле́том.

sun *n* со́лнце ♦ **I'm a person who loves sun, surf and sand.** Я челове́к, лю́бящий со́лнце, прибо́й и песо́к. ♦ **Your love is the sun that awakens life within me.** Твоя́ любо́вь -- э́то со́лнце, пробужда́ющее жизнь во мне.

sunbath *n* со́лнечная ва́нна.

sunbathe *vi* принима́ть со́лнечную ва́нну.

sunbather *n* принима́ющий *m* / принима́ющая *f* со́лнечную ва́нну, загора́ющий *m*, загора́ющая *f*.

sunbathing *n* со́лнечная ва́нна.

sunbeam *n* со́лнечный луч *(pl:* лучи́ *)*, луч со́лнца ♦ **Your letters flood my life with sunbeams.** Твои́ пи́сьма освеща́ют мою́ жизнь со́лнечными луча́ми. ♦ **I see you smile in**

When terms are listed after a main word, a tilde ~
is used to indicate the main word.

all the sunbeams. Я ви́жу твою́ улы́бку в ка́ждом со́лнечном луче́. ♦ **All these sunbeams that flood the day — it is your smile shining down on me.** Твоя́ сия́ющая улы́бка для меня́ -- э́то со́лнечные лучи́, прони́зывающие день. ♦ **The words you write sparkle in my mind like sunbeams.** Слова́, кото́рые ты пи́шешь, сверка́ют в мое́й па́мяти, как со́лнечные лучи́.

sunbleached *adj* вы́горевший, -ая, -ее, -ие.

sun-browned *adj* загоре́лый, -ая, -ое, -ые.

sunburn *n* зага́р.

sunburned / sunburnt *adj* загоре́лый, -ая, -ое, -ые.

Sunday *n* воскресе́нье ♦ **by** ~ к воскресе́нью ♦ **next** ~ в сле́дующее воскресе́нье ♦ **on** ~ в воскресе́нье.

sundress *n* откры́тое ле́тнее пла́тье (без рукаво́в), сарафа́н ♦ **strapless** ~ откры́тое ле́тнее пла́тье без брете́лек.

sunlight *n* со́лнечный свет ♦ **Your blond hair seems to be full of sunlight.** Твои́ све́тлые во́лосы ка́жутся напо́лненными со́лнечным све́том.

sunny *adj* 1. *(sunshiny)* со́лнечный, -ая, -ое, -ые; 2. *(cheerful)* весёлый, -ая, -ое, -ые.

sunrise *n* восхо́д со́лнца.

sunset *n* зака́т ♦ **romantic** ~ романти́ческий зака́т ♦ **I'd love to share sunsets with you.** Я хоте́л *(ж: хоте́ла)* бы наслажда́ться зака́тами с тобо́й. ♦ **Maybe you and I can ride together into the sunset.** Мо́жет быть, мы вме́сте доживём до ста́рости. ♦ **"May there be just enough clouds in your sky to make a beautiful sunset."** *(Anonymous)* «Пусть в твоём не́бе облако́в бу́дет сто́лько, чтобы то́лько созда́ть прекра́сный зака́т.»

sunshine *n* 1. со́лнечный свет; 2. *(term of endearment)* со́лнышко ♦ **You are** *(1)* **...my sunshine. /** *(2)* **...the sunshine of my life.** Ты *(1)* ...мой со́лнечный свет. / *(2)* ...со́лнечный свет мое́й жи́зни. ♦ **You will always be my sunshine.** Ты всегда́ бу́дешь мои́м со́лнечным све́том. ♦ **You bring so much sunshine into my life.** Ты прино́сишь так мно́го со́лнечного све́та в мою́ жизнь. ♦ **You bring sunshine to my spirit.** Ты прино́сишь со́лнечный свет в мою́ ду́шу. ♦ **Sunshine radiates from you.** Со́лнечное сия́ние исхо́дит от тебя́. ♦ **I love the sunshine of your smile.** Я люблю́ со́лнечный свет твое́й улы́бки. ♦ **I want to spend the rest of my days basking in the sunshine of your smile.** Я хочу́ провести́ остальны́е дни, гре́ясь в со́лнечном све́те твое́й улы́бки. ♦ *(1)* **I could... /** *(2)* **I want to... bask forever in the warmth of your sunshine.** *(1)* Я смог *(ж: смогла́)* бы ве́чно... / *(2)* Я хочу́... гре́ться в твои́х со́лнечных луча́х. ♦ **Your letters flood my life with sunshine.** Твои́ пи́сьма затопи́ли мою́ жизнь со́лнечным све́том. ♦ **A letter from you turns the most dismal day into sunshine.** Письмо́ от тебя́ превраща́ет са́мый мра́чный день в день, напо́лненный со́лнечным све́том. ♦ **The sunshine of your** *(1)* **heart /** *(2)* **love has melted away all of my loneliness.** Со́лнечный свет *(1)* ...твоего́ се́рдца... / *(2)* ...твое́й любви́... растопи́л всё моё одино́чество. ♦ **Remember to smile for me in your photos. I want to see the same kind of sunshine on your face that your letters bring to my heart.** Не забу́дь улыба́ться на свои́х фо́то. Я хочу́ ви́деть тако́й же со́лнечный свет на твоём лице́, како́й твои́ пи́сьма прино́сят в моё се́рдце.

sunshine-love *n (term of endearment)* со́лнышко ♦ **Hello, my sunshine-love!** Здра́вствуй, моё со́лнышко!

suntan *n* со́лнечный зага́р ♦ **deep teak** ~ бро́нзовый зага́р.

super *adj (great, wonderful)* великоле́пный, -ая, -ое, -ые, чу́дный, -ая, -ое, -ые.

supercharged *adj* суперэнерги́чный, -ая, -ое, -ые.

supercilious *adj* высокоме́рный, -ая, -ое, -ые.

superficial *adj* пове́рхностный, -ая, -ое, -ые, вне́шний, -яя, -ее, -ие.

A list of abbreviations used in the dictionary is given on page 10.

super-intellectual *n* суперинтеллектуа́л *m*, суперинтеллектуа́лка *f.*

superior *adj* превосхо́дный, -ая, -ое, -ые.

superiority *n* превосхо́дство ♦ **air of** ~ высокоме́рный вид.

super-special *adj* осо́бо специа́льный, -ая, -ое, -ые.

supersmile *n* широ́кая улы́бка.

superstition *n* суеве́рие.

superstitious *adj* суеве́рный, -ая, -ое, -ые.

supine *adj* лежа́щий (-ая, -ее, -ие) на́взничь, лежа́щий (-ая, -ее, -ие) на спине́.

supper *n* у́жин ♦ **wedding** ~ сва́дебный у́жин.

supple *adj* ги́бкий, -ая, -ое, -ие, пласти́чный, -ая, -ое, -ые ♦ **You are so lithe and supple** (*[1]* ...**in the way you move.** / *[2]* ...**in your movements.**). Ты така́я ги́бкая и пласти́чная (*[1]* ...когда́ дви́гаешься. / *[2]* ...в движе́нии.) ♦ **You have such a lithe, supple, beautiful body.** У тебя́ тако́е пода́тливое, ги́бкое, краси́вое те́ло.

suppleness *n* ги́бкость *f*, пла́стика.

support *vt* 1. *(hold up)* подде́рживать / поддержа́ть *(what, whom = acc.)*; 2. *(provide for)* содержа́ть *(whom = acc.)* ♦ ~ **a child** содержа́ть ребёнка ♦ ~ **a family** содержа́ть семью́ ♦ ~ **children** содержа́ть дете́й ♦ **I have to support my** *(1)* ...**son** / *(2)* **father.** / *(3)* ...**daughter** / *(4)* **mother.** / *(5)* ...**children** / *(6)* **parents.** Я до́лжен *(ж: должна́)* содержа́ть *(1)* ...(моего́) сы́на / *(2)* отца́. / *(3)* ...(мою́) дочь / *(4)* мать. / *(5)* ...(мои́х) дете́й / *(6)* роди́телей.

support *n* 1. *(holding up)* подде́ржка; 2. *(financial)* содержа́ние ♦ **child** ~ алиме́нты на ребёнка ♦ **financial** ~ фина́нсовая подде́ржка ♦ **moral** ~ мора́льная подде́ржка ♦ **mutual** ~ взаи́мная подде́ржка ♦ **give** ~ ока́зывать / оказа́ть подде́ржку *(to whom = dat.).*

---
support: *phrases*

I pay (her) for child support every month. Я плачу́ (ей) алиме́нты на ребёнка ка́ждый ме́сяц. ♦ **How much child support do you have to pay?** Ско́лько алиме́нтов на ребёнка ты до́лжен плати́ть? ♦ **You are such a great (moral) support for me.** Ты така́я огро́мная (мора́льная) подде́ржка для меня́. ♦ **You give me a lot of (moral) support.** Ты даёшь мне большу́ю (мора́льную) подде́ржку. ♦ **I'm grateful for your (moral) support.** Я благода́рен *(ж: благода́рна)* за твою́ (мора́льную) подде́ржку. ♦ **I need your (moral) support.** Я нужда́юсь в твое́й (мора́льной) подде́ржке.

supportive *adj* подде́рживаемый, -ая, -ое, -ые ♦ **be** ~ быть подде́рживаемым.

suppose *vi* полага́ть, ду́мать.

sure *adj* уве́рен, -а, -о, -ы *(short forms)* ♦ **for** ~ наверняка́, несомне́нно ♦ **know for** ~ знать наверняка́ ♦ **make** ~ 1. *(see to)* позабо́титься; 2. *(ascertain)* убеди́ться ♦ **Are you sure?** Ты уве́рена *(ж: уве́рен)*? ♦ **I'm (not) sure.** Я (не) уве́рен *(ж: уве́рена).*

sureness *n* уве́ренность *f* ♦ **I sense with such absolute sureness that you are the person in this world that my heart has been yearning to find during these many years.** Я абсолю́тно уве́рен, что ты тот челове́к в э́том ми́ре, кото́рого моё се́рдце жа́ждало найти́ в тече́ние мно́гих лет.

surf *vi* занима́ться сёрфингом.

surf *n* прибо́й ♦ **I'm a person who loves sun, surf and sand.** Я челове́к, лю́бящий со́лнце, прибо́й и песо́к.

surface *n* пове́рхность *f* ♦ **silky** ~ шелкови́стая пове́рхность.

surfing *n* сёрфинг.

surge *vi* вздыма́ться, нахлы́нуть; *(feelings)* нараста́ть / нарасти́ ♦ **I'm going to make waves of exquisite pleasure surge through your body.** Я вы́зову во́лны изы́сканного наслаж-

---

The accents on Russian words are to show how to pronounce them..
You don't have to copy the accents when writing to someone.

де́ния, захлёстывающие твоё те́ло. ♦ **Molten waves of desire surge through** *(1)* **...my entire body...** / *(2)* **...every fiber and cell of my body... whenever I think of your exquisite, luscious beauty**. Бушу́ющие во́лны стра́сти вздыма́ются во *(1)* ...всём моём те́ле,... / *(2)* во всех фи́брах и кле́тках моего́ те́ла, когда́ бы я ни поду́мал о твое́й изы́сканной, со́чной красоте́. ♦ **My lips will rouse flames of** *(1)* **desire** / *(2)* **passion to leap from your soul and surge through your veins**. Мои́ гу́бы пробу́дят пла́мя *(1)* жела́ния / *(2)* стра́сти, кото́рое бу́дет бушева́ть в тебе́ и струи́ться в ве́нах.

surge *n* прили́в, (больша́я) волна́, прито́к ♦ **mighty** ~ могу́чий пото́к ♦ **powerful** ~ могу́чий пото́к ♦ **sudden** ~ внеза́пный прили́в ♦ ~ **of (wild) passion** прили́в (бе́шеной) стра́сти ♦ **Everytime I think about you I feel such a** *(1)* **tremendous** / *(2)* **powerful surge of desire**. Всегда́, когда́ я ду́маю о тебе́, я чу́вствую таку́ю *(1)* огро́мную / *(2)* мо́щную волну́ жела́ния. ♦ **Your touch sends an electrical surge through me**. Твоё прикоснове́ние прони́зывает меня́ электри́ческим и́мпульсом.

surly *adj* ворчли́вый, -ая, -ое, -ые, непривéтливый, -ая, -ое, -ые ♦ **I'm sorry I was so surly (with you)**. Извиня́юсь, я был таки́м непривéтливым *(ж: была́ тако́й непривéтливой)* (с тобо́й).

surmount *vt* преодолева́ть / преодоле́ть *(what = acc.)* ♦ **Side by side I know we can surmount whatever life brings**. Вме́сте, я зна́ю, мы мо́жем преодоле́ть всё, что преподнесёт нам жизнь. ♦ **I cannot surmount the** *(1)* **fierce** / *(2)* **passionate longing in my heart to hold you in my arms (again)**. Я не могу́ преодоле́ть *(1)* неи́стовую / *(2)* стра́стную жа́жду се́рдца (опя́ть) держа́ть тебя́ в объя́тиях.

surpass *vt* превосходи́ть / превзойти́ *(what = + acc.)* ♦ **No one in this whole world can ever surpass you in** *(1)* **loveliness** / *(2)* **beauty** / *(3)* **good-heartedness**. Никто́ на всём све́те не смо́жет превзойти́ тебя́ в *(1,2)* красоте́ / *(3)* добросерде́чности.

surprise *vt* удивля́ть / удиви́ть *(whom = acc.)*, поража́ть *(whom = acc.)* ♦ **I want to surprise you**. Я хочу́ удиви́ть тебя́. ♦ **I may surprise you in bed**. Возмо́жно я поражу́ тебя́ в посте́ли.

surprise *n (something that surprises)* сюрпри́з; *(feeling)* удивле́ние ♦ **element of** ~ элеме́нт неожи́данности ♦ **What a** *(1)* **nice** / *(2)* **pleasant** / *(3)* **happy** / *(4)* **delightful** / *(5)* **lovely** / *(6)* **fabulous** / *(7)* **great** / *(8)* **marvelous** / *(9)* **wonderful** / *(10)* **super** / *(11)* **tremendous** / *(12)* **big surprise!** Что за *(1,2)* прия́тный / *(3)* счастли́вый / *(4)* вохити́тельный / *(5)* прелéстный / *(6,7)* великоле́пный / *(8)* замеча́тельный / *(9)* замеча́тельный / *(10,11)* огро́мный / *(12)* большо́й сюрпри́з! ♦ **You're full of surprises**. Ты полна́ *(ж: по́лон)* сюрпри́зов. ♦ **I've got a (little) surprise for you**. У меня́ для тебя́ есть (ма́ленький) сюрпри́з. ♦ **It's a surprise**. Это сюрпри́з. ♦ **You took me by surprise**. Ты захвати́л *(ж: захвати́ла)* меня́ врасплóх. ♦ **It was a total (and utter) surprise**. Это бы́ло полне́йшим сюрпри́зом. ♦ **I was speechless with surprise**. Я потеря́л *(ж: потеря́ла)* дар ре́чи от удивле́ния.

surprised *adj* удивлён, удивлена́, -ó, -ы́ *(short forms)* ♦ **I was** *(1)* **completely** / *(2)* **totally** / *(3)* **pleasantly surprised**. Я был *(ж: была́)* *(1,2)* совершéнно / *(3)* прия́тно удивлён *(ж: удивлена́)*. ♦ **You'll be (pleasantly) surprised**. Ты бу́дешь (прия́тно) удивлена́ *(ж: удивлён)*.

surrender *vi* 1. *(give up)* сдава́ться / сда́ться *(to what, whom = dat.)*, капитули́ровать; 2. *(give in)* уступа́ть / уступи́ть *(to what, whom = dat.)* ♦ **My heart offers me no alternative but to surrender to my (raging) desire for you**. Моё се́рдце не предлага́ет мне друго́го вы́хода, кро́ме как уступи́ть (бе́шеной) стра́сти к тебе́. ♦ **You're fighting your own desire. Why don't you just surrender to it (for once)?** Ты бо́решься со свое́й стра́стью. Почему́ бы тебе́ про́сто не уступи́ть ей (одна́жды)? ♦ **My mouth is going to do its fer-**

---

*If no accent is shown on a word with a capitalized vowel,
it means that the capitalized vowel is accented.*

vent work on you until the need to surrender invades your whole body. Мой рот бу́дет де́лать свою́ пы́лкую рабо́ту до тех пор, пока́ потре́бность капитули́ровать ни наво́дни́т всё твоё те́ло. ♦ **A wild impulse to surrender is going to seize control of your whole body.** Ди́кое жела́ние капитули́ровать охва́тит всё твоё те́ло. ♦ **Just let yourself go and surrender to your** *(1,2)* **desire.** Про́сто позво́ль себе́ быть само́й собо́й и уступи́ *(1)* ...свое́й стра́сти. / *(2)* ...своему́ жела́нию.

surreptitious *adj* та́йный, -ая, -ое, -ые, скры́тый, -ая, -ое, -ые.

surround *vt* окружа́ть / окружи́ть *(what = acc., with what = instr.)* ♦ **I want to surround you with (***[1]* **endless /** *[2]* **infinite /** *[3]* **ever-lasting /** *[4]* **boundless)** *(5)* **bliss /** *(6)* **happiness.** Я хочу́ окружи́ть тебя́ (*[1,2]* бесконе́чным / *[3]* несконча́емым / *[4]* безграни́чным) *(5)* блаже́нством / *(6)* сча́стьем.

susceptible *adj* 1. *(predisposed to)* подве́рженный, -ая, -ое, -ые; *(easily influenced)* восприи́мчивый, -ая, -ое, -ые; па́дкий, -ая, -ое, -ие, неравноду́шен, -а, -о, -ы *(short forms)*; 2. *(impressionable)* впечатли́тельный, -ая, -ое, -ые, влюбчивый, -ая, -ое, -ые ♦ **~ to flattery** па́дкий на лесть ♦ **I'm susceptible to your female charms.** Я неравноду́шен к твои́м же́нским ча́рам.

suspect *vt* подозрева́ть *(what, whom = acc.)*.

suspicion *n* подозре́ние ♦ **You shouldn't be so prone to suspicion.** Ты не должна́ *(ж: до́лжен)* быть так скло́нна *(ж: скло́нен)* к подозри́тельности.

sustain *vt* подде́рживать / поддержа́ть *(what = acc.)* ♦ **~ a long-term (intimate) relationship** подде́рживать дли́тельные (инти́мные) отноше́ния ♦ **Your letters (really) sustain me through my loneliness.** Твои́ пи́сьма (действи́тельно) подде́рживают меня́ в моём одино́честве. ♦ **I need your letters and the dreams they bring to sustain me through the long, empty nights.** Мне нужны́ твои́ пи́сьма и мечты́, кото́рые они́ прино́сят, что́бы подде́рживать меня́ дли́нными, одино́кими ноча́ми.

svelte *adj* стро́йный, -ая, -ое, -ые ♦ **You look** *(1)* **quite /** *(2)* **very svelte in that dress.** Ты вы́глядишь *(1,2)* о́чень стро́йной в э́том пла́тье.

svelte-looking *adj* вы́глядеть стро́йной *(verb expression)* ♦ **That's a very svelte-looking dress.** Ты вы́глядишь о́чень стро́йной в э́том пла́тье.

swallow *vt* глота́ть / глотну́ть *(what = acc.)*.

swamp *vt* затопля́ть / затопи́ть *(what, whom = acc.)* ♦ **My** *(1)* **emotions /** *(2)* **feelings swamped me so completely that** *(3)* **...I was at a loss for words.** / *(4)* **...I couldn't say anything.** / *(5)* **...I was utterly tongue-tied.** Мои́ *(1)* эмо́ции *(2)* чу́вства затопи́ли меня́ всеце́ло так, что *(3)* ...я потеря́л *(ж: потеря́ла)* дар ре́чи. / *(4)* ...я ничего́ не мог *(ж: могла́)* сказа́ть. / *(5)* ...я был *(ж: была́)* (соверше́нно) безъязы́чным *(ж: безъязы́чной)*.

swankadelic *adj (slang) (real fancy, ultra-modern)* модерно́вый, -ая, -ое, -ые ♦ **~ specs** модерно́вые очки́.

swarthy *adj* сму́глый, -ая, -ое, -ые.

swathed *adj* заку́тан, -а, -о, -ы, завёрнут, -а, -о, -ы *(short forms)* ♦ **You look so incredibly lovely with your (***[1]* **luscious /** *[2]* **svelte /** *[3]* **supple) curves** *(4,5)* **swathed in** *(6)* **silk /** *(7)* **chiffon.** Ты вы́глядишь тако́й невероя́тно краси́вой в *(6)* шёлке / *(7)* шифо́не, *(4)* оку́тывающем / *(5)* покрыва́ющем твои́ (*[1]* роско́шные / *[2]* стро́йные / *[3]* ги́бкие) фо́рмы.

swear *vi* 1. *(solemnly assert)* кля́сться / покля́сться; 2. *(use profanity)* руга́ться ♦ **I swear (it's true).** Я кляну́сь (, э́то пра́вда).

sweat *n* пот.

sweater *n* сви́тер ♦ **tight ~** пло́тно обтя́гивающий сви́тер ♦ **That's a (very) beautiful sweater.** Это (о́чень) краси́вый сви́тер. ♦ **You make that sweater very beautiful.** Ты

Russian has 6 grammatical cases. For an explanation of them, see the grammar appendix on page 686.

делаешь э́тот сви́тер прекра́сным.

sweaty *adj* по́тный, -ая, -ое, -ые.

Swede *n (person)* швед *m*, шве́дка *f (pl:* шве́ды*)*.

Swedish *adj* шве́дский, -ая, -ое, -ие.

Swedish *n (language)* шве́дский язы́к ♦ **speak** ~ говори́ть по-шве́дски.

sweep *vt* 1. *(engulf)* охва́тывать / охвати́ть *whom = acc.)*; 2. *(s.o. off their feet)* смета́ть / смести́ (с ног) *whom = acc.)*, вскружи́ть го́лову *(whom = dat.)*, сража́ть / срази́ть *(whom = acc.)*, покоря́ть / покори́ть *(whom = acc.)* ♦ ~ **away** смета́ть / смести́ (с ног) *(what, whom = acc.)*, покоря́ть / покори́ть *(whom = acc.)*; охва́тывать / охвати́ть *(whom = acc.)*.

---
sweep: phrases
---

(1) **I want...** / *(2)* **My greatest wish is... to sweep you right off your feet.** *(1)* Я хочу́ ... / *(2)* Моё велича́йшее жела́ние... пря́мо смести́ тебя́ с ног. ♦ **You (**[1]** certainly /** [2] **really) swept me** *(3)* **...away.** / *(4)* **...off my feet.** *(ж:)* Ты (*[1]* несомне́нно / *[2]* действи́тельно) *(3)* срази́л / *(4)* покори́л меня́. ♦ **No one ever swept me off my feet like you did.** Ты вскружи́л мне го́лову так, как никому́ никогда́ не удава́лось. ♦ **I'm going to sweep you into my arms (and cover you with kisses).** Я схвачу́ тебя́ в объя́тия (и покро́ю поцелу́ями).

---
sweep away:

You have a magnetism that sweeps me away. У тебя́ тако́й магнети́зм, кото́рый смета́ет меня́ с ног. ♦ **Your (incredible) beauty and (scintillating) charm have completely swept me away.** Твоя́ (невероя́тная) красота́ и (искря́щееся) обая́ние по́лностью покори́ли меня́.

sweep *vi* 1. *(rush)* проноси́ться / пронести́сь; 2. *(through a person)* охва́тывать / охвати́ть *(through whom = acc.)*.

---
sweep: phrases

I love to watch your breasts heave when passion sweeps through you. Я люблю́ смотре́ть, как вздыма́ется твоя́ грудь, когда́ страсть охва́тывает тебя́. ♦ **Oh, what feelings swept over me when your hand enclosed mine.** О, каки́е чу́вства охва́тывали меня́, когда́ моя́ рука́ была́ в твое́й. ♦ *(1)* **Fire sweeps through...** / *(2)* **Molten waves of desire sweep through...** *(3)* **...my entire body...** / *(4)* **...every fiber and cell of my body...** / *(5)* **...my veins... whenever I think of your** *(6)* **...exquisite, luscious beauty.** / *(7)* **...soft, warm, beautiful, luscious body and the oceans of ecstasy that it contains.** *(1)* Ого́нь охва́тывает... / *(2)* Бушу́ющие во́лны стра́сти проно́сятся че́рез... *(3)* ...всё моё те́ло... / *(4)* ...все фи́бры и кле́тки моего́ те́ла,... / *(5)* ...мои ве́ны,... когда́ бы я ни поду́мал о *(6)* ...твое́й изы́сканной, со́чной красоте́. / *(7)* ...твоём мя́гком, тёплом, прекра́сном, со́чном те́ле и океа́нах экста́за, кото́рые оно́ соде́ржит.

sweet *adj* сла́дкий, -ая, -ое, -ие; не́жный, -ая, -ое, -ые ♦ **sweeter** сла́ще ♦ **sugary** ~ слаща́вый, -ая, -ое, -ые ♦ **You are the sweetest** *(1)* **person /** *(2)* **man /** *(3)* **guy in the whole world.** Ты са́мый не́жный *(1)* челове́к / *(2)* мужчи́на / *(3)* па́рень в це́лом ми́ре. ♦ **You are the sweetest** *(1)* **woman /** *(1)* **girl in the whole world.** Ты са́мая не́жная *(1)* же́нщина / *(1)* де́вушка в це́лом ми́ре. ♦ **You are so good and sweet and thoughtful and caring and loving.** Ты така́я хоро́шая *(ж: тако́й хоро́ший)*, не́жная *(ж: не́жный)*, внима́тельная *(ж: внима́тельный)*, забо́тливая *(ж: забо́тливый)* и лю́бящая *(ж: лю́бящий)*.

sweetened *adj* подслащён, подслащена́, -о́ , -ы́ *(short forms)* ♦ **All things around me are sweetened by the magic of your love.** Все ве́щи вокру́г меня́ освещены́ волшебство́м твое́й любви́.

sweetheart *n* возлю́бленный *m;* возлю́бленная *f*; *(name)* дорога́я *f*, дорого́й *m*, ми́лая *f*,

---

There are no articles ("a" or "the") in Russian.

ми́лый *m* ♦ **My greatest joy is having you for / as my sweetheart.** Моя́ велича́йшая ра́дость, что ты моя́ возлю́бленная *(ж: мой возлю́бленный)*. ♦ **Good morning, my dearly loved little sweetheart!** С до́брым у́тром, моя́ дорога́я, ма́ленькая возлю́бленная!

Sweetie *name of endearment* Сла́дкий *m*, Сла́дкая *f*, Ми́лый *m*, Ми́лая *f*, Дорого́й *m*, Дорога́я *f*, люби́мый *m*, люби́мая *f* ♦ **Sweetie, I love you more than anything.** Люби́мая *(ж: Люби́мый)*, я люблю́ тебя́ бо́льше всего́ на све́те. ♦ **As long as we're together, Sweetie, life is wonderful.** Пока́ мы вме́сте, люби́мая, жизнь прекра́сна.

Sweetie Pie *term of endearment* Сла́дкий *m*, Сла́дкая *f*, Ми́лый *m*, Ми́лая *f* ♦ *(1,2)* **Sweetie Pie, I miss you so much.** *(1)* Сла́дкая / *(2)* Ми́лая, я так си́льно скуча́ю по тебе́.

sweet-natured *adj* с прекра́сным хара́ктером.

sweetness *n* 1. *(taste)* сла́дость; 2. *(charm)* обая́ние, пре́лесть; 3. *(affection)* не́жность ♦ **delightful** ~ упои́тельная сла́дость ♦ **enchanting** ~ упои́тельная сла́дость ♦ **exotic** ~ экзоти́ческая пре́лесть ♦ **honey** ~ медо́вая сла́дость ♦ **sensuous** ~ чу́вственная пре́лесть ♦ **sugary** ~ слаща́вость ♦ **~ of your lips** сла́дость твои́х губ ♦ **velvety** ~ барха́тистая сла́дость.

---
sweetness: phrases

I want to revel in the sweetness of your *(1)* **beautiful /** *(2)* **luscious body.** Я хочу́ упива́ться сла́достью твоего́ *(1)* прекра́сного / *(2)* со́чного те́ла. ♦ **You nourish my soul with your sweetness.** Ты пита́ешь мою́ ду́шу свое́й не́жностью. ♦ **To savor the sweetness of your lips is so** *(1)* **divine /** *(2)* **heavenly /** *(3)* **wonderful.** Вкуша́ть сла́дость твои́х губ -- так *(1,2)* замеча́тельно / *(3)* удиви́тельно. ♦ **What a divine ecstasy to savor the sweetness of your lips.** Како́й боже́ственный восто́рг -- вкуша́ть сла́дость твои́х губ. ♦ **You overwhelm me with your sweetness.** Ты ошеломля́ешь меня́ свое́й добро́той. ♦ **In the unbounded vistas of my dreams and fantasies I taste the exquisite sweetness of your lips a thousand, ten thousand, a million times, and each time am only impelled by the sheer ecstasy of the kiss to taste them once again.** В безграни́чной верени́це мои́х снов и фанта́зий я вкуша́ю исключи́тельную сла́дость твои́х губ ты́сячу, де́сять ты́сяч, миллио́н раз, и ка́ждый раз я побуждён и́стинным восто́ргом поцелу́я упива́ться им опя́ть. ♦ **The sweetness of your lips imparidises me.** Сла́дость твои́х губ перено́сит меня́ в рай. ♦ **You impart sweetness to** *(1)* **...everything around you. /** *(2)* **...all my hopes and dreams.** Ты придаёшь не́жность *(1)* ...всему́, окружа́ющему тебя́. / *(2)* ...всем мои́м наде́ждам и мечта́м. ♦ **You'd better save up all your sweetness, because I'm going to be unbelievably greedy with you.** Ты лу́чше *(1)* сохраня́й / *(2)* копи́ всю свою́ сла́дость, потому́ что я бу́ду невероя́тно жа́ден. ♦ **When I read your letters, I feel with my heart how much goodness and sweetness and love there is in you.** Когда́ чита́ю твои́ пи́сьма, я всем се́рдцем чу́вствую, как мно́го в тебе́ доброты́, не́жности и любви́. ♦ **Your body exudes a sweetness like a meadow flower.** От твоего́ те́ла исхо́дит сла́дость, как от луговы́х цвето́в.

sweet-smelling *adj* души́стый, -ая, -ое, -ые, благоуха́нный, -ая, -ое, -ые, благово́нный, -ая, -ое, -ые.

sweet-talk *vt (slang)* говори́ть комплиме́нты *(whom = dat.)*, льстить / польсти́ть *(whom = dat.)*,ума́сливать / ума́слить *(whom = acc.)*, подли́зываться / подлиза́ться *(whom = + к +dat.)* ♦ **You really know how to sweet-talk a person, don't you?** Ты (действи́тельно) зна́ешь, как ума́слить челове́ка, не пра́вда ли? ♦ **Darling, don't think I'm just sweet-talking you. I really mean what I say.** Дорога́я, не ду́май, что я (про́сто) ума́сливаю тебя́. Я говорю́ то, что ду́маю.

sweet-talker *n (slang)* льстец.

This dictionary contains two Russian alphabet pages:
one in Appendix 1, page 685, and a tear-off page on page 799.

swell *n (breast)* вы́пуклость *f* ♦ **How I love to feast my eyes on the creamy, full swell of your breasts.** Как я люблю́ пожира́ть глаза́ми кре́мовую, по́лную вы́пуклость твои́х груде́й.

swept away *adj (emotionally)* охва́чен, -а, -о, -ы *(short forms)*, увлечён, увлечена́, -о́, -ы́ *(short forms)* ♦ **I am** *(1)* **completely /** *(2)* **totally swept away by** *(3)* **...my desire for you. /** *(4)* **...the rapture that you create with your** *(5)* **...skillful hands. /** *(6)* **...ardent kisses. /** *(7)* **...roving lips.** Я *(1)* по́лностью / *(2)* весь *(ж: вся)* охва́чен *(ж: охва́чена) (3)* ...стра́стью к тебе́. / *(4)* ...упое́нием, кото́рое ты создаёшь свои́ми *(5)* ...уме́лыми рука́ми. / *(6)* ...пы́лкими поцелу́ями. / *(7)* ...блужда́ющими губа́ми.

swim *vi* пла́вать ♦ **Do you know how to swim?** Ты уме́ешь пла́вать? ♦ **I love to swim.** Я люблю́ пла́вать.

swimming *n* пла́вание ♦ **Would you like to go swimming (with me)?** Не хоте́ла *(ж: хоте́л)* бы ты попла́вать (со мной)? ♦ **Let's go swimming (together).** Дава́й пойдём пла́вать (вме́сте).

swimsuit *n* купа́льник, купа́льный костю́м ♦ **almost-swimsuit** о́чень ма́ленький купа́льник ♦ **That swimsuit was made for your beautifully contoured body.** Этот купа́льник был со́здан для твоего́ прекра́сного скульпту́рного те́ла.

swine *n* свинья́.

swing *vt (around)* кружи́ть / закружи́ть *(whom = acc.)* ♦ **When we get to our room, I'm going to swing you into my arms and head straight for the bed.** Когда́ мы придём в на́шу ко́мнату, я возьму́ тебя́ на ру́ки и отнесу́ пря́мо в посте́ль. ♦ **When we meet in the airport, I'm going to swing you around (and around) and shower you with kisses.** Когда́ мы встре́тимся в аэропорту́, я закружу́ тебя́ на рука́х и затоплю́ поцелу́ями.

swirl *vt* изгиба́ть *(what = acc.)* ♦ **~ the tongue** изгиба́ть язы́к.

swirl *vi* вихри́ться, верте́ться, враща́ться, проноси́ться ви́хрем, нести́сь ви́хрем, кружи́ться / закружи́ться ♦ **Liquid fire swirls through** *(1)* **...me. /** *(2)* **...every fiber of my body.** Жи́дкий ого́нь прано́сится ви́хрем че́рез *(1)* ...меня́. / *(2)* ...все фи́бры моего́ те́ла. ♦ **You're going to swirl in a kaleidoscope of** *(1)* **passion /** *(2)* **ecstasy.** Ты закру́жишься в калейдоско́пе *(1)* стра́сти / *(2)* экста́за.

swollen *adj* набу́хший, -ая, -ее, -ие ♦ **~ with desire** набу́хший от жела́ния.

swoon *vi* па́дать / упа́сть в о́бморок; замира́ть / замере́ть ♦ **When you get close to me, I almost swoon.** Когда́ ты приближа́ешься ко мне, я почти́ па́даю в о́бморок. ♦ **When our lips met the first time, I almost swooned from ecstasy.** Когда́ на́ши гу́бы встре́тились впервы́е, я за́мер *(ж: замерла́)* от восто́рга.

symbol *n* си́мвол ♦ **~ of enduring love** си́мвол несконча́емой любви́ ♦ **~ of purity** си́мвол чистоты́ ♦ **wedding ~** сва́дебный си́мвол ♦ **~ of fertility** си́мвол плодоро́дия ♦ **phallic ~** фалли́ческий си́мвол ♦ **This is a symbol of a bond between our souls.** Это си́мвол свя́зи на́ших душ. ♦ **This ring is a symbol of our** *(1)* **enduring /** *(2)* **everlasting love.** Это кольцо́ -- си́мвол на́шей *(1)* несконча́емой / *(2)* ве́чной любви́.

symbolize *vt* символизи́ровать *(what = acc.)*.

symmetry *n* симметри́я ♦ **Your body is perfect in its symmetry.** Твоё те́ло так соверше́нно в свое́й симметри́и.

sympathetic *adj* сочу́вственный, -ая, -ое, -ые ♦ **be ~** сочу́вствовать *(to what, whom = dat.)*.

sympathize *vi* сочу́вствовать *(with what, whom = dat.)* ♦ **I (**[1] **deeply /** [2] **truly) sympathize with** *(3)* **...you. /** *(4)* **...your situation.** Я (*[1]* глубоко́ / *[2]* и́скренне) сочу́вствую *(3)* ...тебе́. / *(4)* ...твое́й ситуа́ции.

sympathy *n* сочу́вствие ♦ **arouse ~** пробужда́ть / пробуди́ть сочу́вствие ♦ **drop of ~** ка́пля сочу́вствия ♦ **show ~** сочу́вствовать *(to whom = dat., for what = dat.)* ♦ **I'm full**

Russian verbs conjugate for 6 persons:
I, familiar you, he-she-it, we, polite & plural you, and they.

of sympathy (for *[1]* **...you.** / *[2]* **...your situation.).** Я пóлон *(ж: полнá)* сочýвствия (к *[1]* ...тебé. / *[2]* ...твоéй ситуáции.) ♦ **I'm not trying to** *(1)* **invoke** / *(2)* **arouse (your) sympathy.** Я не пытáюсь *(1)* ...взывáть к (твоему́) сочýвствию. / *(2)* ...пробуди́ть (твоё) сочýвствие.

symphony *n* симфóния ♦ ~ **of pleasure** симфóния наслаждéния ♦ **Through the total orchestration of our bodies you and I together will produce the most beautiful symphony of love anyone has ever known.** Благодаря́ абсолю́тной сы́гранности нáших тел, мы вмéсте создади́м таку́ю прекрáсную симфóнию любви́, котóрую никтó никогдá не знал. ♦ **I want our lives to be an everlasting symphony of love.** Я хочу́, чтóбы нáша жизнь былá бесконéчной симфóнией любви́.

synagogue *n* синагóга.

sync *n (synchronism)* синхрóнность *f*, синхрони́зм ♦ **You and I are so much in sync (together)** Ты и я так подхóдим друг к дру́гу. ♦ **It's wonderful how much in sync we are (together).** Удиви́тельно, как мы подхóдим друг к дру́гу. ♦ **We seem to be out of sync together.** Мы, кáжется, не придём к соглáсию.

synergism *n* синерги́зм, синерги́я.

synergy *n* синерги́я, синерги́зм.

system *n* 1. системá; *(method)* спóсоб, мéтод; 2. *(organism, body)* органи́зм ♦ **Tell me everything. Get it out of your system.** Расскажи́ мне всё. Освободи́ себя́ от э́того.

There are two words for "you" in Russian:
familiar «ты» and polite / plural «вы» (See page 781).

tab -   602   - take

T

tab: ♦ **I try to keep close tab on my emotions.** Я пыта́юсь контроли́ровать свои́ чу́вства.

taboo *n* табу́, запре́т ♦ **social ~** социа́льный запре́т.

tacky *adj (slang)* гру́бый, -ая, -ое, -ые, некульту́рный, -ая, -ое, -ые.

tact *n* такт; такти́чность *f.*

tactful *adj* такти́чный, -ая, -ое, -ые.

tactfully *adv* такти́чно.

tactics *n, pl* та́ктика ♦ **flirting ~s** та́ктика заи́грывания.

tactile *adj* 1. *(relating to touch)* осяза́тельный, -ая, -ое, -ые; 2. *(perceptible by touch)* ощу-ти́мый, -ая, -ое, -ые осяза́емый, -ая, -ое, -ые.

tactless *adj* беста́ктный, -ая, -ое, -ые.

tactlessness *n* беста́ктность *f.*

Tadjik, Tadzhik *adj* таджи́кский, -ая, -ое, -ие.

Tadjik, Tadzhik *n* 1. *(person)* таджи́к *m*, таджи́чка *f (pl:* таджи́ки); 2. *(language)* таджи́к-ский язы́к ♦ **speak ~** говори́ть по-таджи́кски.

tail *n* 1. хвост; 2. *(slang) (buttocks)* за́дница, по́па; *(little)* по́пка ♦ **My tail only wags for you.** Мой хвост ма́шет то́лько для тебя́.

take *vt* брать / взять *(what = acc.)* ♦ **~ after** *(resemble)* быть похо́жим *m* / похо́жей *f (after whom = + на + acc.)* ♦ **~ away** *vt* отнима́ть / отня́ть *(what, whom = acc.)*, отбира́ть / отобра́ть *(what, whom = acc.)* ♦ **~ care** забо́титься / позабо́титься *(of what, whom = + о + prep.)* ♦ **~ in** *(notice)* обраща́ть / обрати́ть внима́ние *(what = + на + acc.)*, замеча́ть / заме́тить *(what = acc.)* ♦ **~ off** *vt* 1. *(time from work)* брать / взять свобо́дный, -ую, -ое, -ые, освобожда́ться / освободи́ться; 2. *(remove)* снима́ть / снять *(what = acc.)* ♦ **~ off clothes** раздева́ться / разде́ться ♦ **~ you out (somewhere)** *vt (socially)* пригласи́ть тебя́ пойти́ (куда́-нибудь), пойти́ (куда́-нибудь) с тобо́й.

take:

(1) **I want to... /** (2) **I'm going to... take you in all kinds of positions.** *(1)* Я хочу́ попро́бовать... / *(2)* Я попро́бую... с тобо́й все пози́ции.

take after:

(1) **You /** (2) **I take after** (3) **your /** (4) **my mother.** *(1)* Ты / *(2)* Я похо́жа на *(3)* твою́ / *(4)* мою́ ма́му. ♦ (1) **You /** (2) **I take after** (3) **your /** (4) **my father.** *(1)* Ты / *(2)* Я похо́ж на *(3)* твоего́ / *(4)* моего́ отца́.

Russian terms of endearment are given in Appendix 13, page 780.

| *take away:* |

I won't let *(1)* **anything / (2) anyone take you away from me (again).** Я не позво́лю *(1)* ничему́ / *(2)* никому́ (опя́ть) отня́ть тебя́ у меня́.

| *take care:* |

I want to take care of you and be your helpmate in every way. Я хочу́ забо́титься о тебе́ и помога́ть тебе́ во всём. ♦ **I'll take care of** *(1)* **it / (2) everything.** Я позабо́чусь *(1)* ...об э́том. / *(2)* ...обо всём.

| *take in:* |

When you walked into the room, I took in everything about you. Когда́ ты вошла́ *(ж: воше́л)* в ко́мнату, я заме́тил *(ж: заме́тила)* в тебе́ всё.

| *take off: get off work* |

Would it be possible for you to *(1,2)* **take** *(3)* **...today / (4) tomorrow / (5) a week off? / (6) ...two / (7) three days off? / (8) ...two / (9) three weeks off?** Смо́жешь ли ты *(1)* ...получи́ть / *(2)* взять *(3)* ...свобо́дный день сего́дня / *(4)* за́втра? / *(5)* ...свобо́дную неде́лю? / *(6)* ...два / *(7)* три свобо́дных дня? / *(8)* ...две / *(9)* три свобо́дных неде́ли?

| *take off: remove* |

I want to take all your clothes off. Я хочу́ снять с тебя́ всю оде́жду. ♦ **I want to take off your panties and kiss everything they're hiding.** Я хочу́ снять с тебя́ тру́сики и целова́ть всё то, что они́ пря́чут.

| *take out:* |

I'd (really) like to take you out (*[1]*...**tonight.** / *[2]* ...**tomorrow night.** /*[3]* ...**Friday night.**). Я (действи́тельно) хоте́л бы пойти́ тобо́й куда́-нибудь (*[1]*...сего́дня ве́чером. / *[2]* ...за́втра ве́чером. / *[3]* ...в пя́тницу ве́чером.). ♦ **I'm going to take you out on the town (when** *[1]* ...**I get there. / [2] ...you get here.**). Я приглашу́ тебя́ пойти́ куда́-нибудь со мной (, когда́ *[1]* ...прие́ду. / *[2]* ...ты прие́дешь сюда́.).

take *n:* ♦ **My take on it is...** То, как я понима́ю э́то,...

take-charge *adj:* ♦ **I'm a take-charge kind of guy.** Я челове́к, беру́щий ли́дерство на себя́.

taken *adj* 1. *(gotten)* взят, -а, -о, -ы *(short forms)*; 2. *(attracted)* привлечён, привлечена́, -о́, -ы́ *(short forms)*; *(charmed, enchanted, captivated)* очаро́ван, -а, -о, -ы *(short forms)*, пленён, пленена́, -о́, -ы́ *(short forms)* ♦ ~**aback** поражён, поражена́, -о́, -ы́ *(short forms)* ♦ **be** ~ *(attracted)* быть привлечённым *m* / привлечённой *f (by / with whom = instr.)* ; *(charmed)* быть очаро́ванным *m* / очаро́ванной *f (by / with whom = instr.)* ♦ **I must** *(1)* **admit / (2) confess, (3,4) I'm very taken by you.** Я до́лжен *(ж: должна́) (1,2)* призна́ться, *(3)* ...ты о́чень привлекла́ *(ж: привлёк)* меня́. / *(4)* ...я соверше́нно очаро́ван тобо́й. ♦ **I was taken aback by the directness of your question.** Я был поражён *(ж: была́ поражена́)* прямото́й твоего́ вопро́са.

taker *n* беру́щий *m*, беру́щая *f* ♦ **I'm a giver, not a taker.** Я даю́щий *(ж: даю́щая)*, а не беру́щий *(ж: беру́щая)*.

talisman *n* талисма́н.

talk *vi* говори́ть *(to whom = dat., with whom = + c + instr..)*; разгова́ривать *(with whom = + c + instr.)* ♦ ~ **about many things** говори́ть о мно́гом ♦ ~ **calmly** говори́ть споко́йно ♦ ~ **continuously** разгова́ривать беспреста́нно ♦ ~ **dirty** скверносло́вить ♦ ~ **fast** говори́ть бы́стро ♦ ~ **louder** говори́ть гро́мче ♦ ~ **loud(ly)** говори́ть гро́мко ♦ ~ **nonstop** разгова́ривать беспреста́нно ♦ ~ **quietly** говори́ть ти́хо ♦ ~ **seriously** говори́ть серьёзно ♦ ~ **sexy** говори́ть сексуа́льно ♦ ~ **slower** говори́ть ме́дленнее ♦ ~ **slowly** говори́ть ме́дленно ♦ ~ **too fast** говори́ть сли́шком бы́стро ♦ ~ **up a storm** о́чень мно́го говори́ть.

Some of the Russian sentences are translations of things we say and are not what Russians themselves would normally say.

talk: *talking with you*

It feels so natural talking to you. Я чу́вствую себя́ так есте́ственно, говоря́ с тобо́й. ♦
I enjoy talking with you. Я наслажда́юсь, говоря́ с тобо́й. ♦ **It's so nice to talk with you.**
Так прия́тно говори́ть с тобо́й. ♦ **I think it would be such a nice feeling to sit close to**
you and talk with you in an intimate way for hours on end. This is going to be my new
dream in the days ahead. Я ду́маю, как бы э́то бы́ло прекра́сно сиде́ть ря́дом с тобо́й
и говори́ть о сокрове́нном бесконе́чные часы́. Это тепе́рь бу́дет мое́й но́вой мечто́й.
♦ **How I hate to stop talking to you.** Я хочу́, чтобы наш разгово́р никогда́ не прерыва́-
ва́лся. ♦ **We have to talk.** Нам ну́жно поговори́ть. ♦ **We need to meet and talk together.**
Нам на́до встре́титься и поговори́ть. ♦ **Darling, I want so very much to see you and talk**
with you and show you love in all the ways that it's possible to show love. Дорога́я *(ж:*
Дорого́й), я так си́льно хочу́ уви́деть тебя́, говори́ть с тобо́й и демонстри́ровать тебе́
любо́вь все́ми возмо́жными спо́собами. ♦ *(1)* **I've been on a cloud...** / *(2)* **My head's**
been in the clouds... ever since I talked with you. *(1)* Я был *(ж: была́)*... / *(2)* Моё се́рдце
бы́ло... на облака́х, с тех пор, как я говори́л *(ж: говори́ла)* с тобо́й. ♦ **When I talk with**
you on the phone, it seems as though I'm never able to convey the love and longing that
I feel in my heart for you. Когда́ я говорю́ с тобо́й по телефо́ну, ка́жется, что я ни-
когда́ не смогу́ переда́ть ту любо́вь к тебе́ и тоску́ по тебе́, кото́рыми полно́ моё
се́рдце. ♦ **You and I could share so many things, make so much wonderful love together,**
talk about so many things together, connect in heart, mind, and spirit so perfectly. Мы
смогли́ бы мно́гим вме́сте наслажда́ться , так мно́го занима́ться любо́вью, говори́ть
о мно́гом друг с дру́гом, так соверше́нно соединя́ться се́рдцем, умо́м и ду́хом.

talk: *I want somebody to talk to*

I want somebody I can talk to and get along with in my old age. Я хочу́ того́, с кем я
смогу́ говори́ть и ла́дить в ста́рости.

talk: *various expressions*

I like the way you talk. Мне нра́вится, как ты говори́шь. ♦ **I don't want to talk about**
it. Я не хочу́ говори́ть об э́том. ♦ **You talk a good game, but that's all.** Ты краси́во
говори́шь, но э́то всё. ♦ **I like it when you talk sexy.** Мне нра́вится, когда́ ты говори́шь
сексуа́льно. ♦ **It's not necessary to talk dirty.** Нет необходи́мости скверносло́вить.

talk *n* разгово́р, бесе́да ♦ **confidential** ~ довери́тельный разгово́р ♦ **dirty** ~ гря́зные
слова́, гря́зный разгово́р ♦ **fascinating** ~ увлека́тельный разгово́р ♦ **friendly** ~ дру́-
жеский разгово́р, дру́жеская бесе́да ♦ **girl** ~ деви́чий разгово́р ♦ **heart-to-heart** ~
задуше́вный разгово́р, разгово́р от се́рдца к се́рдцу ♦ **heavy** ~ серьёзный разгово́р
♦ **interesting** ~ интере́сный разгово́р ♦ **intimate** ~ инти́мный разгово́р ♦ **long** ~**s** до́л-
гие разгово́ры ♦ **nice long** ~**s** прия́тные до́лгие разгово́ры ♦ **nice** ~ прия́тный раз-
гово́р ♦ **pillow** ~ инти́мный разгово́р, инти́мная бесе́да *(в посте́ли)*, разгово́р в по-
сте́ли ♦ **pleasant** ~ прия́тный разгово́р ♦ **serious** ~ серьёзный разгово́р ♦ **sex(y)** ~
сексуа́льный разгово́р ♦ **sexy pillow** ~ сексуа́льный разгово́р в посте́ли ♦ **short** ~
коро́ткий разгово́р ♦ *(1-5)* **small** ~ 1. *(chit-chat)* *(1)* разгово́р о пустя́х, *(2)* сало́нный
/ *(3)* све́тский / *(4)* пусто́й разгово́р; 2. *(short)* *(5)* небольшо́й разгово́р ♦ **sweet** ~ 1. *(ten-*
der talk) не́жный разгово́р; 2. *(idle flattery)*ума́сливание ♦ **woman** ~ же́нский
разгово́р.

talkative *adj* разгово́рчивый, -ая, -ое, -ые.

talking *n* 1. *(speech)* речь; 2. *(conversation)* разгово́р ♦ **deep** ~ серьёзные разгово́ры ♦ **slow**
way of ~ ме́дленная речь.

tall *adj* высо́кий, -ая, -ое, -ие ♦ ~, **dark and handsome** высо́кий, сму́глый и краси́вый ♦
~, **white and handsome** высо́кий, бе́лый и краси́вый.

Counting things in Russian is a bit involved.
See Appendix 4, Numbers, on page 756 .

tallish *adj* дово́льно высо́кий, -ая, -ое, -ие.

tan *n* зага́р ♦ **bronze** ~ бро́нзовый зага́р ♦ **copper** ~ ме́дный зага́р ♦ **dark** ~ тёмный зага́р ♦ **golden** ~ золото́й зага́р ♦ **gorgeous** ~ великоле́пный зага́р ♦ **magnificent** ~ великоле́пный зага́р.

tangle *n*: ♦ ~ **of shining hair** сия́ющие спу́танные во́лосы, копна́ блестя́щих воло́с.

tango *vi* танцева́ть та́нго.

tango *n* та́нго.

tanned *adj* загоре́лый, -ая, -ое, -ые.

tantalizing *adj (teasing, tormenting)* дразня́щий, -ая, -ее, -ие, му́чающий, -ая, -ее, -ие, мучи́тельный, -ая, -ое, -ые; *(enticing, alluring)* маня́щий, -ая, -ее, -ие, привлека́тельный, -ая, -ое, -ые, соблазни́тельный, -ая, -ое, -ые ♦ **The soft curves of your lips are so tantalizing.** Мя́гкие изги́бы твои́х губ таки́е маня́щие. ♦ **All I can think of, day and night, is your tantalizing** *(1)* **mouth** / *(2)* **body.** Всё, о чём я могу́ ду́мать день и ночь, э́то *(1)* ...твой маня́щий рот. / *(2)* ...твоё маня́щее те́ло. ♦ **You have the most tantalizing** *(1)* **mouth** / *(2)* **body I've ever laid eyes on.** У тебя́ *(1)* ...тако́й маня́щий рот,... / *(2)* ...тако́е маня́щее те́ло,... како́го я никогда́ не ви́дел.

tantalizingly *adv* мучи́тельно, дразня́ще.

tap-dance *vi* танцева́ть чечётку ♦ **Your legs are going to be tap-dancing in the air.** Твои́ но́ги бу́дут танцева́ть чечётку в во́здухе.

tart *n* 1. *(prostitute)* у́личная де́вка, проститу́тка; 2. *(loose woman)* распу́тная же́нщина.

taste *vt* 1. *(try)* про́бовать / попро́бовать *(what = acc.)*; 2. *(savor)* вкуша́ть *(what = acc.)* ♦ **In the unbounded vistas of my dreams and fantasies I taste the exquisite sweetness of your lips a thousand, ten thousand, a million times, and each time am only impelled by the sheer ecstasy of the kiss to taste them once again.** В безграни́чной верени́це мои́х снов и фанта́зий я вкуша́ю исключи́тельную сла́дость твои́х губ ты́сячу, де́сять ты́сяч, миллио́н раз, и ка́ждый раз я побужде́н и́стинным восто́ргом поцелу́я упива́ться им опя́ть. ♦ **How I long to taste the warm recesses of your mouth (again).** Как жа́жду я (опя́ть) вкуша́ть тёплые глуби́ны твоего́ рта.

taste *vi* име́ть вкус ♦ **Your lips taste like honey.** У твои́х губ вкус мёда.

taste *n* вкус ♦ **aesthetic** ~ эстети́ческий вкус ♦ **artistic** ~ худо́жественный вкус ♦ **bad** ~ 1. *(preference)* плохо́й вкус; 2. *(food)* дурно́й вкус ♦ **crude** ~s гру́бые вку́сы ♦ **different** ~s ра́зные вку́сы ♦ **eclectic** ~s эклекти́ческие вку́сы ♦ **good** ~ хоро́ший вкус ♦ **impeccable** ~ безупре́чный вкус ♦ **literary** ~ литерату́рный вкус ♦ **modern** ~s совреме́нные вку́сы ♦ **musical** ~ музыка́льный вкус ♦ **nice** ~ *(food)* прия́тный вкус ♦ **personal** ~ ли́чный вкус ♦ **personal** ~s ли́чные вку́сы ♦ **poor** ~ плохо́й вкус ♦ **pretty good** ~ неплохо́й вкус ♦ *(1,2)* **refined** ~ *(1)* утончённый / *(2)* рафини́рованный вкус ♦ **same** ~s одина́ковые вку́сы ♦ **simple** ~s просты́е вку́сы ♦ **sweet** ~ *(food)* сла́дкий вкус ♦ **wonderful** ~ прекра́сный вкус ♦ **in bad** ~ безвку́сно ♦ **in good** ~ со вку́сом.

taste: phrases

I'm a *(1)* **man** / *(2)* **woman** / *(3)* **person of conventional tastes.** Я *(1)* мужчи́на / *(2)* же́нщина / *(3)* челове́к традицио́нных вку́сов. ♦ **I want to devour all the hot, sweet taste of you.** Я хочу́ поглоти́ть весь твой горя́чий, сла́дкий вкус. ♦ **The taste of your kisses is still on my lips.** Вкус твои́х поцелу́ев всё ещё на мои́х губа́х. ♦ *(1)* **You have...** / *(2)* **I must commend you on your...** *(3)* **good** / *(4)* **excellent taste in** *(5)* **clothes** / *(6)* **music** / *(7)* **wine** / *(8)* **art** / *(9)* **decorating.** *(1)* У тебя́ ... / *(2)* Я до́лжен *(ж: должна́)* похвали́ть тебя́ за твой... *(3)* хоро́ший / *(4)* превосхо́дный вкус в *(5)* оде́жде / *(6)* му́зыке / *(7)* вине́ / *(8)* иску́сстве / *(9)* декори́ровании. ♦ **You have good taste in everything.** У тебя́ хоро́ший вкус во всём. ♦ **I have simple tastes.** У меня́ просты́е вку́сы.

Russian has 2 different verbs for "go",
one for "on foot" and the other for "by vehicle".

tattoo *n* татуиро́вка ♦ **navel ~** татуиро́ванный пуп.

tattooed *adj* татуиро́ванный, -ая, -ое, -ые *(short forms:* татуиро́ван, -а, -о, -ы*)* ♦ **tastefully ~** татуиро́ванный со вку́сом.

taunt *vt* насмеха́ться *(whom = + над + instr.).*

Taurus *(Apr. 20 - May 20)* Бык *(20 апре́ля - 20 мáя).*

taut *adj* туго́й, -ая, -ое, -ие, ту́го натя́нутый, -ая, -ое, -ые; плóтно обтя́гивающий, -ая, -ее, -ие.

tautness *n* натя́нутость *f* ♦ **I admire the tautness of your blouse in this photo.** Я восхища́юсь тем, как плóтно обтя́гивает тебя́ блу́зка на э́той фотогра́фии.

tawdry *adj* мишу́рный, -ая, -ое, -ые.

tawny *adj (reddish brown)* рыжева́то-кори́чневый, -ая, -ое, -ые; *(dark yellow)* тёмно-жёлтый, -ая, -ое, -ые.

teach *vt* учи́ть / научи́ть *(whom = acc., what = dat.)* ♦ **Teach me** *(1)* **...what you like best.** / *(2)* **...how to make you happy.** / *(3)* **...what gives you pleasure.** / *(4)* **...how I can give you the most pleasure.** Научи́ меня́, *(1)* ...что тебе́ нра́вится бóльше всего́. / *(2)* ...как сде́лать тебя́ счастли́вой. / *(3)* ...что доставля́ет тебе́ наслажде́ние. / *(4)* ...как я смогу́ доста́вить тебе́ наибóльшее наслажде́ние. ♦ *(1)* **I want to...** / *(2)* **I'm going to... teach you how to** *(3)* **...enjoy (love).** / *(4)* **...let yourself go.** / *(5)* **...ride rainbows.** / *(6)* **...soar through the cosmos.** / *(7)* **...imitate a volcano.** *(1)* Я хочу́ научи́ть... / *(2)* Я научу́... тебя́, как *(3)* ...наслажда́ться (любóвью). / *(4)* ...дать себе́ вóлю. / *(5)* ...скака́ть на ра́дуге. / *(6)* ...взлете́ть в кóсмос. / *(7)* ...подража́ть вулка́ну. ♦ *(1)* **I want to...** / *(2)* **I'm going to... teach you (everything) about love.** *(1)* Я хочу́ научи́ть... / *(2)* Я научу́... тебя́ (всему́) в любви́.

teak-brown *adj* све́тло-кори́чневый, -ая, -ое, -ые.

team *n* кома́нда ♦ **We'll make the best team.** Мы соста́вим наилу́чшую кома́нду. ♦ **We'll make a wonderful team together.** Вме́сте мы соста́вим замеча́тельную кома́нду.

tear *vt* рвать / порва́ть *(what = acc.); (tear up)* разрыва́ть / разорва́ть *(what = acc.); (tear off)* отрыва́ть / оторва́ть *(what = acc.)* ♦ **~ my hair out** рвать на себе́ вóлосы ♦ **I'm tearing my hair out wondering what I did.** Я рву на себе́ вóлосы, поража́ясь, что я наде́лал *(ж: наде́лала).* ♦ **After you read this letter, please tear it up.** Пóсле того́, как ты прочтёшь э́то письмó, пожа́луйста, порви́ его́. ♦ **It tears me apart to think of losing you.** Мысль о потéре тебя́ разрыва́ет меня́ на ча́сти.

tear *n* слеза́ *(pl: слёзы)* ♦ **big ~s** кру́пные слёзы ♦ **bitter ~s** гóрькие слёзы ♦ **crocodile ~s** крокоди́ловые слёзы ♦ **genuine ~s** и́скренние слёзы ♦ **salty ~s** солёные слёзы ♦ **~s of grief** слёзы гóря ♦ **~s of happiness** счастли́вые слёзы, слёзы сча́стья ♦ **~s of joy** слёзы ра́дости, ра́достные слёзы ♦ **shed ~s** пла́кать / запла́кать, пролива́ть / проли́ть слёзы.

> ### tear: phrases

Let me *(1)* **dry** / *(2)* **wipe your tears.** Позвóль мне *(1)* осуши́ть / *(2)* вы́тереть твои́ слёзы. ♦ **I'll kiss away all your tears.** Я осушу́ все твои́ слёзы поцелу́ями. ♦ **At this moment I'm fighting (back) tears.** Сейча́с я пыта́юсь удержа́ть слёзы. ♦ **I was fighting (back) tears (the whole time).** Я (всё врéмя) пыта́лся *(ж: пыта́лась)* удержа́ть слёзы. ♦ **It broke my heart to see your letter stained with tears.** Моё сéрдце разрыва́лось от ви́да твоего́ письма́ с пя́тнами слёз на нём. ♦ **You're crying crocodile tears.** Ты пла́чишь крокоди́ловыми слёзами. ♦ **Please, no tears.** Пожа́луйста, не плачь. ♦ **Please don't burst into tears.** Пожа́луйста, не разража́йся слёзами. ♦ **You don't have to burst into tears about it.** Не на́до пла́кать. ♦ **Spare me the tears.** Изба́вь меня́ от слёз. ♦ **Tears were close to the surface.** Слёзы готóвы бы́ли поли́ться. ♦ **Tears welled up in my eyes.**

> *Dipthongs in Russian are made by adding* й
> *to the end of a vowel (*а, е, ё, о, у, э, ю, *and* я*).*

На мои́х глаза́х вы́ступили слёзы.

tear-stained *adj* запла́канный, -ая, -ое, -ые, со следа́ми слёз.

tease *vt* дразни́ть *(whom = acc.)*; поддра́знивать / поддразни́ть *(whom = acc.)*.

tease *n* люби́тель дразни́ть ♦ **You're (just) a big tease.** Ты всегда́ (то́лько) дра́знишь.

teaser *n* люби́тель дразни́ть.

teasing *adj* дразня́щий, -ая, -ее, -ие ♦ ~ **manner** дразня́щие мане́ры ♦ ~ **remark** поддра́знивающее замеча́ние.

teasing *n* поддра́знивание.

technique *n* те́хника ♦ **lovemaking** ~ те́хника заня́тия любо́вью ♦ **sexual** ~ сексуа́льная те́хника ♦ **You have such** *(1)* **great** / *(2)* **wonderful technique.** У тебя́ така́я *(1)* великоле́пная / *(2)* замеча́тельная те́хника.

teddy *n* 1. *(teddy bear)* медвежёнок; 2. *(negligee)* коро́ткое, прозра́чное, пло́тно облега́ющее неглиже́ *(explanation)*.

telecompanion *n* друг по телефо́ну.

telephone *n* телефо́н.

tell *vt (say)* говори́ть / сказа́ть *(what = acc., to whom = dat.)*; *(relate)* расска́зывать /расска́зать *(what = acc., to whom = dat.)*.

> **tell: you tell me**

Can you *(1,2)* **tell me?** Мо́жешь ты *(1)* сказа́ть / *(2)* рассказа́ть мне? ♦ **Are you going to** *(1,2)* **tell me?** Ты *(1)* ска́жешь / *(2)* расска́жешь мне? ♦ **Tell me** *(1)* **...everything (about it).** / *(2)* **...(all) about yourself.** / *(3)* **...what happened.** / *(4)* **...honestly.** / *(5)* **...what's bothering you.** / *(6)* **...what the matter is.** / / *(7)* **...what's in your heart.** / *(8)* **...your side.** Расскажи́ мне *(1)* ...всё (об э́том). / *(2)* ...всё (о себе́). / *(3)* ..., что случи́лось. / *(4)* ...че́стно. / *(5)* ..., что волну́ет тебя́. / *(6)* ...в чём де́ло. / *(7)* ..., что у тебя́ на се́рдце. / *(8)* ...твой вариа́нт. ♦ **Tell me a little bit (more) about yourself.** Расскажи́ мне немно́го (бо́льше) о себе́. ♦ **Tell me** *(1)* **...the truth.** / *(2)* **...you (still) love me.** / *(3)* **..you'll marry me.** / *(4)* **...what you think.** / *(5)* **...what you like.** / *(6)* **...what to do.** / *(7)* **...where to kiss you.** / *(8)* **...how I can help (you).** / *(9)* **...when.** / *(10)* **...where .** / *(11)* **...why.** Скажи́ мне *(1)* ...пра́вду. / *(2)* ..., что ты (всё ещё) лю́бишь меня́. / *(3)* ..., что ты вы́йдешь за́муж за меня́ *(ж: ...что ты же́нишься на мне)*. / *(4)* ..., что ты ду́маешь. / *(5)* ..., что ты лю́бишь. / *(6)* ..., что де́лать. / *(7)* ..., куда́ поцелова́ть тебя́. / *(8)* ..., как я могу́ помо́чь (тебе́). / *(9)* ..., когда́. / *(10)* ..., где. / *(11)* ..., почему́. ♦ **I think you're just telling me what I want to hear.** Я ду́маю, что ты про́сто говори́шь мне то, что я хочу́ услы́шать.

> **tell: I tell you**

Let me tell you a little bit (more) about myself. Позво́ль мне немно́го (бо́льше) рассказа́ть о себе́. ♦ **I'll** *1,2)* **tell you (later).** Я *(1)* скажу́ / *(2)* расскажу́ тебе́ (позднее́). ♦ **I can't** *(1,2)* **tell you (because...).** Я не могу́ *(1)* сказа́ть / *(2)* рассказа́ть тебе́ (потому́, что...). ♦ *(1)* **I intended...** / *(2)* **It was my intention... to tell you.** *(1)* Я собира́лся *(ж: собира́лась)...* / *(2)* Моё наме́рение бы́ло... сказа́ть тебе́.

> **tell: you tell him / her / them**

Are you going to *(1,2)* **tell** *(3)* **him** / *(4)* **her** / *(5)* **them?** Ты *(1)* ска́жешь / *(2)* расска́жешь *(3)* ему́ / *(4)* ей / *(5)* им? ♦ **Tell** *(1)* **him** / *(2)* **her** / *(3)* **them** *(4)* **...you want a divorce.** / *(5)* **...everything.** / *(6)* **...about us.** / *(7)* **...the truth.** / *(8)* **...you love me.** / *(9,10)* **... you're going to leave.** / *(11)* **...you're going to move out.** / *(12)* **...it's all over.** Скажи́ *(1)* ему́ / *(2)* ей / *(3)* им *(4)* ..., что ты хо́чешь развóда. / *(5)* ...всё. / *(6)* ...о нас. / *(7)* ...пра́вду. / *(8)* ..., что ты лю́бишь меня́. / *(9)* ..., что ты собира́ешься уйти́ *(on foot)* / *(10)* уе́хать *(by veh.)*. / *(11)* ..., что ты уе́дешь. / *(12)* ..., что всё ко́нчено.

> *Some phrases are listed under more than one main word.*

tell: *I tell him / her / them*

I'll *1,2)* **tell** *(3)* **him /** *(4)* **her /** *(5)* **them (later).** Я *(1)* скажу́ / *(2)* расскажу́ *(3)* ему́ / *(4)* ей / *(5)* им (поздне́е). ♦ **It's my intention to tell** *(1)* **him /** *(2)* **her /** *(3)* **them.** Моё наме́рение сказа́ть *(1)* ему́ / *(2)* ей / *(3)* им. ♦ **I can't** *(1,2)* **tell** *(3)* **him /** *(4)* **her /** *(5)* **them (because...).** Я не могу́ *(1)* сказа́ть / *(2)* рассказа́ть *(3)* ему́ / *(4)* ей / *(5)* им (потому́, что...).

temper *n* нрав, хара́ктер ♦ **bad** *(1,2)* ~ дурно́й *(1)* нрав / *(2)* хара́ктер, тяжёлый хара́ктер ♦ **calm** ~ споко́йный нрав ♦ *(1,2)* **even** ~ *(1)* ро́вный / *(2)* уравнове́шенный нрав / хара́ктер ♦ **fiery** *(1,2)* ~ необу́зданный *(1)* нрав / *(2)* хара́ктер ♦ **hot** ~ горя́чий нрав, вспы́льчивость *f* ♦ **nasty** *(1,2)* ~ дурно́й *(1)* нрав / *(2)* хара́ктер ♦ **quick** ~ вспы́льчивый нрав / хара́ктер, вспы́льчивость *f*, горя́чность *f* ♦ **smooth** ~ ро́вный хара́ктер ♦ **sweet** ~ до́брый нрав ♦ **violent** *(1,2)* ~ бе́шеный *(1)* нрав / *(2)* хара́ктер ♦ **lose one's** ~ выходи́ть / вы́йти из себя́.

temper: *phrases*

*(1)***You have... /** *(2)* **He /** *(3)* **She has... a hot temper.** *(1)* Ты вспы́льчивая *(ж: вспы́льчивый)*. / *(2)* Он вспы́льчивый. / *(3)* Она́ вспы́льчивая. ♦ **I'm sorry I lost my temper.** Извиня́юсь, я вы́шел *(ж: вы́шла)* из себя́. ♦ **Control your temper.** Владе́й собо́й.

temperament *n* темпера́мент; нрав, хара́ктер ♦ **conflicting** ~s конфли́ктные хара́ктеры ♦ **creative** ~ тво́рческий темпера́мент ♦ **happy** ~ счастли́вый хара́ктер ♦ **level** ~ уравнове́шенный темпера́мент ♦ **melancholy** ~ меланхоли́ческий темпера́мент ♦ *(1,2)* **nervous** ~ *(1)* нерво́зный / *(2)* беспоко́йный темпера́мент ♦ **quiet** ~ споко́йный нрав.

temperamental *adj* темпера́ментный, -ая, -ое, -ые, стра́стный, -ая, -ое, -ые, бу́йный, -ая, -ое, -ые.

temperature *n* температу́ра ♦ **You send my** *(1,2)* **temperature soaring (when you do that).** *(1)* Я весь *(ж: вся)* горю́,... / *(2)* Моя́ температу́ра взлета́ет,... когда́ ты де́лаешь э́то.

tempest *n* бу́ря ♦ **There is a tempest in my heart** *(1,2)* **caused by your sweet, innocent friendliness.** Твоё ми́лое, неви́нное дружелю́бие *(1)* сотвори́ло / *(2)* вы́звало бу́рю в моём се́рдце. ♦ **You have** *(1)* **created /** *(2)* **caused a tempest in my heart.** Ты *(1)* сотвори́ла / *(2)* вы́звала бу́рю в моём се́рдце.

tempestuous *adj* бу́рный, -ая, -ое, -ые, бу́йный, -ая, -ое, -ые ♦ ~ **lovemaking** бу́рное заня́тие любо́вью ♦ **I am tossed about in a sea of tempestuous emotions.** Я бро́шен *(ж: бро́шена)* в мо́ре бу́рных эмо́ций.

temple *n* 1. *(religious)* храм; 2. *(side of head)* висо́к.

tempt *vt* соблазня́ть / соблазни́ть *(whom = acc.)*, искуша́ть / искуси́ть *(whom = acc.)* ♦ **Don't tempt me.** Не искуша́й меня́. *(иронич.).*

temptation *n* собла́зн, искуше́ние ♦ **incredible** ~ невероя́тный собла́зн ♦ **aura of** ~ а́ура собла́зна ♦ **resist the** ~ устоя́ть пе́ред собла́зном, проти́виться искуше́нию ♦ **succumb to the** ~ поддава́ться / подда́ться собла́зну.

temptation: *phrases*

I can't resist the *(1,2)* **temptation.** Я не могу́ проти́виться *(1)* собла́зну / *(2)* искуше́нию. ♦ **I can never resist the** *(1,2)* **temptation of** *(3)* **...kissing you. /** *(4)* **...making love with you.** Я никогда́ не могу́ устоя́ть пе́ред *(1)* собла́зном / *(2)* искуше́нием *(3)* ...поцелова́ть тебя́. / *(4)* ...заня́ться с тобо́й любо́вью. ♦ **I couldn't resist the temptation.** Я не мог сопротивля́ться искуше́нию. ♦ **I couldn't resist the** *(1,2)* **temptation of** *(3)* **...calling /** *(4)* **contacting /** *(5)* **seeing you (again).** *(6)* **...coming to see you. /** *(7)* **...dropping by.** Я не смог *(ж: смогла́)* устоя́ть пе́ред *(1)* собла́зном / *(2)* искуше́нием *(3)* ...позвони́ть тебе́... / *(4)* ...обща́ться с тобо́й... / *(5)* ...уви́деть тебя́... (опя́ть). / *(6,7)* ...прийти́ к тебе́. ♦ **When we** *(1)* **sat /** *(2)* **stood together there, I could hardly resist the temptation to kiss you.** Когда́ мы *(1)* сиде́ли / *(2)* стоя́ли там вме́сте, я едва́ мог

The singular past tense of Russian verbs ends in -л (m) (usually),
-ла (f) or -ло (n). the plural past tense ends in -li.

сопротивля́ться искуше́нию поцелова́ть тебя́. ♦ **The temptation to** *(1)* **...kiss you...** */ (2)* **...take you in my arms... was almost more than I could bear.** Искуше́ние *(1)* ...целова́ть тебя́... / *(2)* ...заключи́ть тебя́ в объя́тия... бы́ло почти́ невыноси́мо.

tempting *adj* соблазни́тельный, ая, -ое, -ые ♦ **You look so tempting.** Ты вы́глядишь так соблазни́тельно.

temptress *n* соблазни́тельница, искуси́тельница.

ten *n (highest score in various competitions)* де́сять ба́ллов ♦ **You're a "ten" in every respect.** Ты на «де́сять» (ба́ллов) во всех отноше́ниях.

tenacious *adj* 1. *(firm, fast)* це́пкий, -ая, -ое, -ие; *(tight)* кре́пкий, -ая, -ое, -ие; 2. *(persistent, stubborn)* упо́рный, -ая, -ое, -ые, насто́йчивый, -ая, -ое, -ые, упря́мый, -ая, -ое, -ые.

tenaciously *adv* 1. *(firmly, fast)* це́пко; *(tightly)* кре́пко; 2. *(persistently, stubbornly)* упо́рно, насто́йчиво, упря́мо.

tender *adj* не́жный, -ая, -ое, -ые, ла́сковый, -ая, -ое, -ые ♦ **I am the most loving, affectionate, tender male you are ever likely to hear about, much less meet in this world.** Я наибо́лее лю́бящий, не́жный, ла́сковый мужчи́на из всех, о кото́рых ты слы́шала, а тем бо́лее встреча́ла в э́том ми́ре. ♦ **I am the most loving, affectionate, tender female you are ever likely to hear about, much less meet in this world.** Я наибо́лее лю́бящая, не́жная, ла́сковая же́нщиина из всех, о кото́рых ты слы́шал, а тем бо́лее встреча́л в э́том ми́ре.

tenderly *adj* не́жно, ла́сково ♦ **I want to hold you tenderly (in my arms).** Я хочу́ не́жно держа́ть тебя́ (в объя́тиях).

tenderness *n* не́жность *f* ♦ **indescribable** ~ несказа́нная не́жность ♦ **infinite** ~ бесконе́чная не́жность ♦ **sultry** ~ зно́йная не́жность ♦ **act of** ~ не́жное де́йствие.

tenderness: phrases

I need your tenderness. Мне нужна́ твоя́ не́жность. ♦ **I perceive in you a reservoir of warmth and affection and tenderness that is very, very deep.** Я чу́вствую в тебе́ о́чень, о́чень глубо́кий запа́с серде́чности, любви́ и не́жности. ♦ **Your many acts of tenderness have enslaved my heart.** Не́жность, кото́рую ты так ще́дро дари́ла *(ж: дари́л)* мне, поработи́ла моё се́рдце. ♦ **I want to spend endless hours sharing love and tenderness with you.** Я хочу́ проводи́ть бесконе́чные часы́, наслажда́ясь не́жной любо́вью с тобо́й. ♦ *(1)* **I intend...** / *(2)* **I want...** / *(3)* **I'm going... to lavish love and tenderness and adoration upon you such as you have never** *(4)* **...imagined.** / *(5)* **...dreamed of.** *(1)* Я наме́рен... / *(2)* Я хочу́... / *(3)* Я бу́ду... дари́ть тебе́ таки́е любо́вь, не́жность и обожа́ние, о каки́х ты никогда́ не *(4,5)* мечта́ла.

tennis *n* те́ннис ♦ **Would you like to play tennis (with me) ?** Не хоте́ла *(ж: хоте́л)* бы ты сыгра́ть в те́ннис (со мной)? ♦ **(Come on,) I'll teach you how to play tennis.** (Дава́й) я бу́ду учи́ть тебя́ игра́ть в те́ннис.

tense *adj* напряжённый, -ая, -ое, -ые *(short forms:* напряжён, напряжена́, -ó, -ы́) ♦ ~ **silence** напряжённое молча́ние ♦ **Why are you so tense?** Почему́ ты так напряжена́ *(ж: напряжён)*? ♦ **Don't be so tense.** Не будь так напряжена́ *(ж: напряжён)*.

tension *n* напряжённость *f*, напряже́ние ♦ **nervous** ~ не́рвное напряже́ние ♦ **There was a palpable tension.** Чу́вствовалась я́вная напряжённость. ♦ **The air seemed to crackle with tension.** Во́здух, каза́лось, потре́скивал от напряже́ния.

terms *n, pl (relationship)* отноше́ния *pl* ♦ **friendly** ~s прия́тельские отноше́ния ♦ **We're still on friendly terms.** Мы всё ещё в прия́тельских отноше́ниях. ♦ **I hope we can stay on friendly terms.** Я наде́юсь, мы смо́жем оста́ться в прия́тельских отноше́ниях.

terminate *vt* заверша́ть / заверши́ть, прекраща́ть / прекрати́ть, положи́ть коне́ц ♦ **I think we should** *(1,2)* **terminate our relationship.** Я ду́маю, мы должны́ *(1)* ...пре-

---

Please do us a favor:
Fill out and mail in the Feedback Sheet on page 795.

кратить наши отношения. / *(2)* ...положить конец нашим отношениям. ♦ **Do you think we should** *(1,2)* **terminate our relationship.** Ты думаешь, нам следует *(1)* ...прекратить наши отношения? / *(2)* ...положить конец нашим отношениям? ♦ **Do you want to** *(1,2)* **terminate our relationship?** Ты хочешь *(1)* ...прекратить наши отношения? / *(2)* ...положить конец нашим отношениям?

terrible *adj* ужасный, -ая, -ое, -ые, страшный, -ая, -ое, -ые.

terribly *adj* ужасно, страшно.

terrific *adj* потрясающий, -ая, -ее, -ие ♦ **That was (absolutely) terrific.** Это было (совершенно) потрясающе. ♦ **You are (absolutely) terrific.** Ты (совершенно) потрясающая *(ж: потрясающий).* ♦ **You look (absolutely) terrific!** Ты выглядишь (совершенно) потрясающе!

terse *adj* сжатый, -ая, -ое, -ые, краткий, -ая, -ое, -ие, скупой, -ая, -ое, -ые, лаконичный, -ая, -ое, -ые ♦ ~ **letter** краткое письмо ♦ ~ **reply** лаконичный ответ.

test *n* 1. *(trial)* испытание; 2. *(scholastic)* экзамен; 3. *(blood)* анализ ♦ **blood** ~ анализ крови ♦ ~ **of time** испытание временем ♦ **I'm sure that our love will stand the test of time.** Я уверен *(ж: уверена)*, что наша любовь выдержит испытание временем. ♦ **A blood test is (not) required.** Анализ крови (не) требуется. ♦ **We have to get a blood test.** Мы должны сделать анализ крови. ♦ **Where can we get a blood test?** Где мы можем сделать анализ крови? ♦ **We can get a blood test at .....** Мы можем сделать анализ крови в...

testicles *n, pl* яички.

tête-à-tête *n* тет-а-тет, свидание наедине.

texture *n* строение *(ткани)* ♦ **silky** ~ *(of skin)* шёлковистая кожа ♦ **smooth** ~ *(of skin)* гладкая кожа.

thank *vt* благодарить / поблагодарить *(whom = acc., for what = + за + acc.)* ♦ **Thank you with all my heart and soul for coming into my life.** Всем своим сердцем и душой благодарю тебя за приход в мою жизнь.

thankful *adj* благодарен, -благодарна, -о, -ы *(short forms)* ♦ **I am thankful for every day that you are in my life.** Я благодарен *(ж: благодарна)* за каждый наш совместный день. ♦ **I am so thankful for your love.** Я так благодарен *(ж: благодарна)* за твою любовь.

thanks *n, pl* спасибо ♦ **Thanks for being** *(1)* **...mine.** / *(1)* **...there (when I need you).** Спасибо за то, что ты *(1)* ...моя *(ж: мой).* / *(2)* ...всегда рядом(, когда я нуждаюсь в тебе).

theater *n* 1. *(drama)* театр; 2. кинотеатр *(movies).*

thigh *n* бедро *(pl: бёдра)* ♦ **firm** ~s упругие бёдра ♦ **inner** ~s внутренние поверхности бёдер ♦ **lean** ~s поджарые бёдра ♦ **lush** ~s роскошные бёдра ♦ **muscular** ~s мускулистые бёдра ♦ **slender** ~s стройные бёдра ♦ **smooth** ~s гладкие бёдра ♦ **You have such well-muscled thighs.** У тебя такие мускулистые бёдра. ♦ **We'll see what happens, when mouth meets mouth and thigh meets thigh.** Мы увидим, что случится, когда рот встретиться со ртом, а бедро встретится с бедром.

thin *adj* худой, -ая, -ое, -ые, тонкий, -ая, -ое, -ие ♦ **get / grow t.** худеть / похудеть.

thing *n* 1. *(object)* вещь, предмет; 2. *(matter)* дело; *(sometimes expressed by making an adjective neuter - see examples below)*; 3. *(creature)* существо, создание ♦ **another** ~ другое ♦ **appetizing little** ~ аппетитный кусочек ♦ **delectable** ~ лакомый кусочек ♦ **fresh young** ~ молодое существо ♦ **innocent** ~ невинное создание ♦ **lovely** ~ прелестное создание ♦ **most natural** ~ **in the world** самая естественная вещь на свете ♦ **poor (little)** ~ бедняжка *f* ♦ **real** ~ *(slang)* 1. *(true love)* настоящая любовь; 2. *(meaningful relationship)* прочные отношения ♦ **sweet little** ~ прелестная крошка, милая особа ♦

Clock and calender time are discussed in Appendix 5, page 759.

the first ~ пе́рвое ♦ the last ~ после́днее ♦ the most important ~ са́мое ва́жное ♦ the only ~ еди́нственное ♦ wild ~ *(slang)* 1. *(passion, love-making)* страсть, заня́тие любо́вью; 2. *(wild person)* челове́к без ко́мплексов ♦ young *(1,2)* ~ ю́ное *(1)* созда́ние / *(2)* существо́.

| **thing: phrases** |

How are things? Как (обстоя́т) дела́? ♦ How are things going (with you)? Как (иду́т) твои́ дела́? ♦ You're the only thing I have to hold onto (in life). Ты еди́нственное, за что я держу́сь (в жи́зни). ♦ It's all the little things that make me love you so much. Я так си́льно тебя́ люблю́ за все э́ти ма́ленькие зна́ки внима́ния. ♦ You're an appetizing little thing. Ты аппети́тный кусо́чек. ♦ Our love is the real thing. На́ша любо́вь настоя́щая. ♦ The simple things of life are what's important. Просты́е жи́зненные наслажде́ния -- вот что ва́жно. ♦ *(1)* I'm willing to try... / *(2)* I enjoy trying... new things. *(1)* Я хочу́ испыта́ть... / *(2)* Я наслажда́юсь, испы́тывая... но́вое. ♦ We can enjoy life's finer things together. Вме́сте мы мо́жем наслажда́ться пре́лестями жи́зни. ♦ I *(1)* want / *(2)* yearn for someone with whom to share life's finer things. Я *(1)* хочу́ / *(2)* жа́жду того́, с кем бу́ду вме́сте наслажда́ться пре́лестями жи́зни. ♦ When you say intimate things to me, it makes me feel warm all over. Когда́ ты говори́шь мне инти́мные слова́, меня́ всего́ *(ж: всю)* броса́ет в жар. ♦ This is the real thing. Э́то настоя́щее. ♦ They say that love is a many-splendored thing. Говоря́т, что любо́вь -- вещь великоле́пная во мно́гих отноше́ниях. ♦ Little things mean a lot. Ме́лочи зна́чат мно́го. ♦ There are so many things I want to say to you. Я хочу́ сказа́ть тебе́ о мно́гом.

think *vi* ду́мать / поду́мать *(about what, whom = + о + prep.)* ♦ ~ about you ду́мать о тебе́ ♦ ~ a lot ду́мать мно́го ♦ ~ all the time ду́мать всё вре́мя ♦ ~ always ду́мать всегда́ ♦ ~ carefully хорошо́ поду́мать ♦ ~ constantly ду́мать постоя́нно ♦ ~ continuously ду́мать непреры́вно ♦ ~ incessantly ду́мать непреста́нно ♦ ~ often ду́мать ча́сто ♦ ~ seriously ду́мать серьёзно ♦ ~ sometimes ду́мать иногда́ ♦ ~ wistfully ду́мать тоскли́во ♦ begin to ~ нача́ть ду́мать ♦ keep on thinking продолжа́ть ду́мать ♦ stop thinking переста́ть ду́мать.

| **think:** *I think about you - a lot* |

(1) I think... / *(2)* I've been thinking... about you *(3)* ...constantly / *(4)* continuously / *(5)* incessantly. / *(6)* ...every minute of every day. / *(7)* ...day and night. *(1,2)* Я ду́маю о тебе́ *(3)* ...постоя́нно / *(4)* непреры́вно / *(5)* непреста́нно. / *(6)* ...ка́ждую мину́ту ка́ждого дня. / *(7)* ...день и ночь. ♦ I think about you *(1)* ...all the time. / *(2)* ...wherever I am. / *(3,4)* ...wherever I go. / *(5)* ...more than I should. Я ду́маю о тебе́ *(1)* ...всё вре́мя. / *(2)* ...где бы я ни был *(ж: была́)*. / *(3)* ...куда́ бы я ни пое́хал *(by veh.)* *(ж: пое́хала)* / *(4)* пошёл *(on foot)* *(ж: пошла́)* / *(5)* ...бо́льше, чем сле́дует. ♦ I've been thinking about you a lot (lately). (Have you received my brainwaves?) Я мно́го ду́маю о тебе́ (после́днее вре́мя). (Получи́ла *[ж: получи́л]* ли ты мои́ мозговы́е во́лны?) ♦ Not a minute passes that I don't think about you. Не прохо́дит мину́ты, что́бы я не поду́мал *(ж: поду́мала)* о тебе́. ♦ I think about you and think about you and think about you — constantly. Я ду́маю, ду́маю и ду́маю о тебе́ постоя́нно. ♦ I can't think of anyone or anything except you. Я не могу́ ду́мать ни о ком и ни о чём, кро́ме тебя́. ♦ I cannot even breath without thinking of you. Я не могу́ да́же дыша́ть, не ду́мая о тебе́. ♦ I lie awake most of the night thinking about you. Я не сплю́ но́чи напролёт, ду́мая о тебе́. ♦ You can't believe how much I think about you and want you at nighttime before I fall asleep and in the early morning as I wake up. Ты не представля́ешь, как мно́го я ду́маю о тебе́ и как жа́жду тебя́ но́чью пе́ред тем, как засну́ть, и ра́нним у́тром, как то́лько просну́сь.

Reflexive verbs are those that end in -ся *or* -сь.
The -ся *or* -сь *also goes onto a past tense ending.*

♦ **The only two times I think about you are night and day.** То́лько два вре́мени су́ток я ду́маю о тебе́ -- ночь и день. ♦ **Every morning I wake up thinking about you.** Ка́ждое у́тро я просыпа́юсь с мы́слью о тебе́. ♦ **I spend private moments thinking about you, wondering about you, daydreaming about you.** Я провожу́ свои́ свобо́дные мину́ты, ду́мая о тебе́, представля́я себе́, чем ты сейча́с занима́ешься. ♦ **I'm thinking about you all the time and adoring you and wanting you.** Я всё вре́мя ду́маю о тебе́, обожа́ю тебя́ и хочу́ тебя́. ♦ **It's become (extremely)** *(1)* **difficult /** *(2)* **hard not to think about you (all the time).** Ста́ло (чрезвыча́йно) *(1,2)* тру́дно не ду́мать о тебе́ (всё вре́мя). ♦ **My dear, I think about you so** *(1)* **much /** *(2)* **often — at least every five minutes, but usually more often.** Моя́ дорога́я *(ж: Мой дорого́й)*, я ду́маю о тебе́ так *(1)* мно́го / *(2)* ча́сто, по ме́ньшей ме́ре, ка́ждые пять мину́т, но обы́чно ча́ще. ♦ **You're all I think about.** Ты всё, о чём я ду́маю. ♦ **I really think about you a lot and wish with all my heart that I could see you.** Я действи́тельно мно́го ду́маю о тебе́ и всем се́рдцем жела́ю уви́деть тебя́. ♦ **Now I will close my letter, but not before I tell you that I adore you and think about you every day and dream about you every night.** Тепе́рь я зако́нчу своё письмо́, но не ра́ньше, чем скажу́ тебе́, что я обожа́ю тебя́, ду́маю о тебе́ ка́ждый день и мечта́ю о тебе́ ка́ждую ночь.

think: *I thought about you - a lot*

I thought about you and thought about you and thought about you — constantly. Я ду́мал, ду́мал и ду́мал *(ж: ду́мала, ду́мала и ду́мала)* о тебе́ постоя́нно. ♦ **If you had a rose for every time I thought about you, you'd be surrounded by an endless garden.** Е́сли бы с ка́ждой мое́й мы́слью о тебе́ у тебя́ распуска́лась ро́за, ты была́ бы окружена́ *(ж: был бы окружён)* бесконе́чным са́дом. ♦ **There wasn't a single one of those days that I didn't think about you, my darling.** Не́ бы́ло ни одного́ из э́тих дней, когда́ бы я не ду́мал *(ж: ду́мала)* о тебе́, моя́ дорога́я *(ж: мой дорого́й)*. ♦ **I tossed and turned all night long thinking about you.** Я мета́лся и воро́чался всю ночь напролёт, ду́мая о тебе́. ♦ **I was thinking about you so much that I had to stop my work and write this letter to you.** Я так мно́го ду́мал *(ж: ду́мала)* о тебе́, что был вы́нужден *(ж: была́ вы́нуждена)* прекрати́ть рабо́тать и написа́ть тебе́ э́то письмо́.

think: *I 'll be thinking about you*

I'll be thinking and daydreaming about you as I wait for your *(1)* **letter /** *(2)* **call.** Я бу́ду ду́мать и мечта́ть о тебе́ в то вре́мя, пока́ я ожида́ю *(1)* ...твоё письмо́ / *(2)* ...твой звоно́к. ♦ **I'll be thinking of you — warm, tender, affectionate thoughts, full of love.** Мои́ мы́сли бу́дут тёплыми, не́жными и напо́лненными любо́вью. ♦ **I promise you, between now and the day that it happens I'm going to think about nothing else.** Я обеща́ю тебе́, начина́я с сего́дняшнего дня и до того́ дня, когда́ э́то случи́тся, я не бу́ду ду́мать ни о чём друго́м. ♦ **It will be impossible for me not to think about your beautiful** *(1)* **face /** *(2)* **body at all hours of the day and night — especially the night.** Бу́дет невозмо́жно для меня́ не ду́мать о твоём прекра́сном *(1)* лице́ / *(2)* те́ле весь день и всю ночь, осо́бенно но́чью.

think: *can't stop thinking about you*

I can't stop thinking about you. Я не могу́ переста́ть ду́мать о тебе́. ♦ **How can I stop thinking about you when I can't stop looking at your photo?** Как я могу́ переста́ть ду́мать о тебе́, е́сли не могу́ переста́ть смотре́ть на твою́ фотогра́фию?

think: *the way I think about you*

I *(1)* **think /** *(2)* **thought about you in such a tender, loving way.** Я *(1)* ду́маю / *(2)* ду́мал *(ж: ду́мала)* о тебе́ с тако́й не́жностью и любо́вью. ♦ **I can't think about you without instantly feeling love for you.** Сто́ит то́лько поду́мать о тебе́, как то́тчас чу́вство любви́ возника́ет во мне. ♦ **I've been sending you brainwaves all** *(1)* **day /** *(2)* **week long. Surely**

The time zones for many cities of the world
are given in Appendix 6, page 761.

you've gotten some of them. And if you have, then you know how *(3)* tenderly / *(4)* warmly I've been thinking about you. Я *(1)* ...весь день... / *(2)* ...всю неделю... посылаю тебе мозговые волны. Несомненно ты получила *(ж: получил)* некоторые из них. И если ты получила *(ж: получил)*, тогда ты знаешь, как *(3)* нежно / *(4)* тепло я думаю о тебе.

think: *what I feel when I think about you*

Oh, God, whenever I think about you, my throat gets tight, my head gets dizzy, and my knees feel *(1)* **weak** / *(2)* **wobbly.** Боже мой, когда бы я ни подумал *(ж: подумала)* о тебе, комок подходит к горлу, голова кружится и *(1)* ...подкашиваются ноги. / *(2)* ... дрожат колени. ♦ **Whenever I think about you, my body trembles in anticipation.** Когда бы я ни подумал *(ж: подумала)* о тебе, моё тело трепещет в предвкушении. ♦ **I smile to myself thinking of you.** Я улыбаюсь, думая о тебе. ♦ **A flare of desire bursts inside of me any time I even think of you.** Огонь желания вспыхивает во мне, как только я подумаю о тебе. ♦ **It's hard for me to think of you without wanting to hold you tenderly in my arms and kiss you and kiss you and kiss you — ever so lovingly and ever so adoringly.** Мне трудно думать о тебе без желания держать тебя нежно в объятиях и целовать, и целовать, и целовать очень любяще и очень обожающе. ♦ **It makes me tingle all over to think about it.** Сама мысль об этом заставляет меня всего *(ж: всю)* трепетать. ♦ **My heart goes out of control every time I think about you.** Моё сердце выходит из под контроля, когда бы я ни подумал *(ж: подумала)* о тебе. ♦ **If you hear something that sounds like faraway drums, it's just the rapid beat of my heart as I think about you.** Если ты услышишь нечто, звучащее как отдалённый барабан, это только учащённое биение моего сердца, когда я думаю о тебе. ♦ **I get a fluttery feeling in my stomach whenever I think about you.** Моё сердце трепещет всякий раз, когда бы я ни подумал *(ж: подумала)* о тебе.

think: *other phrases*

Do you (really) think so? Ты (действительно) так думаешь? ♦ **I think so.** Думаю, что да. ♦ **I don't think so.** Думаю, что нет. ♦ **Tell me what you think.** Скажи мне, что ты думаешь. ♦ **I have to think about it (carefully).** Мне нужно (хорошо) подумать об этом. ♦ **Please don't think bad about me.** Пожалуйста, не думай плохо обо мне.

thinker *n* мыслитель *m*, думающий (-ая, -ие), размышляющий (-ая, -ие) ♦ **global** *(1,2)*~ *(1)* думающий (-ая, -ие) / *(2)* размышляющий (-ая, -ие) о мировых проблемах ♦ ~ - **doer** думающий и делающий человек.

thinness *n* худоба.

thirst *vi* жаждать *(for what = gen.)* ♦ ~ **for happiness** жаждать счастья.

thirst *n* жажда ♦ ~ **for life** жажда жизни.

thirsty *adj* жаждущий, -ая, -ее, -ие; томимый (-ая, -ое, -ые) жаждой ♦ **I'm thirsty.** Мне хочется пить. ♦ **My heart is thirsty for your kisses.** Моё сердце жаждет твоих поцелуев.

thirtyish *adj (around 30)* около тридцати; *(over 30)* за тридцать.

thong *n* ремень *m*.

thought *n* мысль *f (about what, whom* = + о + *prep.)* ♦ **all my** ~s все мои мысли ♦ **brilliant** ~ блестящая мысль ♦ **constant** ~ постоянная мысль ♦ **deep** ~ глубокая мысль ♦ **dejected** ~s унылые думы ♦ **erotic** ~s эротические мысли ♦ **every** ~ каждая мысль ♦ **gloomy** ~s мрачные мысли ♦ **great** ~ великолепная мысль ♦ **happy** ~ счастливая мысль ♦ *(1,2)* **horrible** ~ *(1)* ужасная / *(2)* страшная мысль ♦ **interesting** ~ интересная мысль ♦ **intimate** ~s интимные мысли ♦ **jealous** ~s ревнивые мысли ♦ **just the** ~ **of you** просто мысль о тебе ♦ **lascivious** ~s похотливые мысли ♦ **love** ~s любовные

Optional parts of sentences are preceded
or followed (or both) by three dots.

мы́сли ♦ **mere** ~ проста́я мысль ♦ **nagging** ~ навя́зчивая мысль ♦ **nice** ~**s** хоро́шие мы́сли ♦ **original** ~ оригина́льная мысль ♦ **painful** ~**s** тя́гостные мы́сли ♦ **relentless** ~ неотсту́пная мысль ♦ **salacious** ~**s** непристо́йные мы́сли ♦ **secret** ~**s** та́йные мы́сли ♦ *(1,2)* **sudden** ~ *(1)* неожи́данная / *(2)* внеза́пная мысль ♦ **tender** ~ не́жная мысль ♦ *(1,2)* **terrible** ~ *(1)* ужа́сная / *(2)* стра́шная мысль ♦ **terrific** ~ великоле́пная мысль ♦ **the very** ~ **of you** сама́ мысль о тебе́ ♦ ~**s full of love** мы́сли, напо́лненные любо́вью *(1 term)* ♦ **touching** ~**s** тро́гательные слова́ ♦ **warm** ~**s** тёплые мы́сли ♦ **wicked** ~**s** нечести́вые мы́сли ♦ **express** *(1)* **my** / *(2)* **your** ~**s** выража́ть / вы́разить *(1,2)* свои́ мы́сли ♦ **write down** *(1)* **my** / *(2)* **your** ~**s** запи́сывать / записа́ть *(1,2)* свои́ мы́сли.

---
thought: *you're in my thoughts*

You are the cynosure of all my thoughts. Ты путево́дная звезда́ всех мои́х мы́слей. ♦ **All my thoughts are filled with love pictures of you.** Все мои́ мы́сли полны́ любо́вными карти́нами о тебе́. ♦ **My thoughts are constantly with you.** Мои́ мы́сли постоя́нно с тобо́й. ♦ **My thoughts constantly drift over to you.** Мои́ мы́сли постоя́нно обраща́ются к тебе́. ♦ **My thoughts have been riveted on you** *(1)* **...since I met you.** / *(2)* **...all day** / *(3)* **week long.** Мои́ мы́сли прико́ваны к тебе́ *(1)* ...с тех пор, как мы встре́тились. / *(2)* ...весь день. / *(3)* ...всю неде́лю. ♦ **My mind is filled with thoughts of you every moment from the time I wake up.** С са́мого моего́ пробужде́ния ка́ждое мгнове́ние все мои́ мы́сли запо́лнены тобо́й. ♦ **I cannot even breath without a thought of you.** Я не могу́ да́же дыша́ть без мы́сли о тебе́. ♦ **My last waking thoughts and all of my dreams are of you.** Мои́ после́дние мы́сли пе́ред сном и все мои́ мечты́ о тебе́. ♦ **My thoughts are constantly drawn to you.** Все мои́ мы́сли постоя́нно о тебе́. ♦ **Everywhere I've gone today, thoughts of you have followed me as if fastened to my head.** Повсю́ду, где бы я ни был *(ж: была́)* сего́дня, мы́сли о тебе́ сле́довали за мной, как привя́занные к мое́й голове́. ♦ **It's not an exaggeration to say that you come into my thoughts at least 50 times a day.** Не бу́дет преувеличе́нием сказа́ть, что ты прихо́дишь в мои́ мы́сли по ме́ньшей ме́ре 50 *(пятьдеся́т)* раз в день.

---
thought: *your vision haunts my thoughts*

The vision of your (alluring, sexy) *(1)* **beauty** / *(2)* **loveliness** *(3)* **...bedevils my thoughts night and day.** / *(4)* **...overwhelms all other thoughts in my mind.** Виде́ние твое́й (зама́нивающей, сексуа́льной) *(1,2)* красоты́ *(3)* ...му́чает меня́ но́чью и днём. / *(4)* ...пода́вля́ет все други́е мы́сли. ♦ **The unsurpassed beauty of your face reigns over all my thoughts.** Непревзойдённая красота́ твоего́ лица́ вла́ствует над все́ми мои́ми по́мыслами. ♦ **I can never shut you out of my thoughts.** Ты всегда́ бу́дешь в мои́х мы́слях. ♦ **I know for sure that your beautiful eyes and face will monopolize my thoughts and dreams in the days ahead.** Я соверше́нно уве́рен, что твои́ прекра́сные глаза́ и лицо́ запо́лнят все мои́ мы́сли и мечты́ на бу́дущие дни.

---
thought: *your name is in my thoughts*

Your (precious) name reverberates *(1)* **through** / *(2)* **in my thoughts like a sacred chant intoned in awed reverence.** Твоё (драгоце́нное) и́мя э́хом отзыва́ется *(1,2)* в мои́х мы́слях, как свяще́нная песнь, интони́рованная с благогове́йным почте́нием. ♦ **Just the thought of your name turns on desire in my body like a light switch.** Про́сто мысль о твоём и́мени включа́ет страсть в моём те́ле, как выключа́тель свет.

---
thought: *you write touching thoughts*

You write me such touching thoughts that I am at a loss to describe my feelings. Ты пи́шешь мне таки́е тро́гательные слова́, что я не в си́лах описа́ть свои́ чу́вства. ♦ **No one has ever written such touching thoughts to me.** Никто́ никогда́ не писа́л мне таки́х тро́гательных слов.

> *If you're not on familiar terms with a person,*
> *the «ты» forms will have to be changed to «Вы».*

thought: *your thought patterns*

The thought patterns that yielded your choice of words and sentences in your ad reveal the exact same raging hunger for love and affection that I harbor within me. Мы́сли, роди́вшие вы́бор слов и предложе́ний в Ва́шем объявле́нии, говоря́т о то́чно тако́й же неи́стовой жа́жде любви́ и не́жности, кото́рая таи́тся во мне.

thought: *thoughts of you brighten my day*

Thoughts of you *(1)* **sparkle /** *(2)* **brighten up my day.** Мы́сли о тебе́ *(1)* озаря́ют / *(2)* освеща́ют мой день. ♦ **Nothing** *(1)* **sparkles /** *(2)* **brightens up my day like thoughts of you.** Ничто́ так не *(1)* озаря́ет / *(2)* освеща́ет мой день, как мы́сли о тебе́.

thought: *loving thoughts of you*

I have such *(1)* **warm /** *(2)* **tender, loving thoughts** *(3)* **about /** *(4)* **of you.** Мои́ мы́сли *(3,4)* о тебе́ напо́лнены тако́й *(1)* теплото́й / *(2)* не́жностью и любо́вью. ♦ **I paint love pictures to you in all my thoughts.** Я рису́ю карти́ны любви́ с тобо́й во всех свои́х мы́слях. ♦ **From far away I send you an endless stream of loving thoughts.** Издалека́ я посыла́ю тебе́ бесконе́чный пото́к любо́вных мы́слей. ♦ **I'll be thinking of you — warm, tender, affectionate thoughts, full of love.** Мои́ мы́сли о тебе́ бу́дут тёплыми, не́жными и напо́лненными любо́вью.

thought: *how thoughts of you affect me*

My heart races (wildly) at the thought of seeing you. Моё се́рдце (бе́шено) коло́тится от мы́сли о встре́че с тобо́й. ♦ **My heart ignites in** *(1)* **celebration /** *(2)* **delight /** *(3)* **ecstasy /** *(4)* **jubilation at the mere thought of you.** Моё се́рдце *(1)* ...загора́ется ра́достью / *(2)* восто́ргом... / *(3)* ...вспы́хивает в экста́зе... / *(4)* ...лику́ет... от просто́й мы́сли о тебе́. ♦ **Forgive me for writing such a steamy letter, but my thoughts of you mixed together with my feelings for you arouse passions in me that are difficult to contain.** Прости́ меня́ за тако́е чу́вственное письмо́, но мои́ мы́сли о тебе́ и чу́вства к тебе́ пробужда́ют во мне страсть, кото́рую тру́дно сдержа́ть. ♦ **The very thought of you sets my heart** *(1)* **aquiver /** *(2)* **aflame.** Сама́ мысль о тебе́ *(1)* ...заставля́ет моё се́рдце трепета́ть. / *(2)* ...наполня́ет моё се́рдце огнём. ♦ **I go away from any encounter with you with my heart spinning wildly and my mind erupting in a fireworks display of love thoughts about you.** По́сле ка́ждой встре́чи с тобо́й я ухожу́ с бе́шено стуча́щим се́рдцем и с це́лым фейерве́рком любо́вных мы́слей о тебе́. ♦ **Your magical green eyes flecked with gold have subjugated all my thoughts.** Твои́ волше́бные зелёные глаза́ с золоты́ми кра́пинками взя́ли в плен все мои́ мы́сли. ♦ **The fierce** *(1)* **passion /** *(2)* **desire I feel for you dominates all my thoughts and attention.** *(1)* Неи́стовая страсть к тебе́... / *(2)* Неи́стовое жела́ние тебя́... госпо́дствует над все́ми мои́ми мы́слями и внима́нием.

thought: *how thoughts of you affect me*

My thoughts go back again and again to our wonderful love-making sessions. Мои́ мы́сли опя́ть и опя́ть возвраща́ются к замеча́тельному вре́мени на́шей бли́зости. ♦ **I try not to be so primitive and carnal in my thoughts about you, but I simply can't help it.** Я пыта́юсь не быть столь первобы́тным и чу́вственным, ду́мая о тебе́, но мне э́то про́сто не удаётся. ♦ **I hope you won't be mad at me when I tell you that I no longer have any thoughts about you that are not erotic.** Я наде́юсь, что ты не рассе́рдишься на меня́, когда́ я скажу́, что у меня́ не оста́лось никаки́х други́х мы́слей о тебе́, кро́ме эроти́ческих.

thought: *penny for your thoughts*

A penny for your thoughts. Что ты ду́маешь?

thought: *quotation*

"One rose, one tender thought of you." *Movie: "Darling Lily"* «Одна́ ро́за -- одна́ не́жная

A list of common places with their grammatical endings is given in Appendix 7, page 763.

мысль о тебе́.» *Фильм «Дорога́я Лили́»*

thoughtful *adj* внима́тельный, -ая, -ое, -ые, забо́тливый, -ая, -ое, -ые, предупреди́тельный, -ая, -ое, -ые ♦ **That was a very thoughtful gesture.** Это был о́чень внима́тельный жест. ♦ **That was so thoughtful of you.** Это бы́ло о́чень внима́тельно с твое́й стороны́. ♦ **Thank you for being so thoughtful.** Спаси́бо за то, что ты была́ так внима́тельна *(ж: был так внима́телен).* ♦ **You are such a thoughtful person.** Ты тако́й внима́тельный челове́к. ♦ **You are so good and sweet and thoughtful and caring and loving.** Ты така́я хоро́шая *(ж: тако́й хоро́ший),* не́жная *(ж: не́жный),* внима́тельная *(ж: внима́тельный),* забо́тливая *(ж: забо́тливый)* и лю́бящая *(ж: лю́бящий).*

thoughtfulness *n* внима́ние; внима́тельность *f* ; забо́тливость *f* ♦ **I appreciate your thoughtfulness (very much).** Я (о́чень) ценю́ твоё внима́ние. ♦ **I must commend you on your thoughtfulness.** Я до́лжен *(ж: должна́)* похвали́ть тебя́ за твою́ внима́тельность. ♦ **You nourish my soul with your thoughtfulness.** Ты пита́ешь мою́ ду́шу свои́м внима́нием. ♦ **I admire you for your thoughtfulness.** Я восхища́юсь твое́й внима́тельностью.

thoughtless *adj* 1. *(inconsiderate)* невнима́тельный, -ая, -ое, -ые; 2. *(careless, unthinking)* беспе́чный, -ая, -ое, -ые, безду́мный, -ая, -ое, -ые, необду́манный, -ая, -ое, -ые.

thoughtlessness *n* 1. *(inconsiderateness)* невнима́тельность *f* ; 2. *(carelessness, not thinking)* беспе́чность *f,* необду́манность *f.*

threat *n* угро́за.

threaten *vt* угрожа́ть *(what, whom = dat.)* ♦ *(1)* **He** / *(2)* **She threatens to ...take our** *(3)* **son** / *(4)* **daughter** / *(5)* **children away from me.** / *(6)* **...kill me.** *(1)* Он / *(2)* Она́ угрожа́ет *(3)* ...забра́ть у меня́ сы́на / *(4)* до́чку / *(5)* дете́й. / *(6)* ...уби́ть меня́. ♦ **Don't threaten me.** Не угрожа́й мне. ♦ **I'm not threatening you.** Я не угрожа́ю тебе́.

threesome *n* три челове́ка вме́сте.

thrifty *adj* эконо́мный, -ая, -ое, -ые; бережли́вый, -ая, -ое, -ые.

thrill *vt* 1. возбужда́ть / возбуди́ть *(what, whom = acc.),* вызыва́ть / вы́звать тре́пет *(what, whom = dat.),* захва́тывать / захвати́ть *(what, whom = acc.);* охва́тывать / охвати́ть *(whom = acc.).*

| **thrill: phrases** |

Your dark exotic beauty thrills me through and through. Твоя́ сму́глая, экзоти́ческая красота́ возбужда́ет всё во мне. ♦ **The dark lambent flame in your eyes thrills me to the core of my being.** Тёмное сверка́ющее пла́мя твои́х глаз возбужда́ет меня́ всего́ *(ж: всю).* ♦ **You thrill me (**[1]**)...like no one ever has.** / **[2] ...through and through.** / **[3] ...to the very core.).** Ты возбужда́ешь меня́ (**[1]**...как никто́ никогда́. / **[2]** ...наскво́зь и наскво́зь. / **[3]** ...всего́ *[ж: всю]*.) ♦ **The exotic touch of your tongue thrills me through and through.** Экзоти́ческое прикоснове́ние твоего́ языка́ пронза́ет меня́ наскво́зь.

thrill *n* 1. *(tremulous)* (не́рвная) дрожь *f,* (не́рвный) тре́пет; (не́рвное) возбужде́ние; 2. *(emotional)* (глубо́кое) волне́ние ♦ **incomparable** ~ несравне́нный тре́пет ♦ **incredible** ~**s** невероя́тное возбужде́ние ♦ **joyous** ~ ра́достное возбужде́ние ♦ **sexual** ~**s** сексуа́льное возбужде́ние ♦ **sweet** ~**s** сла́дкий тре́пет ♦ ~ **of anticipation** тре́петное ожида́ние ♦ **youthful** ~ ю́ношеский тре́пет.

| **thrill: phrases** |

It brings a thrill to my heart whenever the *(1)* **thought** / *(2)* **vision of you creeps into my mind for even a second.** Моё се́рдце трепе́щет вся́кий раз, когда́ *(1)* ...мысль о тебе́... / *(2)* ...твой о́браз... возника́ет пе́редо мной хотя́ бы на мгнове́ние. ♦ **It's such a thrill to gaze into the dark irises of your eyes.** Тако́е возбужде́ние смотре́ть в тёмные зрачки́ твои́х глаз. ♦ **You give me such incredible thrills.** Ты вызыва́ешь во мне тако́е неверо-

---

Common adult heights are given in Appendix 9, page 776.

я́тное возбужде́ние. ♦ **I get a fluttery thrill all over when you do that.** Я весь *(ж: вся)* трепещу́, когда́ ты де́лаешь э́то. ♦ **My lips will send sweet thrills racing through your body.** Мои́ гу́бы пошлю́т сла́дкий тре́пет по всему́ твоему́ те́лу.

thrilled *adj (excited)* возбуждён, возбуждена́, -о́, -ы́ *(short forms)* ♦ *(1,2)* **be ~ 1.** *(1)* испы́тывать / *(2)* чу́вствовать возбужде́ние; 2. *(1)* испы́тывать / *(2)* чу́вствовать глубо́кое волне́ние ♦ *(1,2)* **feel ~** 1. *(1)* испы́тывать / *(2)* чу́вствовать возбужде́ние; 2. *(1)* испы́тывать / *(2)* чу́вствовать глубо́кое волне́ние ♦ **I look at your dark, exotic, sensual eyes and I am thrilled to the very center of my heart.** Я смотрю́ в твои́ тёмные экзоти́ческие, чу́вственные глаза́ и ощуща́ю си́льное волне́ние в своём се́рдце.

thrilling *adj* волну́ющий, -ая, -ее, -ие, захва́тывающий, -ая, -ее, -ие возбужда́ющий, -ая, -ее, -ие.

thrill-seeker *n* и́щущий *m* / и́щущая *f* возбужде́ния.

thrive *vi* процвета́ть; жить ♦ **I thrive on affection.** Я живу́ любо́вью.

throat *n* го́рло, «гло́тка» ♦ *(1)* **She /** *(2)* **He and I are at each other's throats all the time.** Мы с *(1)* ней / *(2)* ним постоя́нно пыта́емся перегры́зть друг дру́гу гло́тку. ♦ **I want to plant dozens of tiny, soft kisses all over the smooth column of your throat.** Я хочу́ покры́ть дю́жиной кро́шечных, не́жных поцелу́ев всю твою́ стро́йную, гла́дкую ше́ю. ♦ **I long to adore the tender grace of your throat with my lips.** Я стра́стно хочу́ губа́ми ощути́ть не́жную грацио́зность твое́й ше́и. ♦ **And then my lips would adore the** *(1)* **creamy /** *(2)* **smooth column of your throat with soft, loving kisses.** А пото́м мои́ гу́бы покро́ют твою́ *(1)* кре́мовую / *(2)* гла́дкую стро́йную ше́ю мя́гкими, любя́щими поцелу́ями.

throb *vi* трепета́ть, пульси́ровать.

through *prep* че́рез, сквозь ♦ *(1)* **Talking to you... /** *(2)* **Hearing your voice... on the phone (just) warms me through and through.** *(1)* Разгово́р с тобо́й... / *(2)* Звук твоего́ го́лоса... по телефо́ну наполня́ет меня́ тепло́м. ♦ **The words you wrote in your letter warmed me through and through.** Слова́ твоего́ письма́ напо́лнили меня́ тепло́м.

throw *vt* броса́ть / бро́сить *(what = acc., to whom = dat.)* ♦ **~ me off balance** выводи́ть / вы́вести меня́ из равнове́сия ♦ **~ oneself** *vi* броса́ться / бро́ситься, отдава́ть / отда́ть себя́ ♦ **~ over** броса́ть / бро́сить *(whom = acc.)*.

┌ *throw off balance:* ┐
You (really) throw me off balance with your wide-eyed innocence. Ты (действи́тельно) выво́дишь меня́ из равнове́сия свое́й наи́вной неви́нностью.

┌ *throw oneself:* ┐
You throw yourself at every man *(woman)* **within reach.** Ты броса́ешься на ка́ждого мужчи́ну *(ж: ка́ждую же́нщину)* в преде́лах досяга́емости. ♦ **I was wrong to throw myself at you (the way I did).** Я ошиба́лся *(ж: ошиба́лась)*, отда́в себя́ тебе́ (таки́м о́бразом).

┌ *throw over:* ┐
She threw me over. Она́ бро́сила меня́. ♦ **He threw me over.** Он бро́сил меня́.

thrust *vt* сова́ть / су́нуть *(what = acc., into what = + в + acc.)*; засо́вывать / засу́нуть*(what = acc., into what = + в + acc.)*, всо́вывать / всу́нуть *(what = acc., into what = + в + acc.)*.

thudding *n* бие́ние ♦ **I was sure you would hear the (** *[1]* **rapid /** *[2]* **wild) thudding of my heart (when** *[3]* **...we met /** *[4]* **danced. /** *[5]* **...I stood next to you.).** Я был уве́рен *(ж: была́ уве́рена)*, что ты слы́шала *(ж: слы́шал)* (*[1]* бы́строе / *[2]* ди́кое) бие́ние моего́ се́рдца (, когда́ *[3]* ...мы встре́тились / *[4]* танцева́ли. / *[5]* ...я стоя́л *[ж: стоя́ла]* ря́дом с тобо́й.)

thumb *n* большо́й па́лец.

Words in parentheses are optional.

Thursday *n* четве́рг ♦ **by** ~ к четвергу́ ♦ **last** ~ в про́шлый четве́рг ♦ **next** ~ в сле́дующий четве́рг ♦ **on** ~ в четве́рг.

tiara *n* тиа́ра ♦ **pearl** ~ жемчу́жная тиа́ра ♦ **wedding** ~ сва́дебная тиа́ра.

ticket *n* биле́т ♦ **ballet** ~(s) биле́т(ы) на бале́т ♦ **bus** ~ авто́бусный биле́т ♦ **concert** ~(s) биле́т(ы) на конце́рт ♦ **extra** ~ ли́шний биле́т ♦ **movie** ~(s) биле́т(ы) на фильм ♦ **plane** ~(s) биле́т(ы) на самолёт ♦ **theater** ~(s) биле́т(ы) в теа́тр ♦ **train** ~(s) биле́т(ы) на по́езд ♦ **buy (a)** ~(s) купи́ть биле́т(ы) ♦ **get (a)** ~(s) доста́ть биле́т(ы) ♦ **order (a)** ~(s) заказа́ть биле́т(ы) ♦ **How much does a ticket cost?** Ско́лько сто́ит биле́т? ♦ **A ticket costs 50 rubles.** Биле́т сто́ит пятьдеся́т (50) рубле́й. ♦ **This is just the ticket.** Это как раз то, что ну́жно.

tide *n* 1. *(ocean) (incoming)* прили́в; *(outgoing)* отли́в; 2. *(feelings)* пото́к ♦ ~ **of passion** прили́в стра́сти ♦ **When I have you in my arms, I'm going to arouse tides of sweet feeling in you that will sweep you into a storm of passion.** Когда́ я заключу́ тебя́ в объя́тия, я разбужу́ в тебе́ пото́к не́жных чу́вств, кото́рый бро́сит тебя́ в бу́рю стра́сти.

tie *n* 1. у́зел; *pl: (bonds)* у́зы; 2. *(necktie)* га́лстук ♦ **broken t~s** обо́рванные свя́зи ♦ **I have no ties.** У меня́ нет уз. ♦ **I have family ties.** У меня́ есть семе́йные у́зы.

tiger *n* тигр ♦ **I'm a warm, loving tiger.** Я тёплый, любя́щий тигрёнок.

tight *adj* 1. *(tightly closed)* пло́тный, -ая, -ое, -ые; 2. *(tight-fitting)* те́сный, -ая, -ое, -ые, у́зкий, -ая, -ое, -ие, облега́ющий, -ая, -ее, -ие, пло́тно обтя́гивающий, -ая, -ее, -ие; 3. *(slang) (drunk)* пья́ный, -ая, -ое, -ые ♦ ~ **vagina** те́сное влага́лище.

tights *n, pl (women's tight pants)* колго́тки.

tigress *n* тигри́ца ♦ **You're a little tigress.** Ты ма́ленькая тигри́ца.

tilt *vt* наклоня́ть / наклони́ть *(what = acc.).*

time *n* 1. *(general)* вре́мя; 2. *(instance)* раз ♦ *(1,2)* **additional** ~ *(1)* доба́вочное / *(2)* допол- ни́тельное вре́мя ♦ **a few** ~**s** не́сколько раз ♦ **agreed-upon** ~ усло́вленное вре́мя ♦ **all the** ~ всё вре́мя, всегда́; *(constantly)* постоя́нно ♦ **a long** ~ до́лго ♦ **a long** ~ **ago** давно́ ♦ **ample** ~ бо́лее чем доста́точно вре́мени ♦ **another** ~ друго́й раз, друго́е вре́мя ♦ **any** ~ любо́е вре́мя ♦ **appointed** ~ назна́ченное вре́мя ♦ **approximate** ~ приблизи́тель- ное вре́мя ♦ **arrival** ~ вре́мя прие́зда ♦ **a short** ~ не до́лго ♦ **awful** ~ ужа́сное вре́мя ♦ **bad** ~ плохо́е вре́мя ♦ **blissful** ~ блаже́нное вре́мя ♦ **certain** ~ определённое вре́мя ♦ **convenient** ~ удо́бное вре́мя ♦ **correct** ~ пра́вильное вре́мя ♦ **definite** ~ определённое вре́мя ♦ **departure** ~ вре́мя отъе́зда ♦ **difficult** ~ тру́дное вре́мя ♦ **each** ~ ка́ждый раз ♦ **enough** ~ доста́точно вре́мени ♦ **evening** ~ вече́рное вре́мя ♦ **every** ~ ка́ждый раз ♦ **exact** ~ то́чное вре́мя ♦ *(1,2)* **extra** ~ *(1)* доба́вочное / *(2)* дополни́тельное вре́мя ♦ **fabulous** ~ потряса́ющее вре́мя ♦ *(1,2)* **fantastic** ~ *(1)* фантасти́ческое / *(2)* велико- ле́пное вре́мя ♦ **favorable** ~ благоприя́тное вре́мя ♦ **free** ~ свобо́дное вре́мя ♦ **fun** ~ весёлое вре́мя ♦ **good** ~ хоро́шее вре́мя ♦ *(1,2)* **great** ~ *(1)* замеча́тельное / *(2)* отли́ч- ное вре́мя ♦ **happy** ~ счастли́вое вре́мя ♦ **heavenly** ~ боже́ственное вре́мя ♦ **how many** ~**s** ско́лько раз ♦ **idyllic** ~ идилли́ческое вре́мя ♦ **incredible** ~ невероя́тное вре́мя ♦ **lack of** ~ отсу́тствие вре́мени ♦ **last** ~ в про́шлый раз ♦ **leisure** ~ свобо́дное вре́мя ♦ **little** ~ ма́ло вре́мени ♦ **local** ~ ме́стное вре́мя ♦ *(1-3)* **long** ~ *(1)* до́лгое / *(2)* дли́тельное вре́мя, *(3)* нема́ло вре́мени ♦ **lousy** ~ ме́рзкое вре́мя ♦ **lovely** ~ о́чень хоро́шее вре́мя ♦ **magical** ~ волше́бное вре́мя ♦ **magnificent** ~ великоле́пное вре́мя ♦ **many** ~**s** мно́го раз ♦ **marvelous** ~ замеча́тельное вре́мя ♦ **meeting** ~ *(time to meet)* вре́мя встре́чи ♦ **Moscow** ~ моско́вское вре́мя ♦ **next** ~ (в) сле́дующий раз ♦ **not enough** ~ недоста́точно вре́мени ♦ **no** ~ нет вре́мени ♦ **not much** ~ ма́ло вре́мени ♦ **one** ~ оди́н раз ♦ **private** ~ ли́чное вре́мя ♦ **rest** ~ вре́мя для о́тдыха ♦ **romantic** ~**s** романти́ческие времена́ ♦ **sad** ~ печа́льное вре́мя ♦ **St. Petersburg** ~ санкт-

---

You can find common clothing sizes in Appendix 11 on page 778.

петербу́ргское вре́мя ♦ **short** ~ коро́ткое вре́мя ♦ **some other** ~ в друго́й раз ♦ **spare** ~ свобо́дное вре́мя ♦ **suitable** ~ подходя́щее вре́мя ♦ **terrible** ~ ужа́сное вре́мя ♦ **this** ~ в э́тот раз ♦ ~ **of day** вре́мя су́ток ♦ ~ **of the month** *(menstrual period)* менструа́ция ♦ ~ **of year** вре́мя го́да ♦ ~ **to** *(1,2)* **think** вре́мя на *(1)* размышле́ние / *(2)* обду́мывание ♦ **two** ~**s** два ра́за ♦ **unforgettable** ~ незабыва́емое вре́мя ♦ **vacation** ~ вре́мя о́тпуска; *(school)* вре́мя кани́кул ♦ **wasted** ~ поте́рянное вре́мя ♦ **waste of** ~ поте́ря вре́мени, пуста́я тра́та вре́мени ♦ **what** ~ како́е вре́мя ♦ **whole** ~ всё вре́мя ♦ *(1,2)* **work(ing)** ~ *(1)* рабо́чее / *(2)* служе́бное вре́мя ♦ *(1,2)* **wonderful** ~ *(1)* удиви́тельное / *(2)* замеча́тельное вре́мя.

time: *verb terms*

cherish the ~ дорожи́ть вре́менем ♦ **choose a** ~ выбира́ть / вы́брать вре́мя ♦ **devote** ~ уделя́ть / удели́ть вре́мя *(to what, whom = dat.)* ♦ **enjoy good** ~**s (together)** наслажда́ться хоро́шим вре́менем (, проведённым вме́сте) ♦ **find** ~ найти́ вре́мя ♦ **have a good** ~ хорошо́ проводи́ть / провести́ вре́мя, весели́ться / повесели́ться ♦ **have** ~ и́меть вре́мя *(I have time:* у меня́ есть вре́мя. *You have time:* у тебя́ есть вре́мя.*)* ♦ **not have** ~ не име́ть вре́мени *(I don't have time:* у меня́ нет вре́мени. *You don't have time:* у тебя́ нет вре́мени.*)* ♦ **save** ~ эконо́мить / сэконо́мить вре́мя ♦ **scrounge (up) the** ~ выкра́ивать / вы́кроить вре́мя ♦ **set a** ~ назнача́ть / назна́чить вре́мя ♦ **share intimate** ~**s** вме́сте наслажда́ться инти́мным вре́менем ♦ **share** ~ проводи́ть / провести́ вре́мя вме́сте ♦ **spend** ~ проводи́ть / провести́ вре́мя ♦ **use** ~ испо́льзовать вре́мя ♦ **wait for the** ~ ждать вре́мени ♦ **waste** ~ теря́ть / потеря́ть вре́мя.

time: *other terms*

(1,2) **all kinds of** ~ *(1)* ма́сса / *(2)* у́йма вре́мени ♦ **a lot of** ~ мно́го вре́мени ♦ **at a** ~ *(simultaneously)* одновреме́нно, за оди́н раз ♦ **at any** ~ в любо́е вре́мя ♦ **at no** ~ никогда́ ♦ **at that** ~ в то вре́мя ♦ **at the present** ~ в настоя́щее вре́мя ♦ **at the same** ~ в то же са́мое вре́мя ♦ **at the** ~ тогда́ ♦ **at this** ~ в э́то вре́мя ♦ **at** ~**s** вре́мя от вре́мени, времена́ми ♦ **by Moscow** ~ по моско́вскому вре́мени ♦ **by that** ~ к тому́ вре́мени ♦ **by this** ~ к э́тому вре́мени ♦ **for the first** ~ впервы́е ♦ **for the** ~ **being** пока́ ♦ **from** ~ **to** ~ вре́мя от вре́мени, времена́ми ♦ **in** ~ 1. *(after a time)* со вре́менем; 2. *(on time)* во́время ♦ *(1,2)* **loads of** ~ *(1)* ма́сса / *(2)* у́йма вре́мени ♦ **lots of** ~ мно́го вре́мени ♦ **lots of** ~**s** мно́го раз ♦ **on** ~ во́время ♦ **since that** ~ с тех пор ♦ ~ **difference** ра́зница во вре́мени ♦ ~ **interval** промежу́ток вре́мени ♦ *(1,2)* **tons of** ~ *(1)* ма́сса / *(2)* у́йма вре́мени.

time: *what time?*

(1,2) **At what time?** *(1)* В како́е вре́мя? / *(2)* В кото́ром часу́? ♦ *(1,2)* **What time** *(3,4)* ...**will you come?** / *(5,6)* ...**shall I come?** / *(7)* ...**do you finish work?** / *(8)* ...**do you get off work?** / *(9)* ...**shall we meet?** / *(10)* ...**will you be there?** / *(11)* ...**shall I call?** / *(12)* ...**will you call?** / *(13)* ...**will the bus** / *(14)* **train** / *(15)* **flight** *(16)* **arrive** / *(17)* **depart?** / *(18-20)* ...**does it** *(21)* **open** / *(22)* **close?** *(1)* Когда́... / *(2)* В како́е вре́мя... ...ты *(3)* *(on foot:)* придёшь / *(4)* *(by veh.:)* прие́дешь? / *(5)* ......до́лжен *(ж: должна́)* я *(on foot:)* прийти́ / *(6)* *(by veh.:)* прие́хать? / *(7)* ...ты ко́нчишь рабо́ту? / *(8)* ...ты уйдёшь с рабо́ты? / *(9)* ...мы встре́тимся? *(10)* ...ты бу́дешь там? / *(11)* ...до́лжен *(ж: должна́)* я позвони́ть? / *(12)* ...ты бу́дешь звони́ть? / *(16)* ...прибу́дет / *(17)* отпра́вится *(13)* авто́бус / *(14)* по́езд / *(15)* самолёт? / ...*(18)* он *m* / *(19)* она́ *f* / *(20)* оно́ *neut* *(21)* открыва́ется / *(22)* закрыва́ется? ♦ **At** *(1)* **one** / *(2)* **two** / *(3)* **three** / *(4)* **four** / *(5)* **five** / *(6)* **six** / *(7)* **seven** / *(8)* **eight** / *(9)* **nine** / *(10)* **ten** / *(11)* **eleven** / *(12)* **twelve o'clock** / **(thirty).** В *(1)* час / *(2)* два / *(3)* три / *(4)* четы́ре / *(5)* пять / *(6)* шесть / *(7)* семь / *(8)* во́семь / *(9)* де́вять / *(10)* де́сять / *(11)* оди́ннадцать / *(12)* двена́дцать (три́дцать). ♦ **It's time.** Пора́.

For general rules of Russian grammar see Appendix 2 on page 686.

---

time: have time

Do you have time? У тебя́ есть вре́мя? ♦ **I have time.** У меня́ есть вре́мя. ♦ **I don't have time.** У меня́ нет вре́мени.

time: someone to share time with

I *(1,2)* **want someone to share** *(3)* **...quality time...** / *(4)* **...intimate times... with.** Я *(1)* хочу́ / *(2)* ищу́ челове́ка для *(3)* хоро́шего / *(4)* инти́много вре́мяпрепровожде́ния. ♦ **I need someone to share the good and bad times.** Мне ну́жен тот, кто бу́дет дели́ть со мной ра́дости и печа́ли. ♦ **I'm looking for someone to share fun times with.** Я ищу́ кого́-нибудь, что́бы вме́сте развлека́ться. ♦ **If you're looking for someone who likes to laugh and have a good time, then write to me.** Если Вы и́щете того́, кто лю́бит смех и хоро́шее вре́мяпрепровожде́ние, тогда́ напиши́те мне.

time: spending time with you

I *(1)* **love** / *(2)* **enjoy spending time with you.** Я *(1)* ...люблю́ проводи́ть вре́мя... / *(2)* ...наслажда́юсь проведе́нием вре́мени... с тобо́й. ♦ **The time we share (together) is** *(1)* **...so precious to me.** / *(2)* **...always special.** Вре́мя, кото́рое мы прово́дим вме́сте, *(1)* ...так до́рого для меня́. / *(2)* ...всегда́ осо́бенное. ♦ **I love the time we share together.** Мне нра́вится вре́мя, кото́рое мы прово́дим вме́сте. ♦ **I feel comfortable spending time with you.** Мне так прия́тно проводи́ть вре́мя с тобо́й. ♦ **It was such an idyllic time with you.** Вре́мя, проведённое с тобо́й, бы́ло идилли́ческим. ♦ **For me, to think of spending time with you in the same house is like imagining what Paradise would be like.** Для меня́ ду́мать о том, что́бы провести́ вре́мя с тобо́й в одно́м до́ме -- э́то воображ́ать, как бу́дет в раю́. ♦ **I want us (always) to spend a lot of time together.** Я хочу́, что́бы мы (всегда́) проводи́ли мно́го вре́мени вме́сте. ♦ **I'm eager to spend unforgettable time with you.** Я жа́жду провести́ с тобо́й незабыва́емое вре́мя. ♦ **It would be nice to share time together.** Бы́ло бы так прия́тно провести́ вре́мя вме́сте.

time: the memory of times shared

The memory of the times we spent together will last forever. Па́мять о вре́мени, проведённом вме́сте, сохрани́тся навсегда́. ♦ **I will always treasure the memory of the wonderful time we spent together.** Я бу́ду всегда́ дорожи́ть па́мятью о замеча́тельном вре́мени, кото́рое мы провели́ вме́сте. ♦ **The memories of those wonderful times (together) assail me night and day.** Воспомина́ния об э́том удиви́тельном вре́мени (, проведённом вме́сте,) не оставля́ют меня́ но́чью и днём.

time: time will have no effect

I'm sure that our love will stand the test of time. Я уве́рен *(ж: уве́рена)*, что на́ша любо́вь вы́держит испыта́ние вре́менем. ♦ **You have a** *(1)* **beauty** / *(2)* **loveliness that time can never** *(3)* **dim** / *(4)* **diminish.** Ты так *(1)* краси́ва / *(2)* милови́дна, что с года́ми твоя́ красота́ не мо́жет *(3)* потускне́ть / *(4)* уме́ньшиться. ♦ **Time and distance will never keep us apart.** Вре́мя и расстоя́ние никогда́ не разлуча́т нас.

time: some other time?

(1) **Can I see you...** / *(2)* **Can we meet... some other time?** *(1)* Могу́ я уви́деть тебя́... / *(2)* Мо́жем мы встре́титься... в друго́е вре́мя?

time: a great time

I had a *(1)* **(very) good** / *(2)* **fantastic** / *(3)* **marvelous** / *(4)* **great** / *(5)* **wonderful time.** Я *(1)* (о́чень) хорошо́ / *(2)* фантасти́чески / *(3,4)* великоле́пно / *(5)* прекра́сно провёл *(ж: провела́)* вре́мя.

time: the first time

Is this the first time for you? Э́то впервы́е для тебя́? ♦ **It's the first time for me.** Э́то впервы́е для меня́. ♦ **It's the first time that I've ever done this.** Впервы́е в свое́й жи́зни

For transitive Russian verbs the cases that they take are shown by means of an = sign and the Russian case. (abbreviated).

я занима́лся *(ж: занима́лась)* э́тим.

> *time: just in time*

You came just in time. Ты пришла́ *(ж: пришёл)* как раз во́время.

> *time: a matter of time*

It's only a matter of time. Это то́лько вопро́с вре́мени.

> *time: not even the time of day*

I wouldn't give *(1)* **him** / *(2)* **her the time of day.** Я не хочу́ име́ть с *(1)* ним / *(2)* ней ничего́ о́бщего.

> *time: make time*

I'm not just trying to make time with you. Я не пыта́юсь про́сто переспа́ть с тобо́й.

> *time: saying*

Time heals all wounds. Вре́мя зале́чивает все ра́ны.

timeless *adj* 1. *(endless, eternal)* бесконе́чный, -ая, -ое, -ые, ве́чный, -ая, -ое, -ые; *(constant)* постоя́нный, -ая, -ое, -ые; 2. *(not restricted to a certain time)* вневре́менный, -ая, -ое, -ые.

timid *adj* ро́бкий, -ая, -ое, -ие.

timidity *n* ро́бость *f* ♦ **girlish ~** деви́чья засте́нчивость.

timing *n* синхрониза́ция, согласо́ванное де́йствие, согласо́ванность *f*, уме́ние вы́брать подходя́щий моме́нт ♦ **Timing is everything.** Уме́ние вы́брать подходя́щий моме́нт -- э́то всё. ♦ **That was** *(1)* **perfect** / *(2)* **great** / *(3)* **bad** / *(4)* **lousy timing.** Что за *(1)* превос-хо́дная / *(2)* замеча́тельная / *(3)* плоха́я / *(4)* мёрзкая согласо́ванность.

timorous *adj* ро́бкий, -ая, -ое, -ие, о́чень боя́зливый, -ая, -ое, -ые.

tinged *adj* с отте́нком ♦ **~ with sadness** с отте́нком печа́ли.

tingle *vi* дрожа́ть, трепета́ть ♦ **Excitement just tingled through me when I** *(1)* **saw** / *(2)* **met** / *(3)* **kissed you.** Я трепета́л *(ж: трепета́ла)* от волне́ния, когда́ *(1)* уви́дел *(ж: уви́де-ла)* / *(2)* встре́тил *(ж: встре́тила)* / *(3)* поцелова́л *(ж: поцелова́ла)* тебя́. ♦ **You make me tingle (all over).** Ты заставля́ешь меня́ всего́ *(ж: всю)* трепета́ть. ♦ **It makes me tingle all over to think about it.** Сама́ мысль об э́том заставля́ет меня́ всего́ *(ж: всю)* трепета́ть.

tingle *n* пока́лывание, пощи́пывание, дрожь *f* ♦ **You make hot tingles run through my body (when you do that).** Ты заставля́ешь горя́чую дрожь пробега́ть по моему́ те́лу (когда́ де́лаешь э́то). ♦ **I'm going to make hot tingles run all through your body.** Я заста́влю горя́чую дрожь пробега́ть по всему́ твоему́ те́лу. ♦ **Hot tingles run through my body every time I think of you.** Жа́ркая дрожь пробега́ет по те́лу вся́кий раз, когда́ я ду́маю о тебе́. ♦ **When you do that, it gives me the tingles all over my body.** Когда́ ты де́лаешь э́то, всё моё те́ло прони́зывает дрожь.

tingling *adj* дрожа́щий, -ая, -ее, -ие, пока́лывающий, -ая, -ее, -ие, пощи́пывающий, -ая, -ее, -ие ♦ **With my lips I'm going to make tingling sensations ripple all through your body.** Мои́ гу́бы вы́зовут во́лны тре́пета, бегу́щие по всему́ твоему́ те́лу. ♦ *(1)* **A hot tingling sensation goes all through my body...** / *(2)* **I feel a hot tingling sensation... when-ever** *(3)* **...you come close to me.** / *(4)* **...you look at me.** / *(5)* **...I think about you.** *(1)* Жа́р-кая дрожь прони́зывает всё моё те́ло... / *(2)* Я чу́вствую жа́ркую дрожь... вся́кий раз, когда́ *(3)* ...ты приближа́ешься ко мне. / 4) ...ты смо́тришь на меня́. / *(5)* ...я ду́маю о тебе́.

tinglingly *adv* тре́петно, трепе́щуще ♦ **You make my body feel so tinglingly alive.** Благо-даря́ тебе́ моё те́ло стано́вится таки́м тре́петно живы́м.

tint *n* кра́ска ♦ **brow ~** кра́ска для брове́й.

tiny *adj* кро́хотный, -ая, -ое, -ые

Russian verbs have 2 forms: imperfective and perfective.
They're given in that order.

tip *n (breast)* кóнчик, рóзочка, бýсинка, бутóн; *(tongue)* кóнчик ♦ **coral ~ of the nipple** корáлловая бýсинка соскá, корáлловый бутóн соскá ♦ **luscious rosy ~s of the nipples** сóчные рóзочки сосков ♦ **rosy ~ of the breast** рóзовый кóнчик груди, рóзочка груди ♦ **soft ~ of the nipple** нéжная бýсинка соскá ♦ **~ of the tongue** кóнчик языкá ♦ **~s of the nipples** бутóнчики сосков ♦ **velvet ~ of the tongue** бархатúстый кóнчик языкá ♦ **I** *(1)* **love /** *(2)* **want to gently caress your breasts, lingering on the tips.** Я *(1)* люблю / *(2)* хочý нéжно ласкáть твою грудь, задéрживаясь на соскáх.

tipsy *adj* навеселé, под мýхой, подвыпивший, -ая, -ее, -ие ♦ **be ~** быть навеселé, быть под мýхой ♦ **get ~** подвыпить, пьянéть / опьянéть ♦ *(1,2)* **Are you tipsy?** *(1)* Ты под мýхой? / *(2)* Ты навеселé? ♦ **(I think) I'm tipsy.** (Кáжется,) я под мýхой. ♦ **I was tipsy.** Я был *(ж: былá)* навеселé. ♦ **I get tipsy easily.** Я легкó пьянéю. ♦ **I think I'm getting tipsy.** (Кáжется,) я пьянéю.

tirade *n* тирáда ♦ **endless ~** бесконéчная тирáда.

tired *adj* устáлый, -ая, -ое, -ые; утомлённый, -ая, -ое, -ые ♦ **~ expression** утомлённое выражéние ♦ **~ eyes** утомлённые глазá ♦ **be ~** уставáть / устáть *(I'm tired:* я устáл *[ж: устáла]. You're tired:* ты устáла *[ж: устáл].)* ♦ **be ~ of** уставáть / устáть *(I'm tired:* я устáл *[ж: устáла]. You're tired:* ты устáла *[ж: устáл].) (of what* = + от + *gen.)* ♦ **get ~** уставáть / устáть ♦ **I'm tired of being alone.** Я устал *(ж: устáла)* от одинóчества.

tireless *adj* неутомúмый, -ая, -ое, -ые

tirelessly *adv* не уставáя, без ýстали.

tiresome *adj* 1. *(irksome)* надоéдливый, -ая, -ое, -ые; 2. *(wearisome, boring)* утомúтельный, -ая, -ое, -ые, скýчный, -ая, -ое, -ые.

tissue *n* бумáжная салфéтка, бумáжный носовóй платóк ♦ **toilet ~** туалéтная бумáга.

TLC *abbrev* = **tender, loving care** любóвь и нéжность.

toad *n (slang) (repulsive person)* гáдина, жáба.

toast *vt* произносúть / произнестú тост *(what, whom* = + за + *acc.),* пить / выпить *(what, whom* = + за + *acc.)* ♦ **Let's toast the** *(1)* **beautiful /** *(2)* **charming bride.** Давáй выпьем за *(1)* прекрáсную / *(2)* очаровáтельную невéсту.

toast *n* тост ♦ **I propose a toast.** Я предлагáю тост.

today *n* сегóдня.

toe *n* пáльчик (на ногé) ♦ **I'd like to kneel in front of you, hold your foot in my hand, and softly caress your toes with my lips.** Я хотéл бы стоять пéред тобóй на колéнях, держáть твою ступню в рукé и мягко ласкáть губáми пáльчики на твоéй ногé.

toenail *n* нóготь на пáльце ноги *(pl:* нóгти на пáльцах ноги) ♦ **beautiful ~s** красúвые нóгти на пáльцах. ♦ **painted ~s** крáшеные нóгти на пáльцах.

together *adv* вмéсте *(with what, whom* = + с + *instr.)* ♦ **get back ~** воссоединяться / воссоединúться. ♦ **Together we can withstand whatever the world throws at us.** Вмéсте мы мóжем выстоять прóтив всегó, что преподнесёт нам жизнь. ♦ **I know that we will be together** *(1)* **soon /** *(2)* **again /** *(3)* **someday, and this** *(4)* **knowledge /** *(5)* **realization fortifies my** *(6)* **soul /** *(7)* **spirit.** Я знáю, что мы *(1)* скóро / *(2)* опять / *(3)* однáжды бýдем вмéсте, и *(4,5)* знáние это укрепляет *(6)* ...мою дýшу. / *(7)* ...мой дух.

togetherness *n* едúнство, единодýшие, духóвная блúзость *f* ♦ **constant ~** постоянная блúзость ♦ **What I** *(1)* **...want... /** *(2)* **...yearn for... most in a relationship is togetherness.** *(1)* Чегó я ...хочý... / *(2)* Чегó я ...жáжду... бóлее всегó в отношéниях -- это духóвной блúзости.

toilet *n* туалéт.

token *n* 1. *(symbol)* сúмвол, знак, 2. *(for subway, etc)* жетóн ♦ **love ~** залóг любвú; сúмвол / знак любвú ♦ *(1)* **This... /** *(2)* **This gift... is just a small token of my unending love for**

How to use the Cyrillic alphabet on the Internet
is the subject of Appendix 20 on page 789.

you. *(1)* Это... / *(2)* Этот пода́рок...-- то́лько ма́ленький знак мое́й несконча́емой любви́ к тебе́. ♦ **This gift is a tiny token of my love (and esteem) for you.** Этот пода́рок -- ма́ленький си́мвол мое́й любви́ (и уваже́ния) к тебе́.

tolerance *n* терпи́мость *f.*

tolerant *adj* терпи́мый, -ая, -ое, -ые.

tolerate *vt* терпе́ть *(what, whom = acc.).*

tomato *n (slang)* «пе́рсик», краси́вая де́вушка / же́нщина.

tomboy *n* сорване́ц.

tomorrow *n* за́втра.

tone *n* тон ♦ **chilly** ~ холо́дный тон ♦ **cool** ~ прохла́дный тон ♦ **deep** ~ глубо́кий тон ♦ **grave** ~ серьёзный тон ♦ **husky** ~ хри́плый тон ♦ **mellifluous** ~ сладкозву́чный тон ♦ **melodious** ~ мелоди́чный тон ♦ **no-nonsense** ~ стро́гий тон ♦ **quavering** ~ дрожа́щий тон ♦ **querulous** ~ жа́лобный го́лос ♦ **rich** ~ бога́тый тон ♦ **skin** ~ тон ко́жи ♦ **soft** ~ мя́гкий тон ♦ **stern** ~ стро́гий тон ♦ **sultry** ~ чу́вственный тон ♦ **warm** ~ тёплый тон.

tone: phrases

Your tone of voice didn't sound very friendly. Тон твоего́ го́лоса звуча́л не сли́шком дру́жески. ♦ **Your tone of voice was rather** *(1)* **chilly** / *(2)* **cool.** Тон твоего́ го́лоса был доста́точно *(1)* холо́дным / *(2)* прохла́дным. ♦ **I love the tone of your voice. It's so** *(1)* **warm** / *(2)* **rich** / *(3)* **melodious** / *(4)* **soft.** Мне нра́вится тон твоего́ го́лоса. Он тако́й *(1)* тёплый / *(2)* бога́тый / *(3)* мелоди́чный / *(4)* мя́гкий.

toned *adj* трениро́ванный, -ая, -ое, -ые, в хоро́шем физи́ческом состоя́нии ♦ **You have a** *(1)* **well** / *(2)* **superbly toned body.** У тебя́ *(1)* хоро́шее / *(2)* мускули́стое те́ло. ♦ **You have a nicely toned body.** У тебя́ хорошо́ трениро́ванное те́ло.

tongue *n* язы́к ♦ *(1,2)* **agile** ~ *(1)* чу́ткий / *(2)* ло́вкий язы́к ♦ **bold** ~ де́рзкий язы́к ♦ **daring** ~ де́рзкий язы́к ♦ **eager** ~ нетерпели́вый язы́к ♦ **insatiable** ~ ненасы́тный язы́к ♦ **insistent** ~ насто́йчивый язы́к ♦ **long** ~ дли́нный язы́к ♦ **loose** ~ небре́жный язы́к ♦ **masterful** ~ ма́стерский язы́к ♦ *(1,2)* **nimble** ~ *(1)* чу́ткий / *(2)* ло́вкий язы́к ♦ **pierced** ~ проко́лотый язы́к ♦ **probing** ~ прощу́пывающий язы́к ♦ **roving** ~ блужда́ющий язы́к ♦ **runaway** ~ *(careless)* небре́жный язы́к ♦ **sharp** ~ о́стрый язы́к ♦ **skilled** / **skillful** ~ уме́лый язы́к ♦ **talented** ~ тала́нтливый язы́к ♦ **(velvet) tip of the** ~ (бархати́стый) ко́нчик языка́.

tongue: my tongue in your mouth

I *(1)* **want** / *(2)* **love to** *(3)* **...caress your tongue with mine.** / *(4)* **...put my tongue in your mouth.** Я *(1)* хочу́ / *(2)* люблю́ *(3)* ...ласка́ть твой язы́к мои́м. / *(4)* ...класть язы́к в твой рот. ♦ **I love it when you part your lips and let my tongue go into your mouth.** Я люблю́, когда́ ты приоткрыва́ешь гу́бы и позволя́ешь моему́ языку́ войти́ в твой рот.

tongue: your tongue in my mouth

I love to feel your tongue in my mouth. Мне нра́вится чу́вствовать во рту твой язы́к. ♦ **When** *(1)* **my** / *(2)* **your tongue slid into** *(3)* **your** / *(4)* **my mouth,** *(5)* **...it was the most wonderful sensation I ever experienced.** / *(6)* **...sweet heat just poured through every part of me.** / *(7)* **...I almost melted away from ecstasy.** Когда́ *(1)* мой / *(2)* твой язы́к скользи́л в *(3)* твой / *(4)* мой рот *(5)* ...э́то бы́ло са́мым замеча́тельным ощуще́нием, испы́танным когда́-либо мной. / *(6)* ...сла́дкое тепло́ напо́лнило ка́ждую мою́ части́цу. / *(7)* ...я почти́ раста́ял *(ж: раста́яла)* от экста́за. ♦ **It's so sensuous to feel your tongue caress my lower lip.** Это так чу́вственно, когда́ твой язы́к ласка́ет мою́ ни́жнюю губу́.

Russian adjectives have long and short forms.
Where short forms are given, they are labeled as such.

tongue: the feel of your tongue

I love the feel of your tongue (there). Мне нра́вится ощуще́ние твоего́ языка́ (там). ♦ **The exotic touch of your tongue thrills me through and through.** Экзоти́ческое прикоснове́ние твоего́ языка́ пронза́ет меня́ насквозь.

tongue: what my tongue will do to you

When my lips and tongue revel on your beautiful, luscious body, they will hear your *(1)* **moans /** *(2)* **screams of** *(3)* **pleasure /** *(4)* **ecstasy in South Africa.** Когда́ мои́ гу́бы и язы́к бу́дут упива́ться твои́м прекра́сным, со́чным те́лом, твои́ *(1)* сто́ны / *(2)* кри́ки *(3)* наслажде́ния / *(4)* экста́за бу́дут слышны́ в Ю́жной А́фрике. ♦ **I'm going to caress every part of your body with my lips and my tongue.** Я бу́ду ласка́ть ка́ждую части́чку твоего́ те́ла губа́ми и языко́м. ♦ **My lips and tongue will give you no** *(1)* **peace /** *(2)* **rest.** Мои́ гу́бы и язы́к не даду́т тебе́ *(1)* поко́я / *(2)* о́тдыха. ♦ **I want to take off your panties with my tongue.** Я хочу́ снять с тебя́ тру́сики свои́м языко́м.

tongue: various phrases

We'll start tongues wagging. Лю́ди начну́т говори́ть о нас. ♦ **You'd better curb your tongue.** Ты бы лу́чше попридержа́ла *(ж: попридержа́л)* свой язы́к. ♦ **Bite your tongue.** Прикуси́ свой язы́к. ♦ **You speak with a forked tongue.** Ты говори́шь одно́, а ду́маешь друго́е. ♦ **Excuse my** *(1)* **loose /** *(2)* **runaway tongue.** Извини́ меня́ за мой *(1,2)* небре́жный язы́к.

tongue-tied *adj* лиши́вшийся (-а́яся, -е́еся, -ие́ся) да́ра ре́чи, безъязы́чный, -ая, -ое, -ые ♦ **You've got me tongue-tied.** Ты лиши́ла *(ж: лиши́л)* меня́ да́ра ре́чи. ♦ **Don't be tongue-tied. Say something!** Не молчи́. Скажи́ что́-нибудь. ♦ **Whenever you come in my presence,** *(1)* **I'm rendered... /** *(2)* **I become... tongue-tied.** Вся́кий раз в твоём прису́тствии *(1,2)* я лиша́юсь да́ра ре́чи. ♦ **My** *(1)* **emotions /** *(2)* **feelings** *(3)* **overwhelmed /** *(4)* **swamped me so completely that I was (utterly) tongue-tied.** *(1)* Эмо́ции / *(2)* Чу́вства *(3)* ошеломи́ли / *(4)* затопи́ли меня́ всеце́ло так, что я был *(ж: была́)* (соверше́нно) безъязы́чным *(ж: безъязы́чной)*.

tonic *n* эликси́р ♦ **It was a tonic for my spirits to get your** *(1)* **call /** *(2)* **letter.** *(1)* Твой звоно́к был... / *(2)* Твоё письмо́ бы́ло... эликси́ром для моего́ ду́ха.

too *adv* 1. *(also)* то́же, та́кже; 2. *(too much)* сли́шком, чересчу́р.

tooth *n* зуб *(pl: зу́бы.)* ♦ **back teeth** за́дние зу́бы ♦ *(1,2)* **buck teeth** *(slang)* *(1)* выступа́ющие / *(2)* торча́щие зу́бы ♦ **crooked teeth** кривы́е зу́бы ♦ **front teeth** пере́дние зу́бы ♦ **gleaming white teeth** ослепи́тельно бе́лые зу́бы ♦ **missing ~** недостаю́щий зуб ♦ *(1,2)* **protruding teeth** *(1)* выступа́ющие / *(2)* торча́щие зу́бы ♦ *(1,2)* **rabbit teeth** *(slang)* *(1)* выступа́ющие / *(2)* торча́щие зу́бы ♦ **sparkling teeth** белосне́жные зу́бы ♦ **straight teeth** прямы́е зу́бы ♦ **white, healthy teeth** бе́лые, здоро́вые зу́бы ♦ **gap in the (front) teeth** расще́лина в (пере́дних) зуба́х.

top *n* 1. *(peak)* верши́на, верху́шка; 2. *(upper part)* верх, ве́рхняя часть; 3. *(highest degree)* вы́сшая сте́пень, верши́на; 4. *(orgasm)* орга́зм, 5. *(upper outer garment)* ве́рхняя оде́жда; ко́фточка; *(blouse)* блу́зка ♦ **lace ~** кружевна́я ко́фточка ♦ **see-through ~** прозра́чная ко́фточка ♦ **skimpy ~** лёгкая ма́йка-ко́фточка ♦ **tank ~** руба́шка с брете́льками, ма́йка ♦ **~ of the head** маку́шка ♦ **tube ~** *(sleeveless, elastic women's upper garment)* эласти́чный топ ♦ **get on ~** залеза́ть / зале́зть на *(of whom = acc.)* ♦ **on ~** *(movement towards)* наве́рх; *(location)* наверху́.

top: phrases

I'm kind of thin on top. Я немно́го лысова́т. ♦ **You took me over the top so beautifully.** Ты так прекра́сно довёл меня́ до орга́зма. ♦ **Oh, Darling, I just love the way you take me over the top every time.** О, дорого́й, я так люблю́ то, как ты ка́ждый раз дово́дишь

Russian nouns are either masculine, feminine or neuter.
Adjectives with them will be the same.

меня́ до орга́зма.

topless *adj* обнажённая (-ые) до по́яса, с обнажённой гру́дью ♦ **I love it when you** *(1)* **go** / *(2)* **walk around topless.** Я люблю́, когда́ ты *(1,2)* хо́дишь с обнажённой гру́дью. ♦ **You were** *(1)* **designed** / *(2)* **made to** *(3)* **go** / *(4)* **walk around topless (all the time).** Ты была́ *(1,2)* со́здана для того́, что́бы *(3,4)* ходи́ть (всё вре́мя) с обнажённой гру́дью.

topography *n* топогра́фия ♦ **I want to become intimately familiar with the sensual topography of your (beautiful) body.** Я хочу́ бли́зко познако́миться с чу́вственной топогра́фией твоего́ (прекра́сного) те́ла.

topsy-turvy *adj* кувырко́м, ши́ворот-навы́ворот, перевёрнутый вверх дном ♦ **My world is topsy-turvy since I met you.** Всё в моём ми́ре пошло́ кувырко́м с тех пор, как я встре́тил *(ж: встре́тила)* тебя́. ♦ **You've turned my whole world topsy-turvy.** Из-за тебя́ весь мой мир пошёл кувырко́м.

torch *n* фа́кел ♦ **I've carried a torch for you for a long time.** Я был заинтересо́ван *(ж: была́ заинтересо́вана)* тобо́й давны́м давно́.

torment *vt* му́чить *(whom = acc.)* ♦ **Do you enjoy tormenting me?** Ты наслажда́ешься, му́чая меня́? ♦ **Do you like to torment me?** Тебе́ нра́вится му́чить меня́?

torment *n* пы́тка, муче́ние ♦ **be in ~** му́читься, страда́ть ♦ **agonizing ~** мучи́тельная пы́тка ♦ **constant ~** постоя́нная пы́тка ♦ **love's ~** любо́вная пы́тка ♦ **unbearable ~** невыноси́мая пы́тка ♦ **My loneliness (without you) is a torment that I can** *(1)* **barely** / *(2)* **scarcely endure.** Моё одино́чество (без тебя́) -- э́то муче́ние, кото́рое я *(1,2)* едва́ выношу́. ♦ **It's a feeling that blends ecstasy and torment.** Это чу́вство -- смесь экста́за и му́ки.

tormented *adj* изму́ченный, -ая, -ое, -ые *(short forms:* изму́чен, -а, -о, -ы*)* ♦ **be ~** му́читься, терза́ться ♦ **My entire being is tormented by the all-consuming need to take you in my arms and revel in the reservoir of your passion.** Я весь изму́чен всепоглоща́ющей жа́ждой заключи́ть тебя́ в объя́тия и упива́ться твое́й стра́стью.

torrent *n* водопа́д ♦ **~ of feelings** водопа́д чувств ♦ **~ of sensations** водопа́д ощуще́ний.

torrid *adj* жа́ркий, -ая, -ое, -ие, зно́йный, -ая, -ое, -ые ♦ **~ dream** жа́ркий сон ♦ **~ embrace** жа́ркое объя́тие ♦ **~ nights** зно́йные но́чи ♦ **Last night I had the most torrid dream about you.** Про́шлой но́чью мне сни́лся жа́ркий сон о тебе́. ♦ **I want to go on a vacation with you and spend** *(1,2)* **torrid days and nights with you in a hotel.** Я хочу́ пое́хать в о́тпуск вме́сте с тобо́й и провести́ *(1)* жа́ркие / *(2)* зно́йные дни и но́чи в оте́ле. ♦ **I want to get you in the most torrid embrace you can imagine.** Я хочу́ заключи́ть тебя́ в са́мые жа́ркие объя́тия, кото́рые ты мо́жешь вообрази́ть. ♦ **One of these days I'm going to teach you the meaning of** *(1,2)* **torrid.** В оди́н из э́тих дней я объясню́ тебе́, что зна́чит *(1)* зно́йный / *(2)* жа́ркий.

torso *n* торс, телосложе́ние ♦ **hard ~** си́льный торс, кре́пкое телосложе́ние ♦ **lean ~** худо́й торс ♦ **muscular ~** мускули́стый торс ♦ **powerful ~** могу́чий торс.

torture *vt* му́чить *(whom = acc.)*, терза́ть *(whom = acc.)*.

torture *n* му́ка, муче́ние, пы́тка ♦ **absolute ~** абсолю́тная пы́тка ♦ **emotional ~** душе́вная му́ка ♦ **sheer ~** су́щая пы́тка ♦ **slow ~** ме́дленная му́ка ♦ *(1,2)* **unbearable ~** *(1)* невыноси́мая / *(2)* нестерпи́мая пы́тка ♦ *(1,2)* **unendurable ~** *(1)* невыноси́мая / *(2)* нестерпи́мая пы́тка.

torture: *phrases*

My loneliness (without you) is a torture that I can *(1)* **barely** / *(2)* **scarcely endure.** Моё одино́чество (без тебя́) -- э́то пы́тка, кото́рую я *(1,2)* едва́ выношу́. ♦ **This being apart from you is sheer torture.** Быть в разлу́ке с тобо́й -- су́щая пы́тка. ♦ **Wanting you and not being able to have you is sheer torture.** Жела́ть тебя́ и не име́ть возмо́жности быть

Learn more about Russian customs in Appendix 15, page 782.

с тобо́й -- су́щая пы́тка. ♦ **You can never know the sheer torture I go through** *(1)* **...being apart from you.** / *(2)* **... wanting you and not being able to have you.** Ты никогда́ не узна́ешь, че́рез каку́ю пы́тку я прохожу́, *(1)* ...бу́дучи в разлу́ке с тобо́й. / *(2)* ...жела́я тебя́ и не име́я возмо́жности быть с тобо́й. ♦ **Two weeks without a letter from you are in reality a long, slow torture.** Две неде́ли без письма́ от тебя́ -- действи́тельно дли́тельная, ме́дленная му́ка. ♦ **It's an absolute torture for me not to be able to fly over there to you this very instant.** Это абсолю́тная пы́тка для меня́ быть не в состоя́нии прилете́ть к тебе́ мгнове́нно.

torturer *n* мучи́тель *m*.

toss *vi* мета́ться ♦ **I tossed and turned all night long thinking about you.** Я мета́лся и воро́чался всю ночь напролёт, ду́мая о тебе́.

total *adj* 1. *(entire)* весь *m*, вся *f*, всё *neut*, все *pl*, це́лый, -ая, -ое, -ые; 2. *(complete)* по́лный, -ая, -ое, -ые, абсолю́тный, -ая, -ое, -ые.

totally *adv* соверше́нно, по́лностью, абсолю́тно, в це́лом ♦ **You are totally beautiful.** Ты соверше́нно прекра́сна.

tote *n* су́мка.

touch *vt* 1. *(with the hand & emotionally)* тро́гать / тро́нуть *(what, whom = + acc.)*; 2. *(come in contact with)* каса́ться / косну́ться *(what, whom = + gen.)* ♦ **~ my heart** растро́гать меня́, тро́нуть моё се́рдце ♦ **~ reverently** благогове́нно тро́гать / тро́нуть ♦ **fierce longing to be ~ed** нейстовая жа́жда прикоснове́ния.

> **touch:** *I love to touch*

I love to kiss, hug, caress, touch, hold hands, nibble, cuddle, rub against, stroke — you just name it. Я люблю́ целова́ть, обнима́ть, ласка́ть, каса́ться, держа́ться за́ руки, поку́сывать, сжима́ть в объя́тиях, тере́ться, гла́дить -- ты то́лько назови́.

> **touch:** *touching you*

I want so much to touch you that even my fingers ache. Я хочу́ косну́ться тебя́ до бо́ли в па́льцах. ♦ **I wanted so much to touch you that it was an actual physical effort to** *(1)* **keep** / *(2)* **hold my hand still.** Я так си́льно хоте́л *(ж: хоте́ла)* косну́ться тебя́, что настоя́щее физи́ческое уси́лие бы́ло *(1,2)* держа́ть ру́ки споко́йными. ♦ **I love the way your body softens when I touch you.** Мне нра́вится, как твоё те́ло расслабля́ется, когда́ я каса́юсь тебя́. ♦ **This is just a short letter to reach across the miles and touch you.** Это то́лько коро́ткое письмо́, кото́рое пройдёт ми́ли и коснётся тебя́.

> **touch:** *touching me*

When you touch me, *(1)* **...I just melt.** / *(2)* **...all my resistance drains out of me.** / *(3)* **...I burst into flames.** / *(4)* **...all my senses come alive.** Когда́ ты каса́ешься меня́, *(1)* ...я про́сто та́ю. / *(2)* ...всё сопротивле́ние исчеза́ет. / *(3)* ...я вспы́хиваю пла́менем. / *(4)* ...все мои́ чу́вства ожива́ют. ♦ **When your lips first met mine, it was like being touched by lightning.** Когда́ твои́ гу́бы впервы́е встре́тились с мои́ми, э́то бы́ло как уда́р мо́лнии. ♦ **Your words really touched my heart.** Твои́ слова́ действи́тельно тро́нули моё се́рдце. ♦ **You have touched my heart in a way no one else ever has.** Ты затро́нула *(ж: затро́нул)* моё се́рдце так, как никто́ никогда́ ещё э́того не де́лал. ♦ **Don't touch me.** Не тро́гай меня́.

touch *n* 1. *(physical contact)* прикоснове́ние; 2. *(communication)* связь ♦ **caressing ~** ла́сковое прикоснове́ние ♦ **erotic ~** эроти́ческое прикоснове́ние ♦ **exotic ~** экзоти́ческое прикоснове́ние ♦ **fantastic ~** фантасти́ческое прикоснове́ние ♦ **feathery ~** лёгкое как пух прикоснове́ние ♦ **feminine ~** же́нственное прикоснове́ние ♦ **heavenly ~** боже́ственное прикоснове́ние ♦ **innocent ~** неви́нное прикоснове́ние ♦ **magic ~** маги́ческое прикоснове́ние ♦ **seductive ~** обольсти́тельное прикоснове́ние ♦ **sensual ~** чу́вствен-

---

A slash always denotes "or."
You can choose the numbered words before and after.

ное прикосновéние ♦ **sensuous** ~ чýвственное прикосновéние ♦ **soothing** ~ успо-кáивающее прикосновéние ♦ **tantalizing** ~ дразнящее прикосновéние ♦ **thrilling** ~ упоительное прикосновéние ♦ **warm human** ~ тёплое человéческое прикосновéние ♦ **wonderful** ~ удивительное прикосновéние ♦ **your** ~ твоё прикосновéние.

> **touch:** *I enjoy touch*

I enjoy touch. Я наслаждáюсь прикосновéниями.

> **touch:** *your wonderful touch*

Your touch *(1)* **...is absolutely wonderful /** *(2)* **fantastic /** *(3)* **heavenly. /** *(4)* **...is raw silk. /** *(5)* **...is like fire. /** *(6)* **...causes sparks. /** *(7)* **...kindles fire in me. /** *(8)* **...scalded me.** Твоё прикосновéние *(1)* ...абсолютно удивительно / *(2)* фантастично / *(3)* божéственно. / *(4)* ...прóсто шёлк. / *(5)* ...подóбно огню. / *(6)* ...вызывáет искры. / *(7)* ...разжигáет во мне огóнь. / *(8)* ...обжигáло меня. ♦ **You have (such) a** *(1)* **wonderful /** *(2)* **fantastic /** *(3)* **heavenly /** *(4)* **magic touch.** У тебя (такóе) *(1)* удивительное / *(2)* фантастическое / *(3)* божéственное / *(4)* магическое прикосновéние. ♦ *(1)* **You have a... /** *(2)* **I love your... feather-soft touch.** *(1)* У тебя... / *(2)* Я люблю твоё... лёгкое, как касáние перá, при-косновéние. ♦ **The touch of your fingers is fire.** Прикосновéние твоих пáльцев -- плáмя. ♦ **You have a touch of fire.** Твоё прикосновéние -- огóнь. ♦ **The exotic touch of your tongue thrills me through and through.** Экзотическое прикосновéние твоегó языкá пронзáет меня насквóзь. ♦ **I love your gentle touch and the warmth I feel at your side.** Мне нрáвится твоё нéжное прикосновéние и теплó, исходящее от тебя. ♦ **I want to feel your touch.** Я хочý почýвствовать твоё прикосновéние. ♦ **I ache (so much) for your touch.** Я (так) жáжду твоих прикосновéний.

> **touch:** *my touch*

I have a feather-soft touch. У меня лёгкое, как касáние перá, прикосновéние. ♦ **I love the way your body comes to life under my touch.** Мне нрáвится, как твоё тéло оживáет под моими рукáми. ♦ **The rich smoothness of your skin excites my touch unimaginably.** Прикосновéние к твоéй изумительно глáдкой кóже невероятно возбуждáет меня.

> **touch:** *getting in touch*

How can I get in touch with you? Как я могý связáться с тобóй? ♦ **Is there some way I can get in touch with you?** Каким óбразом я могý связáться с тобóй? ♦ **You can get in touch with me at** *([1] number or [2] address)* . Ты мóжешь связáться со мной по *(1)* ...телефóну ___. / *(2)* ...áдресу ___. ♦ **I'll get in touch with you** *(1)* **...as soon as I arrive (there). /** *(2)* **...the first chance I get. /** *(3)* **...tomorrow. /** *(4)* **...on Monday /** *etc.* Я свяжýсь с тобóй *(1)* ...срáзу, как приéду (тудá). / *(2)* ...при пéрвой возмóжности. / *(3)* ...зáвтра. / *(4)* ...в понедéльник / *и т.д.* ♦ **Please keep in touch.** Пожáлуйста, держи со мной связь.

touched *adj* растрóганный, -ая, -ое, -ые *(short forms:* растрóган, -а, -о, -ы*)* ♦ **be** ~ быть рас-трóганным *m* / растрóганной *f*; растрóгаться ♦ **I was deeply touched by your** *(1)* **letter /** *(2)* **gift /** *(3)* **concern /** *(4)* **thoughtfulness.** Я был *(ж: былá)* глубокó растрóган *(ж: рас-трóгана)* твоим *(1)* письмóм / *(2)* подáрком / *(3)* учáстием / *(4)* внимáнием. ♦ **I can't tell you how touched I was by your sweet words.** Я не могý вýразить тебé, как растрó-гали меня твои нéжные словá. ♦ **Do you like to have your body touched?** Тебé нрá-вится, когдá касáются твоегó тéла? ♦ **I like to have my body touched (that way).** Мне нрáвится, когдá (так) касáются моегó тéла. ♦ **I want to feel touched by your soul.** Я хочý чýвствовать прикосновéние твоéй души.

touching *adj* трóгательный, -ая, -ое, -ые ♦ **wonderfully** ~ удивительно трóгательный, -ая, -ое, -ые ♦ **You write me such touching thoughts that I am at a loss to describe my feelings.** Ты пишешь мне такие трóгательные словá, что я не в силах описáть свои

Common adult weights are given in Appendix 10, page 777.

чу́вства. ♦ **No one has ever written such touching thoughts to me.** Никто́ никогда́ не писа́л мне таки́х тро́гательных слов. ♦ **That was such a touching letter you wrote.** Ты написа́ла *(ж: написа́л)* тако́е тро́гательное письмо́.

touching *n* прикоснове́ние, каса́ние ♦ **I like lots of touching and caressing and kissing.** Я люблю́ мно́го прикоснове́ний, ласк и поцелу́ев. ♦ **Touching your hand just adds fuel to the fire of my desire for you.** Когда́ я каса́юсь твое́й руки́, ого́нь мое́й стра́сти к тебе́ разжига́ется ещё сильне́е.

touchy *adj* 1. *(irritable)* оби́дчивый, -ая, -ое, -ые, раздражи́тельный, -ая, -ое, -ые; 2. *(highly sensitive)* повы́шенно чувстви́тельный, -ая, -ое, -ые.

tough *adj* 1. *(rugged)* выно́сливый, -ая, -ое, -ые; 2. *(difficult)* тру́дный, -ая, -ое, -ые.

tough-minded *adj* практи́чный, -ая, -ое, -ые, тре́звый, -ая, -ое, -ые, расчётливый, -ая, -ое, -ые.

toupee *n* (небольшо́й) пари́к, накла́дка.

tourist *adj* туристи́ческий, -ая, -ое, -ие.

tourist *n* тури́ст *m*, тури́стка *f.*

towhead *n* белобры́сый челове́к.

towheaded *adj* белобры́сый, -ая, -ое, -ые.

toy *vi* игра́ть *(with what = instr.)* ♦ ~ **with** *(1)* **my** / *(2)* **your feelings** игра́ть *(1)* мои́ми / *(2)* твои́ми чу́вствами.

toy *n* игру́шка.

trace *vt* оче́рчивать / очерти́ть *(what = acc.)* ♦ **My lips are going to softly trace the outline of your** *(1)* **mouth** / *(2)* **body** / *(3)* **breasts.** Мои́ гу́бы мя́гко оче́ртят ко́нтур *(1)* ...твоего́ рта / *(2)* те́ла. / *(3)* ...твое́й груди́.

tradition *n* тради́ция ♦ **old** ~ ста́рая тради́ция ♦ **break with** ~ порыва́ть / порва́ть с тради́цией ♦ **by** ~ по тради́ции.

trail *vi* *(glide)* скользи́ть / скользну́ть; *(travel)* путеше́ствовать ♦ **My mouth will trail along your neck to your shoulder and then down to your breast.** Мой рот бу́дет путеше́ствовать вдоль твое́й ше́и, к твои́м плеча́м и зате́м вниз к твое́й груди́.

trail *n* тропа́; *(kisses)* град ♦ **searing** ~ **of kisses** град обжига́ющих поцелу́ев ♦ **You must have a trail of broken hearts** *(1)* **...behind you.** / *(2)* **...leading from your door.** У тебя́ должна́ быть тропа́, у́стланная разби́тыми сердца́ми *(1)* ...позади́. / *(2)* ...веду́щая от твое́й две́ри. ♦ **The fact that you're not married can only mean that you've left behind a trail of broken hearts.** Тот факт, что ты до сих пор не за́мужем *(ж: жена́т)*, мо́жет означа́ть то́лько, что ты оста́вила *(ж: оста́вил)* позади́ тропу́, у́стланную разби́тыми сердца́ми.

trailer *n*: ♦ ~ **home** дом на колёсах.

train *n* по́езд ♦ **What time will the train** *(1,2)* **arrive** / *(3,4)* **depart?** В како́е вре́мя *(1)* прибу́дет / *(2)* придёт / *(3)* отпра́вится / *(4)* отойдёт по́езд? ♦ **The train will** *(1,2)* **arrive** / *(3,4)* **depart at** *(5)* **one (thirty).** *(See page 759 for other times.)* По́езд *(1)* прибу́дет / *(2)* придёт / *(3)* отпра́вится / *(4)* отойдёт в *(5)* час (три́дцать).

trait *n* (характе́рная) черта́, осо́бенность *f*, сво́йство ♦ **bad** ~**s** плохи́е черты́ ♦ *(1,2)* **family** ~ *(1)* семе́йная / *(2)* фами́льная черта́ ♦ **fine** ~**s** прекра́сные черты́ ♦ **good** ~**s** хоро́шие черты́ ♦ **physical** ~**s** физи́ческие осо́бенности ♦ **similar** *(1-3)* ~**s** похо́жие *(1)* черты́ / *(2)* сво́йства / *(3)* хара́ктеры ♦ **You have many fine traits that I admire.** У тебя́ мно́го прекра́сных черт, кото́рыми я любу́юсь. ♦ **I've got my good traits and my bad traits.** У меня́ есть хоро́шие черты́ и плохи́е черты́.

tramp *n* 1. *(bum)* бродя́жка; 2. *(prostitute)* проститу́тка.

trance *n* транс.

An italicized ж *in parentheses   indicates a woman speaking.*

transcend *vt* 1. *(go beyond the limits, exceed)* выходи́ть / вы́йти за преде́лы *(what = gen.)*, переступа́ть / переступи́ть преде́лы *(what = gen.)*; 2. *(surpass)* превосходи́ть / превзойти́ *(what = acc.)*, превыша́ть / превы́сить *(what = acc.)* ♦ **My love for you transcends (1,2) ...all bounds. / ...(3) all / (4) everything else (in this world).** Моя́ любо́вь к тебе́ превосхо́дит *(1)* ...все преде́лы / *(2)* грани́цы. / *(3,4)* ...всё друго́е (в э́том ми́ре). ♦ **Transcend your pride.** Переступи́ свою́ го́рдость.

transfer *vt (money)* переводи́ть / перевести́ *(to where = + в + acc.)*

transfer *n (money)* перево́д ♦ **money** ~ де́нежный перево́д.

transfixed *adj* пронзён, пронзена́, -о́, -ы́ *(short forms)* ♦ **When I look into the deep blue depths of your eyes, I am (completely) transfixed.** Когда́ я смотрю́ в тёмно-си́нюю глубину́ твои́х глаз, я (соверше́нно) пронзён *(ж: пронзена́)* любо́вью к тебе́.

transgress *vt (violate)* наруша́ть / нару́шить *(what = acc.)*; *(go beyond the limits)* переходи́ть / перейти́ грани́цы *(what = gen.)*.

transgress *vi (sin)* греши́ть / согреши́ть.

transgression *n* 1. *(sin)* грех; прегреше́ние; 2. *(violation)* наруше́ние.

transition *adj (slang) (between relationships)* поко́нчивший (-ая, -ие) с отноше́ниями.

translate *vt* переводи́ть / перевести́ *(what = acc.)* ♦ **~ from English to Russian** переводи́ть / перевести́ с англи́йского на ру́сский ♦ **~ from Russian to English** переводи́ть / перевести́ с ру́сского на англи́йский.

translation *n* перево́д ♦ **accurate** ~ то́чный перево́д ♦ **good** ~ хоро́ший перево́д ♦ **incorrect** ~ непра́вильный перево́д ♦ **literal** ~ буква́льный перево́д ♦ **notarized** ~ нотариа́льно засвиде́тельствованный перево́д ♦ **poor** ~ плохо́й перево́д ♦ **~ from English to Russian** перево́д с англи́йского на ру́сский ♦ **~ from Russian to English** перево́д с ру́сского на англи́йский ♦ **word for word** ~ досло́вный перево́д ♦ **mistake in the** ~ оши́бка в перево́де ♦ **~ fee** пла́та за перево́д.

translator *n* перево́дчик *m*, перево́дчица *f*.

transparent *adj* 1. *(pellucid, sheer)* прозра́чный, -ая, -ое, -ые; 2. *(obvious)* я́вный, -ая, -ое, -ые, очеви́дный, -ая, -ое, -ые ♦ **That's a transparent excuse.** Это я́вная отгово́рка.

transplant *n* 1. транспланта́ция, переса́дка; 2. *(resettled person)* перее́хавший *m*, перее́хавшая *f* ♦ **hair** ~ транспланта́ция воло́с ♦ **New York** ~ перее́хавший *m* / перее́хавшая *f* из Нью-Йо́рка.

transplanted *adj (moved, resettled)* перее́хавший, -ая, -ие ♦ **I'm a transplanted Texan.** Я перее́хал *(ж: перее́хала)* из Теха́са.

transport *vt* переноси́ть / перенести́ *(what, whom = acc.)*; приноси́ть / принести́ *(what, whom = acc.)*; уноси́ть / унести́ *(what, whom = acc.)* ♦ **The soft, warm magic of your body transports me to a cosmic kaleidoscope of ecstasy.** Мя́гкая, тёплая ма́гия твоего́ те́ла перено́сит меня́ в косми́ческий калейдоско́п экста́за. ♦ **You transport me into (1) bliss / (2) ecstasy / (3) paradise.** Ты перено́сишь меня́ в *(1)* блаже́нство / *(2)* экста́з / *(3)* рай.

transport *n* поры́в *(чувства)*, взрыв ♦ **rapturous** ~ взрыв восто́рга.

transvestite *n* трансвести́т *(мужчи́на, нося́щий же́нскую оде́жду)*.

trauma *n* тра́вма ♦ **emotional** ~ эмоциона́льная тра́вма.

travails *n, pl* тяжёлый труд ♦ **share life's** ~s нести́ бре́мя жи́зни вме́сте.

travel *vi* путеше́ствовать ♦ **~ frequently** ча́сто путеше́ствовать ♦ **I have a gypsy heart. I love to travel and enjoy life.** У меня́ цыга́нское се́рдце. Я люблю́ путеше́ствовать и наслажда́ться жи́знью. ♦ **My lips will travel first to one sensitive peak, then to the other.** Мои́ гу́бы бу́дут путеше́ствовать снача́ла к одно́й чувстви́тельной верши́нке, затем к друго́й.

Procedures for getting married to a Russian are outlined in Appendix 18, page 787.

travel *n* путешéствие ♦ **exotic** ~ экзотúческое путешéствие ♦ **foreign** ~ путешéствие загранúцу ♦ **frequent** ~ чáстое путешéствие ♦ ~ **around the world** кругосвéтное путешéствие, путешéствие вокрýг свéта.

traveler *n* путешéствующий, -ая, -ие ♦ **world** ~ путешéствующий (-ая, -ие) по мúру.

treasure *vt* 1. *(preserve)* (бéрежно) хранúть *(what = acc.)*; берéчь, как сокрóвище *(1 term)* *(what = acc.)*; 2. *(regard highly)* высокó ценúть *(what = acc.)*, дорожúть *(what = instr.)*
♦ **I will always treasure the memories of the** *(1)* **times /** *(2)* **moments we shared together.** Я всегдá бýду хранúть воспоминáния о *(1)* ...врéмени, проведённом вдвоём. / *(2)* ...минýтах, проведённых вдвоём. ♦ **I will always treasure the memory of** *(1)* ...**the wonderful time we spent together. /** *(2)* ...**the first time I kissed you. /** *(3)* ...**the day we met.** Я бýду всегдá дорожúть пáмятью *(1)* ...о замечáтельном врéмени, проведённом вмéсте. / *(2)* ...о дне, когдá впервые поцеловáл *(ж: поцеловáла)* тебя. / *(3)* ...о дне, когдá мы встрéтились. ♦ **I will always treasure this memento of the (** *[1]* **wonderful /** *[2]* **happy) time we spent together.** Мне всегдá бýдет дóрого э́то напоминáние о (*[1]* замечáтельном/ *[2]* счастлúвом врéмени, проведённом нáми вмéсте. ♦ **I will treasure** *(1,2)* **it /** *(3)* **this** *(4)* ...**forever. /** *(5)* ...**as long as I live. /** *(6)* ...**until the end of my days.** Я бýду хранúть *(1)* егó *m & neut* / *(2)* её *f* / *(3)* э́то *(4)* ...вéчно. / *(5)* ...всю свою жизнь. / *(6)* ...до концá своúх дней. ♦ **I read your letters over and over again and I never cease to treasure them.** Я перечúтываю твоú пúсьма снóва и снóва и никогдá не перестáну дорожúть úми.

treasure *n* сокрóвище ♦ **hidden** ~**s** скрытые сокрóвища ♦ **priceless** ~ бесцéнное сокрóвище ♦ ~ **of my heart** сокрóвище моегó сéрдца ♦ **My** *(1)* **hungry /** *(2)* **loving /** *(3)* **wandering /** *(4)* **roving lips will seek and find the hidden treasures of your** *(5)* **magnificent /** *(6)* **luscious beauty.** Моú *(1)* голóдные / *(2)* любящие / *(3,4)* блуждáющие гýбы бýдут искáть и находúть скрытые сокрóвища твоéй *(5)* великолéпной / *(6)* сóчной красоты. ♦ **You are the treasure of my heart.** Ты сокрóвище моегó сéрдца.

treasure chest *n (See chest)*.

treat *vt* 1. *(act toward, deal with)* обращáться / обратúться *(whom = + с + instr.)*, обходúться / обойтúсь *(whom = + с + instr.)*; 2. *(provide enjoyment)* угощáть / угостúть *(whom = acc., to what = instr.)* ♦ ~ **badly** плóхо обращáться ♦ ~ **callously** бездýшно обращáться ♦ ~ **gently** нéжно обращáться ♦ ~ **roughly** грýбо обращáться *(whom = + с + instr.)* ♦ ~ **shabbily** некрасúво обращáться ♦ ~ **terribly** ужáсно обращáться ♦ ~ **well** хорошó обращáться.

treat: phrases

That's no way to treat a *(1)* **person /** *(2)* **lady /** *(3)* **woman.** Так нельзя обращáться с *(1)* человéком / *(2,3)* жéнщиной. ♦ **I would never treat you that way.** Я никогдá не бýду с тобóй так обращáться. ♦ **I will always treat you with love and** *(1)* **gentleness /** *(2)* **affection /** *(3)* **understanding /** *(4)* **respect.** Я всегдá бýду относúться к тебé с любóвью и *(1,2)* нéжностью / *(3)* понимáнием / *(4)* уважéнием. ♦ **You treat me like no one else has ever treated me.** Ты обращáешься со мной так, как никтó никогдá прéжде не обращáлся. ♦ **I'm going to treat you to an ever-changing array of pleasurable sensations.** Я бýду угощáть тебя мнóжеством всегдá меняющихся, доставляющих удовóльствие ощущéний. ♦ **I've treated you** *(1)* **badly /** *(2)* **shabbily.** Я обращáлся *(ж: обращáлась)* с тобóй *(1)* плóхо / *(2)* некрасúво. ♦ **I apologize for treating you so** *(1)* **badly /** *(2)* **shabbily.** Я извиняюсь за такóе *(1)* плохóе / *(2)* некрасúвое обхождéние с тобóй. ♦ **You really treated me** *(1)* **badly /** *(2)* **shabbily.** Ты действúтельно обходúлась *(ж: обходúлся)* со мной *(1)* плóхо / *(2)* некрасúво. ♦ **Treat others the same way you want to be treated.** Обращáйся с другúми так, как ты хóчешь, чтóбы другúе обращá-

---

A list of conjugated Russian verbs is given
in Appendix 3 on page 699.

лись с тобо́й. ♦ **I feel so disillusioned by the way you treat me.** Я так разочаро́ван *(ж: разочаро́вана)* тем, как ты обраща́ешься со мной.

treat *n* удово́льствие, наслажде́ние, угоще́ние ♦ **Your breasts are such a treat to the eye.** Твоя́ грудь так ра́дует глаз. ♦ **Heaven holds no sweeter treat than the taste of your beautiful lips.** У небе́с нет бо́лее сла́дкого угоще́ния, чем вкус твои́х прекра́сных губ. ♦ **What a divine treat to see your face beautifully flushed and well-kissed after we make love.** Что за боже́ственное наслажде́ние ви́деть твоё лицо́, прекра́сно раскрасне́вшееся и зацело́ванное по́сле на́шей бли́зости. ♦ **You're in for a treat.** Тебе́ бу́дет прекра́сно.

treatment *n* обраще́ние, обхожде́ние ♦ **kind ~** мя́гкое обраще́ние ♦ **rough ~** гру́бое обраще́ние ♦ **shabby ~** недосто́йное обраще́ние ♦ **I don't think I deserve such treatment.** Я не ду́маю, что заслу́живаю тако́го обраще́ния. ♦ **I'm going to give you the red-carpet treatment when you get here.** Когда́ ты прие́дешь сюда́, я бу́ду де́лать для тебя́ всё.

tremble *vi* дрожа́ть; трепета́ть ♦ **~with delight** трепета́ть от восто́рга ♦ **~with excitement** дрожа́ть от возбужде́ния ♦ **~ with pleasure** дрожа́ть от наслажде́ния ♦ **Whenever I think about you, my body trembles in anticipation.** Когда́ бы я ни поду́мал *(ж: поду́мала)* о тебе́, моё те́ло трепе́щет в предвкуше́нии. ♦ **Whenever you get close to me, my knees begin to tremble.** Вся́кий раз, когда́ ты приближа́ешься ко мне, мои́ коле́ни начина́ют дрожа́ть.

trembling *n* дрожь; тре́пет.

tremendous *adj* огро́мный, -ая, -ое, -ые, грома́дный, -ая, -ое, -ые.

tremendously *adv* огро́мно, чрезвыча́йно, о́чень (и о́чень), исключи́тельно.

tremor *n* дрожь ♦ **~ of passion** дрожь стра́сти.

tremulous *adj* тре́петный, -ая, -ое, -ые.

tremulously *adv* тре́петно.

trendy *adj* мо́дный, -ая, -ое, -ые.

tress *n* ло́кон ♦ **blonde ~s** све́тлые ло́коны ♦ **fiery ~s** о́гненные ло́коны ♦ **golden ~s** золоти́стые ло́коны ♦ **honey-colored ~s** ло́коны цве́та мёда ♦ **long, glistening ~s** дли́нные, блестя́щие ло́коны ♦ **shimmering ~s** блестя́щие ло́коны ♦ **silky ~s** шелкови́стые ло́коны ♦ **thick brown ~s** густы́е кашта́новые ло́коны.

triangle *n* треуго́льник ♦ **love ~** любо́вный треуго́льник ♦ **~ of** *(1)* **golden /** *(2)* **black hair** треуго́льник *(1)* золоти́стых / *(2)* чёрных воло́с.

tribulation *n* невзго́да ♦ **share life's ~s** нести́ тя́готы повседне́вной жи́зни вме́сте ♦ **The greatest happiness I can imagine is to spend my life with you, sharing love and all joys and tribulations.** Са́мое большо́е сча́стье, кото́рое я могу́ себе́ предста́вить, э́то прожи́ть всю жизнь с тобо́й, деля́ любо́вь, ра́дости и невзго́ды.

trick *n* вы́ходка ♦ **artful ~s** иску́сные уло́вки.

trifle *vi (play with)* игра́ть *(with what = instr.)* ♦ **You have trifled with my affections.** Ты игра́ла *(ж: игра́л)* мое́й любо́вью. ♦ **Believe me, I would never trifle with your affections.** Пове́рь мне, я никогда́ не бу́ду игра́ть твое́й любо́вью.

trim *adj* подтя́нутый, -ая, -ое, -ые ♦ **reasonably ~** доста́точно подтя́нутый, -ая, -ое, -ые ♦ **You look (very) trim and fit.** Ты вы́глядишь о́чень подтя́нутой и здоро́вой *(ж: подтя́нутым и здоро́вым).*

trimmed *adj* укра́шен, -а, -о, -ы *(short forms)* ♦ **It's trimmed with** *(1)* **lace /** *(2)* **fur /** *(3)* **red.** Это укра́шено *(1)* кру́жевом / *(2)* ме́хом / *(3)* кра́сным.

trinket *n* брело́к, безделу́шка.

trip *n* пое́здка, путеше́ствие; экску́рсия ♦ **bike** *(1,2)* **~s** *(1)* путеше́ствия / *(2)* пое́здки на

For Russian adjectives, the masculine form is spelled out,
followed by the feminine, neuter and plural endings

велосипе́де ♦ **camping** ~ путеше́ствие с пала́ткой ♦ **honeymoon** ~ сва́дебное путеше́ствие ♦ **motorcycle** *(1,2)* ~s *(1)* путеше́ствия / *(2)* пое́здки на мотоци́кле ♦ **road** ~ путеше́ствие на маши́не ♦ **go on a** ~ путеше́ствовать, отправля́ться / отпра́виться в путеше́ствие, е́хать / пое́хать в путеше́ствие.

trip: phrases

Would you like to go on a trip (with me)? Не хоте́ла *(ж: хоте́л)* бы ты путеше́ствовать (со мной)? ♦ **Let's go on a trip (together) (to** _(name)_ **).** Дава́й пое́дем в путеше́ствие (вме́сте) (в *назва́ние).* ♦ **I like to take short trips (around this area).** Мне нра́вятся коро́ткие путеше́ствия (по э́тому райо́ну). ♦ **We can go on weekend trips to explore new places.** В выходны́е дни мы мо́жем отпра́виться в пое́здку иссле́довать но́вые места́.

tripe *n* чушь *f* ♦ **That's a lot of sentimental tripe.** Всё э́то -- сентимента́льная чушь.

trivial *adj* незначи́тельный, -ая, -ое, -ые, тривиа́льный, -ая, -ое, -ые.

trophy *adj* трофе́йный, -ая, -ое, -ые, наградно́й, -а́я, -о́е, -ы́е, призово́й, -а́я, -о́е, -ы́е ♦ ~ **wife** состоя́тельная жена́.

trophy *n* трофе́й.

trouble *n* 1. *(unpleasantness)* неприя́тность *f*, беда́; 2. *(difficulties)* тру́дности ♦ **I don't want** *(1)* **...to make** / *(2)* **cause any trouble (for you).** / *(3)* **...to put you to a lot of trouble.** Я не хочу́ *(1)* ...доставля́ть / *(2)* причиня́ть (тебе́) никаки́х ли́шних тру́дностей. / *(3)* ...тебя́ си́льно затрудня́ть. ♦ **I've had more than my fair share of trouble.** На мою́ до́лю вы́пало неприя́тностей бо́лее чем доста́точно.

troublemaker *n* смутья́н, наруши́тель споко́йствия.

trousers *n, pl* брю́ки; штаны́ ♦ **pair of** ~s брю́ки; штаны́.

trousseau *n* прида́ное.

true *adj* и́стинный, -ая, -ое, -ые, ве́рный, -ая, -ое, -ые *(short forms:* ве́рен, верна́), пра́вильный, -ая, -ое, -ые ♦ **I promise you, I will be forever true to you.** Я обеща́ю тебе́, я бу́ду всегда́ ве́рен *(ж: верна́)* тебе́. ♦ **I've always been true to you.** Я всегда́ был ве́рен *(ж: была́ верна́)* тебе́. ♦ **I will always be true to you.** Я всегда́ бу́ду ве́рен *(ж: верна́)* тебе́. ♦ **Are you true to me.** Ты верна́ *(ж: ве́рен)* мне? ♦ ***"To thine own self be true."*** Остава́йся сами́м собо́й.

trust *vt* доверя́ть / дове́рить *(what, whom = dat.)* ♦ **(Please) trust me.** (Пожа́луйста,) доверя́й мне. ♦ **I (don't) trust you.** Я (не) доверя́ю тебе́. ♦ **I don't feel that I can trust you.** Я не чу́вствую, что могу́ доверя́ть тебе́. ♦ **I trusted you (and look what happened).** Я доверя́л *(ж: доверя́ла)* тебе́ (и посмотри́, что случи́лось). ♦ **We must always trust each other** *(1)* **...absolutely** / *(2)* **completely** / *(3)* **totally.** / *(4)* **...without reservation.** Мы должны́ всегда́ доверя́ть друг дру́гу *(1)* ...абсолю́тно. / *(2)* по́лностью. / *(3)* ...до конца́. / *(4)* ...безоговоро́чно.

trust *n* дове́рие ♦ **absolute** ~ абсолю́тное дове́рие ♦ **blind** ~ слепо́е дове́рие ♦ **boundless** ~ безграни́чное дове́рие ♦ **complete** ~ по́лное дове́рие ♦ **great** ~ большо́е дове́рие ♦ **infinite** ~ бесконе́чное дове́рие ♦ **mutual** ~ взаи́мное дове́рие ♦ **my** ~ моё дове́рие ♦ **your** ~ *(familiar)* твоё дове́рие; *(polite)* Ва́ше дове́рие.

trust: other terms

betray *(1)* **my** / *(2)* **your** ~ обману́ть *(1)* моё / *(2)* твоё дове́рие ♦ **earn** ~ заслужи́ть твоё дове́рие ♦ **lose** *(1)* **my** / *(2)* **your** ~ потеря́ть *(1)* моё / *(2)* твоё дове́рие ♦ **relationship based on** ~ отноше́ние, осно́ванное на дове́рии *(1 term)* ♦ **win** ~ завоева́ть твоё дове́рие.

trust: phrases

Our love is based on trust and respect and understanding. На́ша любо́вь осно́вана на

See Appendix 19 for notes on sending mail to Russia and Ukraine.

дове́рии, уваже́нии и взаимопонима́нии. ♦ **I want a love based on trust and respect and understanding.** Я хочу́, что́бы в осно́ве любви́ бы́ли дове́рие, уваже́ние и взаимопонима́ние.

trusted *adj* дове́ренный, -ая, -ое, -ые *(short forms:* дове́рен, -а, -о, -ы*)* ♦ **I wonder if you can be trusted.** Я хоте́л *(ж: хоте́ла)* бы знать, могу́ ли я доверя́ть тебе́? ♦ **Can you be trusted?** Мо́жно ли доверя́ть тебе́? ♦ **Yes, I can be trusted.** Да, мне мо́жно доверя́ть. ♦ *(1)* **He's /** *(2)* **She's my trusted friend.** *(1)* Он / *(2)* Она́ мой дове́ренный друг.

trusting *adj* дове́рчивый, -ая, -ое, -ые.

trustworthy *adj* надёжный, -ая, -ое, -ые, заслу́живающий (-ая, -ее, -ие) дове́рия.

truth *n* пра́вда ♦ **bitter** *(1,2)* ~ го́рькая *(1)* пра́вда / *(2)* и́стина ♦ **exact** ~ су́щая пра́вда ♦ **honest** ~ чи́стая пра́вда ♦ **obvious** ~ я́вная и́стина ♦ **plain** ~ чи́стая и́стина ♦ *(1,2)* **real** ~ *(1)* и́стинная / *(2)* су́щая пра́вда ♦ **simple** ~ чи́стая пра́вда ♦ **unadulterated** ~ го́лая пра́вда, неприкра́шенная и́стина ♦ **unvarnished** ~ го́лая пра́вда, неприкра́шенная и́стина ♦ **whole** ~ вся пра́вда ♦ **stretch the** ~ вытя́гивать / вы́тянуть пра́вду ♦ **tell the** ~ говори́ть / сказа́ть пра́вду *(to whom = dat.).*

---
truth: phrases

Are you telling me the truth? Ты говори́шь мне пра́вду? ♦ **You're not telling me the truth.** Ты не говори́шь мне пра́вду. ♦ **I'm telling you the truth.** Я говорю́ тебе́ пра́вду. ♦ **I'll tell you the whole truth.** Я скажу́ тебе́ всю пра́вду. ♦ **Is that the truth?** Э́то пра́вда? ♦ *(1)* **It's /** *(2)* **That's (not) the truth (, I swear it).** *(1,2)* Э́то (не) пра́вда (, кляну́сь тебе́). ♦ **(Please)** *(1,2)* **Tell me the truth.** (Пожа́луйста,) *(1)* Скажи́ *(2)* Расскажи́ мне пра́вду. ♦ **The truth is,** *(1)* **...I'm lost without you. /** *(2)* **...I love you very much.** / *(3)* **...I'm married.** Пра́вда в том, что я *(1)* ...чу́вствую себя́ поте́рянным *(ж: поте́рянной)* без тебя́. / *(2)* ...о́чень люблю́ тебя́. / *(3)* ...жена́т *(ж: за́мужем).* ♦ **You're afraid to confront the truth. (You** *[1]* **love /** *[2]* **want me.)** Ты бои́шься посмотре́ть в лицо́ пра́вде. (Ты *[1]* лю́бишь / *[2]* хо́чешь меня́.)

truthful *adj* правди́вый, -ая, -ое, -ые.

truthfulness *n* правди́вость *f.*

try *vt* про́бовать / попро́бовать *(what = acc.),* испы́тывать / испыта́ть *(what = acc.)* ♦ **I'll** *(1,2)* **try (almost) anything once.** Я (почти́) всё *(1)* попро́бую / *(2)* испыта́ю оди́н раз. ♦ **I want to try everything with you.** Я хочу́ всё испыта́ть с тобо́й.

try *vi* стара́ться / постара́ться, пыта́ться / попыта́ться ♦ **Please, try.** Пожа́луйста, попыта́йся. ♦ **I'll try.** Я попыта́юсь.

tryst *n* любо́вное свида́ние.

tub *n* ва́нна ♦ **hot** ~ масса́жная ва́нна с горя́чей водо́й, джаку́зи ♦ **Roman** ~ ри́мская ва́нна.

tube: ♦ **Our marriage is down the tube.** *(slang)* Наш брак разру́шился.

Tuesday *n* вто́рник ♦ **by** ~ к вто́рнику ♦ **last** ~ в про́шлый вто́рник ♦ **next** ~ в сле́дующий вто́рник ♦ **on** ~ во вто́рник.

tuft *n (of hair)* пучо́к воло́с.

tummy *n (slang)* пу́зо.

tune *vt* настра́ивать / настро́ить *(what = acc.)* ♦ **I want to tune your body with my mouth and hands until it sings.** Я хочу́ настра́ивать твоё те́ло свои́м ртом и рука́ми до тех пор, пока́ оно́ не запоёт.

tune *n* мело́дия, моти́в ♦ **One of these days I'll find someone else and then you're going to sing a different tune.** В оди́н из э́тих дней я найду́ кого́-то друго́го, и тогда́ ты запоёшь по-друго́му.

tuned *adj (verb preferred:)* гармони́ровать ♦ **be** ~ гармони́ровать ♦ **We are so finely tuned**

> *When terms are listed after a main word, a tilde ~*
> *is used to indicate the main word.*

to each other (, don't you think?). Мы так превосхо́дно гармони́руем друг с дру́гом (, не так ли?).

turbulent *adj* бу́рный, -ая, -ое, -ые ♦ ~ **feelings** бу́рные чу́вства ♦ **You** *(1)* **arouse /** *(2)* **cause /** *(3)* **stir up such turbulent feelings in** *(4)* **...me. /** *(5)* **...my heart.** Ты *(1)* пробужда́ешь / *(2)* вызыва́ешь / *(3)* возбужда́ешь таки́е бу́рные чу́вства *(4)* ...во мне. / *(5)* ...в моём се́рдце.

Turkmen(ian) *adj* туркме́нский, -ая, -ое, -ие.

Turkman *n (pl:* **Turkmen)** *(person)* туркме́н *m*, туркме́нка *f (pl:* туркме́ны).

Turkoman *n (language)* туркме́нский язы́к ♦ **speak** ~ говори́ть по-туркме́нски.

turmoil *n* беспоря́док, смяте́ние; сумя́тица ♦ *(1)* **I've been through... /** *(2)* **There is... /** *(3)* **There was... so much (emotional) turmoil (in my** *[4]* **life /** *[5]* **marriage).** *(1)* Я прошёл *(ж: прошла́)* че́рез... / *(2)* Есть... / *(3)* Бы́ло... тако́е си́льное (эмоциона́льное) смяте́ние (в *[4]* ...мое́й жи́зни. / *[5]* ...моём бра́ке).

turn *vt* повора́чивать / поверну́ть *(what = acc.)* ♦ ~ **down** *vt* отка́зывать / отказа́ть *(what, = acc., whom = dat.);* отклоня́ть / отклони́ть *(what = acc.)* ♦ ~ **on** *vt (excite)* возбужда́ть / возбуди́ть *(whom = acc.)* ♦ **You turn everybody's head when you walk into a room.** Ты привлека́ешь к себе́ все взгля́ды, когда́ вхо́дишь в ко́мнату.

> **turn down:**

I was afraid you'd turn me down. Я боя́лся *(ж: боя́лась),* что ты отка́жешь мне. ♦ **I pray that you won't turn me down.** Я молю́сь, что́бы ты не отказа́ла мне.

> **turn on:**

Your (sexy) voice really turns me on. Твой (сексуа́льный) го́лос действи́тельно возбужда́ет меня́. ♦ **You (really) turn me on!** Ты меня́ (действи́тельно) возбужда́ешь! ♦ **No one can turn me on like you do.** Никто́ не мо́жет возбуди́ть меня́ так, как ты.

turn *vi:* ♦ ~ **around** *vi* обора́чиваться / оберну́ться; повора́чиваться / поверну́ться ♦ ~ **away** *vi* отвора́чиваться / отверну́ться ♦ ~ **out** *vi* обора́чиваться / оберну́ться.

> **turn around:**

I see your beautiful face in my thoughts every time I turn around. Что бы я ни де́лал, всегда́ пе́ред мои́ми глаза́ми твоё прекра́сное лицо́.

> **turn away:**

I *(1)* **beg /** *(2)* **beseech you (with all my heart) not to turn away from me.** Я *(1,2)* умоля́ю тебя́ (от всего́ се́рдца) не отвора́чиваться от меня́.

> **turn out:**

Everything turned out differently. Всё оберну́лось по-друго́му.

turned on *adj* возбуждённый, -ая, -ое, -ые ♦ **I** *(1)* **feel /** *(2)* **get turned on whenever** *(3)* **...I look at you. /** *(4)* **...I'm around you. /** *(5)* **...I get close to you. /** *(6)* **...you come close to me. /** *(7)* **...you touch me.** *(1)* Я чу́вствую возбужде́ние... / *(2)* Я возбужда́юсь... всегда́, когда́ бы *(3)* ...ни посмотре́л *(ж: посмотре́ла)* на тебя́. / *(4)* ...ни был *(ж: была́)* ря́дом с тобо́й. / *(5)* ...ни приближа́лся *(ж: приближа́лась)* к тебе́. / *(6)* ...ты ни приближа́лась *(ж: приближа́лся)* ко мне. / *(7)* ...ты ни косну́лась *(ж: косну́лся)* меня́.

turn-on *n* возбужде́ние *(Russian prefers verb* возбужда́ть / возбуди́ть) ♦ **It's a (big) turn-on to me.** Это (о́чень) возбужда́ет меня́.

turquoise *n* бирюза́ ♦ **Your eyes sparkle like burnished turquoise.** Твои́ глаза́ искря́тся, как полиро́ванная бирюза́.

tush *n (slang)* зад, по́па.

tux = **tuxedo** *n* смо́кинг.

tuxedo *n* смо́кинг ♦ **I'm seeking a man who is comfortable in jeans or a tuxedo.** Я ищу́ мужчи́ну, кото́рому одина́ково удо́бно в джи́нсах и в смо́кинге.

A list of abbreviations used in the dictionary is given on page 10.

twaddle *n (slang)* «брехня».

twiddle *vt*: ♦ **sit (around) and ~ one's thumbs** плевáть / плю́нуть в потолóк ♦ **All I do is sit around all day and twiddle my thumbs.** Всё, что я дéлаю цéлый день , -- сижу́ и плюю́ в потолóк.

twin(-size) *adj*: ♦ **~ bed** неширóкая кровáть.

twinge *n* угрызéние *(сóвести)*; укóл; му́ка ♦ **~ of conscience** угрызéние сóвести ♦ **~ of envy** укóл зáвисти ♦ **~ of guilt** му́ки вины́ ♦ **~ of jealousy** му́ки рéвности ♦ **~ of melancholy** при́ступ меланхóлии ♦ **~ of remorse** си́льное раскáяние ♦ **~ of wistfulness** му́ки тоски́ ♦ **I feel a twinge of wistfulness whenever I think of** *(1)* **it** / *(2)* **him** / *(3)* **her** / *(4)* **them.** Я чу́вствую при́ступ тоски́, когдá подýмаю *(1)* ...об э́том / *(2)* о нём / *(3)* о ней / *(4)* о них.

twist *vi* 1. *(dance the twist)* танцевáть твист; 2. *(make love)* занимáться любóвью ♦ **We can twist the night away.** *(make love)* Мы мóжем всю ночь занимáться любóвью.

twist *n (dance)* твист.

two-faced *adj (double-dealing, false)* двули́чный, -ая, -ое, -ые, лжи́вый, -ая, -ое, -ые.

two-time *vt* изменя́ть / измени́ть *(whom = dat.)* ♦ **If you ever two-time me, that's the end.** Если ты тóлько изме́нишь мне, э́то конéц.

two-timer *n (husband)* невéрный муж; *(wife)* невéрная женá; *(lover)* невéрный любóвник *m*, невéрная любóвница *f*.

twosome *n* пáра.

type *n* óбраз, тип, вид ♦ **body ~** тип тéла ♦ *(1,2)* **mellow ~** *(1)* подобрéвший / *(2)* смягчи́вшийся человéк ♦ **moody ~** человéк с перемéнчивым настроéнием ♦ **my ~** мой тип, в моём вкýсе ♦ **silent ~** молчали́вая ли́чность ♦ **that ~** э́тот тип, такóй тип ♦ **this ~** э́тот тип, такóй тип ♦ **what ~** какóй тип ♦ **your ~** *(familiar)* твой тип; *(polite)* Ваш тип ♦ **You have just the body type I look for in a** *(1)* **woman** / *(2)* **man.** У тебя́ как раз такóй тип тéла, котóрый я ищý в *(1)* жéнщине / *(2)* мужчи́не. ♦ **You're the strong, silent type, and that appeals to me.** Ты си́льный, молчали́вый человéк, что импони́рует мне.

The accents on Russian words are to show how to pronounce them..
You don't have to copy the accents when writing to someone.

U

ubiquitous *adj* вездесу́щий, -ая, -ее, -ие.

ugliness *n* уро́дство.

ugly *adj* уро́дливый, -ая, -ое, -ые ♦ ~ **duckling** га́дкий утёнок ♦ **You're not ugly! You're beautiful!** Ты не уро́длива! Ты прекра́сна!

Ukraine *n* Украи́на ♦ **from** ~ с Украи́ны ♦ **in** ~ на Украи́не ♦ **to** ~ на Украи́ну.

Ukrainian *adj* украи́нский, -ая, -ое, -ие.

Ukrainian *n* 1. *(person)* украи́нец *m*, украи́нка *f (pl:* украи́нцы*)*; 2. *(language)* украи́нский язы́к ♦ **speak** ~ говори́ть по-украи́нски ♦ **I (don't) (1) speak / (2) understand Ukrainian.** Я (не) *(1)* говорю́ / *(2)* понима́ю по-украи́нски.

ultimate *adj (maximum)* преде́льный, -ая, -ое, -ые, максима́льный, -ая, -ое, -ые; *(excellent)* превосхо́дный, -ая, -ое, -ые.

ultimatum *n* ультима́тум ♦ **give** *(1)* **me /** *(2)* **you an** ~ ста́вить / поста́вить *(1)* мне / *(2)* тебе́ ультима́тум. ♦ **It sounds like you're giving me an ultimatum.** Это звучи́т так, как бу́дто ты ста́вишь мне ультима́тум.

ultra-feminine *adj* у́льтра-же́нственный, -ая, -ое, -ые.

umbrella *n* зо́нтик.

unabashed *adj* беззасте́нчивый, -ая, -ое, -ые, бессо́вестный, -ая, -ое, -ые.

unable *adj* не в си́лах, не в состоя́нии ♦ **be** ~ не быть в состоя́нии *(I'm unable:* я не в состоя́нии. *You're unable:* ты не в состоя́нии. *)*, не быть в си́лах *(I'm unable:* я не в си́лах. *You're unable:* ты не в си́лах. *)*, не мочь.

unaccompanied *adj* без сопровожде́ния.

unaccustomed *adj*: ♦ **be** ~ не привыка́ть / привы́кнуть *(to what =* + к + *dat.)*.

unadulterated *adj (genuine, pure)* настоя́щий, -ая, -ее, -ие, неподде́льный, -ая, -ое, -ые, чи́стый, -ая, -ое, -ые; *(sheer, utter)* чисте́йший, -ая, -ее, -ие, сплошно́й, -а́я, -о́е, -ы́е ♦ *(1,2)* ~ **joy** *(1)* настоя́щая / *(2)* неподде́льная ра́дость ♦ ~ **pleasure** настоя́щее удово́льствие ♦ **Whenever I look at you, I'm filled with pure, unadulterated desire.** Вся́кий раз, когда́ бы я ни взгляну́л на тебя́, меня́ наполня́ет настоя́щая, и́стинная страсть.

unadventurous *adj* несме́лый, -ая, -ое, -ые, неотва́жный, -ая, -ое, -ые, непредприи́мчивый, -ая, -ое, -ые.

unaffected *adj (without pretense)* неподде́льный, -ая, -ое, -ые, и́скренний, -яя, -ее, -ие ♦ **I admire you for being so natural and unaffected.** Я восхища́юсь твое́й есте́ствен-

---

*If no accent is shown on a word with a capitalized vowel,
it means that the capitalized vowel is accented.*

ностью и искренностью.

unaffectedly *adv* неподдельно, искренне.

unafraid *adj* без страха ♦ **be** ~ не бояться *(of what, whom = gen.).*

unambivalent *adj* недвусмысленный, -ая, -ое, -ые.

unanswered *adj* оставшийся (-аяся, -ееся, -иеся) без ответа, не получивший (-ая, -ее, -ие) ответа ♦ **go** ~ оставаться / остаться без ответа ♦ **My letter went unanswered.** Моё письмо осталось без ответа.

unappealing *adj* непривлекательный, -ая, -ое, -ые.

unappreciated *adj* неоценённый, -ая, -ое, -ые ♦ **feel** ~ чувствовать себя неоценённым *m* / неоценённой *f.*

unapproachable *adj* неприступный, -ая, -ое, -ые; неприветливый, -ая, -ое, -ые.

unashamed *adj* бесстыдный, -ая, -ое, -ые, бессовестный, -ая, -ое, -ые ♦ **be** ~ не стыдиться.

unassuming *adj* скромный, -ая, -ое, -ые.

unattached *adj (alone)* одинок, -а, -и; *(available)* свободен, свободна, -ы; *(unmarried)* не женат *m*, не замужем *f (all short forms)* ♦ **pretend to be** *(1-4)* ~ притворяться *(1)* неженатым *(unmarried, m)* / *(2)* незамужней *(unmarried, f)* / *(3)* свободным *(free, m)* / *(4)* свободной *(free, f).*

⎢ ***unattached: phrases*** ⎥

I'm *(1,2)* **unattached (at the present time).** Я *(1)* свободен / *(2)* не женат *(ж: [1] свободна / [2] не замужем)* (в настоящее время). ♦ **I hope you're** *(1-3)* **unattached. Are you?** Я надеюсь, ты *(1)* не замужем / *(2)* одинока / *(3)* свободна *(ж: [1] не женат / [2] одинок / [3] свободен).* Не так ли? ♦ **You can't imagine how** *(1)* **relieved** / *(2)* **happy** / *(3)* **glad I was when I found out you were unattached.** Ты не можешь вообразить, с *(1)* ...каким облегчением / *(2)* счастьем / *(3)* ...какой радостью... я узнал *(ж: узнала)*, что ты не замужем *(ж: женат).*

unattainable *adj* недостижимый, -ая, -ое, -ые, недосягаемый, -ая, -ое, -ые.

unavoidable *adj* неизбежный, -ая, -ое, -ые.

unaware *adj*: ♦ **be** ~ не знать.

unawares *adv* врасплох ♦ **You caught me completely unawares.** Ты застигла *(ж: застиг)* меня совершенно врасплох.

unbearable *adj* невыносимый, -ая, -ое, -ые *(short forms:* невыносим, -а, -о, -ы), несносный, -ая, -ое, -ые ♦ *(1)* **This waiting...** / *(2)* **This loneliness (without you)... is (absolutely) unbearable.** *(1)* Это ожидание... / *(2)* Это одиночество (без тебя)... (абсолютно) невыносимо. ♦ *(1)* **This being apart (from you)...** / *(2)* **This separation (from you)...** / *(3)* **The longing in my heart for you... is (absolutely) unbearable.** *(1,2)* Эта разлука (с тобой)... / *(3)* Тоска по тебе в моём сердце... (абсолютно) невыносима.

unbecoming *adj* 1. *(unsuitable, inappropriate)* неподходящий, -ая, -ее, -ие, неуместный, -ая, -ее, -ие; 2. *(indecent, improper)* неприличный, -ая, -ое, -ые, неблагопристойный, -ая, -ее, -ие; *(unseemly)* неподобающий, -ая, -ее, -ие; 3. *(unattractive, unflattering)* не (идущий, -ая, -ее, -ие) к лицу.

unbelievable *adj* невероятный, -ая, -ое, -ые.

unbelievably *adv* невероятно.

unbounded *adj* неограниченный, -ая, -ое, -ые, безмерный, -ая, -ое, -ые.

unbridled *adj* необузданный, -ая, -ое, -ые ♦ **Together you and I can experience the ecstasy of unbridled passion.** Вместе ты и я сможем испытать экстаз необузданной страсти.

unbridled *adj (unrestrained)* необузданный, -ая, -ое, -ые.

unburden *vt*: ♦ ~ *(1)* **myself** / *(2)* **yourself** *(1,2)* отводить / отвести душу, *(1,2)* облегчать

⎢ *Russian has 6 grammatical cases. For an explanation of them, see the grammar appendix on page 686.* ⎥

/ облегчи́ть ду́шу ♦ **You can always unburden yourself with me.** Ты всегда́ мо́жешь отвести́ ду́шу со мной.

unbutton *vt* расстёгивать / расстегну́ть *(what = acc.).*

unbuttoned *adj* незастёгнутый, -ая, -ое, -ые.

uncalled-for *adj* 1. *(unnecessary)* нену́жный, -ая, -ое, -ые; *(undeserved)* незаслу́женный, -ая, -ое, -ые; *(for no reason at all)* ни с того́ ни с сего́ *(1 expression)*; 2. *(out of place)* неуме́стный, -ая, -ое, -ые.

unceasing *adj* беспреста́нный, -ая, -ое, -ые, беспреры́вный, -ая, -ое, -ые.

uncensored *adj* не подве́ргнутый (-ая, -ое, -ые) цензу́ре.

uncertain *adj* 1. *(indefinite)* неопределённый, -ая, -ое, -ые; 2. *(unreliable)* ненадёжный, -ая, -ое, -ые, капри́зный, -ая, -ое, -ые; 3. *(unsure)* неуве́ренный, -ая, -ое, -ые; 4. *(doubtful)* сомни́тельный, -ая, -ое, -ые, нея́сный, -ая, -ое, -ые.

uncertainty *n* 1. *(lack of definite information)* неопределённость *f*, неизвестность *f*; 2. *(unreliability)* ненадёжность *f*; 3. *(lack of confidence)* неуве́ренность *f*; 4. *(doubt)* сомне́ние ♦ **I can't endure the uncertainty.** Я не могу́ вы́нести неопределённости.

unchanged *adj* неизме́нный, -ая, -ое, -ые.

unchanging *adj* неизменя́емый, -ая, -ое, -ые.

uncharacteristic *adj* нехаракте́рный, -ая, -ое, -ые.

uncivilized *adj* нецивилизо́ванный, -ая, -ое, -ые.

uncle *n* дя́дя.

unclear *adj* нея́сный, -ая, -ое, -ые.

unclothed *adj* разде́тый, -ая, -ое, -ые, обнажённый, -ая, -ое, -ые, без оде́жды ♦ **You look beautiful in any dress you wear, but I like you better unclothed.** Ты вы́глядишь прекра́сно в любо́м пла́тье, кото́рое ты но́сишь, но мне ты бо́льше нра́вишься без оде́жды.

unclutter *vt* упоря́дочить *(what = acc.)* ♦ ~ **a relationship** упоря́дочить отноше́ния.

uncomfortable *adj* неудо́бный, -ая, -ое, -ые ♦ **It makes me uncomfortable when you** *(1)* **...talk like that.** / *(2)* **...do that.** Мне стано́вится неудо́бно, когда́ ты *(1)* ...говори́шь так. / *(2)* ...э́то де́лаешь.

uncommon *adj* ре́дкий, -ая, -ое, -ие; необыкнове́нный, -ая, -ое, -ые ♦ ~ **beauty** необыкнове́нная красота́.

uncommonly *adv* необыкнове́нно.

unconcerned *adj* 1. *(not worried)* беззабо́тный, -ая, -ое, -ые, беспе́чный, -ая, -ое, -ые; 2. *(indifferent)* равноду́шный, -ая, -ое, -ые.

unconditional *adj* безусло́вный, -ая, -ое, -ые, безогово́рочный, -ая, -ое, -ые ♦ **I give you my unconditional love.** Я безогово́рочно отдаю́ тебе́ мою́ любо́вь.

unconditionally *adv* безусло́вно.

unconscious *adj* 1. *(having lost consciousness)* потеря́вший (-ая, -ее, -ие) созна́ние, в бессозна́тельном состоя́нии; 2. *(involuntary)* непроизво́льный, -ая, -ое, -ые, нево́льный, -ая, -ое, -ые.

unconsciously *adv* непроизво́льно, нево́льно, бессозна́тельно.

uncontrollable *adj* неукроти́мый, -ая, -ое, -ые, неудержи́мый, -ая, -ое, -ые, бесконтро́льный, -ая, -ое, -ые.

unconventional *adj* нетрадицио́нный, -ая, -ое, -ые, необы́чный, -ая, -ое, -ые.

unconvincing *adj* неубеди́тельный, -ая, -ое, -ые.

uncouth *adj* гру́бый, -ая, -ое, -ые.

uncover *vt* раскрыва́ть / раскры́ть *(what = acc.)*, открыва́ть / откры́ть *(what = acc.)* ♦ **My** *(1)* **yearning** / *(2)* **adoring** / *(3)* **roving** / *(4)* **ravenous lips will uncover your most precious**

There are no articles ("a" or "the") in Russian.

secret. Мои *(1)* жа́ждущие / *(2)* обожа́ющие / *(3)* блужда́ющие / *(4)* изголода́вшиеся гу́бы раскро́ют твой са́мый заве́тный секре́т. ♦ **I long for the day when I can uncover all the secrets of your gorgeous body.** Я тоску́ю по дню, когда́ я смогу́ пости́чь все та́йны твоего́ великоле́пного те́ла.

uncultured *adj* некульту́рный, -ая, -ое, -ые.

undated *adj* недати́рованный, -ая, -ое, -ые ♦ ~ **letter** недати́рованное письмо́.

undecided *adj*: ♦ **be** ~ не реши́ть, не приня́ть реше́ние ♦ **I'm still undecided.** Я ещё не реши́л *(ж: реши́ла)*.

undemanding *adj* нетре́бовательный, -ая, -ое, -ые.

undeniable *adj* неоспори́мый, -ая, -ое, -ые.

undeniably *adj* неоспори́мо.

undependable *adj* ненадёжный, -ая, -ое, -ые.

underage(d) *adj* несовершенноле́тний, -яя, -ее, -ие.

underclothes *n, pl* ни́жнее бельё.

underestimate *vt* преуменьша́ть / преуме́ньши́ть *(what, whom = acc.)* ♦ **Never underestimate the power of love.** Никогда́ не преуменьша́й си́лу любви́.

understand *vi* понима́ть / поня́ть *(what, whom = acc.)* ♦ ~ **clearly** я́сно понима́ть / поня́ть ♦ ~ *(1,2)* **correctly** *(1)* пра́вильно / *(2)* ве́рно понима́ть / поня́ть ♦ ~ **differently** понима́ть / поня́ть по-ра́зному ♦ ~ **each other with a half-word** понима́ть / поня́ть друг дру́га с полусло́ва ♦ ~ **each other without words** понима́ть / поня́ть друг дру́га без слов ♦ ~ **incorrectly** непра́вильно понима́ть / поня́ть ♦ **not quite** ~ не совсе́м понима́ть / поня́ть ♦ **not** ~ **well** пло́хо понима́ть / поня́ть ♦ ~ **perfectly** прекра́сно понима́ть / поня́ть ♦ ~ *(1,2)* **right** *(1)* пра́вильно / *(2)* ве́рно понима́ть / поня́ть ♦ ~ **the same (way)** одина́ково понима́ть / поня́ть ♦ ~ **well** хорошо́ понима́ть / поня́ть ♦ **begin to** ~ начина́ть / нача́ть понима́ть ♦ **difficult to** ~ тру́дный (-ая, -ое, -ые) для понима́ния ♦ **failure to** ~ **each other** взаи́мное недопонима́ние ♦ **try to** ~ стара́ться поня́ть.

understand: phrases

You don't seem to understand (*[1]*...**how I feel.** / *[2]* ...**what I mean.**). Ты, ка́жется, не понима́ешь (*[1]*...что я чу́вствую. / *[2]* ...что я име́ю в виду́.) ♦ **How I wish you could understand everything that's in my heart.** Как бы я хоте́л *(ж: хоте́ла)*, чтобы ты смогла́ *(ж: смог)* поня́ть всё, что у меня́ на се́рдце.

understandable *adj* поня́тный, -ая, -ое, -ые ♦ *(1,2)* **completely** ~ *(1)* вполне́ / *(2)* соверше́нно поня́тный, -ая, -ое, -ые.

understandably *adv* поня́тно.

understanding *adj* 1. *(comprehending)* понима́ющий, -ая, -ее, -ие; 2. *(responding, sensitive)* отзы́вчивый, -ая, -ое, -ые, чу́ткий, -ая, -ое, -ие ♦ **If you (really) value our relationship, try to be more understanding.** Если ты (действи́тельно) це́нишь на́ши отноше́ния, попыта́йся быть бо́лее понима́ющей *(ж: понима́ющим)*.

understanding *n* понима́ние ♦ **clear** ~ я́сное понима́ние ♦ **complete** ~ по́лное понима́ние ♦ **correct** ~ пра́вильное понима́ние ♦ **deep** ~ глубо́кое понима́ние ♦ **different** ~ ра́зное понима́ние ♦ **false** ~ ошибо́чное понима́ние ♦ **full** ~ по́лное понима́ние ♦ **fuzzy** ~ сму́тное понима́ние ♦ **good** ~ хоро́шее понима́ние ♦ **mutual** ~ взаимопонима́ние, взаи́мное понима́ние ♦ **perfect** ~ прекра́сное понима́ние ♦ **poor** ~ плохо́е понима́ние ♦ **same** ~ одина́ковое понима́ние ♦ **true** ~ ве́рное понима́ние ♦ **vague** ~ сму́тное понима́ние ♦ **difficulty (in)** ~ тру́дность понима́ния.

understanding: phrases

Our love is based on trust and respect and understanding. На́ша любо́вь осно́вана на дове́рии, уваже́нии и взаимопонима́нии. ♦ **I want a love based on trust and respect**

This dictionary contains two Russian alphabet pages: one in Appendix 1, page 685, and a tear-off page on page 799.

and understanding. Я хочу́, что́бы в осно́ве любви́ бы́ли дове́рие, уваже́ние и взаи-
мопонима́ние.

understatement *n* преуменьше́ние ♦ **To say that you are** *(1)* **...physically appealing...** / *(2)*
...attractive... / *(3)* **...beautiful... is the understatement of the** *(4)* **year** / *(5)* **century.** Ска-
за́ть, что ты про́сто *(1)* ...физи́чески привлека́тельна... / *(2)* ...привлека́тельна... *(3)*
краси́ва -- э́то са́мое невероя́тное преуменьше́ние э́того *(4)* го́да / *(5)* ве́ка. ♦ **To say
that you're (exceptionally)** *(1,2)* **good-looking is a** *(3)* **gross** / *(4)* **huge understatement.**
Сказа́ть, что ты (исключи́тельно) *(1)* краси́ва *(ж: краси́в)* / *(2)* привлека́тельна *(ж:
привлека́телен)* - э́то *(3)* большо́е / *(4)* огро́мное преуменьше́ние. ♦ **Beautiful is a
much-abused word, but it's an understatement when applied to you.** Прекра́сная --
сло́во, кото́рым ча́сто злоупотребля́ют, но э́то преуменьше́ние, когда́ оно́ обращено́
к тебе́.

underthings *n, pl* же́нское (ни́жнее) бельё.

underwear *n, pl* ни́жнее бельё ♦ **How I dream of the day when I can peel away your silk
underwear to reveal the full,** *(1)* **glorious** / *(2)* **magnificent splendor of your of your
beautiful, luscious body.** Как я мечта́ю о том дне, когда́ смогу́ сбро́сить с тебя́ шёлковое бельё, что́бы откры́ть напо́лненную до краёв, *(1)* великоле́пную / *(2)* замеча́-
тельную ро́скошь твоего́ прекра́сного, со́чного те́ла.

undescribable *adj* неопису́емый, -ая, -ое, -ые.

undeserved *adj* незаслу́женный, -ая, -ое, -ые.

undesirable *adj* нежела́тельный, -ая, -ое, -ые.

undies *n, pl (slang) (underpants)* трусы́.

undignified *adj* недосто́йный, -ая, -ое, -ые, лишённый (-ая, -ое, -ые) со́бственного
досто́инства.

undiminishable *adj* неуменьша́емый, -ая, -ое, -ые, неослабева́ющий, -ая, -ее, -ие.

undo *vt (untie)* развя́зывать / развяза́ть *(what = acc.)*; *(unbutton)* расстёгивать / рас-
стегну́ть *(what = acc.)* ♦ ~ **buttons** расстёгивать / расстегну́ть пу́говицы.

undoubtedly *adv* несомне́нно, без сомне́ния.

undress *vt (other)* раздева́ть / разде́ть *(whom = acc.)* ♦ **slowly** ~ ме́дленно раздева́ть ♦ **I
want to undress you slowly.** Я хочу́ ме́дленно разде́ть тебя́. ♦ **You were undressing
her with your eyes.** Ты раздева́л её глаза́ми.

undress *vi (self)* раздева́ться / разде́ться ♦ *(1)* **I'd love to...** / *(2)* **I love to... watch you undress.** *(1)* Я хоте́л бы... / *(2)* Я люблю́... ви́деть, как ты раздева́ешься.

undressed *adj* разде́тый, -ая, -ое, -ые *(short forms:* разде́т, -а, -о, -ы*)* ♦ **get** ~ раздева́ться
/ разде́ться.

undulate *vi* колыха́ться ♦ **I watch your mouth forming sounds, moving and undulating so
supplely, so softly, so enticingly and I am seized with a raging impulse to fuse my own
mouth together with it and once and for all revel in its sweet softness.** Я слежу́, как твой
рот создаёт зву́ки, дви́гаясь и изгиба́ясь так ги́бко, так мя́гко, так соблазни́тельно,
и я захва́чен бе́шеным и́мпульсом соедини́ть мой рот с твои́м, что́бы раз и навсегда́
пирова́ть в его́ сла́дкой не́жности.

undying *adj* бессме́ртный, -ая, -ое, -ые, неумира́ющий, -ая, -ее, -ие ♦ **Yours, with undying love...** *(closing of a letter)* Твой, с неумира́ющей любо́вью... *(коне́ц письма́).*

uneasiness *n* 1. *(awkwardness)* нело́вкость *f*; *(embarrassment)* смуще́ние; 2. *(apprehension)*
беспоко́йство, трево́га ♦ **initial** ~ нача́льная нело́вкость.

uneasy *adj* 1. *(awkward)* нело́вкий, -ая, -ое, -ие; *(embarrassed)* смущённый, -ая, -ое, -ые;
2. *(apprehensive, tense)* беспоко́йный, -ая, -ое, -ые, трево́жный, -ая, -ое, -ые.

unemotional *adj* неэмоциона́льный, -ая, -ое, -ые.

---

*Russian verbs conjugate for 6 persons:
I, familiar you, he-she-it, we, polite & plural you, and they.*

unemployed *adj* безрабо́тный, -ая, -ое, -ые.

unencumbered *adj (having no children, dependents or problems)* необременённый, -ая, -ое, -ые, без дете́й и́ли пробле́м.

unending *adj* бесконе́чный, -ая, -ое, -ые, несконча́емый, -ая, -ое, -ые; *(eternal)* ве́чный, -ая, -ое, -ые ♦ *(1)* This... / *(2)* This gift... is just a small *(3)* expression / *(4)* token of my unending love for you. *(1)* Это... / *(2)* Этот пода́рок... - то́лько ма́ленький *(3)* си́мвол / *(4)* знак мое́й несконча́емой любви́ к тебе́.

unendingly *adv* бесконе́чно.

unenthusiastic *adj* без энтузиа́зма.

unenthusiastically *adv* без энтузиа́зма.

unequal *adj* нера́вный, -ая, -ое, -ые.

unequalled *adj* несравне́нный, -ая, -ое, -ые, бесподо́бный, -ая, -ое, -ые.

uneven *adj (unequal)* нера́вный, -ая, -ое, -ые.

unexceptional *adj* неисключи́тельный, -ая, -ое, -ые.

unexciting *adj* неволну́ющий, -ая, -ее, -ие; ску́чный, -ая, -ое, -ые.

unexpected *adj* неожи́данный, -ая, -ое, -ые ♦ This letter of yours was so unexpected. Your *(1)* sweet / *(2)* beautiful words of love have set my heart completely aquiver. Это письмо́ от тебя́ бы́ло так неожи́данно. Твои́ *(1)* не́жные / *(2)* прекра́сные слова́ любви́ заставля́ют моё се́рдце трепета́ть.

unexpectedly *adj* неожи́данно

unfair *adj* несправедли́вый, -ая, -ое, -ые.

unfairly *adv* несправедли́во.

unfairness *n* несправедли́вость *f.*

unfaithful *adj* неве́рный, -ая, -ое, -ые, вероло́мный, -ая, -ое, -ые be ~ изменя́ть / измени́ть *(to whom = acc.)* ♦ I *(1)* will / *(2)* would never be unfaithful to you. Я никогда́ *(1)* ...не бу́ду изменя́ть... / *(2)* ...не измени́л *(ж: измени́ла)* бы... тебе́. ♦ I have never been unfaithful to you. Я никогда́ не изменя́л *(ж: изменя́ла)* тебе́. / Я всегда́ был ве́рным *(ж: была́ ве́рной)* тебе́. ♦ I will never be unfaithful to you. Я всегда́ бу́ду ве́рен *(ж: верна́)* тебе́. ♦ *(1,2)* I have never been unfaithful to you (in thought or in deed). *(1)* Я всегда́ был ве́рен *(ж: была́ верна́)* тебе́ ... / *(2)* Я никогда́ не изменя́л *(ж: не изменя́ла)* тебе́ ... (в мы́слях или в посту́пках).

unfaltering *adj* непоколеби́мый, -ая, -ое, -ые.

unfamiliar *adj* незнако́мый, -ая, -ое, -ые, чужо́й, -а́я, -о́е, -и́е.

unfasten *vt* расстёгивать / расстегну́ть *(what = acc.).*

unfathomable *adj* необъя́тный, -ая, -ое, -ые.

unfeeling *adj* бесчу́вственный, -ая, -ое, -ые.

unfeminine *adj* неже́нский, -ая, -ое, -ие.

unfettered *adj (unlimited)* неограни́ченный, -ая, -ое, -ые.

unfit *adj* неподходя́щий, -ая, -ее, -ие.

unflappable *adj* невозмути́мый, -ая, -ое, -ые

unforeseen *adj* непредусмо́тренный, -ая, -ое, -ые, непредви́денный, -ая, -ое, -ые

unforgettable *adj* незабве́нный, -ая, -ое, -ые, незабыва́емый, -ая, -ое, -ые ♦ Those *(1)* days / *(2)* hours / *(3)* moments we shared are unforgettable. Те *(1)* дни / *(2)* часы́ / *(3)* моме́нты, кото́рые мы провели́ вме́сте, незабыва́емы.

unforgivable *adj* непрости́тельный, -ая, -ое, -ые.

unforgiving *adj* непроща́ющий, -ая, -ее, -ие.

unfortunate *adj* 1. *(unlucky)* несча́стный, -ая, -ое, -ые; 2. *(regrettable)* неуда́чный, -ая, -ое, -ые.

There are two words for "you" in Russian:
familiar «ты» and polite / plural «вы» (See page 781).

unfortunately *adv* к сожалénию, к несчáстью.

unfriendly *adj* недрýжественный, -ая, -ое, -ые, недружелюбный, -ая, -ое, -ые.

unfulfilled *adj* невыполненный, -ая, -ое, -ые, неиспóлненный, -ая, -ое, -ые, неосуществлённый, -ая, -ое, -ые.

ungallant *adj* негалáнтный, -ая, -ое, -ые.

ungentlemanly *adj* неджентльмéнский, -ая, -ое, -ие.

unglued *adj (slang)* óчень расстрóен, -а, -ы *(short forms)*, опýщен -а, -ы *(short forms)* ♦ **come ~** расстрáиваться / расстрóиться ♦ **Take it easy. Don't come unglued.** Принимáй это лéгче. Не расстрáивайся. ♦ **I didn't tell you, because I knew you'd come unglued.** Я не сказáл *(ж: сказáла)* тебé, потомý что знал *(ж: знáла)*, что ты óчень расстрóишься. ♦ **When I told** *(1)* **her /** *(2)* **him (about it),** *(3)* **she /** *(4)* **he** *(5,6)* **came unglued.** Когдá я расскáзывал *(ж: расскáзывала)* *(1)* ей / *(2)* емý (об этом), *(3)* онá / *(4)* он óчень *(5)* расстрóилась *f* / *(6)* расстрóился *m*.

ungracious *adj* невéжливый, -ая, -ое, -ые.

ungrateful *adj* неблагодáрный, -ая, -ое, -ые.

unhampered *adj* беспрепя́тственный, -ая, -ое, -ые, незатруднённый, -ая, -ое, -ые.

unhappiness *n* несчáстие ♦ **I've had more than my fair share of unhappiness.** На мою́ дóлю вы́пало несчáстий бóлее, чем достáточно.

unhappy *adj* несчáстный, -ая, -ое, -ые ♦ **You seem to be perpetually unhappy.** Ты всегдá вы́глядишь несчáстной *(ж: несчáстным)*.

unhealthy *adj* нездорóвый, -ая, -ое, -ые.

unheard-of *adj* неслы́ханный, -ая, -ое, -ые.

unhook *vt* расстёгивать / расстегнýть (крючки́) *(what = acc.)*.

unhurried *adj* неторопли́вый, -ая, -ое, -ые.

unimaginable *adj* невероя́тный, -ая, -ое, -ые, невообрази́мый, -ая, -ое, -ые.

unimaginably *adv* невероя́тно, невообрази́мо.

unimaginative *adj* лишённый (-ая, -ое, -ые) воображéния.

unimportant *adj* невáжный, -ая, -ое, -ые.

unimpressed: ♦ **I was unimpressed by it.** Это не произвелó на меня́ никакóго впечатлéния.

unimpressive *adj* невпчатля́ющий, -ая, -ее, -ие.

uninhibited *adj* вóльный, -ая, -ое, -ые, раскóванный, -ая, -ое, -ые, нестеснённый, -ая, -ое, -ые, без кóмплексов.

unintelligible *adj* непоня́тный, -ая, -ое, -ые.

unintended *adj* непреднамéренный, -ая, -ое, -ые, неумы́шленный, -ая, -ое, -ые.

unintentional *adj* непреднамéренный, -ая, -ое, -ые, неумы́шленный, -ая, -ое, -ые.

unintentionally *adv* непреднамéренно, неумы́шленно.

uninteresting *adj* неинтерéсный, -ая, -ое, -ые.

union *n* союз ♦ **close ~** тéсный союз ♦ **eternal ~** вéчный союз ♦ **lifelong ~** союз длинóю в жизнь ♦ **strong ~** крéпкий союз ♦ **unbreakable ~** неруши́мый союз.

union: *phrases*

I pray that ours will be a lifelong union. Я молю́сь, чтóбы наш союз был длинóй в жизнь. ♦ **May this union of our hearts last** *(1)* **...forever. /** *(2)* **...throughout our lives.** Пусть этот союз нáших сердéц продолжáется *(1)* ...вéчно. / *(2)* ...всю нáшу жизнь. ♦ **The union of our two spirits was destined to be.** Союз нáших двух душ был предопределён.

unique *adj* уникáльный, -ая, -ое, -ые *(short forms:* уникáлен, уникáльна, -о, -ы*)*, неповтори́мый, -ая, -ое, -ые ♦ **You are indisputably unique and indisputably classic in the**

Russian terms of endearment are given in Appendix 13, page 780.

magnitude of your loveliness. Ты бесспо́рно уника́льна и бесспо́рно класси́чна в свое́й красоте́. ♦ **You are so unique and so special.** Ты так уника́льна *(ж: уника́лен).*
uniquely *adv* уника́льно.
unison *n* 1. унисо́н; 2. *(agreement)* согла́сие ♦ **move in** ~ дви́гаться в унисо́н.
unite *vi* соединя́ться / соедини́ться ♦ **Our two souls have united forever.** На́ши две души́ соедини́лись наве́чно. ♦ **I want to take you as my wife so that we may unite forever in body and soul.** Я хочу́ сде́лать тебя́ свое́й жено́й, что́бы мы могли́ соедини́ться наве́чно те́лом и душо́й.
universe *n* вселе́нная ♦ **I want to explore the universe with you.** Я хочу́ иссле́довать вселе́нную вме́сте с тобо́й.
university-educated *adj* с вы́сшим образова́нием.
unjust *adj* несправедли́вый, -ая, -ое, -ые.
unjustly *adv* несправедли́во.
unjustified *adj* неопра́вданный, -ая, -ое, -ые.
unkempt *adj* 1. *(uncombed)* нечёсаный, -ая, -ое, -ые; 2. *(untidy)* неопря́тный, -ая, -ое, -ые.
unkind *adj* недо́брый, -ая, -ое, -ые, злой, -а́я, -о́е, -ы́е ♦ **I hope I don't sound unkind.** Наде́юсь, я не кажу́сь злым *(ж: злой).*
unknowingly *adv* бессозна́тельно.
unknown *adj* неизве́стный, -ая, -ое, -ые. неизве́данный, -ая, -ое, -ые ♦ **heretofore** неизве́данный дото́ле.
unlovable *adj* не досто́йный (-ая, -ое, -ые) любви́ ♦ **Before I met you, I used to** *(1)* **think** / *(2)* **believe that I was (completely) unlovable.** До встре́чи с тобо́й я привы́к *(ж: привы́кла) (1)* ду́мать / *(2)* ве́рить, что я соверше́нно не досто́ин *(ж: досто́йна)* любви́.
unloved *adj* нелюби́мый, -ая, -ое, -ые ♦ **Until I met you, I felt so (totally) unloved.** До встре́чи с тобо́й я никогда́ не чу́вствовал себя́ люби́мым *(ж: чу́вствовала себя́ люби́мой).*
unlucky *adj* неуда́чный, -ая, -ое, -ые ♦ **I was unlucky.** Мне не везло́.
unmatched *adj* несравни́мый, -ая, -ое, -ые, бесподо́бный, -ая, -ое, -ые ♦ **be** ~ не име́ть себе́ ра́вного, никому́ не уступа́ть.
unmeasurable *adj* неизмери́мый, -ая, -ое, -ые ♦ **My love for you is unmeasurable.** Моя́ любо́вь к тебе́ неизмери́ма.
unmerciful *adj* неща́дный, -ая, -ое, -ые, немилосе́рдный, -ая, -ое, -ые.
unmercifully *adv* неща́дно, немилосе́рдно ♦ **I lie in the dark, thinking about you, and my loin throbs unmercifully.** Я лежу́ в темноте́, ду́мая о тебе́, и моё естество́ трепе́щет неща́дно.
unnatural *adj* 1. неесте́ственный, -ая, -ое, -ые; 2. *(unusual, strange)* необы́чный, -ая, -ое, -ые, стра́нный, -ая, -ое, -ые ♦ ~ **demands** ненорма́льные тре́бования.
unnerve *vt* нерви́ровать *(whom = acc.)*; расстра́ивать / расстро́ить *(whom = acc.).*
unnerved *adj* расстро́енный, -ая, -ое, -ые ♦ **be** ~ расстра́иваться / расстро́иться *(at what* = + из-за + *gen.).*
unpredictable *adj* непредсказу́емый, -ая, -ое, -ые; *(capricious)* капри́зный, -ая, -ое, -ые ♦ ~ **person** непредсказу́емый челове́к.
unpretentious *adj* непритяза́тельный, -ая, -ое, -ые, неприхотли́вый, -ая, -ое, -ые, непретенцио́зный, -ая, -ое, -ые.
unquenchable *adj* неутоли́мый, -ая, -ое, -ые.
unravel *vi (come apart)* распада́ться / распа́сться, разва́ливаться / развали́ться ♦ **I feel like our relationship is beginning to unravel.** Я чу́вствую, как на́ши отноше́ния начина́ют разва́ливаться.

Some of the Russian sentences are translations of things we say
and are not what Russians themselves would normally say.

unreal *adj* нереа́льный, -ая, -ое, -ые.

unrealistic *adj* нереалисти́ческий, -ая, -ое, -ие, нереа́льный, -ая, -ое, -ые ♦ **Your expectations of me are unrealistic.** То, чего́ ты ожида́ешь от меня́, нереа́льно.

unrealistically *adv* нереалисти́чески, нереа́льно.

unrelenting *adj* неумоли́мый, -ая, -ое, -ые.

unremitting *adj* неосла́бный, -ая, -ое, -ые, неослабева́ющий, -ая, -ее, -ие, неосла́бленный, -ая, -ое, -ые; беспреста́нный, -ая, -ое, -ые ♦ **Yours, with unremitting love...** *(ending of a letter)* Твой, с неосла́бной любо́вью... *(коне́ц письма́)*.

unrequited *adj* не по́льзующийся (-аяся, -ееся, -иеся) взаи́мностью, без взаи́мности.

unresisting *adj* несопротивля́ющийся, -аяся, -ееся, -иеся.

unresponsive *adj (sex)* безразли́чный, -ая, -ое, -ые ♦ **My wife is** *(1,2)* **sexually unresponsive.** Моя́ жена́ *(1)* ...сексуа́льно безразли́чная. / *(2)* ...холо́дная. ♦ **My ex-girlfriend was sexually unresponsive before she met me.** Моя́ бы́вшая де́вушка была́ сексуа́льно безразли́чная, пока́ не встре́тила меня́.

unrestrained *adj* несде́ржанный, -ая, -ое, -ые, необу́зданный, -ая, -ое, -ые ♦ **I didn't realize I was capable of such unrestrained passion.** Я не осознава́л *(ж: осознава́ла)*, что был спосо́бен *(ж: была́ спосо́бна)* на таку́ю необу́зданную страсть.

unrivaled *adj* несравне́нный, -ая, -ое, -ые.

unseemly *adj* недосто́йный, -ая, -ое, -ые, неподоба́ющий, -ая, -ее, -ие; неуме́стный, -ая, -ое, -ые ♦ **It would be unseemly to do that.** Бы́ло бы недосто́йно сде́лать э́то.

un-self-conscious *adj* беззасте́нчивый, -ая, -ое, -ые.

unselfish *adj* неэгоисти́чный, -ая, -ое, -ые, бескоры́стный, -ая, -ое, -ые.

unselfishly *adv* неэгоисти́чно, бескоры́стно.

unselfishness *n* неэгоисти́чность *f*, бескоры́стие.

unsettling *adj* беспоко́ящий, -ая, -ее, -ие, трево́жащий, -ая, -ее, -ие.

unsophisticated *adj (inexperienced)* неискушённый, -ая, -ое, -ые; *(ingenuous)* простоду́шный, -ая, -ое, -ые; *(innocent)* неви́нный, -ая, -ое, -ые; *(naive)* наи́вный, -ая, -ое, -ые.

unskinny *adj (slang) (heavy)* по́лный, -ая, -ое, -ые ♦ **pleasantly** ~ прия́тно по́лный, -ая, -ое, -ые

unspoken *adj* невы́сказанный, -ая, -ое, -ые.

unsurpassed *adj* непревзойдённый, -ая, -ое, -ые ♦ **The unsurpassed beauty of your face reigns over all my thoughts.** Непревзойдённая красота́ твоего́ лица́ вла́ствует над все́ми мои́ми по́мыслами.

unswerving *adj* непоколеби́мый, -ая, -ое, -ые, сто́йкий, -ая, -ое, -ие.

unthinking *adj* безду́мный, -ая, -ое, -ые.

untie *vt* развя́зывать / развяза́ть *(what = acc.)*.

until 1. *prep* до *(+ gen.)*; 2. *conj* (до тех пор) пока́ (не).

untrue *adj* неве́рный, -ая, -ое, -ые *(short forms:* неве́рен, неверна́, -о, -ы*)* ♦ **I felt in the pit of my stomach that you were being untrue.** Я чу́вствовал *(ж: чу́вствовала)* в глубине́ души́, что ты была́ неверна́ *(ж: был неве́рен)*.

unwavering *adj* непоколеби́мый, -ая, -ое, -ые, сто́йкий, -ая, -ое, -ие.

unyielding *adj* 1. *(inflexible, intransigent)* непрекло́нный, -ая, -ое, -ые, упо́рный, -ая, -ое, -ые; 2. *(stiff)* неподатливый, -ая, -ое, -ые.

unzip *vt* расстёгивать / расстегну́ть мо́лнию *(what = + на + prep.)* ♦ ~ **your** *(1)* **dress** / *(2)* **skirt** / *(3)* **jeans** / *(4)* **pants** расстёгивать / расстегну́ть мо́лнию на *(1)* ...твоём пла́тье, / *(2)* ...твое́й ю́бке. / *(3)* ...твои́х джи́нсах / *(4)* брю́ках.

unzipped *adj* с расстёгнутой мо́лнией.

up (for) *prep (slang) (ready, willing to try)* гото́в (-а, ы) попро́бовать ♦ **I'm up for (almost)**

Counting things in Russian is a bit involved.
See Appendix 4, Numbers, on page 756 .

anything. Я гото́в *(ж: гото́ва)* попро́бовать (почти́) всё.

upbeat *adj (slang) (positive)* положи́тельный, -ая, -ое, -ые; *(enthusiastic)* оптимисти́ческий, -ая, -ое, -ие; *(cheerful)* бо́дрый, -ая, -ое, -ые .

upbringing *n (condition)* воспи́танность; *(act)* воспита́ние ♦ **I've had a middle-class up-bringing.** У меня́ воспита́ние челове́ка сре́днего кла́сса.

up-front *adj (forthright)* прямо́й, -а́я, -о́е, -ы́е; *(candid)* открове́нный, -ая, -ое, -ые, и́скренний, -яя, -ее, -ие; *(honest)* че́стный, -ая, -ое, -ые.

uplift *vt* поднима́ть / подня́ть ♦ **I can't tell you how much your letters uplift my spirits.** Я да́же не могу́ описа́ть тебе́, как твои́ пи́сьма поднима́ют мой дух. ♦ **How your letter has uplifted my spirits.** Как твоё письмо́ по́дняло мой дух.

uplifted *adj* по́днят, -а́, -о, -ы *(short forms)* ♦ **My spirits are so uplifted by your letters.** Твои́ пи́сьма так поднима́ют мой дух. ♦ **With you by my side I would feel so uplifted and inspired and happy.** С тобо́й я бы чу́вствовал *(ж: чу́вствовала)* тако́й подъём, вдохнове́ние и сча́стье.

uplifting *adj* поднима́ющий, -ая, -ее, -ие ♦ **That's very uplifting news.** Эти но́вости о́чень поднима́ют дух. ♦ **Another of your uplifting letters arrived today.** Ещё одно́ твоё поднима́ющее дух письмо́ пришло́ сего́дня.

up on *idiom (knowledgeable):* ♦ **I'm up on current events.** Я в ку́рсе теку́щих собы́тий.

uppity *adj* высокоме́рный, -ая, -ое, -ые.

upscale *adj* вы́ше сре́днего у́ровня.

upset *adj* расстро́ен, -а, -о, -ы *(short forms)* ♦ **You (1) sound / (2) sounded ([3] a little / [4] rather / [5] very) upset.** Твой го́лос *(1)* звучи́т / *(2)* звуча́л *([3]* немно́го / *[4]* дово́льно / *[5]* о́чень) огорчённо. ♦ **What are you upset about?** Из-за чего́ ты расстро́ена *(ж: расстро́ен)*? ♦ **I'm (not) upset.** Я (не) расстро́ен *(ж: расстро́ена)*.

upset *vt* расстра́ивать / расстро́ить *(whom = acc.)* ♦ **It upset me.** Это расстро́ило меня́.

upstanding *adj* че́стный, -ая, -ое, -ые, открове́нный, -ая, -ое, -ые.

uptight *adj (slang) (tense)* натя́нутый, -ая, -ое, -ые, напряжённый, -ая, -ое, -ые *(short forms:* напряжён, -а́, -о́, -ы́).

upward *adv* вы́ше ♦ **Upward and upward and upward I want to (1) propel / (2) send you into (3) ecstasy / (4) passion.** Я хочу́ *(1,2)* подня́ть тебя́ всё вы́ше, вы́ше и вы́ше к верши́нам *(3)* экста́за / *(4)* стра́сти. ♦ **Upward and upward and upward I want you to soar into ecstasy.** Я хочу́, чтобы ты всё вы́ше, вы́ше и вы́ше пари́ла в экста́зе.

urban *adj* городско́й, -а́я, -о́е, -и́е.

urbane *adj* ве́жливый, -ая, -ое, -ые, обходи́тельный, -ая, -ое, -ые, изы́сканный, -ая, -ое, -ые.

urge *n* побужде́ние, и́мпульс ♦ **overpowering** ~ могу́щественнейшее побужде́ние ♦ **powerful** ~ мо́щное побужде́ние ♦ **primeval** ~ первобы́тный и́мпульс ♦ **tremendous** ~ грома́дный и́мпульс ♦ **uncontrollable** ~ неконтроли́руемый и́мпульс ♦ **I wonder if I could control the urge to kiss you.** Интере́сно, смог *(ж: смогла́)* бы я контроли́ровать побужде́ние поцелова́ть тебя́.

urgency *n* сро́чность *f*, безотлага́тельность *f*, неотло́жность *f*.

urgent *adj* сро́чный, -ая, -ое, -ые, безотлага́тельный, -ая, -ое, -ые, неотло́жный, -ая, -ое, -ые.

use *vt* употребля́ть / употреби́ть *(what = acc.)*, по́льзоваться / воспо́льзоваться *(what = instr.)*, испо́льзовать *(what = acc.)*.

used *adj* 1. *(utilized; exploited)* испо́льзованный, -ая, -ое, -ые *(short forms:* испо́льзован, -а, -о, -ы)*; 2. *(second-hand)* поде́ржанный, -ая, -ое, -ые ♦ **I don't want to be used.** Я не хочу́, чтобы меня́ испо́льзовали. ♦ **I feel like I've been used.** Я чу́вствую, как бу́дто

Russian has 2 different verbs for "go",
one for "on foot" and the other for "by vehicle".

был испо́льзован *(ж: была́ испо́льзована)*.

user *n* по́льзователь *m* ♦ **drug** ~ наркома́н.

usual *adj* обы́чный, -ая, -ое, -ые, обыкнове́нный, -ая, -ое, -ые.

usually *adv* обы́чно, обыкнове́нно.

utter *adj* соверше́нный, -ая, -ое, -ые, по́лный, -ая, -ое, -ые.

utterly *adv* соверше́нно, по́лностью, кра́йне, чрезвыча́йно.

Uzbek *adj* узбе́кский, -ая, -ое, -ие.

Uzbek *n* 1. *(person)* узбе́к *m*, узбе́чка *f (pl:* узбе́ки*)*; 2. *(language)* узбе́кский язы́к ♦ **speak** ~ говори́ть по-узбе́кски.

Dipthongs in Russian are made by adding й
*to the end of a vowel (*а, е, ё, о, у, э, ю, *and* я*).*

V

vacation *n* о́тпуск; *(school)* кани́кулы ♦ **I would just love to take a** *(1,2)* **vacation with you (to** *(place)* . Я бы о́чень хоте́л *(ж: хоте́ла)* провести́ *(1)* о́тпуск / *(2)* кани́кулы с тобо́й в *(назва́ние ме́ста)*. ♦ **Would it be possible for you to take vacation (***[1]* **while I'm here /** *[2]* **there)?** Смо́жешь ли ты взять о́тпуск *([1]* пока́ я здесь / *[2]* там)? ♦ **I can('t) take vacation (at** *[1]* **this /** *[2]* **that time).** Я (не) могу́ взять о́тпуск (в *[1]* э́то / *[2]* то вре́мя). ♦ **It was such an idyllic vacation with you.** Отпуск с тобо́й был иди́ллией.

vacuum *n* пустота́ ♦ **Only you can fill the vacuum of my loneliness.** То́лько ты мо́жешь запо́лнить пустоту́ моего́ одино́чества.

vagabond *n* бродя́га, безде́льник ♦ **cultural** ~ челове́к, интересу́ющийся ра́зными культу́рами *(1 term)*.

vagina *n* влага́лище ♦ **tight** ~ те́сное влага́лище.

vain *adj* 1. *(futile)* тще́тный, -ая, -ое, -ые, напра́сный,-ая, -ое, -ые; 2. *(conceited)* тщесла́вный,-ая, -ое, -ые.

Valentine *n (Caution: Most Russians do not know this holiday.) (Translates into Russian as "beloved")* возлю́бленный *m;* возлю́бленная *f* ♦ **You will always be my Valentine.** Ты всегда́ бу́дешь мое́й возлю́бленной *(ж: мои́м возлю́бленным)*. ♦ *(1,2)* **You are my (year-round) Valentine.** *(1)* Ты моя́ возлю́бленная *(ж: мой возлю́бленный)* (навсегда́). / *(2)* Ты челове́к, кото́рого я люблю́ (навсегда́). ♦ **Let's be Valentines for life.** Дава́й бу́дем возлю́бленными на всю жизнь.

Valentine's Day День Свято́го Валенти́на *(пра́здник возлю́бленных, 14-ое февраля́)*.

valley *n* 1. доли́на; 2. *(breasts)* желобо́к ♦ **lush** ~ роско́шная доли́на ♦ **soft** ~ прия́тный желобо́к ♦ ~ **between the breasts** желобо́к ме́жду грудя́ми ♦ ~ **of paradise** доли́на ра́я.

value *vt* цени́ть *(what = acc.)*, дорожи́ть *(what = instr.) (what = acc.)* ♦ **I value your** *(1)* **friendship /** *(2)* **opinion /** *(3)* **trust.** Я ценю́ *(1)* ...твою́ дру́жбу. / *(2)* ...твоё мне́ние / *(3)* дове́рие. ♦ **If you (really) value our relationship,** *(1)* **...you'll be completely honest with me. /** *(2)* **...you won't hide things from me. /** *(3)* **...you won't do things like that. /** *(4)* **...try to be more loving /** *(5)* **understanding /** *(6)* **sharing /** *(7)* **patient.** Если ты (действи́тельно) це́нишь на́ши отноше́ния, *(1)* ...ты бу́дешь соверше́нно че́стной *(ж: че́стным)* со мной. / *(2)* ...ты не бу́дешь ничего́ от меня́ скрыва́ть. / *(3)* ...ты не бу́дешь де́лать тако́е. *(4)* ...попыта́йся быть бо́лее лю́бящей *(ж: лю́бящим)* / *(5)* понима́ющей *(ж: понима́ющим)* / *(6)* уча́стливой *(ж: уча́стливым)* / *(7)* терпели́вой *(ж: терпели́вым)*.

value *n* це́нность *f* ♦ **artistic** ~**s** худо́жественные це́нности ♦ **Christian** ~**s** христиа́нские

Some phrases are listed under more than one main word.

це́нности ♦ **cultural** ~s культу́рные це́нности ♦ **ethical** ~s мора́льные це́нности ♦ **f amily** ~s семе́йные це́нности ♦ **good moral** ~s высо́кие мора́льные це́нности ♦ **great** ~ больша́я це́нность ♦ **left-of-center** ~s ле́вые полити́ческие взгля́ды ♦ **moral** ~s мора́льные це́нности ♦ **old-fashioned** ~s ста́рая систе́ма це́нностей ♦ **practical** ~s практи́ческие це́нности ♦ **progressive** ~s прогресси́вные це́нности ♦ **solid basic** ~s про́чные це́нности ♦ **spiritual** ~s духо́вные це́нности ♦ **strong family** ~s про́чные семе́йные це́нности ♦ **traditional** ~s **raditional** ~s традицио́нные це́нности ♦ **I'm a** *(1)* **man** */ (2)* **woman** */ (3)* **person of values.** *(1-3)* У меня́ есть свои́ жи́зненные це́нности. ♦ *(1)* **It seems...** */ (2)* **I'm glad... that we share the same values.** *(1)* Похоже,... */ (2)* Я рад *(ж: ра́да)*,... что у нас одина́ковые жи́зненные це́нности.

valve: ♦ **safety** ~ отду́шина.

vamp *n* обольсти́тельница, сире́на.

vampy *adj* обольсти́тельная, соблазни́тельная.

vanity *n* суета́, тщесла́вие.

variety *n* разнообра́зие ♦ **Variety is the** *(1,2)* **spice of life.** Разнообра́зие придаёт жи́зни *(1)* вкус */ (2)* остроту́. ♦ **I don't feel the need for variety when it concerns my love life.** Я не нужда́юсь в разнообра́зии, когда́ э́то каса́ется мое́й любо́вной жи́зни.

vasectomy *n* вазэктоми́я, иссече́ние семявынося́щего прото́ка ♦ **I've had a vasectomy.** У меня́ была́ вазэктоми́я.

vast *adj* обши́рный, -ая, -ое, -ые, огро́мный, -ая, -ое, -ые, грома́дный, -ая, -ое, -ые ♦ ~ **as a savanna** грома́дный как сава́нна ♦ ~ **as the cosmos** грома́дный как ко́смос ♦ **I have such a vast reservoir of tender affection to lavish upon you.** У меня́ тако́й грома́дный запа́с любви́ и не́жности, кото́рый я хочу́ изли́ть на тебя́.

vastness *n* ширь *f* ♦ **There are no words to describe the vastness of the love that I bear in my heart for you.** Нет слов, что́бы описа́ть ту любо́вь к тебе́, кото́рой полно́ моё се́рдце.

vee *n* треуго́льный вы́рез ♦ **the** ~ **of your blouse** треуго́льный вы́рез твое́й блу́зки.

vegan *n (strict vegetarian)* стро́гий вегетериа́нец *m*, стро́гая вегетериа́нка *f*

veganism (= vegetarianism) *n* вегетариа́нство.

vegetarian *n* вегетариа́нец *m*, вегетариа́нка *f*.

vegetarianism *n* вегетариа́нство.

vehement *adj* горя́чий, -ая, -ее, -ие, стра́стный, -ая, -ое, -ые.

vehemently *adv* горячо́, стра́стно.

veil *n* вуа́ль *f* ♦ **bridal** *(1,2)* ~ сва́дебная *(1)* фата́ */ (2)* вуа́ль.

vein *n* ве́на ♦ **Just** *(1)* **...smelling your perfume...** */ (2)* **...being close to you...** */ (3)* **...looking at your photo... sends the blood rushing in my veins.** Кровь начина́ет бе́шено струи́ться в мои́х ве́нах про́сто от *(1)* ...арома́та твои́х духо́в. */ (2)* ...того́, что ты ря́дом. */ (3)* ...взгля́да на твоё фо́то. ♦ **Just to look at your picture sends the blood rushing in my veins.** То́лько взгляд на твою́ фотогра́фию заставля́ет кровь быстре́е бежа́ть в мои́х ве́нах. ♦ **Fire courses through my veins.** Ого́нь струи́тся сквозь мои́ ве́ны.

velcro *n* липу́чка.

velvet(y) *adj* бархати́стый, -ая, -ое, -ые.

venomous *adj* ядови́тый, -ая, -ое, -ые.

Venus *n* Вене́ра.

venusian *(or* **venutian)** *n (hypothetical native or inhabitant of Venus)* венериа́нец *m*, венериа́нка. *f.*

verge *n* грань *f* ♦ **I'm like a volcano on the verge of a full-scale eruption.** Я как вулка́н на гра́ни полномасшта́бного изверже́ния.

The singular past tense of Russian verbs ends in -л (m) (usually), -ла (f) or -ло (n). the plural past tense ends in -li.

verging *adj* бли́зкий, -ая, -ое, -ие *(short forms:* бли́зок, близка́, -о, -и́); почти́, чуть не ♦ **be ~ on beautiful** быть почти́ краси́вой.

verve *n* жи́вость *f*, я́ркость *f*.

very *adv* о́чень.

vest *n* жиле́т.

vestigial *adj* исчеза́ющий, -ая, -ее, -ие.

veteran *n* ветера́н ♦ **military ~** ветера́н вое́нной слу́жбы ♦ **Vietnam ~** ветера́н вьетна́мской войны́ ♦ **war ~** ветера́н войны́.

vibe *n (slang) (feeling)* чу́вство *(pl:* чу́вства*)* ♦ **good ~s** хоро́шие чу́вства ♦ **get** *(1,2)* **a ~ ``(from)** чу́вствовать *(1)* гармони́чность / *(2)* совмести́мость.

vibrant *adj* 1. *(lively, full of life)* живо́й, -а́я, -о́е, -ы́е, по́лный (-ая, -ое, -ые) жи́зни / сил; 2. *(voice)* резони́рующий, -ая, -ее, -ие ♦ **~ colors** живы́е кра́ски ♦ **~ tone** резони́рующий тон.

vibrator *n* вибра́тор.

vicarious *adj* чужо́й, -а́я, -о́е, -и́е, ко́свенный, -ая, -ое, -ые.

victim *n* же́ртва ♦ **~ of incest** же́ртва инце́ста ♦ **~ of rape** же́ртва изнаси́лования.

video *n* ви́део(фильм), фильм ♦ **It would be wonderful to cuddle up with you on the couch and watch a video — until we thought of something else more enjoyable to do.** Бы́ло бы так замеча́тельно прижа́ться друг к дру́гу на дива́не и смотре́ть фильм до тех пор, пока́ мы не поду́маем о том, чтобы заня́ться че́м-то ещё бо́лее прия́тным.

videographer *n* снима́ющий *m* / снима́ющая *f* видеока́мерой.

view *n* 1. *(sight, panorama)* вид; 2. *(conception)* взгляд ♦ **egalitarian ~s** эгалита́рные взгля́ды ♦ **liberal ~s** либера́льные взгля́ды ♦ **personal ~s** ли́чные взгля́ды ♦ **You have a** *(1)* **beautiful /** *(2)* **great rear view.** Ты так *(1)* прекра́сно / *(2)* замеча́тельно вы́глядишь сза́ди.

vigor *n* 1. *(energy)* эне́ргия, жи́вость *f*; 2. *(strength)* си́ла ♦ **full of ~** энерги́чный, -ая, -ое, -ые, живо́й, -а́я, -о́е, -ы́е.

vigorous *adj* энерги́чный, -ая, -ое, -ые, живо́й, -а́я, -о́е, -ы́е.

vigorously *adv* энерги́чно.

vile *adj* гну́сный, -ая, -ое, -ые, по́длый, -ая, -ое, -ые, ни́зкий, -ая, -ое, -ие.

villa *n* ви́лла.

vintage *n* 1. *(wine year)* урожа́й; 2. *(age)* во́зраст; *(generation)* поколе́ние ♦ **rare ~** челове́к ре́дких ка́честв ♦ **someone of similar ~** кто́-то тако́го же во́зраста ♦ **I'm look for someone of similar vintage.** Я ищу́ челове́ка, бли́зкого мне по во́зрасту.

violence *n* наси́лие ♦ **I hate violence.** Я ненави́жу наси́лие.

violent *adj* наси́льственный, -ая, -ое, -ые.

violently *adv* наси́льно.

violet *adj* фиоле́товый, -ая, -ое, -ые.

virgin *n* де́вственница ♦ **Are you a virgin?** Ты де́вственница? ♦ **I'm (not) a virgin.** Я (не) де́вственница.

virginity *n* де́вственность *f* ♦ **take** *(1)* **my /** *(2)* **your virginity** укра́сть *(1)* мою́ / *(2)* твою́ де́вственность.

Virgo *(Aug. 23 - Sep. 22)* Де́ва *(23 а́вгуста - 22 сентября́)*.

virile *adj* 1. *(fully mature)* возмужа́лый, -ая, -ое, -ые; *(sexually mature)* дости́гший (-ая, -ее, -ие) полово́й зре́лости; 2. *(masculine, strong)* му́жественный, -ая, -ое, -ые, си́льный, -ая, -ое, -ые.

virility *n* 1. *(full maturity)* возмужа́лость *f* ; *(sexual maturity)* полова́я зре́лость; 2. *(masculinity)* мужска́я зре́лость, му́жественность *f* ♦ **incredible ~** невероя́тная му́жест-

---

Please do us a favor:
Fill out and mail in the Feedback Sheet on page 795.

венность ♦ **lean, hard** ~ стро́йная, кре́пкая му́жественность ♦ **overpowering** ~ неотрази́мая му́жественность ♦ **rugged** ~ кре́пкая му́жественность.

virtue *n* доброде́тель *f*, досто́инство ♦ **precious** ~ драгоце́нная доброде́тельность ♦ **woman of easy** ~ же́нщина без доброде́тели, проститу́тка ♦ **I'm no paragon of virtue, but I have my principles.** Я не образе́ц доброде́тели, но у меня́ есть свои́ при́нципы.

virtuoso *n* виртуо́з.

virtuous *adj* доброде́тельный, -ая, -ое, -ые.

visa *n* ви́за ♦ **entry** ~ въе́здная ви́за ♦ **exit** ~ вы́ездная ви́за ♦ **fiancé** *m* ~ ви́за для жениха́ ♦ **fiancée** *f* ~ ви́за для неве́сты ♦ **immigration** ~ иммиграцио́нная ви́за ♦ **tourist** ~ туристи́ческая ви́за ♦ **transit** ~ транзи́тная ви́за ♦ **visitor('s)** ~ гостева́я ви́за ♦ **Would it be possible to get my visa extended?** Мо́жно ли бу́дет продли́ть мою́ ви́зу? ♦ **You can('t) get your visa extended.** Ты (не) мо́жешь продли́ть свою́ ви́зу. ♦ **I cling to the hope that** *(1)* **my** / *(2)* **your visa will come through soon.** Я цепля́юсь за наде́жду, что *(1)* моя́ / *(2)* твоя́ ви́за бу́дет полу́чена ско́ро.

vision *n* 1. *(eyesight)* зре́ние; 2. *(mental image)* представле́ние, о́браз, виде́ние, вид, карти́на ♦ **fleeting** ~ мимолётное виде́ние ♦ **With the vision of your beautiful face constantly in my thoughts, I am totally unable to concentrate on anything.** Твоё прекра́сное лицо́ постоя́нно в мои́х мы́слях, и я соверше́нно не в состоя́нии ни на чём сосредото́читься. ♦ **You are a vision of** *(1)* **breath-taking** / *(2)* **exquisite** *(3)* **beauty** / *(4)* **loveliness.** Ты виде́ние *(1)* ,...захва́тывающее дух... / *(2)* ...изы́сканной... *(3,4)* красоты́. ♦ **The vision of your** *(1)* **beauty** / *(2)* **loveliness in my mind overwhelms all other thoughts.** Мы́сли о твое́й *(1,2)* красоте́ подавля́ют все други́е. ♦ **My sleep, shallow and restless, was assailed by visions of your beautiful, voluptuous body.** Мой сон, неглубо́кий и беспоко́йный, был нару́шен виде́нием твоего́ прекра́сного, чу́вственного те́ла. ♦ **The vision of your alluring, sexy loveliness bedevils my thoughts night and day.** Мы́сли о твое́й зама́нивающей, сексуа́льной красоте́ му́чат меня́ но́чью и днём. ♦ **Visions of your voluptuous loveliness send fire licking through my arteries, igniting my entire being into an inferno of passionate desire.** Вид твое́й чу́вственной красоты́ вызыва́ет ого́нь, бушу́ющий в мои́х арте́риях, посыла́ющий всё моё существо́ в ад стра́стного жела́ния. ♦ **An extraordinary heat suffuses my whole body whenever the vision of your perfect loveliness comes into my mind.** Всегда́, когда́ бы я ни поду́мал о твоём прекра́сном сла́достном те́ле, я весь охва́чен жа́ром.

visit *vt* посеща́ть / посети́ть *(what, whom = acc.)* ♦ **Would it be possible to visit you?** Бу́дет ли возмо́жно посети́ть тебя́? ♦ **You can** *(1-3)* **(come) visit me.** Ты мо́жешь *(1)* ...прийти́ *(on foot)* / *(2)* прие́хать *(by veh.)* ко мне. / *(3)* ...посети́ть меня́. ♦ **I want to** *(1-3)* **(come) visit you.** Я хочу́ *(1)* ...прийти́ *(on foot)* / *(2)* прие́хать *(by veh.)* к тебе́. / *(3)* ...посети́ть тебя́. ♦ **I can't** *(1-3)* **(come) visit you (** *[4]* **this** / *[5]* **next** *[6]* **month** / *[7]* **year).** Я не могу́ *(1)* ...прийти́ *(on foot)* / *(2)* прие́хать *(by veh.)* к тебе́... / *(3)* ...посети́ть тебя́... (в *[4]* э́том / *[5]* сле́дующем *[6]* ме́сяце / *[7]* году́). ♦ **Please** *(1,2)* **come visit me.** Пожа́луйста, *(1)* прийди́ *(on foot)* / / *(2)* прие́дь *(by veh.)* ко мне. ♦ **I would be very happy** *(1-3)* **...if you came to visit me.** / *(4-6)* **...to come visit you.** Я был *(ж: была́)* бы о́чень сча́стлив *(ж: сча́стлива)* *(1)* ...е́сли ты придёшь *(on foot)* / *(2)* прие́дешь *(by veh.)* ко мне. / *(3)* ...посети́шь меня́. / *(4)* ...прийти́ *(on foot)* / *(5)* прие́хать *(by veh.)* к тебе́. / *(6)* ...посети́ть тебя́.

visit *n* визи́т, посеще́ние ♦ **forthcoming** ~ предстоя́щий визи́т ♦ *(1,2)* **impromptu** ~ *(1)* неожи́данный / *(2)* случа́йный визи́т ♦ **long** ~ дли́тельный визи́т ♦ **my** ~ мой визи́т ♦ **next** ~ сле́дующий визи́т ♦ **short** ~ коро́ткий визи́т ♦ **social** ~ дру́жеский визи́т, посеще́ние друзе́й ♦ **your** ~ твой визи́т.

vista *n* верени́ца; *(future)* pl: возмо́жности, горизо́нты, перспекти́вы ♦ **In the unbounded**

Clock and calender time are discussed in Appendix 5, page 759.

vistas of my dreams and fantasies I taste the exquisite sweetness of your lips a thousand, ten thousand, a million times, and each time am only impelled by the sheer ecstasy of the kiss to taste them once again. В безграни́чной верени́це мои́х снов и фанта́зий я вкуша́ю исключи́тельную сла́дость твои́х губ ты́сячу, де́сять ты́сяч, миллио́н раз, и ка́ждый раз я побужде́н и́стинным восто́ргом поцелу́я упива́ться им опя́ть.

vital *adj (essential)* кра́йне необходи́мый, -ая, -ое, -ые.

vitality *n (liveliness)* жи́вость *f*; *(energy)* эне́ргия, энерги́чность *f* ♦ **full of** ~ энерги́чный, -ая, -ое, -ые ♦ **You radiate beauty and vitality.** Ты излуча́ешь красоту́ и жи́вость.

vivacious *adj* живо́й, -а́я, -о́е, -ы́е, оживлённый, -ая, -ое, -ые; весёлый, -ая, -ое, -ые, жизнера́достный, -ая, -ое, -ые ♦ ~ **laughter** живо́й смех ♦ **You are the most vivacious woman I have ever met.** Я никогда́ не встреча́л бо́лее живо́й же́нщины, чем ты. ♦ **I am totally bewitched by your vivacious personality.** Твой живо́й хара́ктер про́сто очарова́л меня́. ♦ **You have a very vivacious personality.** У тебя́ о́чень живо́й хара́ктер.

vivacity *n* жи́вость *f*, оживлённость *f*; весёлость *f*, жизнера́достность *f* ♦ **Such sparkle and vivacity I have never** *(1)* **known** / *(2)* **encountered in anyone before.** Таки́х огня́ и жи́вости я никогда́ пре́жде не *(1)* знал / *(2)* встреча́л ни в ком. ♦ **Your vivacity (simply) overwhelms me.** Твоя́ жи́вость (про́сто) покоря́ет меня́. ♦ **You are a paragon of vivacity.** Ты образе́ц жи́вости. ♦ **I am totally captivated by your vivacity and loveliness.** Я соверше́нно очаро́ван твое́й жи́востью и красото́й.

vixen *n* ве́дьма ♦ **black-haired** ~ черноволо́сая ве́дьма ♦ **blonde** ~ белоку́рая ве́дьма ♦ **red-haired** ~ рыжеволо́сая ве́дьма.

v-mail *n (voice mail)* звуково́е сообще́ние.

vodka *n* во́дка.

voice *n* го́лос ♦ **bashful** ~ ро́бкий го́лос ♦ **beautiful** ~ краси́вый го́лос ♦ **beloved** ~ люби́мый го́лос ♦ **broken** ~ лома́ющийся го́лос ♦ **calm** ~ споко́йный го́лос ♦ **cheerful** ~ бо́дрый го́лос ♦ **child's** ~ де́тский го́лос ♦ *(1,2)* **clear** ~ *(1)* зво́нкий / *(2)* чи́стый го́лос ♦ **cold** ~ ледяно́й го́лос ♦ **deep** ~ грудно́й го́лос ♦ **deep-timbered** ~ го́лос глубо́кого те́мбра ♦ **emotional** ~ взволно́ванный го́лос ♦ **even** ~ ро́вный го́лос ♦ **excited** ~ возбуждённый го́лос ♦ **familiar** ~ знако́мый го́лос ♦ **female** ~ же́нский го́лос ♦ **gentle** ~ не́жный го́лос ♦ **good** ~ хоро́ший го́лос ♦ **high** ~ высо́кий го́лос ♦ **high-pitched** ~ то́нкий го́лос ♦ *(1,2)* **hoarse** ~ *(1)* хри́плый / *(2)* си́плый го́лос ♦ **hollow** ~ глухо́й го́лос ♦ **honeyed** ~ медо́вый го́лос ♦ *(1,2)* **husky** ~ *(1)* хри́плый / *(2)* си́плый го́лос ♦ **hypnotic** ~ гипноти́ческий го́лос ♦ **loud** ~ гро́мкий го́лос ♦ **low** ~ ни́зкий го́лос ♦ **low, firm** ~ ни́зкий, твёрдый го́лос ♦ **low-pitched** ~ ни́зкий го́лос ♦ **lyrical** ~ лири́ческий го́лос ♦ **male** ~ мужско́й го́лос ♦ **man's** ~ мужско́й го́лос ♦ *(1,2)* **melodic** ~ *(1)* мелоди́чный / *(2)* певу́чий го́лос ♦ *(1,2)* **melodious** ~ *(1)* мелоди́чный / *(2)* певу́чий го́лос ♦ **my** ~ мой го́лос ♦ **nasal** ~ гнуса́вый го́лос ♦ **nice** ~ хоро́ший го́лос ♦ **pleasant** ~ прия́тный го́лос ♦ **pleasantly deep** ~ прия́тный грудно́й го́лос ♦ **querulous** ~ жа́лобный го́лос ♦ **quiet** ~ ти́хий го́лос ♦ *(1,2)* **resonant** ~ *(1)* зво́нкий / *(2)* зву́чный го́лос ♦ **rich** ~ зву́чный го́лос ♦ **rough** ~ гру́бый го́лос ♦ *(1-3)* **seductive** ~ *(1)* маня́щий / *(2)* обольсти́тельный / *(3)* соблазни́тельный го́лос ♦ **sexy** ~ сексуа́льный го́лос ♦ **sharp** ~ ре́зкий го́лос ♦ **shrill** ~ визгли́вый го́лос ♦ **silky** ~ мя́гкий, не́жный го́лос ♦ **small** ~ небольшо́й го́лос ♦ **soft** ~ мя́гкий го́лос ♦ **sonorous** ~ зву́чный го́лос ♦ **soothing** ~ ла́сковый го́лос ♦ **sophisticated** ~ умудрённый о́пытом го́лос ♦ **squeaky** ~ пискля́вый го́лос ♦ **strange** ~ незнако́мый го́лос ♦ **strong** ~ си́льный го́лос ♦ **subdued** ~ приглушённый го́лос ♦ **sultry** ~ чу́вственный го́лос ♦ **sweet** ~ сла́дкий го́лос ♦ **sweet little** ~ сла́дкий голосо́чек ♦ **tender** ~ ла́сковый го́лос ♦ **trembling** ~ дрожа́щий го́лос ♦ **tremulous** ~ дрожа́щий го́лос ♦ **velvet(y)** ~ бархати́стый го́лос ♦ **warm** ~

Reflexive verbs are those that end in -ся or -сь.
The -ся or -сь also goes onto a past tense ending.

тёплый го́лос ♦ **weak** ~ сла́бый го́лос ♦ **whose** ~ чей го́лос ♦ **woman's** ~ же́нский го́лос ♦ **young** ~ молодо́й го́лос ♦ **your** ~ *(informal)* твой го́лос; *(polite)* Ваш го́лос ♦ **youthful** ~ ю́ношеский го́лос.

> **voice:** *verb terms*

lose *(1)* **my** / *(2)* **your** ~ потеря́ть *(1,2)* го́лос ♦ **lower your** ~ пони́зить го́лос ♦ **raise your** ~ повы́сить го́лос ♦ **recognize** *(1)* **my** / *(2)* **your** ~ узна́ть *(1)* мой / *(2)* твой го́лос.

> **voice:** *other terms*

satiny sound of your ~ ба́рхатный звук твоего́ го́лоса ♦ **with a tear-filled** ~ со слёзами в го́лосе.

> **voice:** *I want to hear yours*

I want to hear your voice. Я хочу́ слы́шать твой го́лос.

> **voice:** *the quality of your voice*

You have such a *(1)* **hypnotic** / *(2)* **sexy** / *(3)* **warm** / *(4)* **rich** / *(5)* **pleasant** / *(6)* **lyrical** / *(7)* **melodic** / *(8)* **melodious** *(9)* **...low, husky...** / *(10)* **deep-timbered voice.** У тебя́ тако́й *(1)* гипноти́ческий / *(2)* сексуа́льный / *(3)* тёплый / *(4)* зву́чный / *(5)* прия́тный / *(6)* лири́ческий / *(7,8)* мелоди́чный *(9)* ...ни́зкий, хри́плый... / *(10)* ...глубо́кого те́мбра... го́лос. ♦ **Your voice is clear as a bell.** Твой го́лос так чист, как колоко́льчик. ♦ **Your voice in my ear is like a serenade of love.** Твой го́лос в мои́х уша́х как сере́нада любви́. ♦ **Your voice is like a lilting musical chime.** Твой го́лос как мелоди́чный музыка́льный колоко́льчик. ♦ **I love the way your voice sounds when you** *(1)* **call** / *(2)* **whisper my name.** Я люблю́ звуча́ние твоего́ го́лоса, когда́ ты *(1)* произно́сишь / *(2)* шёпчешь моё и́мя.

> **voice:** *what your voice does to me*

You have a *(1)* **seductive** / *(2)* **suggestive quality to your voice that really turns me on.** В твоём го́лосе есть *(1)* обольсти́тельное / *(2)* соблазни́тельное звуча́ние, кото́рое действи́тельно заво́дит меня́. ♦ **Your (sexy) voice really turns me on.** Твой (сексуа́льный) го́лос действи́тельно возбужда́ет меня́.

> **voice:** *when I hear your voice*

(1) **Hearing...** / *(2)* **The sound of... your voice (on the phone) (just) warms me** *(3)* **...to my toes.** / *(4)* **...through and through.** / *(5)* **...to the very core.** *(1,2)* Звук твоего́ го́лоса (по телефо́ну) *(3)* ...согрева́ет меня́ до ко́нчиков па́льцев. / *(4)* ...наполня́ет всего́ меня́ тепло́м. / *(5)* ...согрева́ет мне ду́шу. ♦ **When I hear your voice (on the phone) it just adds fuel to the fire of my desire for you.** Когда́ я слы́шу твой го́лос (по телефо́ну), ого́нь мое́й стра́сти к тебе́ разгора́ется ещё сильне́е. ♦ **My heart breaks into rapture whenever I hear your voice on the phone.** Моё се́рдце наполня́ется восто́ргом всегда́, когда́ я слы́шу твой го́лос по телефо́ну.

> **voice:** *when I heard your voice*

It made me feel good to hear your voice full of gentle concern. Мне бы́ло о́чень прия́тно услы́шать твой го́лос, по́лный не́жной забо́ты. ♦ **It really warmed my heart and lifted up my spirits to hear your (beloved) voice on the phone.** Что действи́тельно согре́ло моё се́рдце и по́дняло настрое́ние, так э́то твой люби́мый го́лос по телефо́ну. ♦ **When I heard your voice, I felt shock waves of pure, unadulterated joy.** Когда́ я услы́шал *(ж: услы́шала)* твой го́лос, я ощути́л *(ж: ощути́ла)* во́лны и́стинного, настоя́щего ликова́ния.

> **voice:** *how your voice sounded*

Your voice sounded hollow. Твой го́лос прозвуча́л глу́хо. ♦ **I could hear a catch in your voice.** Я смог *(ж: смогла́)* услы́шать подво́х в твоём го́лосе. ♦ **I noticed a touch of** *(1)* **envy** / *(2)* **resentment** / *(3)* **anger in your voice.** Я заме́тил *(ж: заме́тила)* но́тку *(1)* за́ви-

---

> *The time zones for many cities of the world are given in Appendix 6, page 761.*

сти / *(2)* негодова́ния / *(3)* зло́сти в твоём го́лосе.

void *n* пустота́ ♦ **I feel an aching void (in** *[1]* **...me.** / *[2]* **...my heart).** Я ощуща́ю боле́зненную пустоту́ (*[1]* ...во себе́. / *[2]* ...в своём се́рдце.) ♦ **There is such a void in my life (since you left).** Така́я пустота́ в мое́й жи́зни (с тех пор, как ты уе́хала *[ж: уе́хал]*). ♦ **You fill a (huge) void in my life.** Ты заполня́ешь (огро́мную) пустоту́ в мое́й жи́зни. ♦ **I have a large void in my heart which perhaps you can fill.** В моём се́рдце огро́мная пустота́, кото́рую ты, возмо́жно, смо́жешь запо́лнить. ♦ **Fill my void.** Заполни́ мою́ пустоту́.

volatile *adj* вспы́льчивый, -ая, -ое, -ые.

volcano *n* вулка́н ♦ *(1)* **I want to...** / *(2)* **I'm going to... teach you how to imitate a volcano.** *(1)* Я хочу́ научи́ть... / *(2)* Я научу́... тебя́, как подража́ть вулка́ну. ♦ **I'm like a volcano on the verge of a full-scale eruption.** Я как вулка́н на гра́ни полномасшта́бного изверже́ния.

volleyball *n* волейбо́л.

volts *n, pl* 1. *(elec.)* вольт; 2. *(thrills)* волне́ние, возбужде́ние ♦ **When you kissed me, 6000 volts went straight to my heart.** Когда́ ты поцелова́ла *(ж: поцелова́л)* меня́, 6000 (= *шесть ты́сяч*) вольт пря́мо прошли́ сквозь моё се́рдце. ♦ **When I** *(1)* **hold** / *(2)* **get** / *(3)* **take you in my arms, you're going to learn what 8000 volts feels like.** Когда́ я *(1)* ...бу́ду держа́ть тебя́ в объя́тиях,... / *(2,3)* ...возьму́ тебя́ в объя́тия... ты узна́ешь, что зна́чит 8000 (= *во́семь ты́сяч*) вольт. ♦ **I never felt so many volts in all my life.** Я никогда́ в свое́й жи́зни не чу́вствовал *(ж: чу́вствовала)* тако́го возбужде́ния. ♦ **You're going to feel more volts than you've ever felt in your life.** Ты почу́вствуешь возбужде́ние бо́лее си́льное, чем ты когда́-либо в жи́зни чу́вствовала. ♦ **I'm going to send 10,000 volts of pure** *(1)* **pleasure** / *(2)* **ecstasy through your** *(3)* **veins** / *(4)* **body.** Я пошлю́ 10,000 (= *де́сять ты́сяч*) вольт и́стинного *(1)* наслажде́ния / *(2)* экста́за в *(3)* ...твои́ ве́ны. / *(4)* ...твоё те́ло.

voluntarily *adv* доброво́льно.

voluntary *adj* доброво́льный, -ая, -ое, -ые.

voluptuous *adj* сладостра́стный, -ая, -ое, -ые, чу́вственный, -ая, -ое, -ые, роско́шный, -ая, -ое, -ые ♦ **Visions of your voluptuous loveliness send fire licking through my arteries, igniting my entire being into an inferno of passionate desire.** Вид твое́й чу́вственной красоты́ вызыва́ет ого́нь, бушу́ющий в мои́х арте́риях, посыла́ющий всё моё существо́ в ад стра́стного жела́ния. ♦ **My arms are (so) lonely for your voluptuous charms.** Мои́ ру́ки (так) одино́ки без твои́х сладостра́стных пре́лестей.

voluptuousness *n* чу́вственность *f* ♦ **You are a paragon of voluptuousness.** Ты этало́н чу́вственности.

vortex *n* вихрь *m;* водоворо́т ♦ **When our lips touch even for a brief moment, I am** *(1)* **thrown** / *(2)* **hurled into a vortex of (ineffable) ecstasy.** Когда́ на́ши гу́бы соприкаса́ются да́же на коро́ткое мгнове́ние, я *(1,2)* бро́шен *(ж: бро́шена)* в вихрь (невырази́мого) экста́за. ♦ **When I look into the dark irises of your eyes, I am** *(1)* **drawn** / *(2)* **sucked into a wild vortex of passion.** Когда́ я вгля́дываюсь в тёмную ра́дужную оболо́чку твои́х глаз, меня́ *(1)* втя́гивает / *(2)* заса́сывает в ди́кий вихрь стра́сти. ♦ **Oh, what consummate ecstasy I will bestow upon you when we swirl into the wild vortex of our passion.** О, како́й соверше́нный экста́з я подарю́ тебе́, когда́ мы закру́жимся в бе́шеном водоворо́те стра́сти.

vow *vi* дава́ть / дать обе́т *(to whom = dat.)*, дава́ть / дать кля́тву *(to whom = dat.)*, кля́сться / покля́сться *(to whom = dat.)* ♦ ~ **fidelity** кля́сться / покля́сться в ве́рности ♦ **I vow that I will always love you and be faithful to you.** Кляну́сь, что всегда́ бу́ду люби́ть тебя́

---

*Optional parts of sentences are preceded
or followed (or both) by three dots.*

и бу́ду ве́рным *(ж: ве́рной)* тебе́.

vow *n* обе́т, кля́тва ♦ **marriage** *(1,2)* **~s** бра́чные *(1)* обе́ты / *(2)* кля́твы ♦ **sacred** ~ свято́й обе́т ♦ **solemn** ~ торже́ственная кля́тва ♦ **~ of celibacy** обе́т безбра́чия ♦ **~ of chastity** обе́т безбра́чия ♦ **wedding** *(1,2)* **~s** бра́чные *(1)* обе́ты / *(2)* кля́твы ♦ **break a** *(1,2)* ~ изменя́ть / измени́ть *(1)* обе́ту / *(2)* кля́тве, наруша́ть / нару́шить *(1)* обе́т / *(2)* кля́тву ♦ **exchange ~s** покля́сться друг дру́гу в ве́рности ♦ **keep a** *(1,2)* ~ держа́ть *(1)* обе́т / *(2)* кля́тву ♦ **make a** *(1,2)* ~ дава́ть / дать *(1)* обе́т / *(2)* кля́тву *(to whom = dat.).*

---
vow: phrases

I make this vow to you. Я даю́ э́ту кля́тву тебе́. ♦ **We will repeat our vows in front of the** *(1)* **minister** / *(2)* **priest** / *(3)* **rabbi.** Мы бу́дем повторя́ть на́ши кля́твы пе́ред *(1,2)* свяще́нником / *(3)* равви́ном. ♦ **We must never break our wedding vows.** Мы не должны́ никогда́ изменя́ть на́шим бра́чным обе́там. ♦ **I will never break my (wedding) vows to you.** Я никогда́ не изменю́ свои́м (бра́чным) кля́твам. ♦ **These vows of love that I make to you now will endure for as long as my time on this earth.** Эти обе́ты любви́, кото́рые я даю́ тебе́ сейча́с, бу́дут дли́ться сто́лько, ско́лько моя́ жизнь на э́той земле́. ♦ **My wedding vow is sacred.** Мой сва́дебный обе́т свяще́нен. ♦ **It is my solemn vow to you that I will always** *(1)* **be** / *(2)* **remain faithful to you.** Даю́ тебе́ торже́ственную кля́тву, что всегда́ *(1)* ...бу́ду... / *(2)* ...бу́ду остава́ться... ве́рным *(ж: ве́рной)* тебе́.

vulgar *adj* вульга́рный, -ая, -ое, -ые, гру́бый, -ая, -ое, -ые.

vulgarity *n* вульга́рность *f*, гру́бость *f*.

vulnerability *n* уязви́мость *f*, рани́мость *f*.

vulnerable *adj* уязви́мый, -ая, -ое, -ые, рани́мый, -ая, -ое, -ые ♦ **You took advantage of me when I was vulnerable.** *(ж:)* Ты воспо́льзовался свои́м преиму́ществом на́до мной, когда́ я была́ уязви́ма. ♦ **I think I was vulnerable (at the time).** Я ду́маю, я был уязви́мым *(ж: была́ уязви́мой)* (в э́то вре́мя).

---

wacky *adj (slang)* дура́цкий, -ая, -ое, -ие, идио́тский, -ая, -ое, -ие.

wag *vi* маха́ть *(what = instr.)* ♦ **My tail only wags for you.** Мой хвост ма́шет то́лько для тебя́.

waist *n* та́лия ♦ *(1,2)* **slim ~** *(1)* стро́йная / *(2)* то́нкая та́лия ♦ *(1,2)* **trim ~** *(1)* стро́йная / *(2)* то́нкая та́лия ♦ **wasp-like ~** оси́ная та́лия.

wait *vi* ждать *(for whom = acc., for what = gen.).*

> **wait:** *waiting for you*

You are the woman that I've been waiting for all my life. Ты же́нщина, кото́рую я ждал всю жизнь. ♦ **You are the man that I've been waiting for all my life.** Ты мужчи́на, кото́рого я ждала́ всю жизнь. ♦ **You are the person that I've been waiting for all my life.** Ты челове́к, кото́рого я ждал *(ж: ждала́)* всю жизнь. ♦ **I'll be waiting** *(1)* **...for your letter** / *(2)* **call.** / *(3)* **...to hear from you.** / *(4)* **...for you.** / *(5)* **...for you to come back.** Я буду́ ждать *(1,3)* ...твоего́ письма́. / *(2,3)* ...твоего́ звонка́. / *(4)* ...тебя́. / *(5)* ...твоего́ возвраще́ния. ♦ *(1)* **I can't...** / *(2)* **I can hardly... wait to** *(3)* **...see you (again).** / *(4)* **...be with you (again).** / *(5)* **...hold you in my arms (again).** / *(6)* **...make love with you (again).** *(1)* Я не могу́... / *(2)* Я едва́ могу́... дожда́ться того́ мгнове́ния, когда́ (опя́ть) *(3)*...уви́жу тебя́. / *(4)* ...буду с тобо́й. / *(5)* ...буду держа́ть тебя́ в объя́тиях. / *(6)* ...буду занима́ться любо́вью с тобо́й. ♦ **I'm waiting for you — eagerly, hungrily, full of love, full of tenderness — all yours.** Я жду тебя́ нетерпели́во, жа́дно, по́лный *(ж: по́лная)* любви́, по́лный *(ж: по́лная)* не́жности -- весь твой *(ж: вся твоя́)*.

> **wait:** *other phrases*

Please wait for me. Жди меня́, пожа́луйста. ♦ **I hope you'll wait for me.** Наде́юсь, ты бу́дешь ждать меня́. ♦ **Will you wait for me?** Бу́дешь ли ты ждать меня́? ♦ **I'll wait for you (, I promise).** Я буду ждать тебя́ (, я обеща́ю). ♦ **Wait (a** *[1]* **moment /** *[2]* **minute).** Подожди́ (*[1]* секу́нду / *[2]* мину́ту). ♦ **You probably have someone else waiting in the wings.** У тебя́, вероя́тно, есть кто́-то ещё, жду́щий тебя́.

wait *n* ожида́ние ♦ **It's been a long, agonizing wait.** Это бы́ло до́лгое, мучи́тельное ожида́ние. ♦ **The wait was worth it.** Это сто́ило ожида́ния.

wake up *vt* буди́ть / разбуди́ть *(whom = acc.)*, пробужда́ть / пробуди́ть *(whom = acc.)* ♦ **Do you have any idea how many times you have woken me up in the middle of the night with the power and magic of your beautiful, luscious, sexy body? I couldn't begin to tell you.** Зна́ешь ли ты, как ча́сто ты пробужда́ешь меня́ в середи́не но́чи си́лой и

A list of common places with their grammatical endings is given in Appendix 7, page 763.

волшебство́м твоего́ прекра́сного, со́чного, сексуа́льного тела? Я не зна́ю, как ска-
за́ть тебе́ об э́том.

wake up *vi* просыпа́ться / просну́ться ♦ **Wake up!** Просни́сь! ♦ **I want to wake up and
see your beautiful face every morning.** Ка́ждое у́тро я хочу́ просыпа́ться и ви́деть твоё
прекра́сное лицо́.

walk *vi* 1. *(stroll)* гуля́ть / погуля́ть 2. *(go on foot) (one direction:)* идти́ / пойти́; *(round trip
or repeated)* ходи́ть ♦ **~ hand in hand** идти́ рука́ о́б руку ♦ **May I walk with you?** Могу́
я пойти́ с Ва́ми? ♦ **Yes, you may walk with me.** Да, Вы мо́жете пойти́ со мной. ♦
(Please) walk with me. (Пожа́луйста,) пойдём со мной. ♦ **I've been walking around on
a cloud.** Я вита́ю в облака́х. ♦ **I've been walking around in a dream.** Я предаю́сь меч-
та́м. ♦ **I like the way you walk.** Мне нра́вится, как ты хо́дишь.

walk *n* 1. *(stroll)* прогу́лка; 2. *(way of walking)* похо́дка ♦ **after-dinner** ~ послеобе́ден-
ная прогу́лка ♦ **beach** ~s прогу́лки по пля́жу ♦ **brisk** ~ бы́страя прогу́лка ♦ **cud
dly** ~s **on the beach** прогу́лки в обни́мку по пля́жу ♦ **evening** ~ вече́рняя прогу́лка
♦ **graceful** ~ грацио́зная похо́дка ♦ **long** ~ дли́нная прогу́лка ♦ **lovely** прекра́сная
прогу́лка ♦ *(1,2)* **marvelous** ~ *(1)* удиви́тельная / *(2)* чуде́сная прогу́лка ♦ **moonlit**
~s прогу́лки под луно́й ♦ **morning** ~ у́тренняя прогу́лка ♦ **nature** ~s прогу́лки на
приро́де ♦ **romantic** ~ романти́ческая прогу́лка ♦ **sexy** ~ сексуа́льная похо́дка ♦
(1,2) **short** ~ *(1)* небольша́я / *(2)* коро́ткая прогу́лка ♦ **~ along the beach** прогу́лка
по пля́жу ♦ **~ along the lake** прогу́лка по о́зеру ♦ **~ by the sea** морска́я прогу́лка,
прогу́лка по мо́рю ♦ **~ in the country** заго́родная прогу́лка ♦ **~ in the park** прогу́л-
ка по па́рку ♦ **~ in the woods** прогу́лка в лесу́ ♦ *(1,2)* **wonderful** ~ *(1)* удиви́тельная
/ *(2)* чуде́сная прогу́лка.

| *walk: verb terms* |

enjoy walking наслажда́ться прогу́лками ♦ **go for a ~** 1. *(one time)* пойти́ на прогу́л-
ку, погуля́ть; 2. *(often)* гуля́ть, соверша́ть прогу́лки, ходи́ть на прогу́лку ♦ **go for ~s**
гуля́ть, соверша́ть прогу́лки, ходи́ть на прогу́лку ♦ **take a ~** 1. *(one time)* пойти́ на
прогу́лку, погуля́ть; 2. *(often)* гуля́ть, соверша́ть прогу́лки ♦ **take long ~s** предприни-
ма́ть дли́тельные прогу́лки, ходи́ть на дли́тельные прогу́лки ♦ **take ~s** гуля́ть со-
верша́ть прогу́лки.

| *walk: phrases* |

I want to take a long walk along the beach, holding your hand in mine. Я хочу́ до́лго
гуля́ть по пля́жу, держа́ твою́ ру́ку в свое́й. ♦ **Would you like to go for a walk (with
me)?** Не хоте́ла *(ж: хоте́л)* бы ты пойти́ на прогу́лку (со мной)? ♦ **Let's go for a walk
(together).** Дава́й пойдём на прогу́лку (вме́сте). ♦ **I like brisk walks.** Мне нра́вятся
бы́стрые прогу́лки. ♦ **I love to take long walks on the beach.** Я люблю́ (соверша́ть)
до́лгие прогу́лки по пля́жу.

walking *n* гуля́ние ♦ **I love walking.** Я люблю́ гуля́ть.

wall *n* стена́ ♦ **I seem to have** *(1,2)* **run into a brick wall with you.** Ка́жется, что с то-
бо́й я *(1)* ...упёрся *(ж: упёрлась)* в кирпи́чную сте́ну. / *(2)* ...зашёл *(ж: зашла́)* в
тупи́к.

wallflower *n* де́вушка, не по́льзующаяся успе́хом у мужчи́н *(1 term)* ♦ **I've always
been sort of a wallflower. I never thought anyone would** *(1,2)* **fall in love with me.** *(ж:)*
Я никогда́ не по́льзовалась успе́хом у мужчи́н. Я никогда́ не ду́мала, что кто́-
нибудь мо́жет *(1)* ...влюби́ться в меня́. / *(2)* ...полюби́ть меня́.

wallhugger *n (slang)* засте́нчивая де́вушка.

waltz *vi* вальси́ровать, танцева́ть вальс.

waltz *n* вальс.

Common adult heights are given in Appendix 9, page 776.

wand *n* па́лочка. ♦ **magic ~** волше́бная па́лочка.

wander *vi* броди́ть, скита́ться ♦ **~ aimlessly** броди́ть без це́ли, бесце́льнпрогу́ливать-ся ♦ **~ around town** скита́ться по го́роду.

wanderlust *n* страсть к путеше́ствиям.

wane *vi* уменьша́ться / уме́ньшиться, убыва́ть / убы́ть, слабе́ть / ослабе́ть ♦ **My desire for you never wanes.** Моя́ страсть к тебе́ никогда́ не уме́ньшится.

wannabe *n (slang)* челове́к, кото́рый хо́чет стать ке́м-либо *(definition)*.

want *vt* хоте́ть / захоте́ть *(what [tangible] = acc., what [intangible] = gen., whom = acc.)*
   ♦ **~ more than anything (in the world)** хоте́ть бо́льше всего́ (в жи́зни) ♦ **~ so much** так (си́льно) хоте́ть ♦ **~ (1,2) terribly** *(1)* стра́шно / *(2)* ужа́сно хоте́ть ♦ **~ very much** о́чень хоте́ть ♦ **~ with all my heart** всем се́рдцем хоте́ть.

> **want: what do you want?**

What do you want (me to do)? Что ты хо́чешь (, что́бы я сде́лал *[ж: сде́лала]*)? ♦ **Is that really what you want?** Это действи́тельно то, что ты хо́чешь?

> **want: I want**

That's (not) what I want. Это (не) то, чего́ я хочу́. ♦ **I want (so much)** *(1)* **...to be with you.** / *(2)* **...to hear your voice.** / *(3)* **...to feel your touch.** / *(4)* **...to make love with you (again).** / *(5)* **...to have you by my side (** *[6]***...night and day.** / *[7]* **...always.**). / *(8)* **...to hold you in my arms.** / *(9)* **...to cover you with kisses.** / *(10)* **...to snuggle** / *(11)* **cuddle up with you.** / *(12)* **...to marry you.** / *(13)* **...to kiss you (***[14]***...again and again.** / *[15]* **...all over.** / *[16]* **...endlessly.**) / *(17)* **...to kiss you and kiss you and kiss you..** / *(18)* **...to spend the rest of my life with you.** / *(19)* **...to visit you.** / *(20)* **...to see you (***[21]* **again** / *[22]* **tomorrow** / *[23]* **soon**). / *(24)* **...to see you** *(25)* **...often** / *(26)* **everyday.** Я (так си́льно) хочу́ *(1)* ...быть с тобо́й. / *(2)* ...слы́шать твой го́лос. / *(3)* ...почу́вствовать тво прикоснове́ние. / *(4)* ...(опя́ть) занима́ться с тобо́й любо́вью. / *(5)* ..., что́бы ты была́ *(ж: был)* ря́дом (*[6]*...днём и но́чью. / *[7]* ...всегда́.) / *(8)* ...держа́ть тебя́ в объя́тиях. / *(9)* ...покры́ть тебя́ поцелу́ями. / *(10)* ...приласка́ть тебя́. / *(11)* ...прижа́ться к тебе́. / *(12)* ... жени́ться на тебе́. *(ж: ... вы́йти за тебя́ за́муж.)* / *(13)* ...целова́ть тебя́ (*[14]*...сно́ва и сно́ва. / *[15]* ...всю. / *[16]* ...бесконе́чно.) / *(17)* ...целова́ть, целова́ть и целова́ть тебя́. / *(18)* ...провести́ оста́ток жи́зни с тобо́й. / *(19)* ...прие́хать к тебе́. / *(20)* ...уви́деть тебя́ (*[21]*...опя́ть. / *[22]* ...за́втра. / *[23]* ...вско́ре). / *(24)* ...ви́деть тебя́ *(25)* ...ча́ще. / *(26)* ...ка́ждый день.

> **want: I want you**

I want (only) you. Я хочу́ (то́лько) тебя́. ♦ **I want you so (much).** Я так (си́льно) хочу́ тебя́. ♦ **I have wanted you for a long (, long) time.** Я хоте́л *(ж: хоте́ла)* тебя́ давны́м-давно́. ♦ **I want you** *(1)* **...very much.** / *(2)* **...terribly.** / *(3)* **...more than anything.** / *(4)* **...with all my heart and soul.** / *(5)* **...with every fiber of my body.** *(6)* **...so much I can't bear** / *(7)* **stand it.** / *(8)* **...here, with me.** Я хочу́ тебя́ *(1)* ...о́чень. / *(2)* ...ужа́сно. / *(3)* ...бо́льше всего́ на све́те. / *(4)* ...всем се́рдцем и душо́й. / *(5)* ...все́ми фи́брами своего́ те́ла. / *(6)* ...так си́льно, что не могу́ вы́держать / *(7)* вы́нести э́того. / *(8)* ...здесь со мной. ♦ **How much I want you!** Как си́льно я хочу́ тебя́! ♦ **You are all that I ever want.** Ты всё, чего́ я то́лько хочу́. ♦ **There are no words to describe how I hunger for you, how I ache for you, how I want you.** Нет слов, что́бы описа́ть, как я голо́ден *(ж: голодна́)* по тебе́, как я страда́ю по тебе́, как я хочу́ тебя́. ♦ **You are the only person I want in this whole world.** Ты еди́нственный челове́к, кото́рый ну́жен мне в э́том ми́ре. ♦ **I only have to look at you to want you.** Мне сто́ит то́лько взгляну́ть на тебя́, и мной овладева́ет жела́ние. ♦ **I've never met a woman I wanted as much as I want you.** Я никогда́ не встреча́л же́нщины, кото́рую бы я хоте́л так си́льно, как тебя́. ♦ **Not a minute passes**

Words in parentheses are optional.

that I don't want you. Не прохо́дит и мину́ты, что́бы я не хоте́л *(ж: хоте́ла)* тебя́. ♦ **I'm thinking about you all the time and adoring you and wanting you.** Я всё вре́мя ду́маю о тебе́, обожа́ю тебя́ и хочу́ тебя́. ♦ **You can't believe how much I think about you and want you at nighttime before I fall asleep and in the early morning as I wake up.** Ты не представля́ешь, как мно́го я ду́маю о тебе́ и как хочу́ тебя́ но́чью пе́ред тем, как засну́ть, и ра́нним у́тром, как то́лько проснётесь. ♦ **I want you back.** Я хочу́, что́бы ты верну́лась *(ж: верну́лся).*

> **want: I don't want**

I don't want you *(1)* ...**to call me** *([2]* **anymore** */ [3]* **here** */ [4]* **there).** */ (5)* ...**to come here (anymore).** */ (6)* ...**to tell anyone.** */ (7)* ...**(ever) to leave.** */ (8)* ...**to forget me.** */ (9)* ...**to bother me (anymore).** */ (10)* ...**(ever) to go away.** Я не хочу́, что́бы... *(1)* ты звони́ла *(ж: звони́л)* мне *([2]* бо́льше */ [3]* сюда́ */ [4]* туда́). */ (5)* ...ты приходи́ла *(ж: приходи́л)* (бо́льше). */ (6)* ...говори́ла *(ж: говори́л)* (кому́-нибудь). */ (7)* ...ты (когда́-нибудь) уходи́ла *(ж: уходи́л). / (8)* ...забы́ла *(ж: забы́л)* меня́. */ (9)* ...ты меша́ла *(ж: меша́л)* мне (бо́льше). ♦ **I don't want** *(1)* ...**to make you cry.** */ (2)* ...**to make you feel bad.** */ (3)* ...**to hurt you.** */ (4)* ...**to hurt your feelings.** */ (5,6)* ...**to offend you.** */ (7)* ...**to bother** */ (8)* **disturb you.** */ (9)* ...**to inconvenience you.** */ (10)* ...**to make** */ (11)* **cause any trouble (for you).** */ (12)* ...**to put you to a lot of trouble.** */ (13)* ...**to see you anymore.** */ (14)* ...**to marry you.** */ (15)* ...**to do it.** */ (16)* ...**to make love (with you).** */ (17)*...**to have sex (with you).** */ (18)* ...**to talk about it.** */ (19)* ...**to stop kissing you.** */ (20)* ...**(ever) to lose you.** */ (21,23)* ...**to go** */ (22,24)* **leave.** Я не хочу́ *(1)* ..., что́бы ты пла́кала из-за меня́. */ (2,3)* ...оби́деть тебя́. */ (4)* ...ра́нить твои́ чу́вства. */* ...*(5)* оскорби́ть */ (6)* оби́деть тебя́. */ (7,8)* ...меша́ть тебе́. */ (9)* ...утружда́ть тебя́. */ (10)* ...доставля́ть */ (11)* причиня́ть (тебе́) никаки́х ли́шних тру́дностей. */ (12)* ... тебя́ си́льно затрудня́ть. */ (13)* ...тебя́ бо́льше ви́деть. */ (14)* ...жени́ться на тебе́. *(ж: ...вы́й-ти за тебя́ за́муж.) / (15)* ...э́то де́лать. */ (16)* ...занима́ться любо́вью (с тобо́й). */ (17)* ...се́кса (с тобо́й). */ (18)* ...говори́ть об э́том. */ (19)* ...переста́ть целова́ть тебя́. */ (20)* ...(когда́-нибудь) потеря́ть тебя́. */ (21,22)* ...уходи́ть *(on foot)* / *(23,24)* уезжа́ть *(by veh.).*

wanted *adj* жела́нный, -ая, -ое, -ые ♦ **feel** ~ чу́вствовать себя́ жела́нным *m* / жела́нной *f* ♦ **You make me feel wanted.** С тобо́й я чу́вствую себя́ жела́нным *(ж: жела́нной).* ♦ **You give me such a warm feeling of being wanted.** Ты даёшь мне тако́е сча́стье чу́вствовать себя́ жела́нным *(ж: жела́нной).* ♦ **With you, for the first time in my life, I feel wanted.** С тобо́й, впервы́е в свое́й жи́зни, я чу́вствую себя́ жела́нным *(ж: жела́н-ной).*

wanton *n (lustful)* похотли́вый, -ая, -ое, -ые; *(lewd)* распу́тный, -ая, -ое, -ые; *(bawdy)* непристо́йный, -ая, -ое, -ые; *(sensual)* чу́вственный, -ая, -ое, -ые ♦ **I'm ashamed of my wanton behavior.** Я стыжу́сь своего́ непристо́йного поведе́ния. ♦ **I apologize for my wanton behavior.** Я извиня́юсь за своё непристо́йное поведе́ние.

wantonly *adv (lustfully)* похотли́во; *(lewdly)* распу́тно; *(indecently)* непристо́йно; *(sensually)* чу́вственно ♦ **What a fool I've been to fling myself at you so wantonly.** *(ж:)* Како́й ду́рой я была́, бро́сившись к тебе́ так безу́держно.

wardrobe *n* гардеро́б, запа́с оде́жды ♦ **You (certainly) have a nice wardrobe.** У тебя́ (действи́тельно) прекра́сный гардеро́б.

wariness *n* осторо́жность *f*, осмотри́тельность *f.*

warm *adj* 1. тёплый, -ая, -ое, -ые; 2. серде́чный, -ая, -ое, -ые, горя́чий, -ая, -ее, -ие ♦ ~ **friendship** те́сная дру́жба ♦ *(1,2)* ~ **heart** *(1)* до́брое */ (2)* отзы́вчивое се́рдце ♦ *(1,2)* ~ **welcome** *(1)* тёплый */ (2)* серде́чный приём ♦ ~ **at heart** добросерде́чный, -ая, -ое, -ые ♦ **You are so warm and cuddly.** Ты така́я тёплая и с тобо́й так прия́тно обни-

---

You can find common clothing sizes in Appendix 11 on page 778.

ма́ться.

warm *vt* согрева́ть / согре́ть *(what, whom = acc.)* ♦ *(1)* **Talking to you...** / *(2)* **Hearing your voice...** / *(3)* **The sound of your voice... on the phone (just) warms me** *(3)* **...to my toes.** / *(4)* **...through and through.** / *(5)* **...to the very core.** *(1)* Разгово́р с тобо́й... / *(2,3)* Звук твоего́ го́лоса... по телефо́ну *(3)* ...согрева́ет меня́ до ко́нчиков па́льцев. / *(4)* ...наполня́ет меня́ тепло́м. / *(5)* ...согрева́ет мне ду́шу. ♦ **The words you wrote in your letter warmed me** *(1)* **...to my toes.** / *(2)* **...through and through.** / *(3)* **...to the very core.** Слова́ твоего́ письма́ *(3)* ...согре́ли меня́ до ко́нчиков па́льцев. / *(4)* ...напо́лнили меня́ тепло́м. / *(5)* ...согре́ли мне ду́шу. ♦ **It really warmed my heart and lifted up my spirits to** *(1)* **...get your call** / *(2)* **letter.** / *(3)* **...hear your (beloved) voice on the phone.** / *(4)* **...see you again.** Что действи́тельно согре́ло моё се́рдце и по́дняло настрое́ние, так э́то *(1)* ...твой звоно́к. / *(2)* ...твоё письмо́. / *(3)* ...твой люби́мый го́лос по телефо́ну. / *(4)* ...на́ша после́дняя встре́ча. ♦ **Your letters warm my heart more than you can ever know.** Твои́ пи́сьма согрева́ют моё се́рдце бо́лее, чем ты да́же мо́жешь предста́вить. Звук твоего́ го́лоса согрева́ет меня́ всего́. ♦ **It will help to warm the air.** Это помо́жет сде́лать атмосфе́ру бо́лее непринуждённой. ♦ **Your letter warmed my heart more than I can tell you.** Твоё письмо́ согре́ло моё се́рдце бо́лее, чем я могу́ вы́разить.

warm-hearted *adj* мягкосерде́чный, -ая, -ое, -ые, до́брый, -ая, -ое, -ые, отзы́вчивый, -ая, -ое, -ые.

warm-heartedness *n* мягкосерде́чие, отзы́вчивость *f.*

warmth *n* 1. *(physical)* тепло́, теплота́; 2. *(feelings)* серде́чность *f* ; пыл ♦ **divine** ~ боже́ственное тепло́ ♦ **enticing** ~ маня́щее тепло́ ♦ **genuine** ~ по́длинная теплота́, и́скреннее тепло́ ♦ **hearty** ~ серде́чное тепло́ ♦ **heavenly** ~ боже́ственное тепло́ ♦ **intense** ~ си́льное тепло́ ♦ **luxurious** ~ сладостра́стное тепло́ ♦ **magic** ~ волше́бное тепло́ ♦ **tantalizing** ~ маня́щее тепло́ ♦ **unusual** ~ необыкнове́нное тепло́ ♦ ~ **of your caresses** теплота́ твои́х ласк ♦ **wonderful** ~ замеча́тельное тепло́ ♦ **exude** ~ выделя́ть / вы́делить тепло́ ♦ **full of** ~ по́лный (-ая, -ое, -ые) тепла́ ♦ **radiate** ~ излуча́ть тепло́.

warmth: *you have warmth*

Your *(1)* **blue** / *(2)* **dark eyes and wide smile radiate warmth.** Твои́ *(1)* голу́бые / *(2)* тёмные глаза́ и широ́кая улы́бка излуча́ют тепло́. ♦ **I perceive in you a reservoir of warmth and affection and tenderness that is very, very deep.** Я чу́вствую в тебе́ о́чень, о́чень глубо́кий запа́с серде́чности, любви́ и не́жности. ♦ **I've never met a person so full of warmth and joy (as you).** Я никогда́ не встреча́л *(ж: встреча́ла)* челове́ка так напо́лненного тепло́м и ра́достью(, как ты). ♦ **There is such genuine warmth in your** *(1)* **nature** / *(2)* **personality** / *(3)* **character.** *(1)* В твое́й нату́ре / *(2)* индивидуа́льности... / *(3)* В твоём хара́ктере... така́я и́скренняя теплота́.

warmth: *I've found warmth with you*

With you I have found warmth and compassion and closeness such as I've never known before. В тебе́ я нашёл *(ж: нашла́)* таки́е теплоту́, сострада́ние и отзы́вчивость, каки́х никогда́ пре́жде не знал *(ж: зна́ла)*.

warmth: *the warmth of your love*

What paradise it is to bask in the wonderful warmth of your love. Како́е ра́йское наслажде́ние замеча́тельное тепло́ твое́й любви́.

warmth: *the warmth of your smile*

I never dreamed a smile could fill my life with so much warmth and brightness. Я никогда́ не представля́л *(ж: представля́ла)*, что улы́бка смо́жет наполни́ть мою́ жизнь таки́м тепло́м и све́том.

For general rules of Russian grammar see Appendix 2 on page 686.

---

warmth: *the warmth of your sunshine*

I want to bask in the warmth of your sunshine. Я хочу́ гре́ться в твои́х со́лнечных луча́х. ◆ **I could bask forever in the warmth of your sunshine.** Я смог *(ж: смогла́)* бы ве́чно гре́ться в тепле́ твои́х луче́й.

warmth: *I love your warmth*

I love your gentle touch and the warmth I feel at your side. Мне нра́вится твоё не́жное прикоснове́ние и тепло́, исходя́щее от тебя́.

warmth: *I long for your warmth*

I need your warmth (and softness). Мне нужна́ твоя́ теплота́ (и мя́гкость). ◆ **It would be absolute heaven to lie next to you, hold you tenderly in my arms, look into your beautiful, dark eyes, kiss you ever so lovingly and adoringly, and feel the magic warmth of your body all through the night.** Бы́ло бы соверше́нно боже́ственно лежа́ть ря́дом с тобо́й, держа́ть тебя́ не́жно в объя́тиях, смотре́ть в твои́ прекра́сные тёмные глаза́, целова́ть тебя́ с любо́вью и обожа́нием и чу́вствовать волше́бное тепло́ твоего́ те́ла всю ночь. ◆ **I spend these long, lonely nights yearning and burning for your soft, luscious warmth.** Я провожу́ э́ти до́лгие, одино́кие но́чи, тоску́я и горя́ по твоему́ мя́гкому, ла́сковому теплу́. ◆ **How I want to curl up with you, snuggle against your breast, feel the warmth of you, caress you, love you.** Как бы я хоте́л *(ж: хоте́ла)* обня́ться с тобо́й, прижа́ться к твое́й груди́, чу́вствовать твоё тепло́, ласка́ть тебя́, люби́ть тебя́. ◆ **I want so desperately to be close to you, to hold you in my arms, to feel the warmth of you, to kiss you.** Я отча́янно хочу́ быть ря́дом с тобо́й, держа́ть тебя́ в объя́тиях, чу́вствовать твоё тепло́, целова́ть тебя́.

wary *adj* осторо́жный, -ая, -ое, -ые, осмотри́тельный, -ая, -ое, -ые ◆ **I'm a little wary of** *(1)* **women** / *(2)* **men now.** Я тепе́рь немно́го насторо́женно отношу́сь к *(1)* же́нщинам / *(2)* мужчи́нам.

wash *vi:* ◆ **Every time I think of you, a warm wave of love washes through me.** Вся́кий раз, когда́ бы я ни поду́мал *(ж: поду́мала)* о тебе́, тёплые во́лны любви́ залива́ют меня́.

wasteland *n* пусты́ня ◆ **Your absence makes a wasteland of my whole** *(1)* **day** / *(1)* **evening.** Твоё отсу́тствие де́лает пусты́ней весь мой *(1)* день / *(2)* ве́чер.

water *n* вода́ ◆ **love of ~** любо́вь к воде́ ◆ **play in the ~** игра́ть в воде́ ◆ **Still waters** *(1)* **run** / *(2)* **flow deep.** *(1,2)* В ти́хом о́муте че́рти во́дятся.

waterski *vi* ката́ться на во́дных лы́жах ◆ **I like to waterski.** Мне нра́вится ката́ться на во́дных лы́жах.

waterskiing *n* воднолы́жный спорт.

wave *n* волна́ *(pl:* во́лны*)* ◆ **boundless ~s of ecstasy** безбре́жные во́лны экста́за ◆ **silky ~ of hair** шелкови́стая волна́ воло́с ◆ **soft ~s of hair** мя́гкие во́лны воло́с ◆ **~ of sensuality** волна́ чу́вственности ◆ **~s of ecstasy** во́лны экста́за ◆ **~s of pleasure** во́лны наслажде́ния.

wave: *phrases*

I have never felt such *(1)* **huge** / *(2)* **tremendous** / *(3)* **enormous waves of pleasure.** Я никогда́ не чу́вствовал *(ж: чу́вствовала)* таки́х *(1)* огро́мных / *(2,3)* грома́дных волн наслажде́ния. ◆ **You fill me with such** *(1)* **huge** / *(2)* **tremendous** / *(3)* **enormous waves of pleasure.** Ты наполня́ешь меня́ таки́ми *(1)* огро́мными / *(2,3)* грома́дными во́лнами наслажде́ния. ◆ **I'm going to make waves of exquisite pleasure surge through your body.** Я вы́зову во́лны изы́сканного наслажде́ния, захлёстывающие твоё те́ло. ◆ **Every time I think of you, a warm wave of love washes through me.** Вся́кий раз, когда́ бы я ни поду́мал *(ж: поду́мала)* о тебе́, тёплые во́лны любви́ залива́ют меня́.

wavelength *n* длина́ волны́, волна́ ◆ **You and I are truly on the same wavelength.** Мы с

For transitive Russian verbs the cases that they take are shown by means of an = sign and the Russian case. (abbreviated).

тобо́й действи́тельно настро́ены на одну́ волну́. ♦ **You and I are on such a common wavelength that I really believe neither of us could ever find a more** *(1)* **suitable /** *(2)* **compatible partner.** Мы с тобо́й насто́лько на одно́й волне́, что я уве́рен, ни оди́н из нас не смо́жет найти́ бо́лее *(1,2)* подходя́щего партнёра. ♦ **I'm glad that I've (finally) found someone like you who's on the same wavelength I am.** Я рад *(ж: ра́да)*, что (в конце́ концо́в) нашёл таку́ю *(ж: нашла́ тако́го)*, как ты, с те́ми же мы́слями, стремле́ниями, жела́ниями. ♦ **What a** *(1)* **...pleasure... /** *(2)* **...delight... /** *(3)* **...good feeling... it is to find someone on the same wavelength.** Что за *(1)* ...наслажде́ние... / *(2)* ...ра́дость... / *(3)* ...прия́тное чу́вство... найти́ того́, кто настро́ен на одну́ волну́ с тобо́й.

waver *vi* колеба́ться ♦ **My feelings for you will never waver.** Мои́ чу́вства к тебе́ никогда́ не поколе́блются. ♦ **My love for you will never waver.** Моя́ любо́вь к тебе́ не разве́ется никогда́. ♦ **My love for you has never wavered since the day I met you.** С того́ дня, когда́ я встре́тил *(ж: встре́тила)* тебя́, моя́ любо́вь к тебе́ никогда́ не ослабева́ла.

way *n* 1. *(route)* путь *m*; доро́га; 2. *(direction)* направле́ние; 3. *(manner)* о́браз (де́йствия); *(method)* ме́тод, спо́соб; *(behavior)* мане́ра (поведе́ния), обраще́ние; 4. *(characteristic)* осо́бенность, черта́; *(custom)* обы́чай, привы́чка, укла́д ♦ **different** ~ друго́й спо́соб ♦ **different** ~**s** разли́чные спо́собы ♦ **gentle** ~**s** не́жность *f* ♦ **loving** ~**s** любо́вь *f* ♦ **thoughtful** ~**s** внима́тельность *f.*

way: other terms

in a different ~ по-друго́му ♦ **in a family** ~ *(pregnant)* бере́менная, в интере́сном положе́нии ♦ **in a friendly** ~ по-дру́жески ♦ **in a humane** ~ по-челове́чески ♦ **in a personal** ~ ли́чно ♦ **in** *(1)* **this /** *(2)* **that way** *(1,2)* таки́м о́бразом ♦ **some** ~ не́которым о́бразом ♦ ~ **of life** о́браз жи́зни.

way: your ways

I admire you for your *(1)* **...gentle /** *(2)* **thoughtful ways.** Я восхища́юсь тобо́й за *(1)* ...твою́ не́жность / *(2)* внима́тельность. ♦ **Do you know why I'm so attracted to you? It's your** *(1)* **gentle /** *(2)* **loving ways.** Ты зна́ешь, почему́ я так увлечён *(ж: увлечена́)* тобо́й? За твоё *(1)* не́жное / *(2)* любо́вное обраще́ние. ♦ **You nourish my soul with your loving ways.** Ты пита́ешь мою́ ду́шу свое́й любо́вью. ♦ **You brighten my life with your sweet smile and loving ways.** Ты озаря́ешь мою́ жизнь свое́й не́жной улы́бкой и любо́вью. ♦ **I love your amorous ways.** Мне нра́вится как ты выража́ешь свою́ влюблённость. ♦ **You really have a way with words.** Ты действи́тельно уме́ешь по́льзоваться слова́ми. ♦ **I like the way you** *(1)* **...talk. /** *(2)* **...smile. /** *(3)* **...kiss. /** *(4)* **...hold me. /** *(5)* **...walk. /** *(6)* **...move. /** *(7)* **...look at me. /** *(8)* **...wear your hair.** Мне нра́вится, как ты *(1)* ...говори́шь. / *(2)* ...улыба́ешься. / *(3)* ...целу́ешь. / *(4)* ...де́ржишь меня́. / *(5)* ...хо́дишь. / *(6)* ...дви́жешься. / *(7)* ...смо́тришь на меня́. / *(8)* ...причёсываешь во́лосы. ♦ **I hope you're not set in your ways.** Я наде́юсь, что ты спосо́бна *(ж: спосо́бен)* измени́ться.

way: my ways

(You'll find that) I'm not set in my ways. (Ты уви́дишь, что) я спосо́бен *(ж: спосо́бна)* измени́ться.

way: method

We'll find a way (to do it). Мы найдём возмо́жность (сде́лать э́то). ♦ **Is there some way I can** *(1)* **...reach /** *(2)* **contact you? /** *(3)* **...get in touch with you?** *(1-3)* Каки́м о́бразом я могу́ связа́ться с тобо́й?

way: various phrases

(1,2) **No way!** *(1)* Ни в ко́ем слу́чае! / *(2)* Ни за что! ♦ **By the way, I sent you a package yesterday.** Кста́ти, вчера́ я посла́л *(ж: посла́ла)* тебе́ посы́лку. ♦ **You can't**

Russian verbs have 2 forms: imperfective and perfective.
They're given in that order.

always have your own way. Невозмо́жно всегда́ поступа́ть по-сво́ему. ♦ **What am I supposed to do? Just look the other way?** Что мне де́лать? Про́сто не замеча́ть?

weak *adj* рассла́бленный, -ая, -ое, -ые.

weaken *vt* ослабля́ть / осла́бить *(what = acc.)* ♦ **Nothing will ever weaken this bond between us.** Ничто́ не осла́бит э́тих уз ме́жду на́ми.

weak-kneed *adj (cowardly)* трусли́вый, -ая, -ое, -ые, малоду́шный, -ая, -ое, -ые.

weak-willed *adj* слабово́льный, -ая, -ое, -ые.

wealth *n* бога́тство ♦ **great** ~ большо́е бога́тство ♦ **intellectual** ~ душе́вное бога́тство ♦ **spiritual** ~ духо́вное бога́тство ♦ ~ **of** *(1)* **auburn** / *(2)* **black** / *(3)* **blonde** / *(4)* **chestnut hair** роско́шные *(1)* золоти́сто-кашта́новые / *(2)* чёрные / *(3)* белоку́рые / *(4)* кашта́новые во́лосы ♦ ~ **of ideas** иде́йное бога́тство ♦ ~ **of personality** бога́тство ли́чности ♦ ~ **of spirit** бога́тство души́.

wealthy *adj* бога́тый, -ая, -ое, -ые, состоя́тельный, -ая, -ое, -ые ♦ **My goal is to be healthy, wealthy and wise.** Моя́ цель - быть здоро́вым, бога́тым и му́дрым *(ж: здоро́вой, бога́той и му́дрой).*

weariness *n* 1. *(fatigue)* уста́лость *f*, утомле́ние; 2. *(tedium)* утоми́тельность *f* ; *(ennui)* ску́ка ♦ **bored** ~ ску́ка ♦ **great** ~ больша́я уста́лость.

web *n* 1. *(spider's)* паути́на; 2. *(Internet)* web, веб ♦ **sensual** ~ чу́вственная паути́на ♦ ~ **of desire** паути́на жела́ния.

wed *vt* 1. *(man)* жени́ться *(whom = + на +prep.)*; *(woman)* вы́йти за́муж *f (whom = + за + acc.)*; 2. венча́ть *(whom = acc.)*; сочета́ть бра́ком *(whom = acc.)*; жени́ть *(whom = acc.)* ♦ **We'll be wed in a** *(1)* **church** / *(2)* **chapel** / *(3)* **synagogue.** Мы бу́дем венча́ться в *(1)* це́ркви / *(2)* часо́вне / *(3)* синаго́ге.

wedded *adj* супру́жеский, -ая, -ое, -ие.

wedding *n* сва́дьба ♦ *(1,2)* **church** ~ *(1)* венча́ние / *(2)* сва́дьба в це́ркви ♦ **conventional** ~ традицио́нная сва́дьба ♦ **intimate** ~ инти́мная сва́дьба ♦ **large** ~ больша́я сва́дьба ♦ **one-of-a-kind** ~ уника́льная сва́дьба ♦ **outdoor** ~ сва́дьба на откры́том во́здухе ♦ **shotgun** ~ *(slang)* сва́дьба под ду́лом пистоле́та, вы́нужденная сва́дьба ♦ **small** ~ ма́ленькая сва́дьба ♦ **traditional** ~ традицио́нная сва́дьба ♦ **unique** ~ уника́льная сва́дьба.

---

wedding: *other terms*

call off the ~ отмени́ть сва́дьбу ♦ **celebrate the** ~ **(in a restaurant)** справля́ть / спра́вить сва́дьбу (в рестора́не) ♦ **get out of a** ~ поко́нчить с сва́дьбой ♦ **have the** ~ устро́ить сва́дьбу ♦ **perform the** ~ проводи́ть / провести́ сва́дьбу ♦ **plan the** ~ составля́ть / соста́вить план на сва́дьбу ♦ **postpone the** ~ отложи́ть сва́дьбу ♦ **postponement of the** ~ отсро́чка сва́дьбы ♦ **witness the** ~ быть свиде́телем на сва́дьбе.

---

wedding: *having a wedding*

We need to plan the wedding. Нам на́до соста́вить план на сва́дьбу. ♦ **What kind of wedding do you want to have?** Како́й вид сва́дьбы ты хо́чешь? ♦ **Do you want to have a small wedding or a large one?** Ты хо́чешь име́ть ма́ленькую или большу́ю сва́дьбу? ♦ **Let's have a** *(1)* **big** / *(2)* **small wedding.** Дава́й устро́им *(1)* большу́ю / *(2)* ма́ленькую сва́дьбу. ♦ **I want to have a(n)** *(1)* **small** / *(2)* **intimate** / *(3)* **large wedding.** Я хочу́ *(1)* ма́ленькую / *(2)* инти́мную / *(3)* большу́ю сва́дьбу. ♦ *(1)* **When** / *(2)* **Where shall we** *(3)* **have** / *(4)* **hold the wedding?** *(1)* Когда́ / *(2)* Где *(3,4)* бу́дет на́ша сва́дьба? ♦ **Who should we invite to the wedding?** Кто бу́дет приглашён на сва́дьбу? ♦ **Who will perform the wedding?** Кто бу́дет проводи́ть сва́дьбу? ♦ **Who will witness the wedding for us?** Кто бу́дет свиде́телем у нас на сва́дьбе? ♦ **We can't have the wedding until....** Мы не мо́жем устро́ить сва́дьбу до....

How to use the Cyrillic alphabet on the Internet is the subject of Appendix 20 on page 789.

---

wedding: postponing the wedding

Do you want to postpone the wedding? Ты хо́чешь отложи́ть сва́дьбу? ♦ **I (don't) want to postpone the wedding.** Я (не) хочу́ откла́дывать сва́дьбу. ♦ **We (don't) have to postpone the wedding.** Мы (не) должны́ откла́дывать сва́дьбу. ♦ **We will have to postpone the wedding (until...).** Мы бу́дем должны́ отложи́ть сва́дьбу (до....).

wedding: calling off the wedding

I think we should call off the wedding. Я ду́маю, мы должны́ отмени́ть сва́дьбу. ♦ **I want to call off the wedding.** Я хочу́ отмени́ть сва́дьбу. ♦ **Why do you want to call off the wedding.** Почему́ ты хо́чешь отмени́ть сва́дьбу?

wedlock *n* брак, супру́жество ♦ **out of** ~ внебра́чный, -ая, -ое, -ые.

Wednesday *n* среда́ ♦ **by** ~ к среде́ ♦ **last** ~ в про́шлую сре́ду ♦ **next** ~ в сле́дующую сре́ду ♦ **on** ~ в сре́ду.

weed *n (slang) (marijuana)* марихуа́на.

week *n* неде́ля ♦ **all** ~ всю неде́лю ♦ **every** ~ ка́ждую неде́лю ♦ **for a** ~ 1. *(planned)* на неде́лю; 2. *(spent)* неде́лю ♦ **for one** ~ 1. *(planned)* на одну́ неде́лю; 2. *(spent)* одну́ неде́лю ♦ **for** *(1)* **two** / *(2)* **three** / *(3)* **four** ~**s** 1. *(planned)* на *(1)* две / *(2)* три / *(3)* четы́ре неде́ли; 2. *(spent)* *(1)* две / *(2)* три / *(3)* четы́ре неде́ли ♦ **for five** ~**s** 1. *(planned)* на пять неде́ль; 2. *(spent)* пять неде́ль ♦ **in a** ~ 1. *(after)* че́рез неде́лю; 2. *(in the space of)* за неде́лю ♦ **in** *(1)* **two** / *(2)* **three** / *(2)* **four** ~**s** *(after)* че́рез *(1)* две / *(2)* три / *(3)* четы́ре неде́ли ♦ **in five** ~**s** в пять неде́ль ♦ **in recent** ~**s** в про́шлые неде́ли ♦ **last** ~ на про́шлой неде́ле ♦ *(1,2)* **next** ~ на *(1)* сле́дующей / *(2)* бу́дущей неде́ле ♦ **once a** ~ раз в неде́лю ♦ **this** ~ на э́той неде́ле ♦ **a whole** ~ це́лую неде́лю ♦ **the whole** ~ всю неде́лю ♦ **That** *([1]* **beautiful** / *[2]* **wonderful) week will** *(3)* **stay** / *(4)* **remain indelibly etched in my** *(5)* **mind** / *(6)* **memory** *(7)* **...forever.** / *(8)* **...for as long as I live.** Эта *([1]* прекра́сная / *[2]* замеча́тельная) неде́ля *(3,4)* оста́нется вы́гравированной несмыва́емо в мое́й *(5,6)* па́мяти *(7)* ...навсегда́. / *(8)* ...пока́ я жив *(ж: жива́)*.

weekend *n* выходны́е (дни) *pl* ♦ **next** ~ сле́дующие выходны́е (дни) ♦ **for** *(1)* **a** / *(2)* **the** ~ *(planned)* на *(1,2)* выходны́е дни ♦ **on the** ~ в выходны́е ♦ **on** ~**s** по выходны́м ♦ **It was such an idyllic weekend with you.** Выходны́е с тобо́й бы́ли иди́ллией.

weight *n* вес ♦ **gain** ~прибавля́ть / приба́вить в ве́се; *(get fat)* толсте́ть / потолсте́ть ♦ **lose** ~теря́ть / потеря́ть вес; *(get thin)* худе́ть / похуде́ть ♦ **put on** ~прибавля́ть / приба́вить в ве́се; *(get fat)* толсте́ть / потолсте́ть ♦ **I'm trying to lose weight.** Я пыта́юсь похуде́ть. ♦ **I want to lose some more weight.** Я хочу́ ещё немно́го похуде́ть. ♦ **I gained weight (over the holidays).** Я приба́вил *(ж: приба́вила)* в ве́се (за пра́здники).

weightless *adj* невесо́мый, -ая, -ое, -ые.

weird *adj* стра́нный, -ая, -ое, -ые.

weirdly *adv* стра́нно.

weirdo *n (slang)* чуда́к, приду́рок, челове́к со стра́нностями ♦ **screen out the** ~**s** отсе́ивать / отсе́ять люде́й со стра́нностями.

welcome *vt* приве́тствовать *(what, whom = acc.)*; раду́шно принима́ть / приня́ть *(whom = acc.)*.

welcome *n* приём ♦ **enthusiastic** ~ восто́рженный приём ♦ **friendly** ~ дру́жеский приём ♦ **hearty** ~ серде́чный приём ♦ **joyful** ~ раду́шный приём ♦ **nice** ~ хоро́ший приём ♦ *(1,2)* **warm** ~ *(1)* тёплый / *(2)* серде́чный приём ♦ **Welcome!** *int* Добро́ пожа́ловать! ♦ **Welcome to** *(1)* **America** / *(2)* **New York** / *(3)* **England** / *(4)* **London!** Добро́ пожа́ловать в *(1)* Аме́рику / *(2)* Нью Йо́рк / *(3)* А́нглию / *(4)* Ло́ндон! ♦ **You're welcome!** *(response to thanks)* Пожа́луйста!

well-adjusted *adj* уравнове́шенный, -ая, -ое, -ые.

Russian adjectives have long and short forms. *Where short forms are given, they are labeled as such.*

well-balanced *adj* хорошо уравновéшенный, -ая, -ое, -ые.

well-being *n* благополýчие ♦ **material** ~ материáльное благополýчие.

well-bred *adj* (благо)воспи́танный, -ая, -ое, -ые.

well-built *adj* лáдный, -ая, -ое, -ые.

well-dressed *adj* наря́дный, -ая, -ое, -ые, хорошо одéтый, -ая, -ое, -ые.

well-educated *adj* хорошо образóванный, -ая, -ое, -ые.

well-formed *adj* хорошо слóженный, -ая, -ое, -ые.

well-groomed *adj* хóленый, -ая, -ое, -ые, вы́холенный, -ая, -ое, -ые.

well-grounded *adj (knowledgeable, experienced)* свéдущий, -ая, -ее, -ие; *(well trained)* имé-ющий (-ая, -ее, -ие) хорóшую подготóвку.

well-heeled *adj (affluent)* богáтый, -ая, -ое, -ые, состоя́тельный, -ая, -ое, -ые.

well-informed *adj* хорошо осведомлённый, -ая, -ое, -ые.

well-mannered *adj* (благо)воспи́танный, -ая, -ое, -ые, обходи́тельный, -ая, -ое, -ые.

well-matched *adj* подходя́щий, -ая, -ое, -ые, гармони́рующий, -ая, -ое, -ые ♦ **Never have two people been as well-matched in bed as you.** Никогдá ещё двóе людéй так хорошо не подходи́ли друг дрýгу в постéли, как мы с тобóй.

well-off *adj* состоя́тельный, -ая, -ое, -ые, обеспéченный, -ая, -ое, -ые, богáтый, -ая, -ое, -ые. ♦ **I'm (fairly) well off financially.** Я (довóльно) хорошо финáнсово обеспéчен *(ж: обеспéчена)*.

well-preserved *adj* хорошо сохрани́вшийся, -аяся, -ееся, -иеся ♦ **I think I'm well-pre served for my age.** Я дýмаю, что для моегó вóзраста я хорошо сохрани́лся *(ж: сохрани́лась)*.

well-proportioned *adj* лáдный, -ая, -ое, -ые; пропорционáльно слóженный, -ая, -ое, -ые.

well-put-together *adj* хорошо слóженный, -ая, -ое, -ые.

well-read *adj* начи́танный, -ая, -ое, -ые.

well-rounded *adj* всесторóнний, -яя, -ее, -ие ♦ ~ **education** всесторóннее образовáние ♦ ~ **person** всесторóнний человéк.

well-seasoned *adj* с больши́м óпытом.

well-stacked *adj (slang) (having a great figure)* с великолéпной фигýрой ♦ **You're well-stacked.** У тебя́ великолéпная фигýра.

well-traveled *adj* мнóго путешéствовавший, -ая, -ее, -ие.

well-versed *adj* осведомлённый, -ая, -ое, -ые.

wet *adj* мóкрый, -ая, -ое, -ие ♦ **I'm not some kid, wet behind the ears.** Я не ребёнок, мóкрый по сáмые ýши.

whadaya: ♦ **Whadaya say?** Что ты об э́том дýмаешь?

what *adj (which)* какóй, -áя, -óе, -и́е ♦ ~ **a** какóй, -áя, -óе, -и́е ♦ ~ **kind** какóй, -áя, -óе, -и́е ♦ **What a beautiful face you have!** Какóе у тебя́ краси́вое лицó!.

what *pron* что ♦ **about** ~ *(or* ~ **about***)* о чём ♦ **for** ~ *(or* ~ **for***)* 1. *(reason)* за что; 2. *(use)* для чего ♦ **with** ~ *(or* ~ **with***)* 1. *(by means of)* чем; 2. *(together)* с чем ♦ **What more could I ask for than you (***[1] **...as my life-long partner. /** *[2]* **...as my love in life.).** О чём бóль-шем мог *(ж: моглá)* бы я проси́ть, чем о тебé (*[1]* , ...как о моём спýтнике на всю жизнь. / *[2]* ...как о моéй любви́).

wheelchair *n* крéсло-катáлка, инвали́дная коля́ска ♦ **I use a wheelchair (to get around).** Я пóльзуюсь инвали́дной коля́ской.

where *adv (position)* где; *(motion)* кудá ♦ **Where ...shall we meet? / ...shall I meet you? / ...do you live / work? / ...are you staying? / ...is it? / ...are they?** Где ...мы должны́ встрé-титься? / ...я дóлжен *(ж: должнá)* встрéтить тебя́? / ...Вы живёте? / ...ты останови́-лась *(ж: останови́лся)*? / ...э́то? / ...они́? ♦ **Where are you (1,2) going?** Кудá ты *(1)*

Russian nouns are either masculine, feminine or neuter.
Adjectives with them will be the same.

идёшь *(on foot)* / (2) éдешь *(by veh.)*? ♦ **Where is the train station?** *(See page 763 for other places.)* Где вокзáл?

while *n*: ♦ **(for) a ~** нéкоторое врéмя ♦ **once in a ~** иногдá, врéмя от врéмени.

whim *n* прúхоть *f*; причýда; капрúз ♦ **feminine ~s** жéнские причýды ♦ **~s of fate** капрúзы судьбы́ ♦ **Anything to suit your whims, my love.** Всё для удовлетворéния твоúх причýд, моя́ любóвь.

whimper *vi* хны́кать.

whimper *n* хны́канье.

whimsical *adj* прихотлúвый, -ая, -ое, -ые, капрúзный, -ая, -ое, -ые, причýдливый, -ая, -ое, -ые.

whimsy *n* прúхоть *f*; причýда.

whine *vi* хны́кать, ныть, скулúть.

whiner *n* ны́тик.

whining *n* хны́канье, нытьё ♦ **Stop your** *(1,2)* **whining.** Прекратú *(1)* хны́кать / *(2)* ныть.

whiny *adj* хны́кающий, -ая, -ее, -ие, нóющий, -ая, -ее, -ие.

whipped *adj (slang) (dominated by one's partner)* исполня́ющий (-ая, -ее, -ие) чью́-то вóлю.

whipsmart *adj (slang)* óчень ýмный, -ая, -ое, -ые.

whirl *vt* вращáть *(what, whom = acc.)*, вертéть *(what, whom = acc.)*.

whirl *vi* кружúться, вращáться, вертéться, крутúться ♦ **You set my head to whirling.** Ты вскружúла *(ж: вскружúл)* мне гóлову. ♦ **Your** *(1)* **radiant** / *(2)* **exceptional** / *(3)* **ethereal beauty sets my head to whirling.** Твоя́ *(1)* сия́ющая / *(2)* исключúтельная / *(3)* небéсная красотá вскружúла мою́ гóлову.

whirlpool *n* водоворóт ♦ **I was thrown into a violent whirlpool of emotion.** Я был брóшен *(ж: былá брóшена)* в жýткий водоворóт стрáсти.

whirlwind *n* вихрь *m*.

whiskey *n* вúски *neut* ♦ **mellow ~** вы́держаное вúски ♦ **shot of ~** глотóк вúски.

whisper *vt* шептáть / шепнýть *or* прошептáть *(what = acc.)* ♦ **I want to lie next to you and whisper sweet nothings in your ear.** Я хочý лежáть ря́дом с тобóй и шептáть нéжные словá в твоё ýхо.

whisper *n* шёпот ♦ **passionate ~** стрáстный шёпот ♦ **soft ~** нéжный шёпот ♦ **tremulous ~** трéпетный шёпот.

whistle *vt* свистéть / свúстнуть *(what = acc.)*, насвúстывать *(what = acc.)* ♦ **I'll whistle a tune outside your window.** Я бýду насвúстывать мелóдию под твоúми óкнами.

whistle *n* свист; *(summoning whistle)* прúсвист ♦ **wolf ~** мужскóй восхищённый прúсвист.

whit *n* йóта, кáпелька ♦ **I don't give a whit for what anyone says.** Меня́ ни на йóту не волнýет кто и что говорúт.

white *adj* бéлый, -ая, -ое, -ые ♦ **tall, ~ and handsome** высóкий, бéлый и красúвый.

white-hot *adj* раскалённый, -ая, -ое, -ые.

whiteness *n* белизнá ♦ **creamy ~** слúвочная белизнá ♦ **ivory ~ of your skin** молóчная белизнá твоéй кóжи.

white-skinned *adj* белокóжий, -ая, -ее, -ие.

Whoa! *(1,2) exclamation* (1) Стоя́ть! / (2) Тпру!

whole *adj* цéлый, -ая, -ое, -ые.

wholehearted *adj* беззавéтный, -ая, -ое, -ые.

wholeheartedly *adv* беззавéтно.

wholeness *n* цéльность *f*; цéлость *f*.

wholesome *adj* 1. *(healthy, beneficial)* полéзный, -ая, -ое, -ые, здорóвый, -ая, -ое, -ые; 2.

Learn more about Russian customs in Appendix 15, page 782.

(sensible) здра́вый, -ая, -ое, -ые, здравомы́слящий, -ая, -ее, -ие; 3. *(robust)* цвету́щий, -ая, -ее, -ие, пы́шущий (-ая, -ее, -ие) здоро́вьем.

wholesomeness *n* це́льность *f* ♦ **There is such a wholesomeness** *(1)* **to /** *(2)* **about you.** *(1,2)* В тебе́ така́я це́льность.

wicked *adj (sinful)* гре́шный, -ая, -ое, -ые, нечести́вый, -ая, -ое, -ые ♦ **deliciously ~** восхити́тельно безнра́вственный, -ая, -ое, -ые ♦ **~ thoughts** нечести́вые мы́сли.

wickedly *adv* грешно́.

wide *adj* широ́кий, -ая, -ое, -ие.

wide-eyed *adj* 1. *(eyes opened wide)* с широко́ раскры́тыми глаза́ми; 2. *(naive)* наи́вный, -ая, -ое, -ые.

wide-minded *adj* широкомы́слящий, -ая, -ее, -ие.

widow *n* вдова́ ♦ **attractive ~** привлека́тельная вдова́ ♦ **lonely ~** одино́кая вдова́ ♦ **rich ~** бога́тая вдова́ ♦ **sexy ~** сексапи́льная вдова́ ♦ **wealthy ~** бога́тая вдова́ ♦ **well-to-do ~** состоя́тельная вдова́.

widower *n* вдове́ц ♦ **lonely ~** одино́кий вдове́ц ♦ **sexy ~** сексуа́льный вдове́ц ♦ **wealthy ~** бога́тый вдове́ц.

wife *n* жена́ ♦ **beautiful ~** краси́вая жена́ ♦ **beloved ~** люби́мая жена́ ♦ **caring ~** забо́тливая жена́ ♦ **dear ~** дорога́я жена́ ♦ *(1,2)* **deceased ~** *(1)* уме́ршая / *(2)* поко́йная жена́ ♦ **ex-~** бы́вшая жена́ ♦ **faithful ~** ве́рная жена́ ♦ **first ~** пе́рвая жена́ ♦ **former ~** бы́вшая жена́ ♦ **future ~** бу́дущая жена́ ♦ **good ~** хоро́шая жена́ ♦ **jealous ~** ревни́вая жена́ ♦ *(1,2)* **late ~** *(1)* уме́ршая / *(2)* поко́йная жена́ ♦ **lawfully wedded ~** зако́нная жена́ ♦ **legal ~** зако́нная жена́ ♦ **lovely ~** краси́вая жена́ ♦ **loving ~** лю́бящая жена́ ♦ **model ~** образцо́вая жена́ ♦ **nagging ~** «пила́», сварли́вая жена́ ♦ **perfect ~** образцо́вая жена́ ♦ **second ~** втора́я жена́ ♦ **trophy ~** состоя́тельная жена́ ♦ **unfaithful ~** неве́рная жена́ ♦ **young ~** молода́я жена́.

wife: verb terms

become my ~ стать мое́й жено́й ♦ **divorce my ~** разводи́ться / развести́сь с жено́й ♦ **find a ~** найти́ (себе́) жену́ ♦ **go back to my ~** верну́ться к жене́ ♦ **make up with my ~** помири́ться с жено́й ♦ **search for a ~** иска́ть (себе́) жену́ ♦ **separate from my ~** расходи́ться / разойти́сь с жено́й ♦ **take as a ~** взять в жёны *(whom = acc.)*.

wife: you as my wife

You are the wife of my soul. Ты жена́, кото́рую про́сит моя́ душа́. ♦ **I dream of having you as my wife.** Я мечта́ю о том, что́бы ты была́ мое́й жено́й. ♦ **I want you to be my wife, my friend, my lover.** Я хочу́, что́бы ты была́ мое́й жено́й, мои́м дру́гом, мое́й любо́вницей. ♦ **My greatest happiness would be to have you as my wife.** Как бесконе́чно я был бы сча́стлив, е́сли бы ты ста́ла мое́й жено́й. ♦ **I could never ask for more (in this** *[1]* **life /** *[2]* **world) than to have you as my wife.** Моё са́мое заве́тное жела́ние (в э́той *[1,2]* жи́зни), что́бы ты ста́ла мое́й жено́й. ♦ **This cozy, idyllic, heavenly dream of having you as my loving wife is wonderful beyond any words that I can muster.** Я не могу́ найти́ досто́йных слов, что́бы описа́ть тебе́ свою́ идилли́ческую, боже́ственную мечту́: ты моя́ люби́мая жена́.

wife: I'll be a good wife

I'm going to make every (possible) effort to be a good wife to you. Я приложу́ все (возмо́жные) уси́лия, что́бы быть хоро́шей жено́й.

wife-to-be *n* бу́дущая жена́.

wiggle *vi* пока́чиваться, извива́ться ♦ **~ with pleasure** извива́ться от наслажде́ния ♦ **I like the way you wiggle (when you walk).** Мне нра́вится, как ты пока́чиваешься (при ходьбе́).

A slash always denotes "or."
You can choose the numbered words before and after.

wiggle *n* покачивание ♦ **You have a nice wiggle (when you walk).** Ты приятно покачиваешься (, когда ходишь).

wild *adj (animals)* дикий, -ая, -ое, -ие ♦ **drive** *(1)* **you** / *(2)* **me** ~ доводить / довести *(1)* тебя / *(2)* меня до исступления, сводить / свести *(1)* тебя / *(2)* меня с ума.

wild: phrases

I know so many wonderful ways to drive you wild. Мне известно так много замечательных способов довести тебя до исступления. ♦ **I'm going to do things with you that will drive you (absolutely) wild.** Я сделаю с тобой такое, что доведёт тебя до (полного) исступления. ♦ **You drive me (absolutely) wild.** Ты (совершенно) сводишь меня с ума. ♦ **I promise you, I'm going to drive you (absolutely) wild.** Я обещаю, что я (совершенно) сведу тебя с ума.

wildcat *n (slang)* тигрица.

wiles *n, pl* хитрости ♦ **womanly ~s** женские хитрости.

will *n* 1. *(desire; volition; power)* воля, желание; 2. *(testament)* завещание ♦ **divine ~** воля провидения ♦ **free ~** свобода воли ♦ **good ~** добрая воля ♦ **ill ~** злая воля ♦ **iron ~** железная воля ♦ **strong ~** сильная воля ♦ **weak ~** слабая воля ♦ **of** *(1)* **my** / *(2)* **your own free ~** *(1,2)* по доброй воле, *(1,2)* по собственному желанию.

will: desire; volition; power

It has been set down by a divine will that I am yours and you are mine. Это было волей провидения, что ...я твой и ты моя *(ж: ...я твоя и ты мой).* ♦ *(1)* **With you...** / *(2)* **When I'm around you,... I have no will (at all).** *(1)* С тобой... / *(2)* Когда я рядом с тобой,... у меня (совсем) нет своей воли. ♦ **You take away all my will (to resist).** Ты похитила *(ж: похитил)* всё мою волю (к сопротивлению). ♦ **Where there's a will, there's a way.** Где хотение, там и умение. ♦ **If you have the will, you can do it.** Если у тебя есть воля, ты сможешь сделать это. ♦ **It** *(1)* **is** / *(2)* **was against my will.** *(1)* Это... / *(2)* Это было... против моей воли. ♦ **I don't want to make you do anything against your will.** Я не хочу заставлять тебя делать что-либо вопреки твоей воле. ♦ **I want you to do it of your own free will.** Я хочу, чтобы ты сделала *(ж: сделал)* это по доброй воле.

will: testament

My *(1)* **mother** / *(2)* **father left me the** *(3)* **house** / *(4)* **property** / *(5)* **money in** *(6)* **her** / *(7)* **his will.** *(1)* Моя мать оставила... / *(2)* Мой отец оставил... мне *(3)* дом / *(4)* имущество / *(5)* деньги по *(6,7)* завещанию.

willingness *n* готовность ♦ **I want a partner in life who has a willingness to share (everything).** Я хочу найти спутницу *(ж: спутника)* жизни, которая готова *(ж: который готов)* разделять всё со мной. ♦ **I have the willingness to come there, but not the money.** У меня есть желание приехать туда, но нет денег. ♦ **Whenever I'm in your arms, I feel such a willingness to give up control.** Всякий раз, когда ты обнимаешь меня, я ощущаю такую готовность перестать сдерживаться.

willowy *adj* гибкий, -ая, -ое, -ие, стройный, -ая, -ое, -ые ♦ **Your body has such willowy grace.** В твоём теле есть такая гибкая грация. ♦ **What a** *(1,2)* **willowy figure you have.** Что за *(1)* стройная / *(2)* гибкая фигура у тебя.

will power *n* сила воли ♦ **I can't summon up the will power to say no to you.** У меня не хватает силы воли сказать тебе нет. ♦ **With you I have no will power (at all).** С тобой у меня (совсем) нет силы воли.

wimp *n (slang) (weak person)* безответный человек, баба, тряпка.

wind up *vi* очутиться ♦ **You'll leave me and I'll wind up miserable.** Ты уедешь и я буду несчастен *(ж: несчастна).*

wine *vt* угощать / угостить вином *(whom = acc.),* поить / напоить вином *(whom = acc.)* ♦

Common adult weights are given in Appendix 10, page 777.

I'm going to wine and dine you to your heart's content. Я напою́ тебя́ вино́м и угощу́ обе́дом до отва́ла.

wine *n* вино́ ♦ **good bottle of** *(1)* **red** / *(2)* **white ~** буты́лка хоро́шего *(1)* кра́сного / *(2)* бе́лого вина́.

wing *n* крыло́ *(pl: крылья)* ♦ **~s of ecstasy** кры́лья экста́за.

wink *vi* подми́гивать / подмигну́ть ♦ **I'm glad** *(1)* **...you winked at me.** / *(2)* **...I winked at you.** Я рад *(ж: ра́да)*, что *(1)* ...ты подмигну́ла *(ж: подмигну́л)* мне. / *(2)* ...я подмигну́л *(ж: подмигну́ла)* тебе́. ♦ **My heart went crazy when you winked (back) at me.** Моё се́рдце взбеси́лось, когда́ ты подмигну́ла *(ж: подмигну́л)* мне (в отве́т).

wink *n* подми́гивание, морга́ние ♦ **That was such a sexy wink you gave me.** Ты мне так сексуа́льно подмигну́ла *(ж: подмигну́л)*.

winner *n* завоева́тель *m* ♦ **~ of ladies' hearts** завоева́тель да́мских серде́ц.

winsome *adj* 1. *(pleasant, winning)* прия́тный, -ая, -ое, -ые, привлека́тельный, -ая, -ое, -ые; обая́тельный, -ая, -ое, -ые, располага́ющий, -ая, -ее, -ие; 2. *(cheerful, gay)* весёлый, -ая, -ое, -ые, бо́дрый, -ая, -ое, -ые.

winter *n* зима́ ♦ **in the ~** зимо́й ♦ **last ~** про́шлой зимо́й ♦ **next ~** сле́дующей зимо́й.

wire *n* 1. *(electrical)* про́вод; 2. *(telegram)* телегра́мма ♦ **You're really a live wire.** В тебе́, действи́тельно, бурли́т жизнь.

wiry *adj* жи́листый, -ая, -ое, -ые.

wisdom *n* му́дрость *f* ♦ **I admire you for your wisdom.** Я восхища́юсь твое́й му́дростью. ♦ **I value wisdom, kindness and humor.** Я ценю́ му́дрость, доброту́ и ю́мор.

wise *adj* му́дрый, -ая, -ое, -ые ♦ **My goal is to be healthy, wealthy and wise.** Моя́ цель -- быть здоро́вым, бога́тым и му́дрым *(ж: здоро́вой, бога́той и му́дрой)*.

wish *vt* жела́ть / пожела́ть *(whom = dat., what = gen.)* ♦ **~** *(1,2)* **fervently** *(1)* стра́стно / *(2)* горячо́ жела́ть ♦ **~ sincerely** и́скренне жела́ть ♦ **~ with all my heart** жела́ть от (всей) души́, жела́ть от всего́ се́рдца.

wish: *phrases*

I wish you *(1)* **...(lots of) luck.** / *(2)* **...all the luck in the world.** / *(3)* **...happiness (always).** / *(4)* **...all the best.** Я жела́ю тебе́ *(1)* ...(мно́го) уда́чи. / *(2)* ...всей уда́чи в ми́ре. / *(3)* ...сча́стья (всегда́). / *(4)* ...всего́ наилу́чшего. ♦ **How I wish that I were holding you in my arms at this very minute, covering your beautiful face with adoring kisses.** Как бы я жела́л в э́ту са́мую мину́ту держа́ть тебя́ в объя́тиях, покрыва́я твоё прекра́сное лицо́ обожа́ющими поцелу́ями.

wish *n* жела́ние ♦ **cherished ~** заве́тное жела́ние ♦ *(1,2)* **fervent ~** *(1)* пы́лкое / *(2)* горя́чее жела́ние ♦ **great ~** большо́е жела́ние ♦ **most cherished ~** са́мое заве́тное жела́ние ♦ **my (only) ~** моё (еди́нственное) жела́ние ♦ **secret ~** та́йное жела́ние ♦ **simple ~** просто́е жела́ние ♦ **sincere ~** и́скреннее жела́ние ♦ **your (every) ~** *(familiar)* (ка́ждое) твоё жела́ние; *(polite)* (ка́ждое) Ва́ше жела́ние.

wish: *my wish*

My most cherished wish is *(1)* **...to have you as my wife (husband).** / *(2)* **...to marry you.** / *(3)* **...to make a happy family life with you.** / *(4)* **...to have your love for the rest of my life.** / *(5)* **...to make love with you every night and every day (for the rest of my life).** / *(6)***...to partake of the myriad delights promised by that beautiful body of yours.** Моё са́мое заве́тное жела́ние *(1)* ,...чтобы ты ста́ла мое́й же́ной *(ж: стал мои́м му́жем)*. / *(2)* ...жени́ться на тебе́ *(ж: вы́йти за́муж за тебя́)*. / *(3)* ...созда́ть с тобо́й счастли́вую семью́. / *(4)* ...чтобы ты люби́ла *(ж: люби́л)* меня́ всю оста́вшуюся жизнь. / *(5)* ...занима́ться любо́вью с тобо́й ка́ждую ночь и ка́ждый день (до конца́ жи́зни). / *(6)* ... - испыта́ть мириа́д восто́ргов, обеща́емых твои́м прекра́сным те́лом. ♦ **Will my**

An italicized ж in parentheses   indicates a woman speaking.

(fervent) wish ever come true? Осуществи́тся ли когда́-нибу́дь моё (пы́лкое) жела́-ние? ♦ **I hope that you will grant me this small wish.** Я наде́юсь, что ты позво́лишь мне э́то ма́ленькое жела́ние. ♦ **If I could make three wishes, they would all be to have your love (forever).** Если бы я мог *(ж: могла́)* заду́мать три жела́ния, все они́ бы́ли бы о том, что́бы получи́ть твою́ любо́вь (навсегда́).

> **wish:** *you are my wish come true*

If I were to find Aladdin's lamp, I would just throw it away, because in you I have every-thing a person could wish for. Если бы я нашёл *(ж: нашла́)* ла́мпу Аладди́на, то вы́бро-сил *(ж: вы́бросила)* бы её, потому́ что в тебе́ всё, что челове́к мог бы пожела́ть. ♦ **When you came into my arms, my secret wish came true.** Когда́ ты оказа́лась в мои́х объя́тиях, моё та́йное жела́ние осуществи́лось. ♦ **My secret wish has (finally) come true.** Моё та́йное жела́ние (в конце́ концо́в) осуществи́лось.

> **wish:** *your wish*

Your wish is my command. Твоё жела́ние -- зако́н для меня́. ♦ **Is that (really) your wish?** Это (действи́тельно) твоё жела́ние?

> **wish:** *warmest wishes*

I send you my *(1)* best / *(2)* warmest wishes (for *[3]* ...a happy / *[4]* joyful holiday season. / *[5]* ...a happy and prosperous New Year.). Я посыла́ю тебе́ мои́ *(1)* ...наилу́чшие... / *(2)* ...са́мые серде́чные... пожела́ния (*[3]*...счастли́вого / *[4]* ра́достного вре́мени пра́здников. / *[5]* ...счастли́вого и благоприя́тного Но́вого го́да.)

wisp *n (streak)* стру́йка; *(of smoke)* дымо́к, ды́мка.

wispy *adj* то́нкий, -ая, -ое, -ие.

wistful *adj* 1. *(melancholy)* тоску́ющий, -ая, -ее, -ие, тоскли́вый, -ая, -ое, -ые, томя́щийся, -аяся, -еёся, -иеся; 2. *(pensive)* заду́мчивый, -ая, -ое, -ые, мечта́тельный, -ая, -ое, -ые.

wistfully *adv* 1. *(melancholily)* тоскли́во, с тоско́й; 2. *(pensively)* заду́мчиво, мечта́тельно ♦ **think ~** ду́мать тоскли́во.

wistfulness *n* тоска́ ♦ **I feel a twinge of wistfulness whenever I think of *(1)* it / *(2)* him / *(3)* her / *(4)* them.** Я чу́вствую при́ступ тоски́, когда́ поду́маю о(б) *(1)* ...э́том / *(2)* нём / *(3)* ней / *(4)* них.

wit *n* 1. *(cleverness at humor)* остроу́мие; 2. *(intelligence, sense) (sometimes pl)* ум, ра́зум; 3. *(witty person)* остря́к ♦ **diabolical ~** дья́вольское остро-у́мие ♦ **droll ~** заба́вное остро-у́мие ♦ **ironic ~** ирони́ческое остроу́мие ♦ **keen ~** остроу́мие ♦ **quick ~** остроу́мие ♦ **sarcastic ~** саркасти́ческое остроу́мие ♦ **sharp ~** остроу́мие ♦ **wry ~** то́нкое остро-у́мие.

withdrawn *adj (introverted)* за́мкнутый, -ая, -ое, -ые, углублённый (-ая, -ое, -ые) в себя́; *(remote)* отрешённый, -ая, -ое, -ые ♦ *(1)* **You seem... /** *(2)* **You've been... so withdrawn lately.** Ты ка́жешься... / Ты была́ *(ж: был)*... тако́й отрешённой *(ж: таки́м отрешён-ным)* после́днее вре́мя.

without *prep* без *(+ gen.)* ♦ **Without you, my beloved, I can't see or hear or feel or think — or live.** Без тебя́, моя́ люби́мая *(ж: люби́мый)*, я не могу́ ни ви́деть, ни слы́шать, ни чу́вствовать, ни ду́мать, ни жить. ♦ **I don't know what I would do without you.** Я не зна́ю, что бы я де́лал *(ж: де́лала)* без тебя́. ♦ **Without you my life would be *(1)* so / *(2)* totally / *(3)* completely meaningless.** Без тебя́ моя́ жизнь была́ бы *(1)* так / *(2)* совер-ше́нно / *(3)* по́лностью бессмы́сленна. ♦ **Without you I could not cope (with life).** Без тебя́ я не смог *(ж: смогла́)* бы спра́виться (с жи́знью). ♦ **The last few *(1)* days / *(2)* weeks / *(3)* months without you have been hell.** После́дние *(1)* дни / *(2)* неде́ли / *(3)* меся-цы без тебя́ бы́ли а́дом. ♦ **The thought of being without you *(1)* pierces / *(2)* crushes my very soul.** Мысль быть без тебя́ *(1)* пронза́ет / *(2)* подавля́ет мою́ ду́шу. ♦ **How can**

> *Procedures for getting married to a Russian*
> *are outlined in Appendix 18, page 787.*

I *(1)* **get** / *(2)* **live through another** *(3)* **day** / *(4)* **month** / *(5)* **week without you by my side.**
I cringe at the prospect. Как могу́ я *(1,2)* дожи́ть до *(3)* ...сле́дующего дня / *(4)* ме́ся-
ца... / *(5)* ...сле́дующей неде́ли... без тебя́ ря́дом со мной. Я страшу́сь тако́й
перспекти́вы. ♦ **I don't know how I'm going to last another** *(1)* **day** / *(2)* **month** / *(3)* **week**
without you (here) (by my side). Я не зна́ю, как вы́держу ещё *(1)* ...оди́н день / *(2)* ме́-
сяц... / *(3)* ...одну́ неде́лю... без тебя́ (здесь) (со мной). ♦ **This being without you is**
devastating. Это существова́ние без тебя́ опустоша́ет. ♦ **Life would be so empty**
without you. Жизнь была́ бы так пуста́ без тебя́. ♦ **I'd be lost without you.** Мне бы́ло
бы пло́хо без тебя́. ♦ **I'd be miserable without you.** Без тебя́ я был *(ж: была́)* бы так
несча́стен *(ж: несча́стна)*.

withstand *vt* вы́стоять ♦ **Together we can withstand whatever the world throws at us.**
Вме́сте мы мо́жем вы́стоять про́тив всего́, что преподнесёт нам жизнь.

witness *vt* 1. *(observe)* быть свиде́телем; 2. *(certify a signature)* заверя́ть / заве́рить *(what*
= acc.) ♦ **Who will witness the wedding for us?** Кто бу́дет свиде́телем у нас на сва́дьбе?

witness *n* свиде́тель *m*, свиде́тельница *f* ♦ **We need two witnesses for the wedding.** Нам
на́до двух свиде́телей для бракосочета́ния. ♦ **Who** *(1)* **...will be...** \ *(2)* **...can be... our**
witnesses? Кто *(1)* ...бу́дет... / *(2)* ...мо́жет быть... на́шими свиде́телями?

witty *adj* остроу́мный, -ая, -ое, -ые ♦ **extraordinarily** ~ исключи́тельно остроу́мный,
-ая, -ое, -ые.

wolf *n (slang)* 1. *(womanizer)* ба́бник, волоки́та; 2. *(lustful man)* похотли́вый мужчи́на.

woman *n* же́нщина ♦ **Amazon** ~ амазо́нка ♦ **American** ~ америка́нка ♦ **amiable** ~ приве́т-
ливая же́нщина ♦ **appreciative** ~ высоко́ це́нящая же́нщина ♦ **Armenian** ~ армя́нка
♦ **Asian** ~ азиа́тка ♦ **assertive** ~ напо́ристая же́нщина ♦ **athletic** ~ спорти́вная же́н-
щина ♦ *(1,2)* **attractive** ~ *(1)* интере́сная / *(2)* привлека́тельная же́нщина ♦ **Australian**
~ австрали́йка ♦ **Azerbaijanian** ~ азербайджа́нка ♦ **bad** ~ плоха́я же́нщина ♦ **Belo-**
russian ~ белору́ска ♦ **bereaved** ~ же́нщина, потеря́вшая кого́-то из бли́зких *(1 ex-*
pression) ♦ **big-bosomed** ~ пышногру́дая же́нщина ♦ **bisexual** ~ бисексуа́льная же́н-
щина ♦ **bitchy** ~ сварли́вая же́нщина ♦ **black** ~ чёрная же́нщина ♦ **blue-eyed** ~
синегла́зая же́нщина ♦ **bossy** ~ вла́стная же́нщина ♦ **bubbly** ~ **with a great personality**
сверка́ющая же́нщина с замеча́тельной индивидуа́льностью ♦ **business** ~ делова́я
же́нщина ♦ **Canadian** ~ кана́дка ♦ **caring** ~ забо́тливая же́нщина ♦ **Carribean** ~
же́нщина с Кари́бских острово́в ♦ *(1,2)* **charming** ~ *(1)* обая́тельная / *(2)* очаро-
ва́тельная же́нщина ♦ **cheerful** ~ весёлая же́нщина ♦ **chic** ~ шика́рная же́нщина ♦
Chinese ~ китая́нка ♦ **Christian** ~ христиа́нка ♦ **classy** ~ кла́ссная же́нщина ♦ **college-**
educated ~ же́нщина с вы́сшим образова́нием ♦ *(1,2)* **compassionate** ~ *(1)* состра-
да́тельная / *(2)* чу́ткая же́нщина ♦ **complex** ~ сло́жная же́нщина ♦ **considerate** ~
внима́тельная же́нщина ♦ **cultured** ~ культу́рная же́нщина ♦ **curvaceous** ~ окру́глая
же́нщина ♦ **dark(-complected)** ~ сму́глая же́нщина ♦ **dark-eyed** ~ черногла́зая
же́нщина ♦ **devoted** ~ пре́данная же́нщина ♦ **divorced** ~ разведённая же́нщина ♦
domineering ~ вла́стная же́нщина ♦ **dumb** ~ глу́пая же́нщина ♦ *(1,2)* **educated** ~ *(1)*
образо́ванная / *(2)* интеллиге́нтная же́нщина ♦ *(1,2)* **elderly** ~ *(1)* немолода́я / *(2)*
пожила́я же́нщина ♦ **emotionally generous** ~ эмоциона́льно ще́драя же́нщина ♦
energetic ~ энерги́чная же́нщина ♦ **enlisted** ~ **(EW)** военнослу́жащая ♦ **Estonian** ~
эсто́нка ♦ **experienced** ~ о́пытная же́нщина ♦ **eye-catching** ~ привлека́тельная же́н-
щина ♦ **faithful** ~ ве́рная же́нщина ♦ **fat** ~ то́лстая же́нщина, толсту́ха ♦ **feisty** ~
навя́зчивая же́нщина ♦ **fine quality** ~ прекра́сных ка́честв же́нщина ♦ **Finnish** ~
фи́нка ♦ **fit** ~ спорти́вная же́нщина ♦ **flighty** ~ легкомы́сленная же́нщина ♦ *(1)* **flir-**
tatious / *(2)* **flirty** ~ *(1,2)* коке́тливая же́нщина ♦ **friendly** ~ дружелю́бная же́нщина

A list of conjugated Russian verbs is given
in Appendix 3 on page 699.

♦ **full-figured** ~ по́лная же́нщина ♦ **gentle** ~ мя́гкая же́нщина ♦ **Georgian** ~ грузи́нка ♦ **good** ~ хоро́шая же́нщина ♦ *(1-3)* **good-looking** ~ *(1)* интере́сная / *(2)* привлека́тельная / *(3)* симпати́чная же́нщина ♦ **gracious** ~ грацио́зная же́нщина ♦ **hard-working** ~ трудолюби́вая же́нщина ♦ **heavy(-set)** ~ то́лстая же́нщина ♦ **highly sexed** ~ о́чень сексуа́льная же́нщина ♦ **high-strung** ~ беспоко́йная же́нщина ♦ **Hispanic** ~ лати́но-америка́нка ♦ **honest** ~ че́стная же́нщина ♦ *(1,2)* **hot-blooded** ~ *(1)* пы́лкая / *(2)* стра́стная же́нщина ♦ **Indian** ~ 1. *(India)* индиа́нка 2. *(America)* индиа́нка ♦ **industrious** ~ трудолюби́вая же́нщина ♦ **intelligent** ~ у́мная же́нщина ♦ **interesting** ~ интере́сная же́нщина ♦ **Japanese** ~ япо́нка ♦ **jealous** ~ ревни́вая же́нщина ♦ **Jewish** ~ евре́йка ♦ **Kazakh** ~ каза́шка ♦ **kind** ~ до́брая же́нщина ♦ **kind-hearted** ~ отзы́вчивая же́нщина ♦ **Kirghiz** ~ кирги́зка ♦ **Korean** ~ коре́йка ♦ **Latvian** ~ латы́шка ♦ **lazy** ~ лени́вая же́нщина ♦ **liberated** ~ свобо́дная же́нщина ♦ **Lithuanian** ~ лито́вка ♦ **lonely** ~ одино́кая же́нщина ♦ **loose** ~ безнра́вственная же́нщина ♦ **loud** ~ крикли́вая же́нщина ♦ **lovely** ~ прекра́сная же́нщина ♦ **loving** ~ лю́бящая же́нщина ♦ **married** ~ заму́жняя же́нщина ♦ **mean** ~ зла́я же́нщина ♦ **modern** ~ совреме́нная же́нщина ♦ **modest** ~ скро́мная же́нщина ♦ **Moldovan** ~ молдава́нка ♦ **Mongolian** ~ монго́лка ♦ **moody** ~ капри́зная же́нщина ♦ **multi-dimensional** ~ всесторо́нняя же́нщина ♦ *(1,2)* **neat** ~ *(1)* аккура́тная / *(2)* чистопло́тная же́нщина ♦ **nervous** ~ не́рвная же́нщина ♦ **New Zealand** ~ ново-зела́ндка ♦ **nice** ~ *(1)* ми́лая / *(2)* симпати́чная же́нщина; прия́тная же́нщина ♦ **nurturing** ~ воспи́тывающая же́нщина ♦ **older** ~ же́нщина ста́рше *(than whom = gen.)* ♦ **old** ~ ста́рая же́нщина ♦ **passionate** ~ стра́стная же́нщина ♦ **petite** ~ миниатю́рная же́нщина ♦ **plain** ~ неинтере́сная же́нщина ♦ **pregnant** ~ бере́менная же́нщина ♦ *(1,2)* **pretty** ~ *(1)* хоро́шенькая / *(2)* милови́дная же́нщина ♦ **proud** ~ самолюби́вая же́нщина ♦ **quarrelsome** ~ сварли́вая же́нщина ♦ *(1,2)* **quiet** ~ *(1)* споко́йная / *(2)* ти́хая же́нщина ♦ **refined** ~ культу́рная же́нщина ♦ **remarkable** ~ замеча́тельная же́нщина ♦ **renaissance** ~ ренесса́нсная же́нщина ♦ **respectabe** ~ уважа́ющая себя́ же́нщина ♦ **romantic** ~ романти́ческая же́нщина ♦ **rubenesque** ~ ру́бенсовская же́нщина ♦ **Russian** ~ ру́сская ♦ **scorned** ~ отве́ргнутая же́нщина ♦ **self-assured** ~ самоуве́ренная же́нщина ♦ **self-confident** ~ самоуве́ренная же́нщина ♦ **self-respecting** ~ уважа́ющая себя́ же́нщина ♦ **sensible** ~ разу́мная же́нщина ♦ **sensitive** ~ чувстви́тельная же́нщина ♦ **sensuous** ~ чу́вственная же́нщина ♦ **serious(-minded)** ~ серьёзная же́нщина ♦ **shapely** ~ ста́тная же́нщина ♦ **sharp-minded** ~ остроу́мная же́нщина ♦ **short** ~ невысо́кая же́нщина ♦ **shrewish** ~ сварли́вая же́нщина ♦ **simple** ~ проста́я же́нщина ♦ *(1,2)* **single** ~ *(1)* одино́кая / *(2)* незаму́жняя же́нщина ♦ **slender** ~ стро́йная же́нщина ♦ **slim** ~ стро́йная же́нщина ♦ **sly** ~ хи́трая же́нщина ♦ **small** ~ ма́ленькая же́нщина ♦ **smart** ~ у́мная же́нщина ♦ **sneaky** ~ хи́трая же́нщина ♦ **sophisticated** ~ о́пытная же́нщина ♦ **spiritual** ~ духо́вная же́нщина ♦ **spoiled young** ~ изба́лованная молода́я же́нщина ♦ **strange** ~ 1. *(odd)* стра́нная же́нщина; 2. *(unfamiliar)* незнако́мая же́нщина ♦ **striking** ~ потряса́ющая же́нщина ♦ **strong** ~ си́льная же́нщина ♦ **stubborn** ~ упря́мая же́нщина ♦ **stupid** ~ глу́пая же́нщина ♦ **stylish** ~ мо́дная же́нщина ♦ **submissive** ~ поко́рная же́нщина ♦ **sweet** ~ ми́лая же́нщина ♦ **Tadzhik** ~ таджи́чка ♦ **tall, blonde** ~ высо́кая, светловоло́сая же́нщина ♦ **tanned** ~ загоре́лая же́нщина ♦ **thin** ~ худа́я же́нщина ♦ **thoughtful** ~ внима́тельная же́нщина ♦ **Turkmen** ~ туркме́нка ♦ **Ukrainian** ~ украи́нка ♦ **ultimate** ~ превосхо́дная же́нщина ♦ **unbearable** ~ несно́сная же́нщина ♦ **uninhibited** ~ же́нщина без ко́мплексов ♦ **unique** ~ уника́льная же́нщина ♦ **university-educated** ~ же́нщина с вы́сшим образова́нием ♦ **unpretentious** ~ непритяза́тельная же́нщина ♦ **Uzbek** ~ узбе́чка ♦ **virtuous** ~ доброде́тельная же́нщина ♦ **vivacious** ~ жива́я же́нщина ♦ *(1,2)* **warm-hearted** ~ *(1)* до́брая / *(2)* доброду́шная же́нщина ♦ **weak** ~ сла́бая же́нщина

For Russian adjectives, the masculine form is spelled out,
followed by the feminine, neuter and plural endings

♦ **well-dressed** ~ хорошо́ оде́тая же́нщина ♦ **well-proportioned** ~ хорошо́ сложённая же́нщина ♦ **white** ~ бе́лая же́нщина ♦ **wild** ~ распу́тная же́нщина ♦ **witty** ~ остроу́мная же́нщина ♦ **~ of depth** глубо́кая же́нщина ♦ **~ of exceptional beauty** же́нщина исключи́тельной красоты́ ♦ **~ of experience** о́пытная же́нщина ♦ **~ of extraordinary beauty** же́нщина необыкнове́нной красоты́ ♦ **~ of high energy** чрезвыча́йно энерги́чная же́нщина ♦ **~ of my dreams** же́нщина мое́й мечты́ ♦ **~ of passion** стра́стная же́нщина ♦ **~ of passion** стра́стная же́нщина ♦ **~ with emotional substance** эмоциона́льная же́нщина ♦ **~ with inner beauty** же́нщина с вну́тренней красото́й ♦ *(1,2)* **wonderful** ~ *(1)* замеча́тельная / *(2)* чуде́сная же́нщина ♦ **young** ~ молода́я же́нщина ♦ **zestful** ~ жива́я же́нщина.

woman: *the kind of woman I seek*

What I'm looking for in a woman is... То, что я бы хоте́л найти́ в же́нщине,... ♦ *(1,2)* **You're (exactly) the kind of woman I've been looking for (all my life).** *(1)* Ты *(familiar)* / *(2)* Вы *(polite)* (то́чно) тот тип же́нщины, кото́рый я иска́л (всю жизнь). ♦ **I'm seeking a woman with substance.** Я ищу́ содержа́тельную же́нщину. ♦ **I like older women.** Мне нра́вятся же́нщины, кото́рые ста́рше меня́. ♦ *(1)* **I want...** / *(2)* **I'm looking for... an older woman.** Я *(1,2)* ищу́ же́нщину ста́рше себя́.

woman: *how I relate to women*

(1) **I relate...** / *(2)* **I've always related... well to women.** *(1)* Я отношу́сь... / *(2)* Я всегда́ относи́лся... хорошо́ к же́нщинам. ♦ **I'm not God's gift to women (by any means).** Я (ни ко́им о́бразом) не бо́жий дар для же́нщин.

woman: *you're the woman for me*

You are the woman *(1)* **...of my dreams.** / *(2)* **...that I've been waiting for all my life.** / *(3)* **...that I've been dreaming of all my life.** Ты - же́нщина *(1)* ...мое́й мечты́. / *(2)* ...кото́рую я ждал всю свою́ жизнь. / *(3)* ..., о кото́рой я мечта́л всю свою́ жизнь. ♦ **You are the only woman** *(1)* **...for me.** / *(2)* **...in my life.** Ты - еди́нственная же́нщина *(1)* ...для меня́. / *(2)* ...в мое́й жи́зни. ♦ **You are peerless among women.** Среди́ же́нщин ты несравне́нна. ♦ **How pale and bland all other women are before you.** Как бледны́ и неинтере́сны все други́е же́нщины по сравне́нию с тобо́й. ♦ **You are the only woman I have ever truly loved.** Ты еди́нственная же́нщина, кото́рую я когда́-либо по-настоя́щему люби́л.

woman: *if you were my woman*

If you were my woman, I would fill your life to overflowing with soft, gentle, eager, loving kisses that would awaken all sorts of warm, wonderful, exquisite feelings in you. Если бы ты была́ мое́й же́нщиной, я бы запо́лнил твою́ жизнь до краёв мя́гкими, не́жными, жа́ждущими, лю́бящими поцелу́ями, кото́рые пробуди́ли бы все са́мые тёплые, замеча́тельные, изы́сканные чу́вства в тебе́.

woman: *to feel like a woman*

(1) **I want you to know...** / *(2)* **I'm going to teach you... what it feels like to be a woman.** *(1)* Я хочу́, что́бы ты узна́ла,... / *(2)* Я научу́ тебя́,... что э́то зна́чит чу́вствовать себя́ же́нщиной. ♦ **You don't let yourself be a real woman.** Ты не позволя́ешь себе́ быть реа́льной же́нщиной.

woman: *another woman?*

Is there another woman? Тут заме́шана друга́я же́нщина? ♦ **There's no other woman (in my life).** Нет друго́й же́нщины (в мое́й жи́зни). ♦ **I will never have another woman.** У меня́ никогда́ не бу́дет друго́й же́нщины. ♦ **I don't need another woman.** Друго́й же́нщины мне не ну́жно. ♦ **I'm a one-man woman.** Я однолю́бка.

woman: *a kept woman*

I don't want to be a kept woman. Я не хочу́ быть содержа́нкой.

See Appendix 19 for notes on sending mail to Russia and Ukraine.

woman-hater *n* женоненавистник.

womanhood *n* женственность *f* ♦ **My body aches to feel the fire that rages in the core of your womanhood.** Моё тело жаждет почувствовать огонь, который бушует в глубине твоей женственности. ♦ **I want to open the floodgates of your womanhood.** Я хочу открыть шлюзы твоей женственности. ♦ **You're a prime specimen of womanhood.** Ты эталон женственности.

womanize *vi* путаться с женщинами.

womanizer *n* бабник, волокита; женолюб.

womanliness *n* женственность *f.*

womanly *adj* женственный, -ая, -ое, -ые.

womanness *n* женственность *f* ♦ **Every night my dreams roil in the most torrid scenes of** *(1)* **passionate /** *(2)* **erotic desire for your sweet, warm, wonderful womanness.** Каждую ночь в моих снах роятся самые знойные сцены *(2)* страстного / *(2)* эротического вожделения к твоей сладкой, тёплой, великолепной женственности.

womb *n* матка.

wonder *vi* хотеть знать, интересоваться, *(Note: "I wonder" is most commonly rendered as* Интересно, ...*)* ♦ **I wonder what you're doing right now.** Интересно, чем ты сейчас занимаешься. ♦ **I spend private moments thinking about you, wondering about you, daydreaming about you.** Я провожу свои свободные минуты, думая о тебе, представляя себе, чем ты сейчас занимаешься, мечтая о тебе.

wonder *n* 1. *(miracle)* чудо; 2. *(surprise)* удивление, изумление ♦ **no** ~ не удивительно ♦ **rare** ~ рéдкостная диковина ♦ **I can never get over the wonder and ecstasy of your love.** Я никогда не смогу надивиться чуду и экстазу твоей любви. ♦ **No wonder you're still single — you're constantly** *(1)* **busy /** *(2)* **working.** Не удивительно, что ты всё ещё одна *(ж: один)*, ты постоянно *(1)* занята *(ж: занят)* / *(2)* работаешь. ♦ **It's a feeling that blends ecstasy and wonder.** Это чувство -- смесь экстаза и удивления.

wonderful *adj* удивительный, -ая, -ое, -ые, замечательный, -ая, -ое, -ые, чудесный, -ая, -ое, -ые ♦ **That was (***[1]* **absolutely /** *[2]* **so) wonderful.** Это было (*[1]* совершенно / *[2]* так) замечательно. ♦ **It was wonderful beyond belief.** Это было выше всякого сравнения. ♦ **You are (***[1]* **absolutely /** *[2]* **so) wonderful.** Ты (*[1]* совершенно / *[2]* так) замечательна *(ж: замечателен).* ♦ **Never in my wildest imagination did I ever think I could meet anyone as wonderful as you.** Никогда, даже в самых безумных мечтах, я не думал, что могу встретить кого-либо такого замечательного, как ты. ♦ **You are the most wonderful person that God could ever have brought into my life.** Ты самый замечательный человек, которого Бог мог бы когда-либо послать в мою жизнь. ♦ **The** *(1)* **memory /** *(2)* **thought of your wonderful body never leaves my mind.** *(1)* Воспоминание / *(2)* Мысль о твоём замечательном теле никогда не покидает меня. ♦ **Everything is always (so) wonderful when I'm (together) with you.** Всё всегда (так) замечательно, когда я (вместе) с тобой. ♦ **The image of your wonderful body never leaves my mind.** Видение твоего замечательного тела никогда не покидает меня. ♦ **My wonderful, incredible Anna...** Моя удивительная, невероятная Анна...

wonderfulness *n* чудесность *f.*

wondrous *adj* дивный, -ая, -ое, -ые.

woo *vt* ухаживать *(whom =* + за + *instr.).*

word *n* слово *(pl: слова)* ♦ **admiring** ~**s** восхищённые слова ♦ **adoring** ~**s** обожающие слова ♦ **angry** ~**s** гневные слова ♦ **ardent** ~**s** пылкие слова ♦ **banal** ~**s** банальные слова ♦ **beautiful** ~**s** прекрасные слова ♦ **bitter** ~**s** горькие слова ♦ **contemptuous** ~**s** презрительные слова ♦ **courting** ~**s** слова, произносимые при ухаживании *(explanation)*

When terms are listed after a main word, a tilde ~
is used to indicate the main word.

♦ **cuss** ~ бра́нное сло́во ♦ **devoted** ~s посвящённые слова́ ♦ **dirty** ~s непристо́йные слова́
♦ **English** ~ англи́йское сло́во ♦ **exact** ~s то́чные слова́ ♦ **fancy** ~s напы́щенные слова́
♦ **flowery** ~s цвети́стые слова́ ♦ **heated** ~s горя́чие слова́ ♦ **honeyed** ~s льсти́вые слова́
♦ **hurtful** ~s оби́дные слова́ ♦ **idolizing** ~s идеализи́рующие слова́ ♦ *(1,2)* **loving** ~s *(1)*
слова́ любви́ *(2)* любо́вные слова́ ♦ **mean** ~s злы́е слова́ ♦ **my** ~s мои́ слова́ ♦ *(1,2)* **nasty**
~s *(1)* гря́зные / *(2)* непристо́йные слова́ ♦ **nice** ~s прия́тные слова́ ♦ **rude** ~ гру́бое сло́во
♦ **Russian** ~ ру́сское сло́во ♦ **sharp** ~s о́стрые слова́ ♦ **slang** ~ жарго́нное сло́во ♦ *(1,2)*
soft ~s *(1)* не́жные / *(2)* ла́сковые слова́ ♦ **such** ~s таки́е слова́ ♦ **swear** ~ бра́нное сло́во
♦ *(1,2)* **sweet** ~s *(1)* не́жные / *(2)* ла́сковые слова́ ♦ **sympathetic** ~s уча́стливые слова́ ♦
(1,2) **tender** ~s *(1)* не́жные / *(2)* ла́сковые слова́ ♦ **unkind** ~ гру́бое сло́во ♦ **warm** ~s
тёплые слова́ ♦ **wise** ~ му́дрые слова́ ♦ ~ **of honor** че́стное сло́во ♦ ~s **of encouragement**
слова́ ободре́ния ♦ ~s **of gratitude** слова́ благода́рности ♦ ~s **of love** слова́ любви́ ♦ ~s
of welcome слова́ приве́та ♦ ~s **of sympathy** слова́ сочу́вствия ♦ ~ **that I don't** *(1)* **know**
/ *(2)* **understand** сло́во, кото́рого я не *(1)* зна́ю / *(2)* понима́ю ♦ **your** ~s *(familiar)* твои́
слова́; *(polite)* Ва́ши слова́.

word: *other terms*

beyond ~s вы́ше вся́ких слов, невероя́тно ♦ **convey in** ~s передава́ть / переда́ть слова́ми
(what = acc.) ♦ **express in** ~s выража́ть / вы́разить слова́ми *(what = acc.)* ♦ **find the** ~s
найти́ слова́ ♦ **give you my** ~ дава́ть / дать тебе́ сло́во ♦ **magic set of** ~s волше́бный набо́р
слов ♦ **put into** ~s выража́ть / вы́разить слова́ми *(what = acc.)*.

word: *the way you express yourself*

You have a (*[1]*** great /** *[2]* **marvelous /** *[3]* **wonderful) way with words.** Ты *([1]*
замеча́тельно / *[2]* великоле́пно / *[3]* чуде́сно) владе́ешь языко́м. ♦ **The thought
patterns that yielded your choice of words and sentences in your ad reveal the exact same
raging hunger for love and affection that I harbor within me.** Мы́сли, роди́вшие вы́бор
слов и предложе́ний в Ва́шем объявле́нии, говоря́т о то́чно тако́й же неи́стовой жа́жде
любви́ и не́жности, кото́рая таи́тся во мне.

word: *putting it into words*

I wish I could put into words the (tender) feelings that abound in my heart for you. Я хоте́л
(ж: хоте́ла) бы вы́разить слова́ми *(не́жные)* чу́вства к тебе́, переполня́ющие моё
се́рдце. ♦ **There is no way that I can express in words how (very much) I love you (and** *[1]*
need / *[2]* **want you).** Я не могу́ вы́разить слова́ми, как (о́чень си́льно) я люблю́ тебя́ (и
[1] ...нужда́юсь в тебе́. / *[2]* ...хочу́ тебя́). ♦ **There are no words to describe the** *(1)* **depth**
/ *(2)* **immensity /** *(3)* **intensity /** *(4)* **vastness of the love that I bear in my heart for you.** Нет
слов, что́бы описа́ть *(1)* глубину́ / *(2)* безме́рность / *(3)* си́лу / *(4)* глубину́ той любви́ к
тебе́, кото́рой полно́ моё се́рдце. ♦ **Words alone cannot express the love that I feel for you
in my heart.** Одни́ми слова́ми невозмо́жно вы́разить всю ту любо́вь к тебе́, кото́рую я
чу́вствую. ♦ **Mere words are** *(1)* **...not enough... /** *(2)* **...inadequate...** *(3)* **...to describe your
(***[4]*** ethereal /** *[5]* **incomparable)** *(6)* **beauty /** *(7)* **loveliness. /** *(8)* **...to do justice to your
incredible** *(9)* **beauty /** *(10)* **loveliness.** Про́сто слов *(1,2)* не доста́точно, что́бы *(3)*
...описа́ть твою́ *([4]* небе́сную / *[5]* несравне́нную) *(6,7)* красоту́. / *(8)* ...отда́ть до́лжное
твое́й невероя́тной *(9, 10)* красоте́. ♦ **I search in vain for the right words to tell you how
much** *(1)* **...I love you (and want you). /** *(2)* **...you mean to me.** Я ищу́ напра́сно таки́е слова́,
кото́рые рассказа́ли бы тебе́, *(1)* ...как си́льно я   люблю́ тебя́ (и хочу́
тебя́). / *(2)* ...как мно́го ты зна́чишь для меня́.

word: *beyond words*

(1,2) **You are beautiful beyond words.** *(1)* Твоя́ красота́ вы́ше вся́ких слов. / *(2)* Ты не-
вероя́тно краси́ва. ♦ **The happiness I've found in your** *(1)* **love /** *(2)* **arms is beyond words.**

A list of abbreviations used in the dictionary is given on page 10.

Сча́стье, кото́рое я нашёл *(ж: нашла́)* в *(1)* ...твое́й любви́,... / *(2)* ...твои́х объя́-
тиях,... невозмо́жно вы́разить слова́ми.

word: *your loving words*

**In all my life I have never thought or said to myself so many tender, loving words about
any person on the face of this earth as I do when I** *(1)* **...finish talking to you in person.**
/ *(2)* **...look at your photo.** Никогда́ в жи́зни я не приду́мывал и́ли говори́л так мно́го
не́жных, любо́вных слов кому́-либо на э́той земле́, как я де́лаю, *(1)* ...по́сле разго-
во́ра с тобо́й. / *(2)* ...когда́ смотрю́ на твоё фо́то.

word: *your words have touched me*

Your words *(1)*... **struck deep.** / *(2)* **...warmed my heart.** / *(3)* **...touched my heart.** Твои́
слова́ *(1)* ...глубоко́ порази́ли меня́. / *(2)* ...согре́ли моё се́рдце. / *(3)* ...тро́нули моё
се́рдце. ♦ **The words you wrote in your letter warmed me** *(1)* **...to my toes.** / *(2)* **...through
and through.** / *(3)* **...to the very core.** Слова́ твоего́ письма́ *(3)* ...согре́ли меня́ до ко́нчи-
ков па́льцев. / *(4)* ...напо́лнили меня́ тепло́м. / *(5)* ...согре́ли мне ду́шу. ♦ **The words
you write sparkle in my mind like sunbeams.** Слова́, кото́рые ты пи́шешь, сверка́ют в
мое́й па́мяти как со́лнечные лучи́. ♦ **This letter of yours was so unexpected. Your** *(1)*
sweet / *(2)* **beautiful words of love have set my heart completely aquiver.** Это письмо́ от
тебя́ бы́ло так неожи́данно. Твои́ *(1)* не́жные / *(2)* прекра́сные слова́ любви́ застав-
ля́ют моё се́рдце трепета́ть. ♦ **If these words are true, it would make me the happiest
man in this world.** Е́сли бы э́ти слова́ бы́ли пра́вдой, э́то сде́лало бы меня́ счастли́-
вейшим челове́ком в э́том ми́ре.

word: *word of honor*

I give you my word (of honor). Я даю́ тебе́ моё (че́стное) сло́во. ♦ **I'm a man of my
word.** Я челове́к сло́ва.

word: *heated words*

I regret my heated words. Я сожале́ю, что погорячи́лся *(ж: погорячи́лась)*. ♦ **We had
heated words.** Мы погорячи́лись.

work *vi* рабо́тать ♦ ~ **out** *vi* 1. *(exercise)* тренирова́ться, упражня́ться.; 2. *(succeed)* скла́-
дываться / сложи́ться, получа́ться / получи́ться.

work: *phrases*

Where do you work? Где Вы рабо́таете? ♦ **I work** *(1,2)* **at** *(name)* . Я рабо́таю *(1)* в /
(2) на *(назва́ние)* .

work out: *exercise*

I *(1,2)* **work out regularly (***[3]***...at home.** / *[4]* **...at a health club.).** Я *(1)* трениру́юсь / *(2)*
упражня́юсь. регуля́рно *([3]* ...до́ма. / *[4]* ...в клу́бе здоро́вья.)

work out: *succeed*

Our marriage isn't working (out). Наш брак не скла́дывается. ♦ **Our relationship isn't
working (out).** На́ши отноше́ния не скла́дываются. ♦ **I hope it works (out) between us.**
Я наде́юсь, что у нас бу́дут хоро́шие отноше́ния. ♦ **Things didn't work out (between
us).** Нам не удало́сь разреши́ть на́ши пробле́мы. ♦ **Deep down in my heart I know that
this will (not) work.** В глубине́ своего́ се́рдца я зна́ю, что э́то (не) полу́чится.

work *n* рабо́та ♦ **Are you** *(1)* **busy** / *(2)* **free after work?** Ты (бу́дешь) *(1)* за́нята *(ж: за́нят)*
/ *(2)* свобо́дна *(ж: свобо́ден)* по́сле рабо́ты? ♦ **What are you doing** *(1)* **...after work?** /
(2) **...after you get off work?** Что ты де́лаешь *(1)* ...по́сле рабо́ты? / *(2)* ...по́сле того́, как
зако́нчишь рабо́ту? ♦ *(1,2)* **What time do you** *(3)* **...finish...** / *(4)* **...get off... work?** *(1)*
Когда́... / *(2)* В како́е вре́мя... ты *(3)* ко́нчишь / *(4)* зако́нчишь рабо́ту? ♦ *(1)* **I finish...**
/ *(2)* **I get off... work at one (thirty).** *(See page 759 for other times.)* *(1)* Я око́нчу рабо́ту...
/ *(2)* Я уйду́ с рабо́ты... в час (три́дцать). ♦ **I'm** *(1,2)* **going to work.** Я *(1)* иду́ *(on foot)*

*The accents on Russian words are to show how to pronounce them..
You don't have to copy the accents when writing to someone.*

/ *(2)* éду *(by veh.)* на рабóту. ♦ **I have to** *(1,2)* **go to work.** Я дóлжен *(ж: должнá) (1)* идти *(on foot)* / *(2)* éхать *(by veh.)* на рабóту. ♦ **What kind of work do you do?** Где и кем Вы рабóтаете? ♦ **Work is one piece of who you are**. Рабóта -- э́то тóлько часть твоéй натýры.

workaholic *n* человéк, «горя́щий» на рабóте *(1 term).*

worker *n* 1. *(one who works)* рабóтник *m*, рабóтница *f* ; 2. *(general labor)* рабóчий *m*, рабóчая *f* ; *(office)* слýжащий *m*, слýжащая *f* ♦ **good** ~хорóший рабóтник ♦ **hard** ~ усéрдный рабóтник ♦ **steady** ~имéющий постоя́нную рабóту.

work out *vt (solve)* решáть / реши́ть *(what = acc.)* ♦ **Let's always try to work out our problems together.** Давáй всегдá решáть нáши проблéмы вмéсте. ♦ **I know we can work out our problems if we try.** Я знáю, мы мóжем реши́ть нáши проблéмы, éсли попытáемся.

world *n* мир, свет ♦ **capricious** ~ капри́зный мир ♦ **crazy** ~ безýмный мир ♦ **crowded** ~ мир, напóлненный людьми́ *(1 term)* ♦ **entire** ~ весь мир ♦ **fast-paced** ~бы́стро шагáющий мир ♦ **goofy** ~ дурáцкий мир ♦ **huge** ~ огрóмный мир ♦ **indifferent** ~ равнодýшный мир ♦ **mixed-up** ~ запýтанный мир ♦ **private** ~ сóбственный мир ♦ **vast** ~ громáдный мир ♦ **wacky** ~ дурáцкий мир ♦ **whole** ~ весь мир.

> **world: phrases**

You are the most beautiful woman in this whole world. Ты сáмая прекрáсная жéнщина в цéлом ми́ре. ♦ **You are my world.** Ты мой мир. ♦ **You are the world to me.** Ты для меня́ -- весь мир. ♦ **You mean the world to me.** Ты означáешь весь мир для меня́. ♦ **You are all I want in this world.** Ты всё, чегó я хочý в э́том ми́ре. ♦ **Nothing in this world is more important to me than your love.** Ничтó в э́том ми́ре не вáжно для меня́ так, как твоя́ любóвь. ♦ **I'm looking for someone who can help me cope with this wacky world.** Я ищý тогó, кто смóжет помóчь мне спрáвиться с э́тим сумасшéдшим ми́ром. ♦ **You make my world a** *(1)* **...Garden of Eden.** / *(2)* **...paradise.** / *(3)* **...daily festival of love.** Ты превращáешь мой мир *(1)* ...в рáйский сад. / *(2)* ...в рай. / *(3)* ...в ежеднéвный прáздник любви́. ♦ **We'll** *(1)* **have** / *(2)* **make our own private world.** *(1)* У нас бýдет... / *(2)* Мы создади́м... наш сóбственный мир. ♦ *(1)* **He** / *(2)* **She is in a world of** *(3)* **his** / *(4)* **her own.** *(1)* Он / *(2)* Онá в *(3,4)* своём сóбственном ми́ре. ♦ **I want to share the world with you.** Я хочý дели́ть мир с тобóй. ♦ **My world is a** *(1)* **better** / *(2)* **happier** / *(3)* **brighter place because of you.** Благодаря́ тебé, мой мир стал *(1)* лýчше / *(2)* счастли́вее / *(3)* я́рче.

worldliness *n* суéтность *f.*

worldly *adj* 1. *(of this world, practical)* житéйский, -ая, -ое, -ые, практи́чный, -ая, -ое, -ые; 2. *(worldly-wise)* бывáлый, -ая, -ое, -ые.

world-traveled *adj* путешéствовавший (-ая, -ее, -ие) по всемý ми́ру ♦ **I'm a world-traveled engineer.** Я инженéр, путешéствовавший по всемý ми́ру.

worn out *adj (slang)* 1. *(tired, exhausted)* изнурённый, -ая, -ое, -ые, устáлый, -ая, -ое, -ые; 2. *(dilapidated)* изнóшенный, -ая, -ое, -ые ♦ **I feel worn out.** Я чýвствую себя́ изнурённым *(ж: изнурённой)*. ♦ **I'm emotionally worn out from it all.** Я эмоционáльно устáл *(ж: устáла)* от всегó э́того.

worried *adj* взволнóван, -а, -о, -ы, обеспокóен, -а, -о, -ы *(short forms)* ♦ **Are you** *(1,2)* **worried?** Ты *(1)* взволнóвана *(ж: взволнóван)* / *(2)* обеспокóена *(ж: обеспокóен)*? ♦ **I'm (not)** *(1,2)* **worried.** Я (не) *(1)* взволнóван *(ж: взволнóвана)* / *(2)* обеспокóен *(ж: обеспокóена)*. ♦ **Don't be** *(1-3)* **worried.** Не *(1)* волнýйся / *(2)* переживáй / *(3)* беспокóйся.

worry *vi* волновáться *(about what, whom = + о + acc.)*, тревóжиться *(about what, whom = + о + acc.)*, беспокóиться *(about what, whom = + о + acc.)* ♦ **I (don't) worry (about** *[1]*

If no accent is shown on a word with a capitalized vowel, it means that the capitalized vowel is accented.

you / *[2]* **him** / *[3]* **her** / *[4]* **us** / *[5]* **them** / *[6]* **it).** Я (не) беспоко́юсь (о *[1]* тебе́ / о *[2]* нём / о *[3]* ней / о *[4]* нас / о *[5]* них / об *[6]* э́том). ♦ **Don't** *(1-3)* **worry.** Не *(1)* волну́йся / *(2)* пережива́й / *(3)* беспоко́йся. ♦ **There's nothing to worry about.** Не о чем беспоко́иться.

worry-wart *n (slang)* обеспоко́енный *m*, обеспоко́енная *f*, озабо́ченный *m*, озабо́ченная *f* ♦ **Don't be a worry-wart. Everything will be okay.** Не беспоко́йся. Всё бу́дет хорошо́.

worship *vt* поклоня́ться *(what, whom = dat.)*, обожа́ть *(what, whom = acc.)* ♦ **I want to worship every inch of your body from head to toe.** Я хочу́ поклоня́ться ка́ждому дю́йму твоего́ те́ла с головы́ до па́льчиков ног. ♦ **I'm going to show you every day and every night how much I worship you.** Ка́ждый день и ка́ждую ночь я бу́ду пока́зывать тебе́, как си́льно я обожа́ю тебя́. ♦ **If you only knew how I worship you.** Е́сли бы ты то́лько зна́ла *(ж: знал)*, как я обожа́ю тебя́. ♦ *(1)* **I want to...** / *(2)* **I'm going to... worship every part of your** *(3)* **beautiful** / *(4)* **delectable** / *(5)* **luscious body with my lips.** *(1)* Я хочу́... / *(2)* Я бу́ду... обожа́ть губа́ми ка́ждую части́цу твоего́ *(3)* прекра́сного / *(4)* ла́комого / *(5)* со́чного те́ла. ♦ **I promise you hours and hours of incredible ecstasy as my avid lips totally worship your loveliness.** Я обеща́ю тебе́ часы́ и часы́ невероя́тного экста́за в то вре́мя, как мои́ жа́дные гу́бы бу́дут поклоня́ться твое́й красоте́.

worth *n* цена́; це́нность *f* ♦ **feelings of ~** чу́вства це́нности ♦ **I'm worth your while.** Я сто́ю затра́ченного тобо́й вре́мени. ♦ **You are of infinite worth and importance** *(1)* **...in my life** / *(2)* **...to me.** Ты бесконе́чная це́нность и ва́жность *(1)* ...мое́й жи́зни. / *(2)* ...для меня́.

worthy *adj* досто́йный, -ая, -ое, -ые, заслу́живающий, -ая, -ее, -ие ♦ **I will always** *(1)* **strive** / *(2)* **try to be worthy of your love.** Я всегда́ бу́ду *(1)* стара́ться / *(2)* пыта́ться быть досто́йным *(ж: досто́йной)* твое́й любви́.

wrap around *vi* обви́ться вокру́г *(what = gen.)*.

wretch *n* негодя́й.

wretched *adj* несча́стный, -ая, -ое, -ые, жа́лкий, -ая, -ое, -ие, никуды́шный. -ая, -ое, -ые ♦ **I feel wretched about** *(1)* **...the whole thing.** / *(2)* **...the way I've treated you.** / *(3)* **...not calling** / *(4)* **writing you.** / *(5)* **...what I said.** Я чу́вствую себя́ отврати́тельно *(1)* ...за всё, что случи́лось. / *(2)* ...за то, что так обраща́лся *(ж: обраща́лась)* с тобо́й. / *(3)* ...потому́, что не звони́л *(ж: звони́ла)* / *(4)* писа́л *(ж: писа́ла)* тебе́. / *(5)* ...от того́, что я сказа́л *(ж: сказа́ла)*. ♦ **I feel wretched without you.** Я чу́вствую себя́ ужа́сно без тебя́.

wrist *n* запя́стье.

write *vt* писа́ть / написа́ть *(what = acc., to whom = dat.)* ♦ **~ beautifully** писа́ть краси́во ♦ **~ down** запи́сывать / записа́ть *(what = acc.)* ♦ **~ everyday** писа́ть ка́ждый день ♦ **~ in** *(1)* **English** / *(2)* **Russian** писа́ть / написа́ть на *(1)* англи́йском / *(2)* ру́сском языке́, писа́ть / написа́ть *(1)* по-англи́йски / *(2)* по-ру́сски ♦ **~ me** писа́ть / написа́ть мне ♦ **~ often** писа́ть ча́сто ♦ **~ once a week** писа́ть раз в неде́лю ♦ **~ regularly** писа́ть регуля́рно ♦ **~ right away** писа́ть сра́зу же ♦ **~ seldom** писа́ть ре́дко ♦ **~ soon** писа́ть / написа́ть вско́ре ♦ **~ (to)** *(1,2)* **you** писа́ть / написа́ть *(1)* тебе́ *(familiar)* / *(2)* Вам *(polite)* ♦ **~ well** писа́ть хорошо́.

---
write: *I had to write you*

The minute I read your ad, I knew I had to write to you. В ту мину́ту, когда́ я чита́л *(ж: чита́ла)* Ва́ше объявле́ние, я знал *(ж: зна́ла)*, что до́лжен *(ж: должна́)* написа́ть Вам. ♦ **There were several other ads in the personals that were somewhat interesting, but yours struck an immediate chord in my heart and I knew with a certainty that there was no way I could not write to you.** В отде́ле знако́мств бы́ло не́сколько други́х

Russian has 6 grammatical cases. For an explanation of them, see the grammar appendix on page 686.

объявле́ний, че́м-то интере́сных, но Ва́ше вы́звало неме́дленный о́тклик в моём се́рдце, и я твёрдо знал *(ж: зна́ла)*, что не могу́ не написа́ть Вам. ♦ **The minute I saw your face, *(1)* ...I knew I had to write to you. / *(2)* ...my heart demanded that I write to you.** С той мину́ты, как я уви́дел Ва́ше лицо́, *(1)* ...я знал *(ж: зна́ла)*, что до́лжен *(ж: должна́)* написа́ть Вам. / *(2)* ...моё се́рдце тре́бовало, чтобы я написа́л *(ж: написа́ла)* Вам. ♦ **Just on impulse I decided to write to you.** Я реши́л *(ж: реши́ла)* написа́ть тебе́, про́сто подда́вшись поры́ву.

write: please write

Please write to me (*[1]*...often. / *[2]* ...soon. / *[3]* ...every day / *[4]* week. / *[5]* ...[at least] once or twice a week. / *[6]* ...as soon / *[7]* often as you can. / *[8]* ...when you have time / *[9]* a chance.) Пожа́луйста, пиши́ мне, (*[1]*...ча́сто. / *[2]* ...скоре́е. / *[3]* ...ка́ждый день. / *[4]* ...ка́ждую неде́лю. / *[5]* ...[по кра́йней ме́ре] раз и́ли два в неде́лю. / *[6]* ...как то́лько смо́жешь. / *[7]* ...так ча́сто, как смо́жешь. / *[8]* ...когда́ бу́дет вре́мя / *[9]* возмо́жность.) ♦ **I hope very much that you'll write to me.** Я о́чень наде́юсь, что Вы бу́дете писа́ть мне. ♦ **Write to me whenever you can find the time.** Пиши́ мне всегда́, когда́ у тебя́ бу́дет вре́мя. ♦ **If you don't want me to suffer from a broken heart, you'll write to me at least once a week.** Если ты не хо́чешь, чтобы я страда́л *(ж: страда́ла)* от разби́того се́рдца, ты бу́дешь писа́ть мне по ме́ньшей ме́ре раз в неде́лю.

write: you wrote to me

That was a *(1)* wonderful / *(2)* sweet / *(3)* heart-warming letter that you wrote to me. Письмо́, кото́рое ты написа́ла *(ж: написа́л)* мне, *(1)* ...замеча́тельное. / *(2)* ...ми́лое. / *(3)* ...согрева́ет се́рдце.

write: I wrote to you

I wrote (a *[1]* letter / *[2]* postcard) to you (from...). Did you get *(3,4)* it? Я написа́л *(ж: написа́ла)* тебе́ (*[1]* письмо́ / *[2]* откры́тку) (из...). Ты получи́ла *(ж: получи́л) (3)* его́ / *(4)* её?

write: how I write to you

I write this to you daringly, I know, but I hope that it will reach your heart. Я зна́ю, что пишу́ Вам сме́ло, но наде́юсь, что э́то дойдёт до Ва́шего се́рдца. ♦ **I feel *(1,2)* restricted when I write to you, because I'm afraid *(3)* ...someone... / *(4)*... your mother... / *(5)* ...your father... will read my letters.** Я чу́вствую *(1)* сде́ржанность / *(2)* стеснённость, когда́ пишу́ тебе́, потому́ что бою́сь, что *(3)* ...кто́-то... / *(4)* ...твоя́ ма́ма... / *(5)* ...твой па́па... прочита́ет мои́ пи́сьма. ♦ **I feel (*[1]* rather / *[2]* very) awkward writing a letter to someone I don't know.** Я испы́тываю (*[1]* ...до не́которой сте́пени... / *[2]* ...си́льное...) неудо́бство писа́ть письмо́ челове́ку, кото́рого я не зна́ю.

write: how you write to me

Please never give a thought to how you write to me in English. You write wonderful letters. Пожа́луйста, никогда́ не ду́май о том, как ты пи́шешь мне на англи́йском. Ты пи́шешь великоле́пные пи́сьма. ♦ **The very fact that you write to me at all gives me warm feelings, and then the things you say in your letter intensify those feelings a thousand-fold.** Про́сто факт, что ты пи́шешь мне, вызыва́ет во мне тёплые чу́вства, и зате́м то, что ты говори́шь в свои́х пи́сьмах, уси́ливает э́ти чу́вства в ты́сячу раз. ♦ **The way you write to me makes me want to take you in my arms and hug you and hug you and hug you and cover your sweet face with loving kisses.** То, как ты пи́шешь мне, вызыва́ет во мне жела́ние взять тебя́ на ру́ки, обнима́ть, обнима́ть и обнима́ть тебя́ и покрыва́ть твоё не́жное лицо́ лю́бящими поцелу́ями. ♦ **I marvel at your ability to write *(1)* English / *(2)* Russian.** Я восхища́юсь твое́й спосо́бностью писа́ть *(1)* по-англи́йски / *(2)* по-ру́сски.

There are no articles ("a" or "the") in Russian.

---

write: *I'll write*

(I promise) I'll write to you (*[1]* ...often. / *[2]* ...soon. / *[3]* ...every day / *[4]* week. / *[5]* ...as soon / *[6]* often as I can.** / *[7]* ...[at least] once or twice a week. / *[8]* ...every chance I get.). (Обеща́ю,) Я бу́ду писа́ть тебе́ (*[1]*...ча́сто. / *[2]* ...ско́ро. / *[3]* ...ка́ждый день. / *[4]* ...ка́ждую неде́лю. / *[5]* ...как то́лько смогу́. / *[6]* ...так ча́сто, как смогу́. / *[7]* ...[по кра́йней ме́ре] раз и́ли два в неде́лю. / *[8]* ...ка́ждый раз, когда́ предста́вится слу́чай.).

---

write: *sorry I haven't written*

I'm sorry I haven't written in so long. Прости́, что я не писа́л (*ж: писа́ла*) так до́лго. ♦ **I'm sorry I** *(1)* **didn't /** *(2)* **couldn't write. I was** (*[3]* terribly / *[4]* very / *[5]* so) busy (the whole time). Прости́, что я *(1)* ...не писа́л (*ж: писа́ла*). / *(2)* ...не мог (*ж: могла́*) писа́ть. Я был (*ж: была́*) (*[3]* ужа́сно / *[4]* о́чень / *[5]* так) за́нят (*ж: за́нята*) (всё вре́мя). ♦ **I haven't** *(1)* **...written...,** / *(2)* **...had a chance to write..., because** *(3)* **...I've been very busy.** / *(4)* **...** *(other reason)*. Я не *(1)* ...писа́л (*ж: писа́ла*),... / *(2)* ...име́л (*ж:име́ла*) возмо́жности написа́ть,... потому́ что *(3)* ...был о́чень за́нят (*ж: была́ о́чень занята́*). / *(4)* ...(*друга́я причи́на*). ♦ **I didn't** *(1)* **...have time...** / *(2)* **...get a chance... to write to you. I'm sorry.** У меня́ не́ было *(1)* вре́мени / *(2)* слу́чая написа́ть тебе́. Извини́. ♦ **I'm sorry I didn't write. I lost your address.** Прости́, что не писа́л (*ж: писа́ла*). Я потеря́л (*ж: потеря́ла*) твой а́дрес. ♦ *(1)* **I intended...** / *(2)* **It was my intention... to write you.** *(1)* Я собира́лся *(ж: собира́лась)...* / *(2)* Моё наме́рение бы́ло... написа́ть тебе́.

---

write: *why haven't you written?*

Why haven't you written? Почему́ ты не писа́ла (*ж: писа́л*)? ♦ **Why didn't you write (to me)?** Почему́ ты не написа́ла (*ж: написа́л*) (мне)?

writer *n* писа́тель *m*, писа́тельница *f*

writhe *vi* ко́рчиться.

wrong *adj* непра́вильный, -ая, -ое, -ые, неве́рный, -ая, -ое, -ые, нела́дный, -ая, -ое, -ые ♦ **That's wrong.** Это непра́вильно. ♦ **What's wrong?** В чём де́ло? ♦ **Nothing is wrong.** Всё норма́льно. ♦ **Something is wrong.** Что́-то не так. ♦ **Please don't get the wrong idea (about me).** Не получи́ ло́жного представле́ния (обо мне). ♦ **Somebody may get the wrong idea.** Кто́-то мо́жет получи́ть ло́жное представле́ние. ♦ **I hope** *(1)* **you /** *(2)* **they don't get the wrong idea.** Я наде́юсь, что *(1)* ...ты не полу́чишь... / *(2)* ...они́ не полу́чат... ло́жное представле́ния.

wrong *adv (awry)* неуда́чно, насма́рку ♦ **I hope nothing goes wrong with our plans.** Я наде́юсь, на́ши пла́ны не пойду́т насма́рку. ♦ **I don't want anything to go wrong.** Я не хочу́, чтобы что́-нибудь пошло́ насма́рку. ♦ **Let's hope nothing goes wrong.** Дава́йте наде́яться, что ничто́ не пойдёт насма́рку. ♦ **Everything went wrong.** Всё пошло́ насма́рку.

wrong *vt* нехорошо́ поступа́ть / поступи́ть *(whom =* + с + *instr.)*, быть непра́вым / непра́вой *(whom =* + с + *instr.)* ♦ **(I'm sorry for the way that) I've wronged you.** (Прости́ меня́ за то, что) Я был непра́в (*ж: была́ неправа́*) с тобо́й.

wry *adj* криво́й, -а́я, -о́е, -ы́е, искажённый, -ая, -ое, -ые, переко́шенный, -ая, -ое, -ые.

This dictionary contains two Russian alphabet pages: one in Appendix 1, page 685, and a tear-off page on page 799.

X

XOXO *symbol* = **kiss, hug, kiss, hug** целу́ю, обнима́ю, целу́ю, обнима́ю.

Y

Y = YMCA *abbrev* =**Young Men's Christian Association** Христиа́нский сою́з молоды́х людей.

year *n* год ♦ **every ~** ка́ждый год ♦ **last ~** в про́шлом году́ ♦ *(1,2)* **next ~** в *(1)* сле́дующем / *(2)* бу́дущем году́ ♦ **once a ~** раз в год ♦ **this ~** в э́том году́ ♦ **In what year?** В како́м году́.

yearn *vi* жа́ждать *(for what, whom = gen.)*, стреми́ться *(for whom = + к + dat.)*, стра́стно жела́ть *(for what, whom = gen.)*; тоскова́ть *(for what, whom = + по + dat.)*, томи́ться *(for what, whom = + по + dat.)* ♦ **I yearn for the** *(1)* **paradise / *(2)* heaven of your** *(3)* **precious / *(4)* dear / *(5)* wonderful arms.** Я тоску́ю по *(1)* ра́ю / *(2)* небеса́м твои́х *(3)* драгоце́нных / *(4)* дороги́х / *(5)* удиви́тельных рук. ♦ **I spend these long, lonely nights yearning and burning for** *(1)* **...your soft, luscious warmth. / *(2)* ...the warm, wonderful, heavenly magic of your beautiful body.** Я провожу́ э́ти до́лгие, одино́кие но́чи, сгора́я и тоску́я по *(1)* ...твоему́ мя́гкому ла́сковому теплу́. / *(2)* ...тёплой, удиви́тельной, ра́йской ма́гии твоего́ прекра́сного те́ла. ♦ **I sense with such absolute sureness that you are the person in this world that my heart has been yearning to find during these many years.** Я абсолю́тно уве́рен, что ты тот челове́к в э́том ми́ре, кото́рого моё се́рдце жа́ждало найти́ в тече́ние мно́гих лет. ♦ **Not a minute passes that I don't yearn for you.** Не прохо́дит и мину́ты, что́бы я не тоскова́л *(ж: москова́ла)* по тебе́. ♦ **How my heart yearns to feel the soft pressure of your hand in mine (again).** Как жа́ждет моё се́рдце (опя́ть) ощути́ть не́жное давле́ние твое́й руки́ в мое́й. ♦ **I yearn so** *(1)* **mightily / *(2)* much to explore all the** *(3)* **luscious / *(4)* delicious secrets of your body.** Я *(1,2)* так жа́жду иссле́довать все *(3)* со́чные / *(4)* восхити́тельные секре́ты твоего́ те́ла. ♦ **My heart**

Russian verbs conjugate for 6 persons:
I, familiar you, he-she-it, we, polite & plural you, and they.

yearns to show you my love in an endless stream of warm embraces and soft, *(1)* **adoring / *(2)* loving kisses.** Я всем се́рдцем жа́жду показа́ть тебе́ свою́ любо́вь в бесконе́чном пото́ке тёплых объя́тий и мя́гких, *(1)* обожа́ющих / *(2)* лю́бящих поцелу́ев. ♦ **My heart yearns to be with you (there) right now.** Я всем се́рдцем жа́жду быть с тобо́й (там) пря́мо сейча́с. ♦ **My heart yearns so fiercely to have a partner like you in life, one who combines a gentle spirit with sexuality, good-heartedness, intelligence, and a loving nature.** Я всем се́рдцем неи́стово жа́жду тако́го спу́тника жи́зни, как ты, тако́го, кто соединя́ет мя́гкий хара́ктер с сексуа́льностью, добросерде́чием, интеллиге́нтностью и лю́бящей нату́рой.

yearning *adj* жа́ждущий, -ая, -ее, -ие, си́льно жела́ющий, -ая, -ее, -ие ♦ **My yearning lips will uncover your most precious secret.** Мои́ жа́ждущие гу́бы раскро́ют твой са́мый заве́тный секре́т.

yearning *n (craving)* си́льное жела́ние, жа́жда; *(longing)* тоска́ ♦ **desperate** ~ отча́янное жела́ние ♦ **elemental** ~ стихи́йная жа́жда ♦ **enormous** ~ огро́мная жа́жда ♦ **excruciating** ~ мучи́тельное жела́ние ♦ **fervent** ~ стра́стное жела́ние ♦ **torturous** ~ мучи́тельное жела́ние ♦ **tremendous** ~ грома́дная жа́жда ♦ **unbearable** ~ невыноси́мая жа́жда.

---
yearning: *phrases*

Whenever I look at your beloved face in this photo, I am filled with *(1)* **enormous / *(2)* tremendous / *(2)* unbearable yearning to be with you (again).** Когда́ бы я ни взгляну́л *(ж: взгляну́ла)* на твоё люби́мое лицо́ на э́той фотогра́фии, я перепо́лнен *(1)* огро́мной / *(2)* грома́дной / *(3)* невыноси́мой жа́ждой (опя́ть) быть с тобо́й. ♦ **I am engulfed by a desperate yearning to** *(1)* **...see you. / *(2)* ...be with you. / *(3)* ...hold you in my arms.** Я поглощён *(ж: поглащена́)* отча́янным жела́нием *(1)* ...уви́деть тебя́. / *(2)* ...быть с тобо́й. / *(3)* ...обня́ть тебя́. ♦ **You have no idea with what fervent yearning I wait for each letter from you.** Ты не представля́ешь, с каки́м стра́стным жела́нием я жду ка́ждого твоего́ письма́. ♦ **The yearning in my heart for you is** *(1)* **...more than I can bear. / *(2)* ...an agony that I can hardly bear.** Тоска́ по тебе́ в моём се́рдце *(1)* ...вы́ше мои́х сил. / *(2)* ...- му́ка, кото́рую я едва́ могу́ вы́нести. ♦ **If you have any shred of compassion for me, you'll alleviate the agony of my yearning by sending me more photos of yourself.** Е́сли у тебя́ есть хотя́ бы ма́лая то́лика сострада́ния ко мне, ты облегчи́шь му́ку мое́й тоски́, посла́в мне ещё не́сколько свои́х фотогра́фий. ♦ **The yearning in my heart for you is an inferno that is consuming me.** Тоска́ по тебе́ в моём се́рдце -- э́то ад, поглоща́ющий меня́. ♦ **I am filled with** *(1)* **unbearable / *(2)* torturous / *(3)* excruciating yearning for you.** Я напо́лнен *(ж: напо́лнена)* *(1)* невыноси́мым / *(2,3)* мучи́тельным жела́нием тебя́.

yellow *adj* жёлтый, -ая, -ое, -ые.

yesterday *n* вчера́.

yet *adv* ещё.

yield *vt (produce)* производи́ть / произвести́; *(engender)* рожда́ть / роди́ть ♦ **The thought patterns that yielded your choice of words and sentences in your ad reveal the exact same raging hunger for love and affection that I harbor within me.** Мы́сли, роди́вшие вы́бор слов и предложе́ний в Ва́шем объявле́нии, говоря́т о то́чно тако́й же неи́стовой жа́жде любви́ и не́жности, кото́рая таи́тся во мне.

yoga *n* йо́га.

you *pron (familiar)* ты; *(polite)* Вы ♦ **I want (very much) to** *(1)* **speak / *(1)* write to you with "familiar you."** Я (о́чень) хочу́ *(1)* ...говори́ть с Ва́ми... / *(2)* ...писа́ть Вам... на «ты». ♦ **Can I** *(1)* **speak / *(1)* write to you with "familiar you?"** Могу́ я *(1)* ...говори́ть с Ва́ми...

There are two words for "you" in Russian: familiar «ты» and polite / plural «вы» (See page 781).

/ *(2)* ...писа́ть Вам... на «ты»? ♦ **Would you mind if I used "familiar you with you?"**
I feel such closeness to you and "polite you" seems so formal and distant. Не возража́ете
ли Вы, е́сли я бу́ду с Ва́ми на «ты»? Я чу́вствую таку́ю бли́зость с Ва́ми, и «Вы»
ка́жется сли́шком форма́льным и отдалённым. ♦ **Nothing matters without the joy of**
you. Ничего́ не име́ет значе́ния без тебя́, ра́дости мое́й жи́зни. ♦ **I need you to make**
me a better person than I am. Мне нужна́ *(ж: ну́жен)* ты для того́, что́бы стать лу́чше,
чем я есть. ♦ **I'm the luckiest guy in the world to have you.** Я счастли́вейший челове́к
на све́те потому́, что у меня́ есть ты. ♦ **I'd be lost without you.** Мне бы́ло бы пло́хо
без тебя́. ♦ **I'd be miserable without you.** Без тебя́ я был *(ж: была́)* бы так несча́стен
(ж: несча́стна). ♦ **My days are brighter because of you.** Благодаря́ тебе́ мои́ дни́
ста́ли я́рче.

young *adj* молодо́й, -а́я, -о́е, -ы́е *(short forms:* мо́лод, молода́, мо́лодо, -ы*)* ♦ **eternally ~**
ве́чно молодо́й, -а́я, -о́е, -ы́е ♦ **I'm still (very) young at heart.** Я всё ещё (о́чень) мо́лод
(ж: молода́) се́рдцем. ♦ **Stay young with me.** Будь со мной всегда́ молодо́й *(ж:*
молоды́м).

young-minded *adj* мо́лодо мы́слящий, -ая, -ее, -ие.

your(s) *pron (familiar)* твой, твоя́, твоё, твои́; *(polite)* Ваш, -а, -е, -и ♦ **Ever (1,2) yours,**
(closing of a letter) Всегда́ *(1)* твой *(ж: твоя́) (familiar)* / *(2)* Ваш *(ж: Ва́ша) (polite)* ♦
(1,2) **Yours (**[1] **always** / [2] **forever),** *(Closing of a letter) (1)* Твой *(ж: твоя́) (familiar)*
/ *(2)* Ваш *(ж: Ва́ша) (polite)* (*[1]* всегда́ / *[2]* навсегда́). ♦ **I'm yours in every sense of**
the word. Я твой *(ж: твоя́)* в по́лном смы́сле э́того сло́ва. ♦ **I remain yours always.**
Я навсегда́ оста́нусь твои́м *(ж: твое́й)*.

youth *n* ю́ность *f.*

youthful *adj* молодо́й, -а́я, -о́е, -ы́е, ю́ный, -ая, -ое, -ые; ю́ношеский, -ая, -ое, -ие.

youthfulness *n* мо́лодость *f.*

Z

zaftig *adj (slang, from German "saftig") (luscious)* со́чный, -ая, -ое, -ые.

zealot *n* фана́тик ♦   **religious ~** религио́зный фана́тик.

zero *n* ноль *m* ♦ **(1) He / (2) She is a total zero.** *(1)* Он / *(2)* Она́ абсолю́тный ноль.

zero in *vi* фокуси́ровать *(on what =* + на + *prep.)* ♦ **When you walked in, my eyes zeroed**
in on you. Когда́ ты вошла́, мои́ глаза́ останови́лись на тебе́.

zest *n (gusto, relish)* смак, жар, пыл, энтузиа́зм ♦ **~ for life** жизнелю́бие ♦ **~ for living**
жизнелю́бие ♦ **with ~** со сма́ком, с жа́ром ♦ *(1,2)* **I have a zest for life.** *(1)* У меня́
есть вкус к жи́зни. / *(2)* Я жизнера́достный *(ж: жизнера́достная)*.

zestful *adj* жизнелюби́вый, -ая, -ое, -ые, со сма́ком, с жа́ром.

zestfully *adv* со сма́ком, с жа́ром.

Russian terms of endearment are given in Appendix 13, page 780.

zesty *adj* живо́й, -а́я, -о́е, -ы́е, оживлённый, -ая, -ое, -ые.

zip (up) *vt* застёгивать / застегну́ть мо́лнию *(what = + на + prep.).*

zipped *adj* с застёгнутой мо́лнией.

zipper *n* мо́лния.

zit *n (slang) (blackhead, pimple)* у́горь *m (pl:* угри́*),* пры́щ.

zodiac *n* зодиа́к ♦ **What's your zodiac sign?** Како́й твой знак зодиа́ка? ♦ **My (zodiac) sign is** *(1)* **Capricorn** *(Dec. 22 - Jan. 19)* / *(2)* **Aquarius** *(Jan. 20 - Feb. 18)* / *(3)* **Pisces** *(Feb. 19 - Mar. 20)* / *(4)* **Aries** *(Mar. 21 - Apr. 19)* / *(5)* **Taurus** *(Apr. 20 - May 20)* / *(6)* **Gemini** *(May 21 - Jun. 20)* / *(7)* **Cancer** *(Jun. 21 - Jul. 22)* / *(8)* **Leo** *(Jul. 23 - Aug. 22)* / *(9)* **Virgo** *(Aug. 23 - Sep. 22)* / *(10)* **Libra** *(Sep. 23 - Oct. 22)* / *(11)* **Scorpio** *(Oct. 24 - Nov. 21)* / *(12)* **Sagittarius** *(Nov. 22 - Dec. 21).* Мой знак (зодиа́ка) - *(1)* Козеро́г *(22 декабря́ -19 января́)* / *(2)* Водоле́й *(20 января́ -18 февраля́)* / *(3)* Ры́ба *(19 февраля́ -20 ма́рта)* / *(4)* Ове́н *(21 ма́рта -19 апре́ля)* / *(5)* Бык *(20 апре́ля -20 ма́я)* / *(6)* Близнецы́ *(21ма́я -20 ию́ня)* / *(7)* Рак *(21 ию́ня - 22 ию́ля)* / *(8)* Лев *(23 ию́ля - 22 а́вгуста)* / *(9)* Де́ва *(23 а́вгуста - 22 сентября́)* / *(10)* Весы́ *(23 сентября́ -22 октября́)* / *(11)* Скорпио́н *(23 октября́ -21 ноября́)* / *(12)* Стреле́ц *(22 ноября́ - 21 декабря́).*

zone *n* зо́на ♦ **erogenous** ~ эроге́нная зо́на.

Some of the Russian sentences are translations of things we say and are not what Russians themselves would normally say.

The Russian Alphabet

Printed		Written		Phonetic Value
А	а			**ah** (f<u>a</u>ther, t<u>a</u>lk)
Б	б			**b** (<u>b</u>oy); **p** (sto<u>p</u>)
В	в			**v** (<u>v</u>ote); **f** (cou<u>gh</u>)
Г	г			**g** (<u>g</u>oat); **k** (soa<u>k</u>); **v** (<u>v</u>ote)
Д	д			**d** (<u>d</u>ime); **t** (coa<u>t</u>)
Е	е			**yeh** (<u>y</u>es); **ee** (f<u>ee</u>t)
Ё	ё			**yoh** (<u>yo</u>ke)
Ж	ж			**zh** (lei<u>s</u>ure); **sh** (wa<u>sh</u>)
З	з			**z** (co<u>z</u>y); **s** (ga<u>s</u>)
И	и			**ee** (m<u>ee</u>t)
Й	й			**y** (to<u>y</u>, <u>y</u>ell)
К	к			**k** (<u>c</u>ode, ba<u>ck</u>)
Л	л			**l** (<u>l</u>ow, bal<u>l</u>)
М	м			**m** (<u>m</u>ost, ho<u>m</u>e)
Н	н			**n** (<u>n</u>ote, ma<u>n</u>)
О	о			**oh** (n<u>o</u>te); *(unstressed:)* **ah** (f<u>a</u>ther)
П	п			**p** (sto<u>p</u>, <u>p</u>ork)
Р	р			**r** (bu<u>rr</u>o) *(trilled);* **r** (<u>fr</u>ee)
С	с			**s** (<u>s</u>oak); **z** (<u>z</u>ip)
Т	т			**t** (tes<u>t</u>, <u>t</u>oken)
У	у			**oo** (d<u>oo</u>m, l<u>oo</u>t)
Ф	ф			**f** (<u>f</u>ar, stu<u>ff</u>)
Х	х			**kh** (*Scottish* lo<u>ch</u>, *German* ho<u>ch</u>)
Ц	ц			**ts** (ca<u>ts</u>, ski<u>ts</u>)
Ч	ч			**ch** (<u>ch</u>ess); **sh** (<u>sh</u>ow)
Ш	ш			**sh** (<u>sh</u>ow, ca<u>sh</u>)
Щ	щ			**shch** (ca<u>sh</u> <u>ch</u>eck)
Ъ	ъ			**hard sign** *(hardens preceding letter)*
Ы	ы			**i** *(short i + long e simultaneously deep in throat)*
Ь	ь			**soft sign** *(softens preceding letter)*
Э	э			**eh** (p<u>e</u>t, <u>e</u>gg)
Ю	ю			**yoo** (<u>you</u>, <u>you</u>th)
Я	я			**yah** (<u>ya</u>cht, <u>ya</u>rd)

Russian Grammar

This section will provide you with the general rules of Russian grammar in a very simplified form. For a better treatment of the subject in a concise, easy-to-absorb form we would refer you to the fine manual "Essential Russian Grammar" by Brian Kemple, Dover Publications, NY, C1993 (ISBN 0-486-27375-X).

Accent (Stress)

In Russian, words of more than one syllable have an accent (stress) on one of the syllables. Emphasize this syllable when you pronounce the word.

In this dictionary, accented syllables are shown by an accent mark. However, Russian books, newspapers, and other written material never use accent marks (except for those intended for learners), so you should try to memorize the stress of the word.

*Beware! The accents of some Russian words **shift position** in grammatical cases, in the plural form, in verb conjugation or in the past tense.*

Gender

Russian nouns, adjectives, many pronouns, and the past tenses of verbs have endings that relfect their gender: **masculine, feminine** or **neuter**. They also have **plural** endings. All of these endings (except those of the verbs) change in grammatical cases.

In talking about oneself, a man uses adjectives and past-tense endings (and some nouns) that are masculine, whereas a woman uses the feminine forms.

Articles

There are no articles (**a** and **the**) in Russian. Thus, the word жéнщина (woman) can mean "a woman" or "the woman." If you need more clarity, you can use the words "one," "this" or "that."

Nouns

<u>**Masculine nouns**</u> normally end in a **consonant** or a "**soft sign**" (Russian: **ь**)*. A small number of masculine nouns have feminine endings -- including the word for "man" (!!).

<u>**Feminine nouns**</u> end in **-а, -я, -ия** or a "**soft sign**" (Russian: **ь**)*.

* *Nouns ending in a "**soft sign**" (Russian: **ь**) must be memorized as to whether they are masculine or feminine.*

<u>**Neuter nous**</u> commonly end in **-о, -е, -ие** or **-ё**. A few have the endings **-мя** and **-и**.

The <u>**plurals of masculine and feminine nouns**</u> mostly take the ending **-ы** or **-и**. A small number of masculine nouns, often short ones, have the irregular plural ending of **-а** or **-я**. These irregular plurals are shown in this dictionary.

The **plurals of neuter nouns** usually end in **-a** or **-я**.

Noun Endings

Gender	Singular Ending	Singular Example	Plural Ending	Plural Example
Masculine	**Consonants** (except г, к, х, ж, ч, ш ог щ)	магазѝн	**ы**	магазѝны
	Consonants г, к, х, ж, ч, ш and щ	га́лстук	**и**	га́лстуки
	й	трамва́й	**и**	трамва́и
	ь	день	**и**	дни
Feminine	**a** (except after г, к, х, ж, ч, ш ог щ)	наде́жда	**ы**	наде́жды
	a after г, к, х, ж, ч, ш ог щ	нога́	**и**	но́ги
	я	неде́ля	**и**	неде́ли
	ия	та́лия	**ии**	та́лии
	ь	ночь	**и**	но́чи
Neuter	**o**	лицо́	**a**	ли́ца
	e	по́ле	**я**	поля́
	ие	мне́ние	**ия**	мне́ния
	ё	копьё	**я**	ко́пья
	мя	и́мя	**мена́**	имена́

Adjectives

There are long and short adjectives in Russian. Only the long ones can be put in front of a noun or be used as a noun. The short ones can only be used as predicates, i.e., at the end of a statement, such as "You are **beautiful.**" Long adjectives can also be used as predicates in most cases, but sometimes the short ones are required. Please refer to a grammar manual for the detailed rules on this.

Long Adjective Endings

Gender	Ending	Example
Masculine	-ый	краси́вый
	-ий	после́дний
Feminine	-ая	краси́вая
	-яя	после́дняя
Neuter	-ое	краси́вое
	-ее	после́днее
Plural	-ые	краси́вые
	-ие	после́дние

Short Adjective Endings

Long form	Short M	Short F	Short N	Short Pl
краси́вый	краси́в	краси́ва	краси́во	краси́вы
хоро́ший	хоро́ш	хороша́	хорошо́	хороши́

Comparatives

The **comparative forms of adjectives** are of two kinds: **compound** and **short.**

The **compound comparative** is produced by putting бо́лее (more) or ме́нее (less) in front of the long form of the adjective. This compound is always used in front of a noun and can also be used as the predicate of the verb "to be," as in "You're **more beautiful.**" (Ты бо́лее **краси́вая.**")

The **short comparative** is used only as a predicate or adverbially. In most cases, it is formed by changing the ending of the adjective to -ee. In some, however, -e is added to the mutated stem of the adjective. Since this is a hard rule for the beginner to follow, we show these forms in the dictionary.

A few adjectives have a long comparative form instead of a compound form. These are shown in the dictionary.

The "**than**" in a comparative construction can be rendered one of two ways:

    1) Using "чем" (than) preceded by a comma (with no grammatical changes necessary), or

    2) Putting the compared-to noun into the genitive case. Example: "You're more beautiful than your sister." would be "Ты краси́вее твое́й сестры́.", where "your sister" (твоя́ сестра́) changed in the genitive case to "твое́й сестры́."

Superlatives

The **superlative forms of adjectives** are also of two types: **compound** and **short**.

The **compound superlative** is formed by putting са́мый *(m)*, са́мая *(f)*, са́мое *(neut)* or са́мые *(pl)* (the most) in front of the long form of the adjective (never the short form).

The **simple superlative** is constructed by adding -ейший *(m)*, -ейшая *(f)*, -ейшее *(neut)* or -ейшие *(pl)* (-айший *[m]*, -айшая *[f]*, -айшее *[neut]* or -айшие *[pl]* after ж, ч, ш and щ) to the stem of the adjective (formed by dropping the ending). However, many adjectives do not have a simple superlative form.

Adverbs

Adverbs are mainly formed by dropping the ending of an adjective and adding -о to the resulting stem. Some, however, are made by adding -е or -и.

The **comparative of adverbs** is produced by putting бо́лее (more) or ме́нее (less) in front of the adverb.

Pronouns

The **subject pronouns** in Russian are as follows:

я	I	мы	we
ты	you *(familiar)*	вы	you *(polite and plural)*
он	he *or* it *(masculine)*	они	they
она	she *or* it *(feminine)*		
оно	it *(neuter)*		

Some **possessive pronouns** (1st and 2nd person singular and plural) have different endings for gender the same as adjectives do; others (3rd person singular and plural) have only one form:

Possessive Pronouns

Pronoun	Masculine	Feminine	Neuter	Plural
my	мой	моя́	моё	мои́
your *(familiar)*	твой	твоя́	твоё	твои́
his, its *(masc.)*	его́	его́	его́	его́
her, its *(fem.)*	её	её	её	её
its *(neut.)*	его́	его́	его́	его́
our	наш	на́ша	на́ше	на́ши
your *(polite & plural)*	ваш	ва́ша	ва́ше	ва́ши
their	их	их	их	их
whose	чей	чья	чьё	чьи

The **demonstrative pronouns** (this, that, these, those) and the **adjectival pronoun** **"all"** also have different endings for gender and plural:

Demonstrative & Adjectival Pronouns

Pronoun	Masculine	Feminine	Neuter	Plural
this, that	э́тот	э́та	э́то	э́ти
that *(not this)*	тот	та	то	те
all, the whole	весь	вся	всё	все

Grammatical Cases

There are **6 grammatical cases** in Russian, the names of which are: **nominative, accusative, genitive, dative, instrumental,** and **prepositional** (sometimes called **locative**).

1. Nominative Case *(abbreviated "Nom." in charts)*
    Meaning / Use: This case is for the word as you find it in a dictionary and use it as the subject in a sentence.
    Change of ending: None, unless you use the plural form (which requires the plural ending).

2. Accusative Case *(abbreviated "Acc." in charts)*
    Meaning / Use: The **accusative** (when not used with a preposition) serves most often to denote the direct object of the verb, as in "I love **music**.", where

"music" is the direct object. With motion to, into or onto a place, you use the preposition в or на and put the place in the accusative.

    Change of ending:

        Animate nouns (and their modifying possessive pronouns and adjectives): **Yes,** singular and plural (except singular feminine nouns ending in a soft sign *[-ь]*).

        Inanimate nouns (and their modifying possessive pronouns and adjectives): **Masculine** and **neuter** -- no; **feminine** -- yes (except feminine nouns ending in a soft sign *[-ь]*). *(See declension charts below.)*

        Prepositions taking accusative: в, за, на, над, о(б), под, че́рез

    3.   Genitive Case *(abbreviated "Gen." in charts)*

        Meaning / Use: Major uses of the **genitive** (when not used with a preposition) are to convey the meaning **"of"** ("color of hair"), to show that a word has been **negated** ("there's no time"), and for **counting** things ("5 days"). A few verbs require this case.

        Change of ending: All words, singular and plural. *(See declension charts below.)*

        Prepositions taking genitive: без, вне, внутри́, во вре́мя, вокру́г, для, до, из, кро́ме, напро́тив, о́коло, от, по́сле, с, среди́.

    4.   Dative Case *(abbreviated "Dat." in charts)*

        Meaning / Use: The **dative** (when not used with a preposition) functions largely as **"to,"** as in "I wrote a letter **to my parents**." In Russian, "my parents" would be in the dative case and there would be no separate word "to." A few verbs require this case.

        Change of ending: All words, singular and plural. *(See declension charts below.)*

        Prepositions taking dative: к, по.

    5.   Instrumental Case *(abbreviated "Instr." in charts)*

        Meaning / Use: The **instrumental** case (when not used with a preposition) mainly conveys the idea of "by means of," "with" (e.g., write with a pen), "by" (e.g., send by airmail), and "as" (e.g., work as a secretary). A number of verbs and prepositions require this case.

Change of ending: All words, singular and plural. *(See declension charts below.)*

        Prepositions taking instrumental: за, ме́жду, над, пе́ред, под, с.

    6.   Prepositional Case *(abbreviated "Prep." in charts)*

        Meaning / Use: The **prepositional** case is always used with a preposition, either в (in) or на (on, at) to express fixed location, о (about), or при (in the presence of, with).

        Change of ending: All words, singular and plural. *(See declension charts below.)*

        Prepositions taking prepositional: в, на, о, при.

Declension of Singular Nouns

Gender	Nom. (ending)	First do this	Acc. (add)	Gen. (add)	Dat. (add)	Instr. (add)	Prep. (add)
Masc.	consonant	--	а *(anim.)*	а	у	ом[1]	е
		--	-- *(inanim.)*	"	"	"	"
	-й	*drop* й	я *(anim.)*	я	ю	ем	е
		--	-- *(inanim.)*	"	"	"	"
	-ий	*drop* й	don't drop	я	ю	ем	и
	-ь	*drop* ь	я *(anim.)*	я	ю	ем	е
		--	-- *(inanim.)*	"	"	"	"
Fem.	-а	*drop* а	у	ы[2]	е	ой[3]	е
	-я	*drop* я	ю	и	е	ей	е
	-ия	*drop* я	ю	и	и	ей	и
Neut.	-о[4]	*drop* о	don't drop	а	у	ом	е
	-е[4]	*drop* е	don't drop	я	ю	ем	е
	-ие	*drop* е	don't drop	я	ю	ем	и
	-и	--	--	--	--	--	--
	-мя	*drop* я	don't drop	ени	ени	енем	ени

1 - ем after ж, ч, ш and щ   2 - и after г, ж, к, х, ч, ш and щ
3 - ей after ж, ч, ш and щ   4 - some words of foreign origin do not decline

Declension of Plural Nouns

Gender	Sing. ending	Plural ending	First do this	Acc. (add)	Gen. (add)	Dat. (add)	Instr. (add)	Prep. (add)
Masc.	consonant *(except:)*	-ы[1,2] --	*drop* ы	ов *(anim.)* -- *(inanim.)*	ов	ам	ами	ах
	г, к, х	-и[1]	*drop* и	ов *(anim.)* -- *(inanim.)*	ов	ам	ами	ах
	ж, ч, ш, щ	-и[1]	*drop* и	ей *(anim.)* -- *(inanim.)*	ей	ам	ами	ах
	-й	-и	*drop* и	ев *(anim.)* -- *(inanim.)*	ев	ям	ями	ях
	-ий	-ии	*drop* и	ей *(anim.)* -- *(inanim.)*	ей	ям	ями	ях
	-ь	-и	*drop* и	ей *(anim.)* -- *(inanim.)*	ей	ям	ями	ях
Fem.	-а	-ы --	*drop* ы	-- *(anim.)*[6] -- *(inanim.)*	--	ам	ами	ах
	-а	-и[3] --	*drop* и	--[4] *(anim.)*[6] -- *(inanim.)*	--[4]	ам	ами	ах
	-я	-и --	*drop* и	-- *(anim.)*[6] -- *(inanim.)*	--	ам	ами	ах
	-ия	-ии --	*drop* и	й *(anim.)* -- *(inanim.)*	й	ям	ями	ях
Neut.	-о[2,5]	-а	*drop* а	*don't drop*	--[6]	ам	ами	ах
	-е[5]	-я	*drop* я	*don't drop*	ей	ям	ями	ях
	-ие	-ия	*drop* я	*don't drop*	й	ям	ями	ях
	-и	--	--	--	--	--	--	--
	-мя	-мена́	*drop* ена́	*don't drop*	ён	ена́м	ена́ми	ена́х

1 - some irregular (usually short) nouns take á (stressed) as their plural ending.

2. - some irregular nouns take ья as their plural ending *(gen.:* -ьев; *dat.:* -ьям; *instr.:* -ьями; *prep.:* -ьях*)*.

3 - after г, ж, к, х, ч, ш and щ.

4 - ей after ж, ч, ш and щ.

5 - some words of foreign origin do not decline at all.

6 - if the dropped vowel results in an ending of two incompatible consonants, a vowel (о, е) is added between them.

Declension of Adjectives

Gender	Nom. (ending)	First do this	Acc. (add)	Gen. (add)	Dat. (add)	Instr. (add)	Prep. (add)
Masc.	-ый	*drop* -ый	-ого *(anim.)*[1]	-ого	-ому	-ым	-ом
	-ий *after* г, к, х	*drop* -ий	-ого *(anim.)*[1]	-ого	-ому	-им	-ом
	-ий *after* ж, ч, ш, щ, н	*drop* -ий	-его *(anim.)*[1]	-его	-ему	-им	-ем
	-ой	*drop* -ой	-ого *(anim.)*[1]	-ого	-ому	-ым[1]	-ом
Fem.	-ая	*drop* -ая	-ую	-ой	-ой	-ой	-ой
	-ая *after* ж, ч, ш, щ	*drop* -ая	-ую	-ей	-ей	-ей	-ей
	-яя	*drop* -яя	-юю	-ей	-ей	-ей	-ей
Neut.	-ое	*drop* -ое	*don't drop*	-ого	-ому	-ым[1]	-ом
	-ее	*drop* -ее	*don't drop*	-его	-ему	-им	-ем
Plural	-ые	*drop* -ые	-ых *(anim.)*[1]	-ых	-ым	-ыми	-ых
	-ие *after* г,к,ж х, ч, ш, щ, н[2]	*drop* -ие	-их *(anim.)*[1]	-их	-им	-ими	-их

1 - no change for inanimate. 2 - им after ж, ч, ш and щ.
3 - when masculine singular is -ний.

Declension of Pronouns

Pronoun (Nom.)	Acc.	Gen.	Dat.	Instr.	Prep.
я - I	меня́	меня́	мне	мной	мне
ты - you *(fam.)*	тебя́	тебя́	тебе́	тобо́й	тебе́
он - he	его́[1]	его́[1]	ему́[1]	им[1]	нём
она́ - she	её[1]	ей[1]	ей[1]	ей[1]	ней
оно́ - it	его́[1]	его́[1]	ему́[1]	им[1]	нём
мы - we	нас	нас	нам	на́ми	нас
вы - you *(pol.)*	вас	вас	вам	ва́ми	вас
они́ - they	их[1]	их[1]	им[1]	и́ми[1]	них
что - what	что	чего́	чему́	чем	чём
кто - who	кого́	кого́	кому́	кем	ком

1 - has an н in front when preceded by a preposition.

Declension of Possessive Pronouns

Pronou	Masculine	Feminine	Neuter	Plural
my, mine	мой	моя́	моё	мои́
Accusative	мой	мою́	моё	мои́
Genitive	моего́	мое́й	моего́	мои́х
Dative	моему́	мое́й	моему́	мои́м
Instrumental	мои́м	мое́й	мои́м	мои́ми
Prepositional	моём	мое́й	моём	мои́х
your, yours *(fam.)*	твой	твоя́	твоё	твои́
Accusative	твой	твою́	твоё	твои́
Genitive	твоего́	твое́й	твоего́	твои́х
Dative	твоему́	твое́й	твоему́	твои́м
Instrumental	твои́м	твое́й	твои́м	твои́ми
Prepositional	твоём	твое́й	твоём	твои́х
his, its *(masc.)*	его́	его́	его́	его́
	No changes for any gender or in any case			
her, hers, its *(fem.)*	её	её	её	её
	No changes for any gender or in any case			
its *(neut.)*	его́	его́	его́	его́
	No changes for any gender or in any case			
our, ours	наш	на́ша	на́ше	на́ши
Accusative	наш	на́шу	на́ше	на́ши
Genitive	на́шего	на́шей	на́шего	на́ших
Dative	на́шему	на́шей	на́шему	на́шим
Instrumental	на́шим	на́шей	на́шим	на́шими
Prepositional	на́шем	на́шей	на́шем	на́ших
your, yours *(polite)*	ваш	ва́ша	ва́ше	ва́ши
Accusative	ваш	ва́шу	ва́ше	ва́ши
Genitive	ва́шего	ва́шей	ва́шего	ва́ших
Dative	ва́шему	ва́шей	ва́шему	ва́шим
Instrumental	ва́шим	ва́шей	ва́шим	ва́шими
Prepositional	ва́шем	ва́шей	ва́шем	ва́ших
their, theirs	их	их	их	их
	No changes for any gender or in any case			
whose	чей	чья	чьё	чьи
Accusative	чей	чью	чьё	чьи
Genitive	чьего́	чьей	чьего́	чьих
Dative	чьему́	чьей	чьему́	чьим
Instrumental	чьим	чьей	чьим	чьи́ми
Prepositional	чьём	чьей	чьём	чьих

Verbs

The Russian Verb System in General

The Russian verb system has two forms, called aspects, for practically every verb. These aspects have the names **imperfective** and **perfective.** You can usually tell a pair apart by an added prefix or suffix or by a different spelling of their stems.

Roughly speaking, these two aspects are like two groups of different English tenses. The **imperfective** tenses embody the concepts of **existing states, duration, repetition, and indefiniteness,** whereas the **perfective** tenses apply to **definite, completed or short-duration action**.

Both the imperfective and perfective have past and future tenses, but only the **imperfective** has the **present tense.** (See sections on **Present Tense, Future Tense,** and **Past Tense** below.)

Verbs of Motion

The basic verbs of motion (go *[on foot]*, go *[by vehicle]*, run, fly, sail/swim, crawl, climb, carry, convey/transport, lead/take) each have a family of verbs consisting of the base verb and a number of "cousins" with prefixes. The prefixes give the meanings "in," "out," "over," "up to," etc. The base verb of each family has TWO imperfective forms, in addition to the usual perfective. One of the imperfective forms denotes one-time motion in one direction, and the other form covers round trips, repetition, and indefinite or general action. The "cousins" of the family have the usual set of one imperfective and one perfective.

Reflexive Verbs

Reflexive verbs are those that end in -ся (after consonants or й) or -сь (after vowels). This -ся/-сь ending, which derives from the word "self" (себя), appears throughout the conjugation of the verb and in all tenses and does not change (except for the above-mentioned vowel-consonant rule) in grammatical cases.

This reflexive form is used as follows:

> 1. Passive: "The word **is pronounced** like this." (Слово произно́сится так.)
> 2. Intransitive: "I**'m dressing**." (Я одева́юсь.)
> 3. Reciprocal: "We **hugged (each other)**." (Мы обнима́лись.)
> 4. Impersonal: "I **want** to see it." (Мне хо́чется ви́деть его́.)
> 5. Because only reflexive: "It**'s getting** dark." (Стано́вится темно́.)

Conjugation of Verbs

Both imperfective and perfective verbs have **6 "persons"** to conjugate for:

Person	Typical Ending	Person	Typical Ending
я - I	-у or -ю	мы - we	-ем, ём, им
ты - you *(familiar)*	-ешь, ёшь, ишь	вы - you *(polite)*	-ете, -ёте, ите
он, она, оно - he, she, it	-ет, -ёт, -ит	они - they	-ут, -ют, -ат, ят

When you conjugate the **imperfective** verb, you're in the **present tense**; when you conjugate the **perfective** verb, you're in the **future**.

Please note that there are various conjugation patterns for Russian verbs and that consonants often change in the conjugation. A grammar manual will help you out with the rules. For those not ready for that yet, we've provided an **Appendix of Conjugated Verbs** on pages 699-755, which gives the conjugations of Russian verbs listed in entries in this dictionary.

Present Tense.

The present tense in Russian does duty for the English simple present ("I play the guitar."), the present continuous ("I'm playing the guitar."), the present perfect continuous ("I've been playing the guitar for 5 years."), and sometimes even the present perfect ("I've played the guitar since I was 10.") (i.e., when it's used like the continuous form).

The Russian verb "to be" (**быть**) is not conjugated in the present tense, except for a 3rd-person form, есть, which is used for "there is" and "there are." Thus, to say "She is a doctor.", you literally say "She -- doctor." However, it is conjugated for the future tense and has past-tense forms.

Future Tense.

Russians use the imperfective form to express future ideas like "I'm going to play guitar in that band.", "I'll play the guitar while I wait.", "I'll be playing my guitar in my room if you want me.", or "Tomorrow night I'm playing the guitar at the club." They would turn to the perfective, however, to say something like "I'll play 2 songs for you."

The way to use the imperfective verb in the future tense is to first take Russian "will" (conjugated from the verb **быть** *[to be]* in whichever "person" you need it: I, you, she, etc) and put it in front of the infinitive of the verb. The perfective future, as we have said, is obtained by conjugating the perfective verb. No other word is necessary.

Past Tense.

For both aspects, the past tense forms reflect either the gender of the subject or the plural. They are commonly formed by dropping the -ть or -ти of the infinitive and adding the past tense ending, -л for masculine (there are exceptions), -ла for feminine, -ло for neuter, and -ли for plural.

The differences in the imperfective and perfective past tenses are like this. You would use the imperfective past tense to say such things as "I played for 30 minutes.", "I played the guitar in college.", "I was playing the guitar when you called.", and "I had been playing the guitar." But to say "We already played 3 songs.", you would choose the perfective form.

Negation

To form the negative of a verb, simply put **не** before it.

When negating something, you use the imperfective for complete or long-time negation, and the perfective if an action was expected, but didn't take place.

Negation of direct objects that are intangible will put them in the genitive case.

Imperative

The imperative form of the verb -- the one you use for orders, requests and directions -- is formed in two main ways. Here's how you do it:

1. Take a verb.
2. Conjugate it for "they" (они) (3rd person plural).
3. Drop the the last two letters (a vowel and т).
4. Is there a vowel left?
   a) Yes: add й for familiar use or йте for polite or plural use.
   b) No: add и for familiar use or ите for polite or plural use. (Note: it **could be** a soft sign [ь] instead of an и, if the stress of the word was before the last syllable.)
5. For reflexive imperatives, add -ся to й, and -сь to и and е.

Conditional Mood

The conditional mood (could, would) is easy to form in Russian. Just take the past tense of the verb and put **бы** after it. Example: "I wouldn't think of it." in Russian would be "Я не **подумал бы** об этом." Keep in mind, though, that Russians often just use the future tense where we might use "would."

Participles

You may dimly recall these from high school English. There are two types in English, the -ing type (present participle) and the -ed type (past participle). Russian also has these -- with some variations. (Get out that grammar manual.) The one that gets used most as an adjective is the past participle, which in Russian has long and short forms (just like the adjectives). The long form can be used like a long adjective and like a modifier in a subordinate clause. The short form is used like one of their short adjectives (see the section on **Adjectives**).

The main way you form the long past participle is to drop the vowel ending from the first person of the conjugated verb (transitive verb - the kind that takes a direct object), add (usually) **енн** and then the adjectival ending (**-ый, -ая, -ое** or **-ые**). Like this:

1. Verb: покрасить (to paint) *(perfective)*.
2. First person: я покрашу (I will paint).
3. Drop the vowel ending: покраш - у = покраш.
4. Add енн: покраш + енн = покрашенн.
5. Add an adjectival ending: покрашенн + ый = покрашенный (painted).

The short version of this disposes of the ный ending for the masculine and takes the endings -а, -о and -ы for the feminine, neuter and plural respectively (in the example here: покрашен, покрашена, покрашено, покрашены).

Please realize, this is a **simplified presentation**. There are other types of past participles, but this one will probably be the most useful. Please consult a grammar manual for a more complete treatment of these.`

Russian Verbs Conjugated

On the following pages are the conjugations of Russian verbs that appear in the dictionary as the equivalents of main word entries. The verbs are conjugated for six "persons": 1 - я *(I)*; 2 - ты *(familiar you)*; 3 - он, она́, оно́ *(he, she, it)*; 4 - мы *(we)*; 5 - вы *(polite & plural you)*; and 6 - они *(they)*.

The regular past tense of a verb is formed by removing the -ть and adding -л (or -лся if the verb is reflexive) for masculine, -ла (or -лась) for feminine, -ло (or -лось) for neuter, and -ли (or -лись) for plural. If the past tense form of a verb is irregular or if its accent shifts, it is given after the conjugation. Otherwise, the regular past tense is not shown.

An imperfective verb *(impf)* is conjugated in the present tense; a perfective verb *(pf)* -- in the future. A small number of verbs, such as the first three below, are both imperfective and perfective, i.e., they have the same conjugation for present and future.

List of Conjugated Russian Verbs

аннули́ровать *impf & pf, present & future:* *(1)* аннули́ру-ю, *(2)* -ешь, *(3)* -ет, *(4)* -ем, *(5)* -ете, *(6)* -ют.

апелли́ровать *impf & pf, present & future:* *(1)* апелли́ру-ю, *(2)* -ешь, *(3)* -ет, *(4)* -ем, *(5)* -ете, *(6)* -ют.

арендова́ть *impf & pf, present & future:* *(1)* аренду́-ю, *(2)* -ешь, *(3)* -ет, *(4)* -ем, *(5)* -ете, *(6)* -ют.

бази́роваться *impf, present:* *(1)* бази́ру-юсь, *(2)* -ешься, *(3)* -ется, *(4)* -емся, *(5)* -етесь, *(6)* -ются.

ба́ловать *impf, present:* *(1)* ба́лу-ю, *(2)* -ешь, *(3)* -ет, *(4)* -ем, *(5)* -ете, *(6)* -ют.

бара́хтаться *impf, present:* *(1)* бара́хта-юсь, *(2)* -ешься, *(3)* -ется, *(4)* -емся, *(5)* -етесь, *(6)* -ются.

бе́гать *impf, present:* *(1)* бе́га-ю, *(2)* -ешь, *(3)* -ет, *(4)* -ем, *(5)* -ете, *(6)* -ют.

бежа́ть *impf, present:* *(1)* бегу́, *(2)* беж-и́шь, *(3)* -и́т, *(4)* -и́м, *(5)* -и́те, *(6)* бегу́т.

безде́льничать *impf, present:* *(1)* безде́льнича-ю, *(2)* -ешь, *(3)* -ет, *(4)* -ем, *(5)* -ете, *(6)* -ют.

бере́чь *impf, present:* *(1)* берегу́, *(2)* береж-ёшь, *(3)* -ёт, *(4)* -ём, *(5)* -ёте, *(6)* берегу́т.

беси́ть *impf, present:* *(1)* бешу́, *(2)* бе́с-ишь, *(3)* -ит, *(4)* -им, *(5)* -ите, *(6)* -ят.

беспоко́ить(ся) *impf, present:* *(1)* беспоко́-ю(сь), *(2)* -ишь(ся), *(3)* -ит(ся), *(4)* -им(ся), *(5)* -ите(сь), *(6)* -ят(ся).

би́ть(ся) *impf, present:* *(1)* бь-ю(сь), *(2)* -ёшь(ся), *(3)* -ёт(ся), *(4)* -ём(ся), *(5)* -ёте(сь), *(6)* -ю́т(ся).

благодари́ть *impf, present:* *(1)* благодар-ю́, *(2)* -и́шь, *(3)* -и́т, *(4)* -и́м, *(5)* -и́те, *(6)* -я́т.

благоприя́тствовать *impf, present:* *(1)* благоприя́тству-ю, *(2)* -ешь, *(3)* -ет, *(4)* -ем, *(5)* -ете, *(6)* -ют.

благослови́ть *pf, future:* *(1)* благослов-лю́, *(2)* -и́шь, *(3)* -и́т, *(4)* -и́м, *(5)* -и́те, *(6)* -я́т.

благословля́ть *impf, present:* *(1)* благословля́-ю, *(2)* -ешь, *(3)* -ет, *(4)* -ем, *(5)* -ете, *(6)*-

Persons: 1 = я, 2 = ты, 3 = он, она́, оно́, 4 = мы, 5 = вы, 6 = они́

-ют.

блесте́ть *impf, present:* *(1)* блещу́, *(2)* блест-и́шь, *(3)* -и́т, *(4)* -и́м, *(5)* -и́те, *(6)* -я́т.

боле́ть *(be sick) impf, present:* *(1)* боле́-ю, *(2)* -ешь, *(3)* -ет, *(4)* -ем, *(5)* -ете, *(6)* -ют.

боле́ть *(experience pain) impf, present:* *(3)* бол-и́т, *(6)* -я́т.

болта́ть *impf, present:* *(1)* болта́-ю, *(2)* -ешь, *(3)* -ет, *(4)* -ем, *(5)* -ете, *(6)* -ют.

бормота́ть *impf, present:* *(1)* бормочу́, *(2)* бормо́ч -ешь, *(3)* -ет, *(4)* -ем, *(5)* -ете, *(6)* -ют.

боро́ться *impf, present:* *(1)* борю́сь, *(2)* бо́р-ешься, *(3)* -ется, *(4)* -емся, *(5)* -етесь, *(6)* -ются.

боя́ться *impf, present:* *(1)* бо-ю́сь, *(2)* -и́шься, *(3)* -и́тся, *(4)* -и́мся, *(5)* -и́тесь, *(6)* -я́тся.

брани́ть *impf, present:* *(1)* бран-ю́, *(2)* -и́шь, *(3)* -и́т, *(4)* -и́м, *(5)* -и́те, *(6)* -я́т.

брать *impf, present:* *(1)* бер-у́, *(2)* -ёшь, *(3)* -ёт, *(4)* -ём, *(5)* -ёте, *(6)* -у́т.

бре́дить *impf, present:* *(1)* бре́жу, *(2)* бре́д-ишь, *(3)* -ит, *(4)* -им, *(5)* -ите, *(6)* -ят.

брить *impf, present:* *(1)* бре́-ю, *(2)* -ешь, *(3)* -ет, *(4)* -ем, *(5)* -ете, *(6)* -ют.

бри́ться *impf, present:* *(1)* бре́-юсь, *(2)* -ешься, *(3)* -ется, *(4)* -емся, *(5)* -етесь, *(6)* -ются.

броди́ть *impf, present:* *(1)* брожу́, *(2)* бро́д-ишь, *(3)* -ит, *(4)* -им, *(5)* -ите, *(6)* -ят.

брони́ровать *impf, present:* *(1)* брони́ру-ю, *(2)* -ешь, *(3)* -ет, *(4)* -ем, *(5)* -ете, *(6)* -ют.

броса́ть(ся) *impf, present:* *(1)* броса́-ю(сь), *(2)* -ешь(ся), *(3)* -ет(ся), *(4)* -ем(ся), *(5)* -ете(сь), *(6)* -ют(ся).

бро́сить(ся) *pf, future:* *(1)* бро́шу(сь), *(2)* брос-ишь(ся), *(3)* -ит(ся), *(4)* -им(ся), *(5)* -ите(сь), *(6)* -ят(ся).

буди́ть *impf, present:* *(1)* бужу́, *(2)* бу́д-ишь, *(3)* -ит, *(4)* -им, *(5)* -ите, *(6)* -ят.

бушева́ть *impf, present:* *(1)* бушу́-ю, *(2)* -ешь, *(3)* -ет, *(4)* -ем, *(5)* -ете, *(6)* -ют.

быва́ть *impf, present:* *(1)* быва́-ю, *(2)* -ешь, *(3)* -ет, *(4)* -ем, *(5)* -ете, *(6)* -ют.

быть *impf, present: no present tense; future:* *(1)* бу́д-у, *(2)* -ешь, *(3)* -ет, *(4)* -ем, *(5)* -ете, *(6)* -ут.

вальси́ровать *impf, present:* *(1)* вальси́ру-ю, *(2)* -ешь, *(3)* -ет, *(4)* -ем, *(5)* -ете, *(6)* -ют.

валя́ть(ся) *impf, present:* *(1)* валя́-ю(сь), *(2)* -ешь(ся), *(3)* -ет(ся), *(4)* -ем(ся), *(5)* -ете(сь), *(6)* -ют(ся).

вая́ть *impf, present:* *(1)* вая́-ю, *(2)* -ешь, *(3)* -ет, *(4)* -ем, *(5)* -ете, *(6)* -ют.

ввяза́ться *pf, future:* *(1)* ввяжу́сь, *(2)* ввя́ж-ешься, *(3)* -ется, *(4)* -емся, *(5)* -етесь, *(6)* -утся.

вгля́дываться *impf, present:* *(1)* вгля́дыва-юсь, *(2)* -ешься, *(3)* -ется, *(4)* -емся, *(5)* -етесь, *(6)* -ются.

вдохнови́ть *pf, future:* *(1)* вдохнов-лю́, *(2)* -и́шь, *(3)* -и́т, *(4)* -и́м, *(5)* -и́те, *(6)* -я́т.

вдохновля́ть *impf, present:* *(1)* вдохновля́-ю, *(2)* -ешь, *(3)* -ет, *(4)* -ем, *(5)* -ете, *(6)* -ют.

венча́ть *impf, present:* *(1)* венча́-ю, *(2)* -ешь, *(3)* -ет, *(4)* -ем, *(5)* -ете, *(6)* -ют.

ве́рить *impf, present:* *(1)* ве́р-ю, *(2)* -ишь, *(3)* -ит, *(4)* -им, *(5)* -ите, *(6)* -ят.

верну́ть(ся) *pf, future:* *(1)* верн-у́(сь), *(2)* -ёшь(ся), *(3)* -ёт(ся), *(4)* -ём(ся), *(5)* -ёте(сь), *(6)* -у́т(ся).

верте́ть(ся) *impf, present:* *(1)* верчу́(сь), *(2)* ве́рт-ишь(ся), *(3)* -ит(ся), *(4)* -им(ся), *(5)* -ите(сь), *(6)* -ят(ся).

веселе́ть *impf, present:* *(1)* веселе́-ю, *(2)* -ешь, *(3)* -ет, *(4)* -ем, *(5)* -ете, *(6)* -ют.

весели́ть(ся) *impf, present:* *(1)* весел-ю́(сь), *(2)* -и́шь(ся), *(3)* -и́т(ся), *(4)* -и́м(ся), *(5)* -и́те(сь), *(6)* -я́т(ся).

вести́ *impf, present:* *(1)* вед-у́, *(2)* -ёшь, *(3)* -ёт, *(4)* -ём, *(5)* -ёте, *(6)* -у́т; *past:* вёл, вел-а́, -о́, -и́.

ве́шаться *impf, present:* *(3)* ве́ша-ется, *(6)* -ются.

Persons: 1 = я, 2 = ты, 3 = он, она́, оно́, 4 = мы, 5 = вы, 6 = они́

взбеси́ть *pf, future:* (1) взбешу́, (2) взбе́с-ишь, (3) -ит, (4) -им, (5) -ите, (6) -ят.

взволнова́ть *pf, future:* (1) взволну́-ю, (2) -ешь, (3) -ет, (4) -ем, (5) -ете, (6) -ют.

взгляну́ть *pf, future:* (1) взгляну́, (2) взгля́н-ешь, (3) -ет, (4) -ем, (5) -ете, (6) -ут.

вздохну́ть *pf, future:* (1) вздохн-у́, (2) -ёшь, (3) -ёт, (4) -ём, (5) -ёте, (6) -у́т.

вздыма́ться *impf, present:* (1) вздыма́-юсь, (2) -ешься, (3) -ется, (4) -емся, (5) -етесь, (6) -ются.

вздыха́ть *impf, present:* (1) вздыха́-ю, (2) -ешь, (3) -ет, (4) -ем, (5) -ете, (6) -ют.

взлета́ть *impf, present:* (1) взлета́-ю, (2) -ешь, (3) -ет, (4) -ем, (5) -ете, (6) -ют.

взлете́ть *pf, future:* (1) взлечу́, (2) взлет-и́шь, (3) -и́т, (4) -и́м, (5) -и́те, (6) -я́т.

взмоли́ться *pf, future:* (1) взмолю́сь, (2) взмо́л-ишься, (3) -ится, (4) -имся, (5) -итесь, (6) -ятся.

взмыва́ть *impf, present:* (1) взмыва́-ю, (2) -ешь, (3) -ет, (4) -ем, (5) -ете, (6) -ют.

взмыть *pf, future:* (1) взмо́-ю, (2) -ешь, (3) -ет, (4) -ем, (5) -ете, (6) -ют.

взрасти́ть *pf, future:* (1) взращу́, (2) взраст-и́шь, (3) -и́т, (4) -и́м, (5) -и́те, (6) -я́т.

взра́щивать *impf, present:* (1) взра́щива-ю, (2) -ешь, (3) -ет, (4) -ем, (5) -ете, (6) -ют.

взъеро́шить *pf, future:* (1) взъеро́ш-у, (2) -ишь, (3) -ит, (4) -им, (5) -ите, (6) -ат.

взыва́ть *impf, present:* (1) взыва́-ю, (2) -ешь, (3) -ет, (4) -ем, (5) -ете, (6) -ют.

взять *pf, future:* (1) возьм-у́, (2) -ёшь, (3) -ёт, (4) -ём, (5) -ёте, (6) -у́т.

ви́деть(ся) *impf, present:* (1) ви́жу(сь), (2) ви́д-ишь(ся), (3) -ит(ся), (4) -им(ся), (5) -ите(сь), (6) -ят(ся).

визжа́ть *impf, present:* (1) визж-у́, (2) -и́шь, (3) -и́т, (4) -и́м, (5) -и́те, (6) -а́т.

виля́ть *impf, present:* (1) виля́-ю, (2) -ешь, (3) -ет, (4) -ем, (5) -ете, (6) -ют.

вихри́ться *impf, present:* (3) вихр-и́тся, (6) -я́тся.

вкла́дывать *impf, present:* (1) вкла́дыва-ю, (2) -ешь, (3) -ет, (4) -ем, (5) -ете, (6) -ют.

вкуси́ть *pf, future:* (1) вкушу́, (2) вку́с-ишь, (3) -ит, (4) -им, (5) -ите, (6) -ят.

вкуша́ть *impf, present:* (1) вкуша́-ю, (2) -ешь, (3) -ет, (4) -ем, (5) -ете, (6) -ют.

вла́ствовать *impf, present:* (1) вла́ству-ю, (2) -ешь, (3) -ет, (4) -ем, (5) -ете, (6) -ют.

вложи́ть *pf, future:* (1) вложу́, (2) вло́ж-ишь, (3) -ит, (4) -им, (5) -ите, (6) -ат.

влюби́ться *pf, future:* (1) влюблю́сь, (2) влюб-и́шься, (3) -ится, (4) -имся, (5) -итесь, (6) -ятся.

вля́паться *impf & pf, present & future:* (1) вля́па-юсь, (2) -ешься, (3) -ется, (4) -емся, (5) -етесь, (6) -ются.

вмеша́ться *pf, future:* (1) вмеша́-юсь, (2) -ешься, (3) -ется, (4) -емся, (5) -етесь, (6) -ются.

вме́шиваться *impf, present:* (1) вме́шива-юсь, (2) -ешься, (3) -ется, (4) -емся, (5) -етесь, (6) -ются.

внуша́ть *impf, present:* (1) внуша́-ю, (2) -ешь, (3) -ет, (4) -ем, (5) -ете, (6) -ют.

внуши́ть *pf, future:* (1) внуш-у́, (2) -и́шь, (3) -и́т, (4) -и́м, (5) -и́те, (6) -а́т.

вовлека́ть *impf, present:* (1) вовлека-ю, (2) -ешь, (3) -ет, (4) -ем, (5) -ете, (6) -ют.

вовле́чь *pf, future:* (1) вовлеку́, (2) вовлеч-ёшь, (3) -ёт, (4) -ём, (5) -ёте, (6) вовлеку́т; *past:* вовлёк, вовлекл-а́, -о́, -и́.

води́ть *impf, present:* (1) вожу́, (2) во́д-ишь, (3) -ит, (4) -им, (5) -ите, (6) -ят.

вожделе́ть *impf, present:* (1) вожделе́-ю, (2) -ешь, (3) -ет, (4) -ем, (5) -ете, (6) -ют.

возбуди́ть(ся) *pf, future:* (1) возбужу́(сь), (2) возбуд-и́шь(ся), (3) -и́т(ся), (4) -и́м(ся), (5) -и́те(сь), (6) -я́т(ся).

возбужда́ть(ся) *impf, present:* (1) возбужда́-ю(сь), (2) -ешь(ся), (3) -ет(ся), (4) -ем(ся), (5) -ете(сь), (6) -ют(ся).

возврати́ть(ся) *pf, future:* (1) возвращу́(сь), (2) возврат-и́шь(ся), (3) -и́т(ся), (4) -и́м(ся), (5) -и́те(сь), (6) -я́т(ся).

Persons: 1 = я,   2 = ты,   3 = он, она́, оно́,   4 = мы,   5 = вы,   6 = они́

возвраща́ть(ся) *impf, present:* (*1*) возвраща́-ю(сь), (*2*) -ешь(ся), (*3*) -ет(ся), (*4*) -ем(ся), (*5*) -ете(сь), (*6*) -ют(ся).

возвы́сить *pf, future:* (*1*) возвы́шу, (*2*) возвы́с-ишь, (*3*) -ит, (*4*) -им, (*5*) -ите, (*6*) -ят.

возвыша́ть *impf, present:* (*1*) возвыша́-ю, (*2*) -ешь, (*3*) -ет, (*4*) -ем, (*5*) -ете, (*6*) -ют.

воздержа́ться *pf, future:* (*1*) воздержу́сь, (*2*) воздéрж-ишься, (*3*) -ится, (*4*) -имся, (*5*) -итесь, (*6*) -атся.

воздéрживаться *impf, present:* (*1*) воздéржива-юсь, (*2*) -ешься, (*3*) -ется, (*4*) -емся, (*5*) -етесь, (*6*) -ются.

воззва́ть *pf, future:* (*1*) воззов-у́, (*2*) -ёшь, (*3*) -ёт, (*4*) -ём, (*5*) -ёте, (*6*) -у́т.

во́зиться *impf, present:* (*1*) вожу́сь, (*2*) во́з-ишься, (*3*) -ится, (*4*) -имся, (*5*) -итесь, (*6*) -ятся.

возмести́ть *pf, future:* (*1*) возмещу́, (*2*) возмест-и́шь, (*3*) -и́т, (*4*) -и́м, (*5*) -и́те, (*6*) -я́т.

возмеща́ть *impf, present:* (*1*) возмеща́-ю, (*2*) -ешь, (*3*) -ет, (*4*) -ем, (*5*) -ете, (*6*) -ют.

вознагради́ть *pf, future:* (*1*) вознагражу́, (*2*) вознаград-и́шь, (*3*) -и́т, (*4*) -и́м, (*5*) -и́те, (*6*) -я́т.

вознагражда́ть *impf, present:* (*1*) вознагражда́-ю, (*2*) -ешь, (*3*) -ет, (*4*) -ем, (*5*) -ете, (*6*) -ют.

возража́ть *impf, present:* (*1*) возража́-ю, (*2*) -ешь, (*3*) -ет, (*4*) -ем, (*5*) -ете, (*6*) -ют.

возраста́ть *impf, present:* (*1*) возраста́-ю, (*2*) -ешь, (*3*) -ет, (*4*) -ем, (*5*) -ете, (*6*) -ют.

возрасти́ *pf, future:* (*1*) возраст-у́, (*2*) -ёшь, (*3*) -ёт, (*4*) -ём, (*5*) -ёте, (*6*) -ут; *past:* возро́с, -ла́, -ло́, -ли́.

войти́ *pf, future:* (*1*) войд-у́, (*2*) -ёшь, (*3*) -ёт, (*4*) -ём, (*5*) -ёте, (*6*) -у́т; *past:* во-шёл, -шла́, -шло́, -шли́.

волнова́ть(ся) *impf, present:* (*1*) волну́-ю(сь), (*2*) -ешь(ся), (*3*) -ет(ся), (*4*) -ем(ся), (*5*) -ете(сь), (*6*) -ют(ся).

волочи́ться *impf, present:* (*1*) волочу́сь, (*2*) волоч-и́шься, (*3*) -и́тся, (*4*) -и́мся, (*5*) -и́тесь, (*6*) -а́тся.

вонза́ться *impf, present:* (*1*) вонза́-юсь, (*2*) -ешься, (*3*) -ется, (*4*) -емся, (*5*) -етесь, (*6*) -ются.

вонзи́ться *pf, future:* (*3*) вонз-и́тся, (*6*) -я́тся.

вообража́ть *impf, present:* (*1*) вообража́-ю, (*2*) -ешь, (*3*) -ет, (*4*) -ем, (*5*) -ете, (*6*) -ют.

вообрази́ть *pf, future:* (*1*) воображу́, (*2*) вообраз-и́шь, (*3*) -и́т, (*4*) -и́м, (*5*) -и́те, (*6*) -я́т.

воодушеви́ть *pf, future:* (*1*) воодушев-лю́, (*2*) -и́шь, (*3*) -и́т, (*4*) -и́м, (*5*) -и́те, (*6*) -я́т.

воодушевля́ть *impf, present:* (*1*) воодушевля́-ю, (*2*) -ешь, (*3*) -ет, (*4*) -ем, (*5*) -ете, (*6*) -ют.

вопи́ть *impf, present:* (*1*) воплю́, (*2*) воп-и́шь, (*3*) -и́т, (*4*) -и́м, (*5*) -и́те, (*6*) -я́т.

воплоти́ть *pf, future:* (*1*) воплощу́, (*2*) воплот-и́шь, (*3*) -и́т, (*4*) -и́м, (*5*) -и́те, (*6*) -я́т.

воплоща́ть *impf, present:* (*1*) воплоща́-ю, (*2*) -ешь, (*3*) -ет, (*4*) -ем, (*5*) -ете, (*6*) -ю́т.

ворча́ть *pf, future:* (*1*) ворч-у́, (*2*) -и́шь, (*3*) -и́т, (*4*) -и́м, (*5*) -и́те, (*6*) -а́т.

воспита́ть *pf, future:* (*1*) воспита́-ю, (*2*) -ешь, (*3*) -ет, (*4*) -ем, (*5*) -ете, (*6*) -ют.

воспи́тывать *impf, present:* (*1*) воспи́тыва-ю, (*2*) -ешь, (*3*) -ет, (*4*) -ем, (*5*) -ете, (*6*) -ют.

воспламени́ть *pf, future:* (*1*) воспламен-ю́, (*2*) -и́шь, (*3*) -и́т, (*4*) -и́м, (*5*) -и́те, (*6*) -я́т.

воспламеня́ть *impf, present:* (*1*) воспламеня́-ю, (*2*) -ешь, (*3*) -ет, (*4*) -ем, (*5*) -ете, (*6*) -ют.

воспо́льзоваться *pf, future:* (*1*) воспо́льзу-юсь, (*2*) -ешься, (*3*) -ется, (*4*) -емся, (*5*) -етесь, (*6*) -ются.

воспрепя́тствовать *pf, future:* (*1*) воспрепя́тству-ю, (*2*) -ешь, (*3*) -ет, (*4*) -ем, (*5*) -ете, (*6*) -ют.

воспринима́ть *impf, present:* (*1*) воспринима́-ю, (*2*) -ешь, (*3*) -ет, (*4*) -ем, (*5*) -ете, (*6*)

> *Persons:* 1 = я,   2 = ты,   3 = он, онá, онó,   4 = мы,   5 = вы,   6 = онú

-ют.

восприня́ть *pf, future:* (1) восприму́, (2) восприм-ешь, (3) -ет, (4) -ем, (5) -ете, (6) -ут.

воссоедини́ться *pf, future:* (1) воссоедин-ю́сь, (2) -и́шься, (3) -и́тся, (4) -и́мся, (5) -и́тесь, (6) -я́тся.

воссоединя́ться *impf, present:* (1) воссоединя́-юсь, (2) -ешься, (3) -ется, (4) -емся, (5) -етесь, (6) -ются.

восстана́вливать *impf, present:* (1) восстана́влива-ю, (2) -ешь, (3) -ет, (4) -ем, (5) -ете, (6) -ют.

восстанови́ть *pf, future:* (1) восстановлю́, (2) восстано́в-ишь, (3) -ит, (4) -им, (5) -ите, (6) -ят.

восхити́ть(ся) *pf, future:* (1) восхищу́(сь), (2) восхит-и́шь(ся), (3) -и́т(ся), (4) -и́мся), (5) -и́те(сь), (6) -я́т(ся).

восхища́ть(ся) *impf, present:* (1) восхища́-ю(сь), (2) -ешь(ся), (3) -ет(ся), (4) -ем(ся), (5) -ете(сь), (6) -ют(ся).

впасть *pf, future:* (1) впад-у́, (2) -ёшь, (3) -ёт, (4) -ём, (5) -ёте, (6) -у́т.

вплести́сь *pf, future:* (3) вплет-ётся, (6) -у́тся; *past:* вплёлся, впле-ла́сь, -ло́сь, -ли́сь.

вплета́ться *impf, present:* (1) вплета́-юсь, (2) -ешься, (3) -ется, (4) -емся, (5) -етесь, (6) -ются.

впута́ться *impf, present:* (1) впута́-юсь, (2) -ешься, (3) -ется, (4) -емся, (5) -етесь, (6) -ются.

враща́ть(ся) *impf, present:* (1) враща́-ю(сь), (2) -ешь(ся), (3) -ет(ся), (4) -ем(ся), (5) -ете(сь), (6) -ют(ся).

всколыха́ть *impf, present:* (1) всколыш-у́, (2) всколы́ш -ешь, (3) -ет, (4) -ем, (5) -ете, (6) -ут.

всколыхну́ть *pf, future:* (1) всколыхн-у́, (2) -ёшь, (3) -ёт, (4) -ём, (5) -ёте, (6) -у́т.

вскри́кивать *impf, present:* (1) вскри́кива-ю, (2) -ешь, (3) -ет, (4) -ем, (5) -ете, (6) -ют.

вскри́кнуть *pf, future:* (1) вскри́кн-у, (2) -ешь, (3) -ет, (4) -ем, (5) -ете, (6) -ут.

вскружи́ть *pf, future:* (1) вскружу́, (2) вскруж-и́шь, (3) -и́т, (4) -и́м, (5) -и́те, (6) -а́т.

всо́вывать *impf, present:* (1) всо́выва-ю, (2) -ешь, (3) -ет, (4) -ем, (5) -ете, (6) -ют.

всу́нуть *pf, future:* (1) всу́н-у, (2) -ешь, (3) -ет, (4) -ем, (5) -ете, (6) -ут.

вспа́рхивать *impf, present:* (1) вспа́рхива-ю, (2) -ешь, (3) -ет, (4) -ем, (5) -ете, (6) -ют.

вспомина́ть *impf, present:* (1) вспомина́-ю, (2) -ешь, (3) -ет, (4) -ем, (5) -ете, (6) -ют.

вспо́мнить *pf, future:* (1) вспо́мн-ю, (2) -ишь, (3) -ит, (4) -им, (5) -ите, (6) -ят.

вспорхну́ть *pf, future:* (1) вспорхн-у́, (2) -ёшь, (3) -ёт, (4) -ём, (5) -ёте, (6) -у́т.

вспы́хивать *impf, present:* (1) вспы́хива-ю, (2) -ешь, (3) -ет, (4) -ем, (5) -ете, (6) -ют.

вспы́хнуть *pf, future:* (1) вспы́хн-у, (2) -ешь, (3) -ет, (4) -ем, (5) -ете, (6) -ут.

встава́ть *impf present:* (1) вста-ю́, (2) -ёшь, (3) -ёт, (4) -ём, (5) -ёте, (6) -ю́т.

встать *pf, future:* (1) вста́н-у, (2) -ешь, (3) -ет, (4) -ем, (5) -ете, (6) -ут.

встре́тить(ся) *pf, future:* (1) встре́чу(сь), (2) встре́т-ишь(ся), (3) -ит(ся), (4) -им(ся), (5) -ите(сь), (6) -ят(ся).

встреча́ть(ся) *impf, present:* (1) встреча́-ю(сь), (2) -ешь(ся), (3) -ет(ся), (4) -ем(ся), (5) -ете(сь), (6) -ют(ся).

вступа́ть *impf, present:* (1) вступа́-ю, (2) -ешь, (3) -ет, (4) -ем, (5) -ете, (6) -ют.

вступи́ть *pf, future:* (1) вступлю́, (2) всту́п-ишь, (3) -ит, (4) -им, (5) -ите, (6) -ят.

всхли́пнуть *pf, future:* (1) всхли́пн-у, (2) -ешь, (3) -ет, (4) -ем, (5) -ете, (6) -ут.

всхли́пывать *impf, present:* (1) всхли́пыва-ю, (2) -ешь, (3) -ет, (4) -ем, (5) -ете, (6) -ют.

вторга́ться *impf, present:* (1) вторга́-юсь, (2) -ешься, (3) -ется, (4) -емся, (5) -етесь, (6) -ются.

Persons: 1 = я, 2 = ты, 3 = он, она́, оно́, 4 = мы, 5 = вы, 6 = они́

вто́ргнуться *pf, future:* (1) вто́ргн-усь, (2) -ешься, (3) -ется, (4) -емся, (5) -етесь, (6) -утся; *past:* вто́рг-ся, -лась, -лось, -лись.

входи́ть *impf, present:* (1) вхожу́, (2) вхо́д-ишь, (3) -ит, (4) -им, (5) -ите, (6) -ят.

выбира́ть *impf, present:* (1) выбира́-ю, (2) -ешь, (3) -ет, (4) -ем, (5) -ете, (6) -ют.

выбра́сывать *impf, present:* (1) выбра́сыва-ю, (2) -ешь, (3) -ет, (4) -ем, (5) -ете, (6) -ют.

вы́брать *pf, future:* (1) вы́бер-у, (2) -ешь, (3) -ет, (4) -ем, (5) -ете, (6) -ут.

вы́бросить *pf, future:* (1) вы́брошу, (2) вы́брос-ишь, (3) -ит, (4) -им, (5) -ите, (6) -ят.

вы́вести *pf, future:* (1) вы́вед-у, (2) -ешь, (3) -ет, (4) -ем, (5) -ете, (6) -ут; *past:* вы́ве-л, -ла, -ло, -ли.

выводи́ть *impf, present:* (1) вывожу́, (2) выво́д-ишь, (3) -ит, (4) -им, (5) -ите, (6) -ят.

выгиба́ться *impf, present:* (1) выгиба́-юсь, (2) -ешься, (3) -ется, (4) -емся, (5) -етесь, (6) -ются.

вы́глядеть *impf, present:* (1) вы́гляжу, (2) вы́гляд-ишь, (3) -ит, (4) -им, (5) -ите, (6) -ят.

вы́гнать *pf, future:* (1) вы́гон-ю, (2) -ишь, (3) -ит, (4) -им, (5) -ите, (6) -ят.

вы́гнуться *pf, future:* (1) вы́гн-усь, (2) -ешься, (3) -ется, (4) -емся, (5) -етесь, (6) -утся.

выгоня́ть *impf, present:* (1) выгоня́-ю, (2) -ешь, (3) -ет, (4) -ем, (5) -ете, (6) -ют.

выдава́ть *impf, present:* (1) выда-ю́, (2) -ёшь, (3) -ёт, (4) -ём, (5) -ёте, (6) -ю́т.

выдава́ться *impf, present:* (1) выда-ю́сь, (2) -ёшься, (3) -ётся, (4) -ёмся, (5) -ётесь, (6) -ю́тся.

вы́дать *pf, future:* (1) вы́да-м, (2) -шь, (3) -ст, (4) -дим, (5) -дите, (6) -дут.

вы́делить *pf, future:* (1) вы́дел-ю, (2) -ишь, (3) -ит, (4) -им, (5) -ите, (6) -ят.

выделя́ть *impf, present:* (1) вы́дел-ю, (2) -ешь, (3) -ет, (4) -ем, (5) -ете, (6) -ют.

вы́держать *pf, future:* (1) вы́держ-у, (2) -ишь, (3) -ит, (4) -им, (5) -ите, (6) -ат.

выде́рживать *impf, present:* (1) выде́ржива-ю, (2) -ешь, (3) -ет, (4) -ем, (5) -ете, (6) -ют.

вы́думать *pf, future:* (1) вы́дума-ю, (2) -ешь, (3) -ет, (4) -ем, (5) -ете, (6) -ют.

выду́мывать *impf, present:* (1) выду́мыва-ю, (2) -ешь, (3) -ет, (4) -ем, (5) -ете, (6) -ют.

выезжа́ть *impf, present:* (1) выезжа́-ю, (2) -ешь, (3) -ет, (4) -ем, (5) -ете, (6) -ют.

вы́ехать *pf, future:* (1) вы́ед-у, (2) -ешь, (3) -ет, (4) -ем, (5) -ете, (6) -ут.

вызыва́ть *impf, present:* (1) вызыва́-ю, (2) -ешь, (3) -ет, (4) -ем, (5) -ете, (6) -ют.

вы́звать *pf, future:* (1) вы́зов-у, (2) -ешь, (3) -ет, (4) -ем, (5) -ете, (6) -ут.

вы́йти *pf, future:* (1) вы́йд-у, (2) -ешь, (3) -ет, (4) -ем, (5) -ете, (6) -ут; *past:* вы́-шел, -шла, -шло, -шли.

вы́казать *pf, future:* (1) вы́каж-у, (2) -ешь, (3) -ет, (4) -ем, (5) -ете, (6) -ут.

выка́зывать *impf, present:* (1) выка́зыва-ю, (2) -ешь, (3) -ет, (4) -ем, (5) -ете, (6) -ют.

выкри́кивать *impf, present:* (1) выкри́кива-ю, (2) -ешь, (3) -ет, (4) -ем, (5) -ете, (6) -ют.

выкра́ивать *impf, present:* (1) выкра́ива-ю, (2) -ешь, (3) -ет, (4) -ем, (5) -ете, (6) -ют.

вы́крикнуть *pf, future:* (1) вы́крикн-у, (2) -ешь, (3) -ет, (4) -ем, (5) -ете, (6) -ут.

вы́кроить *pf, future:* (1) вы́кро-ю, (2) -ешь, (3) -ет, (4) -ем, (5) -ете, (6) -ют.

вылеза́ть *impf, present:* (1) вылеза́-ю, (2) -ешь, (3) -ет, (4) -ем, (5) -ете, (6) -ют.

вы́лезти *pf, future:* (1) вы́лез-у, (2) -ешь, (3) -ет, (4) -ем, (5) -ете, (6) -ут; *past:* вы́лез, -ла, -ло, -ли.

вылета́ть *impf, present:* (1) вылета́-ю, (2) -ешь, (3) -ет, (4) -ем, (5) -ете, (6) -ют.

вы́лететь *pf, future:* (1) вы́лечу, (2) вылет-ишь, (3) -ит, (4) -им, (5) -ите, (6) -ят.

вы́мыть *pf, future:* (1) вы́мо-ю, (2) -ешь, (3) -ет, (4) -ем, (5) -ете, (6) -ют.

вы́нести *pf, future:* (1) вы́нес-у, (2) -ешь, (3) -ет, (4) -ем, (5) -ете, (6) -ут; *past:* вы́нес,

> *Persons:* 1 = я, 2 = ты, 3 = он, она́, оно́, 4 = мы, 5 = вы, 6 = они́

-ла, -ло, -ли.

вынима́ть *impf, present:* (1) вынима́-ю, (2) -ешь, (3) -ет, (4) -ем, (5) -ете, (6) -ют.

выноси́ть *impf, present:* (1) выношу́, (2) выно́с-ишь, (3) -ит, (4) -им, (5) -ите, (6) -ят.

вы́нудить *pf, future:* (1) вы́нужу, (2) вы́нуд-ишь, (3) -ит, (4) -им, (5) -ите, (6) -ят.

вынужда́ть *impf, present:* (1) вынужда́-ю, (2) -ешь, (3) -ет, (4) -ем, (5) -ете, (6) -ют.

вы́нуть *pf, future:* (1) вы́н-у, (2) -ешь, (3) -ет, (4) -ем, (5) -ете, (6) -ют.

вы́пить *pf, future:* (1) вы́пь-ю, (2) -ешь, (3) -ет, (4) -ем, (5) -ете, (6) -ют.

вы́плакаться *pf, future:* (1) вы́плач-усь, (2) -ешься, (3) -ется, (4) -емся, (5) -етесь, (6) -утся.

выпла́кивать *impf, present:* (1) выпла́кива-ю, (2) -ешь, (3) -ет, (4) -ем, (5) -ете, (6) -ют.

вы́полнить *pf, future:* (1) вы́полн-ю, (2) -ишь, (3) -ит, (4) -им, (5) -ите, (6) -ят.

выполня́ть *impf, present:* (1) выполня́-ю, (2) -ешь, (3) -ет, (4) -ем, (5) -ете, (6) -ют.

выража́ть *impf, present:* (1) выража́-ю, (2) -ешь, (3) -ет, (4) -ем, (5) -ете, (6) -ют.

вы́разить *pf, future:* (1) вы́ражу, (2) вы́раз-ишь, (3) -ит, (4) -им, (5) -ите, (6) -ят.

выпра́шивать *impf, present:* (1) выпра́шива-ю, (2) -ешь, (3) -ет, (4) -ем, (5) -ете, (6) -ют.

вы́просить *pf, future:* (1) вы́прошу, (2) вы́прос-ишь, (3) -ит, (4) -им, (5) -ите, (6) -ят.

вы́расти *pf, future:* (1) вы́раст-у, (2) -ешь, (3) -ет, (4) -ем, (5) -ете, (6) -ут; *past:* вы́рос, -ла, -ло, -ли.

вы́растить *pf, future:* (1) вы́ращу, (2) вы́раст-ишь, (3) -ит, (4) -им, (5) -ите, (6) -ят.

вырисо́вываться *impf, present:* (1) вырисо́выва-юсь, (2) -ешься, (3) -ется, (4) -емся, (5) -етесь, (6) -ются.

выска́льзывать *impf, present:* (1) выска́льзыва-ю, (2) -ешь, (3) -ет, (4) -ем, (5) -ете, (6) -ют.

вы́скользнуть *pf, future:* (1) вы́скользн-у, (2) -ешь, (3) -ет, (4) -ем, (5) -ете, (6) -ут.

высме́ивать *impf, present:* (1) высме́ива-ю, (2) -ешь, (3) -ет, (4) -ем, (5) -ете, (6) -ют.

вы́смеять *pf, future:* (1) вы́сме-ю, (2) -ешь, (3) -ет, (4) -ем, (5) -ете, (6) -ют.

выставля́ть *impf, present:* (1) выставля́-ю, (2) -ешь, (3) -ет, (4) -ем, (5) -ете, (6) -ют.

вы́стоять *pf, future:* (1) вы́сто-ю, (2) -ишь, (3) -ит, (4) -им, (5) -ите, (6) -ят.

вытя́гивать *impf, present:* (1) вытя́гива-ю, (2) -ешь, (3) -ет, (4) -ем, (5) -ете, (6) -ют.

вы́тянуть *pf, future:* (1) вы́тян-у, (2) -ешь, (3) -ет, (4) -ем, (5) -ете, (6) -ут.

вы́учить *pf, future:* (1) вы́уч-у, (2) -ишь, (3) -ит, (4) -им, (5) -ите, (6) -ат.

выходи́ть *impf, present:* (1) выхожу́, (2) выхо́д-ишь, (3) -ит, (4) -им, (5) -ите, (6) -ят.

вы́яснить *pf, future:* (1) вы́ясн-ю, (2) -ишь, (3) -ит, (4) -им, (5) -ите, (6) -ят.

вя́нуть *impf, present:* (1) вя́н-у, (2) -ешь, (3) -ет, (4) -ем, (5) -ете, (6) -ут.

гаранти́ровать *impf & pf, present & future:* (1) гаранти́ру-ю, (2) -ешь, (3) -ет, (4) -ем, (5) -ете, (6) -ют.

гармони́ровать *impf, present:* (1) гармони́ру-ю, (2) -ешь, (3) -ет, (4) -ем, (5) -ете, (6) -ют.

гаси́ть *impf, present:* (1) гашу́, (2) га́с-ишь, (3) -ит, (4) -им, (5) -ите, (6) -ят.

ги́бнуть *impf, present:* (1) ги́бн-у, (2) -ешь, (3) -ет, (4) -ем, (5) -ете, (6) -ут.

гипнотизи́ровать *impf, present:* (1) гипнотизи́ру-ю, (2) -ешь, (3) -ет, (4) -ем, (5) -ете, (6) -ют.

гла́дить *impf, present:* (1) гла́жу, (2) гла́д-ишь, (3) -ит, (4) -им, (5) -ите, (6) -ят.

глота́ть *impf, present:* (1) глота́-ю, (2) -ешь, (3) -ет, (4) -ем, (5) -ете, (6) -ют.

глотну́ть *pf, future:* (1) глотн-у́, (2) -ёшь, (3) -ёт, (4) -ём, (5) -ёте, (6) -у́т.

гляде́ть *impf, present:* (1) гляжу́, (2) гля́д-ишь, (3) -ит, (4) -им, (5) -ите, (6) -ят.

говори́ть *impf, present:* (1) говор-ю́, (2) -и́шь, (3) -и́т, (4) -и́м, (5) -и́те, (6) -я́т.

Persons: 1 = я,   2 = ты,   3 = он, она́, оно́,   4 = мы,   5 = вы,   6 = они́

гоня́ться *impf, present:* *(1)* гоня́-юсь, *(2)* -ешься, *(3)* -ется, *(4)* -емся, *(5)* -етесь, *(6)* -ются.

горе́ть *impf, present:* *(1)* гор-ю́, *(2)* -и́шь, *(3)* -и́т, *(4)* -и́м, *(5)* -и́те, *(6)* -я́т.

госпо́дствовать *impf, present:* *(1)* госпо́дству-ю, *(2)* -ешь, *(3)* -ет, *(4)* -ем, *(5)* -ете, *(6)* -ют.

гото́вить *impf, present:* *(1)* гото́в-лю, *(2)* -ишь, *(3)* -ит, *(4)* -им, *(5)* -ите, *(6)* -ят.

гре́зить *impf, present:* *(1)* гре́жу, *(2)* гре́з-ишь, *(3)* -ит, *(4)* -им, *(5)* -ите, *(6)* -ят.

гре́ться *impf, present:* *(1)* гре́-юсь, *(2)* -ешься, *(3)* -ется, *(4)* -емся, *(5)* -етесь, *(6)* -ются.

греши́ть *impf, present:* *(1)* греш-у́, *(2)* -и́шь, *(3)* -и́т, *(4)* -и́м, *(5)* -и́те, *(6)* -а́т.

грызть *impf present:* *(1)* грыз-у́, *(2)* -ёшь, *(3)* -ёт, *(4)* -ём, *(5)* -ёте, *(6)* -у́т; *past:* гры́з, -ла, -ло, -ли.

гуля́ть *impf, present:* *(1)* гуля́-ю, *(2)* -ешь, *(3)* -ет, *(4)* -ем, *(5)* -ете, *(6)* -ют.

дава́ть *impf present:* *(1)* да-ю́, *(2)* -ёшь, *(3)* -ёт, *(4)* -ём, *(5)* -ёте, *(6)* -ю́т.

дави́ть *impf, present:* *(1)* давлю́, *(2)* да́в-ишь, *(3)* -ит, *(4)* -им, *(5)* -ите, *(6)* -ят.

дари́ть *impf, present:* *(1)* дарю́, *(2)* да́р-ишь, *(3)* -ит, *(4)* -им, *(5)* -ите, *(6)* -ят.

дать *pf, future:* *(1)* да-м, *(2)* -шь, *(3)* -ст, *(4)* -ди́м, *(5)* -ди́те, *(6)* -ду́т.

дви́гать(ся) *impf, present:* *(1)* дви́га-ю(сь), *(2)* -ешь(ся), *(3)* -ет(ся), *(4)* -ем(ся), *(5)* -ете(сь), *(6)* -ют(ся).

дви́нуть(ся) *pf, future:* *(1)* дви́н-у(с)ь, *(2)* -ешь(ся), *(3)* -ет(ся), *(4)* -ем(ся), *(5)* -ете(сь), *(6)* -ут(ся).

де́йствовать *impf, present:* *(1)* де́йству-ю, *(2)* -ешь, *(3)* -ет, *(4)* -ем, *(5)* -ете, *(6)* -ют.

де́лать *impf, present:* *(1)* де́ла-ю, *(2)* -ешь, *(3)* -ет, *(4)* -ем, *(5)* -ете, *(6)* -ют.

дели́ть *impf, present:* *(1)* делю́, *(2)* де́л-ишь, *(3)* -ит, *(4)* -им, *(5)* -ите, *(6)* -ят.

дели́ться *impf, present:* *(1)* делю́сь, *(2)* де́л-ишься, *(3)* -ится, *(4)* -имся, *(5)* -итесь, *(6)* -ятся.

держа́ть(ся) *impf, present:* *(1)* держу́(сь), *(2)* де́рж-ишь(ся), *(3)* -ит(ся), *(4)* -им(ся), *(5)* -ите(сь), *(6)* -ат(ся).

дискути́ровать *impf, present:* *(1)* дискути́ру-ю, *(2)* -ешь, *(3)* -ет, *(4)* -ем, *(5)* -ете, *(6)* -ют.

доба́вить *pf, future:* *(1)* доба́в-лю, *(2)* -ишь, *(3)* -ит, *(4)* -им, *(5)* -ите, *(6)* -ят.

добавля́ть *impf, present:* *(1)* добавля́-ю, *(2)* -ешь, *(3)* -ет, *(4)* -ем, *(5)* -ете, *(6)* -ют.

добива́ться *impf, present:* *(1)* добива́-юсь, *(2)* -ешься, *(3)* -ется, *(4)* -емся, *(5)* -етесь, *(6)* -ются.

добира́ться *impf, present:* *(1)* добира́-юсь, *(2)* -ешься, *(3)* -ется, *(4)* -емся, *(5)* -етесь, *(6)* -ются.

доби́ться *pf, future:* *(1)* добь-ю́сь, *(2)* -ёшься, *(3)* -ётся, *(4)* -ёмся, *(5)* -ётесь, *(6)* -ю́тся.

добра́ться *pf, future:* *(1)* добер-у́сь, *(2)* -ёшься, *(3)* -ётся, *(4)* -ёмся, *(5)* -ётесь, *(6)* -у́тся; *past:* добра́лся, добрала́сь, добра́лось, -лись.

дове́рить *pf, future:* *(1)* дове́р-ю, *(2)* -ишь, *(3)* -ит, *(4)* -им, *(5)* -ите, *(6)* -ят.

дове́риться *pf, future:* *(1)* дове́р-юсь, *(2)* -ишься, *(3)* -ится, *(4)* -имся, *(5)* -итесь, *(6)* -ятся.

доверя́ть(ся) *impf, present:* *(1)* доверя́-ю(сь), *(2)* -ешь(ся), *(3)* -ет(ся), *(4)* -ем(ся), *(5)* -ете(сь), *(6)* -ют(ся).

довести́ *pf, future:* *(1)* довед-у́, *(2)* -ёшь, *(3)* -ёт, *(4)* -ём, *(5)* -ёте, *(6)* -у́т; *past:* довёл, довел-а́, -о́, -и́.

доводи́ть *impf, present:* *(1)* довожу́, *(2)* дово́д-ишь, *(3)* -ит, *(4)* -им, *(5)* -ите, *(6)* -ят.

доде́лать *pf, future:* *(1)* доде́ла-ю, *(2)* -ешь, *(3)* -ет, *(4)* -ем, *(5)* -ете, *(6)* -ют.

дойти́ *pf, future:* *(1)* дойд-у́, *(2)* -ёшь, *(3)* -ёт, *(4)* -ём, *(5)* -ёте, *(6)* -у́т; *past:* до-шёл, -шла́, -шло́, -шли́.

Persons: 1 = я, 2 = ты, 3 = он, она́, оно́, 4 = мы, 5 = вы, 6 = они́

доказа́ть *pf, future:* *(1)* докажу́, *(2)* дока́ж-ешь, *(3)* -ет, *(4)* -ем, *(5)* -ете, *(6)* -ут.

дока́зывать *impf, present:* *(1)* дока́зыва-ю, *(2)* -ешь, *(3)* -ет, *(4)* -ем, *(5)* -ете, *(6)* -ют.

докуча́ть *impf, present:* *(1)* докуча́-ю, *(2)* -ешь, *(3)* -ет, *(4)* -ем, *(5)* -ете, *(6)* -ют.

допо́лнить *pf, future:* *(1)* допо́лн-ю, *(2)* -ишь, *(3)* -ит, *(4)* -им, *(5)* -ите, *(6)* -ят.

дополня́ть *impf, present:* *(1)* дополня́-ю, *(2)* -ешь, *(3)* -ет, *(4)* -ем, *(5)* -ете, *(6)* -ют.

дорожи́ть *impf, present:* *(1)* дорожу́, *(2)* -и́шь, *(3)* -и́т, *(4)* -и́м, *(5)* -и́те, *(6)* -а́т.

досажда́ть *impf, present:* *(1)* досажда́-ю, *(2)* -ешь, *(3)* -ет, *(4)* -ем, *(5)* -ете, *(6)* -ют.

досади́ть *pf, future:* *(1)* досажу́, *(2)* досад-и́шь, *(3)* -и́т, *(4)* -и́м, *(5)* -и́те, *(6)* -я́т.

достава́ть *impf present:* *(1)* доста-ю́, *(2)* -ёшь, *(3)* -ёт, *(4)* -ём, *(5)* -ёте, *(6)* -ю́т.

доста́вить *pf, future:* *(1)* доста́в-лю, *(2)* -ишь, *(3)* -ит, *(4)* -им, *(5)* -ите, *(6)* -ят.

доставля́ть *impf, present:* *(1)* доставля́-ю, *(2)* -ешь, *(3)* -ет, *(4)* -ем, *(5)* -ете, *(6)* -ют.

доста́ть *pf, future:* *(1)* доста́н-у, *(2)* -ешь, *(3)* -ет, *(4)* -ем, *(5)* -ете, *(6)* -ут.

достига́ть *impf, present:* *(1)* достига́-ю, *(2)* -ешь, *(3)* -ет, *(4)* -ем, *(5)* -ете, *(6)* -ют.

достигнуть *pf, future:* *(1)* дости́гн-у, *(2)* -ешь, *(3)* -ет, *(4)* -ем, *(5)* -ете, *(6)* -ут.

дости́чь *pf, future:* *(1)* дости́гн-у, *(2)* -ешь, *(3)* -ет, *(4)* -ем, *(5)* -ете, *(6)* -ут; *past:* дости́г, -ла, -ло, -ли.

доходи́ть *impf, present:* *(1)* дохожу́, *(2)* дохо́д-ишь, *(3)* -ит, *(4)* -им, *(5)* -ите, *(6)* -ят.

дразни́ть *impf, present:* *(1)* дразню́, *(2)* дра́зн-ишь, *(3)* -ит, *(4)* -им, *(5)* -ите, *(6)* -ят.

драматизи́ровать *impf, present:* *(1)* драматизи́ру-ю, *(2)* -ешь, *(3)* -ет, *(4)* -ем, *(5)* -ете, *(6)* -ют.

дрожа́ть *impf, present:* *(1)* дрож-у́, *(2)* -и́шь, *(3)* -и́т, *(4)* -и́м, *(5)* -и́те, *(6)* -а́т.

дружи́ть *impf, present:* *(1)* дружу́, *(2)* дру́ж-ишь, *(3)* -ит, *(4)* -им, *(5)* -ите, *(6)* -ат.

ду́мать *impf, present:* *(1)* ду́ма-ю, *(2)* -ешь, *(3)* -ет, *(4)* -ем, *(5)* -ете, *(6)* -ют.

дура́чить(ся) *impf, present:* *(1)* дура́ч-у(сь), *(2)* -ишь(ся), *(3)* -ит(ся), *(4)* -им(ся), *(5)* -ите(сь), *(6)* -ат(ся).

ду́ться *impf, present:* *(1)* ду́-юсь, *(2)* -ешься, *(3)* -ется, *(4)* -емся, *(5)* -етесь, *(6)* -ются.

души́ть *impf, present:* *(1)* душу́, *(2)* ду́ш-ишь, *(3)* -ит, *(4)* -им, *(5)* -ите, *(6)* -ат.

дыша́ть *impf, present:* *(1)* дышу́, *(2)* ды́ш-ишь, *(3)* -ит, *(4)* -им, *(5)* -ите, *(6)* -ат.

е́здить *impf, present:* *(1)* е́зжу, *(2)* е́зд-ишь, *(3)* -ит, *(4)* -им, *(5)* -ите, *(6)* -ят.

ёрзать *impf, present:* *(1)* ёрза-ю, *(2)* -ешь, *(3)* -ет, *(4)* -ем, *(5)* -ете, *(6)* -ют.

еро́шить *impf, present:* *(1)* ёрош-у, *(2)* -ишь, *(3)* -ит, *(4)* -им, *(5)* -ите, *(6)* -ат.

есть *impf, present:* *(1)* е-м, *(2)* -шь, *(3)* -ст, *(4)* -ди́м, *(5)* -ди́те, *(6)* -дя́т.

е́хать *impf, present:* *(1)* е́д-у, *(2)* -ешь, *(3)* -ет, *(4)* -ем, *(5)* -ете, *(6)* -ут.

жа́ждать *impf, present:* *(1)* жа́жд-у, *(2)* -ешь, *(3)* -ет, *(4)* -ем, *(5)* -ете, *(6)* -ут.

жале́ть *impf, present:* *(1)* жале́-ю, *(2)* -ешь, *(3)* -ет, *(4)* -ем, *(5)* -ете, *(6)* -ют.

жа́рить *impf, present:* *(1)* жа́р-ю, *(2)* -ишь, *(3)* -ит, *(4)* -им, *(5)* -ите, *(6)* -ят.

ждать *impf present:* *(1)* жд-у, *(2)* -ёшь, *(3)* -ёт, *(4)* -ём, *(5)* -ёте, *(6)* -ут; *past:* ждал, ждала́, жда́л-о, -и.

жела́ть *impf, present:* *(1)* жела́-ю, *(2)* -ешь, *(3)* -ет, *(4)* -ем, *(5)* -ете, *(6)* -ют.

жени́ться *impf & pf, present & future:* *(1)* женю́сь, *(2)* же́н-ишься, *(3)* -ится, *(4)* -имся, *(5)* -итесь, *(6)* -ятся.

же́ртвовать *impf, present:* *(1)* же́ртву-ю, *(2)* -ешь, *(3)* -ет, *(4)* -ем, *(5)* -ете, *(6)* -ют.

жить *impf present:* *(1)* жив-у́, *(2)* -ёшь, *(3)* -ёт, *(4)* -ём, *(5)* -ёте, *(6)* -у́т.

жури́ть *impf, present:* *(1)* жур-ю́, *(2)* -и́шь, *(3)* -и́т, *(4)* -и́м, *(5)* -и́те, *(6)* -я́т.

журча́ть *impf, present:* *(1)* журч-у́, *(2)* -и́шь, *(3)* -и́т, *(4)* -и́м, *(5)* -и́те, *(6)* -а́т.

забавля́ть *impf, present:* *(1)* забавля́-ю, *(2)* -ешь, *(3)* -ет, *(4)* -ем, *(5)* -ете, *(6)* -ют.

забере́менеть *impf, present:* *(1)* забере́мене-ю, *(2)* -ешь, *(3)* -ет, *(4)* -ем, *(5)* -ете, *(6)* -ют.

заболе́ть *pf, future:* *(1)* заболе́-ю, *(2)* -ешь, *(3)* -ет, *(4)* -ем, *(5)* -ете, *(6)* -ют.

> *Persons:* 1 = я,   2 = ты,   3 = он, она́, оно́,   4 = мы,   5 = вы,   6 = они́

забо́титься *impf, present:* *(1)* забо́чусь, *(2)* забот-ишься, *(3)* -ится, *(4)* -имся, *(5)* -итесь, *(6)* -ятся.

заброни́ровать *pf, future:* *(1)* заброни́ру-ю, *(2)* -ешь, *(3)* -ет, *(4)* -ем, *(5)* -ете, *(6)* -ют.

забыва́ть *impf, present:* *(1)* забыва́-ю, *(2)* -ешь, *(3)* -ет, *(4)* -ем, *(5)* -ете, *(6)* -ют.

забы́ть *pf, future:* *(1)* забу́д-у, *(2)* -ешь, *(3)* -ет, *(4)* -ем, *(5)* -ете, *(6)* -ут.

заве́рить *pf, future:* *(1)* заве́р-ю, *(2)* -ишь, *(3)* -ит, *(4)* -им, *(5)* -ите, *(6)* -ят.

заверша́ть *impf, present:* *(1)* заверша́-ю, *(2)* -ешь, *(3)* -ет, *(4)* -ем, *(5)* -ете, *(6)* -ют.

заверши́ть *pf, future:* *(1)* заверш-у́, *(2)* -и́шь, *(3)* -и́т, *(4)* -и́м, *(5)* -и́те, *(6)* -а́т.

заверя́ть *impf, present:* *(1)* заверя́-ю, *(2)* -ешь, *(3)* -ет, *(4)* -ем, *(5)* -ете, *(6)* -ют.

завести́ *pf, future:* *(1)* завед-у́, *(2)* -ёшь, *(3)* -ёт, *(4)* -ём, *(5)* -ёте, *(6)* -у́т; *past:* завёл, завел-а́, -о́, -и́.

зави́довать *impf, present:* *(1)* зави́ду-ю, *(2)* -ешь, *(3)* -ет, *(4)* -ем, *(5)* -ете, *(6)* -ют.

завизжа́ть *pf, future:* *(1)* завизж-у́, *(2)* -ишь, *(3)* -ит, *(4)* -им, *(5)* -ите, *(6)* -ат.

завлека́ть *impf, present:* *(1)* завлека́-ю, *(2)* -ешь, *(3)* -ет, *(4)* -ем, *(5)* -ете, *(6)* -ют.

завле́чь *pf, future:* *(1)* завлеку́, *(2)* завлеч-ёшь, *(3)* -ёт, *(4)* -ём, *(5)* -ёте, *(6)* завлеку́т; *past:* завлёк, завлекл-а́, -о́, -и́.

заводи́ть *impf, present:* *(1)* завожу́, *(2)* заво́д-ишь, *(3)* -ит, *(4)* -им, *(5)* -ите, *(6)* -ят.

завоева́ть *pf, future:* *(1)* завою́-ю, *(2)* -ешь, *(3)* -ет, *(4)* -ем, *(5)* -ете, *(6)* -ют.

завоёвывать *impf, present:* *(1)* завоёвыва-ю, *(2)* -ешь, *(3)* -ет, *(4)* -ем, *(5)* -ете, *(6)* -ют.

завора́живать *impf, present:* *(1)* завора́жива-ю, *(2)* -ешь, *(3)* -ет, *(4)* -ем, *(5)* -ете, *(6)* -ют.

завopoжи́ть *pf, future:* *(1)* заворожу́, *(2)* -и́шь, *(3)* -и́т, *(4)* -и́м, *(5)* -и́те, *(6)* -а́т.

завяза́ть *pf, future:* *(1)* завяжу́, *(2)* завя́ж-ешь, *(3)* -ет, *(4)* -ем, *(5)* -ете, *(6)* -ут.

загипнотизи́ровать *pf, future:* *(1)* загипнотизи́ру-ю, *(2)* -ешь, *(3)* -ет, *(4)* -ем, *(5)* -ете, *(6)* -ют.

загла́дить *pf, future:* *(1)* загла́жу, *(2)* загла́д-ишь, *(3)* -ит, *(4)* -им, *(5)* -ите, *(6)* -ят.

загла́живать *impf, present:* *(1)* загла́жива-ю, *(2)* -ешь, *(3)* -ет, *(4)* -ем, *(5)* -ете, *(6)* -ют.

загора́ться *impf, present:* *(1)* загора́-юсь, *(2)* -ешься, *(3)* -ется, *(4)* -емся, *(5)* -етесь, *(6)* -ются.

загоре́ться *pf, future:* *(1)* загор-ю́сь, *(2)* -и́шься, *(3)* -и́тся, *(4)* -и́мся, *(5)* -и́тесь, *(6)* -я́тся.

зада́бривать *impf, present:* *(1)* зада́брива-ю, *(2)* -ешь, *(3)* -ет, *(4)* -ем, *(5)* -ете, *(6)* -ют.

задава́ть *impf present:* *(1)* зада-ю́, *(2)* -ёшь, *(3)* -ёт, *(4)* -ём, *(5)* -ёте, *(6)* -ю́т.

зада́ть *pf, future:* *(1)* зада́-м, *(2)* -шь, *(3)* -ст, *(4)* -дим, *(5)* -дите, *(6)* -дут.

задева́ть *impf, present:* *(1)* задева́-ю, *(2)* -ешь, *(3)* -ет, *(4)* -ем, *(5)* -ете, *(6)* -ют.

задержа́ть(ся) *pf, future:* *(1)* задержу́с(ь), *(2)* заде́рж-ишь(ся), *(3)* -ит(ся), *(4)* -им(ся), *(5)* -ите(сь), *(6)* -ат(ся).

заде́рживать(ся) *impf, present:* *(1)* заде́ржива-ю(сь), *(2)* -ешь(ся), *(3)* -ет(ся), *(4)* -ем(ся), *(5)* -ете(сь), *(6)* -ют(ся).

заде́ть *pf, future:* *(1)* заде́н-у, *(2)* -ешь, *(3)* -ет, *(4)* -ем, *(5)* -ете, *(6)* -ут.

задо́брить *pf, future:* *(1)* задо́бр-ю, *(2)* -ишь, *(3)* -ит, *(4)* -им, *(5)* -ите, *(6)* -ят.

задохну́ться *pf, future:* *(1)* задохн-у́сь, *(2)* -ёшься, *(3)* -ётся, *(4)* -ёмся, *(5)* -ётесь, *(6)* -у́тся.

заду́мать *pf, future:* *(1)* заду́ма-ю, *(2)* -ешь, *(3)* -ет, *(4)* -ем, *(5)* -ете, *(6)* -ют.

заду́мывать(ся) *impf, present:* *(1)* заду́мыва-ю(сь), *(2)* -ешь(ся), *(3)* -ет(ся), *(4)* -ем(ся), *(5)* -ете(сь), *(6)* -ют(ся).

задуши́ть *pf, future:* *(1)* задушу́, *(2)* заду́ш-ишь, *(3)* -ит, *(4)* -им, *(5)* -ите, *(6)* -ат.

задыха́ться *impf, present:* *(1)* задыха́-юсь, *(2)* -ешься, *(3)* -ется, *(4)* -емся, *(5)* -етесь, *(6)* -ются.

зае́хать *pf, future:* (1) зае́д-у, (2) -ешь, (3) -ет, (4) -ем, (5) -ете, (6) -ут.

зажа́ть *pf, future:* (1) зажм-у́, (2) -ёшь, (3) -ёт, (4) -ём, (5) -ёте, (6) -у́т.

заже́чь(ся) *pf, future:* (1) зажгу́(сь), (2) зажж-ёшь(ся), (3) -ёт(ся), (4) -ём(ся), (5) -ёте(сь), (6) зажгу́т(ся); *past:* зажёг(ся), зажг-ла́(сь), -ло́(сь), -ли́(сь).

зажига́ть(ся) *impf, present:* (1) зажига́-ю(сь), (2) -ешь(ся), (3) -ет(ся), (4) -ем(ся), (5) -ете(сь), (6) -ют(ся).

зажима́ть *impf, present:* (1) зажима́-ю, (2) -ешь, (3) -ет, (4) -ем, (5) -ете, (6) -ют.

заи́грывать *impf, present:* (1) заи́грыва-ю, (2) -ешь, (3) -ет, (4) -ем, (5) -ете, (6) -ют.

заика́ться *impf, present:* (1) заика́-юсь, (2) -ешься, (3) -ется, (4) -емся, (5) -етесь, (6) -ются.

заи́скивать *impf, present:* (1) заи́скива-ю, (2) -ешь, (3) -ет, (4) -ем, (5) -ете, (6) -ют.

заказа́ть *pf, future:* (1) закажу́, (2) зака́ж-ешь, (3) -ет, (4) -ем, (5) -ете, (6) -ут.

зака́зывать *impf, present:* (1) зака́зыва-ю, (2) -ешь, (3) -ет, (4) -ем, (5) -ете, (6) -ют.

заключа́ть *impf, present:* (1) заключа́-ю, (2) -ешь, (3) -ет, (4) -ем, (5) -ете, (6) -ют.

заключи́ть *pf, future:* (1) заключ-у́, (2) -и́шь, (3) -и́т, (4) -и́м, (5) -и́те, (6) -а́т.

заколдова́ть *pf, future:* (1) заколду́-ю, (2) -ешь, (3) -ет, (4) -ем, (5) -ете, (6) -ют.

заколдо́вывать *impf, present:* (1) заколдо́выва-ю, (2) -ешь, (3) -ет, (4) -ем, (5) -ете, (6) -ют.

заколоти́ться *pf, future:* (1) заколочу́сь, (2) заколо́т-ишься, (3) -ится, (4) -имся, (5) -итесь, (6) -ятся.

зако́нчить *pf, future:* (1) зако́нч-у, (2) -ишь, (3) -ит, (4) -им, (5) -ите, (6) -ат.

зако́нчиться *pf, future:* (3) зако́нч-ится, (6) -атся.

закружи́ть(ся) *pf, future:* (1) закружу́(сь), (2) закру́ж-ишь(ся), (3) -ит(ся), (4) -им(ся), (5) -ите(сь), (6) -ат(ся).

закрыва́ться *impf, present:* (1) закрыва́-юсь, (2) -ешься, (3) -ется, (4) -емся, (5) -етесь, (6) -ются.

закры́ться *pf, future:* (1) закро́-юсь, (2) -ешься, (3) -ется, (4) -емся, (5) -етесь, (6) -ются.

залеза́ть *impf, present:* (1) залеза́-ю, (2) -ешь, (3) -ет, (4) -ем, (5) -ете, (6) -ют.

зале́зть *pf, future:* (1) зале́з-у, (2) -ешь, (3) -ет, (4) -ем, (5) -ете, (6) -ут.

зале́чивать *impf, present:* (1) зале́чива-ю, (2) -ешь, (3) -ет, (4) -ем, (5) -ете, (6) -ют.

залечи́ть *pf, future:* (1) залеч-у́, (2) зале́ч-ишь, (3) -ит, (4) -им, (5) -ите, (6) -ат.

залива́ть(ся) *impf, present:* (1) залива́-ю(сь), (2) -ешь(ся), (3) -ет(ся), (4) -ем(ся), (5) -ете(сь), (6) -ют(ся).

зали́ть(ся) *pf, future:* (1) заль-ю́(сь), (2) -ёшь(ся), (3) -ёт(ся), (4) -ём(ся), (5) -ёте(сь), (6) -ю́т(ся); *past:* зали́л(ся), залила́(сь), зали́-ло(сь), -ли́(сь).

зама́нивать *impf, present:* (1) зама́нива-ю, (2) -ешь, (3) -ет, (4) -ем, (5) -ете, (6) -ют.

замани́ть *pf, future:* (1) заманю́, (2) зама́н-ишь, (3) -ит, (4) -им, (5) -ите, (6) -ят.

замаскирова́ть *pf, future:* (1) замаскиру́-ю, (2) -ешь, (3) -ет, (4) -ем, (5) -ете, (6) -ют.

замере́ть *pf, future:* (1) замр-у́, (2) -ёшь, (3) -ёт, (4) -ём, (5) -ёте, (6) -у́т; *past:* за́мер, замерла́, замер-ло́, -ли́.

замерза́ть *impf, present:* (1) замерза́-ю, (2) -ешь, (3) -ет, (4) -ем, (5) -ете, (6) -ют.

замёрзнуть *pf, future:* (1) замёрзн-у, (2) -ешь, (3) -ет, (4) -ем, (5) -ете, (6) -ут.

заме́тить *pf, future:* (1) заме́чу, (2) заме́т-ишь, (3) -ит, (4) -им, (5) -ите, (6) -ят.

замеча́ть *impf, present:* (1) замеча́-ю, (2) -ешь, (3) -ет, (4) -ем, (5) -ете, (6) -ют.

замира́ть *impf, present:* (1) замира́-ю, (2) -ешь, (3) -ет, (4) -ем, (5) -ете, (6) -ют.

замолча́ть *pf, future:* (1) замолч-у́, (2) -и́шь, (3) -и́т, (4) -и́м, (5) -и́те, (6) -а́т.

замыка́ться *impf, present:* (1) замыка́-юсь, (2) -ешься, (3) -ется, (4) -емся, (5) -етесь, (6) -ются.

Persons: 1 = я,   2 = ты,   3 = он, она́, оно́,   4 = мы,   5 = вы,   6 = они́

занима́ть *impf, present:* *(1)* занима́-ю, *(2)* -ешь, *(3)* -ет, *(4)* -ем, *(5)* -ете, *(6)* -ют.

занима́ть(ся) *impf, present:* *(1)* занима́-ю(сь), *(2)* -ешь(ся), *(3)* -ет(ся), *(4)* -ем(ся), *(5)* -ете(сь), *(6)* -ют(ся).

заня́ть *pf, future:* *(1)* займ-у́, *(2)* -ёшь, *(3)* -ёт, *(4)* -ём, *(5)* -ёте, *(6)* -у́т.

заня́ться *pf, future:* *(1)* займ-у́сь, *(2)* -ёшься, *(3)* -ётся, *(4)* -ёмся, *(5)* -ётесь, *(6)* -у́тся.

запере́ть(ся) *pf, future:* *(1)* запр-у́(сь), *(2)* -ёшь(ся), *(3)* -ёт(ся), *(4)* -ём(ся), *(5)* -ёте(сь), *(6)* -у́т(ся); *past:* за́пер(ся), заперла́(сь), за́пер-ло(сь), -ли(сь).

запеча́тать *pf, future:* *(1)* запеча́та-ю, *(2)* -ешь, *(3)* -ет, *(4)* -ем, *(5)* -ете, *(6)* -ют.

запеча́тывать *impf, present:* *(1)* запеча́тыва-ю, *(2)* -ешь, *(3)* -ет, *(4)* -ем, *(5)* -ете, *(6)* -ют.

запина́ться *impf, present:* *(1)* запина́-юсь, *(2)* -ешься, *(3)* -ется, *(4)* -емся, *(5)* -етесь, *(6)* -ются.

запира́ть(ся) *impf, present:* *(1)* запира́-ю(сь), *(2)* -ешь(ся), *(3)* -ет(ся), *(4)* -ем(ся), *(5)* -ете(сь), *(6)* -ют(ся).

запла́кать *pf, future:* *(1)* запла́ч-у, *(2)* -ешь, *(3)* -ет, *(4)* -ем, *(5)* -ете, *(6)* -ут.

заплати́ть *pf, future:* *(1)* заплачу́, *(2)* запла́т-ишь, *(3)* -ит, *(4)* -им, *(5)* -ите, *(6)* -ят.

запну́ться *pf, future:* *(1)* запн-у́сь, *(2)* -ёшься, *(3)* -ётся, *(4)* -ёмся, *(5)* -ётесь, *(6)* -у́тся.

запо́лнить *pf, future:* *(1)* запо́лн-ю *(2)* -ишь, *(3)* -ит, *(4)* -им, *(5)* -ите, *(6)* -ят.

заполня́ть *impf, present:* *(1)* заполня́-ю, *(2)* -ешь, *(3)* -ет, *(4)* -ем, *(5)* -ете, *(6)* -ют.

запрети́ть *pf, future:* *(1)* запрещу́, *(2)* запрет-и́шь, *(3)* -и́т, *(4)* -и́м, *(5)* -и́те, *(6)* -я́т.

запреща́ть *impf, present:* *(1)* запреща́-ю, *(2)* -ешь, *(3)* -ет, *(4)* -ем, *(5)* -ете, *(6)* -ют.

запятна́ть *impf, present:* *(1)* запятна́-ю, *(2)* -ешь, *(3)* -ет, *(4)* -ем, *(5)* -ете, *(6)* -ют.

зараба́тывать *impf, present:* *(1)* зараба́тыва-ю, *(2)* -ешь, *(3)* -ет, *(4)* -ем, *(5)* -ете, *(6)* -ют.

зарабо́тать *pf, future:* *(1)* зарабо́та-ю, *(2)* -ешь, *(3)* -ет, *(4)* -ем, *(5)* -ете, *(6)* -ют.

зарыва́ться *impf, present:* *(1)* зарыва́-юсь, *(2)* -ешься, *(3)* -ется, *(4)* -емся, *(5)* -етесь, *(6)* -ются.

зары́ться *pf, future:* *(1)* заро́-юсь, *(2)* -ешься, *(3)* -ется, *(4)* -емся, *(5)* -етесь, *(6)* -ются.

заряди́ть *pf, future:* *(1)* заряжу́ *(2)* заряд-ишь, *(3)* -ит, *(4)* -им, *(5)* -ите, *(6)* -ят.

заряжа́ть *impf, present:* *(1)* заряжа́-ю, *(2)* -ешь, *(3)* -ет, *(4)* -ем, *(5)* -ете, *(6)* -ют.

заслу́живать *impf, present:* *(1)* заслу́жива-ю, *(2)* -ешь, *(3)* -ет, *(4)* -ем, *(5)* -ете, *(6)* -ют.

заслужи́ть *pf, future:* *(1)* заслужу́, *(2)* заслу́ж-ишь, *(3)* -ит, *(4)* -им, *(5)* -ите, *(6)* -ат.

засо́вывать *impf, present:* *(1)* засо́выва-ю, *(2)* -ешь, *(3)* -ет, *(4)* -ем, *(5)* -ете, *(6)* -ют.

засо́хнуть *pf, future:* *(1)* засо́хн-у, *(2)* -ешь, *(3)* -ет, *(4)* -ем, *(5)* -ете, *(6)* -ут; *past:* засох, -ла, -ло, -ли.

заста́вить *pf, future:* *(1)* заста́в-лю, *(2)* -ишь, *(3)* -ит, *(4)* -им, *(5)* -ите, *(6)* -ят.

заставля́ть *impf, present:* *(1)* заставля́-ю, *(2)* -ешь, *(3)* -ет, *(4)* -ем, *(5)* -ете, *(6)* -ют.

заста́ть *pf, future:* *(1)* заста́н-у, *(2)* -ешь, *(3)* -ет, *(4)* -ем, *(5)* -ете, *(6)* -ут.

застёгивать *impf, present:* *(1)* застёгива-ю, *(2)* -ешь, *(3)* -ет, *(4)* -ем, *(5)* -ете, *(6)* -ют.

застегну́ть *pf, future:* *(1)* застегн-у́, *(2)* -ёшь, *(3)* -ёт, *(4)* -ём, *(5)* -ёте, *(6)* -у́т.

засу́нуть *pf, future:* *(1)* засу́н-у, *(2)* -ешь, *(3)* -ет, *(4)* -ем, *(5)* -ете, *(6)* -ут.

засыпа́ть *impf, present:* *(1)* засыпа́-ю, *(2)* -ешь, *(3)* -ет, *(4)* -ем, *(5)* -ете, *(6)* -ют.

засы́пать *pf, future:* *(1)* засы́пл-ю, *(2)* -ешь, *(3)* -ет, *(4)* -ем, *(5)* -ете, *(6)* -ют.

засыха́ть *impf, present:* *(1)* засыха́-ю, *(2)* -ешь, *(3)* -ет, *(4)* -ем, *(5)* -ете, *(6)* -ют.

зата́ивать *impf, present:* *(1)* зата́ива-ю, *(2)* -ешь, *(3)* -ет, *(4)* -ем, *(5)* -ете, *(6)* -ют.

затаи́ть *pf, future:* *(1)* заста-ю́, *(2)* -и́шь, *(3)* -и́т, *(4)* -и́м, *(5)* -и́те, *(6)* -я́т.

затвердева́ть *impf, present:* *(1)* затвердева́-ю, *(2)* -ешь, *(3)* -ет, *(4)* -ем, *(5)* -ете, *(6)* -ют.

| *Persons:* 1 = я, 2 = ты, 3 = он, она́, оно́, 4 = мы, 5 = вы, 6 = они́ |

затверде́ть *pf, future:* (1) затверде́-ю, (2) -ешь, (3) -ет, (4) -ем, (5) -ете, (6) -ют.

затемни́ть *pf, future:* (1) затемн-ю́, (2) -и́шь, (3) -и́т, (4) -и́м, (5) -и́те, (6) -я́т.

затемня́ть *impf, present:* (1) затемня́-ю, (2) -ешь, (3) -ет, (4) -ем, (5) -ете, (6) -ют.

заткну́ть *pf, future:* (1) заткн- у́, (2) -ёшь, (3) -ёт, (4) -ём, (5) -ёте, (6) -у́т.

затми́ть *pf, future:* (1) not used, (2) затм-и́шь, (3) -и́т, (4) -и́м, (5) -и́те, (6) -я́т.

затмева́ть *impf, present:* (1) затмева́-ю, (2) -ешь, (3) -ет, (4) -ем, (5) -ете, (6) -ют.

затопи́ть *pf, future:* (1) затоплю́, (2) зато́п-ишь, (3) -ит, (4) -им, (5) -ите, (6) -ят.

затопи́ться *pf, future:* (3) зато́п-ится, (6) -ятся.

затопля́ть *impf, present:* (1) затопля́-ю, (2) -ешь, (3) -ет, (4) -ем, (5) -ете, (6) -ют.

затопля́ться *impf, present:* (3) затопля́-ется, (6) -ются.

затра́гивать *impf, present:* (1) затра́гива-ю, (2) -ешь, (3) -ет, (4) -ем, (5) -ете, (6) -ют.

затро́нуть *pf, future:* (1) затро́н-у, (2) -ешь, (3) -ет, (4) -ем, (5) -ете, (6) -ут.

затрудни́ть *pf, future:* (1) затрудн-ю́, (2) -и́шь, (3) -и́т, (4) -и́м, (5) -и́те, (6) -я́т.

затрудня́ть *impf, present:* (1) затрудня́-ю, (2) -ешь, (3) -ет, (4) -ем, (5) -ете, (6) -ют.

захвати́ть *pf, future:* (1) захвачу́, (2) захва́т-ишь, (3) -ит, (4) -им, (5) -ите, (6) -ят.

захва́тывать *impf, present:* (1) захва́тыва-ю, (2) -ешь, (3) -ет, (4) -ем, (5) -ете, (6) -ют.

захоте́ть *pf, future:* (1) захочу́, (2) захо́чешь, (3) захо́чет, (4) захот-и́м, (5)-и́те, (6) -я́т.

зача́ть *pf, future:* (1) зачн-у́, (2) -ёшь, (3) -ёт, (4) -ём, (5) -ёте, (6) -у́т; *fem past:* зачла́.

защити́ть *pf, future:* (1) защищу́, (2) защит-и́шь, (3) -и́т, (4) -и́м, (5) -и́те, (6) -я́т.

защища́ть *impf, present:* (1) защища́-ю, (2) -ешь, (3) -ет, (4) -ем, (5) -ете, (6) -ют.

заяви́ть *pf, future:* (1) заявлю́, (2) заяв-и́шь, (3) -и́т, (4) -и́м, (5) -и́те, (6) -я́т.

заявля́ть *impf, present:* (1) заявля́-ю, (2) -ешь, (3) -ет, (4) -ем, (5) -ете, (6) -ют.

звать *impf, present:* (1) зов-у́, (2) -ёшь, (3) -ёт, (4) -ём, (5) -ёте, (6) -у́т.

звони́ть *impf, present:* (1) звон-ю, (2) -ишь, (3) -ит, (4) -им, (5) -ите, (6) -ят.

звуча́ть *impf, present:* (3) звуч-и́т, (6) -а́т.

злить *impf, present:* (1) зл-ю, (2) -ишь, (3) -ит, (4) -им, (5) -и́те, (6) -ят.

злоупотреби́ть *pf, future:* (1) злоупотреб-лю́, (2) -и́шь, (3) -и́т, (4) -и́м, (5) -и́те, (6) -я́т.

злоупотребля́ть *impf, present:* (1) злоупотребля́-ю, (2) -ешь, (3) -ет, (4) -ем, (5) -ете, (6) -ют.

знако́мить(ся) *impf, present:* (1) знако́м-лю(сь), (2)-ишь(ся), (3) -ит(ся), (4) -им(ся), (5) -ите(сь), (6) -ят(ся).

знать *impf, present:* (1) зна́-ю, (2) -ешь, (3) -ет, (4) -ем, (5) -ете, (6) -ют.

зна́чить *impf, present:* (1) зна́ч-у, (2) -ишь, (3) -ит, (4) -им, (5) -ите, (6) -ат.

игнори́ровать *impf, present:* (1) игнори́ру-ю, (2) -ешь, (3) -ет, (4) -ем, (5) -ете, (6) -ют.

игра́ть *impf, present:* (1) игра́-ю, (2) -ешь, (3) -ет, (4) -ем, (5) -ете, (6) -ют.

идеализи́ровать *impf, present:* (1) идеализи́ру-ю, (2) -ешь, (3) -ет, (4) -ем, (5) -ете, (6) -ют.

идти́ *impf, present:* (1) ид-у́, (2) -ёшь, (3) -ёт, (4) -ём, (5) -ёте, (6) -у́т; *past:* шёл, шла, шло, шли.

избалова́ть *pf, future:* (1) избалу́-ю, (2) -ешь, (3) -ет, (4) -ем, (5) -ете, (6) -ют.

избега́ть *impf, present:* (1) избега́-ю, (2) -ешь, (3) -ет, (4) -ем, (5) -ете, (6) -ют.

избежа́ть *pf, future:* (1) избегу́, (2) избеж-и́шь, (3) -и́т, (4) -и́м, (5) -и́те, (6) избегу́т.

извая́ть *pf, future:* (1) извая́-ю, (2) -ешь, (3) -ет, (4) -ем, (5) -ете, (6) -ют.

изверга́ться *impf, present:* (3) изверга́-ется, (6) -ются.

извести́ть *pf, future:* (1) извещу́, (2) извест-и́шь, (3) -ит, (4) -им, (5) -ите, (6) -ят.

извеща́ть *impf, present:* (1) извеща́-ю, (2) -ешь, (3) -ет, (4) -ем, (5) -ете, (6) -ют.

извиня́ться *impf, present:* (1) извиня́-юсь, (2) -ешься, (3) -ется, (4) -емся, (5) -етесь,

(6) -ются.

извини́ться *pf, future: (1)* извин-ю́сь, *(2)* -и́шься, *(3)* -и́тся, *(4)* -и́мся, *(5)* -и́тесь, *(6)* -я́тся.

извлека́ть *impf, present: (1)* извлека́-ю, *(2)* -ешь, *(3)* -ет, *(4)* -ем, *(5)* -ете, *(6)* -ют.

извле́чь *pf, future: (1)* извлеку́, *(2)* извлеч-ёшь, *(3)* -ёт, *(4)* -ём, *(5)* -ёте, *(6)* извлеку́т; *past:* извлёк, извлекл-а́, -о́, -и́.

изводи́ть(ся) *impf, present: (1)* извожу́(сь), *(2)* изво́д-ишь(ся), *(3)* -ит(ся), *(4)* -им(ся), *(5)* -ите(сь), *(6)* -ят(ся).

изга́дить *pf, future: (1)* изга́ж-у, *(2)* изга́д-ишь, *(3)* -ит, *(4)* -им, *(5)* -ите, *(6)* -ят.

изга́живать *impf, present: (1)* изга́жива-ю, *(2)* -ешь, *(3)* -ет, *(4)* -ем, *(5)* -ете, *(6)* -ют.

изгиба́ть(ся) *impf, present: (1)* изгиба́-ю(сь), *(2)* -ешь(ся), *(3)* -ет(ся), *(4)* -ем(ся), *(5)* -ете(сь), *(6)* -ют(ся).

издава́ть *impf present: (1)* изда-ю́, *(2)* -ёшь, *(3)* -ёт, *(4)* -ём, *(5)* -ёте, *(6)* -ю́т.

изда́ть *pf, future: (1)* изда́-м, *(2)* -шь, *(3)* -ст, *(4)* -дим, *(5)* -дите, *(6)* -дут; *past:* изда́л, издала́, изда́л-о, -и.

изле́чивать *impf, present: (1)* изле́чива-ю, *(2)* -ешь, *(3)* -ет, *(4)* -ем, *(5)* -ете, *(6)* -ют.

излечи́ть *pf, future: (1)* излеч-у́, *(2)* изле́ч-ишь, *(3)* -ит, *(4)* -им, *(5)* -ите, *(6)* -ат.

излива́ть *impf, present: (1)* излива́-ю, *(2)* -ешь, *(3)* -ет, *(4)* -ем, *(5)* -ете, *(6)* -ют.

изли́ть *pf, future: (1)* изоль-ю́, *(2)* -ёшь, *(3)* -ёт, *(4)* -ём, *(5)* -ёте, *(6)* -ю́т; *past:* изли́л, излила́, изли́-ло, -ли.

излуча́ть *impf, present: (1)* излуча́-ю, *(2)* -ешь, *(3)* -ет, *(4)* -ем, *(5)* -ете, *(6)* -ют.

излучи́ть *pf, future: (1)* излуч-у́, *(2)* -и́шь, *(3)* -и́т, *(4)* -и́м, *(5)* -и́те, *(6)* -а́т.

измени́ть *pf, future: (1)* изменю́, *(2)* изме́н-ишь, *(3)* -ит, *(4)* -им, *(5)* -ите, *(6)* -ят.

изменя́ть *impf, present: (1)* изменя́-ю, *(2)* -ешь, *(3)* -ет, *(4)* -ем, *(5)* -ете, *(6)* -ют.

изме́рить *pf, future: (1)* изме́р-ю, *(2)* -ишь, *(3)* -ит, *(4)* -им, *(5)* -ите, *(6)* -ят.

измеря́ть *impf, present: (1)* измеря́-ю, *(2)* -ешь, *(3)* -ет, *(4)* -ем, *(5)* -ете, *(6)* -ют.

изнаси́ловать *pf, future: (1)* изнаси́лу-ю, *(2)* -ешь, *(3)* -ет, *(4)* -ем, *(5)* -ете, *(6)* -ют.

изне́живать *impf, present: (1)* изне́жива-ю, *(2)* -ешь, *(3)* -ет, *(4)* -ем, *(5)* -ете, *(6)* -ют.

изне́жить *pf, future: (1)* изне́ж-у, *(2)* -ишь, *(3)* -ит, *(4)* -им, *(5)* -ите, *(6)* -ат.

изоби́ловать *impf, present: (3)* -ет, *(6)* -ют.

изобража́ть *impf, present: (1)* изобража́-ю, *(2)* -ешь, *(3)* -ет, *(4)* -ем, *(5)* -ете, *(6)* -ют.

изобрази́ть *pf, future: (1)* изображу́, *(2)* изобраз-и́шь, *(3)* -и́т, *(4)* -и́м, *(5)* -и́те, *(6)* -я́т.

изогну́ть(ся) *pf, future: (1)* изогн-у́(сь), *(2)* -ёшь(ся), *(3)* -ёт(ся), *(4)* -ём(ся), *(5)* -ёте(сь), *(6)* -у́т(ся).

изуми́ть *pf, future: (1)* изумлю́, *(2)* изум-и́шь, *(3)* -и́т, *(4)* -и́м, *(5)* -и́те, *(6)* -я́т.

изумля́ть *impf, present: (1)* изумля́-ю, *(2)* -ешь, *(3)* -ет, *(4)* -ем, *(5)* -ете, *(6)* -ют.

изуча́ть *impf, present: (1)* изуча́-ю, *(2)* -ешь, *(3)* -ет, *(4)* -ем, *(5)* -ете, *(6)* -ют.

изучи́ть *pf, future: (1)* изучу́, *(2)* изу́ч-ишь, *(3)* -ит, *(4)* -им, *(5)* -ите, *(6)* -ат.

име́ть *impf, present: (1)* име́-ю, *(2)* -ешь, *(3)* -ет, *(4)* -ем, *(5)* -ете, *(6)* -ют.

име́ться *impf, present: (1)* име́-юсь, *(2)* -ешься, *(3)* -ется, *(4)* -емся, *(5)* -етесь, *(6)* -ются.

интересова́ть(ся) *impf, present: (1)* интересу́-ю(сь), *(2)* -ешь(ся), *(3)* -ет(ся), *(4)* -ем(ся), *(5)* -ете(сь, *(6)* -ют(ся).

интригова́ть *impf, present: (1)* интригу́-ю, *(2)* -ешь, *(3)* -ет, *(4)* -ем, *(5)* -ете, *(6)* -ют.

иска́ть *impf, present: (1)* ищу́, *(2)* и́щ-ешь, *(3)* -ет, *(4)* -ем, *(5)* -ете, *(6)* -ут.

искри́ться *impf, present: (3)* искр-и́тся, *(6)* -я́тся.

искуша́ть *impf, present: (1)* искуша́-ю, *(2)* -ешь, *(3)* -ет, *(4)* -ем, *(5)* -ете, *(6)* -ют.

искуси́ть *pf, future: (1)* искушу́, *(2)* иску́с-ишь, *(3)* -ит, *(4)* -им, *(5)* -ите, *(6)* -ят.

испо́лнить *pf, future: (1)* испо́лн-ю, *(2)* -ишь, *(3)* -ит, *(4)* -им, *(5)* -ите, *(6)* -ят.

исполня́ть *impf, present:* *(1)* исполня́-ю, *(2)* -ешь, *(3)* -ет, *(4)* -ем, *(5)* -ете, *(6)* -ют.

испо́льзовать *impf & pf, present & future:* *(1)* испо́льзу-ю, *(2)* -ешь, *(3)* -ет, *(4)* -ем, *(5)* -ете, *(6)* -ют.

испо́ртить *pf, future:* *(1)* испо́рчу, *(2)* испо́рт-ишь, *(3)* -ит, *(4)* -им, *(5)* -ите, *(6)* -ят.

испра́вить *pf, future:* *(1)* испра́в-лю, *(2)* -ишь, *(3)* -ит, *(4)* -им, *(5)* -ите, *(6)* -ят.

исправля́ть *impf, present:* *(1)* исправля́-ю, *(2)* -ешь, *(3)* -ет, *(4)* -ем, *(5)* -ете, *(6)* -ют.

испуга́ть(ся) *pf, future:* *(1)* испуга́-ю(сь), *(2)* -ешь(ся), *(3)* -ет(ся), *(4)* -ем(ся), *(5)* -ете(сь), *(6)* -ют(ся).

испуска́ть *impf, present:* *(1)* испуска́-ю, *(2)* -ешь, *(3)* -ет, *(4)* -ем, *(5)* -ете, *(6)* -ют.

испусти́ть *pf, future:* *(1)* испущу́, *(2)* испу́ст-ишь, *(3)* -ит, *(4)* -им, *(5)* -ите, *(6)* -ят.

испыта́ть *pf, future:* *(1)* испыта́-ю, *(2)* -ешь, *(3)* -ет, *(4)* -ем, *(5)* -ете, *(6)* -ют.

испы́тывать *impf, present:* *(1)* испы́тыва-ю, *(2)* -ешь, *(3)* -ет, *(4)* -ем, *(5)* -ете, *(6)* -ют.

иссле́довать *impf, present:* *(1)* иссле́ду-ю, *(2)* -ешь, *(3)* -ет, *(4)* -ем, *(5)* -ете, *(6)* -ют.

исстрада́ться *pf, future:* *(1)* исстрада́-юсь, *(2)* -ешься, *(3)* -ется, *(4)* -емся, *(5)* -етесь, *(6)* -ются.

истолкова́ть *pf, future:* *(1)* истолку́-ю, *(2)* -ешь, *(3)* -ет, *(4)* -ем, *(5)* -ете, *(6)* -ют.

истолко́вывать *impf, present:* *(1)* истолко́выва-ю, *(2)* -ешь, *(3)* -ет, *(4)* -ем, *(5)* -ете, *(6)* -ют.

истра́тить *pf, future:* *(1)* истра́чу, *(2)* истра́т-ишь, *(3)* -ит, *(4)* -им, *(5)* -ите, *(6)* -ят.

исходи́ть *impf, present:* *(1)* исхожу́, *(2)* исхо́д-ишь, *(3)* -ит, *(4)* -им, *(5)* -ите, *(6)* -ят.

исчеза́ть *impf, present:* *(1)* исчеза́-ю, *(2)* -ешь, *(3)* -ет, *(4)* -ем, *(5)* -ете, *(6)* -ют.

исче́знуть *pf, future:* *(1)* исче́зн-у, *(2)* -ешь, *(3)* -ет, *(4)* -ем, *(5)* -ете, *(6)* -ут; *past:* исчез, -ла, -ло, -ли.

каза́ться *impf, present:* *(1)* кажу́сь, *(2)* ка́ж-ешься, *(3)* -ется, *(4)* -емся, *(5)* -етесь, *(6)* -утся.

капитули́ровать *impf & pf, present & future:* *(1)* капитули́ру-ю, *(2)* -ешь, *(3)* -ет, *(4)* -ем, *(5)* -ете, *(6)* -ют.

капри́зничать *impf, present:* *(1)* капри́знича-ю, *(2)* -ешь, *(3)* -ет, *(4)* -ем, *(5)* -ете, *(6)* -ют.

каса́ться *impf, present:* *(1)* каса́-юсь, *(2)* -ешься, *(3)* -ется, *(4)* -емся, *(5)* -етесь, *(6)* -ются.

ката́ться *impf, present:* *(1)* ката́-юсь, *(2)* -ешься, *(3)* -ется, *(4)* -емся, *(5)* -етесь, *(6)* -ются.

кати́ться *impf, present:* *(1)* качу́сь, *(2)* ка́т-ишься, *(3)* -ится, *(4)* -имся, *(5)* -итесь, *(6)* -ятся.

кача́ть *impf, present:* *(1)* кача́-ю, *(2)* -ешь, *(3)* -ет, *(4)* -ем, *(5)* -ете, *(6)* -ют.

качну́ть *pf, future:* *(1)* качн-у́, *(2)* -ёшь, *(3)* -ёт, *(4)* -ём, *(5)* -ёте, *(6)* -у́т.

класть *impf, present:* *(1)* клад-у́, *(2)* -ёшь, *(3)* -ёт, *(4)* -ём, *(5)* -ёте, *(6)* -у́т.

клокота́ть *impf, present:* *(1)* клокочу́, *(2)* клоко́ч-ешь, *(3)* -ет, *(4)* -ем, *(5)* -ете, *(6)* -ут.

кля́сться *impf, present:* *(1)* клян-у́сь, *(2)* -ёшься, *(3)* -ётся, *(4)* -ёмся, *(5)* -ётесь, *(6)* -у́тся; *past:* кля́лся, клял-а́сь, -о́сь, -и́сь.

коке́тничать *impf, present:* *(1)* коке́тнича-ю, *(2)* -ешь, *(3)* -ет, *(4)* -ем, *(5)* -ете, *(6)* -ют.

колеба́ться *impf, present:* *(1)* коле́бл-юсь, *(2)* -ешься, *(3)* -ется, *(4)* -емся, *(5)* -етесь, *(6)* -ются.

колоти́ться *impf, present:* *(1)* колочу́сь, *(2)* коло́т-ишься, *(3)* -ится, *(4)* -имся, *(5)* -итесь, *(6)* -ятся.

колыха́ться *impf, present:* *(1)* колы́ш-усь, *(2)* -ешься, *(3)* -ется, *(4)* -емся, *(5)* -етесь, *(6)* -утся.

контроли́ровать *impf, present:* *(1)* контроли́ру-ю, *(2)* -ешь, *(3)* -ет, *(4)* -ем, *(5)* -ете,

---

Persons: 1 = я,   2 = ты,   3 = он, она́, оно́,   4 = мы,   5 = вы,   6 = они́

---

(6) -ют.

конфу́зиться *impf, present:* *(1)* конфу́жусь, *(2)* конфу́з-ишься, *(3)* -ится, *(4)* -имся, *(5)* -итесь, *(6)* -ятся.

концентри́роваться *impf, present:* *(1)* концентри́ру-юсь, *(2)* -ешься, *(3)* -ется, *(4)* -емся, *(5)* -етесь, *(6)* -ются.

конча́ться *impf, present:* *(3)* конча́-ется, *(6)* -ются.

ко́нчить *pf, future:* *(1)* ко́нч-у, *(2)* -ишь, *(3)* -ит, *(4)* -им, *(5)* -ите, *(6)* -ат.

ко́нчиться *pf, future:* *(3)* ко́нч-ится, *(6)* -атся.

корми́ть *impf, present:* *(1)* кормлю́, *(2)* ко́рм-ишь, *(3)* -ит, *(4)* -им, *(5)* -ите, *(6)* -ят.

ко́рчиться *impf, present:* *(1)* ко́рч-усь, *(2)* -ишься, *(3)* -ится, *(4)* -имся, *(5)* -итесь, *(6)* -атся.

косну́ться *pf, future:* *(1)* косн-у́сь, *(2)* -ёшься, *(3)* -ётся, *(4)* -ёмся, *(5)* -ётесь, *(6)* -у́тся.

костене́ть *impf, present:* *(1)* костене́-ю, *(2)* -ешь, *(3)* -ет, *(4)* -ем, *(5)* -ете, *(6)* -ют.

красне́ть *impf, present:* *(1)* красне́-ю, *(2)* -ешь, *(3)* -ет, *(4)* -ем, *(5)* -ете, *(6)* -ют.

красть *impf, present:* *(1)* крад-у́, *(2)* -ёшь, *(3)* -ёт, *(4)* -ём, *(5)* -ёте, *(6)* -у́т; *past:* кра-л, -ла́, -ло́, -ли́.

кри́кнуть *pf, future:* *(1)* кри́кн-у, *(2)* -ешь, *(3)* -ет, *(4)* -ем, *(5)* -ете, *(6)* -ут.

критикова́ть *impf, present:* *(1)* критику́-ю, *(2)* -ешь, *(3)* -ет, *(4)* -ем, *(5)* -ете, *(6)* -ют.

крича́ть *impf, present:* *(1)* крич-у́, *(2)* -и́шь, *(3)* -и́т, *(4)* -и́м, *(5)* -и́те, *(6)* -а́т.

кружи́ть(ся) *impf, present:* *(1)* круж-у́(сь), *(2)* -и́шь(ся), *(3)* -и́т(ся), *(4)* -и́м(ся), *(5)* -и́те(сь), *(6)* -а́т(ся).

крути́ть(ся) *impf, present:* *(1)* кручу́(сь), *(2)* кру́т-ишь(ся), *(3)* -ит(ся), *(4)* -им(ся), *(5)* -ите(сь), *(6)* -ят(ся).

купа́ть *impf, present:* *(1)* купа́-ю, *(2)* -ешь, *(3)* -ет, *(4)* -ем, *(5)* -ете, *(6)* -ют.

купи́ть *pf, future:* *(1)* куплю́, *(2)* ку́п-ишь, *(3)* -ит, *(4)* -им, *(5)* -ите, *(6)* -ят.

куса́ть *impf, present:* *(1)* куса́-ю, *(2)* -ешь, *(3)* -ет, *(4)* -ем, *(5)* -ете, *(6)* -ют.

кути́ть *impf, present:* *(1)* кучу́, *(2)* ку́т-ишь, *(3)* -ит, *(4)* -им, *(5)* -ите, *(6)* -ят.

ла́дить *impf, present:* *(1)* ла́жу, *(2)* ла́д-ишь, *(3)* -ит, *(4)* -им, *(5)* -ите, *(6)* -ят.

ла́комиться *impf, present:* *(1)* ла́ком-люсь, *(2)* -ишься, *(3)* -ится, *(4)* -имся, *(5)* -итесь, *(6)* -ятся.

ла́пать *impf, present:* *(1)* ла́па-ю, *(2)* -ешь, *(3)* -ет, *(4)* -ем, *(5)* -ете, *(6)* -ют.

ласка́ть *impf, present:* *(1)* ласка́-ю, *(2)* -ешь, *(3)* -ет, *(4)* -ем, *(5)* -ете, *(6)* -ют.

лгать *impf, present:* *(1)* лгу, *(2)* лж-ёшь, *(3)* -ёт, *(4)* -ём, *(5)* -ёте, *(6)* лгут; *past:* лгал, лгала́, лга́-ло, -ли.

ледене́ть *impf, present:* *(1)* ледене́-ю, *(2)* -ешь, *(3)* -ет, *(4)* -ем, *(5)* -ете, *(6)* -ют.

лежа́ть *impf, present:* *(1)* леж-у́, *(2)* -и́шь, *(3)* -и́т, *(4)* -и́м, *(5)* -и́те, *(6)* -а́т.

лезть *impf, present:* *(1)* ле́з-у, *(2)* -ешь, *(3)* -ет, *(4)* -ем, *(5)* -ете, *(6)* -ут; *past:* лез, -ла, -ло, -ли.

леле́ять *impf, present:* *(1)* леле́-ю, *(2)* -ешь, *(3)* -ет, *(4)* -ем, *(5)* -ете, *(6)* -ют.

лентя́йничать *impf, present:* *(1)* лентя́йнича-ю, *(2)* -ешь, *(3)* -ет, *(4)* -ем, *(5)* -ете, *(6)* -ют.

лечь *pf, future:* *(1)* ля́гу, *(2)* ля́ж-ешь, *(3)* -ет, *(4)* -ем, *(5)* -ете, *(6)* ля́гут; *past:* лёг, легла́, -ло́, -ли́.

лиза́ть *impf, present:* *(1)* лижу́, *(2)* ли́ж-ешь, *(3)* -ет, *(4)* -ем, *(5)* -ете, *(6)* -ут.

ликова́ть *impf, present:* *(1)* лику́-ю, *(2)* -ешь, *(3)* -ет, *(4)* -ем, *(5)* -ете, *(6)* -ют.

ли́пнуть *impf, present:* *(1)* ли́пн-у, *(2)* -ешь, *(3)* -ет, *(4)* -ем, *(5)* -ете, *(6)* -ут; *past:* ли́пнул, ли́п-ла,-ло, -ли.

ли́ться *impf, present:* *(3)* ль-ётся, *(6)* -ю́тся; *past:* ли́лся, лил-а́сь, ли́л-ось, -ись.

лицеме́рить *impf, present:* *(1)* лицеме́р-ю, *(2)* -ишь, *(3)* -ит, *(4)* -им, *(5)* -ите, *(6)* -ят.

Persons: 1 = я, 2 = ты, 3 = он, она́, оно́, 4 = мы, 5 = вы, 6 = они́

лиши́ться *pf, future:* *(1)* лиш-у́сь, *(2)* -и́шься, *(3)* -и́тся, *(4)* -и́мся, *(5)* -и́тесь, *(6)* -а́тся.

лови́ть *impf, present:* *(1)* ловлю́, *(2)* ло́в-ишь, *(3)* -ит, *(4)* -им, *(5)* -ите, *(6)* -ят.

ложи́ться *impf, present:* *(1)* лож-у́сь, *(2)* -и́шься, *(3)* -и́тся, *(4)* -и́мся, *(5)* -и́тесь, *(6)* -а́тся.

лома́ть *impf, present:* *(1)* лома́-ю, *(2)* -ешь, *(3)* -ет, *(4)* -ем, *(5)* -ете, *(6)* -ют.

лучи́ться *impf, present:* *(3)* луч-и́тся, *(6)* -а́тся.

льнуть *impf, present:* *(1)* льн-у, *(2)* -ёшь, *(3)* -ёт, *(4)* -ём, *(5)* -ёте, *(6)* -ут.

льстить *impf, present:* *(1)* льщу, *(2)* льст-ишь, *(3)* -ит, *(4)* -им, *(5)* -ите, *(6)* -ят.

люби́ть *impf, present:* *(1)* люблю́, *(2)* лю́б-ишь, *(3)* -ит, *(4)* -им, *(5)* -ите, *(6)* -ят.

любова́ться *impf, present:* *(1)* любу́-юсь, *(2)* -ешься, *(3)* -ется, *(4)* -емся, *(5)* -етесь, *(6)* -ются.

манипули́ровать *impf, present:* *(1)* манипули́ру-ю, *(2)* -ешь, *(3)* -ет, *(4)* -ем, *(5)* -ете, *(6)* -ют.

мани́ть *impf, present:* *(1)* маню́, *(2)* ма́н-ишь, *(3)* -ит, *(4)* -им, *(5)* -ите, *(6)* -ят.

маскирова́ть *impf, present:* *(1)* маскиру́-ю, *(2)* -ешь, *(3)* -ет, *(4)* -ем, *(5)* -ете, *(6)* -ют.

массажи́ровать *impf, present:* *(1)* массажи́ру-ю, *(2)* -ешь, *(3)* -ет, *(4)* -ем, *(5)* -ете, *(6)* -ют.

мастурби́ровать *impf, present:* *(1)* мастурби́ру-ю, *(2)* -ешь, *(3)* -ет, *(4)* -ем, *(5)* -ете, *(6)* -ют.

медити́ровать *impf, present:* *(1)* медити́ру-ю, *(2)* -ешь, *(3)* -ет, *(4)* -ем, *(5)* -ете, *(6)* -ют.

ме́длить *impf, present:* *(1)* ме́дл-ю, *(2)* -ишь, *(3)* -ит, *(4)* -им, *(5)* -ите, *(6)* -ят.

меня́ть *impf, present:* *(1)* меня́-ю, *(2)* -ешь, *(3)* -ет, *(4)* -ем, *(5)* -ете, *(6)* -ют.

мёрзнуть *impf, present:* *(1)* мёрзн-у, *(2)* -ешь, *(3)* -ет, *(4)* -ем, *(5)* -ете, *(6)* -ут.

ме́ркнуть *impf, present:* *(3)* ме́ркн-ет, *(6)* -ут.

мерца́ть *impf, present:* *(3)* мерца́-ет, *(6)* -ют.

мести́ *impf, present:* *(1)* мет-у́, *(2)* -ёшь, *(3)* -ёт, *(4)* -ём, *(5)* -ёте, *(6)* -у́т; *past:* мёл, мела́, -ло́, -ли́.

мета́ться *impf, present:* *(1)* мета́-юсь, *(2)* -ешься, *(3)* -ется, *(4)* -емся, *(5)* -етесь, *(6)* -ются.

мечта́ть *impf, present:* *(1)* мечта́-ю, *(2)* -ешь, *(3)* -ет, *(4)* -ем, *(5)* -ете, *(6)* -ют.

меша́ть *impf, present:* *(1)* меша́-ю, *(2)* -ешь, *(3)* -ет, *(4)* -ем, *(5)* -ете, *(6)* -ют.

мига́ть *impf, present:* *(1)* мига́-ю, *(2)* -ешь, *(3)* -ет, *(4)* -ем, *(5)* -ете, *(6)* -ют.

мигну́ть *pf, future:* *(1)* мигн-у́, *(2)* -ёшь, *(3)* -ёт, *(4)* -ём, *(5)* -ёте, *(6)* -у́т.

мири́ться *impf, present:* *(1)* мирю́сь, *(2)* мир-ишься, *(3)* -ится, *(4)* -имся, *(5)* -итесь, *(6)* -ятся.

моли́ться *impf, present:* *(1)* молю́сь, *(2)* мо́л-ишься, *(3)* -ится, *(4)* -имся, *(5)* -итесь, *(6)* -ятся.

молча́ть *impf, present:* *(1)* молч-у́, *(2)* -и́шь, *(3)* -и́т, *(4)* -и́м, *(5)* -и́те, *(6)* -а́т.

морализова́ть *impf, present:* *(1)* морализу́-ю, *(2)* -ешь, *(3)* -ет, *(4)* -ем, *(5)* -ете, *(6)* -ют.

морга́ть *impf, present:* *(1)* морга́-ю, *(2)* -ешь, *(3)* -ет, *(4)* -ем, *(5)* -ете, *(6)* -ют.

моргну́ть *pf, future:* *(1)* моргн-у́, *(2)* -ёшь, *(3)* -ёт, *(4)* -ём, *(5)* -ёте, *(6)* -у́т.

мо́рщить *impf, present:* *(1)* мо́рщ-у, *(2)* -ишь, *(3)* -ит, *(4)* -им, *(5)* -ите, *(6)* -ат.

мочь *impf, present:* *(1)* могу́, *(2)* мо́ж-ешь, *(3)* -ет, *(4)* -ем, *(5)* -ете, *(6)* могут; *past:* мог, -ла́, -ло́, -ли́.

мурлы́кать *impf, present:* *(1)* мурлы́ка-ю, *(2)* -ешь, *(3)* -ет, *(4)* -ем, *(5)* -ете, *(6)* -ют.

му́чить(ся) *impf, present* **(2 conjugations):** *(1)* му́ч-у(сь) *or* -аю(сь), *(2)* -ишь(ся) *or* -аешь(ся), *(3)* -ит(ся) *or* -ает(ся), *(4)* -им(ся) *or* -аем(ся), *(5)* -ите(сь) *or* -аете(сь), *(6)*

> *Persons:* 1 = я,   2 = ты,   3 = он, она́, оно́,   4 = мы,   5 = вы,   6 = они́

-ат(ся) *or* -ают(ся).

мча́ться *impf, present:* *(1)* мч-усь, *(2)* -и́шься, *(3)* -и́тся, *(4)* -и́мся, *(5)* -и́тесь, *(6)* -а́тся.

мыть *impf, present:* *(1)* мо́-ю, *(2)* -ешь, *(3)* -ет, *(4)* -ем, *(5)* -ете, *(6)* -ют.

мя́кнуть *impf, present:* *(3)* мя́кн-ет,   *(6)* -ут; *past:* мя́кнул, мя́к-ла, -ло, -ли.

набира́ться *impf, present:* *(1)* набира́-юсь, *(2)* -ешься, *(3)* -ется, *(4)* -емся, *(5)* -етесь, *(6)* -ются.

наблюда́ть *impf, present:* *(1)* наблюда́-ю, *(2)* -ешь, *(3)* -ет, *(4)* -ем, *(5)* -ете, *(6)* -ют.

набра́сываться *impf, present:* *(1)* набра́сыва-юсь, *(2)* -ешься, *(3)* -ется, *(4)* -емся, *(5)* -етесь, *(6)* -ются.

набра́ться *pf, future:* *(1)* набер-у́сь, *(2)* -ёшься, *(3)* -ётся, *(4)* -ёмся, *(5)* -ётесь, *(6)* -у́тся; *past:* набра́лся, набрала́сь, набра́лось, набра́лись.

набро́ситься *pf, future:* *(1)* набро́шусь, *(2)* набро́с-ишься, *(3)* -ится, *(4)* -имся, *(5)* -итесь, *(6)* -ятся.

наводни́ть *pf, future:* *(1)* наводн-ю́ *(2)* -и́шь, *(3)* -и́т, *(4)* -и́м, *(5)* -и́те, *(6)* -я́т.

наводня́ть *impf, present:* *(1)* наводня́-ю, *(2)* -ешь, *(3)* -ет, *(4)* -ем, *(5)* -ете, *(6)* -ют.

надева́ть *impf, present:* *(1)* надева́-ю, *(2)* -ешь, *(3)* -ет, *(4)* -ем, *(5)* -ете, *(6)* -ют.

надели́ть *pf, future:* *(1)* надел-ю́ *(2)* -и́шь, *(3)* -и́т, *(4)* -и́м, *(5)* -и́те, *(6)* -я́т.

наделя́ть *impf, present:* *(1)* наделя́-ю, *(2)* -ешь, *(3)* -ет, *(4)* -ем, *(5)* -ете, *(6)* -ют.

наде́ть *pf, future:* *(1)* наде́н-у, *(2)* -ешь, *(3)* -ет, *(4)* -ем, *(5)* -ете, *(6)* -ут.

наде́яться *impf, present:* *(1)* наде́-юсь, *(2)* -ешься, *(3)* -ется, *(4)* -емся, *(5)* -етесь, *(6)* -ются.

надиви́ться *pf, future:* *(1)* надив-лю́сь, *(2)* -и́шься, *(3)* -и́тся, *(4)* -и́мся, *(5)* -и́тесь, *(6)* -я́тся.

надоеда́ть *impf, present:* *(1)* надоеда́-ю, *(2)* -ешь, *(3)* -ет, *(4)* -ем, *(5)* -ете, *(6)* -ют.

надое́сть *pf, future:* *(1)* надое́-м, *(2)* -шь, *(3)* -ст, *(4)* -дим, *(5)* -дите, *(6)* -дят.

надува́ть *impf, present:* *(1)* надува́-ю, *(2)* -ешь, *(3)* -ет, *(4)* -ем, *(5)* -ете, *(6)* -ют.

наду́ть *pf, future:* *(1)* наду́-ю, *(2)* -ешь, *(3)* -ет, *(4)* -ем, *(5)* -ете, *(6)* -ют.
-ют.

назва́ть *pf, future:* *(1)* назов-у́, *(2)* -ёшь, *(3)* -ёт, *(4)* -ём, *(5)* -ёте, *(6)* -у́т.

называ́ть *impf, present:* *(1)* называ́-ю, *(2)* -ешь, *(3)* -ет, *(4)* -ем, *(5)* -ете, *(6)* -ют.

найти́ *pf, future:* *(1)* найд-у́, *(2)* -ёшь, *(3)* -ёт, *(4)* -ём, *(5)* -ёте, *(6)* -у́т; *past:* нашёл, наш-ла́, -ло́, -ли́.

нака́пливаться *impf, present:* *(1)* нака́плива-юсь, *(2)* -ешься, *(3)* -ется, *(4)* -емся, *(5)* -етесь, *(6)* -ются.

наки́дывать *impf, present:* *(1)* наки́дыва-ю, *(2)* -ешь, *(3)* -ет, *(4)* -ем, *(5)* -ете, *(6)* -ют.

наки́нуть *pf, future:* *(1)* наки́н-у, *(2)* -ешь, *(3)* -ет, *(4)* -ем, *(5)* -ете, *(6)* -ут.

наклони́ть(ся) *pf, future:* *(1)* наклоню́(сь), *(2)* накло́н-ишь(ся), *(3)* -ит(ся), *(4)* -им(ся), *(5)* -ите(сь), *(6)* -ят(ся).

наклоня́ть(ся) *impf, present:* *(1)* наклоня́-ю(сь), *(2)* -ешь(ся), *(3)* -ет(ся), *(4)* -ем(ся), *(5)* -ете(сь), *(6)* -ют(ся).

накорми́ть *pf, future:* *(1)* накормлю́, *(2)* нако́рм-ишь, *(3)* -ит, *(4)* -им, *(5)* -ите, *(6)* -ят.

нала́дить *pf, future:* *(1)* нала́жу *(2)* нала́д-ишь, *(3)* -ит, *(4)* -им, *(5)* -ите, *(6)* -ят.

нала́живать *impf, present:* *(1)* нала́жива-ю, *(2)* -ешь, *(3)* -ет, *(4)* -ем, *(5)* -ете, *(6)* -ют.

нама́зать *pf, future:* *(1)* нама́ж-у, *(2)* -ешь, *(3)* -ет, *(4)* -ем, *(5)* -ете, *(6)* -ут.

нама́зывать *impf, present:* *(1)* нама́зыва-ю, *(2)* -ешь, *(3)* -ет, *(4)* -ем, *(5)* -ете, *(6)* -ют.

намека́ть *impf, present:* *(1)* намека́-ю, *(2)* -ешь, *(3)* -ет, *(4)* -ем, *(5)* -ете, *(6)* -ют.

намекну́ть *pf, future:* *(1)* намекн-у́, *(2)* -ёшь, *(3)* -ёт, *(4)* -ём, *(5)* -ёте, *(6)* -у́т.

намерева́ться *impf, present:* *(1)* намерева́-юсь, *(2)* -ешься, *(3)* -ется, *(4)* -емся, *(5)* -етесь, *(6)* -ются.

Persons: 1 = я, 2 = ты, 3 = он, она́, оно́, 4 = мы, 5 = вы, 6 = они́

намо́рщить *pf, future:* (1) намо́рщ-у, (2) -ишь, (3) -ит, (4) -им, (5) -ите, (6) -ат.

нанести́ *pf, future:* (1) нанес-у́, (2) -ёшь, (3) -ёт, (4) -ём, (5) -ёте, (6) -у́т; *past:* нанёс, нанес-ла́, -ло́, -ли́.

наноси́ть *impf, present:* (1) наношу́, (2) нано́с-ишь, (3) -ит, (4) -им, (5) -ите, (6) -ят.

напева́ть *impf, present:* (1) напева́-ю, (2) -ешь, (3) -ет, (4) -ем, (5) -ете, (6) -ют.

напе́ть *pf, future:* (1) напо-ю́, (2) -ёшь, (3) -ёт, (4) -ём, (5) -ёте, (6) -ю́т.

напеча́тать *pf, future:* (1) напечата-ю, (2) -ешь, (3) -ет, (4) -ем, (5) -ете, (6) -ют.

напива́ться *impf, present:* (1) напива́-юсь, (2) -ешься, (3) -ется, (4) -емся, (5) -етесь, (6) -ются.

написа́ть *pf, future:* (1) напишу́, (2) напи́ш-ешь, (3) -ет, (4) -ем, (5) -ете, (6) -ут.

напи́ться *pf, future:* (1) напь-ю́сь, (2) -ёшься, (3) -ётся, (4) -ёмся, (5) -ётесь, (6) -ю́тся; *past:* напи́лся, напила́сь, напи́-лось, -лись.

напои́ть *pf, future:* (1) напою́, (2) напо́-ишь, (3) -ит, (4) -им, (5) -ите, (6) -ят.

напо́лнить(ся) *pf, future:* (1) напо́лн-ю(сь), (2) -ишь(ся), (3) -ит(ся), (4) -им(ся), (5) -ите(сь), (6) -ят(ся).

наполня́ть(ся) *impf, present:* (1) наполня́-ю(сь), (2) -ешь(ся), (3) -ет(ся), (4) -ем(ся), (5) -ете(сь), (6) -ют(ся).

напра́вить *pf, future:* (1) напра́влю (2) напра́в-ишь, (3) -ит, (4) -им, (5) -ите, (6) -ят.

направля́ть *impf, present:* (1) направля́-ю, (2) -ешь, (3) -ет, (4) -ем, (5) -ете, (6) -ют.

нараста́ть *impf, present:* (3) нараста́-ет, (6) -ют.

нарасти́ *pf, future:* (3) нараст-ёт, (6) -у́т; *past:* наро́с,нарос -ла́, -ло́, -ли́.

нара́щиваться *impf, present:* (3) нара́щива-ется,(6) -ются.

нарисова́ть *pf, future:* (1) нарису́-ю, (2) -ешь, (3) -ет, (4) -ем, (5) -ете, (6) -ют.

наруша́ть *impf, present:* (1) наруша́-ю, (2) -ешь, (3) -ет, (4) -ем, (5) -ете, (6) -ют.

нару́шить *pf, future:* (1) нару́ш-у (2) -ишь, (3) -ит, (4) -им, (5) -ите, (6) -ат.

насви́стывать *impf, present:* (1) насви́стыва-ю, (2) -ешь, (3) -ет, (4) -ем, (5) -ете, (6) -ют.

наси́ловать *impf, present:* (1) наси́лу-ю, (2) -ешь, (3) -ет, (4) -ем, (5) -ете, (6) -ют.

наску́чить *pf, future:* (1) наску́ч-у (2) -ишь, (3) -ит, (4) -им, (5) -ите, (6) -ат.

наслажда́ться *impf, present:* (1) наслажда́-юсь, (2) -ешься, (3) -ется, (4) -емся, (5) -етесь, (6) -ются.

насмеха́ться *impf, present:* (1) насмеха́-юсь, (2) -ешься, (3) -ется, (4) -емся, (5) -етесь, (6) -ются.

наста́вить *pf, future:* (1) наста́в-лю, (2) -ишь, (3) -ит, (4) -им, (5) -ите, (6) -ят.

наставля́ть *impf, present:* (1) наставля́-ю, (2) -ешь, (3) -ет, (4) -ем, (5) -ете, (6) -ют.

наста́ивать *impf, present:* (1) наста́ива-ю, (2) -ешь, (3) -ет, (4) -ем, (5) -ете, (6) -ют.

настоя́ть *pf, future:* (1) насто-ю́ (2) -и́шь, (3) -и́т, (4) -и́м, (5) -и́те, (6) -я́т.

настра́ивать *impf, present:* (1) настраива-ю, (2) -ешь, (3) -ет, (4) -ем, (5) -ете, (6) -ют.

настро́ить *pf, future:* (1) настро́-ю, (2) -ишь, (3) -ит, (4) -им, (5) -ите, (6) -ят.

насы́титься *pf, future:* (1) насыщу́сь, (2) насы́т-ишься, (3) -ится, (4) -имся, (5) -итесь, (6) -ятся.

насыща́ть(ся) *impf, present:* (1) насыща́-ю(сь), (2) -ешь(ся), (3) -ет(ся), (4) -ем(ся), (5) -ете(сь), (6) -ют(ся).

натя́гивать *impf, present:* (1) натя́гива-ю, (2) -ешь, (3) -ет, (4) -ем, (5) -ете, (6) -ют.

натяну́ть *pf, future:* (1) натяну́, (2) натя́н-ешь, (3) -ет, (4) -ем, (5) -ете, (6) -ут.

научи́ть *pf, future:* (1) научу́, (2) нау́ч-ишь, (3) -ит, (4) -им, (5) -ите, (6) -ат.

научи́ться *pf, future:* (1) научу́сь, (2) нау́ч-ишься, (3) -ится, (4) -имся, (5) -итесь, (6) -атся.

маха́ть *impf, present:* (1) машу́, (2) ма́ш-ешь, (3) -ет, (4) -ем, (5) -ете, (6) -ут.

Persons: 1 = я, 2 = ты, 3 = он, она́, оно́, 4 = мы, 5 = вы, 6 = они́

нахлы́нуть *pf, future:* *(1)* нахлы́н-у, *(2)* -ешь, *(3)* -ет, *(4)* -ем, *(5)* -ете, *(6)* -ут.

нахму́риться *pf, future:* *(1)* нахму́р-юсь, *(2)* -ишься, *(3)* -ится, *(4)* -имся, *(5)* -итесь, *(6)* -ятся.

находи́ть(ся) *impf, present:* *(1)* нахожу́(сь), *(2)* нахо́д-ишь(ся), *(3)* -ит(ся), *(4)* -им(ся), *(5)* -ите(сь), *(6)* -ят(ся).

нача́ть *pf, future:* *(1)* начн-у́, *(2)* -ёшь, *(3)* -ёт, *(4)* -ём, *(5)* -ёте, *(6)* -у́т.

нача́ться *pf, future:* *(3)* начн-ется, *(6)* -утся.

начина́ть *impf, present:* *(1)* начина́-ю, *(2)* -ешь, *(3)* -ет, *(4)* -ем, *(5)* -ете, *(6)* -ют.

начина́ться *impf, present:* *(3)* начина-ется, *(6)* -ются.

нащу́пывать *impf, present:* *(1)* нащу́пыва-ю, *(2)* -ешь, *(3)* -ет, *(4)* -ем, *(5)* -ете, *(6)* -ют.

нерви́ровать *impf, present:* *(1)* нерви́ру-ю, *(2)* -ешь, *(3)* -ет, *(4)* -ем, *(5)* -ете, *(6)* -ют.

негодова́ть *impf, present:* *(1)* негоду́-ю, *(2)* -ешь, *(3)* -ет, *(4)* -ем, *(5)* -ете, *(6)* -ют.

недооце́нивать *impf, present:* *(1)* недооце́нива-ю, *(2)* -ешь, *(3)* -ет, *(4)* -ем, *(5)* -ете, *(6)* -ют.

недооцени́ть *pf, future:* *(1)* недооценю́, *(2)* недооце́н-ишь, *(3)* -ит, *(4)* -им, *(5)* -ите, *(6)* -ят.

недостава́ть *impf, present:(1)* недоста-ю́, *(2)* -ёшь , *(3)* -ёт, *(4)* -ём, *(5)* -ёте, *(6)* -ю́т.

не́жить(ся) *impf, present:* *(1)* не́ж-у(сь), *(2)* -ишь(ся), *(3)* -ит(ся), *(4)* -им(ся), *(5)* -ите(сь), *(6)* -ат(ся).

ненави́деть *impf, present:* *(1)* ненави́жу, *(2)* ненави́д-ишь, *(3)* -ит, *(4)* -им, *(5)* -ите, *(6)* -ят.

нерви́ровать *impf, present:* *(1)* нерви́ру-ю, *(2)* -ешь, *(3)* -ет, *(4)* -ем, *(5)* -ете, *(6)* -ют.

не́рвничать *impf, present:* *(1)* не́рвнича-ю, *(2)* -ешь, *(3)* -ет, *(4)* -ем, *(5)* -ете, *(6)* -ют.

нести́ *impf, present:* *(1)* нес-у́, *(2)* -ёшь, *(3)* -ёт, *(4)* -ём, *(5)* -ёте, *(6)* -у́т; *past:* нёс, несла́, -ло́, -ли́.

нести́сь *impf, present:* *(1)* нес-у́сь, *(2)* -ёшься, *(3)* -ётся, *(4)* -ёмся, *(5)* -ётесь, *(6)* -у́тся; *past:* нёсся, нес-ла́сь, -ло́сь, -ли́сь.

носи́ть *impf, present:* *(1)* ношу́, *(2)* но́с-ишь, *(3)* -ит, *(4)* -им, *(5)* -ите, *(6)* -ят.

нра́виться *impf, present:* *(1)* нра́в-люсь, *(2)* -ишься, *(3)* -ится, *(4)* -имся, *(5)* -итесь, *(6)* -ятся.

нужда́ться *impf, present:* *(1)* нужда́-юсь, *(2)* -ешься, *(3)* -ется, *(4)* -емся, *(5)* -етесь, *(6)* -ются.

нырну́ть *pf, future:* *(1)* нырн-у́, *(2)* -ёшь, *(3)* -ёт, *(4)* -ём, *(5)* -ёте, *(6)* -у́т.

ныря́ть *impf, present:* *(1)* ныря́-ю, *(2)* -ешь, *(3)* -ет, *(4)* -ем, *(5)* -ете, *(6)* -ют.

ныть *impf, present:* *(1)* но́-ю, *(2)* -ешь, *(3)* -ет, *(4)* -ем, *(5)* -ете, *(6)* -ют.

обвенча́ть *pf, future:* *(1)* обвенча́-ю, *(2)* -ешь, *(3)* -ет, *(4)* -ем, *(5)* -ете, *(6)* -ют.

обвива́ться *impf, present:* *(1)* обвива́-юсь, *(2)* -ешься, *(3)* -ется, *(4)* -емся, *(5)* -етесь, *(6)* -ются.

обви́ться *pf, future:* *(1)* обвь-ю́сь, *(2)* -ёшься, *(3)* -ётся, *(4)* -ёмся, *(5)* -ётесь, *(6)* -ю́тся; *past:* обви́лся, обвила́сь, обви́-лось, -лись.

обвини́ть *pf, future:* *(1)* обвин-ю́, *(2)* -и́шь, *(3)* -и́т, *(4)* -и́м, *(5)* -и́те, *(6)* -я́т.

обвиня́ть *impf, present:* *(1)* обвиня́-ю, *(2)* -ешь, *(3)* -ет, *(4)* -ем, *(5)* -ете, *(6)* -ют.

обвола́кивать *impf, present:* *(1)* обвола́кива-ю, *(2)* -ешь, *(3)* -ет, *(4)* -ем, *(5)* -ете, *(6)* -ют.

обвора́живать *impf, present:* *(1)* обвора́жива-ю, *(2)* -ешь, *(3)* -ет, *(4)* -ем, *(5)* -ете, *(6)* -ют.

обворожи́ть *pf, future:* *(1)* обворож-у́, *(2)* -ишь, *(3)* -ит, *(4)* -им, *(5)* -ите, *(6)* -ат.

обду́мать *pf, future:* *(1)* обду́ма-ю, *(2)* -ешь, *(3)* -ет, *(4)* -ем, *(5)* -ете, *(6)* -ют.

обду́мывать *impf, present:* *(1)* обду́мыва-ю, *(2)* -ешь, *(3)* -ет, *(4)* -ем, *(5)* -ете, *(6)* -ют.

Persons: 1 = я,   2 = ты,   3 = он, она́, оно́,   4 = мы,   5 = вы,   6 = они́

обе́дать *impf, present:* *(1)* обе́да-ю, *(2)* -ешь, *(3)* -ет, *(4)* -ем, *(5)* -ете, *(6)* -ют.

обезору́живать *impf, present:* *(1)* обезору́жива-ю, *(2)* -ешь, *(3)* -ет, *(4)* -ем, *(5)* -ете, *(6)* -ют.

обезу́меть *pf, future:* *(1)* обезу́ме-ю, *(2)* -ешь, *(3)* -ет, *(4)* -ем, *(5)* -ете, *(6)* -ют.

оберну́ться *pf, future:* *(1)* оберн-у́сь, *(2)* -ёшься, *(3)* -ётся, *(4)* -ёмся, *(5)* -ётесь, *(6)* -у́тся.

обескура́живать *impf, present:* *(1)* обескура́жива-ю, *(2)* -ешь, *(3)* -ет, *(4)* -ем, *(5)* -ете, *(6)* -ют.

обесси́ливать *impf, present:* *(1)* обесси́лива-ю, *(2)* -ешь, *(3)* -ет, *(4)* -ем, *(5)* -ете, *(6)* -ют.

обесси́лить *pf, future:* *(1)* обесси́л-ю, *(2)* -ишь, *(3)* -ит, *(4)* -им, *(5)* -ите, *(6)* -ат.

обеща́ть *impf, present:* *(1)* обеща́-ю, *(2)* -ешь, *(3)* -ет, *(4)* -ем, *(5)* -ете, *(6)* -ют.

обже́чь *pf, future:* *(1)* обожгу́, *(2)* обожж-ёшь, *(3)* -ёт, *(4)* -ём, *(5)* -ёте, *(6)* обожгу́т; *past:* обжёг, обожг-ла́, -ло́, -ли́.

обжига́ть *impf, present:* *(1)* обжига́-ю, *(2)* -ешь, *(3)* -ет, *(4)* -ем, *(5)* -ете, *(6)* -ют.

оби́деть(ся) *pf, future:* *(1)* оби́жу(сь), *(2)* оби́д-ишь(ся), *(3)* -ит(ся), *(4)* -им(ся), *(5)* -ите(сь), *(6)* -ят(ся).

обижа́ть(ся) *impf, present:* *(1)* обижа́-ю(сь), *(2)* -ешь(ся), *(3)* -ет(ся), *(4)* -ем(ся), *(5)* -ете(сь), *(6)* -ют(ся).

облада́ть *impf, present:* *(1)* облада́-ю, *(2)* -ешь, *(3)* -ет, *(4)* -ем, *(5)* -ете, *(6)* -ют.

облега́ть *impf, present:* *(1)* облега́-ю, *(2)* -ешь, *(3)* -ет, *(4)* -ем, *(5)* -ете, *(6)* -ют.

облегча́ть *impf, present:* *(1)* облегча́-ю, *(2)* -ешь, *(3)* -ет, *(4)* -ем, *(5)* -ете, *(6)* -ют.

облегчи́ть *pf, future:* *(1)* облегч-у́, *(2)* -и́шь, *(3)* -и́т, *(4)* -и́м, *(5)* -и́те, *(6)* -а́т.

обману́ть *pf, future:* *(1)* обману́, *(2)* обма́н-ешь, *(3)* -ет, *(4)* -ем, *(5)* -ете, *(6)* -ут.

обма́нывать *impf, present:* *(1)* обма́ныва-ю, *(2)* -ешь, *(3)* -ет, *(4)* -ем, *(5)* -ете, *(6)* -ют.

обме́ниваться *impf, present:* *(1)* обме́нива-юсь, *(2)* -ешься, *(3)* -ется, *(4)* -емся, *(5)* -етесь, *(6)* -ются.

обменя́ться *pf, future:* *(1)* обменя́-юсь, *(2)* -ешься, *(3)* -ется, *(4)* -емся, *(5)* -етесь, *(6)* -ются.

обнару́жить *pf, future:* *(1)* обнару́ж-у, *(2)* -ишь, *(3)* -ит, *(4)* -им, *(5)* -ите, *(6)* -ат.

обнару́живать *impf, present:* *(1)* обнару́жива-ю, *(2)* -ешь, *(3)* -ет, *(4)* -ем, *(5)* -ете, *(6)* -ют.

обнима́ть(ся) *impf, present:* *(1)* обнима́-ю(сь), *(2)* -ешь(ся), *(3)* -ет(ся), *(4)* -ем(ся), *(5)* -ете(сь), *(6)* -ют(ся).

обня́ть *pf, future:* *(1)* обниму́, *(2)* обни́м-ешь, *(3)* -ет, *(4)* -ем, *(5)* -ете, *(6)* -ут.

обня́ть(ся) *pf, future:* *(1)* обниму́(сь), *(2)* обни́м-ешь(ся), *(3)* -ет(ся), *(4)* -ем(ся), *(5)* -ете(сь), *(6)* -ут(ся); *past:* обня́л(ся), обнял-а́(сь), -ло́(сь), -ли́(сь).

обогаща́ть *impf, present:* *(1)* обогаща́-ю, *(2)* -ешь, *(3)* -ет, *(4)* -ем, *(5)* -ете, *(6)* -ют.

ободри́ть *pf, future:* *(1)* ободр-ю, *(2)* -и́шь, *(3)* -и́т, *(4)* -и́м, *(5)* -и́те, *(6)* -я́т.

ободря́ть *impf, present:* *(1)* ободря́-ю, *(2)* -ешь, *(3)* -ет, *(4)* -ем, *(5)* -ете, *(6)* -ют.

обожа́ть *impf, present:* *(1)* обожа́-ю, *(2)* -ешь, *(3)* -ет, *(4)* -ем, *(5)* -ете, *(6)* -ют.

обойти́сь *pf, future:* *(1)* обойд-у́сь, *(2)* -ёшься, *(3)* -ётся, *(4)* -ёмся, *(5)* -ётесь, *(6)* -у́тся; *past:* обошёлся, обо-шла́сь, -шло́сь, -шли́сь.

обольсти́ть *pf, future:* *(1)* обольщу́, *(2)* обольст-и́шь, *(3)* -и́т, *(4)* -и́м, *(5)* -и́те, *(6)* -я́т.

обольща́ть *impf, present:* *(1)* обольща́-ю, *(2)* -ешь, *(3)* -ет, *(4)* -ем, *(5)* -ете, *(6)* -ют.

обора́чиваться *impf, present:* *(1)* обора́чива-юсь, *(2)* -ешься, *(3)* -ется, *(4)* -емся, *(5)* -етесь, *(6)* -ются.

оборва́ть(ся) *pf, future:* *(1)* оборв-у́(сь), *(2)* -ёшь(ся), *(3)* -ёт(ся), *(4)* -ём(ся), *(5)* -ёте, *(6)* -у́т(ся); *past:* оборва́л(ся), оборвала́(сь), оборва́-ло(сь), -ли(сь).

обосно́вывать *impf, present:* *(1)* обосно́выва-ю, *(2)* -ешь, *(3)* -ет, *(4)* -ем, *(5)* -ете, *(6)* -ют.

обостри́ть *pf, future:* *(1)* обостр-ю́, *(2)* -и́шь, *(3)* -и́т, *(4)* -и́м, *(5)* -и́те, *(6)* -я́т.

обостря́ть *impf, present:* *(1)* обостря́-ю, *(2)* -ешь, *(3)* -ет, *(4)* -ем, *(5)* -ете, *(6)* -ют.

обрабо́тать *pf, future:* *(1)* обрабо́та-ю, *(2)* -ешь, *(3)* -ет, *(4)* -ем, *(5)* -ете, *(6)* -ют.

обра́довать(ся) *pf, future:* *(1)* обра́ду-ю(сь), *(2)* -ешь(ся), *(3)* -ет(ся), *(4)* -ем(ся), *(5)* -ете(сь), *(6)* -ют(ся).

обрати́ть(ся) *pf, future:* *(1)* обращу́(сь), *(2)* обрат-и́шь(ся), *(3)* -и́т(ся), *(4)* -и́м(ся), *(5)* -и́те(сь), *(6)* -я́т(ся).

обраща́ть(ся) *impf, present:* *(1)* обраща́-ю(сь), *(2)* -ешь(ся), *(3)* -ет(ся), *(4)* -ем(ся), *(5)* -ете(сь), *(6)* -ют(ся).

обремени́ть *pf, future:* *(1)* обремен-ю́, *(2)* -ишь, *(3)* -ит, *(4)* -им, *(5)* -ите, *(6)* -ят.

обременя́ть *impf, present:* *(1)* обременя́-ю, *(2)* -ешь, *(3)* -ет, *(4)* -ем, *(5)* -ете, *(6)* -ют.

обрести́ *pf, future:* *(1)* обрет-у́, *(2)* -ёшь, *(3)* -ёт, *(4)* -ём, *(5)* -ёте, *(6)* -у́т.

обрета́ть *impf, present:* *(1)* обрета́-ю, *(2)* -ешь, *(3)* -ет, *(4)* -ем, *(5)* -ете, *(6)* -ют.

оброни́ть *pf, future:* *(1)* оброню́, *(2)* оброн-и́шь, *(3)* -и́т, *(4)* -и́м, *(5)* -и́те, *(6)* -я́т.

обруча́ться *impf, present:* *(1)* обруча́-юсь, *(2)* -ешься, *(3)* -ется, *(4)* -емся, *(5)* -етесь, *(6)* -ются.

обручи́ться *pf, future:* *(1)* обруч-у́сь, *(2)* -и́шься, *(3)* -и́тся, *(4)* -и́мся, *(5)* -и́тесь, *(6)* -а́тся.

обсуди́ть *pf, future:* *(1)* обсужу́, *(2)* обсу́д-ишь, *(3)* -ит, *(4)* -им, *(5)* -ите, *(6)* -ят.

обсужда́ть *impf, present:* *(1)* обсужда́-ю, *(2)* -ешь, *(3)* -ет, *(4)* -ем, *(5)* -ете, *(6)* -ют.

обу́здывать *impf, present:* *(1)* обу́здыва-ю, *(2)* -ешь, *(3)* -ет, *(4)* -ем, *(5)* -ете, *(6)* -ют.

обуча́ть *impf, present:* *(1)* обуча́-ю, *(2)* -ешь, *(3)* -ет, *(4)* -ем, *(5)* -ете, *(6)* -ют.

обучи́ть *pf, future:* *(1)* обучу́, *(2)* обу́ч-ишь, *(3)* -ит, *(4)* -им, *(5)* -ите, *(6)* -ат.

обхвати́ть *pf, future:* *(1)* обхвачу́, *(2)* обхва́т-ишь, *(3)* -ит, *(4)* -им, *(5)* -ите, *(6)* -ят.

обхва́тывать *impf, present:* *(1)* обхва́тыва-ю, *(2)* -ешь, *(3)* -ет, *(4)* -ем, *(5)* -ете, *(6)* -ют.

обходи́ться *impf, present:* *(1)* обхожу́сь, *(2)* обхо́д-ишься, *(3)* -ится, *(4)* -имся, *(5)* -итесь, *(6)* -ятся.

обща́ться *impf, present:* *(1)* обща́-юсь, *(2)* -ешься, *(3)* -ется, *(4)* -емся, *(5)* -етесь, *(6)* -ются.

объяви́ть *pf, future:* *(1)* объявлю́, *(2)* объя́в-ишь, *(3)* -ит, *(4)* -им, *(5)* -ите, *(6)* -ят.

объявля́ть *impf, present:* *(1)* объявля́-ю, *(2)* -ешь, *(3)* -ет, *(4)* -ем, *(5)* -ете, *(6)* -ют.

объясни́ть(ся) *pf, future:* *(1)* объясн-ю́(сь), *(2)* -и́шь(ся), *(3)* -и́т(ся), *(4)* -и́м(ся), *(5)* -и́те(сь), *(6)* -я́т(ся).

объясня́ть(ся) *impf, present:* *(1)* объясня́-ю(сь), *(2)* -ешь(ся), *(3)* -ет(ся), *(4)* -ем(ся), *(5)* -ете(сь), *(6)* -ют(ся).

обяза́ть *pf, future:* *(1)* обяжу́, *(2)* обя́ж-ешь, *(3)* -ет, *(4)* -ем, *(5)* -ете, *(6)* -ут.

обя́зывать *impf, present:* *(1)* обя́зыва-ю, *(2)* -ешь, *(3)* -ет, *(4)* -ем, *(5)* -ете, *(6)* -ют.

овладева́ть *impf, present:* *(1)* овладева́-ю, *(2)* -ешь, *(3)* -ет, *(4)* -ем, *(5)* -ете, *(6)* -ют.

овладе́ть *pf, future:* *(1)* овладе́-ю, *(2)* -ешь, *(3)* -ет, *(4)* -ем, *(5)* -ете, *(6)* -ют.

одари́ть *pf, future:* *(1)* одарю́, *(2)* ода́р-ишь, *(3)* -ит, *(4)* -им, *(5)* -ите, *(6)* -ят.

одаря́ть *impf, present:* *(1)* одаря́-ю, *(2)* -ешь, *(3)* -ет, *(4)* -ем, *(5)* -ете, *(6)* -ют.

одева́ться *impf, present:* *(1)* одева́-юсь, *(2)* -ешься, *(3)* -ется, *(4)* -емся, *(5)* -етесь, *(6)* -ются.

оде́ться *pf, future:* *(1)* оде́н-усь, *(2)* -ешься, *(3)* -ется, *(4)* -емся, *(5)* -етесь, *(6)* -утся.

одержа́ть *pf, future:* *(1)* одержу́, *(2)* оде́рж-ишь, *(3)* -ит, *(4)* -им, *(5)* -ите, *(6)* -ат.

оде́рживать *impf, present:* *(1)* оде́ржива-ю, *(2)* -ешь, *(3)* -ет, *(4)* -ем, *(5)* -ете, *(6)* -ют.

одо́брить *pf, future:* *(1)* одо́бр-ю, *(2)* -ишь, *(3)* -ит, *(4)* -им, *(5)* -ите, *(6)* -ят.

Persons: 1 = я, 2 = ты, 3 = он, она́, оно́, 4 = мы, 5 = вы, 6 = они́

одобря́ть *impf, present: (1)* одобря́-ю, *(2)* -ешь, *(3)* -ет, *(4)* -ем, *(5)* -ете, *(6)* -ют.

одура́чивать *impf, present: (1)* одура́чива-ю, *(2)* -ешь, *(3)* -ет, *(4)* -ем, *(5)* -ете, *(6)* -ют.

одура́чить *impf, future: (1)* дура́ч-у, *(2)* -ишь, *(3)* -ит, *(4)* -им, *(5)* -ите, *(6)* -ат.

ожива́ть *impf, present: (1)* ожива́-ю, *(2)* -ешь, *(3)* -ет, *(4)* -ем, *(5)* -ете, *(6)* -ют.

оживи́ть *pf, future: (1)* ожив-лю́, *(2)* -и́шь, *(3)* -и́т, *(4)* -и́м, *(5)* -и́те, *(6)* -я́т.

оживля́ть *impf, present: (1)* оживля́-ю, *(2)* -ешь, *(3)* -ет, *(4)* -ем, *(5)* -ете, *(6)* -ют.

озада́чивать *impf, present: (1)* озада́чива-ю, *(2)* -ешь, *(3)* -ет, *(4)* -ем, *(5)* -ете, *(6)* -ют.

озада́чить *pf, future: (1)* озада́ч-у, *(2)* -ишь, *(3)* -ит, *(4)* -им, *(5)* -ите, *(6)* -ат.

озари́ть *pf, future: (1)* озар-ю́, *(2)* -ишь, *(3)* -ит, *(4)* -им, *(5)* -ите, *(6)* -я́т.

озаря́ть *impf, present: (1)* озаря́-ю, *(2)* -ешь, *(3)* -ет, *(4)* -ем, *(5)* -ете, *(6)* -ют.

ознако́мить *pf, future: (1)* ознако́м-лю, *(2)* -ишь, *(3)* -ит, *(4)* -им, *(5)* -ите, *(6)* -ят.

ознакомля́ть *impf, present: (1)* ознакомля́-ю, *(2)* -ешь, *(3)* -ет, *(4)* -ем, *(5)* -ете, *(6)* -ют.

означа́ть *impf, present: (3)* означа́-ет, *(6)* -ют.

оказа́ть(ся) *pf, future: (1)* окажу́(сь), *(2)* ока́ж-ешь(ся), *(3)* -ет(ся), *(4)* -ем(ся), *(5)* -ете(сь), *(6)* -ут(ся).

ока́зывать *impf, present: (1)* ока́зыва-ю, *(2)* -ешь, *(3)* -ет, *(4)* -ем, *(5)* -ете, *(6)* -ют.

ока́нчиваться *impf, present: (3)* ока́нчива-ется, *(6)* -ются.

оки́дывать *impf, present: (1)* оки́дыва-ю, *(2)* -ешь, *(3)* -ет, *(4)* -ем, *(5)* -ете, *(6)* -ют.

оки́нуть *pf, future: (1)* оки́н-у, *(2)* -ешь, *(3)* -ет, *(4)* -ем, *(5)* -ете, *(6)* -ут.

околдова́ть *pf, future: (1)* околду́-ю, *(2)* -ешь, *(3)* -ет, *(4)* -ем, *(5)* -ете, *(6)* -ют.

околдо́вывать *impf, present: (1)* околдо́выва-ю, *(2)* -ешь, *(3)* -ет, *(4)* -ем, *(5)* -ете, *(6)* -ют.

окостене́ть *pf, future: (1)* окостене́-ю, *(2)* -ешь, *(3)* -ет, *(4)* -ем, *(5)* -ете, *(6)* -ют.

окочене́ть *pf, future: (1)* окочене́-ю, *(2)* -ешь, *(3)* -ет, *(4)* -ем, *(5)* -ете, *(6)* -ют.

окружа́ть *impf, present: (1)* окружа́-ю, *(2)* -ешь, *(3)* -ет, *(4)* -ем, *(5)* -ете, *(6)* -ют.

окружи́ть *pf, future: (1)* окруж-у́, *(2)* -и́шь, *(3)* -и́т, *(4)* -и́м, *(5)* -и́те, *(6)* -а́т.

оку́тать *pf, future: (1)* оку́та-ю, *(2)* -ешь, *(3)* -ет, *(4)* -ем, *(5)* -ете, *(6)* -ют.

оку́тывать *impf, present: (1)* оку́тыва-ю, *(2)* -ешь, *(3)* -ет, *(4)* -ем, *(5)* -ете, *(6)* -ют.

оледене́ть *pf, future: (1)* оледене́-ю, *(2)* -ешь, *(3)* -ет, *(4)* -ем, *(5)* -ете, *(6)* -ют.

олицетворя́ть *impf, present: (1)* олицетворя́-ю, *(2)* -ешь, *(3)* -ет, *(4)* -ем, *(5)* -ете, *(6)* -ют.

опозда́ть *pf, future: (1)* опозда́-ю, *(2)* -ешь, *(3)* -ет, *(4)* -ем, *(5)* -ете, *(6)* -ют.

опа́здывать *impf, present: (1)* опа́здыва-ю, *(2)* -ешь, *(3)* -ет, *(4)* -ем, *(5)* -ете, *(6)* -ют.

опали́ть *pf, future: (1)* опал-ю́, *(2)* -и́шь, *(3)* -и́т, *(4)* -и́м, *(5)* -и́те, *(6)* -я́т.

описа́ть *pf, future: (1)* опишу́, *(2)* опи́ш-ешь, *(3)* -ет, *(4)* -ем, *(5)* -ете, *(6)* -ут.

опи́сывать *impf, present: (1)* опи́сыва-ю, *(2)* -ешь, *(3)* -ет, *(4)* -ем, *(5)* -ете, *(6)* -ют.

опозда́ть *pf, future: (1)* опозда́-ю, *(2)* -ешь, *(3)* -ет, *(4)* -ем, *(5)* -ете, *(6)* -ют.

опозо́рить *pf, future: (1)* опозо́р-ю, *(2)* -ишь, *(3)* -ит, *(4)* -им, *(5)* -ите, *(6)* -ят.

оправда́ть *pf, future: (1)* оправда́-ю, *(2)* -ешь, *(3)* -ет, *(4)* -ем, *(5)* -ете, *(6)* -ют.

опра́вдывать *impf, present: (1)* опра́вдыва-ю, *(2)* -ешь, *(3)* -ет, *(4)* -ем, *(5)* -ете, *(6)* -ют.

опуска́ть *impf, present: (1)* опуска́-ю, *(2)* -ешь, *(3)* -ет, *(4)* -ем, *(5)* -ете, *(6)* -ют.

опусти́ть *pf, future: (1)* опущу́, *(2)* опу́ст-ишь, *(3)* -ит, *(4)* -им, *(5)* -ите, *(6)* -ят.

опустоша́ть *impf, present: (1)* опустоша́-ю, *(2)* -ешь, *(3)* -ет, *(4)* -ем, *(5)* -ете, *(6)* -ют.

опустоши́ть *pf, future: (1)* опустош-у́, *(2)* -и́шь, *(3)* -и́т, *(4)* -и́м, *(5)* -и́те, *(6)* -а́т.

опыли́ть *pf, future: (1)* опыл-ю́, *(2)* -и́шь, *(3)* -и́т, *(4)* -и́м, *(5)* -и́те, *(6)* -я́т.

опыля́ть *impf, present: (1)* опыля́-ю, *(2)* -ешь, *(3)* -ет, *(4)* -ем, *(5)* -ете, *(6)* -ют.

опьяне́ть *pf, future: (1)* опьяне́-ю, *(2)* -ешь, *(3)* -ет, *(4)* -ем, *(5)* -ете, *(6)* -ют.

Persons: 1 = я,　2 = ты,　3 = он, онá, онó,　4 = мы,　5 = вы,　6 = онú

опьянúть *pf, future:* (*1*) опьян-ю́, (*2*) -úшь, (*3*) -úт, (*4*) -úм, (*5*) -úте, (*6*) -я́т.

опьяня́ть *impf, present:* (*1*) опьяня́-ю, (*2*) -ешь, (*3*) -ет, (*4*) -ем, (*5*) -ете, (*6*) -ют.

освежа́ть *impf, present:* (*1*) освежа́-ю, (*2*) -ешь, (*3*) -ет, (*4*) -ем, (*5*) -ете, (*6*) -ют.

освежúть *pf, future:* (*1*) освеж-у́, (*2*) -úшь, (*3*) -úт, (*4*) -úм, (*5*) -úте, (*6*) -а́т.

осветúть *pf, future:* (*1*) освещу́, (*2*) освет-úшь, (*3*) -úт, (*4*) -úм, (*5*) -úте, (*6*) -я́т.

освеща́ть *impf, present:* (*1*) освеща́-ю, (*2*) -ешь, (*3*) -ет, (*4*) -ем, (*5*) -ете, (*6*) -ют.

освободúть(ся) *pf, future:* (*1*) освобожу́(сь), (*2*) освобод-úшь(ся), (*3*) -úт(ся), (*4*) -úм(ся), (*5*) -úте(сь), (*6*) -ят(ся).

освобожда́ть(ся) *impf, present:* (*1*) освобожда́-ю(сь), (*2*) -ешь(ся), (*3*) -ет(ся), (*4*) -ем(ся), (*5*) -ете(сь), (*6*) -ют(ся).

оскорбúть(ся) *pf, future:* (*1*) оскорб-лю́(сь), (*2*) -úшь(ся), (*3*) -úт(ся), (*4*) -úм(ся), (*5*) -úте(сь), (*6*) -я́т(ся).

оскорбля́ть(ся) *impf, present:* (*1*) оскорбля́-ю(сь), (*2*) -ешь(ся), (*3*) -ет(ся), (*4*) -ем(ся), (*5*) -ете(сь), (*6*) -ют(ся).

ослабева́ть *impf, present:* (*1*) ослабева́-ю, (*2*) -ешь, (*3*) -ет, (*4*) -ем, (*5*) -ете, (*6*) -ют.

ослабе́ть *pf, future:* (*1*) ослабе́-ю, (*2*) -ешь, (*3*) -ет, (*4*) -ем, (*5*) -ете, (*6*) -ют.

осла́бить *pf, future:* (*1*) осла́б-лю, (*2*) -ишь, (*3*) -úт, (*4*) -úм, (*5*) -úте, (*6*) -я́т.

ослепúть *pf, future:* (*1*) ослеп-лю́, (*2*) -úшь, (*3*) -ит, (*4*) -им, (*5*) -ите, (*6*) -ят.

ослабля́ть *impf, present:* (*1*) ослабля́-ю, (*2*) -ешь, (*3*) -ет, (*4*) -ем, (*5*) -ете, (*6*) -ют.

осла́бнуть *pf, future:* (*1*) осла́бн-у, (*2*) -ешь, (*3*) -ет, (*4*) -ем, (*5*) -ете, (*6*) -ут; *past:* осла́б, -ла, -ло, -ли.

ослепля́ть *impf, present:* (*1*) ослепля́-ю, (*2*) -ешь, (*3*) -ет, (*4*) -ем, (*5*) -ете, (*6*) -ют.

осме́ивать *impf, present:* (*1*) осме́ива-ю, (*2*) -ешь, (*3*) -ет, (*4*) -ем, (*5*) -ете, (*6*) -ют.

осме́иваться *impf, present:* (*1*) осме́лива-юсь, (*2*) -ешься, (*3*) -ется, (*4*) -емся, (*5*) -етесь, (*6*) -ются.

осме́литься *pf, future:* (*1*) осме́л-юсь, (*2*) -ишься, (*3*) -ится, (*4*) -имся, (*5*) -итесь, (*6*) -ятся.

осознава́ть *impf, present:* (*1*) осозна-ю́, (*2*) -ёшь, (*3*) -ёт, (*4*) -ём, (*5*) -ёте, (*6*) -ю́т.

осозна́ть *pf, future:* (*1*) осозна́-ю, (*2*) -ешь, (*3*) -ет, (*4*) -ем, (*5*) -ете, (*6*) -ют.

остава́ться *impf, present:* (*1*) оста-ю́сь, (*2*) -ёшься, (*3*) -ётся, (*4*) -ёмся, (*5*) -ётесь, (*6*) -ю́тся.

оста́вить *pf, future:* (*1*) оста́в-лю, (*2*) -ишь, (*3*) -ит, (*4*) -им, (*5*) -ите, (*6*) -ят.

оставля́ть *impf, present:* (*1*) оставля́-ю, (*2*) -ешь, (*3*) -ет, (*4*) -ем, (*5*) -ете, (*6*) -ют.

остана́вливаться *impf, present:* (*1*) остана́влива-юсь, (*2*) -ешься, (*3*) -ется, (*4*) -емся, (*5*) -етесь, (*6*) -ются.

остановúться *pf, future:* (*1*) остановлю́сь, (*2*) остано́в-ишься, (*3*) -ится, (*4*) -имся, (*5*) -итесь, (*6*) -ятся.

оста́ться *pf, future:* (*1*) оста́н-усь, (*2*) -ешься, (*3*) -ется, (*4*) -емся, (*5*) -етесь, (*6*) -утся.

остерега́ться *impf, present:* (*1*) остерега́-юсь, (*2*) -ешься, (*3*) -ется, (*4*) -емся, (*5*) -етесь, (*6*) -ются.

остолбене́ть *pf, future:* (*1*) остолбене́-ю, (*2*) -ешь, (*3*) -ет, (*4*) -ем, (*5*) -ете, (*6*) -ют.

острúчься *impf, present:* (*1*) остригу́сь, (*2*) остриж-ёшься, (*3*) -ётся, (*4*) -ёмся, (*5*) -ётесь, (*6*) остригу́тся; *past:* острúгся, острúг-лась, -лось, -лись.

остыва́ть *impf, present:* (*1*) остыва́-ю, (*2*) -ешь, (*3*) -ет, (*4*) -ем, (*5*) -ете, (*6*) -ют.

осты́ть *pf, future:* (*1*) осты́н-у, (*2*) -ешь, (*3*) -ет, (*4*) -ем, (*5*) -ете, (*6*) -ут.

осудúть *pf, future:* (*1*) осужу́, (*2*) осу́д-ишь, (*3*) -ит, (*4*) -им, (*5*) -ите, (*6*) -ят.

осужда́ть *impf, present:* (*1*) осужда́-ю, (*2*) -ешь, (*3*) -ет, (*4*) -ем, (*5*) -ете, (*6*) -ют.

осуша́ть *impf, present:* (*1*) осуша́-ю, (*2*) -ешь, (*3*) -ет, (*4*) -ем, (*5*) -ете, (*6*) -ют.

осушúть *pf, future:* (*1*) осушу́, (*2*) осу́ш-ишь, (*3*) -ит, (*4*) -им, (*5*) -ите, (*6*) -ат.

Persons: 1 = я,   2 = ты,   3 = он, она́, оно́,   4 = мы,   5 = вы,   6 = они́

осуществи́ть *pf, future:* *(1)* осуществ-лю́, *(2)* -и́шь, *(3)* -и́т, *(4)* -и́м, *(5)* -и́те, *(6)* -я́т.

осуществля́ть *impf, present:* *(1)* осуществля́-ю, *(2)* -ешь, *(3)* -ет, *(4)* -ем, *(5)* -ете, *(6)* -ют.

осыпа́ть *impf, present:* *(1)* осыпа́-ю, *(2)* -ешь, *(3)* -ет, *(4)* -ем, *(5)* -ете, *(6)* -ют.

осы́пать *pf, future:* *(1)* осы́пл-ю, *(2)* -ешь, *(3)* -ет, *(4)* -ем, *(5)* -ете, *(6)* -ют.

отбива́ться *impf, present:* *(1)* отбива́-юсь, *(2)* -ешься, *(3)* -ется, *(4)* -емся, *(5)* -етесь, *(6)* -ются.

отбира́ть *impf, present:* *(1)* отбира́-ю, *(2)* -ешь, *(3)* -ет, *(4)* -ем, *(5)* -ете, *(6)* -ют.

отби́ться *pf, future:* *(1)* отобь-ю́сь, *(2)* -ёшься, *(3)* -ётся, *(4)* -ёмся, *(5)* -ётесь, *(6)* -ю́тся.

отбра́сывать *impf, present:* *(1)* отбра́сыва-ю, *(2)* -ешь, *(3)* -ет, *(4)* -ем, *(5)* -ете, *(6)* -ют.

отбро́сить *pf, future:* *(1)* отбро́шу, *(2)* отброс-ишь, *(3)* -ит, *(4)* -им, *(5)* -ите, *(6)* -ят.

отва́ливать *impf, present:* *(1)* отва́лива-ю, *(2)* -ешь, *(3)* -ет, *(4)* -ем, *(5)* -ете, *(6)* -ют.

отвали́ть *pf, future:* *(1)* отвалю́, *(2)* отва́л-ишь, *(3)* -ит, *(4)* -им, *(5)* -ите, *(6)* -ят.

отверга́ть *impf, present:* *(1)* отверга́-ю, *(2)* -ешь, *(3)* -ет, *(4)* -ем, *(5)* -ете, *(6)* -ют.

отве́ргнуть *pf, future:* *(1)* отве́ргн-у, *(2)* -ешь, *(3)* -ет, *(4)* -ем, *(5)* -ете, *(6)* -ут; *past:* отвверг *or* отвергнул, отверг-ла, -ло, -ли.

отвердева́ть *impf, present:* *(3)* отвердева́-ет, *(6)* -ют.

отверде́ть *pf, future:* *(3)* отверде́-ет, *(6)* -ют.

отверну́ться *pf, future:* *(1)* отверн-у́сь, *(2)* -ёшься, *(3)* -ётся, *(4)* -ёмся, *(5)* -ётесь, *(6)* -у́тся.

отвести́ *pf, future:* *(1)* отвед-у́, *(2)* -ёшь, *(3)* -ёт, *(4)* -ём, *(5)* -ёте, *(6)* -у́т; *past:* отвёл, отвел-а́, -о́, -и́.

отве́тить *pf, future:* *(1)* отве́чу, *(2)* отве́т-ишь, *(3)* -ит, *(4)* -им, *(5)* -ите, *(6)* -ят.

отвеча́ть *impf, present:* *(1)* отвеча́-ю, *(2)* -ешь, *(3)* -ет, *(4)* -ем, *(5)* -ете, *(6)* -ют.

отвлека́ть *impf, present:* *(1)* отвлека́-ю, *(2)* -ешь, *(3)* -ет, *(4)* -ем, *(5)* -ете, *(6)* -ют.

отвле́чь *pf, future:* *(1)* отвлеку́, *(2)* отвлеч-ёшь, *(3)* -ёт, *(4)* -ём, *(5)* -ёте, *(6)* отвлеку́т; *past:* отвлёк, отвлекл-а́, -о́, -и́.

отводи́ть *impf, present:* *(1)* отвожу́, *(2)* отво́д-ишь, *(3)* -ит, *(4)* -им, *(5)* -ите, *(6)* -ят.

отвора́чиваться *impf, present:* *(1)* отвора́чива-юсь, *(2)* -ешься, *(3)* -ется, *(4)* -емся, *(5)* -етесь, *(6)* -ются.

отврати́ть *pf, future:* *(1)* отвращу́, *(2)* отврат-и́шь, *(3)* -и́т, *(4)* -и́м, *(5)* -и́те, *(6)* -я́т.

отвраща́ть *impf, present:* *(1)* отвраща́-ю, *(2)* -ешь, *(3)* -ет, *(4)* -ем, *(5)* -ете, *(6)* -ют.

отгова́ривать *impf, present:* *(1)* отгова́рива-ю, *(2)* -ешь, *(3)* -ет, *(4)* -ем, *(5)* -ете, *(6)* -ют.

отговори́ть *pf, future:* *(1)* отговор-ю́, *(2)* -и́шь, *(3)* -и́т, *(4)* -и́м, *(5)* -и́те, *(6)* -я́т.

отдава́ть(ся) *impf, present:* *(1)* отда-ю́(сь), *(2)* -ёшь(ся), *(3)* -ёт(ся), *(4)* -ём(ся), *(5)* -ёте(сь), *(6)* -ю́т(ся).

отдали́ться *pf, future:* *(1)* отдал-ю́сь, *(2)* -и́шься, *(3)* -и́тся, *(4)* -и́мся, *(5)* -и́тесь, *(6)* -я́тся.

отдаля́ться *impf, present:* *(1)* отдаля́-юсь, *(2)* -ешься, *(3)* -ется, *(4)* -емся, *(5)* -етесь, *(6)* -ются.

отда́ть(ся) *pf, future:* *(1)* отда́-м(ся), *(2)* -шь(ся), *(3)* -ст(ся), *(4)*отда-ди́м(ся), *(5)* -ди́те(сь), *(6)* -ду́т(ся).

отде́латься *pf, future:* *(1)* отде́ла-юсь, *(2)* -ешься, *(3)* -ется, *(4)* -емся, *(5)* -етесь, *(6)* -ются.

отде́лываться *impf, present:* *(1)* отде́лыва-юсь, *(2)* -ешься, *(3)* -ется, *(4)* -емся, *(5)* -етесь, *(6)* -ются.

отдохну́ть *impf, present:* *(1)* отдохн-у́, *(2)* -ёшь, *(3)* -ёт, *(4)* -ём, *(5)* -ёте, *(6)* -у́т.

отдыха́ть *impf, present: (1)* отдыха́-ю, *(2)* -ешь, *(3)* -ет, *(4)* -ем, *(5)* -ете, *(6)* -ют.

отзыва́ться *impf, present: (1)* отзыва́-юсь, *(2)* -ешься, *(3)* -ется, *(4)* -емся, *(5)* -етесь, *(6)* -ются.

отказа́ть(ся) *pf, future: (1)* откажу́(сь), *(2)* отка́ж-ешь(ся), *(3)* -ет(ся), *(4)* -ем(ся), *(5)* -ете(сь), *(6)* -ут(ся).

отка́зывать(ся) *impf, present: (1)* отка́зыва-ю(сь), *(2)* -ешь(ся), *(3)* -ет(ся), *(4)* -ем(ся), *(5)* -ете(сь), *(6)* -ют(ся).

отки́дываться *impf, present: (1)* отки́дыва-юсь, *(2)* -ешься, *(3)* -ется, *(4)* -емся, *(5)* -етесь, *(6)* -ются.

отки́нуться *pf, future: (1)* отки́н-усь, *(2)* -ешься, *(3)* -ется, *(4)* -емся, *(5)* -етесь, *(6)* -утся.

откла́дывать *impf, present: (1)* откла́дыва-ю, *(2)* -ешь, *(3)* -ет, *(4)* -ем, *(5)* -ете, *(6)* -ют.

открика́ться *impf, present: (1)* открика́-юсь, *(2)* -ешься, *(3)* -ется, *(4)* -емся, *(5)* -етесь, *(6)* -ются.

откли́кнуться *pf, future: (1)* откли́кн-усь, *(2)* -ешься, *(3)* -ется, *(4)* -емся, *(5)* -етесь, *(6)* -утся.

отклони́ть(ся) *pf, future: (1)* отклоню́(сь), *(2)* откло́н-ишь(ся), *(3)* -ит(ся), *(4)* -им(ся), *(5)* -ите(сь), *(6)* -ят(ся).

отклоня́ть(ся) *impf, present: (1)* отклоня́-ю(сь), *(2)* -ешь(ся), *(3)* -ет(ся), *(4)* -ем(ся), *(5)* -ете(сь), *(6)* -ют(ся).

открыва́ть(ся) *impf, present: (1)* открыва́-ю(сь), *(2)* -ешь(ся), *(3)* -ет(ся), *(4)* -ем(ся), *(5)* -ете(сь), *(6)* -ют(ся).

откры́ть(ся) *pf, future: (1)* откро́-ю(сь), *(2)* -ешь(ся), *(3)* -ет(ся), *(4)* -ем(ся), *(5)* -ете(сь), *(6)* -ют(ся).

отложи́ть *pf, future: (1)* отложу́, *(2)* отло́ж-ишь, *(3)* -ит, *(4)* -им, *(5)* -ите, *(6)* -ат.

отма́хиваться *impf, present: (1)* отма́хива-юсь, *(2)* -ешься, *(3)* -ется, *(4)* -емся, *(5)* -етесь, *(6)* -ются.

отмахну́ться *impf, present: (1)* отмахн-у́сь, *(2)* -ёшься, *(3)* -ётся, *(4)* -ёмся, *(5)* -ётесь, *(6)* -у́тся.

отмени́ть *pf, future: (1)* отменю́, *(2)* отме́н-ишь, *(3)* -ит, *(4)* -им, *(5)* -ите, *(6)* -ят.

отменя́ть *impf, present: (1)* отменя́-ю, *(2)* -ешь, *(3)* -ет, *(4)* -ем, *(5)* -ете, *(6)* -ют.

отмести́ *pf, future: (1)* отмет-у, *(2)* -ёшь, *(3)* -ёт, *(4)* -ём, *(5)* -ёте, *(6)* -у́т; *past:* отмёл, отме-ла́, -ло́, -ли́.

отмета́ть *impf, present: (1)* отмета́-ю, *(2)* -ешь, *(3)* -ет, *(4)* -ем, *(5)* -ете, *(6)* -ют.

отнести́(сь) *pf, future: (1)* отнес-у́(сь), *(2)* -ёшь(ся), *(3)* -ёт(ся), *(4)* -ём(ся), *(5)* -ёте(сь), *(6)* -у́т(ся); *past:* отнёс(ся), отнес-ла́(сь), -ло́(сь), -ли́(сь).

отнима́ть *impf, present: (1)* отнима́-ю, *(2)* -ешь, *(3)* -ет, *(4)* -ем, *(5)* -ете, *(6)* -ют.

относи́ть(ся) *impf, present: (1)* отношу́(сь), *(2)* отно́с-ишь(ся), *(3)* -ит(ся), *(4)* -им(ся), *(5)* -ите(сь), *(6)* -ат(ся).

отня́ть *pf, future: (1)* отниму́, *(2)* отни́м-ешь, *(3)* -ет, *(4)* -ем, *(5)* -ете, *(6)* -ут; *past:* отнял, отняла, отня-ло, -ли.

отобра́ть *pf, future: (1)* отбер-у́, *(2)* -ёшь, *(3)* -ёт, *(4)* -ём, *(5)* -ёте, *(6)* -ут; *past:* отобра́л, отобрала́, отобра́-ло, -ли.

отожествля́ть *impf, present: (1)* отожествля́-ю, *(2)* -ешь, *(3)* -ет, *(4)* -ем, *(5)* -ете, *(6)* -ют.

отозва́ться *impf, present: (1)* отозову́сь, *(2)* отзов-ёшься, *(3)* -ётся, *(4)* -ёмся, *(5)* -ётесь, *(6)* -у́тся; *past:* отозва́лся, отозвала́сь, отозва́-лось, -лись.

отойти́ *pf, future: (1)* отойд-у́, *(2)* -ёшь, *(3)* -ёт, *(4)* -ём, *(5)* -ёте, *(6)* -у́т; *past:* ото-шёл, шла́, -шло́, -шли́.

оторва́ть *pf, future:* (1) оторв-у́, (2) -ёшь, (3) -ёт, (4) -ём, (5) -ёте, (6) -у́т; *past:* оторва́л, оторвала́, оторва́-ло, -ли.

отпи́ть *pf, future:* (1) отопь-ю́, (2) -ёшь, (3) -ёт, (4) -ём, (5) -ёте, (6) -ю́т.

отпра́вить(ся) *pf, future:* (1) отпра́в-лю(сь), (2) -ишь(ся), (3) -ит(ся), (4) -им(ся), (5) -ите(сь), (6) -ят(ся).

отправля́ть(ся) *impf, present:* (1) отправля́-ю(сь), (2) -ешь(ся), (3) -ет(ся), (4) -ем(ся), (5) -ете(сь), (6) -ют(ся).

отпра́здновать *pf, future:* (1) отпра́здну-ю, (2) -ешь, (3) -ет, (4) -ем, (5) -ете, (6) -ют.

отпуска́ть *impf, present:* (1) отпуска́-ю, (2) -ешь, (3) -ет, (4) -ем, (5) -ете, (6) -ют.

отпусти́ть *pf, future:* (1) отпущу́, (2) отпу́ст-ишь, (3) -ит, (4) -им, (5) -ите, (6) -ят.

отража́ть *impf, present:* (1) отража́-ю, (2) -ешь, (3) -ет, (4) -ем, (5) -ете, (6) -ют.

отрази́ть *pf, future:* (1) отражу́, (2) отраз-и́шь, (3) -и́т, (4) -и́м, (5) -и́те, (6) -я́т.

отреаги́ровать *pf, future:* (1) отреаги́ру-ю, (2) -ешь, (3) -ет, (4) -ем, (5) -ете, (6) -ют.

отрека́ться *impf, present:* (1) отрека́-юсь, (2) -ешься, (3) -ется, (4) -емся, (5) -етесь, (6) -ются.

отремонти́ровать *pf, future:* (1) отремонти́ру-ю, (2) -ешь, (3) -ет, (4) -ем, (5) -ете, (6) -ют.

отре́чься *impf, present:* (1) отрекусь, (2) отреч-ёшься, (3) -ётся, (4) -ёмся, (5) -ётесь, (6) отрекутся.

отрица́ть *impf, present:* (1) отрица́-ю, (2) -ешь, (3) -ет, (4) -ем, (5) -ете, (6) -ют.

отрыва́ть *impf, present:* (1) отрыва́-ю, (2) -ешь, (3) -ет, (4) -ем, (5) -ете, (6) -ют.

отсе́ивать *impf, present:* (1) отсе́ива-ю, (2) -ешь, (3) -ет, (4) -ем, (5) -ете, (6) -ют.

отсе́ять *pf, future:* (1) отсе́-ю, (2) -ешь, (3) -ет, (4) -ем, (5) -ете, (6) -ют.

отсро́чивать *impf, present:* (1) отсро́чива-ю, (2) -ешь, (3) -ет, (4) -ем, (5) -ете, (6) -ют.

отсро́чить *pf, future:* (1) отсро́ч-у, (2) -ишь, (3) -ит, (4) -им, (5) -ите, (6) -ят.

отстава́ть *impf present:* (1) отста-ю́, (2) -ёшь, (3) -ёт, (4) -ём, (5) -ёте, (6) -ю́т.

отста́ть *pf, future:* (1) отста́н-у, (2) -ешь, (3) -ет, (4) -ем, (5) -ете, (6) -ут.

отступа́ть *impf, present:* (1) отступа́-ю, (2) -ешь, (3) -ет, (4) -ем, (5) -ете, (6) -ют.

отступи́ть *pf, future:* (1) отступлю́, (2) отсту́п-ишь, (3) -ит, (4) -им, (5) -ите, (6) -ят.

отта́лкивать(ся) *impf, present:* (1) отта́лкива-ю(сь), (2) -ешь(ся), (3) -ет(ся), (4) -ем(ся), (5) -ете(сь), (6) -ют(ся).

оттолкну́ть(ся) *pf, future:* (1) оттолкн-у(сь), (2) -ёшь(ся), (3) -ёт(ся), (4) -ём(ся), (5) -ёте(сь), (6) -ут(ся).

отходи́ть *impf, present:* (1) отхожу́, (2) отхо́д-ишь, (3) -ит, (4) -им, (5) -ите, (6) -ят.

отчита́ть *impf, present:* (1) отчита́-ю, (2) -ешь, (3) -ет, (4) -ем, (5) -ете, (6) -ют.

отчи́тывать *impf, present:* (1) отчи́тыва-ю, (2) -ешь, (3) -ет, (4) -ем, (5) -ете, (6) -ют.

отчужда́ть *impf, present:* (1) отчужда́-ю, (2) -ешь, (3) -ет, (4) -ем, (5) -ете, (6) -ют.

охвати́ть *pf, future:* (1) охвачу́, (2) охва́т-ишь, (3) -ит, (4) -им, (5) -ите, (6) -ят.

охва́тывать *impf, present:* (1) охва́тыва-ю, (2) -ешь, (3) -ет, (4) -ем, (5) -ете, (6) -ют.

оце́нивать *impf, present:* (1) оце́нива-ю, (2) -ешь, (3) -ет, (4) -ем, (5) -ете, (6) -ют.

оцени́ть *pf, future:* (1) оценю́, (2) оце́н-ишь, (3) -ит, (4) -им, (5) -ите, (6) -ят.

оцепене́ть *pf, future:* (1) оцепене́-ю, (2) -ешь, (3) -ет, (4) -ем, (5) -ете, (6) -ют.

очарова́ть *pf, future:* (1) очару́-ю, (2) -ешь, (3) -ет, (4) -ем, (5) -ете, (6) -ют.

очаро́вывать *impf, present:* (1) очаро́выва-ю, (2) -ешь, (3) -ет, (4) -ем, (5) -ете, (6) -ют.

очерти́ть *pf, future:* (1) очерчу́, (2) очёрт-ишь, (3) -ит, (4) -им, (5) -ите, (6) -ят.

очёрчивать *impf, present:* (1) очерчива-ю, (2) -ешь, (3) -ет, (4) -ем, (5) -ете, (6) -ют.

очи́стить *pf, future:* (1) очи́щу, (2) очи́ст-ишь, (3) -ит, (4) -им, (5) -ите, (6) -ят.

очища́ть *impf, present:* (1) очища́-ю, (2) -ешь, (3) -ет, (4) -ем, (5) -ете, (6) -ют.

Persons: 1 = я, 2 = ты, 3 = он, она́, оно́, 4 = мы, 5 = вы, 6 = они́

очути́ться *pf, future:* *(1) not used,* (2) очу́т-ишься, *(3)* -ится, *(4)* -имся, *(5)* -итесь, *(6)* -ятся.

ошале́ть *pf, future:* *(1)* ошале́-ю, *(2)* -ешь, *(3)* -ет, *(4)* -ем, *(5)* -ете, *(6)* -ют.

ошеломи́ть *pf, future:* *(1)* ошелом-лю́, *(2)* -и́шь, *(3)* -и́т, *(4)* -и́м, *(5)* -и́те, *(6)* -я́т.

ошеломля́ть *impf, present:* *(1)* ошеломля́-ю, *(2)* -ешь, *(3)* -ет, *(4)* -ем, *(5)* -ете, *(6)* -ют.

ошиба́ться *impf, present:* *(1)* ошиба́-юсь, *(2)* -ешься, *(3)* -ется, *(4)* -емся, *(5)* -етесь, *(6)* -ются.

ошиби́ться *pf, future:* *(1)* обшибу́сь, *(2)* -ёшься, *(3)* -ётся, *(4)* -ёмся, *(5)* -ётесь, *(6)* -у́тся.

ощу́пывать *impf, present:* *(1)* ощу́пыва-ю, *(2)* -ешь, *(3)* -ет, *(4)* -ем, *(5)* -ете, *(6)* -ют.

ощути́ть *pf, future:* *(1)* ощущу́, *(2)* ощут-и́шь, *(3)* -и́т, *(4)* -и́м, *(5)* -и́те, *(6)* -я́т.

ощуща́ть *impf, present:* *(1)* ощуща́-ю, *(2)* -ешь, *(3)* -ет, *(4)* -ем, *(5)* -ете, *(6)* -ют.

па́дать *impf, present:* *(1)* па́да-ю, *(2)* -ешь, *(3)* -ет, *(4)* -ем, *(5)* -ете, *(6)* -ют.

пали́ть *impf, present:* *(1)* пал-ю́, *(2)* -и́шь, *(3)* -и́т, *(4)* -и́м, *(5)* -и́те, *(6)* -я́т.

пари́ть *impf, present:* *(1)* пар-ю́, *(2)* -и́шь, *(3)* -и́т, *(4)* -и́м, *(5)* -и́те, *(6)* -я́т.

перебива́ть *impf, present:* *(1)* перебива́-ю, *(2)* -ешь, *(3)* -ет, *(4)* -ем, *(5)* -ете, *(6)* -ют.

переби́ть *pf, future:* *(1)* перебь-ю́, *(2)* -ёшь, *(3)* -ёт, *(4)* -ём, *(5)* -ёте, *(6)* -ю́т.

перевести́ *pf, future:* *(1)* перевед-у́, *(2)* -ёшь, *(3)* -ёт, *(4)* -ём, *(5)* -ёте, *(6)* -у́т; *past:* перевёл, перевел-а́, -о́, -и́.

переводи́ть *impf, present:* *(1)* перевожу́, *(2)* перево́д-ишь, *(3)* -ит, *(4)* -им, *(5)* -ите, *(6)* -ят.

передава́ть *impf present:* *(1)* переда-ю́, *(2)* -ёшь, *(3)* -ёт, *(4)* -ём, *(5)* -ёте, *(6)* -ю́т.

переда́ть *pf, future:* *(1)* переда́-м, *(2)* -шь, *(3)* -ст, *(4)* -дим, *(5)* -дите, *(6)* -дут; *past:* переда́л, передала́, переда́л-о, -и.

переезжа́ть *impf, present:* *(1)* переезжа́-ю, *(2)* -ешь, *(3)* -ет, *(4)* -ем, *(5)* -ете, *(6)* -ют.

перее́хать *pf, future:* *(1)* перее́д-у, *(2)* -ешь, *(3)* -ет, *(4)* -ем, *(5)* -ете, *(6)* -ут.

перезвони́ть *pf, future:* *(1)* перезвон-ю́, *(2)* -и́шь, *(3)* -и́т, *(4)* -и́м, *(5)* -и́те, *(6)* -я́т.

перейти́ *pf, future:* *(1)* перейд-у́, *(2)* -ёшь, *(3)* -ёт, *(4)* -ём, *(5)* -ёте, *(6)* -у́т; *past:* перешёл, -шла́, -шло́, -шли́.

перелива́ться *impf, present:* *(3)* перелива́-ется, *(6)* -ются.

перели́ться *pf, future:* *(3)* перель-ётся, *(6)* -ю́тся; *past:* перели́лся, перелила́сь, перели́-лось, -лись.

перема́нивать *impf, present:* *(1)* перема́нива-ю, *(2)* -ешь, *(3)* -ет, *(4)* -ем, *(5)* -ете, *(6)* -ют.

перемани́ть *pf, future:* *(1)* переманю́, *(2)* перема́н-ишь, *(3)* -ит, *(4)* -им, *(5)* -ите, *(6)* -ят.

перемени́ть *pf, future:* *(1)* переменю́, *(2)* переме́н-ишь, *(3)* -ит, *(4)* -им, *(5)* -ите, *(6)* -ят.

перенести́ *pf, future:* *(1)* перенес-у́, *(2)* -ёшь, *(3)* -ёт, *(4)* -ём, *(5)* -ёте, *(6)* -у́т; *past:* перенёс, перенес-ла́, -ло́, -ли́.

переноси́ть *impf, present:* *(1)* переношу́, *(2)* перено́с-ишь, *(3)* -ит, *(4)* -им, *(5)* -ите, *(6)* -ят.

переодева́ться *impf, present:* *(1)* переодева́-юсь, *(2)* -ешься, *(3)* -ется, *(4)* -емся, *(5)* -етесь, *(6)* -ются.

переоде́ться *pf, future:* *(1)* переоде́н-усь, *(2)* -ешься, *(3)* -ется, *(4)* -емся, *(5)* -етесь, *(6)* -утся.

переписа́ть *pf, future:* *(1)* перепишу́, *(2)* перепи́ш-ешь, *(3)* -ет, *(4)* -ем, *(5)* -ете, *(6)* -ут.

перепи́сывать(ся) *impf, present:* *(1)* перепи́сыва-ю(сь), *(2)* -ешь(ся), *(3)* -ет(ся), *(4)* -ем(ся), *(5)* -ете(сь), *(6)* -ют(ся).

Persons: 1 = я, 2 = ты, 3 = он, она́, оно́, 4 = мы, 5 = вы, 6 = они́

перепо́лниться *pf, future:* *(3)* перепо́лн-ится, *(6)* -ятся.

переполня́ться *impf, present:* *(3)* переполня́-ется, *(6)* -ются.

пересека́ться *impf, present:* *(3)* пересе-чётся, *(6)* -ку́тся.

пересе́чься *pf, future:* *(3)* пересечётся, *(6)* пересеку́тся; *past:* пересе́кся, пересек-ла́сь, -ло́сь, -ли́сь.

пересла́ть *pf, future:* *(1)* перешл-ю́, *(2)* -ёшь, *(3)* -ёт, *(4)* -ём, *(5)* -ёте, *(6)* -ю́т.

переспа́ть *pf, future:* *(1)* пересп-лю́, *(2)* -и́шь, *(3)* -ит, *(4)* -им, *(5)* -ите, *(6)* -ят; *past:* переспа́л, перепала́, переспа́-ло, -ли.

перестра́ивать *impf, present:* *(1)* перестра́ива-ю, *(2)* -ешь, *(3)* -ет, *(4)* -ем, *(5)* -ете, *(6)* -ют.

перестава́ть *impf present:* *(1)* переста-ю́, *(2)* -ёшь, *(3)* -ёт, *(4)* -ём, *(5)* -ёте, *(6)* -ю́т.

перестара́ться *pf, future:* *(1)* перестара́-юсь, *(2)* -ешься, *(3)* -ется, *(4)* -емся, *(5)* -етесь, *(6)* -ются.

переста́ть *pf, future:* *(1)* перестан-у, *(2)* -ешь, *(3)* -ет, *(4)* -ем, *(5)* -ете, *(6)* -ут.

перестро́ить *pf, future:* *(1)* перестро́-ю, *(2)* -ишь, *(3)* -ит, *(4)* -им, *(5)* -ите, *(6)* -ят.

переступа́ть *impf, present:* *(1)* переступа́-ю, *(2)* -ешь, *(3)* -ет, *(4)* -ем, *(5)* -ете, *(6)* -ют.

переступи́ть *pf, future:* *(1)* переступлю́, *(2)* пересту́п-ишь, *(3)* -ит, *(4)* -им, *(5)* -ите, *(6)* -ят.

пересыла́ть *impf, present:* *(1)* пересыла́-ю, *(2)* -ешь, *(3)* -ет, *(4)* -ем, *(5)* -ете, *(6)* -ют.

переходи́ть *impf, present:* *(1)* перехожу́, *(2)* перехо́д-ишь, *(3)* -ит, *(4)* -им, *(5)* -ите, *(6)* -ят.

перечита́ть *pf, future:* *(1)* перечита́-ю, *(2)* -ешь, *(3)* -ет, *(4)* -ем, *(5)* -ете, *(6)* -ют.

перечи́тывать *impf, present:* *(1)* перечи́тыва-ю, *(2)* -ешь, *(3)* -ет, *(4)* -ем, *(5)* -ете, *(6)* -ют.

петь *impf, present:* *(1)* по-ю́, *(2)* -ёшь, *(3)* -ёт, *(4)* -ём, *(5)* -ёте, *(6)* -ю́т.

пили́ть *impf, present:* *(1)* пилю́, *(2)* пи́л-ишь, *(3)* -ит, *(4)* -им, *(5)* -ите, *(6)* -ят.

пирова́ть *impf, present:* *(1)* пиру́-ю, *(2)* -ешь, *(3)* -ет, *(4)* -ем, *(5)* -ете, *(6)* -ют.

писа́ть *impf, present:* *(1)* пишу́, *(2)* пи́ш-ешь, *(3)* -ет, *(4)* -ем, *(5)* -ете, *(6)* -ут.

пита́ть *impf, present:* *(1)* пита́-ю, *(2)* -ешь, *(3)* -ет, *(4)* -ем, *(5)* -ете, *(6)* -ют.

пить *impf, present:* *(1)* пь-ю, *(2)* -ёшь, *(3)* -ёт, *(4)* -ём, *(5)* -ёте, *(6)* -ют.

пла́вать *impf, present:* *(1)* плава-ю, *(2)* -ешь, *(3)* -ет, *(4)* -ем, *(5)* -ете, *(6)* -ют.

пла́виться *impf, present:* *(3)* пла́в-ится, *(6)* -ятся.

пла́кать *impf, present:* *(1)* пла́ч-у, *(2)* -ешь, *(3)* -ет, *(4)* -ем, *(5)* -ете, *(6)* -ут.

плани́ровать *impf, present:* *(1)* плани́ру-ю, *(2)* -ешь, *(3)* -ет, *(4)* -ем, *(5)* -ете, *(6)* -ют.

плати́ть *impf, present:* *(1)* плачу́, *(2)* пла́т-ишь, *(3)* -ит, *(4)* -им, *(5)* -ите, *(6)* -ят.

плева́ть *impf, present:* *(1)* плю-ю́, *(2)* -ёшь, *(3)* -ёт, *(4)* -ём, *(5)* -ёте, *(6)* -ю́т.

плени́ть *pf, future:* *(1)* плен-ю́, *(2)* -ишь, *(3)* -ит, *(4)* -им, *(5)* -ите, *(6)* -ят.

пленя́ть *impf, present:* *(1)* пленя-ю, *(2)* -ешь, *(3)* -ет, *(4)* -ем, *(5)* -ете, *(6)* -ют.

плыть *impf, present:* *(1)* плыв-у, *(2)* -ёшь, *(3)* -ёт, *(4)* -ём, *(5)* -ёте, *(6)* -ут.

плю́нуть *pf, future:* *(1)* плюн-у, *(2)* -ешь, *(3)* -ет, *(4)* -ем, *(5)* -ете, *(6)* -ут.

пляса́ть *impf, present:* *(1)* пляшу́, *(2)* пля́ш-ешь, *(3)* -ет, *(4)* -ем, *(5)* -ете, *(6)* -ут.

победи́ть *pf, future:* *(1)* not used, *(2)* побед-и́шь, *(3)* -ит, *(4)* -им, *(5)* -ите, *(6)* -я́т.

побежа́ть *pf, future:* *(1)* побегу, *(2)* побеж-ишь, *(3)* -ит, *(4)* -им, *(5)* -ите, *(6)* побегут.

побеспоко́ить *pf, future:* *(1)* побеспоко́-ю, *(2)* -ишь, *(3)* -ит, *(4)* -им, *(5)* -ите, *(6)* -ят.

поби́ть *pf, future:* *(1)* побь-ю́, *(2)* -ёшь, *(3)* -ёт, *(4)* -ём, *(5)* -ёте, *(6)* -ю́т.

поблагодари́ть *pf, future:* *(1)* поблагодар-ю́, *(2)* -и́шь, *(3)* -и́т, *(4)* -и́м, *(5)* -и́те, *(6)* -я́т.

поборо́ть *pf, future:* *(1)* поборю́, *(2)* побо́р-ешь, *(3)* -ет, *(4)* -ем, *(5)* -ете, *(6)* -ют.

побрани́ть *pf, future:* *(1)* побран-ю́, *(2)* -и́шь, *(3)* -и́т, *(4)* -и́м, *(5)* -и́те, *(6)* -я́т.

побри́ть *pf, future:* *(1)* побре́-ю, *(2)* -ешь, *(3)* -ет, *(4)* -ем, *(5)* -ете, *(6)* -ют.

побри́ться *pf, future:* *(1)* побре́-юсь, *(2)* -ешься, *(3)* -ется, *(4)* -емся, *(5)* -етесь, *(6)* -ются.

Persons: 1 = я, 2 = ты, 3 = он, она́, оно́, 4 = мы, 5 = вы, 6 = они́

побуди́ть *pf, future:* (1) побужу́, (2) побуд-и́шь, (3) -и́т, (4) -и́м, (5) -и́те, (6) -я́т.

побужда́ть *impf, present:* (1) побужда́-ю, (2) -ешь, (3) -ет, (4) -ем, (5) -ете, (6) -ют.

повенча́ть *pf, future:* (1) повенча́-ю, (2) -ешь, (3) -ет, (4) -ем, (5) -ете, (6) -ют.

пове́рить *pf, future:* (1) пове́р-ю, (2) -ишь, (3) -ит, (4) -им, (5) -ите, (6) -ят.

поверну́ть *impf present:* (1) поверн-у́, (2) -ёшь, (3) -ёт, (4) -ём, (5) -ёте, (6) -у́т.

поверну́ться *pf, future:* (1) поверн-у́сь, (2) -ёшься, (3) -ётся, (4) -ёмся, (5) -ётесь, (6) -у́тся.

повеселе́ть *pf, future:* (1) повеселе́-ю, (2) -ешь, (3) -ет, (4) -ем, (5) -ете, (6) -ют.

повесели́ться *pf, future:* (1) повесел-ю́сь, (2) -и́шься, (3) -и́тся, (4) -и́мся, (5) -и́тесь, (6) -я́тся.

пове́сить *pf, future:* (1) пове́шу, (2) пове́с-ишь, (3) -ит, (4) -им, (5) -ите, (6) -ят.

повести́ *pf, future:* (1) повед-у́, (2) -ёшь, (3) -ёт, (4) -ём, (5) -ёте, (6) -у́т; *past:* повёл, повел-а́, -о́, -и́.

повинова́ться *impf & pf, present & future:* (1) повину́-юсь, (2) -ешься, (3) -ется, (4) -емся, (5) -етесь, (6) -ются.

повора́чивать(ся) *impf, present:* (1) повора́чива-ю(сь), (2) -ешь(ся), (3) -ет(ся), (4) -ем(ся), (5) -ете(сь), (6) -ют(ся).

повы́сить *pf, future:* (1) повы́шу, (2) повы́с-ишь, (3) -ит, (4) -им, (5) -ите, (6) -ят.

повыша́ть *impf, present:* (1) повыша́-ю, (2) -ешь, (3) -ет, (4) -ем, (5) -ете, (6) -ют.

погаси́ть *pf, future:* (1) погашу́, (2) пога́с-ишь, (3) -ит, (4) -им, (5) -ите, (6) -ят.

поги́бнуть *pf, future:* (1) погибн-у, (2) -ешь, (3) -ет, (4) -ем, (5) -ете, (6) -ут; *past:* поги́б, -ла, -ло, -ли.

погла́дить *pf, future:* (1) погла́жу, (2) погла́д-ишь, (3) -ит, (4) -им, (5) -ите, (6) -ят.

погла́живать *impf, present:* (1) погла́жива-ю, (2) -ешь, (3) -ет, (4) -ем, (5) -ете, (6) -ют.

поглоти́ть *pf, future:* (1) поглощу́, (2) поглот-и́шь, (3) -и́т, (4) -и́м, (5) -и́те, (6) -я́т.

поглоща́ть *impf, present:* (1) поглоща́-ю, (2) -ешь, (3) -ет, (4) -ем, (5) -ете, (6) -ют.

поговори́ть *pf, future:* (1) поговор-ю́, (2) -и́шь, (3) -и́т, (4) -и́м, (5) -и́те, (6) -я́т.

погружа́ть(ся) *impf, present:* (1) погружа́-ю(сь), (2) -ешь(ся), (3) -ет(ся), (4) -ем(ся), (5) -ете(сь), (6) -ют(ся).

погрузи́ть(ся) *pf, future:* (1) погружу́(сь), (2) погру́з-ишь(ся), (3) -ит(ся), (4) -им(ся), (5) -ите(сь), (6) -ят(ся).

погуля́ть *pf, future:* (1) погуля́-ю, (2) -ешь, (3) -ет, (4) -ем, (5) -ете, (6) -ют.

подава́ть *impf present:* (1) пода-ю́, (2) -ёшь, (3) -ёт, (4) -ём, (5) -ёте, (6) -ю́т.

подави́ть *pf, future:* (1) подавлю́, (2) пода́в-ишь, (3) -ит, (4) -им, (5) -ите, (6) -ят.

подавля́ть *impf, present:* (1) подавля́-ю, (2) -ешь, (3) -ет, (4) -ем, (5) -ете, (6) -ют.

подари́ть *pf, future:* (1) подарю́, (2) пода́р-ишь, (3) -ит, (4) -им, (5) -ите, (6) -ят.

пода́ть *pf, future:* (1) пода́-м, (2) -шь, (3) -ст, (4) -дим, (5) -дите, (6) -дут; *past:* пода́л, подала́, пода́л-о, -и.

подба́дривать *impf, present:* (1) подба́дрива-ю, (2) -ешь, (3) -ет, (4) -ем, (5) -ете, (6) -ют.

подбодри́ть *pf, future:* (1) подбодр-ю́, (2) -и́шь, (3) -и́т, (4) -и́м, (5) -и́те, (6) -я́т.

подвезти́ *pf, future:* (1) подвез-у́, (2) -ёшь, (3) -ёт, (4) -ём, (5) -ёте, (6) -у́т; *past:* подвёз, подвез-ла́, -ло́, -ли́.

подверга́ть *impf, present:* (1) подверга́-ю, (2) -ешь, (3) -ет, (4) -ем, (5) -ете, (6) -ют.

подве́ргнуть *pf, future:* (1) подве́ргн-у, (2) -ешь, (3) -ет, (4) -ем, (5) -ете, (6) -ут; *past:* подве́рг *or* подве́ргнул, подве́рг-ла, -ло, -ли.

подвести́ *pf, future:* (1) подвед-у́, (2) -ёшь, (3) -ёт, (4) -ём, (5) -ёте, (6) -у́т; *past:* подвёл, подвел-а́, -о́, -и́.

подводи́ть *impf, present:* (1) подвожу́, (2) подво́д-ишь, (3) -ит, (4) -им, (5) -ите, (6) -ят.

подвы́пить *pf, future:* (1) подвы́пь-ю, (2) -ешь, (3) -ет, (4) -ем, (5) -ете, (6) -ют.

поддава́ться *impf, present:* (1) подда-ю́сь, (2) -ёшься, (3) -ётся, (4) -ёмся, (5) -ётесь, (6) -ю́тся.

подда́ться *pf, future:* (1) подда́-мся, (2) -шься, (3) -стся, (4) -димся, (5) -дитесь, (6) -дутся.

подде́лать *pf, future:* (1) подде́ла-ю, (2) -ешь, (3) -ет, (4) -ем, (5) -ете, (6) -ют.

подде́лывать *impf, present:* (1) подде́лыва-ю, (2) -ешь, (3) -ет, (4) -ем, (5) -ете, (6) -ют.

поддержа́ть *pf, future:* (1) поддержу́, (2) подде́рж-ишь, (3) -ит, (4) -им, (5) -ите, (6) -ат.

подде́рживать *impf, present:* (1) подде́ржива-ю, (2) -ешь, (3) -ет, (4) -ем, (5) -ете, (6) -ют.

поддра́знивать *impf, present:* (1) поддра́знива-ю, (2) -ешь, (3) -ет, (4) -ем, (5) -ете, (6) -ют.

поддразни́ть *pf, future:* (1) поддразню́, (2) поддразн-и́шь, (3) -и́т, (4) -и́м, (5) -и́те, (6) -я́т.

подели́ться *pf, future:* (1) поделю́сь, (2) поде́л-ишься, (3) -ится, (4) -имся, (5) -итесь, (6) -ятся.

подзыва́ть *impf, present:* (1) подзыва́-ю, (2) -ешь, (3) -ет, (4) -ем, (5) -ете, (6) -ют.

подлиза́ться *pf, future:* (1) подлижу́сь, (2) подли́ж-ешься, (3) -ется, (4) -емся, (5) -етесь, (6) -утся.

подли́зываться *impf, present:* (1) подли́зыва-юсь, (2) -ешься, (3) -ется, (4) -емся, (5) -етесь, (6) -ются.

подми́гивать *impf, present:* (1) подми́гива-ю, (2) -ешь, (3) -ет, (4) -ем, (5) -ете, (6) -ют.

подмигну́ть *pf, future:* (1) подмигн-у́, (2) -ёшь, (3) -ёт, (4) -ём, (5) -ёте, (6) -у́т.

поднима́ть *impf, present:* (1) поднима́-ю, (2) -ешь, (3) -ет, (4) -ем, (5) -ете, (6) -ют.

подня́ть *pf, future:* (1) подниму́, (2) подни́м-ешь, (3) -ет, (4) -ем, (5) -ете, (6) -ут.

подозва́ть *pf, future:* (1) подзов-у́,(2) -ёшь, (3) -ёт, (4) -ём, (5) -ёте, (6) -у́т.

подозрева́ть *impf, present:* (1) подозрева́-ю, (2) -ешь, (3) -ет, (4) -ем, (5) -ете, (6) -ют.

подойти́ *pf, future:* (1) подойд-у, (2) -ёшь, (3) -ёт, (4) -ём, (5) -ёте, (6) -ут; *past:* подошёл, -шла, -шло, -шли.

подража́ть *impf, present:* (1) подража́-ю, (2) -ешь, (3) -ет, (4) -ем, (5) -ете, (6) -ют.

подразумева́ть *impf, present:* (1) подразумева́-ю, (2) -ешь, (3) -ет, (4) -ем, (5) -ете, (6) -ют.

подружи́ться *pf, future:* (1) подруж-у́сь, (2) подру́ж -ишься, (3) -ится, (4) -имся, (5) -итесь, (6) -атся.

подсказа́ть *pf, future:* (1) подскажу́, (2) подска́ж-ешь, (3) -ет, (4) -ем, (5) -ете, (6) -ут.

подска́зывать *impf, present:* (1) подска́зыва-ю, (2) -ешь, (3) -ет, (4) -ем, (5) -ете, (6) -ют.

подслу́шать *pf, future:* (1) подслу́ша-ю, (2) -ешь, (3) -ет, (4) -ем, (5) -ете, (6) -ют.

подслу́шивать *impf, present:* (1) подслу́шива-ю, (2) -ешь, (3) -ет, (4) -ем, (5) -ете, (6) -ют.

подстрека́ть *impf, present:* (1) подстрека́-ю, (2) -ешь, (3) -ет, (4) -ем, (5) -ете, (6) -ют.

подстрекну́ть *pf, future:* (1) подстрекн-у́, (2) -ёшь, (3) -ёт, (4) -ём, (5) -ёте, (6) -у́т.

подтвержда́ть *impf, present:* (1) подтвержда́-ю, (2) -ешь, (3) -ет, (4) -ем, (5) -ете, (6) -ют.

поду́мать *pf, future:* (1) поду́ма-ю, (2) -ешь, (3) -ет, (4) -ем, (5) -ете, (6) -ют.

подходи́ть *impf, present:* (1) подхожу́, (2) подхо́д-ишь, (3) -ит, (4) -им, (5) -ите, (6) -ят.

подчёркивать *impf, present:* (1) подчёркива-ю, (2) -ешь, (3) -ет, (4) -ем, (5) -ете, (6) -ют.

подчеркну́ть *pf, future:* (1) подчеркн-у́, (2) -ёшь, (3) -ёт, (4) -ём, (5) -ёте, (6) -у́т.

Persons: 1 = я, 2 = ты, 3 = он, она́, оно́, 4 = мы, 5 = вы, 6 = они́

подчини́ть(ся) *pf, future:* *(1)* подчин-ю́(сь), *(2)* -и́шь(ся), *(3)* -и́т(ся), *(4)* -и́м(ся), *(5)* -и́те(сь), *(6)* -я́т(ся).

подчиня́ть(ся) *impf, present:* *(1)* подчиня́-ю(сь), *(2)* -ешь(ся), *(3)* -ет(ся), *(4)* -ем(ся), *(5)* -ете(сь), *(6)* -ют(ся).

подыска́ть *pf, future:* *(1)* подыщу́, *(2)* поды́щ-ешь, *(3)* -ет, *(4)* -ем, *(5)* -ете, *(6)* -ут.

поды́скивать *impf, present:* *(1)* поды́скива-ю, *(2)* -ешь, *(3)* -ет, *(4)* -ем, *(5)* -ете, *(6)* -ют.

подъезжа́ть *impf, present:* *(1)* подъезжа́-ю, *(2)* -ешь, *(3)* -ет, *(4)* -ем, *(5)* -ете, *(6)* -ют.

подъе́хать *pf, future:* *(1)* подъе́д-у, *(2)* -ешь, *(3)* -ет, *(4)* -ем, *(5)* -ете, *(6)* -ут.

пое́сть *pf, future:* (1) по-е́м, (2) -е́шь, (3) -е́ст, (4) поед-и́м, (5) -и́те, (6) -я́т.

пое́хать *pf, future:* *(1)* пое́д-у, *(2)* -ешь, *(3)* -ет, *(4)* -ем, *(5)* -ете, *(6)* -ут.

пожа́рить *pf, future:* *(1)* пожа́р-ю, *(2)* -ишь, *(3)* -ит, *(4)* -им, *(5)* -ите, *(6)* -ят.

пожа́ть *pf, future:* *(1)* пожм-у́, *(2)* -ёшь, *(3)* -ёт, *(4)* -ём, *(5)* -ёте, *(6)* -у́т.

пожела́ть *pf, future:* *(1)* пожела́-ю, *(2)* -ешь, *(3)* -ет, *(4)* -ем, *(5)* -ете, *(6)* -ют.

пожени́ться *pf, future:* *(1)* поженю́сь, *(2)* пожён-ишься, *(3)* -ится, *(4)* -имся, *(5)* -итесь, *(6)* -ятся.

поже́ртвовать *pf, future:* *(1)* поже́ртву-ю, *(2)* -ешь, *(3)* -ет, *(4)* -ем, *(5)* -ете, *(6)* -ют.

пожима́ть *impf, present:* *(1)* пожима́-ю, *(2)* -ешь, *(3)* -ет, *(4)* -ем, *(5)* -ете, *(6)* -ют.

пожира́ть *impf, present:* *(1)* пожира́-ю, *(2)* -ешь, *(3)* -ет, *(4)* -ем, *(5)* -ете, *(6)* -ют.

пожра́ть *pf, future:* *(1)* пожр-у́, *(2)* -ёшь, *(3)* -ёт, *(4)* -ём, *(5)* -ёте, *(6)* -у́т; *past:* пожра́л, пожрала́, пожра́-ло, -ли.

пожури́ть *pf, future:* *(1)* пожур-ю́, *(2)* -ишь, *(3)* -ит, *(4)* -им, *(5)* -ите, *(6)* -я́т.

позабо́тить(ся) *pf, future:* *(1)* позабо́чусь, *(2)* позабо́т-ишься, *(3)* -ится, *(4)* -имся, *(5)* -итесь, *(6)* -ятся.

позави́довать *pf, future:* *(1)* позави́ду-ю, *(2)* -ешь, *(3)* -ет, *(4)* -ем, *(5)* -ете, *(6)* -ю́т.

позва́ть *pf, future:* *(1)* позов-у́, *(2)* -ёшь, *(3)* -ёт, *(4)* -ём, *(5)* -ёте, *(6)* -у́т.

позво́лить *pf, future:* *(1)* позво́л-ю, *(2)* -ишь, *(3)* -ит, *(4)* -им, *(5)* -ите, *(6)* -ят.

позволя́ть *impf, present:* *(1)* позволя́-ю, *(2)* -ешь, *(3)* -ет, *(4)* -ем, *(5)* -ете, *(6)* -ют.

позвони́ть *pf, future:* *(1)* позвон-ю́, *(2)* -и́шь, *(3)* -и́т, *(4)* -и́м, *(5)* -и́те, *(6)* -я́т.

поздра́вить *pf, future:* *(1)* поздра́в-лю, *(2)* -ишь, *(3)* -ит, *(4)* -им, *(5)* -ите, *(6)* -ят.

поздравля́ть *impf, present:* *(1)* поздравля́-ю, *(2)* -ешь, *(3)* -ет, *(4)* -ем, *(5)* -ете, *(6)* -ют.

пози́ровать *impf, present:* *(1)* пози́ру-ю, *(2)* -ешь, *(3)* -ет, *(4)* -ем, *(5)* -ете, *(6)* -ют.

познако́мить(ся) *pf, future:* *(1)* познако́м-лю(сь), *(2)* -ишь(ся), *(3)* -ит(ся), *(4)* -им(ся), *(5)* -ите(сь), *(6)* -ят(ся).

позна́ть *pf, future:* *(1)* позна-ю́, *(2)* -ёшь, *(3)* -ёт, *(4)* -ём, *(5)* -ёте, *(6)* -ю́т.

позо́рить *impf, present:* *(1)* позо́р-ю, *(2)* -ишь, *(3)* -ит, *(4)* -им, *(5)* -ите, *(6)* -ят.

пои́ть *impf, present:* *(1)* пою́, *(2)* по-и́шь, *(3)* -и́т, *(4)* -и́м, *(5)* -и́те, *(6)* -я́т.

пойма́ть *pf, future:* *(1)* пойма́-ю, *(2)* -ешь, *(3)* -ет, *(4)* -ем, *(5)* -ете, *(6)* -ют.

пойти́ *pf, future:* *(1)* пойд-у́, *(2)* -ёшь, *(3)* -ёт, *(4)* -ём, *(5)* -ёте, *(6)* -у́т; *past:* по-шёл, -шла́, -шло́, -шли́.

показа́ть *pf, future:* *(1)* покажу, *(2)* покаж-ешь, *(3)* -ет, *(4)* -ем, *(5)* -ете, *(6)* -ут.

пока́зывать *impf, present:* *(1)* пока́зыва-ю, *(2)* -ешь, *(3)* -ет, *(4)* -ем, *(5)* -ете, *(6)* -ют.

поката́ться *pf, future:* *(1)* поката́-юсь, *(2)* -ешься, *(3)* -ется, *(4)* -емся, *(5)* -етесь, *(6)* -ются.

пока́чиваться *impf, present:* *(1)* пока́чива-юсь, *(2)* -ешься, *(3)* -ется, *(4)* -емся, *(5)* -етесь, *(6)* -ются.

покида́ть *impf, present:* *(1)* покида́-ю, *(2)* -ешь, *(3)* -ет, *(4)* -ем, *(5)* -ете, *(6)* -ют.

поки́нуть *pf, future:* *(1)* поки́н-у, *(2)* -ешь, *(3)* -ет, *(4)* -ем, *(5)* -ете, *(6)* -ут.

поклони́ться *impf, present:* *(1)* поклоня́-юсь, *(2)* -ешься, *(3)* -ется, *(4)* -емся, *(5)* -етесь, *(6)* -ются.

покля́сться *pf, future:* *(1)* поклян-у́сь, *(2)* -ёшься, *(3)* -ётся, *(4)* -ёмся, *(5)* -ётесь, *(6)*

-у́тся; *past:* покля́лся, поклял-а́сь, -о́сь, -и́сь.

поколеба́ться *pf, future:* (1) поколе́бл-юсь, (2) -ешься, (3) -ется, (4) -емся, (5) -етесь, (6) -ются.

поко́нчить *pf, future:* (1) поко́нч-у, (2) -ишь, (3) -ит, (4) -им, (5) -ите, (6) -ат.

покори́ть(ся) *pf, future:* (1) покор-ю́(сь), (2) -и́шь(ся), (3) -и́т(ся), (4) -и́м(ся), (5) -и́те(сь), (6) -я́т(ся).

покоря́ть(ся) *impf, present:* (1) покоря́-ю(сь), (2) -ешь(ся), (3) -ет(ся), (4) -ем(ся), (5) -ете(сь), (6) -ют(ся).

покра́сить *pf, future:* (1) покра́шу, (2) покра́с-ишь, (3) -ит, (4) -им, (5) -ите, (6) -ят.

покрасне́ть *pf, future:* (1) покрасне́-ю, (2) -ешь, (3) -ет, (4) -ем, (5) -ете, (6) -ют.

покрыва́ть *impf, present:* (1) покрыва́-ю, (2) -ешь, (3) -ет, (4) -ем, (5) -ете, (6) -ют.

покры́ть *pf, future:* (1) покро́-ю, (2) -ешь, (3) -ет, (4) -ем, (5) -ете, (6) -ют.

покупа́ть *impf, present:* (1) покупа́-ю, (2) -ешь, (3) -ет, (4) -ем, (5) -ете, (6) -ют.

поку́сывать *impf, present:* (1) поку́сыва-ю, (2) -ешь, (3) -ет, (4) -ем, (5) -ете, (6) -ют.

полага́ть(ся) *pf, future:* (1) полага́-ю(сь), (2) -ешь(ся), (3) -ет(ся), (4) -ем(ся), (5) -ете(сь), (6) -ют(ся).

пола́дить *pf, future:* (1) пола́жу, (2) пола́д-ишь, (3) -ит, (4) -им, (5) -ите, (6) -ят.

пола́комиться *pf, future:* (1) пола́ком-люсь, (2) -ишься, (3) -ится, (4) -имся, (5) -итесь, (6) -ятся.

по́лзать *impf, present:* (1) по́лза-ю, (2) -ешь, (3) -ет, (4) -ем, (5) -ете, (6) -ют.

ползти́ *impf, present:* (1) полз-у́, (2) -ёшь, (3) -ёт, (4) -ём, (5) -ёте, (6) -у́т; *past:* полз, -ла́, -ло́, -ли́.

положи́ть(ся) *pf, future:* (1) положу́(сь), (2) поло́ж-ишь(ся), (3) -ит(ся), (4) -им(ся), (5) -ите(сь), (6) -ят(ся).

получа́ть(ся) *impf, present:* (1) получа́-ю(сь), (2) -ешь(ся), (3) -ет(ся), (4) -ем(ся), (5) -ете(сь), (6) -ют(ся).

получи́ть(ся) *pf, future:* (1) получу́(сь), (2) полу́ч-ишь(ся), (3) -ит(ся), (4) -им(ся), (5) -ите(сь), (6) -ат(ся).

по́льзоваться *impf, present:* (1) по́льзу-юсь, (2) -ешься, (3) -ется, (4) -емся, (5) -етесь, (6) -ются.

польсти́ть *pf, future:* (1) польщу́, (2) польст-и́шь, (3) -и́т, (4) -и́м, (5) -и́те, (6) -я́т.

полюбова́ться *pf, future:* (1) полюбу́-юсь, (2) -ешься, (3) -ется, (4) -емся, (5) -етесь, (6) -ются.

помани́ть *pf, future:* (1) поманю́, (2) пома́н-ишь, (3) -ит, (4) -им, (5) -ите, (6) -ят.

помассажи́ровать *pf, future:* (1) помассажи́ру-ю, (2) -ешь, (3) -ет, (4) -ем, (5) -ете, (6) -ют.

поме́ркнуть *pf, future:* (3) поме́ркн-ет, (6) -ут.

помести́ть *pf, future:* (1) помещу́, (2) помест-и́шь, (3) -и́т, (4) -и́м, (5) -и́те, (6) -я́т.

помеша́ть *pf, future:* (1) помеша́-ю, (2) -ешь, (3) -ет, (4) -ем, (5) -ете, (6) -ют.

помеща́ть *impf, present:* (1) помеща́-ю, (2) -ешь, (3) -ет, (4) -ем, (5) -ете, (6) -ют.

помири́ться *pf, future:* (1) помир-ю́сь, (2) помир -ишься, (3) -ится, (4) -имся, (5) -итесь, (6) -ятся.

помога́ть *impf, present:* (1) помога́-ю, (2) -ешь, (3) -ет, (4) -ем, (5) -ете, (6) -ют.

помо́чь *impf present:* (1) помогу́, (2) помо́ж-ешь, (3) -ет, (4) -ем, (5) -ете, (6) помо́гут; *past:* помо́г, -ла́, -ло́, -ли́.

понести́ *pf, future:* (1) понес-у́, (2) -ёшь, (3) -ёт, (4) -ём, (5) -ёте, (6) -у́т; *past:* понёс, понес-ла́, -ло́, -ли́.

понима́ть *impf, present:* (1) понима́-ю, (2) -ешь, (3) -ет, (4) -ем, (5) -ете, (6) -ют.

понра́виться *pf, future:* (1) понра́в-люсь, (2) -ишься, (3) -ится, (4) -имся, (5) -итесь, (6) -ятся.

поня́ть *pf, future:* (1) пойм-у́, (2) -ёшь, (3) -ёт, (4) -ём, (5) -ёте, (6) -у́т; *past:* по́нял,

> *Persons:* 1 = я, 2 = ты, 3 = он, она́, оно́, 4 = мы, 5 = вы, 6 = они́

поняла́, по́ня-ло, -ли.

пообе́дать *pf, future:* *(1)* пообе́да-ю, *(2)* -ешь, *(3)* -ет, *(4)* -ем, *(5)* -ете, *(6)* -ют.

пообеща́ть *pf, future:* *(1)* пообеща́-ю, *(2)* -ешь, *(3)* -ет, *(4)* -ем, *(5)* -ете, *(6)* -ют.

поощря́ть *impf, present:* *(1)* поощря́-ю, *(2)* -ешь, *(3)* -ет, *(4)* -ем, *(5)* -ете, *(6)* -ют.

попози́ровать *pf, future:* *(1)* попози́ру-ю, *(2)* -ешь, *(3)* -ет, *(4)* -ем, *(5)* -ете, *(6)* -ют.

поползти́ *pf, future:* *(1)* пополз-у́, *(2)* -ёшь, *(3)* -ёт, *(4)* -ём, *(5)* -ёте, *(6)* -у́т; *past:* попо́лз, -ла́, -ло́, -ли́.

попро́бовать *pf, future:* *(1)* попро́бу-ю, *(2)* -ешь, *(3)* -ет, *(4)* -ем, *(5)* -ете, *(6)* -ют.

попроси́ть *pf, future:* *(1)* попрошу́, *(2)* попро́с-ишь, *(3)* -ит, *(4)* -им, *(5)* -ите, *(6)* -ят.

попроша́йничать *impf, present:* *(1)* попроша́йнича-ю, *(2)* -ешь, *(3)* -ет, *(4)* -ем, *(5)* -ете, *(6)* -ют.

попроща́ться *pf, future:* *(1)* попроща́-юсь, *(2)* -ешься, *(3)* -ется, *(4)* -емся, *(5)* -етесь, *(6)* -ются.

попыта́ться *pf, future:* *(1)* попыта́-юсь, *(2)* -ешься, *(3)* -ется, *(4)* -емся, *(5)* -етесь, *(6)* -ются.

поработи́ть *pf, future:* *(1)* порабощу́, *(2)* поработ-и́шь, *(3)* -и́т, *(4)* -и́м, *(5)* -и́те, *(6)* -я́т.

порабоща́ть *impf, present:* *(1)* порабоща-ю, *(2)* -ешь, *(3)* -ет, *(4)* -ем, *(5)* -ете, *(6)* -ют.

поража́ть *impf, present:* *(1)* поража́-ю, *(2)* -ешь, *(3)* -ет, *(4)* -ем, *(5)* -ете, *(6)* -ют.

порази́ть *pf, future:* *(1)* поражу́, *(2)* пораз-и́шь, *(3)* -и́т, *(4)* -и́м, *(5)* -и́те, *(6)* -я́т.

порва́ть *pf, future:* *(1)* порв-у́, *(2)* -ёшь, *(3)* -ёт, *(4)* -ём, *(5)* -ёте, *(6)* -у́т; *past:* порва́л, порвала́, порва́-ло, -ли.

порва́ться *pf, future:* *(3)* порв -ётся, *(6)* -у́тся.

по́ртить *impf, present:* *(1)* по́рчу, *(2)* по́рт-ишь, *(3)* -ит, *(4)* -им, *(5)* -ите, *(6)* -ят.

порха́ть *impf, present:* *(1)* порха́-ю, *(2)* -ешь, *(3)* -ет, *(4)* -ем, *(5)* -ете, *(6)* -ют.

порхну́ть *pf, future:* *(1)* порхн-у́, *(2)* -ёшь, *(3)* -ёт, *(4)* -ём, *(5)* -ёте, *(6)* -у́т.

порыва́ть *impf, present:* *(1)* порыва́-ю, *(2)* -ешь, *(3)* -ет, *(4)* -ем, *(5)* -ете, *(6)* -ют.

посвяти́ть *pf, future:* *(1)* посвящу́, *(2)* посвят-и́шь, *(3)* -и́т, *(4)* -и́м, *(5)* -и́те, *(6)* -я́т.

посвяща́ть *impf, present:* *(1)* посвяща́-ю, *(2)* -ешь, *(3)* -ет, *(4)* -ем, *(5)* -ете, *(6)* -ют.

посети́ть *impf, present:* *(1)* посещу́, *(2)* посет-и́шь, *(3)* -и́т, *(4)* -и́м, *(5)* -и́те, *(6)* -я́т.

посеща́ть *impf, present:* *(1)* посеща́-ю, *(2)* -ешь, *(3)* -ет, *(4)* -ем, *(5)* -ете, *(6)* -ют.

посла́ть *pf, future:* *(1)* пошл-ю́, *(2)* -ёшь, *(3)* -ёт, *(4)* -ём, *(5)* -ёте, *(6)* -ю́т.

после́довать *pf, future:* *(1)* после́ду-ю, *(2)* -ешь, *(3)* -ет, *(4)* -ем, *(5)* -ете, *(6)* -ют.

посме́ть *pf, future:* *(1)* посме́-ю, *(2)* -ешь, *(3)* -ет, *(4)* -ем, *(5)* -ете, *(6)* -ют.

посмотре́ть *pf, future:* *(1)* посмотрю́, *(2)* посмо́тр-ишь, *(3)* -ит, *(4)* -им, *(5)* -ите, *(6)* -ят.

посове́товать(ся) *pf, future:* *(1)* посове́ту-ю(сь), *(2)* -ешь(ся), *(3)* -ет(ся), *(4)* -ем(ся), *(5)* -ете(сь), *(6)* -ют(ся).

поспа́ть *pf, future:* *(1)* посп-лю́, *(2)* -и́шь, *(3)* -и́т, *(4)* -и́м, *(5)* -и́те, *(6)* -я́т; *past:* поспа́л, поспа́ла, поспа́-ло, -ли.

поссо́риться *pf, future:* *(1)* поссо́р-юсь, *(2)* -ишься, *(3)* -ится, *(4)* -имся, *(5)* -итесь, *(6)* -ятся.

поста́вить *pf, future:* *(1)* поста́в-лю, *(2)* -ишь, *(3)* -ит, *(4)* -им, *(5)* -ите, *(6)* -ят.

постара́ться *pf, future:* *(1)* постара́-юсь, *(2)* -ешься, *(3)* -ется, *(4)* -емся, *(5)* -етесь, *(6)* -ются.

постаре́ть *pf, future:* *(1)* постаре́-ю, *(2)* -ешь, *(3)* -ет, *(4)* -ем, *(5)* -ете, *(6)* -ют.

постига́ть *impf, present:* *(1)* постига́-ю, *(2)* -ешь, *(3)* -ет, *(4)* -ем, *(5)* -ете, *(6)* -ют.

пости́гнуть *pf, future:* *(1)* постигн-у, *(2)* -ешь, *(3)* -ет, *(4)* -ем, *(5)* -ете, *(6)* -ут; *past:* пости́г, -ла, -ло, -ли.

пости́чь *pf, future:* *(1)* постигн-у, *(2)* -ешь, *(3)* -ет, *(4)* -ем, *(5)* -ете, *(6)* -ут; *past:* пости́г, -ла, -ло, -ли.

Persons: 1 = я,   2 = ты,   3 = он, она́, оно́,   4 = мы,   5 = вы,   6 = они́

пострада́ть *pf, future:* (1) пострада́-ю, (2) -ешь, (3) -ет, (4) -ем, (5) -ете, (6) -ют.

постре́ливать *impf, present:* (1) постре́лива-ю, (2) -ешь, (3) -ет, (4) -ем, (5) -ете, (6) -ют.

поступа́ть *impf, present:* (1) поступа́-ю, (2) -ешь, (3) -ет, (4) -ем, (5) -ете, (6) -ют.

поступи́ть *pf, future:* (1) поступлю́, (2) посту́п-ишь, (3) -ит, (4) -им, (5) -ите, (6) -ят.

посыла́ть *impf, present:* (1) посыла́-ю, (2) -ешь, (3) -ет, (4) -ем, (5) -ете, (6) -ют.

потере́ть(ся) *pf, future:* (1) потр-у́(сь), (2) -ёшь(ся), (3) -ёт(ся), (4) -ём(ся), (5) -ёте(сь), (6) -у́т(ся); *past:* потёр(ся), потёр-ла(сь), -ло(сь), -ли(сь).

потерпе́ть *pf, future:* (1) потерплю́, (2) поте́рп-ишь, (3) -ит, (4) -им, (5) -ите, (6) -ят.

потеря́ть(ся) *pf, future:* (1) потеря́-ю(сь), (2) -ешь(ся), (3) -ет(ся), (4) -ем(ся), (5) -ете(сь), (6) -ют(ся).

поте́ть *impf, present:* (1) поте́-ю, (2) -ешь, (3) -ет, (4) -ем, (5) -ете, (6) -ют.

потира́ть *impf, present:* (1) потира́-ю, (2) -ешь, (3) -ет, (4) -ем, (5) -ете, (6) -ют.

потолсте́ть *pf, future:* (1) потолсте́-ю, (2) -ешь, (3) -ет, (4) -ем, (5) -ете, (6) -ют.

потону́ть *pf, future:* (1) потону́, (2) пото́н-ешь, (3) -ет, (4) -ем, (5) -ете, (6) -ут.

поторопи́ть *pf, future:* (1) потороплю́, (2) поторо́п-ишь, (3) -ит, (4) -им, (5) -ите, (6) -ят.

потре́бовать *pf, future:* (1) потре́бу-ю, (2) -ешь, (3) -ет, (4) -ем, (5) -ете, (6) -ют.

потряса́ть *impf, present:* (1) потряса́-ю, (2) -ешь, (3) -ет, (4) -ем, (5) -ете, (6) -ют.

потрясти́ *pf, future:* (1) потряс-у́, (2) -ёшь, (3) -ёт, (4) -ём, (5) -ёте, (6) -у́т; *past:* потря́с, -ла́, -ло́, -ли́.

потускне́ть *pf, future:* (1) потускне́-ю, (2) -ешь, (3) -ет, (4) -ем, (5) -ете, (6) -ют.

потя́гиваться *impf, present:* (1) потя́гива-юсь, (2) -ешься, (3) -ется, (4) -емся, (5) -етесь, (6) -ются.

потяну́ть(ся) *pf, future:* (1) потяну́(сь), (2) потя́н-ешь(ся), (3) -ет(ся), (4) -ем(ся), (5) -ете(сь), (6) -ут(ся).

поуча́ть *impf, present:* (1) поуча́-ю, (2) -ешь, (3) -ет, (4) -ем, (5) -ете, (6) -ют.

похвали́ть *pf, future:* (1) похвалю́, (2) похва́л-ишь, (3) -ит, (4) -им, (5) -ите, (6) -ят.

похи́тить *pf, future:* (1) похи́щу, (2) похи́т-ишь, (3) -ит, (4) -им, (5) -ите, (6) -ят.

похуде́ть *pf, future:* (1) похуде́-ю, (2) -ешь, (3) -ет, (4) -ем, (5) -ете, (6) -ют.

поцелова́ть *pf, future:* (1) поцелу́-ю, (2) -ешь, (3) -ет, (4) -ем, (5) -ете, (6) -ют.

починм́ть *pf, future:* (1) починю́, (2) почи́н-ишь, (3) -ит, (4) -им, (5) -ите, (6) -ят.

почи́стить *pf, future:* (1) почи́щу, (2) почи́ст-ишь, (3) -ит, (4) -им, (5) -ите, (6) -ят.

почита́ть *impf, present:* (1) почита́-ю, (2) -ешь, (3) -ет, (4) -ем, (5) -ете, (6) -ют.

почу́вствовать *pf, future:* (1) почу́вству-ю, (2) -ешь, (3) -ет, (4) -ем, (5) -ете, (6) -ют.

почу́ять *pf, future:* (1) почу́-ю, (2) -ешь, (3) -ет, (4) -ем, (5) -ете, (6) -ют.

пошути́ть *pf, future:* (1) пошучу́, (2) пошу́т-ишь, (3) -ит, (4) -им, (5) -ите, (6) -ят.

пра́здновать *impf, present:* (1) праздну-ю, (2) -ешь, (3) -ет, (4) -ем, (5) -ете, (6) -ют.

пребыва́ть *impf, present:* (1) пребыва́-ю, (2) -ешь, (3) -ет, (4) -ем, (5) -ете, (6) -ют.

превзойти́ *pf, future:* (1) превзойд-у́, (2) -ёшь, (3) -ёт, (4) -ём, (5) -ёте, (6) -у́т; *past:* превзо-шёл, -шла́, -шло́, -шли́.

превосходи́ть *impf, present:* (1) превосхожу́, (2) превосхо́д-ишь, (3) -ит, (4) -им, (5) -ите, (6) -ят.

превраща́ться *impf, present:* (1) превраща́-юсь, (2) -ешься, (3) -ется, (4) -емся, (5) -етесь, (6) -ются.

превы́сить *pf, future:* (1) превышу́, (2) превы́с-ишь, (3) -ит, (4) -им, (5) -ите, (6) -ят.

превыша́ть *impf, present:* (1) превыша́-ю, (2) -ешь, (3) -ет, (4) -ем, (5) -ете, (6) -ют.

предава́ть(ся) *impf, present:* (1) преда-ю́(сь), (2) -ёшь(ся), (3) -ёт(ся), (4) -ём(ся), (5) -ёте(сь), (6) -ю́т(ся).

преда́ть(ся) *pf, future:* (1) преда́-м(ся), (2) -шь(ся), (3) -ст(ся), (4) -дим(ся), (5) -дите(сь), (6) -дут(ся).

Persons: 1 = я,   2 = ты,   3 = он, онá, онó,   4 = мы,   5 = вы,   6 = онú

предвúдеть *impf, present:* *(1)* предвúжу, *(2)* предвúд-ишь, *(3)* -ит, *(4)* -им, *(5)* -ите, *(6)* -ят.

предвкушáть *impf, present:* *(1)* предвкушá-ю, *(2)* -ешь, *(3)* -ет, *(4)* -ем, *(5)* -ете, *(6)* -ют.

предлагáть *impf, present:* *(1)* предлагá-ю, *(2)* -ешь, *(3)* -ет, *(4)* -ем, *(5)* -ете, *(6)* -ют.

предложúть *pf, future:* *(1)* предложý, *(2)* предлóж-ишь, *(3)* -ит, *(4)* -им, *(5)* -ите, *(6)* -ат.

предназначáть *impf, present:* *(1)* предназначá-ю, *(2)* -ешь, *(3)* -ет, *(4)* -ем, *(5)* -ете, *(6)* -ют.

предостáвить *pf, future:* *(1)* предостáвл-ю, *(2)* -ишь, *(3)* -ит, *(4)* -им, *(5)* -ите, *(6)* -ят.

предотвратúть *pf, future:* *(1)* предотвращý, *(2)* предотврат-úшь, *(3)* -úт, *(4)* -úм, *(5)* -úте, *(6)* -я́т.

предотвращáть *impf, present:* *(1)* предотвращá-ю, *(2)* -ешь, *(3)* -ет, *(4)* -ем, *(5)* -ете, *(6)* -ют.

предпочитáть *impf, present:* *(1)* предпочитá-ю, *(2)* -ешь, *(3)* -ет, *(4)* -ем, *(5)* -ете, *(6)* -ют.

предпринимáть *impf, present:* *(1)* предпринимá-ю, *(2)* -ешь, *(3)* -ет, *(4)* -ем, *(5)* -ете, *(6)* -ют.

предстáвить *pf, future:* *(1)* предстáв-лю, *(2)* -ишь, *(3)* -ит, *(4)* -им, *(5)* -ите, *(6)* -ят.

представля́ть *impf, present:* *(1)* представля́-ю, *(2)* -ешь, *(3)* -ет, *(4)* -ем, *(5)* -ете, *(6)* -ют.

предусмáтривать *impf, present:* *(1)* предусмáтрива-ю, *(2)* -ешь, *(3)* -ет, *(4)* -ем, *(5)* -ете, *(6)* -ют.

предусмотрéть *pf, future:* *(1)* предусмотрю́, *(2)* предусмóтр-ишь, *(3)* -ит, *(4)* -им, *(5)* -ите, *(6)* -ят.

предчýвствовать *impf, present:* *(1)* предчýвству-ю, *(2)* -ешь, *(3)* -ет, *(4)* -ем, *(5)* -ете, *(6)* -ют.

презирáть *impf, present:* *(1)* презирá-ю, *(2)* -ешь, *(3)* -ет, *(4)* -ем, *(5)* -ете, *(6)* -ют.

прекратúть *pf, future:* *(1)* прекращý, *(2)* прекрат-úшь, *(3)* -úт, *(4)* -úм, *(5)* -úте, *(6)* -я́т.

прекратúться *pf, future:* *(3)* прекрат-úтся, *(6)* -я́тся.

прекращáть *impf, present:* *(1)* прекращá-ю, *(2)* -ешь, *(3)* -ет, *(4)* -ем, *(5)* -ете, *(6)* -ют.

прекращáться *impf, present:* *(3)* прекращá-ется, *(6)* -ются.

прельстúть *pf, future:* *(1)* прельщý, *(2)* прельст-úшь, *(3)* -úт, *(4)* -úм, *(5)* -úте, *(6)* -я́т.

прельщáть *impf, present:* *(1)* прельщá-ю, *(2)* -ешь, *(3)* -ет, *(4)* -ем, *(5)* -ете, *(6)* -ют.

пренебрегáть *impf, present:* *(1)* пренебрегá-ю, *(2)* -ешь, *(3)* -ет, *(4)* -ем, *(5)* -ете, *(6)* -ют.

пренебрéчь *pf, future:* *(1)* пренебрегý, *(2)* пренебреж-ёшь, *(3)* -ёт, *(4)* -ём, *(5)* -ёте, *(6)* пренебрегýт; *past:* пренебрёг, пренебрег-лá, -лó, -лú.

преобладáть *impf, present:* *(1)* преобладá-ю, *(2)* -ешь, *(3)* -ет, *(4)* -ем, *(5)* -ете, *(6)* -ют.

преодолевáть *impf, present:* *(1)* преодолевá-ю, *(2)* -ешь, *(3)* -ет, *(4)* -ем, *(5)* -ете, *(6)* -ют.

преодолéть *pf, future:* *(1)* преодолé-ю, *(2)* -ешь, *(3)* -ет, *(4)* -ем, *(5)* -ете, *(6)* -ют.

препя́тствовать *impf, present:* *(1)* препя́тству-ю, *(2)* -ешь, *(3)* -ет, *(4)* -ем, *(5)* -ете, *(6)* -ют.

прервáть *pf, future:* *(1)* прерв-ý, *(2)* -ёшь, *(3)* -ёт, *(4)* -ём, *(5)* -ёте, *(6)* -ýт; *past:* прервáл, прервалá, прервá-ло, -ли.

прерывáть *impf, present:* *(1)* прерывá-ю, *(2)* -ешь, *(3)* -ет, *(4)* -ем, *(5)* -ете, *(6)* -ют.

прерывáться *impf, present:* *(1)* прерывá-юсь, *(2)* -ешься, *(3)* -ется, *(4)* -емся, *(5)* -етесь, *(6)* -ются.

преслéдовать *impf, present:* *(1)* преслéду-ю, *(2)* -ешь, *(3)* -ет, *(4)* -ем, *(5)* -ете, *(6)* -ют.

| *Persons:* 1 = я,   2 = ты,   3 = он, она́, оно́,   4 = мы,   5 = вы,   6 = они́ |

пресмыка́ться *impf, present:* *(1)* пресмыка́-юсь, *(2)* -ёшься, *(3)* -ётся, *(4)* -ёмся, *(5)* -ётесь, *(6)* -ются.

претвори́ть *pf, future:* *(1)* претвор-ю́, *(2)* -и́шь, *(3)* -и́т, *(4)* -и́м, *(5)* -и́те, *(6)* -я́т.

претворя́ть *impf, present:* *(1)* претворя́-ю, *(2)* -ешь, *(3)* -ет, *(4)* -ем, *(5)* -ете, *(6)* -ют.

преуменьша́ть *impf, present:* *(1)* преуменьша́-ю, *(2)* -ешь, *(3)* -ет, *(4)* -ем, *(5)* -ете, *(6)* -ют.

преуме́ньшить *pf, future:* *(1)* преуме́ньш-у, *(2)* -ишь, *(3)* -ит, *(4)* -им, *(5)* -ите, *(6)* -ат.

приба́вить *pf, future:* *(1)* приба́в-лю, *(2)* -ишь, *(3)* -ит, *(4)* -им, *(5)* -ите, *(6)* -ят.

прибавля́ть *impf, present:* *(1)* прибавля́-ю, *(2)* -ешь, *(3)* -ет, *(4)* -ем, *(5)* -ете, *(6)* -ют.

приближа́ться *impf, present:* *(1)* приближа́-юсь, *(2)* -ешься, *(3)* -ется, *(4)* -емся, *(5)* -етесь, *(6)* -ются.

прибли́зиться *pf, future:* *(1)* прибли́жусь, *(2)* прибли́з-ишься, *(3)* -ится, *(4)* -имся, *(5)* -итесь, *(6)* -ятся.

прибыва́ть *impf, present:* *(1)* прибыва́-ю, *(2)* -ешь, *(3)* -ет, *(4)* -ем, *(5)* -ете, *(6)* -ют.

прибы́ть *pf, future:* *(1)* прибу́д-у, *(2)* -ешь, *(3)* -ет, *(4)* -ем, *(5)* -ете, *(6)* -ут.

привести́ *pf, future:* *(1)* привед-у́, *(2)* -ёшь, *(3)* -ёт, *(4)* -ём, *(5)* -ёте, *(6)* -у́т; *past:* привёл, привел-а́, -о́, -и́.

приве́тствовать *impf, present:* *(1)* приве́тству-ю, *(2)* -ешь, *(3)* -ет, *(4)* -ем, *(5)* -ете, *(6)* -ют.

привлека́ть *impf, present:* *(1)* привлека́-ю, *(2)* -ешь, *(3)* -ет, *(4)* -ем, *(5)* -ете, *(6)* -ют.

привле́чь *pf, future:* *(1)* привлеку́, *(2)* привлеч-ёшь, *(3)* -ёт, *(4)* -ём, *(5)* -ёте, *(6)* привлеку́т; *past:* привлёк, привлекл-а́, -о́, -и́.

приводи́ть *impf, present:* *(1)* привожу́, *(2)* приво́д-ишь, *(3)* -ит, *(4)* -им, *(5)* -ите, *(6)* -ят.

привыка́ть *impf, present:* *(1)* привыка́-ю, *(2)* -ешь, *(3)* -ет, *(4)* -ем, *(5)* -ете, *(6)* -ют.

привы́кнуть *pf, future:* *(1)* привы́кн-у, *(2)* -ешь, *(3)* -ет, *(4)* -ем, *(5)* -ете, *(6)* -ут; *past:* привык, -ла,-ло, -ли.

привяза́ться *pf, future:* *(1)* привяжу́сь, *(2)* привя́ж-ешься, *(3)* -ется, *(4)* -емся, *(5)* -етесь, *(6)* -утся.

привя́зываться *impf, present:* *(1)* привя́зыва-юсь, *(2)* -ешься, *(3)* -ется, *(4)* -емся, *(5)* -етесь, *(6)* -ются.

пригласи́ть *pf, future:* *(1)* приглашу́, *(2)* приглас-и́шь, *(3)* -и́т, *(4)* -и́м, *(5)* -и́те, *(6)* -я́т.

приглаша́ть *impf, present:* *(1)* приглаша́-ю, *(2)* -ешь, *(3)* -ет, *(4)* -ем, *(5)* -ете, *(6)* -ют.

приго́товить *pf, future:* *(1)* приго́тов-лю, *(2)* -ишь, *(3)* -ит, *(4)* -им, *(5)* -ите, *(6)* -ят.

придава́ть *impf present:* *(1)* прида-ю, *(2)* -ёшь, *(3)* -ёт, *(4)* -ём, *(5)* -ёте, *(6)* -ют.

прида́ть *pf, future:* *(1)* прида́-м, *(2)* -шь, *(3)* -ст, *(4)* -дим, *(5)* -дите, *(6)* -дут.

придира́ться *impf, present:* *(1)* придира́-юсь, *(2)* -ешься, *(3)* -ется, *(4)* -емся, *(5)* -етесь, *(6)* -ются.

приду́мать *pf, future:* *(1)* приду́ма-ю, *(2)* -ешь, *(3)* -ет, *(4)* -ем, *(5)* -ете, *(6)* -ют.

приду́мывать *impf, present:* *(1)* приду́мыва-ю, *(2)* -ешь, *(3)* -ет, *(4)* -ем, *(5)* -ете, *(6)* -ют.

приезжа́ть *impf, present:* *(1)* приезжа́-ю, *(2)* -ешь, *(3)* -ет, *(4)* -ем, *(5)* -ете, *(6)* -ют.

прие́хать *pf, future:* *(1)* прие́д-у, *(2)* -ешь, *(3)* -ет, *(4)* -ем, *(5)* -ете, *(6)* -ут.

прижа́ть(ся) *pf, future:* *(1)* прижм-у́(сь), *(2)* -ёшь(ся), *(3)* -ёт(ся), *(4)* -ём(ся), *(5)* -ёте(сь), *(6)* -у́т(ся).

прижима́ть(ся) *impf, present:* *(1)* прижима́-ю(сь), *(2)* -ешь(ся), *(3)* -ет(ся), *(4)* -ем(ся), *(5)* -ете(сь), *(6)* -ют(ся).

признавать(ся) *impf, present:* *(1)* призна-ю́(сь), *(2)* -ёшь(ся), *(3)* -ёт(ся), *(4)* -ём(ся), *(5)* -ёте(сь), *(6)* -ю́т(ся).

призна́ть(ся) *pf, future:* *(1)* призна́-ю(сь), *(2)* -ешь(ся), *(3)* -ет(ся), *(4)* -ем(ся), *(5)*

Persons: 1 = я, 2 = ты, 3 = он, она́, оно́, 4 = мы, 5 = вы, 6 = они́

-ете(сь), *(6)* -ют(ся).

прийти́ *pf, future:* *(1)* прид-у́, *(2)* -ёшь, *(3)* -ёт, *(4)* -ём, *(5)* -ёте, *(6)* -у́т; *past:* при-шёл, -шла́, -шло́, -шли́.

прилага́ть *impf, present:* *(1)* прилага́-ю, *(2)* -ешь, *(3)* -ет, *(4)* -ем, *(5)* -ете, *(6)* -ют.

приласка́ться *impf, present:* *(1)* приласка́-юсь, *(2)* -ешься, *(3)* -ется, *(4)* -емся, *(5)* - етесь, *(6)* -ются.

прилета́ть *impf, present:* *(1)* прилета́-ю, *(2)* -ешь, *(3)* -ет, *(4)* -ем, *(5)* -ете, *(6)* -ют.

прилете́ть *pf, future:* *(1)* прилечу́, *(2)* прилет-и́шь, *(3)* -и́т, *(4)* -и́м, *(5)* -и́те, *(6)* -я́т.

приле́чь *pf, future:* *(1)* приля́-гу, *(2)* приля́ж-ешь, *(3)* -ет, *(4)* -ем, *(5)* -ете, *(6)* приля́гут.

прилипа́ть *impf, present:* *(1)* прилипа́-ю, *(2)* -ешь, *(3)* -ет, *(4)* -ем, *(5)* -ете, *(6)* -ют.

прили́пнуть *pf, future:* *(1)* прили́пн-у, *(2)* -ешь, *(3)* -ет, *(4)* -ем, *(5)* -ете, *(6)* -ут; *past:* прили́п, -ла,-ло, -ли.

приложи́ть *pf, future:* *(1)* приложу́, *(2)* прило́ж-ишь, *(3)* -ит, *(4)* -им, *(5)* -ите, *(6)* -ат.

прильну́ть *pf, future:* *(1)* прильн-у́, *(2)* -ёшь, *(3)* -ёт, *(4)* -ём, *(5)* -ёте, *(6)* -у́т.

примири́ть(ся) *pf, future:* *(1)* примир-ю́(сь), *(2)* -и́шь(ся), *(3)* -и́т(ся), *(4)* -и́м(ся), *(5)* -и́те(сь), *(6)* -я́т(ся).

примиря́ть *impf, present:* *(1)* примиря́-ю, *(2)* -ешь, *(3)* -ет, *(4)* -ем, *(5)* -ете, *(6)* -ют.

примиря́ть(ся) *impf, present:* *(1)* примиря́-ю(сь), *(2)* -ешь(ся), *(3)* -ет(ся), *(4)* -ем(ся), *(5)* -ете(сь), *(6)* -ют(ся).

принадлежа́ть *impf, present:* *(1)* принадлежу́, *(2)* -и́шь, *(3)* -и́т, *(4)* -и́м, *(5)* -и́те, *(6)* -а́т.

принести́ *pf, future:* *(1)* принес-у́, *(2)* -ёшь, *(3)* -ёт, *(4)* -ём, *(5)* -ёте, *(6)* -у́т; *past:* принёс, принес-ла́, -ло́, -ли́.

принима́ть *impf, present:* *(1)* принима́-ю, *(2)* -ешь, *(3)* -ет, *(4)* -ем, *(5)* -ете, *(6)* -ют.

приноси́ть *impf, present:* *(1)* приношу́, *(2)* прино́с-ишь, *(3)* -ит, *(4)* -им, *(5)* -ите, *(6)* -ят.

прину́дить *pf, future:* *(1)* принужу́, *(2)* принуд-и́шь, *(3)* -и́т, *(4)* -и́м, *(5)* -и́те, *(6)* -я́т.

принужда́ть *impf, present:* *(1)* принужда́-ю, *(2)* -ешь, *(3)* -ет, *(4)* -ем, *(5)* -ете, *(6)* -ют.

приня́ть *pf, future:* *(1)* приму́, *(2)* при́м-ешь, *(3)* -ет, *(4)* -ем, *(5)* -ете, *(6)* -ут.

приобрести́ *pf, future:* *(1)* приобрет-у́, *(2)* -ёшь, *(3)* -ёт, *(4)* -ём, *(5)* -ёте, *(6)* -у́т; *past:* приобрёл, приобе-ла́, -ло́, -ли́.

приобрета́ть *impf, present:* *(1)* приобрета́-ю, *(2)* -ешь, *(3)* -ет, *(4)* -ем, *(5)* -ете, *(6)* -ют.

припомина́ть *impf, present:* *(1)* припомина́-ю, *(2)* -ешь, *(3)* -ет, *(4)* -ем, *(5)* -ете, *(6)* -ют.

припо́мнить *pf, future:* *(1)* припо́мн-ю, *(2)* -ишь, *(3)* -ит, *(4)* -им, *(5)* -ите, *(6)* -ят.

приревнова́ть *pf, future:* *(1)* приревну́-ю, *(2)* -ешь, *(3)* -ет, *(4)* -ем, *(5)* -ете, *(6)* -ют.

прислони́ться *pf, future:* *(1)* прислон-ю́сь, *(2)*-и́шься, *(3)* -и́тся, *(4)* -и́мся, *(5)* -и́тесь, *(6)* -я́тся.

прислоня́ться *impf, present:* *(1)* прислоня́-юсь, *(2)* -ешься, *(3)* -ется, *(4)* -емся, *(5)* -етесь, *(6)* -ются.

присма́триваться *impf, present:* *(1)* присма́трива-юсь, *(2)*-ишься, *(3)* -ится, *(4)* -имся, *(5)* -итесь, *(6)* -ются.

присни́ться *pf, future:* *(3)* присн-и́тся, *(6)* -я́тся.

присоедини́ться *pf, future:* *(1)* присоедин-ю́сь, *(2)*-и́шься, *(3)* -и́тся, *(4)* -и́мся, *(5)* -и́тесь, *(6)* -я́тся.

присоединя́ться *impf, present:* *(1)* присоединя́-юсь, *(2)* -ешься, *(3)* -ется, *(4)* -емся, *(5)* -етесь, *(6)* -ются.

приспоса́бливать(ся) *impf, present:* *(1)* приспоса́блива-ю(сь), *(2)* -ешь(ся), *(3)* -ет(ся), *(4)* -ем(ся), *(5)* -ете(сь), *(6)* -ют(ся).

приспосо́бить(ся)*pf, future:* *(1)* приспо́соб-лю(сь), *(2)*-ишь(ся), *(3)* -ит(ся), *(4)*

Persons: 1 = я, 2 = ты, 3 = он, она́, оно́, 4 = мы, 5 = вы, 6 = они́

-им(ся), *(5)* -ите(сь), *(6)* -ят(ся).

приставать *impf present:* *(1)* приста-ю́, *(2)* -ёшь, *(3)* -ёт, *(4)* -ём, *(5)* -ёте, *(6)* -ю́т.

пристать *pf, future:* *(1)* пристан-у, *(2)* -ешь, *(3)* -ет, *(4)* -ем, *(5)* -ете, *(6)* -ут.

пристраститься *pf, future:* *(1)* пристращу́сь, *(2)* пристраст-и́шься, *(3)* -и́тся, *(4)* -и́мся, *(5)* -и́тесь, *(6)* -я́тся.

притвори́ться *pf, future:* *(1)* притвор-ю́сь, *(2)* -и́шься, *(3)* -и́тся, *(4)* -и́мся, *(5)* -и́тесь, *(6)* -я́тся.

притворя́ться *impf, present:* *(1)* притворя́-юсь, *(2)* -ешься, *(3)* -ется, *(4)* -емся, *(5)* -етесь, *(6)* -ются.

притя́гивать *impf, present:* *(1)* притя́гива-ю, *(2)* -ешь, *(3)* -ет, *(4)* -ем, *(5)* -ете, *(6)* -ют.

притяну́ть *pf, future:* *(1)* притяну́, *(2)* притя́н-ешь, *(3)* -ет, *(4)* -ем, *(5)* -ете, *(6)* -ут.

приходи́ть *impf, present:* *(1)* прихожу́, *(2)* прихо́д-ишь, *(3)* -ит, *(4)* -им, *(5)* -ите, *(6)* -ят.

прихора́шиваться *impf, present:* *(1)* прихора́шива-юсь, *(2)* -ешься, *(3)* -ется, *(4)* -емся, *(5)* -етесь, *(6)* -ются.

причеса́ть(ся) *pf, future:* *(1)* причешу́(сь), *(2)* причёш-ешь(ся), *(3)* -ет(ся), *(4)* -ем(ся), *(5)* -ете(сь), *(6)* -ут(с)я.

причёсывать(ся) *impf, present:* *(1)* причёсыва-ю(сь), *(2)* -ешь(ся), *(3)* -ет(ся), *(4)* -ем(ся), *(5)* -ете(сь), *(6)* -ют(ся).

причини́ть *pf, future:* *(1)* причин-ю́, *(2)* -и́шь, *(3)* -и́т, *(4)* -и́м, *(5)* -и́те, *(6)* -я́т.

причиня́ть *impf, present:* *(1)* причиня́-ю, *(2)* -ешь, *(3)* -ет, *(4)* -ем, *(5)* -ете, *(6)* -ют.

пробега́ть *impf, present:* *(1)* пробега́-ю, *(2)* -ешь, *(3)* -ет, *(4)* -ем, *(5)* -ете, *(6)* -ют.

пробежа́ть *pf, future:* *(1)* пробегу́, *(2)* пробеж-и́шь, *(3)* -и́т, *(4)* -и́м, *(5)* -и́те, *(6)* пробегу́т.

про́бовать *impf, present:* *(1)* про́бу-ю, *(2)* -ешь, *(3)* -ет, *(4)* -ем, *(5)* -ете, *(6)* -ют.

пробуди́ть(ся) *pf, future:* *(1)* пробужу́(сь), *(2)* пробу́д-ишь(ся), *(3)* -ит(ся), *(4)* -им(ся), *(5)* -ите(сь), *(6)* -ят(ся).

пробужда́ть(ся) *impf, present:* *(1)* пробужда́-ю(сь), *(2)* -ешь(ся), *(3)* -ет(ся), *(4)* -ем(ся), *(5)* -ете(сь), *(6)* -ют(ся).

прова́ливаться *impf, present:* *(1)* прова́лива-юсь, *(2)* -ешься, *(3)* -ется, *(4)* -емся, *(5)* -етесь, *(6)* -ются.

провали́ться *pf, future:* *(1)* провалю́сь, *(2)* прова́л-ишься, *(3)* -ится, *(4)* -имся, *(5)* -ишься, *(6)* -ятся.

прове́рить *pf, future:* *(1)* прове́р-ю, *(2)* -ишь, *(3)* -ит, *(4)* -им, *(5)* -ите, *(6)* -ят.

проверя́ть *impf, present:* *(1)* проверя́-ю, *(2)* -ешь, *(3)* -ет, *(4)* -ем, *(5)* -ете, *(6)* -ют.

провести́ *pf, future:* *(1)* провед-у́, *(2)* -ёшь, *(3)* -ёт, *(4)* -ём, *(5)* -ёте, *(6)* -у́т; *past:* провёл, провел-а́, -о́, -и́.

проводи́ть *impf, present:* *(1)* провожу́, *(2)* прово́д-ишь, *(3)* -ит, *(4)* -им, *(5)* -ите, *(6)* -ят.

провози́ться *pf, future:* *(1)* провожу́сь, *(2)* прово́з-ишься, *(3)* -ится, *(4)* -имся, *(5)* -итесь, *(6)* -ятся.

прогна́ть *pf, future:* *(1)* прогоню́, *(2)* прого́н-ишь, *(3)* -ит, *(4)* -им, *(5)* -ите, *(6)* -ят; *past:* прогна́л, прогнала́, прогна́л-о, -и.

прогоня́ть *impf, present:* *(1)* прогоня́-ю, *(2)* -ешь, *(3)* -ет, *(4)* -ем, *(5)* -ете, *(6)* -ют.

продлева́ть *impf, present:* *(1)* продлева́-ю, *(2)* -ешь, *(3)* -ет, *(4)* -ем, *(5)* -ете, *(6)* -ют.

продли́ть *pf, future:* *(1)* продл-ю́, *(2)* -и́шь, *(3)* -и́т, *(4)* -и́м, *(5)* -и́те, *(6)* -я́т.

продолжа́ть *impf, present:* *(1)* продолжа́-ю, *(2)* -ешь, *(3)* -ет, *(4)* -ем, *(5)* -ете, *(6)* -ют.

продо́лжить *pf, future:* *(1)* продо́лж-у, *(2)* -ишь, *(3)* -ит, *(4)* -им, *(5)* -ите, *(6)* -ат.

прожи́ть *pf future:* *(1)* прожив-у́, *(2)* -ёшь, *(3)* -ёт, *(4)* -ём, *(5)* -ёте, *(6)* -у́т; *past:* прожи́л, прожила́, прожи́л-о, -и.

произвести́ *pf, future:* *(1)* произвед-у́, *(2)* -ёшь, *(3)* -ёт, *(4)* -ём, *(5)* -ёте, *(6)* -у́т; *past:*

Persons: 1 = я, 2 = ты, 3 = он, она́, оно́, 4 = мы, 5 = вы, 6 = они́

провёл, провел-а́, -о́, -и́.

производи́ть *impf, present:* *(1)* произвожу́, *(2)* произво́д-ишь, *(3)* -ит, *(4)* -им, *(5)* -ите, *(6)* -ят.

произнести́ *pf, future:* *(1)* произнес-у́ *(2)* -ёшь, *(3)* -ёт, *(4)* -ём, *(5)* -ёте, *(6)* -у́т; *past:* произнёс, произнесл-а́, -о́, -и́.

произноси́ть *impf, present:* *(1)* произношу́, *(2)* произно́с-ишь, *(3)* -ит, *(4)* -им, *(5)* -ите, *(6)* -ят.

произойти́ *pf, future:* *(3)* произойд-ёт, *(6)* -у́т; *past:* произо-шёл, -шла́, -шло́, -шли́.

происходи́ть *impf, present:* *(3)* происхо́д-ит, *(6)* -ят.

пройти́ *pf, future:* *(1)* пройд-у́, *(2)* -ёшь, *(3)* -ёт, *(4)* -ём, *(5)* -ёте, *(6)* -у́т; *past:* про-шёл, -шла́, -шло́, -шли́.

прока́лывать *impf, present:* *(1)* прока́лыва-ю, *(2)* -ешь, *(3)* -ет, *(4)* -ем, *(5)* -ете, *(6)* -ют.

прокла́дывать *impf, present:* *(1)* прокла́дыва-ю, *(2)* -ешь, *(3)* -ет, *(4)* -ем, *(5)* -ете, *(6)* -ют.

проколо́ть *pf, future:* *(1)* проколю́, *(2)* проко́л-ешь, *(3)* -ет, *(4)* -ем, *(5)* -ете, *(6)* -ют.

прокра́дываться *impf, present:* *(1)* прокра́дыва-юсь, *(2)* -ешься, *(3)* -ется, *(4)* -емся, *(5)* -етесь, *(6)* -ются.

прокра́сться *pf, future:* *(1)* прокрад-у́сь, *(2)* -ёшься, *(3)* -ётся, *(4)* -ёмся, *(5)* -ётесь, *(6)* -у́тся; *past:* прокра́лся, прокрала́сь, прокра́-лось, -лись.

проложи́ть *pf, future:* *(1)* проложу́, *(2)* проло́ж-ишь, *(3)* -ит, *(4)* -им, *(5)* -ите, *(6)* -ат.

промахну́ться *pf, future:* *(1)* промахн-у́сь, *(2)*-ёшься, *(3)* -ётся, *(4)* -ёмся, *(5)* -ётесь, *(6)* -у́тся.

промча́ться *pf, future:* *(1)* промч-у́сь, *(2)* -и́шься, *(3)* -и́тся, *(4)* -и́мся, *(5)* -и́тесь, *(6)* -а́тся.

пронести́сь *pf, future:* *(1)* принес-у́сь, *(2)* -ёшься, *(3)* -ётся, *(4)* -ёмся, *(5)* -ётесь, *(6)* -у́тся; *past:* принёсся, принес-ла́сь, -ло́сь, -ли́сь.

пронза́ть *impf, present:* *(1)* пронза́-ю, *(2)* -ешь, *(3)* -ет, *(4)* -ем, *(5)* -ете, *(6)* -ют.

пронзи́ть *pf, future:* *(1)* пронжу́, *(2)* пронз-и́шь, *(3)* -и́т, *(4)* -и́м, *(5)* -и́те, *(6)* -я́т.

прони́зывать *impf, present:* *(1)* прони́зыва-ю, *(2)* -ешь, *(3)* -ет, *(4)* -ем, *(5)* -ете, *(6)* -ют.

проника́ть(ся) *impf, present:* *(1)* проника́-ю(сь), *(2)* -ешь(ся), *(3)* -ет(ся), *(4)* -ем(ся), *(5)* -ете(сь), *(6)* -ют(ся).

прони́кнуть(ся) *pf, future:* *(1)* прони́кн-у(сь), *(2)* -ешь(ся), *(3)* -ет(ся), *(4)* -ем(ся), *(5)* -ете(сь), *(6)* -ут(ся); *past:* прони́к(ся), -ла(сь), -ло(сь), -ли(сь).

проноси́ться *impf, present:* *(1)* проношу́сь, *(2)* проно́с-ишься, *(3)* -ится, *(4)* -имся, *(5)* -итесь, *(6)* -ятся.

пропита́ть *pf, future:* *(1)* пропита́-ю, *(2)* -ешь, *(3)* -ет, *(4)* -ем, *(5)* -ете, *(6)* -ют.

пропи́тывать *impf, present:* *(1)* пропи́тыва-ю, *(2)* -ешь, *(3)* -ет, *(4)* -ем, *(5)* -ете, *(6)* -ют.

прореаги́ровать *pf, future:* *(1)* прореаги́ру-ю, *(2)* -ешь, *(3)* -ет, *(4)* -ем, *(5)* -ете, *(6)* -ют.

просвети́ть *pf, future:* *(1)* просвещу́, *(2)* просвет-и́шь, *(3)* -и́т, *(4)* -и́м, *(5)* -и́те, *(6)* -я́т.

просвеща́ть *impf, present:* *(1)* просвеща́-ю, *(2)* -ешь, *(3)* -ет, *(4)* -ем, *(5)* -ете, *(6)* -ют.

проси́ть *impf, present:* *(1)* прошу́, *(2)* про́с-ишь, *(3)* -ит, *(4)* -им, *(5)* -ите, *(6)* -ят.

проска́льзывать *impf, present:* *(1)* проска́льзыва-ю, *(2)* -ешь, *(3)* -ет, *(4)* -ем, *(5)* -ете, *(6)* -ют.

проскользну́ть *pf, future:* *(1)* проскользн-у́, *(2)* -ёшь, *(3)* -ёт, *(4)* -ём, *(5)* -ёте, *(6)* -у́т.

просла́вить *pf, future:* *(1)* просла́в-лю, *(2)* -ишь, *(3)* -ит, *(4)* -им, *(5)* -ите, *(6)* -ят.

прославля́ть *impf, present:* *(1)* прославля́-ю, *(2)* -ешь, *(3)* -ет, *(4)* -ем, *(5)* -ете, *(6)* -ют.

просну́ться *pf, future:* *(1)* просн-у́сь, *(2)* -ёшься, *(3)* -ётся, *(4)* -ёмся, *(5)* -ётесь, *(6)*

Persons: 1 = я, 2 = ты, 3 = он, она́, оно́, 4 = мы, 5 = вы, 6 = они́

-у́тся.

проспа́ть *pf, future:* *(1)* просп-лю́, *(2)* -и́шь, *(3)* -и́т, *(4)* -и́м, *(5)* -и́те, *(6)* -я́т; *past:* проспа́л, проспала́, проспа́-ло, -ли.

прости́ть *pf, future:* *(1)* прощу́, *(2)* прост-и́шь, *(3)* -и́т, *(4)* -и́м, *(5)* -и́те, *(6)* -я́т.

просыпа́ть(ся *)impf, present:* *(1)* просыпа́-ю(сь), *(2)* -ешь(ся), *(3)* -ет(ся), *(4)* -ем(ся), *(5)* -ете(сь), *(6)* -ют(ся).

проходи́ть *impf, present:* *(1)* прохожу́, *(2)* прохо́д-ишь, *(3)* -ит, *(4)* -им, *(5)* -ите, *(6)* -ят.

процвета́ть *impf, present:* *(1)* процвета́-ю, *(2)* -ешь, *(3)* -ет, *(4)* -ем, *(5)* -ете, *(6)* -ют.

прочёсть *pf, future:* *(1)* прочт-у́, *(2)* -ёшь, *(3)* -ёт, *(4)* -ём, *(5)* -ёте, *(6)* -у́т; *past:* прочёл, прочл-а́, -о́, -и́.

прочита́ть *pf, future:* *(1)* прочита́-ю, *(2)* -ешь, *(3)* -ет, *(4)* -ем, *(5)* -ете, *(6)* -ют.

прошепта́ть *pf, future:* *(1)* прошепчу́, *(2)* проше́пч-ешь, *(3)* -ет, *(4)* -ем, *(5)* -ете, *(6)* -ут.

проща́ть(ся) *impf, present:* *(1)* проща́-ю(сь), *(2)* -ешь(ся), *(3)* -ет(ся), *(4)* -ем(ся), *(5)* -етесь, *(6)* -ют(ся).

прощу́пать *pf, future:* *(1)* прощу́па-ю, *(2)* -ешь, *(3)* -ет, *(4)* -ем, *(5)* -ете, *(6)* -ют.

прощу́пывать *impf, present:* *(1)* прощу́пыва-ю, *(2)* -ешь, *(3)* -ет, *(4)* -ем, *(5)* -ете, *(6)* -ют.

прояви́ть *pf, future:* *(1)* прояв-лю́, *(2)* проя́в-ишь, *(3)* -ит, *(4)* -им, *(5)* -ите, *(6)* -ят.

проявля́ть *impf, present:* *(1)* проявля́-ю, *(2)* -ешь, *(3)* -ет, *(4)* -ем, *(5)* -ете, *(6)* -ют.

пры́гать *impf, present:* *(1)* пры́га-ю, *(2)* -ешь, *(3)* -ет, *(4)* -ем, *(5)* -ете, *(6)* -ют.

пры́гнуть *pf, future:* *(1)* пры́гн-у, *(2)* -ешь, *(3)* -ет, *(4)* -ем, *(5)* -ете, *(6)* -ут.

пря́тать(ся) *impf, present:* *(1)* пря́ч-у(сь), *(2)* -ешь(ся), *(3)* -ет(ся), *(4)* -ем(ся), *(5)* -ете(сь), *(6)* -ут(ся).

пуга́ть(ся) *impf, present:* *(1)* пуга́-ю(сь), *(2)* -ешь(ся), *(3)* -ет(ся), *(4)* -ем(ся), *(5)* -ете(сь), *(6)* -ют(ся).

пульси́ровать *impf, present:* *(1)* пульси́ру-ю, *(2)* -ешь, *(3)* -ет, *(4)* -ем, *(5)* -ете, *(6)* -ют.

пу́тать(ся) *impf, present:* *(1)* пу́та-ю(сь), *(2)* -ешь(ся), *(3)* -ет(ся), *(4)* -ем(ся), *(5)* -ете(сь), *(6)*

путеше́ствовать *impf, present:* *(1)* путеше́ству-ю, *(2)* -ешь, *(3)* -ет, *(4)* -ем, *(5)* -ете, *(6)* -ют.

пыла́ть *impf, present:* *(1)* пыла́-ю, *(2)* -ешь, *(3)* -ет, *(4)* -ем, *(5)* -ете, *(6)* -ют.

пыта́ться *impf, present:* *(1)* пыта́-юсь, *(2)* -ешься, *(3)* -ется, *(4)* -емся, *(5)* -етесь, *(6)* -ются.

пьяне́ть *impf, present:* *(1)* пьяне́-ю, *(2)* -ешь, *(3)* -ет, *(4)* -ем, *(5)* -ете, *(6)* -ют.

рабо́тать *impf, present:* *(1)* рабо́та-ю, *(2)* -ешь, *(3)* -ет, *(4)* -ем, *(5)* -ете, *(6)* -ют.

ра́довать(ся) *impf, present:* *(1)* ра́ду-ю(сь), *(2)* -ешь(ся), *(3)* -ет(ся), *(4)* -ем(ся), *(5)* -ете(сь), *(6)* -ют(ся).

разбива́ть *impf, present:* *(1)* разбива́-ю, *(2)* -ешь, *(3)* -ет, *(4)* -ем, *(5)* -ете, *(6)* -ют.

разбира́ться *impf, present:* *(1)* разбира́-юсь, *(2)* -ешься, *(3)* -ется, *(4)* -емся, *(5)* -етесь, *(6)* -ются.

разби́ть *pf, future:* *(1)* разобь-ю́, *(2)* -ёшь, *(3)* -ёт, *(4)* -ём, *(5)* -ёте, *(6)* -ю́т.

разбра́сывать *impf, present:* *(1)* разбра́сыва-ю, *(2)* -ешь, *(3)* -ет, *(4)* -ем, *(5)* -ете, *(6)* -ют.

разброса́ть *pf, future:* *(1)* разброса́-ю, *(2)* -ешь, *(3)* -ет, *(4)* -ем, *(5)* -ете, *(6)* -ют.

разбуди́ть *pf, future:* *(1)* разбужу́, *(2)* разбу́д-ишь, *(3)* -ит, *(4)* -им, *(5)* -ите, *(6)* -ят.

разва́ливаться *impf, present:* *(1)* разва́лива-юсь, *(2)* -ешься, *(3)* -ется, *(4)* -емся, *(5)* -етесь, *(6)* -ются.

развали́ться *pf, future:* *(1)* развалю́сь, *(2)* разва́л-ишься, *(3)* -ится, *(4)* -имся, *(5)* -итесь, *(6)* -ятся.

> *Persons:* 1 = я,   2 = ты,   3 = он, она́, оно́,   4 = мы,   5 = вы,   6 = они́

развесели́ть *pf, future:* *(1)* развесел-ю́, *(2)* -и́шь, *(3)* -и́т, *(4)* -и́м, *(5)* -и́те, *(6)* -я́т.

развести́сь *pf, future:* *(1)* развед-у́сь, *(2)* -ёшься, *(3)* -ётся, *(4)* -ёмся, *(5)* -ётесь, *(6)* -у́тся; *past:* развёлся, разве-ла́сь, -ло́сь, -ли́сь.

разве́ять *pf, future:* *(1)* разве́-ю, *(2)* -ешь, *(3)* -ет, *(4)* -ем, *(5)* -ете, *(6)* -ют.

развива́ть(ся) *impf, present:* *(1)* развива́-ю(сь), *(2)* -ешь(ся), *(3)* -ет(ся), *(4)* -ем(ся), *(5)* -ете(сь), *(6)* -ют(ся).

разви́ть *pf, future:* *(1)* разовь-ю́, *(2)* -ёшь, *(3)* -ёт, *(4)* -ём, *(5)* -ёте, *(6)* -ю́т; *past:* разви́л, развила́, разви́-ло, -ли.

разви́ть(ся) *pf, future:* *(1)* разовь-ю́(сь), *(2)* -ёшь(ся), *(3)* -ёт(ся), *(4)* -ём(ся), *(5)* -ёте(сь), *(6)* -ю́т(ся); *past:* разви́л(ся), разви́-ла(сь),-ло(сь), -ли(сь).

развлека́ть(ся) *impf, present:* *(1)* развлека́-ю(сь), *(2)* -ешь(ся), *(3)* -ет(ся), *(4)* -ем(ся), *(5)* -етесь, *(6)* -ют(ся).

разводи́ться *impf, present:* *(1)* развожу́сь, *(2)* развод-ишься, *(3)* -ится, *(4)* -имся, *(5)* -итесь, *(6)* -ятся.

развра́тничать *impf, present:* *(1)* развра́тнича-ю, *(2)* -ешь, *(3)* -ет, *(4)* -ем, *(5)* -ете, *(6)* -ют.

развяза́ть *pf, future:* *(1)* развяжу́, *(2)* развя́ж-ешь, *(3)* -ет, *(4)* -ем, *(5)* -ете, *(6)* -ут.

развя́зывать *impf, present:* *(1)* развя́зыва-ю, *(2)* -ешь, *(3)* -ет, *(4)* -ем, *(5)* -ете, *(6)* -ют.

разгова́ривать *impf, present:* *(1)* разгова́рива-ю, *(2)* -ешь, *(3)* -ет, *(4)* -ем, *(5)* -ете, *(6)* -ют.

разгоня́ть *impf, present:* *(1)* разгоня́-ю, *(2)* -ешь, *(3)* -ет, *(4)* -ем, *(5)* -ете, *(6)* -ют.

раздави́ть *pf, future:* *(1)* раздавлю́, *(2)* разда́в-ишь, *(3)* -ит, *(4)* -им, *(5)* -ите, *(6)* -ят.

раздева́ть(ся) *impf, present:* *(1)* раздева́-ю(сь), *(2)* -ешь(ся), *(3)* -ет(ся), *(4)* -ем(ся), *(5)* -ете(сь), *(6)* -ют(ся).

раздели́ть *pf, future:* *(1)* разделю́, *(2)* разде́л-ишь, *(3)* -ит, *(4)* -им, *(5)* -ите, *(6)* -ят.

разделя́ть *impf, present:* *(1)* разделя́-ю, *(2)* -ешь, *(3)* -ет, *(4)* -ем, *(5)* -ете, *(6)* -ют.

разде́ть(ся) *pf, future:* *(1)* разде́н-у(сь), *(2)* -ешь(ся), *(3)* -ет(ся), *(4)* -ем(ся), *(5)* -ете(сь), *(6)* -ут(ся).

раздража́ть(ся) *impf, present:* *(1)* раздража́-ю(сь), *(2)* -ешь(ся), *(3)* -ет(ся), *(4)* -ем(ся), *(5)* -ете(сь), *(6)* -ют(ся).
ют(ся).

раздражи́ть *pf, future:* *(1)* раздражу́, *(2)* -ишь, *(3)* -ит, *(4)* -им, *(5)* -ите, *(6)* -ат.

раздува́ть *impf, present:* *(1)* раздува́-ю, *(2)* -ешь, *(3)* -ет, *(4)* -ем, *(5)* -ете, *(6)* -ют.

разду́мывать *impf, present:* *(1)* разду́мыва-ю, *(2)* -ешь, *(3)* -ет, *(4)* -ем, *(5)* -ете, *(6)* -ют.

разду́ть *pf, future:* *(1)* разду́-ю, *(2)* -ешь, *(3)* -ет, *(4)* -ем, *(5)* -ете, *(6)* -ют.

разже́чь *pf, future:* *(1)* разожгу́, *(2)* раззож-ёшь, *(3)* -ёт, *(4)* -ём, *(5)* -ёте, *(6)* разожгу́т; *past:* разжёг, разожг-ла́, -ло́, -ли́.

разжига́ть *impf, present:* *(1)* разжига́-ю, *(2)* -ешь, *(3)* -ет, *(4)* -ем, *(5)* -ете, *(6)* -ют.

разлива́ть *impf, present:* *(1)* разлива́-ю, *(2)* -ешь, *(3)* -ет, *(4)* -ем, *(5)* -ете, *(6)* -ют.

разлива́ться *impf, present:* *(3)* разлива́-ется, *(6)* -ю́тся.

разли́ться *pf, future:* *(3)* разоль-ётся, *(6)* -ю́тся.

разлуча́ться *impf, present:* *(1)* разлуча́-юсь, *(2)* -ешься, *(3)* -ется, *(4)* -емся, *(5)* -етесь, *(6)* -ются.

разлучи́ться *pf, future:* *(1)* разлуч-у́сь, *(2)* -и́шься, *(3)* -и́тся, *(4)* -и́мся, *(5)* -и́тесь, *(6)* -а́тся.

разлюби́ть *pf, future:* *(1)* разлюблю́, *(2)* разлю́б-ишь, *(3)* -ит, *(4)* -им, *(5)* -ите, *(6)* -ят.

размышля́ть *impf, present:* *(1)* размышля́-ю, *(2)* -ешь, *(3)* -ет, *(4)* -ем, *(5)* -ете, *(6)* -ют.

размяка́ть *impf, present:* *(1)* размяка́-ю, *(2)* -ешь, *(3)* -ет, *(4)* -ем, *(5)* -ете, *(6)* -ют.

размя́кнуть *pf, future:* *(1)* размя́кн-у, *(2)* -ешь, *(3)* -ет, *(4)* -ем, *(5)* -ете, *(6)* -ут; *past:* размя́к, -ла, -ло, -ли.

Persons: 1 = я, 2 = ты, 3 = он, онá, онó, 4 = мы, 5 = вы, 6 = онѝ

разобрáться *pf, future:* (1) разбер-ýсь, (2) -ёшься, (3) -ётся, (4) -ёмся, (5) -ётесь, (6) -ýтся.

разогнáть *pf, future:* (1) разгоню́, (2) разгóн-ишь, (3) -ит, (4) -им, (5) -ите, (6) -ят; *past:* разогнáл, разогналá, разогнá-ло, -ли.

разойти́сь *pf, future:* (1) разойд-ýсь, (2) -ёшься, (3) -ётся, (4) -ёмся, (5) -ётесь, (6) -ýтся; *past:* разошёлся, разо-шлáсь, -шлóсь, -шли́сь.

разорвáть(ся) *pf, future:* (1) разорв-ý(сь), (2) -ёшь(ся), (3) -ёт(ся), (4) -ём(ся), (5) -ёте(сь), (6) -ýт(ся).

разори́ть *pf, future:* (1) разор-ю́, (2) -и́шь, (3) -и́т, (4) -и́м, (5) -и́те, (6) -я́т.

разоря́ть *impf, present:* (1) разоря́-ю, (2) -ешь, (3) -ет, (4) -ем, (5) -ете, (6) -ют.

разослáть *pf, future:* (1) разошл-ю́, (2) -ёшь, (3) -ёт, (4) -ём, (5) -ёте, (6) -ю́т.

разочаровáть *pf, future:* (1) разочарý-ю, (2) -ешь, (3) -ет, (4) -ем, (5) -ете, (6) -ют.

разочарóвывать *impf, present:* (1) разочарóвыва-ю, (2) -ешь, (3) -ет, (4) -ем, (5) -ете, (6) -ют.

разрази́ться *pf, future:* (1) разражýсь, (2) разраз-и́шься, (3) -и́тся, (4) -и́мся, (5) -и́тесь, (6) -я́тся.

разрушáть(ся) *impf, present:* (1) разрушá-ю(сь), (2) -ешь(ся), (3) -ет(ся), (4) -ем(ся), (5) -ете(сь), (6) -ют(ся).

разрýшить *pf, future:* (1) разрýш-у, (2) -ишь, (3) -ит, (4) -им, (5) -ите, (6) -ат.

разрýшиться *pf, future:* (3) разрýш-ится, (6) -атся.

разрывáть(ся) *impf, present:* (1) разрывá-ю(сь), (2) -ешь(ся), (3) -ет(ся), (4) -ем(ся), (5) -ете(сь), (6) -ют(ся).

разъяри́ть *pf, future:* (1) разъяр-ю́, (2) -и́шь, (3) -и́т, (4) -и́м, (5) -и́те, (6) -я́т.

разъяря́ть *impf, present:* (1) разъяря́-ю, (2) -ешь, (3) -ет, (4) -ем, (5) -ете, (6) -ют.

разыгрáть *pf, future:* (1) разыгрá-ю, (2) -ешь, (3) -ет, (4) -ем, (5) -ете, (6) -ют.

разы́грывать *impf, present:* (1) разы́грыва-ю, (2) -ешь, (3) -ет, (4) -ем, (5) -ете, (6) -ют.

рáнить *impf, present:* (1) рáн-ю, (2) -ишь, (3) -ит, (4) -им, (5) -ите, (6) -ят.

раскрáсить *pf, future:* (1) раскрáшу, (2) раскрáс-ишь, (3) -ит, (4) -им, (5) -ите, (6) -ят.

раскрáшивать *impf, present:* (1) раскрáшива-ю, (2) -ешь, (3) -ет, (4) -ем, (5) -ете, (6) -ют.

раскрывáть(ся) *impf, present:* (1) раскрывá-ю(сь), (2) -ешь(ся), (3) -ет(ся), (4) -ем(ся), (5) -ете(сь), (6) -ют(ся).

раскры́ть(ся) *pf, future:* (1) раскрó-ю(сь), (2) -ешь(ся), (3) -ет(ся), (4) -ем(ся), (5) -ете(сь), -(6) -ют(ся).

распадáться *impf, present:* (1) распадá-юсь, (2) -ешься, (3) -ется, (4) -емся, (5) -етесь, (6) -ются.

распáсться *pf, future:* (3) распад-ётся, (6) -ýтся; *past:* распá-лся,-лась, -лось, -лись.

распали́ть(ся) *pf, future:* (1) распал-ю́(сь), (2) -и́шь(ся), (3) -и́т(ся), (4) -и́м(ся), (5) -и́те(сь), (6) -я́т(ся).

распаля́ть(ся) *impf, present:* (1) распаля́-ю(сь), (2) -ешь(ся), (3) -ет(ся), (4) -ем(ся), (5) -ете(сь), (6) -ют(ся).

распечáтать *pf, future:* (1) распечáта-ю, (2) -ешь, (3) -ет, (4) -ем, (5) -ете, (6) -ют.

распечáтывать *impf, present:* (1) распечáтыва-ю, (2) -ешь, (3) -ет, (4) -ем, (5) -ете, (6) -ют.

расплáвиться *pf, future:* (3) расплáв-ится, (6) -ятся.

расплавя́ться *impf, present:* (3) расплавля́-ется, (6) -ются.

расположи́ть *pf, future:* (1) расположý, (2) располóж-ишь, (3) -ит, (4) -им, (5) -ите, (6) -ат.

распространи́ться *pf, future:* (3) распростран-и́тся, (4) -и́мся, (5) -и́тесь, (6) -я́тся.

Persons: 1 = я,   2 = ты,   3 = он, она́, оно́,   4 = мы,   5 = вы,   6 = они́

распространя́ться *impf, present:* *(1)* распространя́-юсь, *(2)* -ешься, *(3)* -ется, *(4)* -емся, *(5)* -етесь, *(6)* -ются.

распуска́ть *impf, present:* *(1)* распуска́-ю, *(2)* -ешь, *(3)* -ет, *(4)* -ем, *(5)* -ете, *(6)* -ют.

распусти́ть *pf, future:* *(1)* распущу́, *(2)* распу́ст-ишь, *(3)* -ит, *(4)* -им, *(5)* -ите, *(6)* -ят.

рассе́ивать *impf, present:* *(1)* рассе́ива-ю, *(2)* -ешь, *(3)* -ет, *(4)* -ем, *(5)* -ете, *(6)* -ют.

рассе́иваться *impf, present:* *(3)* рассе́ива -ется,*(6)* -ются.

рассерди́ться *pf, future:* *(1)* рассержу́сь, *(2)* рассерд-ишься, *(3)* -ится, *(4)* -имся, *(5)* -итесь, *(6)* -ятся.

рассе́ять *pf, future:* *(1)* рассе́-ю, *(2)* -ешь, *(3)* -ет, *(4)* -ем, *(5)* -ете, *(6)* -ют.

рассе́яться *pf, future:* *(3)* рассе́-ется, *(6)* -ются.

рассказа́ть *pf, future:* *(1)* расскажу́, *(2)* расска́ж-ешь, *(3)* -ет, *(4)* -ем, *(5)* -ете, *(6)* -ут.

расска́зывать *impf, present:* *(1)* расска́зыва-ю, *(2)* -ешь, *(3)* -ет, *(4)* -ем, *(5)* -ете, *(6)* -ют.

рассла́биться *pf, future:**(1)* рассла́бл-юсь, *(2)* -ишься, *(3)* рассла́б-ится, *(4)* -имся, *(5)* -итесь, *(6)* -ятся.

расслабля́ться *impf, present:* *(1)* расслабля́-юсь, *(2)* -ешься, *(3)* -ется, *(4)* -емся, *(5)* -етесь, *(6)* -ются.

рассма́тривать *impf, present:* *(1)* рассма́трива-ю, *(2)* -ешь, *(3)* -ет, *(4)* -ем, *(5)* -ете, *(6)* -ют.

рассмотре́ть *pf, future:* *(1)* рассмотрю́, *(2)* рассмо́тр-ишь, *(3)* -ит, *(4)* -им, *(5)* -ите, *(6)* -ят.

расстава́ться *impf, present:* *(1)* расста-ю́сь, *(2)* -ёшься, *(3)* -ётся, *(4)* -ёмся, *(5)* -ётесь, *(6)* -ю́тся.

расста́ться *pf, future:* *(1)* расста́н-усь, *(2)* -ешься, *(3)* -ется, *(4)* -емся, *(5)* -етесь, *(6)* -утся.

расстёгивать *impf, present:* *(1)* расстёгива-ю, *(2)* -ешь, *(3)* -ет, *(4)* -ем, *(5)* -ете, *(6)* -ют.

расстегну́ть *pf, future:* *(1)* расстегн-у́, *(2)* -ёшь, *(3)* -ёт, *(4)* -ём, *(5)* -ёте, *(6)* -у́т.

расстра́ивать(ся) *impf, present:* *(1)* расстра́ива-ю(сь), *(2)* -ешь(ся), *(3)* -ет(ся), *(4)* -ем(ся), *(5)* -ете(сь), *(6)* -ют(ся).

расстро́ить(ся) *pf, future:* *(1)* расстро́-ю(сь), *(2)* -ишь(ся), *(3)* -ит(ся), *(4)* -им(ся), *(5)* -ите(сь), *(6)* -ят(ся).

рассыла́ть *impf, present:* *(1)* рассыла́-ю, *(2)* -ешь, *(3)* -ет, *(4)* -ем, *(5)* -ете, *(6)* -ют.

раста́пливать *impf, present:* *(1)* раста́плива-ю, *(2)* -ешь, *(3)* -ет, *(4)* -ем, *(5)* -ете, *(6)* -ют.

раста́ять *pf, future:* *(1)* раста́-ю, *(2)* -ешь, *(3)* -ет, *(4)* -ем, *(5)* -ете, *(6)* -ют.

раствори́ться *pf, future:* *(1)* раствор-ю́сь, *(2)* -и́шься, *(3)* -и́тся, *(4)* -и́мся, *(5)* -и́тесь, *(6)* -я́тся.

растворя́ться *impf, present:* *(3)* растворя́-ется, *(6)* -ются.

растере́ть *pf, future:* *(1)* разотр-у́, *(2)* -ёшь, *(3)* -ёт, *(4)* -ём, *(5)* -ёте, *(6)* -у́т; *past:* растёр, -ла, -ло, -ли.

расти́ *impf, present:* *(1)* раст-у́, *(2)* -ёшь, *(3)* -ёт, *(4)* -ём, *(5)* -ёте, *(6)* -у́т; *past:* рос, -ла́, -ло́, -ли́.

растира́ть *impf, present:* *(1)* растира́-ю, *(2)* -ешь, *(3)* -ет, *(4)* -ем, *(5)* -ете, *(6)* -ют.

расти́ть *impf, present:* *(1)* ращу́, *(2)* раст-и́шь, *(3)* -и́т, *(4)* -и́м, *(5)* -и́те, *(6)* -я́т.

растопи́ть *pf, future:* *(1)* растоплю́, *(2)* расто́п-ишь, *(3)* -ит, *(4)* -им, *(5)* -ите, *(6)* -ят.

растопля́ть *impf, present:* *(1)* растопля́-ю, *(2)* -ешь, *(3)* -ет, *(4)* -ем, *(5)* -ете, *(6)* -ют.

расточа́ть *impf, present:* *(1)* расточа́-ю, *(2)* -ешь, *(3)* -ет, *(4)* -ем, *(5)* -ете, *(6)* -ют.

расточи́ть *pf, future:* *(1)* расточ-у́, *(2)* -и́шь, *(3)* -и́т, *(4)* -и́м, *(5)* -и́те, *(6)* -а́т.

растрави́ть *pf, future:* *(1)* растравлю́, *(2)* растрав-и́шь, *(3)* -и́т, *(4)* -и́м, *(5)* -и́те, *(6)*

> *Persons:* 1 = я, 2 = ты, 3 = он, она́, оно́, 4 = мы, 5 = вы, 6 = они́

-я́т.

растравля́ть *impf, present:* *(1)* растравля́-ю, *(2)* -ешь, *(3)* -ет, *(4)* -ем, *(5)* -ете, *(6)* -ют.

растро́гать(ся) *pf, future:* *(1)* растрога́-ю(сь), *(2)* -ешь(ся), *(3)* -ет(ся), *(4)* -ем(ся), *(5)* -ете(сь), *(6)* -ют(ся).

растя́гивать(ся) *impf, present:* *(1)* растя́гива-ю(сь), *(2)* -ешь(ся), *(3)* -ет(ся), *(4)* -ем(ся), *(5)* -ете(сь), *(6)* -ют(ся).

растяну́ть(ся) *pf, future:* *(1)* растяну́(сь), *(2)* растя́н-ешь(ся), *(3)* -ет(ся), *(4)* -ем(ся), *(5)* -ете(сь), *(6)* -ут(ся).

расходи́ться *impf, present:* *(1)* расхожу́сь, *(2)* расхо́д-ишься, *(3)* -ится, *(4)* -имся, *(5)* -итесь, *(6)* -ятся.

расхохота́ться *impf, present:* *(1)* расхохочу́сь, *(2)* расхохо́ч-ешься, *(3)* -ется, *(4)* -емся, *(5)* -етесь, *(6)* -утся.

расцвести́ *pf, future:* *(1)* расцвет-у́, *(2)* -ёшь, *(3)* -ёт, *(4)* -ём, *(5)* -ёте, *(6)* -у́т; *past:* расцвёл, расцвел-а́, -о́, -и́.

расцвета́ть *impf, present:* *(1)* расцвета́-ю, *(2)* -ешь, *(3)* -ет, *(4)* -ем, *(5)* -ете, *(6)* -ют.

расце́нивать *impf, present:* *(1)* расце́нива-ю, *(2)* -ешь, *(3)* -ет, *(4)* -ем, *(5)* -ете, *(6)* -ют.

расцени́ть *pf, future:* *(1)* расценю́, *(2)* расце́н-ишь, *(3)* -ит, *(4)* -им, *(5)* -ите, *(6)* -ят.

расшата́ть *pf, future:* *(1)* расшата́-ю, *(2)* -ешь, *(3)* -ет, *(4)* -ем, *(5)* -ете, *(6)* -ют.

расша́тывать *impf, present:* *(1)* расша́тыва-ю, *(2)* -ешь, *(3)* -ет, *(4)* -ем, *(5)* -ете, *(6)* -ют.

рвать *impf, present:* *(1)* рв-у, *(2)* -ёшь, *(3)* -ёт, *(4)* -ём, *(5)* -ёте, *(6)* -ут; *past:* рвал, рвала́, рва́-ло, -ли.

реаги́ровать *impf, present:* *(1)* реаги́ру-ю, *(2)* -ешь, *(3)* -ет, *(4)* -ем, *(5)* -ете, *(6)* -ют.

реализова́ть *impf & pf, present & future:* *(1)* реализу́-ю, *(2)* -ешь, *(3)* -ет, *(4)* -ем, *(5)* -ете, *(6)* -ют.

ревнова́ть *impf, present:* *(1)* ревну́-ю, *(2)* -ешь, *(3)* -ет, *(4)* -ем, *(5)* -ете, *(6)* -ют.

резони́ровать *impf, present:* *(1)* резони́ру-ю, *(2)* -ешь, *(3)* -ет, *(4)* -ем, *(5)* -ете, *(6)* -ют.

ремонти́ровать *impf, present:* *(1)* ремонти́ру-ю, *(2)* -ешь, *(3)* -ет, *(4)* -ем, *(5)* -ете, *(6)* -ют.

реша́ть *impf, present:* *(1)* реша́-ю, *(2)* -ешь, *(3)* -ет, *(4)* -ем, *(5)* -ете, *(6)* -ют.

реши́ть(ся) *pf, future:* *(1)* реш-у́(сь), *(2)* -и́шь(ся), *(3)* -и́т(ся), *(4)* -и́м(ся), *(5)* -и́те(сь), *(6)* -а́т(ся).

рискну́ть *pf, future:* *(1)* рискн-у́, *(2)* -ёшь, *(3)* -ёт, *(4)* -ём, *(5)* -ёте, *(6)* -у́т.

рискова́ть *impf, present:* *(1)* риску́-ю, *(2)* -ешь, *(3)* -ет, *(4)* -ем, *(5)* -ете, *(6)* -ют.

рисова́ть *impf, present:* *(1)* рису́-ю, *(2)* -ешь, *(3)* -ет, *(4)* -ем, *(5)* -ете, *(6)* -ют.

роди́ть *pf, future:* *(1)* рожу́, *(2)* род-и́шь, *(3)* -и́т, *(4)* -и́м, *(5)* -и́те, *(6)* -я́т; *past:* роди́л, родила́, роди́л-о, -и.

рожда́ть *impf, present:* *(1)* рожда́-ю, *(2)* -ешь, *(3)* -ет, *(4)* -ем, *(5)* -ете, *(6)* -ют.

ро́иться *impf, present:* *(3)* ро-и́тся, *(6)* -я́тся.

романтизи́ровать *impf, present:* *(1)* романтизи́ру-ю, *(2)* -ешь, *(3)* -ет, *(4)* -ем, *(5)* -ете, *(6)* -ют.

роня́ть *impf, present:* *(1)* роня́-ю, *(2)* -ешь, *(3)* -ет, *(4)* -ем, *(5)* -ете, *(6)* -ют.

руга́ть(ся) *impf, present:* *(1)* руга́-ю(сь), *(2)* -ешь(ся), *(3)* -ет(ся), *(4)* -ем(ся), *(5)* -ете(сь), *(6)* -ют(ся).

ру́шиться *impf, present:* *(3)* ру́ш-ится, *(6)* -атся.

рыда́ть *impf, present:* *(1)* рыда́-ю, *(2)* -ешь, *(3)* -ет, *(4)* -ем, *(5)* -ете, *(6)* -ют.

сади́ться *impf, present:* *(1)* сажу́сь, *(2)* сад-и́шься, *(3)* -и́тся, *(4)* -и́мся, *(5)* -и́тесь, *(6)* -я́тся.

сбежа́ть *pf, future:* *(1)* сбегу́, *(2)* сбеж-и́шь, *(3)* -и́т, *(4)* -и́м, *(5)* -и́те, *(6)* сбегу́т.

сбива́ть *impf, present:* *(1)* сбива́-ю, *(2)* -ешь, *(3)* -ет, *(4)* -ем, *(5)* -ете, *(6)* -ют.

сбить *pf, future:* *(1)* собь-ю́, *(2)* -ёшь, *(3)* -ёт, *(4)* -ём, *(5)* -ёте, *(6)* -ю́т.

Persons: 1 = я,   2 = ты,   3 = он, она́, оно́,   4 = мы,   5 = вы,   6 = они́

сболтну́ть *pf, future:* *(1)* сболтн-у́, *(2)* -ёшь, *(3)* -ёт, *(4)* -ём, *(5)* -ёте, *(6)* -у́т.

сбра́сывать *impf, present:* *(1)* сбра́сыва-ю, *(2)* -ешь, *(3)* -ет, *(4)* -ем, *(5)* -ете, *(6)* -ют.

сбрить *pf, future:* *(1)* сбре́-ю, *(2)* -ешь, *(3)* -ет, *(4)* -ем, *(5)* -ете, *(6)* -ют.

сбро́сить *pf, future:* *(1)* сбро́шу, *(2)* сбро́с-ишь, *(3)* -ит, *(4)* -им, *(5)* -ите, *(6)* -ят.

сверка́ть *impf, present:* *(1)* сверка́-ю, *(2)* -ешь, *(3)* -ет, *(4)* -ем, *(5)* -ете, *(6)* -ют.

сверкну́ть *pf, future:* *(1)* сверкн-у́, *(2)* -ёшь, *(3)* -ёт, *(4)* -ём, *(5)* -ёте, *(6)* -у́т.

сверну́ться *pf, future:* *(1)* сверн-у́сь, *(2)* -ёшься, *(3)* -ётся, *(4)* -ёмся, *(5)* -ётесь, *(6)* -у́тся.

свести́ *pf, future:* *(1)* свед-у́, *(2)* -ёшь, *(3)* -ёт, *(4)* -ём, *(5)* -ёте, *(6)* -у́т; *past:* свёл, свел-а́, -о́, -и́.

свети́ть(ся) *impf, present:* *(1)* свечу́(сь), *(2)* све́т-ишь(ся), *(3)* -ит(ся), *(4)* -им(ся), *(5)* -ите(сь), *(6)* -ят(ся).

светле́ть *impf, present:* *(1)* светле́-ю, *(2)* -ешь, *(3)* -ет, *(4)* -ем, *(5)* -ете, *(6)* -ют.

свисте́ть *impf, present:* *(1)* свищу́, *(2)* свист-и́шь, *(3)* -и́т, *(4)* -и́м, *(5)* -и́те, *(6)* -я́т.

сви́стнуть *pf, future:* *(1)* свистн-у, *(2)* -ешь, *(3)* -ет, *(4)* -ем, *(5)* -ете, *(6)* -ут.

своди́ть *impf, present:* *(1)* свожу́, *(2)* сво́д-ишь, *(3)* -ит, *(4)* -им, *(5)* -ите, *(6)* -ят.

связа́ть(ся) *pf, future:* *(1)* свяжу́(сь), *(2)* свя́ж-ешь(ся), *(3)* -ет(ся), *(4)* -ем(ся), *(5)* -ете(сь), *(6)* -ут(ся).

свя́зывать(ся) *impf, present:* *(1)* свя́зыва-ю(сь), *(2)* -ешь(ся), *(3)* -ет(ся), *(4)* -ем(ся), *(5)* -ете(сь), *(6)* -ют(ся).

сгора́ть *impf, present:* *(1)* сгора́-ю, *(2)* -ешь, *(3)* -ет, *(4)* -ем, *(5)* -ете, *(6)* -ют.

сдава́ться *impf, present:* *(1)* сда-ю́сь, *(2)* -ёшься, *(3)* -ётся, *(4)* -ёмся, *(5)* -ётесь, *(6)* -ю́тся.

сда́ться *pf, future:* *(1)* сда́-мся, *(2)* -шься, *(3)* -стся, *(4)* -димся, *(5)* -дитесь, *(6)* -дутся.

сде́лать *pf, future:* *(1)* сде́ла-ю, *(2)* -ешь, *(3)* -ет, *(4)* -ем, *(5)* -ете, *(6)* -ют.

сдержа́ть(ся) *pf, future:* *(1)* сдержу́(сь), *(2)* сде́рж-ишь(ся), *(3)* -ит(ся), *(4)* -им(ся), *(5)* -ите(сь), *(6)* -ат(ся).

сде́рживать(ся) *impf, present:* *(1)* сде́ржива-ю(сь), *(2)* -ешь(ся), *(3)* -ет(ся), *(4)* -ем(ся), *(5)* -ете(сь), *(6)* -ют(ся).

серди́ться *impf, present:* *(1)* сержу́сь, *(2)* се́рд-ишься, *(3)* -ится, *(4)* -имся, *(5)* -итесь, *(6)* -ятся.

сесть *pf, future:* *(1)* ся́д-у, *(2)* -ешь, *(3)* -ет, *(4)* -ем, *(5)* -ете, *(6)* -ут.

сжать *pf, future:* *(1)* сожм-у́, *(2)* -ёшь, *(3)* -ёт, *(4)* -ём, *(5)* -ёте, *(6)* -у́т.

сжима́ть(ся) *impf, present:* *(1)* сжима́-ю(сь), *(2)* -ешь(ся), *(3)* -ет(ся), *(4)* -ем(ся), *(5)* -ете(сь), *(6)* -ют(ся).

сиде́ть *impf, present:* *(1)* сижу́, *(2)* сид-и́шь, *(3)* -и́т, *(4)* -и́м, *(5)* -и́те, *(6)* -я́т.

символизи́ровать *impf & pf, present & future:* *(1)* символизи́ру-ю, *(2)* -ешь, *(3)* -ет, *(4)* -ем, *(5)* -ете, *(6)* -ют.

сия́ть *impf, present:* *(1)* сия́-ю, *(2)* -ешь, *(3)* -ет, *(4)* -ем, *(5)* -ете, *(6)* -ют.

сказа́ть *pf, future:* *(1)* скажу́, *(2)* ска́ж-ешь, *(3)* -ет, *(4)* -ем, *(5)* -ете, *(6)* -ут.

скака́ть *pf, future:* *(1)* скачу́, *(2)* ска́ч-ешь, *(3)* -ет, *(4)* -ем, *(5)* -ете, *(6)* -ут.

скверносло́вить *impf, present:* *(1)* скверносло́в-лю, *(2)* -ишь, *(3)* -ит, *(4)* -им, *(5)* -ите, *(6)* -ят.

скита́ться *impf, present:* *(1)* скита́-юсь, *(2)* -ешься, *(3)* -ется, *(4)* -емся, *(5)* -етесь, *(6)* -ются.

скла́дываться *impf, present:* *(1)* скла́дыва-юсь, *(2)* -ешься, *(3)* -ется, *(4)* -емся, *(5)* -етесь, *(6)* -ются.

скользи́ть *impf, present:* *(1)* скольжу́, *(2)* скольз-и́шь, *(3)* -и́т, *(4)* -и́м, *(5)* -и́те, *(6)* -я́т.

скользну́ть *pf, future:* *(1)* скользн-у́, *(2)* -ёшь, *(3)* -ёт, *(4)* -ём, *(5)* -ёте, *(6)* -у́т.

ско́рчить(ся) *pf, future:* *(1)* ско́рч-у(сь), *(2)* -ишь(ся), *(3)* -ит(ся), *(4)* -им(ся, *(5)*

Persons: 1 = я, 2 = ты, 3 = он, она́, оно́, 4 = мы, 5 = вы, 6 = они́

-ите(сь), *(6)* -ат(ся).

скрыва́ть(ся) *impf, present: (1)* скрыва́-ю(сь), *(2)* -ешь(ся), *(3)* -ет(ся), *(4)* -ем(ся), *(5)* -ете(сь), *(6)* -ют(ся).

скры́ть(ся) *pf, future: (1)* скро́-ю(сь), *(2)* -ешь(ся), *(3)* -ет(ся), *(4)* -ем(ся), *(5)* -ете(сь), *(6)* -ют(ся).

скули́ть *impf, present: (1)* скул-ю́, *(2)* -и́шь, *(3)* -и́т, *(4)* -и́м, *(5)* -и́те, *(6)* -я́т.

скуча́ть *impf, present: (1)* скуча́-ю, *(2)* -ешь, *(3)* -ет, *(4)* -ем, *(5)* -ете, *(6)* -ют.

слабе́ть *impf, present: (1)* слабе́-ю, *(2)* -ешь, *(3)* -ет, *(4)* -ем, *(5)* -ете, *(6)* -ют.

сле́довать *impf, present: (1)* сле́ду-ю, *(2)* -ешь, *(3)* -ет, *(4)* -ем, *(5)* -ете, *(6)* -ют.

слеза́ть *impf, present: (1)* слеза́-ю, *(2)* -ешь, *(3)* -ет, *(4)* -ем, *(5)* -ете, *(6)* -ют.

слезть *pf, future: (1)* слёз-у, *(2)* -ешь, *(3)* -ет, *(4)* -ем, *(5)* -ете, *(6)* -ут; *past:* слез,слёз -ла, -ло, -ли.

слива́ться *impf, present: (1)* слива́-юсь, *(2)* -ешься, *(3)* -ется, *(4)* -емся, *(5)* -етесь, *(6)* -ются.

сли́ться *pf, future: (1)* соль-ю́сь, *(2)* -ёшься, *(3)* -ётся, *(4)* -ёмся, *(5)* -ётесь, *(6)* -ю́тся; *past:* сли́лся, слила́сь, сли́-лось, -лись.

сложи́ть(ся) *pf, future: (1)* сложу́(сь), *(2)* сло́ж-ишь(ся), *(3)* -ит(ся), *(4)* -им(ся), *(5)* -ите(сь), *(6)* -ат(ся).

слома́ть(ся) *pf, future: (1)* слома́-ю(сь), *(2)* -ешь(ся), *(3)* -ет(ся), *(4)* -ем(ся), *(5)* -ете(сь), *(6)* -ют(ся).

слоня́ться *impf, present: (1)* слоня́-юсь, *(2)* -ешься, *(3)* -ется, *(4)* -емся, *(5)* -етесь, *(6)* -ются.

случа́ться *impf, present: (3)* случа́-ется, *(6)* -ются.

случи́ться *pf, future: (3)* случ-и́тся, *(6)* -а́тся.

слу́шать(ся) *impf, present: (1)* слу́ша-ю(сь), *(2)* -ешь(ся), *(3)* -ет(ся), *(4)* -ем(ся), *(5)* -ете(сь), *(6)* -ют(ся).

слы́шать *impf, present: (1)* слы́ш-у, *(2)* -ишь, *(3)* -ит, *(4)* -им, *(5)* -ите, *(6)* -ат.

смакова́ть *impf, present: (1)* смаку́-ю, *(2)* -ешь, *(3)* -ет, *(4)* -ем, *(5)* -ете, *(6)* -ют.

смеси́ть *pf, future: (1)* not used , *(2)* смес-и́шь, *(3)* -и́т, *(4)* -и́м, *(5)* -и́те, *(6)* -я́т.

смести́ *pf, future: (1)* смет-у́, *(2)* -ёшь, *(3)* -ёт, *(4)* -ём, *(5)* -ёте, *(6)* -у́т; *past:* смёл, смела́, -ло́, -ли́.

смета́ть *impf, present: (1)* смета́-ю, *(2)* -ешь, *(3)* -ет, *(4)* -ем, *(5)* -ете, *(6)* -ют.

сметь *impf, present: (1)* сме́-ю, *(2)* -ешь, *(3)* -ет, *(4)* -ем, *(5)* -ете, *(6)* -ют.

смеша́ться *pf, future: (1)* смеша́-юсь, *(2)* -ешься, *(3)* -ется, *(4)* -емся, *(5)* -етесь, *(6)* -ются.

сме́шивать *impf, present: (1)* сме́шива-ю, *(2)* -ешь, *(3)* -ет, *(4)* -ем, *(5)* -ете, *(6)* -ют.

сме́шиваться *impf, present: (3)* сме́шива-ется, *(6)* -ются.

смея́ться *impf, present: (1)* сме-ю́сь, *(2)* -ёшься, *(3)* -ётся, *(4)* -ёмся, *(5)* -ётесь, *(6)* -ю́тся.

сми́лостивиться *pf, future: (1)* сми́лостив-люсь, *(2)* -ишься, *(3)* -ится, *(4)* -имся, *(5)* -итесь, *(6)* -ятся.

смири́ться *pf, future: (1)* смир-ю́сь, *(2)* -ишься, *(3)* -ится, *(4)* -имся, *(5)* -итесь, *(6)* -ятся.

смиря́ться *impf, present: (1)* смиря́-юсь, *(2)* -ешься, *(3)* -ется, *(4)* -емся, *(5)* -етесь, *(6)* -ются.

смотре́ть(ся) *impf, present: (1)* смотрю́(сь), *(2)* смо́тр-ишь(ся), *(3)* -ит(ся), *(4)* -им(ся), *(5)* -ите(сь), *(6)* -ят(ся).

смочь *impf present: (1)* смогу́, *(2)* смо́ж-ешь, *(3)* -ет, *(4)* -ем, *(5)* -ете, *(6)* смо́гут; *past:* смог, -ла́, -ло́, -ли́.

смути́ть(ся) *pf, future: (1)* смущу́(сь), *(2)* смут-и́шь(ся), *(3)* -и́т(ся), *(4)* -и́м(ся), *(5)* -и́те(сь), *(6)* -я́т(ся).

> *Persons:* 1 = я,   2 = ты,   3 = он, она́, оно́,   4 = мы,   5 = вы,   6 = они́

смуща́ть(ся) *impf, present:* *(1)* смуща́-ю(сь), *(2)* -ешь(ся), *(3)* -ет(ся), *(4)* -ем(ся), *(5)* -ете(сь), *(6)* -ют(ся).

смягча́ть(ся) *impf, present:* *(1)* смягча́-ю(сь), *(2)* -ешь(ся), *(3)* -ет(ся), *(4)* -ем(ся), *(5)* -ете(сь), *(6)* -ют(ся).

смягчи́ть(ся) *pf, future:* *(1)* смягч-у́(сь), *(2)* -и́шь(ся), *(3)* -и́т(ся), *(4)* -и́м(ся), *(5)* -и́те(сь), *(6)* -я́т(ся).

снести́ *pf, future:* *(1)* снес-у́, *(2)* -ёшь, *(3)* -ёт, *(4)* -ём, *(5)* -ёте, *(6)* -у́т; *past:* снёс, снесла́, -ло́, -ли́.

снизойти́ *pf, future:* *(1)* снизойд-у́, *(2)* -ёшь, *(3)* -ёт, *(4)* -ём, *(5)* -ёте, *(6)* -у́т; *past:* снизой-шёл, -шла́, -шло́, -шли́.

снима́ть *impf, present:* *(1)* снима́-ю, *(2)* -ешь, *(3)* -ет, *(4)* -ем, *(5)* -ете, *(6)* -ют.

снисходи́ть *impf, present:* *(1)* снисхожу́, *(2)* снисхо́д-ишь, *(3)* -ит, *(4)* -им, *(5)* -ите, *(6)* -ят.

сни́ться *impf, present:* *(1)* сн-ю́сь, *(2)* -и́шься, *(3)* -и́тся, *(4)* -и́мся, *(5)* -и́тесь, *(6)* -я́тся.

сноси́ть *impf, present:* *(1)* сношу, *(2)* снос-ишь, *(3)* -ит, *(4)* -им, *(5)* -ите, *(6)* -ят.

снять *pf, future:* *(1)* сниму́, *(2)* сни́м-ешь, *(3)* -ет, *(4)* -ем, *(5)* -ете, *(6)* -ут.

собира́ть(ся) *impf, present:* *(1)* собира́-ю(сь), *(2)* -ешь(ся), *(3)* -ет(ся), *(4)* -ем(ся), *(5)* -ете(сь), *(6)* -ют(ся).

соблазни́ть *pf, future:* *(1)* соблазн-ю́, *(2)* -и́шь, *(3)* -и́т, *(4)* -и́м, *(5)* -и́те, *(6)* -я́т.

соблазня́ть *impf, present:* *(1)* соблазня́-ю, *(2)* -ешь, *(3)* -ет, *(4)* -ем, *(5)* -ете, *(6)* -ют.

сова́ть *impf, present:* *(1)* су-ю́, *(2)* -ёшь, *(3)* -ёт, *(4)* -ём, *(5)* -ёте, *(6)* -ю́т.

соверша́ть *impf, present:* *(1)* соверша́-ю, *(2)* -ешь, *(3)* -ет, *(4)* -ем, *(5)* -ете, *(6)* -ют.

сове́товать(ся) *impf, present:* *(1)* сове́ту-ю(сь), *(2)* -ешь(ся), *(3)* -ет(ся), *(4)* -ем(ся), *(5)* -ете(сь), *(6)* -ют(ся).

согласи́ться *pf, future:* *(1)* соглашу́сь, *(2)* соглас-и́шься, *(3)* -и́тся, *(4)* -и́мся, *(5)* -и́тесь, *(6)* -я́тся.

соглаша́ться *impf, present:* *(1)* соглаша́-юсь, *(2)* -ешься, *(3)* -ется, *(4)* -емся, *(5)* -етесь, *(6)* -ются.

согрева́ть(ся) *impf, present:* *(1)* согрева́-ю(сь), *(2)* -ешь(ся), *(3)* -ет(ся), *(4)* -ем(ся), *(5)* -ете(сь), *(6)* -ют(ся).

согре́ть *pf, future:* *(1)* согре́-ю, *(2)* -ешь, *(3)* -ет, *(4)* -ем, *(5)* -ете, *(6)* -ют.

согреши́ть *pf, future:* *(1)* согреш-у́, *(2)* -и́шь, *(3)* -и́т, *(4)* -и́м, *(5)* -и́те, *(6)* -а́т.

содержа́ть *impf, present:* *(1)* содержу́, *(2)* соддерж-ишь, *(3)* -ит, *(4)* -им, *(5)* -ите, *(6)* -ат.

соедини́ть(ся) *pf, future:* *(1)* соедин-ю́(сь), *(2)* -и́шь(ся), *(3)* -и́т(ся), *(4)* -и́м(ся), *(5)* -и́те(сь), *(6)* -я́т(ся).

соединя́ть(ся) *impf, present:* *(1)* соединя́-ю(сь), *(2)* -ешь(ся), *(3)* -ет(ся), *(4)* -ем(ся), *(5)* -ете(сь), *(6)* -ют(ся).

сожале́ть *impf, present:* *(1)* сожале́-ю, *(2)* -ешь, *(3)* -ет, *(4)* -ем, *(5)* -ете, *(6)* -ют.

созва́ниваться *impf, present:* *(1)* созва́нива-юсь, *(2)* -ешься, *(3)* -ется, *(4)* -емся, *(5)* -етесь, *(6)* -ются.

созвони́ться *pf, future:* *(1)* созвон-ю́сь, *(2)* -и́шься, *(3)* -и́тся, *(4)* -и́мся, *(5)* -и́тесь, *(6)* -я́тся.

создава́ть *impf, present:* *(1)* созда-ю́, *(2)* -ёшь, *(3)* -ёт, *(4)* -ём, *(5)* -ёте, *(6)* -ю́т.

созда́ть *pf, future:* *(1)* созда́-м, *(2)* -шь, *(3)* -ст, *(4)* -дим, *(5)* -дите, *(6)* -дут.

созерца́ть *impf, present:* *(1)* созерца́-ю, *(2)* -ешь, *(3)* -ет, *(4)* -ем, *(5)* -ете, *(6)* -ют.

созре́ть *pf, future:* *(1)* созре́-ю, *(2)* -ешь, *(3)* -ет, *(4)* -ем, *(5)* -ете, *(6)* -ют.

сокруша́ть *impf, present:* *(1)* сокруша́-ю, *(2)* -ешь, *(3)* -ет, *(4)* -ем, *(5)* -ете, *(6)* -ют.

сокруши́ть *pf, future:* *(1)* сокруш-у́, *(2)* -и́шь, *(3)* -и́т, *(4)* -и́м, *(5)* -и́те, *(6)* -а́т.

солга́ть *pf, future:* *(1)* солгу́, *(2)* солж-ёшь, *(3)* -ёт, *(4)* -ём, *(5)* -ёте, *(6)* солгу́т; *past:* солга́л, солгала́, солга́-ло, -ли.

> *Persons:* 1 = я,   2 = ты,   3 = он, она́, оно́,   4 = мы,   5 = вы,   6 = они́

сомнева́ться *impf, present:* *(1)* сомнева́-юсь, *(2)* -ешься, *(3)* -ется, *(4)* -емся, *(5)* -етесь, *(6)* -ются.

сообража́ть *impf, present:* *(1)* сообража́-ю, *(2)* -ешь, *(3)* -ет, *(4)* -ем, *(5)* -ете, *(6)* -ют.

сообрази́ть *pf, future:* *(1)* соображу́, *(2)* сообраз-и́шь, *(3)* -и́т, *(4)* -и́м, *(5)* -и́те, *(6)* -я́т.

сообща́ть *impf, present:* *(1)* сообща́-ю, *(2)* -ешь, *(3)* -ет, *(4)* -ем, *(5)* -ете, *(6)* -ют.

сообщи́ть *pf, future:* *(1)* сообщ-у́, *(2)* -и́шь, *(3)* -и́т, *(4)* -и́м, *(5)* -и́те, *(6)* -а́т.

соотве́тствовать *impf, present:* *(1)* соотве́тству-ю, *(2)* -ешь, *(3)* -ет, *(4)* -ем, *(5)* -ете, *(6)* -ют.

сопровожда́ть *impf, present:* *(1)* сопровожда́-ю, *(2)* -ешь, *(3)* -ет, *(4)* -ем, *(5)* -ете, *(6)* -ют.

сопротивля́ться *impf, present:* *(1)* сопротивля́-юсь, *(2)* -ешься, *(3)* -ется, *(4)* -емся, *(5)* -етесь, *(6)* -ются.

сопу́тствовать *impf, present:* *(1)* сопу́тству-ю, *(2)* -ешь, *(3)* -ет, *(4)* -ем, *(5)* -ете, *(6)* -ют.

сорва́ть *pf, future:* *(1)* сорв-у́, *(2)* -ёшь, *(3)* -ёт, *(4)* -ём, *(5)* -ёте, *(6)* -у́т; *past:* сорва́л, сорвала́, сорва́-ло, -ли.

соса́ть *impf, present:* *(1)* сос-у́, *(2)* -ёшь, *(3)* -ёт, *(4)* -ём, *(5)* -ёте, *(6)* -у́т.

соску́читься *pf, future:* *(1)* соску́ч-усь, *(2)* -ишься, *(3)* -ится, *(4)* -имся, *(5)* -итесь, *(6)* -атся.

сосла́ться *pf, future:* *(1)* сошл-ю́сь, *(2)* -ёшься, *(3)* -ётся, *(4)* -ёмся, *(5)* -ётесь, *(6)* -ю́тся.

сосредото́чивать(ся) *impf, present:* *(1)* сосредото́чива-ю(сь), *(2)* -ешь(ся), *(3)* -ет(ся), *(4)* -ем(ся), *(5)* -ете(сь), *(6)* -ют(ся).

сосредото́чить(ся) *pf, future:* *(1)* сосредото́ч-у(сь), *(2)* -ишь(ся), *(3)* -ит(ся), *(4)* -им(ся), *(5)* -ите(сь), *(6)* -ат(ся).

соста́вить *pf, future:* *(1)* соста́в-лю, *(2)* -ишь, *(3)* -ит, *(4)* -им, *(5)* -ите, *(6)* -ят.

составля́ть *impf, present:* *(1)* составля́-ю, *(2)* -ешь, *(3)* -ет, *(4)* -ем, *(5)* -ете, *(6)* -ют.

сосчита́ть *pf, future:* *(1)* сосчита́-ю, *(2)* -ешь, *(3)* -ет, *(4)* -ем, *(5)* -ете, *(6)* -ют.

сохрани́ть *pf, future:* *(1)* сохран-ю́, *(2)* -и́шь, *(3)* -и́т, *(4)* -и́м, *(5)* -и́те, *(6)* -я́т.

сохраня́ть *impf, present:* *(1)* сохраня́-ю, *(2)* -ешь, *(3)* -ет, *(4)* -ем, *(5)* -ете, *(6)* -ют.

сочета́ть(ся) *impf & pf, present & future:* *(1)* сочета́-ю(сь), *(2)* -ешь(ся), *(3)* -ет(ся), *(4)* -ем(ся), *(5)* -ете(сь), *(6)* -ют(ся).

сочини́ть *pf, future:* *(1)* сочин-ю́, *(2)* -и́шь, *(3)* -и́т, *(4)* -и́м, *(5)* -и́те, *(6)* -я́т.

сочиня́ть *impf, present:* *(1)* сочиня-ю, *(2)* -ешь, *(3)* -ет, *(4)* -ем, *(5)* -ете, *(6)* -ют.

сочи́ться *impf, present:* *(3)* соч-и́тся, *(6)* -а́тся.

сочу́вствовать *impf, present:* *(1)* сочу́вству-ю, *(2)* -ешь, *(3)* -ет, *(4)* -ем, *(5)* -ете, *(6)* -ют.

спать *impf, present:* *(1)* сп-лю, *(2)* -ишь, *(3)* -ит, *(4)* -им, *(5)* -ите, *(6)* -ят *past:* спал, спала́, спа́-ло, -ли.

спеть *pf, future:* *(1)* спо-ю́, *(2)* -ёшь, *(3)* -ёт, *(4)* -ём, *(5)* -ёте, *(6)* -ю́т.

спеши́ть *impf, present:* *(1)* спеш-у́, *(2)* -и́шь, *(3)* -и́т, *(4)* -и́м, *(5)* -и́те, *(6)* -а́т.

сплести́сь *pf, future:* *(1)* сплет-у́сь, *(2)* -ёшься, *(3)* -ётся, *(4)* -ёмся, *(5)* -ётесь, *(6)* -у́тся; *past:* сплёлся, спле-ла́сь, -ло́сь, -ли́сь.

сплета́ться *impf, present:* *(1)* сплета́-юсь, *(2)* -ешься, *(3)* -ется, *(4)* -емся, *(5)* -етесь, *(6)* -ются.

спле́тничать *impf, present:* *(1)* спле́тнича-ю, *(2)* -ешь, *(3)* -ет, *(4)* -ем, *(5)* -ете, *(6)* -ют.

спосо́бствовать *impf, present:* *(1)* спосо́бству-ю, *(2)* -ешь, *(3)* -ет, *(4)* -ем, *(5)* -ете, *(6)* -ют.

спра́вить(ся) *pf, future:* *(1)* спра́в-лю(сь), *(2)* -ишь(ся), *(3)* -ит(ся), *(4)* -им(ся), *(5)* -ите(сь), *(6)* -ят(ся).

Persons: 1 = я,   2 = ты,   3 = он, она́, оно́,   4 = мы,   5 = вы,   6 = они́

справля́ть(ся) *impf, present:* (1) справля́-ю(сь), (2) -ешь(ся), (3) -ет(ся), (4) -ем(ся), (5) -ете(сь), (6) -ют(ся).

спра́шивать *impf, present:* (1) спра́шива-ю, (2) -ешь, (3) -ет, (4) -ем, (5) -ете, (6) -ют.

спроси́ть *pf, future:* (1) спрошу́, (2) спро́с-ишь, (3) -ит, (4) -им, (5) -ите, (6) -ят.

спря́тать(ся) *pf, future:* (1) спря́ч-у(сь), (2) -ешь(ся), (3) -ет(ся), (4) -ем(ся), (5) -ете(сь), (6) -ут(ся).

спу́тать(ся) *pf, future:* (1) спу́та-ю(сь), (2) -ешь(ся), (3) -ет(ся), (4) -ем(ся), (5) -ете(сь), (6) -ют(ся).

спу́тываться *impf, present:* (1) спу́тыва-юсь, (2) -ешься, (3) -ется, (4) -емся, (5) -етесь, (6) -ются.

спря́тать *pf, future:* (1) спря́ч-у, (2) -ешь, (3) -ет, (4) -ем, (5) -ете, (6) -ут.

сравни́ть(ся) *pf, future:* (1) сравн-ю́(сь), (2) -ишь(ся), (3) -ит(ся), (4) -им(ся), (5) -ите(сь), (6) -ят(ся).

сража́ть *impf, present:* (1) сража́-ю, (2) -ешь, (3) -ет, (4) -ем, (5) -ете, (6) -ют.

срази́ть *pf, future:* (1) сражу́, (2) сраз-и́шь, (3) -и́т, (4) -и́м, (5) -и́те, (6) -я́т.

ссо́риться *impf, present:* (1) ссо́р-юсь, (2) -ишься, (3) -ится, (4) -имся, (5) -итесь, (6) -ятся.

ссыла́ться *impf, present:* (1) ссыла́-юсь, (2) -ешься, (3) -ется, (4) -емся, (5) -етесь, (6) -ются.

ста́вить *impf, present:* (1) ста́в-лю, (2) -ишь, (3) -ит, (4) -им, (5) -ите, (6) -ят.

станови́ться *impf, present:* (1) становлю́сь, (2) стано́в-ишься, (3) -ится, (4) -имся, (5) -итесь, (6) -ятся.

стара́ться *impf, present:* (1) стара́-юсь, (2) -ешься, (3) -ется, (4) -емся, (5) -етесь, (6) -ются.

старе́ть *impf, present:* (1) старе́-ю, (2) -ешь, (3) -ет, (4) -ем, (5) -ете, (6) -ют.

стать *pf, future:* (1) ста́н-у, (2) -ешь, (3) -ет, (4) -ем, (5) -ете, (6) -ут.

стимули́ровать *impf & pf, present & future:* (1) стимули́ру-ю, (2) -ешь, (3) -ет, (4) -ем, (5) -ете, (6) -ют.

сто́ить *impf, present:* (1) сто́-ю, (2) -ишь, (3) -ит, (4) -им, (5) -ите, (6) -ят.

столбене́ть *impf, present:* (1) столбене́-ю, (2) -ешь, (3) -ет, (4) -ем, (5) -ете, (6) -ют.

стона́ть *impf, present:* (1) стону́, (2) сто́н-ешь, (3) -ет, (4) -ем, (5) -ете, (6) -ут.

стоя́ть *impf, present:* (1) сто-ю́, (2) -и́шь, (3) -и́т, (4) -и́м, (5) -и́те, (6) -я́т.

страда́ть *impf, present:* (1) страда́-ю, (2) -ешь, (3) -ет, (4) -ем, (5) -ете, (6) -ют.

страши́ться *impf, present:* (1) страш-у́сь, (2) -и́шься, (3) -и́тся, (4) -и́мся, (5) -и́тесь, (6) -а́тся.

стреми́ться *impf, present:* (1) стрем-лю́сь, (2) -и́шься, (3) -и́тся, (4) -и́мся, (5) -и́тесь, (6) -я́тся.

стричь(ся) *impf, present:* (1) стригу́(сь), (2) стриж-ёшь(ся), (3) -ёт(ся), (4) -ём(ся), (5) -ёте(сь), (6) стригу́т(ся); *past:* стриг(ся),стри́г -ла(сь), -ло(сь), -ли(сь).

стро́ить *impf, present:* (1) стро́-ю, (2) -ишь, (3) -ит, (4) -им, (5) -ите, (6) -ят.

струи́ться *impf, present:* (3) стру-и́тся, (6) -я́тся.

стру́сить *pf, future:* (1) стру́шу, (2) стру́с-ишь, (3) -ит, (4) -им, (5) -ите, (6) -ят.

стряхну́ть *pf, future:* (1) стряхн-у́, (2) -ёшь, (3) -ёт, (4) -ём, (5) -ёте, (6) -у́т.

стыди́ть(ся) *impf, present:* (1) стыжу́(сь), (2) стыд-и́шь(ся), (3) -и́т(ся), (4) -и́м(ся), (5) -и́те(сь), (6) -я́т(ся).

суди́ть *impf, present:* (1) сужу́, (2) су́д-ишь, (3) -ит, (4) -им, (5) -ите, (6) -ят.

суме́ть *pf, future:* (1) суме́-ю, (2) -ешь, (3) -ет, (4) -ем, (5) -ете, (6) -ют.

су́нуть *pf, future:* (1) су́н-у, (2) -ешь, (3) -ет, (4) -ем, (5) -ете, (6) -ут.

схвати́ть *pf, future:* (1) схвачу́, (2) схва́т-ишь, (3) -ит, (4) -им, (5) -ите, (6) -ят.

схва́тывать *impf, present:* (1) схва́тыва-ю, (2) -ешь, (3) -ет, (4) -ем, (5) -ете, (6) -ют.

сходи́ть *impf, present:* (1) схожу́, (2) схо́д-ишь, (3) -ит, (4) -им, (5) -ите, (6) -ят.

> *Persons:* 1 = я, 2 = ты, 3 = он, она́, оно́, 4 = мы, 5 = вы, 6 = они́

счита́ть *impf, present:* *(1)* счита́-ю, *(2)* -ешь, *(3)* -ет, *(4)* -ем, *(5)* -ете, *(6)* -ют.

съесть *impf, present:* *(1)* съе-м, *(2)* -шь, *(3)* -ст, *(4)* -ди́м, *(5)* -ди́те, *(6)* -дя́т.

таи́ть *impf, present:* *(1)* та-ю́, *(2)* -и́шь, *(3)* -и́т, *(4)* -и́м, *(5)* -и́те, *(6)* -я́т.

танцева́ть *impf, present:* *(1)* танцу́-ю, *(2)* -ешь, *(3)* -ет, *(4)* -ем, *(5)* -ете, *(6)* -ют.

тара́щить *impf, present:* *(1)* тара́щ-у, *(2)* -ишь, *(3)* -ит, *(4)* -им, *(5)* -ите, *(6)* -ат.

тащи́ть *impf, present:* *(1)* тащу́, *(2)* та́щ-ишь, *(3)* -ит, *(4)* -им, *(5)* -ите, *(6)* -ат.

та́ять *impf, present:* *(1)* та́-ю, *(2)* -ешь, *(3)* -ет, *(4)* -ем, *(5)* -ете, *(6)* -ют.

тере́ть(ся) *impf, present:* *(1)* тр-у(сь), *(2)* -ёшь(ся), *(3)* -ёт(ся), *(4)* -ём(ся), *(5)* -ёте(сь), *(6)* -у́т(ся); *past:* тёр(ся), тёр-ла(сь), -ло(сь), -ли(сь).

терза́ть(ся) *impf, present:* *(1)* терза́-ю(сь), *(2)* -ешь(ся), *(3)* -ет(ся), *(4)* -ем(ся), *(5)* -ете(сь), *(6)* -ют(ся).

терпе́ть *impf, present:* *(1)* терплю́, *(2)* те́рп-ишь, *(3)* -ит, *(4)* -им, *(5)* -ите, *(6)* -ят.

теря́ть(ся) *impf, present:* *(1)* теря́-ю(сь), *(2)* -ешь(ся), *(3)* -ет(ся), *(4)* -ем(ся), *(5)* -ете(сь), *(6)* -ют(ся).

течь *impf, present:* *(1)* теку́, *(2)* теч-ёшь, *(3)* -ёт, *(4)* -ём, *(5)* -ёте, *(6)* теку́т; *past:* тёк, текл-а́, -о́, -и́.

тлеть *impf, present:* *(1)* тле́-ю, *(2)* -ешь, *(3)* -ет, *(4)* -ем, *(5)* -ете, *(6)* -ют.

толка́ть *impf, present:* *(1)* толка́-ю, *(2)* -ешь, *(3)* -ет, *(4)* -ем, *(5)* -ете, *(6)* -ют.

толкну́ть *pf, future:* *(1)* толкн-у́, *(2)* -ёшь, *(3)* -ёт, *(4)* -ём, *(5)* -ёте, *(6)* -у́т.

толкова́ть *impf, present:* *(1)* толку́-ю, *(2)* -ешь, *(3)* -ет, *(4)* -ем, *(5)* -ете, *(6)* -ют.

толпи́ться *impf, present:* *(3)* толп-и́тся, *(6)* -я́тся.

толсте́ть *impf, present:* *(1)* толсте́-ю, *(2)* -ешь, *(3)* -ет, *(4)* -ем, *(5)* -ете, *(6)* -ют.

томи́ться *impf, present:* *(1)* том-лю́сь, *(2)* -и́шься, *(3)* -и́тся, *(4)* -и́мся, *(5)* -и́тесь, *(6)* -я́тся.

тону́ть *impf, present:* *(1)* тону́, *(2)* то́н-ешь, *(3)* -ет, *(4)* -ем, *(5)* -ете, *(6)* -ют.

топи́ться *impf, present:* *(3)* то́п-ится, *(6)* -ятся.

торжествова́ть *impf, present:* *(1)* торжеству́-ю, *(2)* -ешь, *(3)* -ет, *(4)* -ем, *(5)* -ете, *(6)* -ют.

торопи́ть(ся) *impf, present:* *(1)* тороплю́(сь), *(2)* торо́п-ишь(ся), *(3)* -ит(ся), *(4)* -им(ся), *(5)* -ите(сь), *(6)* -ят(ся).

торча́ть *pf, future:* *(1)* торч-у́, *(2)* -и́шь, *(3)* -и́т, *(4)* -и́м, *(5)* -и́те, *(6)* -а́т.

тоскова́ть *impf, present:* *(1)* тоску́-ю, *(2)* -ешь, *(3)* -ет, *(4)* -ем, *(5)* -ете, *(6)* -ют.

тра́тить *impf, present:* *(1)* тра́чу, *(2)* тра́т-ишь, *(3)* -ит, *(4)* -им, *(5)* -ите, *(6)* -ят.

тре́бовать *impf, present:* *(1)* тре́бу-ю, *(2)* -ешь, *(3)* -ет, *(4)* -ем, *(5)* -ете, *(6)* -ют.

трево́жить(ся) *impf, present:* *(1)* трево́ж-у(сь), *(2)* -ишь(ся), *(3)* -ит(ся), *(4)* -им(ся), *(5)* -ите(сь), *(6)* -ат(ся).

тренирова́ть(ся) *impf, present:* *(1)* трениру́-ю(сь), *(2)* -ешь(ся), *(3)* -ет(ся), *(4)* -ем(ся), *(5)* -ете(сь), *(6)* -ют(ся).

трепа́ться *impf, present:* *(1)* треплю́сь, *(2)* тре́пл-ешься, *(3)* -ется, *(4)* -емся, *(5)* -етесь, *(6)* -ются.

трепета́ть *impf, present:* *(1)* трепещу́, *(2)* трепещ-ешь, *(3)* -ет, *(4)* -ем, *(5)* -ете, *(6)* -ут.

тро́гать *impf, present:* *(1)* тро́га-ю, *(2)* -ешь, *(3)* -ет, *(4)* -ем, *(5)* -ете, *(6)* -ют.

тро́нуть *pf, future:* *(1)* тро́н-у, *(2)* -ешь, *(3)* -ет, *(4)* -ем, *(5)* -ете, *(6)* -ут.

тру́сить *impf, present:* *(1)* тру́шу, *(2)* тру́с-ишь, *(3)* -ит, *(4)* -им, *(5)* -ите, *(6)* -ят.

трясти́ *impf, present:* *(1)* тряс-у́, *(2)* -ёшь, *(3)* -ёт, *(4)* -ём, *(5)* -ёте, *(6)* -у́т; *past:* тряс, -ла́, -ло́, -ли́.

трясти́сь *impf, present:* *(1)* тряс-у́сь, *(2)* -ёшься, *(3)* -ётся, *(4)* -ёмся, *(5)* -ётесь, *(6)* -у́тся; *past:* тря́сся, тряс-ла́сь, -ло́сь, -ли́сь.

тряхну́ть *pf, future:* *(1)* тряхн-у́, *(2)* -ёшь, *(3)* -ёт, *(4)* -ём, *(5)* -ёте, *(6)* -у́т.

Тускне́ть *impf, present:* *(1)* тускне́-ю, *(2)* -ешь, *(3)* -ет, *(4)* -ем, *(5)* -ете, *(6)* -ют.

Persons: 1 = я,   2 = ты,   3 = он, она́, оно́,   4 = мы,   5 = вы,   6 = они́

ты́каться *impf, present:* *(1)* ты́ч-усь, *(2)* -ешься, *(3)* -ется, *(4)* -емся, *(5)* -етесь, *(6)* -утся.

тя́нуть *impf, present:* *(1)* тяну́, *(2)* тя́н-ешь, *(3)* -ет, *(4)* -ем, *(5)* -ете, *(6)* -ут.

убега́ть *impf, present:* *(1)* убега́-ю, *(2)* -ешь, *(3)* -ет, *(4)* -ем, *(5)* -ете, *(6)* -ют.

убеди́ть(ся) *pf, future:* *(1)* not used *(2)* убед-и́шь(ся), *(3)* -и́т(ся), *(4)* -и́м(ся), *(5)* -и́те(сь), *(6)* -я́т(ся).

убежа́ть *pf, future:* *(1)* убегу́, *(2)* убеж-и́шь, *(3)* -и́т, *(4)* -и́м, *(5)* -и́те, *(6)* убегу́т.

убежда́ть *impf, present:* *(1)* убежда́-ю, *(2)* -ешь, *(3)* -ет, *(4)* -ем, *(5)* -ете, *(6)* -ют.

убива́ть *impf, present:* *(1)* убива́-ю, *(2)* -ешь, *(3)* -ет, *(4)* -ем, *(5)* -ете, *(6)* -ют.

убира́ть(ся) *impf, present:* *(1)* убира́-ю(сь), *(2)* -ешь(ся), *(3)* -ет(ся), *(4)* -ем(ся), *(5)* -ете(сь), *(6)* -ют(ся).

уби́ть *pf, future:* *(1)* убь-ю́, *(2)* -ёшь, *(3)* -ёт, *(4)* -ём, *(5)* -ёте, *(6)* -ю́т.

убра́ть(ся) *pf, future:* *(1)* убер-у́(сь), *(2)* -ёшь(ся), *(3)* -ёт(ся), *(4)* -ём(ся), *(5)* -ёте(сь), *(6)* -у́т(ся); *past:* убра́л(ся), убрала́(сь), убра́-ло(сь), -ли(сь).

убыва́ть *impf, present:* *(1)* убыва́-ю, *(2)* -ешь, *(3)* -ет, *(4)* -ем, *(5)* -ете, *(6)* -ют.

убы́ть *pf, future:* *(1)* убу́д-у, *(2)* -ешь, *(3)* -ет, *(4)* -ем, *(5)* -ете, *(6)* -ут; *past:* у́был, убыла́, у́бы-ло, -ли.

уважа́ть *impf, present:* *(1)* уважа́-ю, *(2)* -ешь, *(3)* -ет, *(4)* -ем, *(5)* -ете, *(6)* -ют.

увели́чивать *impf, present:* *(1)* увели́чива-ю, *(2)* -ешь, *(3)* -ет, *(4)* -ем, *(5)* -ете, *(6)* -ют.

увели́чиваться *impf, present:* *(3)* увели́чива-ется, *(6)* -ются.

увели́чить *pf, future:* *(1)* увели́ч-у, *(2)* -ишь, *(3)* -ит, *(4)* -им, *(5)* -ите, *(6)* -ат.

увели́читься *pf, future:* *(3)* увели́ч-ится, *(6)* -атся.

увенча́ть *pf, future:* *(1)* увенча́-ю, *(2)* -ешь, *(3)* -ет, *(4)* -ем, *(5)* -ете, *(6)* -ют.

уве́рить *pf, future:* *(1)* уве́р-ю, *(2)* -ишь, *(3)* -ит, *(4)* -им, *(5)* -ите, *(6)* -ят.

уверну́ться *pf, future:* *(1)* уверн-у́сь, *(2)* -ёшься, *(3)* -ётся, *(4)* -ёмся, *(5)* -ётесь, *(6)* -у́тся.

увёртываться *impf, present:* *(1)* увёртыва-юсь, *(2)* -ешься, *(3)* -ется, *(4)* -емся, *(5)* -етесь, *(6)* -ются.

уверя́ть *impf, present:* *(1)* уверя́-ю, *(2)* -ешь, *(3)* -ет, *(4)* -ем, *(5)* -ете, *(6)* -ют.

уви́деть *pf, future:* *(1)* уви́жу, *(2)* уви́д-ишь, *(3)* -ит, *(4)* -им, *(5)* -ите, *(6)* -ят.

уви́ливать *impf, present:* *(1)* уви́лива-ю, *(2)* -ешь, *(3)* -ет, *(4)* -ем, *(5)* -ете, *(6)* -ют.

увильну́ть *pf, future:* *(1)* увильн-у́, *(2)* -ёшь, *(3)* -ёт, *(4)* -ём, *(5)* -ёте, *(6)* -у́т.

увлека́ть *impf, present:* *(1)* увлека́-ю, *(2)* -ешь, *(3)* -ет, *(4)* -ем, *(5)* -ете, *(6)* -ют.

увле́чь(ся) *pf, future:* *(1)* увлеку́(сь), *(2)* увлеч-ёшь(ся), *(3)* -ёт(ся), *(4)* -ём(ся), *(5)* -ёте(сь), *(6)* увлеку́т(ся); *past:* увлёк(ся), увлек-ла́(сь), -ло́(сь), -ли́(сь).

увяда́ть *impf, present:* *(1)* увяда́-ю, *(2)* -ешь, *(3)* -ет, *(4)* -ем, *(5)* -ете, *(6)* -ют.

увя́нуть *pf, future:* *(1)* увя́н-у, *(2)* -ешь, *(3)* -ет, *(4)* -ем, *(5)* -ете, *(6)* -ут.

угаса́ть *impf, present:* *(1)* угаса́-ю, *(2)* -ешь, *(3)* -ет, *(4)* -ем, *(5)* -ете, *(6)* -ют.

уга́снуть *pf, future:* *(1)* угásн-у, *(2)* -ешь, *(3)* -ет, *(4)* -ем, *(5)* -ете, *(6)* -ут; *past:* угáс, -ла, -ло, -ли.

углуби́ть(ся) *pf, future:* *(1)* углуб-лю́(сь), *(2)* -и́шь(ся), *(3)* -и́т(ся), *(4)* -и́м(ся), *(5)* -и́те(сь), *(6)* -я́т(ся).

углубля́ть(ся) *impf, present:* *(1)* углубля́-ю(сь), *(2)* -ешь(ся), *(3)* -ет(ся), *(4)* -ем(ся), *(5)* -ете(сь), *(6)* -ют(ся).

угова́ривать *impf, present:* *(1)* угова́рива-ю, *(2)* -ешь, *(3)* -ет, *(4)* -ем, *(5)* -ете, *(6)* -ют.

уговори́ть *pf, future:* *(1)* уговор-ю́, *(2)* -и́шь, *(3)* -и́т, *(4)* -и́м, *(5)* -и́те, *(6)* -я́т.

угоди́ть *pf, future:* *(1)* угожу́, *(2)* угод-и́шь, *(3)* -и́т, *(4)* -и́м, *(5)* -и́те, *(6)* -я́т.

угожда́ть *impf, present:* *(1)* угожда́-ю, *(2)* -ешь, *(3)* -ет, *(4)* -ем, *(5)* -ете, *(6)* -ют.

угости́ть *pf, future:* *(1)* угощу́, *(2)* угост-и́шь, *(3)* -и́т, *(4)* -и́м, *(5)* -и́те, *(6)* -я́т.

угоща́ть(ся) impf, present: *(1)* угоща́-ю(сь), *(2)* -ешь(ся), *(3)* -ет(ся), *(4)* -ем(ся), *(5)* -ете(сь), *(6)* -ют(ся).

Persons: 1 = я,   2 = ты,   3 = он, она́, оно́,   4 = мы,   5 = вы,   6 = они́

угрожа́ть *impf, present: (1)* угрожа́-ю, *(2)* -ешь, *(3)* -ет, *(4)* -ем, *(5)* -ете, *(6)* -ют.

удава́ться *impf, present: (3)* удаётся.

уда́рить *pf, future: (1)* уда́р-ю, *(2)* -ишь, *(3)* -ит, *(4)* -им, *(5)* -ите, *(6)* -ят.

ударя́ть *impf, present: (1)* ударя́-ю, *(2)* -ешь, *(3)* -ет, *(4)* -ем, *(5)* -ете, *(6)* -ют.

уда́ться *pf, future: (3)* уда́стся; *past:* удало́сь.

удели́ть *pf, future: (1)* уделю́, *(2)* удел-и́шь, *(3)* -и́т, *(4)* -и́м, *(5)* -и́те, *(6)* -я́т.

уделя́ть *impf, present: (1)* уделя́-ю, *(2)* -ешь, *(3)* -ет, *(4)* -ем, *(5)* -ете, *(6)* -ют.

удержа́ть(ся) *pf, future: (1)* удержу́(сь), *(2)* уде́рж-ишь(ся), *(3)* -ит(ся), *(4)* -им(ся), *(5)* -ите(сь), *(6)* -ат(ся).

уде́рживать *impf, present: (1)* уде́ржива-ю, *(2)* -ешь, *(3)* -ет, *(4)* -ем, *(5)* -ете, *(6)* -ют.

удиви́ть *pf, future: (1)* удив-лю́, *(2)* -и́шь, *(3)* -и́т, *(4)* -и́м, *(5)* -и́те, *(6)* -я́т.

удивля́ть *impf, present: (1)* удивля́-ю, *(2)* -ешь, *(3)* -ет, *(4)* -ем, *(5)* -ете, *(6)* -ют.

удовлетвори́ть *pf, future: (1)* удовлетвор-ю́, *(2)* -и́шь, *(3)* -и́т, *(4)* -и́м, *(5)* -и́те, *(6)* -я́т.

удовлетворя́ть *impf, present: (1)* удовлетворя́-ю, *(2)* -ешь, *(3)* -ет, *(4)* -ем, *(5)* -ете, *(6)* -ют.

удочери́ть *pf, future: (1)* удочер-ю́, *(2)* -и́шь, *(3)* -и́т, *(4)* -и́м, *(5)* -и́те, *(6)* -я́т.

удочеря́ть *impf, present: (1)* удочеря́-ю, *(2)* -ешь, *(3)* -ет, *(4)* -ем, *(5)* -ете, *(6)* -ют.

удра́ть *pf, future: (1)* удер-у́, *(2)* -ёшь, *(3)* -ёт, *(4)* -ём, *(5)* -ёте, *(6)* -у́т.

удруча́ть *impf, present: (1)* удруча́-ю, *(2)* -ешь, *(3)* -ет, *(4)* -ем, *(5)* -ете, *(6)* -ют.

удручи́ть *pf, future: (1)* удруч-у́, *(2)* -и́шь, *(3)* -и́т, *(4)* -и́м, *(5)* -и́те, *(6)* -а́т.

уедини́ться *pf, future: (1)* уедин-ю́сь, *(2)* -и́шься, *(3)* -и́тся, *(4)* -и́мся, *(5)* -и́тесь, *(6)* -я́тся.

уединя́ться *impf, present: (1)* уединя́-юсь, *(2)* -ешься, *(3)* -ется, *(4)* -емся, *(5)* -етесь, *(6)* -ются.

уезжа́ть *impf, present: (1)* уезжа́-ю, *(2)* -ешь, *(3)* -ет, *(4)* -ем, *(5)* -ете, *(6)* -ют.

уе́хать *pf, future: (1)* уе́д-у, *(2)* -ешь, *(3)* -ет, *(4)* -ем, *(5)* -ете, *(6)* -ут.

узнава́ть *impf, present: (1)* узна-ю́, *(2)* -ёшь, *(3)* -ёт, *(4)* -ём, *(5)* -ёте, *(6)* -ю́т.

узна́ть *pf, future: (1)* узна́-ю, *(2)* -ешь, *(3)* -ет, *(4)* -ем, *(5)* -ете, *(6)* -ют.

уйти́ *pf, future: (1)* уйд-у́, *(2)* -ёшь, *(3)* -ёт, *(4)* -ём, *(5)* -ёте, *(6)* -у́т; *past:* у-шёл, -шла́, -шло́, -шли́.

укла́дывать *impf, present: (1)* укла́дыва-ю, *(2)* -ешь, *(3)* -ет, *(4)* -ем, *(5)* -ете, *(6)* -ют.

уклони́ться *pf, future: (1)* уклон-ю́сь, *(2)* -ишься, *(3)* -ится, *(4)* -имся, *(5)* -итесь, *(6)* -ятся.

уклоня́ться *impf, present: (1)* уклоня́-юсь, *(2)* -ешься, *(3)* -ется, *(4)* -емся, *(5)* -етесь, *(6)* -ются.

укра́сть *pf, future: (1)* украд-у́, *(2)* -ёшь, *(3)* -ёт, *(4)* -ём, *(5)* -ёте, *(6)* -у́т; *past:* укра́-л, -ла, -ло, -ли.

укрепи́ть *pf, future: (1)* укреплю́,(2) -и́шь, *(3)* -и́т, *(4)* -и́м, *(5)* -и́те, *(6)* -я́т.

укрепля́ть *impf, present: (1)* укрепля́-ю, *(2)* -ешь, *(3)* -ет, *(4)* -ем, *(5)* -ете, *(6)* -ют.

укрыва́ть *impf, present: (1)* укрыва́-ю, *(2)* -ешь, *(3)* -ет, *(4)* -ем, *(5)* -ете, *(6)* -ют.

укры́ть *pf, future: (1)* укро́-ю, *(2)* -ешь, *(3)* -ет, *(4)* -ем, *(5)* -ете, *(6)* -ют.

укуси́ть *pf, future: (1)* укушу́, *(2)* уку́с-ишь, *(3)* -ит, *(4)* -им, *(5)* -ите, *(6)* -ят.

ула́вливать *impf, present: (1)* ула́влива-ю, *(2)* -ешь, *(3)* -ет, *(4)* -ем, *(5)* -ете, *(6)* -ют.

улови́ть *pf, future: (1)* уловлю́, *(2)* уло́в-ишь, *(3)* -ит, *(4)* -им, *(5)* -ите, *(6)* -ят.

уложи́ть *pf, future: (1)* уложу, *(2)* уло́ж-ишь, *(3)* -ит, *(4)* -им, *(5)* -ите, *(6)* -ат.

улучша́ть *impf, present: (1)* улучша́-ю, *(2)* -ешь, *(3)* -ет, *(4)* -ем, *(5)* -ете, *(6)* -ют.

улу́чшить *pf, future: (1)* улу́чш-у, *(2)* -ишь, *(3)* -ит, *(4)* -им, *(5)* -ите, *(6)* -ат.

улыба́ться *impf, present: (1)* улыба́-юсь, *(2)* -ешься, *(3)* -ется, *(4)* -емся, *(5)* -етесь, *(6)* -ются.

улыбну́ться *pf, future: (1)* улыбн-у́сь, *(2)* -ёшься, *(3)* -ётся, *(4)* -ёмся, *(5)* -ётесь, *(6)*

> *Persons:* 1 = я,   2 = ты,   3 = он, онá, онó,   4 = мы,   5 = вы,   6 = онѝ

-ýтся.

умáсливать *impf, present: (1)* умáслива-ю, *(2)* -ешь, *(3)* -ет, *(4)* -ем, *(5)* -ете, *(6)* -ют.

умáслить *pf, future: (1)* умáсл-ю, *(2)* -ишь, *(3)* -ит, *(4)* -им, *(5)* -ите, *(6)* -ят.

уменьшáть(ся) *impf, present: (1)* уменьшá-ю(сь), *(2)* -ешь(ся), *(3)* -ет(ся), *(4)* -ем(ся), *(5)* -ете(сь), *(6)* -ют(ся).

умéньшить(ся) *pf, future: (1)* умéньш-у(сь), *(2)* -ишь(ся), *(3)* -ит(ся), *(4)* -им(ся), *(5)* -ите(сь), *(6)* -ат(ся).

умерéть *pf, future: (1)* умр-ý, *(2)* -ёшь, *(3)* -ёт, *(4)* -ём, *(5)* -ёте, *(6)* -ýт; *past:* ýмер, умерлá, ýмер-ло, -ли.

умéть *impf, present: (1)* умé-ю, *(2)* -ешь, *(3)* -ет, *(4)* -ем, *(5)* -ете, *(6)* -ют.

умирáть *impf, present: (1)* умирá-ю, *(2)* -ешь, *(3)* -ет, *(4)* -ем, *(5)* -ете, *(6)* -ют.

умолѝть *pf, future: (1)* умолю́, *(2)* умол-ѝшь, *(3)* -ѝт, *(4)* -ѝм, *(5)* -ѝте, *(6)* -я́т.

умоля́ть *impf, present: (1)* умоля-ю, *(2)* -ешь, *(3)* -ет, *(4)* -ем, *(5)* -ете, *(6)* -ют.

умудрѝться *pf, future: (1)* умудр-ю́сь, *(2)* -ѝшься, *(3)* -ѝтся, *(4)* -ѝмся, *(5)* -ѝтесь, *(6)* -я́тся.

умудря́ться *impf, present: (1)* умудря́-юсь, *(2)* -ешься, *(3)* -ется, *(4)* -емся, *(5)* -етесь, *(6)* -ются.

унестѝ *pf, future: (1)* унес-ý, *(2)* -ёшь, *(3)* -ёт, *(4)* -ём, *(5)* -ёте, *(6)* -ýт; *past:* унёс, унеслá, -лó, -лѝ.

уносѝть *impf, present: (1)* уношý, *(2)* унóс-ишь, *(3)* -ит, *(4)* -им, *(5)* -ите, *(6)* -ят.

унижáть *impf, present: (1)* унижá-ю, *(2)* -ешь, *(3)* -ет, *(4)* -ем, *(5)* -ете, *(6)* -ют.

унѝзить *pf, future: (1)* унѝжу, *(2)* унѝз-ишь, *(3)* -ит, *(4)* -им, *(5)* -ите, *(6)* -ат.

уничтожáть *impf, present: (1)* уничтожá-ю, *(2)* -ешь, *(3)* -ет, *(4)* -ем, *(5)* -ете, *(6)* -ют.

уничтóжить *pf, future: (1)* уничтóж-у, *(2)* -ишь, *(3)* -ит, *(4)* -им, *(5)* -ите, *(6)* -ат.

упáсть *pf, future: (1)* упад-ý, *(2)* -ёшь, *(3)* -ёт, *(4)* -ём, *(5)* -ёте, *(6)* -ýт.

упивáться *impf, present: (1)* упивá-юсь, *(2)* -ешься, *(3)* -ется, *(4)* -емся, *(5)* -етесь, *(6)* -ются.

упоминáть *impf, present: (1)* упоминá-ю, *(2)* -ешь, *(3)* -ет, *(4)* -ем, *(5)* -ете, *(6)* -ют.

упомянýть *pf, future: (1)* упомянý, *(2)* -ёшь, *(3)* -ёт, *(4)* -ём, *(5)* -ёте, *(6)* -ýт.

упоря́дочить *pf, future: (1)* упоря́доч-у, *(2)* -ишь, *(3)* -ит, *(4)* -им, *(5)* -ите, *(6)* -ат.

употребѝть *pf, future: (1)* употреб-лю́, *(2)* -ѝшь, *(3)* -ѝт, *(4)* -ѝм, *(5)* -ѝте, *(6)* -я́т.

употребля́ть *impf, present: (1)* употребля́-ю, *(2)* -ешь, *(3)* -ет, *(4)* -ем, *(5)* -ете, *(6)* -ют.

управля́ть *impf, present: (1)* управля́-ю, *(2)* -ешь, *(3)* -ет, *(4)* -ем, *(5)* -ете, *(6)* -ют.

упражня́ться *impf, present: (1)* упражня́-юсь, *(2)* -ешься, *(3)* -ется, *(4)* -емся, *(5)* -етесь, *(6)* -ются.

упрекáть *impf, present: (1)* упрекá-ю, *(2)* -ешь, *(3)* -ет, *(4)* -ем, *(5)* -ете, *(6)* -ют.

упрекнýть *pf, future: (1)* упрекн-ý, *(2)* -ёшь, *(3)* -ёт, *(4)* -ём, *(5)* -ёте, *(6)* -ýт.

упускáть *impf, present: (1)* упускá-ю, *(2)* -ешь, *(3)* -ет, *(4)* -ем, *(5)* -ете, *(6)* -ют.

упустѝть *pf, future: (1)* упущý, *(2)* упýст-ишь, *(3)* -ит, *(4)* -им, *(5)* -ите, *(6)* -ят.

уронѝть *pf, future: (1)* урон-ю́, *(2)* урóн-ишь, *(3)* -ит, *(4)* -им, *(5)* -ите, *(6)* -ят.

усвáивать *impf, present: (1)* усвáива-ю, *(2)* -ешь, *(3)* -ет, *(4)* -ем, *(5)* -ете, *(6)* -ют.

усвóить *pf, future: (1)* усвó-ю, *(2)* -ишь, *(3)* -ит, *(4)* -им, *(5)* -ите, *(6)* -ят.

усѝлить(ся) *pf, future: (1)* усѝл-ю(сь), *(2)* -ишь(ся), *(3)* -ит(ся), *(4)* -им(ся), *(5)* -ите(сь), *(6)* -ят(ся).

усѝливать(ся) *impf, present: (1)* усѝлива-ю(сь), *(2)* -ешь(ся), *(3)* -ет(ся), *(4)* -ем(ся), *(5)* -ете(сь), *(6)* -ют(ся).

ускользáть *impf, present: (1)* ускользá-ю, *(2)* -ешь, *(3)* -ет, *(4)* -ем, *(5)* -ете, *(6)* -ют.

ускользнýть *pf, future: (1)* ускользн-ý, *(2)* -ёшь, *(3)* -ёт, *(4)* -ём, *(5)* -ёте, *(6)* -ýт.

услы́шать *pf, future: (1)* услы́ш-у, *(2)* -ишь, *(3)* -ит, *(4)* -им, *(5)* -ите, *(6)* -ат.

успевáть *impf, present: (1)* успевá-ю, *(2)* -ешь, *(3)* -ет, *(4)* -ем, *(5)* -ете, *(6)* -ют.

успéть *pf, future: (1)* успé-ю, *(2)* -ешь, *(3)* -ет, *(4)* -ем, *(5)* -ете, *(6)* -ют.

| *Persons:* 1 = я, 2 = ты, 3 = он, она́, оно́, 4 = мы, 5 = вы, 6 = они́ |

успока́ивать(ся) *impf, present:* (1) успока́ива-ю(сь), (2) -ешь(ся), (3) -ет(ся), (4) -ем(ся), (5) -ете(сь), (6) -ют(ся).

успоко́ить(ся) *pf, future:* (1) успоко́-ю(сь), (2) -ишь(ся), (3) -ит(ся), (4) -им(ся), (5) -ите(сь), (6) -ят(ся).

устава́ть *impf, present:* (1) уста-ю́, (2) -ёшь, (3) -ёт, (4) -ём, (5) -ёте, (6) -ю́т.

уста́виться *pf, future:* (1) уста́в-люсь, (2) -ишься, (3) -ится, (4) -имся, (5) -итеся, (6) -ятся.

уставля́ться *impf, present:* (1) уставля́-юсь, (2) -ешься, (3) -ется, (4) -емся, (5) -етесь, (6) -ются.

устана́вливать *impf, present:* (1) устана́влива-ю, (2) -ешь, (3) -ет, (4) -ем, (5) -ете, (6) -ют.

установи́ть *pf, future:* (1) установлю́, (2) устано́в-ишь, (3) -ит, (4) -им, (5) -ите, (6) -ят.

уста́ть *pf, future:* (1) уста́н-у, (2) -ешь, (3) -ет, (4) -ем, (5) -ете, (6) -ут.

устоя́ть *pf, future:* (1) усто-ю́, (2) -ишь, (3) -ит, (4) -им, (5) -ите, (6) -ят.

устра́ивать(ся) *impf, present:* (1) устра́ива-ю(сь), (2) -ешь(ся), (3) -ет(ся), (4) -ем(ся), (5) -ете(сь), (6) -ют(ся).

устрани́ть *pf, future:* (1) устран-ю́, (2) -и́шь, (3) -и́т, (4) -и́м, (5) -и́те, (6) -я́т.

устреми́ться *pf, future:* (1) устрем-лю́сь, (2) -и́шься, (3) -и́тся, (4) -и́мся, (5) -и́тесь, (6) -я́тся.

устремля́ться *impf, present:* (1) устремля́-юсь, (2) -ешься, (3) -ется, (4) -емся, (5) -етесь, (6) -ются.

устро́ить(ся) *pf, future:* (1) урстро́-ю(сь), (2) -ишь(ся), (3) -ит(ся), (4) -им(ся), (5) -ите(сь), (6) -ят(ся).

уступа́ть *impf, present:* (1) уступа́-ю, (2) -ешь, (3) -ет, (4) -ем, (5) -ете, (6) -ют.

уступи́ть *pf, future:* (1) уступлю́, (2) усту́п-ишь, (3) -ит, (4) -им, (5) -ите, (6) -ят.

усынови́ть *pf, future:* (1) усынов-лю́, (2) -и́шь, (3) -и́т, (4) -и́м, (5) -и́те, (6) -я́т.

усыновля́ть *impf, present:* (1) усыновля́-ю, (2) -ешь, (3) -ет, (4) -ем, (5) -ете, (6) -ют.

утверди́ть *pf, future:* (1) утвержу́, (2) утверд-и́шь, (3) -и́т, (4) -и́м, (5) -и́те, (6) -я́т.

утвержда́ть *impf, present:* (1) утвержда́-ю, (2) -ешь, (3) -ет, (4) -ем, (5) -ете, (6) -ют.

утеша́ть *impf, present:* (1) утеша́-ю, (2) -ешь, (3) -ет, (4) -ем, (5) -ете, (6) -ют.

уте́шить *pf, future:* (1) уте́ш-у, (2) -ишь, (3) -ит, (4) -им, (5) -ите, (6) -ат.

утихоми́ривать *impf, present:* (1) утихоми́рива-ю, (2) -ешь, (3) -ет, (4) -ем, (5) -ете, (6) -ют.

утихоми́рить *pf, future:* (1) утихоми́р-ю, (2) -ишь, (3) -ит, (4) -им, (5) -ите, (6) -ят.

утоли́ть *pf, future:* (1) утол-ю́, (2) -и́шь, (3) -и́т, (4) -и́м, (5) -и́те, (6) -я́т.

утоля́ть *impf, present:* (1) утоля́-ю, (2) -ешь, (3) -ет, (4) -ем, (5) -ете, (6) -ют.

утопи́ть *pf, future:* (1) утоп-лю́, (2) уто́п-ишь, (3) -ит, (4) -им, (5) -ите, (6) -ят.

утопи́ться *pf, future:* (3) уто́п-ится, (6) -ятся.

утружда́ть *impf, present:* (1) утружда́-ю, (2) -ешь, (3) -ет, (4) -ем, (5) -ете, (6) -ют.

уха́живать *impf, present:* (1) уха́жива-ю, (2) -ешь, (3) -ет, (4) -ем, (5) -ете, (6) -ют.

ухитри́ться *pf, future:* (1) ухитр-ю́сь, (2) -и́шься, (3) -и́тся, (4) -и́мся, (5) -и́тесь, (6) -я́тся.

ухитря́ться *impf, present:* (1) ухитря́-юсь, (2) -ешься, (3) -ется, (4) -емся, (5) -етесь, (6) -ются.

ухмылну́ться *pf, future:* (1) ухмылн-у́сь, (2) -ёшься, (3) -ётся, (4) -ёмся, (5) -ётесь, (6) -у́тся.

ухмыля́ться *impf, present:* (1) ухмыля́-юсь, (2) -ешься, (3) -ется, (4) -емся, (5) -етесь, (6) -ются.

уходи́ть *impf, present:* (1) ухожу́, (2) ухо́д-ишь, (3) -ит, (4) -им, (5) -ите, (6) -ят.

уцепи́ться *pf, future:* (1) уцеплю́сь, (2) уцеп-ишься, (3) -ится, (4) -имся, (5) -итесь, (6)

> *Persons:* 1 = я,   2 = ты,   3 = он, она́, оно́,   4 = мы,   5 = вы,   6 = они́

-ятся.

участи́ться *pf, future: (3)* участ-и́тся, *(6)* -я́тся.

уча́ствовать *impf, present: (1)* уча́ству-ю, *(2)* -ешь, *(3)* -ет, *(4)* -ем, *(5)* -ете, *(6)* -ют.

учаща́ться *impf, present: (3)* учаща́-ется, *(6)* -ются.

учи́ть(ся) *impf, present: (1)* учу́(сь), *(2)* уч-и́шь(ся), *(3)* -и́т(ся), *(4)* -и́м(ся), *(5)* -и́те(сь), *(6)* -а́т(ся).

ущипну́ть *pf, future: (1)* ущипн-у́, *(2)* -ёшь, *(3)* -ёт, *(4)* -ём, *(5)* -ёте, *(6)* -у́т.

фальсифици́ровать *impf, present: (1)* фальсифици́ру-ю, *(2)* -ешь, *(3)* -ет, *(4)* -ем, *(5)* -ете, *(6)* -ют.

фантази́ровать *impf, present: (1)* фантази́ру-ю, *(2)* -ешь, *(3)* -ет, *(4)* -ем, *(5)* -ете, *(6)* -ют.

флиртова́ть *impf, present: (1)* флирту́-ю, *(2)* -ешь, *(3)* -ет, *(4)* -ем, *(5)* -ете, *(6)* -ют.

фокуси́ровать *impf, present: (1)* фокуси́ру-ю, *(2)* -ешь, *(3)* -ет, *(4)* -ем, *(5)* -ете, *(6)* -ют.

формули́ровать *impf, present: (1)* формули́ру-ю, *(2)* -ешь, *(3)* -ет, *(4)* -ем, *(5)* -ете, *(6)* -ют.

хандри́ть *impf, present: (1)* хандр-ю́, *(2)* -и́шь, *(3)* -и́т, *(4)* -и́м, *(5)* -и́те, *(6)* -я́т.

хвали́ть *impf, present: (1)* хвалю́, *(2)* хва́л-ишь, *(3)* -ит, *(4)* -им, *(5)* -ите, *(6)* -ят.

хва́статься *pf, future: (1)* хва́ста-юсь, *(2)* -ешься, *(3)* -ется, *(4)* -емся, *(5)* -етесь, *(6)* -ются.

хвата́ть *impf, present: (1)* хвата́-ю, *(2)* -ешь, *(3)* -ет, *(4)* -ем, *(5)* -ете, *(6)* -ют.

хитри́ть *impf, present: (1)* хитр-ю́, *(2)* -и́шь, *(3)* -и́т, *(4)* -и́м, *(5)* -и́те, *(6)* -я́т.

хихи́кать *impf, present: (1)* хихи́ка-ю, *(2)* -ешь, *(3)* -ет, *(4)* -ем, *(5)* -ете, *(6)* -ют.

хму́риться *impf, present: (1)* хму́р-юсь, *(2)* -ишься, *(3)* -ится, *(4)* -имся, *(5)* -итесь, *(6)* -ятся.

хны́кать *impf, present (2 conjugations): (1)* хны́-чу *or* -каю, *(2)* -чешь *or* -каешь , *(3)* -чет *or* -кает, *(4)* -чем *or* -каем, *(5)* -чете *or* -каете, *(6)* -чут *or* -кают.

ходи́ть *impf, present: (1)* хожу́, *(2)* хо́д-ишь, *(3)* -ит, *(4)* -им, *(5)* -ите, *(6)* -ят.

хоте́ть *impf, present: (1)* хочу́, *(2)* хо́чешь, *(3)* хо́чет, *(4)* хот-и́м, *(5)* -и́те, *(6)* -я́т.

храни́ть *impf, present: (1)* хран-ю́, *(2)* -и́шь, *(3)* -и́т, *(4)* -и́м, *(5)* -и́те, *(6)* -я́т.

храпе́ть *impf, present: (1)* храп-лю́, *(2)* -и́шь, *(3)* -и́т, *(4)* -и́м, *(5)* -и́те, *(6)* -я́т.

хрома́ть *impf, present: (1)* хрома́-ю, *(2)* -ешь, *(3)* -ет, *(4)* -ем, *(5)* -ете, *(6)* -ют.

худе́ть *impf, present: (1)* худе́-ю, *(2)* -ешь, *(3)* -ет, *(4)* -ем, *(5)* -ете, *(6)* -ют.

цари́ть *impf, present: (1)* цар-ю́, *(2)* -и́шь, *(3)* -и́т, *(4)* -и́м, *(5)* -и́те, *(6)* -я́т.

цвести́ *impf, present: (1)* цвет-у́, *(2)* -ёшь, *(3)* -ёт, *(4)* -ём, *(5)* -ёте, *(6)* -у́т; *past:* цвёл, цвел-а́, -о́, -и́.

целова́ть(ся) *impf, present: (1)* целу́-ю(сь), *(2)* -ешь(ся), *(3)* -ет(ся), *(4)* -ем(ся), *(5)* -ете(сь), *(6)* -ют(ся).

цени́ть *impf, present: (1)* ценю́, *(2)* це́н-ишь, *(3)* -ит, *(4)* -им, *(5)* -ите, *(6)* -ят.

цепене́ть *impf, present: (1)* цепене́-ю, *(2)* -ешь, *(3)* -ет, *(4)* -ем, *(5)* -ете, *(6)* -ют.

цепля́ться *impf, present: (1)* цепля́-юсь, *(2)* -ешься, *(3)* -ется, *(4)* -емся, *(5)* -етесь, *(6)* -ются.

ча́хнуть *impf, present: (1)* ча́хн-у, *(2)* -ешь, *(3)* -ет, *(4)* -ем, *(5)* -ете, *(6)* -ут; *past:* чах *or* ча́хнул, ча́хл-а, -о, -и.

чеса́ть *impf, present: (1)* чешу́, *(2)* чеш-ишь, *(3)* -ит, *(4)* -им, *(5)* -ите, *(6)* -ят.

чини́ть *impf, present: (1)* чиню́, *(2)* чи́н-ишь, *(3)* -ит, *(4)* -им, *(5)* -ите, *(6)* -ят.

чи́стить *impf, present: (1)* чи́щу, *(2)* чи́ст-ишь, *(3)* -ит, *(4)* -им, *(5)* -ите, *(6)* -ят.

чита́ть *impf, present: (1)* чита́-ю, *(2)* -ешь, *(3)* -ет, *(4)* -ем, *(5)* -ете, *(6)* -ют.

чтить *impf, present: (1)* чт-у, *(2)* -ишь, *(3)* -ит, *(4)* -им, *(5)* -ите, *(6)* -ят.

чу́вствовать *impf, present: (1)* чу́вству-ю, *(2)* -ешь, *(3)* -ет, *(4)* -ем, *(5)* -ете, *(6)* -ют.

чу́ять *impf, present: (1)* чу́-ю, *(2)* -ешь, *(3)* -ет, *(4)* -ем, *(5)* -ете, *(6)* -ют.

Persons: 1 = я, 2 = ты, 3 = он, онá, онó, 4 = мы, 5 = вы, 6 = онй

шалéть *impf, present:* *(1)* шалé-ю, *(2)* -ешь, *(3)* -ет, *(4)* -ем, *(5)* -ете, *(6)* -ют.

шантажи́ровать *impf, present:* *(1)* шантажи́ру-ю, *(2)* -ешь, *(3)* -ет, *(4)* -ем, *(5)* -ете, *(6)* -ют.

швырну́ть *pf, future:* *(1)* швырн-ý, *(2)* -ёшь, *(3)* -ёт, *(4)* -ём, *(5)* -ёте, *(6)* -ýт.

швыря́ть *impf, present:* *(1)* швыря́-ю, *(2)* -ешь, *(3)* -ет, *(4)* -ем, *(5)* -ете, *(6)* -ют.

шепну́ть *pf, future:* *(1)* шепн-ý, *(2)* -ёшь, *(3)* -ёт, *(4)* -ём, *(5)* -ёте, *(6)* -ýт.

шепта́ть *impf, present:* *(1)* шепчý, *(2)* шéпч-ешь, *(3)* -ет, *(4)* -ем, *(5)* -ете, *(6)* -ут.

шоки́ровать *impf, present:* *(1)* шоки́ру-ю, *(2)* -ешь, *(3)* -ет, *(4)* -ем, *(5)* -ете, *(6)* -ют.

штрафова́ть *impf, present:* *(1)* штрафý-ю, *(2)* -ешь, *(3)* -ет, *(4)* -ем, *(5)* -ете, *(6)* -ют.

шути́ть *impf, present:* *(1)* шучý, *(2)* шýт-ишь, *(3)* -ит, *(4)* -им, *(5)* -ите, *(6)* -ят.

щебета́ть *impf, present:* *(1)* щебéч-у, *(2)* -ишь, *(3)* -ит, *(4)* -им, *(5)* -ите, *(6)* -ят.

щёлкать *impf, present:* *(1)* щёлка-ю, *(2)* -ешь, *(3)* -ет, *(4)* -ем, *(5)* -ете, *(6)* -ют.

щёлкнуть *pf, future:* *(1)* щёлкн-у, *(2)* -ешь, *(3)* -ет, *(4)* -ем, *(5)* -ете, *(6)* -ут.

эксперименти́ровать *impf, present:* *(1)* эксперименти́ру-ю, *(2)* -ешь, *(3)* -ет, *(4)* -ем, *(5)* -ете, *(6)* -ют.

язви́ть *impf, present:* *(1)* язв-лю́, *(2)*-и́шь, *(3)* -и́т, *(4)* -и́м, *(5)* -и́те, *(6)* -я́т.

Numbers

1	оди́н (одна́, одно́)	21	два́дцать оди́н	500	пятьсо́т
2	два (две)	22	два́дцать два	600	шестьсо́т
3	три	23	два́дцать три	700	семьсо́т
4	четы́ре	24	два́дцать четы́ре	800	восемьсо́т
5	пять	25	два́дцать пять	900	девятьсо́т
6	шесть	26	два́дцать шесть	1000	ты́сяча
7	семь	27	два́дцать семь	2000	две ты́сячи
8	во́семь	28	два́дцать во́семь	3000	три ты́сячи
9	де́вять	29	два́дцать де́вять	4000	четы́ре ты́сячи
10	де́сять	30	три́дцать	5000	пять ты́сяч
11	оди́ннадцать	40	со́рок	6000	шесть ты́сяч
12	двена́дцать	50	пятьдеся́т	7000	семь ты́сяч
13	трина́дцать	60	шестьдеся́т	8000	во́семь ты́сяч
14	четы́рнадцать	70	се́мьдесят	9000	де́вять ты́сяч
15	пятна́дцать	80	во́семьдесят	10,000	де́сять ты́сяч
16	шестна́дцать	90	девяно́сто	100,000	сто ты́сяч
17	семна́дцать	100	сто	1,000,000	оди́н миллио́н
18	восемна́дцать	200	две́сти		
19	девятна́дцать	300	три́ста		
20	два́дцать	400	четы́реста		

Counting Nouns

The following rules apply to counting nouns:

1. **One** (оди́н, одна́, одно́) takes the nominative singular of the noun and agrees in gender with it.

   Examples: оди́н поцелу́й (one kiss) (masculine)

   одна́ звезда́ (one star) (feminine)

   одно́ кольцо́ (one ring) (neuter)

2. **Two** (два, две), **three** (три), **four** (четы́ре), and the word "**both**" (о́ба, о́бе) take the genitive singular of the noun. Два and о́ба are used for masculine and neuter nouns, две and о́бе for feminine. Три and четы́ре are used for all genders.

   Examples: два / о́ба поцелу́я (2 / both kisses) (masculine)

   две / о́бе звезды́ (2 / both stars) (feminine)

   два / о́ба кольца́ (2 / both rings) (neuter)

   три / четы́ре поцелу́я (3,4 kisses) (masculine)

   три / четы́ре звезды́ (3,4 stars) (feminine)

   три / четы́ре кольца́ (3,4 rings) (neuter)

3. Numbers **5 through 20** and **all other numbers ending in 5 though 0** take the genitive plural of the noun. Gender is not a factor. Compare the noun endings with the preceding examples.

    Examples: пять, со́рок, сто поцелу́ев (5, 40, 100 kisses) (masculine)
                    пять, со́рок, сто звёзд (3,4 stars) (feminine)
                    пять, со́рок, сто коле́ц (3,4 rings) (neuter)

4. A number (no matter how large) ending in digits 1 to 0 is subject to the rules for that digit.

    Examples: ты́сяча оди́н поцелу́й (1001 kisses) (masculine)
                    ты́сяча два поцелу́я (1002 kisses) (masculine)
                    ты́сяча три поцелу́я (1003 kisses) (masculine)
                    ты́сяча четы́ре поцелу́я (1004 kisses) (masculine)
                    ты́сяча пять поцелу́ев (1005 kisses) (masculine)

5. Numbers decline in grammatical cases, as shown below. The numbers ты́сяча (thousand) and миллио́н (million) decline like nouns (which see).

Declension of Numbers

Number	Accusative	Genitive	Dative	Instrumental	Prepositional
оди́н	оди́н *	одного́	одному́	одни́м	одно́м
одно́	одно́	одного́	одному́	одни́м	одно́м
одна́	одну́	одно́й	одно́й	одно́й	одно́й
два, две	два, две *	двух	двум	двумя́	двух
о́ба	о́ба *	обо́их	обо́им	обо́ими	обо́их
о́бе	о́бе *	обе́их	обе́им	обе́ими	обе́их
три	три *	трёх	трём	тремя́	трёх
четы́ре	четы́ре *	четырёх	четырём	чеырмя́	четырёх
пять	пять	пяти́	пяти́	пятью́	пяти́
6-20, 30	-ь	-и	-и	-ью	-и
со́рок	со́рок	сорока́	сорока́	сорока́	сорока́
пятьдеся́т	пятьдеся́т	пяти́десяти	пяти́десяти	пятью́десятью	пяти́десяти
шестьдеся́т	шесть-деся́т	шести́десяти	шести́десяти	шестью́десятью	шести́десяти
се́мьдесят	се́мьдесят	семи́десяти	семи́десяти	семью́десятью	семи́десяти
во́семьдесят	во́семьдесят	восьми́десяти	восьми́десяти	восьмью́десятью	восьми́десяти
девяно́сто	девяно́сто	девяно́ста	девянно́ста	девяно́ста	девяно́ста
сто	сто	ста	ста	ста	ста
две́сти	две́сти	двухсо́т	двумста́м	двумяста́ми	двухста́х
три́ста	три́ста	трёхсот	трёмстам	тремястами	трёхстах
пятьсо́т	пятьсо́т	пятисо́т	пятиста́м	пятьюста́ми	пятиста́х

If animate, then same as genitive.

Ordinal Numbers

These are like adjectives. They have different endings for the three genders and the plural and are declined in exactly the same way as adjectives. (See "Declension of Adjectives" on page 694).

Neuter ordinal numbers are used to express **dates** in Russian, and when something occurs on the date, the **genitive form** of the neuter ordinal number is used. Therefore, when you tell someone what date it is or you date a letter, use the nominative form of the neuter ordinal number. When you talk about something happening on a date, use the genitive form. We have given you the first 31 ordinal numbers below.

Ordinal Numbers

Ordinal	Nominitive Forms	Genitive Form
first	пе́рвый, -ая, **-ое**, -ые	пе́рвого
second	второ́й, -а́я, **-о́е**, -ы́е	второ́го
third	тре́тий, -ья, **-ье**, -ьи	тре́тьего
fourth	четвёртый, -ая, **-ое**, -ые	четвёртого
fifth	пя́тый, -ая, **-ое**, -ые	пя́того
sixth	шесто́й, -а́я, **-о́е**, -ы́е	шесто́го
seventh	седьмо́й, -а́я, **-о́е**, -ы́е	седьмо́го
eighth	восьмо́й, -а́я, **-о́е**, -ы́е	восьмо́го
ninth	девя́тый, -ая, **-ое**, -ые	девя́того
tenth	деся́тый, -ая, **-ое**, -ые	деся́того
11th	оди́ннадцатый, -ая, **-ое**, -ые	оди́ннадцатого
12th	двена́дцатый, -ая, **-ое**, -ые	двена́дцатого
13th	трина́дцатый, -ая, **-ое**, -ые	трина́дцатого
14th	четы́рнадцатый, -ая, **-ое**, -ые	четы́рнадцатого
15th	пятна́дцатый, -ая, **-ое**, -ые	пятна́дцатого
16th	шестна́дцатый, -ая, **-ое**, -ые	шестна́дцатого
17th	семна́дцатый, -ая, **-ое**, -ые	семна́дцатого
18th	восемна́дцатый, -ая, **-ое**, -ые	восемна́дцатого
19th	девятна́дцатый, -ая, **-ое**, -ые	девятна́дцатого
20th	двадца́тый, -ая, **-ое**, -ые	двадца́того
21st	два́дцать пе́рвый, -ая, **-ое**, -ые	два́дцать пе́рвого
22nd	два́дцать второ́й, -а́я, **-о́е**, -ы́е	два́дцать второ́го
23rd	два́дцать тре́тий, -ья, **-ье**, -ьи	два́дцать тре́тьего
24th	два́дцать четвёртый, -ая, **-ое**, -ые	два́дцать четвёртого
25th	два́дцать пя́тый, -ая, **-ое**, -ые	два́дцать пя́того
26th	два́дцать шесто́й, -а́я, **-о́е**, -ы́е	два́дцать шесто́го
27th	два́дцать седьмо́й, -а́я, **-о́е**, -ы́е	два́дцать седьмо́го
28th	два́дцать восьмо́й, -а́я, **-о́е**, -ы́е	два́дцать восьмо́го
29h	два́дцать девя́тый, -ая, **-ое**, -ые	два́дцать девя́того
30th	тридца́тый, -ая, **-ое**, -ые	тридца́того
31st	три́дцать пе́рвый, -ая, **-ое**, -ые	три́дцать пе́рвого

Clock & Calendar Time

Clock Time

1:00	час	7:00	семь часо́в
2:00	два часа́	8:00	во́семь часо́в
3:00	три часа́	9:00	де́вять часо́в
4:00	четы́ре часа́	10:00	де́сять часо́в
5:00	пять часо́в	11:00	оди́ннадцать часо́в
6:00	шесть часо́в	12:00	двена́дцать часо́в

To express minutes in addition to the hour, e.g., 4:15, 7:30, 10:45, the simplest way is to drop the word for o'clock (часа́, часо́в) (except for 1:00) and add the minutes.

There is another way to render parts of an hour, but it's a bit complicated and not recommended for beginners. For those interested, please refer to a grammar manual, such as "Essential Russian Grammar," by Brian Kemple.

To say "at" a certain time, just put "в" in front of the time.

To make the time AM or PM, add "утра́" for morning, "дня" for afternoon, "ве́чера" for evening, or "но́чи" for night.

Days of the Week

English Name	Russian Name	On the day
Monday	понеде́льник	в понеде́льник
Tuesday	вто́рник	во вто́рник
Wednesday	среда́	в сре́ду
Thursday	четве́рг	в четве́рг
Friday	пя́тница	в пя́тницу
Saturday	суббо́та	в суббо́ту
Sunday	воскресе́нье	в воскресе́нье

The days of the week are not capitalized in Russian.

"On what day?" or "What day?" in Russian is «В како́й день?»

Dates

The word order for dates in Russian is day, month, year.

The neuter form of ordinal numbers (e.g., first, second, etc) is always used for the day of the month. To state what the date is, the number is in the nominative case, but to say "on" a certain date, the number must go into the genitive case. For a list of the ordinal numbers, see the previous appendix on numbers.

If the month follows the numerical date, it is in the genitive case (expressing "of") (*See* "Months of the Year" *above*).

The year number is a masculine ordinal number (modifying "год" [year], a masculine noun).

> Example: 1998 = ты́сяча девятьсо́т девяно́сто восьмо́й год
> *(one thousand nine hundred ninety **eighth** year)*

If it follows the month, it is also in the genitive case (again, expressing "of").

> Example: March 1998 = март ты́сяча девятьсо́т девяно́сто **восьмо́го го́да**
> *(March of the one thousand nine hundred ninety eighth year)*

If you want to say "in" a year, use "в" and put the last word of the year (and the word "year") in the prepositional case.

> Example: in 1998 = в ты́сяча девятьсо́т девяно́сто **восьмо́м году́**
> *(in the one thousand nine hundred ninety eighth year)*

"In what year?" in Russian is «В како́м году́?»

Months of the Year

English Name	Russian Name	Of the Month	In the Month
January	янва́рь	января́	в январе́
February	февра́ль	февраля́	в феврале́
March	март	ма́рта	в ма́рте
April	апре́ль	апре́ля	в апре́ле
May	май	ма́я	в ма́е
June	ию́нь	ию́ня	в ию́не
July	ию́ль	ию́ля	в ию́ле
August	а́вгуст	а́вгуста	в а́вгусте
September	сентя́брь	сентября́	в сентябре́
October	октя́брь	октября́	в октябре́
November	ноя́брь	ноября́	в ноябре́
December	дека́брь	декабря́	в декабре́

The months of the year are not capitalized in Russian.

"In what month?" or " What month?" in Russian is «В како́м ме́сяце?»

Age

To express a person's age, put the person in the dative case and then say the number of years. The word for year is **год** for any number ending in 1 (except 11), **го́да** for any number ending in 2, 3 and 4 (except 12, 13, 14), and **лет** for any number ending in 5 through 0 (including teens).

Example: I'm 21 / 22 / 25. **Мне 21 год / 22 го́да / 25 лет.**

"How old are you?" in Russian is «Ско́лько Вам лет?» *(polite)*

Time Zones

A = AM, P= PM. For the next 12 hours, change all P's to A and all A's to P. Don't forget a possible change of day. (12PM = noon, 12AM = midnight)

City Time Row:	1	2	3	4	5	6	7	8	9	10	11	12
Almaty +6	6P	7P	8P	9P	10P	11P	12A	1A	2A	3A	4A	5A
Amsterdam +1	1P	2P	3P	4P	5P	6P	7P	8P	9P	10P	llP	12A
Anchorage -9	3A	4A	5A	6A	7A	8A	9A	10A	11A	12P	1P	2P
Ashqabat+5	5P	6P	7P	8P	9P	10P	11P	12A	1A	2A	3A	4A
Atlanta -5	7A	8A	9A	10A	11A	12P	1P	2P	3P	4P	5P	6P
Austin -6	6A	7A	8A	9A	10A	11A	12P	1P	2P	3P	4P	5P
Baku +4	4P	5P	6P	7P	8P	9P	10P	11P	12A	1A	2A	3A
Baltimore -5	7A	8A	9A	10A	11A	12P	1P	2P	3P	4P	5P	6P
Berlin +1	1P	2P	3P	4P	5P	6P	7P	8P	9P	10P	11P	12A
Bishkek +6	6P	7P	8P	9P	10P	11P	12A	1A	2A	3A	4A	5A
Boston -5	7A	8A	9A	10A	11A	12P	1P	2P	3P	4P	5P	6P
Brest +2	2P	3P	4P	5P	6P	7P	8P	9P	10P	11P	12A	1A
Bryansk +3	3P	4P	5P	6P	7P	8P	9P	10P	11P	12A	1A	2A
Chelyabinsk +5	5P	6P	7P	8P	9P	10P	11P	12A	1A	2A	3A	4A
Chicago -6	6A	7A	8A	9A	10A	11A	12P	1P	P	3P	4P	5P
Chisinau +2	2P	3P	4P	5P	6P	7P	8P	9P	10P	11P	12A	1A
Cleveland -5	7A	8A	9A	10A	11A	12P	1P	2P	3P	4P	5P	6P
Copenhagen +1	1P	2P	3P	4P	5P	6P	7P	8P	9P	10P	llP	12A
Dallas -6	6A	7A	8A	9A	10A	11A	12P	1P	2P	3P	4P	5P
Denver -7	5A	6A	7A	8A	9A	10A	11A	12P	1P	2P	3P	4P
Detroit -5	7A	8A	9A	10A	11A	12P	1P	2P	3P	4P	5P	6P
Dnipropetrovsk +2	2P	3P	4P	5P	6P	7P	8P	9P	10P	11P	12A	1A
Donetsk +2	2P	3P	4P	5P	6P	7P	8P	9P	10P	11P	12A	1A
Dublin 01	2P	1P	2P	3P	4P	5P	6P	7P	8P	9P	10P	11P
Dushanbe +6	6P	7P	8P	9P	10P	11P	12A	1A	2A	3A	4A	5A
Helsinki +2	2P	3P	4P	5P	6P	7P	8P	9P	10P	11P	12A	1A
Homyel +2	2P	3P	4P	5P	6P	7P	8P	9P	10P	11P	12A	1A
Honolulu -10	2A	3A	4A	5A	6A	7A	8A	9A	10A	11A	12P	1P
Houston -6	6A	7A	8A	9A	10A	11A	12P	1P	2P	3P	4P	5P
Indianapolis -5	7A	8A	9A	10A	11A	12P	1P	2P	3P	4P	5P	6P
Irkutsk +8	8P	9P	10P	11P	12A	1A	2A	3A	4A	5A	6A	7A
Kaliningrad +2	2P	3P	4P	5P	6P	7P	8P	9P	10P	11P	12A	1A
Kansas City -6	6A	7A	8A	9A	10A	11A	12P	1P	2P	3P	4P	5P
Kazan +3	3P	4P	5P	6P	7P	8P	9P	10P	11P	12A	1A	2A
Khabarovsk +10	10P	11P	12A	1A	2A	3A	4A	5A	6A	7A	8A	9A
Kharkiv +2	2P	3P	4P	5P	6P	7P	8P	9P	10P	11P	12A	1A
Kiev +2	2P	3P	4P	5P	6P	7P	8P	9P	10P	11P	12A	1A
Krasnodar +3	3P	4P	5P	6P	7P	8P	9P	10P	11P	12A	1A	2A
Krasnoyarsk +7	7P	8P	9P	10P	11P	12A	1A	2A	3A	4A	5A	6A
London 0	12P	1P	2P	3P	4P	5P	6P	7P	8P	9P	10P	11P
Los Angeles -8	4A	5A	6A	7A	8A	9A	10A	11A	12P	1P	2P	3P
Lviv +2	2P	3P	4P	5P	6P	7P	8P	9P	10P	11P	12A	1A
Miami -5	7A	8A	9A	10A	11A	12P	1P	2P	3P	4P	5P	6P
Milwaukee -6	6A	7A	8A	9A	10A	11A	12P	1P	2P	3P	4P	5P
Minneapolis -6	6A	7A	8A	9A	10A	11A	12P	1P	2P	3P	4P	5P
Minsk +2	2P	3P	4P	5P	6P	7P	8P	9P	10P	11P	12A	1A

City	Time Row:	1	2	3	4	5	6	7	8	9	10	11	12
Montreal -5		7A	8A	9A	10A	11A	12P	1P	2P	3P	4P	5P	6P
Moscow +3		3P	4P	5P	6P	7P	8P	9P	10P	11P	12A	1A	2A
Murmansk +3		3P	4P	5P	6P	7P	8P	9P	10P	11P	12A	1A	2A
New Orleans -6		6A	7A	8A	9A	10A	11A	12P	1P	2P	3P	4P	5P
New York -5		7A	8A	9A	10A	11A	12P	1P	2P	3P	4P	5P	6P
Nizhny Novgorod +3		3P	4P	5P	6P	7P	8P	9P	10P	11P	12A	1A	2A
Novosibirsk +7		7P	8P	9P	10P	11P	12A	1A	2A	3A	4A	5A	6A
Odesa +2		2P	3P	4P	5P	6P	7P	8P	9P	10P	11P	12A	1A
Omsk +6		6P	7P	8P	9P	10P	11P	12A	1A	2A	3A	4A	5A
Oslo +1		1P	2P	3P	4P	5P	6P	7P	8P	9P	10P	11P	12A
Paris +1		1P	2P	3P	4P	5P	6P	7P	8P	9P	10P	11P	12A
Perm +5		5P	6P	7P	8P	9P	10P	11P	12A	1A	2A	3A	4A
Philadelphia -5		7A	8A	9A	10A	11A	12P	1P	2P	3P	4P	5P	6P
Phoenix -7		5A	6A	7A	8A	9A	10A	11A	12P	1P	2P	3P	4P
Pittsburgh -5		7A	8A	9A	10A	11A	12P	1P	2P	3P	4P	5P	6P
Portland, OR -8		4A	5A	6A	7A	8A	9A	10A	11A	12P	1P	2P	3P
Pskov +3		3P	4P	5P	6P	7P	8P	9P	10P	11P	12A	1A	2A
Riga +2		2P	3P	4P	5P	6P	7P	8P	9P	10P	11P	12A	1A
Rostov +3		3P	4P	5P	6P	7P	8P	9P	10P	11P	12A	1A	2A
Ryazan +3		3P	4P	5P	6P	7P	8P	9P	10P	11P	12A	1A	2A
St. Louis -6		6A	7A	8A	9A	10A	11A	12P	1P	2P	3P	4P	5P
St. Petersburg +3		3P	4P	5P	6P	7P	8P	9P	10P	11P	12A	1A	2A
Salt Lake City -7		5A	6A	7A	8A	9A	10A	11A	12P	1P	2P	3P	4P
Samara +4		4A	5A	6A	7A	8A	9A	10A	11A	12P	1P	2P	3P
San Diego -8		4A	5A	6A	7A	8A	9A	10A	11A	12P	1P	2P	3P
San Francisco -8		4A	5A	6A	7A	8A	9A	10A	11A	12P	1P	2P	3P
Saratov +4		4P	5P	6P	7P	8P	9P	10P	11P	12A	1A	2A	3A
Seattle -8		4A	5A	6A	7A	8A	9A	10A	11A	12P	1P	2P	3P
Sevastopol +3		3P	4P	5P	6P	7P	8P	9P	10P	11P	12A	1A	2A
Stavropol +3		3P	4P	5P	6P	7P	8P	9P	10P	11P	12A	1A	2A
Stockholm +1		1P	2P	3P	4P	5P	6P	7P	8P	9P	10P	11P	12A
Sydney +10		10P	11P	12A	1A	2A	3A	4A	5A	6A	7A	8A	9A
Tallinn +2		2P	3P	4P	5P	6P	7P	8P	9P	10P	11P	12A	1A
Tbilisi +4		4P	5P	6P	7P	8P	9P	10P	11P	12A	1A	2A	3A
Tel Aviv +2		2P	3P	4P	5P	6P	7P	8P	9P	10P	11P	12A	1A
Tokyo +11		11P	12A	1A	2A	3A	4A	5A	6A	7A	8A	9A	10A
Tomsk +7		7P	8P	9P	10P	11P	12A	1A	2A	3A	4A	5A	6A
Toronto -5		7A	8A	9A	10A	11A	12P	1P	2P	3P	4P	5P	6P
Toshkent +6		6P	7P	8P	9P	10P	11P	12A	1A	2A	3A	4A	5A
Tula +3		3P	4P	5P	6P	7P	8P	9P	10P	11P	12A	1A	2A
Ufa +5		5P	6P	7P	8P	9P	10P	11P	12A	1A	2A	3A	4A
Vancouver, BC -8		4A	5A	6A	7A	8A	9A	10A	11A	12P	1P	2P	3P
Vilnius +2		2P	3P	4P	5P	6P	7P	8P	9P	10P	11P	12A	1A
Vladivostok +10		10P	11P	12A	1A	2A	3A	4A	5A	6A	7A	8A	9A
Volgograd +4		4P	5P	6P	7P	8P	9P	10P	11P	12A	1A	2A	3A
Voronezh +3		3P	4P	5P	6P	7P	8P	9P	10P	11P	12A	1A	2A
Washington, DC -5		7A	8A	9A	10A	11A	12P	1P	2P	3P	4P	5P	6P
Wellington +12		12A	1A	2A	3A	4A	5A	6A	7A	8A	9A	10A	11A
Yakutsk +9		9P	10P	11P	12A	1A	2A	3A	4A	5A	6A	7A	8A
Yaroslavl +3		3P	4P	5P	6P	7P	8P	9P	10P	11P	12A	1A	2A
Yekaterinburg +5		5P	6P	7P	8P	9P	10P	11P	12A	1A	2A	3A	4A
Yerevan +2		2P	3P	4P	5P	6P	7P	8P	9P	10P	11P	12A	1A
Zaporizhzhya +2		2P	3P	4P	5P	6P	7P	8P	9P	10P	11P	12A	1A
Zhytomyr+2		2P	3P	4P	5P	6P	7P	8P	9P	10P	11P	12A	1A

Places

Place in English	Russian word	to, into, onto (motion)	in, on, at (location)
air force	военно-воздушные силы	в военно-воздушные силы	в военно-воздушных силах
air terminal	аэровокзал	в аэровокзал	в аэровокзале
air	воздух	в воздух	в воздухе
airplane	самолёт	на самолёт	на самолёте
airport	аэропорт	в аэропорт	в аэропорту
aisle	проход	в проход	в проходе
ambulance	машина скорой помощи	в машину скорой помощи	в машине скорой помощи
Ameican Consulate	американское консульство	в американское консульство	в американском консульстве
America	Америка	в Америку	в Америке
American Embassy	американское посольство	в американское посольство	в американском посольстве
antique shop	антикварный магазин	в антикварный магазин	в антикварном магазине
apartment	квартира	в квартиру	в квартире
armchair	кресло	на кресло	на кресле
Armenia	Армения	в Армению	в Армении
army	армия	в армию	в армии
art gallery	картинная галерея	в картинную галерею	в картинной галерее
ATM	банковский автомат	к банковскому автомату	у банковского автомата
Australia	Австралия	в Австралию	в Австралии
auto parts store	магазин запчастей	в магазин запчастей	в магазине запчастей
avenue	улица	на улицу	на улице
Azerbaijan	Азербайджан	в Азербайджан	в Азербайджане
bakery	пекарня	в пекарню	в пекарне
balcony	балкон	на балкон	на балконе
bank	банк	в банк	в банке
bar	бар	в бар	в баре
barber shop	парикмахерская	в парикмахерскую	в парикмахерской

Place in English	Russian word	to, into, onto (motion)	in, on, at (location)
barn	амба́р; коро́вник	в амба́р; в коро́вник	в амба́ре; в коро́внике
barracks	каза́рма	в каза́рму	в каза́рме
bath	ва́нна	в ва́нну	в ва́нне
bathhouse	купа́льня	в купа́льню	в купа́льне
bathroom	1. *(bathing)* ва́нная;	1. в ва́нную;	1. в ва́нной
	2. *(lavatory)* туале́т	2. в туале́т	2. в туале́те
bay	зали́в	в зали́в	в зали́ве
beach	пляж	на пляж	на пля́же
beauty parlor / shop	же́нский / да́мский	в же́нский /	в же́нском /
	сало́н	да́мский сало́н	да́мском сало́не
bed	крова́ть *f*; посте́ль *f*	на крова́ть;	на крова́ти;
		в посте́ль	в посте́ли
bedroom	спа́льня	в спа́льню	в спа́льне
Belarus	Белару́сь *f*	в Белару́сь	в Белару́си
bicycle	велосипе́д	на велосипе́д	на велосипе́де
billfold	бума́жник	в бума́жник	в бума́жнике
boat	ло́дка	в ло́дку	в ло́дке
book shop	кни́жный магази́н	в кни́жный магази́н	в кни́жном магази́не
boulevard	проспе́кт	на проспе́кт	на проспе́кте
box	я́щик	в я́щик	в я́щике
bridge	мост	на мост	на мосту́
briefcase	портфе́ль *m*	в портфе́ль	в портфе́ле
Britain	Великобрита́ния	в Великобрита́нию	в Великобрита́нии
building	зда́ние	в зда́ние	в зда́нии
bus	авто́бус	в авто́бус	в авто́бусе
bus station	авто́бусная ста́нция	на авто́бусную	на авто́бусной
		ста́нцию	ста́нции
cabinet	шкаф	в шкаф	в шкафу́
cafe	кафе́	в кафе́	в кафе́
cafeteria	кафете́рий	в кафете́рий	в кафете́рии
camp	ла́герь *m*	в ла́герь	в ла́гере
Canada	Кана́да	в Кана́ду	в Кана́де
canal	кана́л	в кана́л	в кана́ле
candy shop / store	конди́терская	в конди́терскую	в конди́терской
car *(auto)*	маши́на	в маши́ну	в маши́не
car *(train)*	ваго́н	в ваго́н	в ваго́не
car dealer	продаве́ц	к продавцу́	у продавца́
	автомоби́лей	автомоби́лей	автомоби́лей
carnival	карнава́л	на карнава́л	на карнава́ле

Place in English	Russian word	to, into, onto (motion)	in, on, at (location)
car rental agency	бюро́ прока́та автомоби́лей	в бюро́ прока́та автомоби́лей	в бюро́ прока́та автомоби́лей
cart *(hand type)*	теле́жка	в теле́жку	в теле́жке
cash machine	ба́нковский автома́т	к ба́нковскому автома́ту	у ба́нковского автома́та
casino	казино́	в казино́	в казино́
castle	за́мок	в за́мок	в за́мке
cathedral	собо́р	в собо́р	в собо́ре
Caucasus	Кавка́з	на Кавка́з	на Кавка́зе
chair	стул	на стул	на сту́ле
child care center	де́тский сад	в де́тский сад	в де́тском саду́
children's clothing store	магази́н де́тской оде́жды	в магази́н де́тской оде́жды	в магази́не де́тской оде́жды
church	це́рковь *f*	в це́рковь	в це́ркви
circus	цирк	в цирк	в ци́рке
city	го́род	в го́род	в го́роде
city administration	городска́я администра́ция	в городску́ю администра́цию	в городско́й администра́ции
class	класс	в класс	в кла́ссе
classroom	класс	в класс	в кла́ссе
cleaners	химчи́стка	в химчи́стку	в химчи́стке
clinic	кли́ника	в кли́нику	в кли́нике
closet	(встро́енный) шкаф	в шкаф	в шкафу́
clothing store	магази́н оде́жды	в магази́н оде́жды	в магази́не оде́жды
club	клуб	в клуб	в клу́бе
coffee shop	кафе́	в кафе́	в кафе́
college	университе́т	в университе́т	в университе́те
commission shop	комисси́онный магази́н	в комисси́онный магази́н	в комисси́онном магази́не
company	фи́рма, компа́ния	в компа́нию / фи́рму	в компа́нии / фи́рме
compartment *(train)*	купе́	в купе́	в купе́
computer shop / store	магази́н компью́теров	в магази́н компью́теров	в магази́не компью́теров
concert	конце́рт	на конце́рт	на конце́рте
condition *(state)*	состоя́ние	в состоя́ние	в состоя́нии
conditions	усло́вия *pl*	в усло́вия	в усло́виях
condo(minium)	со́бственная кварти́ра	в кварти́ру	в кварти́ре
conference	конфере́нция	на конфере́нцию	на конфере́нции

Place in English	*Russian word*	*to, into, onto (motion)*	*in, on, at (location)*
consulate	ко́нсульство	в ко́нсульство	в ко́нсульстве
copy service	копирова́льный сало́н	в копирова́льный сало́н	в копирова́льном сало́не
corner	у́гол	*(in)* в / *(on)* на у́гол	*(in)* в / *(on)* на углу́
corporation	корпора́ция	в корпора́цию	в корпора́ции
couch	дива́н	на дива́н	на дива́не
country	страна́	в страну́	в стране́
court	суд	в суд	в суде́
Crimea	Крым	в Крым	в Крыму́
crowd	толпа́	в толпу́	в толпе́
cruise ship	парохо́д	на парохо́д	на парохо́де
crutches	костыли́	на костыли́	на костыля́х
customs office	тамо́жня	в / на тамо́жню	в / на тамо́жне
dance hall	танцева́льный зал	в танцева́льный зал	в танцева́льном за́ле
delicatessen	гастроно́м	в гастроно́м	в гастроно́ме
dentist	зубно́й врач	к зубно́му врачу́	у зубно́го врача́
department store	универма́г	в универма́г	в универма́ге
desk	пи́сьменный стол	*(in)* в / *(on)* на (пи́сьменный) стол	*(in)* в /*(on)* на (пи́сьменном) столе́
dining room	столо́вая	в столо́вую	в столо́вой
dock	док; при́стань *f*	в док; на при́стань	в до́ке; на при́стани
doctor	врач	к врачу́	у врача́
doctor's office	кабине́т врача́	в кабине́т врача́	в кабине́те врача́
drawer	я́щик	в я́щик	в я́щике
dream *(daydream)*	мечта́	в мечту́	в мечте́
dream *(sleeping)*	сон	в сон	во сне
dressing room	приме́рочная	в приме́рочную	в приме́рочной
dressmaker	ателье́	в ателье́	в ателье́
drug store	апте́ка	в апте́ку	в апте́ке
dry cleaners	химчи́стка	в химчи́стку	в химчи́стке
electrical goods store	магази́н электрото́варов	в магази́н электрото́варов	в магази́не электрото́варов
elementary school	нача́льная шко́ла	в нача́льную шко́лу	в нача́льной шко́ле
embassy	посо́льство	в посо́льство	в посо́льстве
employment agency	бюро́ по трудоустро́йству	в бюро́ по трудоустро́йству	в бюро́ по трудоустро́йству
England	А́нглия	в А́нглию	в А́нглии
entrance	вход	к вхо́ду	у вхо́да
envelope	конве́рт	в конве́рт	в конве́рте

Place in English	Russian word	to, into, onto (motion)	in, on, at (location)
espresso shop	кафе экспрессо	в кафе экспрессо	в кафе экспрессо
Estonia	Эстония	в Эстонию	в Эстонии
Europe	Европа	в Европу	в Европе
exhibit	выставка	на выставку	на выставке
exit	выход	к выходу	у выхода
factory	завод, фабрика	на завод / фабрику	на заводе / фабрике
fair	ярмарка	на ярмарку	на ярмарке
family	семья	в семью	в семье
farm	ферма	на ферму	на ферме
fast food restaurant	закусочная	в закусочную	в закусочной
fax service	факс	--	--
ferry	паром	на паром	на пароме
field	поле	в / на поле	в / на поле
filing cabinet	картотека	в картотеку	в картотеке
fire station	пожарное депо	в пожарное депо	в пожарном депо
fitness club	клуб здоровья	в клуб здоровья	в клубе здоровья
florist (shop)	цветочный магазин	в цветочный магазин	в цветочном магазине
floor	пол	на пол	на полу
forest	лес	в лес	в лесу
front desk *(hotel)*	регистрация	к регистрации	у регистрации
furniture store	мебельный магазин	в мебельный магазин	в мебельном магазине
game	игра	в игру	в игре
garage *(car)*	гараж	в гараж	в гараже
garage *(service)*	авторемонтная мастерская	в авторемонтную мастерскую	в авторемонтной мастерской
garden	сад	в сад	в саду
gas station	бензозаправка	на бензозаправку	на бензозаправке
Georgia	Грузия	в Грузию	в Грузии
gift shop	магазин «Подарки»	в магазин «Подарки»	в магазине «Подарки»
good place to dance	хорошее место потанцевать	в хорошее место потанцевать	в хорошем месте потанцевать
good restaurant	хороший ресторан	в хороший ресторан	в хорошем ресторане
government office	государственная организация	в государственную организацию	в государственной организации
grade school	начальная школа	в начальную школу	в начальной школе
grocery store	продуктовый магазин	в продуктовый магазин	в продуктовом магазине
ground	земля	*(in)* в / *(on)* на землю	*(in)* в / *(on)* на земле

Place in English	Russian word	to, into, onto (motion)	in, on, at (location)
gym(nasium)	гимнасти́ческий зал	в гимнасти́ческий зал	в гимнасти́ческом за́ле
hallway	коридо́р	в коридо́р	в коридо́ре
hand	рука́	в ру́ку	в руке́
handbag	су́мка	в су́мку	в су́мке
harbor	га́вань *f*	в га́вань	в га́вани
hardware store	скобяно́й магази́н	в скобяно́й магази́н	в скобяно́м магази́не
health club	клуб здоро́вья	в клуб здоро́вья	в клу́бе здоро́вья
healthfood store	магази́н диети́ческих проду́ктов	в магази́н диети́ческих проду́ктов	в магази́не диети́ческих проду́ктов
heart	се́рдце	в се́рдце	в се́рдце
heaven	небеса́ *pl*	на небеса́	на небеса́х
her house	её дом; —	в её дом; к ней	в её до́ме; у неё
her place	—	к ней	у неё
high school	сре́дняя шко́ла	в сре́днюю шко́лу	в сре́дней шко́ле
hill	холм	на холм	на холме́
his house	его́ дом; —	в его́ дом; к нему́	в его до́ме; у него́
his place	—	к нему́	у него́
hole	ды́ра; *(small)* ды́рка	в ды́ру; в ды́рку	в ды́ре; в ды́рке
home	дом	домо́й	до́ма
horse	ло́шадь *f*	на ло́шадь	на ло́шади
hospital	го́спиталь *m*	в го́спиталь	в го́спитале
hotel	гости́ница	в гости́ницу	в гости́нице
house	дом	в дом	в до́ме
hut	хи́жина	в хи́жину	в хи́жине
ice cream shop	моро́женица	в моро́женицу	в моро́женице
ice-skating rink	като́к	на като́к	на катке́
institute	институ́т	в институ́т	в институ́те
insurance company	страхово́е аге́нство	в страхово́е аге́нство	в страхово́м аге́нстве
Internet	интерне́т	на интерне́т	на интерне́те
jewelry shop	ювели́рный магази́н	в ювели́рный магази́н	в ювели́рном магази́не
Kazakhstan	Казахста́н	в Казахста́н	в Казахста́не
Kiev	Ки́ев	в Ки́ев	в Ки́еве
kindergarten	подготови́тельный класс	в подготови́тельный класс	в подготови́тельном кла́ссе
kiosk	кио́ск	в кио́ск	в кио́ске
Kirg(h)izia	Кирги́зия	в Кирги́зию	в Кирги́зии

Place in English	Russian word	to, into, onto (motion)	in, on, at (location)
kitchen	ку́хня	в / на ку́хню	в / на ку́хне
laboratory	лаборато́рия	в лаборато́рию	в лаборато́рии
lake	о́зеро	*(in)* в / *(to)* на о́зеро	*(in)* в / *(at)* на о́зере
Latvia	Ла́твия	в Ла́твию	в Ла́твии
laundromat	пра́чечная	в пра́чечную	в пра́чечной
laundry	пра́чечная	в пра́чечную	в пра́чечной
lawyer's office	юриди́ческая конто́ра	в юриди́ческую конто́ру	в юриди́ческой конто́ре
letter	письмо́	в письмо́	в письме́
library	библиоте́ка	в библиоте́ку	в библиоте́ке
liquor store	магази́н спиртны́х напи́тков	в магази́н спирт- ны́х напи́тков	в магази́не спирт- ны́х напи́тков
Lithuania	Литва́	в Литву́	в Литве́
living room	гости́ная	в гости́ную	в гости́ной
lobby	вестибю́ль *m*	в вестибю́ль	в вестибю́ле
lounge	вестибю́ль *m*	в вестибю́ль	в вестибю́ле
magazine	журна́л	в журна́л	в журна́ле
mailbox	почто́вый я́щик	в по́чтовый я́щик	в почто́вом я́щике
massage parlor	кабине́т масса́жа	в кабине́т масса́жа	в кабине́те масса́жа
meadow	луг	на луг	на лугу́
meeting *(group)*	собра́ние	на собра́ние	на собра́нии
men's restroom	мужско́й туале́т	в мужско́й туале́т	в мужско́м туале́те
men's clothing store	магази́н мужско́й оде́жды	в магази́н мужско́й оде́жды	в магази́не муж- ско́й оде́жды
metro	метро́	в метро́	в метро́
middle school	сре́дняя шко́ла	в сре́днюю шко́лу	в сре́дней шко́ле
military installation	вое́нная ба́за	на вое́нную ба́зу	на вое́нной ба́зе
military camp	вое́нный ла́герь	в вое́нный ла́герь	в вое́нном ла́гере
Minsk	Минск	в Минск	в Ми́нске
Moldova	Молдо́ва	в Молдо́ву	в Молдо́ве
money exchange	пункт обме́на валю́ты	в пункт обме́на валю́ты	в пу́нкте обме́на валю́ты
monument	па́мятник	к па́мятнику	у па́мятника
Moscow	Москва́	в Москву́	в Москве́
mosque	мече́ть *f*	в мече́ть	в мече́ти
motel	моте́ль *m*	в моте́ль	в моте́ле
motorboat	мото́рная ло́дка	в мото́рную ло́дку	в мото́рной ло́дке
motorcycle	мотоци́кл	на мотоци́кл	на мотоци́кле
mountain	гора́ *(pl: го́ры)*	*(to)* в / *(on)* на го́ру,	на горе́

Place in English	Russian word	to, into, onto (motion)	in, on, at (location)
		pl: в го́ры	*pl:* гора́х
mouth	рот	в рот	во рту
movie theater	кинотеа́тр	в кинотеа́тр	в кинотеа́тре
museum	музе́й	в музе́й	в музе́е
music store	музыка́льный магази́н	в музыка́льный магази́н	в музыка́льном магази́не
my friend's house / place	дом моего́ дру́га	в дом моего́ дру́га; к моему́ дру́гу	в до́ме моего́ дру́га; у моего́ дру́га
my office	мой о́фис / кабине́т	в мой о́фис / кабине́т	в моём о́фисе / кабине́те
my place	—	ко мне	у меня́
my house	мой дом; —	в мой дом; ко мне	в моём до́ме; у меня́
navy	вое́нно-морско́й флот	в вое́нно-морско́й флот	в вое́нно-морско́м фло́те
newspaper	газе́та	в газе́ту	в газе́те
New Zealand	Но́вая Зела́ндия	в Но́вую Зела́ндию	в Но́вой Зела́ндии
nightclub	ночно́й клуб	в ночно́й клуб	в ночно́м клу́бе
night table	ночно́й сто́лик	на ночно́й сто́лик	на ночно́м сто́лике
nursery	пито́мник	в пито́мник	в пито́мнике
nursing home	дом престаре́лых	в дом престаре́лых	в до́ме престаре́лых
ocean	океа́н	*(on)* на / *(in)* в океа́н	*(on)* на /*(in)* в океа́не
office	о́фис, кабине́т	в о́фис / кабине́т	в о́фисе / кабине́те
office supply store	магази́н канцеля́рских това́ров	в магази́н канцеля́рских това́ров	в магази́не канцеля́рских това́ров
opera	о́пера	в о́перу	в о́пере
orchard	фрукто́вый сад	в фрукто́вый сад	в фрукто́вом саду́
orphanage	де́тский дом	в де́тский дом	в де́тском до́ме
OVIR	ОВИР *abbrev*	в ОВИР	в ОВИРе
palace	дворе́ц	во дворе́ц	во дворце́
park	парк	в парк	в па́рке
parking lot	парко́вка	на парко́вку	на парко́вке
parking garage	гара́ж для парко́вки	в гара́ж для парко́вки	в гараже́ для парко́вки
party	вечери́нка	на вечери́нку	на вечери́нке
passport office	па́спортный стол	в па́спортный стол	в па́спортном столе́
path	тропа́	на тропу́	на тропе́
pawn shop	ломба́рд	в ломба́рд	в ломба́рде
pet shop	зоомагази́н	в зоомагази́н	в зоомагази́не
pharmacy	апте́ка	в апте́ку	в апте́ке

Place in English	Russian word	to, into, onto (motion)	in, on, at (location)
photo studio	фотогра́фия	в фотогра́фию	в фотогра́фии
place	ме́сто	на ме́сто	на ме́сте
plane	самолёт	*(in)* в /*(on)* на самолёт	в / на самолёте
plant	заво́д, фа́брика	на заво́д / фа́брику	на заво́де / фа́брике
play	пье́са	в пье́су	в пье́се
plaza	пло́щадь *f*	на пло́щадь	на пло́щади
pocket	карма́н	в карма́н	в карма́не
police station	мили́ция	в мили́цию	в мили́ции
porch	крыльцо́	на крыльцо́	на крыльце́
port	порт	в порт	в порту́
position	положе́ние	в положе́ние	в положе́нии
post office	по́чта	на по́чту	на по́чте
post office box	абонеме́нтный поч-то́вый я́щик (а/я)	в почто́вый я́щик	в почто́вом я́щике
public telephone	телефо́н-автома́т	в автома́т	в автома́те
purse *(coin)*	кошелёк	в кошелёк	в кошельке́
purse *(handbag)*	су́мка	в су́мку	в су́мке
real estate agency	аге́нство недви́жимости	в аге́нство недви́жимости	в аге́нстве недви́жимости
refrigerator	холоди́льник	в холоди́льник	в холоди́льнике
refugee camp	ла́герь бе́женцев	в ла́герь бе́женцев	в ла́гере бе́женцев
repair shop	ремо́нтная мастерска́я	в ремо́нтную мастерску́ю	в ремо́нтной мастерско́й
restaurant	рестора́н	в рестора́н	в рестора́не
restroom	туале́т	в туале́т	в туале́те
retirement home	дом престаре́лых	в дом престаре́лых	в до́ме престаре́лых
river	река́	*(in)* в / *(on)* на ре́ку	*(in)* в / *(on)* на реке́
road	доро́га	*(in)* в /*(on)* на доро́гу	*(in)* в / *(on)* на доро́ге
roller skating rink	като́к для ката́ния на ро́ликах	на като́к	на катке́
roof	кры́ша	на кры́шу	на кры́ше
room	ко́мната	в ко́мнату	в ко́мнате
row	ряд	в ряд	в ряду́
Russia	Росси́я	в Росси́ю	в Росси́и
safe	сейф	в сейф	в се́йфе
sailboat	па́русник	на па́русник	на па́руснике
sauna	са́уна	в са́уну	в са́уне
school	шко́ла	в шко́лу	в шко́ле
sea	мо́ре	в мо́ре	в мо́ре

Place in English	Russian word	to, into, onto (motion)	in, on, at (location)
seamstress (shop)	ателье́ по пошиву́ оде́жды	в ателье́ по пошиву́ оде́жды	в ателье́ по пошиву́ оде́жды
seat	ме́сто	на ме́сто	на ме́сте
sentence	предложе́ние	в предложе́ние	в предложе́нии
service garage	авторемо́нтная мастерска́я	в авторемо́нтную мастерску́ю	в авторемо́нтной мастерско́й
shed	сара́й	в сара́й	в сара́е
ship *(steamship)*	парохо́д	на парохо́д	на парохо́де
ship *(naval)*	кора́бль *m*	на кора́бль	на корабле́
shoe repair shop	обувна́я мастерска́я	в обувну́ю мастерску́ю	в обувно́й мастерско́й
shoe shop	обувно́й магази́н	в обувно́й магази́н	в обувно́м магази́не
shower	душ	в душ	в ду́ше
Siberia	Сиби́рь *f*	в Сиби́рь	в Сиби́ри
sidewalk	тротуа́р	на тротуа́р	на тротуа́ре
sled	са́ни *pl*	в са́ни	в саня́х
snack bar	заку́сочная	в заку́сочную	в заку́сочной
sofa	дива́н	на дива́н	на дива́не
soul	душа́	в ду́шу	в душе́
spa	куро́рт	на куро́рт	на куро́рте
sporting goods store	магази́н спорти́в- ных това́ров	в магази́н спорти́в- ных това́ров	в магази́не спор- ти́вных това́ров
square	пло́щадь *f*	на пло́щадь	на пло́щади
St. Petersburg	Санкт-Петербу́рг	в Санкт-Петербу́рг	в Санкт-Петербу́рге
stadium	стадио́н	на стадио́н	на стадио́не
stairs	ле́стница	на ле́стницу	на ле́стнице
state *(U.S. type)*	штат	в штат	в шта́те
state *(condition)*	состоя́ние	в состоя́ние	в состоя́нии
station	ста́нция	на ста́нцию	на ста́нции
stationery shop	канцеля́рский магази́н	в канцеля́рский магази́н	в канцеля́рском магази́не
statue	ста́туя	к ста́туе	у ста́туи
steppe	степь *f*	в степь	в степи́
steps	ступе́ни *pl*	к ступе́ням	на ступе́нях
store room	кладова́я	в кладову́ю	в кладово́й
store	магази́н	в магази́н	в магази́не
stove	плита́	на плиту́	на плите́
stream	руче́й	*(to)* к ручью́	*(in)* в ручье́
street	у́лица	на у́лицу	на у́лице

Place in English	Russian word	to, into, onto (motion)	in, on, at (location)
streetcar	трамва́й	на трамва́й	на трамва́е
stretcher	носи́лки *pl*	на носи́лки	на носи́лках
suburb	при́город	в при́город	в при́городе
subway	метро́	*(in)* в /*(on)* на метро́	*(in)* в / *(on)* на метро́
subway station	ста́нция метро́	на ста́нцию метро́	на ста́нции метро́
suitcase	чемода́н	в чемода́н	в чемода́не
supermarket	универса́м	в универса́м	в универса́ме
synagogue	синаго́га	в синаго́гу	в синаго́ге
table	стол	на стол	на столе́
Tadzhikistan	Таджикиста́н	в Таджикиста́н	в Таджикиста́не
taiga	тайга́	в тайгу́	в тайге́
tailor shop	ателье́	в ателье́	в ателье́
tavern	таве́рна	в таве́рну	в таве́рне
taxi stand	стоя́нка такси́	на стоя́нку такси́	на стоя́нке такси́
taxi	такси́	в такси́	на такси́
telephone	телефо́н	к телефо́ну	по телефо́ну
tent	пала́тка	в пала́тку	в пала́тке
terminal *(air)*	термина́л	в термина́л	в термина́ле
theater	теа́тр	в теа́тр	в теа́тре
their place	--	к ним	у них
their house	их дом	в их дом; к ним	в их до́ме; у них
ticket office	биле́тная ка́сса	в биле́тную ка́ссу	в биле́тной ка́ссе
ticket counter	биле́тная сто́йка	в биле́тную сто́йку	в биле́тной сто́йке
tobacco shop	таба́чный магази́н	в таба́чный магази́н	в таба́чном магази́не
toilet	туале́т	в туале́т	в туале́те
town	го́род	в го́род	в го́роде
trail	тропа́	на тропу́	на тропе́
trailer	прице́п	в прице́п	в прице́пе
train	по́езд	*(in)* в /*(on)* на по́езд	*(in)* в / *(on)* на по́езде
train station	вокза́л	на вокза́л	на вокза́ле
travel agency	бюро́ путеше́ствий, турфи́рма	в бюро́ путеше́ствий, в турфи́рму	в бюро́ путеше́ствий, в турфи́рме
travel bag	доро́жная су́мка	в доро́жную су́мку	в доро́жной су́мке
tree	де́рево	на де́рево	на де́реве
troika	тро́йка	на тро́йку	на тро́йке
truck	грузови́к	на грузови́к	на грузовике́
tundra	ту́ндра	в ту́ндру	в ту́ндре
Turkmenistan	Туркмениста́н	в Туркмениста́н	в Туркмениста́не
Ukraine	Украи́на	на Украи́ну	на Украи́не

Place in English	*Russian word*	*to, into, onto (motion)*	*in, on, at (location)*
United States (of America)	Соединённые Шта́ты (Аме́рики)	в Соединённые Шта́ты (Аме́рики)	в Соединённых Шта́тах (Аме́рики)
university	университе́т	в университе́т	в университе́те
USA	США	в США	в США
used car dealer	продаве́ц ста́рых маши́н	к продавцу́ ста́рых маши́н	у продавца́ ста́рых маши́н
Uzbekistan	Узбекиста́н	в Узбекиста́н	в Узбекиста́не
veterinarian	ветерина́р	к ветерина́ру	у ветерина́ра
village	дере́вня	в дере́вню	в дере́вне
visa office	отде́л по оформ-ле́нию виз	в отде́л по оформ-ле́нию виз	в отде́ле по оформ-ле́нию виз
wagon	пово́зка	в пово́зку	в пово́зке
waiting room	ко́мната ожида́ния	в ко́мнату ожида́ния	в ко́мнате ожида́ния
wall	стена́	на сте́ну	на стене́
wallet	бума́жник	в бума́жник	в бума́жнике
Web site	страни́ца на интерне́те	на страни́цу на интерне́т	на страни́це на интерне́те
Web	интерне́т	на интерне́т	на интерне́те
wheelchair	(инвали́дная) коля́ска	в коля́ску	в коля́ске
window	окно́	на / в окно́	на / в окне́
winery	ви́нный заво́д	на ви́нный заво́д	на ви́нном заво́де
women's restroom	же́нский туале́т	в же́нский туале́т	в же́нском туале́те
women's clothing store	магази́н же́нской оде́жды	в магази́н же́нской оде́жды	в магази́не же́н-ской оде́жды
woods	лес	в лес	в лесу́
work	рабо́та	на рабо́ту	на рабо́те
workshop	мастерска́я	в мастерску́ю	в мастерско́й
world	мир	в мир	в ми́ре
yacht	я́хта	на я́хту	на я́хте
your office (familiar)	твой о́фис / кабине́т	в твой о́фис / кабине́т	в твоём о́фисе / кабине́те
your office (polite)	Ваш о́фис / кабине́т	в Ваш о́фис / кабине́т	в Ва́шем о́фисе / кабине́те
your place (fam.)	—	к тебе́	у тебя́
your place (polite)	—	к Вам	у Вас
your house (fam.)	твой дом	в твой дом; к тебе́	в твоём до́ме; у тебя́
your house (polite)	Ваш дом	в Ваш дом; к Вам	в Ва́шем до́ме; у Вас

Metric Measurements

Length

1 millimeter, mm (миллиме́тр, мм) = 0.04 inches
10 mm = 1 centimeter, cm (сантиме́тр, см) = 0.4 inches
1000 mm = 100 cm = 1 meter, m (метр, м) = 3.3 feet
1000 m = 1 kilometer, km (киломе́тр, км) = 0.6 miles
8 km = 5 miles

1 inch = 2.5 centimeters = 25 millimeters
1 foot = 30 centimeters = 300 millimeters
1 yard = 90 centimeters = 0.9 meters
1 mile = 1.6 kilometers = 1609 meters

Weight

1 gram, g (грам, г) = 0.035 ounces
500 g = ½ kilogram (полки́ло) = 1.1 pounds
1000 g = 1 kilogram, kg (килогра́мм, кг) = 2.2 pounds

1 ounce = 28 grams
1 pound = 450 grams = 0.45 kilograms

Volume

1 liter, l (литр, л) = 1.06 quarts
4 liters = 1.06 U.S. gallons

1 quart = 0.95 liters
1 U.S. gallon = 3.8 liters

Temperature

Fahrenheit, F = °Centigrade x 9/5 + 32   *(9/5 = 1.8)*
Centigrade, C = (°Fahrenheit - 32) x 5/9   *(5/9 = 0.5555)*

Boiling point: 212°F = 100°C
Body temperature: 98.6°F = 37°C
Pleasant temperature: 72°F = 22°C
Freezing point: 32°F = 0°C

Appendix 9

Common Adult Heights

The following height equivalents are approximate. 1 inch = 2.54 cm

Russian & European&	American British*	Russian & European	American & British*
150 cm	4' 11"	175 cm	5' 9"
151 cm	4' 11 ½"	176 cm	5' 9"
		177 cm	5' 9 ½"
152 cm	5' 0'		
153 cm	5' 0"	178 cm	5' 10"
154 cm	5' ½"	179 cm	5' 10 ½"
155 cm	5' 1"	180 cm	5' 11"
156 cm	5' 1 ½"	181 cm	5' 11"
		182 cm	5' 11 ½"
157 cm	5' 2"		
158 cm	5' 2"	183 cm	6' 0"
159 cm	5' 2 ½"	184 cm	6' ½"
160 cm	5' 3"	185 cm	6' 1"
161 cm	5' 3 ½"	186 cm	6' 1"
		187 cm	6' 1 ½"
162 cm	5' 4"		
163 cm	5' 4"	188 cm	6' 2"
164 cm	5' 4 ½"	189 cm	6' 2 ½"
165 cm	5' 5"	190 cm	6' 3"
166 cm	5' 5 ½"	191 cm	6' 3"
		192 cm	6' 3 ½"
167 cm	5' 6"		
168 cm	5' 6"	193 cm	6' 4"
169 cm	5' 6 ½"	194 cm	6' 4 ½"
170 cm	5' 7"	195 cm	6' 5"
171 cm	5' 7 ½"	196 cm	6' 5"
		197 cm	6' 5 ½"
172 cm	5' 8"		
173 cm	5' 8"	198 cm	6' 6"
174 cm	5' 8 ½"	199 cm	6' 6 ½"

* Britain now officially uses the metric system.

Appendix 10

Common Adult Weights

The following height equivalents are approximate. 1 kg = 2.2 lbs and 1 lb = 0.455 kg

Russian & European&	American British*	American & British*	Russian & European
40 kg	88 lbs	90 lbs	41 kg
42 kg	92 lbs	95 lbs	43 kg
45 kg	99 lbs	100 lbs	45 kg
47 kg	103 lbs	105 lbs	48 kg
50 kg1	10 lbs	110 lbs	50 kg
52 kg	114 lbs	115 lbs	52 kg
55 kg	121 lbs	120 lbs	55 kg
57 kg	125 lbs	125 lbs	57 kg
60 kg	132 lbs	130 lbs	59 kg
62 kg	136 lbs	135 lbs	61 kg
65 kg	143 lbs	140 lbs	64 kg
67 kg	147 lbs	145 lbs	66 kg
70 kg	154 lbs	150 lbs	68 kg
72 kg	158 lbs	155 lbs	70 kg
75 kg	165 lbs	160 lbs	73 kg
77 kg	169 lbs	165 lbs	75 kg
80 kg	176 lbs	170 lbs	77 kg
82 kg	180 lbs	175 lbs	80 kg
85 kg	187 lbs	180 lbs	82 kg
87 kg	191 lbs	185 lbs	84 kg
90 kg	198 lbs	190 lbs	86 kg
92 kg	202 lbs	195 lbs	89 kg
95 kg	209 lbs	200 lbs	91 kg
97 kg	213 lbs	205 lbs	93 kg
100 kg	220 lbs	210 lbs	95 kg
102 kg	224 lbs	215 lbs	98 kg
105 kg	231 lbs	220 lbs	100 kg
107 kg	235 lbs	225 lbs	102 kg
110 kg	242 lbs	230 lbs	105 kg
112 kg	246 lbs	235 lbs	107 kg
115 kg	253 lbs	240 lbs	109 kg
117 kg	257 lbs	245 lbs	111 kg
120 kg	264 lbs	250 lbs	114 kg

* Britain now officially uses the metric system.

Common Clothing Sizes

Women's Dresses, Coats and Suits:

USA	6	8	10	12	14	16	18	20
Britain	4	6	8	10	12	14	16	18
Europe	34	36	38	40	42	44	46	48
Russia	40	42	44	46	48	50	52	54

Women's Lingerie:

USA	6	8	10	12	14	16	18	20
Britain	22	24	26	28	30	32	34	36
Europe	34	36	38	40	42	44	46	48
Russia	40	42	44	46	48	50	52	54
International		XXS	XS	S	M	L	XL	XXL
Waist, cm	59-62	63-65	66-69	70-74	75-78	79-83	84-89	90-94
Hips, cm	85-88	89-92	93-96	97-101	102-104	105-108	109-112	113-117

Women's Shoes

USA	4	4½	5	5½	6	6½	7	7½	8	8½	9	9½	10
Britain	2½	3	3½	4	4½	5	5½	6	6½	7	7½	8	8½
Europe	35	35	36	36	37	37	38	38	39	39	40	40	41
Russia,	34	35		36		37	38		39		40	41	

Men's Coats and Suits

USA, Britain	36	38	40	42	44	46	48
Russia, Europe	46	48	50	52	54	56	58

Men's Shirts

USA	14	14½	15	15½	16	16½	17	17½
Britain	34	36	38	40	42	44	46	46
Russia, Europe	36	37	38	39	41	42	43	44

Men's Shoes

USA	7	7½	8	8½	9	9½	10	10½	11	11½	12
Britain	6½	7	7½	8	8½	9	9½	10	10½	11	11½
Europe	39	40	41	42	43	43.5	44	44	45	45	46
Russia	39	40		41	42	42	43	43	44	44	45

Common Russian Female Names and Nicknames
(In Russian alphabetical order)

Name	Nickname(s)
Алекса́ндра	Са́ша, Са́шенька, Сашу́рка, Шу́ра, Шу́рочка
А́лла	А́ллочка
А́нна	А́ня, Аню́тка, А́нечка, А́ночка, А́ннушка
Валенти́на	Ва́ля, Валю́ша, Ва́лечка
Ве́ра	Ве́рочка, Веру́нька
Веро́ника	Ни́ка
Викто́рия	Ви́ка
Гали́на	Га́ля, Га́лка, Галчёнок, Га́лочка
Да́рья	Да́ша, Да́шенька
Евге́ния	Же́ня, Же́нечка
Екатери́на	Ка́тя, Ка́тенька, Катю́ша
Еле́на	Ле́на, Алёна, Алёнка, Алёнушка, Ле́ночка, Лено́к
Елизаве́та	Ли́за, Ли́зочка, Ли́зонька
Зинаи́да	Зи́на, Зи́ночка
Зо́я	За́йка, Зо́енька
Ири́на	Ира, Иро́чка, Ири́шка
Ксе́ния	Кса́на, Кса́нка
Лари́са	Ла́ра, Ло́ра, Ла́рочка, Ло́рочка
Ли́дия	Ли́да, Ли́дочка
Любо́вь	Лю́ба, Лю́бочка, Лю́бонька
Людми́ла	Лю́да, Лю́ся, Лю́дочка, Лю́сенька, Ми́ла, Ми́лочка
Маргори́та	Ри́та, Ри́точка, Марго́, Ма́йя, Ма́ечка
Мари́на	Мари́ночка, Мари́шка, Мари́нка
Мари́я	Ма́ша, Ма́шенька, Машу́тка, Ма́ня, Му́ся, Мару́ся
Наде́жда	На́дя, На́денька, Надю́шка
Ната́лия	Ната́ша, Та́ша, На́та, Ната́шенька, Ната́шечка, Ната́шка
Не́ля	Не́ллечка
Ни́на	Ни́ночка
О́льга	О́ля, Оле́чка, Оленька
Поли́на	По́ля, Поли́нка
Светла́на	Све́та, Све́тик, Све́точка
Софи́я	Со́ня, Со́нечка
Тама́ра	Тама́рочка, То́ма
Татья́на	Та́ня, Та́нечка, Таню́шка, Таню́ша
Э́лла	Э́лочка
Э́мма	Э́мочка
Ю́лия	Ю́ля, Ю́лечка

Russian Terms of Endearment

Some of the common Russian terms of endearment are these:

Дорога́я *(M to F)* Dear, Darling
Дорого́й *(F to M)* Dear, Darling

Ми́лая *(M to F)* Dear, Darling, Honey
Ми́лый *(F to M)* Dear, Darling, Honey

Родна́я *(M to F)* Dear, Darling
Родно́й *(F to M)* Dear, Darling

Люби́мая *(M to F)* Beloved, Sweetheart, Darling
Люби́мый *(F to M)* Beloved, Sweetheart, Darling

Со́лнышко *(mostly M to F)* Sunshine

Ки́сонька *(M to F)* Pussy-cat
Ки́са *(M to F)* Pussy-cat

Ры́бонька *(M to F)* "Little Fish" (= Honeybunch, Sweetie-pie)

За́йка *(M to F)* Little Bunny
За́йчик *(mostly M to F)* Little Bunny

Малы́ш *(M to F)* Baby

And like couples the world over, many Russians create their own special, tender nicknames based on some characteristic of a partner or some shared experience. An example in Russian would be «Ла́па» or «Ла́почка» *(M & F)*, which translates as "Little Hand," but which is equivalent to"Honey-bunch" or "Sweetie-pie" in English. The possibilities are infinite. Experiment — but cautiously, on an approval basis.

Russian given names (first names) can also have their endings modified to instill a connotation of endearment. See Appendix 12, "Common Russian Female Names and Nicknames," on the preceding page.

Polite and Familiar "You"

There are two words for "you" in Russian -- «**Вы**» and «**ты**». «**Вы**» is the polite form that you use with strangers, with people who are much older, and with people that you're not on close terms with. Uncapitalized, it is also used for the plural "you." The familiar form «**ты**» is used for family members, loved ones, friends, children, classmates, some colleagues, fellow soldiers, and pets. Young people (teens, 20's) commonly talk to each other with «**ты**».

Crossing the bridge from «**Вы**» to «**ты**» is done by one person suggesting it to the other when they feel they know each other well enough, or simply by beginning to talk to the other person with «**ты**».

When you begin to use «**ты**» with another person, you not only exchange one "you" for another, you exchange a whole set of grammar. The polite (& plural) «**Вы**» takes the 2nd person plural in all verb conjugations, whereas «**ты**» operates with the 2nd person singular. Hence. "Are you going?" is «Вы идёте?» on a polite basis, compared to «Ты идёшь?» when you're on familiar terms. In the past tense, the ending for «**Вы**» is **-ли**, as opposed to that for «**ты**», which will be **-л** when talking to a man, and **-ла** when addressing a woman.

The endings of short (predicate) adjectives will also respond differently to «**Вы**» and «**ты**»: **-ы** serving for «**Вы**», and a **consonant** ending (masculine) or **-а** (feminine) for «**ты**». Thus, "You're very polite." is like this for «**Вы**»: «Вы óчень вéжливы.», but like this for «**ты**»: «Ты óчень вéжлив.» (to a man) or «Ты óчень вéжлива.» (to a woman).

And then, of course, there are differents sets of the possessive pronoun "your" to use for each one.

Hey, no one ever said friendship was easy.

Russian Customs and Etiquette

We give you here a few facts concerning Russian customs and etiquette that we hope will be useful in understanding and adjusting to the culture of the country.

- The wedding ring is worn on the ring finger of the right hand.
- Usually there is no engagement ring.
- A ring worn on the left hand means the person is divorced.

- As in the U.S....
    - a man walking with a woman walks on the street side.
    - a man opens doors for a woman and lets her go first into places. However, it's proper etiquette for him to assume the lead again after she passes through the door.
    - a man gets out of a car, goes around and opens the door for a woman, giving her his hand to get out.
    - in a restaurant, a man moves a chair back from the table for a woman and seats her.
    - when leaving buses, trains or streetcars, a man goes first and then gives his hand to the woman to help her exit.

- When giving flowers, give an odd number of them. An even number is for funerals and certain other occasions. Red is for love. All other colors are okay.
- When meeting for dates, it is common for a woman to come 5-15 minutes late. Punctuality is not viewed as a great virtue as it is in the West.
- "Dutch treat" is not a common practice in Russia. Men almost always pay.

- Friendship is highly valued in Russia.
- Do not expect friendly smiles from strangers in public places.
- With close friends it's appropriate to kiss a person (3 times) on the cheeks.

- During the communist years, titles such as Mr and Mrs were not used. Hence, many Russians find it awkward to use them. However, the practice is gradually coming back, especially in business circles. Mr in Russian is "господи́н," and Mrs is "госпожа́."
- The Russian middle name is a "patronymic," which means that it's derived from the father's first name. For a man, it involves adding **-ович** or **-евицч** to the father's first name; for a woman, **-овна** or **-евна**.
- A woman's last name will have a feminine ending, different from a man's name.

- Birthday parties are often arranged by the person having the birthday.
- Cards and gifts are given on birthdays. But don't give wine as a present to a woman.

- The great majority of Russians are not familiar with Valentine's Day..

- The main meal of the day is dinner .(«обéд»), which is eaten at 1:00 PM.
- Before eating, Russians often say «Прия́тного аппети́та» ("Good appetite").
- It's considered rude to turn down offers of food or drink.
- Before drinking, Russians usually toast. Common toasts are «На здоро́вье!» and «За Ва́ше здоро́вье!». Others are possible. After a toast, most Russians like to clink their glasses together

- Almost all Russians take off their shoes when entering a house.
- Though not a frequent custom, it is polite to give up your seat in a subway train or bus to elderly people or women with small children.
- Before departing home on a trip, Russians customarily sit quietly for a minute.

- The number thirteen is sometimes considered as a bad number.
- Don't shake hands or kiss over a threshold. Russians believe it leads to an argument.
- When you go out of the house, it's considered bad luck to return right away. But this can be counteracted by looking in the mirror before you leave the second time.
- It's not uncommon to be stared at. Don't take offense. It's usually just plain curiosity.

Weddings in Russia were performed exclusively in Wedding Palaces («Дворцы́ бракосочета́ния») during the communist years, but a growing number are now performed in churches and synagogues. Some common wedding customs are:
- Rings are exchanged by the bride and groom.
- Brides wear wedding gowns and carry flowers, as in the West.
- Russians do not know the American custom "something old, something new, something borrowed, something blue."
- Witnesses attend the ceremony, but there is no "best man" or "bridesmaid" in the Western sense.
- A big wedding feast after the wedding is common.
- At the wedding feast there are frequent shouts of «Го́рько!» ("Bitter!"), which is an encouragement to the groom to kiss the bride and thereby sweeten things up.
- Newlyweds go on a honeymoon.
- The groom carries the bride over the threshold of their home.

Russian Holidays & Special Occasions

January 1   **New Years's Day**   **Но́вый год**
People exchange gifts and put up a New Year's tree (ёлка).
Grandfather Frost (Дед Моро́з) and Snow Maiden
(Снегу́роцчка) bring presents for children.
Greeting: «С но́вым го́дом!» ("Happy New Year!")

January 7   **Russian Orthodox Christmas**   **Рождество́**
Quiet religious holiday.

February   **Shrovetide**   **Ма́сленица**
(week before   People make pancakes (бли́ны) and take part
Lent)   in games.

March 8   **International Women's Day**   **Же́нский день**
Men give gifts, especially flowers, to females in family
and pamper them in general.

March / April   **Russian Orthodox Easter**   **Па́схар**
People color eggs (пи́санки) and give them as gifts;
bake Easter cakes (кули́ч), and make па́сха (cottage
cheese dish). Faithful attend elaborate church ceremony
on Easter eve, take part in candlelight procession, then
have big feast at home.

April   **Passover**   **Па́схар**
Jewish religious holiday. People eat matzah (ма́ца).

May 1   **Spring Day**   **Пра́здник весны́**
Formerly Labor Day, now known as Spring Day.

May 9   **Victory Day**   **День побе́ды**
Big military parade is held, as are folk dances, to
show pride in country. Films about WWII on TV.

End of May   **White Nights**   **Вре́мя бе́лых ноче́й**
till end of June   Particularly in St. Petersburg. Stays light until about
midnight, only a few hours are hazy at night. People
stroll along the Neva River.

June 12	**Russian Independence Day** Parades, official meetings, dinners.	**День незави́симости Росси́и**
September	**Yom Kippur** Jewish holiday.	**Ям Кипур**
October 7	**Constitution Day**	**День Конститу́ции**
December	**Hanukka** Jewish holiday.	**Ха́нука**
December 25	**Christmas (Western)** Not widely observed, but government offices are closed.	
December 31	**New Year's Eve**	**Но́вый год**

Russian Laws and Regulations

Here are some of the laws and regulations in Russia that are useful to know:

• The legal age of consent to get married is 18.

• A marriage certificate must be obtained from the Registry of Vital Statistics (ЗАГС = ZAGS) in order to get married. The waiting period for this certificate is 3 months (less if pregnancy is involved).

• An uncontested divorce takes 3 months. To apply for one, a person goes to their local ZAGS office and fills out a form.

• Mothers almost always get custody of the children.

• Permission of a divorced father is needed to adopt a child, unless he has been "deprived of parental rights" (лишён роди́тельских прав).

• A Letter of Invitation (Извеще́ние) is needed in order to visit a private home. One can be obtained by the host through the District OVIR (passport office) (Райо́нный ОВИР). It takes about 24 days.

• Russians can also be invited to the U.S., but it's not easy for them to obtain a tourist visa. If you want to invite someone, it's advisable to send them a letter of invitation that includes your name and address, their name and address, the proposed period of their visit, and a statement to the effect that you will provide them accommodations and help them financially if necessary. The total fee is $140.

• Tourist visas can only be extended in Moscow, through official hotels. It is a rather difficult, time-consuming, and even costly process that requires much patience.

• International driver's licenses are recognized in Russia.

Procedures in Getting Married

Marriage to a Russian in Russia

To get married in Russia you need to do the following:

1. Have your Russian sponsor register your visa at the local or central UVIR (УВИР = Управле́ние виз и регистра́ции иностра́нцев = Office of Foreign Visas and Registration).

2. Prepare a marriage letter (Свиде́тельство = Affadavit) in Russian and have it notarized at a U.S. consulate. The fee is $55 *(Aug 2000)*.

3. Have the marriage letter authenticated at the Ministry of Foreign Affairs (Министе́рство вну́тренних дел) at Neopalimovskiy pereulok, dom 12a, in Moscow. The fee is 85 rubles *(Aug 2000)* for 3-day service, double for next day service.

4. Get an official Russian translation of the information page of your passport. Do this at one of the certified translation centers that has a notary public.

5. Submit your documents for inspection to the ZAGS (ЗАГС = За́пись а́ктов гражда́нского состоя́ния = Civil Registry Office) where your fiancée / fiancé is registered. Copies of all U.S. civil documents submitted must bear U.S. notary seals. A civil wedding will then be scheduled 32 days from the date of registration.

Marriage to a Russian in the U.S.

In order for a U.S. citizen to bring a Russian to the U.S. to get married, the Russian fiancée / fiancé must obtain a K-1 Fiancce Visa, which is valid for 6 months and which has a limit of 90 days from the date of entry into the U.S. The procedure for accomplishing this is rather involved and best deserves an Internet trip to the U.S. Embassy site entitled "Marriage to Foreign Nationals (Fiance(e) Visas)" at http://www.usembassy. state.gov/posts/rs1/wwwhca0. html. The site provides excellent detailed instructions. If you do not have access to the Internet, you can request the necessary instructions from the INS Regional Service Center or the INS office closest to your residence.

Two other very good web sites to visit on this matter are:

1. The web site of the Law Offices of Livingston and Associates at http://homepage.interaccess.com/~jswartz/Overview/Marrying/K1_VISA/k1_visa.html. Provides a wealth of detailed information.

2. http://www.scanna.com/other/visa.html. Here you can find numerous links to other sites with information on the subject.

Notes About Mail

Mail services in Russia, Belarus and Ukraine have improved greatly since the fall of communism, but delivery of an airmail letter from the U.S. can still take 2-3 weeks, especially if it's outside Moscow, St. Petersburg, Minsk or Kiev.

If you have something important to send, it's not a bad idea to send it by **registered** mail (preferably with **Return Receipt Requested**). Putting currency in letters is not recommended, since the metal fibers in most banknotes can be detected.

Postage Rates
The rates for sending **standard airmail letters** to Russia, Belarus and Ukraine are as follows in these countries:

Australia:	Aus$1.50 up to 50 g;
Britain:	44p up to 20 g, 75p up to 50 g;
Canada:	C$0.95 up to 20 g, C$1.45 up to 50 g;
Ireland:	32p up to 25 g, 65p up to 50 g;
New Zealand:	NZ$1.80 up to 200 g.
USA :	$0.60 up to 0.5 oz, $0.40 for each additional 0.5 oz;

Registration
International registration of airmail letters costs $6.00 in the U.S. (plus $1.25 for Return Receipt); Aus$7.91 in Australia; C$9.00 in Canada; £2.50 in Ireland.

International Reply Coupons
International Reply Coupons (IRC's), which enable the recipient to buy a stamp for a standard letter, cost $1.05 each in the U.S.

Writing Addresses
Concerning **addresses**, Russians, Belorussians and Ukrainians put them in the opposite order from what we do in America: they write the country first, then the city, then the street address, and lastly the person's name (family name first, then the given name, and then, optionally, the patronymic, all in the dative case). The U.S. Postal Service does not care how you do it, as long as the last word is the country name in English.

Abbreviations
Some common abbreviations used in Russian addresses are: ул. (у́лица) = street; пр. (проспе́кт) = boulevard; пл. (пло́щадь) = square; наб. (на́бережная) = waterfront; д. (дом) = house, building; кв. (кварти́ра) = apartment; кор. (ко́рпус) = unit; обл. (о́бласть) = region; г. (го́род) = city; д/в (до востре́бования) = general delivery; а/я (абоне́нтский я́щик) = P.O. box.

Using Cyrillic on the Internet

If you have Windows 95 or 98 on your computer, this is a very simple process. All you have to do is install the proper Russian fonts and keyboard, do a couple of clicks, and you're on your way.

The first of these steps, installing the fonts, works like this:

1. Go to **My Computer**, then **Control Panel**, then **Add/Remove Programs**.
2. Choose the **Windows Setup** tab.
3. Put a check in the box next to **Multilingual Support.**
4. Hit **OK.**

Windows may prompt you to put in your original CD ROM disk. If you don't have it, you can download **lang.exe** file from Microsoft and install it per the directions in the Readme file.

This by itself will enable you to **read** Cyrillic messages on the World Wide Web, but in order to **write** Cyrillic, you need to add a Cyrillic keyboard. Here's how you do that:

1. Go to **My Computer**, then **Control Panel**, then **Keyboard.**
2. Choose the **Language** tab.
3. You will see **En English [United States}** listed. If **Ru Russian** is not listed, go to **Add**, find it, and select it.
4. Pick a way to switch languages on your keyboard, either **Left Alt+Shift** or **Ctrl+Shift**. (You can also use your mouse arrow on the language indicator on your desktop taskbar.)
5. Make sure **Enable indicator on taskbar** is checked.
6. Hit **OK.**

The resulting Russian keyboard will have this arrangement:

й ц у к е н г ш щ ъ ё

ф ы в а п р о л д ж э

я ч с м и т ь б ю . , *(the latter two on the same key)*

When reading mail in Internet Explorer 5, go to **Format**, then **Encoding**, then **More**, and then select **Cyrillic (KOI8R)**. If that doesn't work, try **Cyrillic (Windows)**. And make sure your language indicator on the taskbar is switched to **Ru.**

For writing Cyrillic e-mail, do the same as for reading, then choose a font for Russian, such as **Times New Roman Cyr** or **Courier New Cyr**.

To cyrillicize Netscape Communicator, Mac or older versions of Windows, please refer to the following web sites for assistance:

1. http://gwis.circ.gwu.edu/~slavic/cyrilize.html
2. http://koi8.pp.ru
3. http://kulichki.rambler.ru/shura/eng/setup.htm
4. http://www.relcom.ru/English/Russification/WinNetscape/

Introduction Services on the Internet

Introduction services featuring women from Russia, Ukraine, Belarus, and the newly independent states have been springing up on the Wide World Web faster than mushrooms in a rain forest. One need only type in "Russian women" as a query in a search engine to generate a veritable traffic jam of replies.

To give you a concise overview of what's out there in the way of introduction services, we went online and "picked a small basket of mushrooms," gleaning from each site the particulars that we thought would be of interest to you.

Please note that the information provided here concerning these companies does not represent a complete listing of the features of their services. Each commmpany has numerous additional services, the information about which would be too much for us to include on these few pages. You should refer to the web sites themselves for further details.

Also please note that **the listings and descriptions given here are in no way intended as an endorsement or guarantee of the companies or their services.** We have not personally used any of them and cannot in any way vouch for their quality or dependability. We can only attest to the design and navigation features of the sites and present the facts that they themselves have provided for the public.

List of Introduction Services on the Internet

From a design and use standpoint, the site that we liked the best was

"A Pretty Woman" at http://aprettywoman.com/

They have excellent search features that permit you to search for a woman by age, height, weight, children OK?, smoker OK?, beauty, country of residence, English ability, profession, religion, color of hair, and zodiac sign. (Sorry, no shoe size.) Women are shown in groups of six, each with a good-sized lead-off photo that includes her first name, age, date of birth, height in cm and feet/inches, weight in kg and lbs, color of hair, color of eyes, profession, residence, English ability, and available means of communication (phone / e-mail / fax). And all of this up front. Then, by clicking on the photo or the name, you get 2 more photos (one usually a blow-up of the lead-off), more details about the person, including what was given up front, and a short paragraph in the words of the person. Photo uploads and switching from place to place were quite fast.

From **"A Pretty Woman"** you can order addresses in any quantity at varying prices, and they also offer a range of other services, such as personal listings, tours, and women's letters, plus 4 membership plans. Individual addresses can be purchased from them at $15 each for 1-4 addresses, $10 each for 5-9, and $7 each for 10 or more. If you're interested in a larger number of contacts or would like to participate in their tours, the membership plans provide a more economical alternative. Payments can be made by credit card (V, MC, AE) or by money order, personal check or Western Union.

(Information obtained 7-13-2000)

* *

There were some very close runners-up in our personal, unscientific appraisal of these services, among which were:

"Beautiful Dream Network" at http://matchmaking-dating.com

This is a very popular site, which can be slow to reach at certain times of the day, but is well worth the effort. They , too, offer search options for finding the right woman, though not as many as at "A Pretty Woman." Women's profiles include a large photo and many details, plus a self-description. Switching between pages was quite fast.

Addresses from **"Beautiful Dream Network"** cost $14 each for 1-5 addresses, $12 each for 6-9, $10 each for 10-13, and $8 each for 14 or more. Men's addresses are free. They also offer unlimited e-mail service for varying periods at different prices, publishing of personal ads in Russia, membership plans, and tour packages.

(Information obtained 7-7-2000)

* *

"Blue Sapphires" at http://www.bluesapphires.net

Another well-designed site with a versatile search engine, **"Blue Sapphires"** first provides a big lineup of lead-off photos (100 in a block!) and then follows up from each one with 1-3 photos of the woman, various details about her, a description of her, and her description of herself. Switching from page to page is fast. Red lettering on a dark blue background was a bit difficult to read.

Prices for addresses are very reasonable: 1-10 for $10 each, and 10 or more for $5 each. A membership, which permits you to retrieve 10 addresses per month, is $135 per year. **"Blue Sapphires"**, which is based in the UK, also provides a variety of other services, including tours and personal ad listings, and offers the opportunity of entering this business by means of turnkey franchising.

(Information obtained 7-7-2000)

* *

"East Meets West" at http://www.eastmeets west.com

This site appears to be one of the affiliates of **"Blue Sapphires."** Not only are its setup, search engine, and arrangement of lead-off photos and profiles the same, but the women's profiles, as far as we could determine, have the same code numbers. Pricing, however, was structured a bit differently. 1 address goes for $10, 2 for $9 each, 3-5 for $8 each, 6-7 for $7 each, 8-9 for $6 each, 10 or more for $5, and if you buy 20 or more, they have a special offer for you. A 1-year membership is $145.

(Information obtained 7-7-2000)

* *

"Ikar International" at http://www.ikarinter.spb.ru

Features approximately 1500 women, mostly from around St. Petersburg, in two main age categories: under 35 and over 35. Lead-off photos are shown in groups of 6 together with a woman's name and age. A profile page yields 1-3 photos, most of them of excellent quality, plus abundant details about the person.
Fast page links. Includes a search engine. Privilege members can view video clips of some of the women.

Prices for addresses with phone numbers (some with e-mail) are quite reasonable: 1 address - $10, 2 - $19, 3 - $25, 5 - $25, 10 - $45, 15 - $55, 20 - $65.
Some addresses are given FREE.. **"Ikar International"** also offers Ordinary and Privilege memberships, ranging in price from $69 to $199.

(Information obtained 7-7-2000)

* *

"Trueloves.com" at http://www.trueloves.com

You can't beat the price here -- FREE! From a menu of several areas of the world on the first "Search Profiles" page choose "Russia" and then on the next page, "Browse Profiles". This produces a complete 4-page list of the code numbers, names, cities , and ages of over 2,200 women. Selecting one brings up her profile, which includes a photo, personal details, and lengthy description. You can then contact her free by e-mail. A Preferred Membership is available for $5 a month or $14 for 3 months, payable by credit card or check.

(Information obtained 7-13-2000)

* *

Others worthy of note are:

"Absolute Perfection Matchmakers" at http://www.apmatch.com

Has search function and provides 2 photos with each profile, plus essential details. Contacts with women are made through membership. Three packages ranging in price from $39.99 to $499.99. Videos of women available.

(Information obtained 7-7-2000)

* *

"Brides From Russia" at http://www.orc.ru/~brides/

The introduction at the site states that it's possible to contact women free, because the site is sponsored by the women listed on it. Respondents need to fill in name, address, and e-mail address and write a message. "High Priority" messages, which require "High Priority" passwords, are recommended. Such passwords are available at a cost of $9 for 5 H.P. messages, $15 for 10, and $20 for 20.

(Information obtained 7-13-2000)

* *

"Always & Forever Love and Romance"
at   http://sweetshots.com/romance

Features 13 groups of 6 women each. Lead-off photos give name, but no age. Profile page provides one large photo, details, and self-description. A one-month membership is $24.95, payable by credit card, 900-number telephone bill, check or money order (to a U.S. address).

(Information obtained 7-13-2000)

* *

"Amazing Women" at http://www.loveplace.com

A good search engine with numerous options produces a long page with resulting matches in the form of individual photos, names and ages. Selecting one leads to the woman's profile, consisting of a large photo and pertinent details. No self-description. Fairly fast page switching. Addresses are available at the rate of $10 each for 1-5, $9 each for 6-10, and $8 each for 11 or more. Other services are available.

(Information obtained 7-13-2000)

* *

"Cupid Connect" at http://www.cupidconnect.com

Women from St. Petersburg are the focus of this site. You start off with 2 main groups, Russian Ladies A and Russian Ladies B. "A" has 7 "galleries", "B" has 6. Each gallery features the profiles of 10 women. Two photos are shown for each one, with ample details and a self-description. No addresses are sold, instead letter translation and forwardings services are offered at various fees.

(Information obtained 7-13-2000)

* *

"Kazan Marriage Agency" at http://www.zambodia.com

The catalog startup page for this site presents a lineup of 15 thumbnail photos with first names underneath. Unfortunately, ages are not given until you click to a person's profile. The profile page is very nicely designed, with 2 good-sized photos, a description of the person in their own words, and a list of pertinent details. Contact can be made by means of reception, translation and delivery services provided at very low rates.

(Information obtained 7-13-2000)

* *

"Russian Hearts" at http://www.wmellc.com/rhearts

Clicking onto "Women" on the home page, the visitor is greeted with 6 "albums" to choose from, each with 4 pages, each containing 10 thumbnail photos with rather cursory profiles. A click on a photo produces a larger view of the thumbnail, but no more details. Two additional photos are available for most. Addresses can be purchased at the flat rate of $15 each. Tours priced at $4000 are also available.

(Information obtained 7-13-2000)

* *

"Vybor International" at http://www.vybor.com

And here's another FREE one. Just e-mail them the code number and a few details of the person you're interested in, plus your own address and a few details to relay to the person, and contact is made. Most of the profiles of the women include two photos, plus ample details.

(Information obtained 7-13-2000)

* *

"Affectionate Russian Beauties" at http://members.spree.com/romance/russbeauties

This site features around 670 Russian and Ukrainian women in two main age groups, 18-29 and 30-45. Each group has pages of 7 profiles each, consisting of a photo and relevant details. The date of listing is also given. Addresses cost $7 each for 2-5, $6 each for 6-10, $5.50 each for 11-15, and $4.99 each for 16-20. Minimum order is 2. Credit cards accepted.

(Information obtained 7-14-2000)

* *

"Overseas Match" at http://www.overseas-match.com/

Women on this site are grouped under individual ages, with each woman having a small photo, plus her name, age, height, weight, city and country. When selected, her profile page pops up, giving you 1-2 photos, more details, and a personal statement. There are two "catalogues" of listings, one for Y2K and one for 1999. The site has the fastest page switching of any we saw. Addresses are $12 each for 2-9 or $10 each for 10 or more. Memberships are also available. *(Information obtained 7-14-2000)*

Have any comments or contributions?
Please send them to us.

If you have any comments you'd like to make concerning our dictionary or if you wish to contribute any material for the next edition, please write them in the spaces provided below and send them to us at:

Rodnik Publishing Company
P.O. Box 16727
Seattle, WA 98116-0727
U.S.A.

Also, please tell us, where did you buy this book?

Name of store: _____

City / State / Country: _____

_____

Comments and Contributions

_____

_____

_____

_____

_____

_____

_____

Comments and Contributions (continued)

_____

_____

_____

_____

_____

_____

_____

_____

_____

_____

_____

_____

_____

Name & address *(optional)*:

_____

_____

_____

e-mail address: _____

Thank you!

Tear this out and give it to a friend!

ORDER FORM

I'd like to order _____ cy(s) of **"English-Russian Dictionary-Phrasebook of Love"** for just **$24.95** per copy, plus **$3.00** shipping and handling (**$6.00** for airmail outside the U.S.). *(Residents of Washington state please add 8.6% state sales tax.)*

Name: _____

Address: _____

_____

_____

The total for my order is: **$** _____

I wish to pay for this order by:
- ☐   **check** (enclosed).
- ☐   **Visa.**   ☐ **MasterCard.**

Number: _____ Exp: _____

Authorized signature: _____

- ☐   I also wish to be informed of other new Russian language materials published by Rodnik Publishing Company
  - ☐   by mail
  - ☐   by e-mail (*address:* _____)

Mail to: **Rodnik Publishing Company**
P.O. Box 16727
Seattle, WA 98116-0727, USA

Or e-mail your order to: **rodnik2@home.com**

The Russian Alphabet

Printed	Written	Phonetic Value
А а	*Аа*	**ah** (f<u>a</u>ther, t<u>a</u>lk)
Б б	*Бб*	**b** (<u>b</u>oy); **p** (sto<u>p</u>)
В в	*Вв*	**v** (<u>v</u>ote); **f** (coug<u>h</u>)
Г г	*Гг*	**g** (<u>g</u>oat); **k** (soa<u>k</u>); **v** (<u>v</u>ote)
Д д	*Дд*	**d** (<u>d</u>ime); **t** (coa<u>t</u>)
Е е	*Ее*	**yeh** (<u>ye</u>s); **ee** (f<u>ee</u>t)
Ё ё	*Ёё*	**yoh** (<u>yo</u>ke)
Ж ж	*Жж*	**zh** (lei<u>s</u>ure); **sh** (wa<u>sh</u>)
З з	*Зз*	**z** (co<u>z</u>y); **s** (ga<u>s</u>)
И и	*Ии*	**ee** (m<u>ee</u>t)
Й й	*Йй*	**y** (to<u>y</u>, <u>y</u>ell)
К к	*Кк*	**k** (<u>c</u>ode, ba<u>ck</u>)
Л л	*Лл*	**l** (<u>l</u>ow, ba<u>ll</u>)
М м	*Мм*	**m** (<u>m</u>ost, ho<u>m</u>e)
Н н	*Нн*	**n** (<u>n</u>ote, ma<u>n</u>)
О о	*Оо*	**oh** (n<u>o</u>te); *(unstressed:)* **ah** (f<u>a</u>ther)
П п	*Пп*	**p** (sto<u>p</u>, <u>p</u>ork)
Р р	*Рр*	**r** (bu<u>rr</u>o) *(trilled);* **r** (f<u>r</u>ee)
С с	*Сс*	**s** (<u>s</u>oak); **z** (<u>z</u>ip)
Т т	*Тт*	**t** (<u>t</u>est, <u>t</u>oken)
У у	*Уу*	**oo** (d<u>oo</u>m, l<u>oo</u>t)
Ф ф	*Фф*	**f** (<u>f</u>ar, stu<u>ff</u>)
Х х	*Хх*	**kh** (*Scottish* lo<u>ch</u>, *German* ho<u>ch</u>)
Ц ц	*Цц*	**ts** (ca<u>ts</u>, ski<u>ts</u>)
Ч ч	*Чч*	**ch** (<u>ch</u>ess); **sh** (<u>sh</u>ow)
Ш ш	*Шш*	**sh** (<u>sh</u>ow, ca<u>sh</u>)
Щ щ	*Щщ*	**shch** (ca<u>sh ch</u>eck)
Ъ ъ	*ъ*	**hard sign** *(hardens preceding letter)*
Ы ы	*ы*	**i** *(short i + long e simultaneously deep in throat)*
Ь ь	*ь*	**soft sign** *(softens preceding letter)*
Э э	*Ээ*	**eh** (p<u>e</u>t, <u>e</u>gg)
Ю ю	*Юю*	**yoo** (<u>you</u>, <u>you</u>th)
Я я	*Яя*	**yah** (<u>ya</u>cht, <u>ya</u>rd)

The Russian Alphabet

Printed	Written	Phonetic Value
А а	*Аа*	**ah** (f<u>a</u>ther, t<u>a</u>lk)
Б б	*Бб*	**b** (<u>b</u>oy); **p** (sto<u>p</u>)
В в	*Вв*	**v** (<u>v</u>ote); **f** (cou<u>gh</u>)
Г г	*Гг*	**g** (<u>g</u>oat); **k** (soa<u>k</u>); **v** (<u>v</u>ote)
Д д	*Дд*	**d** (<u>d</u>ime); **t** (coa<u>t</u>)
Е е	*Ее*	**yeh** (<u>y</u>es); **ee** (f<u>ee</u>t)
Е ё	*Её*	**yoh** (<u>yo</u>ke)
Ж ж	*Жж*	**zh** (lei<u>s</u>ure); **sh** (wa<u>sh</u>)
З з	*Зз*	**z** (co<u>z</u>y); **s** (ga<u>s</u>)
И и	*Ии*	**ee** (m<u>ee</u>t)
Й й	*Йй*	**y** (to<u>y</u>, <u>y</u>ell)
К к	*Кк*	**k** (<u>c</u>ode, ba<u>ck</u>)
Л л	*Лл*	**l** (<u>l</u>ow, bal<u>l</u>)
М м	*Мм*	**m** (<u>m</u>ost, ho<u>m</u>e)
Н н	*Нн*	**n** (<u>n</u>ote, ma<u>n</u>)
О о	*Оо*	**oh** (n<u>o</u>te); *(unstressed:)* **ah** (f<u>a</u>ther)
П п	*Пп*	**p** (<u>p</u>stop, <u>p</u>ork)
Р р	*Рр*	**r** (bu<u>rr</u>o) *(trilled);* **r** (f<u>r</u>ee)
С с	*Сс*	**s** (<u>s</u>oak); **z** (<u>z</u>ip)
Т т	*Тт*	**t** (<u>t</u>est, <u>t</u>oken)
У у	*Уу*	**oo** (d<u>oo</u>m, l<u>oo</u>t)
Ф ф	*Фф*	**f** (<u>f</u>ar, stu<u>ff</u>)
Х х	*Хх*	**kh** (*Scottish* lo<u>ch</u>, *German* ho<u>ch</u>)
Ц ц	*Цц*	**ts** (ca<u>ts</u>, ski<u>ts</u>)
Ч ч	*Чч*	**ch** (<u>ch</u>ess); **sh** (<u>sh</u>ow)
Ш ш	*Шш*	**sh** (<u>sh</u>ow, ca<u>sh</u>)
Щ щ	*Щщ*	**shch** (ca<u>sh</u> <u>ch</u>eck)
Ъ ъ	*ъ ъ*	**hard sign** (*hardens preceding letter*)
Ы ы	*ы ы*	**i** (*short i + long e simultaneously deep in throat*)
Ь ь	*ь ь*	**soft sign** (*softens preceding letter*)
Э э	*Ээ*	**eh** (p<u>e</u>t, <u>e</u>gg)
Ю ю	*Юю*	**yoo** (<u>you</u>, <u>you</u>th)
Я я	*Яя*	**yah** (<u>ya</u>cht, <u>ya</u>rd)